☞ THE COMPLETE

Crossword

WordFinder ☜

THE COMPLETE
Crossword
WordFinder

Compiled and
Edited by

Diane Emerson Spino

A Perigee Book

A Perigee Book
Published by The Berkley Publishing Group
A member of Penguin Putnam Inc.
375 Hudson Street
New York, New York 10014

G. P. Putnam's Sons edition: October 1997
First Perigee edition: December 1998
Perigee ISBN: 0-399-52451-7

Cover design by Kiley Thompson

Published simultaneously in Canada

The Penguin Putnam Inc. World Wide Web site address is
http://www.penguinputnam.com

The Library of Congress has catalogued the G. P. Putnam's Sons edition as follows:

Spino, Diane.
The complete crossword wordfinder /
compiled and edited by Diane Emerson Spino
        p.   cm.
    ISBN 0-399-14343-2
1. Crossword puzzles—Glossaries, vocabularies, etc. I. Title.
GV1507.C7S63   1997   97-10341 CIP
    793.73'2'03—dc21

Printed in the United States of America

1 2 3 4 5 6 7 8 9 10

Book design by Deborah Kerner

CONTENTS

INTRODUCTION

This word finder will assist you in locating potential solutions to word puzzles. You can use it for crosswords, *Wheel of Fortune* word puzzles, cryptoquotes, and Scrabble. The words are sorted first according to length and then alphabetically according to the first letter, then the second letter, and so forth.

Section 1 of this book contains dictionary words. These are nouns, verbs, adjectives, and other parts of speech, as well as nonpunctuated words, including abbreviations. Prefixes and suffixes that are not stand-alone words are excluded, as are multiword phrases that are defined exclusively as phrases. Plurals of words that are formed by adding *s* or *es* are excluded, but irregular plurals are included. Irregular past-tense verb forms verse are treated similarly.

Section 2 contains nonpunctuated names of famous people. Because crossword puzzle solutions do not use punctuation or spaces, these elements are omitted here. The names listed include famous people in anthropology, archaeology, astronomy, biology, chemistry, earth science, mathematics, medicine, physics, and technology from 600 B.C. to the present, as well as Academy Award winners, U.S. presidents, Nobel Prize winners, Grammy Hall of Famers, Pulitzer Prize winners, modern prolific inventors, and others. (References appear in the bibliography.)

Section 3 contains geographical names, and includes lists of countries, states, their two-letter abbreviations, and their capital cities. At the end of this section is an alphabetical listing of major bodies of water: oceans, seas, lakes, straits, gulfs, bays, sounds, and channels.

How to Look Up Words

STEP 1. Determine the word length by counting the number of letters in the unknown word.

STEP 2. Try to determine at least one of the letters in the unknown word, and its position. Count the number of letters in the unknown word from left to right, up to and including the known letter.

STEP 3. Look in the Contents for the section that contains words of the same *length* as the unknown word. Turn to that section in the text.

STEP 4. Look within the section for the list containing words *sorted according to the same letter position* as that of your known letter.

STEP 5. View the columns of words vertically until the known letter, in its correct position, is located.

STEP 6. Continue to view the columns of words vertically until the last word containing the known letter, in its correct position, is located. (The letter on which the sort is being made appears in **bold** in the text.)

STEP 7. The words located in steps 5 and 6 contain the potential solutions for the word sought in the puzzle.

Helpful Hint

If you discover an extremely large number of possible solutions to your query, try to identify another letter in the unknown word, narrowing down the potential solutions. You can search the sorts for words that meet both criteria; or you can follow steps 2 through 7 using the new letter. For example, there are many potential solutions for words ending in *e*. In such situations, try to identify a consonant or other letter through which to locate a word.

SECTION 1 · DICTIONARY WORDS

2
LETTER WORDS

1st Letter																
	CF	EW	IA	LN	NW	QV	TK	XL	RB	BE	SG	CL	UN	BR	NT	SW
1ST LETTER	CG	EX	IB	LO	NY	QY	TL	XN	SB	CE	VG	EL	XN	CR	OT	UW
AA	CH	FB	IC	LP	NZ	RA	TM	XT	TB	DE	CH	FL	ZN	AO	PT	WW
AB	CI	FD	ID	LR	OB	RB	TN	XU	VB	EE	HH	HL	AO	FR	QT	AX
AC	CJ	FE	IE	LS	OD	RC	TO	YB	WB	HE	IL	BO	GR	RT	BX	
AD	CK	FF	IF	LT	OE	RD	TP	YD	YB	GE	OH	CO	HR	ST	DX	
AF	CL	FI	IG	LU	OF	RE	TR	YE	AC	HE	OH	ML	DO	IR	UT	EX
AG	CM	FM	IL	LV	OG	RF	TV	YR	BC	IE	RH	NL	FO	JR	VT	OX
AK	CN	FN	IP	LZ	OH	RH	TX	YT	CC	ME	EH	PL	GO	KR	WT	PX
AL	CO	FO	IQ	MA	OK	RI	UH	ZN	DC	NE	SH	SL	HO	LR	XT	SX
AM	CP	FP	IR	MB	OM	RM	UK	ZR	HC	OE	TL	TL	JO	MR	TX	
AN	CQ	FR	IS	MC	ON	RN	UN		IC	PE	UH	VL	KO	OR	UX	
AO	CR	FT	IT	MD	OP	RR	UP	**2ND LETTER**	KC	RE	WH	WL	LO	PR	BY	
AP	CS	FY	IV	ME	OR	RS	US	AA	LC	SE	BI	XL	MO	QR	CU	FY
AR	CT	GA	IW	MF	OS	RT	UT	BA	MC	TE	CI	AM	NO	RR	DU	KY
AS	CU	GB	JD	MG	OT	RU	UV	CA	NC	WE	GI	BM	PO	SR	EU	MY
AT	CW	GD	JG	MI	OX	RW	UW	DA	PC	YE	HI	CM	SO	TR	GU	NY
AU	CZ	GE	JN	MK	OZ	SA	UX	EA	QC	AF	MI	EM	TO	YR	LU	QY
AV	DA	GI	JO	ML	PA	SB	VA	GA	RC	BF	NI	FM	WO	ZR	NU	WY
AX	DB	GK	JP	MM	PB	SC	VB	HA	SC	CF	PI	GM	AP	AS	PU	AZ
AZ	DC	GM	JR	MN	PC	SD	VC	IA	TC	DF	RI	HM	BP	BS	QU	CZ
BA	DD	GO	JV	MO	PD	SE	VD	LA	VC	FF	SI	KM	CP	CS	RU	DZ
BB	DE	GP	KC	MP	PE	SF	VF	MA	WC	HF	TI	LM	DP	DS	XU	LZ
BC	DF	GQ	KD	MR	PF	SG	VG	NA	AD	IF	VI	MM	FP	ES	AV	NZ
BD	DG	GR	KG	MS	PG	SH	VI	PA	BD	LF	WI	NM	GP	HS	BV	OZ
BE	DJ	GT	KM	MT	PH	SI	VL	RA	CD	MF	XI	OM	HP	IS	DV	
BF	DK	GU	KN	MV	PI	SJ	VP	SA	DD	NF		PM	IP	KS	HV	
BG	DN	HA	KO	MY	PK	SL	VS	TA	ED	OF	MF	QM	JP	LS	IV	
BI	DP	HB	KR	NA	PL	SM	VT	UA	FD	PF	NF	RM	KP	MS	JV	
BK	DR	HC	KS	NB	PM	SO	VV	WA	GD	QF	OF	SM	LP	NS	KV	
BL	DS	HD	KT	NC	PN	SR	WA		HD	RF	PF	TM	MP	OS	LV	
BM	DU	HE	KW	ND	PO	SS	WB		ID	SF	QF	AN	NP	PS	MV	
BN	DV	HF	KY	NE	PQ	ST	WE		JD	AG	RF	BN	OP	RS	NV	
BO	DX	HG	LA	NF	PR	SV	WH		KD	BG	SF	CN	PP	SS	QV	
BP	DZ	HH	LB	NG	PS	SW	WI		LD	CG	SJ	DN	QP	US	SV	
BR	EA	HI	LC	NH	PT	SX	WK		MD	DG	AN	FN	RP	VS	TV	
BS	ED	HJ	LD	NI	PU	TA	WL		NB	EG	BN	GK	SP	AT	UV	
BU	EE	HL	LF	NJ	PW	TB	WO		OD	FG	CN	IN	TP	CT	VV	
BV	EG	HM	LH	NL	PX	TC	WU		PD	GG	DN	JN	UP	ET	WV	
BX	EG	HO	LK	NM	QC	TD	WW		QD	HG	EN	KN	VP	GT	CW	
BY	EL	HP	LL	NO	QD	TE	WY		RD	JG	FN	MN	CQ	IT	EW	
CA	EM	HQ	LM	NP	QM	TH	XD		SD	KG	GN	NN	EQ	KT	FW	
CB	EQ	HR	LN	NS	QR	TI	XE		TD	LG	JG	PN	HQ	NT	IW	
CC	ES	HS	LK	NT	QT	TE	XI		UD	MG	KG	RN	IQ	IT	KW	
CD	ET	HT	LL	NU	QT	TH	XE		VD	NG	LG	SN	PQ	KT	NW	
CE	EU	HV	LM	NV	QU	TI	XI		XD	OG	WK	TN	SQ	LT	PW	
									YD	PG	AL	AR	MT			RW

3
LETTER WORDS

1st Letter	AMP	BAN	BUG	COG	DDS	DST	ESD	FIN	GIE	HMS	IRA	KKK	LTD	MOL	NIL
	AMT	BAR	BUM	COL	DDT	DTE	ESE	FIO	GIF	HOB	IRE	LAB	LTG	MOM	NIP
AAA	ANC	BAT	BUN	COM	DEB	DUB	ESP	FIR	GIG	HOD	IRK	LAC	LTL	MON	NIT
ABA	AND	BAY	BUR	CON	DEC	DUD	ESQ	FIT	GIN	HOE	IRQ	LAD	LTR	MOO	NIX
ABC	ANN	BBA	BUS	COO	DEF	DUE	EST	FIX	GMC	HOG	IRS	LAG	LUB	MOP	NNE
ABL	ANS	BBB	BUT	COP	DEG	DUG	ETA	FLU	GMT	HON	ISA	LAM	LUG	MOT	NNW
ABM	ANT	BBC	BUY	COR	DEL	DUN	ETC	FLY	GNP	HOP	ISL	LAN	LYE	MOW	NOD
ABP	ANY	BBL	BWI	COS	DEM	DUO	ETD	FOB	GNU	HOR	ISM	LAP	MAC	MPC	NOH
ABR	APB	BBS	BYE	COT	DEN	DUP	ETV	FOC	GOB	HOS	ISO	LAT	MAD	MPG	NOM
ABS	APE	BCD	CAB	COW	DEP	DVM	ETY	FOE	GOD	HOT	ISR	LAW	MAG	MPH	NOR
ACC	API	BCS	CAD	COY	DER	DWT	EUR	FOG	GOO	HOW	ITS	LAX	MAJ	MRS	NOS
ACE	APL	BDL	CAF	CPA	DET	DYE	EVA	FOP	GOP	HRH	IUD	LAY	MAL	MSD	NOT
ACK	APO	BED	CAL	CPD	DEV	EAR	EVE	FOR	GOT	HSB	IVY	LCD	MAN	MSG	NOV
ACT	APP	BEE	CAM	CPL	DEW	EAT	EVG	FOS	GOV	HST	IWW	LCL	MAP	MSL	NOW
ADA	APR	BEF	CAN	CPO	DFC	EBB	EWE	FOT	GPF	HUB	JAB	LDG	MAR	MSS	NPN
ADC	APT	BEG	CAP	CPS	DFM	ECG	EXC	FOX	GPO	HUD	JAG	LEA	MAT	MST	NSA
ADD	ARC	BET	CAR	CPT	DIA	ECM	EXE	FPC	GRO	HUE	JAM	LED	MAW	MTG	NSC
ADJ	ARE	BEY	CAT	CPU	DID	EDP	EXP	FPM	GSA	HUG	JAN	LEE	MAX	MUD	NSF
ADM	ARK	BFA	CAV	CRC	DIE	EDT	EXT	FPO	GTD	HUM	JAP	LEG	MAY	MUG	NSW
ADO	ARM	BHD	CAW	CRT	DIF	EEG	EYE	FPS	GUI	HUN	JAR	LEI	MBA	MUM	NTH
ADV	ARR	BIB	CAY	CRY	DIG	EEL	FAA	FRI	GUM	HUT	JAS	LEK	MDA	MUN	NTP
ADZ	ART	BID	CBC	CSA	DIL	EFF	FAC	FRO	GUN	HVY	JAW	LEM	MED	MUS	NUB
AEC	ARV	BIG	CBS	CSM	DIM	EFT	FAD	FRS	GUT	HWY	JAY	LET	MEG	MVP	NUM
AEF	ASC	BIN	CBW	CST	DIN	EGA	FAG	FRT	GUY	HYP	JCC	LEU	MEM	MVS	NUN
AEQ	ASH	BIT	CCC	CTG	DIP	EGG	FAH	FRY	GYM	IBM	JCL	LEV	MEN	NAB	NUT
AET	ASK	BKG	CCW	CTN	DIR	EGO	FAN	FTC	GYP	ICC	JCS	LGK	MER	NAG	NWT
AFB	ASP	BKS	CDR	CTR	DIV	EHF	FAO	FTP	HAB	ICE	JCT	LHD	MET	NAH	NYC
AFC	ASS	BKT	CEN	CUA	DLL	EKE	FAR	FUN	HAD	ICJ	JER	LIB	MEV	NAK	OAF
AFR	ASV	BLK	CFI	CUB	DLO	EKG	FAS	FUR	HAG	ICY	JET	LID	MEW	NAP	OAK
AFT	ATE	BLT	CGA	CUD	DMA	ELF	FAT	FUT	HAM	IDE	JEW	LIE	MEX	NAS	OAR
AGE	ATL	BMP	CGS	CUE	DMD	ELK	FAX	FWD	HAP	IGY	JIB	LIN	MFA	NAT	OAS
AGO	ATM	BMR	CHG	CUM	DMZ	ELL	FAY	FYI	HAS	IHP	JIG	LIP	MFD	NAV	OAT
AGR	ATN	BOA	CHM	CUP	DNA	ELM	FBI	GAB	HAT	IHS	JOB	LIQ	MFG	NAY	OBI
AGT	ATP	BOB	CIA	CUR	DOA	EMF	FCC	GAD	HAW	ILK	JOG	LIT	MFM	NBC	OBJ
AID	ATT	BOG	CID	CUT	DOB	EMP	FCP	GAG	HAY	ILL	JOT	LLB	MFR	NBS	OBL
AIL	AUD	BOO	CIE	CWO	DOC	EMS	FCY	GAL	HBM	ILS	JOY	LLD	MGR	NCE	OBS
AIM	AUG	BOP	CIF	CWT	DOE	EMU	FDA	GAO	HCL	IMF	JRC	LNG	MGT	NCO	OBV
AIR	AUK	BOQ	CIR	CYC	DOG	ENC	FEB	GAP	HEB	IMP	JUG	LOB	MHZ	NCV	OCR
AKA	AUS	BOR	CIT	CYL	DOL	END	FEC	GAR	HEM	INC	JUL	LOG	MIA	NEB	OCS
AKC	AUX	BOT	CIV	CYO	DOM	ENE	FED	GAS	HEN	IND	JUN	LOP	MIC	NEE	OCT
ALA	AVE	BOW	CLD	DAB	DON	ENG	FEE	GAW	HEP	INF	JUT	LOQ	MID	NEG	ODD
ALC	AVG	BOX	CLK	DAC	DOS	ENL	FEM	GAY	HER	INI	JUV	LOT	MIL	NEH	ODE
ALD	AVO	BOY	CLO	DAD	DOT	ENS	FEN	GAZ	HEW	INK	KEG	LOW	MIN	NEI	OED
ALE	AWE	BPL	CLR	DAM	DOZ	ENV	FET	GCA	HEX	INN	KEN	LOX	MIS	NES	OEM
ALG	AWK	BPS	CLU	DAN	DPI	EOM	FEW	GCT	HGT	INP	KEY	LPG	MIX	NET	OEO
ALK	AWL	BRA	CML	DAR	DPT	EON	FEY	GEL	HHD	INS	KIA	LPI	MKS	NEV	OES
ALL	AWN	BRO	CMS	DAT	DRY	EPH	FEZ	GEM	HIE	INT	KID	LPN	MLD	NEW	OFF
ALP	AYE	BSA	CNO	DAU	DSC	EPS	FHA	GEN	HIM	INV	KIN	LSD	MME	NFS	OFM
ALT	BAD	BSC	CNS	DAY	DSM	ERA	FIB	GER	HIP	ION	KIP	LSS	MNP	NGK	OFS
AMA	BAG	BTU	COB	DBL	DSO	ERE	FIE	GET	HIS	IOU	KIT	LSS	MOB	NHI	OFT
AMB	BAL	BUD	COD	DDE	DSP	ERR	FIG	GHQ	HIT	IPS	KJV	LTC	MOD	NIB	OHM

OIL	PIC	QID	RTE	SON	THE	VAR	WOO	DAT	MAC	TAG	PBX	DDS	HEB	REA	MFA
OJT	PIE	QLD	RUB	SOP	THY	VAT	WOW	DAU	MAD	TAM	RBC	DDT	HEM	REC	MFD
OLD	PIF	QMC	RUE	SOS	TIA	VAX	WPM	DAY	MAG	TAN	RBI	EDP	HEN	RED	MFG
OLE	PIG	QMG	RUG	SOT	TIC	VDT	WPN	EAR	MAJ	TAP	SBA	EDT	HEP	REF	MFM
ONE	PIN	QTO	RUM	SOW	TID	VEL	WRY	EAT	MAL	TAR	TBA	FDA	HER	REG	MFR
ONT	PIP	QTY	RUN	SOX	TIE	VEN	WSW	FAA	MAN	TAT	TBS	IDE	HEW	REL	NFS
OOP	PIS	QUE	RUT	SOY	TIM	VET	WWW	FAC	MAP	TAW	WBC	LDG	HEX	REM	OFF
OPE	PIT	RAD	RWY	SPA	TIN	VEX	XGA	FAD	MAR	TAX	ACC	MDA	JER	REP	OFM
OPP	PIX	RAF	RYE	SPP	TIP	VFD	YAK	FAG	MAT	UAR	ACE	ODD	JET	REQ	OFS
OPT	PKG	RAG	SAA	SPY	TIT	VFW	YAM	FAH	MAW	VAL	ACK	ODE	JEW	RES	OFT
ORB	PKT	RAM	SAC	SRO	TKT	VGA	YAP	FAN	MAX	VAN	ACT	PDA	KEG	RET	PFC
ORD	PLY	RAN	SAD	SSA	TLC	VHF	YAW	FAO	MAY	VAR	BCD	PDD	KEN	REV	PFD
ORE	PMK	RAP	SAG	SSE	TMO	VIA	YEA	FAR	NAB	VAT	BCS	PDQ	KEY	REX	RFD
ORG	PMT	RAT	SAM	SSG	TNC	VIC	YEN	FAS	NAG	VAX	CCC	PDT	LEA	SEA	RFI
OSB	PNP	RAW	SAP	SSP	TNG	VIE	YES	FAT	NAH	WAC	CCW	QDA	LED	SEC	SFC
OSF	POC	RAY	SAT	SSR	TNT	VIL	YET	FAX	NAK	WAD	ECG	TDY	LEE	SEE	UFO
OSI	POD	RBC	SAW	SSS	TOE	VIM	YEW	FAY	NAP	WAF	ECM	VDT	LEG	SEL	VFD
OTS	POE	RBI	SAY	SST	TOG	VIP	YOB	GAB	NAS	WAG	FCC	AEC	LEI	SEM	VFW
OUR	POI	RCT	SBA	SSW	TOM	VIS	YON	GAD	NAT	WAN	FCP	AEF	LEK	SEN	AGE
OUT	POL	REA	SCH	STA	TON	VIZ	YOU	GAG	NAV	WAR	FCY	AEQ	LEM	SEP	AGO
OVA	POP	REC	SCI	STD	TOO	VLB	ZAP	GAL	NAY	WAS	GCA	AET	LET	SEQ	AGR
OWE	POR	RED	SEA	STE	TOP	VOA	ZED	GAO	OAF	WAV	GCT	BED	LEU	SER	AGT
OWL	POS	REF	SEC	STG	TOR	VOC	ZEN	GAP	OAK	WAX	HCL	BEE	LEV	SET	CGA
OWN	POT	REG	SEE	STK	TOT	VOL	ZIP	GAR	OAR	WAY	ICC	BEF	MED	SEW	CGS
PAC	POW	REL	SEL	STP	TOW	VOU	ZOO	GAS	OAS	YAK	ICE	BEG	MEG	SEX	EGA
PAD	POX	REM	SEM	STY	TOY	VOW	ZPG	GAW	OAT	YAM	ICJ	BET	MEM	TEA	EGG
PAL	PPC	REP	SEN	SUB	TPK	VSS		GAY	PAC	YAP	ICY	BEY	MEN	TEE	EGO
PAM	PPD	REQ	SEP	SUE	TRY	WAC		GAZ	PAD	YAW	JCC	CEN	MER	TEL	HGT
PAN	PPM	RES	SEQ	SUM	TSP	WAD	**2ND LETTER**	HAB	PAL	ZAP	JCL	DEB	MET	TEN	IGY
PAP	PPT	RET	SER	SUN	TSR	WAF		HAD	PAM	ABA	JCS	DEC	MEV	TER	LGK
PAR	PRF	REV	SET	SUP	TTL	WAG		HAG	PAN	ABC	JCT	DEF	MEW	TEX	MGR
PAS	PRN	REX	SEW	SVC	TUB	WAN	AAA	HAM	PAP	ABL	LCD	DEG	MEX	VEL	MGT
PAT	PRO	RFD	SEX	SWA	TUG	WAR	BAD	HAP	PAR	ABM	LCL	DEL	NEB	VEN	NGK
PAW	PRP	RFI	SFC	SYL	TUN	WAS	BAG	HAS	PAS	ABP	LCM	DEM	NEE	VET	RGB
PAY	PRY	RGB	SGD	SYM	TVA	WAV	BAL	HAT	PAT	ABR	NCE	DEN	NEG	VEX	SGD
PBX	PSG	RIB	SGT	SYN	TWO	WAX	BAN	HAW	PAW	ABS	NCO	DEP	NEH	WEB	SGT
PCI	PSI	RID	SHE	TAB	TWP	WAY	BAR	HAY	PAY	BBA	NCV	DER	NEI	WED	VGA
PCT	PST	RIG	SHT	TAC	TWX	WBC	BAT	JAB	RAD	BBB	OCR	DET	NES	WEE	XGA
PCX	PTA	RIM	SHY	TAG	UAR	WEB	BAY	JAG	RAF	BBC	OCS	DEV	NET	WEN	BHD
PDA	PTE	RIP	SIC	TAM	UFO	WED	CAB	JAM	RAG	BBL	OCT	DEW	NEV	WET	CHG
PDD	PTG	RIV	SIG	TAN	UHF	WEE	CAD	JAN	RAM	BBS	PCI	EEG	NEW	YEA	CHM
PDQ	PTO	RLL	SIN	TAP	ULT	WEN	CAF	JAP	RAN	CBC	PCT	EEL	OED	YEN	EHF
PDT	PTV	RNA	SIP	TAR	UMT	WET	CAL	JAR	RAP	CBS	PCX	FEB	OEM	YES	FHA
PEA	PUB	RND	SIR	TAT	UPI	WHF	CAM	JAS	RAT	CBW	RCT	FEC	OEO	YET	GHQ
PEG	PUG	ROB	SIT	TAW	URL	WHO	CAN	JAW	RAW	DBL	SCH	FED	OES	YEW	HHD
PEI	PUL	ROD	SIX	TAX	URN	WHS	CAP	JAY	RAY	EBB	SCI	FEE	PEA	ZED	IHP
PEL	PUN	ROE	SJD	TBA	USA	WHY	CAR	LAB	SAA	FBI	ADA	FEM	PEG	ZEN	IHS
PEN	PUP	ROG	SKI	TBS	USE	WID	CAT	LAC	SAC	HBM	ADC	FEN	PEI	AFB	LHD
PEP	PUS	ROM	SKT	TDY	USM	WIG	CAV	LAD	SAD	IBM	ADD	FET	PEL	AFC	MHZ
PER	PUT	ROT	SKY	TEA	USN	WIN	CAW	LAG	SAG	MBA	ADJ	FEW	PEN	AFR	NHI
PET	PVT	ROW	SLD	TEE	USO	WIS	CAY	LAM	SAM	NBC	ADM	FEY	PEP	AFT	OHM
PEW	PYA	RPG	SLY	TEL	USP	WIT	DAB	LAN	SAP	NBS	ADO	FEZ	PER	BFA	PHD
PFC	PYX	RPM	SMA	TEN	USS	WMK	DAC	LAP	SAT	OBI	ADV	GEL	PET	CFI	PHR
PFD	QDA	RPN	SOB	TER	USU	WNW	DAD	LAT	SAW	OBJ	ADZ	GEM	PEW	DFC	PHS
PHD	QED	RPO	SOC	TEX	UTE	WOE	DAM	LAW	SAY	OBL	BDL	GEN	QED	DFM	SHE
PHR	QEF	RPS	SOD	THC	VAL	WOK	DAN	LAX	TAB	OBS	CDR	GER	QEF	EFF	SHT
PHS	QEI	RSV	SOL	THD	VAN	WON	DAR	LAY	TAC	OBV	DDE	GET	QEI	EFT	SHY

C1	C2	C3	C4	C5	C6	C7	C8	C9	C10	C11	C12	C13	C14	C15	C16
THC	KID	VIE	LLB	ENV	DON	NOS	ZOO	ARE	DSP	ATP	CUD	RUE	CYL	MIA	LLB
THD	KIN	VIL	LLD	GNP	DOS	NOT	APB	ARK	ESD	ATT	CUE	RUG	CYO	NSA	LOB
THE	KIP	VIM	MLD	GNU	DOT	NOV	APE	ARM	ESE	BTU	CUM	RUM	DYE	OVA	LUB
THY	KIT	VIP	OLD	INC	DOZ	NOW	API	ARR	ESP	CTG	CUP	RUN	EYE	PDA	MOB
UHF	LIB	VIS	OLE	IND	EOM	OOP	APL	ART	ESQ	CTN	CUR	RUT	FYI	PEA	NAB
VHF	LID	VIZ	PLY	INF	EON	POC	APO	ARV	EST	CTR	CUT	SUB	GYM	PTA	NEB
WHF	LIE	WID	QLD	INI	FOB	POD	APP	BRA	GSA	DTE	DUB	SUE	GYP	PYA	NIB
WHO	LIN	WIG	RLL	INK	FOC	POE	APR	BRO	HSB	ETA	DUD	SUM	HYP	QDA	NUB
WHS	LIP	WIN	SLD	INN	FOE	POI	APT	CRC	HST	ETC	DUE	SUN	LYE	REA	ORB
WHY	LIQ	WIS	SLY	INP	FOG	POL	BPL	CRT	ISA	ETD	DUG	SUP	NYC	RNA	OSB
AID	LIT	WIT	TLC	INS	FOP	POP	BPS	CRY	ISL	ETV	DUN	TUB	PYA	SAA	PUB
AIL	MIA	ZIP	ULT	INT	FOR	POR	CPA	DRY	ISM	ETY	DUO	TUG	PYX	SBA	RGB
AIM	MIC	KJV	VLB	INV	FOS	POS	CPD	ERA	ISO	FTC	DUP	TUN	RYE	SEA	RIB
AIR	MID	OJT	AMA	LNG	FOT	POT	CPL	ERE	ISR	FTP	EUR	AVE	SYL	SMA	ROB
BIB	MIL	SJD	AMB	MNP	FOX	POW	CPO	ERR	LSD	GTD	FUN	AVG	SYM	SPA	RUB
BID	MIN	AKA	AMP	NNE	GOB	POX	CPS	FRI	LSS	ITS	FUR	AVO	SYN	SSA	SOB
BIG	MIS	AKC	BMP	NNW	GOD	ROB	CPT	FRO	MSD	LTC	FUT	DVM		STA	SUB
BIN	MIX	BKG	BMR	ONE	GOO	ROD	CPU	FRS	MSG	LTD	GUI	EVA		SWA	TAB
BIT	NIB	BKS	CML	ONT	GOP	ROE	DPI	FRT	MSL	LTG	GUM	EVE		TBA	TUB
CIA	NIL	BKT	CMS	PNP	GOT	ROG	DPT	FRY	MSS	LTL	GUN	EVG	**3RD LETTER**	TEA	VLB
CID	NIP	EKE	DMA	RNA	GOV	ROM	EPH	GRO	MST	LTR	GUT	HVY		TIA	WEB
CIE	NIT	EKG	DMD	RND	HOB	ROT	EPS	HRH	NSA	MTG	GUY	IVY	AAA	TVA	YOB
CIF	NIX	KKK	DMZ	TNC	HOD	ROW	FPC	IRA	NSC	NTH	HUB	AWE	ABA	USA	ABC
CIR	OIL	MKS	EMC	TNG	HOE	SOB	FPM	IRE	NSF	NTP	HUD	AWK	ADA	VGA	ACC
CIT	PIC	PKG	EMF	TNT	HOG	SOC	FPO	IRK	NSW	OTS	HUE	AWL	AKA	VIA	ADC
CIV	PIE	PKT	EMP	WNW	HON	SOD	FPS	IRQ	OSA	PTA	HUG	AWN	ALA	VOA	AEC
DIA	PIF	SKI	EMS	BOA	HOP	SOL	GPF	IRS	OSB	PTE	HUM	BWI	AMA	XGA	AFC
DID	PIG	SKT	EMU	BOB	HOR	SON	GPO	JRC	OSF	PTG	HUN	CWO	BBA	YEA	AKC
DIE	PIN	SKY	GMC	BOG	HOS	SOP	IPS	MRS	OSI	PTO	HUT	CWT	BFA	AFB	ALC
DIF	PIP	TKT	GMT	BOO	HOT	SOS	LPG	ORB	PSA	PTV	IUD	DWT	BOA	APB	ANC
DIG	PIS	ALA	HMS	BOP	HOW	SOT	LPI	ORD	PSG	QTO	JUG	EWE	BRA	BIB	ARC
DIL	PIT	ALC	IMF	BOQ	ION	SOW	LPN	ORE	PSI	QTY	JUL	FWD	BSA	BOB	ASC
DIM	PIX	ALD	IMP	BOR	IOU	SOX	MPC	ORG	RSV	RTE	JUN	HWY	CGA	DAB	BBC
DIN	QID	ALE	MME	BOT	JOB	SOY	MPG	PRF	SSA	STA	JUT	IWW	CIA	DEB	BSC
DIP	RIB	ALG	PMK	BOW	JOG	TOE	MPH	PRN	SSE	STD	JUV	NWT	CPA	DOB	CBC
DIR	RID	ALK	PMT	BOX	JOT	TOG	NPN	PRO	SSG	STE	LUB	OWE	CSA	DUB	CCC
DIV	RIG	ALL	QMC	BOY	JOY	TOM	OPE	PRP	SSP	STG	LUG	OWL	CUA	EBB	CRC
FIB	RIM	ALP	QMG	COB	LOB	TON	OPP	PRY	SSR	STK	MUD	OWN	DIA	FEB	CYC
FIE	RIP	ALT	SMA	COD	LOG	TOO	OPT	SRO	SSS	STP	MUG	RWY	DMA	FIB	DAC
FIG	RIV	BLK	TMO	COG	LOP	TOP	PPC	TRY	SSW	STY	MUM	SWA	DNA	FOB	DEC
FIN	SIC	BLT	UMT	COL	LOQ	TOR	PPD	URL	TSP	TTL	MUN	TWO	DOA	GAB	DFC
FIO	SIG	CLD	WMK	COM	LOT	TOT	PPM	URN	TSR	UTE	MUS	TWP	EGA	GOB	DOC
FIR	SIN	CLK	ANC	CON	LOW	TOW	PPT	WRY	USA	AUD	NUB	TWX	ERA	HAB	DSC
FIT	SIP	CLO	AND	COO	LOX	TOY	RPG	ASC	USE	AUG	NUM	WWW	ETA	HEB	ENC
FIX	SIR	CLR	ANN	COP	MOB	VOA	RPM	ASH	USM	AUK	NUN	EXC	EVA	HOB	ETC
GIE	SIT	CLU	ANS	COR	MOD	VOC	RPN	ASK	USN	AUS	NUT	EXE	FAA	HSB	EXC
GIF	SIX	DLL	ANT	COS	MOL	VOL	RPO	ASP	USO	AUX	OUR	EXP	FDA	HUB	FAC
GIG	TIA	DLO	ANY	COT	MOM	VOU	RPS	ASS	USP	BUD	OUT	EXT	FHA	JAB	FCC
GIN	TIC	ELF	CNO	COW	MON	VOW	SPA	ASV	USS	BUG	PUB	AYE	GCA	JIB	FEC
HIE	TID	ELK	CNS	COY	MOO	WOE	SPP	BSA	USU	BUM	PUG	BYE	GSA	JOB	FOC
HIM	TIE	ELL	DNA	DOA	MOP	WOK	SPY	BSC	USW	BUN	PUL	CYC	IRA	LAB	FPC
HIP	TIM	ELM	ENC	DOB	MOT	WON	TPK	CSA	VSS	BUR	PUN		ISA	LIB	FTC
HIS	TIN	FLU	END	DOC	MOW	WOO	UPI	CSM	WSW	BUS	PUP		KIA		GMC
HIT	TIP	FLY	ENE	DOE	NOD	WOW	WPM	CST	ATE	BUT	PUS		LEA		ICC
JIB	TIT	ILK	ENG	DOG	NOH	YOB	WPN	DSC	ATL	BUY	PUT		MBA		INC
JIG	VIA	ILL	ENL	DOL	NOM	YON	ZPG	DSM	ATM	CUA	QUE		MDA		JCC
KIA	VIC	ILS	ENS	DOM	NOR	YOU	ARC	DSO	ATN	CUB	RUB		MFA		JRC

LAC	FWD	WED	ROE	DEG	STG	INK	PUL	OFM	MEN	GAO	LAP	BMR	BPS	TBS	HGT
LTC	GAD	WID	RTE	DIG	TAG	IRK	REL	OHM	MIN	GOO	LIP	BOR	BUS	USS	HIT
MAC	GOD	ZED	RUE	DOG	TNG	KKK	RLL	PAM	MON	GPO	LOP	BUR	CBS	VIS	HOT
MIC	GTD	ACE	RYE	DUG	TOG	LEK	SEL	PPM	MUN	GRO	MAP	CAR	CGS	VSS	HST
MPC	HAD	AGE	SEE	ECG	TUG	LGK	SOL	RAM	NPN	ISO	MNP	CDR	CMS	WAS	HUT
NBC	HHD	ALE	SHE	EEG	WAG	NAK	SYL	REM	NUN	MOO	MOP	CIR	CNS	WHS	INT
NSC	HOD	APE	SSE	EGG	WIG	NGK	TEL	RIM	OWN	NCO	MVP	CLR	COS	WIS	JCT
NYC	HUD	ARE	STE	EKG	ZPG	OAK	TTL	ROM	PAN	OEO	NAP	COR	CPS	YES	JET
PAC	IND	ATE	SUE	ENG	ASH	PMK	URL	RPM	PEN	PRO	NIP	CTR	DDS	ACT	JOT
PFC	IUD	AVE	TEE	EVG	EPH	STK	VAL	RUM	PIN	PTO	NTP	CUR	DOS	AET	JUT
PIC	KID	AWE	THE	FAG	FAH	TPK	VEL	SAM	PRN	QTO	OOP	DAR	EMS	AFT	KIT
POC	LAD	AYE	TIE	FIG	HRH	WMK	VIL	SEM	PUN	RPO	OPP	DER	ENS	AGT	LAT
PPC	LCD	BEE	TOE	FOG	MPH	WOK	VOL	SUM	RAN	SRO	PAP	DIR	EPS	ALT	LET
QMC	LED	BYE	USE	GAG	NAH	YAK	ABM	SYM	RUN	TMO	PEP	EAR	FAS	AMT	LIT
RBC	LHD	CIE	UTE	GIG	NEH	ABL	ADM	TAM	SEN	TOO	PHP	ERR	FOS	ANT	LOT
REC	LID	CUE	VIE	HAG	NOH	AIL	AIM	TIM	SIN	TWO	PIP	EUR	FPS	APT	MAT
SAC	LLD	DDE	WEE	HOG	NTH	ALL	ARM	TOM	SON	UFO	PNP	FAR	FRS	ART	MET
SEC	LSD	DIE	WOE	HUG	SCH	APL	ATM	USM	SUN	USO	POP	FIR	GAS	ATT	MGT
SFC	LTD	DOE	AEF	JAG	API	ATL	BUM	VIM	SYN	WHO	PPP	FOR	HAS	BAT	MOT
SIC	MAD	DTE	BEF	JIG	BWI	AWL	CAM	WPM	TAN	WOO	PRP	FUR	HIS	BET	MST
SOC	MED	DUE	CAF	JOG	CFI	BAL	CHM	YAM	TEN	ZOO	PUP	GAR	HMS	BIT	NAT
SVC	MFD	DYE	CIF	JUG	DPI	BBL	COM	ANN	TIN	ABP	RAP	GER	HOS	BKT	NET
TAC	MID	EKE	DEF	KEG	FBI	BDL	CSM	ATN	TON	ALP	REP	HER	IHS	BLT	NIT
THC	MLD	ENE	DIF	LAG	FRI	BPL	CUM	AWN	TUN	AMP	RIP	HOR	ILS	BOT	NOT
TIC	MOD	ERE	EFF	LDG	FYI	CAL	DAM	BAN	URN	APP	SAP	ISR	INS	BUT	NUT
TLC	MSD	ESE	EHF	LEG	GUI	CML	DEM	BIN	USN	ASP	SEP	JAR	IPS	CAT	NWT
TNC	MUD	EVE	ELF	LNG	INI	COL	DFM	BUN	VAN	ATP	SIP	JER	IRS	CIT	OAT
VIC	NOD	EWE	EMF	LOG	LEI	CPL	DIM	CAN	VEN	BMP	SOP	LTR	ITS	COT	OCT
VOC	ODD	EXE	GIF	LPG	LPI	CYL	DOM	CEN	WAN	BOP	SUP	MAR	JAS	CPT	OFT
WAC	OED	EYE	GPF	LTG	NEI	DBL	DSM	CON	WEN	CAP	TAP	MER	JCS	CRT	OJT
WBC	OLD	FEE	IMF	LUG	NHI	DEL	DVM	CTN	WIN	COP	TIP	MFR	LSS	CST	ONT
ADD	ORD	FIE	INF	MAG	OBI	DIL	ECM	DAN	WON	CUP	TOP	MGR	MIS	CUT	OPT
AID	PAD	FOE	NSF	MEG	OSI	DLL	ELM	DEN	WPN	DEP	TSP	NOR	MKS	CWT	OUT
ALD	PDD	GIE	OAF	MFG	PCI	DOL	EOM	DIN	YEN	DIP	TWP	OAR	MRS	DAT	PAT
AND	PFD	HIE	OFF	MPG	PEI	EEL	FEM	DON	YON	DSP	USP	OCR	MSS	DDT	PCT
AUD	PHD	HOE	OSF	MSG	POI	ELL	FPM	DUN	ZEN	DUP	VIP	OUR	MUS	DET	PDT
BAD	POD	HUE	PIF	MTG	PSI	ENL	GEM	EON	ADO	EDP	WIP	PAR	MVS	DOT	PET
BCD	PPD	ICE	PRF	MUG	QEI	GAL	GUM	FAN	AGO	EMP	YAP	PER	NAS	DPT	PIT
BED	QED	IDE	QEF	NAG	RBI	GEL	GYM	FEN	APO	ESP	ZAP	PHR	NBS	DST	PKT
BHD	QID	IRE	RAF	NEG	RFI	HCL	HAM	FIN	AVO	EXP	ZIP	POR	NES	DWT	PMT
BID	QLD	LEE	REF	ORG	SCI	ILL	HBM	FUN	BOO	FCP	AEQ	SER	NFS	EAT	POT
BUD	RAD	LIE	UHF	PEG	SKI	ISL	HEM	GEN	BRO	FOP	BOQ	SIR	NOS	EDT	PPT
CAD	RED	LYE	VHF	PIG	UPI	JCL	HIM	GIN	CEO	FTP	ESQ	TAR	OAS	EFT	PST
CID	RFD	MME	WAF	PKG	ADJ	JUL	HUM	GUN	CLO	GAP	GHQ	TER	OBS	EST	PUT
CLD	RID	NCE	WHF	PSG	ICJ	LCL	IBM	HEN	CNO	GNP	IRQ	TOR	OCS	EXT	PVT
COD	RND	NEE	ALG	PTG	MAJ	LTL	ISM	HON	COO	GOP	LIQ	TSR	OES	FAT	RAT
CPD	ROD	NNE	AUG	PUG	OBJ	MAL	JAM	HUN	CPO	GYP	LOQ	UAR	OFS	FET	RCT
CUD	SAD	ODE	AVG	QMG	ACK	MIL	LAM	INN	CWO	HAP	PDQ	VAR	OTS	FIT	RET
DAD	SGD	OLE	BAG	RAG	ALK	MOL	LCM	ION	CYO	HEP	REQ	WAR	PAS	FOT	ROT
DID	SJD	ONE	BEG	REG	ARK	MSL	LEM	JAN	DLO	HIP	SEQ	ABS	PHS	FRT	RUT
DMD	SLD	OPE	BIG	RIG	ASK	NIL	MEM	JUN	DSO	HOP	ABR	ADS	PIS	FUT	SAT
DUD	SOD	ORE	BKG	ROG	AUK	OBL	MFM	KEN	DUO	HYP	AFR	ANS	POS	GCT	SET
END	STD	OWE	BOG	RPG	AWK	OIL	MOM	KIN	EGO	IHP	AGR	ASS	PUS	GET	SGT
ESD	THD	PIE	BUG	RUG	BLK	OWL	MUM	LAN	FAO	IMP	AIR	AUS	RES	GMT	SHT
ETD	TID	POE	CHG	SAG	CLK	PAL	NOM	LIN	FIO	INP	APR	BBS	RPS	GOT	SIT
FAD	VFD	PTE	COG	SIG	ELK	PEL	NUM	LPN	FPO	JAP	ARR	BCS	SOS	GUT	SKT
FED	WAD	QUE	CTG	SSG	ILK	POL	OEM	MAN	FRO	KIP	BAR	BKS	SSS	HAT	SOT

SST	FEW	TAX	DMZ
TAT	GAW	TEX	DOZ
TIT	HAW	TWX	FEZ
TKT	HEW	VAX	GAZ
TNT	HOW	VEX	MHZ
TOT	IWW	WAX	VIZ
ULT	JAW	ANY	
UMT	JEW	BAY	
VAT	LAW	BEY	
VDT	LOW	BOY	
VET	MAW	BUY	
WET	MEW	CAY	
WIT	MOW	COY	
YET	NEW	CRY	
BTU	NNW	DAY	
CLU	NOW	DRY	
CPU	NSW	ETY	
DAU	PAW	FAY	
EMU	PEW	FCY	
FLU	POW	FEY	
GNU	RAW	FLY	
IOU	ROW	FRY	
LEU	SAW	GAY	
USU	SEW	GUY	
VOU	SOW	HAY	
YOU	SSW	HVY	
ADV	TAW	HWY	
ARV	TOW	ICY	
ASV	VFW	IGY	
CAV	VOW	IVY	
CIV	WNW	JAY	
DEV	WOW	JOY	
DIV	WSW	KEY	
ENV	WWW	LAY	
ETV	YAW	MAY	
GOV	YEW	NAY	
INV	AUX	PAY	
JUV	BOX	PLY	
KJV	FAX	PRY	
LEV	FIX	QTY	
MEV	FOX	RAY	
NAV	HEX	RWY	
NCV	LAX	SAY	
NEV	LOX	SHY	
NOV	MAX	SKY	
OBV	MEX	SLY	
PTV	MIX	SOY	
REV	NIX	SPY	
RIV	PBX	STY	
RSV	PCX	TDY	
WAV	PIX	THY	
BOW	POX	TOY	
CAW	PYX	TRY	
CBW	REX	WAY	
CCW	SEX	WHY	
COW	SIX	WRY	
DEW	SOX	ADZ	

4

LETTER WORDS

1ST LETTER	AMMO	BABY	BEST	BOSH	CALM	CLAM	CONT	CYME	DIDO	DRUG	ENGR	FEET
ABBE	AMOK	BACK	BEVY	BOSS	CAME	CLAN	CONY	CYST	DIET	DRUM	ENVY	FELL
ABBR	ANAL	BADE	BIAS	BOTH	CAMP	CLAP	COOK	CZAR	DIKE	DUAL	EPEE	FELT
ABED	ANAT	BAHT	BIDE	BOUT	CANC	CLAW	COOL	DACE	DILL	DUCK	EPIC	FEND
ABET	ANEW	BAIL	BIER	BOWL	CANE	CLAY	COON	DADA	DIME	DUCT	ERGO	FEPC
ABLE	ANKH	BAIT	BIKE	BPOE	CANT	CLEF	COOP	DAFT	DINE	DUDE	ERIE	FERN
ABUT	ANON	BAKE	BILE	BRAD	CAPE	CLEW	COOT	DAIS	DINT	DUEL	ERST	FETE
ACAD	ANSI	BALD	BILK	BRAE	CAPS	CLIP	COPE	DALE	DIRE	DUET	ESDI	FEUD
ACCT	ANTE	BALE	BILL	BRAG	CAPT	CLOD	COPY	DAME	DIRK	DUKE	ESPY	FIAT
ACHE	ANTI	BALK	BIND	BRAN	CARD	CLOG	CORD	DAMN	DIRT	DULL	ESTH	FICA
ACHY	ANUS	BALL	BIOG	BRAT	CARE	CLOP	CORE	DAMP	DISC	DULY	ETCH	FIDO
ACID	APEX	BALM	BIOL	BRAY	CARP	CLOT	CORK	DANE	DISH	DUMA	EVAP	FIEF
ACME	APPL	BAND	BIOS	BREW	CART	CLOY	CORM	DANK	DISK	DUMB	EVEN	FIFE
ACNE	APPT	BANE	BIRD	BRIG	CASE	CLUB	CORN	DARE	DIST	DUMP	EVER	FIFO
ACRE	APSE	BANG	BITE	BRIM	CASH	CLUE	CORP	DARK	DIVA	DUNE	EVIL	FILE
ACTG	AQUA	BANK	BKGD	BRIO	CASK	CMDG	CORR	DARN	DIVE	DUNG	EWER	FILL
ACTH	ARAB	BARB	BLAB	BRIT	CAST	CMDR	COST	DART	DOCK	DUNK	EXAM	FILM
ADDN	ARCH	BARD	BLDG	BROS	CATV	CMYK	COSY	DASH	DODO	DUPE	EXCH	FILS
ADVT	AREA	BARE	BLDR	BROW	CAUL	COAL	COTE	DATA	DOER	DUSK	EXEC	FIND
AEON	ARIA	BARK	BLEW	BSKT	CAVE	COAT	COUP	DATE	DOES	DUST	EXIT	FINE
AERO	ARID	BARN	BLIP	BTRY	CAVY	COAX	COVE	DAUB	DOFF	DUTY	EXOD	FINK
AERY	ARIZ	BART	BLOB	BUBO	CCTV	COCK	COWL	DAWN	DOGE	DYKE	EXOR	FINN
AFAR	ARMY	BASE	BLOC	BUCK	CEDE	COCO	COZY	DAZE	DOLE	EACH	EXPO	FIRE
AFFT	ARTY	BASH	BLOT	BUFF	CEDI	CODA	CPFF	DEAD	DOLL	EARL	EXPT	FIRM
AFRO	ARUM	BASK	BLOW	BULB	CELL	CODE	CPOM	DEAF	DOLT	EARN	EZEK	FISH
AGAR	ASHY	BASS	BLUE	BULK	CELT	COED	CPOS	DEAL	DOME	EAST	FACE	FIST
AGCY	ASIC	BAST	BLUR	BULL	CENT	COHO	CRAB	DEAN	DONA	EASY	FACT	FIVE
AGED	ASPI	BATE	BLVD	BUMP	CERT	COIF	CRAG	DEAR	DONE	ECCL	FADE	FIZZ
AGOG	ASSN	BATH	BOAR	BUNG	CHAM	COIL	CRAM	DEBT	DONG	ECHO	FADM	FLAB
AGUE	ASSR	BAUD	BOAT	BUNK	CHAP	COIN	CREE	DECK	DOOM	ECOL	FAIL	FLAG
AHOY	ASST	BAWD	BOCK	BUNT	CHAR	COKE	CREW	DEED	DOOR	ECON	FAIN	FLAK
AIDE	ATOM	BAWL	BODE	BUOY	CHAT	COLA	CRIB	DEEM	DOPA	ECRU	FAIR	FLAP
AINU	ATOP	BDRM	BODY	BURL	CHEF	COLD	CRIT	DEEP	DOPE	ECUA	FAKE	FLAT
AIRY	ATTN	BEAD	BOER	BURN	CHEM	COLL	CROP	DEER	DORM	EDAM	FALL	FLAW
AJAR	ATTY	BEAK	BOIL	BURP	CHEW	COLO	CROW	DEFT	DORY	EDDY	FAME	FLAX
AKIN	AULD	BEAM	BOLA	BURR	CHIC	COLT	CRUX	DEFY	DOSE	EDEN	FANE	FLAY
ALEE	AUNT	BEAN	BOLD	BURY	CHIN	COMA	CSSR	DELE	DOTE	EDGE	FANG	FLEA
ALGA	AURA	BEAR	BOLE	BUSH	CHIP	COMB	CTRL	DELI	DOUR	EDGY	FARE	FLEE
ALLY	AUTH	BEAT	BOLL	BUSS	CHIT	COME	CUBE	DELL	DOVE	EDIT	FARM	FLEM
ALMS	AUTO	BEAU	BOLO	BUST	CHON	COML	CUFF	DELY	DOWN	EDUC	FAST	FLEW
ALOE	AVDP	BECK	BOLT	BUSY	CHOP	COMM	CUKE	DENT	DOZE	EGIS	FATE	FLEX
ALSO	AVER	BEEF	BOMB	BUTT	CHOW	COMP	CULL	DENY	DRAB	EISA	FATH	FLIP
ALTA	AVID	BEEN	BOND	BUZZ	CHUB	COMR	CULT	DEPR	DRAG	ELAN	FAUN	FLIT
ALTO	AVOW	BEER	BONE	BYTE	CHUG	CONC	CURB	DEPT	DRAM	ELEC	FAWN	FLOE
ALUM	AWAY	BEET	BOOK	CAFE	CHUM	CONE	CURD	DESK	DRAW	ELEM	FAZE	FLOG
AMAH	AWOL	BELG	BOOM	CAGE	CIAO	CONF	CURE	DEUT	DRAY	ELSE	FEAR	FLOP
AMDT	AWRY	BELL	BOON	CAKE	CICS	CONG	CURL	DHOW	DREG	EMER	FEAT	FLOW
AMEN	AXIS	BELT	BOOR	CALC	CISC	CONJ	CURT	DIAG	DREW	EMIR	FEDN	FLUB
AMER	AXLE	BEND	BOOT	CALF	CITE	CONK	CUSP	DIAL	DRIP	EMIT	FEED	FLUE
AMID	AYAH	BENT	BORE	CALK	CITY	CONN	CUTE	DICE	DROP	ENCY	FEEL	FLUX
	BABE	BERG	BORN	CALL	CLAD	CONS	CYAN	DICT	DRUB			FOAL

FOAM	GATT	GREP	HEFT	HULA	JEEP	KISS	LEND	LOOP	MATT	MIXT	NARD	OKRA
FOGY	GAUD	GREW	HEIR	HULK	JEER	KITE	LENS	LOOT	MAUL	MKTG	NASA	OLEO
FOIL	GAVE	GREY	HELD	HULL	JEHU	KITH	LENT	LOPE	MAXI	MLLE	NATL	OLIO
FOLD	GAWK	GRID	HELL	HUMP	JELL	KIWI	LESS	LORD	MAYA	MOAN	NATO	OMEN
FOLK	GAZE	GRIM	HELM	HUNG	JERK	KNEE	LEST	LORE	MAZE	MOAT	NAUT	OMIT
FOND	GEAR	GRIN	HELP	HUNK	JESS	KNEW	LETT	LORN	MCGA	MOCK	NAVE	ONCE
FONT	GELD	GRIP	HEME	HUNT	JEST	KNIT	LEVY	LOSE	MCPO	MODE	NAVY	ONLY
FOOD	GENE	GRIT	HEMP	HURL	JIBE	KNOB	LEWD	LOSS	MDNT	MOIL	NAZI	ONTO
FOOL	GENL	GROG	HERB	HURT	JILT	KNOT	LIAR	LOST	MDSE	MOLD	NDEA	ONUS
FOOT	GENS	GROT	HERD	HUSH	JINX	KNOW	LICE	LOTH	MEAD	MOLE	NEAP	ONYX
FORA	GENT	GROW	HERE	HUSK	JIVE	KOBO	LICK	LOUD	MEAL	MOLL	NEAR	OOZE
FORD	GEOG	GRUB	HERO	HYMN	JOHN	KOCH	LIDO	LOUR	MEAN	MOLT	NEAT	OPAL
FORE	GEOL	GULF	HERS	HYPE	JOIN	KOOK	LIED	LOUT	MEAS	MOLY	NECK	OPEN
FORK	GEOM	GULL	HGWY	HYPO	JOKE	KUDO	LIEF	LOVE	MEAT	MONK	NEED	OPER
FORM	GERM	GULP	HICK	IAMB	JOLT	KYAT	LIEN	LTJG	MECH	MONO	NEON	OPUS
FORT	GHAT	GURU	HIDE	IBEX	JOSH	LACE	LIEU	LUAU	MEED	MONT	NEST	ORAL
FOUL	GIBE	GUSH	HIGH	IBIS	JOSS	LACK	LIFE	LUBE	MEEK	MOOD	NETH	ORCH
FOUR	GIFT	GUST	HIKE	ICBM	JOUR	LADY	LIFO	LUCK	MEET	MOON	NEUT	OREG
FOWL	GILD	GYRO	HILL	ICKY	JOWL	LAID	LIFT	LUFF	MELD	MOOR	NEWS	ORGY
FOXY	GILL	GYVE	HILT	ICON	JPEG	LAIN	LIKE	LULL	MELT	MOOT	NEWT	ORIG
FRAY	GILT	HACK	HIND	IDEA	JUDG	LAIR	LILT	LUMP	MEMO	MOPE	NEXT	OURS
FREE	GIRD	HAFT	HINT	IDEM	JUDO	LAKE	LILY	LUNG	MEND	MORE	NFLD	OUST
FREQ	GIRL	HAIL	HIRE	IDES	JULY	LAMA	LIMB	LURE	MENU	MORN	NICA	OUZO
FRET	GIST	HAIR	HISS	IDLE	JUMP	LAMB	LIME	LURK	MEOW	MOSS	NICE	OVAL
FROG	GIVE	HAKE	HIST	IDOL	JUNC	LAME	LIMN	LUSH	MERE	MOST	NICK	OVEN
FROM	GLAD	HALE	HIVE	IFFY	JUNE	LAMP	LIMP	LUST	MESA	MOTE	NIGH	OVER
FRWY	GLEE	HALF	HOAX	IKON	JUNK	LAND	LINE	LUTE	MESH	MOTH	NINE	OVUM
FUEL	GLEN	HALL	HOBO	IMHO	JURY	LANE	LING	LYNX	MESS	MOUE	NISI	PACE
FULL	GLIB	HALO	HOCK	IMIT	JUST	LANG	LINK	LYRE	METE	MOVE	NLRB	PACK
FUME	GLOB	HALT	HOKE	INCA	JUTE	LANK	LINT	MACE	MEWS	MPEG	NODE	PACT
FUND	GLOP	HAND	HOLD	INCH	KALE	LAPP	LION	MACH	MICA	MSEC	NOEL	PAGE
FUNK	GLOW	HANG	HOLE	INCL	KAME	LARD	LIRA	MADE	MICE	MSGR	NOES	PAID
FURL	GLUE	HANK	HOLY	INCR	KANA	LARK	LISP	MAGI	MICH	MSGT	NONE	PAIL
FURY	GLUM	HARD	HOME	INFL	KANS	LASH	LIST	MAID	MIDI	MTBF	NOOK	PAIN
FUSE	GLUT	HARE	HOMO	INFO	KART	LASS	LITH	MAIL	MIEN	MTGE	NOON	PAIR
FUSS	GNAT	HARK	HONE	INRI	KAYO	LAST	LIVE	MAIM	MIFF	MUCH	NOPE	PALE
FUZE	GNAW	HARM	HONK	INSP	KBPS	LATE	LOAD	MAIN	MIKE	MUCK	NORM	PALL
FUZZ	GOAD	HARP	HOOD	INST	KEEL	LATH	LOAF	MAKE	MILD	MUFF	NORW	PALM
FWTW	GOAL	HART	HOOF	INTL	KEEN	LAUD	LOAM	MALE	MILE	MULE	NOSE	PANE
GAEL	GOAT	HASH	HOOK	INTO	KEEP	LAVA	LOAN	MALL	MILK	MULL	NOSY	PANG
GAFF	GOLD	HASP	HOOP	IOOF	KELP	LAVE	LOBE	MALT	MILL	MURK	NOTE	PANT
GAGE	GOLF	HATE	HOOT	IOTA	KELT	LAWN	LOCH	MAMA	MILT	MUSE	NOUN	PAPA
GAIN	GONE	HAUL	HOPE	IRBM	KENO	LAZE	LOCK	MANE	MIME	MUSH	NOVA	PARA
GAIT	GONG	HAVE	HOPI	IRIS	KEPI	LAZY	LOCO	MANX	MIND	MUSK	NUDE	PARD
GALA	GOOD	HAWK	HORN	IRON	KERB	LCDR	LODE	MANY	MINE	MUSS	NULL	PARE
GALE	GOOF	HAZE	HORT	ISDN	KERF	LCPL	LOFT	MARE	MINI	MUST	NUMB	PARK
GALL	GOON	HAZY	HOSE	ISLE	KHAN	LEAD	LOGE	MARK	MINK	MUTE	NUTS	PART
GALV	GORE	HDBK	HOSP	ITAL	KICK	LEAF	LOGO	MARL	MINN	MUTT	OATH	PASS
GAME	GORY	HDKF	HOST	ITCH	KILL	LEAK	LOGY	MARS	MINT	MYNA	OBEY	PAST
GAMY	GOTH	HDWE	HOUR	ITEM	KILN	LEAL	LOIN	MART	MINX	MYTH	OBIT	PATE
GANG	GOUT	HEAD	HOVE	IWAY	KILO	LEAN	LOLL	MASC	MIPS	NAIF	OBOE	PATH
GAOL	GOVT	HEAL	HOWL	JACK	KILT	LEAP	LOND	MASH	MIRE	NAIL	ODDS	PAVE
GAPE	GOWN	HEAP	HRZN	JADE	KIND	LECT	LONE	MASK	MISC	NAME	ODOR	PAWL
GARB	GRAB	HEAR	HTML	JAIL	KINE	LEEK	LONG	MASS	MISS	NAND	OGLE	PAWN
GASH	GRAD	HEAT	HTTP	JAMB	KING	LEER	LOOK	MAST	MIST	NANO	OGRE	PAYT
GASP	GRAM	HEED	HUFF	JAPE	KINK	LEES	LOOM	MATE	MITE	NAPE	OINK	PEAK
GATE	GRAY	HEEL	HUGE	JAZZ	KIRK	LEFT	LOON	MATH	MITT	NARC	OKLA	PEAL

P	P	P	R	R	S	S	S	S	T	T	U	W
PEAR	PLUS	PUKE	REAM	ROOD	SCOT	SIKH	SOCK	SUFF	TEEM	TOPS	UPON	WADI
PEAT	PNXT	PULE	REAP	ROOF	SCOW	SILK	SODA	SUIT	TEEN	TORE	URDU	WAFT
PECK	POCK	PULL	REAR	ROOK	SCPO	SILL	SOFA	SULK	TELL	TORN	UREA	WAGE
PEEK	POCO	PULP	RECD	ROOM	SCSI	SILO	SOFT	SUNG	TEMP	TORR	URGE	WAIF
PEEL	POEM	PUMA	RECT	ROOT	SCUD	SILT	SOIL	SUNK	TEND	TORT	URIC	WAIL
PEEN	POET	PUMP	REDO	ROPE	SCUM	SINE	SOLD	SUPP	TENN	TORY	USAF	WAIN
PEEP	POKE	PUNK	REED	ROSE	SEAL	SING	SOLE	SUPT	TENT	TOSS	USCG	WAIT
PEER	POKY	PUNT	REEF	ROSY	SEAM	SINK	SOLN	SURE	TERM	TOTE	USDA	WAKE
PEKE	POLE	PUNY	REEK	ROTC	SEAR	SIRE	SOLO	SURF	TERN	TOUR	USED	WALE
PELF	POLL	PUPA	REEL	ROTE	SEAT	SITE	SOME	SURG	TERR	TOUT	USES	WALK
PELT	POLO	PURE	REFL	ROUE	SECT	SIZE	SONG	SURV	TEST	TOWN	USIA	WALL
PENN	POMP	PURL	REFR	ROUT	SECY	SKAG	SOON	SVGA	TEXT	TRAM	USMC	WAND
PENT	POND	PURR	REGT	ROVE	SEED	SKEW	SOOT	SVGS	THAI	TRAP	USSR	WANE
PEON	PONE	PUSH	REIN	RSVP	SEEK	SKID	SOPH	SWAB	THAN	TRAY	UUCP	WANT
PERF	PONY	PUSS	RELY	RSWC	SEEM	SKIM	SORB	SWAG	THAT	TREE	VADM	WARD
PERH	POOL	PUTT	REND	RTFM	SEEP	SKIN	SORE	SWAM	THAW	TREK	VAIL	WARE
PERK	POOP	PYRE	RENT	RUBY	SEER	SKIP	SORT	SWAN	THEE	TREY	VAIN	WARM
PERM	POOR	QUAD	REPL	RUDE	SELF	SKIT	SOUL	SWAP	THEM	TRIB	VALE	WARN
PERP	POPE	QUAI	REPT	RUFF	SELL	SLAB	SOUP	SWAT	THEN	TRIG	VAMP	WARP
PERS	PORE	QUAY	RESP	RUIN	SEND	SLAG	SOUR	SWAY	THEW	TRIM	VANE	WART
PERT	PORK	QUID	REST	RULE	SENE	SLAM	SPAN	SWED	THEY	TRIO	VARY	WARY
PESO	PORT	QUIP	RETD	RUMP	SENT	SLAN	SPAR	SWIG	THIN	TRIP	VASE	WASH
PEST	POSE	QUIT	REXX	RUNE	SEPN	SLAP	SPAT	SWIM	THIS	TROD	VAST	WASP
PHIL	POSH	QUIZ	RHEA	RUNG	SEPT	SLAT	SPAY	SWUM	THOU	TROT	VEAL	WATS
PHON	POSS	QUOT	RIAL	RUNT	SEQQ	SLAV	SPCA	SYNC	THUD	TROW	VEDA	WATT
PHYS	POST	RAAF	RICE	RUSE	SERA	SLAW	SPCC	SYST	THUG	TROY	VEEP	WAVE
PICA	POSY	RACE	RICH	RUSH	SERB	SLAY	SPEC	TACH	THUS	TRUE	VEER	WAVY
PICE	POUR	RACK	RICK	RUSK	SERE	SLED	SPEW	TACK	TICK	TSAR	VEIL	WAXY
PICK	POUT	RACY	RIDE	RUSS	SERF	SLEW	SPIN	TACO	TIDE	TSGT	VEIN	WCTU
PICO	PPTN	RADM	RIEL	RUST	SERG	SLIM	SPIT	TACT	TIDY	TUBA	VELD	WEAK
PIED	PRAM	RAFT	RIFE	RYFM	SERV	SLIP	SPOT	TAIL	TIER	TUBE	VEND	WEAL
PIER	PRAY	RAGA	RIFF	SACK	SEXY	SLIT	SPRY	TAKA	TIFF	TUCK	VENT	WEAN
PIES	PREC	RAGE	RIFT	SAFE	SGML	SLOB	SPUD	TAKE	TILE	TUES	VERB	WEAR
PIKE	PRED	RAID	RILE	SAGA	SHAD	SLOE	SPUN	TALA	TILL	TUFA	VERT	WEED
PILE	PREF	RAIL	RILL	SAGE	SHAG	SLOP	SPUR	TALC	TILT	TUFF	VERY	WEEK
PILL	PREM	RAIN	RIME	SAGO	SHAH	SLOT	STAB	TALE	TIME	TUFT	VESA	WEEN
PIMP	PREP	RAJA	RIND	SAID	SHAK	SLOW	STAG	TALK	TINE	TUNA	VEST	WEEP
PINE	PRES	RAKE	RING	SAIL	SHAM	SLUE	STAR	TALL	TINT	TUNE	VETO	WEFT
PING	PREV	RAMP	RINK	SAKE	SHED	SLUG	STAT	TAME	TINY	TURF	VIAL	WEIR
PINK	PREY	RAND	RIOT	SALE	SHEW	SLUM	STAY	TAMP	TIRE	TURK	VICE	WELD
PINT	PRIG	RANG	RIPE	SALT	SHIM	SLUR	STBD	TANG	TNPK	TURN	VIDE	WELL
PINX	PRIM	RANI	RISC	SAME	SHIN	SLUT	STEM	TANK	TOAD	TUSK	VIEW	WELT
PIPE	PRIN	RANK	RISE	SAND	SHIP	SMAJ	STEP	TAPE	TOGA	TWIG	VILE	WEND
PITH	PROB	RANT	RISK	SANE	SHIV	SMOG	STER	TAPS	TOGS	TWIN	VINE	WENT
PITY	PROC	RAPE	RITE	SANG	SHOE	SMTP	STEW	TARE	TOIL	TWIT	VIOL	WEPT
PKWY	PROD	RAPT	RIVE	SANK	SHOP	SMUG	STIR	TARN	TOKE	TYKE	VISA	WERE
PLAN	PROF	RARE	ROAD	SANS	SHOT	SMUT	STOL	TARO	TOLD	TYPE	VISE	WEST
PLAT	PROM	RASH	ROAM	SARI	SHOW	SNAG	STOP	TART	TOLE	TYPO	VITA	WHAT
PLAY	PRON	RASP	ROAN	SASH	SHPT	SNAP	STOW	TASK	TOLL	TYRO	VIVA	WHEN
PLEA	PROP	RATE	ROAR	SASK	SHTG	SNIP	STUB	TAUT	TOMB	TZAR	VLSI	WHET
PLOD	PROS	RAVE	ROBE	SATE	SHUN	SNOB	STUD	TAXI	TOME	UGLY	VOID	WHEY
PLOP	PROT	RAZE	ROCK	SAVE	SHUT	SNOW	STUN	TEAK	TONE	ULNA	VOLE	WHIG
PLOT	PROV	RAZZ	RODE	SCAB	SICK	SNUB	SUBJ	TEAL	TONG	UNDO	VOLT	WHIM
PLOW	PROW	RCAF	ROIL	SCAD	SIDE	SNUG	SUCH	TEAM	TOOK	UNIT	VOTE	WHIP
PLOY	PUBL	RCMP	ROLE	SCAN	SIFT	SOAK	SUCK	TEAR	TOOL	UNIV	VTOL	WHIR
PLUG	PUCK	READ	ROLL	SCAR	SIGH	SOAP	SUDS	TEAT	TOOT	UNIX	VULG	WHIT
PLUM	PUFF	REAL	ROMP	SCIL	SIGN	SOAR	SUET	TECH	TOPE	UNTO	WADE	WHIZ

WHOM	YMCA	BARN	DAUB	HALE	LATH	PACK	SAGA	WAIF	ECHO	BEAR	FEUD	LEFT
WICK	YMHA	BART	DAWN	HALF	LAUD	PACT	SAGE	WAIL	ECOL	BEAT	GEAR	LEND
WIDE	YMMV	BASE	DAZE	HALL	LAVA	PAGE	SAGO	WAIN	ECON	BEAU	GELD	LENS
WIFE	YOGA	BASH	EACH	HALO	LAVE	PAID	SAID	WAIT	ECRU	BECK	GENE	LENT
WILD	YOGI	BASK	EARL	HALT	LAWN	PAIL	SAIL	WAKE	ECUA	BEEF	GENL	LESS
WILE	YOKE	BASS	EARN	HAND	LAZE	PAIN	SAKE	WALE	ICBM	BEEN	GENS	LEST
WILL	YOLK	BAST	EASE	HANG	LAZY	PAIR	SALE	WALK	ICKY	BEER	GENT	LETT
WILT	YORE	BATE	EAST	HANK	MACE	PALE	SALT	WALL	ICON	BEET	GEOG	LEVY
WILY	YOUR	BATH	EASY	HARD	MACH	PALL	SAME	WAND	LCDR	BELG	GEOL	LEWD
WIND	YOWL	BAUD	FACE	HARE	MADE	PALM	SAND	WANE	LCPL	BELL	GEOM	MEAD
WINE	YOYO	BAWD	FACT	HARK	MAGI	PANE	SANE	WANT	MCGA	BELT	GERM	MEAL
WING	YRBK	BAWL	FADE	HARM	MAID	PANG	SANG	WARD	MCPO	BEND	HEAD	MEAN
WINK	YUAN	CAFE	FADM	HARP	MAIL	PANT	SANK	WARE	RCAF	BENT	HEAL	MEAS
WINO	YULE	CAGE	FAIL	HART	MAIM	PAPA	SANS	WARM	RCMP	BERG	HEAP	MEAT
WIPE	YURT	CAKE	FAIN	HASH	MAIN	PARA	SARI	WARN	SCAB	BEST	HEAR	MECH
WIRE	YWCA	CALC	FAIR	HASP	MAKE	PARD	SASH	WARP	SCAD	BEVY	HEAT	MEED
WIRY	YWHA	CALF	FAKE	HATE	MALE	PARE	SASK	WART	SCAN	CEDE	HEED	MEEK
WISD	ZANY	CALK	FALL	HAUL	MALL	PARK	SATE	WARY	SCAR	CEDI	HEEL	MEET
WISE	ZEAL	CALL	FAME	HAVE	MALT	PART	SAVE	WASH	SCIL	CELL	HEFT	MELD
WISH	ZEBU	CALM	FANE	HAWK	MAMA	PASS	TACH	WASP	SCOT	CELT	HEIR	MELT
WISP	ZECH	CAME	FANG	HAZE	MANE	PAST	TACK	WATS	SCOW	CENT	HELD	MEMO
WITH	ZEPH	CAMP	FARE	HAZY	MANX	PATE	TACO	WATT	SCPO	CERT	HELL	MEND
WIVE	ZERO	CANC	FARM	IAMB	MANY	PATH	TACT	WAVE	SCSI	DEAD	HELM	MENU
WOAD	ZEST	CANE	FAST	JACK	MARE	PAVE	TAIL	WAVY	SCUD	DEAF	HELP	MEOW
WOKE	ZINC	CANT	FATE	JADE	MARK	PAWL	TAKA	WAXY	SCUM	DEAL	HEME	MERE
WOLD	ZING	CAPE	FATH	JAIL	MARL	PAWN	TAKE	YANK	WCTU	DEAN	HEMP	MESA
WOLF	ZION	CAPS	FAUN	JAMB	MARS	PAYT	TALA	YARD	ADDN	DEAR	HERB	MESH
WOMB	ZONE	CAPT	FAWN	JAPE	MART	RAAF	TALC	YARN	ADVT	DEBT	HERD	MESS
WONT	ZOOL	CARD	FAZE	JAZZ	MASC	RACE	TALE	YAWL	BDRM	DECK	HERE	METE
WOOD	ZOOM	CARE	GAEL	KALE	MASH	RACK	TALK	YAWN	EDAM	DEED	HERO	MEWS
WOOF	ZUNI	CARP	GAFF	KAME	MASK	RACY	TALL	YAWP	EDDY	DEEM	HERS	NEAP
WOOL		CART	GAGE	KANA	MASS	RADM	TAME	YAWS	EDEN	DEEP	JEEP	NEAR
WORD		CASE	GAIN	KANS	MAST	RAFT	TAMP	ZANY	EDGE	DEER	JEER	NEAT
WORE		CASH	GAIT	KART	MATE	RAGA	TANG	ABBE	EDGY	DEFT	JEHU	NECK
WORK	**2ND**	CASK	GALA	KAYO	MATH	RAGE	TANK	ABBR	EDIT	DEFY	JELL	NEED
WORM	**LETTER**	CAST	GALE	LACE	MATT	RAID	TAPE	ABED	EDUC	DELE	JERK	NEON
WORN	BABE	CATV	GALL	LACK	MAUL	RAIL	TAPS	ABET	FDIC	DELI	JESS	NEST
WORT	BABY	CAUL	GALV	LADY	MAXI	RAIN	TARE	ABLE	HDBK	DELL	JEST	NETH
WOVE	BACK	CAVE	GAME	LAID	MAYA	RAJA	TARN	ABUT	HDKF	DELY	KEEL	NEUT
WRAP	BADE	CAVY	GAMY	LAIN	MAZE	RAKE	TARO	IBEX	HDWE	DENT	KEEN	NEWS
WREN	BAHT	DACE	GANG	LAIR	NAIF	RAMP	TART	IBIS	IDEA	DENY	KEEP	NEWT
WRIT	BAIL	DADA	GAOL	LAKE	NAIL	RAND	TASK	KBPS	IDEM	DEPR	KELP	NEXT
WRNT	BAIT	DAFT	GAPE	LAMA	NAME	RANG	TAUT	OBEY	IDES	DEPT	KELT	PEAK
XMAS	BAKE	DAIS	GARB	LAMB	NAND	RANI	TAXI	OBIT	IDLE	DESK	KENO	PEAL
XNTY	BALD	DALE	GASH	LAME	NANO	RANK	VADM	OBOE	IDOL	DEUT	KEPI	PEAR
YANK	BALE	DAME	GASP	LAMP	NAPE	RANT	VAIL	ACAD	MDNT	FEAR	KERB	PEAT
YARD	BALK	DAMN	GATE	LAND	NARC	RAPE	VAIN	ACCT	MDSE	FEAT	KERF	PECK
YARN	BALL	DAMP	GATT	LANE	NARD	RAPT	VALE	ACHE	NDEA	FEDN	LEAD	PEEK
YAWL	BALM	DANE	GAUD	LANG	NASA	RARE	VAMP	ACHY	ODDS	FEED	LEAF	PEEL
YAWN	BAND	DANK	GAVE	LANK	NATL	RASH	VANE	ACID	ODOR	FEEL	LEAK	PEEN
YAWP	BANE	DARE	GAWK	LAPP	NATO	RASP	VARY	ACME	AEON	FEET	LEAL	PEEP
YAWS	BANG	DARK	GAZE	LARD	NAUT	RATE	VASE	ACNE	AERO	FELL	LEAN	PEER
YEAR	BANK	DARN	HACK	LARK	NAVE	RAVE	VAST	ACRE	AERY	FELT	LEAP	PEKE
YEGG	BARB	DART	HAFT	LASH	NAVY	RAZE	WADE	ACTG	BEAD	FEND	LECT	PELF
YELL	BARD	DASH	HAIL	LASS	NAZI	RAZZ	WADI	ACTH	BEAK	FEPC	LEEK	PELT
YELP	BARE	DATA	HAIR	LAST	OATH	SACK	WAFT	CCTV	BEAM	FERN	LEER	PENN
YETI	BARK	DATE	HAKE	LATE	PACE	SAFE	WAGE	ECCL	BEAN	FETE	LEES	PENT

PEON	SERF	YELL	SHIM	CITE	HILT	MIEN	RIFF	WIFE	BLUR	OLIO	SMOG	UNTO
PERF	SERG	YELP	SHIN	CITY	HIND	MIFF	RIFT	WILD	BLVD	PLAN	SMTP	XNTY
PERH	SERV	YETI	SHIP	DIAG	HINT	MIKE	RILE	WILE	CLAD	PLAT	SMUG	BOAR
PERK	SEXY	ZEAL	SHIV	DIAL	HIRE	MILD	RILL	WILL	CLAM	PLAY	SMUT	BOAT
PERM	TEAK	ZEBU	SHOE	DICE	HISS	MILE	RIME	WILT	CLAN	PLEA	XMAS	BOCK
PERP	TEAL	ZECH	SHOP	DICT	HIST	MILK	RIND	WILY	CLAP	PLOD	YMCA	BODE
PERS	TEAM	ZEPH	SHOT	DIDO	HIVE	MILL	RING	WIND	CLAW	PLOP	YMHA	BODY
PERT	TEAR	ZERO	SHOW	DIET	JIBE	MILT	RINK	WINE	CLAY	PLOT	YMMV	BOER
PESO	TEAT	ZEST	SHPT	DIKE	JILT	MIME	RIOT	WING	CLEF	PLOW	ANAL	BOIL
PEST	TECH	AFAR	SHTG	DILL	JINX	MIND	RIPE	WINK	CLEW	PLOY	ANAT	BOLA
READ	TEEM	AFFT	SHUN	DIME	JIVE	MINE	RISC	WINO	CLIP	PLUG	ANEW	BOLD
REAL	TEEN	AFRO	SHUT	DINE	KICK	MINI	RISE	WIPE	CLOD	PLUM	ANKH	BOLE
REAM	TELL	IFFY	THAI	DINT	KILL	MINK	RISK	WIRE	CLOG	PLUS	ANON	BOLL
REAP	TEMP	NFLD	THAN	DIRE	KILN	MINN	RITE	WIRY	CLOP	SLAB	ANSI	BOLO
REAR	TEND	AGAR	THAT	DIRK	KILO	MINT	RIVE	WISD	CLOT	SLAG	ANTE	BOLT
RECD	TENN	AGCY	THAW	DIRT	KILT	MINX	SICK	WISE	CLOY	SLAM	ANTI	BOMB
RECT	TENT	AGED	THEE	DISC	KIND	MIPS	SIDE	WISH	CLUB	SLAN	ANUS	BOND
REDO	TERM	AGOG	THEM	DISH	KINE	MIRE	SIFT	WISP	CLUE	SLAP	ENCY	BONE
REED	TERN	AGUE	THEN	DISK	KING	MISC	SIGH	WITH	ELAN	SLAT	ENGR	BOOK
REEF	TERR	EGIS	THEW	DIST	KINK	MISS	SIGN	WIVE	ELEC	SLAV	ENVY	BOOM
REEK	TEST	HGWY	THEY	DIVA	KIRK	MIST	SIKH	ZINC	ELEM	SLAW	GNAT	BOON
REEL	TEXT	OGLE	THIN	DIVE	KISS	MITE	SILK	ZING	ELSE	SLAY	GNAW	BOOR
REFL	VEAL	OGRE	THIS	EISA	KITE	MITT	SILL	ZION	FLAB	SLED	INCA	BOOT
REFR	VEDA	SGML	THOU	FIAT	KITH	MIXT	SILO	AJAR	FLAG	SLEW	INCH	BORE
REGT	VEEP	UGLY	THUD	FICA	KIWI	NICA	SILT	AKIN	FLAK	SLIM	INCL	BORN
REIN	VEER	AHOY	THUG	FIDO	LIAR	NICE	SINE	BKGD	FLAP	SLIP	INCR	BOSH
RELY	VEIL	CHAM	THUS	FIEF	LICE	NICK	SING	IKON	FLAT	SLIT	INFL	BOSS
REND	VEIN	CHAP	WHAT	FIFE	LICK	NIGH	SINK	MKTG	FLAW	SLOB	INFO	BOTH
RENT	VELD	CHAR	WHEN	FIFO	LIDO	NINE	SIRE	OKLA	FLAX	SLOE	INRI	BOUT
REPL	VEND	CHAT	WHET	FILE	LIED	NISI	SITE	OKRA	FLAY	SLOP	INSP	BOWL
REPT	VENT	CHEF	WHEY	FILL	LIEF	OINK	SIZE	PKWY	FLEA	SLOT	INST	COAL
RESP	VERB	CHEM	WHIG	FILM	LIEN	PICA	TICK	SKAG	FLEE	SLOW	INTL	COAT
REST	VERT	CHEW	WHIM	FILS	LIEU	PICE	TIDE	SKEW	FLEM	SLUE	INTO	COAX
RETD	VERY	CHIC	WHIP	FIND	LIFE	PICK	TIDY	SKID	FLEW	SLUG	KNEE	COCK
REXX	VESA	CHIN	WHIR	FINE	LIFO	PICO	TIER	SKIM	FLEX	SLUM	KNEW	COCO
SEAL	VEST	CHIP	WHIT	FINK	LIFT	PIED	TIFF	SKIN	FLIP	SLUR	KNIT	CODA
SEAM	VETO	CHIT	WHIZ	FINN	LIKE	PIER	TILE	SKIP	FLIT	SLUT	KNOB	CODE
SEAR	WEAK	CHON	WHOM	FIRE	LILT	PIES	TILL	SKIT	FLOE	ULNA	KNOT	COED
SEAT	WEAL	CHOP	AIDE	FIRM	LILY	PIKE	TILT	ALEE	FLOG	VLSI	KNOW	COHO
SECT	WEAN	CHOW	AINU	FISH	LIMB	PILE	TIME	ALGA	FLOP	AMAH	ONCE	COIF
SECY	WEAR	CHUB	AIRY	FIST	LIME	PILL	TINE	ALLY	FLOW	AMDT	ONLY	COIL
SEED	WEED	CHUG	BIAS	FIVE	LIMN	PIMP	TINT	ALMS	FLUB	AMEN	ONTO	COIN
SEEK	WEEK	CHUM	BIDE	FIZZ	LIMP	PINE	TINY	ALOE	FLUE	AMER	ONUS	COKE
SEEM	WEEN	DHOW	BIER	GIBE	LINE	PING	TIRE	ALSO	FLUX	AMID	ONYX	COLA
SEEP	WEEP	GHAT	BIKE	GIFT	LING	PINK	VIAL	ALTA	GLAD	AMMO	PNXT	COLD
SEER	WEFT	KHAN	BILE	GILD	LINK	PINT	VICE	ALTO	GLEE	AMOK	SNAG	COLL
SELF	WEIR	PHIL	BILK	GILL	LINT	PINX	VIDE	ALUM	GLIB	CMDG	SNAP	COLO
SELL	WELD	PHON	BILL	GILT	LION	PIPE	VIEW	BLAB	GLEN	CMDR	SNIP	COLT
SEND	WELL	PHYS	BIND	GIRD	LIRA	PITH	VILE	BLDG	GLOB	CMYK	SNOB	COMA
SENE	WELT	RHEA	BIOG	GIRL	LISP	PITY	VINE	BLDR	GLOP	EMER	SNOW	COMB
SENT	WEND	SHAD	BIOL	GIST	LIST	RIAL	VIOL	BLEW	GLOW	EMIR	SNUB	COME
SEPN	WENT	SHAG	BIOS	GIVE	LITH	RICE	VISA	BLIP	GLUE	EMIT	SNUG	COML
SEPT	WEPT	SHAH	BIRD	HICK	LIVE	RICH	VISE	BLOB	GLUM	IMHO	TNPK	COMM
SEQQ	WERE	SHAK	BITE	HIDE	MICA	RICK	VITA	BLOC	GLUT	IMIT	UNDO	COMP
SERA	WEST	SHAM	CIAO	HIGH	MICE	RIDE	VIVA	BLOT	MLLE	OMEN	UNIT	COMR
SERB	YEAR	SHED	CICS	HIKE	MICH	RIEL	WICK	BLOW	NLRB	OMIT	UNIV	CONC
SERE	YEGG	SHEW	CISC	HILL	MIDI	RIFE	WIDE	BLUE	OLEO	SMAJ	UNIX	CONE

CONF	FOIL	HOUR	MOLE	POSS	TOLD	BPOE	CRIB	PREM	MSEC	BULB	FUSE	MUTE
CONG	FOLD	HOVE	MOLL	POST	TOLE	CPFF	CRIT	PREP	MSGR	BULK	FUSS	MUTT
CONJ	FOLK	HOWL	MOLT	POSY	TOLL	CPOM	CROP	PRES	MSGT	BULL	FUZE	NUDE
CONK	FOND	IOOF	MOLY	POUR	TOMB	CPOS	CROW	PREV	RSVP	BUMP	FUZZ	NULL
CONN	FONT	IOTA	MONK	POUT	TOME	EPEE	CRUX	PREY	RSWC	BUNG	GULF	NUMB
CONS	FOOD	JOHN	MONO	ROAD	TONE	EPIC	DRAB	PRIG	TSAR	BUNK	GULL	NUTS
CONT	FOOL	JOIN	MONT	ROAM	TONG	JPEG	DRAG	PRIM	TSGT	BUNT	GULP	OURS
CONY	FOOT	JOKE	MOOD	ROAN	TOOK	MPEG	DRAM	PRIN	USAF	BUOY	GURU	OUST
COOK	FORA	JOLT	MOON	ROAR	TOOL	OPAL	DRAW	PROB	USCG	BURL	GUSH	OUZO
COOL	FORD	JOSH	MOOR	ROBE	TOOT	OPEN	DRAY	PROC	USDA	BURN	GUST	PUBL
COON	FORE	JOSS	MOOT	ROCK	TOPE	OPER	DREG	PROD	USED	BURP	HUFF	PUCK
COOP	FORK	JOUR	MOPE	RODE	TOPS	OPUS	DREW	PROF	USES	BURR	HUGE	PUFF
COOT	FORM	JOWL	MORE	ROIL	TORE	PPTN	DRIP	PROM	USIA	BURY	HULA	PUKE
COPE	FORT	KOBO	MORN	ROLE	TORN	SPAN	DROP	PRON	USMC	BUSH	HULK	PULE
COPY	FOUL	KOCH	MOSS	ROLL	TORR	SPAR	DRUB	PROP	USSR	BUSS	HULL	PULL
CORD	FOUR	KOOK	MOST	ROMP	TORT	SPAT	DRUG	PROS	ATOM	BUST	HUMP	PULP
CORE	FOWL	LOAD	MOTE	ROOD	TORY	SPAY	DRUM	PROT	ATOP	BUSY	HUNG	PUMA
CORK	FOXY	LOAF	MOTH	ROOF	TOSS	SPCA	ERGO	PROV	ATTN	BUTT	HUNK	PUMP
CORM	GOAD	LOAM	MOUE	ROOK	TOTE	SPCC	ERIE	PROW	ATTY	BUZZ	HURL	PUNK
CORN	GOAL	LOAN	MOVE	ROOM	TOUR	SPEC	ERST	TRAM	BTRY	CUBE	HURT	PUNT
CORP	GOAT	LOBE	MOWN	ROOT	TOUT	SPEW	FRAY	TRAP	CTRL	CUFF	HUSH	PUNY
CORR	GOLD	LOCH	NODE	ROPE	TOWN	SPIN	FREE	TRAY	ETCH	CUKE	HUSK	PUPA
COST	GOLF	LOCK	NOEL	ROSE	TOYS	SPIT	FREQ	TREE	HTML	CULL	JUDG	PURE
COSY	GONE	LOCO	NOES	ROSY	VOID	SPOT	FRET	TREK	HTTP	CULT	JUDO	PURL
COTE	GONG	LODE	NONE	ROTC	VOLE	SPRY	FROG	TREY	ITAL	CURB	JULY	PURR
COUP	GOOD	LOFT	NOOK	ROTE	VOLT	SPUD	FROM	TRIB	ITCH	CURD	JUMP	PUSH
COVE	GOOF	LOGE	NOON	ROUE	VOTE	SPUN	FRWY	TRIG	ITEM	CURE	JUNC	PUSS
COWL	GOON	LOGO	NOPE	ROUT	WOAD	SPUR	GRAB	TRIM	LTJG	CURL	JUNE	PUTT
COZY	GORE	LOGY	NORM	ROVE	WOKE	UPON	GRAD	TRIO	MTBF	CURT	JUNK	QUAD
DOCK	GORY	LOIN	NOSE	SOAK	WOLD	AQUA	GRAM	TRIP	MTGE	CUSP	JURY	QUAI
DODO	GOTH	LOLL	NOSY	SOAP	WOLF	ARAB	GRAY	TROD	RTFM	CUTE	JUST	QUAY
DOER	GOUT	LOND	NOTE	SOAR	WOMB	ARCH	GREP	TROT	STAB	DUAL	JUTE	QUID
DOES	GOVT	LONE	NOUN	SOCK	WONT	AREA	GREW	TROW	STAG	DUCK	KUDO	QUIP
DOFF	GOWN	LONG	NOVA	SODA	WOOD	ARIA	GREY	TROY	STAR	DUCT	KUDU	QUIT
DOGE	HOAX	LOOK	OOZE	SOFA	WOOF	ARID	GRID	TRUE	STAT	DUDE	LUAU	QUIZ
DOLE	HOBO	LOOM	POCK	SOFT	WOOL	ARIZ	GRIM	URDU	STAY	DUEL	LUBE	QUOT
DOLL	HOCK	LOON	POCO	SOIL	WORD	ARMY	GRIN	UREA	STBD	DUET	LUCK	RUBY
DOLT	HOKE	LOOP	POEM	SOLD	WORE	ARTY	GRIP	URGE	STEM	DUKE	LUFF	RUDE
DOME	HOLD	LOOT	POET	SOLE	WORK	ARUM	GRIT	URIC	STEP	DULL	LULL	RUFF
DONA	HOLE	LOPE	POKE	SOLN	WORM	BRAD	GROG	WRAP	STER	DULY	LUMP	RUIN
DONE	HOLY	LORD	POKY	SOLO	WORN	BRAE	GROT	WREN	STEW	DUMA	LUNG	RULE
DONG	HOME	LORE	POLE	SOME	WORT	BRAG	GROW	WRIT	STIR	DUMB	LURE	RUMP
DOOM	HOMO	LORN	POLL	SONG	WOVE	BRAN	GRUB	WRNT	STOL	DUMP	LURK	RUNE
DOOR	HONE	LOSE	POLO	SOON	YOGA	BRAT	HRZN	YRBK	STOP	DUNE	LUSH	RUNG
DOPA	HONK	LOSS	POMP	SOOT	YOGI	BRAY	IRBM	ASHY	STOW	DUNG	LUST	RUNT
DOPE	HOOD	LOST	POND	SOPH	YOKE	BREW	IRIS	ASIC	STUB	DUNK	LUTE	RUSE
DORM	HOOF	LOTH	PONE	SORB	YOLK	BRIG	IRON	ASPI	STUD	DUPE	MUCH	RUSH
DORY	HOOK	LOUD	PONY	SORE	YORE	BRIM	ORAL	ASSN	STUN	DUSK	MUCK	RUSK
DOSE	HOOP	LOUR	POOL	SORT	YOWL	BRIO	ORCH	ASSR	VTOL	DUST	MUFF	RUSS
DOTE	HOOT	LOUT	POOP	SOUL	YOYO	BRIT	OREG	ASST	AULD	DUTY	MULE	RUST
DOUR	HOPE	LOVE	POOR	SOUP	ZONE	BROS	ORGY	BSKT	AUNT	FUEL	MULL	SUBJ
DOVE	HOPI	MOAN	POPE	SOUR	ZOOL	BROW	ORIG	CSSR	AURA	FULL	MURK	SUCH
DOWN	HORN	MOAT	PORE	TOAD	ZOOM	CRAB	PRAM	ESDI	AUTH	FUME	MUSE	SUCK
DOZE	HORT	MOCK	PORK	TOGA	APEX	CRAG	PRAY	ESPY	AUTO	FUND	MUSH	SUDS
FOAL	HOSE	MODE	PORT	TOGS	APPL	CRAM	PREC	ESTH	BUBO	FUNK	MUSK	SUET
FOAM	HOSP	MOIL	POSE	TOIL	APPT	CREE	PRED	ISDN	BUCK	FURL	MUSS	SUFF
FOGY	HOST	MOLD	POSH	TOKE	APSE	CREW	PREF	ISLE	BUFF	FURY	MUST	SUIT

SULK	SWIM	AWAY	FIAT	ORAL	SPAT	LOBE	MACE	ZECH	VEDA	FLEE	PEEP	VIEW
SUNG	SWUM	AYAH	FLAB	OVAL	SPAY	LUBE	MACH	ADDN	VIDE	FLEM	PEER	WEED
SUNK	TWIG	BEAD	FLAG	PEAK	STAB	MTBF	MECH	AIDE	WADE	FLEW	PIED	WEEK
SUPP	TWIN	BEAK	FLAK	PEAL	STAG	PUBL	MICA	AMDT	WADI	FLEX	PIER	WEEN
SUPT	TWIT	BEAM	FLAP	PEAR	STAR	ROBE	MICE	AVDP	WIDE	FREE	PIES	WEEP
SURE	YWCA	BEAN	FLAT	PEAT	STAT	RUBY	MICH	BADE	ABED	FREQ	PLEA	WHEN
SURF	YWHA	BEAR	FLAW	PLAN	STAY	STBD	MOCK	BIDE	ABET	FRET	POEM	WHET
SURG	AXIS	BEAT	FLAX	PLAT	SWAB	SUBJ	MUCH	BLDG	AGED	FUEL	POET	WHEY
SURV	AXLE	BEAU	FLAY	PLAY	SWAG	TUBA	MUCK	BLDR	ALEE	GAEL	PREC	WREN
TUBA	EXAM	BIAS	FOAL	PRAM	SWAM	TUBE	NECK	BODE	AMEN	GLEE	PRED	AFFT
TUBE	EXCH	BLAB	FOAM	PRAY	SWAN	YRBK	NICA	BODY	AMER	GLEN	PREF	BUFF
TUCK	EXEC	BOAR	FRAY	QUAD	SWAP	ZEBU	NICE	CEDE	ANEW	GREP	PREM	CAFE
TUES	EXIT	BOAT	GEAR	QUAI	SWAT	ACCT	NICK	CEDI	APEX	GREW	PREP	CPFF
TUFA	EXOD	BRAD	GHAT	QUAY	SWAY	AGCY	ONCE	CMDG	AREA	GREY	PRES	CUFF
TUFF	EXOR	BRAE	GLAD	RAAF	TEAK	ARCH	ORCH	CMDR	AVER	HEED	PREV	DAFT
TUFT	EXPO	BRAG	GNAT	RCAF	TEAL	BACK	PACE	CODA	BEEF	HEEL	PREY	DEFT
TUNA	EXPT	BRAN	GNAW	READ	TEAM	BECK	PACK	CODE	BEEN	IBEX	REED	DEFY
TUNE	AYAH	BRAT	GOAD	REAL	TEAR	BOCK	PACT	DADA	BEER	IDEA	REEF	DOFF
TURF	BYTE	BRAY	GOAL	REAM	TEAT	BUCK	PECK	DIDO	BEET	IDEM	REEK	FIFE
TURK	CYAN	CHAM	GOAT	REAP	THAI	CICS	PICA	DODO	BIER	IDES	REEL	FIFO
TURN	CYME	CHAP	GRAB	REAR	THAN	COCK	PICE	DUDE	BLEW	ITEM	RHEA	GAFF
TUSK	CYST	CHAR	GRAD	RIAL	THAT	COCO	PICK	EDDY	BOER	JEEP	RIEL	GIFT
UUCP	DYKE	CHAT	GRAM	ROAD	THAW	DACE	PICO	ESDI	BREW	JEER	SEED	HAFT
VULG	GYRO	CIAO	GRAY	ROAM	TOAD	DECK	POCK	FADE	CHEF	JPEG	SEEK	HEFT
YUAN	GYVE	CLAD	HEAD	ROAN	TRAM	DICE	POCO	FADM	CHEM	KEEL	SEEM	HUFF
YULE	HYMN	CLAM	HEAL	ROAR	TRAP	DICT	PUCK	FEDN	CHEW	KEEN	SEEP	IFFY
YURT	HYPE	CLAN	HEAP	SCAB	TRAY	DOCK	RACE	FIDO	CLEF	KEEP	SEER	INFL
ZUNI	HYPO	CLAP	HEAR	SCAD	TSAR	DUCK	RACK	HIDE	CLEW	KNEE	SHED	INFO
AVDP	KYAT	CLAW	HEAT	SCAN	TZAR	DUCT	RACY	ISDN	COED	KNEW	SHEW	LEFT
AVER	LYNX	CLAY	HOAX	SCAR	USAF	EACH	RECD	JADE	CREE	LEEK	SKEW	LIFE
AVID	LYRE	COAL	ITAL	SEAL	VEAL	ECCL	RECT	JUDG	CREW	LEER	SLED	LIFO
AVOW	MYNA	COAT	IWAY	SEAM	VIAL	ENCY	RICE	JUDO	DEED	LEES	SLEW	LIFT
EVAP	MYTH	COAX	KHAN	SEAR	WEAK	ETCH	RICH	KUDO	DEEM	LIED	SPEC	LOFT
EVEN	PYRE	CRAB	KYAT	SEAT	WEAL	EXCH	RICK	LADY	DEEP	LIEF	SPEW	LUFF
EVER	RYFM	CRAG	LEAD	SHAD	WEAN	FACE	ROCK	LCDR	DEER	LIEN	STEM	MIFF
EVIL	SYNC	CRAM	LEAF	SHAG	WEAR	FACT	SACK	LIDO	DIET	LIEU	STEP	MUFF
OVAL	SYST	CYAN	LEAK	SHAH	WHAT	FICA	SECT	LODE	DOER	MEED	STER	PUFF
OVEN	TYKE	CZAR	LEAL	SHAK	WOAD	HACK	SECY	MADE	DOES	MEEK	STEW	RAFT
OVER	TYPE	DEAD	LEAN	SHAM	WRAP	HICK	SICK	MIDI	DREG	MEET	SUET	REFL
OVUM	TYPO	DEAF	LEAP	SKAG	XMAS	HOCK	SOCK	MODE	DREW	MIEN	SWED	REFR
SVGA	TYRO	DEAL	LIAR	SLAB	YEAR	INCA	SPCA	NODE	DUEL	MPEG	TEEM	RIFE
SVGS	CZAR	DEAN	LOAD	SLAG	YUAN	INCH	SPCC	NUDE	DUET	MSEC	TEEN	RIFF
AWAY	EZEK	DEAR	LOAF	SLAM	ZEAL	INCL	SUCH	ODDS	EDEN	NDEA	THEE	RIFT
AWOL	TZAR	DIAG	LOAM	SLAN	ABBE	INCR	SUCK	RADM	ELEC	NEED	THEM	RTFM
AWRY		DIAL	LOAN	SLAP	ABBR	ITCH	TACH	REDO	ELEM	NOEL	THEN	RUFF
EWER		DRAB	LUAU	SLAT	BABE	JACK	TACK	RIDE	EMER	NOES	THEW	RYFM
FWTW		DRAG	MEAD	SLAV	BABY	KICK	TACO	RODE	EPEE	OBEY	THEY	SAFE
IWAY	3RD LETTER	DRAM	MEAL	SLAW	BUBO	KOCH	TACT	RUDE	EVEN	OLEO	TIER	SIFT
SWAB	ACAD	DRAW	MEAN	SLAY	CUBE	LACE	TECH	SIDE	EVER	OMEN	TREE	SOFA
SWAG	AFAR	DRAY	MEAS	SMAJ	DEBT	LACK	TICK	SODA	EWER	OPEN	TREK	SOFT
SWAM	AGAR	DUAL	MEAT	SNAG	GIBE	LECT	TUCK	SUDS	EXEC	OPER	TREY	SUFF
SWAN	AJAR	EDAM	MOAN	SNAP	HDBK	LICE	USCG	TIDE	EZEK	OREG	TUES	TIFF
SWAP	AMAH	ELAN	MOAT	SOAK	HOBO	LICK	UUCP	TIDY	FEED	OVEN	UREA	TUFA
SWAT	ANAL	EVAP	NEAP	SOAP	ICBM	LOCH	VICE	UNDO	FEEL	OVER	USED	TUFF
SWAY	ANAT	EXAM	NEAR	SOAR	IRBM	LOCK	WICK	URDU	FEET	PEEK	USES	TUFT
SWED	ARAB	FEAR	NEAT	SPAN	JIBE	LOCO	YMCA	USDA	FIEF	PEEL	VEEP	WAFT
SWIG		FEAT	OPAL	SPAR	KOBO	LUCK	YWCA	VADM	FLEA	PEEN	VEER	WEFT

WIFE	ARID	LAID	THIN	PIKE	DILL	KILO	SOLE	DAMN	YMMV	GENT	NAND	TONE
ALGA	ARIZ	LAIN	THIS	POKE	DOLE	KILT	SOLN	DAMP	ACNE	GONE	NANO	TONG
BKGD	ASIC	LAIR	TOIL	POKY	DOLL	LILT	SOLO	DIME	AINU	GONG	NINE	TUNA
CAGE	AVID	LOIN	TRIB	PUKE	DOLT	LILY	SULK	DOME	AUNT	HAND	NONE	TUNE
DOGE	AXIS	MAID	TRIG	RAKE	DULL	LOLL	TALA	DUMA	BAND	HANG	OINK	ULNA
EDGE	BAIL	MAIL	TRIM	SAKE	DULY	LULL	TALC	DUMB	BANE	HANK	PANE	VANE
EDGY	BAIT	MAIM	TRIO	SIKH	FALL	MALE	TALE	DUMP	BANG	HIND	PANG	VEND
ENGR	BLIP	MAIN	TRIP	TAKA	FELL	MALL	TALK	FAME	BANK	HINT	PANT	VENT
ERGO	BOIL	MOIL	TWIG	TAKE	FELT	MALT	TALL	FUME	BEND	HONE	PENN	VINE
FOGY	BRIG	NAIF	TWIN	TOKE	FILE	MELD	TELL	GAME	BENT	HONK	PENT	WAND
GAGE	BRIM	NAIL	TWIT	TYKE	FILL	MELT	TILE	GAMY	BIND	HUNG	PINE	WANE
HIGH	BRIO	OBIT	UNIT	WAKE	FILM	MILD	TILL	HEME	BOND	HUNK	PING	WANT
HUGE	BRIT	OLIO	UNIV	WOKE	FILS	MILE	TILT	HEMP	BONE	HUNT	PINK	WEND
LOGE	CHIC	OMIT	UNIX	YOKE	FOLD	MILK	TOLD	HOME	BUNG	JINX	PINT	WENT
LOGO	CHIN	ORIG	URIC	ABLE	FOLK	MILL	TOLE	HOMO	BUNK	JUNC	PINX	WIND
LOGY	CHIP	PAID	USIA	ALLY	FULL	MILT	TOLL	HTML	BUNT	JUNE	POND	WINE
MAGI	CHIT	PAIL	VAIL	AULD	GALA	MLLE	UGLY	HUMP	CANC	JUNK	PONE	WING
MCGA	CLIP	PAIN	VAIN	AXLE	GALE	MOLD	VALE	HYMN	CANE	KANA	PONY	WINK
MSGR	COIF	PAIR	VEIL	BALD	GALL	MOLE	VELD	IAMB	CANT	KANS	PUNK	WINO
MSGT	COIL	PHIL	VEIN	BALE	GALV	MOLL	VILE	JAMB	CENT	KENO	PUNT	WONT
MTGE	COIN	PRIG	VOID	BALK	GELD	MOLT	VOLE	JUMP	CONC	KIND	PUNY	WRNT
NIGH	CRIB	PRIM	WAIF	BALL	GILD	MOLY	VOLT	KAME	CONE	KINE	RAND	YANK
ORGY	CRIT	PRIN	WAIL	BALM	GILL	MULE	VULG	LAMA	CONF	KING	RANG	ZANY
PAGE	DAIS	QUID	WAIN	BELG	GILT	MULL	WALE	LAMB	CONG	KINK	RANI	ZINC
RAGA	DRIP	QUIP	WAIT	BELL	GOLD	NFLD	WALK	LAME	CONJ	LAND	RANK	ZING
RAGE	EDIT	QUIT	WEIR	BELT	GOLF	NULL	WALL	LAMP	CONK	LANE	RANT	ZONE
REGT	EGIS	QUIZ	WHIG	BILE	GULF	OGLE	WELD	LIMB	CONN	LANG	REND	ZUNI
SAGA	EMIR	RAID	WHIM	BILK	GULL	OKLA	WELL	LIME	CONS	LANK	RENT	AEON
SAGE	EMIT	RAIL	WHIP	BILL	GULP	ONLY	WELT	LIMN	CONT	LEND	RIND	AGOG
SAGO	EPIC	RAIN	WHIR	BOLA	HALE	PALE	WILD	LIMP	CONY	LENS	RING	AHOY
SIGH	ERIE	REIN	WHIT	BOLD	HALF	PALL	WILE	LUMP	DANE	LENT	RINK	ALOE
SIGN	EVIL	ROIL	WHIZ	BOLE	HALL	PALM	WILL	MAMA	DANK	LING	RUNE	AMOK
SVGA	EXIT	RUIN	WRIT	BOLL	HALO	PELF	WILT	MEMO	DENT	LINK	RUNG	ANON
SVGS	FAIL	SAID	LTJG	BOLO	HALT	PELT	WILY	MIME	DENY	LINK	RUNT	ATOM
TOGA	FAIN	SAIL	RAJA	BOLT	HELD	PILE	WOLD	NAME	DINE	LINT	SAND	ATOP
TOGS	FAIR	SCIL	ANKH	BULB	HELL	PILL	WOLF	NUMB	DINT	LOND	SANE	AVOW
TSGT	FDIC	SHIM	BAKE	BULK	HELM	POLE	YELL	PIMP	DONA	LONE	SANG	AWOL
URGE	FLIP	SHIN	BIKE	BULL	HELP	POLL	YELP	POMP	DONE	LONG	SANK	BIOG
WAGE	FLIT	SHIP	BSKT	CALC	HILL	POLO	YOLK	PUMA	DONG	LUNG	SANS	BIOL
YEGG	FOIL	SHIV	CAKE	CALF	HILT	PULE	YULE	PUMP	DUNE	LYNX	SEND	BIOS
YOGA	GAIN	SKID	COKE	CALK	HOLD	PULL	ACME	RAMP	DUNG	MANE	SENE	BLOB
YOGI	GAIT	SKIM	CUKE	CALL	HOLE	PULP	ALMS	RCMP	DUNK	MANX	SENT	BLOC
ACHE	GLIB	SKIN	DIKE	CALM	HOLY	RELY	AMMO	RIME	FANE	MANY	SINE	BLOT
ACHY	GRID	SKIP	DUKE	CELL	HULA	RILE	ARMY	ROMP	FANG	MDNT	SING	BLOW
ASHY	GRIM	SKIT	DYKE	CELT	HULK	RILL	BOMB	RUMP	FEND	MEND	SINK	BOOK
BAHT	GRIN	SLIM	FAKE	COLA	HULL	ROLE	BUMP	SAME	FIND	MENU	SONG	BOOM
COHO	GRIP	SLIP	HAKE	COLD	IDLE	ROLL	CAME	SGML	FINE	MIND	SUNG	BOON
ECHO	GRIT	SLIT	HDKF	COLL	ISLE	RULE	CAMP	SOME	FINK	MINE	SUNK	BOOR
IMHO	HAIL	SNIP	HIKE	COLO	JELL	SALE	COMA	TAME	FINN	MINI	SYNC	BOOT
JEHU	HAIR	SOIL	HOKE	COLT	JILT	SALT	COMB	TAMP	FOND	MINK	TANG	BPOE
JOHN	HEIR	SPIN	ICKY	CULL	JOLT	SELF	COME	TEMP	FONT	MINN	TANK	BROS
YMHA	IBIS	SPIT	JOKE	CULT	JULY	SELL	COML	TIME	FUND	MINT	TEND	BROW
YWHA	IMIT	STIR	LAKE	DALE	KALE	SILK	COMM	TOMB	FUNK	MINX	TENN	BUOY
ACID	IRIS	SUIT	LIKE	DELE	KELP	SILL	COMP	TOME	GANG	MONK	TENT	CHON
AKIN	JAIL	SWIG	MAKE	DELI	KELT	SILO	COMR	USMC	GENE	MONO	TINE	CHOP
AMID	JOIN	SWIM	MIKE	DELL	KILL	SILT	CYME	VAMP	GENL	MONT	TINT	CHOW
ARIA	KNIT	TAIL	PEKE	DELY	KILN	SOLD	DAME	WOMB	GENS	MYNA	TINY	CLOD

CLOG	LION	SNOW	NOPE	CERT	HERS	PURR	YARN	HASH	PEST	BATE	PATE	FOUL
CLOP	LOOK	SOON	PAPA	CORD	HIRE	PYRE	YORE	HASP	POSE	BATH	PATH	FOUR
CLOT	LOOM	SOOT	PIPE	CORE	HORN	RARE	YURT	HISS	POSH	BITE	PITH	GAUD
CLOY	LOON	SPOT	POPE	CORK	HORT	SARI	ZERO	HIST	POSS	BOTH	PITY	GLUE
COOK	LOOP	STOL	PUPA	CORM	HURL	SERA	ALSO	HOSE	POST	BUTT	PPTN	GLUM
COOL	LOOT	STOP	RAPE	CORN	HURT	SERB	ANSI	HOSP	POSY	BYTE	PUTT	GLUT
COON	MEOW	STOW	RAPT	CORP	INRI	SERE	APSE	HOST	PUSH	CATV	RATE	GOUT
COOP	MOOD	THOU	REPL	CORR	JERK	SERF	ASSN	HUSH	PUSS	CCTV	RETD	GRUB
COOT	MOON	TOOK	REPT	CTRL	JURY	SERG	ASSR	HUSK	RASH	CITE	RITE	HAUL
CPOM	MOOR	TOOL	RIPE	CURB	KART	SERV	ASST	INSP	RASP	CITY	ROTC	HOUR
CPOS	MOOT	TOOT	ROPE	CURD	KERB	SIRE	BASE	INST	RESP	COTE	ROTE	JOUR
CROP	NEON	TROD	SCPO	CURE	KERF	SORB	BASH	JESS	REST	CUTE	SATE	LAUD
CROW	NOOK	TROT	SEPN	CURL	KIRK	SORE	BASK	JEST	RISC	DATA	SHTG	LOUD
DHOW	NOON	TROW	SEPT	CURT	LARD	SORT	BASS	JOSH	RISE	DATE	SITE	LOUR
DOOM	OBOE	TROY	SHPT	DARE	LARK	SPRY	BAST	JOSS	RISK	DOTE	SMTP	LOUT
DOOR	ODOR	UPON	SOPH	DARK	LIRA	SURE	BEST	JUST	ROSE	DUTY	UNTO	MAUL
DROP	PEON	VIOL	SUPP	DARN	LORD	SURF	BOSH	KISS	ROSY	ESTH	VETO	MOUE
ECOL	PHON	VTOL	SUPT	DART	LORE	SURG	BOSS	LASH	RUSE	FATE	VITA	NAUT
ECON	PLOD	WHOM	TAPE	DIRE	LORN	SURV	BUSH	LASS	RUSH	FATH	VOTE	NEUT
EXOD	PLOP	WOOD	TAPS	DIRK	LURE	TARE	BUSS	LAST	RUSK	FETE	WATS	NOUN
EXOR	PLOT	WOOF	TNPK	DIRT	LURK	TARN	BUST	LESS	RUSS	FWTW	WATT	ONUS
FLOE	PLOW	WOOL	TOPE	DORM	LYRE	TARO	BUSY	LEST	RUST	GATE	WCTU	OPUS
FLOG	PLOY	ZION	TOPS	DORY	MARE	TART	CASE	LISP	SASH	GATT	WITH	OVUM
FLOP	POOL	ZOOL	TYPE	EARL	MARK	TERM	CASH	LIST	SASK	GOTH	XNTY	PLUG
FLOW	POOP	ZOOM	TYPO	EARN	MARL	TERN	CASK	LOSE	SCSI	HATE	YETI	PLUM
FOOD	POOR	APPL	WEPT	ECRU	MARS	TERR	CAST	LOSS	SYST	HTTP	ABUT	PLUS
FOOL	PROB	APPT	WIPE	FARE	MART	TIRE	CISC	LOST	TASK	INTL	AGUE	POUR
FOOT	PROC	ASPI	ZEPH	FARM	MERE	TORE	COST	LUSH	TEST	INTO	ALUM	POUT
FROG	PROD	CAPE	SEQQ	FERN	MIRE	TORN	COSY	LUST	TOSS	IOTA	ANUS	ROUE
FROM	PROF	CAPS	ACRE	FIRE	MORE	TORR	CSSR	MASC	TUSK	JUTE	AQUA	ROUT
GAOL	PROM	CAPT	AERO	FIRM	MORN	TORT	CUSP	MASH	USSR	KITE	ARUM	SCUD
GEOG	PRON	COPE	AERY	FORA	MURK	TORY	CYST	MASK	VASE	KITH	BAUD	SCUM
GEOL	PROP	COPY	AFRO	FORD	NARC	TURF	DASH	MASS	VAST	LATE	BLUE	SHUN
GEOM	PROS	DEPR	AIRY	FORE	NARD	TURK	DESK	MAST	VESA	LATH	BLUR	SHUT
GLOB	PROT	DEPT	AURA	FORK	NLRB	TURN	DISC	MDSE	VEST	LETT	BOUT	SLUE
GLOP	PROV	DOPA	AWRY	FORM	NORM	TYRO	DISH	MESA	VISA	LITH	CAUL	SLUG
GLOW	PROW	DOPE	BARB	FORT	NORW	VARY	DISK	MESH	VISE	LOTH	CHUB	SLUM
GOOD	QUOT	DUPE	BARD	FURL	OGRE	VERB	DIST	MESS	VLSI	LUTE	CHUG	SLUR
GOOF	RIOT	ESPY	BARE	FURY	OKRA	VERT	DOSE	MISC	WASH	MATE	CHUM	SLUT
GOON	ROOD	EXPO	BARK	GARB	OURS	VERY	DUSK	MISS	WASP	MATH	CLUB	SMUG
GROG	ROOF	EXPT	BARN	GERM	PARA	WARD	DUST	MIST	WEST	MATT	CLUE	SMUT
GROT	ROOK	FEPC	BART	GIRD	PARD	WARE	EASE	MOSS	WISD	METE	COUP	SNUB
GROW	ROOM	GAPE	BDRM	GIRL	PARE	WARM	EAST	MOST	WISE	MITE	CRUX	SNUG
HOOD	ROOT	HOPE	BERG	GORE	PARK	WARN	EASY	MUSE	WISH	MITT	DAUB	SOUL
HOOF	SCOT	HOPI	BIRD	GORY	PART	WARP	EISA	MUSH	WISP	MKTG	DEUT	SOUP
HOOK	SCOW	HYPE	BORE	GURU	PERF	WART	ELSE	MUSK	ZEST	MOTE	DOUR	SOUR
HOOP	SHOE	HYPO	BORN	GYRO	PERH	WARY	ERST	MUSS	ACTG	MOTH	DRUB	SPUD
HOOT	SHOP	JAPE	BTRY	HARD	PERK	WERE	FAST	MUST	ACTH	MUTE	DRUG	SPUN
ICON	SHOT	KBPS	BURL	HARE	PERM	WIRE	FISH	NASA	ALTA	MUTT	DRUM	SPUR
IDOL	SHOW	KEPI	BURN	HARK	PERP	WIRY	FIST	NEST	ALTO	MYTH	ECUA	STUB
IKON	SLOB	LAPP	BURP	HARM	PERS	WORD	FUSE	NISI	ANTE	NATL	EDUC	STUD
IOOF	SLOE	LCPL	BURR	HARP	PERT	WORE	FUSS	NOSE	ANTI	NATO	FAUN	STUN
IRON	SLOP	LOPE	BURY	HART	PORE	WORK	GASH	NOSY	ARTY	NETH	FEUD	SWUM
KNOB	SLOT	MCPO	CARD	HERB	PORK	WORM	GASP	OUST	ATTN	NOTE	FLUB	TAUT
KNOT	SLOW	MIPS	CARE	HERD	PORT	WORN	GIST	PASS	ATTY	NUTS	FLUE	THUD
KNOW	SMOG	MOPE	CARP	HERE	PURE	WORT	GUSH	PAST	AUTH	OATH	FLUE	THUG
KOOK	SNOB	NAPE	CART	HERO	PURL	YARD	GUST	PESO	AUTO	ONTO	FLUX	THUS

C1	C2	C3	C4	C5	C6	C7	C8	C9	C10	C11	C12	C13
TOUR	HOWL	**4TH**	SPCA	SLAB	BEND	LORD	VOID	CITE	FETE	JOKE	MOUE	RIME
TOUT	JOWL	**LETTER**	SVGA	SLOB	BIND	LOUD	WAND	CLUE	FIFE	JUNE	MOVE	RIPE
TRUE	KIWI	ALGA	TAKA	SNOB	BIRD	MAID	WARD	CODE	FILE	JUTE	MTGE	RISE
YOUR	LAWN	ALTA	TALA	SNUB	BKGD	PAID	WEED	COKE	FINE	KALE	MULE	RITE
ADVT	LEWD	AQUA	TOGA	SORB	MEAD	PARD	WELD	COME	FIRE	KAME	MUSE	RIVE
BEVY	MEWS	AREA	TUBA	STAB	MEED	PIED	WEND	CONE	FIVE	KINE	MUTE	ROBE
BLVD	NEWS	ARIA	TUFA	STUB	MELD	PLOD	WILD	COPE	FLEE	KITE	NAME	RODE
CAVE	NEWT	AURA	TUNA	SWAB	MEND	POND	WIND	CORE	FLOE	KNEE	NAPE	ROLE
CAVY	PAWL	BOLA	ULNA	TOMB	MILD	PRED	WISD	COTE	FLUE	LACE	NAVE	ROPE
COVE	PAWN	CODA	UREA	TRIB	MIND	PROD	WOAD	COVE	FORE	LAKE	NICE	ROSE
DIVA	PKWY	COLA	USDA	VERB	MOLD	QUAD	WOLD	CREE	FREE	LAME	NINE	ROTE
DIVE	RSWC	COMA	USIA	WOMB	MOOD	QUID	WOOD	CUBE	FUME	LANE	NODE	ROUE
DOVE	TOWN	DADA	VEDA	ASIC	NAND	RAID	WORD	CUKE	FUSE	LATE	NONE	ROVE
ENVY	YAWL	DATA	VESA	BLOC	NARD	RAND	YARD	CURE	FUZE	LAVE	NOPE	RUDE
FIVE	YAWN	DIVA	VISA	CALC	NEED	READ	ABBE	CUTE	GAGE	LAZE	NOSE	RULE
GAVE	YAWP	DONA	VITA	CANC	NFLD	RECD	ABLE	CYME	GALE	LICE	NOTE	RUNE
GIVE	YAWS	DOPA	VIVA	CHIC	DEAD	REED	ACHE	DACE	GAME	LIFE	NUDE	RUSE
GOVT	YOWL	DUMA	YMCA	CISC	DEED	REND	ACME	DALE	GAPE	LIKE	OBOE	SAFE
GYVE	FOXY	ECUA	YMHA	CONC	EXOD	RETD	ACNE	DAME	GATE	LIME	OGLE	SAGE
HAVE	MAXI	EISA	YOGA	DISC	FEED	RIND	ACRE	DANE	GAVE	LINE	OGRE	SAKE
HIVE	MIXT	FICA	YWCA	EDUC	FEND	ROAD	AGUE	DARE	GAZE	LIVE	ONCE	SALE
HOVE	NEXT	FLEA	YWHA	ELEC	FEUD	ROOD	AIDE	DATE	GENE	LOBE	OOZE	SAME
JIVE	PNXT	FORA	ARAB	EPIC	FIND	SAID	ALEE	DAZE	GIBE	LODE	PACE	SANE
LAVA	REXX	GALA	BARB	EXEC	FOLD	SAND	ALOE	DELE	GIVE	LOGE	PAGE	SATE
LAVE	SEXY	HULA	BLAB	FDIC	FOND	SCAD	ANTE	DICE	GLEE	LONE	PALE	SAVE
LEVY	TAXI	IDEA	BLOB	FEPC	FOOD	SCUD	APSE	DIKE	GLUE	LOPE	PANE	SENE
LIVE	TEXT	INCA	BOMB	JUNC	FORD	SEED	AXLE	DIME	GONE	LORE	PARE	SERE
LOVE	WAXY	IOTA	BULB	MASC	FUND	SEND	BABE	DINE	GORE	LOSE	PATE	SHOE
MOVE	CMYK	KANA	CHUB	MISC	GAUD	SHAD	BADE	DIRE	GYVE	LOVE	PAVE	SIDE
NAVE	KAYO	LAMA	CLUB	MSEC	GELD	SHED	BAKE	DIVE	HAKE	LUBE	PEKE	SINE
NAVY	MAYA	LAVA	COMB	NARC	GILD	SKID	BALE	DOGE	HALE	LURE	PICE	SIRE
NOVA	ONYX	LIRA	CRAB	PREC	GIRD	SLED	BANE	DOLE	HARE	LUTE	PIKE	SITE
PAVE	PAYT	MAMA	CRIB	PROC	GLAD	SOLD	BARE	DOME	HATE	LYRE	PILE	SIZE
RAVE	PHYS	MAYA	CURB	RISC	GOAD	SPUD	BASE	DONE	HAVE	MACE	PINE	SLOE
RIVE	YOYO	MCGA	DAUB	ROTC	GOLD	STBD	BATE	DOPE	HAZE	MADE	PIPE	SLUE
ROVE	BUZZ	MESA	DRAB	RSWC	GOOD	STUD	BIDE	DOSE	HDWE	MAKE	POKE	SOLE
RSVP	COZY	MICA	DRUB	SPCC	GRAD	SWED	BIKE	DOTE	HEME	MALE	POLE	SOME
SAVE	DAZE	MYNA	DUMB	SPEC	GRID	TEND	BILE	DOVE	HERE	MANE	PONE	SORE
VIVA	DOZE	NASA	FLAB	SYNC	HAND	THUD	BITE	DOZE	HIDE	MARE	POPE	SURE
WAVE	FAZE	NDEA	FLUB	TALC	HARD	TOAD	BLUE	DUDE	HIKE	MATE	PORE	TAKE
WAVY	FIZZ	NICA	GARB	URIC	HEAD	TOLD	BODE	DUKE	HIRE	MAZE	POSE	TALE
WIVE	FUZE	NOVA	GLIB	USMC	HEED	TROD	BOLE	DUNE	HIVE	MDSE	PUKE	TAME
WOVE	FUZZ	OKLA	GLOB	ZINC	HELD	USED	BONE	DUPE	HOKE	MERE	PULE	TAPE
BAWD	GAZE	OKRA	GRAB	ABED	HERD	VELD	BORE	DYKE	HOLE	METE	PURE	TARE
BAWL	HAZE	PAPA	GRUB	ACAD	HIND	VEND	BPOE	EASE	HOME	MICE	PYRE	THEE
BOWL	HAZY	PARA	HERB	ACID	HOLD		BRAE	EDGE	HONE	MIKE	RACE	TIDE
COWL	HRZN	PICA	IAMB	AGED	HOOD		BYTE	ELSE	HOPE	MILE	RAGE	TILE
DAWN	JAZZ	PLEA	JAMB	AMID	KIND		CAFE	EPEE	HOSE	MIME	RAKE	TIME
DOWN	LAZE	PUMA	KERB	ARID	LAID		CAGE	ERIE	HOVE	MINE	RAPE	TINE
FAWN	LAZY	PUPA	KNOB	AULD	LAND		CAKE	FACE	HUGE	MIRE	RARE	TIRE
FOWL	MAZE	RAGA	LAMB	AVID	LARD		CAME	FADE	HYPE	MITE	RATE	TOKE
FRWY	NAZI	RAJA	LIMB	BALD	LAUD		CANE	FAKE	IDLE	MLLE	RAVE	TOLE
GAWK	OOZE	RHEA	NLRB	BAND	LEAD		CAPE	FAME	ISLE	MODE	RAZE	TOME
GOWN	OUZO	SAGA	NUMB	BARD	LEND		CARE	FANE	JADE	MOLE	RICE	TONE
HAWK	RAZE	SERA	PROB	BAUD	LEWD		CASE	FARE	JAPE	MOPE	RIDE	TOPE
HDWE	RAZZ	SODA	SCAB	BEAD	LIED		CAVE	FATE	JIBE	MORE	RIFE	TORE
HGWY	SIZE	SOFA	SERB		LOND	VEND	CEDE	FAZE	JIVE	MOTE	RILE	TOTE

TREE	HDKF	FLAG	ACTH	RICH	BULK	MASK	TURK	FOUL	PAWL	BALM	ROOM	EDEN
TRUE	HOOF	FLOG	AMAH	RUSH	BUNK	MEEK	TUSK	FOWL	PEAL	BDRM	RTFM	ELAN
TUBE	HUFF	FROG	ANKH	SASH	CALK	MILK	WALK	FUEL	PEEL	BEAM	RYFM	EVEN
TUNE	IOOF	GANG	ARCH	SHAH	CASK	MINK	WEAK	FULL	PHIL	BOOM	SCUM	FAIN
TYKE	KERF	GEOG	AUTH	SIGH	CMYK	MOCK	WEEK	FURL	PILL	BRIM	SEAM	FAUN
TYPE	LEAF	GONG	AYAH	SIKH	COCK	MONK	WICK	GAEL	POLL	CALM	SEEM	FAWN
URGE	LIEF	GROG	BASH	SOPH	CONK	MUCK	WINK	GALL	POOL	CHAM	SHAM	FEDN
VALE	LOAF	HANG	BATH	SUCH	COOK	MURK	WORK	GAOL	PUBL	CHEM	SHIM	FERN
VANE	LUFF	HUNG	BOSH	TACH	CORK	MUSK	YANK	GENL	PULL	CHUM	SKIM	FINN
VASE	MIFF	JPEG	BOTH	TECH	DANK	NECK	YOLK	GEOL	PURL	CLAM	SLAM	GAIN
VICE	MTBF	JUDG	BUSH	WASH	DARK	NICK	YRBK	GILL	RAIL	COMM	SLIM	GLEN
VIDE	MUFF	KING	CASH	WISH	DECK	NOOK	ANAL	GIRL	REAL	CORM	SLUM	GOON
VILE	NAIF	LANG	DASH	WITH	DESK	OINK	APPL	GOAL	REEL	CPOM	STEM	GOWN
VINE	PELF	LING	DISH	ZECH	DIRK	PACK	AWOL	GULL	REFL	CRAM	SWAM	GRIN
VISE	PERF	LONG	EACH	ZEPH	DISK	PARK	BAIL	HAIL	REPL	DEEM	SWIM	HORN
VOLE	PREF	LTJG	ESTH	ANSI	DOCK	PEAK	BALL	HALL	RIAL	DOOM	SWUM	HRZN
VOTE	PROF	LUNG	ETCH	ANTI	DUCK	PECK	BAWL	HAUL	RIEL	DORM	TEAM	HYMN
WADE	PUFF	MKTG	EXCH	ASPI	DUNK	PEEK	BELL	HEAL	RILL	DRAM	TEEM	ICON
WAGE	RAAF	MPEG	FATH	CEDI	DUSK	PERK	BILL	HEEL	ROIL	DRUM	TERM	IKON
WAKE	RCAF	OREG	FISH	DELI	EZEK	PICK	BIOL	HELL	ROLL	EDAM	THEM	IRON
WALE	REEF	ORIG	GASH	ESDI	FINK	PINK	BOIL	HILL	SAIL	ELEM	TRAM	ISDN
WANE	RIFF	PANG	GOTH	HOPI	FLAK	POCK	BOLL	HOWL	SCIL	EXAM	TRIM	JOHN
WARE	ROOF	PING	GUSH	INRI	FOLK	PORK	BOWL	HTML	SEAL	FADM	VADM	JOIN
WAVE	RUFF	PLUG	HASH	KEPI	FORK	PUCK	BULL	HULL	SELL	FARM	WARM	KEEN
WERE	SELF	PRIG	HIGH	KIWI	FUNK	PUNK	BURL	HURL	SGML	FILM	WHIM	KHAN
WIDE	SERF	RANG	HUSH	MAGI	GAWK	RACK	CALL	IDOL	SILL	FIRM	WHOM	KILN
WIFE	SUFF	RING	INCH	MAXI	HACK	RANK	CAUL	INCL	SOIL	FLEM	WORM	LAIN
WILE	SURF	RUNG	ITCH	MIDI	HANK	REEK	CELL	INFL	SOUL	FOAM	ZOOM	LAWN
WINE	TIFF	SANG	JOSH	MINI	HARK	RICK	COAL	INTL	STOL	FORM	ADDN	LEAN
WIPE	TUFF	SERG	KITH	NAZI	HAWK	RINK	COIL	ITAL	TAIL	FROM	AEON	LIEN
WIRE	TURF	SHAG	KOCH	NISI	HDBK	RISK	COLL	JAIL	TALL	GEOM	AKIN	LIMN
WISE	USAF	SHTG	LASH	QUAI	HICK	ROCK	COML	JELL	TEAL	GERM	AMEN	LION
WIVE	WAIF	SING	LATH	RANI	HOCK	ROOK	COOL	JOWL	TELL	GLUM	ANON	LOAN
WOKE	WOLF	SKAG	LITH	SARI	HONK	RUSK	COWL	KEEL	TILL	GRAM	ASSN	LOIN
WORE	WOOF	SLAG	LOCH	SCSI	HOOK	SACK	CTRL	KILL	TOIL	GRIM	ATTN	LOON
WOVE	ACTG	SLUG	LOTH	TAXI	HULK	SANK	CULL	LCPL	TOLL	HARM	BARN	LORN
YOKE	AGOG	SMOG	LUSH	THAI	HUNK	SASK	CURL	LEAL	TOOL	HELM	BEAN	MAIN
YORE	BANG	SMUG	MACH	VLSI	HUSK	SEEK	DEAL	LOLL	VAIL	ICBM	BEEN	MEAN
YULE	BELG	SNAG	MASH	WADI	JACK	SHAK	DELL	LULL	VEAL	IDEM	BOON	MIEN
ZONE	BERG	SNUG	MATH	YETI	JERK	SICK	DIAL	MAIL	VEIL	IRBM	BORN	MINN
BEEF	BIOG	SONG	MECH	YOGI	JUNK	SILK	DILL	MALL	VIAL	ITEM	BRAN	MOAN
BUFF	BLDG	STAG	MESH	ZUNI	KICK	SINK	DOLL	MARL	VIOL	LOAM	BURN	MOON
CALF	BRAG	SUNG	MICH	CONJ	KINK	SOAK	DUAL	MAUL	VTOL	LOOM	CHIN	MORN
CHEF	BRIG	SURG	MOTH	SMAJ	KIRK	SOCK	DUEL	MEAL	WAIL	MAIM	CHON	NEON
CLEF	BUNG	SWAG	MUCH	SUBJ	KOOK	SUCK	DULL	MILL	WALL	NORM	CLAN	NOON
COIF	CHUG	SWIG	MUSH	AMOK	LACK	SULK	EARL	MOIL	WEAL	OVUM	COIN	NOUN
CONF	CLOG	TANG	MYTH	BACK	LANK	SUNK	ECCL	MOLL	WELL	PALM	CONN	OMEN
CPFF	CMDG	THUG	NETH	BALK	LARK	TACK	ECOL	MULL	WILL	PERM	COON	OPEN
CUFF	CONG	TONG	NIGH	BANK	LEAK	TALK	EVIL	NAIL	WOOL	PLUM	CORN	OVEN
DEAF	CRAG	TRIG	OATH	BARK	LEEK	TANK	FAIL	NATL	YAWL	POEM	CYAN	PAIN
DOFF	DIAG	TWIG	ORCH	BASK	LICK	TASK	FALL	NOEL	YELL	PRAM	DAMN	PAWN
FIEF	DONG	USCG	PATH	BEAK	LINK	TEAK	FEEL	NULL	YOWL	PREM	DARN	PEEN
GAFF	DRAG	VULG	PERH	BECK	LOCK	TICK	FELL	OPAL	ZEAL	PRIM	DAWN	PENN
GOLF	DREG	WHIG	PITH	BILK	LOOK	TNPK	FILL	ORAL	ZOOL	PROM	DEAN	PEON
GOOF	DRUG	WING	POSH	BOCK	LUCK	TOOK	FOAL	OVAL	ALUM	RADM	DOWN	PHON
GULF	DUNG	YEGG	PUSH	BOOK	LURK	TREK	FOIL	PAIL	ARUM	REAM	EARN	PLAN
HALF	FANG	ZING	RASH	BUCK	MARK	TUCK	FOOL	PALL	ATOM	ROAM	ECON	PPTN

PRIN	COLO	AVDP	PLOP	BEER	ROAR	LENS	BEAT	FACT	LEST	POST	THAT	UNIV
PRON	DIDO	BLIP	POMP	BIER	SCAR	LESS	BEET	FAST	LETT	POUT	TILT	YMMV
RAIN	DODO	BUMP	POOP	BLDR	SEAR	LOSS	BELT	FEAT	LIFT	PROT	TINT	ANEW
REIN	ECHO	BURP	PREP	BLUR	SEER	MARS	BENT	FEET	LILT	PUNT	TOOT	AVOW
ROAN	ERGO	CAMP	PROP	BOAR	SLUR	MASS	BEST	FELT	LINT	PUTT	TORT	BLEW
RUIN	EXPO	CARP	PULP	BOER	SOAR	MEAS	BLOT	FIAT	LIST	QUIT	TOUT	BLOW
SCAN	FIDO	CHAP	PUMP	BOOR	SOUR	MESS	BOAT	FIST	LOFT	QUOT	TROT	BREW
SEPN	FIFO	CHIP	QUIP	BURR	SPAR	MEWS	BOLT	FLAT	LOOT	RAFT	TSGT	BROW
SHIN	GYRO	CHOP	RAMP	CHAR	SPUR	MIPS	BOOT	FLIT	LOST	RANT	TUFT	CHEW
SHUN	HALO	CLAP	RASP	CMDR	STAR	MISS	BOUT	FONT	LOUT	RAPT	TWIT	CHOW
SIGN	HERO	CLIP	RCMP	COMR	STER	MOSS	BRAT	FOOT	LUST	RECT	UNIT	CLAW
SKIN	HOBO	CLOP	REAP	CORR	STIR	MUSS	BRIT	FORT	MALT	REGT	VAST	CLEW
SLAN	HOMO	COMP	RESP	CSSR	TEAR	NEWS	BSKT	FRET	MART	RENT	VENT	CREW
SOLN	HYPO	COOP	ROMP	CZAR	TERR	NOES	BUNT	GAIT	MAST	REPT	VERT	CROW
SOON	IMHO	CORP	RSVP	DEAR	TIER	NUTS	BUST	GATT	MATT	REST	VEST	DHOW
SPAN	INFO	COUP	RUMP	DEER	TORR	ODDS	BUTT	GENT	MDNT	RIFT	VOLT	DRAW
SPIN	INTO	CROP	SEEP	DEPR	TOUR	ONUS	CANT	GHAT	MEAT	RIOT	WAFT	DREW
SPUN	JUDO	CUSP	SHIP	DOER	TSAR	OPUS	CAPT	GIFT	MEET	ROOT	WAIT	FLAW
STUN	KAYO	DAMP	SHOP	DOOR	TZAR	OURS	CART	GILT	MELT	ROUT	WANT	FLEW
SWAN	KENO	DEEP	SKIP	DOUR	USSR	PASS	CAST	GIST	MILT	RUNT	WART	FLOW
TARN	KILO	DRIP	SLAP	EMER	VEER	PERS	CELT	GLUT	MINT	RUST	WATT	FWTW
TEEN	KOBO	DROP	SLIP	EMIR	WEAR	PHYS	CENT	GNAT	MIST	SALT	WEFT	GLOW
TENN	KUDO	DUMP	SLOP	ENGR	WEIR	PIES	CERT	GOAT	MITT	SCOT	WELT	GNAW
TERN	LIDO	EVAP	SMTP	EVER	WHIR	PLUS	CHAT	GOUT	MIXT	SEAT	WENT	GREW
THAN	LIFO	FLAP	SNAP	EWER	YEAR	POSS	CHIT	GOVT	MOAT	SECT	WEPT	GROW
THEN	LOCO	FLIP	SNIP	EXOR	YOUR	PRES	CLOT	GRIT	MOLT	SENT	WEST	KNEW
THIN	LOGO	FLOP	SOAP	FAIR	ALMS	PROS	COAT	GROT	MONT	SEPT	WHAT	KNOW
TORN	MCPO	GASP	SOUP	FEAR	ANUS	PUSS	COLT	GUST	MOOT	SHOT	WHET	MEOW
TOWN	MEMO	GLOP	STEP	FOUR	AXIS	RUSS	CONT	HAFT	MOST	SHPT	WHIT	NORW
TURN	MONO	GREP	STOP	GEAR	BASS	SANS	COOT	HALT	MSGT	SHUT	WILT	PLOW
TWIN	NANO	GRIP	SUPP	HAIR	BIAS	SUDS	COST	HART	MUST	SIFT	WONT	PROW
UPON	NATO	GULP	SWAP	HEAR	BIOS	SVGS	CRIT	HEAT	MUTT	SILT	WORT	SCOW
VAIN	OLEO	HARP	TAMP	HEIR	BOSS	TAPS	CULT	HEFT	NAUT	SKIT	WRIT	SHEW
VEIN	OLIO	HASP	TEMP	HOUR	BROS	THIS	CURT	HILT	NEAT	SLAT	WRNT	SHOW
WAIN	ONTO	HEAP	TRAP	INCR	BUSS	THUS	CYST	HINT	NEST	SLIT	YURT	SKEW
WARN	OUZO	HELP	TRIP	JEER	CAPS	TOGS	DAFT	HIST	NEUT	SLOT	ZEST	SLAW
WEAN	PESO	HEMP	UUCP	JOUR	CICS	TOPS	DART	HOOT	NEWT	SLUT	AINU	SLEW
WEEN	PICO	HOOP	VAMP	LAIR	CONS	TOSS	DEBT	HORT	NEXT	SMUT	BEAU	SLOW
WHEN	POCO	HOSP	VEEP	LCDR	CPOS	TUES	DEFT	HOST	OBIT	SOFT	ECRU	SNOW
WORN	POLO	HTTP	WARP	LEER	DAIS	USES	DENT	HUNT	OMIT	SOOT	GURU	SPEW
WREN	REDO	HUMP	WASP	LIAR	DOES	WATS	DEPT	HURT	OUST	SORT	JEHU	STEW
YARN	SAGO	INSP	WEEP	LOUR	EGIS	XMAS	DEUT	IMIT	PACT	SPAT	LIEU	STOW
YAWN	SCPO	JEEP	WHIP	MOOR	FILS	YAWS	DICT	INST	PANT	SPIT	LUAU	THAW
YUAN	SILO	JUMP	WISP	MSGR	FUSS	ABET	DIET	JEST	PART	SPOT	MENU	THEW
ZION	SOLO	KEEP	WRAP	NEAR	GENS	ABUT	DINT	JILT	PAST	STAT	THOU	TROW
AERO	TACO	KELP	YAWP	ODOR	HERS	ACCT	DIRT	JOLT	PAYT	SUET	URDU	VIEW
AFRO	TARO	LAMP	YELP	OPER	HISS	ADVT	DIST	JUST	PEAT	SUIT	WCTU	APEX
ALSO	TRIO	LAPP	FREQ	OVER	IBIS	AFFT	DOLT	KART	PELT	SUPT	ZEBU	COAX
ALTO	TYPO	LEAP	SEQQ	PAIR	IDES	AMDT	DUCT	KELT	PENT	SWAT	CATV	CRUX
AMMO	TYRO	LIMP	ABBR	PEAR	IRIS	ANAT	DUET	KILT	PERT	SYST	CCTV	FLAX
AUTO	UNDO	LISP	AFAR	PEER	JESS	APPT	DUST	KNIT	PEST	TACT	GALV	FLEX
BOLO	UNTO	LOOP	AGAR	PIER	JOSS	ASST	EAST	KNOT	PINT	TART	PREV	FLUX
BRIO	VETO	LUMP	AJAR	POOR	KANS	AUNT	EDIT	KYAT	PLAT	TAUT	PROV	HOAX
BUBO	WINO	NEAP	AMER	POUR	KBPS	BAHT	EMIT	LAST	PLOT	TEAT	SERV	IBEX
CIAO	YOYO	PEEP	ASSR	PURR	KISS	BAIT	ERST	LECT	PNXT	TENT	SHIV	JINX
COCO	ZERO	PERP	AVER	REAR	LASS	BART	EXIT	LEFT	POET	TEST	SLAV	LYNX
COHO	ATOP	PIMP	BEAR	REFR	LEES	BAST	EXPT	LENT	PORT	TEXT	SURV	MANX

MINX	HGWY	XNTY
ONYX	HOLY	ZANY
PINX	ICKY	ARIZ
REXX	IFFY	BUZZ
UNIX	IWAY	FIZZ
ACHY	JULY	FUZZ
AERY	JURY	JAZZ
AGCY	LADY	QUIZ
AHOY	LAZY	RAZZ
AIRY	LEVY	WHIZ
ALLY	LILY	
ARMY	LOGY	
ARTY	MANY	
ASHY	MOLY	
ATTY	NAVY	
AWAY	NOSY	
AWRY	OBEY	
BABY	ONLY	
BEVY	ORGY	
BODY	PITY	
BRAY	PKWY	
BTRY	PLAY	
BUOY	PLOY	
BURY	POKY	
BUSY	PONY	
CAVY	POSY	
CITY	PRAY	
CLAY	PREY	
CLOY	PUNY	
CONY	QUAY	
COPY	RACY	
COSY	RELY	
COZY	ROSY	
DEFY	RUBY	
DELY	SECY	
DENY	SEXY	
DORY	SLAY	
DRAY	SPAY	
DULY	SPRY	
DUTY	STAY	
EASY	SWAY	
EDDY	THEY	
EDGY	TIDY	
ENCY	TINY	
ENVY	TORY	
ESPY	TRAY	
FLAY	TREY	
FOGY	TROY	
FOXY	UGLY	
FRAY	VARY	
FRWY	VERY	
FURY	WARY	
GAMY	WAVY	
GORY	WAXY	
GRAY	WHEY	
GREY	WILY	
HAZY	WIRY	

5

LETTER WORDS

1st Letter											
	AGATE	ANENT	ASSAY	BARGE	BIDDY	BOGUS	BRINK	CALVE	CHEEK	CLASP	CONST
ABACK	AGAVE	ANGEL	ASSET	BARON	BIDET	BOLUS	BRISK	CALYX	CHEEP	CLASS	CONTD
ABAFT	AGENT	ANGER	ASSOC	BASAL	BIGHT	BONER	BROAD	CAMEL	CHEER	CLEAN	CONTG
ABASE	AGILE	ANGLE	ASTER	BASIC	BIGOT	BONGO	BROIL	CAMEO	CHELA	CLEAR	CONTR
ABASH	AGLOW	ANGLO	ASTIR	BASIL	BILGE	BONNY	BROKE	CANAL	CHERT	CLEAT	COPRA
ABATE	AGONY	ANGRY	ATILT	BASIN	BILLY	BONUS	BROOD	CANDY	CHESS	CLEFT	COPSE
ABBEY	AGORA	ANGST	ATLAS	BASIS	BINGE	BONZE	BROOK	CANNA	CHEST	CLERK	CORAL
ABBOT	AGREE	ANGUS	ATOLL	BASSO	BINGO	BOOBY	BROOM	CANNY	CHEWY	CLICK	CORNY
ABEAM	AHEAD	ANION	ATONE	BASTE	BIPED	BOOST	BROTH	CANOE	CHIAO	CLIFF	CORPS
ABHOR	AISLE	ANISE	ATTAR	BATCH	BIRCH	BOOTH	BROWN	CANON	CHICK	CLIMB	COUCH
ABIDE	ALARM	ANKLE	ATTIC	BATHE	BIRTH	BOOTY	BRUIN	CANTO	CHIDE	CLIME	COUGH
ABODE	ALBUM	ANNEX	AUDIO	BATIK	BISON	BOOZE	BRUIT	CAPER	CHIEF	CLING	COULD
ABORT	ALDER	ANNOY	AUDIT	BATON	BITCH	BORAX	BRUNT	CAPON	CHILD	CLINK	COUNT
ABOUT	ALERT	ANNUL	AUGER	BATTY	BLACK	BORNE	BRUSH	CARAT	CHILI	CLOAK	COUPE
ABOVE	ALGOL	ANODE	AUGHT	BAWDY	BLADE	BORON	BRUTE	CARET	CHILL	CLOCK	COURT
ABSTR	ALIAS	ANTIC	AUGUR	BAYOU	BLAIN	BOSKY	BUDDY	CARGO	CHIME	CLONE	COVEN
ABUSE	ALIBI	ANVIL	AURAL	BEACH	BLAME	BOSOM	BUDGE	CARNY	CHIMP	CLOSE	COVER
ABYSM	ALIEN	AORTA	AURAR	BEANO	BLAND	BOSUN	BUGGY	CAROL	CHINA	CLOTH	COVET
ABYSS	ALIGN	APACE	AUXIN	BEARD	BLANK	BOTCH	BUGLE	CAROM	CHINE	CLOUD	COVEY
ACORN	ALIKE	APART	AVAIL	BEAST	BLARE	BOUGH	BUILD	CARRY	CHINK	CLOUT	COWER
ACRID	ALIVE	APEAK	AVAST	BEDEW	BLASE	BOULE	BULGE	CARVE	CHINO	CLOVE	COYPU
ACTOR	ALKYD	APHID	AVERT	BEECH	BLAST	BOUND	BULKY	CASTE	CHIRP	CLOWN	COZEN
ACUTE	ALLAH	APHIS	AVGAS	BEEFY	BLAZE	BOURN	BULLY	CATCH	CHIVE	CLUCK	CRACK
ADAGE	ALLAY	APORT	AVIAN	BEFIT	BLEAK	BOWEL	BUNCH	CATER	CHOCK	CLUMP	CRAFT
ADAPT	ALLEY	APPLE	AVOID	BEFOG	BLEAR	BOWER	BUNCO	CATTY	CHOIR	CLUNG	CRAMP
ADDER	ALLOT	APPLY	AWAIT	BEGET	BLEAT	BOXER	BUNNY	CAULK	CHOKE	CMSGT	CRANE
ADDLE	ALLOW	APRIL	AWAKE	BEGIN	BLEED	BRACE	BURGH	CAUSE	CHOMP	COACH	CRANK
ADDNL	ALLOY	APRON	AWARD	BEGUM	BLEND	BRACT	BURLY	CAVIL	CHOPS	COAST	CRAPE
ADEPT	ALOFT	ARBOR	AWARE	BEIGE	BLESS	BRAID	BURRO	CCITT	CHORD	COBOL	CRAPS
ADIEU	ALOHA	ARDOR	AWASH	BEING	BLIMP	BRAIN	BURST	CEASE	CHORE	COBRA	CRASH
ADIOS	ALONE	ARENA	AWFUL	BELAY	BLIND	BRAKE	BUSBY	CECUM	CHOSE	COCKY	CRASS
ADMAN	ALONG	ARGON	AXIAL	BELCH	BLINK	BRAND	BUTTE	CEDAR	CHRON	COCOA	CRATE
ADMIN	ALOOF	ARGOT	AXIOM	BELIE	BLISS	BRASH	BUTUT	CELLO	CHUCK	CODEC	CRAVE
ADMIT	ALOUD	ARGUE	AZTEC	BELLE	BLITZ	BRASS	BUXOM	CHAFE	CHUMP	CODEX	CRAWL
ADMIX	ALTAR	ARISE	AZURE	BELLS	BLOAT	BRAVE	BYLAW	CHAFF	CHUNK	COLIC	CRAZE
ADOBE	ALTER	ARITH	BABEL	BELLY	BLOCK	BRAVO	BYWAY	CHAIN	CHURL	COLON	CRAZY
ADOPT	AMAIN	ARMOR	BACON	BELOW	BLOND	BRAWL	CABAL	CHAIR	CHURN	COLOR	CREAK
ADORE	AMASS	AROMA	BADGE	BENCH	BLOOD	BRAWN	CABBY	CHALK	CHUTE	COMBO	CREAM
ADORN	AMAZE	ARRAS	BAGEL	BENNY	BLOOM	BRAZE	CABIN	CHAMP	CIDER	COMDG	CREDO
ADULT	AMBER	ARRAY	BAGGY	BERET	BLOWY	BREAD	CABLE	CHANT	CIGAR	COMDR	CREED
AEGIS	AMBLE	ARROW	BAIRN	BERRY	BLUES	BREAK	CACAO	CHAOS	CINCH	COMDT	CREEK
AERIE	AMEBA	ARSON	BAIZA	BERTH	BLUET	BREAM	CACHE	CHAPS	CIRCA	COMER	CREEL
AFAIK	AMEND	ARYAN	BAIZE	BERYL	BLUFF	BREED	CADDY	CHARD	CIVET	COMET	CREEP
AFAIR	AMISS	ASCII	BALKY	BESET	BLUNT	BRIAR	CADET	CHARM	CIVIC	COMFY	CREME
AFFIX	AMITY	ASCOT	BALMY	BESOM	BLURB	BRIBE	CADGE	CHART	CIVIL	COMIC	CREPE
AFIRE	AMONG	ASHEN	BALSA	BESOT	BLURT	BRICK	CADRE	CHARY	CLACK	COMMA	CRESC
AFOOT	AMOUR	ASIAN	BANAL	BETEL	BLUSH	BRIDE	CAGEY	CHASE	CLAIM	COMMO	CRESS
AFTER	AMPLE	ASIDE	BANDY	BEVEL	BOARD	BRIEF	CAIRN	CHASM	CLAMP	CONCH	CREST
AGAIN	AMPUL	ASKEW	BANJO	BEZEL	BOAST	BRIER	CAJUN	CHEAP	CLANG	CONEY	CRICK
AGAPE	AMUCK	ASPEN	BANNS	BHANG	BOBBY	BRINE	CALIF	CHEAT	CLANK	CONGA	CRIER
	AMUSE	ASPIC	BANTU	BIBLE	BOGEY	BRING	CALLA	CHECK	CLASH	CONIC	CRIME

CRIMP	DEFER	DOWEL	ECLAT	ERUPT	FETUS	FLUNG	GABLE	GORGE	GULCH	HOGAN	INEPT
CRISP	DEFOG	DOWER	EDEMA	ESSAY	FEVER	FLUNK	GAFFE	GORSE	GULLY	HOIST	INERT
CROAK	DEGAS	DOWNY	EDICT	ESTER	FEWER	FLUSH	GAILY	GOUDA	GUMBO	HOKUM	INFER
CROCK	DEICE	DOWRY	EDLIN	ETHER	FIBER	FLUTE	GAMIN	GOUGE	GUNNY	HOLLO	INGLE
CRONE	DEIFY	DOWSE	EDUCE	ETHOS	FICHE	FLYBY	GAMMA	GOURD	GUPPY	HOLLY	INGOT
CRONY	DEIGN	DOYEN	EERIE	ETHYL	FICHU	FLYER	GAMUT	GRACE	GUSHY	HOMER	INLAY
CROOK	DEISM	DOZEN	EGRET	ETUDE	FIELD	FOCUS	GANTT	GRADE	GUSTO	HOMEY	INLET
CROON	DEITY	DRAFT	EIDER	EVADE	FIEND	FOEHN	GAUDY	GRAFT	GUTTY	HONEY	INNER
CROSS	DELAY	DRAIN	EIGHT	EVENT	FIERY	FOIST	GAUGE	GRAIL	GUYOT	HONOR	INPUT
CROUP	DELFT	DRAKE	EJECT	EVERY	FIFTH	FOLIO	GAUNT	GRAIN	GYPSY	HOOEY	INSET
CROWD	DELTA	DRAMA	ELAND	EVICT	FIFTY	FOLLY	GAUSS	GRAND	HABIT	HORDE	INSOL
CROWN	DELVE	DRANK	ELATE	EVOKE	FIGHT	FORAY	GAUZE	GRANT	HADES	HORSE	INSTR
CRUDE	DEMON	DRAPE	ELBOW	EXACT	FILAR	FORCE	GAVEL	GRAPE	HAIKU	HOTEL	INTEL
CRUEL	DEMUR	DRAWL	ELDER	EXALT	FILCH	FORGE	GAWKY	GRAPH	HAIRY	HOUND	INTER
CRUET	DENIM	DREAD	ELECT	EXCEL	FILLY	FORGO	GEESE	GRASP	HAJJI	HOURI	INURE
CRUMB	DENSE	DREAM	ELEGY	EXERT	FILTH	FORTE	GELID	GRASS	HALER	HOUSE	INURN
CRUSE	DEPOT	DREAR	ELIDE	EXILE	FINAL	FORTH	GENIE	GRATE	HALLO	HOVEL	IRAQI
CRUSH	DEPTH	DRESS	ELITE	EXIST	FINCH	FORTY	GENRE	GRAVE	HALVE	HOVER	IRATE
CRUST	DERBY	DRIER	ELOPE	EXPEL	FINIS	FORUM	GENUS	GRAVY	HANDY	HUMAN	IRISH
CRYPT	DERIV	DRIFT	ELUDE	EXPTL	FINNY	FOUND	GEODE	GRAZE	HAOLE	HUMID	IRONY
CRYST	DETER	DRILL	ELVER	EXTOL	FIORD	FOUNT	GETUP	GREAT	HAPLY	HUMOR	IRREG
CUBAN	DEUCE	DRILY	ELVES	EXTRA	FIRST	FOXED	GHOST	GREBE	HAPPY	HUMUS	ISLAM
CUBIC	DEVIL	DRINK	EMAIL	EXUDE	FIRTH	FOYER	GHOUL	GREED	HARDY	HUNCH	ISLET
CUBIT	DIARY	DRIVE	EMBED	EXULT	FISHY	FRAIL	GIANT	GREEK	HAREM	HURON	ISSUE
CUPID	DIGIT	DROLL	EMBER	EXURB	FIXED	FRAME	GIDDY	GREEN	HARPY	HURRY	IVORY
CURIA	DINAR	DRONE	EMCEE	EYRIE	FJORD	FRANC	GIMPY	GREET	HARRY	HUSKY	JABOT
CURIO	DINER	DROOL	EMEND	EYRIR	FLAIL	FRANK	GIPSY	GRIEF	HARSH	HUSSY	JADED
CURRY	DINGO	DROOP	EMERY	FABLE	FLAIR	FRAUD	GIRTH	GRILL	HASTE	HUTCH	JALAP
CURSE	DINGY	DROSS	EMOTE	FACET	FLAKE	FREAK	GIVEN	GRIME	HATCH	HYDRA	JAPAN
CURVE	DINKY	DROVE	EMPTY	FAGOT	FLAME	FRESH	GIZMO	GRIND	HAUNT	HYDRO	JAUNT
CUTUP	DIODE	DROWN	ENACT	FAINT	FLANK	FRIAR	GLAND	GRIPE	HAVEN	HYENA	JAZZY
CYCLE	DIRGE	DRUID	ENDOW	FAIRY	FLARE	FRILL	GLANS	GRIST	HAVOC	HYING	JEANS
CYNIC	DIRTY	DRUNK	ENDUE	FAITH	FLASH	FRISK	GLARE	GRITS	HAYES	HYMEN	JELLY
CZECH	DISCO	DRUPE	ENEMA	FAKIR	FLASK	FRIZZ	GLASS	GROAN	HAZEL	ICHOR	JENNY
DACHA	DISTN	DRYAD	ENEMY	FALSE	FLECK	FROCK	GLAZE	GROAT	HEADY	ICING	JETTY
DADDY	DISTR	DRYER	ENIAC	FANCY	FLEER	FROND	GLEAM	GROIN	HEART	ICTUS	JEWEL
DAFFY	DITCH	DUCAL	ENJOY	FARCE	FLEET	FRONT	GLEAN	GROOM	HEATH	IDEAL	JEWRY
DAILY	DITTO	DUCAT	ENNUI	FATAL	FLESH	FROST	GLEBE	GROPE	HEAVE	IDIOM	JIFFY
DAIRY	DITTY	DUCHY	ENSUE	FATED	FLICK	FROTH	GLIDE	GROSS	HEAVY	IDIOT	JIHAD
DAISY	DIVAN	DUMMY	ENTER	FATTY	FLIED	FROWN	GLINT	GROSZ	HEDGE	IDYLL	JIMMY
DALLY	DIVOT	DUMPS	ENTOM	FAULT	FLIER	FROZE	GLOAT	GROUP	HEFTY	IGLOO	JOINT
DANCE	DIZZY	DUMPY	ENTRY	FAUNA	FLING	FRUIT	GLOBE	GROUT	HEIST	ILEUM	JOIST
DANDY	DLITT	DUNCE	ENVOI	FAVOR	FLINT	FRYER	GLOOM	GROVE	HELIX	IMAGE	JOKER
DATED	DODGE	DUPLE	ENVOY	FEAST	FLIRT	FSLIC	GLORY	GROWL	HELLO	IMAGO	JOLLY
DATUM	DOGGY	DUSKY	EPOCH	FEAZE	FLOAT	FUDGE	GLOSS	GRUEL	HELOT	IMBED	JOULE
DAUNT	DOGIE	DUTCH	EPOXY	FECES	FLOCK	FUGUE	GLOVE	GRUFF	HELVE	IMBUE	JOUST
DAVIT	DOGMA	DWARF	EPROM	FEIGN	FLOOD	FULLY	GLOZE	GRUNT	HENCE	IMPEL	JUDGE
DEATH	DOILY	DWELL	EPSON	FEINT	FLOOR	FUNKY	GLYPH	GUANO	HENNA	IMPER	JUICE
DEBAR	DOLLY	DYING	EQUAL	FELLY	FLORA	FUNNY	GNARL	GUARD	HERON	IMPLY	JUICY
DEBIT	DOLOR	EAGER	EQUIP	FELON	FLOSS	FUROR	GNASH	GUAVA	HERTZ	INANE	JULEP
DEBUG	DONOR	EAGLE	EQUIV	FEMUR	FLOUR	FURRY	GNOME	GUESS	HINDI	INCOG	JUMBO
DEBUT	DONUT	EARED	ERASE	FENCE	FLOUT	FURZE	GODLY	GUEST	HINGE	INCUR	JUMPY
DECAL	DOPEY	EARLY	ERECT	FERAL	FLOWN	FUSEE	GONAD	GUIDE	HITCH	INCUS	JUNCO
DECAY	DOUBT	EARTH	ERGOT	FERRY	FLUFF	FUSSY	GONER	GUILD	HIVES	INDEF	JUNTA
DECOR	DOUGH	EASEL	ERISA	FETAL	FLUID	FUSTY	GOODY	GUILE	HOARD	INDEX	JUNTO
DECOY	DOUSE	EAVES	ERODE	FETCH	FLUKE	FUZZY	GOOFY	GUILT	HOARY	INDIC	JUROR
DECRY	DOWDY	EBONY	ERROR	FETID	FLUME	GABBY	GOOSE	GUISE	HOBBY	INDUE	KABOB

KANJI	LATCH	LOESS	MAUVE	MOTEL	NICAD	ORGAN	PEACE	PLANK	PRONE	QUOIT	RHYME
KAPOK	LATEX	LOFTY	MAVEN	MOTET	NICHE	ORIEL	PEACH	PLANT	PRONG	QUOTA	RIDER
KAPUT	LATHE	LOGIC	MAVIS	MOTIF	NIECE	ORRIS	PEARL	PLASH	PROOF	QUOTE	RIDGE
KARAT	LATIN	LONER	MAXIM	MOTOR	NIFTY	OSAGE	PECAN	PLATE	PROSE	QUOTH	RIFLE
KARMA	LAUGH	LOONY	MAYBE	MOTTO	NIGHT	OSIER	PEDAL	PLATY	PROSY	QURSH	RIGHT
KARST	LAYER	LOOSE	MAYOR	MOULD	NINNY	OTHER	PEEVE	PLAYA	PROUD	RABBI	RIGID
KAYAK	LAZAR	LORRY	MCCOY	MOULT	NIPPY	OTTER	PEKOE	PLAZA	PROVE	RABID	RIGOR
KAZOO	LEACH	LOTUS	MECCA	MOUND	NISEI	OUGHT	PENAL	PLEAD	PROWL	RADAR	RINSE
KEBAB	LEARN	LOUSE	MEDAL	MOUNT	NITER	OUNCE	PENCE	PLEAT	PROXY	RADII	RIPEN
KEDGE	LEASE	LOUSY	MEDIA	MOURN	NITRO	OUTDO	PENIS	PLEBE	PRUDE	RADIO	RISER
KETCH	LEASH	LOWER	MEDIC	MOUSE	NOBLE	OUTER	PENNI	PLEBS	PRUNE	RADIX	RIVAL
KHAKI	LEAST	LOWLY	MELEE	MOUSY	NODDY	OUTGO	PENNY	PLUCK	PSALM	RADON	RIVER
KIOSK	LEAVE	LOYAL	MELON	MOUTH	NOHOW	OUTRE	PEONY	PLUMB	PSEUD	RAISE	RIVET
KIOWA	LEDGE	LUCID	MERCY	MOVER	NOISE	OVARY	PERCH	PLUME	PSYCH	RALLY	RIYAL
KITTY	LEECH	LUCKY	MERGE	MOVIE	NOISY	OVATE	PERIL	PLUMP	PUBES	RAMIE	RNZAF
KLUGE	LEERY	LUCRE	MERIT	MUCUS	NOMAD	OVERT	PESKY	PLUNK	PUBIC	RANCH	ROACH
KNACK	LEGAL	LUNAR	MERRY	MUFTI	NONCE	OVOID	PETAL	PLUSH	PUBIS	RANGE	ROAST
KNAVE	LEGGY	LUNCH	METAL	MUGGY	NONES	OVULE	PETER	PLUTO	PUDGY	RANGY	ROBIN
KNEAD	LEGIS	LUNGE	METER	MULCH	NOOSE	OWING	PETTY	POACH	PUFFY	RAPID	ROBOT
KNEEL	LEGIT	LURCH	METRE	MULCT	NORSE	OWLET	PEWEE	POESY	PUKKA	RATIO	RODEO
KNELL	LEMON	LURID	METRO	MUMMY	NORTH	OXBOW	PHAGE	POILU	PULSE	RATTY	ROGER
KNIFE	LEMUR	LUSTY	MIAMI	MUMPS	NOTCH	OXIDE	PHARM	POINT	PUNCH	RAVEL	ROGUE
KNISH	LEONE	LYING	MICRO	MUNCH	NOTED	OZONE	PHASE	POISE	PUPIL	RAVEN	ROMAN
KNOCK	LEPER	LYMPH	MIDDY	MURAL	NOVEL	PACER	PHIAL	POKER	PUPPY	RAYON	ROOST
KNOLL	LETUP	LYNCH	MIDGE	MUSHY	NOWAY	PADDY	PHLOX	POLAR	PUREE	RAZOR	ROSIN
KNOUT	LEVEE	LYRIC	MIDST	MUSIC	NUDGE	PADRE	PHONE	POLIO	PURGE	REACH	ROTOR
KNURL	LEVEL	MACAW	MIGHT	MUSTY	NUMIS	PAEAN	PHONO	POLIT	PURIM	REACT	ROUGE
KOALA	LEVER	MACRO	MILCH	MYRRH	NURSE	PAGAN	PHONY	POLKA	PURSE	READY	ROUGH
KOOKY	LIBEL	MADAM	MIMIC	NAACP	NUTTY	PAINT	PHOTO	POLYP	PUSHY	REALM	ROUND
KORAN	LICIT	MAFIA	MINCE	NABOB	NYLON	PAISA	PIANO	POOCH	PUSSY	REBEL	ROUSE
KRAAL	LIEGE	MAGIC	MINIM	NACRE	NYMPH	PALMY	PICKY	POPPY	PUTTY	REBUS	ROUTE
KRAUT	LIEUT	MAGMA	MINOR	NADIR	OAKUM	PALSY	PICOT	PORCH	PYGMY	REBUT	ROWDY
KRONA	LIFER	MAIZE	MINUS	NAIAD	OASIS	PAMPA	PIECE	POSER	PYLON	RECAP	ROWEL
KRONE	LIGHT	MAJOR	MIRTH	NAIRA	OBESE	PANDA	PIETY	POSIT	QUACK	RECIP	ROYAL
KUDOS	LIKEN	MALAY	MISER	NAIVE	OCCAS	PANEL	PIGMY	POSSE	QUAFF	RECTO	RUBLE
KULAK	LILAC	MAMBO	MISTY	NAKED	OCCUR	PANIC	PIKER	POUCH	QUAIL	RECUR	RUDDY
KURUS	LIMBO	MANES	MITER	NARIS	OCEAN	PANSY	PILAF	POULT	QUAKE	REEVE	RUGBY
LABEL	LIMIT	MANGE	MIXER	NASAL	OCHER	PANTS	PILES	POUND	QUALM	REFER	RULER
LABOR	LINEN	MANGO	MLLES	NASTY	OCTAL	PAPAL	PILOT	POWER	QUART	REGAL	RUMBA
LADEN	LINER	MANIA	MODEL	NATAL	OCTET	PAPAW	PINCH	PRANK	QUASH	REIGN	RUMMY
LADLE	LINGO	MANIC	MODEM	NATTY	ODIUM	PAPER	PINON	PRATE	QUASI	RELAX	RUMOR
LAGER	LINKS	MANLY	MODIF	NAVAL	OFFAL	PARCH	PINTO	PRAWN	QUEAN	RELAY	RUNNY
LAIRD	LISLE	MANNA	MOGUL	NAVEL	OFFER	PARKA	PINUP	PREEN	QUEEN	RELIC	RUPEE
LAITY	LISTS	MANOR	MOIRE	NEEDS	OFTEN	PARRY	PIOUS	PRESS	QUELL	RELIG	RURAL
LAMIA	LITER	MANSE	MOIST	NEEDY	OLDEN	PARSE	PIQUE	PRICE	QUERY	REMIT	SABER
LANAI	LITHE	MANTA	MOLAR	NEGRO	OLDIE	PARTY	PITCH	PRICK	QUEST	RENAL	SABLE
LANCE	LIVEN	MANUF	MONEY	NEGUS	OLIVE	PASHA	PITHY	PRIDE	QUEUE	RENEW	SAINT
LANKY	LIVER	MAORI	MONGO	NEIGH	OMAHA	PASSE	PITON	PRIME	QUICK	REPAY	SALAD
LAPEL	LIVES	MAPLE	MONTH	NERVE	ONION	PASTA	PIVOT	PRIMP	QUIET	REPEL	SALLY
LAPIN	LIVID	MARCH	MOODY	NERVY	ONSET	PASTE	PIXEL	PRINK	QUILL	REPLY	SALON
LAPSE	LLAMA	MARGE	MOOSE	NEVER	OPERA	PASTY	PIXIE	PRINT	QUILT	RERUN	SALVE
LARCH	LLANO	MARRY	MORAL	NEVUS	OPINE	PATCH	PIZZA	PRIOR	QUINT	RESIN	SALVO
LARGE	LOATH	MARSH	MORAY	NEWEL	OPIUM	PATEN	PLACE	PRISM	QUIRE	RETCH	SANIT
LARGO	LOBBY	MASER	MOREL	NEWLY	OPTIC	PATIO	PLAID	PRIVY	QUIRK	REVEL	SAPPY
LARVA	LOCAL	MASON	MORES	NEWSY	ORATE	PATSY	PLAIN	PRIZE	QUIRT	REVUE	SASSY
LASER	LOCUS	MATCH	MORON	NEXUS	ORBIT	PATTY	PLAIT	PROBE	QUITE	RHEUM	SATAN
LASSO	LODGE	MATZO	MOSEY	NGWEE	ORDER	PAUSE	PLANE	PROEM	QUITS	RHINO	SATIN

SATYR	SEPIA	SHREW	SLUNK	SPASM	STANK	STUNT	TACIT	THIRD	TOWER	TWANG	VALOR
SAUCE	SERGE	SHRUB	SLURP	SPATE	STARE	STYLE	TACKY	THOLE	TOXIC	TWEAK	VALSE
SAUCY	SERIF	SHRUG	SLUSH	SPAWN	STARK	SUAVE	TAFFY	THONG	TOXIN	TWEED	VALUE
SAUNA	SERUM	SHUCK	SMACK	SPEAK	START	SUCRE	TAIGA	THORN	TRACE	TWEEN	VALVE
SAUTE	SERVE	SHUNT	SMALL	SPEAR	STASH	SUEDE	TAINT	THORP	TRACK	TWEET	VAPID
SAVOR	SERVO	SIBYL	SMART	SPECK	STATE	SUGAR	TALER	THOSE	TRACT	TWICE	VAPOR
SAVVY	SETUP	SIDLE	SMASH	SPEED	STAVE	SUITE	TALLY	THREE	TRADE	TWILL	VARIA
SCALD	SEVEN	SIEGE	SMEAR	SPELL	STEAD	SULFA	TALON	THREW	TRAIL	TWINE	VASTY
SCALE	SEVER	SIEVE	SMELL	SPEND	STEAK	SULKY	TALUS	THROB	TRAIN	TWIRL	VATIC
SCALP	SEWER	SIGHT	SMELT	SPENT	STEAL	SULLY	TANGO	THROE	TRAIT	TWIST	VAULT
SCAMP	SHACK	SIGMA	SMILE	SPERM	STEAM	SUMAC	TANSY	THROW	TRAMP	TWIXT	VAUNT
SCAND	SHADE	SILLY	SMIRK	SPICE	STEED	SUNUP	TAPER	THRUM	TRANS	TYING	VEERY
SCANF	SHAFT	SINCE	SMITE	SPIEL	STEEL	SUPER	TAPIR	THUMB	TRAPS	UDDER	VELAR
SCANT	SHAKE	SINEW	SMITH	SPIKE	STEEP	SUPRA	TARDY	THUMP	TRASH	UKASE	VELUM
SCARE	SHAKY	SINGE	SMOCK	SPILL	STEER	SUPVR	TAROT	THURS	TRAWL	ULCER	VENAL
SCARF	SHALE	SINUS	SMOKE	SPINE	STEIN	SURGE	TARRY	THYME	TREAD	ULTRA	VENOM
SCARP	SHALL	SIOUX	SMOTE	SPIRE	STERE	SURLY	TASTE	TIARA	TREAS	UMBEL	VENUE
SCENE	SHAME	SIREN	SMSGT	SPIRT	STERN	SWAGE	TASTY	TIBIA	TREAT	UMBER	VENUS
SCENT	SHANK	SIRUP	SNACK	SPITE	STICK	SWAIN	TAUNT	TICAL	TREND	UMBRA	VERGE
SCION	SHAPE	SISAL	SNAIL	SPLAY	STIFF	SWAMI	TAUPE	TIGER	TRESS	UMIAK	VERSE
SCOFF	SHARD	SISSY	SNAKE	SPLIT	STILE	SWAMP	TAWNY	TIGHT	TRIAD	UNARM	VERSO
SCOLD	SHARE	SITAR	SNARE	SPOIL	STILL	SWANK	TEACH	TILDE	TRIAL	UNBAR	VERST
SCONE	SHARK	SIXTY	SNARL	SPOKE	STILT	SWARD	TEASE	TILTH	TRIBE	UNCAP	VERVE
SCOOP	SHARP	SKATE	SNEAK	SPOOF	STING	SWARM	TEENS	TIMES	TRICE	UNCLE	VETCH
SCOOT	SHAVE	SKEET	SNEER	SPOOK	STINK	SWART	TEENY	TIMID	TRICK	UNCUT	VIAND
SCOPE	SHAWL	SKEIN	SNIDE	SPOOL	STINT	SWASH	TEETH	TINCT	TRIED	UNDER	VIBES
SCORE	SHEAF	SKIFF	SNIFF	SPOON	STOAT	SWATH	TELEG	TINGE	TRILL	UNDUE	VICAR
SCORN	SHEAR	SKILL	SNIPE	SPOOR	STOCK	SWEAR	TELEX	TINNY	TRINE	UNFIT	VIDEO
SCOTS	SHEEN	SKIMP	SNIPS	SPORE	STOIC	SWEAT	TEMPO	TIPSY	TRIPE	UNFIX	VIGIL
SCOUR	SHEEP	SKIRT	SNOOP	SPORT	STOKE	SWEDE	TEMPT	TIRED	TRITE	UNIFY	VIGOR
SCOUT	SHEER	SKULK	SNORE	SPOUT	STOLE	SWEEP	TENET	TITAN	TROLL	UNION	VILLA
SCOWL	SHEET	SKULL	SNORT	SPRAT	STOMP	SWEET	TENON	TITHE	TROMP	UNITE	VINYL
SCRAM	SHELF	SKUNK	SNOUT	SPRAY	STONE	SWELL	TENOR	TITLE	TROOP	UNITY	VIOLA
SCRAP	SHELL	SLACK	SNOWY	SPREE	STOOD	SWEPT	TENSE	TIZZY	TROPE	UNMAN	VIPER
SCREW	SHIER	SLAIN	SNUCK	SPRIG	STOOL	SWIFT	TEPEE	TOADY	TROTH	UNPEG	VIRAL
SCRIM	SHIFT	SLAKE	SNUFF	SPUME	STOOP	SWILL	TEPID	TOAST	TROUT	UNPIN	VIREO
SCRIP	SHILL	SLANG	SOBER	SPUNK	STORE	SWINE	TERRY	TODAY	TRUCE	UNRWA	VIRTU
SCROD	SHINE	SLANT	SOGGY	SPURN	STORK	SWING	TERSE	TODDY	TRUCK	UNSAY	VIRUS
SCRUB	SHINY	SLASH	SOLAR	SPURT	STORM	SWIPE	TESTY	TOKAY	TRUMP	UNTIE	VISIT
SCUBA	SHIPT	SLATE	SOLID	SQUAB	STORY	SWIRL	THANE	TOKEN	TRUNK	UNTIL	VISOR
SCUFF	SHIRE	SLAVE	SOLON	SQUAD	STOUT	SWISH	THANK	TONER	TRUSS	UNZIP	VISTA
SCULL	SHIRK	SLEEK	SOLVE	SQUAT	STOVE	SWISS	THEAT	TONGS	TRUST	UPEND	VITAL
SCURF	SHIRR	SLEEP	SONAR	SQUAW	STRAP	SWITZ	THEFT	TONIC	TRUTH	UPPER	VIVID
SEAMY	SHIRT	SLEET	SONIC	SQUIB	STRAW	SWOON	THEGN	TOOTH	TRYST	UPSET	VIXEN
SEATO	SHOAL	SLICE	SOOTH	SQUID	STRAY	SWOOP	THEIR	TOPAZ	TUBER	URBAN	VIZOR
SEDAN	SHOAT	SLICK	SORRY	STACK	STREW	SWORD	THEME	TOPER	TULIP	URINE	VOCAB
SEDGE	SHOCK	SLIDE	SOUGH	STAFF	STRIA	SWORE	THEOL	TOPIC	TULLE	USAGE	VOCAL
SEEDY	SHONE	SLIER	SOUND	STAGE	STRIP	SWORN	THERE	TOPOG	TUMID	USHER	VODKA
SEINE	SHOOK	SLIME	SOUPY	STAID	STROP	SWUNG	THERM	TOQUE	TUMMY	USUAL	VOGUE
SEISM	SHOOT	SLING	SOUSE	STAIN	STRUM	SYLPH	THESE	TORAH	TUMOR	USURP	VOICE
SEIZE	SHORE	SLINK	SOUTH	STAIR	STRUT	SYNOD	THESS	TORCH	TUNIC	USURY	VOILE
SEMEN	SHORN	SLOOP	SPACE	STAKE	STUCK	SYRUP	THICK	TORSO	TUNNY	UTILE	VOMIT
SENGI	SHORT	SLOPE	SPADE	STALE	STUDY	SYSOP	THIEF	TOTAL	TUQUE	UTTER	VOUCH
SENNA	SHOUT	SLOSH	SPANK	STALK	STUFF	TABBY	THIGH	TOTEM	TURBO	UVULA	VOWEL
SENSE	SHOVE	SLOTH	SPARC	STALL	STUMP	TABLE	THINE	TOUCH	TURPS	VAGUE	VULVA
SENTI	SHOWY	SLUMP	SPARE	STAMP	STUNG	TABOO	THING	TOUGH	TUTOR	VALET	VYING
SEPAL	SHRED	SLUNG	SPARK	STAND	STUNK	TABOR	THINK	TOWEL	TWAIN	VALID	WACKY

		2ND LETTER									
WADER	WIGHT	BABEL	CANOE	GABLE	LAGER	MAXIM	RADII	TASTE	OBESE	ADDLE	BEVEL
WAFER	WINCE	BACON	CANON	GAFFE	LAIRD	MAYBE	RADIO	TASTY	ACORN	ADDNL	BEZEL
WAGER	WINCH	BADGE	CANTO	GAILY	LAITY	MAYOR	RADIX	TAUNT	ACRID	ADEPT	CEASE
WAGON	WINDY	BAGEL	CAPER	GAMIN	LAMIA	NAACP	RADON	TAUPE	ACTOR	ADIEU	CECUM
WAHOO	WITCH	BAGGY	CAPON	GAMMA	LANAI	NABOB	RAISE	TAWNY	ACUTE	ADIOS	CEDAR
WAIST	WITHE	BAIRN	CARAT	GAMUT	LANCE	NACRE	RALLY	VAGUE	CCITT	ADMAN	CELLO
WAIVE	WITHY	BAIZA	CARET	GANTT	LANKY	NADIR	RAMIE	VALET	ECLAT	ADMIN	DEATH
WAKEN	WITTY	BAIZE	CARGO	GAUDY	LAPEL	NAIAD	RANCH	VALID	ICHOR	ADMIT	DEBAR
WALTZ	WIVES	BALKY	CARNY	GAUGE	LAPIN	NAIRA	RANGE	VALOR	ICING	ADMIX	DEBIT
WASHY	WOKEN	BALMY	CAROL	GAUNT	LAPSE	NAIVE	RANGY	VALSE	ICTUS	ADOBE	DEBUG
WASTE	WOMAN	BALSA	CAROM	GAUSS	LARCH	NAKED	RAPID	VALUE	MCCOY	ADOPT	DEBUT
WATCH	WOODY	BANAL	CARRY	GAUZE	LARGE	NARIS	RATIO	VALVE	OCCAS	ADORE	DECAL
WATER	WOOZY	BANDY	CARVE	GAVEL	LARGO	NASAL	RATTY	VAPID	OCCUR	ADORN	DECAY
WAVER	WORDY	BANJO	CASTE	GAWKY	LARVA	NASTY	RAVEL	VAPOR	OCEAN	ADULT	DECOR
WAXEN	WORLD	BANNS	CATCH	HABIT	LASER	NATAL	RAVEN	VARIA	OCHER	EDEMA	DECOY
WEALD	WORRY	BANTU	CATER	HADES	LASSO	NATTY	RAYON	VASTY	OCTAL	EDICT	DECRY
WEARY	WORSE	BARGE	CATTY	HAIKU	LATCH	NAVAL	RAZOR	VATIC	OCTET	EDLIN	DEFER
WEAVE	WORST	BARON	CAULK	HAIRY	LATEX	NAVEL	SABER	VAULT	SCALD	EDUCE	DEFOG
WEDGE	WORTH	BASAL	CAUSE	HAJJI	LATHE	OAKUM	SABLE	VAUNT	SCALE	IDEAL	DEGAS
WEEDY	WOULD	BASIC	CAVIL	HALER	LATIN	OASIS	SAINT	WACKY	SCALP	IDIOM	DEICE
WEENY	WOUND	BASIL	DACHA	HALLO	LAUGH	PACER	SALAD	WADER	SCAMP	IDIOT	DEIFY
WEEPY	WOVEN	BASIN	DADDY	HALVE	LAYER	PADDY	SALLY	WAFER	SCAND	IDYLL	DEIGN
WEIGH	WRACK	BASIS	DAFFY	HANDY	LAZAR	PADRE	SALON	WAGER	SCANF	ODIUM	DEISM
WEIRD	WRATH	BASSO	DAILY	HAOLE	MACAW	PAEAN	SALVE	WAGON	SCANT	UDDER	DEITY
WELCH	WREAK	BASTE	DAIRY	HAPLY	MACRO	PAGAN	SALVO	WAHOO	SCARE	AEGIS	DELAY
WELSH	WRECK	BATCH	DAISY	HAPPY	MADAM	PAINT	SANIT	WAIST	SCARF	AERIE	DELFT
WENCH	WREST	BATHE	DALLY	HARDY	MAFIA	PAISA	SAPPY	WAIVE	SCARP	BEACH	DELTA
WHACK	WRING	BATIK	DANCE	HAREM	MAGIC	PALMY	SASSY	WAKEN	SCENE	BEANO	DELVE
WHALE	WRIST	BATON	DANDY	HARPY	MAGMA	PALSY	SATAN	WALTZ	SCENT	BEARD	DEMON
WHARF	WRITE	BATTY	DATED	HARRY	MAIZE	PAMPA	SATIN	WASHY	SCION	BEAST	DEMUR
WHEAL	WRONG	BAWDY	DATUM	HARSH	MAJOR	PANDA	SATYR	WASTE	SCOFF	BEDEW	DENIM
WHEAT	WROTE	BAYOU	DAUNT	HASTE	MALAY	PANEL	SAUCE	WATCH	SCOLD	BEECH	DENSE
WHEEL	WROTH	CABAL	DAVIT	HATCH	MAMBO	PANIC	SAUCY	WATER	SCONE	BEEFY	DEPOT
WHELK	WRUNG	CABBY	EAGER	HAUNT	MANES	PANSY	SAUNA	WAVER	SCOOP	BEFIT	DEPTH
WHELM	WURST	CABIN	EAGLE	HAVEN	MANGE	PANTS	SAUTE	WAXEN	SCOOT	BEFOG	DERBY
WHELP	XCOPY	CABLE	EARED	HAVOC	MANGO	PAPAL	SAVOR	YACHT	SCOPE	BEGET	DERIV
WHERE	XEBEC	CACAO	EARLY	HAYES	MANIA	PAPAW	SAVVY	YAHOO	SCORE	BEGIN	DETER
WHICH	XENON	CACHE	EARTH	HAZEL	MANIC	PAPER	TABBY	ZAIRE	SCORN	BEGUM	DEUCE
WHIFF	XERIC	CADDY	EASEL	JABOT	MANLY	PARCH	TABLE	ABACK	SCOTS	BEIGE	DEVIL
WHILE	XYLEM	CADET	EAVES	JADED	MANNA	PARKA	TABOO	ABAFT	SCOUR	BEING	EERIE
WHINE	YACHT	CADGE	FABLE	JALAP	MANOR	PARRY	TABOR	ABASE	SCOUT	BELAY	FEAST
WHIRL	YAHOO	CADRE	FACET	JAPAN	MANSE	PARSE	TACIT	ABASH	SCOWL	BELCH	FEAZE
WHISH	YEARN	CAGEY	FAGOT	JAUNT	MANTA	PARTY	TACKY	ABATE	SCRAM	BELIE	FECES
WHISK	YEAST	CAIRN	FAINT	JAZZY	MANUF	PASHA	TAFFY	ABBEY	SCRAP	BELLE	FEIGN
WHIST	YIELD	CAJUN	FAIRY	KABOB	MAORI	PASSE	TAIGA	ABBOT	SCREW	BELLS	FEINT
WHITE	YODEL	CALIF	FAITH	KANJI	MAPLE	PASTA	TAINT	ABEAM	SCRIM	BELLY	FELLY
WHOLE	YOKEL	CALLA	FAKIR	KAPOK	MARCH	PASTE	TALER	ABHOR	SCRIP	BELOW	FELON
WHOOP	YOUNG	CALIF	FALSE	KAPUT	MARGE	PASTY	TALLY	ABIDE	SCROD	BENCH	FEMUR
WHORE	YOURS	CALLA	FANCY	KARAT	MARRY	PATCH	TALON	ABODE	SCRUB	BENNY	FENCE
WHORL	YOUTH	CALVE	FARCE	KARMA	MARSH	PATEN	TALUS	ABORT	SCUBA	BERET	FERAL
WHOSE	YUCCA	CALYX	FATAL	KARST	MASER	PATIO	TANGO	ABOUT	SCUFF	BERRY	FERRY
WHOSO	YUMMY	CAMEL	FATED	KAYAK	MASON	PATSY	TANSY	ABOVE	SCULL	BERTH	FETAL
WHSLE	ZAIRE	CAMEO	FATTY	KAZOO	MATCH	PATTY	TAPER	ABSTR	SCURF	BERYL	FETCH
WIDEN	ZEBRA	CANAL	FAULT	LABEL	MATZO	PAUSE	TAPIR	ABUSE	XCOPY	BESET	FETID
WIDOW	ZIPPY	CANDY	FAUNA	LABOR	MAUVE	RABBI	TARDY	ABYSM	ADAGE	BESOM	FETUS
WIDTH	ZLOTY	CANNA	FAVOR	LADEN	MAVEN	RABID	TAROT	ABYSS	ADAPT	BESOT	FEVER
WIELD	ZONAL	CANNY	GABBY	LADLE	MAVIS	RADAR	TARRY	EBONY	ADDER	BETEL	FEWER

GEESE	MELEE	REIGN	TESTY	CHAFF	KHAKI	SHOVE	WHISH	FIELD	LIVID	RINSE	VISIT
GELID	MELON	RELAX	VEERY	CHAIN	PHAGE	SHOWY	WHISK	FIEND	MIAMI	RIPEN	VISOR
GENIE	MERCY	RELAY	VELAR	CHAIR	PHARM	SHRED	WHIST	FIERY	MICRO	RISER	VISTA
GENRE	MERGE	RELIC	VELUM	CHALK	PHASE	SHREW	WHITE	FIFTH	MIDDY	RIVAL	VITAL
GENUS	MERIT	RELIG	VENAL	CHAMP	PHIAL	SHRUB	WHOLE	FIFTY	MIDGE	RIVER	VIVID
GEODE	MERRY	REMIT	VENOM	CHANT	PHLOX	SHRUG	WHOOP	FIGHT	MIDST	RIVET	VIXEN
GETUP	METAL	RENAL	VENUE	CHAOS	PHONE	SHUCK	WHORE	FILAR	MIGHT	RIYAL	VIZOR
HEADY	METER	RENEW	VENUS	CHAPS	PHONO	SHUNT	WHORL	FILCH	MILCH	SIBYL	WIDEN
HEART	METRE	REPAY	VERGE	CHARD	PHONY	THANE	WHOSE	FILLY	MIMIC	SIDLE	WIDOW
HEATH	METRO	REPEL	VERSE	CHARM	PHOTO	THANK	WHOSO	FILTH	MINCE	SIEGE	WIDTH
HEAVE	NEEDS	REPLY	VERSO	CHART	RHEUM	THEAT	WHSLE	FINAL	MINIM	SIEVE	WIELD
HEAVY	NEEDY	RERUN	VERST	CHARY	RHINO	THEFT	AISLE	FINCH	MINOR	SIGHT	WIGHT
HEDGE	NEGRO	RESIN	VERVE	CHASE	RHYME	THEGN	BIBLE	FINIS	MINUS	SIGMA	WINCE
HEFTY	NEGUS	RETCH	VETCH	CHASM	SHACK	THEIR	BIDDY	FINNY	MIRTH	SILLY	WINCH
HEIST	NEIGH	REVEL	WEALD	CHEAP	SHADE	THEME	BIDET	FIORD	MISER	SINCE	WINDY
HELIX	NERVE	REVUE	WEARY	CHEAT	SHAFT	THEOL	BIGHT	FIRST	MISTY	SINEW	WITCH
HELLO	NERVY	SEAMY	WEAVE	CHECK	SHAKE	THERE	BIGOT	FIRTH	MITER	SINGE	WITHE
HELOT	NEVER	SEATO	WEDGE	CHEEK	SHAKY	THERM	BILGE	FISHY	MIXER	SINUS	WITHY
HELVE	NEVUS	SEDAN	WEEDY	CHEEP	SHALE	THESE	BILLY	FIXED	NICAD	SIOUX	WITTY
HENCE	NEWEL	SEDGE	WEENY	CHEER	SHALL	THESS	BINGE	GIANT	NICHE	SIREN	WIVES
HENNA	NEWLY	SEEDY	WEEPY	CHELA	SHAME	THICK	BINGO	GIDDY	NIECE	SIRUP	YIELD
HERON	NEWSY	SEINE	WEIGH	CHERT	SHANK	THIEF	BIPED	GIMPY	NIFTY	SISAL	ZIPPY
HERTZ	NEXUS	SEISM	WEIRD	CHESS	SHAPE	THIGH	BIRCH	GIPSY	NIGHT	SISSY	EJECT
JEANS	PEACE	SEIZE	WELCH	CHEST	SHARD	THINE	BIRTH	GIRTH	NINNY	SITAR	FJORD
JELLY	PEACH	SEMEN	WELSH	CHEWY	SHARE	THING	BISON	GIVEN	NIPPY	SIXTY	SKATE
JENNY	PEARL	SENGI	WENCH	CHIAO	SHARK	THINK	BITCH	GIZMO	NISEI	TIARA	SKEET
JETTY	PECAN	SENNA	XEBEC	CHICK	SHARP	THIRD	CIDER	HINDI	NITER	TIBIA	SKEIN
JEWEL	PEDAL	SENSE	XENON	CHIDE	SHAVE	THOLE	CIGAR	HINGE	NITRO	TICAL	SKIFF
JEWRY	PEEVE	SENTI	XERIC	CHIEF	SHAWL	THONG	CINCH	HITCH	PIANO	TIGER	SKILL
KEBAB	PEKOE	SEPAL	YEARN	CHILD	SHEAF	THORN	CIRCA	HIVES	PICKY	TIGHT	SKIMP
KEDGE	PENAL	SEPIA	YEAST	CHILI	SHEAR	THORP	CIVET	JIFFY	PICOT	TILDE	SKIRT
KETCH	PENCE	SERGE	ZEBRA	CHILL	SHEEN	THOSE	CIVIC	JIHAD	PIECE	TILTH	SKULK
LEACH	PENIS	SERIF	AFAIK	CHIME	SHEEP	THREE	CIVIL	JIMMY	PIETY	TIMES	SKULL
LEARN	PENNI	SERUM	AFAIR	CHIMP	SHEER	THREW	DIARY	KIOSK	PIGMY	TIMID	SKUNK
LEASE	PENNY	SERVE	AFFIX	CHINA	SHEET	THROB	DIGIT	KIOWA	PIKER	TINCT	UKASE
LEASH	PEONY	SERVO	AFIRE	CHINE	SHELF	THROE	DINAR	KITTY	PILAF	TINGE	ALARM
LEAST	PERCH	SETUP	AFOOT	CHINK	SHELL	THROW	DINER	LIBEL	PILES	TINNY	ALBUM
LEAVE	PERIL	SEVEN	AFTER	CHINO	SHIER	THRUM	DINGO	LICIT	PILOT	TIPSY	ALDER
LEDGE	PESKY	SEVER	OFFAL	CHIRP	SHIFT	THUMB	DINGY	LIEGE	PINCH	TIRED	ALERT
LEECH	PETAL	SEWER	OFFER	CHIVE	SHILL	THUMP	DINKY	LIEUT	PINON	TITAN	ALGOL
LEERY	PETER	TEACH	OFTEN	CHOCK	SHINE	THURS	DIODE	LIFER	PINTO	TITHE	ALIAS
LEGAL	PETTY	TEASE	AGAIN	CHOIR	SHINY	THYME	DIRGE	LIGHT	PINUP	TITLE	ALIBI
LEGGY	PEWEE	TEENS	AGAPE	CHOKE	SHIPT	WHACK	DIRTY	LIKEN	PIOUS	TIZZY	ALIEN
LEGIS	REACH	TEENY	AGATE	CHOMP	SHIRE	WHALE	DISCO	LILAC	PIQUE	VIAND	ALIGN
LEGIT	REACT	TEETH	AGAVE	CHOPS	SHIRK	WHARF	DISTN	LIMBO	PITCH	VIBES	ALIKE
LEMON	READY	TELEG	AGENT	CHORD	SHIRR	WHEAL	DISTR	LIMIT	PITHY	VICAR	ALIVE
LEMUR	REALM	TELEX	AGILE	CHORE	SHIRT	WHEAT	DITCH	LINEN	PITON	VIDEO	ALKYD
LEONE	REBEL	TEMPO	AGLOW	CHOSE	SHOAL	WHEEL	DITTO	LINER	PIVOT	VIGIL	ALLAH
LEPER	REBUS	TEMPT	AGONY	CHRON	SHOAT	WHELK	DITTY	LINGO	PIXEL	VIGOR	ALLAY
LETUP	REBUT	TENET	AGORA	CHUCK	SHOCK	WHELM	DIVAN	LINKS	PIXIE	VILLA	ALLEY
LEVEE	RECAP	TENON	AGREE	CHUMP	SHONE	WHELP	DIVOT	LISLE	PIZZA	VINYL	ALLOT
LEVEL	RECIP	TENOR	EGRET	CHUNK	SHOOK	WHERE	DIZZY	LISTS	RIDER	VIOLA	ALLOW
LEVER	RECTO	TENSE	IGLOO	CHURL	SHOOT	WHICH	EIDER	LITER	RIDGE	VIPER	ALLOY
MECCA	RECUR	TEPEE	NGWEE	CHURN	SHORE	WHIFF	EIGHT	LITHE	RIFLE	VIRAL	ALOFT
MEDAL	REEVE	TEPID	AHEAD	CHUTE	SHORN	WHILE	FIBER	LIVEN	RIGHT	VIREO	ALOHA
MEDIA	REFER	TERRY	BHANG	GHOST	SHORT	WHINE	FICHE	LIVER	RIGID	VIRTU	ALONE
MEDIC	REGAL	TERSE	CHAFE	GHOUL	SHOUT	WHIRL	FICHU	LIVES	RIGOR	VIRUS	ALONG

ALOOF	CLOAK	FLUNK	SLANG	IMPLY	INCUR	UNCLE	COLIC	DOWSE	JOUST	NOHOW	SOLON
ALOUD	CLOCK	FLUSH	SLANT	OMAHA	INCUS	UNCUT	COLON	DOYEN	KOALA	NOISE	SOLVE
ALTAR	CLONE	FLUTE	SLASH	SMACK	INDEF	UNDER	COLOR	DOZEN	KOOKY	NOISY	SONAR
ALTER	CLOSE	FLYBY	SLATE	SMALL	INDEX	UNDUE	COMBO	FOCUS	KORAN	NOMAD	SONIC
BLACK	CLOTH	FLYER	SLAVE	SMART	INDIC	UNFIT	COMDG	FOEHN	LOATH	NONCE	SOOTH
BLADE	CLOUD	GLAND	SLEEK	SMASH	INDUE	UNFIX	COMDR	FOIST	LOBBY	NONES	SORRY
BLAIN	CLOUT	GLANS	SLEEP	SMEAR	INEPT	UNIFY	COMDT	FOLIO	LOCAL	NOOSE	SOUGH
BLAME	CLOVE	GLARE	SLEET	SMELL	INERT	UNION	COMER	FOLLY	LOCUS	NORSE	SOUND
BLAND	CLOWN	GLASS	SLICE	SMELT	INFER	UNITE	COMET	FORAY	LODGE	NORTH	SOUPY
BLANK	CLUCK	GLAZE	SLICK	SMILE	INGLE	UNITY	COMFY	FORCE	LOESS	NOTCH	SOUSE
BLARE	CLUMP	GLEAM	SLIDE	SMIRK	INGOT	UNMAN	COMIC	FORGE	LOFTY	NOTED	SOUTH
BLASE	CLUNG	GLEAN	SLIER	SMITE	INLAY	UNPEG	COMMA	FORGO	LOGIC	NOVEL	TOADY
BLAST	DLITT	GLEBE	SLIME	SMITH	INLET	UNPIN	COMMO	FORTE	LONER	NOWAY	TOAST
BLAZE	ELAND	GLIDE	SLING	SMOCK	INNER	UNRWA	CONCH	FORTH	LOONY	POACH	TODAY
BLEAK	ELATE	GLINT	SLINK	SMOKE	INPUT	UNSAY	CONEY	FORTY	LOOSE	POESY	TODDY
BLEAR	ELBOW	GLOAT	SLOOP	SMOTE	INSET	UNTIE	CONGA	FORUM	LORRY	POILU	TOKAY
BLEAT	ELDER	GLOBE	SLOPE	SMSGT	INSOL	UNTIL	CONIC	FOUND	LOTUS	POINT	TOKEN
BLEED	ELECT	GLOOM	SLOSH	UMBEL	INSTR	UNZIP	CONST	FOUNT	LOUSE	POISE	TONER
BLEND	ELEGY	GLORY	SLOTH	UMBER	INTEL	AORTA	CONTD	FOXED	LOUSY	POKER	TONGS
BLESS	ELIDE	GLOSS	SLUMP	UMBRA	INTER	BOARD	CONTG	FOYER	LOWER	POLAR	TONIC
BLIMP	ELITE	GLOVE	SLUNG	UMIAK	INURE	BOAST	CONTR	GODLY	LOWLY	POLIO	TOOTH
BLIND	ELOPE	GLOZE	SLUNK	ANENT	INURN	BOBBY	COPRA	GONAD	LOYAL	POLIT	TOPAZ
BLINK	ELUDE	GLYPH	SLURP	ANGEL	KNACK	BOGEY	COPSE	GONER	MODEL	POLKA	TOPER
BLISS	ELVER	ILEUM	SLUSH	ANGER	KNAVE	BOGUS	CORAL	GOODY	MODEM	POLYP	TOPIC
BLITZ	ELVES	KLUGE	ULCER	ANGLE	KNEAD	BOLUS	CORNY	GOOFY	MODIF	POOCH	TOPOG
BLOAT	FLAIL	LLAMA	ULTRA	ANGLO	KNEEL	BONER	CORPS	GOOSE	MOGUL	POPPY	TOQUE
BLOCK	FLAIR	LLANO	ZLOTY	ANGRY	KNELL	BONGO	COUCH	GORGE	MOIRE	PORCH	TORAH
BLOND	FLAKE	MLLES	AMAIN	ANGST	KNIFE	BONNY	COUGH	GORSE	MOIST	POSER	TORCH
BLOOD	FLAME	OLDEN	AMASS	ANGUS	KNISH	BONUS	COULD	GOUDA	MOLAR	POSIT	TORSO
BLOOM	FLANK	OLDIE	AMAZE	ANION	KNOCK	BONZE	COUNT	GOUGE	MONEY	POSSE	TOTAL
BLOWY	FLARE	OLIVE	AMBER	ANISE	KNOLL	BOOBY	COUPE	GOURD	MONGO	POUCH	TOTEM
BLUES	FLASH	PLACE	AMBLE	ANKLE	KNOUT	BOOST	COURT	HOARD	MONTH	POULT	TOUCH
BLUET	FLASK	PLAID	AMEBA	ANNEX	KNURL	BOOTH	COVEN	HOARY	MOODY	POUND	TOUGH
BLUFF	FLECK	PLAIN	AMEND	ANNOY	ONION	BOOTY	COVER	HOBBY	MOOSE	POWER	TOWEL
BLUNT	FLEER	PLAIT	AMISS	ANNUL	ONSET	BOOZE	COVET	HOGAN	MORAL	ROACH	TOWER
BLURB	FLEET	PLANE	AMITY	ANODE	RNZAF	BORAX	COVEY	HOIST	MORAY	ROAST	TOXIC
BLURT	FLESH	PLANK	AMONG	ANTIC	SNACK	BORNE	COWER	HOKUM	MOREL	ROBIN	TOXIN
BLUSH	FLICK	PLANT	AMOUR	ANVIL	SNAIL	BORON	COYPU	HOLLO	MORES	ROBOT	VOCAB
CLACK	FLIED	PLASH	AMPLE	ENACT	SNAKE	BOSKY	COZEN	HOLLY	MORON	RODEO	VOCAL
CLAIM	FLIER	PLATE	AMPUL	ENDOW	SNARE	BOSOM	DODGE	HOMER	MOSEY	ROGER	VODKA
CLAMP	FLING	PLATY	AMUCK	ENDUE	SNARL	BOSUN	DOGGY	HOMEY	MOTEL	ROGUE	VOGUE
CLANG	FLINT	PLAYA	AMUSE	ENEMA	SNEAK	BOTCH	DOGIE	HONEY	MOTET	ROMAN	VOICE
CLANK	FLIRT	PLAZA	CMSGT	ENEMY	SNEER	BOUGH	DOGMA	HONOR	MOTIF	ROOST	VOILE
CLASH	FLOAT	PLEAD	EMAIL	ENIAC	SNIDE	BOULE	DOILY	HOOEY	MOTOR	ROSIN	VOMIT
CLASP	FLOCK	PLEAT	EMBED	ENJOY	SNIFF	BOUND	DOLLY	HORDE	MOTTO	ROTOR	VOUCH
CLASS	FLOOD	PLEBE	EMBER	ENNUI	SNIPE	BOURN	DOLOR	HORSE	MOULD	ROUGE	VOWEL
CLEAN	FLOOR	PLEBS	EMCEE	ENSUE	SNIPS	BOWEL	DONOR	HOTEL	MOULT	ROUGH	WOKEN
CLEAR	FLORA	PLUCK	EMEND	ENTER	SNOOP	BOWER	DONUT	HOUND	MOUND	ROUND	WOMAN
CLEAT	FLOSS	PLUMB	EMERY	ENTOM	SNORE	BOXER	DOPEY	HOURI	MOUNT	ROUSE	WOODY
CLEFT	FLOUR	PLUME	EMOTE	ENTRY	SNORT	COACH	DOUBT	HOUSE	MOURN	ROUTE	WOOZY
CLERK	FLOUT	PLUMP	EMPTY	ENVOI	SNOUT	COAST	DOUGH	HOVEL	MOUSE	ROWDY	WORDY
CLICK	FLOWN	PLUNK	IMAGE	ENVOY	SNOWY	COBOL	DOUSE	HOVER	MOUSY	ROWEL	WORLD
CLIFF	FLUFF	PLUSH	IMAGO	GNARL	SNUCK	COBRA	DOWDY	JOINT	MOUTH	ROYAL	WORRY
CLIMB	FLUID	PLUTO	IMBED	GNASH	SNUFF	COCKY	DOWEL	JOIST	MOVER	SOBER	WORSE
CLIME	FLUKE	SLACK	IMBUE	GNOME	UNARM	COCOA	DOWER	JOKER	MOVIE	SOGGY	WORST
CLING	FLUME	SLAIN	IMPEL	INANE	UNBAR	CODEC	DOWNY	JOLLY	NOBLE	SOLAR	WORTH
CLINK	FLUNG	SLAKE	IMPER	INCOG	UNCAP	CODEX	DOWRY	JOULE	NODDY	SOLID	WOULD

WOUND	SPOOL	BREED	CRONE	FRAUD	GRUNT	TREAD	ESTER	STICK	BULKY	GUMBO	OUTDO
WOVEN	SPOON	BRIAR	CRONY	FREAK	IRAQI	TREAS	FSLIC	STIFF	BULLY	GUNNY	OUTER
YODEL	SPOOR	BRIBE	CROOK	FRESH	IRATE	TREAT	ISLAM	STILE	BUNCH	GUPPY	OUTGO
YOKEL	SPORE	BRICK	CROON	FRIAR	IRISH	TREND	ISLET	STILL	BUNCO	GUSHY	OUTRE
YOUNG	SPORT	BRIDE	CROSS	FRILL	IRONY	TRESS	ISSUE	STILT	BUNNY	GUSTO	PUBES
YOURS	SPOUT	BRIEF	CROUP	FRISK	IRREG	TRIAD	OSAGE	STING	BURGH	GUTTY	PUBIC
YOUTH	SPRAT	BRIER	CROWD	FRIZZ	KRAAL	TRIAL	OSIER	STINK	BURLY	GUYOT	PUBIS
ZONAL	SPRAY	BRINE	CROWN	FROCK	KRAUT	TRIBE	PSALM	STINT	BURRO	HUMAN	PUDGY
APACE	SPREE	BRING	CRUDE	FROND	KRONA	TRICE	PSEUD	STOAT	BURST	HUMID	PUKKA
APART	SPRIG	BRINK	CRUEL	FRONT	KRONE	TRICK	PSYCH	STOCK	BUSBY	HUMOR	PULSE
APEAK	SPUME	BRISK	CRUET	FROST	ORATE	TRIED	USAGE	STOIC	BUTTE	HUMUS	PUNCH
APHID	SPUNK	BROAD	CRUMB	FROTH	ORBIT	TRILL	USHER	STOKE	BUTUT	HUNCH	PUPIL
APHIS	SPURN	BROIL	CRUSE	FROWN	ORDER	TRINE	USUAL	STOLE	BUXOM	HURON	PUPPY
APORT	SPURT	BROKE	CRUSH	FROZE	ORGAN	TRIPE	USURP	STOMP	CUBAN	HURRY	PUREE
APPLE	UPEND	BROOD	CRUST	FRUIT	ORIEL	TRITE	USURY	STONE	CUBIC	HUSKY	PURGE
APPLY	UPPER	BROOK	CRYPT	FRYER	ORRIS	TROLL	ATILT	STOOD	CUBIT	HUSSY	PURIM
APRIL	UPSET	BROOM	CRYST	GRACE	PRANK	TROMP	ATLAS	STOOL	CUPID	HUTCH	PURSE
APRON	EQUAL	BROTH	DRAFT	GRADE	PRATE	TROOP	ATOLL	STOOP	CURIA	JUDGE	PUSHY
EPOCH	EQUIP	BROWN	DRAIN	GRAFT	PRAWN	TROPE	ATONE	STORE	CURIO	JUICE	PUSSY
EPOXY	EQUIV	BRUIN	DRAKE	GRAIL	PREEN	TROTH	ATTAR	STORK	CURRY	JUICY	PUTTY
EPROM	SQUAB	BRUIT	DRAMA	GRAIN	PRESS	TROUT	ATTIC	STORM	CURSE	JULEP	QUACK
EPSON	SQUAD	BRUNT	DRANK	GRAND	PRICE	TRUCE	ETHER	STORY	CURVE	JUMBO	QUAFF
OPERA	SQUAT	BRUSH	DRAPE	GRANT	PRICK	TRUCK	ETHOS	STOUT	CUTUP	JUMPY	QUAIL
OPINE	SQUAW	BRUTE	DRAWL	GRAPE	PRIDE	TRUMP	ETHYL	STOVE	DUCAL	JUNCO	QUAKE
OPIUM	SQUIB	CRACK	DREAD	GRAPH	PRIME	TRUNK	ETUDE	STRAP	DUCAT	JUNTA	QUALM
OPTIC	SQUID	CRAFT	DREAM	GRASP	PRIMP	TRUSS	OTHER	STRAW	DUCHY	JUNTO	QUART
SPACE	ARBOR	CRAMP	DREAR	GRASS	PRINK	TRUST	OTTER	STRAY	DUMMY	JUROR	QUASH
SPADE	ARDOR	CRANE	DRESS	GRATE	PRINT	TRUTH	STACK	STREW	DUMPS	KUDOS	QUASI
SPANK	ARENA	CRANK	DRIER	GRAVE	PRIOR	TRYST	STAFF	STRIA	DUMPY	KULAK	QUEAN
SPARC	ARGON	CRAPE	DRIFT	GRAVY	PRISM	URBAN	STAGE	STRIP	DUNCE	KURUS	QUEEN
SPARE	ARGOT	CRAPS	DRILL	GRAZE	PRIVY	URINE	STAID	STROP	DUPLE	LUCID	QUEER
SPARK	ARGUE	CRASH	DRILY	GREAT	PRIZE	WRACK	STAIN	STRUM	DUSKY	LUCKY	QUELL
SPASM	ARISE	CRASS	DRINK	GREBE	PROBE	WRATH	STAIR	STRUT	DUTCH	LUCRE	QUERY
SPATE	ARITH	CRATE	DRIVE	GREED	PROEM	WREAK	STAKE	STUCK	FUDGE	LUNAR	QUEST
SPAWN	ARMOR	CRAVE	DROLL	GREEK	PRONE	WRECK	STALE	STUDY	FUGUE	LUNCH	QUEUE
SPEAK	AROMA	CRAWL	DRONE	GREEN	PRONG	WREST	STALK	STUFF	FULLY	LUNGE	QUICK
SPEAR	ARRAS	CRAZE	DROOL	GREET	PROOF	WRING	STALL	STUMP	FUNKY	LURCH	QUIET
SPECK	ARRAY	CRAZY	DROOP	GRIEF	PROSE	WRIST	STAMP	STUNG	FUNNY	LURID	QUILL
SPEED	ARROW	CREAK	DROSS	GRILL	PROSY	WRITE	STAND	STUNK	FUROR	LUSTY	QUILT
SPELL	ARSON	CREAM	DROVE	GRIME	PROUD	WRONG	STANK	STUNT	FURRY	MUCUS	QUINT
SPEND	ARYAN	CREDO	DROWN	GRIND	PROVE	WROTE	STARE	STYLE	FURZE	MUFTI	QUIRE
SPENT	BRACE	CREED	DRUID	GRIPE	PROWL	WROTH	STARK	UTILE	FUSEE	MUGGY	QUIRK
SPERM	BRACT	CREEK	DRUNK	GRIST	PROXY	WRUNG	START	UTTER	FUSSY	MULCH	QUIRT
SPICE	BRAID	CREEL	DRUPE	GRITS	PRUDE	ASCII	STASH	AUDIO	FUSTY	MULCT	QUITE
SPIEL	BRAIN	CREEP	DRYAD	GROAN	PRUNE	ASCOT	STATE	AUDIT	FUZZY	MUMMY	QUITS
SPIKE	BRAKE	CREME	DRYER	GROAT	TRACE	ASHEN	STAVE	AUGER	GUANO	MUMPS	QUOIT
SPILL	BRAND	CREPE	ERASE	GROIN	TRACK	ASIAN	STEAD	AUGHT	GUARD	MUNCH	QUOTA
SPINE	BRASH	CRESC	ERECT	GROOM	TRACT	ASIDE	STEAK	AUGUR	GUAVA	MURAL	QUOTE
SPIRE	BRASS	CRESS	ERGOT	GROPE	TRADE	ASKEW	STEAL	AURAL	GUESS	MUSHY	QUOTH
SPIRT	BRAVE	CREST	ERISA	GROSS	TRAIL	ASPEN	STEAM	AURAR	GUEST	MUSIC	QURSH
SPITE	BRAVO	CRICK	ERODE	GROSZ	TRAIN	ASPIC	STEED	AUXIN	GUIDE	MUSTY	RUBLE
SPLAY	BRAWL	CRIER	ERROR	GROUP	TRAIT	ASSAY	STEEL	BUDDY	GUILD	NUDGE	RUDDY
SPLIT	BRAWN	CRIME	ERUPT	GROUT	TRAMP	ASSET	STEEP	BUDGE	GUILE	NUMIS	RUGBY
SPOIL	BRAZE	CRIMP	FRAIL	GROVE	TRANS	ASSOC	STEER	BUGGY	GUILT	NURSE	RULER
SPOKE	BREAD	CRISP	FRAME	GROWL	TRAPS	ASTER	STEIN	BUGLE	GUISE	NUTTY	RUMBA
SPOOF	BREAK	CROAK	FRANC	GRUEL	TRASH	ASTIR	STERE	BUILD	GULCH	OUGHT	RUMMY
SPOOK	BREAM	CROCK	FRANK	GRUFF	TRAWL	ESSAY	STERN	BULGE	GULLY	OUNCE	RUMOR

RUNNY	AWFUL	EXPEL	AGAPE	CHARM	FRAIL	LLANO	SEAMY	STANK	AMBLE	TABOO	PACER
RUPEE	DWARF	EXPTL	AGATE	CHART	FRAME	LOATH	SEATO	STARE	ARBOR	TABOR	PECAN
RURAL	DWELL	EXTOL	AGAVE	CHARY	FRANC	MIAMI	SHACK	STARK	BABEL	TIBIA	PICKY
SUAVE	OWING	EXTRA	ALARM	CHASE	FRANK	NAACP	SHADE	START	BIBLE	TUBER	PICOT
SUCRE	OWLET	EXUDE	AMAIN	CHASM	FRAUD	OMAHA	SHAFT	STASH	BOBBY	UMBEL	RECAP
SUEDE	SWAGE	EXULT	AMASS	CLACK	GIANT	ORATE	SHAKE	STATE	CABAL	UMBER	RECIP
SUGAR	SWAIN	EXURB	AMAZE	CLAIM	GLAND	OSAGE	SHAKY	STAVE	CABBY	UMBRA	RECTO
SUITE	SWAMI	OXBOW	APACE	CLAMP	GLANS	OVARY	SHALE	SUAVE	CABIN	UNBAR	RECUR
SULFA	SWAMP	OXIDE	APART	CLANG	GLARE	OVATE	SHALL	SWAGE	CABLE	URBAN	SUCRE
SULKY	SWANK	BYLAW	AVAIL	CLANK	GLASS	PEACE	SHAME	SWAIN	COBOL	VIBES	TACIT
SULLY	SWARD	BYWAY	AVAST	CLASH	GLAZE	PEACH	SHANK	SWAMI	COBRA	XEBEC	TACKY
SUMAC	SWARM	CYCLE	AWAIT	CLASP	GNARL	PEARL	SHAPE	SWAMP	CUBAN	ZEBRA	TICAL
SUNUP	SWART	CYNIC	AWAKE	CLASS	GNASH	PHAGE	SHARD	SWANK	CUBIC	ASCII	ULCER
SUPER	SWASH	DYING	AWARD	COACH	GRACE	PHARM	SHARE	SWARD	CUBIT	ASCOT	UNCAP
SUPRA	SWATH	EYRIE	AWARE	COAST	GRADE	PHASE	SHARK	SWARM	DEBAR	BACON	UNCLE
SUPVR	SWEAR	EYRIR	AWASH	CRACK	GRAFT	PIANO	SHARP	SWART	DEBIT	CACAO	UNCUT
SURGE	SWEAT	GYPSY	BEACH	CRAFT	GRAIL	PLACE	SHAVE	SWASH	DEBUG	CACHE	VICAR
SURLY	SWEDE	HYDRA	BEANO	CRAMP	GRAIN	PLAID	SHAWL	SWATH	DEBUT	CECUM	VOCAB
TUBER	SWEEP	HYDRO	BEARD	CRANE	GRAND	PLAIN	SKATE	TEACH	ELBOW	COCKY	VOCAL
TULIP	SWEET	HYENA	BEAST	CRANK	GRANT	PLAIT	SLACK	TEASE	EMBED	COCOA	WACKY
TULLE	SWELL	HYING	BHANG	CRAPE	GRAPE	PLANE	SLAIN	THANE	EMBER	CYCLE	YACHT
TUMID	SWEPT	HYMEN	BLACK	CRAPS	GRAPH	PLANK	SLAKE	THANK	FABLE	DACHA	YUCCA
TUMMY	SWIFT	LYING	BLADE	CRASH	GRASP	PLANT	SLANG	TIARA	FIBER	DECAL	ADDER
TUMOR	SWILL	LYMPH	BLAIN	CRASS	GRASS	PLASH	SLANT	TOADY	GABBY	DECAY	ADDLE
TUNIC	SWINE	LYNCH	BLAME	CRATE	GRATE	PLATE	SLASH	TOAST	GABLE	DECOR	ADDNL
TUNNY	SWING	LYRIC	BLAND	CRAVE	GRAVE	PLATY	SLATE	TRACE	HABIT	DECOY	ALDER
TUQUE	SWIPE	MYRRH	BLANK	CRAWL	GRAVY	PLAYA	SLAVE	TRACK	HOBBY	DECRY	ARDOR
TURBO	SWIRL	NYLON	BLARE	CRAZE	GRAZE	PLAZA	SMACK	TRACT	IMBED	DUCAL	AUDIO
TURPS	SWISH	NYMPH	BLASE	CRAZY	GUANO	POACH	SMALL	TRADE	IMBUE	DUCAT	AUDIT
TUTOR	SWISS	PYGMY	BLAST	DEATH	GUARD	PRANK	SMART	TRAIL	JABOT	DUCHY	BADGE
VULVA	SWITZ	PYLON	BLAZE	DIARY	GUAVA	PRATE	SMASH	TRAIN	KABOB	EMCEE	BEDEW
WURST	SWOON	SYLPH	BOARD	DRAFT	HEADY	PRAWN	SNACK	TRAIT	KEBAB	EXCEL	BIDDY
YUCCA	SWOOP	SYNOD	BOAST	DRAIN	HEART	PSALM	SNAIL	TRAMP	LABEL	FACET	BIDET
YUMMY	SWORD	SYRUP	BRACE	DRAKE	HEATH	QUACK	SNAKE	TRANS	LABOR	FECES	BUDDY
AVAIL	SWORE	SYSOP	BRACT	DRAMA	HEAVE	QUAFF	SNARE	TRAPS	LIBEL	FICHE	BUDGE
AVAST	SWORN	TYING	BRAID	DRANK	HEAVY	QUAIL	SNARL	TRASH	LOBBY	FICHU	CADDY
AVERT	SWUNG	VYING	BRAIN	DRAPE	HOARD	QUAKE	SPACE	TRAWL	NABOB	FOCUS	CADET
AVGAS	TWAIN	XYLEM	BRAKE	DRAWL	HOARY	QUALM	SPADE	TWAIN	NOBLE	INCOG	CADGE
AVIAN	TWANG	AZTEC	BRAND	DWARF	IMAGE	QUART	SPANK	TWANG	ORBIT	INCUR	CADRE
AVOID	TWEAK	AZURE	BRASH	ELAND	IMAGO	QUASH	SPARC	UKASE	OXBOW	INCUS	CEDAR
EVADE	TWEED	CZECH	BRASS	ELATE	INANE	QUASI	SPARE	UNARM	PUBES	LICIT	CIDER
EVENT	TWEEN	OZONE	BRAVE	EMAIL	IRAQI	REACH	SPARK	USAGE	PUBIC	LOCAL	CODEC
EVERY	TWEET		BRAVO	ENACT	IRATE	REACT	SPASM	VIAND	PUBIS	LOCUS	CODEX
EVICT	TWICE		BRAWL	ERASE	JEANS	READY	SPATE	WEALD	RABBI	LUCID	DADDY
EVOKE	TWILL		BRAWN	EVADE	KHAKI	REALM	SPAWN	WEARY	RABID	LUCKY	DODGE
IVORY	TWINE	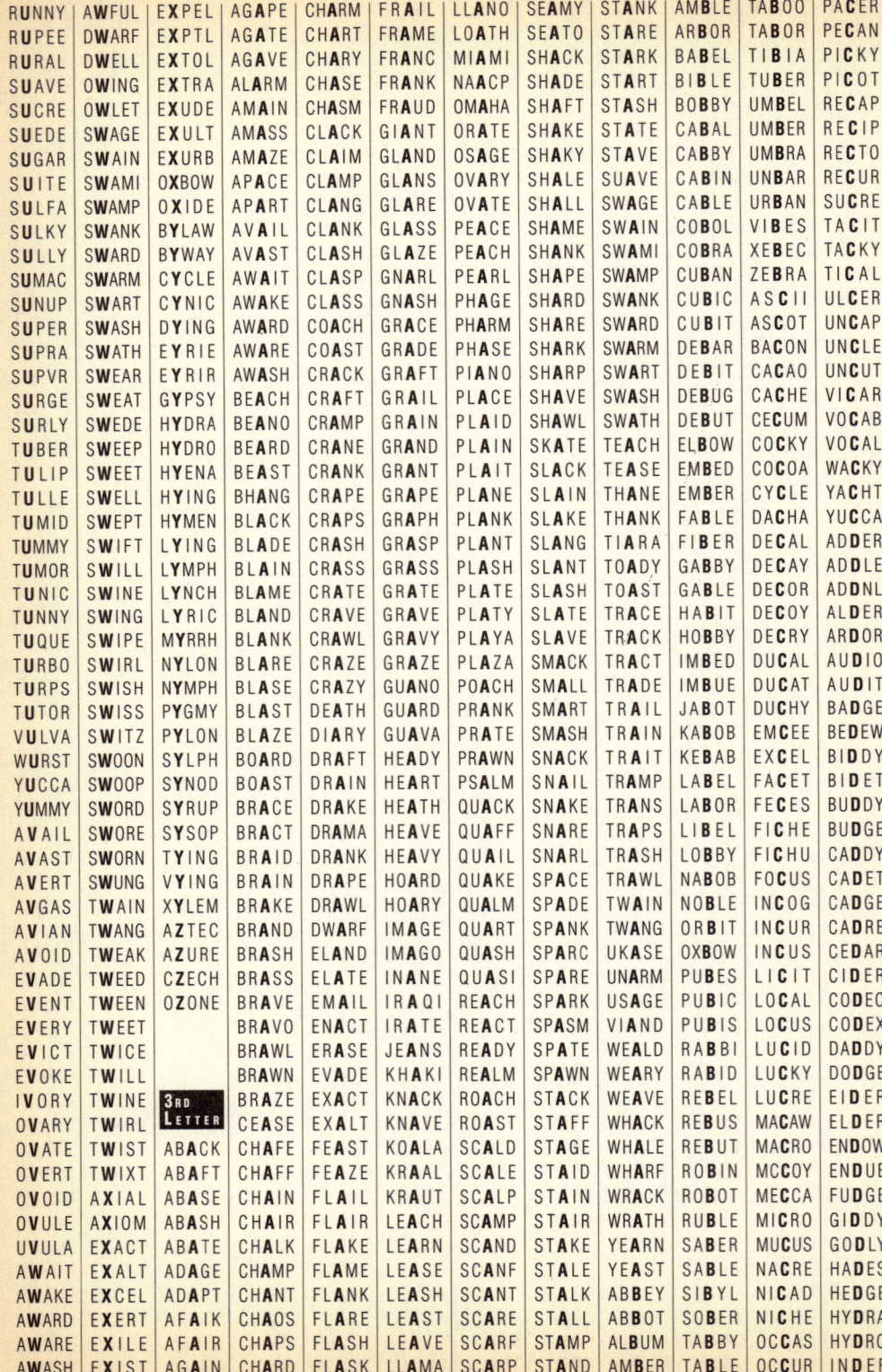 3RD LETTER	BRAZE	EXACT	KNACK	ROACH	STACK	WEAVE	REBEL	LUCRE	EIDER
OVARY	TWIRL	ABACK	CEASE	EXALT	KNAVE	ROAST	STAFF	WHACK	REBUS	MACAW	ELDER
OVATE	TWIST	ABAFT	CHAFE	FEAST	KOALA	SCALD	STAGE	WHALE	REBUT	MACRO	ENDOW
OVERT	TWIXT	ABASE	CHAFF	FEAZE	KRAAL	SCALE	STAID	WHARF	ROBIN	MCCOY	ENDUE
OVOID	AXIAL	ABASH	CHAIN	FLAIL	KRAUT	SCALP	STAIN	WRACK	ROBOT	MECCA	FUDGE
OVULE	AXIOM	ABATE	CHAIR	FLAIR	LEACH	SCAMP	STAIR	WRATH	RUBLE	MICRO	GIDDY
UVULA	EXACT	ADAGE	CHALK	FLAKE	LEARN	SCAND	STAKE	YEARN	SABER	MUCUS	GODLY
AWAIT	EXALT	ADAPT	CHAMP	FLAME	LEASE	SCANF	STALE	YEAST	SABLE	NACRE	HADES
AWAKE	EXCEL	AFAIK	CHANT	FLANK	LEASH	SCANT	STALK	ABBEY	SIBYL	NICAD	HEDGE
AWARD	EXERT	AFAIR	CHAOS	FLARE	LEAST	SCARE	STALL	ABBOT	SOBER	NICHE	HYDRA
AWARE	EXILE	AGAIN	CHAPS	FLASH	LEAVE	SCARF	STAMP	ALBUM	TABBY	OCCAS	HYDRO
AWASH	EXIST		CHARD	FLASK	LLAMA	SCARP	STAND	AMBER	TABLE	OCCUR	INDEF

INDEX	ADEPT	EJECT	PLEAD	STERE	FIFTY	FIGHT	USHER	CHIMP	FRISK	POINT	SNIFF
INDIC	AGENT	ELECT	PLEAT	STERN	GAFFE	FUGUE	WAHOO	CHINA	FRIZZ	POISE	SNIPE
INDUE	AHEAD	ELEGY	PLEBE	SUEDE	HEFTY	HOGAN	YAHOO	CHINE	GAILY	PRICE	SNIPS
JADED	ALERT	EMEND	PLEBS	SWEAR	INFER	INGLE	ABIDE	CHINK	GLIDE	PRICK	SPICE
JUDGE	AMEBA	EMERY	POESY	SWEAT	JIFFY	INGOT	ADIEU	CHINO	GLINT	PRIDE	SPIEL
KEDGE	AMEND	ENEMA	PREEN	SWEDE	LIFER	LAGER	ADIOS	CHIRP	GRIEF	PRIME	SPIKE
KUDOS	ANENT	ENEMY	PRESS	SWEEP	LOFTY	LEGAL	AFIRE	CHIVE	GRILL	PRIMP	SPILL
LADEN	APEAK	ERECT	PSEUD	SWEET	MAFIA	LEGGY	AGILE	CLICK	GRIME	PRINK	SPINE
LADLE	ARENA	EVENT	QUEAN	SWELL	MUFTI	LEGIS	ALIAS	CLIFF	GRIND	PRINT	SPIRE
LEDGE	AVERT	EVERY	QUEEN	SWEPT	NIFTY	LEGIT	ALIBI	CLIMB	GRIPE	PRIOR	SPIRT
LODGE	BEECH	EXERT	QUEER	TEENS	OFFAL	LIGHT	ALIEN	CLIME	GRIST	PRISM	SPITE
MADAM	BEEFY	FIELD	QUELL	TEENY	OFFER	LOGIC	ALIGN	CLING	GRITS	PRIVY	STICK
MEDAL	BLEAK	FIEND	QUERY	TEETH	REFER	MAGIC	ALIKE	CLINK	GUIDE	PRIZE	STIFF
MEDIA	BLEAR	FIERY	QUEST	THEAT	RIFLE	MAGMA	ALIVE	CRICK	GUILD	QUICK	STILE
MEDIC	BLEAT	FLECK	QUEUE	THEFT	TAFFY	MIGHT	AMISS	CRIER	GUILE	QUIET	STILL
MIDDY	BLEED	FLEER	REEVE	THEGN	UNFIT	MOGUL	AMITY	CRIME	GUILT	QUILL	STILT
MIDGE	BLEND	FLEET	RHEUM	THEIR	UNFIX	MUGGY	ANION	CRIMP	GUISE	QUILT	STING
MIDST	BLESS	FLESH	SCENE	THEME	WAFER	NEGRO	ANISE	CRISP	HAIKU	QUINT	STINK
MODEL	BREAD	FOEHN	SCENT	THEOL	AEGIS	NEGUS	ARISE	DAILY	HAIRY	QUIRE	STINT
MODEM	BREAK	FREAK	SEEDY	THERE	ALGOL	NIGHT	ARITH	DAIRY	HEIST	QUIRK	SUITE
MODIF	BREAM	FRESH	SHEAF	THERM	ANGEL	ORGAN	ASIAN	DAISY	HOIST	QUIRT	SWIFT
NADIR	BREED	GEESE	SHEAR	THESE	ANGER	OUGHT	ASIDE	DEICE	HYING	QUITE	SWILL
NODDY	CHEAP	GLEAM	SHEEN	THESS	ANGLE	PAGAN	ATILT	DEIFY	ICING	QUITS	SWINE
NUDGE	CHEAT	GLEAN	SHEEP	TREAD	ANGLO	PIGMY	AVIAN	DEIGN	IDIOM	RAISE	SWING
OLDEN	CHECK	GLEBE	SHEER	TREAS	ANGRY	PYGMY	AXIAL	DEISM	IDIOT	REIGN	SWIPE
OLDIE	CHEEK	GREAT	SHEET	TREAT	ANGST	REGAL	AXIOM	DEITY	IRISH	RHINO	SWIRL
ORDER	CHEEP	GREBE	SHELF	TREND	ANGUS	RIGHT	BAIRN	DLITT	JOINT	SAINT	SWISH
PADDY	CHEER	GREED	SHELL	TRESS	ARGON	RIGID	BAIZA	DOILY	JOIST	SCION	SWISS
PADRE	CHELA	GREEK	SIEGE	TWEAK	ARGOT	RIGOR	BAIZE	DRIER	JUICE	SEINE	SWITZ
PEDAL	CHERT	GREEN	SIEVE	TWEED	ARGUE	ROGER	BEIGE	DRIFT	JUICY	SEISM	TAIGA
PUDGY	CHESS	GREET	SKEET	TWEEN	AUGER	ROGUE	BEING	DRILL	KNIFE	SEIZE	TAINT
RADAR	CHEST	GUESS	SKEIN	TWEET	AUGHT	RUGBY	BLIMP	DRILY	KNISH	SHIER	THICK
RADII	CHEWY	GUEST	SLEEK	UPEND	AUGUR	SIGHT	BLIND	DRINK	LAIRD	SHIFT	THIEF
RADIO	CLEAN	HYENA	SLEEP	VEERY	AVGAS	SIGMA	BLINK	DRIVE	LAITY	SHILL	THIGH
RADIX	CLEAR	IDEAL	SLEET	WEEDY	BAGEL	SOGGY	BLISS	DYING	LYING	SHINE	THINE
RADON	CLEAT	ILEUM	SMEAR	WEENY	BAGGY	SUGAR	BLITZ	EDICT	MAIZE	SHINY	THING
RIDER	CLEFT	INEPT	SMELL	WEEPY	BEGET	TIGER	BRIAR	ELIDE	MOIRE	SHIPT	THINK
RIDGE	CLERK	INERT	SMELT	WHEAL	BEGIN	TIGHT	BRIBE	ELITE	MOIST	SHIRE	THIRD
RODEO	CREAK	KNEAD	SNEAK	WHEAT	BEGUM	VAGUE	BRICK	ENIAC	NAIAD	SHIRK	TRIAD
RUDDY	CREAM	KNEEL	SNEER	WHEEL	BIGHT	VIGIL	BRIDE	ERISA	NAIRA	SHIRR	TRIAL
SEDAN	CREDO	KNELL	SPEAK	WHELK	BIGOT	VIGOR	BRIEF	EVICT	NAIVE	SHIRT	TRIBE
SEDGE	CREED	LEECH	SPEAR	WHELM	BOGEY	VOGUE	BRIER	EXILE	NEIGH	SKIFF	TRICE
SIDLE	CREEK	LEERY	SPECK	WHELP	BOGUS	WAGER	BRINE	EXIST	NOISE	SKILL	TRICK
TODAY	CREEL	LIEGE	SPEED	WHERE	BUGGY	WAGON	BRING	FAINT	NOISY	SKIMP	TRIED
TODDY	CREEP	LIEUT	SPELL	WIELD	BUGLE	WIGHT	BRINK	FAIRY	ODIUM	SKIRT	TRILL
UDDER	CREME	LOESS	SPEND	WREAK	CAGEY	ABHOR	BRISK	FAITH	OLIVE	SLICE	TRINE
UNDER	CREPE	NEEDS	SPENT	WRECK	CIGAR	APHID	BUILD	FEIGN	ONION	SLICK	TRIPE
UNDUE	CRESC	NEEDY	SPERM	WREST	DEGAS	APHIS	CAIRN	FEINT	OPINE	SLIDE	TRITE
VIDEO	CRESS	NIECE	STEAD	YIELD	DIGIT	ASHEN	CCITT	FLICK	OPIUM	SLIER	TWICE
VODKA	CREST	OBESE	STEAK	AFFIX	DOGGY	ETHER	CHIAO	FLIED	ORIEL	SLIME	TWILL
WADER	CZECH	OCEAN	STEAL	AWFUL	DOGIE	ETHOS	CHICK	FLIER	OSIER	SLING	TWINE
WEDGE	DREAD	OPERA	STEAM	BEFIT	DOGMA	ETHYL	CHIDE	FLING	OWING	SLINK	TWIRL
WIDEN	DREAM	OVERT	STEED	BEFOG	EAGER	ICHOR	CHIEF	FLINT	OXIDE	SMILE	TWIST
WIDOW	DREAR	PAEAN	STEEL	DAFFY	EAGLE	JIHAD	CHILD	FLIRT	PAINT	SMIRK	TWIXT
WIDTH	DRESS	PEEVE	STEEP	DEFER	EIGHT	NOHOW	CHILI	FOIST	PAISA	SMITE	TYING
YODEL	DWELL	PIECE	STEER	DEFOG	ERGOT	OCHER	CHILL	FRIAR	PHIAL	SMITH	UMIAK
ABEAM	EDEMA	PIETY	STEIN	FIFTH	FAGOT	OTHER	CHIME	FRILL	POILU	SNIDE	UNIFY

UNION	BALSA	INLET	TALUS	JUMBO	CANNA	LANAI	SANIT	AMOUR	DROOP	IVORY	SHOOK
UNITE	BELAY	ISLAM	TELEG	JUMPY	CANNY	LANCE	SENGI	ANODE	DROSS	KIOSK	SHOOT
UNITY	BELCH	ISLET	TELEX	LAMIA	CANOE	LANKY	SENNA	APORT	DROVE	KIOWA	SHORE
URINE	BELIE	JALAP	TILDE	LEMON	CANON	LINEN	SENSE	AROMA	DROWN	KNOCK	SHORN
UTILE	BELLE	JELLY	TILTH	LEMUR	CANTO	LINER	SENTI	ATOLL	EBONY	KNOLL	SHORT
VOICE	BELLS	JOLLY	TULIP	LIMBO	CINCH	LINGO	SINCE	ATONE	ELOPE	KNOUT	SHOUT
VOILE	BELLY	JULEP	TULLE	LIMIT	CONCH	LINKS	SINEW	AVOID	EMOTE	KOOKY	SHOVE
VYING	BELOW	KULAK	VALET	LYMPH	CONEY	LONER	SINGE	BLOAT	EPOCH	KRONA	SHOWY
WAIST	BILGE	LILAC	VALID	MAMBO	CONGA	LUNAR	SINUS	BLOCK	EPOXY	KRONE	SIOUX
WAIVE	BILLY	MALAY	VALOR	MIMIC	CONIC	LUNCH	SONAR	BLOND	ERODE	LEONE	SLOOP
WEIGH	BOLUS	MELEE	VALSE	MUMMY	CONST	LUNGE	SONIC	BLOOD	EVOKE	LOONY	SLOPE
WEIRD	BULGE	MELON	VALUE	MUMPS	CONTD	LYNCH	SUNUP	BLOOM	FIORD	LOOSE	SLOSH
WHICH	BULKY	MILCH	VALVE	NOMAD	CONTG	MANES	SYNOD	BLOWY	FJORD	MAORI	SLOTH
WHIFF	BULLY	MLLES	VELAR	NUMIS	CONTR	MANGE	TANGO	BOOBY	FLOAT	MOODY	SMOCK
WHILE	BYLAW	MOLAR	VELUM	NYMPH	CYNIC	MANGO	TANSY	BOOST	FLOCK	MOOSE	SMOKE
WHINE	CALIF	MULCH	VILLA	PAMPA	DANCE	MANIA	TENET	BOOTH	FLOOD	NOOSE	SMOTE
WHIRL	CALLA	MULCT	VULVA	RAMIE	DANDY	MANIC	TENON	BOOTY	FLOOR	OVOID	SNOOP
WHISH	CALVE	NYLON	WALTZ	REMIT	DENIM	MANLY	TENOR	BOOZE	FLORA	OZONE	SNORE
WHISK	CALYX	OWLET	WELCH	ROMAN	DENSE	MANNA	TENSE	BROAD	FLOSS	PEONY	SNORT
WHIST	CELLO	PALMY	WELSH	RUMBA	DINAR	MANOR	TINCT	BROIL	FLOUR	PHONE	SNOUT
WHITE	COLIC	PALSY	XYLEM	RUMMY	DINER	MANSE	TINGE	BROKE	FLOUT	PHONO	SNOWY
WRING	COLON	PHLOX	ADMAN	RUMOR	DINGO	MANTA	TINNY	BROOD	FLOWN	PHONY	SOOTH
WRIST	COLOR	PILAF	ADMIN	SEMEN	DINGY	MANUF	TONER	BROOK	FROCK	PHOTO	SPOIL
WRITE	DALLY	PILES	ADMIT	SUMAC	DINKY	MINCE	TONGS	BROOM	FROND	PIOUS	SPOKE
ZAIRE	DELAY	PILOT	ADMIX	TEMPO	DONOR	MINIM	TONIC	BROTH	FRONT	POOCH	SPOOF
CAJUN	DELFT	POLAR	ARMOR	TEMPT	DONUT	MINOR	TUNIC	BROWN	FROST	PROBE	SPOOK
ENJOY	DELTA	POLIO	CAMEL	TIMES	DUNCE	MINUS	TUNNY	CHOCK	FROTH	PROEM	SPOOL
HAJJI	DELVE	POLIT	CAMEO	TIMID	ENNUI	MONEY	VENAL	CHOIR	FROWN	PRONE	SPOON
MAJOR	DOLLY	POLKA	COMBO	TUMID	FANCY	MONGO	VENOM	CHOKE	FROZE	PRONG	SPOOR
ALKYD	DOLOR	POLYP	COMDG	TUMMY	FENCE	MONTH	VENUE	CHOMP	GEODE	PROOF	SPORE
ANKLE	ECLAT	PULSE	COMDR	TUMOR	FINAL	MUNCH	VENUS	CHOPS	GHOST	PROSE	SPORT
ASKEW	EDLIN	PYLON	COMDT	UNMAN	FINCH	NINNY	VINYL	CHORD	GHOUL	PROSY	SPOUT
FAKIR	FALSE	RALLY	COMER	VOMIT	FINIS	NONCE	WENCH	CHORE	GLOAT	PROUD	STOAT
HOKUM	FELLY	RELAX	COMET	WOMAN	FINNY	NONES	WINCE	CHOSE	GLOBE	PROVE	STOCK
JOKER	FELON	RELAY	COMFY	YUMMY	FUNKY	OUNCE	WINCH	CLOAK	GLOOM	PROWL	STOIC
LIKEN	FILAR	RELIC	COMIC	ANNEX	FUNNY	PANDA	WINDY	CLOCK	GLORY	PROXY	STOKE
NAKED	FILCH	RELIG	COMMA	ANNOY	GANTT	PANEL	XENON	CLONE	GLOSS	QUOIT	STOLE
OAKUM	FILLY	RULER	COMMO	ANNUL	GENIE	PANIC	ZONAL	CLOSE	GLOVE	QUOTA	STOMP
PEKOE	FILTH	SALAD	DEMON	BANAL	GENRE	PANSY	ABODE	CLOTH	GLOZE	QUOTE	STONE
PIKER	FOLIO	SALLY	DEMUR	BANDY	GENUS	PANTS	ABORT	CLOUD	GNOME	QUOTH	STOOD
POKER	FOLLY	SALON	DUMMY	BANJO	GONAD	PENAL	ABOUT	CLOUT	GOODY	ROOST	STOOL
PUKKA	FSLIC	SALVE	DUMPS	BANNS	GONER	PENCE	ABOVE	CLOVE	GOOFY	SCOFF	STOOP
TOKAY	FULLY	SALVO	DUMPY	BANTU	GUNNY	PENIS	ACORN	CLOWN	GOOSE	SCOLD	STORE
TOKEN	GELID	SILLY	FEMUR	BENCH	HANDY	PENNI	ADOBE	CROAK	GROAN	SCONE	STORK
WAKEN	GULCH	SOLAR	GAMIN	BENNY	HENCE	PENNY	ADOPT	CROCK	GROAT	SCOOP	STORM
WOKEN	GULLY	SOLID	GAMMA	BINGE	HENNA	PINCH	ADORE	CRONE	GROIN	SCOOT	STORY
YOKEL	HALER	SOLON	GAMUT	BINGO	HINDI	PINON	ADORN	CRONY	GROOM	SCOPE	STOUT
AGLOW	HALLO	SOLVE	GIMPY	BONER	HINGE	PINTO	AFOOT	CROOK	GROPE	SCORE	STOVE
ALLAH	HALVE	SPLAY	GUMBO	BONGO	HONEY	PINUP	AGONY	CROON	GROSS	SCORN	SWOON
ALLAY	HELIX	SPLIT	HOMER	BONNY	HONOR	PUNCH	AGORA	CROSS	GROSZ	SCOTS	SWOOP
ALLEY	HELLO	SULFA	HOMEY	BONUS	HUNCH	RANCH	ALOFT	CROUP	GROUP	SCOUR	SWORD
ALLOT	HELOT	SULKY	HUMAN	BONZE	INNER	RANGE	ALOHA	CROWD	GROUT	SCOUT	SWORE
ALLOW	HELVE	SULLY	HUMID	BUNCH	JENNY	RANGY	ALONE	CROWN	GROVE	SCOWL	SWORN
ALLOY	HOLLO	SYLPH	HUMOR	BUNCO	JUNCO	RENAL	ALONG	DIODE	GROWL	SHOAL	THOLE
ATLAS	HOLLY	TALER	HUMUS	BUNNY	JUNTA	RENEW	ALOOF	DROLL	HAOLE	SHOAT	THONG
BALKY	IGLOO	TALLY	HYMEN	CANAL	JUNTO	RINSE	ALOUD	DRONE	HOOEY	SHOCK	THORN
BALMY	INLAY	TALON	JIMMY	CANDY	KANJI	RUNNY	AMONG	DROOL	IRONY	SHONE	THORP

THOSE	MAPLE	BIRTH	GORSE	PORCH	TORSO	GUSHY	WHSLE	LATCH	TITAN	COURT	JOULE
TOOTH	NIPPY	BORAX	HARDY	PUREE	TURBO	GUSTO	ACTOR	LATEX	TITHE	CRUDE	JOUST
TROLL	PAPAL	BORNE	HAREM	PURGE	TURPS	HASTE	AFTER	LATHE	TITLE	CRUEL	KLUGE
TROMP	PAPAW	BORON	HARPY	PURIM	UNRWA	HUSKY	ALTAR	LATIN	TOTAL	CRUET	KNURL
TROOP	PAPER	BURGH	HARRY	PURSE	VARIA	HUSSY	ALTER	LETUP	TOTEM	CRUMB	LAUGH
TROPE	POPPY	BURLY	HARSH	QURSH	VERGE	INSET	ANTIC	LITER	TUTOR	CRUSE	LOUSE
TROTH	PUPIL	BURRO	HERON	RERUN	VERSE	INSOL	ASTER	LITHE	ULTRA	CRUSH	LOUSY
TROUT	PUPPY	BURST	HERTZ	RURAL	VERSO	INSTR	ASTIR	LOTUS	UNTIE	CRUST	MAUVE
VIOLA	RAPID	CARAT	HORDE	SCRAM	VERST	ISSUE	ATTAR	MATCH	UNTIL	DAUNT	MOULD
WHOLE	REPAY	CARET	HORSE	SCRAP	VERVE	LASER	ATTIC	MATZO	UTTER	DEUCE	MOULT
WHOOP	REPEL	CARGO	HURON	SCREW	VIRAL	LASSO	AZTEC	METAL	VATIC	DOUBT	MOUND
WHORE	REPLY	CARNY	HURRY	SCRIM	VIREO	LISLE	BATCH	METER	VETCH	DOUGH	MOUNT
WHORL	RIPEN	CAROL	IRREG	SCRIP	VIRTU	LISTS	BATHE	METRE	VITAL	DOUSE	MOURN
WHOSE	RUPEE	CAROM	JUROR	SCROD	VIRUS	LUSTY	BATIK	METRO	WATCH	DRUID	MOUSE
WHOSO	SAPPY	CARRY	KARAT	SCRUB	WORDY	MASER	BATON	MITER	WATER	DRUNK	MOUSY
WOODY	SEPAL	CARVE	KARMA	SERGE	WORLD	MASON	BATTY	MOTEL	WITCH	DRUPE	MOUTH
WOOZY	SEPIA	CHRON	KARST	SERIF	WORRY	MISER	BETEL	MOTET	WITHE	EDUCE	OVULE
WRONG	SUPER	CIRCA	KORAN	SERUM	WORSE	MISTY	BITCH	MOTIF	WITHY	ELUDE	PAUSE
WROTE	SUPRA	CORAL	KURUS	SERVE	WORST	MOSEY	BOTCH	MOTOR	WITTY	EQUAL	PLUCK
WROTH	SUPVR	CORNY	LARCH	SERVO	WORTH	MUSHY	BUTTE	MOTTO	ABUSE	EQUIP	PLUMB
XCOPY	TAPER	CORPS	LARGE	SHRED	WURST	MUSIC	BUTUT	NATAL	ACUTE	EQUIV	PLUME
ZLOTY	TAPIR	CURIA	LARGO	SHREW	XERIC	MUSTY	CATCH	NATTY	ADULT	ERUPT	PLUMP
AMPLE	TEPEE	CURIO	LARVA	SHRUB	ABSTR	NASAL	CATER	NITER	AMUCK	ETUDE	PLUNK
AMPUL	TEPID	CURRY	LORRY	SHRUG	AISLE	NASTY	CATTY	NITRO	AMUSE	EXUDE	PLUSH
APPLE	TIPSY	CURSE	LURCH	SIREN	ARSON	NISEI	CUTUP	NOTCH	AZURE	EXULT	PLUTO
APPLY	TOPAZ	CURVE	LURID	SIRUP	ASSAY	OASIS	DATED	NOTED	BLUES	EXURB	POUCH
ASPEN	TOPER	DERBY	LYRIC	SORRY	ASSET	ONSET	DATUM	NUTTY	BLUET	FAULT	POULT
ASPIC	TOPIC	DERIV	MARCH	SPRAT	ASSOC	PASHA	DETER	OCTAL	BLUFF	FAUNA	POUND
BIPED	TOPOG	DIRGE	MARGE	SPRAY	BASAL	PASSE	DITCH	OCTET	BLUNT	FLUFF	PRUDE
CAPER	UNPEG	DIRTY	MARRY	SPREE	BASIC	PASTA	DITTO	OFTEN	BLURB	FLUID	PRUNE
CAPON	UNPIN	EARED	MARSH	SPRIG	BASIL	PASTE	DITTY	OPTIC	BLURT	FLUKE	ROUGE
COPRA	UPPER	EARLY	MERCY	STRAP	BASIN	PASTY	OPTIC	OTTER	BLUSH	FLUME	ROUGH
COPSE	VAPID	EARTH	MERGE	STRAW	BASIS	PESKY	OTTER	OUTDO	BOUGH	FLUNG	ROUND
CUPID	VAPOR	EERIE	MERIT	STRAY	BASSO	POSER	OUTER	OUTER	BOULE	FLUNK	ROUSE
DEPOT	VIPER	EGRET	MERRY	STREW	BASTE	POSIT	OUTGO	OUTGO	BOUND	FLUSH	ROUTE
DEPTH	ZIPPY	EPROM	MIRTH	STRIA	BESET	POSSE	OUTRE	OUTRE	BOURN	FLUTE	SAUCE
DOPEY	PIQUÉ	ERROR	MORAL	STRIP	BESOM	PUSHY	PATCH	PATCH	BRUIN	FOUND	SAUCY
DUPLE	TOQUE	EYRIE	MORAY	STROP	BESOT	PUSSY	PATEN	PATEN	BRUIT	FOUNT	SAUNA
EMPTY	TUQUE	EYRIR	MOREL	STRUM	BISON	RESIN	PATIO	PATIO	BRUNT	FRUIT	SAUTE
EXPEL	ACRID	FARCE	MORES	STRUT	BOSKY	RISER	PATSY	PATSY	BRUSH	GAUDY	SCUBA
EXPTL	AERIE	FERAL	MORON	SURGE	BOSOM	ROSIN	PATTY	PATTY	BRUTE	GAUGE	SCUFF
GIPSY	AGREE	FERRY	MURAL	SURLY	BOSUN	SASSY	PETAL	PETAL	CAULK	GAUNT	SCULL
GUPPY	AORTA	FIRST	MYRRH	SYRUP	BUSBY	SISAL	PETER	PETER	CAUSE	GAUSS	SCURF
GYPSY	APRIL	FIRTH	NARIS	TARDY	CASTE	SISSY	PETTY	PETTY	CHUCK	GAUZE	SHUCK
HAPLY	APRON	FORAY	NERVE	TAROT	CMSGT	SMSGT	PITCH	PITCH	CHUMP	GOUDA	SHUNT
HAPPY	ARRAS	FORCE	NERVY	TARRY	DISCO	SYSOP	PITON	PITON	CHUNK	GOUGE	SKULK
IMPEL	ARRAY	FORGE	NORSE	TERRY	DISTN	TASTE	GUTTY	PUTTY	CHURL	GOURD	SKULL
IMPER	ARROW	FORGO	NORTH	TERSE	DISTR	TASTY	HATCH		CHURN	GRUEL	SKUNK
IMPLY	AURAL	FORTE	NURSE	THREE	DUSKY	TESTY	HITCH	RATIO	CHUTE	GRUFF	SLUMP
INPUT	AURAR	FORTH	ORRIS	THREW	EASEL	UNSAY	HOTEL	RATTY	CLUCK	GRUNT	SLUNG
JAPAN	BARGE	FORTY	PARCH	THROB	ENSUE	UPSET	HUTCH	RETCH	CLUMP	HAUNT	SLUNK
KAPOK	BARON	FORUM	PARKA	THROE	EPSON	VASTY	ICTUS	ROTOR	CLUNG	HOUND	SLURP
KAPUT	BERET	FUROR	PARRY	THROW	ESSAY	VISIT	INTEL	SATAN	COUCH	HOURI	SLUSH
LAPEL	BERRY	FURRY	PARSE	THRUM	FISHY	VISOR	INTER	SATIN	COUGH	HOUSE	SNUCK
LAPIN	BERTH	FURZE	PARTY	TIRED	FUSEE	VISTA	JETTY	SATYR	COULD	INURE	SNUFF
LAPSE	BERYL	GIRTH	PERCH	TORAH	FUSSY	WASHY	KETCH	SETUP	COUNT	INURN	SOUGH
LEPER	BIRCH	GORGE	PERIL	TORCH	FUSTY	WASTE	KITTY	SITAR	COUPE	JAUNT	SOUND

SOUPY	COVEY	DOWEL	IDYLL	BELAY	GLEAM	PETAL	THEAT	PLEBS	EPOCH	PINCH	WENCH
SOUSE	DAVIT	DOWER	KAYAK	BLEAK	GLEAN	PHIAL	TICAL	PROBE	ERECT	PITCH	WHACK
SOUTH	DEVIL	DOWNY	LAYER	BLEAR	GLOAT	PILAF	TITAN	RABBI	EVICT	PLACE	WHICH
SPUME	DIVAN	DOWRY	LOYAL	BLEAT	GONAD	PLEAD	TODAY	RUGBY	EXACT	PLUCK	WINCE
SPUNK	DIVOT	DOWSE	MAYBE	BLOAT	GREAT	PLEAT	TOKAY	RUMBA	FANCY	POACH	WINCH
SPURN	EAVES	FEWER	MAYOR	BORAX	GROAN	POLAR	TOPAZ	SCUBA	FARCE	POOCH	WITCH
SPURT	ELVER	GAWKY	PSYCH	BREAD	GROAT	QUEAN	TORAH	TABBY	FENCE	PORCH	WRACK
SQUAB	ELVES	JEWEL	RAYON	BREAK	HOGAN	RADAR	TOTAL	TRIBE	FETCH	POUCH	WRECK
SQUAD	ENVOI	JEWRY	RHYME	BREAM	HUMAN	RECAP	TREAD	TURBO	FILCH	PRICE	YUCCA
SQUAT	ENVOY	LOWER	RIYAL	BRIAR	IDEAL	REGAL	TREAS	ABACK	FINCH	PRICK	ABIDE
SQUAW	FAVOR	LOWLY	ROYAL	BROAD	INLAY	RELAX	TREAT	AMUCK	FLECK	PSYCH	ABODE
SQUIB	FEVER	NEWEL	STYLE	BYLAW	ISLAM	RELAY	TRIAD	APACE	FLICK	PUNCH	ANODE
SQUID	GAVEL	NEWLY	THYME	BYWAY	JALAP	RENAL	TRIAL	BATCH	FLOCK	QUACK	ASIDE
STUCK	GIVEN	NEWSY	TRYST	CABAL	JAPAN	REPAY	TWEAK	BEACH	FORCE	QUICK	BANDY
STUDY	HAVEN	NGWEE	BEZEL	CACAO	JIHAD	RIVAL	UMIAK	BEECH	FROCK	RANCH	BAWDY
STUFF	HAVOC	NOWAY	COZEN	CANAL	KARAT	RIYAL	UNBAR	BELCH	GRACE	REACH	BIDDY
STUMP	HIVES	PEWEE	DIZZY	CARAT	KAYAK	RNZAF	UNCAP	BENCH	GULCH	REACT	BLADE
STUNG	HOVEL	POWER	DOZEN	CEDAR	KEBAB	ROMAN	UNMAN	BIRCH	HATCH	RETCH	BRIDE
STUNK	HOVER	ROWDY	FUZZY	CHEAP	KNEAD	ROYAL	UNSAY	BITCH	HENCE	ROACH	BUDDY
STUNT	LEVEE	ROWEL	GIZMO	CHEAT	KORAN	RURAL	URBAN	BLACK	HITCH	SAUCE	CADDY
SWUNG	LEVEL	SEWER	HAZEL	CHIAO	KRAAL	SALAD	USUAL	BLOCK	HUNCH	SAUCY	CANDY
TAUNT	LEVER	TAWNY	JAZZY	CIGAR	KULAK	SATAN	VELAR	BOTCH	HUTCH	SHACK	CHIDE
TAUPE	LIVEN	TOWEL	KAZOO	CLEAN	LANAI	SCRAM	VENAL	BRACE	JUICE	SHOCK	COMDG
THUMB	LIVER	TOWER	LAZAR	CLEAR	LAZAR	SCRAP	VICAR	BRACT	JUICY	SHUCK	COMDR
THUMP	LIVES	VOWEL	PIZZA	CLEAT	LEGAL	SEDAN	VIRAL	BRICK	JUNCO	SINCE	COMDT
THURS	LIVID	AUXIN	RAZOR	CLOAK	LILAC	SEPAL	VITAL	BUNCH	KETCH	SLACK	CREDO
TOUCH	MAVEN	BOXER	RNZAF	CORAL	LOCAL	SHEAF	VOCAB	BUNCO	KNACK	SLICE	CRUDE
TOUGH	MAVIS	BUXOM	TIZZY	CREAK	LOYAL	SHEAR	VOCAL	CATCH	KNOCK	SLICK	DADDY
TRUCE	MOVER	FIXED	UNZIP	CREAM	LUNAR	SHOAL	WHEAL	CHECK	LANCE	SMACK	DANDY
TRUCK	MOVIE	FOXED	VIZOR	CROAK	MACAW	SHOAT	WHEAT	CHICK	LARCH	SMOCK	DIODE
TRUMP	NAVAL	MAXIM		CUBAN	MADAM	SISAL	WOMAN	CHOCK	LATCH	SNACK	DOWDY
TRUNK	NAVEL	MIXER		DEBAR	MALAY	SITAR	WREAK	CHUCK	LEACH	SNUCK	ELIDE
TRUSS	NEVER	NEXUS		DECAL	MEDAL	SMEAR	ZONAL	CINCH	LEECH	SPACE	ELUDE
TRUST	NEVUS	PIXEL	4TH LETTER	DECAY	METAL	SNEAK	ADOBE	CIRCA	LUNCH	SPECK	ERODE
TRUTH	NOVEL	PIXIE		DEGAS	MOLAR	SOLAR	ALIBI	CLACK	LURCH	SPICE	ETUDE
USUAL	PIVOT	SIXTY	ABEAM	DELAY	MORAL	SONAR	AMEBA	CLICK	LYNCH	STACK	EVADE
USURP	RAVEL	TOXIC	ADMAN	DINAR	MORAY	SPEAK	BOBBY	CLOCK	MARCH	STICK	EXUDE
USURY	RAVEN	TOXIN	AHEAD	DIVAN	MURAL	SPEAR	BOOBY	CLUCK	MATCH	STOCK	GAUDY
UVULA	REVEL	VIXEN	ALIAS	DREAD	NAIAD	SPLAY	BRIBE	COACH	MECCA	STUCK	GEODE
VAULT	REVUE	WAXEN	ALLAH	DREAM	NASAL	SPRAT	BUSBY	CONCH	MERCY	TEACH	GIDDY
VAUNT	RIVAL	ABYSM	ALLAY	DREAR	NATAL	SPRAY	CABBY	COUCH	MILCH	THICK	GLIDE
VOUCH	RIVER	ABYSS	ALTAR	DRYAD	NAVAL	SQUAB	COMBO	CRACK	MINCE	TINCT	GOODY
WOULD	RIVET	ARYAN	APEAK	DUCAL	NICAD	SQUAD	DERBY	CRICK	MULCH	TORCH	GOUDA
WOUND	SAVOR	BAYOU	ARRAS	DUCAT	NOMAD	SQUAT	DOUBT	CROCK	MULCT	TOUCH	GRADE
WRUNG	SAVVY	COYPU	ARRAY	ECLAT	NOWAY	SQUAW	FLYBY	CZECH	MUNCH	TRACE	GUIDE
YOUNG	SEVEN	CRYPT	ARYAN	ENIAC	OCCAS	STEAD	GABBY	DANCE	NAACP	TRACK	HANDY
YOURS	SEVER	CRYST	ASIAN	EQUAL	OCEAN	STEAK	GLEBE	DEICE	NIECE	TRACT	HARDY
YOUTH	VIVID	DOYEN	ASSAY	ESSAY	OCTAL	STEAL	GLOBE	DEUCE	NONCE	TRICE	HEADY
ANVIL	WAVER	DRYAD	ATLAS	FATAL	OFFAL	STEAM	GREBE	DISCO	NOTCH	TRICK	HINDI
BEVEL	WIVES	DRYER	ATTAR	FERAL	ORGAN	STOAT	GUMBO	DITCH	OUNCE	TRUCE	HORDE
CAVIL	WOVEN	FLYBY	AURAL	FETAL	PAEAN	STRAP	HOBBY	DUNCE	PARCH	TRUCK	MIDDY
CIVET	BAWDY	FLYER	AURAR	FILAR	PAGAN	STRAW	JUMBO	DUTCH	PATCH	TWICE	MOODY
CIVIC	BOWEL	FOYER	AVGAS	FINAL	PAPAL	STRAY	LIMBO	EDICT	PEACE	VETCH	NEEDS
CIVIL	BOWER	FRYER	AVIAN	FLOAT	PAPAW	SUGAR	LOBBY	EDUCE	PEACH	VOICE	NEEDY
COVEN	BYWAY	GLYPH	AXIAL	FORAY	PECAN	SUMAC	MAMBO	EJECT	PENCE	VOUCH	NODDY
COVER	COWER	GUYOT	BANAL	FREAK	PEDAL	SWEAR	MAYBE	ELECT	PERCH	WATCH	OUTDO
COVET	DOWDY	HAYES	BASAL	FRIAR	PENAL	SWEAT	PLEBE	ENACT	PIECE	WELCH	OXIDE

PADDY	BLUET	ELDER	INLET	NISEI	SEVEN	UNDER	SNIFF	LEGGY	FIGHT	BEGIN	GROIN
PANDA	BOGEY	ELVER	INNER	NITER	SEVER	UNPEG	SNUFF	LIEGE	FISHY	BELIE	HABIT
PRIDE	BONER	ELVES	INSET	NONES	SEWER	UPPER	STAFF	LINGO	FOEHN	BLAIN	HELIX
PRUDE	BOWEL	EMBED	INTEL	NOTED	SHEEN	UPSET	STIFF	LODGE	GUSHY	BRAID	HUMID
READY	BOWER	EMBER	INTER	NOVEL	SHEEP	USHER	STUFF	LUNGE	LATHE	BRAIN	INDIC
ROWDY	BOXER	EMCEE	IRREG	OCHER	SHEER	UTTER	SULFA	MANGE	LIGHT	BROIL	LAMIA
RUDDY	BREED	ENTER	ISLET	OCTET	SHEET	VALET	SWIFT	MANGO	LITHE	BRUIN	LAPIN
SEEDY	BRIEF	ESTER	JADED	OFFER	SHIER	VIBES	TAFFY	MARGE	MIGHT	BRUIT	LATIN
SHADE	BRIER	ETHER	JEWEL	OFTEN	SHRED	VIDEO	THEFT	MERGE	MUSHY	CABIN	LEGIS
SLIDE	CADET	EXCEL	JOKER	OLDEN	SHREW	VIPER	UNIFY	MIDGE	NICHE	CALIF	LEGIT
SNIDE	CAGEY	EXPEL	JULEP	ONSET	SINEW	VIREO	WHIFF	MONGO	NIGHT	CAVIL	LICIT
SPADE	CAMEL	FACET	KNEEL	ORDER	SIREN	VIXEN	ADAGE	MUGGY	OMAHA	CHAIN	LIMIT
STUDY	CAMEO	FATED	LABEL	ORIEL	SKEET	VOWEL	ALIGN	NEIGH	OUGHT	CHAIR	LIVID
SUEDE	CAPER	FECES	LADEN	OSIER	SLEEK	WADER	BADGE	NUDGE	PASHA	CHOIR	LOGIC
SWEDE	CARET	FEVER	LAGER	OTHER	SLEEP	WAFER	BAGGY	OSAGE	PITHY	CIVIC	LUCID
TARDY	CATER	FEWER	LAPEL	OTTER	SLEET	WAGER	BARGE	OUTGO	PUSHY	CIVIL	LURID
TILDE	CHEEK	FIBER	LASER	OUTER	SLIER	WAKEN	BEIGE	PHAGE	RIGHT	CLAIM	LYRIC
TOADY	CHEEP	FIXED	LATEX	OWLET	SNEER	WATER	BILGE	PUDGY	SIGHT	COLIC	MAFIA
TODDY	CHEER	FLEER	LAYER	PACER	SOBER	WAVER	BINGE	PURGE	TIGHT	COMIC	MAGIC
TRADE	CHIEF	FLEET	LEPER	PANEL	SPEED	WAXEN	BINGO	RANGE	TITHE	CONIC	MANIA
WEEDY	CIDER	FLIED	LEVEE	PAPER	SPIEL	WHEEL	BONGO	RANGY	WASHY	CUBIC	MANIC
WINDY	CIVET	FLIER	LEVEL	PATEN	SPREE	WIDEN	BOUGH	REIGN	WIGHT	CUBIT	MAVIS
WOODY	CODEC	FLYER	LEVER	PETER	STEED	WIVES	BUDGE	RIDGE	WITHE	CUPID	MAXIM
WORDY	CODEX	FOXED	LIBEL	PEWEE	STEEL	WOKEN	BUGGY	ROUGE	WITHY	CURIA	MEDIA
ABBEY	COMER	FOYER	LIFER	PIKER	STEEP	WOVEN	BULGE	ROUGH	YACHT	CURIO	MEDIC
ADDER	COMET	FRYER	LIKEN	PILES	STEER	XEBEC	BURGH	SEDGE	ACRID	CYNIC	MERIT
ADIEU	CONEY	FUSEE	LINEN	PIXEL	STREW	XYLEM	CADGE	SENGI	ADMIN	DAVIT	MIMIC
AFTER	COVEN	GAVEL	LINER	POKER	SUPER	YODEL	CARGO	SERGE	ADMIT	DEBIT	MINIM
AGREE	COVER	GIVEN	LITER	POSER	SWEEP	YOKEL	CMSGT	SIEGE	ADMIX	DENIM	MODIF
ALDER	COVET	GONER	LIVEN	POWER	SWEET	ABAFT	CONGA	SINGE	AEGIS	DERIV	MOTIF
ALIEN	COVEY	GREED	LIVER	PREEN	TALER	ALOFT	COUGH	SMSGT	AERIE	DEVIL	MOVIE
ALLEY	COWER	GREEK	LIVES	PROEM	TAPER	BEEFY	DEIGN	SOGGY	AFAIK	DIGIT	MUSIC
ALTER	COZEN	GREEN	LONER	PUBES	TELEG	BLUFF	DINGO	SOUGH	AFAIR	DOGIE	NADIR
AMBER	CREED	GREET	LOWER	PUREE	TELEX	CHAFE	DINGY	STAGE	AFFIX	DRAIN	NARIS
ANGEL	CREEK	GRIEF	MANES	QUEEN	TENET	CHAFF	DIRGE	SURGE	AGAIN	DRUID	NUMIS
ANGER	CREEL	GRUEL	MASER	QUEER	TEPEE	CLEFT	DODGE	SWAGE	AMAIN	EDLIN	OASIS
ANNEX	CREEP	HADES	MAVEN	QUIET	THIEF	CLIFF	DOGGY	TAIGA	ANTIC	EERIE	OLDIE
ASHEN	CRIER	HALER	MELEE	RAVEL	THREE	COMFY	DOUGH	TANGO	ANVIL	EMAIL	OPTIC
ASKEW	CRUEL	HAREM	METER	RAVEN	THREW	CRAFT	ELEGY	THEGN	APHID	EQUIP	ORBIT
ASPEN	CRUET	HAVEN	MISER	REBEL	TIGER	DAFFY	FEIGN	THIGH	APHIS	EQUIV	ORRIS
ASSET	DATED	HAYES	MITER	REFER	TIMES	DEIFY	FORGE	TINGE	APRIL	EYRIE	OVOID
ASTER	DEFER	HAZEL	MIXER	RENEW	TIRED	DELFT	FORGO	TONGS	ASCII	EYRIR	PANIC
AUGER	DETER	HIVES	MLLES	REPEL	TOKEN	DRAFT	FUDGE	TOUGH	ASPIC	FAKIR	PATIO
AZTEC	DINER	HOMER	MODEL	REVEL	TONER	DRIFT	GAUGE	USAGE	ASTIR	FETID	PENIS
BABEL	DOPEY	HOMEY	MODEM	RIDER	TOPER	FLUFF	GORGE	VERGE	ATTIC	FINIS	PERIL
BAGEL	DOWEL	HONEY	MONEY	RIPEN	TOTEM	GAFFE	GOUGE	WEDGE	AUDIO	PIXIE	PIXIE
BEDEW	DOWER	HOOEY	MOREL	RISER	TOWEL	GOOFY	HEDGE	WEIGH	AUDIT	FLAIR	PLAID
BEGET	DOYEN	HOTEL	MORES	RIVER	TOWER	GRAFT	HINGE	ALOHA	AUXIN	FLUID	PLAIN
BERET	DOZEN	HOVEL	MOSEY	RIVET	TRIED	GRUFF	IMAGE	AUGHT	AVAIL	FOLIO	PLAIT
BESET	DRIER	HOVER	MOTEL	RODEO	TUBER	JIFFY	IMAGO	BATHE	AVOID	FRAIL	POLIO
BETEL	DRYER	HYMEN	MOTET	ROGER	TWEED	KNIFE	JUDGE	BIGHT	AWAIT	FRUIT	POLIT
BEVEL	EAGER	IMBED	MOVER	ROWEL	TWEEN	QUAFF	KEDGE	CACHE	BASIC	FSLIC	POSIT
BEZEL	EARED	IMPEL	NAKED	RULER	TWEET	SCOFF	KLUGE	DACHA	BASIL	GAMIN	PUBIC
BIDET	EASEL	IMPER	NAVEL	RUPEE	UDDER	SCUFF	LARGE	DUCHY	BASIN	GELID	PUBIS
BIPED	EAVES	INDEF	NEVER	SABER	ULCER	SHAFT	LARGO	EIGHT	BASIS	GENIE	PUPIL
BLEED	EGRET	INDEX	NEWEL	SCREW	UMBEL	SHIFT	LAUGH	FICHE	BATIK	GRAIL	PURIM
BLUES	EIDER	INFER	NGWEE	SEMEN	UMBER	SKIFF	LEDGE	FICHU	BEFIT	GRAIN	QUAIL

QUOIT	UNFIT	SULKY	FOLLY	SHELF	CHAMP	SWAMP	COUNT	KRONE	SLUNK	AGLOW	DONOR
RABID	UNFIX	TACKY	FRILL	SHELL	CHIME	THEME	CRANE	LEONE	SOUND	ALGOL	DROOL
RADII	UNPIN	VODKA	FULLY	SHILL	CHIMP	THUMB	CRANK	LLANO	SPANK	ALLOT	DROOP
RADIO	UNTIE	WACKY	GABLE	SIDLE	CHOMP	THUMP	CRONE	LOONY	SPEND	ALLOW	ELBOW
RADIX	UNTIL	ADDLE	GAILY	SILLY	CHUMP	THYME	CRONY	LYING	SPENT	ALLOY	ENDOW
RAMIE	UNZIP	ADULT	GODLY	SKILL	CLAMP	TRAMP	DAUNT	MANNA	SPINE	ALOOF	ENJOY
RAPID	VALID	AGILE	GRILL	SKULK	CLIMB	TROMP	DOWNY	MOUND	SPUNK	ANION	ENTOM
RATIO	VAPID	AISLE	GUILD	SKULL	CLIME	TRUMP	DRANK	MOUNT	STAND	ANNOY	ENVOI
RECIP	VARIA	AMBLE	GUILE	SMALL	CLUMP	TUMMY	DRINK	NINNY	STANK	APRON	ENVOY
RELIC	VATIC	AMPLE	GUILT	SMELL	COMMA	YUMMY	DRONE	OPINE	STING	ARBOR	EPROM
RELIG	VIGIL	ANGLE	GULLY	SMELT	COMMO	ADDNL	DRUNK	OWING	STINK	ARDOR	EPSON
REMIT	VISIT	ANGLO	HALLO	SMILE	CRAMP	AGENT	DYING	OZONE	STINT	ARGON	ERGOT
RESIN	VIVID	ANKLE	HAOLE	SPELL	CREME	AGONY	EBONY	PAINT	STONE	ARGOT	ERROR
RIGID	VOMIT	APPLE	HAPLY	SPILL	CRIME	ALONE	ELAND	PENNI	STUNG	ARMOR	ETHOS
ROBIN	XERIC	APPLY	HELLO	STALE	CRIMP	ALONG	EMEND	PENNY	STUNK	ARROW	EXTOL
ROSIN	BANJO	ATILT	HOLLO	STALK	CRUMB	AMEND	EVENT	PEONY	STUNT	ARSON	FAGOT
SANIT	HAJJI	ATOLL	HOLLY	STALL	DOGMA	AMONG	FAINT	PHONE	SWANK	ASCOT	FAVOR
SATIN	KANJI	BELLE	IDYLL	STILE	DRAMA	ANENT	FAUNA	PHONO	SWINE	ASSOC	FELON
SCRIM	ALIKE	BELLS	IMPLY	STILL	DUMMY	ARENA	FEINT	PHONY	SWING	AXIOM	FLOOD
SCRIP	AWAKE	BELLY	INGLE	STILT	EDEMA	ATONE	FIEND	PIANO	SWUNG	BACON	FLOOR
SEPIA	BALKY	BIBLE	JELLY	STOLE	ENEMA	BANNS	FINNY	PLANE	TAINT	BARON	FUROR
SERIF	BOSKY	BILLY	JOLLY	STYLE	ENEMY	BEANO	FLANK	PLANK	TAUNT	BATON	GLOOM
SKEIN	BRAKE	BOULE	JOULE	SULLY	FLAME	BEING	FLING	PLANT	TAWNY	BAYOU	GROOM
SLAIN	BROKE	BUGLE	KNELL	SURLY	FLUME	BENNY	FLINT	PLUNK	TEENS	BEFOG	GUYOT
SNAIL	BULKY	BUILD	KNOLL	SWELL	FRAME	BHANG	FLUNG	POINT	TEENY	BELOW	HAVOC
SOLID	CHOKE	BULLY	KOALA	SWILL	GAMMA	BLAND	FLUNK	POUND	THANE	BESOM	HELOT
SONIC	COCKY	BURLY	LADLE	TABLE	GIZMO	BLANK	FOUND	PRANK	THANK	BESOT	HERON
SPLIT	DINKY	CABLE	LISLE	TALLY	GNOME	BLEND	FOUNT	PRINK	THINE	BIGOT	HONOR
SPOIL	DRAKE	CALLA	LOWLY	THOLE	GRIME	BLIND	FRANC	PRINT	THING	BISON	HUMOR
SPRIG	DUSKY	CAULK	MANLY	TITLE	JIMMY	BLINK	FRANK	PRONE	THINK	BLOOD	HURON
SQUIB	EVOKE	CELLO	MAPLE	TRILL	KARMA	BLOND	FROND	PRONG	THONG	BLOOM	ICHOR
SQUID	FLAKE	CHALK	MOULD	TROLL	LLAMA	BLUNT	FRONT	PRUNE	TINNY	BORON	IDIOM
STAID	FLUKE	CHELA	MOULT	TULLE	MAGMA	BONNY	FUNNY	QUINT	TRANS	BOSOM	IDIOT
STAIN	FUNKY	CHILD	NEWLY	TWILL	MIAMI	BORNE	GAUNT	RHINO	TREND	BROOD	IGLOO
STAIR	GAWKY	CHILI	NOBLE	UNCLE	MUMMY	BOUND	GIANT	ROUND	TRINE	BROOK	INCOG
STEIN	HAIKU	CHILL	OVULE	UTILE	PALMY	BRAND	GLAND	RUNNY	TRUNK	BROOM	INGOT
STOIC	HUSKY	COULD	POILU	UVULA	PIGMY	BRINE	GLANS	SAINT	TUNNY	BUXOM	INSOL
STRIA	KHAKI	CYCLE	POULT	VAULT	PLUMB	BRING	GLINT	SAUNA	TWANG	CANOE	JABOT
STRIP	KOOKY	DAILY	PSALM	VILLA	PLUME	BRINK	GRAND	SCAND	TWINE	CANON	JUROR
SWAIN	LANKY	DALLY	QUALM	VIOLA	PLUMP	BRUNT	GRANT	SCANF	TYING	CAPON	KABOB
TACIT	LINKS	DOILY	QUELL	VOILE	PRIME	BUNNY	GRIND	SCANT	UPEND	CAROL	KAPOK
TAPIR	LUCKY	DOLLY	QUILL	WEALD	PRIMP	CANNA	GRUNT	SCENE	URINE	CAROM	KAZOO
TEPID	PARKA	DRILL	QUILT	WHALE	PYGMY	CANNY	GUANO	SCENT	VAUNT	CHAOS	KUDOS
THEIR	PESKY	DRILY	RALLY	WHELK	RHYME	CARNY	GUNNY	SCONE	VIAND	CHRON	LABOR
TIBIA	PICKY	DROLL	REALM	WHELM	RUMMY	CHANT	HAUNT	SEINE	VYING	COBOL	LEMON
TIMID	POLKA	DUPLE	REPLY	WHELP	SCAMP	CHINA	HENNA	SENNA	WEENY	COCOA	MAJOR
TONIC	PUKKA	DWELL	RIFLE	WHILE	SEAMY	CHINE	HOUND	SHANK	WHINE	COLON	MANOR
TOPIC	QUAKE	EAGLE	RUBLE	WHOLE	SHAME	CHINK	HYENA	SHINE	WOUND	COLOR	MASON
TOXIC	SHAKE	EARLY	SABLE	WHSLE	SIGMA	CHINO	HYING	SHINY	WRING	CROOK	MAYOR
TOXIN	SHAKY	EXALT	SALLY	WIELD	SKIMP	CHUNK	ICING	SHONE	WRONG	CROON	MCCOY
TRAIL	SLAKE	EXILE	SCALD	WORLD	SLIME	CLANG	INANE	SHUNT	WRUNG	DECOR	MELON
TRAIN	SMOKE	EXULT	SCALE	WOULD	SLUMP	CLANK	IRONY	SKUNK	YOUNG	DECOY	MINOR
TRAIT	SNAKE	FABLE	SCALP	YIELD	SPUME	CLING	JAUNT	SLANG	ABBOT	DEFOG	MORON
TULIP	SPIKE	FAULT	SCOLD	AROMA	STAMP	CLINK	JEANS	SLANT	ABHOR	DEMON	MOTOR
TUMID	SPOKE	FELLY	SCULL	BALMY	STOMP	CLONE	JENNY	SLING	ACTOR	DEPOT	NABOB
TUNIC	STAKE	FIELD	SHALE	BLAME	STUMP	CLUNG	JOINT	SLINK	ADIOS	DIVOT	NOHOW
TWAIN	STOKE	FILLY	SHALL	BLIMP	SWAMI	CORNY	KRONA	SLUNG	AFOOT	DOLOR	NYLON

ONION	UNION	SOUPY	DAIRY	NAIRA	STORE	BLASE	FRESH	PAISA	TRYST	DLITT	PASTA
OXBOW	VALOR	SWEPT	DECRY	NEGRO	STORK	BLAST	FRISK	PALSY	TWIST	EARTH	PASTE
PEKOE	VAPOR	SWIPE	DIARY	NITRO	STORM	BLESS	FROST	PANSY	UKASE	ELATE	PASTY
PHLOX	VENOM	SYLPH	DOWRY	OPERA	STORY	BLISS	FUSSY	PARSE	VALSE	ELITE	PATTY
PICOT	VIGOR	TAUPE	DWARF	OUTRE	SUCRE	BLUSH	GAUSS	PASSE	VERSE	EMOTE	PETTY
PILOT	VISOR	TEMPO	EMERY	OVARY	SUPRA	BOAST	GEESE	PATSY	VERSO	EMPTY	PHOTO
PINON	VIZOR	TEMPT	ENTRY	OVERT	SWARD	BOOST	GHOST	PAUSE	VERST	EXPTL	PIETY
PITON	WAGON	TRAPS	EVERY	PADRE	SWARM	BRASH	GIPSY	PHASE	WAIST	FAITH	PINTO
PIVOT	WAHOO	TRIPE	EXERT	PARRY	SWART	BRASS	GLASS	PLASH	WELSH	FATTY	PLATE
PRIOR	WHOOP	TROPE	EXTRA	PEARL	SWIRL	BRISK	GLOSS	PLUSH	WHISH	FIFTH	PLATY
PROOF	WIDOW	TURPS	EXURB	PHARM	SWORD	BRUSH	GNASH	POESY	WHISK	FIFTY	PLUTO
PYLON	XENON	WEEPY	FAIRY	QUART	SWORE	BURST	GOOSE	POISE	WHIST	FILTH	PRATE
RADON	YAHOO	XCOPY	FERRY	QUERY	SWORN	CAUSE	GORSE	POSSE	WHOSE	FIRTH	PUTTY
RAYON	ADAPT	ZIPPY	FIERY	QUIRE	TARRY	CEASE	GRASP	PRESS	WHOSO	FLUTE	QUITE
RAZOR	ADEPT	IRAQI	FIORD	QUIRK	TERRY	CHASE	GRASS	PRISM	WORSE	FORTE	QUITS
RIGOR	ADOPT	ABORT	FJORD	QUIRT	THERE	CHASM	GRIST	PROSE	WORST	FORTH	QUOTA
ROBOT	AGAPE	ACORN	FLARE	SCARE	THERM	CHESS	GROSS	PROSY	WREST	FORTY	QUOTE
ROTOR	CHAPS	ADORE	FLIRT	SCARF	THIRD	CHEST	GROSZ	PULSE	WRIST	FROTH	QUOTH
RUMOR	CHOPS	ADORN	FLORA	SCARP	THORN	CHOSE	GUESS	PURSE	WURST	FUSTY	RATTY
SALON	CORPS	AFIRE	FURRY	SCORE	THORP	CLASH	GUEST	PUSSY	YEAST	GANTT	RECTO
SAVOR	COUPE	AGORA	GENRE	SCORN	THURS	CLASP	GUISE	QUASH	ABATE	GIRTH	ROUTE
SCION	COYPU	ALARM	GLARE	SCURF	TIARA	CLASS	GYPSY	QUASI	ABSTR	GRATE	SAUTE
SCOOP	CRAPE	ALERT	GLORY	SHARD	TWIRL	CLOSE	HARSH	QUEST	ACUTE	GRITS	SCOTS
SCOOT	CRAPS	ANGRY	GNARL	SHARE	ULTRA	COAST	HEIST	QURSH	AGATE	GUSTO	SEATO
SCROD	CREPE	APART	GOURD	SHARK	UMBRA	CONST	HOIST	RAISE	AMITY	GUTTY	SENTI
SHOOK	CRYPT	APORT	GUARD	SHARP	UNARM	COPSE	HORSE	RINSE	AORTA	HASTE	SIXTY
SHOOT	DRAPE	AVERT	HAIRY	SHIRE	USURP	CRASH	HOUSE	ROAST	ARITH	HEATH	SKATE
SLOOP	DRUPE	AWARD	HARRY	SHIRK	USURY	CRASS	HUSSY	ROOST	BANTU	HEFTY	SLATE
SNOOP	DUMPS	AWARE	HEART	SHIRR	VEERY	CRESC	IRISH	ROUSE	BASTE	HERTZ	SLOTH
SOLON	DUMPY	AZURE	HOARD	SHIRT	WEARY	CRESS	JOIST	SASSY	BATTY	INSTR	SMITE
SPOOF	ELOPE	BAIRN	HOARY	SHORE	WEIRD	CREST	JOUST	SEISM	BERTH	IRATE	SMITH
SPOOK	ERUPT	BEARD	HOURI	SHORN	WHARF	CRISP	KARST	SENSE	BIRTH	JETTY	SMOTE
SPOOL	GIMPY	BERRY	HURRY	SHORT	WHERE	CROSS	KIOSK	SISSY	BLITZ	JUNTA	SOOTH
SPOON	GLYPH	BLARE	HYDRA	SKIRT	WHIRL	CRUSE	KNISH	SLASH	BOOTH	JUNTO	SOUTH
SPOOR	GRAPE	BLURB	HYDRO	SLURP	WHORE	CRUSH	LAPSE	SLOSH	BOOTY	KITTY	SPATE
STOOD	GRAPH	BLURT	INERT	SMART	WHORL	CRUST	LASSO	SLUSH	BROTH	LAITY	SPITE
STOOL	GRIPE	BOARD	INURE	SMIRK	WORRY	CRYST	LEASE	SMASH	BRUTE	LISTS	STATE
STOOP	GROPE	BOURN	INURN	SNARE	YEARN	CURSE	LEASH	SOUSE	BUTTE	LOATH	SUITE
STROP	GUPPY	BURRO	IVORY	SNARL	YOURS	DAISY	LEAST	SPASM	CANTO	LOFTY	SWATH
SWOON	HAPPY	CADRE	JEWRY	SNORE	ZAIRE	DEISM	LOESS	STASH	CASTE	LUSTY	SWITZ
SWOOP	HARPY	CAIRN	KNURL	SNORT	ZEBRA	DENSE	LOOSE	SWASH	CATTY	MANTA	TASTE
SYNOD	INEPT	CARRY	LAIRD	SORRY	ABASE	DOUSE	LOUSE	SWISH	CCITT	MIRTH	TASTY
SYSOP	JUMPY	CHARD	LEARN	SPARC	ABASH	DOWSE	LOUSY	SWISS	CHUTE	MISTY	TEETH
TABOO	LYMPH	CHARM	LEERY	SPARE	ABUSE	DRESS	MANSE	TANSY	CLOTH	MONTH	TESTY
TABOR	MUMPS	CHART	LORRY	SPARK	ABYSM	DROSS	MARSH	TEASE	CONTD	MOTTO	TILTH
TALON	NIPPY	CHARY	LUCRE	SPERM	ABYSS	ERASE	MIDST	TENSE	CONTG	MOUTH	TOOTH
TAROT	NYMPH	CHERT	MACRO	SPIRE	AMASS	ERISA	MOIST	TERSE	CONTR	MUFTI	TRITE
TENON	PAMPA	CHIRP	MAORI	SPIRT	AMISS	EXIST	MOOSE	THESE	CRATE	MUSTY	TROTH
TENOR	POPPY	CHORD	MARRY	SPORE	AMUSE	FALSE	MOUSE	THESS	DEATH	NASTY	TRUTH
THEOL	PUPPY	CHORE	MERRY	SPORT	ANGST	FEAST	MOUSY	THOSE	DEITY	NATTY	UNITE
THROB	SAPPY	CHURL	METRE	SPURN	ANISE	FIRST	NEWSY	TIPSY	DELTA	NIFTY	UNITY
THROE	SCOPE	CHURN	METRO	SPURT	ARISE	FLASH	NOISE	TOAST	DEPTH	NORTH	VASTY
THROW	SHAPE	CLERK	MICRO	STARE	AVAST	FLASK	NOISY	TORSO	DIRTY	NUTTY	VIRTU
TOPOG	SHIPT	COBRA	MOIRE	STARK	AWASH	FLESH	NOOSE	TRASH	DISTN	ORATE	VISTA
TROOP	SLOPE	COPRA	MOURN	START	BALSA	FLOSS	NORSE	TRESS	DISTR	OVATE	WALTZ
TUMOR	SNIPE	COURT	MYRRH	STERE	BASSO	FLUSH	NURSE	TRUSS	DITTO	PANTS	WASTE
TUTOR	SNIPS	CURRY	NACRE	STERN	BEAST	FOIST	OBESE	TRUST	DITTY	PARTY	WHITE

WIDTH	IMBUE	TALUS	SLAVE	FEAZE	HYENA	CRUMB	ALKYD	GOURD	TIMID	AWARE	CLOSE
WITTY	INCUR	THRUM	SOLVE	FRIZZ	JUNTA	EXURB	ALOUD	GRAND	TIRED	AZURE	CLOVE
WORTH	INCUS	TOQUE	STAVE	FROZE	KARMA	KABOB	AMEND	GREED	TREAD	BADGE	COPSE
WRATH	INDUE	TROUT	STOVE	FURZE	KIOWA	KEBAB	APHID	GRIND	TREND	BAIZE	COUPE
WRITE	INPUT	TUQUE	SUAVE	FUZZY	KOALA	NABOB	AVOID	GUARD	TRIAD	BARGE	CRANE
WROTE	ISSUE	UNCUT	SUPVR	GAUZE	KRONA	PLUMB	AWARD	GUILD	TRIED	BASTE	CRAPE
WROTH	KAPUT	UNDUE	VALVE	GLAZE	LAMIA	SCRUB	BEARD	HOARD	TUMID	BATHE	CRATE
YOUTH	KNOUT	VAGUE	VERVE	GLOZE	LARVA	SHRUB	BIPED	HOUND	TWEED	BEIGE	CRAVE
ZLOTY	KRAUT	VALUE	VULVA	GRAZE	LLAMA	SQUAB	BLAND	HUMID	UPEND	BELIE	CRAZE
ABOUT	KURUS	VELUM	WAIVE	JAZZY	MAFIA	SQUIB	BLEED	IMBED	VALID	BELLE	CREME
ALBUM	LEMUR	VENUE	WEAVE	MAIZE	MAGMA	THROB	BLEND	JADED	VAPID	BIBLE	CREPE
ALOUD	LETUP	VENUS	BLOWY	MATZO	MANIA	THUMB	BLIND	JIHAD	VIAND	BILGE	CRIME
AMOUR	LIEUT	VIRUS	BRAWL	PIZZA	MANNA	VOCAB	BLOND	KNEAD	VIVID	BINGE	CRONE
AMPUL	LOCUS	VOGUE	BRAWN	PLAZA	MANTA	ANTIC	BLOOD	LAIRD	WEALD	BLADE	CRUDE
ANGUS	LOTUS	ABOVE	BROWN	PRIZE	MECCA	ASPIC	BOARD	LIVID	WEIRD	BLAME	CRUSE
ANNUL	MANUF	AGAVE	CHEWY	SEIZE	MEDIA	ASSOC	BOUND	LUCID	WIELD	BLARE	CURSE
ARGUE	MINUS	ALIVE	CLOWN	TIZZY	NAIRA	ATTIC	BRAID	LURID	WORLD	BLASE	CURVE
AUGUR	MOGUL	BRAVE	CRAWL	WOOZY	OMAHA	AZTEC	BRAND	MOULD	WOULD	BLAZE	CYCLE
AWFUL	MUCUS	BRAVO	CROWD		OPERA	BASIC	BREAD	MOUND	WOUND	BONZE	DANCE
BEGUM	NEGUS	CALVE	CROWN		PAISA	CIVIC	BREED	NAIAD	YIELD	BOOZE	DEICE
BOGUS	NEVUS	CARVE	DRAWL		PAMPA	CODEC	BROAD	NAKED	ABASE	BORNE	DELVE
BOLUS	NEXUS	CHIVE	DROWN	**5TH LETTER**	PANDA	COLIC	BROOD	NICAD	ABATE	BOULE	DENSE
BONUS	OAKUM	CLOVE	FLOWN		PARKA	COMIC	BUILD	NOMAD	ABIDE	BRACE	DEUCE
BOSUN	OCCUR	CRAVE	FROWN	AGORA	PASHA	CONIC	CHARD	NOTED	ABODE	BRAKE	DIODE
BUTUT	ODIUM	CURVE	GROWL	ALOHA	PASTA	CRESC	CHILD	OVOID	ABOVE	BRAVE	DIRGE
CAJUN	OPIUM	DELVE	KIOWA	AMEBA	PIZZA	CUBIC	CHORD	PLAID	ABUSE	BRAZE	DODGE
CECUM	PINUP	DRIVE	PRAWN	AORTA	PLAYA	CYNIC	CLOUD	PLEAD	ACUTE	BRIBE	DOGIE
CLOUD	PIOUS	DROVE	PROWL	ARENA	PLAZA	ENIAC	CONTD	POUND	ADAGE	BRIDE	DOUSE
CLOUT	PIQUE	GLOVE	SCOWL	AROMA	POLKA	FRANC	COULD	PROUD	ADDLE	BRINE	DOWSE
CROUP	PROUD	GRAVE	SHAWL	BAIZA	PUKKA	FSLIC	CREED	PSEUD	ADOBE	BROKE	DRAKE
CUTUP	PSEUD	GRAVY	SHOWY	BALSA	QUOTA	HAVOC	CROWD	RABID	ADORE	BRUTE	DRAPE
DATUM	QUEUE	GROVE	SNOWY	CALLA	RUMBA	INDIC	CUPID	RAPID	AERIE	BUDGE	DRIVE
DEBUG	REBUS	GUAVA	SPAWN	CANNA	SAUNA	LILAC	DATED	RIGID	AFIRE	BUGLE	DRONE
DEBUT	REBUT	HALVE	TRAWL	CHELA	SCUBA	LOGIC	DREAD	ROUND	AGAPE	BULGE	DROVE
DEMUR	RECUR	HEAVE	UNRWA	CHINA	SENNA	LYRIC	DRUID	SALAD	AGATE	BUTTE	DRUPE
DONUT	RERUN	HEAVY	EPOXY	CIRCA	SEPIA	MAGIC	DRYAD	SCALD	AGAVE	CABLE	DUNCE
ENDUE	REVUE	HELVE	PROXY	COBRA	SIGMA	MANIC	EARED	SCAND	AGILE	CACHE	DUPLE
ENNUI	RHEUM	KNAVE	TWIXT	COCOA	STRIA	MEDIC	ELAND	SCOLD	AGREE	CADGE	EAGLE
ENSUE	ROGUE	LARVA	ALKYD	COMMA	SULFA	MIMIC	EMBED	SCROD	AISLE	CADRE	EDUCE
FEMUR	SCOUR	LEAVE	BERYL	CONGA	SUPRA	MUSIC	EMEND	SHARD	ALIKE	CALVE	EERIE
FETUS	SCOUT	MAUVE	CALYX	COPRA	TAIGA	OPTIC	FATED	SHRED	ALIVE	CANOE	ELATE
FLOUR	SCRUB	NAIVE	ETHYL	CURIA	TIARA	PANIC	FETID	SOLID	ALONE	CARVE	ELIDE
FLOUT	SERUM	NERVE	PLAYA	DACHA	TIBIA	PUBIC	FIELD	SOUND	AMAZE	CASTE	ELITE
FOCUS	SETUP	NERVY	POLYP	DELTA	ULTRA	RELIC	FIEND	SPEED	AMBLE	CAUSE	ELOPE
FORUM	SHOUT	OLIVE	SATYR	DOGMA	UMBRA	SONIC	FIORD	SPEND	AMPLE	CEASE	ELUDE
FRAUD	SHRUB	PEEVE	SIBYL	DRAMA	UNRWA	SPARC	FIXED	SQUAD	AMUSE	CHAFE	EMCEE
FUGUE	SHRUG	PRIVY	VINYL	EDEMA	UVULA	STOIC	FJORD	SQUID	ANGLE	CHASE	EMOTE
GAMUT	SINUS	PROVE	AMAZE	ENEMA	VARIA	SUMAC	FLIED	STAID	ANISE	CHIDE	ENDUE
GENUS	SIOUX	REEVE	BAIZA	ERISA	VILLA	TONIC	FLOOD	STAND	ANKLE	CHIME	ENSUE
GETUP	SIRUP	SALVE	BAIZE	EXTRA	VIOLA	TOPIC	FLUID	STEAD	ANODE	CHINE	ERASE
GHOUL	SNOUT	SALVO	BLAZE	FAUNA	VISTA	TOXIC	FOUND	STEED	APACE	CHIVE	ERODE
GROUP	SPOUT	SAVVY	BONZE	FLORA	VODKA	TUNIC	FOXED	STOOD	APPLE	CHOKE	ETUDE
GROUT	STOUT	SERVE	BOOZE	GAMMA	VULVA	VATIC	FRAUD	SWARD	ARGUE	CHORE	EVADE
HOKUM	STRUM	SERVO	BRAZE	GOUDA	YUCCA	XEBEC	FROND	SWORD	ARISE	CHOSE	EVOKE
HUMUS	STRUT	SHAVE	CRAZE	GUAVA	ZEBRA	XERIC	GELID	SYNOD	ASIDE	CHUTE	EXILE
ICTUS	SUNUP	SHOVE	CRAZY	HENNA	BLURB	ACRID	GLAND	TEPID	ATONE	CLIME	EXUDE
ILEUM	SYRUP	SIEVE	DIZZY	HYDRA	CLIMB	AHEAD	GONAD	THIRD	AWAKE	CLONE	EYRIE

FABLE	HASTE	MOUSE	PROSE	SIEGE	SWINE	WAIVE	AMONG	BLUSH	LEACH	SYLPH	BLACK
FALSE	HEAVE	MOVIE	PROVE	SIEVE	SWIPE	WASTE	BEFOG	BOOTH	LEASH	TEACH	BLANK
FARCE	HEDGE	NACRE	PRUDE	SINCE	SWORE	WEAVE	BEING	BOTCH	LEECH	TEETH	BLEAK
FEAZE	HELVE	NAIVE	PRUNE	SINGE	TABLE	WEDGE	BHANG	BOUGH	LOATH	THIGH	BLINK
FENCE	HENCE	NERVE	PULSE	SKATE	TASTE	WHALE	BRING	BRASH	LUNCH	TILTH	BLOCK
FICHE	HINGE	NGWEE	PUREE	SLAKE	TAUPE	WHERE	CLANG	BROTH	LURCH	TOOTH	BREAK
FLAKE	HORDE	NICHE	PURGE	SLATE	TEASE	WHILE	CLING	BRUSH	LYMPH	TORAH	BRICK
FLAME	HORSE	NIECE	PURSE	SLAVE	TENSE	WHINE	CLUNG	BUNCH	LYNCH	TORCH	BRINK
FLARE	HOUSE	NOBLE	QUAKE	SLICE	TEPEE	WHITE	COMDG	BURGH	MARCH	TOUCH	BRISK
FLUKE	IMAGE	NOISE	QUEUE	SLIDE	TERSE	WHOLE	CONTG	CATCH	MARSH	TOUGH	BROOK
FLUME	IMBUE	NONCE	QUIRE	SLIME	THANE	WHORE	DEBUG	CINCH	MILCH	TRASH	CAULK
FLUTE	INANE	NOOSE	QUITE	SLOPE	THEME	WHOSE	DEFOG	CLASH	MIRTH	TROTH	CHALK
FORCE	INDUE	NORSE	QUOTE	SMILE	THERE	WHSLE	DYING	CLOTH	MONTH	TRUTH	CHECK
FORGE	INGLE	NUDGE	RAISE	SMITE	THESE	WINCE	FLING	COACH	MOUTH	VETCH	CHEEK
FORTE	INURE	NURSE	RAMIE	SMOKE	THINE	WITHE	FLUNG	CONCH	MULCH	VOUCH	CHICK
FRAME	IRATE	OBESE	RANGE	SMOTE	THOLE	WORSE	GOING	COUCH	MUNCH	WATCH	CHINK
FROZE	ISSUE	OLDIE	REEVE	SNAKE	THOSE	WRITE	HYING	COUGH	MYRRH	WEIGH	CHOCK
FUDGE	JOULE	OLIVE	REVUE	SNARE	THREE	WROTE	ICING	CRASH	NEIGH	WELCH	CHUCK
FUGUE	JUDGE	OPINE	RHYME	SNIDE	THROE	ZAIRE	INCOG	CRUSH	NINTH	WELSH	CHUNK
FURZE	JUICE	ORATE	RIDGE	SNIPE	THYME	ALOOF	IRREG	CZECH	NORTH	WENCH	CLACK
FUSEE	KEDGE	OSAGE	RIFLE	SNORE	TILDE	BLUFF	LYING	DEATH	NOTCH	WHICH	CLANK
GABLE	KLUGE	OUNCE	RINSE	SOLVE	TINGE	BRIEF	OWING	DEPTH	NYMPH	WHISH	CLERK
GAFFE	KNAVE	OUTRE	ROGUE	SOUSE	TITHE	CALIF	PRONG	DITCH	PARCH	WIDTH	CLICK
GAUGE	KNIFE	OVATE	ROUGE	SPACE	TITLE	CHAFF	RELIG	DOUGH	PATCH	WINCH	CLINK
GAUZE	KRONE	OVULE	ROUSE	SPADE	TOQUE	CHIEF	SHRUG	DUTCH	PEACH	WITCH	CLOAK
GEESE	LADLE	OXIDE	ROUTE	SPARE	TRACE	CLIFF	SLANG	EARTH	PERCH	WORTH	CLOCK
GENIE	LANCE	OZONE	RUBLE	SPATE	TRADE	DWARF	SLING	EPOCH	PINCH	WRATH	CLUCK
GENRE	LAPSE	PADRE	RUPEE	SPICE	TRIBE	FLUFF	SLUNG	FAITH	PITCH	WROTH	CRACK
GEODE	LARGE	PARSE	SABLE	SPIKE	TRICE	GRIEF	SPRIG	FETCH	PLASH	YOUTH	CRANK
GLARE	LATHE	PASSE	SALVE	SPINE	TRINE	GRUFF	STING	FIFTH	PLUSH	ALIBI	CREAK
GLAZE	LEASE	PASTE	SAUCE	SPIRE	TRIPE	INDEF	STUNG	FILCH	POACH	ASCII	CREEK
GLEBE	LEAVE	PAUSE	SAUTE	SPITE	TRITE	MANUF	SWING	FILTH	POOCH	CHILI	CRICK
GLIDE	LEDGE	PEACE	SCALE	SPOKE	TROPE	MODIF	SWUNG	FINCH	PORCH	ENNUI	CROAK
GLOBE	LEONE	PEEVE	SCARE	SPORE	TRUCE	MOTIF	TELEG	FIRTH	POUCH	ENVOI	CROCK
GLOVE	LEVEE	PEKOE	SCENE	SPREE	TULLE	PILAF	THING	FLASH	PSYCH	HAJJI	CROOK
GLOZE	LIEGE	PENCE	SCONE	SPUME	TUQUE	PROOF	THONG	FLESH	PUNCH	HINDI	DRANK
GNOME	LISLE	PEWEE	SCOPE	STAGE	TWICE	QUAFF	TOPOG	FLUSH	QUASH	HOURI	DRINK
GOOSE	LITHE	PHAGE	SCORE	STAKE	TWINE	RNZAF	TWANG	FORTH	QUOTH	IRAQI	DRUNK
GORGE	LODGE	PHASE	SEDGE	STALE	UKASE	SCANF	TYING	FRESH	RANCH	KANJI	FLANK
GORSE	LOOSE	PHONE	SEINE	STARE	UNCLE	SCARF	UNPEG	FROTH	REACH	KHAKI	FLASK
GOUGE	LOUSE	PIECE	SEIZE	STATE	UNDUE	SCOFF	VYING	GIRTH	RETCH	LANAI	FLECK
GRACE	LUCRE	PIQUE	SENSE	STAVE	UNITE	SCUFF	WRING	GLYPH	ROACH	MAORI	FLICK
GRADE	LUNGE	PIXIE	SERGE	STERE	UNTIE	SCURF	WRONG	GNASH	ROUGH	MIAMI	FLOCK
GRAPE	MAIZE	PLACE	SERVE	STILE	URINE	SERIF	YOUNG	GRAPH	SIXTH	MUFTI	FLUNK
GRATE	MANGE	PLANE	SHADE	STOKE	USAGE	SHEAF	ABASH	GULCH	SLASH	NISEI	FRANK
GRAVE	MANSE	PLATE	SHAKE	STOLE	UTILE	SHELF	ALLAH	HARSH	SLOSH	PENNI	FREAK
GRAZE	MAPLE	PLEBE	SHALE	STONE	VAGUE	SKIFF	ARITH	HATCH	SLOTH	QUASI	FRISK
GREBE	MARGE	PLUME	SHAME	STORE	VALSE	SNIFF	AWASH	HEATH	SLUSH	RABBI	FROCK
GRIME	MAUVE	POISE	SHAPE	STOVE	VALUE	SNUFF	BATCH	HITCH	SMASH	RADII	GREEK
GRIPE	MAYBE	POSSE	SHARE	STYLE	VALVE	SPOOF	BEACH	HUNCH	SMITH	SENGI	KAPOK
GROPE	MELEE	PRATE	SHAVE	SUAVE	VENUE	STAFF	BEECH	HUTCH	SOOTH	SENTI	KAYAK
GROVE	MERGE	PRICE	SHINE	SUCRE	VERGE	STIFF	BELCH	IRISH	SOUGH	SWAMI	KIOSK
GUIDE	METRE	PRIDE	SHIRE	SUEDE	VERSE	STUFF	BENCH	KETCH	SOUTH	ABACK	KNACK
GUILE	MIDGE	PRIME	SHONE	SUITE	VERVE	THIEF	BERTH	KNISH	STASH	AFAIK	KNOCK
GUISE	MINCE	PRIZE	SHORE	SURGE	VOGUE	WHARF	BIRCH	LARCH	SWASH	AMUCK	KULAK
HALVE	MOIRE	PROBE	SHOVE	SWAGE	VOICE	WHIFF	BIRTH	LATCH	SWATH	APEAK	PLANK
HAOLE	MOOSE	PRONE	SIDLE	SWEDE	VOILE	ALONG	BITCH	LAUGH	SWISH	BATIK	PLUCK

PLUNK	WRACK	FATAL	PERIL	TROLL	OAKUM	BOURN	LIKEN	SWOON	HELLO	CHIRP	THORP
PRANK	WREAK	FERAL	PETAL	TWILL	ODIUM	BRAIN	LINEN	SWORN	HOLLO	CHOMP	THUMP
PRICK	WRECK	FETAL	PHIAL	TWIRL	OPIUM	BRAWN	LIVEN	TALON	HYDRO	CHUMP	TRAMP
PRINK	ADDNL	FINAL	PIXEL	UMBEL	PHARM	BROWN	MASON	TENON	IGLOO	CLAMP	TROMP
QUACK	ALGOL	FLAIL	PROWL	UNTIL	PRISM	BRUIN	MAVEN	THEGN	IMAGO	CLASP	TROOP
QUICK	AMPUL	FRAIL	PUPIL	USUAL	PROEM	CABIN	MELON	THORN	JUMBO	CLUMP	TRUMP
QUIRK	ANGEL	FRILL	QUAIL	VENAL	PSALM	CAIRN	MORON	TITAN	JUNCO	CRAMP	TULIP
SHACK	ANNUL	GAVEL	QUELL	VIGIL	PURIM	CAJUN	MOURN	TOKEN	JUNTO	CREEP	UNCAP
SHANK	ANVIL	GHOUL	QUILL	VINYL	QUALM	CANON	NYLON	TOXIN	KAZOO	CRIMP	UNZIP
SHARK	APRIL	GNARL	RAVEL	VIRAL	REALM	CAPON	OCEAN	TRAIN	LARGO	CRISP	USURP
SHIRK	ATOLL	GRAIL	REBEL	VITAL	RHEUM	CHAIN	OFTEN	TWAIN	LASSO	CROUP	WHELP
SHOCK	AURAL	GRILL	REGAL	VOCAL	SCRAM	CHRON	OLDEN	TWEEN	LIMBO	CUTUP	WHOOP
SHOOK	AVAIL	GROWL	RENAL	VOWEL	SCRIM	CHURN	ONION	UNION	LINGO	DROOP	ABHOR
SHUCK	AWFUL	GRUEL	REPEL	WHEAL	SEISM	CLEAN	ORGAN	UNMAN	LLANO	EQUIP	ABSTR
SKULK	AXIAL	HAZEL	REVEL	WHEEL	SERUM	CLOWN	PAEAN	UNPIN	MACRO	GETUP	ACTOR
SKUNK	BABEL	HOTEL	RIVAL	WHIRL	SPASM	COLON	PAGAN	URBAN	MAMBO	GRASP	ADDER
SLACK	BAGEL	HOVEL	RIYAL	WHORL	SPERM	COVEN	PATEN	VIXEN	MANGO	GROUP	AFAIR
SLEEK	BANAL	IDEAL	ROWEL	YODEL	STEAM	COZEN	PECAN	WAGON	MATZO	JALAP	AFTER
SLICK	BASAL	IDYLL	ROYAL	YOKEL	STORM	CROON	PINON	WAKEN	METRO	JULEP	ALDER
SLINK	BASIL	IMPEL	RURAL	ZONAL	STRUM	CROWN	PITON	WAXEN	MICRO	LETUP	ALTAR
SLUNK	BERYL	INSOL	SCOWL	ABEAM	SWARM	CUBAN	PLAIN	WIDEN	MONGO	NAACP	ALTER
SMACK	BETEL	INTEL	SCULL	ABYSM	THERM	DEIGN	PRAWN	WOKEN	MOTTO	PINUP	AMBER
SMIRK	BEVEL	JEWEL	SEPAL	ALARM	THRUM	DEMON	PREEN	WOMAN	NEGRO	PLUMP	AMOUR
SMOCK	BEZEL	KNEEL	SHALL	ALBUM	TOTEM	DISTN	PYLON	WOVEN	NITRO	POLYP	ANGER
SNACK	BOWEL	KNELL	SHAWL	AXIOM	UNARM	DIVAN	QUEAN	XENON	OUTDO	PRIMP	ARBOR
SNEAK	BRAWL	KNOLL	SHELL	BEGUM	VELUM	DOYEN	QUEEN	YEARN	OUTGO	RECAP	ARDOR
SNUCK	BROIL	KNURL	SHILL	BESOM	VENOM	DOZEN	RADON	ANGLO	PATIO	RECIP	ARMOR
SPANK	CABAL	KRAAL	SHOAL	BLOOM	WHELM	DRAIN	RAVEN	AUDIO	PHONO	SCALP	ASTER
SPARK	CAMEL	LABEL	SIBYL	BOSOM	XYLEM	DROWN	RAYON	BANJO	PHOTO	SCAMP	ASTIR
SPEAK	CANAL	LAPEL	SISAL	BREAM	ACORN	EDLIN	REIGN	BASSO	PIANO	SCARP	ATTAR
SPECK	CAROL	LEGAL	SKILL	BROOM	ADMAN	EPSON	RERUN	BEANO	PINTO	SCOOP	AUGER
SPOOK	CAVIL	LEVEL	SKULL	BUXOM	ADMIN	FEIGN	RESIN	BINGO	PLUTO	SCRAP	AUGUR
SPUNK	CHILL	LIBEL	SMALL	CAROM	ADORN	FELON	RIPEN	BONGO	POLIO	SCRIP	AURAR
STACK	CHURL	LOCAL	SMELL	CECUM	AGAIN	FLOWN	ROBIN	BRAVO	RADIO	SETUP	BLEAR
STALK	CIVIL	LOYAL	SNAIL	CHARM	ALIEN	FOEHN	ROMAN	BUNCO	RATIO	SHARP	BONER
STANK	COBOL	MEDAL	SNARL	CHASM	ALIGN	FROWN	ROSIN	BURRO	RECTO	SHEEP	BOWER
STARK	CORAL	METAL	SPELL	CLAIM	AMAIN	GAMIN	SALON	CACAO	RHINO	SIRUP	BOXER
STEAK	CRAWL	MODEL	SPIEL	CREAM	ANION	GIVEN	SATAN	CAMEO	RODEO	SKIMP	BRIAR
STICK	CREEL	MOGUL	SPILL	DATUM	APRON	GLEAN	SATIN	CANTO	SALVO	SLEEP	BRIER
STINK	CRUEL	MORAL	SPOIL	DEISM	ARGON	GRAIN	SCION	CARGO	SEATO	SLOOP	CAPER
STOCK	DECAL	MOREL	SPOOL	DENIM	ARSON	GREEN	SCORN	CELLO	SERVO	SLUMP	CATER
STORK	DEVIL	MOTEL	STALL	DREAM	ARYAN	GROAN	SEDAN	CHIAO	TABOO	SLURP	CEDAR
STUCK	DOWEL	MURAL	STEAL	ENTOM	ASHEN	GROIN	SEMEN	CHINO	TANGO	SNOOP	CHAIR
STUNK	DRAWL	NASAL	STEEL	EPROM	ASIAN	HAVEN	SEVEN	COMBO	TEMPO	STAMP	CHEER
SWANK	DRILL	NATAL	STILL	FORUM	ASPEN	HERON	SHEEN	COMMO	TORSO	STEEP	CHOIR
THANK	DROLL	NAVAL	STOOL	GLEAM	AUXIN	HOGAN	SHORN	CREDO	TURBO	STOMP	CIDER
THICK	DROOL	NAVEL	SWELL	GLOOM	AVIAN	HUMAN	SIREN	CURIO	VERSO	STOOP	CIGAR
THINK	DUCAL	NEWEL	SWILL	GROOM	BACON	HURON	SKEIN	DINGO	VIDEO	STRAP	CLEAR
TRACK	DWELL	NOVEL	SWIRL	HAREM	BAIRN	HYMEN	SLAIN	DISCO	VIREO	STRIP	COLOR
TRICK	EASEL	OCTAL	THEOL	HOKUM	BARON	INURN	SOLON	DITTO	WAHOO	STROP	COMDR
TRUCK	EMAIL	OFFAL	TICAL	IDIOM	BASIN	JAPAN	SPAWN	FOLIO	WHOSO	STUMP	COMER
TRUNK	EQUAL	ORIEL	TOTAL	ILEUM	BATON	KORAN	SPOON	FORGO	YAHOO	SUNUP	CONTR
TWEAK	ETHYL	PANEL	TOWEL	ISLAM	BEGIN	LADEN	SPURN	GIZMO	BLIMP	SWAMP	COVER
UMIAK	EXCEL	PAPAL	TRAIL	MADAM	BISON	LAPIN	STAIN	GUANO	CHAMP	SWEEP	COWER
WHACK	EXPEL	PEARL	TRAWL	MAXIM	BLAIN	LATIN	STEIN	GUMBO	CHEAP	SWOOP	CRIER
WHELK	EXPTL	PEDAL	TRIAL	MINIM	BORON	LEARN	STERN	GUSTO	CHEEP	SYRUP	DEBAR
WHISK	EXTOL	PENAL	TRILL	MODEM	BOSUN	LEMON	SWAIN	HALLO	CHIMP	SYSOP	DECOR

DEFER	LAYER	SABER	WATER	HUMUS	VIBES	CHANT	FAINT	KRAUT	SHIFT	TWIXT	CALYX
DEMUR	LAZAR	SATYR	WAVER	ICTUS	VIRUS	CHART	FAULT	LEAST	SHIPT	UNCUT	CODEX
DETER	LEMUR	SAVOR	ABYSS	INCUS	WIVES	CHEAT	FEAST	LEGIT	SHIRT	UNFIT	HELIX
DINAR	LEPER	SCOUR	ADIOS	JEANS	YOURS	CHERT	FEINT	LICIT	SHOAT	UPSET	INDEX
DINER	LEVER	SEVER	AEGIS	KUDOS	ABAFT	CHEST	FIGHT	LIEUT	SHOOT	VALET	LATEX
DISTR	LIFER	SEWER	ALIAS	KURUS	ABBOT	CIVET	FIRST	LIGHT	SHORT	VAULT	PHLOX
DOLOR	LINER	SHEAR	AMASS	LEGIS	ABORT	CLEAT	FLEET	LIMIT	SHOUT	VAUNT	RADIX
DONOR	LITER	SHEER	AMISS	LINKS	ABOUT	CLEFT	FLINT	MERIT	SHUNT	VERST	RELAX
DOWER	LIVER	SHIER	ANGUS	LISTS	ADAPT	CLOUT	FLIRT	MIDST	SIGHT	VISIT	SIOUX
DREAR	LONER	SHIRR	APHIS	LIVES	ADEPT	CMSGT	FLOAT	MIGHT	SKEET	VOMIT	TELEX
DRIER	LOWER	SITAR	ARRAS	LOCUS	ADMIT	COAST	FLOUT	MOIST	SKIRT	WAIST	UNFIX
DRYER	LUNAR	SLIER	ATLAS	LOESS	ADOPT	COMDT	FOIST	MOTET	SLANT	WHEAT	ABBEY
EAGER	MAJOR	SMEAR	AVGAS	LOTUS	ADULT	COMET	FOUNT	MOULT	SLEET	WHIST	AGONY
EIDER	MANOR	SNEER	BANNS	MANES	AFOOT	CONST	FRONT	MOUNT	SMART	WIGHT	ALLAY
ELDER	MASER	SOBER	BASIS	MAVIS	AGENT	COUNT	FROST	MULCT	SMELT	WORST	ALLEY
ELVER	MAYOR	SOLAR	BELLS	MINUS	ALERT	COURT	FRUIT	NIGHT	SMSGT	WREST	ALLOY
EMBER	METER	SONAR	BLESS	MLLES	ALLOT	COVET	GAMUT	OCTET	SNORT	WRIST	AMITY
ENTER	MINOR	SPEAR	BLISS	MORES	ALOFT	CRAFT	GANTT	ONSET	SNOUT	WURST	ANGRY
ERROR	MISER	SPOOR	BLUES	MUCUS	ANENT	CREST	GAUNT	ORBIT	SPENT	YACHT	ANNOY
ESTER	MITER	STAIR	BOGUS	MUMPS	ANGST	CRUET	GHOST	OUGHT	SPIRT	YEAST	APPLY
ETHER	MIXER	STEER	BOLUS	NARIS	APART	CRUST	GIANT	OVERT	SPLIT	ADIEU	ARRAY
EYRIR	MOLAR	SUGAR	BONUS	NEEDS	APORT	CRYPT	GLINT	OWLET	SPORT	BANTU	ASSAY
FAKIR	MOTOR	SUPER	BRASS	NEGUS	ARGOT	CRYST	GLOAT	PAINT	SPOUT	BAYOU	BAGGY
FAVOR	MOVER	SUPVR	CHAOS	NEVUS	ASCOT	CUBIT	GRAFT	PICOT	SPRAT	COYPU	BALKY
FEMUR	NADIR	SWEAR	CHAPS	NEXUS	ASSET	DAUNT	GRANT	PILOT	SPURT	FICHU	BALMY
FEVER	NEVER	TABOR	CHESS	NONES	ATILT	DAVIT	GREAT	PIVOT	SQUAT	HAIKU	BANDY
FEWER	NITER	TALER	CHOPS	NUMIS	AUDIT	DEBIT	GREET	PLAIT	START	POILU	BATTY
FIBER	OCCUR	TAPER	CLASS	OASIS	AUGHT	DEBUT	GRIST	PLANT	STILT	VIRTU	BAWDY
FILAR	OCHER	TAPIR	CORPS	OCCAS	AVAST	DELFT	GROAT	PLEAT	STINT	DERIV	BEEFY
FLAIR	OFFER	TENOR	CRAPS	ORRIS	AVERT	DEPOT	GROUT	POINT	STOAT	EQUIV	BELAY
FLEER	ORDER	THEIR	CRASS	PANTS	AWAIT	DIGIT	GRUNT	POLIT	STOUT	AGLOW	BELLY
FLIER	OSIER	TIGER	CRESS	PENIS	BEAST	DIVOT	GUEST	POSIT	STRUT	ALLOW	BENNY
FLOOR	OTHER	TONER	CROSS	PILES	BEFIT	DLITT	GUILT	POULT	STUNT	ARROW	BERRY
FLOUR	OTTER	TOPER	DEGAS	PIOUS	BEGET	DONUT	GUYOT	PRINT	SWART	ASKEW	BIDDY
FLYER	OUTER	TOWER	DRESS	PLEBS	BERET	DOUBT	HABIT	QUART	SWEAT	BEDEW	BILLY
FOYER	PACER	TUBER	DROSS	PRESS	BESET	DRAFT	HAUNT	QUEST	SWEET	BELOW	BLOWY
FRIAR	PAPER	TUMOR	DUMPS	PUBES	BESOT	DRIFT	HEART	QUIET	SWEPT	BYLAW	BOBBY
FRYER	PETER	TUTOR	EAVES	PUBIS	BIDET	DUCAT	HEIST	QUILT	SWIFT	ELBOW	BOGEY
FUROR	PIKER	UDDER	ELVES	QUITS	BIGHT	ECLAT	HELOT	QUINT	TACIT	ENDOW	BONNY
GONER	POKER	ULCER	ETHOS	REBUS	BIGOT	EDICT	HOIST	QUIRT	TAINT	MACAW	BOOBY
HALER	POLAR	UMBER	FECES	SCOTS	BLAST	EGRET	IDIOT	QUOIT	TAROT	NOHOW	BOOTY
HOMER	POSER	UNBAR	FETUS	SINUS	BLEAT	EIGHT	INEPT	REACT	TAUNT	OXBOW	BOSKY
HONOR	POWER	UNDER	FINIS	SNIPS	BLOAT	EJECT	INERT	REBUT	TEMPT	PAPAW	BUDDY
HOVER	PRIOR	UPPER	FLOSS	SWISS	BLUET	ELECT	INGOT	REMIT	TENET	RENEW	BUGGY
HUMOR	QUEER	USHER	FOCUS	TALUS	BLUNT	ENACT	INLET	RIGHT	THEAT	SCREW	BULKY
ICHOR	RADAR	UTTER	GAUSS	TEENS	BLURT	ERECT	INPUT	RIVET	THEFT	SHREW	BULLY
IMPER	RAZOR	VALOR	GENUS	THESS	BOAST	ERGOT	INSET	ROAST	TIGHT	SINEW	BUNNY
INCUR	RECUR	VAPOR	GLANS	THURS	BOOST	ERUPT	ISLET	ROBOT	TINCT	SQUAW	BURLY
INFER	REFER	VELAR	GLASS	TIMES	BRACT	EVENT	JABOT	ROOST	TOAST	STRAW	BUSBY
INNER	RIDER	VICAR	GLOSS	TONGS	BRUIT	EVICT	JAUNT	SAINT	TRACT	STREW	BYWAY
INSTR	RIGOR	VIGOR	GRASS	TRANS	BRUNT	EXACT	JOINT	SANIT	TRAIT	THREW	CABBY
INTER	RISER	VIPER	GRITS	TRAPS	BURST	EXALT	JOIST	SCANT	TREAT	THROW	CADDY
JOKER	RIVER	VISOR	GROSS	TREAS	BUTUT	EXERT	JOUST	SCENT	TROUT	WIDOW	CAGEY
JUROR	ROGER	VIZOR	GUESS	TRESS	CADET	EXIST	KAPUT	SCOOT	TRUST	ADMIX	CANDY
LABOR	ROTOR	WADER	HADES	TRUSS	CARAT	EXULT	KARAT	SCOUT	TRYST	AFFIX	CANNY
LAGER	RULER	WAFER	HAYES	TURPS	CARET	FACET	KARST	SHAFT	TWEET	ANNEX	CARNY
LASER	RUMOR	WAGER	HIVES	VENUS	CCITT	FAGOT	KNOUT	SHEET	TWIST	BORAX	CARRY

CATTY	FATTY	INLAY	OVARY	SNOWY	FRIZZ
CHARY	FELLY	IRONY	PADDY	SOGGY	GROSZ
CHEWY	FERRY	IVORY	PALMY	SORRY	HERTZ
COCKY	FIERY	JAZZY	PALSY	SOUPY	SWITZ
COMFY	FIFTY	JELLY	PANSY	SPLAY	TOPAZ
CONEY	FILLY	JENNY	PARRY	SPRAY	WALTZ
CORNY	FINNY	JETTY	PARTY	STORY	
COVEY	FISHY	JEWRY	PASTY	STRAY	
CRAZY	FLYBY	JIFFY	PATSY	STUDY	
CRONY	FOLLY	JIMMY	PATTY	SULKY	
CURRY	FORAY	JOLLY	PENNY	SULLY	
DADDY	FORTY	JUICY	PEONY	SURLY	
DAFFY	FULLY	JUMPY	PESKY	TABBY	
DAILY	FUNKY	KITTY	PETTY	TACKY	
DAIRY	FUNNY	KOOKY	PHONY	TAFFY	
DAISY	FURRY	LAITY	PICKY	TALLY	
DALLY	FUSSY	LANKY	PIETY	TANSY	
DANDY	FUSTY	LEERY	PIGMY	TARDY	
DECAY	FUZZY	LEGGY	PITHY	TARRY	
DECOY	GABBY	LOBBY	PLATY	TASTY	
DECRY	GAILY	LOFTY	POESY	TAWNY	
DEIFY	GAUDY	LOONY	POPPY	TEENY	
DEITY	GAWKY	LORRY	PRIVY	TERRY	
DELAY	GIDDY	LOUSY	PROSY	TESTY	
DERBY	GIMPY	LOWLY	PROXY	TINNY	
DIARY	GIPSY	LUCKY	PUDGY	TIPSY	
DINGY	GLORY	LUSTY	PUPPY	TIZZY	
DINKY	GODLY	MALAY	PUSHY	TOADY	
DIRTY	GOODY	MANLY	PUSSY	TODAY	
DITTY	GOOFY	MARRY	PUTTY	TODDY	
DIZZY	GRAVY	MCCOY	PYGMY	TOKAY	
DOGGY	GULLY	MERCY	QUERY	TUMMY	
DOILY	GUNNY	MERRY	RALLY	TUNNY	
DOLLY	GUPPY	MIDDY	RANGY	UNIFY	
DOPEY	GUSHY	MISTY	RATTY	UNITY	
DOWDY	GUTTY	MONEY	READY	UNSAY	
DOWNY	GYPSY	MOODY	RELAY	USURY	
DOWRY	HAIRY	MORAY	REPAY	VASTY	
DRILY	HANDY	MOSEY	REPLY	VEERY	
DUCHY	HAPLY	MOUSY	ROWDY	WACKY	
DUMMY	HAPPY	MUGGY	RUDDY	WASHY	
DUMPY	HARDY	MUMMY	RUGBY	WEARY	
DUSKY	HARPY	MUSHY	RUMMY	WEEDY	
EARLY	HARRY	MUSTY	RUNNY	WEENY	
EBONY	HEADY	NASTY	SALLY	WEEPY	
ELEGY	HEAVY	NATTY	SAPPY	WINDY	
EMERY	HEFTY	NEEDY	SASSY	WITHY	
EMPTY	HOARY	NERVY	SAUCY	WITTY	
ENEMY	HOBBY	NEWLY	SAVVY	WOODY	
ENJOY	HOLLY	NEWSY	SEAMY	WOOZY	
ENTRY	HOMEY	NIFTY	SEEDY	WORDY	
ENVOY	HONEY	NINNY	SHAKY	WORRY	
EPOXY	HOOEY	NIPPY	SHINY	XCOPY	
ESSAY	HURRY	NODDY	SHOWY	YUMMY	
EVERY	HUSKY	NOISY	SILLY	ZIPPY	
FAIRY	HUSSY	NOWAY	SISSY	ZLOTY	
FANCY	IMPLY	NUTTY	SIXTY	BLITZ	

1ST LETTER

ABACUS	ADVERB	ANADEM	ARMFUL	ATTUNE	BARELY	BELFRY	BLAZON	BRANDY	BURSAR
ABATIS	ADVERT	ANALOG	ARMLET	AUBURN	BARFLY	BELIEF	BLEACH	BRAZEN	BUSBOY
ABBACY	ADVICE	ANCHOR	ARMORY	AUGURY	BARIUM	BELIKE	BLEARY	BREACH	BUSHED
ABBESS	ADVISE	ANEMIA	ARMPIT	AUGUST	BARKER	BELLOW	BLENCH	BREAST	BUSHEL
ABDUCT	AERATE	ANGINA	ARNICA	AURORA	BARLEY	BELONG	BLIGHT	BREATH	BUSILY
ABJECT	AERIAL	ANGORA	AROUND	AUTHOR	BARRED	BELUGA	BLITHE	BREECH	BUSKIN
ABJURE	AFFAIR	ANIMAL	AROUSE	AUTISM	BARREL	BEMIRE	BLOTCH	BREEZE	BUSTLE
ABLAZE	AFFECT	ANIMUS	ARRANT	AUTUMN	BARREN	BEMOAN	BLOUSE	BREVET	BUTANE
ABLOOM	AFFIRM	ANKLET	ARREST	AVATAR	BARRIO	BEMUSE	BLOWSY	BRIDAL	BUTLER
ABNAKI	AFFORD	ANNALS	ARRIVE	AVAUNT	BARROW	BENDER	BLOWUP	BRIDGE	BUTTER
ABOARD	AFFRAY	ANNEAL	ARROYO	AVENGE	BARTER	BENIGN	BLUING	BRIDLE	BUTTON
ABOUND	AFGHAN	ANNUAL	ARTERY	AVENUE	BASALT	BENUMB	BLUISH	BRIGHT	BUZZER
ABRADE	AFIELD	ANOINT	ARTFUL	AVERSE	BASKET	BENZOL	BOATER	BRITON	BYGONE
ABROAD	AFLAME	ANSWER	ARTIST	AVIARY	BASQUE	BERATE	BOBBIN	BROACH	BYPASS
ABRUPT	AFLOAT	ANTHEM	ASCEND	AVOCET	BATEAU	BERBER	BOBBLE	BROGAN	BYPATH
ABSENT	AFRAID	ANTHER	ASCENT	AVOUCH	BATHOS	BEREFT	BOBCAT	BROGUE	BYPLAY
ABSORB	AFRESH	ANTLER	ASHLAR	AWAKEN	BATMAN	BESEEM	BOCCIE	BROKEN	BYWORD
ABSURD	AGENCY	ANTRUM	ASHORE	AWEARY	BATTEN	BESIDE	BODICE	BROKER	CABALA
ACACIA	AGENDA	ANYHOW	ASHRAM	AWEIGH	BATTER	BESTIR	BODILY	BRONCO	CABANA
ACCEDE	AGHAST	ANYONE	ASLANT	AWHILE	BATTLE	BESTOW	BODKIN	BRONZE	CACHET
ACCENT	AGLEAM	ANYWAY	ASLEEP	AWHIRL	BAUBLE	BETAKE	BOGGLE	BROOCH	CACKLE
ACCEPT	AIDMAN	APACHE	ASPECT	AWNING	BAZAAR	BETHEL	BOILER	BROWSE	CACTUS
ACCESS	AIRMAN	APATHY	ASPIRE	AZALEA	BEACON	BETIDE	BOLERO	BRUISE	CADDIE
ACCORD	AIRWAY	APERCU	ASSAIL	BABBLE	BEADLE	BETRAY	BOMBER	BRUNCH	CAECUM
ACCOST	AKIMBO	APIARY	ASSENT	BABOON	BEAGLE	BETTER	BONBON	BRUNET	CAESAR
ACCRUE	ALBEIT	APICAL	ASSERT	BACKER	BEAKER	BETTOR	BONITO	BRUTAL	CAFTAN
ACCUSE	ALBINO	APIECE	ASSESS	BACKUP	BEANIE	BEWAIL	BONNET	BUBBLE	CAHOOT
ACETIC	ALCOVE	APLOMB	ASSIGN	BADGER	BEAUTY	BEWARE	BONSAI	BUCKET	CAIMAN
ACQUIT	ALIGHT	APOGEE	ASSIST	BAFFLE	BEAVER	BEYOND	BOODLE	BUCKLE	CAJOLE
ACROSS	ALKALI	APPALL	ASSIZE	BAGMAN	BECALM	BICEPS	BOOKIE	BUDGET	CALCIC
ACTING	ALLEGE	APPEAL	ASSORT	BAGNIO	BECKON	BICKER	BOOTEE	BUDGIE	CALICO
ACTION	ALLIED	APPEAR	ASSUME	BAKERY	BECOME	BIGAMY	BORATE	BUFFER	CALIPH
ACTIVE	ALLUDE	APPEND	ASSURE	BALBOA	BEDAUB	BIGWIG	BORDER	BUFFET	CALLOW
ACTUAL	ALLURE	APPLET	ASTERN	BALEEN	BEDBUG	BIKINI	BOREAL	BULBUL	CALLUS
ACUITY	ALMOND	APPROX	ASTHMA	BALLAD	BEDECK	BILLET	BORROW	BULLET	CALVES
ACUMEN	ALMOST	ARABIC	ASTRAL	BALLET	BEDLAM	BILLOW	BOTANY	BUMMER	CAMBER
ADAGIO	ALPACA	ARABLE	ASTRAY	BALLOT	BEDPAN	BINARY	BOTHER	BUMPER	CAMERA
ADDEND	ALPINE	ARCADE	ASTROL	BALSAM	BEETLE	BINHEX	BOTTLE	BUNDLE	CAMPER
ADDICT	ALTAIR	ARCANE	ASTRON	BAMBOO	BEFALL	BIOPSY	BOTTOM	BUNGLE	CAMPUS
ADDUCE	ALUMNA	ARCCOS	ASTUTE	BANANA	BEFORE	BIOTIC	BOUGHT	BUNION	CANAPE
ADHERE	ALWAYS	ARCHON	ASYLUM	BANDED	BEFOUL	BIOTIN	BOUNCE	BUNKER	CANARD
ADJOIN	AMAZON	ARCNET	ATOMIC	BANDIT	BEGGAR	BIRDIE	BOUNTY	BUNKUM	CANARY
ADJURE	AMBUSH	ARCSIN	ATONAL	BANGLE	BEGONE	BISECT	BOURSE	BUQSHA	CANCAN
ADJUST	AMENDS	ARCTAN	ATRIUM	BANISH	BEHALF	BISHOP	BOVINE	BURDEN	CANCEL
ADMIRE	AMERCE	ARCTIC	ATTACH	BANNER	BEHAVE	BISQUE	BOWLEG	BUREAU	CANCER
ADRIFT	AMOEBA	ARDENT	ATTACK	BANTAM	BEHEAD	BISTRO	BOWLER	BURGEE	CANDID
ADROIT	AMORAL	ARGENT	ATTAIN	BANTER	BEHEST	BITING	BOWMAN	BURGLE	CANDLE
ADSORB	AMOUNT	ARGOSY	ATTEND	BANYAN	BEHIND	BITNET	BOXCAR	BURIAL	CANDOR
ADVENT	AMPERE	ARGYLE	ATTEST	BANZAI	BEHOLD	BITTER	BOXING	BURLAP	CANINE
	AMULET	ARIGHT	ATTIRE	BAOBAB	BEHOOF	BLANCH	BRAISE	BURNER	CANKER
	AMVETS	ARMADA	ATTRIB	BARBER	BELDAM	BLAZER	BRANCH	BURROW	CANNED

CANNON	CAYUGA	CHUMMY	COGENT	CORRAL	CUNNER	DEBRIS	DERMIS	DITHER	DUPLEX
CANNOT	CAYUSE	CHUNKY	COGNAC	CORSET	CUPOLA	DEBTOR	DERRIS	DIVERS	DURESS
CANOPY	CELERY	CHURCH	COHEIR	CORTEX	CURATE	DEBUNK	DESALT	DIVERT	DURING
CANTER	CELLAR	CICADA	COHERE	CORYZA	CURDLE	DECADE	DESCRY	DIVEST	DUSTER
CANTLE	CEMENT	CILIUM	COHORT	COSINE	CURFEW	DECAMP	DESERT	DIVIDE	DYBBUK
CANTON	CENSER	CINDER	COITUS	COSMIC	CURIUM	DECANT	DESIGN	DIVINE	DYNAMO
CANTOR	CENSOR	CINEMA	COLLAR	COSMOS	CURLEW	DECEIT	DESIRE	DOBBIN	EAGLET
CANVAS	CENSUS	CIPHER	COLLAT	COSTLY	CURSOR	DECENT	DESIST	DOCENT	EARTHY
CANYON	CENTER	CIRCLE	COLLIE	COTTER	CURTSY	DECIDE	DESKEW	DOCILE	EARWAX
CAPFUL	CENTRE	CIRCUS	COLLOQ	COTTON	CURVET	DECODE	DESPOT	DOCKET	EARWIG
CAPTOR	CEREAL	CIRQUE	COLONY	COUGAR	CUSPID	DECREE	DETACH	DOCTOR	EASTER
CARAFE	CEREUS	CIRRUS	COLUMN	COULEE	CUSTOM	DEDUCE	DETAIL	DODDER	EATERY
CARBON	CERISE	CITIFY	COMBAT	COUNTY	CUTLER	DEDUCT	DETAIN	DOGGED	EBCDIC
CARBOY	CERIUM	CITRON	COMBER	COUPLE	CUTLET	DEEJAY	DETECT	DOGLEG	ECCLES
CAREEN	CERMET	CITRUS	COMDEX	COUPON	CUTOFF	DEEPEN	DETEST	DOINGS	ECCLUS
CAREER	CERVIX	CIVICS	COMEDY	COURSE	CUTOUT	DEFACE	DETOUR	DOLLAR	ECLAIR
CARESS	CESIUM	CLAMMY	COMELY	COUSIN	CUTTER	DEFAME	DEVICE	DOLLOP	ECZEMA
CARHOP	CHAFER	CLAMOR	COMFIT	COVERT	CYGNET	DEFEAT	DEVISE	DOLMEN	EDGING
CARIES	CHAISE	CLAQUE	COMING	COWARD	CYMBAL	DEFECT	DEVOID	DOMAIN	EDIBLE
CARNAL	CHALET	CLARET	COMITY	COWBOY	DABBLE	DEFEND	DEVOIR	DOMINO	EEPROM
CARPAL	CHANCE	CLASSY	COMMIT	COWMAN	DACTYL	DEFILE	DEVOTE	DONATE	EFFACE
CARPEL	CHANCY	CLAUSE	COMMON	COWPOX	DAEMON	DEFINE	DEVOUR	DONKEY	EFFECT
CARPET	CHANGE	CLEAVE	COMPAQ	COYOTE	DAGGER	DEFORM	DEVOUT	DOODAD	EFFETE
CARREL	CHAPEL	CLENCH	COMPAR	CRABBY	DAHLIA	DEFRAY	DEWLAP	DOODLE	EFFIGY
CARROT	CHARGE	CLERGY	COMPEL	CRADLE	DAINTY	DEFUSE	DIADEM	DOPANT	EFFORT
CARTEL	CHASER	CLERIC	COMPLY	CRAFTY	DAKOTA	DEGREE	DIAPER	DORMER	EGGNOG
CARTON	CHASTE	CLEVER	CONCUR	CRANKY	DALASI	DEHORN	DIATOM	DORSAL	EGOISM
CARTOP	CHATTY	CLEVIS	CONDOM	CRANNY	DAMAGE	DELETE	DIBBLE	DOTAGE	EGRESS
CASABA	CHAUNT	CLICHE	CONDOR	CRATER	DAMASK	DELUDE	DICKER	DOTARD	EIGHTY
CASEIN	CHEEKY	CLIENT	CONFAB	CRATON	DAMPEN	DELUGE	DICKEY	DOTTLE	EITHER
CASHEW	CHEERY	CLIMAX	CONFED	CRAVAT	DAMPER	DELUXE	DICTUM	DOUBLE	ELAPSE
CASING	CHEESE	CLINCH	CONFER	CRAVEN	DAMSEL	DEMAND	DIESEL	DOUBLY	ELDEST
CASINO	CHEQUE	CLINIC	CONSOL	CRAYON	DAMSON	DEMEAN	DIFFER	DOUCHE	ELEVEN
CASKET	CHERRY	CLIQUE	CONSTR	CREASE	DANDER	DEMISE	DIGEST	DOWNER	ELICIT
CASQUE	CHERUB	CLOCHE	CONSUL	CREATE	DANDLE	DEMODE	DILATE	DRAFTY	ELIXIR
CASSIA	CHICHI	CLOSET	CONVEX	CRECHE	DANGER	DEMOTE	DILUTE	DRAGON	EMBALM
CASTER	CHICLE	CLOTHE	CONVEY	CREDIT	DANGLE	DEMURE	DIMITY	DRAPER	EMBANK
CASTLE	CHILLY	CLOVEN	CONVOY	CREEPY	DANISH	DENGUE	DIMMER	DRAWER	EMBARK
CASUAL	CHINTZ	CLOVER	COOKIE	CREOLE	DAPPER	DENIAL	DIMPLE	DREARY	EMBLEM
CATCHY	CHISEL	CLUMSY	COOLER	CRETIN	DAPPLE	DENIER	DINGHY	DREDGE	EMBODY
CATGUT	CHITIN	CLUTCH	COOLIE	CREWEL	DARING	DENOTE	DINGLE	DRENCH	EMBOSS
CATION	CHOICE	COARSE	COOPER	CRINGE	DARKEN	DENTAL	DINGUS	DRESSY	EMBRYO
CATKIN	CHOKER	COBALT	COOTIE	CRISIS	DARNEL	DENTIN	DINNER	DRIVEL	EMERGE
CATNAP	CHOLER	COBBLE	COPIER	CRITIC	DARTER	DENUDE	DIPPER	DRIVER	EMETIC
CATNIP	CHOOSE	COBWEB	COPING	CROCUS	DASHER	DEODAR	DIRECT	DROGUE	EMIGRE
CATSUP	CHOOSY	COCCUS	COPPER	CROTCH	DATIVE	DEPART	DIRHAM	DROPSY	EMPIRE
CATTLE	CHOPPY	COCCYX	COPTER	CROUCH	DAWDLE	DEPEND	DIRNDL	DROVER	EMPLOY
CAUCUS	CHORAL	COCKLE	COPULA	CRUISE	DAYBED	DEPICT	DISARM	DROWSE	ENABLE
CAUDAL	CHOREA	COCOON	COQUET	CRUMMY	DAZZLE	DEPLOY	DISBAR	DROWSY	ENAMEL
CAUGHT	CHORUS	CODDLE	CORBEL	CRUNCH	DEACON	DEPORT	DISCUS	DRUDGE	ENAMOR
CAUSAL	CHOSEN	CODGER	CORDON	CRUTCH	DEADEN	DEPOSE	DISHED	DUBBIN	ENCAMP
CAVEAT	CHRISM	CODIFY	CORNEA	CUBISM	DEADLY	DEPUTE	DISMAL	DUENDE	ENCASE
CAVERN	CHRIST	COERCE	CORNER	CUCKOO	DEAFEN	DEPUTY	DISMAY	DUENNA	ENCODE
CAVIAR	CHROME	COEVAL	CORNET	CUDDLE	DEARTH	DERAIL	DISOWN	DUFFER	ENCORE
CAVITY	CHROMO	COFFEE	CORONA	CUDGEL	DEBARK	DERIDE	DISPEL	DUGOUT	ENCYST
CAVORT	CHUBBY	COFFER	CORPSE	CUESTA	DEBASE	DERIVE	DISTAL	DULCET	ENDEAR
CAYMAN	CHUKKA	COFFIN	CORPUS	CUMBER	DEBATE	DERMAL	DISUSE	DUMDUM	ENDING

ENDIVE	EUREKA	FAUCET	FLAGON	FRIDAY	GARNER	GOPHER	HALITE	HIATUS	IBIDEM
ENDRIN	EVINCE	FAVOUR	FLANGE	FRIEND	GARNET	GOSPEL	HALLOW	HICCUP	ICEBOX
ENDURE	EVOLVE	FEALTY	FLASHY	FRIEZE	GARRET	GOSSIP	HALTER	HIJACK	ICEMAN
ENERGY	EXCEED	FECUND	FLATUS	FRIGHT	GARTER	GOTHIC	HALVES	HINDER	ICICLE
ENFOLD	EXCEPT	FEDORA	FLAUNT	FRIGID	GASKET	GOTTEN	HAMLET	HIPPED	IDIOCY
ENGAGE	EXCESS	FEEBLE	FLAVOR	FRINGE	GATHER	GOURDE	HAMMER	HIPPIE	IGNITE
ENGINE	EXCISE	FEELER	FLAXEN	FRISKY	GAUCHE	GOVERN	HAMPER	HITHER	IGNORE
ENGRAM	EXCITE	FELINE	FLEECE	FROLIC	GAUCHO	GRABEN	HANDLE	HOAGIE	IGUANA
ENGULF	EXCUSE	FELLAH	FLESHY	FROWSY	GAYETY	GRADER	HANGAR	HOARSE	ILLUME
ENIGMA	EXEMPT	FELLOW	FLIGHT	FROZEN	GAZEBO	GRAINY	HANKER	HOBBLE	ILLUST
ENISLE	EXHALE	FELONY	FLIMSY	FRUGAL	GEEZER	GRANGE	HANSEL	HOBNOB	IMBIBE
ENJOIN	EXHORT	FEMALE	FLINCH	FRUITY	GEISHA	GRATIS	HANSOM	HOCKEY	IMBRUE
ENLIST	EXHUME	FENDER	FLITCH	FRUMPY	GENDER	GRAVEL	HAPPEN	HOLDUP	IMMUNE
ENMESH	EXODUS	FENIAN	FLOOZY	FUDDLE	GENERA	GRAVID	HARASS	HOLLER	IMMURE
ENMITY	EXOTIC	FENNEL	FLOPPY	FUHRER	GENIAL	GRAYED	HARBOR	HOLLOW	IMPACT
ENOUGH	EXPAND	FERRET	FLORAL	FUMBLE	GENIUS	GREASE	HARDEN	HOMAGE	IMPAIR
ENRAGE	EXPECT	FERRIC	FLORID	FUNGUS	GENTLE	GRIEVE	HARDLY	HOMELY	IMPALA
ENRICH	EXPEND	FERULE	FLORIN	FUNNEL	GENTRY	GRILLE	HARKEN	HOMILY	IMPALE
ENROLL	EXPERT	FERVID	FLOSSY	FURORE	GERBIL	GRIPPE	HARLOT	HOMINY	IMPART
ENSIGN	EXPIRE	FERVOR	FLOWER	FURROW	GERMAN	GRISLY	HARROW	HONEST	IMPEDE
ENSILE	EXPORT	FESTAL	FLUENT	FUSION	GERUND	GROCER	HASSLE	HONOUR	IMPEND
ENSURE	EXPOSE	FESTER	FLUFFY	FUTILE	GEWGAW	GROGGY	HASTEN	HOODOO	IMPERF
ENTAIL	EXTANT	FETISH	FLUNKY	FUTURE	GEYSER	GROOVE	HATBOX	HOOKAH	IMPISH
ENTICE	EXTEND	FETTER	FLURRY	GABBLE	GHETTO	GROOVY	HATRED	HOOKER	IMPORT
ENTIRE	EXTENT	FETTLE	FLYWAY	GABBRO	GIBBER	GROTTO	HATTER	HOOKUP	IMPOSE
ENTITY	EXTERN	FEUDAL	FODDER	GADFLY	GIBBET	GROUCH	HAUNCH	HOOPLA	IMPOST
ENTOMB	EXTORT	FIANCE	FOEMAN	GADGET	GIBBON	GROUND	HAWKER	HOPPER	IMPUGN
ENTRAP	EYELET	FIASCO	FOETAL	GAELIC	GIBSON	GROUSE	HAWSER	HORNET	IMPURE
ENTREE	EYELID	FIBRIL	FOIBLE	GAFFER	GIFTED	GROVEL	HAYMOW	HORRID	IMPUTE
ENZYME	FABIAN	FIBRIN	FOLDER	GAGGLE	GIGGLE	GROWTH	HAZARD	HORROR	INBORN
EOLIAN	FABLED	FIBULA	FOLKSY	GAIETY	GIGOLO	GRUBBY	HEALTH	HORSEY	INBRED
EQUATE	FABRIC	FICKLE	FOLLOW	GAITER	GIMBAL	GRUDGE	HEARSE	HOSTEL	INCASE
EQUINE	FACADE	FIDDLE	FOMENT	GALAXY	GIMLET	GRUMPY	HEARTH	HOTBED	INCEST
EQUITY	FACIAL	FIDGET	FONDLE	GALENA	GINGER	GUFFAW	HEARTY	HOTBOX	INCISE
ERBIUM	FACILE	FIERCE	FONDUE	GALLEY	GINKGO	GUIDON	HEAVEN	HOWDAH	INCITE
ERMINE	FACING	FIESTA	FOOTED	GALLIC	GIRDER	GUILTY	HEBREW	HOWLER	INCOME
EROTIC	FACTOR	FIGURE	FORAGE	GALLON	GIRDLE	GUINEA	HECKLE	HOYDEN	INDEED
ERRAND	FACULA	FILIAL	FORBID	GALLOP	GLANCE	GUITAR	HECTIC	HUBBUB	INDENT
ERRANT	FAECAL	FILING	FOREGO	GALORE	GLIDER	GULDEN	HECTOR	HUBCAP	INDIAN
ERRATA	FAERIE	FILLER	FOREST	GALOSH	GLITCH	GULLET	HEGIRA	HUBRIS	INDICT
ERSATZ	FAGGOT	FILLET	FORGET	GAMBIT	GLOBAL	GUNMAN	HEIFER	HUDDLE	INDIGO
ESCAPE	FAILLE	FILLIP	FORINT	GAMBLE	GLOSSY	GUNNER	HEIGHT	HUMANE	INDITE
ESCHEW	FAIRLY	FILTER	FORKED	GAMBOL	GLOWER	GURGLE	HELIUM	HUMBLE	INDIUM
ESCORT	FALCON	FINALE	FORMAL	GAMETE	GLUTEN	GURKHA	HELMET	HUMBUG	INDOOR
ESCROW	FALLOW	FINDER	FORMAT	GAMINE	GNEISS	GUSHER	HEPCAT	HUMOUR	INDUCE
ESCUDO	FALTER	FINERY	FORMER	GAMMER	GOALIE	GUSSET	HERALD	HUNGER	INDUCT
ESKIMO	FAMILY	FINGER	FOSSIL	GAMMON	GOATEE	GUTTER	HEREBY	HUNKER	INFAMY
ESPRIT	FAMINE	FINIAL	FOSTER	GANDER	GOBBET	GUZZLE	HEREIN	HURDLE	INFANT
ESTATE	FAMISH	FINISH	FOUGHT	GANNET	GOBBLE	GYPSUM	HEREOF	HURRAH	INFECT
ESTEEM	FAMOUS	FINITE	FOURTH	GANTRY	GOBLET	GYRATE	HEREON	HURTLE	INFEST
ETHANE	FARINA	FISCAL	FRACAS	GARAGE	GOBLIN	HACKER	HERESY	HUSSAR	INFIRM
ETHICS	FARROW	FISHER	FRAPPE	GARBLE	GODSON	HACKIE	HERETO	HUSTLE	INFLOW
ETHNIC	FASTEN	FITFUL	FREEZE	GARCON	GOGGLE	HACKLE	HERMIT	HUZZAH	INFLUX
ETHNOL	FATHER	FIXITY	FRENCH	GARDEN	GOITER	HAGGIS	HERNIA	HYAENA	INFOLD
EUCHRE	FATHOM	FIZZLE	FRENZY	GARGLE	GOLDEN	HAGGLE	HEROIN	HYBRID	INFORM
EULOGY	FATTEN	FLABBY	FRESCO	GARISH	GOOBER	HAIRDO	HERPES	HYPHEN	INFUSE
EUNUCH	FAUCES	FLACON	FRIARY	GARLIC	GOODLY	HALALA	HEYDAY	HYSSOP	INGEST

INHALE	JAGGED	KIBOSH	LAWYER	LINTEL	MAGNET	MASTER	MILLET	MOTIVE	NESTLE
INHERE	JAGUAR	KIDNAP	LAYMAN	LIQUID	MAGPIE	MASTIC	MIMOSA	MOTLEY	NETHER
INHUME	JAILER	KIDNEY	LAYOFF	LIQUOR	MAGYAR	MATINS	MINDED	MOTTLE	NETTLE
INJECT	JALOPY	KILTER	LAYOUT	LISTEN	MAHOUT	MATRIX	MINGLE	MOUSER	NEURAL
INJURE	JANGLE	KIMONO	LEADEN	LITANY	MAIDEN	MATRON	MINION	MOUSSE	NEUROL
INJURY	JARGON	KINDLE	LEADER	LITCHI	MAILED	MATTER	MINNOW	MOUTON	NEURON
INKJET	JASPER	KINDLY	LEAFED	LITMUS	MAKEUP	MATURE	MINUET	MSCDEX	NEUTER
INLAID	JAUNTY	KIPPER	LEAGUE	LITTER	MAKUTA	MAYFLY	MINUTE	MUDDLE	NEWTON
INLAND	JAYCEE	KIRTLE	LEAVED	LITTLE	MALADY	MAYHEM	MIRAGE	MUFFIN	NIACIN
INMATE	JAYGEE	KISMET	LEAVEN	LIVELY	MALIAN	MEADOW	MIRROR	MUFFLE	NIBBLE
INMOST	JAYVEE	KISSER	LEAVES	LIVERY	MALICE	MEAGER	MISCUE	MUKLUK	NICETY
INNATE	JEJUNE	KITSCH	LECTOR	LIVING	MALIGN	MEASLY	MISERY	MULLET	NICKEL
INNING	JENNET	KITTEN	LEDGER	LIZARD	MALLET	MEDDLE	MISFIT	MUMBLE	NICKER
INROAD	JERKIN	KLATCH	LEEWAY	LOADED	MALLOW	MEDIAL	MISHAP	MUMMER	NIMBLE
INRUSH	JERSEY	KNIGHT	LEGACY	LOADER	MAMMAL	MEDIAN	MISLAY	MURDER	NIMBUS
INSANE	JESTER	KOBOLD	LEGATE	LOATHE	MAMMON	MEDICO	MISSAL	MURMUR	NIMROD
INSEAM	JETSAM	KOPECK	LEGATO	LOBULE	MANAGE	MEDIUM	MISTER	MUSCLE	NINETY
INSECT	JIGGER	KOREAN	LEGEND	LOCALE	MANANA	MEDLEY	MISUSE	MUSEUM	NIPPER
INSERT	JIGGLE	KORUNA	LEGION	LOCATE	MANEGE	MEGOHM	MITTEN	MUSKEG	NIPPLE
INSIDE	JIGSAW	KOSHER	LEGMAN	LOCKER	MANFUL	MELLOW	MIZZEN	MUSKET	NITRIC
INSIST	JINGLE	KOWTOW	LEGUME	LOCKET	MANGER	MELODY	MOBILE	MUSLIM	NITWIT
INSOLE	JITNEY	KWACHA	LENGTH	LOCKUP	MANGLE	MEMBER	MODERN	MUSLIN	NOBODY
INSTEP	JOBBER	LABIAL	LENITY	LOCUST	MANIAC	MEMOIR	MODEST	MUSSEL	NODDLE
INSULT	JOCKEY	LABILE	LENTIL	LODGER	MANIOC	MEMORY	MODIFY	MUSTER	NODULE
INSURE	JOCOSE	LABIUM	LEPTON	LOGGIA	MANNED	MENACE	MODISH	MUTANT	NOGGIN
INTACT	JOCUND	LABOUR	LESION	LOGJAM	MANNER	MENAGE	MODULE	MUTATE	NONAGE
INTAKE	JOGGLE	LACKEY	LESSEE	LOITER	MANQUE	MENIAL	MOHAIR	MUTINY	NONCOM
INTEND	JOHNNY	LACTIC	LESSEN	LONELY	MANTEL	MENINX	MOHAWK	MUTTER	NONFAT
INTENT	JOINER	LACUNA	LESSER	LOOPER	MANTIS	MENSES	MOIETY	MUTTON	NOODLE
INTERJ	JOSTLE	LADDER	LESSON	LOOSEN	MANTLE	MENTAL	MOLDER	MUTUAL	NORDIC
INTERN	JOUNCE	LADDIE	LESSOR	LORDLY	MANTRA	MENTOR	MOLEST	MUUMUU	NORMAL
INTONE	JOVIAL	LADING	LETHAL	LOTION	MANUAL	MERCER	MOLTEN	MUZZLE	NORMAN
INTROD	JOYFUL	LAGOON	LETTER	LOUNGE	MANURE	MERGER	MOMENT	MYOPIA	NORTON
INTUIT	JOYOUS	LAMENT	LEVITY	LOUVER	MAOISM	MERINO	MONDAY	MYRIAD	NOTICE
INVADE	JUDAIC	LAMINA	LIABLE	LOVELY	MARACA	MERMAN	MONGER	MYRTLE	NOTIFY
INVENT	JUGGLE	LANCER	LIBIDO	LOVING	MARAUD	MESCAL	MONISM	MYSELF	NOTION
INVERT	JUICER	LANCET	LIBYAN	LOWERY	MARBLE	MESSRS	MONKEY	MYSTIC	NOUGAT
INVEST	JUJUBE	LANDAU	LICHEE	LUBBER	MARCEL	METEOR	MONODY	NAMELY	NOUGHT
INVITE	JUMBLE	LANDED	LICHEN	LUCENT	MARGIN	METHOD	MOPPET	NAPALM	NOVELL
INVOKE	JUMPER	LANDER	LIGATE	LUMBAR	MARINA	METHYL	MORALE	NAPERY	NOVENA
INWARD	JUNGLE	LAPDOG	LIGHTS	LUMBER	MARINE	METIER	MORBID	NAPKIN	NOVICE
IODIDE	JUNIOR	LAPPET	LIKELY	LUMMOX	MARKED	METRIC	MORGAN	NARROW	NOWISE
IODINE	JUNKER	LAPTOP	LIKING	LUNACY	MARKET	METTLE	MORGUE	NATION	NOZZLE
IODIZE	JUNKET	LARDER	LIKUTA	LUPINE	MARKKA	MIASMA	MORMON	NATIVE	NUANCE
IONIZE	JUNKIE	LARIAT	LIMBER	LUSTER	MARKUP	MICMAC	MOROSE	NATURE	NUBBIN
IPECAC	JURIST	LARYNX	LIMPET	LUXURY	MARLIN	MICRON	MORRIS	NAUGHT	NUBBLE
IRENIC	KABUKI	LASCAR	LIMPID	LYCEUM	MARMOT	MIDAIR	MORROW	NAUSEA	NUBILE
IRONIC	KAISER	LASSIE	LINAGE	MACAPP	MAROON	MIDDAY	MORSEL	NAUTCH	NUDISM
IRRUPT	KAOLIN	LATENT	LINDEN	MACRON	MARROW	MIDDEN	MORTAL	NAVAHO	NUGGET
ISLAND	KARATE	LATHER	LINEAL	MADAME	MARTEN	MIDDLE	MORTAR	NEARBY	NUMBER
ISOBAR	KEGLER	LATTER	LINEAR	MADCAP	MARTIN	MIDGET	MOSAIC	NEBULA	NUNCIO
ISOMER	KELVIN	LAUNCH	LINEUP	MADDEN	MARTYR	MIDWAY	MOSLEM	NECTAR	NUTMEG
ITALIC	KENNEL	LAUREL	LINGER	MADDER	MARVEL	MIGHTY	MOSQUE	NEEDLE	NUTRIA
ITSELF	KERMIT	LAVAGE	LINING	MADMAN	MASCON	MIKADO	MOSTLY	NEGATE	NUZZLE
JABBER	KERNEL	LAVISH	LINKED	MADRAS	MASCOT	MILDEW	MOTHER	NELSON	OBJECT
JACKAL	KETTLE	LAWFUL	LINKUP	MAENAD	MASQUE	MILIEU	MOTILE	NEPHEW	OBLATE
JACKET	KIBBLE	LAWMAN	LINNET	MAGGOT	MASSIF	MILLER	MOTION	NEREID	OBLIGE

OBLONG	OUTFIT	PARSON	PEWTER	PLEDGE	POWDER	PURITY	RANDOM	REFUND	RETARD
OBSESS	OUTFOX	PARTLY	PEYOTE	PLENTY	POWWOW	PURPLE	RANGER	REFUSE	RETINA
OBTAIN	OUTGUN	PASCAL	PHAROS	PLENUM	PRAISE	PURSER	RANKLE	REFUTE	RETIRE
OBTUSE	OUTING	PASSEL	PHENOL	PLEXUS	PRANCE	PURSUE	RANSOM	REGAIN	RETORT
OCCULT	OUTLAW	PASSIM	PHILOS	PLIANT	PRAYER	PURVEY	RAPIER	REGALE	RETURN
OCCUPY	OUTLAY	PASTEL	PHLEGM	PLIERS	PREACH	PUSHER	RAPINE	REGARD	REVAMP
OCELOT	OUTLET	PASTOR	PHLOEM	PLIGHT	PRECIS	PUTOUT	RAPPEN	REGENT	REVEAL
OCTANE	OUTPUT	PASTRY	PHOBIA	PLINTH	PREFAB	PUTRID	RAREFY	REGIME	REVERB
OCTAVE	OUTRUN	PATACA	PHOEBE	PLOVER	PREFER	PUTSCH	RARING	REGION	REVERE
OCTAVO	OUTSET	PATENT	PHONIC	PLUCKY	PREFIX	PUTTEE	RASCAL	REGNAL	REVERS
OCULAR	OUTWIT	PATHOS	PHOTOG	PLUNGE	PRELIM	PUTTER	RASHER	REGRET	REVERT
ODDITY	OVERDO	PATINA	PHOTON	PLURAL	PREMED	PUZZLE	RASTER	REHASH	REVIEW
ODIOUS	OVERLY	PATOIS	PHRASE	PLUTON	PREMIX	PYRITE	RATHER	REJECT	REVILE
OEUVRE	OXFORD	PATROL	PHYLUM	POCKET	PREPAY	PYTHON	RATIFY	REJOIN	REVISE
OFFEND	OXYGEN	PATRON	PHYSIC	PODIUM	PRESET	QBASIC	RATING	RELATE	REVIVE
OFFICE	OYSTER	PATTER	PIAZZA	POETRY	PRESTO	QINTAR	RATION	RELENT	REVOKE
OFFING	PACIFY	PAUNCH	PICKAX	POGROM	PRETTY	QIVIUT	RATTAN	RELICT	REVOLT
OFFISH	PACKER	PAUPER	PICKET	POISON	PREWAR	QUAHOG	RATTER	RELIEF	REWARD
OFFSET	PACKET	PAVING	PICKLE	POLDER	PRIEST	QUAINT	RATTLE	RELISH	RHYTHM
OJIBWA	PADDLE	PAWNEE	PICKUP	POLEAX	PRIMAL	QUAKER	RAVAGE	RELIVE	RIBALD
OMELET	PAGODA	PAWPAW	PICNIC	POLICE	PRIMER	QUARRY	RAVINE	REMAIN	RIBAND
ONEIDA	PAIUTE	PAYOFF	PIDDLE	POLICY	PRINCE	QUARTO	RAVISH	REMAND	RIBBON
ONRUSH	PALACE	PCMCIA	PIDGIN	POLISH	PRINTF	QUARTZ	REALLY	REMARK	RICHES
ONWARD	PALATE	PEAHEN	PIERCE	POLITE	PRIORY	QUASAR	REALTY	REMEDY	RIDDEN
OODLES	PALEON	PEAKED	PIFFLE	POLITY	PRISON	QUAVER	REAMER	REMIND	RIDDLE
OOLITE	PALING	PEANUT	PIGEON	POLLEN	PRISSY	QUEASY	REASON	REMISS	RIGGER
OPAQUE	PALLET	PEBBLE	PIGLET	POMADE	PRIVET	QUENCH	REBATE	REMORA	RINGER
OPIATE	PALLID	PECTIN	PIGNUT	POMMEL	PROFIT	QUINCE	REBORN	REMOTE	RIPPLE
OPPOSE	PALLOR	PEDANT	PIGPEN	POMPON	PROLIX	QUINSY	REBUFF	REMOVE	RIPSAW
OPTICS	PALMER	PEDDLE	PIGSTY	PONCHO	PROLOG	QUIVER	REBUKE	RENDER	RISQUE
OPTION	PALTER	PEEWEE	PILFER	PONDER	PROMPT	QUORUM	RECALL	RENEGE	RITUAL
ORACLE	PALTRY	PELAGE	PILING	PONGEE	PRONTO	RABBET	RECANT	RENNET	RLOGIN
ORANGE	PAMPER	PELLET	PILLAR	POODLE	PROPEL	RABBIT	RECEDE	RENNIN	ROBBER
ORATOR	PANAMA	PELVIS	PILLOW	POPGUN	PROPER	RABBLE	RECENT	RENOWN	ROBUST
ORCHID	PANDER	PENCIL	PIMPLE	POPLAR	PROTON	RABIES	RECESS	RENTAL	ROCKER
ORDAIN	PANTIE	PENMAN	PINCER	POPLIN	PSEUDO	RACEME	RECIPE	REPAIR	ROCKET
ORDEAL	PANTRY	PENNON	PINEAL	POPPER	PSYCHE	RACISM	RECITE	REPAST	RODENT
ORDURE	PAPACY	PENURY	PINION	PORKER	PSYCHO	RACKET	RECKON	REPEAL	ROLLER
ORGASM	PAPAIN	PEOPLE	PINKIE	POROUS	PUBLIC	RADIAL	RECOIL	REPEAT	ROMANO
ORIENT	PAPAYA	PEPPER	PIPING	PORTAL	PUCKER	RADIAN	RECORD	REPENT	ROMPER
ORIGIN	PAPIST	PEPSIN	PIPKIN	PORTER	PUDDLE	RADISH	RECOUP	REPINE	ROOKIE
ORIOLE	PAPULE	PEPTIC	PIPPIN	PORTLY	PUEBLO	RADIUM	RECTAL	REPLAY	ROSARY
ORISON	PARADE	PEQUOT	PIQUET	POSEUR	PUFFIN	RADIUS	RECTOR	REPORT	ROSTER
ORMOLU	PARCEL	PERIOD	PIRACY	POSSUM	PULLET	RAFFIA	RECTUM	REPOSE	ROTARY
ORNATE	PARDON	PERISH	PIRATE	POSTAL	PULLEY	RAFFLE	REDACT	REPUTE	ROTATE
ORNERY	PARENT	PERMIT	PISTIL	POSTER	PULPIT	RAFTER	REDCAP	RESALE	ROTTEN
ORNITH	PARIAH	PERSON	PISTOL	POTAGE	PULSAR	RAGGED	REDDEN	RESCUE	ROTUND
ORPHAN	PARING	PERUKE	PISTON	POTASH	PUMICE	RAGLAN	REDEEM	RESENT	ROUBLE
OSMIUM	PARISH	PERUSE	PLACER	POTATO	PUMMEL	RAGOUT	REDUCE	RESIDE	RUBBER
OSPREY	PARITY	PESETA	PLACID	POTBOY	PUNDIT	RAISIN	REEFER	RESIGN	RUBBLE
OSSIFY	PARLAY	PESEWA	PLAGUE	POTEEN	PUNISH	RAKISH	REFILL	RESIST	RUBRIC
OSTLER	PARLEY	PESTER	PLAINT	POTENT	PUNKIN	RAMBLE	REFINE	RESORT	RUCKUS
OTIOSE	PARLOR	PESTLE	PLANET	POTHER	PUPPET	RAMIFY	REFLEX	RESULT	RUDDER
OTTAWA	PARODY	PETARD	PLAQUE	POTION	PURDAH	RAMROD	REFLUX	RESUME	RUFFLE
OUSTER	PAROLE	PETITE	PLASMA	POTPIE	PURIFY	RANCHO	REFORM	RETAIL	RUGGED
OUTBID	PARROT	PETREL	PLATEN	POTTER	PURINE	RANCID	REFRIG	RETAIN	RUMBLE
OUTCRY	PARSEC	PETROL	PLEASE	POUNCE	PURISM	RANCOR	REFUGE	RETAKE	RUMPLE

RUMPUS	SCORIA	SETTEE	SILVER	SOCIOL	SPRUNG	STROBE	SVELTE	TENPIN	TISSUE
RUNLET	SCOTCH	SETTER	SIMIAN	SOCKET	SPURGE	STRODE	SWATCH	TENURE	TITBIT
RUNNEL	SCRAPE	SETTLE	SIMILE	SODDEN	SPUTUM	STROKE	SWATHE	TEREDO	TITLED
RUNNER	SCRAWL	SEVERE	SIMMER	SODIUM	SQUALL	STROLL	SWERVE	TERROR	TITTER
RUNOFF	SCREAM	SEWAGE	SIMONY	SODOMY	SQUARE	STRONG	SWITCH	TESTER	TITTLE
RUNWAY	SCREEN	SEWING	SIMPER	SOEVER	SQUASH	STROVE	SWIVEL	TESTIS	TOCSIN
RUPIAH	SCREWY	SEXISM	SIMPLE	SOFTEN	SQUAWK	STRUCK	SYLVAN	TETCHY	TODDLE
RUSSET	SCRIBE	SEXPOT	SINFUL	SOIGNE	SQUEAK	STRUNG	SYMBOL	TETHER	TOFFEE
RUSTIC	SCRIMP	SEXTET	SINGLE	SOIREE	SQUEAL	STUBBY	SYNTAX	THANKS	TOGGLE
RUSTLE	SCRIPT	SEXTON	SINKER	SOLACE	SQUINT	STUCCO	SYPHON	THATCH	TOILET
SACHEM	SCROLL	SEXUAL	SIPHON	SOLDER	SQUIRE	STUDIO	SYSTEM	THEIRS	TOMATO
SACHET	SCRUFF	SHABBY	SISTER	SOLEMN	SQUIRM	STUFFY	TABLET	THEISM	TOMBOY
SACRED	SCULPT	SHADOW	SIZZLE	SOMBER	SQUIRT	STUPID	TACKLE	THENCE	TOMCAT
SACRUM	SCURRY	SHAGGY	SKETCH	SONATA	STABLE	STUPOR	TACTIC	THEORY	TOMTIT
SADDEN	SCURVY	SHAKER	SKEWER	SONNET	STAMEN	STURDY	TAILOR	THESIS	TONGUE
SADDLE	SCUZZY	SHAMAN	SKIMPY	SOOTHE	STANCE	STYLUS	TAKING	THIEVE	TONSIL
SADISM	SCYTHE	SHANTY	SKINNY	SORDID	STANCH	STYMIE	TALENT	THIRST	TOOTHY
SAFARI	SEABED	SHAVER	SKYCAP	SORREL	STANZA	SUBDUE	TALLOW	THIRTY	TOPPLE
SAFETY	SEALER	SHAVES	SLALOM	SORROW	STAPES	SUBLET	TALMUD	THORAX	TORERO
SAILOR	SEAMAN	SHEATH	SLAVER	SORTIE	STAPLE	SUBMIT	TAMALE	THOUGH	TORPID
SALAAM	SEANCE	SHEAVE	SLAVIC	SOUGHT	STARCH	SUBORN	TAMPER	THRALL	TORPOR
SALAMI	SEARCH	SHEIKH	SLEAZY	SOURCE	STARVE	SUBSET	TAMPON	THRASH	TORQUE
SALARY	SEASON	SHELVE	SLEDGE	SOVIET	STATIC	SUBTLE	TANDEM	THREAD	TORRID
SALINE	SEAWAY	SHERRY	SLEEPY	SPADIX	STATUE	SUBURB	TANGLE	THREAT	TOTTER
SALIVA	SECEDE	SHIELD	SLEEVE	SPARSE	STATUS	SUBWAY	TANKER	THRESH	TOUCAN
SALLOW	SECOND	SHIEST	SLEIGH	SPATHE	STAVES	SUCCOR	TANNER	THRICE	TOUCHE
SALMON	SECRET	SHIFTY	SLEUTH	SPAVIN	STEADY	SUCKER	TANNIN	THRIFT	TOUCHY
SALOON	SECTOR	SHIMMY	SLIDER	SPECIE	STENCH	SUCKLE	TAOISM	THRILL	TOUPEE
SALUTE	SECURE	SHINER	SLIEST	SPECIF	STEPPE	SUDDEN	TAPPET	THRIVE	TOUSLE
SALVER	SEDATE	SHINNY	SLIGHT	SPEECH	STEREO	SUFFER	TARGET	THROAT	TOWARD
SAMPAN	SEDUCE	SHINTO	SLIPUP	SPHERE	STICKY	SUFFIX	TARIFF	THRONE	TOWHEE
SAMPLE	SEEMLY	SHIVER	SLIVER	SPHINX	STIFLE	SUITOR	TARPON	THRONG	TRADER
SANDAL	SEESAW	SHODDY	SLOGAN	SPIDER	STIGMA	SULFUR	TARSUS	THROVE	TRAGIC
SANITY	SEETHE	SHOULD	SLOPPY	SPIGOT	STINGY	SULLEN	TARTAN	THRUSH	TRANCE
SARONG	SELDOM	SHOVEL	SLOUCH	SPINAL	STITCH	SULTAN	TARTAR	THRUST	TRANSL
SASHAY	SELECT	SHOWER	SLOUGH	SPINEL	STOCKY	SULTRY	TASSEL	THWACK	TRANSP
SATANG	SELVES	SHREWD	SLOVEN	SPINET	STODGY	SUMMER	TATTER	THWART	TRAUMA
SATEEN	SEMITE	SHRIEK	SLUDGE	SPIRAL	STOLEN	SUMMIT	TATTLE	THYMUS	TRAVEL
SATIRE	SENATE	SHRIFT	SLUICE	SPIREA	STOLID	SUMMON	TATTOO	TICKER	TREATY
SATRAP	SENECA	SHRIKE	SLURRY	SPIRIT	STOLON	SUNDAE	TAUGHT	TICKET	TREBLE
SATURN	SENILE	SHRILL	SMILAX	SPLASH	STONED	SUNDAY	TAVERN	TICKLE	TREMOR
SAUCER	SENIOR	SHRIMP	SMIRCH	SPLEEN	STOOGE	SUNDER	TAWDRY	TIDBIT	TRENCH
SAVAGE	SENITI	SHRINE	SMITHY	SPLICE	STRAFE	SUNDRY	TEACUP	TIFFIN	TREPAN
SAVANT	SENSOR	SHRINK	SMOOCH	SPLINE	STRAIN	SUNKEN	TEAPOT	TIGHTS	TRIAGE
SAVIOR	SENTRY	SHRIVE	SMOOTH	SPLINT	STRAIT	SUNLIT	TEASEL	TILLER	TRICKY
SAYING	SEPSIS	SHROUD	SMUDGE	SPOKEN	STRAND	SUNSET	TEDIUM	TIMBER	TRIFLE
SCAMPI	SEPTIC	SICKEN	SMUTCH	SPONGE	STREAK	SUNTAN	TEEPEE	TIMBRE	TRIODE
SCANTY	SEQUEL	SICKLE	SNATCH	SPOTTY	STREAM	SUPERB	TEETER	TIMELY	TRIPLE
SCARAB	SEQUIN	SIDING	SNEEZE	SPOUSE	STREET	SUPINE	TEETHE	TINDER	TRIPLY
SCARCE	SERAPE	SIERRA	SNIPPY	SPRAIN	STRESS	SUPPER	TELLER	TINGLE	TRIPOD
SCHEME	SERAPH	SIESTA	SNITCH	SPRAWL	STRICT	SUPPLE	TELNET	TINKER	TRITON
SCHISM	SERENE	SIGILL	SNIVEL	SPREAD	STRIDE	SUPPLY	TEMPER	TINKLE	TRIUNE
SCHIST	SERIAL	SIGNAL	SNOBOL	SPRING	STRIFE	SURETY	TEMPLE	TINSEL	TRIVET
SCHOOL	SERIES	SIGNET	SNOOTY	SPRINT	STRIKE	SURREY	TENANT	TIPPET	TRIVIA
SCHUSS	SERMON	SILAGE	SNOOZE	SPRITE	STRING	SURTAX	TENDER	TIPPLE	TROCHE
SCONCE	SERVER	SILENT	SOCCER	SPROUT	STRIPE	SURVEY	TENDON	TIPTOE	TROIKA
SCORCH	SESAME	SILICA	SOCIAL	SPRUCE	STRIVE	SUTURE	TENNIS	TIRADE	TROJAN

TROPHY	UNCOIL	UNWIND	VARIED	VOLUTE	WHINNY	YANQUI	BAOBAB	CANNED	CAYMAN
TROPIC	UNCORK	UNWISE	VARLET	VOODOO	WHITEN	YARROW	BARBER	CANNON	CAYUGA
TROUGH	UNCURL	UNWRAP	VASSAL	VORTEX	WHOLLY	YEARLY	BARELY	CANNOT	CAYUSE
TROUPE	UNDIES	UNYOKE	VECTOR	VOTARY	WICKED	YEASTY	BARFLY	CANOPY	DABBLE
TROWEL	UNDULY	UPBEAT	VELLUM	VOTIVE	WICKER	YELLOW	BARIUM	CANTER	DACTYL
TRUANT	UNEASY	UPDATE	VELOUR	VOYAGE	WICKET	YEOMAN	BARKER	CANTLE	DAEMON
TRUDGE	UNESCO	UPHILL	VELVET	VOYEUR	WIENER	YMODEM	BARLEY	CANTON	DAGGER
TRUISM	UNEVEN	UPHOLD	VENDEE	VULGAR	WIGGLE	YOGURT	BARRED	CANTOR	DAHLIA
TRUSTY	UNFAIR	UPKEEP	VENDER	WABBLE	WIGGLY	YONDER	BARREL	CANVAS	DAINTY
TRYING	UNFOLD	UPLAND	VENDOR	WADDLE	WIGLET	ZEALOT	BARREN	CANYON	DAKOTA
TSETSE	UNFURL	UPLIFT	VENEER	WAFFLE	WIGWAG	ZENANA	BARRIO	CAPFUL	DALASI
TUBING	UNGIRD	UPLOAD	VENIAL	WAGGLE	WIGWAM	ZENITH	BARROW	CAPTOR	DAMAGE
TUBULE	UNHAND	UPMOST	VENIRE	WAHINE	WILLOW	ZEPHYR	BARTER	CARAFE	DAMASK
TUCKER	UNHOLY	UPPISH	VENOUS	WAITER	WIMBLE	ZIGZAG	BASALT	CARBON	DAMPEN
TUGRIK	UNHOOK	UPPITY	VERBAL	WAIVER	WIMPLE	ZINNIA	BASKET	CARBOY	DAMPER
TUMBLE	UNICEF	UPREAR	VERGER	WALLET	WINDER	ZIPPER	BASQUE	CAREEN	DAMSEL
TUMULT	UNIQUE	UPROAR	VERIFY	WALLOP	WINDOW	ZIRCON	BATEAU	CAREER	DAMSON
TUNDRA	UNISEX	UPROOT	VERILY	WALLOW	WINDUP	ZITHER	BATHOS	CARESS	DANDER
TUNNEL	UNISON	UPRUSH	VERITY	WALNUT	WINGED	ZMODEM	BATMAN	CARHOP	DANDLE
TURBAN	UNITED	UPSHOT	VERMIN	WALRUS	WINKER	ZODIAC	BATTEN	CARIES	DANGER
TURBID	UNJUST	UPSIDE	VERNAL	WAMBLE	WINKLE	ZOMBIE	BATTER	CARNAL	DANGLE
TURBOT	UNKIND	UPTAKE	VERSED	WAMPUM	WINNER	ZONKED	BATTLE	CARPAL	DANISH
TUREEN	UNLACE	UPTOWN	VERSUS	WANDER	WINNOW	ZOUAVE	BAUBLE	CARPEL	DAPPER
TURGID	UNLADE	UPTURN	VERTEX	WANGLE	WINTER	ZOUNDS	BAZAAR	CARPET	DAPPLE
TURING	UNLESS	UPWARD	VESPER	WANTON	WINTRY	ZOYSIA	CABALA	CARREL	DARING
TURKEY	UNLIKE	UPWELL	VESSEL	WAPITI	WIRING	ZYGOTE	CABANA	CARROT	DARKEN
TURNER	UNLOAD	UPWIND	VESTAL	WARBLE	WISDOM		CACHET	CARTEL	DARNEL
TURNIP	UNLOCK	URACIL	VESTEE	WARDEN	WITHAL		CACKLE	CARTON	DARTER
TURRET	UNMASK	URANIC	VESTRY	WARDER	WITHER		CACTUS	CARTOP	DASHER
TURTLE	UNMEET	URANUS	VIABLE	WARMTH	WITHIN	**2ND**	CADDIE	CASABA	DATIVE
TURVES	UNMOOR	URBANE	VICTIM	WARREN	WITTED	**LETTER**	CAECUM	CASEIN	DAWDLE
TUSKER	UNPACK	URCHIN	VICTOR	WASHER	WIZARD		CAESAR	CASHEW	DAYBED
TUSSLE	UNPILE	UREMIA	VICUNA	WATERY	WOBBLE	BABBLE	CAFTAN	CASING	DAZZLE
TUXEDO	UNPLUG	URETER	VIKING	WATTLE	WOEFUL	BABOON	CAHOOT	CASINO	EAGLET
TWEEDY	UNREAD	URGENT	VILIFY	WAYLAY	WOMBAT	BACKER	CAIMAN	CASKET	EARTHY
TWELVE	UNREAL	URINAL	VILLUS	WEAKEN	WONDER	BACKUP	CAJOLE	CASQUE	EARWAX
TWENTY	UNREEL	URSINE	VINOUS	WEAKLY	WONTED	BADGER	CALCIC	CASSIA	EARWIG
TWINGE	UNREST	USABLE	VIOLET	WEALTH	WOODED	BAFFLE	CALICO	CASTER	EASTER
TWITCH	UNRIPE	USEFUL	VIOLIN	WEAPON	WOODEN	BAGMAN	CALIPH	CASTLE	EATERY
TYCOON	UNROBE	USENET	VIRAGO	WEASEL	WOODSY	BAGNIO	CALLOW	CASUAL	FABIAN
TYPHUS	UNROLL	USURER	VIRGIN	WEBBED	WOOFER	BAKERY	CALLUS	CATCHY	FABLED
TYPIFY	UNROOF	UTERUS	VIRILE	WEEKLY	WOOLEN	BALBOA	CALVES	CATGUT	FABRIC
TYPIST	UNRULY	UTMOST	VIRION	WEEVIL	WOOLLY	BALEEN	CAMBER	CATION	FACADE
TYRANT	UNSEAL	UTOPIA	VIRTUE	WEIGHT	WORKER	BALLAD	CAMERA	CATKIN	FACIAL
ULLAGE	UNSEAT	VACANT	VISAGE	WELKIN	WORSEN	BALLET	CAMPER	CATNAP	FACILE
ULSTER	UNSHIP	VACATE	VISCID	WELTER	WORTHY	BALLOT	CAMPUS	CATNIP	FACING
ULTIMO	UNSHOD	VACUUM	VISCUS	WESKIT	WRAITH	BALSAM	CANAPE	CATSUP	FACTOR
ULTRIX	UNSNAP	VAGARY	VISION	WETHER	WRASSE	BAMBOO	CANARD	CATTLE	FACULA
UMPIRE	UNSTOP	VAGINA	VISUAL	WHALER	WREATH	BANANA	CANARY	CAUCUS	FAECAL
UNABLE	UNSUNG	VAGROM	VITALS	WHAMMY	WRENCH	BANDED	CANCAN	CAUDAL	FAERIE
UNBEND	UNTOLD	VALISE	VIVACE	WHEEZE	WRETCH	BANDIT	CANCEL	CAUGHT	FAGGOT
UNBIND	UNTRUE	VALLEY	VIVIFY	WHEEZY	WRITER	BANGLE	CANCER	CAUSAL	FAILLE
UNBOLT	UNTUNE	VALUED	VIZARD	WHENCE	WRITHE	BANISH	CANDID	CAVEAT	FAIRLY
UNBORN	UNUSED	VANDAL	VIZIER	WHERRY	XMODEM	BANNER	CANDLE	CAVERN	FALCON
UNCIAL	UNVEIL	VANISH	VOICED	WHILOM	YAHWEH	BANTAM	CANDOR	CAVIAR	FALLOW
UNCLAD	UNWELL	VANITY	VOLLEY	WHILST	YAMMER	BANTER	CANINE	CAVITY	FALTER
UNCLOG	UNWEPT	VAPORY	VOLUME	WHIMSY	YANKEE	BANZAI	CANKER	CAVORT	FAMILY

FAMINE	HACKIE	LABOUR	MALIGN	NAPERY	PASTOR	RATION	TANNER	WATERY	ECZEMA
FAMISH	HACKLE	LACKEY	MALLET	NAPKIN	PASTRY	RATTAN	TANNIN	WATTLE	ICEBOX
FAMOUS	HAGGIS	LACTIC	MALLOW	NARROW	PATACA	RATTER	TAOISM	WAYLAY	ICEMAN
FARINA	HAGGLE	LACUNA	MAMMAL	NATION	PATENT	RATTLE	TAPPET	WAYWEH	ICICLE
FARROW	HAIRDO	LADDER	MAMMON	NATIVE	PATHOS	RAVAGE	TARGET	YAMMER	OCCULT
FASTEN	HALALA	LADDIE	MANAGE	NATURE	PATINA	RAVINE	TARIFF	YANKEE	OCCUPY
FATHER	HALITE	LADING	MANANA	NAUGHT	PATOIS	RAVISH	TARPON	YANQUI	OCELOT
FATHOM	HALLOW	LAGOON	MANEGE	NAUSEA	PATROL	SACHEM	TARSUS	YARROW	OCTANE
FATTEN	HALTER	LAMENT	MANFUL	NAUTCH	PATRON	SACHET	TARTAN	ABACUS	OCTAVE
FAUCES	HALVES	LAMINA	MANGER	NAVAHO	PATTER	SACRED	TARTAR	ABATIS	OCTAVO
FAUCET	HAMLET	LANCER	MANGLE	PACIFY	PAUNCH	SACRUM	TASSEL	ABBACY	OCULAR
FAVOUR	HAMMER	LANCET	MANIAC	PACKER	PAUPER	SADDEN	TATTER	ABBESS	PCMCIA
GABBLE	HAMPER	LANDAU	MANIOC	PACKET	PAVING	SADDLE	TATTLE	ABDUCT	SCAMPI
GABBRO	HANDLE	LANDED	MANNED	PADDLE	PAWNEE	SADISM	TATTOO	ABJECT	SCANTY
GADFLY	HANGAR	LANDER	MANNER	PAGODA	PAWPAW	SAFARI	TAUGHT	ABJURE	SCARAB
GADGET	HANKER	LAPDOG	MANQUE	PAIUTE	PAYOFF	SAFETY	TAVERN	ABLAZE	SCARCE
GAELIC	HANSEL	LAPPET	MANTEL	PALACE	RABBET	SAILOR	TAWDRY	ABLOOM	SCHEME
GAFFER	HANSOM	LAPTOP	MANTIS	PALATE	RABBIT	SALAAM	VACANT	ABNAKI	SCHISM
GAGGLE	HAPPEN	LARDER	MANTLE	PALEON	RABBLE	SALAMI	VACATE	ABOARD	SCHIST
GAIETY	HARASS	LARIAT	MANTRA	PALING	RABIES	SALARY	VACUUM	ABOUND	SCHOOL
GAITER	HARBOR	LARYNX	MANUAL	PALLET	RACEME	SALINE	VAGARY	ABRADE	SCHUSS
GALAXY	HARDEN	LASCAR	MANURE	PALLID	RACISM	SALIVA	VAGINA	ABROAD	SCONCE
GALENA	HARDLY	LASSIE	MAOISM	PALLOR	RACKET	SALLOW	VAGROM	ABRUPT	SCORCH
GALLEY	HARKEN	LATENT	MARACA	PALMER	RADIAL	SALMON	VALISE	ABSENT	SCORIA
GALLIC	HARLOT	LATHER	MARAUD	PALTER	RADIAN	SALOON	VALLEY	ABSORB	SCOTCH
GALLON	HARROW	LATTER	MARBLE	PALTRY	RADISH	SALUTE	VALUED	ABSURD	SCRAPE
GALLOP	HASSLE	LAUNCH	MARCEL	PAMPER	RADIUM	SALVER	VANDAL	EBCDIC	SCRAWL
GALORE	HASTEN	LAUREL	MARGIN	PANAMA	RADIUS	SAMPAN	VANISH	IBIDEM	SCREAM
GALOSH	HATBOX	LAVAGE	MARINA	PANDER	RAFFIA	SAMPLE	VANITY	OBJECT	SCREEN
GAMBIT	HATRED	LAVISH	MARINE	PANTIE	RAFFLE	SANDAL	VAPORY	OBLATE	SCREWY
GAMBLE	HATTER	LAWFUL	MARKED	PANTRY	RAFTER	SANITY	VARIED	OBLIGE	SCRIBE
GAMBOL	HAUNCH	LAWMAN	MARKET	PAPACY	RAGGED	SARONG	VARLET	OBLONG	SCRIMP
GAMETE	HAWKER	LAWYER	MARKKA	PAPAIN	RAGLAN	SASHAY	VASSAL	OBSESS	SCRIPT
GAMINE	HAWSER	LAYMAN	MARKUP	PAPAYA	RAGOUT	SATANG	WABBLE	OBTAIN	SCROLL
GAMMER	HAYMOW	LAYOFF	MARLIN	PAPIST	RAISIN	SATEEN	WADDLE	OBTUSE	SCRUFF
GAMMON	HAZARD	LAYOUT	MARMOT	PAPULE	RAKISH	SATIRE	WAFFLE	QBASIC	SCULPT
GANDER	JABBER	MACAPP	MAROON	PARADE	RAMBLE	SATRAP	WAGGLE	ACACIA	SCURRY
GANNET	JACKAL	MACRON	MARROW	PARCEL	RAMIFY	SATURN	WAHINE	ACCEDE	SCURVY
GANTRY	JACKET	MADAME	MARTEN	PARDON	RAMROD	SAUCER	WAITER	ACCENT	SCUZZY
GARAGE	JAGGED	MADCAP	MARTIN	PARENT	RANCHO	SAVAGE	WAIVER	ACCEPT	SCYTHE
GARBLE	JAGUAR	MADDEN	MARTYR	PARIAH	RANCID	SAVANT	WALLET	ACCESS	ADAGIO
GARCON	JAILER	MADDER	MARVEL	PARING	RANCOR	SAVIOR	WALLOP	ACCORD	ADDEND
GARDEN	JALOPY	MADMAN	MASCON	PARISH	RANDOM	SAYING	WALLOW	ACCOST	ADDICT
GARGLE	JANGLE	MADRAS	MASCOT	PARITY	RANGER	TABLET	WALNUT	ACCRUE	ADDUCE
GARISH	JARGON	MAENAD	MASQUE	PARLAY	RANKLE	TACKLE	WALRUS	ACCUSE	ADHERE
GARLIC	JASPER	MAGGOT	MASSIF	PARLEY	RANSOM	TACTIC	WAMBLE	ACETIC	ADJOIN
GARNER	JAUNTY	MAGNET	MASTER	PARLOR	RAPIER	TAILOR	WAMPUM	ACQUIT	ADJURE
GARNET	JAYCEE	MAGPIE	MASTIC	PARODY	RAPINE	TAKING	WANDER	ACROSS	ADJUST
GARRET	JAYGEE	MAGYAR	MATINS	PAROLE	RAPPEN	TALENT	WANGLE	ACTING	ADMIRE
GARTER	JAYVEE	MAHOUT	MATRIX	PARROT	RAREFY	TALLOW	WANTON	ACTION	ADRIFT
GASKET	KABUKI	MAIDEN	MATRON	PARSEC	RARING	TALMUD	WAPITI	ACTIVE	ADROIT
GATHER	KAISER	MAILED	MATTER	PARSON	RASCAL	TAMALE	WARBLE	ACTUAL	ADSORB
GAUCHE	KAOLIN	MAKEUP	MATURE	PARTLY	RASHER	TAMPER	WARDEN	ACUITY	ADVENT
GAUCHO	KARATE	MAKUTA	MAYFLY	PASCAL	RASTER	TAMPON	WARDER	ACUMEN	ADVERB
GAYETY	LABIAL	MALADY	MAYHEM	PASSEL	RATHER	TANDEM	WARMTH	ECCLES	ADVERT
GAZEBO	LABILE	MALIAN	NAMELY	PASSIM	RATIFY	TANGLE	WARREN	ECCLUS	ADVICE
HACKER	LABIUM	MALICE	NAPALM	PASTEL	RATING	TANKER	WASHER	ECLAIR	ADVISE

EDGING	BETHEL	DEHORN	FECUND	HERETO	MEGOHM	PEOPLE	REFUSE	RETINA	SETTEE
EDIBLE	BETIDE	DELETE	FEDORA	HERMIT	MELLOW	PEPPER	REFUTE	RETIRE	SETTER
IDIOCY	BETRAY	DELUDE	FEEBLE	HERNIA	MELODY	PEPSIN	REGAIN	RETORT	SETTLE
ODDITY	BETTER	DELUGE	FEELER	HEROIN	MEMBER	PEPTIC	REGALE	RETURN	SEVERE
ODIOUS	BETTOR	DELUXE	FELINE	HERPES	MEMOIR	PEQUOT	REGARD	REVAMP	SEWAGE
AERATE	BEWAIL	DEMAND	FELLAH	HEYDAY	MEMORY	PERIOD	REGENT	REVEAL	SEWING
AERIAL	BEWARE	DEMEAN	FELLOW	JEJUNE	MENACE	PERISH	REGIME	REVERB	SEXISM
BEACON	BEYOND	DEMISE	FELONY	JENNET	MENAGE	PERMIT	REGION	REVERE	SEXPOT
BEADLE	CELERY	DEMODE	FEMALE	JERKIN	MENIAL	PERSON	REGNAL	REVERS	SEXTET
BEAGLE	CELLAR	DEMOTE	FENDER	JERSEY	MENINX	PERUKE	REGRET	REVERT	SEXTON
BEAKER	CEMENT	DEMURE	FENIAN	JESTER	MENSES	PERUSE	REHASH	REVIEW	SEXUAL
BEANIE	CENSER	DENGUE	FENNEL	JETSAM	MENTAL	PESETA	REJECT	REVILE	TEACUP
BEAUTY	CENSOR	DENIAL	FERRET	KEGLER	MENTOR	PESEWA	REJOIN	REVISE	TEAPOT
BEAVER	CENSUS	DENIER	FERRIC	KELVIN	MERCER	PESTER	RELATE	REVIVE	TEASEL
BECALM	CENTER	DENOTE	FERULE	KENNEL	MERGER	PESTLE	RELENT	REVOKE	TEDIUM
BECKON	CENTRE	DENTAL	FERVID	KERMIT	MERINO	PETARD	RELICT	REVOLT	TEEPEE
BECOME	CEREAL	DENTIN	FERVOR	KERNEL	MERMAN	PETITE	RELIEF	REWARD	TEETER
BEDAUB	CEREUS	DENUDE	FESTAL	KETTLE	MESCAL	PETREL	RELISH	SEABED	TEETHE
BEDBUG	CERISE	DEODAR	FESTER	LEADEN	MESSRS	PETROL	RELIVE	SEALER	TELLER
BEDECK	CERIUM	DEPART	FETISH	LEADER	METEOR	PEWTER	REMAIN	SEAMAN	TELNET
BEDLAM	CERMET	DEPEND	FETTER	LEAFED	METHOD	PEYOTE	REMAND	SEANCE	TEMPER
BEDPAN	CERVIX	DEPICT	FETTLE	LEAGUE	METHYL	REALLY	REMARK	SEARCH	TEMPLE
BEETLE	CESIUM	DEPLOY	FEUDAL	LEAVED	METIER	REALTY	REMEDY	SEASON	TENANT
BEFALL	DEACON	DEPORT	GEEZER	LEAVEN	METRIC	REAMER	REMIND	SEAWAY	TENDER
BEFORE	DEADEN	DEPOSE	GEISHA	LEAVES	METTLE	REASON	REMISS	SECEDE	TENDON
BEFOUL	DEADLY	DEPUTE	GENDER	LECTOR	NEARBY	REBATE	REMORA	SECOND	TENNIS
BEGGAR	DEAFEN	DEPUTY	GENERA	LEDGER	NEBULA	REBORN	REMOTE	SECRET	TENPIN
BEGONE	DEARTH	DERAIL	GENIAL	LEEWAY	NECTAR	REBUFF	REMOVE	SECTOR	TENURE
BEHALF	DEBARK	DERIDE	GENIUS	LEGACY	NEEDLE	REBUKE	RENDER	SECURE	TEREDO
BEHAVE	DEBASE	DERIVE	GENTLE	LEGATE	NEGATE	RECALL	RENEGE	SEDATE	TERROR
BEHEAD	DEBATE	DERMAL	GENTRY	LEGATO	NELSON	RECANT	RENNET	SEDUCE	TESTER
BEHEST	DEBRIS	DERMIS	GERBIL	LEGEND	NEPHEW	RECEDE	RENNIN	SEEMLY	TESTIS
BEHIND	DEBTOR	DERRIS	GERMAN	LEGION	NEREID	RECENT	RENOWN	SEESAW	TETCHY
BEHOLD	DEBUNK	DESALT	GERUND	LEGMAN	NESTLE	RECESS	RENTAL	SEETHE	TETHER
BEHOOF	DECADE	DESCRY	GEWGAW	LEGUME	NETHER	RECIPE	REPAIR	SELDOM	VECTOR
BELDAM	DECAMP	DESERT	GEYSER	LENGTH	NETTLE	RECITE	REPAST	SELECT	VELLUM
BELFRY	DECANT	DESIGN	HEALTH	LENITY	NEURAL	RECKON	REPEAL	SELVES	VELOUR
BELIEF	DECEIT	DESIRE	HEARSE	LENTIL	NEUROL	RECOIL	REPEAT	SEMITE	VELVET
BELIKE	DECENT	DESIST	HEARTH	LEPTON	NEURON	RECORD	REPENT	SENATE	VENDEE
BELLOW	DECIDE	DESKEW	HEARTY	LESION	NEUTER	RECOUP	REPINE	SENECA	VENDER
BELONG	DECODE	DESPOT	HEAVEN	LESSEE	NEWTON	RECTAL	REPLAY	SENILE	VENDOR
BELUGA	DECREE	DETACH	HEBREW	LESSEN	OEUVRE	RECTOR	REPORT	SENIOR	VENEER
BEMIRE	DEDUCE	DETAIL	HECKLE	LESSER	PEAHEN	RECTUM	REPOSE	SENITI	VENIAL
BEMOAN	DEDUCT	DETAIN	HECTIC	LESSON	PEAKED	REDACT	REPUTE	SENSOR	VENIRE
BEMUSE	DEEJAY	DETECT	HECTOR	LESSOR	PEANUT	REDCAP	RESALE	SENTRY	VENOUS
BENDER	DEEPEN	DETEST	HEGIRA	LETHAL	PEBBLE	REDDEN	RESCUE	SEPSIS	VERBAL
BENIGN	DEFACE	DETOUR	HEIFER	LETTER	PECTIN	REDEEM	RESENT	SEPTIC	VERGER
BENUMB	DEFAME	DEVICE	HEIGHT	LEVITY	PEDANT	REDUCE	RESIDE	SEQUEL	VERIFY
BENZOL	DEFEAT	DEVISE	HELIUM	MEADOW	PEDDLE	REEFER	RESIGN	SEQUIN	VERILY
BERATE	DEFECT	DEVOID	HELMET	MEAGER	PEEWEE	REFILL	RESIST	SERAPE	VERITY
BERBER	DEFEND	DEVOIR	HEPCAT	MEASLY	PELAGE	REFINE	RESORT	SERAPH	VERMIN
BEREFT	DEFILE	DEVOTE	HERALD	MEDDLE	PELLET	REFLEX	RESULT	SERENE	VERNAL
BESEEM	DEFINE	DEVOUR	HEREBY	MEDIAL	PELVIS	REFLUX	RESUME	SERIAL	VERSED
BESIDE	DEFORM	DEVOUT	HEREIN	MEDIAN	PENCIL	REFORM	RETAIL	SERIES	VERSUS
BESTIR	DEFRAY	DEWLAP	HEREOF	MEDICO	PENMAN	REFRIG	RETAIN	SERMON	VERTEX
BESTOW	DEFUSE	EEPROM	HEREON	MEDIUM	PENNON	REFUGE	RETAKE	SERVER	VESPER
BETAKE	DEGREE	FEALTY	HERESY	MEDLEY	PENURY	REFUND	RETARD	SESAME	VESSEL

VESTAL	CHALET	SHADOW	THRONG	DIATOM	FINDER	LIKELY	MISLAY	RICHES	VIABLE
VESTEE	CHANCE	SHAGGY	THROVE	DIBBLE	FINERY	LIKING	MISSAL	RIDDEN	VICTIM
VESTRY	CHANCY	SHAKER	THRUSH	DICKER	FINGER	LIKUTA	MISTER	RIDDLE	VICTOR
WEAKEN	CHANGE	SHAMAN	THRUST	DICKEY	FINIAL	LIMBER	MISUSE	RIGGER	VICUNA
WEAKLY	CHAPEL	SHANTY	THWACK	DICTUM	FINISH	LIMPET	MITTEN	RINGER	VIKING
WEALTH	CHARGE	SHAVER	THWART	DIESEL	FINITE	LIMPID	MIZZEN	RIPPLE	VILIFY
WEAPON	CHASER	SHAVES	THYMUS	DIFFER	FISCAL	LINAGE	NIACIN	RIPSAW	VILLUS
WEASEL	CHASTE	SHEATH	WHALER	DIGEST	FISHER	LINDEN	NIBBLE	RISQUE	VINOUS
WEBBED	CHATTY	SHEAVE	WHAMMY	DILATE	FITFUL	LINEAL	NICETY	RITUAL	VIOLET
WEEKLY	CHAUNT	SHEIKH	WHEEZE	DILUTE	FIXITY	LINEAR	NICKEL	SICKEN	VIOLIN
WEEVIL	CHEEKY	SHELVE	WHEEZY	DIMITY	FIZZLE	LINEUP	NICKER	SICKLE	VIRAGO
WEIGHT	CHEERY	SHERRY	WHENCE	DIMMER	GIBBER	LINGER	NIMBLE	SIDING	VIRGIN
WELKIN	CHEESE	SHIELD	WHERRY	DIMPLE	GIBBET	LINING	NIMBUS	SIERRA	VIRILE
WELTER	CHEQUE	SHIEST	WHILOM	DINGHY	GIBBON	LINKED	NIMROD	SIESTA	VIRION
WESKIT	CHERRY	SHIFTY	WHILST	DINGLE	GIBSON	LINKUP	NINETY	SIGILL	VIRTUE
WETHER	CHERUB	SHIMMY	WHIMSY	DINGUS	GIFTED	LINNET	NIPPER	SIGNAL	VISAGE
YEARLY	CHICHI	SHINER	WHINNY	DINNER	GIGGLE	LINTEL	NIPPLE	SIGNET	VISCID
YEASTY	CHICLE	SHINNY	WHITEN	DIPPER	GIGOLO	LIQUID	NITRIC	SILAGE	VISCUS
YELLOW	CHILLY	SHINTO	WHOLLY	DIRECT	GIMBAL	LIQUOR	NITWIT	SILENT	VISION
YEOMAN	CHINTZ	SHIVER	AIDMAN	DIRHAM	GIMLET	LISTEN	PIAZZA	SILICA	VISUAL
ZEALOT	CHISEL	SHODDY	AIRMAN	DIRNDL	GINGER	LITANY	PICKAX	SILVER	VITALS
ZENANA	CHITIN	SHOULD	AIRWAY	DISARM	GINKGO	LITCHI	PICKET	SIMIAN	VIVACE
ZENITH	CHOICE	SHOVEL	BICEPS	DISBAR	GIRDER	LITMUS	PICKLE	SIMILE	VIVIFY
ZEPHYR	CHOKER	SHOWER	BICKER	DISCUS	GIRDLE	LITTER	PICKUP	SIMMER	VIZARD
AFFAIR	CHOLER	SHREWD	BIGAMY	DISHED	HIATUS	LITTLE	PICNIC	SIMONY	VIZIER
AFFECT	CHOOSE	SHRIEK	BIGWIG	DISMAL	HICCUP	LIVELY	PIDDLE	SIMPER	WICKED
AFFIRM	CHOOSY	SHRIFT	BIKINI	DISMAY	HIJACK	LIVERY	PIDGIN	SIMPLE	WICKER
AFFORD	CHOPPY	SHRIKE	BILLET	DISOWN	HINDER	LIVING	PIERCE	SINFUL	WICKET
AFFRAY	CHORAL	SHRILL	BILLOW	DISPEL	HIPPED	LIZARD	PIFFLE	SINGLE	WIENER
AFGHAN	CHOREA	SHRIMP	BINARY	DISTAL	HIPPIE	MIASMA	PIGEON	SINKER	WIGGLE
AFIELD	CHORUS	SHRINE	BINHEX	DISUSE	HITHER	MICMAC	PIGLET	SIPHON	WIGGLY
AFLAME	CHOSEN	SHRINK	BIOPSY	DITHER	JIGGER	MICRON	PIGNUT	SISTER	WIGLET
AFLOAT	CHRISM	SHRIVE	BIOTIC	DIVERS	JIGGLE	MIDAIR	PIGPEN	SIZZLE	WIGWAG
AFRAID	CHRIST	SHROUD	BIOTIN	DIVERT	JIGSAW	MIDDAY	PIGSTY	TICKER	WIGWAM
AFRESH	CHROME	THANKS	BIRDIE	DIVEST	JINGLE	MIDDEN	PILFER	TICKET	WILLOW
EFFACE	CHROMO	THATCH	BISECT	DIVIDE	JITNEY	MIDDLE	PILING	TICKLE	WIMBLE
EFFECT	CHUBBY	THEIRS	BISHOP	DIVINE	KIBBLE	MIDGET	PILLAR	TIDBIT	WIMPLE
EFFETE	CHUKKA	THEISM	BISQUE	EIGHTY	KIBOSH	MIDWAY	PILLOW	TIFFIN	WINDER
EFFIGY	CHUMMY	THENCE	BISTRO	EITHER	KIDNAP	MIGHTY	PIMPLE	TIGHTS	WINDOW
EFFORT	CHUNKY	THEORY	BITING	FIANCE	KIDNEY	MIKADO	PINCER	TILLER	WINDUP
OFFEND	CHURCH	THESIS	BITNET	FIASCO	KILTER	MILDEW	PINEAL	TIMBER	WINGED
OFFICE	GHETTO	THIEVE	BITTER	FIBRIL	KIMONO	MILIEU	PINION	TIMBRE	WINKER
OFFING	PHAROS	THIRST	CICADA	FIBRIN	KINDLE	MILLER	PINKIE	TIMELY	WINKLE
OFFISH	PHENOL	THIRTY	CILIUM	FIBULA	KINDLY	MILLET	PIPING	TINDER	WINNER
OFFSET	PHILOS	THORAX	CINDER	FICKLE	KIPPER	MIMOSA	PIPKIN	TINGLE	WINNOW
AGENCY	PHLEGM	THOUGH	CINEMA	FIDDLE	KIRTLE	MINDED	PIPPIN	TINKER	WINTER
AGENDA	PHLOEM	THRALL	CIPHER	FIDGET	KISMET	MINGLE	PIQUET	TINKLE	WINTRY
AGHAST	PHOBIA	THRASH	CIRCLE	FIERCE	KISSER	MINION	PIRACY	TINSEL	WIRING
AGLEAM	PHOEBE	THREAD	CIRCUS	FIESTA	KITSCH	MINNOW	PIRATE	TIPPET	WISDOM
EGGNOG	PHONIC	THREAT	CIRQUE	FIGURE	KITTEN	MINUET	PISTIL	TIPPLE	WITHAL
EGOISM	PHOTOG	THRESH	CIRRUS	FILIAL	LIABLE	MINUTE	PISTOL	TIPTOE	WITHER
EGRESS	PHOTON	THRICE	CITIFY	FILING	LIBIDO	MIRAGE	PISTON	TIRADE	WITHIN
IGNITE	PHRASE	THRIFT	CITRON	FILLER	LIBYAN	MIRROR	QINTAR	TISSUE	WITTED
IGNORE	PHYLUM	THRILL	CITRUS	FILLET	LICHEE	MISCUE	QIVIUT	TITBIT	WIZARD
IGUANA	PHYSIC	THRIVE	CIVICS	FILLIP	LICHEN	MISERY	RIBALD	TITLED	ZIGZAG
CHAFER	RHYTHM	THROAT	DIADEM	FILTER	LIGATE	MISFIT	RIBAND	TITTER	ZINNIA
CHAISE	SHABBY	THRONE	DIAPER	FINALE	LIGHTS	MISHAP	RIBBON	TITTLE	ZIPPER

ZIRCON	CLOCHE	PLEASE	EMBRYO	ANYWAY	INDOOR	ONRUSH	UNROBE	BOXCAR	COOLER
ZITHER	CLOSET	PLEDGE	EMERGE	ENABLE	INDUCE	ONWARD	UNROLL	BOXING	COOLIE
OJIBWA	CLOTHE	PLENTY	EMETIC	ENAMEL	INDUCT	SNATCH	UNROOF	COARSE	COOPER
AKIMBO	CLOVEN	PLENUM	EMIGRE	ENAMOR	INFAMY	SNEEZE	UNRULY	COBALT	COOTIE
SKETCH	CLOVER	PLEXUS	EMPIRE	ENCAMP	INFANT	SNIPPY	UNSEAL	COBBLE	COPIER
SKEWER	CLUMSY	PLIANT	EMPLOY	ENCASE	INFECT	SNITCH	UNSEAT	COBWEB	COPING
SKIMPY	CLUTCH	PLIERS	IMBIBE	ENCODE	INFEST	SNIVEL	UNSHIP	COCCUS	COPPER
SKINNY	ELAPSE	PLIGHT	IMBRUE	ENCORE	INFIRM	SNOBOL	UNSHOD	COCCYX	COPTER
SKYCAP	ELDEST	PLINTH	IMMUNE	ENCYST	INFLOW	SNOOTY	UNSNAP	COCKLE	COPULA
ALBEIT	ELEVEN	PLOVER	IMMURE	ENDEAR	INFLUX	SNOOZE	UNSTOP	COCOON	COQUET
ALBINO	ELICIT	PLUCKY	IMPACT	ENDING	INFOLD	UNABLE	UNSUNG	CODDLE	CORBEL
ALCOVE	ELIXIR	PLUNGE	IMPAIR	ENDIVE	INFORM	UNBEND	UNTOLD	CODGER	CORDON
ALIGHT	FLABBY	PLURAL	IMPALA	ENDRIN	INFUSE	UNBIND	UNTRUE	CODIFY	CORNEA
ALKALI	FLACON	PLUTON	IMPALE	ENDURE	INGEST	UNBOLT	UNTUNE	COERCE	CORNER
ALLEGE	FLAGON	RLOGIN	IMPART	ENDURO	INHALE	UNBORN	UNUSED	COEVAL	CORNET
ALLIED	FLANGE	SLALOM	IMPEDE	ENERGY	INHERE	UNCIAL	UNVEIL	COFFEE	CORONA
ALLUDE	FLASHY	SLAVER	IMPEND	ENFOLD	INHUME	UNCLAD	UNWELL	COFFER	CORPSE
ALLURE	FLATUS	SLAVIC	IMPERF	ENGAGE	INJECT	UNCLOG	UNWEPT	COFFIN	CORPUS
ALMOND	FLAUNT	SLEAZY	IMPISH	ENGINE	INJURE	UNCOIL	UNWIND	COGENT	CORRAL
ALMOST	FLAVOR	SLEDGE	IMPORT	ENGRAM	INJURY	UNCORK	UNWISE	COGNAC	CORSET
ALPACA	FLAXEN	SLEEPY	IMPOSE	ENGULF	INKJET	UNCURL	UNWRAP	COHEIR	CORTEX
ALPINE	FLEECE	SLEEVE	IMPOST	ENIGMA	INLAID	UNDIES	UNYOKE	COHERE	CORYZA
ALTAIR	FLESHY	SLEIGH	IMPUGN	ENISLE	INLAND	UNDULY	BOATER	COHORT	COSINE
ALUMNA	FLIGHT	SLEUTH	IMPURE	ENJOIN	INMATE	UNEASY	BOBBIN	COITUS	COSMIC
ALWAYS	FLIMSY	SLIDER	IMPUTE	ENLIST	INMOST	UNESCO	BOBBLE	COLLAR	COSMOS
BLANCH	FLINCH	SLIEST	OMELET	ENMESH	INNATE	UNEVEN	BOBCAT	COLLAT	COSTLY
BLAZER	FLITCH	SLIGHT	SMILAX	ENMITY	INNING	UNFAIR	BOCCIE	COLLIE	COTTER
BLAZON	FLOOZY	SLIPUP	SMIRCH	ENOUGH	INROAD	UNFOLD	BODICE	COLLOQ	COTTON
BLEACH	FLOPPY	SLIVER	SMITHY	ENRAGE	INRUSH	UNFURL	BODILY	COLONY	COUGAR
BLEARY	FLORAL	SLOGAN	SMOOCH	ENRICH	INSANE	UNGIRD	BODKIN	COLUMN	COULEE
BLENCH	FLORID	SLOPPY	SMOOTH	ENROLL	INSEAM	UNHAND	BOGGLE	COMBAT	COUNTY
BLIGHT	FLORIN	SLOUCH	SMUDGE	ENSIGN	INSECT	UNHOLY	BOILER	COMBER	COUPLE
BLITHE	FLOSSY	SLOUGH	SMUTCH	ENSILE	INSERT	UNHOOK	BOLERO	COMDEX	COUPON
BLOTCH	FLOWER	SLOVEN	UMPIRE	ENSURE	INSIDE	UNICEF	BOMBER	COMEDY	COURSE
BLOUSE	FLUENT	SLUDGE	XMODEM	ENTAIL	INSIST	UNIQUE	BONBON	COMELY	COUSIN
BLOWSY	FLUFFY	SLUICE	YMODEM	ENTICE	INSOLE	UNISEX	BONITO	COMFIT	COVERT
BLOWUP	FLUNKY	SLURRY	ZMODEM	ENTIRE	INSTEP	UNISON	BONNET	COMING	COWARD
BLUING	FLURRY	ULLAGE	ANADEM	ENTITY	INSULT	UNITED	BONSAI	COMITY	COWBOY
BLUISH	FLYWAY	ULSTER	ANALOG	ENTOMB	INSURE	UNJUST	BOODLE	COMMIT	COWMAN
CLAMMY	GLANCE	ULTIMO	ANCHOR	ENTRAP	INTACT	UNKIND	BOOKIE	COMMON	COWPOX
CLAMOR	GLIDER	ULTRIX	ANEMIA	ENTREE	INTAKE	UNLACE	BOOTEE	COMPAQ	COYOTE
CLAQUE	GLITCH	AMAZON	ANGINA	ENZYME	INTEND	UNLADE	BORATE	COMPAR	DOBBIN
CLARET	GLOBAL	AMBUSH	ANGORA	GNEISS	INTENT	UNLESS	BORDER	COMPEL	DOCENT
CLASSY	GLOSSY	AMENDS	ANIMAL	INBORN	INTERJ	UNLIKE	BOREAL	COMPLY	DOCILE
CLAUSE	GLOWER	AMERCE	ANIMUS	INBRED	INTERN	UNLOAD	BORROW	CONCUR	DOCKET
CLEAVE	GLUTEN	AMOEBA	ANKLET	INCASE	INTONE	UNLOCK	BOTANY	CONDOM	DOCTOR
CLENCH	ILLUME	AMORAL	ANNALS	INCEST	INTROD	UNMASK	BOTHER	CONDOR	DODDER
CLERGY	ILLUST	AMOUNT	ANNEAL	INCISE	INTUIT	UNMEET	BOTTLE	CONFAB	DOGGED
CLERIC	KLATCH	AMPERE	ANNUAL	INCITE	INVADE	UNMOOR	BOTTOM	CONFED	DOGLEG
CLEVER	PLACER	AMULET	ANOINT	INCOME	INVENT	UNPACK	BOUGHT	CONFER	DOINGS
CLEVIS	PLACID	AMVETS	ANSWER	INDEED	INVERT	UNPILE	BOUNCE	CONSOL	DOLLAR
CLICHE	PLAGUE	EMBALM	ANTHEM	INDENT	INVEST	UNPLUG	BOUNTY	CONSTR	DOLLOP
CLIENT	PLAINT	EMBANK	ANTHER	INDIAN	INVITE	UNREAD	BOURSE	CONSUL	DOLMEN
CLIMAX	PLANET	EMBARK	ANTLER	INDICT	INVOKE	UNREAL	BOVINE	CONVEX	DOMAIN
CLINCH	PLAQUE	EMBLEM	ANTRUM	INDIGO	INWARD	UNREEL	BOWLEG	CONVEY	DOMINO
CLINIC	PLASMA	EMBODY	ANYHOW	INDITE	KNIGHT	UNREST	BOWLER	CONVOY	DONATE
CLIQUE	PLATEN	EMBOSS	ANYONE	INDIUM	ONEIDA	UNRIPE	BOWMAN	COOKIE	DONKEY

DOODAD	HOAGIE	LOCATE	MOTLEY	PORTLY	SOURCE	ZOUAVE	SPRUNG	ARMORY	CREWEL
DOODLE	HOARSE	LOCKER	MOTTLE	POSEUR	SOVIET	ZOUNDS	SPURGE	ARMPIT	CRINGE
DOPANT	HOBBLE	LOCKET	MOUSER	POSSUM	TOCSIN	ZOYSIA	SPUTUM	ARNICA	CRISIS
DORMER	HOBNOB	LOCKUP	MOUSSE	POSTAL	TODDLE	APACHE	UPBEAT	AROUND	CRITIC
DORSAL	HOCKEY	LOCUST	MOUTON	POSTER	TOFFEE	APATHY	UPDATE	AROUSE	CROCUS
DOTAGE	HOLDUP	LODGER	NOBODY	POTAGE	TOGGLE	APERCU	UPHILL	ARRANT	CROTCH
DOTARD	HOLLER	LOGGIA	NODDLE	POTASH	TOILET	APIARY	UPHOLD	ARREST	CROUCH
DOTTLE	HOLLOW	LOGJAM	NODULE	POTATO	TOMATO	APICAL	UPKEEP	ARRIVE	CRUISE
DOUBLE	HOMAGE	LOITER	NOGGIN	POTBOY	TOMBOY	APIECE	UPLAND	ARROYO	CRUMMY
DOUBLY	HOMELY	LONELY	NONAGE	POTEEN	TOMCAT	APLOMB	UPLIFT	ARTERY	CRUNCH
DOUCHE	HOMILY	LOOPER	NONCOM	POTENT	TOMTIT	APOGEE	UPLOAD	ARTFUL	CRUTCH
DOWNER	HOMINY	LOOSEN	NONFAT	POTHER	TONGUE	APPALL	UPMOST	ARTIST	DRAFTY
EOLIAN	HONEST	LORDLY	NOODLE	POTION	TONSIL	APPEAL	UPPISH	BRAISE	DRAGON
FODDER	HONOUR	LOTION	NORDIC	POTPIE	TOOTHY	APPEAR	UPPITY	BRANCH	DRAPER
FOEMAN	HOODOO	LOUNGE	NORMAL	POTTER	TOPPLE	APPEND	UPREAR	BRANDY	DRAWER
FOETAL	HOOKAH	LOUVER	NORMAN	POUNCE	TORERO	APPLET	UPROAR	BRAZEN	DREARY
FOIBLE	HOOKER	LOVELY	NORTON	POWDER	TORPID	APPROX	UPROOT	BREACH	DREDGE
FOLDER	HOOKUP	LOVING	NOTICE	POWWOW	TORPOR	IPECAC	UPRUSH	BREAST	DRENCH
FOLKSY	HOOPLA	LOWERY	NOTIFY	ROBBER	TORQUE	OPAQUE	UPSHOT	BREATH	DRESSY
FOLLOW	HOPPER	MOBILE	NOTION	ROBUST	TORRID	OPIATE	UPSIDE	BREECH	DRIVEL
FOMENT	HORNET	MODERN	NOUGAT	ROCKER	TOTTER	OPPOSE	UPTAKE	BREEZE	DRIVER
FONDLE	HORRID	MODEST	NOUGHT	ROCKET	TOUCAN	OPTICS	UPTOWN	BREVET	DROGUE
FONDUE	HORROR	MODIFY	NOVELL	RODENT	TOUCHE	OPTION	UPTURN	BRIDAL	DROPSY
FOOTED	HORSEY	MODISH	NOVENA	ROLLER	TOUCHY	SPADIX	UPWARD	BRIDGE	DROVER
FORAGE	HOSTEL	MODULE	NOVICE	ROMANO	TOUPEE	SPARSE	UPWELL	BRIDLE	DROWSE
FORBID	HOTBED	MOHAIR	NOWISE	ROMPER	TOUSLE	SPATHE	UPWIND	BRIGHT	DROWSY
FOREGO	HOTBOX	MOHAWK	NOZZLE	ROOKIE	TOWARD	SPAVIN	EQUATE	BRITON	DRUDGE
FOREST	HOWDAH	MOIETY	OODLES	ROSARY	TOWHEE	SPECIE	EQUINE	BROACH	ERBIUM
FORGET	HOWLER	MOLDER	OOLITE	ROSTER	VOICED	SPECIF	EQUITY	BROGAN	ERMINE
FORINT	HOYDEN	MOLEST	POCKET	ROTARY	VOLLEY	SPEECH	SQUALL	BROGUE	EROTIC
FORKED	IODIDE	MOLTEN	PODIUM	ROTATE	VOLUME	SPHERE	SQUARE	BROKEN	ERRAND
FORMAL	IODINE	MOMENT	POETRY	ROTTEN	VOLUTE	SPHINX	SQUASH	BROKER	ERRANT
FORMAT	IODIZE	MONDAY	POGROM	ROTUND	VOODOO	SPIDER	SQUAWK	BRONCO	ERRATA
FORMER	IONIZE	MONGER	POISON	ROUBLE	VORTEX	SPIGOT	SQUEAK	BRONZE	ERSATZ
FOSSIL	JOBBER	MONISM	POLDER	SOCCER	VOTARY	SPINAL	SQUEAL	BROOCH	FRACAS
FOSTER	JOCKEY	MONKEY	POLEAX	SOCIAL	VOTIVE	SPINEL	SQUINT	BROWSE	FRAPPE
FOUGHT	JOCOSE	MONODY	POLICE	SOCIOL	VOYAGE	SPINET	SQUIRE	BRUISE	FREEZE
FOURTH	JOCUND	MOPPET	POLICY	SOCKET	VOYEUR	SPIRAL	SQUIRM	BRUNCH	FRENCH
GOALIE	JOGGLE	MORALE	POLISH	SODDEN	WOBBLE	SPIREA	SQUIRT	BRUNET	FRENZY
GOATEE	JOHNNY	MORBID	POLITE	SODIUM	WOEFUL	SPIRIT	ARABIC	BRUTAL	FRESCO
GOBBET	JOINER	MORGAN	POLITY	SODOMY	WOMBAT	SPLASH	ARABLE	CRABBY	FRIARY
GOBBLE	JOSTLE	MORGUE	POLLEN	SOEVER	WONDER	SPLEEN	ARCADE	CRADLE	FRIDAY
GOBLET	JOUNCE	MORMON	POMADE	SOFTEN	WONTED	SPLICE	ARCANE	CRAFTY	FRIEND
GOBLIN	JOVIAL	MOROSE	POMMEL	SOIGNE	WOODED	SPLINE	ARCCOS	CRANKY	FRIEZE
GODSON	JOYFUL	MORRIS	POMPON	SOIREE	WOODEN	SPLINT	ARCHON	CRANNY	FRIGHT
GOGGLE	JOYOUS	MORROW	PONCHO	SOLACE	WOODSY	SPOKEN	ARCNET	CRATER	FRIGID
GOITER	KOBOLD	MORSEL	PONDER	SOLDER	WOOFER	SPONGE	ARCSIN	CRATON	FRINGE
GOLDEN	KOPECK	MORTAL	PONGEE	SOLEMN	WOOLEN	SPOTTY	ARCTAN	CRAVAT	FRISKY
GOOBER	KOREAN	MORTAR	POODLE	SOMBER	WOOLLY	SPOUSE	ARCTIC	CRAVEN	FROLIC
GOODLY	KORUNA	MOSAIC	POPGUN	SONATA	WORKER	SPRAIN	ARDENT	CRAYON	FROWSY
GOPHER	KOSHER	MOSLEM	POPLAR	SONNET	WORSEN	SPRAWL	ARGENT	CREASE	FROZEN
GOSPEL	KOWTOW	MOSQUE	POPLIN	SOOTHE	WORTHY	SPREAD	ARGOSY	CREATE	FRUGAL
GOSSIP	LOADED	MOSTLY	POPPER	SORDID	YOGURT	SPRING	ARGYLE	CRECHE	FRUITY
GOTHIC	LOADER	MOTHER	PORKER	SORREL	YONDER	SPRINT	ARIGHT	CREDIT	FRUMPY
GOTTEN	LOATHE	MOTILE	POROUS	SORROW	ZODIAC	SPRITE	ARMADA	CREEPY	GRABEN
GOURDE	LOBULE	MOTION	PORTAL	SORTIE	ZOMBIE	SPROUT	ARMFUL	CREOLE	GRADER
GOVERN	LOCALE	MOTIVE	PORTER	SOUGHT	ZONKED	SPRUCE	ARMLET	CRETIN	GRAINY

GRANGE	PRETTY	URANUS	OSSIFY	STOOGE	BUNKER	EUCHRE	LUBBER	OUTSET	RUNLET
GRATIS	PREWAR	URBANE	OSTLER	STRAFE	BUNKUM	EULOGY	LUCENT	OUTWIT	RUNNEL
GRAVEL	PRIEST	URCHIN	PSEUDO	STRAIN	BUQSHA	EUNUCH	LUMBAR	PUBLIC	RUNNER
GRAVID	PRIMAL	UREMIA	PSYCHE	STRAIT	BURDEN	EUREKA	LUMBER	PUCKER	RUNOFF
GRAYED	PRIMER	URETER	PSYCHO	STRAND	BUREAU	EUNUCH	LUMMOX	PUDDLE	RUNWAY
GREASE	PRINCE	URGENT	TSETSE	STREAK	BURGEE	FUDDLE	LUNACY	PUEBLO	RUPIAH
GRIEVE	PRINTF	URINAL	USABLE	STREAM	BURGLE	FUHRER	LUPINE	PUFFIN	RUSSET
GRILLE	PRIORY	URSINE	USEFUL	STREET	BURIAL	FUMBLE	LUSTER	PULLET	RUSTIC
GRIPPE	PRISON	WRAITH	USENET	STRESS	BURLAP	FUNGUS	LUXURY	PULLEY	RUSTLE
GRISLY	PRISSY	WRASSE	USURER	STRICT	BURNER	FUNNEL	MUDDLE	PULPIT	SUBDUE
GROCER	PRIVET	WREATH	ATOMIC	STRIDE	BURROW	FURORE	MUFFIN	PULSAR	SUBLET
GROGGY	PROFIT	WRENCH	ATONAL	STRIFE	BURSAR	FURROW	MUFFLE	PUMICE	SUBMIT
GROOVE	PROLIX	WRETCH	ATRIUM	STRIKE	BUSBOY	FUSION	MUKLUK	PUMMEL	SUBORN
GROOVY	PROLOG	WRITER	ATTACH	STRING	BUSHED	FUTILE	MULLET	PUNDIT	SUBSET
GROTTO	PROMPT	WRITHE	ATTACK	STRIPE	BUSHEL	FUTURE	MUMBLE	PUNISH	SUBTLE
GROUCH	PRONTO	ASCEND	ATTAIN	STRIVE	BUSILY	GUFFAW	MUMMER	PUNKIN	SUBURB
GROUND	PROPEL	ASCENT	ATTEND	STROBE	BUSKIN	GUIDON	MURDER	PUPPET	SUBWAY
GROUSE	PROPER	ASHLAR	ATTEST	STRODE	BUSTLE	GUILTY	MURMUR	PURDAH	SUCCOR
GROVEL	PROTON	ASHORE	ATTIRE	STROKE	BUTANE	GUINEA	MUSCLE	PURIFY	SUCKER
GROWTH	TRADER	ASHRAM	ATTRIB	STROLL	BUTLER	GUITAR	MUSEUM	PURINE	SUCKLE
GRUBBY	TRAGIC	ASLANT	ATTUNE	STRONG	BUTTER	GULDEN	MUSKEG	PURISM	SUDDEN
GRUDGE	TRANCE	ASLEEP	ETHANE	STROVE	BUTTON	GULLET	MUSKET	PURITY	SUFFER
GRUMPY	TRANSL	ASPECT	ETHICS	STRUCK	BUZZER	GUNMAN	MUSLIM	PURPLE	SUFFIX
IRENIC	TRANSP	ASPIRE	ETHNIC	STRUNG	CUBISM	GUNNER	MUSLIN	PURSER	SUITOR
IRONIC	TRAUMA	ASSAIL	ETHNOL	STUBBY	CUCKOO	GURGLE	MUSSEL	PURSUE	SULFUR
IRRUPT	TRAVEL	ASSENT	ITALIC	STUCCO	CUDDLE	GURKHA	MUSTER	PURVEY	SULLEN
ORACLE	TREATY	ASSERT	ITSELF	STUDIO	CUDGEL	GUSHER	MUTANT	PUSHER	SULTAN
ORANGE	TREBLE	ASSESS	OTIOSE	STUFFY	CUESTA	GUSSET	MUTATE	PUTOUT	SULTRY
ORATOR	TREMOR	ASSIGN	OTTAWA	STUPID	CUMBER	GUTTER	MUTINY	PUTRID	SUMMER
ORCHID	TRENCH	ASSIST	STABLE	STUPOR	CUNNER	GUZZLE	MUTTER	PUTSCH	SUMMIT
ORDAIN	TREPAN	ASSIZE	STAMEN	STURDY	CUPOLA	HUBBUB	MUTTON	PUTTEE	SUMMON
ORDEAL	TRIAGE	ASSORT	STANCE	STYLUS	CURATE	HUBCAP	MUTUAL	PUTTER	SUNDAE
ORDURE	TRICKY	ASSUME	STANCH	STYMIE	CURDLE	HUBRIS	MUUMUU	PUZZLE	SUNDAY
ORGASM	TRIFLE	ASSURE	STANZA	UTERUS	CURFEW	HUDDLE	MUZZLE	QUAHOG	SUNDER
ORIENT	TRIODE	ASTERN	STAPES	UTMOST	CURIUM	HUMANE	NUANCE	QUAINT	SUNDRY
ORIGIN	TRIPLE	ASTHMA	STAPLE	UTOPIA	CURLEW	HUMBLE	NUBBIN	QUAKER	SUNKEN
ORIOLE	TRIPLY	ASTRAL	STARCH	AUBURN	CURSOR	HUMBUG	NUBBLE	QUARRY	SUNLIT
ORISON	TRIPOD	ASTRAY	STARVE	AUGURY	CURTSY	HUMOUR	NUBILE	QUARTO	SUNSET
ORMOLU	TRITON	ASTROL	STATIC	AUGUST	CURVET	HUNGER	NUDISM	QUARTZ	SUNTAN
ORNATE	TRIUNE	ASTRON	STATUE	AURORA	CUSPID	HUNKER	NUGGET	QUASAR	SUPERB
ORNERY	TRIVET	ASTUTE	STATUS	AUTHOR	CUSTOM	HURDLE	NUMBER	QUAVER	SUPINE
ORNITH	TRIVIA	ASYLUM	STAVES	AUTISM	CUTLER	HURRAH	NUNCIO	QUEASY	SUPPER
ORPHAN	TROCHE	ESCAPE	STEADY	AUTUMN	CUTLET	HURTLE	NUTMEG	QUENCH	SUPPLE
PRAISE	TROIKA	ESCHEW	STENCH	BUBBLE	CUTOFF	HUSSAR	NUTRIA	QUINCE	SUPPLY
PRANCE	TROJAN	ESCORT	STEPPE	BUCKET	CUTOUT	HUSTLE	NUZZLE	QUINSY	SURETY
PRAYER	TROPHY	ESCROW	STEREO	BUCKLE	CUTTER	HUZZAH	OUSTER	QUIVER	SURREY
PREACH	TROPIC	ESCUDO	STICKY	BUDGET	DUBBIN	JUDAIC	OUTBID	QUORUM	SURTAX
PRECIS	TROUGH	ESKIMO	STIFLE	BUDGIE	DUENDE	JUGGLE	OUTCRY	RUBBER	SURVEY
PREFAB	TROUPE	ESPRIT	STIGMA	BUFFER	DUENNA	JUICER	OUTFIT	RUBBLE	SUTURE
PREFER	TROWEL	ESTATE	STINGY	BUFFET	DUFFER	JUJUBE	OUTFOX	RUBRIC	TUBING
PREFIX	TRUANT	ESTEEM	STITCH	BULBUL	DUGOUT	JUMBLE	OUTGUN	RUCKUS	TUBULE
PRELIM	TRUDGE	ISLAND	STOCKY	BULLET	DULCET	JUMPER	OUTING	RUDDER	TUCKER
PREMED	TRUISM	ISOBAR	STODGY	BUMMER	DUMDUM	JUNGLE	OUTLAW	RUFFLE	TUGRIK
PREMIX	TRUSTY	ISOMER	STOLEN	BUMPER	DUPLEX	JUNIOR	OUTLAY	RUGGED	TUMBLE
PREPAY	TRYING	MSCDEX	STOLID	BUNDLE	DURESS	JUNKER	OUTLET	RUMBLE	TUMULT
PRESET	URACIL	OSMIUM	STOLON	BUNGLE	DURING	JUNKET	OUTPUT	RUMPLE	TUNDRA
PRESTO	URANIC	OSPREY	STONED	BUNION	DUSTER	JURIST	OUTRUN	RUMPUS	TUNNEL

		3RD LETTER →							
TURBAN	EXOTIC		CRATON	LEADEN	SEAMAN	WEAPON	GIBSON	SUBMIT	DACTYL
TURBID	EXPAND		CRAVAT	LEADER	SEANCE	WEASEL	GOBBET	SUBORN	DECADE
TURBOT	EXPECT	ABACUS	CRAVEN	LEAFED	SEARCH	WHALER	GOBBLE	SUBSET	DECAMP
TUREEN	EXPEND	ABATIS	CRAYON	LEAGUE	SEASON	WHAMMY	GOBLET	SUBTLE	DECANT
TURGID	EXPERT	ACACIA	DEACON	LEAVED	SEAWAY	WRAITH	GOBLIN	SUBURB	DECEIT
TURING	EXPIRE	ADAGIO	DEADEN	LEAVEN	SHABBY	WRASSE	HEBREW	SUBWAY	DECENT
TURKEY	EXPORT	AMAZON	DEADLY	LEAVES	SHADOW	YEARLY	HOBBLE	TABLET	DECIDE
TURNER	EXPOSE	ANADEM	DEAFEN	LIABLE	SHAGGY	YEASTY	HOBNOB	TUBING	DECODE
TURNIP	EXTANT	ANALOG	DEARTH	LOADED	SHAKER	ZEALOT	HUBBUB	TUBULE	DECREE
TURRET	EXTEND	APACHE	DIADEM	LOADER	SHAMAN	ABBACY	HUBCAP	UNBEND	DICKER
TURTLE	EXTENT	APATHY	DIAPER	LOATHE	SHANTY	ABBESS	HUBRIS	UNBIND	DICKEY
TURVES	EXTERN	ARABIC	DIATOM	MEADOW	SHAVER	ALBEIT	HYBRID	UNBOLT	DICTUM
TUSKER	EXTORT	ARABLE	DRAFTY	MEAGER	SHAVES	ALBINO	IMBIBE	UNBORN	DOCENT
TUSSLE	OXFORD	AVATAR	DRAGON	MEASLY	SLALOM	AMBUSH	IMBRUE	UPBEAT	DOCILE
TUXEDO	OXYGEN	AVAUNT	DRAPER	MIASMA	SLAVER	AUBURN	INBORN	URBANE	DOCKET
VULGAR	BYGONE	AWAKEN	DRAWER	NEARBY	SLAVIC	BABBLE	INBRED	WABBLE	DOCTOR
AVATAR	BYPASS	AZALEA	ELAPSE	NIACIN	SNATCH	BABOON	JABBER	WEBBED	EBCDIC
AVAUNT	BYPATH	BEACON	ENABLE	NUANCE	SPADIX	BOBBIN	JOBBER	WOBBLE	ECCLES
AVENGE	BYPLAY	BEADLE	ENAMEL	OPAQUE	SPARSE	BOBBLE	KABUKI	ACCEDE	ECCLUS
AVENUE	BYWORD	BEAGLE	ENAMOR	ORACLE	SPATHE	BOBCAT	KIBBLE	ACCENT	ENCAMP
AVERSE	CYGNET	BEAKER	FEALTY	ORANGE	SPAVIN	BUBBLE	KIBOSH	ACCEPT	ENCASE
AVIARY	CYMBAL	BEANIE	FIANCE	ORATOR	STABLE	CABALA	KOBOLD	ACCESS	ENCODE
AVOCET	DYBBUK	BEAUTY	FIASCO	PEAHEN	STAMEN	CABANA	LABIAL	ACCORD	ENCORE
AVOUCH	DYNAMO	BEAVER	FLABBY	PEAKED	STANCE	COBALT	LABILE	ACCOST	ENCYST
EVINCE	EYELET	BLANCH	FLACON	PEANUT	STANCH	COBBLE	LABIUM	ACCRUE	ESCAPE
EVOLVE	EYELID	BLAZER	FLAGON	PHAROS	STANZA	COBWEB	LABOUR	ACCUSE	ESCHEW
OVERDO	GYPSUM	BLAZON	FLANGE	PIAZZA	STAPES	CUBISM	LIBIDO	ALCOVE	ESCORT
OVERLY	GYRATE	BOATER	FLASHY	PLACER	STAPLE	DABBLE	LIBYAN	ANCHOR	ESCROW
SVELTE	HYAENA	BRAISE	FLATUS	PLACID	STARCH	DEBARK	LOBULE	ARCADE	ESCUDO
AWAKEN	HYBRID	BRANCH	FLAUNT	PLAGUE	STARVE	DEBASE	LUBBER	ARCANE	EUCHRE
AWEARY	HYPHEN	BRANDY	FLAVOR	PLAINT	STATIC	DEBATE	MOBILE	ARCCOS	EXCEED
AWEIGH	HYSSOP	BRAZEN	FLAXEN	PLANET	STATUE	DEBRIS	NEBULA	ARCHON	EXCEPT
AWHILE	LYCEUM	CHAFER	FRACAS	PLAQUE	STATUS	DEBTOR	NIBBLE	ARCNET	EXCESS
AWHIRL	MYOPIA	CHAISE	FRAPPE	PLASMA	STAVES	DEBUNK	NOBODY	ARCSIN	EXCISE
AWNING	MYRIAD	CHALET	GLANCE	PLATEN	SWATCH	DIBBLE	NUBBIN	ARCTAN	EXCITE
KWACHA	MYRTLE	CHANCE	GOALIE	PRAISE	SWATHE	DOBBIN	NUBBLE	ARCTIC	EXCUSE
SWATCH	MYSELF	CHANCY	GOATEE	PRANCE	TEACUP	DUBBIN	NUBILE	ASCEND	FACADE
SWATHE	MYSTIC	CHANGE	GRABEN	PRAYER	TEAPOT	DYBBUK	PEBBLE	ASCENT	FACIAL
SWERVE	OYSTER	CHAPEL	GRADER	QBASIC	TEASEL	EMBALM	PUBLIC	BACKER	FACILE
SWITCH	PYRITE	CHARGE	GRAINY	QUAHOG	THANKS	EMBANK	RABBET	BACKUP	FACING
SWIVEL	PYTHON	CHASER	GRANGE	QUAINT	THATCH	EMBARK	RABBIT	BECALM	FACTOR
TWEEDY	SYLVAN	CHASTE	GRATIS	QUAKER	TRADER	EMBLEM	RABBLE	BECKON	FACULA
TWELVE	SYMBOL	CHATTY	GRAVEL	QUARRY	TRAGIC	EMBODY	RABIES	BECOME	FECUND
TWENTY	SYNTAX	CHAUNT	GRAVID	QUARTO	TRANCE	EMBOSS	REBATE	BICEPS	FICKLE
TWINGE	SYPHON	CLAMMY	GRAYED	QUARTZ	TRANSL	EMBRYO	REBORN	BICKER	HACKER
TWITCH	SYSTEM	CLAMOR	HEALTH	QUASAR	TRANSP	ERBIUM	REBUFF	BOCCIE	HACKIE
EXCEED	TYCOON	CLAQUE	HEARSE	QUAVER	TRAUMA	FABIAN	REBUKE	BUCKET	HACKLE
EXCEPT	TYPHUS	CLARET	HEARTH	REALLY	TRAVEL	FABLED	RIBALD	BUCKLE	HECKLE
EXCESS	TYPIFY	CLASSY	HEARTY	REALTY	UNABLE	FABRIC	RIBAND	CACHET	HECTIC
EXCISE	TYPIST	CLAUSE	HEAVEN	REAMER	URACIL	FIBRIL	RIBBON	CACKLE	HECTOR
EXCITE	TYRANT	COARSE	HIATUS	REASON	URANIC	FIBRIN	ROBBER	CACTUS	HICCUP
EXCUSE	ZYGOTE	CRABBY	HOAGIE	SCAMPI	URANUS	FIBULA	ROBUST	CICADA	HOCKEY
EXEMPT	AZALEA	CRADLE	HOARSE	SCANTY	USABLE	GABBLE	RUBBER	COCCUS	INCASE
EXHALE		CRAFTY	HYAENA	SCARAB	VIABLE	GABBRO	RUBBLE	COCCYX	INCEST
EXHORT		CRANKY	ITALIC	SCARCE	WEAKEN	GIBBER	RUBRIC	COCKLE	INCISE
EXHUME		CRANNY	KLATCH	SEABED	WEAKLY	GIBBET	SUBDUE	COCOON	INCITE
EXODUS		CRATER	KWACHA	SEALER	WEALTH	GIBBON	SUBLET	CUCKOO	INCOME

JACKAL	RECTOR	BEDBUG	MADDEN	SODDEN	CREWEL	PLEXUS	TREATY	EFFETE	ARGYLE
JACKET	RECTUM	BEDECK	MADDER	SODIUM	CUESTA	POETRY	TREBLE	EFFIGY	AUGURY
JOCKEY	RICHES	BEDLAM	MADMAN	SODOMY	DAEMON	PREACH	TREMOR	EFFORT	AUGUST
JOCOSE	ROCKER	BEDPAN	MADRAS	SUDDEN	DEEJAY	PRECIS	TRENCH	ENFOLD	BAGMAN
JOCUND	ROCKET	BODICE	MEDDLE	TEDIUM	DEEPEN	PREFAB	TREPAN	GAFFER	BAGNIO
LACKEY	RUCKUS	BODILY	MEDIAL	TIDBIT	DIESEL	PREFER	TSETSE	GIFTED	BEGGAR
LACTIC	SACHEM	BODKIN	MEDIAN	TODDLE	DREARY	PREFIX	TWEEDY	GUFFAW	BEGONE
LACUNA	SACHET	BUDGET	MEDICO	UNDIES	DREDGE	PRELIM	TWELVE	INFAMY	BIGAMY
LECTOR	SACRED	BUDGIE	MEDIUM	UNDULY	DRENCH	PREMED	TWENTY	INFANT	BIGWIG
LICHEE	SACRUM	CADDIE	MEDLEY	UPDATE	DRESSY	PREMIX	UNEASY	INFECT	BOGGLE
LICHEN	SECEDE	CODDLE	MIDAIR	WADDLE	DUENDE	PREPAY	UNESCO	INFEST	BYGONE
LOCALE	SECOND	CODGER	MIDDAY	ZODIAC	DUENNA	PRESET	UNEVEN	INFIRM	COGENT
LOCATE	SECRET	CODIFY	MIDDEN	ACETIC	ELEVEN	PRESTO	UREMIA	INFLOW	COGNAC
LOCKER	SECTOR	CUDDLE	MIDDLE	AGENCY	EMERGE	PRETTY	URETER	INFLUX	CYGNET
LOCKET	SECURE	CUDGEL	MIDGET	AGENDA	EMETIC	PREWAR	USEFUL	INFOLD	DAGGER
LOCKUP	SICKEN	DEDUCE	MIDWAY	AMENDS	ENERGY	PSEUDO	USENET	INFORM	DEGREE
LOCUST	SICKLE	DEDUCT	MODERN	AMERCE	EXEMPT	PUEBLO	UTERUS	INFUSE	DIGEST
LUCENT	SOCCER	DODDER	MODEST	ANEMIA	EYELET	QUEASY	WEEKLY	MUFFIN	DOGGED
LYCEUM	SOCIAL	ELDEST	MODIFY	APERCU	EYELID	QUENCH	WEEVIL	MUFFLE	DOGLEG
MACAPP	SOCIOL	ENDEAR	MODISH	AVENGE	FAECAL	REEFER	WHEEZE	OFFEND	DUGOUT
MACRON	SOCKET	ENDING	MODULE	AVENUE	FAERIE	SEEMLY	WHEEZY	OFFICE	EAGLET
MICMAC	SUCCOR	ENDIVE	MUDDLE	AVERSE	FEEBLE	SEESAW	WHENCE	OFFING	EDGING
MICRON	SUCKER	ENDRIN	NODDLE	AWEARY	FEELER	SEETHE	WHERRY	OFFISH	EGGNOG
MSCDEX	SUCKLE	ENDURE	NODULE	AWEIGH	FIERCE	SHEATH	WIENER	OFFSET	EIGHTY
NECTAR	TACKLE	ENDURO	NUDISM	BEETLE	FIESTA	SHEAVE	WOEFUL	OXFORD	ENGAGE
NICETY	TACTIC	FEDORA	ODDITY	BLEACH	FLEECE	SHEIKH	WREATH	PIFFLE	ENGINE
NICKEL	TICKER	FIDDLE	OODLES	BLEARY	FLESHY	SHELVE	WRENCH	PUFFIN	ENGRAM
NICKER	TICKET	FIDGET	ORDAIN	BLENCH	FOEMAN	SHERRY	WRETCH	RAFFIA	ENGULF
OCCULT	TICKLE	FODDER	ORDEAL	BREACH	FOETAL	SIERRA	AFFAIR	RAFFLE	FAGGOT
OCCUPY	TOCSIN	FUDDLE	ORDURE	BREAST	FREEZE	SIESTA	AFFECT	RAFTER	FIGURE
ORCHID	TUCKER	GADFLY	PADDLE	BREATH	FRENCH	SKETCH	AFFIRM	REFILL	GAGGLE
PACIFY	TYCOON	GADGET	PEDANT	BREECH	FRENZY	SKEWER	AFFORD	REFINE	GIGGLE
PACKER	UNCIAL	GODSON	PEDDLE	BREEZE	FRESCO	SLEAZY	AFFRAY	REFLEX	GIGOLO
PACKET	UNCLAD	HUDDLE	PIDDLE	BREVET	GAELIC	SLEDGE	BAFFLE	REFLUX	GOGGLE
PECTIN	UNCLOG	INDEED	PIDGIN	CAECUM	GEEZER	SLEEPY	BEFALL	REFORM	HAGGIS
PICKAX	UNCOIL	INDENT	PODIUM	CAESAR	GHETTO	SLEEVE	BEFORE	REFRIG	HAGGLE
PICKET	UNCORK	INDIAN	PUDDLE	CHEEKY	GNEISS	SLEIGH	BEFOUL	REFUGE	HEGIRA
PICKLE	UNCURL	INDICT	RADIAL	CHEERY	GREASE	SLEUTH	BUFFER	REFUND	INGEST
PICKUP	URCHIN	INDIGO	RADIAN	CHEESE	ICEBOX	SNEEZE	BUFFET	REFUSE	JAGGED
PICNIC	VACANT	INDITE	RADISH	CHEQUE	ICEMAN	SOEVER	CAFTAN	REFUTE	JAGUAR
POCKET	VACATE	INDIUM	RADIUM	CHERRY	IPECAC	SPECIE	COFFEE	RUFFLE	JIGGER
PUCKER	VACUUM	INDOOR	RADIUS	CHERUB	IRENIC	SPECIF	COFFER	SAFARI	JIGGLE
RACEME	VECTOR	INDUCE	REDACT	CLEAVE	LEEWAY	SPEECH	COFFIN	SAFETY	JIGSAW
RACISM	VICTIM	INDUCT	REDCAP	CLENCH	MAENAD	STEADY	DEFACE	SOFTEN	JOGGLE
RACKET	VICTOR	IODIDE	REDDEN	CLERGY	NEEDLE	STENCH	DEFAME	SUFFER	JUGGLE
RECALL	VICUNA	IODINE	REDEEM	CLERIC	OCELOT	STEPPE	DEFEAT	SUFFIX	KEGLER
RECANT	WICKED	IODIZE	REDUCE	CLEVER	OMELET	STEREO	DEFECT	TIFFIN	LAGOON
RECEDE	WICKER	JUDAIC	RIDDEN	CLEVIS	ONEIDA	SVELTE	DEFEND	TOFFEE	LEGACY
RECENT	WICKET	KIDNAP	RIDDLE	COERCE	OVERDO	SWERVE	DEFILE	UNFAIR	LEGATE
RECESS	ABDUCT	KIDNEY	RODENT	COEVAL	OVERLY	TEEPEE	DEFINE	UNFOLD	LEGATO
RECIPE	ADDEND	LADDER	RUDDER	CREASE	PEEWEE	TEETER	DEFORM	UNFURL	LEGEND
RECITE	ADDICT	LADDIE	SADDEN	CREATE	PHENOL	TEETHE	DEFRAY	WAFFLE	LEGION
RECKON	ADDUCE	LADING	SADDLE	CRECHE	PIERCE	THEIRS	DEFUSE	AFGHAN	LEGMAN
RECOIL	AIDMAN	LEDGER	SADISM	CREDIT	PLEASE	THEISM	DIFFER	ANGINA	LEGUME
RECORD	ARDENT	LODGER	SEDATE	CREEPY	PLEDGE	THENCE	DUFFER	ANGORA	LIGATE
RECOUP	BADGER	MADAME	SEDUCE	CREOLE	PLENTY	THEORY	EFFACE	ARGENT	LIGHTS
RECTAL	BEDAUB	MADCAP	SIDING	CRETIN	PLENUM	THESIS	EFFECT	ARGOSY	LOGGIA

LOGJAM	AWHIRL	BRIDAL	GRISLY	SKIMPY	WAIVER	BALBOA	FILLER	PALACE	SOLEMN
MAGGOT	BEHALF	BRIDGE	GUIDON	SKINNY	WEIGHT	BALEEN	FILLET	PALATE	SPLASH
MAGNET	BEHAVE	BRIDLE	GUILTY	SLIDER	WHILOM	BALLAD	FILLIP	PALEON	SPLEEN
MAGPIE	BEHEAD	BRIGHT	GUINEA	SLIEST	WHILST	BALLET	FILTER	PALING	SPLICE
MAGYAR	BEHEST	BRITON	GUITAR	SLIGHT	WHIMSY	BALLOT	FOLDER	PALLET	SPLINE
MEGOHM	BEHIND	CAIMAN	HAIRDO	SLIPUP	WHINNY	BALSAM	FOLKSY	PALLID	SPLINT
MIGHTY	BEHOLD	CHICHI	HEIFER	SLIVER	WHITEN	BELDAM	FOLLOW	PALLOR	SULFUR
NEGATE	BEHOOF	CHICLE	HEIGHT	SMILAX	WRITER	BELFRY	GALAXY	PALMER	SULLEN
NOGGIN	CAHOOT	CHILLY	IBIDEM	SMIRCH	WRITHE	BELIEF	GALENA	PALTER	SULTAN
NUGGET	COHEIR	CHINTZ	ICICLE	SMITHY	ABJECT	BELIKE	GALLEY	PALTRY	SULTRY
ORGASM	COHERE	CHISEL	IDIOCY	SNIPPY	ABJURE	BELLOW	GALLIC	PELAGE	SYLVAN
PAGODA	COHORT	CHITIN	JAILER	SNITCH	ADJOIN	BELONG	GALLON	PELLET	TALENT
PIGEON	DAHLIA	CLICHE	JOINER	SNIVEL	ADJURE	BELUGA	GALLOP	PELVIS	TALLOW
PIGLET	DEHORN	CLIENT	JUICER	SOIGNE	ADJUST	BILLET	GALORE	PHLEGM	TALMUD
PIGNUT	ETHANE	CLIMAX	KAISER	SOIREE	CAJOLE	BILLOW	GALOSH	PHLOEM	TELLER
PIGPEN	ETHICS	CLINCH	KNIGHT	SPIDER	ENJOIN	BOLERO	GOLDEN	PILFER	TELNET
PIGSTY	ETHNIC	CLINIC	LOITER	SPIGOT	HIJACK	BULBUL	GULDEN	PILING	TILLER
POGROM	ETHNOL	CLIQUE	MAIDEN	SPINAL	INJECT	BULLET	GULLET	PILLAR	ULLAGE
RAGGED	EXHALE	COITUS	MAILED	SPINEL	INJURE	CALCIC	HALALA	PILLOW	UNLACE
RAGLAN	EXHORT	CRINGE	MOIETY	SPINET	INJURY	CALICO	HALITE	POLDER	UNLADE
RAGOUT	EXHUME	CRISIS	ODIOUS	SPIRAL	JEJUNE	CALIPH	HALLOW	POLEAX	UNLESS
REGAIN	FUHRER	CRITIC	OJIBWA	SPIREA	JUJUBE	CALLOW	HALTER	POLICE	UNLIKE
REGALE	INHALE	DAINTY	OPIATE	SPIRIT	OBJECT	CALLUS	HALVES	POLICY	UNLOAD
REGARD	INHERE	DOINGS	ORIENT	STICKY	REJECT	CALVES	HELIUM	POLISH	UNLOCK
REGENT	INHUME	DRIVEL	ORIGIN	STIFLE	REJOIN	CELERY	HELMET	POLITE	UPLAND
REGIME	JOHNNY	DRIVER	ORIOLE	STIGMA	UNJUST	CELLAR	HOLDUP	POLITY	UPLIFT
REGION	MAHOUT	EDIBLE	ORISON	STINGY	ALKALI	CILIUM	HOLLER	POLLEN	UPLOAD
REGNAL	MOHAIR	ELICIT	OTIOSE	STITCH	ANKLET	COLLAR	HOLLOW	PULLET	VALISE
REGRET	MOHAWK	ELIXIR	PAIUTE	SUITOR	BAKERY	COLLAT	ILLUME	PULLEY	VALLEY
RIGGER	REHASH	EMIGRE	PHILOS	SWITCH	BIKINI	COLLIE	ILLUST	PULPIT	VALUED
RUGGED	SCHEME	ENIGMA	PLIANT	SWIVEL	DAKOTA	COLLOQ	INLAID	PULSAR	VELLUM
SIGILL	SCHISM	ENISLE	PLIERS	TAILOR	ESKIMO	COLONY	INLAND	RELATE	VELOUR
SIGNAL	SCHIST	EVINCE	PLIGHT	THIEVE	INKJET	COLUMN	ISLAND	RELENT	VELVET
SIGNET	SCHOOL	FAILLE	PLINTH	THIRST	LIKELY	DALASI	JALOPY	RELICT	VILIFY
TIGHTS	SCHUSS	FAIRLY	POISON	THIRTY	LIKING	DELETE	KELVIN	RELIEF	VILLUS
TOGGLE	SPHERE	FLIGHT	PRIEST	TOILET	LIKUTA	DELUDE	KILTER	RELISH	VOLLEY
TUGRIK	SPHINX	FLIMSY	PRIMAL	TRIAGE	MAKEUP	DELUGE	MALADY	RELIVE	VOLUME
UNGIRD	UNHAND	FLINCH	PRIMER	TRICKY	MAKUTA	DELUXE	MALIAN	ROLLER	VOLUTE
URGENT	UNHOLY	FLITCH	PRINCE	TRIFLE	MIKADO	DILATE	MALICE	SALAAM	VULGAR
VAGARY	UNHOOK	FOIBLE	PRINTF	TRIODE	MUKLUK	DILUTE	MALIGN	SALAMI	WALLET
VAGINA	UPHILL	FRIARY	PRIORY	TRIPLE	RAKISH	DOLLAR	MALLET	SALARY	WALLOP
VAGROM	UPHOLD	FRIDAY	PRISON	TRIPLY	TAKING	DOLLOP	MALLOW	SALINE	WALLOW
WAGGLE	WAHINE	FRIEND	PRISSY	TRIPOD	UNKIND	DOLMEN	MELLOW	SALIVA	WALNUT
WIGGLE	YAHWEH	FRIEZE	PRIVET	TRITON	UPKEEP	DULCET	MELODY	SALLOW	WALRUS
WIGGLY	AFIELD	FRIGHT	QUINCE	TRIUNE	VIKING	ECLAIR	MILDEW	SALMON	WELKIN
WIGLET	AKIMBO	FRIGID	QUINSY	TRIVET	ABLAZE	ENLIST	MILIEU	SALOON	WELTER
WIGWAG	ALIGHT	FRINGE	QUIVER	TRIVIA	ABLOOM	EOLIAN	MILLER	SALUTE	WILLOW
WIGWAM	ANIMAL	FRISKY	RAISIN	TWINGE	AFLAME	EULOGY	MILLET	SALVER	YELLOW
YOGURT	ANIMUS	GAIETY	SAILOR	TWITCH	AFLOAT	FALCON	MOLDER	SELDOM	ADMIRE
ZIGZAG	APIARY	GAITER	SHIELD	UNICEF	AGLEAM	FALLOW	MOLEST	SELECT	ALMOND
ZYGOTE	APICAL	GEISHA	SHIEST	UNIQUE	ALLEGE	FALTER	MOLTEN	SELVES	ALMOST
ADHERE	APIECE	GLIDER	SHIFTY	UNISEX	ALLIED	FELINE	MULLET	SILAGE	ARMADA
AGHAST	ARIGHT	GLITCH	SHIMMY	UNISON	ALLUDE	FELLAH	NELSON	SILENT	ARMFUL
ASHLAR	AVIARY	GOITER	SHINER	UNITED	ALLURE	FELLOW	OBLATE	SILICA	ARMLET
ASHORE	BLIGHT	GRIEVE	SHINNY	URINAL	APLOMB	FELONY	OBLIGE	SILVER	ARMORY
ASHRAM	BLITHE	GRILLE	SHINTO	VOICED	ASLANT	FILIAL	OBLONG	SOLACE	ARMPIT
AWHILE	BOILER	GRIPPE	SHIVER	WAITER	ASLEEP	FILING	OOLITE	SOLDER	BAMBOO

BEMIRE	GAMBOL	RAMBLE	ABNAKI	CINDER	GENTRY	MANGLE	RANCHO	TINSEL	BLOWSY
BEMOAN	GAMETE	RAMIFY	ANNALS	CINEMA	GINGER	MANIAC	RANCID	TONGUE	BLOWUP
BEMUSE	GAMINE	RAMROD	ANNEAL	CONCUR	GINKGO	MANIOC	RANCOR	TONSIL	BOODLE
BOMBER	GAMMER	REMAIN	ANNUAL	CONDOM	GUNMAN	MANNED	RANDOM	TUNDRA	BOOKIE
BUMMER	GAMMON	REMAND	ARNICA	CONDOR	GUNNER	MANNER	RANGER	TUNNEL	BOOTEE
BUMPER	GIMBAL	REMARK	AWNING	CONFAB	HANDLE	MANQUE	RANKLE	VANDAL	BROACH
CAMBER	GIMLET	REMEDY	BANANA	CONFED	HANGAR	MANTEL	RANSOM	VANISH	BROGAN
CAMERA	HAMLET	REMIND	BANDED	CONFER	HANKER	MANTIS	RENDER	VANITY	BROGUE
CAMPER	HAMMER	REMISS	BANDIT	CONSOL	HANSEL	MANTLE	RENEGE	VENDEE	BROKEN
CAMPUS	HAMPER	REMORA	BANGLE	CONSTR	HANSOM	MANTRA	RENNET	VENDER	BROKER
CEMENT	HOMAGE	REMOTE	BANISH	CONSUL	HINDER	MANUAL	RENNIN	VENDOR	BRONCO
COMBAT	HOMELY	REMOVE	BANNER	CONVEX	HONEST	MANURE	RENOWN	VENEER	BRONZE
COMBER	HOMILY	ROMANO	BANTAM	CONVEY	HONOUR	MENACE	RENTAL	VENIAL	BROOCH
COMDEX	HOMINY	ROMPER	BANTER	CONVOY	HUNGER	MENAGE	RENTAL	VENIRE	BROWSE
COMEDY	HUMANE	RUMBLE	BANYAN	CUNNER	HUNKER	MENIAL	RINGER	VENOUS	CHOICE
COMELY	HUMBLE	RUMPLE	BANZAI	DANDER	IGNITE	MENINX	RUNLET	VINOUS	CHOKER
COMFIT	HUMBUG	RUMPUS	BENDER	DANDLE	IGNORE	MENSES	RUNNEL	WANDER	CHOLER
COMING	HUMOUR	SAMPAN	BENIGN	DANGER	INNATE	MENTAL	RUNNER	WANGLE	CHOOSE
COMITY	IMMUNE	SAMPLE	BENUMB	DANGLE	INNING	MENTOR	RUNOFF	WANTON	CHOOSY
COMMIT	IMMURE	SEMITE	BENZOL	DANISH	IONIZE	MINDED	RUNWAY	WINDER	CHOPPY
COMMON	INMATE	SIMIAN	BINARY	DENGUE	JANGLE	MINGLE	SANDAL	WINDOW	CHORAL
COMPAQ	INMOST	SIMILE	BINHEX	DENIAL	JENNET	MINION	SANITY	WINDUP	CHOREA
COMPAR	JUMBLE	SIMMER	BONBON	DENIER	JINGLE	MINNOW	SENATE	WINGED	CHORUS
COMPEL	JUMPER	SIMONY	BONITO	DENOTE	JUNGLE	MINUET	SENECA	WINKER	CHOSEN
COMPLY	KIMONO	SIMPER	BONNET	DENTAL	JUNIOR	MINUTE	SENILE	WINKLE	CLOCHE
CUMBER	LAMENT	SIMPLE	BONSAI	DENTIN	JUNKER	MONDAY	SENIOR	WINNER	CLOSET
CYMBAL	LAMINA	SOMBER	BUNDLE	DENUDE	JUNKET	MONGER	SENITI	WINNOW	CLOTHE
DAMAGE	LIMBER	SUMMER	BUNGLE	DINGHY	JUNKIE	MONISM	SENSOR	WINTER	CLOVEN
DAMASK	LIMPET	SUMMIT	BUNION	DINGLE	KENNEL	MONKEY	SENTRY	WINTRY	CLOVER
DAMPEN	LIMPID	SUMMON	BUNKER	DINGUS	KINDLE	MONODY	SINFUL	WONDER	COOKIE
DAMPER	LUMBAR	SYMBOL	BUNKUM	DINNER	KINDLY	NINETY	SINGLE	WONTED	COOLER
DAMSEL	LUMBER	TAMALE	CANAPE	DONATE	LANCER	NONAGE	SINKER	YANKEE	COOLIE
DAMSON	LUMMOX	TAMPER	CANARD	DONKEY	LANCET	NONCOM	SONATA	YANQUI	COOPER
DEMAND	MAMMAL	TAMPON	CANARY	DYNAMO	LANDAU	NONFAT	SONNET	YONDER	COOTIE
DEMEAN	MAMMON	TEMPER	CANCAN	EUNUCH	LANDED	NUNCIO	SUNDAE	ZENANA	CROCUS
DEMISE	MEMBER	TEMPLE	CANCEL	FENDER	LANDER	ORNATE	SUNDAY	ZENITH	CROTCH
DEMODE	MEMOIR	TIMBER	CANCER	FENIAN	LENGTH	ORNERY	SUNDER	ZINNIA	CROUCH
DEMOTE	MEMORY	TIMBRE	CANDID	FENNEL	LENITY	ORNITH	SUNDRY	ZONKED	DEODAR
DEMURE	MIMOSA	TIMELY	CANDLE	FINALE	LENTIL	PANAMA	SUNKEN	ABOARD	DOODAD
DIMITY	MOMENT	TOMATO	CANDOR	FINDER	LINAGE	PANDER	SUNLIT	ABOUND	DOODLE
DIMMER	MUMBLE	TOMBOY	CANINE	FINERY	LINDEN	PANTIE	SUNSET	AMOEBA	DROGUE
DIMPLE	MUMMER	TOMCAT	CANKER	FINGER	LINEAL	PANTRY	SUNTAN	AMORAL	DROPSY
DOMAIN	NAMELY	TOMTIT	CANNED	FINIAL	LINEAR	PENCIL	SYNTAX	AMOUNT	DROVER
DOMINO	NIMBLE	TUMBLE	CANNON	FINISH	LINEUP	PENMAN	TANDEM	ANOINT	DROWSE
DUMDUM	NIMBUS	TUMULT	CANNOT	FINITE	LINGER	PENNON	TANGLE	APOGEE	DROWSY
ENMESH	NIMROD	UNMASK	CANOPY	FONDLE	LINING	PENURY	TANKER	AROUND	EGGISM
ENMITY	NUMBER	UNMEET	CANTER	FONDUE	LINKED	PINCER	TANNER	AROUSE	ENOUGH
ERMINE	ORMOLU	UNMOOR	CANTLE	FUNGUS	LINKUP	PINEAL	TANNIN	ATOMIC	EROTIC
FAMILY	OSMIUM	UPMOST	CANTON	FUNNEL	LINNET	PINION	TENANT	ATONAL	EVOLVE
FAMINE	PAMPER	UTMOST	CANTOR	GANDER	LINTEL	PINKIE	TENDER	AVOCET	EXODUS
FAMISH	PCMCIA	WAMBLE	CANVAS	GANNET	LONELY	PINCHO	TENDON	AVOUCH	EXOTIC
FAMOUS	PIMPLE	WAMPUM	CANYON	GANTRY	LUNACY	PONDER	TENNIS	BAOBAB	FLOOZY
FEMALE	POMADE	WIMBLE	CENSER	GENDER	MANAGE	PONGEE	TENPIN	BIOPSY	FLOPPY
FOMENT	POMMEL	WIMPLE	CENSOR	GENERA	MANANA	PUNDIT	TENURE	BIOTIC	FLORAL
FUMBLE	POMPON	WOMBAT	CENSUS	GENIAL	MANEGE	PUNISH	TINDER	BIOTIN	FLORID
GAMBIT	PUMICE	YAMMER	CENTER	GENIUS	MANFUL	PUNKIN	TINGLE	BLOTCH	FLORIN
GAMBLE	PUMMEL	ZOMBIE	CENTRE	GENTLE	MANGER	QINTAR	TINKER	BLOUSE	FLOSSY

FLOWER	SHODDY	APPEAL	IMPEND	RUPIAH	BARFLY	CIRRUS	FORBID	IRRUPT	NORDIC
FOOTED	SHOULD	APPEAR	IMPERF	SEPSIS	BARIUM	CORBEL	FOREGO	JARGON	NORMAL
FROLIC	SHOVEL	APPEND	IMPISH	SEPTIC	BARKER	CORDON	FOREST	JERKIN	NORMAN
FROWSY	SHOWER	APPLET	IMPORT	SIPHON	BARLEY	CORNEA	FORGET	JERSEY	NORTON
FROZEN	SLOGAN	APPROX	IMPOSE	SUPERB	BARRED	CORNER	FORINT	JURIST	ONRUSH
GLOBAL	SLOPPY	ASPECT	IMPOST	SUPINE	BARREL	CORNET	FORKED	KARATE	PARADE
GLOSSY	SLOUCH	ASPIRE	IMPUGN	SUPPER	BARREN	CORONA	FORMAL	KERMIT	PARCEL
GLOWER	SLOUGH	BYPASS	IMPURE	SUPPLE	BARRIO	CORPSE	FORMAT	KERNEL	PARDON
GOOBER	SLOVEN	BYPATH	IMPUTE	SUPPLY	BARROW	CORPUS	FORMER	KIRTLE	PARENT
GOODLY	SMOOCH	BYPLAY	KIPPER	SYPHON	BARTER	CORRAL	FURORE	KOREAN	PARIAH
GROCER	SMOOTH	CAPFUL	KOPECK	TAPPET	BERATE	CORSET	FURROW	KORUNA	PARING
GROGGY	SNOBOL	CAPTOR	LAPDOG	TIPPET	BERBER	CORTEX	GARAGE	LARDER	PARISH
GROOVE	SNOOTY	CIPHER	LAPPET	TIPPLE	BEREFT	CORYZA	GARBLE	LARIAT	PARITY
GROOVY	SNOOZE	COPIER	LAPTOP	TIPTOE	BIRDIE	CURATE	GARCON	LARYNX	PARLAY
GROTTO	SOOTHE	COPING	LEPTON	TOPPLE	BORATE	CURDLE	GARDEN	LORDLY	PARLEY
GROUCH	SPOKEN	COPPER	LUPINE	TYPHUS	BORDER	CURFEW	GARGLE	MARACA	PARLOR
GROUND	SPONGE	COPTER	MOPPET	TYPIFY	BOREAL	CURIUM	GARISH	MARAUD	PARODY
GROUSE	SPOTTY	COPULA	NAPALM	TYPIST	BORROW	CURLEW	GARLIC	MARBLE	PAROLE
GROVEL	SPOUSE	CUPOLA	NAPERY	UMPIRE	BURDEN	CURSOR	GARNER	MARCEL	PARROT
GROWTH	STOCKY	DAPPER	NAPKIN	UNPACK	BUREAU	CURTSY	GARNET	MARGIN	PARSEC
HOODOO	STODGY	DAPPLE	NEPHEW	UNPILE	BURGEE	CURVET	GARRET	MARINA	PARSON
HOOKAH	STOLEN	DEPART	NIPPER	UNPLUG	BURGLE	DARING	GARTER	MARINE	PARTLY
HOOKER	STOLID	DEPEND	NIPPLE	UPPISH	BURIAL	DARKEN	GERBIL	MARKED	PERIOD
HOOKUP	STOLON	DEPICT	OPPOSE	UPPITY	BURLAP	DARNEL	GERMAN	MARKET	PERISH
HOOPLA	STONED	DEPLOY	ORPHAN	VAPORY	BURNER	DARTER	GERUND	MARKKA	PERMIT
IRONIC	STOOGE	DEPORT	OSPREY	WAPITI	BURROW	DERAIL	GIRDER	MARKUP	PERSON
ISOBAR	TAOISM	DEPOSE	PAPACY	ZEPHYR	BURSAR	DERIDE	GIRDLE	MARLIN	PERUKE
ISOMER	THORAX	DEPUTE	PAPAIN	ZIPPER	CARAFE	DERIVE	GURGLE	MARMOT	PERUSE
KAOLIN	THOUGH	DEPUTY	PAPAYA	ACQUIT	CARBON	DERMAL	GURKHA	MAROON	PHRASE
LOOPER	TOOTHY	DIPPER	PAPIST	BUQSHA	CARBOY	DERMIS	GYRATE	MARROW	PIRACY
LOOSEN	TROCHE	DOPANT	PAPULE	COQUET	CAREEN	DERRIS	HARASS	MARTEN	PIRATE
MAOISM	TROIKA	DUPLEX	PEPPER	LIQUID	CAREER	DIRECT	HARBOR	MARTIN	PORKER
MYOPIA	TROJAN	EEPROM	PEPSIN	LIQUOR	CARESS	DIRHAM	HARDEN	MARTYR	POROUS
NOODLE	TROPHY	EMPIRE	PEPTIC	PEQUOT	CARHOP	DIRNDL	HARDLY	MARVEL	PORTAL
PEOPLE	TROPIC	EMPLOY	PIPING	PIQUET	CARIES	DORMER	HARKEN	MERCER	PORTER
PHOBIA	TROUGH	ESPRIT	PIPKIN	SEQUEL	CARNAL	DORSAL	HARLOT	MERGER	PORTLY
PHOEBE	TROUPE	EXPAND	PIPPIN	SEQUIN	CARPAL	DURESS	HARROW	MERINO	PURDAH
PHONIC	TROWEL	EXPECT	POPGUN	ABRADE	CARPEL	DURING	HERALD	MERMAN	PURIFY
PHOTOG	UTOPIA	EXPEND	POPLAR	ABROAD	CARPET	EARTHY	HEREBY	MIRAGE	PURINE
PHOTON	VIOLET	EXPERT	POPLIN	ABRUPT	CARREL	EARWAX	HEREIN	MIRROR	PURISM
PLOVER	VIOLIN	EXPIRE	POPPER	ACROSS	CARROT	EARWIG	HEREOF	MORALE	PURITY
POODLE	VOODOO	EXPORT	PUPPET	ADRIFT	CARTEL	EGRESS	HEREON	MORBID	PURPLE
PROFIT	WHOLLY	EXPOSE	RAPIER	ADROIT	CARTON	ENRAGE	HERESY	MORGAN	PURSER
PROLIX	WOODED	GOPHER	RAPINE	AERATE	CARTOP	ENRICH	HERETO	MORGUE	PURSUE
PROLOG	WOODEN	GYPSUM	RAPPEN	AERIAL	CEREAL	ENROLL	HERMIT	MORMON	PURVEY
PROMPT	WOODSY	HAPPEN	REPAIR	AFRAID	CEREUS	ERRAND	HERNIA	MOROSE	PYRITE
PRONTO	WOOFER	HEPCAT	REPAST	AFRESH	CERISE	ERRANT	HEROIN	MORRIS	RAREFY
PROPEL	WOOLEN	HIPPED	REPEAL	AIRMAN	CERIUM	ERRATA	HERPES	MORROW	RARING
PROPER	WOOLLY	HIPPIE	REPEAT	AIRWAY	CERMET	EUREKA	HORNET	MORSEL	SARONG
PROTON	XMODEM	HOPPER	REPENT	ARRANT	CERVIX	FARINA	HORRID	MORTAL	SCRAPE
QUORUM	YEOMAN	HYPHEN	REPINE	ARREST	CHRISM	FARROW	HORROR	MORTAR	SCRAWL
RLOGIN	YMODEM	IMPACT	REPLAY	ARRIVE	CHRIST	FERRET	HORSEY	MURDER	SCREAM
ROOKIE	ZMODEM	IMPAIR	REPORT	ARROYO	CHROME	FERRIC	HURDLE	MURMUR	SCREEN
SCONCE	ALPACA	IMPALA	REPOSE	ATRIUM	CHROMO	FERULE	HURRAH	MYRIAD	SCREWY
SCORCH	ALPINE	IMPALE	REPUTE	AURORA	CIRCLE	FERVID	HURTLE	MYRTLE	SCRIBE
SCORIA	AMPERE	IMPART	RIPPLE	BARBER	CIRCUS	FERVOR	INROAD	NARROW	SCRIMP
SCOTCH	APPALL	IMPEDE	RIPSAW	BARELY	CIRQUE	FORAGE	INRUSH	NEREID	SCRIPT

SCROLL	SURTAX	VARIED	BUSHEL	GOSSIP	MUSEUM	TISSUE	AUTUMN	ENTIRE	MATRIX
SCRUFF	SURVEY	VARLET	BUSILY	GUSHER	MUSKEG	TUSKER	BATEAU	ENTITY	MATRON
SERAPE	TARGET	VERBAL	BUSKIN	GUSSET	MUSKET	TUSSLE	BATHOS	ENTOMB	MATTER
SERAPH	TARIFF	VERGER	BUSTLE	HASSLE	MUSLIM	ULSTER	BATMAN	ENTRAP	MATURE
SERENE	TARPON	VERIFY	CASABA	HASTEN	MUSLIN	UNSEAL	BATTEN	ENTREE	METEOR
SERIAL	TARSUS	VERILY	CASEIN	HOSTEL	MUSSEL	UNSEAT	BATTER	ESTATE	METHOD
SERIES	TARTAN	VERITY	CASHEW	HUSSAR	MUSTER	UNSHIP	BATTLE	ESTEEM	METHYL
SERMON	TARTAR	VERMIN	CASING	HUSTLE	MYSELF	UNSHOD	BETAKE	EXTANT	METIER
SERVER	TEREDO	VERNAL	CASINO	HYSSOP	MYSTIC	UNSNAP	BETHEL	EXTEND	METRIC
SHREWD	TERROR	VERSED	CASKET	INSANE	NESTLE	UNSTOP	BETIDE	EXTENT	METTLE
SHRIEK	THRALL	VERSUS	CASQUE	INSEAM	OBSESS	UNSUNG	BETRAY	EXTERN	MITTEN
SHRIFT	THRASH	VERTEX	CASSIA	INSECT	OSSIFY	UPSHOT	BETTER	EXTORT	MOTHER
SHRIKE	THREAD	VIRAGO	CASTER	INSERT	OUSTER	UPSIDE	BETTOR	FATHER	MOTILE
SHRILL	THREAT	VIRGIN	CASTLE	INSIDE	OYSTER	URSINE	BITING	FATHOM	MOTION
SHRIMP	THRESH	VIRILE	CASUAL	INSIST	PASCAL	VASSAL	BITNET	FATTEN	MOTIVE
SHRINE	THRICE	VIRION	CESIUM	INSOLE	PASSEL	VESPER	BITTER	FETISH	MOTLEY
SHRINK	THRIFT	VIRTUE	COSINE	INSTEP	PASSIM	VESSEL	BOTANY	FETTER	MOTTLE
SHRIVE	THRILL	VORTEX	COSMIC	INSULT	PASTEL	VESTAL	BOTHER	FETTLE	MUTANT
SHROUD	THRIVE	WARBLE	COSMOS	INSURE	PASTOR	VESTEE	BOTTLE	FITFUL	MUTATE
SORDID	THROAT	WARDEN	COSTLY	ITSELF	PASTRY	VESTRY	BOTTOM	FUTILE	MUTINY
SORREL	THRONE	WARDER	CUSPID	JASPER	PESETA	VISAGE	BUTANE	FUTURE	MUTTER
SORROW	THRONG	WARMTH	CUSTOM	JESTER	PESEWA	VISCID	BUTLER	GATHER	MUTTON
SORTIE	THROVE	WARREN	DASHER	JOSTLE	PESTER	VISCUS	BUTTER	GOTHIC	MUTUAL
SPRAIN	THRUSH	WIRING	DESALT	KISMET	PESTLE	VISION	BUTTON	GOTTEN	NATION
SPRAWL	THRUST	WORKER	DESCRY	KISSER	PISTIL	VISUAL	CATCHY	GUTTER	NATIVE
SPREAD	TIRADE	WORSEN	DESERT	KOSHER	PISTOL	WASHER	CATGUT	HATBOX	NATURE
SPRING	TORERO	WORTHY	DESIGN	LASCAR	PISTON	WESKIT	CATION	HATRED	NETHER
SPRINT	TORPID	YARROW	DESIRE	LASSIE	POSEUR	WISDOM	CATKIN	HATTER	NETTLE
SPRITE	TORPOR	ZIRCON	DESIST	LESION	POSSUM	ACTING	CATNAP	HITHER	NITRIC
SPROUT	TORQUE	ABSENT	DESKEW	LESSEE	POSTAL	ACTION	CATNIP	HOTBED	NITWIT
SPRUCE	TORRID	ABSORB	DESPOT	LESSEN	POSTER	ACTIVE	CATSUP	HOTBOX	NOTICE
SPRUNG	TURBAN	ABSURD	DISARM	LESSER	PUSHER	ACTUAL	CATTLE	INTACT	NOTIFY
STRAFE	TURBID	ADSORB	DISBAR	LESSON	RASCAL	ALTAIR	CITIFY	INTAKE	NOTION
STRAIN	TURBOT	ANSWER	DISCUS	LESSOR	RASHER	ANTHEM	CITRON	INTEND	NUTMEG
STRAIT	TUREEN	ASSAIL	DISHED	LISTEN	RASTER	ANTHER	CITRUS	INTENT	NUTRIA
STRAND	TURGID	ASSENT	DISMAL	LUSTER	RESALE	ANTLER	COTTER	INTERJ	OBTAIN
STREAK	TURING	ASSERT	DISMAY	MASCON	RESCUE	ANTRUM	COTTON	INTERN	OBTUSE
STREAM	TURKEY	ASSESS	DISOWN	MASCOT	RESENT	ARTERY	CUTLER	INTONE	OCTANE
STREET	TURNER	ASSIGN	DISPEL	MASQUE	RESIDE	ARTFUL	CUTLET	INTROD	OCTAVE
STRESS	TURNIP	ASSIST	DISTAL	MASSIF	RESIGN	ARTIST	CUTOFF	INTUIT	OCTAVO
STRICT	TURRET	ASSIZE	DISUSE	MASTER	RESIST	ASTERN	CUTOUT	JETSAM	OPTICS
STRIDE	TURTLE	ASSORT	DUSTER	MASTIC	RESORT	ASTHMA	CUTTER	JITNEY	OPTION
STRIFE	TURVES	ASSUME	EASTER	MESCAL	RESULT	ASTRAL	DATIVE	KETTLE	OSTLER
STRIKE	TYRANT	ASSURE	ENSIGN	MESSRS	RESUME	ASTRAY	DETACH	KITSCH	OTTAWA
STRING	UNREAD	BASALT	ENSILE	MISCUE	RISQUE	ASTROL	DETAIL	KITTEN	OUTBID
STRIPE	UNREAL	BASKET	ENSURE	MISERY	ROSARY	ASTRON	DETAIN	LATENT	OUTCRY
STRIVE	UNREEL	BASQUE	ERSATZ	MISFIT	ROSTER	ASTUTE	DETECT	LATHER	OUTFIT
STROBE	UNREST	BESEEM	FASTEN	MISHAP	RUSSET	ATTACH	DETEST	LATTER	OUTFOX
STRODE	UNRIPE	BESIDE	FESTAL	MISLAY	RUSTIC	ATTACK	DETOUR	LETHAL	OUTGUN
STROKE	UNROBE	BESTIR	FESTER	MISSAL	RUSTLE	ATTAIN	DITHER	LETTER	OUTING
STROLL	UNROLL	BESTOW	FISCAL	MISTER	SASHAY	ATTEND	DOTAGE	LITANY	OUTLAW
STRONG	UNROOF	BISECT	FISHER	MISUSE	SESAME	ATTEST	DOTARD	LITCHI	OUTLAY
STROVE	UNRULY	BISHOP	FOSSIL	MOSAIC	SISTER	ATTIRE	DOTTLE	LITMUS	OUTLET
STRUCK	UPREAR	BISQUE	FOSTER	MOSLEM	SYSTEM	ATTRIB	EATERY	LITTER	OUTPUT
STRUNG	UPROAR	BISTRO	FUSION	MOSQUE	TASSEL	ATTUNE	EITHER	LITTLE	OUTRUN
SURETY	UPROOT	BUSBOY	GASKET	MOSTLY	TESTER	AUTHOR	ENTAIL	LOTION	OUTSET
SURREY	UPRUSH	BUSHED	GOSPEL	MUSCLE	TESTIS	AUTISM	ENTICE	MATINS	OUTWIT

PATACA	TATTER	COUNTY	OEUVRE	ADVICE	REVISE	UNWISE	VOYAGE	BANANA	DILATE
PATENT	TATTLE	COUPLE	PAUNCH	ADVISE	REVIVE	UNWRAP	VOYEUR	BASALT	DISARM
PATHOS	TATTOO	COUPON	PAUPER	AMVETS	REVOKE	UPWARD	WAYLAY	BAZAAR	DOMAIN
PATINA	TETCHY	COURSE	PLUCKY	BOVINE	REVOLT	UPWELL	ZOYSIA	BECALM	DONATE
PATOIS	TETHER	COUSIN	PLUNGE	CAVEAT	SAVAGE	UPWIND	BAZAAR	BEDAUB	DOPANT
PATROL	TITBIT	CRUISE	PLURAL	CAVERN	SAVANT	BOXCAR	BEFALL	DOTAGE
PATRON	TITLED	CRUMMY	PLUTON	CAVIAR	SAVIOR	BOXING	DAZZLE	BEHALF	DOTARD
PATTER	TITTER	CRUNCH	POUNCE	CAVITY	SEVERE	FIXITY	ECZEMA	BEHAVE	DREARY
PETARD	TITTLE	CRUTCH	ROUBLE	CAVORT	SOVIET	LUXURY	ENZYME	BERATE	DYNAMO
PETITE	TOTTER	DOUBLE	SAUCER	CIVICS	TAVERN	SEXISM	FIZZLE	BETAKE	ECLAIR
PETREL	ULTIMO	DOUBLY	SCULPT	COVERT	UNVEIL	SEXPOT	GAZEBO	BEWAIL	EFFACE
PETROL	ULTRIX	DOUCHE	SCURRY	DEVICE	VIVACE	SEXTET	GUZZLE	BEWARE	EMBALM
POTAGE	UNTOLD	DRUDGE	SCURVY	DEVISE	VIVIFY	SEXTON	HAZARD	BIGAMY	EMBANK
POTASH	UNTRUE	EQUATE	SCUZZY	DEVOID	ALWAYS	SEXUAL	HUZZAH	BINARY	EMBARK
POTATO	UNTUNE	EQUINE	SLUDGE	DEVOIR	BEWAIL	TUXEDO	LIZARD	BLEACH	ENCAMP
POTBOY	UPTAKE	EQUITY	SLUICE	DEVOTE	BEWARE	ANYHOW	MIZZEN	BLEARY	ENCASE
POTEEN	UPTOWN	FAUCES	SLURRY	DEVOUR	BOWLEG	ANYONE	MUZZLE	BORATE	ENGAGE
POTENT	UPTURN	FAUCET	SMUDGE	DEVOUT	BOWLER	ANYWAY	NOZZLE	BOTANY	ENRAGE
POTHER	VITALS	FEUDAL	SMUTCH	DIVERS	BOWMAN	ASYLUM	NUZZLE	BREACH	ENTAIL
POTION	VOTARY	FLUENT	SOUGHT	DIVERT	BYWORD	BEYOND	PUZZLE	BREAST	EQUATE
POTPIE	VOTIVE	FLUFFY	SOURCE	DIVEST	COWARD	CAYMAN	SIZZLE	BREATH	ERRAND
POTTER	WATERY	FLUNKY	SPURGE	DIVIDE	COWBOY	CAYUGA	VIZARD	BROACH	ERRANT
PUTOUT	WATTLE	FLURRY	SPUTUM	DIVINE	COWMAN	CAYUSE	VIZIER	BUTANE	ERRATA
PUTRID	WETHER	FOUGHT	SQUALL	FAVOUR	COWPOX	COYOTE	WIZARD	BYPASS	ERSATZ
PUTSCH	WITHAL	FOURTH	SQUARE	GOVERN	DAWDLE	DAYBED		BYPATH	ESCAPE
PUTTEE	WITHER	FRUGAL	SQUASH	INVADE	DEWLAP	FLYWAY		CABALA	ESTATE
PUTTER	WITHIN	FRUITY	SQUAWK	INVENT	DOWNER	GAYETY		CABANA	ETHANE
PYTHON	WITTED	FRUMPY	SQUEAK	INVERT	GEWGAW	GEYSER	**4TH LETTER**	CANAPE	EXHALE
RATHER	ZITHER	GAUCHE	SQUEAL	INVEST	HAWKER	HAYMOW		CANARD	EXPAND
RATIFY	ACUITY	GAUCHO	SQUINT	INVITE	HAWSER	HEYDAY	ABBACY	CANARY	EXTANT
RATING	ACUMEN	GLUTEN	SQUIRE	INVOKE	HOWDAH	HOYDEN	ABLAZE	CARAFE	FACADE
RATION	ALUMNA	GOURDE	SQUIRM	JOVIAL	HOWLER	JAYCEE	ABNAKI	CASABA	FEMALE
RATTAN	AMULET	GRUBBY	SQUIRT	LAVAGE	INWARD	JAYGEE	ABOARD	CICADA	FINALE
RATTER	BAUBLE	GRUDGE	STUBBY	LAVISH	KOWTOW	JAYVEE	ABRADE	CLEAVE	FORAGE
RATTLE	BLUING	GRUMPY	STUCCO	LEVITY	LAWFUL	JOYFUL	AERATE	COBALT	FRIARY
RETAIL	BLUISH	HAUNCH	STUDIO	LIVELY	LAWMAN	JOYOUS	AFFAIR	COWARD	GALAXY
RETAIN	BOUGHT	IGUANA	STUFFY	LIVERY	LAWYER	LAYMAN	AFLAME	CREASE	GARAGE
RETAKE	BOUNCE	JAUNTY	STUPID	LIVING	LOWERY	LAYOFF	AFRAID	CREATE	GREASE
RETARD	BOUNTY	JOUNCE	STUPOR	LOVELY	NEWTON	LAYOUT	AGHAST	CURATE	GYRATE
RETINA	BOURSE	LAUNCH	STURDY	LOVING	NOWISE	MAYFLY	ALKALI	DALASI	HALALA
RETIRE	BRUISE	LAUREL	TAUGHT	NAVAHO	ONWARD	MAYHEM	ALPACA	DAMAGE	HARASS
RETORT	BRUNCH	LOUNGE	TOUCAN	NOVELL	PAWNEE	OXYGEN	ALTAIR	DAMASK	HAZARD
RETURN	BRUNET	LOUVER	TOUCHE	NOVENA	PAWPAW	PAYOFF	ALWAYS	DEBARK	HERALD
RITUAL	BRUTAL	MOUSER	TOUCHY	NOVICE	PEWTER	PEYOTE	ANNALS	DEBASE	HIJACK
ROTARY	CAUCUS	MOUSSE	TOUPEE	PAVING	POWDER	PHYLUM	APIARY	DEBATE	HOMAGE
ROTATE	CAUDAL	MOUTON	TOUSLE	QIVIUT	POWWOW	PHYSIC	APPALL	DECADE	HUMANE
ROTTEN	CAUGHT	MUUMUU	TRUANT	RAVAGE	REWARD	PSYCHE	ARCADE	DECAMP	IGUANA
ROTUND	CAUSAL	NAUGHT	TRUDGE	RAVINE	SEWAGE	PSYCHO	ARCANE	DECANT	IMPACT
SATANG	CHUBBY	NAUSEA	TRUISM	RAVISH	SEWING	RHYTHM	ARMADA	DEFACE	IMPAIR
SATEEN	CHUKKA	NAUTCH	TRUSTY	REVAMP	TAWDRY	SAYING	ARRANT	DEFAME	IMPALA
SATIRE	CHUMMY	NEURAL	UNUSED	REVEAL	THWACK	SCYTHE	ASLANT	DEMAND	IMPALE
SATRAP	CHUNKY	NEUROL	USURER	REVERB	THWART	SKYCAP	ASSAIL	DEPART	IMPART
SATURN	CHURCH	NEURON	ZOUAVE	REVERE	TOWARD	STYLUS	ATTACH	DERAIL	INCASE
SETTEE	CLUMSY	NEUTER	ZOUNDS	REVERS	TOWHEE	STYMIE	ATTACK	DESALT	INFAMY
SETTER	CLUTCH	NOUGAT	ADVENT	REVERT	UNWELL	THYMUS	ATTAIN	DETACH	INFANT
SETTLE	COUGAR	NOUGHT	ADVERB	REVIEW	UNWEPT	TRYING	AVIARY	DETAIL	INHALE
SUTURE	COULEE	OCULAR	ADVERT	REVILE	UNWIND	UNYOKE	AWEARY	DETAIN	INLAID

INLAND	PANAMA	SEDATE	VIZARD	GARBLE	SEABED	DEACON	RASCAL	DAWDLE	LEADER
INMATE	PAPACY	SENATE	VOTARY	GERBIL	SHABBY	DESCRY	REDCAP	DEADEN	LINDEN
INNATE	PAPAIN	SERAPE	VOYAGE	GIBBER	SNOBOL	DISCUS	RESCUE	DEADLY	LOADED
INSANE	PAPAYA	SERAPH	WIZARD	GIBBET	SOMBER	DOUCHE	SAUCER	DEODAR	LOADER
INTACT	PARADE	SESAME	WREATH	GIBBON	STABLE	DULCET	SKYCAP	DIADEM	LORDLY
INTAKE	PATACA	SEWAGE	ZENANA	GIMBAL	STUBBY	ELICIT	SOCCER	DODDER	MADDEN
INVADE	PEDANT	SHEATH	ZOUAVE	GLOBAL	SYMBOL	FAECAL	SPECIE	DOODAD	MADDER
INWARD	PELAGE	SHEAVE	ARABIC	GOBBET	TIDBIT	FALCON	SPECIF	DOODLE	MAIDEN
ISLAND	PETARD	SILAGE	ARABLE	GOBBLE	TIMBER	FAUCES	STICKY	DREDGE	MEADOW
JUDAIC	PHRASE	SLEAZY	BABBLE	GOOBER	TIMBRE	FAUCET	STOCKY	DRUDGE	MEDDLE
KARATE	PIRACY	SOLACE	BALBOA	GRABEN	TITBIT	FISCAL	STUCCO	DUMDUM	MIDDAY
LAVAGE	PIRATE	SONATA	BAMBOO	GRUBBY	TOMBOY	FLACON	SUCCOR	EBCDIC	MIDDEN
LEGACY	PLEASE	SPLASH	BAOBAB	HARBOR	TREBLE	FRACAS	TEACUP	EXODUS	MIDDLE
LEGATE	PLIANT	SPRAIN	BARBER	HATBOX	TUMBLE	GARCON	TETCHY	FENDER	MILDEW
LEGATO	POMADE	SPRAWL	BAUBLE	HOBBLE	TURBAN	GAUCHE	TOMCAT	FEUDAL	MINDED
LIGATE	POTAGE	SQUALL	BEDBUG	HOTBED	TURBID	GAUCHO	TOUCAN	FIDDLE	MOLDER
LINAGE	POTASH	SQUARE	BERBER	HOTBOX	TURBOT	GROCER	TOUCHE	FINDER	MONDAY
LITANY	POTATO	SQUASH	BOBBIN	HUBBUB	UNABLE	HEPCAT	TOUCHY	FODDER	MSCDEX
LIZARD	PREACH	SQUAWK	BOBBLE	HUMBLE	USABLE	HICCUP	TRICKY	FOLDER	MUDDLE
LOCALE	QUEASY	STEADY	BOMBER	HUMBUG	VERBAL	HUBCAP	TROCHE	FONDLE	MURDER
LOCATE	RAVAGE	STRAFE	BONBON	ICEBOX	VIABLE	ICICLE	UNICEF	FONDUE	NEEDLE
LUNACY	REBATE	STRAIN	BUBBLE	ISOBAR	WABBLE	IPECAC	URACIL	FRIDAY	NODDLE
MACAPP	RECALL	STRAIT	BULBUL	JABBER	WAMBLE	JAYCEE	VISCID	FUDDLE	NOODLE
MADAME	RECANT	STRAND	BUSBOY	JOBBER	WARBLE	JUICER	VISCUS	GANDER	NORDIC
MALADY	REDACT	TAMALE	CAMBER	JUMBLE	WEBBED	KWACHA	VOICED	GARDEN	PADDLE
MANAGE	REGAIN	TENANT	CARBON	KIBBLE	WIMBLE	LANCER	ZIRCON	GENDER	PANDER
MANANA	REGALE	THRALL	CARBOY	LIABLE	WOBBLE	LANCET	ANADEM	GIRDER	PARDON
MARACA	REGARD	THRASH	CHUBBY	LIMBER	WOMBAT	LASCAR	BANDED	GIRDLE	PEDDLE
MARAUD	REHASH	THWACK	COBBLE	LUBBER	ZOMBIE	LITCHI	BANDIT	GLIDER	PIDDLE
MENACE	RELATE	THWART	COMBAT	LUMBAR	ABACUS	MADCAP	BEADLE	GOLDEN	PLEDGE
MENAGE	REMAIN	TIRADE	COMBER	LUMBER	ACACIA	MARCEL	BELDAM	GOODLY	POLDER
MIDAIR	REMAND	TOMATO	CORBEL	MARBLE	APACHE	MASCON	BENDER	GRADER	PONDER
MIKADO	REMARK	TOWARD	COWBOY	MEMBER	APICAL	MASCOT	BIRDIE	GRUDGE	POODLE
MIRAGE	REPAIR	TREATY	CRABBY	MORBID	ARCCOS	MERCER	BOODLE	GUIDON	POWDER
MOHAIR	REPAST	TRIAGE	CUMBER	MUMBLE	AVOCET	MESCAL	BORDER	GULDEN	PUDDLE
MOHAWK	RESALE	TRUANT	CYMBAL	NIBBLE	BEACON	MISCUE	BRIDAL	HANDLE	PUNDIT
MORALE	RETAIL	TYRANT	DABBLE	NIMBLE	BOBCAT	MUSCLE	BRIDGE	HARDEN	PURDAH
MOSAIC	RETAIN	ULLAGE	DAYBED	NIMBUS	BOCCIE	NIACIN	BRIDLE	HARDLY	RANDOM
MUTANT	RETAKE	UNEASY	DIBBLE	NUBBIN	BOXCAR	NONCOM	BUNDLE	HEYDAY	REDDEN
MUTATE	RETARD	UNFAIR	DISBAR	NUBBLE	CAECUM	NUNCIO	BURDEN	HINDER	RENDER
NAPALM	REVAMP	UNHAND	DOBBIN	NUMBER	CALCIC	ORACLE	CADDIE	HOLDUP	RIDDEN
NAVAHO	REWARD	UNLACE	DOUBLE	OJIBWA	CANCAN	OUTCRY	CANDID	HOODOO	RIDDLE
NEGATE	RIBALD	UNLADE	DOUBLY	OUTBID	CANCEL	PARCEL	CANDLE	HOWDAH	RUDDER
NONAGE	RIBAND	UNMASK	DUBBIN	PEBBLE	CANCER	PASCAL	CANDOR	HOYDEN	SADDEN
OBLATE	ROMANO	UNPACK	DYBBUK	PHOBIA	CATCHY	PCMCIA	CAUDAL	HUDDLE	SADDLE
OBTAIN	ROSARY	UPDATE	EDIBLE	POTBOY	CAUCUS	PENCIL	CINDER	HURDLE	SANDAL
OCTANE	ROTARY	UPLAND	ENABLE	PUEBLO	CHICHI	PINCER	CODDLE	IBIDEM	SELDOM
OCTAVE	ROTATE	UPTAKE	FEEBLE	RABBET	CHICLE	PLACER	CODDLE	KINDLE	SHADOW
OCTAVO	SAFARI	UPWARD	FLABBY	RABBIT	CIRCLE	PLACID	COMDEX	KINDLY	SHODDY
ONWARD	SALAAM	URBANE	FOIBLE	RABBLE	CIRCUS	PLUCKY	CONDOM	LADDER	SLEDGE
OPIATE	SALAMI	VACANT	FORBID	RAMBLE	CLICHE	PONCHO	CONDOR	LADDIE	SLIDER
ORDAIN	SALARY	VACATE	FUMBLE	RIBBON	CLOCHE	PRECIS	CORDON	LANDAU	SLUDGE
ORGASM	SATANG	VAGARY	GABBLE	ROBBER	COCCUS	PSYCHE	CRADLE	LANDED	SMUDGE
ORNATE	SAVAGE	VIRAGO	GABBRO	ROUBLE	COCCYX	PSYCHO	CREDIT	LANDER	SODDEN
OTTAWA	SAVANT	VISAGE	GAMBIT	RUBBER	CONCUR	RANCHO	CUDDLE	LAPDOG	SOLDER
PALACE	SCRAPE	VITALS	GAMBLE	RUBBLE	CRECHE	RANCID	CURDLE	LARDER	SORDID
PALATE	SCRAWL	VIVACE	GAMBOL	RUMBLE	CROCUS	RANCOR	DANDLE	LEADEN	SPADIX

SPIDER	AMOEBA	COMEDY	GRIEVE	MUSEUM	SECEDE	WATERY	SUFFER	GADGET	RANGER
STODGY	AMPERE	COMELY	HEREBY	MYSELF	SELECT	WHEEZE	SUFFIX	GAGGLE	RIGGER
STUDIO	AMVETS	COVERT	HEREIN	NAMELY	SENECA	WHEEZY	SULFUR	GARGLE	RINGER
SUBDUE	ANNEAL	CREEPY	HEREOF	NAPERY	SERENE	ARMFUL	TIFFIN	GEWGAW	RLOGIN
SUDDEN	APIECE	DECEIT	HEREON	NEREID	SEVERE	ARTFUL	TOFFEE	GIGGLE	RUGGED
SUNDAE	APPEAL	DECENT	HERESY	NICETY	SHIELD	BAFFLE	TRIFLE	GINGER	SHAGGY
SUNDAY	APPEAR	DEFEAT	HERETO	NINETY	SHIEST	BARFLY	USEFUL	GOGGLE	SINGLE
SUNDER	APPEND	DEFECT	HOMELY	NOVELL	SHREWD	BELFRY	WAFFLE	GROGGY	SLIGHT
SUNDRY	ARDENT	DEFEND	HONEST	NOVENA	SILENT	BUFFER	WOEFUL	GURGLE	SLOGAN
TANDEM	ARGENT	DELETE	HYAENA	OBJECT	SLEEPY	BUFFET	WOOFER	HAGGIS	SOIGNE
TAWDRY	ARREST	DEMEAN	IMPEDE	OBSESS	SLEEVE	CAPFUL	ADAGIO	HAGGLE	SOUGHT
TENDER	ARTERY	DEPEND	IMPEND	OFFEND	SLIEST	CHAFER	ALIGHT	HANGAR	SPIGOT
TENDON	ASCEND	DESERT	IMPERF	ORDEAL	SNEEZE	COFFEE	APOGEE	HEIGHT	STIGMA
TINDER	ASCENT	DETECT	INCEST	ORIENT	SOLEMN	COFFER	ARIGHT	HOAGIE	TANGLE
TODDLE	ASLEEP	DETEST	INDEED	ORNERY	SPEECH	COFFIN	BADGER	HUNGER	TARGET
TRADER	ASPECT	DIGEST	INDENT	PALEON	SPHERE	COMFIT	BANGLE	JAGGED	TAUGHT
TRUDGE	ASSENT	DIRECT	INFECT	PARENT	SPLEEN	CONFAB	BEAGLE	JANGLE	TINGLE
TUNDRA	ASSERT	DIVERS	INFEST	PATENT	SPREAD	CONFED	BEGGAR	JARGON	TOGGLE
VANDAL	ASSESS	DIVERT	INGEST	PESETA	SQUEAK	CONFER	BLIGHT	JAYGEE	TONGUE
VENDEE	ASTERN	DIVEST	INHERE	PESEWA	SQUEAL	CRAFTY	BOGGLE	JIGGER	TRAGIC
VENDER	ATTEND	DOCENT	INJECT	PHLEGM	STREAK	CURFEW	BOUGHT	JIGGLE	TURGID
VENDOR	ATTEST	DURESS	INSEAM	PHOEBE	STREAM	DEAFEN	BRIGHT	JINGLE	VERGER
VOODOO	BAKERY	EATERY	INSECT	PIGEON	STREET	DIFFER	BROGAN	JOGGLE	VIRGIN
WADDLE	BALEEN	ECZEMA	INSERT	PINEAL	STRESS	DRAFTY	BROGUE	JUGGLE	VULGAR
WANDER	BARELY	EFFECT	INTEND	PLIERS	SUPERB	DUFFER	BUDGET	JUNGLE	WAGGLE
WARDEN	BATEAU	EFFETE	INTENT	POLEAX	SURETY	FITFUL	BUDGIE	KNIGHT	WANGLE
WARDER	BEDECK	EGRESS	INTERJ	POSEUR	TALENT	FLUFFY	BUNGLE	LEAGUE	WEIGHT
WINDER	BEHEAD	ELDEST	INTERN	POTEEN	TAVERN	GADFLY	BURGEE	LEDGER	WIGGLE
WINDOW	BEHEST	ENDEAR	INVENT	POTENT	TEREDO	GAFFER	BURGLE	LENGTH	WIGGLY
WINDUP	BEREFT	ENMESH	INVERT	PRIEST	THIEVE	GUFFAW	CATGUT	LINGER	WINGED
WISDOM	BESEEM	ESTEEM	INVEST	RACEME	THREAD	HEIFER	CAUGHT	LODGER	AFGHAN
WONDER	BICEPS	EUREKA	ITSELF	RAREFY	THREAT	JOYFUL	CODGER	LOGGIA	ANCHOR
WOODED	BISECT	EXCEED	KOPECK	RECEDE	THRESH	LAWFUL	COUGAR	MAGGOT	ANTHEM
WOODEN	BOLERO	EXCEPT	KOREAN	RECENT	TIMELY	LEAFED	CUDGEL	MANGER	ANTHER
WOODSY	BOREAL	EXCESS	LAMENT	RECESS	TORERO	MANFUL	DAGGER	MANGLE	ANYHOW
XMODEM	BREECH	EXPECT	LATENT	REDEEM	TUREEN	MAYFLY	DANGER	MARGIN	ARCHON
YMODEM	BREEZE	EXPEND	LEGEND	REGENT	TUXEDO	MISFIT	DANGLE	MEAGER	ASTHMA
YONDER	BUREAU	EXPERT	LIKELY	REJECT	TWEEDY	MUFFIN	DENGUE	MERGER	AUTHOR
ZMODEM	CAMERA	EXTEND	LINEAL	RELENT	UNBEND	MUFFLE	DINGHY	MIDGET	BATHOS
ABBESS	CAREEN	EXTENT	LINEAR	REMEDY	UNLESS	NONFAT	DINGLE	MINGLE	BETHEL
ABJECT	CAREER	EXTERN	LINEUP	RENEGE	UNMEET	OUTFIT	DINGUS	MONGER	BINHEX
ABSENT	CARESS	FINERY	LIVELY	REPEAL	UNREAD	OUTFOX	DOGGED	MORGAN	BISHOP
ACCEDE	CASEIN	FLEECE	LIVERY	REPEAT	UNREAL	PIFFLE	DRAGON	MORGUE	BOTHER
ACCENT	CAVEAT	FLUENT	LONELY	REPENT	UNREEL	PILFER	DROGUE	NAUGHT	BUSHED
ACCEPT	CAVERN	FOMENT	LOVELY	RESENT	UNREST	PREFAB	EMIGRE	NOGGIN	BUSHEL
ACCESS	CELERY	FOREGO	LOWERY	REVEAL	UNSEAL	PREFER	ENIGMA	NOUGAT	CACHET
ADDEND	CEMENT	FOREST	LUCENT	REVERB	UNSEAT	PREFIX	FAGGOT	NOUGHT	CARHOP
ADHERE	CEREAL	FREEZE	LYCEUM	REVERE	UNVEIL	PROFIT	FIDGET	NUGGET	CASHEW
ADVENT	CEREUS	FRIEND	MAKEUP	REVERS	UNWELL	PUFFIN	FINGER	ORIGIN	CIPHER
ADVERB	CHEEKY	FRIEZE	MANEGE	REVERT	UNWEPT	RAFFIA	FLAGON	OUTGUN	DASHER
ADVERT	CHEERY	GAIETY	METEOR	RODENT	UPBEAT	RAFFLE	FLIGHT	OXYGEN	DIRHAM
AFFECT	CHEESE	GALENA	MISERY	SAFETY	UPKEEP	REEFER	FORGET	PIDGIN	DISHED
AFIELD	CINEMA	GAMETE	MODERN	SATEEN	UPREAR	RUFFLE	FOUGHT	PLAGUE	DITHER
AFRESH	CLIENT	GAYETY	MODEST	SCHEME	UPWELL	SHIFTY	FRIGHT	PLIGHT	EIGHTY
AGLEAM	COGENT	GAZEBO	MOIETY	SCREAM	URGENT	SINFUL	FRIGID	PONGEE	EITHER
ALBEIT	COHEIR	GENERA	MOLEST	SCREEN	VENEER	STIFLE	FRUGAL	POPGUN	ESCHEW
ALLEGE	COHERE	GOVERN	MOMENT	SCREWY	VOYEUR	STUFFY	FUNGUS	RAGGED	EUCHRE

FATHER	ACUITY	CAVIAR	ENTIRE	INSIST	NOTICE	RADISH	SHRIEK	UNBIND	BUCKET
FATHOM	ADDICT	CAVITY	ENTITY	INVITE	NOTIFY	RADIUM	SHRIFT	UNCIAL	BUCKLE
FISHER	ADMIRE	CERISE	EOLIAN	IODIDE	NOTION	RADIUS	SHRIKE	UNDIES	BUNKER
GATHER	ADRIFT	CERIUM	EQUINE	IODINE	NOVICE	RAKISH	SHRILL	UNGIRD	BUNKUM
GOPHER	ADVICE	CESIUM	EQUITY	IODIZE	NOWISE	RAMIFY	SHRIMP	UNKIND	BUSKIN
GOTHIC	ADVISE	CHAISE	ERBIUM	IONIZE	NUBILE	RAPIER	SHRINE	UNLIKE	CACKLE
GUSHER	AERIAL	CHOICE	ERMINE	JOVIAL	NUDISM	RAPINE	SHRINK	UNPILE	CANKER
HITHER	AFFIRM	CHRISM	ESKIMO	JUNIOR	OBLIGE	RARING	SHRIVE	UNRIPE	CASKET
HYPHEN	ALBINO	CHRIST	ETHICS	JURIST	ODDITY	RATIFY	SIDING	UNWIND	CATKIN
KOSHER	ALLIED	CILIUM	EXCISE	LABIAL	OFFICE	RATING	SIGILL	UNWISE	CHOKER
LATHER	ALPINE	CITIFY	EXCITE	LABILE	OFFING	RATION	SILICA	UPHILL	CHUKKA
LETHAL	ANGINA	CIVICS	EXPIRE	LABIUM	OFFISH	RAVINE	SIMIAN	UPLIFT	COCKLE
LICHEE	ANOINT	CODIFY	FABIAN	LADING	ONEIDA	RAVISH	SIMILE	UPPISH	COOKIE
LICHEN	ARNICA	COMING	FACIAL	LAMINA	OOLITE	RECIPE	SLEIGH	UPPITY	CUCKOO
LIGHTS	ARRIVE	COMITY	FACILE	LARIAT	OPTICS	RECITE	SLUICE	UPSIDE	DARKEN
MAYHEM	ARTIST	COPIER	FACING	LAVISH	OPTION	REFILL	SOCIAL	UPWIND	DESKEW
METHOD	ASPIRE	COPING	FAMILY	LEGION	ORNITH	REFINE	SOCIOL	URSINE	DICKER
METHYL	ASSIGN	COSINE	FAMINE	LENITY	OSMIUM	REGIME	SODIUM	VAGINA	DICKEY
MIGHTY	ASSIST	CRUISE	FAMISH	LESION	OSSIFY	REGION	SOVIET	VALISE	DOCKET
MISHAP	ASSIZE	CUBISM	FARINA	LEVITY	OUTING	RELICT	SPHINX	VANISH	DONKEY
MOTHER	ATRIUM	CURIUM	FELINE	LIBIDO	PACIFY	RELIEF	SPLICE	VANITY	FICKLE
NEPHEW	ATTIRE	DANISH	FENIAN	LIKING	PALING	RELISH	SPLINE	VARIED	FOLKSY
NETHER	AUTISM	DARING	FETISH	LINING	PAPIST	RELIVE	SPLINT	VENIAL	FORKED
ORCHID	AWEIGH	DATIVE	FILIAL	LIVING	PARIAH	REMIND	SPRING	VENIRE	GASKET
ORPHAN	AWHILE	DECIDE	FILING	LOTION	PARING	REMISS	SPRINT	VERIFY	GINKGO
PATHOS	AWHIRL	DEFILE	FINIAL	LOVING	PARISH	REPINE	SPRITE	VERILY	GURKHA
PEAHEN	AWNING	DEFINE	FINISH	LUPINE	PARITY	RESIDE	SQUINT	VERITY	HACKER
POTHER	BANISH	DEMISE	FINITE	MALIAN	PATINA	RESIGN	SQUIRE	VIKING	HACKIE
PUSHER	BARIUM	DENIAL	FIXITY	MALICE	PAVING	RESIST	SQUIRM	VILIFY	HACKLE
PYTHON	BEHIND	DENIER	FORINT	MALIGN	PERIOD	RETINA	SQUIRT	VIRILE	HANKER
QUAHOG	BELIEF	DEPICT	FRUITY	MANIAC	PERISH	RETIRE	STRICT	VIRION	HARKEN
RASHER	BELIKE	DERIDE	FUSION	MANIOC	PETITE	REVIEW	STRIDE	VISION	HAWKER
RATHER	BEMIRE	DERIVE	FUTILE	MAOISM	PILING	REVILE	STRIFE	VIVIFY	HECKLE
RICHES	BENIGN	DESIGN	GAMINE	MARINA	PINION	REVISE	STRIKE	VIZIER	HOCKEY
SACHEM	BESIDE	DESIRE	GARISH	MARINE	PIPING	REVIVE	STRING	VOTIVE	HOOKAH
SACHET	BETIDE	DESIST	GENIAL	MATINS	PLAINT	RUPIAH	STRIPE	WAHINE	HOOKER
SASHAY	BIKINI	DEVICE	GENIUS	MEDIAL	PODIUM	SADISM	STRIVE	WAPITI	HOOKUP
SIPHON	BITING	DEVISE	GNEISS	MEDIAN	POLICE	SALINE	SUPINE	WIRING	HUNKER
SYPHON	BLUING	DIMITY	GRAINY	MEDICO	POLICY	SALIVA	TAKING	WRAITH	JACKAL
TETHER	BLUISH	DIVIDE	HALITE	MEDIUM	POLISH	SANITY	TAOISM	ZENITH	JACKET
TIGHTS	BODICE	DIVINE	HEGIRA	MENIAL	POLITE	SATIRE	TARIFF	ZODIAC	JERKIN
TOWHEE	BODILY	DOCILE	HELIUM	MENINX	POLITY	SAVIOR	TEDIUM	DEEJAY	JOCKEY
TYPHUS	BONITO	DOMINO	HOMILY	MERINO	POTION	SAYING	THEIRS	INKJET	JUNKER
UNSHIP	BOVINE	DURING	HOMINY	METIER	PRAISE	SCHISM	THEISM	LOGJAM	JUNKET
UNSHOD	BOXING	EDGING	IGNITE	MILIEU	PUMICE	SCHIST	THRICE	TROJAN	JUNKIE
UPSHOT	BRAISE	EFFIGY	IMBIBE	MINION	PUNISH	SCRIBE	THRIFT	AWAKEN	LACKEY
URCHIN	BRUISE	EGOISM	IMPISH	MOBILE	PURIFY	SCRIMP	THRILL	BACKER	LINKED
WASHER	BUNION	EMPIRE	INCISE	MODIFY	PURINE	SCRIPT	THRIVE	BACKUP	LINKUP
WETHER	BURIAL	ENDING	INCITE	MODISH	PURISM	SEMITE	TROIKA	BARKER	LOCKER
WITHAL	BUSILY	ENDIVE	INDIAN	MONISM	PURITY	SENILE	TRUISM	BASKET	LOCKET
WITHER	CALICO	ENGINE	INDICT	MOTILE	PYRITE	SENIOR	TRYING	BEAKER	LOCKUP
WITHIN	CALIPH	ENLIST	INDIGO	MOTION	QIVIUT	SENITI	TUBING	BECKON	MARKED
ZEPHYR	CANINE	ENMITY	INDITE	MOTIVE	QUAINT	SERIAL	TURING	BICKER	MARKET
ZITHER	CARIES	ENRICH	INDIUM	MUTINY	RABIES	SERIES	TYPIFY	BODKIN	MARKKA
ACTING	CASING	ENSIGN	INFIRM	MYRIAD	RACISM	SEWING	TYPIST	BOOKIE	MARKUP
ACTION	CASINO	ENSILE	INNING	NATION	RADIAL	SEXISM	ULTIMO	BROKEN	MONKEY
ACTIVE	CATION	ENTICE	INSIDE	NATIVE	RADIAN	SHEIKH	UMPIRE	BROKER	MUSKEG

MUSKET	AMULET	FALLOW	OUTLAY	VALLEY	ENAMEL	SHIMMY	CORNEA	LOUNGE	TELNET
NAPKIN	ANALOG	FEALTY	OUTLET	VARLET	ENAMOR	SIMMER	CORNER	MAENAD	TENNIS
NICKEL	ANKLET	FEELER	PALLET	VELLUM	EXEMPT	SKIMPY	CORNET	MAGNET	THANKS
NICKER	ANTLER	FELLAH	PALLID	VILLUS	FLIMSY	STAMEN	COUNTY	MANNED	THENCE
PACKER	APPLET	FELLOW	PALLOR	VIOLET	FOEMAN	STYMIE	CRANKY	MANNER	TRANCE
PACKET	ARMLET	FILLER	PARLAY	VIOLIN	FORMAL	SUBMIT	CRANNY	MINNOW	TRANSL
PEAKED	ASHLAR	FILLET	PARLEY	VOLLEY	FORMAT	SUMMER	CRINGE	NUANCE	TRANSP
PICKAX	ASYLUM	FILLIP	PARLOR	WALLET	FORMER	SUMMIT	CRUNCH	ORANGE	TRENCH
PICKET	AZALEA	FOLLOW	PELLET	WALLOP	FRUMPY	SUMMON	CUNNER	PAUNCH	TUNNEL
PICKLE	BALLAD	FROLIC	PHILOS	WALLOW	GAMMER	TALMUD	CYGNET	PAWNEE	TURNER
PICKUP	BALLET	GAELIC	PHYLUM	WAYLAY	GAMMON	THYMUS	DAINTY	PEANUT	TURNIP
PINKIE	BALLOT	GALLEY	PIGLET	WEALTH	GERMAN	TREMOR	DARNEL	PENNON	TWENTY
PIPKIN	BARLEY	GALLIC	PILLAR	WHALER	GRUMPY	UREMIA	DINNER	PHENOL	TWINGE
POCKET	BEDLAM	GALLON	PILLOW	WHILOM	GUNMAN	VERMIN	DIRNDL	PHONIC	UNSNAP
PORKER	BELLOW	GALLOP	POLLEN	WHILST	HAMMER	WARMTH	DOINGS	PICNIC	URANIC
PUCKER	BILLET	GARLIC	POPLAR	WHOLLY	HAYMOW	WHAMMY	DOWNER	PIGNUT	URANUS
PUNKIN	BILLOW	GIMLET	POPLIN	WIGLET	HELMET	WHIMSY	DRENCH	PLANET	URINAL
QUAKER	BOILER	GOALIE	PRELIM	WILLOW	HERMIT	YAMMER	DUENDE	PLENTY	USENET
RACKET	BOWLEG	GOBLET	PROLIX	WOOLEN	ICEMAN	YEOMAN	DUENNA	PLENUM	VERNAL
RANKLE	BOWLER	GOBLIN	PROLOG	WOOLLY	ISOMER	AGENCY	EGGNOG	PLINTH	WALNUT
RECKON	BULLET	GRILLE	PUBLIC	YELLOW	KERMIT	AGENDA	ETHNIC	PLUNGE	WHENCE
ROCKER	BURLAP	GUILTY	PULLET	ZEALOT	KISMET	AMENDS	ETHNOL	POUNCE	WHINNY
ROCKET	BUTLER	GULLET	PULLEY	ACUMEN	LAWMAN	ARCNET	EVINCE	PRANCE	WIENER
ROOKIE	BYPLAY	HALLOW	RAGLAN	AIDMAN	LAYMAN	ATONAL	FENNEL	PRINCE	WINNER
RUCKUS	CALLOW	HAMLET	REALLY	AIRMAN	LEGMAN	AVENGE	FIANCE	PRINTF	WINNOW
SHAKER	CALLUS	HARLOT	REALTY	AKIMBO	LITMUS	AVENUE	FLANGE	PRONTO	WRENCH
SICKEN	CELLAR	HEALTH	REFLEX	ALUMNA	LUMMOX	BAGNIO	FLINCH	QUENCH	ZINNIA
SICKLE	CHALET	HOLLER	REFLUX	ANEMIA	MADMAN	BANNER	FLUNKY	QUINCE	ZOUNDS
SINKER	CHILLY	HOLLOW	REPLAY	ANIMAL	MAMMAL	BEANIE	FRENCH	QUINSY	ABLOOM
SOCKET	CHOLER	HOWLER	ROLLER	ANIMUS	MAMMON	BITNET	FRENZY	REGNAL	ABROAD
SPOKEN	COLLAR	INFLOW	RUNLET	ATOMIC	MARMOT	BLANCH	FRINGE	RENNET	ABSORB
SUCKER	COLLAT	INFLUX	SAILOR	BAGMAN	MERMAN	BLENCH	FUNNEL	RENNIN	ACCORD
SUCKLE	COLLIE	ITALIC	SALLOW	BATMAN	MICMAC	BONNET	GANNET	RUNNEL	ACCOST
SUNKEN	COLLOQ	JAILER	SCULPT	BOWMAN	MORMON	BOUNCE	GARNER	RUNNER	ACROSS
TACKLE	COOLER	KAOLIN	SEALER	BUMMER	MUMMER	BOUNTY	GARNET	SCANTY	ADJOIN
TANKER	COOLIE	KEGLER	SHELVE	CAIMAN	MURMUR	BRANCH	GLANCE	SCONCE	ADROIT
TICKER	COULEE	MAILED	SLALOM	CAYMAN	MUUMUU	BRANDY	GRANGE	SEANCE	ADSORB
TICKET	CURLEW	MALLET	SMILAX	CERMET	NORMAL	BRONCO	GUINEA	SHANTY	AFFORD
TICKLE	CUTLER	MALLOW	STOLEN	CHUMMY	NORMAN	BRONZE	GUNNER	SHINER	AFLOAT
TINKER	CUTLET	MARLIN	STOLID	CLAMMY	NUTMEG	BRUNCH	HAUNCH	SHINNY	ALCOVE
TINKLE	DAHLIA	MEDLEY	STOLON	CLAMOR	PALMER	BRUNET	HERNIA	SHINTO	ALMOND
TUCKER	DEPLOY	MELLOW	STYLUS	CLIMAX	PENMAN	BURNER	HOBNOB	SIGNAL	ALMOST
TURKEY	DEWLAP	MILLER	SUBLET	CLUMSY	PERMIT	CANNED	HORNET	SIGNET	ANGORA
TUSKER	DOGLEG	MILLET	SULLEN	COMMIT	POMMEL	CANNON	IRENIC	SKINNY	ANYONE
WEAKEN	DOLLAR	MISLAY	SUNLIT	COMMON	PREMED	CANNOT	IRONIC	SONNET	APLOMB
WEAKLY	DOLLOP	MOSLEM	SVELTE	COSMIC	PREMIX	CARNAL	JAUNTY	SPINAL	ARGOSY
WEEKLY	DUPLEX	MOTLEY	TABLET	COSMOS	PRIMAL	CATNAP	JENNET	SPINEL	ARMORY
WELKIN	EAGLET	MUKLUK	TAILOR	COWMAN	PRIMER	CATNIP	JITNEY	SPINET	ARROYO
WESKIT	ECCLES	MULLET	TALLOW	CRUMMY	PROMPT	CHANCE	JOHNNY	SPONGE	ASHORE
WICKED	ECCLUS	MUSLIM	TELLER	DAEMON	PUMMEL	CHANCY	JOINER	STANCE	ASSORT
WICKER	EMBLEM	MUSLIN	TILLER	DERMAL	REAMER	CHANGE	JOUNCE	STANCH	AURORA
WICKET	EMPLOY	OCELOT	TITLED	DERMIS	SALMON	CHINTZ	KENNEL	STANZA	BABOON
WINKER	EVOLVE	OCULAR	TOILET	DIMMER	SCAMPI	CHUNKY	KERNEL	STENCH	BECOME
WINKLE	EYELET	OMELET	TWELVE	DISMAL	SEAMAN	CLENCH	KIDNAP	STINGY	BEFORE
WORKER	EYELID	OODLES	UNCLAD	DISMAY	SEEMLY	CLINCH	KIDNEY	STONED	BEFOUL
YANKEE	FABLED	OSTLER	UNCLOG	DOLMEN	SERMON	CLINIC	LAUNCH	TANNER	BEGONE
ZONKED	FAILLE	OUTLAW	UNPLUG	DORMER	SHAMAN	COGNAC	LINNET	TANNIN	BEHOLD

BEHOOF	FAVOUR	PAROLE	UNCORK	DRAPER	STAPES	APPROX	FERRIC	PHAROS	WARREN
BELONG	FEDORA	PATOIS	UNFOLD	DROPSY	STAPLE	ASHRAM	FIBRIL	PIERCE	WHERRY
BEMOAN	FELONY	PAYOFF	UNHOLY	ELAPSE	STEPPE	ASTRAL	FIBRIN	PLURAL	YARROW
BEYOND	FLOOZY	PEYOTE	UNHOOK	FLOPPY	STUPID	ASTRAY	FIERCE	POGROM	YEARLY
BROOCH	FURORE	PHLOEM	UNLOAD	FRAPPE	STUPOR	ASTROL	FLORAL	PUTRID	ARCSIN
BYGONE	GALORE	POROUS	UNLOCK	GOSPEL	SUPPER	ASTRON	FLORID	QUARRY	BALSAM
BYWORD	GALOSH	PRIORY	UNMOOR	GRIPPE	SUPPLE	ATTRIB	FLORIN	QUARTO	BONSAI
CAHOOT	GIGOLO	PUTOUT	UNROBE	HAMPER	SUPPLY	AVERSE	FLURRY	QUARTZ	BUQSHA
CAJOLE	GROOVE	RAGOUT	UNROLL	HAPPEN	TAMPER	BARRED	FOURTH	QUORUM	BURSAR
CANOPY	GROOVY	REBORN	UNROOF	HERPES	TAMPON	BARREL	FUHRER	RAMROD	CAESAR
CAVORT	HEROIN	RECOIL	UNTOLD	HIPPED	TAPPET	BARREN	FURROW	REFRIG	CASSIA
CHOOSE	HONOUR	RECORD	UNYOKE	HIPPIE	TARPON	BARRIO	GARRET	REGRET	CATSUP
CHOOSY	HUMOUR	RECOUP	UPHOLD	HOOPLA	TEAPOT	BARROW	GOURDE	RUBRIC	CAUSAL
CHROME	IDIOCY	REFORM	UPLOAD	HOPPER	TEEPEE	BETRAY	HAIRDO	SACRED	CENSER
CHROMO	IGNORE	REJOIN	UPMOST	JASPER	TEMPER	BORROW	HARROW	SACRUM	CENSOR
COCOON	IMPORT	REMORA	UPROAR	JUMPER	TEMPLE	BOURSE	HATRED	SATRAP	CENSUS
COHORT	IMPOSE	REMOTE	UPROOT	KIPPER	TENPIN	BURROW	HEARSE	SCARAB	CHASER
COLONY	IMPOST	REMOVE	UPTOWN	LAPPET	TIPPET	CARREL	HEARTH	SCARCE	CHASTE
CORONA	INBORN	RENOWN	UTMOST	LIMPET	TIPPLE	CARROT	HEARTY	SCORCH	CHISEL
COYOTE	INCOME	REPORT	VAPORY	LIMPID	TOPPLE	CHARGE	HEBREW	SCORIA	CHOSEN
CREOLE	INDOOR	REPOSE	VELOUR	LOOPER	TORPID	CHERRY	HOARSE	SCURRY	CLASSY
CUPOLA	INFOLD	RESORT	VENOUS	MAGPIE	TORPOR	CHERUB	HORRID	SCURVY	CLOSET
CUTOFF	INFORM	RETORT	VINOUS	MOPPET	TOUPEE	CHORAL	HORROR	SEARCH	CONSOL
CUTOUT	INMOST	REVOKE	ZYGOTE	MYOPIA	TREPAN	CHOREA	HUBRIS	SECRET	CONSTR
DAKOTA	INROAD	REVOLT	ARMPIT	NIPPER	TRIPLE	CHORUS	HURRAH	SHERRY	CONSUL
DECODE	INSOLE	RUNOFF	BEDPAN	NIPPLE	TRIPLY	CHURCH	HYBRID	SIERRA	CORSET
DEFORM	INTONE	SALOON	BIOPSY	OUTPUT	TRIPOD	CIRRUS	IMBRUE	SLURRY	COUSIN
DEHORN	INVOKE	SARONG	BUMPER	PAMPER	TROPHY	CITRON	INBRED	SMIRCH	CRISIS
DEMODE	JALOPY	SCHOOL	CAMPER	PAUPER	TROPIC	CITRUS	INTROD	SOIREE	CUESTA
DEMOTE	JOCOSE	SCROLL	CAMPUS	PAWPAW	UTOPIA	CLARET	LAUREL	SORREL	CURSOR
DENOTE	JOYOUS	SECOND	CARPAL	PEOPLE	VESPER	CLERGY	MACRON	SORROW	DAMSEL
DEPORT	KIBOSH	SHROUD	CARPEL	PEPPER	WAMPUM	CLERIC	MADRAS	SOURCE	DAMSON
DEPOSE	KIMONO	SIMONY	CARPET	PIGPEN	WEAPON	COARSE	MARROW	SPARSE	DIESEL
DETOUR	KOBOLD	SMOOCH	CHAPEL	PIMPLE	WIMPLE	COERCE	MATRIX	SPIRAL	DORSAL
DEVOID	LABOUR	SMOOTH	CHOPPY	PIPPIN	ZIPPER	CORRAL	MATRON	SPIREA	DRESSY
DEVOIR	LAGOON	SNOOTY	COMPAQ	POMPON	BASQUE	COURSE	METRIC	SPIRIT	ENISLE
DEVOTE	LAYOFF	SNOOZE	COMPAR	POPPER	BISQUE	DEARTH	MICRON	SPURGE	FIASCO
DEVOUR	LAYOUT	SODOMY	COMPEL	POTPIE	CASQUE	DEBRIS	MIRROR	STARCH	FIESTA
DEVOUT	MAHOUT	SPROUT	COMPLY	PREPAY	CHEQUE	DECREE	MORRIS	STARVE	FLASHY
DISOWN	MAROON	STOOGE	COOPER	PROPEL	CIRQUE	DEFRAY	MORROW	STEREO	FLESHY
DUGOUT	MEGOHM	STROBE	COPPER	PROPER	CLAQUE	DEGREE	NARROW	STURDY	FLOSSY
EFFORT	MELODY	STRODE	CORPSE	PULPIT	CLIQUE	DERRIS	NEARBY	SURREY	FOSSIL
EMBODY	MEMOIR	STROKE	CORPUS	PUPPET	MANQUE	EEPROM	NEURAL	SWERVE	FRESCO
EMBOSS	MEMORY	STROLL	COUPLE	PURPLE	MASQUE	EMBRYO	NEUROL	TERROR	FRISKY
ENCODE	MIMOSA	STRONG	COUPON	RAPPEN	MOSQUE	EMERGE	NEURON	THIRST	GEISHA
ENCORE	MONODY	STROVE	COWPOX	RIPPLE	OPAQUE	ENDRIN	NIMROD	THIRTY	GEYSER
ENFOLD	MOROSE	SUBORN	CUSPID	ROMPER	PLAQUE	ENERGY	NITRIC	THORAX	GIBSON
ENJOIN	NOBODY	THEORY	DAMPEN	RUMPLE	RISQUE	ENGRAM	NUTRIA	TORRID	GLOSSY
ENROLL	OBLONG	THROAT	DAMPER	RUMPUS	TORQUE	ENTRAP	OSPREY	TUGRIK	GODSON
ENTOMB	ODIOUS	THRONE	DAPPER	SAMPAN	UNIQUE	ENTREE	OUTRUN	TURRET	GOSSIP
ESCORT	OPPOSE	THRONG	DAPPLE	SAMPLE	YANQUI	ESCROW	OVERDO	ULTRIX	GRISLY
EULOGY	ORIOLE	THROVE	DEEPEN	SEXPOT	ACCRUE	ESPRIT	OVERLY	UNTRUE	GUSSET
EXHORT	ORMOLU	TRIODE	DESPOT	SIMPER	AFFRAY	FABRIC	PARROT	UNWRAP	GYPSUM
EXPORT	OTIOSE	TYCOON	DIAPER	SIMPLE	AMERCE	FAERIE	PATROL	USURER	HANSEL
EXPOSE	OXFORD	UNBOLT	DIMPLE	SLIPUP	AMORAL	FAIRLY	PATRON	UTERUS	HANSOM
EXTORT	PAGODA	UNBORN	DIPPER	SLOPPY	ANTRUM	FARROW	PETREL	VAGROM	HASSLE
FAMOUS	PARODY	UNCOIL	DISPEL	SNIPPY	APERCU	FERRET	PETROL	WALRUS	HAWSER

HORSEY	SEASON	BOTTOM	FACTOR	LITTER	PISTIL	STITCH	WRITER	ENDURE	MINUTE
HUSSAR	SEESAW	BRITON	FALTER	LITTLE	PISTOL	SUBTLE	WRITHE	ENDURO	MISUSE
HYSSOP	SENSOR	BRUTAL	FASTEN	LOATHE	PISTON	SUITOR	ABDUCT	ENGULF	MODULE
JERSEY	SEPSIS	BUSTLE	FATTEN	LOITER	PLATEN	SULTAN	ABJURE	ENOUGH	MUTUAL
JETSAM	SIESTA	BUTTER	FESTAL	LUSTER	PLUTON	SULTRY	ABOUND	ENSURE	NATURE
JIGSAW	SUBSET	BUTTON	FESTER	MANTEL	POETRY	SUNTAN	ABRUPT	ESCUDO	NEBULA
KAISER	SUNSET	CACTUS	FETTER	MANTIS	PORTAL	SURTAX	ABSURD	EUNUCH	NODULE
KISSER	TARSUS	CAFTAN	FETTLE	MANTLE	PORTER	SWATCH	ACCUSE	EXCUSE	OBTUSE
KITSCH	TASSEL	CANTER	FILTER	MANTRA	PORTLY	SWATHE	ACQUIT	EXHUME	OCCULT
LASSIE	TEASEL	CANTLE	FLATUS	MARTEN	POSTAL	SWITCH	ACTUAL	FACULA	OCCUPY
LESSEE	THESIS	CANTON	FLITCH	MARTIN	POSTER	SYNTAX	ADDUCE	FECUND	ONRUSH
LESSEN	TINSEL	CANTOR	FOETAL	MARTYR	POTTER	SYSTEM	ADJURE	FERULE	ORDURE
LESSER	TISSUE	CAPTOR	FOOTED	MASTER	PRETTY	TACTIC	ADJUST	FIBULA	PAIUTE
LESSON	TOCSIN	CARTEL	FOSTER	MASTIC	PROTON	TARTAN	ALLUDE	FIGURE	PAPULE
LESSOR	TONSIL	CARTON	GAITER	MATTER	PUTTEE	TARTAR	ALLURE	FLAUNT	PENURY
LOOSEN	TOUSLE	CARTOP	GANTRY	MENTAL	PUTTER	TATTER	AMBUSH	FUTURE	PEQUOT
MASSIF	TRUSTY	CASTER	GARTER	MENTOR	QINTAR	TATTLE	AMOUNT	GERUND	PERUKE
MEASLY	TUSSLE	CASTLE	GENTLE	METTLE	RAFTER	TATTOO	ANNUAL	GROUCH	PERUSE
MENSES	UNESCO	CATTLE	GENTRY	MISTER	RASTER	TEETER	AROUND	GROUND	PIQUET
MESSRS	UNISEX	CENTER	GHETTO	MITTEN	RATTAN	TEETHE	AROUSE	GROUSE	PSEUDO
MIASMA	UNISON	CENTRE	GIFTED	MOLTEN	RATTER	TESTER	ASSUME	ILLUME	REBUFF
MISSAL	UNUSED	CHATTY	GLITCH	MORTAL	RATTLE	TESTIS	ASSURE	ILLUST	REBUKE
MORSEL	VASSAL	CHITIN	GLUTEN	MORTAR	RECTAL	THATCH	ASTUTE	IMMUNE	REDUCE
MOUSER	VERSED	CLOTHE	GOATEE	MOSTLY	RECTOR	TIPTOE	ATTUNE	IMMURE	REFUGE
MOUSSE	VERSUS	CLUTCH	GOITER	MOTTLE	RECTUM	TITTER	AUBURN	IMPUGN	REFUND
MUSSEL	VESSEL	COITUS	GOTTEN	MOUTON	RENTAL	TITTLE	AUGURY	IMPURE	REFUSE
NAUSEA	WEASEL	COOTIE	GRATIS	MUSTER	RHYTHM	TOMTIT	AUGUST	IMPUTE	REFUTE
NELSON	WORSEN	COPTER	GROTTO	MUTTER	ROSTER	TOOTHY	AUTUMN	INDUCE	REPUTE
OFFSET	WRASSE	CORTEX	GUITAR	MUTTON	ROTTEN	TOTTER	AVAUNT	INDUCT	RESULT
ORISON	YEASTY	COSTLY	GUTTER	MYRTLE	RUSTIC	TRITON	AVOUCH	INFUSE	RESUME
OUTSET	ZOYSIA	COTTER	HALTER	MYSTIC	RUSTLE	TSETSE	BEAUTY	INHUME	RETURN
PARSEC	ABATIS	COTTON	HASTEN	NAUTCH	SCOTCH	TURTLE	BELUGA	INJURE	RITUAL
PARSON	ACETIC	CRATER	HATTER	NECTAR	SCYTHE	TWITCH	BEMUSE	INJURY	ROBUST
PASSEL	APATHY	CRATON	HECTIC	NESTLE	SECTOR	ULSTER	BENUMB	INRUSH	ROTUND
PASSIM	ARCTAN	CRETIN	HECTOR	NETTLE	SEETHE	UNITED	BLOUSE	INSULT	SALUTE
PEPSIN	ARCTIC	CRITIC	HIATUS	NEUTER	SENTRY	UNSTOP	CASUAL	INSURE	SATURN
PERSON	AVATAR	CROTCH	HOSTEL	NEWTON	SEPTIC	URETER	CAYUGA	INTUIT	SCHUSS
PHYSIC	BANTAM	CRUTCH	HURTLE	NORTON	SETTEE	VECTOR	CAYUSE	IRRUPT	SCRUFF
PIGSTY	BANTER	CURTSY	HUSTLE	ORATOR	SETTER	VERTEX	CHAUNT	JAGUAR	SECURE
PLASMA	BARTER	CUSTOM	INSTEP	OUSTER	SETTLE	VESTAL	CLAUSE	JEJUNE	SEDUCE
POISON	BATTEN	CUTTER	JESTER	OYSTER	SEXTET	VESTEE	COLUMN	JOCUND	SEQUEL
POSSUM	BATTER	DACTYL	JOSTLE	PALTER	SEXTON	VESTRY	COPULA	JUJUBE	SEQUIN
PRESET	BATTLE	DARTER	KETTLE	PALTRY	SISTER	VICTIM	COQUET	KABUKI	SEXUAL
PRESTO	BEETLE	DEBTOR	KILTER	PANTIE	SKETCH	VICTOR	CROUCH	KORUNA	SHOULD
PRISON	BESTIR	DENTAL	KIRTLE	PANTRY	SMITHY	VIRTUE	DEBUNK	LACUNA	SLEUTH
PRISSY	BESTOW	DENTIN	KITTEN	PARTLY	SMUTCH	VORTEX	DEDUCE	LEGUME	SLOUCH
PULSAR	BETTER	DIATOM	KLATCH	PASTEL	SNATCH	WAITER	DEDUCT	LIKUTA	SLOUGH
PURSER	BETTOR	DICTUM	KOWTOW	PASTOR	SNITCH	WANTON	DEFUSE	LIQUID	SPOUSE
PURSUE	BIOTIC	DISTAL	LACTIC	PASTRY	SOFTEN	WATTLE	DELUDE	LIQUOR	SPRUCE
PUTSCH	BIOTIN	DOCTOR	LAPTOP	PATTER	SOOTHE	WELTER	DELUGE	LOBULE	SPRUNG
QBASIC	BISTRO	DOTTLE	LATTER	PECTIN	SORTIE	WHITEN	DELUXE	LOCUST	STRUCK
QUASAR	BITTER	DUSTER	LECTOR	PEPTIC	SPATHE	WINTER	DEMURE	LUXURY	STRUNG
RAISIN	BLITHE	EARTHY	LENTIL	PESTER	SPOTTY	WINTRY	DENUDE	MAKUTA	SUBURB
RANSOM	BLOTCH	EASTER	LEPTON	PESTLE	SPUTUM	WITTED	DEPUTE	MANUAL	SUTURE
REASON	BOATER	EMETIC	LETTER	PEWTER	STATIC	WONTED	DEPUTY	MANURE	TENURE
RIPSAW	BOOTEE	EROTIC	LINTEL	PHOTOG	STATUE	WORTHY	DILUTE	MATURE	THOUGH
RUSSET	BOTTLE	EXOTIC	LISTEN	PHOTON	STATUS	WRETCH	DISUSE	MINUET	THRUSH

THRUST	MARVEL	OUTWIT	AERIAL	CANVAS	FINIAL	MADRAS	RADIAL	TOMCAT	ADDUCE
TRAUMA	OEUVRE	PEEWEE	AFFRAY	CARNAL	FISCAL	MAENAD	RADIAN	TOUCAN	ADVICE
TRIUNE	PELVIS	POWWOW	AFGHAN	CARPAL	FLORAL	MAGYAR	RAGLAN	TREPAN	AFFECT
TROUGH	PLOVER	PREWAR	AFLOAT	CASUAL	FLYWAY	MALIAN	RASCAL	TROJAN	AGENCY
TROUPE	PRIVET	RUNWAY	AGLEAM	CATNAP	FOEMAN	MAMMAL	RATTAN	TURBAN	ALPACA
TUBULE	PURVEY	SEAWAY	AIDMAN	CAUDAL	FOETAL	MANIAC	RECTAL	UNCIAL	AMERCE
TUMULT	QUAVER	SHOWER	AIRMAN	CAUSAL	FORMAL	MANUAL	REDCAP	UNCLAD	APERCU
UNCURL	QUIVER	SKEWER	AIRWAY	CAVEAT	FORMAT	MEDIAL	REGNAL	UNLOAD	APIECE
UNDULY	SALVER	SUBWAY	AMORAL	CAVIAR	FRACAS	MEDIAN	RENTAL	UNREAD	ARNICA
UNFURL	SELVES	TROWEL	ANIMAL	CAYMAN	FRIDAY	MENIAL	REPEAL	UNREAL	ASPECT
UNJUST	SERVER	WIGWAG	ANNEAL	CELLAR	FRUGAL	MENTAL	REPEAT	UNSEAL	ATTACH
UNRULY	SHAVER	WIGWAM	ANNUAL	CEREAL	GENIAL	MERMAN	REPLAY	UNSEAT	ATTACK
UNSUNG	SHAVES	YAHWEH	ANYWAY	CHORAL	GERMAN	MESCAL	REVEAL	UNSNAP	AVOUCH
UNTUNE	SHIVER	ELIXIR	APICAL	CLIMAX	GEWGAW	MICMAC	RIPSAW	UNWRAP	BEDECK
UPRUSH	SHOVEL	FLAXEN	APPEAL	COEVAL	GIMBAL	MIDDAY	RITUAL	UPBEAT	BISECT
UPTURN	SILVER	PLEXUS	APPEAR	COGNAC	GLOBAL	MIDWAY	RUNWAY	UPLOAD	BLANCH
VACUUM	SLAVER	ARGYLE	ARCTAN	COLLAR	GUFFAW	MISHAP	RUPIAH	UPREAR	BLEACH
VALUED	SLAVIC	BANYAN	ASHLAR	COLLAT	GUITAR	MISLAY	SALAAM	UPROAR	BLENCH
VICUNA	SLIVER	CANYON	ASHRAM	COMBAT	GUNMAN	MISSAL	SAMPAN	URINAL	BLOTCH
VISUAL	SLOVEN	CORYZA	ASTRAL	COMPAQ	HANGAR	MONDAY	SANDAL	VANDAL	BODICE
VOLUME	SNIVEL	CRAYON	ASTRAY	COMPAR	HEPCAT	MORGAN	SASHAY	VASSAL	BOUNCE
VOLUTE	SOEVER	ENCYST	ATONAL	CONFAB	HEYDAY	MORTAL	SATRAP	VENIAL	BRANCH
YOGURT	SPAVIN	ENZYME	AVATAR	CORRAL	HOOKAH	MORTAR	SCARAB	VERBAL	BREACH
BEAVER	STAVES	GRAYED	BAGMAN	COUGAR	HOWDAH	MUTUAL	SCREAM	VERNAL	BREECH
BREVET	SURVEY	LARYNX	BALLAD	COWMAN	HUBCAP	MYRIAD	SEAMAN	VESTAL	BROACH
CALVES	SWIVEL	LAWYER	BALSAM	CRAVAT	HURRAH	NECTAR	SEAWAY	VISUAL	BRONCO
CANVAS	SYLVAN	LIBYAN	BANTAM	CYMBAL	HUSSAR	NEURAL	SEESAW	VULGAR	BROOCH
CERVIX	TRAVEL	MAGYAR	BANYAN	DEEJAY	HUZZAH	NONFAT	SERIAL	WAYLAY	BRUNCH
CLEVER	TRIVET	PRAYER	BANZAI	DEFEAT	ICEMAN	NORMAL	SEXUAL	WIGWAG	CALICO
CLEVIS	TRIVIA	AMAZON	BAOBAB	DEFRAY	INDIAN	NORMAN	SHAMAN	WIGWAM	CHANCE
CLOVEN	TURVES	BANZAI	BATEAU	DEMEAN	INROAD	NOUGAT	SIGNAL	WITHAL	CHANCY
CLOVER	UNEVEN	BENZOL	BATMAN	DENIAL	INSEAM	OCULAR	SIMIAN	WOMBAT	CHOICE
COEVAL	VELVET	BLAZER	BAZAAR	DENTAL	IPECAC	ORDEAL	SKYCAP	YEOMAN	CHURCH
CONVEX	WAIVER	BLAZON	BEDLAM	DEODAR	ISOBAR	ORPHAN	SLOGAN	ZIGZAG	CIVICS
CONVEY	WEEVIL	BRAZEN	BEDPAN	DERMAL	JACKAL	OUTLAW	SMILAX	ZODIAC	CLENCH
CONVOY	AIRWAY	BUZZER	BEGGAR	DEWLAP	JAGUAR	OUTLAY	SOCIAL	AKIMBO	CLINCH
CRAVAT	ANSWER	DAZZLE	BEHEAD	DIRHAM	JETSAM	PARIAH	SPINAL	AMOEBA	CLUTCH
CRAVEN	ANYWAY	FIZZLE	BELDAM	DISBAR	JIGSAW	PARLAY	SPIRAL	CASABA	COERCE
CURVET	BIGWIG	FROZEN	BEMOAN	DISMAL	JOVIAL	PASCAL	SPREAD	CHUBBY	CROTCH
DRIVEL	BLOWSY	GEEZER	BETRAY	DISMAY	KIDNAP	PAWPAW	SQUEAK	CRABBY	CROUCH
DRIVER	BLOWUP	GUZZLE	BOBCAT	DISTAL	KOREAN	PENMAN	SQUEAL	FLABBY	CRUNCH
DROVER	BROWSE	HUZZAH	BONSAI	DOLLAR	LABIAL	PICKAX	STREAK	GAZEBO	CRUTCH
ELEVEN	COBWEB	MIZZEN	BOREAL	DOODAD	LANDAU	PILLAR	STREAM	GRUBBY	DEDUCE
FERVID	CREWEL	MUZZLE	BOWMAN	DORSAL	LARIAT	PINEAL	SUBWAY	HEREBY	DEDUCT
FERVOR	DRAWER	NOZZLE	BOXCAR	EARWAX	LASCAR	PLURAL	SULTAN	IMBIBE	DEFACE
FLAVOR	DROWSE	NUZZLE	BRIDAL	ENDEAR	LAWMAN	POLEAX	SUNDAE	JUJUBE	DEFECT
GRAVEL	DROWSY	PIAZZA	BROGAN	ENGRAM	LAYMAN	POPLAR	SUNDAY	NEARBY	DEPICT
GRAVID	EARWAX	PUZZLE	BRUTAL	ENTRAP	LEEWAY	PORTAL	SUNTAN	PHOEBE	DETACH
GROVEL	EARWIG	SCUZZY	BUREAU	EOLIAN	LEGMAN	POSTAL	SURTAX	SCRIBE	DETECT
HALVES	FLOWER	SIZZLE	BURIAL	FABIAN	LETHAL	PREFAB	SYLVAN	SHABBY	DEVICE
HEAVEN	FLYWAY	ZIGZAG	BURLAP	FACIAL	LIBYAN	PREPAY	SYNTAX	STROBE	DIRECT
JAYVEE	FROWSY		BURSAR	FAECAL	LINEAL	PREWAR	TARTAN	STUBBY	DRENCH
KELVIN	GLOWER		BYPLAY	FELLAH	LINEAR	PRIMAL	TARTAR	UNROBE	EFFACE
LEAVED	GROWTH	**5TH LETTER**	CAESAR	FENIAN	LOGJAM	PULSAR	THORAX	ABBACY	EFFECT
LEAVEN	LEEWAY	ABROAD	CAFTAN	FESTAL	LUMBAR	PURDAH	THREAD	ABDUCT	ENRICH
LEAVES	MIDWAY	ACTUAL	CAIMAN	FEUDAL	MADCAP	QINTAR	THREAT	ABJECT	ENTICE
LOUVER	NITWIT		CANCAN	FILIAL	MADMAN	QUASAR	THROAT	ADDICT	ETHICS

EUNUCH	QUENCH	ALLUDE	UPSIDE	BOWLEG	CLEVER	DEEPEN	FETTER	GRAVEL	JAILER
EVINCE	QUINCE	AMENDS	ZOUNDS	BOWLER	CLOSET	DEGREE	FIDGET	GRAYED	JASPER
EXPECT	REDACT	ARCADE	ACUMEN	BRAZEN	CLOVEN	DENIER	FILLER	GROCER	JAYCEE
FIANCE	REDUCE	ARMADA	ALLIED	BREVET	CLOVER	DESKEW	FILLET	GROVEL	JAYGEE
FIASCO	REJECT	BESIDE	AMULET	BROKEN	COBWEB	DIADEM	FILTER	GUINEA	JAYVEE
FIERCE	RELICT	BETIDE	ANADEM	BROKER	CODGER	DIAPER	FINDER	GULDEN	JENNET
FLEECE	SCARCE	BRANDY	ANKLET	BRUNET	COFFEE	DICKER	FINGER	GULLET	JERSEY
FLINCH	SCONCE	CICADA	ANSWER	BUCKET	COFFER	DICKEY	FISHER	GUNNER	JESTER
FLITCH	SCORCH	COMEDY	ANTHEM	BUDGET	COMBER	DIESEL	FLAXEN	GUSHER	JIGGER
FRENCH	SCOTCH	DECADE	ANTHER	BUFFER	COMDEX	DIFFER	FLOWER	GUSSET	JITNEY
FRESCO	SEANCE	DECIDE	ANTLER	BUFFET	COMPEL	DIMMER	FODDER	GUTTER	JOBBER
GLANCE	SEARCH	DECODE	APOGEE	BULLET	CONFED	DINNER	FOLDER	HACKER	JOCKEY
GLITCH	SEDUCE	DELUDE	APPLET	BUMMER	CONFER	DIPPER	FOOTED	HALTER	JOINER
GROUCH	SELECT	DEMODE	ARCNET	BUMPER	CONVEX	DISHED	FORGET	HALVES	JUICER
HAUNCH	SENECA	DENUDE	ARMLET	BUNKER	CONVEY	DISPEL	FORKED	HAMLET	JUMPER
HIJACK	SILICA	DERIDE	ASLEEP	BURDEN	COOLER	DITHER	FORMER	HAMMER	JUNKER
IDIOCY	SKETCH	DIRNDL	AVOCET	BURGEE	COOPER	DOCKET	FOSTER	HAMPER	JUNKET
IMPACT	SLOUCH	DIVIDE	AWAKEN	BURNER	COPIER	DODDER	FROZEN	HANKER	KAISER
INDICT	SLUICE	DUENDE	AZALEA	BUSHED	COPPER	DOGGED	FUHRER	HANSEL	KEGLER
INDUCE	SMIRCH	EMBODY	BACKER	BUSHEL	COPTER	DOGLEG	FUNNEL	HAPPEN	KENNEL
INDUCT	SMOOCH	ENCODE	BADGER	BUTLER	COQUET	DOLMEN	GADGET	HARDEN	KERNEL
INFECT	SMUTCH	ESCUDO	BALEEN	BUTTER	CORBEL	DONKEY	GAFFER	HARKEN	KIDNEY
INJECT	SNATCH	FACADE	BALLET	BUZZER	CORNEA	DORMER	GAITER	HASTEN	KILTER
INSECT	SNITCH	GOURDE	BANDED	CACHET	CORNER	DOWNER	GALLEY	HATRED	KIPPER
INTACT	SOLACE	HAIRDO	BANNER	CALVES	CORNET	DRAPER	GAMMER	HATTER	KISMET
JOUNCE	SOURCE	IMPEDE	BANTER	CAMBER	CORSET	DRAWER	GANDER	HAWKER	KISSER
KITSCH	SPEECH	INSIDE	BARBER	CAMPER	CORTEX	DRIVEL	GANNET	HAWSER	KITTEN
KLATCH	SPLICE	INVADE	BARKER	CANCEL	COTTER	DRIVER	GARDEN	HEAVEN	KOSHER
KOPECK	SPRUCE	IODIDE	BARLEY	CANCER	COULEE	DROVER	GARNER	HEBREW	LACKEY
LAUNCH	STANCE	LIBIDO	BARRED	CANKER	CRATER	DUFFER	GARNET	HEIFER	LADDER
LEGACY	STANCH	MALADY	BARREL	CANNED	CRAVEN	DULCET	GARRET	HELMET	LANCER
LUNACY	STARCH	MELODY	BARREN	CANTER	CREWEL	DUPLEX	GARTER	HERPES	LANCET
MALICE	STENCH	MIKADO	BARTER	CAREEN	CUDGEL	DUSTER	GASKET	HINDER	LANDED
MARACA	STITCH	MONODY	BASKET	CAREER	CUMBER	EAGLET	GATHER	HIPPED	LANDER
MEDICO	STRICT	NOBODY	BATTEN	CARIES	CUNNER	EASTER	GEEZER	HITHER	LAPPET
MENACE	STRUCK	ONEIDA	BATTER	CARPEL	CURFEW	ECCLES	GENDER	HOCKEY	LARDER
NAUTCH	STUCCO	OVERDO	BEAKER	CARPET	CURLEW	EITHER	GEYSER	HOLLER	LATHER
NOTICE	SWATCH	PAGODA	BEAVER	CARREL	CURVET	ELEVEN	GIBBER	HOOKER	LATTER
NOVICE	SWITCH	PARADE	BELIEF	CARTEL	CUTLER	EMBLEM	GIBBET	HOPPER	LAUREL
NUANCE	THATCH	PARODY	BENDER	CASHEW	CUTLET	ENAMEL	GIFTED	HORNET	LAWYER
OBJECT	THENCE	POMADE	BERBER	CASKET	CUTTER	ENTREE	GIMLET	HORSEY	LEADEN
OFFICE	THRICE	PSEUDO	BESEEM	CASTER	CYGNET	ESCHEW	GINGER	HOSTEL	LEADER
OPTICS	THWACK	RECEDE	BETHEL	CENSER	DAGGER	ESTEEM	GIRDER	HOTBED	LEAFED
PALACE	TRANCE	REMEDY	BETTER	CENTER	DAMPEN	EXCEED	GLIDER	HOWLER	LEAVED
PAPACY	TRENCH	RESIDE	BICKER	CERMET	DAMPER	EYELET	GLOWER	HOYDEN	LEAVEN
PATACA	TWITCH	SECEDE	BILLET	CHAFER	DAMSEL	FABLED	GLUTEN	HUNGER	LEAVES
PAUNCH	UNESCO	SHODDY	BINHEX	CHALET	DANDER	FALTER	GOATEE	HUNKER	LEDGER
PIERCE	UNLACE	STEADY	BITNET	CHAPEL	DANGER	FASTEN	GOBBET	HYPHEN	LESSEE
PIRACY	UNLOCK	STRIDE	BITTER	CHASER	DAPPER	FATHER	GOBLET	IBIDEM	LESSEN
POLICE	UNPACK	STRODE	BLAZER	CHISEL	DARKEN	FATTEN	GOITER	INBRED	LESSER
POLICY	VIVACE	STURDY	BOATER	CHOKER	DARNEL	FAUCES	GOLDEN	INDEED	LETTER
POUNCE	WHENCE	TEREDO	BOILER	CHOLER	DARTER	FAUCET	GOOBER	INKJET	LICHEE
PRANCE	WRENCH	TIRADE	BOMBER	CHOREA	DASHER	FEELER	GOPHER	INSTEP	LICHEN
PREACH	WRETCH	TRIODE	BONNET	CHOSEN	DAYBED	FENDER	GOSPEL	ISOMER	LIMBER
PRINCE	ABRADE	TUXEDO	BOOTEE	CINDER	DEADEN	FENNEL	GOTTEN	JABBER	LIMPET
PUMICE	ACCEDE	TWEEDY	BORDER	CIPHER	DEAFEN	FERRET	GRABEN	JACKET	LINDEN
PUTSCH	AGENDA	UNLADE	BOTHER	CLARET	DECREE	FESTER	GRADER	JAGGED	LINGER

LINKED	MOPPET	PEWTER	RATHER	SIGNET	TARGET	VENDEE	ZITHER	ENOUGH	VISAGE
LINNET	MORSEL	PHLOEM	RATTER	SILVER	TASSEL	VENDER	ZMODEM	ENRAGE	VOYAGE
LINTEL	MOSLEM	PICKET	REAMER	SIMMER	TATTER	VENEER	ZONKED	ENSIGN	ALIGHT
LISTEN	MOTHER	PIGLET	REDDEN	SIMPER	TEASEL	VERGER	ADRIFT	EULOGY	APACHE
LITTER	MOTLEY	PIGPEN	REDEEM	SINKER	TEEPEE	VERSED	BEREFT	FLANGE	APATHY
LOADED	MOUSER	PILFER	REEFER	SISTER	TEETER	VERTEX	CARAFE	FORAGE	ARIGHT
LOADER	MSCDEX	PINCER	REFLEX	SKEWER	TELLER	VESPER	CITIFY	FOREGO	BLIGHT
LOCKER	MULLET	PIQUET	REGRET	SLAVER	TELNET	VESSEL	CODIFY	FRINGE	BLITHE
LOCKET	MUMMER	PLACER	RELIEF	SLIDER	TEMPER	VESTEE	CUTOFF	GARAGE	BOUGHT
LODGER	MURDER	PLANET	RENDER	SLIVER	TENDER	VIOLET	FLUFFY	GINKGO	BRIGHT
LOITER	MUSKEG	PLATEN	RENNET	SLOVEN	TESTER	VIZIER	LAYOFF	GRANGE	BUQSHA
LOOPER	MUSKET	PLOVER	REVIEW	SNIVEL	TETHER	VOICED	MODIFY	GROGGY	CATCHY
LOOSEN	MUSSEL	POCKET	RICHES	SOCCER	TICKER	VOLLEY	NOTIFY	GRUDGE	CAUGHT
LOUVER	MUSTER	POLDER	RIDDEN	SOCKET	TICKET	VORTEX	OSSIFY	HOMAGE	CHICHI
LUBBER	MUTTER	POLLEN	RIGGER	SODDEN	TILLER	WAITER	PACIFY	IMPUGN	CLICHE
LUMBER	NAUSEA	POMMEL	RINGER	SOEVER	TIMBER	WAIVER	PAYOFF	INDIGO	CLOCHE
LUSTER	NEPHEW	PONDER	ROBBER	SOFTEN	TINDER	WALLET	PURIFY	LAVAGE	CLOTHE
MADDEN	NETHER	PONGEE	ROCKER	SOIREE	TINKER	WANDER	RAMIFY	LINAGE	CRECHE
MADDER	NEUTER	POPPER	ROCKET	SOLDER	TINSEL	WARDEN	RAREFY	LOUNGE	DINGHY
MAGNET	NICKEL	PORKER	ROLLER	SOMBER	TIPPET	WARDER	RATIFY	MALIGN	DOUCHE
MAIDEN	NICKER	PORTER	ROMPER	SONNET	TITLED	WARREN	REBUFF	MANAGE	EARTHY
MAILED	NIPPER	POSTER	ROSTER	SORREL	TITTER	WASHER	RUNOFF	MANEGE	FLASHY
MALLET	NUGGET	POTEEN	ROTTEN	SOVIET	TOFFEE	WEAKEN	SCRUFF	MENAGE	FLESHY
MANGER	NUMBER	POTHER	RUBBER	SPIDER	TOILET	WEASEL	SHRIFT	MIRAGE	FLIGHT
MANNED	NUTMEG	POTTER	RUDDER	SPINEL	TOTTER	WEBBED	STRAFE	NONAGE	FOUGHT
MANNER	OFFSET	POWDER	RUGGED	SPINET	TOUPEE	WELTER	STRIFE	OBLIGE	FRIGHT
MANTEL	OMELET	PRAYER	RUNLET	SPIREA	TOWHEE	WETHER	STUFFY	ORANGE	GAUCHE
MARCEL	OODLES	PREFER	RUNNEL	SPLEEN	TRADER	WHALER	TARIFF	PELAGE	GAUCHO
MARKED	OSPREY	PREMED	RUNNER	SPOKEN	TRAVEL	WHITEN	THRIFT	PHLEGM	GEISHA
MARKET	OSTLER	PRESET	RUSSET	STAMEN	TRIVET	WICKED	TYPIFY	PLEDGE	GURKHA
MARTEN	OUSTER	PRIMER	SACHEM	STAPES	TROWEL	WICKER	UPLIFT	PLUNGE	HEIGHT
MARVEL	OUTLET	PRIVET	SACHET	STAVES	TUCKER	WICKET	VERIFY	POTAGE	KNIGHT
MASTER	OUTSET	PROPEL	SACRED	STEREO	TUNNEL	WIENER	VILIFY	RAVAGE	KWACHA
MATTER	OXYGEN	PROPER	SADDEN	STOLEN	TUREEN	WIGLET	VIVIFY	REFUGE	LITCHI
MAYHEM	OYSTER	PUCKER	SALVER	STONED	TURKEY	WINDER	ALLEGE	RENEGE	LOATHE
MEAGER	PACKER	PULLET	SATEEN	STREET	TURNER	WINGED	ASSIGN	RESIGN	MEGOHM
MEDLEY	PACKET	PULLEY	SAUCER	SUBLET	TURRET	WINKER	AVENGE	SAVAGE	NAUGHT
MEMBER	PALLET	PUMMEL	SCREEN	SUBSET	TURVES	WINNER	AWEIGH	SEWAGE	NAVAHO
MENSES	PALMER	PUPPET	SEABED	SUCKER	TUSKER	WINTER	BELUGA	SHAGGY	NOUGHT
MERCER	PALTER	PURSER	SEALER	SUDDEN	ULSTER	WITHER	BENIGN	SILAGE	PLIGHT
MERGER	PAMPER	PURVEY	SECRET	SUFFER	UNDIES	WITTED	BRIDGE	SLEDGE	PONCHO
METIER	PANDER	PUSHER	SELVES	SULLEN	UNEVEN	WONDER	CAYUGA	SLEIGH	PSYCHE
MIDDEN	PARCEL	PUTTEE	SEQUEL	SUMMER	UNICEF	WONTED	CHANGE	SLOUGH	PSYCHO
MIDGET	PARLEY	PUTTER	SERIES	SUNDER	UNISEX	WOODED	CHARGE	SLUDGE	RANCHO
MILDEW	PARSEC	QUAKER	SERVER	SUNKEN	UNITED	WOODEN	CLERGY	SMUDGE	RHYTHM
MILIEU	PASSEL	QUAVER	SETTEE	SUNSET	UNMEET	WOOFER	CRINGE	SPONGE	SCYTHE
MILLER	PASTEL	QUIVER	SETTER	SUPPER	UNREEL	WOOLEN	DAMAGE	SPURGE	SEETHE
MILLET	PATTER	RABBET	SEXTET	SURREY	UNUSED	WORKER	DELUGE	STINGY	SLIGHT
MINDED	PAUPER	RABIES	SHAKER	SURVEY	UPKEEP	WORSEN	DESIGN	STODGY	SMITHY
MINUET	PAWNEE	RACKET	SHAVER	SWIVEL	URETER	WRITER	DOINGS	STOOGE	SOOTHE
MISTER	PEAHEN	RAFTER	SHAVES	SYSTEM	USENET	XMODEM	DOTAGE	THOUGH	SOUGHT
MITTEN	PEAKED	RAGGED	SHINER	TABLET	USURER	YAHWEH	DREDGE	TRIAGE	SPATHE
MIZZEN	PEEWEE	RANGER	SHIVER	TAMPER	VALLEY	YAMMER	DRUDGE	TROUGH	SWATHE
MOLDER	PELLET	RAPIER	SHOVEL	TANDEM	VALUED	YANKEE	EFFIGY	TRUDGE	TAUGHT
MOLTEN	PEPPER	RAPPEN	SHOWER	TANKER	VARIED	YMODEM	EMERGE	TWINGE	TEETHE
MONGER	PESTER	RASHER	SHRIEK	TANNER	VARLET	YONDER	ENERGY	ULLAGE	TETCHY
MONKEY	PETREL	RASTER	SICKEN	TAPPET	VELVET	ZIPPER	ENGAGE	VIRAGO	TOOTHY

TOUCHE	COLLIE	GARLIC	MUSLIN	RABBIT	TROPIC	UPTAKE	CUDDLE	GIRDLE	MANGLE
TOUCHY	COMFIT	GERBIL	MYOPIA	RAFFIA	TUGRIK	AFIELD	CUPOLA	GOBBLE	MANTLE
TROCHE	COMMIT	GOALIE	MYSTIC	RAISIN	TURBID	ALKALI	CURDLE	GOGGLE	MARBLE
TROPHY	COOKIE	GOBLIN	NAPKIN	RANCID	TURGID	ANNALS	DABBLE	GOODLY	MAYFLY
WEIGHT	COOLIE	GOSSIP	NEREID	RECOIL	TURNIP	APPALL	DANDLE	GRILLE	MEASLY
WORTHY	COOTIE	GOTHIC	NIACIN	REFRIG	ULTRIX	ARABLE	DANGLE	GRISLY	MEDDLE
WRITHE	COSMIC	GRATIS	NITRIC	REGAIN	UNCOIL	ARGYLE	DAPPLE	GURGLE	METTLE
ABATIS	COUSIN	GRAVID	NITWIT	REJOIN	UNFAIR	AWHILE	DAWDLE	GUZZLE	MIDDLE
ACACIA	CREDIT	HACKIE	NOGGIN	REMAIN	UNSHIP	BABBLE	DAZZLE	HACKLE	MINGLE
ACETIC	CRETIN	HAGGIS	NORDIC	RENNIN	UNVEIL	BAFFLE	DEADLY	HAGGLE	MOBILE
ACQUIT	CRISIS	HECTIC	NUBBIN	REPAIR	URACIL	BANGLE	DEFILE	HALALA	MODULE
ADAGIO	CRITIC	HEREIN	NUNCIO	RETAIL	URANIC	BARELY	DESALT	HANDLE	MORALE
ADJOIN	CUSPID	HERMIT	NUTRIA	RETAIN	URCHIN	BARFLY	DIBBLE	HARDLY	MOSTLY
ADROIT	DAHLIA	HERNIA	OBTAIN	RLOGIN	UREMIA	BASALT	DIMPLE	HASSLE	MOTILE
AFFAIR	DEBRIS	HEROIN	ORCHID	ROOKIE	UTOPIA	BATTLE	DINGLE	HECKLE	MOTTLE
AFRAID	DECEIT	HIPPIE	ORDAIN	RUBRIC	VERMIN	BAUBLE	DOCILE	HERALD	MUDDLE
ALBEIT	DENTIN	HOAGIE	ORIGIN	RUSTIC	VICTIM	BEADLE	DOODLE	HOBBLE	MUFFLE
ALTAIR	DERAIL	HORRID	OUTBID	SCORIA	VIOLIN	BEAGLE	DOTTLE	HOMELY	MUMBLE
ANEMIA	DERMIS	HUBRIS	OUTFIT	SEPSIS	VIRGIN	BECALM	DOUBLE	HOMILY	MUSCLE
ARABIC	DERRIS	HYBRID	OUTWIT	SEPTIC	VISCID	BEETLE	DOUBLY	HOOPLA	MUZZLE
ARCSIN	DETAIL	IMPAIR	PALLID	SEQUIN	WEEVIL	BEFALL	EDIBLE	HUDDLE	MYRTLE
ARCTIC	DETAIN	INLAID	PANTIE	SLAVIC	WELKIN	BEHALF	EMBALM	HUMBLE	MYSELF
ARMPIT	DEVOID	INTUIT	PAPAIN	SORDID	WESKIT	BEHOLD	ENABLE	HURDLE	NAMELY
ASSAIL	DEVOIR	IRENIC	PASSIM	SORTIE	WITHIN	BOBBLE	ENFOLD	HURTLE	NAPALM
ATOMIC	DOBBIN	IRONIC	PATOIS	SPADIX	ZINNIA	BODILY	ENGULF	HUSTLE	NEBULA
ATTAIN	DOMAIN	ITALIC	PCMCIA	SPAVIN	ZOMBIE	BOGGLE	ENISLE	ICICLE	NEEDLE
ATTRIB	DUBBIN	JERKIN	PECTIN	SPECIE	ZOYSIA	BOODLE	ENROLL	IMPALA	NESTLE
BAGNIO	EARWIG	JUDAIC	PELVIS	SPECIF	ABNAKI	BOTTLE	ENSILE	IMPALE	NETTLE
BANDIT	EBCDIC	JUNKIE	PENCIL	SPIRIT	BELIKE	BRIDLE	EXHALE	INFOLD	NIBBLE
BARRIO	ECLAIR	KAOLIN	PEPSIN	SPRAIN	BETAKE	BUBBLE	FACILE	INHALE	NIMBLE
BEANIE	ELICIT	KELVIN	PEPTIC	STATIC	CHEEKY	BUCKLE	FACULA	INSOLE	NIPPLE
BESTIR	ELIXIR	KERMIT	PERMIT	STOLID	CHUKKA	BUNDLE	FAILLE	INSULT	NODDLE
BEWAIL	EMETIC	LACTIC	PHOBIA	STRAIN	CHUNKY	BUNGLE	FAIRLY	ITSELF	NODULE
BIGWIG	ENDRIN	LADDIE	PHONIC	STRAIT	CRANKY	BURGLE	FAMILY	JANGLE	NOODLE
BIOTIC	ENJOIN	LASSIE	PHYSIC	STUDIO	EUREKA	BUSILY	FEEBLE	JIGGLE	NOVELL
BIOTIN	ENTAIL	LENTIL	PICNIC	STUPID	FLUNKY	BUSTLE	FEMALE	JINGLE	NOZZLE
BIRDIE	EROTIC	LIMPID	PIDGIN	STYMIE	FRISKY	CABALA	FERULE	JOGGLE	NUBBLE
BOBBIN	ESPRIT	LIQUID	PINKIE	SUBMIT	INTAKE	CACKLE	FETTLE	JOSTLE	NUBILE
BOCCIE	ETHNIC	LOGGIA	PIPKIN	SUFFIX	INVOKE	CAJOLE	FIBULA	JUGGLE	NUZZLE
BODKIN	EXOTIC	MAGPIE	PIPPIN	SUMMIT	KABUKI	CANDLE	FICKLE	JUMBLE	OCCULT
BOOKIE	EYELID	MANTIS	PISTIL	SUNLIT	MARKKA	CANTLE	FIDDLE	JUNGLE	ORACLE
BUDGIE	FABRIC	MARGIN	PLACID	TACTIC	PERUKE	CASTLE	FINALE	KETTLE	ORIOLE
BUSKIN	FAERIE	MARLIN	POPLIN	TANNIN	PLUCKY	CATTLE	FIZZLE	KIBBLE	ORMOLU
CADDIE	FERRIC	MARTIN	POTPIE	TENNIS	REBUKE	CHICLE	FOIBLE	KINDLE	OVERLY
CALCIC	FERVID	MASSIF	PRECIS	TENPIN	RETAKE	CHILLY	FONDLE	KINDLY	PADDLE
CANDID	FIBRIL	MASTIC	PREFIX	TESTIS	REVOKE	CIRCLE	FUDDLE	KIRTLE	PAPULE
CASEIN	FIBRIN	MATRIX	PRELIM	THESIS	SHEIKH	COBALT	FUMBLE	KOBOLD	PAROLE
CASSIA	FILLIP	MEMOIR	PREMIX	TIDBIT	SHRIKE	COBBLE	FUTILE	LABILE	PARTLY
CATKIN	FLORID	METRIC	PROFIT	TIFFIN	STICKY	COCKLE	GABBLE	LIABLE	PEBBLE
CATNIP	FLORIN	MIDAIR	PROLIX	TITBIT	STOCKY	CODDLE	GADFLY	LIKELY	PEDDLE
CERVIX	FORBID	MISFIT	PUBLIC	TOCSIN	STRIKE	COMELY	GAGGLE	LITTLE	PEOPLE
CHITIN	FOSSIL	MOHAIR	PUFFIN	TOMTIT	STROKE	COMPLY	GAMBLE	LIVELY	PESTLE
CLERIC	FRIGID	MORBID	PULPIT	TONSIL	THANKS	COPULA	GARBLE	LOBULE	PICKLE
CLEVIS	FROLIC	MORRIS	PUNDIT	TORPID	TRICKY	COSTLY	GARGLE	LOCALE	PIDDLE
CLINIC	GAELIC	MOSAIC	PUNKIN	TORRID	TROIKA	COUPLE	GENTLE	LONELY	PIFFLE
COFFIN	GALLIC	MUFFIN	PUTRID	TRAGIC	UNLIKE	CRADLE	GIGGLE	LORDLY	PIMPLE
COHEIR	GAMBIT	MUSLIM	QBASIC	TRIVIA	UNYOKE	CREOLE	GIGOLO	LOVELY	POODLE

PORTLY	THRILL	AFLAME	ALBINO	DIVINE	KIMONO	REMIND	URBANE	CARBOY	GALLON
PUDDLE	TICKLE	APLOMB	ALMOND	DOCENT	KORUNA	REPENT	URGENT	CARHOP	GALLOP
PUEBLO	TIMELY	ASSUME	ALPINE	DOMINO	LACUNA	REPINE	URSINE	CARROT	GAMBOL
PURPLE	TINGLE	ASTHMA	ALUMNA	DOPANT	LADING	RESENT	VACANT	CARTON	GAMMON
PUZZLE	TINKLE	AUTUMN	AMOUNT	DUENNA	LAMENT	RETINA	VAGINA	CARTOP	GARCON
RABBLE	TIPPLE	BECOME	ANGINA	DURING	LAMINA	RIBAND	VICUNA	CATION	GIBBON
RAFFLE	TITTLE	BENUMB	ANOINT	EDGING	LARYNX	RODENT	VIKING	CENSOR	GIBSON
RAMBLE	TODDLE	BIGAMY	ANYONE	EMBANK	LATENT	ROMANO	WAHINE	CITRON	GODSON
RANKLE	TOGGLE	CHROME	APPEND	ENDING	LEGEND	ROTUND	WHINNY	CLAMOR	GUIDON
RATTLE	TOPPLE	CHROMO	ARCANE	ENGINE	LIKING	SALINE	WIRING	COCOON	HALLOW
REALLY	TOUSLE	CHUMMY	ARDENT	EQUINE	LINING	SARONG	ZENANA	COLLOQ	HANSOM
RECALL	TREBLE	CINEMA	ARGENT	ERMINE	LITANY	SATANG	ABLOOM	COMMON	HARBOR
REFILL	TRIFLE	CLAMMY	AROUND	ERRAND	LIVING	SAVANT	ACTION	CONDOM	HARLOT
REGALE	TRIPLE	COLUMN	ARRANT	ERRANT	LOVING	SAYING	AMAZON	CONDOR	HARROW
RESALE	TRIPLY	CRUMMY	ASCEND	ETHANE	LUCENT	SECOND	ANALOG	CONSOL	HATBOX
RESULT	TUBULE	DECAMP	ASCENT	EXPAND	LUPINE	SERENE	ANCHOR	CONVOY	HAYMOW
REVILE	TUMBLE	DEFAME	ASLANT	EXPEND	MANANA	SEWING	ANYHOW	CORDON	HECTOR
REVOLT	TUMULT	DYNAMO	ASSENT	EXTANT	MARINA	SHINNY	APPROX	COSMOS	HEREOF
RIBALD	TURTLE	ECZEMA	ATTEND	EXTEND	MARINE	SHRINE	ARCCOS	COTTON	HEREON
RIDDLE	TUSSLE	ENCAMP	ATTUNE	EXTENT	MATINS	SHRINK	ARCHON	COUPON	HOBNOB
RIPPLE	UNABLE	ENIGMA	AVAUNT	FACING	MENINX	SIDING	ASTROL	COWBOY	HOLLOW
ROUBLE	UNBOLT	ENTOMB	AWNING	FAMINE	MERINO	SILENT	ASTRON	COWPOX	HOODOO
RUBBLE	UNDULY	ENZYME	BANANA	FARINA	MOMENT	SIMONY	AUTHOR	CRATON	HORROR
RUFFLE	UNFOLD	ESKIMO	BEGONE	FECUND	MUTANT	SKINNY	BABOON	CRAYON	HOTBOX
RUMBLE	UNHOLY	EXHUME	BEHIND	FELINE	MUTINY	SOIGNE	BALBOA	CUCKOO	HYSSOP
RUMPLE	UNPILE	ILLUME	BELONG	FELONY	NOVENA	SPHINX	BALLOT	CURSOR	ICEBOX
RUSTLE	UNROLL	INCOME	BEYOND	FILING	OBLONG	SPLINE	BAMBOO	CUSTOM	INDOOR
SADDLE	UNRULY	INFAMY	BIKINI	FLAUNT	OCTANE	SPLINT	BARROW	DAEMON	INFLOW
SAMPLE	UNTOLD	INHUME	BITING	FLUENT	OFFEND	SPRING	BATHOS	DAMSON	INTROD
SCROLL	UNWELL	LEGUME	BLUING	FOMENT	OFFING	SPRINT	BEACON	DEACON	JARGON
SEEMLY	UPHILL	MADAME	BOTANY	FORINT	ORIENT	SPRUNG	BECKON	DEBTOR	JUNIOR
SENILE	UPHOLD	MIASMA	BOVINE	FRIEND	OUTING	SQUINT	BEHOOF	DEPLOY	KOWTOW
SETTLE	UPWELL	PANAMA	BOXING	GALENA	PALING	STRAND	BELLOW	DESPOT	LAGOON
SHIELD	USABLE	PLASMA	BUTANE	GAMINE	PARENT	STRING	BENZOL	DIATOM	LAPDOG
SHOULD	VERILY	RACEME	BYGONE	GERUND	PARING	STRONG	BESTOW	DOCTOR	LAPTOP
SHRILL	VIABLE	REGIME	CABANA	GRAINY	PATENT	STRUNG	BETTOR	DOLLOP	LECTOR
SICKLE	VIRILE	RESUME	CANINE	GROUND	PATINA	SUPINE	BILLOW	DRAGON	LEGION
SIGILL	VITALS	REVAMP	CASING	HOMINY	PAVING	TAKING	BISHOP	EEPROM	LEPTON
SIMILE	WABBLE	SALAMI	CASINO	HUMANE	PEDANT	TALENT	BLAZON	EGGNOG	LESION
SIMPLE	WADDLE	SCHEME	CEMENT	HYAENA	PILING	TENANT	BONBON	EMPLOY	LESSON
SINGLE	WAFFLE	SCRIMP	CHAUNT	IGUANA	PIPING	THRONE	BORROW	ENAMOR	LESSOR
SIZZLE	WAGGLE	SESAME	CLIENT	IMMUNE	PLAINT	THRONG	BOTTOM	ESCROW	LIQUOR
SQUALL	WAMBLE	SHIMMY	COGENT	IMPEND	PLIANT	TRIUNE	BRITON	ETHNOL	LOTION
STABLE	WANGLE	SHRIMP	COLONY	INDENT	POTENT	TRUANT	BUNION	FACTOR	LUMMOX
STAPLE	WARBLE	SODOMY	COMING	INFANT	PURINE	TRYING	BURROW	FAGGOT	MACRON
STIFLE	WATTLE	SOLEMN	COPING	INLAND	QUAINT	TUBING	BUSBOY	FALCON	MAGGOT
STROLL	WEAKLY	STIGMA	CORONA	INNING	RAPINE	TURING	BUTTON	FALLOW	MALLOW
SUBTLE	WEEKLY	TRAUMA	COSINE	INSANE	RARING	TYRANT	CAHOOT	FARROW	MAMMON
SUCKLE	WHOLLY	ULTIMO	CRANNY	INTEND	RATING	UNBEND	CALLOW	FATHOM	MANIOC
SUPPLE	WIGGLE	VOLUME	DARING	INTENT	RAVINE	UNBIND	CANDOR	FELLOW	MARMOT
SUPPLY	WIGGLY	WHAMMY	DEBUNK	INTONE	RECANT	UNHAND	CANNON	FERVOR	MAROON
TACKLE	WIMBLE	ABOUND	DECANT	INVENT	RECENT	UNKIND	CANNOT	FLACON	MARROW
TAMALE	WIMPLE	ABSENT	DECENT	IODINE	REFINE	UNSUNG	CANTON	FLAGON	MASCON
TANGLE	WINKLE	ACCENT	DEFEND	ISLAND	REFUND	UNTUNE	CANTOR	FLAVOR	MASCOT
TATTLE	WOBBLE	ACTING	DEFINE	JEJUNE	REGENT	UNWIND	CANYON	FOLLOW	MATRON
TEMPLE	WOOLLY	ADDEND	DEMAND	JOCUND	RELENT	UPLAND	CAPTOR	FURROW	MEADOW
THRALL	YEARLY	ADVENT	DEPEND	JOHNNY	REMAND	UPWIND	CARBON	FUSION	MELLOW

MENTOR	POTION	TRIPOD	SCRIPT	CANARY	HEGIRA	RETORT	WINTRY	DAMASK	INFUSE
METEOR	POWWOW	TRITON	SCULPT	CAVERN	IGNORE	RETURN	WIZARD	DANISH	INGEST
METHOD	PRISON	TURBOT	SERAPE	CAVORT	IMMURE	REVERB	YOGURT	DEBASE	INMOST
MICRON	PROLOG	TYCOON	SERAPH	CELERY	IMPART	REVERE	ABBESS	DEFUSE	INRUSH
MINION	PROTON	UNCLOG	SKIMPY	CENTRE	IMPERF	REVERS	ACCESS	DEMISE	INSIST
MINNOW	PYTHON	UNHOOK	SLEEPY	CHEERY	IMPORT	REVERT	ACCOST	DEPOSE	INVEST
MIRROR	QUAHOG	UNISON	SLOPPY	CHERRY	IMPURE	REWARD	ACCUSE	DESIST	JOCOSE
MORMON	RAMROD	UNMOOR	SNIPPY	COHERE	INBORN	ROSARY	ACROSS	DETEST	JURIST
MORROW	RANCOR	UNROOF	STEPPE	COHORT	INFIRM	ROTARY	ADJUST	DEVISE	KIBOSH
MOTION	RANDOM	UNSHOD	STRIPE	COVERT	INFORM	SAFARI	ADVISE	DIGEST	LAVISH
MOUTON	RANSOM	UNSTOP	TROUPE	COWARD	INHERE	SALARY	AFRESH	DISUSE	LOCUST
MUTTON	RATION	UPROOT	UNRIPE	DEBARK	INJURE	SATIRE	AGHAST	DIVEST	MAOISM
NARROW	REASON	UPSHOT	UNWEPT	DEFORM	INJURY	SATURN	ALMOST	DRESSY	MIMOSA
NATION	RECKON	VAGROM	ABJURE	DEHORN	INSERT	SCURRY	AMBUSH	DROPSY	MISUSE
NELSON	RECTOR	VECTOR	ABOARD	DEMURE	INSURE	SECURE	ARGOSY	DROWSE	MODEST
NEUROL	REGION	VENDOR	ABSORB	DEPART	INTERJ	SENTRY	AROUSE	DROWSY	MODISH
NEURON	RIBBON	VICTOR	ABSURD	DEPORT	INTERN	SEVERE	ARREST	DURESS	MOLEST
NEWTON	SAILOR	VIRION	ACCORD	DESCRY	INVERT	SHERRY	ARTIST	EGOISM	MONISM
NIMROD	SALLOW	VISION	ADHERE	DESERT	INWARD	SIERRA	ASSESS	EGRESS	MOROSE
NONCOM	SALMON	VOODOO	ADJURE	DESIRE	LIVERY	SLURRY	ASSIST	ELAPSE	MOUSSE
NORTON	SALOON	WALLOP	ADMIRE	DISARM	LIZARD	SPHERE	ATTEST	ELDEST	NOWISE
NOTION	SAVIOR	WALLOW	ADSORB	DIVERS	LOWERY	SQUARE	AUGUST	EMBOSS	NUDISM
OCELOT	SCHOOL	WANTON	ADVERB	DIVERT	LUXURY	SQUIRE	AUTISM	ENCASE	OBSESS
OPTION	SEASON	WEAPON	ADVERT	DOTARD	MANTRA	SQUIRM	AVERSE	ENCYST	OBTUSE
ORATOR	SECTOR	WHILOM	AFFIRM	DREARY	MANURE	SQUIRT	BANISH	ENLIST	OFFISH
ORISON	SELDOM	WILLOW	AFFORD	EATERY	MATURE	SUBORN	BEHEST	ENMESH	ONRUSH
OUTFOX	SENIOR	WINDOW	ALLURE	EFFORT	MEMORY	SUBURB	BEMUSE	EXCESS	OPPOSE
PALEON	SENSOR	WINNOW	AMPERE	EMBARK	MESSRS	SULTRY	BIOPSY	EXCISE	ORGASM
PALLOR	SERMON	WISDOM	ANGORA	EMIGRE	MISERY	SUNDRY	BLOUSE	EXCUSE	OTIOSE
PARDON	SEXPOT	YARROW	APIARY	EMPIRE	MODERN	SUPERB	BLOWSY	EXPOSE	PAPIST
PARLOR	SEXTON	YELLOW	ARMORY	ENCORE	NAPERY	SUTURE	BLUISH	FAMISH	PARISH
PARROT	SHADOW	ZEALOT	ARTERY	ENDURE	NATURE	TAVERN	BOURSE	FETISH	PERISH
PARSON	SIPHON	ZIRCON	ASHORE	ENDURO	OEUVRE	TAWDRY	BRAISE	FINISH	PERUSE
PASTOR	SLALOM	ABRUPT	ASPIRE	ENSURE	ONWARD	TENURE	BREAST	FLIMSY	PHRASE
PATHOS	SNOBOL	ACCEPT	ASSERT	ENTIRE	ORDURE	THEIRS	BROWSE	FLOSSY	PLEASE
PATROL	SOCIOL	BICEPS	ASSORT	ESCORT	ORNERY	THEORY	BRUISE	FOLKSY	POLISH
PATRON	SORROW	CALIPH	ASSURE	EUCHRE	OUTCRY	THWART	BYPASS	FOREST	POTASH
PENNON	SPIGOT	CANAPE	ASTERN	EXHORT	OXFORD	TIMBRE	CARESS	FROWSY	PRAISE
PEQUOT	STOLON	CANOPY	ATTIRE	EXPERT	PALTRY	TORERO	CAYUSE	GALOSH	PRIEST
PERIOD	STUPOR	CHOPPY	AUBURN	EXPIRE	PANTRY	TOWARD	CERISE	GARISH	PRISSY
PERSON	SUCCOR	CREEPY	AUGURY	EXPORT	PASTRY	TUNDRA	CHAISE	GLOSSY	PUNISH
PETROL	SUITOR	ESCAPE	AURORA	EXTERN	PENURY	UMPIRE	CHEESE	GNEISS	PURISM
PHAROS	SUMMON	EXCEPT	AVIARY	EXTORT	PETARD	UNBORN	CHOOSE	GREASE	QUEASY
PHENOL	SYMBOL	EXEMPT	AWEARY	FEDORA	PLIERS	UNCORK	CHOOSY	GROUSE	QUINSY
PHILOS	SYPHON	FLOPPY	AWHIRL	FIGURE	POETRY	UNCURL	CHRISM	HARASS	RACISM
PHOTOG	TAILOR	FRAPPE	BAKERY	FINERY	PRIORY	UNFURL	CHRIST	HEARSE	RADISH
PHOTON	TALLOW	FRUMPY	BEFORE	FLURRY	QUARRY	UNGIRD	CLASSY	HERESY	RAKISH
PIGEON	TAMPON	GRIPPE	BELFRY	FRIARY	REBORN	UPTURN	CLAUSE	HOARSE	RAVISH
PILLOW	TARPON	GRUMPY	BEMIRE	FURORE	RECORD	UPWARD	CLUMSY	HONEST	RECESS
PINION	TATTOO	IRRUPT	BEWARE	FUTURE	REFORM	VAGARY	COARSE	ILLUST	REFUSE
PISTOL	TEAPOT	JALOPY	BINARY	GABBRO	REGARD	VAPORY	CORPSE	IMPISH	REHASH
PISTON	TENDON	MACAPP	BISTRO	GALORE	REMARK	VENIRE	COURSE	IMPOSE	RELISH
PLUTON	TERROR	OCCUPY	BLEARY	GANTRY	REMORA	VESTRY	CREASE	IMPOST	REMISS
POGROM	TIPTOE	PROMPT	BOLERO	GENERA	REPORT	VIZARD	CRUISE	INCASE	REPAST
POISON	TOMBOY	RECIPE	BYWORD	GENTRY	RESORT	VOTARY	CUBISM	INCEST	REPOSE
POMPON	TORPOR	SCAMPI	CAMERA	GOVERN	RETARD	WATERY	CURTSY	INCISE	RESIST
POTBOY	TREMOR	SCRAPE	CANARD	HAZARD	RETIRE	WHERRY	DALASI	INFEST	REVISE

ROBUST	CONSTR	INVITE	SANITY	BULBUL	HICCUP	PURSUE	ACTIVE	ZEPHYR	CUPOLA
SADISM	COUNTY	JAUNTY	SCANTY	BUNKUM	HOLDUP	PUTOUT	ALCOVE	ABLAZE	DAHLIA
SCHISM	COYOTE	KARATE	SEDATE	CACTUS	HONOUR	QIVIUT	ARRIVE	ASSIZE	DAKOTA
SCHIST	CRAFTY	LEGATE	SEMITE	CAECUM	HOOKUP	QUORUM	BEHAVE	BREEZE	DUENNA
SCHUSS	CREATE	LEGATO	SENATE	CALLUS	HUBBUB	RADIUM	CLEAVE	BRONZE	ECZEMA
SEXISM	CUESTA	LENGTH	SENITI	CAMPUS	HUMBUG	RADIUS	DATIVE	CORYZA	ENIGMA
SHIEST	CURATE	LENITY	SHANTY	CAPFUL	HUMOUR	RAGOUT	DERIVE	FLOOZY	ERRATA
SLIEST	DAINTY	LEVITY	SHEATH	CASQUE	IMBRUE	RECOUP	ENDIVE	FREEZE	EUREKA
SPARSE	DAKOTA	LIGATE	SHIFTY	CATGUT	INDIUM	RECTUM	EVOLVE	FRENZY	FACULA
SPLASH	DEARTH	LIGHTS	SHINTO	CATSUP	INFLUX	REFLUX	GRIEVE	FRIEZE	FARINA
SPOUSE	DEBATE	LIKUTA	SIESTA	CAUCUS	JOYFUL	RESCUE	GROOVE	IODIZE	FEDORA
SQUASH	DELETE	LOCATE	SLEUTH	CENSUS	JOYOUS	RISQUE	GROOVY	IONIZE	FIBULA
STRESS	DEMOTE	MAKUTA	SMOOTH	CEREUS	LABIUM	RUCKUS	MOTIVE	PIAZZA	FIESTA
TAOISM	DENOTE	MIGHTY	SNOOTY	CERIUM	LABOUR	RUMPUS	NATIVE	SCUZZY	GALENA
THEISM	DEPUTE	MINUTE	SONATA	CESIUM	LAWFUL	SACRUM	OCTAVE	SLEAZY	GEISHA
THIRST	DEPUTY	MOIETY	SPOTTY	CHEQUE	LAYOUT	SHROUD	OCTAVO	SNEEZE	GENERA
THRASH	DEVOTE	MUTATE	SPRITE	CHERUB	LEAGUE	SINFUL	RELIVE	SNOOZE	GUINEA
THRESH	DILATE	NEGATE	SURETY	CHORUS	LINEUP	SLIPUP	REMOVE	STANZA	GURKHA
THRUSH	DILUTE	NICETY	SVELTE	CILIUM	LINKUP	SODIUM	REVIVE	WHEEZE	HALALA
THRUST	DIMITY	NINETY	THIRTY	CIRCUS	LITMUS	SPROUT	SALIVA	WHEEZY	HEGIRA
TRANSL	DONATE	OBLATE	TIGHTS	CIRQUE	LOCKUP	SPUTUM	SCURVY	**6TH LETTER**	HERNIA
TRANSP	DRAFTY	ODDITY	TOMATO	CIRRUS	LYCEUM	STATUE	SHEAVE		HOOPLA
TRUISM	EFFETE	OOLITE	TREATY	CITRUS	MAHOUT	STATUS	SHELVE		HYAENA
TSETSE	EIGHTY	OPIATE	TRUSTY	CLAQUE	MAKEUP	STYLUS	SHRIVE		IGUANA
TYPIST	ENMITY	ORNATE	TWENTY	CLIQUE	MANFUL	SUBDUE	SLEEVE		IMPALA
UNEASY	ENTITY	ORNITH	UPDATE	COCCUS	MANQUE	SULFUR	STARVE	ACACIA	KORUNA
UNJUST	EQUATE	PAIUTE	UPPITY	COITUS	MARAUD	TALMUD	STRIVE	AGENDA	KWACHA
UNLESS	EQUITY	PALATE	VACATE	CONCUR	MARKUP	TARSUS	STROVE	ALPACA	LACUNA
UNMASK	ERRATA	PARITY	VANITY	CONSUL	MASQUE	TEACUP	SWERVE	ALUMNA	LAMINA
UNREST	ERSATZ	PESETA	VERITY	CORPUS	MEDIUM	TEDIUM	THIEVE	AMOEBA	LIKUTA
UNWISE	ESTATE	PETITE	VOLUTE	CROCUS	MISCUE	THYMUS	THRIVE	ANEMIA	LOGGIA
UPMOST	EXCITE	PEYOTE	WAPITI	CURIUM	MORGUE	TISSUE	THROVE	ANGINA	MAKUTA
UPPISH	FEALTY	PIGSTY	WARMTH	CUTOUT	MOSQUE	TONGUE	TWELVE	ANGORA	MANANA
UPRUSH	FIESTA	PIRATE	WEALTH	DENGUE	MUKLUK	TORQUE	VOTIVE	ARMADA	MANTRA
UTMOST	FINITE	PLENTY	WRAITH	DETOUR	MURMUR	TYPHUS	ZOUAVE	ARNICA	MARACA
VALISE	FIXITY	PLINTH	WREATH	DEVOUR	MUSEUM	UNIQUE	DISOWN	ASTHMA	MARINA
VANISH	FOURTH	POLITE	YEASTY	DEVOUT	MUUMUU	UNPLUG	MOHAWK	AURORA	MARKKA
WHILST	FRUITY	POLITY	ZENITH	DICTUM	NIMBUS	UNTRUE	OJIBWA	AZALEA	MIASMA
WHIMSY	GAIETY	POTATO	ZYGOTE	DINGUS	ODIOUS	URANUS	OTTAWA	BALBOA	MIMOSA
WOODSY	GAMETE	PRESTO	ABACUS	DISCUS	OPAQUE	USEFUL	PESEWA	BANANA	MYOPIA
WRASSE	GAYETY	PRETTY	ACCRUE	DROGUE	OSMIUM	UTERUS	RENOWN	BELUGA	NAUSEA
ACUITY	GHETTO	PRINTF	ANIMUS	DUGOUT	OUTGUN	VACUUM	SCRAWL	BUQSHA	NEBULA
AERATE	GROTTO	PRONTO	ANTRUM	DUMDUM	OUTPUT	VELLUM	SCREWY	CABALA	NOVENA
AMVETS	GROWTH	PURITY	ARMFUL	DYBBUK	OUTRUN	VELOUR	SHREWD	CABANA	NUTRIA
ASTUTE	GUILTY	PYRITE	ARTFUL	ECCLUS	PEANUT	VENOUS	SPRAWL	CAMERA	OJIBWA
BEAUTY	GYRATE	QUARTO	ASYLUM	ERBIUM	PHYLUM	VERSUS	SQUAWK	CASABA	ONEIDA
BERATE	HALITE	QUARTZ	ATRIUM	EXODUS	PICKUP	VILLUS	UPTOWN	CASSIA	OTTAWA
BONITO	HEALTH	REALTY	AVENUE	FAMOUS	PIGNUT	VINOUS	DELUXE	CAYUGA	PAGODA
BORATE	HEARTH	REBATE	BACKUP	FAVOUR	PLAGUE	VIRTUE	GALAXY	CHOREA	PANAMA
BOUNTY	HEARTY	RECITE	BARIUM	FITFUL	PLAQUE	VISCUS	ALWAYS	CHUKKA	PAPAYA
BREATH	HERETO	REFUTE	BASQUE	FLATUS	PLENUM	VOYEUR	ARROYO	CICADA	PATACA
BYPATH	IGNITE	RELATE	BEDAUB	FONDUE	PLEXUS	WALNUT	COCCYX	CINEMA	PATINA
CAVITY	IMPUTE	REMOTE	BEDBUG	FUNGUS	PODIUM	WALRUS	DACTYL	COPULA	PCMCIA
CHASTE	INCITE	REPUTE	BEFOUL	GENIUS	POPGUN	WAMPUM	EMBRYO	CORNEA	PESETA
CHATTY	INDITE	ROTATE	BISQUE	GYPSUM	POROUS	WINDUP	MARTYR	CORONA	PESEWA
CHINTZ	INMATE	SAFETY	BLOWUP	HELIUM	POSEUR	WOEFUL	METHYL	CORYZA	PHOBIA
COMITY	INNATE	SALUTE	BROGUE	HIATUS	POSSUM	YANQUI	PAPAYA	CUESTA	PIAZZA

PLASMA	EROTIC	ATTEND	INLAID	SEABED	ACCEDE	BEMUSE	CHARGE	DECREE	ENCORE
RAFFIA	ETHNIC	BALLAD	INLAND	SECOND	ACCRUE	BERATE	CHASTE	DEDUCE	ENDIVE
REMORA	EXOTIC	BANDED	INROAD	SHIELD	ACCUSE	BESIDE	CHEESE	DEFACE	ENDURE
RETINA	FABRIC	BARRED	INTEND	SHOULD	ACTIVE	BETAKE	CHEQUE	DEFAME	ENGAGE
SALIVA	FERRIC	BEHEAD	INTROD	SHREWD	ADDUCE	BETIDE	CHICLE	DEFILE	ENGINE
SCORIA	FROLIC	BEHIND	INWARD	SHROUD	ADHERE	BEWARE	CHOICE	DEFINE	ENISLE
SENECA	GAELIC	BEHOLD	ISLAND	SORDID	ADJURE	BIRDIE	CHOOSE	DEFUSE	ENRAGE
SIERRA	GALLIC	BEYOND	JAGGED	SPREAD	ADMIRE	BISQUE	CHROME	DEGREE	ENSILE
SIESTA	GARLIC	BUSHED	JOCUND	STOLID	ADVICE	BLITHE	CIRCLE	DELETE	ENSURE
SILICA	GOTHIC	BYWORD	KOBOLD	STONED	ADVISE	BLOUSE	CIRQUE	DELUDE	ENTICE
SONATA	HECTIC	CANARD	LANDED	STRAND	AERATE	BOBBLE	CLAQUE	DELUGE	ENTIRE
SPIREA	IPECAC	CANDID	LEAFED	STUPID	AFLAME	BOCCIE	CLAUSE	DELUXE	ENTREE
STANZA	IRENIC	CANNED	LEAVED	TALMUD	ALCOVE	BODICE	CLEAVE	DEMISE	ENZYME
STIGMA	IRONIC	CONFED	LEGEND	THREAD	ALLEGE	BOGGLE	CLICHE	DEMODE	EQUATE
TRAUMA	ITALIC	COWARD	LIMPID	TITLED	ALLUDE	BOODLE	CLIQUE	DEMOTE	EQUINE
TRIVIA	JUDAIC	CUSPID	LINKED	TORPID	ALLURE	BOOKIE	CLOCHE	DEMURE	ERMINE
TROIKA	LACTIC	DAYBED	LIQUID	TORRID	ALPINE	BOOTEE	CLOTHE	DENGUE	ESCAPE
TUNDRA	MANIAC	DEFEND	LIZARD	TOWARD	AMERCE	BORATE	COARSE	DENOTE	ESTATE
UREMIA	MANIOC	DEMAND	LOADED	TRIPOD	AMPERE	BOTTLE	COBBLE	DENUDE	ETHANE
UTOPIA	MASTIC	DEPEND	MAENAD	TURBID	ANYONE	BOUNCE	COCKLE	DEPOSE	EUCHRE
VAGINA	METRIC	DEVOID	MAILED	TURGID	APACHE	BOURSE	CODDLE	DEPUTE	EVINCE
VICUNA	MICMAC	DISHED	MANNED	UNBEND	APIECE	BOVINE	COERCE	DERIDE	EVOLVE
ZENANA	MOSAIC	DOGGED	MARAUD	UNBIND	APOGEE	BRAISE	COFFEE	DERIVE	EXCISE
ZINNIA	MYSTIC	DOODAD	MARKED	UNCLAD	ARABLE	BREEZE	COHERE	DESIRE	EXCITE
ZOYSIA	NITRIC	DOTARD	METHOD	UNFOLD	ARCADE	BRIDGE	COLLIE	DEVICE	EXCUSE
ABSORB	NORDIC	ENFOLD	MINDED	UNGIRD	ARCANE	BRIDLE	COOKIE	DEVISE	EXHALE
ADSORB	PARSEC	ERRAND	MORBID	UNHAND	ARGYLE	BROGUE	COOLIE	DEVOTE	EXHUME
ADVERB	PEPTIC	EXCEED	MYRIAD	UNITED	AROUSE	BRONZE	COOTIE	DIBBLE	EXPIRE
APLOMB	PHONIC	EXPAND	NEREID	UNKIND	ARRIVE	BROWSE	CORPSE	DILATE	EXPOSE
ATTRIB	PHYSIC	EXPEND	NIMROD	UNLOAD	ASHORE	BRUISE	COSINE	DILUTE	FACADE
BAOBAB	PICNIC	EXTEND	OFFEND	UNREAD	ASPIRE	BUBBLE	COULEE	DIMPLE	FACILE
BEDAUB	PUBLIC	EYELID	ONWARD	UNSHOD	ASSIZE	BUCKLE	COUPLE	DINGLE	FAERIE
BENUMB	QBASIC	FABLED	ORCHID	UNTOLD	ASSUME	BUDGIE	COURSE	DISUSE	FAILLE
CHERUB	RUBRIC	FECUND	OUTBID	UNUSED	ASSURE	BUNDLE	COYOTE	DIVIDE	FAMINE
COBWEB	RUSTIC	FERVID	OXFORD	UNWIND	ASTUTE	BUNGLE	CRADLE	DIVINE	FEEBLE
CONFAB	SEPTIC	FLORID	PALLID	UPHOLD	ATTIRE	BURGEE	CREASE	DOCILE	FELINE
ENTOMB	SLAVIC	FOOTED	PEAKED	UPLAND	ATTUNE	BURGLE	CREATE	DONATE	FEMALE
HOBNOB	STATIC	FORBID	PERIOD	UPLOAD	AVENGE	BUSTLE	CRECHE	DOODLE	FERULE
HUBBUB	TACTIC	FORKED	PETARD	UPWARD	AVENUE	BUTANE	CREOLE	DOTAGE	FETTLE
PREFAB	TRAGIC	FRIEND	PLACID	UPWIND	AVERSE	BYGONE	CRINGE	DOTTLE	FIANCE
REVERB	TROPIC	FRIGID	PREMED	VALUED	AWHILE	CACKLE	CRUISE	DOUBLE	FICKLE
SCARAB	URANIC	GERUND	PUTRID	VARIED	BABBLE	CADDIE	CUDDLE	DOUCHE	FIDDLE
SUBURB	ZODIAC	GIFTED	RAGGED	VERSED	BAFFLE	CAJOLE	CURATE	DREDGE	FIERCE
SUPERB	ABOARD	GRAVID	RAMROD	VISCID	BANGLE	CANAPE	CURDLE	DROGUE	FIGURE
ACETIC	ABOUND	GRAYED	RANCID	VIZARD	BASQUE	CANDLE	DABBLE	DROWSE	FINALE
ARABIC	ABROAD	GROUND	RECORD	VOICED	BATTLE	CANINE	DAMAGE	DRUDGE	FINITE
ARCTIC	ABSURD	HATRED	REFUND	WEBBED	BAUBLE	CANTLE	DANDLE	DUENDE	FIZZLE
ATOMIC	ACCORD	HAZARD	REGARD	WICKED	BEADLE	CARAFE	DANGLE	EDIBLE	FLANGE
BIOTIC	ADDEND	HERALD	REMAND	WINGED	BEAGLE	CASQUE	DAPPLE	EFFACE	FLEECE
CALCIC	AFFORD	HIPPED	REMIND	WITTED	BEANIE	CASTLE	DATIVE	EFFETE	FOIBLE
CLERIC	AFIELD	HORRID	RETARD	WIZARD	BECOME	CATTLE	DAWDLE	ELAPSE	FONDLE
CLINIC	AFRAID	HOTBED	REWARD	WONTED	BEETLE	CAYUSE	DAZZLE	EMERGE	FONDUE
COGNAC	ALLIED	HYBRID	RIBALD	WOODED	BEFORE	CENTRE	DEBASE	EMIGRE	FORAGE
COSMIC	ALMOND	IMPEND	RIBAND	ZONKED	BEGONE	CERISE	DEBATE	EMPIRE	FRAPPE
CRITIC	APPEND	INBRED	ROTUND	ABJURE	BEHAVE	CHAISE	DECADE	ENABLE	FREEZE
EBCDIC	AROUND	INDEED	RUGGED	ABLAZE	BELIKE	CHANCE	DECIDE	ENCASE	FRIEZE
EMETIC	ASCEND	INFOLD	SACRED	ABRADE	BEMIRE	CHANGE	DECODE	ENCODE	FRINGE

FUDDLE	ILLUME	LABILE	MUZZLE	PETITE	REGIME	SEVERE	STYMIE	TURTLE	ZOMBIE
FUMBLE	IMBIBE	LADDIE	MYRTLE	PEYOTE	RELATE	SEWAGE	SUBDUE	TUSSLE	ZOUAVE
FURORE	IMBRUE	LASSIE	NATIVE	PHOEBE	RELIVE	SHEAVE	SUBTLE	TWELVE	ZYGOTE
FUTILE	IMMUNE	LAVAGE	NATURE	PHRASE	REMOTE	SHELVE	SUCKLE	TWINGE	BEHALF
FUTURE	IMMURE	LEAGUE	NEEDLE	PICKLE	REMOVE	SHRIKE	SUNDAE	ULLAGE	BEHOOF
GABBLE	IMPALE	LEGATE	NEGATE	PIDDLE	RENEGE	SHRINE	SUPINE	UMPIRE	BELIEF
GAGGLE	IMPEDE	LEGUME	NESTLE	PIERCE	REPINE	SHRIVE	SUPPLE	UNABLE	CUTOFF
GALORE	IMPOSE	LESSEE	NETTLE	PIFFLE	REPOSE	SICKLE	SUTURE	UNIQUE	ENGULF
GAMBLE	IMPURE	LIABLE	NIBBLE	PIMPLE	REPUTE	SILAGE	SVELTE	UNLACE	HEREOF
GAMETE	IMPUTE	LICHEE	NIMBLE	PINKIE	RESALE	SIMILE	SWATHE	UNLADE	IMPERF
GAMINE	INCASE	LIGATE	NIPPLE	PIRATE	RESCUE	SIMPLE	SWERVE	UNLIKE	ITSELF
GARAGE	INCISE	LINAGE	NODDLE	PLAGUE	RESIDE	SINGLE	TACKLE	UNPILE	LAYOFF
GARBLE	INCITE	LITTLE	NODULE	PLAQUE	RESUME	SIZZLE	TAMALE	UNRIPE	MASSIF
GARGLE	INCOME	LOATHE	NONAGE	PLEASE	RETAKE	SLEDGE	TANGLE	UNROBE	MYSELF
GAUCHE	INDITE	LOBULE	NOODLE	PLEDGE	RETIRE	SLEEVE	TATTLE	UNTRUE	PAYOFF
GENTLE	INDUCE	LOCALE	NOTICE	PLUNGE	REVERE	SLUDGE	TEEPEE	UNTUNE	PRINTF
GIGGLE	INFUSE	LOCATE	NOVICE	POLICE	REVILE	SLUICE	TEETHE	UNWISE	REBUFF
GIRDLE	INHALE	LOUNGE	NOWISE	POLITE	REVISE	SMUDGE	TEMPLE	UNYOKE	RELIEF
GLANCE	INHERE	LUPINE	NOZZLE	POMADE	REVIVE	SNEEZE	TENURE	UPDATE	RUNOFF
GOALIE	INHUME	MADAME	NUANCE	PONGEE	REVOKE	SNOOZE	THENCE	UPSIDE	SCRUFF
GOATEE	INJURE	MAGPIE	NUBBLE	POODLE	RIDDLE	SOIGNE	THIEVE	UPTAKE	SPECIF
GOBBLE	INMATE	MALICE	NUBILE	POTAGE	RIPPLE	SOIREE	THRICE	URBANE	TARIFF
GOGGLE	INNATE	MANAGE	NUZZLE	POTPIE	RISQUE	SOLACE	THRIVE	URSINE	UNICEF
GOURDE	INSANE	MANEGE	OBLATE	POUNCE	ROOKIE	SOOTHE	THRONE	USABLE	UNROOF
GRANGE	INSIDE	MANGLE	OBLIGE	PRAISE	ROTATE	SORTIE	THROVE	VACATE	ACTING
GREASE	INSOLE	MANQUE	OBTUSE	PRANCE	ROUBLE	SOURCE	TICKLE	VALISE	ANALOG
GRIEVE	INSURE	MANTLE	OCTANE	PRINCE	RUBBLE	SPARSE	TIMBRE	VENDEE	AWNING
GRILLE	INTAKE	MANURE	OCTAVE	PSYCHE	RUFFLE	SPATHE	TINGLE	VENIRE	BEDBUG
GRIPPE	INTONE	MARBLE	OEUVRE	PUDDLE	RUMBLE	SPECIE	TINKLE	VESTEE	BELONG
GROOVE	INVADE	MARINE	OFFICE	PUMICE	RUMPLE	SPHERE	TIPPLE	VIABLE	BIGWIG
GROUSE	INVITE	MASQUE	OOLITE	PURINE	RUSTLE	SPLICE	TIPTOE	VIRILE	BITING
GRUDGE	INVOKE	MATURE	OPAQUE	PURPLE	SADDLE	SPLINE	TIRADE	VIRTUE	BLUING
GURGLE	IODIDE	MEDDLE	OPIATE	PURSUE	SALINE	SPONGE	TISSUE	VISAGE	BOWLEG
GUZZLE	IODINE	MENACE	OPPOSE	PUTTEE	SALUTE	SPOUSE	TITTLE	VIVACE	BOXING
GYRATE	IODIZE	MENAGE	ORACLE	PUZZLE	SAMPLE	SPRITE	TODDLE	VOLUME	CASING
HACKIE	IONIZE	METTLE	ORANGE	PYRITE	SATIRE	SPRUCE	TOFFEE	VOLUTE	COMING
HACKLE	JANGLE	MIDDLE	ORDURE	QUINCE	SAVAGE	SPURGE	TOGGLE	VOTIVE	COPING
HAGGLE	JAYCEE	MINGLE	ORIOLE	RABBLE	SCARCE	SQUARE	TONGUE	VOYAGE	DARING
HALITE	JAYGEE	MINUTE	ORNATE	RACEME	SCHEME	SQUIRE	TOPPLE	WABBLE	DOGLEG
HANDLE	JAYVEE	MIRAGE	OTIOSE	RAFFLE	SCONCE	STABLE	TORQUE	WADDLE	DURING
HASSLE	JEJUNE	MISCUE	PADDLE	RAMBLE	SCRAPE	STANCE	TOUCHE	WAFFLE	EARWIG
HEARSE	JIGGLE	MISUSE	PAIUTE	RANKLE	SCRIBE	STAPLE	TOUPEE	WAGGLE	EDGING
HECKLE	JINGLE	MOBILE	PALACE	RAPINE	SCYTHE	STARVE	TOUSLE	WAHINE	EGGNOG
HIPPIE	JOCOSE	MODULE	PALATE	RATTLE	SEANCE	STATUE	TOWHEE	WAMBLE	ENDING
HOAGIE	JOGGLE	MORALE	PANTIE	RAVAGE	SECEDE	STEPPE	TRANCE	WANGLE	FACING
HOARSE	JOSTLE	MORGUE	PAPULE	RAVINE	SECURE	STIFLE	TREBLE	WARBLE	FILING
HOBBLE	JOUNCE	MOROSE	PARADE	REBATE	SEDATE	STOOGE	TRIAGE	WATTLE	HUMBUG
HOMAGE	JUGGLE	MOSQUE	PAROLE	REBUKE	SEDUCE	STRAFE	TRIFLE	WHEEZE	INNING
HUDDLE	JUJUBE	MOTILE	PAWNEE	RECEDE	SEETHE	STRIDE	TRIODE	WHENCE	LADING
HUMANE	JUMBLE	MOTIVE	PEBBLE	RECIPE	SEMITE	STRIFE	TRIPLE	WIGGLE	LAPDOG
HUMBLE	JUNGLE	MOTTLE	PEDDLE	RECITE	SENATE	STRIKE	TRIUNE	WIMBLE	LIKING
HURDLE	JUNKIE	MOUSSE	PEEWEE	REDUCE	SENILE	STRIPE	TROCHE	WIMPLE	LINING
HURTLE	KARATE	MUDDLE	PELAGE	REFINE	SERAPE	STRIVE	TROUPE	WINKLE	LIVING
HUSTLE	KETTLE	MUFFLE	PEOPLE	REFUGE	SERENE	STROBE	TRUDGE	WOBBLE	LOVING
ICICLE	KIBBLE	MUMBLE	PERUKE	REFUSE	SESAME	STRODE	TSETSE	WRASSE	MUSKEG
IGNITE	KINDLE	MUSCLE	PERUSE	REFUTE	SETTEE	STROKE	TUBULE	WRITHE	NUTMEG
IGNORE	KIRTLE	MUTATE	PESTLE	REGALE	SETTLE	STROVE	TUMBLE	YANKEE	OBLONG

OFFIN**G**	CLIN**C**H	PUTS**C**H	BONSA**I**	BENZO**L**	FILIA**L**	PASTE**L**	THRAL**L**	CHRIS**M**	RACIS**M**
OUTIN**G**	CLUT**C**H	QUEN**C**H	CHICH**I**	BETHE**L**	FINIA**L**	PATRO**L**	THRIL**L**	CILIU**M**	RADIU**M**
PALIN**G**	CROT**C**H	RADIS**H**	DALAS**I**	BEWAI**L**	FISCA**L**	PENCI**L**	TINSE**L**	CONDO**M**	RANDO**M**
PARIN**G**	CROU**C**H	RAKIS**H**	KABUK**I**	BOREA**L**	FITFU**L**	PETRE**L**	TONSI**L**	CUBIS**M**	RANSO**M**
PAVIN**G**	CRUN**C**H	RAVIS**H**	LITCH**I**	BRIDA**L**	FLORA**L**	PETRO**L**	TRANS**L**	CURIU**M**	RECTU**M**
PHOTO**G**	CRUT**C**H	REHAS**H**	SAFAR**I**	BRUTA**L**	FOETA**L**	PHENO**L**	TRAVE**L**	CUSTO**M**	REDEE**M**
PILIN**G**	DANIS**H**	RELIS**H**	SALAM**I**	BULBU**L**	FORMA**L**	PINEA**L**	TROWE**L**	DEFOR**M**	REFOR**M**
PIPIN**G**	DEART**H**	RUPIA**H**	SCAMP**I**	BURIA**L**	FOSSI**L**	PISTI**L**	TUNNE**L**	DIADE**M**	RHYTH**M**
PROLO**G**	DETA**C**H	SCOR**C**H	SENIT**I**	BUSHE**L**	FRUGA**L**	PISTO**L**	UNCIA**L**	DIATO**M**	SACHE**M**
QUAHO**G**	DREN**C**H	SCOT**C**H	WAPIT**I**	CANCE**L**	FUNNE**L**	PLURA**L**	UNCOI**L**	DICTU**M**	SACRU**M**
RARIN**G**	ENMES**H**	SEAR**C**H	YANQU**I**	CAPFU**L**	GAMBO**L**	POMME**L**	UNCUR**L**	DIRHA**M**	SADIS**M**
RATIN**G**	ENOUG**H**	SERAP**H**	INTER**J**	CARNA**L**	GENIA**L**	PORTA**L**	UNFUR**L**	DISAR**M**	SALAA**M**
REFRI**G**	ENRI**C**H	SHEAT**H**	ATTAC**K**	CARPA**L**	GERBI**L**	POSTA**L**	UNREA**L**	DUMDU**M**	SCHIS**M**
SARON**G**	EUNU**C**H	SHEIK**H**	BEDEC**K**	CARPE**L**	GIMBA**L**	PRIMA**L**	UNREE**L**	EEPRO**M**	SCREA**M**
SATAN**G**	FAMIS**H**	SKET**C**H	DAMAS**K**	CARRE**L**	GLOBA**L**	PROPE**L**	UNROL**L**	EGOIS**M**	SELDO**M**
SAYIN**G**	FELLA**H**	SLEIG**H**	DEBAR**K**	CARTE**L**	GOSPE**L**	PUMME**L**	UNSEA**L**	EMBAL**M**	SEXIS**M**
SEWIN**G**	FETIS**H**	SLEUT**H**	DEBUN**K**	CASUA**L**	GRAVE**L**	RADIA**L**	UNVEI**L**	EMBLE**M**	SLALO**M**
SIDIN**G**	FINIS**H**	SLOU**C**H	DYBBU**K**	CAUDA**L**	GROVE**L**	RASCA**L**	UNWEL**L**	ENGRA**M**	SODIU**M**
SPRIN**G**	FLIN**C**H	SLOUG**H**	EMBAN**K**	CAUSA**L**	HANSE**L**	RECAL**L**	UPHIL**L**	ERBIU**M**	SPUTU**M**
SPRUN**G**	FLIT**C**H	SMIR**C**H	EMBAR**K**	CEREA**L**	HOSTE**L**	RECOI**L**	UPWEL**L**	ESTEE**M**	SQUIR**M**
STRIN**G**	FOURT**H**	SMOO**C**H	HIJAC**K**	CHAPE**L**	JACKA**L**	RECTA**L**	URACI**L**	FATHO**M**	STREA**M**
STRON**G**	FREN**C**H	SMOOT**H**	KOPEC**K**	CHISE**L**	JOVIA**L**	REFIL**L**	URINA**L**	GYPSU**M**	SYSTE**M**
STRUN**G**	GALOS**H**	SMUT**C**H	MOHAW**K**	CHORA**L**	JOYFU**L**	REGNA**L**	USEFU**L**	HANSO**M**	TANDE**M**
TAKIN**G**	GARIS**H**	SNAT**C**H	MUKLU**K**	COEVA**L**	KENNE**L**	RENTA**L**	VANDA**L**	HELIU**M**	TAOIS**M**
THRON**G**	GLIT**C**H	SNIT**C**H	REMAR**K**	COMPE**L**	KERNE**L**	REPEA**L**	VASSA**L**	IBIDE**M**	TEDIU**M**
TRYIN**G**	GROU**C**H	SPEE**C**H	SHRIE**K**	CONSO**L**	LABIA**L**	RETAI**L**	VENIA**L**	INDIU**M**	THEIS**M**
TUBIN**G**	GROWT**H**	SPLAS**H**	SHRIN**K**	CONSU**L**	LAURE**L**	REVEA**L**	VERBA**L**	INFIR**M**	TRUIS**M**
TURIN**G**	HAUN**C**H	SQUAS**H**	SQUAW**K**	CORBE**L**	LAWFU**L**	RITUA**L**	VERNA**L**	INFOR**M**	VACUU**M**
UNCLO**G**	HEALT**H**	STAN**C**H	SQUEA**K**	CORRA**L**	LENTI**L**	RUNNE**L**	VESSE**L**	INSEA**M**	VAGRO**M**
UNPLU**G**	HEART**H**	STAR**C**H	STREA**K**	CREWE**L**	LETHA**L**	SANDA**L**	VESTA**L**	JETSA**M**	VELLU**M**
UNSUN**G**	HOOKA**H**	STEN**C**H	STRUC**K**	CUDGE**L**	LINEA**L**	SCHOO**L**	VISUA**L**	LABIU**M**	VICTI**M**
VIKIN**G**	HOWDA**H**	STIT**C**H	THWAC**K**	CYMBA**L**	LINTE**L**	SCRAW**L**	WEASE**L**	LOGJA**M**	WAMPU**M**
WIGWA**G**	HURRA**H**	SWAT**C**H	TUGRI**K**	DACTY**L**	MAMMA**L**	SCROL**L**	WEEVI**L**	LYCEU**M**	WHILO**M**
WIRIN**G**	HUZZA**H**	SWIT**C**H	UNCOR**K**	DAMSE**L**	MANFU**L**	SEQUE**L**	WITHA**L**	MAOIS**M**	WIGWA**M**
ZIGZA**G**	IMPIS**H**	THAT**C**H	UNHOO**K**	DARNE**L**	MANTE**L**	SERIA**L**	WOEFU**L**	MAYHE**M**	WISDO**M**
AFRES**H**	INRUS**H**	THOUG**H**	UNLOC**K**	DENIA**L**	MANUA**L**	SEXUA**L**	ABLOO**M**	MEDIU**M**	XMODE**M**
AMBUS**H**	KIBOS**H**	THRAS**H**	UNMAS**K**	DENTA**L**	MARCE**L**	SHOVE**L**	AFFIR**M**	MEGOH**M**	YMODE**M**
ATTA**C**H	KITS**C**H	THRES**H**	UNPAC**K**	DERAI**L**	MARVE**L**	SHRIL**L**	AGLEA**M**	MONIS**M**	ZMODE**M**
AVOU**C**H	KLAT**C**H	THRUS**H**	ACTUA**L**	DERMA**L**	MEDIA**L**	SIGIL**L**	ANADE**M**	MOSLE**M**	ACTIO**N**
AWEIG**H**	LAUN**C**H	TREN**C**H	AERIA**L**	DETAI**L**	MENIA**L**	SIGNA**L**	ANTHE**M**	MUSEU**M**	ACUME**N**
BANIS**H**	LAVIS**H**	TROUG**H**	AMORA**L**	DIESE**L**	MENTA**L**	SINFU**L**	ANTRU**M**	MUSLI**M**	ADJOI**N**
BLAN**C**H	LENGT**H**	TWIT**C**H	ANIMA**L**	DIRND**L**	MESCA**L**	SNIVE**L**	ASHRA**M**	NAPAL**M**	AFGHA**N**
BLEA**C**H	MODIS**H**	UPPIS**H**	ANNEA**L**	DISMA**L**	METHY**L**	SNOBO**L**	ASYLU**M**	NONCO**M**	AIDMA**N**
BLEN**C**H	NAUT**C**H	UPRUS**H**	ANNUA**L**	DISPE**L**	MISSA**L**	SOCIA**L**	ATRIU**M**	NUDIS**M**	AIRMA**N**
BLOT**C**H	OFFIS**H**	VANIS**H**	APICA**L**	DISTA**L**	MORSE**L**	SOCIO**L**	AUTIS**M**	ORGAS**M**	AMAZO**N**
BLUIS**H**	ONRUS**H**	WARMT**H**	APPAL**L**	DORSA**L**	MORTA**L**	SORRE**L**	BALSA**M**	OSMIU**M**	ARCHO**N**
BRAN**C**H	ORNIT**H**	WEALT**H**	APPEA**L**	DRIVE**L**	MUSSE**L**	SPINA**L**	BANTA**M**	PASSI**M**	ARCSI**N**
BREA**C**H	PARIA**H**	WRAIT**H**	ARMFU**L**	ENAME**L**	MUTUA**L**	SPINE**L**	BARIU**M**	PHLEG**M**	ARCTA**N**
BREAT**H**	PARIS**H**	WREAT**H**	ARTFU**L**	ENROL**L**	NEURA**L**	SPIRA**L**	BECAL**M**	PHLOE**M**	ASSIG**N**
BREE**C**H	PAUN**C**H	WREN**C**H	ASSAI**L**	ENTAI**L**	NEURO**L**	SPRAW**L**	BEDLA**M**	PHYLU**M**	ASTER**N**
BROA**C**H	PERIS**H**	WRET**C**H	ASTRA**L**	ETHNO**L**	NICKE**L**	SQUAL**L**	BELDA**M**	PLENU**M**	ASTRO**N**
BROO**C**H	PLINT**H**	YAHWE**H**	ASTRO**L**	FACIA**L**	NORMA**L**	SQUEA**L**	BESEE**M**	PODIU**M**	ATTAI**N**
BRUN**C**H	POLIS**H**	ZENIT**H**	ATONA**L**	FAECA**L**	NOVEL**L**	STROL**L**	BOTTO**M**	POGRO**M**	AUBUR**N**
BYPAT**H**	POTAS**H**	ABNAK**I**	AWHIR**L**	FENNE**L**	ORDEA**L**	SWIVE**L**	BUNKU**M**	POSSU**M**	AUTUM**N**
CALIP**H**	PREA**C**H	ALKAL**I**	BARRE**L**	FESTA**L**	PARCE**L**	SYMBO**L**	CAECU**M**	PRELI**M**	AWAKE**N**
CHUR**C**H	PUNIS**H**	BANZA**I**	BEFAL**L**	FEUDA**L**	PASCA**L**	TASSE**L**	CERIU**M**	PURIS**M**	BABOO**N**
CLEN**C**H	PURDA**H**	BIKIN**I**	BEFOU**L**	FIBRI**L**	PASSE**L**	TEASE**L**	CESIU**M**	QUORU**M**	BAGMA**N**

BALEEN	DAMSON	HEAVEN	MORGAN	PUFFIN	SULLEN	BRONCO	VOODOO	ALTAIR	CAVIAR
BANYAN	DARKEN	HEREIN	MORMON	PUNKIN	SULTAN	CALICO	ASLEEP	ANCHOR	CELLAR
BARREN	DEACON	HEREON	MOTION	PYTHON	SUMMON	CASINO	BACKUP	ANSWER	CENSER
BATMAN	DEADEN	HEROIN	MOUTON	RADIAN	SUNKEN	CHROMO	BISHOP	ANTHER	CENSOR
BATTEN	DEAFEN	HOYDEN	MUFFIN	RAGLAN	SUNTAN	CUCKOO	BLOWUP	ANTLER	CENTER
BEACON	DEEPEN	HYPHEN	MUSLIN	RAISIN	SYLVAN	DOMINO	BURLAP	APPEAR	CHAFER
BECKON	DEHORN	ICEMAN	MUTTON	RAPPEN	SYPHON	DYNAMO	CARHOP	ASHLAR	CHASER
BEDPAN	DEMEAN	IMPUGN	NAPKIN	RATION	TAMPON	EMBRYO	CARTOP	AUTHOR	CHOKER
BEMOAN	DENTIN	INBORN	NATION	RATTAN	TANNIN	ENDURO	CATNAP	AVATAR	CHOLER
BENIGN	DESIGN	INDIAN	NELSON	REASON	TARPON	ESCUDO	CATNIP	BACKER	CINDER
BIOTIN	DETAIN	INTERN	NEURON	REBORN	TARTAN	ESKIMO	CATSUP	BADGER	CIPHER
BLAZON	DISOWN	JARGON	NEWTON	RECKON	TAVERN	FIASCO	DECAMP	BANNER	CLAMOR
BOBBIN	DOBBIN	JERKIN	NIACIN	REDDEN	TENDON	FOREGO	DEWLAP	BANTER	CLEVER
BODKIN	DOLMEN	KAOLIN	NOGGIN	REGAIN	TENPIN	FRESCO	DOLLOP	BARBER	CLOVER
BONBON	DOMAIN	KELVIN	NORMAN	REGION	TIFFIN	GABBRO	ENCAMP	BARKER	CODGER
BOWMAN	DRAGON	KITTEN	NORTON	REJOIN	TOCSIN	GAUCHO	ENTRAP	BARTER	COFFER
BRAZEN	DUBBIN	KOREAN	NOTION	REMAIN	TOUCAN	GAZEBO	FILLIP	BATTER	COHEIR
BRITON	ELEVEN	LAGOON	NUBBIN	RENNIN	TREPAN	GHETTO	GALLOP	BAZAAR	COLLAR
BROGAN	ENDRIN	LAWMAN	OBTAIN	RENOWN	TRITON	GIGOLO	GOSSIP	BEAKER	COMBER
BROKEN	ENJOIN	LAYMAN	OPTION	RESIGN	TROJAN	GINKGO	HICCUP	BEAVER	COMPAR
BUNION	ENSIGN	LEADEN	ORDAIN	RETAIN	TURBAN	GROTTO	HOLDUP	BEGGAR	CONCUR
BURDEN	EOLIAN	LEAVEN	ORIGIN	RETURN	TUREEN	HAIRDO	HOOKUP	BENDER	CONDOR
BUSKIN	EXTERN	LEGION	ORISON	RIBBON	TYCOON	HERETO	HUBCAP	BERBER	CONFER
BUTTON	FABIAN	LEGMAN	ORPHAN	RIDDEN	UNBORN	HOODOO	HYSSOP	BESTIR	CONSTR
CAFTAN	FALCON	LEPTON	OUTGUN	RLOGIN	UNEVEN	INDIGO	INSTEP	BETTER	COOLER
CAIMAN	FASTEN	LESION	OUTRUN	ROTTEN	UNISON	KIMONO	KIDNAP	BETTOR	COOPER
CANCAN	FATTEN	LESSEN	OXYGEN	SADDEN	UPTOWN	LEGATO	LAPTOP	BICKER	COPIER
CANNON	FENIAN	LESSON	PALEON	SALMON	UPTURN	LIBIDO	LINEUP	BITTER	COPPER
CANTON	FIBRIN	LIBYAN	PAPAIN	SALOON	URCHIN	MEDICO	LINKUP	BLAZER	COPTER
CANYON	FLACON	LICHEN	PARDON	SAMPAN	VERMIN	MERINO	LOCKUP	BOATER	CORNER
CARBON	FLAGON	LINDEN	PARSON	SATEEN	VIOLIN	MIKADO	MACAPP	BOILER	COTTER
CAREEN	FLAXEN	LISTEN	PATRON	SATURN	VIRGIN	NAVAHO	MADCAP	BOMBER	COUGAR
CARTON	FLORIN	LOOSEN	PEAHEN	SCREEN	VIRION	NUNCIO	MAKEUP	BORDER	CRATER
CASEIN	FOEMAN	LOTION	PECTIN	SEAMAN	VISION	OCTAVO	MARKUP	BOTHER	CUMBER
CATION	FROZEN	MACRON	PENMAN	SEASON	WANTON	OVERDO	MISHAP	BOWLER	CUNNER
CATKIN	FUSION	MADDEN	PENNON	SEQUIN	WARDEN	PONCHO	PICKUP	BOXCAR	CURSOR
CAVERN	GALLON	MADMAN	PEPSIN	SERMON	WARREN	POTATO	RECOUP	BROKER	CUTLER
CAYMAN	GAMMON	MAIDEN	PERSON	SEXTON	WEAKEN	PRESTO	REDCAP	BUFFER	CUTTER
CHITIN	GARCON	MALIAN	PHOTON	SHAMAN	WEAPON	PRONTO	REVAMP	BUMMER	DAGGER
CHOSEN	GARDEN	MALIGN	PIDGIN	SICKEN	WELKIN	PSEUDO	SATRAP	BUMPER	DAMPER
CITRON	GERMAN	MAMMON	PIGEON	SIMIAN	WHITEN	PSYCHO	SCRIMP	BUNKER	DANDER
CLOVEN	GIBBON	MARGIN	PIGPEN	SIPHON	WITHIN	PUEBLO	SHRIMP	BURNER	DANGER
COCOON	GIBSON	MARLIN	PINION	SLOGAN	WOODEN	QUARTO	SKYCAP	BURSAR	DAPPER
COFFIN	GLUTEN	MAROON	PIPKIN	SLOVEN	WOOLEN	RANCHO	SLIPUP	BUTLER	DARTER
COLUMN	GOBLIN	MARTEN	PIPPIN	SODDEN	WORSEN	ROMANO	TEACUP	BUTTER	DASHER
COMMON	GODSON	MARTIN	PISTON	SOFTEN	YEOMAN	SHINTO	TRANSP	BUZZER	DEBTOR
CORDON	GOLDEN	MASCON	PLATEN	SOLEMN	ZIRCON	STEREO	TURNIP	CAESAR	DENIER
COTTON	GOTTEN	MATRON	PLUTON	SPAVIN	ADAGIO	STUCCO	UNSHIP	CAMBER	DEODAR
COUPON	GOVERN	MEDIAN	POISON	SPLEEN	AKIMBO	STUDIO	UNSNAP	CAMPER	DETOUR
COUSIN	GRABEN	MERMAN	POLLEN	SPOKEN	ALBINO	TATTOO	UNSTOP	CANCER	DEVOIR
COWMAN	GUIDON	MICRON	POMPON	SPRAIN	ARROYO	TEREDO	UNWRAP	CANDOR	DEVOUR
CRATON	GULDEN	MIDDEN	POPGUN	STAMEN	BAGNIO	TOMATO	UPKEEP	CANKER	DIAPER
CRAVEN	GUNMAN	MINION	POPLIN	STOLEN	BAMBOO	TORERO	WALLOP	CANTER	DICKER
CRAYON	HAPPEN	MITTEN	POTEEN	STOLON	BARRIO	TUXEDO	WINDUP	CANTOR	DIFFER
CRETIN	HARDEN	MIZZEN	POTION	STRAIN	BISTRO	ULTIMO	COLLOQ	CAPTOR	DIMMER
DAEMON	HARKEN	MODERN	PRISON	SUBORN	BOLERO	UNESCO	COMPAQ	CAREER	DINNER
DAMPEN	HASTEN	MOLTEN	PROTON	SUDDEN	BONITO	VIRAGO	AFFAIR	CASTER	DIPPER

DISBAR	GOPHER	LARDER	NETHER	RAPIER	SUPPER	WINNER	ECCLES	SHAVES	ARMLET
DITHER	GRADER	LASCAR	NEUTER	RASHER	TAILOR	WINTER	ECCLUS	STAPES	ARMPIT
DOCTOR	GROCER	LATHER	NICKER	RASTER	TAMPER	WITHER	EGRESS	STATUS	ARRANT
DODDER	GUITAR	LATTER	NIPPER	RATHER	TANKER	WONDER	EMBOSS	STAVES	ARREST
DOLLAR	GUNNER	LAWYER	NUMBER	RATTER	TANNER	WOOFER	ETHICS	STRESS	ARTIST
DORMER	GUSHER	LEADER	OCULAR	REAMER	TARTAR	WORKER	EXCESS	STYLUS	ASCENT
DOWNER	GUTTER	LECTOR	ORATOR	RECTOR	TATTER	WRITER	EXODUS	TARSUS	ASLANT
DRAPER	HACKER	LEDGER	OSTLER	REEFER	TEETER	YAMMER	FAMOUS	TENNIS	ASPECT
DRAWER	HALTER	LESSER	OUSTER	RENDER	TELLER	YONDER	FAUCES	TESTIS	ASSENT
DRIVER	HAMMER	LESSOR	OYSTER	REPAIR	TEMPER	ZEPHYR	FLATUS	THANKS	ASSERT
DROVER	HAMPER	LETTER	PACKER	RIGGER	TENDER	ZIPPER	FRACAS	THEIRS	ASSIST
DUFFER	HANGAR	LIMBER	PALLOR	RINGER	TERROR	ZITHER	FUNGUS	THESIS	ASSORT
DUSTER	HANKER	LINEAR	PALMER	ROBBER	TESTER	ABACUS	GENIUS	THYMUS	ATTEST
EASTER	HARBOR	LINGER	PALTER	ROCKER	TETHER	ABATIS	GNEISS	TIGHTS	AUGUST
ECLAIR	HATTER	LIQUOR	PAMPER	ROLLER	TICKER	ABBESS	GRATIS	TURVES	AVAUNT
EITHER	HAWKER	LITTER	PANDER	ROMPER	TILLER	ACCESS	HAGGIS	TYPHUS	AVOCET
ELIXIR	HAWSER	LOADER	PARLOR	ROSTER	TIMBER	ACROSS	HALVES	UNDIES	BALLET
ENAMOR	HECTOR	LOCKER	PASTOR	RUBBER	TINDER	ALWAYS	HARASS	UNLESS	BALLOT
ENDEAR	HEIFER	LODGER	PATTER	RUDDER	TINKER	AMENDS	HERPES	URANUS	BANDIT
FACTOR	HINDER	LOITER	PAUPER	RUNNER	TITTER	AMVETS	HIATUS	UTERUS	BASALT
FALTER	HITHER	LOOPER	PEPPER	SAILOR	TORPOR	ANIMUS	HUBRIS	VENOUS	BASKET
FATHER	HOLLER	LOUVER	PESTER	SALVER	TOTTER	ANNALS	JOYOUS	VERSUS	BEHEST
FAVOUR	HONOUR	LUBBER	PEWTER	SAUCER	TRADER	ARCCOS	LEAVES	VILLUS	BEREFT
FEELER	HOOKER	LUMBAR	PILFER	SAVIOR	TREMOR	ASSESS	LIGHTS	VINOUS	BILLET
FENDER	HOPPER	LUMBER	PILLAR	SEALER	TUCKER	BATHOS	LITMUS	VISCUS	BISECT
FERVOR	HORROR	LUSTER	PINCER	SECTOR	TURNER	BICEPS	MADRAS	VITALS	BITNET
FESTER	HOWLER	MADDER	PLACER	SENIOR	TUSKER	BYPASS	MANTIS	WALRUS	BLIGHT
FETTER	HUMOUR	MAGYAR	PLOVER	SENSOR	ULSTER	CACTUS	MATINS	ZOUNDS	BOBCAT
FILLER	HUNGER	MANGER	POLDER	SERVER	UNFAIR	CALLUS	MENSES	ABDUCT	BONNET
FILTER	HUNKER	MANNER	PONDER	SETTER	UNMOOR	CALVES	MESSRS	ABJECT	BOUGHT
FINDER	HUSSAR	MARTYR	POPLAR	SHAKER	UPREAR	CAMPUS	MORRIS	ABRUPT	BREAST
FINGER	IMPAIR	MASTER	POPPER	SHAVER	UPROAR	CANVAS	NIMBUS	ABSENT	BREVET
FISHER	INDOOR	MATTER	PORKER	SHINER	URETER	CARESS	OBSESS	ACCENT	BRIGHT
FLAVOR	ISOBAR	MEAGER	PORTER	SHIVER	USURER	CARIES	ODIOUS	ACCEPT	BRUNET
FLOWER	ISOMER	MEMBER	POSEUR	SHOWER	VECTOR	CAUCUS	OODLES	ACCOST	BUCKET
FODDER	JABBER	MEMOIR	POSTER	SILVER	VELOUR	CENSUS	OPTICS	ACQUIT	BUDGET
FOLDER	JAGUAR	MENTOR	POTHER	SIMMER	VENDER	CEREUS	PATHOS	ADDICT	BUFFET
FORMER	JAILER	MERCER	POTTER	SIMPER	VENDOR	CHORUS	PATOIS	ADJUST	BULLET
FOSTER	JASPER	MERGER	POWDER	SINKER	VENEER	CIRCUS	PELVIS	ADRIFT	CACHET
FUHRER	JESTER	METEOR	PRAYER	SISTER	VERGER	CIRRUS	PHAROS	ADROIT	CAHOOT
GAFFER	JIGGER	METIER	PREFER	SKEWER	VESPER	CITRUS	PHILOS	ADVENT	CANNOT
GAITER	JOBBER	MIDAIR	PREWAR	SLAVER	VICTOR	CIVICS	PLEXUS	ADVERT	CARPET
GAMMER	JOINER	MILLER	PRIMER	SLIDER	VIZIER	CLEVIS	PLIERS	AFFECT	CARROT
GANDER	JUICER	MIRROR	PROPER	SLIVER	VOYEUR	COCCUS	POROUS	AFLOAT	CASKET
GARNER	JUMPER	MISTER	PUCKER	SOCCER	VULGAR	COITUS	PRECIS	AGHAST	CATGUT
GARTER	JUNIOR	MOHAIR	PULSAR	SOEVER	WAITER	CORPUS	RABIES	ALBEIT	CAUGHT
GATHER	JUNKER	MOLDER	PURSER	SOLDER	WAIVER	COSMOS	RADIUS	ALIGHT	CAVEAT
GEEZER	KAISER	MONGER	PUSHER	SOMBER	WANDER	CRISIS	RECESS	ALMOST	CAVORT
GENDER	KEGLER	MORTAR	PUTTER	SPIDER	WARDER	CROCUS	REMISS	AMOUNT	CEMENT
GEYSER	KILTER	MOTHER	QINTAR	STUPOR	WASHER	DEBRIS	REVERS	AMULET	CERMET
GIBBER	KIPPER	MOUSER	QUAKER	SUCCOR	WELTER	DERMIS	RICHES	ANKLET	CHALET
GINGER	KISSER	MUMMER	QUASAR	SUCKER	WETHER	DERRIS	RUCKUS	ANOINT	CHAUNT
GIRDER	KOSHER	MURDER	QUAVER	SUFFER	WHALER	DINGUS	RUMPUS	APPLET	CHRIST
GLIDER	LABOUR	MURMUR	QUIVER	SUITOR	WICKER	DISCUS	SCHUSS	ARCNET	CLARET
GLOWER	LADDER	MUSTER	RAFTER	SULFUR	WIENER	DIVERS	SELVES	ARDENT	CLIENT
GOITER	LANCER	MUTTER	RANCOR	SUMMER	WINDER	DOINGS	SEPSIS	ARGENT	CLOSET
GOOBER	LANDER	NECTAR	RANGER	SUNDER	WINKER	DURESS	SERIES	ARIGHT	COBALT

COGENT	EXTANT	INSIST	OUTFIT	RESORT	THROAT	BORROW	CORTEX	BLEARY	DIMITY
COHORT	EXTENT	INSULT	OUTLET	RESULT	THRUST	BURROW	COWPOX	BLOWSY	DINGHY
COLLAT	EXTORT	INTACT	OUTPUT	RETORT	THWART	CALLOW	DUPLEX	BODILY	DISMAY
COMBAT	EYELET	INTENT	OUTSET	REVERT	TICKET	CASHEW	EARWAX	BOTANY	DONKEY
COMFIT	FAGGOT	INTUIT	OUTWIT	REVOLT	TIDBIT	CURFEW	HATBOX	BOUNTY	DOUBLY
COMMIT	FAUCET	INVENT	PACKET	ROBUST	TIPPET	CURLEW	HOTBOX	BRANDY	DRAFTY
COQUET	FERRET	INVERT	PALLET	ROCKET	TITBIT	DESKEW	ICEBOX	BUSBOY	DREARY
CORNET	FIDGET	INVEST	PAPIST	RODENT	TOILET	ESCHEW	INFLUX	BUSILY	DRESSY
CORSET	FILLET	IRRUPT	PARENT	RUNLET	TOMCAT	ESCROW	LARYNX	BYPLAY	DROPSY
COVERT	FLAUNT	JACKET	PARROT	RUSSET	TOMTIT	FALLOW	LUMMOX	CANARY	DROWSY
CRAVAT	FLIGHT	JENNET	PATENT	SACHET	TRIVET	FARROW	MATRIX	CANOPY	EARTHY
CREDIT	FLUENT	JUNKET	PEANUT	SAVANT	TRUANT	FELLOW	MENINX	CARBOY	EATERY
CURVET	FOMENT	JURIST	PEDANT	SCHIST	TUMULT	FOLLOW	MSCDEX	CATCHY	EFFIGY
CUTLET	FOREST	KERMIT	PELLET	SCRIPT	TURBOT	FURROW	OUTFOX	CAVITY	EIGHTY
CUTOUT	FORGET	KISMET	PEQUOT	SCULPT	TURRET	GEWGAW	PICKAX	CELERY	EMBODY
CYGNET	FORINT	KNIGHT	PERMIT	SECRET	TYPIST	GUFFAW	POLEAX	CHANCY	EMPLOY
DECANT	FORMAT	LAMENT	PICKET	SELECT	TYRANT	GUFFAW	PREFIX	CHATTY	ENERGY
DECEIT	FOUGHT	LANCET	PIGLET	SEXPOT	UNBOLT	HALLOW	PREMIX	CHEEKY	ENMITY
DECENT	FRIGHT	LAPPET	PIGNUT	SEXTET	UNJUST	HARROW	PROLIX	CHEERY	ENTITY
DEDUCT	GADGET	LARIAT	PIQUET	SHIEST	UNMEET	HAYMOW	REFLEX	CHERRY	EQUITY
DEFEAT	GAMBIT	LATENT	PLAINT	SHRIFT	UNREST	HEBREW	REFLUX	CHILLY	EULOGY
DEFECT	GANNET	LAYOUT	PLANET	SIGNET	UNSEAT	HOLLOW	SMILAX	CHOOSY	FAIRLY
DEPART	GARNET	LIMPET	PLIANT	SILENT	UNWEPT	INFLOW	SPADIX	CHOPPY	FAMILY
DEPICT	GARRET	LINNET	PLIGHT	SLIEST	UPBEAT	JIGSAW	SPHINX	CHUBBY	FEALTY
DEPORT	GASKET	LOCKET	POCKET	SLIGHT	UPLIFT	KOWTOW	SUFFIX	CHUMMY	FELONY
DESALT	GIBBET	LOCUST	POTENT	SOCKET	UPMOST	MALLOW	SURTAX	CHUNKY	FINERY
DESERT	GIMLET	LUCENT	PRESET	SONNET	UPROOT	MARROW	SYNTAX	CITIFY	FIXITY
DESIST	GOBBET	MAGGOT	PRIEST	SOUGHT	UPSHOT	MEADOW	THORAX	CLAMMY	FLABBY
DESPOT	GOBLET	MAGNET	PRIVET	SOVIET	URGENT	MELLOW	ULTRIX	CLASSY	FLASHY
DETECT	GULLET	MAHOUT	PROFIT	SPIGOT	USENET	MILDEW	UNISEX	CLERGY	FLESHY
DETEST	GUSSET	MALLET	PROMPT	SPINET	UTMOST	MINNOW	VERTEX	CLUMSY	FLIMSY
DEVOUT	HAMLET	MARKET	PULLET	SPIRIT	VACANT	MORROW	VORTEX	CODIFY	FLOOZY
DIGEST	HARLOT	MARMOT	PULPIT	SPLINT	VARLET	NARROW	ABBACY	COLONY	FLOPPY
DIRECT	HEIGHT	MASCOT	PUNDIT	SPRINT	VELVET	NEPHEW	ACUITY	COMEDY	FLOSSY
DIVERT	HELMET	MIDGET	PUPPET	SPROUT	VIOLET	OUTLAW	AFFRAY	COMELY	FLUFFY
DIVEST	HEPCAT	MILLET	PUTOUT	SQUINT	WALLET	PAWPAW	AGENCY	COMITY	FLUNKY
DOCENT	HERMIT	MINUET	QIVIUT	SQUIRT	WALNUT	PILLOW	AIRWAY	COMPLY	FLURRY
DOCKET	HONEST	MISFIT	QUAINT	STRAIT	WEIGHT	POWWOW	ANYWAY	CONVEY	FLYWAY
DOPANT	HORNET	MODEST	RABBET	STREET	WESKIT	REVIEW	APATHY	CONVOY	FOLKSY
DUGOUT	ILLUST	MOLEST	RABBIT	STRICT	WHILST	RIPSAW	APIARY	COSTLY	FRENZY
DULCET	IMPACT	MOMENT	RACKET	SUBLET	WICKET	SALLOW	ARGOSY	COUNTY	FRIARY
EAGLET	IMPART	MOPPET	RAGOUT	SUBMIT	WIGLET	SEESAW	ARMORY	COWBOY	FRIDAY
EFFECT	IMPORT	MULLET	RECANT	SUBSET	WOMBAT	SHADOW	ARTERY	CRABBY	FRISKY
EFFORT	IMPOST	MUSKET	RECENT	SUMMIT	YOGURT	SORROW	ASTRAY	CRAFTY	FROWSY
ELDEST	INCEST	MUTANT	REDACT	SUNLIT	ZEALOT	TALLOW	AUGURY	CRANKY	FRUITY
ELICIT	INDENT	NAUGHT	REGENT	SUNSET	APERCU	WALLOW	AVIARY	CRANNY	FRUMPY
ENCYST	INDICT	NITWIT	REGRET	TABLET	BATEAU	WILLOW	AWEARY	CREEPY	GADFLY
ENLIST	INDUCT	NONFAT	REJECT	TALENT	BUREAU	WINDOW	BAKERY	CRUMMY	GAIETY
ERRANT	INFANT	NOUGAT	RELENT	TAPPET	LANDAU	WINNOW	BARELY	CURTSY	GALAXY
ESCORT	INFECT	NOUGHT	RELICT	TARGET	MILIEU	YARROW	BARFLY	DAINTY	GALLEY
ESPRIT	INFEST	NUGGET	RENNET	TAUGHT	MUUMUU	YELLOW	BARLEY	DEADLY	GANTRY
EXCEPT	INGEST	OBJECT	REPAST	TEAPOT	ORMOLU	APPROX	BEAUTY	DEEJAY	GAYETY
EXEMPT	INJECT	OCCULT	REPEAT	TELNET	ANYHOW	BINHEX	BELFRY	DEFRAY	GENTRY
EXHORT	INKJET	OCELOT	REPENT	TENANT	BARROW	CERVIX	BETRAY	DEPLOY	GLOSSY
EXPECT	INMOST	OFFSET	REPORT	THIRST	BELLOW	CLIMAX	BIGAMY	DEPUTY	GOODLY
EXPERT	INSECT	OMELET	RESENT	THREAT	BESTOW	COCCYX	BINARY	DESCRY	GRAINY
EXPORT	INSERT	ORIENT	RESIST	THRIFT	BILLOW	CONVEX	BIOPSY	DICKEY	GRISLY

GROGGY	MOSTLY	ROTARY	TOUCHY
GROOVY	MOTLEY	RUNWAY	TREATY
GRUBBY	MUTINY	SAFETY	TRICKY
GRUMPY	NAMELY	SALARY	TRIPLY
GUILTY	NAPERY	SANITY	TROPHY
HARDLY	NEARBY	SASHAY	TRUSTY
HEARTY	NICETY	SCANTY	TURKEY
HEREBY	NINETY	SCREWY	TWEEDY
HERESY	NOBODY	SCURRY	TWENTY
HEYDAY	NOTIFY	SCURVY	TYPIFY
HOCKEY	OCCUPY	SCUZZY	UNDULY
HOMELY	ODDITY	SEAWAY	UNEASY
HOMILY	ORNERY	SEEMLY	UNHOLY
HOMINY	OSPREY	SENTRY	UNRULY
HORSEY	OSSIFY	SHABBY	UPPITY
IDIOCY	OUTCRY	SHAGGY	VAGARY
INFAMY	OUTLAY	SHANTY	VALLEY
INJURY	OVERLY	SHERRY	VANITY
JALOPY	PACIFY	SHIFTY	VAPORY
JAUNTY	PALTRY	SHIMMY	VERIFY
JERSEY	PANTRY	SHINNY	VERILY
JITNEY	PAPACY	SHODDY	VERITY
JOCKEY	PARITY	SIMONY	VESTRY
JOHNNY	PARLAY	SKIMPY	VILIFY
KIDNEY	PARLEY	SKINNY	VIVIFY
KINDLY	PARODY	SLEAZY	VOLLEY
LACKEY	PARTLY	SLEEPY	VOTARY
LEEWAY	PASTRY	SLOPPY	WATERY
LEGACY	PENURY	SLURRY	WAYLAY
LENITY	PIGSTY	SMITHY	WEAKLY
LEVITY	PIRACY	SNIPPY	WEEKLY
LIKELY	PLENTY	SNOOTY	WHAMMY
LITANY	PLUCKY	SODOMY	WHEEZY
LIVELY	POETRY	SPOTTY	WHERRY
LIVERY	POLICY	STEADY	WHIMSY
LONELY	POLITY	STICKY	WHINNY
LORDLY	PORTLY	STINGY	WHOLLY
LOVELY	POTBOY	STOCKY	WIGGLY
LOWERY	PREPAY	STODGY	WINTRY
LUNACY	PRETTY	STUBBY	WOODSY
LUXURY	PRIORY	STUFFY	WOOLLY
MALADY	PRISSY	STURDY	WORTHY
MAYFLY	PULLEY	SUBWAY	YEARLY
MEASLY	PURIFY	SULTRY	YEASTY
MEDLEY	PURITY	SUNDAY	CHINTZ
MELODY	PURVEY	SUNDRY	ERSATZ
MEMORY	QUARRY	SUPPLY	QUARTZ
MIDDAY	QUEASY	SURETY	
MIDWAY	QUINSY	SURREY	
MIGHTY	RAMIFY	SURVEY	
MISERY	RAREFY	TAWDRY	
MISLAY	RATIFY	TETCHY	
MODIFY	REALLY	THEORY	
MOIETY	REALTY	THIRTY	
MONDAY	REMEDY	TIMELY	
MONKEY	REPLAY	TOMBOY	
MONODY	ROSARY	TOOTHY	

7
LETTER WORDS

1st Letter								
	AEROSOL	AMERIND	APHASIA	ASSAULT	BANDBOX	BEGUILE	BISCUIT	BOULDER
	AFFABLE	AMIABLE	APOLOGY	ASSUAGE	BANNOCK	BEGUINE	BISMUTH	BOUNCER
ABALONE	AFFLICT	AMMETER	APOLUNE	ASSURED	BANQUET	BEHOOVE	BITTERN	BOUNDEN
ABANDON	AFFRONT	AMMONIA	APOSTLE	ASTOUND	BANSHEE	BELABOR	BITTERS	BOUQUET
ABDOMEN	AFGHANI	AMNESIA	APPAREL	ASTRIDE	BAPTISM	BELATED	BITUMEN	BOURBON
ABILITY	AFRICAN	AMNESTY	APPEASE	ASUNDER	BAPTIST	BELGIAN	BIVALVE	BOWLDER
ABOLISH	AGAINST	AMOROUS	APPLAUD	ATAVISM	BAPTIZE	BELIEVE	BIVOUAC	BOWLINE
ABREAST	AGELESS	AMPHORA	APPLIED	ATELIER	BARBELL	BELLBOY	BIZARRE	BOWLING
ABRIDGE	AGITATE	AMPLIFY	APPOINT	ATHEIST	BARGAIN	BELLHOP	BLACKEN	BOYCOTT
ABSCESS	AGONIZE	AMPUTEE	APPRISE	ATHIRST	BARONET	BELLOWS	BLADDER	BRACERO
ABSCOND	AGROUND	AMYLASE	APPROVE	ATHLETE	BAROQUE	BELOVED	BLANKET	BRACKEN
ABSENCE	AILERON	ANAEMIA	APRICOT	ATHWART	BARRAGE	BELTWAY	BLARNEY	BRACKET
ABSOLVE	AILMENT	ANAGRAM	APROPOS	ATOMIZE	BARRIER	BENEATH	BLATANT	BRAHMAN
ABSTAIN	AIMLESS	ANALOGY	AQUATIC	ATROPHY	BARRING	BENEFIT	BLATHER	BRAHMIN
ABYSMAL	AIRDROP	ANALYZE	AQUAVIT	ATTACHE	BARROOM	BENISON	BLEEDER	BRAILLE
ABYSSAL	AIRFLOW	ANAPEST	AQUEOUS	ATTAINT	BASHFUL	BENTHIC	BLEMISH	BRAMBLE
ACADEME	AIRFOIL	ANARCHY	AQUIFER	ATTEMPT	BASSOON	BENTHOS	BLESSED	BRAVADO
ACADEMY	AIRLIFT	ANATOMY	ARAPAHO	ATTRACT	BASTARD	BENZENE	BLINDER	BRAVERY
ACCLAIM	AIRLINE	ANCHOVY	ARBITER	AUCTION	BASTION	BENZINE	BLINKER	BRAVURA
ACCOUNT	AIRMAIL	ANCIENT	ARBUTUS	AUDIBLE	BATHTUB	BENZOIN	BLINTZE	BRAZIER
ACCUSAL	AIRPORT	ANDANTE	ARCHAIC	AUDITOR	BATISTE	BEQUEST	BLISTER	BREADTH
ACCUSED	AIRPOST	ANDIRON	ARCHERY	AUGMENT	BATSMAN	BERSERK	BLOATER	BREAKER
ACETATE	AIRSHIP	ANDROID	ARCHIVE	AUREATE	BATTERY	BESEECH	BLOODED	BREAKUP
ACETONE	AIRSICK	ANEMONE	ARCHWAY	AUREOLE	BATTING	BESHREW	BLOOPER	BREATHE
ACHIEVE	AIRWAVE	ANGUISH	ARDUOUS	AURICLE	BAUXITE	BESIDES	BLOSSOM	BRECCIA
ACIDIFY	ALBUMEN	ANGULAR	AREAWAY	AUSPICE	BAYONET	BESIEGE	BLOTTER	BREVITY
ACOLYTE	ALBUMIN	ANILINE	ARMHOLE	AUSTERE	BAZOOKA	BESMEAR	BLOWGUN	BRIGADE
ACONITE	ALCALDE	ANIMATE	ARMORER	AUSTRAL	BEARING	BESPEAK	BLOWOUT	BRIGAND
ACQUIRE	ALCAZAR	ANIMISM	ARMREST	AUTOPSY	BEASTLY	BESTIAL	BLUBBER	BRIMFUL
ACREAGE	ALCHEMY	ANNUITY	ARPANET	AVARICE	BEATIFY	BETHINK	BLUCHER	BRIOCHE
ACROBAT	ALCOHOL	ANNULAR	ARRAIGN	AVERAGE	BEATNIK	BETIMES	BLUNDER	BRISKET
ACRONYM	ALEMBIC	ANODIZE	ARRANGE	AVOCADO	BECAUSE	BETOKEN	BLUSTER	BRISTLE
ACRYLIC	ALEWIFE	ANODYNE	ARREARS	AWKWARD	BECLOUD	BETROTH	BOATMAN	BRITISH
ACTUARY	ALFALFA	ANOMALY	ARRIVAL	AZIMUTH	BEDDING	BETWEEN	BOBSLED	BRITTLE
ACTUATE	ALGEBRA	ANOTHER	ARSENAL	BACKING	BEDEVIL	BETWIXT	BOLIVAR	BROADEN
ADAMANT	ALIMENT	ANTACID	ARSENIC	BACKLIT	BEDFAST	BEWITCH	BOLOGNA	BROCADE
ADAPTER	ALIMONY	ANTENNA	ARTICLE	BACKLOG	BEDIZEN	BIBELOT	BOLSTER	BROIDER
ADDRESS	ALLEGRO	ANTHILL	ARTISAN	BADLAND	BEDOUIN	BICYCLE	BOMBARD	BROILER
ADENINE	ALLERGY	ANTHRAX	ARTISTE	BAGASSE	BEDPOST	BIFOCAL	BOMBAST	BROMIDE
ADENOID	ALMANAC	ANTHROP	ARTLESS	BAGGAGE	BEDROCK	BIGHORN	BONANZA	BROMINE
ADIPOSE	ALMONER	ANTIGEN	ASCETIC	BAGPIPE	BEDROLL	BIKEWAY	BONDAGE	BROODER
ADJOURN	ALREADY	ANTIQUE	ASCRIBE	BAILIFF	BEDROOM	BILIOUS	BONDMAN	BROTHEL
ADJUDGE	ALRIGHT	ANTONYM	ASEPTIC	BALANCE	BEDSIDE	BILLION	BONFIRE	BROTHER
ADJUNCT	ALUMINA	ANXIETY	ASEXUAL	BALCONY	BEDSORE	BIMETAL	BOOKEND	BROUGHT
ADMIRAL	ALUMNUS	ANXIOUS	ASHAMED	BALDING	BEDTIME	BINDING	BOOKISH	BROWNIE
ADRENAL	AMALGAM	ANYBODY	ASHTRAY	BALDRIC	BEEHIVE	BIOLOGY	BOOKLET	BROWSER
ADULATE	AMATEUR	ANYMORE	ASIATIC	BALEFUL	BEELINE	BIOTITE	BOOTLEG	BRUISER
ADVANCE	AMATIVE	ANYTIME	ASININE	BALLAST	BEESWAX	BIPLANE	BOREDOM	BRUSQUE
ADVERSE	AMATORY	ANYWISE	ASKANCE	BALLOON	BEGGARY	BIPOLAR	BOROUGH	BRUTISH
ADVISED	AMBIENT	APANAGE	ASPHALT	BALONEY	BEGONIA	BIRCHER	BORSCHT	BUCKEYE
AEROBIC	AMENITY	APATITE	ASPIRIN	BANDAGE	BEGRIME	BIRETTA	BOUDOIR	BUCKLER

BUCKRAM	CANASTA	CATCHER	CHATTEL	CLEANSE	COMPEER	CONTENT	COWLICK	CUSTARD
BUCKSAW	CANDIED	CATCHUP	CHATTER	CLEANUP	COMPETE	CONTEST	COWLING	CUSTODY
BUCOLIC	CANNERY	CATFISH	CHEAPEN	CLEAVER	COMPILE	CONTEXT	COWPOKE	CUTBACK
BUFFALO	CANNULA	CATHODE	CHECKER	CLEMENT	COMPLEX	CONTORT	COWSLIP	CUTICLE
BUFFOON	CANTATA	CATLIKE	CHECKUP	CLIMATE	COMPORT.	CONTOUR	COXCOMB	CUTLASS
BUGABOO	CANTEEN	CATTAIL	CHEDDAR	CLINKER	COMPOSE	CONTRIB	CRABBED	CUTLERY
BUGBEAR	CANVASS	CATWALK	CHEETAH	CLIPPER	COMPOST	CONTROL	CRACKER	CUTTING
BULLDOG	CAPABLE	CAUSTIC	CHEMISE	CLOBBER	COMPOTE	CONVENE	CRACKLE	CUTWORM
BULLION	CAPITAL	CAUTION	CHEMIST	CLOSURE	COMPUTE	CONVENT	CRANIUM	CYANIDE
BULLOCK	CAPITOL	CAVALRY	CHERISH	CLOTHES	COMRADE	CONVERT	CRAVING	CYCLIST
BULRUSH	CAPRICE	CAVEMAN	CHEROOT	CLOTURE	CONCAVE	CONVICT	CREATOR	CYCLONE
BULWARK	CAPSIZE	CEDILLA	CHEVIOT	CLUSTER	CONCEAL	CONVOKE	CREMATE	CYPRESS
BUMPKIN	CAPSTAN	CEILING	CHEVRON	CLUTTER	CONCEDE	COOKERY	CREVICE	CZARINA
BUNTING	CAPSULE	CELESTA	CHIANTI	COARSEN	CONCEIT	COOKOUT	CRICKET	DANDIFY
BURDOCK	CAPTAIN	CELSIUS	CHICANE	COATING	CONCEPT	COOLANT	CRIMSON	DARLING
BURETTE	CAPTION	CEMBALO	CHICANO	COAXIAL	CONCERN	COPILOT	CRINKLE	DASHIKI
BURGEON	CAPTIVE	CENSURE	CHICKEN	COBBLER	CONCERT	COPIOUS	CRIPPLE	DASHING
BURGESS	CAPTURE	CENTARE	CHICORY	COCAINE	CONCISE	COPPICE	CRITTER	DASHPOT
BURGHER	CARABAO	CENTAUR	CHIFFON	COCHLEA	CONCOCT	COPYBOY	CROCHET	DASTARD
BURMESE	CARAMEL	CENTAVO	CHIGGER	COCKADE	CONCORD	COPYCAT	CROOKED	DAUPHIN
BURNISH	CARAVAN	CENTIME	CHIGNON	COCKEYE	CONDEMN	CORACLE	CROPPER	DAYBOOK
BURNOUT	CARAVEL	CENTIMO	CHIMERA	COCKNEY	CONDIGN	CORDAGE	CROQUET	DAYTIME
BUSHING	CARAWAY	CENTRAL	CHIMNEY	COCKPIT	CONDOLE	CORDIAL	CROSIER	DEADPAN
BUTCHER	CARBIDE	CENTURY	CHINESE	COCONUT	CONDONE	CORDITE	CROUTON	DEALING
BUTTOCK	CARBINE	CERAMIC	CHINOOK	CODEINE	CONDUCE	CORDOBA	CROWBAR	DEANERY
BUZZARD	CARCASS	CERTAIN	CHINTZY	CODFISH	CONDUCT	CORINTH	CRUCIAL	DEATHLY
CABARET	CARDBUS	CERTIFY	CHIPPER	CODICIL	CONDUIT	CORNCOB	CRUCIFY	DEBACLE
CABBAGE	CARDIAC	CERUMEN	CHOCTAW	CODLING	CONDYLE	CORNICE	CRUISER	DEBAUCH
CABINET	CAREFUL	CESSION	CHOLERA	COEQUAL	CONFESS	COROLLA	CRULLER	DEBOUCH
CABOOSE	CARFARE	CHABLIS	CHOPPER	COEXIST	CONFIDE	CORONAL	CRUMBLE	DEBRIEF
CADAVER	CARIBOU	CHADIAN	CHORALE	COGNATE	CONFINE	CORONER	CRUMPET	DECAGON
CADENCE	CARIOUS	CHAFFER	CHORTLE	COHABIT	CONFIRM	CORONET	CRUMPLE	DECEASE
CADENZA	CARLOAD	CHAGRIN	CHOWDER	COINAGE	CONFLUX	CORRECT	CRUSADE	DECEIVE
CADMIUM	CARMINE	CHALICE	CHROMIC	COLLAGE	CONFORM	CORRODE	CRYBABY	DECENCY
CAESURA	CARNAGE	CHALLIS	CHRONIC	COLLARD	CONFUSE	CORRUPT	CRYPTIC	DECIBEL
CAISSON	CAROTID	CHAMBER	CHUCKLE	COLLATE	CONFUTE	CORSAGE	CRYSTAL	DECIDED
CAITIFF	CAROUSE	CHAMFER	CHUKKER	COLLECT	CONGEAL	CORSAIR	CUBICLE	DECIMAL
CALCIFY	CARPORT	CHAMOIS	CHUTNEY	COLLEEN	CONGEST	CORTEGE	CUCKOLD	DECLAIM
CALCINE	CARRIER	CHANCEL	CILIATE	COLLEGE	CONICAL	COSSACK	CUISINE	DECLARE
CALCITE	CARRION	CHANCRE	CIRCLET	COLLIDE	CONIFER	COSTIVE	CULOTTE	DECLINE
CALCIUM	CARRYON	CHANNEL	CIRCUIT	COLLIER	CONJOIN	COSTUME	CULPRIT	DECODER
CALDERA	CARSICK	CHANSON	CISTERN	COLLOID	CONJURE	COTERIE	CULTURE	DECORUM
CALDRON	CARTAGE	CHANTEY	CITADEL	COLOGNE	CONNECT	COTTAGE	CULVERT	DEERFLY
CALENDS	CARTOON	CHANTRY	CITIZEN	COLONEL	CONNIVE	COULOMB	CUMULUS	DEFAULT
CALIBER	CASCADE	CHAPEAU	CIVILLY	COLORED	CONNOTE	COUNCIL	CUNNING	DEFENSE
CALIPER	CASCARA	CHAPLET	CIVVIES	COMBINE	CONQUER	COUNSEL	CUPCAKE	DEFIANT
CALLING	CASHIER	CHAPMAN	CLAMBER	COMFORT	CONSENT	COUNTER	CUPRITE	DEFICIT
CALLOUS	CASSAVA	CHAPTER	CLANGOR	COMMAND	CONSIGN	COUNTRY	CURATOR	DEFLATE
CALOMEL	CASSOCK	CHARGER	CLAPPER	COMMEND	CONSIST	COUPLET	CURBING	DEFLECT
CALORIC	CASTING	CHARIOT	CLARIFY	COMMENT	CONSOLE	COURAGE	CURIOUS	DEFRAUD
CALORIE	CASTLED	CHARITY	CLARION	COMMODE	CONSORT	COURIER	CURRANT	DEFROST
CALUMET	CATALOG	CHARMER	CLARITY	COMMUNE	CONSULT	COURSER	CURRENT	DEFUNCT
CALUMNY	CATALPA	CHARNEL	CLASSIC	COMMUTE	CONSUME	COURTLY	CURSIVE	DEGAUSS
CALYPSO	CATARRH	CHARTER	CLASTIC	COMPACT	CONTACT	COUTURE	CURSORY	DEGRADE
CAMBIUM	CATBIRD	CHASSIS	CLATTER	COMPANY	CONTAIN	COWBIRD	CURTAIL	DELIGHT
CAMBRIC	CATBOAT	CHASTEN	CLAVIER	COMPARE	CONTEMN	COWHAND	CURTAIN	DELIMIT
CAMPHOR	CATCALL	CHATEAU	CLEANLY	COMPASS	CONTEND	COWHIDE	CUSHION	DELIVER

DELOUSE	DIFFUSE	DOLEFUL	EARTHLY	ENGLISH	EXAMINE	FATUITY	FLATCAR	FOUNDRY
DEMERIT	DIGITAL	DOLPHIN	EASTERN	ENGRAFT	EXAMPLE	FATUOUS	FLATTEN	FOXHOLE
DEMESNE	DIGNIFY	DOMINIE	EBONITE	ENGRAVE	EXCERPT	FAUVISM	FLATTER	FRACTAL
DEMIGOD	DIGNITY	DOORMAN	ECHELON	ENGROSS	EXCLAIM	FEARFUL	FLATTOP	FRAGILE
DEMONIC	DIGRAPH	DOORMAT	ECLIPSE	ENHANCE	EXCLUDE	FEATHER	FLAVOUR	FRAILTY
DEMOTIC	DIGRESS	DOORWAY	ECLOGUE	ENLARGE	EXCRETA	FEATURE	FLEMING	FRANTIC
DENIZEN	DILEMMA	DORMANT	ECOLOGY	ENLIVEN	EXCRETE	FEBRILE	FLEMISH	FRAUGHT
DENSITY	DILUENT	DOSSIER	ECONOMY	ENNOBLE	EXECUTE	FEDERAL	FLESHLY	FRAZZLE
DENTATE	DINETTE	DOUBLET	ECSTASY	ENPLANE	EXEGETE	FEEDLOT	FLEXURE	FRECKLE
DENTIST	DIOCESE	DOUGHTY	EDIFICE	ENQUIRE	EXHAUST	FEELING	FLICKER	FREEBIE
DENTURE	DIPLOID	DOWAGER	EDITION	ENSLAVE	EXHIBIT	FENCING	FLIGHTY	FREEDOM
DEPLANE	DIPLOMA	DOYENNE	EDUCATE	ENSNARE	EXPANSE	FERMENT	FLIPPER	FREEMAN
DEPLETE	DIREFUL	DRACHMA	EFFENDI	ENTENTE	EXPENSE	FERMIUM	FLIVVER	FREEWAY
DEPLORE	DISABLE	DRAGNET	EGGHEAD	ENTHUSE	EXPIATE	FERNERY	FLORIST	FREEZER
DEPOSIT	DISAVOW	DRAGOON	EGOTISM	ENTITLE	EXPLAIN	FERROUS	FLOTSAM	FREIGHT
DEPRAVE	DISBAND	DRAPERY	EIDOLON	ENTRAIN	EXPLODE	FERRULE	FLOUNCE	FRESHEN
DEPRESS	DISCARD	DRASTIC	ELASTIC	ENTRANT	EXPLOIT	FERTILE	FLOWERY	FRESHET
DEPRIVE	DISCERN	DRAUGHT	ELDERLY	ENTREAT	EXPLORE	FERVENT	FLUSTER	FRETFUL
DERANGE	DISCORD	DRAWING	ELECTOR	ENTROPY	EXPOUND	FESTIVE	FLUTIST	FRETSAW
DERRICK	DISCUSS	DRESSER	ELEGIAC	ENTRUST	EXPRESS	FESTOON	FLUTTER	FRIABLE
DERVISH	DISDAIN	DRIBBLE	ELEMENT	ENTWINE	EXPUNGE	FETLOCK	FLYABLE	FRIGATE
DESCANT	DISEASE	DRIBLET	ELEVATE	ENVELOP	EXTINCT	FIANCEE	FLYLEAF	FRITTER
DESCEND	DISEUSE	DRIFTER	ELISION	ENVENOM	EXTRACT	FIBROID	FOGHORN	FRIZZLE
DESCENT	DISGUST	DRIZZLE	ELITISM	ENVIOUS	EXTREME	FICTION	FOLDOUT	FROGMAN
DESERVE	DISHRAG	DROPLET	ELLIPSE	EPAULET	EXTRUDE	FIFTEEN	FOLIAGE	FROWARD
DESKTOP	DISJOIN	DROPPER	ELUSIVE	EPERGNE	EYEBALL	FIGHTER	FOLKWAY	FRUSTUM
DESPAIR	DISLIKE	DROUGHT	ELYSIUM	EPICURE	EYEBROW	FIGMENT	FONDANT	FUCHSIA
DESPISE	DISMISS	DRUMLIN	EMANATE	EPIGRAM	EYELASH	FILBERT	FOOLERY	FULCRUM
DESPITE	DISOBEY	DRUMMER	EMBARGO	EPISODE	EYESORE	FILLING	FOOLISH	FULFILL
DESPOIL	DISPLAY	DRUNKEN	EMBASSY	EPISTLE	EYEWASH	FILMDOM	FOOTAGE	FULSOME
DESPOND	DISPORT	DUBIETY	EMBOWER	EPITAPH	FACTION	FINAGLE	FOOTING	FUNERAL
DESSERT	DISPOSE	DUBIOUS	EMBRACE	EPITHET	FACTORY	FINANCE	FOOTMAN	FURBISH
DESTINE	DISPUTE	DUCHESS	EMBROIL	EPITOME	FACTUAL	FINDING	FOOTPAD	FURIOUS
DESTINY	DISROBE	DUCKPIN	EMBRYOL	EQUABLE	FACULTY	FINESSE	FORBEAR	FURLONG
DESTROY	DISRUPT	DUCTILE	EMERALD	EQUATOR	FAIENCE	FINFISH	FORBODE	FURNACE
DETENTE	DISSECT	DUDGEON	EMERITA	EQUERRY	FAILING	FINICKY	FORCEPS	FURNISH
DETRACT	DISSENT	DULLARD	EMINENT	EQUINOX	FAILURE	FINNISH	FOREARM	FURRIER
DETRAIN	DISTAFF	DUMPING	EMITTER	ERELONG	FAIRING	FIREARM	FOREIGN	FURRING
DEVALUE	DISTANT	DUNGEON	EMOTION	EREMITE	FAIRWAY	FIREBOX	FORELEG	FURTHER
DEVELOP	DISTEND	DURABLE	EMPATHY	EROSION	FALLACY	FIREBUG	FOREMAN	FURTIVE
DEVIANT	DISTICH	DURANCE	EMPEROR	EROSIVE	FALLOUT	FIREFLY	FORESEE	FUSTIAN
DEVIATE	DISTILL	DUSTPAN	EMPOWER	ERRATIC	FALSIFY	FIREMAN	FORETOP	GABFEST
DEVILRY	DISTORT	DUTEOUS	EMPRESS	ERRATUM	FANATIC	FIRSTLY	FOREVER	GAINFUL
DEVIOUS	DISTURB	DUTIFUL	EMULATE	ESCAPEE	FANCIER	FISHERY	FORFEIT	GAINSAY
DEVOLVE	DIURNAL	DWINDLE	ENAMOUR	ESQUIRE	FANFARE	FISHING	FORFEND	GALLANT
DEVOTED	DIVERGE	DYNAMIC	ENCHAIN	ESSENCE	FANTAIL	FISSILE	FORGING	GALLEON
DEVOTEE	DIVERSE	DYNASTY	ENCHANT	ESTHETE	FANTASY	FISSION	FORGIVE	GALLERY
DEWCLAW	DIVIDER	EARACHE	ENCLAVE	ESTUARY	FARAWAY	FISSURE	FORLORN	GALLIUM
DEWDROP	DIVISOR	EARDRUM	ENCLOSE	ETCHING	FARMING	FISTFUL	FORMULA	GALLOWS
DEXTRIN	DIVORCE	EARLOBE	ENCRUST	ETERNAL	FARRAGO	FISTULA	FORSAKE	GAMBIAN
DIAGRAM	DIVULGE	EARMARK	ENDEMIC	ETHANOL	FARRIER	FITTING	FORTIFY	GANGWAY
DIALECT	DOCKAGE	EARMUFF	ENDLESS	ETHICAL	FARTHER	FIXTURE	FORTRAN	GANTLET
DIAMOND	DOGBANE	EARNEST	ENDMOST	EUPHONY	FASCISM	FLACCID	FORTUNE	GARBAGE
DIARIST	DOGCART	EARPLUG	ENDORSE	EVACUEE	FASHION	FLANKER	FORWARD	GARFISH
DICTATE	DOGFISH	EARRING	ENDWAYS	EVASION	FATBACK	FLANNEL	FOULARD	GARLAND
DICTION	DOGTROT	EARSHOT	ENDWISE	EVENING	FATEFUL	FLAPPER	FOULING	GARMENT
DIEHARD	DOGWOOD	EARTHEN	ENFORCE	EVIDENT	FATIGUE	FLATBED	FOUNDER	GARNISH

GARROTE	GONDOLA	HAFNIUM	HEADWAY	HOPHEAD	IMPIETY	INSIDER	JOLLITY	LAMINAR
GASTRIC	GOODMAN	HAGGARD	HEALTHY	HORIZON	IMPINGE	INSIGHT	JONQUIL	LAMPOON
GATEWAY	GORILLA	HAIRCUT	HEARING	HORMONE	IMPIOUS	INSIPID	JOTTING	LAMPREY
GAVOTTE	GOSHAWK	HAIRPIN	HEARKEN	HORRIFY	IMPLODE	INSPECT	JOURNAL	LANDING
GAZELLE	GOSLING	HALBERD	HEARSAY	HOSANNA	IMPLORE	INSPIRE	JOURNEY	LANGUID
GAZETTE	GOULASH	HALCYON	HEARTEN	HOSIERY	IMPOUND	INSTALL	JOYANCE	LANGUOR
GEARBOX	GOURMET	HALFWAY	HEATHEN	HOSPICE	IMPRESS	INSTANT	JOYRIDE	LANOLIN
GELATIN	GRACKLE	HALIBUT	HEATHER	HOSTAGE	IMPRINT	INSTATE	JUBILEE	LANTANA
GELDING	GRADUAL	HALLWAY	HECTARE	HOSTESS	IMPROVE	INSTEAD	JUDAISM	LANTERN
GENERAL	GRAMMAR	HALTING	HEINOUS	HOSTILE	IMPULSE	INSTILL	JUGULAR	LANYARD
GENERIC	GRANARY	HALVERS	HEIRESS	HOSTLER	INBOARD	INSULAR	JUJITSU	LAOTIAN
GENESIS	GRANDAM	HALYARD	HELICAL	HOTCAKE	INBOUND	INSULIN	JUKEBOX	LAPWING
GENETIC	GRANDEE	HAMMOCK	HELLCAT	HOTFOOT	INCENSE	INSURED	JUNIPER	LARCENY
GENITAL	GRANITE	HAMSTER	HELLENE	HOTSHOT	INCISOR	INSURER	JUPITER	LARGESS
GENTEEL	GRANTEE	HANDBAG	HELLION	HOUSING	INCLINE	INTEGER	JUSTICE	LASAGNA
GENTIAN	GRANULE	HANDCAR	HELPING	HOWBEIT	INCLOSE	INTENSE	JUSTIFY	LATAKIA
GENTILE	GRAPHIC	HANDFUL	HEMLINE	HOWEVER	INCLUDE	INTERIM	KADDISH	LATCHET
GENUINE	GRAPNEL	HANDGUN	HEMLOCK	HOWLING	INCRUST	INTRANS	KARAKUL	LATERAL
GEODESY	GRAPPLE	HANDOUT	HENPECK	HULKING	INCUBUS	INTROIT	KATYDID	LATRINE
GEOLOGY	GRATIFY	HANDSAW	HEPARIN	HUMDRUM	INDEXED	INTRUDE	KEELSON	LATTICE
GERMANE	GRATING	HANDSEL	HEPATIC	HUMERUS	INDICIA	INTRUST	KEEPING	LATVIAN
GESTAPO	GRAUPEL	HANDSET	HERBAGE	HUMIDOR	INDOORS	INVALID	KERATIN	LAUNDER
GESTURE	GRAVITY	HANGDOG	HEROICS	HUMMOCK	INDORSE	INVEIGH	KERNING	LAUNDRY
GETAWAY	GRAVURE	HANGING	HEROINE	HUNDRED	INDULGE	INVERSE	KETCHUP	LAWLESS
GHASTLY	GRAZIER	HANGMAN	HEROISM	HUNKERS	INDWELL	INVOICE	KEYHOLE	LAWSUIT
GHERKIN	GRECIAN	HANGOUT	HERRING	HUSBAND	INERTIA	INVOLVE	KEYNOTE	LAYAWAY
GIBBOUS	GREMLIN	HAPLESS	HERSELF	HUSKING	INEXACT	IRANIAN	KHEDIVE	LAYETTE
GIBLETS	GRENADE	HAPLOID	HEXAGON	HUTMENT	INFANCY	IRIDIUM	KIBBUTZ	LEADING
GIMMICK	GRIDDLE	HAPPILY	HEXAPOD	HYDRANT	INFARCT	IRKSOME	KICKOFF	LEAFAGE
GINGHAM	GRIMACE	HARBOUR	HIBACHI	HYDRATE	INFERNO	IRONING	KIDSKIN	LEAFLET
GINSENG	GRINDER	HARDPAN	HICKORY	HYDROUS	INFIDEL	ISOLATE	KILLING	LEAGUER
GIRAFFE	GRISTLE	HARDTOP	HIDALGO	HYGIENE	INFIELD	ISOTOPE	KILLJOY	LEAKAGE
GIZZARD	GRIZZLY	HARELIP	HIDEOUS	HYMNODY	INFLAME	ISRAELI	KILOTON	LEARNED
GLACIAL	GROMMET	HARMONY	HIDEOUT	ICEBERG	INFLATE	ISTHMUS	KINDRED	LEATHER
GLACIER	GROUPER	HARNESS	HIGHBOY	ICEBOAT	INFLECT	ITALIAN	KINETIC	LECHERY
GLADDEN	GROUPIE	HARPOON	HIGHWAY	IDEALLY	INFLICT	ITEMIZE	KINFOLK	LECTERN
GLAMOUR	GRUMBLE	HARRIER	HILLOCK	IDOLIZE	INGENUE	ITERATE	KINGDOM	LECTURE
GLAZIER	GRUNION	HARVARD	HILLTOP	IGNEOUS	INGRAFT	JACINTH	KINGPIN	LEEWARD
GLEEMAN	GUANINE	HARVEST	HIMSELF	IGNOBLE	INGRAIN	JACKASS	KINSHIP	LEFTISM
GLIMMER	GUARANI	HASHING	HINTING	ILEITIS	INGRATE	JACKDAW	KINSMAN	LEGATEE
GLIMPSE	GUERDON	HASHISH	HIPBONE	ILLEGAL	INGRESS	JACKLEG	KITCHEN	LEGGING
GLISTEN	GUILDER	HASSOCK	HIPSTER	ILLICIT	INGROWN	JACKPOT	KNEECAP	LEGHORN
GLISTER	GUMBOIL	HATCHET	HIRSUTE	ILLNESS	INHABIT	JANITOR	KNOCKER	LEGIBLE
GLITTER	GUMDROP	HAUBERK	HISTORY	IMAGERY	INHALER	JANUARY	KNOWING	LEISURE
GLOBULE	GUMSHOE	HAUGHTY	HOBNAIL	IMAGINE	INHERIT	JASMINE	KNUCKLE	LEMMING
GLORIFY	GUNBOAT	HAULAGE	HOECAKE	IMAGISM	INHIBIT	JAVELIN	KREMLIN	LEMPIRA
GLOTTIS	GUNFIRE	HAUTEUR	HOEDOWN	IMITATE	INHUMAN	JAYBIRD	KRYPTON	LENIENT
GLUCOSE	GUNLOCK	HAYCOCK	HOGBACK	IMMENSE	INITIAL	JAYWALK	KUMQUAT	LEONINE
GLUTTON	GUNNERY	HAYFORK	HOGWASH	IMMERSE	INKHORN	JEALOUS	LABORED	LEOPARD
GOBBLER	GUNSHOT	HAYLOFT	HOLDING	IMMORAL	INKLING	JEHOVAH	LACONIC	LEOTARD
GODDESS	GUNWALE	HAYRICK	HOLIDAY	IMPANEL	INKWELL	JEJUNUM	LACQUER	LEPROSY
GODHEAD	HABITAT	HAYSEED	HOLMIUM	IMPASSE	INNARDS	JETPORT	LACTATE	LESBIAN
GODHOOD	HABITUE	HAYWIRE	HOLSTER	IMPASTO	INNINGS	JEWELER	LACTEAL	LETDOWN
GODLESS	HACKMAN	HEADING	HOMBURG	IMPEACH	INQUEST	JEWELRY	LACTOSE	LETTUCE
GODLIKE	HACKNEY	HEADMAN	HOMONYM	IMPEARL	INQUIRE	JITTERS	LADYBUG	LEXICON
GODSEND	HACKSAW	HEADPIN	HOODLUM	IMPERIL	INQUIRY	JOCULAR	LAGGARD	LIAISON
GOGGLES	HADDOCK	HEADSET	HOOSIER	IMPETUS	INSHORE	JODHPUR	LAMBENT	LIBERAL

LIBERTY	MAFIOSO	MASTIFF	MILLION	MORNING	NITRITE	ODDMENT	OUTLINE	PANNIER
LIBRARY	MAGENTA	MASTOID	MIMESIS	MOROCCO	NOCUOUS	ODYSSEY	OUTLIVE	PANOPLY
LICENSE	MAGNATE	MATADOR	MIMETIC	MORPHIA	NOISOME	OEDIPAL	OUTLOOK	PANTHER
LIGHTEN	MAGNETO	MATINEE	MIMICRY	MORTIFY	NOMADIC	OFFBEAT	OUTPLAY	PAPILLA
LIGHTER	MAGNIFY	MATTINS	MINARET	MORTISE	NOMINAL	OFFENSE	OUTPOST	PAPOOSE
LIGNIFY	MAHATMA	MATTOCK	MINDFUL	MOUNTIE	NOMINEE	OFFHAND	OUTPULL	PAPRIKA
LIGNITE	MAHICAN	MAUDLIN	MINERAL	MUDROOM	NONBOOK	OFFICER	OUTRAGE	PAPYRUS
LIMBECK	MAILBOX	MAUNDER	MINIBUS	MUEZZIN	NONHERO	OFFSIDE	OUTRANK	PARABLE
LIMEADE	MAILMAN	MAWKISH	MINIMAL	MUFFLER	NONPLUS	OILSKIN	OUTSELL	PARADOX
LIMITED	MAINTOP	MAXILLA	MINIMUM	MUGWUMP	NONSKED	OLDSTER	OUTSIDE	PARAGON
LINEAGE	MAJESTY	MAXIMAL	MINSTER	MULATTO	NONSTOP	OLIVINE	OUTSIZE	PARAPET
LINEMAN	MAKINGS	MAXIMUM	MINUEND	MULLEIN	NONUSER	OMINOUS	OUTSTAY	PARASOL
LINGUAL	MALAISE	MAYPOLE	MINUTIA	MULLION	NOONDAY	OMNIBUS	OUTVOTE	PARBOIL
LINKAGE	MALARIA	MAZURKA	MIRACLE	MUNDANE	NORTHER	ONEROUS	OUTWARD	PARESIS
LINSEED	MALEFIC	MEANDER	MISCALL	MURRAIN	NOSEGAY	ONESELF	OUTWEAR	PARFAIT
LIONIZE	MALISON	MEANING	MISDEED	MUSETTE	NOSTRIL	ONETIME	OUTWORK	PARKWAY
LIQUEFY	MALLARD	MEASLES	MISFILE	MUSICAL	NOSTRUM	ONGOING	OUTWORN	PARLOUR
LIQUEUR	MALLEUS	MEASURE	MISFIRE	MUSKRAT	NOTABLE	ONSHORE	OVATION	PARLOUS
LISSOME	MALMSEY	MEATMAN	MISLEAD	MUSTANG	NOTHING	OPACITY	OVERACT	PARQUET
LISTING	MALTOSE	MEDIATE	MISLIKE	MUSTARD	NOURISH	OPENING	OVERAGE	PARSING
LITERAL	MAMMARY	MEDICAL	MISNAME	MUTABLE	NOVELLA	OPERATE	OVERALL	PARSLEY
LITHIUM	MAMMOTH	MEDULLA	MISPLAY	MYSTERY	NOVELTY	OPINION	OVERARM	PARSNIP
LITURGY	MANACLE	MEETING	MISREAD	MYSTIFY	NOWHERE	OPOSSUM	OVERAWE	PARTAKE
LIVABLE	MANAGER	MEGATON	MISRULE	NACELLE	NOXIOUS	OPPRESS	OVERFLY	PARTIAL
LOATHLY	MANDATE	MEIOSIS	MISSEND	NAIVETE	NUCLEAR	OPTICAL	OVERJOY	PARTING
LOBSTER	MANDREL	MELANGE	MISSILE	NAIVETY	NUCLEON	OPTIMAL	OVERLAP	PARTITE
LOCATOR	MANDRIL	MELANIC	MISSING	NANKEEN	NUCLEUS	OPTIMUM	OVERLAY	PARTNER
LOCKJAW	MANHOLE	MELANIN	MISSION	NAPHTHA	NUCLIDE	OPULENT	OVERRUN	PARTWAY
LOCKNUT	MANHOOD	MEMENTO	MISSIVE	NARRATE	NULLIFY	ORATION	OVERSEA	PARVENU
LOCKOUT	MANHUNT	MENFOLK	MISSTEP	NARTHEX	NUMERAL	ORATORY	OVERSEE	PASSAGE
LODGING	MANIKIN	MENTHOL	MISTAKE	NARWHAL	NUMERIC	ORBITER	OVERTOP	PASSING
LONGBOW	MANKIND	MENTION	MISTRAL	NASCENT	NUPTIAL	ORCHARD	OVIDUCT	PASSION
LONGING	MANLIKE	MERCURY	MITOSIS	NATURAL	NURSERY	ORDERLY	OVULATE	PASSIVE
LOOKOUT	MANNISH	MERMAID	MIXTURE	NAUGHTY	NURTURE	ORDINAL	OXBLOOD	PASSKEY
LOTTERY	MANSARD	MESSAGE	MOBSTER	NECKTIE	NUTPICK	OREGANO	OXIDANT	PASTERN
LOWBROW	MANSION	MESSIAH	MODICUM	NEEDFUL	OARLOCK	ORGANDY	OXIDIZE	PASTIME
LOWDOWN	MANTEAU	MESTIZO	MODISTE	NEGLECT	OARSMAN	ORGANIC	PABULUM	PASTURE
LOWLAND	MANUMIT	METHANE	MODULAR	NEITHER	OATCAKE	ORGANZA	PACIFIC	PATELLA
LOZENGE	MARGENT	MEXICAN	MOHEGAN	NEMESIS	OATMEAL	ORIFICE	PACKAGE	PATHWAY
LUCERNE	MARIMBA	MICROBE	MOHICAN	NEOLOGY	OBELISK	ORIGAMI	PACKING	PATIENT
LUCIFER	MARINER	MIDLAND	MOISTEN	NEPTUNE	OBLIQUE	OROGENY	PADDING	PATRIOT
LUGGAGE	MARITAL	MIDMOST	MOLDING	NERVOUS	OBLOQUY	OROTUND	PADDOCK	PATROON
LULLABY	MARPLOT	MIDRIFF	MOLLIFY	NETTING	OBSCENE	ORTOLAN	PADLOCK	PATTERN
LUMBAGO	MARQUEE	MIDTOWN	MOLLUSK	NETWARE	OBSCURE	OSMOSIS	PAGEANT	PAUCITY
LUNATIC	MARQUIS	MIDWEEK	MONADIC	NETWORK	OBSEQUY	OSSUARY	PAGEBOY	PAYLOAD
LUNETTE	MARSHAL	MIDWIFE	MONARCH	NEUTRAL	OBSERVE	OSTMARK	PAISLEY	PAYMENT
LUSTRAL	MARTIAL	MIDYEAR	MONEYED	NEUTRON	OBTRUDE	OSTRICH	PAJAMAS	PAYROLL
MACABRE	MARTIAN	MIGRANT	MONGREL	NEWBORN	OBVERSE	OTTOMAN	PALADIN	PEACOCK
MACADAM	MARTINI	MIGRATE	MONITOR	NEWSBOY	OBVIATE	OUTCAST	PALAVER	PEAFOWL
MACAQUE	MARXISM	MILEAGE	MONOCLE	NEWSMAN	OBVIOUS	OUTCOME	PALETTE	PEASANT
MACDRAW	MASCARA	MILITIA	MONOMER	NIAGARA	OCARINA	OUTCROP	PALFREY	PECCARY
MACHETE	MASONIC	MILKMAN	MONSOON	NIGGARD	OCCLUDE	OUTDOOR	PALMATE	PECCAVI
MACHINE	MASONRY	MILKSOP	MONSTER	NIGHTLY	OCTAGON	OUTDRAW	PALPATE	PEDICAB
MACRAME	MASSAGE	MILLAGE	MONTAGE	NIOBIUM	OCTOBER	OUTFACE	PANACEA	PEELING
MADDING	MASSEUR	MILLDAM	MOORING	NIRVANA	OCTOPUS	OUTFLOW	PANACHE	PEEVISH
MADEIRA	MASSIVE	MILLIME	MORAINE	NITRATE	OCULIST	OUTGROW	PANCAKE	PELAGIC
MAESTRO	MASTERY	MILLING	MORDANT	NITRIFY	ODDBALL	OUTLAST	PANICLE	PELICAN

PENALTY	PIEBALD	POINTER	PREFECT	PRORATE	RACCOON	REDOUBT	RESPITE	RUBELLA
PENANCE	PIGGISH	POLARIS	PREFORM	PROSAIC	RACEWAY	REDOUND	RESPOND	RUFFIAN
PENATES	PIGMENT	POLECAT	PREHEAT	PROSODY	RADIANT	REDRESS	RESTIVE	RUINOUS
PENDANT	PIGSKIN	POLEMIC	PRELATE	PROSPER	RADIATE	REDSKIN	RESTORE	RUMMAGE
PENDENT	PIGTAIL	POLITIC	PRELUDE	PROTEAN	RADICAL	REDWOOD	RETINUE	RUNAWAY
PENDING	PILGRIM	POLLACK	PREMIER	PROTECT	RAFFISH	REENTRY	RETIRED	RUNDOWN
PENGUIN	PILLAGE	POLLUTE	PREMISE	PROTEGE	RAGTIME	REFEREE	RETIREE	RUNNING
PENNANT	PILLBOX	POLYGON	PREMIUM	PROTEIN	RAGWEED	REFINED	RETOUCH	RUPTURE
PENSION	PILLION	POLYMER	PREPARE	PROTEST	RAILING	REFLECT	RETRACE	RUSSIAN
PENSIVE	PILLORY	POMPANO	PREPUCE	PROVERB	RAILWAY	REFRACT	RETRACT	SABBATH
PENTIUM	PILSNER	POMPOUS	PRESAGE	PROVIDE	RAIMENT	REFRAIN	RETREAD	SADIRON
PEPPERY	PIMENTO	PONIARD	PRESENT	PROVISO	RAINBOW	REFRESH	RETREAT	SAFFRON
PERCALE	PINHOLE	PONTIFF	PRESIDE	PROVOKE	RAMBLER	REFUGEE	REUNION	SAGUARO
PERCENT	PINKEYE	PONTOON	PRESOAK	PROVOST	RAMPAGE	REGALIA	REVENGE	SAILING
PERCEPT	PINNACE	POPCORN	PRESUME	PROWESS	RAMPANT	REGATTA	REVENUE	SAINTLY
PERFECT	PINNATE	POPOVER	PRETEEN	PROXIMO	RAMPART	REGENCY	REVERIE	SALIENT
PERFIDY	PINWORM	POPULAR	PRETEND	PRUDENT	RANKING	REGIMEN	REVERSE	SALTBOX
PERFORM	PIONEER	PORCINE	PRETEXT	PSALTER	RANSACK	REGNANT	REVIVAL	SALTINE
PERFUME	PIPETTE	PORTAGE	PRETZEL	PSYCHIC	RAPPORT	REGRESS	REVOLVE	SALVAGE
PERGOLA	PIQUANT	PORTEND	PREVAIL	PSYCHOL	RAPTURE	REGROUP	RHENIUM	SAMOVAR
PERHAPS	PIRANHA	PORTENT	PREVENT	PUBERTY	RAREBIT	REGULAR	RHIZOME	SAMPLER
PERIGEE	PISMIRE	PORTICO	PREVIEW	PUBLISH	RATCHET	REJOICE	RHODIUM	SAMURAI
PERIQUE	PITCHER	PORTION	PRICKER	PUDDING	RATLINE	RELAPSE	RHOMBUS	SANCTUM
PERIWIG	PITEOUS	PORTRAY	PRICKLE	PUERILE	RATTLER	RELATED	RHUBARB	SANDBAG
PERJURY	PITFALL	POSSESS	PRIMACY	PULLMAN	RATTRAP	RELATOR	RICKETS	SANDBAR
PERLITE	PITIFUL	POSTAGE	PRIMARY	PULLOUT	RAUCOUS	RELEASE	RICKETY	SANDHOG
PERPLEX	PIZZAZZ	POSTBOY	PRIMATE	PULSATE	RAUNCHY	RELIEVE	RICKSHA	SANDLOT
PERSIAN	PLACARD	POSTERN	PRITHEE	PUMPKIN	RAVIOLI	RELIQUE	RIGGING	SANDMAN
PERSIST	PLACATE	POSTMAN	PRIVACY	PUNGENT	RAWHIDE	REMAINS	RIGHTLY	SAPIENT
PERTAIN	PLACEBO	POSTURE	PRIVATE	PUNSTER	REACTOR	REMNANT	RINGLET	SAPLING
PERTURB	PLACKET	POSTWAR	PROBATE	PURITAN	READING	REMODEL	RIPOSTE	SAPWOOD
PERVADE	PLANTAR	POTABLE	PROBITY	PURLIEU	READOUT	REMORSE	RISIBLE	SARCASM
PERVERT	PLANTER	POTHEAD	PROBLEM	PURLOIN	REAGENT	REMOUNT	RIVALRY	SARDINE
PETIOLE	PLASTER	POTHERB	PROCEED	PURPORT	REALISM	RENEWAL	RIVULET	SATANIC
PETRIFY	PLASTIC	POTHOLE	PROCESS	PURPOSE	REALITY	REPLACE	ROADBED	SATCHEL
PETTISH	PLATEAU	POTHOOK	PROCTOR	PURSUIT	REALIZE	REPLETE	ROADWAY	SATIATE
PETUNIA	PLATING	POTLUCK	PROCURE	PURVIEW	REBIRTH	REPLICA	ROASTER	SATIETY
PFENNIG	PLATOON	POTSHOT	PRODIGY	PUSTULE	REBOUND	REPRESS	ROBBERY	SATISFY
PHAETON	PLATTER	POTTAGE	PRODUCE	PUTREFY	REBUILD	REPRINT	ROEBUCK	SAUNTER
PHALANX	PLAUDIT	POTTERY	PRODUCT	PYJAMAS	RECEIPT	REPRISE	ROISTER	SAUSAGE
PHALLIC	PLAYBOY	POULTRY	PROFANE	PYRAMID	RECEIVE	REPROOF	ROLLICK	SAVANNA
PHALLUS	PLAYLET	POVERTY	PROFESS	PYRITES	RECENCY	REPROVE	ROMANCE	SAWDUST
PHANTOM	PLAYPEN	PRAETOR	PROFFER	QUALIFY	RECITAL	REPTILE	ROOFTOP	SAWMILL
PHARAOH	PLENARY	PRAIRIE	PROFILE	QUALITY	RECLAIM	REPULSE	ROOKERY	SCALLOP
PHARYNX	PLIABLE	PRALINE	PROFUSE	QUANTUM	RECLAME	REPUTED	ROOSTER	SCALPEL
PHILTER	PLOTTER	PRATTLE	PROGENY	QUARREL	RECLINE	REQUEST	ROOTLET	SCAMPER
PHOENIX	PLOWBOY	PRAYING	PROGMAN	QUARTER	RECLUSE	REQUIEM	ROSEATE	SCANDAL
PHONEME	PLOWMAN	PREBEND	PROGRAM	QUARTET	RECOUNT	REQUIRE	ROSEBUD	SCANNER
PHONICS	PLUMAGE	PRECEDE	PROJECT	QUETZAL	RECOVER	REQUITE	ROSETTE	SCAPULA
PHRENIC	PLUMBER	PRECEPT	PROLONG	QUIBBLE	RECRUIT	REREDOS	ROSTRUM	SCARIFY
PHYSICS	PLUMMET	PRECISE	PROMISE	QUICKEN	RECTIFY	RESCIND	ROTUNDA	SCARLET
PHYSIOL	PLUNDER	PRECOOK	PROMOTE	QUICKIE	RECTORY	RESEDIT	ROUGHEN	SCATTER
PIANIST	PLUNGER	PREDATE	PRONOUN	QUIETUS	RECYCLE	RESERVE	ROUNDUP	SCENERY
PIASTER	PLUVIAL	PREDICT	PROPANE	QUININE	REDCOAT	RESIDUE	ROUTINE	SCEPTER
PIBROCH	PLYWOOD	PREEMIE	PROPHET	QUINTAL	REDDISH	RESOLVE	ROWBOAT	SCEPTIC
PICCOLO	POCOSIN	PREEMPT	PROPMAN	QUINTET	REDHEAD	RESOUND	ROYALTY	SCHOLAR
PICTURE	POINTED	PREFACE	PROPOSE	QUONDAM	REDLINE	RESPECT	RUBBISH	SCIENCE

SCOOTER	SHACKLE	SKIPPER	SPARROW	STIFFEN	SUNDOWN	TAPSTER	THYMINE	TRAFFIC
SCOURGE	SHADING	SKITTER	SPASTIC	STILTED	SUNFISH	TARNISH	THYROID	TRAGEDY
SCRAPPY	SHALLOP	SKIWEAR	SPATIAL	STILTON	SUNLAMP	TATTING	THYSELF	TRAILER
SCRATCH	SHALLOW	SKYLARK	SPATTER	STIPEND	SUNRISE	TAXICAB	TIBETAN	TRAINEE
SCRAWNY	SHAMBLE	SKYLINE	SPATULA	STIPPLE	SUNROOF	TECHNIC	TICKING	TRAIPSE
SCREECH	SHAMPOO	SKYWARD	SPEAKER	STIRRUP	SUNSPOT	TEDIOUS	TIDINGS	TRAITOR
SCROTUM	SHAPELY	SLACKEN	SPECIAL	STOMACH	SUPPORT	TEENAGE	TIEBACK	TRAMMEL
SCRUFFY	SHARPEN	SLACKER	SPECIES	STOPGAP	SUPPOSE	TEKTITE	TIGHTEN	TRAMPLE
SCRUPLE	SHARPER	SLANDER	SPECIFY	STOPPER	SUPREME	TELLING	TILLAGE	TRANSIT
SCUFFLE	SHARPIE	SLATHER	SPECKLE	STORAGE	SURFACE	TEMPERA	TIMBREL	TRANSOM
SCUPPER	SHATTER	SLAVERY	SPECTER	STORIED	SURFEIT	TEMPEST	TIMOTHY	TRAPEZE
SCUTTLE	SHAVING	SLAVISH	SPEEDUP	STRANGE	SURGEON	TENABLE	TIMPANI	TRAVAIL
SEABIRD	SHAWNEE	SLEEPER	SPELLER	STRATUM	SURGERY	TENANCY	TINFOIL	TREACLE
SEAFOOD	SHEATHE	SLEIGHT	SPICULE	STRETCH	SURMISE	TENDRIL	TINWARE	TREADLE
SEALANT	SHEBANG	SLENDER	SPINACH	STRINGY	SURNAME	TENFOLD	TIPSTER	TREASON
SEAPORT	SHELLAC	SLICKER	SPINDLE	STROPHE	SURPASS	TENSILE	TITANIC	TREFOIL
SEASICK	SHELTER	SLIPPER	SPINDLY	STRUDEL	SURPLUS	TENSION	TITULAR	TRELLIS
SEASIDE	SHERBET	SLITHER	SPIRANT	STUBBLE	SURTOUT	TENUOUS	TOASTER	TREMBLE
SEATING	SHERIFF	SLOBBER	SPITTLE	STUDENT	SURVIVE	TENURED	TOBACCO	TREMOLO
SEAWALL	SHIMMER	SLUMBER	SPLENIC	STUDIED	SUSPECT	TEQUILA	TOEHOLD	TRESTLE
SEAWARD	SHINGLE	SMELTER	SPLOTCH	STUFFIT	SUSPEND	TERBIUM	TOENAIL	TRIBUNE
SEAWEED	SHOCKER	SMIDGEN	SPLURGE	STUMBLE	SUSTAIN	TERMITE	TOGGERY	TRIBUTE
SECLUDE	SHORING	SMOLDER	SPOILER	STUPEFY	SWADDLE	TERNARY	TOLUENE	TRICEPS
SECRECY	SHORTEN	SMOTHER	SPONSOR	STUTTER	SWAGGER	TERRACE	TONIGHT	TRICKLE
SECRETE	SHORTLY	SMUGGLE	SPOTTER	STYLING	SWAHILI	TERRAIN	TONNAGE	TRIDENT
SECTARY	SHOTGUN	SNAFFLE	SPOUSAL	STYLISH	SWALLOW	TERRIER	TONNEAU	TRIGGER
SECTION	SHOWMAN	SNEAKER	SPUMONI	STYLIST	SWARTHY	TERRIFY	TONSURE	TRILOGY
SECULAR	SHRIVEL	SNICKER	SPUTNIK	STYLIZE	SWEATER	TESTATE	TOOLBOX	TRINITY
SEEMING	SHUDDER	SNIFFLE	SPUTTER	STYPTIC	SWEDISH	TESTIFY	TOPCOAT	TRINKET
SEGMENT	SHUFFLE	SNORKEL	SQUALID	SUBJECT	SWEETEN	TETANUS	TOPICAL	TRIPLET
SEISMIC	SHUTOUT	SNUFFLE	SQUALOR	SUBJOIN	SWELTER	TEXTILE	TOPKNOT	TRIPLEX
SELFISH	SHUTTER	SNUGGLE	SQUEEZE	SUBLIME	SWINDLE	TEXTURE	TOPLESS	TRIREME
SELTZER	SHUTTLE	SOCIETY	SQUELCH	SUBSIDE	SWOLLEN	THEATER	TOPMAST	TRISECT
SELVAGE	SHYLOCK	SOJOURN	STABILE	SUBSIDY	SYMPTOM	THEOREM	TOPMOST	TRITIUM
SEMINAL	SHYSTER	SOLARIS	STADIUM	SUBSIST	SYNAPSE	THERAPY	TOPPING	TRIUMPH
SEMINAR	SIAMESE	SOLDIER	STAFFER	SUBSOIL	SYNCOPE	THEREAT	TOPSAIL	TRIVIAL
SENATOR	SIBLING	SOLICIT	STAGGER	SUBTILE	SYNONYM	THEREBY	TOPSIDE	TRIVIUM
SENSORY	SICKBED	SOLUBLE	STAGING	SUBVERT	SYRINGE	THEREIN	TOPSOIL	TROCHEE
SENSUAL	SIDEARM	SOLVENT	STAMINA	SUCCEED	SYSTOLE	THEREOF	TORMENT	TRODDEN
SENTIMO	SIDECAR	SOMEDAY	STAMMER	SUCCESS	TABLEAU	THEREON	TORNADO	TROLLEY
SEQUENT	SIDELIT	SOMEHOW	STANDBY	SUCCUMB	TABLOID	THERETO	TORPEDO	TROLLOP
SEQUOIA	SIDEMAN	SOMEONE	STARTLE	SUCROSE	TABULAR	THERMAL	TORRENT	TROOPER
SERIOUS	SIGHTED	SOPHISM	STARTUP	SUCTION	TACTICS	THERMOS	TORSION	TROPISM
SERPENT	SIGHTLY	SOPHIST	STATELY	SUFFICE	TACTILE	THICKEN	TORTONI	TROUBLE
SERRATE	SIGNIFY	SOPRANO	STATION	SUFFUSE	TADPOLE	THICKET	TORTURE	TROUNCE
SERRIED	SILENCE	SORCERY	STATURE	SUGGEST	TAFFETA	THIMBLE	TOUGHEN	TRUCKLE
SERVANT	SILICON	SORGHUM	STATUTE	SUICIDE	TAKEOFF	THINNER	TOURIST	TRUFFLE
SERVICE	SIMILAR	SOUFFLE	STAUNCH	SUITING	TALLYHO	THISTLE	TOURNEY	TRUMPET
SERVILE	SINCERE	SOULFUL	STEALTH	SULFATE	TAMBALA	THITHER	TOWBOAT	TRUNDLE
SERVING	SINUOUS	SOUNDER	STEEPLE	SULFIDE	TANAGER	THORIUM	TOWHEAD	TRUSTEE
SESSILE	SIRLOIN	SOUPCON	STELLAR	SULTANA	TANBARK	THOUGHT	TOWPATH	TSUNAMI
SESSION	SIROCCO	SOYBEAN	STENCIL	SUMMARY	TANGENT	THREADY	TOXEMIA	TUBULAR
SETBACK	SIXTEEN	SPANGLE	STEPSON	SUMMONS	TANNERY	THROATY	TRACERY	TUESDAY
SETTING	SIZABLE	SPANIEL	STERILE	SUNBATH	TANTRUM	THROUGH	TRACHEA	TUGBOAT
SEVENTY	SKEPTIC	SPANISH	STERNUM	SUNBEAM	TAPIOCA	THRUWAY	TRACING	TUITION
SEVERAL	SKIFFLE	SPARING	STEWARD	SUNBURN	TAPROOM	THULIUM	TRACTOR	TUMBLER
SEXTANT	SKILLET	SPARKLE	STICKER	SUNDIAL	TAPROOT	THUNDER	TRADUCE	TUMBREL

TUNABLE	UNHEARD	UTILITY	VICEROY	WARLORD	WHITHER	WRINKLE	BASHFUL	CAPTAIN
TUNEFUL	UNHINGE	UTILIZE	VICINAL	WARNING	WHITING	WRITING	BASSOON	CAPTION
TURBINE	UNHITCH	UTOPIAN	VICIOUS	WARPATH	WHITISH	WRONGLY	BASTARD	CAPTIVE
TURKISH	UNHORSE	VACANCY	VICTORY	WARRANT	WHITLOW	WROUGHT	BASTION	CAPTURE
TURMOIL	UNICORN	VACCINE	VICTUAL	WARRIOR	WHITTLE	WRYNECK	BATHTUB	CARABAO
TURNERY	UNIFORM	VACUITY	VILLAGE	WARSHIP	WHOEVER	WYSIWYG	BATISTE	CARAMEL
TURNING	UNITARY	VACUOLE	VILLAIN	WARTHOG	WHOOPLA	YARDAGE	BATSMAN	CARAVAN
TURNKEY	UNITIZE	VACUOUS	VILLEIN	WARTIME	WHOPPER	YARDARM	BATTERY	CARAVEL
TURNOFF	UNKEMPT	VAGRANT	VILLOUS	WASHING	WHORLED	YARDMAN	BATTING	CARAWAY
TURNOUT	UNKNOWN	VALANCE	VINEGAR	WASHOUT	WICKIUP	YESHIVA	BAUXITE	CARBIDE
TUSSOCK	UNLATCH	VALENCE	VINTAGE	WASHTUB	WIDGEON	YIDDISH	BAYONET	CARBINE
TUTELAR	UNLEARN	VALIANT	VINTNER	WASPISH	WIDOWER	YOUNKER	BAZOOKA	CARCASS
TWADDLE	UNLEASH	VALUATE	VIOLATE	WASSAIL	WIGGLER	YTTRIUM	CABARET	CARDBUS
TWEETER	UNLOOSE	VAMOOSE	VIOLENT	WASTAGE	WILDCAT	ZAMBIAN	CABBAGE	CARDIAC
TWIDDLE	UNLUCKY	VAMPIRE	VIRGULE	WASTREL	WILLFUL	ZEALOUS	CABINET	CAREFUL
TWILLED	UNMANLY	VANDYKE	VIRTUAL	WATTAGE	WILLIES	ZEOLITE	CABOOSE	CARFARE
TWINKLE	UNMORAL	VANILLA	VISCERA	WAVELET	WILLING	ZILLION	CADAVER	CARIBOU
TWISTER	UNMOVED	VANTAGE	VISCOSE	WAXWING	WILLOWY	ZIONISM	CADENCE	CARIOUS
TWITTER	UNNERVE	VANWARD	VISCOUS	WAXWORK	WINDAGE	ZOOLOGY	CADENZA	CARLOAD
TWOSOME	UNQUIET	VAQUERO	VISIBLE	WAYBILL	WINDBAG	ZYMURGY	CADMIUM	CARMINE
TYPHOID	UNQUOTE	VARIANT	VISITOR	WAYSIDE	WINDING		CAESURA	CARNAGE
TYPHOON	UNRAVEL	VARIETY	VITAMIN	WAYWARD	WINDOWS		CAISSON	CAROTID
TYPICAL	UNSAVED	VARIOUS	VITIATE	WAYWORN	WINDROW		CAITIFF	CAROUSE
TYRANNY	UNSCREW	VARMINT	VITRIFY	WEALTHY	WINNING	**2ND LETTER**	CALCIFY	CARPORT
UKULELE	UNSLING	VARNISH	VITRIOL	WEASAND	WINSOME		CALCINE	CARRIER
ULULATE	UNSNARL	VARSITY	VITTLES	WEATHER	WIRETAP	BACKING	CALCITE	CARRION
UMBRAGE	UNSOUND	VATICAN	VOCABLE	WEBBING	WISHFUL	BACKLIT	CALCIUM	CARRYON
UMPTEEN	UNSTRAP	VAULTED	VOCALIC	WEDDING	WISTFUL	BACKLOG	CALDERA	CARSICK
UNARMED	UNTRIED	VEDANTA	VOGUISH	WEDLOCK	WITHERS	BADLAND	CALDRON	CARTAGE
UNAWARE	UNTRUTH	VEGETAL	VOLCANO	WEEKDAY	WITHOUT	BAGASSE	CALENDS	CARTOON
UNBLOCK	UNTWINE	VEGETAL	VOLTAGE	WEEKEND	WITLESS	BAGGAGE	CALIBER	CASCADE
UNBOSOM	UNTWIST	VEILING	VOLTAIC	WEEPING	WITNESS	BAGPIPE	CALIPER	CASCARA
UNBOWED	UNUSUAL	VENISON	VOLUBLE	WEIGHTY	WITTING	BAILIFF	CALLING	CASHIER
UNCANNY	UNWEAVE	VENTRAL	VOUCHER	WELCOME	WIZENED	BALANCE	CALLOUS	CASSAVA
UNCHAIN	UPBRAID	VENTURE	VULGATE	WELFARE	WOLFRAM	BALCONY	CALOMEL	CASSOCK
UNCIVIL	UPCHUCK	VERANDA	VULPINE	WESTERN	WOMANLY	BALDING	CALORIC	CASTING
UNCLASP	UPDRAFT	VERBENA	VULTURE	WETBACK	WOODCUT	BALDRIC	CALORIE	CASTLED
UNCLEAN	UPGRADE	VERBOSE	WADABLE	WETLAND	WOODLOT	BALEFUL	CALUMET	CATALOG
UNCLOAK	UPRAISE	VERDANT	WADDING	WHATNOT	WOODMAN	BALLAST	CALUMNY	CATALPA
UNCLOSE	UPRIGHT	VERDICT	WAGGERY	WHEEDLE	WORDAGE	BALLOON	CALYPSO	CATARRH
UNCOUTH	UPRIVER	VERDURE	WAGGISH	WHEELER	WORDING	BALONEY	CAMBIUM	CATBIRD
UNCOVER	UPSHIFT	VERMEIL	WAGONER	WHEREAS	WORKBAG	BANDAGE	CAMBRIC	CATBOAT
UNCROSS	UPSTAGE	VERNIER	WAGTAIL	WHEREAT	WORKBOX	BANDBOX	CAMPHOR	CATCALL
UNCTION	UPSTART	VERSIFY	WAILFUL	WHEREBY	WORKDAY	BANNOCK	CANASTA	CATCHER
UNDERGO	UPSTATE	VERSION	WAKEFUL	WHEREIN	WORKING	BANQUET	CANDIED	CATCHUP
UNDOING	UPSURGE	VERTIGO	WALKOUT	WHEREOF	WORKMAN	BANSHEE	CANNERY	CATFISH
UNDRESS	UPSWEPT	VERVAIN	WALKWAY	WHEREON	WORKOUT	BAPTISM	CANNULA	CATHODE
UNDYING	UPSWING	VESICLE	WALLABY	WHERETO	WORLDLY	BAPTIST	CANTATA	CATLIKE
UNEARTH	UPTIGHT	VESPERS	WALLEYE	WHETHER	WORSHIP	BAPTIZE	CANTEEN	CATTAIL
UNEQUAL	URANIUM	VESTIGE	WALLOON	WHICKER	WORSTED	BARBELL	CANVASS	CATWALK
UNERASE	URANOUS	VESTING	WANTING	WHIMPER	WRANGLE	BARGAIN	CAPABLE	CAUSTIC
UNFROCK	URETHRA	VESTURE	WARBLER	WHIPPET	WRAPPER	BARONET	CAPITAL	CAUTION
UNGODLY	URINARY	VETERAN	WARFARE	WHIPSAW	WREATHE	BAROQUE	CAPITOL	CAVALRY
UNGROUP	URINATE	VIADUCT	WARHEAD	WHISKER	WRECKER	BARRAGE	CAPRICE	CAVEMAN
UNGUENT	UROLOGY	VIBRANT	WARLESS	WHISKEY	WRESTLE	BARRIER	CAPSIZE	DANDIFY
UNHANDY	USELESS	VIBRATE	WARLIKE	WHISPER	WRIGGLE	BARRING	CAPSTAN	DARLING
UNHAPPY	UTENSIL	VIBRATO	WARLOCK	WHISTLE	WRINGER	BARROOM	CAPSULE	DASHIKI

DASHING	GANGWAY	HARVEST	LATTICE	MARIMBA	PAJAMAS	PAYROLL	SATIETY	WAGGISH
DASHPOT	GANTLET	HASHING	LATVIAN	MARINER	PALADIN	RACCOON	SATISFY	WAGONER
DASTARD	GARBAGE	HASHISH	LAUNDER	MARITAL	PALAVER	RACEWAY	SAUNTER	WAGTAIL
DAUPHIN	GARFISH	HASSOCK	LAUNDRY	MARPLOT	PALETTE	RADIANT	SAUSAGE	WAILFUL
DAYBOOK	GARLAND	HATCHET	LAWLESS	MARQUEE	PALFREY	RADIATE	SAVANNA	WAKEFUL
DAYTIME	GARMENT	HAUBERK	LAWSUIT	MARQUIS	PALMATE	RADICAL	SAWDUST	WALKOUT
EARACHE	GARNISH	HAUGHTY	LAYAWAY	MARSHAL	PALPATE	RAFFISH	SAWMILL	WALKWAY
EARDRUM	GARROTE	HAULAGE	LAYETTE	MARTIAL	PANACEA	RAGTIME	TABLEAU	WALLABY
EARLOBE	GASTRIC	HAUTEUR	MACABRE	MARTIAN	PANACHE	RAGWEED	TABLOID	WALLEYE
EARMARK	GATEWAY	HAYCOCK	MACADAM	MARTINI	PANCAKE	RAILING	TABULAR	WALLOON
EARMUFF	GAVOTTE	HAYFORK	MACAQUE	MARXISM	PANICLE	RAILWAY	TACTICS	WANTING
EARNEST	GAZELLE	HAYLOFT	MACDRAW	MASCARA	PANNIER	RAIMENT	TACTILE	WARBLER
EARPLUG	GAZETTE	HAYRICK	MACHETE	MASONIC	PANOPLY	RAINBOW	TADPOLE	WARFARE
EARRING	HABITAT	HAYSEED	MACHINE	MASONRY	PANTHER	RAMBLER	TAFFETA	WARHEAD
EARSHOT	HABITUE	HAYWIRE	MACRAME	MASSAGE	PAPILLA	RAMPAGE	TAKEOFF	WARLESS
EARTHEN	HACKMAN	JACINTH	MADDING	MASSEUR	PAPOOSE	RAMPANT	TALLYHO	WARLIKE
EARTHLY	HACKNEY	JACKASS	MADEIRA	MASSIVE	PAPRIKA	RAMPART	TAMBALA	WARLOCK
EASTERN	HACKSAW	JACKDAW	MAESTRO	MASTERY	PAPYRUS	RANKING	TANAGER	WARLORD
FACTION	HADDOCK	JACKLEG	MAFIOSO	MASTIFF	PARABLE	RANSACK	TANBARK	WARNING
FACTORY	HAFNIUM	JACKPOT	MAGENTA	MASTOID	PARADOX	RAPPORT	TANGENT	WARPATH
FACTUAL	HAGGARD	JANITOR	MAGNATE	MATADOR	PARAGON	RAPTURE	TANNERY	WARRANT
FACULTY	HAIRCUT	JANUARY	MAGNETO	MATINEE	PARAPET	RAREBIT	TANTRUM	WARRIOR
FAIENCE	HAIRPIN	JASMINE	MAGNIFY	MATTINS	PARASOL	RATCHET	TAPIOCA	WARSHIP
FAILING	HALBERD	JAVELIN	MAHATMA	MATTOCK	PARBOIL	RATLINE	TAPROOM	WARTHOG
FAILURE	HALCYON	JAYBIRD	MAHICAN	MAUDLIN	PARESIS	RATTLER	TAPROOT	WARTIME
FAIRING	HALFWAY	JAYWALK	MAILBOX	MAUNDER	PARFAIT	RATTRAP	TAPSTER	WASHING
FAIRWAY	HALIBUT	KADDISH	MAILMAN	MAWKISH	PARKWAY	RAUCOUS	TARNISH	WASHOUT
FALLACY	HALLWAY	KARAKUL	MAINTOP	MAXILLA	PARLOUR	RAUNCHY	TATTING	WASHTUB
FALLOUT	HALTING	KATYDID	MAJESTY	MAXIMAL	PARLOUS	RAVIOLI	TAXICAB	WASPISH
FALSIFY	HALVERS	LABORED	MAKINGS	MAXIMUM	PARQUET	RAWHIDE	VACANCY	WASSAIL
FANATIC	HALYARD	LACONIC	MALAISE	MAYPOLE	PARSING	SABBATH	VACCINE	WASTAGE
FANCIER	HAMMOCK	LACQUER	MALARIA	MAZURKA	PARSLEY	SADIRON	VACUITY	WASTREL
FANFARE	HAMSTER	LACTATE	MALEFIC	NACELLE	PARSNIP	SAFFRON	VACUOLE	WATTAGE
FANTAIL	HANDBAG	LACTEAL	MALISON	NAIVETE	PARTAKE	SAGUARO	VACUOUS	WAVELET
FANTASY	HANDCAR	LACTOSE	MALLARD	NAIVETY	PARTIAL	SAILING	VAGRANT	WAXWING
FARAWAY	HANDFUL	LADYBUG	MALLEUS	NANKEEN	PARTING	SAINTLY	VALANCE	WAXWORK
FARMING	HANDGUN	LAGGARD	MALMSEY	NAPHTHA	PARTITE	SALIENT	VALENCE	WAYBILL
FARRAGO	HANDOUT	LAMBENT	MALTOSE	NARRATE	PARTNER	SALTBOX	VALENCE	WAYSIDE
FARRIER	HANDSAW	LAMINAR	MAMMARY	NARTHEX	PARTWAY	SALTINE	VALIANT	WAYWARD
FARTHER	HANDSEL	LAMPOON	MAMMOTH	NARWHAL	PARVENU	SALVAGE	VALUATE	WAYWORN
FASCISM	HANDSET	LAMPREY	MANACLE	NASCENT	PASSAGE	SAMOVAR	VAMOOSE	YARDAGE
FASHION	HANGDOG	LANDING	MANAGER	NATURAL	PASSING	SAMPLER	VAMPIRE	YARDARM
FATBACK	HANGING	LANGUID	MANDATE	NAUGHTY	PASSION	SAMURAI	VANDYKE	YARDMAN
FATEFUL	HANGMAN	LANGUOR	MANDREL	OARLOCK	PASSIVE	SANCTUM	VANILLA	ZAMBIAN
FATIGUE	HANGOUT	LANOLIN	MANDRIL	OARSMAN	PASSKEY	SANDBAG	VANTAGE	ABALONE
FATUITY	HAPLESS	LANTANA	MANHOLE	OATCAKE	PASTERN	SANDBAR	VANWARD	ABANDON
FATUOUS	HAPLOID	LANTERN	MANHOOD	OATMEAL	PASTIME	SANDHOG	VAQUERO	ABDOMEN
FAUVISM	HAPPILY	LANYARD	MANHUNT	PABULUM	PASTURE	SANDLOT	VARIANT	ABILITY
GABFEST	HARBOUR	LAOTIAN	MANIKIN	PACIFIC	PATELLA	SANDMAN	VARIETY	ABOLISH
GAINFUL	HARDPAN	LAPWING	MANKIND	PACKAGE	PATHWAY	SAPIENT	VARIOUS	ABREAST
GAINSAY	HARDTOP	LARCENY	MANLIKE	PACKING	PATIENT	SAPLING	VARMINT	ABRIDGE
GALLANT	HARELIP	LARGESS	MANNISH	PADDING	PATRIOT	SAPWOOD	VARNISH	ABSCESS
GALLEON	HARMONY	LASAGNA	MANSARD	PADDOCK	PATROON	SARCASM	VARSITY	ABSCOND
GALLERY	HARNESS	LATAKIA	MANSION	PADLOCK	PATTERN	SARDINE	VATICAN	ABSENCE
GALLIUM	HARPOON	LATCHET	MANTEAU	PAGEANT	PAUCITY	SATANIC	VAULTED	ABSOLVE
GALLOWS	HARRIER	LATERAL	MANUMIT	PAGEBOY	PAYLOAD	SATCHEL	WADABLE	ABSTAIN
GAMBIAN	HARVARD	LATRINE	MARGENT	PAISLEY	PAYMENT	SATIATE	WADDING	ABYSMAL

ABYSSAL	SCEPTIC	BEDTIME	CERTAIN	DERANGE	GENITAL	LEADING	NEMESIS	PETRIFY
EBONITE	SCHOLAR	BEEHIVE	CERTIFY	DERRICK	GENTEEL	LEAFAGE	NEOLOGY	PETTISH
OBELISK	SCIENCE	BEELINE	CERUMEN	DERVISH	GENTIAN	LEAFLET	NEPTUNE	PETUNIA
OBLIQUE	SCOOTER	BEESWAX	CESSION	DESCANT	GENTILE	LEAGUER	NERVOUS	REACTOR
OBLOQUY	SCOURGE	BEGGARY	DEADPAN	DESCEND	GENUINE	LEAKAGE	NETTING	READING
OBSCENE	SCRAPPY	BEGONIA	DEALING	DESCENT	GEODESY	LEARNED	NETWARE	READOUT
OBSCURE	SCRATCH	BEGRIME	DEANERY	DESERVE	GEOLOGY	LEATHER	NETWORK	REAGENT
OBSEQUY	SCRAWNY	BEGUILE	DEATHLY	DESKTOP	GERMANE	LECHERY	NEUTRAL	REALISM
OBSERVE	SCREECH	BEGUINE	DEBACLE	DESPAIR	GESTAPO	LECTERN	NEUTRON	REALITY
OBTRUDE	SCROTUM	BEHOOVE	DEBAUCH	DESPISE	GESTURE	LECTURE	NEWBORN	REALIZE
OBVERSE	SCRUFFY	BELABOR	DEBOUCH	DESPITE	GETAWAY	LEEWARD	NEWSBOY	REBIRTH
OBVIATE	SCRUPLE	BELATED	DEBRIEF	DESPOIL	HEADING	LEFTISM	NEWSMAN	REBOUND
OBVIOUS	SCUFFLE	BELGIAN	DECAGON	DESPOND	HEADMAN	LEGATEE	OEDIPAL	REBUILD
ACADEME	SCUPPER	BELIEVE	DECEASE	DESSERT	HEADPIN	LEGGING	PEACOCK	RECEIPT
ACADEMY	SCUTTLE	BELLBOY	DECEIVE	DESTINE	HEADSET	LEGHORN	PEAFOWL	RECEIVE
ACCLAIM	ADAMANT	BELLHOP	DECENCY	DESTINY	HEADWAY	LEGIBLE	PEASANT	RECENCY
ACCOUNT	ADAPTER	BELLOWS	DECIBEL	DESTROY	HEALTHY	LEISURE	PECCARY	RECITAL
ACCUSAL	ADDRESS	BELOVED	DECIDED	DETENTE	HEARING	LEMMING	PECCAVI	RECLAIM
ACCUSED	ADENINE	BELTWAY	DECIMAL	DETRACT	HEARKEN	LEMPIRA	PEDICAB	RECLAME
ACETATE	ADENOID	BENEATH	DECLAIM	DETRAIN	HEARSAY	LENIENT	PEELING	RECLINE
ACETONE	ADIPOSE	BENEFIT	DECLARE	DEVALUE	HEARTEN	LEONINE	PEEVISH	RECLUSE
ACHIEVE	ADJOURN	BENISON	DECLINE	DEVELOP	HEATHEN	LEOPARD	PELAGIC	RECOUNT
ACIDIFY	ADJUDGE	BENTHIC	DECODER	DEVIANT	HEATHER	LEOTARD	PELICAN	RECOVER
ACOLYTE	ADJUNCT	BENTHOS	DECORUM	DEVIATE	HECTARE	LEPROSY	PENALTY	RECRUIT
ACONITE	ADMIRAL	BENZENE	DEERFLY	DEVILRY	HEINOUS	LESBIAN	PENANCE	RECTIFY
ACQUIRE	ADRENAL	BENZINE	DEFAULT	DEVIOUS	HEIRESS	LETDOWN	PENATES	RECTORY
ACREAGE	ADULATE	BENZOIN	DEFENSE	DEVOLVE	HELICAL	LETTUCE	PENDANT	RECYCLE
ACROBAT	ADVANCE	BEQUEST	DEFIANT	DEVOTED	HELLCAT	LEXICON	PENDENT	REDCOAT
ACRONYM	ADVERSE	BERSERK	DEFICIT	DEVOTEE	HELLENE	MEANDER	PENDING	REDDISH
ACRYLIC	ADVISED	BESEECH	DEFLATE	DEWCLAW	HELLION	MEANING	PENGUIN	REDHEAD
ACTUARY	EDIFICE	BESHREW	DEFLECT	DEWDROP	HELPING	MEASLES	PENNANT	REDLINE
ACTUATE	EDITION	BESIDES	DEFRAUD	DEXTRIN	HEMLINE	MEASURE	PENSION	REDOUBT
ECHELON	EDUCATE	BESIEGE	DEFROST	FEARFUL	HEMLOCK	MEATMAN	PENSIVE	REDOUND
ECLIPSE	IDEALLY	BESMEAR	DEFUNCT	FEATHER	HENPECK	MEDIATE	PENTIUM	REDRESS
ECLOGUE	IDOLIZE	BESPEAK	DEGAUSS	FEATURE	HEPARIN	MEDICAL	PEPPERY	REDSKIN
ECOLOGY	ODDBALL	BESTIAL	DEGRADE	FEBRILE	HEPATIC	MEDULLA	PERCALE	REDWOOD
ECONOMY	ODDMENT	BETHINK	DELIGHT	FEDERAL	HERBAGE	MEETING	PERCENT	REENTRY
ECSTASY	ODYSSEY	BETIMES	DELIMIT	FEEDLOT	HEROICS	MEGATON	PERCEPT	REFEREE
ICEBERG	AEROBIC	BETOKEN	DELIVER	FEELING	HEROINE	MEIOSIS	PERFECT	REFINED
ICEBOAT	AEROSOL	BETROTH	DELOUSE	FENCING	HEROISM	MELANGE	PERFIDY	REFLECT
OCARINA	BEARING	BETWEEN	DEMERIT	FERMENT	HERRING	MELANIC	PERFORM	REFRACT
OCCLUDE	BEASTLY	BETWIXT	DEMESNE	FERMIUM	HERSELF	MELANIN	PERFUME	REFRAIN
OCTAGON	BEATIFY	BEWITCH	DEMIGOD	FERNERY	HEXAGON	MEMENTO	PERGOLA	REFRESH
OCTOBER	BEATNIK	CEDILLA	DEMONIC	FERROUS	HEXAPOD	MENFOLK	PERHAPS	REFUGEE
OCTOPUS	BECAUSE	CEILING	DEMOTIC	FERRULE	JEALOUS	MENTHOL	PERIGEE	REGALIA
OCULIST	BECLOUD	CELESTA	DENIZEN	FERTILE	JEHOVAH	MENTION	PERIQUE	REGATTA
SCALLOP	BEDDING	CELSIUS	DENSITY	FERVENT	JEJUNUM	MERCURY	PERIWIG	REGENCY
SCALPEL	BEDEVIL	CEMBALO	DENTATE	FESTIVE	JETPORT	MERMAID	PERJURY	REGIMEN
SCAMPER	BEDFAST	CENSURE	DENTIST	FESTOON	JEWELER	MESSAGE	PERLITE	REGNANT
SCANDAL	BEDIZEN	CENTARE	DENTURE	FETLOCK	JEWELRY	MESSIAH	PERPLEX	REGRESS
SCANNER	BEDOUIN	CENTAUR	DEPLANE	GEARBOX	KEELSON	MESTIZO	PERSIAN	REGROUP
SCAPULA	BEDPOST	CENTAVO	DEPLETE	GELATIN	KEEPING	METHANE	PERSIST	REGULAR
SCARIFY	BEDROCK	CENTIME	DEPLORE	GELDING	KERATIN	MEXICAN	PERTAIN	REJOICE
SCARLET	BEDROLL	CENTIMO	DEPOSIT	GENERAL	KERNING	NECKTIE	PERTURB	RELAPSE
SCATTER	BEDROOM	CENTRAL	DEPRAVE	GENERIC	KETCHUP	NEEDFUL	PERVADE	RELATED
SCENERY	BEDSIDE	CENTURY	DEPRESS	GENESIS	KEYHOLE	NEGLECT	PERVERT	RELATOR
SCEPTER	BEDSORE	CERAMIC	DEPRIVE	GENETIC	KEYNOTE	NEITHER	PETIOLE	RELEASE

RELIEVE	SEAWALL	TERRACE	EFFENDI	CHIANTI	SHATTER	WHEREAT	BITUMEN	DISTANT
RELIQUE	SEAWARD	TERRAIN	OFFBEAT	CHICANE	SHAVING	WHEREBY	BIVALVE	DISTEND
REMAINS	SEAWEED	TERRIER	OFFENSE	CHICANO	SHAWNEE	WHEREIN	BIVOUAC	DISTICH
REMNANT	SECLUDE	TERRIFY	OFFHAND	CHICKEN	SHEATHE	WHEREOF	BIZARRE	DISTILL
REMODEL	SECRECY	TESTATE	OFFICER	CHICORY	SHEBANG	WHEREON	CILIATE	DISTORT
REMORSE	SECRETE	TESTIFY	OFFSIDE	CHIFFON	SHELLAC	WHERETO	CIRCLET	DISTURB
REMOUNT	SECTARY	TETANUS	PFENNIG	CHIGGER	SHELTER	WHETHER	CIRCUIT	DIURNAL
RENEWAL	SECTION	TEXTILE	AGAINST	CHIGNON	SHERBET	WHICKER	CISTERN	DIVERGE
REPLACE	SECULAR	TEXTURE	AGELESS	CHIMERA	SHERIFF	WHIMPER	CITADEL	DIVERSE
REPLETE	SEEMING	VEDANTA	AGITATE	CHIMNEY	SHIMMER	WHIPPET	CITIZEN	DIVIDER
REPLICA	SEGMENT	VEGETAL	AGONIZE	CHINESE	SHINGLE	WHIPSAW	CIVILLY	DIVISOR
REPRESS	SEISMIC	VEHICLE	AGROUND	CHINOOK	SHOCKER	WHISKER	CIVVIES	DIVORCE
REPRINT	SELFISH	VEILING	EGGHEAD	CHINTZY	SHORING	WHISKEY	DIAGRAM	DIVULGE
REPRISE	SELTZER	VENISON	EGOTISM	CHIPPER	SHORTEN	WHISPER	DIALECT	EIDOLON
REPROOF	SELVAGE	VENTRAL	IGNEOUS	CHOCTAW	SHORTLY	WHISTLE	DIAMOND	FIANCEE
REPROVE	SEMINAL	VENTURE	IGNOBLE	CHOLERA	SHOTGUN	WHITHER	DIARIST	FIBROID
REPTILE	SEMINAR	VERANDA	CHABLIS	CHOPPER	SHOWMAN	WHITING	DICTATE	FICTION
REPULSE	SENATOR	VERBENA	CHADIAN	CHORALE	SHRIVEL	WHITISH	DICTION	FIFTEEN
REPUTED	SENSORY	VERBOSE	CHAFFER	CHORTLE	SHUDDER	WHITLOW	DIEHARD	FIGHTER
REQUEST	SENSUAL	VERDANT	CHAGRIN	CHOWDER	SHUFFLE	WHITTLE	DIFFUSE	FIGMENT
REQUIEM	SENTIMO	VERDICT	CHALICE	CHROMIC	SHUTOUT	WHOEVER	DIGITAL	FILBERT
REQUIRE	SEQUENT	VERDURE	CHALLIS	CHRONIC	SHUTTER	WHOOPLA	DIGNIFY	FILLING
REQUITE	SEQUOIA	VERMEIL	CHAMBER	CHUCKLE	SHUTTLE	WHOPPER	DIGNITY	FILMDOM
REREDOS	SERIOUS	VERNIER	CHAMFER	CHUKKER	SHYLOCK	WHORLED	DIGRAPH	FINAGLE
RESCIND	SERPENT	VERSIFY	CHAMOIS	CHUTNEY	SHYSTER	AILERON	DIGRESS	FINANCE
RESEDIT	SERRATE	VERSION	CHANCEL	GHASTLY	THEATER	AILMENT	DILEMMA	FINDING
RESERVE	SERRIED	VERTIGO	CHANCRE	GHERKIN	THEOREM	AIMLESS	DILUENT	FINESSE
RESIDUE	SERVANT	VERVAIN	CHANNEL	KHEDIVE	THERAPY	AIRDROP	DINETTE	FINFISH
RESOLVE	SERVICE	VESICLE	CHANSON	PHAETON	THEREAT	AIRFLOW	DIOCESE	FINICKY
RESOUND	SERVILE	VESPERS	CHANTEY	PHALANX	THEREBY	AIRFOIL	DIPLOID	FINNISH
RESPECT	SERVING	VESTIGE	CHANTRY	PHALLIC	THEREIN	AIRLIFT	DIPLOMA	FIREARM
RESPITE	SESSILE	VESTING	CHAPEAU	PHALLUS	THEREOF	AIRLINE	DIREFUL	FIREBOX
RESPOND	SESSION	VESTURE	CHAPLET	PHANTOM	THEREON	AIRMAIL	DISABLE	FIREBUG
RESTIVE	SETBACK	VETERAN	CHAPMAN	PHARAOH	THERETO	AIRPORT	DISAVOW	FIREFLY
RESTORE	SETTING	WEALTHY	CHAPTER	PHARYNX	THERMAL	AIRPOST	DISBAND	FIREMAN
RETINUE	SEVENTY	WEASAND	CHARGER	PHILTER	THERMOS	AIRSHIP	DISCARD	FIRSTLY
RETIRED	SEVERAL	WEATHER	CHARIOT	PHOENIX	THICKEN	AIRSICK	DISCERN	FISHERY
RETIREE	SEXTANT	WEBBING	CHARITY	PHONEME	THICKET	AIRWAVE	DISCORD	FISHING
RETOUCH	TECHNIC	WEDDING	CHARMER	PHONICS	THIMBLE	BIBELOT	DISCUSS	FISSILE
RETRACE	TEDIOUS	WEDLOCK	CHARNEL	PHRENIC	THINNER	BICYCLE	DISDAIN	FISSION
RETRACT	TEENAGE	WEEKDAY	CHARTER	PHYSICS	THISTLE	BIFOCAL	DISEASE	FISSURE
RETREAD	TEKTITE	WEEKEND	CHASSIS	PHYSIOL	THITHER	BIGHORN	DISEUSE	FISTFUL
RETREAT	TELLING	WEEPING	CHASTEN	RHENIUM	THORIUM	BIKEWAY	DISGUST	FISTULA
REUNION	TEMPERA	WEIGHTY	CHATEAU	RHIZOME	THOUGHT	BILIOUS	DISHRAG	FITTING
REVENGE	TEMPEST	WELCOME	CHATTEL	RHODIUM	THREADY	BILLION	DISJOIN	FIXTURE
REVENUE	TENABLE	WELFARE	CHATTER	RHOMBUS	THROATY	BIMETAL	DISLIKE	GIBBOUS
REVERIE	TENANCY	WESTERN	CHEAPEN	RHUBARB	THROUGH	BINDING	DISMISS	GIBLETS
REVERSE	TENDRIL	WETBACK	CHECKER	SHACKLE	THRUWAY	BIOLOGY	DISOBEY	GIMMICK
REVIVAL	TENFOLD	WETLAND	CHECKUP	SHADING	THULIUM	BIOTITE	DISPLAY	GINGHAM
REVOLVE	TENSILE	YESHIVA	CHEDDAR	SHALLOP	THUNDER	BIPLANE	DISPORT	GINSENG
SEABIRD	TENSION	ZEALOUS	CHEETAH	SHALLOW	THYMINE	BIPOLAR	DISPOSE	GIRAFFE
SEAFOOD	TENUOUS	ZEOLITE	CHEMISE	SHAMBLE	THYROID	BIRCHER	DISPUTE	GIZZARD
SEALANT	TENURED	AFFABLE	CHEMIST	SHAMPOO	THYSELF	BIRETTA	DISROBE	HIBACHI
SEAPORT	TEQUILA	AFFLICT	CHERISH	SHAPELY	WHATNOT	BISCUIT	DISRUPT	HICKORY
SEASICK	TERBIUM	AFFRONT	CHEROOT	SHARPEN	WHEEDLE	BISMUTH	DISSECT	HIDALGO
SEASIDE	TERMITE	AFGHANI	CHEVIOT	SHARPER	WHEELER	BITTERN	DISSENT	HIDEOUS
SEATING	TERNARY	AFRICAN	CHEVRON	SHARPIE	WHEREAS	BITTERS	DISTAFF	HIDEOUT

HIGHBOY	MIDWIFE	PIBROCH	SIXTEEN	WINDING	BLINKER	FLATTOP	PLENARY	EMPEROR
HIGHWAY	MIDYEAR	PICCOLO	SIZABLE	WINDOWS	BLINTZE	FLAVOUR	PLIABLE	EMPOWER
HILLOCK	MIGRANT	PICTURE	TIBETAN	WINDROW	BLISTER	FLEMING	PLOTTER	EMPRESS
HILLTOP	MIGRATE	PIEBALD	TICKING	WINNING	BLOATER	FLEMISH	PLOWBOY	EMULATE
HIMSELF	MILEAGE	PIGGISH	TIDINGS	WINSOME	BLOODED	FLESHLY	PLOWMAN	IMAGERY
HINTING	MILITIA	PIGMENT	TIEBACK	WIRETAP	BLOOPER	FLEXURE	PLUMAGE	IMAGINE
HIPBONE	MILKMAN	PIGSKIN	TIGHTEN	WISHFUL	BLOSSOM	FLICKER	PLUMBER	IMAGISM
HIPSTER	MILKSOP	PIGTAIL	TILLAGE	WISTFUL	BLOTTER	FLIGHTY	PLUMMET	IMITATE
HIRSUTE	MILLAGE	PILGRIM	TIMBREL	WITHERS	BLOWGUN	FLIPPER	PLUNDER	IMMENSE
HISTORY	MILLDAM	PILLAGE	TIMOTHY	WITHOUT	BLOWOUT	FLIVVER	PLUNGER	IMMERSE
JITTERS	MILLIME	PILLBOX	TIMPANI	WITLESS	BLUBBER	FLORIST	PLUVIAL	IMMORAL
KIBBUTZ	MILLING	PILLION	TINFOIL	WITNESS	BLUCHER	FLOTSAM	PLYWOOD	IMPANEL
KICKOFF	MILLION	PILLORY	TINWARE	WITTING	BLUNDER	FLOUNCE	SLACKEN	IMPASSE
KIDSKIN	MIMESIS	PILSNER	TIPSTER	WIZENED	BLUSTER	FLOWERY	SLACKER	IMPASTO
KILLING	MIMETIC	PIMENTO	TITANIC	YIDDISH	CLAMBER	FLUSTER	SLANDER	IMPEACH
KILLJOY	MIMICRY	PINHOLE	TITULAR	ZILLION	CLANGOR	FLUTIST	SLATHER	IMPEARL
KILOTON	MINARET	PINKEYE	VIADUCT	ZIONISM	CLAPPER	FLUTTER	SLAVERY	IMPERIL
KINDRED	MINDFUL	PINNACE	VIBRANT	SKEPTIC	CLARIFY	FLYABLE	SLAVISH	IMPETUS
KINETIC	MINERAL	PINNATE	VIBRATE	SKIFFLE	CLARION	FLYLEAF	SLEEPER	IMPIETY
KINFOLK	MINIBUS	PINWORM	VIBRATO	SKILLET	CLARITY	GLACIAL	SLEIGHT	IMPINGE
KINGDOM	MINIMAL	PIONEER	VICEROY	SKIPPER	CLASSIC	GLACIER	SLENDER	IMPIOUS
KINGPIN	MINIMUM	PIPETTE	VICINAL	SKITTER	CLASTIC	GLADDEN	SLICKER	IMPLODE
KINSHIP	MINSTER	PIQUANT	VICIOUS	SKIWEAR	CLATTER	GLAMOUR	SLIPPER	IMPLORE
KINSMAN	MINUEND	PIRANHA	VICTORY	SKYLARK	CLAVIER	GLAZIER	SLITHER	IMPOUND
KITCHEN	MINUTIA	PISMIRE	VICTUAL	SKYLINE	CLEANLY	GLEEMAN	SLOBBER	IMPRESS
LIAISON	MIRACLE	PITCHER	VILLAGE	SKYWARD	CLEANSE	GLIMMER	SLUMBER	IMPRINT
LIBERAL	MISCALL	PITEOUS	VILLAIN	UKULELE	CLEANUP	GLIMPSE	ULULATE	IMPROVE
LIBERTY	MISDEED	PITFALL	VILLEIN	ALBUMEN	CLEAVER	GLISTEN	AMALGAM	IMPULSE
LIBRARY	MISFILE	PITIFUL	VILLOUS	ALBUMIN	CLEMENT	GLISTER	AMATEUR	OMINOUS
LICENSE	MISFIRE	PIZZAZZ	VINEGAR	ALCALDE	CLIMATE	GLITTER	AMATIVE	OMNIBUS
LIGHTEN	MISLEAD	RICKETS	VINTAGE	ALCAZAR	CLINKER	GLOBULE	AMATORY	SMELTER
LIGHTER	MISLIKE	RICKETY	VINTNER	ALCHEMY	CLIPPER	GLORIFY	AMBIENT	SMIDGEN
LIGNIFY	MISNAME	RICKSHA	VIOLATE	ALCOHOL	CLOBBER	GLOTTIS	AMENITY	SMOLDER
LIGNITE	MISPLAY	RIGGING	VIOLENT	ALEMBIC	CLOSURE	GLUCOSE	AMERIND	SMOTHER
LIMBECK	MISREAD	RIGHTLY	VIRGULE	ALEWIFE	CLOTHES	GLUTTON	AMIABLE	SMUGGLE
LIMEADE	MISRULE	RINGLET	VIRTUAL	ALFALFA	CLOTURE	ILEITIS	AMMETER	UMBRAGE
LIMITED	MISSEND	RIPOSTE	VISCERA	ALGEBRA	CLUSTER	ILLEGAL	AMMONIA	UMPTEEN
LINEAGE	MISSILE	RISIBLE	VISCOSE	ALIMENT	CLUTTER	ILLICIT	AMNESIA	ANAEMIA
LINEMAN	MISSING	RIVALRY	VISCOUS	ALIMONY	ELASTIC	ILLNESS	AMNESTY	ANAGRAM
LINGUAL	MISSION	RIVULET	VISIBLE	ALLEGRO	ELDERLY	OLDSTER	AMOROUS	ANALOGY
LINKAGE	MISSIVE	SIAMESE	VISITOR	ALLERGY	ELECTOR	OLIVINE	AMPHORA	ANALYZE
LINSEED	MISSTEP	SIBLING	VITAMIN	ALMANAC	ELEGIAC	PLACARD	AMPLIFY	ANAPEST
LIONIZE	MISTAKE	SICKBED	VITIATE	ALMONER	ELEMENT	PLACATE	AMPUTEE	ANARCHY
LIQUEFY	MISTRAL	SIDEARM	VITRIFY	ALREADY	ELEVATE	PLACEBO	AMYLASE	ANATOMY
LIQUEUR	MITOSIS	SIDECAR	VITRIOL	ALRIGHT	ELISION	PLACKET	EMANATE	ANCHOVY
LISSOME	MIXTURE	SIDELIT	VITTLES	ALUMINA	ELITISM	PLANTAR	EMBARGO	ANCIENT
LISTING	NIAGARA	SIDEMAN	WICKIUP	ALUMNUS	ELLIPSE	PLANTER	EMBASSY	ANDANTE
LITERAL	NIGGARD	SIGHTED	WIDGEON	BLACKEN	ELUSIVE	PLASTER	EMBOWER	ANDIRON
LITHIUM	NIGHTLY	SIGHTLY	WIDOWER	BLADDER	ELYSIUM	PLASTIC	EMBRACE	ANDROID
LITURGY	NIOBIUM	SIGNIFY	WIGGLER	BLANKET	FLACCID	PLATEAU	EMBROIL	ANEMONE
LIVABLE	NIRVANA	SILENCE	WILDCAT	BLARNEY	FLANKER	PLATING	EMBRYOL	ANGUISH
MICROBE	NITRATE	SILICON	WILLFUL	BLATANT	FLANNEL	PLATOON	EMERALD	ANGULAR
MIDLAND	NITRIFY	SIMILAR	WILLIES	BLATHER	FLAPPER	PLATTER	EMERITA	ANILINE
MIDMOST	NITRITE	SINCERE	WILLING	BLEEDER	FLATBED	PLAUDIT	EMINENT	ANIMATE
MIDRIFF	OILSKIN	SINUOUS	WILLOWY	BLEMISH	FLATCAR	PLAYBOY	EMITTER	ANIMISM
MIDTOWN	PIANIST	SIRLOIN	WINDAGE	BLESSED	FLATTEN	PLAYLET	EMOTION	ANNUITY
MIDWEEK	PIASTER	SIROCCO	WINDBAG	BLINDER	FLATTER	PLAYPEN	EMPATHY	ANNULAR

ANODIZE	INCENSE	INSURED	UNHANDY	BOUNDEN	COMPOST	CONTROL	DOGBANE	GODHOOD
ANODYNE	INCISOR	INSURER	UNHAPPY	BOUQUET	COMPOTE	CONVENE	DOGCART	GODLESS
ANOMALY	INCLINE	INTEGER	UNHEARD	BOURBON	COMPUTE	CONVENT	DOGFISH	GODLIKE
ANOTHER	INCLOSE	INTENSE	UNHINGE	BOWLDER	COMRADE	CONVERT	DOGTROT	GODSEND
ANTACID	INCLUDE	INTERIM	UNHITCH	BOWLINE	CONCAVE	CONVICT	DOGWOOD	GOGGLES
ANTENNA	INCRUST	INTRANS	UNHORSE	BOWLING	CONCEAL	CONVOKE	DOLEFUL	GONDOLA
ANTHILL	INCUBUS	INTROIT	UNICORN	BOYCOTT	CONCEDE	COOKERY	DOLPHIN	GOODMAN
ANTHRAX	INDEXED	INTRUDE	UNIFORM	COARSEN	CONCEIT	COOKOUT	DOMINIE	GORILLA
ANTHROP	INDICIA	INTRUST	UNITARY	COATING	CONCEPT	COOLANT	DOORMAN	GOSHAWK
ANTIGEN	INDOORS	INVALID	UNITIZE	COAXIAL	CONCERN	COPILOT	DOORMAT	GOSLING
ANTIQUE	INDORSE	INVEIGH	UNKEMPT	COBBLER	CONCERT	COPIOUS	DOORWAY	GOULASH
ANTONYM	INDULGE	INVERSE	UNKNOWN	COCAINE	CONCISE	COPPICE	DORMANT	GOURMET
ANXIETY	INDWELL	INVOICE	UNLATCH	COCHLEA	CONCOCT	COPYBOY	DOSSIER	HOBNAIL
ANXIOUS	INERTIA	INVOLVE	UNLEARN	COCKADE	CONCORD	COPYCAT	DOUBLET	HOECAKE
ANYBODY	INEXACT	KNEECAP	UNLEASH	COCKEYE	CONDEMN	CORACLE	DOUGHTY	HOEDOWN
ANYMORE	INFANCY	KNOCKER	UNLOOSE	COCKNEY	CONDIGN	CORDAGE	DOWAGER	HOGBACK
ANYTIME	INFARCT	KNOWING	UNLUCKY	COCKPIT	CONDOLE	CORDIAL	DOYENNE	HOGWASH
ANYWISE	INFERNO	KNUCKLE	UNMANLY	COCONUT	CONDONE	CORDITE	FOGHORN	HOLDING
ENAMOUR	INFIDEL	ONEROUS	UNMORAL	CODEINE	CONDUCE	CORDOBA	FOLDOUT	HOLIDAY
ENCHAIN	INFIELD	ONESELF	UNMOVED	CODFISH	CONDUCT	CORINTH	FOLIAGE	HOLMIUM
ENCHANT	INFLAME	ONETIME	UNNERVE	CODICIL	CONDUIT	CORNCOB	FOLKWAY	HOLSTER
ENCLAVE	INFLATE	ONGOING	UNQUIET	CODLING	CONDYLE	CORNICE	FONDANT	HOMBURG
ENCLOSE	INFLECT	ONSHORE	UNQUOTE	COEQUAL	CONFESS	COROLLA	FOOLERY	HOMONYM
ENCRUST	INFLICT	SNAFFLE	UNRAVEL	COEXIST	CONFIDE	CORONAL	FOOLISH	HOODLUM
ENDEMIC	INGENUE	SNEAKER	UNSAVED	COGNATE	CONFINE	CORONER	FOOTAGE	HOOSIER
ENDLESS	INGRAFT	SNICKER	UNSCREW	COHABIT	CONFIRM	CORONET	FOOTING	HOPHEAD
ENDMOST	INGRAIN	SNIFFLE	UNSLING	COINAGE	CONFLUX	CORRECT	FOOTMAN	HORIZON
ENDORSE	INGRATE	SNORKEL	UNSNARL	COLLAGE	CONFORM	CORRODE	FOOTPAD	HORMONE
ENDWAYS	INGRESS	SNUFFLE	UNSOUND	COLLARD	CONFUSE	CORRUPT	FORBEAR	HORRIFY
ENDWISE	INGROWN	SNUGGLE	UNSTRAP	COLLATE	CONFUTE	CORSAGE	FORBODE	HOSANNA
ENFORCE	INHABIT	UNARMED	UNTRIED	COLLECT	CONGEAL	CORSAIR	FORCEPS	HOSIERY
ENGLISH	INHALER	UNAWARE	UNTRUTH	COLLEEN	CONGEST	CORTEGE	FOREARM	HOSPICE
ENGRAFT	INHERIT	UNBLOCK	UNTWINE	COLLEGE	CONICAL	COSSACK	FOREIGN	HOSTAGE
ENGRAVE	INHIBIT	UNBOSOM	UNTWIST	COLLIDE	CONIFER	COSTIVE	FORELEG	HOSTESS
ENGROSS	INHUMAN	UNBOWED	UNUSUAL	COLLIER	CONJOIN	COSTUME	FOREMAN	HOSTILE
ENHANCE	INITIAL	UNCANNY	UNWEAVE	COLLOID	CONJURE	COTERIE	FORESEE	HOSTLER
ENLARGE	INKHORN	UNCHAIN	BOATMAN	COLOGNE	CONNECT	COTTAGE	FORETOP	HOTCAKE
ENLIVEN	INKLING	UNCIVIL	BOBSLED	COLONEL	CONNIVE	COULOMB	FOREVER	HOTFOOT
ENNOBLE	INKWELL	UNCLASP	BOLIVAR	COLORED	CONNOTE	COUNCIL	FORFEIT	HOTSHOT
ENPLANE	INNARDS	UNCLEAN	BOLOGNA	COMBINE	CONQUER	COUNSEL	FORFEND	HOUSING
ENQUIRE	INNINGS	UNCLOAK	BOLSTER	COMFORT	CONSENT	COUNTER	FORGING	HOWBEIT
ENSLAVE	INQUEST	UNCLOSE	BOMBARD	COMMAND	CONSIGN	COUNTRY	FORGIVE	HOWEVER
ENSNARE	INQUIRE	UNCOUTH	BOMBAST	COMMEND	CONSIST	COUPLET	FORLORN	HOWLING
ENTENTE	INQUIRY	UNCOVER	BONANZA	COMMENT	CONSOLE	COURAGE	FORMULA	JOCULAR
ENTHUSE	INSHORE	UNCROSS	BONDAGE	COMMODE	CONSORT	COURIER	FORSAKE	JODHPUR
ENTITLE	INSIDER	UNCTION	BONDMAN	COMMUNE	CONSULT	COURSER	FORTIFY	JOLLITY
ENTRAIN	INSIGHT	UNDERGO	BONFIRE	COMMUTE	CONSUME	COURTLY	FORTRAN	JONQUIL
ENTRANT	INSIPID	UNDOING	BOOKEND	COMPACT	CONTACT	COUTURE	FORTUNE	JOTTING
ENTREAT	INSPECT	UNDRESS	BOOKISH	COMPANY	CONTAIN	COWBIRD	FORWARD	JOURNAL
ENTROPY	INSPIRE	UNDYING	BOOKLET	COMPARE	CONTEMN	COWHAND	FOULARD	JOURNEY
ENTRUST	INSTALL	UNEARTH	BOOTLEG	COMPASS	CONTEND	COWHIDE	FOULING	JOYANCE
ENTWINE	INSTANT	UNEQUAL	BOREDOM	COMPEER	CONTENT	COWLICK	FOUNDER	JOYRIDE
ENVELOP	INSTATE	UNERASE	BOROUGH	COMPETE	CONTEST	COWLING	FOUNDRY	LOATHLY
ENVENOM	INSTEAD	UNFROCK	BORSCHT	COMPILE	CONTEXT	COWPOKE	FOXHOLE	LOBSTER
ENVIOUS	INSTILL	UNGODLY	BOUDOIR	COMPLEX	CONTORT	COWSLIP	GOBBLER	LOCATOR
INBOARD	INSULAR	UNGROUP	BOULDER	COMPORT	CONTOUR	COXCOMB	GODDESS	LOCKJAW
INBOUND	INSULIN	UNGUENT	BOUNCER	COMPOSE	CONTRIB	DOCKAGE	GODHEAD	LOCKNUT

LOCKOUT	NOURISH	ROOFTOP	TORPEDO	EPISODE	UPSTAGE	BRECCIA	DRAGNET	GRAPNEL
LODGING	NOVELLA	ROOKERY	TORRENT	EPISTLE	UPSTART	BREVITY	DRAGOON	GRAPPLE
LONGBOW	NOVELTY	ROOSTER	TORSION	EPITAPH	UPSTATE	BRIGADE	DRAPERY	GRATIFY
LONGING	NOWHERE	ROOTLET	TORTONI	EPITHET	UPSURGE	BRIGAND	DRASTIC	GRATING
LOOKOUT	NOXIOUS	ROSEATE	TORTURE	EPITOME	UPSWEPT	BRIMFUL	DRAUGHT	GRAUPEL
LOTTERY	POCOSIN	ROSEBUD	TOUGHEN	OPACITY	UPSWING	BRIOCHE	DRAWING	GRAVITY
LOWBROW	POINTED	ROSETTE	TOURIST	OPENING	UPTIGHT	BRISKET	DRESSER	GRAVURE
LOWDOWN	POINTER	ROSTRUM	TOURNEY	OPERATE	AQUATIC	BRISTLE	DRIBBLE	GRAZIER
LOWLAND	POLARIS	ROTUNDA	TOWBOAT	OPINION	AQUAVIT	BRITISH	DRIBLET	GRECIAN
LOZENGE	POLECAT	ROUGHEN	TOWHEAD	OPOSSUM	AQUEOUS	BRITTLE	DRIFTER	GREMLIN
MOBSTER	POLEMIC	ROUNDUP	TOWPATH	OPPRESS	AQUIFER	BROADEN	DRIZZLE	GRENADE
MODICUM	POLITIC	ROUTINE	TOXEMIA	OPTICAL	EQUABLE	BROCADE	DROPLET	GRIDDLE
MODISTE	POLLACK	ROWBOAT	VOCABLE	OPTIMAL	EQUATOR	BROIDER	DROPPER	GRIMACE
MODULAR	POLLUTE	ROYALTY	VOCALIC	OPTIMUM	EQUERRY	BROILER	DROUGHT	GRINDER
MOHEGAN	POLYGON	SOCIETY	VOGUISH	OPULENT	EQUINOX	BROMIDE	DRUMLIN	GRISTLE
MOHICAN	POLYMER	SOJOURN	VOLCANO	SPANGLE	SQUALID	BROMINE	DRUMMER	GRIZZLY
MOISTEN	POMPANO	SOLARIS	VOLTAGE	SPANIEL	SQUALOR	BROODER	DRUNKEN	GROMMET
MOLDING	POMPOUS	SOLDIER	VOLTAIC	SPANISH	SQUEEZE	BROTHEL	ERELONG	GROUPER
MOLLIFY	PONIARD	SOLICIT	VOLUBLE	SPARING	SQUELCH	BROTHER	EREMITE	GROUPIE
MOLLUSK	PONTIFF	SOLUBLE	VOUCHER	SPARKLE	ARAPAHO	BROUGHT	EROSION	GRUMBLE
MONADIC	PONTOON	SOLVENT	WOLFRAM	SPARROW	ARBITER	BROWNIE	EROSIVE	GRUNION
MONARCH	POPCORN	SOMEDAY	WOMANLY	SPASTIC	ARBUTUS	BROWSER	ERRATIC	IRANIAN
MONEYED	POPOVER	SOMEHOW	WOODCUT	SPATIAL	ARCHAIC	BRUISER	ERRATUM	IRIDIUM
MONGREL	POPULAR	SOMEONE	WOODLOT	SPATTER	ARCHERY	BRUSQUE	FRACTAL	IRKSOME
MONITOR	PORCINE	SOPHISM	WOODMAN	SPATULA	ARCHIVE	BRUTISH	FRAGILE	IRONING
MONOCLE	PORTAGE	SOPHIST	WORDAGE	SPEAKER	ARCHWAY	CRABBED	FRAILTY	KREMLIN
MONOMER	PORTEND	SOPRANO	WORDING	SPECIAL	ARDUOUS	CRACKER	FRANTIC	KRYPTON
MONSOON	PORTENT	SORCERY	WORKBAG	SPECIES	AREAWAY	CRACKLE	FRAUGHT	ORATION
MONSTER	PORTICO	SORGHUM	WORKBOX	SPECIFY	ARMHOLE	CRANIUM	FRAZZLE	ORATORY
MONTAGE	PORTION	SOUFFLE	WORKDAY	SPECKLE	ARMORER	CRAVING	FRECKLE	ORBITER
MOORING	PORTRAY	SOULFUL	WORKING	SPECTER	ARMREST	CREATOR	FREEBIE	ORCHARD
MORAINE	POSSESS	SOUNDER	WORKMAN	SPEEDUP	ARPANET	CREMATE	FREEDOM	ORDERLY
MORDANT	POSTAGE	SOUPCON	WORKOUT	SPELLER	ARRAIGN	CREVICE	FREEMAN	ORDINAL
MORNING	POSTBOY	SOYBEAN	WORLDLY	SPICULE	ARRANGE	CRICKET	FREEWAY	OREGANO
MOROCCO	POSTERN	TOASTER	WORSHIP	SPINACH	ARREARS	CRIMSON	FREEZER	ORGANDY
MORPHIA	POSTMAN	TOBACCO	WORSTED	SPINDLE	ARRIVAL	CRINKLE	FREIGHT	ORGANIC
MORTIFY	POSTURE	TOEHOLD	YOUNKER	SPINDLY	ARSENAL	CRIPPLE	FRESHEN	ORGANZA
MORTISE	POSTWAR	TOENAIL	ZOOLOGY	SPIRANT	ARSENIC	CRITTER	FRESHET	ORIFICE
MOUNTIE	POTABLE	TOGGERY	APANAGE	SPITTLE	ARTICLE	CROCHET	FRETFUL	ORIGAMI
NOCUOUS	POTHEAD	TOLUENE	APATITE	SPLENIC	ARTISAN	CROOKED	FRETSAW	OROGENY
NOISOME	POTHERB	TONIGHT	APHASIA	SPLOTCH	ARTISTE	CROPPER	FRIABLE	OROTUND
NOMADIC	POTHOLE	TONNAGE	APOLOGY	SPLURGE	ARTLESS	CROQUET	FRIGATE	ORTOLAN
NOMINAL	POTHOOK	TONNEAU	APOLUNE	SPOILER	BRACERO	CROSIER	FRITTER	PRAETOR
NOMINEE	POTLUCK	TONSURE	APOSTLE	SPONSOR	BRACKEN	CROUTON	FRIZZLE	PRAIRIE
NONBOOK	POTSHOT	TOOLBOX	APPAREL	SPOTTER	BRACKET	CROWBAR	FROGMAN	PRALINE
NONHERO	POTTAGE	TOPCOAT	APPEASE	SPOUSAL	BRAHMAN	CRUCIAL	FROWARD	PRATTLE
NONPLUS	POTTERY	TOPICAL	APPLAUD	SPUMONI	BRAHMIN	CRUCIFY	FRUSTUM	PRAYING
NONSKED	POULTRY	TOPKNOT	APPLIED	SPUTNIK	BRAILLE	CRUISER	GRACKLE	PREBEND
NONSTOP	POVERTY	TOPLESS	APPOINT	SPUTTER	BRAMBLE	CRULLER	GRADUAL	PRECEDE
NONUSER	ROADBED	TOPMAST	APPRISE	UPBRAID	BRAVADO	CRUMBLE	GRAMMAR	PRECEPT
NOONDAY	ROADWAY	TOPMOST	APPROVE	UPCHUCK	BRAVERY	CRUMPET	GRANARY	PRECISE
NORTHER	ROASTER	TOPPING	APRICOT	UPDRAFT	BRAVURA	CRUMPLE	GRANDAM	PRECOOK
NOSEGAY	ROBBERY	TOPSAIL	APROPOS	UPGRADE	BRAZIER	CRUSADE	GRANDEE	PREDATE
NOSTRIL	ROEBUCK	TOPSIDE	EPAULET	UPRAISE	BREADTH	CRYBABY	GRANITE	PREDICT
NOSTRUM	ROISTER	TOPSOIL	EPERGNE	UPRIGHT	BREAKER	CRYPTIC	GRANTEE	PREEMIE
NOTABLE	ROLLICK	TORMENT	EPICURE	UPRIVER	BREAKUP	CRYSTAL	GRANULE	PREEMPT
NOTHING	ROMANCE	TORNADO	EPIGRAM	UPSHIFT	BREATHE	DRACHMA	GRAPHIC	PREFACE

PREFECT	PRORATE	TRIVIAL	ISRAELI	STILTON	BUMPKIN	EUPHONY	MUDROOM	PULLOUT
PREFORM	PROSAIC	TRIVIUM	ISTHMUS	STIPEND	BUNTING	FUCHSIA	MUEZZIN	PULSATE
PREHEAT	PROSODY	TROCHEE	OSMOSIS	STIPPLE	BURDOCK	FULCRUM	MUFFLER	PUMPKIN
PRELATE	PROSPER	TRODDEN	OSSUARY	STIRRUP	BURETTE	FULFILL	MUGWUMP	PUNGENT
PRELUDE	PROTEAN	TROLLEY	OSTMARK	STOMACH	BURGEON	FULSOME	MULATTO	PUNSTER
PREMIER	PROTECT	TROLLOP	OSTRICH	STOPGAP	BURGESS	FUNERAL	MULLEIN	PURITAN
PREMISE	PROTEGE	TROOPER	PSALTER	STOPPER	BURGHER	FURBISH	MULLION	PURLIEU
PREMIUM	PROTEIN	TROPISM	PSYCHIC	STORAGE	BURMESE	FURIOUS	MUNDANE	PURLOIN
PREPARE	PROTEST	TROUBLE	PSYCHOL	STORIED	BURNISH	FURLONG	MURRAIN	PURPORT
PREPUCE	PROVERB	TROUNCE	TSUNAMI	STRANGE	BURNOUT	FURNACE	MUSETTE	PURPOSE
PRESAGE	PROVIDE	TRUCKLE	USELESS	STRATUM	BUSHING	FURNISH	MUSICAL	PURSUIT
PRESENT	PROVISO	TRUFFLE	ATAVISM	STRETCH	BUTCHER	FURRIER	MUSKRAT	PURVIEW
PRESIDE	PROVOKE	TRUMPET	ATELIER	STRINGY	BUTTOCK	FURRING	MUSTANG	PUSTULE
PRESOAK	PROVOST	TRUNDLE	ATHEIST	STROPHE	BUZZARD	FURTHER	MUSTARD	PUTREFY
PRESUME	PROWESS	TRUSTEE	ATHIRST	STRUDEL	CUBICLE	FURTIVE	MUTABLE	QUALIFY
PRETEEN	PROXIMO	URANIUM	ATHLETE	STUBBLE	CUCKOLD	FUSTIAN	NUCLEAR	QUALITY
PRETEND	PRUDENT	URANOUS	ATHWART	STUDENT	CUISINE	GUANINE	NUCLEON	QUANTUM
PRETEXT	TRACERY	URETHRA	ATOMIZE	STUDIED	CULOTTE	GUARANI	NUCLEUS	QUARREL
PRETZEL	TRACHEA	URINARY	ATROPHY	STUFFIT	CULPRIT	GUERDON	NUCLIDE	QUARTER
PREVAIL	TRACING	URINATE	ATTACHE	STUMBLE	CULTURE	GUILDER	NULLIFY	QUARTET
PREVENT	TRACTOR	UROLOGY	ATTAINT	STUPEFY	CULVERT	GUMBOIL	NUMERAL	QUETZAL
PREVIEW	TRADUCE	WRANGLE	ATTEMPT	STUTTER	CUMULUS	GUMDROP	NUMERIC	QUIBBLE
PRICKER	TRAFFIC	WRAPPER	ATTRACT	STYLING	CUNNING	GUMSHOE	NUPTIAL	QUICKEN
PRICKLE	TRAGEDY	WREATHE	ETCHING	STYLISH	CUPCAKE	GUNBOAT	NURSERY	QUICKIE
PRIMACY	TRAILER	WRECKER	ETERNAL	STYLIST	CUPRITE	GUNFIRE	NURTURE	QUIETUS
PRIMARY	TRAINEE	WRESTLE	ETHANOL	STYLIZE	CURATOR	GUNLOCK	NUTPICK	QUININE
PRIMATE	TRAIPSE	WRIGGLE	ETHICAL	STYPTIC	CURBING	GUNNERY	OUTCAST	QUINTAL
PRITHEE	TRAITOR	WRINGER	ITALIAN	UTENSIL	CURIOUS	GUNSHOT	OUTCOME	QUINTET
PRIVACY	TRAMMEL	WRINKLE	ITEMIZE	UTILITY	CURRANT	GUNWALE	OUTCROP	QUONDAM
PRIVATE	TRAMPLE	WRITING	ITERATE	UTILIZE	CURRENT	HULKING	OUTDOOR	RUBBISH
PROBATE	TRANSIT	WRONGLY	OTTOMAN	UTOPIAN	CURSIVE	HUMDRUM	OUTDRAW	RUBELLA
PROBITY	TRANSOM	WROUGHT	STABILE	YTTRIUM	CURSORY	HUMERUS	OUTFACE	RUFFIAN
PROBLEM	TRAPEZE	WRYNECK	STADIUM	AUCTION	CURTAIL	HUMIDOR	OUTFLOW	RUINOUS
PROCEED	TRAVAIL	ASCETIC	STAFFER	AUDIBLE	CURTAIN	HUMMOCK	OUTGROW	RUMMAGE
PROCESS	TREACLE	ASCRIBE	STAGGER	AUDITOR	CUSHION	HUNDRED	OUTLAST	RUNAWAY
PROCTOR	TREADLE	ASEPTIC	STAGING	AUGMENT	CUSTARD	HUNKERS	OUTLINE	RUNDOWN
PROCURE	TREASON	ASEXUAL	STAMINA	AUREATE	CUSTODY	HUSBAND	OUTLIVE	RUNNING
PRODIGY	TREFOIL	ASHAMED	STAMMER	AUREOLE	CUTBACK	HUSKING	OUTLOOK	RUPTURE
PRODUCE	TRELLIS	ASHTRAY	STANDBY	AURICLE	CUTICLE	HUTMENT	OUTPLAY	RUSSIAN
PRODUCT	TREMBLE	ASIATIC	STARTLE	AUSPICE	CUTLASS	JUBILEE	OUTPOST	SUBJECT
PROFANE	TREMOLO	ASININE	STARTUP	AUSTERE	CUTLERY	JUDAISM	OUTPULL	SUBJOIN
PROFESS	TRESTLE	ASKANCE	STATELY	AUSTRAL	CUTTING	JUGULAR	OUTRAGE	SUBLIME
PROFFER	TRIBUNE	ASPHALT	STATION	AUTOPSY	CUTWORM	JUJITSU	OUTRANK	SUBSIDE
PROFILE	TRIBUTE	ASPIRIN	STATURE	BUCKEYE	DUBIETY	JUKEBOX	OUTSELL	SUBSIDY
PROFUSE	TRICEPS	ASSAULT	STATUTE	BUCKLER	DUBIOUS	JUNIPER	OUTSIDE	SUBSIST
PROGENY	TRICKLE	ASSUAGE	STAUNCH	BUCKRAM	DUCHESS	JUPITER	OUTSIZE	SUBSOIL
PROGMAN	TRIDENT	ASSURED	STEALTH	BUCKSAW	DUCKPIN	JUSTICE	OUTSTAY	SUBTILE
PROGRAM	TRIGGER	ASTOUND	STEEPLE	BUCOLIC	DUCTILE	JUSTIFY	OUTVOTE	SUBVERT
PROJECT	TRILOGY	ASTRIDE	STELLAR	BUFFALO	DUDGEON	KUMQUAT	OUTWARD	SUCCEED
PROLONG	TRINITY	ASUNDER	STENCIL	BUFFOON	DULLARD	LUCERNE	OUTWEAR	SUCCESS
PROMISE	TRINKET	ESCAPEE	STEPSON	BUGABOO	DUMPING	LUCIFER	OUTWORK	SUCCUMB
PROMOTE	TRIPLET	ESQUIRE	STERILE	BUGBEAR	DUNGEON	LUGGAGE	OUTWORN	SUCROSE
PRONOUN	TRIPLEX	ESSENCE	STERNUM	BULLDOG	DURABLE	LULLABY	PUBERTY	SUCTION
PROPANE	TRIREME	ESTHETE	STEWARD	BULLION	DURANCE	LUMBAGO	PUBLISH	SUFFICE
PROPHET	TRISECT	ESTUARY	STICKER	BULLOCK	DUSTPAN	LUNATIC	PUDDING	SUFFUSE
PROPMAN	TRITIUM	ISOLATE	STIFFEN	BULRUSH	DUTEOUS	LUNETTE	PUERILE	SUGGEST
PROPOSE	TRIUMPH	ISOTOPE	STILTED	BULWARK	DUTIFUL	LUSTRAL	PULLMAN	SUICIDE

SUITING	EVASION	EXPLORE	AGAINST	CHAPTER	FEATURE	IMAGERY	PRATTLE	SLAVISH
SULFATE	EVENING	EXPOUND	AMALGAM	CHARGER	FIANCEE	IMAGINE	PRAYING	SNAFFLE
SULFIDE	EVIDENT	EXPRESS	AMATEUR	CHARIOT	FLACCID	IMAGISM	PSALTER	SPANGLE
SULTANA	OVATION	EXPUNGE	AMATIVE	CHARITY	FLANKER	IRANIAN	QUALIFY	SPANIEL
SUMMARY	OVERACT	EXTINCT	AMATORY	CHARMER	FLANNEL	ITALIAN	QUALITY	SPANISH
SUMMONS	OVERAGE	EXTRACT	ANAEMIA	CHARNEL	FLAPPER	JEALOUS	QUANTUM	SPARING
SUNBATH	OVERALL	EXTREME	ANAGRAM	CHARTER	FLATBED	LEADING	QUARREL	SPARKLE
SUNBEAM	OVERARM	EXTRUDE	ANALOGY	CHASSIS	FLATCAR	LEAFAGE	QUARTER	SPARROW
SUNBURN	OVERAWE	OXBLOOD	ANALYZE	CHASTEN	FLATTEN	LEAFLET	QUARTET	SPASTIC
SUNDIAL	OVERFLY	OXIDANT	ANAPEST	CHATEAU	FLATTER	LEAGUER	REACTOR	SPATIAL
SUNDOWN	OVERJOY	OXIDIZE	ANARCHY	CHATTEL	FLATTOP	LEAKAGE	READING	SPATTER
SUNFISH	OVERLAP	CYANIDE	ANATOMY	CHATTER	FLAVOUR	LEARNED	READOUT	SPATULA
SUNLAMP	OVERLAY	CYCLIST	APANAGE	CLAMBER	FRACTAL	LEATHER	REAGENT	STABILE
SUNRISE	OVERRUN	CYCLONE	APATITE	CLANGOR	FRAGILE	LIAISON	REALISM	STADIUM
SUNROOF	OVERSEA	CYPRESS	ARAPAHO	CLAPPER	FRAILTY	LOATHLY	REALITY	STAFFER
SUNSPOT	OVERSEE	DYNAMIC	ATAVISM	CLARIFY	FRANTIC	MEANDER	REALIZE	STAGGER
SUPPORT	OVERTOP	DYNASTY	AVARICE	CLARION	FRAUGHT	MEANING	ROADBED	STAGING
SUPPOSE	OVIDUCT	EYEBALL	BEARING	CLARITY	FRAZZLE	MEASLES	ROADWAY	STAMINA
SUPREME	OVULATE	EYEBROW	BEASTLY	CLASSIC	GEARBOX	MEASURE	ROASTER	STAMMER
SURFACE	AWKWARD	EYELASH	BEATIFY	CLASTIC	GHASTLY	MEATMAN	SCALLOP	STANDBY
SURFEIT	DWINDLE	EYESORE	BEATNIK	CLATTER	GLACIAL	NIAGARA	SCALPEL	STARTLE
SURGEON	SWADDLE	EYEWASH	BLACKEN	CLAVIER	GLACIER	OCARINA	SCAMPER	STARTUP
SURGERY	SWAGGER	HYDRANT	BLADDER	COARSEN	GLADDEN	OPACITY	SCANDAL	STATELY
SURMISE	SWAHILI	HYDRATE	BLANKET	COATING	GLAMOUR	ORATION	SCANNER	STATION
SURNAME	SWALLOW	HYDROUS	BLARNEY	COAXIAL	GLAZIER	ORATORY	SCAPULA	STATURE
SURPASS	SWARTHY	HYGIENE	BLATANT	CRABBED	GRACKLE	OVATION	SCARIFY	STATUTE
SURPLUS	SWEATER	HYMNODY	BLATHER	CRACKER	GRADUAL	PEACOCK	SCARLET	STAUNCH
SURTOUT	SWEDISH	MYSTERY	BOATMAN	CRACKLE	GRAMMAR	PEAFOWL	SCATTER	SWADDLE
SURVIVE	SWEETEN	MYSTIFY	BRACERO	CRANIUM	GRANARY	PEASANT	SEABIRD	SWAGGER
SUSPECT	SWELTER	PYJAMAS	BRACKEN	CRAVING	GRANDAM	PHAETON	SEAFOOD	SWAHILI
SUSPEND	SWINDLE	PYRAMID	BRACKET	CYANIDE	GRANDEE	PHALANX	SEALANT	SWALLOW
SUSTAIN	SWOLLEN	PYRITES	BRAHMAN	CZARINA	GRANITE	PHALLIC	SEAPORT	SWARTHY
TUBULAR	TWADDLE	SYMPTOM	BRAHMIN	DEADPAN	GRANTEE	PHALLUS	SEASICK	TOASTER
TUESDAY	TWEETER	SYNAPSE	BRAILLE	DEALING	GRANULE	PHANTOM	SEASIDE	TRACERY
TUGBOAT	TWIDDLE	SYNCOPE	BRAMBLE	DEANERY	GRAPHIC	PHARAOH	SEATING	TRACHEA
TUITION	TWILLED	SYNONYM	BRAVADO	DEATHLY	GRAPNEL	PHARYNX	SEAWALL	TRACING
TUMBLER	TWINKLE	SYRINGE	BRAVERY	DIAGRAM	GRAPPLE	PIANIST	SEAWARD	TRACTOR
TUMBREL	TWISTER	SYSTOLE	BRAVURA	DIALECT	GRATIFY	PIASTER	SEAWEED	TRADUCE
TUNABLE	TWITTER	TYPHOID	BRAZIER	DIAMOND	GRATING	PLACARD	SHACKLE	TRAFFIC
TUNEFUL	TWOSOME	TYPHOON	CHABLIS	DIARIST	GRAUPEL	PLACATE	SHADING	TRAGEDY
TURBINE	EXAMINE	TYPICAL	CHADIAN	DRACHMA	GRAVITY	PLACEBO	SHALLOP	TRAILER
TURKISH	EXAMPLE	TYRANNY	CHAFFER	DRAGNET	GRAVURE	PLACKET	SHALLOW	TRAINEE
TURMOIL	EXCERPT	WYSIWYG	CHAGRIN	DRAGOON	GRAZIER	PLANTAR	SHAMBLE	TRAIPSE
TURNERY	EXCLAIM	ZYMURGY	CHALICE	DRAPERY	GUANINE	PLANTER	SHAMPOO	TRAITOR
TURNING	EXCLUDE	AZIMUTH	CHALLIS	DRASTIC	GUARANI	PLASTER	SHAPELY	TRAMMEL
TURNKEY	EXCRETA	CZARINA	CHAMBER	DRAUGHT	HEADING	PLASTIC	SHARPEN	TRAMPLE
TURNOFF	EXCRETE		CHAMFER	DRAWING	HEADMAN	PLATEAU	SHARPER	TRANSIT
TURNOUT	EXECUTE		CHAMOIS	ELASTIC	HEADPIN	PLATING	SHARPIE	TRANSOM
TUSSOCK	EXEGETE		CHANCEL	EMANATE	HEADSET	PLATOON	SHATTER	TRAPEZE
TUTELAR	EXHAUST	3RD LETTER	CHANCRE	ENAMOUR	HEADWAY	PLATTER	SHAVING	TRAVAIL
VULGATE	EXHIBIT		CHANNEL	EPAULET	HEALTHY	PLAUDIT	SHAWNEE	TWADDLE
VULPINE	EXPANSE	ABALONE	CHANSON	EVACUEE	HEARING	PLAYBOY	SIAMESE	UNARMED
VULTURE	EXPENSE	ABANDON	CHANTEY	EVASION	HEARKEN	PLAYLET	SLACKEN	UNAWARE
AVARICE	EXPIATE	ACADEME	CHANTRY	EXAMINE	HEARSAY	PLAYPEN	SLACKER	URANIUM
AVERAGE	EXPLAIN	ACADEMY	CHAPEAU	EXAMPLE	HEARTEN	PRAETOR	SLANDER	URANOUS
AVOCADO	EXPLODE	ADAMANT	CHAPLET	FEARFUL	HEATHEN	PRAIRIE	SLATHER	VIADUCT
EVACUEE	EXPLOIT	ADAPTER	CHAPMAN	FEATHER	HEATHER	PRALINE	SLAVERY	WEALTHY

WEASAND	REBIRTH	BUCKRAM	INCLOSE	RECLAIM	ANDANTE	JODHPUR	UPDRAFT	CREVICE
WEATHER	REBOUND	BUCKSAW	INCLUDE	RECLAME	ANDIRON	JUDAISM	VEDANTA	DEERFLY
WHATNOT	REBUILD	BUCOLIC	INCRUST	RECLINE	ANDROID	KADDISH	WADABLE	DIEHARD
WRANGLE	ROBBERY	COCAINE	INCUBUS	RECLUSE	ARDUOUS	KIDSKIN	WADDING	DRESSER
WRAPPER	RUBBISH	COCHLEA	JACINTH	RECOUNT	AUDIBLE	LADYBUG	WEDDING	ELECTOR
ZEALOUS	RUBELLA	COCKADE	JACKASS	RECOVER	AUDITOR	LODGING	WEDLOCK	ELEGIAC
ALBUMEN	SABBATH	COCKEYE	JACKDAW	RECRUIT	BADLAND	MADDING	WIDGEON	ELEMENT
ALBUMIN	SIBLING	COCKNEY	JACKLEG	RECTIFY	BEDDING	MADEIRA	WIDOWER	ELEVATE
AMBIENT	SUBJECT	COCKPIT	JACKPOT	RECTORY	BEDEVIL	MEDIATE	YIDDISH	EMERALD
ARBITER	SUBJOIN	COCONUT	JOCULAR	RECYCLE	BEDFAST	MEDICAL	ACETATE	EMERITA
ARBUTUS	SUBLIME	CUCKOLD	KICKOFF	RICKETS	BEDIZEN	MEDULLA	ACETONE	EPERGNE
BIBELOT	SUBSIDE	CYCLIST	LACONIC	RICKETY	BEDOUIN	MIDLAND	ADENINE	ERELONG
BOBSLED	SUBSIDY	CYCLONE	LACQUER	RICKSHA	BEDPOST	MIDMOST	ADENOID	EREMITE
CABARET	SUBSIST	DECAGON	LACTATE	SECLUDE	BEDROCK	MIDRIFF	AGELESS	ETERNAL
CABBAGE	SUBSOIL	DECEASE	LACTEAL	SECRECY	BEDROLL	MIDTOWN	ALEMBIC	EVENING
CABINET	SUBTILE	DECEIVE	LACTOSE	SECRETE	BEDROOM	MIDWEEK	ALEWIFE	EXECUTE
CABOOSE	SUBVERT	DECENCY	LECHERY	SECTARY	BEDSIDE	MIDWIFE	AMENITY	EXEGETE
COBBLER	TABLEAU	DECIBEL	LECTERN	SECTION	BEDSORE	MIDYEAR	AMERIND	EYEBALL
CUBICLE	TABLOID	DECIDED	LECTURE	SECULAR	BEDTIME	MODICUM	ANEMONE	EYEBROW
DEBACLE	TABULAR	DECIMAL	LICENSE	SICKBED	CADAVER	MODISTE	AREAWAY	EYELASH
DEBAUCH	TIBETAN	DECLAIM	LOCATOR	SOCIETY	CADENCE	MODULAR	ASEPTIC	EYESORE
DEBOUCH	TOBACCO	DECLARE	LOCKJAW	SUCCEED	CADENZA	MUDROOM	ASEXUAL	EYEWASH
DEBRIEF	TUBULAR	DECLINE	LOCKNUT	SUCCESS	CADMIUM	ODDBALL	ATELIER	FEEDLOT
DUBIETY	UMBRAGE	DECODER	LOCKOUT	SUCCUMB	CEDILLA	ODDMENT	AVERAGE	FEELING
DUBIOUS	UNBLOCK	DECORUM	LUCERNE	SUCROSE	CODEINE	OEDIPAL	BEEHIVE	FLEMING
EMBARGO	UNBOSOM	DICTATE	LUCIFER	SUCTION	CODFISH	OLDSTER	BEELINE	FLEMISH
EMBASSY	UNBOWED	DICTION	MACABRE	TACTICS	CODICIL	ORDERLY	BEESWAX	FLESHLY
EMBOWER	UPBRAID	DOCKAGE	MACADAM	TACTILE	CODLING	ORDINAL	BLEEDER	FLEXURE
EMBRACE	VIBRANT	DUCHESS	MACAQUE	TECHNIC	DUDGEON	PADDING	BLEMISH	FRECKLE
EMBROIL	VIBRATE	DUCKPIN	MACDRAW	TICKING	EIDOLON	PADDOCK	BLESSED	FREEBIE
EMBRYOL	VIBRATO	DUCTILE	MACHETE	UNCANNY	ELDERLY	PADLOCK	BREADTH	FREEDOM
FEBRILE	WEBBING	ENCHAIN	MACHINE	UNCHAIN	ENDEMIC	PEDICAB	BREAKER	FREEMAN
FIBROID	ACCLAIM	ENCHANT	MACRAME	UNCIVIL	ENDLESS	PUDDING	BREAKUP	FREEWAY
GABFEST	ACCOUNT	ENCLAVE	MICROBE	UNCLASP	ENDMOST	RADIANT	BREATHE	FREEZER
GIBBOUS	ACCUSAL	ENCLOSE	NACELLE	UNCLEAN	ENDORSE	RADIATE	BRECCIA	FREIGHT
GIBLETS	ACCUSED	ENCRUST	NECKTIE	UNCLOAK	ENDWAYS	RADICAL	BREVITY	FRESHEN
GOBBLER	ALCALDE	ESCAPEE	NOCUOUS	UNCLOSE	ENDWISE	REDCOAT	CAESURA	FRESHET
HABITAT	ALCAZAR	ETCHING	NUCLEAR	UNCOUTH	FEDERAL	REDDISH	CHEAPEN	FRETFUL
HABITUE	ALCHEMY	EXCERPT	NUCLEON	UNCOVER	GODDESS	REDHEAD	CHECKER	FRETSAW
HIBACHI	ALCOHOL	EXCLAIM	NUCLEUS	UNCROSS	GODHEAD	REDLINE	CHECKUP	GHERKIN
HOBNAIL	ANCHOVY	EXCLUDE	NUCLIDE	UNCTION	GODHOOD	REDOUBT	CHEDDAR	GLEEMAN
INBOARD	ANCIENT	EXCRETA	OCCLUDE	UPCHUCK	GODLESS	REDOUND	CHEETAH	GRECIAN
INBOUND	ARCHAIC	EXCRETE	ORCHARD	VACANCY	GODLIKE	REDRESS	CHEMISE	GREMLIN
JUBILEE	ARCHERY	FACTION	PACIFIC	VACCINE	GODSEND	REDSKIN	CHEMIST	GRENADE
KIBBUTZ	ARCHIVE	FACTORY	PACKAGE	VACUITY	HADDOCK	REDWOOD	CHERISH	GUERDON
LABORED	ARCHWAY	FACTUAL	PACKING	VACUOLE	HIDALGO	SADIRON	CHEROOT	HOECAKE
LIBERAL	ASCETIC	FACULTY	PECCARY	VACUOUS	HIDEOUS	SIDEARM	CHEVIOT	HOEDOWN
LIBERTY	ASCRIBE	FICTION	PECCAVI	VICEROY	HIDEOUT	SIDECAR	CHEVRON	ICEBERG
LIBRARY	AUCTION	FUCHSIA	PICCOLO	VICINAL	HYDRANT	SIDELIT	CLEANLY	ICEBOAT
LOBSTER	BACKING	HACKMAN	PICTURE	VICIOUS	HYDRATE	SIDEMAN	CLEANSE	IDEALLY
MOBSTER	BACKLIT	HACKNEY	POCOSIN	VICTORY	HYDROUS	TADPOLE	CLEANUP	ILEITIS
ORBITER	BACKLOG	HACKSAW	RACCOON	VICTUAL	INDEXED	TEDIOUS	CLEAVER	INERTIA
OXBLOOD	BECAUSE	HECTARE	RACEWAY	VOCABLE	INDICIA	TIDINGS	CLEMENT	INEXACT
PABULUM	BECLOUD	HICKORY	RECEIPT	VOCALIC	INDOORS	UNDERGO	COEQUAL	ITEMIZE
PIBROCH	BICYCLE	INCENSE	RECEIVE	WICKIUP	INDORSE	UNDOING	COEXIST	ITERATE
PUBERTY	BUCKEYE	INCISOR	RECENCY	ABDOMEN	INDULGE	UNDRESS	CREATOR	KEELSON
PUBLISH	BUCKLER	INCLINE	RECITAL	ADDRESS	INDWELL	UNDYING	CREMATE	KEEPING

KHEDIVE	PRESUME	THEREON	ENFORCE	DIGRESS	PIGSKIN	MAHATMA	CLIPPER	IMITATE
KNEECAP	PRETEEN	THERETO	FIFTEEN	DOGBANE	PIGTAIL	MAHICAN	COINAGE	INITIAL
KREMLIN	PRETEND	THERMAL	HAFNIUM	DOGCART	RAGTIME	MOHEGAN	CRICKET	IRIDIUM
LEEWARD	PRETEXT	THERMOS	INFANCY	DOGFISH	RAGWEED	MOHICAN	CRIMSON	LEISURE
MAESTRO	PRETZEL	TIEBACK	INFARCT	DOGTROT	REGALIA	SCHOLAR	CRINKLE	MAILBOX
MEETING	PREVAIL	TOEHOLD	INFERNO	DOGWOOD	REGATTA	UNHANDY	CRIPPLE	MAILMAN
MUEZZIN	PREVENT	TOENAIL	INFIDEL	EGGHEAD	REGENCY	UNHAPPY	CRITTER	MAINTOP
NEEDFUL	PREVIEW	TREACLE	INFIELD	ENGLISH	REGIMEN	UNHEARD	CUISINE	MEIOSIS
OBELISK	PUERILE	TREADLE	INFLAME	ENGRAFT	REGNANT	UNHINGE	DRIBBLE	MOISTEN
ONEROUS	QUETZAL	TREASON	INFLATE	ENGRAVE	REGRESS	UNHITCH	DRIBLET	NAIVETE
ONESELF	REENTRY	TREFOIL	INFLECT	ENGROSS	REGROUP	UNHORSE	DRIFTER	NAIVETY
ONETIME	RHENIUM	TRELLIS	INFLICT	FIGHTER	REGULAR	VEHICLE	DRIZZLE	NEITHER
OPENING	ROEBUCK	TREMBLE	LEFTISM	FIGMENT	RIGGING	ABILITY	DWINDLE	NOISOME
OPERATE	SCENERY	TREMOLO	MAFIOSO	FOGHORN	RIGHTLY	ACIDIFY	EDIFICE	OLIVINE
OREGANO	SCEPTER	TRESTLE	MUFFLER	GOGGLES	SAGUARO	ADIPOSE	EDITION	OMINOUS
OVERACT	SCEPTIC	TUESDAY	OFFBEAT	HAGGARD	SEGMENT	AGITATE	ELISION	OPINION
OVERAGE	SEEMING	TWEETER	OFFENSE	HIGHBOY	SIGHTED	ALIMENT	ELITISM	ORIFICE
OVERALL	SHEATHE	UNEARTH	OFFHAND	HIGHWAY	SIGHTLY	ALIMONY	EMINENT	ORIGAMI
OVERARM	SHEBANG	UNEQUAL	OFFICER	HOGBACK	SIGNIFY	AMIABLE	EMITTER	OVIDUCT
OVERAWE	SHELLAC	UNERASE	OFFSIDE	HOGWASH	SUGGEST	ANILINE	EPICURE	OXIDANT
OVERFLY	SHELTER	URETHRA	RAFFISH	HYGIENE	TIGHTEN	ANIMATE	EPIGRAM	OXIDIZE
OVERJOY	SHERBET	USELESS	REFEREE	INGENUE	TOGGERY	ANIMISM	EPISODE	PAISLEY
OVERLAP	SHERIFF	UTENSIL	REFINED	INGRAFT	TUGBOAT	ASIATIC	EPISTLE	PHILTER
OVERLAY	SKEPTIC	WEEKDAY	REFLECT	INGRAIN	UNGODLY	ASININE	EPITAPH	PLIABLE
OVERRUN	SLEEPER	WEEKEND	REFRACT	INGRATE	UNGROUP	AZIMUTH	EPITHET	POINTED
OVERSEA	SLEIGHT	WEEPING	REFRAIN	INGRESS	UNGUENT	BAILIFF	EPITOME	POINTER
OVERSEE	SLENDER	WHEEDLE	REFRESH	INGROWN	UPGRADE	BLINDER	EVIDENT	PRICKER
OVERTOP	SMELTER	WHEELER	REFUGEE	JUGULAR	VAGRANT	BLINKER	FAIENCE	PRICKLE
PEELING	SNEAKER	WHEREAS	RUFFIAN	LAGGARD	VEGETAL	BLINTZE	FAILING	PRIMACY
PEEVISH	SPEAKER	WHEREAT	SAFFRON	LEGATEE	VOGUISH	BLISTER	FAILURE	PRIMARY
PFENNIG	SPECIAL	WHEREBY	SUFFICE	LEGGING	WAGGERY	BRIGADE	FAIRING	PRIMATE
PIEBALD	SPECIES	WHEREIN	SUFFUSE	LEGHORN	WAGGISH	BRIGAND	FAIRWAY	PRITHEE
PLENARY	SPECIFY	WHEREOF	TAFFETA	LEGIBLE	WAGONER	BRIMFUL	FLICKER	PRIVACY
PREBEND	SPECKLE	WHEREON	UNFROCK	LIGHTEN	WAGTAIL	BRIOCHE	FLIGHTY	PRIVATE
PRECEDE	SPECTER	WHERETO	AFGHANI	LIGHTER	WIGGLER	BRISKET	FLIPPER	QUIBBLE
PRECEPT	SPEEDUP	WHETHER	ALGEBRA	LIGNIFY	ACHIEVE	BRISTLE	FLIVVER	QUICKEN
PRECISE	SPELLER	WREATHE	ANGUISH	LIGNITE	APHASIA	BRITISH	FRIABLE	QUICKIE
PRECOOK	STEALTH	WRECKER	ANGULAR	LUGGAGE	ASHAMED	BRITTLE	FRIGATE	QUIETUS
PREDATE	STEEPLE	WRESTLE	AUGMENT	MAGENTA	ASHTRAY	CAISSON	FRITTER	QUININE
PREDICT	STELLAR	AFFABLE	BAGASSE	MAGNATE	ATHEIST	CAITIFF	FRIZZLE	QUINTAL
PREEMIE	STENCIL	AFFLICT	BAGGAGE	MAGNETO	ATHIRST	CEILING	GAINFUL	QUINTET
PREEMPT	STEPSON	AFFRONT	BAGPIPE	MAGNIFY	ATHLETE	CHIANTI	GAINSAY	RAILING
PREFACE	STERILE	ALFALFA	BEGGARY	MEGATON	ATHWART	CHICANE	GLIMMER	RAILWAY
PREFECT	STERNUM	BIFOCAL	BEGONIA	MIGRANT	BEHOOVE	CHICANO	GLIMPSE	RAIMENT
PREFORM	STEWARD	BUFFALO	BEGRIME	MIGRATE	COHABIT	CHICKEN	GLISTEN	RAINBOW
PREHEAT	SWEATER	BUFFOON	BEGUILE	MUGWUMP	ECHELON	CHICORY	GLISTER	RHIZOME
PRELATE	SWEDISH	DEFAULT	BEGUINE	NEGLECT	ENHANCE	CHIFFON	GLITTER	ROISTER
PRELUDE	SWEETEN	DEFENSE	BIGHORN	NIGGARD	ETHANOL	CHIGGER	GRIDDLE	RUINOUS
PREMIER	SWELTER	DEFIANT	BUGABOO	NIGHTLY	ETHICAL	CHIGNON	GRIMACE	SAILING
PREMISE	TEENAGE	DEFICIT	BUGBEAR	ONGOING	EXHAUST	CHIMERA	GRINDER	SAINTLY
PREMIUM	THEATER	DEFLATE	COGNATE	ORGANDY	EXHIBIT	CHIMNEY	GRISTLE	SCIENCE
PREPARE	THEOREM	DEFLECT	DEGAUSS	ORGANIC	INHABIT	CHINESE	GRIZZLY	SEISMIC
PREPUCE	THERAPY	DEFRAUD	DEGRADE	ORGANZA	INHALER	CHINOOK	GUILDER	SHIMMER
PRESAGE	THEREAT	DEFROST	DIGITAL	PAGEANT	INHERIT	CHINTZY	HAIRCUT	SHINGLE
PRESENT	THEREBY	DEFUNCT	DIGNIFY	PAGEBOY	INHIBIT	CHIPPER	HAIRPIN	SKIFFLE
PRESIDE	THEREIN	DIFFUSE	DIGNITY	PIGGISH	INHUMAN	CLIMATE	HEINOUS	SKILLET
PRESOAK	THEREOF	EFFENDI	DIGRAPH	PIGMENT	JEHOVAH	CLINKER	HEIRESS	SKIPPER

SKITTER	URINARY	BALLAST	CULVERT	JOLLITY	PULLMAN	WALLEYE	DUMPING	REMOUNT
SKIWEAR	URINATE	BALLOON	DELIGHT	KILLING	PULLOUT	WALLOON	GAMBIAN	ROMANCE
SLICKER	UTILITY	BALONEY	DELIMIT	KILLJOY	PULSATE	WELCOME	GIMMICK	RUMMAGE
SLIPPER	UTILIZE	BELABOR	DELIVER	KILOTON	RELAPSE	WELFARE	GUMBOIL	SAMOVAR
SLITHER	VEILING	BELATED	DELOUSE	LULLABY	RELATED	WILDCAT	GUMDROP	SAMPLER
SMIDGEN	WAILFUL	BELGIAN	DILEMMA	MALAISE	RELATOR	WILLFUL	GUMSHOE	SAMURAI
SNICKER	WEIGHTY	BELIEVE	DILUENT	MALARIA	RELEASE	WILLIES	HAMMOCK	SEMINAL
SNIFFLE	WHICKER	BELLBOY	DOLEFUL	MALEFIC	RELIEVE	WILLING	HAMSTER	SEMINAR
SPICULE	WHIMPER	BELLHOP	DOLPHIN	MALISON	RELIQUE	WILLOWY	HEMLINE	SIMILAR
SPINACH	WHIPPET	BELLOWS	DULLARD	MALLARD	ROLLICK	WOLFRAM	HEMLOCK	SOMEDAY
SPINDLE	WHIPSAW	BELOVED	ECLIPSE	MALLEUS	SALIENT	ZILLION	HIMSELF	SOMEHOW
SPINDLY	WHISKER	BELTWAY	ECLOGUE	MALMSEY	SALTBOX	ADMIRAL	HOMBURG	SOMEONE
SPIRANT	WHISKEY	BILIOUS	ELLIPSE	MALTOSE	SALTINE	AIMLESS	HOMONYM	SUMMARY
SPITTLE	WHISPER	BILLION	ENLARGE	MELANGE	SALVAGE	ALMANAC	HUMDRUM	SUMMONS
STICKER	WHISTLE	BOLIVAR	ENLIVEN	MELANIC	SELFISH	ALMONER	HUMERUS	SYMPTOM
STIFFEN	WHITHER	BOLOGNA	FALLACY	MELANIN	SELTZER	AMMETER	HUMIDOR	TAMBALA
STILTED	WHITING	BOLSTER	FALLOUT	MILEAGE	SELVAGE	AMMONIA	HUMMOCK	TEMPERA
STILTON	WHITISH	BULLDOG	FALSIFY	MILITIA	SILENCE	ARMHOLE	HYMNODY	TEMPEST
STIPEND	WHITLOW	BULLION	FILBERT	MILKMAN	SILICON	ARMORER	IMMENSE	TIMBREL
STIPPLE	WHITTLE	BULLOCK	FILLING	MILKSOP	SOLARIS	ARMREST	IMMERSE	TIMOTHY
STIRRUP	WRIGGLE	BULRUSH	FILMDOM	MILLAGE	SOLDIER	BIMETAL	IMMORAL	TIMPANI
SUICIDE	WRINGER	BULWARK	FOLDOUT	MILLDAM	SOLICIT	BOMBARD	KUMQUAT	TUMBLER
SUITING	WRINKLE	CALCIFY	FOLIAGE	MILLIME	SOLUBLE	BOMBAST	LAMBENT	TUMBREL
SWINDLE	WRITING	CALCINE	FOLKWAY	MILLING	SOLVENT	BUMPKIN	LAMINAR	UNMANLY
THICKEN	ADJOURN	CALCITE	FULCRUM	MILLION	SPLENIC	CAMBIUM	LAMPOON	UNMORAL
THICKET	ADJUDGE	CALCIUM	FULFILL	MOLDING	SPLOTCH	CAMBRIC	LAMPREY	UNMOVED
THIMBLE	ADJUNCT	CALDERA	FULSOME	MOLLIFY	SPLURGE	CAMPHOR	LEMMING	VAMOOSE
THINNER	JEJUNUM	CALDRON	GALLANT	MOLLUSK	SULFATE	CEMBALO	LEMPIRA	VAMPIRE
THISTLE	JUJITSU	CALENDS	GALLEON	MULATTO	SULFIDE	COMBINE	LIMBECK	WOMANLY
THITHER	MAJESTY	CALIBER	GALLERY	MULLEIN	SULTANA	COMFORT	LIMEADE	ZAMBIAN
TRIBUNE	PAJAMAS	CALIPER	GALLIUM	MULLION	TALLYHO	COMMAND	LIMITED	ZYMURGY
TRIBUTE	PYJAMAS	CALLING	GALLOWS	NULLIFY	TELLING	COMMEND	LUMBAGO	AMNESIA
TRICEPS	REJOICE	CALLOUS	GELATIN	OBLIQUE	TILLAGE	COMMENT	MAMMARY	AMNESTY
TRICKLE	SOJOURN	CALOMEL	GELDING	OBLOQUY	TOLUENE	COMMODE	MAMMOTH	ANNUITY
TRIDENT	ASKANCE	CALORIC	HALBERD	OILSKIN	UNLATCH	COMMUNE	MEMENTO	ANNULAR
TRIGGER	AWKWARD	CALORIE	HALCYON	PALADIN	UNLEARN	COMMUTE	MIMESIS	BANDAGE
TRILOGY	BIKEWAY	CALUMET	HALFWAY	PALAVER	UNLEASH	COMPACT	MIMETIC	BANDBOX
TRINITY	INKHORN	CALUMNY	HALIBUT	PALETTE	UNLOOSE	COMPANY	MIMICRY	BANNOCK
TRINKET	INKLING	CALYPSO	HALLWAY	PALFREY	UNLUCKY	COMPARE	NEMESIS	BANQUET
TRIPLET	INKWELL	CELESTA	HALTING	PALMATE	VALANCE	COMPASS	NOMADIC	BANSHEE
TRIPLEX	IRKSOME	CELSIUS	HALVERS	PALPATE	VALENCE	COMPEER	NOMINAL	BENEATH
TRIREME	JUKEBOX	CILIATE	HALYARD	PELAGIC	VALIANT	COMPETE	NOMINEE	BENEFIT
TRISECT	MAKINGS	COLLAGE	HELICAL	PELICAN	VALUATE	COMPILE	NUMERAL	BENISON
TRITIUM	TAKEOFF	COLLARD	HELLCAT	PILGRIM	VILLAGE	COMPLEX	NUMERIC	BENTHIC
TRIUMPH	TEKTITE	COLLATE	HELLENE	PILLAGE	VILLAIN	COMPORT	OSMOSIS	BENTHOS
TRIVIAL	UNKEMPT	COLLECT	HELLION	PILLBOX	VILLEIN	COMPOSE	PIMENTO	BENZENE
TRIVIUM	UNKNOWN	COLLEEN	HELPING	PILLION	VILLOUS	COMPOST	POMPANO	BENZINE
TUITION	WAKEFUL	COLLEGE	HILLOCK	PILLORY	VOLCANO	COMPOTE	POMPOUS	BENZOIN
TWIDDLE	AILERON	COLLIDE	HILLTOP	PILSNER	VOLTAGE	COMPUTE	PUMPKIN	BINDING
TWILLED	AILMENT	COLLIER	HOLDING	POLARIS	VOLTAIC	COMRADE	RAMBLER	BONANZA
TWINKLE	ALLEGRO	COLLOID	HOLIDAY	POLECAT	VOLUBLE	CUMULUS	RAMPAGE	BONDAGE
TWISTER	ALLERGY	COLOGNE	HOLMIUM	POLEMIC	VULGATE	DEMERIT	RAMPANT	BONDMAN
TWITTER	BALANCE	COLONEL	HOLSTER	POLITIC	VULPINE	DEMESNE	RAMPART	BONFIRE
UNICORN	BALCONY	COLORED	HULKING	POLLACK	VULTURE	DEMIGOD	REMAINS	BUNTING
UNIFORM	BALDING	CULOTTE	ILLEGAL	POLLUTE	WALKOUT	DEMONIC	REMNANT	CANASTA
UNITARY	BALDRIC	CULPRIT	ILLICIT	POLYGON	WALKWAY	DEMOTIC	REMODEL	CANDIED
UNITIZE	BALEFUL	CULTURE	ILLNESS	POLYMER	WALLABY	DOMINIE	REMORSE	CANNERY

CANNULA	CONTEMN	GUNLOCK	MANHOLE	PENSION	TENURED	BROIDER	GEOLOGY	PROMOTE
CANTATA	CONTEND	GUNNERY	MANHOOD	PENSIVE	TINFOIL	BROILER	GLOBULE	PRONOUN
CANTEEN	CONTENT	GUNSHOT	MANHUNT	PENTIUM	TINWARE	BROMIDE	GLORIFY	PROPANE
CANVASS	CONTEST	GUNWALE	MANIKIN	PINHOLE	TONIGHT	BROMINE	GLOTTIS	PROPHET
CENSURE	CONTEXT	HANDBAG	MANKIND	PINKEYE	TONNAGE	BROODER	GOODMAN	PROPMAN
CENTARE	CONTORT	HANDCAR	MANLIKE	PINNACE	TONNEAU	BROTHEL	GROMMET	PROPOSE
CENTAUR	CONTOUR	HANDFUL	MANNISH	PINNATE	TONSURE	BROTHER	GROUPER	PRORATE
CENTAVO	CONTRIB	HANDGUN	MANSARD	PINWORM	TUNABLE	BROUGHT	GROUPIE	PROSAIC
CENTIME	CONTROL	HANDOUT	MANSION	PONIARD	TUNEFUL	BROWNIE	HOODLUM	PROSODY
CENTIMO	CONVENE	HANDSAW	MANTEAU	PONTIFF	UNNERVE	BROWSER	HOOSIER	PROSPER
CENTRAL	CONVENT	HANDSEL	MANUMIT	PONTOON	VANDYKE	CHOCTAW	IDOLIZE	PROTEAN
CENTURY	CONVERT	HANDSET	MENFOLK	PUNGENT	VANILLA	CHOLERA	IRONING	PROTECT
CONCAVE	CONVICT	HANGDOG	MENTHOL	PUNSTER	VANTAGE	CHOPPER	ISOLATE	PROTEGE
CONCEAL	CONVOKE	HANGING	MENTION	RANKING	VANWARD	CHORALE	ISOTOPE	PROTEIN
CONCEDE	CUNNING	HANGMAN	MINARET	RANSACK	VENISON	CHORTLE	KNOCKER	PROTEST
CONCEIT	DANDIFY	HANGOUT	MINDFUL	RENEWAL	VENTRAL	CHOWDER	KNOWING	PROVERB
CONCEPT	DENIZEN	HENPECK	MINERAL	RINGLET	VENTURE	CLOBBER	LAOTIAN	PROVIDE
CONCERN	DENSITY	HINTING	MINIBUS	RUNAWAY	VINEGAR	CLOSURE	LEONINE	PROVISO
CONCERT	DENTATE	HUNDRED	MINIMAL	RUNDOWN	VINTAGE	CLOTHES	LEOPARD	PROVOKE
CONCISE	DENTIST	HUNKERS	MINIMUM	RUNNING	VINTNER	CLOTURE	LEOTARD	PROVOST
CONCOCT	DENTURE	IGNEOUS	MINSTER	SANCTUM	WANTING	COOKERY	LIONIZE	PROWESS
CONCORD	DINETTE	IGNOBLE	MINUEND	SANDBAG	WINDAGE	COOKOUT	LOOKOUT	PROXIMO
CONDEMN	DUNGEON	INNARDS	MINUTIA	SANDBAR	WINDBAG	COOLANT	MOORING	QUONDAM
CONDIGN	DYNAMIC	INNINGS	MONADIC	SANDHOG	WINDING	CROCHET	NEOLOGY	RHODIUM
CONDOLE	DYNASTY	JANITOR	MONARCH	SANDLOT	WINDOWS	CROOKED	NIOBIUM	RHOMBUS
CONDONE	ENNOBLE	JANUARY	MONEYED	SANDMAN	WINDROW	CROPPER	NOONDAY	ROOFTOP
CONDUCE	FANATIC	JONQUIL	MONGREL	SENATOR	WINNING	CROQUET	OPOSSUM	ROOKERY
CONDUCT	FANCIER	JUNIPER	MONITOR	SENSORY	WINSOME	CROSIER	OROGENY	ROOSTER
CONDUIT	FANFARE	KINDRED	MONOCLE	SENSUAL	ABOLISH	CROUTON	OROTUND	ROOTLET
CONDYLE	FANTAIL	KINETIC	MONOMER	SENTIMO	ACOLYTE	CROWBAR	PHOENIX	SCOOTER
CONFESS	FANTASY	KINFOLK	MONSOON	SINCERE	ACONITE	DIOCESE	PHONEME	SCOURGE
CONFIDE	FENCING	KINGDOM	MONSTER	SINUOUS	AGONIZE	DOORMAN	PHONICS	SHOCKER
CONFINE	FINAGLE	KINGPIN	MONTAGE	SUNBATH	AMOROUS	DOORMAT	PIONEER	SHORING
CONFIRM	FINANCE	KINSHIP	MUNDANE	SUNBEAM	ANODIZE	DOORWAY	PLOTTER	SHORTEN
CONFLUX	FINDING	KINSMAN	NANKEEN	SUNBURN	ANODYNE	DROPLET	PLOWBOY	SHORTLY
CONFORM	FINESSE	LANDING	NONBOOK	SUNDIAL	ANOMALY	DROPPER	PLOWMAN	SHOTGUN
CONFUSE	FINFISH	LANGUID	NONHERO	SUNDOWN	ANOTHER	DROUGHT	PROBATE	SHOWMAN
CONFUTE	FINICKY	LANGUOR	NONPLUS	SUNFISH	APOLOGY	EBONITE	PROBITY	SLOBBER
CONGEAL	FINNISH	LANOLIN	NONSKED	SUNLAMP	APOLUNE	ECOLOGY	PROBLEM	SMOLDER
CONGEST	FONDANT	LANTANA	NONSTOP	SUNRISE	APOSTLE	ECONOMY	PROCEED	SMOTHER
CONICAL	FUNERAL	LANTERN	NONUSER	SUNROOF	ATOMIZE	EGOTISM	PROCESS	SNORKEL
CONIFER	GANGWAY	LANYARD	OMNIBUS	SUNSPOT	AVOCADO	EMOTION	PROCTOR	SPOILER
CONJOIN	GANTLET	LENIENT	PANACEA	SYNAPSE	BIOLOGY	EROSION	PROCURE	SPONSOR
CONJURE	GENERAL	LINEAGE	PANACHE	SYNCOPE	BIOTITE	EROSIVE	PRODIGY	SPOTTER
CONNECT	GENERIC	LINEMAN	PANCAKE	SYNONYM	BLOATER	FLORIST	PRODUCE	SPOUSAL
CONNIVE	GENESIS	LINGUAL	PANICLE	TANAGER	BLOODED	FLOTSAM	PRODUCT	STOMACH
CONNOTE	GENETIC	LINKAGE	PANNIER	TANBARK	BLOOPER	FLOUNCE	PROFANE	STOPGAP
CONQUER	GENITAL	LINSEED	PANOPLY	TANGENT	BLOSSOM	FLOWERY	PROFESS	STOPPER
CONSENT	GENTEEL	LONGBOW	PANTHER	TANNERY	BLOTTER	FOOLERY	PROFFER	STORAGE
CONSIGN	GENTIAN	LONGING	PENALTY	TANTRUM	BLOWGUN	FOOLISH	PROFILE	STORIED
CONSIST	GENTILE	LUNATIC	PENANCE	TENABLE	BLOWOUT	FOOTAGE	PROFUSE	SWOLLEN
CONSOLE	GENUINE	LUNETTE	PENATES	TENANCY	BOOKEND	FOOTING	PROGENY	THORIUM
CONSORT	GINGHAM	MANACLE	PENDANT	TENDRIL	BOOKISH	FOOTMAN	PROGMAN	THOUGHT
CONSULT	GINSENG	MANAGER	PENDENT	TENFOLD	BOOKLET	FOOTPAD	PROGRAM	TOOLBOX
CONSUME	GONDOLA	MANDATE	PENDING	TENSILE	BOOTLEG	FROGMAN	PROJECT	TROCHEE
CONTACT	GUNBOAT	MANDREL	PENGUIN	TENSION	BROADEN	FROWARD	PROLONG	TRODDEN
CONTAIN	GUNFIRE	MANDRIL	PENNANT	TENUOUS	BROCADE	GEODESY	PROMISE	TROLLEY

TROLLOP	CUPRITE	NUPTIAL	ESQUIRE	BARRING	CORNICE	FIREMAN	HIRSUTE	PARSNIP
TROOPER	CYPRESS	OPPRESS	INQUEST	BARROOM	COROLLA	FIRSTLY	HORIZON	PARTAKE
TROPISM	DEPLANE	PAPILLA	INQUIRE	BERSERK	CORONAL	FORBEAR	HORMONE	PARTIAL
TROUBLE	DEPLETE	PAPOOSE	INQUIRY	BIRCHER	CORONER	FORBODE	HORRIFY	PARTING
TROUNCE	DEPLORE	PAPRIKA	LIQUEFY	BIRETTA	CORONET	FORCEPS	ISRAELI	PARTITE
TWOSOME	DEPOSIT	PAPYRUS	LIQUEUR	BOREDOM	CORRECT	FOREARM	KARAKUL	PARTNER
UROLOGY	DEPRAVE	PEPPERY	PIQUANT	BOROUGH	CORRODE	FOREIGN	KERATIN	PARTWAY
UTOPIAN	DEPRESS	PIPETTE	REQUEST	BORSCHT	CORRUPT	FORELEG	KERNING	PARVENU
VIOLATE	DEPRIVE	POPCORN	REQUIEM	BURDOCK	CORSAGE	FOREMAN	LARCENY	PERCALE
VIOLENT	DIPLOID	POPOVER	REQUIRE	BURETTE	CORSAIR	FORESEE	LARGESS	PERCENT
WHOEVER	DIPLOMA	POPULAR	REQUITE	BURGEON	CORTEGE	FORETOP	MARGENT	PERCEPT
WHOOPLA	EMPATHY	RAPPORT	SEQUENT	BURGESS	CURATOR	FOREVER	MARIMBA	PERFECT
WHOPPER	EMPEROR	RAPTURE	SEQUOIA	BURGHER	CURBING	FORFEIT	MARINER	PERFIDY
WHORLED	EMPOWER	REPLACE	TEQUILA	BURMESE	CURIOUS	FORFEND	MARITAL	PERFORM
WOODCUT	EMPRESS	REPLETE	UNQUIET	BURNISH	CURRANT	FORGING	MARPLOT	PERFUME
WOODLOT	ENPLANE	REPLICA	UNQUOTE	BURNOUT	CURRENT	FORGIVE	MARQUEE	PERGOLA
WOODMAN	EUPHONY	REPRESS	VAQUERO	CARABAO	CURSIVE	FORLORN	MARQUIS	PERHAPS
WRONGLY	EXPANSE	REPRINT	ABREAST	CARAMEL	CURSORY	FORMULA	MARSHAL	PERIGEE
WROUGHT	EXPENSE	REPRISE	ABRIDGE	CARAVAN	CURTAIL	FORSAKE	MARTIAL	PERIQUE
ZEOLITE	EXPIATE	REPROOF	ACREAGE	CARAVEL	CURTAIN	FORTIFY	MARTIAN	PERIWIG
ZIONISM	EXPLAIN	REPROVE	ACROBAT	CARAWAY	DARLING	FORTRAN	MARTINI	PERJURY
ZOOLOGY	EXPLODE	REPTILE	ACRONYM	CARBIDE	DERANGE	FORTUNE	MARXISM	PERLITE
AMPHORA	EXPLOIT	REPULSE	ACRYLIC	CARBINE	DERRICK	FORWARD	MERCURY	PERPLEX
AMPLIFY	EXPLORE	REPUTED	ADRENAL	CARCASS	DERVISH	FURBISH	MERMAID	PERSIAN
AMPUTEE	EXPOUND	RIPOSTE	AEROBIC	CARDBUS	DIREFUL	FURIOUS	MIRACLE	PERSIST
APPAREL	EXPRESS	RUPTURE	AEROSOL	CARDIAC	DORMANT	FURLONG	MORAINE	PERTAIN
APPEASE	EXPUNGE	SAPIENT	AFRICAN	CAREFUL	DURABLE	FURNACE	MORDANT	PERTURB
APPLAUD	HAPLESS	SAPLING	AGROUND	CARFARE	DURANCE	FURNISH	MORNING	PERVADE
APPLIED	HAPLOID	SAPWOOD	AIRDROP	CARIBOU	EARACHE	FURRIER	MOROCCO	PERVERT
APPOINT	HAPPILY	SOPHISM	AIRFLOW	CARIOUS	EARDRUM	FURRING	MORPHIA	PHRENIC
APPRISE	HEPARIN	SOPHIST	AIRFOIL	CARLOAD	EARLOBE	FURTHER	MORTIFY	PIRANHA
APPROVE	HEPATIC	SOPRANO	AIRLIFT	CARMINE	EARMARK	FURTIVE	MORTISE	PORCINE
ARPANET	HIPBONE	SUPPORT	AIRLINE	CARNAGE	EARMUFF	GARBAGE	MURRAIN	PORTAGE
ASPHALT	HIPSTER	SUPPOSE	AIRMAIL	CAROTID	EARNEST	GARFISH	NARRATE	PORTEND
ASPIRIN	HOPHEAD	SUPREME	AIRPORT	CAROUSE	EARPLUG	GARLAND	NARTHEX	PORTENT
BAPTISM	IMPANEL	TAPIOCA	AIRPOST	CARPORT	EARRING	GARMENT	NARWHAL	PORTICO
BAPTIST	IMPASSE	TAPROOM	AIRSHIP	CARRIER	EARSHOT	GARNISH	NERVOUS	PORTION
BAPTIZE	IMPASTO	TAPROOT	AIRSICK	CARRION	EARTHEN	GARROTE	NIRVANA	PORTRAY
BIPLANE	IMPEACH	TAPSTER	AIRWAVE	CARRYON	EARTHLY	GERMANE	NORTHER	PURITAN
BIPOLAR	IMPEARL	TIPSTER	ALREADY	CARSICK	ERRATIC	GIRAFFE	NURSERY	PURLIEU
CAPABLE	IMPERIL	TOPCOAT	ALRIGHT	CARTAGE	ERRATUM	GORILLA	NURTURE	PURLOIN
CAPITAL	IMPETUS	TOPICAL	APRICOT	CARTOON	FARAWAY	HARBOUR	OARLOCK	PURPORT
CAPITOL	IMPIETY	TOPKNOT	APROPOS	CERAMIC	FARMING	HARDPAN	OARSMAN	PURPOSE
CAPRICE	IMPINGE	TOPLESS	ARRAIGN	CERTAIN	FARRAGO	HARDTOP	PARABLE	PURSUIT
CAPSIZE	IMPIOUS	TOPMAST	ARRANGE	CERTIFY	FARRIER	HARELIP	PARADOX	PURVIEW
CAPSTAN	IMPLODE	TOPMOST	ARREARS	CERUMEN	FARTHER	HARMONY	PARAGON	PYRAMID
CAPSULE	IMPLORE	TOPPING	ARRIVAL	CHROMIC	FERMENT	HARNESS	PARAPET	PYRITES
CAPTAIN	IMPOUND	TOPSAIL	ATROPHY	CHRONIC	FERMIUM	HARPOON	PARASOL	RAREBIT
CAPTION	IMPRESS	TOPSIDE	AUREATE	CIRCLET	FERNERY	HARRIER	PARBOIL	REREDOS
CAPTIVE	IMPRINT	TOPSOIL	AUREOLE	CIRCUIT	FERROUS	HARVARD	PARESIS	SARCASM
CAPTURE	IMPROVE	TYPHOID	AURICLE	CORACLE	FERRULE	HARVEST	PARFAIT	SARDINE
COPILOT	IMPULSE	TYPHOON	BARBELL	CORDAGE	FERTILE	HERBAGE	PARKWAY	SCRAPPY
COPIOUS	JUPITER	TYPICAL	BARGAIN	CORDIAL	FERVENT	HEROICS	PARLOUR	SCRATCH
COPPICE	LAPWING	UMPTEEN	BARONET	CORDITE	FIREARM	HEROINE	PARLOUS	SCRAWNY
COPYBOY	LEPROSY	ACQUIRE	BAROQUE	CORDOBA	FIREBOX	HEROISM	PARQUET	SCREECH
COPYCAT	NAPHTHA	BEQUEST	BARRAGE	CORINTH	FIREBUG	HERRING	PARSING	SCROTUM
CUPCAKE	NEPTUNE	ENQUIRE	BARRIER	CORNCOB	FIREFLY	HERSELF	PARSLEY	SCRUFFY

SCRUPLE	TURNOUT	ABSENCE	DESTROY	HASHISH	MISSEND	ROSTRUM	ARTISAN	ENTRAIN
SERIOUS	TYRANNY	ABSOLVE	DISABLE	HASSOCK	MISSILE	RUSSIAN	ARTISTE	ENTRANT
SERPENT	UNRAVEL	ABSTAIN	DISAVOW	HISTORY	MISSING	SESSILE	ARTLESS	ENTREAT
SERRATE	UPRAISE	ARSENAL	DISBAND	HOSANNA	MISSION	SESSION	ASTOUND	ENTROPY
SERRIED	UPRIGHT	ARSENIC	DISCARD	HOSIERY	MISSIVE	SUSPECT	ASTRIDE	ENTRUST
SERVANT	UPRIVER	ASSAULT	DISCERN	HOSPICE	MISSTEP	SUSPEND	ATTACHE	ENTWINE
SERVICE	VARIANT	ASSUAGE	DISCORD	HOSTAGE	MISTAKE	SUSTAIN	ATTAINT	ESTHETE
SERVILE	VARIETY	ASSURED	DISCUSS	HOSTESS	MISTRAL	SYSTOLE	ATTEMPT	ESTUARY
SERVING	VARIOUS	AUSPICE	DISDAIN	HOSTILE	MUSETTE	TESTATE	ATTRACT	EXTINCT
SHRIVEL	VARMINT	AUSTERE	DISEASE	HOSTLER	MUSICAL	TESTIFY	AUTOPSY	EXTRACT
SIRLOIN	VARNISH	AUSTRAL	DISEUSE	HUSBAND	MUSKRAT	TUSSOCK	BATHTUB	EXTREME
SIROCCO	VARSITY	BASHFUL	DISGUST	HUSKING	MUSTANG	UNSAVED	BATISTE	EXTRUDE
SORCERY	VERANDA	BASSOON	DISHRAG	INSHORE	MUSTARD	UNSCREW	BATSMAN	FATBACK
SORGHUM	VERBENA	BASTARD	DISJOIN	INSIDER	MYSTERY	UNSLING	BATTERY	FATEFUL
STRANGE	VERBOSE	BASTION	DISLIKE	INSIGHT	MYSTIFY	UNSNARL	BATTING	FATIGUE
STRATUM	VERDANT	BESEECH	DISMISS	INSIPID	NASCENT	UNSOUND	BETHINK	FATUITY
STRETCH	VERDICT	BESHREW	DISOBEY	INSPECT	NOSEGAY	UNSTRAP	BETIMES	FATUOUS
STRINGY	VERDURE	BESIDES	DISPLAY	INSPIRE	NOSTRIL	UPSHIFT	BETOKEN	FETLOCK
STROPHE	VERMEIL	BESIEGE	DISPORT	INSTALL	NOSTRUM	UPSTAGE	BETROTH	FITTING
STRUDEL	VERNIER	BESMEAR	DISPOSE	INSTANT	OBSCENE	UPSTART	BETWEEN	GATEWAY
SURFACE	VERSIFY	BESPEAK	DISPUTE	INSTATE	OBSCURE	UPSTATE	BETWIXT	GETAWAY
SURFEIT	VERSION	BESTIAL	DISROBE	INSTEAD	OBSEQUY	UPSURGE	BITTERN	HATCHET
SURGEON	VERTIGO	BISCUIT	DISRUPT	INSTILL	OBSERVE	UPSWEPT	BITTERS	HOTCAKE
SURGERY	VERVAIN	BISMUTH	DISSECT	INSULAR	ONSHORE	UPSWING	BITUMEN	HOTFOOT
SURMISE	VIRGULE	BUSHING	DISSENT	INSULIN	OSSUARY	VESICLE	BUTCHER	HOTSHOT
SURNAME	VIRTUAL	CASCADE	DISTAFF	INSURED	PASSAGE	VESPERS	BUTTOCK	HUTMENT
SURPASS	WARBLER	CASCARA	DISTANT	INSURER	PASSING	VESTIGE	CATALOG	INTEGER
SURPLUS	WARFARE	CASHIER	DISTEND	JASMINE	PASSION	VESTING	CATALPA	INTENSE
SURTOUT	WARHEAD	CASSAVA	DISTICH	JUSTICE	PASSIVE	VESTURE	CATARRH	INTERIM
SURVIVE	WARLESS	CASSOCK	DISTILL	JUSTIFY	PASSKEY	VISCERA	CATBIRD	INTRANS
SYRINGE	WARLIKE	CASTING	DISTORT	LASAGNA	PASTERN	VISCOSE	CATBOAT	INTROIT
TARNISH	WARLOCK	CASTLED	DISTURB	LESBIAN	PASTIME	VISCOUS	CATCALL	INTRUDE
TERBIUM	WARLORD	CESSION	DOSSIER	LISSOME	PASTURE	VISIBLE	CATCHER	INTRUST
TERMITE	WARNING	CISTERN	DUSTPAN	LISTING	PISMIRE	VISITOR	CATCHUP	ISTHMUS
TERNARY	WARPATH	COSSACK	EASTERN	LUSTRAL	POSSESS	WASHING	CATFISH	JETPORT
TERRACE	WARRANT	COSTIVE	ECSTASY	MASCARA	POSTAGE	WASHOUT	CATHODE	JITTERS
TERRAIN	WARRIOR	COSTUME	ENSLAVE	MASONIC	POSTBOY	WASHTUB	CATLIKE	JOTTING
TERRIER	WARSHIP	CUSHION	ENSNARE	MASONRY	POSTERN	WASPISH	CATTAIL	KATYDID
TERRIFY	WARTHOG	CUSTARD	ESSENCE	MASSAGE	POSTMAN	WASSAIL	CATWALK	KETCHUP
THREADY	WARTIME	CUSTODY	FASCISM	MASSEUR	POSTURE	WASTAGE	CITADEL	KITCHEN
THROATY	WIRETAP	DASHIKI	FASHION	MASSIVE	POSTWAR	WASTREL	CITIZEN	LATAKIA
THROUGH	WORDAGE	DASHING	FESTIVE	MASTERY	PUSTULE	WESTERN	COTERIE	LATCHET
THRUWAY	WORDING	DASHPOT	FESTOON	MASTIFF	RESCIND	WISHFUL	COTTAGE	LATERAL
TORMENT	WORKBAG	DASTARD	FISHERY	MASTOID	RESEDIT	WISTFUL	CUTBACK	LATRINE
TORNADO	WORKBOX	DESCANT	FISHING	MESSAGE	RESERVE	WYSIWYG	CUTICLE	LATTICE
TORPEDO	WORKDAY	DESCEND	FISSILE	MESSIAH	RESIDUE	YESHIVA	CUTLASS	LATVIAN
TORRENT	WORKING	DESCENT	FISSION	MESTIZO	RESOLVE	ACTUARY	CUTLERY	LETDOWN
TORSION	WORKMAN	DESERVE	FISSURE	MISCALL	RESOUND	ACTUATE	CUTTING	LETTUCE
TORTONI	WORKOUT	DESKTOP	FISTFUL	MISDEED	RESPECT	ANTACID	CUTWORM	LITERAL
TORTURE	WORLDLY	DESPAIR	FISTULA	MISFILE	RESPITE	ANTENNA	DETENTE	LITHIUM
TURBINE	WORSHIP	DESPISE	FUSTIAN	MISFIRE	RESPOND	ANTHILL	DETRACT	LITURGY
TURKISH	WORSTED	DESPITE	GASTRIC	MISLEAD	RESTIVE	ANTHRAX	DETRAIN	LOTTERY
TURMOIL	YARDAGE	DESPOIL	GESTAPO	MISLIKE	RESTORE	ANTHROP	DUTEOUS	MATADOR
TURNERY	YARDARM	DESPOND	GESTURE	MISNAME	RISIBLE	ANTIGEN	DUTIFUL	MATINEE
TURNING	YARDMAN	DESSERT	GOSHAWK	MISPLAY	ROSEATE	ANTIQUE	ENTENTE	MATTINS
TURNKEY	ABSCESS	DESTINE	GOSLING	MISREAD	ROSEBUD	ANTONYM	ENTHUSE	MATTOCK
TURNOFF	ABSCOND	DESTINY	HASHING	MISRULE	ROSETTE	ARTICLE	ENTITLE	METHANE

MITOSIS	PETIOLE	WETLAND	DOUBLET	RAUNCHY	ADVISED	COWHAND	AMYLASE	WAYSIDE
MUTABLE	PETRIFY	WITHERS	DOUGHTY	REUNION	BIVALVE	COWHIDE	ANYBODY	WAYWARD
NATURAL	PETTISH	WITHOUT	DRUMLIN	RHUBARB	BIVOUAC	COWLICK	ANYMORE	WAYWORN
NETTING	PETUNIA	WITLESS	DRUMMER	ROUGHEN	CAVALRY	COWLING	ANYTIME	WRYNECK
NETWARE	PITCHER	WITNESS	DRUNKEN	ROUNDUP	CAVEMAN	COWPOKE	ANYWISE	BAZOOKA
NETWORK	PITEOUS	WITTING	EDUCATE	ROUTINE	CIVILLY	COWSLIP	BAYONET	BIZARRE
NITRATE	PITFALL	YTTRIUM	ELUSIVE	SAUNTER	CIVVIES	DEWCLAW	BOYCOTT	BUZZARD
NITRIFY	PITIFUL	ADULATE	EMULATE	SAUSAGE	DEVALUE	DEWDROP	CRYBABY	GAZELLE
NITRITE	POTABLE	ALUMINA	EQUABLE	SCUFFLE	DEVELOP	DOWAGER	CRYPTIC	GAZETTE
NOTABLE	POTHEAD	ALUMNUS	EQUATOR	SCUPPER	DEVIANT	HOWBEIT	CRYSTAL	GIZZARD
NOTHING	POTHERB	AQUATIC	EQUERRY	SCUTTLE	DEVIATE	HOWEVER	DAYBOOK	LOZENGE
NUTPICK	POTHOLE	AQUAVIT	EQUINOX	SHUDDER	DEVILRY	HOWLING	DAYTIME	MAZURKA
OATCAKE	POTHOOK	AQUEOUS	FAUVISM	SHUFFLE	DEVIOUS	JEWELER	DOYENNE	PIZZAZZ
OATMEAL	POTLUCK	AQUIFER	FLUSTER	SHUTOUT	DEVOLVE	JEWELRY	ELYSIUM	SIZABLE
OBTRUDE	POTSHOT	ASUNDER	FLUTIST	SHUTTER	DEVOTED	LAWLESS	FLYABLE	WIZENED
OCTAGON	POTTAGE	BAUXITE	FLUTTER	SHUTTLE	DEVOTEE	LAWSUIT	FLYLEAF	
OCTOBER	POTTERY	BLUBBER	FOULARD	SLUMBER	DIVERGE	LOWBROW	HAYCOCK	
OCTOPUS	PUTREFY	BLUCHER	FOULING	SMUGGLE	DIVERSE	LOWDOWN	HAYFORK	
OPTICAL	RATCHET	BLUNDER	FOUNDER	SNUFFLE	DIVIDER	LOWLAND	HAYLOFT	**4TH LETTER**
OPTIMAL	RATLINE	BLUSTER	FOUNDRY	SNUGGLE	DIVISOR	MAWKISH	HAYRICK	
OPTIMUM	RATTLER	BOUDOIR	FRUSTUM	SOUFFLE	DIVORCE	NEWBORN	HAYSEED	ADVANCE
ORTOLAN	RATTRAP	BOULDER	GLUCOSE	SOULFUL	DIVULGE	NEWSBOY	HAYWIRE	AFFABLE
OSTMARK	RETINUE	BOUNCER	GLUTTON	SOUNDER	ENVELOP	NEWSMAN	JAYBIRD	ALCALDE
OSTRICH	RETIRED	BOUNDEN	GOULASH	SOUPCON	ENVENOM	NOWHERE	JAYWALK	ALCAZAR
OTTOMAN	RETIREE	BOUQUET	GOURMET	SPUMONI	ENVIOUS	RAWHIDE	JOYANCE	ALFALFA
OUTCAST	RETOUCH	BOURBON	GRUMBLE	SPUTNIK	GAVOTTE	ROWBOAT	JOYRIDE	ALMANAC
OUTCOME	RETRACE	BRUISER	GRUNION	SPUTTER	INVALID	SAWDUST	KEYHOLE	AMIABLE
OUTCROP	RETRACT	BRUSQUE	HAUBERK	SQUALID	INVEIGH	SAWMILL	KEYNOTE	ANDANTE
OUTDOOR	RETREAD	BRUTISH	HAUGHTY	SQUALOR	INVERSE	TOWBOAT	KRYPTON	ANTACID
OUTDRAW	RETREAT	CAUSTIC	HAULAGE	SQUEEZE	INVOICE	TOWHEAD	LAYAWAY	APHASIA
OUTFACE	ROTUNDA	CAUTION	HAUTEUR	SQUELCH	INVOLVE	TOWPATH	LAYETTE	APPAREL
OUTFLOW	SATANIC	CHUCKLE	HOUSING	STUBBLE	JAVELIN	UNWEAVE	MAYPOLE	AQUATIC
OUTGROW	SATCHEL	CHUKKER	JOURNAL	STUDENT	LIVABLE	ANXIETY	ODYSSEY	AQUAVIT
OUTLAST	SATIATE	CHUTNEY	JOURNEY	STUDIED	NOVELLA	ANXIOUS	PAYLOAD	AREAWAY
OUTLINE	SATIETY	CLUSTER	KNUCKLE	STUFFIT	NOVELTY	COXCOMB	PAYMENT	ARPANET
OUTLIVE	SATISFY	CLUTTER	LAUNDER	STUMBLE	OBVERSE	DEXTRIN	PAYROLL	ARRAIGN
OUTLOOK	SETBACK	COULOMB	LAUNDRY	STUPEFY	OBVIATE	FIXTURE	PHYSICS	ARRANGE
OUTPLAY	SETTING	COUNCIL	MAUDLIN	STUTTER	OBVIOUS	FOXHOLE	PHYSIOL	ASHAMED
OUTPOST	TATTING	COUNSEL	MAUNDER	THULIUM	POVERTY	HEXAGON	PLYWOOD	ASIATIC
OUTPULL	TETANUS	COUNTER	MOUNTIE	THUNDER	RAVIOLI	HEXAPOD	PSYCHIC	ASKANCE
OUTRAGE	TITANIC	COUNTRY	NAUGHTY	TOUGHEN	REVENGE	LEXICON	PSYCHOL	ASSAULT
OUTRANK	TITULAR	COUPLET	NEUTRAL	TOURIST	REVENUE	MAXILLA	ROYALTY	ATTACHE
OUTSELL	TUTELAR	COURAGE	NEUTRON	TOURNEY	REVERIE	MAXIMAL	SHYLOCK	ATTAINT
OUTSIDE	UNTRIED	COURIER	NOURISH	TRUCKLE	REVERSE	MAXIMUM	SHYSTER	BAGASSE
OUTSIZE	UNTRUTH	COURSER	OCULIST	TRUFFLE	REVIVAL	MEXICAN	SKYLARK	BALANCE
OUTSTAY	UNTWINE	COURTLY	OPULENT	TRUMPET	REVOLVE	MIXTURE	SKYLINE	BECAUSE
OUTVOTE	UNTWIST	COUTURE	OVULATE	TRUNDLE	RIVALRY	NOXIOUS	SKYWARD	BELABOR
OUTWARD	UPTIGHT	CRUCIAL	PAUCITY	TRUSTEE	RIVULET	SEXTANT	SOYBEAN	BELATED
OUTWEAR	VATICAN	CRUCIFY	PLUMAGE	TSUNAMI	SAVANNA	SIXTEEN	STYLING	BIVALVE
OUTWORK	VETERAN	CRUISER	PLUMBER	UKULELE	SEVENTY	TAXICAB	STYLISH	BIZARRE
OUTWORN	VITAMIN	CRULLER	PLUMMET	ULULATE	SEVERAL	TEXTILE	STYLIST	BLOATER
PATELLA	VITIATE	CRUMBLE	PLUNDER	UNUSUAL	WAVELET	TEXTURE	STYLIZE	BONANZA
PATHWAY	VITRIFY	CRUMPET	PLUNGER	VAULTED	BEWITCH	TOXEMIA	STYPTIC	BREADTH
PATIENT	VITRIOL	CRUMPLE	PLUVIAL	VOUCHER	BOWLDER	WAXWING	THYMINE	BREAKER
PATRIOT	VITTLES	CRUSADE	POULTRY	YOUNKER	BOWLINE	WAXWORK	THYROID	BREAKUP
PATROON	WATTAGE	DAUPHIN	PRUDENT	ADVANCE	BOWLING	ABYSMAL	THYSELF	BREATHE
PATTERN	WETBACK	DIURNAL	RAUCOUS	ADVERSE	COWBIRD	ABYSSAL	WAYBILL	BROADEN

BUGABOO	FINAGLE	NOTABLE	THEATER	EYEBROW	SUNBATH	CONCAVE	LARCENY	SLICKER
CABARET	FINANCE	OCTAGON	TITANIC	FATBACK	SUNBEAM	CONCEAL	LATCHET	SNICKER
CADAVER	FLYABLE	ORGANDY	TOBACCO	FILBERT	SUNBURN	CONCEDE	MASCARA	SORCERY
CANASTA	FRIABLE	ORGANIC	TREACLE	FORBEAR	TAMBALA	CONCEIT	MERCURY	SPECIAL
CAPABLE	GELATIN	ORGANZA	TREADLE	FORBODE	TANBARK	CONCEPT	MISCALL	SPECIES
CARABAO	GETAWAY	PAJAMAS	TREASON	FURBISH	TERBIUM	CONCERN	NASCENT	SPECIFY
CARAMEL	GIRAFFE	PALADIN	TUNABLE	GAMBIAN	TIEBACK	CONCERT	OATCAKE	SPECKLE
CARAVAN	HEPARIN	PALAVER	TYRANNY	GARBAGE	TIMBREL	CONCISE	OBSCENE	SPECTER
CARAVEL	HEPATIC	PANACEA	UNCANNY	GIBBOUS	TOWBOAT	CONCOCT	OBSCURE	SPICULE
CARAWAY	HEXAGON	PANACHE	UNEARTH	GLOBULE	TRIBUNE	CONCORD	OPACITY	STICKER
CATALOG	HEXAPOD	PARABLE	UNHANDY	GOBBLER	TRIBUTE	COXCOMB	OUTCAST	SUCCEED
CATALPA	HIBACHI	PARADOX	UNHAPPY	GUMBOIL	TUGBOAT	CRACKER	OUTCOME	SUCCESS
CATARRH	HIDALGO	PARAGON	UNLATCH	GUNBOAT	TUMBLER	CRACKLE	OUTCROP	SUCCUMB
CAVALRY	HOSANNA	PARAPET	UNMANLY	HALBERD	TUMBREL	CRICKET	PANCAKE	SUICIDE
CERAMIC	IDEALLY	PARASOL	UNRAVEL	HARBOUR	TURBINE	CROCHET	PAUCITY	SYNCOPE
CHEAPEN	IMPANEL	PELAGIC	UNSAVED	HAUBERK	VERBENA	CRUCIAL	PEACOCK	THICKEN
CHIANTI	IMPASSE	PENALTY	UPRAISE	HERBAGE	VERBOSE	CRUCIFY	PECCARY	THICKET
CITADEL	IMPASTO	PENANCE	VACANCY	HIPBONE	WARBLER	CUPCAKE	PECCAVI	TOPCOAT
CLEANLY	INFANCY	PENATES	VALANCE	HOGBACK	WAYBILL	DESCANT	PERCALE	TRACERY
CLEANSE	INFARCT	PIRANHA	VEDANTA	HOMBURG	WEBBING	DESCEND	PERCENT	TRACHEA
CLEANUP	INHABIT	PLIABLE	VERANDA	HOWBEIT	WETBACK	DESCENT	PERCEPT	TRACING
CLEAVER	INHALER	POLARIS	VITAMIN	HUSBAND	ZAMBIAN	DEWCLAW	PICCOLO	TRACTOR
COCAINE	INNARDS	POTABLE	VOCABLE	ICEBERG	ABSCESS	DIOCESE	PITCHER	TRICEPS
COHABIT	INVALID	PYJAMAS	VOCALIC	ICEBOAT	ABSCOND	DISCARD	PLACARD	TRICKLE
CORACLE	ISRAELI	PYRAMID	WADABLE	JAYBIRD	AVOCADO	DISCERN	PLACATE	TROCHEE
CREATOR	JOYANCE	REGALIA	WOMANLY	KIBBUTZ	BALCONY	DISCORD	PLACEBO	TRUCKLE
CURATOR	JUDAISM	REGATTA	WREATHE	LAMBENT	BIRCHER	DISCUSS	PLACKET	UNICORN
DEBACLE	KARAKUL	RELAPSE	ANYBODY	LESBIAN	BISCUIT	DOGCART	POPCORN	UNSCREW
DEBAUCH	KERATIN	RELATED	BARBELL	LIMBECK	BLACKEN	DRACHMA	PORCINE	VACCINE
DECAGON	LASAGNA	RELATOR	BLUBBER	LOWBROW	BLUCHER	EDUCATE	PRECEDE	VISCERA
DEFAULT	LATAKIA	REMAINS	BOMBARD	LUMBAGO	BOYCOTT	ELECTOR	PRECEPT	VISCOSE
DEGAUSS	LAYAWAY	RIVALRY	BOMBAST	NEWBORN	BRACERO	EPICURE	PRECISE	VISCOUS
DERANGE	LEGATEE	ROMANCE	BUGBEAR	NIOBIUM	BRACKEN	EVACUEE	PRECOOK	VOLCANO
DEVALUE	LIVABLE	ROYALTY	CABBAGE	NONBOOK	BRACKET	EXECUTE	PRICKER	VOUCHER
DISABLE	LOCATOR	RUNAWAY	CAMBIUM	ODDBALL	BRECCIA	FANCIER	PRICKLE	WELCOME
DISAVOW	LUNATIC	SATANIC	CAMBRIC	OFFBEAT	BROCADE	FASCISM	PROCEED	WHICKER
DOWAGER	MACABRE	SAVANNA	CARBIDE	PARBOIL	BUTCHER	FENCING	PROCESS	WRECKER
DURABLE	MACADAM	SCRAPPY	CARBINE	PIEBALD	CALCIFY	FLACCID	PROCTOR	ACADEME
DURANCE	MACAQUE	SCRATCH	CATBIRD	PREBEND	CALCINE	FLICKER	PROCURE	ACADEMY
DYNAMIC	MAHATMA	SCRAWNY	CATBOAT	PROBATE	CALCITE	FORCEPS	PSYCHIC	ACIDIFY
DYNASTY	MALAISE	SENATOR	CEMBALO	PROBITY	CALCIUM	FRACTAL	PSYCHOL	AIRDROP
EARACHE	MALARIA	SHEATHE	CHABLIS	PROBLEM	CARCASS	FRECKLE	QUICKEN	ANODIZE
EMBARGO	MANACLE	SIZABLE	CLOBBER	QUIBBLE	CASCADE	FULCRUM	QUICKIE	ANODYNE
EMBASSY	MANAGER	SNEAKER	COBBLER	RAMBLER	CASCARA	GLACIAL	RACCOON	BALDING
EMPATHY	MATADOR	SOLARIS	COMBINE	RHUBARB	CATCALL	GLACIER	RATCHET	BALDRIC
ENHANCE	MEGATON	SPEAKER	COWBIRD	ROBBERY	CATCHER	GLUCOSE	RAUCOUS	BANDAGE
ENLARGE	MELANGE	SQUALID	CRABBED	ROEBUCK	CATCHUP	GRACKLE	REACTOR	BANDBOX
EQUABLE	MELANIC	SQUALOR	CRYBABY	ROWBOAT	CHECKER	GRECIAN	REDCOAT	BEDDING
EQUATOR	MELANIN	STEALTH	CURBING	RUBBISH	CHECKUP	HALCYON	RESCIND	BINDING
ERRATIC	MINARET	STRANGE	CUTBACK	SABBATH	CHICANE	HATCHET	SANCTUM	BLADDER
ERRATUM	MIRACLE	STRATUM	DAYBOOK	SEABIRD	CHICANO	HAYCOCK	SARCASM	BONDAGE
ESCAPEE	MONADIC	SWEATER	DISBAND	SETBACK	CHICKEN	HOECAKE	SATCHEL	BONDMAN
ETHANOL	MONARCH	SYNAPSE	DOGBANE	SHEBANG	CHICORY	HOTCAKE	SHACKLE	BOUDOIR
EXHAUST	MORAINE	TANAGER	DOUBLET	SLOBBER	CHOCTAW	KETCHUP	SHOCKER	BURDOCK
EXPANSE	MULATTO	TENABLE	DRIBBLE	SOYBEAN	CHUCKLE	KITCHEN	SINCERE	CALDERA
FANATIC	MUTABLE	TENANCY	DRIBLET	STABILE	CIRCLET	KNOCKER	SLACKEN	CALDRON
FARAWAY	NOMADIC	TETANUS	EYEBALL	STUBBLE	CIRCUIT	KNUCKLE	SLACKER	CANDIED

CARDBUS	KADDISH	SUNDIAL	BALEFUL	FIREBOX	LIBERTY	REFEREE	WHEELER	PREFACE
CARDIAC	KHEDIVE	SUNDOWN	BEDEVIL	FIREBUG	LICENSE	REGENCY	WHOEVER	PREFECT
CHADIAN	KINDRED	SWADDLE	BENEATH	FIREFLY	LIMEADE	RELEASE	WIRETAP	PREFORM
CHEDDAR	LANDING	SWEDISH	BENEFIT	FIREMAN	LINEAGE	RENEWAL	WIZENED	PROFANE
CONDEMN	LEADING	TENDRIL	BESEECH	FOREARM	LINEMAN	REREDOS	AIRFLOW	PROFESS
CONDIGN	LETDOWN	TRADUCE	BIBELOT	FOREIGN	LITERAL	RESEDIT	AIRFOIL	PROFFER
CONDOLE	LOWDOWN	TRIDENT	BIKEWAY	FORELEG	LOZENGE	RESERVE	BEDFAST	PROFILE
CONDONE	MACDRAW	TRODDEN	BIMETAL	FOREMAN	LUCERNE	REVENGE	BONFIRE	PROFUSE
CONDUCE	MADDING	TWADDLE	BIRETTA	FORESEE	LUNETTE	REVENUE	BUFFALO	RAFFISH
CONDUCT	MANDATE	TWIDDLE	BLEEDER	FORETOP	MADEIRA	REVERIE	BUFFOON	ROOFTOP
CONDUIT	MANDREL	VANDYKE	BOREDOM	FOREVER	MAGENTA	REVERSE	CARFARE	RUFFIAN
CONDYLE	MANDRIL	VERDANT	BURETTE	FREEBIE	MAJESTY	ROSEATE	CATFISH	SAFFRON
CORDAGE	MAUDLIN	VERDICT	CADENCE	FREEDOM	MALEFIC	ROSEBUD	CHAFFER	SCUFFLE
CORDIAL	MINDFUL	VERDURE	CADENZA	FREEMAN	MEMENTO	ROSETTE	CHIFFON	SEAFOOD
CORDITE	MISDEED	VIADUCT	CALENDS	FREEWAY	MILEAGE	RUBELLA	CODFISH	SELFISH
CORDOBA	MOLDING	WADDING	CAREFUL	FREEZER	MIMESIS	SCIENCE	COMFORT	SHUFFLE
DANDIFY	MORDANT	WEDDING	CAVEMAN	FUNERAL	MIMETIC	SCREECH	CONFESS	SKIFFLE
DEADPAN	MUNDANE	WILDCAT	CELESTA	GATEWAY	MINERAL	SEVENTY	CONFIDE	SNAFFLE
DEWDROP	NEEDFUL	WINDAGE	CHEETAH	GAZELLE	MOHEGAN	SEVERAL	CONFINE	SNIFFLE
DISDAIN	OUTDOOR	WINDBAG	CODEINE	GAZETTE	MONEYED	SIDEARM	CONFIRM	SNUFFLE
EARDRUM	OUTDRAW	WINDING	COTERIE	GENERAL	MUSETTE	SIDECAR	CONFLUX	SOUFFLE
EVIDENT	OVIDUCT	WINDOWS	DECEASE	GENERIC	NACELLE	SIDELIT	CONFORM	STAFFER
FEEDLOT	OXIDANT	WINDROW	DECEIVE	GENESIS	NEMESIS	SIDEMAN	CONFUSE	STIFFEN
FINDING	OXIDIZE	WOODCUT	DECENCY	GENETIC	NOSEGAY	SILENCE	CONFUTE	STUFFIT
FOLDOUT	PADDING	WOODLOT	DEFENSE	GLEEMAN	NOVELLA	SLEEPER	DIFFUSE	SUFFICE
FONDANT	PADDOCK	WOODMAN	DEMERIT	HARELIP	NOVELTY	SOMEDAY	DOGFISH	SUFFUSE
GELDING	PENDANT	WORDAGE	DEMESNE	HIDEOUS	NUMERAL	SOMEHOW	DRIFTER	SULFATE
GEODESY	PENDENT	WORDING	DESERVE	HIDEOUT	NUMERIC	SOMEONE	EDIFICE	SULFIDE
GLADDEN	PENDING	YARDAGE	DETENTE	HOWEVER	OBSEQUY	SPEEDUP	FANFARE	SUNFISH
GODDESS	PREDATE	YARDARM	DEVELOP	HUMERUS	OBSERVE	SPLENIC	FINFISH	SURFACE
GONDOLA	PREDICT	YARDMAN	DILEMMA	IGNEOUS	OBVERSE	SQUEEZE	FORFEIT	SURFEIT
GOODMAN	PRODIGY	YIDDISH	DINETTE	ILLEGAL	OFFENSE	SQUELCH	FORFEND	TAFFETA
GRADUAL	PRODUCE	ABREAST	DIREFUL	IMMENSE	ORDERLY	STEEPLE	FULFILL	TENFOLD
GRIDDLE	PRODUCT	ABSENCE	DISEASE	IMMERSE	PAGEANT	STRETCH	GABFEST	TINFOIL
GUMDROP	PRUDENT	ACREAGE	DISEUSE	IMPEACH	PAGEBOY	SWEETEN	GARFISH	TRAFFIC
HADDOCK	PUDDING	ADRENAL	DIVERGE	IMPEARL	PALETTE	TAKEOFF	GUNFIRE	TREFOIL
HANDBAG	READING	ADVERSE	DIVERSE	IMPERIL	PARESIS	THREADY	HALFWAY	TRUFFLE
HANDCAR	READOUT	AILERON	DOLEFUL	IMPETUS	PATELLA	TIBETAN	HAYFORK	UNIFORM
HANDFUL	REDDISH	ALGEBRA	DOYENNE	INCENSE	PHAETON	TOXEMIA	HOTFOOT	WARFARE
HANDGUN	RHODIUM	ALLEGRO	DUTEOUS	INDEXED	PHOENIX	TUNEFUL	KINFOLK	WELFARE
HANDOUT	ROADBED	ALLERGY	ECHELON	INFERNO	PHRENIC	TUTELAR	LEAFAGE	WOLFRAM
HANDSAW	ROADWAY	ALREADY	EFFENDI	INGENUE	PIMENTO	TWEETER	LEAFLET	ANAGRAM
HANDSEL	RUNDOWN	AMMETER	ELDERLY	INHERIT	PIPETTE	UNDERGO	MENFOLK	BAGGAGE
HANDSET	SANDBAG	AMNESIA	EMPEROR	INTEGER	PITEOUS	UNHEARD	MISFILE	BARGAIN
HARDPAN	SANDBAR	AMNESTY	ENDEMIC	INTENSE	POLECAT	UNKEMPT	MISFIRE	BEGGARY
HARDTOP	SANDHOG	ANAEMIA	ENTENTE	INTERIM	POLEMIC	UNLEARN	MUFFLER	BELGIAN
HEADING	SANDLOT	ANTENNA	ENVELOP	INVEIGH	POVERTY	UNLEASH	ORIFICE	BRIGADE
HEADMAN	SANDMAN	APPEASE	ENVENOM	INVERSE	PRAETOR	UNNERVE	OUTFACE	BRIGAND
HEADPIN	SARDINE	AQUEOUS	EQUERRY	JAVELIN	PREEMIE	UNWEAVE	OUTFLOW	BURGEON
HEADSET	SAWDUST	ARREARS	ESSENCE	JEWELER	PREEMPT	VALENCE	PALFREY	BURGESS
HEADWAY	SHADING	ARSENAL	EXCERPT	JEWELRY	PUBERTY	VEGETAL	PARFAIT	BURGHER
HOEDOWN	SHUDDER	ARSENIC	EXPENSE	JUKEBOX	QUIETUS	VETERAN	PEAFOWL	CHAGRIN
HOLDING	SMIDGEN	ASCETIC	FAIENCE	KINETIC	RACEWAY	VICEROY	PERFECT	CHIGGER
HOODLUM	SOLDIER	ATHEIST	FATEFUL	KNEECAP	RAREBIT	VINEGAR	PERFIDY	CHIGNON
HUMDRUM	STADIUM	ATTEMPT	FEDERAL	LATERAL	RECEIPT	WAKEFUL	PERFORM	CONGEAL
HUNDRED	STUDENT	AUREATE	FINESSE	LAYETTE	RECEIVE	WAVELET	PERFUME	CONGEST
IRIDIUM	STUDIED	AUREOLE	FIREARM	LIBERAL	RECENCY	WHEEDLE	PITFALL	DIAGRAM

DISGUST	REAGENT	DIEHARD	RAWHIDE	BETIMES	EXHIBIT	MAXIMAL	RETIRED	PERJURY
DOUGHTY	RIGGING	DISHRAG	REDHEAD	BEWITCH	EXPIATE	MAXIMUM	RETIREE	PROJECT
DRAGNET	RINGLET	DUCHESS	RIGHTLY	BILIOUS	EXTINCT	MEDIATE	REVIVAL	SUBJECT
DRAGOON	ROUGHEN	EGGHEAD	SIGHTED	BOLIVAR	FATIGUE	MEDICAL	RISIBLE	SUBJOIN
DUDGEON	SMUGGLE	ENCHAIN	SIGHTLY	BRAILLE	FINICKY	MEXICAN	SADIRON	BACKING
DUNGEON	SNUGGLE	ENCHANT	SOPHISM	BROIDER	FOLIAGE	MILITIA	SALIENT	BACKLIT
ELEGIAC	SORGHUM	ENTHUSE	SOPHIST	BROILER	FRAILTY	MIMICRY	SAPIENT	BACKLOG
EPIGRAM	STAGGER	ESTHETE	SWAHILI	BRUISER	FREIGHT	MINIBUS	SATIATE	BOOKEND
EXEGETE	STAGING	ETCHING	TECHNIC	CABINET	FURIOUS	MINIMAL	SATIETY	BOOKISH
FLIGHTY	SUGGEST	EUPHONY	TIGHTEN	CALIBER	GENITAL	MINIMUM	SATISFY	BOOKLET
FORGING	SURGEON	FASHION	TOEHOLD	CALIPER	GORILLA	MODICUM	SEMINAL	BUCKEYE
FORGIVE	SURGERY	FIGHTER	TOWHEAD	CAPITAL	HABITAT	MODISTE	SEMINAR	BUCKLER
FRAGILE	SWAGGER	FISHERY	TYPHOID	CAPITOL	HABITUE	MOHICAN	SERIOUS	BUCKRAM
FRIGATE	TANGENT	FISHING	TYPHOON	CARIBOU	HALIBUT	MONITOR	SHRIVEL	BUCKSAW
FROGMAN	TOGGERY	FOGHORN	UNCHAIN	CARIOUS	HELICAL	MUSICAL	SILICON	CHUKKER
GANGWAY	TOUGHEN	FOXHOLE	UPCHUCK	CEDILLA	HOLIDAY	NOMINAL	SIMILAR	COCKADE
GINGHAM	TRAGEDY	FUCHSIA	UPSHIFT	CILIATE	HORIZON	NOMINEE	SLEIGHT	COCKEYE
GOGGLES	TRIGGER	GODHEAD	WARHEAD	CITIZEN	HOSIERY	NOXIOUS	SOCIETY	COCKNEY
HAGGARD	VIRGULE	GODHOOD	WASHING	CIVILLY	HUMIDOR	OBLIQUE	SOLICIT	COCKPIT
HANGDOG	VULGATE	GOSHAWK	WASHOUT	CODICIL	HYGIENE	OBVIATE	SPOILER	COOKERY
HANGING	WAGGERY	HASHING	WASHTUB	CONICAL	ILEITIS	OBVIOUS	STRINGY	COOKOUT
HANGMAN	WAGGISH	HASHISH	WISHFUL	CONIFER	ILLICIT	OEDIPAL	SYRINGE	CUCKOLD
HANGOUT	WEIGHTY	HIGHBOY	WITHERS	COPILOT	IMPIETY	OFFICER	TAPIOCA	DESKTOP
HAUGHTY	WIDGEON	HIGHWAY	WITHOUT	COPIOUS	IMPINGE	OMNIBUS	TAXICAB	DOCKAGE
IMAGERY	WIGGLER	HOPHEAD	YESHIVA	CORINTH	IMPIOUS	OPTICAL	TEDIOUS	DUCKPIN
IMAGINE	WRIGGLE	INKHORN	ABRIDGE	CRUISER	INCISOR	OPTIMAL	TIDINGS	FOLKWAY
IMAGISM	AFGHANI	INSHORE	ACHIEVE	CUBICLE	INDICIA	OPTIMUM	TONIGHT	HACKMAN
KINGDOM	ALCHEMY	ISTHMUS	ADMIRAL	CURIOUS	INFIDEL	ORBITER	TOPICAL	HACKNEY
KINGPIN	AMPHORA	JODHPUR	ADVISED	CUTICLE	INFIELD	ORDINAL	TRAILER	HACKSAW
LAGGARD	ANCHOVY	KEYHOLE	AFRICAN	DECIBEL	INHIBIT	PACIFIC	TRAINEE	HICKORY
LANGUID	ANTHILL	LECHERY	AGAINST	DECIDED	INNINGS	PANICLE	TRAIPSE	HULKING
LANGUOR	ANTHRAX	LEGHORN	ALRIGHT	DECIMAL	INSIDER	PAPILLA	TRAITOR	HUNKERS
LARGESS	ANTHROP	LIGHTEN	AMBIENT	DEFIANT	INSIGHT	PATIENT	TYPICAL	HUSKING
LEAGUER	ARCHAIC	LIGHTER	ANCIENT	DEFICIT	INSIPID	PEDICAB	UNCIVIL	JACKASS
LEGGING	ARCHERY	LITHIUM	ANDIRON	DELIGHT	JACINTH	PELICAN	UNHINGE	JACKDAW
LINGUAL	ARCHIVE	MACHETE	ANTIGEN	DELIMIT	JANITOR	PERIGEE	UNHITCH	JACKLEG
LODGING	ARCHWAY	MACHINE	ANTIQUE	DELIVER	JUBILEE	PERIQUE	UPRIGHT	JACKPOT
LONGBOW	ARMHOLE	MANHOLE	ANXIETY	DEMIGOD	JUJITSU	PERIWIG	UPRIVER	KICKOFF
LONGING	ASPHALT	MANHOOD	ANXIOUS	DENIZEN	JUNIPER	PETIOLE	UPTIGHT	LEAKAGE
LUGGAGE	BASHFUL	MANHUNT	APRICOT	DEVIANT	JUPITER	PITIFUL	VALIANT	LINKAGE
MARGENT	BATHTUB	METHANE	AQUIFER	DEVIATE	LAMINAR	POLITIC	VANILLA	LOCKJAW
MONGREL	BEEHIVE	NAPHTHA	ARBITER	DEVILRY	LEGIBLE	PONIARD	VARIANT	LOCKNUT
NAUGHTY	BESHREW	NIGHTLY	ARRIVAL	DEVIOUS	LENIENT	PRAIRIE	VARIETY	LOCKOUT
NIAGARA	BETHINK	NONHERO	ARTICLE	DIGITAL	LEXICON	PURITAN	VARIOUS	LOOKOUT
NIGGARD	BIGHORN	NOTHING	ARTISAN	DIVIDER	LIAISON	PYRITES	VATICAN	MANKIND
OREGANO	BRAHMAN	NOWHERE	ARTISTE	DIVISOR	LIMITED	RADIANT	VEHICLE	MAWKISH
ORIGAMI	BRAHMIN	OFFHAND	ASPIRIN	DOMINIE	LUCIFER	RADIATE	VENISON	MILKMAN
OROGENY	BUSHING	ONSHORE	ATHIRST	DUBIETY	MAFIOSO	RADICAL	VESICLE	MILKSOP
OUTGROW	CASHIER	ORCHARD	AUDIBLE	DUBIOUS	MAHICAN	RAVIOLI	VICINAL	MUSKRAT
PENGUIN	CATHODE	PATHWAY	AUDITOR	DUTIFUL	MAKINGS	REBIRTH	VICIOUS	NANKEEN
PERGOLA	COCHLEA	PERHAPS	AURICLE	ECLIPSE	MALISON	RECITAL	VISIBLE	NECKTIE
PIGGISH	COWHAND	PINHOLE	BATISTE	ELLIPSE	MANIKIN	REFINED	VISITOR	PACKAGE
PILGRIM	COWHIDE	POTHEAD	BEDIZEN	ENLIVEN	MARIMBA	REGIMEN	VITIATE	PACKING
PROGENY	CUSHION	POTHERB	BELIEVE	ENTITLE	MARINER	RELIEVE	WYSIWYG	PARKWAY
PROGMAN	DASHIKI	POTHOLE	BENISON	ENVIOUS	MARITAL	RELIQUE	CONJOIN	PINKEYE
PROGRAM	DASHING	POTHOOK	BESIDES	EQUINOX	MATINEE	RESIDUE	CONJURE	RANKING
PUNGENT	DASHPOT	PREHEAT	BESIEGE	ETHICAL	MAXILLA	RETINUE	DISJOIN	RICKETS

RICKETY	BOWLING	EXCLUDE	INFLICT	PILLAGE	STILTED	WILLING	DORMANT	PREMIUM
RICKSHA	BULLDOG	EXPLAIN	INKLING	PILLBOX	STILTON	WILLOWY	DRUMLIN	PRIMACY
ROOKERY	BULLION	EXPLODE	ISOLATE	PILLION	STYLING	WITLESS	DRUMMER	PRIMARY
SICKBED	BULLOCK	EXPLOIT	ITALIAN	PILLORY	STYLISH	WORLDLY	EARMARK	PRIMATE
TICKING	CALLING	EXPLORE	JEALOUS	POLLACK	STYLIST	ZEALOUS	EARMUFF	PROMISE
TOPKNOT	CALLOUS	EYELASH	JOLLITY	POLLUTE	STYLIZE	ZEOLITE	ELEMENT	PROMOTE
TURKISH	CARLOAD	FAILING	KEELSON	POTLUCK	SUBLIME	ZILLION	ENAMOUR	RAIMENT
WALKOUT	CATLIKE	FAILURE	KILLING	POULTRY	SUNLAMP	ZOOLOGY	ENDMOST	RHOMBUS
WALKWAY	CEILING	FALLACY	KILLJOY	PRALINE	SWALLOW	ADAMANT	EREMITE	RUMMAGE
WEEKDAY	CHALICE	FALLOUT	LAWLESS	PRELATE	SWELTER	AILMENT	EXAMINE	SAWMILL
WEEKEND	CHALLIS	FEELING	LOWLAND	PRELUDE	SWOLLEN	AIRMAIL	EXAMPLE	SCAMPER
WICKIUP	CHOLERA	FETLOCK	LULLABY	PROLONG	TABLEAU	ALEMBIC	FARMING	SEEMING
WORKBAG	CODLING	FILLING	MAILBOX	PSALTER	TABLOID	ALIMENT	FERMENT	SEGMENT
WORKBOX	COLLAGE	FLYLEAF	MAILMAN	PUBLISH	TALLYHO	ALIMONY	FERMIUM	SHAMBLE
WORKDAY	COLLARD	FOOLERY	MALLARD	PULLMAN	TELLING	ALUMINA	FIGMENT	SHAMPOO
WORKING	COLLATE	FOOLISH	MALLEUS	PULLOUT	THULIUM	ALUMNUS	FILMDOM	SHIMMER
WORKMAN	COLLECT	FORLORN	MANLIKE	PURLIEU	TILLAGE	ANEMONE	FLEMING	SIAMESE
WORKOUT	COLLEEN	FOULARD	MIDLAND	PURLOIN	TOOLBOX	ANIMATE	FLEMISH	SLUMBER
ABALONE	COLLEGE	FOULING	MILLAGE	QUALIFY	TOPLESS	ANIMISM	FORMULA	SPUMONI
ABILITY	COLLIDE	FURLONG	MILLDAM	QUALITY	TRELLIS	ANOMALY	GARMENT	STAMINA
ABOLISH	COLLIER	GALLANT	MILLIME	RAILING	TRILOGY	ANYMORE	GERMANE	STAMMER
ACCLAIM	COLLOID	GALLEON	MILLING	RAILWAY	TROLLEY	ATOMIZE	GIMMICK	STOMACH
ACOLYTE	COOLANT	GALLERY	MILLION	RATLINE	TROLLOP	AUGMENT	GLAMOUR	STUMBLE
ADULATE	COULOMB	GALLIUM	MISLEAD	REALISM	TWILLED	AZIMUTH	GLIMMER	SUMMARY
AFFLICT	COWLICK	GALLOWS	MISLIKE	REALITY	UKULELE	BESMEAR	GLIMPSE	SUMMONS
AGELESS	COWLING	GARLAND	MOLLIFY	REALIZE	ULULATE	BISMUTH	GRAMMAR	SURMISE
AIMLESS	CRULLER	GEOLOGY	MOLLUSK	RECLAIM	UNBLOCK	BLEMISH	GREMLIN	TERMITE
AIRLIFT	CUTLASS	GIBLETS	MULLEIN	RECLAME	UNCLASP	BRAMBLE	GRIMACE	THIMBLE
AIRLINE	CUTLERY	GODLESS	MULLION	RECLINE	UNCLEAN	BRIMFUL	GROMMET	THYMINE
AMALGAM	CYCLIST	GODLIKE	NEGLECT	RECLUSE	UNCLOAK	BROMIDE	GRUMBLE	TOPMAST
AMPLIFY	CYCLONE	GOSLING	NEOLOGY	REDLINE	UNCLOSE	BROMINE	HAMMOCK	TOPMOST
AMYLASE	DARLING	GOULASH	NUCLEAR	REFLECT	UNSLING	BURMESE	HARMONY	TORMENT
ANALOGY	DEALING	GUILDER	NUCLEON	REPLACE	UROLOGY	CADMIUM	HOLMIUM	TRAMMEL
ANALYZE	DECLAIM	GUNLOCK	NUCLEUS	REPLETE	USELESS	CARMINE	HORMONE	TRAMPLE
ANILINE	DECLARE	HALLWAY	NUCLIDE	REPLICA	UTILITY	CHAMBER	HUMMOCK	TREMBLE
APOLOGY	DECLINE	HAPLESS	NULLIFY	ROLLICK	UTILIZE	CHAMFER	HUTMENT	TREMOLO
APOLUNE	DEFLATE	HAPLOID	OARLOCK	SAILING	VAULTED	CHAMOIS	ITEMIZE	TRUMPET
APPLAUD	DEFLECT	HAULAGE	OBELISK	SAPLING	VEILING	CHEMISE	JASMINE	TURMOIL
APPLIED	DEPLANE	HAYLOFT	OCCLUDE	SCALLOP	VILLAGE	CHEMIST	KREMLIN	VARMINT
ARTLESS	DEPLETE	HEALTHY	OCULIST	SCALPEL	VILLAIN	CHIMERA	LEMMING	VERMEIL
ATELIER	DEPLORE	HELLCAT	OPULENT	SEALANT	VILLEIN	CHIMNEY	MALMSEY	WHIMPER
ATHLETE	DIALECT	HELLENE	OUTLAST	SECLUDE	VILLOUS	CLAMBER	MAMMARY	ABANDON
BADLAND	DIPLOID	HELLION	OUTLINE	SHALLOP	VIOLATE	CLEMENT	MAMMOTH	ACONITE
BAILIFF	DIPLOMA	HEMLINE	OUTLIVE	SHALLOW	VIOLENT	CLIMATE	MERMAID	ADENINE
BALLAST	DISLIKE	HEMLOCK	OUTLOOK	SHELLAC	WAILFUL	COMMAND	MIDMOST	ADENOID
BALLOON	DULLARD	HILLOCK	OVULATE	SHELTER	WALLABY	COMMEND	OATMEAL	AGONIZE
BECLOUD	EARLOBE	HILLTOP	OXBLOOD	SHYLOCK	WALLEYE	COMMENT	ODDMENT	AMENITY
BEELINE	ECOLOGY	HOWLING	PADLOCK	SIBLING	WALLOON	COMMODE	OSTMARK	APANAGE
BELLBOY	EMULATE	IDOLIZE	PARLOUR	SIRLOIN	WARLESS	COMMUNE	PALMATE	ASININE
BELLHOP	ENCLAVE	IMPLODE	PARLOUS	SKILLET	WARLIKE	COMMUTE	PAYMENT	ASUNDER
BELLOWS	ENCLOSE	IMPLORE	PAYLOAD	SKYLARK	WARLOCK	CREMATE	PIGMENT	BANNOCK
BILLION	ENDLESS	INCLINE	PEELING	SKYLINE	WARLORD	CRIMSON	PISMIRE	BLANKET
BIOLOGY	ENGLISH	INCLOSE	PERLITE	SMELTER	WEALTHY	CRUMBLE	PLUMAGE	BLINDER
BIPLANE	ENPLANE	INCLUDE	PHALANX	SMOLDER	WEDLOCK	CRUMPET	PLUMBER	BLINKER
BOULDER	ENSLAVE	INFLAME	PHALLIC	SOULFUL	WETLAND	CRUMPLE	PLUMMET	BLINTZE
BOWLDER	ERELONG	INFLATE	PHALLUS	SPELLER	WILLFUL	DIAMOND	PREMIER	BLUNDER
BOWLINE	EXCLAIM	INFLECT	PHILTER	STELLAR	WILLIES	DISMISS	PREMISE	BOUNCER

BOUNDEN	GRANARY	POINTED	TURNKEY	BOLOGNA	JEHOVAH	UNHORSE	DISPLAY	RESPITE
BURNISH	GRANDAM	POINTER	TURNOFF	BOROUGH	KILOTON	UNLOOSE	DISPORT	RESPOND
BURNOUT	GRANDEE	PRONOUN	TURNOUT	BRIOCHE	LABORED	UNMORAL	DISPOSE	SAMPLER
CANNERY	GRANITE	QUANTUM	TWINKLE	BROODER	LACONIC	UNMOVED	DISPUTE	SCAPULA
CANNULA	GRANTEE	QUININE	UNKNOWN	BUCOLIC	LANOLIN	UNSOUND	DOLPHIN	SCEPTER
CARNAGE	GRANULE	QUINTAL	UNSNARL	CABOOSE	MASONIC	VAMOOSE	DRAPERY	SCEPTIC
CHANCEL	GRENADE	QUINTET	URANIUM	CALOMEL	MASONRY	WAGONER	DROPLET	SCUPPER
CHANCRE	GRINDER	QUONDAM	URANOUS	CALORIC	MEIOSIS	WHOOPLA	DROPPER	SEAPORT
CHANNEL	GRUNION	RAINBOW	URINARY	CALORIE	MITOSIS	WIDOWER	DUMPING	SERPENT
CHANSON	GUANINE	RAUNCHY	URINATE	CAROTID	MONOCLE	ADAPTER	EARPLUG	SHAPELY
CHANTEY	GUNNERY	REENTRY	UTENSIL	CAROUSE	MONOMER	ADIPOSE	FLAPPER	SKEPTIC
CHANTRY	HAFNIUM	REGNANT	VARNISH	CHROMIC	MOROCCO	AIRPORT	FLIPPER	SKIPPER
CHINESE	HARNESS	REMNANT	VERNIER	CHRONIC	OBLOQUY	AIRPOST	GRAPHIC	SLIPPER
CHINOOK	HEINOUS	REUNION	WARNING	COCONUT	OCTOBER	ANAPEST	GRAPNEL	SOUPCON
CHINTZY	HOBNAIL	RHENIUM	WINNING	COLOGNE	OCTOPUS	ARAPAHO	GRAPPLE	STEPSON
CLANGOR	HYMNODY	ROUNDUP	WITNESS	COLONEL	ONGOING	ASEPTIC	HAPPILY	STIPEND
CLINKER	ILLNESS	RUINOUS	WRANGLE	COLORED	ORTOLAN	AUSPICE	HARPOON	STIPPLE
COGNATE	IRANIAN	RUNNING	WRINGER	COROLLA	OSMOSIS	BAGPIPE	HELPING	STOPGAP
COINAGE	IRONING	SAINTLY	WRINKLE	CORONAL	OTTOMAN	BEDPOST	HENPECK	STOPPER
CONNECT	KERNING	SAUNTER	WRONGLY	CORONER	PANOPLY	BESPEAK	HOSPICE	STUPEFY
CONNIVE	KEYNOTE	SCANDAL	WRYNECK	CORONET	PAPOOSE	BUMPKIN	INSPECT	STYPTIC
CONNOTE	LAUNDER	SCANNER	YOUNKER	CROOKED	POCOSIN	CAMPHOR	INSPIRE	SUPPORT
CORNCOB	LAUNDRY	SCENERY	ZIONISM	CULOTTE	POPOVER	CARPORT	JETPORT	SUPPOSE
CORNICE	LEONINE	SHINGLE	ABDOMEN	DEBOUCH	REBOUND	CHAPEAU	KEEPING	SURPASS
COUNCIL	LIGNIFY	SIGNIFY	ABSOLVE	DECODER	RECOUNT	CHAPLET	KRYPTON	SURPLUS
COUNSEL	LIGNITE	SLANDER	ACCOUNT	DECORUM	RECOVER	CHAPMAN	LAMPOON	SUSPECT
COUNTER	LIONIZE	SLENDER	ACROBAT	DELOUSE	REDOUBT	CHAPTER	LAMPREY	SUSPEND
COUNTRY	MAGNATE	SOUNDER	ACRONYM	DEMONIC	REDOUND	CHIPPER	LEMPIRA	SYMPTOM
CRANIUM	MAGNETO	SPANGLE	ADJOURN	DEMOTIC	REJOICE	CHOPPER	LEOPARD	TADPOLE
CRINKLE	MAGNIFY	SPANIEL	AEROBIC	DEPOSIT	REMODEL	CLAPPER	MARPLOT	TEMPERA
CUNNING	MAINTOP	SPANISH	AEROSOL	DEVOLVE	REMORSE	CLIPPER	MAYPOLE	TEMPEST
CYANIDE	MANNISH	SPINACH	AGROUND	DEVOTED	REMOUNT	COMPACT	MISPLAY	TIMPANI
DEANERY	MAUNDER	SPINDLE	ALCOHOL	DEVOTEE	RESOLVE	COMPANY	MORPHIA	TOPPING
DIGNIFY	MEANDER	SPINDLY	ALMONER	DISOBEY	RESOUND	COMPARE	NONPLUS	TORPEDO
DIGNITY	MEANING	SPONSOR	AMMONIA	DIVORCE	RETOUCH	COMPASS	NUTPICK	TOWPATH
DRUNKEN	MISNAME	STANDBY	ANTONYM	ECLOGUE	REVOLVE	COMPEER	OUTPLAY	TRAPEZE
DWINDLE	MORNING	STENCIL	APPOINT	EIDOLON	RIPOSTE	COMPETE	OUTPOST	TRIPLET
EARNEST	MOUNTIE	SURNAME	APROPOS	EMBOWER	SAMOVAR	COMPILE	OUTPULL	TRIPLEX
EBONITE	NOONDAY	SWINDLE	ARMORER	EMPOWER	SCHOLAR	COMPLEX	PALPATE	TROPISM
ECONOMY	OMINOUS	TANNERY	ASTOUND	ENDORSE	SCOOTER	COMPORT	PEPPERY	UTOPIAN
EMANATE	OPENING	TARNISH	ATROPHY	ENFORCE	SCROTUM	COMPOSE	PERPLEX	VAMPIRE
EMINENT	OPINION	TEENAGE	AUTOPSY	ENNOBLE	SIROCCO	COMPOST	POMPANO	VESPERS
ENSNARE	PANNIER	TERNARY	BALONEY	EXPOUND	SOJOURN	COMPOTE	POMPOUS	VULPINE
EVENING	PENNANT	THINNER	BARONET	GAVOTTE	SPLOTCH	COMPUTE	PREPARE	WARPATH
FERNERY	PFENNIG	THUNDER	BAROQUE	HEROICS	STROPHE	COPPICE	PREPUCE	WASPISH
FIANCEE	PHANTOM	TOENAIL	BAYONET	HEROINE	SYNONYM	COUPLET	PROPANE	WEEPING
FINNISH	PHONEME	TONNAGE	BAZOOKA	HEROISM	THEOREM	COWPOKE	PROPHET	WHIPPET
FLANKER	PHONICS	TONNEAU	BEDOUIN	HOMONYM	THROATY	CRIPPLE	PROPMAN	WHIPSAW
FLANNEL	PIANIST	TORNADO	BEGONIA	IGNOBLE	THROUGH	CROPPER	PROPOSE	WHOPPER
FOUNDER	PINNACE	TRANSIT	BEHOOVE	IMMORAL	TIMOTHY	CRYPTIC	PUMPKIN	WRAPPER
FOUNDRY	PINNATE	TRANSOM	BELOVED	IMPOUND	TROOPER	CULPRIT	PURPORT	BANQUET
FRANTIC	PIONEER	TRINITY	BETOKEN	INBOARD	UNBOSOM	DAUPHIN	PURPOSE	BOUQUET
FURNACE	PLANTAR	TRINKET	BIFOCAL	INBOUND	UNBOWED	DESPAIR	RAMPAGE	COEQUAL
FURNISH	PLANTER	TRUNDLE	BIPOLAR	INDOORS	UNCOUTH	DESPISE	RAMPANT	CONQUER
GAINFUL	PLENARY	TSUNAMI	BIVOUAC	INDORSE	UNCOVER	DESPITE	RAMPART	CROQUET
GAINSAY	PLUNDER	TURNERY	BLOODED	INVOICE	UNDOING	DESPOIL	RAPPORT	JONQUIL
GARNISH	PLUNGER	TURNING	BLOOPER	INVOLVE	UNGODLY	DESPOND	RESPECT	KUMQUAT

LACQUER	COURTLY	FERRULE	MURRAIN	SCARIFY	UNERASE	CELSIUS	GINSENG	OFFSIDE
MARQUEE	CUPRITE	FIBROID	NARRATE	SCARLET	UNFROCK	CENSURE	GLISTEN	OILSKIN
MARQUIS	CURRANT	FLORIST	NITRATE	SECRECY	UNGROUP	CESSION	GLISTER	OLDSTER
PARQUET	CURRENT	FURRIER	NITRIFY	SECRETE	UNTRIED	CHASSIS	GODSEND	ONESELF
UNEQUAL	CYPRESS	FURRING	NITRITE	SERRATE	UNTRUTH	CHASTEN	GRISTLE	OPOSSUM
ADDRESS	CZARINA	GARROTE	NOURISH	SERRIED	UPBRAID	CLASSIC	GUMSHOE	OUTSELL
AFFRONT	DEBRIEF	GEARBOX	OBTRUDE	SHARPEN	UPDRAFT	CLASTIC	GUNSHOT	OUTSIDE
AMERIND	DEERFLY	GHERKIN	OCARINA	SHARPER	UPGRADE	CLOSURE	HAMSTER	OUTSIZE
AMOROUS	DEFRAUD	GLORIFY	ONEROUS	SHARPIE	VAGRANT	CLUSTER	HASSOCK	OUTSTAY
ANARCHY	DEFROST	GOURMET	OPERATE	SHERBET	VIBRANT	CONSENT	HAYSEED	PAISLEY
ANDROID	DEGRADE	GUARANI	OPPRESS	SHERIFF	VIBRATE	CONSIGN	HERSELF	PARSING
APPRISE	DEPRAVE	GUERDON	OSTRICH	SHORING	VIBRATO	CONSIST	HIMSELF	PARSLEY
APPROVE	DEPRESS	HAIRCUT	OUTRAGE	SHORTEN	VITRIFY	CONSOLE	HIPSTER	PARSNIP
ARMREST	DEPRIVE	HAIRPIN	OUTRANK	SHORTLY	VITRIOL	CONSORT	HIRSUTE	PASSAGE
ASCRIBE	DERRICK	HARRIER	OVERACT	SNORKEL	WARRANT	CONSULT	HOLSTER	PASSING
ASTRIDE	DETRACT	HAYRICK	OVERAGE	SOPRANO	WARRIOR	CONSUME	HOOSIER	PASSION
ATTRACT	DETRAIN	HEARING	OVERALL	SPARING	WHEREAS	CORSAGE	HOTSHOT	PASSIVE
AVARICE	DIARIST	HEARKEN	OVERARM	SPARKLE	WHEREAT	CORSAIR	HOUSING	PASSKEY
AVERAGE	DIGRAPH	HEARSAY	OVERAWE	SPARROW	WHEREBY	COSSACK	IRKSOME	PEASANT
BARRAGE	DIGRESS	HEARTEN	OVERFLY	SPIRANT	WHEREIN	COWSLIP	KIDSKIN	PENSION
BARRIER	DISROBE	HEIRESS	OVERJOY	STARTLE	WHEREOF	CROSIER	KINSHIP	PENSIVE
BARRING	DISRUPT	HERRING	OVERLAP	STARTUP	WHEREON	CRUSADE	KINSMAN	PERSIAN
BARROOM	DIURNAL	HORRIFY	OVERLAY	STERILE	WHERETO	CRYSTAL	LAWSUIT	PERSIST
BEARING	DOORMAN	HYDRANT	OVERRUN	STERNUM	WHORLED	CUISINE	LEISURE	PHYSICS
BEDROCK	DOORMAT	HYDRATE	OVERSEA	STIRRUP	YTTRIUM	CURSIVE	LINSEED	PHYSIOL
BEDROLL	DOORWAY	HYDROUS	OVERSEE	STORAGE	ABYSMAL	CURSORY	LISSOME	PIASTER
BEDROOM	EARRING	IMPRESS	OVERTOP	STORIED	ABYSSAL	DENSITY	LOBSTER	PIGSKIN
BEGRIME	EMBRACE	IMPRINT	PAPRIKA	SUCROSE	AIRSHIP	DESSERT	MAESTRO	PILSNER
BETROTH	EMBROIL	IMPROVE	PATRIOT	SUNRISE	AIRSICK	DISSECT	MANSARD	PLASTER
BLARNEY	EMBRYOL	INCRUST	PATROON	SUNROOF	APOSTLE	DISSENT	MANSION	PLASTIC
BOURBON	EMERALD	INERTIA	PAYROLL	SUPREME	BANSHEE	DOSSIER	MARSHAL	POSSESS
BULRUSH	EMERITA	INGRAFT	PETRIFY	SWARTHY	BASSOON	DRASTIC	MASSAGE	POTSHOT
CAPRICE	EMPRESS	INGRAIN	PHARAOH	TAPROOM	BATSMAN	DRESSER	MASSEUR	PRESAGE
CARRIER	ENCRUST	INGRATE	PHARYNX	TAPROOT	BEASTLY	EARSHOT	MASSIVE	PRESENT
CARRION	ENGRAFT	INGRESS	PIBROCH	TERRACE	BEDSIDE	ELASTIC	MEASLES	PRESIDE
CARRYON	ENGRAVE	INGROWN	PRORATE	TERRAIN	BEDSORE	ELISION	MEASURE	PRESOAK
CHARGER	ENGROSS	INTRANS	PUERILE	TERRIER	BEESWAX	ELUSIVE	MESSAGE	PRESUME
CHARIOT	ENTRAIN	INTROIT	PUTREFY	TERRIFY	BERSERK	ELYSIUM	MESSIAH	PROSAIC
CHARITY	ENTRANT	INTRUDE	QUARREL	THERAPY	BLESSED	EPISODE	MINSTER	PROSODY
CHARMER	ENTREAT	INTRUST	QUARTER	THEREAT	BLISTER	EPISTLE	MISSEND	PROSPER
CHARNEL	ENTROPY	ITERATE	QUARTET	THEREBY	BLOSSOM	EROSION	MISSILE	PULSATE
CHARTER	ENTRUST	JOURNAL	RECRUIT	THEREIN	BLUSTER	EROSIVE	MISSING	PUNSTER
CHERISH	EPERGNE	JOURNEY	REDRESS	THEREOF	BOBSLED	EVASION	MISSION	PURSUIT
CHEROOT	ETERNAL	JOYRIDE	REFRACT	THEREON	BOLSTER	EYESORE	MISSIVE	RANSACK
CHORALE	EXCRETA	LATRINE	REFRAIN	THERETO	BORSCHT	FALSIFY	MISSTEP	REDSKIN
CHORTLE	EXCRETE	LEARNED	REFRESH	THERMAL	BRISKET	FIRSTLY	MOBSTER	ROASTER
CLARIFY	EXPRESS	LEPROSY	REGRESS	THERMOS	BRISTLE	FISSILE	MOISTEN	ROISTER
CLARION	EXTRACT	LIBRARY	REGROUP	THORIUM	BRUSQUE	FISSION	MONSOON	ROOSTER
CLARITY	EXTREME	MACRAME	REPRESS	THYROID	CAESURA	FISSURE	MONSTER	RUSSIAN
COARSEN	EXTRUDE	MICROBE	REPRINT	TORRENT	CAISSON	FLESHLY	NEWSBOY	SAUSAGE
COMRADE	FAIRING	MIDRIFF	REPRISE	TOURIST	CAPSIZE	FLUSTER	NEWSMAN	SEASICK
CORRECT	FAIRWAY	MIGRANT	REPROOF	TOURNEY	CAPSTAN	FORSAKE	NOISOME	SEASIDE
CORRODE	FARRAGO	MIGRATE	REPROVE	TRIREME	CAPSULE	FRESHEN	NONSKED	SEISMIC
CORRUPT	FARRIER	MISREAD	RETRACE	UMBRAGE	CARSICK	FRESHET	NONSTOP	SENSORY
COURAGE	FEARFUL	MISRULE	RETRACT	UNARMED	CASSAVA	FRUSTUM	NURSERY	SENSUAL
COURIER	FEBRILE	MOORING	RETREAD	UNCROSS	CASSOCK	FULSOME	OARSMAN	SESSILE
COURSER	FERROUS	MUDROOM	RETREAT	UNDRESS	CAUSTIC	GHASTLY	ODYSSEY	SESSION

SHYSTER	BAPTISM	CLOTHES	EMOTION	HEATHER	MORTIFY	POSTWAR	STATELY	WASTREL
SPASTIC	BAPTIST	CLOTURE	EPITAPH	HECTARE	MORTISE	POTTAGE	STATION	WATTAGE
SUBSIDE	BAPTIZE	CLUTTER	EPITHET	HINTING	MUSTANG	POTTERY	STATURE	WEATHER
SUBSIDY	BASTARD	COATING	EPITOME	HISTORY	MUSTARD	PRATTLE	STATUTE	WESTERN
SUBSIST	BASTION	CONTACT	FACTION	HOSTAGE	MYSTERY	PRETEEN	STUTTER	WHATNOT
SUBSOIL	BATTERY	CONTAIN	FACTORY	HOSTESS	MYSTIFY	PRETEND	SUBTILE	WHETHER
SUNSPOT	BATTING	CONTEMN	FACTUAL	HOSTILE	NARTHEX	PRETEXT	SUCTION	WHITHER
TAPSTER	BEATIFY	CONTEND	FANTAIL	HOSTLER	NEITHER	PRETZEL	SUITING	WHITING
TENSILE	BEATNIK	CONTENT	FANTASY	IMITATE	NEPTUNE	PRITHEE	SULTANA	WHITISH
TENSION	BEDTIME	CONTEST	FARTHER	INITIAL	NETTING	PROTEAN	SURTOUT	WHITLOW
THISTLE	BELTWAY	CONTEXT	FEATHER	INSTALL	NEUTRAL	PROTECT	SUSTAIN	WHITTLE
THYSELF	BENTHIC	CONTORT	FEATURE	INSTANT	NEUTRON	PROTEGE	SYSTOLE	WISTFUL
TIPSTER	BENTHOS	CONTOUR	FERTILE	INSTATE	NORTHER	PROTEIN	TACTICS	WITTING
TOASTER	BESTIAL	CONTRIB	FESTIVE	INSTEAD	NOSTRIL	PROTEST	TACTILE	WRITING
TONSURE	BIOTITE	CONTROL	FESTOON	INSTILL	NOSTRUM	PUSTULE	TANTRUM	ACCUSAL
TOPSAIL	BITTERN	CORTEGE	FICTION	ISOTOPE	NUPTIAL	QUETZAL	TATTING	ACCUSED
TOPSIDE	BITTERS	COSTIVE	FIFTEEN	JITTERS	NURTURE	RAGTIME	TEKTITE	ACQUIRE
TOPSOIL	BLATANT	COSTUME	FISTFUL	JOTTING	ONETIME	RAPTURE	TESTATE	ACTUARY
TORSION	BLATHER	COTTAGE	FISTULA	JUSTICE	ORATION	RATTLER	TESTIFY	ACTUATE
TRESTLE	BLOTTER	COUTURE	FITTING	JUSTIFY	ORATORY	RATTRAP	TEXTILE	ADJUDGE
TRISECT	BOATMAN	CRITTER	FIXTURE	LACTATE	OROTUND	RECTIFY	TEXTURE	ADJUNCT
TRUSTEE	BOOTLEG	CULTURE	FLATBED	LACTEAL	OVATION	RECTORY	THITHER	ALBUMEN
TUESDAY	BRITISH	CURTAIL	FLATCAR	LACTOSE	PANTHER	REPTILE	TORTONI	ALBUMIN
TUSSOCK	BRITTLE	CURTAIN	FLATTEN	LANTANA	PARTAKE	RESTIVE	TORTURE	AMPUTEE
TWISTER	BROTHEL	CUSTARD	FLATTER	LANTERN	PARTIAL	RESTORE	TRITIUM	ANGUISH
TWOSOME	BROTHER	CUSTODY	FLATTOP	LAOTIAN	PARTING	ROOTLET	TUITION	ANGULAR
UNUSUAL	BRUTISH	CUTTING	FLOTSAM	LATTICE	PARTITE	ROSTRUM	TWITTER	ANNUITY
VARSITY	BUNTING	DASTARD	FLUTIST	LEATHER	PARTNER	ROUTINE	UMPTEEN	ANNULAR
VERSIFY	BUTTOCK	DAYTIME	FLUTTER	LECTERN	PARTWAY	RUPTURE	UNCTION	ARBUTUS
VERSION	CAITIFF	DEATHLY	FOOTAGE	LECTURE	PASTERN	SALTBOX	UNITARY	ARDUOUS
WARSHIP	CANTATA	DENTATE	FOOTING	LEFTISM	PASTIME	SALTINE	UNITIZE	ASSUAGE
WASSAIL	CANTEEN	DENTIST	FOOTMAN	LEOTARD	PASTURE	SCATTER	UNSTRAP	ASSURED
WAYSIDE	CAPTAIN	DENTURE	FOOTPAD	LETTUCE	PATTERN	SCUTTLE	UPSTAGE	BEGUILE
WEASAND	CAPTION	DESTINE	FORTIFY	LISTING	PENTIUM	SEATING	UPSTART	BEGUINE
WHISKER	CAPTIVE	DESTINY	FORTRAN	LOATHLY	PERTAIN	SECTARY	UPSTATE	BEQUEST
WHISKEY	CAPTURE	DESTROY	FORTUNE	LOTTERY	PERTURB	SECTION	URETHRA	BITUMEN
WHISPER	CARTAGE	DEXTRIN	FRETFUL	LUSTRAL	PETTISH	SELTZER	VANTAGE	BROUGHT
WHISTLE	CARTOON	DICTATE	FRETSAW	MALTOSE	PICTURE	SENTIMO	VENTRAL	CALUMET
WINSOME	CASTING	DICTION	FRITTER	MANTEAU	PIGTAIL	SETTING	VENTURE	CALUMNY
WORSHIP	CASTLED	DISTAFF	FURTHER	MARTIAL	PLATEAU	SEXTANT	VERTIGO	CERUMEN
WORSTED	CATTAIL	DISTANT	FURTIVE	MARTIAN	PLATING	SHATTER	VESTIGE	CROUTON
WRESTLE	CAUTION	DISTEND	FUSTIAN	MARTINI	PLATOON	SHOTGUN	VESTING	CUMULUS
ABSTAIN	CENTARE	DISTICH	GANTLET	MASTERY	PLATTER	SHUTOUT	VESTURE	DEFUNCT
ACETATE	CENTAUR	DISTILL	GASTRIC	MASTIFF	PLOTTER	SHUTTER	VICTORY	DILUENT
ACETONE	CENTAVO	DISTORT	GENTEEL	MASTOID	PONTIFF	SHUTTLE	VICTUAL	DIVULGE
AGITATE	CENTIME	DISTURB	GENTIAN	MATTINS	PONTOON	SIXTEEN	VINTAGE	DRAUGHT
AMATEUR	CENTIMO	DOGTROT	GENTILE	MATTOCK	PORTAGE	SKITTER	VINTNER	DROUGHT
AMATIVE	CENTRAL	DUCTILE	GESTAPO	MEATMAN	PORTEND	SLATHER	VIRTUAL	ENQUIRE
AMATORY	CENTURY	DUSTPAN	GESTURE	MEETING	PORTENT	SLITHER	VITTLES	EPAULET
ANATOMY	CERTAIN	EARTHEN	GLITTER	MENTHOL	PORTICO	SMOTHER	VOLTAGE	ESQUIRE
ANOTHER	CERTIFY	EARTHLY	GLOTTIS	MENTION	PORTION	SPATIAL	VOLTAIC	ESTUARY
ANYTIME	CHATEAU	EASTERN	GLUTTON	MESTIZO	PORTRAY	SPATTER	VULTURE	EXPUNGE
APATITE	CHATTEL	ECSTASY	GRATIFY	MIDTOWN	POSTAGE	SPATULA	WAGTAIL	FACULTY
ASHTRAY	CHATTER	EDITION	GRATING	MISTAKE	POSTBOY	SPITTLE	WANTING	FATUITY
AUCTION	CHUTNEY	EGOTISM	HALTING	MISTRAL	POSTERN	SPOTTER	WARTHOG	FATUOUS
AUSTERE	CISTERN	ELITISM	HAUTEUR	MIXTURE	POSTMAN	SPUTNIK	WARTIME	FLOUNCE
AUSTRAL	CLATTER	EMITTER	HEATHEN	MONTAGE	POSTURE	SPUTTER	WASTAGE	FRAUGHT

GENUINE	SOLUBLE	HALVERS	CUTWORM	BAUXITE	AIRMAIL	CENTARE	DEVIANT	FOULARD
GRAUPEL	SPLURGE	HARVARD	DOGWOOD	COAXIAL	AIRWAVE	CENTAUR	DEVIATE	FRIGATE
GROUPER	SPOUSAL	HARVEST	DRAWING	COEXIST	ALREADY	CENTAVO	DICTATE	FROWARD
GROUPIE	STAUNCH	LATVIAN	ENDWAYS	FLEXURE	AMYLASE	CERTAIN	DIEHARD	FURNACE
IMPULSE	STRUDEL	NAIVETE	ENDWISE	INEXACT	ANIMATE	CHICANE	DIGRAPH	GALLANT
INCUBUS	TABULAR	NAIVETY	ENTWINE	MARXISM	ANOMALY	CHICANO	DISBAND	GARBAGE
INDULGE	TENUOUS	NERVOUS	EYEWASH	PROXIMO	APANAGE	CHORALE	DISCARD	GARLAND
INHUMAN	TENURED	NIRVANA	FLOWERY	ACRYLIC	APPEASE	CILIATE	DISDAIN	GERMANE
INQUEST	TEQUILA	OLIVINE	FORWARD	BICYCLE	APPLAUD	CLIMATE	DISEASE	GESTAPO
INQUIRE	THOUGHT	OUTVOTE	FROWARD	CALYPSO	ARAPAHO	COCKADE	DISTAFF	GIZZARD
INQUIRY	THRUWAY	PARVENU	GUNWALE	COPYBOY	ARCHAIC	COGNATE	DISTANT	GOSHAWK
INSULAR	TITULAR	PEEVISH	HAYWIRE	COPYCAT	ARREARS	COINAGE	DOCKAGE	GOULASH
INSULIN	TOLUENE	PERVADE	HOGWASH	HALYARD	ASPHALT	COLLAGE	DOGBANE	GRANARY
INSURED	TRIUMPH	PERVERT	INDWELL	KATYDID	ASSUAGE	COLLARD	DOGCART	GRENADE
INSURER	TROUBLE	PLUVIAL	INKWELL	LADYBUG	ATHWART	COLLATE	DORMANT	GRIMACE
JANUARY	TROUNCE	PREVAIL	JAYWALK	LANYARD	ATTRACT	COMMAND	DULLARD	GUARANI
JEJUNUM	TUBULAR	PREVENT	KNOWING	MIDYEAR	AUREATE	COMPACT	EARMARK	GUNWALE
JOCULAR	UNGUENT	PREVIEW	LAPWING	PAPYRUS	AVERAGE	COMPANY	ECSTASY	HAGGARD
JUGULAR	UNLUCKY	PRIVACY	LEEWARD	PLAYBOY	AVOCADO	COMPARE	EDUCATE	HALYARD
LIQUEFY	UNQUIET	PRIVATE	MIDWEEK	PLAYLET	AWKWARD	COMPASS	ELEVATE	HARVARD
LIQUEUR	UNQUOTE	PROVERB	MIDWIFE	PLAYPEN	BADLAND	COMRADE	EMANATE	HAULAGE
LITURGY	UPSURGE	PROVIDE	MUGWUMP	POLYGON	BAGGAGE	CONCAVE	EMBRACE	HECTARE
MANUMIT	VACUITY	PROVISO	NARWHAL	POLYMER	BALLAST	CONTACT	EMERALD	HERBAGE
MAZURKA	VACUOLE	PROVOKE	NETWARE	PRAYING	BANDAGE	CONTAIN	EMULATE	HOBNAIL
MEDULLA	VACUOUS	PROVOST	NETWORK	RECYCLE	BARGAIN	COOLANT	ENCHAIN	HOECAKE
MINUEND	VALUATE	PURVIEW	OUTWARD	UNDYING	BARRAGE	CORDAGE	ENCHANT	HOGBACK
MINUTIA	VAQUERO	SALVAGE	OUTWEAR	BENZENE	BASTARD	CORSAGE	ENCLAVE	HOGWASH
MODULAR	VOGUISH	SELVAGE	OUTWORK	BENZINE	BEDFAST	CORSAIR	ENDWAYS	HOSTAGE
NATURAL	VOLUBLE	SERVANT	OUTWORN	BENZOIN	BEGGARY	COSSACK	ENGRAFT	HOTCAKE
NOCUOUS	WROUGHT	SERVICE	PINWORM	BRAZIER	BENEATH	COTTAGE	ENGRAVE	HUSBAND
NONUSER	ZYMURGY	SERVILE	PLOWBOY	BUZZARD	BIPLANE	COURAGE	ENPLANE	HYDRANT
OSSUARY	ATAVISM	SERVING	PLOWMAN	DRIZZLE	BLATANT	COWHAND	ENSLAVE	HYDRATE
PABULUM	BRAVADO	SHAVING	PLYWOOD	FRAZZLE	BOMBARD	CREMATE	ENSNARE	IMITATE
PETUNIA	BRAVERY	SLAVERY	PROWESS	FRIZZLE	BOMBAST	CRUSADE	ENTRAIN	IMPEACH
PIQUANT	BRAVURA	SLAVISH	RAGWEED	GIZZARD	BONDAGE	CRYBABY	ENTRANT	IMPEARL
PLAUDIT	BREVITY	SOLVENT	REDWOOD	GLAZIER	BRAVADO	CUPCAKE	EPITAPH	INBOARD
POPULAR	CANVASS	SUBVERT	SAPWOOD	GRAZIER	BRIGADE	CURRANT	ESTUARY	INEXACT
REBUILD	CHEVIOT	SURVIVE	SEAWALL	GRIZZLY	BRIGAND	CURTAIL	EXCLAIM	INFLAME
REFUGEE	CHEVRON	TRAVAIL	SEAWARD	MUEZZIN	BROCADE	CURTAIN	EXPIATE	INFLATE
REGULAR	CIVVIES	TRIVIAL	SEAWEED	PIZZAZZ	BUFFALO	CUSTARD	EXPLAIN	INGRAFT
REPULSE	CLAVIER	TRIVIUM	SHAWNEE	RHIZOME	BULWARK	CUTBACK	EXTRACT	INGRAIN
REPUTED	CONVENE	VERVAIN	SHOWMAN		BUZZARD	CUTLASS	EYEBALL	INGRATE
REQUEST	CONVENT	AIRWAVE	SKIWEAR		CABBAGE	DASTARD	EYELASH	INSTALL
REQUIEM	CONVERT	ALEWIFE	SKYWARD		CANTATA	DECEASE	EYEWASH	INSTANT
REQUIRE	CONVICT	ANYWISE	STEWARD	**5TH LETTER**	CANVASS	DECLAIM	FALLACY	INSTATE
REQUITE	CONVOKE	ATHWART	TINWARE		CAPTAIN	DECLARE	FANFARE	INTRANS
RIVULET	CRAVING	AWKWARD	UNAWARE	ABREAST	CARCASS	DEFIANT	FANTAIL	ISOLATE
ROTUNDA	CREVICE	BETWEEN	UNTWINE	ABSTAIN	CARFARE	DEFLATE	FANTASY	ITERATE
SAGUARO	CULVERT	BETWIXT	UNTWIST	ACCLAIM	CARNAGE	DEFRAUD	FARRAGO	JACKASS
SAMURAI	DERVISH	BLOWGUN	UPSWEPT	ACETATE	CARTAGE	DEGRADE	FATBACK	JANUARY
SCOURGE	ELEVATE	BLOWOUT	UPSWING	ACREAGE	CASCADE	DENTATE	FIREARM	JAYWALK
SCRUFFY	FAUVISM	BROWNIE	VANWARD	ACTUARY	CASCARA	DEPLANE	FOLIAGE	LACTATE
SCRUPLE	FERVENT	BROWSER	WAXWING	ACTUATE	CASSAVA	DEPRAVE	FONDANT	LAGGARD
SECULAR	FLAVOUR	BULWARK	WAXWORK	ADAMANT	CATCALL	DESCANT	FOOTAGE	LANTANA
SEQUENT	FLIVVER	CATWALK	WAYWARD	ADULATE	CATTAIL	DESPAIR	FOREARM	LANYARD
SEQUOIA	GRAVITY	CHOWDER	WAYWORN	AFGHANI	CATWALK	DETRACT	FORSAKE	LEAFAGE
SINUOUS	GRAVURE	CROWBAR	ASEXUAL	AGITATE	CEMBALO	DETRAIN	FORWARD	LEAKAGE

LEEWARD	OUTRANK	PROBATE	SURPASS	VINTAGE	EQUABLE	STUMBLE	MEXICAN	CITADEL
LEOPARD	OUTWARD	PROFANE	SUSTAIN	VIOLATE	EXHIBIT	TENABLE	MIMICRY	DECIDED
LEOTARD	OVERACT	PROPANE	TAMBALA	VITIATE	FIREBOX	THIMBLE	MIRACLE	DECODER
LIBRARY	OVERAGE	PRORATE	TANBARK	VOLCANO	FIREBUG	TOOLBOX	MODICUM	DIVIDER
LIMEADE	OVERALL	PROSAIC	TEENAGE	VOLTAGE	FLATBED	TREMBLE	MOHICAN	DWINDLE
LINEAGE	OVERARM	PULSATE	TERNARY	VOLTAIC	FLYABLE	TROUBLE	MONOCLE	FILMDOM
LINKAGE	OVERAWE	RADIANT	TERRACE	VULGATE	FREEBIE	TUNABLE	MOROCCO	FOUNDER
LOWLAND	OVULATE	RADIATE	TERRAIN	WAGTAIL	FRIABLE	VISIBLE	MUSICAL	FOUNDRY
LUGGAGE	OXIDANT	RAMPAGE	TESTATE	WALLABY	GEARBOX	VOCABLE	OFFICER	FREEDOM
LULLABY	PACKAGE	RAMPANT	THERAPY	WARFARE	GRUMBLE	VOLUBLE	OPTICAL	GLADDEN
LUMBAGO	PAGEANT	RAMPART	THREADY	WARPATH	HALIBUT	WADABLE	PANACEA	GRANDAM
MACRAME	PALMATE	RANSACK	THROATY	WARRANT	HANDBAG	WINDBAG	PANACHE	GRANDEE
MAGNATE	PALPATE	RECLAIM	TIEBACK	WASSAIL	HIGHBOY	WORKBAG	PANICLE	GRIDDLE
MALLARD	PANCAKE	RECLAME	TILLAGE	WASTAGE	IGNOBLE	WORKBOX	PEDICAB	GRINDER
MAMMARY	PARFAIT	REFRACT	TIMPANI	WATTAGE	INCUBUS	AFRICAN	PELICAN	GUERDON
MANDATE	PARTAKE	REFRAIN	TINWARE	WAYWARD	INHABIT	ANARCHY	POLECAT	GUILDER
MANSARD	PASSAGE	REGNANT	TOENAIL	WEASAND	INHIBIT	ANTACID	RADICAL	HANGDOG
MASCARA	PEASANT	RELEASE	TONNAGE	WELFARE	JUKEBOX	APRICOT	RAUNCHY	HOLIDAY
MASSAGE	PECCARY	REMNANT	TOPMAST	WETBACK	LADYBUG	ARTICLE	RECYCLE	HUMIDOR
MEDIATE	PECCAVI	REPLACE	TOPSAIL	WETLAND	LEGIBLE	ATTACHE	SIDECAR	INFIDEL
MERMAID	PENDANT	RETRACE	TORNADO	WINDAGE	LIVABLE	AURICLE	SILICON	INSIDER
MESSAGE	PENNANT	RETRACT	TOWPATH	WORDAGE	LONGBOW	BICYCLE	SIROCCO	JACKDAW
METHANE	PERCALE	RHUBARB	TRAVAIL	YARDAGE	MACABRE	BIFOCAL	SOLICIT	KATYDID
MIDLAND	PERHAPS	ROSEATE	TSUNAMI	YARDARM	MAILBOX	BORSCHT	SOUPCON	KINGDOM
MIGRANT	PERTAIN	RUMMAGE	ULULATE	ACROBAT	MINIBUS	BOUNCER	STENCIL	LAUNDER
MIGRATE	PERVADE	SABBATH	UMBRAGE	AEROBIC	MUTABLE	BRECCIA	TAXICAB	LAUNDRY
MILEAGE	PHALANX	SAGUARO	UNAWARE	AFFABLE	NEWSBOY	BRIOCHE	TOBACCO	MACADAM
MILLAGE	PHARAOH	SALVAGE	UNCHAIN	ALEMBIC	NOTABLE	CHANCEL	TOPICAL	MATADOR
MISCALL	PIEBALD	SARCASM	UNCLASP	ALGEBRA	OCTOBER	CHANCRE	TREACLE	MAUNDER
MISNAME	PIGTAIL	SATIATE	UNERASE	AMIABLE	OMNIBUS	CODICIL	TYPICAL	MEANDER
MISTAKE	PILLAGE	SAUSAGE	UNHEARD	AUDIBLE	PAGEBOY	CONICAL	UNLUCKY	MILLDAM
MONTAGE	PINNACE	SEALANT	UNITARY	BANDBOX	PARABLE	COPYCAT	VATICAN	MONADIC
MORDANT	PINNATE	SEAWALL	UNLEARN	BELABOR	PILLBOX	CORACLE	VEHICLE	NOMADIC
MUNDANE	PIQUANT	SEAWARD	UNLEASH	BELLBOY	PLAYBOY	CORNCOB	VESICLE	NOONDAY
MURRAIN	PITFALL	SECTARY	UNSNARL	BLUBBER	PLIABLE	COUNCIL	WILDCAT	PALADIN
MUSTANG	PIZZAZZ	SELVAGE	UNWEAVE	BOURBON	PLOWBOY	CUBICLE	WOODCUT	PARADOX
MUSTARD	PLACARD	SERRATE	UPBRAID	BRAMBLE	PLUMBER	CUTICLE	ABANDON	PLAUDIT
NARRATE	PLACATE	SERVANT	UPDRAFT	BUGABOO	POSTBOY	DEBACLE	ABRIDGE	PLUNDER
NETWARE	PLENARY	SETBACK	UPGRADE	CALIBER	POTABLE	DEFICIT	ADJUDGE	QUONDAM
NIAGARA	PLUMAGE	SEXTANT	UPSTAGE	CAPABLE	QUIBBLE	EARACHE	ASUNDER	REMODEL
NIGGARD	POLLACK	SHEBANG	UPSTART	CARABAO	RAINBOW	ETHICAL	BESIDES	REREDOS
NIRVANA	POMPANO	SIDEARM	UPSTATE	CARDBUS	RAREBIT	FIANCEE	BLADDER	RESEDIT
NITRATE	PONIARD	SKYLARK	URINARY	CARIBOU	RHOMBUS	FINICKY	BLEEDER	RESIDUE
OATCAKE	PORTAGE	SKYWARD	URINATE	CHAMBER	RISIBLE	FLACCID	BLINDER	ROUNDUP
OBVIATE	POSTAGE	SOPRANO	VAGRANT	CLAMBER	ROADBED	FLATCAR	BLOODED	SCANDAL
ODDBALL	POTTAGE	SPINACH	VALIANT	CLOBBER	ROSEBUD	HAIRCUT	BLUNDER	SHUDDER
OFFHAND	PREDATE	SPIRANT	VALUATE	COHABIT	SALTBOX	HANDCAR	BOREDOM	SLANDER
OPERATE	PREFACE	STEWARD	VANTAGE	COPYBOY	SANDBAG	HELICAL	BOULDER	SLENDER
ORCHARD	PRELATE	STOMACH	VANWARD	CRABBED	SANDBAR	HELLCAT	BOUNDEN	SMOLDER
OREGANO	PREPARE	STORAGE	VARIANT	CROWBAR	SHAMBLE	HIBACHI	BOWLDER	SOMEDAY
ORIGAMI	PRESAGE	SULFATE	VERDANT	CRUMBLE	SHERBET	ILLICIT	BREADTH	SOUNDER
OSSUARY	PREVAIL	SULTANA	VERVAIN	DECIBEL	SICKBED	INDICIA	BROADEN	SPEEDUP
OSTMARK	PRIMACY	SUMMARY	VIBRANT	DISABLE	SIZABLE	KNEECAP	BROIDER	SPINDLE
OUTCAST	PRIMARY	SUNBATH	VIBRATE	DISOBEY	SLOBBER	LEXICON	BROODER	SPINDLY
OUTFACE	PRIMATE	SUNLAMP	VIBRATO	DRIBBLE	SLUMBER	MAHICAN	BULLDOG	STANDBY
OUTLAST	PRIVACY	SURFACE	VILLAGE	DURABLE	SOLUBLE	MANACLE	CHEDDAR	STRUDEL
OUTRAGE	PRIVATE	SURNAME	VILLAIN	ENNOBLE	STUBBLE	MEDICAL	CHOWDER	SWADDLE

SWINDLE	CANTEEN	DISTEND	HELLENE	NAIVETY	PROGENY	SUBJECT	WALLEYE	STIFFEN
THUNDER	CHAPEAU	DRAPERY	HENPECK	NANKEEN	PROJECT	SUBVERT	WARHEAD	STUFFIT
TREADLE	CHATEAU	DUBIETY	HERSELF	NASCENT	PROTEAN	SUCCEED	WARLESS	TRAFFIC
TRODDEN	CHIMERA	DUCHESS	HIMSELF	NEGLECT	PROTECT	SUCCESS	WEEKEND	TRUFFLE
TRUNDLE	CHINESE	DUDGEON	HOPHEAD	NONHERO	PROTEGE	SUGGEST	WESTERN	TUNEFUL
TUESDAY	CHOLERA	DUNGEON	HOSIERY	NOWHERE	PROTEIN	SUNBEAM	WHEREAS	WAILFUL
TWADDLE	CISTERN	EARNEST	HOSTESS	NUCLEAR	PROTEST	SUPREME	WHEREAT	WAKEFUL
TWIDDLE	CLEMENT	EASTERN	HOWBEIT	NUCLEON	PROVERB	SURFEIT	WHEREBY	WILLFUL
UNGODLY	COCKEYE	EGGHEAD	HUNKERS	NUCLEUS	PROWESS	SURGEON	WHEREIN	WISHFUL
WEEKDAY	COLLECT	ELEMENT	HUTMENT	NURSERY	PRUDENT	SURGERY	WHEREOF	WISTFUL
WHEEDLE	COLLEEN	EMINENT	HYGIENE	OATMEAL	PUNGENT	SUSPECT	WHEREON	ALLEGRO
WORKDAY	COLLEGE	EMPRESS	ICEBERG	OBSCENE	PUTREFY	SUSPEND	WHERETO	ALRIGHT
WORLDLY	COMMEND	ENDLESS	ILLNESS	ODDMENT	RAGWEED	TABLEAU	WIDGEON	AMALGAM
ABSCESS	COMMENT	ENTREAT	IMAGERY	OFFBEAT	RAIMENT	TAFFETA	WITHERS	ANTIGEN
ACADEME	COMPEER	ESTHETE	IMPIETY	ONESELF	REAGENT	TANGENT	WITLESS	BLOWGUN
ACADEMY	COMPETE	EVIDENT	IMPRESS	OPPRESS	REDHEAD	TANNERY	WITNESS	BOLOGNA
ACHIEVE	CONCEAL	EXCRETA	INDWELL	OPULENT	REDRESS	TEMPERA	WRYNECK	BROUGHT
ADDRESS	CONCEDE	EXCRETE	INFIELD	OROGENY	REFLECT	TEMPEST	AQUIFER	CHARGER
AGELESS	CONCEIT	EXEGETE	INFLECT	OUTSELL	REFRESH	THEREAT	BALEFUL	CHIGGER
AILMENT	CONCEPT	EXPRESS	INGRESS	OUTWEAR	REGRESS	THEREBY	BASHFUL	CLANGOR
AIMLESS	CONCERN	EXTREME	INKWELL	PARVENU	RELIEVE	THEREIN	BENEFIT	COLOGNE
ALCHEMY	CONCERT	FERMENT	INQUEST	PASTERN	REPLETE	THEREOF	BRIMFUL	DECAGON
ALIMENT	CONDEMN	FERNERY	INSPECT	PATIENT	REPRESS	THEREON	CAREFUL	DELIGHT
AMATEUR	CONFESS	FERVENT	INSTEAD	PATTERN	REQUEST	THERETO	CHAFFER	DEMIGOD
AMBIENT	CONGEAL	FIFTEEN	ISRAELI	PAYMENT	RESPECT	THYSELF	CHAMFER	DOWAGER
ANAPEST	CONGEST	FIGMENT	JITTERS	PENDENT	RETREAD	TOGGERY	CHIFFON	DRAUGHT
ANCIENT	CONNECT	FILBERT	LACTEAL	PEPPERY	RETREAT	TOLUENE	CONIFER	DROUGHT
ANXIETY	CONSENT	FISHERY	LAMBENT	PERCENT	RICKETS	TONNEAU	DEERFLY	ECLOGUE
ARCHERY	CONTEMN	FLOWERY	LANTERN	PERCEPT	RICKETY	TOPLESS	DIREFUL	EPERGNE
ARMREST	CONTEND	FLYLEAF	LARCENY	PERFECT	ROBBERY	TORMENT	DOLEFUL	FATIGUE
ARTLESS	CONTENT	FOOLERY	LARGESS	PERVERT	ROOKERY	TORPEDO	DUTIFUL	FINAGLE
ATHLETE	CONTEST	FORBEAR	LAWLESS	PHONEME	SALIENT	TORRENT	FATEFUL	FRAUGHT
AUGMENT	CONTEXT	FORCEPS	LECHERY	PIGMENT	SAPIENT	TOWHEAD	FEARFUL	FREIGHT
AUSTERE	CONVENE	FORFEIT	LECTERN	PINKEYE	SATIETY	TRACERY	FIREFLY	HANDGUN
BARBELL	CONVENT	FORFEND	LENIENT	PIONEER	SCENERY	TRAGEDY	FISTFUL	HEXAGON
BATTERY	CONVERT	GABFEST	LIMBECK	PLACEBO	SCREECH	TRAPEZE	FRETFUL	ILLEGAL
BELIEVE	COOKERY	GALLEON	LINSEED	PLATEAU	SEAWEED	TRICEPS	GAINFUL	INSIGHT
BENZENE	CORRECT	GALLERY	LIQUEFY	PORTEND	SECRECY	TRIDENT	GIRAFFE	INTEGER
BEQUEST	CORTEGE	GARMENT	LIQUEUR	PORTENT	SECRETE	TRIREME	HANDFUL	LASAGNA
BERSERK	CULVERT	GENTEEL	LOTTERY	POSSESS	SEGMENT	TRISECT	LUCIFER	MANAGER
BESEECH	CURRENT	GEODESY	MACHETE	POSTERN	SEQUENT	TURNERY	MALEFIC	MOHEGAN
BESIEGE	CUTLERY	GIBLETS	MAGNETO	POTHEAD	SERPENT	UKULELE	MINDFUL	NOSEGAY
BESMEAR	CYPRESS	GINSENG	MALLEUS	POTHERB	SHAPELY	UMPTEEN	NEEDFUL	OCTAGON
BESPEAK	DEANERY	GODDESS	MANTEAU	POTTERY	SIAMESE	UNCLEAN	OVERFLY	PARAGON
BETWEEN	DEFLECT	GODHEAD	MARGENT	PREBEND	SINCERE	UNDRESS	PACIFIC	PELAGIC
BITTERN	DEPLETE	GODLESS	MASSEUR	PRECEDE	SIXTEEN	UNGUENT	PITIFUL	PERIGEE
BITTERS	DEPRESS	GODSEND	MASTERY	PRECEPT	SKIWEAR	UPSWEPT	PROFFER	PLUNGER
BOOKEND	DESCEND	GUNNERY	MIDWEEK	PREFECT	SLAVERY	USELESS	SCRUFFY	POLYGON
BRACERO	DESCENT	HALBERD	MIDYEAR	PREHEAT	SOCIETY	VAQUERO	SCUFFLE	REFUGEE
BRAVERY	DESSERT	HALVERS	MINUEND	PRESENT	SOLVENT	VARIETY	SHUFFLE	SHINGLE
BUCKEYE	DIALECT	HAPLESS	MISDEED	PRETEEN	SORCERY	VERBENA	SKIFFLE	SHOTGUN
BUGBEAR	DIGRESS	HARNESS	MISLEAD	PRETEND	SOYBEAN	VERMEIL	SNAFFLE	SLEIGHT
BURGEON	DILUENT	HARVEST	MISREAD	PRETEXT	SQUEEZE	VESPERS	SNIFFLE	SMIDGEN
BURGESS	DIOCESE	HAUBERK	MISSEND	PREVENT	STATELY	VILLEIN	SNUFFLE	SMUGGLE
BURMESE	DISCERN	HAUTEUR	MULLEIN	PROCEED	STIPEND	VIOLENT	SOUFFLE	SNUGGLE
CALDERA	DISSECT	HAYSEED	MYSTERY	PROCESS	STUDENT	VISCERA	SOULFUL	SPANGLE
CANNERY	DISSENT	HEIRESS	NAIVETE	PROFESS	STUPEFY	WAGGERY	STAFFER	STAGGER

STOPGAP	HOTSHOT	AMATIVE	BINDING	CIVVIES	DEBRIEF	FASHION	GRECIAN	JUDAISM
SWAGGER	KETCHUP	AMENITY	BIOTITE	CLARIFY	DECEIVE	FATUITY	GRUNION	JUSTICE
TANAGER	KINSHIP	AMERIND	BLEMISH	CLARION	DECLINE	FAUVISM	GUANINE	JUSTIFY
THOUGHT	KITCHEN	AMPLIFY	BONFIRE	CLARITY	DENSITY	FEBRILE	GUNFIRE	KADDISH
TONIGHT	LATCHET	ANGUISH	BOOKISH	CLAVIER	DENTIST	FEELING	HAFNIUM	KEEPING
TRIGGER	LEATHER	ANILINE	BOWLINE	COATING	DEPRIVE	FENCING	HALTING	KERNING
UPRIGHT	LOATHLY	ANIMISM	BOWLING	COAXIAL	DERRICK	FERMIUM	HANGING	KHEDIVE
UPTIGHT	MARSHAL	ANNUITY	BRAZIER	COCAINE	DERVISH	FERTILE	HAPPILY	KILLING
VINEGAR	MENTHOL	ANODIZE	BREVITY	CODEINE	DESPISE	FESTIVE	HARRIER	KNOWING
WRANGLE	MORPHIA	ANTHILL	BRITISH	CODFISH	DESPITE	FICTION	HASHING	LANDING
WRIGGLE	NARTHEX	ANYTIME	BROMIDE	CODLING	DESTINE	FILLING	HASHISH	LAOTIAN
WRINGER	NARWHAL	ANYWISE	BROMINE	COEXIST	DESTINY	FINDING	HAYRICK	LAPWING
WRONGLY	NAUGHTY	APATITE	BRUTISH	COLLIDE	DIARIST	FINFISH	HAYWIRE	LATRINE
WROUGHT	NEITHER	APPLIED	BULLION	COLLIER	DICTION	FINNISH	HEADING	LATTICE
AIRSHIP	NORTHER	APPOINT	BUNTING	COMBINE	DIGNIFY	FISHING	HEARING	LATVIAN
ALCOHOL	PANTHER	APPRISE	BURNISH	COMPILE	DIGNITY	FISSILE	HELLION	LEADING
ANOTHER	PITCHER	ARCHIVE	BUSHING	CONCISE	DISLIKE	FISSION	HELPING	LEFTISM
BANSHEE	POTSHOT	ARRAIGN	CADMIUM	CONDIGN	DISMISS	FITTING	HEMLINE	LEGGING
BELLHOP	PRITHEE	ASCRIBE	CAITIFF	CONFIDE	DISTICH	FLEMING	HEROICS	LEMMING
BENTHIC	PROPHET	ASININE	CALCIFY	CONFINE	DISTILL	FLEMISH	HEROINE	LEMPIRA
BENTHOS	PSYCHIC	ASTRIDE	CALCINE	CONFIRM	DOGFISH	FLORIST	HEROISM	LEONINE
BIRCHER	PSYCHOL	ATAVISM	CALCITE	CONNIVE	DOSSIER	FLUTIST	HERRING	LESBIAN
BLATHER	RATCHET	ATELIER	CALCIUM	CONSIGN	DRAWING	FOOLISH	HINTING	LIGNIFY
BLUCHER	ROUGHEN	ATHEIST	CALLING	CONSIST	DUCTILE	FOOTING	HOLDING	LIGNITE
BROTHEL	SANDHOG	ATOMIZE	CAMBIUM	CONVICT	DUMPING	FOREIGN	HOLMIUM	LIONIZE
BROTHER	SATCHEL	ATTAINT	CANDIED	COPPICE	EARRING	FORGING	HOOSIER	LISTING
BURGHER	SLATHER	AUCTION	CAPRICE	CORDIAL	EBONITE	FORGIVE	HORRIFY	LITHIUM
BUTCHER	SLITHER	AUSPICE	CAPSIZE	CORDITE	EDIFICE	FORTIFY	HOSPICE	LODGING
CAMPHOR	SMOTHER	AVARICE	CAPTION	CORNICE	EDITION	FOULING	HOSTILE	LONGING
CATCHER	SOMEHOW	BACKING	CAPTIVE	COSTIVE	EGOTISM	FRAGILE	HOUSING	MACHINE
CATCHUP	SORGHUM	BAGPIPE	CARBIDE	COURIER	ELEGIAC	FULFILL	HOWLING	MADDING
CLOTHES	THITHER	BAILIFF	CARBINE	COWBIRD	ELISION	FURBISH	HULKING	MADEIRA
CROCHET	TOUGHEN	BALDING	CARDIAC	COWHIDE	ELITISM	FURNISH	HUSKING	MAGNIFY
DAUPHIN	TRACHEA	BAPTISM	CARMINE	COWLICK	ELUSIVE	FURRIER	IDOLIZE	MALAISE
DEATHLY	TROCHEE	BAPTIST	CARRIER	COWLING	ELYSIUM	FURRING	IMAGINE	MANKIND
DOLPHIN	URETHRA	BAPTIZE	CARRION	CRANIUM	EMERITA	FURTIVE	IMAGISM	MANLIKE
DOUGHTY	VOUCHER	BARRIER	CARSICK	CRAVING	EMOTION	FUSTIAN	IMPRINT	MANNISH
DRACHMA	WARSHIP	BARRING	CASHIER	CREVICE	ENDWISE	GALLIUM	INCLINE	MANSION
EARSHOT	WARTHOG	BASTION	CASTING	CROSIER	ENGLISH	GAMBIAN	INFLICT	MARTIAL
EARTHEN	WEATHER	BATTING	CATBIRD	CRUCIAL	ENQUIRE	GARFISH	INITIAL	MARTIAN
EARTHLY	WEIGHTY	BAUXITE	CATFISH	CRUCIFY	ENTWINE	GARNISH	INKLING	MARTINI
EPITHET	WHETHER	BEARING	CATLIKE	CUISINE	EREMITE	GELDING	INQUIRE	MARXISM
FARTHER	WHITHER	BEATIFY	CAUTION	CUNNING	EROSION	GENTIAN	INQUIRY	MASSIVE
FEATHER	WORSHIP	BEDDING	CEILING	CUPRITE	EROSIVE	GENTILE	INSPIRE	MASTIFF
FLESHLY	ABILITY	BEDSIDE	CELSIUS	CURBING	ESQUIRE	GENUINE	INSTILL	MATTINS
FLIGHTY	ABOLISH	BEDTIME	CENTIME	CURSIVE	ETCHING	GIMMICK	INVEIGH	MAWKISH
FRESHEN	ACIDIFY	BEEHIVE	CENTIMO	CUSHION	EVASION	GLACIAL	INVOICE	MEANING
FRESHET	ACONITE	BEELINE	CERTIFY	CUTTING	EVENING	GLACIER	IRANIAN	MEETING
FURTHER	ACQUIRE	BEGRIME	CESSION	CYANIDE	EXAMINE	GLAZIER	IRIDIUM	MENTION
GINGHAM	ADENINE	BEGUILE	CHADIAN	CYCLIST	FACTION	GLORIFY	IRONING	MESSIAH
GRAPHIC	AFFLICT	BEGUINE	CHALICE	CZARINA	FAILING	GODLIKE	ITALIAN	MESTIZO
GUMSHOE	AGONIZE	BELGIAN	CHARIOT	DANDIFY	FAIRING	GOSLING	ITEMIZE	MIDRIFF
GUNSHOT	AIRLIFT	BENZINE	CHARITY	DARLING	FALSIFY	GRANITE	JASMINE	MIDWIFE
HATCHET	AIRLINE	BESTIAL	CHEMISE	DASHIKI	FANCIER	GRATIFY	JAYBIRD	MILLIME
HAUGHTY	AIRSICK	BETHINK	CHEMIST	DASHING	FARMING	GRATING	JOLLITY	MILLING
HEATHEN	ALEWIFE	BETWIXT	CHERISH	DAYTIME	FARRIER	GRAVITY	JOTTING	MILLION
HEATHER	ALUMINA	BILLION	CHEVIOT	DEALING	FASCISM	GRAZIER	JOYRIDE	MISFILE

MISFIRE	PAUCITY	REALISM	SIBLING	TEXTILE	WARNING	GHERKIN	BOBSLED	IDEALLY
MISLIKE	PEELING	REALITY	SIGNIFY	THORIUM	WARRIOR	GRACKLE	BOOKLET	IMPULSE
MISSILE	PEEVISH	REALIZE	SKYLINE	THULIUM	WARTIME	HEARKEN	BOOTLEG	INDULGE
MISSING	PENDING	REBUILD	SLAVISH	THYMINE	WASHING	KARAKUL	BRAILLE	INHALER
MISSION	PENSION	RECEIPT	SOLDIER	TICKING	WASPISH	KIDSKIN	BROILER	INSULAR
MISSIVE	PENSIVE	RECEIVE	SOPHISM	TOPPING	WAXWING	KNOCKER	BUCKLER	INSULIN
MOLDING	PENTIUM	RECLINE	SOPHIST	TOPSIDE	WAYBILL	KNUCKLE	BUCOLIC	INVALID
MOLLIFY	PERFIDY	RECTIFY	SPANIEL	TORSION	WAYSIDE	LATAKIA	CASTLED	INVOLVE
MOORING	PERLITE	REDDISH	SPANISH	TOURIST	WEBBING	MANIKIN	CATALOG	JACKLEG
MORAINE	PERSIAN	REDLINE	SPARING	TRACING	WEDDING	NONSKED	CATALPA	JAVELIN
MORNING	PERSIST	REJOICE	SPATIAL	TRINITY	WEEPING	OILSKIN	CAVALRY	JEWELER
MORTIFY	PETRIFY	REMAINS	SPECIAL	TRITIUM	WHITING	PASSKEY	CEDILLA	JEWELRY
MORTISE	PETTISH	REPLICA	SPECIES	TRIVIAL	WHITISH	PIGSKIN	CHABLIS	JOCULAR
MULLION	PHONICS	REPRINT	SPECIFY	TRIVIUM	WICKIUP	PLACKET	CHALLIS	JUBILEE
MYSTIFY	PHYSICS	REPRISE	STABILE	TROPISM	WILLIES	PRICKER	CHAPLET	JUGULAR
NETTING	PHYSIOL	REPTILE	STADIUM	TUITION	WILLING	PRICKLE	CIRCLET	KREMLIN
NIOBIUM	PIANIST	REQUIEM	STAGING	TURBINE	WINDING	PUMPKIN	CIVILLY	LANOLIN
NITRIFY	PIGGISH	REQUIRE	STAMINA	TURKISH	WINNING	QUICKEN	COBBLER	LEAFLET
NITRITE	PILLION	REQUITE	STATION	TURNING	WITTING	QUICKIE	COCHLEA	MARPLOT
NOTHING	PISMIRE	RESCIND	STERILE	UNCTION	WORDING	REDSKIN	COMPLEX	MAUDLIN
NOURISH	PLATING	RESPITE	STORIED	UNDOING	WORKING	SHACKLE	CONFLUX	MAXILLA
NUCLIDE	PLUVIAL	RESTIVE	STUDIED	UNDYING	WRITING	SHOCKER	COPILOT	MEASLES
NULLIFY	PONTIFF	REUNION	STYLING	UNITIZE	YESHIVA	SLACKEN	COROLLA	MEDULLA
NUPTIAL	PORCINE	RHENIUM	STYLISH	UNQUIET	YIDDISH	SLACKER	COUPLET	MISPLAY
NUTPICK	PORTICO	RHODIUM	STYLIST	UNSLING	YTTRIUM	SLICKER	COWSLIP	MODULAR
OBELISK	PORTION	RIGGING	STYLIZE	UNTRIED	ZAMBIAN	SNEAKER	CRULLER	MUFFLER
OCARINA	PRALINE	ROLLICK	SUBLIME	UNTWINE	ZEOLITE	SNICKER	CUMULUS	NACELLE
OCULIST	PRAYING	ROUTINE	SUBSIDE	UNTWIST	ZILLION	SNORKEL	DEVALUE	NONPLUS
OFFSIDE	PRECISE	RUBBISH	SUBSIDY	UPRAISE	ZIONISM	SPARKLE	DEVELOP	NOVELLA
OLIVINE	PREDICT	RUFFIAN	SUBSIST	UPSHIFT	KILLJOY	SPEAKER	DEVILRY	NOVELTY
ONETIME	PREMIER	RUNNING	SUBTILE	UPSWING	LOCKJAW	SPECKLE	DEVOLVE	ORTOLAN
ONGOING	PREMISE	RUSSIAN	SUCTION	URANIUM	OVERJOY	STICKER	DEWCLAW	OUTFLOW
OPACITY	PREMIUM	SAILING	SUFFICE	UTILITY	BETOKEN	THICKEN	DISPLAY	OUTPLAY
OPENING	PRESIDE	SALTINE	SUICIDE	UTILIZE	BLACKEN	THICKET	DIVULGE	OVERLAP
OPINION	PREVIEW	SAPLING	SUITING	UTOPIAN	BLANKET	TRICKLE	DOUBLET	OVERLAY
ORATION	PROBITY	SARDINE	SULFIDE	VACCINE	BLINKER	TRINKET	DRIBLET	PABULUM
ORIFICE	PRODIGY	SAWMILL	SUNDIAL	VACUITY	BRACKEN	TRUCKLE	DROPLET	PAISLEY
OSTRICH	PROFILE	SCARIFY	SUNFISH	VAMPIRE	BRACKET	TURNKEY	DRUMLIN	PAPILLA
OUTLINE	PROMISE	SEABIRD	SUNRISE	VARMINT	BREAKER	TWINKLE	EARPLUG	PARSLEY
OUTLIVE	PROVIDE	SEASICK	SURMISE	VARNISH	BREAKUP	WHICKER	ECHELON	PATELLA
OUTSIDE	PROVISO	SEASIDE	SURVIVE	VARSITY	BRISKET	WHISKER	EIDOLON	PENALTY
OUTSIZE	PROXIMO	SEATING	SWAHILI	VEILING	BUMPKIN	WHISKEY	ENVELOP	PERPLEX
OVATION	PUBLISH	SECTION	SWEDISH	VERDICT	CHECKER	WRECKER	EPAULET	PHALLIC
OXIDIZE	PUDDING	SEEMING	TACTICS	VERNIER	CHECKUP	WRINKLE	FACULTY	PHALLUS
PACKING	PUERILE	SELFISH	TACTILE	VERSIFY	CHICKEN	YOUNKER	FEEDLOT	PLAYLET
PADDING	PURLIEU	SENTIMO	TARNISH	VERSION	CHUCKLE	ABSOLVE	FORELEG	POPULAR
PANNIER	PURVIEW	SERRIED	TATTING	VERTIGO	CHUKKER	ACRYLIC	FRAILTY	PROBLEM
PAPRIKA	QUALIFY	SERVICE	TEKTITE	VESTIGE	CLINKER	AIRFLOW	GANTLET	RAMBLER
PARSING	QUALITY	SERVILE	TELLING	VESTING	CRACKER	ALCALDE	GAZELLE	RATTLER
PARTIAL	QUININE	SERVING	TENSILE	VITRIFY	CRACKLE	ALFALFA	GOBBLER	REGALIA
PARTING	RAFFISH	SESSILE	TENSION	VITRIOL	CRICKET	ANGULAR	GOGGLES	REGULAR
PARTITE	RAGTIME	SESSION	TEQUILA	VOGUISH	CRINKLE	ANNULAR	GORILLA	REPULSE
PASSING	RAILING	SETTING	TERBIUM	VULPINE	CROOKED	BACKLIT	GREMLIN	RESOLVE
PASSION	RANKING	SHADING	TERMITE	WADDING	DRUNKEN	BACKLOG	HARELIP	REVOLVE
PASSIVE	RATLINE	SHAVING	TERRIER	WAGGISH	FLANKER	BIBELOT	HIDALGO	RINGLET
PASTIME	RAWHIDE	SHERIFF	TERRIFY	WANTING	FLICKER	BIPOLAR	HOODLUM	RIVALRY
PATRIOT	READING	SHORING	TESTIFY	WARLIKE	FRECKLE	BIVALVE	HOSTLER	RIVULET

ROOTLET	BOATMAN	PLUMMET	CADENCE	INNINGS	SPLENIC	AQUEOUS	CONNOTE	FALLOUT
ROYALTY	BONDMAN	POLEMIC	CADENZA	INTENSE	SPUTNIK	ARDUOUS	CONSOLE	FATUOUS
RUBELLA	BRAHMAN	POLYMER	CALENDS	JACINTH	STAUNCH	ARMHOLE	CONSORT	FERROUS
SAMPLER	BRAHMIN	POSTMAN	CHANNEL	JEJUNUM	STERNUM	AUREOLE	CONTORT	FESTOON
SANDLOT	CALOMEL	PREEMIE	CHARNEL	JOURNAL	STRANGE	BALCONY	CONTOUR	FETLOCK
SCALLOP	CALUMET	PREEMPT	CHIANTI	JOURNEY	STRINGY	BALLOON	CONVOKE	FIBROID
SCARLET	CALUMNY	PROGMAN	CHIGNON	JOYANCE	SYNONYM	BANNOCK	COOKOUT	FLAVOUR
SCHOLAR	CARAMEL	PROPMAN	CHIMNEY	LACONIC	SYRINGE	BARROOM	COPIOUS	FOGHORN
SECULAR	CAVEMAN	PULLMAN	CHRONIC	LAMINAR	TECHNIC	BASSOON	CORDOBA	FOLDOUT
SHALLOP	CERAMIC	PYJAMAS	CHUTNEY	LEARNED	TENANCY	BAZOOKA	CORRODE	FORBODE
SHALLOW	CERUMEN	PYRAMID	CLEANLY	LICENSE	TETANUS	BECLOUD	COULOMB	FORLORN
SHELLAC	CHAPMAN	REGIMEN	CLEANSE	LOCKNUT	THINNER	BEDPOST	COWPOKE	FOXHOLE
SIDELIT	CHARMER	SANDMAN	CLEANUP	LOZENGE	TIDINGS	BEDROCK	COXCOMB	FULSOME
SIMILAR	CHROMIC	SEISMIC	COCKNEY	MAGENTA	TITANIC	BEDROLL	CUCKOLD	FURIOUS
SKILLET	DECIMAL	SHIMMER	COCONUT	MAKINGS	TOPKNOT	BEDROOM	CURIOUS	FURLONG
SPELLER	DELIMIT	SHOWMAN	COLONEL	MARINER	TOURNEY	BEDSORE	CURSORY	GALLOWS
SPOILER	DILEMMA	SIDEMAN	CORINTH	MASONIC	TRAINEE	BEHOOVE	CUSTODY	GARROTE
SQUALID	DOORMAN	STAMMER	CORONAL	MASONRY	TROUNCE	BELLOWS	CUTWORM	GEOLOGY
SQUALOR	DOORMAT	THERMAL	CORONER	MATINEE	TYRANNY	BENZOIN	CYCLONE	GIBBOUS
SQUELCH	DRUMMER	THERMOS	CORONET	MELANGE	UNCANNY	BETROTH	DAYBOOK	GLAMOUR
STEALTH	DYNAMIC	TOXEMIA	DECENCY	MELANIC	UNHANDY	BIGHORN	DEFROST	GLUCOSE
STELLAR	ENDEMIC	TRAMMEL	DEFENSE	MELANIN	UNHINGE	BILIOUS	DEPLORE	GODHOOD
SURPLUS	FIREMAN	TRIUMPH	DEFUNCT	MEMENTO	UNMANLY	BIOLOGY	DESPOIL	GONDOLA
SWALLOW	FOOTMAN	UNARMED	DEMONIC	NOMINAL	VACANCY	BLOWOUT	DESPOND	GUMBOIL
SWOLLEN	FOREMAN	UNKEMPT	DERANGE	NOMINEE	VALANCE	BOUDOIR	DEVIOUS	GUNBOAT
TABULAR	FREEMAN	VITAMIN	DETENTE	OFFENSE	VALENCE	BOYCOTT	DIAMOND	GUNLOCK
TITULAR	FROGMAN	WOODMAN	DIURNAL	ORDINAL	VEDANTA	BUFFOON	DIPLOID	HADDOCK
TRAILER	GLEEMAN	WORKMAN	DOMINIE	ORGANDY	VERANDA	BULLOCK	DIPLOMA	HAMMOCK
TRELLIS	GLIMMER	YARDMAN	DOYENNE	ORGANIC	VICINAL	BURDOCK	DISCORD	HANDOUT
TRIPLET	GOODMAN	ABSENCE	DRAGNET	ORGANZA	VINTNER	BURNOUT	DISJOIN	HANGOUT
TRIPLEX	GOURMET	ACRONYM	DURANCE	PARSNIP	WAGONER	BUTTOCK	DISPORT	HAPLOID
TROLLEY	GRAMMAR	ADJUNCT	EFFENDI	PARTNER	WHATNOT	CABOOSE	DISPOSE	HARBOUR
TROLLOP	GROMMET	ADRENAL	ENHANCE	PENANCE	WIZENED	CALLOUS	DISROBE	HARMONY
TUBULAR	HACKMAN	ADVANCE	ENTENTE	PETUNIA	WOMANLY	CARIOUS	DISTORT	HARPOON
TUMBLER	HANGMAN	AGAINST	ENVENOM	PFENNIG	ABALONE	CARLOAD	DOGWOOD	HASSOCK
TUTELAR	HEADMAN	ALMANAC	EQUINOX	PHOENIX	ABSCOND	CARPORT	DRAGOON	HAYCOCK
TWILLED	INHUMAN	ALMONER	ESSENCE	PHRENIC	ACETONE	CARTOON	DUBIOUS	HAYFORK
VANILLA	ISTHMUS	ALUMNUS	ETERNAL	PILSNER	ADENOID	CASSOCK	DUTEOUS	HAYLOFT
VITTLES	KINSMAN	AMMONIA	ETHANOL	PIMENTO	ADIPOSE	CATBOAT	EARLOBE	HEINOUS
VOCALIC	LINEMAN	ANDANTE	EXPANSE	PIRANHA	AFFRONT	CATHODE	ECOLOGY	HEMLOCK
WARBLER	MAILMAN	ANTENNA	EXPENSE	RECENCY	AIRFOIL	CHAMOIS	ECONOMY	HICKORY
WAVELET	MANUMIT	ANTONYM	EXPUNGE	REFINED	AIRPORT	CHEROOT	EMBROIL	HIDEOUS
WHEELER	MARIMBA	ARPANET	EXTINCT	REGENCY	AIRPOST	CHICORY	ENAMOUR	HIDEOUT
WHITLOW	MAXIMAL	ARRANGE	FAIENCE	RETINUE	ALIMONY	CHINOOK	ENCLOSE	HILLOCK
WHORLED	MAXIMUM	ARSENAL	FINANCE	REVENGE	AMATORY	COLLOID	ENDMOST	HIPBONE
WIGGLER	MEATMAN	ARSENIC	FLANNEL	REVENUE	AMOROUS	COMFORT	ENGROSS	HISTORY
WOODLOT	MILKMAN	ASKANCE	FLOUNCE	ROMANCE	AMPHORA	COMMODE	ENTROPY	HOEDOWN
ABDOMEN	MINIMAL	BALANCE	GRAPNEL	ROTUNDA	ANALOGY	COMPORT	ENVIOUS	HORMONE
ABYSMAL	MINIMUM	BALONEY	HACKNEY	SATANIC	ANATOMY	COMPOSE	EPISODE	HOTFOOT
ALBUMEN	MONOMER	BARONET	HOMONYM	SAVANNA	ANCHOVY	COMPOST	EPITOME	HUMMOCK
ALBUMIN	NEWSMAN	BAYONET	HOSANNA	SCANNER	ANDROID	COMPOTE	ERELONG	HYDROUS
ANAEMIA	OARSMAN	BEATNIK	IMMENSE	SCIENCE	ANEMONE	CONCOCT	EUPHONY	HYMNODY
ASHAMED	OPTIMAL	BEGONIA	IMPANEL	SEMINAL	ANXIOUS	CONCORD	EXPLODE	ICEBOAT
ATTEMPT	OPTIMUM	BLARNEY	IMPINGE	SEMINAR	ANYBODY	CONDOLE	EXPLOIT	IGNEOUS
BATSMAN	OTTOMAN	BONANZA	INCENSE	SEVENTY	ANYMORE	CONDONE	EXPLORE	IMPIOUS
BETIMES	PAJAMAS	BROWNIE	INFANCY	SHAWNEE	APOLOGY	CONFORM	EYESORE	IMPLODE
BITUMEN	PLOWMAN	CABINET	INGENUE	SILENCE	APPROVE	CONJOIN	FACTORY	IMPLORE

IMPROVE	OUTWORK	RHIZOME	UNCLOSE	DUSTPAN	WRAPPER	ELDERLY	NEUTRAL	VETERAN
INCLOSE	OUTWORN	ROWBOAT	UNCROSS	ECLIPSE	ANTIQUE	EMBARGO	NEUTRON	VICEROY
INDOORS	OXBLOOD	RUINOUS	UNFROCK	ELLIPSE	BAROQUE	EMPEROR	NOSTRIL	WASTREL
INGROWN	PADDOCK	RUNDOWN	UNGROUP	ESCAPEE	BRUSQUE	ENDORSE	NOSTRUM	WINDROW
INKHORN	PADLOCK	SAPWOOD	UNICORN	EXAMPLE	MACAQUE	ENFORCE	NUMERAL	WOLFRAM
INSHORE	PAPOOSE	SEAFOOD	UNIFORM	FLAPPER	OBLIQUE	ENLARGE	NUMERIC	ZYMURGY
INTROIT	PARBOIL	SEAPORT	UNKNOWN	FLIPPER	OBLOQUY	EPIGRAM	OBSERVE	ABYSSAL
IRKSOME	PARLOUR	SENSORY	UNLOOSE	FOOTPAD	OBSEQUY	EQUERRY	OBVERSE	ACCUSAL
ISOTOPE	PARLOUS	SEQUOIA	UNQUOTE	GLIMPSE	PERIQUE	EXCERPT	ORDERLY	ACCUSED
JEALOUS	PATROON	SERIOUS	URANOUS	GRAPPLE	RELIQUE	EYEBROW	OUTCROP	ADVISED
JETPORT	PAYLOAD	SHUTOUT	UROLOGY	GRAUPEL	ADMIRAL	FEDERAL	OUTDRAW	AEROSOL
KEYHOLE	PAYROLL	SHYLOCK	VACUOLE	GROUPER	ADVERSE	FORTRAN	OUTGROW	AMNESIA
KEYNOTE	PEACOCK	SINUOUS	VACUOUS	GROUPIE	AILERON	FULCRUM	OVERRUN	AMNESTY
KICKOFF	PEAFOWL	SIRLOIN	VAMOOSE	HAIRPIN	AIRDROP	FUNERAL	PALFREY	APHASIA
KINFOLK	PERFORM	SOMEONE	VARIOUS	HARDPAN	ALLERGY	GASTRIC	PAPYRUS	ARTISAN
LACTOSE	PERGOLA	SPUMONI	VERBOSE	HEADPIN	ANAGRAM	GENERAL	PILGRIM	ARTISTE
LAMPOON	PETIOLE	SUBJOIN	VICIOUS	HEXAPOD	ANDIRON	GENERIC	POLARIS	BAGASSE
LEGHORN	PIBROCH	SUBSOIL	VICTORY	INSIPID	ANTHRAX	GUMDROP	PORTRAY	BATISTE
LEPROSY	PICCOLO	SUCROSE	VILLOUS	JACKPOT	ANTHROP	HEPARIN	POVERTY	BENISON
LETDOWN	PILLORY	SUMMONS	VISCOSE	JODHPUR	APPAREL	HUMDRUM	PRAIRIE	BLESSED
LISSOME	PINHOLE	SUNDOWN	VISCOUS	JUNIPER	ARMORER	HUMERUS	PROGRAM	BLOSSOM
LOCKOUT	PINWORM	SUNROOF	WALKOUT	KINGPIN	ASHTRAY	HUNDRED	PUBERTY	BROWSER
LOOKOUT	PITEOUS	SUPPORT	WALLOON	OCTOPUS	ASPIRIN	IMMERSE	QUARREL	BRUISER
LOWDOWN	PLATOON	SUPPOSE	WARLOCK	OEDIPAL	ASSURED	IMMORAL	RATTRAP	BUCKSAW
MAFIOSO	PLYWOOD	SURTOUT	WARLORD	PANOPLY	ATHIRST	IMPERIL	REBIRTH	CAISSON
MALTOSE	POMPOUS	SYNCOPE	WASHOUT	PARAPET	AUSTRAL	INDORSE	REFEREE	CANASTA
MAMMOTH	PONTOON	SYSTOLE	WAXWORK	PLAYPEN	BALDRIC	INFARCT	REMORSE	CELESTA
MANHOLE	POPCORN	TABLOID	WAYWORN	PROSPER	BESHREW	INFERNO	RESERVE	CHANSON
MANHOOD	POTHOLE	TADPOLE	WEDLOCK	RELAPSE	BIZARRE	INHERIT	RETIRED	CHASSIS
MASTOID	POTHOOK	TAKEOFF	WELCOME	SCALPEL	BUCKRAM	INNARDS	RETIREE	CLASSIC
MATTOCK	PRECOOK	TAPIOCA	WILLOWY	SCAMPER	CABARET	INSURED	REVERIE	COARSEN
MAYPOLE	PREFORM	TAPROOM	WINDOWS	SCRAPPY	CALDRON	INSURER	REVERSE	COUNSEL
MENFOLK	PRESOAK	TAPROOT	WINSOME	SCRUPLE	CALORIC	INTERIM	ROSTRUM	COURSER
MICROBE	PROLONG	TEDIOUS	WITHOUT	SCUPPER	CALORIE	INVERSE	SADIRON	CRIMSON
MIDMOST	PROMOTE	TENFOLD	WORKOUT	SHAMPOO	CAMBRIC	KINDRED	SAFFRON	CRUISER
MIDTOWN	PRONOUN	TENUOUS	ZEALOUS	SHARPEN	CATARRH	LABORED	SAMURAI	DEMESNE
MONSOON	PROPOSE	THYROID	ZOOLOGY	SHARPER	CENTRAL	LAMPREY	SCOURGE	DEPOSIT
MUDROOM	PROSODY	TINFOIL	APROPOS	SHARPIE	CHAGRIN	LATERAL	SEVERAL	DIVISOR
NEOLOGY	PROVOKE	TOEHOLD	ATROPHY	SKIPPER	CHEVRON	LIBERAL	SOLARIS	DRESSER
NERVOUS	PROVOST	TOPCOAT	AUTOPSY	SLEEPER	COLORED	LIBERTY	SPARROW	DYNASTY
NETWORK	PULLOUT	TOPMOST	BLOOPER	SLIPPER	CONTRIB	LITERAL	SPLURGE	EMBASSY
NEWBORN	PURLOIN	TOPSOIL	CALIPER	STEEPLE	CONTROL	LITURGY	STIRRUP	FINESSE
NOCUOUS	PURPORT	TORTONI	CALYPSO	STIPPLE	COTERIE	LOWBROW	TANTRUM	FLOTSAM
NOISOME	PURPOSE	TOWBOAT	CHEAPEN	STOPPER	CULPRIT	LUCERNE	TENDRIL	FORESEE
NONBOOK	RACCOON	TREFOIL	CHIPPER	STROPHE	DECORUM	LUSTRAL	TENURED	FRETSAW
NOXIOUS	RAPPORT	TREMOLO	CHOPPER	SUNSPOT	DEMERIT	MACDRAW	THEOREM	FUCHSIA
OARLOCK	RAUCOUS	TRILOGY	CLAPPER	SYNAPSE	DESERVE	MALARIA	TIMBREL	GAINSAY
OBVIOUS	RAVIOLI	TUGBOAT	CLIPPER	TRAIPSE	DESTROY	MANDREL	TUMBREL	GENESIS
OMINOUS	READOUT	TURMOIL	COCKPIT	TRAMPLE	DEWDROP	MANDRIL	UNDERGO	HACKSAW
ONEROUS	RECTORY	TURNOFF	CRIPPLE	TROOPER	DEXTRIN	MAZURKA	UNEARTH	HANDSAW
ONSHORE	REDCOAT	TURNOUT	CROPPER	TRUMPET	DIAGRAM	MINARET	UNHORSE	HANDSEL
ORATORY	REDWOOD	TUSSOCK	CRUMPET	UNHAPPY	DISHRAG	MINERAL	UNMORAL	HANDSET
OUTCOME	REGROUP	TWOSOME	CRUMPLE	WHIMPER	DIVERGE	MISTRAL	UNNERVE	HEADSET
OUTDOOR	REPROOF	TYPHOID	DASHPOT	WHIPPET	DIVERSE	MONARCH	UNSCREW	HEARSAY
OUTLOOK	REPROVE	TYPHOON	DEADPAN	WHISPER	DIVORCE	MONGREL	UNSTRAP	IMPASSE
OUTPOST	RESPOND	UNBLOCK	DROPPER	WHOOPLA	DOGTROT	MUSKRAT	UPSURGE	IMPASTO
OUTVOTE	RESTORE	UNCLOAK	DUCKPIN	WHOPPER	EARDRUM	NATURAL	VENTRAL	INCISOR

KEELSON	BRISTLE	FLUTTER	MISSTEP	ROOSTER	TRUSTEE	CONSUME	LANGUID	SCAPULA
LIAISON	BRITTLE	FORETOP	MOBSTER	ROSETTE	TWEETER	CORRUPT	LANGUOR	SECLUDE
MAJESTY	BURETTE	FRACTAL	MOISTEN	SAINTLY	TWISTER	COSTUME	LAWSUIT	SENSUAL
MALISON	CAPITAL	FRANTIC	MONITOR	SANCTUM	TWITTER	COUTURE	LEAGUER	SOJOURN
MALMSEY	CAPITOL	FRITTER	MONSTER	SAUNTER	UNHITCH	CROQUET	LECTURE	SPATULA
MEIOSIS	CAPSTAN	FRUSTUM	MOUNTIE	SCATTER	UNLATCH	CULTURE	LEISURE	SPICULE
MILKSOP	CAROTID	GAVOTTE	MULATTO	SCEPTER	VAULTED	DEBAUCH	LETTUCE	STATURE
MIMESIS	CAUSTIC	GAZETTE	MUSETTE	SCEPTIC	VEGETAL	DEBOUCH	LINGUAL	STATUTE
MITOSIS	CHANTEY	GELATIN	NAPHTHA	SCOOTER	VISITOR	DEFAULT	MANHUNT	SUCCUMB
MODISTE	CHANTRY	GENETIC	NECKTIE	SCRATCH	WASHTUB	DEGAUSS	MARQUEE	SUFFUSE
NEMESIS	CHAPTER	GENITAL	NIGHTLY	SCROTUM	WEALTHY	DELOUSE	MARQUIS	SUNBURN
NONUSER	CHARTER	GHASTLY	NONSTOP	SCUTTLE	WHISTLE	DENTURE	MEASURE	TEXTURE
ODYSSEY	CHASTEN	GLISTEN	OLDSTER	SENATOR	WHITTLE	DIFFUSE	MERCURY	THROUGH
OPOSSUM	CHATTEL	GLISTER	ORBITER	SHATTER	WIRETAP	DISCUSS	MISRULE	TONSURE
OSMOSIS	CHATTER	GLITTER	OUTSTAY	SHEATHE	WORSTED	DISEUSE	MIXTURE	TORTURE
OVERSEA	CHEETAH	GLOTTIS	OVERTOP	SHELTER	WREATHE	DISGUST	MOLLUSK	TRADUCE
OVERSEE	CHINTZY	GLUTTON	PALETTE	SHORTEN	WRESTLE	DISPUTE	MUGWUMP	TRIBUNE
PARASOL	CHOCTAW	GRANTEE	PENATES	SHORTLY	ACCOUNT	DISRUPT	NEPTUNE	TRIBUTE
PARESIS	CHORTLE	GRISTLE	PHAETON	SHUTTER	ADJOURN	DISTURB	NURTURE	UNCOUTH
POCOSIN	CLASTIC	HABITAT	PHANTOM	SHUTTLE	AGROUND	EARMUFF	OBSCURE	UNEQUAL
RICKSHA	CLATTER	HABITUE	PHILTER	SHYSTER	APOLUNE	ENCRUST	OBTRUDE	UNSOUND
RIPOSTE	CLUSTER	HAMSTER	PIASTER	SIGHTED	ASEXUAL	ENTHUSE	OCCLUDE	UNTRUTH
SATISFY	CLUTTER	HARDTOP	PIPETTE	SIGHTLY	ASSAULT	ENTRUST	OROTUND	UNUSUAL
SPONSOR	COUNTER	HEALTHY	PLANTAR	SKEPTIC	ASTOUND	EPICURE	OUTPULL	UPCHUCK
SPOUSAL	COUNTRY	HEARTEN	PLANTER	SKITTER	AZIMUTH	EVACUEE	OVIDUCT	VENTURE
STEPSON	COURTLY	HEPATIC	PLASTER	SMELTER	BANQUET	EXCLUDE	PARQUET	VERDURE
TRANSIT	CREATOR	HILLTOP	PLASTIC	SPASTIC	BECAUSE	EXECUTE	PASTURE	VESTURE
TRANSOM	CRITTER	HIPSTER	PLATTER	SPATTER	BEDOUIN	EXHAUST	PENGUIN	VIADUCT
TREASON	CROUTON	HOLSTER	PLOTTER	SPECTER	BISCUIT	EXPOUND	PERFUME	VICTUAL
UNBOSOM	CRYPTIC	ILEITIS	POINTED	SPITTLE	BISMUTH	FACTUAL	PERJURY	VIRGULE
UTENSIL	CRYSTAL	IMPETUS	POINTER	SPLOTCH	BIVOUAC	FAILURE	PERTURB	VIRTUAL
VENISON	CULOTTE	INERTIA	POLITIC	SPOTTER	BOROUGH	FEATURE	PICTURE	VULTURE
WHIPSAW	CURATOR	JANITOR	POULTRY	SPUTTER	BOUQUET	FERRULE	POLLUTE	AQUAVIT
ADAPTER	DEMOTIC	JUJITSU	PRAETOR	STARTLE	BRAVURA	FISSURE	POSTURE	ARRIVAL
AMMETER	DESKTOP	JUPITER	PRATTLE	STARTUP	BULRUSH	FISTULA	POTLUCK	BEDEVIL
AMPUTEE	DEVOTED	KERATIN	PROCTOR	STILTED	CAESURA	FIXTURE	PRELUDE	BELOVED
APOSTLE	DEVOTEE	KILOTON	PSALTER	STILTON	CANNULA	FLEXURE	PREPUCE	BOLIVAR
AQUATIC	DIGITAL	KINETIC	PUNSTER	STRATUM	CAPSULE	FORMULA	PRESUME	CADAVER
ARBITER	DINETTE	KRYPTON	PURITAN	STRETCH	CAPTURE	FORTUNE	PROCURE	CARAVAN
ARBUTUS	DRASTIC	LAYETTE	PYRITES	STUTTER	CAROUSE	GESTURE	PRODUCE	CARAVEL
ASCETIC	DRIFTER	LEGATEE	QUANTUM	STYPTIC	CENSURE	GLOBULE	PRODUCT	CLEAVER
ASEPTIC	ELASTIC	LIGHTEN	QUARTER	SWARTHY	CENTURY	GRADUAL	PROFUSE	DELIVER
ASIATIC	ELECTOR	LIGHTER	QUARTET	SWEATER	CIRCUIT	GRANULE	PURSUIT	DISAVOW
AUDITOR	EMITTER	LIMITED	QUIETUS	SWEETEN	CLOSURE	GRAVURE	PUSTULE	ENLIVEN
BATHTUB	EMPATHY	LOBSTER	QUINTAL	SWELTER	CLOTURE	HIRSUTE	RAPTURE	FLIVVER
BEASTLY	ENTITLE	LOCATOR	QUINTET	SYMPTOM	COEQUAL	HOMBURG	REBOUND	FOREVER
BELATED	EPISTLE	LUNATIC	REACTOR	TAPSTER	COMMUNE	IMPOUND	RECLUSE	HOWEVER
BEWITCH	EQUATOR	LUNETTE	RECITAL	THEATER	COMMUTE	INBOUND	RECOUNT	JEHOVAH
BIMETAL	ERRATIC	MAESTRO	REENTRY	THISTLE	COMPUTE	INCLUDE	RECRUIT	PALAVER
BIRETTA	ERRATUM	MAHATMA	REGATTA	TIBETAN	CONDUCE	INCRUST	REDOUBT	POPOVER
BLINTZE	FANATIC	MAINTOP	RELATED	TIGHTEN	CONDUCT	INTRUDE	REDOUND	RECOVER
BLISTER	FIGHTER	MARITAL	RELATOR	TIMOTHY	CONDUIT	INTRUST	REMOUNT	REVIVAL
BLOATER	FIRSTLY	MEGATON	REPUTED	TIPSTER	CONFUSE	JONQUIL	RESOUND	SAMOVAR
BLOTTER	FLATTEN	MILITIA	RIGHTLY	TOASTER	CONFUTE	KIBBUTZ	RETOUCH	SHRIVEL
BLUSTER	FLATTER	MIMETIC	ROASTER	TRACTOR	CONJURE	KUMQUAT	ROEBUCK	UNCIVIL
BOLSTER	FLATTOP	MINSTER	ROISTER	TRAITOR	CONQUER	KWMQUAT	RUPTURE	UNCOVER
BREATHE	FLUSTER	MINUTIA	ROOFTOP	TRESTLE	CONSULT	LACQUER	SAWDUST	UNMOVED

UNRAVEL	DRIZZLE	CAPSTAN	FOREMAN	JOURNAL	OATMEAL	ROADWAY	UTOPIAN	CAPRICE
UNSAVED	FRAZZLE	CARABAO	FORTRAN	JUGULAR	OEDIPAL	ROWBOAT	VATICAN	CARSICK
UPRIVER	FREEZER	CARAVAN	FRACTAL	KINSMAN	OFFBEAT	RUFFIAN	VEGETAL	CASSOCK
WHOEVER	FRIZZLE	CARAWAY	FREEMAN	KNEECAP	OPTICAL	RUNAWAY	VENTRAL	CHALICE
ARCHWAY	GRIZZLY	CARDIAC	FREEWAY	KUMQUAT	OPTIMAL	RUSSIAN	VETERAN	COLLECT
AREAWAY	HORIZON	CARLOAD	FRETSAW	LACTEAL	ORDINAL	SAMOVAR	VICINAL	COMPACT
BEESWAX	MUEZZIN	CATBOAT	FROGMAN	LAMINAR	ORTOLAN	SAMURAI	VICTUAL	CONCOCT
BELTWAY	PRETZEL	CAVEMAN	FUNERAL	LAOTIAN	OTTOMAN	SANDBAG	VINEGAR	CONDUCE
BIKEWAY	QUETZAL	CENTRAL	FUSTIAN	LATERAL	OUTDRAW	SANDBAR	VIRTUAL	CONDUCT
CARAWAY	SELTZER	CHADIAN	GAINSAY	LATVIAN	OUTPLAY	SANDMAN	WALKWAY	CONNECT
DOORWAY		CHAPEAU	GAMBIAN	LAYAWAY	OUTSTAY	SCANDAL	WARHEAD	CONTACT
EMBOWER		CHAPMAN	GANGWAY	LESBIAN	OUTWEAR	SCHOLAR	WEEKDAY	CONVICT
EMPOWER		CHATEAU	GATEWAY	LIBERAL	OVERLAP	SECULAR	WHEREAS	COPPICE
FAIRWAY	**6TH LETTER**	CHEDDAR	GENERAL	LINEMAN	OVERLAY	SEMINAL	WHEREAT	CORNICE
FARAWAY		CHEETAH	GENITAL	LINGUAL	PAJAMAS	SEMINAR	WHIPSAW	CORRECT
FOLKWAY	ABYSMAL	CHOCTAW	GENTIAN	LITERAL	PARKWAY	SENSUAL	WILDCAT	COSSACK
FREEWAY	ABYSSAL	COAXIAL	GETAWAY	LOCKJAW	PARTIAL	SEVERAL	WINDBAG	COWLICK
GANGWAY	ACCUSAL	COEQUAL	GINGHAM	LUSTRAL	PARTWAY	SHELLAC	WIRETAP	CREVICE
GATEWAY	ACROBAT	CONCEAL	GLACIAL	MACADAM	PATHWAY	SHOWMAN	WOLFRAM	CUTBACK
GETAWAY	ADMIRAL	CONGEAL	GLEEMAN	MACDRAW	PAYLOAD	SIDECAR	WOODMAN	DEBAUCH
HALFWAY	ADRENAL	CONICAL	GODHEAD	MAHICAN	PEDICAB	SIDEMAN	WORKBAG	DEBOUCH
HALLWAY	AFRICAN	COPYCAT	GOODMAN	MAILMAN	PELICAN	SIMILAR	WORKDAY	DECENCY
HEADWAY	ALCAZAR	CORDIAL	GRADUAL	MANTEAU	PERSIAN	SKIWEAR	WORKMAN	DEFLECT
HIGHWAY	ALMANAC	CORONAL	GRAMMAR	MARITAL	PLANTAR	SOMEDAY	YARDMAN	DEFUNCT
LAYAWAY	AMALGAM	CROWBAR	GRANDAM	MARSHAL	PLATEAU	SOYBEAN	ZAMBIAN	DERRICK
PARKWAY	ANAGRAM	CRUCIAL	GRECIAN	MARTIAL	PLOWMAN	SPATIAL	ASCRIBE	DETRACT
PARTWAY	ANGULAR	CRYSTAL	GUNBOAT	MARTIAN	PLUVIAL	SPECIAL	CORDOBA	DIALECT
PATHWAY	ANNULAR	DEADPAN	HABITAT	MAXIMAL	POLECAT	SPOUSAL	CRYBABY	DISSECT
PERIWIG	ANTHRAX	DECIMAL	HACKMAN	MEATMAN	POPULAR	STELLAR	DISROBE	DISTICH
POSTWAR	ARCHWAY	DEWCLAW	HACKSAW	MEDICAL	PORTRAY	STOPGAP	EARLOBE	DIVORCE
RACEWAY	AREAWAY	DIAGRAM	HALFWAY	MESSIAH	POSTMAN	SUNBEAM	LULLABY	DURANCE
RAILWAY	ARRIVAL	DIGITAL	HALLWAY	MEXICAN	POSTWAR	SUNDIAL	MARIMBA	EDIFICE
RENEWAL	ARSENAL	DISHRAG	HANDBAG	MIDYEAR	POTHEAD	TABLEAU	MICROBE	EMBRACE
ROADWAY	ARTISAN	DISPLAY	HANDCAR	MILKMAN	PREHEAT	TABULAR	PLACEBO	ENFORCE
RUNAWAY	ASEXUAL	DIURNAL	HANDSAW	MILLDAM	PRESOAK	TAXICAB	REDOUBT	ENHANCE
SCRAWNY	ASHTRAY	DOORMAN	HANGMAN	MINERAL	PROGMAN	THEREAT	STANDBY	ESSENCE
THRUWAY	AUSTRAL	DOORMAT	HARDPAN	MINIMAL	PROGRAM	THERMAL	THEREBY	EXTINCT
UNBOWED	BATSMAN	DUSTPAN	HEADMAN	MISLEAD	PROPMAN	THRUWAY	WALLABY	EXTRACT
WALKWAY	BEESWAX	DOORWAY	HEADWAY	MISPLAY	PROTEAN	TIBETAN	WHEREBY	FAIENCE
WIDOWER	BELGIAN	EGGHEAD	HEARSAY	MISREAD	PULLMAN	TITULAR	ABSENCE	FALLACY
WYSIWYG	BELTWAY	ELEGIAC	HELICAL	MISTRAL	PURITAN	TONNEAU	ADJUNCT	FATBACK
INDEXED	BESMEAR	ENTREAT	HELLCAT	MODULAR	PYJAMAS	TOPCOAT	ADVANCE	FETLOCK
ACOLYTE	BESPEAK	EPIGRAM	HIGHWAY	MOHEGAN	QUETZAL	TOPICAL	AFFLICT	FINANCE
ANALYZE	BESTIAL	ETERNAL	HOLIDAY	MOHICAN	QUINTAL	TOWBOAT	AIRSICK	FLOUNCE
ANODYNE	BIFOCAL	ETHICAL	HOPHEAD	MUSICAL	QUONDAM	TOWHEAD	ASKANCE	FURNACE
CARRYON	BIKEWAY	FACTUAL	ICEBOAT	MUSKRAT	RACEWAY	TRIVIAL	ATTRACT	GIMMICK
CONDYLE	BIMETAL	FAIRWAY	ILLEGAL	NARWHAL	RADICAL	TUBULAR	AUSPICE	GRIMACE
EMBRYOL	BIPOLAR	FARAWAY	IMMORAL	NATURAL	RAILWAY	TUESDAY	AVARICE	GUNLOCK
HALCYON	BIVOUAC	FEDERAL	INHUMAN	NEUTRAL	RATTRAP	TUGBOAT	BALANCE	HADDOCK
MONEYED	BOATMAN	FIREMAN	INITIAL	NEWSMAN	RECITAL	TUTELAR	BANNOCK	HAMMOCK
PHARYNX	BOLIVAR	FLATCAR	INSTEAD	NOMINAL	REDCOAT	TYPICAL	BEDROCK	HASSOCK
TALLYHO	BONDMAN	FLOTSAM	INSULAR	NOONDAY	REDHEAD	UNCLEAN	BESEECH	HAYCOCK
VANDYKE	BRAHMAN	FLYLEAF	IRANIAN	NOSEGAY	REGULAR	UNCLOAK	BEWITCH	HAYRICK
ALCAZAR	BUCKRAM	FOLKWAY	ITALIAN	NUCLEAR	RENEWAL	UNEQUAL	BULLOCK	HEMLOCK
BEDIZEN	BUCKSAW	FOOTMAN	JACKDAW	NUMERAL	RETREAD	UNMORAL	BURDOCK	HENPECK
CITIZEN	BUGBEAR	FOOTPAD	JEHOVAH	NUPTIAL	RETREAT	UNSTRAP	BUTTOCK	HEROICS
DENIZEN	CAPITAL	FORBEAR	JOCULAR	OARSMAN	REVIVAL	UNUSUAL	CADENCE	HILLOCK

HOGBACK	RESPECT	BRAVADO	TORNADO	BLUBBER	CHASTEN	CRULLER	FRITTER	KITCHEN
HOSPICE	RETOUCH	BRIGADE	TORPEDO	BLUCHER	CHATTEL	CRUMPET	FURRIER	KNOCKER
HUMMOCK	RETRACE	BROCADE	TRAGEDY	BLUNDER	CHATTER	DEBRIEF	FURTHER	LABORED
IMPEACH	RETRACT	BROMIDE	UNHANDY	BLUSTER	CHEAPEN	DECIBEL	GANTLET	LACQUER
INEXACT	ROEBUCK	CALENDS	UPGRADE	BOBSLED	CHECKER	DECIDED	GENTEEL	LAMPREY
INFANCY	ROLLICK	CARBIDE	VERANDA	BOLSTER	CHICKEN	DECODER	GLACIER	LATCHET
INFARCT	ROMANCE	CASCADE	WAYSIDE	BOOKLET	CHIGGER	DELIVER	GLADDEN	LAUNDER
INFLECT	SCIENCE	CATHODE	ABDOMEN	BOOTLEG	CHIMNEY	DENIZEN	GLAZIER	LEAFLET
INFLICT	SCRATCH	COCKADE	ACCUSED	BOULDER	CHIPPER	DEVOTED	GLIMMER	LEAGUER
INSPECT	SCREECH	COLLIDE	ADAPTER	BOUNCER	CHOPPER	DEVOTEE	GLISTEN	LEARNED
INVOICE	SEASICK	COMMODE	ADVISED	BOUNDEN	CHOWDER	DISOBEY	GLISTER	LEATHER
JOYANCE	SECRECY	COMRADE	ALBUMEN	BOUQUET	CHUKKER	DIVIDER	GLITTER	LEGATEE
JUSTICE	SERVICE	CONCEDE	ALMONER	BOWLDER	CHUTNEY	DOSSIER	GOBBLER	LIGHTEN
LATTICE	SETBACK	CONFIDE	AMMETER	BRACKEN	CIRCLET	DOUBLET	GOGGLES	LIGHTER
LETTUCE	SHYLOCK	CORRODE	AMPUTEE	BRACKET	CITADEL	DOWAGER	GOURMET	LIMITED
LIMBECK	SILENCE	COWHIDE	ANOTHER	BRAZIER	CITIZEN	DRAGNET	GRANDEE	LINSEED
MATTOCK	SIROCCO	CRUSADE	ANTIGEN	BREAKER	CIVVIES	DRESSER	GRANTEE	LOBSTER
MONARCH	SPINACH	CUSTODY	APPAREL	BRISKET	CLAMBER	DRIBLET	GRAPNEL	LUCIFER
MOROCCO	SPLOTCH	CYANIDE	APPLIED	BROADEN	CLAPPER	DRIFTER	GRAUPEL	MALMSEY
NEGLECT	SQUELCH	DEGRADE	AQUIFER	BROIDER	CLATTER	DROPLET	GRAZIER	MANAGER
NUTPICK	STAUNCH	EFFENDI	ARBITER	BROILER	CLAVIER	DROPPER	GRINDER	MANDREL
OARLOCK	STOMACH	EPISODE	ARMORER	BROODER	CLEAVER	DRUMMER	GROMMET	MARINER
ORIFICE	STRETCH	EXCLUDE	ARPANET	BROTHEL	CLINKER	DRUNKEN	GROUPER	MARQUEE
OSTRICH	SUBJECT	EXPLODE	ASHAMED	BROTHER	CLIPPER	EARTHEN	GUILDER	MATINEE
OUTFACE	SUFFICE	EXTRUDE	ASSURED	BROWSER	CLOBBER	EMBOWER	HACKNEY	MAUNDER
OVERACT	SURFACE	FORBODE	ASUNDER	BRUISER	CLOTHES	EMITTER	HAMSTER	MEANDER
OVIDUCT	SUSPECT	GRENADE	ATELIER	BUCKLER	CLUSTER	EMPOWER	HANDSEL	MEASLES
PADDOCK	TACTICS	HYMNODY	BALONEY	BURGHER	CLUTTER	ENLIVEN	HANDSET	MIDWEEK
PADLOCK	TAPIOCA	IMPLODE	BANQUET	BUTCHER	COARSEN	EPAULET	HARRIER	MINARET
PEACOCK	TENANCY	INCLUDE	BANSHEE	CABARET	COBBLER	EPITHET	HATCHET	MINSTER
PENANCE	TERRACE	INNARDS	BARONET	CABINET	COCHLEA	ESCAPEE	HAYSEED	MISDEED
PERFECT	TIEBACK	INTRUDE	BARRIER	CADAVER	COCKNEY	EVACUEE	HEADSET	MISSTEP
PHONICS	TOBACCO	JOYRIDE	BAYONET	CALIBER	COLLEEN	FANCIER	HEARKEN	MOBSTER
PHYSICS	TRADUCE	LIMEADE	BEDIZEN	CALIPER	COLLIER	FARRIER	HEARTEN	MOISTEN
PIBROCH	TRISECT	NUCLIDE	BELATED	CALOMEL	COLONEL	FARTHER	HEATHEN	MONEYED
PINNACE	TROUNCE	OBTRUDE	BELOVED	CALUMET	COLORED	FEATHER	HEATHER	MONGREL
POLLACK	TUSSOCK	OCCLUDE	BESHREW	CANDIED	COMPEER	FIANCEE	HIPSTER	MONOMER
PORTICO	UNBLOCK	OFFSIDE	BESIDES	CANTEEN	COMPLEX	FIFTEEN	HOLSTER	MONSTER
POTLUCK	UNFROCK	ORGANDY	BETIMES	CARAMEL	CONIFER	FIGHTER	HOOSIER	MUFFLER
PREDICT	UNHITCH	OUTSIDE	BETOKEN	CARAVEL	CONQUER	FLANKER	HOSTLER	NANKEEN
PREFACE	UNLATCH	PERFIDY	BETWEEN	CARRIER	CORONER	FLANNEL	HOWEVER	NARTHEX
PREFECT	UPCHUCK	PERVADE	BIRCHER	CASHIER	CORONET	FLAPPER	HUNDRED	NEITHER
PREPUCE	VACANCY	PRECEDE	BITUMEN	CASTLED	COUNSEL	FLATBED	IMPANEL	NOMINEE
PRIMACY	VALANCE	PRELUDE	BLACKEN	CATCHER	COUNTER	FLATTEN	INDEXED	NONSKED
PRIVACY	VALENCE	PRESIDE	BLADDER	CERUMEN	COUPLET	FLATTER	INFIDEL	NONUSER
PRODUCE	VERDICT	PROSODY	BLANKET	CHAFFER	COURIER	FLICKER	INHALER	NORTHER
PRODUCT	VIADUCT	PROVIDE	BLARNEY	CHAMBER	COURSER	FLIPPER	INSIDER	OCTOBER
PROJECT	WARLOCK	RAWHIDE	BLATHER	CHAMFER	CRABBED	FLIVVER	INSURED	ODYSSEY
PROTECT	WEDLOCK	ROTUNDA	BLEEDER	CHANCEL	CRACKER	FLUSTER	INSURER	OFFICER
RANSACK	WETBACK	SEASIDE	BLESSED	CHANNEL	CRICKET	FLUTTER	INTEGER	OLDSTER
RECENCY	WRYNECK	SECLUDE	BLINDER	CHANTEY	CRITTER	FORELEG	JACKLEG	ORBITER
REFLECT	ALCALDE	SUBSIDE	BLINKER	CHAPLET	CROCHET	FORESEE	JEWELER	OVERSEA
REFRACT	ALREADY	SUBSIDY	BLISTER	CHAPTER	CROOKED	FOREVER	JOURNEY	OVERSEE
REGENCY	ANYBODY	SUICIDE	BLOATER	CHARGER	CROPPER	FOUNDER	JUBILEE	PAISLEY
REJOICE	ASTRIDE	SULFIDE	BLOODED	CHARMER	CROQUET	FREEZER	JUNIPER	PALAVER
REPLACE	AVOCADO	THREADY	BLOOPER	CHARNEL	CROSIER	FRESHEN	JUPITER	PALFREY
REPLICA	BEDSIDE	TOPSIDE	BLOTTER	CHARTER	CRUISER	FRESHET	KINDRED	PANACEA

PANNIER	REFINED	SLIPPER	TRAILER	WORSTED	TESTIFY	INNINGS	VILLAGE	AMMONIA
PANTHER	REFUGEE	SLITHER	TRAINEE	WRAPPER	TURNOFF	INVEIGH	VINTAGE	AMNESIA
PARAPET	REGIMEN	SLOBBER	TRAMMEL	WRECKER	UPDRAFT	LEAFAGE	VOLTAGE	ANAEMIA
PARQUET	RELATED	SLUMBER	TRIGGER	WRINGER	UPSHIFT	LEAKAGE	WASTAGE	ANDROID
PARSLEY	REMODEL	SMELTER	TRINKET	YOUNKER	VERSIFY	LINEAGE	WATTAGE	ANTACID
PARTNER	REPUTED	SMIDGEN	TRIPLET	ACIDIFY	VITRIFY	LINKAGE	WINDAGE	APHASIA
PASSKEY	REQUIEM	SMOLDER	TRIPLEX	AIRLIFT	ABRIDGE	LITURGY	WORDAGE	AQUATIC
PENATES	RETIRED	SMOTHER	TROCHEE	ALEWIFE	ACREAGE	LOZENGE	YARDAGE	AQUAVIT
PERIGEE	RETIREE	SNEAKER	TRODDEN	ALFALFA	ADJUDGE	LUGGAGE	ZOOLOGY	ARCHAIC
PERPLEX	RINGLET	SNICKER	TROLLEY	AMPLIFY	ALLERGY	LUMBAGO	ZYMURGY	ARSENIC
PHILTER	RIVULET	SNORKEL	TROOPER	BAILIFF	ANALOGY	MAKINGS	ALRIGHT	ASCETIC
PIASTER	ROADBED	SOLDIER	TRUMPET	BEATIFY	APANAGE	MASSAGE	ANARCHY	ASEPTIC
PILSNER	ROASTER	SOUNDER	TRUSTEE	CAITIFF	APOLOGY	MELANGE	ARAPAHO	ASIATIC
PIONEER	ROISTER	SPANIEL	TUMBLER	CALCIFY	ARRAIGN	MESSAGE	ATROPHY	ASPIRIN
PITCHER	ROOSTER	SPATTER	TUMBREL	CERTIFY	ARRANGE	MILEAGE	ATTACHE	BACKLIT
PLACKET	ROOTLET	SPEAKER	TURNKEY	CLARIFY	ASSUAGE	MILLAGE	BORSCHT	BALDRIC
PLANTER	ROUGHEN	SPECIES	TWEETER	CRUCIFY	AVERAGE	MONTAGE	BREATHE	BARGAIN
PLASTER	SAMPLER	SPECTER	TWILLED	DANDIFY	BAGGAGE	NEOLOGY	BRIOCHE	BEATNIK
PLATTER	SATCHEL	SPELLER	TWISTER	DIGNIFY	BANDAGE	OUTRAGE	BROUGHT	BEDEVIL
PLAYLET	SAUNTER	SPOILER	TWITTER	DISTAFF	BARRAGE	OVERAGE	DELIGHT	BEDOUIN
PLAYPEN	SCALPEL	SPOTTER	UMPTEEN	EARMUFF	BESIEGE	PACKAGE	DRAUGHT	BEGONIA
PLOTTER	SCAMPER	SPUTTER	UNARMED	ENGRAFT	BIOLOGY	PASSAGE	DROUGHT	BENEFIT
PLUMBER	SCANNER	STAFFER	UNBOWED	FALSIFY	BONDAGE	PILLAGE	EARACHE	BENTHIC
PLUMMET	SCARLET	STAGGER	UNCOVER	FORTIFY	BOROUGH	PLUMAGE	EMPATHY	BENZOIN
PLUNDER	SCATTER	STAMMER	UNMOVED	GIRAFFE	CABBAGE	PORTAGE	FRAUGHT	BISCUIT
PLUNGER	SCEPTER	STICKER	UNQUIET	GLORIFY	CARNAGE	POSTAGE	FREIGHT	BOUDOIR
POINTED	SCOOTER	STIFFEN	UNRAVEL	GRATIFY	CARTAGE	POTTAGE	HEALTHY	BRAHMIN
POINTER	SCUPPER	STILTED	UNSAVED	HAYLOFT	COINAGE	PRESAGE	HIBACHI	BRECCIA
POLYMER	SEAWEED	STOPPER	UNSCREW	HORRIFY	COLLAGE	PRODIGY	INSIGHT	BROWNIE
POPOVER	SELTZER	STORIED	UNTRIED	INGRAFT	COLLEGE	PROTEGE	NAPHTHA	BUCOLIC
PREMIER	SERRIED	STRUDEL	UPRIVER	JUSTIFY	CONDIGN	RAMPAGE	PANACHE	BUMPKIN
PRETEEN	SHARPEN	STUDIED	VAULTED	KICKOFF	CONSIGN	REVENGE	PIRANHA	CALORIC
PRETZEL	SHARPER	STUTTER	VERNIER	LIGNIFY	CORDAGE	RUMMAGE	RAUNCHY	CALORIE
PREVIEW	SHATTER	SUCCEED	VINTNER	LIQUEFY	CORSAGE	SALVAGE	RICKSHA	CAMBRIC
PRICKER	SHAWNEE	SWAGGER	VITTLES	MAGNIFY	CORTEGE	SAUSAGE	SHEATHE	CAPTAIN
PRITHEE	SHELTER	SWEATER	VOUCHER	MASTIFF	COTTAGE	SCOURGE	SLEIGHT	CAROTID
PROBLEM	SHERBET	SWEETEN	WAGONER	MIDRIFF	COURAGE	SELVAGE	STROPHE	CATTAIL
PROCEED	SHIMMER	SWELTER	WARBLER	MIDWIFE	DERANGE	SPLURGE	SWARTHY	CAUSTIC
PROFFER	SHOCKER	SWOLLEN	WASTREL	MOLLIFY	DIVERGE	STORAGE	TALLYHO	CERAMIC
PROPHET	SHORTEN	TANAGER	WAVELET	MORTIFY	DIVULGE	STRANGE	THOUGHT	CERTAIN
PROSPER	SHRIVEL	TAPSTER	WEATHER	MYSTIFY	DOCKAGE	STRINGY	TIMOTHY	CHABLIS
PSALTER	SHUDDER	TENURED	WHEELER	NITRIFY	ECOLOGY	SYRINGE	TONIGHT	CHAGRIN
PUNSTER	SHUTTER	TERRIER	WHETHER	NULLIFY	EMBARGO	TEENAGE	UPRIGHT	CHALLIS
PURLIEU	SHYSTER	THEATER	WHICKER	PETRIFY	ENLARGE	THROUGH	UPTIGHT	CHAMOIS
PURVIEW	SICKBED	THEOREM	WHIMPER	PONTIFF	EXPUNGE	TIDINGS	WEALTHY	CHASSIS
PYRITES	SIGHTED	THICKEN	WHIPPET	PUTREFY	FARRAGO	TILLAGE	WREATHE	CHROMIC
QUARREL	SIXTEEN	THICKET	WHISKER	QUALIFY	FOLIAGE	TONNAGE	WROUGHT	CHRONIC
QUARTER	SKILLET	THINNER	WHISKEY	RECTIFY	FOOTAGE	TRILOGY	ABSTAIN	CIRCUIT
QUARTET	SKIPPER	THITHER	WHISPER	SATISFY	FOREIGN	UMBRAGE	ACCLAIM	CLASSIC
QUICKEN	SKITTER	THUNDER	WHITHER	SCARIFY	GARBAGE	UNDERGO	ACRYLIC	CLASTIC
QUINTET	SLACKEN	TIGHTEN	WHOEVER	SCRUFFY	GEOLOGY	UNHINGE	ADENOID	COCKPIT
RAGWEED	SLACKER	TIMBREL	WHOPPER	SHERIFF	HAULAGE	UPSTAGE	AEROBIC	CODICIL
RAMBLER	SLANDER	TIPSTER	WHORLED	SIGNIFY	HERBAGE	UPSURGE	AIRFOIL	COHABIT
RATCHET	SLATHER	TOASTER	WIDOWER	SPECIFY	HIDALGO	UROLOGY	AIRMAIL	COLLOID
RATTLER	SLEEPER	TOUGHEN	WIGGLER	STUPEFY	HOSTAGE	VANTAGE	AIRSHIP	CONCEIT
RECOVER	SLENDER	TOURNEY	WILLIES	TAKEOFF	IMPINGE	VERTIGO	ALBUMIN	CONDUIT
REFEREE	SLICKER	TRACHEA	WIZENED	TERRIFY	INDULGE	VESTIGE	ALEMBIC	CONJOIN

CONTAIN	GREMLIN	MITOSIS	REVERIE	BAZOOKA	CLEANLY	GHASTLY	PAPILLA	SPICULE
CONTRIB	GROUPIE	MONADIC	SATANIC	CATLIKE	COMPILE	GLOBULE	PARABLE	SPINDLE
CORSAIR	GUMBOIL	MORPHIA	SCEPTIC	CONVOKE	CONDOLE	GONDOLA	PATELLA	SPINDLY
COTERIE	HAIRPIN	MOUNTIE	SEISMIC	COWPOKE	CONDYLE	GORILLA	PAYROLL	SPITTLE
COUNCIL	HAPLOID	MUEZZIN	SEQUOIA	CUPCAKE	CONSOLE	GRACKLE	PERCALE	STABILE
COWSLIP	HARELIP	MULLEIN	SHARPIE	DASHIKI	CONSULT	GRANULE	PERGOLA	STARTLE
CRYPTIC	HEADPIN	MURRAIN	SIDELIT	DISLIKE	CORACLE	GRAPPLE	PETIOLE	STATELY
CULPRIT	HEPARIN	NECKTIE	SIRLOIN	FINICKY	COROLLA	GRIDDLE	PICCOLO	STEEPLE
CURTAIL	HEPATIC	NEMESIS	SKEPTIC	FORSAKE	COURTLY	GRISTLE	PIEBALD	STERILE
CURTAIN	HOBNAIL	NOMADIC	SOLARIS	GODLIKE	CRACKLE	GRIZZLY	PINHOLE	STIPPLE
DAUPHIN	HOWBEIT	NOSTRIL	SOLICIT	HOECAKE	CRINKLE	GRUMBLE	PITFALL	STUBBLE
DECLAIM	ILEITIS	NUMERIC	SPASTIC	HOTCAKE	CRIPPLE	GUNWALE	PLIABLE	STUMBLE
DEFICIT	ILLICIT	OILSKIN	SPLENIC	MANLIKE	CRUMBLE	HAPPILY	POTABLE	SUBTILE
DELIMIT	IMPERIL	ORGANIC	SPUTNIK	MAZURKA	CRUMPLE	HERSELF	POTHOLE	SWADDLE
DEMERIT	INDICIA	OSMOSIS	SQUALID	MISLIKE	CUBICLE	HIMSELF	PRATTLE	SWAHILI
DEMONIC	INERTIA	PACIFIC	STENCIL	MISTAKE	CUCKOLD	HOSTILE	PRICKLE	SWINDLE
DEMOTIC	INGRAIN	PALADIN	STUFFIT	OATCAKE	CUTICLE	IDEALLY	PROFILE	SYSTOLE
DEPOSIT	INHABIT	PARBOIL	STYPTIC	PANCAKE	DEATHLY	IGNOBLE	PUERILE	TACTILE
DESPAIR	INHERIT	PARESIS	SUBJOIN	PAPRIKA	DEBACLE	INDWELL	PUSTULE	TADPOLE
DESPOIL	INHIBIT	PARFAIT	SUBSOIL	PARTAKE	DEERFLY	INFIELD	QUIBBLE	TAMBALA
DETRAIN	INSIPID	PARSNIP	SURFEIT	PROVOKE	DEFAULT	INKWELL	RAVIOLI	TENABLE
DEXTRIN	INSULIN	PELAGIC	SUSTAIN	UNLUCKY	DISABLE	INSTALL	REBUILD	TENFOLD
DIPLOID	INTERIM	PENGUIN	TABLOID	VANDYKE	DISTILL	INSTILL	RECYCLE	TENSILE
DISDAIN	INTROIT	PERIWIG	TECHNIC	WARLIKE	DRIBBLE	ISRAELI	REPTILE	TEQUILA
DISJOIN	INVALID	PERTAIN	TENDRIL	AFFABLE	DRIZZLE	JAYWALK	RIGHTLY	TEXTILE
DOLPHIN	JAVELIN	PETUNIA	TERRAIN	AMIABLE	DUCTILE	KEYHOLE	RISIBLE	THIMBLE
DOMINIE	JONQUIL	PFENNIG	THEREIN	ANOMALY	DURABLE	KINFOLK	RUBELLA	THISTLE
DRASTIC	KATYDID	PHALLIC	THYROID	ANTHILL	DWINDLE	KNUCKLE	SAINTLY	THYSELF
DRUMLIN	KERATIN	PHOENIX	TINFOIL	APOSTLE	EARTHLY	LEGIBLE	SAWMILL	TOEHOLD
DUCKPIN	KIDSKIN	PHRENIC	TITANIC	ARMHOLE	ELDERLY	LIVABLE	SCAPULA	TRAMPLE
DYNAMIC	KINETIC	PIGSKIN	TOENAIL	ARTICLE	EMERALD	LOATHLY	SCRUPLE	TREACLE
ELASTIC	KINGPIN	PIGTAIL	TOPSAIL	ASPHALT	ENNOBLE	MANACLE	SCUFFLE	TREADLE
EMBROIL	KINSHIP	PILGRIM	TOPSOIL	ASSAULT	ENTITLE	MANHOLE	SCUTTLE	TREMBLE
ENCHAIN	KREMLIN	PLASTIC	TOXEMIA	AUDIBLE	EPISTLE	MAXILLA	SEAWALL	TREMOLO
ENDEMIC	LACONIC	PLAUDIT	TRAFFIC	AUREOLE	EQUABLE	MAYPOLE	SERVILE	TRESTLE
ENTRAIN	LANGUID	POCOSIN	TRANSIT	AURICLE	EXAMPLE	MEDULLA	SESSILE	TRICKLE
ERRATIC	LANOLIN	POLARIS	TRAVAIL	BARBELL	EYEBALL	MENFOLK	SHACKLE	TROUBLE
EXCLAIM	LATAKIA	POLEMIC	TREFOIL	BEASTLY	FEBRILE	MIRACLE	SHAMBLE	TRUCKLE
EXHIBIT	LAWSUIT	POLITIC	TRELLIS	BEDROLL	FERRULE	MISCALL	SHAPELY	TRUFFLE
EXPLAIN	LUNATIC	PRAIRIE	TURMOIL	BEGUILE	FERTILE	MISFILE	SHINGLE	TRUNDLE
EXPLOIT	MALARIA	PREEMIE	TYPHOID	BICYCLE	FINAGLE	MISRULE	SHORTLY	TUNABLE
FANATIC	MALEFIC	PREVAIL	UNCHAIN	BRAILLE	FIREFLY	MISSILE	SHUFFLE	TWADDLE
FANTAIL	MANDRIL	PROSAIC	UNCIVIL	BRAMBLE	FIRSTLY	MONOCLE	SHUTTLE	TWIDDLE
FIBROID	MANIKIN	PROTEIN	UPBRAID	BRISTLE	FISSILE	MUTABLE	SIGHTLY	TWINKLE
FLACCID	MANUMIT	PSYCHIC	UTENSIL	BRITTLE	FISTULA	NACELLE	SIZABLE	UKULELE
FORFEIT	MARQUIS	PUMPKIN	VERMEIL	BUFFALO	FLESHLY	NIGHTLY	SKIFFLE	UNGODLY
FRANTIC	MASONIC	PURLOIN	VERVAIN	CANNULA	FLYABLE	NOTABLE	SMUGGLE	UNMANLY
FREEBIE	MASTOID	PURSUIT	VILLAIN	CAPABLE	FORMULA	NOVELLA	SNAFFLE	VACUOLE
FUCHSIA	MAUDLIN	PYRAMID	VILLEIN	CAPSULE	FOXHOLE	ODDBALL	SNIFFLE	VANILLA
GASTRIC	MEIOSIS	QUICKIE	VITAMIN	CATCALL	FRAGILE	ONESELF	SNUFFLE	VEHICLE
GELATIN	MELANIC	RAREBIT	VOCALIC	CATWALK	FRAZZLE	ORDERLY	SNUGGLE	VESICLE
GENERIC	MELANIN	RECLAIM	VOLTAIC	CEDILLA	FRECKLE	OUTPULL	SOLUBLE	VIRGULE
GENESIS	MERMAID	RECRUIT	WAGTAIL	CEMBALO	FRIABLE	OUTSELL	SOUFFLE	VISIBLE
GENETIC	MILITIA	REDSKIN	WARSHIP	CHORALE	FRIZZLE	OVERALL	SPANGLE	VOCABLE
GHERKIN	MIMESIS	REFRAIN	WASSAIL	CHORTLE	FULFILL	OVERFLY	SPARKLE	VOLUBLE
GLOTTIS	MIMETIC	REGALIA	WHEREIN	CHUCKLE	GAZELLE	PANICLE	SPATULA	WADABLE
GRAPHIC	MINUTIA	RESEDIT	WORSHIP	CIVILLY	GENTILE	PANOPLY	SPECKLE	WAYBILL

WHEEDLE	SUNLAMP	BROMINE	DIAMOND	GUANINE	LOWLAND	PENDING	SCRAWNY	VACCINE
WHISTLE	SUPREME	BUNTING	DILUENT	GUARANI	LUCERNE	PENNANT	SEALANT	VAGRANT
WHITTLE	SURNAME	BUSHING	DISBAND	HALTING	MACHINE	PERCENT	SEATING	VALIANT
WHOOPLA	TRIREME	CALCINE	DISSENT	HANGING	MADDING	PHALANX	SEEMING	VARIANT
WOMANLY	TSUNAMI	CALLING	DISTANT	HARMONY	MANHUNT	PHARYNX	SEGMENT	VARMINT
WORLDLY	TWOSOME	CALUMNY	DISTEND	HASHING	MANKIND	PIGMENT	SEQUENT	VEILING
WRANGLE	WARTIME	CARBINE	DOGBANE	HEADING	MARGENT	PIQUANT	SERPENT	VERBENA
WRESTLE	WELCOME	CARMINE	DORMANT	HEARING	MARTINI	PLATING	SERVANT	VERDANT
WRIGGLE	WINSOME	CASTING	DOYENNE	HELLENE	MATTINS	POMPANO	SERVING	VESTING
WRINKLE	ABALONE	CEILING	DRAWING	HELPING	MEANING	PORCINE	SETTING	VIBRANT
WRONGLY	ABSCOND	CHICANE	DUMPING	HEMLINE	MEETING	PORTEND	SEXTANT	VIOLENT
ACADEME	ACCOUNT	CHICANO	EARRING	HEROINE	METHANE	PORTENT	SHADING	VOLCANO
ACADEMY	ACETONE	CLEMENT	ELEMENT	HERRING	MIDLAND	PRALINE	SHAVING	VULPINE
ALCHEMY	ADAMANT	COATING	EMINENT	HINTING	MIGRANT	PRAYING	SHEBANG	WADDING
ANATOMY	ADENINE	COCAINE	ENCHANT	HIPBONE	MILLING	PREBEND	SHORING	WANTING
ANYTIME	AFFRONT	CODEINE	ENPLANE	HOLDING	MINUEND	PRESENT	SIBLING	WARNING
BEDTIME	AFGHANI	CODLING	ENTRANT	HORMONE	MISSEND	PRETEND	SKYLINE	WARRANT
BEGRIME	AGROUND	COLOGNE	ENTWINE	HOSANNA	MISSING	PREVENT	SOLVENT	WASHING
CENTIME	AILMENT	COMBINE	EPERGNE	HOUSING	MOLDING	PROFANE	SOMEONE	WAXWING
CENTIMO	AIRLINE	COMMAND	ERELONG	HOWLING	MOORING	PROGENY	SOPRANO	WEASAND
CONDEMN	ALIMENT	COMMEND	ETCHING	HULKING	MORAINE	PROLONG	SPARING	WEBBING
CONSUME	ALIMONY	COMMENT	EUPHONY	HUSBAND	MORDANT	PROPANE	SPIRANT	WEDDING
CONTEMN	ALUMINA	COMMUNE	EVENING	HUSKING	MORNING	PRUDENT	SPUMONI	WEEKEND
COSTUME	AMBIENT	COMPANY	EVIDENT	HUTMENT	MUNDANE	PUDDING	STAGING	WEEPING
COULOMB	AMERIND	CONDONE	EXAMINE	HYDRANT	MUSTANG	PUNGENT	STAMINA	WETLAND
COXCOMB	ANCIENT	CONFINE	EXPOUND	HYGIENE	NASCENT	QUININE	STIPEND	WHITING
DAYTIME	ANEMONE	CONSENT	FAILING	IMAGINE	NEPTUNE	RADIANT	STUDENT	WILLING
DILEMMA	ANILINE	CONTEND	FAIRING	IMPOUND	NETTING	RAILING	STYLING	WINDING
DIPLOMA	ANODYNE	CONTENT	FARMING	IMPRINT	NIRVANA	RAIMENT	SUITING	WINNING
DRACHMA	ANTENNA	CONVENE	FEELING	INBOUND	NOTHING	RAMPANT	SULTANA	WITTING
ECONOMY	APOLUNE	CONVENT	FENCING	INCLINE	OBSCENE	RANKING	SUMMONS	WORDING
EPITOME	APPOINT	COOLANT	FERMENT	INFERNO	OCARINA	RATLINE	SUSPEND	WORKING
EXTREME	ASININE	COWHAND	FERVENT	INKLING	ODDMENT	READING	TANGENT	WRITING
FULSOME	ASTOUND	COWLING	FIGMENT	INSTANT	OFFHAND	REAGENT	TATTING	ABANDON
INFLAME	ATTAINT	CRAVING	FILLING	INTRANS	OLIVINE	REBOUND	TELLING	AEROSOL
IRKSOME	AUGMENT	CUISINE	FINDING	IRONING	ONGOING	RECLINE	THYMINE	AILERON
LISSOME	BACKING	CUNNING	FISHING	JASMINE	OPENING	RECOUNT	TICKING	AIRDROP
MACRAME	BADLAND	CURBING	FITTING	JOTTING	OPULENT	REDLINE	TIMPANI	AIRFLOW
MAHATMA	BALCONY	CURRANT	FLEMING	KEEPING	OREGANO	REDOUND	TOLUENE	ALCOHOL
MILLIME	BALDING	CURRENT	FONDANT	KERNING	OROGENY	REGNANT	TOPPING	ANDIRON
MISNAME	BARRING	CUTTING	FOOTING	KILLING	OROTUND	REMAINS	TORMENT	ANTHROP
MUGWUMP	BATTING	CYCLONE	FORFEND	KNOWING	OUTLINE	REMNANT	TORRENT	APRICOT
NOISOME	BEARING	CZARINA	FORGING	LAMBENT	OUTRANK	REMOUNT	TORTONI	APROPOS
ONETIME	BEDDING	DARLING	FORTUNE	LANDING	OXIDANT	REPRINT	TRACING	AUCTION
ORIGAMI	BEELINE	DASHING	FOULING	LANTANA	PACKING	RESCIND	TRIBUNE	AUDITOR
OUTCOME	BEGUINE	DEALING	FURLONG	LAPWING	PADDING	RESOUND	TRIDENT	BACKLOG
PASTIME	BENZENE	DECLINE	FURRING	LARCENY	PAGEANT	RESPOND	TURBINE	BALLOON
PERFUME	BENZINE	DEFIANT	GALLANT	LASAGNA	PARSING	RIGGING	TURNING	BANDBOX
PHONEME	BETHINK	DEMESNE	GARLAND	LATRINE	PARTING	ROUTINE	TYRANNY	BARROOM
PRESUME	BINDING	DEPLANE	GARMENT	LEADING	PARVENU	RUNNING	UNCANNY	BASSOON
PROXIMO	BIPLANE	DESCANT	GELDING	LEGGING	PASSING	SAILING	UNDOING	BASTION
RAGTIME	BLATANT	DESCEND	GENUINE	LEMMING	PATIENT	SALIENT	UNDYING	BEDROOM
RECLAME	BOLOGNA	DESCENT	GERMANE	LENIENT	PAYMENT	SALTINE	UNGUENT	BELABOR
RHIZOME	BOOKEND	DESPOND	GINSENG	LEONINE	PEASANT	SAPIENT	UNSLING	BELLBOY
SENTIMO	BOWLINE	DESTINE	GODSEND	LISTING	PEELING	SAPLING	UNSOUND	BELLHOP
SUBLIME	BOWLING	DESTINY	GOSLING	LODGING	PENDANT	SARDINE	UNTWINE	BENISON
SUCCUMB	BRIGAND	DEVIANT	GRATING	LONGING	PENDENT	SAVANNA	UPSWING	BENTHOS

BIBELOT	EARSHOT	KINGDOM	PLATOON	THERMOS	ACTUARY	CONFIRM	FOREARM	LOTTERY
BILLION	ECHELON	KRYPTON	PLAYBOY	TOOLBOX	ADJOURN	CONFORM	FORLORN	MACABRE
BLOSSOM	EDITION	LAMPOON	PLOWBOY	TOPKNOT	AIRPORT	CONJURE	FORWARD	MADEIRA
BOREDOM	EIDOLON	LANGUOR	PLYWOOD	TORSION	ALGEBRA	CONSORT	FOULARD	MAESTRO
BOURBON	ELECTOR	LEXICON	POLYGON	TRACTOR	ALLEGRO	CONTORT	FOUNDRY	MALLARD
BUFFOON	ELISION	LIAISON	PONTOON	TRAITOR	AMATORY	CONVERT	FROWARD	MAMMARY
BUGABOO	EMBRYOL	LOCATOR	PORTION	TRANSOM	AMPHORA	COOKERY	GALLERY	MANSARD
BULLDOG	EMOTION	LONGBOW	POSTBOY	TREASON	ANYMORE	COUNTRY	GESTURE	MASCARA
BULLION	EMPEROR	LOWBROW	POTHOOK	TROLLOP	ARCHERY	COUTURE	GIZZARD	MASONRY
BURGEON	ENVELOP	MAILBOX	POTSHOT	TUITION	ARREARS	COWBIRD	GRANARY	MASTERY
CAISSON	ENVENOM	MAINTOP	PRAETOR	TYPHOON	ATHWART	CULTURE	GRAVURE	MEASURE
CALDRON	EQUATOR	MALISON	PRECOOK	UNBOSOM	AUSTERE	CULVERT	GUNFIRE	MERCURY
CAMPHOR	EQUINOX	MANHOOD	PROCTOR	UNCTION	AWKWARD	CURSORY	GUNNERY	MIMICRY
CAPITOL	EROSION	MANSION	PSYCHOL	VENISON	BASTARD	CUSTARD	HAGGARD	MISFIRE
CAPTION	ETHANOL	MARPLOT	RACCOON	VERSION	BATTERY	CUTLERY	HALBERD	MIXTURE
CARIBOU	EVASION	MATADOR	RAINBOW	VICEROY	BEDSORE	CUTWORM	HALVERS	MUSTARD
CARRION	EYEBROW	MEGATON	REACTOR	VISITOR	BEGGARY	DASTARD	HALYARD	MYSTERY
CARRYON	FACTION	MENTHOL	REDWOOD	VITRIOL	BERSERK	DEANERY	HARVARD	NETWARE
CARTOON	FASHION	MENTION	RELATOR	WALLOON	BIGHORN	DECLARE	HAUBERK	NETWORK
CATALOG	FEEDLOT	MILKSOP	REPROOF	WARRIOR	BITTERN	DENTURE	HAYFORK	NEWBORN
CAUTION	FESTOON	MILLION	REREDOS	WARTHOG	BITTERS	DEPLORE	HAYWIRE	NIAGARA
CESSION	FICTION	MISSION	REUNION	WHATNOT	BIZARRE	DESSERT	HECTARE	NIGGARD
CHANSON	FILMDOM	MONITOR	ROOFTOP	WHEREOF	BOMBARD	DEVILRY	HICKORY	NONHERO
CHARIOT	FIREBOX	MONSOON	SADIRON	WHEREON	BONFIRE	DIEHARD	HISTORY	NOWHERE
CHEROOT	FISSION	MUDROOM	SAFFRON	WHITLOW	BRACERO	DISCARD	HOMBURG	NURSERY
CHEVIOT	FLATTOP	MULLION	SALTBOX	WIDGEON	BRAVERY	DISCERN	HOSIERY	NURTURE
CHEVRON	FORETOP	NEUTRON	SANDHOG	WINDROW	BRAVURA	DISCORD	HUNKERS	OBSCURE
CHIFFON	FREEDOM	NEWSBOY	SANDLOT	WOODLOT	BULWARK	DISPORT	ICEBERG	ONSHORE
CHIGNON	GALLEON	NONBOOK	SAPWOOD	WORKBOX	BUZZARD	DISTORT	IMAGERY	ORATORY
CHINOOK	GEARBOX	NONSTOP	SCALLOP	ZILLION	CAESURA	DISTURB	IMPEARL	ORCHARD
CLANGOR	GLUTTON	NUCLEON	SEAFOOD	ATTEMPT	CALDERA	DOGCART	IMPLORE	OSSUARY
CLARION	GODHOOD	OCTAGON	SECTION	BAGPIPE	CANNERY	DRAPERY	INBOARD	OSTMARK
CONTROL	GRUNION	OPINION	SENATOR	CATALPA	CAPTURE	DULLARD	INDOORS	OUTWARD
COPILOT	GUERDON	ORATION	SESSION	CONCEPT	CARFARE	EARMARK	INKHORN	OUTWORK
COPYBOY	GUMDROP	OUTCROP	SHALLOP	CORRUPT	CARPORT	EASTERN	INQUIRE	OUTWORN
CORNCOB	GUMSHOE	OUTDOOR	SHALLOW	DIGRAPH	CASCARA	ENQUIRE	INQUIRY	OVERARM
CREATOR	GUNSHOT	OUTFLOW	SHAMPOO	DISRUPT	CATARRH	ENSNARE	INSHORE	PASTERN
CRIMSON	HALCYON	OUTGROW	SILICON	ENTROPY	CATBIRD	EPICURE	INSPIRE	PASTURE
CROUTON	HANGDOG	OUTLOOK	SOMEHOW	EPITAPH	CAVALRY	EQUERRY	JANUARY	PECCARY
CURATOR	HARDTOP	OVATION	SOUPCON	EXCERPT	CENSURE	ESQUIRE	JAYBIRD	PEPPERY
CUSHION	HARPOON	OVERJOY	SPARROW	FORCEPS	CENTARE	ESTUARY	JETPORT	PERFORM
DASHPOT	HELLION	OVERTOP	SPONSOR	GESTAPO	CENTURY	EXPLORE	JEWELRY	PERJURY
DAYBOOK	HEXAGON	OXBLOOD	SQUALOR	ISOTOPE	CHANCRE	EYESORE	JITTERS	PERTURB
DECAGON	HEXAPOD	PAGEBOY	STATION	PERCEPT	CHANTRY	FACTORY	LAGGARD	PERVERT
DEMIGOD	HIGHBOY	PARADOX	STEPSON	PERHAPS	CHICORY	FAILURE	LANTERN	PICTURE
DESKTOP	HILLTOP	PARAGON	STILTON	PRECEPT	CHIMERA	FANFARE	LANYARD	PILLORY
DESTROY	HORIZON	PARASOL	SUCTION	PREEMPT	CHOLERA	FEATURE	LAUNDRY	PINWORM
DEVELOP	HOTFOOT	PASSION	SUNROOF	RECEIPT	CISTERN	FERNERY	LECHERY	PISMIRE
DEWDROP	HOTSHOT	PATRIOT	SUNSPOT	SCRAPPY	CLOSURE	FILBERT	LECTERN	PLACARD
DICTION	HUMIDOR	PATROON	SURGEON	SYNCOPE	CLOTURE	FIREARM	LECTURE	PLENARY
DISAVOW	INCISOR	PENSION	SWALLOW	THERAPY	COLLARD	FISHERY	LEEWARD	PONIARD
DIVISOR	JACKPOT	PHAETON	SYMPTOM	TRICEPS	COMFORT	FISSURE	LEGHORN	POPCORN
DOGTROT	JANITOR	PHANTOM	TAPROOM	TRIUMPH	COMPARE	FIXTURE	LEISURE	POSTERN
DOGWOOD	JUKEBOX	PHARAOH	TAPROOT	UNHAPPY	COMPORT	FLEXURE	LEMPIRA	POSTURE
DRAGOON	KEELSON	PHYSIOL	TENSION	UNKEMPT	CONCERN	FLOWERY	LEOPARD	POTHERB
DUDGEON	KILLJOY	PILLBOX	THEREOF	UPSWEPT	CONCERT	FOGHORN	LEOTARD	POTTERY
DUNGEON	KILOTON	PILLION	THEREON	ACQUIRE	CONCORD	FOOLERY	LIBRARY	

POULTRY	UNSNARL	BOOKISH	EGOTISM	INCENSE	RAFFISH	USELESS	COMPUTE	ITERATE
PREFORM	UPSTART	BRITISH	ELITISM	INCLOSE	REALISM	VAMOOSE	CONFUTE	JACINTH
PREPARE	URETHRA	BRUTISH	ELLIPSE	INCRUST	RECLUSE	VARNISH	CONNOTE	JOLLITY
PRIMARY	URINARY	BULRUSH	EMBASSY	INDORSE	REDDISH	VERBOSE	CORDITE	KEYNOTE
PROCURE	VAMPIRE	BURGESS	EMPRESS	INGRESS	REDRESS	VISCOSE	CORINTH	KIBBUTZ
PROVERB	VANWARD	BURMESE	ENCLOSE	INQUEST	REFRESH	VOGUISH	CREMATE	LACTATE
PURPORT	VAQUERO	BURNISH	ENCRUST	INTENSE	REGRESS	WAGGISH	CULOTTE	LAYETTE
RAMPART	VENTURE	CABOOSE	ENDLESS	INTRUST	RELAPSE	WARLESS	CUPRITE	LIBERTY
RAPPORT	VERDURE	CALYPSO	ENDMOST	INVERSE	RELEASE	WASPISH	DEFLATE	LIGNITE
RAPTURE	VESPERS	CANVASS	ENDORSE	JACKASS	REMORSE	WHITISH	DENSITY	LUNETTE
RECTORY	VESTURE	CARCASS	ENDWISE	JUDAISM	REPRESS	WITLESS	DENTATE	MACHETE
REENTRY	VICTORY	CAROUSE	ENGLISH	JUJITSU	REPRISE	WITNESS	DEPLETE	MAGENTA
REQUIRE	VISCERA	CATFISH	ENGROSS	KADDISH	REPULSE	YIDDISH	DESPITE	MAGNATE
RESTORE	VULTURE	CHEMISE	ENTHUSE	LACTOSE	REQUEST	ZIONISM	DETENTE	MAGNETO
RHUBARB	WAGGERY	CHEMIST	ENTRUST	LARGESS	REVERSE	ABILITY	DEVIATE	MAJESTY
RIVALRY	WARFARE	CHERISH	EXHAUST	LAWLESS	RUBBISH	ACETATE	DICTATE	MAMMOTH
ROBBERY	WARLORD	CHINESE	EXPANSE	LEFTISM	SARCASM	ACOLYTE	DIGNITY	MANDATE
ROOKERY	WAXWORK	CLEANSE	EXPENSE	LEPROSY	SAWDUST	ACONITE	DINETTE	MEDIATE
RUPTURE	WAYWARD	CODFISH	EXPRESS	LICENSE	SELFISH	ACTUATE	DISPUTE	MEMENTO
SAGUARO	WAYWORN	COEXIST	EYELASH	MAFIOSO	SIAMESE	ADULATE	DOUGHTY	MIGRATE
SCENERY	WELFARE	COMPASS	EYEWASH	MALAISE	SLAVISH	AGITATE	DUBIETY	MODISTE
SEABIRD	WESTERN	COMPOSE	FANTASY	MALTOSE	SOPHISM	AMENITY	DYNASTY	MULATTO
SEAPORT	WITHERS	COMPOST	FASCISM	MANNISH	SOPHIST	AMNESTY	EBONITE	MUSETTE
SEAWARD	YARDARM	CONCISE	FAUVISM	MARXISM	SPANISH	ANDANTE	EDUCATE	NAIVETE
SECTARY	ABOLISH	CONFESS	FINESSE	MAWKISH	STYLISH	ANIMATE	ELEVATE	NAIVETY
SENSORY	ABREAST	CONFUSE	FINFISH	MIDMOST	STYLIST	ANNUITY	EMANATE	NARRATE
SIDEARM	ABSCESS	CONGEST	FINNISH	MOLLUSK	SUBSIST	ANXIETY	EMERITA	NAUGHTY
SINCERE	ADDRESS	CONSIST	FLEMISH	MORTISE	SUCCESS	APATITE	EMULATE	NITRATE
SKYLARK	ADIPOSE	CONTEST	FLORIST	NOURISH	SUCROSE	ARTISTE	ENTENTE	NITRITE
SKYWARD	ADVERSE	CUTLASS	FLUTIST	OBELISK	SUFFUSE	ATHLETE	EREMITE	NOVELTY
SLAVERY	AGAINST	CYCLIST	FOOLISH	OBVERSE	SUGGEST	AUREATE	ESTHETE	OBVIATE
SOJOURN	AGELESS	CYPRESS	FURBISH	OCULIST	SUNFISH	AZIMUTH	EXCRETA	OPACITY
SORCERY	AIMLESS	DECEASE	FURNISH	OFFENSE	SUNRISE	BATISTE	EXCRETE	OPERATE
STATURE	AIRPOST	DEFENSE	GABFEST	OPPRESS	SUPPOSE	BAUXITE	EXECUTE	OUTVOTE
STEWARD	AMYLASE	DEFROST	GARFISH	OUTCAST	SURMISE	BENEATH	EXEGETE	OVULATE
SUBVERT	ANAPEST	DEGAUSS	GARNISH	OUTLAST	SURPASS	BETROTH	EXPIATE	PALETTE
SUMMARY	ANGUISH	DELOUSE	GEODESY	OUTPOST	SWEDISH	BIOTITE	FACULTY	PALMATE
SUNBURN	ANIMISM	DENTIST	GLIMPSE	PAPOOSE	SYNAPSE	BIRETTA	FATUITY	PALPATE
SUPPORT	ANYWISE	DEPRESS	GLUCOSE	PEEVISH	TARNISH	BISMUTH	FLIGHTY	PARTITE
SURGERY	APPEASE	DERVISH	GODDESS	PERSIST	TEMPEST	BOYCOTT	FRAILTY	PAUCITY
TANBARK	APPRISE	DESPISE	GODLESS	PETTISH	TOPLESS	BREADTH	FRIGATE	PENALTY
TANNERY	ARMREST	DIARIST	GOULASH	PIANIST	TOPMAST	BREVITY	GARROTE	PERLITE
TEMPERA	ARTLESS	DIFFUSE	HAPLESS	PIGGISH	TOPMOST	BURETTE	GAVOTTE	PIMENTO
TERNARY	ATAVISM	DIGRESS	HARNESS	POSSESS	TOURIST	CALCITE	GAZETTE	PINNATE
TEXTURE	ATHEIST	DIOCESE	HARVEST	PRECISE	TRAIPSE	CANASTA	GIBLETS	PIPETTE
TINWARE	ATHIRST	DISCUSS	HASHISH	PREMISE	TROPISM	CANTATA	GRANITE	PLACATE
TOGGERY	AUTOPSY	DISEASE	HEIRESS	PROCESS	TURKISH	CELESTA	GRAVITY	POLLUTE
TONSURE	BAGASSE	DISEUSE	HEROISM	PROFESS	UNCLASP	CHARITY	HAUGHTY	POVERTY
TORTURE	BALLAST	DISGUST	HOGWASH	PROFUSE	UNCLOSE	CHIANTI	HIRSUTE	PREDATE
TRACERY	BAPTISM	DISMISS	HOSTESS	PROMISE	UNCROSS	CILIATE	HYDRATE	PRELATE
TURNERY	BAPTIST	DISPOSE	ILLNESS	PROPOSE	UNDRESS	CLARITY	IMITATE	PRIMATE
UNAWARE	BECAUSE	DIVERSE	IMAGISM	PROTEST	UNERASE	CLIMATE	IMPASTO	PRIVATE
UNHEARD	BEDFAST	DOGFISH	IMMENSE	PROVISO	UNHORSE	COGNATE	IMPIETY	PROBATE
UNICORN	BEDPOST	DUCHESS	IMMERSE	PROVOST	UNLEASH	COLLATE	INFLATE	PROBITY
UNIFORM	BEQUEST	EARNEST	IMPASSE	PROWESS	UNLOOSE	COMMUTE	INGRATE	PROMOTE
UNITARY	BLEMISH	ECLIPSE	IMPRESS	PUBLISH	UNTWIST	COMPETE	INSTATE	PRORATE
UNLEARN	BOMBAST	ECSTASY	IMPULSE	PURPOSE	UPRAISE	COMPOTE	ISOLATE	PUBERTY

PULSATE	ALUMNUS	FALLOUT	MASSEUR	SHOTGUN	CAPTIVE	CONTEXT	CADENZA	PERGOLA
QUALITY	AMATEUR	FATEFUL	MAXIMUM	SHUTOUT	CASSAVA	PRETEXT	CAESURA	PETUNIA
RADIATE	AMOROUS	FATIGUE	MINDFUL	SINUOUS	CENTAVO	ACRONYM	CALDERA	PIRANHA
REALITY	ANTIQUE	FATUOUS	MINIBUS	SORGHUM	CONCAVE	ANTONYM	CANASTA	REGALIA
REBIRTH	ANXIOUS	FEARFUL	MINIMUM	SOULFUL	CONNIVE	BUCKEYE	CANNULA	REGATTA
REGATTA	APPLAUD	FERMIUM	MODICUM	SPEEDUP	COSTIVE	COCKEYE	CANTATA	REPLICA
REPLETE	AQUEOUS	FERROUS	NEEDFUL	STADIUM	CURSIVE	ENDWAYS	CASCARA	RICKSHA
REQUITE	ARBUTUS	FIREBUG	NERVOUS	STARTUP	DECEIVE	HOMONYM	CASSAVA	ROTUNDA
RESPITE	ARDUOUS	FISTFUL	NIOBIUM	STERNUM	DEPRAVE	PINKEYE	CATALPA	RUBELLA
RICKETS	BALEFUL	FLAVOUR	NOCUOUS	STIRRUP	DEPRIVE	SYNONYM	CEDILLA	SAVANNA
RICKETY	BAROQUE	FOLDOUT	NONPLUS	STRATUM	DESERVE	WALLEYE	CELESTA	SCAPULA
RIPOSTE	BASHFUL	FRETFUL	NOSTRUM	SURPLUS	DEVOLVE	WYSIWYG	CHIMERA	SEQUOIA
ROSEATE	BATHTUB	FRUSTUM	NOXIOUS	SURTOUT	ELUSIVE	AGONIZE	CHOLERA	SPATULA
ROSETTE	BECLOUD	FULCRUM	NUCLEUS	TANTRUM	ENCLAVE	ANALYZE	COCHLEA	STAMINA
ROYALTY	BILIOUS	FURIOUS	OBLIQUE	TEDIOUS	ENGRAVE	ANODIZE	CORDOBA	SULTANA
SABBATH	BLOWGUN	GAINFUL	OBLOQUY	TENUOUS	ENSLAVE	ATOMIZE	COROLLA	TAFFETA
SATIATE	BLOWOUT	GALLIUM	OBSEQUY	TERBIUM	EROSIVE	BAPTIZE	CZARINA	TAMBALA
SATIETY	BREAKUP	GIBBOUS	OBVIOUS	TETANUS	FESTIVE	BLINTZE	DILEMMA	TAPIOCA
SECRETE	BRIMFUL	GLAMOUR	OCTOPUS	THORIUM	FORGIVE	BONANZA	DIPLOMA	TEMPERA
SERRATE	BRUSQUE	HABITUE	OMINOUS	THULIUM	FURTIVE	CADENZA	DRACHMA	TEQUILA
SEVENTY	BURNOUT	HAFNIUM	OMNIBUS	TRITIUM	IMPROVE	CAPSIZE	EMERITA	TOXEMIA
SOCIETY	CADMIUM	HAIRCUT	ONEROUS	TRIVIUM	INVOLVE	CHINTZY	EXCRETA	TRACHEA
STATUTE	CALCIUM	HALIBUT	OPOSSUM	TUNEFUL	KHEDIVE	IDOLIZE	FISTULA	URETHRA
STEALTH	CALLOUS	HANDFUL	OPTIMUM	TURNOUT	MASSIVE	ITEMIZE	FORMULA	VANILLA
SULFATE	CAMBIUM	HANDGUN	OVERRUN	UNGROUP	MISSIVE	LIONIZE	FUCHSIA	VEDANTA
SUNBATH	CARDBUS	HANDOUT	PABULUM	URANIUM	OBSERVE	MESTIZO	GONDOLA	VERANDA
TAFFETA	CAREFUL	HANGOUT	PAPYRUS	URANOUS	OUTLIVE	ORGANZA	GORILLA	VERBENA
TEKTITE	CARIOUS	HARBOUR	PARLOUR	VACUOUS	PASSIVE	OUTSIZE	HOSANNA	VISCERA
TERMITE	CATCHUP	HAUTEUR	PARLOUS	VARIOUS	PECCAVI	OXIDIZE	INDICIA	WHOOPLA
TESTATE	CELSIUS	HEINOUS	PENTIUM	VICIOUS	PENSIVE	PIZZAZZ	INERTIA	YESHIVA
THERETO	CENTAUR	HIDEOUS	PERIQUE	VILLOUS	RECEIVE	REALIZE	LANTANA	BATHTUB
THROATY	CHECKUP	HIDEOUT	PHALLUS	VISCOUS	RELIEVE	SQUEEZE	LASAGNA	CONTRIB
TOWPATH	CLEANUP	HOLMIUM	PITEOUS	WAILFUL	REPROVE	STYLIZE	LATAKIA	CORNCOB
TRIBUTE	COCONUT	HOODLUM	PITIFUL	WAKEFUL	RESERVE	TRAPEZE	LEMPIRA	COULOMB
TRINITY	CONFLUX	HUMDRUM	POMPOUS	WALKOUT	RESTIVE	UNITIZE	MADEIRA	COXCOMB
ULULATE	CONTOUR	HUMERUS	PREMIUM	WASHOUT	REVOLVE	UTILIZE	MAGENTA	DISTURB
UNCOUTH	COOKOUT	HYDROUS	PRONOUN	WASHTUB	SURVIVE		MAHATMA	PEDICAB
UNEARTH	COPIOUS	IGNEOUS	PULLOUT	WICKIUP	UNNERVE		MALARIA	PERTURB
UNQUOTE	CRANIUM	IMPETUS	QUANTUM	WILLFUL	UNWEAVE		MARIMBA	POTHERB
UNTRUTH	CUMULUS	IMPIOUS	QUIETUS	WISHFUL	YESHIVA		MASCARA	PROVERB
UPSTATE	CURIOUS	INCUBUS	RAUCOUS	WISTFUL	**7TH LETTER**		MAXILLA	RHUBARB
URINATE	DECORUM	INGENUE	READOUT	WITHOUT	BELLOWS	ALFALFA	MAZURKA	SUCCUMB
UTILITY	DEFRAUD	IRIDIUM	REGROUP	WOODCUT	GALLOWS	ALGEBRA	MEDULLA	TAXICAB
VACUITY	DEVALUE	ISTHMUS	RELIQUE	WORKOUT	GOSHAWK	ALUMINA	MILITIA	WASHTUB
VALUATE	DEVIOUS	JEALOUS	RESIDUE	YTTRIUM	HOEDOWN	AMMONIA	MINUTIA	ACRYLIC
VARIETY	DIREFUL	JEJUNUM	RETINUE	ZEALOUS	INGROWN	AMNESIA	MORPHIA	AEROBIC
VARSITY	DOLEFUL	JODHPUR	REVENUE	ABSOLVE	LETDOWN	AMPHORA	NAPHTHA	ALEMBIC
VEDANTA	DUBIOUS	KARAKUL	RHENIUM	ACHIEVE	LOWDOWN	ANAEMIA	NIAGARA	ALMANAC
VIBRATE	DUTEOUS	KETCHUP	RHODIUM	AIRWAVE	MIDTOWN	ANTENNA	NIRVANA	AQUATIC
VIBRATO	DUTIFUL	LADYBUG	RHOMBUS	AMATIVE	OVERAWE	APHASIA	NOVELLA	ARCHAIC
VIOLATE	EARDRUM	LIQUEUR	ROSEBUD	ANCHOVY	PEAFOWL	BAZOOKA	OCARINA	ARSENIC
VITIATE	EARPLUG	LITHIUM	ROSTRUM	APPROVE	RUNDOWN	BEGONIA	ORGANZA	ASCETIC
VULGATE	ECLOGUE	LOCKNUT	ROUNDUP	ARCHIVE	SUNDOWN	BIRETTA	OVERSEA	ASEPTIC
WARPATH	ELYSIUM	LOCKOUT	RUINOUS	BEEHIVE	UNKNOWN	BOLOGNA	PANACEA	ASIATIC
WEIGHTY	ENAMOUR	LOOKOUT	SANCTUM	BEHOOVE	WILLOWY	BONANZA	PAPILLA	BALDRIC
WHERETO	ENVIOUS	MACAQUE	SCROTUM	BELIEVE	WINDOWS	BRAVURA	PAPRIKA	BENTHIC
ZEOLITE	ERRATUM	MALLEUS	SERIOUS	BIVALVE	BETWIXT	BRECCIA	PATELLA	BIVOUAC

BUCOLIC	VOCALIC	DISCARD	MANSARD	STILTED	ALCALDE	BEDSIDE	CATHODE	CONVOKE
CALORIC	VOLTAIC	DISCORD	MASTOID	STIPEND	ALEWIFE	BEDSORE	CATLIKE	COPPICE
CAMBRIC	ABSCOND	DISTEND	MERMAID	STORIED	AMATIVE	BEDTIME	CENSURE	CORACLE
CARDIAC	ACCUSED	DOGWOOD	MIDLAND	STUDIED	AMIABLE	BEEHIVE	CENTARE	CORDAGE
CAUSTIC	ADENOID	DULLARD	MINUEND	SUCCEED	AMPUTEE	BEELINE	CENTIME	CORDITE
CERAMIC	ADVISED	EGGHEAD	MISDEED	SUSPEND	AMYLASE	BEGRIME	CHALICE	CORNICE
CHROMIC	AGROUND	EMERALD	MISLEAD	TABLOID	ANALYZE	BEGUILE	CHANCRE	CORRODE
CHRONIC	AMERIND	EXPOUND	MISREAD	TENFOLD	ANDANTE	BEGUINE	CHEMISE	CORSAGE
CLASSIC	ANDROID	FIBROID	MISSEND	TENURED	ANEMONE	BEHOOVE	CHICANE	CORTEGE
CLASTIC	ANTACID	FLACCID	MONEYED	THYROID	ANILINE	BELIEVE	CHINESE	COSTIVE
CRYPTIC	APPLAUD	FLATBED	MUSTARD	TOEHOLD	ANIMATE	BENZENE	CHORALE	COSTUME
DEMONIC	APPLIED	FOOTPAD	NIGGARD	TOWHEAD	ANODIZE	BENZINE	CHORTLE	COTERIE
DEMOTIC	ASHAMED	FORFEND	NONSKED	TWILLED	ANODYNE	BESIEGE	CHUCKLE	COTTAGE
DRASTIC	ASSURED	FORWARD	OFFHAND	TYPHOID	ANTIQUE	BICYCLE	CILIATE	COURAGE
DYNAMIC	ASTOUND	FOULARD	ORCHARD	UNARMED	ANYMORE	BIOTITE	CLEANSE	COUTURE
ELASTIC	AWKWARD	FROWARD	OROTUND	UNBOWED	ANYTIME	BIPLANE	CLIMATE	COWHIDE
ELEGIAC	BADLAND	GARLAND	OUTWARD	UNHEARD	ANYWISE	BIVALVE	CLOSURE	COWPOKE
ENDEMIC	BASTARD	GIZZARD	OXBLOOD	UNMOVED	APANAGE	BIZARRE	CLOTURE	CRACKLE
ERRATIC	BECLOUD	GODHEAD	PAYLOAD	UNSAVED	APATITE	BLINTZE	COCAINE	CREMATE
FANATIC	BELATED	GODHOOD	PIEBALD	UNSOUND	APOLUNE	BONDAGE	COCKADE	CREVICE
FRANTIC	BELOVED	GODSEND	PLACARD	UNTRIED	APOSTLE	BONFIRE	COCKEYE	CRINKLE
GASTRIC	BLESSED	HAGGARD	PLYWOOD	UPBRAID	APPEASE	BOWLINE	CODEINE	CRIPPLE
GENERIC	BLOODED	HALBERD	POINTED	VANWARD	APPRISE	BRAILLE	COGNATE	CRUMBLE
GENETIC	BOBSLED	HALYARD	PONIARD	VAULTED	APPROVE	BRAMBLE	COINAGE	CRUMPLE
GRAPHIC	BOMBARD	HAPLOID	PORTEND	WARHEAD	ARCHIVE	BREATHE	COLLAGE	CRUSADE
HEPATIC	BOOKEND	HARVARD	POTHEAD	WARLORD	ARMHOLE	BRIGADE	COLLATE	CUBICLE
KINETIC	BRIGAND	HAYSEED	PREBEND	WAYWARD	ARRANGE	BRIOCHE	COLLEGE	CUISINE
LACONIC	BUZZARD	HEXAPOD	PRETEND	WEASAND	ARTICLE	BRISTLE	COLLIDE	CULOTTE
LUNATIC	CANDIED	HOPHEAD	PROCEED	WEEKEND	ARTISTE	BRITTLE	COLOGNE	CULTURE
MALEFIC	CARLOAD	HUNDRED	PYRAMID	WETLAND	ASCRIBE	BROCADE	COMBINE	CUPCAKE
MASONIC	CAROTID	HUSBAND	RAGWEED	WHORLED	ASININE	BROMIDE	COMMODE	CUPRITE
MELANIC	CASTLED	IMPOUND	REBOUND	WIZENED	ASKANCE	BROMINE	COMMUNE	CURSIVE
MIMETIC	CATBIRD	INBOARD	REBUILD	WORSTED	ASSUAGE	BROWNIE	COMMUTE	CUTICLE
MONADIC	COLLARD	INBOUND	REDHEAD	ABALONE	ASTRIDE	BRUSQUE	COMPARE	CYANIDE
NOMADIC	COLLOID	INDEXED	REDOUND	ABRIDGE	ATHLETE	BUCKEYE	COMPETE	CYCLONE
NUMERIC	COLORED	INFIELD	REDWOOD	ABSENCE	ATOMIZE	BURETTE	COMPILE	DAYTIME
ORGANIC	COMMAND	INSIPID	REFINED	ABSOLVE	ATTACHE	BURMESE	COMPOSE	DEBACLE
PACIFIC	COMMEND	INSTEAD	RELATED	ACADEME	AUDIBLE	CABBAGE	COMPOTE	DECEASE
PELAGIC	CONCORD	INSURED	REPUTED	ACETATE	AUREATE	CABOOSE	COMPUTE	DECEIVE
PHALLIC	CONTEND	INVALID	RESCIND	ACETONE	AUREOLE	CADENCE	COMRADE	DECLARE
PHRENIC	COWBIRD	JAYBIRD	RESOUND	ACHIEVE	AURICLE	CALCINE	CONCAVE	DECLINE
PLASTIC	COWHAND	KATYDID	RESPOND	ACOLYTE	AUSPICE	CALCITE	CONCEDE	DEFENSE
POLEMIC	CRABBED	KINDRED	RETIRED	ACONITE	AUSTERE	CALORIE	CONCISE	DEFLATE
POLITIC	CROOKED	LABORED	RETREAD	ACQUIRE	AVARICE	CAPABLE	CONDOLE	DEGRADE
PROSAIC	CUCKOLD	LAGGARD	ROADBED	ACREAGE	AVERAGE	CAPRICE	CONDONE	DELOUSE
PSYCHIC	CUSTARD	LANGUID	ROSEBUD	ACTUATE	BAGASSE	CAPSIZE	CONDUCE	DEMESNE
SATANIC	DASTARD	LANYARD	SAPWOOD	ADENINE	BAGGAGE	CAPSULE	CONDYLE	DENTATE
SCEPTIC	DECIDED	LEARNED	SEABIRD	ADIPOSE	BAGPIPE	CAPTIVE	CONFIDE	DENTURE
SEISMIC	DEFRAUD	LEEWARD	SEAFOOD	ADJUDGE	BALANCE	CAPTURE	CONFINE	DEPLANE
SHELLAC	DEMIGOD	LEOPARD	SEAWARD	ADULATE	BANDAGE	CARBIDE	CONFUSE	DEPLETE
SKEPTIC	DESCEND	LEOTARD	SEAWEED	ADVANCE	BANSHEE	CARBINE	CONFUTE	DEPLORE
SPASTIC	DESPOND	LIMITED	SERRIED	ADVERSE	BAPTIZE	CARFARE	CONJURE	DEPRAVE
SPLENIC	DEVOTED	LINSEED	SICKBED	AFFABLE	BAROQUE	CARMINE	CONNIVE	DEPRIVE
STYPTIC	DIAMOND	LOWLAND	SIGHTED	AGITATE	BARRAGE	CARNAGE	CONNOTE	DERANGE
TECHNIC	DIEHARD	MALLARD	SKYWARD	AGONIZE	BATISTE	CAROUSE	CONSOLE	DESERVE
TITANIC	DIPLOID	MANHOOD	SQUALID	AIRLINE	BAUXITE	CARTAGE	CONSUME	DESPISE
TRAFFIC	DISBAND	MANKIND	STEWARD	AIRWAVE	BECAUSE	CASCADE	CONVENE	DESPITE

DESTINE	ENTENTE	FORTUNE	HOSTILE	LEGATEE	MONTAGE	PAPOOSE	PROBATE	RETIREE
DETENTE	ENTHUSE	FOXHOLE	HOTCAKE	LEGIBLE	MORAINE	PARABLE	PROCURE	RETRACE
DEVALUE	ENTITLE	FRAGILE	HYDRATE	LEISURE	MORTISE	PARTAKE	PRODUCE	REVENGE
DEVIATE	ENTWINE	FRAZZLE	HYGIENE	LEONINE	MOUNTIE	PARTITE	PROFANE	REVENUE
DEVOLVE	EPERGNE	FRECKLE	IDOLIZE	LETTUCE	MUNDANE	PASSAGE	PROFILE	REVERIE
DEVOTEE	EPICURE	FREEBIE	IGNOBLE	LICENSE	MUSETTE	PASSIVE	PROFUSE	REVERSE
DICTATE	EPISODE	FRIABLE	IMAGINE	LIGNITE	MUTABLE	PASTIME	PROMISE	REVOLVE
DIFFUSE	EPISTLE	FRIGATE	IMITATE	LIMEADE	NACELLE	PASTURE	PROMOTE	RHIZOME
DINETTE	EPITOME	FRIZZLE	IMMENSE	LINEAGE	NAIVETE	PENANCE	PROPANE	RIPOSTE
DIOCESE	EQUABLE	FULSOME	IMMERSE	LINKAGE	NARRATE	PENSIVE	PROPOSE	RISIBLE
DISABLE	EREMITE	FURNACE	IMPASSE	LIONIZE	NECKTIE	PERCALE	PRORATE	ROMANCE
DISEASE	EROSIVE	FURTIVE	IMPINGE	LISSOME	NEPTUNE	PERFUME	PROTEGE	ROSEATE
DISEUSE	ESCAPEE	GARBAGE	IMPLODE	LIVABLE	NETWARE	PERIGEE	PROVIDE	ROSETTE
DISLIKE	ESQUIRE	GARROTE	IMPLORE	LOZENGE	NITRATE	PERIQUE	PROVOKE	ROUTINE
DISPOSE	ESSENCE	GAVOTTE	IMPROVE	LUCERNE	NITRITE	PERLITE	PUERILE	RUMMAGE
DISPUTE	ESTHETE	GAZELLE	IMPULSE	LUGGAGE	NOISOME	PERVADE	PULSATE	RUPTURE
DISROBE	EVACUEE	GAZETTE	INCENSE	LUNETTE	NOMINEE	PETIOLE	PURPOSE	SALTINE
DIVERGE	EXAMINE	GENTILE	INCLINE	MACABRE	NOTABLE	PHONEME	PUSTULE	SALVAGE
DIVERSE	EXAMPLE	GENUINE	INCLOSE	MACAQUE	NOWHERE	PICTURE	QUIBBLE	SARDINE
DIVORCE	EXCLUDE	GERMANE	INCLUDE	MACHETE	NUCLIDE	PILLAGE	QUICKIE	SATIATE
DIVULGE	EXCRETE	GESTURE	INDORSE	MACHINE	NURTURE	PINHOLE	QUININE	SAUSAGE
DOCKAGE	EXECUTE	GIRAFFE	INDULGE	MACRAME	OATCAKE	PINKEYE	RADIATE	SCIENCE
DOGBANE	EXEGETE	GLIMPSE	INFLAME	MAGNATE	OBLIQUE	PINNACE	RAGTIME	SCOURGE
DOMINIE	EXPANSE	GLOBULE	INFLATE	MALAISE	OBSCENE	PINNATE	RAMPAGE	SCRUPLE
DOYENNE	EXPENSE	GLUCOSE	INGENUE	MALTOSE	OBSCURE	PIPETTE	RAPTURE	SCUFFLE
DRIBBLE	EXPIATE	GODLIKE	INGRATE	MANACLE	OBSERVE	PISMIRE	RATLINE	SCUTTLE
DRIZZLE	EXPLODE	GRACKLE	INQUIRE	MANDATE	OBTRUDE	PLACATE	RAWHIDE	SEASIDE
DUCTILE	EXPLORE	GRANDEE	INSHORE	MANHOLE	OBVERSE	PLIABLE	REALIZE	SECLUDE
DURABLE	EXPUNGE	GRANITE	INSPIRE	MANLIKE	OBVIATE	PLUMAGE	RECEIVE	SECRETE
DURANCE	EXTREME	GRANTEE	INSTATE	MARQUEE	OCCLUDE	POLLUTE	RECLAME	SELVAGE
DWINDLE	EXTRUDE	GRANULE	INTENSE	MASSAGE	OFFENSE	PORCINE	RECLINE	SERRATE
EARACHE	EYESORE	GRAPPLE	INTRUDE	MASSIVE	OFFSIDE	PORTAGE	RECLUSE	SERVICE
EARLOBE	FAIENCE	GRAVURE	INVERSE	MATINEE	OLIVINE	POSTAGE	RECYCLE	SERVILE
EBONITE	FAILURE	GRENADE	INVOICE	MAYPOLE	ONETIME	POSTURE	REDLINE	SESSILE
ECLIPSE	FANFARE	GRIDDLE	INVOLVE	MEASURE	ONSHORE	POTABLE	REFEREE	SHACKLE
ECLOGUE	FATIGUE	GRIMACE	IRKSOME	MEDIATE	OPERATE	POTHOLE	REFUGEE	SHAMBLE
EDIFICE	FEATURE	GRISTLE	ISOLATE	MELANGE	ORIFICE	POTTAGE	REJOICE	SHARPIE
EDUCATE	FEBRILE	GROUPIE	ISOTOPE	MESSAGE	OUTCOME	PRAIRIE	RELAPSE	SHAWNEE
ELEVATE	FERRULE	GRUMBLE	ITEMIZE	METHANE	OUTFACE	PRALINE	RELEASE	SHEATHE
ELLIPSE	FERTILE	GUANINE	ITERATE	MICROBE	OUTLINE	PRATTLE	RELIEVE	SHINGLE
ELUSIVE	FESTIVE	GUMSHOE	JASMINE	MIDWIFE	OUTLIVE	PRECEDE	RELIQUE	SHUFFLE
EMANATE	FIANCEE	GUNFIRE	JOYANCE	MIGRATE	OUTRAGE	PRECISE	REMORSE	SHUTTLE
EMBRACE	FINAGLE	GUNWALE	JOYRIDE	MILEAGE	OUTSIDE	PREDATE	REPLACE	SIAMESE
EMULATE	FINANCE	HABITUE	JUBILEE	MILLAGE	OUTSIZE	PREEMIE	REPLETE	SILENCE
ENCLAVE	FINESSE	HAULAGE	JUSTICE	MILLIME	OUTVOTE	PREFACE	REPRISE	SINCERE
ENCLOSE	FISSILE	HAYWIRE	KEYHOLE	MIRACLE	OVERAGE	PRELATE	REPROVE	SIZABLE
ENDORSE	FISSURE	HECTARE	KEYNOTE	MISFILE	OVERAWE	PRELUDE	REPTILE	SKIFFLE
ENDWISE	FIXTURE	HELLENE	KHEDIVE	MISFIRE	OVERSEE	PREMISE	REPULSE	SKYLINE
ENFORCE	FLEXURE	HEMLINE	KNUCKLE	MISLIKE	OVULATE	PREPARE	REQUIRE	SMUGGLE
ENGRAVE	FLOUNCE	HERBAGE	LACTATE	MISNAME	OXIDIZE	PREPUCE	REQUITE	SNAFFLE
ENHANCE	FLYABLE	HEROINE	LACTOSE	MISRULE	PACKAGE	PRESAGE	RESERVE	SNIFFLE
ENLARGE	FOLIAGE	HIPBONE	LATRINE	MISSILE	PALETTE	PRESIDE	RESIDUE	SNUFFLE
ENNOBLE	FOOTAGE	HIRSUTE	LATTICE	MISSIVE	PALMATE	PRESUME	RESOLVE	SNUGGLE
ENPLANE	FORBODE	HOECAKE	LAYETTE	MISTAKE	PALPATE	PRICKLE	RESPITE	SOLUBLE
ENQUIRE	FORESEE	HORMONE	LEAFAGE	MIXTURE	PANACHE	PRIMATE	RESTIVE	SOMEONE
ENSLAVE	FORGIVE	HOSPICE	LEAKAGE	MODISTE	PANCAKE	PRITHEE	RESTORE	SOUFFLE
ENSNARE	FORSAKE	HOSTAGE	LECTURE	MONOCLE	PANICLE	PRIVATE	RETINUE	SPANGLE

SPARKLE	TINWARE	VALUATE	KICKOFF	FITTING	ONGOING	WEEPING	JACINTH	AFGHANI
SPECKLE	TOLUENE	VAMOOSE	MASTIFF	FLEMING	OPENING	WHITING	JEHOVAH	CHIANTI
SPICULE	TONNAGE	VAMPIRE	MIDRIFF	FOOTING	PACKING	WILLING	KADDISH	DASHIKI
SPINDLE	TONSURE	VANDYKE	ONESELF	FORELEG	PADDING	WINDBAG	MAMMOTH	EFFENDI
SPITTLE	TOPSIDE	VANTAGE	PONTIFF	FORGING	PARSING	WINDING	MANNISH	GUARANI
SPLURGE	TORTURE	VEHICLE	REPROOF	FOULING	PARTING	WINNING	MAWKISH	HIBACHI
SQUEEZE	TRADUCE	VENTURE	SHERIFF	FURLONG	PASSING	WITTING	MESSIAH	ISRAELI
STABILE	TRAINEE	VERBOSE	SUNROOF	FURRING	PEELING	WORDING	MONARCH	MARTINI
STARTLE	TRAIPSE	VERDURE	TAKEOFF	GELDING	PENDING	WORKBAG	NOURISH	ORIGAMI
STATURE	TRAMPLE	VESICLE	THEREOF	GINSENG	PERIWIG	WORKING	OSTRICH	PECCAVI
STATUTE	TRAPEZE	VESTIGE	THYSELF	GOSLING	PFENNIG	WRITING	PEEVISH	RAVIOLI
STEEPLE	TREACLE	VESTURE	TURNOFF	GRATING	PLATING	WYSIWYG	PETTISH	SAMURAI
STERILE	TREADLE	VIBRATE	WHEREOF	HALTING	PRAYING	ABOLISH	PHARAOH	SPUMONI
STIPPLE	TREMBLE	VILLAGE	BACKING	HANDBAG	PROLONG	ANGUISH	PIBROCH	SWAHILI
STORAGE	TRESTLE	VINTAGE	BACKLOG	HANGDOG	PUDDING	AZIMUTH	PIGGISH	TIMPANI
STRANGE	TRIBUNE	VIOLATE	BALDING	HANGING	RAILING	BENEATH	PUBLISH	TORTONI
STROPHE	TRIBUTE	VIRGULE	BARRING	HASHING	RANKING	BESEECH	RAFFISH	TSUNAMI
STUBBLE	TRICKLE	VISCOSE	BATTING	HEADING	READING	BETROTH	REBIRTH	AIRSICK
STUMBLE	TRIREME	VISIBLE	BEARING	HEARING	RIGGING	BEWITCH	REDDISH	BANNOCK
STYLIZE	TROCHEE	VITIATE	BEDDING	HELPING	RUNNING	BISMUTH	REFRESH	BEATNIK
SUBLIME	TROUBLE	VOCABLE	BINDING	HERRING	SAILING	BLEMISH	RETOUCH	BEDROCK
SUBSIDE	TROUNCE	VOLTAGE	BOOTLEG	HINTING	SANDBAG	BOOKISH	RUBBISH	BERSERK
SUBTILE	TRUCKLE	VOLUBLE	BOWLING	HOLDING	SANDHOG	BOROUGH	SABBATH	BESPEAK
SUCROSE	TRUFFLE	VULGATE	BULLDOG	HOMBURG	SAPLING	BREADTH	SCRATCH	BETHINK
SUFFICE	TRUNDLE	VULPINE	BUNTING	HOUSING	SEATING	BRITISH	SCREECH	BULLOCK
SUFFUSE	TRUSTEE	VULTURE	BUSHING	HOWLING	SEEMING	BRUTISH	SELFISH	BULWARK
SUICIDE	TUNABLE	WADABLE	CALLING	HULKING	SERVING	BULRUSH	SLAVISH	BURDOCK
SULFATE	TURBINE	WALLEYE	CASTING	HUSKING	SETTING	BURNISH	SPANISH	BUTTOCK
SULFIDE	TWADDLE	WARFARE	CATALOG	ICEBERG	SHADING	CATARRH	SPINACH	CARSICK
SUNRISE	TWIDDLE	WARLIKE	CEILING	INKLING	SHAVING	CATFISH	SPLOTCH	CASSOCK
SUPPOSE	TWINKLE	WARTIME	COATING	IRONING	SHEBANG	CHEETAH	SQUELCH	CATWALK
SUPREME	TWOSOME	WASTAGE	CODLING	JACKLEG	SHORING	CHERISH	STAUNCH	CHINOOK
SURFACE	UKULELE	WATTAGE	COWLING	JOTTING	SIBLING	CODFISH	STEALTH	COSSACK
SURMISE	ULULATE	WAYSIDE	CRAVING	KEEPING	SPARING	CORINTH	STOMACH	COWLICK
SURNAME	UMBRAGE	WELCOME	CUNNING	KERNING	STAGING	DEBAUCH	STRETCH	CUTBACK
SURVIVE	UNAWARE	WELFARE	CURBING	KILLING	STYLING	DEBOUCH	STYLISH	DAYBOOK
SWADDLE	UNCLOSE	WHEEDLE	CUTTING	KNOWING	SUITING	DERVISH	SUNBATH	DERRICK
SWINDLE	UNERASE	WHISTLE	DARLING	LADYBUG	TATTING	DIGRAPH	SUNFISH	EARMARK
SYNAPSE	UNHINGE	WHITTLE	DASHING	LANDING	TELLING	DISTICH	SWEDISH	FATBACK
SYNCOPE	UNHORSE	WINDAGE	DEALING	LAPWING	TICKING	DOGFISH	TARNISH	FETLOCK
SYRINGE	UNITIZE	WINSOME	DISHRAG	LEADING	TOPPING	ENGLISH	THROUGH	GIMMICK
SYSTOLE	UNLOOSE	WORDAGE	DRAWING	LEGGING	TRACING	EPITAPH	TOWPATH	GOSHAWK
TACTILE	UNNERVE	WRANGLE	DUMPING	LEMMING	TURNING	EYELASH	TRIUMPH	GUNLOCK
TADPOLE	UNQUOTE	WREATHE	EARPLUG	LISTING	UNDOING	EYEWASH	TURKISH	HADDOCK
TEENAGE	UNTWINE	WRESTLE	EARRING	LODGING	UNDYING	FINFISH	UNCOUTH	HAMMOCK
TEKTITE	UNWEAVE	WRIGGLE	ERELONG	LONGING	UNSLING	FINNISH	UNEARTH	HASSOCK
TENABLE	UPGRADE	WRINKLE	ETCHING	MADDING	UPSWING	FLEMISH	UNHITCH	HAUBERK
TENSILE	UPRAISE	YARDAGE	EVENING	MEANING	VEILING	FOOLISH	UNLATCH	HAYCOCK
TERMITE	UPSTAGE	ZEOLITE	FAILING	MEETING	VESTING	FURBISH	UNLEASH	HAYFORK
TERRACE	UPSTATE	BAILIFF	FAIRING	MILLING	WADDING	FURNISH	UNTRUTH	HAYRICK
TESTATE	UPSURGE	CAITIFF	FARMING	MISSING	WANTING	GARFISH	VARNISH	HEMLOCK
TEXTILE	URINATE	DEBRIEF	FEELING	MOLDING	WARNING	GARNISH	VOGUISH	HENPECK
TEXTURE	UTILIZE	DISTAFF	FENCING	MOORING	WARTHOG	GOULASH	WAGGISH	HILLOCK
THIMBLE	VACCINE	EARMUFF	FILLING	MORNING	WASHING	HASHISH	WARPATH	HOGBACK
THISTLE	VACUOLE	FLYLEAF	FINDING	MUSTANG	WAXWING	HOGWASH	WASPISH	HUMMOCK
THYMINE	VALANCE	HERSELF	FIREBUG	NETTING	WEBBING	IMPEACH	WHITISH	JAYWALK
TILLAGE	VALENCE	HIMSELF	FISHING	NOTHING	WEDDING	INVEIGH	YIDDISH	KINFOLK

LIMBECK	BALEFUL	FEARFUL	NATURAL	THERMAL	CUTWORM	PREFORM	BASSOON	COLLEEN
MATTOCK	BARBELL	FEDERAL	NEEDFUL	TIMBREL	DECLAIM	PREMIUM	BASTION	CONCERN
MENFOLK	BASHFUL	FISTFUL	NEUTRAL	TINFOIL	DECORUM	PROBLEM	BATSMAN	CONDEMN
MIDWEEK	BEDEVIL	FLANNEL	NOMINAL	TOENAIL	DIAGRAM	PROGRAM	BEDIZEN	CONDIGN
MOLLUSK	BEDROLL	FRACTAL	NOSTRIL	TOPICAL	EARDRUM	QUANTUM	BEDOUIN	CONJOIN
NETWORK	BESTIAL	FRETFUL	NUMERAL	TOPSAIL	EGOTISM	QUONDAM	BELGIAN	CONSIGN
NONBOOK	BIFOCAL	FULFILL	NUPTIAL	TOPSOIL	ELITISM	REALISM	BENISON	CONTAIN
NUTPICK	BIMETAL	FUNERAL	OATMEAL	TRAMMEL	ELYSIUM	RECLAIM	BENZOIN	CONTEMN
OARLOCK	BRIMFUL	GAINFUL	ODDBALL	TRAVAIL	ENVENOM	REQUIEM	BETOKEN	CRIMSON
OBELISK	BROTHEL	GENERAL	OEDIPAL	TREFOIL	EPIGRAM	RHENIUM	BETWEEN	CROUTON
OSTMARK	CALOMEL	GENITAL	OPTICAL	TRIVIAL	ERRATUM	RHODIUM	BIGHORN	CURTAIN
OUTLOOK	CAPITAL	GENTEEL	OPTIMAL	TUMBREL	EXCLAIM	ROSTRUM	BILLION	CUSHION
OUTRANK	CAPITOL	GLACIAL	ORDINAL	TUNEFUL	FASCISM	SANCTUM	BITTERN	DAUPHIN
OUTWORK	CARAMEL	GRADUAL	OUTPULL	TURMOIL	FAUVISM	SARCASM	BITUMEN	DEADPAN
PADDOCK	CARAVEL	GRAPNEL	OUTSELL	TYPICAL	FERMIUM	SCROTUM	BLACKEN	DECAGON
PADLOCK	CAREFUL	GRAUPEL	OVERALL	UNCIVIL	FILMDOM	SIDEARM	BLOWGUN	DENIZEN
PEACOCK	CATCALL	GUMBOIL	PARASOL	UNEQUAL	FIREARM	SOPHISM	BOATMAN	DETRAIN
POLLACK	CATTAIL	HANDFUL	PARBOIL	UNMORAL	FLOTSAM	SORGHUM	BONDMAN	DEXTRIN
POTHOOK	CENTRAL	HANDSEL	PARTIAL	UNRAVEL	FOREARM	STADIUM	BOUNDEN	DICTION
POTLUCK	CHANCEL	HELICAL	PAYROLL	UNSNARL	FREEDOM	STERNUM	BOURBON	DISCERN
PRECOOK	CHANNEL	HOBNAIL	PEAFOWL	UNUSUAL	FRUSTUM	STRATUM	BRACKEN	DISDAIN
PRESOAK	CHARNEL	ILLEGAL	PHYSIOL	UTENSIL	FULCRUM	SUNBEAM	BRAHMAN	DISJOIN
RANSACK	CHATTEL	IMMORAL	PIGTAIL	VEGETAL	GALLIUM	SYMPTOM	BRAHMIN	DOLPHIN
ROEBUCK	CITADEL	IMPANEL	PITFALL	VENTRAL	GINGHAM	SYNONYM	BROADEN	DOORMAN
ROLLICK	COAXIAL	IMPEARL	PITIFUL	VERMEIL	GRANDAM	TANTRUM	BUFFOON	DRAGOON
SEASICK	CODICIL	IMPERIL	PLUVIAL	VICINAL	HAFNIUM	TAPROOM	BULLION	DRUMLIN
SETBACK	COEQUAL	INDWELL	PRETZEL	VICTUAL	HEROISM	TERBIUM	BUMPKIN	DRUNKEN
SHYLOCK	COLONEL	INFIDEL	PREVAIL	VIRTUAL	HOLMIUM	THEOREM	BURGEON	DUCKPIN
SKYLARK	CONCEAL	INITIAL	PSYCHOL	VITRIOL	HOMONYM	THORIUM	CAISSON	DUDGEON
SPUTNIK	CONGEAL	INKWELL	QUARREL	WAGTAIL	HOODLUM	THULIUM	CALDRON	DUNGEON
TANBARK	CONICAL	INSTALL	QUETZAL	WAILFUL	HUMDRUM	TRANSOM	CANTEEN	DUSTPAN
TIEBACK	CONTROL	INSTILL	QUINTAL	WAKEFUL	IMAGISM	TRITIUM	CAPSTAN	EARTHEN
TUSSOCK	CORDIAL	JONQUIL	RADICAL	WASSAIL	INTERIM	TRIVIUM	CAPTAIN	EASTERN
UNBLOCK	CORONAL	JOURNAL	RECITAL	WASTREL	IRIDIUM	TROPISM	CAPTION	ECHELON
UNCLOAK	COUNCIL	KARAKUL	REMODEL	WAYBILL	JEJUNUM	UNBOSOM	CARAVAN	EDITION
UNFROCK	COUNSEL	LACTEAL	RENEWAL	WILLFUL	JUDAISM	UNIFORM	CARRION	EIDOLON
UPCHUCK	CRUCIAL	LATERAL	REVIVAL	WISHFUL	KINGDOM	URANIUM	CARRYON	ELISION
WARLOCK	CRYSTAL	LIBERAL	SATCHEL	WISTFUL	LEFTISM	WOLFRAM	CARTOON	EMOTION
WAXWORK	CURTAIL	LINGUAL	SAWMILL	ACCLAIM	LITHIUM	YARDARM	CAUTION	ENCHAIN
WEDLOCK	DECIBEL	LITERAL	SCALPEL	ACRONYM	MACADAM	YTTRIUM	CAVEMAN	ENLIVEN
WETBACK	DECIMAL	LUSTRAL	SCANDAL	AMALGAM	MARXISM	ZIONISM	CERTAIN	ENTRAIN
WRYNECK	DESPOIL	MANDREL	SEAWALL	ANAGRAM	MAXIMUM	ABANDON	CERUMEN	EROSION
ABYSMAL	DIGITAL	MANDRIL	SEMINAL	ANIMISM	MILLDAM	ABDOMEN	CESSION	EVASION
ABYSSAL	DIREFUL	MARITAL	SENSUAL	ANTONYM	MINIMUM	ABSTAIN	CHADIAN	EXPLAIN
ACCUSAL	DISTILL	MARSHAL	SEVERAL	ATAVISM	MODICUM	ADJOURN	CHAGRIN	FACTION
ADMIRAL	DIURNAL	MARTIAL	SHRIVEL	BAPTISM	MUDROOM	AFRICAN	CHANSON	FASHION
ADRENAL	DOLEFUL	MAXIMAL	SNORKEL	BARROOM	NIOBIUM	AILERON	CHAPMAN	FESTOON
AEROSOL	DUTIFUL	MEDICAL	SOULFUL	BEDROOM	NOSTRUM	ALBUMEN	CHASTEN	FICTION
AIRFOIL	EMBROIL	MENTHOL	SPANIEL	BLOSSOM	OPOSSUM	ALBUMIN	CHEAPEN	FIFTEEN
AIRMAIL	EMBRYOL	MINDFUL	SPATIAL	BOREDOM	OPTIMUM	ANDIRON	CHEVRON	FIREMAN
ALCOHOL	ETERNAL	MINERAL	SPECIAL	BUCKRAM	OVERARM	ANTIGEN	CHICKEN	FISSION
ANTHILL	ETHANOL	MINIMAL	SPOUSAL	CADMIUM	PABULUM	ARRAIGN	CHIFFON	FLATTEN
APPAREL	ETHICAL	MISCALL	STENCIL	CALCIUM	PENTIUM	ARTISAN	CHIGNON	FOGHORN
ARRIVAL	EYEBALL	MISTRAL	STRUDEL	CAMBIUM	PERFORM	ASPIRIN	CISTERN	FOOTMAN
ARSENAL	FACTUAL	MONGREL	SUBSOIL	CONFIRM	PHANTOM	AUCTION	CITIZEN	FOREIGN
ASEXUAL	FANTAIL	MUSICAL	SUNDIAL	CONFORM	PILGRIM	BALLOON	CLARION	FOREMAN
AUSTRAL	FATEFUL	NARWHAL	TENDRIL	CRANIUM	PINWORM	BARGAIN	COARSEN	FORLORN

FORTRAN	LATVIAN	PENSION	STILTON	CARABAO	ENVELOP	BLADDER	CLATTER	FLIPPER
FREEMAN	LECTERN	PERSIAN	SUBJOIN	CEMBALO	FLATTOP	BLATHER	CLAVIER	FLIVVER
FRESHEN	LEGHORN	PERTAIN	SUCTION	CENTAVO	FORETOP	BLEEDER	CLEAVER	FLUSTER
FROGMAN	LESBIAN	PHAETON	SUNBURN	CENTIMO	GUMDROP	BLINDER	CLINKER	FLUTTER
FUSTIAN	LETDOWN	PIGSKIN	SUNDOWN	CHICANO	HARDTOP	BLINKER	CLIPPER	FORBEAR
GALLEON	LEXICON	PILLION	SURGEON	EMBARGO	HARELIP	BLISTER	CLOBBER	FOREVER
GAMBIAN	LIAISON	PLATOON	SUSTAIN	FARRAGO	HILLTOP	BLOATER	CLUSTER	FOUNDER
GELATIN	LIGHTEN	PLAYPEN	SWEETEN	GESTAPO	KETCHUP	BLOOPER	CLUTTER	FREEZER
GENTIAN	LINEMAN	PLOWMAN	SWOLLEN	HIDALGO	KINSHIP	BLOTTER	COBBLER	FRITTER
GHERKIN	LOWDOWN	POCOSIN	TENSION	IMPASTO	KNEECAP	BLUBBER	COLLIER	FURRIER
GLADDEN	MAHICAN	POLYGON	TERRAIN	INFERNO	MAINTOP	BLUCHER	COMPEER	FURTHER
GLEEMAN	MAILMAN	POPCORN	THEREIN	LUMBAGO	MILKSOP	BLUNDER	CONIFER	GLACIER
GLISTEN	MALISON	PORTION	THEREON	MAESTRO	MISSTEP	BLUSTER	CONQUER	GLAMOUR
GLUTTON	MANIKIN	POSTERN	THICKEN	MAFIOSO	MUGWUMP	BOLIVAR	CONTOUR	GLAZIER
GOODMAN	MANSION	POSTMAN	TIBETAN	MAGNETO	NONSTOP	BOLSTER	CORONER	GLIMMER
GRECIAN	MARTIAN	PRETEEN	TIGHTEN	MEMENTO	OUTCROP	BOUDOIR	CORSAIR	GLISTER
GREMLIN	MAUDLIN	PROGMAN	TORSION	MESTIZO	OVERLAP	BOULDER	COUNTER	GLITTER
GRUNION	MEATMAN	PRONOUN	TOUGHEN	MOROCCO	OVERTOP	BOUNCER	COURIER	GOBBLER
GUERDON	MEGATON	PROPMAN	TREASON	MULATTO	PARSNIP	BOWLDER	COURSER	GRAMMAR
HACKMAN	MELANIN	PROTEAN	TRODDEN	NONHERO	RATTRAP	BRAZIER	CRACKER	GRAZIER
HAIRPIN	MENTION	PROTEIN	TUITION	OREGANO	REGROUP	BREAKER	CREATOR	GRINDER
HALCYON	MEXICAN	PROTEIN	TYPHOON	PICCOLO	ROOFTOP	BROIDER	CRITTER	GROUPER
HANDGUN	MIDTOWN	PULLMAN	UMPTEEN	PIMENTO	ROUNDUP	BROILER	CROPPER	GUILDER
HANGMAN	MILKMAN	PUMPKIN	UNCHAIN	PLACEBO	SCALLOP	BROODER	CROSIER	HAMSTER
HARDPAN	MILLION	PURITAN	UNCLEAN	POMPANO	SHALLOP	BROTHER	CROWBAR	HANDCAR
HARPOON	MISSION	PURLOIN	UNCTION	PORTICO	SPEEDUP	BROWSER	CRUISER	HARBOUR
HEADMAN	MOHEGAN	QUICKEN	UNICORN	PROVISO	STARTUP	BRUISER	CRULLER	HARRIER
HEADPIN	MOHICAN	RACCOON	UNKNOWN	PROXIMO	STIRRUP	BUCKLER	CURATOR	HAUTEUR
HEARKEN	MOISTEN	REDSKIN	UNLEARN	SAGUARO	STOPGAP	BUGBEAR	DECODER	HEATHER
HEARTEN	MONSOON	REFRAIN	UTOPIAN	SENTIMO	SUNLAMP	BURGHER	DELIVER	HIPSTER
HEATHEN	MUEZZIN	REGIMEN	VATICAN	SHAMPOO	TROLLOP	BUTCHER	DESPAIR	HOLSTER
HELLION	MULLEIN	REUNION	VENISON	SIROCCO	UNCLASP	CADAVER	DIVIDER	HOOSIER
HEPARIN	MULLION	ROUGHEN	VERSION	SOPRANO	UNGROUP	CALIBER	DIVISOR	HOSTLER
HEXAGON	MURRAIN	RUFFIAN	VERVAIN	TALLYHO	UNSTRAP	CALIPER	DOSSIER	HOWEVER
HOEDOWN	NANKEEN	RUNDOWN	VETERAN	THERETO	WARSHIP	CAMPHOR	DOWAGER	HUMIDOR
HORIZON	NEUTRON	RUSSIAN	VILLAIN	TOBACCO	WICKIUP	CARRIER	DRESSER	INCISOR
INGRAIN	NEWBORN	SADIRON	VILLEIN	TORNADO	WIRETAP	CASHIER	DRIFTER	INHALER
INGROWN	NEWSMAN	SAFFRON	VITAMIN	TORPEDO	WORSHIP	CATCHER	DROPPER	INSIDER
INHUMAN	NUCLEON	SANDMAN	WALLOON	TREMOLO	ADAPTER	CENTAUR	DRUMMER	INSULAR
INKHORN	OARSMAN	SECTION	WAYWORN	UNDERGO	ALCAZAR	CHAFFER	ELECTOR	INSURER
INSULIN	OCTAGON	SESSION	WESTERN	VAQUERO	ALMONER	CHAMBER	EMBOWER	INTEGER
IRANIAN	OILSKIN	SHARPEN	WHEREIN	VERTIGO	AMATEUR	CHAMFER	EMITTER	JANITOR
ITALIAN	OPINION	SHORTEN	WHEREON	VIBRATO	AMMETER	CHAPTER	EMPEROR	JEWELER
JAVELIN	ORATION	SHOTGUN	WIDGEON	VOLCANO	ANGULAR	CHARGER	EMPOWER	JOCULAR
KEELSON	ORTOLAN	SHOWMAN	WOODMAN	WHERETO	ANNULAR	CHARMER	ENAMOUR	JODHPUR
KERATIN	OTTOMAN	SIDEMAN	WORKMAN	AIRDROP	ANOTHER	CHARTER	EQUATOR	JUGULAR
KIDSKIN	OUTWORN	SILICON	YARDMAN	AIRSHIP	AQUIFER	CHATTER	FANCIER	JUNIPER
KILOTON	OVATION	SIRLOIN	ZAMBIAN	ANTHROP	ARBITER	CHECKER	FARRIER	JUPITER
KINGPIN	OVERRUN	SIXTEEN	ZILLION	BELLHOP	ARMORER	CHEDDAR	FARTHER	KNOCKER
KINSMAN	PALADIN	SLACKEN	ALLEGRO	BREAKUP	ASUNDER	CHIGGER	FEATHER	LACQUER
KITCHEN	PARAGON	SMIDGEN	ARAPAHO	CATCHUP	ATELIER	CHIPPER	FIGHTER	LAMINAR
KREMLIN	PASSION	SOJOURN	AVOCADO	CHECKUP	AUDITOR	CHOPPER	FLANKER	LANGUOR
KRYPTON	PASTERN	SOUPCON	BRACERO	CLEANUP	BARRIER	CHOWDER	FLAPPER	LAUNDER
LAMPOON	PATROON	SOYBEAN	BRAVADO	COWSLIP	BELABOR	CHUKKER	FLATCAR	LEAGUER
LANOLIN	PATTERN	STATION	BUFFALO	DESKTOP	BESMEAR	CLAMBER	FLATTER	LEATHER
LANTERN	PELICAN	STEPSON	BUGABOO	DEVELOP	BIPOLAR	CLANGOR	FLAVOUR	LIGHTER
LAOTIAN	PENGUIN	STIFFEN	CALYPSO	DEWDROP	BIRCHER	CLAPPER	FLICKER	LIQUEUR

LOBSTER	PUNSTER	SPEAKER	WHITHER	DUTEOUS	NEMESIS	TRICEPS	BEDFAST	CONTEXT
LOCATOR	QUARTER	SPECTER	WHOEVER	EMPRESS	NERVOUS	UNCROSS	BEDPOST	CONTORT
LUCIFER	RAMBLER	SPELLER	WHOPPER	ENDLESS	NOCUOUS	UNDRESS	BENEFIT	CONVENT
MANAGER	RATTLER	SPOILER	WIDOWER	ENDWAYS	NONPLUS	URANOUS	BEQUEST	CONVERT
MARINER	REACTOR	SPONSOR	WIGGLER	ENGROSS	NOXIOUS	USELESS	BETWIXT	CONVICT
MASSEUR	RECOVER	SPOTTER	WRAPPER	ENVIOUS	NUCLEUS	VACUOUS	BIBELOT	COOKOUT
MATADOR	REGULAR	SPUTTER	WRECKER	EXPRESS	OBVIOUS	VARIOUS	BISCUIT	COOLANT
MAUNDER	RELATOR	SQUALOR	WRINGER	FATUOUS	OCTOPUS	VESPERS	BLANKET	COPILOT
MEANDER	ROASTER	STAFFER	YOUNKER	FERROUS	OMINOUS	VICIOUS	BLATANT	COPYCAT
MIDYEAR	ROISTER	STAGGER	ABSCESS	FORCEPS	OMNIBUS	VILLOUS	BLOWOUT	CORONET
MINSTER	ROOSTER	STAMMER	ADDRESS	FURIOUS	ONEROUS	VISCOUS	BOMBAST	CORRECT
MOBSTER	SAMOVAR	STELLAR	AGELESS	GALLOWS	OPPRESS	VITTLES	BOOKLET	CORRUPT
MODULAR	SAMPLER	STICKER	AIMLESS	GENESIS	OSMOSIS	WARLESS	BORSCHT	COUPLET
MONITOR	SANDBAR	STOPPER	ALUMNUS	GIBBOUS	PAJAMAS	WHEREAS	BOUQUET	CRICKET
MONOMER	SAUNTER	STUTTER	AMOROUS	GIBLETS	PAPYRUS	WILLIES	BOYCOTT	CROCHET
MONSTER	SCAMPER	SWAGGER	ANXIOUS	GLOTTIS	PARESIS	WINDOWS	BRACKET	CROQUET
MUFFLER	SCANNER	SWEATER	APROPOS	GODDESS	PARLOUS	WITHERS	BRISKET	CRUMPET
NEITHER	SCATTER	SWELTER	AQUEOUS	GODLESS	PENATES	WITLESS	BROUGHT	CULPRIT
NONUSER	SCEPTER	TABULAR	ARBUTUS	GOGGLES	PERHAPS	WITNESS	BURNOUT	CULVERT
NORTHER	SCHOLAR	TANAGER	ARDUOUS	HALVERS	PHALLUS	ZEALOUS	CABARET	CURRANT
NUCLEAR	SCOOTER	TAPSTER	ARREARS	HAPLESS	PHONICS	ABREAST	CABINET	CURRENT
OCTOBER	SCUPPER	TERRIER	ARTLESS	HARNESS	PHYSICS	ACCOUNT	CALUMET	CYCLIST
OFFICER	SECULAR	THEATER	BELLOWS	HEINOUS	PITEOUS	ACROBAT	CARPORT	DASHPOT
OLDSTER	SELTZER	THINNER	BENTHOS	HEIRESS	POLARIS	ADAMANT	CATBOAT	DEFAULT
ORBITER	SEMINAR	THITHER	BESIDES	HEROICS	POMPOUS	ADJUNCT	CHAPLET	DEFIANT
OUTDOOR	SENATOR	THUNDER	BETIMES	HIDEOUS	POSSESS	AFFLICT	CHARIOT	DEFICIT
OUTWEAR	SHARPER	TIPSTER	BILIOUS	HOSTESS	PROCESS	AFFRONT	CHEMIST	DEFLECT
PALAVER	SHATTER	TITULAR	BITTERS	HUMERUS	PROFESS	AGAINST	CHEROOT	DEFROST
PANNIER	SHELTER	TOASTER	BURGESS	HUNKERS	PROWESS	AILMENT	CHEVIOT	DEFUNCT
PANTHER	SHIMMER	TRACTOR	CALENDS	HYDROUS	PYJAMAS	AIRLIFT	CIRCLET	DELIGHT
PARLOUR	SHOCKER	TRAILER	CALLOUS	IGNEOUS	PYRITES	AIRPORT	CIRCUIT	DELIMIT
PARTNER	SHUDDER	TRAITOR	CANVASS	ILEITIS	QUIETUS	AIRPOST	CLEMENT	DEMERIT
PHILTER	SHUTTER	TRIGGER	CARCASS	ILLNESS	RAUCOUS	ALIMENT	COCKPIT	DENTIST
PIASTER	SHYSTER	TROOPER	CARDBUS	IMPETUS	REDRESS	ALRIGHT	COCONUT	DEPOSIT
PILSNER	SIDECAR	TUBULAR	CARIOUS	IMPIOUS	REGRESS	AMBIENT	COEXIST	DESCANT
PIONEER	SIMILAR	TUMBLER	CELSIUS	IMPRESS	REMAINS	ANAPEST	COHABIT	DESCENT
PITCHER	SKIPPER	TUTELAR	CHABLIS	INCUBUS	REPRESS	ANCIENT	COLLECT	DESSERT
PLANTAR	SKITTER	TWEETER	CHALLIS	INDOORS	REREDOS	APPOINT	COMFORT	DETRACT
PLANTER	SKIWEAR	TWISTER	CHAMOIS	INGRESS	RHOMBUS	APRICOT	COMMENT	DEVIANT
PLASTER	SLACKER	TWITTER	CHASSIS	INNARDS	RICKETS	AQUAVIT	COMPACT	DIALECT
PLATTER	SLANDER	UNCOVER	CIVVIES	INNINGS	RUINOUS	ARMREST	COMPORT	DIARIST
PLOTTER	SLATHER	UPRIVER	CLOTHES	INTRANS	SERIOUS	ARPANET	COMPOST	DILUENT
PLUMBER	SLEEPER	VERNIER	COMPASS	ISTHMUS	SINUOUS	ASPHALT	CONCEIT	DISGUST
PLUNDER	SLENDER	VINEGAR	CONFESS	JACKASS	SOLARIS	ASSAULT	CONCEPT	DISPORT
PLUNGER	SLICKER	VINTNER	COPIOUS	JEALOUS	SPECIES	ATHEIST	CONCERT	DISRUPT
POINTER	SLIPPER	VISITOR	CUMULUS	JITTERS	SUCCESS	ATHIRST	CONCOCT	DISSECT
POLYMER	SLITHER	VOUCHER	CURIOUS	LARGESS	SUMMONS	ATHWART	CONDUCT	DISSENT
POPOVER	SLOBBER	WAGONER	CUTLASS	LAWLESS	SURPASS	ATTAINT	CONDUIT	DISTANT
POPULAR	SLUMBER	WARBLER	CYPRESS	MAKINGS	SURPLUS	ATTEMPT	CONGEST	DISTORT
POSTWAR	SMELTER	WARRIOR	DEGAUSS	MALLEUS	TACTICS	ATTRACT	CONNECT	DOGCART
PRAETOR	SMOLDER	WEATHER	DEPRESS	MARQUIS	TEDIOUS	AUGMENT	CONSENT	DOGTROT
PREMIER	SMOTHER	WHEELER	DEVIOUS	MATTINS	TENUOUS	BACKLIT	CONSIST	DOORMAT
PRICKER	SNEAKER	WHETHER	DIGRESS	MEASLES	TETANUS	BALLAST	CONSORT	DORMANT
PROCTOR	SNICKER	WHICKER	DISCUSS	MEIOSIS	THERMOS	BANQUET	CONSULT	DOUBLET
PROFFER	SOLDIER	WHIMPER	DISMISS	MIMESIS	TIDINGS	BAPTIST	CONTACT	DRAGNET
PROSPER	SOUNDER	WHISKER	DUBIOUS	MINIBUS	TOPLESS	BARONET	CONTENT	DRAUGHT
PSALTER	SPATTER	WHISPER	DUCHESS	MITOSIS	TRELLIS	BAYONET	CONTEST	DRIBLET

DROPLET	HOTSHOT	PARQUET	REDOUBT	TOPKNOT	AIRFLOW	ALREADY	CRUCIFY	GALLERY
DROUGHT	HOWBEIT	PATIENT	REFLECT	TOPMAST	BESHREW	AMATORY	CRYBABY	GANGWAY
EARNEST	HUTMENT	PATRIOT	REFRACT	TOPMOST	BUCKSAW	AMENITY	CURSORY	GATEWAY
EARSHOT	HYDRANT	PAYMENT	REGNANT	TORMENT	CHOCTAW	AMNESTY	CUSTODY	GEODESY
ELEMENT	ICEBOAT	PEASANT	REMNANT	TORRENT	DEWCLAW	AMPLIFY	CUTLERY	GEOLOGY
EMINENT	ILLICIT	PENDANT	REMOUNT	TOURIST	DISAVOW	ANALOGY	DANDIFY	GETAWAY
ENCHANT	IMPRINT	PENDENT	REPRINT	TOWBOAT	EYEBROW	ANARCHY	DEANERY	GHASTLY
ENCRUST	INCRUST	PENNANT	REQUEST	TRANSIT	FRETSAW	ANATOMY	DEATHLY	GLORIFY
ENDMOST	INEXACT	PERCENT	RESEDIT	TRIDENT	HACKSAW	ANCHOVY	DECENCY	GRANARY
ENGRAFT	INFARCT	PERCEPT	RESPECT	TRINKET	HANDSAW	ANNUITY	DEERFLY	GRATIFY
ENTRANT	INFLECT	PERFECT	RETRACT	TRIPLET	JACKDAW	ANOMALY	DENSITY	GRAVITY
ENTREAT	INFLICT	PERSIST	RETREAT	TRISECT	LOCKJAW	ANXIETY	DESTINY	GRIZZLY
ENTRUST	INGRAFT	PERVERT	RINGLET	TRUMPET	LONGBOW	ANYBODY	DESTROY	GUNNERY
EPAULET	INHABIT	PIANIST	RIVULET	TUGBOAT	LOWBROW	APOLOGY	DEVILRY	HACKNEY
EPITHET	INHERIT	PIGMENT	ROOTLET	TURNOUT	MACDRAW	ARCHERY	DIGNIFY	HALFWAY
EVIDENT	INHIBIT	PIQUANT	ROWBOAT	UNGUENT	OUTDRAW	ARCHWAY	DIGNITY	HALLWAY
EXCERPT	INQUEST	PLACKET	SALIENT	UNKEMPT	OUTFLOW	AREAWAY	DISOBEY	HAPPILY
EXHAUST	INSIGHT	PLAUDIT	SANDLOT	UNQUIET	OUTGROW	ASHTRAY	DISPLAY	HARMONY
EXHIBIT	INSPECT	PLAYLET	SAPIENT	UNTWIST	PREVIEW	ATROPHY	DOORWAY	HAUGHTY
EXPLOIT	INSTANT	PLUMMET	SAWDUST	UPDRAFT	PURVIEW	AUTOPSY	DOUGHTY	HEADWAY
EXTINCT	INTROIT	POLECAT	SCARLET	UPRIGHT	RAINBOW	BALCONY	DRAPERY	HEALTHY
EXTRACT	INTRUST	PORTENT	SEALANT	UPSHIFT	SHALLOW	BALONEY	DUBIETY	HEARSAY
FALLOUT	JACKPOT	POTSHOT	SEAPORT	UPSTART	SOMEHOW	BATTERY	DYNASTY	HICKORY
FEEDLOT	JETPORT	PRECEPT	SEGMENT	UPSWEPT	SPARROW	BEASTLY	EARTHLY	HIGHBOY
FERMENT	KUMQUAT	PREDICT	SEQUENT	UPTIGHT	SWALLOW	BEATIFY	ECOLOGY	HIGHWAY
FERVENT	LAMBENT	PREEMPT	SERPENT	VAGRANT	UNSCREW	BEGGARY	ECONOMY	HISTORY
FIGMENT	LATCHET	PREFECT	SERVANT	VALIANT	WHIPSAW	BELLBOY	ECSTASY	HOLIDAY
FILBERT	LAWSUIT	PREHEAT	SEXTANT	VARIANT	WHITLOW	BELTWAY	ELDERLY	HORRIFY
FLORIST	LEAFLET	PRESENT	SHERBET	VARMINT	WINDROW	BIKEWAY	EMBASSY	HOSIERY
FLUTIST	LENIENT	PRETEXT	SHUTOUT	VERDANT	ANTHRAX	BIOLOGY	EMPATHY	HYMNODY
FOLDOUT	LOCKNUT	PREVENT	SIDELIT	VERDICT	BANDBOX	BLARNEY	ENTROPY	IDEALLY
FONDANT	LOCKOUT	PRODUCT	SKILLET	VIADUCT	BEESWAX	BRAVERY	EQUERRY	IMAGERY
FORFEIT	LOOKOUT	PROJECT	SLEIGHT	VIBRANT	COMPLEX	BREVITY	ESTUARY	IMPIETY
FRAUGHT	MANHUNT	PROPHET	SOLICIT	VIOLENT	CONFLUX	CALCIFY	EUPHONY	INFANCY
FREIGHT	MANUMIT	PROTECT	SOLVENT	WALKOUT	EQUINOX	CALUMNY	FACTORY	INQUIRY
FRESHET	MARGENT	PROTEST	SOPHIST	WARRANT	FIREBOX	CANNERY	FACULTY	JANUARY
GABFEST	MARPLOT	PROVOST	SPIRANT	WASHOUT	GEARBOX	CARAWAY	FAIRWAY	JEWELRY
GALLANT	MIDMOST	PRUDENT	STUDENT	WAVELET	JUKEBOX	CAVALRY	FALLACY	JOLLITY
GANTLET	MIGRANT	PULLOUT	STUFFIT	WHATNOT	MAILBOX	CENTURY	FALSIFY	JOURNEY
GARMENT	MINARET	PUNGENT	STYLIST	WHEREAT	NARTHEX	CERTIFY	FANTASY	JUSTIFY
GOURMET	MORDANT	PURPORT	SUBJECT	WHIPPET	PARADOX	CHANTEY	FARAWAY	KILLJOY
GROMMET	MUSKRAT	PURSUIT	SUBSIST	WILDCAT	PERPLEX	CHANTRY	FATUITY	LAMPREY
GUNBOAT	NASCENT	QUARTET	SUBVERT	WITHOUT	PHALANX	CHARITY	FERNERY	LARCENY
GUNSHOT	NEGLECT	QUINTET	SUGGEST	WOODCUT	PHARYNX	CHICORY	FINICKY	LAUNDRY
HABITAT	OCULIST	RADIANT	SUNSPOT	WOODLOT	PHOENIX	CHIMNEY	FIREFLY	LAYAWAY
HAIRCUT	ODDMENT	RAIMENT	SUPPORT	WORKOUT	PILLBOX	CHINTZY	FIRSTLY	LECHERY
HALIBUT	OFFBEAT	RAMPANT	SURFEIT	WROUGHT	SALTBOX	CHUTNEY	FISHERY	LEPROSY
HANDOUT	OPULENT	RAMPART	SURTOUT	CARIBOU	TOOLBOX	CIVILLY	FLESHLY	LIBERTY
HANDSET	OUTCAST	RAPPORT	SUSPECT	CHAPEAU	TRIPLEX	CLARIFY	FLIGHTY	LIBRARY
HANGOUT	OUTLAST	RAREBIT	TANGENT	CHATEAU	WORKBOX	CLARITY	FLOWERY	LIGNIFY
HARVEST	OUTPOST	RATCHET	TAPROOT	JUJITSU	ABILITY	CLEANLY	FOLKWAY	LIQUEFY
HATCHET	OVERACT	READOUT	TEMPEST	MANTEAU	ACADEMY	COCKNEY	FOOLERY	LITURGY
HAYLOFT	OVIDUCT	REAGENT	THEREAT	PARVENU	ACIDIFY	COMPANY	FORTIFY	LOATHLY
HEADSET	OXIDANT	RECEIPT	THICKET	PLATEAU	ACTUARY	COOKERY	FOUNDRY	LOTTERY
HELLCAT	PAGEANT	RECOUNT	THOUGHT	PURLIEU	ALCHEMY	COPYBOY	FRAILTY	LULLABY
HIDEOUT	PARAPET	RECRUIT	TONIGHT	TABLEAU	ALIMONY	COUNTRY	FREEWAY	MAGNIFY
HOTFOOT	PARFAIT	REDCOAT	TOPCOAT	TONNEAU	ALLERGY	COURTLY	GAINSAY	MAJESTY

MALMSEY	POSTBOY	STUPEFY	WRONGLY
MAMMARY	POTTERY	SUBSIDY	ZOOLOGY
MASONRY	POULTRY	SUMMARY	ZYMURGY
MASTERY	POVERTY	SURGERY	KIBBUTZ
MERCURY	PRIMACY	SWARTHY	PIZZAZZ
MIMICRY	PRIMARY	TANNERY	
MISPLAY	PRIVACY	TENANCY	
MOLLIFY	PROBITY	TERNARY	
MORTIFY	PRODIGY	TERRIFY	
MYSTERY	PROGENY	TESTIFY	
MYSTIFY	PROSODY	THERAPY	
NAIVETY	PUBERTY	THEREBY	
NAUGHTY	PUTREFY	THREADY	
NEOLOGY	QUALIFY	THROATY	
NEWSBOY	QUALITY	THRUWAY	
NIGHTLY	RACEWAY	TIMOTHY	
NITRIFY	RAILWAY	TOGGERY	
NOONDAY	RAUNCHY	TOURNEY	
NOSEGAY	REALITY	TRACERY	
NOVELTY	RECENCY	TRAGEDY	
NULLIFY	RECTIFY	TRILOGY	
NURSERY	RECTORY	TRINITY	
OBLOQUY	REENTRY	TROLLEY	
OBSEQUY	REGENCY	TUESDAY	
ODYSSEY	RICKETY	TURNERY	
OPACITY	RIGHTLY	TURNKEY	
ORATORY	RIVALRY	TYRANNY	
ORDERLY	ROADWAY	UNCANNY	
ORGANDY	ROBBERY	UNGODLY	
OROGENY	ROOKERY	UNHANDY	
OSSUARY	ROYALTY	UNHAPPY	
OUTPLAY	RUNAWAY	UNITARY	
OUTSTAY	SAINTLY	UNLUCKY	
OVERFLY	SATIETY	UNMANLY	
OVERJOY	SATISFY	URINARY	
OVERLAY	SCARIFY	UROLOGY	
PAGEBOY	SCENERY	UTILITY	
PAISLEY	SCRAPPY	VACANCY	
PALFREY	SCRAWNY	VACUITY	
PANOPLY	SCRUFFY	VARIETY	
PARKWAY	SECRECY	VARSITY	
PARSLEY	SECTARY	VERSIFY	
PARTWAY	SENSORY	VICEROY	
PASSKEY	SEVENTY	VICTORY	
PATHWAY	SHAPELY	VITRIFY	
PAUCITY	SHORTLY	WAGGERY	
PECCARY	SIGHTLY	WALKWAY	
PENALTY	SIGNIFY	WALLABY	
PEPPERY	SLAVERY	WEALTHY	
PERFIDY	SOCIETY	WEEKDAY	
PERJURY	SOMEDAY	WEIGHTY	
PETRIFY	SORCERY	WHEREBY	
PILLORY	SPECIFY	WHISKEY	
PLAYBOY	SPINDLY	WILLOWY	
PLENARY	STANDBY	WOMANLY	
PLOWBOY	STATELY	WORKDAY	
PORTRAY	STRINGY	WORLDLY	

8 LETTER WORDS

1ST LETTER							
AARDVARK	ADHESIVE	ALIENATE	ANTELOPE	ARROGANT	BACKHAND	BATHROOM	BIRDSEED
AABATTOIR	ADJACENT	ALIENIST	ANTERIOR	ARROGATE	BACKLASH	BAYBERRY	BIRTHDAY
AARDVARK	ADJUTANT	ALIZARIN	ANTEROOM	ARTERIAL	BACKPACK	BEANBALL	BISEXUAL
ABATTOIR	ADJUVANT	ALKALOID	ANTHROPO	ARTIFACT	BACKREST	BEARSKIN	BITSTOCK
ABDICATE	ADMONISH	ALLEGORY	ANTIBODY	ARTIFICE	BACKSIDE	BEATIFIC	BIWEEKLY
ABEYANCE	ADOPTIVE	ALLELUIA	ANTIDOTE	ARTISTIC	BACKSLAP	BEAUTIFY	BIYEARLY
ABLATION	ADORABLE	ALLERGEN	ANTIMONY	ARTISTRY	BACKSPIN	BECHUANA	BLACKING
ABLATIVE	ADULTERY	ALLEYWAY	ANTINOMY	ASBESTOS	BACKSTOP	BECOMING	BLACKOUT
ABLUTION	ADVISORY	ALLIANCE	ANTIPODE	ASPERITY	BACKWARD	BEDAZZLE	BLACKTOP
ABNEGATE	ADVOCATE	ALLOCATE	ANTIPOPE	ASPHODEL	BACKWASH	BEDSTEAD	BLESSING
ABNORMAL	AEROLOGY	ALLSPICE	ANYPLACE	ASPHYXIA	BADINAGE	BEECHNUT	BLISSFUL
ABORNING	AERONAUT	ALLUVIUM	ANYTHING	ASPIRANT	BAEDEKER	BEFRIEND	BLIZZARD
ABORTION	AESTHETE	ALMIGHTY	ANYWHERE	ASPIRATE	BAGUETTE	BEFUDDLE	BLOCKADE
ABRASIVE	AFFECTED	ALOPECIA	APERITIF	ASSASSIN	BAILABLE	BEGGARLY	BLOOMERS
ABROGATE	AFFERENT	ALPHABET	APERTURE	ASSEMBLE	BAILSMAN	BEGRUDGE	BLOWPIPE
ABSCISSA	AFFIANCE	ALTHOUGH	APHANITE	ASSEMBLY	BAKESHOP	BEHAVIOR	BLUDGEON
ABSENTEE	AFFINITY	ALTITUDE	APHELION	ASSORTED	BALLROOM	BEHEMOTH	BLUEBELL
ABSINTHE	AFFLATUS	ALTRUISM	APHORISM	ASSTATINE	BALLYHOO	BEHOLDEN	BLUEBIRD
ABSOLUTE	AFFRIGHT	ALUMINUM	APOLOGIA	ASTERISK	BALUSTER	BELITTLE	BLUEFISH
ABSTRACT	AFLUTTER	AMARANTH	APOPLEXY	ASTEROID	BANDANNA	BENEDICT	BLUENOSE
ABSTRUSE	AFTERTAX	AMBIENCE	APOSTASY	ASTONISH	BANISTER	BENEFICE	BOASTFUL
ABUNDANT	AGERATUM	AMBITION	APOTHEGM	ATHLETIC	BANKBOOK	BENTWOOD	BOBOLINK
ABUTMENT	AGGRIEVE	AMBROSIA	APPANAGE	ATOMIZER	BANKROLL	BENZOATE	BOBWHITE
ABUTTALS	AGITPROP	AMBULANT	APPARENT	ATROCITY	BANKRUPT	BEQUEATH	BODILESS
ACADEMIC	AGLITTER	AMENABLE	APPELLEE	ATROPINE	BANTLING	BERCEUSE	BODYWORK
ACANTHUS	AGNOSTIC	AMERICAN	APPENDIX	ATTITUDE	BARBARIC	BEREAVED	BOGEYMAN
ACCIDENT	AGRARIAN	AMETHYST	APPETITE	ATTORNEY	BARBECUE	BERIBERI	BOHEMIAN
ACCOLADE	AGRONOMY	AMICABLE	APPLAUSE	ATYPICAL	BARBERRY	BERMUDAS	BOLDFACE
ACCOUTRE	AIGRETTE	AMMONIUM	APPLIQUE	AUDIENCE	BARBICAN	BESMIRCH	BOLLWORM
ACCREDIT	AIRBORNE	AMOEBOID	APPOSITE	AUDITION	BARBITAL	BESTIARY	BONDSMAN
ACCURATE	AIRBRUSH	AMORTIZE	APPRAISE	AUDITORY	BAREBACK	BESTRIDE	BONHOMIE
ACCURSED	AIRCRAFT	AMPERAGE	APPROACH	AUSTRIAN	BAREFOOT	BETATRON	BOOKCASE
ACCUSTOM	AIRDROME	AMPUTATE	APPROVAL	AUTOBAHN	BARITONE	BEVERAGE	BOOKMARK
ACERBATE	AIRFIELD	ANACONDA	APTITUDE	AUTOGIRO	BARNACLE	BEWILDER	BOOKWORM
ACERBITY	AIRFRAME	ANAEROBE	AQUACADE	AUTOJOIN	BARNYARD	BIANNUAL	BOOTLESS
ACIDHEAD	AIRLINER	ANALOGUE	AQUANAUT	AUTOMATE	BARONAGE	BIATHLON	BORDELLO
ACIDOSIS	AIRPLANE	ANALYSIS	AQUARIUM	AVERMENT	BARONESS	BIBULOUS	BOTULISM
ACOUSTIC	AIRSPACE	ANATHEMA	AQUEDUCT	AVERSION	BAROUCHE	BICONVEX	BOUFFANT
ACQUAINT	AIRSPEED	ANCESTOR	AQUILINE	AVIATION	BARRACKS	BICUSPID	BOUILLON
ACRIMONY	AIRSTRIP	ANCESTRY	ARACHNID	AVIATRIX	BARRATRY	BIDDABLE	BOUNDARY
ACROSTIC	AIRTIGHT	ANDROGEN	ARBALEST	AVIONICS	BARRETTE	BIENNIAL	BOUTIQUE
ACTINISM	ALACRITY	ANECDOTE	ARBOREAL	AXLETREE	BASEBALL	BIENNIUM	BOWSPRIT
ACTINIUM	ALARMIST	ANECHOIC	ARCHDUKE	BABUSHKA	BASEBORN	BIFOCALS	BRACELET
ACTIVATE	ALBACORE	ANGELICA	ARGUABLE	BACCARAT	BASELESS	BILLFOLD	BRACKISH
ACTIVISM	ALBANIAN	ANGLICAN	ARGUMENT	BACHELOR	BASELINE	BILLHEAD	BRAGGART
ACTIVITY	ALDERMAN	ANGSTROM	ARMAMENT	BACILLUS	BASEMENT	BINAURAL	BRAKEMAN
ADDENDUM	ALEATORY	ANISETTE	ARMATURE	BACKACHE	BASILICA	BINNACLE	BRANDISH
ADDITION	ALEHOUSE	ANNOTATE	ARMCHAIR	BACKBITE	BASILISK	BIOCIDAL	BREAKAGE
ADDITIVE	ALFRESCO	ANNOUNCE	ARMORIAL	BACKBONE	BASSINET	BIRACIAL	BREAKOUT
ADEQUATE	ALGERIAN	ANTEATER	ARMYWORM	BACKDROP	BASSWOOD	BIRDBATH	BREEDING
ADHESION	ALIASING	ANTEDATE	ARPEGGIO	BACKFIRE	BATHROBE	BIRDLIME	BRETHREN

BREVIARY	CAMSHAFT	CELIBATE	CHUTZPAH	COLLIERY	CONTRIVE	CROPLAND	DECISION
BRICKBAT	CANADIAN	CELLULAR	CICATRIX	COLLOQUY	CONVERGE	CROSSBAR	DECISIVE
BRIGHTEN	CANAILLE	CEMENTUM	CICERONE	COLONIAL	CONVERSE	CROSSBOW	DECKHAND
BRINDLED	CANALIZE	CEMETERY	CINCHONA	COLONIST	CONVINCE	CROSSCUT	DECORATE
BRISLING	CANISTER	CENOBITE	CINCTURE	COLONIZE	CONVULSE	CROSSING	DECOROUS
BRITCHES	CANNABIS	CENOTAPH	CINNABAR	COLOPHON	COOKBOOK	CROTCHET	DECREASE
BROCCOLI	CANNIBAL	CENTERED	CINNAMON	COLOSSAL	COONSKIN	CROUPIER	DECREPIT
BROCHURE	CANONIZE	CENTRIST	CIRCUITY	COLOSSUS	COPPERAS	CROWFOOT	DEDICATE
BROMIDIC	CANTICLE	CEPHALIC	CIRCULAR	COMANCHE	COPULATE	CRUCIBLE	DEERSKIN
BRONCHUS	CAPACITY	CERAMIST	CISLUNAR	COMBINGS	COPYBOOK	CRUCIFIX	DEFECATE
BROOKLET	CAPESKIN	CEREBRUM	CITATION	COMEBACK	COPYDESK	CRUZEIRO	DEFIANCE
BROUGHAM	CAPRIOLE	CEREMENT	CIVILIAN	COMEDIAN	COQUETTE	CRYOLITE	DEFINITE
BROUHAHA	CAPSICUM	CEREMONY	CIVILITY	COMEDOWN	CORDLESS	CUCUMBER	DEFLOWER
BROWBEAT	CAPSULAR	CERULEAN	CIVILIZE	COMMANDO	CORDOVAN	CULINARY	DEFOREST
BROWNOUT	CAPTIOUS	CERVICAL	CLAIMANT	COMMENCE	CORDUROY	CULPABLE	DEIONIZE
BUCKSHOT	CAPUCHIN	CESAREAN	CLAMBAKE	COMMERCE	CORNCRIB	CUPBOARD	DEJECTED
BUCKSKIN	CARACOLE	CESSPOOL	CLAPTRAP	COMMONER	CORNMEAL	CUPIDITY	DEKAGRAM
BUDDHISM	CARAPACE	CHAIRMAN	CLARINET	COMMUNAL	CORONACH	CURATIVE	DELAWARE
BUILDING	CARDAMOM	CHAMBRAY	CLASSIFY	COMPILER	CORONARY	CURLICUE	DELEGATE
BULKHEAD	CARDIGAN	CHAMPION	CLAVICLE	COMPLAIN	CORPORAL	CURRENCY	DELICACY
BULLDOZE	CARDINAL	CHANCERY	CLAYMORE	COMPLEAT	CORPSMAN	CUSPIDOR	DELICATE
BULLETIN	CAREFREE	CHANDLER	CLEARING	COMPLETE	CORRIDOR	CUSTOMER	DELIRIUM
BULLFROG	CARELESS	CHANUKAH	CLEAVAGE	COMPOUND	CORUNDUM	CYCLAMEN	DELIVERY
BULLHEAD	CAREWORN	CHAPBOOK	CLEMATIS	COMPRESS	CORVETTE	CYLINDER	DELUSION
BUNDLING	CARILLON	CHAPERON	CLEMENCY	COMPRISE	COSIGNER	CYNOSURE	DEMARCHE
BUNGALOW	CARNAUBA	CHAPLAIN	CLERICAL	COMPUTER	COSMETIC	CYTOLOGY	DEMEANOR
BUNGHOLE	CARNIVAL	CHARADES	CLINCHER	CONCEIVE	COUCHANT	CYTOSINE	DEMENTED
BUOYANCY	CAROTENE	CHARCOAL	CLINICAL	CONCERTO	COUNTESS	DAFFODIL	DEMENTIA
BURGLARY	CAROUSAL	CHARISMA	CLIPPING	CONCLAVE	COUPLING	DAIQUIRI	DEMIBOLD
BURGUNDY	CAROUSEL	CHARMING	CLITORIS	CONCLUDE	COURTESY	DAIRYING	DEMIJOHN
BURNOOSE	CARRIAGE	CHASTISE	CLOISTER	CONCRETE	COURTIER	DAIRYMAN	DEMOCRAT
BURSITIS	CARRYALL	CHASTITY	CLOSEOUT	CONDENSE	COVENANT	DAMNABLE	DEMOLISH
BUSINESS	CARYATID	CHASUBLE	CLOTHIER	CONFETTI	COVERAGE	DANDRUFF	DEMONIAC
BUSYBODY	CASEMENT	CHECKERS	CLOTHING	CONFINES	COVERALL	DANSEUSE	DEMURRER
BUSYWORK	CASEWORK	CHECKOFF	CLOUDLET	CONFLICT	COVERLET	DARKLING	DENATURE
BUTTRESS	CASHMERE	CHECKOUT	CLUBFOOT	CONFOCAL	COXSWAIN	DARKROOM	DENOUNCE
CABOCHON	CASSETTE	CHECKSUM	COACHMAN	CONFOUND	CRACKPOT	DARKSOME	DEPONENT
CABSTAND	CASTAWAY	CHEERFUL	COAGULUM	CONFRERE	CRAWFISH	DATABASE	DEPUTIZE
CADUCEUS	CASTRATE	CHEMICAL	COALESCE	CONFRONT	CRAYFISH	DATELESS	DERELICT
CAFFEINE	CASUALTY	CHEMURGY	COAUTHOR	CONGENER	CREAMERY	DATELINE	DEROGATE
CAGELING	CATACOMB	CHENILLE	COCKATOO	CONGRESS	CREATION	DAUGHTER	DERRIERE
CAKEWALK	CATALYZE	CHEROKEE	COCKCROW	CONJUGAL	CREATURE	DAYBREAK	DESCRIBE
CALABASH	CATAPULT	CHESTNUT	COCKEREL	CONJUNCT	CREDENCE	DAYDREAM	DESELECT
CALADIUM	CATARACT	CHEYENNE	COCKSURE	CONQUEST	CREDENZA	DAYLIGHT	DESIROUS
CALAMINE	CATCHALL	CHIPMUNK	COCKTAIL	CONSERVE	CREDIBLE	DEADBEAT	DESOLATE
CALAMITY	CATCHING	CHIPPEWA	COGITATE	CONSIDER	CREDITOR	DEADLINE	DESPATCH
CALCULUS	CATEGORY	CHITCHAT	COGNOMEN	CONSOMME	CREEPING	DEADLOCK	DESTRUCT
CALENDAR	CATHETER	CHIVALRY	COGWHEEL	CONSPIRE	CREMAINS	DEADWOOD	DETACHED
CALENDER	CATHOLIC	CHLORIDE	COHERENT	CONSTANT	CREOSOTE	DEATHBED	DETHRONE
CALFSKIN	CAUDILLO	CHLORINE	COHESION	CONSTRUE	CRESCENT	DEBILITY	DETONATE
CALLBACK	CAULDRON	CHLORITE	COIFFEUR	CONTEMPT	CRETONNE	DEBONAIR	DETOXIFY
CALLIOPE	CAUSERIE	CHOIRBOY	COIFFURE	CONTINUE	CREVASSE	DECANTER	DETRITUS
CAMELLIA	CAUSEWAY	CHOLERIC	COINCIDE	CONTRACT	CRIBBAGE	DECEDENT	DEVILISH
CAMISOLE	CAUTIOUS	CHOWCHOW	COLANDER	CONTRAIL	CRIMINAL	DECEMBER	DEVOTION
CAMOMILE	CAVALIER	CHRISTEN	COLESLAW	CONTRARY	CRITICAL	DECIGRAM	DEWBERRY
CAMPAIGN	CELERITY	CHRISTIE	COLISEUM	CONTRAST	CRITIQUE	DECIMATE	DEXTROSE
CAMPOREE	CELIBACY	CHROMIUM	COLLAPSE	CONTRITE	CROCKERY	DECIPHER	DIABETES

DIABOLIC	DISSEVER	DRAGOMAN	EMERITUS	ESCALLOP	EYEPIECE	FILTRATE	FOLDAWAY
DIAGONAL	DISSOLVE	DRAINAGE	EMIGRATE	ESCAPADE	EYESIGHT	FINALIST	FOLDBOAT
DIALOGUE	DISSUADE	DRAUGHTS	EMINENCE	ESCAPISM	EYETOOTH	FINALIZE	FOLDEROL
DIALYSIS	DISTANCE	DRAWBACK	EMISSARY	ESCAROLE	FABULOUS	FINESPUN	FOLIATED
DIAMETER	DISTASTE	DREADFUL	EMOTICON	ESOTERIC	FACEDOWN	FIREBALL	FOLKLORE
DIANTHUS	DISTINCT	DRESSAGE	EMPHASIS	ESPALIER	FACILITY	FIREBOAT	FOLLICLE
DIAPASON	DISTRACT	DRESSING	EMPHATIC	ESPECIAL	FACTIOUS	FIREBOMB	FOOLSCAP
DIARRHEA	DISTRAIT	DRIVEWAY	EMPLOYEE	ESPOUSAL	FACTOTUM	FIRECLAY	FOOTBALL
DIASTOLE	DISTRESS	DROPKICK	EMPORIUM	ESPRESSO	FADELESS	FIREDAMP	FOOTFALL
DIATOMIC	DISTRICT	DRUGGIST	EMPYREAN	ESTIMATE	FAGOTING	FIREPLUG	FOOTHILL
DIATRIBE	DISTRUST	DRUMBEAT	EMULSIFY	ESTONIAN	FALCHION	FIRESIDE	FOOTHOLD
DICTATOR	DISUNITE	DRUNKARD	EMULSION	ESTRANGE	FALLIBLE	FIRETRAP	FOOTLESS
DIDACTIC	DISUNITY	DUCKBILL	ENCEINTE	ESTROGEN	FALSETTO	FIREWOOD	FOOTLING
DIELDRIN	DIURETIC	DUCKLING	ENCIPHER	ETERNITY	FALTBOAT	FIREWORK	FOOTNOTE
DILATORY	DIVAGATE	DULCIMER	ENCIRCLE	ETHEREAL	FAMILIAL	FIRMWARE	FOOTPATH
DILIGENT	DIVIDEND	DUMBBELL	ENCOMIUM	ETHERNET	FAMILIAR	FISHBOWL	FOOTRACE
DIMINISH	DIVINITY	DUMPLING	ENCROACH	ETHOLOGY	FANCIFUL	FISHHOOK	FOOTREST
DINGBATS	DIVISION	DUNGAREE	ENCUMBER	ETIOLOGY	FANDANGO	FISHWIFE	FOOTSORE
DINOSAUR	DIVISIVE	DUNGHILL	ENDANGER	ETRUSCAN	FANLIGHT	FIXATION	FOOTSTEP
DIPLOMAT	DIVORCEE	DUODENUM	ENDEAVOR	EUGENICS	FANTASIA	FIXATIVE	FOOTWEAR
DIPSTICK	DOCKHAND	DURATION	ENERGIZE	EUPHORIA	FAREWELL	FLAGPOLE	FOOTWORK
DIRECTOR	DOCKYARD	DUTIABLE	ENERVATE	EURASIAN	FARMHAND	FLAGRANT	FORCIBLE
DISABUSE	DOCTRINE	DWELLING	ENFEEBLE	EUROBOND	FARMLAND	FLAGSHIP	FOREBEAR
DISAGREE	DOCUMENT	DYESTUFF	ENFILADE	EUROPEAN	FARMYARD	FLAMBEAU	FOREBODE
DISALLOW	DOGFIGHT	DYNAMITE	ENGAGING	EUROPIUM	FAROUCHE	FLAMENCO	FORECAST
DISARRAY	DOGGEREL	DYSLEXIA	ENGENDER	EVACUATE	FARTHEST	FLAMEOUT	FOREDOOM
DISASTER	DOGHOUSE	EARNINGS	ENGINEER	EVALUATE	FARTHING	FLAMINGO	FOREFEND
DISBURSE	DOLDRUMS	EARPHONE	ENORMITY	EVENSONG	FASCICLE	FLAPJACK	FOREFOOT
DISCIPLE	DOLOMITE	ECLIPTIC	ENORMOUS	EVENTIDE	FASCISTA	FLASHGUN	FOREGONE
DISCLAIM	DOMESTIC	ECONOMIC	ENSCONCE	EVENTUAL	FASTBACK	FLASHING	FOREHAND
DISCLOSE	DOMICILE	EDGEWAYS	ENSEMBLE	EVERMORE	FASTNESS	FLATBOAT	FOREHEAD
DISCOLOR	DOMINATE	EDUCABLE	ENSHRINE	EVERYDAY	FATALISM	FLATFISH	FOREKNOW
DISCOUNT	DOMINEER	EFFERENT	ENSHROUD	EVERYONE	FATALITY	FLATFOOT	FORELADY
DISCOVER	DOMINION	EFFUSION	ENSILAGE	EVIDENCE	FAUBOURG	FLATHEAD	FORELAND
DISCREET	DONATION	EGGPLANT	ENTANGLE	EXACTING	FAVORITE	FLATIRON	FORELIMB
DISCRETE	DOOMSDAY	EGGSHELL	ENTHRALL	EXCAVATE	FEARLESS	FLATLAND	FORELOCK
DISFAVOR	DOORJAMB	EGYPTIAN	ENTHRONE	EXCHANGE	FEARSOME	FLATTERY	FOREMAST
DISGORGE	DOORKNOB	EIGHTEEN	ENTIRETY	EXCURSUS	FEASIBLE	FLATWARE	FOREMOST
DISGRACE	DOORSTEP	EKISTICS	ENTRAILS	EXECRATE	FEBRUARY	FLAUTIST	FORENAME
DISGUISE	DOORYARD	ELECTION	ENTRANCE	EXECUTOR	FECKLESS	FLEABANE	FORENOON
DISHEVEL	DORMOUSE	ELECTIVE	ENTRENCH	EXEGESIS	FEDERATE	FLEABITE	FORENSIC
DISHONOR	DOUBLOON	ELECTRIC	ENURESIS	EXEMPLAR	FEEDBACK	FLEETING	FOREPART
DISINTER	DOUBTFUL	ELECTRON	ENVELOPE	EXERCISE	FELDSPAR	FLESHPOT	FORESAIL
DISJOINT	DOUGHBOY	ELEGANCE	ENVIABLE	EXIGENCY	FELICITY	FLEXIBLE	FORESKIN
DISKETTE	DOUGHNUT	ELEPHANT	ENVIRONS	EXIGUOUS	FELLATIO	FLIMFLAM	FORESTRY
DISLODGE	DOVETAIL	ELEVATOR	ENVISAGE	EXORCISE	FEMININE	FLIPPANT	FORETELL
DISLOYAL	DOWNBEAT	ELIGIBLE	EPIDEMIC	EXORDIUM	FEMINISM	FLOTILLA	FOREWARN
DISMOUNT	DOWNCAST	ELLIPSIS	EPILEPSY	EXPEDITE	FEROCITY	FLOUNDER	FOREWORD
DISORDER	DOWNFALL	ELONGATE	EPILOGUE	EXPLICIT	FERVENCY	FLOURISH	FORKLIFT
DISPATCH	DOWNHILL	ELOQUENT	EPIPHANY	EXPLODED	FESTIVAL	FLUIDRAM	FORMERLY
DISPENSE	DOWNLOAD	EMACIATE	EQUALIZE	EXPONENT	FETCHING	FLUORIDE	FORMLESS
DISPERSE	DOWNPOUR	EMBATTLE	EQUATION	EXPOSURE	FIBROSIS	FLUORINE	FORSOOTH
DISPIRIT	DOWNTOWN	EMBEZZLE	EQUIPAGE	EXTERIOR	FIDELITY	FLUORITE	FORSWEAR
DISPLACE	DOWNTURN	EMBITTER	ERECTILE	EXTERNAL	FIGURINE	FLYBLOWN	FORTRESS
DISPOSAL	DOWNWARD	EMBLAZON	ERECTION	EXTRADOS	FILAMENT	FLYPAPER	FORTUITY
DISPROVE	DOWNWIND	EMBOLDEN	ERYTHEMA	EYEGLASS	FILIGREE	FLYSPECK	FORWARDS
DISQUIET	DOXOLOGY	EMBOLISM	ESCALATE	EYELINER	FILIPINO	FLYWHEEL	FOUNTAIN

FOURFOLD	GARRISON	GRAFFITO	HARDHACK	HERMETIC	HUGUENOT	IMPROPER	INSTINCT
FOURSOME	GASLIGHT	GRANDEUR	HARDSHIP	HESITANT	HUMANISM	IMPUDENT	INSTRUCT
FOURTEEN	GASOLINE	GRANDSON	HARDTACK	HESITATE	HUMANITY	IMPUNITY	INSULATE
FOXGLOVE	GASWORKS	GRANULAR	HARDWARE	HIBISCUS	HUMANIZE	INCHOATE	INTAGLIO
FOXHOUND	GATEPOST	GRAPHITE	HARDWOOD	HIDEAWAY	HUMANOID	INCHWORM	INTEGRAL
FRACTION	GAUNTLET	GRASPING	HAREBELL	HIGHBALL	HUMIDIFY	INCIDENT	INTENDED
FRACTURE	GEMINATE	GRATEFUL	HARMONIC	HIGHBORN	HUMIDITY	INCISION	INTERCOM
FRAGMENT	GEMOLOGY	GRATUITY	HARRIDAN	HIGHBRED	HUMILITY	INCISIVE	INTEREST
FRAGRANT	GEMSTONE	GRAVAMEN	HATCHING	HIGHBROW	HUMPBACK	INCOMING	INTERIOR
FRANCIUM	GENDARME	GRAYLING	HATCHWAY	HIGHLAND	HUNTRESS	INCREASE	INTERMIT
FREEBORN	GENERATE	GREEKING	HAUTBOIS	HIGHNESS	HUNTSMAN	INCUBATE	INTERMIX
FREEDMAN	GENEROUS	GREENERY	HAWAIIAN	HIGHROAD	HUSTINGS	INCUMBER	INTERNAL
FREEHAND	GENETICS	GREETING	HAWKWEED	HIGHTAIL	HYACINTH	INDEBTED	INTERNEE
FREEHOLD	GENITALS	GRIDIRON	HAWTHORN	HILLSIDE	HYDROGEN	INDECENT	INTERNET
FREELOAD	GENITIVE	GRIEVOUS	HAYSTACK	HINDMOST	HYMENEAL	INDIAMAN	INTERROG
FREEWILL	GENOCIDE	GRIZZLED	HEADACHE	HINDUISM	HYPNOSIS	INDICATE	INTERVAL
FRENETIC	GEODESIC	GROSBEAK	HEADBAND	HIRELING	HYPNOTIC	INDIGENT	INTIMATE
FREQUENT	GEOMETRY	GROSCHEN	HEADGEAR	HISPANIC	HYSTERIA	INDIRECT	INTRADOS
FRESHMAN	GERANIUM	GROUNDER	HEADLAND	HITHERTO	ICEBOUND	INDOLENT	INTRENCH
FRETWORK	GERMINAL	GRUELING	HEADLINE	HOARDING	ICEHOUSE	INDURATE	INTREPID
FRICTION	GHANAIAN	GRUESOME	HEADLOCK	HOGSHEAD	IDEALISM	INDUCTEE	INTRIGUE
FRIGHTEN	GIGABYTE	GUARANTY	HEADLONG	HOLDOVER	IDEALIZE	INDUSTRY	INTROMIT
FRIPPERY	GIGANTIC	GUARDIAN	HEADREST	HOLINESS	IDEATION	INEDITED	INUNDATE
FRONTAGE	GIMCRACK	GUERNSEY	HEADROOM	HOLOGRAM	IDENTIFY	INERRANT	INVASION
FRONTIER	GINGERLY	GUIDANCE	HEADSHIP	HOLSTEIN	IDENTITY	INEXPERT	INVEIGLE
FROSTING	GIVEAWAY	GUMPTION	HEADSMAN	HOMEBODY	IDEOGRAM	INFAMOUS	INVERTER
FROUFROU	GLABROUS	GUNFIGHT	HEADWORD	HOMEBRED	IDEOLOGY	INFANTRY	INVIABLE
FRUCTIFY	GLACIATE	GUNPOINT	HEADWORK	HOMELAND	IDOLATER	INFERIOR	INVITING
FRUITION	GLADSOME	GUNSMITH	HEAVYSET	HOMEMADE	IDOLATRY	INFERNAL	INVOLUTE
FUGITIVE	GLASSFUL	GUTTURAL	HEBRAISM	HOMEROOM	IGNITION	INFINITE	INVOLVED
FULLBACK	GLAUCOMA	GUYANESE	HECATOMB	HOMESICK	IGNORANT	INFINITY	INWARDLY
FUMAROLE	GLOAMING	GYMKHANA	HEDGEHOG	HOMESPUN	ILLINOIS	INFOBAHN	IRONCLAD
FUMIGANT	GLOBULIN	HABANERA	HEDGEHOP	HOMEWARD	ILLUMINE	INFORMAL	IRONWARE
FUMIGATE	GLORIOUS	HABITANT	HEDGEROW	HOMEWORK	ILLUSION	INFORMED	IRONWEED
FUNCTION	GLOSSARY	HABITUAL	HEDONISM	HOMICIDE	ILLUSIVE	INFORMER	IRONWOOD
FUNERARY	GLOWWORM	HACIENDA	HEGEMONY	HONEYDEW	ILLUSORY	INFRADIG	IRONWORK
FUNEREAL	GLOXINIA	HACKWORD	HEIGHTEN	HONORARY	IMBECILE	INFRARED	IROQUOIS
FURBELOW	GLYCERIN	HAIRLINE	HEIRLOOM	HOODWINK	IMITABLE	INFRINGE	IRRIGATE
FURLOUGH	GLYCEROL	HALFBACK	HELICOID	HOOKWORM	IMMANENT	INGUINAL	IRRITATE
FURTHEST	GLYCOGEN	HALFTONE	HELIPORT	HOOLIGAN	IMMATURE	INHALANT	ISLANDER
FUSELAGE	GOALPOST	HALLMARK	HELLHOLE	HOOSEGOW	IMMINENT	INHERENT	ISOPRENE
FUTILITY	GOATHERD	HANDBALL	HELMSMAN	HORMONAL	IMMOBILE	INHUMANE	ISOSTASY
FUTURISM	GOATSKIN	HANDBILL	HELPMATE	HORNBOOK	IMMODEST	INIMICAL	ISOTHERM
FUTURITY	GODCHILD	HANDBOOK	HELPMEET	HORNPIPE	IMMOLATE	INIQUITY	ISOTONIC
GADABOUT	GOLDFISH	HANDCUFF	HEMATITE	HOROLOGY	IMMORTAL	INITIATE	ISSUANCE
GALLUSES	GONFALON	HANDICAP	HENCHMAN	HORRIBLE	IMMOTILE	INKSTAND	ISTHMIAN
GAMECOCK	GOODNESS	HANDMADE	HEPATICA	HORSEFLY	IMMUNIZE	INNOCENT	JACKBOOT
GAMESOME	GOODWIFE	HANDPICK	HERALDIC	HORSEMAN	IMPACTED	INNOVATE	JACQUARD
GAMESTER	GOODWILL	HANDRAIL	HERALDRY	HOSPITAL	IMPELLER	INNUENDO	JAILBIRD
GANGLAND	GOOFBALL	HANDSOME	HERCULES	HOSTELRY	IMPERIAL	INSCRIBE	JALOUSIE
GANGLING	GORGEOUS	HANDYMAN	HERDSMAN	HOTHOUSE	IMPETIGO	INSECURE	JAMBOREE
GANGLION	GOSSAMER	HANGNAIL	HEREDITY	HOUSEBOY	IMPLICIT	INSIGNIA	JAPANESE
GANGPLOW	GOURMAND	HANGOVER	HEREFORD	HOUSEFLY	IMPOLITE	INSOLENT	JAUNDICE
GANGRENE	GOVERNOR	HANUKKAH	HEREUNTO	HOUSETOP	IMPOSING	INSOMNIA	JEOPARDY
GANGSTER	GRACIOUS	HARANGUE	HEREUPON	HOWITZER	IMPOSTOR	INSOMUCH	JEREMIAD
GARDENIA	GRADIENT	HARDBACK	HEREWITH	HUARACHE	IMPOTENT	INSPIRIT	JETTISON
GARGOYLE	GRADUATE	HARDBALL	HERITAGE	HUCKSTER	IMPRISON	INSTANCE	JINGOISM

JONGLEUR	LANDFORM	LINCHPIN	MACKINAW	MARQUESS	MICROBUS	MODULATE	MUSHROOM
JOYSTICK	LANDLORD	LINESMAN	MACPAINT	MARQUISE	MIDDLING	MOISTURE	MUSICALE
JUBILANT	LANDMARK	LINGERIE	MADHOUSE	MARRIAGE	MIDNIGHT	MOLASSES	MUSICIAN
JUDGMENT	LANDMASS	LINGUIST	MADRIGAL	MARTINET	MIDPOINT	MOLECULE	MUSKETRY
JUDICIAL	LANDSMAN	LINIMENT	MAGAZINE	MARZIPAN	MIDSHIPS	MOLEHILL	MUSTACHE
JUNCTION	LANDWARD	LINOLEUM	MAGDALEN	MASSACRE	MIGRAINE	MOLESKIN	MUTATION
JUNCTURE	LANGUAGE	LIPSTICK	MAGICIAN	MASSEUSE	MILEPOST	MOMENTUM	MUTILATE
JURISTIC	LANGUISH	LISTLESS	MAGNESIA	MASSLESS	MILESIMO	MONARCHY	MYCOLOGY
JUVENILE	LAPBOARD	LITERARY	MAGNETIC	MASTERLY	MILITANT	MONASTIC	MYELITIS
KAMAAINA	LAPIDARY	LITERATE	MAGNOLIA	MASTHEAD	MILITARY	MONAURAL	MYRMIDON
KAMIKAZE	LARBOARD	LITERATI	MAHARAJA	MASTODON	MILITATE	MONETARY	MYSTICAL
KANGAROO	LARKSPUR	LITIGANT	MAHARANI	MATERIAL	MILKMAID	MONGOOSE	MYSTIQUE
KATAKANA	LASERJET	LITIGATE	MAHOGANY	MATERIEL	MILKWEED	MONITION	NAINSOOK
KEELBOAT	LATCHKEY	LITTORAL	MAINLAND	MATERNAL	MILLIARD	MONITORY	NAMELESS
KEELHAUL	LATITUDE	LIVELONG	MAINLINE	MATTRESS	MILLIBAR	MONOGAMY	NAMESAKE
KEEPSAKE	LAUDANUM	LIVERISH	MAINMAST	MATURATE	MILLIEME	MONOGRAM	NAPOLEON
KERCHIEF	LAUGHTER	LOANWORD	MAINSAIL	MATURITY	MILLINER	MONOLITH	NARCOSIS
KEROSINE	LAUNCHER	LOATHING	MAINSTAY	MAVERICK	MILLPOND	MONOPOLY	NARCOTIC
KEYBOARD	LAUREATE	LOBOTOMY	MAINTAIN	MAXIMIZE	MILLRACE	MONORAIL	NASALIZE
KEYPUNCH	LAVATORY	LOCALITY	MAJOLICA	MAYAPPLE	MINATORY	MONOTONE	NATALITY
KEYSTONE	LAVENDER	LOCALIZE	MAJORITY	MEALTIME	MINDLESS	MONOXIDE	NATIONAL
KEYWORDS	LAWGIVER	LOCATION	MALAMUTE	MEALYBUG	MINIBIKE	MONSIEUR	NATIVISM
KIBITZER	LAWMAKER	LOCKSTEP	MALAPERT	MEANTIME	MINIMIZE	MONUMENT	NATIVITY
KICKBACK	LAXATIVE	LOCOWEED	MALARKEY	MEATBALL	MINISTER	MOONBEAM	NAUSEATE
KICKSHAW	LAYERING	LOCUTION	MALAWIAN	MECHANIC	MINISTRY	MOORLAND	NAUTICAL
KIELBASA	LEAPFROG	LODESTAR	MALINGER	MEDALIST	MINORITY	MORALIST	NAUTILUS
KILLDEER	LEARNING	LODGMENT	MALTREAT	MEDICAID	MINSTREL	MORALITY	NAVIGATE
KILOBYTE	LEAVINGS	LOGOTYPE	MALTSTER	MEDICARE	MISAPPLY	MORALIZE	NEBULIZE
KILOGRAM	LECITHIN	LOLLIPOP	MANCIPLE	MEDICATE	MISBRAND	MOREOVER	NEBULOUS
KILOVOLT	LEFTOVER	LOLLYGAG	MANDAMUS	MEDICINE	MISCARRY	MORIBUND	NECKLACE
KILOWATT	LEGALISM	LONESOME	MANDARIN	MEDIEVAL	MISCHIEF	MOROCCAN	NECKLINE
KINDLING	LEGATION	LONGBOAT	MANDIBLE	MEDIOCRE	MISCIBLE	MORPHEME	NECROSIS
KINETICS	LEMONADE	LONGHAIR	MANDOLIN	MEDITATE	MISCOUNT	MORPHINE	NEEDLESS
KINGBOLT	LENGTHEN	LONGHAND	MANDRAKE	MEGABYTE	MISDOING	MORTGAGE	NEGATION
KNAPSACK	LENITIVE	LONGHORN	MANEUVER	MEGALITH	MISJUDGE	MORTUARY	NEGATIVE
KNEEHOLE	LETHARGY	LONGTIME	MANGROVE	MELANISM	MISLABEL	MOSQUITO	NEGLIGEE
KNICKERS	LEUKEMIA	LONGUEUR	MANIACAL	MELANOMA	MISMATCH	MOSSBACK	NEIGHBOR
KNITWEAR	LEVERAGE	LOOPHOLE	MANICURE	MELODEON	MISMATCH	MOTHBALL	NEMATODE
KNOCKOUT	LEVITATE	LOPSIDED	MANIFEST	MEMBRANE	MISNOMER	MOTIVATE	NEONATAL
KNOTHOLE	LIBATION	LORDSHIP	MANIFOLD	MEMORIAL	MISPLACE	MOTORCAR	NEOPHYTE
KOHLRABI	LIBERATE	LOVEBIRD	MANNERED	MEMORIZE	MISPRINT	MOTORIZE	NEOPLASM
KOLINSKY	LIBRETTO	LOVELORN	MANNERLY	MENHADEN	MISQUOTE	MOTORMAN	NEPENTHE
LABURNUM	LICENSEE	LOVESICK	MANTELET	MENISCUS	MISSHAPE	MOTOROLA	NEPOTISM
LACERATE	LICORICE	LOYALIST	MANTILLA	MEPHITIC	MISSPELL	MOUNTAIN	NESTLING
LACEWING	LIFEBOAT	LUKEWARM	MANTISSA	MERCHANT	MISSPEND	MOUNTING	NEURITIS
LACRIMAL	LIFELINE	LUMINARY	MANYFOLD	MERCURIC	MISSTATE	MOURNFUL	NEUROSIS
LACROSSE	LIFELONG	LUMINOUS	MARATHON	MERIDIAN	MISTAKEN	MOURNING	NEUROTIC
LADYBIRD	LIFETIME	LUNCHEON	MARBLING	MERINGUE	MISTREAT	MOVEMENT	NEUTRINO
LADYLIKE	LIFEWORK	LUSCIOUS	MARGRAVE	MESDAMES	MISTRESS	MUCILAGE	NEWCOMER
LADYLOVE	LIGAMENT	LUTETIUM	MARIACHI	MESHWORK	MISTRIAL	MUDGUARD	NEWFOUND
LADYSHIP	LIGATURE	LUTHERAN	MARIGOLD	MESQUITE	MISTRUST	MUENSTER	NEWLYWED
LAMASERY	LIGNEOUS	LYMPHOID	MARINATE	MESSMATE	MISUSAGE	MULBERRY	NEWSCAST
LAMBASTE	LIKENESS	MACARONI	MARITIME	METAFILE	MITIGATE	MULETEER	NEWSREEL
LAMBSKIN	LIKEWISE	MACAROON	MARJORAM	METAPHOR	MNEMONIC	MULTIPLE	NICKNAME
LAMPBACK	LIMEKILN	MACERATE	MARKDOWN	METEORIC	MOBILIZE	MULTIPLY	NICOTINE
LANDFALL	LIMERICK	MACHISMO	MARKSMAN	METHANOL	MOCCASIN	MUNITION	NIGERIAN
LANDFILL	LIMONITE	MACKEREL	MARMOSET	METRICAL	MODERATE	MUSCATEL	NIGEROIS

NIGGLING	OFFSTAGE	OVENBIRD	PARABOLA	PENITENT	PLANKING	POSTLUDE	PROSPECT
NIHILISM	OHMMETER	OVERALLS	PARADIGM	PENKNIFE	PLANKTON	POSTMARK	PROSTATE
NINEPINS	OILCLOTH	OVERCAST	PARADISE	PENLIGHT	PLANTAIN	POSTPAID	PROTOCOL
NINETEEN	OINTMENT	OVERCOAT	PARAFFIN	PENOLOGY	PLATFORM	POSTPONE	PROTRACT
NITROGEN	OLEANDER	OVERCOME	PARAKEET	PENSTOCK	PLATINUM	POTATION	PROTRUDE
NOBELIST	ONCOMING	OVERDRAW	PARALLAX	PENTAGON	PLATYPUS	POTBELLY	PROVIDED
NOBELIUM	ONLOOKER	OVERFLOW	PARALLEL	PENUMBRA	PLAYBACK	POTSHERD	PROVINCE
NOBILITY	ONONDAGA	OVERGROW	PARALYZE	PERCEIVE	PLAYBILL	POULTICE	PRURIENT
NOBLEMAN	OPENWORK	OVERHAND	PARAMOUR	PERFECTO	PLAYBOOK	POUNDAGE	PSALMODY
NOCTURNE	OPERABLE	OVERHANG	PARANOIA	PERFORCE	PLAYGOER	PRACTICE	PTOMAINE
NOMINATE	OPERANDS	OVERHAUL	PARASITE	PERILUNE	PLAYMATE	PRATFALL	PUBLICAN
NONDAIRY	OPERETTA	OVERHEAD	PARDONER	PERIODIC	PLAYSUIT	PRATIQUE	PUDDLING
NONESUCH	OPPONENT	OVERHEAR	PARFOCAL	PERMEATE	PLEASANT	PREAMBLE	PUDENDUM
NONEVENT	OPPOSITE	OVERKILL	PARIETAL	PEROXIDE	PLEASING	PRECINCT	PUFFBALL
NONMETAL	OPTICIAN	OVERLAID	PARLANCE	PERSONAL	PLEASURE	PRECIOUS	PUGILISM
NONRIGID	OPTIMISM	OVERLAND	PARMESAN	PERSPIRE	PLEBEIAN	PRECLUDE	PULLBACK
NONSENSE	OPUSCULE	OVERLEAP	PAROXYSM	PERSUADE	PLECTRUM	PREEXIST	PULLOVER
NONSTICK	ORANGERY	OVERLOOK	PARTERRE	PERVERSE	PLETHORA	PREGNANT	PULMOTOR
NONUNION	ORATORIO	OVERLORD	PARTIBLE	PETITION	PLEURISY	PREJUDGE	PULPWOOD
NOONTIDE	ORDINARY	OVERMUCH	PARTICLE	PETTIFOG	PLUMBING	PREMIERE	PUNCHEON
NOONTIME	ORDINATE	OVERPASS	PARTISAN	PETULANT	POCKMARK	PREMOLAR	PUNCTUAL
NORSEMAN	ORDNANCE	OVERPLAY	PASSABLE	PHANTASM	PODIATRY	PRENATAL	PUNCTURE
NOTARIAL	ORGANISM	OVERRIDE	PASSBOOK	PHANTASY	POIGNANT	PREPRESS	PUNITIVE
NOTARIZE	ORGANIST	OVERRULE	PASSOVER	PHARISEE	POKEWEED	PRESENCE	PURBLIND
NOTATION	ORGANIZE	OVERSEAS	PASSPORT	PHARMACY	POLARITY	PRESERVE	PURCHASE
NOTEBOOK	ORGULOUS	OVERSHOE	PASSWORD	PHASEOUT	POLARIZE	PRESIDIO	PUREBRED
NOTIONAL	ORIENTAL	OVERSIZE	PASTICHE	PHEASANT	POLESTAR	PRESSING	PURSLANE
NOVELIZE	ORIGINAL	OVERSTAY	PASTILLE	PHENOLIC	POLITICK	PRESSMAN	PURULENT
NOVEMBER	ORNAMENT	OVERSTEP	PASTORAL	PHOSPHOR	POLITICO	PRESSURE	PUSHCART
NOWADAYS	ORTHODOX	OVERTAKE	PASTRAMI	PHRASING	POLITICS	PRESTIGE	PUSHDOWN
NUCLEATE	ORTHOEPY	OVERTIME	PATERNAL	PHYSICAL	POLLIWOG	PRETENSE	PUSHOVER
NUGATORY	OSCULATE	OVERTONE	PATHETIC	PHYSIQUE	POLLSTER	PRETERIT	PUSSYCAT
NUISANCE	OUTBOARD	OVERTURE	PATHOGEN	PICAYUNE	POLONIUM	PRETTIFY	PUTATIVE
NUMERATE	OUTBOUND	OVERTURN	PATIENCE	PICKEREL	POLTROON	PREVIOUS	PYORRHEA
NUMEROUS	OUTBREAK	OVERVIEW	PAVEMENT	PICKINGS	POLYGAMY	PRIMEVAL	QUADRANT
NUMSKULL	OUTBURST	PACIFIER	PAVILION	PICKLOCK	POLYGLOT	PRIMROSE	QUADROON
NURSLING	OUTCLASS	PACIFISM	PAWNSHOP	PIDDLING	POLYMATH	PRINCESS	QUAGMIRE
NUTHATCH	OUTDATED	PAGINATE	PAYCHECK	PIEPLANT	PONYTAIL	PRINTING	QUALMISH
NUTRIENT	OUTDOORS	PAINTING	PECTORAL	PILASTER	POPINJAY	PRINTOUT	QUANDARY
NUTSHELL	OUTFIELD	PALATINE	PECULATE	PILCHARD	POPULACE	PRISONER	QUANTITY
OBDURATE	OUTFIGHT	PALEFACE	PECULIAR	PILOTAGE	POPULATE	PRISTINE	QUANTIZE
OBEDIENT	OUTFLANK	PALINODE	PEDAGOGY	PIMIENTO	POPULIST	PROBABLE	QUATRAIN
OBITUARY	OUTGOING	PALISADE	PEDERAST	PINAFORE	POPULOUS	PROCAINE	QUESTION
OBLATION	OUTGUESS	PALLIATE	PEDESTAL	PINNACLE	PORPHYRY	PROCEEDS	QUIETUDE
OBLIGATE	OUTHOUSE	PALMETTO	PEDICURE	PINOCHLE	PORPOISE	PROCLAIM	QUISLING
OBLIVION	OUTLYING	PALOMINO	PEDIGREE	PINPOINT	PORRIDGE	PRODIGAL	QUIXOTIC
OBSIDIAN	OUTMODED	PALPABLE	PEDIMENT	PINPRICK	PORTABLE	PROFOUND	QUOTABLE
OBSOLETE	OUTPOINT	PAMPHLET	PEDUNCLE	PINWHEEL	PORTHOLE	PROGRESS	QUOTIENT
OBSTACLE	OUTREACH	PANATELA	PEEPHOLE	PIPELINE	PORTIERE	PROHIBIT	RADIATOR
OBSTRUCT	OUTRIDER	PANCREAS	PEERLESS	PITCHMAN	PORTRAIT	PROLIFIC	RADIOMAN
OCCASION	OUTRIGHT	PANDEMIC	PEIGNOIR	PITIABLE	POSITION	PROLOGUE	RAILLERY
OCCUPANT	OUTSHINE	PANDOWDY	PELLAGRA	PITILESS	POSITIVE	PROMOTER	RAILROAD
ODOMETER	OUTSIDER	PANELING	PELLUCID	PITTANCE	POSITRON	PROPERTY	RAINCOAT
OFFICIAL	OUTSMART	PANELIST	PEMMICAN	PIXELATE	POSSIBLE	PROPHECY	RAINDROP
OFFPRINT	OUTSPEND	PANORAMA	PENALIZE	PIZZERIA	POSTCARD	PROPHESY	RAINFALL
OFFSHOOT	OUTSTRIP	PANTHEON	PENCHANT	PLACENTA	POSTDATE	PROPOUND	RATIONAL
OFFSHORE	OUTWEIGH	PANTSUIT	PENDULUM	PLANGENT	POSTHOLE	PROROGUE	RATTLING

RAVENING	RESIDENT	ROSEMARY	SCHEDULE	SERGEANT	SINGULAR	SPACEMAN	STOCKING
RAVENOUS	RESIDUAL	ROSEWOOD	SCHMALTZ	SEROLOGY	SINISTER	SPACIOUS	STOPPAGE
RAWBONED	RESIDUUM	ROUGHAGE	SCHOONER	SERVITOR	SINKHOLE	SPANIARD	STOTINKA
REACTANT	RESIGNED	ROULETTE	SCIATICA	SETSCREW	SITUATED	SPANKING	STOWAWAY
REACTION	RESISTOR	ROUTEMAN	SCILICET	SEWERAGE	SIXPENCE	SPECIFIC	STRADDLE
REACTIVE	RESOLUTE	ROYALIST	SCIMITAR	SHAMBLES	SKELETON	SPECIMEN	STRAGGLE
REARWARD	RESONANT	RUBICUND	SCISSORS	SHAMROCK	SKILLFUL	SPECIOUS	STRAIGHT
REASSURE	RESONATE	RUBIDIUM	SCOFFLAW	SHANGHAI	SKIMMING	SPECTRAL	STRAITEN
REBUTTAL	RESORTER	RUDIMENT	SCORPION	SHANTUNG	SKIRMISH	SPECTRUM	STRANGER
RECEIVER	RESOURCE	RUMANIAN	SCOTTISH	SHEEPISH	SKITTISH	SPEEDWAY	STRANGLE
RECEPTOR	RESPONSE	RUMBLING	SCRABBLE	SHEETING	SKULLCAP	SPHAGNUM	STRATEGY
RECKLESS	RESTLESS	RUMINANT	SCRAGGLY	SHELVING	SKYLIGHT	SPHEROID	STRATIFY
RECORDER	RESTRAIN	RUMINATE	SCRAMBLE	SHEPHERD	SLATTERN	SPILLWAY	STREAMER
RECOURSE	RESTRICT	RUNABOUT	SCRIBBLE	SHILINGI	SLIPKNOT	SPINSTER	STRENGTH
RECREANT	RETAINER	RUNAGATE	SCROFULA	SHILLING	SLIPPERY	SPIRITED	STRICKEN
RECREATE	RETARDED	RUTABAGA	SCROUNGE	SHINBONE	SLIPSHOD	SPITBALL	STRIDENT
REDOLENT	RETICENT	RUTHLESS	SCRUTINY	SHINGLES	SLOVENLY	SPITTOON	STRIKING
REFERENT	RETIRING	SABOTAGE	SCULLERY	SHIPMATE	SLUGGARD	SPLATTER	STRINGED
REFERRAL	RETRENCH	SABOTEUR	SCULLION	SHIPMENT	SLUGGISH	SPLENDID	STRINGER
REFINERY	RETRIEVE	SACRISTY	SCULPTOR	SHIPPING	SLUMLORD	SPLENDOR	STRUGGLE
REFOREST	RETROFIT	SADDUCEE	SEABOARD	SHIPWORM	SMALLPOX	SPLINTER	STRUMPET
REFORMER	RETURNEE	SAGAMORE	SEACOAST	SHIPYARD	SNAPSHOT	SPLUTTER	STUBBORN
REGICIDE	REVANCHE	SAILBOAT	SEAFARER	SHIRRING	SNOBBERY	SPOOLING	STUDBOOK
REGIMENT	REVEILLE	SAILFISH	SEAGOING	SHIRTING	SNOWBALL	SPORADIC	STUDDING
REGIONAL	REVENUER	SALESMAN	SEALSKIN	SHOCKING	SNOWBANK	SPRINKLE	STUDIOUS
REGISTER	REVEREND	SALIVATE	SEAMOUNT	SHOELACE	SNOWDROP	SPROCKET	STUFFING
REGISTRY	REVERENT	SALUTARY	SEAPLANE	SHOPLIFT	SNOWFALL	SPURIOUS	STULTIFY
REGOLITH	REVERSAL	SAMARIUM	SEASCAPE	SHOPWORN	SNOWPLOW	SPYGLASS	STUNNING
REGULATE	REVIEWER	SANCTIFY	SEASHORE	SHORTAGE	SNOWSHOE	SQUABBLE	STURGEON
REHEARSE	REVIVIFY	SANCTION	SEAWATER	SHORTCUT	SOBRIETY	SQUADRON	SUBMERGE
REINDEER	REVOLVER	SANCTITY	SECURITY	SHOSHONE	SOCIABLE	SQUANDER	SUBMERSE
RELATION	RHAPSODY	SANDBANK	SEDATIVE	SHOULDER	SOFTBALL	SQUEEGEE	SUBPOENA
RELATIVE	RHEOLOGY	SANDWICH	SEDIMENT	SHOWCASE	SOFTWARE	SQUIRREL	SUBSONIC
RELAXANT	RHEOSTAT	SANGUINE	SEDITION	SHOWDOWN	SOFTWOOD	STACCATO	SUBTITLE
RELEGATE	RHETORIC	SANITARY	SEDULOUS	SHRAPNEL	SOLARIUM	STAGNANT	SUBTRACT
RELEVANT	RHOMBOID	SANITIZE	SEEDLING	SHREWISH	SOLDIERY	STAGNATE	SUBURBIA
RELIABLE	RHYOLITE	SANSKRIT	SEEDTIME	SHUTDOWN	SOLECISM	STAIRWAY	SUCCINCT
RELIANCE	RIBOSOME	SAPPHIRE	SEIGNEUR	SIBILANT	SOLENOID	STAKEOUT	SUCHLIKE
RELIGION	RICOCHET	SARDONIC	SELECTEE	SICKNESS	SOLIDIFY	STALLION	SUCKLING
RELOCATE	RIDICULE	SATURATE	SELENITE	SIDEKICK	SOLITARY	STALWART	SUFFRAGE
REMEDIAL	RIFFRAFF	SATURDAY	SELENIUM	SIDELONG	SOLITUDE	STAMPEDE	SUITABLE
REMEMBER	RIGHTFUL	SAUCEPAN	SELFLESS	SIDEREAL	SOLSTICE	STANDARD	SUITCASE
REMITTAL	RINGWORM	SAUTERNE	SELFSAME	SIDERITE	SOLUTION	STANDING	SUKIYAKI
RENEGADE	RIPARIAN	SAWHORSE	SEMANTIC	SIDESHOW	SOLVENCY	STANDOFF	SULFURIC
RENOUNCE	RIVERBED	SCABBARD	SEMESTER	SIDESTEP	SOMBRERO	STANDOUT	SUNDRIES
RENOVATE	ROADSIDE	SCABROUS	SEMINARY	SIDEWALK	SOMEBODY	STARFISH	SUNLIGHT
REPARTEE	ROADSTER	SCAFFOLD	SEMINOLE	SIDEWALL	SOMERSET	STARLING	SUNSHADE
REPEATED	ROADWORK	SCALABLE	SEMISOFT	SIDEWAYS	SOMETIME	STATUARY	SUNSHINE
REPORTER	ROCKETRY	SCALAWAG	SENSIBLE	SIGNPOST	SOMEWHAT	STEALTHY	SUPEREGO
REPRIEVE	ROCKFALL	SCALEPAN	SENSUOUS	SILENCER	SONATINA	STEERAGE	SUPERIOR
REPRISAL	ROLLBACK	SCALLION	SENTENCE	SILICATE	SONGBIRD	STERLING	SUPERJET
REPROACH	ROMANIAN	SCANDIUM	SENTIENT	SILICIFY	SONGSTER	STICKLER	SUPERNAL
REPUBLIC	ROMANTIC	SCAPULAR	SENTINEL	SILICONE	SONOROUS	STILETTO	SUPPLANT
RESCRIPT	ROOFTREE	SCARCELY	SEPARATE	SIMONIZE	SORORITY	STIMULUS	SUPPOSED
RESEARCH	ROOMETTE	SCATHING	SEQUENCE	SIMPLIFY	SORPTION	STINKBUG	SUPPRESS
RESEMBLE	ROOMMATE	SCAVENGE	SERAGLIO	SIMULATE	SOUTHPAW	STIRRING	SURCEASE
RESERVED	ROSEBUSH	SCENARIO	SERENADE	SINECURE	SOUVENIR	STOCKADE	SUREFIRE

SURGICAL	TELLTALE	TOGETHER	TRIUMVIR	UNDERBID	UPGROWTH	VERTICAL	WASHROOM
SURMOUNT	TEMERITY	TOILETRY	TROMBONE	UNDERCUT	UPHEAVAL	VESICANT	WATCHDOG
SURPLICE	TEMPLATE	TOILETTE	TROUSERS	UNDERDOG	UPPERCUT	VESTMENT	WATCHFUL
SURPRISE	TEMPORAL	TOILWORN	TRUCKAGE	UNDERFUR	UPRISING	VEXATION	WATCHMAN
SURROUND	TENANTRY	TOKENISM	TRUETYPE	UNDERLIE	UPSTAIRS	VIATICUM	WATERLOO
SUSPENSE	TENDENCY	TOLERATE	TRUMPERY	UNDERLIP	UPSTREAM	VIBURNUM	WATERWAY
SUZERAIN	TENEMENT	TOLLBOTH	TRUNCATE	UNDERPAY	UPSTROKE	VICARAGE	WAYFARER
SWASTIKA	TENPENNY	TOLLGATE	TRUSTFUL	UNDERSEA	UPTHRUST	VICINAGE	WEAKFISH
SWAYBACK	TENTACLE	TOMAHAWK	TRUTHFUL	UNDERTOW	URBANITE	VICINITY	WEAKLING
SWEEPING	TEOSINTE	TOMORROW	TUBERCLE	UNDULANT	URBANIZE	VICTORIA	WEAKNESS
SWELLING	TERMINAL	TONALITY	TUBEROSE	UNDULATE	USUFRUCT	VIETCONG	WEAPONRY
SWIMMING	TERMINUS	TOPOLOGY	TUBEROUS	UNEARNED	USURIOUS	VIGILANT	WELDMENT
SYBARITE	TERRAPIN	TOPSIDES	TUNELESS	UNENDING	UUDECODE	VIGNETTE	WELLBORN
SYCAMORE	TERRIBLE	TOREADOR	TUNGSTEN	UNERRING	UUENCODE	VIGOROUS	WELLHEAD
SYLLABLE	TERRIFIC	TORTILLA	TUNISIAN	UNFASTEN	UXORIOUS	VILLAGER	WEREWOLF
SYLLABUS	TERTIARY	TORTOISE	TURBOFAN	UNFETTER	VACATION	VILLAINY	WHARFAGE
SYMBOLIC	TESTATOR	TORTUOUS	TURBOJET	UNFILIAL	VACCINIA	VINCIBLE	WHATEVER
SYMMETRY	TESTICLE	TOTALITY	TURMERIC	UNFORMED	VAGABOND	VINEGARY	WHENEVER
SYMPATHY	TEUTONIC	TOUCHING	TURNCOAT	UNFREEZE	VAGRANCY	VINEYARD	WHEREVER
SYMPHONY	TEXTBOOK	TOWELING	TURNOVER	UNGAINLY	VALIDATE	VIOLABLE	WHIPCORD
SYNDROME	THALAMUS	TOWERING	TURNPIKE	UNGULATE	VALUABLE	VIOLENCE	WHIPLASH
SYNOPSIS	THALLIUM	TOWNSHIP	TURNSPIT	UNIAXIAL	VALVULAR	VIRGINAL	WHITECAP
SYNOPTIC	THANKFUL	TOWNSMAN	TUTELAGE	UNICYCLE	VANADIUM	VIROLOGY	WHITEFLY
SYPHILIS	THEOLOGY	TRACKAGE	TUTELARY	UNIONISM	VANGUARD	VIRTUOSO	WHODUNIT
SYSADMIN	THEORIZE	TRACTATE	TUTORIAL	UNIONIZE	VANQUISH	VIRTUOUS	WHOMEVER
SYSTEMIC	THEREFOR	TRACTION	TWEEZERS	UNIVALVE	VAPORING	VIRULENT	WHOPPING
TABULATE	THESPIAN	TRAINING	TWILIGHT	UNIVERSE	VAPORISH	VISCERAL	WILDFIRE
TACITURN	THIAMINE	TRAINMAN	TWOPENCE	UNKINDLY	VAPORIZE	VISCOUNT	WILDFOWL
TAFFRAIL	THICKSET	TRANQUIL	TWOPENNY	UNLAWFUL	VAPOROUS	VISICALC	WILDLIFE
TAHITIAN	THIEVERY	TRANSACT	TYMPANUM	UNLEADED	VARIABLE	VISITANT	WILDWOOD
TAILCOAT	THIRTEEN	TRANSEPT	TYPECAST	UNLIKELY	VARIANCE	VITALITY	WILLIWAW
TAILGATE	THOROUGH	TRANSFER	TYPEFACE	UNLIMBER	VARICOSE	VITALIZE	WINDBURN
TAILSPIN	THOUSAND	TRANSFIX	ULCERATE	UNLOOSEN	VARIETAL	VITREOUS	WINDFALL
TALESMAN	THRASHER	TRANSMIT	ULTERIOR	UNLOVELY	VARIORUM	VIVACITY	WINDLASS
TALISMAN	THREATEN	TRAPDOOR	ULTIMATE	UNMUZZLE	VARISTOR	VIVARIUM	WINDMILL
TAMARACK	THRENODY	TRAPPING	UMBRELLA	UNPERSON	VASCULAR	VOCALIST	WINDPIPE
TAMARIND	THROMBUS	TRAPROCK	UNAWARES	UNRIDDLE	VAULTING	VOCALIZE	WINDWARD
TANGIBLE	THROTTLE	TRAVERSE	UNBEATEN	UNSADDLE	VEGANISM	VOCATION	WINESHOP
TANTALUM	THRUSTER	TRAVESTY	UNBELIEF	UNSAVORY	VEGETATE	VOCATIVE	WINGDING
TAPESTRY	THURSDAY	TREASURE	UNBIASED	UNSEEMLY	VEHEMENT	VOLATILE	WINGSPAN
TAPEWORM	TICKLISH	TREASURY	UNBIDDEN	UNSETTLE	VELLEITY	VOLCANIC	WIREDRAW
TARRAGON	TIDELAND	TREATISE	UNBODIED	UNSHAPED	VELOCITY	VOLITION	WIREHAIR
TAXONOMY	TIGHTWAD	TRENCHER	UNBOLTED	UNSOUGHT	VENATION	VOLPLANE	WIRELESS
TAXPAYER	TIMBERED	TRESPASS	UNBROKEN	UNSPRUNG	VENDETTA	VOYAGEUR	WIREWORM
TEACHING	TIMELESS	TRIANGLE	UNBUCKLE	UNSTABLE	VENERATE	WAINSCOT	WISEACRE
TEAMSTER	TIMEWORN	TRIBUNAL	UNBURDEN	UNSTEADY	VENEREAL	WAITRESS	WISHBONE
TEAMWORK	TIMOROUS	TRICHINA	UNBUTTON	UNSTRUNG	VENGEFUL	WALKAWAY	WISTARIA
TEASPOON	TINCTURE	TRICKERY	UNCHASTE	UNTANGLE	VENOMOUS	WALKOVER	WISTERIA
TEETHING	TINPLATE	TRICOLOR	UNCHURCH	UNTAUGHT	VENUSIAN	WARDROBE	WITCHERY
TEETOTAL	TINSMITH	TRICYCLE	UNCLENCH	UNTIMELY	VERACITY	WARDROOM	WITCHING
TELECAST	TIRELESS	TRIFLING	UNCLOTHE	UNTOWARD	VERBATIM	WARDSHIP	WITHDRAW
TELEFILM	TIRESOME	TRILLION	UNCOMMON	UNVOICED	VERBIAGE	WAREROOM	WITHHOLD
TELEGRAM	TITANIUM	TRILLIUM	UNCOUPLE	UNWIELDY	VERBOTEN	WARFARIN	WIZARDRY
TELEPLAY	TITILATE	TRIMARAN	UNCTUOUS	UNWONTED	VERMOUTH	WARPLANE	WOMANISH
TELETHON	TITIVATE	TRIMETER	UNDERACT	UNWORTHY	VERONICA	WARRANTY	WONDROUS
TELEVIEW	TITMOUSE	TRIMMING	UNDERAGE	UNZIPPED	VERSICLE	WASHABLE	WOODBINE
TELEVISE	TOBOGGAN	TRIPTYCH	UNDERARM	UPCOMING	VERTEBRA	WASHBOWL	WOODCOCK

WOODLAND	BACKDROP	CADUCEUS	CASTRATE	FAROUCHE	HARDTACK	LAUREATE	MANYFOLD
WOODNOTE	BACKFIRE	CAFFEINE	CASUALTY	FARTHEST	HARDWARE	LAVATORY	MARATHON
WOODPILE	BACKHAND	CAGELING	CATACOMB	FARTHING	HARDWOOD	LAVENDER	MARBLING
WOODRUFF	BACKLASH	CAKEWALK	CATALYZE	FASCICLE	HAREBELL	LAWGIVER	MARGRAVE
WOODSHED	BACKPACK	CALABASH	CATAPULT	FASCISTA	HARMONIC	LAWMAKER	MARIACHI
WOODSMAN	BACKREST	CALADIUM	CATARACT	FASTBACK	HARRIDAN	LAXATIVE	MARIGOLD
WOODWIND	BACKSIDE	CALAMINE	CATCHALL	FASTNESS	HATCHING	LAYERING	MARINATE
WOODWORK	BACKSLAP	CALAMITY	CATCHING	FATALISM	HATCHWAY	MACARONI	MARITIME
WOOLSACK	BACKSPIN	CALCULUS	CATEGORY	FATALITY	HAUTBOIS	MACAROON	MARJORAM
WORDBOOK	BACKSTOP	CALENDAR	CATHETER	FAUBOURG	HAWAIIAN	MACERATE	MARKDOWN
WORDPLAY	BACKWARD	CALENDER	CATHOLIC	FAVORITE	HAWKWEED	MACHISMO	MARKSMAN
WORDSTAR	BACKWASH	CALFSKIN	CAUDILLO	GADABOUT	HAWTHORN	MACKEREL	MARMOSET
WORKABLE	BADINAGE	CALLBACK	CAULDRON	GALLUSES	HAYSTACK	MACKINAW	MARQUESS
WORKADAY	BAEDEKER	CALLIOPE	CAUSERIE	GAMECOCK	JACKBOOT	MACPAINT	MARQUISE
WORKBOOK	BAGUETTE	CAMELLIA	CAUSEWAY	GAMESOME	JACQUARD	MADHOUSE	MARRIAGE
WORKROOM	BAILABLE	CAMISOLE	CAUTIOUS	GAMESTER	JAILBIRD	MADRIGAL	MARTINET
WORKSHOP	BAILSMAN	CAMOMILE	CAVALIER	GANGLAND	JALOUSIE	MAGAZINE	MARZIPAN
WORMHOLE	BAKESHOP	CAMPAIGN	DAFFODIL	GANGLING	JAMBOREE	MAGDALEN	MASSACRE
WORMWOOD	BALLROOM	CAMPOREE	DAIQUIRI	GANGLION	JAPANESE	MAGICIAN	MASSEUSE
WRAPPING	BALLYHOO	CAMSHAFT	DAIRYING	GANGPLOW	JAUNDICE	MAGNESIA	MASSLESS
WRATHFUL	BALUSTER	CANADIAN	DAIRYMAN	GANGRENE	KAMAAINA	MAGNETIC	MASTERLY
WRECKAGE	BANDANNA	CANAILLE	DAMNABLE	GANGSTER	KAMIKAZE	MAGNOLIA	MASTHEAD
WRETCHED	BANISTER	CANALIZE	DANDRUFF	GARDENIA	KANGAROO	MAHARAJA	MASTODON
WRIGGLER	BANKBOOK	CANISTER	DANSEUSE	GARGOYLE	KATAKANA	MAHARANI	MATERIAL
WRISTLET	BANKROLL	CANNABIS	DARKLING	GARRISON	LABURNUM	MAHOGANY	MATERIEL
WRONGFUL	BANKRUPT	CANNIBAL	DARKROOM	GASLIGHT	LACERATE	MAINLAND	MATERNAL
XENOLITH	BANTLING	CANONIZE	DARKSOME	GASOLINE	LACEWING	MAINLINE	MATTRESS
YACHTING	BARBARIC	CANTICLE	DATABASE	GASWORKS	LACRIMAL	MAINMAST	MATURATE
YEARBOOK	BARBECUE	CAPACITY	DATELESS	GATEPOST	LACROSSE	MAINSAIL	MATURITY
YEARLING	BARBERRY	CAPESKIN	DATELINE	GAUNTLET	LADYBIRD	MAINSTAY	MAVERICK
YEARLONG	BARBICAN	CAPRIOLE	DAUGHTER	HABANERA	LADYLIKE	MAINTAIN	MAXIMIZE
YEARNING	BARBITAL	CAPSICUM	DAYBREAK	HABITANT	LADYLOVE	MAJOLICA	MAYAPPLE
YEOMANRY	BAREBACK	CAPSULAR	DAYDREAM	HABITUAL	LADYSHIP	MAJORITY	NAINSOOK
YIELDING	BAREFOOT	CAPTIOUS	DAYLIGHT	HACIENDA	LAMASERY	MALAMUTE	NAMELESS
YOUNGISH	BARITONE	CAPUCHIN	EARNINGS	HACKWORD	LAMBASTE	MALAPERT	NAMESAKE
YOURSELF	BARNACLE	CARACOLE	EARPHONE	HAIRLINE	LAMBSKIN	MALARKEY	NAPOLEON
YOUTHFUL	BARNYARD	CARAPACE	FABULOUS	HALFBACK	LAMPBACK	MALAWIAN	NARCOSIS
YUGOSLAV	BARONAGE	CARDAMOM	FACEDOWN	HALFTONE	LANDFALL	MALINGER	NARCOTIC
YULETIDE	BARONESS	CARDIGAN	FACILITY	HALLMARK	LANDFILL	MALTREAT	NASALIZE
ZEPPELIN	BAROUCHE	CARDINAL	FACTIOUS	HANDBALL	LANDFORM	MALTSTER	NATALITY
ZOOPHYTE	BARRACKS	CAREFREE	FACTOTUM	HANDBILL	LANDLORD	MANCIPLE	NATIONAL
ZOOSPORE	BARRATRY	CARELESS	FADELESS	HANDBOOK	LANDMARK	MANDAMUS	NATIVISM
ZUCCHINI	BARRETTE	CAREWORN	FAGOTING	HANDCUFF	LANDMASS	MANDARIN	NATIVITY
ZWIEBACK	BASEBALL	CARILLON	FALCHION	HANDICAP	LANDSMAN	MANDIBLE	NAUSEATE
	BASEBORN	CARNAUBA	FALLIBLE	HANDMADE	LANDWARD	MANDOLIN	NAUTICAL
	BASELESS	CARNIVAL	FALSETTO	HANDPICK	LANGUAGE	MANDRAKE	NAUTILUS
	BASELINE	CAROTENE	FALTBOAT	HANDRAIL	LANGUISH	MANEUVER	NAVIGATE
	BASEMENT	CAROUSAL	FAMILIAL	HANDSOME	LAPBOARD	MANGROVE	PACIFIER
	BASILICA	CAROUSEL	FAMILIAR	HANDYMAN	LAPIDARY	MANIACAL	PACIFISM
2ND LETTER	BASILISK	CARRIAGE	FANCIFUL	HANGNAIL	LARBOARD	MANICURE	PAGINATE
AARDVARK	BASSINET	CARRYALL	FANDANGO	HANGOVER	LARKSPUR	MANIFEST	PAINTING
BABUSHKA	BASSWOOD	CARYATID	FANLIGHT	HANUKKAH	LASERJET	MANIFOLD	PALATINE
BACCARAT	BATHROBE	CASEMENT	FANTASIA	HARANGUE	LATCHKEY	MANNERED	PALEFACE
BACHELOR	BATHROOM	CASEWORK	FAREWELL	HARDBACK	LATITUDE	MANNERLY	PALINODE
BACILLUS	BAYBERRY	CASHMERE	FARMHAND	HARDBALL	LAUDANUM	MANTELET	PALISADE
BACKACHE	CABOCHON	CASSETTE	FARMLAND	HARDHACK	LAUGHTER	MANTILLA	PALLIATE
BACKBITE	CABSTAND	CASTAWAY	FARMYARD	HARDSHIP	LAUNCHER	MANTISSA	PALMETTO
BACKBONE							

PALOMINO	RATIONAL	VANADIUM	OBDURATE	SCISSORS	BEHAVIOR	DECREPIT	FELDSPAR
PALPABLE	RATTLING	VANGUARD	OBEDIENT	SCOFFLAW	BEHEMOTH	DEDICATE	FELICITY
PAMPHLET	RAVENING	VANQUISH	OBITUARY	SCORPION	BEHOLDEN	DEERSKIN	FELLATIO
PANATELA	RAVENOUS	VAPORING	OBLATION	SCOTTISH	BELITTLE	DEFECATE	FEMININE
PANCREAS	RAWBONED	VAPORISH	OBLIGATE	SCRABBLE	BENEDICT	DEFIANCE	FEMINISM
PANDEMIC	SABOTAGE	VAPORIZE	OBLIVION	SCRAGGLY	BENEFICE	DEFINITE	FEROCITY
PANDOWDY	SABOTEUR	VAPOROUS	OBSIDIAN	SCRAMBLE	BENTWOOD	DEFLOWER	FERVENCY
PANELING	SACRISTY	VARIABLE	OBSOLETE	SCRIBBLE	BENZOATE	DEFOREST	FESTIVAL
PANELIST	SADDUCEE	VARIANCE	OBSTACLE	SCROFULA	BEQUEATH	DEIONIZE	FETCHING
PANORAMA	SAGAMORE	VARICOSE	OBSTRUCT	SCROUNGE	BERCEUSE	DEJECTED	GEMINATE
PANTHEON	SAILBOAT	VARIETAL	ACADEMIC	SCRUTINY	BEREAVED	DEKAGRAM	GEMOLOGY
PANTSUIT	SAILFISH	VARIORUM	ACANTHUS	SCULLERY	BERIBERI	DELAWARE	GEMSTONE
PARABOLA	SALESMAN	VARISTOR	ACCIDENT	SCULLION	BERMUDAS	DELEGATE	GENDARME
PARADIGM	SALIVATE	VASCULAR	ACCOLADE	SCULPTOR	BESMIRCH	DELICACY	GENERATE
PARADISE	SALUTARY	VAULTING	ACCOUTRE	ADDENDUM	BESTIARY	DELICATE	GENEROUS
PARAFFIN	SAMARIUM	WAINSCOT	ACCREDIT	ADDITION	BESTRIDE	DELIRIUM	GENETICS
PARAKEET	SANCTIFY	WAITRESS	ACCURATE	ADDITIVE	BETATRON	DELIVERY	GENITALS
PARALLAX	SANCTION	WALKAWAY	ACCURSED	ADEQUATE	BEVERAGE	DELUSION	GENITIVE
PARALLEL	SANCTITY	WALKOVER	ACCUSTOM	ADHESION	BEWILDER	DEMARCHE	GENOCIDE
PARALYZE	SANDBANK	WARDROBE	ACERBATE	ADHESIVE	CELERITY	DEMEANOR	GEODESIC
PARAMOUR	SANDWICH	WARDROOM	ACERBITY	ADJACENT	CELIBACY	DEMENTED	GEOMETRY
PARANOIA	SANGUINE	WARDSHIP	ACIDHEAD	ADJUTANT	CELIBATE	DEMENTIA	GERANIUM
PARASITE	SANITARY	WAREROOM	ACIDOSIS	ADJUVANT	CELLULAR	DEMIBOLD	GERMINAL
PARDONER	SANITIZE	WARFARIN	ACOUSTIC	ADMONISH	CEMENTUM	DEMIJOHN	HEADACHE
PARFOCAL	SANSKRIT	WARPLANE	ACQUAINT	ADOPTIVE	CEMETERY	DEMOCRAT	HEADBAND
PARIETAL	SAPPHIRE	WARRANTY	ACRIMONY	ADORABLE	CENOBITE	DEMOLISH	HEADGEAR
PARLANCE	SARDONIC	WASHABLE	ACROSTIC	ADULTERY	CENOTAPH	DEMONIAC	HEADLAND
PARMESAN	SATURATE	WASHBOWL	ACTINISM	ADVISORY	CENTERED	DEMURRER	HEADLINE
PAROXYSM	SATURDAY	WASHROOM	ACTINIUM	ADVOCATE	CENTRIST	DENATURE	HEADLOCK
PARTERRE	SAUCEPAN	WATCHDOG	ACTIVATE	EDGEWAYS	CEPHALIC	DENOUNCE	HEADLONG
PARTIBLE	SAUTERNE	WATCHFUL	ACTIVISM	EDUCABLE	CERAMIST	DEPONENT	HEADREST
PARTICLE	SAWHORSE	WATCHMAN	ACTIVITY	IDEALISM	CEREBRUM	DEPUTIZE	HEADROOM
PARTISAN	TABULATE	WATERLOO	ECLIPTIC	IDEALIZE	CEREMENT	DERELICT	HEADSHIP
PASSABLE	TACITURN	WATERWAY	ECONOMIC	IDEATION	CEREMONY	DEROGATE	HEADSMAN
PASSBOOK	TAFFRAIL	WAYFARER	ICEBOUND	IDENTIFY	CERULEAN	DERRIERE	HEADWORD
PASSOVER	TAHITIAN	YACHTING	ICEHOUSE	IDENTITY	CERVICAL	DESCRIBE	HEADWORK
PASSPORT	TAILCOAT	ABATTOIR	OCCASION	IDEOGRAM	CESAREAN	DESELECT	HEAVYSET
PASSWORD	TAILGATE	ABDICATE	OCCUPANT	IDEOLOGY	CESSPOOL	DESIROUS	HEBRAISM
PASTICHE	TAILSPIN	ABEYANCE	SCABBARD	IDOLATER	DEADBEAT	DESOLATE	HECATOMB
PASTILLE	TALESMAN	ABLATION	SCABROUS	IDOLATRY	DEADLINE	DESPATCH	HEDGEHOG
PASTORAL	TALISMAN	ABLATIVE	SCAFFOLD	ODOMETER	DEADLOCK	DESTRUCT	HEDGEHOP
PASTRAMI	TAMARACK	ABLUTION	SCALABLE	AEROLOGY	DEADWOOD	DETACHED	HEDGEROW
PATERNAL	TAMARIND	ABNEGATE	SCALAWAG	AERONAUT	DEATHBED	DETHRONE	HEDONISM
PATHETIC	TANGIBLE	ABNORMAL	SCALEPAN	AESTHETE	DEBILITY	DETONATE	HEGEMONY
PATHOGEN	TANTALUM	ABORNING	SCALLION	BEANBALL	DEBONAIR	DETOXIFY	HEIGHTEN
PATIENCE	TAPESTRY	ABORTION	SCANDIUM	BEARSKIN	DECANTER	DETRITUS	HEIRLOOM
PAVEMENT	TAPEWORM	ABRASIVE	SCAPULAR	BEATIFIC	DECEDENT	DEVILISH	HELICOID
PAVILION	TARRAGON	ABROGATE	SCARCELY	BEAUTIFY	DECEMBER	DEVOTION	HELIPORT
PAWNSHOP	TAXONOMY	ABSCISSA	SCATHING	BECHUANA	DECIGRAM	DEWBERRY	HELLHOLE
PAYCHECK	TAXPAYER	ABSENTEE	SCAVENGE	BECOMING	DECIMATE	DEXTROSE	HELMSMAN
RADIATOR	VACATION	ABSINTHE	SCENARIO	BEDAZZLE	DECIPHER	FEARLESS	HELPMATE
RADIOMAN	VACCINIA	ABSOLUTE	SCHEDULE	BEDSTEAD	DECISION	FEARSOME	HELPMEET
RAILLERY	VAGABOND	ABSTRACT	SCHMALTZ	BEECHNUT	DECISIVE	FEASIBLE	HEMATITE
RAILROAD	VAGRANCY	ABSTRUSE	SCHOONER	BEFRIEND	DECKHAND	FEBRUARY	HENCHMAN
RAINCOAT	VALIDATE	ABUNDANT	SCIATICA	BEFUDDLE	DECORATE	FECKLESS	HEPATICA
RAINDROP	VALUABLE	ABUTMENT	SCILICET	BEGGARLY	DECOROUS	FEDERATE	HERALDIC
RAINFALL	VALVULAR	ABUTTALS	SCIMITAR	BEGRUDGE	DECREASE	FEEDBACK	HERALDRY

HERCULES	MEMORIZE	PELLUCID	RELEGATE	SEAGOING	TENDENCY	AFFINITY	CHLORITE
HERDSMAN	MENHADEN	PEMMICAN	RELEVANT	SEALSKIN	TENEMENT	AFFLATUS	CHOIRBOY
HEREDITY	MENISCUS	PENALIZE	RELIABLE	SEAMOUNT	TENPENNY	AFFRIGHT	CHOLERIC
HEREFORD	MEPHITIC	PENCHANT	RELIANCE	SEAPLANE	TENTACLE	AFLUTTER	CHOWCHOW
HEREUNTO	MERCHANT	PENDULUM	RELIGION	SEASCAPE	TEOSINTE	AFTERTAX	CHRISTEN
HEREUPON	MERCURIC	PENITENT	RELOCATE	SEASHORE	TERMINAL	EFFERENT	CHRISTIE
HEREWITH	MERIDIAN	PENKNIFE	REMEDIAL	SEAWATER	TERMINUS	EFFUSION	CHROMIUM
HERITAGE	MERINGUE	PENLIGHT	REMEMBER	SECURITY	TERRAPIN	OFFICIAL	CHUTZPAH
HERMETIC	MESDAMES	PENOLOGY	REMITTAL	SEDATIVE	TERRIBLE	OFFPRINT	GHANAIAN
HESITANT	MESHWORK	PENSTOCK	RENEGADE	SEDIMENT	TERRIFIC	OFFSHOOT	OHMMETER
HESITATE	MESQUITE	PENTAGON	RENOUNCE	SEDITION	TERTIARY	OFFSHORE	PHANTASM
JEOPARDY	MESSMATE	PENUMBRA	RENOVATE	SEDULOUS	TESTATOR	OFFSTAGE	PHANTASY
JEREMIAD	METAFILE	PERCEIVE	REPARTEE	SEEDLING	TESTICLE	AGERATUM	PHARISEE
JETTISON	METAPHOR	PERFECTO	REPEATED	SEEDTIME	TEUTONIC	AGGRIEVE	PHARMACY
KEELBOAT	METEORIC	PERFORCE	REPORTER	SEIGNEUR	TEXTBOOK	AGITPROP	PHASEOUT
KEELHAUL	METHANOL	PERILUNE	REPRIEVE	SELECTEE	VEGANISM	AGLITTER	PHEASANT
KEEPSAKE	METRICAL	PERIODIC	REPRISAL	SELENITE	VEGETATE	AGNOSTIC	PHENOLIC
KERCHIEF	NEBULIZE	PERMEATE	REPROACH	SELENIUM	VEHEMENT	AGRARIAN	PHOSPHOR
KEROSINE	NEBULOUS	PEROXIDE	REPUBLIC	SELFLESS	VELLEITY	AGRONOMY	PHRASING
KEYBOARD	NECKLACE	PERSONAL	RESCRIPT	SELFSAME	VELOCITY	EGGPLANT	PHYSICAL
KEYPUNCH	NECKLINE	PERSPIRE	RESEARCH	SEMANTIC	VENATION	EGGSHELL	PHYSIQUE
KEYSTONE	NECROSIS	PERSUADE	RESEMBLE	SEMESTER	VENDETTA	EGYPTIAN	RHAPSODY
KEYWORDS	NEEDLESS	PERVERSE	RESERVED	SEMINARY	VENERATE	IGNITION	RHEOLOGY
LEAPFROG	NEGATION	PETITION	RESIDENT	SEMINOLE	VENEREAL	IGNORANT	RHEOSTAT
LEARNING	NEGATIVE	PETTIFOG	RESIDUAL	SEMISOFT	VENGEFUL	CHAIRMAN	RHETORIC
LEAVINGS	NEGLIGEE	PETULANT	RESIDUUM	SENSIBLE	VENOMOUS	CHAMBRAY	RHOMBOID
LECITHIN	NEIGHBOR	REACTANT	RESIGNED	SENSUOUS	VENUSIAN	CHAMPION	RHYOLITE
LEFTOVER	NEMATODE	REACTION	RESISTOR	SENTENCE	VERACITY	CHANCERY	SHAMBLES
LEGALISM	NEONATAL	REACTIVE	RESOLUTE	SENTIENT	VERBATIM	CHANDLER	SHAMROCK
LEGATION	NEOPHYTE	REARWARD	RESONANT	SENTINEL	VERBIAGE	CHANUKAH	SHANGHAI
LEMONADE	NEOPLASM	REASSURE	RESONATE	SEPARATE	VERBOTEN	CHAPBOOK	SHANTUNG
LENGTHEN	NEPENTHE	REBUTTAL	RESORTER	SEQUENCE	VERMOUTH	CHAPERON	SHEEPISH
LENITIVE	NEPOTISM	RECEIVER	RESOURCE	SERAGLIO	VERONICA	CHAPLAIN	SHEETING
LETHARGY	NESTLING	RECEPTOR	RESPONSE	SERENADE	VERSICLE	CHARADES	SHELVING
LEUKEMIA	NEURITIS	RECKLESS	RESTLESS	SERGEANT	VERTEBRA	CHARCOAL	SHEPHERD
LEVERAGE	NEUROSIS	RECORDER	RESTRAIN	SEROLOGY	VERTICAL	CHARISMA	SHILINGI
LEVITATE	NEUROTIC	RECOURSE	RESTRICT	SERVITOR	VESICANT	CHARMING	SHILLING
MEALTIME	NEUTRINO	RECREANT	RETAINER	SETSCREW	VESTMENT	CHASTISE	SHINBONE
MEALYBUG	NEWCOMER	RECREATE	RETARDED	SEWERAGE	VEXATION	CHASTITY	SHINGLES
MEANTIME	NEWFOUND	REDOLENT	RETICENT	TEACHING	WEAKFISH	CHASUBLE	SHIPMATE
MEATBALL	NEWLYWED	REFERENT	RETIRING	TEAMSTER	WEAKLING	CHECKERS	SHIPMENT
MECHANIC	NEWSCAST	REFERRAL	RETRENCH	TEAMWORK	WEAKNESS	CHECKOFF	SHIPPING
MEDALIST	NEWSREEL	REFINERY	RETRIEVE	TEASPOON	WEAPONRY	CHECKOUT	SHIPWORM
MEDICAID	PECTORAL	REFOREST	RETROFIT	TEETHING	WELDMENT	CHECKSUM	SHIPYARD
MEDICARE	PECULATE	REFORMER	RETURNEE	TEETOTAL	WELLBORN	CHEERFUL	SHIRRING
MEDICATE	PECULIAR	REGICIDE	REVANCHE	TELECAST	WELLHEAD	CHEMICAL	SHIRTING
MEDICINE	PEDAGOGY	REGIMENT	REVEILLE	TELEFILM	WEREWOLF	CHEMURGY	SHOCKING
MEDIEVAL	PEDERAST	REGIONAL	REVENUER	TELEGRAM	XENOLITH	CHENILLE	SHOELACE
MEDIOCRE	PEDESTAL	REGISTER	REVEREND	TELEPLAY	YEARBOOK	CHEROKEE	SHOPLIFT
MEDITATE	PEDICURE	REGISTRY	REVERENT	TELETHON	YEARLING	CHESTNUT	SHOPWORN
MEGABYTE	PEDIGREE	REGOLITH	REVERSAL	TELEVIEW	YEARLONG	CHEYENNE	SHORTAGE
MEGALITH	PEDIMENT	REGULATE	REVIEWER	TELEVISE	YEARNING	CHIPMUNK	SHORTCUT
MELANISM	PEDUNCLE	REHEARSE	REVIVIFY	TELLTALE	YEOMANRY	CHIPPEWA	SHOSHONE
MELANOMA	PEEPHOLE	REINDEER	REVOLVER	TEMERITY	ZEPPELIN	CHITCHAT	SHOULDER
MELODEON	PEERLESS	RELATION	SEABOARD	TEMPLATE	AFFECTED	CHIVALRY	SHOWCASE
MEMBRANE	PEIGNOIR	RELATIVE	SEACOAST	TEMPORAL	AFFERENT	CHLORIDE	SHOWDOWN
MEMORIAL	PELLAGRA	RELAXANT	SEAFARER	TENANTRY	AFFIANCE	CHLORINE	SHRAPNEL

SHREWISH	BINAURAL	DISCOLOR	FIREBALL	LIFELONG	MISCHIEF	RIBOSOME	VIGNETTE
SHUTDOWN	BINNACLE	DISCOUNT	FIREBOAT	LIFETIME	MISCIBLE	RICOCHET	VIGOROUS
THALAMUS	BIOCIDAL	DISCOVER	FIREBOMB	LIFEWORK	MISCOUNT	RIDICULE	VILLAGER
THALLIUM	BIRACIAL	DISCREET	FIRECLAY	LIGAMENT	MISDOING	RIFFRAFF	VILLAINY
THANKFUL	BIRDBATH	DISCRETE	FIREDAMP	LIGATURE	MISJUDGE	RIGHTFUL	VINCIBLE
THEOLOGY	BIRDLIME	DISFAVOR	FIREPLUG	LIGNEOUS	MISLABEL	RINGWORM	VINEGARY
THEORIZE	BIRDSEED	DISGORGE	FIRESIDE	LIKENESS	MISMATCH	RIPARIAN	VINEYARD
THEREFOR	BIRTHDAY	DISGRACE	FIRETRAP	LIKEWISE	MISNOMER	RIVERBED	VIOLABLE
THESPIAN	BISEXUAL	DISGUISE	FIREWOOD	LIMEKILN	MISPLACE	SIBILANT	VIOLENCE
THIAMINE	BITSTOCK	DISHEVEL	FIREWORK	LIMERICK	MISPRINT	SICKNESS	VIRGINAL
THICKSET	BIWEEKLY	DISHONOR	FIRMWARE	LIMONITE	MISQUOTE	SIDEKICK	VIROLOGY
THIEVERY	BIYEARLY	DISINTER	FISHBOWL	LINCHPIN	MISSHAPE	SIDELONG	VIRTUOSO
THIRTEEN	CICATRIX	DISJOINT	FISHHOOK	LINESMAN	MISSPELL	SIDEREAL	VIRTUOUS
THOROUGH	CICERONE	DISKETTE	FISHWIFE	LINGERIE	MISSPEND	SIDERITE	VIRULENT
THOUSAND	CINCHONA	DISLODGE	FIXATION	LINGUIST	MISSTATE	SIDESHOW	VISCERAL
THRASHER	CINCTURE	DISLOYAL	FIXATIVE	LINIMENT	MISTAKEN	SIDESTEP	VISCOUNT
THREATEN	CINNABAR	DISMOUNT	GIGABYTE	LINOLEUM	MISTREAT	SIDEWALK	VISICALC
THRENODY	CINNAMON	DISORDER	GIGANTIC	LIPSTICK	MISTRESS	SIDEWALL	VISITANT
THROMBUS	CIRCUITY	DISPATCH	GIMCRACK	LISTLESS	MISTRIAL	SIDEWAYS	VITALITY
THROTTLE	CIRCULAR	DISPENSE	GINGERLY	LITERARY	MISTRIAL	SIGNPOST	VITALIZE
THRUSTER	CISLUNAR	DISPERSE	GIVEAWAY	LITERATE	MISTRUST	SILENCER	VITREOUS
THURSDAY	CITATION	DISPIRIT	HIBISCUS	LITERATI	MISUSAGE	SILICATE	VIVACITY
WHARFAGE	CIVILIAN	DISPLACE	HIDEAWAY	LITIGANT	MITIGATE	SILICIFY	VIVARIUM
WHATEVER	CIVILITY	DISPOSAL	HIGHBALL	LITIGATE	NICKNAME	SILICONE	WILDFIRE
WHENEVER	CIVILIZE	DISPROVE	HIGHBORN	LITTORAL	NICOTINE	SIMONIZE	WILDFOWL
WHEREVER	DIABETES	DISQUIET	HIGHBRED	LIVELONG	NIGERIAN	SIMPLIFY	WILDLIFE
WHIPCORD	DIABOLIC	DISSEVER	HIGHBROW	LIVERISH	NIGEROIS	SIMULATE	WILDWOOD
WHIPLASH	DIAGONAL	DISSOLVE	HIGHLAND	MICROBUS	NIGGLING	SINECURE	WILLIWAW
WHITECAP	DIALOGUE	DISSUADE	HIGHNESS	MIDDLING	NIHILISM	SINGULAR	WINDBURN
WHITEFLY	DIALYSIS	DISTANCE	HIGHROAD	MIDNIGHT	NINEPINS	SINISTER	WINDFALL
WHODUNIT	DIAMETER	DISTASTE	HIGHTAIL	MIDPOINT	NINETEEN	SINKHOLE	WINDLASS
WHOMEVER	DIANTHUS	DISTINCT	HILLSIDE	MIDSHIPS	NITROGEN	SITUATED	WINDMILL
WHOPPING	DIAPASON	DISTRACT	HINDMOST	MIGRAINE	OILCLOTH	SIXPENCE	WINDPIPE
AIGRETTE	DIARRHEA	DISTRAIT	HINDUISM	MILEPOST	OINTMENT	TICKLISH	WINDWARD
AIRBORNE	DIASTOLE	DISTRESS	HIRELING	MILESIMO	PICAYUNE	TIDELAND	WINESHOP
AIRBRUSH	DIATOMIC	DISTRICT	HISPANIC	MILITANT	PICKEREL	TIGHTWAD	WINGDING
AIRCRAFT	DIATRIBE	DISTRUST	HITHERTO	MILITARY	PICKINGS	TIMBERED	WINGSPAN
AIRDROME	DICTATOR	DISUNITE	JINGOISM	MILITATE	PICKLOCK	TIMELESS	WIREDRAW
AIRFIELD	DIDACTIC	DISUNITY	KIBITZER	MILKMAID	PIDDLING	TIMEWORN	WIREHAIR
AIRFRAME	DIELDRIN	DIURETIC	KICKBACK	MILKWEED	PIEPLANT	TIMOROUS	WIRELESS
AIRLINER	DILATORY	DIVAGATE	KICKSHAW	MILLIARD	PILASTER	TINCTURE	WIREWORM
AIRPLANE	DILIGENT	DIVIDEND	KIELBASA	MILLIBAR	PILCHARD	TINPLATE	WISEACRE
AIRSPACE	DIMINISH	DIVINITY	KILLDEER	MILLIEME	PILOTAGE	TINSMITH	WISHBONE
AIRSPEED	DINGBATS	DIVISION	KILOBYTE	MILLINER	PIMIENTO	TIRELESS	WISTARIA
AIRSTRIP	DINOSAUR	DIVISIVE	KILOGRAM	MILLPOND	PINAFORE	TIRESOME	WISTERIA
AIRTIGHT	DIPLOMAT	DIVORCEE	KILOVOLT	MILLRACE	PINNACLE	TITANIUM	WITCHERY
BIANNUAL	DIPSTICK	EIGHTEEN	KILOWATT	MINATORY	PINOCHLE	TITILATE	WITCHING
BIATHLON	DIRECTOR	FIBROSIS	KINDLING	MINDLESS	PINPOINT	TITIVATE	WITHDRAW
BIBULOUS	DISABUSE	FIDELITY	KINETICS	MINIBIKE	PINPRICK	TITMOUSE	WITHHOLD
BICONVEX	DISAGREE	FIGURINE	KINGBOLT	MINIMIZE	PINWHEEL	VIATICUM	WIZARDRY
BICUSPID	DISALLOW	FILAMENT	LIBATION	MINISTER	PIPELINE	VIBURNUM	YIELDING
BIDDABLE	DISARRAY	FILIGREE	LIBERATE	MINISTRY	PITCHMAN	VICARAGE	EKISTICS
BIENNIAL	DISASTER	FILIPINO	LIBRETTO	MINORITY	PITIABLE	VICINAGE	SKELETON
BIENNIUM	DISBURSE	FILTRATE	LICENSEE	MINSTREL	PITILESS	VICINITY	SKILLFUL
BIFOCALS	DISCIPLE	FINALIST	LICORICE	MISAPPLY	PITTANCE	VICTORIA	SKIMMING
BILLFOLD	DISCLAIM	FINALIZE	LIFEBOAT	MISBRAND	PIXELATE	VIETCONG	SKIRMISH
BILLHEAD	DISCLOSE	FINESPUN	LIFELINE	MISCARRY	PIZZERIA	VIGILANT	SKITTISH

SKULLCAP	CLINCHER	FLYWHEEL	AMBROSIA	ANAEROBE	ENTRANCE	INSOMNIA	UNBIDDEN
SKYLIGHT	CLINICAL	GLABROUS	AMBULANT	ANALOGUE	ENTRENCH	INSOMUCH	UNBODIED
ALACRITY	CLIPPING	GLACIATE	AMENABLE	ANALYSIS	ENURESIS	INSPIRIT	UNBOLTED
ALARMIST	CLITORIS	GLADSOME	AMERICAN	ANATHEMA	ENVELOPE	INSTANCE	UNBROKEN
ALBACORE	CLOISTER	GLASSFUL	AMETHYST	ANCESTOR	ENVIABLE	INSTINCT	UNBUCKLE
ALBANIAN	CLOSEOUT	GLAUCOMA	AMICABLE	ANCESTRY	ENVIRONS	INSTRUCT	UNBURDEN
ALDERMAN	CLOTHIER	GLOAMING	AMMONIUM	ANDROGEN	ENVISAGE	INSULATE	UNBUTTON
ALEATORY	CLOTHING	GLOBULIN	AMOEBOID	ANECDOTE	INCHOATE	INTAGLIO	UNCHASTE
ALEHOUSE	CLOUDLET	GLORIOUS	AMORTIZE	ANECHOIC	INCHWORM	INTEGRAL	UNCHURCH
ALFRESCO	CLUBFOOT	GLOSSARY	AMPERAGE	ANGELICA	INCIDENT	INTENDED	UNCLENCH
ALGERIAN	ELECTION	GLOWWORM	AMPUTATE	ANGLICAN	INCISION	INTERCOM	UNCLOTHE
ALIASING	ELECTIVE	GLOXINIA	EMACIATE	ANGSTROM	INCISIVE	INTEREST	UNCOMMON
ALIENATE	ELECTRIC	GLYCERIN	EMBATTLE	ANISETTE	INCOMING	INTERIOR	UNCOUPLE
ALIENIST	ELECTRON	GLYCEROL	EMBEZZLE	ANNOTATE	INCREASE	INTERMIT	UNCTUOUS
ALIZARIN	ELEGANCE	GLYCOGEN	EMBITTER	ANNOUNCE	INCUBATE	INTERMIX	UNDERACT
ALKALOID	ELEPHANT	ILLINOIS	EMBLAZON	ANTEATER	INCUMBER	INTERNAL	UNDERAGE
ALLEGORY	ELEVATOR	ILLUMINE	EMBOLDEN	ANTEDATE	INDEBTED	INTERNEE	UNDERARM
ALLELUIA	ELIGIBLE	ILLUSION	EMBOLISM	ANTELOPE	INDECENT	INTERNET	UNDERBID
ALLERGEN	ELLIPSIS	ILLUSIVE	EMERITUS	ANTERIOR	INDIAMAN	INTERROG	UNDERCUT
ALLEYWAY	ELONGATE	ILLUSORY	EMIGRATE	ANTEROOM	INDICATE	INTERVAL	UNDERDOG
ALLIANCE	ELOQUENT	OLEANDER	EMINENCE	ANTHROPO	INDIGENT	INTIMATE	UNDERFUR
ALLOCATE	FLAGPOLE	PLACENTA	EMISSARY	ANTIBODY	INDIRECT	INTRADOS	UNDERLIE
ALLSPICE	FLAGRANT	PLANGENT	EMOTICON	ANTIDOTE	INDOLENT	INTRENCH	UNDERLIP
ALLUVIUM	FLAGSHIP	PLANKING	EMPHASIS	ANTIMONY	INDUCTEE	INTREPID	UNDERPAY
ALMIGHTY	FLAMBEAU	PLANKTON	EMPHATIC	ANTINOMY	INDURATE	INTRIGUE	UNDERSEA
ALOPECIA	FLAMENCO	PLANTAIN	EMPLOYEE	ANTIPODE	INDUSTRY	INTROMIT	UNDERTOW
ALPHABET	FLAMEOUT	PLATFORM	EMPORIUM	ANTIPOPE	INEDITED	INUNDATE	UNDULANT
ALTHOUGH	FLAMINGO	PLATINUM	EMPYREAN	ANYPLACE	INERRANT	INVASION	UNDULATE
ALTITUDE	FLAPJACK	PLATYPUS	EMULSIFY	ANYTHING	INEXPERT	INVEIGLE	UNEARNED
ALTRUISM	FLASHGUN	PLAYBACK	EMULSION	ANYWHERE	INFAMOUS	INVERTER	UNENDING
ALUMINUM	FLASHING	PLAYBILL	IMBECILE	ENCEINTE	INFANTRY	INVIABLE	UNERRING
BLACKING	FLATBOAT	PLAYBOOK	IMITABLE	ENCIPHER	INFERIOR	INVITING	UNFASTEN
BLACKOUT	FLATFISH	PLAYGOER	IMMANENT	ENCIRCLE	INFERNAL	INVOLUTE	UNFETTER
BLACKTOP	FLATFOOT	PLAYMATE	IMMATURE	ENCOMIUM	INFINITE	INVOLVED	UNFILIAL
BLESSING	FLATHEAD	PLAYSUIT	IMMINENT	ENCROACH	INFINITY	INWARDLY	UNFORMED
BLISSFUL	FLATIRON	PLEASANT	IMMOBILE	ENCUMBER	INFOBAHN	KNAPSACK	UNFREEZE
BLIZZARD	FLATLAND	PLEASING	IMMODEST	ENDANGER	INFORMAL	KNEEHOLE	UNGAINLY
BLOCKADE	FLATTERY	PLEASURE	IMMOLATE	ENDEAVOR	INFORMED	KNICKERS	UNGULATE
BLOOMERS	FLATWARE	PLEBEIAN	IMMORTAL	ENERGIZE	INFORMER	KNITWEAR	UNIAXIAL
BLOWPIPE	FLAUTIST	PLECTRUM	IMMOTILE	ENERVATE	INFRADIG	KNOCKOUT	UNICYCLE
BLUDGEON	FLEABANE	PLETHORA	IMMUNIZE	ENFEEBLE	INFRARED	KNOTHOLE	UNIONISM
BLUEBELL	FLEABITE	PLEURISY	IMPACTED	ENFILADE	INFRINGE	MNEMONIC	UNIONIZE
BLUEBIRD	FLEETING	PLUMBING	IMPELLER	ENGAGING	INGUINAL	ONCOMING	UNIVALVE
BLUEFISH	FLESHPOT	SLATTERN	IMPERIAL	ENGENDER	INHALANT	ONLOOKER	UNIVERSE
BLUENOSE	FLEXIBLE	SLIPKNOT	IMPETIGO	ENGINEER	INHERENT	ONONDAGA	UNKINDLY
CLAIMANT	FLIMFLAM	SLIPPERY	IMPLICIT	ENORMITY	INHUMANE	SNAPSHOT	UNLAWFUL
CLAMBAKE	FLIPPANT	SLIPSHOD	IMPOLITE	ENORMOUS	INIMICAL	SNOBBERY	UNLEADED
CLAPTRAP	FLOTILLA	SLOVENLY	IMPOSING	ENSCONCE	INIQUITY	SNOWBALL	UNLIKELY
CLARINET	FLOUNDER	SLUGGARD	IMPOSTOR	ENSEMBLE	INITIATE	SNOWBANK	UNLIMBER
CLASSIFY	FLOURISH	SLUGGISH	IMPOTENT	ENSHRINE	INKSTAND	SNOWDROP	UNLOOSEN
CLAVICLE	FLUIDRAM	SLUMLORD	IMPRISON	ENSHROUD	INNOCENT	SNOWFALL	UNLOVELY
CLAYMORE	FLUORIDE	ULCERATE	IMPROPER	ENSILAGE	INNOVATE	SNOWPLOW	UNMUZZLE
CLEARING	FLUORINE	ULTERIOR	IMPUDENT	ENTANGLE	INNUENDO	SNOWSHOE	UNPERSON
CLEAVAGE	FLUORITE	ULTIMATE	IMPUNITY	ENTHRALL	INSCRIBE	UNAWARES	UNRIDDLE
CLEMATIS	FLYBLOWN	AMARANTH	SMALLPOX	ENTHRONE	INSECURE	UNBEATEN	UNSADDLE
CLEMENCY	FLYPAPER	AMBIENCE	UMBRELLA	ENTIRETY	INSIGNIA	UNBELIEF	UNSAVORY
CLERICAL	FLYSPECK	AMBITION	ANACONDA	ENTRAILS	INSOLENT	UNBIASED	UNSEEMLY

UNSETTLE	COLISEUM	CONTRAST	DOORYARD	FORENOON	HOOLIGAN	MOMENTUM	NOONTIME
UNSHAPED	COLLAPSE	CONTRITE	DORMOUSE	FORENSIC	HOOSEGOW	MONARCHY	NORSEMAN
UNSOUGHT	COLLIERY	CONTRIVE	DOUBLOON	FOREPART	HORMONAL	MONASTIC	NOTARIAL
UNSPRUNG	COLLOQUY	CONVERGE	DOUBTFUL	FORESAIL	HORNBOOK	MONAURAL	NOTARIZE
UNSTABLE	COLONIAL	CONVERSE	DOUGHBOY	FORESKIN	HORNPIPE	MONETARY	NOTATION
UNSTEADY	COLONIST	CONVINCE	DOUGHNUT	FORESTRY	HOROLOGY	MONGOOSE	NOTEBOOK
UNSTRUNG	COLONIZE	CONVULSE	DOVETAIL	FORETELL	HORRIBLE	MONITION	NOTIONAL
UNTANGLE	COLOPHON	COOKBOOK	DOWNBEAT	FOREWARN	HORSEFLY	MONITORY	NOVELIZE
UNTAUGHT	COLOSSAL	COONSKIN	DOWNCAST	FOREWORD	HORSEMAN	MONOGAMY	NOVEMBER
UNTIMELY	COLOSSUS	COPPERAS	DOWNFALL	FORKLIFT	HOSPITAL	MONOGRAM	NOWADAYS
UNTOWARD	COMANCHE	COPULATE	DOWNHILL	FORMERLY	HOSTELRY	MONOLITH	POCKMARK
UNVOICED	COMBINGS	COPYBOOK	DOWNLOAD	FORMLESS	HOTHOUSE	MONOPOLY	PODIATRY
UNWIELDY	COMEBACK	COPYDESK	DOWNPOUR	FORSOOTH	HOUSEBOY	MONORAIL	POIGNANT
UNWONTED	COMEDIAN	COQUETTE	DOWNTOWN	FORSWEAR	HOUSEFLY	MONOTONE	POKEWEED
UNWORTHY	COMEDOWN	CORDLESS	DOWNTURN	FORTRESS	HOUSETOP	MONOXIDE	POLARITY
UNZIPPED	COMMANDO	CORDOVAN	DOWNWARD	FORTUITY	HOWITZER	MONSIEUR	POLARIZE
BOASTFUL	COMMENCE	CORDUROY	DOWNWIND	FORWARDS	JONGLEUR	MONUMENT	POLESTAR
BOBOLINK	COMMERCE	CORNCRIB	DOXOLOGY	FOUNTAIN	JOYSTICK	MOONBEAM	POLITICK
BOBWHITE	COMMONER	CORNMEAL	FOLDAWAY	FOURFOLD	KOHLRABI	MOORLAND	POLITICO
BODILESS	COMMUNAL	CORONACH	FOLDBOAT	FOURSOME	KOLINSKY	MORALIST	POLITICS
BODYWORK	COMPILER	CORONARY	FOLDEROL	FOURTEEN	LOANWORD	MORALITY	POLLIWOG
BOGEYMAN	COMPLAIN	CORPORAL	FOLIATED	FOXGLOVE	LOATHING	MORALIZE	POLLSTER
BOHEMIAN	COMPLEAT	CORPSMAN	FOLKLORE	FOXHOUND	LOBOTOMY	MOREOVER	POLONIUM
BOLDFACE	COMPLETE	CORRIDOR	FOLLICLE	GOALPOST	LOCALITY	MORIBUND	POLTROON
BOLLWORM	COMPOUND	CORUNDUM	FOOLSCAP	GOATHERD	LOCALIZE	MOROCCAN	POLYGAMY
BONDSMAN	COMPRESS	CORVETTE	FOOTBALL	GOATSKIN	LOCATION	MORPHEME	POLYGLOT
BONHOMIE	COMPRISE	COSIGNER	FOOTFALL	GODCHILD	LOCKSTEP	MORPHINE	POLYMATH
BOOKCASE	COMPUTER	COSMETIC	FOOTHILL	GOLDFISH	LOCOWEED	MORTGAGE	PONYTAIL
BOOKMARK	CONCEIVE	COUCHANT	FOOTHOLD	GONFALON	LOCUTION	MORTUARY	POPINJAY
BOOKWORM	CONCERTO	COUNTESS	FOOTLESS	GOODNESS	LODESTAR	MOSQUITO	POPULACE
BOOTLESS	CONCLAVE	COUPLING	FOOTLING	GOODWIFE	LODGMENT	MOSSBACK	POPULATE
BORDELLO	CONCLUDE	COURTESY	FOOTNOTE	GOODWILL	LOGOTYPE	MOTHBALL	POPULIST
BOTULISM	CONCRETE	COURTIER	FOOTPATH	GOOFBALL	LOLLIPOP	MOTIVATE	POPULOUS
BOUFFANT	CONDENSE	COVENANT	FOOTRACE	GORGEOUS	LOLLYGAG	MOTORCAR	PORPHYRY
BOUILLON	CONFETTI	COVERAGE	FOOTREST	GOSSAMER	LONESOME	MOTORIZE	PORPOISE
BOUNDARY	CONFINES	COVERALL	FOOTSORE	GOURMAND	LONGBOAT	MOTORMAN	PORRIDGE
BOUTIQUE	CONFLICT	COVERLET	FOOTSTEP	GOVERNOR	LONGHAIR	MOTOROLA	PORTABLE
BOWSPRIT	CONFOCAL	COXSWAIN	FOOTWEAR	HOARDING	LONGHAND	MOUNTAIN	PORTHOLE
COACHMAN	CONFOUND	DOCKHAND	FOOTWORK	HOGSHEAD	LONGHORN	MOUNTING	PORTIERE
COAGULUM	CONFRERE	DOCKYARD	FORCIBLE	HOLDOVER	LONGTIME	MOURNFUL	PORTRAIT
COALESCE	CONFRONT	DOCTRINE	FOREBEAR	HOLINESS	LONGUEUR	MOURNING	PORTRAIT
COAUTHOR	CONGENER	DOCUMENT	FOREBODE	HOLOGRAM	LOOPHOLE	MOVEMENT	POSITION
COCKATOO	CONGRESS	DOGFIGHT	FORECAST	HOLSTEIN	LOPSIDED	NOBELIST	POSITIVE
COCKCROW	CONJUGAL	DOGGEREL	FOREDOOM	HOMEBODY	LORDSHIP	NOBELIUM	POSITRON
COCKEREL	CONJUNCT	DOGHOUSE	FOREFEND	HOMEBRED	LOVEBIRD	NOBILITY	POSSIBLE
COCKSURE	CONQUEST	DOLDRUMS	FOREFOOT	HOMELAND	LOVELORN	NOBLEMAN	POSTCARD
COCKTAIL	CONSERVE	DOLOMITE	FOREGONE	HOMEMADE	LOVESICK	NOCTURNE	POSTDATE
COGITATE	CONSIDER	DOMESTIC	FOREHAND	HOMEROOM	LOYALIST	NOMINATE	POSTHOLE
COGNOMEN	CONSOMME	DOMICILE	FOREHEAD	HOMESICK	MOBILIZE	NONDAIRY	POSTLUDE
COGWHEEL	CONSPIRE	DOMINATE	FOREKNOW	HOMESPUN	MOCCASIN	NONESUCH	POSTMARK
COHERENT	CONSTANT	DOMINEER	FORELADY	HOMEWARD	MODERATE	NONEVENT	POSTPAID
COHESION	CONSTRUE	DOMINION	FORELAND	HOMEWORK	MODULATE	NONMETAL	POSTPONE
COIFFEUR	CONTEMPT	DONATION	FORELIMB	HOMICIDE	MOISTURE	NONRIGID	POTATION
COIFFURE	CONTINUE	DOOMSDAY	FORELOCK	HONEYDEW	MOLASSES	NONSENSE	POTBELLY
COINCIDE	CONTRACT	DOORJAMB	FOREMAST	HONORARY	MOLECULE	NONSTICK	POTSHERD
COLANDER	CONTRAIL	DOORKNOB	FOREMOST	HOODWINK	MOLEHILL	NONUNION	POULTICE
COLESLAW	CONTRARY	DOORSTEP	FORENAME	HOOKWORM	MOLESKIN	NOONTIDE	POUNDAGE

ROADSIDE

ROADSTER	TOPOLOGY	APOTHEGM	UPPERCUT	BROOKLET	FRANCIUM	ORGANISM	PROSPECT
ROADWORK	TOPSIDES	APPANAGE	UPRISING	BROUGHAM	FREEBORN	ORGANIST	PROSTATE
ROCKETRY	TOREADOR	APPARENT	UPSTAIRS	BROUHAHA	FREEDMAN	ORGANIZE	PROTOCOL
ROCKFALL	TORTILLA	APPELLEE	UPSTREAM	BROWBEAT	FREEHAND	ORGULOUS	PROTRACT
ROLLBACK	TORTOISE	APPENDIX	UPSTROKE	BROWNOUT	FREEHOLD	ORIENTAL	PROTRUDE
ROMANIAN	TORTUOUS	APPETITE	UPTHRUST	CRACKPOT	FREELOAD	ORIGINAL	PROVIDED
ROMANTIC	TOTALITY	APPLAUSE	AQUACADE	CRAWFISH	FREEWILL	ORNAMENT	PROVINCE
ROOFTREE	TOUCHING	APPLIQUE	AQUANAUT	CRAYFISH	FRENETIC	ORTHODOX	PRURIENT
ROOMETTE	TOWELING	APPOSITE	AQUARIUM	CREAMERY	FREQUENT	ORTHOEPY	TRACKAGE
ROOMMATE	TOWERING	APPRAISE	AQUEDUCT	CREATION	FRESHMAN	PRACTICE	TRACTATE
ROSEBUSH	TOWNSHIP	APPROACH	AQUILINE	CREATURE	FRETWORK	PRATFALL	TRACTION
ROSEMARY	TOWNSMAN	APPROVAL	EQUALIZE	CREDENCE	FRICTION	PRATIQUE	TRAINING
ROSEWOOD	VOCALIST	APTITUDE	EQUATION	CREDENZA	FRIGHTEN	PREAMBLE	TRAINMAN
ROUGHAGE	VOCALIZE	EPIDEMIC	EQUIPAGE	CREDIBLE	FRIPPERY	PRECINCT	TRANQUIL
ROULETTE	VOCATION	EPILEPSY	SQUABBLE	CREDITOR	FRONTAGE	PRECIOUS	TRANSACT
ROUTEMAN	VOCATIVE	EPILOGUE	SQUADRON	CREEPING	FRONTIER	PRECLUDE	TRANSEPT
ROYALIST	VOLATILE	EPIPHANY	SQUANDER	CREMAINS	FROSTING	PREEXIST	TRANSFER
SOBRIETY	VOLCANIC	OPENWORK	SQUEEGEE	CREOSOTE	FROUFROU	PREGNANT	TRANSFIX
SOCIABLE	VOLITION	OPERABLE	SQUIRREL	CRESCENT	FRUCTIFY	PREJUDGE	TRANSMIT
SOFTBALL	VOLPLANE	OPERANDS	ARACHNID	CRETONNE	FRUITION	PREMIERE	TRAPDOOR
SOFTWARE	VOYAGEUR	OPERETTA	ARBALEST	CREVASSE	GRACIOUS	PREMOLAR	TRAPPING
SOFTWOOD	WOMANISH	OPPONENT	ARBOREAL	CRIBBAGE	GRADIENT	PRENATAL	TRAPROCK
SOLARIUM	WONDROUS	OPPOSITE	ARCHDUKE	CRIMINAL	GRADUATE	PREPRESS	TRAVERSE
SOLDIERY	WOODBINE	OPTICIAN	ARGUABLE	CRITICAL	GRAFFITO	PRESENCE	TRAVESTY
SOLECISM	WOODCOCK	OPTIMISM	ARGUMENT	CRITIQUE	GRANDEUR	PRESERVE	TREASURE
SOLENOID	WOODLAND	OPUSCULE	ARMAMENT	CROCKERY	GRANDSON	PRESIDIO	TREASURY
SOLIDIFY	WOODNOTE	SPACEMAN	ARMATURE	CROPLAND	GRANULAR	PRESSING	TREATISE
SOLITARY	WOODPILE	SPACIOUS	ARMCHAIR	CROSSBAR	GRAPHITE	PRESSMAN	TRENCHER
SOLITUDE	WOODRUFF	SPANIARD	ARMORIAL	CROSSBOW	GRASPING	PRESSURE	TRESPASS
SOLSTICE	WOODSHED	SPANKING	ARMYWORM	CROSSCUT	GRATEFUL	PRESTIGE	TRIANGLE
SOLUTION	WOODSMAN	SPECIFIC	ARPEGGIO	CROSSING	GRATUITY	PRETENSE	TRIBUNAL
SOLVENCY	WOODWIND	SPECIMEN	ARROGANT	CROTCHET	GRAVAMEN	PRETERIT	TRICHINA
SOMBRERO	WOODWORK	SPECIOUS	ARROGATE	CROUPIER	GRAYLING	PRETTIFY	TRICKERY
SOMEBODY	WOOLSACK	SPECTRAL	ARTERIAL	CROWFOOT	GREEKING	PREVIOUS	TRICOLOR
SOMERSET	WORDBOOK	SPECTRUM	ARTIFACT	CRUCIBLE	GREENERY	PRIMEVAL	TRICYCLE
SOMETIME	WORDPLAY	SPEEDWAY	ARTIFICE	CRUCIFIX	GREETING	PRIMROSE	TRIFLING
SOMEWHAT	WORDSTAR	SPHAGNUM	ARTISTIC	CRUZEIRO	GRIDIRON	PRINCESS	TRILLION
SONATINA	WORKABLE	SPHEROID	ARTISTRY	CRYOLITE	GRIEVOUS	PRINTING	TRILLIUM
SONGBIRD	WORKADAY	SPILLWAY	BRACELET	DRAGOMAN	GRIZZLED	PRINTOUT	TRIMARAN
SONGSTER	WORKBOOK	SPINSTER	BRACKISH	DRAINAGE	GROSBEAK	PRISONER	TRIMETER
SONOROUS	WORKROOM	SPIRITED	BRAGGART	DRAUGHTS	GROSCHEN	PRISTINE	TRIMMING
SORORITY	WORKSHOP	SPITBALL	BRAKEMAN	DRAWBACK	GROUNDER	PROBABLE	TRIPTYCH
SORPTION	WORMHOLE	SPITTOON	BRANDISH	DREADFUL	GRUELING	PROCAINE	TRIUMVIR
SOUTHPAW	WORMWOOD	SPLATTER	BREAKAGE	DRESSAGE	GRUESOME	PROCEEDS	TROMBONE
SOUVENIR	YOUNGISH	SPLENDID	BREAKOUT	DRESSING	IRONCLAD	PROCLAIM	TROUSERS
TOBOGGAN	YOURSELF	SPLENDOR	BREEDING	DRIVEWAY	IRONWARE	PRODIGAL	TRUCKAGE
TOGETHER	YOUTHFUL	SPLINTER	BRETHREN	DROPKICK	IRONWEED	PROFOUND	TRUETYPE
TOILETRY	ZOOPHYTE	SPLUTTER	BREVIARY	DRUGGIST	IRONWOOD	PROGRESS	TRUMPERY
TOILETTE	ZOOSPORE	SPOOLING	BRICKBAT	DRUMBEAT	IRONWORK	PROHIBIT	TRUNCATE
TOILWORN	APERITIF	SPORADIC	BRIGHTEN	DRUNKARD	IROQUOIS	PROLIFIC	TRUSTFUL
TOKENISM	APERTURE	SPRINKLE	BRINDLED	ERECTILE	IRRIGATE	PROLOGUE	TRUTHFUL
TOLERATE	APHANITE	SPROCKET	BRISLING	ERECTION	IRRITATE	PROMOTER	URBANITE
TOLLBOTH	APHELION	SPURIOUS	BRITCHES	ERYTHEMA	ORANGERY	PROPERTY	URBANIZE
TOLLGATE	APHORISM	SPYGLASS	BROCCOLI	FRACTION	ORATORIO	PROPHECY	WRAPPING
TOMAHAWK	APOLOGIA	UPCOMING	BROCHURE	FRACTURE	ORDINARY	PROPHESY	WRATHFUL
TOMORROW	APOPLEXY	UPGROWTH	BROMIDIC	FRAGMENT	ORDINATE	PROPOUND	WRECKAGE
TONALITY	APOSTASY	UPHEAVAL	BRONCHUS	FRAGRANT	ORDNANCE	PROROGUE	WRETCHED

WRIGGLER	STAGNANT	AUTOGIRO	FUNEREAL	MUSICIAN	PURULENT	SURCEASE	OVERKILL
WRISTLET	STAGNATE	AUTOJOIN	FURBELOW	MUSKETRY	PUSHCART	SUREFIRE	OVERLAID
WRONGFUL	STAIRWAY	AUTOMATE	FURLOUGH	MUSTACHE	PUSHDOWN	SURGICAL	OVERLAND
ASBESTOS	STAKEOUT	BUCKSHOT	FURTHEST	MUSTANG	PUSHOVER	SURMOUNT	OVERLEAP
ASPERITY	STALLION	BUCKSKIN	FUSELAGE	MUTATION	PUSSYCAT	SURPLICE	OVERLOOK
ASPHODEL	STALWART	BUDDHISM	FUTILITY	MUTILATE	PUTATIVE	SURPRISE	OVERLORD
ASPHYXIA	STAMPEDE	BUILDING	FUTURISM	NUCLEATE	QUADRANT	SURROUND	OVERMUCH
ASPIRANT	STANDARD	BULKHEAD	FUTURITY	NUGATORY	QUADROON	SUSPENSE	OVERPASS
ASPIRATE	STANDING	BULLDOZE	GUARANTY	NUISANCE	QUAGMIRE	SUZERAIN	OVERPLAY
ASSASSIN	STANDOFF	BULLETIN	GUARDIAN	NUMERATE	QUALMISH	TUBERCLE	OVERRIDE
ASSEMBLE	STANDOUT	BULLFROG	GUERNSEY	NUMEROUS	QUANDARY	TUBEROSE	OVERRULE
ASSEMBLY	STARFISH	BULLHEAD	GUIDANCE	NUMSKULL	QUANTITY	TUBEROUS	OVERSEAS
ASSORTED	STARLING	BUNDLING	GUMPTION	NURSLING	QUANTIZE	TUNELESS	OVERSHOE
ASTATINE	STATUARY	BUNGALOW	GUNFIGHT	NUTHATCH	QUATRAIN	TUNGSTEN	OVERSIZE
ASTERISK	STEALTHY	BUNGHOLE	GUNPOINT	NUTRIENT	QUESTION	TUNISIAN	OVERSTAY
ASTEROID	STEERAGE	BUOYANCY	GUNSMITH	NUTSHELL	QUIETUDE	TURBOFAN	OVERSTEP
ASTONISH	STERLING	BURGLARY	GUTTURAL	OUTBOARD	QUISLING	TURBOJET	OVERTAKE
ESCALATE	STICKLER	BURGUNDY	GUYANESE	OUTBOUND	QUIXOTIC	TURMERIC	OVERTIME
ESCALLOP	STILETTO	BURNOOSE	HUARACHE	OUTBREAK	QUOTABLE	TURNCOAT	OVERTONE
ESCAPADE	STIMULUS	BURSITIS	HUCKSTER	OUTBURST	QUOTIENT	TURNOVER	OVERTURE
ESCAPISM	STINKBUG	BUSINESS	HUGUENOT	OUTCLASS	RUBICUND	TURNPIKE	OVERTURN
ESCAROLE	STIRRING	BUSYBODY	HUMANISM	OUTDATED	RUBIDIUM	TURNSPIT	OVERVIEW
ESOTERIC	STOCKADE	BUSYWORK	HUMANITY	OUTDOORS	RUDIMENT	TUTELAGE	DWELLING
ESPALIER	STOCKING	BUTTRESS	HUMANIZE	OUTFIELD	RUMANIAN	TUTELARY	SWASTIKA
ESPECIAL	STOPPAGE	CUCUMBER	HUMANOID	OUTFIGHT	RUMBLING	TUTORIAL	SWAYBACK
ESPOUSAL	STOTINKA	CULINARY	HUMIDIFY	OUTFLANK	RUMINANT	UUDECODE	SWEEPING
ESPRESSO	STOWAWAY	CULPABLE	HUMIDITY	OUTGOING	RUMINATE	UUENCODE	SWELLING
ESTIMATE	STRADDLE	CUPBOARD	HUMILITY	OUTGUESS	RUNABOUT	YUGOSLAV	SWIMMING
ESTONIAN	STRAGGLE	CUPIDITY	HUMPBACK	OUTHOUSE	RUNAGATE	YULETIDE	TWEEZERS
ESTRANGE	STRAIGHT	CURATIVE	HUNTRESS	OUTLYING	RUTABAGA	ZUCCHINI	TWILIGHT
ESTROGEN	STRAITEN	CURLICUE	HUNTSMAN	OUTMODED	RUTHLESS	AVERMENT	TWOPENCE
ISLANDER	STRANGER	CURRENCY	HUSTINGS	OUTPOINT	SUBMERGE	AVERSION	TWOPENNY
ISOPRENE	STRANGLE	CUSPIDOR	JUBILANT	OUTREACH	SUBMERSE	AVIATION	ZWIEBACK
ISOSTASY	STRATEGY	CUSTOMER	JUDGMENT	OUTRIDER	SUBPOENA	AVIATRIX	AXLETREE
ISOTHERM	STRATIFY	DUCKBILL	JUDICIAL	OUTRIGHT	SUBSONIC	AVIONICS	EXACTING
ISOTONIC	STREAMER	DUCKLING	JUNCTION	OUTSHINE	SUBTITLE	EVACUATE	EXCAVATE
ISSUANCE	STRENGTH	DULCIMER	JUNCTURE	OUTSIDER	SUBTRACT	EVALUATE	EXCHANGE
ISTHMIAN	STRICKEN	DUMBBELL	JURISTIC	OUTSMART	SUBURBIA	EVENSONG	EXCURSUS
OSCULATE	STRIDENT	DUMPLING	JUVENILE	OUTSPEND	SUCCINCT	EVENTIDE	EXECRATE
PSALMODY	STRIKING	DUNGAREE	LUKEWARM	OUTSTRIP	SUCHLIKE	EVENTUAL	EXECUTOR
USUFRUCT	STRINGED	DUNGHILL	LUMINARY	OUTWEIGH	SUCKLING	EVERMORE	EXEGESIS
USURIOUS	STRINGER	DUODENUM	LUMINOUS	PUBLICAN	SUFFRAGE	EVERYDAY	EXEMPLAR
ATHLETIC	STRUGGLE	DURATION	LUNCHEON	PUDDLING	SUITABLE	EVERYONE	EXERCISE
ATOMIZER	STRUMPET	DUTIABLE	LUSCIOUS	PUDENDUM	SUITCASE	EVIDENCE	EXIGENCY
ATROCITY	STUBBORN	EUGENICS	LUTETIUM	PUFFBALL	SUKIYAKI	EXIGUOUS	EXIGUOUS
ATROPINE	STUDBOOK	EUPHORIA	LUTHERAN	PUGILISM	SULFURIC	OVENBIRD	EXORCISE
ATTITUDE	STUDDING	EURASIAN	MUCILAGE	PULLBACK	SUNDRIES	OVERALLS	EXORDIUM
ATTORNEY	STUDIOUS	EUROBOND	MUDGUARD	PULLOVER	SUNLIGHT	OVERCAST	EXPEDITE
ATYPICAL	STUFFING	EUROPEAN	MUENSTER	PULMOTOR	SUNSHADE	OVERCOAT	EXPLICIT
ETERNITY	STULTIFY	EUROPIUM	MULBERRY	PULPWOOD	SUNSHINE	OVERCOME	EXPLODED
ETHEREAL	STUNNING	FUGITIVE	MULETEER	PUNCHEON	SUPEREGO	OVERDRAW	EXPONENT
ETHERNET	STURGEON	FULLBACK	MULTIPLE	PUNCTUAL	SUPERIOR	OVERFLOW	EXPOSURE
ETHOLOGY	AUDIENCE	FUMAROLE	MULTIPLY	PUNCTURE	SUPERJET	OVERGROW	EXTERIOR
ETIOLOGY	AUDITION	FUMIGANT	MUNITION	PUNITIVE	SUPERNAL	OVERHAND	EXTERNAL
ETRUSCAN	AUDITORY	FUMIGATE	MUSCATEL	PURBLIND	SUPPLANT	OVERHANG	EXTRADOS
PTOMAINE	AUSTRIAN	FUNCTION	MUSHROOM	PURCHASE	SUPPOSED	OVERHAUL	UXORIOUS
STACCATO	AUTOBAHN	FUNERARY	MUSICALE	PUREBRED	SUPPRESS	OVERHEAD	CYCLAMEN

CYLINDER	ANALYSIS	DIALYSIS	GRANDSON	PLAYSUIT	STAGNATE	AMBULANT	SYBARITE
CYNOSURE	ANATHEMA	DIAMETER	GRANULAR	PRACTICE	STAIRWAY	ARBALEST	TABULATE
CYTOLOGY	ARACHNID	DIANTHUS	GRAPHITE	PRATFALL	STAKEOUT	ARBOREAL	TOBOGGAN
CYTOSINE	BEANBALL	DIAPASON	GRASPING	PRATIQUE	STALLION	ASBESTOS	TUBERCLE
DYESTUFF	BEARSKIN	DIARRHEA	GRATEFUL	PSALMODY	STALWART	BABUSHKA	TUBEROSE
DYNAMITE	BEATIFIC	DIASTOLE	GRATUITY	QUADRANT	STAMPEDE	BIBULOUS	TUBEROUS
DYSLEXIA	BEAUTIFY	DIATOMIC	GRAVAMEN	QUADROON	STANDARD	BOBOLINK	UMBRELLA
EYEGLASS	BIANNUAL	DIATRIBE	GRAYLING	QUAGMIRE	STANDING	BOBWHITE	UNBEATEN
EYELINER	BIATHLON	DRAGOMAN	GUARANTY	QUALMISH	STANDOFF	CABOCHON	UNBELIEF
EYEPIECE	BLACKING	DRAINAGE	GUARDIAN	QUANDARY	STANDOUT	CABSTAND	UNBIASED
EYESIGHT	BLACKOUT	DRAUGHTS	HEADACHE	QUANTITY	STARFISH	DEBILITY	UNBIDDEN
EYETOOTH	BLACKTOP	DRAWBACK	HEADBAND	QUANTIZE	STARLING	DEBONAIR	UNBODIED
GYMKHANA	BOASTFUL	EMACIATE	HEADGEAR	QUATRAIN	STATUARY	EMBATTLE	UNBOLTED
HYACINTH	BRACELET	EVACUATE	HEADLAND	REACTANT	SWASTIKA	EMBEZZLE	UNBROKEN
HYDROGEN	BRACKISH	EVALUATE	HEADLINE	REACTION	SWAYBACK	EMBITTER	UNBUCKLE
HYMENEAL	BRAGGART	EXACTING	HEADLOCK	REACTIVE	TEACHING	EMBLAZON	UNBURDEN
HYPNOSIS	BRAKEMAN	FEARLESS	HEADLONG	REARWARD	TEAMSTER	EMBOLDEN	UNBUTTON
HYPNOTIC	BRANDISH	FEARSOME	HEADREST	REASSURE	TEAMWORK	EMBOLISM	URBANITE
HYSTERIA	CHAIRMAN	FEASIBLE	HEADROOM	RHAPSODY	TEASPOON	FABULOUS	URBANIZE
LYMPHOID	CHAMBRAY	FLAGPOLE	HEADSHIP	ROADSIDE	THALAMUS	FEBRUARY	VIBURNUM
MYCOLOGY	CHAMPION	FLAGRANT	HEADSMAN	ROADSTER	THALLIUM	FIBROSIS	ACCIDENT
MYELITIS	CHANCERY	FLAGSHIP	HEADWORD	ROADWORK	THANKFUL	HABANERA	ACCOLADE
MYRMIDON	CHANDLER	FLAMBEAU	HEADWORK	SCABBARD	TRACKAGE	HABITANT	ACCOUTRE
MYSTICAL	CHANUKAH	FLAMENCO	HEAVYSET	SCABROUS	TRACTATE	HABITUAL	ACCREDIT
MYSTIQUE	CHAPBOOK	FLAMEOUT	HOARDING	SCAFFOLD	TRACTION	HEBRAISM	ACCURATE
PYORRHEA	CHAPERON	FLAMINGO	HUARACHE	SCALABLE	TRAINING	HIBISCUS	ACCURSED
SYBARITE	CHAPLAIN	FLAPJACK	HYACINTH	SCALAWAG	TRAINMAN	IMBECILE	ACCUSTOM
SYCAMORE	CHARADES	FLASHGUN	KNAPSACK	SCALEPAN	TRANQUIL	JUBILANT	ANCESTOR
SYLLABLE	CHARCOAL	FLASHING	LEAPFROG	SCALLION	TRANSACT	KIBITZER	ANCESTRY
SYLLABUS	CHARISMA	FLATBOAT	LEARNING	SCANDIUM	TRANSEPT	LABURNUM	ARCHDUKE
SYMBOLIC	CHARMING	FLATFISH	LEAVINGS	SCAPULAR	TRANSFER	LIBATION	BACCARAT
SYMMETRY	CHASTISE	FLATFOOT	LOANWORD	SCARCELY	TRANSFIX	LIBERATE	BACHELOR
SYMPATHY	CHASTITY	FLATHEAD	LOATHING	SCATHING	TRANSMIT	LIBRETTO	BACILLUS
SYMPHONY	CHASUBLE	FLATIRON	MEALTIME	SCAVENGE	TRAPDOOR	LOBOTOMY	BACKACHE
SYNDROME	CLAIMANT	FLATLAND	MEALYBUG	SEABOARD	TRAPPING	MOBILIZE	BACKBITE
SYNOPSIS	CLAMBAKE	FLATTERY	MEANTIME	SEACOAST	TRAPROCK	NEBULIZE	BACKBONE
SYNOPTIC	CLAPTRAP	FLATWARE	MEATBALL	SEAFARER	TRAVERSE	NEBULOUS	BACKDROP
SYPHILIS	CLARINET	FLAUTIST	ORANGERY	SEAGOING	TRAVESTY	NOBELIST	BACKFIRE
SYSADMIN	CLASSIFY	FRACTION	ORATORIO	SEALSKIN	UNAWARES	NOBELIUM	BACKHAND
SYSTEMIC	CLAVICLE	FRACTURE	PHANTASM	SEAMOUNT	VIATICUM	NOBILITY	BACKLASH
TYMPANUM	CLAYMORE	FRAGMENT	PHANTASY	SEAPLANE	WEAKFISH	NOBLEMAN	BACKPACK
TYPECAST	COACHMAN	FRAGRANT	PHARISEE	SEASCAPE	WEAKLING	PUBLICAN	BACKREST
TYPEFACE	COAGULUM	FRANCIUM	PHARMACY	SEASHORE	WEAKNESS	REBUTTAL	BACKSIDE
	COALESCE	GHANAIAN	PHASEOUT	SEAWATER	WEAPONRY	RIBOSOME	BACKSLAP
	COAUTHOR	GLABROUS	PLACENTA	SHAMBLES	WHARFAGE	RUBICUND	BACKSPIN
	CRACKPOT	GLACIATE	PLANGENT	SHAMROCK	WHATEVER	RUBIDIUM	BACKSTOP
3RD LETTER	CRAWFISH	GLADSOME	PLANKING	SHANGHAI	WRAPPING	SABOTAGE	BACKWARD
	CRAYFISH	GLASSFUL	PLANKTON	SHANTUNG	WRATHFUL	SABOTEUR	BACKWASH
ABATTOIR	DEADBEAT	GLAUCOMA	PLANTAIN	SLATTERN	YEARBOOK	SIBILANT	BECHUANA
ACADEMIC	DEADLINE	GOALPOST	PLATFORM	SMALLPOX	YEARLING	SOBRIETY	BECOMING
ACANTHUS	DEADLOCK	GOATHERD	PLATINUM	SNAPSHOT	YEARLONG	SUBMERGE	BICONVEX
ALACRITY	DEADWOOD	GOATSKIN	PLATYPUS	SPACEMAN	YEARNING	SUBMERSE	BICUSPID
ALARMIST	DEATHBED	GRACIOUS	PLAYBACK	SPACIOUS	ALBACORE	SUBPOENA	BUCKSHOT
AMARANTH	DIABETES	GRADIENT	PLAYBILL	SPANIARD	ALBANIAN	SUBSONIC	BUCKSKIN
ANACONDA	DIABOLIC	GRADUATE	PLAYBOOK	SPANKING	AMBIENCE	SUBTITLE	CICATRIX
ANAEROBE	DIAGONAL	GRAFFITO	PLAYGOER	STACCATO	AMBITION	SUBTRACT	CICERONE
ANALOGUE	DIALOGUE	GRANDEUR	PLAYMATE	STAGNANT	AMBROSIA	SUBURBIA	COCKATOO

COCKCROW	INCUMBER	RECREATE	FEDERATE	PODIATRY	BIENNIUM	EVENTIDE	OLEANDER
COCKEREL	JACKBOOT	RICOCHET	FIDELITY	PUDDLING	BLESSING	EVENTUAL	OPENWORK
COCKSURE	JACQUARD	ROCKETRY	GADABOUT	PUDENDUM	BREAKAGE	EVERMORE	OPERABLE
COCKTAIL	KICKBACK	ROCKFALL	GODCHILD	RADIATOR	BREAKOUT	EVERYDAY	OPERANDS
CUCUMBER	KICKSHAW	SACRISTY	HEDGEHOG	RADIOMAN	BREEDING	EVERYONE	OPERETTA
CYCLAMEN	LACERATE	SECURITY	HEDGEHOP	REDOLENT	BRETHREN	EXECRATE	OVENBIRD
DECANTER	LACEWING	SICKNESS	HEDGEROW	RIDICULE	BREVIARY	EXECUTOR	OVERALLS
DECEDENT	LACRIMAL	SOCIABLE	HEDONISM	RUDIMENT	CHECKERS	EXEGESIS	OVERCAST
DECEMBER	LACROSSE	SUCCINCT	HIDEAWAY	SADDUCEE	CHECKOFF	EXEMPLAR	OVERCOAT
DECIGRAM	LECITHIN	SUCHLIKE	HYDROGEN	SEDATIVE	CHECKOUT	EXERCISE	OVERCOME
DECIMATE	LICENSEE	SUCKLING	INDEBTED	SEDIMENT	CHECKSUM	EYEGLASS	OVERDRAW
DECIPHER	LICORICE	SYCAMORE	INDECENT	SEDITION	CHEERFUL	EYELINER	OVERFLOW
DECISION	LOCALITY	TACITURN	INDIAMAN	SEDULOUS	CHEMICAL	EYEPIECE	OVERGROW
DECISIVE	LOCALIZE	TICKLISH	INDICATE	SIDEKICK	CHEMURGY	EYESIGHT	OVERHAND
DECKHAND	LOCATION	ULCERATE	INDIGENT	SIDELONG	CHENILLE	EYETOOTH	OVERHANG
DECORATE	LOCKSTEP	UNCHASTE	INDIRECT	SIDEREAL	CHEROKEE	FEEDBACK	OVERHAUL
DECOROUS	LOCOWEED	UNCHURCH	INDOLENT	SIDERITE	CHESTNUT	FLEABANE	OVERHEAD
DECREASE	LOCUTION	UNCLENCH	INDUCTEE	SIDESHOW	CHEYENNE	FLEABITE	OVERHEAR
DECREPIT	MACARONI	UNCLOTHE	INDURATE	SIDESTEP	CLEARING	FLEETING	OVERKILL
DICTATOR	MACAROON	UNCOMMON	INDUSTRY	SIDEWALK	CLEAVAGE	FLESHPOT	OVERLAID
DOCKHAND	MACERATE	UNCOUPLE	JUDGMENT	SIDEWALL	CLEMATIS	FLEXIBLE	OVERLAND
DOCKYARD	MACHISMO	UNCTUOUS	JUDICIAL	SIDEWAYS	CLEMENCY	FREEBORN	OVERLEAP
DOCTRINE	MACKEREL	UPCOMING	LADYBIRD	TIDELAND	CLERICAL	FREEDMAN	OVERLOOK
DOCUMENT	MACKINAW	VACATION	LADYLIKE	UNDERACT	CREAMERY	FREEHAND	OVERLORD
DUCKBILL	MACPAINT	VACCINIA	LADYLOVE	UNDERAGE	CREATION	FREEHOLD	OVERMUCH
DUCKLING	MECHANIC	VICARAGE	LADYSHIP	UNDERARM	CREATURE	FREELOAD	OVERPASS
ENCEINTE	MICROBUS	VICINAGE	LODESTAR	UNDERBID	CREDENCE	FREEWILL	OVERPLAY
ENCIPHER	MOCCASIN	VICINITY	LODGMENT	UNDERCUT	CREDENZA	FRENETIC	OVERRIDE
ENCIRCLE	MUCILAGE	VICTORIA	MADHOUSE	UNDERDOG	CREDIBLE	FREQUENT	OVERRULE
ENCOMIUM	MYCOLOGY	VOCALIST	MADRIGAL	UNDERFUR	CREDITOR	FRESHMAN	OVERSEAS
ENCROACH	NECKLACE	VOCALIZE	MEDALIST	UNDERLIE	CREEPING	FRETWORK	OVERSHOE
ENCUMBER	NECKLINE	VOCATION	MEDICAID	UNDERLIP	CREMAINS	GREEKING	OVERSIZE
ESCALATE	NECROSIS	VOCATIVE	MEDICARE	UNDERPAY	CREOSOTE	GREENERY	OVERSTAY
ESCALLOP	NICKNAME	YACHTING	MEDICATE	UNDERSEA	CRESCENT	GREETING	OVERSTEP
ESCAPADE	NICOTINE	ZUCCHINI	MEDICINE	UNDERTOW	CRETONNE	GUERNSEY	OVERTAKE
ESCAPISM	NOCTURNE	ABDICATE	MEDIEVAL	UNDULANT	CREVASSE	ICEBOUND	OVERTIME
ESCAROLE	NUCLEATE	ADDENDUM	MEDIOCRE	UNDULATE	DEERSKIN	ICEHOUSE	OVERTONE
EXCAVATE	OCCASION	ADDITION	MEDITATE	UUDECODE	DIELDRIN	IDEALISM	OVERTURE
EXCHANGE	OCCUPANT	ADDITIVE	MIDDLING	ABEYANCE	DREADFUL	IDEALIZE	OVERTURN
EXCURSUS	ONCOMING	ALDERMAN	MIDNIGHT	ACERBATE	DRESSAGE	IDEATION	OVERVIEW
FACEDOWN	OSCULATE	ANDROGEN	MIDPOINT	ACERBITY	DRESSING	IDENTIFY	PEEPHOLE
FACILITY	PACIFIER	AUDIENCE	MIDSHIPS	ADEQUATE	DWELLING	IDENTITY	PEERLESS
FACTIOUS	PACIFISM	AUDITION	MODERATE	AGERATUM	DYESTUFF	IDEOGRAM	PHEASANT
FACTOTUM	PECTORAL	AUDITORY	MODULATE	ALEATORY	ELECTION	IDEOLOGY	PHENOLIC
FECKLESS	PECULATE	BADINAGE	MUDGUARD	ALEHOUSE	ELECTIVE	INEDITED	PIEPLANT
HACIENDA	PECULIAR	BEDAZZLE	OBDURATE	AMENABLE	ELECTRIC	INERRANT	PLEASANT
HACKWORD	PICAYUNE	BEDSTEAD	ORDINARY	AMERICAN	ELECTRON	INEXPERT	PLEASING
HECATOMB	PICKEREL	BIDDABLE	ORDINATE	AMETHYST	ELEGANCE	KEELBOAT	PLEASURE
HUCKSTER	PICKINGS	BODILESS	ORDNANCE	ANECDOTE	ELEPHANT	KEELHAUL	PLEBEIAN
INCHOATE	PICKLOCK	BODYWORK	PEDAGOGY	ANECHOIC	ELEVATOR	KEEPSAKE	PLECTRUM
INCHWORM	POCKMARK	BUDDHISM	PEDERAST	APERITIF	EMERITUS	KIELBASA	PLETHORA
INCIDENT	RECEIVER	CADUCEUS	PEDESTAL	APERTURE	ENERGIZE	KNEEHOLE	PLEURISY
INCISION	RECEPTOR	DEDICATE	PEDICURE	AVERMENT	ENERVATE	MNEMONIC	PREAMBLE
INCISIVE	RECKLESS	DIDACTIC	PEDIGREE	AVERSION	ERECTILE	MUENSTER	PRECINCT
INCOMING	RECORDER	ENDANGER	PEDIMENT	BAEDEKER	ERECTION	MYELITIS	PRECIOUS
INCREASE	RECOURSE	ENDEAVOR	PEDUNCLE	BEECHNUT	ETERNITY	NEEDLESS	PRECLUDE
INCUBATE	RECREANT	FADELESS	PIDDLING	BIENNIAL	EVENSONG	OBEDIENT	PREEXIST

PREGNANT	WHENEVER	SOFTBALL	LIGATURE	BOHEMIAN	CRIMINAL	PRIMROSE	THICKSET
PREJUDGE	WHEREVER	SOFTWARE	LIGNEOUS	COHERENT	CRITICAL	PRINCESS	THIEVERY
PREMIERE	WRECKAGE	SOFTWOOD	LOGOTYPE	COHESION	CRITIQUE	PRINTING	THIRTEEN
PREMOLAR	WRETCHED	SUFFRAGE	MAGAZINE	ETHEREAL	DAIQUIRI	PRINTOUT	TOILETRY
PRENATAL	YIELDING	TAFFRAIL	MAGDALEN	ETHERNET	DAIRYING	PRISONER	TOILETTE
PREPRESS	AFFECTED	UNFASTEN	MAGICIAN	ETHOLOGY	DAIRYMAN	PRISTINE	TOILWORN
PRESENCE	AFFERENT	UNFETTER	MAGNESIA	INHALANT	DEIONIZE	QUIETUDE	TRIANGLE
PRESERVE	AFFIANCE	UNFILIAL	MAGNETIC	INHERENT	DRIVEWAY	QUISLING	TRIBUNAL
PRESIDIO	AFFINITY	UNFORMED	MAGNOLIA	INHUMANE	EKISTICS	QUIXOTIC	TRICHINA
PRESSING	AFFLATUS	UNFREEZE	MEGABYTE	KOHLRABI	ELIGIBLE	RAILLERY	TRICKERY
PRESSMAN	AFFRIGHT	AGGRIEVE	MEGALITH	MAHARAJA	EMIGRATE	RAILROAD	TRICOLOR
PRESSURE	ALFRESCO	AIGRETTE	MIGRAINE	MAHARANI	EMINENCE	RAINCOAT	TRICYCLE
PRESTIGE	BEFRIEND	ALGERIAN	NEGATION	MAHOGANY	EMISSARY	RAINDROP	TRIFLING
PRETENSE	BEFUDDLE	ANGELICA	NEGATIVE	NIHILISM	EPIDEMIC	RAINFALL	TRILLION
PRETERIT	BIFOCALS	ANGLICAN	NEGLIGEE	REHEARSE	EPILEPSY	REINDEER	TRILLIUM
PRETTIFY	CAFFEINE	ANGSTROM	NIGERIAN	SCHEDULE	EPILOGUE	SAILBOAT	TRIMARAN
PREVIOUS	DAFFODIL	ARGUABLE	NIGEROIS	SCHMALTZ	EPIPHANY	SAILFISH	TRIMETER
QUESTION	DEFECATE	ARGUMENT	NIGGLING	SCHOONER	ETIOLOGY	SCIATICA	TRIMMING
RHEOLOGY	DEFIANCE	BAGUETTE	NUGATORY	SPHAGNUM	EVIDENCE	SCILICET	TRIPTYCH
RHEOSTAT	DEFINITE	BEGGARLY	ORGANISM	SPHEROID	EXIGENCY	SCIMITAR	TRIUMVIR
RHETORIC	DEFLOWER	BEGRUDGE	ORGANIST	TAHITIAN	EXIGUOUS	SCISSORS	TWILIGHT
SCENARIO	DEFOREST	BOGEYMAN	ORGANIZE	UPHEAVAL	FLIMFLAM	SEIGNEUR	UNIAXIAL
SEEDLING	EFFERENT	CAGELING	ORGULOUS	VEHEMENT	FLIPPANT	SHILINGI	UNICYCLE
SEEDTIME	EFFUSION	COGITATE	PAGINATE	ACIDHEAD	FRICTION	SHILLING	UNIONISM
SHEEPISH	ENFEEBLE	COGNOMEN	PUGILISM	ACIDOSIS	FRIGHTEN	SHINBONE	UNIONIZE
SHEETING	ENFILADE	COGWHEEL	REGICIDE	AGITPROP	FRIPPERY	SHINGLES	UNIVALVE
SHELVING	INFAMOUS	DOGFIGHT	REGIMENT	ALIASING	GRIDIRON	SHIPMATE	UNIVERSE
SHEPHERD	INFANTRY	DOGGEREL	REGIONAL	ALIENATE	GRIEVOUS	SHIPMENT	WAINSCOT
SKELETON	INFERIOR	DOGHOUSE	REGISTER	ALIENIST	GRIZZLED	SHIPPING	WAITRESS
SPECIFIC	INFERNAL	EDGEWAYS	REGISTRY	ALIZARIN	GUIDANCE	SHIPWORM	WHIPCORD
SPECIMEN	INFINITE	EGGPLANT	REGOLITH	AMICABLE	HAIRLINE	SHIPYARD	WHIPLASH
SPECIOUS	INFINITY	EGGSHELL	REGULATE	ANISETTE	HEIGHTEN	SHIRRING	WHITECAP
SPECTRAL	INFOBAHN	EIGHTEEN	RIGHTFUL	AVIATION	HEIRLOOM	SHIRTING	WHITEFLY
SPECTRUM	INFORMAL	ENGAGING	SAGAMORE	AVIATRIX	IMITABLE	SKILLFUL	WRIGGLER
SPEEDWAY	INFORMED	ENGENDER	SIGNPOST	AVIONICS	INIMICAL	SKIMMING	WRISTLET
STEALTHY	INFORMER	ENGINEER	TIGHTWAD	BAILABLE	INIQUITY	SKIRMISH	ZWIEBACK
STEERAGE	INFRADIG	EUGENICS	TOGETHER	BAILSMAN	INITIATE	SKITTISH	ADJACENT
STERLING	INFRARED	FAGOTING	UNGAINLY	BLISSFUL	JAILBIRD	SLIPKNOT	ADJUTANT
SWEEPING	INFRINGE	FIGURINE	UNGULATE	BLIZZARD	KNICKERS	SLIPPERY	ADJUVANT
SWELLING	LEFTOVER	FUGITIVE	UPGROWTH	BRICKBAT	KNITWEAR	SLIPSHOD	DEJECTED
TEETHING	LIFEBOAT	GIGABYTE	VAGABOND	BRIGHTEN	MAINLAND	SPILLWAY	MAJOLICA
TEETOTAL	LIFELINE	GIGANTIC	VAGRANCY	BRINDLED	MAINLINE	SPINSTER	MAJORITY
THEOLOGY	LIFELONG	HEGEMONY	VEGANISM	BRISLING	MAINMAST	SPIRITED	ALKALOID
THEORIZE	LIFETIME	HIGHBALL	VEGETATE	BRITCHES	MAINSAIL	SPITBALL	BAKESHOP
THEREFOR	LIFEWORK	HIGHBORN	VIGILANT	BUILDING	MAINSTAY	SPITTOON	CAKEWALK
THESPIAN	OFFICIAL	HIGHBRED	VIGNETTE	CHIPMUNK	MAINTAIN	STICKLER	DEKAGRAM
TREASURE	OFFPRINT	HIGHBROW	VIGOROUS	CHIPPEWA	MOISTURE	STILETTO	INKSTAND
TREASURY	OFFSHOOT	HIGHLAND	YUGOSLAV	CHITCHAT	NAINSOOK	STIMULUS	LIKENESS
TREATISE	OFFSHORE	HIGHNESS	ADHESION	CHIVALRY	NEIGHBOR	STINKBUG	LIKEWISE
TRENCHER	OFFSTAGE	HIGHROAD	ADHESIVE	CLINCHER	NUISANCE	STIRRING	LUKEWARM
TRESPASS	PUFFBALL	HIGHTAIL	APHANITE	CLINICAL	OBITUARY	SUITABLE	POKEWEED
TWEEZERS	REFERENT	HOGSHEAD	APHELION	CLIPPING	ORIENTAL	SUITCASE	SUKIYAKI
UNEARNED	REFERRAL	HUGUENOT	APHORISM	CLITORIS	ORIGINAL	SWIMMING	TOKENISM
UNENDING	REFINERY	INGUINAL	ATHLETIC	COIFFEUR	PAINTING	TAILCOAT	UNKINDLY
UNERRING	REFOREST	LEGALISM	BEHAVIOR	COIFFURE	PEIGNOIR	TAILGATE	ABLATION
UUENCODE	REFORMER	LEGATION	BEHEMOTH	COINCIDE	POIGNANT	TAILSPIN	ABLATIVE
VIETCONG	RIFFRAFF	LIGAMENT	BEHOLDEN	CRIBBAGE	PRIMEVAL	THIAMINE	ABLUTION

AFLUTTER	DELEGATE	KILOVOLT	POLITICK	TELEFILM	COMEDIAN	HOMESPUN	RUMBLING
AGLITTER	DELICACY	KILOWATT	POLITICO	TELEGRAM	COMEDOWN	HOMEWARD	RUMINANT
ALLEGORY	DELICATE	KOLINSKY	POLITICS	TELEPLAY	COMMANDO	HOMEWORK	RUMINATE
ALLELUIA	DELIRIUM	LOLLIPOP	POLLIWOG	TELETHON	COMMENCE	HOMICIDE	SAMARIUM
ALLERGEN	DELIVERY	LOLLYGAG	POLLSTER	TELEVIEW	COMMERCE	HUMANISM	SEMANTIC
ALLEYWAY	DELUSION	MALAMUTE	POLONIUM	TELEVISE	COMMONER	HUMANITY	SEMESTER
ALLIANCE	DILATORY	MALAPERT	POLTROON	TELLTALE	COMMUNAL	HUMANIZE	SEMINARY
ALLOCATE	DILIGENT	MALARKEY	POLYGAMY	TOLERATE	COMPILER	HUMANOID	SEMINOLE
ALLSPICE	DOLDRUMS	MALAWIAN	POLYGLOT	TOLLBOTH	COMPLAIN	HUMIDIFY	SEMISOFT
ALLUVIUM	DOLOMITE	MALINGER	POLYMATH	TOLLGATE	COMPLEAT	HUMIDITY	SIMONIZE
AXLETREE	DULCIMER	MALTREAT	PULLBACK	UNLAWFUL	COMPLETE	HUMILITY	SIMPLIFY
BALLROOM	ECLIPTIC	MALTSTER	PULLOVER	UNLEADED	COMPOUND	HUMPBACK	SIMULATE
BALLYHOO	ELLIPSIS	MELANISM	PULMOTOR	UNLIKELY	COMPRESS	HYMENEAL	SOMBRERO
BALUSTER	FALCHION	MELANOMA	PULPWOOD	UNLIMBER	COMPRISE	IMMANENT	SOMEBODY
BELITTLE	FALLIBLE	MELODEON	RELATION	UNLOOSEN	COMPUTER	IMMATURE	SOMERSET
BILLFOLD	FALSETTO	MILEPOST	RELATIVE	UNLOVELY	DAMNABLE	IMMINENT	SOMETIME
BILLHEAD	FALTBOAT	MILESIMO	RELAXANT	VALIDATE	DEMARCHE	IMMOBILE	SOMEWHAT
BOLDFACE	FELDSPAR	MILITANT	RELEGATE	VALUABLE	DEMEANOR	IMMODEST	SYMBOLIC
BOLLWORM	FELICITY	MILITARY	RELEVANT	VALVULAR	DEMENTED	IMMOLATE	SYMMETRY
BULKHEAD	FELLATIO	MILITATE	RELIABLE	VELLEITY	DEMENTIA	IMMORTAL	SYMPATHY
BULLDOZE	FILAMENT	MILKMAID	RELIANCE	VELOCITY	DEMIBOLD	IMMOTILE	SYMPHONY
BULLETIN	FILIGREE	MILKWEED	RELIGION	VILLAGER	DEMIJOHN	IMMUNIZE	TAMARACK
BULLFROG	FILIPINO	MILLIARD	RELOCATE	VILLAINY	DEMOCRAT	JAMBOREE	TAMARIND
BULLHEAD	FILTRATE	MILLIBAR	ROLLBACK	VOLATILE	DEMOLISH	KAMAAINA	TEMERITY
CALABASH	FOLDAWAY	MILLIEME	SALESMAN	VOLCANIC	DEMONIAC	KAMIKAZE	TEMPLATE
CALADIUM	FOLDBOAT	MILLINER	SALIVATE	VOLITION	DEMURRER	LAMASERY	TEMPORAL
CALAMINE	FOLDEROL	MILLPOND	SALUTARY	VOLPLANE	DIMINISH	LAMBASTE	TIMBERED
CALAMITY	FOLIATED	MILLRACE	SELECTEE	WALKAWAY	DOMESTIC	LAMBSKIN	TIMELESS
CALCULUS	FOLKLORE	MOLASSES	SELENITE	WALKOVER	DOMICILE	LAMPBACK	TIMEWORN
CALENDAR	FOLLICLE	MOLECULE	SELENIUM	WELDMENT	DOMINATE	LEMONADE	TIMOROUS
CALENDER	FULLBACK	MOLEHILL	SELFLESS	WELLBORN	DOMINEER	LIMEKILN	TOMAHAWK
CALFSKIN	GALLUSES	MOLESKIN	SELFSAME	WELLHEAD	DOMINION	LIMERICK	TOMORROW
CALLBACK	GOLDFISH	MULBERRY	SILENCER	WILDFIRE	DUMBBELL	LIMONITE	TYMPANUM
CALLIOPE	HALFBACK	MULETEER	SILICATE	WILDFOWL	DUMPLING	LUMINARY	UNMUZZLE
CELERITY	HALFTONE	MULTIPLE	SILICIFY	WILDLIFE	FAMILIAL	LUMINOUS	WOMANISH
CELIBACY	HALLMARK	MULTIPLY	SILICONE	WILDWOOD	FAMILIAR	LYMPHOID	ABNEGATE
CELIBATE	HELICOID	OBLATION	SOLARIUM	WILLIWAW	FEMININE	MEMBRANE	ABNORMAL
CELLULAR	HELIPORT	OBLIGATE	SOLDIERY	YULETIDE	FEMINISM	MEMORIAL	AGNOSTIC
CHLORIDE	HELLHOLE	OBLIVION	SOLECISM	ADMONISH	FUMAROLE	MEMORIZE	ANNOTATE
CHLORINE	HELMSMAN	OILCLOTH	SOLENOID	ALMIGHTY	FUMIGANT	MOMENTUM	ANNOUNCE
CHLORITE	HELPMATE	ONLOOKER	SOLIDIFY	AMMONIUM	FUMIGATE	NAMELESS	BANDANNA
COLANDER	HELPMEET	PALATINE	SOLITARY	ARMAMENT	GAMECOCK	NAMESAKE	BANISTER
COLESLAW	HILLSIDE	PALEFACE	SOLITUDE	ARMATURE	GAMESOME	NEMATODE	BANKBOOK
COLISEUM	HOLDOVER	PALINODE	SOLSTICE	ARMCHAIR	GAMESTER	NOMINATE	BANKROLL
COLLAPSE	HOLINESS	PALISADE	SOLUTION	ARMORIAL	GEMINATE	NUMERATE	BANKRUPT
COLLIERY	HOLOGRAM	PALLIATE	SOLVENCY	ARMYWORM	GEMOLOGY	NUMEROUS	BANTLING
COLLOQUY	HOLSTEIN	PALMETTO	SPLATTER	CAMELLIA	GEMSTONE	NUMSKULL	BENEDICT
COLONIAL	ILLINOIS	PALOMINO	SPLENDID	CAMISOLE	GIMCRACK	OHMMETER	BENEFICE
COLONIST	ILLUMINE	PALPABLE	SPLENDOR	CAMOMILE	GUMPTION	PAMPHLET	BENTWOOD
COLONIZE	ILLUSION	PELLAGRA	SPLINTER	CAMPAIGN	GYMKHANA	PEMMICAN	BENZOATE
COLOPHON	ILLUSIVE	PELLUCID	SPLUTTER	CAMPOREE	HEMATITE	PIMIENTO	BINAURAL
COLOSSAL	ILLUSORY	PILASTER	SULFURIC	CAMSHAFT	HOMEBODY	REMEDIAL	BINNACLE
COLOSSUS	ISLANDER	PILCHARD	SYLLABLE	CEMENTUM	HOMEBRED	REMEMBER	BONDSMAN
CULINARY	JALOUSIE	PILOTAGE	SYLLABUS	CEMETERY	HOMELAND	REMITTAL	BONHOMIE
CULPABLE	KILLDEER	POLARITY	TALESMAN	COMANCHE	HOMEMADE	ROMANIAN	BUNDLING
CYLINDER	KILOBYTE	POLARIZE	TALISMAN	COMBINGS	HOMEROOM	ROMANTIC	BUNGALOW
DELAWARE	KILOGRAM	POLESTAR	TELECAST	COMEBACK	HOMESICK	RUMANIAN	BUNGHOLE

CANADIAN	DINGBATS	INNOVATE	MINDLESS	PINOCHLE	TUNISIAN	CHOLERIC	GEOMETRY
CANAILLE	DINOSAUR	INNUENDO	MINIBIKE	PINPOINT	VANADIUM	CHOWCHOW	GLOAMING
CANALIZE	DONATION	JINGOISM	MINIMIZE	PINPRICK	VANGUARD	CLOISTER	GLOBULIN
CANISTER	DUNGAREE	JONGLEUR	MINISTER	PINWHEEL	VANQUISH	CLOSEOUT	GLORIOUS
CANNABIS	DUNGHILL	JUNCTION	MINISTRY	PONYTAIL	VENATION	CLOTHIER	GLOSSARY
CANNIBAL	DYNAMITE	JUNCTURE	MINORITY	PUNCHEON	VENDETTA	CLOTHING	GLOWWORM
CANONIZE	FANCIFUL	KANGAROO	MINSTREL	PUNCTUAL	VENERATE	CLOUDLET	GLOXINIA
CANTICLE	FANDANGO	KINDLING	MONARCHY	PUNCTURE	VENEREAL	COOKBOOK	GOODNESS
CENOBITE	FANLIGHT	KINETICS	MONASTIC	PUNITIVE	VENGEFUL	COONSKIN	GOODWIFE
CENOTAPH	FANTASIA	KINGBOLT	MONAURAL	RENEGADE	VENOMOUS	CROCKERY	GOODWILL
CENTERED	FINALIST	LANDFALL	MONETARY	RENOUNCE	VENUSIAN	CROPLAND	GOOFBALL
CENTRIST	FINALIZE	LANDFILL	MONGOOSE	RENOVATE	VINCIBLE	CROSSBAR	GROSBEAK
CINCHONA	FINESPUN	LANDFORM	MONITION	RINGWORM	VINEGARY	CROSSBOW	GROSCHEN
CINCTURE	FUNCTION	LANDLORD	MONITORY	RUNABOUT	VINEYARD	CROSSCUT	GROUNDER
CINNABAR	FUNERARY	LANDMARK	MONOGAMY	RUNAGATE	WINDBURN	CROSSING	HOODWINK
CINNAMON	FUNEREAL	LANDMASS	MONOGRAM	SANCTIFY	WINDFALL	CROTCHET	HOOKWORM
CONCEIVE	GANGLAND	LANDSMAN	MONOLITH	SANCTION	WINDLASS	CROUPIER	HOOLIGAN
CONCERTO	GANGLING	LANDWARD	MONOPOLY	SANCTITY	WINDMILL	CROWFOOT	HOOSEGOW
CONCLAVE	GANGLION	LANGUAGE	MONORAIL	SANDBANK	WINDPIPE	DOOMSDAY	IDOLATER
CONCLUDE	GANGPLOW	LANGUISH	MONOTONE	SANDWICH	WINDWARD	DOORJAMB	IDOLATRY
CONCRETE	GANGRENE	LENGTHEN	MONOXIDE	SANGUINE	WINESHOP	DOORKNOB	IRONCLAD
CONDENSE	GANGSTER	LENITIVE	MONSIEUR	SANITARY	WINGDING	DOORSTEP	IRONWARE
CONFETTI	GENDARME	LINCHPIN	MONUMENT	SANITIZE	WINGSPAN	DOORYARD	IRONWEED
CONFINES	GENERATE	LINESMAN	MUNITION	SANSKRIT	WONDROUS	DROPKICK	IRONWOOD
CONFLICT	GENEROUS	LINGERIE	NINEPINS	SENSIBLE	XENOLITH	DUODENUM	IRONWORK
CONFOCAL	GENETICS	LINGUIST	NINETEEN	SENSUOUS	ABORNING	ECONOMIC	IROQUOIS
CONFOUND	GENITALS	LINIMENT	NONDAIRY	SENTENCE	ABORTION	ELONGATE	ISOPRENE
CONFRERE	GENITIVE	LINOLEUM	NONESUCH	SENTIENT	ACOUSTIC	ELOQUENT	ISOSTASY
CONFRONT	GENOCIDE	LONESOME	NONEVENT	SENTINEL	ADOPTIVE	EMOTICON	ISOTHERM
CONGENER	GINGERLY	LONGBOAT	NONMETAL	SINECURE	ADORABLE	ENORMITY	ISOTONIC
CONGRESS	GONFALON	LONGHAIR	NONRIGID	SINGULAR	ALOPECIA	ENORMOUS	JEOPARDY
CONJUGAL	GUNFIGHT	LONGHAND	NONSENSE	SINISTER	AMOEBOID	ESOTERIC	KNOCKOUT
CONJUNCT	GUNPOINT	LONGHORN	NONSTICK	SINKHOLE	AMORTIZE	EXORCISE	KNOTHOLE
CONQUEST	GUNSMITH	LONGTIME	NONUNION	SONATINA	APOLOGIA	EXORDIUM	LOOPHOLE
CONSERVE	HANDBALL	LONGUEUR	OINTMENT	SONGBIRD	APOPLEXY	FLOTILLA	MOONBEAM
CONSIDER	HANDBILL	LUNCHEON	ORNAMENT	SONGSTER	APOSTASY	FLOUNDER	MOORLAND
CONSOMME	HANDBOOK	MANCIPLE	PANATELA	SONOROUS	APOTHEGM	FLOURISH	NEONATAL
CONSPIRE	HANDCUFF	MANDAMUS	PANCREAS	SUNDRIES	ATOMIZER	FOOLSCAP	NEOPHYTE
CONSTANT	HANDICAP	MANDARIN	PANDEMIC	SUNLIGHT	BIOCIDAL	FOOTBALL	NEOPLASM
CONSTRUE	HANDMADE	MANDIBLE	PANDOWDY	SUNSHADE	BLOCKADE	FOOTFALL	NOONTIDE
CONTEMPT	HANDPICK	MANDOLIN	PANELING	SUNSHINE	BLOOMERS	FOOTHILL	NOONTIME
CONTINUE	HANDRAIL	MANDRAKE	PANELIST	SYNDROME	BLOWPIPE	FOOTHOLD	ODOMETER
CONTRACT	HANDSOME	MANEUVER	PANORAMA	SYNOPSIS	BOOKCASE	FOOTLESS	ONONDAGA
CONTRAIL	HANDYMAN	MANGROVE	PANTHEON	SYNOPTIC	BOOKMARK	FOOTLING	PHOSPHOR
CONTRARY	HANGNAIL	MANIACAL	PANTSUIT	TANGIBLE	BOOKWORM	FOOTNOTE	PROBABLE
CONTRAST	HANGOVER	MANICURE	PENALIZE	TANTALUM	BOOTLESS	FOOTPATH	PROCAINE
CONTRITE	HANUKKAH	MANIFEST	PENCHANT	TENANTRY	BROCCOLI	FOOTRACE	PROCEEDS
CONTRIVE	HENCHMAN	MANIFOLD	PENDULUM	TENDENCY	BROCHURE	FOOTREST	PROCLAIM
CONVERGE	HINDMOST	MANNERED	PENITENT	TENEMENT	BROMIDIC	FOOTSORE	PRODIGAL
CONVERSE	HINDUISM	MANNERLY	PENKNIFE	TENPENNY	BRONCHUS	FOOTSTEP	PROFOUND
CONVINCE	HONEYDEW	MANTELET	PENLIGHT	TENTACLE	BROOKLET	FOOTWEAR	PROGRESS
CONVULSE	HONORARY	MANTILLA	PENOLOGY	TINCTURE	BROUGHAM	FOOTWORK	PROHIBIT
CYNOSURE	HUNTRESS	MANTISSA	PENSTOCK	TINPLATE	BROUHAHA	FRONTAGE	PROLIFIC
DANDRUFF	HUNTSMAN	MANYFOLD	PENTAGON	TINSMITH	BROWBEAT	FRONTIER	PROLOGUE
DANSEUSE	IGNITION	MENHADEN	PENUMBRA	TONALITY	BROWNOUT	FROSTING	PROMOTER
DENATURE	IGNORANT	MENISCUS	PINAFORE	TUNELESS	BUOYANCY	FROUFROU	PROPERTY
DENOUNCE	INNOCENT	MINATORY	PINNACLE	TUNGSTEN	CHOIRBOY	GEODESIC	PROPHECY

PROPHESY	WHOMEVER	EMPLOYEE	SUPERIOR	BARNACLE	CORPORAL	FORELIMB	HOROLOGY
PROPOUND	WHOPPING	EMPORIUM	SUPERJET	BARNYARD	CORPSMAN	FORELOCK	HORRIBLE
PROROGUE	WOODBINE	EMPYREAN	SUPERNAL	BARONAGE	CORRIDOR	FOREMAST	HORSEFLY
PROSPECT	WOODCOCK	ESPALIER	SUPPLANT	BARONESS	CORUNDUM	FOREMOST	HORSEMAN
PROSTATE	WOODLAND	ESPECIAL	SUPPOSED	BAROUCHE	CORVETTE	FORENAME	IRRIGATE
PROTOCOL	WOODNOTE	ESPOUSAL	SUPPRESS	BARRACKS	CURATIVE	FORENOON	IRRITATE
PROTRACT	WOODPILE	ESPRESSO	SYPHILIS	BARRATRY	CURLICUE	FORENSIC	JEREMIAD
PROTRUDE	WOODRUFF	EUPHORIA	TAPESTRY	BARRETTE	CURRENCY	FOREPART	JURISTIC
PROVIDED	WOODSHED	EXPEDITE	TAPEWORM	BERCEUSE	DARKLING	FORESAIL	KERCHIEF
PROVINCE	WOODSMAN	EXPLICIT	TOPOLOGY	BEREAVED	DARKROOM	FORESKIN	KEROSINE
PTOMAINE	WOODWIND	EXPLODED	TOPSIDES	BERIBERI	DARKSOME	FORESTRY	LARBOARD
PYORRHEA	WOODWORK	EXPONENT	TYPECAST	BERMUDAS	DERELICT	FORETELL	LARKSPUR
QUOTABLE	WOOLSACK	EXPOSURE	TYPEFACE	BIRACIAL	DEROGATE	FOREWARN	LORDSHIP
QUOTIENT	WRONGFUL	HEPATICA	UNPERSON	BIRDBATH	DERRIERE	FOREWORD	MARATHON
RHOMBOID	YEOMANRY	HYPNOSIS	UPPERCUT	BIRDLIME	DIRECTOR	FORKLIFT	MARBLING
ROOFTREE	ZOOPHYTE	HYPNOTIC	VAPORING	BIRDSEED	DORMOUSE	FORMERLY	MARGRAVE
ROOMETTE	ZOOSPORE	IMPACTED	VAPORISH	BIRTHDAY	DURATION	FORMLESS	MARIACHI
ROOMMATE	ALPHABET	IMPELLER	VAPORIZE	BORDELLO	EARNINGS	FORSOOTH	MARIGOLD
SCOFFLAW	AMPERAGE	IMPERIAL	VAPOROUS	BURGLARY	EARPHONE	FORSWEAR	MARINATE
SCORPION	AMPUTATE	IMPETIGO	ZEPPELIN	BURGUNDY	ETRUSCAN	FORTRESS	MARITIME
SCOTTISH	APPANAGE	IMPLICIT	ACQUAINT	BURNOOSE	EURASIAN	FORTUITY	MARJORAM
SHOCKING	APPARENT	IMPOLITE	BEQUEATH	BURSITIS	EUROBOND	FORWARDS	MARKDOWN
SHOELACE	APPELLEE	IMPOSING	COQUETTE	CARACOLE	EUROPEAN	FURBELOW	MARKSMAN
SHOPLIFT	APPENDIX	IMPOSTOR	SEQUENCE	CARAPACE	EUROPIUM	FURLOUGH	MARMOSET
SHOPWORN	APPETITE	IMPOTENT	AARDVARK	CARDAMOM	FAREWELL	FURTHEST	MARQUESS
SHORTAGE	APPLAUSE	IMPRISON	ABRASIVE	CARDIGAN	FARMHAND	GARDENIA	MARQUISE
SHORTCUT	APPLIQUE	IMPROPER	ABROGATE	CARDINAL	FARMLAND	GARGOYLE	MARRIAGE
SHOSHONE	APPOSITE	IMPUDENT	ACRIMONY	CAREFREE	FARMYARD	GARRISON	MARTINET
SHOULDER	APPRAISE	IMPUNITY	ACROSTIC	CARELESS	FAROUCHE	GERANIUM	MARZIPAN
SHOWCASE	APPROACH	JAPANESE	AEROLOGY	CAREWORN	FARTHEST	GERMINAL	MERCHANT
SHOWDOWN	APPROVAL	LAPBOARD	AERONAUT	CARILLON	FARTHING	GORGEOUS	MERCURIC
SLOVENLY	ARPEGGIO	LAPIDARY	AGRARIAN	CARNAUBA	FEROCITY	HARANGUE	MERIDIAN
SNOBBERY	ASPERITY	LIPSTICK	AGRONOMY	CARNIVAL	FERVENCY	HARDBACK	MERINGUE
SNOWBALL	ASPHODEL	LOPSIDED	AIRBORNE	CAROTENE	FIREBALL	HARDBALL	MORALIST
SNOWBANK	ASPHYXIA	MEPHITIC	AIRBRUSH	CAROUSAL	FIREBOAT	HARDHACK	MORALITY
SNOWDROP	ASPIRANT	NAPOLEON	AIRCRAFT	CAROUSEL	FIREBOMB	HARDSHIP	MORALIZE
SNOWFALL	ASPIRATE	NEPENTHE	AIRDROME	CARRIAGE	FIRECLAY	HARDTACK	MOREOVER
SNOWPLOW	CAPACITY	NEPOTISM	AIRFIELD	CARRYALL	FIREDAMP	HARDWARE	MORIBUND
SNOWSHOE	CAPESKIN	OPPONENT	AIRFRAME	CARYATID	FIREPLUG	HARDWOOD	MOROCCAN
SPOOLING	CAPRIOLE	OPPOSITE	AIRLINER	CERAMIST	FIRESIDE	HAREBELL	MORPHEME
SPORADIC	CAPSICUM	PIPELINE	AIRPLANE	CEREBRUM	FIRETRAP	HARMONIC	MORPHINE
STOCKADE	CAPSULAR	POPINJAY	AIRSPACE	CEREMENT	FIREWOOD	HARRIDAN	MORTGAGE
STOCKING	CAPTIOUS	POPULACE	AIRSPEED	CEREMONY	FIREWORK	HERALDIC	MORTUARY
STOPPAGE	CAPUCHIN	POPULATE	AIRSTRIP	CERULEAN	FIRMWARE	HERALDRY	MYRMIDON
STOTINKA	CEPHALIC	POPULIST	AIRTIGHT	CERVICAL	FORCIBLE	HERCULES	NARCOSIS
STOWAWAY	COPPERAS	POPULOUS	ARROGANT	CHRISTEN	FOREBEAR	HERDSMAN	NARCOTIC
TEOSINTE	COPULATE	REPARTEE	ARROGATE	CHRISTIE	FOREBODE	HEREDITY	NORSEMAN
THOROUGH	COPYBOOK	REPEATED	ATROCITY	CHROMIUM	FORECAST	HEREFORD	NURSLING
THOUSAND	COPYDESK	REPORTER	ATROPINE	CIRCUITY	FOREDOOM	HEREUNTO	PARABOLA
TROMBONE	CUPBOARD	REPRIEVE	BARBARIC	CIRCULAR	FOREFEND	HEREUPON	PARADIGM
TROUSERS	CUPIDITY	REPRISAL	BARBECUE	CORDLESS	FOREFOOT	HEREWITH	PARADISE
TWOPENCE	DEPONENT	REPROACH	BARBERRY	CORDOVAN	FOREGONE	HERITAGE	PARAFFIN
TWOPENNY	DEPUTIZE	REPUBLIC	BARBICAN	CORDUROY	FOREHAND	HERMETIC	PARAKEET
UXORIOUS	DIPLOMAT	RIPARIAN	BARBITAL	CORNCRIB	FOREHEAD	HIRELING	PARALLAX
VIOLABLE	DIPSTICK	SAPPHIRE	BAREBACK	CORNMEAL	FOREKNOW	HORMONAL	PARALLEL
VIOLENCE	EMPHASIS	SEPARATE	BAREFOOT	CORONACH	FORELADY	HORNBOOK	PARALYZE
WHODUNIT	EMPHATIC	SUPEREGO	BARITONE	CORONARY	FORELAND	HORNPIPE	PARAMOUR

PARANOIA	STRAIGHT	VERBATIM	BESTIARY	DISPLACE	LUSCIOUS	PASTICHE	UPSTROKE
PARASITE	STRAITEN	VERBIAGE	BESTRIDE	DISPOSAL	MASSACRE	PASTILLE	VASCULAR
PARDONER	STRANGER	VERBOTEN	BISEXUAL	DISPROVE	MASSEUSE	PASTORAL	VESICANT
PARFOCAL	STRANGLE	VERMOUTH	BUSINESS	DISQUIET	MASSLESS	PASTRAMI	VESTMENT
PARIETAL	STRATEGY	VERONICA	BUSYBODY	DISSEVER	MASTERLY	POSITION	VISCERAL
PARLANCE	STRATIFY	VERSICLE	BUSYWORK	DISSOLVE	MASTHEAD	POSITIVE	VISCOUNT
PARMESAN	STREAMER	VERTEBRA	CASEMENT	DISSUADE	MASTODON	POSITRON	VISICALC
PAROXYSM	STRENGTH	VERTICAL	CASEWORK	DISTANCE	MESDAMES	POSSIBLE	VISITANT
PARTERRE	STRICKEN	VIRGINAL	CASHMERE	DISTASTE	MESHWORK	POSTCARD	WASHABLE
PARTIBLE	STRIDENT	VIROLOGY	CASSETTE	DISTINCT	MESQUITE	POSTDATE	WASHBOWL
PARTICLE	STRIKING	VIRTUOSO	CASTAWAY	DISTRACT	MESSMATE	POSTHOLE	WASHROOM
PARTISAN	STRINGED	VIRTUOUS	CASTRATE	DISTRAIT	MISAPPLY	POSTLUDE	WISEACRE
PERCEIVE	STRINGER	VIRULENT	CASUALTY	DISTRESS	MISBRAND	POSTMARK	WISHBONE
PERFECTO	STRUGGLE	WARDROBE	CESAREAN	DISTRICT	MISCARRY	POSTPAID	WISTARIA
PERFORCE	STRUMPET	WARDROOM	CESSPOOL	DISTRUST	MISCHIEF	POSTPONE	WISTERIA
PERILUNE	SURCEASE	WARDSHIP	CISLUNAR	DISUNITE	MISCIBLE	PUSHCART	ACTINISM
PERIODIC	SUREFIRE	WAREROOM	COSIGNER	DISUNITY	MISCOUNT	PUSHDOWN	ACTINIUM
PERMEATE	SURGICAL	WARFARIN	COSMETIC	DYSLEXIA	MISDOING	PUSHOVER	ACTIVATE
PEROXIDE	SURMOUNT	WARPLANE	CUSPIDOR	ENSCONCE	MISHMASH	PUSSYCAT	ACTIVISM
PERSONAL	SURPLICE	WARRANTY	CUSTOMER	ENSEMBLE	MISJUDGE	RESCRIPT	ACTIVITY
PERSPIRE	SURPRISE	WEREWOLF	DESCRIBE	ENSHRINE	MISLABEL	RESEARCH	AFTERTAX
PERSUADE	SURROUND	WIREDRAW	DESELECT	ENSHROUD	MISMATCH	RESEMBLE	ALTHOUGH
PERVERSE	TARRAGON	WIREHAIR	DESIROUS	ENSILAGE	MISNOMER	RESERVED	ALTITUDE
PHRASING	TERMINAL	WIRELESS	DESOLATE	FASCICLE	MISPLACE	RESIDENT	ALTRUISM
PORPHYRY	TERMINUS	WIREWORM	DESPATCH	FASCISTA	MISPRINT	RESIDUAL	ANTEATER
PORPOISE	TERRAPIN	WORDBOOK	DESTRUCT	FASTBACK	MISQUOTE	RESIDUUM	ANTEDATE
PORRIDGE	TERRIBLE	WORDPLAY	DISABUSE	FASTNESS	MISSHAPE	RESIGNED	ANTELOPE
PORTABLE	TERRIFIC	WORDSTAR	DISAGREE	FESTIVAL	MISSPELL	RESISTOR	ANTERIOR
PORTHOLE	TERTIARY	WORKABLE	DISALLOW	FISHBOWL	MISSPEND	RESOLUTE	ANTEROOM
PORTIERE	THRASHER	WORKADAY	DISARRAY	FISHHOOK	MISSTATE	RESONANT	ANTHROPO
PORTRAIT	THREATEN	WORKBOOK	DISASTER	FISHWIFE	MISTAKEN	RESONATE	ANTIBODY
PURBLIND	THRENODY	WORKROOM	DISBURSE	FUSELAGE	MISTREAT	RESORTER	ANTIDOTE
PURCHASE	THROMBUS	WORKSHOP	DISCIPLE	GASLIGHT	MISTRESS	RESOURCE	ANTIMONY
PUREBRED	THROTTLE	WORMHOLE	DISCLAIM	GASOLINE	MISTRIAL	RESPONSE	ANTINOMY
PURSLANE	THRUSTER	WORMWOOD	DISCLOSE	GASWORKS	MISTRUST	RESTLESS	ANTIPODE
PURULENT	TIRELESS	ABSCISSA	DISCOLOR	GOSSAMER	MISUSAGE	RESTRAIN	ANTIPOPE
SARDONIC	TIRESOME	ABSENTEE	DISCOUNT	HESITANT	MOSQUITO	RESTRICT	APTITUDE
SCRABBLE	TOREADOR	ABSINTHE	DISCOVER	HESITATE	MOSSBACK	ROSEBUSH	ARTERIAL
SCRAGGLY	TORTILLA	ABSOLUTE	DISCREET	HISPANIC	MUSCATEL	ROSEMARY	ARTIFACT
SCRAMBLE	TORTOISE	ABSTRACT	DISCRETE	HOSPITAL	MUSHROOM	ROSEWOOD	ARTIFICE
SCRIBBLE	TORTUOUS	ABSTRUSE	DISFAVOR	HOSTELRY	MUSICALE	SUSPENSE	ARTISTIC
SCROFULA	TURBOFAN	AESTHETE	DISGORGE	HUSTINGS	MUSICIAN	SYSADMIN	ARTISTRY
SCROUNGE	TURBOJET	ASSASSIN	DISGRACE	HYSTERIA	MUSKETRY	SYSTEMIC	ASTATINE
SCRUTINY	TURMERIC	ASSEMBLE	DISGUISE	INSCRIBE	MUSTACHE	TESTATOR	ASTERISK
SERAGLIO	TURNCOAT	ASSEMBLY	DISHEVEL	INSECURE	MYSTICAL	TESTICLE	ASTEROID
SERENADE	TURNOVER	ASSORTED	DISHONOR	INSIGNIA	MYSTIQUE	UNSADDLE	ASTONISH
SERGEANT	TURNPIKE	AUSTRIAN	DISINTER	INSOLENT	NASALIZE	UNSAVORY	ATTITUDE
SEROLOGY	TURNSPIT	BASEBALL	DISJOINT	INSOMNIA	NESTLING	UNSEEMLY	ATTORNEY
SERVITOR	UNRIDDLE	BASEBORN	DISKETTE	INSOMUCH	OBSIDIAN	UNSETTLE	AUTOBAHN
SHRAPNEL	UPRISING	BASELESS	DISLODGE	INSPIRIT	OBSOLETE	UNSHAPED	AUTOGIRO
SHREWISH	VARIABLE	BASELINE	DISLOYAL	INSTANCE	OBSTACLE	UNSOUGHT	AUTOJOIN
SORORITY	VARIANCE	BASEMENT	DISMOUNT	INSTINCT	OBSTRUCT	UNSPRUNG	AUTOMATE
SORPTION	VARICOSE	BASILICA	DISORDER	INSTRUCT	PASSABLE	UNSTABLE	BATHROBE
SPRINKLE	VARIETAL	BASILISK	DISPATCH	INSULATE	PASSBOOK	UNSTEADY	BATHROOM
SPROCKET	VARIORUM	BASSINET	DISPENSE	ISSUANCE	PASSOVER	UNSTRUNG	BETATRON
STRADDLE	VARISTOR	BASSWOOD	DISPERSE	LASERJET	PASSPORT	UPSTAIRS	BITSTOCK
STRAGGLE	VERACITY	BESMIRCH	DISPIRIT	LISTLESS	PASSWORD	UPSTREAM	BOTULISM

BUTTRESS	INTERNEE	OPTICIAN	SATURDAY	COUNTESS	NEUROSIS	CIVILITY	RIVERBED
CATACOMB	INTERNET	OPTIMISM	SETSCREW	COUPLING	NEUROTIC	CIVILIZE	UNVOICED
CATALYZE	INTERROG	ORTHODOX	SITUATED	COURTESY	NEUTRINO	COVENANT	VIVACITY
CATAPULT	INTERVAL	ORTHOEPY	TITANIUM	COURTIER	OPUSCULE	COVERAGE	VIVARIUM
CATARACT	INTIMATE	OUTBOARD	TITILATE	CRUCIBLE	PLUMBING	COVERALL	BEWILDER
CATCHALL	INTRADOS	OUTBOUND	TITIVATE	CRUCIFIX	POULTICE	COVERLET	BIWEEKLY
CATCHING	INTRENCH	OUTBREAK	TITMOUSE	CRUZEIRO	POUNDAGE	DEVILISH	BOWSPRIT
CATEGORY	INTREPID	OUTBURST	TOTALITY	DAUGHTER	PRURIENT	DEVOTION	DEWBERRY
CATHETER	INTRIGUE	OUTCLASS	TUTELAGE	DIURETIC	ROUGHAGE	DIVAGATE	DOWNBEAT
CATHOLIC	INTROMIT	OUTDATED	TUTELARY	DOUBLOON	ROULETTE	DIVIDEND	DOWNCAST
CITATION	ISTHMIAN	OUTDOORS	TUTORIAL	DOUBTFUL	ROUTEMAN	DIVINITY	DOWNFALL
CYTOLOGY	JETTISON	OUTFIELD	ULTERIOR	DOUGHBOY	SAUCEPAN	DIVISION	DOWNHILL
CYTOSINE	KATAKANA	OUTFIGHT	ULTIMATE	DOUGHNUT	SAUTERNE	DIVISIVE	DOWNLOAD
DATABASE	LATCHKEY	OUTFLANK	UNTANGLE	DRUGGIST	SCULLERY	DIVORCEE	DOWNPOUR
DATELESS	LATITUDE	OUTGOING	UNTAUGHT	DRUMBEAT	SCULLION	DOVETAIL	DOWNTOWN
DATELINE	LETHARGY	OUTGUESS	UNTIMELY	DRUNKARD	SCULPTOR	ENVELOPE	DOWNTURN
DETACHED	LITERARY	OUTHOUSE	UNTOWARD	EDUCABLE	SHUTDOWN	ENVIABLE	DOWNWARD
DETHRONE	LITERATE	OUTLYING	UPTHRUST	EMULSIFY	SKULLCAP	ENVIRONS	DOWNWIND
DETONATE	LITERATI	OUTMODED	VITALITY	EMULSION	SLUGGARD	ENVISAGE	HAWAIIAN
DETOXIFY	LITIGANT	OUTPOINT	VITALIZE	ENURESIS	SLUGGISH	FAVORITE	HAWKWEED
DETRITUS	LITIGATE	OUTREACH	VITREOUS	EQUALIZE	SLUMLORD	GIVEAWAY	HAWTHORN
DUTIABLE	LITTORAL	OUTRIDER	WATCHDOG	EQUATION	SOUTHPAW	GOVERNOR	HOWITZER
ENTANGLE	LUTETIUM	OUTRIGHT	WATCHFUL	EQUIPAGE	SOUVENIR	INVASION	INWARDLY
ENTHRALL	LUTHERAN	OUTSHINE	WATCHMAN	FAUBOURG	SPURIOUS	INVEIGLE	LAWGIVER
ENTHRONE	MATERIAL	OUTSIDER	WATERLOO	FLUIDRAM	SQUABBLE	INVERTER	LAWMAKER
ENTIRETY	MATERIEL	OUTSMART	WATERWAY	FLUORIDE	SQUADRON	INVIABLE	NEWCOMER
ENTRAILS	MATERNAL	OUTSPEND	WITCHERY	FLUORINE	SQUANDER	INVITING	NEWFOUND
ENTRANCE	MATTRESS	OUTSTRIP	WITCHING	FLUORITE	SQUEEGEE	INVOLUTE	NEWLYWED
ENTRENCH	MATURATE	OUTWEIGH	WITHDRAW	FOUNTAIN	SQUIRREL	INVOLVED	NEWSCAST
ESTIMATE	MATURITY	PATERNAL	WITHHOLD	FOURFOLD	STUBBORN	JUVENILE	NEWSREEL
ESTONIAN	METAFILE	PATHETIC	ABUNDANT	FOURSOME	STUDBOOK	LAVATORY	NOWADAYS
ESTRANGE	METAPHOR	PATHOGEN	ABUTMENT	FOURTEEN	STUDDING	LAVENDER	PAWNSHOP
ESTROGEN	METEORIC	PATIENCE	ABUTTALS	FRUCTIFY	STUDIOUS	LEVERAGE	RAWBONED
EXTERIOR	METHANOL	PETITION	ADULTERY	FRUITION	STUFFING	LEVITATE	SAWHORSE
EXTERNAL	METRICAL	PETTIFOG	ALUMINUM	GAUNTLET	STULTIFY	LIVELONG	SEWERAGE
EXTRADOS	MITIGATE	PETULANT	AQUACADE	GOURMAND	STUNNING	LIVERISH	TOWELING
FATALISM	MOTHBALL	PITCHMAN	AQUANAUT	GRUELING	STURGEON	LOVEBIRD	TOWERING
FATALITY	MOTIVATE	PITIABLE	AQUARIUM	GRUESOME	TEUTONIC	LOVELORN	TOWNSHIP
FETCHING	MOTORCAR	PITILESS	AQUEDUCT	HAUTBOIS	THURSDAY	LOVESICK	TOWNSMAN
FUTILITY	MOTORIZE	PITTANCE	AQUILINE	HOUSEBOY	TOUCHING	MAVERICK	UNWIELDY
FUTURISM	MOTORMAN	POTATION	BLUDGEON	HOUSEFLY	TRUCKAGE	MOVEMENT	UNWONTED
FUTURITY	MOTOROLA	POTBELLY	BLUEBELL	HOUSETOP	TRUETYPE	NAVIGATE	UNWORTHY
GATEPOST	MUTATION	POTSHERD	BLUEBIRD	INUNDATE	TRUMPERY	NOVELIZE	COXSWAIN
GUTTURAL	MUTILATE	PUTATIVE	BLUEFISH	JAUNDICE	TRUNCATE	NOVEMBER	DEXTROSE
HATCHING	NATALITY	RATIONAL	BLUENOSE	LAUDANUM	TRUSTFUL	PAVEMENT	DOXOLOGY
HATCHWAY	NATIONAL	RATTLING	BOUFFANT	LAUGHTER	TRUTHFUL	PAVILION	FIXATION
HITHERTO	NATIVISM	RETAINER	BOUILLON	LAUNCHER	USUFRUCT	RAVENING	FIXATIVE
HOTHOUSE	NATIVITY	RETARDED	BOUNDARY	LAUREATE	USURIOUS	RAVENOUS	FOXGLOVE
INTAGLIO	NITROGEN	RETICENT	BOUTIQUE	LEUKEMIA	VAULTING	REVANCHE	FOXHOUND
INTEGRAL	NOTARIAL	RETIRING	CAUDILLO	MOUNTAIN	YOUNGISH	REVEILLE	LAXATIVE
INTENDED	NOTARIZE	RETRENCH	CAULDRON	MOUNTING	YOURSELF	REVENUER	MAXIMIZE
INTERCOM	NOTATION	RETRIEVE	CAUSERIE	MOURNFUL	YOUTHFUL	REVEREND	PIXELATE
INTEREST	NOTEBOOK	RETROFIT	CAUSEWAY	MOURNING	ADVISORY	REVERENT	SIXPENCE
INTERIOR	NOTIONAL	RETURNEE	CAUTIOUS	NAUSEATE	ADVOCATE	REVERSAL	TAXONOMY
INTERMIT	NUTHATCH	RUTABAGA	CHUTZPAH	NAUTICAL	BEVERAGE	REVIEWER	TAXPAYER
INTERMIX	NUTRIENT	RUTHLESS	CLUBFOOT	NAUTILUS	CAVALIER	REVIVIFY	TEXTBOOK
INTERNAL	NUTSHELL	SATURATE	COUCHANT	NEURITIS	CIVILIAN	REVOLVER	VEXATION

ANYPLACE	APHANITE	DISAGREE	INFAMOUS	NOTATION	SCRAGGLY	VICARAGE	RAWBONED
ANYTHING	APPANAGE	DISALLOW	INFANTRY	NOWADAYS	SCRAMBLE	VITALITY	RUMBLING
ANYWHERE	APPARENT	DISARRAY	INHALANT,	NUGATORY	SEDATIVE	VITALIZE	SCABBARD
ATYPICAL	AQUACADE	DISASTER	INTAGLIO	OBLATION	SEMANTIC	VIVACITY	SCABROUS
BAYBERRY	AQUANAUT	DIVAGATE	INVASION	OCCASION	SEPARATE	VIVARIUM	SEABOARD
BIYEARLY	AQUARIUM	DONATION	INWARDLY	OLEANDER	SERAGLIO	VOCALIST	SNOBBERY
CRYOLITE	ARBALEST	DREADFUL	ISLANDER	ORGANISM	SHRAPNEL	VOCALIZE	SOMBRERO
DAYBREAK	ARMAMENT	DURATION	JAPANESE	ORGANIST	SOLARIUM	VOCATION	STUBBORN
DAYDREAM	ARMATURE	DYNAMITE	KAMAAINA	ORGANIZE	SONATINA	VOCATIVE	SYMBOLIC
DAYLIGHT	ASSASSIN	EMBATTLE	KATAKANA	ORNAMENT	SPHAGNUM	VOLATILE	TIMBERED
EGYPTIAN	ASTATINE	ENDANGER	LAMASERY	PALATINE	SPLATTER	VOYAGEUR	TRIBUNAL
ERYTHEMA	AVIATION	ENGAGING	LAVATORY	PANATELA	SQUABBLE	WIZARDRY	TURBOFAN
FLYBLOWN	AVIATRIX	ENTANGLE	LAXATIVE	PARABOLA	SQUADRON	WOMANISH	TURBOJET
FLYPAPER	BEDAZZLE	EQUALIZE	LEGALISM	PARADIGM	SQUANDER	AIRBORNE	VERBATIM
FLYSPECK	BEHAVIOR	EQUATION	LEGATION	PARADISE	STEALTHY	AIRBRUSH	VERBIAGE
FLYWHEEL	BETATRON	ESCALATE	LIBATION	PARAFFIN	STRADDLE	BARBARIC	VERBOTEN
GLYCERIN	BINAURAL	ESCALLOP	LIGAMENT	PARAKEET	STRAGGLE	BARBECUE	ABSCISSA
GLYCEROL	BIRACIAL	ESCAPADE	LIGATURE	PARALLAX	STRAIGHT	BARBERRY	AIRCRAFT
GLYCOGEN	BREAKAGE	ESCAPISM	LOCALITY	PARALLEL	STRAITEN	BARBICAN	ALACRITY
GUYANESE	BREAKOUT	ESCAROLE	LOCALIZE	PARALYZE	STRANGER	BARBITAL	AMICABLE
HAYSTACK	CALABASH	ESPALIER	LOCATION	PARAMOUR	STRANGLE	BAYBERRY	ANACONDA
JOYSTICK	CALADIUM	EURASIAN	LOYALIST	PARANOIA	STRATEGY	CLUBFOOT	ANECDOTE
KEYBOARD	CALAMINE	EXCAVATE	MACARONI	PARASITE	STRATIFY	COMBINGS	ANECHOIC
KEYPUNCH	CALAMITY	FATALISM	MACAROON	PEDAGOGY	SYBARITE	CRIBBAGE	ARACHNID
KEYSTONE	CANADIAN	FATALITY	MAGAZINE	PENALIZE	SYCAMORE	CUPBOARD	ARMCHAIR
KEYWORDS	CANAILLE	FILAMENT	MAHARAJA	PHEASANT	SYSADMIN	DAYBREAK	BACCARAT
LAYERING	CANALIZE	FINALIST	MAHARANI	PHRASING	TAMARACK	DEWBERRY	BEECHNUT
LOYALIST	CAPACITY	FINALIZE	MALAMUTE	PICAYUNE	TAMARIND	DIABETES	BERCEUSE
MAYAPPLE	CARACOLE	FIXATION	MALAPERT	PILASTER	TENANTRY	DIABOLIC	BIOCIDAL
PAYCHECK	CARAPACE	FIXATIVE	MALARKEY	PINAFORE	THIAMINE	DISBURSE	BLACKING
PHYSICAL	CATACOMB	FLEABANE	MALAWIAN	PLEASANT	THRASHER	DOUBLOON	BLACKOUT
PHYSIQUE	CATALYZE	FLEABITE	MARATHON	PLEASING	TITANIUM	DOUBTFUL	BLACKTOP
RHYOLITE	CATAPULT	FUMAROLE	MAYAPPLE	PLEASURE	TOMAHAWK	DUMBBELL	BLOCKADE
ROYALIST	CATARACT	GADABOUT	MEDALIST	POLARITY	TONALITY	FAUBOURG	BRACELET
SKYLIGHT	CAVALIER	GERANIUM	MEGABYTE	POLARIZE	TOTALITY	FLYBLOWN	BRACKISH
SPYGLASS	CERAMIST	GIGABYTE	MEGALITH	POTATION	TREASURE	FURBELOW	BRICKBAT
VOYAGEUR	CESAREAN	GIGANTIC	MELANISM	PREAMBLE	TREASURY	GLABROUS	BROCCOLI
WAYFARER	CICATRIX	GLOAMING	MELANOMA	PUTATIVE	TREATISE	GLOBULIN	BROCHURE
PIZZERIA	CITATION	GUYANESE	METAFILE	RELATION	TRIANGLE	ICEBOUND	CALCULUS
SUZERAIN	CLEARING	HABANERA	METAPHOR	RELATIVE	UNEARNED	JAMBOREE	CATCHALL
UNZIPPED	CLEAVAGE	HARANGUE	MINATORY	RELAXANT	UNFASTEN	KEYBOARD	CATCHING
WIZARDRY	COLANDER	HAWAIIAN	MISAPPLY	REPARTEE	UNGAINLY	LAMBASTE	CHECKERS
	COMANCHE	HECATOMB	MOLASSES	RETAINER	UNIAXIAL	LAMBSKIN	CHECKOFF
	CREAMERY	HEMATITE	MONARCHY	RETARDED	UNLAWFUL	LAPBOARD	CHECKOUT
	CREATION	HEPATICA	MONASTIC	REVANCHE	UNSADDLE	LARBOARD	CHECKSUM
4TH LETTER	CREATURE	HERALDIC	MONAURAL	RIPARIAN	UNSAVORY	MARBLING	CINCHONA
	CURATIVE	HERALDRY	MORALIST	ROMANIAN	UNTANGLE	MEMBRANE	CINCTURE
ABLATION	DATABASE	HUMANISM	MORALITY	ROMANTIC	UNTAUGHT	MISBRAND	CIRCUITY
ABLATIVE	DECANTER	HUMANITY	MORALIZE	ROYALIST	URBANITE	MULBERRY	CIRCULAR
ABRASIVE	DEKAGRAM	HUMANIZE	MUTATION	RUMANIAN	URBANIZE	OUTBOARD	COACHMAN
ADJACENT	DELAWARE	HUMANOID	NASALIZE	RUNABOUT	VACATION	OUTBOUND	CONCEIVE
AGRARIAN	DEMARCHE	IDEALISM	NATALITY	RUNAGATE	VAGABOND	OUTBREAK	CONCERTO
ALBACORE	DENATURE	IDEALIZE	NEGATION	RUTABAGA	VANADIUM	OUTBURST	CONCLAVE
ALBANIAN	DETACHED	IDEATION	NEGATIVE	SAGAMORE	VEGANISM	PLEBEIAN	CONCLUDE
ALEATORY	DIDACTIC	IMMANENT	NEMATODE	SAMARIUM	VENATION	POTBELLY	CONCRETE
ALIASING	DILATORY	IMMATURE	NOTARIAL	SCIATICA	VERACITY	PROBABLE	COUCHANT
ALKALOID	DISABUSE	IMPACTED	NOTARIZE	SCRABBLE	VEXATION	PURBLIND	CRACKPOT

CROCKERY	LUNCHEON	SURCEASE	DAYDREAM	HERDSMAN	VENDETTA	APHELION	COHERENT
CRUCIBLE	LUSCIOUS	TEACHING	DEADBEAT	HINDMOST	WARDROBE	APPELLEE	COHESION
CRUCIFIX	MANCIPLE	THICKSET	DEADLINE	HINDUISM	WARDROOM	APPENDIX	COLESLAW
DESCRIBE	MERCHANT	TINCTURE	DEADLOCK	HOLDOVER	WARDSHIP	APPETITE	COMEBACK
DISCIPLE	MERCURIC	TOUCHING	DEADWOOD	HOODWINK	WELDMENT	AQUEDUCT	COMEDIAN
DISCLAIM	MISCARRY	TRACKAGE	DOLDRUMS	INEDITED	WHODUNIT	ARPEGGIO	COMEDOWN
DISCLOSE	MISCHIEF	TRACTATE	DUODENUM	KINDLING	WILDFIRE	ARTERIAL	COVENANT
DISCOLOR	MISCIBLE	TRACTION	EPIDEMIC	LANDFALL	WILDFOWL	ASBESTOS	COVERAGE
DISCOUNT	MISCOUNT	TRICHINA	EVIDENCE	LANDFILL	WILDLIFE	ASPERITY	COVERALL
DISCOVER	MOCCASIN	TRICKERY	FANDANGO	LANDFORM	WILDWOOD	ASSEMBLE	COVERLET
DISCREET	MUSCATEL	TRICOLOR	FEEDBACK	LANDLORD	WINDBURN	ASSEMBLY	CREEPING
DISCRETE	NARCOSIS	TRICYCLE	FELDSPAR	LANDMARK	WINDFALL	ASTERISK	DATELESS
DULCIMER	NARCOTIC	TRUCKAGE	FOLDAWAY	LANDMASS	WINDLASS	ASTEROID	DATELINE
EDUCABLE	NEWCOMER	UNICYCLE	FOLDBOAT	LANDSMAN	WINDMILL	AXLETREE	DECEDENT
ELECTION	OILCLOTH	VACCINIA	FOLDEROL	LANDWARD	WINDPIPE	BAKESHOP	DECEMBER
ELECTIVE	OUTCLASS	VASCULAR	GARDENIA	LAUDANUM	WINDWARD	BAREBACK	DEFECATE
ELECTRIC	PANCREAS	VINCIBLE	GENDARME	LORDSHIP	WONDROUS	BAREFOOT	DEJECTED
ELECTRON	PAYCHECK	VISCERAL	GEODESIC	MAGDALEN	WOODBINE	BASEBALL	DELEGATE
EMACIATE	PENCHANT	VISCOUNT	GLADSOME	MANDAMUS	WOODCOCK	BASEBORN	DEMEANOR
ENSCONCE	PERCEIVE	VOLCANIC	GOLDFISH	MANDARIN	WOODLAND	BASELESS	DEMENTED
ERECTILE	PILCHARD	WATCHDOG	GOODNESS	MANDIBLE	WOODNOTE	BASELINE	DEMENTIA
ERECTION	PITCHMAN	WATCHFUL	GOODWIFE	MANDOLIN	WOODPILE	BASEMENT	DERELICT
EVACUATE	PLACENTA	WATCHMAN	GOODWILL	MANDRAKE	WOODRUFF	BEHEMOTH	DESELECT
EXACTING	PLECTRUM	WITCHERY	GRADIENT	MESDAMES	WOODSHED	BENEDICT	DIRECTOR
EXECRATE	PRACTICE	WITCHING	GRADUATE	MIDDLING	WOODSMAN	BENEFICE	DOMESTIC
EXECUTOR	PRECINCT	WRECKAGE	GRIDIRON	MINDLESS	WOODWIND	BEREAVED	DOVETAIL
FALCHION	PRECIOUS	ZUCCHINI	GUIDANCE	MISDOING	WOODWORK	BEVERAGE	EDGEWAYS
FANCIFUL	PRECLUDE	AARDVARK	HANDBALL	NEEDLESS	WORDBOOK	BISEXUAL	EFFERENT
FASCICLE	PROCAINE	ACADEMIC	HANDBILL	NONDAIRY	WORDPLAY	BIWEEKLY	EMBEZZLE
FASCISTA	PROCEEDS	ACIDHEAD	HANDBOOK	OBEDIENT	WORDSTAR	BIYEARLY	ENCEINTE
FETCHING	PROCLAIM	ACIDOSIS	HANDCUFF	OUTDATED	ABNEGATE	BLUEBELL	ENDEAVOR
FORCIBLE	PUNCHEON	AIRDROME	HANDICAP	OUTDOORS	ABSENTEE	BLUEBIRD	ENFEEBLE
FRACTION	PUNCTUAL	BAEDEKER	HANDMADE	PANDEMIC	ADDENDUM	BLUEFISH	ENGENDER
FRACTURE	PUNCTURE	BANDANNA	HANDPICK	PANDOWDY	ADHESION	BLUENOSE	ENSEMBLE
FRICTION	PURCHASE	BIDDABLE	HANDRAIL	PARDONER	ADHESIVE	BOGEYMAN	ENVELOPE
FRUCTIFY	REACTANT	BIRDBATH	HANDSOME	PENDULUM	AFFECTED	BOHEMIAN	ESPECIAL
FUNCTION	REACTION	BIRDLIME	HANDYMAN	PIDDLING	AFFERENT	BREEDING	ETHEREAL
GIMCRACK	REACTIVE	BIRDSEED	HARDBACK	PRODIGAL	AFTERTAX	CAGELING	ETHERNET
GLACIATE	RESCRIPT	BLUDGEON	HARDBALL	PUDDLING	ALDERMAN	CAKEWALK	EUGENICS
GLYCERIN	SANCTIFY	BOLDFACE	HARDHACK	QUADRANT	ALGERIAN	CALENDAR	EXPEDITE
GLYCEROL	SANCTION	BONDSMAN	HARDSHIP	QUADROON	ALIENATE	CALENDER	EXTERIOR
GLYCOGEN	SANCTITY	BORDELLO	HARDTACK	ROADSIDE	ALIENIST	CAMELLIA	EXTERNAL
GODCHILD	SAUCEPAN	BUDDHISM	HARDWARE	ROADSTER	ALLEGORY	CAPESKIN	FACEDOWN
GRACIOUS	SEACOAST	BUNDLING	HARDWOOD	ROADWORK	ALLELUIA	CAREFREE	FADELESS
HATCHING	SHOCKING	CARDAMOM	HEADACHE	SADDUCEE	ALLERGEN	CARELESS	FAREWELL
HATCHWAY	SPACEMAN	CARDIGAN	HEADBAND	SANDBANK	ALLEYWAY	CAREWORN	FEDERATE
HENCHMAN	SPACIOUS	CARDINAL	HEADGEAR	SANDWICH	AMOEBOID	CASEMENT	FIDELITY
HERCULES	SPECIFIC	CAUDILLO	HEADLAND	SARDONIC	AMPERAGE	CASEWORK	FINESPUN
HYACINTH	SPECIMEN	CONDENSE	HEADLINE	SEEDLING	ANAEROBE	CATEGORY	FIREBALL
INSCRIBE	SPECIOUS	CORDLESS	HEADLOCK	SEEDTIME	ANCESTOR	CELERITY	FIREBOAT
JUNCTION	SPECTRAL	CORDOVAN	HEADLONG	SOLDIERY	ANCESTRY	CEMENTUM	FIREBOMB
JUNCTURE	SPECTRUM	CORDUROY	HEADREST	STUDBOOK	ANGELICA	CEMETERY	FIRECLAY
KERCHIEF	STACCATO	CREDENCE	HEADROOM	STUDDING	ANTEATER	CEREBRUM	FIREDAMP
KNICKERS	STICKLER	CREDENZA	HEADSHIP	STUDIOUS	ANTEDATE	CEREMENT	FIREPLUG
KNOCKOUT	STOCKADE	CREDIBLE	HEADSMAN	SUNDRIES	ANTELOPE	CEREMONY	FIRESIDE
LATCHKEY	STOCKING	CREDITOR	HEADWORD	SYNDROME	ANTERIOR	CHEERFUL	FIRETRAP
LINCHPIN	SUCCINCT	DANDRUFF	HEADWORK	TENDENCY	ANTEROOM	CICERONE	FIREWOOD

FIREWORK	HEREUPON	LIKEWISE	PEDESTAL	SOLECISM	ULCERATE	DISFAVOR	EMIGRATE
FLEETING	HEREWITH	LIMEKILN	PIPELINE	SOLENOID	ULTERIOR	DOGFIGHT	EXEGESIS
FOREBEAR	HIDEAWAY	LIMERICK	PIXELATE	SOMEBODY	UNBEATEN	GONFALON	EXIGENCY
FOREBODE	HIRELING	LINESMAN	POKEWEED	SOMERSET	UNBELIEF	GOOFBALL	EXIGUOUS
FORECAST	HOMEBODY	LITERARY	POLESTAR	SOMETIME	UNDERACT	GRAFFITO	EYEGLASS
FOREDOOM	HOMEBRED	LITERATE	PREEXIST	SOMEWHAT	UNDERAGE	GUNFIGHT	FLAGPOLE
FOREFEND	HOMELAND	LITERATI	PUDENDUM	SPEEDWAY	UNDERARM	HALFBACK	FLAGRANT
FOREFOOT	HOMEMADE	LIVELONG	PUREBRED	SPHEROID	UNDERBID	HALFTONE	FLAGSHIP
FOREGONE	HOMEROOM	LIVERISH	QUIETUDE	SPLENDID	UNDERCUT	NEWFOUND	FOXGLOVE
FOREHAND	HOMESICK	LODESTAR	RAVENING	SPLENDOR	UNDERDOG	OUTFIELD	FRAGMENT
FOREHEAD	HOMESPUN	LONESOME	RAVENOUS	SQUEEGEE	UNDERFUR	OUTFIGHT	FRAGRANT
FOREKNOW	HOMEWARD	LOVEBIRD	RECEIVER	STEERAGE	UNDERLIE	OUTFLANK	FRIGHTEN
FORELADY	HOMEWORK	LOVELORN	RECEPTOR	STREAMER	UNDERLIP	PARFOCAL	GANGLAND
FORELAND	HONEYDEW	LOVESICK	REFERENT	STRENGTH	UNDERPAY	PERFECTO	GANGLING
FORELIMB	HYMENEAL	LUKEWARM	REFERRAL	SUPEREGO	UNDERSEA	PERFORCE	GANGLION
FORELOCK	IMBECILE	LUTETIUM	REHEARSE	SUPERIOR	UNDERTOW	PROFOUND	GANGPLOW
FOREMAST	IMPELLER	MACERATE	RELEGATE	SUPERJET	UNFETTER	PUFFBALL	GANGRENE
FOREMOST	IMPERIAL	MANEUVER	RELEVANT	SUPERNAL	UNLEADED	RIFFRAFF	GANGSTER
FORENAME	IMPETIGO	MATERIAL	REMEDIAL	SUREFIRE	UNPERSON	ROOFTREE	GARGOYLE
FORENOON	INDEBTED	MATERIEL	REMEMBER	SUZERAIN	UNSEEMLY	SCAFFOLD	GINGERLY
FORENSIC	INDECENT	MATERNAL	RENEGADE	SWEEPING	UNSETTLE	SCOFFLAW	GORGEOUS
FOREPART	INFERIOR	MAVERICK	REPEATED	TALESMAN	UPHEAVAL	SEAFARER	HANGNAIL
FORESAIL	INFERNAL	METEORIC	RESEARCH	TAPESTRY	UPPERCUT	SELFLESS	HANGOVER
FORESKIN	INHERENT	MILEPOST	RESEMBLE	TAPEWORM	UUDECODE	SELFSAME	HEDGEHOG
FORESTRY	INSECURE	MILESIMO	RESERVED	TELECAST	VEGETATE	STUFFING	HEDGEHOP
FORETELL	INTEGRAL	MODERATE	REVEILLE	TELEFILM	VEHEMENT	SUFFRAGE	HEDGEROW
FOREWARN	INTENDED	MOLECULE	REVENUER	TELEGRAM	VENERATE	SULFURIC	HEIGHTEN
FOREWORD	INTERCOM	MOLEHILL	REVEREND	TELEPLAY	VENEREAL	TAFFRAIL	JINGOISM
FREEBORN	INTEREST	MOLESKIN	REVERENT	TELETHON	VINEGARY	TRIFLING	JONGLEUR
FREEDMAN	INTERIOR	MOMENTUM	REVERSAL	TELEVIEW	VINEYARD	USUFRUCT	JUDGMENT
FREEHAND	INTERMIT	MONETARY	RIVERBED	TELEVISE	WAREROOM	WARFARIN	KANGAROO
FREEHOLD	INTERMIX	MOREOVER	ROSEBUSH	TEMERITY	WATERLOO	WAYFARER	KINGBOLT
FREELOAD	INTERNAL	MOVEMENT	ROSEMARY	TENEMENT	WATERWAY	BEGGARLY	LANGUAGE
FREEWILL	INTERNEE	MULETEER	ROSEWOOD	THIEVERY	WEREWOLF	BRAGGART	LANGUISH
FUNERARY	INTERNET	NAMELESS	SALESMAN	THREATEN	WINESHOP	BRIGHTEN	LAUGHTER
FUNEREAL	INTERROG	NAMESAKE	SCHEDULE	THRENODY	WIREDRAW	BUNGALOW	LAWGIVER
FUSELAGE	INTERVAL	NEPENTHE	SELECTEE	TIDELAND	WIREHAIR	BUNGHOLE	LENGTHEN
GAMECOCK	INVEIGLE	NIGERIAN	SELENITE	TIMELESS	WIRELESS	BURGLARY	LINGERIE
GAMESOME	INVERTER	NIGEROIS	SELENIUM	TIMEWORN	WIREWORM	BURGUNDY	LINGUIST
GAMESTER	JEREMIAD	NINEPINS	SEMESTER	TIRELESS	WISEACRE	COAGULUM	LODGMENT
GATEPOST	JUVENILE	NINETEEN	SERENADE	TIRESOME	YULETIDE	CONGENER	LONGBOAT
GENERATE	KINETICS	NOBELIST	SEWERAGE	TOGETHER	ZWIEBACK	CONGRESS	LONGHAIR
GENEROUS	KNEEHOLE	NOBELIUM	SHEEPISH	TOKENISM	AIRFIELD	DAUGHTER	LONGHAND
GENETICS	LACERATE	NONESUCH	SHEETING	TOLERATE	AIRFRAME	DIAGONAL	LONGHORN
GIVEAWAY	LACEWING	NONEVENT	SHOELACE	TOREADOR	BOUFFANT	DINGBATS	LONGTIME
GOVERNOR	LASERJET	NOTEBOOK	SHREWISH	TOWELING	CAFFEINE	DISGORGE	LONGUEUR
GREEKING	LAVENDER	NOVELIZE	SIDEKICK	TOWERING	CALFSKIN	DISGRACE	MANGROVE
GREENERY	LAYERING	NOVEMBER	SIDELONG	TRUETYPE	COIFFEUR	DISGUISE	MARGRAVE
GREETING	LEVERAGE	NUMERATE	SIDEREAL	TUBERCLE	COIFFURE	DOGGEREL	MONGOOSE
GRIEVOUS	LIBERATE	NUMEROUS	SIDERITE	TUBEROSE	CONFETTI	DOUGHBOY	MUDGUARD
GRUELING	LICENSEE	ORIENTAL	SIDESHOW	TUBEROUS	CONFINES	DOUGHNUT	NEIGHBOR
GRUESOME	LIFEBOAT	PALEFACE	SIDESTEP	TUNELESS	CONFLICT	DRAGOMAN	NIGGLING
HAREBELL	LIFELINE	PANELING	SIDEWALK	TUTELAGE	CONFOCAL	DRUGGIST	ORIGINAL
HEGEMONY	LIFELONG	PANELIST	SIDEWALL	TUTELARY	CONFOUND	DUNGAREE	OUTGOING
HEREDITY	LIFETIME	PATERNAL	SIDEWAYS	TWEEZERS	CONFRERE	DUNGHILL	OUTGUESS
HEREFORD	LIFEWORK	PAVEMENT	SILENCER	TYPECAST	CONFRONT	ELEGANCE	PEIGNOIR
HEREUNTO	LIKENESS	PEDERAST	SINECURE	TYPEFACE	DAFFODIL	ELIGIBLE	POIGNANT

PREGNANT	FISHWIFE	ACCIDENT	CIVILIAN	FAMILIAR	LECITHIN	OBSIDIAN	RUBICUND
PROGRESS	FOXHOUND	ACRIMONY	CIVILITY	FELICITY	LENITIVE	OFFICIAL	RUBIDIUM
QUAGMIRE	HIGHBALL	ACTINISM	CIVILIZE	FEMININE	LEVITATE	OPTICIAN	RUDIMENT
RINGWORM	HIGHBORN	ACTINIUM	CLAIMANT	FEMINISM	LINIMENT	OPTIMISM	RUMINANT
ROUGHAGE	HIGHBRED	ACTIVATE	CLOISTER	FILIGREE	LITIGANT	OPTIMISM	RUMINATE
SANGUINE	HIGHBROW	ACTIVISM	COGITATE	FILIPINO	LITIGATE	ORDINARY	SALIVATE
SEAGOING	HIGHLAND	ACTIVITY	COLISEUM	FLUIDRAM	LUMINARY	ORDINATE	SANITARY
SEIGNEUR	HIGHNESS	ADDITION	COSIGNER	FOLIATED	LUMINOUS	PACIFIER	SANITIZE
SERGEANT	HIGHROAD	ADDITIVE	CULINARY	FRUITION	MAGICIAN	PACIFISM	SCRIBBLE
SINGULAR	HIGHTAIL	ADVISORY	CUPIDITY	FUGITIVE	MALINGER	PAGINATE	SEDIMENT
SLUGGARD	HITHERTO	AFFIANCE	CYLINDER	FUMIGANT	MANIACAL	PALINODE	SEDITION
SLUGGISH	HOTHOUSE	AFFINITY	DEBILITY	FUMIGATE	MANICURE	PALISADE	SEMINARY
SONGBIRD	ICEHOUSE	AGLITTER	DECIGRAM	FUTILITY	MANIFEST	PARIETAL	SEMINOLE
SONGSTER	INCHOATE	ALLIANCE	DECIMATE	GEMINATE	MANIFOLD	PATIENCE	SEMISOFT
SPYGLASS	INCHWORM	ALMIGHTY	DECIPHER	GENITALS	MARIACHI	PAVILION	SIBILANT
STAGNANT	ISTHMIAN	ALTITUDE	DECISION	GENITIVE	MARIGOLD	PEDICURE	SILICATE
STAGNATE	LETHARGY	AMBIENCE	DECISIVE	HABITANT	MARINATE	PEDIGREE	SILICIFY
SURGICAL	LUTHERAN	AMBITION	DEDICATE	HABITUAL	MARITIME	PEDIMENT	SILICONE
TANGIBLE	MACHISMO	ANTIBODY	DEFIANCE	HACIENDA	MAXIMIZE	PENITENT	SINISTER
TUNGSTEN	MADHOUSE	ANTIDOTE	DEFINITE	HELICOID	MEDICAID	PERILUNE	SOCIABLE
VANGUARD	MECHANIC	ANTIMONY	DELICACY	HELIPORT	MEDICARE	PERIODIC	SOLIDIFY
VENGEFUL	MENHADEN	ANTINOMY	DELICATE	HERITAGE	MEDICATE	PETITION	SOLITARY
VIRGINAL	MEPHITIC	ANTIPODE	DELIRIUM	HESITANT	MEDICINE	PIMIENTO	SOLITUDE
WINGDING	MESHWORK	ANTIPOPE	DELIVERY	HESITATE	MEDIEVAL	PITIABLE	SPLINTER
WINGSPAN	METHANOL	APTITUDE	DEMIBOLD	HIBISCUS	MEDIOCRE	PITILESS	SPRINKLE
WRIGGLER	MISHMASH	AQUILINE	DEMIJOHN	HOLINESS	MEDITATE	PODIATRY	SQUIRREL
ALEHOUSE	MOTHBALL	ARTIFACT	DESIROUS	HOMICIDE	MENISCUS	POLITICK	STAIRWAY
ALPHABET	MUSHROOM	ARTIFICE	DEVILISH	HOWITZER	MERIDIAN	POLITICO	STRICKEN
ALTHOUGH	NUTHATCH	ARTISTIC	DILIGENT	HUMIDIFY	MERINGUE	POLITICS	STRIDENT
ANTHROPO	ORTHODOX	ARTISTRY	DIMINISH	HUMIDITY	MILITANT	POPINJAY	STRIKING
ARCHDUKE	ORTHOEPY	ASPIRANT	DISINTER	HUMILITY	MILITARY	POSITION	STRINGED
ASPHODEL	OUTHOUSE	ASPIRATE	DIVIDEND	IGNITION	MILITATE	POSITIVE	STRINGER
ASPHYXIA	PATHETIC	ATTITUDE	DIVINITY	ILLINOIS	MINIBIKE	POSITRON	SUKIYAKI
BACHELOR	PATHOGEN	AUDIENCE	DIVISION	IMMINENT	MINIMIZE	PUGILISM	TACITURN
BATHROBE	PROHIBIT	AUDITION	DIVISIVE	INCIDENT	MINISTER	PUNITIVE	TAHITIAN
BATHROOM	PUSHCART	AUDITORY	DOMICILE	INCISION	MINISTRY	RADIATOR	TALISMAN
BECHUANA	PUSHDOWN	BACILLUS	DOMINATE	INCISIVE	MITIGATE	RADIOMAN	TITILATE
BONHOMIE	PUSHOVER	BADINAGE	DOMINEER	INDIAMAN	MOBILIZE	RATIONAL	TITIVATE
CASHMERE	RIGHTFUL	BANISTER	DOMINION	INDICATE	MONITION	REFINERY	TRAINING
CATHETER	RUTHLESS	BARITONE	DRAINAGE	INDIGENT	MONITORY	REGICIDE	TRAINMAN
CATHOLIC	SAWHORSE	BASILICA	DUTIABLE	INDIRECT	MORIBUND	REGIMENT	TUNISIAN
CEPHALIC	SUCHLIKE	BASILISK	ECLIPTIC	INFINITE	MOTIVATE	REGIONAL	ULTIMATE
DETHRONE	SYPHILIS	BELITTLE	ELLIPSIS	INFINITY	MUCILAGE	REGISTER	UNBIASED
DISHEVEL	TIGHTWAD	BERIBERI	EMBITTER	INSIGNIA	MUNITION	REGISTRY	UNBIDDEN
DISHONOR	UNCHASTE	BEWILDER	ENCIPHER	INTIMATE	MUSICALE	RELIABLE	UNFILIAL
DOGHOUSE	UNCHURCH	BODILESS	ENCIRCLE	INVIABLE	MUSICIAN	RELIANCE	UNKINDLY
EIGHTEEN	UNSHAPED	BOUILLON	ENFILADE	INVITING	MUTILATE	RELIGION	UNLIKELY
EMPHASIS	UPTHRUST	BUSINESS	ENGINEER	IRRIGATE	NATIONAL	REMITTAL	UNLIMBER
EMPHATIC	WASHABLE	CAMISOLE	ENSILAGE	IRRITATE	NATIVISM	RESIDENT	UNRIDDLE
ENSHRINE	WASHBOWL	CANISTER	ENTIRETY	JUBILANT	NATIVITY	RESIDUAL	UNTIMELY
ENSHROUD	WASHROOM	CARILLON	ENVIABLE	JUDICIAL	NAVIGATE	RESIDUUM	UNWIELDY
ENTHRALL	WISHBONE	CELIBACY	ENVIRONS	JURISTIC	NIHILISM	RESIGNED	UNZIPPED
ENTHRONE	WITHDRAW	CELIBATE	ENVISAGE	KAMIKAZE	NOBILITY	RESISTOR	UPRISING
EUPHORIA	WITHHOLD	CHAIRMAN	EQUIPAGE	KIBITZER	NOMINATE	RETICENT	VALIDATE
EXCHANGE	YACHTING	CHOIRBOY	ESTIMATE	KOLINSKY	NOTIONAL	RETIRING	VARIABLE
FISHBOWL	ABDICATE	CHRISTEN	FACILITY	LAPIDARY	OBLIGATE	REVIEWER	VARIANCE
FISHHOOK	ABSINTHE	CHRISTIE	FAMILIAL	LATITUDE	OBLIVION	RIDICULE	VARICOSE

VARIETAL	FOLKLORE	BAILSMAN	IDOLATER	SHILINGI	COMMERCE	SHAMBLES	CORNCRIB
VARIORUM	FORKLIFT	BALLROOM	IDOLATRY	SHILLING	COMMONER	SHAMROCK	CORNMEAL
VARISTOR	GYMKHANA	BALLYHOO	IMPLICIT	SKELETON	COMMUNAL	SKIMMING	COUNTESS
VESICANT	HACKWORD	BILLFOLD	JAILBIRD	SKILLFUL	COSMETIC	SLUMLORD	DAMNABLE
VICINAGE	HAWKWEED	BILLHEAD	KEELBOAT	SKULLCAP	CREMAINS	STAMPEDE	DIANTHUS
VICINITY	HOOKWORM	BOLLWORM	KEELHAUL	SKYLIGHT	CRIMINAL	STIMULUS	DOWNBEAT
VIGILANT	HUCKSTER	BUILDING	KIELBASA	SMALLPOX	DIAMETER	SUBMERGE	DOWNCAST
VISICALC	JACKBOOT	BULLDOZE	KILLDEER	SPILLWAY	DISMOUNT	SUBMERSE	DOWNFALL
VISITANT	KICKBACK	BULLETIN	KOHLRABI	STALLION	DOOMSDAY	SURMOUNT	DOWNHILL
VOLITION	KICKSHAW	BULLFROG	LOLLIPOP	STALWART	DORMOUSE	SWIMMING	DOWNLOAD
CONJUGAL	LARKSPUR	BULLHEAD	LOLLYGAG	STILETTO	DRUMBEAT	SYMMETRY	DOWNPOUR
CONJUNCT	LEUKEMIA	CALLBACK	MEALTIME	STULTIFY	EXEMPLAR	TEAMSTER	DOWNTOWN
DISJOINT	LOCKSTEP	CALLIOPE	MEALYBUG	SUNLIGHT	FARMHAND	TEAMWORK	DOWNTURN
MARJORAM	MACKEREL	CAULDRON	MILLIARD	SWELLING	FARMLAND	TERMINAL	DOWNWARD
MISJUDGE	MACKINAW	CELLULAR	MILLIBAR	SYLLABLE	FARMYARD	TERMINUS	DOWNWIND
PREJUDGE	MARKDOWN	CHOLERIC	MILLIEME	SYLLABUS	FIRMWARE	TITMOUSE	DRUNKARD
BACKACHE	MARKSMAN	CISLUNAR	MILLINER	TAILCOAT	FLAMBEAU	TRIMARAN	EARNINGS
BACKBITE	MILKMAID	COALESCE	MILLPOND	TAILGATE	FLAMENCO	TRIMETER	ECONOMIC
BACKBONE	MILKWEED	COLLAPSE	MILLRACE	TAILSPIN	FLAMEOUT	TRIMMING	ELONGATE
BACKDROP	MUSKETRY	COLLIERY	MISLABEL	TELLTALE	FLAMINGO	TROMBONE	EMINENCE
BACKFIRE	NECKLACE	COLLOQUY	MYELITIS	THALAMUS	FLIMFLAM	TRUMPERY	EVENSONG
BACKHAND	NECKLINE	CURLICUE	NEGLIGEE	THALLIUM	FORMERLY	TURMERIC	EVENTIDE
BACKLASH	NICKNAME	CYCLAMEN	NEWLYWED	TOILETRY	FORMLESS	VERMOUTH	EVENTUAL
BACKPACK	PENKNIFE	DAYLIGHT	NOBLEMAN	TOILETTE	GEOMETRY	WHOMEVER	FOUNTAIN
BACKREST	PICKEREL	DEFLOWER	NUCLEATE	TOILWORN	GERMINAL	WORMHOLE	FRANCIUM
BACKSIDE	PICKINGS	DIALOGUE	OUTLYING	TOLLBOTH	HARMONIC	WORMWOOD	FRENETIC
BACKSLAP	PICKLOCK	DIALYSIS	PALLIATE	TOLLGATE	HELMSMAN	YEOMANRY	FRONTAGE
BACKSPIN	POCKMARK	DIELDRIN	PARLANCE	TRILLION	HERMETIC	ABUNDANT	FRONTIER
BACKSTOP	RECKLESS	DIPLOMAT	PELLAGRA	TRILLIUM	HORMONAL	ACANTHUS	GAUNTLET
BACKWARD	ROCKETRY	DISLODGE	PELLUCID	TWILIGHT	INIMICAL	AMENABLE	GHANAIAN
BACKWASH	ROCKFALL	DISLOYAL	PENLIGHT	UNCLENCH	LAWMAKER	BARNACLE	GRANDEUR
BANKBOOK	SICKNESS	DWELLING	POLLIWOG	UNCLOTHE	MARMOSET	BARNYARD	GRANDSON
BANKROLL	SINKHOLE	DYSLEXIA	POLLSTER	VAULTING	MISMATCH	BEANBALL	GRANULAR
BANKRUPT	STAKEOUT	EMBLAZON	POULTICE	VELLEITY	MNEMONIC	BIANNUAL	HORNBOOK
BOOKCASE	SUCKLING	EMPLOYEE	PROLIFIC	VILLAGER	MYRMIDON	BIENNIAL	HORNPIPE
BOOKMARK	TICKLISH	EMULSIFY	PROLOGUE	VILLAINY	NONMETAL	BIENNIUM	HYPNOSIS
BOOKWORM	WALKAWAY	EMULSION	PSALMODY	VIOLABLE	ODOMETER	BINNACLE	HYPNOTIC
BRAKEMAN	WALKOVER	EPILEPSY	PUBLICAN	VIOLENCE	OHMMETER	BOUNDARY	IDENTIFY
BUCKSHOT	WEAKFISH	EPILOGUE	PULLBACK	WELLBORN	OUTMODED	BRANDISH	IDENTITY
BUCKSKIN	WEAKLING	EVALUATE	PULLOVER	WELLHEAD	PALMETTO	BRINDLED	INUNDATE
BULKHEAD	WEAKNESS	EXPLICIT	QUALMISH	WILLIWAW	PARMESAN	BRONCHUS	IRONCLAD
COCKATOO	WORKABLE	EXPLODED	RAILLERY	WOOLSACK	PEMMICAN	BURNOOSE	IRONWARE
COCKCROW	WORKADAY	EYELINER	RAILROAD	YIELDING	PERMEATE	CANNABIS	IRONWEED
COCKEREL	WORKBOOK	FALLIBLE	ROLLBACK	ALUMINUM	PLUMBING	CANNIBAL	IRONWOOD
COCKSURE	WORKROOM	FANLIGHT	ROULETTE	ATOMIZER	PREMIERE	CARNAUBA	IRONWORK
COCKTAIL	WORKSHOP	FELLATIO	SAILBOAT	BERMUDAS	PREMOLAR	CARNIVAL	JAUNDICE
COOKBOOK	ADULTERY	FOLLICLE	SAILFISH	BESMIRCH	PRIMEVAL	CHANCERY	LAUNCHER
DARKLING	AFFLATUS	FOOLSCAP	SCALABLE	BROMIDIC	PRIMROSE	CHANDLER	LIGNEOUS
DARKROOM	AIRLINER	FULLBACK	SCALAWAG	CHAMBRAY	PROMOTER	CHANUKAH	LOANWORD
DARKSOME	ANALOGUE	FURLOUGH	SCALEPAN	CHAMPION	PTOMAINE	CHENILLE	MAGNESIA
DECKHAND	ANALYSIS	GALLUSES	SCALLION	CHEMICAL	PULMOTOR	CINNABAR	MAGNETIC
DISKETTE	ANGLICAN	GASLIGHT	SCILICET	CHEMURGY	RHOMBOID	CINNAMON	MAGNOLIA
DOCKHAND	APOLOGIA	GOALPOST	SCULLERY	CLAMBAKE	ROOMETTE	CLINCHER	MAINLAND
DOCKYARD	APPLAUSE	HALLMARK	SCULLION	CLEMATIS	ROOMMATE	CLINICAL	MAINLINE
DUCKBILL	APPLIQUE	HELLHOLE	SCULPTOR	CLEMENCY	SCHMALTZ	COGNOMEN	MAINMAST
DUCKLING	ATHLETIC	HILLSIDE	SEALSKIN	COMMANDO	SCIMITAR	COINCIDE	MAINSAIL
FECKLESS	BAILABLE	HOOLIGAN	SHELVING	COMMENCE	SEAMOUNT	COONSKIN	MAINSTAY

MAINTAIN	THANKFUL	BECOMING	ESTONIAN	LOBOTOMY	RHYOLITE	ATYPICAL	KEEPSAKE
MANNERED	TOWNSHIP	BEHOLDEN	ETHOLOGY	LOCOWEED	RIBOSOME	CAMPAIGN	KEYPUNCH
MANNERLY	TOWNSMAN	BICONVEX	ETIOLOGY	LOGOTYPE	RICOCHET	CAMPOREE	KNAPSACK
MEANTIME	TRANQUIL	BIFOCALS	EUROBOND	MAHOGANY	SABOTAGE	CHAPBOOK	LAMPBACK
MIDNIGHT	TRANSACT	BLOOMERS	EUROPEAN	MAJOLICA	SABOTEUR	CHAPERON	LEAPFROG
MISNOMER	TRANSEPT	BOBOLINK	EUROPIUM	MAJORITY	SCHOONER	CHAPLAIN	LOOPHOLE
MOONBEAM	TRANSFER	BROOKLET	EXPONENT	MELODEON	SCROFULA	CHIPMUNK	LYMPHOID
MOUNTAIN	TRANSFIX	CABOCHON	EXPOSURE	MEMORIAL	SCROUNGE	CHIPPEWA	MACPAINT
MOUNTING	TRANSMIT	CAMOMILE	FAGOTING	MEMORIZE	SEROLOGY	CLAPTRAP	MIDPOINT
MUENSTER	TRENCHER	CANONIZE	FAROUCHE	MINORITY	SIMONIZE	CLIPPING	MISPLACE
NAINSOOK	TRUNCATE	CAROTENE	FAVORITE	MONOGAMY	SONOROUS	COMPILER	MISPRINT
NEONATAL	TURNCOAT	CAROUSAL	FEROCITY	MONOGRAM	SORORITY	COMPLAIN	MORPHEME
NOONTIDE	TURNOVER	CAROUSEL	FLUORIDE	MONOLITH	SPOOLING	COMPLEAT	MORPHINE
NOONTIME	TURNPIKE	CENOBITE	FLUORINE	MONOPOLY	SPROCKET	COMPLETE	NEOPHYTE
ONONDAGA	TURNSPIT	CENOTAPH	FLUORITE	MONORAIL	SYNOPSIS	COMPOUND	NEOPLASM
OPENWORK	UNENDING	CHLORIDE	GASOLINE	MONOTONE	SYNOPTIC	COMPRESS	OFFPRINT
ORANGERY	UUENCODE	CHLORINE	GEMOLOGY	MONOXIDE	TAXONOMY	COMPRISE	OUTPOINT
ORDNANCE	VIGNETTE	CHLORITE	GENOCIDE	MOROCCAN	THEOLOGY	COMPUTER	PALPABLE
OVENBIRD	WAINSCOT	CHROMIUM	HEDONISM	MOTORCAR	THEORIZE	COPPERAS	PAMPHLET
PAINTING	WHENEVER	COLONIAL	HOLOGRAM	MOTORIZE	THROMBUS	CORPORAL	PEEPHOLE
PAWNSHOP	WRONGFUL	COLONIST	HONORARY	MOTORMAN	THROTTLE	CORPSMAN	PIEPLANT
PHANTASM	YOUNGISH	COLONIZE	HOROLOGY	MOTOROLA	TIMOROUS	COUPLING	PINPOINT
PHANTASY	ABNORMAL	COLOPHON	IDEOGRAM	MYCOLOGY	TOBOGGAN	CROPLAND	PINPRICK
PHENOLIC	ABROGATE	COLOSSAL	IDEOLOGY	NAPOLEON	TOMORROW	CULPABLE	PORPHYRY
PINNACLE	ABSOLUTE	COLOSSUS	IGNORANT	NEPOTISM	TOPOLOGY	CUSPIDOR	PORPOISE
PLANGENT	ACCOLADE	CORONACH	IMMOBILE	NICOTINE	TUTORIAL	DESPATCH	PREPRESS
PLANKING	ACCOUTRE	CORONARY	IMMODEST	OBSOLETE	UNBODIED	DIAPASON	PROPERTY
PLANKTON	ACROSTIC	CREOSOTE	IMMOLATE	ONCOMING	UNBOLTED	DISPATCH	PROPHECY
PLANTAIN	ADMONISH	CRYOLITE	IMMORTAL	ONLOOKER	UNCOMMON	DISPENSE	PROPHESY
POUNDAGE	ADVOCATE	CYNOSURE	IMMOTILE	OPPONENT	UNCOUPLE	DISPERSE	PROPOUND
PRENATAL	AEROLOGY	CYTOLOGY	IMPOLITE	OPPOSITE	UNFORMED	DISPIRIT	PULPWOOD
PRINCESS	AERONAUT	CYTOSINE	IMPOSING	PALOMINO	UNIONISM	DISPLACE	RESPONSE
PRINTING	AGNOSTIC	DEBONAIR	IMPOSTOR	PANORAMA	UNIONIZE	DISPOSAL	RHAPSODY
PRINTOUT	AGRONOMY	DECORATE	IMPOTENT	PAROXYSM	UNLOOSEN	DISPROVE	SAPPHIRE
QUANDARY	ALLOCATE	DECOROUS	INCOMING	PENOLOGY	UNLOVELY	DROPKICK	SCAPULAR
QUANTITY	AMMONIUM	DEFOREST	INDOLENT	PEROXIDE	UNSOUGHT	DUMPLING	SEAPLANE
QUANTIZE	ANNOTATE	DEIONIZE	INFOBAHN	PILOTAGE	UNTOWARD	EARPHONE	SHEPHERD
RAINCOAT	ANNOUNCE	DEMOCRAT	INFORMAL	PINOCHLE	UNVOICED	EGGPLANT	SHIPMATE
RAINDROP	APHORISM	DEMOLISH	INFORMED	POLONIUM	UNWONTED	EGYPTIAN	SHIPMENT
RAINFALL	APPOSITE	DEMONIAC	INFORMER	RECORDER	UNWORTHY	ELEPHANT	SHIPPING
REINDEER	ARBOREAL	DENOUNCE	INNOCENT	RECOURSE	UPCOMING	EPIPHANY	SHIPWORM
SCANDIUM	ARMORIAL	DEPONENT	INNOVATE	REDOLENT	VAPORING	EYEPIECE	SHIPYARD
SCENARIO	ARROGANT	DEROGATE	INSOLENT	REFOREST	VAPORISH	FLAPJACK	SHOPLIFT
SHANGHAI	ARROGATE	DESOLATE	INSOMNIA	REFORMER	VAPORIZE	FLIPPANT	SHOPWORN
SHANTUNG	ASSORTED	DETONATE	INSOMUCH	REGOLITH	VAPOROUS	FLYPAPER	SIMPLIFY
SHINBONE	ASTONISH	DETOXIFY	INVOLUTE	RELOCATE	VELOCITY	FRIPPERY	SIXPENCE
SHINGLES	ATROCITY	DEVOTION	INVOLVED	RENOUNCE	VENOMOUS	GRAPHITE	SLIPKNOT
SIGNPOST	ATROPINE	DINOSAUR	JALOUSIE	RENOVATE	VERONICA	GUMPTION	SLIPPERY
SPANIARD	ATTORNEY	DISORDER	KEROSINE	REPORTER	VIGOROUS	GUNPOINT	SLIPSHOD
SPANKING	AUTOBAHN	DIVORCEE	KILOBYTE	RESOLUTE	VIROLOGY	HELPMATE	SNAPSHOT
SPINSTER	AUTOGIRO	DOLOMITE	KILOGRAM	RESONANT	XENOLITH	HELPMEET	SORPTION
STANDARD	AUTOJOIN	DOXOLOGY	KILOVOLT	RESONATE	YUGOSLAV	HISPANIC	STOPPAGE
STANDING	AUTOMATE	EMBOLDEN	KILOWATT	RESORTER	ADOPTIVE	HOSPITAL	SUBPOENA
STANDOFF	AVIONICS	EMBOLISM	LEMONADE	RESOURCE	AIRPLANE	HUMPBACK	SUPPLANT
STANDOUT	BARONAGE	EMPORIUM	LICORICE	REVOLVER	ALOPECIA	INSPIRIT	SUPPOSED
STINKBUG	BARONESS	ENCOMIUM	LIMONITE	RHEOLOGY	ANYPLACE	ISOPRENE	SUPPRESS
STUNNING	BAROUCHE	ESPOUSAL	LINOLEUM	RHEOSTAT	APOPLEXY	JEOPARDY	SURPLICE

SURPRISE	AMORTIZE	EVERYDAY	NONRIGID	RETROFIT	BOASTFUL	GRASPING	PERSONAL
SUSPENSE	ANDROGEN	EVERYONE	NUTRIENT	SACRISTY	BOWSPRIT	GROSBEAK	PERSPIRE
SYMPATHY	APERITIF	EXERCISE	OPERABLE	SCARCELY	BRISLING	GROSCHEN	PERSUADE
SYMPHONY	APERTURE	EXORCISE	OPERANDS	SCORPION	BURSITIS	GUNSMITH	PHASEOUT
TAXPAYER	APPRAISE	EXORDIUM	OPERETTA	SHIRRING	CABSTAND	HAYSTACK	PHOSPHOR
TEMPLATE	APPROACH	EXTRADOS	OUTREACH	SHIRTING	CAMSHAFT	HOGSHEAD	PHYSICAL
TEMPORAL	APPROVAL	FEARLESS	OUTRIDER	SHORTAGE	CAPSICUM	HOLSTEIN	PHYSIQUE
TENPENNY	AVERMENT	FEARSOME	OUTRIGHT	SHORTCUT	CAPSULAR	HOOSEGOW	POSSIBLE
TINPLATE	AVERSION	FEBRUARY	OVERALLS	SKIRMISH	CASSETTE	HORSEFLY	POTSHERD
TRAPDOOR	BARRACKS	FIBROSIS	OVERCAST	SOBRIETY	CAUSERIE	HORSEMAN	PRESENCE
TRAPPING	BARRATRY	FOURFOLD	OVERCOAT	SPIRITED	CAUSEWAY	HOUSEBOY	PRESERVE
TRAPROCK	BARRETTE	FOURSOME	OVERCOME	SPORADIC	CESSPOOL	HOUSEFLY	PRESIDIO
TRIPTYCH	BEARSKIN	FOURTEEN	OVERDRAW	SPURIOUS	CHASTISE	HOUSETOP	PRESSING
TWOPENCE	BEFRIEND	GARRISON	OVERFLOW	STARFISH	CHASTITY	INKSTAND	PRESSMAN
TWOPENNY	BEGRUDGE	GLORIOUS	OVERGROW	STARLING	CHASUBLE	ISOSTASY	PRESSURE
TYMPANUM	CAPRIOLE	GOURMAND	OVERHAND	STERLING	CHESTNUT	JOYSTICK	PRESTIGE
UNSPRUNG	CARRIAGE	GUARANTY	OVERHANG	STIRRING	CLASSIFY	KEYSTONE	PRISONER
VOLPLANE	CARRYALL	GUARDIAN	OVERHAUL	STURGEON	CLOSEOUT	LIPSTICK	PRISTINE
WARPLANE	CHARADES	GUERNSEY	OVERHEAD	SURROUND	CONSERVE	LOPSIDED	PROSPECT
WEAPONRY	CHARCOAL	HAIRLINE	OVERHEAR	TARRAGON	CONSIDER	MASSACRE	PROSTATE
WHIPCORD	CHARISMA	HARRIDAN	OVERKILL	TERRAPIN	CONSOMME	MASSEUSE	PURSLANE
WHIPLASH	CHARMING	HEBRAISM	OVERLAID	TERRIBLE	CONSPIRE	MASSLESS	PUSSYCAT
WHOPPING	CHEROKEE	HEIRLOOM	OVERLAND	TERRIFIC	CONSTANT	MESSMATE	QUESTION
WRAPPING	CLARINET	HOARDING	OVERLEAP	THEREFOR	CONSTRUE	MIDSHIPS	QUISLING
ZEPPELIN	CLERICAL	HORRIBLE	OVERLOOK	THIRTEEN	COXSWAIN	MINSTREL	REASSURE
ZOOPHYTE	CORRIDOR	HUARACHE	OVERLORD	THOROUGH	CRESCENT	MISSHAPE	SANSKRIT
ADEQUATE	COURTESY	HYDROGEN	OVERMUCH	THURSDAY	CROSSBAR	MISSPELL	SCISSORS
CONQUEST	COURTIER	IMPRISON	OVERPASS	UMBRELLA	CROSSBOW	MISSPEND	SEASCAPE
DAIQUIRI	CURRENCY	IMPROPER	OVERPLAY	UNBROKEN	CROSSCUT	MISSTATE	SEASHORE
DISQUIET	DAIRYING	INCREASE	OVERRIDE	UNERRING	CROSSING	MOISTURE	SENSIBLE
ELOQUENT	DAIRYMAN	INERRANT	OVERRULE	UNFREEZE	DANSEUSE	MONSIEUR	SENSUOUS
FREQUENT	DECREASE	INFRADIG	OVERSEAS	UPGROWTH	DIASTOLE	MOSSBACK	SETSCREW
INIQUITY	DECREPIT	INFRARED	OVERSHOE	USURIOUS	DIPSTICK	NAUSEATE	SHOSHONE
IROQUOIS	DEERSKIN	INFRINGE	OVERSIZE	UXORIOUS	DISSEVER	NEWSCAST	SOLSTICE
JACQUARD	DERRIERE	INTRADOS	OVERSTAY	VAGRANCY	DISSOLVE	NEWSREEL	SUBSONIC
MARQUESS	DETRITUS	INTRENCH	OVERSTEP	VITREOUS	DISSUADE	NONSENSE	SUNSHADE
MARQUISE	DIARRHEA	INTREPID	OVERTAKE	WARRANTY	DRESSAGE	NONSTICK	SUNSHINE
MESQUITE	DIURETIC	INTRIGUE	OVERTIME	WHARFAGE	DRESSING	NORSEMAN	SWASTIKA
MISQUOTE	DOORJAMB	INTROMIT	OVERTONE	WHEREVER	DYESTUFF	NUISANCE	TEASPOON
MOSQUITO	DOORKNOB	LACRIMAL	OVERTURE	YEARBOOK	EGGSHELL	NUMSKULL	TEOSINTE
VANQUISH	DOORSTEP	LACROSSE	OVERTURN	YEARLING	EKISTICS	NURSLING	THESPIAN
ABORNING	DOORYARD	LAUREATE	OVERVIEW	YEARLONG	EMISSARY	NUTSHELL	TINSMITH
ABORTION	EMERITUS	LEARNING	PEERLESS	YEARNING	EYESIGHT	OFFSHOOT	TOPSIDES
ACCREDIT	ENCROACH	LIBRETTO	PHARISEE	YOURSELF	FALSETTO	OFFSHORE	TRESPASS
ACERBATE	ENERGIZE	MADRIGAL	PHARMACY	AIRSPACE	FEASIBLE	OFFSTAGE	TRUSTFUL
ACERBITY	ENERVATE	MARRIAGE	PORRIDGE	AIRSPEED	FLASHGUN	OPUSCULE	VERSICLE
ADORABLE	ENORMITY	METRICAL	PROROGUE	AIRSTRIP	FLASHING	OUTSHINE	WRISTLET
AFFRIGHT	ENORMOUS	MICROBUS	PRURIENT	ALLSPICE	FLESHPOT	OUTSIDER	ZOOSPORE
AGERATUM	ENTRAILS	MIGRAINE	PYORRHEA	ANGSTROM	FLYSPECK	OUTSMART	ABATTOIR
AGGRIEVE	ENTRANCE	MOORLAND	REARWARD	ANISETTE	FORSOOTH	OUTSPEND	ABSTRACT
AIGRETTE	ENTRENCH	MOURNFUL	RECREANT	APOSTASY	FORSWEAR	OUTSTRIP	ABSTRUSE
ALARMIST	ENURESIS	MOURNING	RECREATE	BASSINET	FRESHMAN	PASSABLE	ABUTMENT
ALFRESCO	ESPRESSO	NECROSIS	REPRIEVE	BASSWOOD	FROSTING	PASSBOOK	ABUTTALS
ALTRUISM	ESTRANGE	NEURITIS	REPRISAL	BEDSTEAD	GEMSTONE	PASSOVER	AESTHETE
AMARANTH	ESTROGEN	NEUROSIS	REPROACH	BITSTOCK	GLASSFUL	PASSPORT	AGITPROP
AMBROSIA	ETERNITY	NEUROTIC	RETRENCH	BLESSING	GLOSSARY	PASSWORD	AIRTIGHT
AMERICAN	EVERMORE	NITROGEN	RETRIEVE	BLISSFUL	GOSSAMER	PENSTOCK	AMETHYST

ANATHEMA	ERYTHEMA	ISOTHERM	PLATINUM	TENTACLE	BROUGHAM	MISUSAGE	CERVICAL
ANYTHING	ESOTERIC	ISOTONIC	PLATYPUS	TERTIARY	BROUHAHA	MODULATE	CHIVALRY
APOTHEGM	EYETOOTH	JETTISON	PLETHORA	TESTATOR	CADUCEUS	MONUMENT	CLAVICLE
AUSTRIAN	FACTIOUS	KNITWEAR	POLTROON	TESTICLE	CAPUCHIN	NEBULIZE	CONVERGE
BANTLING	FACTOTUM	KNOTHOLE	PORTABLE	TEUTONIC	CASUALTY	NEBULOUS	CONVERSE
BEATIFIC	FALTBOAT	LEFTOVER	PORTHOLE	TEXTBOOK	CERULEAN	NONUNION	CONVINCE
BENTWOOD	FANTASIA	LISTLESS	PORTIERE	TORTILLA	CLOUDLET	OBDURATE	CONVULSE
BESTIARY	FARTHEST	LITTORAL	PORTRAIT	TORTOISE	COAUTHOR	OCCUPANT	CORVETTE
BESTRIDE	FARTHING	LOATHING	POSTCARD	TORTUOUS	COPULATE	ORGULOUS	CREVASSE
BIATHLON	FASTBACK	MALTREAT	POSTDATE	TRUTHFUL	COQUETTE	OSCULATE	DRIVEWAY
BIRTHDAY	FASTNESS	MALTSTER	POSTHOLE	UNCTUOUS	CORUNDUM	PECULATE	ELEVATOR
BOOTLESS	FESTIVAL	MANTELET	POSTLUDE	UNSTABLE	CROUPIER	PECULIAR	FERVENCY
BOUTIQUE	FILTRATE	MANTILLA	POSTMARK	UNSTEADY	CUCUMBER	PEDUNCLE	GRAVAMEN
BRETHREN	FLATBOAT	MANTISSA	POSTPAID	UNSTRUNG	DELUSION	PENUMBRA	HEAVYSET
BRITCHES	FLATFISH	MARTINET	POSTPONE	UPSTAIRS	DEMURRER	PETULANT	LEAVINGS
BUTTRESS	FLATFOOT	MASTERLY	PRATFALL	UPSTREAM	DEPUTIZE	PLEURISY	PERVERSE
CANTICLE	FLATHEAD	MASTHEAD	PRATIQUE	UPSTROKE	DISUNITE	POPULACE	PREVIOUS
CAPTIOUS	FLATIRON	MASTODON	PRETENSE	VERTEBRA	DISUNITY	POPULATE	PROVIDED
CASTAWAY	FLATLAND	MATTRESS	PRETERIT	VERTICAL	DOCUMENT	POPULIST	PROVINCE
CASTRATE	FLATTERY	MEATBALL	PRETTIFY	VESTMENT	DRAUGHTS	POPULOUS	SCAVENGE
CAUTIOUS	FLATWARE	MISTAKEN	PROTOCOL	VIATICUM	EFFUSION	PURULENT	SERVITOR
CENTERED	FLOTILLA	MISTREAT	PROTRACT	VICTORIA	ENCUMBER	REBUTTAL	SLOVENLY
CENTRIST	FOOTBALL	MISTRESS	PROTRUDE	VIETCONG	ETRUSCAN	REGULATE	SOLVENCY
CHITCHAT	FOOTFALL	MISTRIAL	QUATRAIN	VIRTUOSO	EXCURSUS	REPUBLIC	SOUVENIR
CHUTZPAH	FOOTHILL	MISTRUST	QUOTABLE	VIRTUOUS	FABULOUS	RETURNEE	TRAVERSE
CLITORIS	FOOTHOLD	MORTGAGE	QUOTIENT	WAITRESS	FIGURINE	SALUTARY	TRAVESTY
CLOTHIER	FOOTLESS	MORTUARY	RATTLING	WHATEVER	FLAUTIST	SATURATE	UNIVALVE
CLOTHING	FOOTLING	MULTIPLE	RESTLESS	WHITECAP	FLOUNDER	SATURDAY	UNIVERSE
CONTEMPT	FOOTNOTE	MULTIPLY	RESTRAIN	WHITEFLY	FLOURISH	SCRUTINY	VALVULAR
CONTINUE	FOOTPATH	MUSTACHE	RESTRICT	WISTARIA	FROUFROU	SECURITY	ANYWHERE
CONTRACT	FOOTRACE	MYSTICAL	RHETORIC	WISTERIA	FUTURISM	SEDULOUS	BLOWPIPE
CONTRAIL	FOOTREST	MYSTIQUE	ROUTEMAN	WRATHFUL	FUTURITY	SEQUENCE	BOBWHITE
CONTRARY	FOOTSORE	NAUTICAL	SAUTERNE	WRETCHED	GLAUCOMA	SHOULDER	BROWBEAT
CONTRAST	FOOTSTEP	NAUTILUS	SCATHING	YOUTHFUL	GROUNDER	SIMULATE	BROWNOUT
CONTRITE	FOOTWEAR	NESTLING	SCOTTISH	ABLUTION	HANUKKAH	SITUATED	CHOWCHOW
CONTRIVE	FOOTWORK	NEUTRINO	SENTENCE	ACCURATE	HUGUENOT	SOLUTION	COGWHEEL
CRETONNE	FORTRESS	NOCTURNE	SENTIENT	ACCURSED	ILLUMINE	SPLUTTER	CRAWFISH
CRITICAL	FORTUITY	OBITUARY	SENTINEL	ACCUSTOM	ILLUSION	STRUGGLE	CROWFOOT
CRITIQUE	FRETWORK	OBSTACLE	SHUTDOWN	ACOUSTIC	ILLUSIVE	STRUMPET	DRAWBACK
CROTCHET	FURTHEST	OBSTRUCT	SKITTISH	ACQUAINT	ILLUSORY	SUBURBIA	FLYWHEEL
CUSTOMER	GOATHERD	OINTMENT	SLATTERN	ADJUTANT	IMMUNIZE	TABULATE	FORWARDS
DEATHBED	GOATSKIN	ORATORIO	SOFTBALL	ADJUVANT	IMPUDENT	THOUSAND	GASWORKS
DESTRUCT	GRATEFUL	PANTHEON	SOFTWARE	AFLUTTER	IMPUNITY	THRUSTER	GLOWWORM
DEXTROSE	GRATUITY	PANTSUIT	SOFTWOOD	ALLUVIUM	INCUBATE	TRIUMVIR	KEYWORDS
DIATOMIC	GUTTURAL	PARTERRE	SOUTHPAW	AMBULANT	INCUMBER	TROUSERS	OUTWEIGH
DIATRIBE	HAUTBOIS	PARTIBLE	SPITBALL	AMPUTATE	INDUCTEE	UNBUCKLE	PINWHEEL
DICTATOR	HAWTHORN	PARTICLE	SPITTOON	ARGUABLE	INDURATE	UNBURDEN	SEAWATER
DISTANCE	HOSTELRY	PARTISAN	STATUARY	ARGUMENT	INDUSTRY	UNBUTTON	SHOWCASE
DISTASTE	HUNTRESS	PASTICHE	STOTINKA	BABUSHKA	INGUINAL	UNDULANT	SHOWDOWN
DISTINCT	HUNTSMAN	PASTILLE	SUBTITLE	BAGUETTE	INHUMANE	UNDULATE	SNOWBALL
DISTRACT	HUSTINGS	PASTORAL	SUBTRACT	BALUSTER	INNUENDO	UNGULATE	SNOWBANK
DISTRAIT	HYSTERIA	PASTRAMI	SUITABLE	BEAUTIFY	INSULATE	UNMUZZLE	SNOWDROP
DISTRESS	IMITABLE	PECTORAL	SUITCASE	BEFUDDLE	ISSUANCE	VALUABLE	SNOWFALL
DISTRICT	INITIATE	PENTAGON	SYSTEMIC	BEQUEATH	LABURNUM	VENUSIAN	SNOWPLOW
DISTRUST	INSTANCE	PETTIFOG	TANTALUM	BIBULOUS	LOCUTION	VIBURNUM	SNOWSHOE
DOCTRINE	INSTINCT	PITTANCE	TEETHING	BICUSPID	MATURATE	VIRULENT	STOWAWAY
EMOTICON	INSTRUCT	PLATFORM	TEETOTAL	BOTULISM	MATURITY	BREVIARY	UNAWARES

FLEXIBLE	AMICABLE	EMPHATIC	MISCARRY	TERRAPIN	CELIBATE	HORNBOOK	STUBBORN
GLOXINIA	ANTEATER	ENDEAVOR	MISLABEL	TESTATOR	CENOBITE	HUMPBACK	STUDBOOK
INEXPERT	APPLAUSE	ENTRAILS	MISMATCH	THALAMUS	CEREBRUM	IMMOBILE	SWAYBACK
QUIXOTIC	APPRAISE	ENTRANCE	MISTAKEN	THREATEN	CHAMBRAY	INCUBATE	TEXTBOOK
ABEYANCE	ARGUABLE	ENVIABLE	MOCCASIN	TOREADOR	CHAPBOOK	INDEBTED	TOLLBOTH
ARMYWORM	BACCARAT	ESTRANGE	MUSCATEL	TRIMARAN	CLAMBAKE	INFOBAHN	TROMBONE
BODYWORK	BACKACHE	EXCHANGE	MUSTACHE	TYMPANUM	COMEBACK	JACKBOOT	VAGABOND
BUOYANCY	BAILABLE	EXTRADOS	NEONATAL	UNAWARES	COOKBOOK	JAILBIRD	WASHBOWL
BUSYBODY	BANDANNA	FANDANGO	NONDAIRY	UNBEATEN	COPYBOOK	KEELBOAT	WELLBORN
BUSYWORK	BARBARIC	FANTASIA	NUISANCE	UNBIASED	CRIBBAGE	KICKBACK	WINDBURN
CARYATID	BARNACLE	FELLATIO	NUTHATCH	UNCHASTE	DATABASE	KIELBASA	WISHBONE
CHEYENNE	BARRACKS	FLYPAPER	OBSTACLE	UNIVALVE	DEADBEAT	KILOBYTE	WOODBINE
CLAYMORE	BARRATRY	FOLDAWAY	OPERABLE	UNLEADED	DEMIBOLD	KINGBOLT	WORDBOOK
COPYBOOK	BEGGARLY	FOLIATED	OPERANDS	UNSHAPED	DINGBATS	LADYBIRD	WORKBOOK
COPYDESK	BEREAVED	FORWARDS	ORDNANCE	UNSTABLE	DISABUSE	LAMPBACK	YEARBOOK
CRAYFISH	BIDDABLE	GENDARME	OUTDATED	UPHEAVAL	DOWNBEAT	LIFEBOAT	ZWIEBACK
EMPYREAN	BINNACLE	GHANAIAN	OVERALLS	UPSTAIRS	DRAWBACK	LONGBOAT	ABDICATE
GRAYLING	BIYEARLY	GIVEAWAY	PALPABLE	VAGRANCY	DRUMBEAT	LOVEBIRD	ADJACENT
LADYBIRD	BUNGALOW	GONFALON	PARLANCE	VALUABLE	DUCKBILL	MEATBALL	ADVOCATE
LADYLIKE	BUOYANCY	GOSSAMER	PASSABLE	VARIABLE	DUMBBELL	MEGABYTE	AFFECTED
LADYLOVE	CAMPAIGN	GRAVAMEN	PELLAGRA	VARIANCE	EUROBOND	MINIBIKE	ALBACORE
LADYSHIP	CANNABIS	GUARANTY	PENTAGON	VERBATIM	FALTBOAT	MOONBEAM	ALLOCATE
MANYFOLD	CARDAMOM	GUIDANCE	PINNACLE	VILLAGER	FASTBACK	MORIBUND	AQUACADE
PLAYBACK	CARNAUBA	HEADACHE	PITIABLE	VILLAINY	FEEDBACK	MOSSBACK	ATROCITY
PLAYBILL	CARYATID	HEBRAISM	PITTANCE	VIOLABLE	FIREBALL	MOTHBALL	BIFOCALS
PLAYBOOK	CASTAWAY	HIDEAWAY	PODIATRY	VOLCANIC	FIREBOAT	NOTEBOOK	BIRACIAL
PLAYGOER	CASUALTY	HISPANIC	PORTABLE	WALKAWAY	FIREBOMB	OVENBIRD	BOOKCASE
PLAYMATE	CEPHALIC	HUARACHE	PRENATAL	WARFARIN	FISHBOWL	PARABOLA	BRITCHES
PLAYSUIT	CHARADES	IDOLATER	PROBABLE	WARRANTY	FLAMBEAU	PASSBOOK	BROCCOLI
POLYGAMY	CHIVALRY	IDOLATRY	PROCAINE	WASHABLE	FLATBOAT	PLAYBACK	BRONCHUS
POLYGLOT	CINNABAR	IMITABLE	PTOMAINE	WAYFARER	FLEABANE	PLAYBILL	CABOCHON
POLYMATH	CINNAMON	INDIAMAN	QUOTABLE	WISEACRE	FLEABITE	PLAYBOOK	CADUCEUS
PONYTAIL	CLEMATIS	INFRADIG	RADIATOR	WISTARIA	FOLDBOAT	PLUMBING	CAPACITY
SWAYBACK	COCKATOO	INFRARED	REHEARSE	WORKABLE	FOOTBALL	PUFFBALL	CAPUCHIN
ALIZARIN	COLLAPSE	INSTANCE	RELIABLE	WORKADAY	FOREBEAR	PULLBACK	CARACOLE
BENZOATE	COMMANDO	INTRADOS	RELIANCE	YEOMANRY	FOREBODE	PUREBRED	CATACOMB
BLIZZARD	CREMAINS	INVIABLE	REPEATED	ACERBATE	FREEBORN	REPUBLIC	CHANCERY
CRUZEIRO	CREVASSE	ISSUANCE	RESEARCH	ACERBITY	FULLBACK	RHOMBOID	CHARCOAL
GRIZZLED	CULPABLE	JEOPARDY	SCALABLE	AMOEBOID	GADABOUT	ROLLBACK	CHITCHAT
MARZIPAN	CYCLAMEN	KAMAAINA	SCALAWAG	ANTIBODY	GIGABYTE	ROSEBUSH	CHOWCHOW
PIZZERIA	DAMNABLE	KANGAROO	SCENARIO	AUTOBAHN	GOOFBALL	RUNABOUT	CLINCHER
	DEFIANCE	LAMBASTE	SCHMALTZ	BACKBITE	GROSBEAK	RUTABAGA	COCKCROW
	DEMEANOR	LAUDANUM	SEAFARER	BACKBONE	HALFBACK	SAILBOAT	COINCIDE
	DESPATCH	LAWMAKER	SEAWATER	BANKBOOK	HANDBALL	SANDBANK	CORNCRIB
5TH LETTER	DIAPASON	LETHARGY	SITUATED	BAREBACK	HANDBILL	SCABBARD	CRESCENT
	DICTATOR	MACPAINT	SOCIABLE	BASEBALL	HANDBOOK	SCRABBLE	CROTCHET
ABEYANCE	DISFAVOR	MAGDALEN	SPORADIC	BASEBORN	HARDBACK	SCRIBBLE	DEDICATE
ACQUAINT	DISPATCH	MANDAMUS	STOWAWAY	BEANBALL	HARDBALL	SHAMBLES	DEFECATE
ADORABLE	DISTANCE	MANDARIN	STREAMER	BERIBERI	HAREBELL	SHINBONE	DEJECTED
AFFIANCE	DISTASTE	MANIACAL	SUITABLE	BIRDBATH	HAUTBOIS	SNOBBERY	DELICACY
AFFLATUS	DUNGAREE	MARIACHI	SYLLABLE	BLUEBELL	HEADBAND	SNOWBALL	DELICATE
AGERATUM	DUTIABLE	MASSACRE	SYLLABUS	BLUEBIRD	HIGHBALL	SNOWBANK	DEMOCRAT
ALIZARIN	EDUCABLE	MECHANIC	SYMPATHY	BROWBEAT	HIGHBORN	SOFTBALL	DETACHED
ALLIANCE	ELEGANCE	MENHADEN	TANTALUM	BUSYBODY	HIGHBRED	SOMEBODY	DIDACTIC
ALPHABET	ELEVATOR	MESDAMES	TARRAGON	CALABASH	HIGHBROW	SONGBIRD	DIRECTOR
AMARANTH	EMBLAZON	METHANOL	TAXPAYER	CALLBACK	HOMEBODY	SPITBALL	DOMICILE
AMENABLE	EMPHASIS	MIGRAINE	TENTACLE	CELIBACY	HOMEBRED	SQUABBLE	DOWNCAST

ESPECIAL	SETSCREW	DIVIDEND	STUDDING	CONSERVE	HEDGEHOP	PICKEREL	UNFREEZE
EXERCISE	SHOWCASE	DREADFUL	SYSADMIN	CONTEMPT	HEDGEROW	PIMIENTO	UNIVERSE
EXORCISE	SILICATE	EXORDIUM	TRAPDOOR	CONVERGE	HERMETIC	PIZZERIA	UNSEEMLY
FELICITY	SILICIFY	EXPEDITE	UNBIDDEN	CONVERSE	HITHERTO	PLACENTA	UNSTEADY
FEROCITY	SILICONE	FACEDOWN	UNBODIED	COPPERAS	HOOSEGOW	PLEBEIAN	UNWIELDY
FIRECLAY	SINECURE	FIREDAMP	UNENDING	COQUETTE	HORSEFLY	POTBELLY	VARIETAL
FORECAST	SOLECISM	FLUIDRAM	UNRIDDLE	CORVETTE	HORSEMAN	PRESENCE	VELLEITY
FRANCIUM	SPROCKET	FOREDOOM	UNSADDLE	COSMETIC	HOSTELRY	PRESERVE	VENDETTA
GAMECOCK	STACCATO	FREEDMAN	VALIDATE	CREDENCE	HOUSEBOY	PRETENSE	VENGEFUL
GENOCIDE	STRICKEN	GRANDEUR	VANADIUM	CREDENZA	HOUSEFLY	PRETERIT	VERTEBRA
GLAUCOMA	SUITCASE	GRANDSON	WINGDING	CRUZEIRO	HOUSETOP	PRIMEVAL	VIGNETTE
GROSCHEN	TAILCOAT	GUARDIAN	WIREDRAW	CURRENCY	HUGUENOT	PROCEEDS	VIOLENCE
HANDCUFF	TELECAST	HEREDITY	WITHDRAW	DANSEUSE	HYSTERIA	PROPERTY	VISCERAL
HELICOID	TRENCHER	HOARDING	YIELDING	DECREASE	INCREASE	RECREANT	VITREOUS
HOMICIDE	TRUNCATE	HUMIDIFY	ACADEMIC	DECREPIT	INNUENDO	RECREATE	WHATEVER
IMBECILE	TURNCOAT	HUMIDITY	ACCREDIT	DEWBERRY	INTRENCH	RETRENCH	WHENEVER
IMPACTED	TYPECAST	IMMODEST	AIGRETTE	DIABETES	INTREPID	REVIEWER	WHEREVER
INDECENT	UNBUCKLE	IMPUDENT	ALFRESCO	DIAMETER	LAUREATE	ROCKETRY	WHITECAP
INDICATE	UUDECODE	INCIDENT	ALOPECIA	DISHEVEL	LEUKEMIA	ROOMETTE	WHITEFLY
INDUCTEE	UUENCODE	INUNDATE	AMBIENCE	DISKETTE	LIBRETTO	ROULETTE	WHOMEVER
INNOCENT	VARICOSE	JAUNDICE	ANISETTE	DISPENSE	LIGNEOUS	ROUTEMAN	WISTERIA
INSECURE	VELOCITY	KILLDEER	ATHLETIC	DISPERSE	LINGERIE	SAUCEPAN	ZEPPELIN
IRONCLAD	VERACITY	LAPIDARY	AUDIENCE	DISSEVER	LUTHERAN	SAUTERNE	ARTIFACT
JUDICIAL	VESICANT	MARKDOWN	BACHELOR	DIURETIC	MACKEREL	SCALEPAN	ARTIFICE
LAUNCHER	VIETCONG	MELODEON	BAEDEKER	DOGGEREL	MAGNESIA	SCAVENGE	BACKFIRE
MAGICIAN	VISICALC	MERIDIAN	BAGUETTE	DRIVEWAY	MAGNETIC	SENTENCE	BAREFOOT
MANICURE	VIVACITY	NOWADAYS	BARBECUE	DUODENUM	MANNERED	SEQUENCE	BENEFICE
MEDICAID	WHIPCORD	OBSIDIAN	BARBERRY	DYSLEXIA	MANNERLY	SERGEANT	BILLFOLD
MEDICARE	WOODCOCK	ONONDAGA	BARRETTE	EMINENCE	MANTELET	SIXPENCE	BLUEFISH
MEDICATE	WRETCHED	OVERDRAW	BAYBERRY	ENFEEBLE	MASSEUSE	SKELETON	BOLDFACE
MEDICINE	ABUNDANT	PARADIGM	BEQUEATH	ENTRENCH	MASTERLY	SLOVENLY	BOUFFANT
MOLECULE	ACCIDENT	PARADISE	BERCEUSE	ENURESIS	MEDIEVAL	SOLVENCY	BULLFROG
MOROCCAN	ANECDOTE	POSTDATE	BIWEEKLY	EPIDEMIC	MULBERRY	SOUVENIR	CAREFREE
MUSICALE	ANTEDATE	POUNDAGE	BORDELLO	EPILEPSY	MUSKETRY	SPACEMAN	CLUBFOOT
MUSICIAN	ANTIDOTE	PUSHDOWN	BRACELET	ESOTERIC	NAUSEATE	SQUEEGEE	COIFFEUR
NEWSCAST	AQUEDUCT	QUANDARY	BRAKEMAN	ESPRESSO	NOBLEMAN	STAKEOUT	COIFFURE
OFFICIAL	ARCHDUKE	RAINDROP	BULLETIN	EVIDENCE	NONMETAL	STILETTO	CRAWFISH
OPTICIAN	BACKDROP	REINDEER	CAFFEINE	EXEGESIS	NONSENSE	SUBMERGE	CRAYFISH
OPUSCULE	BEFUDDLE	REMEDIAL	CASSETTE	EXIGENCY	NORSEMAN	SUBMERSE	CROWFOOT
OVERCAST	BENEDICT	RESIDENT	CATHETER	FALSETTO	NUCLEATE	SURCEASE	DOWNFALL
OVERCOAT	BOUNDARY	RESIDUAL	CAUSERIE	FERVENCY	ODOMETER	SUSPENSE	FLATFISH
OVERCOME	BRANDISH	RESIDUUM	CAUSEWAY	FLAMENCO	OHMMETER	SYMMETRY	FLATFOOT
PEDICURE	BREEDING	RUBIDIUM	CENTERED	FLAMEOUT	OPERETTA	SYSTEMIC	FLIMFLAM
PINOCHLE	BRINDLED	SCANDIUM	CHAPERON	FOLDEROL	OUTREACH	TENDENCY	FOOTFALL
POSTCARD	BUILDING	SCHEDULE	CHEYENNE	FORMERLY	OUTWEIGH	TENPENNY	FOREFEND
PRINCESS	BULLDOZE	SHOWDOWN	CHOLERIC	FRENETIC	PALMETTO	THEREFOR	FOREFOOT
PUSHCART	CALADIUM	SHUTDOWN	CLEMENCY	FURBELOW	PANDEMIC	TIMBERED	FOURFOLD
RAINCOAT	CANADIAN	SNOWDROP	CLOSEOUT	GARDENIA	PARIETAL	TOILETRY	FROUFROU
REGICIDE	CAULDRON	SOLIDIFY	COALESCE	GEODESIC	PARMESAN	TOILETTE	GOLDFISH
RELOCATE	CHANDLER	SPEEDWAY	COCKEREL	GEOMETRY	PARTERRE	TRAVERSE	GRAFFITO
RETICENT	CLOUDLET	SQUADRON	COMMENCE	GINGERLY	PATHETIC	TRAVESTY	HEREFORD
RICOCHET	COMEDIAN	STANDARD	COMMERCE	GLYCERIN	PATIENCE	TRIMETER	LANDFALL
RIDICULE	COMEDOWN	STANDING	CONCEIVE	GLYCEROL	PERCEIVE	TURMERIC	LANDFILL
RUBICUND	COPYDESK	STANDOFF	CONCERTO	GORGEOUS	PERFECTO	TWOPENCE	LANDFORM
SCARCELY	CUPIDITY	STANDOUT	CONDENSE	GRATEFUL	PERMEATE	TWOPENNY	LEAPFROG
SEASCAPE	DECEDENT	STRADDLE	CONFETTI	HACIENDA	PERVERSE	UMBRELLA	MANIFEST
SELECTEE	DIELDRIN	STRIDENT	CONGENER	HEDGEHOG	PHASEOUT	UNCLENCH	MANIFOLD

MANYFOLD	HOLOGRAM	APOTHEGM	FRIGHTEN	PORPHYRY	BESTIARY	ENCEINTE	MADRIGAL
METAFILE	IDEOGRAM	ARACHNID	FURTHEST	PORTHOLE	BIOCIDAL	EXPLICIT	MANCIPLE
OVERFLOW	INDIGENT	ARMCHAIR	GOATHERD	POSTHOLE	BOUTIQUE	EYELINER	MANDIBLE
PACIFIER	INSIGNIA	BACKHAND	GODCHILD	POTSHERD	BREVIARY	EYEPIECE	MANTILLA
PACIFISM	INTAGLIO	BEECHNUT	GRAPHITE	PROPHECY	BROMIDIC	EYESIGHT	MANTISSA
PALEFACE	INTEGRAL	BIATHLON	GYMKHANA	PROPHESY	BURSITIS	FACTIOUS	MARRIAGE
PARAFFIN	IRRIGATE	BILLHEAD	HARDHACK	PUNCHEON	CALLIOPE	FALLIBLE	MARTINET
PINAFORE	KILOGRAM	BIRTHDAY	HATCHING	PURCHASE	CANAILLE	FANCIFUL	MARZIPAN
PLATFORM	LITIGANT	BOBWHITE	HATCHWAY	ROUGHAGE	CANNIBAL	FANLIGHT	MEPHITIC
PRATFALL	LITIGATE	BRETHREN	HAWTHORN	SAPPHIRE	CANTICLE	FASCICLE	METRICAL
RAINFALL	MAHOGANY	BRIGHTEN	HEIGHTEN	SCATHING	CAPRIOLE	FASCISTA	MIDNIGHT
ROCKFALL	MARIGOLD	BROCHURE	HELLHOLE	SEASHORE	CAPSICUM	FEASIBLE	MILLIARD
SAILFISH	MITIGATE	BROUHAHA	HENCHMAN	SHEPHERD	CAPTIOUS	FESTIVAL	MILLIBAR
SCAFFOLD	MONOGAMY	BUDDHISM	HOGSHEAD	SHOSHONE	CARDIGAN	FLAMINGO	MILLIEME
SCOFFLAW	MONOGRAM	BULKHEAD	ISOTHERM	SINKHOLE	CARDINAL	FLATIRON	MILLINER
SCROFULA	MORTGAGE	BULLHEAD	KEELHAUL	SOUTHPAW	CARNIVAL	FLEXIBLE	MISCIBLE
SNOWFALL	NAVIGATE	BUNGHOLE	KERCHIEF	SUNSHADE	CARRIAGE	FLOTILLA	MONSIEUR
STARFISH	OBLIGATE	CAMSHAFT	KNEEHOLE	SUNSHINE	CAUDILLO	FOLLICLE	MULTIPLE
STUFFING	ORANGERY	CATCHALL	KNOTHOLE	SYMPHONY	CAUTIOUS	FORCIBLE	MULTIPLY
SUREFIRE	OVERGROW	CATCHING	LATCHKEY	TEACHING	CERVICAL	GARRISON	MYELITIS
TELEFILM	PEDAGOGY	CINCHONA	LAUGHTER	TEETHING	CHARISMA	GASLIGHT	MYRMIDON
TYPEFACE	PEDIGREE	CLOTHIER	LINCHPIN	TOMAHAWK	CHEMICAL	GERMINAL	MYSTICAL
WEAKFISH	PLANGENT	CLOTHING	LOATHING	TOUCHING	CHENILLE	GLACIATE	MYSTIQUE
WHARFAGE	PLAYGOER	COACHMAN	LONGHAIR	TRICHINA	CLARINET	GLORIOUS	NAUTICAL
WILDFIRE	POLYGAMY	COGWHEEL	LONGHAND	TRUTHFUL	CLAVICLE	GLOXINIA	NAUTILUS
WILDFOWL	POLYGLOT	COUCHANT	LONGHORN	WATCHDOG	CLERICAL	GRACIOUS	NEGLIGEE
WINDFALL	RELEGATE	DAUGHTER	LOOPHOLE	WATCHFUL	CLINICAL	GRADIENT	NEURITIS
ABNEGATE	RELIGION	DEATHBED	LUNCHEON	WATCHMAN	COLLIERY	GRIDIRON	NONRIGID
ABROGATE	RENEGADE	DECKHAND	LYMPHOID	WELLHEAD	COMBINGS	GUNFIGHT	NUTRIENT
ALLEGORY	RESIGNED	DOCKHAND	MASTHEAD	WIREHAIR	COMPILER	HANDICAP	OBEDIENT
ALMIGHTY	RUNAGATE	DOUGHBOY	MERCHANT	WITCHERY	CONFINES	HARRIDAN	ORIGINAL
ARPEGGIO	SCRAGGLY	DOUGHNUT	MIDSHIPS	WITCHING	CONSIDER	HAWAIIAN	OUTFIELD
ARROGANT	SERAGLIO	DOWNHILL	MISCHIEF	WITHHOLD	CONTINUE	HOOLIGAN	OUTFIGHT
ARROGATE	SHANGHAI	DUNGHILL	MISSHAPE	WORMHOLE	CONVINCE	HORRIBLE	OUTRIDER
AUTOGIRO	SHINGLES	EARPHONE	MOLEHILL	WRATHFUL	CORRIDOR	HOSPITAL	OUTRIGHT
BLUDGEON	SLUGGARD	EGGSHELL	MORPHEME	YOUTHFUL	CREDIBLE	HUSTINGS	OUTSIDER
BRAGGART	SLUGGISH	ELEPHANT	MORPHINE	ZOOPHYTE	CREDITOR	HYACINTH	PALLIATE
BROUGHAM	SPHAGNUM	EPIPHANY	NEIGHBOR	ZUCCHINI	CRIMINAL	IMPLICIT	PARTIBLE
CATEGORY	STRAGGLE	ERYTHEMA	NEOPHYTE	ABSCISSA	CRITICAL	IMPRISON	PARTICLE
COSIGNER	STRUGGLE	FALCHION	NUTSHELL	AFFRIGHT	CRITIQUE	INEDITED	PARTISAN
DECIGRAM	STURGEON	FARMHAND	OFFSHOOT	AGGRIEVE	CRUCIBLE	INFRINGE	PASTICHE
DEKAGRAM	TAILGATE	FARTHEST	OFFSHORE	AIRFIELD	CRUCIFIX	INGUINAL	PASTILLE
DELEGATE	TELEGRAM	FARTHING	OUTSHINE	AIRLINER	CURLICUE	INIMICAL	PEMMICAN
DEROGATE	TOBOGGAN	FETCHING	OVERHAND	AIRTIGHT	CUSPIDOR	INITIATE	PENLIGHT
DILIGENT	TOLLGATE	FISHHOOK	OVERHANG	ALUMINUM	DAYLIGHT	INSPIRIT	PETTIFOG
DISAGREE	VINEGARY	FLASHGUN	OVERHAUL	AMERICAN	DERRIERE	INSTINCT	PHARISEE
DIVAGATE	VOYAGEUR	FLASHING	OVERHEAD	ANGLICAN	DETRITUS	INTRIGUE	PHYSICAL
DRAUGHTS	WRIGGLER	FLATHEAD	OVERHEAR	APERITIF	DISCIPLE	INVEIGLE	PHYSIQUE
DRUGGIST	WRONGFUL	FLESHPOT	PAMPHLET	APPLIQUE	DISPIRIT	JETTISON	PICKINGS
ELONGATE	YOUNGISH	FLYWHEEL	PANTHEON	ATOMIZER	DISTINCT	LACRIMAL	PLATINUM
ENERGIZE	ACIDHEAD	FOOTHILL	PAYCHECK	ATYPICAL	DOGFIGHT	LAWGIVER	POLLIWOG
ENGAGING	AESTHETE	FOOTHOLD	PEEPHOLE	BARBICAN	DULCIMER	LEAVINGS	PORRIDGE
FILIGREE	AMETHYST	FOREHAND	PENCHANT	BARBITAL	EARNINGS	LOLLIPOP	PORTIERE
FOREGONE	ANATHEMA	FOREHEAD	PILCHARD	BASSINET	ELIGIBLE	LOPSIDED	POSSIBLE
FUMIGANT	ANECHOIC	FREEHAND	PINWHEEL	BEATIFIC	EMACIATE	LUSCIOUS	PRATIQUE
FUMIGATE	ANYTHING	FREEHOLD	PITCHMAN	BEFRIEND	EMERITUS	MACHISMO	PRECINCT
HEADGEAR	ANYWHERE	FRESHMAN	PLETHORA	BESMIRCH	EMOTICON	MACKINAW	PRECIOUS

PREMIERE	USURIOUS	TRACKAGE	COPULATE	FOOTLING	LOVELORN	PECULATE	SKULLCAP
PRESIDIO	UXORIOUS	TRICKERY	CORDLESS	FORELADY	LOYALIST	PECULIAR	SLUMLORD
PREVIOUS	VACCINIA	TRUCKAGE	COUPLING	FORELAND	MAINLAND	PEERLESS	SMALLPOX
PRODIGAL	VERBIAGE	UNLIKELY	CROPLAND	FORELIMB	MAINLINE	PENALIZE	SPILLWAY
PROHIBIT	VERSICLE	WRECKAGE	CRYOLITE	FORELOCK	MAJOLICA	PENOLOGY	SPOOLING
PROLIFIC	VERTICAL	ABSOLUTE	CYTOLOGY	FORKLIFT	MARBLING	PERILUNE	SPYGLASS
PROVIDED	VIATICUM	ACCOLADE	DARKLING	FORMLESS	MASSLESS	PETULANT	STALLION
PROVINCE	VINCIBLE	AEROLOGY	DATELESS	FOXGLOVE	MEDALIST	PICKLOCK	STARLING
PRURIENT	VIRGINAL	AIRPLANE	DATELINE	FREELOAD	MEGALITH	PIDDLING	STEALTHY
PUBLICAN	WILLIWAW	ALKALOID	DEADLINE	FUSELAGE	MIDDLING	PIEPLANT	STERLING
QUOTIENT	AUTOJOIN	ALLELUIA	DEADLOCK	FUTILITY	MINDLESS	PIPELINE	SUCHLIKE
RECEIVER	DEMIJOHN	AMBULANT	DEBILITY	GANGLAND	MISPLACE	PITILESS	SUCKLING
REPRIEVE	DOORJAMB	ANGELICA	DEMOLISH	GANGLING	MOBILIZE	PIXELATE	SUPPLANT
REPRISAL	FLAPJACK	ANTELOPE	DERELICT	GANGLION	MODULATE	POPULACE	SURPLICE
RETAINER	BLACKING	ANYPLACE	DESELECT	GASOLINE	MONOLITH	POPULATE	SWELLING
RETRIEVE	BLACKOUT	APHELION	DESOLATE	GEMOLOGY	MORALIST	POPULIST	TABULATE
REVEILLE	BLACKTOP	APOPLEXY	DEVILISH	GRAYLING	MORALITY	POPULOUS	TEMPLATE
SACRISTY	BLOCKADE	APPELLEE	DISALLOW	GRUELING	MORALIZE	POSTLUDE	THALLIUM
SCILICET	BRACKISH	AQUILINE	DISCLAIM	HAIRLINE	MUCILAGE	PRECLUDE	THEOLOGY
SCIMITAR	BREAKAGE	ARBALEST	DISCLOSE	HEADLAND	MUTILATE	PROCLAIM	TICKLISH
SENSIBLE	BREAKOUT	BACILLUS	DISPLACE	HEADLINE	MYCOLOGY	PUDDLING	TIDELAND
SENTIENT	BRICKBAT	BACKLASH	DOUBLOON	HEADLOCK	NAMELESS	PUGILISM	TIMELESS
SENTINEL	BROOKLET	BANTLING	DOWNLOAD	HEADLONG	NAPOLEON	PURBLIND	TINPLATE
SERVITOR	CHECKERS	BASELESS	DOXOLOGY	HEIRLOOM	NASALIZE	PURSLANE	TIRELESS
SHILINGI	CHECKOFF	BASELINE	DUCKLING	HERALDIC	NATALITY	PURULENT	TITILATE
SKYLIGHT	CHECKOUT	BASILICA	DUMPLING	HERALDRY	NEBULIZE	QUISLING	TONALITY
SOBRIETY	CHECKSUM	BASILISK	DWELLING	HIGHLAND	NEBULOUS	RAILLERY	TOPOLOGY
SOLDIERY	CRACKPOT	BEHOLDEN	EGGPLANT	HIRELING	NECKLACE	RATTLING	TOTALITY
SPACIOUS	CROCKERY	BEWILDER	EMBOLDEN	HOMELAND	NECKLINE	RECKLESS	TOWELING
SPANIARD	DOORKNOB	BIBULOUS	EMBOLISM	HOROLOGY	NEEDLESS	REDOLENT	TRIFLING
SPECIFIC	DROPKICK	BIRDLIME	ENFILADE	HUMILITY	NEOPLASM	REGOLITH	TRILLION
SPECIMEN	DRUNKARD	BOBOLINK	ENSILAGE	IDEALISM	NESTLING	REGULATE	TRILLIUM
SPECIOUS	FOREKNOW	BODILESS	ENVELOPE	IDEALIZE	NIGGLING	RESOLUTE	TUNELESS
SPIRITED	GREEKING	BOOTLESS	EQUALIZE	IDEOLOGY	NIHILISM	RESTLESS	TUTELAGE
SPURIOUS	HANUKKAH	BOTULISM	ESCALATE	IMMOLATE	NOBELIST	REVOLVER	TUTELARY
STOTINKA	KAMIKAZE	BOUILLON	ESCALLOP	IMPELLER	NOBELIUM	RHEOLOGY	UNBELIEF
STRAIGHT	KATAKANA	BRISLING	ESPALIER	IMPOLITE	NOBILITY	RHYOLITE	UNBOLTED
STRAITEN	KNICKERS	BUNDLING	ETHOLOGY	INDOLENT	NOVELIZE	ROYALIST	UNDULANT
STUDIOUS	KNOCKOUT	BURGLARY	ETIOLOGY	INHALANT	NURSLING	RUMBLING	UNDULATE
SUBTITLE	LIMEKILN	CAGELING	EYEGLASS	INSOLENT	OBSOLETE	RUTHLESS	UNFILIAL
SUCCINCT	NUMSKULL	CAMELLIA	FABULOUS	INSULATE	OILCLOTH	SCALLION	UNGULATE
SUNLIGHT	OVERKILL	CANALIZE	FACILITY	INVOLUTE	ORGULOUS	SCULLERY	VIGILANT
SURGICAL	PARAKEET	CARELESS	FADELESS	INVOLVED	OSCULATE	SCULLION	VIROLOGY
SYPHILIS	PLANKING	CARILLON	FAMILIAL	JONGLEUR	OUTCLASS	SEAPLANE	VIRULENT
TANGIBLE	PLANKTON	CATALYZE	FAMILIAR	JUBILANT	OUTFLANK	SEDULOUS	VITALITY
TEOSINTE	SANSKRIT	CAVALIER	FARMLAND	KINDLING	OVERLAID	SEEDLING	VITALIZE
TERMINAL	SHOCKING	CERULEAN	FATALISM	LADYLIKE	OVERLAND	SELFLESS	VOCALIST
TERMINUS	SIDEKICK	CHAPLAIN	FATALITY	LADYLOVE	OVERLEAP	SEROLOGY	VOCALIZE
TERRIBLE	SLIPKNOT	CIVILIAN	FEARLESS	LANDLORD	OVERLOOK	SHILLING	VOLPLANE
TERRIFIC	SPANKING	CIVILITY	FECKLESS	LEGALISM	OVERLORD	SHOELACE	WARPLANE
TERTIARY	STICKLER	CIVILIZE	FIDELITY	LIFELINE	PANELING	SHOPLIFT	WEAKLING
TESTICLE	STINKBUG	COMPLAIN	FINALIST	LIFELONG	PANELIST	SHOULDER	WHIPLASH
TOPSIDES	STOCKADE	COMPLEAT	FINALIZE	LINOLEUM	PARALLAX	SIBILANT	WILDLIFE
TORTILLA	STOCKING	COMPLETE	FLATLAND	LISTLESS	PARALLEL	SIDELONG	WINDLASS
TWILIGHT	STRIKING	CONCLAVE	FLYBLOWN	LIVELONG	PARALYZE	SIMPLIFY	WIRELESS
UNGAINLY	THANKFUL	CONCLUDE	FOLKLORE	LOCALITY	PARALYZE	SIMULATE	WOODLAND
UNVOICED	THICKSET	CONFLICT	FOOTLESS	LOCALIZE	PAVILION	SKILLFUL	XENOLITH

YEARLING	HELPMEET	SEDIMENT	CANONIZE	HARANGUE	POLONIUM	VICINAGE	DRAGOMAN
YEARLONG	HINDMOST	SHIPMATE	CEMENTUM	HEDONISM	POPINJAY	VICINITY	ECONOMIC
ABUTMENT	HOMEMADE	SHIPMENT	COLANDER	HIGHNESS	PREGNANT	WEAKNESS	EMPLOYEE
ACRIMONY	ILLUMINE	SKIMMING	COLONIAL	HOLINESS	PUDENDUM	WOMANISH	ENCROACH
ALARMIST	INCOMING	SKIRMISH	COLONIST	HUMANISM	RAVENING	WOODNOTE	ENSCONCE
ANTIMONY	INCUMBER	STRUMPET	COLONIZE	HUMANITY	RAVENOUS	YEARNING	EPILOGUE
ARGUMENT	INFAMOUS	SWIMMING	COMANCHE	HUMANIZE	REFINERY	ACIDOSIS	ESTROGEN
ARMAMENT	INHUMANE	SYCAMORE	CORONACH	HUMANOID	RESONANT	AIRBORNE	EUPHORIA
ASSEMBLE	INSOMNIA	TENEMENT	CORONARY	HYMENEAL	RESONATE	ALEHOUSE	EXPLODED
ASSEMBLY	INSOMUCH	THIAMINE	CORUNDUM	ILLINOIS	REVANCHE	ALTHOUGH	EYETOOTH
AUTOMATE	INTIMATE	THROMBUS	COVENANT	IMMANENT	REVENUER	AMBROSIA	FACTOTUM
AVERMENT	ISTHMIAN	TINSMITH	CULINARY	IMMINENT	ROMANIAN	ANACONDA	FAUBOURG
BASEMENT	JEREMIAD	TRIMMING	CYLINDER	IMMUNIZE	ROMANTIC	ANALOGUE	FIBROSIS
BECOMING	JUDGMENT	TRIUMVIR	DEBONAIR	IMPUNITY	RUMANIAN	ANDROGEN	FORSOOTH
BEHEMOTH	LANDMARK	ULTIMATE	DECANTER	INFANTRY	RUMINANT	APOLOGIA	FOXHOUND
BLOOMERS	LANDMASS	UNCOMMON	DEFINITE	INFINITE	RUMINATE	APPROACH	FURLOUGH
BOHEMIAN	LIGAMENT	UNLIMBER	DEIONIZE	INFINITY	SEIGNEUR	APPROVAL	GARGOYLE
BOOKMARK	LINIMENT	UNTIMELY	DEMENTED	INTENDED	SELENITE	ASPHODEL	GASWORKS
CALAMINE	LODGMENT	UPCOMING	DEMENTIA	ISLANDER	SELENIUM	BENZOATE	GLYCOGEN
CALAMITY	MAINMAST	VEHEMENT	DEMONIAC	JAPANESE	SEMANTIC	BONHOMIE	GUNPOINT
CAMOMILE	MALAMUTE	VENOMOUS	DEPONENT	JUVENILE	SEMINARY	BURNOOSE	HANGOVER
CASEMENT	MAXIMIZE	VESTMENT	DETONATE	KOLINSKY	SEMINOLE	CAMPOREE	HARMONIC
CASHMERE	MESSMATE	WELDMENT	DIMINISH	LAVENDER	SERENADE	CATHOLIC	HOLDOVER
CERAMIST	MILKMAID	WINDMILL	DISINTER	LEARNING	SICKNESS	CHEROKEE	HORMONAL
CEREMENT	MINIMIZE	ABORNING	DISUNITE	LEMONADE	SILENCER	CLITORIS	HOTHOUSE
CEREMONY	MISHMASH	ABSENTEE	DISUNITY	LICENSEE	SIMONIZE	COGNOMEN	HYDROGEN
CHARMING	MONUMENT	ABSINTHE	DIVINITY	LIKENESS	SOLENOID	COLLOQUY	HYPNOSIS
CHIPMUNK	MOVEMENT	ACTINISM	DOMINATE	LIMONITE	SPLENDID	COMMONER	HYPNOTIC
CHROMIUM	NOVEMBER	ACTINIUM	DOMINEER	LUMINARY	SPLENDOR	COMPOUND	ICEBOUND
CLAIMANT	OINTMENT	ADDENDUM	DOMINION	LUMINOUS	SPLINTER	CONFOCAL	ICEHOUSE
CLAYMORE	ONCOMING	ADMONISH	DRAINAGE	MALINGER	SPRINKLE	CONFOUND	IMPROPER
CORNMEAL	OPTIMISM	AERONAUT	ENDANGER	MARINATE	SQUANDER	CONSOMME	INCHOATE
CREAMERY	ORNAMENT	AFFINITY	ENGENDER	MELANISM	STAGNANT	CORDOVAN	INTROMIT
CUCUMBER	OUTSMART	AGRONOMY	ENGINEER	MELANOMA	STAGNATE	CORPORAL	ISOTONIC
DECEMBER	OVERMUCH	ALBANIAN	ENTANGLE	MERINGUE	STRANGER	CRETONNE	JAMBOREE
DECIMATE	PALOMINO	ALIENATE	ESTONIAN	MOMENTUM	STRANGLE	CUPBOARD	JINGOISM
DOCUMENT	PARAMOUR	ALIENIST	ETERNITY	MOURNFUL	STRENGTH	CUSTOMER	KEYBOARD
DOLOMITE	PAVEMENT	AMMONIUM	EUGENICS	MOURNING	STRINGED	DAFFODIL	KEYWORDS
DYNAMITE	PEDIMENT	ANTINOMY	EXPONENT	NEPENTHE	STRINGER	DEFLOWER	LACROSSE
ENCOMIUM	PENUMBRA	APHANITE	FASTNESS	NICKNAME	STUNNING	DIABOLIC	LAPBOARD
ENCUMBER	PHARMACY	APPANAGE	FEMININE	NOMINATE	TAXONOMY	DIAGONAL	LARBOARD
ENORMITY	PLAYMATE	APPENDIX	FEMINISM	NONUNION	TENANTRY	DIALOGUE	LEFTOVER
ENORMOUS	POCKMARK	AQUANAUT	FLOUNDER	OLEANDER	THRENODY	DIATOMIC	LITTORAL
ENSEMBLE	POLYMATH	ASTONISH	FOOTNOTE	OPPONENT	TITANIUM	DIPLOMAT	MADHOUSE
ESTIMATE	POSTMARK	AVIONICS	FORENAME	ORDINARY	TOKENISM	DISCOLOR	MAGNOLIA
EVERMORE	PREAMBLE	BADINAGE	FORENOON	ORDINATE	TRAINING	DISCOUNT	MANDOLIN
FILAMENT	PSALMODY	BARONAGE	FORENSIC	ORGANISM	TRAINMAN	DISCOVER	MARJORAM
FOREMAST	QUAGMIRE	BARONESS	GEMINATE	ORGANIST	TRIANGLE	DISGORGE	MARMOSET
FOREMOST	QUALMISH	BIANNUAL	GERANIUM	ORGANIZE	UNIONISM	DISHONOR	MASTODON
FRAGMENT	REGIMENT	BICONVEX	GIGANTIC	ORIENTAL	UNIONIZE	DISJOINT	MEDIOCRE
GLOAMING	REMEMBER	BIENNIAL	GOODNESS	PAGINATE	UNKINDLY	DISLODGE	METEORIC
GOURMAND	RESEMBLE	BIENNIUM	GREENERY	PALINODE	UNTANGLE	DISLOYAL	MICROBUS
GUNSMITH	ROOMMATE	BLUENOSE	GROUNDER	PARANOIA	UNWONTED	DISMOUNT	MIDPOINT
HALLMARK	ROSEMARY	BROWNOUT	GUERNSEY	PEDUNCLE	URBANITE	DISPOSAL	MISCOUNT
HANDMADE	RUDIMENT	BUSINESS	GUYANESE	PEIGNOIR	URBANIZE	DISSOLVE	MISDOING
HEGEMONY	SAGAMORE	CALENDAR	HABANERA	PENKNIFE	VEGANISM	DOGHOUSE	MISNOMER
HELPMATE	SCRAMBLE	CALENDER	HANGNAIL	POIGNANT	VERONICA	DORMOUSE	MNEMONIC

MONGOOSE	SAWHORSE	ENCIPHER	TEASPOON	BEVERAGE	DISTRICT	INDIRECT	MEMORIZE
MOREOVER	SCHOONER	EQUIPAGE	TELEPLAY	BUTTRESS	DISTRUST	INDURATE	MILLRACE
NARCOSIS	SEABOARD	ESCAPADE	THESPIAN	CASTRATE	DIVORCEE	INERRANT	MINORITY
NARCOTIC	SEACOAST	ESCAPISM	TRAPPING	CATARACT	DOCTRINE	INFERIOR	MISBRAND
NATIONAL	SEAGOING	EUROPEAN	TRESPASS	CELERITY	DOLDRUMS	INFERNAL	MISPRINT
NECROSIS	SEAMOUNT	EUROPIUM	TRUMPERY	CENTRIST	EFFERENT	INFORMAL	MISTREAT
NEUROSIS	SUBPOENA	EXEMPLAR	TURNPIKE	CESAREAN	EMIGRATE	INFORMED	MISTRESS
NEUROTIC	SUBSONIC	FILIPINO	UNZIPPED	CHAIRMAN	EMPORIUM	INFORMER	MISTRIAL
NEWCOMER	SUPPOSED	FIREPLUG	WHOPPING	CHEERFUL	EMPYREAN	INHERENT	MISTRUST
NEWFOUND	SURMOUNT	FLAGPOLE	WINDPIPE	CHLORIDE	ENCIRCLE	INSCRIBE	MODERATE
NITROGEN	SURROUND	FLIPPANT	WOODPILE	CHLORINE	ENSHRINE	INSTRUCT	MONARCHY
NOTIONAL	SYMBOLIC	FLYSPECK	WORDPLAY	CHLORITE	ENSHROUD	INTERCOM	MONORAIL
ONLOOKER	TEETOTAL	FOOTPATH	WRAPPING	CHOIRBOY	ENTHRALL	INTEREST	MOTORCAR
ORATORIO	TEMPORAL	FOREPART	ZOOSPORE	CICERONE	ENTHRONE	INTERIOR	MOTORIZE
ORTHODOX	TEUTONIC	FRIPPERY	TRANQUIL	CLEARING	ENTIRETY	INTERMIT	MOTORMAN
ORTHOEPY	THOROUGH	GANGPLOW	ABNORMAL	COHERENT	ENVIRONS	INTERMIX	MOTOROLA
OUTBOARD	TITMOUSE	GATEPOST	ABSTRACT	COMPRESS	ESCAROLE	INTERNAL	MUSHROOM
OUTBOUND	TORTOISE	GOALPOST	ABSTRUSE	COMPRISE	ETHEREAL	INTERNEE	NEUTRINO
OUTDOORS	TRICOLOR	GRASPING	ACCURATE	CONCRETE	ETHERNET	INTERNET	NEWSREEL
OUTGOING	TURBOFAN	HANDPICK	ACCURSED	CONFRERE	EXCURSUS	INTERROG	NIGERIAN
OUTHOUSE	TURBOJET	HELIPORT	AFFERENT	CONFRONT	EXECRATE	INTERVAL	NIGEROIS
OUTMODED	TURNOVER	HORNPIPE	AFTERTAX	CONGRESS	EXTERIOR	INVERTER	NOTARIAL
OUTPOINT	UNBROKEN	INEXPERT	AGRARIAN	CONTRACT	EXTERNAL	INWARDLY	NOTARIZE
PANDOWDY	UNCLOTHE	MALAPERT	AIRBRUSH	CONTRAIL	FAVORITE	ISOPRENE	NUMERATE
PARDONER	UNLOOSEN	MAYAPPLE	AIRCRAFT	CONTRARY	FEDERATE	KOHLRABI	NUMEROUS
PARFOCAL	UPGROWTH	METAPHOR	AIRDROME	CONTRAST	FIGURINE	LABURNUM	OBDURATE
PASSOVER	VARIORUM	MILEPOST	AIRFRAME	CONTRITE	FILTRATE	LACERATE	OBSTRUCT
PASTORAL	VERBOTEN	MILLPOND	ALACRITY	CONTRIVE	FLAGRANT	LASERJET	OFFPRINT
PATHOGEN	VERMOUTH	MISAPPLY	ALDERMAN	COVERAGE	FLOURISH	LAYERING	OUTBREAK
PECTORAL	VICTORIA	MISSPELL	ALGERIAN	COVERALL	FLUORIDE	LEVERAGE	OVERRIDE
PERFORCE	VISCOUNT	MISSPEND	ALLERGEN	COVERLET	FLUORINE	LIBERATE	OVERRULE
PERIODIC	WALKOVER	MONOPOLY	AMPERAGE	DANDRUFF	FLUORITE	LICORICE	PANCREAS
PERSONAL	WEAPONRY	NINEPINS	ANAEROBE	DARKROOM	FOOTRACE	LIMERICK	PANORAMA
PHENOLIC	AGITPROP	OCCUPANT	ANTERIOR	DAYBREAK	FOOTREST	LITERARY	PASTRAMI
PINPOINT	AIRSPACE	OUTSPEND	ANTEROOM	DAYDREAM	FORTRESS	LITERATE	PATERNAL
PORPOISE	AIRSPEED	OVERPASS	ANTHROPO	DECORATE	FRAGRANT	LITERATI	PEDERAST
PREMOLAR	ALLSPICE	OVERPLAY	APHORISM	DECOROUS	FUMAROLE	LIVERISH	PINPRICK
PRISONER	ANTIPODE	PASSPORT	APPARENT	DEFOREST	FUNERARY	MACARONI	PLEURISY
PROFOUND	ANTIPOPE	PERSPIRE	AQUARIUM	DELIRIUM	FUNEREAL	MACAROON	POLARITY
PROLOGUE	ATROPINE	PHOSPHOR	ARBOREAL	DEMARCHE	FUTURISM	MACERATE	POLARIZE
PROMOTER	BACKPACK	POSTPAID	ARMORIAL	DEMURRER	FUTURITY	MAHARAJA	POLTROON
PROPOUND	BLOWPIPE	POSTPONE	ARTERIAL	DESCRIBE	GANGRENE	MAHARANI	PORTRAIT
PROROGUE	BOWSPRIT	PROSPECT	ASPERITY	DESIROUS	GENERATE	MAJORITY	PREPRESS
PROTOCOL	CARAPACE	RECEPTOR	ASPIRANT	DESTRUCT	GENEROUS	MALARKEY	PRIMROSE
PULLOVER	CATAPULT	SCORPION	ASPIRATE	DETHRONE	GIMCRACK	MALTREAT	PROGRESS
PULMOTOR	CESSPOOL	SCULPTOR	ASSORTED	DEXTROSE	GLABROUS	MANDRAKE	PROTRACT
PUSHOVER	CHAMPION	SHEEPISH	ASTERISK	DIARRHEA	GOVERNOR	MANGROVE	PROTRUDE
QUIXOTIC	CHIPPEWA	SHIPPING	ASTEROID	DIATRIBE	HANDRAIL	MARGRAVE	PYORRHEA
RADIOMAN	CLIPPING	SHRAPNEL	ATTORNEY	DISARRAY	HEADREST	MATERIAL	QUADRANT
RATIONAL	COLOPHON	SIGNPOST	AUSTRIAN	DISCREET	HEADROOM	MATERIEL	QUADROON
RAWBONED	CONSPIRE	SLIPPERY	BACKREST	DISCRETE	HIGHROAD	MATERNAL	QUATRAIN
REGIONAL	CREEPING	SNOWPLOW	BALLROOM	DISGRACE	HOMEROOM	MATTRESS	RAILROAD
REPROACH	CROUPIER	STAMPEDE	BANKROLL	DISORDER	HONORARY	MATURATE	RECORDER
RESPONSE	DECIPHER	STOPPAGE	BANKRUPT	DISPROVE	HUNTRESS	MATURITY	REFERENT
RETROFIT	DOWNPOUR	SWEEPING	BATHROBE	DISTRACT	IGNORANT	MAVERICK	REFERRAL
RHETORIC	ECLIPTIC	SYNOPSIS	BATHROOM	DISTRAIT	IMMORTAL	MEMBRANE	REFOREST
SARDONIC	ELLIPSIS	SYNOPTIC	BESTRIDE	DISTRESS	IMPERIAL	MEMORIAL	REFORMER

REPARTEE	TOMORROW	ACOUSTIC	DECISIVE	IMPOSTOR	POLLSTER	WINGSPAN	CINCTURE
REPORTER	TOWERING	ACROSTIC	DEERSKIN	INCISION	PRESSING	WOODSHED	CITATION
RESCRIPT	TRAPROCK	ADHESION	DELUSION	INCISIVE	PRESSMAN	WOODSMAN	CLAPTRAP
RESERVED	TUBERCLE	ADHESIVE	DINOSAUR	INDUSTRY	PRESSURE	WOOLSACK	COAUTHOR
RESORTER	TUBEROSE	ADVISORY	DISASTER	INVASION	REASSURE	WORDSTAR	COCKTAIL
RESTRAIN	TUBEROUS	AGNOSTIC	DIVISION	JURISTIC	REGISTER	WORKSHOP	COGITATE
RESTRICT	TUTORIAL	ALIASING	DIVISIVE	KEEPSAKE	REGISTRY	YOURSELF	CONSTANT
RETARDED	ULCERATE	ANCESTOR	DOMESTIC	KEROSINE	RESISTOR	YUGOSLAV	CONSTRUE
RETIRING	ULTERIOR	ANCESTRY	DOOMSDAY	KICKSHAW	RHAPSODY	ABATTOIR	COUNTESS
RETURNEE	UNBURDEN	APPOSITE	DOORSTEP	KNAPSACK	RHEOSTAT	ABLATION	COURTESY
REVEREND	UNDERACT	ARTISTIC	DRESSAGE	LADYSHIP	RIBOSOME	ABLATIVE	COURTIER
REVERENT	UNDERAGE	ARTISTRY	DRESSING	LAMASERY	ROADSIDE	ABLUTION	CREATION
REVERSAL	UNDERARM	ASBESTOS	EFFUSION	LAMBSKIN	ROADSTER	ABORTION	CREATURE
RIFFRAFF	UNDERBID	ASSASSIN	EMISSARY	LANDSMAN	SALESMAN	ABUTTALS	CURATIVE
RIPARIAN	UNDERCUT	AVERSION	EMULSIFY	LARKSPUR	SCISSORS	ACANTHUS	DENATURE
RIVERBED	UNDERDOG	BABUSHKA	EMULSION	LINESMAN	SEALSKIN	ADDITION	DEPUTIZE
SAMARIUM	UNDERFUR	BACKSIDE	ENVISAGE	LOCKSTEP	SELFSAME	ADDITIVE	DEVOTION
SATURATE	UNDERLIE	BACKSLAP	ETRUSCAN	LODESTAR	SEMESTER	ADJUTANT	DIANTHUS
SATURDAY	UNDERLIP	BACKSPIN	EURASIAN	LONESOME	SEMISOFT	ADOPTIVE	DIASTOLE
SCABROUS	UNDERPAY	BACKSTOP	EVENSONG	LORDSHIP	SIDESHOW	ADULTERY	DILATORY
SECURITY	UNDERSEA	BAILSMAN	EXPOSURE	LOVESICK	SIDESTEP	AFLUTTER	DIPSTICK
SEPARATE	UNDERTOW	BAKESHOP	FEARSOME	MAINSAIL	SINISTER	AGLITTER	DONATION
SEWERAGE	UNEARNED	BALUSTER	FELDSPAR	MAINSTAY	SLIPSHOD	AIRSTRIP	DOUBTFUL
SHAMROCK	UNERRING	BANISTER	FINESPUN	MALTSTER	SNAPSHOT	ALEATORY	DOVETAIL
SHIRRING	UNFORMED	BEARSKIN	FIRESIDE	MARKSMAN	SNOWSHOE	ALTITUDE	DOWNTOWN
SIDEREAL	UNPERSON	BICUSPID	FLAGSHIP	MENISCUS	SONGSTER	AMBITION	DOWNTURN
SIDERITE	UNSPRUNG	BIRDSEED	FOOLSCAP	MILESIMO	SPINSTER	AMORTIZE	DURATION
SOLARIUM	UNSTRUNG	BLESSING	FOOTSORE	MINISTER	TAILSPIN	AMPUTATE	DYESTUFF
SOMBRERO	UNWORTHY	BLISSFUL	FOOTSTEP	MINISTRY	TALESMAN	ANGSTROM	EGYPTIAN
SOMERSET	UPPERCUT	BONDSMAN	FORESAIL	MISUSAGE	TALISMAN	ANNOTATE	EIGHTEEN
SONOROUS	UPSTREAM	BUCKSHOT	FORESKIN	MOLASSES	TAPESTRY	APERTURE	EKISTICS
SORORITY	UPSTROKE	BUCKSKIN	FORESTRY	MOLESKIN	TEAMSTER	APOSTASY	ELECTION
SPHEROID	UPTHRUST	CALFSKIN	FOURSOME	MONASTIC	THOUSAND	APPETITE	ELECTIVE
SQUIRREL	USUFRUCT	CAMISOLE	GAMESOME	MUENSTER	THRASHER	APTITUDE	ELECTRIC
STAIRWAY	VAPORING	CANISTER	GAMESTER	NAINSOOK	THRUSTER	ARMATURE	ELECTRON
STEERAGE	VAPORISH	CAPESKIN	GANGSTER	NAMESAKE	THURSDAY	ASTATINE	EMBATTLE
STIRRING	VAPORIZE	CHRISTEN	GLADSOME	NONESUCH	TIRESOME	ATTITUDE	EMBITTER
SUBTRACT	VAPOROUS	CHRISTIE	GLASSFUL	OCCASION	TOWNSHIP	AUDITION	EQUATION
SUBURBIA	VENERATE	CLASSIFY	GLOSSARY	OPPOSITE	TOWNSMAN	AUDITORY	ERECTILE
SUFFRAGE	VENEREAL	CLOISTER	GOATSKIN	OVERSEAS	TRANSACT	AVIATION	ERECTION
SUNDRIES	VIBURNUM	COCKSURE	GRUESOME	OVERSHOE	TRANSEPT	AVIATRIX	EVENTIDE
SUPEREGO	VICARAGE	COHESION	HANDSOME	OVERSIZE	TRANSFER	AXLETREE	EVENTUAL
SUPERIOR	VIGOROUS	COLESLAW	HARDSHIP	OVERSTAY	TRANSFIX	BARITONE	EXACTING
SUPERJET	VIVARIUM	COLISEUM	HEADSHIP	OVERSTEP	TRANSMIT	BEAUTIFY	FAGOTING
SUPERNAL	WAITRESS	COLOSSAL	HEADSMAN	PALISADE	TREASURE	BEDSTEAD	FIRETRAP
SUPPRESS	WARDROBE	COLOSSUS	HELMSMAN	PANTSUIT	TREASURY	BELITTLE	FIXATION
SURPRISE	WARDROOM	COONSKIN	HERDSMAN	PARASITE	TROUSERS	BETATRON	FIXATIVE
SUZERAIN	WAREROOM	CORPSMAN	HIBISCUS	PAWNSHOP	TUNGSTEN	BITSTOCK	FLATTERY
SYBARITE	WASHROOM	CREOSOTE	HILLSIDE	PEDESTAL	TUNISIAN	BOASTFUL	FLAUTIST
SYNDROME	WATERLOO	CROSSBAR	HOMESICK	PHEASANT	TURNSPIT	CABSTAND	FLEETING
TAFFRAIL	WATERWAY	CROSSBOW	HOMESPUN	PHRASING	UNFASTEN	CAROTENE	FORETELL
TAMARACK	WIZARDRY	CROSSCUT	HUCKSTER	PILASTER	UPRISING	CEMETERY	FOUNTAIN
TAMARIND	WONDROUS	CROSSING	HUNTSMAN	PLAYSUIT	VARISTOR	CENOTAPH	FOURTEEN
TEMERITY	WOODRUFF	CYNOSURE	ILLUSION	PLEASANT	VENUSIAN	CHASTISE	FRACTION
THEORIZE	WORKROOM	CYTOSINE	ILLUSIVE	PLEASING	WAINSCOT	CHASTITY	FRACTURE
TIMOROUS	ABRASIVE	DARKSOME	ILLUSORY	PLEASURE	WARDSHIP	CHESTNUT	FRICTION
TOLERATE	ACCUSTOM	DECISION	IMPOSING	POLESTAR	WINESHOP	CICATRIX	FRONTAGE

FRONTIER	LOBOTOMY	PLECTRUM	SOLSTICE	CAROUSAL	MISJUDGE	NONEVENT	HOODWINK
FROSTING	LOCATION	POLITICK	SOLUTION	CAROUSEL	MISQUOTE	OBLIVION	HOOKWORM
FRUCTIFY	LOCUTION	POLITICO	SOMETIME	CELLULAR	MONAURAL	OVERVIEW	INCHWORM
FRUITION	LOGOTYPE	POLITICS	SONATINA	CHANUKAH	MORTUARY	RELEVANT	IRONWARE
FUGITIVE	LONGTIME	PONYTAIL	SORPTION	CHASUBLE	MOSQUITO	RENOVATE	IRONWEED
FUNCTION	LUTETIUM	POSITION	SPECTRAL	CHEMURGY	MUDGUARD	REVIVIFY	IRONWOOD
GAUNTLET	MAINTAIN	POSITIVE	SPECTRUM	CIRCUITY	NOCTURNE	SALIVATE	IRONWORK
GEMSTONE	MARATHON	POSITRON	SPITTOON	CIRCULAR	OBITUARY	SHELVING	KILOWATT
GENETICS	MARITIME	POTATION	SPLATTER	CISLUNAR	OUTBURST	TELEVIEW	KNITWEAR
GENITALS	MEALTIME	POULTICE	SPLUTTER	COAGULUM	OUTGUESS	TELEVISE	LACEWING
GENITIVE	MEANTIME	PRACTICE	STRATEGY	COMMUNAL	PELLUCID	THIEVERY	LANDWARD
GREETING	MEDITATE	PRESTIGE	STRATIFY	COMPUTER	PENDULUM	TITIVATE	LIFEWORK
GUMPTION	MILITANT	PRETTIFY	STULTIFY	CONJUGAL	PERSUADE	UNLOVELY	LIKEWISE
HABITANT	MILITARY	PRINTING	SWASTIKA	CONJUNCT	PREJUDGE	UNSAVORY	LOANWORD
HABITUAL	MILITATE	PRINTOUT	TACITURN	CONQUEST	RECOURSE	ARMYWORM	LOCOWEED
HALFTONE	MINATORY	PRISTINE	TAHITIAN	CONVULSE	RENOUNCE	BACKWARD	LUKEWARM
HARDTACK	MINSTREL	PROSTATE	TELETHON	CORDUROY	RESOURCE	BACKWASH	MALAWIAN
HAYSTACK	MISSTATE	PUNCTUAL	TELLTALE	DAIQUIRI	SADDUCEE	BASSWOOD	MESHWORK
HECATOMB	MOISTURE	PUNCTURE	THIRTEEN	DENOUNCE	SANGUINE	BENTWOOD	MILKWEED
HEMATITE	MONETARY	PUNITIVE	THROTTLE	DISBURSE	SCAPULAR	BODYWORK	OPENWORK
HEPATICA	MONITION	PUTATIVE	TIGHTWAD	DISGUISE	SCROUNGE	BOLLWORM	PASSWORD
HERITAGE	MONITORY	QUANTITY	TINCTURE	DISQUIET	SENSUOUS	BOOKWORM	POKEWEED
HESITANT	MONOTONE	QUANTIZE	TOGETHER	DISSUADE	SINGULAR	BUSYWORK	PULPWOOD
HESITATE	MOUNTAIN	QUESTION	TRACTATE	ELOQUENT	STATUARY	CAKEWALK	REARWARD
HIGHTAIL	MOUNTING	QUIETUDE	TRACTION	ESPOUSAL	STIMULUS	CAREWORN	RINGWORM
HOLSTEIN	MULETEER	REACTANT	TREATISE	EVACUATE	SULFURIC	CASEWORK	ROADWORK
HOWITZER	MUNITION	REACTION	TRIPTYCH	EVALUATE	TORTUOUS	COXSWAIN	ROSEWOOD
IDEATION	MUTATION	REACTIVE	TRUETYPE	EXECUTOR	TRIBUNAL	DEADWOOD	SANDWICH
IDENTIFY	NEGATION	REBUTTAL	TRUSTFUL	EXIGUOUS	UNCHURCH	DELAWARE	SHIPWORM
IDENTITY	NEGATIVE	RELATION	UNBUTTON	FAROUCHE	UNCOUPLE	DOWNWARD	SHOPWORN
IGNITION	NEMATODE	RELATIVE	UNFETTER	FEBRUARY	UNCTUOUS	DOWNWIND	SHREWISH
IMMATURE	NEPOTISM	REMITTAL	UNSETTLE	FORTUITY	UNSOUGHT	EDGEWAYS	SIDEWALK
IMMOTILE	NICOTINE	RIGHTFUL	VACATION	FREQUENT	UNTAUGHT	FAREWELL	SIDEWALL
IMPETIGO	NINETEEN	ROOFTREE	VAULTING	GALLUSES	VALVULAR	FIREWOOD	SIDEWAYS
IMPOTENT	NONSTICK	SABOTAGE	VEGETATE	GLOBULIN	VANGUARD	FIREWORK	SOFTWARE
INKSTAND	NOONTIDE	SABOTEUR	VENATION	GRADUATE	VANQUISH	FIRMWARE	SOFTWOOD
INVITING	NOONTIME	SALUTARY	VEXATION	GRANULAR	VASCULAR	FISHWIFE	SOMEWHAT
IRRITATE	NOTATION	SANCTIFY	VISITANT	GRATUITY	VIRTUOSO	FLATWARE	STALWART
ISOSTASY	NUGATORY	SANCTION	VOCATION	GUTTURAL	VIRTUOUS	FOOTWEAR	TAPEWORM
JOYSTICK	OBLATION	SANCTITY	VOCATIVE	HERCULES	WHODUNIT	FOOTWORK	TEAMWORK
JUNCTION	OFFSTAGE	SANITARY	VOLATILE	HEREUNTO	AARDVARK	FOREWARN	TIMEWORN
JUNCTURE	OUTSTRIP	SANITIZE	VOLITION	HEREUPON	ACTIVATE	FOREWORD	TOILWORN
KEYSTONE	OVERTAKE	SCIATICA	WRISTLET	HINDUISM	ACTIVISM	FORSWEAR	UNLAWFUL
KIBITZER	OVERTIME	SCOTTISH	YACHTING	INIQUITY	ACTIVITY	FREEWILL	UNTOWARD
KINETICS	OVERTONE	SCRUTINY	YULETIDE	IROQUOIS	ADJUVANT	FRETWORK	WEREWOLF
LATITUDE	OVERTURE	SEDATIVE	ACCOUTRE	JACQUARD	ALLUVIUM	GLOWWORM	WILDWOOD
LAVATORY	OVERTURN	SEDITION	ADEQUATE	JALOUSIE	BEHAVIOR	GOODWIFE	WINDWARD
LAXATIVE	PAINTING	SEEDTIME	ALTRUISM	KEYPUNCH	CLEAVAGE	GOODWILL	WIREWORM
LECITHIN	PALATINE	SHANTUNG	ANNOUNCE	LANGUAGE	DELIVERY	HACKWORD	WOODWIND
LEGATION	PANATELA	SHEETING	BAROUCHE	LANGUISH	ENERVATE	HARDWARE	WOODWORK
LENGTHEN	PENITENT	SHIRTING	BECHUANA	LINGUIST	EXCAVATE	HARDWOOD	WORMWOOD
LENITIVE	PENSTOCK	SHORTAGE	BEGRUDGE	LONGUEUR	GRIEVOUS	HAWKWEED	BISEXUAL
LEVITATE	PETITION	SHORTCUT	BERMUDAS	MANEUVER	INNOVATE	HEADWORD	DETOXIFY
LIBATION	PHANTASM	SKITTISH	BINAURAL	MARQUESS	KILOVOLT	HEADWORK	MONOXIDE
LIFETIME	PHANTASY	SLATTERN	BURGUNDY	MARQUISE	MOTIVATE	HEREWITH	PAROXYSM
LIGATURE	PILOTAGE	SOLITARY	CALCULUS	MERCURIC	NATIVISM	HOMEWARD	PEROXIDE
LIPSTICK	PLANTAIN	SOLITUDE	CAPSULAR	MESQUITE	NATIVITY	HOMEWORK	PREEXIST

RELAXANT	ADJUTANT	BROUHAHA	DINGBATS	FLAPJACK	HIGHBALL	LITERATE	MUTILATE
UNIAXIAL	ADJUVANT	BURGLARY	DINOSAUR	FLATLAND	HIGHLAND	LITERATI	NAMESAKE
ALLEYWAY	ADVOCATE	CABSTAND	DISCLAIM	FLATWARE	HIGHTAIL	LITIGANT	NAUSEATE
ANALYSIS	AERONAUT	CAKEWALK	DISGRACE	FLEABANE	HOMELAND	LITIGATE	NAVIGATE
ASPHYXIA	AIRCRAFT	CALABASH	DISPLACE	FLIPPANT	HOMEMADE	LONGHAIR	NECKLACE
BALLYHOO	AIRFRAME	CALLBACK	DISSUADE	FOOTBALL	HOMEWARD	LONGHAND	NEOPLASM
BARNYARD	AIRPLANE	CAMSHAFT	DISTRACT	FOOTFALL	HONORARY	LUKEWARM	NEWSCAST
BOGEYMAN	AIRSPACE	CARAPACE	DISTRAIT	FOOTPATH	HUMPBACK	LUMINARY	NICKNAME
CARRYALL	ALIENATE	CARRIAGE	DIVAGATE	FOOTRACE	IGNORANT	MACERATE	NOMINATE
DAIRYING	ALLOCATE	CARRYALL	DOCKHAND	FORECAST	IMMOLATE	MAHARAJA	NOWADAYS
DAIRYMAN	AMBULANT	CASTRATE	DOCKYARD	FOREHAND	INCHOATE	MAHARANI	NUCLEATE
DIALYSIS	AMPERAGE	CATARACT	DOMINATE	FORELADY	INCREASE	MAHOGANY	NUMERATE
DOCKYARD	AMPUTATE	CATCHALL	DOORJAMB	FORELAND	INCUBATE	MAINLAND	OBDURATE
DOORYARD	ANNOTATE	CELIBACY	DOORYARD	FOREMAST	INDICATE	MAINMAST	OBITUARY
EVERYDAY	ANTEDATE	CELIBATE	DOVETAIL	FORENAME	INDURATE	MAINSAIL	OBLIGATE
EVERYONE	ANYPLACE	CENOTAPH	DOWNCAST	FOREPART	INERRANT	MAINTAIN	OCCUPANT
FARMYARD	APOSTASY	CHAPLAIN	DOWNFALL	FORESAIL	INFOBAHN	MANDRAKE	OFFSTAGE
HANDYMAN	APPANAGE	CLAIMANT	DOWNWARD	FOREWARN	INHALANT	MARGRAVE	ONONDAGA
HEAVYSET	APPROACH	CLAMBAKE	DRAINAGE	FOUNTAIN	INHUMANE	MARINATE	ORDINARY
HONEYDEW	AQUACADE	CLEAVAGE	DRAWBACK	FRAGRANT	INITIATE	MARRIAGE	ORDINATE
LOLLYGAG	AQUANAUT	COCKTAIL	DRESSAGE	FREEHAND	INKSTAND	MATURATE	OSCULATE
MEALYBUG	ARMCHAIR	COGITATE	DRUNKARD	FRONTAGE	INNOVATE	MEATBALL	OUTBOARD
NEWLYWED	ARROGANT	COMEBACK	EDGEWAYS	FULLBACK	INSULATE	MEDICAID	OUTCLASS
OUTLYING	ARROGATE	COMPLAIN	EGGPLANT	FUMIGANT	INTIMATE	MEDICARE	OUTFLANK
PICAYUNE	ARTIFACT	CONCLAVE	ELEPHANT	FUMIGATE	INUNDATE	MEDICATE	OUTREACH
PLATYPUS	ASPIRANT	CONSTANT	ELONGATE	FUNERARY	IRONWARE	MEDITATE	OUTSMART
PUSSYCAT	ASPIRATE	CONTRACT	EMACIATE	FUSELAGE	IRRIGATE	MEMBRANE	OVERCAST
SHIPYARD	AUTOBAHN	CONTRAIL	EMIGRATE	GANGLAND	IRRITATE	MERCHANT	OVERHAND
SUKIYAKI	AUTOMATE	CONTRARY	EMISSARY	GEMINATE	ISOSTASY	MESSMATE	OVERHANG
TRICYCLE	BACKHAND	CONTRAST	ENCROACH	GENERATE	JACQUARD	MILITANT	OVERHAUL
UNICYCLE	BACKLASH	COPULATE	ENERVATE	GENITALS	JUBILANT	MILITARY	OVERLAID
VINEYARD	BACKPACK	CORONACH	ENFILADE	GIMCRACK	KAMIKAZE	MILITATE	OVERLAND
BEDAZZLE	BACKWARD	CORONARY	ENSILAGE	GLACIATE	KATAKANA	MILKMAID	OVERPASS
BLIZZARD	BACKWASH	COUCHANT	ENTHRALL	GLOSSARY	KEELHAUL	MILLIARD	OVERTAKE
CHUTZPAH	BADINAGE	COVENANT	ENVISAGE	GOOFBALL	KEEPSAKE	MILLRACE	PAGINATE
EMBEZZLE	BAREBACK	COVERAGE	EPIPHANY	GOURMAND	KEYBOARD	MISBRAND	PALEFACE
GRIZZLED	BARNYARD	COVERALL	EQUIPAGE	GRADUATE	KICKBACK	MISHMASH	PALISADE
MAGAZINE	BARONAGE	COXSWAIN	ESCALATE	GYMKHANA	KIELBASA	MISPLACE	PALLIATE
TWEEZERS	BASEBALL	CRIBBAGE	ESCAPADE	HABITANT	KILOWATT	MISSHAPE	PANORAMA
UNMUZZLE	BEANBALL	CROPLAND	ESTIMATE	HALFBACK	KNAPSACK	MISSTATE	PASTRAMI
	BECHUANA	CULINARY	EVACUATE	HALLMARK	KOHLRABI	MISUSAGE	PECULATE
	BENZOATE	CUPBOARD	EVALUATE	HANDBALL	LACERATE	MITIGATE	PEDERAST
	BEQUEATH	DATABASE	EXCAVATE	HANDMADE	LAMPBACK	MODERATE	PENCHANT
6TH LETTER	BESTIARY	DEBONAIR	EXECRATE	HANDRAIL	LANDFALL	MODULATE	PERMEATE
	BEVERAGE	DECIMATE	EYEGLASS	HANGNAIL	LANDMARK	MONETARY	PERSUADE
AARDVARK	BIFOCALS	DECKHAND	FARMHAND	HARDBACK	LANDMASS	MONOGAMY	PETULANT
ABDICATE	BIRDBATH	DECORATE	FARMLAND	HARDBALL	LANDWARD	MONORAIL	PHANTASM
ABNEGATE	BLIZZARD	DECREASE	FARMYARD	HARDHACK	LANGUAGE	MOORLAND	PHANTASY
ABROGATE	BLOCKADE	DEDICATE	FASTBACK	HARDTACK	LAPBOARD	MORTGAGE	PHARMACY
ABSTRACT	BOLDFACE	DEFECATE	FEBRUARY	HARDWARE	LAPIDARY	MORTUARY	PHEASANT
ABUNDANT	BOOKCASE	DELAWARE	FEDERATE	HAYSTACK	LARBOARD	MOSSBACK	PIEPLANT
ABUTTALS	BOOKMARK	DELEGATE	FEEDBACK	HEADBAND	LAUREATE	MOTHBALL	PILCHARD
ACCOLADE	BOUFFANT	DELICACY	FILTRATE	HEADLAND	LEMONADE	MOTIVATE	PILOTAGE
ACCURATE	BOUNDARY	DELICATE	FIREBALL	HELPMATE	LEVERAGE	MOUNTAIN	PIXELATE
ACERBATE	BRAGGART	DEROGATE	FIREDAMP	HERITAGE	LEVITATE	MUCILAGE	PLANTAIN
ACTIVATE	BREAKAGE	DESOLATE	FIRMWARE	HESITANT	LIBERATE	MUDGUARD	PLAYBACK
ADEQUATE	BREVIARY	DETONATE	FLAGRANT	HESITATE	LITERARY	MUSICALE	PLAYMATE

PLEASANT	SANITARY	TELLTALE	ALPHABET	PROBABLE	EMOTICON	VIATICUM	PORRIDGE
POCKMARK	SATURATE	TEMPLATE	AMENABLE	PROHIBIT	ENCIRCLE	WAINSCOT	PREJUDGE
POIGNANT	SCABBARD	TERTIARY	AMICABLE	QUOTABLE	ETRUSCAN	WHITECAP	PRESIDIO
POLYGAMY	SEABOARD	THOUSAND	ARGUABLE	RELIABLE	EXPLICIT	WISEACRE	PROVIDED
POLYMATH	SEACOAST	TIDELAND	ASSEMBLE	REMEMBER	FAROUCHE	ACCREDIT	PUDENDUM
PONYTAIL	SEAPLANE	TINPLATE	ASSEMBLY	RESEMBLE	FASCICLE	ADDENDUM	RECORDER
POPULACE	SEASCAPE	TITILATE	BAILABLE	RIVERBED	FOLLICLE	APPENDIX	RETARDED
POPULATE	SELFSAME	TITIVATE	BIDDABLE	SCALABLE	FOOLSCAP	ASPHODEL	SATURDAY
PORTRAIT	SEMINARY	TOLERATE	BRICKBAT	SCRABBLE	HANDICAP	BEFUDDLE	SHOULDER
POSTCARD	SEPARATE	TOLLGATE	CANNABIS	SCRAMBLE	HEADACHE	BEGRUDGE	SPLENDID
POSTDATE	SERENADE	TOMAHAWK	CANNIBAL	SCRIBBLE	HIBISCUS	BEHOLDEN	SPLENDOR
POSTMARK	SERGEANT	TRACKAGE	CHASUBLE	SENSIBLE	HUARACHE	BERMUDAS	SPORADIC
POSTPAID	SEWERAGE	TRACTATE	CHOIRBOY	SOCIABLE	IMPLICIT	BEWILDER	SQUANDER
POUNDAGE	SHIPMATE	TRANSACT	CINNABAR	SQUABBLE	INIMICAL	BIOCIDAL	STRADDLE
PRATFALL	SHIPYARD	TRESPASS	CREDIBLE	STINKBUG	INTERCOM	BIRTHDAY	THURSDAY
PREGNANT	SHOELACE	TRUCKAGE	CROSSBAR	SUBURBIA	MANIACAL	BROMIDIC	TOPSIDES
PROCLAIM	SHORTAGE	TRUNCATE	CROSSBOW	SUITABLE	MARIACHI	CALENDAR	TOREADOR
PROSTATE	SHOWCASE	TUTELAGE	CRUCIBLE	SYLLABLE	MASSACRE	CALENDER	UNBIDDEN
PROTRACT	SIBILANT	TUTELARY	CUCUMBER	SYLLABUS	MEDIOCRE	CHARADES	UNBURDEN
PUFFBALL	SIDEWALK	TYPECAST	CULPABLE	TANGIBLE	MENISCUS	COLANDER	UNDERDOG
PULLBACK	SIDEWALL	TYPEFACE	DAMNABLE	TERRIBLE	METRICAL	CONSIDER	UNKINDLY
PURCHASE	SIDEWAYS	ULCERATE	DEATHBED	THROMBUS	MONARCHY	CORRIDOR	UNLEADED
PURSLANE	SILICATE	ULTIMATE	DECEMBER	UNDERBID	MOROCCAN	CORUNDUM	UNRIDDLE
PUSHCART	SIMULATE	UNDERACT	DOUGHBOY	UNLIMBER	MOTORCAR	CUSPIDOR	UNSADDLE
QUADRANT	SLUGGARD	UNDERAGE	DUTIABLE	UNSTABLE	MUSTACHE	CYLINDER	WATCHDOG
QUANDARY	SNOWBALL	UNDERARM	EDUCABLE	VALUABLE	MYSTICAL	DAFFODIL	WIZARDRY
QUATRAIN	SNOWBANK	UNDULANT	ELIGIBLE	VARIABLE	NAUTICAL	DISLODGE	WORKADAY
RAINFALL	SNOWFALL	UNDULATE	ENCUMBER	VERTEBRA	OBSTACLE	DISORDER	ABUTMENT
REACTANT	SOFTBALL	UNGULATE	ENFEEBLE	VINCIBLE	PARFOCAL	DOOMSDAY	ACCIDENT
REARWARD	SOFTWARE	UNSTEADY	ENSEMBLE	VIOLABLE	PARTICLE	EMBOLDEN	ACIDHEAD
RECREANT	SOLITARY	UNTOWARD	ENVIABLE	WASHABLE	PASTICHE	ENGENDER	ADJACENT
RECREATE	SPANIARD	VALIDATE	FALLIBLE	WORKABLE	PEDUNCLE	EVERYDAY	ADULTERY
REGULATE	SPITBALL	VANGUARD	FEASIBLE	ALOPECIA	PELLUCID	EXPLODED	AESTHETE
RELAXANT	SPYGLASS	VEGETATE	FLEXIBLE	AMERICAN	PEMMICAN	EXTRADOS	AFFERENT
RELEGATE	STACCATO	VENERATE	FORCIBLE	ANGLICAN	PERFECTO	FLOUNDER	AGGRIEVE
RELEVANT	STAGNANT	VERBIAGE	HORRIBLE	ATYPICAL	PHYSICAL	GROUNDER	AIRFIELD
RELOCATE	STAGNATE	VESICANT	HOUSEBOY	BACKACHE	PINNACLE	HARRIDAN	AIRSPEED
RENEGADE	STALWART	VICARAGE	IMITABLE	BARBECUE	PROTOCOL	HERALDIC	ANATHEMA
RENOVATE	STANDARD	VICINAGE	INCUMBER	BARBICAN	PUBLICAN	HERALDRY	ANYWHERE
REPROACH	STATUARY	VIGILANT	INVIABLE	BARNACLE	PUSSYCAT	HONEYDEW	APOPLEXY
RESONANT	STEERAGE	VINEGARY	MANDIBLE	BAROUCHE	REVANCHE	INFRADIG	APOTHEGM
RESONATE	STOCKADE	VINEYARD	MEALYBUG	BARRACKS	SADDUCEE	INTENDED	APPARENT
RESTRAIN	STOPPAGE	VISICALC	MICROBUS	BINNACLE	SCILICET	INTRADOS	ARBALEST
RIFFRAFF	SUBTRACT	VISITANT	MILLIBAR	CANTICLE	SHORTCUT	INWARDLY	ARBOREAL
ROCKFALL	SUFFRAGE	VOLPLANE	MISCIBLE	CAPSICUM	SILENCER	ISLANDER	ARGUMENT
ROLLBACK	SUITCASE	WARPLANE	MISLABEL	CERVICAL	SKULLCAP	LAVENDER	ARMAMENT
ROOMMATE	SUKIYAKI	WHARFAGE	NEIGHBOR	CHEMICAL	SURGICAL	LOPSIDED	AVERMENT
ROSEMARY	SUNSHADE	WHIPLASH	NOVEMBER	CLAVICLE	TENTACLE	MASTODON	BACKREST
ROUGHAGE	SUPPLANT	WINDFALL	OPERABLE	CLERICAL	TESTICLE	MENHADEN	BARONESS
RUMINANT	SURCEASE	WINDLASS	PALPABLE	CLINICAL	TRICYCLE	MISJUDGE	BASELESS
RUMINATE	SUZERAIN	WINDWARD	PARTIBLE	COMANCHE	TUBERCLE	MYRMIDON	BASEMENT
RUNAGATE	SWAYBACK	WIREHAIR	PASSABLE	CONFOCAL	UNDERCUT	OLEANDER	BEDSTEAD
RUTABAGA	TABULATE	WOODLAND	PENUMBRA	CRITICAL	UNICYCLE	ORTHODOX	BEFRIEND
SABOTAGE	TAFFRAIL	WOOLSACK	PITIABLE	CROSSCUT	UNVOICED	OUTMODED	BERIBERI
SALIVATE	TAILGATE	WRECKAGE	PORTABLE	CURLICUE	UPPERCUT	OUTRIDER	BILLHEAD
SALUTARY	TAMARACK	ZWIEBACK	POSSIBLE	DEMARCHE	VERSICLE	OUTSIDER	BIRDSEED
SANDBANK	TELECAST	ADORABLE	PREAMBLE	DIVORCEE	VERTICAL	PERIODIC	BLOOMERS

BLUDGEON	DOMINEER	HELPMEET	MONUMENT	REDOLENT	VESTMENT	DOGFIGHT	BAKESHOP
BLUEBELL	DOWNBEAT	HIGHNESS	MOONBEAM	REFERENT	VIRULENT	ENDANGER	BALLYHOO
BODILESS	DRUMBEAT	HOGSHEAD	MORPHEME	REFINERY	VOYAGEUR	ENTANGLE	BRITCHES
BOOTLESS	DUMBBELL	HOLINESS	MOVEMENT	REFOREST	WAITRESS	EPILOGUE	BRONCHUS
BROWBEAT	EFFERENT	HOLSTEIN	MULETEER	REGIMENT	WEAKNESS	ESTROGEN	BROUGHAM
BULKHEAD	EGGSHELL	HUNTRESS	NAMELESS	REINDEER	WELDMENT	EYESIGHT	BUCKSHOT
BULLHEAD	EIGHTEEN	HYMENEAL	NAPOLEON	REPRIEVE	WELLHEAD	FANLIGHT	CABOCHON
BUSINESS	ELOQUENT	IMMANENT	NEEDLESS	RESIDENT	WIRELESS	FLASHGUN	CAPUCHIN
BUTTRESS	EMPYREAN	IMMINENT	NEWSREEL	RESTLESS	WITCHERY	GASLIGHT	CHITCHAT
CADUCEUS	ENGINEER	IMMODEST	NINETEEN	RETICENT	YOURSELF	GLYCOGEN	CHOWCHOW
CARELESS	ENTIRETY	IMPOTENT	NONEVENT	RETRIEVE	BEATIFIC	GUNFIGHT	CLINCHER
CAROTENE	ERYTHEMA	IMPUDENT	NUTRIENT	REVEREND	BLISSFUL	HARANGUE	COAUTHOR
CASEMENT	ETHEREAL	INCIDENT	NUTSHELL	REVERENT	BOASTFUL	HOOLIGAN	COLOPHON
CASHMERE	EUROPEAN	INDECENT	OBEDIENT	RUDIMENT	CHEERFUL	HOOSEGOW	CROTCHET
CEMETERY	EXPONENT	INDIGENT	OBSOLETE	RUTHLESS	CRUCIFIX	HYDROGEN	DECIPHER
CEREMENT	EYEPIECE	INDIRECT	OINTMENT	SABOTEUR	DOUBTFUL	INTRIGUE	DETACHED
CERULEAN	FADELESS	INDOLENT	OPPONENT	SCARCELY	DREADFUL	INVEIGLE	DIANTHUS
CESAREAN	FAREWELL	INEXPERT	ORANGERY	SCULLERY	FANCIFUL	LOLLYGAG	DIARRHEA
CHANCERY	FARTHEST	INHERENT	ORNAMENT	SEDIMENT	GLASSFUL	MADRIGAL	DRAUGHTS
CHECKERS	FASTNESS	INNOCENT	ORTHOEPY	SEIGNEUR	GRATEFUL	MALINGER	ENCIPHER
CHIPPEWA	FEARLESS	INSOLENT	OUTBREAK	SELFLESS	HORSEFLY	MERINGUE	FLAGSHIP
COGWHEEL	FECKLESS	INTEREST	OUTFIELD	SENTIENT	HOUSEFLY	MIDNIGHT	GROSCHEN
COHERENT	FILAMENT	IRONWEED	OUTGUESS	SHEPHERD	MOURNFUL	NEGLIGEE	HARDSHIP
COIFFEUR	FLAMBEAU	ISOPRENE	OUTSPEND	SHIPMENT	PARAFFIN	NITROGEN	HEADSHIP
COLISEUM	FLATHEAD	ISOTHERM	OVERHEAD	SICKNESS	PETTIFOG	NONRIGID	HEDGEHOG
COLLIERY	FLATTERY	JAPANESE	OVERHEAR	SIDEREAL	PROLIFIC	OUTFIGHT	HEDGEHOP
COMPLEAT	FLYSPECK	JONGLEUR	OVERLEAP	SLATTERN	RETROFIT	OUTRIGHT	KICKSHAW
COMPLETE	FLYWHEEL	JUDGMENT	OVERSEAS	SLIPPERY	RIGHTFUL	PATHOGEN	LADYSHIP
COMPRESS	FOOTLESS	KILLDEER	PANATELA	SNOBBERY	SKILLFUL	PELLAGRA	LAUNCHER
CONCRETE	FOOTREST	KNICKERS	PANCREAS	SOBRIETY	SPECIFIC	PENLIGHT	LECITHIN
CONFRERE	FOOTWEAR	KNITWEAR	PANTHEON	SOLDIERY	TERRIFIC	PENTAGON	LENGTHEN
CONGRESS	FOREBEAR	LAMASERY	PARAKEET	SOMBRERO	THANKFUL	PRODIGAL	LORDSHIP
CONQUEST	FOREFEND	LIGAMENT	PAVEMENT	STAMPEDE	THEREFOR	PROLOGUE	MARATHON
COPYDESK	FOREHEAD	LIKENESS	PAYCHECK	STRATEGY	TRANSFER	PROROGUE	METAPHOR
CORDLESS	FORETELL	LINIMENT	PEDIMENT	STRIDENT	TRANSFIX	SCRAGGLY	OVERSHOE
CORNMEAL	FORMLESS	LINOLEUM	PEERLESS	STURGEON	TRUSTFUL	SKYLIGHT	PAWNSHOP
COUNTESS	FORSWEAR	LISTLESS	PENITENT	SUBPOENA	TRUTHFUL	SQUEEGEE	PHOSPHOR
COURTESY	FORTRESS	LOCOWEED	PINWHEEL	SUPEREGO	TURBOFAN	STRAGGLE	PINOCHLE
CREAMERY	FOURTEEN	LODGMENT	PITILESS	SUPPRESS	UNDERFUR	STRAIGHT	PYORRHEA
CRESCENT	FRAGMENT	LONGUEUR	PLANGENT	TENEMENT	UNLAWFUL	STRANGER	RICOCHET
CROCKERY	FREQUENT	LUNCHEON	POKEWEED	THIEVERY	VENGEFUL	STRANGLE	SHANGHAI
DATELESS	FRIPPERY	MALAPERT	PORTIERE	THIRTEEN	WATCHFUL	STRENGTH	SIDESHOW
DAYBREAK	FUNEREAL	MALTREAT	POTSHERD	TIMELESS	WHITEFLY	STRINGED	SLIPSHOD
DAYDREAM	FURTHEST	MANIFEST	PREMIERE	TIRELESS	WRATHFUL	STRINGER	SNAPSHOT
DEADBEAT	GANGRENE	MARQUESS	PREPRESS	TRANSEPT	WRONGFUL	STRUGGLE	SNOWSHOE
DECEDENT	GOATHERD	MASSLESS	PRINCESS	TRICKERY	YOUTHFUL	SUNLIGHT	SOMEWHAT
DEFOREST	GOODNESS	MASTHEAD	PROCEEDS	TROUSERS	AFFRIGHT	TARRAGON	TELETHON
DELIVERY	GRADIENT	MATTRESS	PROGRESS	TRUMPERY	AIRTIGHT	TOBOGGAN	THRASHER
DEPONENT	GRANDEUR	MELODEON	PROPHECY	TUNELESS	ALLERGEN	TRIANGLE	TOGETHER
DERRIERE	GREENERY	MILKWEED	PROPHESY	TWEEZERS	ANALOGUE	TWILIGHT	TOWNSHIP
DESELECT	GROSBEAK	MILLIEME	PROSPECT	UNFREEZE	ANDROGEN	UNSOUGHT	TRENCHER
DILIGENT	GUYANESE	MINDLESS	PRURIENT	UNLIKELY	APOLOGIA	UNTANGLE	WARDSHIP
DISCREET	HABANERA	MISSPELL	PUNCHEON	UNLOVELY	ARPEGGIO	UNTAUGHT	WINESHOP
DISCRETE	HAREBELL	MISSPEND	PURULENT	UNTIMELY	CARDIGAN	VILLAGER	WOODSHED
DISTRESS	HAWKWEED	MISTREAT	QUOTIENT	UPSTREAM	CONJUGAL	ACANTHUS	WORKSHOP
DIVIDEND	HEADGEAR	MISTRESS	RAILLERY	VEHEMENT	DAYLIGHT	ALMIGHTY	WRETCHED
DOCUMENT	HEADREST	MONSIEUR	RECKLESS	VENEREAL	DIALOGUE	BABUSHKA	ABLATION

ABLATIVE	BACKBITE	CHROMIUM	DIATRIBE	EXACTING	GANGLION	ILLUSION	LIVERISH
ABLUTION	BACKFIRE	CIRCUITY	DIMINISH	EXERCISE	GASOLINE	ILLUSIVE	LOATHING
ABORNING	BACKSIDE	CITATION	DIPSTICK	EXORCISE	GENETICS	IMBECILE	LOCALITY
ABORTION	BANTLING	CIVILIAN	DISGUISE	EXORDIUM	GENITIVE	IMMOBILE	LOCALIZE
ABRASIVE	BASELINE	CIVILITY	DISJOINT	EXPEDITE	GENOCIDE	IMMOTILE	LOCATION
ACERBITY	BASILICA	CIVILIZE	DISQUIET	EXTERIOR	GERANIUM	IMMUNIZE	LOCUTION
ACQUAINT	BASILISK	CLASSIFY	DISTRICT	FACILITY	GHANAIAN	IMPERIAL	LONGTIME
ACTINISM	BEAUTIFY	CLEARING	DISUNITE	FAGOTING	GLOAMING	IMPETIGO	LOVEBIRD
ACTINIUM	BECOMING	CLIPPING	DISUNITY	FALCHION	GODCHILD	IMPOLITE	LOVESICK
ACTIVISM	BEHAVIOR	CLOTHIER	DIVINITY	FAMILIAL	GOLDFISH	IMPOSING	LOYALIST
ACTIVITY	BENEDICT	CLOTHING	DIVISION	FAMILIAR	GOODWIFE	IMPUNITY	LUTETIUM
ADDITION	BENEFICE	COHESION	DIVISIVE	FARTHING	GOODWILL	INCISION	MACPAINT
ADDITIVE	BESTRIDE	COINCIDE	DOCTRINE	FATALISM	GRAFFITO	INCISIVE	MAGAZINE
ADHESION	BIENNIAL	COLONIAL	DOLOMITE	FATALITY	GRAPHITE	INCOMING	MAGICIAN
ADHESIVE	BIENNIUM	COLONIST	DOMICILE	FAVORITE	GRASPING	INFERIOR	MAINLINE
ADMONISH	BIRACIAL	COLONIZE	DOMINION	FELICITY	GRATUITY	INFINITE	MAJOLICA
ADOPTIVE	BIRDLIME	COMEDIAN	DONATION	FEMININE	GRAYLING	INFINITY	MAJORITY
AFFINITY	BLACKING	COMPRISE	DOWNHILL	FEMINISM	GREEKING	INIQUITY	MALAWIAN
AGRARIAN	BLESSING	CONCEIVE	DOWNWIND	FEROCITY	GREETING	INSCRIBE	MARBLING
ALACRITY	BLOWPIPE	CONFLICT	DRESSING	FETCHING	GRUELING	INTERIOR	MARITIME
ALARMIST	BLUEBIRD	CONSPIRE	DROPKICK	FIDELITY	GUARDIAN	INVASION	MARQUISE
ALBANIAN	BLUEFISH	CONTRITE	DRUGGIST	FIGURINE	GUMPTION	INVITING	MATERIAL
ALGERIAN	BOBOLINK	CONTRIVE	DUCKBILL	FILIPINO	GUNPOINT	ISTHMIAN	MATERIEL
ALIASING	BOBWHITE	COUPLING	DUCKLING	FINALIST	GUNSMITH	JAILBIRD	MATURITY
ALIENIST	BOHEMIAN	COURTIER	DUMPLING	FINALIZE	HAIRLINE	JAUNDICE	MAVERICK
ALLSPICE	BOTULISM	CRAWFISH	DUNGHILL	FIRESIDE	HANDBILL	JEREMIAD	MAXIMIZE
ALLUVIUM	BRACKISH	CRAYFISH	DURATION	FISHWIFE	HANDPICK	JINGOISM	MEALTIME
ALTRUISM	BRANDISH	CREATION	DWELLING	FIXATION	HATCHING	JOYSTICK	MEANTIME
AMBITION	BREEDING	CREEPING	DYNAMITE	FIXATIVE	HAWAIIAN	JUDICIAL	MEDALIST
AMMONIUM	BRISLING	CREMAINS	EFFUSION	FLASHING	HEADLINE	JUNCTION	MEDICINE
AMORTIZE	BUDDHISM	CROSSING	EGYPTIAN	FLATFISH	HEBRAISM	JUVENILE	MEGALITH
ANGELICA	BUILDING	CROUPIER	EKISTICS	FLAUTIST	HEDONISM	KAMAAINA	MELANISM
ANTERIOR	BUNDLING	CRUZEIRO	ELECTION	FLEABITE	HEMATITE	KERCHIEF	MEMORIAL
ANYTHING	CAFFEINE	CRYOLITE	ELECTIVE	FLEETING	HEPATICA	KEROSINE	MEMORIZE
APHANITE	CAGELING	CUPIDITY	EMBOLISM	FLOURISH	HEREDITY	KINDLING	MERIDIAN
APHELION	CALADIUM	CURATIVE	EMPORIUM	FLUORIDE	HEREWITH	KINETICS	MESQUITE
APHORISM	CALAMINE	CYTOSINE	EMULSIFY	FLUORINE	HILLSIDE	LACEWING	METAFILE
APPETITE	CALAMITY	DAIQUIRI	EMULSION	FLUORITE	HINDUISM	LADYBIRD	MIDDLING
APPOSITE	CAMOMILE	DAIRYING	ENCOMIUM	FOOTHILL	HIRELING	LADYLIKE	MIDPOINT
APPRAISE	CAMPAIGN	DARKLING	ENERGIZE	FOOTLING	HOARDING	LANDFILL	MIDSHIPS
AQUARIUM	CANADIAN	DATELINE	ENGAGING	FORELIMB	HOMESICK	LANGUISH	MIGRAINE
AQUILINE	CANALIZE	DEADLINE	ENORMITY	FORKLIFT	HOMICIDE	LAXATIVE	MILESIMO
ARMORIAL	CANONIZE	DEBILITY	ENSHRINE	FORTUITY	HOODWINK	LAYERING	MINIBIKE
ARTERIAL	CAPACITY	DECISION	ENTRAILS	FRACTION	HORNPIPE	LEARNING	MINIMIZE
ARTIFICE	CATCHING	DECISIVE	EQUALIZE	FRANCIUM	HUMANISM	LEGALISM	MINORITY
ASPERITY	CAVALIER	DEFINITE	EQUATION	FREEWILL	HUMANITY	LEGATION	MISCHIEF
ASTATINE	CELERITY	DEIONIZE	ERECTILE	FRICTION	HUMANIZE	LENITIVE	MISDOING
ASTERISK	CENOBITE	DELIRIUM	ERECTION	FRONTIER	HUMIDIFY	LIBATION	MISPRINT
ASTONISH	CENTRIST	DELUSION	ESCAPISM	FROSTING	HUMIDITY	LICORICE	MISTRIAL
ATROCITY	CERAMIST	DEMOLISH	ESPALIER	FRUCTIFY	HUMILITY	LIFELINE	MOBILIZE
ATROPINE	CHAMPION	DEMONIAC	ESPECIAL	FRUITION	IDEALISM	LIFETIME	MOLEHILL
AUDITION	CHARMING	DEPUTIZE	ESTONIAN	FUGITIVE	IDEALIZE	LIKEWISE	MONITION
AUSTRIAN	CHASTISE	DERELICT	ETERNITY	FUNCTION	IDEATION	LIMEKILN	MONOLITH
AUTOGIRO	CHASTITY	DESCRIBE	EUGENICS	FUTILITY	IDENTIFY	LIMERICK	MONOXIDE
AVERSION	CHLORIDE	DETOXIFY	EURASIAN	FUTURISM	IDENTITY	LIMONITE	MORALIST
AVIATION	CHLORINE	DEVILISH	EUROPIUM	FUTURITY	IGNITION	LINGUIST	MORALITY
AVIONICS	CHLORITE	DEVOTION	EVENTIDE	GANGLING	ILLUMINE	LIPSTICK	MORALIZE

MORPHINE	OVERRIDE	PURBLIND	SHELVING	TEACHING	VENUSIAN	LAWMAKER	GRANULAR
MOSQUITO	OVERSIZE	PUTATIVE	SHILLING	TEETHING	VERACITY	MALARKEY	GRIZZLED
MOTORIZE	OVERTIME	QUAGMIRE	SHIPPING	TELEFILM	VERONICA	MISTAKEN	HERCULES
MOUNTING	OVERVIEW	QUALMISH	SHIRRING	TELEVIEW	VEXATION	MOLESKIN	HOSTELRY
MOURNING	PACIFIER	QUANTITY	SHIRTING	TELEVISE	VICINITY	ONLOOKER	IMPELLER
MUNITION	PACIFISM	QUANTIZE	SHOCKING	TEMERITY	VILLAINY	SEALSKIN	INTAGLIO
MUSICIAN	PAINTING	QUESTION	SHOPLIFT	THALLIUM	VITALITY	SPRINKLE	IRONCLAD
MUTATION	PALATINE	QUISLING	SHREWISH	THEORIZE	VITALIZE	SPROCKET	MAGDALEN
NASALIZE	PALOMINO	RATTLING	SIDEKICK	THESPIAN	VIVACITY	STRICKEN	MAGNOLIA
NATALITY	PANELING	RAVENING	SIDERITE	THIAMINE	VIVARIUM	UNBROKEN	MANDOLIN
NATIVISM	PANELIST	REACTION	SILICIFY	TICKLISH	VOCALIST	UNBUCKLE	MANTELET
NATIVITY	PARADIGM	REACTIVE	SIMONIZE	TINSMITH	VOCALIZE	APPELLEE	MANTILLA
NEBULIZE	PARADISE	REGICIDE	SIMPLIFY	TITANIUM	VOCATION	BACHELOR	NAUTILUS
NECKLINE	PARASITE	REGOLITH	SKIMMING	TOKENISM	VOCATIVE	BACILLUS	OVERALLS
NEGATION	PAVILION	RELATION	SKIRMISH	TONALITY	VOLATILE	BACKSLAP	OVERFLOW
NEGATIVE	PECULIAR	RELATIVE	SKITTISH	TORTOISE	VOLITION	BIATHLON	OVERPLAY
NEPOTISM	PENALIZE	RELIGION	SLUGGISH	TOTALITY	WEAKFISH	BORDELLO	PAMPHLET
NESTLING	PENKNIFE	REMEDIAL	SOLARIUM	TOUCHING	WEAKLING	BOUILLON	PARALLAX
NEUTRINO	PERCEIVE	RESCRIPT	SOLECISM	TOWELING	WHOPPING	BRACELET	PARALLEL
NICOTINE	PEROXIDE	RESTRICT	SOLIDIFY	TOWERING	WILDFIRE	BRINDLED	PASTILLE
NIGERIAN	PERSPIRE	RETIRING	SOLSTICE	TRACTION	WILDLIFE	BROOKLET	PENDULUM
NIGGLING	PETITION	REVIVIFY	SOLUTION	TRAINING	WINDMILL	BUNGALOW	PHENOLIC
NIHILISM	PHRASING	RHYOLITE	SOMETIME	TRAPPING	WINDPIPE	CALCULUS	POLYGLOT
NINEPINS	PIDDLING	RIPARIAN	SONATINA	TREATISE	WINGDING	CAMELLIA	POTBELLY
NOBELIST	PINPOINT	ROADSIDE	SONGBIRD	TRICHINA	WITCHING	CANAILLE	PREMOLAR
NOBELIUM	PINPRICK	ROMANIAN	SORORITY	TRIFLING	WOMANISH	CAPSULAR	REPUBLIC
NOBILITY	PIPELINE	ROYALIST	SORPTION	TRILLION	WOODBINE	CARILLON	REVEILLE
NONDAIRY	PLANKING	RUBIDIUM	SPANKING	TRILLIUM	WOODPILE	CASUALTY	SCAPULAR
NONSTICK	PLAYBILL	RUMANIAN	SPOOLING	TRIMMING	WOODWIND	CATHOLIC	SCHMALTZ
NONUNION	PLEASING	RUMBLING	STALLION	TUNISIAN	WRAPPING	CAUDILLO	SCOFFLAW
NOONTIDE	PLEBEIAN	SAILFISH	STANDING	TURNPIKE	XENOLITH	CELLULAR	SERAGLIO
NOONTIME	PLEURISY	SAMARIUM	STARFISH	TUTORIAL	YACHTING	CEPHALIC	SHAMBLES
NOTARIAL	PLUMBING	SANCTIFY	STARLING	ULTERIOR	YEARLING	CHANDLER	SHINGLES
NOTARIZE	POLARITY	SANCTION	STERLING	UNBELIEF	YEARNING	CHENILLE	SINGULAR
NOTATION	POLARIZE	SANCTITY	STIRRING	UNBODIED	YIELDING	CHIVALRY	SNOWPLOW
NOVELIZE	POLITICK	SANDWICH	STOCKING	UNENDING	YOUNGISH	CIRCULAR	STICKLER
NURSLING	POLITICO	SANGUINE	STRATIFY	UNERRING	YULETIDE	CLOUDLET	STIMULUS
OBLATION	POLITICS	SANITIZE	STRIKING	UNFILIAL	ZUCCHINI	COAGULUM	SYMBOLIC
OBLIVION	POLONIUM	SAPPHIRE	STUDDING	UNIAXIAL	LASERJET	COLESLAW	SYPHILIS
OBSIDIAN	POPULIST	SCALLION	STUFFING	UNIONISM	POPINJAY	COMPILER	TANTALUM
OCCASION	PORPOISE	SCANDIUM	STULTIFY	UNIONIZE	SUPERJET	CONVULSE	TELEPLAY
OFFICIAL	POSITION	SCATHING	STUNNING	UPCOMING	TURBOJET	COVERLET	TORTILLA
OFFPRINT	POSITIVE	SCIATICA	SUCHLIKE	UPRISING	BAEDEKER	DIABOLIC	TRICOLOR
ONCOMING	POTATION	SCORPION	SUCKLING	UPSTAIRS	BEARSKIN	DISALLOW	UMBRELLA
OPPOSITE	POULTICE	SCOTTISH	SUNDRIES	URBANITE	BIWEEKLY	DISCOLOR	UNDERLIE
OPTICIAN	PRACTICE	SCRUTINY	SUNSHINE	URBANIZE	BUCKSKIN	DISSOLVE	UNDERLIP
OPTIMISM	PREEXIST	SCULLION	SUPERIOR	VACATION	CALFSKIN	ESCALLOP	UNIVALVE
ORGANISM	PRESSING	SEAGOING	SUREFIRE	VANADIUM	CAPESKIN	EXEMPLAR	UNWIELDY
ORGANIST	PRESTIGE	SECURITY	SURPLICE	VANQUISH	CHANUKAH	FIRECLAY	VALVULAR
ORGANIZE	PRETTIFY	SEDATIVE	SURPRISE	VAPORING	CHEROKEE	FIREPLUG	VASCULAR
OUTGOING	PRINTING	SEDITION	SWASTIKA	VAPORISH	COONSKIN	FLIMFLAM	WATERLOO
OUTLYING	PRISTINE	SEEDLING	SWEEPING	VAPORIZE	DEERSKIN	FLOTILLA	WORDPLAY
OUTPOINT	PROCAINE	SEEDTIME	SWELLING	VAULTING	FORESKIN	FURBELOW	WRIGGLER
OUTSHINE	PTOMAINE	SELENITE	SWIMMING	VEGANISM	GOATSKIN	GANGPLOW	WRISTLET
OUTWEIGH	PUDDLING	SELENIUM	SYBARITE	VELLEITY	HANUKKAH	GAUNTLET	YUGOSLAV
OVENBIRD	PUGILISM	SHEEPISH	TAHITIAN	VELOCITY	LAMBSKIN	GLOBULIN	ZEPPELIN
OVERKILL	PUNITIVE	SHEETING	TAMARIND	VENATION	LATCHKEY	GONFALON	ABNORMAL

ACADEMIC	RADIOMAN	CRETONNE	INTERNET	SLIPKNOT	ARMYWORM	CREOSOTE	FOOTSORE
ALDERMAN	REFORMER	CRIMINAL	INTRENCH	SLOVENLY	ASTEROID	CROWFOOT	FOOTWORK
BAILSMAN	ROUTEMAN	CURRENCY	ISOTONIC	SOLVENCY	AUDITORY	CYTOLOGY	FOREBODE
BOGEYMAN	SALESMAN	DEFIANCE	ISSUANCE	SOUVENIR	AUTOJOIN	DARKROOM	FOREDOOM
BONDSMAN	SPACEMAN	DEMEANOR	KEYPUNCH	SPHAGNUM	BACKBONE	DARKSOME	FOREFOOT
BONHOMIE	SPECIMEN	DENOUNCE	LABURNUM	STOTINKA	BALLROOM	DEADLOCK	FOREGONE
BRAKEMAN	STREAMER	DIAGONAL	LAUDANUM	SUBSONIC	BANKBOOK	DEADWOOD	FORELOCK
CARDAMOM	SYSADMIN	DISHONOR	LEAVINGS	SUCCINCT	BANKROLL	DECOROUS	FOREMOST
CHAIRMAN	SYSTEMIC	DISPENSE	MACKINAW	SUPERNAL	BAREFOOT	DEMIBOLD	FORENOON
CINNAMON	TALESMAN	DISTANCE	MARTINET	SUSPENSE	BARITONE	DEMIJOHN	FOREWORD
COACHMAN	TALISMAN	DISTINCT	MATERNAL	TENDENCY	BASEBORN	DESIROUS	FORSOOTH
COGNOMEN	THALAMUS	DOORKNOB	MECHANIC	TENPENNY	BASSWOOD	DETHRONE	FOURFOLD
CONSOMME	TOWNSMAN	DOUGHNUT	METHANOL	TEOSINTE	BATHROBE	DEXTROSE	FOURSOME
CONTEMPT	TRAINMAN	DUODENUM	MILLINER	TERMINAL	BATHROOM	DIASTOLE	FOXGLOVE
CORPSMAN	TRANSMIT	EARNINGS	MNEMONIC	TERMINUS	BEHEMOTH	DILATORY	FREEBORN
CUSTOMER	UNCOMMON	ELEGANCE	NATIONAL	TEUTONIC	BENTWOOD	DISCLOSE	FREEHOLD
CYCLAMEN	UNFORMED	EMINENCE	NONSENSE	TRIBUNAL	BIBULOUS	DISPROVE	FREELOAD
DAIRYMAN	UNSEEMLY	ENCEINTE	NOTIONAL	TWOPENCE	BILLFOLD	DOUBLOON	FRETWORK
DIATOMIC	WATCHMAN	ENSCONCE	NUISANCE	TWOPENNY	BITSTOCK	DOWNLOAD	FUMAROLE
DIPLOMAT	WOODSMAN	ENTRANCE	OPERANDS	TYMPANUM	BLACKOUT	DOWNPOUR	GADABOUT
DRAGOMAN	ABEYANCE	ENTRENCH	ORDNANCE	UNCLENCH	BLUENOSE	DOWNTOWN	GAMECOCK
DULCIMER	AFFIANCE	ESTRANGE	ORIGINAL	UNEARNED	BODYWORK	DOXOLOGY	GAMESOME
ECONOMIC	AIRLINER	ETHERNET	PARDONER	UNGAINLY	BOLLWORM	EARPHONE	GATEPOST
EPIDEMIC	ALLIANCE	EVIDENCE	PARLANCE	VACCINIA	BOOKWORM	ENORMOUS	GEMOLOGY
FREEDMAN	ALUMINUM	EXCHANGE	PATERNAL	VAGRANCY	BREAKOUT	ENSHROUD	GEMSTONE
FRESHMAN	AMARANTH	EXIGENCY	PATIENCE	VARIANCE	BROCCOLI	ENTHRONE	GENEROUS
GOSSAMER	AMBIENCE	EXTERNAL	PERSONAL	VIBURNUM	BROWNOUT	ENVELOPE	GLABROUS
GRAVAMEN	ANACONDA	EYELINER	PICKINGS	VIOLENCE	BULLDOZE	ENVIRONS	GLADSOME
HANDYMAN	ANNOUNCE	FANDANGO	PIMIENTO	VIRGINAL	BUNGHOLE	ESCAROLE	GLAUCOMA
HEADSMAN	ARACHNID	FERVENCY	PITTANCE	VOLCANIC	BURNOOSE	ETHOLOGY	GLORIOUS
HELMSMAN	ATTORNEY	FLAMENCO	PLACENTA	WARRANTY	BUSYBODY	ETIOLOGY	GLOWWORM
HENCHMAN	AUDIENCE	FLAMINGO	PLATINUM	WEAPONRY	BUSYWORK	EUROBOND	GOALPOST
HERDSMAN	BANDANNA	FOREKNOW	PRECINCT	WHODUNIT	CALLIOPE	EVENSONG	GORGEOUS
HORSEMAN	BASSINET	GARDENIA	PRESENCE	YEOMANRY	CAMISOLE	EVERMORE	GRACIOUS
HUNTSMAN	BEECHNUT	GERMINAL	PRETENSE	ABATTOIR	CAPRIOLE	EVERYONE	GRIEVOUS
INDIAMAN	BUOYANCY	GLOXINIA	PRISONER	ACRIMONY	CAPTIOUS	EXIGUOUS	GRUESOME
INFORMAL	BURGUNDY	GOVERNOR	PROVINCE	ADVISORY	CARACOLE	EYETOOTH	HACKWORD
INFORMED	CARDINAL	GUARANTY	RATIONAL	AEROLOGY	CAREWORN	FABULOUS	HALFTONE
INFORMER	CHESTNUT	GUIDANCE	RAWBONED	AGRONOMY	CASEWORK	FACEDOWN	HANDBOOK
INTERMIT	CHEYENNE	HACIENDA	REGIONAL	AIRDROME	CATACOMB	FACTIOUS	HANDSOME
INTERMIX	CISLUNAR	HARMONIC	RELIANCE	ALBACORE	CATEGORY	FALTBOAT	HARDWOOD
INTROMIT	CLARINET	HEREUNTO	RENOUNCE	ALEATORY	CAUTIOUS	FEARSOME	HAUTBOIS
LACRIMAL	CLEMENCY	HISPANIC	RESIGNED	ALKALOID	CEREMONY	FIREBOAT	HAWTHORN
LANDSMAN	COMBINGS	HORMONAL	RESPONSE	ALLEGORY	CESSPOOL	FIREBOMB	HEADLOCK
LEUKEMIA	COMMANDO	HUGUENOT	RETAINER	AMOEBOID	CHAPBOOK	FIREWOOD	HEADLONG
LINESMAN	COMMENCE	HUSTINGS	RETRENCH	ANAEROBE	CHARCOAL	FIREWORK	HEADROOM
MANDAMUS	COMMONER	HYACINTH	RETURNEE	ANECDOTE	CHECKOFF	FISHBOWL	HEADWORD
MARKSMAN	COMMUNAL	INFERNAL	SARDONIC	ANECHOIC	CHECKOUT	FISHHOOK	HEADWORK
MESDAMES	CONDENSE	INFRINGE	SCAVENGE	ANTELOPE	CICERONE	FLAGPOLE	HECATOMB
MISNOMER	CONFINES	INGUINAL	SCHOONER	ANTEROOM	CINCHONA	FLAMEOUT	HEGEMONY
MOTORMAN	CONGENER	INNUENDO	SCROUNGE	ANTHROPO	CLAYMORE	FLATBOAT	HEIRLOOM
NEWCOMER	CONJUNCT	INSIGNIA	SENTENCE	ANTIBODY	CLOSEOUT	FLATFOOT	HELICOID
NOBLEMAN	CONTINUE	INSOMNIA	SENTINEL	ANTIDOTE	CLUBFOOT	FLYBLOWN	HELIPORT
NORSEMAN	CONVINCE	INSTANCE	SEQUENCE	ANTIMONY	COMEDOWN	FOLDBOAT	HELLHOLE
PANDEMIC	COSIGNER	INSTINCT	SHILINGI	ANTINOMY	CONFRONT	FOLKLORE	HEREFORD
PITCHMAN	CREDENCE	INTERNAL	SHRAPNEL	ANTIPODE	COOKBOOK	FOOTHOLD	HIGHBORN
PRESSMAN	CREDENZA	INTERNEE	SIXPENCE	ANTIPOPE	COPYBOOK	FOOTNOTE	HIGHROAD

HINDMOST	MONITORY	RAINCOAT	THEOLOGY	BACKSPIN	BAYBERRY	FORMERLY	PICKEREL
HOMEBODY	MONOPOLY	RAVENOUS	THRENODY	BICUSPID	BEGGARLY	FORWARDS	PIZZERIA
HOMEROOM	MONOTONE	RHAPSODY	TIMEWORN	CHUTZPAH	BESMIRCH	FROUFROU	PLECTRUM
HOMEWORK	MOTOROLA	RHEOLOGY	TIMOROUS	COLLAPSE	BETATRON	GASWORKS	POSITRON
HOOKWORM	MUSHROOM	RHOMBOID	TIRESOME	CRACKPOT	BINAURAL	GENDARME	PRESERVE
HORNBOOK	MYCOLOGY	RIBOSOME	TOILWORN	DECREPIT	BIYEARLY	GINGERLY	PRETERIT
HOROLOGY	NAINSOOK	RINGWORM	TOLLBOTH	DISCIPLE	BOWSPRIT	GLYCERIN	PROPERTY
HUMANOID	NEBULOUS	ROADWORK	TOPOLOGY	EPILEPSY	BRETHREN	GLYCEROL	PUREBRED
IDEOLOGY	NEMATODE	ROSEWOOD	TORTUOUS	FELDSPAR	BULLFROG	GRIDIRON	RAINDROP
ILLINOIS	NIGEROIS	RUNABOUT	TRAPDOOR	FINESPUN	CAMPOREE	GUTTURAL	RECOURSE
ILLUSORY	NOTEBOOK	SAGAMORE	TRAPROCK	FLESHPOT	CAREFREE	HEDGEROW	REFERRAL
INCHWORM	NUGATORY	SAILBOAT	TROMBONE	FLYPAPER	CAULDRON	HIGHBRED	REHEARSE
INFAMOUS	NUMEROUS	SCABROUS	TUBEROSE	HEREUPON	CAUSERIE	HIGHBROW	RESEARCH
IRONWOOD	OFFSHOOT	SCAFFOLD	TUBEROUS	HOMESPUN	CENTERED	HITHERTO	RESOURCE
IRONWORK	OFFSHORE	SCISSORS	TURNCOAT	IMPROPER	CEREBRUM	HOLOGRAM	RHETORIC
IROQUOIS	OILCLOTH	SEASHORE	UNCTUOUS	INTREPID	CHAMBRAY	HOMEBRED	ROOFTREE
JACKBOOT	OPENWORK	SEDULOUS	UNSAVORY	LARKSPUR	CHAPERON	HYSTERIA	SANSKRIT
KEELBOAT	ORGULOUS	SEMINOLE	UPSTROKE	LINCHPIN	CHEMURGY	IDEOGRAM	SAUTERNE
KEYSTONE	OUTDOORS	SEMISOFT	USURIOUS	LOLLIPOP	CHOLERIC	INFRARED	SAWHORSE
KILOVOLT	OVERCOAT	SENSUOUS	UUDECODE	MANCIPLE	CICATRIX	INSPIRIT	SCENARIO
KINGBOLT	OVERCOME	SEROLOGY	UUENCODE	MARZIPAN	CLAPTRAP	INTEGRAL	SEAFARER
KNEEHOLE	OVERLOOK	SHAMROCK	UXORIOUS	MAYAPPLE	CLITORIS	INTERROG	SETSCREW
KNOCKOUT	OVERLORD	SHINBONE	VAGABOND	MISAPPLY	COCKCROW	JAMBOREE	SNOWDROP
KNOTHOLE	OVERTONE	SHIPWORM	VAPOROUS	MULTIPLE	COCKEREL	JEOPARDY	SPECTRAL
LADYLOVE	PALINODE	SHOPWORN	VARICOSE	MULTIPLY	COMMERCE	KANGAROO	SPECTRUM
LANDFORM	PARABOLA	SHOSHONE	VENOMOUS	PLATYPUS	CONCERTO	KEYWORDS	SQUADRON
LANDLORD	PARAMOUR	SHOWDOWN	VIETCONG	SAUCEPAN	CONSERVE	KILOGRAM	SQUIRREL
LAVATORY	PARANOIA	SHUTDOWN	VIGOROUS	SCALEPAN	CONSTRUE	LEAPFROG	SUBMERGE
LIFEBOAT	PASSBOOK	SIDELONG	VIROLOGY	SMALLPOX	CONVERGE	LETHARGY	SUBMERSE
LIFELONG	PASSPORT	SIGNPOST	VIRTUOSO	SOUTHPAW	CONVERSE	LINGERIE	SULFURIC
LIFEWORK	PASSWORD	SILICONE	VIRTUOUS	STRUMPET	COPPERAS	LITTORAL	TELEGRAM
LIGNEOUS	PEDAGOGY	SINKHOLE	VITREOUS	TAILSPIN	CORDUROY	LUTHERAN	TEMPORAL
LIVELONG	PEEPHOLE	SLUMLORD	WARDROBE	TERRAPIN	CORNCRIB	MACKEREL	TIMBERED
LOANWORD	PEIGNOIR	SOFTWOOD	WARDROOM	TURNSPIT	CORPORAL	MANDARIN	TOMORROW
LOBOTOMY	PENOLOGY	SOLENOID	WAREROOM	UNCOUPLE	DECIGRAM	MANNERED	TRAVERSE
LONESOME	PENSTOCK	SOMEBODY	WASHBOWL	UNDERPAY	DEKAGRAM	MANNERLY	TRIMARAN
LONGBOAT	PHASEOUT	SONOROUS	WASHROOM	UNSHAPED	DEMOCRAT	MARJORAM	TURMERIC
LONGHORN	PICKLOCK	SPACIOUS	WELLBORN	UNZIPPED	DEMURRER	MASTERLY	UNAWARES
LOOPHOLE	PINAFORE	SPECIOUS	WEREWOLF	WINGSPAN	DEWBERRY	MERCURIC	UNCHURCH
LOVELORN	PLATFORM	SPHEROID	WHIPCORD	APPLIQUE	DIELDRIN	METEORIC	UNIVERSE
LUMINOUS	PLAYBOOK	SPITTOON	WILDFOWL	BOUTIQUE	DISAGREE	MINSTREL	VARIORUM
LUSCIOUS	PLAYGOER	SPURIOUS	WILDWOOD	COLLOQUY	DISARRAY	MISCARRY	VICTORIA
LYMPHOID	PLETHORA	STAKEOUT	WIREWORM	CRITIQUE	DISBURSE	MONAURAL	VISCERAL
MACARONI	POLTROON	STANDOFF	WISHBONE	MYSTIQUE	DISGORGE	MONOGRAM	WARFARIN
MACAROON	POPULOUS	STANDOUT	WITHHOLD	PHYSIQUE	DISPERSE	MULBERRY	WAYFARER
MANGROVE	PORTHOLE	STUBBORN	WONDROUS	PRATIQUE	DISPIRIT	NOCTURNE	WIREDRAW
MANIFOLD	POSTHOLE	STUDBOOK	WOODCOCK	AGITPROP	DOGGEREL	ORATORIO	WISTARIA
MANYFOLD	POSTPONE	STUDIOUS	WOODNOTE	AIRBORNE	DUNGAREE	OUTBURST	WISTERIA
MARIGOLD	PRECIOUS	SYCAMORE	WOODWORK	AIRSTRIP	ELECTRIC	OUTSTRIP	WITHDRAW
MARKDOWN	PREVIOUS	SYMPHONY	WORDBOOK	ALIZARIN	ELECTRON	OVERDRAW	ABSCISSA
MELANOMA	PRIMROSE	SYNDROME	WORKBOOK	ANGSTROM	ESOTERIC	OVERGROW	ACCURSED
MESHWORK	PRINTOUT	TAILCOAT	WORKROOM	AVIATRIX	EUPHORIA	PARTERRE	ACIDOSIS
MILEPOST	PSALMODY	TAPEWORM	WORMHOLE	AXLETREE	FILIGREE	PASTORAL	ALFRESCO
MILLPOND	PULPWOOD	TAXONOMY	WORMWOOD	BACCARAT	FIRETRAP	PECTORAL	AMBROSIA
MINATORY	PUSHDOWN	TEAMWORK	YEARBOOK	BACKDROP	FLATIRON	PEDIGREE	ANALYSIS
MISQUOTE	QUADROON	TEASPOON	YEARLONG	BARBARIC	FLUIDRAM	PERFORCE	ASSASSIN
MONGOOSE	RAILROAD	TEXTBOOK	ZOOSPORE	BARBERRY	FOLDEROL	PERVERSE	CAROUSAL

CAROUSEL	UNCHASTE	DECANTER	LOCKSTEP	ROOMETTE	AIRBRUSH	JUNCTURE	TITMOUSE
CHARISMA	UNDERSEA	DEJECTED	LODESTAR	ROULETTE	ALEHOUSE	LATITUDE	TRANQUIL
CHECKSUM	UNLOOSEN	DEMENTED	MAGNETIC	SCIMITAR	ALLELUIA	LIGATURE	TREASURE
COALESCE	UNPERSON	DEMENTIA	MAINSTAY	SCULPTOR	ALTHOUGH	MADHOUSE	TREASURY
COLOSSAL	ABSENTEE	DESPATCH	MALTSTER	SEAWATER	ALTITUDE	MALAMUTE	UNSPRUNG
COLOSSUS	ABSINTHE	DETRITUS	MEPHITIC	SELECTEE	APERTURE	MANICURE	UNSTRUNG
CREVASSE	ACCOUTRE	DIABETES	MINISTER	SEMANTIC	APPLAUSE	MASSEUSE	UPTHRUST
DIALYSIS	ACCUSTOM	DIAMETER	MINISTRY	SEMESTER	APTITUDE	MISCOUNT	USUFRUCT
DIAPASON	ACOUSTIC	DICTATOR	MISMATCH	SERVITOR	AQUEDUCT	MISTRUST	VERMOUTH
DISPOSAL	ACROSTIC	DIDACTIC	MOMENTUM	SIDESTEP	ARCHDUKE	MOISTURE	VISCOUNT
DISTASTE	AFFECTED	DIRECTOR	MONASTIC	SINISTER	ARMATURE	MOLECULE	WINDBURN
ELLIPSIS	AFFLATUS	DISASTER	MUENSTER	SITUATED	ATTITUDE	MORIBUND	WOODRUFF
EMPHASIS	AFLUTTER	DISINTER	MUSCATEL	SKELETON	BANKRUPT	NEWFOUND	APPROVAL
ENURESIS	AFTERTAX	DISKETTE	MUSKETRY	SONGSTER	BERCEUSE	NONESUCH	BEREAVED
ESPOUSAL	AGERATUM	DISPATCH	MYELITIS	SPINSTER	BIANNUAL	NUMSKULL	BICONVEX
ESPRESSO	AGLITTER	DIURETIC	NARCOTIC	SPIRITED	BISEXUAL	OBSTRUCT	CARNIVAL
EXCURSUS	AGNOSTIC	DOMESTIC	NEONATAL	SPLATTER	BROCHURE	OPUSCULE	CORDOVAN
EXEGESIS	AIGRETTE	DOORSTEP	NEPENTHE	SPLINTER	CARNAUBA	OUTBOUND	DISCOVER
FANTASIA	ANCESTOR	ECLIPTIC	NEURITIS	SPLUTTER	CATAPULT	OUTHOUSE	DISFAVOR
FASCISTA	ANCESTRY	ELEVATOR	NEUROTIC	STEALTHY	CHIPMUNK	OVERMUCH	DISHEVEL
FIBROSIS	ANISETTE	EMBATTLE	NONMETAL	STILETTO	CINCTURE	OVERRULE	DISSEVER
FORENSIC	ANTEATER	EMBITTER	NUTHATCH	STRAITEN	COCKSURE	OVERTURE	ENDEAVOR
GALLUSES	APERITIF	EMERITUS	ODOMETER	SUBTITLE	COIFFURE	OVERTURN	FESTIVAL
GARRISON	ARTISTIC	EMPHATIC	OHMMETER	SYMMETRY	COMPOUND	PANTSUIT	HANGOVER
GEODESIC	ARTISTRY	EXECUTOR	OPERETTA	SYMPATHY	CONCLUDE	PEDICURE	HOLDOVER
GRANDSON	ASBESTOS	FACTOTUM	ORIENTAL	SYNOPTIC	CONFOUND	PERILUNE	INTERVAL
GUERNSEY	ASSORTED	FALSETTO	OUTDATED	TAPESTRY	CREATURE	PICAYUNE	INVOLVED
HEAVYSET	ATHLETIC	FELLATIO	OVERSTAY	TEAMSTER	CYNOSURE	PLAYSUIT	LAWGIVER
HYPNOSIS	BACKSTOP	FOLIATED	OVERSTEP	TEETOTAL	DANDRUFF	PLEASURE	LEFTOVER
IMPRISON	BAGUETTE	FOOTSTEP	PALMETTO	TENANTRY	DANSEUSE	POSTLUDE	MANEUVER
JALOUSIE	BALUSTER	FORESTRY	PARIETAL	TESTATOR	DENATURE	PRECLUDE	MEDIEVAL
JETTISON	BANISTER	FRENETIC	PATHETIC	THREATEN	DESTRUCT	PRESSURE	MOREOVER
KOLINSKY	BARBITAL	FRIGHTEN	PEDESTAL	THROTTLE	DISABUSE	PROFOUND	PASSOVER
LACROSSE	BARRATRY	GAMESTER	PILASTER	THRUSTER	DISCOUNT	PROPOUND	PRIMEVAL
LAMBASTE	BARRETTE	GANGSTER	PLANKTON	TOILETRY	DISMOUNT	PROTRUDE	PULLOVER
LICENSEE	BELITTLE	GEOMETRY	PODIATRY	TOILETTE	DISTRUST	PUNCTUAL	PUSHOVER
MACHISMO	BLACKTOP	GIGANTIC	POLESTAR	TRIMETER	DOGHOUSE	PUNCTURE	RECEIVER
MAGNESIA	BRIGHTEN	HEIGHTEN	POLLSTER	TUNGSTEN	DOLDRUMS	QUIETUDE	RESERVED
MANTISSA	BULLETIN	HERMETIC	PRENATAL	UNBEATEN	DORMOUSE	REASSURE	REVOLVER
MARMOSET	BURSITIS	HOSPITAL	PROMOTER	UNBOLTED	DOWNTURN	RESIDUAL	TRIUMVIR
MOCCASIN	CANISTER	HOUSETOP	PULMOTOR	UNBUTTON	DYESTUFF	RESIDUUM	TURNOVER
MOLASSES	CARYATID	HUCKSTER	QUIXOTIC	UNCLOTHE	EVENTUAL	RESOLUTE	UPHEAVAL
NARCOSIS	CASSETTE	HYPNOTIC	RADIATOR	UNDERTOW	EXPOSURE	REVENUER	WALKOVER
NECROSIS	CATHETER	IDOLATER	REBUTTAL	UNFASTEN	FAUBOURG	RIDICULE	WHATEVER
NEUROSIS	CEMENTUM	IDOLATRY	RECEPTOR	UNFETTER	FOXHOUND	ROSEBUSH	WHENEVER
PARMESAN	CHRISTEN	IMMORTAL	REGISTER	UNSETTLE	FRACTURE	RUBICUND	WHEREVER
PARTISAN	CHRISTIE	IMPACTED	REGISTRY	UNWONTED	FURLOUGH	SCHEDULE	WHOMEVER
PHARISEE	CLEMATIS	IMPOSTOR	REMITTAL	UNWORTHY	HABITUAL	SCROFULA	ALLEYWAY
REPRISAL	CLOISTER	INDEBTED	REPARTEE	VARIETAL	HANDCUFF	SEAMOUNT	CASTAWAY
REVERSAL	COCKATOO	INDUCTEE	REPEATED	VARISTOR	HOTHOUSE	SHANTUNG	CAUSEWAY
SACRISTY	COMPUTER	INDUSTRY	REPORTER	VENDETTA	ICEBOUND	SINECURE	DEFLOWER
SOMERSET	CONFETTI	INEDITED	RESISTOR	VERBATIM	ICEHOUSE	SOLITUDE	DRIVEWAY
SUPPOSED	COQUETTE	INFANTRY	RESORTER	VERBOTEN	IMMATURE	SURMOUNT	FOLDAWAY
SYNOPSIS	CORVETTE	INVERTER	RHEOSTAT	VIGNETTE	INSECURE	SURROUND	GIVEAWAY
THICKSET	COSMETIC	JURISTIC	ROADSTER	WORDSTAR	INSOMUCH	TACITURN	HATCHWAY
TRAVESTY	CREDITOR	LAUGHTER	ROCKETRY	ABSOLUTE	INSTRUCT	THOROUGH	HIDEAWAY
UNBIASED	DAUGHTER	LIBRETTO	ROMANTIC	ABSTRUSE	INVOLUTE	TINCTURE	NEWLYWED

PANDOWDY	ARTERIAL	COLONIAL	FLATHEAD	JUDICIAL	OVERCOAT	SCAPULAR	WINGSPAN
POLLIWOG	ATYPICAL	COLOSSAL	FLIMFLAM	KEELBOAT	OVERDRAW	SCIMITAR	WIREDRAW
REVIEWER	AUSTRIAN	COMEDIAN	FLUIDRAM	KICKSHAW	OVERHEAD	SCOFFLAW	WITHDRAW
SCALAWAG	BACCARAT	COMMUNAL	FOLDAWAY	KILOGRAM	OVERHEAR	SHANGHAI	WOODSMAN
SPEEDWAY	BACKSLAP	COMPLEAT	FOLDBOAT	KNITWEAR	OVERLEAP	SIDEREAL	WORDPLAY
SPILLWAY	BAILSMAN	CONFOCAL	FOOLSCAP	LACRIMAL	OVERPLAY	SINGULAR	WORDSTAR
STAIRWAY	BARBICAN	CONJUGAL	FOOTWEAR	LANDSMAN	OVERSEAS	SKULLCAP	WORKADAY
STOWAWAY	BARBITAL	COPPERAS	FOREBEAR	LIFEBOAT	OVERSTAY	SOMEWHAT	YUGOSLAV
TIGHTWAD	BEDSTEAD	CORDOVAN	FOREHEAD	LINESMAN	PANCREAS	SOUTHPAW	ANAEROBE
UPGROWTH	BERMUDAS	CORNMEAL	FORSWEAR	LITTORAL	PARALLAX	SPACEMAN	BATHROBE
WALKAWAY	BIANNUAL	CORPORAL	FREEDMAN	LODESTAR	PARFOCAL	SPECTRAL	CARNAUBA
WATERWAY	BIENNIAL	CORPSMAN	FREELOAD	LOLLYGAG	PARIETAL	SPEEDWAY	DESCRIBE
WILLIWAW	BILLHEAD	CRIMINAL	FRESHMAN	LONGBOAT	PARMESAN	SPILLWAY	DIATRIBE
ASPHYXIA	BINAURAL	CRITICAL	FUNEREAL	LUTHERAN	PARTISAN	STAIRWAY	INSCRIBE
DYSLEXIA	BIOCIDAL	CROSSBAR	GERMINAL	MACKINAW	PASTORAL	STOWAWAY	KOHLRABI
AMETHYST	BIRACIAL	DAIRYMAN	GHANAIAN	MADRIGAL	PATERNAL	SUPERNAL	WARDROBE
CATALYZE	BIRTHDAY	DAYBREAK	GIVEAWAY	MAGICIAN	PECTORAL	SURGICAL	ABEYANCE
DISLOYAL	BISEXUAL	DAYDREAM	GRANULAR	MAINSTAY	PECULIAR	TAHITIAN	ABSTRACT
EMPLOYEE	BOGEYMAN	DEADBEAT	GROSBEAK	MALAWIAN	PEDESTAL	TAILCOAT	AFFIANCE
GARGOYLE	BOHEMIAN	DECIGRAM	GUARDIAN	MALTREAT	PEMMICAN	TALESMAN	AIRSPACE
GIGABYTE	BONDSMAN	DEKAGRAM	GUTTURAL	MANIACAL	PERSONAL	TALISMAN	ALFRESCO
KILOBYTE	BRAKEMAN	DEMOCRAT	HABITUAL	MARJORAM	PHYSICAL	TEETOTAL	ALLIANCE
LOGOTYPE	BRICKBAT	DEMONIAC	HANDICAP	MARKSMAN	PITCHMAN	TELEGRAM	ALLSPICE
MEGABYTE	BROUGHAM	DIAGONAL	HANDYMAN	MARZIPAN	PLEBEIAN	TELEPLAY	AMBIENCE
NEOPHYTE	BROWBEAT	DIPLOMAT	HANUKKAH	MASTHEAD	POLESTAR	TEMPORAL	ANGELICA
PARALYZE	BULKHEAD	DISARRAY	HARRIDAN	MATERIAL	POPINJAY	TERMINAL	ANNOUNCE
PAROXYSM	BULLHEAD	DISLOYAL	HATCHWAY	MATERNAL	PREMOLAR	THESPIAN	ANYPLACE
PORPHYRY	CALENDAR	DISPOSAL	HAWAIIAN	MEDIEVAL	PRENATAL	THURSDAY	APPROACH
TAXPAYER	CANADIAN	DOOMSDAY	HEADGEAR	MEMORIAL	PRESSMAN	TIGHTWAD	AQUEDUCT
TRIPTYCH	CANNIBAL	DOWNBEAT	HEADSMAN	MERIDIAN	PRIMEVAL	TOBOGGAN	ARTIFACT
TRUETYPE	CAPSULAR	DOWNLOAD	HELMSMAN	METRICAL	PRODIGAL	TOWNSMAN	ARTIFICE
ZOOPHYTE	CARDIGAN	DRAGOMAN	HENCHMAN	MILLIBAR	PUBLICAN	TRAINMAN	AUDIENCE
ATOMIZER	CARDINAL	DRIVEWAY	HERDSMAN	MISTREAT	PUNCTUAL	TRIBUNAL	AVIONICS
BEDAZZLE	CARNIVAL	DRUMBEAT	HIDEAWAY	MISTRIAL	PUSSYCAT	TRIMARAN	BACKPACK
EMBEZZLE	CAROUSAL	EGYPTIAN	HIGHROAD	MONAURAL	RADIOMAN	TUNISIAN	BAREBACK
EMBLAZON	CASTAWAY	EMPYREAN	HOGSHEAD	MONOGRAM	RAILROAD	TURBOFAN	BASILICA
HOWITZER	CAUSEWAY	ESPECIAL	HOLOGRAM	MOONBEAM	RAINCOAT	TURNCOAT	BENEDICT
KIBITZER	CELLULAR	ESPOUSAL	HOOLIGAN	MOROCCAN	RATIONAL	TUTORIAL	BENEFICE
UNMUZZLE	CERULEAN	ESTONIAN	HORMONAL	MOTORCAR	REBUTTAL	UNDERPAY	BESMIRCH
	CERVICAL	ETHEREAL	HORSEMAN	MOTORMAN	REFERRAL	UNFILIAL	BITSTOCK
	CESAREAN	ETRUSCAN	HOSPITAL	MUSICIAN	REGIONAL	UNIAXIAL	BOLDFACE
	CHAIRMAN	EURASIAN	HUNTSMAN	MYSTICAL	REMEDIAL	UPHEAVAL	BUOYANCY
	CHAMBRAY	EUROPEAN	HYMENEAL	NATIONAL	REMITTAL	UPSTREAM	CALLBACK
7TH LETTER	CHANUKAH	EVENTUAL	IDEOGRAM	NAUTICAL	REPRISAL	VALVULAR	CARAPACE
	CHARCOAL	EVERYDAY	IMMORTAL	NEONATAL	RESIDUAL	VARIETAL	CATARACT
ABNORMAL	CHEMICAL	EXEMPLAR	IMPERIAL	NIGERIAN	REVERSAL	VASCULAR	CELIBACY
ACIDHEAD	CHITCHAT	EXTERNAL	INDIAMAN	NOBLEMAN	RHEOSTAT	VENEREAL	CLEMENCY
AFTERTAX	CHUTZPAH	FALTBOAT	INFERNAL	NONMETAL	RIPARIAN	VENUSIAN	COALESCE
AGRARIAN	CINNABAR	FAMILIAL	INFORMAL	NORSEMAN	ROMANIAN	VERTICAL	COMEBACK
ALBANIAN	CIRCULAR	FAMILIAR	INGUINAL	NOTARIAL	ROUTEMAN	VIRGINAL	COMMENCE
ALDERMAN	CISLUNAR	FELDSPAR	INIMICAL	NOTIONAL	RUMANIAN	VISCERAL	COMMERCE
ALGERIAN	CIVILIAN	FESTIVAL	INTEGRAL	OBSIDIAN	SAILBOAT	WALKAWAY	CONFLICT
ALLEYWAY	CLAPTRAP	FIREBOAT	INTERNAL	OFFICIAL	SALESMAN	WATCHMAN	CONJUNCT
AMERICAN	CLERICAL	FIRECLAY	INTERVAL	OPTICIAN	SATURDAY	WATERWAY	CONTRACT
ANGLICAN	CLINICAL	FIRETRAP	IRONCLAD	ORIENTAL	SAUCEPAN	WELLHEAD	CONVINCE
ARBOREAL	COACHMAN	FLAMBEAU	ISTHMIAN	ORIGINAL	SCALAWAG	WHITECAP	CORONACH
ARMORIAL	COLESLAW	FLATBOAT	JEREMIAD	OUTBREAK	SCALEPAN	WILLIWAW	CREDENCE

CURRENCY	INSTRUCT	RESOURCE	FIRESIDE	ALPHABET	CUSTOMER	GAUNTLET	MAGDALEN
DEADLOCK	INTRENCH	RESTRICT	FLUORIDE	ANDROGEN	CYCLAMEN	GLYCOGEN	MALARKEY
DEFIANCE	ISSUANCE	RETRENCH	FOREBODE	ANTEATER	CYLINDER	GOSSAMER	MALINGER
DELICACY	JAUNDICE	ROLLBACK	FORELADY	APPELLEE	DAUGHTER	GRAVAMEN	MALTSTER
DENOUNCE	JOYSTICK	SANDWICH	FORWARDS	ASPHODEL	DEATHBED	GRIZZLED	MANEUVER
DERELICT	KEYPUNCH	SCIATICA	GENOCIDE	ASSORTED	DECANTER	GROSCHEN	MANNERED
DESELECT	KICKBACK	SENTENCE	HACIENDA	ATOMIZER	DECEMBER	GROUNDER	MANTELET
DESPATCH	KINETICS	SEQUENCE	HANDMADE	ATTORNEY	DECIPHER	GUERNSEY	MARMOSET
DESTRUCT	KNAPSACK	SHAMROCK	HILLSIDE	AXLETREE	DEFLOWER	HANGOVER	MARTINET
DIPSTICK	LAMPBACK	SHOELACE	HOMEBODY	BAEDEKER	DEJECTED	HAWKWEED	MATERIEL
DISGRACE	LICORICE	SIDEKICK	HOMEMADE	BALUSTER	DEMENTED	HEAVYSET	MENHADEN
DISPATCH	LIMERICK	SIXPENCE	HOMICIDE	BANISTER	DEMURRER	HEIGHTEN	MESDAMES
DISPLACE	LIPSTICK	SOLSTICE	INNUENDO	BASSINET	DETACHED	HELPMEET	MILKWEED
DISTANCE	LOVESICK	SOLVENCY	JEOPARDY	BEHOLDEN	DIABETES	HERCULES	MILLINER
DISTINCT	MAJOLICA	SUBTRACT	KEYWORDS	BEREAVED	DIAMETER	HIGHBRED	MINISTER
DISTRACT	MAVERICK	SUCCINCT	LATITUDE	BEWILDER	DIARRHEA	HOLDOVER	MINSTREL
DISTRICT	MILLRACE	SURPLICE	LEMONADE	BICONVEX	DISAGREE	HOMEBRED	MISCHIEF
DRAWBACK	MISMATCH	SWAYBACK	MONOXIDE	BIRDSEED	DISASTER	HONEYDEW	MISLABEL
DROPKICK	MISPLACE	TAMARACK	NEMATODE	BRACELET	DISCOVER	HOWITZER	MISNOMER
EKISTICS	MOSSBACK	TENDENCY	NOONTIDE	BRETHREN	DISCREET	HUCKSTER	MISTAKEN
ELEGANCE	NECKLACE	TRANSACT	OPERANDS	BRIGHTEN	DISHEVEL	HYDROGEN	MOLASSES
EMINENCE	NONESUCH	TRAPROCK	OVERRIDE	BRINDLED	DISINTER	IDOLATER	MOREOVER
ENCROACH	NONSTICK	TRIPTYCH	PALINODE	BRITCHES	DISORDER	IMPACTED	MUENSTER
ENSCONCE	NUISANCE	TWOPENCE	PALISADE	BROOKLET	DISQUIET	IMPELLER	MULETEER
ENTRANCE	NUTHATCH	TYPEFACE	PANDOWDY	CALENDER	DISSEVER	IMPROPER	MUSCATEL
ENTRENCH	OBSTRUCT	UNCHURCH	PEROXIDE	CAMPOREE	DIVORCEE	INCUMBER	NEGLIGEE
EUGENICS	ORDNANCE	UNCLENCH	PERSUADE	CANISTER	DOGGEREL	INDEBTED	NEWCOMER
EVIDENCE	OUTREACH	UNDERACT	POSTLUDE	CAREFREE	DOMINEER	INDUCTEE	NEWLYWED
EXIGENCY	OVERMUCH	USUFRUCT	PRECLUDE	CAROUSEL	DOORSTEP	INEDITED	NEWSREEL
EYEPIECE	PALEFACE	VAGRANCY	PROCEEDS	CATHETER	DULCIMER	INFORMED	NINETEEN
FASTBACK	PARLANCE	VARIANCE	PROTRUDE	CAVALIER	DUNGAREE	INFORMER	NITROGEN
FEEDBACK	PATIENCE	VERONICA	PSALMODY	CENTERED	EIGHTEEN	INFRARED	NOVEMBER
FERVENCY	PAYCHECK	VIOLENCE	QUIETUDE	CHANDLER	EMBITTER	INTENDED	ODOMETER
FLAMENCO	PENSTOCK	WOODCOCK	REGICIDE	CHARADES	EMBOLDEN	INTERNEE	OHMMETER
FLAPJACK	PERFORCE	WOOLSACK	RENEGADE	CHEROKEE	EMPLOYEE	INTERNET	OLEANDER
FLYSPECK	PHARMACY	ZWIEBACK	RHAPSODY	CHRISTEN	ENCIPHER	INVERTER	ONLOOKER
FOOTRACE	PICKLOCK	ACCOLADE	ROADSIDE	CLARINET	ENCUMBER	INVOLVED	OUTDATED
FORELOCK	PINPRICK	ALTITUDE	SERENADE	CLINCHER	ENDANGER	IRONWEED	OUTMODED
FULLBACK	PITTANCE	ANACONDA	SOLITUDE	CLOISTER	ENGENDER	ISLANDER	OUTRIDER
GAMECOCK	PLAYBACK	ANTIBODY	SOMEBODY	CLOTHIER	ENGINEER	JAMBOREE	OUTSIDER
GENETICS	POLITICK	ANTIPODE	STAMPEDE	CLOUDLET	ESPALIER	KERCHIEF	OVERSTEP
GIMCRACK	POLITICO	APTITUDE	STOCKADE	COCKEREL	ESTROGEN	KIBITZER	OVERVIEW
GUIDANCE	POLITICS	AQUACADE	SUNSHADE	COGNOMEN	ETHERNET	KILLDEER	PACIFIER
HALFBACK	POPULACE	ATTITUDE	THRENODY	COGWHEEL	EXPLODED	LASERJET	PAMPHLET
HANDPICK	POULTICE	BACKSIDE	UNSTEADY	COLANDER	EYELINER	LATCHKEY	PARAKEET
HARDBACK	PRACTICE	BESTRIDE	UNWIELDY	COMMONER	FILIGREE	LAUGHTER	PARALLEL
HARDHACK	PRECINCT	BLOCKADE	UUDECODE	COMPILER	FLOUNDER	LAUNCHER	PARDONER
HARDTACK	PRESENCE	BURGUNDY	UUENCODE	COMPUTER	FLYPAPER	LAVENDER	PASSOVER
HAYSTACK	PROPHECY	BUSYBODY	YULETIDE	CONFINES	FLYWHEEL	LAWGIVER	PATHOGEN
HEADLOCK	PROSPECT	CHLORIDE	ABSENTEE	CONGENER	FOLIATED	LAWMAKER	PEDIGREE
HEPATICA	PROTRACT	COINCIDE	ACCURSED	CONSIDER	FOOTSTEP	LEFTOVER	PHARISEE
HOMESICK	PROVINCE	COMMANDO	AFFECTED	COSIGNER	FOURTEEN	LENGTHEN	PICKEREL
HUMPBACK	PULLBACK	CONCLUDE	AFLUTTER	COURTIER	FRIGHTEN	LICENSEE	PILASTER
INDIRECT	RELIANCE	DISSUADE	AGLITTER	COVERLET	FRONTIER	LOCKSTEP	PINWHEEL
INSOMUCH	RENOUNCE	ENFILADE	AIRLINER	CROTCHET	GALLUSES	LOCOWEED	PLAYGOER
INSTANCE	REPROACH	ESCAPADE	AIRSPEED	CROUPIER	GAMESTER	LOPSIDED	POKEWEED
INSTINCT	RESEARCH	EVENTIDE	ALLERGEN	CUCUMBER	GANGSTER	MACKEREL	POLLSTER

PRISONER	SQUEEGEE	WHEREVER	DISLODGE	STOPPAGE	UNWORTHY	COMPLAIN	HEADSHIP
PROMOTER	SQUIRREL	WHOMEVER	DOXOLOGY	STRATEGY	ABATTOIR	CONTRAIL	HELICOID
PROVIDED	STICKLER	WOODSHED	DRAINAGE	SUBMERGE	ACADEMIC	COONSKIN	HERALDIC
PULLOVER	STRAITEN	WRETCHED	DRESSAGE	SUFFRAGE	ACCREDIT	CORNCRIB	HERMETIC
PUREBRED	STRANGER	WRIGGLER	EARNINGS	SUPEREGO	ACIDOSIS	COSMETIC	HIGHTAIL
PUSHOVER	STREAMER	WRISTLET	ENSILAGE	THEOLOGY	ACOUSTIC	COXSWAIN	HISPANIC
PYORRHEA	STRICKEN	AIRCRAFT	ENVISAGE	THOROUGH	ACROSTIC	CRUCIFIX	HOLSTEIN
RAWBONED	STRINGED	BEAUTIFY	EQUIPAGE	TOPOLOGY	AGNOSTIC	DAFFODIL	HUMANOID
RECEIVER	STRINGER	CAMSHAFT	ESTRANGE	TRACKAGE	AIRSTRIP	DEBONAIR	HYPNOSIS
RECORDER	STRUMPET	CHECKOFF	ETHOLOGY	TRUCKAGE	ALIZARIN	DECREPIT	HYPNOTIC
REFORMER	SUNDRIES	CLASSIFY	ETIOLOGY	TUTELAGE	ALKALOID	DEERSKIN	HYSTERIA
REGISTER	SUPERJET	DANDRUFF	EXCHANGE	UNDERAGE	ALLELUIA	DEMENTIA	ILLINOIS
REINDEER	SUPPOSED	DETOXIFY	FANDANGO	VERBIAGE	ALOPECIA	DIABOLIC	IMPLICIT
REMEMBER	TAXPAYER	DYESTUFF	FLAMINGO	VICARAGE	AMBROSIA	DIALYSIS	INFRADIG
REPARTEE	TEAMSTER	EMULSIFY	FRONTAGE	VICINAGE	AMOEBOID	DIATOMIC	INSIGNIA
REPEATED	TELEVIEW	FISHWIFE	FURLOUGH	VIROLOGY	ANALYSIS	DIDACTIC	INSOMNIA
REPORTER	THICKSET	FORKLIFT	FUSELAGE	WHARFAGE	ANECHOIC	DIELDRIN	INSPIRIT
RESERVED	THIRTEEN	FRUCTIFY	GEMOLOGY	WRECKAGE	APERITIF	DISCLAIM	INTAGLIO
RESIGNED	THRASHER	GOODWIFE	HERITAGE	ABSINTHE	APOLOGIA	DISPIRIT	INTERMIT
RESORTER	THREATEN	HANDCUFF	HOROLOGY	AFFRIGHT	APPENDIX	DISTRAIT	INTERMIX
RETAINER	THRUSTER	HUMIDIFY	HUSTINGS	AIRTIGHT	ARACHNID	DIURETIC	INTREPID
RETARDED	TIMBERED	IDENTIFY	IDEOLOGY	AUTOBAHN	ARMCHAIR	DOMESTIC	INTROMIT
RETURNEE	TOGETHER	PENKNIFE	IMPETIGO	BACKACHE	ARPEGGIO	DOVETAIL	IROQUOIS
REVENUER	TOPSIDES	PRETTIFY	INFRINGE	BAROUCHE	ARTISTIC	DYSLEXIA	ISOTONIC
REVIEWER	TRANSFER	REVIVIFY	LANGUAGE	BROUHAHA	ASPHYXIA	ECLIPTIC	JALOUSIE
REVOLVER	TRENCHER	RIFFRAFF	LEAVINGS	COMANCHE	ASSASSIN	ECONOMIC	JURISTIC
RICOCHET	TRIMETER	SANCTIFY	LETHARGY	DAYLIGHT	ASTEROID	ELECTRIC	LADYSHIP
RIVERBED	TUNGSTEN	SEMISOFT	LEVERAGE	DEMARCHE	ATHLETIC	ELLIPSIS	LAMBSKIN
ROADSTER	TURBOJET	SHOPLIFT	MARRIAGE	DEMIJOHN	AUTOJOIN	EMPHASIS	LECITHIN
ROOFTREE	TURNOVER	SILICIFY	MISJUDGE	DOGFIGHT	AVIATRIX	EMPHATIC	LEUKEMIA
SADDUCEE	UNAWARES	SIMPLIFY	MISUSAGE	EYESIGHT	BACKSPIN	ENURESIS	LINCHPIN
SCHOONER	UNBEATEN	SOLIDIFY	MORTGAGE	FANLIGHT	BARBARIC	EPIDEMIC	LINGERIE
SCILICET	UNBELIEF	STANDOFF	MUCILAGE	FAROUCHE	BEARSKIN	ESOTERIC	LONGHAIR
SEAFARER	UNBIASED	STRATIFY	MYCOLOGY	GASLIGHT	BEATIFIC	EUPHORIA	LORDSHIP
SEAWATER	UNBIDDEN	STULTIFY	OFFSTAGE	GUNFIGHT	BICUSPID	EXEGESIS	LYMPHOID
SELECTEE	UNBODIED	WILDLIFE	ONONDAGA	HEADACHE	BONHOMIE	EXPLICIT	MAGNESIA
SEMESTER	UNBOLTED	WOODRUFF	OUTWEIGH	HUARACHE	BOWSPRIT	FANTASIA	MAGNETIC
SENTINEL	UNBROKEN	AEROLOGY	PARADIGM	INFOBAHN	BROMIDIC	FELLATIO	MAGNOLIA
SETSCREW	UNBURDEN	ALTHOUGH	PEDAGOGY	MARIACHI	BUCKSKIN	FIBROSIS	MAINSAIL
SHAMBLES	UNDERSEA	AMPERAGE	PENOLOGY	MIDNIGHT	BULLETIN	FLAGSHIP	MAINTAIN
SHINGLES	UNEARNED	APOTHEGM	PICKINGS	MONARCHY	BURSITIS	FORENSIC	MANDARIN
SHOULDER	UNFASTEN	APPANAGE	PILOTAGE	MUSTACHE	CALFSKIN	FORESAIL	MANDOLIN
SHRAPNEL	UNFETTER	BADINAGE	PORRIDGE	NEPENTHE	CAMELLIA	FORESKIN	MECHANIC
SIDESTEP	UNFORMED	BARONAGE	POUNDAGE	OUTFIGHT	CANNABIS	FOUNTAIN	MEDICAID
SILENCER	UNLEADED	BEGRUDGE	PREJUDGE	OUTRIGHT	CAPESKIN	FRENETIC	MEPHITIC
SINISTER	UNLIMBER	BEVERAGE	PRESTIGE	PASTICHE	CAPUCHIN	GARDENIA	MERCURIC
SITUATED	UNLOOSEN	BREAKAGE	RHEOLOGY	PENLIGHT	CARYATID	GEODESIC	METEORIC
SOMERSET	UNSHAPED	CAMPAIGN	ROUGHAGE	REVANCHE	CATHOLIC	GIGANTIC	MILKMAID
SONGSTER	UNVOICED	CARRIAGE	RUTABAGA	SKYLIGHT	CAUSERIE	GLOBULIN	MNEMONIC
SPECIMEN	UNWONTED	CHEMURGY	SABOTAGE	STEALTHY	CEPHALIC	GLOXINIA	MOCCASIN
SPINSTER	UNZIPPED	CLEAVAGE	SCAVENGE	STRAIGHT	CHAPLAIN	GLYCERIN	MOLESKIN
SPIRITED	VERBOTEN	COMBINGS	SCROUNGE	SUNLIGHT	CHOLERIC	GOATSKIN	MONASTIC
SPLATTER	VILLAGER	CONVERGE	SEROLOGY	SYMPATHY	CHRISTIE	HANDRAIL	MONORAIL
SPLINTER	WALKOVER	COVERAGE	SEWERAGE	TWILIGHT	CICATRIX	HANGNAIL	MOUNTAIN
SPLUTTER	WAYFARER	CRIBBAGE	SHILINGI	UNCLOTHE	CLEMATIS	HARDSHIP	MYELITIS
SPROCKET	WHATEVER	CYTOLOGY	SHORTAGE	UNSOUGHT	CLITORIS	HARMONIC	NARCOSIS
SQUANDER	WHENEVER	DISGORGE	STEERAGE	UNTAUGHT	COCKTAIL	HAUTBOIS	NARCOTIC

NECROSIS	SYSADMIN	BARNACLE	ENVIABLE	MANNERLY	SCAFFOLD	VARIABLE	OVERCOME
NEURITIS	SYSTEMIC	BASEBALL	ERECTILE	MANTILLA	SCALABLE	VERSICLE	OVERTIME
NEUROSIS	TAFFRAIL	BEANBALL	ESCAROLE	MANYFOLD	SCARCELY	VINCIBLE	PANORAMA
NEUROTIC	TAILSPIN	BEDAZZLE	FALLIBLE	MARIGOLD	SCHEDULE	VIOLABLE	PASTRAMI
NIGEROIS	TERRAPIN	BEFUDDLE	FAREWELL	MASTERLY	SCRABBLE	VISICALC	POLYGAMY
NONRIGID	TERRIFIC	BEGGARLY	FASCICLE	MAYAPPLE	SCRAGGLY	VOLATILE	RIBOSOME
ORATORIO	TEUTONIC	BELITTLE	FEASIBLE	MEATBALL	SCRAMBLE	WASHABLE	SEEDTIME
OUTSTRIP	TOWNSHIP	BIDDABLE	FIREBALL	METAFILE	SCRIBBLE	WEREWOLF	SELFSAME
OVERLAID	TRANQUIL	BIFOCALS	FLAGPOLE	MISAPPLY	SCROFULA	WHITEFLY	SOMETIME
PANDEMIC	TRANSFIX	BILLFOLD	FLEXIBLE	MISCIBLE	SEMINOLE	WINDFALL	SYNDROME
PANTSUIT	TRANSMIT	BINNACLE	FLOTILLA	MISSPELL	SENSIBLE	WINDMILL	TAXONOMY
PARAFFIN	TRIUMVIR	BIWEEKLY	FOLLICLE	MOLECULE	SIDEWALK	WITHHOLD	TIRESOME
PARANOIA	TURMERIC	BIYEARLY	FOOTBALL	MOLEHILL	SIDEWALL	WOODPILE	ABORNING
PATHETIC	TURNSPIT	BLUEBELL	FOOTFALL	MONOPOLY	SINKHOLE	WORKABLE	ABUNDANT
PEIGNOIR	UNDERBID	BORDELLO	FOOTHILL	MOTHBALL	SLOVENLY	WORMHOLE	ABUTMENT
PELLUCID	UNDERLIE	BROCCOLI	FOOTHOLD	MOTOROLA	SNOWBALL	YOURSELF	ACCIDENT
PERIODIC	UNDERLIP	BUNGHOLE	FORCIBLE	MULTIPLE	SNOWFALL	AGRONOMY	ACQUAINT
PHENOLIC	VACCINIA	CAKEWALK	FORETELL	MULTIPLY	SOCIABLE	AIRDROME	ACRIMONY
PIZZERIA	VERBATIM	CAMISOLE	FORMERLY	MUSICALE	SOFTBALL	AIRFRAME	ADJACENT
PLANTAIN	VICTORIA	CAMOMILE	FOURFOLD	NUMSKULL	SPITBALL	ANATHEMA	ADJUTANT
PLAYSUIT	VOLCANIC	CANAILLE	FREEHOLD	NUTSHELL	SPRINKLE	ANTINOMY	ADJUVANT
PONYTAIL	WARDSHIP	CANTICLE	FREEWILL	OBSTACLE	SQUABBLE	BIRDLIME	AFFERENT
PORTRAIT	WARFARIN	CAPRIOLE	FUMAROLE	OPERABLE	STRADDLE	CATACOMB	AIRBORNE
POSTPAID	WHODUNIT	CARACOLE	GARGOYLE	OPUSCULE	STRAGGLE	CHARISMA	AIRPLANE
PRESIDIO	WIREHAIR	CARRYALL	GENITALS	OUTFIELD	STRANGLE	CONSOMME	ALIASING
PRETERIT	WISTARIA	CATAPULT	GINGERLY	OVERALLS	STRUGGLE	DARKSOME	AMBULANT
PROCLAIM	WISTERIA	CATCHALL	GODCHILD	OVERKILL	SUBTITLE	DOLDRUMS	ANTIMONY
PROHIBIT	ZEPPELIN	CAUDILLO	GOODWILL	OVERRULE	SUITABLE	DOORJAMB	ANYTHING
PROLIFIC	MAHARAJA	CHASUBLE	GOOFBALL	PALPABLE	SYLLABLE	ERYTHEMA	APPARENT
QUATRAIN	ARCHDUKE	CHENILLE	HANDBALL	PANATELA	TANGIBLE	FEARSOME	AQUILINE
QUIXOTIC	BABUSHKA	CLAVICLE	HANDBILL	PARABOLA	TELEFILM	FIREBOMB	ARGUMENT
REPUBLIC	BARRACKS	COVERALL	HARDBALL	PARTIBLE	TELLTALE	FIREDAMP	ARMAMENT
RESTRAIN	CLAMBAKE	CREDIBLE	HAREBELL	PARTICLE	TENTACLE	FORELIMB	ARROGANT
RETROFIT	GASWORKS	CRUCIBLE	HELLHOLE	PASSABLE	TERRIBLE	FORENAME	ASPIRANT
RHETORIC	KEEPSAKE	CULPABLE	HIGHBALL	PASTILLE	TESTICLE	FOURSOME	ASTATINE
RHOMBOID	KOLINSKY	DAMNABLE	HORRIBLE	PEDUNCLE	THROTTLE	GAMESOME	ATROPINE
ROMANTIC	LADYLIKE	DEMIBOLD	HORSEFLY	PEEPHOLE	TORTILLA	GENDARME	AVERMENT
SANSKRIT	MANDRAKE	DIASTOLE	HOUSEFLY	PINNACLE	TRIANGLE	GLADSOME	BACKBONE
SARDONIC	MINIBIKE	DISCIPLE	IMBECILE	PINOCHLE	TRICYCLE	GLAUCOMA	BACKHAND
SCENARIO	NAMESAKE	DOMICILE	IMITABLE	PITIABLE	TUBERCLE	GRUESOME	BANDANNA
SEALSKIN	OVERTAKE	DOWNFALL	IMMOBILE	PLAYBILL	UMBRELLA	HANDSOME	BANTLING
SEMANTIC	STOTINKA	DOWNHILL	IMMOTILE	PORTABLE	UNBUCKLE	HECATOMB	BARITONE
SERAGLIO	SUCHLIKE	DUCKBILL	INVEIGLE	PORTHOLE	UNCOUPLE	LIFETIME	BASELINE
SOLENOID	SUKIYAKI	DUMBBELL	INVIABLE	POSSIBLE	UNGAINLY	LOBOTOMY	BASEMENT
SOUVENIR	SWASTIKA	DUNGHILL	INWARDLY	POSTHOLE	UNICYCLE	LONESOME	BECHUANA
SPECIFIC	TURNPIKE	DUTIABLE	JUVENILE	POTBELLY	UNKINDLY	LONGTIME	BECOMING
SPHEROID	UPSTROKE	EDUCABLE	KILOVOLT	PRATFALL	UNLIKELY	MACHISMO	BEFRIEND
SPLENDID	ABUTTALS	EGGSHELL	KINGBOLT	PREAMBLE	UNLOVELY	MARITIME	BLACKING
SPORADIC	ADORABLE	ELIGIBLE	KNEEHOLE	PROBABLE	UNMUZZLE	MEALTIME	BLESSING
SUBSONIC	AIRFIELD	EMBATTLE	KNOTHOLE	PUFFBALL	UNRIDDLE	MEANTIME	BOBOLINK
SUBURBIA	AMENABLE	EMBEZZLE	LANDFALL	QUOTABLE	UNSADDLE	MELANOMA	BOUFFANT
SULFURIC	AMICABLE	ENCIRCLE	LANDFILL	RAINFALL	UNSEEMLY	MILESIMO	BREEDING
SUZERAIN	ARGUABLE	ENFEEBLE	LIMEKILN	RELIABLE	UNSETTLE	MILLIEME	BRISLING
SYMBOLIC	ASSEMBLE	ENSEMBLE	LOOPHOLE	RESEMBLE	UNSTABLE	MONOGAMY	BUILDING
SYNOPSIS	ASSEMBLY	ENTANGLE	MANCIPLE	REVEILLE	UNTANGLE	MORPHEME	BUNDLING
SYNOPTIC	BAILABLE	ENTHRALL	MANDIBLE	RIDICULE	UNTIMELY	NICKNAME	CABSTAND
SYPHILIS	BANKROLL	ENTRAILS	MANIFOLD	ROCKFALL	VALUABLE	NOONTIME	CAFFEINE

CAGELING	ELOQUENT	HATCHING	MAHOGANY	PANELING	SANGUINE	THOUSAND	ANCESTOR
CALAMINE	ENGAGING	HEADBAND	MAINLAND	PAVEMENT	SAUTERNE	TIDELAND	ANGSTROM
CAROTENE	ENSHRINE	HEADLAND	MAINLINE	PEDIMENT	SCATHING	TOUCHING	ANTERIOR
CASEMENT	ENTHRONE	HEADLINE	MARBLING	PENCHANT	SCRUTINY	TOWELING	ANTEROOM
CATCHING	ENVIRONS	HEADLONG	MEDICINE	PENITENT	SEAGOING	TOWERING	APHELION
CEREMENT	EPIPHANY	HEGEMONY	MEMBRANE	PERILUNE	SEAMOUNT	TRAINING	ASBESTOS
CEREMONY	EUROBOND	HESITANT	MERCHANT	PETULANT	SEAPLANE	TRAPPING	AUDITION
CHARMING	EVENSONG	HIGHLAND	MIDDLING	PHEASANT	SEDIMENT	TRICHINA	AVERSION
CHEYENNE	EVERYONE	HIRELING	MIDPOINT	PHRASING	SEEDLING	TRIFLING	AVIATION
CHIPMUNK	EXACTING	HOARDING	MIGRAINE	PICAYUNE	SENTIENT	TRIMMING	BACHELOR
CHLORINE	EXPONENT	HOMELAND	MILITANT	PIDDLING	SERGEANT	TROMBONE	BACKDROP
CICERONE	FAGOTING	HOODWINK	MILLPOND	PIEPLANT	SHANTUNG	TWOPENNY	BACKSTOP
CINCHONA	FARMHAND	ICEBOUND	MISBRAND	PINPOINT	SHEETING	UNDULANT	BAKESHOP
CLAIMANT	FARMLAND	IGNORANT	MISCOUNT	PIPELINE	SHELVING	UNENDING	BALLROOM
CLEARING	FARTHING	ILLUMINE	MISDOING	PLANGENT	SHILLING	UNERRING	BALLYHOO
CLIPPING	FEMININE	IMMANENT	MISPRINT	PLANKING	SHINBONE	UNSPRUNG	BANKBOOK
CLOTHING	FETCHING	IMMINENT	MISSPEND	PLEASANT	SHIPMENT	UNSTRUNG	BAREFOOT
COHERENT	FIGURINE	IMPOSING	MONOTONE	PLEASING	SHIPPING	UPCOMING	BASSWOOD
COMPOUND	FILAMENT	IMPOTENT	MONUMENT	PLUMBING	SHIRRING	UPRISING	BATHROOM
CONFOUND	FILIPINO	IMPUDENT	MOORLAND	POIGNANT	SHIRTING	VAGABOND	BEHAVIOR
CONFRONT	FLAGRANT	INCIDENT	MORIBUND	POSTPONE	SHOCKING	VAPORING	BENTWOOD
CONSTANT	FLASHING	INCOMING	MORPHINE	PREGNANT	SHOSHONE	VAULTING	BETATRON
COUCHANT	FLATLAND	INDECENT	MOUNTING	PRESSING	SIBILANT	VEHEMENT	BIATHLON
COUPLING	FLEABANE	INDIGENT	MOURNING	PRINTING	SIDELONG	VESICANT	BLACKTOP
COVENANT	FLEETING	INDOLENT	MOVEMENT	PRISTINE	SILICONE	VESTMENT	BLUDGEON
CREEPING	FLIPPANT	INERRANT	NECKLINE	PROCAINE	SKIMMING	VIETCONG	BOUILLON
CREMAINS	FLUORINE	INHALANT	NESTLING	PROFOUND	SNOWBANK	VIGILANT	BUCKSHOT
CRESCENT	FOOTLING	INHERENT	NEUTRINO	PROPOUND	SONATINA	VILLAINY	BULLFROG
CRETONNE	FOREFEND	INHUMANE	NEWFOUND	PRURIENT	SPANKING	VIRULENT	BUNGALOW
CROPLAND	FOREGONE	INKSTAND	NICOTINE	PTOMAINE	SPOOLING	VISCOUNT	CABOCHON
CROSSING	FOREHAND	INNOCENT	NIGGLING	PUDDLING	STAGNANT	VISITANT	CARDAMOM
CYTOSINE	FORELAND	INSOLENT	NINEPINS	PURBLIND	STANDING	VOLPLANE	CARILLON
DAIRYING	FOXHOUND	INVITING	NOCTURNE	PURSLANE	STARLING	WARPLANE	CAULDRON
DARKLING	FRAGMENT	ISOPRENE	NONEVENT	PURULENT	STERLING	WEAKLING	CESSPOOL
DATELINE	FRAGRANT	JUBILANT	NURSLING	QUADRANT	STIRRING	WELDMENT	CHAMPION
DEADLINE	FREEHAND	JUDGMENT	NUTRIENT	QUISLING	STOCKING	WHOPPING	CHAPBOOK
DECEDENT	FREQUENT	KAMAAINA	OBEDIENT	QUOTIENT	STRIDENT	WINGDING	CHAPERON
DECKHAND	FROSTING	KATAKANA	OCCUPANT	RATTLING	STRIKING	WISHBONE	CHOIRBOY
DEPONENT	FUMIGANT	KEROSINE	OFFPRINT	RAVENING	STUDDING	WITCHING	CHOWCHOW
DETHRONE	GANGLAND	KEYSTONE	OINTMENT	REACTANT	STUFFING	WOODBINE	CINNAMON
DILIGENT	GANGLING	KINDLING	ONCOMING	RECREANT	STUNNING	WOODLAND	CITATION
DISCOUNT	GANGRENE	LACEWING	OPPONENT	REDOLENT	SUBPOENA	WOODWIND	CLUBFOOT
DISJOINT	GASOLINE	LAYERING	ORNAMENT	REFERENT	SUCKLING	WRAPPING	COAUTHOR
DISMOUNT	GEMSTONE	LEARNING	OUTBOUND	REGIMENT	SUNSHINE	YACHTING	COCKATOO
DIVIDEND	GLOAMING	LIFELINE	OUTFLANK	RELAXANT	SUPPLANT	YEARLING	COCKCROW
DOCKHAND	GOURMAND	LIFELONG	OUTGOING	RELEVANT	SURMOUNT	YEARLONG	COHESION
DOCTRINE	GRADIENT	LIGAMENT	OUTLYING	RESIDENT	SURROUND	YEARNING	COLOPHON
DOCUMENT	GRASPING	LINIMENT	OUTPOINT	RESONANT	SWEEPING	YIELDING	COOKBOOK
DOWNWIND	GRAYLING	LITIGANT	OUTSHINE	RETICENT	SWELLING	ZUCCHINI	COPYBOOK
DRESSING	GREEKING	LIVELONG	OUTSPEND	RETIRING	SWIMMING	ABLATION	CORDUROY
DUCKLING	GREETING	LOATHING	OVERHAND	REVEREND	SYMPHONY	ABLUTION	CORRIDOR
DUMPLING	GRUELING	LODGMENT	OVERHANG	REVERENT	TAMARIND	ABORTION	CRACKPOT
DWELLING	GUNPOINT	LONGHAND	OVERLAND	RUBICUND	TEACHING	ACCUSTOM	CREATION
EARPHONE	GYMKHANA	MACARONI	OVERTONE	RUDIMENT	TEETHING	ADDITION	CREDITOR
EFFERENT	HABITANT	MACPAINT	PAINTING	RUMBLING	TENEMENT	ADHESION	CROSSBOW
EGGPLANT	HAIRLINE	MAGAZINE	PALATINE	RUMINANT	TENPENNY	AGITPROP	CROWFOOT
ELEPHANT	HALFTONE	MAHARANI	PALOMINO	SANDBANK	THIAMINE	AMBITION	CUSPIDOR

DARKROOM	GOVERNOR	NEIGHBOR	SNOWPLOW	CONTEMPT	CINCTURE	HALLMARK	MINATORY
DEADWOOD	GRANDSON	NONUNION	SNOWSHOE	ENVELOPE	CLAYMORE	HARDWARE	MINISTRY
DECISION	GRIDIRON	NOTATION	SOFTWOOD	HORNPIPE	COCKSURE	HAWTHORN	MISCARRY
DELUSION	GUMPTION	NOTEBOOK	SOLUTION	LOGOTYPE	COIFFURE	HEADWORD	MOISTURE
DEMEANOR	HANDBOOK	OBLATION	SORPTION	MIDSHIPS	COLLIERY	HEADWORK	MONETARY
DEVOTION	HARDWOOD	OBLIVION	SPITTOON	MISSHAPE	CONFRERE	HELIPORT	MONITORY
DIAPASON	HEADROOM	OCCASION	SPLENDOR	ORTHOEPY	CONSPIRE	HERALDRY	MORTUARY
DICTATOR	HEDGEHOG	OFFSHOOT	SQUADRON	RESCRIPT	CONTRARY	HEREFORD	MUDGUARD
DIRECTOR	HEDGEHOP	ORTHODOX	STALLION	SEASCAPE	CORONARY	HIGHBORN	MULBERRY
DISALLOW	HEDGEROW	OVERFLOW	STUDBOOK	TRANSEPT	CREAMERY	HOMEWARD	MUSKETRY
DISCOLOR	HEIRLOOM	OVERGROW	STURGEON	TRUETYPE	CREATURE	HOMEWORK	NONDAIRY
DISFAVOR	HEREUPON	OVERLOOK	SUPERIOR	WINDPIPE	CROCKERY	HONORARY	NUGATORY
DISHONOR	HIGHBROW	OVERSHOE	TARRAGON	AARDVARK	CRUZEIRO	HOOKWORM	OBITUARY
DIVISION	HOMEROOM	PANTHEON	TEASPOON	ACCOUTRE	CULINARY	HOSTELRY	OFFSHORE
DOMINION	HOOSEGOW	PASSBOOK	TELETHON	ADULTERY	CUPBOARD	IDOLATRY	OPENWORK
DONATION	HORNBOOK	PAVILION	TESTATOR	ADVISORY	CYNOSURE	ILLUSORY	ORANGERY
DOORKNOB	HOUSEBOY	PAWNSHOP	TEXTBOOK	ALBACORE	DAIQUIRI	IMMATURE	ORDINARY
DOUBLOON	HOUSETOP	PENTAGON	THEREFOR	ALEATORY	DELAWARE	INCHWORM	OUTBOARD
DOUGHBOY	HUGUENOT	PETITION	TOMORROW	ALLEGORY	DELIVERY	INDUSTRY	OUTDOORS
DURATION	IDEATION	PETTIFOG	TOREADOR	ANCESTRY	DENATURE	INEXPERT	OUTSMART
EFFUSION	IGNITION	PHOSPHOR	TRACTION	ANYWHERE	DERRIERE	INFANTRY	OVENBIRD
ELECTION	ILLUSION	PLANKTON	TRAPDOOR	APERTURE	DEWBERRY	INSECURE	OVERLORD
ELECTRON	IMPOSTOR	PLAYBOOK	TRICOLOR	ARMATURE	DILATORY	IRONWARE	OVERTURE
ELEVATOR	IMPRISON	POLLIWOG	TRILLION	ARMYWORM	DOCKYARD	IRONWORK	OVERTURN
EMBLAZON	INCISION	POLTROON	ULTERIOR	ARTISTRY	DOORYARD	ISOTHERM	PARTERRE
EMOTICON	INFERIOR	POLYGLOT	UNBUTTON	AUDITORY	DOWNTURN	JACQUARD	PASSPORT
EMULSION	INTERCOM	POSITION	UNCOMMON	AUTOGIRO	DOWNWARD	JAILBIRD	PASSWORD
ENDEAVOR	INTERIOR	POSITRON	UNDERDOG	BACKFIRE	DRUNKARD	JUNCTURE	PEDICURE
EQUATION	INTERROG	POTATION	UNDERTOW	BACKWARD	EMISSARY	KEYBOARD	PELLAGRA
ERECTION	INTRADOS	PROTOCOL	UNPERSON	BARBERRY	EVERMORE	KNICKERS	PENUMBRA
ESCALLOP	INVASION	PULMOTOR	VACATION	BARNYARD	EXPOSURE	LADYBIRD	PERSPIRE
EXECUTOR	IRONWOOD	PULPWOOD	VARISTOR	BARRATRY	FARMYARD	LAMASERY	PILCHARD
EXTERIOR	JACKBOOT	PUNCHEON	VENATION	BASEBORN	FAUBOURG	LANDFORM	PINAFORE
EXTRADOS	JETTISON	QUADROON	VEXATION	BAYBERRY	FEBRUARY	LANDLORD	PLATFORM
FALCHION	JUNCTION	QUESTION	VOCATION	BERIBERI	FIREWORK	LANDMARK	PLEASURE
FIREWOOD	KANGAROO	RADIATOR	VOLITION	BESTIARY	FIRMWARE	LANDWARD	PLETHORA
FISHHOOK	LEAPFROG	RAINDROP	WAINSCOT	BLIZZARD	FLATTERY	LAPBOARD	POCKMARK
FIXATION	LEGATION	REACTION	WARDROOM	BLOOMERS	FLATWARE	LAPIDARY	PODIATRY
FLATFOOT	LIBATION	RECEPTOR	WAREROOM	BLUEBIRD	FOLKLORE	LARBOARD	PORPHYRY
FLATIRON	LOCATION	RELATION	WASHROOM	BODYWORK	FOOTSORE	LAVATORY	PORTIERE
FLESHPOT	LOCUTION	RELIGION	WATCHDOG	BOLLWORM	FOOTWORK	LIFEWORK	POSTCARD
FOLDEROL	LOLLIPOP	RESISTOR	WATERLOO	BOOKMARK	FOREPART	LIGATURE	POSTMARK
FOREDOOM	LUNCHEON	ROSEWOOD	WILDWOOD	BOOKWORM	FORESTRY	LITERARY	POTSHERD
FOREFOOT	MACAROON	SANCTION	WINESHOP	BOUNDARY	FOREWARN	LOANWORD	PREMIERE
FOREKNOW	MARATHON	SCALLION	WORDBOOK	BRAGGART	FOREWORD	LONGHORN	PRESSURE
FORENOON	MASTODON	SCORPION	WORKBOOK	BREVIARY	FRACTURE	LOVEBIRD	PUNCTURE
FRACTION	MELODEON	SCULLION	WORKROOM	BROCHURE	FREEBORN	LOVELORN	PUSHCART
FRICTION	METAPHOR	SCULPTOR	WORKSHOP	BURGLARY	FRETWORK	LUKEWARM	QUAGMIRE
FROUFROU	METHANOL	SEDITION	WORMWOOD	BUSYWORK	FRIPPERY	LUMINARY	QUANDARY
FRUITION	MONITION	SERVITOR	YEARBOOK	CAREWORN	FUNERARY	MALAPERT	RAILLERY
FUNCTION	MUNITION	SIDESHOW	ANTELOPE	CASEWORK	GEOMETRY	MANICURE	REARWARD
FURBELOW	MUSHROOM	SKELETON	ANTHROPO	CASHMERE	GLOSSARY	MASSACRE	REASSURE
GANGLION	MUTATION	SLIPKNOT	ANTIPOPE	CATEGORY	GLOWWORM	MEDICARE	REFINERY
GANGPLOW	MYRMIDON	SLIPSHOD	BANKRUPT	CEMETERY	GOATHERD	MEDIOCRE	REGISTRY
GARRISON	NAINSOOK	SMALLPOX	BLOWPIPE	CHANCERY	GREENERY	MESHWORK	RINGWORM
GLYCEROL	NAPOLEON	SNAPSHOT	CALLIOPE	CHECKERS	HABANERA	MILITARY	ROADWORK
GONFALON	NEGATION	SNOWDROP	CENOTAPH	CHIVALRY	HACKWORD	MILLIARD	ROCKETRY

ROSEMARY	VERTEBRA	CHASTISE	FOOTLESS	MISTRESS	SEACOAST	ACTIVATE	CUPIDITY
SAGAMORE	VINEGARY	COLLAPSE	FOOTREST	MISTRUST	SELFLESS	ACTIVITY	DEBILITY
SALUTARY	VINEYARD	COLONIST	FORECAST	MONGOOSE	SHEEPISH	ADEQUATE	DECIMATE
SANITARY	WEAPONRY	COMPRESS	FOREMAST	MORALIST	SHOWCASE	ADVOCATE	DECORATE
SAPPHIRE	WELLBORN	COMPRISE	FOREMOST	NAMELESS	SHREWISH	AESTHETE	DEDICATE
SCABBARD	WHIPCORD	CONDENSE	FORMLESS	NATIVISM	SICKNESS	AFFINITY	DEFECATE
SCISSORS	WILDFIRE	CONGRESS	FORTRESS	NEEDLESS	SIGNPOST	AIGRETTE	DEFINITE
SCULLERY	WINDBURN	CONQUEST	FURTHEST	NEOPLASM	SKIRMISH	ALACRITY	DELEGATE
SEABOARD	WINDWARD	CONTRAST	FUTURISM	NEPOTISM	SKITTISH	ALIENATE	DELICATE
SEASHORE	WIREWORM	CONVERSE	GATEPOST	NEWSCAST	SLUGGISH	ALLOCATE	DEROGATE
SEMINARY	WISEACRE	CONVULSE	GOALPOST	NIHILISM	SOLECISM	ALMIGHTY	DESOLATE
SHEPHERD	WITCHERY	COPYDESK	GOLDFISH	NOBELIST	SPYGLASS	AMARANTH	DETONATE
SHIPWORM	WIZARDRY	CORDLESS	GOODNESS	NONSENSE	STARFISH	AMPUTATE	DINGBATS
SHIPYARD	WOODWORK	COUNTESS	GUYANESE	OPTIMISM	SUBMERSE	ANECDOTE	DISCRETE
SHOPWORN	YEOMANRY	COURTESY	HEADREST	ORGANISM	SUITCASE	ANISETTE	DISKETTE
SINECURE	ZOOSPORE	CRAWFISH	HEBRAISM	ORGANIST	SUPPRESS	ANNOTATE	DISTASTE
SLATTERN	ABSCISSA	CRAYFISH	HEDONISM	OUTBURST	SURCEASE	ANTEDATE	DISUNITE
SLIPPERY	ABSTRUSE	CREVASSE	HIGHNESS	OUTCLASS	SURPRISE	ANTIDOTE	DISUNITY
SLUGGARD	ACTINISM	DANSEUSE	HINDMOST	OUTGUESS	SUSPENSE	APHANITE	DIVAGATE
SLUMLORD	ACTIVISM	DATABASE	HINDUISM	OUTHOUSE	TELECAST	APPETITE	DIVINITY
SNOBBERY	ADMONISH	DATELESS	HOLINESS	OVERCAST	TELEVISE	APPOSITE	DOLOMITE
SOFTWARE	AIRBRUSH	DECREASE	HOTHOUSE	OVERPASS	TICKLISH	ARROGATE	DOMINATE
SOLDIERY	ALARMIST	DEFOREST	HUMANISM	PACIFISM	TIMELESS	ASPERITY	DRAUGHTS
SOLITARY	ALEHOUSE	DEMOLISH	HUNTRESS	PANELIST	TIRELESS	ASPIRATE	DYNAMITE
SOMBRERO	ALIENIST	DEVILISH	ICEHOUSE	PARADISE	TITMOUSE	ATROCITY	ELONGATE
SONGBIRD	ALTRUISM	DEXTROSE	IDEALISM	PAROXYSM	TOKENISM	AUTOMATE	EMACIATE
SPANIARD	AMETHYST	DIMINISH	IMMODEST	PEDERAST	TORTOISE	BACKBITE	EMIGRATE
STALWART	APHORISM	DISABUSE	INCREASE	PEERLESS	TRAVERSE	BAGUETTE	ENCEINTE
STANDARD	APOSTASY	DISBURSE	INTEREST	PERVERSE	TREATISE	BARRETTE	ENERVATE
STATUARY	APPLAUSE	DISCLOSE	ISOSTASY	PHANTASM	TRESPASS	BEHEMOTH	ENORMITY
STUBBORN	APPRAISE	DISGUISE	JAPANESE	PHANTASY	TUBEROSE	BENZOATE	ENTIRETY
SUREFIRE	ARBALEST	DISPENSE	JINGOISM	PITILESS	TUNELESS	BEQUEATH	ESCALATE
SYCAMORE	ASTERISK	DISPERSE	KIELBASA	PLEURISY	TYPECAST	BIRDBATH	ESTIMATE
SYMMETRY	ASTONISH	DISTRESS	LACROSSE	POPULIST	UNIONISM	BOBWHITE	ETERNITY
TACITURN	BACKLASH	DISTRUST	LANDMASS	PORPOISE	UNIVERSE	CALAMITY	EVACUATE
TAPESTRY	BACKREST	DOGHOUSE	LANGUISH	PREEXIST	UPTHRUST	CAPACITY	EVALUATE
TAPEWORM	BACKWASH	DORMOUSE	LEGALISM	PREPRESS	VANQUISH	CASSETTE	EXCAVATE
TEAMWORK	BARONESS	DOWNCAST	LIKENESS	PRETENSE	VAPORISH	CASTRATE	EXECRATE
TENANTRY	BASELESS	DRUGGIST	LIKEWISE	PRIMROSE	VARICOSE	CASUALTY	EXPEDITE
TERTIARY	BASILISK	EMBOLISM	LINGUIST	PRINCESS	VEGANISM	CELERITY	EYETOOTH
THIEVERY	BERCEUSE	EPILEPSY	LISTLESS	PROGRESS	VIRTUOSO	CELIBATE	FACILITY
TIMEWORN	BLUEFISH	ESCAPISM	LIVERISH	PROPHESY	VOCALIST	CENOBITE	FALSETTO
TINCTURE	BLUENOSE	ESPRESSO	LOYALIST	PUGILISM	WAITRESS	CHASTITY	FASCISTA
TOILETRY	BODILESS	EXERCISE	MADHOUSE	PURCHASE	WEAKFISH	CHLORITE	FATALITY
TOILWORN	BOOKCASE	EXORCISE	MAINMAST	QUALMISH	WEAKNESS	CIRCUITY	FAVORITE
TREASURE	BOOTLESS	EYEGLASS	MANIFEST	RECKLESS	WHIPLASH	CIVILITY	FEDERATE
TREASURY	BOTULISM	FADELESS	MANTISSA	RECOURSE	WINDLASS	COGITATE	FELICITY
TRICKERY	BRACKISH	FARTHEST	MARQUESS	REFOREST	WIRELESS	COMPLETE	FEROCITY
TROUSERS	BRANDISH	FASTNESS	MARQUISE	REHEARSE	WOMANISH	CONCERTO	FIDELITY
TRUMPERY	BUDDHISM	FATALISM	MASSEUSE	RESPONSE	YOUNGISH	CONCRETE	FILTRATE
TUTELARY	BURNOOSE	FEARLESS	MASSLESS	RESTLESS	ABDICATE	CONFETTI	FLEABITE
TWEEZERS	BUSINESS	FECKLESS	MATTRESS	ROSEBUSH	ABNEGATE	CONTRITE	FLUORITE
UNDERARM	BUTTRESS	FEMINISM	MEDALIST	ROYALIST	ABROGATE	COPULATE	FOOTNOTE
UNSAVORY	CALABASH	FINALIST	MELANISM	RUTHLESS	ABSOLUTE	COQUETTE	FOOTPATH
UNTOWARD	CARELESS	FLATFISH	MILEPOST	SAILFISH	ACCURATE	CORVETTE	FORSOOTH
UPSTAIRS	CENTRIST	FLAUTIST	MINDLESS	SAWHORSE	ACERBATE	CREOSOTE	FORTUITY
VANGUARD	CERAMIST	FLOURISH	MISHMASH	SCOTTISH	ACERBITY	CRYOLITE	FUMIGATE

FUTILITY	MALAMUTE	RECREATE	URBANITE	COIFFEUR	JONGLEUR	SKILLFUL	AGGRIEVE
FUTURITY	MARINATE	REGOLITH	VALIDATE	COLISEUM	KEELHAUL	SOLARIUM	CONCEIVE
GEMINATE	MATURATE	REGULATE	VEGETATE	COLLOQUY	KNOCKOUT	SONOROUS	CONCLAVE
GENERATE	MATURITY	RELEGATE	VELLEITY	COLOSSUS	LABURNUM	SPACIOUS	CONSERVE
GIGABYTE	MEDICATE	RELOCATE	VELOCITY	CONSTRUE	LARKSPUR	SPECIOUS	CONTRIVE
GLACIATE	MEDITATE	RENOVATE	VENDETTA	CONTINUE	LAUDANUM	SPECTRUM	CURATIVE
GRADUATE	MEGABYTE	RESOLUTE	VENERATE	CORUNDUM	LIGNEOUS	SPHAGNUM	DECISIVE
GRAFFITO	MEGALITH	RESONATE	VERACITY	CRITIQUE	LINOLEUM	SPURIOUS	DISPROVE
GRAPHITE	MESQUITE	RHYOLITE	VERMOUTH	CROSSCUT	LONGUEUR	STAKEOUT	DISSOLVE
GRATUITY	MESSMATE	ROOMETTE	VICINITY	CURLICUE	LUMINOUS	STANDOUT	DIVISIVE
GUARANTY	MILITATE	ROOMMATE	VIGNETTE	DECOROUS	LUSCIOUS	STIMULUS	ELECTIVE
GUNSMITH	MINORITY	ROULETTE	VITALITY	DELIRIUM	LUTETIUM	STINKBUG	FIXATIVE
HELPMATE	MISQUOTE	RUMINATE	VIVACITY	DESIROUS	MANDAMUS	STUDIOUS	FOXGLOVE
HEMATITE	MISSTATE	RUNAGATE	WARRANTY	DETRITUS	MEALYBUG	SYLLABUS	FUGITIVE
HEREDITY	MITIGATE	SACRISTY	WOODNOTE	DIALOGUE	MENISCUS	TANTALUM	GENITIVE
HEREUNTO	MODERATE	SALIVATE	XENOLITH	DIANTHUS	MERINGUE	TERMINUS	ILLUSIVE
HEREWITH	MODULATE	SANCTITY	ZOOPHYTE	DINOSAUR	MICROBUS	THALAMUS	INCISIVE
HESITATE	MONOLITH	SATURATE	ACANTHUS	DOUBTFUL	MOMENTUM	THALLIUM	LADYLOVE
HITHERTO	MORALITY	SCHMALTZ	ACTINIUM	DOUGHNUT	MONSIEUR	THANKFUL	LAXATIVE
HUMANITY	MOSQUITO	SECURITY	ADDENDUM	DOWNPOUR	MOURNFUL	THROMBUS	LENITIVE
HUMIDITY	MOTIVATE	SELENITE	AERONAUT	DREADFUL	MYSTIQUE	TIMOROUS	MANGROVE
HUMILITY	MUTILATE	SEPARATE	AFFLATUS	DUODENUM	NAUTILUS	TITANIUM	MARGRAVE
HYACINTH	NATALITY	SHIPMATE	AGERATUM	EMERITUS	NEBULOUS	TORTUOUS	NEGATIVE
IDENTITY	NATIVITY	SIDERITE	ALLUVIUM	EMPORIUM	NOBELIUM	TRILLIUM	PERCEIVE
IMMOLATE	NAUSEATE	SILICATE	ALUMINUM	ENCOMIUM	NUMEROUS	TRUSTFUL	POSITIVE
IMPOLITE	NAVIGATE	SIMULATE	AMMONIUM	ENORMOUS	ORGULOUS	TRUTHFUL	PRESERVE
IMPUNITY	NEOPHYTE	SOBRIETY	ANALOGUE	ENSHROUD	OVERHAUL	TUBEROUS	PUNITIVE
INCHOATE	NOBILITY	SORORITY	APPLIQUE	EPILOGUE	PARAMOUR	TYMPANUM	PUTATIVE
INCUBATE	NOMINATE	STACCATO	AQUANAUT	EUROPIUM	PENDULUM	UNCTUOUS	REACTIVE
INDICATE	NUCLEATE	STAGNATE	AQUARIUM	EXCURSUS	PHASEOUT	UNDERCUT	RELATIVE
INDURATE	NUMERATE	STILETTO	BACILLUS	EXIGUOUS	PHYSIQUE	UNDERFUR	REPRIEVE
INFINITE	OBDURATE	STRENGTH	BARBECUE	EXORDIUM	PLATINUM	UNLAWFUL	RETRIEVE
INFINITY	OBLIGATE	SYBARITE	BEECHNUT	FABULOUS	PLATYPUS	UPPERCUT	SEDATIVE
INIQUITY	OBSOLETE	TABULATE	BIBULOUS	FACTIOUS	PLECTRUM	USURIOUS	UNIVALVE
INITIATE	OILCLOTH	TAILGATE	BIENNIUM	FACTOTUM	POLONIUM	UXORIOUS	VOCATIVE
INNOVATE	OPERETTA	TEMERITY	BLACKOUT	FANCIFUL	POPULOUS	VANADIUM	CHIPPEWA
INSULATE	OPPOSITE	TEMPLATE	BLISSFUL	FINESPUN	PRATIQUE	VAPOROUS	COMEDOWN
INTIMATE	ORDINATE	TEOSINTE	BOASTFUL	FIREPLUG	PRECIOUS	VARIORUM	DOWNTOWN
INUNDATE	OSCULATE	TINPLATE	BOUTIQUE	FLAMEOUT	PREVIOUS	VENGEFUL	FACEDOWN
INVOLUTE	PAGINATE	TINSMITH	BREAKOUT	FLASHGUN	PRINTOUT	VENOMOUS	FISHBOWL
IRRIGATE	PALLIATE	TITILATE	BRONCHUS	FRANCIUM	PROLOGUE	VIATICUM	FLYBLOWN
IRRITATE	PALMETTO	TITIVATE	BROWNOUT	GADABOUT	PROROGUE	VIBURNUM	MARKDOWN
KILOBYTE	PARASITE	TOILETTE	CADUCEUS	GENEROUS	PUDENDUM	VIGOROUS	PUSHDOWN
KILOWATT	PECULATE	TOLERATE	CALADIUM	GERANIUM	RAVENOUS	VIRTUOUS	SHOWDOWN
LACERATE	PERFECTO	TOLLBOTH	CALCULUS	GLABROUS	RESIDUUM	VITREOUS	SHUTDOWN
LAMBASTE	PERMEATE	TOLLGATE	CAPSICUM	GLASSFUL	RIGHTFUL	VIVARIUM	TOMAHAWK
LAUREATE	PIMIENTO	TONALITY	CAPTIOUS	GLORIOUS	RUBIDIUM	VOYAGEUR	WASHBOWL
LEVITATE	PIXELATE	TOTALITY	CAUTIOUS	GORGEOUS	RUNABOUT	WATCHFUL	WILDFOWL
LIBERATE	PLACENTA	TRACTATE	CEMENTUM	GRACIOUS	SABOTEUR	WONDROUS	APOPLEXY
LIBRETTO	PLAYMATE	TRAVESTY	CEREBRUM	GRANDEUR	SAMARIUM	WRATHFUL	EDGEWAYS
LIMONITE	POLARITY	TRUNCATE	CHECKOUT	GRATEFUL	SCABROUS	WRONGFUL	NOWADAYS
LITERATE	POLYMATH	ULCERATE	CHECKSUM	GRIEVOUS	SCANDIUM	YOUTHFUL	SIDEWAYS
LITERATI	POPULATE	ULTIMATE	CHEERFUL	HARANGUE	SEDULOUS	ABLATIVE	AMORTIZE
LITIGATE	POSTDATE	UNCHASTE	CHESTNUT	HIBISCUS	SEIGNEUR	ABRASIVE	BULLDOZE
LOCALITY	PROPERTY	UNDULATE	CHROMIUM	HOMESPUN	SELENIUM	ADDITIVE	CANALIZE
MACERATE	PROSTATE	UNGULATE	CLOSEOUT	INFAMOUS	SENSUOUS	ADHESIVE	CANONIZE
MAJORITY	QUANTITY	UPGROWTH	COAGULUM	INTRIGUE	SHORTCUT	ADOPTIVE	CATALYZE

CIVILIZE	CAMELLIA	TRICHINA	MERCURIC	CARYATID	HIGHROAD	OUTMODED	TIMBERED
COLONIZE	CARNAUBA	UMBRELLA	METEORIC	CENTERED	HOGSHEAD	OUTSPEND	UNBIASED
CREDENZA	CHARISMA	UNDERSEA	MNEMONIC	COMPOUND	HOMEBRED	OVENBIRD	UNBODIED
DEIONIZE	CHIPPEWA	VACCINIA	MONASTIC	CONFOUND	HOMELAND	OVERHAND	UNBOLTED
DEPUTIZE	CINCHONA	VENDETTA	NARCOTIC	CROPLAND	HOMEWARD	OVERHEAD	UNDERBID
ENERGIZE	CREDENZA	VERONICA	NEUROTIC	CUPBOARD	HUMANOID	OVERLAID	UNEARNED
EQUALIZE	DEMENTIA	VERTEBRA	PANDEMIC	DEADWOOD	ICEBOUND	OVERLAND	UNFORMED
FINALIZE	DIARRHEA	VICTORIA	PATHETIC	DEATHBED	IMPACTED	OVERLORD	UNLEADED
HUMANIZE	DYSLEXIA	WISTARIA	PERIODIC	DECKHAND	INDEBTED	PASSWORD	UNSHAPED
IDEALIZE	ERYTHEMA	WISTERIA	PHENOLIC	DEJECTED	INEDITED	PELLUCID	UNTOWARD
IMMUNIZE	EUPHORIA	CATACOMB	PROLIFIC	DEMENTED	INFORMED	PILCHARD	UNVOICED
KAMIKAZE	FANTASIA	CORNCRIB	QUIXOTIC	DEMIBOLD	INFRARED	POKEWEED	UNWONTED
LOCALIZE	FASCISTA	DOORJAMB	REPUBLIC	DETACHED	INKSTAND	POSTCARD	UNZIPPED
MAXIMIZE	FLOTILLA	DOORKNOB	RHETORIC	DIVIDEND	INTENDED	POSTPAID	VAGABOND
MEMORIZE	GARDENIA	FIREBOMB	ROMANTIC	DOCKHAND	INTREPID	POTSHERD	VANGUARD
MINIMIZE	GLAUCOMA	FORELIMB	SARDONIC	DOCKYARD	INVOLVED	PROFOUND	VINEYARD
MOBILIZE	GLOXINIA	HECATOMB	SEMANTIC	DOORYARD	IRONCLAD	PROPOUND	WELLHEAD
MORALIZE	GYMKHANA	ACADEMIC	SPECIFIC	DOWNLOAD	IRONWEED	PROVIDED	WHIPCORD
MOTORIZE	HABANERA	ACOUSTIC	SPORADIC	DOWNWARD	IRONWOOD	PULPWOOD	WILDWOOD
NASALIZE	HACIENDA	ACROSTIC	SUBSONIC	DOWNWIND	JACQUARD	PURBLIND	WINDWARD
NEBULIZE	HEPATICA	AGNOSTIC	SULFURIC	DRUNKARD	JAILBIRD	PUREBRED	WITHHOLD
NOTARIZE	HYSTERIA	ANECHOIC	SYMBOLIC	ENSHROUD	JEREMIAD	RAILROAD	WOODLAND
NOVELIZE	INSIGNIA	ARTISTIC	SYNOPTIC	EUROBOND	KEYBOARD	RAWBONED	WOODSHED
ORGANIZE	INSOMNIA	ATHLETIC	SYSTEMIC	EXPLODED	LADYBIRD	REARWARD	WOODWIND
OVERSIZE	KAMAAINA	BARBARIC	TERRIFIC	FARMHAND	LANDLORD	REPEATED	WORMWOOD
PARALYZE	KATAKANA	BEATIFIC	TEUTONIC	FARMLAND	LANDWARD	RESERVED	WRETCHED
PENALIZE	KIELBASA	BROMIDIC	TURMERIC	FARMYARD	LAPBOARD	RESIGNED	ABDICATE
POLARIZE	LEUKEMIA	CATHOLIC	VISICALC	FIREWOOD	LARBOARD	RETARDED	ABEYANCE
QUANTIZE	MAGNESIA	CEPHALIC	VOLCANIC	FLATHEAD	LOANWORD	REVEREND	ABLATIVE
SANITIZE	MAGNOLIA	CHOLERIC	ACCURSED	FLATLAND	LOCOWEED	RHOMBOID	ABNEGATE
SIMONIZE	MAHARAJA	COSMETIC	ACIDHEAD	FOLIATED	LONGHAND	RIVERBED	ABRASIVE
THEORIZE	MAJOLICA	DEMONIAC	AFFECTED	FOOTHOLD	LOPSIDED	ROSEWOOD	ABROGATE
UNFREEZE	MANTILLA	DIABOLIC	AIRFIELD	FOREFEND	LOVEBIRD	RUBICUND	ABSENTEE
UNIONIZE	MANTISSA	DIATOMIC	AIRSPEED	FOREHAND	LYMPHOID	SCABBARD	ABSINTHE
URBANIZE	MELANOMA	DIDACTIC	ALKALOID	FOREHEAD	MAINLAND	SCAFFOLD	ABSOLUTE
VAPORIZE	MOTOROLA	DIURETIC	AMOEBOID	FORELAND	MANIFOLD	SEABOARD	ABSTRUSE
VITALIZE	ONONDAGA	DOMESTIC	ARACHNID	FOREWORD	MANNERED	SHEPHERD	ACCOLADE
VOCALIZE	OPERETTA	ECLIPTIC	ASSORTED	FOURFOLD	MANYFOLD	SHIPYARD	ACCOUTRE
	PANATELA	ECONOMIC	ASTEROID	FOXHOUND	MARIGOLD	SITUATED	ACCURATE
	PANORAMA	ELECTRIC	BACKHAND	FREEHAND	MASTHEAD	SLIPSHOD	ACERBATE
	PARABOLA	EMPHATIC	BACKWARD	FREEHOLD	MEDICAID	SLUGGARD	ACTIVATE
	PARANOIA	EPIDEMIC	BARNYARD	FREELOAD	MILKMAID	SLUMLORD	ADDITIVE
8TH LETTER	PELLAGRA	ESOTERIC	BASSWOOD	GANGLAND	MILKWEED	SOFTWOOD	ADEQUATE
ABSCISSA	PENUMBRA	FORENSIC	BEDSTEAD	GOATHERD	MILLIARD	SOLENOID	ADHESIVE
ALLELUIA	PIZZERIA	FRENETIC	BEFRIEND	GODCHILD	MILLPOND	SONGBIRD	ADOPTIVE
ALOPECIA	PLACENTA	GEODESIC	BENTWOOD	GOURMAND	MISBRAND	SPANIARD	ADORABLE
AMBROSIA	PLETHORA	GIGANTIC	BEREAVED	GRIZZLED	MISSPEND	SPHEROID	ADVOCATE
ANACONDA	PYORRHEA	HARMONIC	BICUSPID	HACKWORD	MOORLAND	SPIRITED	AESTHETE
ANATHEMA	RUTABAGA	HERALDIC	BILLFOLD	HARDWOOD	MORIBUND	SPLENDID	AFFIANCE
ANGELICA	SCIATICA	HERMETIC	BILLHEAD	HAWKWEED	MUDGUARD	STANDARD	AGGRIEVE
APOLOGIA	SCROFULA	HISPANIC	BIRDSEED	HEADBAND	NEWFOUND	STRINGED	AIGRETTE
ASPHYXIA	SONATINA	HYPNOTIC	BLIZZARD	HEADLAND	NEWLYWED	SUPPOSED	AIRBORNE
BABUSHKA	STOTINKA	ISOTONIC	BLUEBIRD	HEADWORD	NONRIGID	SURROUND	AIRDROME
BANDANNA	SUBPOENA	JURISTIC	BRINDLED	HELICOID	OUTBOARD	TAMARIND	AIRFRAME
BASILICA	SUBURBIA	MAGNETIC	BULKHEAD	HEREFORD	OUTBOUND	THOUSAND	AIRPLANE
BECHUANA	SWASTIKA	MECHANIC	BULLHEAD	HIGHBRED	OUTDATED	TIDELAND	AIRSPACE
BROUHAHA	TORTILLA	MEPHITIC	CABSTAND	HIGHLAND	OUTFIELD	TIGHTWAD	ALBACORE

ALEHOUSE	BAILABLE	CHASTISE	CRUCIBLE	DISTASTE	EVERYONE	GENDARME	INNOVATE
ALIENATE	BARBECUE	CHASUBLE	CRYOLITE	DISUNITE	EVIDENCE	GENERATE	INSCRIBE
ALLIANCE	BARITONE	CHENILLE	CULPABLE	DIVAGATE	EXCAVATE	GENITIVE	INSECURE
ALLOCATE	BARNACLE	CHEROKEE	CURATIVE	DIVISIVE	EXCHANGE	GENOCIDE	INSTANCE
ALLSPICE	BARONAGE	CHEYENNE	CURLICUE	DIVORCEE	EXECRATE	GIGABYTE	INSULATE
ALTITUDE	BAROUCHE	CHLORIDE	CYNOSURE	DOCTRINE	EXERCISE	GLACIATE	INTERNEE
AMBIENCE	BARRETTE	CHLORINE	CYTOSINE	DOGHOUSE	EXORCISE	GLADSOME	INTIMATE
AMENABLE	BASELINE	CHLORITE	DAMNABLE	DOLOMITE	EXPEDITE	GOODWIFE	INTRIGUE
AMICABLE	BATHROBE	CHRISTIE	DANSEUSE	DOMICILE	EXPOSURE	GRADUATE	INUNDATE
AMORTIZE	BEDAZZLE	CICERONE	DARKSOME	DOMINATE	EYEPIECE	GRAPHITE	INVEIGLE
AMPERAGE	BEFUDDLE	CINCTURE	DATABASE	DORMOUSE	FALLIBLE	GRUESOME	INVIABLE
AMPUTATE	BEGRUDGE	CIVILIZE	DATELINE	DRAINAGE	FAROUCHE	GUIDANCE	INVOLUTE
ANAEROBE	BELITTLE	CLAMBAKE	DEADLINE	DRESSAGE	FASCICLE	GUYANESE	IRONWARE
ANALOGUE	BENEFICE	CLAVICLE	DECIMATE	DUNGAREE	FAVORITE	HAIRLINE	IRRIGATE
ANECDOTE	BENZOATE	CLAYMORE	DECISIVE	DUTIABLE	FEARSOME	HALFTONE	IRRITATE
ANISETTE	BERCEUSE	CLEAVAGE	DECORATE	DYNAMITE	FEASIBLE	HANDMADE	ISOPRENE
ANNOTATE	BESTRIDE	COALESCE	DECREASE	EARPHONE	FEDERATE	HANDSOME	ISSUANCE
ANNOUNCE	BEVERAGE	COCKSURE	DEDICATE	EDUCABLE	FEMININE	HARANGUE	JALOUSIE
ANTEDATE	BIDDABLE	COGITATE	DEFECATE	ELECTIVE	FIGURINE	HARDWARE	JAMBOREE
ANTELOPE	BINNACLE	COIFFURE	DEFIANCE	ELEGANCE	FILIGREE	HEADACHE	JAPANESE
ANTIDOTE	BIRDLIME	COINCIDE	DEFINITE	ELIGIBLE	FILTRATE	HEADLINE	JAUNDICE
ANTIPODE	BLOCKADE	COLLAPSE	DEIONIZE	ELONGATE	FINALIZE	HELLHOLE	JUNCTURE
ANTIPOPE	BLOWPIPE	COLONIZE	DELAWARE	EMACIATE	FIRESIDE	HELPMATE	JUVENILE
ANYPLACE	BLUENOSE	COMANCHE	DELEGATE	EMBATTLE	FIRMWARE	HEMATITE	KAMIKAZE
ANYWHERE	BOBWHITE	COMMENCE	DELICATE	EMBEZZLE	FISHWIFE	HERITAGE	KEEPSAKE
APERTURE	BOLDFACE	COMMERCE	DEMARCHE	EMIGRATE	FIXATIVE	HESITATE	KEROSINE
APHANITE	BONHOMIE	COMPLETE	DENATURE	EMINENCE	FLAGPOLE	HILLSIDE	KEYSTONE
APPANAGE	BOOKCASE	COMPRISE	DENOUNCE	EMPLOYEE	FLATWARE	HOMEMADE	KILOBYTE
APPELLEE	BOUTIQUE	CONCEIVE	DEPUTIZE	ENCEINTE	FLEABANE	HOMICIDE	KNEEHOLE
APPETITE	BREAKAGE	CONCLAVE	DEROGATE	ENCIRCLE	FLEABITE	HORNPIPE	KNOTHOLE
APPLAUSE	BROCHURE	CONCLUDE	DERRIERE	ENERGIZE	FLEXIBLE	HORRIBLE	LACERATE
APPLIQUE	BULLDOZE	CONCRETE	DESCRIBE	ENERVATE	FLUORIDE	HOTHOUSE	LACROSSE
APPOSITE	BUNGHOLE	CONDENSE	DESOLATE	ENFEEBLE	FLUORINE	HUARACHE	LADYLIKE
APPRAISE	BURNOOSE	CONFRERE	DETHRONE	ENFILADE	FLUORITE	HUMANIZE	LADYLOVE
APTITUDE	CAFFEINE	CONSERVE	DETONATE	ENSCONCE	FOLKLORE	ICEHOUSE	LAMBASTE
AQUACADE	CALAMINE	CONSOMME	DEXTROSE	ENSEMBLE	FOLLICLE	IDEALIZE	LANGUAGE
AQUILINE	CALLIOPE	CONSPIRE	DIALOGUE	ENSHRINE	FOOTNOTE	ILLUMINE	LATITUDE
ARCHDUKE	CAMISOLE	CONSTRUE	DIASTOLE	ENSILAGE	FOOTRACE	ILLUSIVE	LAUREATE
ARGUABLE	CAMOMILE	CONTINUE	DIATRIBE	ENTANGLE	FOOTSORE	IMBECILE	LAXATIVE
ARMATURE	CAMPOREE	CONTRITE	DISABUSE	ENTHRONE	FORCIBLE	IMITABLE	LEMONADE
ARROGATE	CANAILLE	CONTRIVE	DISAGREE	ENTRANCE	FOREBODE	IMMATURE	LENITIVE
ARTIFICE	CANALIZE	CONVERGE	DISBURSE	ENVELOPE	FOREGONE	IMMOBILE	LEVERAGE
ASPIRATE	CANONIZE	CONVERSE	DISCIPLE	ENVIABLE	FORENAME	IMMOLATE	LEVITATE
ASSEMBLE	CANTICLE	CONVINCE	DISCLOSE	ENVISAGE	FOURSOME	IMMOTILE	LIBERATE
ASTATINE	CAPRIOLE	CONVULSE	DISCRETE	EPILOGUE	FOXGLOVE	IMMUNIZE	LICENSEE
ATROPINE	CARACOLE	COPULATE	DISGORGE	EQUALIZE	FRACTURE	IMPOLITE	LICORICE
ATTITUDE	CARAPACE	COQUETTE	DISGRACE	EQUIPAGE	FRONTAGE	INCHOATE	LIFELINE
AUDIENCE	CAREFREE	CORVETTE	DISGUISE	ERECTILE	FUGITIVE	INCISIVE	LIFETIME
AUTOMATE	CAROTENE	COVERAGE	DISKETTE	ESCALATE	FUMAROLE	INCREASE	LIGATURE
AXLETREE	CARRIAGE	CREATURE	DISLODGE	ESCAPADE	FUMIGATE	INCUBATE	LIKEWISE
BACKACHE	CASHMERE	CREDENCE	DISPENSE	ESCAROLE	FUSELAGE	INDICATE	LIMONITE
BACKBITE	CASSETTE	CREDIBLE	DISPERSE	ESTIMATE	GAMESOME	INDUCTEE	LINGERIE
BACKBONE	CASTRATE	CREOSOTE	DISPLACE	ESTRANGE	GANGRENE	INDURATE	LITERATE
BACKFIRE	CATALYZE	CRETONNE	DISPROVE	EVACUATE	GARGOYLE	INFINITE	LITIGATE
BACKSIDE	CAUSERIE	CREVASSE	DISSOLVE	EVALUATE	GASOLINE	INFRINGE	LOCALIZE
BADINAGE	CELIBATE	CRIBBAGE	DISSUADE	EVENTIDE	GEMINATE	INHUMANE	LOGOTYPE
BAGUETTE	CENOBITE	CRITIQUE	DISTANCE	EVERMORE	GEMSTONE	INITIATE	LONESOME

LONGTIME	MONOXIDE	OVERTAKE	PORTIERE	RESOLUTE	SIDERITE	TINCTURE	VARIANCE
LOOPHOLE	MORALIZE	OVERTIME	POSITIVE	RESONATE	SILICATE	TINPLATE	VARICOSE
MACERATE	MORPHEME	OVERTONE	POSSIBLE	RESOURCE	SILICONE	TIRESOME	VEGETATE
MADHOUSE	MORPHINE	OVERTURE	POSTDATE	RESPONSE	SIMONIZE	TITILATE	VENERATE
MAGAZINE	MORTGAGE	PAGINATE	POSTHOLE	RETRIEVE	SIMULATE	TITIVATE	VERBIAGE
MAINLINE	MOTIVATE	PALATINE	POSTLUDE	RETURNEE	SINECURE	TITMOUSE	VERSICLE
MALAMUTE	MOTORIZE	PALEFACE	POSTPONE	REVANCHE	SINKHOLE	TOILETTE	VICARAGE
MANCIPLE	MUCILAGE	PALINODE	POULTICE	REVEILLE	SIXPENCE	TOLERATE	VICINAGE
MANDIBLE	MULTIPLE	PALISADE	POUNDAGE	RHYOLITE	SNOWSHOE	TOLLGATE	VIGNETTE
MANDRAKE	MUSICALE	PALLIATE	PRACTICE	RIBOSOME	SOCIABLE	TORTOISE	VINCIBLE
MANGROVE	MUSTACHE	PALPABLE	PRATIQUE	RIDICULE	SOFTWARE	TRACKAGE	VIOLABLE
MANICURE	MUTILATE	PARADISE	PREAMBLE	ROADSIDE	SOLITUDE	TRACTATE	VIOLENCE
MARGRAVE	MYSTIQUE	PARALYZE	PRECLUDE	ROOFTREE	SOLSTICE	TRAVERSE	VITALIZE
MARINATE	NAMESAKE	PARASITE	PREJUDGE	ROOMETTE	SOMETIME	TREASURE	VOCALIZE
MARITIME	NASALIZE	PARLANCE	PREMIERE	ROOMMATE	SPRINKLE	TREATISE	VOCATIVE
MARQUISE	NAUSEATE	PARTERRE	PRESENCE	ROUGHAGE	SQUABBLE	TRIANGLE	VOLATILE
MARRIAGE	NAVIGATE	PARTIBLE	PRESERVE	ROULETTE	SQUEEGEE	TRICYCLE	VOLPLANE
MASSACRE	NEBULIZE	PARTICLE	PRESSURE	RUMINATE	STAGNATE	TROMBONE	WARDROBE
MASSEUSE	NECKLACE	PASSABLE	PRESTIGE	RUNAGATE	STAMPEDE	TRUCKAGE	WARPLANE
MATURATE	NECKLINE	PASTICHE	PRETENSE	SABOTAGE	STEERAGE	TRUETYPE	WASHABLE
MAXIMIZE	NEGATIVE	PASTILLE	PRIMROSE	SADDUCEE	STOCKADE	TRUNCATE	WHARFAGE
MAYAPPLE	NEGLIGEE	PATIENCE	PRISTINE	SAGAMORE	STOPPAGE	TUBERCLE	WILDFIRE
MEALTIME	NEMATODE	PECULATE	PROBABLE	SALIVATE	STRADDLE	TUBEROSE	WILDLIFE
MEANTIME	NEOPHYTE	PEDICURE	PROCAINE	SANGUINE	STRAGGLE	TURNPIKE	WINDPIPE
MEDICARE	NEPENTHE	PEDIGREE	PROLOGUE	SANITIZE	STRANGLE	TUTELAGE	WISEACRE
MEDICATE	NICKNAME	PEDUNCLE	PROROGUE	SAPPHIRE	STRUGGLE	TWOPENCE	WISHBONE
MEDICINE	NICOTINE	PEEPHOLE	PROSTATE	SATURATE	SUBMERGE	TYPEFACE	WOODBINE
MEDIOCRE	NOCTURNE	PENALIZE	PROTRUDE	SAUTERNE	SUBMERSE	ULCERATE	WOODNOTE
MEDITATE	NOMINATE	PENKNIFE	PROVINCE	SAWHORSE	SUBTITLE	ULTIMATE	WOODPILE
MEGABYTE	NONSENSE	PERCEIVE	PTOMAINE	SCALABLE	SUCHLIKE	UNBUCKLE	WORKABLE
MEMBRANE	NOONTIDE	PERFORCE	PUNCTURE	SCAVENGE	SUFFRAGE	UNCHASTE	WORMHOLE
MEMORIZE	NOONTIME	PERILUNE	PUNITIVE	SCHEDULE	SUITABLE	UNCLOTHE	WRECKAGE
MERINGUE	NOTARIZE	PERMEATE	PURCHASE	SCRABBLE	SUITCASE	UNCOUPLE	YULETIDE
MESQUITE	NOVELIZE	PEROXIDE	PURSLANE	SCRAMBLE	SUNSHADE	UNDERAGE	ZOOPHYTE
MESSMATE	NUCLEATE	PERSPIRE	PUTATIVE	SCRIBBLE	SUNSHINE	UNDERLIE	ZOOSPORE
METAFILE	NUISANCE	PERSUADE	QUAGMIRE	SCROUNGE	SURCEASE	UNDULATE	APERITIF
MIGRAINE	NUMERATE	PERVERSE	QUANTIZE	SEAPLANE	SUREFIRE	UNFREEZE	CHECKOFF
MILITATE	OBDURATE	PHARISEE	QUIETUDE	SEASCAPE	SURPLICE	UNGULATE	DANDRUFF
MILLIEME	OBLIGATE	PHYSIQUE	QUOTABLE	SEASHORE	SURPRISE	UNICYCLE	DYESTUFF
MILLRACE	OBSOLETE	PICAYUNE	REACTIVE	SEDATIVE	SUSPENSE	UNIONIZE	HANDCUFF
MINIBIKE	OBSTACLE	PILOTAGE	REASSURE	SEEDTIME	SYBARITE	UNIVALVE	KERCHIEF
MINIMIZE	OFFSHORE	PINAFORE	RECOURSE	SELECTEE	SYCAMORE	UNIVERSE	MISCHIEF
MISCIBLE	OFFSTAGE	PINNACLE	RECREATE	SELENITE	SYLLABLE	UNMUZZLE	RIFFRAFF
MISJUDGE	OPERABLE	PINOCHLE	REGICIDE	SELFSAME	SYNDROME	UNRIDDLE	STANDOFF
MISPLACE	OPPOSITE	PIPELINE	REGULATE	SEMINOLE	TABULATE	UNSADDLE	UNBELIEF
MISQUOTE	OPUSCULE	PITIABLE	REHEARSE	SENSIBLE	TAILGATE	UNSETTLE	WEREWOLF
MISSHAPE	ORDINATE	PITTANCE	RELATIVE	SENTENCE	TANGIBLE	UNSTABLE	WOODRUFF
MISSTATE	ORDNANCE	PIXELATE	RELEGATE	SEPARATE	TELEVISE	UNTANGLE	YOURSELF
MISUSAGE	ORGANIZE	PLAYMATE	RELIABLE	SEQUENCE	TELLTALE	UPSTROKE	ABORNING
MITIGATE	OSCULATE	PLEASURE	RELIANCE	SERENADE	TEMPLATE	URBANITE	ALIASING
MOBILIZE	OUTHOUSE	POLARIZE	RELOCATE	SEWERAGE	TENTACLE	URBANIZE	ANYTHING
MODERATE	OUTSHINE	POPULACE	RENEGADE	SHINBONE	TEOSINTE	UUDECODE	BANTLING
MODULATE	OVERCOME	POPULATE	RENOUNCE	SHIPMATE	TERRIBLE	UUENCODE	BECOMING
MOISTURE	OVERRIDE	PORPOISE	RENOVATE	SHOELACE	TESTICLE	VALIDATE	BLACKING
MOLECULE	OVERRULE	PORRIDGE	REPARTEE	SHORTAGE	THEORIZE	VALUABLE	BLESSING
MONGOOSE	OVERSHOE	PORTABLE	REPRIEVE	SHOSHONE	THIAMINE	VAPORIZE	BREEDING
MONOTONE	OVERSIZE	PORTHOLE	RESEMBLE	SHOWCASE	THROTTLE	VARIABLE	BRISLING

BUILDING	MEALYBUG	SWELLING	DIMINISH	VERMOUTH	GROSBEAK	TEAMWORK	CRIMINAL
BULLFROG	MIDDLING	SWIMMING	DISPATCH	WEAKFISH	HALFBACK	TEXTBOOK	CRITICAL
BUNDLING	MISDOING	TEACHING	ENCROACH	WHIPLASH	HALLMARK	TOMAHAWK	DAFFODIL
CAGELING	MOUNTING	TEETHING	ENTRENCH	WOMANISH	HANDBOOK	TRAPROCK	DIAGONAL
CATCHING	MOURNING	TOUCHING	EYETOOTH	XENOLITH	HANDPICK	WOODCOCK	DISHEVEL
CHARMING	NESTLING	TOWELING	FLATFISH	YOUNGISH	HARDBACK	WOODWORK	DISLOYAL
CLEARING	NIGGLING	TOWERING	FLOURISH	BERIBERI	HARDHACK	WOOLSACK	DISPOSAL
CLIPPING	NURSLING	TRAINING	FOOTPATH	BROCCOLI	HARDTACK	WORDBOOK	DOGGEREL
CLOTHING	ONCOMING	TRAPPING	FORSOOTH	CONFETTI	HAYSTACK	WORKBOOK	DOUBTFUL
COUPLING	OUTGOING	TRIFLING	FURLOUGH	DAIQUIRI	HEADLOCK	YEARBOOK	DOVETAIL
CREEPING	OUTLYING	TRIMMING	GOLDFISH	KOHLRABI	HEADWORK	ZWIEBACK	DOWNFALL
CROSSING	OVERHANG	UNDERDOG	GUNSMITH	LITERATI	HOMESICK	ABNORMAL	DOWNHILL
DAIRYING	PAINTING	UNENDING	HANUKKAH	MACARONI	HOMEWORK	APPROVAL	DREADFUL
DARKLING	PANELING	UNERRING	HEREWITH	MAHARANI	HOODWINK	ARBOREAL	DUCKBILL
DRESSING	PETTIFOG	UNSPRUNG	HYACINTH	MARIACHI	HORNBOOK	ARMORIAL	DUMBBELL
DUCKLING	PHRASING	UNSTRUNG	INSOMUCH	PASTRAMI	HUMPBACK	ARTERIAL	DUNGHILL
DUMPLING	PIDDLING	UPCOMING	INTRENCH	SHANGHAI	IRONWORK	ASPHODEL	EGGSHELL
DWELLING	PLANKING	UPRISING	KEYPUNCH	SHILINGI	JOYSTICK	ATYPICAL	ENTHRALL
ENGAGING	PLEASING	VAPORING	LANGUISH	SUKIYAKI	KICKBACK	BANKROLL	ESPECIAL
EVENSONG	PLUMBING	VAULTING	LIVERISH	ZUCCHINI	KNAPSACK	BARBITAL	ESPOUSAL
EXACTING	POLLIWOG	VIETCONG	MEGALITH	AARDVARK	LAMPBACK	BASEBALL	ETHEREAL
FAGOTING	PRESSING	WATCHDOG	MISHMASH	ASTERISK	LANDMARK	BEANBALL	EVENTUAL
FARTHING	PRINTING	WEAKLING	MISMATCH	BACKPACK	LIFEWORK	BIANNUAL	EXTERNAL
FAUBOURG	PUDDLING	WHOPPING	MONOLITH	BANKBOOK	LIMERICK	BIENNIAL	FAMILIAL
FETCHING	QUISLING	WINGDING	NONESUCH	BAREBACK	LIPSTICK	BINAURAL	FANCIFUL
FIREPLUG	RATTLING	WITCHING	NUTHATCH	BASILISK	LOVESICK	BIOCIDAL	FAREWELL
FLASHING	RAVENING	WRAPPING	OILCLOTH	BITSTOCK	MAVERICK	BIRACIAL	FESTIVAL
FLEETING	RETIRING	YACHTING	OUTREACH	BOBOLINK	MESHWORK	BISEXUAL	FIREBALL
FOOTLING	RUMBLING	YEARLING	OUTWEIGH	BODYWORK	MOSSBACK	BLISSFUL	FISHBOWL
FROSTING	SCALAWAG	YEARLONG	OVERMUCH	BOOKMARK	NAINSOOK	BLUEBELL	FLYWHEEL
GANGLING	SCATHING	YEARNING	POLYMATH	BUSYWORK	NONSTICK	BOASTFUL	FOLDEROL
GLOAMING	SEAGOING	YIELDING	QUALMISH	CAKEWALK	NOTEBOOK	CANNIBAL	FOOTBALL
GRASPING	SEEDLING	ADMONISH	REGOLITH	CALLBACK	OPENWORK	CARDINAL	FOOTFALL
GRAYLING	SHANTUNG	AIRBRUSH	REPROACH	CASEWORK	OUTBREAK	CARNIVAL	FOOTHILL
GREEKING	SHEETING	ALTHOUGH	RESEARCH	CHAPBOOK	OUTFLANK	CAROUSAL	FORESAIL
GREETING	SHELVING	AMARANTH	RETRENCH	CHIPMUNK	OVERLOOK	CAROUSEL	FORETELL
GRUELING	SHILLING	APPROACH	ROSEBUSH	COMEBACK	PASSBOOK	CARRYALL	FREEWILL
HATCHING	SHIPPING	ASTONISH	SAILFISH	COOKBOOK	PAYCHECK	CATCHALL	FUNEREAL
HEADLONG	SHIRRING	BACKLASH	SANDWICH	COPYBOOK	PENSTOCK	CERVICAL	GERMINAL
HEDGEHOG	SHIRTING	BACKWASH	SCOTTISH	COPYDESK	PICKLOCK	CESSPOOL	GLASSFUL
HIRELING	SHOCKING	BEHEMOTH	SHEEPISH	DAYBREAK	PINPRICK	CHARCOAL	GLYCEROL
HOARDING	SIDELONG	BEQUEATH	SHREWISH	DEADLOCK	PLAYBACK	CHEERFUL	GOODWILL
IMPOSING	SKIMMING	BESMIRCH	SKIRMISH	DIPSTICK	PLAYBOOK	CHEMICAL	GOOFBALL
INCOMING	SPANKING	BIRDBATH	SKITTISH	DRAWBACK	POCKMARK	CLERICAL	GRATEFUL
INFRADIG	SPOOLING	BLUEFISH	SLUGGISH	DROPKICK	POLITICK	CLINICAL	GUTTURAL
INTERROG	STANDING	BRACKISH	STARFISH	FASTBACK	POSTMARK	COCKEREL	HABITUAL
INVITING	STARLING	BRANDISH	STRENGTH	FEEDBACK	PULLBACK	COCKTAIL	HANDBALL
KINDLING	STERLING	CALABASH	THOROUGH	FIREWORK	ROADWORK	COGWHEEL	HANDBILL
LACEWING	STINKBUG	CENOTAPH	TICKLISH	FISHHOOK	ROLLBACK	COLONIAL	HANDRAIL
LAYERING	STIRRING	CHANUKAH	TINSMITH	FLAPJACK	SANDBANK	COLOSSAL	HANGNAIL
LEAPFROG	STOCKING	CHUTZPAH	TOLLBOTH	FLYSPECK	SHAMROCK	COMMUNAL	HARDBALL
LEARNING	STRIKING	CORONACH	TRIPTYCH	FOOTWORK	SIDEKICK	CONFOCAL	HAREBELL
LIFELONG	STUDDING	CRAWFISH	UNCHURCH	FORELOCK	SIDEWALK	CONJUGAL	HIGHBALL
LIVELONG	STUFFING	CRAYFISH	UNCLENCH	FRETWORK	SNOWBANK	CONTRAIL	HIGHTAIL
LOATHING	STUNNING	DEMOLISH	UPGROWTH	FULLBACK	STUDBOOK	CORNMEAL	HORMONAL
LOLLYGAG	SUCKLING	DESPATCH	VANQUISH	GAMECOCK	SWAYBACK	CORPORAL	HOSPITAL
MARBLING	SWEEPING	DEVILISH	VAPORISH	GIMCRACK	TAMARACK	COVERALL	HYMENEAL

IMMORTAL	PECTORAL	VERTICAL	EXORDIUM	PUDENDUM	AUTOJOIN	DELUSION	GONFALON
IMPERIAL	PEDESTAL	VIRGINAL	FACTOTUM	PUGILISM	AVERSION	DEMIJOHN	GRANDSON
INFERNAL	PERSONAL	VISCERAL	FATALISM	RESIDUUM	AVIATION	DEVOTION	GRAVAMEN
INFORMAL	PHYSICAL	WASHBOWL	FEMINISM	RINGWORM	BACKSPIN	DIAPASON	GRIDIRON
INGUINAL	PICKEREL	WATCHFUL	FLIMFLAM	RUBIDIUM	BAILSMAN	DIELDRIN	GROSCHEN
INIMICAL	PINWHEEL	WILDFOWL	FLUIDRAM	SAMARIUM	BARBICAN	DIVISION	GUARDIAN
INTEGRAL	PLAYBILL	WINDFALL	FOREDOOM	SCANDIUM	BASEBORN	DOMINION	GUMPTION
INTERNAL	PONYTAIL	WINDMILL	FRANCIUM	SELENIUM	BEARSKIN	DONATION	HANDYMAN
INTERVAL	PRATFALL	WRATHFUL	FUTURISM	SHIPWORM	BEHOLDEN	DOUBLOON	HARRIDAN
JUDICIAL	PRENATAL	WRONGFUL	GERANIUM	SOLARIUM	BETATRON	DOWNTOWN	HAWAIIAN
KEELHAUL	PRIMEVAL	YOUTHFUL	GLOWWORM	SOLECISM	BIATHLON	DOWNTURN	HAWTHORN
LACRIMAL	PRODIGAL	ACCUSTOM	HEADROOM	SPECTRUM	BLUDGEON	DRAGOMAN	HEADSMAN
LANDFALL	PROTOCOL	ACTINISM	HEBRAISM	SPHAGNUM	BOGEYMAN	DURATION	HEIGHTEN
LANDFILL	PUFFBALL	ACTINIUM	HEDONISM	TANTALUM	BOHEMIAN	EFFUSION	HELMSMAN
LITTORAL	PUNCTUAL	ACTIVISM	HEIRLOOM	TAPEWORM	BONDSMAN	EGYPTIAN	HENCHMAN
MACKEREL	RAINFALL	ADDENDUM	HINDUISM	TELEFILM	BOUILLON	EIGHTEEN	HERDSMAN
MADRIGAL	RATIONAL	AGERATUM	HOLOGRAM	TELEGRAM	BRAKEMAN	ELECTION	HEREUPON
MAINSAIL	REBUTTAL	ALLUVIUM	HOMEROOM	THALLIUM	BRETHREN	ELECTRON	HIGHBORN
MANIACAL	REFERRAL	ALTRUISM	HOOKWORM	TITANIUM	BRIGHTEN	EMBLAZON	HOLSTEIN
MATERIAL	REGIONAL	ALUMINUM	HUMANISM	TOKENISM	BUCKSKIN	EMBOLDEN	HOMESPUN
MATERIEL	REMEDIAL	AMMONIUM	IDEALISM	TRILLIUM	BULLETIN	EMOTICON	HOOLIGAN
MATERNAL	REMITTAL	ANGSTROM	IDEOGRAM	TYMPANUM	CABOCHON	EMPYREAN	HORSEMAN
MEATBALL	REPRISAL	ANTEROOM	INCHWORM	UNDERARM	CALFSKIN	EMULSION	HUNTSMAN
MEDIEVAL	RESIDUAL	APHORISM	INTERCOM	UNIONISM	CAMPAIGN	EQUATION	HYDROGEN
MEMORIAL	REVERSAL	APOTHEGM	ISOTHERM	UPSTREAM	CANADIAN	ERECTION	IDEATION
METHANOL	RIGHTFUL	AQUARIUM	JINGOISM	VANADIUM	CAPESKIN	ESTONIAN	IGNITION
METRICAL	ROCKFALL	ARMYWORM	KILOGRAM	VARIORUM	CAPUCHIN	ESTROGEN	ILLUSION
MINSTREL	SENTINEL	BALLROOM	LABURNUM	VEGANISM	CARDIGAN	ETRUSCAN	IMPRISON
MISLABEL	SHRAPNEL	BATHROOM	LANDFORM	VERBATIM	CAREWORN	EURASIAN	INCISION
MISSPELL	SIDEREAL	BIENNIUM	LAUDANUM	VIATICUM	CARILLON	EUROPEAN	INDIAMAN
MISTRIAL	SIDEWALL	BOLLWORM	LEGALISM	VIBURNUM	CAULDRON	FACEDOWN	INFOBAHN
MOLEHILL	SKILLFUL	BOOKWORM	LINOLEUM	VIVARIUM	CERULEAN	FALCHION	INVASION
MONAURAL	SNOWBALL	BOTULISM	LUKEWARM	WARDROOM	CESAREAN	FINESPUN	ISTHMIAN
MONORAIL	SNOWFALL	BROUGHAM	LUTETIUM	WAREROOM	CHAIRMAN	FIXATION	JETTISON
MOTHBALL	SOFTBALL	BUDDHISM	MARJORAM	WASHROOM	CHAMPION	FLASHGUN	JUNCTION
MOURNFUL	SPECTRAL	CALADIUM	MELANISM	WIREWORM	CHAPERON	FLATIRON	LAMBSKIN
MUSCATEL	SPITBALL	CAPSICUM	MOMENTUM	WORKROOM	CHAPLAIN	FLYBLOWN	LANDSMAN
MYSTICAL	SQUIRREL	CARDAMOM	MONOGRAM	ABLATION	CHRISTEN	FORENOON	LECITHIN
NATIONAL	SUPERNAL	CEMENTUM	MOONBEAM	ABLUTION	CINNAMON	FORESKIN	LEGATION
NAUTICAL	SURGICAL	CEREBRUM	MUSHROOM	ABORTION	CITATION	FOREWARN	LENGTHEN
NEONATAL	TAFFRAIL	CHECKSUM	NATIVISM	ADDITION	CIVILIAN	FOUNTAIN	LIBATION
NEWSREEL	TEETOTAL	CHROMIUM	NEOPLASM	ADHESION	COACHMAN	FOURTEEN	LIMEKILN
NONMETAL	TEMPORAL	COAGULUM	NEPOTISM	AGRARIAN	COGNOMEN	FRACTION	LINCHPIN
NOTARIAL	TERMINAL	COLISEUM	NIHILISM	ALBANIAN	COHESION	FREEBORN	LINESMAN
NOTIONAL	THANKFUL	CORUNDUM	NOBELIUM	ALDERMAN	COLOPHON	FREEDMAN	LOCATION
NUMSKULL	TRANQUIL	DARKROOM	OPTIMISM	ALGERIAN	COMEDIAN	FRESHMAN	LOCUTION
NUTSHELL	TRIBUNAL	DAYDREAM	ORGANISM	ALIZARIN	COMEDOWN	FRICTION	LONGHORN
OFFICIAL	TRUSTFUL	DECIGRAM	PACIFISM	ALLERGEN	COMPLAIN	FRIGHTEN	LOVELORN
ORIENTAL	TRUTHFUL	DEKAGRAM	PARADIGM	AMBITION	COONSKIN	FRUITION	LUNCHEON
ORIGINAL	TUTORIAL	DELIRIUM	PAROXYSM	AMERICAN	CORDOVAN	FUNCTION	LUTHERAN
OVERHAUL	UNFILIAL	DISCLAIM	PENDULUM	ANDROGEN	CORPSMAN	GANGLION	MACAROON
OVERKILL	UNIAXIAL	DUODENUM	PHANTASM	ANGLICAN	COXSWAIN	GARRISON	MAGDALEN
PARALLEL	UNLAWFUL	EMBOLISM	PLATFORM	APHELION	CREATION	GHANAIAN	MAGICIAN
PARFOCAL	UPHEAVAL	EMPORIUM	PLATINUM	ASSASSIN	CYCLAMEN	GLOBULIN	MAINTAIN
PARIETAL	VARIETAL	ENCOMIUM	PLECTRUM	AUDITION	DAIRYMAN	GLYCERIN	MALAWIAN
PASTORAL	VENEREAL	ESCAPISM	POLONIUM	AUSTRIAN	DECISION	GLYCOGEN	MANDARIN
PATERNAL	VENGEFUL	EUROPIUM	PROCLAIM	AUTOBAHN	DEERSKIN	GOATSKIN	MANDOLIN

MARATHON	QUESTION	TUNGSTEN	PALMETTO	ANTEATER	DISFAVOR	LAUNCHER	RESISTOR
MARKDOWN	RADIOMAN	TUNISIAN	PALOMINO	ANTERIOR	DISHONOR	LAVENDER	RESORTER
MARKSMAN	REACTION	TURBOFAN	PERFECTO	ARMCHAIR	DISINTER	LAWGIVER	RETAINER
MARZIPAN	RELATION	UNBEATEN	PIMIENTO	ATOMIZER	DISORDER	LAWMAKER	REVENUER
MASTODON	RELIGION	UNBIDDEN	POLITICO	BACHELOR	DISSEVER	LEFTOVER	REVIEWER
MELODEON	RESTRAIN	UNBROKEN	PRESIDIO	BAEDEKER	DOMINEER	LODESTAR	REVOLVER
MENHADEN	RIPARIAN	UNBURDEN	SCENARIO	BALUSTER	DOWNPOUR	LONGHAIR	ROADSTER
MERIDIAN	ROMANIAN	UNBUTTON	SERAGLIO	BANISTER	DULCIMER	LONGUEUR	SABOTEUR
MISTAKEN	ROUTEMAN	UNCOMMON	SOMBRERO	BEHAVIOR	ELEVATOR	MALINGER	SCAPULAR
MOCCASIN	RUMANIAN	UNFASTEN	STACCATO	BEWILDER	EMBITTER	MALTSTER	SCHOONER
MOLESKIN	SALESMAN	UNLOOSEN	STILETTO	CALENDAR	ENCIPHER	MANEUVER	SCIMITAR
MONITION	SANCTION	UNPERSON	SUPEREGO	CALENDER	ENCUMBER	METAPHOR	SCULPTOR
MOROCCAN	SAUCEPAN	VACATION	VIRTUOSO	CANISTER	ENDANGER	MILLIBAR	SEAFARER
MOTORMAN	SCALEPAN	VENATION	WATERLOO	CAPSULAR	ENDEAVOR	MILLINER	SEAWATER
MOUNTAIN	SCALLION	VENUSIAN	AGITPROP	CATHETER	ENGENDER	MINISTER	SEIGNEUR
MUNITION	SCORPION	VERBOTEN	AIRSTRIP	CAVALIER	ENGINEER	MISNOMER	SEMESTER
MUSICIAN	SCULLION	VEXATION	BACKDROP	CELLULAR	ESPALIER	MONSIEUR	SERVITOR
MUTATION	SEALSKIN	VOCATION	BACKSLAP	CHANDLER	EXECUTOR	MOREOVER	SHOULDER
MYRMIDON	SEDITION	VOLITION	BACKSTOP	CINNABAR	EXEMPLAR	MOTORCAR	SILENCER
NAPOLEON	SHOPWORN	WARFARIN	BAKESHOP	CIRCULAR	EXTERIOR	MUENSTER	SINGULAR
NEGATION	SHOWDOWN	WATCHMAN	BLACKTOP	CISLUNAR	EYELINER	MULETEER	SINISTER
NIGERIAN	SHUTDOWN	WELLBORN	CLAPTRAP	CLINCHER	FAMILIAR	NEIGHBOR	SONGSTER
NINETEEN	SKELETON	WINDBURN	DOORSTEP	CLOISTER	FELDSPAR	NEWCOMER	SOUVENIR
NITROGEN	SLATTERN	WINGSPAN	ESCALLOP	CLOTHIER	FLOUNDER	NOVEMBER	SPINSTER
NOBLEMAN	SOLUTION	WOODSMAN	FIREDAMP	COAUTHOR	FLYPAPER	ODOMETER	SPLATTER
NONUNION	SORPTION	ZEPPELIN	FIRETRAP	COIFFEUR	FOOTWEAR	OHMMETER	SPLENDOR
NORSEMAN	SPACEMAN	ALFRESCO	FLAGSHIP	COLANDER	FOREBEAR	OLEANDER	SPLINTER
NOTATION	SPECIMEN	ANTHROPO	FOOLSCAP	COMMONER	FORSWEAR	ONLOOKER	SPLUTTER
OBLATION	SPITTOON	ARPEGGIO	FOOTSTEP	COMPILER	FRONTIER	OUTRIDER	SQUANDER
OBLIVION	SQUADRON	AUTOGIRO	HANDICAP	COMPUTER	GAMESTER	OUTSIDER	STICKLER
OBSIDIAN	STALLION	BALLYHOO	HARDSHIP	CONGENER	GANGSTER	OVERHEAR	STRANGER
OCCASION	STRAITEN	BORDELLO	HEADSHIP	CONSIDER	GOSSAMER	PACIFIER	STREAMER
OPTICIAN	STRICKEN	CAUDILLO	HEDGEHOP	CORRIDOR	GOVERNOR	PARAMOUR	STRINGER
OVERTURN	STUBBORN	COCKATOO	HOUSETOP	COSIGNER	GRANDEUR	PARDONER	SUPERIOR
PANTHEON	STURGEON	COMMANDO	LADYSHIP	COURTIER	GRANULAR	PASSOVER	TAXPAYER
PARAFFIN	SUZERAIN	CONCERTO	LOCKSTEP	CREDITOR	GROUNDER	PECULIAR	TEAMSTER
PARMESAN	SYSADMIN	CRUZEIRO	LOLLIPOP	CROSSBAR	HANGOVER	PEIGNOIR	TESTATOR
PARTISAN	TACITURN	ESPRESSO	LORDSHIP	CROUPIER	HEADGEAR	PHOSPHOR	THEREFOR
PATHOGEN	TAHITIAN	FALSETTO	OUTSTRIP	CUCUMBER	HOLDOVER	PILASTER	THRASHER
PAVILION	TAILSPIN	FANDANGO	OVERLEAP	CUSPIDOR	HOWITZER	PLAYGOER	THRUSTER
PEMMICAN	TALESMAN	FELLATIO	OVERSTEP	CUSTOMER	HUCKSTER	POLESTAR	TOGETHER
PENTAGON	TALISMAN	FILIPINO	PAWNSHOP	CYLINDER	IDOLATER	POLLSTER	TOREADOR
PETITION	TARRAGON	FLAMENCO	RAINDROP	DAUGHTER	IMPELLER	PREMOLAR	TRANSFER
PITCHMAN	TEASPOON	FLAMINGO	SIDESTEP	DEBONAIR	IMPOSTOR	PRISONER	TRAPDOOR
PLANKTON	TELETHON	GRAFFITO	SKULLCAP	DECANTER	IMPROPER	PROMOTER	TRENCHER
PLANTAIN	TERRAPIN	HEREUNTO	SNOWDROP	DECEMBER	INCUMBER	PULLOVER	TRICOLOR
PLEBEIAN	THESPIAN	HITHERTO	TOWNSHIP	DECIPHER	INFERIOR	PULMOTOR	TRIMETER
POLTROON	THIRTEEN	IMPETIGO	UNDERLIP	DEFLOWER	INFORMER	PUSHOVER	TRIUMVIR
POSITION	THREATEN	INNUENDO	WARDSHIP	DEMEANOR	INTERIOR	RADIATOR	TURNOVER
POSITRON	TIMEWORN	INTAGLIO	WHITECAP	DEMURRER	INVERTER	RECEIVER	ULTERIOR
POTATION	TOBOGGAN	KANGAROO	WINESHOP	DIAMETER	ISLANDER	RECEPTOR	UNDERFUR
PRESSMAN	TOILWORN	LIBRETTO	WORKSHOP	DICTATOR	JONGLEUR	RECORDER	UNFETTER
PUBLICAN	TOWNSMAN	MACHISMO	ABATTOIR	DINOSAUR	KIBITZER	REFORMER	UNLIMBER
PUNCHEON	TRACTION	MILESIMO	AFLUTTER	DIRECTOR	KILLDEER	REGISTER	VALVULAR
PUSHDOWN	TRAINMAN	MOSQUITO	AGLITTER	DISASTER	KNITWEAR	REINDEER	VARISTOR
QUADROON	TRILLION	NEUTRINO	AIRLINER	DISCOLOR	LARKSPUR	REMEMBER	VASCULAR
QUATRAIN	TRIMARAN	ORATORIO	ANCESTOR	DISCOVER	LAUGHTER	REPORTER	VILLAGER

VOYAGEUR	DIANTHUS	KNICKERS	SCABROUS	ADJUVANT	COMPLEAT	FARTHEST	INSOLENT
WALKOVER	DINGBATS	LANDMASS	SCISSORS	AERONAUT	CONFLICT	FILAMENT	INSPIRIT
WAYFARER	DISTRESS	LEAVINGS	SEDULOUS	AFFERENT	CONFRONT	FINALIST	INSTINCT
WHATEVER	DOLDRUMS	LIGNEOUS	SELFLESS	AFFRIGHT	CONJUNCT	FIREBOAT	INSTRUCT
WHENEVER	DRAUGHTS	LIKENESS	SENSUOUS	AIRCRAFT	CONQUEST	FLAGRANT	INTEREST
WHEREVER	EARNINGS	LISTLESS	SHAMBLES	AIRTIGHT	CONSTANT	FLAMEOUT	INTERMIT
WHOMEVER	EDGEWAYS	LUMINOUS	SHINGLES	ALARMIST	CONTEMPT	FLATBOAT	INTERNET
WIREHAIR	EKISTICS	LUSCIOUS	SICKNESS	ALIENIST	CONTRACT	FLATFOOT	INTROMIT
WORDSTAR	ELLIPSIS	MANDAMUS	SIDEWAYS	ALPHABET	CONTRAST	FLAUTIST	JACKBOOT
WRIGGLER	EMERITUS	MARQUESS	SONOROUS	AMBULANT	COUCHANT	FLESHPOT	JUBILANT
ABUTTALS	EMPHASIS	MASSLESS	SPACIOUS	AMETHYST	COVENANT	FLIPPANT	JUDGMENT
ACANTHUS	ENORMOUS	MATTRESS	SPECIOUS	APPARENT	COVERLET	FOLDBOAT	KEELBOAT
ACIDOSIS	ENTRAILS	MENISCUS	SPURIOUS	AQUANAUT	CRACKPOT	FOOTREST	KILOVOLT
AFFLATUS	ENURESIS	MESDAMES	SPYGLASS	AQUEDUCT	CRESCENT	FORECAST	KILOWATT
ANALYSIS	ENVIRONS	MICROBUS	STIMULUS	ARBALEST	CROSSCUT	FOREFOOT	KINGBOLT
ASBESTOS	EUGENICS	MIDSHIPS	STUDIOUS	ARGUMENT	CROTCHET	FOREMAST	KNOCKOUT
AVIONICS	EXCURSUS	MINDLESS	SUNDRIES	ARMAMENT	CROWFOOT	FOREMOST	LASERJET
BACILLUS	EXEGESIS	MISTRESS	SUPPRESS	ARROGANT	DAYLIGHT	FOREPART	LIFEBOAT
BARONESS	EXIGUOUS	MOLASSES	SYLLABUS	ARTIFACT	DEADBEAT	FORKLIFT	LIGAMENT
BARRACKS	EXTRADOS	MYELITIS	SYNOPSIS	ASPIRANT	DECEDENT	FRAGMENT	LINGUIST
BASELESS	EYEGLASS	NAMELESS	SYPHILIS	AVERMENT	DECREPIT	FRAGRANT	LINIMENT
BERMUDAS	FABULOUS	NARCOSIS	TERMINUS	BACCARAT	DEFOREST	FREQUENT	LITIGANT
BIBULOUS	FACTIOUS	NAUTILUS	THALAMUS	BACKREST	DEMOCRAT	FUMIGANT	LODGMENT
BIFOCALS	FADELESS	NEBULOUS	THROMBUS	BANKRUPT	DEPONENT	FURTHEST	LONGBOAT
BLOOMERS	FASTNESS	NECROSIS	TIMELESS	BAREFOOT	DERELICT	GADABOUT	LOYALIST
BODILESS	FEARLESS	NEEDLESS	TIMOROUS	BASEMENT	DESELECT	GASLIGHT	MACPAINT
BOOTLESS	FECKLESS	NEURITIS	TIRELESS	BASSINET	DESTRUCT	GATEPOST	MAINMAST
BRITCHES	FIBROSIS	NEUROSIS	TOPSIDES	BEECHNUT	DILIGENT	GAUNTLET	MALAPERT
BRONCHUS	FOOTLESS	NIGEROIS	TORTUOUS	BENEDICT	DIPLOMAT	GOALPOST	MALTREAT
BURSITIS	FORMLESS	NINEPINS	TRESPASS	BLACKOUT	DISCOUNT	GRADIENT	MANIFEST
BUSINESS	FORTRESS	NOWADAYS	TROUSERS	BOUFFANT	DISCREET	GUNFIGHT	MANTELET
BUTTRESS	FORWARDS	NUMEROUS	TUBEROUS	BOWSPRIT	DISJOINT	GUNPOINT	MARMOSET
CADUCEUS	GALLUSES	OPERANDS	TUNELESS	BRACELET	DISMOUNT	HABITANT	MARTINET
CALCULUS	GASWORKS	ORGULOUS	TWEEZERS	BRAGGART	DISPIRIT	HEADREST	MEDALIST
CANNABIS	GENEROUS	OUTCLASS	UNAWARES	BREAKOUT	DISQUIET	HEAVYSET	MERCHANT
CAPTIOUS	GENETICS	OUTDOORS	UNCTUOUS	BRICKBAT	DISTINCT	HELIPORT	MIDNIGHT
CARELESS	GENITALS	OUTGUESS	UPSTAIRS	BROOKLET	DISTRACT	HELPMEET	MIDPOINT
CAUTIOUS	GLABROUS	OVERALLS	USURIOUS	BROWBEAT	DISTRAIT	HESITANT	MILEPOST
CHARADES	GLORIOUS	OVERPASS	UXORIOUS	BROWNOUT	DISTRICT	HINDMOST	MILITANT
CHECKERS	GOODNESS	OVERSEAS	VAPOROUS	BUCKSHOT	DISTRUST	HUGUENOT	MISCOUNT
CLEMATIS	GORGEOUS	PANCREAS	VENOMOUS	CAMSHAFT	DOCUMENT	IGNORANT	MISPRINT
CLITORIS	GRACIOUS	PEERLESS	VIGOROUS	CASEMENT	DOGFIGHT	IMMANENT	MISTREAT
COLOSSUS	GRIEVOUS	PICKINGS	VIRTUOUS	CATAPULT	DOUGHNUT	IMMINENT	MISTRUST
COMBINGS	HAUTBOIS	PITILESS	VITREOUS	CATARACT	DOWNBEAT	IMMODEST	MONUMENT
COMPRESS	HERCULES	PLATYPUS	WAITRESS	CENTRIST	DOWNCAST	IMPLICIT	MORALIST
CONFINES	HIBISCUS	POLITICS	WEAKNESS	CERAMIST	DRUGGIST	IMPOTENT	MOVEMENT
CONGRESS	HIGHNESS	POPULOUS	WINDLASS	CEREMENT	DRUMBEAT	IMPUDENT	NEWSCAST
COPPERAS	HOLINESS	PRECIOUS	WIRELESS	CHECKOUT	EFFERENT	INCIDENT	NOBELIST
CORDLESS	HUNTRESS	PREPRESS	WONDROUS	CHESTNUT	EGGPLANT	INDECENT	NONEVENT
COUNTESS	HUSTINGS	PREVIOUS	ABSTRACT	CHITCHAT	ELEPHANT	INDIGENT	NUTRIENT
CREMAINS	HYPNOSIS	PRINCESS	ABUNDANT	CLAIMANT	ELOQUENT	INDIRECT	OBEDIENT
DATELESS	ILLINOIS	PROCEEDS	ABUTMENT	CLARINET	ETHERNET	INDOLENT	OBSTRUCT
DECOROUS	INFAMOUS	PROGRESS	ACCIDENT	CLOSEOUT	EXPLICIT	INERRANT	OCCUPANT
DESIROUS	INTRADOS	RAVENOUS	ACCREDIT	CLOUDLET	EXPONENT	INEXPERT	OFFPRINT
DETRITUS	IROQUOIS	RECKLESS	ACQUAINT	CLUBFOOT	EYESIGHT	INHALANT	OFFSHOOT
DIABETES	KEYWORDS	RESTLESS	ADJACENT	COHERENT	FALTBOAT	INHERENT	OINTMENT
DIALYSIS	KINETICS	RUTHLESS	ADJUTANT	COLONIST	FANLIGHT	INNOCENT	OPPONENT

ORGANIST	RESONANT	UNDERCUT	CRUCIFIX	CHANCERY	FORMERLY	MAJORITY	RHEOLOGY
ORNAMENT	RESTRICT	UNDULANT	INTERMIX	CHASTITY	FORTUITY	MALARKEY	ROCKETRY
OUTBURST	RETICENT	UNSOUGHT	ORTHODOX	CHEMURGY	FRIPPERY	MANNERLY	ROSEMARY
OUTFIGHT	RETROFIT	UNTAUGHT	PARALLAX	CHIVALRY	FRUCTIFY	MASTERLY	SACRISTY
OUTPOINT	REVERENT	UPPERCUT	SMALLPOX	CHOIRBOY	FUNERARY	MATURITY	SALUTARY
OUTRIGHT	RHEOSTAT	UPTHRUST	TRANSFIX	CIRCUITY	FUTILITY	MILITARY	SANCTIFY
OUTSMART	RICOCHET	USUFRUCT	ACERBITY	CIVILITY	FUTURITY	MINATORY	SANCTITY
OVERCAST	ROYALIST	VEHEMENT	ACRIMONY	CLASSIFY	GEMOLOGY	MINISTRY	SANITARY
OVERCOAT	RUDIMENT	VESICANT	ACTIVITY	CLEMENCY	GEOMETRY	MINORITY	SATURDAY
PAMPHLET	RUMINANT	VESTMENT	ADULTERY	COLLIERY	GINGERLY	MISAPPLY	SCARCELY
PANELIST	RUNABOUT	VIGILANT	ADVISORY	COLLOQUY	GIVEAWAY	MISCARRY	SCRAGGLY
PANTSUIT	SAILBOAT	VIRULENT	AEROLOGY	CONTRARY	GLOSSARY	MONARCHY	SCRUTINY
PARAKEET	SANSKRIT	VISCOUNT	AFFINITY	CORDUROY	GRATUITY	MONETARY	SCULLERY
PASSPORT	SCILICET	VISITANT	AGRONOMY	CORONARY	GREENERY	MONITORY	SECURITY
PAVEMENT	SEACOAST	VOCALIST	ALACRITY	COURTESY	GUARANTY	MONOGAMY	SEMINARY
PEDERAST	SEAMOUNT	WAINSCOT	ALEATORY	CREAMERY	GUERNSEY	MONOPOLY	SEROLOGY
PEDIMENT	SEDIMENT	WELDMENT	ALLEGORY	CROCKERY	HATCHWAY	MORALITY	SILICIFY
PENCHANT	SEMISOFT	WHODUNIT	ALLEYWAY	CULINARY	HEGEMONY	MORTUARY	SIMPLIFY
PENITENT	SENTIENT	WRISTLET	ALMIGHTY	CUPIDITY	HERALDRY	MULBERRY	SLIPPERY
PENLIGHT	SERGEANT	FLAMBEAU	ANCESTRY	CURRENCY	HEREDITY	MULTIPLY	SLOVENLY
PETULANT	SHIPMENT	FROUFROU	ANTIBODY	CYTOLOGY	HIDEAWAY	MUSKETRY	SNOBBERY
PHASEOUT	SHOPLIFT	YUGOSLAV	ANTIMONY	DEBILITY	HOMEBODY	MYCOLOGY	SOBRIETY
PHEASANT	SHORTCUT	BUNGALOW	ANTINOMY	DELICACY	HONORARY	NATALITY	SOLDIERY
PIEPLANT	SIBILANT	CHOWCHOW	APOPLEXY	DELIVERY	HOROLOGY	NATIVITY	SOLIDIFY
PINPOINT	SIGNPOST	COCKCROW	APOSTASY	DETOXIFY	HORSEFLY	NOBILITY	SOLITARY
PLANGENT	SKYLIGHT	COLESLAW	ARTISTRY	DEWBERRY	HOSTELRY	NONDAIRY	SOLVENCY
PLAYSUIT	SLIPKNOT	CROSSBOW	ASPERITY	DILATORY	HOUSEBOY	NUGATORY	SOMEBODY
PLEASANT	SNAPSHOT	DISALLOW	ASSEMBLY	DISARRAY	HOUSEFLY	OBITUARY	SORORITY
POIGNANT	SOMERSET	FOREKNOW	ATROCITY	DISUNITY	HUMANITY	ORANGERY	SPEEDWAY
POLYGLOT	SOMEWHAT	FURBELOW	ATTORNEY	DIVINITY	HUMIDIFY	ORDINARY	SPILLWAY
POPULIST	SPROCKET	GANGPLOW	AUDITORY	DOOMSDAY	HUMIDITY	ORTHOEPY	STAIRWAY
PORTRAIT	STAGNANT	HEDGEROW	BARBERRY	DOUGHBOY	HUMILITY	OVERPLAY	STATUARY
PRECINCT	STAKEOUT	HIGHBROW	BARRATRY	DOXOLOGY	IDENTIFY	OVERSTAY	STEALTHY
PREEXIST	STALWART	HONEYDEW	BAYBERRY	DRIVEWAY	IDENTITY	PANDOWDY	STOWAWAY
PREGNANT	STANDOUT	HOOSEGOW	BEAUTIFY	EMISSARY	IDEOLOGY	PEDAGOGY	STRATEGY
PRETERIT	STRAIGHT	KICKSHAW	BEGGARLY	EMULSIFY	IDOLATRY	PENOLOGY	STRATIFY
PRINTOUT	STRIDENT	MACKINAW	BESTIARY	ENORMITY	ILLUSORY	PHANTASY	STULTIFY
PROHIBIT	STRUMPET	OVERDRAW	BIRTHDAY	ENTIRETY	IMPUNITY	PHARMACY	SYMMETRY
PROSPECT	SUBTRACT	OVERFLOW	BIWEEKLY	EPILEPSY	INDUSTRY	PLEURISY	SYMPATHY
PROTRACT	SUCCINCT	OVERGROW	BIYEARLY	EPIPHANY	INFANTRY	PODIATRY	SYMPHONY
PRURIENT	SUNLIGHT	OVERVIEW	BOUNDARY	ETERNITY	INFINITY	POLARITY	TAPESTRY
PURULENT	SUPERJET	SCOFFLAW	BREVIARY	ETHOLOGY	INIQUITY	POLYGAMY	TAXONOMY
PUSHCART	SUPPLANT	SETSCREW	BUOYANCY	ETIOLOGY	INWARDLY	POPINJAY	TELEPLAY
PUSSYCAT	SURMOUNT	SIDESHOW	BURGLARY	EVERYDAY	ISOSTASY	PORPHYRY	TEMERITY
QUADRANT	TAILCOAT	SNOWPLOW	BURGUNDY	EXIGENCY	JEOPARDY	POTBELLY	TENANTRY
QUOTIENT	TELECAST	SOUTHPAW	BUSYBODY	FACILITY	KOLINSKY	PRETTIFY	TENDENCY
RAINCOAT	TENEMENT	TELEVIEW	CALAMITY	FATALITY	LAMASERY	PROPERTY	TENPENNY
REACTANT	THICKSET	TOMORROW	CAPACITY	FEBRUARY	LAPIDARY	PROPHECY	TERTIARY
RECREANT	TRANSACT	UNDERTOW	CASTAWAY	FELICITY	LATCHKEY	PROPHESY	THEOLOGY
REDOLENT	TRANSEPT	WILLIWAW	CASUALTY	FEROCITY	LAVATORY	PSALMODY	THIEVERY
REFERENT	TRANSMIT	WIREDRAW	CATEGORY	FERVENCY	LETHARGY	QUANDARY	THRENODY
REFOREST	TURBOJET	WITHDRAW	CAUSEWAY	FIDELITY	LITERARY	QUANTITY	THURSDAY
REGIMENT	TURNCOAT	AFTERTAX	CELERITY	FIRECLAY	LOBOTOMY	RAILLERY	TOILETRY
RELAXANT	TURNSPIT	APPENDIX	CELIBACY	FLATTERY	LOCALITY	REFINERY	TONALITY
RELEVANT	TWILIGHT	AVIATRIX	CEMETERY	FOLDAWAY	LUMINARY	REGISTRY	TOPOLOGY
RESCRIPT	TYPECAST	BICONVEX	CEREMONY	FORELADY	MAHOGANY	REVIVIFY	TOTALITY
RESIDENT	UNDERACT	CICATRIX	CHAMBRAY	FORESTRY	MAINSTAY	RHAPSODY	TRAVESTY

TREASUR**Y**
TRICKER**Y**
TRUMPER**Y**
TUTELAR**Y**
TWOPENN**Y**
UNDERPA**Y**
UNGAINL**Y**
UNKINDL**Y**
UNLIKEL**Y**
UNLOVEL**Y**
UNSAVOR**Y**
UNSEEML**Y**
UNSTEAD**Y**
UNTIMEL**Y**
UNWIELD**Y**
UNWORTH**Y**
VAGRANC**Y**
VELLEIT**Y**
VELOCIT**Y**
VERACIT**Y**
VICINIT**Y**
VILLAIN**Y**
VINEGAR**Y**
VIROLOG**Y**
VITALIT**Y**
VIVACIT**Y**
WALKAWA**Y**
WARRANT**Y**
WATERWA**Y**
WEAPONR**Y**
WHITEFL**Y**
WITCHER**Y**
WIZARDR**Y**
WORDPLA**Y**
WORKADA**Y**
YEOMANR**Y**
SCHMALT**Z**

9
LETTER WORDS

1ST LETTER							
ABANDONED	AFFLUENCE	ANALGESIA	APPLETALK	ATHENAEUM	BANDSTAND	BILLBOARD	BOULEVARD
ABATEMENT	AFORESAID	ANALGESIC	APPLIANCE	ATHLETICS	BANDWAGON	BILLIARDS	BOUNTEOUS
ABHORRENT	AFRIKAANS	ANALOGOUS	APPLICANT	ATONEMENT	BANDWIDTH	BIMONTHLY	BOUNTIFUL
ABOMINATE	AFTERCARE	ANARCHISM	APPOINTEE	ATROCIOUS	BANQUETTE	BINOCULAR	BOURGEOIS
ABORIGINE	AFTERDECK	ANATOMIZE	APPORTION	ATTAINDER	BANTUSTAN	BINOMINAL	BOWSTRING
ABSORBENT	AFTERGLOW	ANCHORAGE	APPREHEND	ATTENDANT	BARBARIAN	BIOGRAPHY	BRASSERIE
ACCESSION	AFTERLIFE	ANCHORITE	AQUAPLANE	ATTENTION	BARBARISM	BIOSPHERE	BRASSIERE
ACCESSORY	AFTERMATH	ANCHORMAN	ARABESQUE	ATTENUATE	BARBAROUS	BIPARTITE	BRAZILIAN
ACCIDENCE	AFTERNOON	ANCILLARY	ARBITRARY	ATTRIBUTE	BARCAROLE	BIRDHOUSE	BREAKDOWN
ACCLIMATE	AFTERWARD	ANGELFISH	ARBITRATE	ATTRITION	BAREFACED	BIRTHMARK	BREAKFAST
ACCLIVITY	AGGRAVATE	ANGLEWORM	ARBORETUM	AUCTORIAL	BARKEEPER	BIRTHRATE	BREEZEWAY
ACCOMPANY	AGGREGATE	ANGLICIZE	ARCHANGEL	AUDACIOUS	BARNSTORM	BISHOPRIC	BRIEFCASE
ACCORDION	AGREEABLE	ANGUISHED	ARCHENEMY	AUDIOLOGY	BAROGRAPH	BLACKBALL	BRILLIANT
ACCRETION	AGREEMENT	ANHYDROUS	ARCHETYPE	AURICULAR	BAROMETER	BLACKBIRD	BRIMSTONE
ACETYLENE	AILANTHUS	ANIMALISM	ARCHFIEND	AUTHENTIC	BARRACUDA	BLACKBODY	BRIQUETTE
ACIDULATE	AIRMOBILE	ANIMATION	ARCHITECT	AUTHORITY	BARRICADE	BLACKFOOT	BRITANNIC
ACIDULOUS	AIRWORTHY	ANIMOSITY	ARCHIVIST	AUTHORIZE	BARRISTER	BLACKHEAD	BROADBAND
ACOUSTICS	ALABASTER	ANKLEBONE	ARGENTINE	AUTOCRACY	BARTENDER	BLACKJACK	BROADCAST
ACQUIESCE	ALBATROSS	ANNOUNCER	ARGENTITE	AUTOGRAPH	BASEBOARD	BLACKLIST	BROADLOOM
ACROPOLIS	ALCOHOLIC	ANNOYANCE	ARMADILLO	AUTOMATIC	BASTINADO	BLACKMAIL	BROADSIDE
ADDICTION	ALEATORIC	ANNUITANT	ARMISTICE	AUTOMATON	BATHHOUSE	BLASPHEME	BROADTAIL
ADDRESSEE	ALGONQUIN	ANOMALOUS	ARROWHEAD	AUTOTRACE	BATHOLITH	BLASPHEMY	BROCHETTE
ADIABATIC	ALGORITHM	ANONYMOUS	ARROWROOT	AUXILIARY	BATTALION	BLEACHERS	BROKERAGE
ADJECTIVE	ALIENABLE	ANOPHELES	ARTERIOLE	AVAILABLE	BEACHHEAD	BLINDFOLD	BRONCHIAL
ADJOINING	ALLERGIST	ANTARCTIC	ARTHRITIS	AVALANCHE	BEATITUDE	BLOCKHEAD	BRUSHWOOD
ADMIRABLE	ALLEVIATE	ANTECHOIR	ARTHROPOD	AVOCATION	BEAUTEOUS	BLOODBATH	BRUTALIZE
ADMIRALTY	ALLIGATOR	ANTHOLOGY	ARTICHOKE	AVUNCULAR	BEAUTIFUL	BLOODLINE	BUCCANEER
ADMISSION	ALLOWANCE	ANTICLINE	ARTICULAR	AWESTRUCK	BEDFELLOW	BLOODROOT	BUCKBOARD
ADMIXTURE	ALMANDITE	ANTIKNOCK	ARTIFICER	BACCHANAL	BEDRIDDEN	BLOODSHED	BUCKTOOTH
ADSORBATE	ALMSHOUSE	ANTINOVEL	ARTILLERY	BACKBOARD	BEDSPREAD	BLOODSHOT	BUCKWHEAT
ADSORBENT	ALONGSIDE	ANTIPASTO	ASAFETIDA	BACKFIELD	BEEFEATER	BLOWTORCH	BULGARIAN
ADUMBRATE	ALTERNATE	ANTIPATHY	ASCENDANT	BACKPEDAL	BEEFSTEAK	BLUEBERRY	BULLFIGHT
ADVANTAGE	ALTIMETER	ANTIQUARY	ASCENDERS	BACKSLASH	BEEKEEPER	BLUEBLACK	BULLFINCH
ADVENTURE	ALUMINIUM	ANTIQUITY	ASCENSION	BACKSLIDE	BELEAGUER	BLUEGRASS	BUMBLEBEE
ADVERSARY	ALUMINIZE	ANTISERUM	ASCERTAIN	BACKSTAGE	BELLICOSE	BLUEPOINT	BUMPTIOUS
ADVERSITY	AMARYLLIS	ANTITOXIN	ASPARAGUS	BACKSWEPT	BELLYACHE	BLUEPRINT	BURLESQUE
ADVERTISE	AMBERGRIS	ANTITUMOR	ASPERSION	BACKTRACK	BELVEDERE	BOARDWALK	BURUNDIAN
ADVISABLE	AMBIGUOUS	ANTIVENIN	ASSEMBLER	BACKWATER	BENIGHTED	BOATSWAIN	BUSHWHACK
AERIALIST	AMBITIOUS	APARTHEID	ASSERTION	BACKWOODS	BENIGNANT	BODYGUARD	BUTTERCUP
AERODROME	AMBULANCE	APARTMENT	ASSIDUOUS	BACTERIUM	BENTONITE	BOLSHEVIK	BUTTERFAT
AEROPAUSE	AMBUSCADE	APOCRYPHA	ASSISTANT	BADMINTON	BERKELIUM	BOMBAZINE	BUTTERFLY
AEROPLANE	AMENDMENT	APOLOGIZE	ASSOCIATE	BAGATELLE	BERYLLIUM	BOMBPROOF	BUTTERNUT
AEROSPACE	AMERICANA	APOSTOLIC	ASSONANCE	BAILIWICK	BESETTING	BOMBSHELL	BYSTANDER
AESTHETIC	AMERICIUM	APPALOOSA	ASSURANCE	BAKSHEESH	BESPANGLE	BOMBSIGHT	CABLEGRAM
AESTIVATE	AMIDSHIPS	APPARATUS	ASTRADDLE	BALALAIKA	BESPATTER	BONDWOMAN	CABRIOLET
AFFECTING	AMORPHOUS	APPELLANT	ASTRAKHAN	BALDACHIN	BETROTHED	BOOKMAKER	CACOPHONY
AFFECTION	AMPERSAND	APPELLATE	ASTROLABE	BALLADEER	BICAMERAL	BOOKPLATE	CAFETERIA
AFFIDAVIT	AMPHIBIAN	APPENDAGE	ASTROLOGY	BALLERINA	BICONCAVE	BOOKSHELF	CALABOOSE
AFFILIATE	AMPHIBOLE	APPERTAIN	ASTRONAUT	BAMBOOZLE	BIFURCATE	BOOMERANG	CALCIMINE
	AMPLITUDE	APPETIZER	ASTRONOMY	BANDEROLE	BILATERAL	BOONDOCKS	CALCULATE
	ANAEROBIC	APPLEJACK	ASYMPTOTE	BANDOLIER	BILINGUAL	BOOTBLACK	CALENDULA

CALIBRATE	CATCHWORD	CHIROPODY	COLLEGIUM	CONTENTED	CROQUETTE	DECORATOR	DETERGENT
CALLOSITY	CATECHISM	CHIVALRIC	COLLIMATE	CONTINENT	CROSSOVER	DECOUPAGE	DETERMINE
CALORIFIC	CATERWAUL	CHLORDANE	COLLODION	CONTINUAL	CROSSROAD	DECREMENT	DETERRENT
CALVINISM	CATHARSIS	CHOCOLATE	COLLUSION	CONTINUUM	CROSSWALK	DEDUCTION	DETONATOR
CAMELBACK	CATHARTIC	CHONDRITE	COLLUVIUM	CONTRALTO	CROSSWAYS	DEFEATISM	DETRIMENT
CAMEMBERT	CATHEDRAL	CHONDRULE	COLONNADE	CONTUMELY	CROSSWISE	DEFECTIVE	DEUTERIUM
CAMPANILE	CAUCASIAN	CHOPHOUSE	COLORCAST	CONTUSION	CRUCIFORM	DEFENDANT	DEVASTATE
CAMPSTOOL	CAUSATION	CHOPSTICK	COLORFAST	CONUNDRUM	CRYOGENIC	DEFENSIVE	DEVILMENT
CANALBOAT	CAUTERIZE	CHORISTER	COLUMBINE	CONVIVIAL	CUBBYHOLE	DEFERENCE	DEXTERITY
CANDIDACY	CAVALCADE	CHRISTIAN	COLUMNIST	COONHOUND	CULLENDER	DEFERMENT	DEXTEROUS
CANDIDATE	CEASELESS	CHRISTMAS	COMFORTER	COOPERATE	CULMINATE	DEFICIENT	DHRYSTONE
CANDLEMAS	CELANDINE	CHROMATIC	COMMANDER	COPARTNER	CULTIVATE	DEFLATION	DIACRITIC
CANDLEPIN	CELEBRATE	CHRONICLE	COMMINGLE	COPYRIGHT	CUNEIFORM	DEFOLIANT	DIAERESIS
CANEBRAKE	CELEBRITY	CHRYSALIS	COMMISSAR	CORELDRAW	CUPBEARER	DEFOLIATE	DIAGNOSIS
CANNONADE	CELESTIAL	CHUCKHOLE	COMMITTEE	CORIANDER	CURETTAGE	DEFORMITY	DIALECTIC
CANNONEER	CELLARAGE	CHURCHMAN	COMMODITY	CORKSCREW	CURRYCOMB	DEHYDRATE	DIAMETRIC
CANONICAL	CELLULOSE	CIGARETTE	COMMODORE	CORMORANT	CURVATURE	DEJECTION	DIAPHRAGM
CANTABILE	CENTENARY	CIGARILLO	COMMOTION	CORNSTALK	CUSTODIAL	DEKALITER	DIATHERMY
CANTHARIS	CENTESIMO	CIRCADIAN	COMMUNION	COROLLARY	CUSTODIAN	DEKAMETER	DIATOMITE
CAPACIOUS	CENTIGRAM	CIRCUITRY	COMMUNISM	CORPORATE	CUSTOMARY	DEKASTERE	DICHOTOMY
CAPACITOR	CENTIPEDE	CIRCULATE	COMMUNITY	CORPOREAL	CUSTOMIZE	DELFTWARE	DIETETICS
CAPARISON	CENTURION	CIRRHOSIS	COMPANION	CORPUSCLE	CUTANEOUS	DELICIOUS	DIFFERENT
CAPILLARY	CEREBRATE	CITIZENRY	COMPETENT	CORRELATE	CUTTHROAT	DELIGHTED	DIFFICULT
CAPITALLY	CERECLOTH	CLAMSHELL	COMPLAINT	CORRUGATE	CYCLAMATE	DELIMITER	DIFFIDENT
CAPRICCIO	CERTAINTY	CLAPBOARD	COMPONENT	CORTISONE	CYCLOTRON	DELINEATE	DIGITALIS
CAPSULATE	CERTITUDE	CLASSICAL	COMPOSITE	CORUSCATE	CYTOPLASM	DEMAGOGUE	DIGITIZED
CAPTIVATE	CESSATION	CLASSMATE	COMPOSURE	COSMOGONY	DACHSHUND	DEMARCATE	DIGNIFIED
CARBONATE	CHAFFINCH	CLASSROOM	CONCERNED	COSMOLOGY	DAIRYMAID	DEMIMONDE	DIGNITARY
CARBUNCLE	CHALKBORD	CLEARANCE	CONCERTED	COSMONAUT	DALMATION	DEMITASSE	DIMENSION
CARBURIZE	CHALLENGE	CLERGYMAN	CONCIERGE	COSPONSOR	DAMASCENE	DEMOCRACY	DIMORPHIC
CARCINOMA	CHAMELEON	CLIENTELE	CONCORDAT	COTILLION	DAMNATION	DEMULCENT	DIPHTHONG
CARDBOARD	CHAMOMILE	CLINICIAN	CONCOURSE	COTYLEDON	DAMSELFLY	DEMURRAGE	DIPLOMACY
CARETAKER	CHAMPAGNE	CLIPBOARD	CONCUBINE	COUNSELOR	DANDELION	DENIGRATE	DIPTEROUS
CARIBBEAN	CHAMPAIGN	CLIPSHEET	CONDENSER	COUNTDOWN	DANGEROUS	DENTITION	DIRECTION
CARNATION	CHANCROID	CLOCKWISE	CONDIMENT	COUNTLESS	DAREDEVIL	DEODORANT	DIRECTIVE
CARNELIAN	CHANTEUSE	CLOCKWORK	CONDITION	COURTEOUS	DARWINISM	DEODORIZE	DIRECTORY
CARNIVORA	CHAPARRAL	CLOISONNE	CONDUCTOR	COURTESAN	DASHBOARD	DEOXIDIZE	DIRIGIBLE
CARNIVORE	CHARABANC	CLUBHOUSE	CONESTOGA	COURTROOM	DAUNTLESS	DEPARTURE	DISAFFECT
CARPENTER	CHARACTER	COADJUTOR	CONFESSOR	COURTSHIP	DAVENPORT	DEPENDENT	DISAPPEAR
CARPETBAG	CHARLATAN	COAGULANT	CONFIDANT	COURTYARD	DEATHBLOW	DEPRECATE	DISBURDEN
CARPETING	CHARWOMAN	COAGULATE	CONFUSION	COUTURIER	DEATHLESS	DEPRESSED	DISCHARGE
CARROUSEL	CHAUFFEUR	COALFIELD	CONGENIAL	COVALENCE	DEBENTURE	DERRINGER	DISCOMFIT
CARTILAGE	CHECKBOOK	COALITION	CONGERIES	CRABGRASS	DEBUTANTE	DESCENDER	DISCOURSE
CARTRIDGE	CHECKLIST	COASTLINE	CONGRUITY	CRACKDOWN	DECADENCE	DESECRATE	DISCREDIT
CARTWHEEL	CHECKMATE	COCHINEAL	CONJUGATE	CRAFTSMAN	DECALOGUE	DESICCANT	DISEMBARK
CASSEROLE	CHECKROOM	COCKATIEL	CONNUBIAL	CRANBERRY	DECATHLON	DESICCATE	DISEMBODY
CASSOWARY	CHEEKBONE	COCKFIGHT	CONSCIOUS	CRANKCASE	DECEITFUL	DESIGNATE	DISENGAGE
CASTANETS	CHEERLESS	COCKROACH	CONSCRIPT	CREDULOUS	DECENNIAL	DESIGNING	DISESTEEM
CASTIGATE	CHEMISTRY	COFEATURE	CONSENSUS	CREMATORY	DECEPTION	DESIRABLE	DISFIGURE
CASUISTRY	CHEVALIER	COFFEEPOT	CONSONANT	CRESCENDO	DECIDUOUS	DESPERADO	DISHCLOTH
CATACLYSM	CHICANERY	COFFERDAM	CONSTABLE	CRETINISM	DECILITER	DESPERATE	DISHONEST
CATALEPSY	CHICKADEE	COGNITION	CONSTANCY	CRINOLINE	DECIMETER	DESTITUTE	DISHWATER
CATALYSIS	CHICKASAW	COIFFEUSE	CONSTRAIN	CRITERION	DECISTERE	DESTROYER	DISINFECT
CATAMARAN	CHICKWEED	COLLATION	CONSTRICT	CRITICISM	DECLIVITY	DESUETUDE	DISLOCATE
CATAMOUNT	CHIEFTAIN	COLLEAGUE	CONSTRUCT	CRITICIZE	DECOLLETE	DESULTORY	DISMANTLE
CATATONIC	CHILBLAIN	COLLECTED	CONTAGION	CROCODILE	DECOMPOSE	DETECTIVE	DISMEMBER
CATCHMENT	CHILDHOOD	COLLEGIAN	CONTAINER	CROISSANT	DECONTROL	DETENTION	DISOBLIGE

DISORIENT	EARTHWORM	ENRAPTURE	EXCULPATE	FAVORABLE	FOOTLOOSE	GALACTOSE	GRASSLAND
DISPARAGE	EASYGOING	ENSHEATHE	EXCURSION	FEBRIFUGE	FOOTPRINT	GALLANTRY	GRATICULE
DISPARATE	EAVESDROP	ENTERITIS	EXCURSIVE	FECUNDATE	FOOTSTOOL	GALLINULE	GRATITUDE
DISPLEASE	EBULLIENT	ENTERTAIN	EXECRABLE	FEEDSTOCK	FORECLOSE	GALLIVANT	GRAVEYARD
DISPRAISE	ECCENTRIC	ENTOURAGE	EXECUTIVE	FEEDSTUFF	FOREFRONT	GALLSTONE	GRAVITATE
DISPUTANT	ECONOMICS	ENUMERATE	EXECUTRIX	FELLOWMAN	FOREGOING	GALVANISM	GRAYBEARD
DISREGARD	ECONOMIZE	ENUNCIATE	EXEMPLARY	FEROCIOUS	FOREIGNER	GALVANIZE	GREATCOAT
DISREPAIR	ECOSYSTEM	ENWREATHE	EXEMPLIFY	FERRYBOAT	FORENAMED	GANGPLANK	GREENBACK
DISREPUTE	EDELWEISS	EPHEDRINE	EXISTENCE	FERTILIZE	FORESHEET	GARNISHEE	GREENBELT
DISSECTED	EDITORIAL	EPHEMERAL	EXOGENOUS	FESTIVITY	FORESHORE	GARNITURE	GREENHORN
DISSEMBLE	EDUCATION	EPICENTER	EXONERATE	FETISHISM	FORESIGHT	GARRULOUS	GREENROOM
DISSENTER	EFFECTIVE	EPICUREAN	EXOSPHERE	FEUDALISM	FORESTALL	GASTRITIS	GREENWOOD
DISSIDENT	EFFECTUAL	EPIDERMIS	EXPANSION	FEUDATORY	FORESWEAR	GASTROPOD	GRENADIER
DISSIPATE	EFFICIENT	EPIGRAPHY	EXPANSIVE	FIDUCIARY	FORETASTE	GAUCHERIE	GRENADINE
DISSOLUTE	EFFLUENCE	EPISCOPAL	EXPATIATE	FILMSTRIP	FORETOKEN	GAZETTEER	GREYHOUND
DISTEMPER	EFFLUVIUM	EQUIPMENT	EXPECTANT	FINANCIAL	FOREWOMAN	GEARSHIFT	GRIEVANCE
DISTURBED	EGGBEATER	EQUIPOISE	EXPEDIENT	FINANCIER	FORGATHER	GELIGNITE	GRILLWORK
DITHERING	EGLANTINE	EQUITABLE	EXPEDITER	FINGERING	FORGIVING	GENEALOGY	GRISTMILL
DIVERSIFY	EGREGIOUS	EQUIVOCAL	EXPENSIVE	FINGERTIP	FORMALISM	GENERATOR	GROOMSMAN
DIVERSION	EIDERDOWN	ERADICATE	EXPERTISE	FINICKING	FORMALITY	GENITALIA	GROSGRAIN
DIVERSITY	EJACULATE	EROGENOUS	EXPIATORY	FIREBRAND	FORMALIZE	GENTILITY	GROTESQUE
DIVISIBLE	ELABORATE	ERRONEOUS	EXPLETIVE	FIREBREAK	FORMATION	GENTLEMAN	GROUNDHOG
DIXIELAND	ELASTOMER	ERSTWHILE	EXPLICATE	FIREBRICK	FORMATIVE	GENUFLECT	GROUNDING
DOBSONFLY	ELBOWROOM	ERUDITION	EXPLOSION	FIREHOUSE	FORMULATE	GEOGRAPHY	GROUPWARE
DOCTORATE	ELECTRIFY	ESCALATOR	EXPLOSIVE	FIREPLACE	FORSYTHIA	GERIATRIC	GRUBSTAKE
DOGMATISM	ELECTRODE	ESOPHAGUS	EXPOSITOR	FIREPOWER	FORTHWITH	GERMANIUM	GUARANTEE
DOMINANCE	ELEVATION	ESPERANTO	EXPULSION	FIREPROOF	FORTITUDE	GERMICIDE	GUARANTOR
DOORPLATE	ELIMINATE	ESPIONAGE	EXPURGATE	FIREWATER	FORTNIGHT	GERMINATE	GUARDROOM
DORMITORY	ELLIPSOID	ESPLANADE	EXQUISITE	FIRMAMENT	FORTUNATE	GESTATION	GUARDSMAN
DOSIMETER	ELOCUTION	ESSENTIAL	EXTEMPORE	FIRSTBORN	FORWARDER	GIBBERISH	GUERRILLA
DOUBTLESS	ELSEWHERE	ESTABLISH	EXTENSION	FIRSTHAND	FOUNDLING	GIMMICKRY	GUIDEBOOK
DOWITCHER	ELUCIDATE	ESTAMINET	EXTENSIVE	FIRSTLING	FOURSCORE	GLADIATOR	GUIDELINE
DOWNGRADE	EMBARRASS	ESTIMABLE	EXTENUATE	FISHERMAN	FRACTIOUS	GLADIOLUS	GUNCOTTON
DOWNRANGE	EMBAYMENT	ETHIOPIAN	EXTIRPATE	FLAGELLUM	FRAMEWORK	GLADSTONE	GUNNYSACK
DOWNRIGHT	EMBELLISH	ETHNOLOGY	EXTRADITE	FLAGEOLET	FRANCHISE	GLAMORIZE	GUNPOWDER
DOWNSHIFT	EMBRASURE	ETIQUETTE	EXTRAVERT	FLAGSTAFF	FRANGIBLE	GLEANINGS	GUSTATORY
DOWNSTAGE	EMBROCATE	ETYMOLOGY	EXTREMISM	FLAGSTONE	FRATERNAL	GLENGARRY	GYMNASIUM
DOWNSWING	EMBROIDER	EUCHARIST	EXTREMITY	FLAMMABLE	FREEBOARD	GLISSANDO	GYRFALCON
DRAFTSMAN	EMERGENCY	EUCLIDEAN	EXTRICATE	FLASHBACK	FREEMASON	GLUTINOUS	GYROSCOPE
DRAGONFLY	EMOLLIENT	EUPHEMISM	EXTRINSIC	FLASHBULB	FREESTONE	GLYCOSIDE	HABITABLE
DRAINPIPE	EMOLUMENT	EUTHENICS	EXTRUSIVE	FLASHCUBE	FREEWHEEL	GODFATHER	HABITUATE
DRAMATIZE	EMPENNAGE	EUTROPHIC	EXUBERANT	FLASHTUBE	FREQUENCY	GODMOTHER	HACKNEYED
DREAMLAND	EMPHASIZE	EVAPORATE	EYESTRAIN	FLATULENT	FRICASSEE	GODPARENT	HAILSTONE
DRIFTWOOD	EMPHYSEMA	EVAPORITE	FABRICATE	FLAVORING	FRIEDCAKE	GOLDBRICK	HAILSTORM
DROMEDARY	EMPIRICAL	EVENTUATE	FACETIOUS	FLEDGLING	FRIGHTFUL	GOLDENROD	HAIRBRUSH
DRUGSTORE	ENCHILADA	EVERGLADE	FACSIMILE	FLINTLOCK	FRIVOLOUS	GOLDFIELD	HAIRCLOTH
DRUMSTICK	ENCOMPASS	EVERGREEN	FACTORIAL	FLOODGATE	FROSTBITE	GOLDFINCH	HAIRPIECE
DUCKBOARD	ENCOUNTER	EVERYBODY	FAIRYLAND	FLOPHOUSE	FRUITCAKE	GOLDSMITH	HAIRSTYLE
DUMBFOUND	ENCOURAGE	EVOLUTION	FALSEHOOD	FLOTATION	FRUITERER	GONDOLIER	HALFPENNY
DUPLICATE	ENDOCRINE	EXCELLENT	FANCYWORK	FLOWCHART	FRUSTRATE	GONORRHEA	HALITOSIS
DUPLICITY	ENDOSCOPE	EXCELSIOR	FANTASIZE	FLOWERPOT	FULMINATE	GOVERNESS	HALLOWEEN
DYSENTERY	ENDURANCE	EXCEPTION	FANTASTIC	FLUCTUATE	FUNGICIDE	GRADATION	HAMADRYAD
DYSPEPSIA	ENERGETIC	EXCHEQUER	FARMHOUSE	FOLLOWING	FUNICULAR	GRANDIOSE	HAMBURGER
DYSTROPHY	ENERGIZER	EXCITABLE	FARMSTEAD	FOODSTUFF	FURNITURE	GRANTSMAN	HAMMERTOE
EARTHLING	ENGRAVING	EXCLUSIVE	FARSEEING	FOOLHARDY	FUSILLADE	GRANULATE	HAMSTRING
EARTHWARD	ENIGMATIC	EXCORIATE	FASCINATE	FOOLPROOF	GABARDINE	GRAPESHOT	HANDCLASP
EARTHWORK	ENLIGHTEN	EXCREMENT	FASTENING	FOOTBOARD	GABERDINE	GRAPEVINE	HANDCRAFT

HANDIWORK	HEURISTIC	HYDRANGEA	INCARNATE	INOCULATE	INTROVERT	LAMINATED	LUCRATIVE
HANDSHAKE	HEXAMETER	HYDRAULIC	INCENTIVE	INORGANIC	INTUITION	LANDOWNER	LUDICROUS
HANDSPIKE	HIBERNATE	HYDROFOIL	INCEPTION	INPATIENT	INTUMESCE	LANDSCAPE	LUNCHROOM
HANDSTAND	HIDEBOUND	HYDROLOGY	INCESSANT	INSATIATE	INVECTIVE	LANDSLIDE	LUXURIANT
HANDWOVEN	HIERARCHY	HYDROXIDE	INCIDENCE	INSENSATE	INVENTION	LANTHANUM	LUXURIATE
HAPHAZARD	HIGHLIGHT	HYPERBOLA	INCIPIENT	INSERTION	INVENTIVE	LASSITUDE	MACHINERY
HAPPENING	HILARIOUS	HYPERBOLE	INCLEMENT	INSIDIOUS	INVENTORY	LATECOMER	MACHINIST
HAPPINESS	HILLBILLY	HYPERCARD	INCOGNITO	INSINCERE	INVERNESS	LAUDATORY	MACINTOSH
HARBINGER	HINDRANCE	HYPERTEXT	INCOMMODE	INSINUATE	INVERSION	LAUNCHPAD	MACROCOSM
HARBORAGE	HINDSIGHT	HYPHENATE	INCORRECT	INSISTENT	INVIDIOUS	LAVALIERE	MAELSTROM
HARDBOARD	HISTAMINE	HYPOCRISY	INCREMENT	INSOLUBLE	INVIOLATE	LAZYBONES	MAGISTRAL
HARDBOUND	HISTOGRAM	HYSTERICS	INCUBATOR	INSOLVENT	INVISIBLE	LEAFSTALK	MAGNESIUM
HARDCOVER	HISTORIAN	ICELANDER	INCULCATE	INSTANTER	INVOLUCRE	LEASEHOLD	MAGNETISM
HARDIHOOD	HITCHHIKE	ICELANDIC	INCULPATE	INSTANTLY	IRASCIBLE	LEASTWISE	MAGNETITE
HARDSTAND	HOARFROST	IDENTICAL	INCUMBENT	INSTIGATE	IRONBOUND	LEAVENING	MAGNETIZE
HARLEQUIN	HOBGOBLIN	IGNORANCE	INCURABLE	INSTITUTE	IRONSTONE	LEGENDARY	MAGNIFICO
HARMONICA	HOLLYHOCK	ILLEGIBLE	INCURIOUS	INSURABLE	IRRADIATE	LEGISLATE	MAGNITUDE
HARMONICS	HOLOCAUST	ILLIBERAL	INCURSION	INSURANCE	IRREGULAR	LEITMOTIV	MAHARISHI
HARMONIUM	HOLOGRAPH	ILLOGICAL	INDELIBLE	INSURGENT	IRRITABLE	LEUKOCYTE	MAINFRAME
HARMONIZE	HOLYSTONE	IMAGINARY	INDEMNIFY	INTEGRATE	ISINGLASS	LEVIATHAN	MAJORDOMO
HARTSHORN	HOMEGROWN	IMBALANCE	INDEMNITY	INTEGRITY	ISOSCELES	LIABILITY	MAJORETTE
HATCHMENT	HOMEMAKER	IMBROGLIO	INDENTION	INTELLECT	ISRAELITE	LIBERTINE	MAJUSCULE
HAVERSACK	HOMESTEAD	IMITATION	INDENTURE	INTENDANT	ITALICIZE	LIBRARIAN	MAKESHIFT
HEADBOARD	HOMOGRAPH	IMITATIVE	INDIGNANT	INTENSIFY	ITERATION	LIFEBLOOD	MALACHITE
HEADDRESS	HOMOPHONE	IMMEDIACY	INDIGNITY	INTENSITY	ITINERANT	LIFEGUARD	MALADROIT
HEADFIRST	HONEYCOMB	IMMEDIATE	INDUCTION	INTENSIVE	ITINERARY	LIGHTFACE	MALATHION
HEADLIGHT	HONEYMOON	IMMIGRANT	INDUCTIVE	INTENTION	JACARANDA	LIGHTNING	MALAYSIAN
HEADPHONE	HONORABLE	IMMIGRATE	INEBRIATE	INTERCEDE	JACKKNIFE	LIGHTSHIP	MALIGNANT
HEADPIECE	HONORIFIC	IMMOVABLE	INEFFABLE	INTERCEPT	JACKSCREW	LIGHTSOME	MALLEABLE
HEADSTALL	HOPSCOTCH	IMMUTABLE	INELEGANT	INTERDICT	JACKSTRAW	LIMBURGER	MANDATORY
HEADSTONE	HOREHOUND	IMPARTIAL	INFANTILE	INTERFACE	JAILBREAK	LIMELIGHT	MANGANESE
HEADWATER	HOROSCOPE	IMPASSIVE	INFATUATE	INTERFERE	JAUNDICED	LIMESTONE	MANHANDLE
HEALTHFUL	HORSEBACK	IMPATIENS	INFECTION	INTERFUSE	JELLYFISH	LIMOUSINE	MANHATTAN
HEARTACHE	HORSEHAIR	IMPATIENT	INFERENCE	INTERJECT	JERKWATER	LINEAMENT	MANIFESTO
HEARTBEAT	HORSEHIDE	IMPEDANCE	INFERTILE	INTERLACE	JESSAMINE	LIQUIDATE	MANNEQUIN
HEARTBURN	HORSEPLAY	IMPERFECT	INFIRMARY	INTERLARD	JEWELWEED	LITERATIM	MANNERISM
HEARTFELT	HORSESHOE	IMPERIOUS	INFIRMITY	INTERLEAF	JINRIKSHA	LITHESOME	MANOEUVRE
HEARTLESS	HORSETAIL	IMPETUOUS	INFLATION	INTERLINE	JITTERBUG	LITHOLOGY	MANOMETER
HEARTSICK	HORSEWHIP	IMPLEMENT	INFLEXION	INTERLINK	JOBHOLDER	LITIGIOUS	MANSLAYER
HEARTWOOD	HORTATIVE	IMPLICATE	INFLUENCE	INTERLOCK	JUDICIARY	LITTERBUG	MARGARINE
HECTOGRAM	HORTATORY	IMPOLITIC	INFLUENZA	INTERLOPE	JUDICIOUS	LIVERWORT	MARIJUANA
HELLEBORE	HOTHEADED	IMPORTANT	INFORMANT	INTERLUDE	JURIDICAL	LIVERYMAN	MARMALADE
HELLENISM	HOURGLASS	IMPORTUNE	INFURIATE	INTERMENT	JUXTAPOSE	LIVESTOCK	MARMOREAL
HELVETIAN	HOUSEBOAT	IMPOSTURE	INFUSIBLE	INTERNIST	KICKSTAND	LOADSTONE	MARQUETRY
HELVETICA	HOUSECOAT	IMPRECATE	INGENIOUS	INTERNODE	KILOCYCLE	LOATHSOME	MARSUPIAL
HEMISTICH	HOUSEHOLD	IMPRECISE	INGENUITY	INTERPLAY	KILOHERTZ	LOCKSMITH	MARTYRDOM
HEMSTITCH	HOUSEMAID	IMPROMPTU	INGENUOUS	INTERPOSE	KILOLITER	LOCOMOTOR	MARVELOUS
HEPATITIS	HOUSEWIFE	IMPROVISE	INGLENOOK	INTERPRET	KILOMETER	LODESTONE	MASCULINE
HERBALIST	HOUSEWORK	IMPRUDENT	INGROWING	INTERRUPT	KINESCOPE	LOGARITHM	MASOCHISM
HERBARIUM	HOWSOEVER	IMPULSION	INHALATOR	INTERSECT	KINSWOMAN	LOGISTICS	MASTERFUL
HERBICIDE	HUMANKIND	IMPULSIVE	INJECTION	INTERVENE	KNOCKDOWN	LOINCLOTH	MASTICATE
HERCULEAN	HUMDINGER	INABILITY	INJUSTICE	INTERVIEW	KNOWLEDGE	LONGEVITY	MATCHBOOK
HEREAFTER	HUMILIATE	INAMORATA	INNERMOST	INTESTATE	LABORIOUS	LONGITUDE	MATCHLOCK
HEREUNDER	HUNCHBACK	INANIMATE	INNERSOLE	INTESTINE	LABYRINTH	LORGNETTE	MATCHWOOD
HERITABLE	HUNGARIAN	INANITION	INNKEEPER	INTRICATE	LACCOLITH	LOWERCASE	MATERNITY
HERMITAGE	HURRICANE	INAUGURAL	INNOCENCE	INTRINSIC	LAGNIAPPE	LUBRICANT	MATRIARCH
HETERODOX	HUSBANDRY	INCAPABLE	INNOCUOUS	INTRODUCE	LAMEBRAIN	LUBRICATE	MATRICIDE

MATRIMONY	MILLIGRAM	MULTIFORM	NORTHWEST	OUTNUMBER	PARSIMONY	PESSIMISM	POETASTER
MATUTINAL	MILLINERY	MULTISCAN	NORWEGIAN	OUTRIGGER	PARSONAGE	PESTHOUSE	POINCIANA
MAUSOLEUM	MILLIPEDE	MULTISPIN	NOSEBLEED	OUTSKIRTS	PARTITION	PESTICIDE	POLICEMAN
MAYFLOWER	MILLIVOLT	MULTISYNC	NOSEPIECE	OUTSPOKEN	PARTITIVE	PESTILENT	POLITBURO
MEANWHILE	MILLSTONE	MULTITUDE	NOSTALGIA	OUTSPREAD	PARTRIDGE	PETROLEUM	POLITESSE
MECHANICS	MINCEMEAT	MUNICIPAL	NOTCHBACK	OUTWARDLY	PASSENGER	PETROLOGY	POLITICAL
MECHANISM	MINELAYER	MURDEROUS	NOTORIOUS	OVERBLOWN	PASSERINE	PETTICOAT	POLYESTER
MECHANIZE	MINIATURE	MUSKMELON	NOVELETTE	OVERBOARD	PASTORALE	PHALAROPE	POLYGRAPH
MEDALLION	MINISCULE	MUSSULMAN	NOVITIATE	OVERCLOUD	PASTURAGE	PHEROMONE	POLYPHONY
MEDICABLE	MINISKIRT	MYSTICISM	NUMERATOR	OVERDRAFT	PATCHWORK	PHILANDER	POMPADOUR
MEDICINAL	MINISTATE	MYTHOLOGY	NUMERICAL	OVERDRIVE	PATERNITY	PHILATELY	PONDEROUS
MEGACYCLE	MINUSCULE	NAMEPLATE	NURSEMAID	OVERMATCH	PATHOLOGY	PHILIPPIC	POORHOUSE
MEGADEATH	MINUTEMAN	NANOMETER	NUTRIMENT	OVERNIGHT	PATRIARCH	PHILOLOGY	POPPYCOCK
MEGAHERTZ	MISBEHAVE	NARCISSUS	NUTRITION	OVERPOWER	PATRICIAN	PHLEBITIS	PORCELAIN
MEGAPHONE	MISCHANCE	NARCOTIZE	OBBLIGATO	OVERPRINT	PATRICIDE	PHONETICS	PORCUPINE
MEGAPIXEL	MISCREANT	NARRATIVE	OBEISANCE	OVERREACH	PATRIMONY	PHONOLOGY	PORRINGER
MELIORATE	MISDIRECT	NATURALLY	OBFUSCATE	OVERSEXED	PATRISTIC	PHOSPHATE	PORTFOLIO
MELODIOUS	MISERABLE	NAVIGABLE	OBJECTIFY	OVERSHOOT	PATROLMAN	PHOTOCELL	PORTULACA
MELODRAMA	MISGIVING	NECESSARY	OBJECTIVE	OVERSIGHT	PATRONAGE	PHOTOCOPY	POSTERIOR
MELTWATER	MISGOVERN	NECESSITY	OBJURGATE	OVERSLEEP	PATRONIZE	PHOTOPLAY	POSTERITY
MEMORABLE	MISHANDLE	NECROLOGY	OBLIVIOUS	OVERSTATE	PAYMASTER	PHRENETIC	POSTHASTE
MENAGERIE	MISINFORM	NECTARINE	OBNOXIOUS	OVERTHROW	PEACETIME	PHYSICIAN	POSTILION
MENDICANT	MISMANAGE	NEFARIOUS	OBSERVANT	OVERTRICK	PECUNIARY	PHYSICIST	POSTNATAL
MENOPAUSE	MISORIENT	NEGLIGENT	OBSESSION	OVERWEIGH	PEDAGOGUE	PICKABACK	POSTULANT
MENTALITY	MISSILERY	NEGOTIANT	OBSTINATE	OVERWHELM	PEDOMETER	PICTORIAL	POSTULATE
MERCENARY	MISSIONER	NEGOTIATE	OCCULTISM	OVERWRITE	PEGMATITE	PIECEMEAL	POTASSIUM
MERCERIZE	MISTLETOE	NEGRITUDE	OCCUPANCY	OVIPAROUS	PEKINGESE	PIECEWORK	POTBOILER
MERCURIAL	MODERATOR	NEODYMIUM	OFFENSIVE	OXIDATION	PENDULOUS	PIGGYBACK	POTENTATE
MERCUROUS	MODERNISM	NEOLOGISM	OFFERTORY	OXYGENATE	PENEPLAIN	PIGHEADED	POTENTIAL
MERGANSER	MODERNIZE	NEPHRITIC	OFFICIANT	PACEMAKER	PENETRATE	PIKESTAFF	POTPOURRI
MERRIMENT	MOLDBOARD	NEPHRITIS	OFFICIATE	PACHYDERM	PENHOLDER	PIMPERNEL	POULTERER
MESCALINE	MOMENTARY	NEPTUNIUM	OFFICIOUS	PACKHORSE	PENINSULA	PINEAPPLE	POURBOIRE
MESMERIZE	MOMENTOUS	NEURALGIA	OFFSPRING	PAGEMAKER	PENTECOST	PINSTRIPE	POWERBOAT
MESSENGER	MONASTERY	NEUROLOGY	OLFACTORY	PAKISTANI	PENTHOUSE	PIROUETTE	PRACTICAL
MESSIEURS	MONGOLIAN	NEVERMORE	OLIGARCHY	PALAESTRA	PENURIOUS	PISTACHIO	PRAGMATIC
METALWARE	MONGOLISM	NEWSPAPER	OMBUDSMAN	PALANQUIN	PERCHANCE	PITCHFORK	PRAYERFUL
METALWORK	MONGOLOID	NEWSPRINT	ONIONSKIN	PALATABLE	PERCOLATE	PITUITARY	PRECANCEL
METEORITE	MONKSHOOD	NEWSSTAND	ONSLAUGHT	PALLADIUM	PERDITION	PIZZICATO	PRECEDENT
METEOROID	MONOGRAPH	NICOTINIC	OPERATION	PALMISTRY	PERENNIAL	PLACEKICK	PRECEDING
METHADONE	MONOLOGUE	NIGHTCLUB	OPERATIVE	PALPITATE	PERFORATE	PLACEMENT	PRECENTOR
METHODIST	MONOMANIA	NIGHTFALL	OPPORTUNE	PANEGYRIC	PERFUMERY	PLAINTIFF	PRECEPTOR
METHODIZE	MONOPLANE	NIGHTGOWN	OPTOMETRY	PANHANDLE	PERIMETER	PLAINTIVE	PRECIPICE
METRICIZE	MONOSPACE	NIGHTHAWK	ORANGEADE	PANTHEISM	PERIPHERY	PLANELOAD	PRECISION
METROLOGY	MONSIGNOR	NIGHTLIFE	ORCHESTRA	PANTOMIME	PERISCOPE	PLANETOID	PRECURSOR
METRONOME	MOONLIGHT	NIGHTMARE	ORDINANCE	PAPERBACK	PERISTYLE	PLATITUDE	PREDATION
MEZZANINE	MOONSCAPE	NIGHTTIME	ORGIASTIC	PAPILLOTE	PERMANENT	PLAUSIBLE	PREDATORY
MICROCOPY	MOONSHINE	NIGRITUDE	ORIENTATE	PARACHUTE	PERMEABLE	PLAYHOUSE	PREDICATE
MICROCOSM	MOONSTONE	NOCTURNAL	ORIFLAMME	PARAGRAPH	PERPETUAL	PLAYTHING	PREFIGURE
MICROFILM	MORTICIAN	NONCREDIT	ORIGINATE	PARALYSIS	PERPLEXED	PLENITUDE	PREFLIGHT
MICROGRAM	MOTORBIKE	NONENTITY	ORPHANAGE	PARAMETER	PERSECUTE	PLENTEOUS	PREGNABLE
MICROSOFT	MOTORBOAT	NONPAREIL	OSCILLATE	PARAMOUNT	PERSEVERE	PLENTIFUL	PREJUDICE
MICROWAVE	MOTORCADE	NONPERSON	OSTRACIZE	PARATHION	PERSIMMON	PLOWSHARE	PRELAUNCH
MIDDLEMAN	MOUSETRAP	NONPROFIT	OTHERWISE	PARCHMENT	PERSONAGE	PLURALITY	PREMATURE
MIDSTREAM	MOUSTACHE	NONREADER	OUBLIETTE	PAREGORIC	PERSONATE	PLURALIZE	PREOCCUPY
MIDSUMMER	MOUTHPART	NORMALIZE	OURSELVES	PAROCHIAL	PERSONIFY	PLUTONIUM	PREORDAIN
MIDWINTER	MOUTHWASH	NORMATIVE	OUTERMOST	PARQUETRY	PERSONNEL	PNEUMATIC	PRERECORD
MILESTONE	MUCKRAKER	NORTHEAST	OUTGROWTH	PARRICIDE	PERTINENT	PNEUMONIA	PRESBYTER

PRESCHOOL	PSEUDONYM	RANGELAND	RENCONTRE	ROUGHNECK	SCREWBALL	SHIPSHAPE	SOLILOQUY
PRESCRIBE	PSORIASIS	RAPACIOUS	RENDITION	ROUMANIAN	SCRIMMAGE	SHIPWRECK	SOLITAIRE
PRESENTLY	PSYCHOSIS	RASPBERRY	REPAIRMAN	ROUNDELAY	SCRIMSHAW	SHOEMAKER	SOMETHING
PRESHRUNK	PTARMIGAN	RASTERIZE	REPELLENT	ROUNDWORM	SCRIPTURE	SHOREBIRD	SOMETIMES
PRESIDENT	PUBESCENT	RATIONALE	REPERTORY	RUINATION	SCRIVENER	SHORTCAKE	SOMEWHERE
PRESIDIUM	PUBLICIST	RAUWOLFIA	REPLENISH	RUMRUNNER	SCULPTURE	SHORTHAND	SOMNOLENT
PRESSROOM	PUBLICITY	REACTANCE	REPLETION	RUNAROUND	SCUTCHEON	SHORTHORN	SOPHISTIC
PRESTRESS	PUBLICIZE	REBELLION	REPLICATE	RUSTICATE	SEAFARING	SHORTSTOP	SOPHISTRY
PREVALENT	PUERPERAL	RECEPTION	REPORTAGE	RUTHENIUM	SEASONING	SHORTWAVE	SOPHOMORE
PREVERBAL	PUISSANCE	RECEPTIVE	REPOSSESS	SACCHARIN	SEAWORTHY	SHOWPIECE	SOPORIFIC
PREVISION	PULMONARY	RECESSION	REPREHEND	SACKCLOTH	SEBACEOUS	SHOWPLACE	SOUBRETTE
PRICELESS	PULVERIZE	RECESSIVE	REPRESENT	SACRAMENT	SECESSION	SHRINKAGE	SOUTHEAST
PRIMARILY	PUNCTILIO	RECHERCHE	REPRIMAND	SACRIFICE	SECLUSION	SHRUBBERY	SOUTHWEST
PRIMITIVE	PUNCTUATE	RECIPIENT	REPROBATE	SACRILEGE	SECONDARY	SIDEBOARD	SOVEREIGN
PRINCIPAL	PUPPETEER	RECKONING	REPRODUCE	SACRISTAN	SECRETARY	SIDEBURNS	SPACESHIP
PRINCIPLE	PUREBLOOD	RECOGNIZE	REPUDIATE	SADDLEBOW	SECRETION	SIDEPIECE	SPAGHETTI
PRINTABLE	PURGATION	RECOLLECT	REPUGNANT	SAFEGUARD	SECRETIVE	SIDESWIPE	SPEAKEASY
PRIVATEER	PURGATIVE	RECOMMEND	REPULSION	SAFFLOWER	SECTARIAN	SIDETRACK	SPEARHEAD
PRIVATION	PURGATORY	RECONCILE	REPULSIVE	SAGACIOUS	SECTIONAL	SIGNALIZE	SPEARMINT
PRIVILEGE	PURSUANCE	RECONDITE	REPUTABLE	SAGEBRUSH	SEDENTARY	SIGNALMAN	SPECIALTY
PROBATION	PUSSYFOOT	RECORDING	REQUISITE	SAILCLOTH	SEGREGATE	SIGNATORY	SPECTACLE
PROBATIVE	PYRETHRUM	RECORDIST	RESECTION	SAILPLANE	SELECTION	SIGNATURE	SPECTATOR
PROBOSCIS	PYROLYSIS	RECTANGLE	RESERPINE	SALACIOUS	SELECTMAN	SIGNBOARD	SPECULATE
PROCEDURE	PYROMANIA	RECTIFIER	RESERVIST	SALESGIRL	SEMANTICS	SILICEOUS	SPEEDBOAT
PROCESSOR	PYROMETER	RECTITUDE	RESERVOIR	SALTPETER	SEMAPHORE	SILICOSIS	SPEEDWELL
PROCONSUL	QUADRATIC	RECUMBENT	RESHUFFLE	SALTWATER	SEMBLANCE	SILTSTONE	SPELUNKER
PROCREATE	QUADRILLE	RECURSION	RESIDENCE	SALVATION	SEMICOLON	SIMPATICO	SPHINCTER
PROFANITY	QUADRUPED	REDACTION	RESIDENCY	SANCTUARY	SEMIFINAL	SIMPLETON	SPICEBUSH
PROFESSOR	QUADRUPLE	REDBREAST	RESIDUARY	SANDBLAST	SEMIFLUID	SINGLETON	SPINDLING
PROFITEER	QUARTERLY	REDUCTION	RESISTANT	SANDPAPER	SEMILUNAR	SINUSITIS	SPINDRIFT
PROGNOSIS	QUARTZITE	REDUNDANT	RESONANCE	SANDPIPER	SEMIWORKS	SITUATION	SPINNAKER
PROJECTOR	QUERULOUS	REENFORCE	RESONATOR	SANDSTONE	SENIORITY	SKIMOBILE	SPIRITUAL
PROMENADE	QUICKDRAW	REENTRANT	RESTRAINT	SANDSTORM	SENSATION	SKINFLINT	SPLENETIC
PROMINENT	QUICKLIME	REFECTION	RESURRECT	SANGFROID	SENSITIVE	SKINTIGHT	SPLITTING
PROMISING	QUICKSAND	REFECTORY	RETALIATE	SAPSUCKER	SENSITIZE	SKYDIVING	SPOKESMAN
PRONGHORN	QUICKSORT	REFERENCE	RETARDATE	SARTORIAL	SENTIMENT	SKYJACKER	SPOONBILL
PRONOUNCE	QUICKSTEP	REFLECTOR	RETENTION	SASSAFRAS	SEPARABLE	SKYLOUNGE	SPORTSMAN
PROOFREAD	QUICKTIME	REFLEXIVE	RETENTIVE	SATELLITE	SEPARATOR	SKYROCKET	SPOTLIGHT
PROPAGATE	QUIESCENT	REFRACTOR	RETRIEVER	SATINWOOD	SEPTEMBER	SLAUGHTER	SPRIGHTLY
PROPELLER	QUINTUPLE	REFURBISH	RETROFIRE	SATURNINE	SEPULCHER	SLINGSHOT	SQUEAMISH
PROPHETIC	QUITTANCE	REGARDING	REVERENCE	SAXIFRAGE	SEPULTURE	SLUICEWAY	STABILIZE
PROPONENT	QUIZZICAL	REGISTRAR	REVERSION	SAXOPHONE	SEQUESTER	SMALLTALK	STAIRCASE
PROPRIETY	QUOTIDIAN	REHEARING	REVOCABLE	SCANTLING	SERIGRAPH	SNAKEBIRD	STAIRWELL
PROSCRIBE	RABBINATE	REHEARSAL	REVOLTING	SCAPEGOAT	SERVITUDE	SNAKEBITE	STALEMATE
PROSECUTE	RACEHORSE	REIMBURSE	REVULSION	SCARECROW	SEVENTEEN	SNOWDRIFT	STAMINATE
PROSELYTE	RACETRACK	REINFORCE	RHEOMETER	SCAVENGER	SHADOWBOX	SNOWFIELD	STANCHION
PROSTRATE	RACIALISM	REINSTATE	RIDGEPOLE	SCHEELITE	SHAKEDOWN	SNOWFLAKE	STANDPIPE
PROTECTOR	RACKETEER	REITERATE	RIGHTEOUS	SCHEMATIC	SHAPELESS	SNOWSTORM	STARBOARD
PROTOTYPE	RACONTEUR	REJOINDER	RIGMAROLE	SCHILLING	SHAREWARE	SOAPSTONE	STARLIGHT
PROTOZOAN	RADIOGRAM	RELEVANCE	RIVERBANK	SCHLEMIEL	SHARKSKIN	SOBRIQUET	STARTLING
PROVENCAL	RADIOLOGY	RELEVANCY	RIVERBOAT	SCHNAUZER	SHEATHING	SOCIALISM	STATEMENT
PROVENDER	RAGPICKER	RELIGIOUS	RIVERSIDE	SCHOOLBOY	SHEEPFOLD	SOCIALITE	STATEROOM
PROVIDENT	RAINSPOUT	RELIQUARY	ROADBLOCK	SCINTILLA	SHEEPSKIN	SOCIALIZE	STATESIDE
PROVISION	RAINSTORM	RELUCTANT	ROADSTEAD	SCLEROSIS	SHELLFIRE	SOCIOLOGY	STATESMAN
PROVOLONE	RAINWATER	REMAINDER	ROCKBOUND	SCOUNDREL	SHELLFISH	SOFTBOUND	STATIONER
PROXIMATE	RANCHLAND	REMINISCE	ROOTSTOCK	SCRAPBOOK	SHIFTLESS	SOLEMNIZE	STATISTIC
PROXIMITY	RANDOMIZE	REMISSION	ROSEWATER	SCREENING	SHIPBOARD	SOLICITOR	STATUETTE

STATUTORY	SUNBONNET	TECHNIQUE	TOLLHOUSE	TUSCARORA	UNFLEDGED	VELVETEEN	WAGONETTE
STEADFAST	SUNFLOWER	TECTONICS	TOMBSTONE	TWINKLING	UNFOUNDED	VENERABLE	WAISTBAND
STEAMBOAT	SUNSEEKER	TECTONISM	TONSORIAL	TYPEWRITE	UNGUARDED	VENGEANCE	WAISTCOAT
STEAMSHIP	SUNSTROKE	TELEGENIC	TOOTHACHE	TYRANNIZE	UNHARNESS	VENIREMAN	WAISTLINE
STEELYARD	SUPERNOVA	TELEGRAPH	TOOTHPICK	TYRANNOUS	UNHEALTHY	VENTILATE	WALLBOARD
STEPCHILD	SUPERPOSE	TELEMETER	TOOTHSOME	UKRAINIAN	UNISEXUAL	VENTRICLE	WALLOPING
STERILIZE	SUPERSEDE	TELEPATHY	TOUCHDOWN	ULTIMATUM	UNITARIAN	VENTUROUS	WALLPAPER
STEVEDORE	SUPERVENE	TELEPHONE	TOWNSFOLK	ULTRAHIGH	UNIVALENT	VERACIOUS	WARBONNET
STILLBORN	SUPERVISE	TELEPHONY	TRACKBALL	ULTRAPURE	UNIVERSAL	VERBALIZE	WAREHOUSE
STIMULANT	SUPPLIANT	TELEPHOTO	TRACTABLE	UMBILICUS	UNKNOWING	VERDIGRIS	WARMONGER
STIMULATE	SUPPOSING	TELESCOPE	TRADEMARK	UNADVISED	UNLEARNED	VERIDICAL	WASHBASIN
STIPULATE	SUPPURATE	TELLURIUM	TRADESMAN	UNALIGNED	UNMEANING	VERITABLE	WASHBOARD
STOCKPILE	SUPREMACY	TEMPERATE	TRADITION	UNALLOYED	UNMINDFUL	VERMIFORM	WASHCLOTH
STOCKYARD	SURCHARGE	TEMPORARY	TRAGEDIAN	UNANIMOUS	UNNATURAL	VERMIFUGE	WASHHOUSE
STOMACHER	SURCINGLE	TEMPORIZE	TRAINLOAD	UNBEKNOWN	UNPLUMBED	VERMILION	WASHSTAND
STOMACHIC	SURFBOARD	TENACIOUS	TRANSCEND	UNBENDING	UNPOPULAR	VERNALIZE	WASHWOMAN
STOPLIGHT	SURRENDER	TENDERIZE	TRANSDUCE	UNBLESSED	UNRIVALED	VERSATILE	WASTELAND
STOPWATCH	SURROGATE	TENEBROUS	TRANSFORM	UNBOUNDED	UNRUFFLED	VERTEBRAL	WATCHBAND
STOREROOM	SURVEYING	TENTATIVE	TRANSFUSE	UNBRIDLED	UNSCATHED	VESTIBULE	WATCHCASE
STRAPLESS	SUSPENDER	TERMAGANT	TRANSIENT	UNCEASING	UNSELFISH	VESTRYMAN	WATCHWORD
STRAPPING	SUSPICION	TERMINATE	TRANSLATE	UNCERTAIN	UNSETTLED	VEXATIOUS	WATERFALL
STRATAGEM	SWAMPLAND	TERRARIUM	TRANSMUTE	UNCHARTED	UNSHACKLE	VIBRATION	WATERFOWL
STREAMBED	SWANSDOWN	TERRITORY	TRANSONIC	UNCLEANLY	UNSHEATHE	VIBRATORY	WATERLINE
STREAMLET	SWEATSHOP	TERRORISM	TRANSPIRE	UNCONCERN	UNSIGHTLY	VICARIOUS	WATERMARK
STREETCAR	SWEETMEAT	TERRORIZE	TRANSPORT	UNCOUNTED	UNSKILLED	VICENNIAL	WATERSHED
STRENUOUS	SWELLHEAD	TESTAMENT	TRANSPOSE	UNDAUNTED	UNSPARING	VICEREGAL	WATERSIDE
STRETCHER	SWITCHMAN	TESTIMONY	TRANSSHIP	UNDECEIVE	UNSPOTTED	VICTIMIZE	WAVETABLE
STRICTURE	SWORDFISH	THANKLESS	TRAPEZOID	UNDECIDED	UNSTUDIED	VICTORIAN	WEARISOME
STRIKEOUT	SWORDPLAY	THEATRICS	TRAPPINGS	UNDERBODY	UNTUTORED	VICTUALER	WEDNESDAY
STRIPLING	SWORDSMAN	THEOCRACY	TREACHERY	UNDERBRED	UNWILLING	VIDELICET	WHALEBOAT
STRONTIUM	SWORDTAIL	THEOSOPHY	TREADMILL	UNDERCOAT	UNWITTING	VIDEOTAPE	WHALEBONE
STRUCTURE	SYCOPHANT	THEREFORE	TREASURER	UNDERDONE	UNWORLDLY	VIEWPOINT	WHEELBASE
SUBALPINE	SYLLABIFY	THEREFROM	TREATMENT	UNDERFEED	UNWRITTEN	VIGESIMAL	WHEREFORE
SUBALTERN	SYLLOGISM	THEREUNTO	TREMATODE	UNDERFOOT	UPANISHAD	VIGILANCE	WHEREUPON
SUBATOMIC	SYMBIOSIS	THEREUPON	TREMULOUS	UNDERGIRD	UPHOLSTER	VIGILANTE	WHEREWITH
SUBDIVIDE	SYMBOLISM	THEREWITH	TRENCHANT	UNDERHAND	UPPERCASE	VILLENAGE	WHETSTONE
SUBJUGATE	SYMBOLIZE	THESAURUS	TRIBESMAN	UNDERLINE	UPPERMOST	VINDICATE	WHICHEVER
SUBLIMATE	SYMPOSIUM	THICKNESS	TRIBUTARY	UNDERLING	URTICARIA	VIOLATION	WHIMSICAL
SUBLUNARY	SYNAGOGUE	THIGHBONE	TRICKSTER	UNDERMINE	UTTERANCE	VIRGINITY	WHIRLIGIG
SUBMARINE	SYNDICATE	THRALLDOM	TRIENNIAL	UNDERMOST	UTTERMOST	VISCOSITY	WHIRLPOOL
SUBNORMAL	SYNERGISM	THREEFOLD	TRIFOCALS	UNDERPART	VACCINATE	VISIONARY	WHIRLWIND
SUBSCRIBE	SYNTHESIS	THREESOME	TRIMESTER	UNDERPASS	VACILLATE	VISUALIZE	WHITEBAIT
SUBSCRIPT	SYNTHETIC	THRESHOLD	TRITURATE	UNDERPLAY	VAGARIOUS	VIVACIOUS	WHITEFISH
SUBSIDIZE	SYSTEMIZE	THROWAWAY	TRIWEEKLY	UNDERRATE	VAGINITIS	VOICELESS	WHITEHALL
SUBSTANCE	TABLELAND	THROWBACK	TROOPSHIP	UNDERSELL	VAINGLORY	VOLCANISM	WHITEHEAD
SUCCESSOR	TABLEWARE	THUMBNAIL	TROUSSEAU	UNDERSHOT	VALENTINE	VOLTMETER	WHITENESS
SUCCOTASH	TAILLIGHT	THUMBTACK	TRUCKLOAD	UNDERSIDE	VALUATION	VOLUNTARY	WHITETAIL
SUCCULENT	TALKATIVE	THYROXINE	TRUCULENT	UNDERTAKE	VANDALISM	VOLUNTEER	WHITEWALL
SUFFERING	TANGERINE	TIDEWATER	TRUNCHEON	UNDERTONE	VANDALIZE	VOODOOISM	WHITEWASH
SUFFOCATE	TANTALIZE	TIGHTROPE	TULAREMIA	UNDERWEAR	VAPORIZER	VORACIOUS	WHITEWOOD
SUFFRAGAN	TANZANIAN	TIMBERING	TURBOPROP	UNDERWOOD	VAPORWARE	VOUCHSAFE	WHOLESALE
SUGARCANE	TARANTULA	TIMEPIECE	TURBULENT	UNDOUBTED	VARIATION	VULCANISM	WHOLESOME
SUGARPLUM	TARPAULIN	TIMETABLE	TURNABOUT	UNEARTHLY	VARIEGATE	VULGARIAN	WHOSOEVER
SULFUROUS	TAUTOLOGY	TINDERBOX	TURNSTILE	UNEQUALED	VASECTOMY	VULGARISM	WILLPOWER
SUMMARIZE	TAXIDERMY	TOADSTOOL	TURNTABLE	UNFAILING	VASSALAGE	VULGARITY	WINDBLOWN
SUMMATION	TEAKETTLE	TOLERABLE	TURPITUDE	UNFEELING	VEGETABLE	VULGARIZE	WINDBREAK
SUMPTUOUS	TECHNICAL	TOLERANCE	TURQUOISE	UNFEIGNED	VEHEMENCE		WINDCHILL

WINDPROOF	BACKPEDAL	CAMPANILE	CAUCASIAN	HACKNEYED	LAUDATORY	MATUTINAL	PATRONIZE
WINDSTORM	BACKSLASH	CAMPSTOOL	CAUSATION	HAILSTONE	LAUNCHPAD	MAUSOLEUM	PAYMASTER
WINDSWEPT	BACKSLIDE	CANALBOAT	CAUTERIZE	HAILSTORM	LAVALIERE	MAYFLOWER	RABBINATE
WINEPRESS	BACKSTAGE	CANDIDACY	CAVALCADE	HAIRBRUSH	LAZYBONES	NAMEPLATE	RACEHORSE
WINTERIZE	BACKSWEPT	CANDIDATE	DACHSHUND	HAIRCLOTH	MACHINERY	NANOMETER	RACETRACK
WIREFRAME	BACKTRACK	CANDLEMAS	DAIRYMAID	HAIRPIECE	MACHINIST	NARCISSUS	RACIALISM
WISECRACK	BACKWATER	CANDLEPIN	DALMATION	HAIRSTYLE	MACINTOSH	NARCOTIZE	RACKETEER
WITHDRAWN	BACKWOODS	CANEBRAKE	DAMASCENE	HALFPENNY	MACROCOSM	NARRATIVE	RACONTEUR
WITHSTAND	BACTERIUM	CANNONADE	DAMNATION	HALITOSIS	MAELSTROM	NATURALLY	RADIOGRAM
WITTICISM	BADMINTON	CANNONEER	DAMSELFLY	HALLOWEEN	MAGISTRAL	NAVIGABLE	RADIOLOGY
WOEBEGONE	BAGATELLE	CANONICAL	DANDELION	HAMADRYAD	MAGNESIUM	PACEMAKER	RAGPICKER
WOLFHOUND	BAILIWICK	CANTABILE	DANGEROUS	HAMBURGER	MAGNETISM	PACHYDERM	RAINSPOUT
WOLFSBANE	BAKSHEESH	CANTHARIS	DAREDEVIL	HAMMERTOE	MAGNETITE	PACKHORSE	RAINSTORM
WOLVERINE	BALALAIKA	CAPACIOUS	DARWINISM	HAMSTRING	MAGNETIZE	PAGEMAKER	RAINWATER
WOMANHOOD	BALDACHIN	CAPACITOR	DASHBOARD	HANDCLASP	MAGNIFICO	PAKISTANI	RANCHLAND
WOMANKIND	BALLADEER	CAPARISON	DAUNTLESS	HANDCRAFT	MAGNITUDE	PALAESTRA	RANDOMIZE
WOMANLIKE	BALLERINA	CAPILLARY	DAVENPORT	HANDIWORK	MAHARISHI	PALANQUIN	RANGELAND
WOMENFOLK	BAMBOOZLE	CAPITALLY	EARTHLING	HANDSHAKE	MAINFRAME	PALATABLE	RAPACIOUS
WONDERFUL	BANDEROLE	CAPRICCIO	EARTHWARD	HANDSPIKE	MAJORDOMO	PALLADIUM	RASPBERRY
WOODBLOCK	BANDOLIER	CAPSULATE	EARTHWORK	HANDSTAND	MAJORETTE	PALMISTRY	RASTERIZE
WOODCHUCK	BANDSTAND	CAPTIVATE	EARTHWORM	HANDWOVEN	MAJUSCULE	PALPITATE	RATIONALE
WOODCRAFT	BANDWAGON	CARBONATE	EASYGOING	HAPHAZARD	MAKESHIFT	PANEGYRIC	RAUWOLFIA
WORKBENCH	BANDWIDTH	CARBUNCLE	EAVESDROP	HAPPENING	MALACHITE	PANHANDLE	SACCHARIN
WORKGROUP	BANQUETTE	CARBURIZE	FABRICATE	HAPPINESS	MALADROIT	PANTHEISM	SACKCLOTH
WORKHORSE	BANTUSTAN	CARCINOMA	FACETIOUS	HARBINGER	MALATHION	PANTOMIME	SACRAMENT
WORKHOUSE	BARBARIAN	CARDBOARD	FACSIMILE	HARBORAGE	MALAYSIAN	PAPERBACK	SACRIFICE
WORKPLACE	BARBARISM	CARETAKER	FACTORIAL	HARDBOARD	MALIGNANT	PAPILLOTE	SACRILEGE
WORKTABLE	BARBAROUS	CARIBBEAN	FAIRYLAND	HARDBOUND	MALLEABLE	PARACHUTE	SACRISTAN
WORLDLING	BARCAROLE	CARNATION	FALSEHOOD	HARDCOVER	MANDATORY	PARAGRAPH	SADDLEBOW
WORLDWIDE	BAREFACED	CARNELIAN	FANCYWORK	HARDIHOOD	MANGANESE	PARALYSIS	SAFEGUARD
WORRISOME	BARKEEPER	CARNIVORA	FANTASIZE	HARDSTAND	MANHANDLE	PARAMETER	SAFFLOWER
WORRYWART	BARNSTORM	CARNIVORE	FANTASTIC	HARLEQUIN	MANHATTAN	PARAMOUNT	SAGACIOUS
WORTHLESS	BAROGRAPH	CARPENTER	FARMHOUSE	HARMONICA	MANIFESTO	PARATHION	SAGEBRUSH
WRESTLING	BAROMETER	CARPETBAG	FARMSTEAD	HARMONICS	MANNEQUIN	PARCHMENT	SAILCLOTH
WRISTBAND	BARRACUDA	CARPETING	FARSEEING	HARMONIUM	MANNERISM	PAREGORIC	SAILPLANE
WRONGDOER	BARRICADE	CARROUSEL	FASCINATE	HARMONIZE	MANOEUVRE	PAROCHIAL	SALACIOUS
XANTHIPPE	BARRISTER	CARTILAGE	FASTENING	HARTSHORN	MANOMETER	PARQUETRY	SALESGIRL
XEROPHYTE	BARTENDER	CARTRIDGE	FAVORABLE	HATCHMENT	MANSLAYER	PARRICIDE	SALTPETER
XYLOPHONE	BASEBOARD	CARTWHEEL	GABARDINE	HAVERSACK	MARGARINE	PARSIMONY	SALTWATER
YACHTSMAN	BASTINADO	CASSEROLE	GABERDINE	JACARANDA	MARIJUANA	PARSONAGE	SALVATION
YARDSTICK	BATHHOUSE	CASSOWARY	GALACTOSE	JACKKNIFE	MARMALADE	PARTITION	SANCTUARY
YESTERDAY	BATHOLITH	CASTANETS	GALLANTRY	JACKSCREW	MARMOREAL	PARTITIVE	SANDBLAST
YOUNGLING	BATTALION	CASTIGATE	GALLINULE	JACKSTRAW	MARQUETRY	PARTRIDGE	SANDPAPER
YOUNGSTER	CABLEGRAM	CASUISTRY	GALLIVANT	JAILBREAK	MARSUPIAL	PASSENGER	SANDPIPER
YTTERBIUM	CABRIOLET	CATACLYSM	GALLSTONE	JAUNDICED	MARTYRDOM	PASSERINE	SANDSTONE
ZEITGEIST	CACOPHONY	CATALEPSY	GALVANISM	LABORIOUS	MARVELOUS	PASTORALE	SANDSTORM
ZIRCONIUM	CAFETERIA	CATALYSIS	GALVANIZE	LABYRINTH	MASCULINE	PASTURAGE	SANGFROID
ZUCCHETTO	CALABOOSE	CATAMARAN	GANGPLANK	LACCOLITH	MASOCHISM	PATCHWORK	SAPSUCKER
ZWINGLIAN	CALCIMINE	CATAMOUNT	GARNISHEE	LAGNIAPPE	MASTERFUL	PATERNITY	SARTORIAL
	CALCULATE	CATATONIC	GARNITURE	LAMEBRAIN	MASTICATE	PATHOLOGY	SATINWOOD
	CALENDULA	CATCHMENT	GARRULOUS	LAMINATED	MATCHBOOK	PATRIARCH	SATURNINE
	CALIBRATE	CATCHWORD	GASTRITIS	LANDOWNER	MATCHLOCK	PATRICIAN	SAXIFRAGE
2ND LETTER	CALLOSITY	CATECHISM	GASTROPOD	LANDSCAPE	MATCHWOOD	PATRICIDE	SASSAFRAS
	CALORIFIC	CATERWAUL	GAUCHERIE	LANDSLIDE	MATERNITY	PATRIMONY	SATELLITE
BACCHANAL	CALVINISM	CATHARSIS	GAZETTEER	LANTHANUM	MATRIARCH	PATRISTIC	SAXOPHONE
BACKBOARD	CAMELBACK	CATHARTIC	HABITABLE	LASSITUDE	MATRICIDE	PATROLMAN	TABLELAND
BACKFIELD	CAMEMBERT	CATHEDRAL	HABITUATE	LATECOMER	MATRIMONY	PATRONAGE	TABLEWARE

TAILLIGHT	ABOMINATE	SCULPTURE	CELEBRITY	DEMAGOGUE	GENERATOR	LEITMOTIV	NEPHRITIS
TALKATIVE	ABORIGINE	SCUTCHEON	CELESTIAL	DEMARCATE	GENITALIA	LEUKOCYTE	NEPTUNIUM
TANGERINE	ABSORBENT	ADDICTION	CELLARAGE	DEMIMONDE	GENTILITY	LEVIATHAN	NEURALGIA
TANTALIZE	EBULLIENT	ADDRESSEE	CELLULOSE	DEMITASSE	GENTLEMAN	MEANWHILE	NEUROLOGY
TANZANIAN	OBBLIGATO	ADIABATIC	CENTENARY	DEMOCRACY	GENUFLECT	MECHANICS	NEVERMORE
TARANTULA	OBEISANCE	ADJECTIVE	CENTESIMO	DEMULCENT	GEOGRAPHY	MECHANISM	NEWSPAPER
TARPAULIN	OBFUSCATE	ADJOINING	CENTIGRAM	DEMURRAGE	GERIATRIC	MECHANIZE	NEWSPRINT
TAUTOLOGY	OBJECTIFY	ADMIRABLE	CENTIPEDE	DENIGRATE	GERMANIUM	MEDALLION	NEWSSTAND
TAXIDERMY	OBJECTIVE	ADMIRALTY	CENTURION	DENTITION	GERMICIDE	MEDICABLE	PEACETIME
VACCINATE	OBJURGATE	ADMISSION	CEREBRATE	DEODORANT	GERMINATE	MEDICINAL	PECUNIARY
VACILLATE	OBLIVIOUS	ADMIXTURE	CERECLOTH	DEODORIZE	GESTATION	MEGACYCLE	PEDAGOGUE
VAGARIOUS	OBNOXIOUS	ADSORBATE	CERTAINTY	DEOXIDIZE	HEADBOARD	MEGADEATH	PEDOMETER
VAGINITIS	OBSERVANT	ADSORBENT	CERTITUDE	DEPARTURE	HEADDRESS	MEGAHERTZ	PEGMATITE
VAINGLORY	OBSESSION	ADUMBRATE	CESSATION	DEPENDENT	HEADFIRST	MEGAPHONE	PEKINGESE
VALENTINE	OBSTINATE	ADVANTAGE	DEATHBLOW	DEPRECATE	HEADLIGHT	MEGAPIXEL	PENDULOUS
VALUATION	ACCESSION	ADVENTURE	DEATHLESS	DEPRESSED	HEADPHONE	MELIORATE	PENEPLAIN
VANDALISM	ACCESSORY	ADVERSARY	DEBENTURE	DERRINGER	HEADPIECE	MELODIOUS	PENETRATE
VANDALIZE	ACCIDENCE	ADVERSITY	DEBUTANTE	DESCENDER	HEADSTALL	MELODRAMA	PENHOLDER
VAPORIZER	ACCLIMATE	ADVERTISE	DECADENCE	DESECRATE	HEADSTONE	MELTWATER	PENINSULA
VAPORWARE	ACCLIVITY	ADVISABLE	DECALOGUE	DESICCANT	HEADWATER	MEMORABLE	PENTECOST
VARIATION	ACCOMPANY	EDELWEISS	DECATHLON	DESICCATE	HEALTHFUL	MENAGERIE	PENTHOUSE
VARIEGATE	ACCORDION	EDITORIAL	DECEITFUL	DESIGNATE	HEARTACHE	MENDICANT	PENURIOUS
VASECTOMY	ACCRETION	EDUCATION	DECENNIAL	DESIGNING	HEARTBEAT	MENOPAUSE	PERCHANCE
VASSALAGE	ACETYLENE	IDENTICAL	DECEPTION	DESIRABLE	HEARTBURN	MENTALITY	PERCOLATE
WAGONETTE	ACIDULATE	AERIALIST	DECIDUOUS	DESPERADO	HEARTFELT	MERCENARY	PERDITION
WAISTBAND	ACIDULOUS	AERODROME	DECILITER	DESPERATE	HEARTLESS	MERCERIZE	PERENNIAL
WAISTCOAT	ACOUSTICS	AEROPAUSE	DECIMETER	DESTITUTE	HEARTSICK	MERCURIAL	PERFORATE
WAISTLINE	ACQUIESCE	AEROPLANE	DECISTERE	DESTROYER	HEARTWOOD	MERCUROUS	PERFUMERY
WALLBOARD	ACROPOLIS	AEROSPACE	DECLIVITY	DESUETUDE	HECTOGRAM	MERGANSER	PERIMETER
WALLOPING	ECCENTRIC	AESTHETIC	DECOLLETE	DESULTORY	HELLEBORE	MERRIMENT	PERIPHERY
WALLPAPER	ECONOMICS	AESTIVATE	DECOMPOSE	DETECTIVE	HELLENISM	MESCALINE	PERISCOPE
WARBONNET	ECONOMIZE	BEACHHEAD	DECONTROL	DETENTION	HELVETIAN	MESMERIZE	PERISTYLE
WAREHOUSE	ECOSYSTEM	BEATITUDE	DECORATOR	DETERGENT	HELVETICA	MESSENGER	PERMANENT
WARMONGER	ICELANDER	BEAUTEOUS	DECOUPAGE	DETERMINE	HEMISTICH	MESSIEURS	PERMEABLE
WASHBASIN	ICELANDIC	BEAUTIFUL	DECREMENT	DETERRENT	HEMSTITCH	METALWARE	PERPETUAL
WASHBOARD	OCCULTISM	BEDFELLOW	DEDUCTION	DETONATOR	HEPATITIS	METALWORK	PERPLEXED
WASHCLOTH	OCCUPANCY	BEDRIDDEN	DEFEATISM	DETRIMENT	HERBALIST	METEORITE	PERSECUTE
WASHHOUSE	SCANTLING	BEDSPREAD	DEFECTIVE	DEUTERIUM	HERBARIUM	METEOROID	PERSEVERE
WASHSTAND	SCAPEGOAT	BEEFEATER	DEFENDANT	DEVASTATE	HERBICIDE	METHADONE	PERSIMMON
WASHWOMAN	SCARECROW	BEEFSTEAK	DEFENSIVE	DEVILMENT	HERCULEAN	METHODIST	PERSONAGE
WASTELAND	SCAVENGER	BEEKEEPER	DEFERENCE	DEXTERITY	HEREAFTER	METHODIZE	PERSONATE
WATCHBAND	SCHEELITE	BELEAGUER	DEFERMENT	DEXTEROUS	HEREUNDER	METRICIZE	PERSONIFY
WATCHCASE	SCHEMATIC	BELLICOSE	DEFICIENT	FEBRIFUGE	HERITABLE	METROLOGY	PERSONNEL
WATCHWORD	SCHILLING	BELLYACHE	DEFLATION	FECUNDATE	HERMITAGE	METRONOME	PERTINENT
WATERFALL	SCHLEMIEL	BELVEDERE	DEFOLIANT	FEEDSTOCK	HETERODOX	MEZZANINE	PESSIMISM
WATERFOWL	SCHNAUZER	BENIGHTED	DEFOLIATE	FEEDSTUFF	HEURISTIC	NECESSARY	PESTHOUSE
WATERLINE	SCHOOLBOY	BENIGNANT	DEFORMITY	FELLOWMAN	HEXAMETER	NECESSITY	PESTICIDE
WATERMARK	SCINTILLA	BENTONITE	DEHYDRATE	FEROCIOUS	JELLYFISH	NECROLOGY	PESTILENT
WATERSHED	SCLEROSIS	BERKELIUM	DEJECTION	FERRYBOAT	JERKWATER	NECTARINE	PETROLEUM
WATERSIDE	SCOUNDREL	BERYLLIUM	DEKALITER	FERTILIZE	JESSAMINE	NEFARIOUS	PETROLOGY
WAVETABLE	SCRAPBOOK	BESETTING	DEKAMETER	FESTIVITY	JEWELWEED	NEGLIGENT	PETTICOAT
XANTHIPPE	SCREENING	BESPANGLE	DEKASTERE	FETISHISM	LEAFSTALK	NEGOTIANT	REACTANCE
YACHTSMAN	SCREWBALL	BESPATTER	DELFTWARE	FEUDALISM	LEASEHOLD	NEGOTIATE	REBELLION
YARDSTICK	SCRIMMAGE	BETROTHED	DELICIOUS	FEUDATORY	LEASTWISE	NEGRITUDE	RECEPTION
ABANDONED	SCRIMSHAW	CEASELESS	DELIGHTED	GEARSHIFT	LEAVENING	NEODYMIUM	RECEPTIVE
ABATEMENT	SCRIPTURE	CELANDINE	DELIMETER	GELIGNITE	LEGENDARY	NEOLOGISM	RECESSION
ABHORRENT	SCRIVENER	CELEBRATE	DELINEATE	GENEALOGY	LEGISLATE	NEPHRITIC	RECESSIVE

RECHERCHE	REPRIMAND	SENIORITY	VERMIFORM	CHARABANC	SHAREWARE	WHITEHALL	DIPLOMACY
RECIPIENT	REPROBATE	SENSATION	VERMIFUGE	CHARACTER	SHARKSKIN	WHITEHEAD	DIPTEROUS
RECKONING	REPRODUCE	SENSITIVE	VERMILION	CHARLATAN	SHEATHING	WHITENESS	DIRECTION
RECOGNIZE	REPUDIATE	SENSITIZE	VERNALIZE	CHARWOMAN	SHEEPFOLD	WHITETAIL	DIRECTIVE
RECOLLECT	REPUGNANT	SENTIMENT	VERSATILE	CHAUFFEUR	SHEEPSKIN	WHITEWALL	DIRECTORY
RECOMMEND	REPULSION	SEPARABLE	VERTEBRAL	CHECKBOOK	SHELLFIRE	WHITEWASH	DIRIGIBLE
RECONCILE	REPULSIVE	SEPARATOR	VESTIBULE	CHECKLIST	SHELLFISH	WHITEWOOD	DISAFFECT
RECONDITE	REPUTABLE	SEPTEMBER	VESTRYMAN	CHECKMATE	SHIFTLESS	WHOLESALE	DISAPPEAR
RECORDING	REQUISITE	SEPULCHER	VEXATIOUS	CHECKROOM	SHIPBOARD	WHOLESOME	DISBURDEN
RECORDIST	RESECTION	SEPULTURE	WEARISOME	CHEEKBONE	SHIPSHAPE	WHOSOEVER	DISCHARGE
RECTANGLE	RESERPINE	SEQUESTER	WEDNESDAY	CHEERLESS	SHIPWRECK	AILANTHUS	DISCOMFIT
RECTIFIER	RESERVIST	SERIGRAPH	XEROPHYTE	CHEMISTRY	SHOEMAKER	AIRMOBILE	DISCOURSE
RECTITUDE	RESERVOIR	SERVITUDE	YESTERDAY	CHEVALIER	SHOREBIRD	AIRWORTHY	DISCREDIT
RECUMBENT	RESHUFFLE	SEVENTEEN	ZEITGEIST	CHICANERY	SHORTCAKE	BICAMERAL	DISEMBARK
RECURSION	RESIDENCE	TEAKETTLE	AFFECTING	CHICKADEE	SHORTHAND	BICONCAVE	DISEMBODY
REDACTION	RESIDENCY	TECHNICAL	AFFECTION	CHICKASAW	SHORTHORN	BIFURCATE	DISENGAGE
REDBREAST	RESIDUARY	TECHNIQUE	AFFIDAVIT	CHICKWEED	SHORTSTOP	BILATERAL	DISESTEEM
REDUCTION	RESISTANT	TECTONICS	AFFILIATE	CHIEFTAIN	SHORTWAVE	BILINGUAL	DISFIGURE
REDUNDANT	RESONANCE	TECTONISM	AFFLUENCE	CHILBLAIN	SHOWPIECE	BILLBOARD	DISHCLOTH
REENFORCE	RESONATOR	TELEGENIC	AFORESAID	CHILDHOOD	SHOWPLACE	BILLIARDS	DISHONEST
REENTRANT	RESTRAINT	TELEGRAPH	AFRIKAANS	CHIROPODY	SHRINKAGE	BIMONTHLY	DISHWATER
REFECTION	RESURRECT	TELEMETER	AFTERCARE	CHIVALRIC	SHRUBBERY	BINOCULAR	DISINFECT
REFECTORY	RETALIATE	TELEPATHY	AFTERDECK	CHLORDANE	THANKLESS	BINOMINAL	DISLOCATE
REFERENCE	RETARDATE	TELEPHONE	AFTERGLOW	CHOCOLATE	THEATRICS	BIOGRAPHY	DISMANTLE
REFLECTOR	RETENTION	TELEPHONY	AFTERLIFE	CHONDRITE	THEOCRACY	BIOSPHERE	DISMEMBER
REFLEXIVE	RETENTIVE	TELEPHOTO	AFTERMATH	CHONDRULE	THEOSOPHY	BIPARTITE	DISOBLIGE
REFRACTOR	RETRIEVER	TELESCOPE	AFTERNOON	CHOPHOUSE	THEREFORE	BIRDHOUSE	DISORIENT
REFURBISH	RETROFIRE	TELLURIUM	AFTERWARD	CHOPSTICK	THEREFROM	BIRTHMARK	DISPARAGE
REGARDING	REVERENCE	TEMPERATE	EFFECTIVE	CHORISTER	THEREUNTO	BIRTHRATE	DISPARATE
REGISTRAR	REVERSION	TEMPORARY	EFFECTUAL	CHRISTIAN	THEREUPON	BISHOPRIC	DISPLEASE
REHEARING	REVOCABLE	TEMPORIZE	EFFICIENT	CHRISTMAS	THEREWITH	CIGARETTE	DISPRAISE
REHEARSAL	REVOLTING	TENACIOUS	EFFLUENCE	CHROMATIC	THESAURUS	CIGARILLO	DISPUTANT
REIMBURSE	REVULSION	TENDERIZE	EFFLUVIUM	CHRONICLE	THICKNESS	CIRCADIAN	DISREGARD
REINFORCE	SEAFARING	TENEBROUS	OFFENSIVE	CHRYSALIS	THIGHBONE	CIRCUITRY	DISREPAIR
REINSTATE	SEASONING	TENTATIVE	OFFERTORY	CHUCKHOLE	THRALLDOM	CIRCULATE	DISREPUTE
REITERATE	SEAWORTHY	TERMAGANT	OFFICIANT	CHURCHMAN	THREEFOLD	CIRRHOSIS	DISSECTED
REJOINDER	SEBACEOUS	TERMINATE	OFFICIATE	DHRYSTONE	THREESOME	CITIZENRY	DISSEMBLE
RELEVANCE	SECESSION	TERRARIUM	OFFICIOUS	PHALAROPE	THRESHOLD	DIACRITIC	DISSENTER
RELEVANCY	SECLUSION	TERRITORY	OFFSPRING	PHEROMONE	THROWAWAY	DIAERESIS	DISSIDENT
RELIGIOUS	SECONDARY	TERRORISM	AGGRAVATE	PHILANDER	THROWBACK	DIAGNOSIS	DISSIPATE
RELIQUARY	SECRETARY	TERRORIZE	AGGREGATE	PHILATELY	THUMBNAIL	DIALECTIC	DISSOLUTE
RELUCTANT	SECRETION	TESTAMENT	AGREEABLE	PHILIPPIC	THUMBTACK	DIAMETRIC	DISTEMPER
REMAINDER	SECRETIVE	TESTIMONY	AGREEMENT	PHILOLOGY	THYROXINE	DIAPHRAGM	DISTURBED
REMINISCE	SECTARIAN	VEGETABLE	EGGBEATER	PHLEBITIS	WHALEBOAT	DIATHERMY	DITHERING
REMISSION	SECTIONAL	VEHEMENCE	EGLANTINE	PHONETICS	WHALEBONE	DIATOMITE	DIVERSIFY
RENCONTRE	SEDENTARY	VELVETEEN	EGREGIOUS	PHONOLOGY	WHEELBASE	DICHOTOMY	DIVERSION
RENDITION	SEGREGATE	VENERABLE	IGNORANCE	PHOSPHATE	WHEREFORE	DIETETICS	DIVERSITY
REPAIRMAN	SELECTION	VENGEANCE	CHAFFINCH	PHOTOCELL	WHEREUPON	DIFFERENT	DIVISIBLE
REPELLENT	SELECTMAN	VENIREMAN	CHALKBORD	PHOTOCOPY	WHEREWITH	DIFFICULT	DIXIELAND
REPERTORY	SEMANTICS	VENTILATE	CHALLENGE	PHOTOPLAY	WHETSTONE	DIFFIDENT	EIDERDOWN
REPLENISH	SEMAPHORE	VENTRICLE	CHAMELEON	PHRENETIC	WHICHEVER	DIGITALIS	FIDUCIARY
REPLETION	SEMBLANCE	VENTUROUS	CHAMOMILE	PHYSICIAN	WHIMSICAL	DIGITIZED	FILMSTRIP
REPLICATE	SEMICOLON	VERACIOUS	CHAMPAGNE	PHYSICIST	WHIRLIGIG	DIGNIFIED	FINANCIAL
REPORTAGE	SEMIFINAL	VERBALIZE	CHAMPAIGN	RHEOMETER	WHIRLPOOL	DIGNITARY	FINANCIER
REPOSSESS	SEMIFLUID	VERDIGRIS	CHANCROID	SHADOWBOX	WHIRLWIND	DIMENSION	FINGERING
REPREHEND	SEMILUNAR	VERIDICAL	CHANTEUSE	SHAKEDOWN	WHITEBAIT	DIMORPHIC	FINGERTIP
REPRESENT	SEMIWORKS	VERITABLE	CHAPARRAL	SHAPELESS	WHITEFISH	DIPHTHONG	FINICKING

FIREBRAND	LIVERYMAN	PINEAPPLE	VISUALIZE	BLOODBATH	GLADIOLUS	EMERGENCY	ANIMALISM
FIREBREAK	LIVESTOCK	PINSTRIPE	VIVACIOUS	BLOODLINE	GLADSTONE	EMOLLIENT	ANIMATION
FIREBRICK	MICROCOPY	PIROUETTE	WILLPOWER	BLOODROOT	GLAMORIZE	EMOLUMENT	ANIMOSITY
FIREHOUSE	MICROCOSM	PISTACHIO	WINDBLOWN	BLOODSHED	GLEANINGS	EMPENNAGE	ANKLEBONE
FIREPLACE	MICROFILM	PITCHFORK	WINDBREAK	BLOODSHOT	GLENGARRY	EMPHASIZE	ANNOUNCER
FIREPOWER	MICROGRAM	PITUITARY	WINDCHILL	BLOWTORCH	GLISSANDO	EMPHYSEMA	ANNOYANCE
FIREPROOF	MICROSOFT	PIZZICATO	WINDPROOF	BLUEBERRY	GLUTINOUS	EMPIRICAL	ANNUITANT
FIREWATER	MICROWAVE	RIDGEPOLE	WINDSTORM	BLUEBLACK	GLYCOSIDE	IMAGINARY	ANOMALOUS
FIRMAMENT	MIDDLEMAN	RIGHTEOUS	WINDSWEPT	BLUEGRASS	ILLEGIBLE	IMBALANCE	ANONYMOUS
FIRSTBORN	MIDSTREAM	RIGMAROLE	WINEPRESS	BLUEPOINT	ILLIBERAL	IMBROGLIO	ANOPHELES
FIRSTHAND	MIDSUMMER	RIVERBANK	WINTERIZE	BLUEPRINT	ILLOGICAL	IMITATION	ANTARCTIC
FIRSTLING	MIDWINTER	RIVERBOAT	WIREFRAME	CLAMSHELL	OLFACTORY	IMITATIVE	ANTECHOIR
FISHERMAN	MILESTONE	RIVERSIDE	WISECRACK	CLAPBOARD	OLIGARCHY	IMMEDIACY	ANTHOLOGY
GIBBERISH	MILLIGRAM	SIDEBOARD	WITHDRAWN	CLASSICAL	PLACEKICK	IMMEDIATE	ANTICLINE
GIMMICKRY	MILLINERY	SIDEBURNS	WITHSTAND	CLASSMATE	PLACEMENT	IMMIGRANT	ANTIKNOCK
HIBERNATE	MILLIPEDE	SIDEPIECE	WITTICISM	CLASSROOM	PLAINTIFF	IMMIGRATE	ANTINOVEL
HIDEBOUND	MILLIVOLT	SIDESWIPE	ZIRCONIUM	CLEARANCE	PLAINTIVE	IMMOVABLE	ANTIPASTO
HIERARCHY	MILLSTONE	SIDETRACK	EJACULATE	CLERGYMAN	PLANELOAD	IMMUTABLE	ANTIPATHY
HIGHLIGHT	MINCEMEAT	SIGNALIZE	SKIMOBILE	CLIENTELE	PLANETOID	IMPARTIAL	ANTIQUARY
HILARIOUS	MINELAYER	SIGNALMAN	SKINFLINT	CLINICIAN	PLATITUDE	IMPASSIVE	ANTIQUITY
HILLBILLY	MINIATURE	SIGNATORY	SKINTIGHT	CLIPBOARD	PLAUSIBLE	IMPATIENS	ANTISERUM
HINDRANCE	MINISCULE	SIGNATURE	SKYDIVING	CLIPSHEET	PLAYHOUSE	IMPATIENT	ANTITOXIN
HINDSIGHT	MINISKIRT	SIGNBOARD	SKYJACKER	CLOCKWISE	PLAYTHING	IMPEDANCE	ANTITUMOR
HISTAMINE	MINISTATE	SILICEOUS	SKYLOUNGE	CLOCKWORK	PLENITUDE	IMPERFECT	ANTIVENIN
HISTOGRAM	MINUSCULE	SILICOSIS	SKYROCKET	CLOISONNE	PLENTEOUS	IMPERIOUS	ENCHILADA
HISTORIAN	MINUTEMAN	SILTSTONE	UKRAINIAN	CLUBHOUSE	PLENTIFUL	IMPETUOUS	ENCOMPASS
HITCHHIKE	MISBEHAVE	SIMPATICO	ALABASTER	ELABORATE	PLOWSHARE	IMPLEMENT	ENCOUNTER
JINRIKSHA	MISCHANCE	SIMPLETON	ALBATROSS	ELASTOMER	PLURALITY	IMPLICATE	ENCOURAGE
JITTERBUG	MISCREANT	SINGLETON	ALCOHOLIC	ELBOWROOM	PLURALIZE	IMPOLITIC	ENDOCRINE
KICKSTAND	MISDIRECT	SINUSITIS	ALEATORIC	ELECTRIFY	PLUTONIUM	IMPORTANT	ENDOSCOPE
KILOCYCLE	MISERABLE	SITUATION	ALGONQUIN	ELECTRODE	SLAUGHTER	IMPORTUNE	ENDURANCE
KILOHERTZ	MISGIVING	TIDEWATER	ALGORITHM	ELEVATION	SLINGSHOT	IMPOSTURE	ENERGETIC
KILOLITER	MISGOVERN	TIGHTROPE	ALIENABLE	ELIMINATE	SLUICEWAY	IMPRECATE	ENERGIZER
KILOMETER	MISHANDLE	TIMBERING	ALLERGIST	ELLIPSOID	ULTIMATUM	IMPRECISE	ENGRAVING
KINESCOPE	MISINFORM	TIMEPIECE	ALLEVIATE	ELOCUTION	ULTRAHIGH	IMPROMPTU	ENIGMATIC
KINSWOMAN	MISMANAGE	TIMETABLE	ALLIGATOR	ELSEWHERE	ULTRAPURE	IMPROVISE	ENLIGHTEN
LIABILITY	MISORIENT	TINDERBOX	ALLOWANCE	ELUCIDATE	AMARYLLIS	IMPRUDENT	ENRAPTURE
LIBERTINE	MISSILERY	VIBRATION	ALMANDITE	FLAGELLUM	AMBERGRIS	IMPULSION	ENSHEATHE
LIBRARIAN	MISSIONER	VIBRATORY	ALMSHOUSE	FLAGEOLET	AMBIGUOUS	IMPULSIVE	ENTERITIS
LIFEBLOOD	MISTLETOE	VICARIOUS	ALONGSIDE	FLAGSTAFF	AMBITIOUS	OMBUDSMAN	ENTERTAIN
LIFEGUARD	NICOTINIC	VICENNIAL	ALTERNATE	FLAGSTONE	AMBULANCE	SMALLTALK	ENTOURAGE
LIGHTFACE	NIGHTCLUB	VICEREGAL	ALTIMETER	FLAMMABLE	AMBUSCADE	UMBILICUS	ENUMERATE
LIGHTNING	NIGHTFALL	VICTIMIZE	ALUMINIUM	FLASHBACK	AMENDMENT	ANAEROBIC	ENUNCIATE
LIGHTSHIP	NIGHTGOWN	VICTORIAN	ALUMINIZE	FLASHBULB	AMERICANA	ANALGESIA	ENWREATHE
LIGHTSOME	NIGHTHAWK	VICTUALER	BLACKBALL	FLASHCUBE	AMERICIUM	ANALGESIC	INABILITY
LIMBURGER	NIGHTLIFE	VIDELICET	BLACKBIRD	FLASHTUBE	AMIDSHIPS	ANALOGOUS	INAMORATA
LIMELIGHT	NIGHTMARE	VIDEOTAPE	BLACKBODY	FLATULENT	AMORPHOUS	ANARCHISM	INANIMATE
LIMESTONE	NIGHTTIME	VIEWPOINT	BLACKFOOT	FLAVORING	AMPERSAND	ANATOMIZE	INANITION
LIMOUSINE	NIGRITUDE	VIGESIMAL	BLACKHEAD	FLEDGLING	AMPHIBIAN	ANCHORAGE	INAUGURAL
LINEAMENT	PICKABACK	VIGILANCE	BLACKJACK	FLINTLOCK	AMPHIBOLE	ANCHORITE	INCAPABLE
LIQUIDATE	PICTORIAL	VIGILANTE	BLACKLIST	FLOODGATE	AMPLITUDE	ANCHORMAN	INCARNATE
LITERATIM	PIECEMEAL	VILLENAGE	BLACKMAIL	FLOPHOUSE	EMBARRASS	ANCILLARY	INCENTIVE
LITHESOME	PIECEWORK	VINDICATE	BLASPHEME	FLOTATION	EMBAYMENT	ANGELFISH	INCEPTION
LITHOLOGY	PIGGYBACK	VIOLATION	BLASPHEMY	FLOWCHART	EMBELLISH	ANGLEWORM	INCESSANT
LITIGIOUS	PIGHEADED	VIRGINITY	BLEACHERS	FLOWERPOT	EMBRASURE	ANGLICIZE	INCIDENCE
LITTERBUG	PIKESTAFF	VISCOSITY	BLINDFOLD	FLUCTUATE	EMBROCATE	ANGUISHED	INCIPIENT
LIVERWORT	PIMPERNEL	VISIONARY	BLOCKHEAD	GLADIATOR	EMBROIDER	ANHYDROUS	INCLEMENT

INCOGNITO	INSINCERE	INVERNESS	UNDERWEAR	BOUNTEOUS	CONDIMENT	COUNTLESS	FORWARDER
INCOMMODE	INSINUATE	INVERSION	UNDERWOOD	BOUNTIFUL	CONDITION	COURTEOUS	FOUNDLING
INCORRECT	INSISTENT	INVIDIOUS	UNDOUBTED	BOURGEOIS	CONDUCTOR	COURTESAN	FOURSCORE
INCREMENT	INSOLUBLE	INVIOLATE	UNEARTHLY	BOWSTRING	CONESTOGA	COURTROOM	GODFATHER
INCUBATOR	INSOLVENT	INVISIBLE	UNEQUALED	COADJUTOR	CONFESSOR	COURTSHIP	GODMOTHER
INCULCATE	INSTANTER	INVOLUCRE	UNFAILING	COAGULANT	CONFIDANT	COURTYARD	GODPARENT
INCULPATE	INSTANTLY	KNOCKDOWN	UNFEELING	COAGULATE	CONFUSION	COUTURIER	GOLDBRICK
INCUMBENT	INSTIGATE	KNOWLEDGE	UNFEIGNED	COALFIELD	CONGENIAL	COVALENCE	GOLDENROD
INCURABLE	INSTITUTE	ONIONSKIN	UNFLEDGED	COALITION	CONGERIES	DOBSONFLY	GOLDFIELD
INCURIOUS	INSURABLE	ONSLAUGHT	UNFOUNDED	COASTLINE	CONGRUITY	DOCTORATE	GOLDFINCH
INCURSION	INSURANCE	PNEUMATIC	UNGUARDED	COCHINEAL	CONJUGATE	DOGMATISM	GOLDSMITH
INDELIBLE	INSURGENT	PNEUMONIA	UNHARNESS	COCKATIEL	CONNUBIAL	DOMINANCE	GONDOLIER
INDEMNIFY	INTEGRATE	SNAKEBIRD	UNHEALTHY	COCKFIGHT	CONSCIOUS	DOORPLATE	GONORRHEA
INDEMNITY	INTEGRITY	SNAKEBITE	UNISEXUAL	COCKROACH	CONSCRIPT	DORMITORY	GOVERNESS
INDENTION	INTELLECT	SNOWDRIFT	UNITARIAN	COFEATURE	CONSENSUS	DOSIMETER	HOARFROST
INDENTURE	INTENDANT	SNOWFIELD	UNIVALENT	COFFEEPOT	CONSONANT	DOUBTLESS	HOBGOBLIN
INDIGNANT	INTENSIFY	SNOWFLAKE	UNIVERSAL	COFFERDAM	CONSTABLE	DOWITCHER	HOLLYHOCK
INDIGNITY	INTENSITY	SNOWSTORM	UNKNOWING	COGNITION	CONSTANCY	DOWNGRADE	HOLOCAUST
INDUCTION	INTENSIVE	UNADVISED	UNLEARNED	COIFFEUSE	CONSTRAIN	DOWNRANGE	HOLOGRAPH
INDUCTIVE	INTENTION	UNALIGNED	UNMEANING	COLLATION	CONSTRICT	DOWNRIGHT	HOLYSTONE
INEBRIATE	INTERCEDE	UNALLOYED	UNMINDFUL	COLLEAGUE	CONSTRUCT	DOWNSHIFT	HOMEGROWN
INEFFABLE	INTERCEPT	UNANIMOUS	UNNATURAL	COLLEGIAN	CONTAGION	DOWNSTAGE	HOMEMAKER
INELEGANT	INTERDICT	UNBEKNOWN	UNPLUMBED	COLLEGIUM	CONTAINER	DOWNSWING	HOMESTEAD
INFANTILE	INTERFACE	UNBENDING	UNPOPULAR	COLLIMATE	CONTENTED	FOLLOWING	HOMOGRAPH
INFATUATE	INTERFERE	UNBLESSED	UNRIVALED	COLLODION	CONTINENT	FOODSTUFF	HOMOPHONE
INFECTION	INTERFUSE	UNBOUNDED	UNRUFFLED	COLLUSION	CONTINUAL	FOOLHARDY	HONEYCOMB
INFERENCE	INTERJECT	UNBRIDLED	UNSCATHED	COLLUVIUM	CONTINUUM	FOOLPROOF	HONEYMOON
INFERTILE	INTERLACE	UNCEASING	UNSELFISH	COLONNADE	CONTRALTO	FOOTBOARD	HONORABLE
INFIRMARY	INTERLARD	UNCERTAIN	UNSETTLED	COLORCAST	CONTUMELY	FOOTLOOSE	HONORIFIC
INFIRMITY	INTERLEAF	UNCHARTED	UNSHACKLE	COLORFAST	CONTUSION	FOOTPRINT	HOPSCOTCH
INFLATION	INTERLINE	UNCLEANLY	UNSHEATHE	COLUMBINE	CONUNDRUM	FOOTSTOOL	HOREHOUND
INFLEXION	INTERLINK	UNCONCERN	UNSIGHTLY	COLUMNIST	CONVIVIAL	FORECLOSE	HOROSCOPE
INFLUENCE	INTERLOCK	UNCOUNTED	UNSKILLED	COMFORTER	COONHOUND	FOREFRONT	HORSEBACK
INFLUENZA	INTERLOPE	UNDAUNTED	UNSPARING	COMMANDER	COOPERATE	FOREGOING	HORSEHAIR
INFORMANT	INTERLUDE	UNDECEIVE	UNSPOTTED	COMMINGLE	COPARTNER	FOREIGNER	HORSEHIDE
INFURIATE	INTERMENT	UNDECIDED	UNSTUDIED	COMMISSAR	COPYRIGHT	FORENAMED	HORSEPLAY
INFUSIBLE	INTERNIST	UNDERBODY	UNTUTORED	COMMITTEE	CORELDRAW	FORESHEET	HORSESHOE
INGENIOUS	INTERNODE	UNDERBRED	UNWILLING	COMMODITY	CORIANDER	FORESHORE	HORSETAIL
INGENUITY	INTERPLAY	UNDERCOAT	UNWITTING	COMMODORE	CORKSCREW	FORESIGHT	HORSEWHIP
INGENUOUS	INTERPOSE	UNDERDONE	UNWORLDLY	COMMOTION	CORMORANT	FORESTALL	HORTATIVE
INGLENOOK	INTERPRET	UNDERFEED	UNWRITTEN	COMMUNION	COROLLARY	FORESWEAR	HORTATORY
INGROWING	INTERRUPT	UNDERFOOT	BOARDWALK	COMMUNISM	CORPORATE	FORETASTE	HOTHEADED
INHALATOR	INTERSECT	UNDERGIRD	BOATSWAIN	COMMUNITY	CORPOREAL	FORETOKEN	HOURGLASS
INJECTION	INTERVENE	UNDERHAND	BODYGUARD	COMPANION	CORPUSCLE	FOREWOMAN	HOUSEBOAT
INJUSTICE	INTERVIEW	UNDERLINE	BOLSHEVIK	COMPETENT	CORRELATE	FORGATHER	HOUSECOAT
INNERMOST	INTESTATE	UNDERLING	BOMBAZINE	COMPLAINT	CORRUGATE	FORGIVING	HOUSEHOLD
INNERSOLE	INTESTINE	UNDERMINE	BOMBPROOF	COMPONENT	CORTISONE	FORMALISM	HOUSEMAID
INNKEEPER	INTRICATE	UNDERMOST	BOMBSHELL	COMPOSITE	CORUSCATE	FORMALITY	HOUSEWIFE
INNOCENCE	INTRINSIC	UNDERPART	BOMBSIGHT	COMPOSURE	COSMOGONY	FORMALIZE	HOUSEWORK
INNOCUOUS	INTRODUCE	UNDERPASS	BONDWOMAN	CONCERNED	COSMOLOGY	FORMATION	HOWSOEVER
INOCULATE	INTROVERT	UNDERPLAY	BOOKMAKER	CONCERTED	COSMONAUT	FORMATIVE	JOBHOLDER
INORGANIC	INTUITION	UNDERRATE	BOOKPLATE	CONCIERGE	COSPONSOR	FORMULATE	LOADSTONE
INPATIENT	INTUMESCE	UNDERSELL	BOOKSHELF	CONCORDAT	COTILLION	FORSYTHIA	LOATHSOME
INSATIATE	INVECTIVE	UNDERSHOT	BOOMERANG	CONCOURSE	COTYLEDON	FORTHWITH	LOCKSMITH
INSENSATE	INVENTION	UNDERSIDE	BOONDOCKS	CONCUBINE	COUNSELOR	FORTITUDE	LOCOMOTOR
INSERTION	INVENTIVE	UNDERTAKE	BOOTBLACK	CONDENSER	COUNTDOWN	FORTNIGHT	LODESTONE
INSIDIOUS	INVENTORY	UNDERTONE	BOULEVARD			FORTUNATE	LOGARITHM

LOGISTICS	POLITBURO	SOPORIFIC	APPELLATE	ARABESQUE	CROCODILE	GREENHORN	PRESHRUNK
LOINCLOTH	POLITESSE	SOUBRETTE	APPENDAGE	ARBITRARY	CROISSANT	GREENROOM	PRESIDENT
LONGEVITY	POLITICAL	SOUTHEAST	APPERTAIN	ARBITRATE	CROQUETTE	GREENWOOD	PRESIDIUM
LONGITUDE	POLYESTER	SOUTHWEST	APPETIZER	ARBORETUM	CROSSOVER	GRENADIER	PRESSROOM
LORGNETTE	POLYGRAPH	SOVEREIGN	APPLEJACK	ARCHANGEL	CROSSROAD	GRENADINE	PRESTRESS
LOWERCASE	POLYPHONY	TOADSTOOL	APPLETALK	ARCHENEMY	CROSSWALK	GREYHOUND	PREVALENT
MODERATOR	POMPADOUR	TOLERABLE	APPLIANCE	ARCHETYPE	CROSSWAYS	GRIEVANCE	PREVERBAL
MODERNISM	PONDEROUS	TOLERANCE	APPLICANT	ARCHFIEND	CROSSWISE	GRILLWORK	PREVISION
MODERNIZE	POORHOUSE	TOLLHOUSE	APPOINTEE	ARCHITECT	CRUCIFORM	GRISTMILL	PRICELESS
MOLDBOARD	POPPYCOCK	TOMBSTONE	APPORTION	ARCHIVIST	CRYOGENIC	GROOMSMAN	PRIMARILY
MOMENTARY	PORCELAIN	TONSORIAL	APPREHEND	ARGENTINE	DRAFTSMAN	GROSGRAIN	PRIMITIVE
MOMENTOUS	PORCUPINE	TOOTHACHE	EPHEDRINE	ARGENTITE	DRAGONFLY	GROSQUE	PRINCIPAL
MONASTERY	PORRINGER	TOOTHPICK	EPHEMERAL	ARMADILLO	DRAINPIPE	GROTESQUE	PRINCIPLE
MONGOLIAN	PORTFOLIO	TOOTHSOME	EPICENTER	ARMISTICE	DRAMATIZE	GROUNDHOG	PRINTABLE
MONGOLISM	PORTULACA	TOUCHDOWN	EPICUREAN	ARROWHEAD	DREAMLAND	GROUNDING	PRIVATEER
MONGOLOID	POSTERIOR	TOWNSFOLK	EPIDERMIS	ARROWROOT	DRIFTWOOD	GROUPWARE	PRIVATION
MONKSHOOD	POSTERITY	VOICELESS	EPIGRAPHY	ARTERIOLE	DROMEDARY	GRUBSTAKE	PRIVILEGE
MONOGRAPH	POSTHASTE	VOLCANISM	EPISCOPAL	ARTHRITIS	DRUGSTORE	IRASCIBLE	PROBATION
MONOLOGUE	POSTILION	VOLTMETER	OPERATION	ARTHROPOD	DRUMSTICK	IRONBOUND	PROBATIVE
MONOMANIA	POSTNATAL	VOLUNTARY	OPERATIVE	ARTICHOKE	ERADICATE	IRONSTONE	PROBOSCIS
MONOPLANE	POSTULANT	VOLUNTEER	OPPORTUNE	ARTICULAR	EROGENOUS	IRRADIATE	PROCEDURE
MONOSPACE	POSTULATE	VOODOOISM	OPTOMETRY	ARTIFICER	ERRONEOUS	IRREGULAR	PROCESSOR
MONSIGNOR	POTASSIUM	VORACIOUS	SPACESHIP	ARTILLERY	ERSTWHILE	IRRITABLE	PROCONSUL
MOONLIGHT	POTBOILER	VOUCHSAFE	SPAGHETTI	BRASSERIE	ERUDITION	ORANGEADE	PROCREATE
MOONSCAPE	POTENTATE	WOEBEGONE	SPEAKEASY	BRASSIERE	FRACTIOUS	ORCHESTRA	PROFANITY
MOONSHINE	POTENTIAL	WOLFHOUND	SPEARHEAD	BRAZILIAN	FRAMEWORK	ORDINANCE	PROFESSOR
MOONSTONE	POTPOURRI	WOLFSBANE	SPEARMINT	BREAKDOWN	FRANCHISE	ORGIASTIC	PROFITEER
MORTICIAN	POULTERER	WOLVERINE	SPECIALTY	BREAKFAST	FRANGIBLE	ORIENTATE	PROGNOSIS
MOTORBIKE	POURBOIRE	WOMANHOOD	SPECTACLE	BREEZEWAY	FRATERNAL	ORIFLAMME	PROJECTOR
MOTORBOAT	POWERBOAT	WOMANKIND	SPECTATOR	BRIEFCASE	FREEBOARD	ORIGINATE	PROMENADE
MOTORCADE	ROADBLOCK	WOMANLIKE	SPECULATE	BRILLIANT	FREEMASON	ORPHANAGE	PROMINENT
MOUSETRAP	ROADSTEAD	WOMENFOLK	SPEEDBOAT	BRIMSTONE	FREESTONE	PRACTICAL	PROMISING
MOUSTACHE	ROCKBOUND	WONDERFUL	SPEEDWELL	BRIQUETTE	FREEWHEEL	PRAGMATIC	PRONGHORN
MOUTHPART	ROOTSTOCK	WOODBLOCK	SPELUNKER	BRITANNIC	FREQUENCY	PRAYERFUL	PRONOUNCE
MOUTHWASH	ROSEWATER	WOODCHUCK	SPHINCTER	BROADBAND	FRICASSEE	PRECANCEL	PROOFREAD
NOCTURNAL	ROUGHNECK	WOODCRAFT	SPICEBUSH	BROADCAST	FRIEDCAKE	PRECEDENT	PROPAGATE
NONCREDIT	ROUMANIAN	WORKBENCH	SPINDLING	BROADLOOM	FRIGHTFUL	PRECEDING	PROPELLER
NONENTITY	ROUNDELAY	WORKGROUP	SPINDRIFT	BROADSIDE	FRIVOLOUS	PRECENTOR	PROPHETIC
NONPAREIL	ROUNDWORM	WORKHORSE	SPINNAKER	BROADTAIL	FROSTBITE	PRECEPTOR	PROPONENT
NONPERSON	SOAPSTONE	WORKHOUSE	SPIRITUAL	BROCHETTE	FRUITCAKE	PRECIPICE	PROPRIETY
NONPROFIT	SOBRIQUET	WORKPLACE	SPLENETIC	BROKERAGE	FRUITERER	PRECISION	PROSCRIBE
NONREADER	SOCIALISM	WORKTABLE	SPLITTING	BRONCHIAL	FRUSTRATE	PRECURSOR	PROSECUTE
NORMALIZE	SOCIALITE	WORLDLING	SPOKESMAN	BRUSHWOOD	GRADATION	PREDATION	PROSELYTE
NORMATIVE	SOCIALIZE	WORLDWIDE	SPOONBILL	BRUTALIZE	GRANDIOSE	PREDATORY	PROSTRATE
NORTHEAST	SOCIOLOGY	WORRISOME	SPORTSMAN	CRABGRASS	GRANTSMAN	PREDICATE	PROTECTOR
NORTHWEST	SOFTBOUND	WORRYWART	SPOTLIGHT	CRACKDOWN	GRANULATE	PREFIGURE	PROTOTYPE
NORWEGIAN	SOLEMNIZE	WORTHLESS	SPRIGHTLY	CRAFTSMAN	GRAPESHOT	PREFLIGHT	PROTOZOAN
NOSEBLEED	SOLICITOR	YOUNGLING	UPANISHAD	CRANBERRY	GRAPEVINE	PREGNABLE	PROVENCAL
NOSEPIECE	SOLILOQUY	YOUNGSTER	UPHOLSTER	CRANKCASE	GRASSLAND	PREJUDICE	PROVENDER
NOSTALGIA	SOLITAIRE	APARTHEID	UPPERCASE	CREDULOUS	GRATICULE	PRELAUNCH	PROVIDENT
NOTCHBACK	SOMETHING	APARTMENT	UPPERMOST	CREMATORY	GRATITUDE	PREMATURE	PROVISION
NOTORIOUS	SOMETIMES	APOCRYPHA	AQUAPLANE	CRESCENDO	GRAVEYARD	PREOCCUPY	PROVOLONE
NOVELETTE	SOMEWHERE	APOLOGIZE	EQUIPMENT	CRETINISM	GRAVITATE	PREORDAIN	PROXIMATE
NOVITIATE	SOMNOLENT	APOSTOLIC	EQUIPOISE	CRINOLINE	GRAYBEARD	PRERECORD	PROXIMITY
POETASTER	SOPHISTIC	APPALOOSA	EQUITABLE	CRITERION	GREATCOAT	PRESBYTER	TRACKBALL
POINCIANA	SOPHISTRY	APPARATUS	EQUIVOCAL	CRITICISM	GREENBACK	PRESCHOOL	TRACTABLE
POLICEMAN	SOPHOMORE	APPELLANT	SQUEAMISH	CRITICIZE	GREENBELT	PRESENTLY	TRADEMARK

TRADESMAN	ASTRAKHAN	STATIONER	BULLFINCH	JUDICIARY	QUARTERLY	SURCHARGE	SWAMPLAND
TRADITION	ASTROLABE	STATISTIC	BUMBLEBEE	JUDICIOUS	QUARTZITE	SURCINGLE	SWANSDOWN
TRAGEDIAN	ASTROLOGY	STATUETTE	BUMPTIOUS	JURIDICAL	QUERULOUS	SURFBOARD	SWEATSHOP
TRAINLOAD	ASTRONAUT	STATUTORY	BURLESQUE	JUXTAPOSE	QUICKDRAW	SURRENDER	SWEETMEAT
TRANSCEND	ASTRONOMY	STEADFAST	BURUNDIAN	LUBRICANT	QUICKLIME	SURROGATE	SWELLHEAD
TRANSDUCE	ASYMPTOTE	STEAMBOAT	BUSHWHACK	LUBRICATE	QUICKSAND	SURVEYING	SWITCHMAN
TRANSFORM	ESCALATOR	STEAMSHIP	BUTTERCUP	LUCRATIVE	QUICKSORT	SUSPENDER	SWORDFISH
TRANSFUSE	ESOPHAGUS	STEELYARD	BUTTERFAT	LUDICROUS	QUICKSTEP	SUSPICION	SWORDPLAY
TRANSIENT	ESPERANTO	STEPCHILD	BUTTERFLY	LUNCHROOM	QUICKTIME	TULAREMIA	SWORDSMAN
TRANSLATE	ESPIONAGE	STERILIZE	BUTTERNUT	LUXURIANT	QUIESCENT	TURBOPROP	SWORDTAIL
TRANSMUTE	ESPLANADE	STEVEDORE	CUBBYHOLE	LUXURIATE	QUINTUPLE	TURBULENT	TWINKLING
TRANSONIC	ESSENTIAL	STILLBORN	CULLENDER	MUCKRAKER	QUITTANCE	TURNABOUT	ZWINGLIAN
TRANSPIRE	ESTABLISH	STIMULANT	CULMINATE	MULTIFORM	QUIZZICAL	TURNSTILE	EXCELLENT
TRANSPORT	ESTAMINET	STIMULATE	CULTIVATE	MULTISCAN	QUOTIDIAN	TURNTABLE	EXCELSIOR
TRANSPOSE	ESTIMABLE	STIPULATE	CUNEIFORM	MULTISPIN	RUINATION	TURPITUDE	EXCEPTION
TRANSSHIP	ISINGLASS	STOCKPILE	CUPBEARER	MULTISYNC	RUMRUNNER	TURQUOISE	EXCHEQUER
TRAPEZOID	ISOSCELES	STOCKYARD	CURETTAGE	MULTITUDE	RUNAROUND	TUSCARORA	EXCITABLE
TRAPPINGS	ISRAELITE	STOMACHER	CURRYCOMB	MUNICIPAL	RUSTICATE	VULCANISM	EXCLUSIVE
TREACHERY	OSCILLATE	STOMACHIC	CURVATURE	MURDEROUS	RUTHENIUM	VULCANIZE	EXCORIATE
TREADMILL	OSTRACIZE	STOPLIGHT	CUSTODIAL	MUSKMELON	SUBALPINE	VULGARIAN	EXCREMENT
TREASURER	PSEUDONYM	STOPWATCH	CUSTODIAN	MUSSULMAN	SUBALTERN	VULGARISM	EXCULPATE
TREATMENT	PSORIASIS	STOREROOM	CUSTOMARY	NUMERATOR	SUBATOMIC	VULGARITY	EXCURSION
TREMATODE	PSYCHOSIS	STRAPLESS	CUSTOMIZE	NUMERICAL	SUBDIVIDE	VULGARIZE	EXCURSIVE
TREMULOUS	ATHENAEUM	STRAPPING	CUTANEOUS	NURSEMAID	SUBJUGATE	ZUCCHETTO	EXECRABLE
TRENCHANT	ATHLETICS	STRATAGEM	CUTTHROAT	NUTRIMENT	SUBLIMATE	AVAILABLE	EXECUTIVE
TRIBESMAN	ATONEMENT	STREAMBED	DUCKBOARD	NUTRITION	SUBLUNARY	AVALANCHE	EXECUTRIX
TRIBUTARY	ATROCIOUS	STREAMLET	DUMBFOUND	OUBLIETTE	SUBMARINE	AVOCATION	EXEMPLARY
TRICKSTER	ATTAINDER	STREETCAR	DUPLICATE	OURSELVES	SUBNORMAL	AVUNCULAR	EXEMPLIFY
TRIENNIAL	ATTENDANT	STRENUOUS	DUPLICITY	OUTERMOST	SUBSCRIBE	EVAPORATE	EXISTENCE
TRIFOCALS	ATTENTION	STRETCHER	EUCHARIST	OUTGROWTH	SUBSCRIPT	EVAPORITE	EXOGENOUS
TRIMESTER	ATTENUATE	STRICTURE	EUCLIDEAN	OUTNUMBER	SUBSIDIZE	EVENTUATE	EXONERATE
TRITURATE	ATTRIBUTE	STRIKEOUT	EUPHEMISM	OUTRIGGER	SUBSTANCE	EVERGLADE	EXOSPHERE
TRIWEEKLY	ATTRITION	STRIPLING	EUTHENICS	OUTSKIRTS	SUCCESSOR	EVERGREEN	EXPANSION
TROOPSHIP	ETHIOPIAN	STRONTIUM	EUTROPHIC	OUTSPOKEN	SUCCOTASH	EVERYBODY	EXPANSIVE
TROUSSEAU	ETHNOLOGY	STRUCTURE	FULMINATE	OUTSPREAD	SUCCULENT	EVOLUTION	EXPATIATE
TRUCKLOAD	ETIQUETTE	UTTERANCE	FUNGICIDE	OUTWARDLY	SUFFERING	OVERBLOWN	EXPECTANT
TRUCULENT	ETYMOLOGY	UTTERMOST	FUNICULAR	PUBESCENT	SUFFOCATE	OVERBOARD	EXPEDIENT
TRUNCHEON	ITALICIZE	YTTERBIUM	FURNITURE	PUBLICIST	SUFFRAGAN	OVERCLOUD	EXPEDITER
URTICARIA	ITERATION	AUCTORIAL	FUSILLADE	PUBLICITY	SUGARCANE	OVERDRAFT	EXPENSIVE
WRESTLING	ITINERANT	AUDACIOUS	GUARANTEE	PUBLICIZE	SUGARPLUM	OVERDRIVE	EXPERTISE
WRISTBAND	ITINERARY	AUDIOLOGY	GUARANTOR	PUERPERAL	SULFUROUS	OVERMATCH	EXPIATORY
WRONGDOER	OTHERWISE	AURICULAR	GUARDROOM	PUISSANCE	SUMMARIZE	OVERNIGHT	EXPLETIVE
ASAFETIDA	PTARMIGAN	AUTHENTIC	GUARDSMAN	PULMONARY	SUMMATION	OVERPOWER	EXPLICATE
ASCENDANT	STABILIZE	AUTHORITY	GUERRILLA	PULVERIZE	SUMPTUOUS	OVERPRINT	EXPLOSION
ASCENDERS	STAIRCASE	AUTHORIZE	GUIDEBOOK	PUNCTILIO	SUNBONNET	OVERREACH	EXPLOSIVE
ASCENSION	STAIRWELL	AUTOCRACY	GUIDELINE	PUNCTUATE	SUNFLOWER	OVERSEXED	EXPOSITOR
ASCERTAIN	STALEMATE	AUTOGRAPH	GUNCOTTON	PUPPETEER	SUNSEEKER	OVERSHOOT	EXPULSION
ASPARAGUS	STAMINATE	AUTOMATIC	GUNNYSACK	PUREBLOOD	SUNSTROKE	OVERSIGHT	EXPURGATE
ASPERSION	STANCHION	AUTOMATON	GUNPOWDER	PURGATION	SUPERNOVA	OVERSLEEP	EXQUISITE
ASSEMBLER	STANDPIPE	AUTOTRACE	GUSTATORY	PURGATIVE	SUPERPOSE	OVERSTATE	EXTEMPORE
ASSERTION	STARBOARD	AUXILIARY	HUMANKIND	PURGATORY	SUPERSEDE	OVERTHROW	EXTENSION
ASSIDUOUS	STARLIGHT	BUCCANEER	HUMDINGER	PURSUANCE	SUPERVENE	OVERTRICK	EXTENSIVE
ASSISTANT	STARTLING	BUCKBOARD	HUMILIATE	PUSSYFOOT	SUPERVISE	OVERWEIGH	EXTENUATE
ASSOCIATE	STATEMENT	BUCKTOOTH	HUNCHBACK	QUADRATIC	SUPPLIANT	OVERWHELM	EXTIRPATE
ASSONANCE	STATEROOM	BUCKWHEAT	HUNGARIAN	QUADRILLE	SUPPOSING	OVERWRITE	EXTRADITE
ASSURANCE	STATESIDE	BULGARIAN	HURRICANE	QUADRUPED	SUPPURATE	OVIPAROUS	EXTRAVERT
ASTRADDLE	STATESMAN	BULLFIGHT	HUSBANDRY	QUADRUPLE	SUPREMACY	AWESTRUCK	EXTREMISM

	3RD LETTER						
EXTREMITY		CLASSROOM	GRAPESHOT	PLAYHOUSE	TRACKBALL	HABITUATE	ANCHORMAN
EXTRICATE		COADJUTOR	GRAPEVINE	PLAYTHING	TRACTABLE	HIBERNATE	ANCILLARY
EXTRINSIC	ABANDONED	COAGULANT	GRASSLAND	PRACTICAL	TRADEMARK	HOBGOBLIN	ARCHANGEL
EXTRUSIVE	ABATEMENT	COAGULATE	GRATICULE	PRAGMATIC	TRADESMAN	IMBALANCE	ARCHENEMY
EXUBERANT	ALABASTER	COALFIELD	GRATITUDE	PRAYERFUL	TRADITION	IMBROGLIO	ARCHETYPE
OXIDATION	AMARYLLIS	COALITION	GRAVEYARD	PTARMIGAN	TRAGEDIAN	JOBHOLDER	ARCHFIEND
OXYGENATE	ANAEROBIC	COASTLINE	GRAVITATE	QUADRATIC	TRAINLOAD	LABORIOUS	ARCHITECT
BYSTANDER	ANALGESIA	CRABGRASS	GRAYBEARD	QUADRILLE	TRANSCEND	LABYRINTH	ARCHIVIST
CYCLAMATE	ANALGESIC	CRACKDOWN	GUARANTEE	QUADRUPED	TRANSDUCE	LIBERTINE	ASCENDANT
CYCLOTRON	ANALOGOUS	CRAFTSMAN	GUARANTOR	QUADRUPLE	TRANSFORM	LIBRARIAN	ASCENDERS
CYTOPLASM	ANARCHISM	CRANBERRY	GUARDROOM	QUARTERLY	TRANSFUSE	LUBRICANT	ASCENSION
DYSENTERY	ANATOMIZE	CRANKCASE	GUARDSMAN	QUARTZITE	TRANSIENT	LUBRICATE	ASCERTAIN
DYSPEPSIA	APARTHEID	DEATHBLOW	HEADBOARD	REACTANCE	TRANSLATE	OBBLIGATO	AUCTORIAL
DYSTROPHY	APARTMENT	DEATHLESS	HEADDRESS	ROADBLOCK	TRANSMUTE	OMBUDSMAN	BACCHANAL
EYESTRAIN	ARABESQUE	DIACRITIC	HEADFIRST	ROADSTEAD	TRANSONIC	OUBLIETTE	BACKBOARD
GYMNASIUM	ASAFETIDA	DIAERESIS	HEADLIGHT	SCANTLING	TRANSPIRE	PUBESCENT	BACKFIELD
GYRFALCON	AVAILABLE	DIAGNOSIS	HEADPHONE	SCAPEGOAT	TRANSPORT	PUBLICIST	BACKPEDAL
GYROSCOPE	AVALANCHE	DIALECTIC	HEADPIECE	SCARECROW	TRANSPOSE	PUBLICITY	BACKSLASH
HYDRANGEA	BEACHHEAD	DIAMETRIC	HEADSTALL	SCAVENGER	TRANSSHIP	PUBLICIZE	BACKSLIDE
HYDRAULIC	BEATITUDE	DIAPHRAGM	HEADSTONE	SEAFARING	TRAPEZOID	RABBINATE	BACKSTAGE
HYDROFOIL	BEAUTEOUS	DIATHERMY	HEADWATER	SEASONING	TRAPPINGS	REBELLION	BACKSWEPT
HYDROLOGY	BEAUTIFUL	DIATOMITE	HEALTHFUL	SEAWORTHY	UNADVISED	SEBACEOUS	BACKTRACK
HYDROXIDE	BLACKBALL	DRAFTSMAN	HEARTACHE	SHADOWBOX	UNALIGNED	SOBRIQUET	BACKWATER
HYPERBOLA	BLACKBIRD	DRAGONFLY	HEARTBEAT	SHAKEDOWN	UNALLOYED	SUBALPINE	BACKWOODS
HYPERBOLE	BLACKBODY	DRAINPIPE	HEARTBURN	SHAPELESS	UNANIMOUS	SUBALTERN	BACTERIUM
HYPERCARD	BLACKFOOT	DRAMATIZE	HEARTFELT	SHAREWARE	UPANISHAD	SUBATOMIC	BICAMERAL
HYPERTEXT	BLACKHEAD	EJACULATE	HEARTLESS	SHARKSKIN	WEARISOME	SUBDIVIDE	BICONCAVE
HYPHENATE	BLACKJACK	ELABORATE	HEARTSICK	SLAUGHTER	WHALEBOAT	SUBJUGATE	BUCCANEER
HYPOCRISY	BLACKLIST	ELASTOMER	HEARTWOOD	SMALLTALK	WHALEBONE	SUBLIMATE	BUCKBOARD
HYSTERICS	BLACKMAIL	ERADICATE	HOARFROST	SNAKEBIRD	ALBATROSS	SUBLUNARY	BUCKTOOTH
MYSTICISM	BLASPHEME	EVAPORATE	IMAGINARY	SNAKEBITE	AMBERGRIS	SUBMARINE	BUCKWHEAT
MYTHOLOGY	BLASPHEMY	EVAPORITE	INABILITY	SOAPSTONE	AMBIGUOUS	SUBNORMAL	CACOPHONY
PYRETHRUM	BOARDWALK	FLAGELLUM	INAMORATA	SPACESHIP	AMBITIOUS	SUBSCRIBE	COCHINEAL
PYROLYSIS	BOATSWAIN	FLAGEOLET	INANIMATE	SPAGHETTI	AMBULANCE	SUBSCRIPT	COCKATIEL
PYROMANIA	BRASSERIE	FLAGSTAFF	INANITION	STABILIZE	AMBUSCADE	SUBSIDIZE	COCKFIGHT
PYROMETER	BRASSIERE	FLAGSTONE	INAUGURAL	STAIRCASE	ARBITRARY	SUBSTANCE	COCKROACH
SYCOPHANT	BRAZILIAN	FLAMMABLE	IRASCIBLE	STAIRWELL	ARBITRATE	TABLELAND	CYCLAMATE
SYLLABIFY	CEASELESS	FLASHBACK	ITALICIZE	STALEMATE	ARBORETUM	TABLEWARE	CYCLOTRON
SYLLOGISM	CHAFFINCH	FLASHBULB	LEAFSTALK	STAMINATE	CABLEGRAM	UMBILICUS	DACHSHUND
SYMBIOSIS	CHALKBORD	FLASHCUBE	LEASEHOLD	STANCHION	CABRIOLET	UNBEKNOWN	DECADENCE
SYMBOLISM	CHALLENGE	FLASHTUBE	LEASTWISE	STANDPIPE	CUBBYHOLE	UNBENDING	DECALOGUE
SYMBOLIZE	CHAMELEON	FLATULENT	LEAVENING	STARBOARD	DEBENTURE	UNBLESSED	DECATHLON
SYMPOSIUM	CHAMOMILE	FLAVORING	LIABILITY	STARLIGHT	DEBUTANTE	UNBOUNDED	DECEITFUL
SYNAGOGUE	CHAMPAGNE	FRACTIOUS	LOADSTONE	STARTLING	DOBSONFLY	UNBRIDLED	DECENNIAL
SYNDICATE	CHAMPAIGN	FRAMEWORK	LOATHSOME	STATEMENT	ELBOWROOM	VIBRATION	DECEPTION
SYNERGISM	CHANCROID	FRANCHISE	MEANWHILE	STATEROOM	EMBARRASS	VIBRATORY	DECIDUOUS
SYNTHESIS	CHANTEUSE	FRANGIBLE	ORANGEADE	STATESIDE	EMBAYMENT	ACCESSION	DECILITER
SYNTHETIC	CHAPARRAL	FRATERNAL	PEACETIME	STATESMAN	EMBELLISH	ACCESSORY	DECIMETER
SYSTEMIZE	CHARABANC	GEARSHIFT	PHALAROPE	STATIONER	EMBRASURE	ACCIDENCE	DECISTERE
TYPEWRITE	CHARACTER	GLADIATOR	PLACEKICK	STATISTIC	EMBROCATE	ACCLIMATE	DECLIVITY
TYRANNIZE	CHARLATAN	GLADIOLUS	PLACEMENT	STATUETTE	EMBROIDER	ACCLIVITY	DECOLLETE
TYRANNOUS	CHARWOMAN	GLADSTONE	PLAINTIFF	STATUTORY	FABRICATE	ACCOMPANY	DECOMPOSE
XYLOPHONE	CHAUFFEUR	GLAMORIZE	PLAINTIVE	SWAMPLAND	FEBRIFUGE	ACCORDION	DECONTROL
	CLAMSHELL	GRADATION	PLANELOAD	SWANSDOWN	GABARDINE	ACCRETION	DECORATOR
	CLAPBOARD	GRANDIOSE	PLANETOID	TEAKETTLE	GABERDINE	ALCOHOLIC	DECOUPAGE
	CLASSICAL	GRANTSMAN	PLATITUDE	THANKLESS	GIBBERISH	ANCHORAGE	DECREMENT
	CLASSMATE	GRANULATE	PLAUSIBLE	TOADSTOOL	HABITABLE	ANCHORITE	DICHOTOMY

DOCTORATE	MACINTOSH	SACRILEGE	HYDRANGEA	UNDERLINE	EVERGREEN	OVERWEIGH	SPEARMINT
DUCKBOARD	MACROCOSM	SACRISTAN	HYDRAULIC	UNDERLING	EVERYBODY	OVERWHELM	SPECIALTY
ECCENTRIC	MECHANICS	SECESSION	HYDROFOIL	UNDERMINE	EXECRABLE	OVERWRITE	SPECTACLE
ENCHILADA	MECHANISM	SECLUSION	HYDROLOGY	UNDERMOST	EXECUTIVE	PHEROMONE	SPECTATOR
ENCOMPASS	MECHANIZE	SECONDARY	HYDROXIDE	UNDERPART	EXECUTRIX	PIECEMEAL	SPECULATE
ENCOUNTER	MICROCOPY	SECRETARY	INDELIBLE	UNDERPASS	EXEMPLARY	PIECEWORK	SPEEDBOAT
ENCOURAGE	MICROCOSM	SECRETION	INDEMNIFY	UNDERPLAY	EXEMPLIFY	PLENITUDE	SPEEDWELL
ESCALATOR	MICROFILM	SECRETIVE	INDEMNITY	UNDERRATE	EYESTRAIN	PLENTEOUS	SPELUNKER
EUCHARIST	MICROGRAM	SECTARIAN	INDENTION	UNDERSELL	FEEDSTOCK	PLENTIFUL	STEADFAST
EUCLIDEAN	MICROSOFT	SECTIONAL	INDENTURE	UNDERSHOT	FEEDSTUFF	PNEUMATIC	STEAMBOAT
EXCELLENT	MICROWAVE	SOCIALISM	INDIGNANT	UNDERSIDE	FLEDGLING	PNEUMONIA	STEAMSHIP
EXCELSIOR	MUCKRAKER	SOCIALITE	INDIGNITY	UNDERTAKE	FREEBOARD	POETASTER	STEELYARD
EXCEPTION	NECESSARY	SOCIALIZE	INDUCTION	UNDERTONE	FREEMASON	PRECANCEL	STEPCHILD
EXCHEQUER	NECESSITY	SOCIOLOGY	INDUCTIVE	UNDERWEAR	FREESTONE	PRECEDENT	STERILIZE
EXCITABLE	NECROLOGY	SUCCESSOR	JUDICIARY	UNDERWOOD	FREEWHEEL	PRECEDING	STEVEDORE
EXCLUSIVE	NECTARINE	SUCCOTASH	JUDICIOUS	UNDOUBTED	FREQUENCY	PRECENTOR	SWEATSHOP
EXCORIATE	NICOTINIC	SUCCULENT	LODESTONE	VIDELICET	GLEANINGS	PRECEPTOR	SWEETMEAT
EXCREMENT	NOCTURNAL	SYCOPHANT	LUDICROUS	VIDEOTAPE	GLENGARRY	PRECIPICE	SWELLHEAD
EXCULPATE	OCCULTISM	TECHNICAL	MEDALLION	WEDNESDAY	GREATCOAT	PRECISION	THEATRICS
EXCURSION	OCCUPANCY	TECHNIQUE	MEDICABLE	ACETYLENE	GREENBACK	PRECURSOR	THEOCRACY
EXCURSIVE	ORCHESTRA	TECTONICS	MEDICINAL	ALEATORIC	GREENBELT	PREDATION	THEOSOPHY
FACETIOUS	OSCILLATE	TECTONISM	MIDDLEMAN	AMENDMENT	GREENHORN	PREDATORY	THEREFORE
FACSIMILE	PACEMAKER	UNCEASING	MIDSTREAM	AMERICANA	GREENROOM	PREDICATE	THEREFROM
FACTORIAL	PACHYDERM	UNCERTAIN	MIDSUMMER	AMERICIUM	GREENWOOD	PREFIGURE	THEREUNTO
FECUNDATE	PACKHORSE	UNCHARTED	MIDWINTER	AWESTRUCK	GRENADIER	PREFLIGHT	THEREUPON
HACKNEYED	PECUNIARY	UNCLEANLY	MODERATOR	BEEFEATER	GRENADINE	PREGNABLE	THEREWITH
HECTOGRAM	PICKABACK	UNCONCERN	MODERNISM	BEEFSTEAK	GREYHOUND	PREJUDICE	THESAURUS
INCAPABLE	PICTORIAL	UNCOUNTED	MODERNIZE	BEEKEEPER	GUERRILLA	PRELAUNCH	TREACHERY
INCARNATE	RACEHORSE	VACCINATE	ORDINANCE	BLEACHERS	HIERARCHY	PREMATURE	TREADMILL
INCENTIVE	RACETRACK	VACILLATE	PEDAGOGUE	BREAKDOWN	ICELANDER	PREOCCUPY	TREASURER
INCEPTION	RACIALISM	VICARIOUS	PEDOMETER	BREAKFAST	ICELANDIC	PREORDAIN	TREATMENT
INCESSANT	RACKETEER	VICENNIAL	RADIOGRAM	BREEZEWAY	IDENTICAL	PRERECORD	TREMATODE
INCIDENCE	RACONTEUR	VICEREGAL	RADIOLOGY	CHECKBOOK	INEBRIATE	PRESBYTER	TREMULOUS
INCIPIENT	RECEPTION	VICTIMIZE	REDACTION	CHECKLIST	INEFFABLE	PRESCHOOL	TRENCHANT
INCLEMENT	RECEPTIVE	VICTORIAN	REDBREAST	CHECKMATE	INELEGANT	PRESCRIBE	UNEARTHLY
INCOGNITO	RECESSION	VICTUALER	REDUCTION	CHECKROOM	ITERATION	PRESENTLY	UNEQUALED
INCOMMODE	RECESSIVE	YACHTSMAN	REDUNDANT	CHEEKBONE	MAELSTROM	PRESHRUNK	VIEWPOINT
INCORRECT	RECHERCHE	ZUCCHETTO	RIDGEPOLE	CHEERLESS	OBEISANCE	PRESIDENT	WHEELBASE
INCREMENT	RECIPIENT	ADDICTION	SADDLEBOW	CHEMISTRY	OPERATION	PRESIDIUM	WHEREFORE
INCUBATOR	RECKONING	ADDRESSEE	SEDENTARY	CHEVALIER	OPERATIVE	PRESSROOM	WHEREUPON
INCULCATE	RECOGNIZE	AUDACIOUS	SIDEBOARD	CLEARANCE	OVERBLOWN	PRESTRESS	WHEREWITH
INCULPATE	RECOLLECT	AUDIOLOGY	SIDEBURNS	CLERGYMAN	OVERBOARD	PREVALENT	WHETSTONE
INCUMBENT	RECOMMEND	BADMINTON	SIDEPIECE	CREDULOUS	OVERCLOUD	PREVERBAL	WOEBEGONE
INCURABLE	RECONCILE	BEDFELLOW	SIDESWIPE	CREMATORY	OVERDRAFT	PREVISION	WRESTLING
INCURIOUS	RECONDITE	BEDRIDDEN	SIDETRACK	CRESCENDO	OVERDRIVE	PSEUDONYM	AFFECTING
INCURSION	RECORDING	BEDSPREAD	TIDEWATER	CRETINISM	OVERMATCH	PUERPERAL	AFFECTION
JACARANDA	RECORDIST	BODYGUARD	UNDAUNTED	DIETETICS	OVERNIGHT	QUERULOUS	AFFIDAVIT
JACKKNIFE	RECTANGLE	DEDUCTION	UNDECEIVE	DREAMLAND	OVERPOWER	REENFORCE	AFFILIATE
JACKSCREW	RECTIFIER	EIDERDOWN	UNDECIDED	EDELWEISS	OVERPRINT	REENTRANT	AFFLUENCE
JACKSTRAW	RECTITUDE	ENDOCRINE	UNDERBODY	ELECTRIFY	OVERREACH	RHEOMETER	BIFURCATE
KICKSTAND	RECUMBENT	ENDOSCOPE	UNDERBRED	ELECTRODE	OVERSEXED	SHEATHING	CAFETERIA
LACCOLITH	RECURSION	ENDURANCE	UNDERCOAT	ELEVATION	OVERSHOOT	SHEEPFOLD	COFEATURE
LOCKSMITH	ROCKBOUND	FIDUCIARY	UNDERDONE	EMERGENCY	OVERSIGHT	SHEEPSKIN	COFFEEPOT
LOCOMOTOR	SACCHARIN	GODFATHER	UNDERFEED	ENERGETIC	OVERSLEEP	SHELLFIRE	COFFERDAM
LUCRATIVE	SACKCLOTH	GODMOTHER	UNDERFOOT	ENERGIZER	OVERSTATE	SHELLFISH	DEFEATISM
MACHINERY	SACRAMENT	GODPARENT	UNDERGIRD	EVENTUATE	OVERTHROW	SPEAKEASY	DEFECTIVE
MACHINIST	SACRIFICE	HIDEBOUND	UNDERHAND	EVERGLADE	OVERTRICK	SPEARHEAD	DEFENDANT

DEFENSIVE	UNFLEDGED	NIGHTHAWK	UPHOLSTER	GUIDEBOOK	SAILCLOTH	ZEITGEIST	CELLARAGE
DEFERENCE	UNFOUNDED	NIGHTLIFE	VEHEMENCE	GUIDELINE	SAILPLANE	ZWINGLIAN	CELLULOSE
DEFERMENT	AGGRAVATE	NIGHTMARE	ACIDULATE	HAILSTONE	SCINTILLA	ADJECTIVE	CHLORDANE
DEFICIENT	AGGREGATE	NIGHTTIME	ACIDULOUS	HAILSTORM	SHIFTLESS	ADJOINING	COLLATION
DEFLATION	ALGONQUIN	NIGRITUDE	ADIABATIC	HAIRBRUSH	SHIPBOARD	DEJECTION	COLLEAGUE
DEFOLIANT	ALGORITHM	ORGIASTIC	ALIENABLE	HAIRCLOTH	SHIPSHAPE	INJECTION	COLLECTED
DEFOLIATE	ANGELFISH	PAGEMAKER	AMIDSHIPS	HAIRPIECE	SHIPWRECK	INJUSTICE	COLLEGIAN
DEFORMITY	ANGLEWORM	PEGMATITE	ANIMALISM	HAIRSTYLE	SKIMOBILE	MAJORDOMO	COLLEGIUM
DIFFERENT	ANGLICIZE	PIGGYBACK	ANIMATION	IMITATION	SKINFLINT	MAJORETTE	COLLIMATE
DIFFICULT	ANGUISHED	PIGHEADED	ANIMOSITY	IMITATIVE	SKINTIGHT	MAJUSCULE	COLLODION
DIFFIDENT	ARGENTINE	RAGPICKER	BAILIWICK	ISINGLASS	SLINGSHOT	OBJECTIFY	COLLUSION
EFFECTIVE	ARGENTITE	REGARDING	BLINDFOLD	ITINERANT	SPICEBUSH	OBJECTIVE	COLLUVIUM
EFFECTUAL	BAGATELLE	REGISTRAR	BRIEFCASE	ITINERARY	SPINDLING	OBJURGATE	COLONNADE
EFFICIENT	CIGARETTE	RIGHTEOUS	BRILLIANT	JAILBREAK	SPINDRIFT	REJOINDER	COLORCAST
EFFLUENCE	CIGARILLO	RIGMAROLE	BRIMSTONE	LEITMOTIV	SPINNAKER	ANKLEBONE	COLORFAST
EFFLUVIUM	COGNITION	SAGACIOUS	BRIQUETTE	LOINCLOTH	SPIRITUAL	BAKSHEESH	COLUMBINE
INFANTILE	DIGITALIS	SAGEBRUSH	BRITANNIC	MAINFRAME	STILLBORN	DEKALITER	COLUMNIST
INFATUATE	DIGITIZED	SEGREGATE	CHICANERY	OLIGARCHY	STIMULANT	DEKAMETER	CULLENDER
INFECTION	DIGNIFIED	SIGNALIZE	CHICKADEE	ONIONSKIN	STIMULATE	DEKASTERE	CULMINATE
INFERENCE	DIGNITARY	SIGNALMAN	CHICKASAW	ORIENTATE	STIPULATE	MAKESHIFT	CULTIVATE
INFERTILE	DOGMATISM	SIGNATORY	CHICKWEED	ORIFLAMME	SWITCHMAN	PAKISTANI	DALMATION
INFIRMARY	EGGBEATER	SIGNATURE	CHIEFTAIN	ORIGINATE	TAILLIGHT	PEKINGESE	DELFTWARE
INFIRMITY	ENGRAVING	SIGNBOARD	CHILBLAIN	OVIPAROUS	THICKNESS	PIKESTAFF	DELICIOUS
INFLATION	HIGHLIGHT	SUGARCANE	CHILDHOOD	OXIDATION	THIGHBONE	UNKNOWING	DELIGHTED
INFLEXION	INGENIOUS	SUGARPLUM	CHIROPODY	PHILANDER	TRIBESMAN	AILANTHUS	DELIMITER
INFLUENCE	INGENUITY	TIGHTROPE	CHIVALRIC	PHILATELY	TRIBUTARY	ALLERGIST	DELINEATE
INFLUENZA	INGENUOUS	UNGUARDED	CLIENTELE	PHILIPPIC	TRICKSTER	ALLEVIATE	EGLANTINE
INFORMANT	INGLENOOK	VAGARIOUS	CLINICIAN	PHILOLOGY	TRIENNIAL	ALLIGATOR	ELLIPSOID
INFURIATE	INGROWING	VAGINITIS	CLIPBOARD	POINCIANA	TRIFOCALS	ALLOWANCE	ENLIGHTEN
INFUSIBLE	LAGNIAPPE	VEGETABLE	CLIPSHEET	PRICELESS	TRIMESTER	BALALAIKA	FALSEHOOD
LIFEBLOOD	LEGENDARY	VIGESIMAL	COIFFEUSE	PRIMARILY	TRITURATE	BALDACHIN	FELLOWMAN
LIFEGUARD	LEGISLATE	VIGILANCE	CRINOLINE	PRIMITIVE	TRIWEEKLY	BALLADEER	FILMSTRIP
NEFARIOUS	LIGHTFACE	VIGILANTE	CRITERION	PRINCIPAL	TWINKLING	BALLERINA	FOLLOWING
OBFUSCATE	LIGHTNING	WAGONETTE	CRITICISM	PRINCIPLE	UNISEXUAL	BELEAGUER	FULMINATE
OFFENSIVE	LIGHTSHIP	ABHORRENT	CRITICIZE	PRINTABLE	UNITARIAN	BELLICOSE	GALACTOSE
OFFERTORY	LIGHTSOME	ANHYDROUS	DAIRYMAID	PRIVATEER	UNIVALENT	BELLYACHE	GALLANTRY
OFFICIANT	LOGARITHM	ATHENAEUM	DRIFTWOOD	PRIVATION	UNIVERSAL	BELVEDERE	GALLINULE
OFFICIATE	LOGISTICS	ATHLETICS	EDITORIAL	PRIVILEGE	VAINGLORY	BILATERAL	GALLIVANT
OFFICIOUS	MAGISTRAL	DEHYDRATE	ELIMINATE	PUISSANCE	VOICELESS	BILINGUAL	GALLSTONE
OFFSPRING	MAGNESIUM	EPHEDRINE	ENIGMATIC	QUICKDRAW	WAISTBAND	BILLBOARD	GALVANISM
OLFACTORY	MAGNETISM	EPHEMERAL	EPICENTER	QUICKLIME	WAISTCOAT	BILLIARDS	GALVANIZE
REFECTION	MAGNETITE	ETHIOPIAN	EPICUREAN	QUICKSAND	WAISTLINE	BOLSHEVIK	GELIGNITE
REFECTORY	MAGNETIZE	ETHNOLOGY	EPIDERMIS	QUICKSORT	WHICHEVER	BULGARIAN	GOLDBRICK
REFERENCE	MAGNIFICO	INHALATOR	EPIGRAPHY	QUICKSTEP	WHIMSICAL	BULLFIGHT	GOLDENROD
REFLECTOR	MAGNITUDE	MAHARISHI	EPISCOPAL	QUICKTIME	WHIRLIGIG	BULLFINCH	GOLDFIELD
REFLEXIVE	MEGACYCLE	OTHERWISE	ETIQUETTE	QUIESCENT	WHIRLPOOL	CALABOOSE	GOLDFINCH
REFRACTOR	MEGADEATH	REHEARING	EXISTENCE	QUINTUPLE	WHIRLWIND	CALCIMINE	GOLDSMITH
REFURBISH	MEGAHERTZ	REHEARSAL	FAIRYLAND	QUITTANCE	WHITEBAIT	CALCULATE	HALFPENNY
SAFEGUARD	MEGAPHONE	SCHEELITE	FLINTLOCK	QUIZZICAL	WHITEFISH	CALENDULA	HALITOSIS
SAFFLOWER	MEGAPIXEL	SCHEMATIC	FRICASSEE	RAINSPOUT	WHITEHALL	CALIBRATE	HALLOWEEN
SOFTBOUND	NEGLIGENT	SCHILLING	FRIEDCAKE	RAINSTORM	WHITEHEAD	CALLOSITY	HELLEBORE
SUFFERING	NEGOTIANT	SCHLEMIEL	FRIGHTFUL	RAINWATER	WHITENESS	CALORIFIC	HELLENISM
SUFFOCATE	NEGOTIATE	SCHNAUZER	FRIVOLOUS	REIMBURSE	WHITETAIL	CALVINISM	HELVETIAN
SUFFRAGAN	NEGRITUDE	SCHOOLBOY	GLISSANDO	REINFORCE	WHITEWALL	CELANDINE	HELVETICA
UNFAILING	NIGHTCLUB	SPHINCTER	GRIEVANCE	REINSTATE	WHITEWASH	CELEBRATE	HILARIOUS
UNFEELING	NIGHTFALL	UNHARNESS	GRILLWORK	REITERATE	WHITEWOOD	CELEBRITY	HILLBILLY
UNFEIGNED	NIGHTGOWN	UNHEALTHY	GRISTMILL	RUINATION	WRISTBAND	CELESTIAL	HOLLYHOCK

HOLOCAUST	SALTPETER	ADMISSION	HOMEGROWN	TIMEPIECE	CONGRUITY	HINDRANCE	MONSIGNOR
HOLOGRAPH	SALTWATER	ADMIXTURE	HOMEMAKER	TIMETABLE	CONJUGATE	HINDSIGHT	MUNICIPAL
HOLYSTONE	SALVATION	ALMANDITE	HOMESTEAD	TOMBSTONE	CONNUBIAL	HONEYCOMB	NANOMETER
ILLEGIBLE	SCLEROSIS	ALMSHOUSE	HOMOGRAPH	UNMEANING	CONSCIOUS	HONEYMOON	NONCREDIT
ILLIBERAL	SELECTION	ARMADILLO	HOMOPHONE	UNMINDFUL	CONSCRIPT	HONORABLE	NONENTITY
ILLOGICAL	SELECTMAN	ARMISTICE	HUMANKIND	WOMANHOOD	CONSENSUS	HONORIFIC	NONPAREIL
JELLYFISH	SILICEOUS	BAMBOOZLE	HUMDINGER	WOMANKIND	CONSONANT	HUNCHBACK	NONPERSON
KILOCYCLE	SILICOSIS	BIMONTHLY	HUMILIATE	WOMANLIKE	CONSTABLE	HUNGARIAN	NONPROFIT
KILOHERTZ	SILTSTONE	BOMBAZINE	IMMEDIACY	WOMENFOLK	CONSTANCY	IGNORANCE	NONREADER
KILOLITER	SOLEMNIZE	BOMBPROOF	IMMEDIATE	ANNOUNCER	CONSTRAIN	INNERMOST	OBNOXIOUS
KILOMETER	SOLICITOR	BOMBSHELL	IMMIGRANT	ANNOYANCE	CONSTRICT	INNERSOLE	PANEGYRIC
MALACHITE	SOLILOQUY	BOMBSIGHT	IMMIGRATE	ANNUITANT	CONSTRUCT	INNKEEPER	PANHANDLE
MALADROIT	SOLITAIRE	BUMBLEBEE	IMMOVABLE	BANDEROLE	CONTAGION	INNOCENCE	PANTHEISM
MALATHION	SPLENETIC	BUMPTIOUS	IMMUTABLE	BANDOLIER	CONTAINER	INNOCUOUS	PANTOMIME
MALAYSIAN	SPLITTING	CAMELBACK	LAMEBRAIN	BANDSTAND	CONTENTED	JINRIKSHA	PENDULOUS
MALIGNANT	SULFUROUS	CAMEMBERT	LAMINATED	BANDWAGON	CONTINENT	KINESCOPE	PENEPLAIN
MALLEABLE	SYLLABIFY	CAMPANILE	LIMBURGER	BANDWIDTH	CONTINUAL	KINSWOMAN	PENETRATE
MELIORATE	SYLLOGISM	CAMPSTOOL	LIMELIGHT	BANQUETTE	CONTINUUM	LANDOWNER	PENHOLDER
MELODIOUS	TALKATIVE	COMFORTER	LIMESTONE	BANTUSTAN	CONTRALTO	LANDSCAPE	PENINSULA
MELODRAMA	TELEGENIC	COMMANDER	LIMOUSINE	BENIGHTED	CONTUMELY	LANDSLIDE	PENTECOST
MELTWATER	TELEGRAPH	COMMINGLE	MEMORABLE	BENIGNANT	CONTUSION	LANTHANUM	PENTHOUSE
MILESTONE	TELEMETER	COMMISSAR	MOMENTARY	BENTONITE	CONUNDRUM	LINEAMENT	PENURIOUS
MILLIGRAM	TELEPATHY	COMMITTEE	MOMENTOUS	BINOCULAR	CONVIVIAL	LONGEVITY	PINEAPPLE
MILLINERY	TELEPHONE	COMMODITY	NAMEPLATE	BINOMINAL	CUNEIFORM	LONGITUDE	PINSTRIPE
MILLIPEDE	TELEPHONY	COMMODORE	NUMERATOR	BONDWOMAN	DANDELION	LUNCHROOM	PONDEROUS
MILLIVOLT	TELEPHOTO	COMMOTION	NUMERICAL	CANALBOAT	DANGEROUS	MANDATORY	PUNCTILIO
MILLSTONE	TELESCOPE	COMMUNION	PIMPERNEL	CANDIDACY	DENIGRATE	MANGANESE	PUNCTUATE
MOLDBOARD	TELLURIUM	COMMUNISM	POMPADOUR	CANDIDATE	DENTITION	MANHANDLE	RANCHLAND
MULTIFORM	TOLERABLE	COMMUNITY	REMAINDER	CANDLEMAS	FANCYWORK	MANHATTAN	RANDOMIZE
MULTISCAN	TOLERANCE	COMPANION	REMINISCE	CANDLEPIN	FANTASIZE	MANIFESTO	RANGELAND
MULTISPIN	TOLLHOUSE	COMPETENT	REMISSION	CANEBRAKE	FANTASTIC	MANNEQUIN	RENCONTRE
MULTISYNC	TULAREMIA	COMPLAINT	RUMRUNNER	CANNONADE	FINANCIAL	MANNERISM	RENDITION
MULTITUDE	UNLEARNED	COMPONENT	SEMANTICS	CANNONEER	FINANCIER	MANOEUVRE	RUNAROUND
OBLIVIOUS	VALENTINE	COMPOSITE	SEMAPHORE	CANONICAL	FINGERING	MANOMETER	SANCTUARY
PALAESTRA	VALUATION	COMPOSURE	SEMBLANCE	CANTABILE	FINGERTIP	MANSLAYER	SANDBLAST
PALANQUIN	VELVETEEN	DAMASCENE	SEMICOLON	CANTHARIS	FINICKING	MENAGERIE	SANDPAPER
PALATABLE	VILLENAGE	DAMNATION	SEMIFINAL	CENTENARY	FUNGICIDE	MENDICANT	SANDPIPER
PALLADIUM	VOLCANISM	DAMSELFLY	SEMIFLUID	CENTESIMO	FUNICULAR	MENOPAUSE	SANDSTONE
PALMISTRY	VOLTMETER	DEMAGOGUE	SEMILUNAR	CENTIGRAM	GANGPLANK	MENTALITY	SANDSTORM
PALPITATE	VOLUNTARY	DEMARCATE	SEMIWORKS	CENTIPEDE	GENEALOGY	MINCEMEAT	SANGFROID
PHLEBITIS	VOLUNTEER	DEMIMONDE	SIMPATICO	CENTURION	GENERATOR	MINELAYER	SENIORITY
POLICEMAN	VULCANISM	DEMITASSE	SIMPLETON	CONCERNED	GENITALIA	MINIATURE	SENSATION
POLITBURO	VULCANIZE	DEMOCRACY	SOMETHING	CONCERTED	GENTILITY	MINISCULE	SENSITIVE
POLITESSE	VULGARIAN	DEMULCENT	SOMETIMES	CONCIERGE	GENTLEMAN	MINISKIRT	SENSITIZE
POLITICAL	VULGARISM	DEMURRAGE	SOMEWHERE	CONCORDAT	GENUFLECT	MINISTATE	SENTIMENT
POLYESTER	VULGARITY	DIMENSION	SOMNOLENT	CONCOURSE	GONDOLIER	MINUSCULE	SINGLETON
POLYGRAPH	VULGARIZE	DIMORPHIC	SUMMARIZE	CONCUBINE	GONORRHEA	MINUTEMAN	SINUSITIS
POLYPHONY	WALLBOARD	DOMINANCE	SUMMATION	CONDENSER	GUNCOTTON	MONASTERY	SUNBONNET
PULMONARY	WALLOPING	DUMBFOUND	SUMPTUOUS	CONDIMENT	GUNNYSACK	MONGOLIAN	SUNFLOWER
PULVERIZE	WALLPAPER	GIMMICKRY	SYMBIOSIS	CONDITION	GUNPOWDER	MONGOLISM	SUNSEEKER
RELEVANCE	WILLPOWER	GYMNASIUM	SYMBOLISM	CONDUCTOR	HANDCLASP	MONGOLOID	SUNSTROKE
RELEVANCY	WOLFHOUND	HAMADRYAD	SYMBOLIZE	CONESTOGA	HANDCRAFT	MONKSHOOD	SYNAGOGUE
RELIGIOUS	WOLFSBANE	HAMBURGER	SYMPOSIUM	CONFESSOR	HANDIWORK	MONOGRAPH	SYNDICATE
RELIQUARY	WOLVERINE	HAMMERTOE	TEMPERATE	CONFIDANT	HANDSHAKE	MONOLOGUE	SYNERGISM
RELUCTANT	XYLOPHONE	HAMSTRING	TEMPORARY	CONFUSION	HANDSPIKE	MONOMANIA	SYNTHESIS
SALACIOUS	ADMIRABLE	HEMISTICH	TEMPORIZE	CONGENIAL	HANDSTAND	MONOPLANE	SYNTHETIC
SALESGIRL	ADMIRALTY	HEMSTITCH	TIMBERING	CONGERIES	HANDWOVEN	MONOSPACE	TANGERINE

TANTALIZE	BROADBAND	GEOGRAPHY	PROTOZOAN	AMPLITUDE	EXPLOSION	REPRESENT	BARBAROUS
TANZANIAN	BROADCAST	GROOMSMAN	PROVENCAL	APPALOOSA	EXPLOSIVE	REPRIMAND	BARCAROLE
TENACIOUS	BROADLOOM	GROSGRAIN	PROVENDER	APPARATUS	EXPOSITOR	REPROBATE	BAREFACED
TENDERIZE	BROADSIDE	GROTESQUE	PROVIDENT	APPELLANT	EXPULSION	REPRODUCE	BARKEEPER
TENEBROUS	BROADTAIL	GROUNDHOG	PROVISION	APPELLATE	EXPURGATE	REPUDIATE	BARNSTORM
TENTATIVE	BROCHETTE	GROUNDING	PROVOLONE	APPENDAGE	HAPHAZARD	REPUGNANT	BAROGRAPH
TINDERBOX	BROKERAGE	GROUPWARE	PROXIMATE	APPERTAIN	HAPPENING	REPULSION	BAROMETER
TONSORIAL	BRONCHIAL	INOCULATE	PROXIMITY	APPETIZER	HAPPINESS	REPULSIVE	BARRACUDA
UNNATURAL	CHOCOLATE	INORGANIC	PSORIASIS	APPLEJACK	HEPATITIS	REPUTABLE	BARRICADE
VANDALISM	CHONDRITE	IRONBOUND	QUOTIDIAN	APPLETALK	HOPSCOTCH	SAPSUCKER	BARRISTER
VANDALIZE	CHONDRULE	IRONSTONE	ROOTSTOCK	APPLIANCE	HYPERBOLA	SEPARABLE	BARTENDER
VENERABLE	CHOPHOUSE	ISOSCELES	SCOUNDREL	APPLICANT	HYPERBOLE	SEPARATOR	BERKELIUM
VENGEANCE	CHOPSTICK	KNOCKDOWN	SHOEMAKER	APPOINTEE	HYPERCARD	SEPTEMBER	BERYLLIUM
VENIREMAN	CHORISTER	KNOWLEDGE	SHOREBIRD	APPORTION	HYPERTEXT	SEPULCHER	BIRDHOUSE
VENTILATE	CLOCKWISE	MOONLIGHT	SHORTCAKE	APPREHEND	HYPHENATE	SEPULTURE	BIRTHMARK
VENTRICLE	CLOCKWORK	MOONSCAPE	SHORTHAND	ASPARAGUS	HYPOCRISY	SOPHISTIC	BIRTHRATE
VENTUROUS	CLOISONNE	MOONSHINE	SHORTHORN	ASPERSION	IMPARTIAL	SOPHISTRY	BURLESQUE
VINDICATE	COONHOUND	MOONSTONE	SHORTSTOP	BIPARTITE	IMPASSIVE	SOPHOMORE	BURUNDIAN
WINDBLOWN	COOPERATE	NEODYMIUM	SHORTWAVE	CAPACIOUS	IMPATIENS	SOPORIFIC	CARBONATE
WINDBREAK	CROCODILE	NEOLOGISM	SHOWPIECE	CAPACITOR	IMPATIENT	SUPERNOVA	CARBUNCLE
WINDCHILL	CROISSANT	PHONETICS	SHOWPLACE	CAPARISON	IMPEDANCE	SUPERPOSE	CARBURIZE
WINDPROOF	CROQUETTE	PHONOLOGY	SNOWDRIFT	CAPILLARY	IMPERFECT	SUPERSEDE	CARCINOMA
WINDSTORM	CROSSOVER	PHOSPHATE	SNOWFIELD	CAPITALLY	IMPERIOUS	SUPERVENE	CARDBOARD
WINDSWEPT	CROSSROAD	PHOTOCELL	SNOWFLAKE	CAPRICCIO	IMPETUOUS	SUPERVISE	CARETAKER
WINEPRESS	CROSSWALK	PHOTOCOPY	SNOWSTORM	CAPSULATE	IMPLEMENT	SUPPLIANT	CARIBBEAN
WINTERIZE	CROSSWAYS	PHOTOPLAY	SPOKESMAN	CAPTIVATE	IMPLICATE	SUPPOSING	CARNATION
WONDERFUL	CROSSWISE	PLOWSHARE	SPOONBILL	COPARTNER	IMPOLITIC	SUPPURATE	CARNELIAN
XANTHIPPE	DEODORANT	POORHOUSE	SPORTSMAN	COPYRIGHT	IMPORTANT	SUPREMACY	CARNIVORA
ABOMINATE	DEODORIZE	PROBATION	SPOTLIGHT	CUPBEARER	IMPORTUNE	TYPEWRITE	CARNIVORE
ABORIGINE	DEOXIDIZE	PROBATIVE	STOCKPILE	DEPARTURE	IMPOSTURE	UNPLUMBED	CARPENTER
ACOUSTICS	DOORPLATE	PROBOSCIS	STOCKYARD	DEPENDENT	IMPRECATE	UNPOPULAR	CARPETBAG
AFORESAID	DROMEDARY	PROCEDURE	STOMACHER	DEPRECATE	IMPRECISE	UPPERCASE	CARPETING
ALONGSIDE	ECONOMICS	PROCESSOR	STOMACHIC	DEPRESSED	IMPROMPTU	UPPERMOST	CARROUSEL
AMORPHOUS	ECONOMIZE	PROCONSUL	STOPLIGHT	DIPHTHONG	IMPROVISE	VAPORIZER	CARTILAGE
ANOMALOUS	ECOSYSTEM	PROCREATE	STOPWATCH	DIPLOMACY	IMPRUDENT	VAPORWARE	CARTRIDGE
ANONYMOUS	ELOCUTION	PROFANITY	STOREROOM	DIPTEROUS	IMPULSION	ACQUIESCE	CARTWHEEL
ANOPHELES	EMOLLIENT	PROFESSOR	SWORDFISH	DUPLICATE	IMPULSIVE	EXQUISITE	CEREBRATE
APOCRYPHA	EMOLUMENT	PROFITEER	SWORDPLAY	DUPLICITY	INPATIENT	LIQUIDATE	CERECLOTH
APOLOGIZE	EROGENOUS	PROGNOSIS	SWORDSMAN	EMPENNAGE	NEPHRITIC	REQUISITE	CERTAINTY
APOSTOLIC	ESOPHAGUS	PROJECTOR	SWORDTAIL	EMPHASIZE	NEPHRITIS	SEQUESTER	CERTITUDE
ATONEMENT	EVOLUTION	PROMENADE	TOOTHACHE	EMPHYSEMA	NEPTUNIUM	ACROPOLIS	CHRISTIAN
AVOCATION	EXOGENOUS	PROMINENT	TOOTHPICK	EMPIRICAL	OPPORTUNE	AERIALIST	CHRISTMAS
BIOGRAPHY	EXONERATE	PROMISING	TOOTHSOME	ESPERANTO	ORPHANAGE	AERODROME	CHROMATIC
BIOSPHERE	EXOSPHERE	PRONGHORN	TROOPSHIP	ESPIONAGE	PAPERBACK	AEROPAUSE	CHRONICLE
BLOCKHEAD	FLOODGATE	PRONOUNCE	TROUSSEAU	ESPLANADE	PAPILLOTE	AEROPLANE	CHRYSALIS
BLOODBATH	FLOPHOUSE	PROOFREAD	VIOLATION	EUPHEMISM	POPPYCOCK	AEROSPACE	CIRCADIAN
BLOODLINE	FLOTATION	PROPAGATE	VOODOOISM	EXPANSION	PUPPETEER	AFRIKAANS	CIRCUITRY
BLOODROOT	FLOWCHART	PROPELLER	WHOLESALE	EXPANSIVE	RAPACIOUS	AGREEABLE	CIRCULATE
BLOODSHED	FLOWERPOT	PROPHETIC	WHOLESOME	EXPATIATE	REPAIRMAN	AGREEMENT	CIRRHOSIS
BLOODSHOT	FOODSTUFF	PROPONENT	WHOSOEVER	EXPECTANT	REPELLENT	AIRMOBILE	CORELDRAW
BLOWTORCH	FOOLHARDY	PROPRIETY	WOODBLOCK	EXPEDIENT	REPERTORY	AIRWORTHY	CORIANDER
BOOKMAKER	FOOLPROOF	PROSCRIBE	WOODCHUCK	EXPEDITER	REPLENISH	ARROWHEAD	CORKSCREW
BOOKPLATE	FOOTBOARD	PROSECUTE	WOODCRAFT	EXPENSIVE	REPLETION	ARROWROOT	CORMORANT
BOOKSHELF	FOOTLOOSE	PROSELYTE	WRONGDOER	EXPERTISE	REPLICATE	ATROCIOUS	CORNSTALK
BOOMERANG	FOOTPRINT	PROSTRATE	AMPERSAND	EXPIATORY	REPORTAGE	AURICULAR	COROLLARY
BOONDOCKS	FOOTSTOOL	PROTECTOR	AMPHIBIAN	EXPLETIVE	REPOSSESS	BARBARIAN	CORPORATE
BOOTBLACK	FROSTBITE	PROTOTYPE	AMPHIBOLE	EXPLICATE	REPREHEND	BARBARISM	CORPOREAL

CORPUSCLE	FORMALISM	IRRITABLE	PERMANENT	SURRENDER	WORRYWART	DISCOMFIT	INSENSATE
CORRELATE	FORMALITY	ISRAELITE	PERMEABLE	SURROGATE	WORTHLESS	DISCOURSE	INSERTION
CORRUGATE	FORMALIZE	JERKWATER	PERPETUAL	SURVEYING	XEROPHYTE	DISCREDIT	INSIDIOUS
CORTISONE	FORMATION	JURIDICAL	PERPLEXED	TARANTULA	YARDSTICK	DISEMBARK	INSINCERE
CORUSCATE	FORMATIVE	LORGNETTE	PERSECUTE	TARPAULIN	ZIRCONIUM	DISEMBODY	INSINUATE
CURETTAGE	FORMULATE	MARGARINE	PERSEVERE	TERMAGANT	ABSORBENT	DISENGAGE	INSISTENT
CURRYCOMB	FORSYTHIA	MARIJUANA	PERSIMMON	TERMINATE	ADSORBATE	DISESTEEM	INSOLUBLE
CURVATURE	FORTHWITH	MARMALADE	PERSONAGE	TERRARIUM	ADSORBENT	DISFIGURE	INSOLVENT
DAREDEVIL	FORTITUDE	MARMOREAL	PERSONATE	TERRITORY	AESTHETIC	DISHCLOTH	INSTANTER
DARWINISM	FORTNIGHT	MARQUETRY	PERSONIFY	TERRORISM	AESTIVATE	DISHONEST	INSTANTLY
DERRINGER	FORTUNATE	MARSUPIAL	PERSONNEL	TERRORIZE	ASSEMBLER	DISHWATER	INSTIGATE
DHRYSTONE	FORWARDER	MARTYRDOM	PERTINENT	THRALLDOM	ASSERTION	DISINFECT	INSTITUTE
DIRECTION	FURNITURE	MARVELOUS	PHRENETIC	THREEFOLD	ASSIDUOUS	DISLOCATE	INSURABLE
DIRECTIVE	GARNISHEE	MERCENARY	PIROUETTE	THREESOME	ASSISTANT	DISMANTLE	INSURANCE
DIRECTORY	GARNITURE	MERCERIZE	PORCELAIN	THRESHOLD	ASSOCIATE	DISMEMBER	INSURGENT
DIRIGIBLE	GARRULOUS	MERCURIAL	PORCUPINE	THROWAWAY	ASSONANCE	DISOBLIGE	JESSAMINE
DORMITORY	GERIATRIC	MERCUROUS	PORRINGER	THROWBACK	ASSURANCE	DISORIENT	LASSITUDE
EARTHLING	GERMANIUM	MERGANSER	PORTFOLIO	TURBOPROP	BASEBOARD	DISPARAGE	MASCULINE
EARTHWARD	GERMICIDE	MERRIMENT	PORTULACA	TURBULENT	BASTINADO	DISPARATE	MASOCHISM
EARTHWORK	GERMINATE	MORTICIAN	PUREBLOOD	TURNABOUT	BESETTING	DISPLEASE	MASTERFUL
EARTHWORM	GYRFALCON	MURDEROUS	PURGATION	TURNSTILE	BESPANGLE	DISPRAISE	MASTICATE
EGREGIOUS	GYROSCOPE	NARCISSUS	PURGATIVE	TURNTABLE	BESPATTER	DISPUTANT	MESCALINE
ENRAPTURE	HARBINGER	NARCOTIZE	PURGATORY	TURPITUDE	BISHOPRIC	DISREGARD	MESMERIZE
ERRONEOUS	HARBORAGE	NARRATIVE	PURSUANCE	TURQUOISE	BUSHWHACK	DISREPAIR	MESSENGER
FARMHOUSE	HARDBOARD	NORMALIZE	PYRETHRUM	TYRANNIZE	BYSTANDER	DISREPUTE	MESSIEURS
FARMSTEAD	HARDBOUND	NORMATIVE	PYROLYSIS	TYRANNOUS	CASSEROLE	DISSECTED	MISBEHAVE
FARSEEING	HARDCOVER	NORTHEAST	PYROMANIA	UKRAINIAN	CASSOWARY	DISSEMBLE	MISCHANCE
FEROCIOUS	HARDIHOOD	NORTHWEST	PYROMETER	UNRIVALED	CASTANETS	DISSENTER	MISCREANT
FERRYBOAT	HARDSTAND	NORWEGIAN	SARTORIAL	UNRUFFLED	CASTIGATE	DISSIDENT	MISDIRECT
FERTILIZE	HARLEQUIN	NURSEMAID	SCRAPBOOK	VARIATION	CASUISTRY	DISSIPATE	MISERABLE
FIREBRAND	HARMONICA	OURSELVES	SCREENING	VARIEGATE	CESSATION	DISSOLUTE	MISGIVING
FIREBREAK	HARMONICS	PARACHUTE	SCREWBALL	VERACIOUS	COSMOGONY	DISTEMPER	MISGOVERN
FIREBRICK	HARMONIUM	PARAGRAPH	SCRIMMAGE	VERBALIZE	COSMOLOGY	DISTURBED	MISHANDLE
FIREHOUSE	HARMONIZE	PARALYSIS	SCRIMSHAW	VERDIGRIS	COSMONAUT	DOSIMETER	MISINFORM
FIREPLACE	HARTSHORN	PARAMETER	SCRIPTURE	VERIDICAL	COSPONSOR	DYSENTERY	MISMANAGE
FIREPOWER	HERBALIST	PARAMOUNT	SCRIVENER	VERITABLE	CUSTODIAL	DYSPEPSIA	MISORIENT
FIREPROOF	HERBARIUM	PARATHION	SERIGRAPH	VERMIFORM	CUSTODIAN	DYSTROPHY	MISSILERY
FIREWATER	HERBICIDE	PARCHMENT	SERVITUDE	VERMIFUGE	CUSTOMARY	EASYGOING	MISSIONER
FIRMAMENT	HERCULEAN	PAREGORIC	SHRINKAGE	VERMILION	CUSTOMIZE	ELSEWHERE	MISTLETOE
FIRSTBORN	HEREAFTER	PAROCHIAL	SHRUBBERY	VERNALIZE	DASHBOARD	ENSHEATHE	MUSKMELON
FIRSTHAND	HEREUNDER	PARQUETRY	SPRIGHTLY	VERSATILE	DESCENDER	ERSTWHILE	MUSSULMAN
FIRSTLING	HERITABLE	PARRICIDE	STRAPLESS	VERTEBRAL	DESECRATE	ESSENTIAL	MYSTICISM
FORECLOSE	HERMITAGE	PARSIMONY	STRAPPING	VIRGINITY	DESICCANT	FASCINATE	NOSEBLEED
FOREFRONT	HOREHOUND	PARSONAGE	STRATAGEM	VORACIOUS	DESICCATE	FASTENING	NOSEPIECE
FOREGOING	HOROSCOPE	PARTITION	STREAMBED	WARBONNET	DESIGNATE	FESTIVITY	NOSTALGIA
FOREIGNER	HORSEBACK	PARTITIVE	STREAMLET	WAREHOUSE	DESIGNING	FISHERMAN	OBSERVANT
FORENAMED	HORSEHAIR	PARTRIDGE	STREETCAR	WARMONGER	DESIRABLE	FUSILLADE	OBSESSION
FORESHEET	HORSEHIDE	PERCHANCE	STRENUOUS	WIREFRAME	DESPERADO	GASTRITIS	OBSTINATE
FORESHORE	HORSEPLAY	PERCOLATE	STRETCHER	WORKBENCH	DESPERATE	GASTROPOD	ONSLAUGHT
FORESIGHT	HORSESHOE	PERDITION	STRICTURE	WORKGROUP	DESTITUTE	GESTATION	PASSENGER
FORESTALL	HORSETAIL	PERENNIAL	STRIKEOUT	WORKHORSE	DESTROYER	GUSTATORY	PASSERINE
FORESWEAR	HORSEWHIP	PERFORATE	STRIPLING	WORKHOUSE	DESUETUDE	HISTAMINE	PASTORALE
FORETASTE	HORTATIVE	PERFUMERY	STRONTIUM	WORKPLACE	DESULTORY	HISTOGRAM	PASTURAGE
FORETOKEN	HORTATORY	PERIMETER	STRUCTURE	WORKTABLE	DISAFFECT	HISTORIAN	PESSIMISM
FOREWOMAN	HURRICANE	PERIPHERY	SURCHARGE	WORLDLING	DISAPPEAR	HUSBANDRY	PESTHOUSE
FORGATHER	IRRADIATE	PERISCOPE	SURCINGLE	WORLDWIDE	DISBURDEN	HYSTERICS	PESTICIDE
FORGIVING	IRREGULAR	PERISTYLE	SURFBOARD	WORRISOME	DISCHARGE	INSATIATE	PESTILENT

PISTACHIO	WASTELAND	BETROTHED	HOTHEADED	MATUTINAL	RETRIEVER	COURTYARD	ROUMANIAN
POSTERIOR	WISECRACK	BUTTERCUP	INTEGRATE	METALWARE	RETROFIRE	COUTURIER	ROUNDELAY
POSTERITY	YESTERDAY	BUTTERFAT	INTEGRITY	METALWORK	RUTHENIUM	CRUCIFORM	ROUNDWORM
POSTHASTE	AFTERCARE	BUTTERFLY	INTELLECT	METEORITE	SATELLITE	DAUNTLESS	SCULPTURE
POSTILION	AFTERDECK	BUTTERNUT	INTENDANT	METEOROID	SATINWOOD	DEUTERIUM	SCUTCHEON
POSTNATAL	AFTERGLOW	CATACLYSM	INTENSIFY	METHADONE	SATURNINE	DOUBTLESS	SLUICEWAY
POSTULANT	AFTERLIFE	CATALEPSY	INTENSITY	METHODIST	SITUATION	DRUGSTORE	SOUBRETTE
POSTULATE	AFTERMATH	CATALYSIS	INTENSIVE	METHODIZE	ULTIMATUM	DRUMSTICK	SOUTHEAST
PUSSYFOOT	AFTERNOON	CATAMARAN	INTENTION	METRICIZE	ULTRAHIGH	EBULLIENT	SOUTHWEST
RASPBERRY	AFTERWARD	CATAMOUNT	INTERCEDE	METROLOGY	ULTRAPURE	EDUCATION	SQUEAMISH
RASTERIZE	ALTERNATE	CATATONIC	INTERCEPT	METRONOME	UNTUTORED	ELUCIDATE	TAUTOLOGY
RESECTION	ALTIMETER	CATCHMENT	INTERDICT	MOTORBIKE	URTICARIA	ENUMERATE	THUMBNAIL
RESERPINE	ANTARCTIC	CATCHWORD	INTERFACE	MOTORBOAT	UTTERANCE	ENUNCIATE	THUMBTACK
RESERVIST	ANTECHOIR	CATECHISM	INTERFERE	MOTORCADE	UTTERMOST	EQUIPMENT	TOUCHDOWN
RESERVOIR	ANTHOLOGY	CATERWAUL	INTERFUSE	MYTHOLOGY	WATCHBAND	EQUIPOISE	TRUCKLOAD
RESHUFFLE	ANTICLINE	CATHARSIS	INTERJECT	NATURALLY	WATCHCASE	EQUITABLE	TRUCULENT
RESIDENCE	ANTIKNOCK	CATHARTIC	INTERLACE	NOTCHBACK	WATCHWORD	EQUIVOCAL	TRUNCHEON
RESIDENCY	ANTINOVEL	CATHEDRAL	INTERLARD	NOTORIOUS	WATERFALL	ERUDITION	VOUCHSAFE
RESIDUARY	ANTIPASTO	CITIZENRY	INTERLEAF	NUTRIMENT	WATERFOWL	EXUBERANT	YOUNGLING
RESISTANT	ANTIPATHY	COTILLION	INTERLINE	NUTRITION	WATERLINE	FEUDALISM	YOUNGSTER
RESONANCE	ANTIQUARY	COTYLEDON	INTERLINK	OPTOMETRY	WATERMARK	FEUDATORY	ADVANTAGE
RESONATOR	ANTIQUITY	CUTANEOUS	INTERLOCK	OSTRACIZE	WATERSHED	FLUCTUATE	ADVENTURE
RESTRAINT	ANTISERUM	CUTTHROAT	INTERLOPE	OUTERMOST	WATERSIDE	FOUNDLING	ADVERSARY
RESURRECT	ANTITOXIN	CYTOPLASM	INTERLUDE	OUTGROWTH	WITHDRAWN	FOURSCORE	ADVERSITY
ROSEWATER	ANTITUMOR	DETECTIVE	INTERMENT	OUTNUMBER	WITHSTAND	FRUITCAKE	ADVERTISE
RUSTICATE	ANTIVENIN	DETENTION	INTERNIST	OUTRIGGER	WITTICISM	FRUITERER	ADVISABLE
SASSAFRAS	ARTERIOLE	DETERGENT	INTERNODE	OUTSKIRTS	YTTERBIUM	FRUSTRATE	CAVALCADE
SUSPENDER	ARTHRITIS	DETERMINE	INTERPLAY	OUTSPOKEN	ADUMBRATE	GAUCHERIE	COVALENCE
SUSPICION	ARTHROPOD	DETERRENT	INTERPOSE	OUTSPREAD	ALUMINIUM	GLUTINOUS	DAVENPORT
SYSTEMIZE	ARTICHOKE	DETONATOR	INTERPRET	OUTWARDLY	ALUMINIZE	GRUBSTAKE	DEVASTATE
TESTAMENT	ARTICULAR	DETRIMENT	INTERRUPT	PATCHWORK	AQUAPLANE	HEURISTIC	DEVILMENT
TESTIMONY	ARTIFICER	DITHERING	INTERSECT	PATERNITY	AVUNCULAR	HOURGLASS	DIVERSIFY
TUSCARORA	ARTILLERY	ENTERITIS	INTERVENE	PATHOLOGY	BLUEBERRY	HOUSEBOAT	DIVERSION
UNSCATHED	ASTRADDLE	ENTERTAIN	INTERVIEW	PATRIARCH	BLUEBLACK	HOUSECOAT	DIVERSITY
UNSELFISH	ASTRAKHAN	ENTOURAGE	INTESTATE	PATRICIAN	BLUEGRASS	HOUSEHOLD	DIVISIBLE
UNSETTLED	ASTROLABE	ESTABLISH	INTESTINE	PATRICIDE	BLUEPOINT	HOUSEMAID	EAVESDROP
UNSHACKLE	ASTROLOGY	ESTAMINET	INTRICATE	PATRIMONY	BLUEPRINT	HOUSEWIFE	FAVORABLE
UNSHEATHE	ASTRONAUT	ESTIMABLE	INTRINSIC	PATRISTIC	BOULEVARD	HOUSEWORK	GOVERNESS
UNSIGHTLY	ASTRONOMY	EUTHENICS	INTRODUCE	PATROLMAN	BOUNTEOUS	JAUNDICED	HAVERSACK
UNSKILLED	ATTAINDER	EUTROPHIC	INTROVERT	PATRONAGE	BOUNTIFUL	LAUDATORY	INVECTIVE
UNSPARING	ATTENDANT	EXTEMPORE	INTUITION	PATRONIZE	BOURGEOIS	LAUNCHPAD	INVENTION
UNSPOTTED	ATTENTION	EXTENSION	INTUMESCE	PETROLEUM	BRUSHWOOD	LEUKOCYTE	INVENTIVE
UNSTUDIED	ATTENUATE	EXTENSIVE	JITTERBUG	PETROLOGY	BRUTALIZE	MAUSOLEUM	INVENTORY
VASECTOMY	ATTRIBUTE	EXTENUATE	LATECOMER	PETTICOAT	CAUCASIAN	MOUSETRAP	INVERNESS
VASSALAGE	ATTRITION	EXTIRPATE	LITERATIM	PITCHFORK	CAUSATION	MOUSTACHE	INVERSION
VESTIBULE	AUTHENTIC	EXTRADITE	LITHESOME	PITUITARY	CAUTERIZE	MOUTHPART	INVIDIOUS
VESTRYMAN	AUTHORITY	EXTRAVERT	LITHOLOGY	POTASSIUM	CHUCKHOLE	MOUTHWASH	INVIOLATE
VISCOSITY	AUTHORIZE	EXTREMISM	LITIGIOUS	POTBOILER	CHURCHMAN	NEURALGIA	INVISIBLE
VISIONARY	AUTOCRACY	EXTREMITY	LITTERBUG	POTENTATE	CLUBHOUSE	NEUROLOGY	INVOLUCRE
VISUALIZE	AUTOGRAPH	EXTRICATE	MATCHBOOK	POTENTIAL	COUNSELOR	PLURALITY	LAVALIERE
WASHBASIN	AUTOMATIC	EXTRINSIC	MATCHLOCK	POTPOURRI	COUNTDOWN	PLURALIZE	LEVIATHAN
WASHBOARD	AUTOMATON	EXTRUSIVE	MATCHWOOD	RATIONALE	COUNTLESS	PLUTONIUM	LIVERWORT
WASHCLOTH	AUTOTRACE	FETISHISM	MATERNITY	RETALIATE	COURTEOUS	POULTERER	LIVERYMAN
WASHHOUSE	BATHHOUSE	HATCHMENT	MATRIARCH	RETARDATE	COURTESAN	POURBOIRE	LIVESTOCK
WASHSTAND	BATHOLITH	HETERODOX	MATRICIDE	RETENTION	COURTROOM	RAUWOLFIA	NAVIGABLE
WASHWOMAN	BATTALION	HITCHHIKE	MATRIMONY	RETENTIVE	COURTSHIP	ROUGHNECK	NEVERMORE

NOVELETTE	PSYCHOSIS	CIGARILLO	LOGARITHM	SUBALTERN	GIBBERISH	CATCHWORD	KNOCKDOWN
NOVITIATE	SKYDIVING	CLEARANCE	MAHARISHI	SUBATOMIC	GRUBSTAKE	CAUCASIAN	LACCOLITH
REVERENCE	SKYJACKER	COPARTNER	MALACHITE	SUGARCANE	HAMBURGER	CHECKBOOK	LUNCHROOM
REVERSION	SKYLOUNGE	COVALENCE	MALADROIT	SUGARPLUM	HARBINGER	CHECKLIST	MASCULINE
REVOCABLE	SKYROCKET	CUTANEOUS	MALATHION	SWEATSHOP	HARBORAGE	CHECKMATE	MATCHBOOK
REVOLTING	THYROXINE	DAMASCENE	MALAYSIAN	SYNAGOGUE	HERBALIST	CHECKROOM	MATCHLOCK
REVULSION	GAZETTEER	DECADENCE	MEDALLION	TARANTULA	HERBARIUM	CHICANERY	MATCHWOOD
RIVERBANK	LAZYBONES	DECALOGUE	MEGACYCLE	TENACIOUS	HERBICIDE	CHICKADEE	MERCENARY
RIVERBOAT	MEZZANINE	DECATHLON	MEGADEATH	THEATRICS	HUSBANDRY	CHICKASAW	MERCERIZE
RIVERSIDE	PIZZICATO	DEKALITER	MEGAHERTZ	THRALLDOM	INABILITY	CHICKWEED	MERCURIAL
SEVENTEEN		DEKAMETER	MEGAPHONE	TREACHERY	INEBRIATE	CHOCOLATE	MERCUROUS
SOVEREIGN		DEKASTERE	MEGAPIXEL	TREADMILL	LIABILITY	CHUCKHOLE	MESCALINE
VIVACIOUS		DEMAGOGUE	MENAGERIE	TREASURER	LIMBURGER	CIRCADIAN	MINCEMEAT
WAVETABLE	**4TH LETTER**	DEMARCATE	METALWARE	TREATMENT	MISBEHAVE	CIRCUITRY	MISCHANCE
BOWSTRING		DEPARTURE	METALWORK	TULAREMIA	POTBOILER	CIRCULATE	MISCREANT
DOWITCHER	ADIABATIC	DEVASTATE	MONASTERY	TYRANNIZE	PROBATION	CLOCKWISE	NARCISSUS
DOWNGRADE	ADVANTAGE	DISAFFECT	NEFARIOUS	TYRANNOUS	PROBATIVE	CLOCKWORK	NARCOTIZE
DOWNRANGE	AILANTHUS	DISAPPEAR	OLFACTORY	UKRAINIAN	PROBOSCIS	CONCERNED	NONCREDIT
DOWNRIGHT	ALBATROSS	DREAMLAND	PALAESTRA	UNDAUNTED	RABBINATE	CONCERTED	NOTCHBACK
DOWNSHIFT	ALEATORIC	EGLANTINE	PALANQUIN	UNEARTHLY	REDBREAST	CONCIERGE	PARCHMENT
DOWNSTAGE	ALMANDITE	EMBARRASS	PALATABLE	UNFAILING	SEMBLANCE	CONCORDAT	PATCHWORK
DOWNSWING	ANTARCTIC	EMBAYMENT	PARACHUTE	UNHARNESS	SOUBRETTE	CONCOURSE	PEACETIME
ENWREATHE	APPALOOSA	ENRAPTURE	PARAGRAPH	UNNATURAL	STABILIZE	CONCUBINE	PERCHANCE
HOWSOEVER	APPARATUS	ESCALATOR	PARALYSIS	VAGARIOUS	SUNBONNET	CRACKDOWN	PERCOLATE
JEWELWEED	AQUAPLANE	ESTABLISH	PARAMETER	VERACIOUS	SYMBIOSIS	CROCODILE	PIECEMEAL
LOWERCASE	ARMADILLO	ESTAMINET	PARAMOUNT	VEXATIOUS	SYMBOLISM	CRUCIFORM	PIECEWORK
NEWSPAPER	ASPARAGUS	EXPANSION	PARATHION	VICARIOUS	SYMBOLIZE	DESCENDER	PITCHFORK
NEWSPRINT	ATTAINDER	EXPANSIVE	PEDAGOGUE	VIVACIOUS	TIMBERING	DIACRITIC	PLACEKICK
NEWSSTAND	AUDACIOUS	EXPATIATE	POTASSIUM	VORACIOUS	TOMBSTONE	DISCHARGE	PLACEMENT
POWERBOAT	BAGATELLE	FINANCIAL	RAPACIOUS	WOMANHOOD	TRIBESMAN	DISCOMFIT	PORCELAIN
TOWNSFOLK	BALALAIKA	FINANCIER	REDACTION	WOMANKIND	TRIBUTARY	DISCOURSE	PORCUPINE
UNWILLING	BICAMERAL	GABARDINE	REGARDING	WOMANLIKE	TURBOPROP	DISCREDIT	PRACTICAL
UNWITTING	BILATERAL	GALACTOSE	REMAINDER	ALABASTER	TURBULENT	EDUCATION	PRECANCEL
UNWORLDLY	BIPARTITE	GLEANINGS	REPAIRMAN	ARABESQUE	VERBALIZE	EJACULATE	PRECEDENT
UNWRITTEN	BLEACHERS	GREATCOAT	RETALIATE	BAMBOOZLE	WARBONNET	ELECTRIFY	PRECEDING
AUXILIARY	BREAKDOWN	HAMADRYAD	RETARDATE	BARBARIAN	WOEBEGONE	ELECTRODE	PRECENTOR
DEXTERITY	BREAKFAST	HEPATITIS	RUNAROUND	BARBARISM	APOCRYPHA	ELOCUTION	PRECEPTOR
DEXTEROUS	BROADBAND	HEXAMETER	SAGACIOUS	BARBAROUS	AVOCATION	ELUCIDATE	PRECIPICE
DIXIELAND	BROADCAST	HILARIOUS	SALACIOUS	BOMBAZINE	BACCHANAL	EPICENTER	PRECISION
HEXAMETER	BROADLOOM	HUMANKIND	SCRAPBOOK	BOMBPROOF	BARCAROLE	EPICUREAN	PRECURSOR
JUXTAPOSE	BROADSIDE	IMBALANCE	SEBACEOUS	BOMBSHELL	BEACHHEAD	EXECRABLE	PRICELESS
LUXURIANT	BROADTAIL	IMPARTIAL	SEMANTICS	BOMBSIGHT	BLACKBALL	EXECUTIVE	PROCEDURE
LUXURIATE	CALABOOSE	IMPASSIVE	SEMAPHORE	BUMBLEBEE	BLACKBIRD	EXECUTRIX	PROCESSOR
SAXIFRAGE	CANALBOAT	IMPATIENS	SEPARABLE	CARBONATE	BLACKBODY	FANCYWORK	PROCONSUL
SAXOPHONE	CAPACIOUS	IMPATIENT	SEPARATOR	CARBUNCLE	BLACKFOOT	FASCINATE	PROCREATE
TAXIDERMY	CAPACITOR	INCAPABLE	SHEATHING	CARBURIZE	BLACKHEAD	FLUCTUATE	PSYCHOSIS
VEXATIOUS	CAPARISON	INCARNATE	SPEAKEASY	CLUBHOUSE	BLACKJACK	FRACTIOUS	PUNCTILIO
ASYMPTOTE	CATACLYSM	INFANTILE	SPEARHEAD	CRABGRASS	BLACKLIST	FRICASSEE	PUNCTUATE
CRYOGENIC	CATALEPSY	INFATUATE	SPEARMINT	CUBBYHOLE	BLACKMAIL	GAUCHERIE	QUICKDRAW
ETYMOLOGY	CATALYSIS	INHALATOR	STEADFAST	CUPBEARER	BLOCKHEAD	GLYCOSIDE	QUICKLIME
GLYCOSIDE	CATAMARAN	INPATIENT	STEAMBOAT	DISBURDEN	BROCHETTE	GUNCOTTON	QUICKSAND
MAYFLOWER	CATAMOUNT	INSATIATE	STEAMSHIP	DOUBTLESS	BUCCANEER	HATCHMENT	QUICKSORT
OXYGENATE	CATATONIC	IRRADIATE	STRAPLESS	DUMBFOUND	CALCIMINE	HERCULEAN	QUICKSTEP
PAYMASTER	CAVALCADE	ISRAELITE	STRAPPING	EGGBEATER	CALCULATE	HITCHHIKE	QUICKTIME
PHYSICIAN	CELANDINE	JACARANDA	STRATAGEM	ELABORATE	CARCINOMA	HUNCHBACK	RANCHLAND
PHYSICIST	CIGARETTE	LAVALIERE	SUBALPINE	EXUBERANT	CATCHMENT	INOCULATE	REACTANCE

RENCONTRE	CONDITION	MENDICANT	ADVENTURE	CAMEMBERT	EIDERDOWN	GREENROOM	INTERFERE
SACCHARIN	CONDUCTOR	MIDDLEMAN	ADVERSARY	CANEBRAKE	ELSEWHERE	GREENWOOD	INTERFUSE
SANCTUARY	CREDULOUS	MISDIRECT	ADVERSITY	CARETAKER	EMBELLISH	GRIEVANCE	INTERJECT
SPACESHIP	DANDELION	MOLDBOARD	ADVERTISE	CATECHISM	EMPENNAGE	HAVERSACK	INTERLACE
SPECIALTY	DEODORANT	MURDEROUS	AFFECTING	CATERWAUL	ENTERITIS	HEREAFTER	INTERLARD
SPECTACLE	DEODORIZE	NEODYMIUM	AFFECTION	CELEBRATE	ENTERTAIN	HEREUNDER	INTERLEAF
SPECTATOR	EPIDERMIS	OXIDATION	AFTERCARE	CELEBRITY	EPHEDRINE	HETERODOX	INTERLINE
SPECULATE	ERADICATE	PENDULOUS	AFTERDECK	CELESTIAL	EPHEMERAL	HIBERNATE	INTERLINK
SPICEBUSH	ERUDITION	PERDITION	AFTERGLOW	CEREBRATE	ESPERANTO	HIDEBOUND	INTERLOCK
STOCKPILE	FEEDSTOCK	PONDEROUS	AFTERLIFE	CERECLOTH	ESSENTIAL	HOMEGROWN	INTERLOPE
STOCKYARD	FEEDSTUFF	PREDATION	AFTERMATH	CHEEKBONE	EXCELLENT	HOMEMAKER	INTERLUDE
SUCCESSOR	FEUDALISM	PREDATORY	AFTERNOON	CHEERLESS	EXCELSIOR	HOMESTEAD	INTERMENT
SUCCOTASH	FEUDATORY	PREDICATE	AFTERWARD	CHIEFTAIN	EXCEPTION	HONEYCOMB	INTERNIST
SUCCULENT	FLEDGLING	QUADRATIC	AGREEABLE	CLIENTELE	EXPECTANT	HONEYMOON	INTERNODE
SURCHARGE	FOODSTUFF	QUADRILLE	AGREEMENT	COFEATURE	EXPEDIENT	HOREHOUND	INTERPLAY
SURCINGLE	GLADIATOR	QUADRUPED	ALIENABLE	CONESTOGA	EXPEDITER	HYPERBOLA	INTERPOSE
THICKNESS	GLADIOLUS	QUADRUPLE	ALLERGIST	CORELDRAW	EXPENSIVE	HYPERBOLE	INTERPRET
TOUCHDOWN	GLADSTONE	RANDOMIZE	ALLEVIATE	CUNEIFORM	EXPERTISE	HYPERCARD	INTERRUPT
TRACKBALL	GOLDBRICK	RENDITION	ALTERNATE	CURETTAGE	EXTEMPORE	HYPERTEXT	INTERSECT
TRACTABLE	GOLDENROD	ROADBLOCK	AMBERGRIS	DAREDEVIL	EXTENSION	ILLEGIBLE	INTERVENE
TRICKSTER	GOLDFIELD	ROADSTEAD	AMPERSAND	DAVENPORT	EXTENSIVE	IMMEDIACY	INTERVIEW
TRUCKLOAD	GOLDFINCH	SADDLEBOW	ANAEROBIC	DEBENTURE	EXTENUATE	IMMEDIATE	INTESTATE
TRUCULENT	GOLDSMITH	SANDBLAST	ANGELFISH	DECEITFUL	FACETIOUS	IMPEDANCE	INTESTINE
TUSCARORA	GONDOLIER	SANDPAPER	ANTECHOIR	DECENNIAL	FIREBRAND	IMPERFECT	INVECTIVE
UNSCATHED	GRADATION	SANDPIPER	APPELLANT	DECEPTION	FIREBREAK	IMPERIOUS	INVENTION
VACCINATE	GUIDEBOOK	SANDSTONE	APPELLATE	DEFEATISM	FIREBRICK	IMPETUOUS	INVENTIVE
VISCOSITY	GUIDELINE	SANDSTORM	APPENDAGE	DEFECTIVE	FIREHOUSE	INCENTIVE	INVENTORY
VOICELESS	HANDCLASP	SHADOWBOX	APPERTAIN	DEFENDANT	FIREPLACE	INCEPTION	INVERNESS
VOLCANISM	HANDCRAFT	SKYDIVING	APPETIZER	DEFENSIVE	FIREPOWER	INCESSANT	INVERSION
VOUCHSAFE	HANDIWORK	SUBDIVIDE	ARGENTINE	DEFERENCE	FIREPROOF	INDELIBLE	IRREGULAR
VULCANISM	HANDSHAKE	SYNDICATE	ARGENTITE	DEFERMENT	FIREWATER	INDEMNIFY	JEWELWEED
VULCANIZE	HANDSPIKE	TENDERIZE	ARTERIOLE	DEJECTION	FORECLOSE	INDEMNITY	KINESCOPE
WATCHBAND	HANDSTAND	TINDERBOX	ASCENDANT	DEPENDENT	FOREFRONT	INDENTION	LAMEBRAIN
WATCHCASE	HANDWOVEN	TOADSTOOL	ASCENDERS	DESECRATE	FOREGOING	INDENTURE	LATECOMER
WATCHWORD	HARDBOARD	TRADEMARK	ASCENSION	DETECTIVE	FOREIGNER	INFECTION	LEGENDARY
WHICHEVER	HARDBOUND	TRADESMAN	ASCERTAIN	DETENTION	FORENAMED	INFERENCE	LIBERTINE
ZIRCONIUM	HARDCOVER	TRADITION	ASPERSION	DETERGENT	FORESHEET	INFERTILE	LIFEBLOOD
ZUCCHETTO	HARDIHOOD	UNADVISED	ASSEMBLER	DETERMINE	FORESHORE	INGENIOUS	LIFEGUARD
ACIDULATE	HARDSTAND	VANDALISM	ASSERTION	DETERRENT	FORESIGHT	INGENUITY	LIMELIGHT
ACIDULOUS	HEADBOARD	VANDALIZE	ATHENAEUM	DIAERESIS	FORESTALL	INGENUOUS	LIMESTONE
AMIDSHIPS	HEADDRESS	VERDIGRIS	ATTENDANT	DIMENSION	FORESWEAR	INJECTION	LINEAMENT
BALDACHIN	HEADFIRST	VINDICATE	ATTENTION	DIRECTION	FORETASTE	INNERMOST	LITERATIM
BANDEROLE	HEADLIGHT	VOODOOISM	ATTENUATE	DIRECTIVE	FORETOKEN	INNERSOLE	LIVERWORT
BANDOLIER	HEADPHONE	WINDBLOWN	BAREFACED	DIRECTORY	FOREWOMAN	INSENSATE	LIVERYMAN
BANDSTAND	HEADPIECE	WINDBREAK	BASEBOARD	DISEMBARK	FREEBOARD	INSERTION	LIVESTOCK
BANDWAGON	HEADSTALL	WINDCHILL	BELEAGUER	DISEMBODY	FREEMASON	INTEGRATE	LODESTONE
BANDWIDTH	HEADSTONE	WINDPROOF	BESETTING	DISENGAGE	FREESTONE	INTEGRITY	LOWERCASE
BIRDHOUSE	HEADWATER	WINDSTORM	BLUEBERRY	DISESTEEM	FREEWHEEL	INTELLECT	MAKESHIFT
BONDWOMAN	HINDRANCE	WINDSWEPT	BLUEBLACK	DIVERSIFY	FRIEDCAKE	INTENDANT	MATERNITY
CANDIDACY	HINDSIGHT	WONDERFUL	BLUEGRASS	DIVERSION	GABERDINE	INTENSIFY	METEORITE
CANDIDATE	HUMDINGER	WOODBLOCK	BLUEPOINT	DIVERSITY	GAZETTEER	INTENSITY	METEOROID
CANDLEMAS	LANDOWNER	WOODCHUCK	BLUEPRINT	DYSENTERY	GENEALOGY	INTENSIVE	MILESTONE
CANDLEPIN	LANDSCAPE	WOODCRAFT	BREEZEWAY	EAVESDROP	GENERATOR	INTENTION	MINELAYER
CARDBOARD	LANDSLIDE	YARDSTICK	BRIEFCASE	ECCENTRIC	GOVERNESS	INTERCEDE	MISERABLE
COADJUTOR	LAUDATORY	ACCESSION	CAFETERIA	EFFECTIVE	GREENBACK	INTERCEPT	MODERATOR
CONDENSER	LOADSTONE	ACCESSORY	CALENDULA	EFFECTUAL	GREENBELT	INTERDICT	MODERNISM
CONDIMENT	MANDATORY	ADJECTIVE	CAMELBACK	EGREGIOUS	GREENHORN	INTERFACE	MODERNIZE

MOMENTARY	RESECTION	TELEGRAPH	UTTERMOST	PROFESSOR	OUTGROWTH	EMPHASIZE	TIGHTROPE
MOMENTOUS	RESERPINE	TELEMETER	VALENTINE	PROFITEER	OXYGENATE	EMPHYSEMA	UNCHARTED
NAMEPLATE	RESERVIST	TELEPATHY	VASECTOMY	SAFFLOWER	PIGGYBACK	ENCHILADA	UNSHACKLE
NECESSARY	RESERVOIR	TELEPHONE	VEGETABLE	SEAFARING	PRAGMATIC	ENSHEATHE	UNSHEATHE
NECESSITY	RETENTION	TELEPHONY	VEHEMENCE	SHIFTLESS	PREGNABLE	EUCHARIST	WASHBASIN
NEVERMORE	RETENTIVE	TELEPHOTO	VENERABLE	SUFFERING	PROGNOSIS	EUPHEMISM	WASHBOARD
NONENTITY	REVERENCE	TELESCOPE	VICENNIAL	SUFFOCATE	PURGATION	EUTHENICS	WASHCLOTH
NOSEBLEED	REVERSION	TENEBROUS	VICEREGAL	SUFFRAGAN	PURGATIVE	EXCHEQUER	WASHHOUSE
NOSEPIECE	RIVERBANK	THREEFOLD	VIDELICET	SULFUROUS	PURGATORY	FISHERMAN	WASHSTAND
NOVELETTE	RIVERBOAT	THREESOME	VIDEOTAPE	SUNFLOWER	RANGELAND	HAPHAZARD	WASHWOMAN
NUMERATOR	RIVERSIDE	THRESHOLD	VIGESIMAL	SURFBOARD	RIDGEPOLE	HIGHLIGHT	WITHDRAWN
NUMERICAL	ROSEWATER	TIDEWATER	WAREHOUSE	TRIFOCALS	ROUGHNECK	HOTHEADED	WITHSTAND
OBJECTIFY	SAFEGUARD	TIMEPIECE	WATERFALL	WOLFHOUND	SANGFROID	HYPHENATE	YACHTSMAN
OBJECTIVE	SAGEBRUSH	TIMETABLE	WATERFOWL	WOLFSBANE	SINGLETON	JOBHOLDER	ACCIDENCE
OBSERVANT	SALESGIRL	TOLERABLE	WATERLINE	BIOGRAPHY	SPAGHETTI	LIGHTFACE	ADDICTION
OBSESSION	SATELLITE	TOLERANCE	WATERMARK	BULGARIAN	TANGERINE	LIGHTNING	ADMIRABLE
OFFENSIVE	SCHEELITE	TRIENNIAL	WATERSHED	COAGULANT	THIGHBONE	LIGHTSHIP	ADMIRALTY
OFFERTORY	SCHEMATIC	TYPEWRITE	WATERSIDE	COAGULATE	TRAGEDIAN	LIGHTSOME	ADMISSION
ORIENTATE	SCLEROSIS	UNBEKNOWN	WAVETABLE	CONGENIAL	VENGEANCE	LITHESOME	ADMIXTURE
OTHERWISE	SCREENING	UNBENDING	WHEELBASE	CONGERIES	VIRGINITY	LITHOLOGY	ADVISABLE
OUTERMOST	SCREWBALL	UNCEASING	WINEPRESS	CONGRUITY	VULGARIAN	MACHINERY	AERIALIST
PACEMAKER	SECESSION	UNCERTAIN	WIREFRAME	DANGEROUS	VULGARISM	MACHINIST	AFFIDAVIT
PAGEMAKER	SEDENTARY	UNDECEIVE	WISECRACK	DIAGNOSIS	VULGARITY	MANHANDLE	AFFILIATE
PANEGYRIC	SELECTION	UNDECIDED	WOMENFOLK	DRAGONFLY	VULGARIZE	MANHATTAN	AFRIKAANS
PAPERBACK	SELECTMAN	UNDERBODY	YTTERBIUM	DRUGSTORE	AMPHIBIAN	MECHANICS	ALLIGATOR
PAREGORIC	SEVENTEEN	UNDERBRED	ASAFETIDA	ENIGMATIC	AMPHIBOLE	MECHANISM	ALTIMETER
PATERNITY	SHEEPFOLD	UNDERCOAT	BEDFELLOW	EPIGRAPHY	ANCHORAGE	MECHANIZE	AMBIGUOUS
PENEPLAIN	SHEEPSKIN	UNDERDONE	BEEFEATER	EROGENOUS	ANCHORITE	METHADONE	AMBITIOUS
PENETRATE	SHOEMAKER	UNDERFEED	BEEFSTEAK	EXOGENOUS	ANCHORMAN	METHODIST	ANCILLARY
PERENNIAL	SIDEBOARD	UNDERFOOT	CHAFFINCH	FINGERING	ANTHOLOGY	METHODIZE	ANTICLINE
PHLEBITIS	SIDEBURNS	UNDERGIRD	COFFEEPOT	FINGERTIP	ARCHANGEL	MISHANDLE	ANTIKNOCK
PHRENETIC	SIDEPIECE	UNDERHAND	COFFERDAM	FLAGELLUM	ARCHENEMY	MYTHOLOGY	ANTINOVEL
PIKESTAFF	SIDESWIPE	UNDERLINE	COIFFEUSE	FLAGEOLET	ARCHETYPE	NEPHRITIC	ANTIPASTO
PINEAPPLE	SIDETRACK	UNDERLING	COMFORTER	FLAGSTAFF	ARCHFIEND	NEPHRITIS	ANTIPATHY
POTENTATE	SOLEMNIZE	UNDERMINE	CONFESSOR	FLAGSTONE	ARCHITECT	NIGHTCLUB	ANTIQUARY
POTENTIAL	SOMETHING	UNDERMOST	CONFIDANT	FORGATHER	ARCHIVIST	NIGHTFALL	ANTIQUITY
POWERBOAT	SOMETIMES	UNDERPART	CONFUSION	FORGIVING	ARTHRITIS	NIGHTGOWN	ANTISERUM
PUBESCENT	SOMEWHERE	UNDERPASS	CRAFTSMAN	FRIGHTFUL	ARTHROPOD	NIGHTHAWK	ANTITOXIN
PUREBLOOD	SOVEREIGN	UNDERPLAY	DELFTWARE	FUNGICIDE	AUTHENTIC	NIGHTLIFE	ANTITUMOR
PYRETHRUM	SPEEDBOAT	UNDERRATE	DIFFERENT	GANGPLANK	AUTHORITY	NIGHTMARE	ANTIVENIN
QUIESCENT	SPEEDWELL	UNDERSELL	DIFFICULT	GEOGRAPHY	AUTHORIZE	NIGHTTIME	ARBITRARY
RACEHORSE	SPLENETIC	UNDERSHOT	DIFFIDENT	HOBGOBLIN	BATHHOUSE	ORCHESTRA	ARBITRATE
RACETRACK	SQUEAMISH	UNDERSIDE	DISFIGURE	HUNGARIAN	BATHOLITH	ORPHANAGE	ARMISTICE
REBELLION	STEELYARD	UNDERTAKE	DRAFTSMAN	IMAGINARY	BISHOPRIC	PACHYDERM	ARTICHOKE
RECEPTION	STREAMBED	UNDERTONE	DRIFTWOOD	LONGEVITY	BUSHWHACK	PANHANDLE	ARTICULAR
RECEPTIVE	STREAMLET	UNDERWEAR	GODFATHER	LONGITUDE	CATHARSIS	PATHOLOGY	ARTIFICER
RECESSION	STREETCAR	UNDERWOOD	GYRFALCON	LORGNETTE	CATHARTIC	PENHOLDER	ARTILLERY
RECESSIVE	STRENUOUS	UNFEELING	HALFPENNY	MANGANESE	CATHEDRAL	PIGHEADED	ASSIDUOUS
REFECTION	STRETCHER	UNFEIGNED	INEFFABLE	MARGARINE	COCHINEAL	RECHERCHE	ASSISTANT
REFECTORY	SUPERNOVA	UNHEALTHY	LEAFSTALK	MERGANSER	DACHSHUND	RESHUFFLE	AUDIOLOGY
REFERENCE	SUPERPOSE	UNLEARNED	MAYFLOWER	MISGIVING	DASHBOARD	RIGHTEOUS	AURICULAR
REHEARING	SUPERSEDE	UNMEANING	ORIFLAMME	MISGOVERN	DICHOTOMY	RUTHENIUM	AUXILIARY
REHEARSAL	SUPERVENE	UNSELFISH	PERFORATE	MONGOLIAN	DIPHTHONG	SOPHISTIC	AVAILABLE
RELEVANCE	SUPERVISE	UNSETTLED	PERFUMERY	MONGOLISM	DISHCLOTH	SOPHISTRY	BENIGHTED
RELEVANCY	SWEETMEAT	UPPERCASE	PREFIGURE	MONGOLOID	DISHONEST	SOPHOMORE	BENIGNANT
REPELLENT	SYNERGISM	UPPERMOST	PREFLIGHT	OLIGARCHY	DISHWATER	TECHNICAL	BILINGUAL
REPERTORY	TELEGENIC	UTTERANCE	PROFANITY	ORIGINATE	DITHERING	TECHNIQUE	CALIBRATE

CAPILLARY	FUSILLADE	ORDINANCE	SPLITTING	HACKNEYED	BULLFIGHT	HALLOWEEN	SMALLTALK
CAPITALLY	GELIGNITE	ORGIASTIC	SPRIGHTLY	INNKEEPER	BULLFINCH	HARLEQUIN	SPELUNKER
CARIBBEAN	GENITALIA	OSCILLATE	STAIRCASE	JACKKNIFE	BURLESQUE	HEALTHFUL	STALEMATE
CHRISTIAN	GERIATRIC	PAKISTANI	STAIRWELL	JACKSCREW	CABLEGRAM	HELLEBORE	STILLBORN
CHRISTMAS	HABITABLE	PAPILLOTE	STRICTURE	JACKSTRAW	CALLOSITY	HELLENISM	SUBLIMATE
CITIZENRY	HABITUATE	PEKINGESE	STRIKEOUT	JERKWATER	CELLARAGE	HILLBILLY	SUBLUNARY
CLOISONNE	HALITOSIS	PENINSULA	STRIPLING	KICKSTAND	CELLULOSE	HOLLYHOCK	SWELLHEAD
CORIANDER	HEMISTICH	PERIMETER	TAXIDERMY	LEUKOCYTE	CHALKBORD	ICELANDER	SYLLABIFY
COTILLION	HERITABLE	PERIPHERY	TRAINLOAD	LOCKSMITH	CHALLENGE	ICELANDIC	SYLLOGISM
CROISSANT	HUMILIATE	PERISCOPE	ULTIMATUM	MONKSHOOD	CHILBLAIN	IMPLEMENT	TABLELAND
DECIDUOUS	ILLIBERAL	PERISTYLE	UMBILICUS	MUCKRAKER	CHILDHOOD	IMPLICATE	TABLEWARE
DECILITER	IMMIGRANT	PLAINTIFF	UNMINDFUL	MUSKMELON	COALFIELD	INCLEMENT	TAILLIGHT
DECIMETER	IMMIGRATE	PLAINTIVE	UNRIVALED	PACKHORSE	COALITION	INELEGANT	TELLURIUM
DECISTERE	INCIDENCE	POLICEMAN	UNSIGHTLY	PICKABACK	COLLATION	INFLATION	TOLLHOUSE
DEFICIENT	INCIPIENT	POLITBURO	UNWILLING	RACKETEER	COLLEAGUE	INFLEXION	UNALIGNED
DELICIOUS	INDIGNANT	POLITESSE	UNWITTING	RECKONING	COLLECTED	INFLUENCE	UNALLOYED
DELIGHTED	INDIGNITY	POLITICAL	URTICARIA	ROCKBOUND	COLLEGIAN	INFLUENZA	UNBLESSED
DELIMITER	INFIRMARY	RACIALISM	VACILLATE	SACKCLOTH	COLLEGIUM	INGLENOOK	UNCLEANLY
DELINEATE	INFIRMITY	RADIOGRAM	VAGINITIS	SHAKEDOWN	COLLIMATE	ITALICIZE	UNFLEDGED
DEMIMONDE	INSIDIOUS	RADIOLOGY	VARIATION	SNAKEBIRD	COLLODION	JAILBREAK	UNPLUMBED
DEMITASSE	INSINCERE	RATIONALE	VARIEGATE	SNAKEBITE	COLLUSION	JELLYFISH	VILLENAGE
DENIGRATE	INSINUATE	RECIPIENT	VENIREMAN	SPOKESMAN	COLLUVIUM	MAELSTROM	VIOLATION
DESICCANT	INSISTENT	REGISTRAR	VERIDICAL	TALKATIVE	CULLENDER	MALLEABLE	WALLBOARD
DESICCATE	INVIDIOUS	RELIGIOUS	VERITABLE	TEAKETTLE	CYCLAMATE	MILLIGRAM	WALLOPING
DESIGNATE	INVIOLATE	RELIQUARY	VIGILANCE	UNSKILLED	CYCLOTRON	MILLINERY	WALLPAPER
DESIGNING	INVISIBLE	REMINISCE	VIGILANTE	WORKBENCH	DECLIVITY	MILLIPEDE	WHALEBOAT
DESIRABLE	IRRITABLE	REMISSION	VISIONARY	WORKGROUP	DEFLATION	MILLIVOLT	WHALEBONE
DEVILMENT	JUDICIARY	RESIDENCE	CONJUGATE	WORKHORSE	DIALECTIC	MILLSTONE	WHOLESALE
DIGITALIS	JUDICIOUS	RESIDENCY	PREJUDICE	WORKHOUSE	DIPLOMACY	NEGLIGENT	WHOLESOME
DIGITIZED	JURIDICAL	RESIDUARY	PROJECTOR	WORKPLACE	DISLOCATE	NEOLOGISM	WILLPOWER
DIRIGIBLE	LAMINATED	RESISTANT	SKYJACKER	WORKTABLE	DUPLICATE	OBBLIGATO	WORLDLING
DISINFECT	LEGISLATE	SATINWOOD	SUBJUGATE	ACCLIMATE	DUPLICITY	ONSLAUGHT	WORLDWIDE
DIVISIBLE	LEVIATHAN	SAXIFRAGE	BACKBOARD	ACCLIVITY	EBULLIENT	OUBLIETTE	ABOMINATE
DIXIELAND	LITIGIOUS	SCHILLING	BACKFIELD	AFFLUENCE	EDELWEISS	PALLADIUM	ADUMBRATE
DOMINANCE	LOGISTICS	SCRIMMAGE	BACKPEDAL	AMPLITUDE	EFFLUENCE	PHALAROPE	AIRMOBILE
DOSIMETER	LUDICROUS	SCRIMSHAW	BACKSLASH	ANALGESIA	EFFLUVIUM	PHILANDER	ALUMINIUM
DOWITCHER	MACINTOSH	SCRIPTURE	BACKSLIDE	ANALGESIC	EMOLLIENT	PHILATELY	ALUMINIZE
DRAINPIPE	MAGISTRAL	SCRIVENER	BACKSTAGE	ANALOGOUS	EMOLUMENT	PHILIPPIC	ANIMALISM
EFFICIENT	MALIGNANT	SEMICOLON	BACKSWEPT	ANGLEWORM	ESPLANADE	PHILOLOGY	ANIMATION
ELLIPSOID	MANIFESTO	SEMIFINAL	BACKTRACK	ANGLICIZE	EUCLIDEAN	POULTERER	ANIMOSITY
EMPIRICAL	MARIJUANA	SEMIFLUID	BACKWATER	ANKLEBONE	EVOLUTION	PRELAUNCH	ANOMALOUS
ENLIGHTEN	MEDICABLE	SEMILUNAR	BACKWOODS	APOLOGIZE	EXCLUSIVE	PUBLICIST	ASYMPTOTE
EQUIPMENT	MEDICINAL	SEMIWORKS	BARKEEPER	APPLEJACK	EXPLETIVE	PUBLICITY	BADMINTON
EQUIPOISE	MELIORATE	SENIORITY	BEEKEEPER	APPLETALK	EXPLICATE	PUBLICIZE	BOOMERANG
EQUITABLE	MINIATURE	SERIGRAPH	BERKELIUM	APPLIANCE	EXPLOSION	REFLECTOR	BRIMSTONE
EQUIVOCAL	MINISCULE	SHRINKAGE	BOOKMAKER	APPLICANT	EXPLOSIVE	REFLEXIVE	CHAMELEON
ESPIONAGE	MINISKIRT	SILICEOUS	BOOKPLATE	ATHLETICS	FELLOWMAN	REPLENISH	CHAMOMILE
ESTIMABLE	MINISTATE	SILICOSIS	BOOKSHELF	AVALANCHE	FOLLOWING	REPLETION	CHAMPAGNE
ETHIOPIAN	MISINFORM	SLUICEWAY	BROKERAGE	BAILIWICK	FOOLHARDY	REPLICATE	CHAMPAIGN
EXCITABLE	MUNICIPAL	SOCIALISM	BUCKBOARD	BALLADEER	FOOLPROOF	SAILCLOTH	CHEMISTRY
EXPIATORY	NAVIGABLE	SOCIALITE	BUCKTOOTH	BALLERINA	GALLANTRY	SAILPLANE	CLAMSHELL
EXTIRPATE	NOVITIATE	SOCIALIZE	BUCKWHEAT	BELLICOSE	GALLINULE	SCHLEMIEL	COMMANDER
FETISHISM	OBEISANCE	SOCIOLOGY	COCKATIEL	BELLYACHE	GALLIVANT	SCULPTURE	COMMINGLE
FINICKING	OBLIVIOUS	SOLICITOR	COCKFIGHT	BILLBOARD	GALLSTONE	SECLUSION	COMMISSAR
FRUITCAKE	OFFICIANT	SOLILOQUY	COCKROACH	BILLIARDS	GRILLWORK	SHELLFIRE	COMMITTEE
FRUITERER	OFFICIATE	SOLITAIRE	CORKSCREW	BOULEVARD	HAILSTONE	SHELLFISH	COMMODITY
FUNICULAR	OFFICIOUS	SPHINCTER	DUCKBOARD	BRILLIANT	HAILSTORM	SKYLOUNGE	COMMODORE

COMMOTION	PAYMASTER	CHONDRULE	MAGNETITE	THANKLESS	AUTOGRAPH	HOLOGRAPH	PAROCHIAL
COMMUNION	PEGMATITE	CLINICIAN	MAGNETIZE	TOWNSFOLK	AUTOMATIC	HOMOGRAPH	PEDOMETER
COMMUNISM	PERMANENT	COGNITION	MAGNIFICO	TRANSCEND	AUTOMATON	HOMOPHONE	PIROUETTE
COMMUNITY	PERMEABLE	CONNUBIAL	MAGNITUDE	TRANSDUCE	AUTOTRACE	HONORABLE	PREOCCUPY
CORMORANT	PREMATURE	COONHOUND	MAINFRAME	TRANSFORM	BAROGRAPH	HONORIFIC	PREORDAIN
COSMOGONY	PRIMARILY	CORNSTALK	MANNEQUIN	TRANSFUSE	BAROMETER	HOROSCOPE	PROOFREAD
COSMOLOGY	PRIMITIVE	COUNSELOR	MANNERISM	TRANSIENT	BICONCAVE	HYPOCRISY	PYROLYSIS
COSMONAUT	PROMENADE	COUNTDOWN	MEANWHILE	TRANSLATE	BIMONTHLY	IGNORANCE	PYROMANIA
CREMATORY	PROMINENT	COUNTLESS	MOONLIGHT	TRANSMUTE	BINOCULAR	ILLOGICAL	PYROMETER
CULMINATE	PROMISING	CRANBERRY	MOONSCAPE	TRANSONIC	BINOMINAL	IMMOVABLE	RACONTEUR
DALMATION	PULMONARY	CRANKCASE	MOONSHINE	TRANSPIRE	BLOODBATH	IMPOLITIC	RECOGNIZE
DIAMETRIC	REIMBURSE	CRINOLINE	MOONSTONE	TRANSPORT	BLOODLINE	IMPORTANT	RECOLLECT
DISMANTLE	RIGMAROLE	DAMNATION	ORANGEADE	TRANSPOSE	BLOODROOT	IMPORTUNE	RECOMMEND
DISMEMBER	ROUMANIAN	DAUNTLESS	OUTNUMBER	TRANSSHIP	BLOODSHED	IMPOSTURE	RECONCILE
DOGMATISM	SKIMOBILE	DIGNIFIED	PHONETICS	TRENCHANT	BLOODSHOT	INCOGNITO	RECONDITE
DORMITORY	STAMINATE	DIGNITARY	PHONOLOGY	TRUNCHEON	CACOPHONY	INCOMMODE	RECORDING
DRAMATIZE	STIMULANT	DOWNGRADE	PLANELOAD	TURNABOUT	CALORIFIC	INCORRECT	RECORDIST
DROMEDARY	STIMULATE	DOWNRANGE	PLANETOID	TURNSTILE	CANONICAL	INFORMANT	REJOINDER
DRUMSTICK	STOMACHER	DOWNRIGHT	PLENITUDE	TURNTABLE	CHLORDANE	INNOCENCE	REPORTAGE
ELIMINATE	STOMACHIC	DOWNSHIFT	PLENTEOUS	TWINKLING	CHROMATIC	INNOCUOUS	REPOSSESS
ENUMERATE	SUBMARINE	DOWNSTAGE	PLENTIFUL	UNANIMOUS	CHRONICLE	INSOLUBLE	RESONANCE
ETYMOLOGY	SUMMARIZE	DOWNSWING	POINCIANA	UNKNOWING	COLONNADE	INSOLVENT	RESONATOR
EXEMPLARY	SUMMATION	ECONOMICS	PRINCIPAL	UPANISHAD	COLORCAST	INVOLUCRE	REVOCABLE
EXEMPLIFY	SWAMPLAND	ECONOMIZE	PRINCIPLE	VAINGLORY	COLORFAST	KILOCYCLE	REVOLTING
FARMHOUSE	TERMAGANT	ENUNCIATE	PRINTABLE	VERNALIZE	COROLLARY	KILOHERTZ	RHEOMETER
FARMSTEAD	TERMINATE	ETHNOLOGY	PRONGHORN	WEDNESDAY	CRYOGENIC	KILOLITER	SAXOPHONE
FILMSTRIP	THUMBNAIL	EVENTUATE	PRONOUNCE	WRONGDOER	CYTOPLASM	KILOMETER	SCHOOLBOY
FIRMAMENT	THUMBTACK	EXONERATE	QUINTUPLE	YOUNGLING	DECOLLETE	LABORIOUS	SECONDARY
FLAMMABLE	TREMATODE	FLINTLOCK	RAINSPOUT	YOUNGSTER	DECOMPOSE	LIMOUSINE	SOPORIFIC
FORMALISM	TREMULOUS	FOUNDLING	RAINSTORM	ZWINGLIAN	DECONTROL	LOCOMOTOR	SPOONBILL
FORMALITY	TRIMESTER	FRANCHISE	RAINWATER	ABHORRENT	DECORATOR	MAJORDOMO	STRONTIUM
FORMALIZE	VERMIFORM	FRANGIBLE	REENFORCE	ABSORBENT	DECOUPAGE	MAJORETTE	SYCOPHANT
FORMATION	VERMIFUGE	FURNITURE	REENTRANT	ACCOMPANY	DEFOLIANT	MANOEUVRE	THEOCRACY
FORMATIVE	VERMILION	GARNISHEE	REINFORCE	ACCORDION	DEFOLIATE	MANOMETER	THEOSOPHY
FORMULATE	WARMONGER	GARNITURE	REINSTATE	ACROPOLIS	DEFORMITY	MASOCHISM	THROWAWAY
FRAMEWORK	WHIMSICAL	GLENGARRY	ROUNDELAY	ADJOINING	DEMOCRACY	MELODIOUS	THROWBACK
FULMINATE	ABANDONED	GRANDIOSE	ROUNDWORM	ADSORBATE	DETONATOR	MELODRAMA	TROOPSHIP
GERMANIUM	ALONGSIDE	GRANTSMAN	RUINATION	ADSORBENT	DIMORPHIC	MEMORABLE	UNBOUNDED
GERMICIDE	AMENDMENT	GRANULATE	SCANTLING	AERODROME	DISOBLIGE	MENOPAUSE	UNCONCERN
GERMINATE	ANONYMOUS	GRENADIER	SCHNAUZER	AEROPAUSE	DISORIENT	MISORIENT	UNCOUNTED
GIMMICKRY	ATONEMENT	GRENADINE	SCINTILLA	AEROPLANE	ELBOWROOM	MONOGRAPH	UNDOUBTED
GLAMORIZE	AVUNCULAR	GUNNYSACK	SIGNALIZE	AEROSPACE	ENCOMPASS	MONOLOGUE	UNFOUNDED
GODMOTHER	BARNSTORM	GYMNASIUM	SIGNALMAN	ALCOHOLIC	ENCOUNTER	MONOMANIA	UNPOPULAR
HAMMERTOE	BLINDFOLD	IDENTICAL	SIGNATORY	ALGONQUIN	ENCOURAGE	MONOPLANE	UNWORLDLY
HARMONICA	BOONDOCKS	INANIMATE	SIGNATURE	ALGORITHM	ENDOCRINE	MONOSPACE	UPHOLSTER
HARMONICS	BOUNTEOUS	INANITION	SIGNBOARD	ALLOWANCE	ENDOSCOPE	MOTORBIKE	VAPORIZER
HARMONIUM	BOUNTIFUL	IRONBOUND	SKINFLINT	ANNOUNCER	ENTOURAGE	MOTORBOAT	VAPORWARE
HARMONIZE	BRONCHIAL	IRONSTONE	SKINTIGHT	ANNOYANCE	ERRONEOUS	MOTORCADE	WAGONETTE
HERMITAGE	CANNONADE	ISINGLASS	SLINGSHOT	APPOINTEE	EXCORIATE	NANOMETER	XEROPHYTE
INAMORATA	CANNONEER	ITINERANT	SOMNOLENT	APPORTION	EXPOSITOR	NEGOTIANT	XYLOPHONE
MARMALADE	CARNATION	ITINERARY	SPINDLING	ARBORETUM	FAVORABLE	NEGOTIATE	ANOPHELES
MARMOREAL	CARNELIAN	JAUNDICED	SPINDRIFT	ARROWHEAD	FEROCIOUS	NICOTINIC	BESPANGLE
MESMERIZE	CARNIVORA	LAGNIAPPE	SPINNAKER	ARROWROOT	FLOODGATE	NOTORIOUS	BESPATTER
MISMANAGE	CARNIVORE	LAUNCHPAD	STANCHION	ASSOCIATE	GONORRHEA	OBNOXIOUS	BUMPTIOUS
NORMALIZE	CHANCROID	LOINCLOTH	STANDPIPE	ASSONANCE	GROOMSMAN	ONIONSKIN	CAMPANILE
NORMATIVE	CHANTEUSE	MAGNESIUM	SUBNORMAL	ATROCIOUS	GYROSCOPE	OPPORTUNE	CAMPSTOOL
PALMISTRY	CHONDRITE	MAGNETISM	SWANSDOWN	AUTOCRACY	HOLOCAUST	OPTOMETRY	CARPENTER

CARPETBAG	SCAPEGOAT	ATTRIBUTE	EXTRINSIC	MATRIMONY	PLURALIZE	THEREFORE	CROSSWAYS
CARPETING	SHAPELESS	ATTRITION	EXTRUSIVE	MERRIMENT	POORHOUSE	THEREFROM	CROSSWISE
CHAPARRAL	SHIPBOARD	BARRACUDA	FABRICATE	METRICIZE	PORRINGER	THEREUNTO	DAMSELFLY
CHOPHOUSE	SHIPSHAPE	BARRICADE	FAIRYLAND	METROLOGY	POURBOIRE	THEREUPON	DISSECTED
CHOPSTICK	SHIPWRECK	BARRISTER	FEBRIFUGE	METRONOME	PRERECORD	THEREWITH	DISSEMBLE
CLAPBOARD	SIMPATICO	BEDRIDDEN	FERRYBOAT	MICROCOPY	PSORIASIS	THYROXINE	DISSENTER
CLIPBOARD	SIMPLETON	BETROTHED	FOURSCORE	MICROCOSM	PTARMIGAN	ULTRAHIGH	DISSIDENT
CLIPSHEET	SOAPSTONE	BOARDWALK	GARRULOUS	MICROFILM	PUERPERAL	ULTRAPURE	DISSIPATE
COMPANION	STEPCHILD	BOURGEOIS	GEARSHIFT	MICROGRAM	QUARTERLY	UNBRIDLED	DISSOLUTE
COMPETENT	STIPULATE	CABRIOLET	GUARANTEE	MICROSOFT	QUARTZITE	UNWRITTEN	DOBSONFLY
COMPLAINT	STOPLIGHT	CAPRICCIO	GUARANTOR	MICROWAVE	QUERULOUS	VIBRATION	ECOSYSTEM
COMPONENT	STOPWATCH	CARROUSEL	GUARDROOM	NARRATIVE	REFRACTOR	VIBRATORY	ELASTOMER
COMPOSITE	SUMPTUOUS	CHARABANC	GUARDSMAN	NECROLOGY	REPREHEND	WEARISOME	EPISCOPAL
COMPOSURE	SUPPLIANT	CHARACTER	GUERRILLA	NEGRITUDE	REPRESENT	WHEREFORE	EXISTENCE
COOPERATE	SUPPOSING	CHARLATAN	HAIRBRUSH	NEURALGIA	REPRIMAND	WHEREUPON	EXOSPHERE
CORPORATE	SUPPURATE	CHARWOMAN	HAIRCLOTH	NEUROLOGY	REPROBATE	WHEREWITH	EYESTRAIN
CORPOREAL	SUSPENDER	CHIROPODY	HAIRPIECE	NIGRITUDE	REPRODUCE	WHIRLIGIG	FACSIMILE
CORPUSCLE	SUSPICION	CHORISTER	HAIRSTYLE	NONREADER	RETRIEVER	WHIRLPOOL	FALSEHOOD
COSPONSOR	SYMPOSIUM	CHURCHMAN	HEARTACHE	NUTRIMENT	RETROFIRE	WHIRLWIND	FARSEEING
DESPERADO	TARPAULIN	CIRRHOSIS	HEARTBEAT	NUTRITION	RUMRUNNER	WORRISOME	FIRSTBORN
DESPERATE	TEMPERATE	CLERGYMAN	HEARTBURN	OPERATION	SACRAMENT	WORRYWART	FIRSTHAND
DIAPHRAGM	TEMPORARY	CORRELATE	HEARTFELT	OPERATIVE	SACRIFICE	ALMSHOUSE	FIRSTLING
DISPARAGE	TEMPORIZE	CORRUGATE	HEARTLESS	OSTRACIZE	SACRILEGE	APOSTOLIC	FLASHBACK
DISPARATE	TRAPEZOID	COURTEOUS	HEARTSICK	OUTRIGGER	SACRISTAN	AWESTRUCK	FLASHBULB
DISPLEASE	TRAPPINGS	COURTESAN	HEARTWOOD	OVERBLOWN	SCARECROW	BAKSHEESH	FLASHCUBE
DISPRAISE	TURPITUDE	COURTROOM	HEURISTIC	OVERBOARD	SECRETARY	BEDSPREAD	FLASHTUBE
DISPUTANT	UNSPARING	COURTSHIP	HIERARCHY	OVERCLOUD	SECRETION	BIOSPHERE	FORSYTHIA
DYSPEPSIA	UNSPOTTED	COURTYARD	HOARFROST	OVERDRAFT	SECRETIVE	BLASPHEME	FROSTBITE
ESOPHAGUS	BANQUETTE	CURRYCOMB	HOURGLASS	OVERDRIVE	SEGREGATE	BLASPHEMY	FRUSTRATE
EVAPORATE	BRIQUETTE	DAIRYMAID	HURRICANE	OVERMATCH	SHAREWARE	BOLSHEVIK	GLISSANDO
EVAPORITE	CROQUETTE	DECREMENT	HYDRANGEA	OVERNIGHT	SHARKSKIN	BOWSTRING	GRASSLAND
FLOPHOUSE	ETIQUETTE	DEPRECATE	HYDRAULIC	OVERPOWER	SHOREBIRD	BRASSERIE	GRISTMILL
GODPARENT	FREQUENCY	DEPRESSED	HYDROFOIL	OVERPRINT	SHORTCAKE	BRASSIERE	GROSGRAIN
GRAPESHOT	MARQUETRY	DERRINGER	HYDROLOGY	OVERREACH	SHORTHAND	BRUSHWOOD	HAMSTRING
GRAPEVINE	PARQUETRY	DETRIMENT	HYDROXIDE	OVERSEXED	SHORTHORN	CAPSULATE	HEMSTITCH
GUNPOWDER	TURQUOISE	DISREGARD	IMBROGLIO	OVERSHOOT	SHORTSTOP	CASSEROLE	HOPSCOTCH
HAPPENING	UNEQUALED	DISREPAIR	IMPRECATE	OVERSIGHT	SHORTWAVE	CASSOWARY	HORSEBACK
HAPPINESS	ABORIGINE	DISREPUTE	IMPRECISE	OVERSLEEP	SKYROCKET	CAUSATION	HORSEHAIR
NONPAREIL	ACCRETION	DOORPLATE	IMPROMPTU	OVERSTATE	SOBRIQUET	CEASELESS	HORSEHIDE
NONPERSON	ADDRESSEE	EMBRASURE	IMPROVISE	OVERTHROW	SPIRITUAL	CESSATION	HORSEPLAY
NONPROFIT	AFORESAID	EMBROCATE	IMPRUDENT	OVERTRICK	SPORTSMAN	CLASSICAL	HORSESHOE
OVIPAROUS	AGGRAVATE	EMBROIDER	INCREMENT	OVERWEIGH	STARBOARD	CLASSMATE	HORSETAIL
PALPITATE	AGGREGATE	EMERGENCY	INGROWING	OVERWHELM	STARLIGHT	CLASSROOM	HORSEWHIP
PERPETUAL	AMARYLLIS	ENERGETIC	INORGANIC	OVERWRITE	STARTLING	COASTLINE	HOUSEBOAT
PERPLEXED	AMERICANA	ENERGIZER	INTRICATE	PARRICIDE	STERILIZE	CONSCIOUS	HOUSECOAT
PIMPERNEL	AMERICIUM	ENGRAVING	INTRINSIC	PATRIARCH	STOREROOM	CONSCRIPT	HOUSEHOLD
POMPADOUR	AMORPHOUS	ENWREATHE	INTRODUCE	PATRICIAN	SUPREMACY	CONSENSUS	HOUSEMAID
POPPYCOCK	ANARCHISM	EUTROPHIC	INTROVERT	PATRICIDE	SURRENDER	CONSONANT	HOUSEWIFE
POTPOURRI	APARTHEID	EVERGLADE	ITERATION	PATRIMONY	SURROGATE	CONSTABLE	HOUSEWORK
PROPAGATE	APARTMENT	EVERGREEN	JINRIKSHA	PATRISTIC	SWORDFISH	CONSTANCY	HOWSOEVER
PROPELLER	APPREHEND	EVERYBODY	LIBRARIAN	PATROLMAN	SWORDPLAY	CONSTRAIN	IRASCIBLE
PROPHETIC	ASTRADDLE	EXCREMENT	LUBRICANT	PATRONAGE	SWORDSMAN	CONSTRICT	ISOSCELES
PROPONENT	ASTRAKHAN	EXTRADITE	LUBRICATE	PATRONIZE	SWORDTAIL	CONSTRUCT	JESSAMINE
PROPRIETY	ASTROLABE	EXTRAVERT	LUCRATIVE	PETROLEUM	TERRARIUM	CRESCENDO	KINSWOMAN
PUPPETEER	ASTROLOGY	EXTREMISM	MACROCOSM	PETROLOGY	TERRITORY	CROSSOVER	LASSITUDE
RAGPICKER	ASTRONAUT	EXTREMITY	MATRIARCH	PHEROMONE	TERRORISM	CROSSROAD	LEASEHOLD
RASPBERRY	ASTRONOMY	EXTRICATE	MATRICIDE	PLURALITY	TERRORIZE	CROSSWALK	LEASTWISE

MANSLAYER	SENSATION	CENTURION	FOOTSTOOL	OBSTINATE	SPOTLIGHT	ANGUISHED	MATUTINAL
MARSUPIAL	SENSITIVE	CERTAINTY	FORTHWITH	PANTHEISM	STATEMENT	ANNUITANT	MINUSCULE
MAUSOLEUM	SENSITIZE	CERTITUDE	FORTITUDE	PANTOMIME	STATEROOM	ASSURANCE	MINUTEMAN
MESSENGER	SUBSCRIBE	CONTAGION	FORTNIGHT	PARTITION	STATESIDE	BEAUTEOUS	NATURALLY
MESSIEURS	SUBSCRIPT	CONTAINER	FORTUNATE	PARTITIVE	STATESMAN	BEAUTIFUL	OBFUSCATE
MIDSTREAM	SUBSIDIZE	CONTENTED	FRATERNAL	PARTRIDGE	STATIONER	BIFURCATE	OBJURGATE
MIDSUMMER	SUBSTANCE	CONTINENT	GASTRITIS	PASTORALE	STATISTIC	BURUNDIAN	OCCULTISM
MISSILERY	SUNSEEKER	CONTINUAL	GASTROPOD	PASTURAGE	STATUETTE	CASUISTRY	OCCUPANCY
MISSIONER	SUNSTROKE	CONTINUUM	GENTILITY	PENTECOST	STATUTORY	CHAUFFEUR	OMBUDSMAN
MONSIGNOR	THESAURUS	CONTRALTO	GENTLEMAN	PENTHOUSE	SWITCHMAN	COLUMBINE	PECUNIARY
MOUSETRAP	TONSORIAL	CONTUMELY	GESTATION	PERTINENT	SYNTHESIS	COLUMNIST	PENURIOUS
MOUSTACHE	UNISEXUAL	CONTUSION	GLUTINOUS	PESTHOUSE	SYNTHETIC	CONUNDRUM	PITUITARY
MUSSULMAN	VASSALAGE	CORTISONE	GRATICULE	PESTICIDE	SYSTEMIZE	CORUSCATE	PLAUSIBLE
NEWSPAPER	VERSATILE	COUTURIER	GRATITUDE	PESTILENT	TANTALIZE	DEBUTANTE	PNEUMATIC
NEWSPRINT	WAISTBAND	CRETINISM	GROTESQUE	PETTICOAT	TAUTOLOGY	DEDUCTION	PNEUMONIA
NEWSSTAND	WAISTCOAT	CRITERION	GUSTATORY	PHOTOCELL	TECTONICS	DEMULCENT	PSEUDONYM
NURSEMAID	WAISTLINE	CRITICISM	HARTSHORN	PHOTOCOPY	TECTONISM	DEMURRAGE	RECUMBENT
OFFSPRING	WHOSOEVER	CRITICIZE	HECTOGRAM	PHOTOPLAY	TENTATIVE	DESUETUDE	RECURSION
OURSELVES	WRESTLING	CULTIVATE	HISTAMINE	PICTORIAL	TESTAMENT	DESULTORY	REDUCTION
OUTSKIRTS	WRISTBAND	CUSTODIAL	HISTOGRAM	PISTACHIO	TESTIMONY	ENDURANCE	REDUNDANT
OUTSPOKEN	ABATEMENT	CUSTODIAN	HISTORIAN	PLATITUDE	TOOTHACHE	EXCULPATE	REFURBISH
OUTSPREAD	ACETYLENE	CUSTOMARY	HORTATIVE	PLUTONIUM	TOOTHPICK	EXCURSION	RELUCTANT
PARSIMONY	AESTHETIC	CUSTOMIZE	HORTATORY	POETASTER	TOOTHSOME	EXCURSIVE	REPUDIATE
PARSONAGE	AESTIVATE	CUTTHROAT	HYSTERICS	PORTFOLIO	TRITURATE	EXPULSION	REPUGNANT
PASSENGER	ANATOMIZE	DEATHBLOW	IMITATION	PORTULACA	UNITARIAN	EXPURGATE	REPULSION
PASSERINE	AUCTORIAL	DEATHLESS	IMITATIVE	POSTERIOR	UNSTUDIED	EXQUISITE	REPULSIVE
PERSECUTE	BACTERIUM	DENTITION	INSTANTER	POSTERITY	VENTILATE	FECUNDATE	REPUTABLE
PERSEVERE	BANTUSTAN	DESTITUTE	INSTANTLY	POSTHASTE	VENTRICLE	FIDUCIARY	REQUISITE
PERSIMMON	BARTENDER	DESTROYER	INSTIGATE	POSTILION	VENTUROUS	GENUFLECT	RESURRECT
PERSONAGE	BASTINADO	DEUTERIUM	INSTITUTE	POSTNATAL	VERTEBRAL	GROUNDHOG	REVULSION
PERSONATE	BATTALION	DEXTERITY	JITTERBUG	POSTULANT	VESTIBULE	GROUNDING	SATURNINE
PERSONIFY	BEATITUDE	DEXTEROUS	JUXTAPOSE	POSTULATE	VESTRYMAN	GROUPWARE	SCOUNDREL
PERSONNEL	BENTONITE	DIATHERMY	LANTHANUM	PROTECTOR	VICTIMIZE	IMMUTABLE	SEPULCHER
PESSIMISM	BIRTHMARK	DIATOMITE	LEITMOTIV	PROTOTYPE	VICTORIAN	IMPULSION	SEPULTURE
PHOSPHATE	BIRTHRATE	DIETETICS	LITTERBUG	PROTOZOAN	VICTUALER	IMPULSIVE	SEQUESTER
PHYSICIAN	BOATSWAIN	DIPTEROUS	LOATHSOME	QUITTANCE	VOLTMETER	INAUGURAL	SHRUBBERY
PHYSICIST	BOOTBLACK	DISTEMPER	MARTYRDOM	QUOTIDIAN	WASTELAND	INCUBATOR	SINUSITIS
PINSTRIPE	BRITANNIC	DISTURBED	MASTERFUL	RASTERIZE	WHETSTONE	INCULCATE	SITUATION
PRESBYTER	BRUTALIZE	DOCTORATE	MASTICATE	RECTANGLE	WHITEBAIT	INCULPATE	SLAUGHTER
PRESCHOOL	BUTTERCUP	DYSTROPHY	MELTWATER	RECTIFIER	WHITEFISH	INCUMBENT	STRUCTURE
PRESCRIBE	BUTTERFAT	EARTHLING	MENTALITY	RECTITUDE	WHITEHALL	INCURABLE	TROUSSEAU
PRESENTLY	BUTTERFLY	EARTHWARD	MISTLETOE	REITERATE	WHITEHEAD	INCURIOUS	UNGUARDED
PRESHRUNK	BUTTERNUT	EARTHWORK	MORTICIAN	RESTRAINT	WHITENESS	INCURSION	UNRUFFLED
PRESIDENT	BYSTANDER	EARTHWORM	MOUTHPART	ROOTSTOCK	WHITETAIL	INDUCTION	UNTUTORED
PRESIDIUM	CANTABILE	EDITORIAL	MOUTHWASH	RUSTICATE	WHITEWALL	INDUCTIVE	VALUATION
PRESSROOM	CANTHARIS	ERSTWHILE	MULTIFORM	SALTPETER	WHITEWASH	INFURIATE	VISUALIZE
PRESTRESS	CAPTIVATE	FACTORIAL	MULTISCAN	SALTWATER	WHITEWOOD	INFUSIBLE	VOLUNTARY
PROSCRIBE	CARTILAGE	FANTASIZE	MULTISPIN	SARTORIAL	WINTERIZE	INJUSTICE	VOLUNTEER
PROSECUTE	CARTRIDGE	FANTASTIC	MULTISYNC	SCUTCHEON	WITTICISM	INSURABLE	BELVEDERE
PROSELYTE	CARTWHEEL	FASTENING	MULTITUDE	SECTARIAN	WORTHLESS	INSURANCE	CALVINISM
PROSTRATE	CASTANETS	FERTILIZE	MYSTICISM	SECTIONAL	XANTHIPPE	INSURGENT	CHEVALIER
PUISSANCE	CASTIGATE	FESTIVITY	NECTARINE	SENTIMENT	YESTERDAY	INTUITION	CHIVALRIC
PURSUANCE	CAUTERIZE	FLATULENT	NEPTUNIUM	SEPTEMBER	ZEITGEIST	INTUMESCE	CONVIVIAL
PUSSYFOOT	CENTENARY	FLOTATION	NOCTURNAL	SILTSTONE	ACOUSTICS	LIQUIDATE	CURVATURE
SAPSUCKER	CENTESIMO	FOOTBOARD	NORTHEAST	SOFTBOUND	ACQUIESCE	LUXURIANT	ELEVATION
SASSAFRAS	CENTIGRAM	FOOTLOOSE	NORTHWEST	SOUTHEAST	AMBULANCE	LUXURIATE	FLAVORING
SEASONING	CENTIPEDE	FOOTPRINT	NOSTALGIA	SOUTHWEST	AMBUSCADE	MAJUSCULE	FRIVOLOUS

GALVANISM	COPYRIGHT	CASTANETS	FORWARDER	MESCALINE	REHEARING	VANDALISM	INCUBATOR
GALVANIZE	COTYLEDON	CATHARSIS	FRICASSEE	METHADONE	REHEARSAL	VANDALIZE	IRONBOUND
GRAVEYARD	DEHYDRATE	CATHARTIC	GALLANTRY	MEZZANINE	RIGMAROLE	VARIATION	JAILBREAK
GRAVITATE	DHRYSTONE	CAUCASIAN	GALVANISM	MINIATURE	ROUMANIAN	VASSALAGE	LAMEBRAIN
HELVETIAN	EASYGOING	CAUSATION	GALVANIZE	MISHANDLE	RUINATION	VERBALIZE	LAZYBONES
HELVETICA	GRAYBEARD	CELLARAGE	GENEALOGY	MISMANAGE	SACRAMENT	VERNALIZE	LIFEBLOOD
LEAVENING	GREYHOUND	CERTAINTY	GERIATRIC	NARRATIVE	SALVATION	VERSATILE	MOLDBOARD
MARVELOUS	HOLYSTONE	CESSATION	GERMANIUM	NECTARINE	SASSAFRAS	VIBRATION	NOSEBLEED
PREVALENT	LABYRINTH	CHAPARRAL	GESTATION	NEURALGIA	SCHNAUZER	VIBRATORY	OVERBLOWN
PREVERBAL	LAZYBONES	CHARABANC	GODFATHER	NONPAREIL	SEAFARING	VIOLATION	OVERBOARD
PREVISION	PLAYHOUSE	CHARACTER	GODPARENT	NORMALIZE	SECTARIAN	VISUALIZE	PHLEBITIS
PRIVATEER	PLAYTHING	CHEVALIER	GRADATION	NORMATIVE	SENSATION	VOLCANISM	POURBOIRE
PRIVATION	POLYESTER	CHICANERY	GRENADIER	NOSTALGIA	SIGNALIZE	VULCANISM	PRESBYTER
PRIVILEGE	POLYGRAPH	CHIVALRIC	GRENADINE	OLIGARCHY	SIGNALMAN	VULCANIZE	PUREBLOOD
PROVENCAL	POLYPHONY	CIRCADIAN	GUARANTEE	ONSLAUGHT	SIGNATORY	VULGARIAN	RASPBERRY
PROVENDER	PRAYERFUL	COCKATIEL	GUARANTOR	OPERATION	SIGNATURE	VULGARISM	REIMBURSE
PROVIDENT	BRAZILIAN	COFEATURE	GUSTATORY	OPERATIVE	SIMPATICO	VULGARITY	ROADBLOCK
PROVISION	MEZZANINE	COLLATION	GYMNASIUM	ORGIASTIC	SITUATION	VULGARIZE	ROCKBOUND
PROVOLONE	PIZZICATO	COMMANDER	GYRFALCON	ORPHANAGE	SKYJACKER	ADIABATIC	SAGEBRUSH
PULVERIZE	QUIZZICAL	COMPANION	HAPHAZARD	OSTRACIZE	SOCIALISM	ADUMBRATE	SANDBLAST
SALVATION	TANZANIAN	CONTAGION	HERBALIST	OUTWARDLY	SOCIALITE	BACKBOARD	SHIPBOARD
SCAVENGER		CONTAINER	HERBARIUM	OVIPAROUS	SOCIALIZE	BASEBOARD	SHRUBBERY
SERVITUDE		CORIANDER	HEREAFTER	OXIDATION	SQUEAMISH	BILLBOARD	SIDEBOARD
STEVEDORE		CREMATORY	HIERARCHY	PALLADIUM	STOMACHER	BLUEBERRY	SIDEBURNS
SURVEYING	**5TH LETTER**	CURVATURE	HISTAMINE	PANHANDLE	STOMACHIC	BLUEBLACK	SIGNBOARD
UNIVALENT		CYCLAMATE	HORTATIVE	PAYMASTER	STREAMBED	BOOTBLACK	SOFTBOUND
UNIVERSAL	AERIALIST	DALMATION	HORTATORY	PEGMATITE	STREAMLET	BUCKBOARD	STARBOARD
VELVETEEN	AGGRAVATE	DAMNATION	HUNGARIAN	PERMANENT	SUBMARINE	CALABOOSE	SURFBOARD
WOLVERINE	ALABASTER	DEFEATISM	HUSBANDRY	PHALAROPE	SUMMARIZE	CALIBRATE	TENEBROUS
AIRWORTHY	ANIMALISM	DEFLATION	HYDRANGEA	PHILANDER	SUMMATION	CANEBRAKE	THUMBNAIL
BLOWTORCH	ANIMATION	DISMANTLE	HYDRAULIC	PHILATELY	SYLLABIFY	CARDBOARD	THUMBTACK
DARWINISM	ANOMALOUS	DISPARAGE	ICELANDER	PICKABACK	TALKATIVE	CARIBBEAN	WALLBOARD
FLOWCHART	ARCHANGEL	DISPARATE	ICELANDIC	PINEAPPLE	TANTALIZE	CELEBRATE	WASHBASIN
FLOWERPOT	ASTRADDLE	DOGMATISM	IMITATION	PISTACHIO	TANZANIAN	CELEBRITY	WASHBOARD
FORWARDER	ASTRAKHAN	DRAMATIZE	IMITATIVE	PLURALITY	TARPAULIN	CEREBRATE	WINDBLOWN
KNOWLEDGE	AVALANCHE	EDUCATION	INFLATION	PLURALIZE	TENTATIVE	CHILBLAIN	WINDBREAK
MIDWINTER	AVOCATION	ELEVATION	INSTANTER	POETASTER	TERMAGANT	CLAPBOARD	WOODBLOCK
NORWEGIAN	BALDACHIN	EMBRASURE	INSTANTLY	POMPADOUR	TERRARIUM	CLIPBOARD	WORKBENCH
OUTWARDLY	BALLADEER	EMPHASIZE	ITERATION	PRECANCEL	TESTAMENT	CRANBERRY	ADDICTION
PLOWSHARE	BARBARIAN	ENGRAVING	JESSAMINE	PREDATION	THESAURUS	DASHBOARD	ADJECTIVE
RAUWOLFIA	BARBARISM	ESPLANADE	JUXTAPOSE	PREDATORY	TREMATODE	DISOBLIGE	AFFECTING
SEAWORTHY	BARBAROUS	EUCHARIST	LAUDATORY	PRELAUNCH	TURNABOUT	DUCKBOARD	AFFECTION
SHOWPIECE	BARCAROLE	EXPIATORY	LEVIATHAN	PREMATURE	TUSCARORA	ESTABLISH	ANARCHISM
SHOWPLACE	BARRACUDA	EXTRADITE	LIBRARIAN	PREVALENT	ULTRAHIGH	FIREBRAND	ANTECHOIR
SNOWDRIFT	BATTALION	EXTRAVERT	LINEAMENT	PRIMARILY	ULTRAPURE	FIREBREAK	ANTICLINE
SNOWFIELD	BELEAGUER	FANTASIZE	LUCRATIVE	PRIVATEER	UNCEASING	FIREBRICK	ARTICHOKE
SNOWFLAKE	BESPANGLE	FANTASTIC	MANDATORY	PRIVATION	UNCHARTED	FOOTBOARD	ARTICULAR
SNOWSTORM	BESPATTER	FEUDALISM	MANGANESE	PROBATION	UNGUARDED	FREEBOARD	ASSOCIATE
TRIWEEKLY	BOMBAZINE	FEUDATORY	MANHANDLE	PROBATIVE	UNHEALTHY	GOLDBRICK	ATROCIOUS
VIEWPOINT	BRITANNIC	FIRMAMENT	MANHATTAN	PROFANITY	UNITARIAN	GRAYBEARD	AUDACIOUS
DEOXIDIZE	BRUTALIZE	FLOTATION	MARGARINE	PROPAGATE	UNIVALENT	HAIRBRUSH	AURICULAR
PROXIMATE	BUCCANEER	FORGATHER	MARMALADE	PURGATION	UNLEARNED	HARDBOARD	AUTOCRACY
PROXIMITY	BULGARIAN	FORMALISM	MECHANICS	PURGATIVE	UNMEANING	HARDBOUND	AVUNCULAR
ANHYDROUS	BYSTANDER	FORMALITY	MECHANISM	PURGATORY	UNSCATHED	HEADBOARD	BINOCULAR
BERYLLIUM	CAMPANILE	FORMALIZE	MECHANIZE	RACIALISM	UNSHACKLE	HIDEBOUND	BLEACHERS
BODYGUARD	CANTABILE	FORMATION	MENTALITY	RECTANGLE	UNSPARING	HILLBILLY	BRONCHIAL
CHRYSALIS	CARNATION	FORMATIVE	MERGANSER	REFRACTOR	VALUATION	ILLIBERAL	CAPACIOUS

CAPACITOR	LATECOMER	TREACHERY	INCIDENCE	BALLERINA	DESPERATE	GUIDELINE	MISBEHAVE
CATACLYSM	LAUNCHPAD	TRENCHANT	INSIDIOUS	BANDEROLE	DESUETUDE	HAMMERTOE	MOUSETRAP
CATECHISM	LOINCLOTH	TRUNCHEON	INVIDIOUS	BARKEEPER	DEUTERIUM	HAPPENING	MURDEROUS
CERECLOTH	LUDICROUS	UNDECEIVE	IRRADIATE	BARTENDER	DEXTERITY	HARLEQUIN	NONPERSON
CHANCROID	MALACHITE	UNDECIDED	JAUNDICED	BEDFELLOW	DEXTEROUS	HELLEBORE	NONREADER
CHURCHMAN	MASOCHISM	URTICARIA	JURIDICAL	BEEFEATER	DIALECTIC	HELLENISM	NORWEGIAN
CONSCIOUS	MEDICABLE	VASECTOMY	MALADROIT	BEEKEEPER	DIAMETRIC	HELVETIAN	NURSEMAID
CONSCRIPT	MEDICINAL	VERACIOUS	MEGADEATH	BELVEDERE	DIETETICS	HELVETICA	ORCHESTRA
CRESCENDO	MEGACYCLE	VIVACIOUS	MELODIOUS	BERKELIUM	DIFFERENT	HORSEBACK	OURSELVES
DEDUCTION	MUNICIPAL	VORACIOUS	MELODRAMA	BOOMERANG	DIPTEROUS	HORSEHAIR	OXYGENATE
DEFECTIVE	OBJECTIFY	WASHCLOTH	OMBUDSMAN	BOULEVARD	DISMEMBER	HORSEHIDE	PALAESTRA
DEFICIENT	OBJECTIVE	WINDCHILL	OVERDRAFT	BROKERAGE	DISREGARD	HORSEPLAY	PASSENGER
DEJECTION	OFFICIANT	WISECRACK	OVERDRIVE	BURLESQUE	DISREPAIR	HORSESHOE	PASSERINE
DELICIOUS	OFFICIATE	WOODCHUCK	PSEUDONYM	BUTTERCUP	DISREPUTE	HORSETAIL	PEACETIME
DEMOCRACY	OFFICIOUS	WOODCRAFT	REPUDIATE	BUTTERFAT	DISSECTED	HORSEWHIP	PENTECOST
DESECRATE	OLFACTORY	ABANDONED	RESIDENCE	BUTTERFLY	DISSEMBLE	HOTHEADED	PERMEABLE
DESICCANT	OVERCLOUD	ACCIDENCE	RESIDENCY	BUTTERNUT	DISSENTER	HOUSEBOAT	PERPETUAL
DESICCATE	PARACHUTE	AERODROME	RESIDUARY	CABLEGRAM	DISTEMPER	HOUSECOAT	PERSECUTE
DETECTIVE	PAROCHIAL	AFFIDAVIT	ROUNDELAY	CARNELIAN	DITHERING	HOUSEHOLD	PERSEVERE
DIRECTION	POINCIANA	AMENDMENT	ROUNDWORM	CARPENTER	DIXIELAND	HOUSEMAID	PHONETICS
DIRECTIVE	POLICEMAN	ANHYDROUS	SNOWDRIFT	CARPETBAG	DROMEDARY	HOUSEWIFE	PIECEMEAL
DIRECTORY	PREOCCUPY	ARMADILLO	SPEEDBOAT	CARPETING	DYSPEPSIA	HOUSEWORK	PIECEWORK
DISHCLOTH	PRESCHOOL	ASSIDUOUS	SPEEDWELL	CASSEROLE	EGGBEATER	HYPHENATE	PIGHEADED
EFFECTIVE	PRESCRIBE	BLINDFOLD	SPINDLING	CATHEDRAL	ENSHEATHE	HYSTERICS	PIMPERNEL
EFFECTUAL	PRINCIPAL	BLOODBATH	SPINDRIFT	CAUTERIZE	ENUMERATE	IMPLEMENT	PLACEKICK
EFFICIENT	PRINCIPLE	BLOODLINE	STANDPIPE	CEASELESS	ENWREATHE	IMPRECATE	PLACEMENT
ENDOCRINE	PROSCRIBE	BLOODROOT	STEADFAST	CENTENARY	EPICENTER	IMPRECISE	PLANELOAD
ENUNCIATE	RAPACIOUS	BLOODSHED	SWORDFISH	CENTESIMO	EPIDERMIS	INCLEMENT	PLANETOID
EPISCOPAL	REDACTION	BLOODSHOT	SWORDPLAY	CHAMELEON	EROGENOUS	INCREMENT	POLYESTER
EXPECTANT	REDUCTION	BOARDWALK	SWORDSMAN	COFFEEPOT	EUPHEMISM	INELEGANT	PONDEROUS
FEROCIOUS	REFECTION	BOONDOCKS	SWORDTAIL	COFFERDAM	EUTHENICS	INFLEXION	PORCELAIN
FIDUCIARY	REFECTORY	BROADBAND	TAXIDERMY	COLLEAGUE	EXCHEQUER	INGLENOOK	POSTERIOR
FINICKING	RELUCTANT	BROADCAST	TREADMILL	COLLECTED	EXCREMENT	INNKEEPER	POSTERITY
FLOWCHART	RESECTION	BROADLOOM	VERIDICAL	COLLEGIAN	EXOGENOUS	ISRAELITE	PRAYERFUL
FORECLOSE	REVOCABLE	BROADSIDE	WITHDRAWN	COLLEGIUM	EXONERATE	ITINERANT	PRECEDENT
FRANCHISE	SACKCLOTH	BROADTAIL	WORLDLING	COMPETENT	EXPLETIVE	ITINERARY	PRECEDING
FUNICULAR	SAGACIOUS	CHILDHOOD	WORLDWIDE	CONCERNED	EXTREMISM	JITTERBUG	PRECENTOR
GALACTOSE	SAILCLOTH	CHONDRITE	ABATEMENT	CONCERTED	EXTREMITY	LEASEHOLD	PRECEPTOR
HAIRCLOTH	SALACIOUS	CHONDRULE	ACCRETION	CONDENSER	EXUBERANT	LEAVENING	PRERECORD
HANDCLASP	SCUTCHEON	DAREDEVIL	ADDRESSEE	CONFESSOR	FALSEHOOD	LITHESOME	PRESENTLY
HANDCRAFT	SEBACEOUS	DECADENCE	AFORESAID	CONGENIAL	FARSEEING	LITTERBUG	PREVERBAL
HARDCOVER	SELECTION	DECIDUOUS	AGGREGATE	CONGERIES	FASTENING	LONGEVITY	PRICELESS
HOLOCAUST	SELECTMAN	DEHYDRATE	AGREEABLE	CONSENSUS	FINGERING	MAGNESIUM	PROCEDURE
HOPSCOTCH	SEMICOLON	EPHEDRINE	AGREEMENT	CONTENTED	FINGERTIP	MAGNETISM	PROCESSOR
HYPOCRISY	SILICEOUS	EXPEDIENT	ANGLEWORM	COOPERATE	FISHERMAN	MAGNETITE	PROFESSOR
INDUCTION	SILICOSIS	EXPEDITER	ANKLEBONE	CORRELATE	FLAGELLUM	MAGNETIZE	PROJECTOR
INDUCTIVE	SLUICEWAY	FLOODGATE	APPLEJACK	CRITERION	FLAGEOLET	MALLEABLE	PROMENADE
INFECTION	SOLICITOR	FOUNDLING	APPLETALK	CULLENDER	FLOWERPOT	MANNEQUIN	PROPELLER
INJECTION	STANCHION	FRIEDCAKE	APPREHEND	CUPBEARER	FRAMEWORK	MANNERISM	PROSECUTE
INNOCENCE	STEPCHILD	GRANDIOSE	ARABESQUE	DAMSELFLY	FRATERNAL	MANOEUVRE	PROSELYTE
INNOCUOUS	STRICTURE	GUARDROOM	ARCHENEMY	DANDELION	GIBBERISH	MARVELOUS	PROTECTOR
INVECTIVE	STRUCTURE	GUARDSMAN	ARCHETYPE	DANGEROUS	GOLDENROD	MASTERFUL	PROVENCAL
IRASCIBLE	SUBSCRIBE	HAMADRYAD	ASAFETIDA	DECREMENT	GRAPESHOT	MERCENARY	PROVENDER
ISOSCELES	SUBSCRIPT	HEADDRESS	ATHLETICS	DEPRECATE	GRAPEVINE	MERCERIZE	PULVERIZE
JUDICIARY	SWITCHMAN	IMMEDIACY	ATONEMENT	DEPRESSED	GRAVEYARD	MESMERIZE	PUPPETEER
JUDICIOUS	TENACIOUS	IMMEDIATE	AUTHENTIC	DESCENDER	GROTESQUE	MESSENGER	RACKETEER
KILOCYCLE	THEOCRACY	IMPEDANCE	BACTERIUM	DESPERADO	GUIDEBOOK	MINCEMEAT	RANGELAND

RASTERIZE	THEREUPON	CHAUFFEUR	EVERGLADE	AESTHETIC	MOUTHPART	AMERICANA	CONTINUAL
RECHERCHE	THEREWITH	CHIEFTAIN	EVERGREEN	ALCOHOLIC	MOUTHWASH	AMERICIUM	CONTINUUM
REFLECTOR	THREEFOLD	COALFIELD	FLEDGLING	ALMSHOUSE	NORTHEAST	AMPHIBIAN	CONVIVIAL
REFLEXIVE	THREESOME	COCKFIGHT	FOREGOING	ANOPHELES	NORTHWEST	AMPHIBOLE	CORTISONE
REITERATE	TIMBERING	COIFFEUSE	FRANGIBLE	BACCHANAL	NOTCHBACK	AMPLITUDE	CRETINISM
REPLENISH	TINDERBOX	DISAFFECT	GELIGNITE	BAKSHEESH	PACKHORSE	ANGLICIZE	CRITICISM
REPLETION	TRADEMARK	DUMBFOUND	GLENGARRY	BATHHOUSE	PANTHEISM	ANGUISHED	CRITICIZE
REPREHEND	TRADESMAN	FOREFRONT	GROSGRAIN	BEACHHEAD	PARCHMENT	ANNUITANT	CRUCIFORM
REPRESENT	TRAGEDIAN	GENUFLECT	HOLOGRAPH	BIRDHOUSE	PATCHWORK	APPLIANCE	CULMINATE
RIDGEPOLE	TRAPEZOID	GOLDFIELD	HOMEGROWN	BIRTHMARK	PENTHOUSE	APPLICANT	CULTIVATE
RUTHENIUM	TRIBESMAN	GOLDFINCH	HOMOGRAPH	BIRTHRATE	PERCHANCE	APPOINTEE	CUNEIFORM
SCAPEGOAT	TRIMESTER	HEADFIRST	HOURGLASS	BOLSHEVIK	PESTHOUSE	ARCHITECT	DARWINISM
SCARECROW	TRIWEEKLY	HOARFROST	ILLEGIBLE	BROCHETTE	PITCHFORK	ARCHIVIST	DECEITFUL
SCAVENGER	UNBLESSED	INEFFABLE	ILLOGICAL	BRUSHWOOD	PLAYHOUSE	ATTAINDER	DECLIVITY
SCHEELITE	UNCLEANLY	MAINFRAME	IMMIGRANT	CANTHARIS	POORHOUSE	ATTRIBUTE	DENTITION
SCHLEMIEL	UNFEELING	MANIFESTO	IMMIGRATE	CATCHMENT	POSTHASTE	ATTRITION	DEOXIDIZE
SCREENING	UNFLEDGED	PORTFOLIO	INAUGURAL	CATCHWORD	PRESHRUNK	BADMINTON	DERRINGER
SECRETARY	UNISEXUAL	PROOFREAD	INCOGNITO	CHOPHOUSE	PROPHETIC	BAILIWICK	DESTITUTE
SECRETION	UNIVERSAL	REENFORCE	INDIGNANT	CIRRHOSIS	PSYCHOSIS	BARRICADE	DETRIMENT
SECRETIVE	UNSHEATHE	REINFORCE	INDIGNITY	CLUBHOUSE	RACEHORSE	BARRISTER	DIFFICULT
SEGREGATE	VARIEGATE	SANGFROID	INORGANIC	COONHOUND	RANCHLAND	BASTINADO	DIFFIDENT
SEPTEMBER	VELVETEEN	SAXIFRAGE	INTEGRATE	CUTTHROAT	ROUGHNECK	BEATITUDE	DIGNIFIED
SEQUESTER	VENGEANCE	SEMIFINAL	INTEGRITY	DEATHBLOW	SACCHARIN	BEDRIDDEN	DIGNITARY
SHAKEDOWN	VERTEBRAL	SEMIFLUID	IRREGULAR	DEATHLESS	SOUTHEAST	BELLICOSE	DISFIGURE
SHAPELESS	VILLENAGE	SKINFLINT	ISINGLASS	DIAPHRAGM	SOUTHWEST	BILLIARDS	DISSIDENT
SHAREWARE	VOICELESS	SNOWFIELD	LIFEGUARD	DIATHERMY	SPAGHETTI	BRAZILIAN	DISSIPATE
SHOREBIRD	WASTELAND	SNOWFLAKE	LITIGIOUS	DISCHARGE	SURCHARGE	CABRIOLET	DORMITORY
SNAKEBIRD	WEDNESDAY	UNRUFFLED	MALIGNANT	EARTHLING	SYNTHESIS	CALCIMINE	DUPLICATE
SNAKEBITE	WHALEBOAT	WIREFRAME	MENAGERIE	EARTHWARD	SYNTHETIC	CALVINISM	DUPLICITY
SPACESHIP	WHALEBONE	ALLIGATOR	MONOGRAPH	EARTHWORK	THIGHBONE	CANDIDACY	ELIMINATE
SPICEBUSH	WHEREFORE	ALONGSIDE	NAVIGABLE	EARTHWORM	TOLLHOUSE	CANDIDATE	ELUCIDATE
SPOKESMAN	WHEREUPON	AMBIGUOUS	ORANGEADE	ESOPHAGUS	TOOTHACHE	CAPRICCIO	ENCHILADA
STALEMATE	WHEREWITH	ANALGESIA	PANEGYRIC	FARMHOUSE	TOOTHPICK	CAPTIVATE	ERADICATE
STATEMENT	WHITEBAIT	ANALGESIC	PARAGRAPH	FIREHOUSE	TOOTHSOME	CARCINOMA	ERUDITION
STATEROOM	WHITEFISH	AUTOGRAPH	PAREGORIC	FLASHBACK	TOUCHDOWN	CARNIVORA	EUCLIDEAN
STATESIDE	WHITEHALL	BAROGRAPH	PEDAGOGUE	FLASHBULB	VOUCHSAFE	CARNIVORE	EXPLICATE
STATESMAN	WHITEHEAD	BENIGHTED	POLYGRAPH	FLASHCUBE	WAREHOUSE	CARTILAGE	EXQUISITE
STEVEDORE	WHITENESS	BENIGNANT	PRONGHORN	FLASHTUBE	WASHHOUSE	CASTIGATE	EXTRICATE
STOREROOM	WHITETAIL	BLUEGRASS	RECOGNIZE	FLOPHOUSE	WATCHBAND	CASUISTRY	EXTRINSIC
STREETCAR	WHITEWALL	BODYGUARD	RELIGIOUS	FOOLHARDY	WATCHCASE	CENTIGRAM	FABRICATE
SUCCESSOR	WHITEWASH	BOURGEOIS	REPUGNANT	FORTHWITH	WATCHWORD	CENTIPEDE	FACSIMILE
SUFFERING	WHITEWOOD	CLERGYMAN	SAFEGUARD	FRIGHTFUL	WHICHEVER	CERTITUDE	FASCINATE
SUNSEEKER	WHOLESALE	CRABGRASS	SERIGRAPH	GAUCHERIE	WOLFHOUND	CHEMISTRY	FEBRIFUGE
SUPREMACY	WHOLESOME	CRYOGENIC	SLAUGHTER	GREYHOUND	WORKHORSE	CHORISTER	FERTILIZE
SURRENDER	WINTERIZE	DELIGHTED	SLINGSHOT	HATCHMENT	WORKHOUSE	CLINICIAN	FESTIVITY
SURVEYING	WOEBEGONE	DEMAGOGUE	SPRIGHTLY	HITCHHIKE	WORTHLESS	COALITION	FOREIGNER
SUSPENDER	WOLVERINE	DENIGRATE	SYNAGOGUE	HOREHOUND	XANTHIPPE	COCHINEAL	FORGIVING
SYSTEMIZE	WONDERFUL	DESIGNATE	TELEGENIC	HUNCHBACK	ZUCCHETTO	COGNITION	FORTITUDE
TABLELAND	YESTERDAY	DESIGNING	TELEGRAPH	KILOHERTZ	ABOMINATE	COLLIMATE	FULMINATE
TABLEWARE	ARCHFIEND	DIRIGIBLE	UNSIGHTLY	LANTHANUM	ABORIGINE	COMMINGLE	FUNGICIDE
TANGERINE	ARTIFICER	DOWNGRADE	VAINGLORY	LOATHSOME	ACCLIMATE	COMMISSAR	FURNITURE
TEAKETTLE	BACKFIELD	EASYGOING	WORKGROUP	LUNCHROOM	ACCLIVITY	COMMITTEE	GALLINULE
TEMPERATE	BAREFACED	EGREGIOUS	WRONGDOER	MATCHBOOK	ACQUIESCE	CONCIERGE	GALLIVANT
TENDERIZE	BRIEFCASE	EMERGENCY	YOUNGLING	MATCHLOCK	ADJOINING	CONDIMENT	GARNISHEE
THEREFORE	BULLFIGHT	ENERGETIC	YOUNGSTER	MATCHWOOD	AESTIVATE	CONDITION	GARNITURE
THEREFROM	BULLFINCH	ENERGIZER	ZEITGEIST	MEGAHERTZ	ALUMINIUM	CONFIDANT	GENTILITY
THEREUNTO	CHAFFINCH	ENLIGHTEN	ZWINGLIAN	MISCHANCE	ALUMINIZE	CONTINENT	GERMICIDE

GERMINATE	MONSIGNOR	PROMISING	UNBRIDLED	SHARKSKIN	EXCELSIOR	SCHILLING	DISEMBODY
GIMMICKRY	MORTICIAN	PROVIDENT	UNFAILING	SPEAKEASY	EXCULPATE	SEMBLANCE	DOSIMETER
GLADIATOR	MULTIFORM	PROVISION	UNFEIGNED	STOCKPILE	EXPULSION	SEMILUNAR	DREAMLAND
GLADIOLUS	MULTISCAN	PROXIMATE	UNSKILLED	STOCKYARD	FOOTLOOSE	SEPULCHER	ENCOMPASS
GLUTINOUS	MULTISPIN	PROXIMITY	UNWRITTEN	STRIKEOUT	FUSILLADE	SEPULTURE	ENIGMATIC
GRATICULE	MULTISYNC	PSORIASIS	UPANISHAD	THANKLESS	GENTLEMAN	SHELLFIRE	EPHEMERAL
GRATITUDE	MULTITUDE	PUBLICIST	VACCINATE	THICKNESS	GRILLWORK	SHELLFISH	ESTAMINET
GRAVITATE	MYSTICISM	PUBLICITY	VENTILATE	TRACKBALL	HEADLIGHT	SIMPLETON	ESTIMABLE
HANDIWORK	NARCISSUS	PUBLICIZE	VERDIGRIS	TRICKSTER	HIGHLIGHT	SINGLETON	EXTEMPORE
HAPPINESS	NEGLIGENT	QUOTIDIAN	VERMIFORM	TRUCKLOAD	HUMILIATE	SMALLTALK	FLAMMABLE
HARBINGER	NEGRITUDE	RABBINATE	VERMIFUGE	TWINKLING	IMBALANCE	SOLILOQUY	FREEMASON
HARDIHOOD	NIGRITUDE	RAGPICKER	VERMILION	UNBEKNOWN	IMPOLITIC	SPOTLIGHT	GROOMSMAN
HERBICIDE	NUTRIMENT	RECTIFIER	VESTIBULE	AFFILIATE	IMPULSION	STARLIGHT	HEXAMETER
HERMITAGE	NUTRITION	RECTITUDE	VICTIMIZE	AMBULANCE	IMPULSIVE	STEELYARD	HOMEMAKER
HEURISTIC	OBBLIGATO	REJOINDER	VINDICATE	ANCILLARY	INCULCATE	STILLBORN	INCOMMODE
HUMDINGER	OBSTINATE	REMAINDER	VIRGINITY	ANGELFISH	INCULPATE	STOPLIGHT	INCUMBENT
HURRICANE	ORIGINATE	RENDITION	WEARISOME	APPALOOSA	INDELIBLE	SUBALPINE	INDEMNIFY
IMAGINARY	OUBLIETTE	REPAIRMAN	WITTICISM	APPELLANT	INHALATOR	SUBALTERN	INDEMNITY
IMPLICATE	OUTRIGGER	REPLICATE	WORRISOME	APPELLATE	INSOLUBLE	SUNFLOWER	INTUMESCE
INABILITY	PALMISTRY	REPRIMAND	COADJUTOR	ARTILLERY	INSOLVENT	SUPPLIANT	KILOMETER
INANIMATE	PALPITATE	REQUISITE	MARIJUANA	AUXILIARY	INTELLECT	SWELLHEAD	LEITMOTIV
INANITION	PARRICIDE	RETRIEVER	AFRIKAANS	AVAILABLE	INVOLUCRE	TAILLIGHT	LOCOMOTOR
INSTIGATE	PARSIMONY	RUSTICATE	ANTIKNOCK	BALALAIKA	JEWELWEED	THRALLDOM	MANOMETER
INSTITUTE	PARTITION	SACRIFICE	BLACKBALL	BERYLLIUM	KILOLITER	UMBILICUS	MONOMANIA
INTRICATE	PARTITIVE	SACRILEGE	BLACKBIRD	BRILLIANT	KNOWLEDGE	UNALLOYED	MUSKMELON
INTRINSIC	PATRIARCH	SACRISTAN	BLACKBODY	BUMBLEBEE	LAVALIERE	UNSELFISH	NANOMETER
INTUITION	PATRICIAN	SECTIONAL	BLACKFOOT	CAMELBACK	LIMELIGHT	UNWILLING	OPTOMETRY
ITALICIZE	PATRICIDE	SENSITIVE	BLACKHEAD	CANALBOAT	MANSLAYER	UPHOLSTER	OVERMATCH
JINRIKSHA	PATRIMONY	SENSITIZE	BLACKJACK	CANDLEMAS	MAYFLOWER	VACILLATE	PACEMAKER
LAGNIAPPE	PATRISTIC	SENTIMENT	BLACKLIST	CANDLEPIN	MEDALLION	VIDELICET	PAGEMAKER
LASSITUDE	PERDITION	SERVITUDE	BLACKMAIL	CAPILLARY	METALWARE	VIGILANCE	PARAMETER
LIABILITY	PERSIMMON	SKYDIVING	BLOCKHEAD	CATALEPSY	METALWORK	VIGILANTE	PARAMOUNT
LIQUIDATE	PERTINENT	SOBRIQUET	BREAKDOWN	CATALYSIS	MIDDLEMAN	WHEELBASE	PEDOMETER
LONGITUDE	PESSIMISM	SOPHISTIC	BREAKFAST	CAVALCADE	MINELAYER	WHIRLIGIG	PERIMETER
LUBRICANT	PESTICIDE	SOPHISTRY	CHALKBORD	CHALLENGE	MISTLETOE	WHIRLPOOL	PNEUMATIC
LUBRICATE	PESTILENT	SPECIALTY	CHECKBOOK	CHARLATAN	MONOLOGUE	WHIRLWIND	PNEUMONIA
MACHINERY	PETTICOAT	SPIRITUAL	CHECKLIST	COMPLAINT	MOONLIGHT	ACCOMPANY	PRAGMATIC
MACHINIST	PHILIPPIC	STABILIZE	CHECKMATE	CORELDRAW	NOVELETTE	ALTIMETER	PTARMIGAN
MAGNIFICO	PHYSICIAN	STAMINATE	CHECKROOM	COROLLARY	OCCULTISM	ASSEMBLER	PYROMANIA
MAGNITUDE	PHYSICIST	STATIONER	CHEEKBONE	COTILLION	ORIFLAMME	AUTOMATIC	PYROMETER
MASTICATE	PITUITARY	STATISTIC	CHICKADEE	COTYLEDON	OSCILLATE	AUTOMATON	RECOMMEND
MATRIARCH	PIZZICATO	STERILIZE	CHICKASAW	COVALENCE	PAPILLOTE	BAROMETER	RECUMBENT
MATRICIDE	PLATITUDE	SUBDIVIDE	CHICKWEED	DECALOGUE	PARALYSIS	BICAMERAL	RHEOMETER
MATRIMONY	PLENITUDE	SUBLIMATE	CHUCKHOLE	DECILITER	PERPLEXED	BINOMINAL	SCHEMATIC
MENDICANT	PORRINGER	SUBSIDIZE	CLOCKWISE	DECOLLETE	PREFLIGHT	BOOKMAKER	SCRIMMAGE
MERRIMENT	POSTILION	SURCINGLE	CLOCKWORK	DEFOLIANT	PYROLYSIS	CAMEMBERT	SCRIMSHAW
MESSIEURS	PRECIPICE	SUSPICION	CRACKDOWN	DEFOLIATE	REBELLION	CATAMARAN	SHOEMAKER
METRICIZE	PRECISION	SYMBIOSIS	CRANKCASE	DEKALITER	RECOLLECT	CATAMOUNT	SOLEMNIZE
MIDWINTER	PREDICATE	SYNDICATE	JACKKNIFE	DEMULCENT	REPELLENT	CHROMATIC	STEAMBOAT
MILLIGRAM	PREFIGURE	TERMINATE	KNOCKDOWN	DESULTORY	REPULSION	COLUMBINE	STEAMSHIP
MILLINERY	PRESIDENT	TERRITORY	OUTSKIRTS	DEVILMENT	REPULSIVE	COLUMNIST	TELEMETER
MILLIPEDE	PRESIDIUM	TESTIMONY	QUICKDRAW	DISPLEASE	RETALIATE	DECIMETER	ULTIMATUM
MILLIVOLT	PREVISION	TRADITION	QUICKLIME	EBULLIENT	REVOLTING	DECOMPOSE	VEHEMENCE
MISDIRECT	PRIMITIVE	TURPITUDE	QUICKSAND	EMBELLISH	REVULSION	DEKAMETER	VOLTMETER
MISGIVING	PRIVILEGE	UKRAINIAN	QUICKSORT	EMOLLIENT	SADDLEBOW	DELIMITER	ADVANTAGE
MISSILERY	PROFITEER	UNALIGNED	QUICKSTEP	ESCALATOR	SAFFLOWER	DEMIMONDE	ADVENTURE
MISSIONER	PROMINENT	UNANIMOUS	QUICKTIME	EXCELLENT	SATELLITE	DISEMBARK	AILANTHUS

ALGONQUIN	FINANCIER	RACONTEUR	AUDIOLOGY	ECONOMIZE	METEOROID	RATIONALE	ANTIPATHY
ALIENABLE	FORENAMED	RECONCILE	AUTHORITY	EDITORIAL	METHODIST	RAUWOLFIA	AQUAPLANE
ALMANDITE	FORTNIGHT	RECONDITE	AUTHORIZE	ELABORATE	METHODIZE	RECKONING	ASYMPTOTE
ANTINOVEL	GLEANINGS	REDUNDANT	BAMBOOZLE	EMBROCATE	METROLOGY	RENCONTRE	BACKPEDAL
APPENDAGE	GREENBACK	REMINISCE	BANDOLIER	EMBROIDER	METRONOME	REPROBATE	BEDSPREAD
ARGENTINE	GREENBELT	RESONANCE	BATHOLITH	ESPIONAGE	MICROCOPY	REPRODUCE	BIOSPHERE
ARGENTITE	GREENHORN	RESONATOR	BENTONITE	ETHIOPIAN	MICROCOSM	RETROFIRE	BLASPHEME
ASCENDANT	GREENROOM	RETENTION	BETROTHED	ETHNOLOGY	MICROFILM	SARTORIAL	BLASPHEMY
ASCENDERS	GREENWOOD	RETENTIVE	BISHOPRIC	ETYMOLOGY	MICROGRAM	SCHOOLBOY	BLUEPOINT
ASCENSION	GROUNDHOG	SATINWOOD	CALLOSITY	EUTROPHIC	MICROSOFT	SEASONING	BLUEPRINT
ASSONANCE	GROUNDING	SCOUNDREL	CANNONADE	EVAPORATE	MICROWAVE	SEAWORTHY	BOMBPROOF
ATHENAEUM	HACKNEYED	SECONDARY	CANNONEER	EVAPORITE	MISGOVERN	SENIORITY	BOOKPLATE
ATTENDANT	HUMANKIND	SEDENTARY	CARBONATE	EXPLOSION	MONGOLIAN	SHADOWBOX	CACOPHONY
ATTENTION	INCENTIVE	SEMANTICS	CARROUSEL	EXPLOSIVE	MONGOLISM	SKIMOBILE	CHAMPAGNE
ATTENUATE	INDENTION	SEVENTEEN	CASSOWARY	FACTORIAL	MONGOLOID	SKYLOUNGE	CHAMPAIGN
BICONCAVE	INDENTURE	SHRINKAGE	CHAMOMILE	FELLOWMAN	MYTHOLOGY	SKYROCKET	CYTOPLASM
BILINGUAL	INFANTILE	SPHINCTER	CHIROPODY	FLAVORING	NARCOTIZE	SOCIOLOGY	DECEPTION
BIMONTHLY	INGENIOUS	SPINNAKER	CHOCOLATE	FOLLOWING	NECROLOGY	SOMNOLENT	DISAPPEAR
BURUNDIAN	INGENUITY	SPLENETIC	COLLODION	FRIVOLOUS	NEOLOGISM	SOPHOMORE	DOORPLATE
CALENDULA	INGENUOUS	SPOONBILL	COMFORTER	GLAMORIZE	NEUROLOGY	SUBNORMAL	ELLIPSOID
CANONICAL	INSENSATE	STRENUOUS	COMMODITY	GLYCOSIDE	PANTOMIME	SUCCOTASH	ENRAPTURE
CELANDINE	INSINCERE	STRONTIUM	COMMODORE	GODMOTHER	PARSONAGE	SUFFOCATE	EQUIPMENT
CHRONICLE	INSINUATE	TARANTULA	COMMOTION	GONDOLIER	PASTORALE	SUNBONNET	EQUIPOISE
CLIENTELE	INTENDANT	TECHNICAL	COMPONENT	GUNCOTTON	PATHOLOGY	SUPPOSING	EXCEPTION
COLONNADE	INTENSIFY	TECHNIQUE	COMPOSITE	GUNPOWDER	PATROLMAN	SURROGATE	EXEMPLARY
CONUNDRUM	INTENSITY	TRAINLOAD	COMPOSURE	HALLOWEEN	PATRONAGE	SYLLOGISM	EXEMPLIFY
CUTANEOUS	INTENSIVE	TRIENNIAL	CONCORDAT	HARBORAGE	PATRONIZE	SYMBOLISM	EXOSPHERE
DAVENPORT	INTENTION	TYRANNIZE	CONCOURSE	HARMONICA	PENHOLDER	SYMBOLIZE	FIREPLACE
DEBENTURE	INVENTION	TYRANNOUS	CONSONANT	HARMONICS	PERCOLATE	SYMPOSIUM	FIREPOWER
DECENNIAL	INVENTIVE	UNBENDING	CORMORANT	HARMONIUM	PERFORATE	TAUTOLOGY	FIREPROOF
DECONTROL	INVENTORY	UNCONCERN	CORPORATE	HARMONIZE	PERSONAGE	TECTONICS	FOOLPROOF
DEFENDANT	LAMINATED	UNMINDFUL	CORPOREAL	HECTOGRAM	PERSONATE	TECTONISM	FOOTPRINT
DEFENSIVE	LEGENDARY	VAGINITIS	COSMOGONY	HISTOGRAM	PERSONIFY	TEMPORARY	GANGPLANK
DELINEATE	LORGNETTE	VALENTINE	COSMOLOGY	HISTORIAN	PERSONNEL	TEMPORIZE	GROUPWARE
DEPENDENT	MACINTOSH	VICENNIAL	COSMONAUT	HOBGOBLIN	PETROLEUM	TERRORISM	HAIRPIECE
DETENTION	MISINFORM	VOLUNTARY	COSPONSOR	HOWSOEVER	PETROLOGY	TERRORIZE	HALFPENNY
DETONATOR	MOMENTARY	VOLUNTEER	CRINOLINE	HYDROFOIL	PHEROMONE	THYROXINE	HEADPHONE
DIAGNOSIS	MOMENTOUS	WAGONETTE	CROCODILE	HYDROLOGY	PHILOLOGY	TONSORIAL	HEADPIECE
DIMENSION	NONENTITY	WOMANHOOD	CUSTODIAL	HYDROXIDE	PHONOLOGY	TRIFOCALS	HOMOPHONE
DISENGAGE	OFFENSIVE	WOMANKIND	CUSTODIAN	IMBROGLIO	PHOTOCELL	TURBOPROP	INCAPABLE
DISINFECT	ONIONSKIN	WOMANLIKE	CUSTOMARY	IMPROMPTU	PHOTOCOPY	UNKNOWING	INCEPTION
DOMINANCE	ORDINANCE	WOMENFOLK	CUSTOMIZE	IMPROVISE	PHOTOPLAY	UNSPOTTED	INCIPIENT
DRAINPIPE	ORIENTATE	AIRMOBILE	CYCLOTRON	INAMORATA	PICTORIAL	VICTORIAN	MEGAPHONE
DYSENTERY	OVERNIGHT	AIRWORTHY	DEODORANT	INGROWING	PLUTONIUM	VIDEOTAPE	MEGAPIXEL
ECCENTRIC	PALANQUIN	ANALOGOUS	DEODORIZE	INTRODUCE	POTBOILER	VISCOSITY	MENOPAUSE
EGLANTINE	PECUNIARY	ANATOMIZE	DIATOMITE	INTROVERT	POTPOURRI	VISIONARY	MONOPLANE
EMPENNAGE	PEKINGESE	ANCHORAGE	DICHOTOMY	INVIOLATE	PROBOSCIS	VOODOOISM	NAMEPLATE
ERRONEOUS	PENINSULA	ANCHORITE	DIPLOMACY	JOBHOLDER	PROCONSUL	WALLOPING	NEWSPAPER
ESSENTIAL	PERENNIAL	ANCHORMAN	DISCOMFIT	LACCOLITH	PRONOUNCE	WARBONNET	NEWSPRINT
EXPANSION	PHRENETIC	ANIMOSITY	DISCOURSE	LANDOWNER	PROPONENT	WARMONGER	NOSEPIECE
EXPANSIVE	PLAINTIFF	ANTHOLOGY	DISHONEST	LEUKOCYTE	PROTOTYPE	WHOSOEVER	OCCUPANCY
EXPENSIVE	PLAINTIVE	APOLOGIZE	DISLOCATE	LITHOLOGY	PROTOZOAN	ZIRCONIUM	OFFSPRING
EXTENSION	POSTNATAL	ASTROLABE	DISSOLUTE	MACROCOSM	PROVOLONE	ACROPOLIS	OUTSPOKEN
EXTENSIVE	POTENTATE	ASTROLOGY	DOBSONFLY	MARMOREAL	PULMONARY	AEROPAUSE	OUTSPREAD
EXTENUATE	POTENTIAL	ASTRONAUT	DOCTORATE	MAUSOLEUM	RADIOGRAM	AEROPLANE	OVERPOWER
FECUNDATE	PREGNABLE	ASTRONOMY	DRAGONFLY	MELIORATE	RADIOLOGY	AMORPHOUS	OVERPRINT
FINANCIAL	PROGNOSIS	AUCTORIAL	ECONOMICS	METEORITE	RANDOMIZE	ANTIPASTO	PENEPLAIN

PERIPHERY	AFTERGLOW	DIAERESIS	INCURSION	MISCREANT	RIVERBANK	UTTERMOST	CORUSCATE
PHOSPHATE	AFTERLIFE	DIMORPHIC	INEBRIATE	MISERABLE	RIVERBOAT	VAGARIOUS	COUNSELOR
POLYPHONY	AFTERMATH	DISCREDIT	INFERENCE	MISORIENT	RIVERSIDE	VAPORIZER	CROISSANT
PUERPERAL	AFTERNOON	DISORIENT	INFERTILE	MODERATOR	RUNAROUND	VAPORWARE	CROSSOVER
RECEPTION	AFTERWARD	DISPRAISE	INFIRMARY	MODERNISM	SATURNINE	VENERABLE	CROSSROAD
RECEPTIVE	ALGORITHM	DIVERSIFY	INFIRMITY	MODERNIZE	SCLEROSIS	VENIREMAN	CROSSWALK
RECIPIENT	ALLERGIST	DIVERSION	INFORMANT	MOTORBIKE	SEPARABLE	VENTRICLE	CROSSWAYS
SAILPLANE	ALTERNATE	DIVERSITY	INFURIATE	MOTORBOAT	SEPARATOR	VESTRYMAN	CROSSWISE
SALTPETER	AMBERGRIS	DOWNRANGE	INNERMOST	MOTORCADE	SOPORIFIC	VICARIOUS	DACHSHUND
SANDPAPER	AMPERSAND	DOWNRIGHT	INNERSOLE	MUCKRAKER	SOUBRETTE	VICEREGAL	DAMASCENE
SANDPIPER	ANAEROBIC	DYSTROPHY	INSERTION	NATURALLY	SOVEREIGN	WATERFALL	DECISTERE
SAXOPHONE	ANTARCTIC	EIDERDOWN	INSURABLE	NEFARIOUS	SPEARHEAD	WATERFOWL	DEKASTERE
SCRAPBOOK	APOCRYPHA	EMBARRASS	INSURANCE	NEPHRITIC	SPEARMINT	WATERLINE	DEVASTATE
SCRIPTURE	APPARATUS	EMPIRICAL	INSURGENT	NEPHRITIS	STAIRCASE	WATERMARK	DHRYSTONE
SCULPTURE	APPERTAIN	ENDURANCE	INTERCEDE	NEVERMORE	STAIRWELL	WATERSHED	DISESTEEM
SEMAPHORE	APPORTION	ENTERITIS	INTERCEPT	NONCREDIT	SUFFRAGAN	WATERSIDE	DIVISIBLE
SHEEPFOLD	ARBORETUM	ENTERTAIN	INTERDICT	NONPROFIT	SUGARCANE	YTTERBIUM	DOWNSHIFT
SHEEPSKIN	ARTERIOLE	EPIGRAPHY	INTERFACE	NOTORIOUS	SUGARPLUM	ACCESSION	DOWNSTAGE
SHOWPIECE	ARTHRITIS	ESPERANTO	INTERFERE	NUMERATOR	SUPERNOVA	ACCESSORY	DOWNSWING
SHOWPLACE	ARTHROPOD	EXCORIATE	INTERFUSE	NUMERICAL	SUPERPOSE	ACOUSTICS	DRUGSTORE
SIDEPIECE	ASCERTAIN	EXCURSION	INTERJECT	OBJURGATE	SUPERSEDE	ADMISSION	DRUMSTICK
STRAPLESS	ASPARAGUS	EXCURSIVE	INTERLACE	OBSERVANT	SUPERVENE	ADVISABLE	EAVESDROP
STRAPPING	ASPERSION	EXECRABLE	INTERLARD	OFFERTORY	SUPERVISE	AEROSPACE	ENDOSCOPE
STRIPLING	ASSERTION	EXPERTISE	INTERLEAF	OPPORTUNE	SYNERGISM	AMBUSCADE	EXPOSITOR
SWAMPLAND	ASSURANCE	EXPURGATE	INTERLINE	OTHERWISE	TOLERABLE	AMIDSHIPS	FARMSTEAD
SYCOPHANT	BIFURCATE	EXTIRPATE	INTERLINK	OUTERMOST	TOLERANCE	ANTISERUM	FEEDSTOCK
TELEPATHY	BIOGRAPHY	FAVORABLE	INTERLOCK	OUTGROWTH	TULAREMIA	ARMISTICE	FEEDSTUFF
TELEPHONE	BIPARTITE	GABARDINE	INTERLOPE	OVERREACH	UNCERTAIN	ASSISTANT	FETISHISM
TELEPHONY	CALORIFIC	GABERDINE	INTERLUDE	PAPERBACK	UNDERBODY	BACKSLASH	FILMSTRIP
TELEPHOTO	CAPARISON	GASTRITIS	INTERMENT	PARTRIDGE	UNDERBRED	BACKSLIDE	FLAGSTAFF
TIMEPIECE	CARTRIDGE	GASTROPOD	INTERNIST	PATERNITY	UNDERCOAT	BACKSTAGE	FLAGSTONE
TRAPPINGS	CATERWAUL	GENERATOR	INTERNODE	PENURIOUS	UNDERDONE	BACKSWEPT	FOODSTUFF
TROOPSHIP	CHEERLESS	GEOGRAPHY	INTERPLAY	POWERBOAT	UNDERFEED	BANDSTAND	FOOTSTOOL
UNPOPULAR	CHLORDANE	GONORRHEA	INTERPOSE	PREORDAIN	UNDERFOOT	BARNSTORM	FORESHEET
VIEWPOINT	CIGARETTE	GOVERNESS	INTERPRET	PROCREATE	UNDERGIRD	BEEFSTEAK	FORESHORE
WALLPAPER	CIGARILLO	GUERRILLA	INTERRUPT	PROPRIETY	UNDERHAND	BOATSWAIN	FORESIGHT
WILLPOWER	CLEARANCE	HAVERSACK	INTERSECT	QUADRATIC	UNDERLINE	BOMBSHELL	FORESTALL
WINDPROOF	COCKROACH	HETERODOX	INTERVENE	QUADRILLE	UNDERLING	BOMBSIGHT	FORESWEAR
WINEPRESS	COLORCAST	HIBERNATE	INTERVIEW	QUADRUPED	UNDERMINE	BOOKSHELF	FOURSCORE
WORKPLACE	COLORFAST	HILARIOUS	INVERNESS	QUADRUPLE	UNDERMOST	BRASSERIE	FREESTONE
XEROPHYTE	CONGRUITY	HINDRANCE	INVERSION	RECORDING	UNDERPART	BRASSIERE	GALLSTONE
XYLOPHONE	CONTRALTO	HONORABLE	JACARANDA	RECORDIST	UNDERPASS	BRIMSTONE	GEARSHIFT
ANTIQUARY	COPARTNER	HONORIFIC	LABORIOUS	RECURSION	UNDERPLAY	CAMPSTOOL	GLADSTONE
ANTIQUITY	COPYRIGHT	HYPERBOLA	LABYRINTH	REDBREAST	UNDERRATE	CELESTIAL	GLISSANDO
RELIQUARY	DECORATOR	HYPERBOLE	LIBERTINE	REFERENCE	UNDERSELL	CHOPSTICK	GOLDSMITH
ABHORRENT	DEFERENCE	HYPERCARD	LITERATIM	REFURBISH	UNDERSHOT	CHRISTIAN	GRASSLAND
ABSORBENT	DEFERMENT	HYPERTEXT	LIVERWORT	REGARDING	UNDERSIDE	CHRISTMAS	GRUBSTAKE
ACCORDION	DEFORMITY	IGNORANCE	LIVERYMAN	REPERTORY	UNDERTAKE	CHRYSALIS	GYROSCOPE
ADMIRABLE	DEMARCATE	IMPARTIAL	LOGARITHM	REPORTAGE	UNDERTONE	CLAMSHELL	HAILSTONE
ADMIRALTY	DEMURRAGE	IMPERFECT	LOWERCASE	RESERPINE	UNDERWEAR	CLASSICAL	HAILSTORM
ADSORBATE	DEPARTURE	IMPERIOUS	LUXURIANT	RESERVIST	UNDERWOOD	CLASSMATE	HAIRSTYLE
ADSORBENT	DESIRABLE	IMPORTANT	LUXURIATE	RESERVOIR	UNEARTHLY	CLASSROOM	HANDSHAKE
ADVERSARY	DESTROYER	IMPORTUNE	MAHARISHI	RESTRAINT	UNHARNESS	CLIPSHEET	HANDSPIKE
ADVERSITY	DETERGENT	INCARNATE	MAJORDOMO	RESURRECT	UNWORLDLY	CLOISONNE	HANDSTAND
ADVERTISE	DETERMINE	INCORRECT	MAJORETTE	RETARDATE	UPPERCASE	CONESTOGA	HARDSTAND
AFTERCARE	DETERRENT	INCURABLE	MATERNITY	REVERENCE	UPPERMOST	CORKSCREW	HARTSHORN
AFTERDECK	DIACRITIC	INCURIOUS	MEMORABLE	REVERSION	UTTERANCE	CORNSTALK	HEADSTALL

HEADSTONE	PAKISTANI	WHIMSICAL	DIGITIZED	LEASTWISE	SHORTHORN	COAGULANT	MERCUROUS
HEMISTICH	PERISCOPE	WINDSTORM	DIPHTHONG	LIGHTFACE	SHORTSTOP	COAGULATE	MIDSUMMER
HINDSIGHT	PERISTYLE	WINDSWEPT	DOUBTLESS	LIGHTNING	SHORTWAVE	COLLUSION	MUSSULMAN
HOLYSTONE	PIKESTAFF	WITHSTAND	DOWITCHER	LIGHTSHIP	SIDETRACK	COLLUVIUM	NEPTUNIUM
HOMESTEAD	PLAUSIBLE	WOLFSBANE	DRAFTSMAN	LIGHTSOME	SKINTIGHT	COMMUNION	NOCTURNAL
HOROSCOPE	PLOWSHARE	YARDSTICK	DRIFTWOOD	MALATHION	SOLITAIRE	COMMUNISM	OUTNUMBER
IMPASSIVE	POTASSIUM	ALBATROSS	ELASTOMER	MATUTINAL	SOMETHING	COMMUNITY	PARQUETRY
IMPOSTURE	PRESSROOM	ALEATORIC	ELECTRIFY	MIDSTREAM	SOMETIMES	CONCUBINE	PASTURAGE
INCESSANT	PUBESCENT	AMBITIOUS	ELECTRODE	MINUTEMAN	SPECTACLE	CONDUCTOR	PENDULOUS
INFUSIBLE	PUISSANCE	ANTITOXIN	EQUITABLE	MOUSTACHE	SPECTATOR	CONFUSION	PERFUMERY
INJUSTICE	QUIESCENT	ANTITUMOR	EVENTUATE	NEGOTIANT	SPLITTING	CONJUGATE	PIROUETTE
INSISTENT	RAINSPOUT	APARTHEID	EXCITABLE	NEGOTIATE	SPORTSMAN	CONNUBIAL	PORCUPINE
INTESTATE	RAINSTORM	APARTMENT	EXISTENCE	NICOTINIC	STARTLING	CONTUMELY	PORTULACA
INTESTINE	RECESSION	APOSTOLIC	EXPATIATE	NIGHTCLUB	STRATAGEM	CONTUSION	POSTULANT
INVISIBLE	RECESSIVE	APPETIZER	EYESTRAIN	NIGHTFALL	STRETCHER	CORPUSCLE	POSTULATE
IRONSTONE	REGISTRAR	ARBITRARY	FACETIOUS	NIGHTGOWN	SUBATOMIC	CORRUGATE	PRECURSOR
JACKSCREW	REINSTATE	ARBITRATE	FIRSTBORN	NIGHTHAWK	SUBSTANCE	COUTURIER	PREJUDICE
JACKSTRAW	REMISSION	AUTOTRACE	FIRSTHAND	NIGHTLIFE	SUMPTUOUS	CREDULOUS	PURSUANCE
KICKSTAND	REPOSSESS	AWESTRUCK	FIRSTLING	NIGHTMARE	SUNSTROKE	CROQUETTE	QUERULOUS
KINESCOPE	RESISTANT	BACKTRACK	FLINTLOCK	NIGHTTIME	SWEATSHOP	DECOUPAGE	RESHUFFLE
LANDSCAPE	ROADSTEAD	BAGATELLE	FLUCTUATE	NOVITIATE	SWEETMEAT	DISBURDEN	RUMRUNNER
LANDSLIDE	ROOTSTOCK	BEAUTEOUS	FORETASTE	OVERTHROW	THEATRICS	DISPUTANT	SAPSUCKER
LEAFSTALK	SALESGIRL	BEAUTIFUL	FORETOKEN	OVERTRICK	TIGHTROPE	DISTURBED	SECLUSION
LEGISLATE	SANDSTONE	BESETTING	FRACTIOUS	PALATABLE	TIMETABLE	EFFLUENCE	SPECULATE
LIMESTONE	SANDSTORM	BILATERAL	FROSTBITE	PARATHION	TRACTABLE	EFFLUVIUM	SPELUNKER
LIVESTOCK	SECESSION	BLOWTORCH	FRUITCAKE	PENETRATE	TREATMENT	EJACULATE	STATUETTE
LOADSTONE	SHIPSHAPE	BOUNTEOUS	FRUITERER	PINSTRIPE	TURNTABLE	ELOCUTION	STATUTORY
LOCKSMITH	SIDESWIPE	BOUNTIFUL	FRUSTRATE	PLAYTHING	UNNATURAL	EMOLUMENT	STIMULANT
LODESTONE	SILTSTONE	BOWSTRING	GAZETTEER	PLENTEOUS	UNSETTLED	ENCOUNTER	STIMULATE
LOGISTICS	SINUSITIS	BUCKTOOTH	GENITALIA	PLENTIFUL	UNTUTORED	ENCOURAGE	STIPULATE
MAELSTROM	SNOWSTORM	BUMPTIOUS	GRANTSMAN	POLITBURO	UNWITTING	ENTOURAGE	SUBJUGATE
MAGISTRAL	SOAPSTONE	CAFETERIA	GREATCOAT	POLITESSE	VEGETABLE	EPICUREAN	SUBLUNARY
MAJUSCULE	SWANSDOWN	CAPITALLY	GRISTMILL	POLITICAL	VERITABLE	ETIQUETTE	SUCCULENT
MAKESHIFT	TELESCOPE	CARETAKER	HABITABLE	POULTERER	VEXATIOUS	EVOLUTION	SULFUROUS
MILESTONE	THEOSOPHY	CATATONIC	HABITUATE	PRACTICAL	WAISTBAND	EXCLUSIVE	SUPPURATE
MILLSTONE	THRESHOLD	CHANTEUSE	HALITOSIS	PRESTRESS	WAISTCOAT	EXECUTIVE	TELLURIUM
MINISCULE	TOADSTOOL	COASTLINE	HAMSTRING	PRINTABLE	WAISTLINE	EXECUTRIX	TREMULOUS
MINISKIRT	TOMBSTONE	CONSTABLE	HEALTHFUL	PROSTRATE	WAVETABLE	EXTRUSIVE	TRIBUTARY
MINISTATE	TOWNSFOLK	CONSTANCY	HEARTACHE	PUNCTILIO	WORKTABLE	FLATULENT	TRITURATE
MINUSCULE	TRANSCEND	CONSTRAIN	HEARTBEAT	PUNCTUATE	WRESTLING	FORMULATE	TRUCULENT
MONASTERY	TRANSDUCE	CONSTRICT	HEARTBURN	PYRETHRUM	WRISTBAND	FORTUNATE	TURBULENT
MONKSHOOD	TRANSFORM	CONSTRUCT	HEARTFELT	QUARTERLY	YACHTSMAN	FREQUENCY	TURQUOISE
MONOSPACE	TRANSFUSE	COUNTDOWN	HEARTLESS	QUARTZITE	ACIDULATE	GARRULOUS	UNBOUNDED
MOONSCAPE	TRANSIENT	COUNTLESS	HEARTSICK	QUINTUPLE	ACIDULOUS	GRANULATE	UNCOUNTED
MOONSHINE	TRANSLATE	COURTEOUS	HEARTWOOD	QUITTANCE	AFFLUENCE	HAMBURGER	UNDAUNTED
MOONSTONE	TRANSMUTE	COURTESAN	HEMSTITCH	RACETRACK	ANNOUNCER	HERCULEAN	UNDOUBTED
NECESSARY	TRANSONIC	COURTROOM	HEPATITIS	REACTANCE	BANQUETTE	HEREUNDER	UNEQUALED
NECESSITY	TRANSPIRE	COURTSHIP	HERITABLE	REENTRANT	BANTUSTAN	IMPRUDENT	UNFOUNDED
NEWSSTAND	TRANSPORT	COURTYARD	IDENTICAL	REPUTABLE	BRIQUETTE	INFLUENCE	UNPLUMBED
OBEISANCE	TRANSPOSE	CRAFTSMAN	IMMUTABLE	RIGHTEOUS	CALCULATE	INFLUENZA	UNSTUDIED
OBFUSCATE	TRANSSHIP	CURETTAGE	IMPATIENS	SANCTUARY	CAPSULATE	INOCULATE	VENTUROUS
OBSESSION	TREASURER	DAUNTLESS	IMPATIENT	SCANTLING	CARBUNCLE	LIMBURGER	VICTUALER
OVERSEXED	TROUSSEAU	DEBUTANTE	IMPETUOUS	SCINTILLA	CARBURIZE	LIMOUSINE	ALLEVIATE
OVERSHOOT	TURNSTILE	DECATHLON	INFATUATE	SHEATHING	CELLULOSE	MARQUETRY	ANTIVENIN
OVERSIGHT	VIGESIMAL	DELFTWARE	INPATIENT	SHIFTLESS	CENTURION	MARSUPIAL	EQUIVOCAL
OVERSLEEP	WASHSTAND	DEMITASSE	INSATIATE	SHORTCAKE	CIRCUITRY	MASCULINE	GRIEVANCE
OVERSTATE	WHETSTONE	DIGITALIS	IRRITABLE	SHORTHAND	CIRCULATE	MERCURIAL	IMMOVABLE

OBLIVIOUS	DAIRYMAID	BANDWAGON	GENITALIA	ORIFLAMME	TURNTABLE	HEARTBEAT	AMERICANA
RELEVANCE	ECOSYSTEM	BAREFACED	GEOGRAPHY	OVERMATCH	ULTIMATUM	HEARTBURN	AMERICIUM
RELEVANCY	EMBAYMENT	BEEFEATER	GLADIATOR	PACEMAKER	UNCLEANLY	HELLEBORE	ANGLICIZE
SCRIVENER	EMPHYSEMA	BELLYACHE	GLENGARRY	PAGEMAKER	UNEQUALED	HOBGOBLIN	ANTARCTIC
UNADVISED	EVERYBODY	BILLIARDS	GLISSANDO	PALATABLE	UNRIVALED	HORSEBACK	APPLICANT
UNRIVALED	FAIRYLAND	BIOGRAPHY	GRIEVANCE	PATRIARCH	UNSHEATHE	HOUSEBOAT	BALDACHIN
ALLOWANCE	FANCYWORK	BOOKMAKER	HABITABLE	PERCHANCE	URTICARIA	HUNCHBACK	BARRACUDA
ARROWHEAD	FERRYBOAT	CANTHARIS	HEADWATER	PERMEABLE	UTTERANCE	HYPERBOLA	BARRICADE
ARROWROOT	FORSYTHIA	CAPITALLY	HEARTACHE	PIGHEADED	VEGETABLE	HYPERBOLE	BELLICOSE
BACKWATER	GUNNYSACK	CARETAKER	HERITABLE	PNEUMATIC	VENERABLE	INCUMBENT	BICONCAVE
BACKWOODS	HOLLYHOCK	CATAMARAN	HINDRANCE	POSTHASTE	VENGEANCE	MATCHBOOK	BIFURCATE
BANDWAGON	HONEYCOMB	CHAMPAGNE	HOLOCAUST	POSTNATAL	VERITABLE	MOTORBIKE	BRIEFCASE
BANDWIDTH	HONEYMOON	CHAMPAIGN	HOMEMAKER	PRAGMATIC	VICTUALER	MOTORBOAT	BROADCAST
BONDWOMAN	JELLYFISH	CHARLATAN	HONORABLE	PREGNABLE	VIGILANCE	NOTCHBACK	CAPRICCIO
BUCKWHEAT	MALAYSIAN	CHICKADEE	HOTHEADED	PRINTABLE	VIGILANTE	PAPERBACK	CAVALCADE
BUSHWHACK	MARTYRDOM	CHICKASAW	IGNORANCE	PSORIASIS	WALLPAPER	PICKABACK	CHARACTER
CARTWHEEL	NEODYMIUM	CHROMATIC	IMBALANCE	PUISSANCE	WASHBASIN	PIGGYBACK	CLINICIAN
CHARWOMAN	PACHYDERM	CHRYSALIS	IMMOVABLE	PURSUANCE	WAVETABLE	POLITBURO	COLLECTED
DISHWATER	PIGGYBACK	CLEARANCE	IMMUTABLE	PYROMANIA	WORKTABLE	POWERBOAT	COLORCAST
EDELWEISS	POPPYCOCK	COLLEAGUE	IMPEDANCE	QUADRATIC	ABSORBENT	RECUMBENT	CONDUCTOR
ELBOWROOM	PUSSYFOOT	COMPLAINT	INCAPABLE	QUITTANCE	ADSORBATE	REFURBISH	CORKSCREW
ELSEWHERE	WORRYWART	CONSTABLE	INCUBATOR	RAINWATER	ADSORBENT	REPROBATE	CORUSCATE
ERSTWHILE	BREEZEWAY	CONSTANCY	INCURABLE	REACTANCE	AIRMOBILE	RIVERBANK	CRANKCASE
FIREWATER	CITIZENRY	CONTRALTO	INEFFABLE	RELEVANCE	AMPHIBIAN	RIVERBOAT	CRITICISM
FOREWOMAN	QUIZZICAL	CUPBEARER	INHALATOR	RELEVANCY	AMPHIBOLE	SCRAPBOOK	CRITICIZE
FREEWHEEL		DEBUTANTE	INORGANIC	REPUTABLE	ANKLEBONE	SCREWBALL	CURRYCOMB
HANDWOVEN		DECORATOR	INSURABLE	RESONANCE	ASSEMBLER	SHOREBIRD	DAMASCENE
HEADWATER	**6TH LETTER**	DEMITASSE	INSURANCE	RESONATOR	ATTRIBUTE	SHRUBBERY	DEMARCATE
JERKWATER		DESIRABLE	IRRITABLE	RESTRAINT	BLACKBALL	SKIMOBILE	DEMULCENT
KINSWOMAN		DETONATOR	JACARANDA	REVOCABLE	BLACKBIRD	SNAKEBIRD	DEPRECATE
MEANWHILE	ADIABATIC	DIGITALIS	JERKWATER	ROSEWATER	BLACKBODY	SNAKEBITE	DESICCANT
MELTWATER	ADMIRABLE	DISCHARGE	LAGNIAPPE	SACCHARIN	BLOODBATH	SPEEDBOAT	DESICCATE
OVERWEIGH	ADMIRALTY	DISHWATER	LAMINATED	SALTWATER	BROADBAND	SPICEBUSH	DIALECTIC
OVERWHELM	ADVISABLE	DISPRAISE	LANTHANUM	SANDPAPER	CAMELBACK	SPOONBILL	DIFFICULT
OVERWRITE	AEROPAUSE	DOMINANCE	LITERATIM	SCHEMATIC	CAMEMBERT	STEAMBOAT	DISLOCATE
RAINWATER	AFFIDAVIT	DOWNRANGE	MALLEABLE	SEMBLANCE	CANALBOAT	STILLBORN	DISSECTED
ROSEWATER	AFRIKAANS	EGGBEATER	MANSLAYER	SEPARABLE	CANTABILE	SYLLABIFY	DOWITCHER
SALTWATER	AGREEABLE	ENDURANCE	MATRIARCH	SEPARATOR	CARIBBEAN	THIGHBONE	DUPLICATE
SCREWBALL	ALIENABLE	ENIGMATIC	MEDICABLE	SHOEMAKER	CHALKBORD	THROWBACK	DUPLICITY
SEMIWORKS	ALLIGATOR	ENSHEATHE	MELTWATER	SOLITAIRE	CHARABANC	TRACKBALL	EMBROCATE
SHIPWRECK	ALLOWANCE	ENWREATHE	MEMORABLE	SPECIALTY	CHECKBOOK	TURNABOUT	ENDOSCOPE
SOMEWHERE	AMBULANCE	EPIGRAPHY	MENOPAUSE	SPECTACLE	CHEEKBONE	UNDERBODY	ERADICATE
STOPWATCH	ANNOYANCE	EQUITABLE	MINELAYER	SPECTATOR	COLUMBINE	UNDERBRED	EXPLICATE
THROWAWAY	ANTIPASTO	ESCALATOR	MISCHANCE	SPINNAKER	CONCUBINE	UNDOUBTED	EXTRICATE
THROWBACK	ANTIPATHY	ESOPHAGUS	MISERABLE	STOPWATCH	CONNUBIAL	VERTEBRAL	FABRICATE
TIDEWATER	APPARATUS	ESPERANTO	MODERATOR	STRATAGEM	DEATHBLOW	VESTIBULE	FINANCIAL
TYPEWRITE	APPLIANCE	ESTIMABLE	MONOMANIA	SUBSTANCE	DISEMBARK	WAISTBAND	FINANCIER
WASHWOMAN	ASPARAGUS	EXCITABLE	MOUSTACHE	SUFFRAGAN	DISEMBODY	WATCHBAND	FLASHCUBE
ADMIXTURE	ASSONANCE	EXECRABLE	MUCKRAKER	SURCHARGE	EVERYBODY	WHALEBOAT	FOURSCORE
OBNOXIOUS	ASSURANCE	FAVORABLE	NATURALLY	TELEPATHY	FERRYBOAT	WHALEBONE	FRIEDCAKE
ACETYLENE	ATHENAEUM	FIREWATER	NAVIGABLE	THROWAWAY	FIRSTBORN	WHEELBASE	FRUITCAKE
AMARYLLIS	AUTOMATIC	FLAMMABLE	NEWSPAPER	TIDEWATER	FLASHBACK	WHITEBAIT	FUNGICIDE
ANNOYANCE	AUTOMATON	FOOLHARDY	NONREADER	TIMETABLE	FLASHBULB	WOLFSBANE	GERMICIDE
ANONYMOUS	AVAILABLE	FORENAMED	NUMERATOR	TOLERABLE	FROSTBITE	WRISTBAND	GIMMICKRY
BELLYACHE	BACCHANAL	FORETASTE	OBEISANCE	TOLERANCE	GREENBACK	YTTERBIUM	GRATICULE
CUBBYHOLE	BACKWATER	FREEMASON	OCCUPANCY	TOOTHACHE	GREENBELT	AFTERCARE	GREATCOAT
CURRYCOMB	BALALAIKA	GENERATOR	ORDINANCE	TRACTABLE	GUIDEBOOK	AMBUSCADE	GYROSCOPE

HERBICIDE	PROJECTOR	CELANDINE	RECORDING	CHANTEUSE	LORGNETTE	SINGLETON	RECTIFIER
HONEYCOMB	PROSECUTE	CHLORDANE	RECORDIST	CIGARETTE	MAJORETTE	SLUICEWAY	RESHUFFLE
HOROSCOPE	PROTECTOR	CIRCADIAN	REDUNDANT	CITIZENRY	MANIFESTO	SOUBRETTE	RETROFIRE
HOUSECOAT	PUBESCENT	COLLODION	REGARDING	COFFEEPOT	MANOMETER	SOUTHEAST	SACRIFICE
HURRICANE	PUBLICIST	COMMODITY	REPRODUCE	COIFFEUSE	MARQUETRY	SOVEREIGN	SASSAFRAS
HYPERCARD	PUBLICITY	COMMODORE	RETARDATE	CONCIERGE	MEGADEATH	SPAGHETTI	SHEEPFOLD
IMPLICATE	PUBLICIZE	CONFIDANT	SCOUNDREL	COTYLEDON	MEGAHERTZ	SPEAKEASY	SHELLFIRE
IMPRECATE	QUIESCENT	CONUNDRUM	SECONDARY	COUNSELOR	MENAGERIE	SPLENETIC	SHELLFISH
IMPRECISE	RAGPICKER	CORELDRAW	SHAKEDOWN	COURTEOUS	MESSIEURS	STATUETTE	STEADFAST
INCULCATE	RECONCILE	COUNTDOWN	STEVEDORE	COURTESAN	MIDDLEMAN	STRIKEOUT	SWORDFISH
INSINCERE	REFLECTOR	CRACKDOWN	SUBSIDIZE	COVALENCE	MINUTEMAN	SUNSEEKER	THEREFORE
INTERCEDE	REFRACTOR	CROCODILE	SWANSDOWN	CRANBERRY	MISCREANT	SYNTHESIS	THEREFROM
INTERCEPT	REPLICATE	CUSTODIAL	TOUCHDOWN	CRESCENDO	MISTLETOE	SYNTHETIC	THREEFOLD
INTRICATE	RUSTICATE	CUSTODIAN	TRAGEDIAN	CROQUETTE	MUSKMELON	TAXIDERMY	TOWNSFOLK
ITALICIZE	SAPSUCKER	DEFENDANT	TRANSDUCE	CRYOGENIC	NANOMETER	TELEGENIC	TRANSFORM
JACKSCREW	SCARECROW	DEOXIDIZE	UNBENDING	CUTANEOUS	NONCREDIT	TELEMETER	TRANSFUSE
KINESCOPE	SEPULCHER	DEPENDENT	UNBRIDLED	DAREDEVIL	NORTHEAST	TRIWEEKLY	UNDERFEED
LANDSCAPE	SHORTCAKE	DIFFIDENT	UNDERDONE	DECADENCE	NOVELETTE	TULAREMIA	UNDERFOOT
LEUKOCYTE	SKYJACKER	DISSIDENT	UNFLEDGED	DECIMETER	OPTOMETRY	UNDECEIVE	UNRUFFLED
LOWERCASE	SKYROCKET	DROMEDARY	UNMINDFUL	DEFERENCE	ORANGEADE	VEHEMENCE	UNSELFISH
LUBRICANT	SPHINCTER	EAVESDROP	UNSTUDIED	DEKAMETER	OUBLIETTE	VENIREMAN	VERMIFORM
LUBRICATE	STAIRCASE	EIDERDOWN	WRONGDOER	DELINEATE	OVERREACH	VICEREGAL	VERMIFUGE
MACROCOSM	STOMACHER	ELUCIDATE	ACCIDENCE	DIAERESIS	OVERSEXED	VOLTMETER	WATERFALL
MAJUSCULE	STOMACHIC	EUCLIDEAN	ACQUIESCE	DIATHERMY	OVERWEIGH	WAGONETTE	WATERFOWL
MASTICATE	STRETCHER	EXTRADITE	AESTHETIC	DISCREDIT	PANTHEISM	WHICHEVER	WHEREFORE
MATRICIDE	SUFFOCATE	FECUNDATE	AFFLUENCE	DISPLEASE	PARAMETER	WHOSOEVER	WHITEFISH
MENDICANT	SUGARCANE	GABARDINE	ALTIMETER	DOSIMETER	PARQUETRY	WORKBENCH	WOMENFOLK
METRICIZE	SUSPICION	GABERDINE	ANALGESIA	EDELWEISS	PEDOMETER	ZEITGEIST	ABORIGINE
MICROCOPY	SYNDICATE	GRENADIER	ANALGESIC	EFFLUENCE	PERIMETER	ZUCCHETTO	AFTERGLOW
MICROCOSM	TELESCOPE	GRENADINE	ANOPHELES	EMERGENCY	PERPLEXED	ANGELFISH	AGGREGATE
MINISCULE	TRANSCEND	GROUNDHOG	ANTISERUM	ENERGETIC	PHRENETIC	BLACKFOOT	ALLERGIST
MINUSCULE	TRIFOCALS	GROUNDING	ANTIVENIN	EPHEMERAL	PIROUETTE	BLINDFOLD	AMBERGRIS
MOONSCAPE	UNCONCERN	IMPRUDENT	ARBORETUM	ERRONEOUS	PLENTEOUS	BREAKFAST	ANALOGOUS
MORTICIAN	UNDERCOAT	INTENDANT	BACKPEDAL	ETIQUETTE	POLICEMAN	CHAUFFEUR	APOLOGIZE
MOTORCADE	UNSHACKLE	INTERDICT	BAGATELLE	EXISTENCE	POLITESSE	COLORFAST	BELEAGUER
MYSTICISM	UPPERCASE	INTRODUCE	BAKSHEESH	FARSEEING	POULTERER	CRUCIFORM	BILINGUAL
NIGHTCLUB	VINDICATE	KNOCKDOWN	BANQUETTE	FREQUENCY	PROCREATE	CUNEIFORM	CABLEGRAM
OBFUSCATE	WAISTCOAT	LEGENDARY	BARKEEPER	FRUITERER	PROPHETIC	DIGNIFIED	CASTIGATE
OSTRACIZE	WATCHCASE	LIQUIDATE	BAROMETER	GAUCHERIE	PUERPERAL	DISAFFECT	CENTIGRAM
PARRICIDE	WITTICISM	MAJORDOMO	BEAUTEOUS	GENTLEMAN	PYROMETER	DISINFECT	COLLEGIAN
PATRICIAN	ACCORDION	METHADONE	BEEKEEPER	GRAYBEARD	QUARTERLY	FEBRIFUGE	COLLEGIUM
PATRICIDE	AFTERDECK	METHODIST	BICAMERAL	HACKNEYED	RASPBERRY	HEARTFELT	CONJUGATE
PENTECOST	ALMANDITE	METHODIZE	BILATERAL	HALFPENNY	REDBREAST	HEREAFTER	CONTAGION
PERISCOPE	APPENDAGE	PACHYDERM	BLUEBERRY	HEXAMETER	REFERENCE	HYDROFOIL	CORRUGATE
PERSECUTE	ASCENDANT	PALLADIUM	BOLSHEVIK	HOWSOEVER	RESIDENCE	IMPERFECT	COSMOGONY
PESTICIDE	ASCENDERS	POMPADOUR	BOUNTEOUS	ILLIBERAL	RESIDENCY	INTERFACE	DETERGENT
PETTICOAT	ASTRADDLE	PRECEDENT	BOURGEOIS	INCIDENCE	RETRIEVER	INTERFERE	DISENGAGE
PHOTOCELL	ATTENDANT	PRECEDING	BRASSERIE	INFERENCE	REVERENCE	INTERFUSE	DISFIGURE
PHOTOCOPY	BALLADEER	PREJUDICE	BREEZEWAY	INFLUENCE	RHEOMETER	JELLYFISH	DISREGARD
PHYSICIAN	BEDRIDDEN	PREORDAIN	BRIQUETTE	INFLUENZA	RIGHTEOUS	LIGHTFACE	EXPURGATE
PHYSICIST	BELVEDERE	PRESIDENT	BROCHETTE	INNKEEPER	ROUNDELAY	MAGNIFICO	FLOODGATE
PISTACHIO	BREAKDOWN	PRESIDIUM	BUMBLEBEE	INNOCENCE	SADDLEBOW	MICROFILM	FOREIGNER
PIZZICATO	BURUNDIAN	PROCEDURE	CAFETERIA	INTUMESCE	SALTPETER	MISINFORM	HECTOGRAM
POPPYCOCK	CALENDULA	PROVIDENT	CANDLEMAS	ISOSCELES	SCRIVENER	MULTIFORM	HISTOGRAM
PREDICATE	CANDIDACY	QUICKDRAW	CANDLEPIN	KILOHERTZ	SEBACEOUS	NIGHTFALL	IMBROGLIO
PREOCCUPY	CANDIDATE	QUOTIDIAN	CATALEPSY	KILOMETER	SILICEOUS	PITCHFORK	INELEGANT
PRERECORD	CATHEDRAL	RECONDITE	CHALLENGE	KNOWLEDGE	SIMPLETON	PUSSYFOOT	INSTIGATE

INSURGENT	CLIPSHEET	PYRETHRUM	BRILLIANT	GLEANINGS	MELODIOUS	SOMETIMES	ARTILLERY
MICROGRAM	CUBBYHOLE	REPREHEND	BULLFIGHT	GOLDFIELD	MISORIENT	SOPORIFIC	ASTROLABE
MILLIGRAM	DACHSHUND	SAXOPHONE	BULLFINCH	GOLDFINCH	MOONLIGHT	SPOTLIGHT	ASTROLOGY
MONSIGNOR	DECATHLON	SCUTCHEON	BUMPTIOUS	GRANDIOSE	MUNICIPAL	STARLIGHT	AUDIOLOGY
NEGLIGENT	DELIGHTED	SEMAPHORE	CALORIFIC	GUERRILLA	NEFARIOUS	STOPLIGHT	BACKSLASH
NEOLOGISM	DIPHTHONG	SHEATHING	CANONICAL	HAIRPIECE	NEGOTIANT	SUPPLIANT	BACKSLIDE
NIGHTGOWN	DOWNSHIFT	SHIPSHAPE	CAPACIOUS	HEADFIRST	NEGOTIATE	TAILLIGHT	BANDOLIER
NORWEGIAN	ELSEWHERE	SHORTHAND	CAPACITOR	HEADLIGHT	NEPHRITIC	TECHNICAL	BATHOLITH
OBBLIGATO	ENLIGHTEN	SHORTHORN	CAPARISON	HEADPIECE	NEPHRITIS	TECHNIQUE	BATTALION
OBJURGATE	ERSTWHILE	SLAUGHTER	CARTRIDGE	HEMSTITCH	NICOTINIC	TENACIOUS	BEDFELLOW
OUTRIGGER	EXOSPHERE	SOMETHING	CERTAINTY	HEPATITIS	NOSEPIECE	TIMEPIECE	BERKELIUM
PEKINGESE	FALSEHOOD	SOMEWHERE	CHAFFINCH	HIGHLIGHT	NOTORIOUS	TRANSIENT	BERYLLIUM
PREFIGURE	FETISHISM	SPEARHEAD	CHRONICLE	HILARIOUS	NOVITIATE	TRAPPINGS	BLACKLIST
PROPAGATE	FIRSTHAND	SPRIGHTLY	CIGARILLO	HILLBILLY	NUMERICAL	UMBILICUS	BLOODLINE
RADIOGRAM	FLOWCHART	STANCHION	CIRCUITRY	HINDSIGHT	OBLIVIOUS	UNADVISED	BLUEBLACK
SALESGIRL	FORESHEET	STEPCHILD	CLASSICAL	HONORIFIC	OBNOXIOUS	UNDECIDED	BOOKPLATE
SCAPEGOAT	FORESHORE	SWELLHEAD	COALFIELD	HUMILIATE	OFFICIANT	VAGARIOUS	BOOTBLACK
SEGREGATE	FRANCHISE	SWITCHMAN	COCKFIGHT	IDENTICAL	OFFICIATE	VAGINITIS	BRAZILIAN
SUBJUGATE	FREEWHEEL	SYCOPHANT	CONSCIOUS	ILLEGIBLE	OFFICIOUS	VAPORIZER	BROADLOOM
SURROGATE	GEARSHIFT	TELEPHONE	CONTAINER	ILLOGICAL	OUTSKIRTS	VENTRICLE	BRUTALIZE
SYLLOGISM	GREENHORN	TELEPHONY	COPYRIGHT	IMMEDIACY	OVERNIGHT	VERACIOUS	CALCULATE
SYNERGISM	HANDSHAKE	TELEPHOTO	DECILITER	IMMEDIATE	OVERSIGHT	VERIDICAL	CAPILLARY
TERMAGANT	HARDIHOOD	THRESHOLD	DEFICIENT	IMPATIENS	PARTRIDGE	VEXATIOUS	CAPSULATE
UNALIGNED	HARTSHORN	TREACHERY	DEFOLIANT	IMPATIENT	PECUNIARY	VICARIOUS	CARNELIAN
UNDERGIRD	HEADPHONE	TRENCHANT	DEFOLIATE	IMPERIOUS	PENURIOUS	VIDELICET	CARTILAGE
UNFEIGNED	HEALTHFUL	TRUNCHEON	DEKALITER	IMPOLITIC	PHLEBITIS	VIGESIMAL	CATACLYSM
VARIEGATE	HITCHHIKE	ULTRAHIGH	DELICIOUS	INCIPIENT	PLAUSIBLE	VIVACIOUS	CEASELESS
VERDIGRIS	HOLLYHOCK	UNDERHAND	DELIMITER	INCURIOUS	PLENTIFUL	VORACIOUS	CELLULOSE
WOEBEGONE	HOMOPHONE	UNSIGHTLY	DIACRITIC	INDELIBLE	POINCIANA	WHIMSICAL	CERECLOTH
AMIDSHIPS	HORSEHAIR	WHITEHALL	DIGITIZED	INEBRIATE	POLITICAL	WHIRLIGIG	CHAMELEON
AMORPHOUS	HORSEHIDE	WHITEHEAD	DIRIGIBLE	INFURIATE	POTBOILER	XANTHIPPE	CHECKLIST
ANARCHISM	HOUSEHOLD	WINDCHILL	DISORIENT	INFUSIBLE	PRACTICAL	APPLEJACK	CHEERLESS
ANTECHOIR	LAUNCHPAD	WOMANHOOD	DIVISIBLE	INGENIOUS	PREFLIGHT	BLACKJACK	CHEVALIER
APARTHEID	LEASEHOLD	WOODCHUCK	DOWNRIGHT	INPATIENT	PRINCIPAL	INTERJECT	CHILBLAIN
APPREHEND	MAKESHIFT	XEROPHYTE	EBULLIENT	INSATIATE	PRINCIPLE	ASTRAKHAN	CHIVALRIC
ARROWHEAD	MALACHITE	XYLOPHONE	EFFICIENT	INSIDIOUS	PROPRIETY	FINICKING	CHOCOLATE
ARTICHOKE	MALATHION	AFFILIATE	EGREGIOUS	INVIDIOUS	PTARMIGAN	HUMANKIND	CIRCULATE
BEACHHEAD	MASOCHISM	ALGORITHM	EMBROIDER	INVISIBLE	PUNCTILIO	JINRIKSHA	COAGULANT
BENIGHTED	MEANWHILE	ALLEVIATE	EMOLLIENT	IRASCIBLE	QUADRILLE	MINISKIRT	COAGULATE
BIOSPHERE	MEGAPHONE	AMBITIOUS	EMPIRICAL	IRRADIATE	QUIZZICAL	PLACEKICK	COASTLINE
BLACKHEAD	MISBEHAVE	APPETIZER	ENERGIZER	JAUNDICED	RAPACIOUS	SHRINKAGE	COROLLARY
BLASPHEME	MONKSHOOD	ARCHFIEND	ENTERITIS	JUDICIARY	RECIPIENT	WOMANKIND	CORRELATE
BLASPHEMY	MOONSHINE	ARMADILLO	ENUNCIATE	JUDICIOUS	RELIGIOUS	ACETYLENE	COSMOLOGY
BLEACHERS	NIGHTHAWK	ARTERIOLE	ESTAMINET	JURIDICAL	REMINISCE	ACIDULATE	COTILLION
BLOCKHEAD	OVERSHOOT	ARTHRITIS	EXCORIATE	KILOLITER	REPUDIATE	ACIDULOUS	COUNTLESS
BOMBSHELL	OVERTHROW	ARTIFICER	EXPATIATE	LABORIOUS	RETALIATE	AERIALIST	CREDULOUS
BOOKSHELF	OVERWHELM	ASSOCIATE	EXPEDIENT	LABYRINTH	SAGACIOUS	AEROPLANE	CRINOLINE
BRONCHIAL	PARACHUTE	ATROCIOUS	EXPEDITER	LAVALIERE	SALACIOUS	AFTERLIFE	CYTOPLASM
BUCKWHEAT	PARATHION	AUDACIOUS	EXPOSITOR	LIMELIGHT	SANDPIPER	AMARYLLIS	DAMSELFLY
BUSHWHACK	PAROCHIAL	AUXILIARY	FACETIOUS	LITIGIOUS	SCINTILLA	ANCILLARY	DANDELION
CACOPHONY	PERIPHERY	BACKFIELD	FEROCIOUS	LOGARITHM	SEMIFINAL	ANIMALISM	DAUNTLESS
CARTWHEEL	PHOSPHATE	BANDWIDTH	FIDUCIARY	LUXURIANT	SHOWPIECE	ANOMALOUS	DEATHLESS
CATECHISM	PLAYTHING	BEAUTIFUL	FORESIGHT	LUXURIATE	SIDEPIECE	ANTHOLOGY	DECOLLETE
CHILDHOOD	PLOWSHARE	BINOMINAL	FORTNIGHT	MAHARISHI	SINUSITIS	ANTICLINE	DISHCLOTH
CHUCKHOLE	POLYPHONY	BOMBSIGHT	FRACTIOUS	MATUTINAL	SKINTIGHT	APPELLANT	DISOBLIGE
CHURCHMAN	PRESCHOOL	BOUNTIFUL	FRANGIBLE	MEDICINAL	SNOWFIELD	APPELLATE	DISSOLUTE
CLAMSHELL	PRONGHORN	BRASSIERE	GASTRITIS	MEGAPIXEL	SOLICITOR	AQUAPLANE	DIXIELAND

DOORPLATE	INTERLOPE	PORCELAIN	SWAMPLAND	BIRTHMARK	MATRIMONY	ADJOINING	CULLENDER
DOUBTLESS	INTERLUDE	PORTULACA	SYMBOLISM	BLACKMAIL	MERRIMENT	AFTERNOON	CULMINATE
DREAMLAND	INVIOLATE	POSTILION	SYMBOLIZE	CALCIMINE	MIDSUMMER	ALTERNATE	DARWINISM
EARTHLING	ISINGLASS	POSTULANT	TABLELAND	CATCHMENT	MINCEMEAT	ALUMINIUM	DECENNIAL
EJACULATE	ISRAELITE	POSTULATE	TANTALIZE	CHAMOMILE	NEODYMIUM	ALUMINIZE	DERRINGER
EMBELLISH	JOBHOLDER	PREVALENT	TAUTOLOGY	CHECKMATE	NEVERMORE	ANNOUNCER	DESCENDER
ENCHILADA	LACCOLITH	PRICELESS	THANKLESS	CLASSMATE	NIGHTMARE	ANTIKNOCK	DESIGNATE
ESTABLISH	LANDSLIDE	PRIVILEGE	THRALLDOM	COLLIMATE	NURSEMAID	APPOINTEE	DESIGNING
ETHNOLOGY	LEGISLATE	PROPELLER	TRAINLOAD	CONDIMENT	NUTRIMENT	ARCHANGEL	DISHONEST
ETYMOLOGY	LIABILITY	PROSELYTE	TRANSLATE	CONTUMELY	OUTERMOST	ARCHENEMY	DISMANTLE
EVERGLADE	LIFEBLOOD	PROVOLONE	TREMULOUS	CUSTOMARY	OUTNUMBER	ASTRONAUT	DISSENTER
EXCELLENT	LITHOLOGY	PUREBLOOD	TRUCKLOAD	CUSTOMIZE	PANTOMIME	ASTRONOMY	DOBSONFLY
EXEMPLARY	LOINCLOTH	QUERULOUS	TRUCULENT	CYCLAMATE	PARCHMENT	ATTAINDER	DRAGONFLY
EXEMPLIFY	MARMALADE	QUICKLIME	TURBULENT	DAIRYMAID	PARSIMONY	AUTHENTIC	ELIMINATE
FAIRYLAND	MARVELOUS	RACIALISM	TWINKLING	DECREMENT	PATRIMONY	AVALANCHE	EMPENNAGE
FERTILIZE	MASCULINE	RADIOLOGY	UNDERLINE	DEFERMENT	PERFUMERY	BADMINTON	ENCOUNTER
FEUDALISM	MATCHLOCK	RANCHLAND	UNDERLING	DEFORMITY	PERSIMMON	BARTENDER	EPICENTER
FIREPLACE	MAUSOLEUM	RANGELAND	UNFAILING	DETERMINE	PESSIMISM	BASTINADO	EROGENOUS
FIRSTLING	MEDALLION	RAUWOLFIA	UNFEELING	DETRIMENT	PHEROMONE	BENIGNANT	ESPIONAGE
FLAGELLUM	MENTALITY	REBELLION	UNHEALTHY	DEVILMENT	PIECEMEAL	BENTONITE	ESPLANADE
FLATULENT	MESCALINE	RECOLLECT	UNIVALENT	DIATOMITE	PLACEMENT	BESPANGLE	EUTHENICS
FLEDGLING	METROLOGY	REPELLENT	UNSKILLED	DIPLOMACY	PROXIMATE	BRITANNIC	EXOGENOUS
FLINTLOCK	MISSILERY	ROADBLOCK	UNWILLING	DISCOMFIT	PROXIMITY	BUCCANEER	EXTRINSIC
FORECLOSE	MONGOLIAN	SACKCLOTH	UNWORLDLY	DISMEMBER	RANDOMIZE	BYSTANDER	FASCINATE
FORMALISM	MONGOLISM	SACRILEGE	VACILLATE	DISSEMBLE	RECOMMEND	CALVINISM	FASTENING
FORMALITY	MONGOLOID	SAILCLOTH	VAINGLORY	DISTEMPER	REPRIMAND	CAMPANILE	FORTUNATE
FORMALIZE	MONOPLANE	SAILPLANE	VANDALISM	ECONOMICS	SACRAMENT	CANNONADE	FULMINATE
FORMULATE	MUSSULMAN	SANDBLAST	VANDALIZE	ECONOMIZE	SCHLEMIEL	CANNONEER	GALLANTRY
FOUNDLING	MYTHOLOGY	SATELLITE	VASSALAGE	EMBAYMENT	SCRIMMAGE	CARBONATE	GALLINULE
FRIVOLOUS	NAMEPLATE	SCANTLING	VENTILATE	EMOLUMENT	SENTIMENT	CARBUNCLE	GALVANISM
FUSILLADE	NECROLOGY	SCHEELITE	VERBALIZE	EQUIPMENT	SEPTEMBER	CARCINOMA	GALVANIZE
GANGPLANK	NEURALGIA	SCHILLING	VERMILION	EUPHEMISM	SOPHOMORE	CARPENTER	GELIGNITE
GARRULOUS	NEUROLOGY	SCHOOLBOY	VERNALIZE	EXCREMENT	SPEARMINT	CASTANETS	GERMANIUM
GENEALOGY	NIGHTLIFE	SEMIFLUID	VISUALIZE	EXTREMISM	SQUEAMISH	CENTENARY	GERMINATE
GENTILITY	NORMALIZE	SHAPELESS	VOICELESS	EXTREMITY	STALEMATE	CHICANERY	GLUTINOUS
GENUFLECT	NOSEBLEED	SHIFTLESS	WAISTLINE	FACSIMILE	STATEMENT	COCHINEAL	GOLDENROD
GONDOLIER	NOSTALGIA	SHOWPLACE	WASHCLOTH	FIRMAMENT	STREAMBED	COLONNADE	GOVERNESS
GRANULATE	OSCILLATE	SIGNALIZE	WASTELAND	GOLDSMITH	STREAMLET	COLUMNIST	GUARANTEE
GRASSLAND	OURSELVES	SIGNALMAN	WATERLINE	GRISTMILL	SUBLIMATE	COMMANDER	GUARANTOR
GUIDELINE	OVERBLOWN	SKINFLINT	WINDBLOWN	HATCHMENT	SUPREMACY	COMMINGLE	HAPPENING
GYRFALCON	OVERCLOUD	SNOWFLAKE	WOMANLIKE	HISTAMINE	SWEETMEAT	COMMUNION	HAPPINESS
HAIRCLOTH	OVERSLEEP	SOCIALISM	WOODBLOCK	HONEYMOON	SYSTEMIZE	COMMUNISM	HARBINGER
HANDCLASP	PAPILLOTE	SOCIALITE	WORKPLACE	HOUSEMAID	TESTAMENT	COMMUNITY	HARMONICA
HEARTLESS	PATHOLOGY	SOCIALIZE	WORLDLING	IMPLEMENT	TESTIMONY	COMPANION	HARMONICS
HERBALIST	PATROLMAN	SOCIOLOGY	WORTHLESS	IMPROMPTU	TRADEMARK	COMPONENT	HARMONIUM
HERCULEAN	PENDULOUS	SOMNOLENT	WRESTLING	INANIMATE	TRANSMUTE	CONDENSER	HARMONIZE
HOURGLASS	PENEPLAIN	SPECULATE	YOUNGLING	INCLEMENT	TREADMILL	CONGENIAL	HELLENISM
HYDROLOGY	PENHOLDER	SPINDLING	ZWINGLIAN	INCOMMODE	TREATMENT	CONSENSUS	HEREUNDER
INABILITY	PERCOLATE	STABILIZE	ABATEMENT	INCREMENT	UNANIMOUS	CONSONANT	HIBERNATE
INOCULATE	PESTILENT	STARTLING	ACCLIMATE	INFIRMARY	UNDERMINE	CONTENTED	HUMDINGER
INTELLECT	PETROLEUM	STERILIZE	AFTERMATH	INFIRMITY	UNDERMOST	CONTINENT	HUSBANDRY
INTERLACE	PETROLOGY	STIMULANT	AGREEMENT	INFORMANT	UNPLUMBED	CONTINUAL	HYDRANGEA
INTERLARD	PHILOLOGY	STIMULATE	AMENDMENT	INNERMOST	UPPERMOST	CONTINUUM	HYPHENATE
INTERLEAF	PHONOLOGY	STIPULATE	ANATOMIZE	INTERMENT	UTTERMOST	CORIANDER	ICELANDER
INTERLINE	PLANELOAD	STRAPLESS	ANONYMOUS	JESSAMINE	VICTIMIZE	COSMONAUT	ICELANDIC
INTERLINK	PLURALITY	STRIPLING	APARTMENT	LINEAMENT	WATERMARK	COSPONSOR	IMAGINARY
INTERLOCK	PLURALIZE	SUCCULENT	ATONEMENT	LOCKSMITH	ABOMINATE	CRETINISM	INCARNATE

INCOGNITO	PRECENTOR	VIRGINITY	EASYGOING	PSYCHOSIS	ETHIOPIAN	ANHYDROUS	CONGERIES
INDEMNIFY	PRESENTLY	VISIONARY	ELASTOMER	RACEHORSE	EUTROPHIC	ARBITRARY	CONSCRIPT
INDEMNITY	PROCONSUL	VOLCANISM	EPISCOPAL	REENFORCE	EXCULPATE	ARBITRATE	CONSTRAIN
INDIGNANT	PROFANITY	VULCANISM	EQUIPOISE	REINFORCE	EXTEMPORE	ARROWROOT	CONSTRICT
INDIGNITY	PROMENADE	VULCANIZE	EQUIVOCAL	ROCKBOUND	EXTIRPATE	AUCTORIAL	CONSTRUCT
INGLENOOK	PROMINENT	WARBONNET	FARMHOUSE	RUNAROUND	HANDSPIKE	AUTHORITY	COOPERATE
INSTANTER	PROPONENT	WARMONGER	FIREHOUSE	SAFFLOWER	HORSEPLAY	AUTHORIZE	CORMORANT
INSTANTLY	PROVENCAL	WHITENESS	FIREPOWER	SCLEROSIS	INCULPATE	AUTOCRACY	CORPORATE
INTERNIST	PROVENDER	ZIRCONIUM	FLAGEOLET	SECTIONAL	INTERPLAY	AUTOGRAPH	CORPOREAL
INTERNODE	PULMONARY	ABANDONED	FLOPHOUSE	SEMICOLON	INTERPOSE	AUTOTRACE	COURTROOM
INTRINSIC	RABBINATE	ACROPOLIS	FOOTBOARD	SEMIWORKS	INTERPRET	AWESTRUCK	COUTURIER
INVERNESS	RATIONALE	ALCOHOLIC	FOOTLOOSE	SHIPBOARD	JUXTAPOSE	BACKTRACK	CRABGRASS
JACKKNIFE	RECKONING	ALEATORIC	FOREGOING	SIDEBOARD	MARSUPIAL	BACTERIUM	CRITERION
LEAVENING	RECOGNIZE	ALMSHOUSE	FORETOKEN	SIGNBOARD	MILLIPEDE	BALLERINA	CROSSROAD
LIGHTNING	RECTANGLE	ANAEROBIC	FOREWOMAN	SILICOSIS	MONOSPACE	BANDEROLE	CUTTHROAT
MACHINERY	REJOINDER	ANTINOVEL	FREEBOARD	SOFTBOUND	MOUTHPART	BARBARIAN	DANGEROUS
MACHINIST	REMAINDER	ANTITOXIN	GASTROPOD	SOLILOQUY	PHILIPPIC	BARBARISM	DEHYDRATE
MALIGNANT	RENCONTRE	APOSTOLIC	GLADIOLUS	STARBOARD	PHOTOPLAY	BARBAROUS	DEMOCRACY
MANGANESE	REPLENISH	APPALOOSA	GREYHOUND	STATIONER	PINEAPPLE	BARCAROLE	DEMURRAGE
MANHANDLE	REPUGNANT	ARTHROPOD	HALITOSIS	SUBATOMIC	PORCUPINE	BAROGRAPH	DENIGRATE
MATERNITY	ROUGHNECK	BACKBOARD	HANDWOVEN	SUNFLOWER	PRECEPTOR	BEDSPREAD	DEODORANT
MECHANICS	ROUMANIAN	BACKWOODS	HARDBOARD	SURFBOARD	PRECIPICE	BIRTHRATE	DEODORIZE
MECHANISM	RUMRUNNER	BAMBOOZLE	HARDBOUND	SYMBIOSIS	RAINSPOUT	BLOODROOT	DESECRATE
MECHANIZE	RUTHENIUM	BASEBOARD	HARDCOVER	SYNAGOGUE	RESERPINE	BLUEGRASS	DESPERADO
MERCENARY	SATURNINE	BATHHOUSE	HEADBOARD	THEOSOPHY	RIDGEPOLE	BLUEPRINT	DESPERATE
MERGANSER	SCAVENGER	BILLBOARD	HETERODOX	TOLLHOUSE	STANDPIPE	BOMBPROOF	DETERRENT
MESSENGER	SCREENING	BIRDHOUSE	HIDEBOUND	TRANSONIC	STOCKPILE	BOOMERANG	DEUTERIUM
METRONOME	SEASONING	BLOWTORCH	HOPSCOTCH	TURQUOISE	STRAPPING	BOWSTRING	DEXTERITY
MEZZANINE	SOLEMNIZE	BLUEPOINT	HOREHOUND	UNALLOYED	SUBALPINE	BROKERAGE	DEXTEROUS
MIDWINTER	SPELUNKER	BONDWOMAN	IRONBOUND	UNTUTORED	SUGARPLUM	BULGARIAN	DIAPHRAGM
MILLINERY	STAMINATE	BOONDOCKS	KINSWOMAN	VIEWPOINT	SUPERPOSE	BUTTERCUP	DIFFERENT
MISHANDLE	SUBLUNARY	BUCKBOARD	LATECOMER	VOODOOISM	SWORDPLAY	BUTTERFAT	DIPTEROUS
MISMANAGE	SUNBONNET	BUCKTOOTH	LAZYBONES	WALLBOARD	TOOTHPICK	BUTTERFLY	DISBURDEN
MODERNISM	SUPERNOVA	CABRIOLET	LEITMOTIV	WAREHOUSE	TRANSPIRE	BUTTERNUT	DISPARAGE
MODERNIZE	SURCINGLE	CALABOOSE	LOCOMOTOR	WASHBOARD	TRANSPORT	CALIBRATE	DISPARATE
NEPTUNIUM	SURRENDER	CARDBOARD	MAYFLOWER	WASHHOUSE	TRANSPOSE	CANEBRAKE	DISTURBED
OBSTINATE	SUSPENDER	CATAMOUNT	MISSIONER	WASHWOMAN	TURBOPROP	CARBURIZE	DITHERING
ORIGINATE	TANZANIAN	CATATONIC	MOLDBOARD	WILLPOWER	ULTRAPURE	CASSEROLE	DOCTORATE
ORPHANAGE	TECTONICS	CHARWOMAN	MONOLOGUE	WOLFHOUND	UNDERPART	CATHARSIS	DOWNGRADE
OXYGENATE	TECTONISM	CHOPHOUSE	NONPROFIT	WORKHORSE	UNDERPASS	CATHARTIC	EDITORIAL
PANHANDLE	TERMINATE	CIRRHOSIS	OUTGROWTH	WORKHOUSE	UNDERPLAY	CAUTERIZE	ELABORATE
PARSONAGE	THICKNESS	CLAPBOARD	OUTSPOKEN	ACCOMPANY	WALLOPING	CELEBRATE	ELBOWROOM
PASSENGER	THUMBNAIL	CLIPBOARD	OVERBOARD	AEROSPACE	WHIRLPOOL	CELEBRITY	ELECTRIFY
PATERNITY	TRIENNIAL	CLOISONNE	OVERPOWER	BISHOPRIC	ALGONQUIN	CELLARAGE	ELECTRODE
PATRONAGE	TYRANNIZE	CLUBHOUSE	PACKHORSE	CENTIPEDE	EXCHEQUER	CENTURION	EMBARRASS
PATRONIZE	TYRANNOUS	COCKROACH	PARAMOUNT	CHIROPODY	HARLEQUIN	CEREBRATE	ENCOURAGE
PERENNIAL	UKRAINIAN	COONHOUND	PAREGORIC	DAVENPORT	MANNEQUIN	CHANCROID	ENDOCRINE
PERMANENT	UNBEKNOWN	CROSSOVER	PEDAGOGUE	DECOMPOSE	PALANQUIN	CHAPARRAL	ENTOURAGE
PERSONAGE	UNBOUNDED	DASHBOARD	PENTHOUSE	DECOUPAGE	SOBRIQUET	CHECKROOM	ENUMERATE
PERSONATE	UNCOUNTED	DECALOGUE	PESTHOUSE	DIMORPHIC	ABHORRENT	CHONDRITE	EPHEDRINE
PERSONIFY	UNDAUNTED	DEMAGOGUE	PLAYHOUSE	DISAPPEAR	ADUMBRATE	CHONDRULE	EPICUREAN
PERSONNEL	UNFOUNDED	DEMIMONDE	PNEUMONIA	DISREPAIR	AERODROME	CLASSROOM	EPIDERMIS
PERTINENT	UNHARNESS	DESTROYER	POORHOUSE	DISREPUTE	AIRWORTHY	COFFERDAM	EUCHARIST
PHILANDER	UNMEANING	DIAGNOSIS	PORTFOLIO	DISSIPATE	ALBATROSS	COMFORTER	EVAPORATE
PLUTONIUM	VACCINATE	DUCKBOARD	POURBOIRE	DRAINPIPE	ANCHORAGE	CONCERNED	EVAPORITE
PORRINGER	VICENNIAL	DUMBFOUND	PROGNOSIS	DYSPEPSIA	ANCHORITE	CONCERTED	EVERGREEN
PRECANCEL	VILLENAGE	DYSTROPHY	PSEUDONYM	ENCOMPASS	ANCHORMAN	CONCORDAT	EXONERATE

EXUBERANT	LIMBURGER	PRESTRESS	TONSORIAL	COMMISSAR	INCURSION	RIVERSIDE	ADVANTAGE
EYESTRAIN	LITTERBUG	PREVERBAL	TRITURATE	COMPOSITE	INNERSOLE	SACRISTAN	ADVENTURE
FACTORIAL	LUDICROUS	PRIMARILY	TUSCARORA	COMPOSURE	INSENSATE	SCRIMSHAW	ADVERTISE
FINGERING	LUNCHROOM	PROOFREAD	TYPEWRITE	CONFESSOR	INTENSIFY	SECESSION	AFFECTING
FINGERTIP	MAINFRAME	PROSCRIBE	UNCHARTED	CONFUSION	INTENSITY	SECLUSION	AFFECTION
FIREBRAND	MALADROIT	PROSTRATE	UNDERRATE	CONTUSION	INTENSIVE	SEQUESTER	AILANTHUS
FIREBREAK	MANNERISM	PULVERIZE	UNGUARDED	CORPUSCLE	INTERSECT	SHARKSKIN	AMPLITUDE
FIREBRICK	MARGARINE	RACETRACK	UNITARIAN	CORTISONE	INVERSION	SHEEPSKIN	ANIMATION
FIREPROOF	MARMOREAL	RASTERIZE	UNIVERSAL	COURTSHIP	LIGHTSHIP	SHORTSTOP	ANNUITANT
FISHERMAN	MARTYRDOM	RECHERCHE	UNLEARNED	CRAFTSMAN	LIGHTSOME	SLINGSHOT	APPERTAIN
FLAVORING	MASTERFUL	REENTRANT	UNSPARING	CROISSANT	LIMOUSINE	SOPHISTIC	APPLETALK
FLOWERPOT	MELIORATE	REHEARING	VENTUROUS	DEFENSIVE	LITHESOME	SOPHISTRY	APPORTION
FOOLPROOF	MELODRAMA	REHEARSAL	VICTORIAN	DEPRESSED	LOATHSOME	SPACESHIP	ARCHETYPE
FOOTPRINT	MERCERIZE	REITERATE	VULGARIAN	DIMENSION	MAGNESIUM	SPOKESMAN	ARCHITECT
FOREFRONT	MERCURIAL	REPAIRMAN	VULGARISM	DIVERSIFY	MALAYSIAN	SPORTSMAN	ARGENTINE
FORWARDER	MERCUROUS	RESURRECT	VULGARITY	DIVERSION	MICROSOFT	STATESIDE	ARGENTITE
FRATERNAL	MESMERIZE	RIGMAROLE	VULGARIZE	DIVERSITY	MULTISCAN	STATESMAN	ARMISTICE
FRUSTRATE	METEORITE	SAGEBRUSH	WINDBREAK	DRAFTSMAN	MULTISPIN	STATISTIC	ASAFETIDA
GIBBERISH	METEOROID	SANGFROID	WINDPROOF	ECOSYSTEM	MULTISYNC	STEAMSHIP	ASCERTAIN
GLAMORIZE	MIDSTREAM	SARTORIAL	WINEPRESS	ELLIPSOID	NARCISSUS	SUCCESSOR	ASSERTION
GODPARENT	MISDIRECT	SAXIFRAGE	WINTERIZE	EMBRASURE	NECESSARY	SUPERSEDE	ASSISTANT
GOLDBRICK	MONOGRAPH	SEAFARING	WIREFRAME	EMPHASIZE	NECESSITY	SUPPOSING	ASYMPTOTE
GONORRHEA	MURDEROUS	SEAWORTHY	WISECRACK	EMPHYSEMA	OBSESSION	SWEATSHOP	ATHLETICS
GREENROOM	NECTARINE	SECTARIAN	WITHDRAWN	EXCELSIOR	OFFENSIVE	SWORDSMAN	ATTENTION
GROSGRAIN	NEWSPRINT	SENIORITY	WOLVERINE	EXCLUSIVE	OMBUDSMAN	SYMPOSIUM	ATTRITION
GUARDROOM	NOCTURNAL	SERIGRAPH	WONDERFUL	EXCURSION	ONIONSKIN	THREESOME	AVOCATION
HAIRBRUSH	NONPAREIL	SHIPWRECK	WOODCRAFT	EXCURSIVE	ORCHESTRA	TOOTHSOME	BACKSTAGE
HAMADRYAD	NONPERSON	SIDETRACK	WORKGROUP	EXPANSION	ORGIASTIC	TRADESMAN	BANDSTAND
HAMBURGER	OFFSPRING	SNOWDRIFT	YESTERDAY	EXPANSIVE	PALAESTRA	TRANSSHIP	BARNSTORM
HAMMERTOE	OLIGARCHY	SPINDRIFT	ACCESSION	EXPENSIVE	PALMISTRY	TRIBESMAN	BEATITUDE
HAMSTRING	OUTSPREAD	STATEROOM	ACCESSORY	EXPLOSION	PATRISTIC	TRICKSTER	BEEFSTEAK
HANDCRAFT	OUTWARDLY	STOREROOM	ADDRESSEE	EXPLOSIVE	PAYMASTER	TRIMESTER	BESETTING
HARBORAGE	OVERDRAFT	SUBMARINE	ADMISSION	EXPULSION	PENINSULA	TROOPSHIP	BESPATTER
HEADDRESS	OVERDRIVE	SUBNORMAL	ADVERSARY	EXQUISITE	POETASTER	TROUSSEAU	BETROTHED
HERBARIUM	OVERPRINT	SUBSCRIBE	ADVERSITY	EXTENSION	POLYESTER	UNBLESSED	BIMONTHLY
HIERARCHY	OVERTRICK	SUBSCRIPT	AFORESAID	EXTENSIVE	POTASSIUM	UNCEASING	BIPARTITE
HISTORIAN	OVERWRITE	SUFFERING	ALABASTER	EXTRUSIVE	PRECISION	UNDERSELL	BRIMSTONE
HOARFROST	OVIPAROUS	SULFUROUS	ALONGSIDE	FANTASIZE	PREVISION	UNDERSHOT	BROADTAIL
HOLOGRAPH	PARAGRAPH	SUMMARIZE	AMPERSAND	FANTASTIC	PROBOSCIS	UNDERSIDE	CAMPSTOOL
HOMEGROWN	PASSERINE	SUNSTROKE	ANGUISHED	FRICASSEE	PROCESSOR	UPANISHAD	CARNATION
HOMOGRAPH	PASTORALE	SUPPURATE	ANIMOSITY	GARNISHEE	PROFESSOR	UPHOLSTER	CARPETBAG
HUNGARIAN	PASTURAGE	TANGERINE	ARABESQUE	GLYCOSIDE	PROMISING	VISCOSITY	CARPETING
HYPOCRISY	PENETRATE	TELEGRAPH	ASCENSION	GRANTSMAN	PROVISION	VOUCHSAFE	CAUSATION
HYSTERICS	PERFORATE	TELLURIUM	ASPERSION	GRAPESHOT	QUICKSAND	WATERSHED	CELESTIAL
IMMIGRANT	PHALAROPE	TEMPERATE	BANTUSTAN	GROOMSMAN	QUICKSORT	WATERSIDE	CERTITUDE
IMMIGRATE	PICTORIAL	TEMPORARY	BARRISTER	GROTESQUE	QUICKSTEP	WEARISOME	CESSATION
INAMORATA	PIMPERNEL	TEMPORIZE	BLOODSHED	GUARDSMAN	RECESSION	WEDNESDAY	CHIEFTAIN
INCORRECT	PINSTRIPE	TENDERIZE	BLOODSHOT	GUNNYSACK	RECESSIVE	WHOLESALE	CHOPSTICK
INTEGRATE	POLYGRAPH	TENEBROUS	BROADSIDE	GYMNASIUM	RECURSION	WHOLESOME	CHRISTIAN
INTEGRITY	PONDEROUS	TERRARIUM	BURLESQUE	HAVERSACK	REMISSION	WORRISOME	CHRISTMAS
INTERRUPT	POSTERIOR	TERRORISM	CALLOSITY	HEARTSICK	REPOSSESS	YACHTSMAN	CLIENTELE
ITINERANT	POSTERITY	TERRORIZE	CASUISTRY	HEURISTIC	REPRESENT	YOUNGSTER	COALITION
ITINERARY	PRAYERFUL	THEATRICS	CAUCASIAN	HORSESHOE	REPULSION	ACCRETION	COCKATIEL
JAILBREAK	PRECURSOR	THEOCRACY	CENTESIMO	IMPASSIVE	REPULSIVE	ACOUSTICS	COFEATURE
JITTERBUG	PRESCRIBE	TIGHTROPE	CHEMISTRY	IMPULSION	REQUISITE	ADDICTION	COGNITION
LAMEBRAIN	PRESHRUNK	TIMBERING	CHORISTER	IMPULSIVE	REVERSION	ADJECTIVE	COLLATION
LIBRARIAN	PRESSROOM	TINDERBOX	COLLUSION	INCESSANT	REVULSION	ADMIXTURE	COMMITTEE

COMMOTION	ERUDITION	HOMESTEAD	MAGNITUDE	PRIVATEER	SIMPATICO	ANTIQUARY	THESAURUS
COMPETENT	ESSENTIAL	HORSETAIL	MANDATORY	PRIVATION	SITUATION	ANTIQUITY	TREASURER
CONDITION	EVOLUTION	HORTATIVE	MANHATTAN	PROBATION	SMALLTALK	ANTITUMOR	UNNATURAL
CONESTOGA	EXCEPTION	HORTATORY	MILESTONE	PROBATIVE	SNOWSTORM	ARTICULAR	UNPOPULAR
COPARTNER	EXECUTIVE	HYPERTEXT	MILLSTONE	PROFITEER	SOAPSTONE	ASSIDUOUS	WHEREUPON
CORNSTALK	EXECUTRIX	IMITATION	MINIATURE	PROTOTYPE	SPIRITUAL	ATTENUATE	ACCLIVITY
CREMATORY	EXPECTANT	IMITATIVE	MINISTATE	PUPPETEER	SPLITTING	AURICULAR	AESTIVATE
CURETTAGE	EXPERTISE	IMPARTIAL	MOMENTARY	PURGATION	STATUTORY	AVUNCULAR	AGGRAVATE
CURVATURE	EXPIATORY	IMPORTANT	MOMENTOUS	PURGATIVE	STREETCAR	BINOCULAR	ARCHIVIST
CYCLOTRON	EXPLETIVE	IMPORTUNE	MONASTERY	PURGATORY	STRICTURE	BODYGUARD	BOULEVARD
DALMATION	FARMSTEAD	IMPOSTURE	MOONSTONE	QUICKTIME	STRONTIUM	CARROUSEL	CAPTIVATE
DAMNATION	FEEDSTOCK	INANITION	MOUSETRAP	RACKETEER	STRUCTURE	COADJUTOR	CARNIVORA
DEBENTURE	FEEDSTUFF	INCENTIVE	MULTITUDE	RACONTEUR	SUBALTERN	CONCOURSE	CARNIVORE
DECEITFUL	FEUDATORY	INCEPTION	NARCOTIZE	RAINSTORM	SUCCOTASH	CONGRUITY	COLLUVIUM
DECEPTION	FILMSTRIP	INDENTION	NARRATIVE	RECEPTION	SUMMATION	DECIDUOUS	CONVIVIAL
DECISTERE	FLAGSTAFF	INDENTURE	NEGRITUDE	RECEPTIVE	SWORDTAIL	DISCOURSE	CULTIVATE
DECONTROL	FLAGSTONE	INDUCTION	NEWSSTAND	RECTITUDE	TALKATIVE	EVENTUATE	DECLIVITY
DEDUCTION	FLASHTUBE	INDUCTIVE	NIGHTTIME	REDACTION	TARANTULA	EXTENUATE	EFFLUVIUM
DEFEATISM	FLOTATION	INFANTILE	NIGRITUDE	REDUCTION	TEAKETTLE	FLUCTUATE	ENGRAVING
DEFECTIVE	FOODSTUFF	INFECTION	NONENTITY	REFECTION	TENTATIVE	FUNICULAR	EXTRAVERT
DEFLATION	FOOTSTOOL	INFERTILE	NORMATIVE	REFECTORY	TERRITORY	HABITUATE	FESTIVITY
DEJECTION	FORESTALL	INFLATION	NUTRITION	REGISTRAR	THUMBTACK	HYDRAULIC	FORGIVING
DEKASTERE	FORGATHER	INJECTION	OBJECTIFY	REINSTATE	TOADSTOOL	IMPETUOUS	GALLIVANT
DENTITION	FORMATION	INJUSTICE	OBJECTIVE	RELUCTANT	TOMBSTONE	INAUGURAL	GRAPEVINE
DEPARTURE	FORMATIVE	INSERTION	OCCULTISM	RENDITION	TRADITION	INFATUATE	IMPROVISE
DESTITUTE	FORSYTHIA	INSISTENT	OFFERTORY	REPERTORY	TREMATODE	INGENUITY	INSOLVENT
DESUETUDE	FORTITUDE	INSTITUTE	OLFACTORY	REPLETION	TRIBUTARY	INGENUOUS	INTERVENE
DESULTORY	FREESTONE	INTENTION	OPERATION	REPORTAGE	TURNSTILE	INNOCUOUS	INTERVIEW
DETECTIVE	FRIGHTFUL	INTESTATE	OPERATIVE	RESECTION	TURPITUDE	INSINUATE	INTROVERT
DETENTION	FURNITURE	INTESTINE	OPPORTUNE	RESISTANT	UNCERTAIN	INSOLUBLE	LONGEVITY
DEVASTATE	GALACTOSE	INTUITION	ORIENTATE	RETENTION	UNDERTAKE	INVOLUCRE	MILLIVOLT
DHRYSTONE	GALLSTONE	INVECTIVE	OVERSTATE	RETENTIVE	UNDERTONE	IRREGULAR	MISGIVING
DIAMETRIC	GARNITURE	INVENTION	OXIDATION	REVOLTING	UNEARTHLY	LIFEGUARD	MISGOVERN
DICHOTOMY	GAZETTEER	INVENTIVE	PAKISTANI	ROADSTEAD	UNSCATHED	MANOEUVRE	OBSERVANT
DIETETICS	GERIATRIC	INVENTORY	PALPITATE	ROOTSTOCK	UNSETTLED	MARIJUANA	PERSEVERE
DIGNITARY	GESTATION	IRONSTONE	PARTITION	RUINATION	UNSPOTTED	ONSLAUGHT	RESERVIST
DIRECTION	GLADSTONE	ITERATION	PARTITIVE	SALVATION	UNWITTING	POTPOURRI	RESERVOIR
DIRECTIVE	GODFATHER	JACKSTRAW	PEACETIME	SANDSTONE	UNWRITTEN	PRELAUNCH	SKYDIVING
DIRECTORY	GODMOTHER	KICKSTAND	PEGMATITE	SANDSTORM	VALENTINE	PRONOUNCE	SUBDIVIDE
DISESTEEM	GRADATION	LASSITUDE	PERDITION	SCRIPTURE	VALUATION	PUNCTUATE	SUPERVENE
DISPUTANT	GRATITUDE	LAUDATORY	PERISTYLE	SCULPTURE	VARIATION	QUADRUPED	SUPERVISE
DOGMATISM	GRAVITATE	LEAFSTALK	PERPETUAL	SECRETARY	VASECTOMY	QUADRUPLE	AFTERWARD
DORMITORY	GRUBSTAKE	LEVIATHAN	PHILATELY	SECRETION	VELVETEEN	QUINTUPLE	ANGLEWORM
DOWNSTAGE	GUNCOTTON	LIBERTINE	PHONETICS	SECRETIVE	VERSATILE	REIMBURSE	BACKSWEPT
DRAMATIZE	GUSTATORY	LIMESTONE	PIKESTAFF	SEDENTARY	VIBRATION	RELIQUARY	BAILIWICK
DRUGSTORE	HAILSTONE	LIVESTOCK	PITUITARY	SELECTION	VIBRATORY	RESIDUARY	BOARDWALK
DRUMSTICK	HAILSTORM	LOADSTONE	PLAINTIFF	SELECTMAN	VIDEOTAPE	SAFEGUARD	BOATSWAIN
DYSENTERY	HAIRSTYLE	LODESTONE	PLAINTIVE	SEMANTICS	VIOLATION	SANCTUARY	BRUSHWOOD
ECCENTRIC	HANDSTAND	LOGISTICS	PLANETOID	SENSATION	VOLUNTARY	SCHNAUZER	CASSOWARY
EDUCATION	HARDSTAND	LONGITUDE	PLATITUDE	SENSITIVE	VOLUNTEER	SEMILUNAR	CATCHWORD
EFFECTIVE	HEADSTALL	LUCRATIVE	PLENITUDE	SENSITIZE	WASHSTAND	SIDEBURNS	CATERWAUL
EFFECTUAL	HEADSTONE	MACINTOSH	POTENTATE	SEPULTURE	WHETSTONE	SKYLOUNGE	CHICKWEED
EGLANTINE	HELVETIAN	MAELSTROM	POTENTIAL	SERVITUDE	WHITETAIL	STRENUOUS	CLOCKWISE
ELEVATION	HELVETICA	MAGISTRAL	PREDATION	SEVENTEEN	WINDSTORM	SUMPTUOUS	CLOCKWORK
ELOCUTION	HEMISTICH	MAGNETISM	PREDATORY	SIGNATORY	WITHSTAND	TARPAULIN	CROSSWALK
ENRAPTURE	HERMITAGE	MAGNETITE	PREMATURE	SIGNATURE	YARDSTICK	THEREUNTO	CROSSWAYS
ENTERTAIN	HOLYSTONE	MAGNETIZE	PRIMITIVE	SILTSTONE	AMBIGUOUS	THEREUPON	CROSSWISE

DELFTWARE	WINDSWEPT	AMPERSAND	BRILLIANT	COSMONAUT	EARTHWARD	GALLIVANT	INFIRMARY
DOWNSWING	WORLDWIDE	ANCHORAGE	BROADBAND	COURTYARD	EJACULATE	GANGPLANK	INFORMANT
DRIFTWOOD	WORRYWART	ANCILLARY	BROADCAST	CRABGRASS	ELABORATE	GERMINATE	INFURIATE
EARTHWARD	HYDROXIDE	ANNUITANT	BROADTAIL	CRANKCASE	ELIMINATE	GRANULATE	INOCULATE
EARTHWORK	INFLEXION	ANTIQUARY	BROKERAGE	CROISSANT	ELUCIDATE	GRASSLAND	INSATIATE
EARTHWORM	REFLEXIVE	APPELLANT	BUCKBOARD	CROSSWALK	EMBARRASS	GRAVEYARD	INSENSATE
FANCYWORK	THYROXINE	APPELLATE	BUSHWHACK	CROSSWAYS	EMBROCATE	GRAVITATE	INSINUATE
FELLOWMAN	UNISEXUAL	APPENDAGE	CALCULATE	CULMINATE	EMPENNAGE	GRAYBEARD	INSTIGATE
FOLLOWING	APOCRYPHA	APPERTAIN	CALIBRATE	CULTIVATE	ENCHILADA	GREENBACK	INTEGRATE
FORESWEAR	CATALYSIS	APPLEJACK	CAMELBACK	CURETTAGE	ENCOMPASS	GROSGRAIN	INTENDANT
FORTHWITH	CLERGYMAN	APPLETALK	CANDIDACY	CUSTOMARY	ENCOURAGE	GROUPWARE	INTERFACE
FRAMEWORK	COURTYARD	APPLICANT	CANDIDATE	CYCLAMATE	ENTERTAIN	GRUBSTAKE	INTERLACE
GREENWOOD	GRAVEYARD	AQUAPLANE	CANEBRAKE	CYTOPLASM	ENTOURAGE	GUNNYSACK	INTERLARD
GRILLWORK	KILOCYCLE	ARBITRARY	CANNONADE	DAIRYMAID	ENUMERATE	HABITUATE	INTESTATE
GROUPWARE	LIVERYMAN	ARBITRATE	CAPILLARY	DASHBOARD	ENUNCIATE	HANDCLASP	INTRICATE
GUNPOWDER	MEGACYCLE	ASCENDANT	CAPSULATE	DECOUPAGE	ERADICATE	HANDCRAFT	INVIOLATE
HALLOWEEN	PANEGYRIC	ASCERTAIN	CAPTIVATE	DEFENDANT	ESPIONAGE	HANDSHAKE	IRRADIATE
HANDIWORK	PARALYSIS	ASSISTANT	CARBONATE	DEFOLIANT	ESPLANADE	HANDSTAND	ISINGLASS
HEARTWOOD	PRESBYTER	ASSOCIATE	CARDBOARD	DEFOLIATE	EVAPORATE	HAPHAZARD	ITINERANT
HORSEWHIP	PYROLYSIS	ASTROLABE	CARTILAGE	DEHYDRATE	EVENTUATE	HARBORAGE	ITINERARY
HOUSEWIFE	STEELYARD	ASTRONAUT	CASSOWARY	DELINEATE	EVERGLADE	HARDBOARD	JUDICIARY
HOUSEWORK	STOCKYARD	ATTENDANT	CASTIGATE	DEMARCATE	EXCORIATE	HARDSTAND	KICKSTAND
INGROWING	SURVEYING	ATTENUATE	CATERWAUL	DEMOCRACY	EXCULPATE	HAVERSACK	LAMEBRAIN
JEWELWEED	VESTRYMAN	AUTOCRACY	CAVALCADE	DEMURRAGE	EXEMPLARY	HEADBOARD	LANDSCAPE
LANDOWNER	BOMBAZINE	AUTOGRAPH	CELEBRATE	DENIGRATE	EXONERATE	HEADSTALL	LEAFSTALK
LEASTWISE	HAPHAZARD	AUTOTRACE	CELLARAGE	DEODORANT	EXPATIATE	HERMITAGE	LEGENDARY
LIVERWORT	PROTOZOAN	AUXILIARY	CENTENARY	DEPRECATE	EXPECTANT	HIBERNATE	LEGISLATE
MATCHWOOD	QUARTZITE	BACKBOARD	CEREBRATE	DESECRATE	EXPLICATE	HOLOGRAPH	LIFEGUARD
METALWARE	TRAPEZOID	BACKSLASH	CHARABANC	DESICCANT	EXPURGATE	HOMOGRAPH	LIGHTFACE
METALWORK		BACKSTAGE	CHECKMATE	DESICCATE	EXTENUATE	HORSEBACK	LIQUIDATE
MICROWAVE		BACKTRACK	CHIEFTAIN	DESIGNATE	EXTIRPATE	HORSEHAIR	LOWERCASE
MOUTHWASH		BANDSTAND	CHILBLAIN	DESPERADO	EXTRICATE	HORSETAIL	LUBRICANT
NORTHWEST	**7TH LETTER**	BAROGRAPH	CHLORDANE	DESPERATE	EXUBERANT	HOURGLASS	LUBRICATE
OTHERWISE		BARRICADE	CHOCOLATE	DEVASTATE	EYESTRAIN	HOUSEMAID	LUXURIANT
PATCHWORK	ABOMINATE	BASEBOARD	CIRCULATE	DIAPHRAGM	FABRICATE	HUMILIATE	LUXURIATE
PIECEWORK	ACCLIMATE	BASTINADO	CLAPBOARD	DIGNITARY	FAIRYLAND	HUNCHBACK	MAINFRAME
ROUNDWORM	ACCOMPANY	BENIGNANT	CLASSMATE	DIPLOMACY	FASCINATE	HURRICANE	MALIGNANT
SATINWOOD	ACIDULATE	BICONCAVE	CLIPBOARD	DISEMBARK	FECUNDATE	HYPERCARD	MARIJUANA
SHADOWBOX	ADSORBATE	BIFURCATE	COAGULANT	DISENGAGE	FIDUCIARY	HYPHENATE	MARMALADE
SHAREWARE	ADUMBRATE	BILLBOARD	COAGULATE	DISLOCATE	FIREBRAND	IMAGINARY	MASTICATE
SHORTWAVE	ADVANTAGE	BIRTHMARK	COCKROACH	DISPARAGE	FIREPLACE	IMMEDIACY	MEGADEATH
SIDESWIPE	ADVERSARY	BIRTHRATE	COLLIMATE	DISPARATE	FIRSTHAND	IMMEDIATE	MELIORATE
SOUTHWEST	AEROPLANE	BLACKBALL	COLONNADE	DISPLEASE	FLAGSTAFF	IMMIGRANT	MELODRAMA
SPEEDWELL	AEROSPACE	BLACKJACK	COLORCAST	DISPUTANT	FLASHBACK	IMMIGRATE	MENDICANT
STAIRWELL	AESTIVATE	BLACKMAIL	COLORFAST	DISREGARD	FLOODGATE	IMPLICATE	MERCENARY
TABLEWARE	AFFILIATE	BLOODBATH	CONFIDANT	DISREPAIR	FLOWCHART	IMPORTANT	METALWARE
THEREWITH	AFORESAID	BLUEBLACK	CONJUGATE	DISSIPATE	FLUCTUATE	IMPRECATE	MICROWAVE
UNDERWEAR	AFRIKAANS	BLUEGRASS	CONSONANT	DIXIELAND	FOOTBOARD	INAMORATA	MINISTATE
UNDERWOOD	AFTERCARE	BOARDWALK	CONSTRAIN	DOCTORATE	FORESTALL	INANIMATE	MISBEHAVE
UNKNOWING	AFTERMATH	BOATSWAIN	COOPERATE	DOORPLATE	FORMULATE	INCARNATE	MISCREANT
VAPORWARE	AFTERWARD	BODYGUARD	CORMORANT	DOWNGRADE	FORTUNATE	INCESSANT	MISMANAGE
WATCHWORD	AGGRAVATE	BOOKPLATE	CORNSTALK	DOWNSTAGE	FREEBOARD	INCULCATE	MOLDBOARD
WHEREWITH	AGGREGATE	BOOMERANG	COROLLARY	DOWNSTAGE	FRIEDCAKE	INCULPATE	MOMENTARY
WHIRLWIND	ALLEVIATE	BOOTBLACK	CORPORATE	DREAMLAND	FRUITCAKE	INDIGNANT	MONOGRAPH
WHITEWALL	ALTERNATE	BOULEVARD	CORRELATE	DROMEDARY	FRUSTRATE	INEBRIATE	MONOPLANE
WHITEWASH	AMBUSCADE	BREAKFAST	CORRUGATE	DUCKBOARD	FULMINATE	INELEGANT	MONOSPACE
WHITEWOOD	AMERICANA	BRIEFCASE	CORUSCATE	DUPLICATE	FUSILLADE	INFATUATE	MOONSCAPE

MOTORCADE	PORTULACA	SHRINKAGE	UNDERTAKE	EXECRABLE	BELLYACHE	DISBURDEN	BACKSWEPT
MOUTHPART	POSTULANT	SIDEBOARD	UPPERCASE	FAVORABLE	BOONDOCKS	DISCREDIT	BAKSHEESH
MOUTHWASH	POSTULATE	SIDETRACK	VACCINATE	FLAMMABLE	BUTTERCUP	EMBROIDER	BALLADEER
NAMEPLATE	POTENTATE	SIGNBOARD	VACILLATE	FRANGIBLE	CANONICAL	FORWARDER	BEACHHEAD
NECESSARY	PREDICATE	SMALLTALK	VAPORWARE	HABITABLE	CAPRICCIO	GUNPOWDER	BEDSPREAD
NEGOTIANT	PREORDAIN	SNOWFLAKE	VARIEGATE	HERITABLE	CARBUNCLE	HEREUNDER	BEEFSTEAK
NEGOTIATE	PROCREATE	SOUTHEAST	VASSALAGE	HONORABLE	CHRONICLE	HETERODOX	BELVEDERE
NEWSSTAND	PROMENADE	SPEAKEASY	VENTILATE	ILLEGIBLE	CLASSICAL	HOTHEADED	BIOSPHERE
NIGHTFALL	PROPAGATE	SPECULATE	VIDEOTAPE	IMMOVABLE	CORPUSCLE	HUSBANDRY	BLACKHEAD
NIGHTHAWK	PROSTRATE	STAIRCASE	VILLENAGE	IMMUTABLE	EMPIRICAL	ICELANDER	BLASPHEME
NIGHTMARE	PROXIMATE	STALEMATE	VINDICATE	INCAPABLE	EQUIVOCAL	ICELANDIC	BLASPHEMY
NORTHEAST	PULMONARY	STAMINATE	VISIONARY	INCURABLE	GYRFALCON	JOBHOLDER	BLEACHERS
NOTCHBACK	PUNCTUATE	STARBOARD	VOLUNTARY	INDELIBLE	HEARTACHE	KNOWLEDGE	BLOCKHEAD
NOVITIATE	QUICKSAND	STEADFAST	VOUCHSAFE	INEFFABLE	HIERARCHY	MANHANDLE	BOMBSHELL
NURSEMAID	RABBINATE	STEELYARD	WAISTBAND	INFUSIBLE	IDENTICAL	MARTYRDOM	BOOKSHELF
OBBLIGATO	RACETRACK	STIMULANT	WALLBOARD	INSOLUBLE	ILLOGICAL	MISHANDLE	BRASSIERE
OBFUSCATE	RANCHLAND	STIMULATE	WASHBOARD	INSURABLE	INVOLUCRE	NONCREDIT	BUCCANEER
OBJURGATE	RANGELAND	STIPULATE	WASHSTAND	INVISIBLE	JAUNDICED	NONREADER	BUCKWHEAT
OBSERVANT	RATIONALE	STOCKYARD	WASTELAND	IRASCIBLE	JURIDICAL	OUTWARDLY	CAMEMBERT
OBSTINATE	REDBREAST	SUBJUGATE	WATCHBAND	IRRITABLE	KILOCYCLE	PANHANDLE	CANNONEER
OFFICIANT	REDUNDANT	SUBLIMATE	WATCHCASE	JITTERBUG	MEGACYCLE	PARTRIDGE	CARIBBEAN
OFFICIATE	REENTRANT	SUBLUNARY	WATERFALL	LITTERBUG	MOUSTACHE	PENHOLDER	CARTWHEEL
ORANGEADE	REINSTATE	SUCCOTASH	WATERMARK	MALLEABLE	MULTISCAN	PHILANDER	CASTANETS
ORIENTATE	REITERATE	SUFFOCATE	WHEELBASE	MEDICABLE	NUMERICAL	PIGHEADED	CATCHMENT
ORIGINATE	RELIQUARY	SUGARCANE	WHITEBAIT	MEMORABLE	OLIGARCHY	PROVENDER	CEASELESS
ORPHANAGE	RELUCTANT	SUPPLIANT	WHITEHALL	MISERABLE	POLITICAL	REJOINDER	CENTIPEDE
OSCILLATE	REPLICATE	SUPPURATE	WHITETAIL	NAVIGABLE	PRACTICAL	REMAINDER	CHAMELEON
OVERBOARD	REPORTAGE	SUPREMACY	WHITEWALL	OUTNUMBER	PRECANCEL	SURRENDER	CHAUFFEUR
OVERDRAFT	REPRIMAND	SURFBOARD	WHITEWASH	PALATABLE	PROBOSCIS	SUSPENDER	CHEERLESS
OVERREACH	REPROBATE	SURROGATE	WHOLESALE	PERMEABLE	PROVENCAL	THRALLDOM	CHICANERY
OVERSTATE	REPUDIATE	SWAMPLAND	WIREFRAME	PLAUSIBLE	QUIZZICAL	UNBOUNDED	CHICKWEED
OXYGENATE	REPUGNANT	SWORDTAIL	WISECRACK	PREGNABLE	RECHERCHE	UNDECIDED	CLAMSHELL
PAKISTANI	RESIDUARY	SYCOPHANT	WITHDRAWN	PREVERBAL	SPECTACLE	UNFOUNDED	CLIENTELE
PALPITATE	RESISTANT	SYNDICATE	WITHSTAND	PRINTABLE	STREETCAR	UNGUARDED	CLIPSHEET
PAPERBACK	RETALIATE	TABLELAND	WOLFSBANE	REPUTABLE	TECHNICAL	UNWORLDLY	COALFIELD
PARAGRAPH	RETARDATE	TABLEWARE	WOODCRAFT	REVOCABLE	TOOTHACHE	WEDNESDAY	COCHINEAL
PARSONAGE	RIVERBANK	TELEGRAPH	WORKPLACE	SADDLEBOW	UMBILICUS	YESTERDAY	COMPETENT
PASTORALE	RUSTICATE	TEMPERATE	WORRYWART	SCHOOLBOY	VENTRICLE	ABATEMENT	COMPONENT
PASTURAGE	SAFEGUARD	TEMPORARY	WRISTBAND	SEPARABLE	VERIDICAL	ABHORRENT	CONDIMENT
PATRONAGE	SAILPLANE	TERMAGANT	ADMIRABLE	SEPTEMBER	VIDELICET	ABSORBENT	CONTINENT
PECUNIARY	SANCTUARY	TERMINATE	ADVISABLE	SHADOWBOX	WHIMSICAL	ACETYLENE	CONTUMELY
PENEPLAIN	SANDBLAST	THEOCRACY	AGREEABLE	STREAMBED	ASTRADDLE	ADSORBENT	CORPOREAL
PENETRATE	SAXIFRAGE	THROWBACK	ALIENABLE	TIMETABLE	ATTAINDER	AFTERDECK	COUNTLESS
PERCOLATE	SCREWBALL	THUMBNAIL	ANAEROBIC	TINDERBOX	BACKPEDAL	AGREEMENT	DAMASCENE
PERFORATE	SCRIMMAGE	THUMBTACK	AVAILABLE	TOLERABLE	BANDWIDTH	AMENDMENT	DAUNTLESS
PERSONAGE	SECONDARY	TRACKBALL	BUMBLEBEE	TRACTABLE	BARTENDER	APARTHEID	DEATHLESS
PERSONATE	SECRETARY	TRADEMARK	CARPETBAG	TURNTABLE	BEDRIDDEN	APARTMENT	DECISTERE
PHOSPHATE	SEDENTARY	TRANSLATE	CONSTABLE	UNPLUMBED	BYSTANDER	APPREHEND	DECOLLETE
PICKABACK	SEGREGATE	TRENCHANT	DESIRABLE	VEGETABLE	CARTRIDGE	ARCHENEMY	DECREMENT
PIGGYBACK	SERIGRAPH	TRIBUTARY	DIRIGIBLE	VENERABLE	CHICKADEE	ARCHFIEND	DEFERMENT
PIKESTAFF	SHAREWARE	TRIFOCALS	DISMEMBER	VERITABLE	COFFERDAM	ARCHITECT	DEFICIENT
PITUITARY	SHIPBOARD	TRITURATE	DISSEMBLE	WAVETABLE	COMMANDER	ARROWHEAD	DEKASTERE
PIZZICATO	SHIPSHAPE	UNCERTAIN	DISTURBED	WORKTABLE	CONCORDAT	ARTILLERY	DEMULCENT
PLOWSHARE	SHORTCAKE	UNDERHAND	DIVISIBLE	ANNOUNCER	CORIANDER	ASCENDERS	DEPENDENT
POINCIANA	SHORTHAND	UNDERPART	EQUITABLE	ARTIFICER	COTYLEDON	ATHENAEUM	DETERGENT
POLYGRAPH	SHORTWAVE	UNDERPASS	ESTIMABLE	AVALANCHE	CULLENDER	ATONEMENT	DETERRENT
PORCELAIN	SHOWPLACE	UNDERRATE	EXCITABLE	BAREFACED	DESCENDER	BACKFIELD	DETRIMENT

DEVILMENT	IMPRUDENT	PESTILENT	SUPERSEDE	BOMBSIGHT	BIMONTHLY	ALUMINIZE	BULGARIAN
DIFFERENT	INCIPIENT	PETROLEUM	SUPERVENE	BULLFIGHT	BLOODSHED	AMERICIUM	BURUNDIAN
DIFFIDENT	INCLEMENT	PHILATELY	SWEETMEAT	CHAMPAGNE	BLOODSHOT	AMIDSHIPS	CALCIMINE
DISAFFECT	INCORRECT	PHOTOCELL	SWELLHEAD	COCKFIGHT	COURTSHIP	AMPHIBIAN	CALLOSITY
DISAPPEAR	INCREMENT	PIECEMEAL	TESTAMENT	COLLEAGUE	DIMORPHIC	ANARCHISM	CALVINISM
DISESTEEM	INCUMBENT	PLACEMENT	THANKLESS	COMMINGLE	DOWITCHER	ANATOMIZE	CAMPANILE
DISHONEST	INPATIENT	PRECEDENT	THICKNESS	COPYRIGHT	EUTROPHIC	ANCHORITE	CANTABILE
DISINFECT	INSINCERE	PRESIDENT	TIMEPIECE	DECALOGUE	FORGATHER	ANGELFISH	CARBURIZE
DISORIENT	INSISTENT	PRESTRESS	TRANSCEND	DEMAGOGUE	FORSYTHIA	ANGLICIZE	CARNATION
DISSIDENT	INSOLVENT	PREVALENT	TRANSIENT	DERRINGER	GARNISHEE	ANIMALISM	CARNELIAN
DOUBTLESS	INSURGENT	PRICELESS	TREACHERY	DOWNRIGHT	GODFATHER	ANIMATION	CARPETING
DYSENTERY	INTELLECT	PRIVATEER	TREATMENT	ESOPHAGUS	GODMOTHER	ANIMOSITY	CATECHISM
EBULLIENT	INTERCEDE	PRIVILEGE	TROUSSEAU	FORESIGHT	GONORRHEA	ANTICLINE	CAUCASIAN
EFFICIENT	INTERCEPT	PROFITEER	TRUCULENT	FORTNIGHT	GRAPESHOT	ANTIQUITY	CAUSATION
ELSEWHERE	INTERFERE	PROMINENT	TRUNCHEON	HAMBURGER	GROUNDHOG	APOLOGIZE	CAUTERIZE
EMBAYMENT	INTERJECT	PROOFREAD	TURBULENT	HARBINGER	HORSESHOE	APPORTION	CELANDINE
EMOLLIENT	INTERLEAF	PROPONENT	UNCONCERN	HEADLIGHT	HORSEWHIP	ARCHIVIST	CELEBRITY
EMOLUMENT	INTERMENT	PROPRIETY	UNDERFEED	HIGHLIGHT	LEVIATHAN	ARGENTINE	CELESTIAL
EMPHYSEMA	INTERSECT	PROVIDENT	UNDERSELL	HINDSIGHT	LIGHTSHIP	ARGENTITE	CENTESIMO
EPICUREAN	INTERVENE	PUBESCENT	UNDERWEAR	HUMDINGER	PISTACHIO	ARMISTICE	CENTURION
EQUIPMENT	INTROVERT	PUPPETEER	UNHARNESS	HYDRANGEA	SCRIMSHAW	ASAFETIDA	CESSATION
EUCLIDEAN	INVERNESS	QUIESCENT	UNIVALENT	LIMBURGER	SEPULCHER	ASCENSION	CHAMOMILE
EVERGREEN	JAILBREAK	RACKETEER	VELVETEEN	LIMELIGHT	SLINGSHOT	ASPERSION	CHAMPAIGN
EXCELLENT	JEWELWEED	RACONTEUR	VOICELESS	MESSENGER	SPACESHIP	ASSERTION	CHECKLIST
EXCREMENT	LAVALIERE	RECIPIENT	VOLUNTEER	MONOLOGUE	STEAMSHIP	ATHLETICS	CHEVALIER
EXOSPHERE	LINEAMENT	RECOLLECT	WHITEHEAD	MOONLIGHT	STOMACHER	ATTENTION	CHONDRITE
EXPEDIENT	MACHINERY	RECOMMEND	WHITENESS	NEURALGIA	STOMACHIC	ATTRITION	CHOPSTICK
EXTRAVERT	MANGANESE	RECUMBENT	WINDBREAK	NOSTALGIA	STRETCHER	AUCTORIAL	CHRISTIAN
FARMSTEAD	MARMOREAL	REPELLENT	WINDSWEPT	ONSLAUGHT	SWEATSHOP	AUTHORITY	CIRCADIAN
FIREBREAK	MAUSOLEUM	REPOSSESS	WINEPRESS	OUTRIGGER	TRANSSHIP	AUTHORIZE	CLINICIAN
FIRMAMENT	MERRIMENT	REPREHEND	WORTHLESS	OVERNIGHT	TROOPSHIP	AVOCATION	CLOCKWISE
FLATULENT	MIDSTREAM	REPRESENT	BEAUTIFUL	OVERSIGHT	UNDERSHOT	BACKSLIDE	COALITION
FORESHEET	MILLINERY	RESURRECT	BOUNTIFUL	PASSENGER	UNEARTHLY	BACTERIUM	COASTLINE
FORESWEAR	MILLIPEDE	ROADSTEAD	BUTTERFAT	PEDAGOGUE	UNSCATHED	BAILIWICK	COCKATIEL
FREEWHEEL	MINCEMEAT	ROUGHNECK	BUTTERFLY	PORRINGER	UPANISHAD	BALALAIKA	COGNITION
GAZETTEER	MISDIRECT	SACRAMENT	CALORIFIC	PREFLIGHT	WATERSHED	BALLERINA	COLLATION
GENUFLECT	MISGOVERN	SACRILEGE	DAMSELFLY	PTARMIGAN	ABORIGINE	BANDOLIER	COLLEGIAN
GODPARENT	MISORIENT	SCUTCHEON	DECEITFUL	RECTANGLE	ACCESSION	BARBARIAN	COLLEGIUM
GOLDFIELD	MISSILERY	SENTIMENT	DISCOMFIT	SCAVENGER	ACCLIVITY	BARBARISM	COLLODION
GOVERNESS	MONASTERY	SEVENTEEN	DOBSONFLY	SKINTIGHT	ACCORDION	BATHOLITH	COLLUSION
GREENBELT	NEGLIGENT	SHAPELESS	DRAGONFLY	SPOTLIGHT	ACCRETION	BATTALION	COLLUVIUM
HAIRPIECE	NONPAREIL	SHIFTLESS	FRIGHTFUL	STARLIGHT	ACOUSTICS	BENTONITE	COLUMBINE
HALLOWEEN	NORTHWEST	SHIPWRECK	HEALTHFUL	STOPLIGHT	ADDICTION	BERKELIUM	COLUMNIST
HAPPINESS	NOSEBLEED	SHOWPIECE	HONORIFIC	STRATAGEM	ADJECTIVE	BERYLLIUM	COMMODITY
HATCHMENT	NOSEPIECE	SHRUBBERY	MASTERFUL	SUFFRAGAN	ADJOINING	BESETTING	COMMOTION
HEADDRESS	NUTRIMENT	SIDEPIECE	NONPROFIT	SURCINGLE	ADMISSION	BIPARTITE	COMMUNION
HEADPIECE	OUTSPREAD	SNOWFIELD	PLENTIFUL	SYNAGOGUE	ADVERSITY	BLACKBIRD	COMMUNISM
HEARTBEAT	OVERSLEEP	SOMEWHERE	PRAYERFUL	TAILLIGHT	ADVERTISE	BLACKLIST	COMMUNITY
HEARTFELT	OVERWHELM	SOMNOLENT	RAUWOLFIA	UNFLEDGED	AERIALIST	BLOODLINE	COMPANION
HEARTLESS	PACHYDERM	SOUTHWEST	RESHUFFLE	VICEREGAL	AFFECTING	BLUEPOINT	COMPLAINT
HERCULEAN	PARCHMENT	SPEARHEAD	SOPORIFIC	WARMONGER	AFFECTION	BLUEPRINT	COMPOSITE
HOMESTEAD	PEKINGESE	SPEEDWELL	UNMINDFUL	WHIRLIGIG	AFTERLIFE	BOMBAZINE	CONCUBINE
HYPERTEXT	PERFUMERY	STAIRWELL	WONDERFUL	AILANTHUS	AIRMOBILE	BOWSTRING	CONDITION
IMPATIENS	PERIPHERY	STATEMENT	ARCHANGEL	ANGUISHED	ALLERGIST	BRAZILIAN	CONFUSION
IMPATIENT	PERMANENT	STRAPLESS	ASPARAGUS	ASTRAKHAN	ALMANDITE	BROADSIDE	CONGENIAL
IMPERFECT	PERSEVERE	SUBALTERN	BANDWAGON	BALDACHIN	ALONGSIDE	BRONCHIAL	CONGERIES
IMPLEMENT	PERTINENT	SUCCULENT	BESPANGLE	BETROTHED	ALUMINIUM	BRUTALIZE	CONGRUITY

CONNUBIAL	DRAMATIZE	FARSEEING	HARMONICS	INTENTION	MESMERIZE	PATERNITY	QUOTIDIAN
CONSCRIPT	DRUMSTICK	FASTENING	HARMONIUM	INTERDICT	METEORITE	PATRICIAN	RACIALISM
CONSTRICT	DUPLICITY	FERTILIZE	HARMONIZE	INTERLINE	METHODIST	PATRICIDE	RANDOMIZE
CONTAGION	EARTHLING	FESTIVITY	HEARTSICK	INTERLINK	METHODIZE	PATRONIZE	RASTERIZE
CONTUSION	EASYGOING	FETISHISM	HELLENISM	INTERNIST	METRICIZE	PEACETIME	REBELLION
CONVIVIAL	ECONOMICS	FEUDALISM	HELVETIAN	INTERVIEW	MEZZANINE	PEGMATITE	RECEPTION
COTILLION	ECONOMIZE	FINANCIAL	HELVETICA	INTESTINE	MICROFILM	PERDITION	RECEPTIVE
COUTURIER	EDELWEISS	FINANCIER	HEMISTICH	INTUITION	MINISKIRT	PERENNIAL	RECESSION
CRETINISM	EDITORIAL	FINGERING	HERBALIST	INVECTIVE	MISGIVING	PERSONIFY	RECESSIVE
CRINOLINE	EDUCATION	FINICKING	HERBARIUM	INVENTION	MODERNISM	PESSIMISM	RECKONING
CRITERION	EFFECTIVE	FIREBRICK	HERBICIDE	INVENTIVE	MODERNIZE	PESTICIDE	RECOGNIZE
CRITICISM	EFFLUVIUM	FIRSTLING	HISTAMINE	INVERSION	MONGOLIAN	PHONETICS	RECONCILE
CRITICIZE	EGLANTINE	FLAVORING	HISTORIAN	ISRAELITE	MONGOLISM	PHYSICIAN	RECONDITE
CROCODILE	ELECTRIFY	FLEDGLING	HITCHHIKE	ITALICIZE	MOONSHINE	PHYSICIST	RECORDING
CROSSWISE	ELEVATION	FLOTATION	HORSEHIDE	ITERATION	MORTICIAN	PICTORIAL	RECORDIST
CUSTODIAL	ELOCUTION	FOLLOWING	HORTATIVE	JACKKNIFE	MOTORBIKE	PINSTRIPE	RECTIFIER
CUSTODIAN	EMBELLISH	FOOTPRINT	HOUSEWIFE	JELLYFISH	MYSTICISM	PLACEKICK	RECURSION
CUSTOMIZE	EMPHASIZE	FOREGOING	HUMANKIND	JESSAMINE	NARCOTIZE	PLAINTIFF	REDACTION
DALMATION	ENDOCRINE	FORGIVING	HUNGARIAN	LACCOLITH	NARRATIVE	PLAINTIVE	REDUCTION
DAMNATION	ENGRAVING	FORMALISM	HYDROXIDE	LANDSLIDE	NECESSITY	PLAYTHING	REFECTION
DANDELION	EPHEDRINE	FORMALITY	HYPOCRISY	LEASTWISE	NECTARINE	PLURALITY	REFLEXIVE
DARWINISM	EQUIPOISE	FORMALIZE	HYSTERICS	LEAVENING	NEODYMIUM	PLURALIZE	REFURBISH
DECENNIAL	ERSTWHILE	FORMATION	IMITATION	LIABILITY	NEOLOGISM	PLUTONIUM	REGARDING
DECEPTION	ERUDITION	FORMATIVE	IMITATIVE	LIBERTINE	NEPTUNIUM	PORCUPINE	REHEARING
DECLIVITY	ESSENTIAL	FORTHWITH	IMPARTIAL	LIBRARIAN	NEWSPRINT	POSTERIOR	REMISSION
DEDUCTION	ESTABLISH	FOUNDLING	IMPASSIVE	LIGHTNING	NIGHTLIFE	POSTERITY	RENDITION
DEFEATISM	ETHIOPIAN	FRANCHISE	IMPRECISE	LIMOUSINE	NIGHTTIME	POSTILION	REPLENISH
DEFECTIVE	EUCHARIST	FROSTBITE	IMPROVISE	LOCKSMITH	NONENTITY	POTASSIUM	REPLETION
DEFENSIVE	EUPHEMISM	FUNGICIDE	IMPULSION	LOGISTICS	NORMALIZE	POTENTIAL	REPULSION
DEFLATION	EUTHENICS	GABARDINE	IMPULSIVE	LONGEVITY	NORMATIVE	POURBOIRE	REPULSIVE
DEFORMITY	EVAPORITE	GABERDINE	INABILITY	LUCRATIVE	NORWEGIAN	PRECEDING	REQUISITE
DEJECTION	EVOLUTION	GALVANISM	INANITION	MACHINIST	NUTRITION	PRECIPICE	RESECTION
DENTITION	EXCELSIOR	GALVANIZE	INCENTIVE	MAGNESIUM	OBJECTIFY	PRECISION	RESERPINE
DEODORIZE	EXCEPTION	GEARSHIFT	INCEPTION	MAGNETISM	OBJECTIVE	PREDATION	RESERVIST
DEOXIDIZE	EXCLUSIVE	GELIGNITE	INCOGNITO	MAGNETITE	OBSESSION	PREJUDICE	RESTRAINT
DESIGNING	EXCURSION	GENTILITY	INCURSION	MAGNETIZE	OCCULTISM	PRESCRIBE	RETENTION
DETECTIVE	EXCURSIVE	GERMANIUM	INDEMNIFY	MAGNIFICO	OFFENSIVE	PRESIDIUM	RETENTIVE
DETENTION	EXECUTIVE	GERMICIDE	INDEMNITY	MAKESHIFT	OFFSPRING	PREVISION	RETROFIRE
DETERMINE	EXEMPLIFY	GESTATION	INDENTION	MALACHITE	OPERATION	PRIMARILY	REVERSION
DEUTERIUM	EXPANSION	GIBBERISH	INDIGNITY	MALATHION	OPERATIVE	PRIMITIVE	REVOLTING
DEXTERITY	EXPANSIVE	GLAMORIZE	INDUCTION	MALAYSIAN	OSTRACIZE	PRIVATION	REVULSION
DIATOMITE	EXPENSIVE	GLYCOSIDE	INDUCTIVE	MANNERISM	OTHERWISE	PROBATION	RIVERSIDE
DIETETICS	EXPERTISE	GOLDBRICK	INFANTILE	MARGARINE	OVERDRIVE	PROBATIVE	ROUMANIAN
DIGNIFIED	EXPLETIVE	GOLDSMITH	INFECTION	MARSUPIAL	OVERPRINT	PROFANITY	RUINATION
DIMENSION	EXPLOSION	GONDOLIER	INFERTILE	MASCULINE	OVERTRICK	PROMISING	RUTHENIUM
DIRECTION	EXPLOSIVE	GRADATION	INFIRMITY	MASOCHISM	OVERWEIGH	PROSCRIBE	SACRIFICE
DIRECTIVE	EXPULSION	GRAPEVINE	INFLATION	MATERNITY	OVERWRITE	PROVISION	SALESGIRL
DISOBLIGE	EXQUISITE	GRENADIER	INFLEXION	MATRICIDE	OXIDATION	PROXIMITY	SALVATION
DISPRAISE	EXTENSION	GRENADINE	INGENUITY	MEANWHILE	PALLADIUM	PUBLICIST	SARTORIAL
DITHERING	EXTENSIVE	GRISTMILL	INGROWING	MECHANICS	PANTHEISM	PUBLICITY	SATELLITE
DIVERSIFY	EXTRADITE	GROUNDING	INJECTION	MECHANISM	PANTOMIME	PUBLICIZE	SATURNINE
DIVERSION	EXTREMISM	GUIDELINE	INJUSTICE	MECHANIZE	PARATHION	PULVERIZE	SCANTLING
DIVERSITY	EXTREMITY	GYMNASIUM	INSERTION	MEDALLION	PAROCHIAL	PURGATION	SCHEELITE
DOGMATISM	EXTRUSIVE	HAMSTRING	INTEGRITY	MENTALITY	PARRICIDE	PURGATIVE	SCHILLING
DOWNSHIFT	FACSIMILE	HANDSPIKE	INTENSIFY	MERCERIZE	PARTITION	QUARTZITE	SCHLEMIEL
DOWNSWING	FACTORIAL	HAPPENING	INTENSITY	MERCURIAL	PARTITIVE	QUICKLIME	SCREENING
DRAINPIPE	FANTASIZE	HARMONICA	INTENSIVE	MESCALINE	PASSERINE	QUICKTIME	SEAFARING

SEASONING	SUMMARIZE	UNMEANING	GIMMICKRY	MUSKMELON	POLICEMAN	ENDURANCE	REVERENCE
SECESSION	SUMMATION	UNSELFISH	HOMEMAKER	NATURALLY	REPAIRMAN	ESPERANTO	RUMRUNNER
SECLUSION	SUPERVISE	UNSPARING	MUCKRAKER	NIGHTCLUB	SELECTMAN	ESTAMINET	SCRIVENER
SECRETION	SUPPOSING	UNSTUDIED	ONIONSKIN	PHOTOPLAY	SIGNALMAN	EXISTENCE	SECTIONAL
SECRETIVE	SURVEYING	UNWILLING	OUTSPOKEN	PORTFOLIO	SOMETIMES	FOREIGNER	SEMBLANCE
SECTARIAN	SUSPICION	UNWITTING	PACEMAKER	POTBOILER	SPOKESMAN	FRATERNAL	SEMIFINAL
SELECTION	SWORDFISH	VALENTINE	PAGEMAKER	PROPELLER	SPORTSMAN	FREQUENCY	SEMILUNAR
SEMANTICS	SYLLABIFY	VALUATION	RAGPICKER	PUNCTILIO	STATESMAN	GLEANINGS	SKYLOUNGE
SENIORITY	SYLLOGISM	VANDALISM	SAPSUCKER	QUADRILLE	SUBATOMIC	GLISSANDO	STATIONER
SENSATION	SYMBOLISM	VANDALIZE	SHARKSKIN	ROUNDELAY	SUBNORMAL	GOLDFINCH	SUBSTANCE
SENSITIVE	SYMBOLIZE	VARIATION	SHEEPSKIN	SCINTILLA	SWITCHMAN	GRIEVANCE	SUNBONNET
SENSITIZE	SYMPOSIUM	VERBALIZE	SHOEMAKER	SEMICOLON	SWORDSMAN	HALFPENNY	TELEGENIC
SHEATHING	SYNERGISM	VERMILION	SKYJACKER	SPECIALTY	TRADESMAN	HINDRANCE	THEREUNTO
SHELLFIRE	SYSTEMIZE	VERNALIZE	SKYROCKET	STREAMLET	TRIBESMAN	IGNORANCE	TOLERANCE
SHELLFISH	TALKATIVE	VERSATILE	SPELUNKER	SUGARPLUM	TULAREMIA	IMBALANCE	TRANSONIC
SHOREBIRD	TANGERINE	VIBRATION	SPINNAKER	SWORDPLAY	VENIREMAN	IMPEDANCE	TRAPPINGS
SIDESWIPE	TANTALIZE	VICENNIAL	SUNSEEKER	TARPAULIN	VESTRYMAN	INCIDENCE	UNALIGNED
SIGNALIZE	TANZANIAN	VICTIMIZE	TRIWEEKLY	UNBRIDLED	VIGESIMAL	INFERENCE	UNCLEANLY
SIMPATICO	TECTONICS	VICTORIAN	UNSHACKLE	UNDERPLAY	WASHWOMAN	INFLUENCE	UNFEIGNED
SITUATION	TECTONISM	VIEWPOINT	ACROPOLIS	UNEQUALED	YACHTSMAN	INFLUENZA	UNLEARNED
SKIMOBILE	TELLURIUM	VIOLATION	ADMIRALTY	UNPOPULAR	ABANDONED	INNOCENCE	UTTERANCE
SKINFLINT	TEMPORIZE	VIRGINITY	AFTERGLOW	UNRIVALED	ACCIDENCE	INORGANIC	VEHEMENCE
SKYDIVING	TENDERIZE	VISCOSITY	ALCOHOLIC	UNRUFFLED	AFFLUENCE	INSURANCE	VENGEANCE
SNAKEBIRD	TENTATIVE	VISUALIZE	AMARYLLIS	UNSETTLED	ALLOWANCE	JACARANDA	VIGILANCE
SNAKEBITE	TERRARIUM	VOLCANISM	ANOPHELES	UNSKILLED	AMBULANCE	LABYRINTH	VIGILANTE
SNOWDRIFT	TERRORISM	VOODOOISM	APOSTOLIC	VICTUALER	ANNOYANCE	LANDOWNER	WARBONNET
SOCIALISM	TERRORIZE	VULCANISM	ARMADILLO	ANCHORMAN	ANTIVENIN	LANTHANUM	WORKBENCH
SOCIALITE	THEATRICS	VULCANIZE	ARTICULAR	ANTITUMOR	APPLIANCE	LAZYBONES	ACCESSORY
SOCIALIZE	THEREWITH	VULGARIAN	ASSEMBLER	BONDWOMAN	ASSONANCE	MATUTINAL	ACIDULOUS
SOLEMNIZE	THYROXINE	VULGARISM	AURICULAR	CANDLEMAS	ASSURANCE	MEDICINAL	AERODROME
SOLITAIRE	TIMBERING	VULGARITY	AVUNCULAR	CHARWOMAN	BACCHANAL	MISCHANCE	AFTERNOON
SOMETHING	TONSORIAL	VULGARIZE	BAGATELLE	CHRISTMAS	BINOMINAL	MISSIONER	ALBATROSS
SOVEREIGN	TOOTHPICK	WAISTLINE	BEDFELLOW	CHURCHMAN	BRITANNIC	MONOMANIA	AMBIGUOUS
SPEARMINT	TRADITION	WALLOPING	BINOCULAR	CLERGYMAN	BULLFINCH	MONSIGNOR	AMBITIOUS
SPINDLING	TRAGEDIAN	WATERLINE	CABRIOLET	CRAFTSMAN	BUTTERNUT	NICOTINIC	AMORPHOUS
SPINDRIFT	TRANSPIRE	WATERSIDE	CAPITALLY	DRAFTSMAN	CATATONIC	NOCTURNAL	AMPHIBOLE
SPLITTING	TREADMILL	WHEREWITH	CHRYSALIS	ELASTOMER	CERTAINTY	OBEISANCE	ANALOGOUS
SPOONBILL	TRIENNIAL	WHIRLWIND	CIGARILLO	EPIDERMIS	CHAFFINCH	OCCUPANCY	ANGLEWORM
SQUEAMISH	TURNSTILE	WHITEFISH	CONTRALTO	FELLOWMAN	CHALLENGE	ORDINANCE	ANHYDROUS
STABILIZE	TURQUOISE	WINDCHILL	COUNSELOR	FISHERMAN	CITIZENRY	PERCHANCE	ANKLEBONE
STANCHION	TWINKLING	WINTERIZE	DEATHBLOW	FORENAMED	CLEARANCE	PERSONNEL	ANOMALOUS
STANDPIPE	TYPEWRITE	WITTICISM	DECATHLON	FOREWOMAN	CLOISONNE	PIMPERNEL	ANONYMOUS
STARTLING	TYRANNIZE	WOLVERINE	DIGITALIS	GENTLEMAN	CONCERNED	PNEUMONIA	ANTECHOIR
STATESIDE	UKRAINIAN	WOMANKIND	FLAGELLUM	GRANTSMAN	CONSTANCY	PRELAUNCH	ANTHOLOGY
STEPCHILD	ULTRAHIGH	WOMANLIKE	FLAGEOLET	GROOMSMAN	CONTAINER	PRONOUNCE	ANTIKNOCK
STERILIZE	UNBENDING	WORLDLING	FUNICULAR	GUARDSMAN	COPARTNER	PSEUDONYM	APPALOOSA
STOCKPILE	UNCEASING	WORLDWIDE	GENITALIA	KINSWOMAN	COVALENCE	PUISSANCE	ARROWROOT
STRAPPING	UNDECEIVE	WRESTLING	GLADIOLUS	LATECOMER	CRESCENDO	PURSUANCE	ARTERIOLE
STRIPLING	UNDERGIRD	YARDSTICK	GUERRILLA	LIVERYMAN	CRYOGENIC	PYROMANIA	ARTICHOKE
STRONTIUM	UNDERLINE	YOUNGLING	HILLBILLY	MIDDLEMAN	DEBUTANTE	QUITTANCE	ASSIDUOUS
SUBALPINE	UNDERLING	YTTERBIUM	HOBGOBLIN	MIDSUMMER	DECADENCE	REACTANCE	ASTROLOGY
SUBDIVIDE	UNDERMINE	ZEITGEIST	HORSEPLAY	MINUTEMAN	DEFERENCE	REFERENCE	ASTRONOMY
SUBMARINE	UNDERSIDE	ZIRCONIUM	HYDRAULIC	MUSSULMAN	DEMIMONDE	RELEVANCE	ASYMPTOTE
SUBSCRIBE	UNFAILING	ZWINGLIAN	IMBROGLIO	OMBUDSMAN	DOMINANCE	RELEVANCY	ATROCIOUS
SUBSCRIPT	UNFEELING	BOOKMAKER	INTERPLAY	ORIFLAMME	DOWNRANGE	RESIDENCE	AUDACIOUS
SUBSIDIZE	UNITARIAN	CARETAKER	IRREGULAR	PATROLMAN	EFFLUENCE	RESIDENCY	AUDIOLOGY
SUFFERING	UNKNOWING	FORETOKEN	ISOSCELES	PERSIMMON	EMERGENCY	RESONANCE	BACKWOODS

BANDEROLE	CURRYCOMB	FRIVOLOUS	INTERLOPE	MULTIFORM	RADIOLOGY	TELESCOPE	WHETSTONE
BARBAROUS	CUTANEOUS	GALACTOSE	INTERNODE	MURDEROUS	RAINSPOUT	TENACIOUS	WHIRLPOOL
BARCAROLE	CUTTHROAT	GALLSTONE	INTERPOSE	MYTHOLOGY	RAINSTORM	TENEBROUS	WHITEWOOD
BARNSTORM	DANGEROUS	GARRULOUS	INVENTORY	NECROLOGY	RAPACIOUS	TERRITORY	WHOLESOME
BEAUTEOUS	DAVENPORT	GENEALOGY	INVIDIOUS	NEFARIOUS	REFECTORY	TESTIMONY	WINDBLOWN
BELLICOSE	DECIDUOUS	GLADSTONE	IRONSTONE	NEUROLOGY	RELIGIOUS	THEREFORE	WINDPROOF
BLACKBODY	DECOMPOSE	GLUTINOUS	JUDICIOUS	NEVERMORE	REPERTORY	THIGHBONE	WINDSTORM
BLACKFOOT	DELICIOUS	GRANDIOSE	JUXTAPOSE	NIGHTGOWN	RESERVOIR	THREEFOLD	WOEBEGONE
BLINDFOLD	DESULTORY	GREATCOAT	KINESCOPE	NOTORIOUS	RIDGEPOLE	THREESOME	WOMANHOOD
BLOODROOT	DEXTEROUS	GREENHORN	KNOCKDOWN	OBLIVIOUS	RIGHTEOUS	THRESHOLD	WOMENFOLK
BOMBPROOF	DHRYSTONE	GREENROOM	LABORIOUS	OBNOXIOUS	RIGMAROLE	TIGHTROPE	WOODBLOCK
BOUNTEOUS	DICHOTOMY	GREENWOOD	LAUDATORY	OFFERTORY	RIVERBOAT	TOADSTOOL	WORKGROUP
BOURGEOIS	DIPHTHONG	GRILLWORK	LEASEHOLD	OFFICIOUS	ROADBLOCK	TOMBSTONE	WORRISOME
BREAKDOWN	DIPTEROUS	GUARDROOM	LIFEBLOOD	OLFACTORY	ROOTSTOCK	TOOTHSOME	WRONGDOER
BRIMSTONE	DIRECTORY	GUIDEBOOK	LIGHTSOME	OUTERMOST	ROUNDWORM	TOUCHDOWN	XYLOPHONE
BROADLOOM	DISEMBODY	GUSTATORY	LIMESTONE	OVERBLOWN	SACKCLOTH	TOWNSFOLK	APOCRYPHA
BRUSHWOOD	DISHCLOTH	GYROSCOPE	LITHESOME	OVERCLOUD	SAGACIOUS	TRAINLOAD	ARTHROPOD
BUCKTOOTH	DORMITORY	HAILSTONE	LITHOLOGY	OVERSHOOT	SAILCLOTH	TRANSFORM	BARKEEPER
BUMPTIOUS	DRIFTWOOD	HAILSTORM	LITIGIOUS	OVIPAROUS	SALACIOUS	TRANSPORT	BEEKEEPER
CACOPHONY	DRUGSTORE	HAIRCLOTH	LIVERWORT	PAPILLOTE	SANDSTONE	TRANSPOSE	BIOGRAPHY
CALABOOSE	EARTHWORK	HANDIWORK	LIVESTOCK	PARSIMONY	SANDSTORM	TRAPEZOID	CANDLEPIN
CAMPSTOOL	EARTHWORM	HARDIHOOD	LOADSTONE	PATCHWORK	SANGFROID	TREMATODE	CATALEPSY
CANALBOAT	EGREGIOUS	HARTSHORN	LOATHSOME	PATHOLOGY	SATINWOOD	TREMULOUS	COFFEEPOT
CAPACIOUS	EIDERDOWN	HEADPHONE	LODESTONE	PATRIMONY	SAXOPHONE	TRUCKLOAD	DISTEMPER
CARCINOMA	ELBOWROOM	HEADSTONE	LOINCLOTH	PENDULOUS	SCAPEGOAT	TURNABOUT	DYSTROPHY
CARNIVORA	ELECTRODE	HEARTWOOD	LUDICROUS	PENTECOST	SCRAPBOOK	TUSCARORA	EPIGRAPHY
CARNIVORE	ELLIPSOID	HELLEBORE	LUNCHROOM	PENURIOUS	SEBACEOUS	TYRANNOUS	EPISCOPAL
CASSEROLE	ENDOSCOPE	HILARIOUS	MACINTOSH	PERISCOPE	SEMAPHORE	UNANIMOUS	FLOWERPOT
CATCHWORD	EROGENOUS	HOARFROST	MACROCOSM	PETROLOGY	SHAKEDOWN	UNBEKNOWN	GASTROPOD
CELLULOSE	ERRONEOUS	HOLLYHOCK	MAJORDOMO	PETTICOAT	SHEEPFOLD	UNDERBODY	GEOGRAPHY
CERECLOTH	ETHNOLOGY	HOLYSTONE	MALADROIT	PHALAROPE	SHORTHORN	UNDERCOAT	IMPROMPTU
CHALKBORD	ETYMOLOGY	HOMEGROWN	MANDATORY	PHEROMONE	SIGNATORY	UNDERDONE	INNKEEPER
CHANCROID	EVERYBODY	HOMOPHONE	MARVELOUS	PHILOLOGY	SILICEOUS	UNDERFOOT	LAGNIAPPE
CHECKBOOK	EXOGENOUS	HONEYCOMB	MATCHBOOK	PHONOLOGY	SILTSTONE	UNDERMOST	LAUNCHPAD
CHECKROOM	EXPIATORY	HONEYMOON	MATCHLOCK	PHOTOCOPY	SNOWSTORM	UNDERTONE	MULTISPIN
CHEEKBONE	EXTEMPORE	HOROSCOPE	MATCHWOOD	PIECEWORK	SOAPSTONE	UNDERWOOD	MUNICIPAL
CHILDHOOD	FACETIOUS	HORTATORY	MATRIMONY	PITCHFORK	SOCIOLOGY	UPPERMOST	NEWSPAPER
CHIROPODY	FALSEHOOD	HOUSEBOAT	MEGAPHONE	PLANELOAD	SOPHOMORE	UTTERMOST	PHILIPPIC
CHUCKHOLE	FANCYWORK	HOUSECOAT	MELODIOUS	PLANETOID	SPEEDBOAT	VAGARIOUS	PINEAPPLE
CLASSROOM	FEEDSTOCK	HOUSEHOLD	MERCUROUS	PLENTEOUS	STATEROOM	VAINGLORY	PRINCIPAL
CLOCKWORK	FEROCIOUS	HOUSEWORK	METALWORK	POLYPHONY	STATUTORY	VASECTOMY	PRINCIPLE
COMMODORE	FERRYBOAT	HYDROFOIL	METEOROID	POMPADOUR	STEAMBOAT	VENTUROUS	QUADRUPED
CONESTOGA	FEUDATORY	HYDROLOGY	METHADONE	PONDEROUS	STEVEDORE	VERACIOUS	QUADRUPLE
CONSCIOUS	FIREPROOF	HYPERBOLA	METROLOGY	POPPYCOCK	STILLBORN	VERMIFORM	QUINTUPLE
CORTISONE	FIRSTBORN	HYPERBOLE	METRONOME	POWERBOAT	STOREROOM	VEXATIOUS	SANDPAPER
COSMOGONY	FLAGSTONE	IMPERIOUS	MICROCOPY	PREDATORY	STRENUOUS	VIBRATORY	SANDPIPER
COSMOLOGY	FLINTLOCK	IMPETUOUS	MICROCOSM	PRERECORD	STRIKEOUT	VICARIOUS	THEOSOPHY
COUNTDOWN	FOOLPROOF	INCOMMODE	MICROSOFT	PRESCHOOL	SULFUROUS	VIVACIOUS	THEREUPON
COURTEOUS	FOOTLOOSE	INCURIOUS	MILESTONE	PRESSROOM	SUMPTUOUS	VORACIOUS	WALLPAPER
COURTROOM	FOOTSTOOL	INGENIOUS	MILLIVOLT	PRONGHORN	SUNSTROKE	WAISTCOAT	WHEREUPON
CRACKDOWN	FORECLOSE	INGENUOUS	MILLSTONE	PROTOZOAN	SUPERNOVA	WASHCLOTH	XANTHIPPE
CREDULOUS	FOREFRONT	INGLENOOK	MISINFORM	PROVOLONE	SUPERPOSE	WATCHWORD	ARABESQUE
CREMATORY	FORESHORE	INNERMOST	MOMENTOUS	PUREBLOOD	SWANSDOWN	WATERFOWL	BURLESQUE
CROSSROAD	FOURSCORE	INNERSOLE	MONGOLOID	PURGATORY	TAUTOLOGY	WEARISOME	GROTESQUE
CRUCIFORM	FRACTIOUS	INNOCUOUS	MONKSHOOD	PUSSYFOOT	TELEPHONE	WHALEBOAT	SOLILOQUY
CUBBYHOLE	FRAMEWORK	INSIDIOUS	MOONSTONE	QUERULOUS	TELEPHONY	WHALEBONE	TECHNIQUE
CUNEIFORM	FREESTONE	INTERLOCK	MOTORBOAT	QUICKSORT	TELEPHOTO	WHEREFORE	ALEATORIC

AMBERGRIS	MOUSETRAP	DEPRESSED	BANQUETTE	FANTASTIC	PERIMETER	ULTIMATUM	ENRAPTURE
ANTISERUM	OUTSKIRTS	DIAERESIS	BANTUSTAN	FINGERTIP	PHLEBITIS	UNCHARTED	EXCHEQUER
BICAMERAL	OVERTHROW	DIAGNOSIS	BAROMETER	FIREWATER	PHRENETIC	UNCOUNTED	FARMHOUSE
BILATERAL	PACKHORSE	DYSPEPSIA	BARRISTER	GALLANTRY	PIROUETTE	UNDAUNTED	FEBRIFUGE
BILLIARDS	PANEGYRIC	EXTRINSIC	BEEFEATER	GASTRITIS	PNEUMATIC	UNDOUBTED	FEEDSTUFF
BISHOPRIC	PAREGORIC	FORETASTE	BENIGHTED	GENERATOR	POETASTER	UNHEALTHY	FIREHOUSE
BLOWTORCH	PATRIARCH	FREEMASON	BESPATTER	GLADIATOR	POLYESTER	UNSHEATHE	FLASHBULB
BLUEBERRY	POTPOURRI	FRICASSEE	BRIQUETTE	GUARANTEE	POSTNATAL	UNSIGHTLY	FLASHCUBE
BRASSERIE	POULTERER	HALITOSIS	BROCHETTE	GUARANTOR	PRAGMATIC	UNSPOTTED	FLASHTUBE
CABLEGRAM	PUERPERAL	INTRINSIC	CAPACITOR	GUNCOTTON	PRECENTOR	UNWRITTEN	FLOPHOUSE
CAFETERIA	PYRETHRUM	INTUMESCE	CARPENTER	HAMMERTOE	PRECEPTOR	UPHOLSTER	FOODSTUFF
CANTHARIS	QUARTERLY	JINRIKSHA	CASUISTRY	HEADWATER	PRESBYTER	VAGINITIS	FORTITUDE
CATAMARAN	QUICKDRAW	MAHARISHI	CATHARTIC	HEMSTITCH	PRESENTLY	VOLTMETER	FURNITURE
CATHEDRAL	RACEHORSE	MANIFESTO	CHARACTER	HEPATITIS	PROJECTOR	WAGONETTE	GALLINULE
CENTIGRAM	RADIOGRAM	MERGANSER	CHARLATAN	HEREAFTER	PROPHETIC	YOUNGSTER	GARNITURE
CHAPARRAL	RASPBERRY	NARCISSUS	CHEMISTRY	HEURISTIC	PROTECTOR	ZUCCHETTO	GRATICULE
CHIVALRIC	REENFORCE	NONPERSON	CHORISTER	HEXAMETER	PYROMETER	ADMIXTURE	GRATITUDE
CONCIERGE	REGISTRAR	PARALYSIS	CHROMATIC	HOPSCOTCH	QUADRATIC	ADVENTURE	GREYHOUND
CONCOURSE	REIMBURSE	POLITESSE	CIGARETTE	IMPOLITIC	QUICKSTEP	AEROPAUSE	HAIRBRUSH
CONUNDRUM	REINFORCE	POSTHASTE	CIRCUITRY	INCUBATOR	RAINWATER	ALGONQUIN	HARDBOUND
CORELDRAW	SACCHARIN	PRECURSOR	COADJUTOR	INHALATOR	REFLECTOR	ALMSHOUSE	HARLEQUIN
CORKSCREW	SASSAFRAS	PROCESSOR	COLLECTED	INSTANTER	REFRACTOR	AMPLITUDE	HEARTBURN
CRANBERRY	SCARECROW	PROCONSUL	COMFORTER	INSTANTLY	RENCONTRE	ATTRIBUTE	HIDEBOUND
CUPBEARER	SCOUNDREL	PROFESSOR	COMMITTEE	JERKWATER	RESONATOR	AWESTRUCK	HOLOCAUST
CYCLOTRON	SEMIWORKS	PROGNOSIS	CONCERTED	KILOLITER	RHEOMETER	BARRACUDA	HOREHOUND
DECONTROL	SIDEBURNS	PSORIASIS	CONDUCTOR	KILOMETER	ROSEWATER	BATHHOUSE	IMPORTUNE
DIAMETRIC	SURCHARGE	PSYCHOSIS	CONTENTED	LAMINATED	SACRISTAN	BEATITUDE	IMPOSTURE
DIATHERMY	TAXIDERMY	PYROLYSIS	CROQUETTE	LEITMOTIV	SALTPETER	BELEAGUER	INDENTURE
DISCHARGE	THEREFROM	REHEARSAL	DECILITER	LITERATIM	SALTWATER	BILINGUAL	INSTITUTE
DISCOURSE	THESAURUS	REMINISCE	DECIMETER	LOCOMOTOR	SCHEMATIC	BIRDHOUSE	INTERFUSE
EAVESDROP	TREASURER	SCLEROSIS	DECORATOR	LOGARITHM	SEAWORTHY	CALENDULA	INTERLUDE
ECCENTRIC	TURBOPROP	SILICOSIS	DEKALITER	LORGNETTE	SEPARATOR	CATAMOUNT	INTERRUPT
EPHEMERAL	UNDERBRED	SUCCESSOR	DEKAMETER	MAJORETTE	SEQUESTER	CERTITUDE	INTRODUCE
EXECUTRIX	UNNATURAL	SYMBIOSIS	DELIGHTED	MANHATTAN	SHORTSTOP	CHANTEUSE	IRONBOUND
FILMSTRIP	UNTUTORED	SYNTHESIS	DELIMETER	MANOMETER	SIMPLETON	CHONDRULE	LASSITUDE
FOOLHARDY	URTICARIA	UNADVISED	DETONATOR	MARQUETRY	SINGLETON	CHOPHOUSE	LONGITUDE
FRUITERER	VERDIGRIS	UNBLESSED	DIACRITIC	MELTWATER	SINUSITIS	CLUBHOUSE	MAGNITUDE
GAUCHERIE	VERTEBRAL	UNIVERSAL	DIALECTIC	MIDWINTER	SLAUGHTER	COFEATURE	MAJUSCULE
GERIATRIC	WORKHORSE	WASHBASIN	DISHWATER	MISTLETOE	SOLICITOR	COIFFEUSE	MANNEQUIN
GLENGARRY	ACQUIESCE	ADIABATIC	DISMANTLE	MODERATOR	SOPHISTIC	COMPOSURE	MENOPAUSE
GOLDENROD	ADDRESSEE	AESTHETIC	DISSECTED	NANOMETER	SOPHISTRY	CONSTRUCT	MESSIEURS
HEADFIRST	ANALGESIA	AIRWORTHY	DISSENTER	NEPHRITIC	SOUBRETTE	CONTINUAL	MINIATURE
HECTOGRAM	ANALGESIC	ALABASTER	DOSIMETER	NEPHRITIS	SPAGHETTI	CONTINUUM	MINISCULE
HISTOGRAM	ANTIPASTO	ALGORITHM	ECOSYSTEM	NOVELETTE	SPECTATOR	COONHOUND	MINUSCULE
ILLIBERAL	CAPARISON	ALLIGATOR	EGGBEATER	NUMERATOR	SPHINCTER	CURVATURE	MULTITUDE
INAUGURAL	CARROUSEL	ALTIMETER	ENCOUNTER	OPTOMETRY	SPLENETIC	DACHSHUND	NEGRITUDE
INTERPRET	CATALYSIS	ANTARCTIC	ENERGETIC	ORCHESTRA	SPRIGHTLY	DEBENTURE	NIGRITUDE
JACKSCREW	CATHARSIS	ANTIPATHY	ENIGMATIC	ORGIASTIC	STATISTIC	DEPARTURE	OPPORTUNE
JACKSTRAW	CHICKASAW	APPARATUS	ENLIGHTEN	OUBLIETTE	STATUETTE	DESTITUTE	PALANQUIN
KILOHERTZ	CIRRHOSIS	APPOINTEE	ENSHEATHE	OVERMATCH	STOPWATCH	DESUETUDE	PARACHUTE
MAELSTROM	COMMISSAR	ARBORETUM	ENTERITIS	PALAESTRA	SYNTHETIC	DIFFICULT	PARAMOUNT
MAGISTRAL	CONDENSER	ARTHRITIS	ENWREATHE	PALMISTRY	TEAKETTLE	DISFIGURE	PENINSULA
MATRIARCH	CONFESSOR	AUTHENTIC	EPICENTER	PARAMETER	TELEMETER	DISREPUTE	PENTHOUSE
MEGAHERTZ	CONSENSUS	AUTOMATIC	ESCALATOR	PARQUETRY	TELEPATHY	DISSOLUTE	PERPETUAL
MENAGERIE	COSPONSOR	AUTOMATON	ETIQUETTE	PATRISTIC	TIDEWATER	DUMBFOUND	PERSECUTE
MICROGRAM	COURTESAN	BACKWATER	EXPEDITER	PAYMASTER	TRICKSTER	EFFECTUAL	PESTHOUSE
MILLIGRAM	DEMITASSE	BADMINTON	EXPOSITOR	PEDOMETER	TRIMESTER	EMBRASURE	PLATITUDE

PLAYHOUSE	MAYFLOWER	BINOMINAL	EPHEMERAL	MEDICINAL	SASSAFRAS	WEDNESDAY	DISAFFECT
PLENITUDE	OUTGROWTH	BLACKHEAD	EPICUREAN	MERCURIAL	SCAPEGOAT	WHALEBOAT	DISINFECT
POLITBURO	OVERPOWER	BLOCKHEAD	EPISCOPAL	MICROGRAM	SCRIMSHAW	WHIMSICAL	DOMINANCE
POORHOUSE	SAFFLOWER	BONDWOMAN	EQUIVOCAL	MIDDLEMAN	SECTARIAN	WHITEHEAD	DRUMSTICK
PREFIGURE	SLUICEWAY	BRAZILIAN	ESSENTIAL	MIDSTREAM	SECTIONAL	WINDBREAK	ECONOMICS
PREMATURE	SUNFLOWER	BREEZEWAY	ETHIOPIAN	MILLIGRAM	SELECTMAN	YACHTSMAN	EFFLUENCE
PREOCCUPY	THROWAWAY	BRONCHIAL	EUCLIDEAN	MINCEMEAT	SEMIFINAL	YESTERDAY	EMERGENCY
PRESHRUNK	WILLPOWER	BUCKWHEAT	FACTORIAL	MINUTEMAN	SEMILUNAR	ZWINGLIAN	ENDURANCE
PROCEDURE	ANTITOXIN	BULGARIAN	FARMSTEAD	MONGOLIAN	SIGNALMAN	ASTROLABE	EUTHENICS
PROSECUTE	MEGAPIXEL	BURUNDIAN	FELLOWMAN	MORTICIAN	SLUICEWAY	FLASHCUBE	EXISTENCE
RECTITUDE	OVERSEXED	BUTTERFAT	FERRYBOAT	MOTORBOAT	SPEARHEAD	FLASHTUBE	FEEDSTOCK
REPRODUCE	PERPLEXED	CABLEGRAM	FINANCIAL	MOUSETRAP	SPEEDBOAT	PRESCRIBE	FIREBRICK
ROCKBOUND	ARCHETYPE	CANALBOAT	FIREBREAK	MULTISCAN	SPIRITUAL	PROSCRIBE	FIREPLACE
RUNAROUND	CATACLYSM	CANDLEMAS	FISHERMAN	MUNICIPAL	SPOKESMAN	SUBSCRIBE	FLASHBACK
SAGEBRUSH	DESTROYER	CANONICAL	FORESWEAR	MUSSULMAN	SPORTSMAN	ACCIDENCE	FLINTLOCK
SCRIPTURE	HACKNEYED	CARIBBEAN	FOREWOMAN	NOCTURNAL	STATESMAN	ACOUSTICS	FREQUENCY
SCULPTURE	HAIRSTYLE	CARNELIAN	FRATERNAL	NORWEGIAN	STEAMBOAT	ACQUIESCE	GENUFLECT
SEMIFLUID	HAMADRYAD	CARPETBAG	FUNICULAR	NUMERICAL	STREETCAR	AEROSPACE	GOLDBRICK
SEPULTURE	LEUKOCYTE	CATAMARAN	GENTLEMAN	OMBUDSMAN	SUBNORMAL	AFFLUENCE	GOLDFINCH
SERVITUDE	MANSLAYER	CATHEDRAL	GRANTSMAN	OUTSPREAD	SUFFRAGAN	AFTERDECK	GREENBACK
SIGNATURE	MINELAYER	CAUCASIAN	GREATCOAT	PAROCHIAL	SWEETMEAT	ALLOWANCE	GRIEVANCE
SOBRIQUET	MULTISYNC	CELESTIAL	GROOMSMAN	PATRICIAN	SWELLHEAD	AMBULANCE	GUNNYSACK
SOFTBOUND	PERISTYLE	CENTIGRAM	GUARDSMAN	PATROLMAN	SWITCHMAN	ANNOYANCE	HAIRPIECE
SPICEBUSH	PROSELYTE	CHAPARRAL	HAMADRYAD	PERENNIAL	SWORDPLAY	ANTIKNOCK	HARMONICA
SPIRITUAL	PROTOTYPE	CHARLATAN	HEARTBEAT	PERPETUAL	SWORDSMAN	APPLEJACK	HARMONICS
STRICTURE	UNALLOYED	CHARWOMAN	HECTOGRAM	PETTICOAT	TANZANIAN	APPLIANCE	HAVERSACK
STRUCTURE	XEROPHYTE	CHICKASAW	HELVETIAN	PHOTOPLAY	TECHNICAL	ARCHITECT	HEADPIECE
TARANTULA	APPETIZER	CHRISTIAN	HERCULEAN	PHYSICIAN	THROWAWAY	ARMISTICE	HEARTSICK
TOLLHOUSE	BAMBOOZLE	CHRISTMAS	HISTOGRAM	PICTORIAL	TONSORIAL	ASSONANCE	HELVETICA
TRANSDUCE	DIGITIZED	CHURCHMAN	HISTORIAN	PIECEMEAL	TRADESMAN	ASSURANCE	HEMISTICH
TRANSFUSE	ENERGIZER	CIRCADIAN	HOMESTEAD	PLANELOAD	TRAGEDIAN	ATHLETICS	HEMSTITCH
TRANSMUTE	SCHNAUZER	CLASSICAL	HORSEPLAY	POLICEMAN	TRAINLOAD	AUTOCRACY	HINDRANCE
TURPITUDE	VAPORIZER	CLERGYMAN	HOUSEBOAT	POLITICAL	TRIBESMAN	AUTOTRACE	HOLLYHOCK
ULTRAPURE		CLINICIAN	HOUSECOAT	POSTNATAL	TRIENNIAL	AWESTRUCK	HOPSCOTCH
UNISEXUAL		COCHINEAL	HUNGARIAN	POTENTIAL	TROUSSEAU	BACKTRACK	HORSEBACK
VERMIFUGE		COFFERDAM	IDENTICAL	POWERBOAT	TRUCKLOAD	BAILIWICK	HUNCHBACK
VESTIBULE	**8TH LETTER**	COLLEGIAN	ILLIBERAL	PRACTICAL	UKRAINIAN	BLACKJACK	HYSTERICS
WAREHOUSE		COMMISSAR	ILLOGICAL	PREVERBAL	UNDERCOAT	BLOWTORCH	IGNORANCE
WASHHOUSE	AMPHIBIAN	CONCORDAT	IMPARTIAL	PRINCIPAL	UNDERPLAY	BLUEBLACK	IMBALANCE
WOLFHOUND	ANCHORMAN	CONGENIAL	INAUGURAL	PROOFREAD	UNDERWEAR	BOOTBLACK	IMMEDIACY
WOODCHUCK	ARROWHEAD	CONNUBIAL	INTERLEAF	PROTOZOAN	UNISEXUAL	BULLFINCH	IMPEDANCE
WORKHOUSE	ARTICULAR	CONTINUAL	INTERPLAY	PROVENCAL	UNITARIAN	BUSHWHACK	IMPERFECT
AFFIDAVIT	ASTRAKHAN	CONVIVIAL	IRREGULAR	PTARMIGAN	UNIVERSAL	CAMELBACK	INCIDENCE
ANTINOVEL	AUCTORIAL	CORELDRAW	JACKSTRAW	PUERPERAL	UNNATURAL	CANDIDACY	INCORRECT
BOLSHEVIK	AURICULAR	CORPOREAL	JAILBREAK	QUICKDRAW	UNPOPULAR	CHAFFINCH	INFERENCE
CROSSOVER	AVUNCULAR	COURTESAN	JURIDICAL	QUIZZICAL	UPANISHAD	CHOPSTICK	INFLUENCE
DAREDEVIL	BACCHANAL	CRAFTSMAN	KINSWOMAN	QUOTIDIAN	VENIREMAN	CLEARANCE	INJUSTICE
HANDWOVEN	BACKPEDAL	CROSSROAD	LAUNCHPAD	RADIOGRAM	VERIDICAL	COCKROACH	INNOCENCE
HARDCOVER	BANTUSTAN	CUSTODIAL	LEVIATHAN	REGISTRAR	VERTEBRAL	CONSTANCY	INSURANCE
HOWSOEVER	BARBARIAN	CUSTODIAN	LIBRARIAN	REHEARSAL	VESTRYMAN	CONSTRICT	INTELLECT
MANOEUVRE	BEACHHEAD	CUTTHROAT	LIVERYMAN	REPAIRMAN	VICENNIAL	CONSTRUCT	INTERDICT
OURSELVES	BEDSPREAD	DECENNIAL	MAGISTRAL	RIVERBOAT	VICEREGAL	COVALENCE	INTERFACE
RETRIEVER	BEEFSTEAK	DISAPPEAR	MALAYSIAN	ROADSTEAD	VICTORIAN	DECADENCE	INTERJECT
WHICHEVER	BICAMERAL	DRAFTSMAN	MANHATTAN	ROUMANIAN	VIGESIMAL	DEFERENCE	INTERLACE
WHOSOEVER	BILATERAL	EDITORIAL	MARMOREAL	ROUNDELAY	VULGARIAN	DEMOCRACY	INTERLOCK
BREEZEWAY	BILINGUAL	EFFECTUAL	MARSUPIAL	SACRISTAN	WASHWOMAN	DIETETICS	INTERSECT
FIREPOWER	BINOCULAR	EMPIRICAL	MATUTINAL	SARTORIAL	WAISTCOAT	DIPLOMACY	INTRODUCE

INTUMESCE	SHOWPIECE	FOOLHARDY	ARTIFICER	DELIGHTED	HARDCOVER	PENHOLDER	STOMACHER
LIGHTFACE	SHOWPLACE	FORTITUDE	ASSEMBLER	DELIMITER	HEADWATER	PERIMETER	STRATAGEM
LIVESTOCK	SIDEPIECE	FUNGICIDE	ATTAINDER	DEPRESSED	HEREAFTER	PERPLEXED	STREAMBED
LOGISTICS	SIDETRACK	FUSILLADE	BACKWATER	DERRINGER	HEREUNDER	PERSONNEL	STREAMLET
MAGNIFICO	SIMPATICO	GERMICIDE	BALLADEER	DESCENDER	HEXAMETER	PHILANDER	STRETCHER
MATCHLOCK	STOPWATCH	GLISSANDO	BANDOLIER	DESTROYER	HOMEMAKER	PIGHEADED	SUNBONNET
MATRIARCH	SUBSTANCE	GLYCOSIDE	BAREFACED	DIGITIZED	HOTHEADED	PIMPERNEL	SUNFLOWER
MECHANICS	SUPREMACY	GRATITUDE	BARKEEPER	DIGNIFIED	HOWSOEVER	POETASTER	SUNSEEKER
MISCHANCE	TECTONICS	HERBICIDE	BAROMETER	DISBURDEN	HUMDINGER	POLYESTER	SURRENDER
MISDIRECT	THEATRICS	HORSEHIDE	BARRISTER	DISESTEEM	HYDRANGEA	PORRINGER	SUSPENDER
MONOSPACE	THEOCRACY	HYDROXIDE	BARTENDER	DISHWATER	ICELANDER	POTBOILER	TELEMETER
NOSEPIECE	THROWBACK	INCOMMODE	BEDRIDDEN	DISMEMBER	INNKEEPER	POULTERER	TIDEWATER
NOTCHBACK	THUMBTACK	INTERCEDE	BEEFEATER	DISSECTED	INSTANTER	PRECANCEL	TREASURER
OBEISANCE	TIMEPIECE	INTERLUDE	BEEKEEPER	DISSENTER	INTERPRET	PRESBYTER	TRICKSTER
OCCUPANCY	TOLERANCE	INTERNODE	BELEAGUER	DISTEMPER	INTERVIEW	PRIVATEER	TRIMESTER
ORDINANCE	TOOTHPICK	JACARANDA	BENIGHTED	DISTURBED	ISOSCELES	PROFITEER	UNADVISED
OVERMATCH	TRANSDUCE	LANDSLIDE	BESPATTER	DOSIMETER	JACKSCREW	PROPELLER	UNALIGNED
OVERREACH	UTTERANCE	LASSITUDE	BETROTHED	DOWITCHER	JAUNDICED	PROVENDER	UNALLOYED
OVERTRICK	VEHEMENCE	LONGITUDE	BLOODSHED	ECOSYSTEM	JERKWATER	PUPPETEER	UNBLESSED
PAPERBACK	VENGEANCE	MAGNITUDE	BOOKMAKER	EGGBEATER	JEWELWEED	PYROMETER	UNBOUNDED
PATRIARCH	VIGILANCE	MARMALADE	BUCCANEER	ELASTOMER	JOBHOLDER	QUADRUPED	UNBRIDLED
PERCHANCE	WISECRACK	MATRICIDE	BUMBLEBEE	EMBROIDER	KILOLITER	QUICKSTEP	UNCHARTED
PHONETICS	WOODBLOCK	MILLIPEDE	BYSTANDER	ENCOUNTER	KILOMETER	RACKETEER	UNCOUNTED
PICKABACK	WOODCHUCK	MOTORCADE	CABRIOLET	ENERGIZER	LAMINATED	RAGPICKER	UNDAUNTED
PIGGYBACK	WORKBENCH	MULTITUDE	CANNONEER	ENLIGHTEN	LANDOWNER	RAINWATER	UNDECIDED
PLACEKICK	WORKPLACE	NEGRITUDE	CARETAKER	EPICENTER	LATECOMER	RECTIFIER	UNDERBRED
POPPYCOCK	YARDSTICK	NIGRITUDE	CARPENTER	ESTAMINET	LAZYBONES	REJOINDER	UNDERFEED
PORTULACA	ALONGSIDE	ORANGEADE	CARROUSEL	EVERGREEN	LIMBURGER	REMAINDER	UNDOUBTED
PRECIPICE	AMBUSCADE	PARRICIDE	CARTWHEEL	EXCHEQUER	MANOMETER	RETRIEVER	UNEQUALED
PREJUDICE	AMPLITUDE	PATRICIDE	CHARACTER	EXPEDITER	MANSLAYER	RHEOMETER	UNFEIGNED
PRELAUNCH	ASAFETIDA	PESTICIDE	CHEVALIER	FINANCIER	MAYFLOWER	ROSEWATER	UNFLEDGED
PRONOUNCE	BACKSLIDE	PLATITUDE	CHICKADEE	FIREPOWER	MEGAPIXEL	RUMRUNNER	UNFOUNDED
PUISSANCE	BACKWOODS	PLENITUDE	CHICKWEED	FIREWATER	MELTWATER	SAFFLOWER	UNGUARDED
PURSUANCE	BARRACUDA	PROMENADE	CHORISTER	FLAGEOLET	MERGANSER	SALTPETER	UNLEARNED
QUITTANCE	BARRICADE	RECTITUDE	CLIPSHEET	FOREIGNER	MESSENGER	SALTWATER	UNPLUMBED
RACETRACK	BASTINADO	RIVERSIDE	COCKATIEL	FORENAMED	MIDSUMMER	SANDPAPER	UNRIVALED
REACTANCE	BEATITUDE	SERVITUDE	COLLECTED	FORESHEET	MIDWINTER	SANDPIPER	UNRUFFLED
RECOLLECT	BILLIARDS	STATESIDE	COMFORTER	FORETOKEN	MINELAYER	SAPSUCKER	UNSCATHED
REENFORCE	BLACKBODY	SUBDIVIDE	COMMANDER	FORGATHER	MISSIONER	SCAVENGER	UNSETTLED
REFERENCE	BROADSIDE	SUPERSEDE	COMMITTEE	FORWARDER	MUCKRAKER	SCHLEMIEL	UNSKILLED
REINFORCE	CANNONADE	TREMATODE	CONCERNED	FREEWHEEL	NANOMETER	SCHNAUZER	UNSPOTTED
RELEVANCE	CAVALCADE	TURPITUDE	CONCERTED	FRICASSEE	NEWSPAPER	SCOUNDREL	UNSTUDIED
RELEVANCY	CENTIPEDE	UNDERBODY	CONDENSER	FRUITERER	NONREADER	SCRIVENER	UNTUTORED
REMINISCE	CERTITUDE	UNDERSIDE	CONGERIES	GARNISHEE	NOSEBLEED	SEPTEMBER	UNWRITTEN
REPRODUCE	CHIROPODY	WATERSIDE	CONTAINER	GAZETTEER	OURSELVES	SEPULCHER	UPHOLSTER
RESIDENCE	COLONNADE	WORLDWIDE	CONTENTED	GODFATHER	OUTNUMBER	SEQUESTER	VAPORIZER
RESIDENCY	CRESCENDO	ABANDONED	COPARTNER	GODMOTHER	OUTRIGGER	SEVENTEEN	VELVETEEN
RESONANCE	DEMIMONDE	ADDRESSEE	CORIANDER	GONDOLIER	OUTSPOKEN	SHOEMAKER	VICTUALER
RESURRECT	DESPERADO	ALABASTER	CORKSCREW	GONORRHEA	OVERPOWER	SKYJACKER	VIDELICET
REVERENCE	DESUETUDE	ALTIMETER	COUTURIER	GRENADIER	OVERSEXED	SKYROCKET	VOLTMETER
ROADBLOCK	DISEMBODY	ANGUISHED	CROSSOVER	GUARANTEE	OVERSLEEP	SLAUGHTER	VOLUNTEER
ROOTSTOCK	DOWNGRADE	ANNOUNCER	CULLENDER	GUNPOWDER	PACEMAKER	SOBRIQUET	WALLPAPER
ROUGHNECK	ELECTRODE	ANOPHELES	CUPBEARER	HACKNEYED	PAGEMAKER	SOMETIMES	WARBONNET
SACRIFICE	ENCHILADA	ANTINOVEL	DECILITER	HALLOWEEN	PARAMETER	SPELUNKER	WARMONGER
SEMANTICS	ESPLANADE	APPETIZER	DECIMETER	HAMBURGER	PASSENGER	SPHINCTER	WATERSHED
SEMBLANCE	EVERGLADE	APPOINTEE	DEKALITER	HANDWOVEN	PAYMASTER	SPINNAKER	WHICHEVER
SHIPWRECK	EVERYBODY	ARCHANGEL	DEKAMETER	HARBINGER	PEDOMETER	STATIONER	WHOSOEVER

WILLPOWER	ENCOURAGE	DOWNRIGHT	ASCERTAIN	FINGERTIP	PNEUMATIC	CANEBRAKE	CROCODILE
WRONGDOER	ENTOURAGE	DYSTROPHY	AUTHENTIC	FORSYTHIA	PNEUMONIA	FRIEDCAKE	CROSSWALK
YOUNGSTER	ESPIONAGE	ENSHEATHE	AUTOMATIC	GASTRITIS	PORCELAIN	FRUITCAKE	CUBBYHOLE
AFTERLIFE	ETHNOLOGY	ENWREATHE	BALDACHIN	GAUCHERIE	PORTFOLIO	GRUBSTAKE	DAMSELFLY
DIVERSIFY	ETYMOLOGY	EPIGRAPHY	BISHOPRIC	GENITALIA	PRAGMATIC	HANDSHAKE	DESIRABLE
DOWNSHIFT	FEBRIFUGE	FORESIGHT	BLACKMAIL	GERIATRIC	PREORDAIN	HANDSPIKE	DIFFICULT
ELECTRIFY	GENEALOGY	FORTNIGHT	BOATSWAIN	GROSGRAIN	PROBOSCIS	HITCHHIKE	DIRIGIBLE
EXEMPLIFY	GLEANINGS	GEOGRAPHY	BOLSHEVIK	HALITOSIS	PROGNOSIS	MOTORBIKE	DISMANTLE
FEEDSTUFF	HARBORAGE	HEADLIGHT	BOURGEOIS	HARLEQUIN	PROPHETIC	SEMIWORKS	DISSEMBLE
FLAGSTAFF	HERMITAGE	HEARTACHE	BRASSERIE	HEPATITIS	PSORIASIS	SHORTCAKE	DIVISIBLE
FOODSTUFF	HYDROLOGY	HIERARCHY	BRITANNIC	HEURISTIC	PSYCHOSIS	SNOWFLAKE	DOBSONFLY
GEARSHIFT	KNOWLEDGE	HIGHLIGHT	BROADTAIL	HOBGOBLIN	PUNCTILIO	SUNSTROKE	DRAGONFLY
HANDCRAFT	LITHOLOGY	HINDSIGHT	CAFETERIA	HONORIFIC	PYROLYSIS	UNDERTAKE	EQUITABLE
HOUSEWIFE	METROLOGY	JINRIKSHA	CALORIFIC	HORSEHAIR	PYROMANIA	WOMANLIKE	ERSTWHILE
INDEMNIFY	MISMANAGE	LIMELIGHT	CANDLEPIN	HORSETAIL	QUADRATIC	ADMIRABLE	ESTIMABLE
INTENSIFY	MYTHOLOGY	LOGARITHM	CANTHARIS	HORSEWHIP	RAUWOLFIA	ADVISABLE	EXCITABLE
JACKKNIFE	NECROLOGY	MAHARISHI	CAPRICCIO	HOUSEMAID	RESERVOIR	AGREEABLE	EXECRABLE
MAKESHIFT	NEUROLOGY	MOONLIGHT	CATALYSIS	HYDRAULIC	SACCHARIN	AIRMOBILE	FACSIMILE
MICROSOFT	ORPHANAGE	MOUSTACHE	CATATONIC	HYDROFOIL	SANGFROID	ALIENABLE	FAVORABLE
NIGHTLIFE	OVERWEIGH	OLIGARCHY	CATHARSIS	ICELANDIC	SCHEMATIC	AMPHIBOLE	FLAMMABLE
OBJECTIFY	PARSONAGE	ONSLAUGHT	CATHARTIC	IMBROGLIO	SCLEROSIS	APPLETALK	FLASHBULB
OVERDRAFT	PARTRIDGE	OVERNIGHT	CHANCROID	IMPOLITIC	SEMIFLUID	ARMADILLO	FORESTALL
PERSONIFY	PASTURAGE	OVERSIGHT	CHIEFTAIN	INORGANIC	SHARKSKIN	ARTERIOLE	FRANGIBLE
PIKESTAFF	PATHOLOGY	PREFLIGHT	CHILBLAIN	INTRINSIC	SHEEPSKIN	ASTRADDLE	GALLINULE
PLAINTIFF	PATRONAGE	RECHERCHE	CHIVALRIC	LAMEBRAIN	SILICOSIS	AVAILABLE	GOLDFIELD
SNOWDRIFT	PERSONAGE	SEAWORTHY	CHROMATIC	LEITMOTIV	SINUSITIS	BACKFIELD	GRATICULE
SPINDRIFT	PETROLOGY	SKINTIGHT	CHRYSALIS	LIGHTSHIP	SOPHISTIC	BAGATELLE	GREENBELT
SYLLABIFY	PHILOLOGY	SPOTLIGHT	CIRRHOSIS	LITERATIM	SOPORIFIC	BAMBOOZLE	GRISTMILL
VOUCHSAFE	PHONOLOGY	STARLIGHT	CONSTRAIN	MALADROIT	SPACESHIP	BANDEROLE	GUERRILLA
WOODCRAFT	PRIVILEGE	STOPLIGHT	COURTSHIP	MANNEQUIN	SPLENETIC	BARCAROLE	HABITABLE
ADVANTAGE	RADIOLOGY	TAILLIGHT	CRYOGENIC	MENAGERIE	STATISTIC	BESPANGLE	HAIRSTYLE
ANCHORAGE	REPORTAGE	TELEPATHY	DAIRYMAID	METEOROID	STEAMSHIP	BIMONTHLY	HEADSTALL
ANTHOLOGY	SACRILEGE	THEOSOPHY	DAREDEVIL	MONGOLOID	STOMACHIC	BLACKBALL	HEARTFELT
APPENDAGE	SAXIFRAGE	TOOTHACHE	DIACRITIC	MONOMANIA	SUBATOMIC	BLINDFOLD	HERITABLE
ASTROLOGY	SCRIMMAGE	UNHEALTHY	DIAERESIS	MULTISPIN	SWORDTAIL	BOARDWALK	HILLBILLY
AUDIOLOGY	SHRINKAGE	UNSHEATHE	DIAGNOSIS	NEPHRITIC	SYMBIOSIS	BOMBSHELL	HONORABLE
BACKSTAGE	SKYLOUNGE	ACROPOLIS	DIALECTIC	NEPHRITIS	SYNTHESIS	BOOKSHELF	HOUSEHOLD
BROKERAGE	SOCIOLOGY	ADIABATIC	DIAMETRIC	NEURALGIA	SYNTHETIC	BUTTERFLY	HYPERBOLA
CARTILAGE	SOVEREIGN	AESTHETIC	DIGITALIS	NICOTINIC	TARPAULIN	CALENDULA	HYPERBOLE
CARTRIDGE	SURCHARGE	AFFIDAVIT	DIMORPHIC	NONCREDIT	TELEGENIC	CAMPANILE	ILLEGIBLE
CELLARAGE	TAUTOLOGY	AFORESAID	DISCOMFIT	NONPAREIL	THUMBNAIL	CANTABILE	IMMOVABLE
CHALLENGE	TRAPPINGS	ALCOHOLIC	DISCREDIT	NONPROFIT	TRANSONIC	CAPITALLY	IMMUTABLE
CHAMPAIGN	ULTRAHIGH	ALEATORIC	DISREPAIR	NOSTALGIA	TRANSSHIP	CARBUNCLE	INCAPABLE
CONCIERGE	VASSALAGE	ALGONQUIN	DYSPEPSIA	NURSEMAID	TRAPEZOID	CASSEROLE	INCURABLE
CONESTOGA	VERMIFUGE	AMARYLLIS	ECCENTRIC	ONIONSKIN	TROOPSHIP	CHAMOMILE	INDELIBLE
COSMOLOGY	VILLENAGE	AMBERGRIS	ELLIPSOID	ORGIASTIC	TULAREMIA	CHONDRULE	INEFFABLE
CURETTAGE	AIRWORTHY	ANAEROBIC	ENERGETIC	PALANQUIN	UNCERTAIN	CHRONICLE	INFANTILE
DECOUPAGE	ALGORITHM	ANALGESIA	ENIGMATIC	PANEGYRIC	URTICARIA	CHUCKHOLE	INFERTILE
DEMURRAGE	ANTIPATHY	ANALGESIC	ENTERITIS	PARALYSIS	VAGINITIS	CIGARILLO	INFUSIBLE
DIAPHRAGM	APOCRYPHA	ANTARCTIC	ENTERTAIN	PAREGORIC	VERDIGRIS	CLAMSHELL	INNERSOLE
DISCHARGE	AVALANCHE	ANTECHOIR	EPIDERMIS	PATRISTIC	WASHBASIN	CLIENTELE	INSOLUBLE
DISENGAGE	BELLYACHE	ANTITOXIN	EUTROPHIC	PENEPLAIN	WHIRLIGIG	COALFIELD	INSTANTLY
DISOBLIGE	BIOGRAPHY	ANTIVENIN	EXECUTRIX	PHILIPPIC	WHITEBAIT	COMMINGLE	INSURABLE
DISPARAGE	BOMBSIGHT	APARTHEID	EXTRINSIC	PHLEBITIS	WHITETAIL	CONSTABLE	INVISIBLE
DOWNRANGE	BULLFIGHT	APOSTOLIC	EYESTRAIN	PHRENETIC	ARTICHOKE	CONTUMELY	IRASCIBLE
DOWNSTAGE	COCKFIGHT	APPERTAIN	FANTASTIC	PISTACHIO	BALALAIKA	CORNSTALK	IRRITABLE
EMPENNAGE	COPYRIGHT	ARTHRITIS	FILMSTRIP	PLANETOID	BOONDOCKS	CORPUSCLE	KILOCYCLE

LEAFSTALK	SPRIGHTLY	METRONOME	CACOPHONY	EARTHLING	HATCHMENT	MENDICANT	RECKONING
LEASEHOLD	STAIRWELL	NIGHTTIME	CALCIMINE	EASYGOING	HEADPHONE	MERRIMENT	RECOMMEND
MAJUSCULE	STEPCHILD	ORIFLAMME	CARPETING	EBULLIENT	HEADSTONE	MESCALINE	RECORDING
MALLEABLE	STOCKPILE	PANTOMIME	CATAMOUNT	EFFICIENT	HIDEBOUND	METHADONE	RECUMBENT
MANHANDLE	SURCINGLE	PEACETIME	CATCHMENT	EGLANTINE	HISTAMINE	MEZZANINE	REDUNDANT
MEANWHILE	TARANTULA	QUICKLIME	CELANDINE	EMBAYMENT	HOLYSTONE	MILESTONE	REENTRANT
MEDICABLE	TEAKETTLE	QUICKTIME	CHAMPAGNE	EMOLLIENT	HOMOPHONE	MILLSTONE	REGARDING
MEGACYCLE	THREEFOLD	TAXIDERMY	CHARABANC	EMOLUMENT	HOREHOUND	MISCREANT	REHEARING
MEMORABLE	THRESHOLD	THREESOME	CHEEKBONE	ENDOCRINE	HUMANKIND	MISGIVING	RELUCTANT
MICROFILM	TIMETABLE	TOOTHSOME	CHLORDANE	ENGRAVING	HURRICANE	MISORIENT	REPELLENT
MILLIVOLT	TOLERABLE	VASECTOMY	CLOISONNE	EPHEDRINE	IMMIGRANT	MONOPLANE	REPREHEND
MINISCULE	TOWNSFOLK	WEARISOME	COAGULANT	EQUIPMENT	IMPATIENS	MOONSHINE	REPRESENT
MINUSCULE	TRACKBALL	WHOLESOME	COASTLINE	EXCELLENT	IMPATIENT	MOONSTONE	REPRIMAND
MISERABLE	TRACTABLE	WIREFRAME	COLUMBINE	EXCREMENT	IMPLEMENT	MULTISYNC	REPUGNANT
MISHANDLE	TREADMILL	WORRISOME	COMPETENT	EXPECTANT	IMPORTANT	NECTARINE	RESERPINE
NATURALLY	TRIFOCALS	ABATEMENT	COMPLAINT	EXPEDIENT	IMPORTUNE	NEGLIGENT	RESISTANT
NAVIGABLE	TRIWEEKLY	ABHORRENT	COMPONENT	EXUBERANT	IMPRUDENT	NEGOTIANT	RESTRAINT
NIGHTFALL	TURNSTILE	ABORIGINE	CONCUBINE	FAIRYLAND	INCESSANT	NEWSPRINT	REVOLTING
OUTWARDLY	TURNTABLE	ABSORBENT	CONDIMENT	FARSEEING	INCIPIENT	NEWSSTAND	RIVERBANK
OVERWHELM	UNCLEANLY	ACCOMPANY	CONFIDANT	FASTENING	INCLEMENT	NUTRIMENT	ROCKBOUND
PALATABLE	UNDERSELL	ACETYLENE	CONSONANT	FINGERING	INCREMENT	OBSERVANT	RUNAROUND
PANHANDLE	UNEARTHLY	ADJOINING	CONTINENT	FINICKING	INCUMBENT	OFFICIANT	SACRAMENT
PASTORALE	UNSHACKLE	ADSORBENT	COONHOUND	FIREBRAND	INDIGNANT	OFFSPRING	SAILPLANE
PENINSULA	UNSIGHTLY	AEROPLANE	CORMORANT	FIRMAMENT	INELEGANT	OPPORTUNE	SANDSTONE
PERISTYLE	UNWORLDLY	AFFECTING	CORTISONE	FIRSTHAND	INFORMANT	OVERPRINT	SATURNINE
PERMEABLE	VEGETABLE	AFRIKAANS	COSMOGONY	FIRSTLING	INGROWING	PAKISTANI	SAXOPHONE
PHILATELY	VENERABLE	AGREEMENT	CRINOLINE	FLAGSTONE	INPATIENT	PARAMOUNT	SCANTLING
PHOTOCELL	VENTRICLE	AMENDMENT	CROISSANT	FLATULENT	INSISTENT	PARCHMENT	SCHILLING
PINEAPPLE	VERITABLE	AMERICANA	DACHSHUND	FLAVORING	INSOLVENT	PARSIMONY	SCREENING
PLAUSIBLE	VERSATILE	AMPERSAND	DAMASCENE	FLEDGLING	INSURGENT	PASSERINE	SEAFARING
PREGNABLE	VESTIBULE	ANKLEBONE	DECREMENT	FOLLOWING	INTENDANT	PATRIMONY	SEASONING
PRESENTLY	WATERFALL	ANNUITANT	DEFENDANT	FOOTPRINT	INTERLINE	PERMANENT	SENTIMENT
PRIMARILY	WAVETABLE	ANTICLINE	DEFERMENT	FOREFRONT	INTERLINK	PERTINENT	SHEATHING
PRINCIPLE	WHITEHALL	APARTMENT	DEFICIENT	FOREGOING	INTERMENT	PESTILENT	SHORTHAND
PRINTABLE	WHITEWALL	APPELLANT	DEFOLIANT	FORGIVING	INTERVENE	PHEROMONE	SIDEBURNS
QUADRILLE	WHOLESALE	APPLICANT	DEMULCENT	FOUNDLING	INTESTINE	PLACEMENT	SILTSTONE
QUADRUPLE	WINDCHILL	APPREHEND	DEODORANT	FREESTONE	IRONBOUND	PLAYTHING	SKINFLINT
QUARTERLY	WOMENFOLK	AQUAPLANE	DEPENDENT	GABARDINE	IRONSTONE	POINCIANA	SKYDIVING
QUINTUPLE	WORKTABLE	ARCHFIEND	DESICCANT	GABERDINE	ITINERANT	POLYPHONY	SOAPSTONE
RATIONALE	AERODROME	ARGENTINE	DESIGNING	GALLIVANT	JESSAMINE	PORCUPINE	SOFTBOUND
RECONCILE	ARCHENEMY	ASCENDANT	DETERGENT	GALLSTONE	KICKSTAND	POSTULANT	SOMETHING
RECTANGLE	ASTRONOMY	ASSISTANT	DETERMINE	GANGPLANK	LEAVENING	PRECEDENT	SOMNOLENT
REPUTABLE	BLASPHEME	ATONEMENT	DETERRENT	GLADSTONE	LIBERTINE	PRECEDING	SPEARMINT
RESHUFFLE	BLASPHEMY	ATTENDANT	DETRIMENT	GODPARENT	LIGHTNING	PRESHRUNK	SPINDLING
REVOCABLE	CARCINOMA	BALLERINA	DEVILMENT	GRAPEVINE	LIMESTONE	PRESIDENT	SPLITTING
RIDGEPOLE	CENTESIMO	BANDSTAND	DHRYSTONE	GRASSLAND	LIMOUSINE	PREVALENT	STARTLING
RIGMAROLE	CURRYCOMB	BENIGNANT	DIFFERENT	GRENADINE	LINEAMENT	PROMINENT	STATEMENT
SCINTILLA	DIATHERMY	BESETTING	DIFFIDENT	GREYHOUND	LOADSTONE	PROMISING	STIMULANT
SCREWBALL	DICHOTOMY	BLOODLINE	DIPHTHONG	GROUNDING	LODESTONE	PROPONENT	STRAPPING
SEPARABLE	EMPHYSEMA	BLUEPOINT	DISORIENT	GUIDELINE	LUBRICANT	PROVIDENT	STRIPLING
SHEEPFOLD	HONEYCOMB	BLUEPRINT	DISPUTANT	HAILSTONE	LUXURIANT	PROVOLONE	SUBALPINE
SKIMOBILE	LIGHTSOME	BOMBAZINE	DISSIDENT	HALFPENNY	MALIGNANT	PUBESCENT	SUBMARINE
SMALLTALK	LITHESOME	BOOMERANG	DITHERING	HAMSTRING	MARGARINE	QUICKSAND	SUCCULENT
SNOWFIELD	LOATHSOME	BOWSTRING	DIXIELAND	HANDSTAND	MARIJUANA	QUIESCENT	SUFFERING
SPECTACLE	MAINFRAME	BRILLIANT	DOWNSWING	HAPPENING	MASCULINE	RANCHLAND	SUGARCANE
SPEEDWELL	MAJORDOMO	BRIMSTONE	DREAMLAND	HARDBOUND	MATRIMONY	RANGELAND	SUPERVENE
SPOONBILL	MELODRAMA	BROADBAND	DUMBFOUND	HARDSTAND	MEGAPHONE	RECIPIENT	SUPPLIANT

SUPPOSING	WRESTLING	CONDITION	GESTATION	OPERATION	SELECTION	LANDSCAPE	CATCHWORD
SURVEYING	WRISTBAND	CONDUCTOR	GLADIATOR	OVERSHOOT	SEMICOLON	MICROCOPY	CENTENARY
SWAMPLAND	XYLOPHONE	CONFESSOR	GOLDENROD	OVERTHROW	SENSATION	MONOGRAPH	CHALKBORD
SYCOPHANT	YOUNGLING	CONFUSION	GRADATION	OXIDATION	SEPARATOR	MOONSCAPE	CHEMISTRY
TABLELAND	ACCESSION	CONTAGION	GRAPESHOT	PARATHION	SHADOWBOX	PARAGRAPH	CHICANERY
TANGERINE	ACCORDION	CONTUSION	GREENROOM	PARTITION	SHORTSTOP	PERISCOPE	CIRCUITRY
TELEPHONE	ACCRETION	COSPONSOR	GREENWOOD	PERDITION	SIMPLETON	PHALAROPE	CITIZENRY
TELEPHONY	ADDICTION	COTILLION	GROUNDHOG	PERSIMMON	SINGLETON	PHOTOCOPY	CLAPBOARD
TERMAGANT	ADMISSION	COTYLEDON	GUARANTOR	POSTERIOR	SITUATION	PINSTRIPE	CLIPBOARD
TESTAMENT	AFFECTION	COUNSELOR	GUARDROOM	POSTILION	SLINGSHOT	POLYGRAPH	CLOCKWORK
TESTIMONY	AFTERGLOW	COURTROOM	GUIDEBOOK	PRECENTOR	SOLICITOR	PREOCCUPY	COFEATURE
THIGHBONE	AFTERNOON	CRITERION	GUNCOTTON	PRECEPTOR	SPECTATOR	PROTOTYPE	COMMODORE
THYROXINE	ALLIGATOR	CYCLOTRON	GYRFALCON	PRECISION	STANCHION	SERIGRAPH	COMPOSURE
TIMBERING	ANIMATION	DALMATION	HAMMERTOE	PRECURSOR	STATEROOM	SHIPSHAPE	COROLLARY
TOMBSTONE	ANTITUMOR	DAMNATION	HARDIHOOD	PREDATION	STOREROOM	SIDESWIPE	COURTYARD
TRANSCEND	APPORTION	DANDELION	HEARTWOOD	PRESCHOOL	SUCCESSOR	STANDPIPE	CRANBERRY
TRANSIENT	ARROWROOT	DEATHBLOW	HETERODOX	PRESSROOM	SUMMATION	SUBSCRIPT	CREMATORY
TREATMENT	ARTHROPOD	DECATHLON	HONEYMOON	PREVISION	SUSPICION	TELEGRAPH	CRUCIFORM
TRENCHANT	ASCENSION	DECEPTION	HORSESHOE	PRIVATION	SWEATSHOP	TELESCOPE	CUNEIFORM
TRUCULENT	ASPERSION	DECONTROL	IMITATION	PROBATION	THEREFROM	TIGHTROPE	CURVATURE
TURBULENT	ASSERTION	DECORATOR	IMPULSION	PROCESSOR	THEREUPON	VIDEOTAPE	CUSTOMARY
TWINKLING	ATTENTION	DEDUCTION	INANITION	PROFESSOR	THRALLDOM	WINDSWEPT	DASHBOARD
UNBENDING	ATTRITION	DEFLATION	INCEPTION	PROJECTOR	TINDERBOX	XANTHIPPE	DAVENPORT
UNCEASING	AUTOMATON	DEJECTION	INCUBATOR	PROTECTOR	TOADSTOOL	ACCESSORY	DEBENTURE
UNDERDONE	AVOCATION	DENTITION	INCURSION	PROVISION	TRADITION	ADMIXTURE	DECISTERE
UNDERHAND	BADMINTON	DETENTION	INDENTION	PUREBLOOD	TRUNCHEON	ADVENTURE	DEKASTERE
UNDERLINE	BANDWAGON	DETONATOR	INDUCTION	PURGATION	TURBOPROP	ADVERSARY	DELFTWARE
UNDERLING	BATTALION	DIMENSION	INFECTION	PUSSYFOOT	UNDERFOOT	AFTERCARE	DEPARTURE
UNDERMINE	BEDFELLOW	DIRECTION	INFLATION	REBELLION	UNDERSHOT	AFTERWARD	DESULTORY
UNDERTONE	BLACKFOOT	DIVERSION	INFLEXION	RECEPTION	UNDERWOOD	ANCILLARY	DIGNITARY
UNFAILING	BLOODROOT	DRIFTWOOD	INGLENOOK	RECESSION	VALUATION	ANGLEWORM	DIRECTORY
UNFEELING	BLOODSHOT	EAVESDROP	INHALATOR	RECURSION	VARIATION	ANTIQUARY	DISEMBARK
UNIVALENT	BOMBPROOF	EDUCATION	INJECTION	REDACTION	VERMILION	ARBITRARY	DISFIGURE
UNKNOWING	BROADLOOM	ELBOWROOM	INSERTION	REDUCTION	VIBRATION	ARTILLERY	DISREGARD
UNMEANING	BRUSHWOOD	ELEVATION	INTENTION	REFECTION	VIOLATION	ASCENDERS	DORMITORY
UNSPARING	CAMPSTOOL	ELOCUTION	INTUITION	REFLECTOR	WHEREUPON	AUXILIARY	DROMEDARY
UNWILLING	CAPACITOR	ERUDITION	INVENTION	REFRACTOR	WHIRLPOOL	BACKBOARD	DRUGSTORE
UNWITTING	CAPARISON	ESCALATOR	INVERSION	REMISSION	WHITEWOOD	BARNSTORM	DUCKBOARD
VALENTINE	CARNATION	EVOLUTION	ITERATION	RENDITION	WINDPROOF	BASEBOARD	DYSENTERY
VIEWPOINT	CAUSATION	EXCELSIOR	LIFEBLOOD	REPLETION	WOMANHOOD	BELVEDERE	EARTHWARD
WAISTBAND	CENTURION	EXCEPTION	LOCOMOTOR	REPULSION	AMIDSHIPS	BILLBOARD	EARTHWORK
WAISTLINE	CESSATION	EXCURSION	LUNCHROOM	RESECTION	ARCHETYPE	BIOSPHERE	EARTHWORM
WALLOPING	CHAMELEON	EXPANSION	MAELSTROM	RESONATOR	AUTOGRAPH	BIRTHMARK	ELSEWHERE
WASHSTAND	CHECKBOOK	EXPLOSION	MALATHION	RETENTION	BACKSWEPT	BLACKBIRD	EMBRASURE
WASTELAND	CHECKROOM	EXPOSITOR	MARTYRDOM	REVERSION	BAROGRAPH	BLEACHERS	ENRAPTURE
WATCHBAND	CHILDHOOD	EXPULSION	MATCHBOOK	REVULSION	CONSCRIPT	BLUEBERRY	EXEMPLARY
WATERLINE	CLASSROOM	EXTENSION	MATCHWOOD	RUINATION	DRAINPIPE	BODYGUARD	EXOSPHERE
WHALEBONE	COADJUTOR	FALSEHOOD	MEDALLION	SADDLEBOW	ENDOSCOPE	BOULEVARD	EXPIATORY
WHETSTONE	COALITION	FIREPROOF	MISTLETOE	SALVATION	GYROSCOPE	BRASSIERE	EXTEMPORE
WHIRLWIND	COFFEEPOT	FLOTATION	MODERATOR	SATINWOOD	HOLOGRAPH	BUCKBOARD	EXTRAVERT
WITHSTAND	COGNITION	FLOWERPOT	MONKSHOOD	SCARECROW	HOMOGRAPH	CAMEMBERT	FANCYWORK
WOEBEGONE	COLLATION	FOOLPROOF	MONSIGNOR	SCHOOLBOY	HOROSCOPE	CAPILLARY	FEUDATORY
WOLFHOUND	COLLODION	FOOTSTOOL	MUSKMELON	SCRAPBOOK	INTERCEPT	CARDBOARD	FIDUCIARY
WOLFSBANE	COLLUSION	FORMATION	NONPERSON	SCUTCHEON	INTERLOPE	CARNIVORA	FIRSTBORN
WOLVERINE	COMMOTION	FREEMASON	NUMERATOR	SECESSION	INTERRUPT	CARNIVORE	FLOWCHART
WOMANKIND	COMMUNION	GASTROPOD	NUTRITION	SECLUSION	KINESCOPE	CASSOWARY	FOOTBOARD
WORLDLING	COMPANION	GENERATOR	OBSESSION	SECRETION	LAGNIAPPE	CASUISTRY	FORESHORE

FOURSCORE	MOLDBOARD	SEPULTURE	AERIALIST	DOGMATISM	MECHANISM	SYNERGISM	ARGENTITE
FRAMEWORK	MOMENTARY	SHAREWARE	AEROPAUSE	DOUBTLESS	MENOPAUSE	TECTONISM	ASSOCIATE
FREEBOARD	MONASTERY	SHELLFIRE	ALBATROSS	EDELWEISS	METHODIST	TERRORISM	ASYMPTOTE
FURNITURE	MOUTHPART	SHIPBOARD	ALLERGIST	EMBARRASS	MICROCOSM	THANKLESS	ATTENUATE
GALLANTRY	MULTIFORM	SHOREBIRD	ALMSHOUSE	EMBELLISH	MODERNISM	THICKNESS	ATTRIBUTE
GARNITURE	NECESSARY	SHORTHORN	ANARCHISM	ENCOMPASS	MONGOLISM	TOLLHOUSE	AUTHORITY
GIMMICKRY	NEVERMORE	SHRUBBERY	ANGELFISH	EQUIPOISE	MOUTHWASH	TRANSFUSE	BANDWIDTH
GLENGARRY	NIGHTMARE	SIDEBOARD	ANIMALISM	ESTABLISH	MYSTICISM	TRANSPOSE	BANQUETTE
GRAVEYARD	OFFERTORY	SIGNATORY	APPALOOSA	EUCHARIST	NEOLOGISM	TURQUOISE	BATHOLITH
GRAYBEARD	OLFACTORY	SIGNATURE	ARCHIVIST	EUPHEMISM	NORTHEAST	UNDERMOST	BENTONITE
GREENHORN	OPTOMETRY	SIGNBOARD	BACKSLASH	EXPERTISE	NORTHWEST	UNDERPASS	BIFURCATE
GRILLWORK	ORCHESTRA	SNAKEBIRD	BAKSHEESH	EXTREMISM	OCCULTISM	UNHARNESS	BIPARTITE
GROUPWARE	OVERBOARD	SNOWSTORM	BARBARISM	FARMHOUSE	OTHERWISE	UNSELFISH	BIRTHRATE
GUSTATORY	PACHYDERM	SOLITAIRE	BATHHOUSE	FETISHISM	OUTERMOST	UPPERCASE	BLOODBATH
HAILSTORM	PALAESTRA	SOMEWHERE	BELLICOSE	FEUDALISM	PACKHORSE	UPPERMOST	BOOKPLATE
HANDIWORK	PALMISTRY	SOPHISTRY	BIRDHOUSE	FIREHOUSE	PANTHEISM	UTTERMOST	BRIQUETTE
HAPHAZARD	PARQUETRY	SOPHOMORE	BLACKLIST	FLOPHOUSE	PEKINGESE	VANDALISM	BROCHETTE
HARDBOARD	PATCHWORK	STARBOARD	BLUEGRASS	FOOTLOOSE	PENTECOST	VOICELESS	BUCKTOOTH
HARTSHORN	PECUNIARY	STATUTORY	BREAKFAST	FORECLOSE	PENTHOUSE	VOLCANISM	CALCULATE
HEADBOARD	PERFUMERY	STEELYARD	BRIEFCASE	FORMALISM	PESSIMISM	VOODOOISM	CALIBRATE
HEARTBURN	PERIPHERY	STEVEDORE	BROADCAST	FRANCHISE	PESTHOUSE	VULCANISM	CALLOSITY
HELLEBORE	PERSEVERE	STILLBORN	CALABOOSE	GALACTOSE	PHYSICIST	VULGARISM	CANDIDATE
HORTATORY	PIECEWORK	STOCKYARD	CALVINISM	GALVANISM	PLAYHOUSE	WAREHOUSE	CAPSULATE
HOUSEWORK	PITCHFORK	STRICTURE	CATACLYSM	GIBBERISH	POLITESSE	WASHHOUSE	CAPTIVATE
HUSBANDRY	PITUITARY	STRUCTURE	CATALEPSY	GOVERNESS	POORHOUSE	WATCHCASE	CARBONATE
HYPERCARD	PLOWSHARE	SUBALTERN	CATECHISM	GRANDIOSE	PRESTRESS	WHEELBASE	CASTANETS
IMAGINARY	POLITBURO	SUBLUNARY	CEASELESS	HAIRBRUSH	PRICELESS	WHITEFISH	CASTIGATE
IMPOSTURE	POTPOURRI	SURFBOARD	CELLULOSE	HANDCLASP	PUBLICIST	WHITENESS	CELEBRATE
INDENTURE	POURBOIRE	TABLEWARE	CHANTEUSE	HAPPINESS	RACEHORSE	WHITEWASH	CELEBRITY
INFIRMARY	PREDATORY	TEMPORARY	CHECKLIST	HEADDRESS	RACIALISM	WINEPRESS	CEREBRATE
INSINCERE	PREFIGURE	TERRITORY	CHEERLESS	HEADFIRST	RECORDIST	WITTICISM	CERECLOTH
INTERFERE	PREMATURE	THEREFORE	CHOPHOUSE	HEARTLESS	REDBREAST	WORKHORSE	CERTAINTY
INTERLARD	PRERECORD	TRADEMARK	CLOCKWISE	HELLENISM	REFURBISH	WORKHOUSE	CHECKMATE
INTROVERT	PROCEDURE	TRANSFORM	CLUBHOUSE	HERBALIST	REIMBURSE	WORTHLESS	CHOCOLATE
INVENTORY	PRONGHORN	TRANSPIRE	COIFFEUSE	HOARFROST	REPLENISH	ZEITGEIST	CHONDRITE
INVOLUCRE	PULMONARY	TRANSPORT	COLORCAST	HOLOCAUST	REPOSSESS	ABOMINATE	CIGARETTE
ITINERARY	PURGATORY	TREACHERY	COLORFAST	HOURGLASS	RESERVIST	ACCLIMATE	CIRCULATE
JUDICIARY	QUICKSORT	TRIBUTARY	COLUMNIST	HYPOCRISY	SAGEBRUSH	ACCLIVITY	CLASSMATE
LAUDATORY	RAINSTORM	TUSCARORA	COMMUNISM	IMPRECISE	SANDBLAST	ACIDULATE	COAGULATE
LAVALIERE	RASPBERRY	ULTRAPURE	CONCOURSE	IMPROVISE	SHAPELESS	ADMIRALTY	COLLIMATE
LEGENDARY	REFECTORY	UNCONCERN	COUNTLESS	INNERMOST	SHELLFISH	ADSORBATE	COMMODITY
LIFEGUARD	RELIQUARY	UNDERGIRD	CRABGRASS	INTERFUSE	SHIFTLESS	ADUMBRATE	COMMUNITY
LIVERWORT	RENCONTRE	UNDERPART	CRANKCASE	INTERNIST	SOCIALISM	ADVERSITY	COMPOSITE
MACHINERY	REPERTORY	VAINGLORY	CRETINISM	INTERPOSE	SOUTHEAST	AESTIVATE	CONGRUITY
MANDATORY	RESIDUARY	VAPORWARE	CRITICISM	INVERNESS	SOUTHWEST	AFFILIATE	CONJUGATE
MANOEUVRE	RETROFIRE	VERMIFORM	CROSSWISE	ISINGLASS	SPEAKEASY	AFTERMATH	CONTRALTO
MARQUETRY	ROUNDWORM	VIBRATORY	CYTOPLASM	JELLYFISH	SPICEBUSH	AGGRAVATE	COOPERATE
MERCENARY	SAFEGUARD	VISIONARY	DARWINISM	JUXTAPOSE	SQUEAMISH	AGGREGATE	CORPORATE
MESSIEURS	SALESGIRL	VOLUNTARY	DAUNTLESS	LEASTWISE	STAIRCASE	ALLEVIATE	CORRELATE
METALWARE	SANCTUARY	WALLBOARD	DEATHLESS	LOWERCASE	STEADFAST	ALMANDITE	CORRUGATE
METALWORK	SANDSTORM	WASHBOARD	DECOMPOSE	MACHINIST	STRAPLESS	ALTERNATE	CORUSCATE
MILLINERY	SCRIPTURE	WATCHWORD	DEFEATISM	MACINTOSH	SUCCOTASH	ANCHORITE	CROQUETTE
MINIATURE	SCULPTURE	WATERMARK	DEMITASSE	MACROCOSM	SUPERPOSE	ANIMOSITY	CULMINATE
MINISKIRT	SECONDARY	WHEREFORE	DISCOURSE	MAGNETISM	SUPERVISE	ANTIPASTO	CULTIVATE
MISGOVERN	SECRETARY	WINDSTORM	DISHONEST	MANGANESE	SWORDFISH	ANTIQUITY	CYCLAMATE
MISINFORM	SEDENTARY	WORRYWART	DISPLEASE	MANNERISM	SYLLOGISM	APPELLATE	DEBUTANTE
MISSILERY	SEMAPHORE	ADVERTISE	DISPRAISE	MASOCHISM	SYMBOLISM	ARBITRATE	DECLIVITY

DECOLLETE	FLUCTUATE	LEUKOCYTE	POSTULATE	TYPEWRITE	CONTINUUM	MERCUROUS	TURNABOUT
DEFOLIATE	FORETASTE	LIABILITY	POTENTATE	UNDERRATE	CONUNDRUM	MOMENTOUS	TYRANNOUS
DEFORMITY	FORMALITY	LIQUIDATE	PREDICATE	VACCINATE	COSMONAUT	MONOLOGUE	ULTIMATUM
DEHYDRATE	FORMULATE	LOCKSMITH	PROCREATE	VACILLATE	COURTEOUS	MURDEROUS	UMBILICUS
DELINEATE	FORTHWITH	LOINCLOTH	PROFANITY	VARIEGATE	CREDULOUS	NARCISSUS	UNANIMOUS
DEMARCATE	FORTUNATE	LONGEVITY	PROPAGATE	VENTILATE	CUTANEOUS	NEFARIOUS	UNMINDFUL
DENIGRATE	FROSTBITE	LORGNETTE	PROPRIETY	VIGILANTE	DANGEROUS	NEODYMIUM	VAGARIOUS
DEPRECATE	FRUSTRATE	LUBRICATE	PROSECUTE	VINDICATE	DECALOGUE	NEPTUNIUM	VENTUROUS
DESECRATE	FULMINATE	LUXURIATE	PROSELYTE	VIRGINITY	DECEITFUL	NIGHTCLUB	VERACIOUS
DESICCATE	GELIGNITE	MAGNETITE	PROSTRATE	VISCOSITY	DECIDUOUS	NOTORIOUS	VEXATIOUS
DESIGNATE	GENTILITY	MAJORETTE	PROXIMATE	VULGARITY	DELICIOUS	OBLIVIOUS	VICARIOUS
DESPERATE	GERMINATE	MALACHITE	PROXIMITY	WAGONETTE	DEMAGOGUE	OBNOXIOUS	VIVACIOUS
DESTITUTE	GOLDSMITH	MANIFESTO	PUBLICITY	WASHCLOTH	DEUTERIUM	OFFICIOUS	VORACIOUS
DEVASTATE	GRANULATE	MASTICATE	PUNCTUATE	WHEREWITH	DEXTEROUS	OVERCLOUD	WONDERFUL
DEXTERITY	GRAVITATE	MATERNITY	QUARTZITE	XEROPHYTE	DIPTEROUS	OVIPAROUS	WORKGROUP
DIATOMITE	HABITUATE	MEGADEATH	RABBINATE	ZUCCHETTO	EFFLUVIUM	PALLADIUM	YTTERBIUM
DISHCLOTH	HAIRCLOTH	MEGAHERTZ	RECONDITE	ACIDULOUS	EGREGIOUS	PEDAGOGUE	ZIRCONIUM
DISLOCATE	HIBERNATE	MELIORATE	REINSTATE	AILANTHUS	EROGENOUS	PENDULOUS	ADJECTIVE
DISPARATE	HUMILIATE	MENTALITY	REITERATE	ALUMINIUM	ERRONEOUS	PENURIOUS	BICONCAVE
DISREPUTE	HYPHENATE	METEORITE	REPLICATE	AMBIGUOUS	ESOPHAGUS	PETROLEUM	DEFECTIVE
DISSIPATE	IMMEDIATE	MINISTATE	REPROBATE	AMBITIOUS	EXOGENOUS	PLENTEOUS	DEFENSIVE
DISSOLUTE	IMMIGRATE	NAMEPLATE	REPUDIATE	AMERICIUM	FACETIOUS	PLENTIFUL	DETECTIVE
DIVERSITY	IMPLICATE	NECESSITY	REQUISITE	AMORPHOUS	FEROCIOUS	PLUTONIUM	DIRECTIVE
DOCTORATE	IMPRECATE	NEGOTIATE	RETALIATE	ANALOGOUS	FLAGELLUM	POMPADOUR	EFFECTIVE
DOORPLATE	IMPROMPTU	NONENTITY	RETARDATE	ANHYDROUS	FRACTIOUS	PONDEROUS	EXCLUSIVE
DUPLICATE	INABILITY	NOVELETTE	RUSTICATE	ANOMALOUS	FRIGHTFUL	POTASSIUM	EXCURSIVE
DUPLICITY	INAMORATA	NOVITIATE	SACKCLOTH	ANONYMOUS	FRIVOLOUS	PRAYERFUL	EXECUTIVE
EJACULATE	INANIMATE	OBBLIGATO	SAILCLOTH	ANTISERUM	GARRULOUS	PRESIDIUM	EXPANSIVE
ELABORATE	INCARNATE	OBFUSCATE	SATELLITE	APPARATUS	GERMANIUM	PROCONSUL	EXPENSIVE
ELIMINATE	INCOGNITO	OBJURGATE	SCHEELITE	ARABESQUE	GLADIOLUS	PYRETHRUM	EXPLETIVE
ELUCIDATE	INCULCATE	OBSTINATE	SEGREGATE	ARBORETUM	GLUTINOUS	QUERULOUS	EXPLOSIVE
EMBROCATE	INCULPATE	OFFICIATE	SENIORITY	ASPARAGUS	GROTESQUE	RACONTEUR	EXTENSIVE
ENUMERATE	INDEMNITY	ORIENTATE	SNAKEBITE	ASSIDUOUS	GYMNASIUM	RAINSPOUT	EXTRUSIVE
ENUNCIATE	INDIGNITY	ORIGINATE	SOCIALITE	ASTRONAUT	HARMONIUM	RAPACIOUS	FORMATIVE
ERADICATE	INEBRIATE	OSCILLATE	SOUBRETTE	ATHENAEUM	HEALTHFUL	RELIGIOUS	HORTATIVE
ESPERANTO	INFATUATE	OUBLIETTE	SPAGHETTI	ATROCIOUS	HERBARIUM	RIGHTEOUS	IMITATIVE
ETIQUETTE	INFIRMITY	OUTGROWTH	SPECIALTY	AUDACIOUS	HILARIOUS	RUTHENIUM	IMPASSIVE
EVAPORATE	INFURIATE	OUTSKIRTS	SPECULATE	BACTERIUM	IMPERIOUS	SAGACIOUS	IMPULSIVE
EVAPORITE	INGENUITY	OVERSTATE	STALEMATE	BARBAROUS	IMPETUOUS	SALACIOUS	INCENTIVE
EVENTUATE	INOCULATE	OVERWRITE	STAMINATE	BEAUTEOUS	INCURIOUS	SEBACEOUS	INDUCTIVE
EXCORIATE	INSATIATE	OXYGENATE	STATUETTE	BEAUTIFUL	INGENIOUS	SILICEOUS	INTENSIVE
EXCULPATE	INSENSATE	PALPITATE	STIMULATE	BERKELIUM	INGENUOUS	SOLILOQUY	INVECTIVE
EXONERATE	INSINUATE	PAPILLOTE	STIPULATE	BERYLLIUM	INNOCUOUS	STRENUOUS	INVENTIVE
EXPATIATE	INSTIGATE	PARACHUTE	SUBJUGATE	BOUNTEOUS	INSIDIOUS	STRIKEOUT	LUCRATIVE
EXPLICATE	INSTITUTE	PATERNITY	SUBLIMATE	BOUNTIFUL	INVIDIOUS	STRONTIUM	MICROWAVE
EXPURGATE	INTEGRATE	PEGMATITE	SUFFOCATE	BUMPTIOUS	JITTERBUG	SUGARPLUM	MISBEHAVE
EXQUISITE	INTEGRITY	PENETRATE	SUPPURATE	BURLESQUE	JUDICIOUS	SULFUROUS	NARRATIVE
EXTENUATE	INTENSITY	PERCOLATE	SURROGATE	BUTTERCUP	LABORIOUS	SUMPTUOUS	NORMATIVE
EXTIRPATE	INTESTATE	PERFORATE	SYNDICATE	BUTTERNUT	LANTHANUM	SYMPOSIUM	OBJECTIVE
EXTRADITE	INTRICATE	PERSECUTE	TELEPHOTO	CAPACIOUS	LITIGIOUS	SYNAGOGUE	OFFENSIVE
EXTREMITY	INVIOLATE	PERSONATE	TEMPERATE	CATERWAUL	LITTERBUG	TECHNIQUE	OPERATIVE
EXTRICATE	IRRADIATE	PHOSPHATE	TERMINATE	CHAUFFEUR	LUDICROUS	TELLURIUM	OVERDRIVE
FABRICATE	ISRAELITE	PIROUETTE	THEREUNTO	COLLEAGUE	MAGNESIUM	TENACIOUS	PARTITIVE
FASCINATE	KILOHERTZ	PIZZICATO	THEREWITH	COLLEGIUM	MARVELOUS	TENEBROUS	PLAINTIVE
FECUNDATE	LABYRINTH	PLURALITY	TRANSLATE	COLLUVIUM	MASTERFUL	TERRARIUM	PRIMITIVE
FESTIVITY	LACCOLITH	POSTERITY	TRANSMUTE	CONSCIOUS	MAUSOLEUM	THESAURUS	PROBATIVE
FLOODGATE	LEGISLATE	POSTHASTE	TRITURATE	CONSENSUS	MELODIOUS	TREMULOUS	PURGATIVE

RECEPTIVE	MESMERIZE	ENCHILADA	DIAMETRIC	BETROTHED	GRAVEYARD	REPRIMAND	UNRUFFLED
RECESSIVE	METHODIZE	FORSYTHIA	DIMORPHIC	BILLBOARD	GRAYBEARD	ROADSTEAD	UNSCATHED
REFLEXIVE	METRICIZE	GENITALIA	ECCENTRIC	BLACKBIRD	GREENWOOD	ROCKBOUND	UNSETTLED
REPULSIVE	MODERNIZE	GONORRHEA	ENERGETIC	BLACKHEAD	GREYHOUND	RUNAROUND	UNSKILLED
RETENTIVE	NARCOTIZE	GUERRILLA	ENIGMATIC	BLINDFOLD	HACKNEYED	SAFEGUARD	UNSPOTTED
SECRETIVE	NORMALIZE	HARMONICA	EUTROPHIC	BLOCKHEAD	HAMADRYAD	SANGFROID	UNSTUDIED
SENSITIVE	OSTRACIZE	HELVETICA	EXTRINSIC	BLOODSHED	HANDSTAND	SATINWOOD	UNTUTORED
SHORTWAVE	PATRONIZE	HYDRANGEA	FANTASTIC	BODYGUARD	HAPHAZARD	SEMIFLUID	UPANISHAD
SUPERNOVA	PLURALIZE	HYPERBOLA	GERIATRIC	BOULEVARD	HARDBOARD	SHEEPFOLD	WAISTBAND
TALKATIVE	PUBLICIZE	INAMORATA	HEURISTIC	BROADBAND	HARDBOUND	SHIPBOARD	WALLBOARD
TENTATIVE	PULVERIZE	INFLUENZA	HONORIFIC	BRUSHWOOD	HARDIHOOD	SHOREBIRD	WASHBOARD
UNDECEIVE	RANDOMIZE	JACARANDA	HYDRAULIC	BUCKBOARD	HARDSTAND	SHORTHAND	WASHSTAND
BREAKDOWN	RASTERIZE	JINRIKSHA	ICELANDIC	CARDBOARD	HEADBOARD	SIDEBOARD	WASTELAND
COUNTDOWN	RECOGNIZE	MARIJUANA	IMPOLITIC	CATCHWORD	HEARTWOOD	SIGNBOARD	WATCHBAND
CRACKDOWN	SENSITIZE	MELODRAMA	INORGANIC	CHALKBORD	HIDEBOUND	SNAKEBIRD	WATCHWORD
EIDERDOWN	SIGNALIZE	MONOMANIA	INTRINSIC	CHANCROID	HOMESTEAD	SNOWFIELD	WATERSHED
HOMEGROWN	SOCIALIZE	NEURALGIA	MULTISYNC	CHICKWEED	HOREHOUND	SOFTBOUND	WHIRLWIND
KNOCKDOWN	SOLEMNIZE	NOSTALGIA	NEPHRITIC	CHILDHOOD	HOTHEADED	SPEARHEAD	WHITEHEAD
NIGHTGOWN	STABILIZE	ORCHESTRA	NICOTINIC	CLAPBOARD	HOUSEHOLD	STARBOARD	WHITEWOOD
NIGHTHAWK	STERILIZE	PALAESTRA	ORGIASTIC	CLIPBOARD	HOUSEMAID	STEELYARD	WITHSTAND
OVERBLOWN	SUBSIDIZE	PENINSULA	PANEGYRIC	COALFIELD	HUMANKIND	STEPCHILD	WOLFHOUND
SHAKEDOWN	SUMMARIZE	PNEUMONIA	PAREGORIC	COLLECTED	HYPERCARD	STOCKYARD	WOMANHOOD
SWANSDOWN	SYMBOLIZE	POINCIANA	PATRISTIC	CONCERNED	INTERLARD	STREAMBED	WOMANKIND
TOUCHDOWN	SYSTEMIZE	PORTULACA	PHILIPPIC	CONCERTED	IRONBOUND	SURFBOARD	WRISTBAND
UNBEKNOWN	TANTALIZE	PYROMANIA	PHRENETIC	CONTENTED	JAUNDICED	SWAMPLAND	ABOMINATE
WATERFOWL	TEMPORIZE	RAUWOLFIA	PNEUMATIC	COONHOUND	JEWELWEED	SWELLHEAD	ABORIGINE
WINDBLOWN	TENDERIZE	SCINTILLA	PRAGMATIC	COURTYARD	KICKSTAND	TABLELAND	ACCIDENCE
WITHDRAWN	TERRORIZE	SUPERNOVA	PROPHETIC	CROSSROAD	LAMINATED	THREEFOLD	ACCLIMATE
HYPERTEXT	TYRANNIZE	TARANTULA	QUADRATIC	DACHSHUND	LAUNCHPAD	THRESHOLD	ACETYLENE
CROSSWAYS	VANDALIZE	TULAREMIA	SCHEMATIC	DAIRYMAID	LEASEHOLD	TRAINLOAD	ACIDULATE
PSEUDONYM	VERBALIZE	TUSCARORA	SOPHISTIC	DASHBOARD	LIFEBLOOD	TRANSCEND	ACQUIESCE
ALUMINIZE	VERNALIZE	URTICARIA	SOPORIFIC	DELIGHTED	LIFEGUARD	TRAPEZOID	ADDRESSEE
ANATOMIZE	VICTIMIZE	CURRYCOMB	SPLENETIC	DEPRESSED	MATCHWOOD	TRUCKLOAD	ADJECTIVE
ANGLICIZE	VISUALIZE	FLASHBULB	STATISTIC	DIGITIZED	METEOROID	UNADVISED	ADMIRABLE
APOLOGIZE	VULCANIZE	HONEYCOMB	STOMACHIC	DIGNIFIED	MOLDBOARD	UNALIGNED	ADMIXTURE
AUTHORIZE	VULGARIZE	NIGHTCLUB	SUBATOMIC	DISREGARD	MONGOLOID	UNALLOYED	ADSORBATE
BRUTALIZE	WINTERIZE	ADIABATIC	SYNTHETIC	DISSECTED	MONKSHOOD	UNBLESSED	ADUMBRATE
CARBURIZE		AESTHETIC	TELEGENIC	DISTURBED	NEWSSTAND	UNBOUNDED	ADVANTAGE
CAUTERIZE		ALCOHOLIC	TRANSONIC	DIXIELAND	NOSEBLEED	UNBRIDLED	ADVENTURE
CRITICIZE		ALEATORIC	ABANDONED	DREAMLAND	NURSEMAID	UNCHARTED	ADVERTISE
CUSTOMIZE	**9TH LETTER**	ANAEROBIC	AFORESAID	DRIFTWOOD	OUTSPREAD	UNCOUNTED	ADVISABLE
DEODORIZE		ANALGESIC	AFTERWARD	DUCKBOARD	OVERBOARD	UNDAUNTED	AERODROME
DEOXIDIZE	AMERICANA	ANTARCTIC	AMPERSAND	DUMBFOUND	OVERCLOUD	UNDECIDED	AEROPAUSE
DRAMATIZE	ANALGESIA	APOSTOLIC	ANGUISHED	EARTHWARD	OVERSEXED	UNDERBRED	AEROPLANE
ECONOMIZE	APOCRYPHA	AUTHENTIC	APARTHEID	ELLIPSOID	PERPLEXED	UNDERFEED	AEROSPACE
EMPHASIZE	APPALOOSA	AUTOMATIC	APPREHEND	FAIRYLAND	PIGHEADED	UNDERGIRD	AESTIVATE
FANTASIZE	ASAFETIDA	BISHOPRIC	ARCHFIEND	FALSEHOOD	PLANELOAD	UNDERHAND	AFFILIATE
FERTILIZE	BALALAIKA	BRITANNIC	ARROWHEAD	FARMSTEAD	PLANETOID	UNDERWOOD	AFFLUENCE
FORMALIZE	BALLERINA	CALORIFIC	ARTHROPOD	FIREBRAND	PRERECORD	UNDOUBTED	AFTERCARE
GALVANIZE	BARRACUDA	CATATONIC	BACKBOARD	FIRSTHAND	PROOFREAD	UNEQUALED	AFTERLIFE
GLAMORIZE	CAFETERIA	CATHARTIC	BACKFIELD	FOOTBOARD	PUREBLOOD	UNFEIGNED	AGGRAVATE
HARMONIZE	CALENDULA	CHARABANC	BANDSTAND	FORENAMED	QUADRUPED	UNFLEDGED	AGGREGATE
INFLUENZA	CARCINOMA	CHIVALRIC	BAREFACED	FREEBOARD	QUICKSAND	UNFOUNDED	AGREEABLE
ITALICIZE	CARNIVORA	CHROMATIC	BASEBOARD	GASTROPOD	RANCHLAND	UNGUARDED	AIRMOBILE
MAGNETIZE	CONESTOGA	CRYOGENIC	BEACHHEAD	GOLDENROD	RANGELAND	UNLEARNED	ALIENABLE
MECHANIZE	DYSPEPSIA	DIACRITIC	BEDSPREAD	GOLDFIELD	RECOMMEND	UNPLUMBED	ALLEVIATE
MERCERIZE	EMPHYSEMA	DIALECTIC	BENIGHTED	GRASSLAND	REPREHEND	UNRIVALED	ALLOWANCE

ALMANDITE	BICONCAVE	CHOCOLATE	DECALOGUE	DOWNRANGE	EXPLETIVE	GALVANIZE	HYPERBOLE
ALMSHOUSE	BIFURCATE	CHONDRITE	DECISTERE	DOWNSTAGE	EXPLICATE	GARNISHEE	HYPHENATE
ALONGSIDE	BIOSPHERE	CHONDRULE	DECOLLETE	DRAINPIPE	EXPLOSIVE	GARNITURE	IGNORANCE
ALTERNATE	BIPARTITE	CHOPHOUSE	DECOMPOSE	DRAMATIZE	EXPURGATE	GAUCHERIE	ILLEGIBLE
ALUMINIZE	BIRDHOUSE	CHRONICLE	DECOUPAGE	DRUGSTORE	EXQUISITE	GELIGNITE	IMBALANCE
AMBULANCE	BIRTHRATE	CHUCKHOLE	DEFECTIVE	DUPLICATE	EXTEMPORE	GERMICIDE	IMITATIVE
AMBUSCADE	BLASPHEME	CIGARETTE	DEFENSIVE	ECONOMIZE	EXTENSIVE	GERMINATE	IMMEDIATE
AMPHIBOLE	BLOODLINE	CIRCULATE	DEFERENCE	EFFECTIVE	EXTENUATE	GLADSTONE	IMMIGRATE
AMPLITUDE	BOMBAZINE	CLASSMATE	DEFOLIATE	EFFLUENCE	EXTIRPATE	GLAMORIZE	IMMOVABLE
ANATOMIZE	BOOKPLATE	CLEARANCE	DEHYDRATE	EGLANTINE	EXTRADITE	GLYCOSIDE	IMMUTABLE
ANCHORAGE	BRASSERIE	CLIENTELE	DEKASTERE	EJACULATE	EXTRICATE	GRANDIOSE	IMPASSIVE
ANCHORITE	BRASSIERE	CLOCKWISE	DELFTWARE	ELABORATE	EXTRUSIVE	GRANULATE	IMPEDANCE
ANGLICIZE	BRIEFCASE	CLOISONNE	DELINEATE	ELECTRODE	FABRICATE	GRAPEVINE	IMPLICATE
ANKLEBONE	BRIMSTONE	CLUBHOUSE	DEMAGOGUE	ELIMINATE	FACSIMILE	GRATICULE	IMPORTUNE
ANNOYANCE	BRIQUETTE	COAGULATE	DEMARCATE	ELSEWHERE	FANTASIZE	GRATITUDE	IMPOSTURE
ANTICLINE	BROADSIDE	COASTLINE	DEMIMONDE	ELUCIDATE	FARMHOUSE	GRAVITATE	IMPRECATE
APOLOGIZE	BROCHETTE	COFEATURE	DEMITASSE	EMBRASURE	FASCINATE	GRENADINE	IMPRECISE
APPELLATE	BROKERAGE	COIFFEUSE	DEMURRAGE	EMBROCATE	FAVORABLE	GRIEVANCE	IMPROVISE
APPENDAGE	BRUTALIZE	COLLEAGUE	DENIGRATE	EMPENNAGE	FEBRIFUGE	GROTESQUE	IMPULSIVE
APPLIANCE	BUMBLEBEE	COLLIMATE	DEODORIZE	EMPHASIZE	FECUNDATE	GROUPWARE	INANIMATE
APPOINTEE	BURLESQUE	COLONNADE	DEOXIDIZE	ENCOURAGE	FERTILIZE	GRUBSTAKE	INCAPABLE
AQUAPLANE	CALABOOSE	COLUMBINE	DEPARTURE	ENDOCRINE	FIREHOUSE	GUARANTEE	INCARNATE
ARABESQUE	CALCIMINE	COMMINGLE	DEPRECATE	ENDOSCOPE	FIREPLACE	GUIDELINE	INCENTIVE
ARBITRATE	CALCULATE	COMMITTEE	DESECRATE	ENDURANCE	FLAGSTONE	GYROSCOPE	INCIDENCE
ARCHETYPE	CALIBRATE	COMMODORE	DESICCATE	ENRAPTURE	FLAMMABLE	HABITABLE	INCOMMODE
ARGENTINE	CAMPANILE	COMPOSITE	DESIGNATE	ENSHEATHE	FLASHCUBE	HABITUATE	INCULCATE
ARGENTITE	CANDIDATE	COMPOSURE	DESIRABLE	ENTOURAGE	FLASHTUBE	HAILSTONE	INCULPATE
ARMISTICE	CANEBRAKE	CONCIERGE	DESPERATE	ENUMERATE	FLOODGATE	HAIRPIECE	INCURABLE
ARTERIOLE	CANNONADE	CONCOURSE	DESTITUTE	ENUNCIATE	FLOPHOUSE	HAIRSTYLE	INDELIBLE
ARTICHOKE	CANTABILE	CONCUBINE	DESUETUDE	ENWREATHE	FLUCTUATE	HAMMERTOE	INDENTURE
ASSOCIATE	CAPSULATE	CONJUGATE	DETECTIVE	EPHEDRINE	FOOTLOOSE	HANDSHAKE	INDUCTIVE
ASSONANCE	CAPTIVATE	CONSTABLE	DETERMINE	EQUIPOISE	FORECLOSE	HANDSPIKE	INEBRIATE
ASSURANCE	CARBONATE	COOPERATE	DEVASTATE	EQUITABLE	FORESHORE	HARBORAGE	INEFFABLE
ASTRADDLE	CARBUNCLE	CORPORATE	DHRYSTONE	ERADICATE	FORETASTE	HARMONIZE	INFANTILE
ASTROLABE	CARBURIZE	CORPUSCLE	DIATOMITE	ERSTWHILE	FORMALIZE	HEADPHONE	INFATUATE
ASYMPTOTE	CARNIVORE	CORRELATE	DIRECTIVE	ESPIONAGE	FORMATIVE	HEADPIECE	INFERENCE
ATTENUATE	CARTILAGE	CORRUGATE	DIRIGIBLE	ESPLANADE	FORMULATE	HEADSTONE	INFERTILE
ATTRIBUTE	CARTRIDGE	CORTISONE	DISCHARGE	ESTIMABLE	FORTITUDE	HEARTACHE	INFLUENCE
AUTHORIZE	CASSEROLE	CORUSCATE	DISCOURSE	ETIQUETTE	FORTUNATE	HELLEBORE	INFURIATE
AUTOTRACE	CASTIGATE	COVALENCE	DISENGAGE	EVAPORATE	FOURSCORE	HERBICIDE	INFUSIBLE
AVAILABLE	CAUTERIZE	CRANKCASE	DISFIGURE	EVAPORITE	FRANCHISE	HERITABLE	INJUSTICE
AVALANCHE	CAVALCADE	CRINOLINE	DISLOCATE	EVENTUATE	FRANGIBLE	HERMITAGE	INNERSOLE
BACKSLIDE	CELANDINE	CRITICIZE	DISMANTLE	EVERGLADE	FREESTONE	HIBERNATE	INNOCENCE
BACKSTAGE	CELEBRATE	CROCODILE	DISOBLIGE	EXCITABLE	FRICASSEE	HINDRANCE	INOCULATE
BAGATELLE	CELLARAGE	CROQUETTE	DISPARAGE	EXCLUSIVE	FRIEDCAKE	HISTAMINE	INSATIATE
BAMBOOZLE	CELLULOSE	CROSSWISE	DISPARATE	EXCORIATE	FROSTBITE	HITCHHIKE	INSENSATE
BANDEROLE	CENTIPEDE	CUBBYHOLE	DISPLEASE	EXCULPATE	FRUITCAKE	HOLYSTONE	INSINCERE
BANQUETTE	CEREBRATE	CULMINATE	DISPRAISE	EXCURSIVE	FRUSTRATE	HOMOPHONE	INSINUATE
BARCAROLE	CERTITUDE	CULTIVATE	DISREPUTE	EXECRABLE	FULMINATE	HONORABLE	INSOLUBLE
BARRICADE	CHALLENGE	CURETTAGE	DISSEMBLE	EXECUTIVE	FUNGICIDE	HOROSCOPE	INSTIGATE
BATHHOUSE	CHAMOMILE	CURVATURE	DISSIPATE	EXISTENCE	FURNITURE	HORSEHIDE	INSTITUTE
BEATITUDE	CHAMPAGNE	CUSTOMIZE	DISSOLUTE	EXONERATE	FUSILLADE	HORSESHOE	INSURABLE
BELLICOSE	CHANTEUSE	CYCLAMATE	DIVISIBLE	EXOSPHERE	GABARDINE	HORTATIVE	INSURANCE
BELLYACHE	CHECKMATE	DAMASCENE	DOCTORATE	EXPANSIVE	GABERDINE	HOUSEWIFE	INTEGRATE
BELVEDERE	CHEEKBONE	DEBENTURE	DOMINANCE	EXPATIATE	GALACTOSE	HUMILIATE	INTENSIVE
BENTONITE	CHICKADEE	DEBUTANTE	DOORPLATE	EXPENSIVE	GALLINULE	HURRICANE	INTERCEDE
BESPANGLE	CHLORDANE	DECADENCE	DOWNGRADE	EXPERTISE	GALLSTONE	HYDROXIDE	INTERFACE

INTERFERE	MAGNITUDE	MULTITUDE	PATRONIZE	PROSECUTE	RETENTIVE	STAIRCASE	TIMETABLE
INTERFUSE	MAINFRAME	NAMEPLATE	PEACETIME	PROSELYTE	RETROFIRE	STALEMATE	TOLERABLE
INTERLACE	MAJORETTE	NARCOTIZE	PEDAGOGUE	PROSTRATE	REVERENCE	STAMINATE	TOLERANCE
INTERLINE	MAJUSCULE	NARRATIVE	PEGMATITE	PROTOTYPE	REVOCABLE	STANDPIPE	TOLLHOUSE
INTERLOPE	MALACHITE	NAVIGABLE	PEKINGESE	PROVOLONE	RIDGEPOLE	STATESIDE	TOMBSTONE
INTERLUDE	MALLEABLE	NECTARINE	PENETRATE	PROXIMATE	RIGMAROLE	STATUETTE	TOOTHACHE
INTERNODE	MANGANESE	NEGOTIATE	PENTHOUSE	PUBLICIZE	RIVERSIDE	STERILIZE	TOOTHSOME
INTERPOSE	MANHANDLE	NEGRITUDE	PERCHANCE	PUISSANCE	RUSTICATE	STEVEDORE	TRACTABLE
INTERVENE	MANOEUVRE	NEVERMORE	PERCOLATE	PULVERIZE	SACRIFICE	STIMULATE	TRANSDUCE
INTESTATE	MARGARINE	NIGHTLIFE	PERFORATE	PUNCTUATE	SACRILEGE	STIPULATE	TRANSFUSE
INTESTINE	MARMALADE	NIGHTMARE	PERISCOPE	PURGATIVE	SAILPLANE	STOCKPILE	TRANSLATE
INTRICATE	MASCULINE	NIGHTTIME	PERISTYLE	PURSUANCE	SANDSTONE	STRICTURE	TRANSMUTE
INTRODUCE	MASTICATE	NIGRITUDE	PERMEABLE	QUADRILLE	SATELLITE	STRUCTURE	TRANSPIRE
INTUMESCE	MATRICIDE	NORMALIZE	PERSECUTE	QUADRUPLE	SATURNINE	SUBALPINE	TRANSPOSE
INVECTIVE	MEANWHILE	NORMATIVE	PERSEVERE	QUARTZITE	SAXIFRAGE	SUBDIVIDE	TREMATODE
INVENTIVE	MECHANIZE	NOSEPIECE	PERSONAGE	QUICKLIME	SAXOPHONE	SUBJUGATE	TRITURATE
INVIOLATE	MEDICABLE	NOVELETTE	PERSONATE	QUICKTIME	SCHEELITE	SUBLIMATE	TURNSTILE
INVISIBLE	MEGACYCLE	NOVITIATE	PESTHOUSE	QUINTUPLE	SCRIMMAGE	SUBMARINE	TURNTABLE
INVOLUCRE	MEGAPHONE	OBEISANCE	PESTICIDE	QUITTANCE	SCRIPTURE	SUBSCRIBE	TURPITUDE
IRASCIBLE	MELIORATE	OBFUSCATE	PHALAROPE	RABBINATE	SCULPTURE	SUBSIDIZE	TURQUOISE
IRONSTONE	MEMORABLE	OBJECTIVE	PHEROMONE	RACEHORSE	SECRETIVE	SUBSTANCE	TYPEWRITE
IRRADIATE	MENAGERIE	OBJURGATE	PHOSPHATE	RANDOMIZE	SEGREGATE	SUFFOCATE	TYRANNIZE
IRRITABLE	MENOPAUSE	OBSTINATE	PINEAPPLE	RASTERIZE	SEMAPHORE	SUGARCANE	ULTRAPURE
ISRAELITE	MERCERIZE	OFFENSIVE	PINSTRIPE	RATIONALE	SEMBLANCE	SUMMARIZE	UNDECEIVE
ITALICIZE	MESCALINE	OFFICIATE	PIROUETTE	REACTANCE	SENSITIVE	SUNSTROKE	UNDERDONE
JACKKNIFE	MESMERIZE	OPERATIVE	PLAINTIVE	RECEPTIVE	SENSITIZE	SUPERPOSE	UNDERLINE
JESSAMINE	METALWARE	OPPORTUNE	PLATITUDE	RECESSIVE	SEPARABLE	SUPERSEDE	UNDERMINE
JUXTAPOSE	METEORITE	ORANGEADE	PLAUSIBLE	RECHERCHE	SEPULTURE	SUPERVENE	UNDERRATE
KILOCYCLE	METHADONE	ORDINANCE	PLAYHOUSE	RECOGNIZE	SERVITUDE	SUPERVISE	UNDERSIDE
KINESCOPE	METHODIZE	ORIENTATE	PLENITUDE	RECONCILE	SHAREWARE	SUPPURATE	UNDERTAKE
KNOWLEDGE	METRICIZE	ORIFLAMME	PLOWSHARE	RECONDITE	SHELLFIRE	SURCHARGE	UNDERTONE
LAGNIAPPE	METRONOME	ORIGINATE	PLURALIZE	RECTANGLE	SHIPSHAPE	SURCINGLE	UNSHACKLE
LANDSCAPE	MEZZANINE	ORPHANAGE	POLITESSE	RECTITUDE	SHORTCAKE	SURROGATE	UNSHEATHE
LANDSLIDE	MICROWAVE	OSCILLATE	POORHOUSE	REENFORCE	SHORTWAVE	SYMBOLIZE	UPPERCASE
LASSITUDE	MILESTONE	OSTRACIZE	PORCUPINE	REFERENCE	SHOWPIECE	SYNAGOGUE	UTTERANCE
LAVALIERE	MILLIPEDE	OTHERWISE	POSTHASTE	REFLEXIVE	SHOWPLACE	SYNDICATE	VACCINATE
LEASTWISE	MILLSTONE	OUBLIETTE	POSTULATE	REIMBURSE	SHRINKAGE	SYSTEMIZE	VACILLATE
LEGISLATE	MINIATURE	OVERDRIVE	POTENTATE	REINFORCE	SIDEPIECE	TABLEWARE	VALENTINE
LEUKOCYTE	MINISCULE	OVERSTATE	POURBOIRE	REINSTATE	SIDESWIPE	TALKATIVE	VANDALIZE
LIBERTINE	MINISTATE	OVERWRITE	PRECIPICE	REITERATE	SIGNALIZE	TANGERINE	VAPORWARE
LIGHTFACE	MINUSCULE	OXYGENATE	PREDICATE	RELEVANCE	SIGNATURE	TANTALIZE	VARIEGATE
LIGHTSOME	MISBEHAVE	PACKHORSE	PREFIGURE	REMINISCE	SILTSTONE	TEAKETTLE	VASSALAGE
LIMESTONE	MISCHANCE	PALATABLE	PREGNABLE	RENCONTRE	SKIMOBILE	TECHNIQUE	VEGETABLE
LIMOUSINE	MISERABLE	PALPITATE	PREJUDICE	REPLICATE	SKYLOUNGE	TELEPHONE	VEHEMENCE
LIQUIDATE	MISHANDLE	PANHANDLE	PREMATURE	REPORTAGE	SNAKEBITE	TELESCOPE	VENERABLE
LITHESOME	MISMANAGE	PANTOMIME	PRESCRIBE	REPROBATE	SNOWFLAKE	TEMPERATE	VENGEANCE
LOADSTONE	MISTLETOE	PAPILLOTE	PRIMITIVE	REPRODUCE	SOAPSTONE	TEMPORIZE	VENTILATE
LOATHSOME	MODERNIZE	PARACHUTE	PRINCIPLE	REPUDIATE	SOCIALITE	TENDERIZE	VENTRICLE
LODESTONE	MONOLOGUE	PARRICIDE	PRINTABLE	REPULSIVE	SOCIALIZE	TENTATIVE	VERBALIZE
LONGITUDE	MONOPLANE	PARSONAGE	PRIVILEGE	REPUTABLE	SOLEMNIZE	TERMINATE	VERITABLE
LORGNETTE	MONOSPACE	PARTITIVE	PROBATIVE	REQUISITE	SOLITAIRE	TERRORIZE	VERMIFUGE
LOWERCASE	MOONSCAPE	PARTRIDGE	PROCEDURE	RESERPINE	SOMEWHERE	THEREFORE	VERNALIZE
LUBRICATE	MOONSHINE	PASSERINE	PROCREATE	RESHUFFLE	SOPHOMORE	THIGHBONE	VERSATILE
LUCRATIVE	MOONSTONE	PASTORALE	PROMENADE	RESIDENCE	SOUBRETTE	THREESOME	VESTIBULE
LUXURIATE	MOTORBIKE	PASTURAGE	PRONOUNCE	RESONANCE	SPECTACLE	THYROXINE	VICTIMIZE
MAGNETITE	MOTORCADE	PATRICIDE	PROPAGATE	RETALIATE	SPECULATE	TIGHTROPE	VIDEOTAPE
MAGNETIZE	MOUSTACHE	PATRONAGE	PROSCRIBE	RETARDATE	STABILIZE	TIMEPIECE	VIGILANCE

VIGILANTE	DITHERING	UNFEELING	PRELAUNCH	GANGPLANK	AUCTORIAL	ILLOGICAL	TRACKBALL
VILLENAGE	DOWNSWING	UNKNOWING	REFURBISH	GOLDBRICK	BACCHANAL	IMPARTIAL	TREADMILL
VINDICATE	EARTHLING	UNMEANING	REPLENISH	GREENBACK	BACKPEDAL	INAUGURAL	TRIENNIAL
VISUALIZE	EASYGOING	UNSPARING	SACKCLOTH	GRILLWORK	BEAUTIFUL	JURIDICAL	UNDERSELL
VOUCHSAFE	ENGRAVING	UNWILLING	SAGEBRUSH	GUIDEBOOK	BICAMERAL	MAGISTRAL	UNISEXUAL
VULCANIZE	FARSEEING	UNWITTING	SAILCLOTH	GUNNYSACK	BILATERAL	MARMOREAL	UNIVERSAL
VULGARIZE	FASTENING	WALLOPING	SERIGRAPH	HANDIWORK	BILINGUAL	MARSUPIAL	UNMINDFUL
WAGONETTE	FINGERING	WHIRLIGIG	SHELLFISH	HAVERSACK	BINOMINAL	MASTERFUL	UNNATURAL
WAISTLINE	FINICKING	WORLDLING	SPICEBUSH	HEARTSICK	BLACKBALL	MATUTINAL	VERIDICAL
WAREHOUSE	FIRSTLING	WRESTLING	SQUEAMISH	HOLLYHOCK	BLACKMAIL	MEDICINAL	VERTEBRAL
WASHHOUSE	FLAVORING	YOUNGLING	STOPWATCH	HORSEBACK	BOMBSHELL	MEGAPIXEL	VICENNIAL
WATCHCASE	FLEDGLING	AFTERMATH	SUCCOTASH	HOUSEWORK	BOUNTIFUL	MERCURIAL	VICEREGAL
WATERLINE	FOLLOWING	ANGELFISH	SWORDFISH	HUNCHBACK	BROADTAIL	MUNICIPAL	VIGESIMAL
WATERSIDE	FOREGOING	AUTOGRAPH	TELEGRAPH	INGLENOOK	BRONCHIAL	NIGHTFALL	WATERFALL
WAVETABLE	FORGIVING	BACKSLASH	THEREWITH	INTERLINK	CAMPSTOOL	NOCTURNAL	WATERFOWL
WEARISOME	FOUNDLING	BAKSHEESH	ULTRAHIGH	INTERLOCK	CANONICAL	NONPAREIL	WHIMSICAL
WHALEBONE	GROUNDHOG	BANDWIDTH	UNSELFISH	JAILBREAK	CARROUSEL	NUMERICAL	WHIRLPOOL
WHEELBASE	GROUNDING	BAROGRAPH	WASHCLOTH	LEAFSTALK	CARTWHEEL	PAROCHIAL	WHITEHALL
WHEREFORE	HAMSTRING	BATHOLITH	WHEREWITH	LIVESTOCK	CATERWAUL	PERENNIAL	WHITETAIL
WHETSTONE	HAPPENING	BLOODBATH	WHITEFISH	MATCHBOOK	CATHEDRAL	PERPETUAL	WHITEWALL
WHOLESALE	INGROWING	BLOWTORCH	WHITEWASH	MATCHLOCK	CELESTIAL	PERSONNEL	WINDCHILL
WHOLESOME	JITTERBUG	BUCKTOOTH	WORKBENCH	METALWORK	CHAPARRAL	PHOTOCELL	WONDERFUL
WINTERIZE	LEAVENING	BULLFINCH	MAHARISHI	NIGHTHAWK	CLAMSHELL	PICTORIAL	ALGORITHM
WIREFRAME	LIGHTNING	CERECLOTH	PAKISTANI	NOTCHBACK	CLASSICAL	PIECEMEAL	ALUMINIUM
WOEBEGONE	LITTERBUG	CHAFFINCH	POTPOURRI	OVERTRICK	COCHINEAL	PIMPERNEL	AMERICIUM
WOLFSBANE	MISGIVING	COCKROACH	SPAGHETTI	PAPERBACK	COCKATIEL	PLENTIFUL	ANARCHISM
WOLVERINE	OFFSPRING	DISHCLOTH	AFTERDECK	PATCHWORK	CONGENIAL	POLITICAL	ANGLEWORM
WOMANLIKE	PLAYTHING	EMBELLISH	ANTIKNOCK	PICKABACK	CONNUBIAL	POSTNATAL	ANIMALISM
WORKHORSE	PRECEDING	ESTABLISH	APPLEJACK	PIECEWORK	CONTINUAL	POTENTIAL	ANTISERUM
WORKHOUSE	PROMISING	FORTHWITH	APPLETALK	PIGGYBACK	CONVIVIAL	PRACTICAL	ARBORETUM
WORKPLACE	RECKONING	GIBBERISH	AWESTRUCK	PITCHFORK	CORPOREAL	PRAYERFUL	ATHENAEUM
WORKTABLE	RECORDING	GOLDFINCH	BACKTRACK	PLACEKICK	CUSTODIAL	PRECANCEL	BACTERIUM
WORLDWIDE	REGARDING	GOLDSMITH	BAILIWICK	POPPYCOCK	DAREDEVIL	PRESCHOOL	BARBARISM
WORRISOME	REHEARING	HAIRBRUSH	BEEFSTEAK	PRESHRUNK	DECEITFUL	PREVERBAL	BARNSTORM
XANTHIPPE	REVOLTING	HAIRCLOTH	BIRTHMARK	RACETRACK	DECENNIAL	PRINCIPAL	BERKELIUM
XEROPHYTE	SCANTLING	HEMISTICH	BLACKJACK	RIVERBANK	DECONTROL	PROCONSUL	BERYLLIUM
XYLOPHONE	SCHILLING	HEMSTITCH	BLUEBLACK	ROADBLOCK	EDITORIAL	PROVENCAL	BROADLOOM
BOMBPROOF	SCREENING	HOLOGRAPH	BOARDWALK	ROOTSTOCK	EFFECTUAL	PUERPERAL	CABLEGRAM
BOOKSHELF	SEAFARING	HOMOGRAPH	BOLSHEVIK	ROUGHNECK	EMPIRICAL	QUIZZICAL	CALVINISM
FEEDSTUFF	SEASONING	HOPSCOTCH	BOOTBLACK	SCRAPBOOK	EPHEMERAL	REHEARSAL	CATACLYSM
FIREPROOF	SHEATHING	JELLYFISH	BUSHWHACK	SHIPWRECK	EPISCOPAL	SALESGIRL	CATECHISM
FLAGSTAFF	SKYDIVING	LABYRINTH	CAMELBACK	SIDETRACK	EQUIVOCAL	SARTORIAL	CENTIGRAM
FOODSTUFF	SOMETHING	LACCOLITH	CHECKBOOK	SMALLTALK	ESSENTIAL	SCHLEMIEL	CHECKROOM
FOOLPROOF	SPINDLING	LOCKSMITH	CHOPSTICK	THROWBACK	FACTORIAL	SCOUNDREL	CLASSROOM
INTERLEAF	SPLITTING	LOINCLOTH	CLOCKWORK	THUMBTACK	FINANCIAL	SCREWBALL	COFFERDAM
PIKESTAFF	STARTLING	MACINTOSH	CORNSTALK	TOOTHPICK	FOOTSTOOL	SECTIONAL	COLLEGIUM
PLAINTIFF	STRAPPING	MATRIARCH	CROSSWALK	TOWNSFOLK	FORESTALL	SEMIFINAL	COLLUVIUM
WINDPROOF	STRIPLING	MEGADEATH	DISEMBARK	TRADEMARK	FRATERNAL	SPEEDWELL	COMMUNISM
ADJOINING	SUFFERING	MONOGRAPH	DRUMSTICK	WATERMARK	FREEWHEEL	SPIRITUAL	CONTINUUM
AFFECTING	SUPPOSING	MOUTHWASH	EARTHWORK	WINDBREAK	FRIGHTFUL	SPOONBILL	CONUNDRUM
BESETTING	SURVEYING	OUTGROWTH	FANCYWORK	WISECRACK	GRISTMILL	STAIRWELL	COURTROOM
BOOMERANG	TIMBERING	OVERMATCH	FEEDSTOCK	WOMENFOLK	HEADSTALL	SUBNORMAL	CRETINISM
BOWSTRING	TWINKLING	OVERREACH	FIREBREAK	WOODBLOCK	HEALTHFUL	SWORDTAIL	CRITICISM
CARPETBAG	UNBENDING	OVERWEIGH	FIREBRICK	WOODCHUCK	HORSETAIL	TECHNICAL	CRUCIFORM
CARPETING	UNCEASING	PARAGRAPH	FLASHBACK	YARDSTICK	HYDROFOIL	THUMBNAIL	CUNEIFORM
DESIGNING	UNDERLING	PATRIARCH	FLINTLOCK	ANTINOVEL	IDENTICAL	TOADSTOOL	CYTOPLASM
DIPHTHONG	UNFAILING	POLYGRAPH	FRAMEWORK	ARCHANGEL	ILLIBERAL	TONSORIAL	DARWINISM

DEFEATISM	PESSIMISM	APPORTION	CONTUSION	GROOMSMAN	NUTRITION	SECTARIAN	YACHTSMAN
DEUTERIUM	PETROLEUM	ASCENSION	COTILLION	GROSGRAIN	OBSESSION	SELECTION	ZWINGLIAN
DIAPHRAGM	PLUTONIUM	ASCERTAIN	COTYLEDON	GUARDSMAN	OMBUDSMAN	SELECTMAN	ANTIPASTO
DISESTEEM	POTASSIUM	ASPERSION	COUNTDOWN	GUNCOTTON	ONIONSKIN	SEMICOLON	ARMADILLO
DOGMATISM	PRESIDIUM	ASSERTION	COURTESAN	GYRFALCON	OPERATION	SENSATION	BASTINADO
EARTHWORM	PRESSROOM	ASTRAKHAN	CRACKDOWN	HALLOWEEN	OUTSPOKEN	SEVENTEEN	CAPRICCIO
ECOSYSTEM	PSEUDONYM	ATTENTION	CRAFTSMAN	HANDWOVEN	OVERBLOWN	SHAKEDOWN	CENTESIMO
EFFLUVIUM	PYRETHRUM	ATTRITION	CRITERION	HARLEQUIN	OXIDATION	SHARKSKIN	CIGARILLO
ELBOWROOM	RACIALISM	AUTOMATON	CUSTODIAN	HARTSHORN	PALANQUIN	SHEEPSKIN	CONTRALTO
EUPHEMISM	RADIOGRAM	AVOCATION	CYCLOTRON	HEARTBURN	PARATHION	SHORTHORN	CRESCENDO
EXTREMISM	RAINSTORM	BADMINTON	DALMATION	HELVETIAN	PARTITION	SIGNALMAN	DESPERADO
FETISHISM	ROUNDWORM	BALDACHIN	DAMNATION	HERCULEAN	PATRICIAN	SIMPLETON	ESPERANTO
FEUDALISM	RUTHENIUM	BANDWAGON	DANDELION	HISTORIAN	PATROLMAN	SINGLETON	GLISSANDO
FLAGELLUM	SANDSTORM	BANTUSTAN	DECATHLON	HOBGOBLIN	PENEPLAIN	SITUATION	IMBROGLIO
FORMALISM	SNOWSTORM	BARBARIAN	DECEPTION	HOMEGROWN	PERDITION	SOVEREIGN	INCOGNITO
GALVANISM	SOCIALISM	BATTALION	DEDUCTION	HONEYMOON	PERSIMMON	SPOKESMAN	MAGNIFICO
GERMANIUM	STATEROOM	BEDRIDDEN	DEFLATION	HUNGARIAN	PHYSICIAN	SPORTSMAN	MAJORDOMO
GREENROOM	STOREROOM	BOATSWAIN	DEJECTION	IMITATION	POLICEMAN	STANCHION	MANIFESTO
GUARDROOM	STRATAGEM	BONDWOMAN	DENTITION	IMPULSION	PORCELAIN	STATESMAN	OBBLIGATO
GYMNASIUM	STRONTIUM	BRAZILIAN	DETENTION	INANITION	POSTILION	STILLBORN	PISTACHIO
HAILSTORM	SUGARPLUM	BREAKDOWN	DIMENSION	INCEPTION	PRECISION	SUBALTERN	PIZZICATO
HARMONIUM	SYLLOGISM	BULGARIAN	DIRECTION	INCURSION	PREDATION	SUFFRAGAN	POLITBURO
HECTOGRAM	SYMBOLISM	BURUNDIAN	DISBURDEN	INDENTION	PREORDAIN	SUMMATION	PORTFOLIO
HELLENISM	SYMPOSIUM	CANDLEPIN	DIVERSION	INDUCTION	PREVISION	SUSPICION	PUNCTILIO
HERBARIUM	SYNERGISM	CAPARISON	DRAFTSMAN	INFECTION	PRIVATION	SWANSDOWN	SIMPATICO
HISTOGRAM	TECTONISM	CARIBBEAN	EDUCATION	INFLATION	PROBATION	SWITCHMAN	TELEPHOTO
LANTHANUM	TELLURIUM	CARNATION	EIDERDOWN	INFLEXION	PRONGHORN	SWORDSMAN	THEREUNTO
LITERATIM	TERRARIUM	CARNELIAN	ELEVATION	INJECTION	PROTOZOAN	TANZANIAN	ZUCCHETTO
LOGARITHM	TERRORISM	CATAMARAN	ELOCUTION	INSERTION	PROVISION	TARPAULIN	BUTTERCUP
LUNCHROOM	THEREFROM	CAUCASIAN	ENLIGHTEN	INTENTION	PTARMIGAN	THEREUPON	COURTSHIP
MACROCOSM	THRALLDOM	CAUSATION	ENTERTAIN	INTUITION	PURGATION	TOUCHDOWN	EAVESDROP
MAELSTROM	TRANSFORM	CENTURION	EPICUREAN	INVENTION	QUOTIDIAN	TRADESMAN	FILMSTRIP
MAGNESIUM	ULTIMATUM	CESSATION	ERUDITION	INVERSION	REBELLION	TRADITION	FINGERTIP
MAGNETISM	VANDALISM	CHAMELEON	ETHIOPIAN	ITERATION	RECEPTION	TRAGEDIAN	HANDCLASP
MANNERISM	VERMIFORM	CHAMPAIGN	EUCLIDEAN	KINSWOMAN	RECESSION	TRIBESMAN	HORSEWHIP
MARTYRDOM	VOLCANISM	CHARLATAN	EVERGREEN	KNOCKDOWN	RECURSION	TRUNCHEON	LIGHTSHIP
MASOCHISM	VOODOOISM	CHARWOMAN	EVOLUTION	LAMEBRAIN	REDACTION	UKRAINIAN	MOUSETRAP
MAUSOLEUM	VULCANISM	CHIEFTAIN	EXCEPTION	LEVIATHAN	REDUCTION	UNBEKNOWN	OVERSLEEP
MECHANISM	VULGARISM	CHILBLAIN	EXCURSION	LIBRARIAN	REFECTION	UNCERTAIN	QUICKSTEP
MICROCOSM	WINDSTORM	CHRISTIAN	EXPANSION	LIVERYMAN	REMISSION	UNCONCERN	SHORTSTOP
MICROFILM	WITTICISM	CHURCHMAN	EXPLOSION	MALATHION	RENDITION	UNITARIAN	SPACESHIP
MICROGRAM	YTTERBIUM	CIRCADIAN	EXPULSION	MALAYSIAN	REPAIRMAN	UNWRITTEN	STEAMSHIP
MIDSTREAM	ZIRCONIUM	CLERGYMAN	EXTENSION	MANHATTAN	REPLETION	VALUATION	SWEATSHOP
MILLIGRAM	ACCESSION	CLINICIAN	EYESTRAIN	MANNEQUIN	REPULSION	VARIATION	TRANSSHIP
MISINFORM	ACCORDION	COALITION	FELLOWMAN	MEDALLION	RESECTION	VELVETEEN	TROOPSHIP
MODERNISM	ACCRETION	COGNITION	FIRSTBORN	MIDDLEMAN	RETENTION	VENIREMAN	TURBOPROP
MONGOLISM	ADDICTION	COLLATION	FISHERMAN	MINUTEMAN	REVERSION	VERMILION	WORKGROUP
MULTIFORM	ADMISSION	COLLEGIAN	FLOTATION	MISGOVERN	REVULSION	VESTRYMAN	ALABASTER
MYSTICISM	AFFECTION	COLLODION	FORETOKEN	MONGOLIAN	ROUMANIAN	VIBRATION	ALLIGATOR
NEODYMIUM	AFTERNOON	COLLUSION	FOREWOMAN	MORTICIAN	RUINATION	VICTORIAN	ALTIMETER
NEOLOGISM	ALGONQUIN	COMMOTION	FORMATION	MULTISCAN	SACCHARIN	VIOLATION	ANNOUNCER
NEPTUNIUM	AMPHIBIAN	COMMUNION	FREEMASON	MULTISPIN	SACRISTAN	VULGARIAN	ANTECHOIR
OCCULTISM	ANCHORMAN	COMPANION	GENTLEMAN	MUSKMELON	SALVATION	WASHBASIN	ANTITUMOR
OVERWHELM	ANIMATION	CONDITION	GESTATION	MUSSULMAN	SCUTCHEON	WASHWOMAN	APPETIZER
PACHYDERM	ANTITOXIN	CONFUSION	GRADATION	NIGHTGOWN	SECESSION	WHEREUPON	ARTICULAR
PALLADIUM	ANTIVENIN	CONSTRAIN	GRANTSMAN	NONPERSON	SECLUSION	WINDBLOWN	ARTIFICER
PANTHEISM	APPERTAIN	CONTAGION	GREENHORN	NORWEGIAN	SECRETION	WITHDRAWN	ASSEMBLER

ATTAINDER	DISTEMPER	MANOMETER	REGISTRAR	WRONGDOER	DANGEROUS	LAZYBONES	SUMPTUOUS
AURICULAR	DOSIMETER	MANSLAYER	REJOINDER	YOUNGSTER	DAUNTLESS	LITIGIOUS	SYMBIOSIS
AVUNCULAR	DOWITCHER	MAYFLOWER	REMAINDER	ACIDULOUS	DEATHLESS	LOGISTICS	SYNTHESIS
BACKWATER	EGGBEATER	MELTWATER	RESERVOIR	ACOUSTICS	DECIDUOUS	LUDICROUS	TECTONICS
BALLADEER	ELASTOMER	MERGANSER	RESONATOR	ACROPOLIS	DELICIOUS	MARVELOUS	TENACIOUS
BANDOLIER	EMBROIDER	MESSENGER	RETRIEVER	AFRIKAANS	DEXTEROUS	MECHANICS	TENEBROUS
BARKEEPER	ENCOUNTER	MIDSUMMER	RHEOMETER	AILANTHUS	DIAERESIS	MELODIOUS	THANKLESS
BAROMETER	ENERGIZER	MIDWINTER	ROSEWATER	ALBATROSS	DIAGNOSIS	MERCUROUS	THEATRICS
BARRISTER	EPICENTER	MINELAYER	RUMRUNNER	AMARYLLIS	DIETETICS	MESSIEURS	THESAURUS
BARTENDER	ESCALATOR	MISSIONER	SAFFLOWER	AMBERGRIS	DIGITALIS	MOMENTOUS	THICKNESS
BEEFEATER	EXCELSIOR	MODERATOR	SALTPETER	AMBIGUOUS	DIPTEROUS	MURDEROUS	TRAPPINGS
BEEKEEPER	EXCHEQUER	MONSIGNOR	SALTWATER	AMBITIOUS	DOUBTLESS	NARCISSUS	TREMULOUS
BELEAGUER	EXPEDITER	MUCKRAKER	SANDPAPER	AMIDSHIPS	ECONOMICS	NEFARIOUS	TRIFOCALS
BESPATTER	EXPOSITOR	NANOMETER	SANDPIPER	AMORPHOUS	EDELWEISS	NEPHRITIS	TYRANNOUS
BINOCULAR	FINANCIER	NEWSPAPER	SAPSUCKER	ANALOGOUS	EGREGIOUS	NOTORIOUS	UMBILICUS
BOOKMAKER	FIREPOWER	NONREADER	SCAVENGER	ANHYDROUS	EMBARRASS	OBLIVIOUS	UNANIMOUS
BUCCANEER	FIREWATER	NUMERATOR	SCHNAUZER	ANOMALOUS	ENCOMPASS	OBNOXIOUS	UNDERPASS
BYSTANDER	FOREIGNER	OUTNUMBER	SCRIVENER	ANONYMOUS	ENTERITIS	OFFICIOUS	UNHARNESS
CANNONEER	FORESWEAR	OUTRIGGER	SEMILUNAR	ANOPHELES	EPIDERMIS	OURSELVES	VAGARIOUS
CAPACITOR	FORGATHER	OVERPOWER	SEPARATOR	APPARATUS	EROGENOUS	OUTSKIRTS	VAGINITIS
CARETAKER	FORWARDER	PACEMAKER	SEPTEMBER	ARTHRITIS	ERRONEOUS	OVIPAROUS	VENTUROUS
CARPENTER	FRUITERER	PAGEMAKER	SEPULCHER	ASCENDERS	ESOPHAGUS	PARALYSIS	VERACIOUS
CHARACTER	FUNICULAR	PARAMETER	SEQUESTER	ASPARAGUS	EUTHENICS	PENDULOUS	VERDIGRIS
CHAUFFEUR	GAZETTEER	PASSENGER	SHOEMAKER	ASSIDUOUS	EXOGENOUS	PENURIOUS	VEXATIOUS
CHEVALIER	GENERATOR	PAYMASTER	SKYJACKER	ATHLETICS	FACETIOUS	PHLEBITIS	VICARIOUS
CHORISTER	GLADIATOR	PEDOMETER	SLAUGHTER	ATROCIOUS	FEROCIOUS	PHONETICS	VIVACIOUS
COADJUTOR	GODFATHER	PENHOLDER	SOLICITOR	AUDACIOUS	FRACTIOUS	PLENTEOUS	VOICELESS
COMFORTER	GODMOTHER	PERIMETER	SPECTATOR	BACKWOODS	FRIVOLOUS	PONDEROUS	VORACIOUS
COMMANDER	GONDOLIER	PHILANDER	SPELUNKER	BARBAROUS	GARRULOUS	PRESTRESS	WHITENESS
COMMISSAR	GRENADIER	POETASTER	SPHINCTER	BEAUTEOUS	GASTRITIS	PRICELESS	WINEPRESS
CONDENSER	GUARANTOR	POLYESTER	SPINNAKER	BILLIARDS	GLADIOLUS	PROBOSCIS	WORTHLESS
CONDUCTOR	GUNPOWDER	POMPADOUR	STATIONER	BLEACHERS	GLEANINGS	PROGNOSIS	ABATEMENT
CONFESSOR	HAMBURGER	PORRINGER	STOMACHER	BLUEGRASS	GLUTINOUS	PSORIASIS	ABHORRENT
CONTAINER	HARBINGER	POSTERIOR	STREETCAR	BOONDOCKS	GOVERNESS	PSYCHOSIS	ABSORBENT
COPARTNER	HARDCOVER	POTBOILER	STRETCHER	BOUNTEOUS	HALITOSIS	PYROLYSIS	ADSORBENT
CORIANDER	HEADWATER	POULTERER	SUCCESSOR	BOURGEOIS	HAPPINESS	QUERULOUS	AERIALIST
COSPONSOR	HEREAFTER	PRECENTOR	SUNFLOWER	BUMPTIOUS	HARMONICS	RAPACIOUS	AFFIDAVIT
COUNSELOR	HEREUNDER	PRECEPTOR	SUNSEEKER	CANDLEMAS	HEADDRESS	RELIGIOUS	AGREEMENT
COUTURIER	HEXAMETER	PRECURSOR	SURRENDER	CANTHARIS	HEARTLESS	REPOSSESS	ALLERGIST
CROSSOVER	HOMEMAKER	PRESBYTER	SUSPENDER	CAPACIOUS	HEPATITIS	RIGHTEOUS	AMENDMENT
CULLENDER	HORSEHAIR	PRIVATEER	TELEMETER	CASTANETS	HILARIOUS	SAGACIOUS	ANNUITANT
CUPBEARER	HOWSOEVER	PROCESSOR	TIDEWATER	CATALYSIS	HOURGLASS	SALACIOUS	APARTMENT
DECILITER	HUMDINGER	PROFESSOR	TREASURER	CATHARSIS	HYSTERICS	SASSAFRAS	APPELLANT
DECIMETER	ICELANDER	PROFITEER	TRICKSTER	CEASELESS	IMPATIENS	SCLEROSIS	APPLICANT
DECORATOR	INCUBATOR	PROJECTOR	TRIMESTER	CHEERLESS	IMPERIOUS	SEBACEOUS	ARCHITECT
DEKALITER	INHALATOR	PROPELLER	UNDERWEAR	CHRISTMAS	IMPETUOUS	SEMANTICS	ARCHIVIST
DEKAMETER	INNKEEPER	PROTECTOR	UNPOPULAR	CHRYSALIS	INCURIOUS	SEMIWORKS	ARROWROOT
DELIMITER	INSTANTER	PROVENDER	UPHOLSTER	CIRRHOSIS	INGENIOUS	SHAPELESS	ASCENDANT
DERRINGER	IRREGULAR	PUPPETEER	VAPORIZER	CONGERIES	INGENUOUS	SHIFTLESS	ASSISTANT
DESCENDER	JERKWATER	PYROMETER	VICTUALER	CONSCIOUS	INNOCUOUS	SIDEBURNS	ASTRONAUT
DESTROYER	JOBHOLDER	RACKETEER	VOLTMETER	CONSENSUS	INSIDIOUS	SILICEOUS	ATONEMENT
DETONATOR	KILOLITER	RACONTEUR	VOLUNTEER	COUNTLESS	INVERNESS	SILICOSIS	ATTENDANT
DISAPPEAR	KILOMETER	RAGPICKER	WALLPAPER	COURTEOUS	INVIDIOUS	SINUSITIS	BACKSWEPT
DISHWATER	LANDOWNER	RAINWATER	WARMONGER	CRABGRASS	ISINGLASS	SOMETIMES	BENIGNANT
DISMEMBER	LATECOMER	RECTIFIER	WHICHEVER	CREDULOUS	ISOSCELES	STRAPLESS	BLACKFOOT
DISREPAIR	LIMBURGER	REFLECTOR	WHOSOEVER	CROSSWAYS	JUDICIOUS	STRENUOUS	BLACKLIST
DISSENTER	LOCOMOTOR	REFRACTOR	WILLPOWER	CUTANEOUS	LABORIOUS	SULFUROUS	BLOODROOT

BLOODSHOT	DISAFFECT	IMPATIENT	NONPROFIT	SKINFLINT	LEITMOTIV	CENTENARY	GENTILITY
BLUEPOINT	DISCOMFIT	IMPERFECT	NORTHEAST	SKINTIGHT	AFTERGLOW	CERTAINTY	GEOGRAPHY
BLUEPRINT	DISCREDIT	IMPLEMENT	NORTHWEST	SKYROCKET	BEDFELLOW	CHEMISTRY	GIMMICKRY
BOMBSIGHT	DISHONEST	IMPORTANT	NUTRIMENT	SLINGSHOT	CHICKASAW	CHICANERY	GLENGARRY
BREAKFAST	DISINFECT	IMPRUDENT	OBSERVANT	SNOWDRIFT	CORELDRAW	CHIROPODY	GUSTATORY
BRILLIANT	DISORIENT	INCESSANT	OFFICIANT	SOBRIQUET	CORKSCREW	CIRCUITRY	HALFPENNY
BROADCAST	DISPUTANT	INCIPIENT	ONSLAUGHT	SOMNOLENT	DEATHBLOW	CITIZENRY	HIERARCHY
BUCKWHEAT	DISSIDENT	INCLEMENT	OUTERMOST	SOUTHEAST	INTERVIEW	COMMODITY	HILLBILLY
BULLFIGHT	DOWNRIGHT	INCORRECT	OVERDRAFT	SOUTHWEST	JACKSCREW	COMMUNITY	HORSEPLAY
BUTTERFAT	DOWNSHIFT	INCREMENT	OVERNIGHT	SPEARMINT	JACKSTRAW	CONGRUITY	HORTATORY
BUTTERNUT	EBULLIENT	INCUMBENT	OVERPRINT	SPEEDBOAT	OVERTHROW	CONSTANCY	HUSBANDRY
CABRIOLET	EFFICIENT	INDIGNANT	OVERSHOOT	SPINDRIFT	QUICKDRAW	CONTUMELY	HYDROLOGY
CAMEMBERT	EMBAYMENT	INELEGANT	OVERSIGHT	SPOTLIGHT	SADDLEBOW	COROLLARY	HYPOCRISY
CANALBOAT	EMOLLIENT	INFORMANT	PARAMOUNT	STARLIGHT	SCARECROW	COSMOGONY	IMAGINARY
CATAMOUNT	EMOLUMENT	INNERMOST	PARCHMENT	STATEMENT	SCRIMSHAW	COSMOLOGY	IMMEDIACY
CATCHMENT	EQUIPMENT	INPATIENT	PENTECOST	STEADFAST	EXECUTRIX	CRANBERRY	INABILITY
CHECKLIST	ESTAMINET	INSISTENT	PERMANENT	STEAMBOAT	HETERODOX	CREMATORY	INDEMNIFY
CLIPSHEET	EUCHARIST	INSOLVENT	PERTINENT	STIMULANT	SHADOWBOX	CUSTOMARY	INDEMNITY
COAGULANT	EXCELLENT	INSURGENT	PESTILENT	STOPLIGHT	TINDERBOX	DAMSELFLY	INDIGNITY
COCKFIGHT	EXCREMENT	INTELLECT	PETTICOAT	STREAMLET	ACCESSORY	DECLIVITY	INFIRMARY
COFFEEPOT	EXPECTANT	INTENDANT	PHYSICIST	STRIKEOUT	ACCLIVITY	DEFORMITY	INFIRMITY
COLORCAST	EXPEDIENT	INTERCEPT	PLACEMENT	SUBSCRIPT	ACCOMPANY	DEMOCRACY	INGENUITY
COLORFAST	EXTRAVERT	INTERDICT	POSTULANT	SUCCULENT	ADMIRALTY	DESULTORY	INSTANTLY
COLUMNIST	EXUBERANT	INTERJECT	POWERBOAT	SUNBONNET	ADVERSARY	DEXTERITY	INTEGRITY
COMPETENT	FERRYBOAT	INTERMENT	PRECEDENT	SUPPLIANT	ADVERSITY	DIATHERMY	INTENSIFY
COMPLAINT	FIRMAMENT	INTERNIST	PREFLIGHT	SWEETMEAT	AIRWORTHY	DICHOTOMY	INTENSITY
COMPONENT	FLAGEOLET	INTERPRET	PRESIDENT	SYCOPHANT	ANCILLARY	DIGNITARY	INTERPLAY
CONCORDAT	FLATULENT	INTERRUPT	PREVALENT	TAILLIGHT	ANIMOSITY	DIPLOMACY	INVENTORY
CONDIMENT	FLOWCHART	INTERSECT	PROMINENT	TERMAGANT	ANTHOLOGY	DIRECTORY	ITINERARY
CONFIDANT	FLOWERPOT	INTROVERT	PROPONENT	TESTAMENT	ANTIPATHY	DISEMBODY	JUDICIARY
CONSCRIPT	FOOTPRINT	ITINERANT	PROVIDENT	TRANSIENT	ANTIQUARY	DIVERSIFY	LAUDATORY
CONSONANT	FOREFRONT	LIMELIGHT	PUBESCENT	TRANSPORT	ANTIQUITY	DIVERSITY	LEGENDARY
CONSTRICT	FORESHEET	LINEAMENT	PUBLICIST	TREATMENT	ARBITRARY	DOBSONFLY	LIABILITY
CONSTRUCT	FORESIGHT	LIVERWORT	PUSSYFOOT	TRENCHANT	ARCHENEMY	DORMITORY	LITHOLOGY
CONTINENT	FORTNIGHT	LUBRICANT	QUICKSORT	TRUCULENT	ARTILLERY	DRAGONFLY	LONGEVITY
COPYRIGHT	GALLIVANT	LUXURIANT	QUIESCENT	TURBULENT	ASTROLOGY	DROMEDARY	MACHINERY
CORMORANT	GEARSHIFT	MACHINIST	RAINSPOUT	TURNABOUT	ASTRONOMY	DUPLICITY	MANDATORY
COSMONAUT	GENUFLECT	MAKESHIFT	RECIPIENT	UNDERCOAT	AUDIOLOGY	DYSENTERY	MARQUETRY
CROISSANT	GODPARENT	MALADROIT	RECOLLECT	UNDERFOOT	AUTHORITY	DYSTROPHY	MATERNITY
CUTTHROAT	GRAPESHOT	MALIGNANT	RECORDIST	UNDERMOST	AUTOCRACY	ELECTRIFY	MATRIMONY
DAVENPORT	GREATCOAT	MENDICANT	RECUMBENT	UNDERPART	AUXILIARY	EMERGENCY	MENTALITY
DECREMENT	GREENBELT	MERRIMENT	REDBREAST	UNDERSHOT	BIMONTHLY	EPIGRAPHY	MERCENARY
DEFENDANT	HANDCRAFT	METHODIST	REDUNDANT	UNIVALENT	BIOGRAPHY	ETHNOLOGY	METROLOGY
DEFERMENT	HATCHMENT	MICROSOFT	REENTRANT	UPPERMOST	BLACKBODY	ETYMOLOGY	MICROCOPY
DEFICIENT	HEADFIRST	MILLIVOLT	RELUCTANT	UTTERMOST	BLASPHEMY	EVERYBODY	MILLINERY
DEFOLIANT	HEADLIGHT	MINCEMEAT	REPELLENT	VIDELICET	BLUEBERRY	EXEMPLARY	MISSILERY
DEMULCENT	HEARTBEAT	MINISKIRT	REPRESENT	VIEWPOINT	BREEZEWAY	EXEMPLIFY	MOMENTARY
DEODORANT	HEARTFELT	MISCREANT	REPUGNANT	WAISTCOAT	BUTTERFLY	EXPIATORY	MONASTERY
DEPENDENT	HERBALIST	MISDIRECT	RESERVIST	WARBONNET	CACOPHONY	EXTREMITY	MYTHOLOGY
DESICCANT	HIGHLIGHT	MISORIENT	RESISTANT	WHALEBOAT	CALLOSITY	FESTIVITY	NATURALLY
DETERGENT	HINDSIGHT	MOONLIGHT	RESTRAINT	WHITEBAIT	CANDIDACY	FEUDATORY	NECESSARY
DETERRENT	HOARFROST	MOTORBOAT	RESURRECT	WINDSWEPT	CAPILLARY	FIDUCIARY	NECESSITY
DETRIMENT	HOLOCAUST	MOUTHPART	RIVERBOAT	WOODCRAFT	CAPITALLY	FOOLHARDY	NECROLOGY
DEVILMENT	HOUSEBOAT	NEGLIGENT	SACRAMENT	WORRYWART	CASSOWARY	FORMALITY	NEUROLOGY
DIFFERENT	HOUSECOAT	NEGOTIANT	SANDBLAST	ZEITGEIST	CASUISTRY	FREQUENCY	NONENTITY
DIFFICULT	HYPERTEXT	NEWSPRINT	SCAPEGOAT	IMPROMPTU	CATALEPSY	GALLANTRY	OBJECTIFY
DIFFIDENT	IMMIGRANT	NONCREDIT	SENTIMENT	TROUSSEAU	CELEBRITY	GENEALOGY	OCCUPANCY

OFFERTORY	SOPHISTRY
OLFACTORY	SPEAKEASY
OLIGARCHY	SPECIALTY
OPTOMETRY	SPRIGHTLY
OUTWARDLY	STATUTORY
PALMISTRY	SUBLUNARY
PARQUETRY	SUPREMACY
PARSIMONY	SWORDPLAY
PATERNITY	SYLLABIFY
PATHOLOGY	TAUTOLOGY
PATRIMONY	TAXIDERMY
PECUNIARY	TELEPATHY
PERFUMERY	TELEPHONY
PERIPHERY	TEMPORARY
PERSONIFY	TERRITORY
PETROLOGY	TESTIMONY
PHILATELY	THEOCRACY
PHILOLOGY	THEOSOPHY
PHONOLOGY	THROWAWAY
PHOTOCOPY	TREACHERY
PHOTOPLAY	TRIBUTARY
PITUITARY	TRIWEEKLY
PLURALITY	UNCLEANLY
POLYPHONY	UNDERBODY
POSTERITY	UNDERPLAY
PREDATORY	UNEARTHLY
PREOCCUPY	UNHEALTHY
PRESENTLY	UNSIGHTLY
PRIMARILY	UNWORLDLY
PROFANITY	VAINGLORY
PROPRIETY	VASECTOMY
PROXIMITY	VIBRATORY
PUBLICITY	VIRGINITY
PULMONARY	VISCOSITY
PURGATORY	VISIONARY
QUARTERLY	VOLUNTARY
RADIOLOGY	VULGARITY
RASPBERRY	WEDNESDAY
REFECTORY	YESTERDAY
RELEVANCY	KILOHERTZ
RELIQUARY	MEGAHERTZ
REPERTORY	
RESIDENCY	
RESIDUARY	
ROUNDELAY	
SANCTUARY	
SCHOOLBOY	
SEAWORTHY	
SECONDARY	
SECRETARY	
SEDENTARY	
SENIORITY	
SHRUBBERY	
SIGNATORY	
SLUICEWAY	
SOCIOLOGY	
SOLILOQUY	

1ST LETTER						
	AIRFREIGHT	ANTISEPTIC	AURIFEROUS	BIRTHPLACE	BRONTOSAUR	CENSORSHIP
	ALBUMINOUS	ANTISOCIAL	AUSPICIOUS	BIRTHRIGHT	BROWNSTONE	CENTENNIAL
ABBREVIATE	ALCOHOLISM	ANTITHESIS	AUSTRALIAN	BIRTHSTONE	BUDGERIGAR	CENTESIMAL
ABERRATION	ALIMENTARY	APOCALYPSE	AUTHORSHIP	BITUMINOUS	BULLHEADED	CENTIGRADE
ABOMINABLE	ALKALINIZE	APOCRYPHAL	AUTOMATION	BLACKAMOOR	BUSHMASTER	CENTILITER
ABORIGINAL	ALLEGIANCE	APOLITICAL	AUTOMATIZE	BLACKBERRY	BUTTERMILK	CENTIMETER
ABOVEBOARD	ALLHALLOWS	APOLOGETIC	AUTOMOBILE	BLACKBOARD	BUTTONHOLE	CENTRALIZE
ABSCISSION	ALLITERATE	APOSTROPHE	AUTOMOTIVE	BLACKGUARD	BUTTONHOOK	CENTRIFUGE
ABSOLUTION	ALONGSHORE	APOTHECARY	AUTONOMOUS	BLACKSMITH	CACCIATORE	CEREBELLUM
ABSOLUTISM	ALPHABETIC	APOTHEOSIS	AUTOSTRADA	BLACKTHORN	CADAVEROUS	CEREMONIAL
ABSORPTION	ALTARPIECE	APPARITION	BACKGAMMON	BLANCMANGE	CALCAREOUS	CHALCEDONY
ABSTEMIOUS	ALTERNATOR	APPEARANCE	BACKGROUND	BLITZKRIEG	CALCULATED	CHANCELLOR
ABSTINENCE	ALTOGETHER	APPETIZING	BACKHANDED	BLOCKHOUSE	CALUMNIATE	CHANDELIER
ACCELERATE	AMALGAMATE	APPLICABLE	BACKSTAIRS	BLOODHOUND	CAMELOPARD	CHANGELING
ACCENTUATE	AMANUENSIS	APPLICATOR	BACKSTROKE	BLOODSTAIN	CAMOUFLAGE	CHANGEOVER
ACCEPTABLE	AMBASSADOR	APPOINTIVE	BALBRIGGAN	BLOODSTONE	CAMPHORATE	CHANNELIZE
ACCEPTANCE	AMBULATORY	APPOSITION	BALDERDASH	BLUEBONNET	CANDELABRA	CHAPFALLEN
ACCESSIBLE	AMELIORATE	APPOSITIVE	BALLISTICS	BLUEBOTTLE	CANDESCENT	CHARACTERY
ACCIDENTAL	AMERINDIAN	APPRECIATE	BALUSTRADE	BLUECOLLAR	CANDLEWICK	CHARITABLE
ACCOMPLICE	AMMUNITION	APPRENTICE	BAPTISTERY	BLUEJACKET	CANKERWORM	CHARLESTON
ACCOMPLISH	AMPHIBIOUS	AQUALUNGER	BAREHEADED	BOISTEROUS	CANNONBALL	CHARTREUSE
ACCORDANCE	ANEMOMETER	AQUAMARINE	BASKETBALL	BOLSHEVISM	CANONICALS	CHATELAINE
ACCOUNTANT	ANESTHESIA	ARBITRATOR	BASTARDIZE	BOMBARDIER	CANTALOUPE	CHATTERBOX
ACCOUNTING	ANESTHETIC	ARBORVITAE	BATHYSCAPH	BONDHOLDER	CANTILEVER	CHAUVINISM
ACCUMULATE	ANGIOSPERM	ARCHBISHOP	BATRACHIAN	BOOKKEEPER	CANTONMENT	CHEAPSKATE
ACCUSATIVE	ANGLOPHILE	ARCHDEACON	BATTLEMENT	BOOKMOBILE	CANVASBACK	CHECKPOINT
ACCUSTOMED	ANGLOPHOBE	ARCHITRAVE	BATTLESHIP	BOOKSELLER	CAOUTCHOUC	CHEESECAKE
ACHROMATIC	ANIMADVERT	ARITHMETIC	BEAUJOLAIS	BOONDOGGLE	CAPACITATE	CHIFFONIER
ACROBATICS	ANIMALCULE	ARMAGEDDON	BEAUTICIAN	BORDERLAND	CAPITALISM	CHILDBIRTH
ACROPHOBIA	ANNIHILATE	ARTICULATE	BEDCLOTHES	BOTTLENECK	CAPITALIST	CHIMERICAL
ACTIONABLE	ANNUNCIATE	ARTIFICIAL	BEDRAGGLED	BOTTOMLAND	CAPITALIZE	CHIMPANZEE
ADDITIONAL	ANSWERABLE	ASCENDANCY	BEFOREHAND	BOWDLERIZE	CAPITATION	CHINCHILLA
ADJUDICATE	ANTAGONISM	ASPHYXIATE	BEHINDHAND	BRAHMANISM	CAPITULATE	CHIROMANCY
ADMINISTER	ANTAGONIST	ASPIRATION	BELLADONNA	BRAINCHILD	CAPOREGIME	CHIVALROUS
ADMISSIBLE	ANTAGONIZE	ASSEMBLAGE	BELLETRIST	BRAINSTORM	CARABINEER	CHLORINATE
ADMITTANCE	ANTEBELLUM	ASSEVERATE	BELLWETHER	BREADBOARD	CARBOLATED	CHLOROFORM
ADRENALINE	ANTECEDENT	ASSIGNMENT	BELONGINGS	BREADFRUIT	CARBURETOR	CHROMOSOME
ADULTERANT	ANTEPENULT	ASSIMILATE	BENCHMARKS	BREADSTUFF	CARCINOGEN	CHRONOLOGY
ADULTERATE	ANTHRACITE	ASSORTMENT	BENEFACTOR	BREAKFRONT	CARDIOGRAM	CHRYSOLITE
ADVENTURER	ANTHROPOID	ASSUMPTION	BENEFICENT	BREAKWATER	CARDIOLOGY	CHURCHGOER
ADVISEMENT	ANTIBIOTIC	ASTRINGENT	BENEFICIAL	BREASTBONE	CARICATURE	CHURCHLESS
AEROBATICS	ANTICANCER	ASYMMETRIC	BESPRINKLE	BREASTWORK	CATABOLISM	CHURCHYARD
AESTHETICS	ANTICHRIST	ATMOSPHERE	BESTIALITY	BRICKLAYER	CATAFALQUE	CINERARIUM
AFFLICTIVE	ANTICIPATE	ATTACHMENT	BETTERMENT	BRIDEGROOM	CATCHPENNY	CINQUEFOIL
AFICIONADO	ANTICLIMAX	ATTAINMENT	BICHLORIDE	BRIDESMAID	CATECHUMEN	CIRCUITOUS
AFTERBIRTH	ANTIFREEZE	ATTENDANCE	BIMETALLIC	BRIDGEHEAD	CATEGORIZE	CIRCUMCISE
AFTERIMAGE	ANTIMATTER	ATTRACTANT	BIOMEDICAL	BRIDGEWORK	CAVITATION	CIRCUMFLEX
AFTERTASTE	ANTINOMIAN	ATTRACTION	BIOPHYSICS	BRIGANTINE	CELEBRATED	CIRCUMVENT
AGGRANDIZE	ANTIPHONAL	AUCTIONEER	BIPARENTAL	BROADCLOTH	CELLARETTE	CITRONELLA
AGGRESSION	ANTIPROTON	AUDIOPHILE	BIPARIETAL	BROADSWORD	CELLOPHANE	CLASSICISM
AGGRESSIVE	ANTIQUATED	AUDITORIUM	BIPARTISAN	BRONCHITIS	CENSORIOUS	CLASSIFIED

CLAVICHORD	CONCENTRIC	CONVENTION	DEBILITATE	DEROGATORY	DISSATISFY	ENDEARMENT
CLERESTORY	CONCEPTION	CONVERSANT	DECAPITATE	DESALINATE	DISSENSION	ENDOGENOUS
CLINGSTONE	CONCERNING	CONVERSION	DECELERATE	DESALINIZE	DISSERVICE	ENGAGEMENT
CLODHOPPER	CONCERTINA	CONVEYANCE	DECIMALIZE	DESCENDANT	DISSIMILAR	ENJAMBMENT
CLOTHESPIN	CONCESSION	CONVICTION	DECLASSIFY	DESERVEDLY	DISSOCIATE	ENTERPRISE
CLOUDBURST	CONCESSIVE	CONVOLUTED	DECLENSION	DESOLATION	DISSONANCE	ENTHUSIASM
CLOVERLEAF	CONCILIATE	CONVULSION	DECOLORIZE	DESPICABLE	DISTILLATE	ENTOMOLOGY
COCKATRICE	CONCLUSION	COORDINATE	DECOMPRESS	DESTRUCTOR	DISTRAUGHT	EPIGLOTTIS
COGNIZANCE	CONCORDANT	COPPERHEAD	DECORATION	DETACHMENT	DISTRIBUTE	EPISCOPACY
COINCIDENT	CONCRETION	COPYREADER	DECORATIVE	DETERMINED	DIVINATION	EPISCOPATE
COLLARBONE	CONCURRENT	COPYWRITER	DECRYPTION	DETERRENCE	DOCKWORKER	EPITHELIUM
COLLATERAL	CONCUSSION	CORDILLERA	DEFINITION	DEVITALIZE	DOGCATCHER	EQUANIMITY
COLLECTIVE	CONDENSATE	CORDWAINER	DEFINITIVE	DIAPHANOUS	DOMINATION	EQUESTRIAN
COLLOQUIAL	CONDESCEND	CORNFLOWER	DEFLAGRATE	DICTIONARY	DONNYBROOK	EQUITATION
COLLOQUIUM	CONDUCTIVE	CORNSTARCH	DEGENERACY	DIELECTRIC	DOORKEEPER	EQUIVALENT
COLORATION	CONFECTION	CORNUCOPIA	DEGENERATE	DIFFERENCE	DOWNSTAIRS	EQUIVOCATE
COLORATURA	CONFERENCE	CORONATION	DEGRADABLE	DIFFICULTY	DOWNSTREAM	ERGONOMICS
COLPORTEUR	CONFESSION	CORPULENCE	DEHUMANIZE	DILETTANTE	DOWNSTROKE	ERGOSTEROL
COMBUSTION	CONFIDENCE	CORRESPOND	DEHUMIDIFY	DILLYDALLY	DRAWBRIDGE	ERYSIPELAS
COMEDIENNE	CONFISCATE	CORRIGIBLE	DELECTABLE	DIMINUENDO	DRAWSTRING	ESCARPMENT
COMESTIBLE	CONFLUENCE	COSMOPOLIS	DELEGATION	DIMINUTIVE	DREAMWORLD	ESCRITOIRE
COMMANDANT	CONFORMITY	COTERMINAL	DELIBERATE	DINNERWARE	DUMBWAITER	ESCUTCHEON
COMMANDEER	CONGENITAL	COTTONSEED	DELINQUENT	DIPHTHERIA	DUNDERHEAD	ESPADRILLE
COMMENTARY	CONGREGATE	COTTONTAIL	DELIQUESCE	DIPSOMANIA	DUODECIMAL	ESTIMATION
COMMERCIAL	CONGRUENCE	COTTONWOOD	DELPHINIUM	DISAPPOINT	DUPLICATOR	EUCALYPTUS
COMMISSARY	CONGRUENCY	COUNTERACT	DEMOBILIZE	DISAPPROVE	DYSPROSIUM	EUPHONIOUS
COMMISSION	CONJECTURE	COUNTERMAN	DEMOCRATIC	DISARRANGE	EARTHQUAKE	EURODOLLAR
COMMODIOUS	CONNECTION	COUNTERSPY	DEMOGRAPHY	DISBELIEVE	EBULLITION	EUTHANASIA
COMMONALTY	CONNECTIVE	COUNTRYMAN	DEMOISELLE	DISCERNING	ECONOMICAL	EVANESCENT
COMMONWEAL	CONNIPTION	COURTHOUSE	DEMOLITION	DISCIPLINE	ECUMENICAL	EVANGELISM
COMMUNIQUE	CONSCIENCE	COWPUNCHER	DEMONETIZE	DISCOMFORT	EFFECTUATE	EVANGELIST
COMMUTATOR	CONSECRATE	CRADLESONG	DEMONOLOGY	DISCOMMODE	EFFEMINATE	EVANGELIZE
COMPARABLE	CONSEQUENT	CRANKSHAFT	DEMORALIZE	DISCOMPOSE	EFFERVESCE	EVENHANDED
COMPARISON	CONSISTORY	CREDENTIAL	DENDROLOGY	DISCONCERT	EFFICIENCY	EVERYTHING
COMPASSION	CONSONANCE	CREDITABLE	DENOMINATE	DISCONNECT	EFFLORESCE	EVERYWHERE
COMPATIBLE	CONSORTIUM	CRENELLATE	DENOTATIVE	DISCONTENT	EFFRONTERY	EVISCERATE
COMPATRIOT	CONSPECTUS	CRETACEOUS	DENOUEMENT	DISCOURAGE	EFFULGENCE	EXACERBATE
COMPENDIUM	CONSPIRACY	CRISSCROSS	DENTIFRICE	DISCREPANT	EGOCENTRIC	EXACTITUDE
COMPENSATE	CONSTITUTE	CROSSBONES	DEPARTMENT	DISCRETION	EISTEDDFOD	EXAGGERATE
COMPETENCE	CONSTRAINT	CROSSBREED	DEPENDABLE	DISCURSIVE	ELDERBERRY	EXASPERATE
COMPETENCY	CONSUMMATE	CROSSPIECE	DEPENDENCE	DISCUSSANT	ELECTORATE	EXCELLENCE
COMPETITOR	CONTAGIOUS	CRUSTACEAN	DEPENDENCY	DISEMBOWEL	ELECTRONIC	EXCELLENCY
COMPLECTED	CONTENTION	CRYOGENICS	DEPILATORY	DISENCHANT	ELEMENTARY	EXCITEMENT
COMPLEMENT	CONTIGUOUS	CRYPTOGRAM	DEPLORABLE	DISGRUNTLE	EMANCIPATE	EXCOGITATE
COMPLEXION	CONTINENCE	CUMMERBUND	DEPOLARIZE	DISHABILLE	EMASCULATE	EXHAUSTION
COMPLIANCE	CONTINGENT	CUMULATIVE	DEPOPULATE	DISHARMONY	EMBANKMENT	EXHAUSTIVE
COMPLIANCY	CONTINUITY	CURRICULUM	DEPORTMENT	DISHEARTEN	EMBONPOINT	EXHILARATE
COMPLICATE	CONTINUOUS	CURVACEOUS	DEPOSITION	DISHWASHER	EMBOUCHURE	EXOBIOLOGY
COMPLICITY	CONTRABAND	CUTTLEFISH	DEPOSITORY	DISINCLINE	EMBROIDERY	EXORBITANT
COMPLIMENT	CONTRADICT	CYBERSPACE	DEPRECIATE	DISINHERIT	EMBRYOLOGY	EXOTHERMIC
COMPOSITOR	CONTRAVENE	CYCLOMETER	DEPRESSANT	DISJOINTED	EMPIRICISM	EXPATRIATE
COMPREHEND	CONTRIBUTE	CYCLOPEDIA	DEPRESSION	DISORDERLY	EMPLOYMENT	EXPECTANCY
COMPROMISE	CONTROLLER	DATAMATION	DEPRESSIVE	DISPENSARY	EMULSIFIER	EXPEDIENCE
COMPULSION	CONTROVERT	DEACTIVATE	DEPUTATION	DISPOSABLE	ENAMELWARE	EXPEDIENCY
COMPULSIVE	CONVALESCE	DEADWEIGHT	DERIVATION	DISPOSSESS	ENCRYPTION	EXPEDITION
COMPULSORY	CONVECTION	DEALERSHIP	DERIVATIVE	DISQUALIFY	ENCYCLICAL	EXPERIENCE
COMPUSERVE	CONVENIENT	DEATHWATCH	DERMATITIS	DISRESPECT	ENDANGERED	EXPERIMENT

EXPLICABLE	FOOTLIGHTS	GOVERNMENT	HEREDITARY	IMMORALITY	INEVITABLE	INTINCTION
EXPOSITION	FOOTLOCKER	GRADUALISM	HERETOFORE	IMMUNOLOGY	INEXORABLE	INTOLERANT
EXPRESSION	FORBIDDING	GRADUATION	HIEROPHANT	IMPALPABLE	INEXPIABLE	INTONATION
EXPRESSMAN	FORECASTLE	GRAINFIELD	HIGHLANDER	IMPASSABLE	INFALLIBLE	INTOXICANT
EXPRESSWAY	FOREFATHER	GRAMOPHONE	HIGHWAYMAN	IMPASSIBLE	INFIDELITY	INTOXICATE
EXTINGUISH	FOREFINGER	GRANDCHILD	HINTERLAND	IMPATIENCE	INFIGHTING	INTRAMURAL
EXTRAMURAL	FOREGATHER	GRANDSTAND	HIPPODROME	IMPECCABLE	INFILTRATE	INTRASTATE
EXTRANEOUS	FOREGROUND	GRAPEFRUIT	HISTRIONIC	IMPEDIMENT	INFINITIVE	INVALIDATE
EXURBANITE	FOREHANDED	GRATUITOUS	HOBBYHORSE	IMPENITENT	INFINITUDE	INVALUABLE
EYEDROPPER	FOREORDAIN	GRAVESTONE	HODGEPODGE	IMPERATIVE	INFLECTION	INVARIABLE
EYEWITNESS	FORERUNNER	GRAVIMETER	HOLLOWWARE	IMPERSONAL	INFLEXIBLE	INVESTMENT
FACILITATE	FORESHADOW	GREENHOUSE	HOLOGRAPHY	IMPERVIOUS	INFRACTION	INVETERATE
FACTITIOUS	FORFEITURE	GREENSWARD	HOMECOMING	IMPLACABLE	INFRASONIC	INVIGORATE
FAHRENHEIT	FORMIDABLE	GREGARIOUS	HOMEOPATHY	IMPORTANCE	INFREQUENT	INVINCIBLE
FAIRGROUND	FORTHRIGHT	GRINDSTONE	HOMOGENIZE	IMPOSSIBLE	INGLORIOUS	INVIOLABLE
FALLACIOUS	FORTISSIMO	GROUNDLING	HOMOLOGOUS	IMPOVERISH	INGRATIATE	INVOCATION
FAMILARIZE	FORTUITOUS	GROUNDMASS	HOMOSEXUAL	IMPREGNATE	INGREDIENT	INVOLUTION
FARFETCHED	FOSTERLING	GROUNDWORK	HONORARIUM	IMPRESARIO	INHABITANT	IONOSPHERE
FARSIGHTED	FOUNDATION	GUARDHOUSE	HOOTENANNY	IMPRESSION	INHIBITION	IRRATIONAL
FASTIDIOUS	FOURSQUARE	GUILLOTINE	HORIZONTAL	IMPRESSIVE	INHUMANITY	IRRELEVANT
FATHERLAND	FRANCHISEE	GUNSLINGER	HORRENDOUS	IMPRIMATUR	INIMITABLE	IRRESOLUTE
FATHOMLESS	FRANCHISER	GYMNASTICS	HORSEFLESH	IMPROBABLE	INITIATIVE	ISOMETRICS
FAVORITISM	FRANCHISOR	GYMNOSPERM	HORSELAUGH	INACTIVATE	INITIATORY	ISOTHERMAL
FEDERALISM	FRATERNITY	GYNECOLOGY	HORSEPOWER	INADEQUATE	INJUNCTION	JACKANAPES
FEDERALIST	FRATERNIZE	HABILIMENT	HORSEWOMAN	INAPTITUDE	INNOMINATE	JACKHAMMER
FEDERALIZE	FRATRICIDE	HABITATION	HOSPITABLE	INAUGURATE	INNOVATION	JACKRABBIT
FEDERATION	FRAUDULENT	HALLELUJAH	HOUSECLEAN	INBREEDING	INOPERABLE	JARDINIERE
FELICITATE	FREEBOOTER	HAMMERHEAD	HOUSEWARES	INCAPACITY	INORDINATE	JAWBREAKER
FELICITOUS	FRESHWATER	HAMMERLOCK	HULLABALOO	INCENDIARY	INQUIETUDE	JIMSONWEED
FELLOWSHIP	FUSSBUDGET	HANDBARROW	HUSBANDMAN	INCIDENTAL	INSATIABLE	JINRIKISHA
FERTILIZER	FUTURISTIC	HANDICRAFT	HYDRAULICS	INCINERATE	INSEMINATE	JOURNALESE
FIBERBOARD	GADOLINIUM	HANDLEBARS	HYDROLYSIS	INCIVILITY	INSENSIBLE	JOURNALISM
FIBERGLASS	GAMEKEEPER	HANDMAIDEN	HYDROMETER	INCLINABLE	INSENTIENT	JOURNEYMAN
FIBRINOGEN	GARGANTUAN	HANDSPRING	HYDROPHONE	INCOHERENT	INSISTENCE	JUBILATION
FICTITIOUS	GASTRONOMY	HARDHEADED	HYDROPLANE	INCOMPLETE	INSOLATION	JUDICATURE
FIELDPIECE	GATEKEEPER	HARMONIOUS	HYGROMETER	INCONSTANT	INSOLVABLE	JUGGERNAUT
FIGURATION	GENERALITY	HEADMASTER	HYPERBARIC	INCREDIBLE	INSTRUCTOR	KETTLEDRUM
FIGURATIVE	GENERALIZE	HEADSTRONG	HYPOCENTER	INCULPABLE	INSTRUMENT	KIESELGUHR
FIGUREHEAD	GENERATION	HEADWAITER	HYPODERMIC	INCUMBENCY	INTANGIBLE	KINEMATICS
FILIBUSTER	GENTLEFOLK	HEARTBREAK	HYPOTENUSE	INDECISION	INTEGUMENT	KINGFISHER
FINGERLING	GEOCENTRIC	HEARTHSIDE	HYPOTHESIS	INDECISIVE	INTERBLOCK	KNICKKNACK
FINGERNAIL	GEOPHYSICS	HEARTTHROB	ICEBREAKER	INDECOROUS	INTERBREED	KNIGHTHOOD
FISTICUFFS	GEOSCIENCE	HEATSTROKE	ICONOCLASM	INDEFINITE	INTERFAITH	KNOCKWURST
FLAGELLATE	GEOTHERMAL	HECTOLITER	ICONOCLAST	INDELICATE	INTERFERON	KRUGERRAND
FLAGITIOUS	GERIATRICS	HECTOMETER	IDIOPATHIC	INDICATIVE	INTERLEAVE	LABORATORY
FLAMBOYANT	GESUNDHEIT	HELICOPTER	IGNORAMOUS	INDIGENOUS	INTERLUNAR	LACHRYMOSE
FLASHLIGHT	GHOSTWRITE	HELIOGRAPH	ILLITERATE	INDISCREET	INTERMARRY	LACKLUSTER
FLOODLIGHT	GINGERSNAP	HELIOTROPE	ILLUMINATE	INDISPOSED	INTERMEZZO	LADYFINGER
FLOODPLAIN	GINGIVITIS	HEMATOLOGY	ILLUSTRATE	INDISTINCT	INTERNMENT	LANDHOLDER
FLOODWATER	GLACIOLOGY	HEMISPHERE	IMAGINABLE	INDIVIDUAL	INTERSTATE	LANDLOCKED
FLOORBOARD	GOALKEEPER	HEMOGLOBIN	IMBIBITION	INDONESIAN	INTERSTICE	LANDLUBBER
FLUIDOUNCE	GOLDBEATER	HEMOPHILIA	IMMACULATE	INDUCEMENT	INTERTIDAL	LARYNGITIS
FLUORIDATE	GONOCOCCUS	HEMORRHAGE	IMMATERIAL	INDUCTANCE	INTERTWINE	LASCIVIOUS
FLUORINATE	GOOSEBERRY	HEMORRHOID	IMMEMORIAL	INDULGENCE	INTERTWIST	LAWBREAKER
FLYCATCHER	GOOSEFLESH	HENCEFORTH	IMMISCIBLE	INDUSTRIAL	INTERURBAN	LAWRENCIUM
FOLKSINGER	GORGONZOLA	HEPTAMETER	IMMOBILIZE	INELIGIBLE	INTERWEAVE	LEAFHOPPER
FOOTBRIDGE	GORMANDIZE	HEREABOUTS	IMMODERATE	INEQUALITY	INTIMIDATE	LEDERHOSEN

LEGITIMATE	MARGINALIA	MINESTRONE	NEIGHBORLY	ORDINATION	PERCENTAGE	PILGRIMAGE
LENGTHWISE	MARGUERITE	MINISCROLL	NEOCLASSIC	ORGANGUTAN	PERCENTILE	PILLOWCASE
LEPRECHAUN	MARIONETTE	MINISTRANT	NETHERMOST	OSTENSIBLE	PERCEPTION	PILOTHOUSE
LETTERHEAD	MARROWBONE	MISALIGNED	NETTLESOME	OSTEOPATHY	PERCEPTIVE	PINCUSHION
LIBERALISM	MARTINGALE	MISCELLANY	NEUTRALISM	OTHERWORLD	PERCEPTUAL	PINFEATHER
LIBIDINOUS	MASQUERADE	MISCONDUCT	NEUTRALITY	OUTBALANCE	PERCIPIENT	PLAGIARIZE
LICENTIATE	MASTERMIND	MISFORTUNE	NEUTRALIZE	OUTGENERAL	PERCUSSION	PLANTATION
LICENTIOUS	MASTERSHIP	MISOGAMIST	NEWFANGLED	OUTLANDISH	PERDURABLE	PLAYACTING
LIEUTENANT	MASTERWORK	MISOGYNIST	NEWSGROUPS	OUTPATIENT	PEREMPTORY	PLAYGROUND
LIFESAVING	MATCHMAKER	MISSILEMAN	NEWSLETTER	OUTPERFORM	PERFECTION	PLAYWRIGHT
LIGHTHOUSE	MATURATION	MISSIONARY	NEWSWORTHY	OUTPOURING	PERIHELION	PLEASANTRY
LIGHTPROOF	MAYONNAISE	MISTAKABLE	NIGHTDRESS	OUTRAGEOUS	PERIODICAL	PLEBISCITE
LIKELIHOOD	MEADOWLARK	MIZZENMAST	NIGHTSHADE	OVERCHARGE	PERIPHERAL	PLUPERFECT
LINEBACKER	MECHANICAL	MOHAMMEDAN	NIGHTSHIRT	OVERMASTER	PERISHABLE	PLUTOCRACY
LIPREADING	MEDDLESOME	MOLYBDENUM	NIGHTSTICK	OVERSHADOW	PERITONEUM	POCKETBOOK
LITERALISM	MEDICAMENT	MONARCHIST	NINCOMPOOP	OVERSPREAD	PERIWINKLE	POINSETTIA
LITERATURE	MEERSCHAUM	MONOCHROME	NOISEMAKER	OVERWINTER	PERMAFROST	POLITICIAN
LITHUANIAN	MELANCHOLY	MONOPHONIC	NOMINATIVE	PACKSADDLE	PERMISSION	POLYCLINIC
LIVELIHOOD	MELANESIAN	MONOTHEISM	NONCHALANT	PACKTHREAD	PERMISSIVE	POLYHEDRON
LIVERWURST	MEMBERSHIP	MONOTONOUS	NONDRINKER	PAGINATION	PERNICIOUS	POLYNESIAN
LOCOMOTION	MEMORANDUM	MONSTRANCE	NONSTARTER	PAINKILLER	PERORATION	POLYTHEISM
LOCOMOTIVE	MENDACIOUS	MONUMENTAL	NONSUPPORT	PAINTBRUSH	PERPETRATE	POPULATION
LOGANBERRY	MENINGITIS	MOONSTRUCK	NOTABILITY	PALATALIZE	PERPETUATE	PORTCULLIS
LOGGERHEAD	MENSURABLE	MORATORIUM	NOTEWORTHY	PALATINATE	PERPETUITY	PORTENTOUS
LOGROLLING	MERCANTILE	MORPHOLOGY	NOTICEABLE	PALIMPSEST	PERQUISITE	PORTUGUESE
LOQUACIOUS	MESOSPHERE	MOTHERHOOD	NOURISHING	PALINDROME	PERSIFLAGE	POSSESSION
LOVEMAKING	METABOLISM	MOTHERLAND	NUCLEONICS	PALLBEARER	PERSONABLE	POSSESSIVE
LUBRICIOUS	METABOLITE	MOTORCYCLE	NUMBERLESS	PANJANDRUM	PERSONALTY	POSTHUMOUS
LUGUBRIOUS	METACARPUS	MOTORTRUCK	NUMEROLOGY	PANTALOONS	PERSUASION	POSTMASTER
LUMBERJACK	METAGALAXY	MOUNTEBANK	NURSERYMAN	PANTYWAIST	PERVERSION	POSTMORTEM
LUMBERYARD	METALLURGY	MOUTHPIECE	NUTCRACKER	PAPERBOARD	PESTILENCE	POSTPARTUM
MACKINTOSH	METASTASIS	MOZZARELLA	OBLIGATION	PARAMECIUM	PETNAPPING	POSTSCRIPT
MAGISTRATE	METATARSAL	MUDSLINGER	OBLITERATE	PARAPHRASE	PETROLATUM	POTENTIATE
MAIDENHAIR	METATARSUS	MUHAMMADAN	OBSEQUIOUS	PARAPLEGIA	PHENOMENON	POULTRYMAN
MAIDENHEAD	METICULOUS	MULTILEVEL	OBSERVABLE	PARATROOPS	PHILISTINE	POURPARLER
MAIDENHOOD	METROPOLIS	MULTIMEDIA	OBSERVANCE	PARLIAMENT	PHILOSOPHY	POWERHOUSE
MAINSPRING	METTLESOME	MULTIPLIER	OBSTETRICS	PARMIGIANA	PHLEBOTOMY	POWERLINES
MAINSTREAM	MICROFICHE	MULTISENSE	OCCASIONAL	PARTICIPLE	PHLEGMATIC	PRAGMATISM
MAISONETTE	MICROGRAPH	MULTISTAGE	OCCIDENTAL	PARTICULAR	PHONOGRAPH	PREARRANGE
MALADAPTED	MICROMETER	MULTISTORY	OCCUPATION	PASSAGEWAY	PHOSPHORUS	PREBENDARY
MALAPROPOS	MICROPHONE	MUNIFICENT	OCCURRENCE	PASTEBOARD	PHOTOFLASH	PRECARIOUS
MALCONTENT	MICROPROBE	MUSICOLOGY	OCEANARIUM	PASTEURIZE	PHOTOGENIC	PRECAUTION
MALEFACTOR	MICROSCOPE	MYRIAMETER	OCEANFRONT	PATHFINDER	PHOTOGRAPH	PRECEDENCE
MALEFICENT	MICROSTATE	NANOSECOND	OCEANGOING	PATRONYMIC	PHOTOMETER	PRECESSION
MALEVOLENT	MIDDLEBROW	NAPOLEONIC	OCEANOLOGY	PAWNBROKER	PHOTOMURAL	PRECIOSITY
MALODOROUS	MIDSHIPMAN	NASTURTIUM	OCTOTHORPE	PEACEMAKER	PHOTOPAINT	PRECOCIOUS
MALTHUSIAN	MIGNONETTE	NATATORIUM	OESOPHAGUS	PEASHOOTER	PHRENOLOGY	PREDACEOUS
MANAGEMENT	MILITARISM	NATIONWIDE	OFTENTIMES	PECCADILLO	PHYLACTERY	PREDECEASE
MANDELBROT	MILITARIZE	NATURALISM	OLEAGINOUS	PEDESTRIAN	PHYSIOLOGY	PREDESTINE
MANDRAGORA	MILLENNIUM	NATURALIST	OMNIPOTENT	PEDIATRICS	PIANISSIMO	PREDICABLE
MANICURIST	MILLILITER	NATURALIZE	OMNISCIENT	PEJORATIVE	PIANOFORTE	PREDISPOSE
MANIPULATE	MILLIMETER	NEBULOSITY	OMNIVOROUS	PENICILLIN	PICARESQUE	PREEMINENT
MANSERVANT	MILLSTREAM	NECROMANCY	OPALESCENT	PENMANSHIP	PICCALILLI	PREEMPTIVE
MANSUETUDE	MILLWRIGHT	NECROPOLIS	OPHTHALMIC	PENNYROYAL	PICKANINNY	PREFERENCE
MANTLEROCK	MIMEOGRAPH	NEEDLEWORK	OPPRESSION	PENTAMETER	PICKPOCKET	PREFERMENT
MANUSCRIPT	MINERALIZE	NEGATIVISM	OPPROBRIUM	PEPPERCORN	PICOSECOND	PREHENSILE
MARASCHINO	MINERALOGY	NEGLIGIBLE	ORATORICAL	PEPPERMINT	PIGEONHOLE	PREMARITAL

PREMEDICAL	PROVINCIAL	REGRESSION	RINGLEADER	SEPARATIVE	SPORTSCAST	SUPERCARGO
PREPACKAGE	PSEUDOCODE	REGULATION	RINGMASTER	SEPTICEMIA	SPRINGTIME	SUPERSONIC
PREPOSSESS	PSYCHIATRY	REJUVENATE	RISIBILITY	SEPTUAGINT	SPRINKLING	SUPERTWIST
PRESBYOPIA	PSYCHOLOGY	RELATIONAL	ROADRUNNER	SEPULCHRAL	STAGECOACH	SUPPLEMENT
PRESBYTERY	PSYCHOPATH	RELATIVITY	ROLLERBALL	SERPENTINE	STALACTITE	SUPPLICANT
PRESCIENCE	PUBESCENCE	RELAXATION	ROLLICKING	SERVICEMAN	STALAGMITE	SUPPLICATE
PRESSURIZE	PUGNACIOUS	RELENTLESS	ROTISSERIE	SERVOMOTOR	STANDPOINT	SURREALISM
PRESUPPOSE	PUNISHMENT	RELINQUISH	ROUGHHOUSE	SETTLEMENT	STANDSTILL	SUSPENSION
PRIMORDIAL	PUTRESCENT	RELUCTANCE	ROUNDABOUT	SHAMEFACED	STARVELING	SUSPENSORY
PRINCELING	PYRIMIDINE	REMARKABLE	ROUNDHOUSE	SHENANIGAN	STATECRAFT	SUSPICIOUS
PRINCIPLED	QUADRANGLE	REMEDIABLE	ROUSTABOUT	SHIBBOLETH	STATEHOUSE	SUSTENANCE
PRIVILEGED	QUADRATICS	REMITTANCE	RUBBERNECK	SHILLELAGH	STATIONARY	SWEETBREAD
PRIZEFIGHT	QUADRIVIUM	REMUNERATE	SACCHARINE	SHIPFITTER	STATIONERY	SWEETBRIER
PROCEEDING	QUADRUPLET	RENASCENCE	SACERDOTAL	SHIPWRIGHT	STATISTICS	SWEETHEART
PROCESSION	QUARANTINE	RENDEZVOUS	SACROILIAC	SHOESTRING	STATUESQUE	SWITCHBACK
PROCLIVITY	QUATREFOIL	REPAGINATE	SACROSANCT	SHOPKEEPER	STENTORIAN	SYMPATHIZE
PROCURATOR	QUICKBASIC	REPARATION	SALAMANDER	SHORTENING	STEPFATHER	TABERNACLE
PRODIGIOUS	QUINTUPLET	REPARATIVE	SALESWOMAN	SHUNPIKING	STEPLADDER	TABLECLOTH
PRODUCTION	RACECOURSE	REPATRIATE	SALTCELLAR	SHUTTERBUG	STEPMOTHER	TABLESPOON
PROFESSION	RADARSCOPE	REPERTOIRE	SALUBRIOUS	SIDESTROKE	STEPPARENT	TACHOMETER
PROFICIENT	RADICALIZE	REPETITION	SALUTATION	SIDEWINDER	STEPSISTER	TAMBOURINE
PROFLIGATE	RADIOGENIC	REPETITIVE	SANATORIUM	SILHOUETTE	STEREOTYPE	TANTAMOUNT
PROGENITOR	RADIOGRAPH	REPORTEDLY	SANDALWOOD	SILVERFISH	STIGMATIZE	TARANTELLA
PROGNOSTIC	RADIOMETER	REPOSITORY	SANGUINARY	SILVERWARE	STILLBIRTH	TASKMASTER
PROGRAMMED	RADIOPHONE	REPUBLICAN	SANITARIAN	SIMILITUDE	STOCHASTIC	TATTERSALL
PROGRAMMER	RADIOSONDE	REPUGNANCE	SANITARIUM	SIMPLICITY	STOREHOUSE	TATTLETALE
PROJECTILE	RAGAMUFFIN	REPUTATION	SANITATION	SIMPLISTIC	STRAIGHTEN	TEARJERKER
PROMETHIUM	RAINMAKING	RESILIENCE	SAPROPHYTE	SINGLETREE	STRAWBERRY	TECHNETIUM
PROMINENCE	RAMSHACKLE	RESILIENCY	SAUERKRAUT	SISTERHOOD	STRENGTHEN	TECHNICIAN
PROMISSORY	RATTLETRAP	RESISTANCE	SCAPEGRACE	SKATEBOARD	STRINGENCY	TECHNOLOGY
PROMONTORY	REACTIVATE	RESOLUTION	SCARLATINA	SKEPTICISM	STRIPTEASE	TEETHRIDGE
PROMPTBOOK	READERSHIP	RESORPTION	SCHISMATIC	SKYSCRAPER	STRONGHOLD	TELEGRAPHY
PROMULGATE	REASONABLE	RESOUNDING	SCHOLASTIC	SKYWRITING	STRYCHNINE	TELESCOPIC
PRONOUNCED	REBELLIOUS	RESPECTING	SCHOOLGIRL	SLENDERIZE	STUPENDOUS	TELEVISION
PROPAGANDA	RECEIVABLE	RESPECTIVE	SCHOOLMARM	SLIPSTREAM	SUBCOMPACT	TEMPERANCE
PROPELLANT	RECEPTACLE	RESPIRATOR	SCHOOLMATE	SLUMBEROUS	SUBJECTIVE	TEMPTATION
PROPENSITY	RECIDIVISM	RESPONDENT	SCHOOLROOM	SMATTERING	SUBLIMINAL	TENDERFOOT
PROPERTIED	RECIPROCAL	RESPONSIVE	SCRUTINIZE	SMOKESTACK	SUBORBITAL	TENDERLOIN
PROPITIATE	RECITATION	RESTAURANT	SCURRILOUS	SNAPDRAGON	SUBROUTINE	TENEBRIOUS
PROPITIOUS	RECOILLESS	RESTORABLE	SEAMANSHIP	SNOWMOBILE	SUBSEQUENT	TERMINATOR
PROPORTION	RECOMPENSE	RESTRAINED	SEAMSTRESS	SOLICITOUS	SUBSIDIARY	TESSELLATE
PROPRIETOR	RECONSIDER	RESURGENCE	SEARCHWARE	SOLICITUDE	SUBSTATION	TETRAMETER
PROPRINTER	RECREATION	RETRACTILE	SEASONABLE	SOLIDARITY	SUBSTITUTE	THEATRICAL
PROPULSION	RECUPERATE	RETROGRADE	SECONDHAND	SOMERSAULT	SUBSTRATUM	THEMSELVES
PROSCENIUM	REDEMPTION	RETROGRESS	SECULARISM	SOOTHSAYER	SUBSURFACE	THEREAFTER
PROSPECTUS	REDISTRICT	RETROSPECT	SECULARIZE	SOPHOMORIC	SUBTERFUGE	THERMISTOR
PROSPERITY	REDUNDANCY	REVELATION	SEERSUCKER	SPACECRAFT	SUBTRAHEND	THERMOSTAT
PROSPEROUS	REFERENDUM	REVITALIZE	SEISMOGRAM	SPECIALIST	SUBVENTION	THOUGHTFUL
PROSTHESIS	REFINEMENT	REVOCATION	SEISMOLOGY	SPECIALIZE	SUCCESSION	THREADBARE
PROSTITUTE	REFRACTION	REVOLUTION	SELENOLOGY	SPELLBOUND	SUCCESSIVE	THREEPENCE
PROTECTION	REFRACTORY	RHEUMATISM	SEMIDRYING	SPIRITUOUS	SUFFERANCE	THREESCORE
PROTESTANT	REFRINGENT	RHINESTONE	SEMPSTRESS	SPIROCHETE	SUFFICIENT	THROMBOSIS
PROTOPLASM	REFULGENCE	RHINOCEROS	SENEGALESE	SPITTLEBUG	SUFFRAGIST	THROUGHOUT
PROTRACTOR	REGENERACY	RIBOFLAVIN	SENESCENCE	SPLASHDOWN	SUGGESTION	THROUGHPUT
PROVENANCE	REGENERATE	RICKETTSIA	SEPARATION	SPOILSPORT	SUGGESTIVE	THROUGHWAY
PROVIDENCE	REGISTRANT	RIDICULOUS	SEPARATIST	SPOLIATION	SUNGLASSES	THUMBSCREW

THUNDEROUS	UNAFFECTED	UNILATERAL	VULNERABLE	WOODCUTTER	CAPITALIST	LACKLUSTER
TIMBERLINE	UNASSUMING	UNIVERSITY	WAINWRIGHT	WOODENWARE	CAPITALIZE	LADYFINGER
TIMEKEEPER	UNATTACHED	UNLETTERED	WALLFLOWER	WOODPECKER	CAPITATION	LANDHOLDER
TOMFOOLERY	UNAVAILING	UNMANNERLY	WANDERLUST	WORKBASKET	CAPITULATE	LANDLOCKED
TOOTHBRUSH	UNBALANCED	UNMERCIFUL	WASTEPAPER	WORKINGMAN	CAPOREGIME	LANDLUBBER
TOOTHPASTE	UNBEARABLE	UNNUMBERED	WATCHMAKER	WORSHIPFUL	CARABINEER	LARYNGITIS
TOPOGRAPHY	UNBEATABLE	UNOCCUPIED	WATCHTOWER	WORTHWHILE	CARBOLATED	LASCIVIOUS
TORRENTIAL	UNBECOMING	UNPLEASANT	WATERBORNE	WRAPAROUND	CARBURETOR	LAWBREAKER
TOUCHSTONE	UNBELIEVER	UNREASONED	WATERCOLOR	WRISTWATCH	CARCINOGEN	LAWRENCIUM
TOURMALINE	UNBLUSHING	UNRESERVED	WATERCRAFT	XENOPHOBIA	CARDIOGRAM	MACKINTOSH
TOURNAMENT	UNCRITICAL	UNSCHOOLED	WATERCRESS	XEROGRAPHY	CARDIOLOGY	MAGISTRATE
TOURNIQUET	UNDENIABLE	UNSCRAMBLE	WATERFRONT	YARDMASTER	CARICATURE	MAIDENHAIR
TOXICOLOGY	UNDERBELLY	UNSKILLFUL	WATERMELON	YESTERYEAR	CATABOLISM	MAIDENHEAD
TRAJECTORY	UNDERBRUSH	UNSUITABLE	WATERPOWER		CATAFALQUE	MAIDENHOOD
TRAMPOLINE	UNDERCOVER	UNTHINKING	WATERPROOF		CATCHPENNY	MAINSPRING
TRANSCRIBE	UNDERCROFT	UNYIELDING	WATERSPOUT		CATECHUMEN	MAINSTREAM
TRANSCRIPT	UNDERLYING	UPBRINGING	WATERTIGHT	**2**ND **LETTER**	CATEGORIZE	MAISONETTE
TRANSDUCER	UNDERNEATH	UPHOLSTERY	WATERWHEEL		CAVITATION	MALADAPTED
TRANSGRESS	UNDERPANTS	UPROARIOUS	WATERWORKS	BACKGAMMON	DATAMATION	MALAPROPOS
TRANSISTOR	UNDERSCORE	UPSTANDING	WAVELENGTH	BACKGROUND	EARTHQUAKE	MALCONTENT
TRANSITION	UNDERSEXED	URETHRITIS	WEAPONLESS	BACKHANDED	FACILITATE	MALEFACTOR
TRANSITIVE	UNDERSHIRT	URINALYSIS	WEATHERING	BACKSTAIRS	FACTITIOUS	MALEFICENT
TRANSITORY	UNDERSHOOT	UROGENITAL	WEATHERMAN	BACKSTROKE	FAHRENHEIT	MALEVOLENT
TRANSPLANT	UNDERSIZED	VARICOSITY	WEIGHTLESS	BALBRIGGAN	FAIRGROUND	MALODOROUS
TRANSPOLAR	UNDERSKIRT	VAUDEVILLE	WELLSPRING	BALDERDASH	FALLACIOUS	MALTHUSIAN
TRANSVERSE	UNDERSLUNG	VEGETARIAN	WESTERNIZE	BALLISTICS	FAMILARIZE	MANAGEMENT
TRAVELOGUE	UNDERSTAND	VEGETATION	WHARFINGER	BALUSTRADE	FARFETCHED	MANDELBROT
TRAVERTINE	UNDERSTATE	VEGETATIVE	WHATSOEVER	BAPTISTERY	FARSIGHTED	MANDRAGORA
TREMENDOUS	UNDERSTOOD	VELOCIPEDE	WHEELCHAIR	BAREHEADED	FASTIDIOUS	MANICURIST
TRIFOLIATE	UNDERSTORY	VERMICELLI	WHEELHORSE	BASKETBALL	FATHERLAND	MANIPULATE
TRIMONTHLY	UNDERSTUDY	VERNACULAR	WHEELHOUSE	BASTARDIZE	FATHOMLESS	MANSERVANT
TRIPARTITE	UNDERTAKER	VERTEBRATE	WHENSOEVER	BATHYSCAPH	FAVORITISM	MANSUETUDE
TRIPLICATE	UNDERTRICK	VESPERTINE	WHIRLYBIRD	BATRACHIAN	GADOLINIUM	MANTLEROCK
TROLLEYBUS	UNDERVALUE	VETERINARY	WHITSUNDAY	BATTLEMENT	GAMEKEEPER	MANUSCRIPT
TROUBADOUR	UNDERWAIST	VIBRAPHONE	WHOMSOEVER	BATTLESHIP	GARGANTUAN	MARASCHINO
TRUNCATION	UNDERWATER	VICEGERENT	WICKERWORK	CACCIATORE	GASTRONOMY	MARGINALIA
TUBERCULAR	UNDERWORLD	VICTORIOUS	WIDESPREAD	CADAVEROUS	GATEKEEPER	MARGUERITE
TUBERCULIN	UNDERWRITE	VICTUALLER	WILDEBEEST	CALCAREOUS	HABILIMENT	MARIONETTE
TUMBLEDOWN	UNDULATION	VIDEOPHONE	WILDERNESS	CALCULATED	HABITATION	MARROWBONE
TUMBLEWEED	UNEMPLOYED	VIETNAMESE	WILLOWWARE	CALUMNIATE	HALLELUJAH	MARTINGALE
TUMULTUOUS	UNEVENTFUL	VILLAINOUS	WINCHESTER	CAMELOPARD	HAMMERHEAD	MASQUERADE
TURBULENCE	UNEXAMPLED	VINDICTIVE	WINDFLOWER	CAMOUFLAGE	HAMMERLOCK	MASTERMIND
TURNBUCKLE	UNEXPECTED	VIRTUOSITY	WINDJAMMER	CAMPHORATE	HANDBARROW	MASTERSHIP
TURPENTINE	UNFAITHFUL	VISIBILITY	WINDOWPANE	CANDELABRA	HANDICRAFT	MASTERWORK
TURTLEDOVE	UNFAMILIAR	VISITATION	WINDOWSILL	CANDESCENT	HANDLEBARS	MATCHMAKER
TURTLENECK	UNFRIENDLY	VITUPERATE	WINDSHIELD	CANDLEWICK	HANDMAIDEN	MATURATION
TYPESCRIPT	UNFRUITFUL	VIVIPAROUS	WINEGROWER	CANKERWORM	HANDSPRING	MAYONNAISE
TYPESETTER	UNGENEROUS	VOCABULARY	WINGSPREAD	CANNONBALL	HARDHEADED	NANOSECOND
TYPEWRITER	UNGRACEFUL	VOCIFERATE	WINTERTIDE	CANONICALS	HARMONIOUS	NAPOLEONIC
TYPOGRAPHY	UNGRACIOUS	VOCIFEROUS	WINTERTIME	CANTALOUPE	JACKANAPES	NARCISSISM
TYRANNICAL	UNGRATEFUL	VOICEPRINT	WIREHAIRED	CANTILEVER	JACKHAMMER	NASTURTIUM
UBIQUITOUS	UNGROUNDED	VOLLEYBALL	WITCHCRAFT	CANTONMENT	JACKRABBIT	NATATORIUM
ULTRASHORT	UNHALLOWED	VOLUMETRIC	WITCHGRASS	CANVASBACK	JARDINIERE	NATIONWIDE
ULTRASONIC	UNHANDSOME	VOLUMINOUS	WITHDRAWAL	CAOUTCHOUC	JAWBREAKER	NATURALISM
ULTRASOUND	UNICAMERAL	VOLUPTUARY	WONDERLAND	CAPACITATE	LABORATORY	NATURALIST
UNABRIDGED	UNIFORMITY	VOLUPTUOUS	WONDERMENT	CAPITALISM	LACHRYMOSE	NATURALIZE

PACKSADDLE	TABERNACLE	ACCOMPLICE	BELLWETHER	DEMONETIZE	HEADMASTER	NECROPOLIS
PACKTHREAD	TABLECLOTH	ACCOMPLISH	BELONGINGS	DEMONOLOGY	HEADSTRONG	NEEDLEWORK
PAGINATION	TABLESPOON	ACCORDANCE	BENCHMARKS	DEMORALIZE	HEADWAITER	NEGATIVISM
PAINKILLER	TACHOMETER	ACCOUNTANT	BENEFACTOR	DENDROLOGY	HEARTBREAK	NEGLIGIBLE
PAINTBRUSH	TAMBOURINE	ACCOUNTING	BENEFICENT	DENOMINATE	HEARTHSIDE	NEIGHBORLY
PALATALIZE	TANTAMOUNT	ACCUMULATE	BENEFICIAL	DENOTATIVE	HEARTTHROB	NEOCLASSIC
PALATINATE	TARANTELLA	ACCUSATIVE	BESPRINKLE	DENOUEMENT	HEATSTROKE	NETHERMOST
PALIMPSEST	TASKMASTER	ACCUSTOMED	BESTIALITY	DENTIFRICE	HECTOLITER	NETTLESOME
PALINDROME	TATTERSALL	ACHROMATIC	BETTERMENT	DEPARTMENT	HECTOMETER	NEUTRALISM
PALLBEARER	TATTLETALE	ACROBATICS	CELEBRATED	DEPENDABLE	HELICOPTER	NEUTRALITY
PANJANDRUM	VARICOSITY	ACROPHOBIA	CELLARETTE	DEPENDENCE	HELIOGRAPH	NEUTRALIZE
PANTALOONS	VAUDEVILLE	ACTIONABLE	CELLOPHANE	DEPENDENCY	HELIOTROPE	NEWFANGLED
PANTYWAIST	WAINWRIGHT	ECONOMICAL	CENSORIOUS	DEPILATORY	HEMATOLOGY	NEWSGROUPS
PAPERBOARD	WALLFLOWER	ECUMENICAL	CENSORSHIP	DEPLORABLE	HEMISPHERE	NEWSLETTER
PARAMECIUM	WANDERLUST	ICEBREAKER	CENTENNIAL	DEPOLARIZE	HEMOGLOBIN	NEWSWORTHY
PARAPHRASE	WASTEPAPER	ICONOCLASM	CENTESIMAL	DEPOPULATE	HEMOPHILIA	OESOPHAGUS
PARAPLEGIA	WATCHMAKER	ICONOCLAST	CENTIGRADE	DEPORTMENT	HEMORRHAGE	PEACEMAKER
PARATROOPS	WATCHTOWER	OCCASIONAL	CENTILITER	DEPOSITION	HEMORRHOID	PEASHOOTER
PARLIAMENT	WATERBORNE	OCCIDENTAL	CENTIMETER	DEPOSITORY	HENCEFORTH	PECCADILLO
PARMIGIANA	WATERCOLOR	OCCUPATION	CENTRALIZE	DEPRECIATE	HEPTAMETER	PEDESTRIAN
PARTICIPLE	WATERCRAFT	OCCURRENCE	CENTRIFUGE	DEPRESSANT	HEREABOUTS	PEDIATRICS
PARTICULAR	WATERCRESS	OCEANARIUM	CEREBELLUM	DEPRESSION	HEREDITARY	PEJORATIVE
PASSAGEWAY	WATERFRONT	OCEANFRONT	CEREMONIAL	DEPRESSIVE	HERETOFORE	PENICILLIN
PASTEBOARD	WATERMELON	OCEANGOING	DEACTIVATE	DEPUTATION	KETTLEDRUM	PENMANSHIP
PASTEURIZE	WATERPOWER	OCEANOLOGY	DEADWEIGHT	DERIVATION	LEAFHOPPER	PENNYROYAL
PATHFINDER	WATERPROOF	OCTOTHORPE	DEALERSHIP	DERIVATIVE	LEDERHOSEN	PENTAMETER
PATRONYMIC	WATERSPOUT	SCAPEGRACE	DEATHWATCH	DERMATITIS	LEGITIMATE	PEPPERCORN
PAWNBROKER	WATERTIGHT	SCARLATINA	DEBILITATE	DEROGATORY	LENGTHWISE	PEPPERMINT
RACECOURSE	WATERWHEEL	SCHISMATIC	DECAPITATE	DESALINATE	LEPRECHAUN	PERCENTAGE
RADARSCOPE	WATERWORKS	SCHOLASTIC	DECELERATE	DESALINIZE	LETTERHEAD	PERCENTILE
RADICALIZE	WAVELENGTH	SCHOOLGIRL	DECIMALIZE	DESCENDANT	MEADOWLARK	PERCEPTION
RADIOGENIC	YARDMASTER	SCHOOLMARM	DECLASSIFY	DESERVEDLY	MECHANICAL	PERCEPTIVE
RADIOGRAPH	ABBREVIATE	SCHOOLMATE	DECLENSION	DESOLATION	MEDDLESOME	PERCEPTUAL
RADIOMETER	ABERRATION	SCHOOLROOM	DECOLORIZE	DESPICABLE	MEDICAMENT	PERCIPIENT
RADIOPHONE	ABOMINABLE	SCRUTINIZE	DECOMPRESS	DESTRUCTOR	MEERSCHAUM	PERCUSSION
RADIOSONDE	ABORIGINAL	SCURRILOUS	DECORATION	DETACHMENT	MELANCHOLY	PERDURABLE
RAGAMUFFIN	ABOVEBOARD	ADDITIONAL	DECORATIVE	DETERMINED	MELANESIAN	PEREMPTORY
RAINMAKING	ABSCISSION	ADJUDICATE	DECRYPTION	DETERRENCE	MEMBERSHIP	PERFECTION
RAMSHACKLE	ABSOLUTION	ADMINISTER	DEFINITION	DEVITALIZE	MEMORANDUM	PERIHELION
RATTLETRAP	ABSOLUTISM	ADMISSIBLE	DEFINITIVE	FEDERALISM	MENDACIOUS	PERIODICAL
SACCHARINE	ABSORPTION	ADMITTANCE	DEFLAGRATE	FEDERALIST	MENINGITIS	PERIPHERAL
SACERDOTAL	ABSTEMIOUS	ADRENALINE	DEGENERACY	FEDERALIZE	MENSURABLE	PERISHABLE
SACROILIAC	ABSTINENCE	ADULTERANT	DEGENERATE	FEDERATION	MERCANTILE	PERITONEUM
SACROSANCT	EBULLITION	ADULTERATE	DEGRADABLE	FELICITATE	MESOSPHERE	PERIWINKLE
SALAMANDER	OBLIGATION	ADVENTURER	DEHUMANIZE	FELICITOUS	METABOLISM	PERMAFROST
SALESWOMAN	OBLITERATE	ADVISEMENT	DEHUMIDIFY	FELLOWSHIP	METABOLITE	PERMISSION
SALTCELLAR	OBSEQUIOUS	IDIOPATHIC	DELECTABLE	FERTILIZER	METACARPUS	PERMISSIVE
SALUBRIOUS	OBSERVABLE	AEROBATICS	DELEGATION	GENERALITY	METAGALAXY	PERNICIOUS
SALUTATION	OBSERVANCE	AESTHETICS	DELIBERATE	GENERALIZE	METALLURGY	PERORATION
SANATORIUM	OBSTETRICS	BEAUJOLAIS	DELINQUENT	GENERATION	METASTASIS	PERPETRATE
SANDALWOOD	UBIQUITOUS	BEAUTICIAN	DELIQUESCE	GENTLEFOLK	METATARSAL	PERPETUATE
SANGUINARY	ACCELERATE	BEDCLOTHES	DELPHINIUM	GEOCENTRIC	METATARSUS	PERPETUITY
SANITARIAN	ACCENTUATE	BEDRAGGLED	DEMOBILIZE	GEOPHYSICS	METICULOUS	PERQUISITE
SANITARIUM	ACCEPTABLE	BEFOREHAND	DEMOCRATIC	GEOSCIENCE	METROPOLIS	PERSIFLAGE
SANITATION	ACCEPTANCE	BEHINDHAND	DEMOGRAPHY	GEOTHERMAL	METTLESOME	PERSONABLE
SAPROPHYTE	ACCESSIBLE	BELLADONNA	DEMOISELLE	GERIATRICS	NEBULOSITY	PERSONALTY
SAUERKRAUT	ACCIDENTAL	BELLETRIST	DEMOLITION	GESUNDHEIT	NECROMANCY	PERSUASION

PERVERSION	RESILIENCE	TEMPTATION	CHEAPSKATE	THREESCORE	DISCONNECT	KINEMATICS
PESTILENCE	RESILIENCY	TENDERFOOT	CHECKPOINT	THROMBOSIS	DISCONTENT	KINGFISHER
PETNAPPING	RESISTANCE	TENDERLOIN	CHEESECAKE	THROUGHOUT	DISCOURAGE	LIBERALISM
PETROLATUM	RESOLUTION	TENEBRIOUS	CHIFFONIER	THROUGHPUT	DISCREPANT	LIBIDINOUS
REACTIVATE	RESORPTION	TERMINATOR	CHILDBIRTH	THROUGHWAY	DISCRETION	LICENTIATE
READERSHIP	RESOUNDING	TESSELLATE	CHIMERICAL	THUMBSCREW	DISCURSIVE	LICENTIOUS
REASONABLE	RESPECTING	TETRAMETER	CHIMPANZEE	THUNDEROUS	DISCUSSANT	LIEUTENANT
REBELLIOUS	RESPECTIVE	VEGETARIAN	CHINCHILLA	WHARFINGER	DISEMBOWEL	LIFESAVING
RECEIVABLE	RESPIRATOR	VEGETATION	CHIROMANCY	WHATSOEVER	DISENCHANT	LIGHTHOUSE
RECEPTACLE	RESPONDENT	VEGETATIVE	CHIVALROUS	WHEELCHAIR	DISGRUNTLE	LIGHTPROOF
RECIDIVISM	RESPONSIVE	VELOCIPEDE	CHLORINATE	WHEELHORSE	DISHABILLE	LIKELIHOOD
RECIPROCAL	RESTAURANT	VERMICELLI	CHLOROFORM	WHEELHOUSE	DISHARMONY	LINEBACKER
RECITATION	RESTORABLE	VERNACULAR	CHROMOSOME	WHENSOEVER	DISHEARTEN	LIPREADING
RECOILLESS	RESTRAINED	VERTEBRATE	CHRONOLOGY	WHIRLYBIRD	DISHWASHER	LITERALISM
RECOMPENSE	RESURGENCE	VESPERTINE	CHRYSOLITE	WHITSUNDAY	DISINCLINE	LITERATURE
RECONSIDER	RETRACTILE	VETERINARY	CHURCHGOER	WHOMSOEVER	DISINHERIT	LITHUANIAN
RECREATION	RETROGRADE	WEAPONLESS	CHURCHLESS	AIRFREIGHT	DISJOINTED	LIVELIHOOD
RECUPERATE	RETROGRESS	WEATHERING	CHURCHYARD	BICHLORIDE	DISORDERLY	LIVERWURST
REDEMPTION	RETROSPECT	WEATHERMAN	GHOSTWRITE	BIMETALLIC	DISPENSARY	MICROFICHE
REDISTRICT	REVELATION	WEIGHTLESS	PHENOMENON	BIOMEDICAL	DISPOSABLE	MICROGRAPH
REDUNDANCY	REVITALIZE	WELLSPRING	PHILISTINE	BIOPHYSICS	DISPOSSESS	MICROMETER
REFERENDUM	REVOCATION	WESTERNIZE	PHILOSOPHY	BIPARENTAL	DISQUALIFY	MICROPHONE
REFINEMENT	REVOLUTION	XENOPHOBIA	PHLEBOTOMY	BIPARIETAL	DISRESPECT	MICROPROBE
REFRACTION	SEAMANSHIP	XEROGRAPHY	PHLEGMATIC	BIPARTISAN	DISSATISFY	MICROSCOPE
REFRACTORY	SEAMSTRESS	YESTERYEAR	PHONOGRAPH	BIRTHPLACE	DISSENSION	MICROSTATE
REFRINGENT	SEARCHWARE	AFFLICTIVE	PHOSPHORUS	BIRTHRIGHT	DISSERVICE	MIDDLEBROW
REFULGENCE	SEASONABLE	AFICIONADO	PHOTOFLASH	BIRTHSTONE	DISSIMILAR	MIDSHIPMAN
REGENERACY	SECONDHAND	AFTERBIRTH	PHOTOGENIC	BITUMINOUS	DISSOCIATE	MIGNONETTE
REGENERATE	SECULARISM	AFTERIMAGE	PHOTOGRAPH	CINERARIUM	DISSONANCE	MILITARISM
REGISTRANT	SECULARIZE	AFTERTASTE	PHOTOMETER	CINQUEFOIL	DISTILLATE	MILITARIZE
REGRESSION	SEERSUCKER	EFFECTUATE	PHOTOMURAL	CIRCUITOUS	DISTRAUGHT	MILLENNIUM
REGULATION	SEISMOGRAM	EFFEMINATE	PHOTOPAINT	CIRCUMCISE	DISTRIBUTE	MILLILITER
REJUVENATE	SEISMOLOGY	EFFERVESCE	PHRENOLOGY	CIRCUMFLEX	DIVINATION	MILLIMETER
RELATIONAL	SELENOLOGY	EFFICIENCY	PHYLACTERY	CIRCUMVENT	EISTEDDFOD	MILLSTREAM
RELATIVITY	SEMIDRYING	EFFLORESCE	PHYSIOLOGY	CITRONELLA	FIBERBOARD	MILLWRIGHT
RELAXATION	SEMPSTRESS	EFFRONTERY	RHEUMATISM	DIAPHANOUS	FIBERGLASS	MIMEOGRAPH
RELENTLESS	SENEGALESE	EFFULGENCE	RHINESTONE	DICTIONARY	FIBRINOGEN	MINERALIZE
RELINQUISH	SENESCENCE	OFTENTIMES	RHINOCEROS	DIELECTRIC	FICTITIOUS	MINERALOGY
RELUCTANCE	SEPARATION	AGGRANDIZE	SHAMEFACED	DIFFERENCE	FIELDPIECE	MINESTRONE
REMARKABLE	SEPARATIST	AGGRESSION	SHENANIGAN	DIFFICULTY	FIGURATION	MINISCROLL
REMEDIABLE	SEPARATIVE	AGGRESSIVE	SHIBBOLETH	DILETTANTE	FIGURATIVE	MINISTRANT
REMITTANCE	SEPTICEMIA	EGOCENTRIC	SHILLELAGH	DILLYDALLY	FIGUREHEAD	MISALIGNED
REMUNERATE	SEPTUAGINT	IGNORAMOUS	SHIPFITTER	DIMINUENDO	FILIBUSTER	MISCELLANY
RENASCENCE	SEPULCHRAL	CHALCEDONY	SHIPWRIGHT	DIMINUTIVE	FINGERLING	MISCONDUCT
RENDEZVOUS	SERPENTINE	CHANCELLOR	SHOESTRING	DINNERWARE	FINGERNAIL	MISFORTUNE
REPAGINATE	SERVICEMAN	CHANDELIER	SHOPKEEPER	DIPHTHERIA	FISTICUFFS	MISOGAMIST
REPARATION	SERVOMOTOR	CHANGELING	SHORTENING	DIPSOMANIA	GINGERSNAP	MISOGYNIST
REPARATIVE	SETTLEMENT	CHANGEOVER	SHUNPIKING	DISAPPOINT	GINGIVITIS	MISSILEMAN
REPATRIATE	TEARJERKER	CHANNELIZE	SHUTTERBUG	DISAPPROVE	HIEROPHANT	MISSIONARY
REPERTOIRE	TECHNETIUM	CHAPFALLEN	THEATRICAL	DISARRANGE	HIGHLANDER	MISTAKABLE
REPETITION	TECHNICIAN	CHARACTERY	THEMSELVES	DISBELIEVE	HIGHWAYMAN	MIZZENMAST
REPETITIVE	TECHNOLOGY	CHARITABLE	THEREAFTER	DISCERNING	HINTERLAND	NIGHTDRESS
REPORTEDLY	TEETHRIDGE	CHARLESTON	THERMISTOR	DISCIPLINE	HIPPODROME	NIGHTSHADE
REPOSITORY	TELEGRAPHY	CHARTREUSE	THERMOSTAT	DISCOMFORT	HISTRIONIC	NIGHTSHIRT
REPUBLICAN	TELESCOPIC	CHATELAINE	THOUGHTFUL	DISCOMMODE	JIMSONWEED	NIGHTSTICK
REPUGNANCE	TELEVISION	CHATTERBOX	THREADBARE	DISCOMPOSE	JINRIKISHA	NINCOMPOOP
REPUTATION	TEMPERANCE	CHAUVINISM	THREEPENCE	DISCONCERT	KIESELGUHR	PIANISSIMO

PIANOFORTE	WINTERTIME	FLOORBOARD	IMPECCABLE	ENDANGERED	INGLORIOUS	INVIOLABLE
PICARESQUE	WIREHAIRED	FLUIDOUNCE	IMPEDIMENT	ENDEARMENT	INGRATIATE	INVOCATION
PICCALILLI	WITCHCRAFT	FLUORIDATE	IMPENITENT	ENDOGENOUS	INGREDIENT	INVOLUTION
PICKANINNY	WITCHGRASS	FLUORINATE	IMPERATIVE	ENGAGEMENT	INHABITANT	KNICKKNACK
PICKPOCKET	WITHDRAWAL	FLYCATCHER	IMPERSONAL	ENJAMBMENT	INHIBITION	KNIGHTHOOD
PICOSECOND	SKATEBOARD	GLACIOLOGY	IMPERVIOUS	ENTERPRISE	INHUMANITY	KNOCKWURST
PIGEONHOLE	SKEPTICISM	ILLITERATE	IMPLACABLE	ENTHUSIASM	INIMITABLE	SNAPDRAGON
PILGRIMAGE	SKYSCRAPER	ILLUMINATE	IMPORTANCE	ENTOMOLOGY	INITIATIVE	SNOWMOBILE
PILLOWCASE	SKYWRITING	ILLUSTRATE	IMPOSSIBLE	INACTIVATE	INITIATORY	UNABRIDGED
PILOTHOUSE	ALBUMINOUS	OLEAGINOUS	IMPOVERISH	INADEQUATE	INJUNCTION	UNAFFECTED
PINCUSHION	ALCOHOLISM	PLAGIARIZE	IMPREGNATE	INAPTITUDE	INNOMINATE	UNASSUMING
PINFEATHER	ALIMENTARY	PLANTATION	IMPRESARIO	INAUGURATE	INNOVATION	UNATTACHED
RIBOFLAVIN	ALKALINIZE	PLAYACTING	IMPRESSION	INBREEDING	INOPERABLE	UNAVAILING
RICKETTSIA	ALLEGIANCE	PLAYGROUND	IMPRESSIVE	INCAPACITY	INORDINATE	UNBALANCED
RIDICULOUS	ALLHALLOWS	PLAYWRIGHT	IMPRIMATUR	INCENDIARY	INQUIETUDE	UNBEARABLE
RINGLEADER	ALLITERATE	PLEASANTRY	IMPROBABLE	INCIDENTAL	INSATIABLE	UNBEATABLE
RINGMASTER	ALONGSHORE	PLEBISCITE	OMNIPOTENT	INCINERATE	INSEMINATE	UNBECOMING
RISIBILITY	ALPHABETIC	PLUPERFECT	OMNISCIENT	INCIVILITY	INSENSIBLE	UNBELIEVER
SIDESTROKE	ALTARPIECE	PLUTOCRACY	OMNIVOROUS	INCLINABLE	INSENTIENT	UNBLUSHING
SIDEWINDER	ALTERNATOR	SLENDERIZE	SMATTERING	INCOHERENT	INSISTENCE	UNCRITICAL
SILHOUETTE	ALTOGETHER	SLIPSTREAM	SMOKESTACK	INCOMPLETE	INSOLATION	UNDENIABLE
SILVERFISH	BLACKAMOOR	SLUMBEROUS	ANEMOMETER	INCONSTANT	INSOLVABLE	UNDERBELLY
SILVERWARE	BLACKBERRY	ULTRASHORT	ANESTHESIA	INCREDIBLE	INSTRUCTOR	UNDERBRUSH
SIMILITUDE	BLACKBOARD	ULTRASONIC	ANESTHETIC	INCULPABLE	INSTRUMENT	UNDERCOVER
SIMPLICITY	BLACKGUARD	ULTRASOUND	ANGIOSPERM	INCUMBENCY	INTANGIBLE	UNDERCROFT
SIMPLISTIC	BLACKSMITH	AMALGAMATE	ANGLOPHILE	INDECISION	INTEGUMENT	UNDERLYING
SINGLETREE	BLACKTHORN	AMANUENSIS	ANGLOPHOBE	INDECISIVE	INTERBLOCK	UNDERNEATH
SISTERHOOD	BLANCMANGE	AMBASSADOR	ANIMADVERT	INDECOROUS	INTERBREED	UNDERPANTS
TIMBERLINE	BLITZKRIEG	AMBULATORY	ANIMALCULE	INDEFINITE	INTERFAITH	UNDERSCORE
TIMEKEEPER	BLOCKHOUSE	AMELIORATE	ANNIHILATE	INDELICATE	INTERFERON	UNDERSEXED
VIBRAPHONE	BLOODHOUND	AMERINDIAN	ANNUNCIATE	INDICATIVE	INTERLEAVE	UNDERSHIRT
VICEGERENT	BLOODSTAIN	AMMUNITION	ANSWERABLE	INDIGENOUS	INTERLUNAR	UNDERSHOOT
VICTORIOUS	BLOODSTONE	AMPHIBIOUS	ANTAGONISM	INDISCREET	INTERMARRY	UNDERSIZED
VICTUALLER	BLUEBONNET	EMANCIPATE	ANTAGONIST	INDISPOSED	INTERMEZZO	UNDERSKIRT
VIDEOPHONE	BLUEBOTTLE	EMASCULATE	ANTAGONIZE	INDISTINCT	INTERNMENT	UNDERSLUNG
VIETNAMESE	BLUECOLLAR	EMBANKMENT	ANTEBELLUM	INDIVIDUAL	INTERSTATE	UNDERSTAND
VILLAINOUS	BLUEJACKET	EMBONPOINT	ANTECEDENT	INDONESIAN	INTERSTICE	UNDERSTATE
VINDICTIVE	CLASSICISM	EMBOUCHURE	ANTEPENULT	INDUCEMENT	INTERTIDAL	UNDERSTOOD
VIRTUOSITY	CLASSIFIED	EMBROIDERY	ANTHRACITE	INDUCTANCE	INTERTWINE	UNDERSTORY
VISIBILITY	CLAVICHORD	EMBRYOLOGY	ANTHROPOID	INDULGENCE	INTERTWIST	UNDERSTUDY
VISITATION	CLERESTORY	EMPIRICISM	ANTIBIOTIC	INDUSTRIAL	INTERURBAN	UNDERTAKER
VITUPERATE	CLINGSTONE	EMPLOYMENT	ANTICANCER	INELIGIBLE	INTERWEAVE	UNDERTRICK
VIVIPAROUS	CLODHOPPER	EMULSIFIER	ANTICHRIST	INEQUALITY	INTIMIDATE	UNDERVALUE
WICKERWORK	CLOTHESPIN	IMAGINABLE	ANTICIPATE	INEVITABLE	INTINCTION	UNDERWAIST
WIDESPREAD	CLOUDBURST	IMBIBITION	ANTICLIMAX	INEXORABLE	INTOLERANT	UNDERWATER
WILDEBEEST	CLOVERLEAF	IMMACULATE	ANTIFREEZE	INEXPIABLE	INTONATION	UNDERWORLD
WILDERNESS	ELDERBERRY	IMMATERIAL	ANTIMATTER	INFALLIBLE	INTOXICANT	UNDERWRITE
WILLOWWARE	ELECTORATE	IMMEMORIAL	ANTINOMIAN	INFIDELITY	INTOXICATE	UNDULATION
WINCHESTER	ELECTRONIC	IMMISCIBLE	ANTIPHONAL	INFIGHTING	INTRAMURAL	UNEMPLOYED
WINDFLOWER	ELEMENTARY	IMMOBILIZE	ANTIPROTON	INFILTRATE	INTRASTATE	UNEVENTFUL
WINDJAMMER	FLAGELLATE	IMMODERATE	ANTIQUATED	INFINITIVE	INVALIDATE	UNEXAMPLED
WINDOWPANE	FLAGITIOUS	IMMORALITY	ANTISEPTIC	INFINITUDE	INVALUABLE	UNEXPECTED
WINDOWSILL	FLAMBOYANT	IMMUNOLOGY	ANTISOCIAL	INFLECTION	INVARIABLE	UNFAITHFUL
WINDSHIELD	FLASHLIGHT	IMPALPABLE	ANTITHESIS	INFLEXIBLE	INVESTMENT	UNFAMILIAR
WINEGROWER	FLOODLIGHT	IMPASSABLE	ENAMELWARE	INFRACTION	INVETERATE	UNFRIENDLY
WINGSPREAD	FLOODPLAIN	IMPASSIBLE	ENCRYPTION	INFRASONIC	INVIGORATE	UNFRUITFUL
WINTERTIDE	FLOODWATER	IMPATIENCE	ENCYCLICAL	INFREQUENT	INVINCIBLE	UNGENEROUS

UNGRACEFUL	COMMONALTY	CONNECTIVE	COUNTRYMAN	HORSEWOMAN	POSTHUMOUS	APOTHECARY
UNGRACIOUS	COMMONWEAL	CONNIPTION	COURTHOUSE	HOSPITABLE	POSTMASTER	APOTHEOSIS
UNGRATEFUL	COMMUNIQUE	CONSCIENCE	COWPUNCHER	HOUSECLEAN	POSTMORTEM	APPARITION
UNGROUNDED	COMMUTATOR	CONSECRATE	DOCKWORKER	HOUSEWARES	POSTPARTUM	APPEARANCE
UNHALLOWED	COMPARABLE	CONSEQUENT	DOGCATCHER	IONOSPHERE	POSTSCRIPT	APPETIZING
UNHANDSOME	COMPARISON	CONSISTORY	DOMINATION	JOURNALESE	POTENTIATE	APPLICABLE
UNICAMERAL	COMPASSION	CONSONANCE	DONNYBROOK	JOURNALISM	POULTRYMAN	APPLICATOR
UNIFORMITY	COMPATIBLE	CONSORTIUM	DOORKEEPER	JOURNEYMAN	POURPARLER	APPOINTIVE
UNILATERAL	COMPATRIOT	CONSPECTUS	DOWNSTAIRS	LOCOMOTION	POWERHOUSE	APPOSITION
UNIVERSITY	COMPENDIUM	CONSPIRACY	DOWNSTREAM	LOCOMOTIVE	POWERLINES	APPOSITIVE
UNLETTERED	COMPENSATE	CONSTITUTE	DOWNSTROKE	LOGANBERRY	ROADRUNNER	APPRECIATE
UNMANNERLY	COMPETENCE	CONSTRAINT	FOLKSINGER	LOGGERHEAD	ROLLERBALL	APPRENTICE
UNMERCIFUL	COMPETENCY	CONSUMMATE	FOOTBRIDGE	LOGROLLING	ROLLICKING	EPIGLOTTIS
UNNUMBERED	COMPETITOR	CONTAGIOUS	FOOTLIGHTS	LOQUACIOUS	ROTISSERIE	EPISCOPACY
UNOCCUPIED	COMPLECTED	CONTENTION	FOOTLOCKER	LOVEMAKING	ROUGHHOUSE	EPISCOPATE
UNPLEASANT	COMPLEMENT	CONTIGUOUS	FORBIDDING	MOHAMMEDAN	ROUNDABOUT	EPITHELIUM
UNREASONED	COMPLEXION	CONTINENCE	FORECASTLE	MOLYBDENUM	ROUNDHOUSE	OPALESCENT
UNRESERVED	COMPLIANCE	CONTINGENT	FOREFATHER	MONARCHIST	ROUSTABOUT	OPHTHALMIC
UNSCHOOLED	COMPLIANCY	CONTINUITY	FOREFINGER	MONOCHROME	SOLICITOUS	OPPRESSION
UNSCRAMBLE	COMPLICATE	CONTINUOUS	FOREGATHER	MONOPHONIC	SOLICITUDE	OPPROBRIUM
UNSKILLFUL	COMPLICITY	CONTRABAND	FOREGROUND	MONOTHEISM	SOLIDARITY	SPACECRAFT
UNSUITABLE	COMPLIMENT	CONTRADICT	FOREHANDED	MONOTONOUS	SOMERSAULT	SPECIALIST
UNTHINKING	COMPOSITOR	CONTRAVENE	FOREORDAIN	MONSTRANCE	SOOTHSAYER	SPECIALIZE
UNYIELDING	COMPREHEND	CONTRIBUTE	FORERUNNER	MONUMENTAL	SOPHOMORIC	SPELLBOUND
BOISTEROUS	COMPROMISE	CONTROLLER	FORESHADOW	MOONSTRUCK	TOMFOOLERY	SPIRITUOUS
BOLSHEVISM	COMPULSION	CONTROVERT	FORFEITURE	MORATORIUM	TOOTHBRUSH	SPIROCHETE
BOMBARDIER	COMPULSIVE	CONVALESCE	FORMIDABLE	MORPHOLOGY	TOOTHPASTE	SPITTLEBUG
BONDHOLDER	COMPULSORY	CONVECTION	FORTHRIGHT	MOTHERHOOD	TOPOGRAPHY	SPLASHDOWN
BOOKKEEPER	COMPUSERVE	CONVENIENT	FORTISSIMO	MOTHERLAND	TORRENTIAL	SPOILSPORT
BOOKMOBILE	CONCENTRIC	CONVENTION	FORTUITOUS	MOTORCYCLE	TOUCHSTONE	SPOLIATION
BOOKSELLER	CONCEPTION	CONVERSANT	FOSTERLING	MOTORTRUCK	TOURMALINE	SPORTSCAST
BOONDOGGLE	CONCERNING	CONVERSION	FOUNDATION	MOUNTEBANK	TOURNAMENT	SPRINGTIME
BORDERLAND	CONCERTINA	CONVEYANCE	FOURSQUARE	MOUTHPIECE	TOURNIQUET	SPRINKLING
BOTTLENECK	CONCESSION	CONVICTION	GOALKEEPER	MOZZARELLA	TOXICOLOGY	UPBRINGING
BOTTOMLAND	CONCESSIVE	CONVOLUTED	GOLDBEATER	NOISEMAKER	VOCABULARY	UPHOLSTERY
BOWDLERIZE	CONCILIATE	CONVULSION	GONOCOCCUS	NOMINATIVE	VOCIFERATE	UPROARIOUS
COCKATRICE	CONCLUSION	COORDINATE	GOOSEBERRY	NONCHALANT	VOCIFEROUS	UPSTANDING
COGNIZANCE	CONCORDANT	COPPERHEAD	GOOSEFLESH	NONDRINKER	VOICEPRINT	AQUALUNGER
COINCIDENT	CONCRETION	COPYREADER	GORGONZOLA	NONSTARTER	VOLLEYBALL	AQUAMARINE
COLLARBONE	CONCURRENT	COPYWRITER	GORMANDIZE	NONSUPPORT	VOLUMETRIC	EQUANIMITY
COLLATERAL	CONCUSSION	CORDILLERA	GOVERNMENT	NOTABILITY	VOLUMINOUS	EQUESTRIAN
COLLECTIVE	CONDENSATE	CORDWAINER	HOBBYHORSE	NOTEWORTHY	VOLUPTUARY	EQUITATION
COLLOQUIAL	CONDESCEND	CORNFLOWER	HODGEPODGE	NOTICEABLE	VOLUPTUOUS	EQUIVALENT
COLLOQUIUM	CONDUCTIVE	CORNSTARCH	HOLLOWWARE	NOURISHING	WONDERLAND	EQUIVOCATE
COLORATION	CONFECTION	CORNUCOPIA	HOLOGRAPHY	POCKETBOOK	WONDERMENT	ARBITRATOR
COLORATURA	CONFERENCE	CORONATION	HOMECOMING	POINSETTIA	WOODCUTTER	ARBORVITAE
COLPORTEUR	CONFESSION	CORPULENCE	HOMEOPATHY	POLITICIAN	WOODENWARE	ARCHBISHOP
COMBUSTION	CONFIDENCE	CORRESPOND	HOMOGENIZE	POLYCLINIC	WOODPECKER	ARCHDEACON
COMEDIENNE	CONFISCATE	CORRIGIBLE	HOMOLOGOUS	POLYHEDRON	WORKBASKET	ARCHITRAVE
COMESTIBLE	CONFLUENCE	COSMOPOLIS	HOMOSEXUAL	POLYNESIAN	WORKINGMAN	ARITHMETIC
COMMANDANT	CONFORMITY	COTERMINAL	HONORARIUM	POLYTHEISM	WORSHIPFUL	ARMAGEDDON
COMMANDEER	CONGENITAL	COTTONSEED	HOOTENANNY	POPULATION	WORTHWHILE	ARTICULATE
COMMENTARY	CONGREGATE	COTTONTAIL	HORIZONTAL	PORTCULLIS	APOCALYPSE	ARTIFICIAL
COMMERCIAL	CONGRUENCE	COTTONWOOD	HORRENDOUS	PORTENTOUS	APOCRYPHAL	BRAHMANISM
COMMISSARY	CONGRUENCY	COUNTERACT	HORSEFLESH	PORTUGUESE	APOLITICAL	BRAINCHILD
COMMISSION	CONJECTURE	COUNTERMAN	HORSELAUGH	POSSESSION	APOLOGETIC	BRAINSTORM
COMMODIOUS	CONNECTION	COUNTERSPY	HORSEPOWER	POSSESSIVE	APOSTROPHE	BREADBOARD

BREADFRUIT	GREGARIOUS	PROGRAMMER	UROGENITAL	STRAIGHTEN	MULTIMEDIA	SUPPLEMENT
BREADSTUFF	GRINDSTONE	PROJECTILE	WRAPAROUND	STRAWBERRY	MULTIPLIER	SUPPLICANT
BREAKFRONT	GROUNDLING	PROMETHIUM	WRISTWATCH	STRENGTHEN	MULTISENSE	SUPPLICATE
BREAKWATER	GROUNDMASS	PROMINENCE	ASCENDANCY	STRINGENCY	MULTISTAGE	SURREALISM
BREASTBONE	GROUNDWORK	PROMISSORY	ASPHYXIATE	STRIPTEASE	MULTISTORY	SUSPENSION
BREASTWORK	IRRATIONAL	PROMONTORY	ASPIRATION	STRONGHOLD	MUNIFICENT	SUSPENSORY
BRICKLAYER	IRRELEVANT	PROMPTBOOK	ASSEMBLAGE	STRYCHNINE	MUSICOLOGY	SUSPICIOUS
BRIDEGROOM	IRRESOLUTE	PROMULGATE	ASSEVERATE	STUPENDOUS	NUCLEONICS	SUSTENANCE
BRIDESMAID	KRUGERRAND	PRONOUNCED	ASSIGNMENT	AUCTIONEER	NUMBERLESS	TUBERCULAR
BRIDGEHEAD	ORATORICAL	PROPAGANDA	ASSIMILATE	AUDIOPHILE	NUMEROLOGY	TUBERCULIN
BRIDGEWORK	ORDINATION	PROPELLANT	ASSORTMENT	AUDITORIUM	NURSERYMAN	TUMBLEDOWN
BRIGANTINE	ORGANGUTAN	PROPENSITY	ASSUMPTION	AURIFEROUS	NUTCRACKER	TUMBLEWEED
BROADCLOTH	PRAGMATISM	PROPERTIED	ASTRINGENT	AUSPICIOUS	OUTBALANCE	TUMULTUOUS
BROADSWORD	PREARRANGE	PROPITIATE	ASYMMETRIC	AUSTRALIAN	OUTGENERAL	TURBULENCE
BRONCHITIS	PREBENDARY	PROPITIOUS	ESCARPMENT	AUTHORSHIP	OUTLANDISH	TURNBUCKLE
BRONTOSAUR	PRECARIOUS	PROPORTION	ESCRITOIRE	AUTOMATION	OUTPATIENT	TURPENTINE
BROWNSTONE	PRECAUTION	PROPRIETOR	ESCUTCHEON	AUTOMATIZE	OUTPERFORM	TURTLEDOVE
CRADLESONG	PRECEDENCE	PROPRINTER	ESPADRILLE	AUTOMOBILE	OUTPOURING	TURTLENECK
CRANKSHAFT	PRECESSION	PROPULSION	ESTIMATION	AUTOMOTIVE	OUTRAGEOUS	VULNERABLE
CREDENTIAL	PRECIOSITY	PROSCENIUM	ISOMETRICS	AUTONOMOUS	PUBESCENCE	EVANESCENT
CREDITABLE	PRECOCIOUS	PROSPECTUS	ISOTHERMAL	AUTOSTRADA	PUGNACIOUS	EVANGELISM
CRENELLATE	PREDACEOUS	PROSPERITY	OSTENSIBLE	BUDGERIGAR	PUNISHMENT	EVANGELIST
CRETACEOUS	PREDECEASE	PROSPEROUS	OSTEOPATHY	BULLHEADED	PUTRESCENT	EVANGELIZE
CRISSCROSS	PREDESTINE	PROSTHESIS	PSEUDOCODE	BUSHMASTER	QUADRANGLE	EVENHANDED
CROSSBONES	PREDICABLE	PROSTITUTE	PSYCHIATRY	BUTTERMILK	QUADRATICS	EVERYTHING
CROSSBREED	PREDISPOSE	PROTECTION	PSYCHOLOGY	BUTTONHOLE	QUADRIVIUM	EVERYWHERE
CROSSPIECE	PREEMINENT	PROTESTANT	PSYCHOPATH	BUTTONHOOK	QUADRUPLET	EVISCERATE
CRUSTACEAN	PREEMPTIVE	PROTOPLASM	ATMOSPHERE	CUMMERBUND	QUARANTINE	OVERCHARGE
CRYOGENICS	PREFERENCE	PROTRACTOR	ATTACHMENT	CUMULATIVE	QUATREFOIL	OVERMASTER
CRYPTOGRAM	PREFERMENT	PROVENANCE	ATTAINMENT	CURRICULUM	QUICKBASIC	OVERSHADOW
DRAWBRIDGE	PREHENSILE	PROVIDENCE	ATTENDANCE	CURVACEOUS	QUINTUPLET	OVERSPREAD
DRAWSTRING	PREMARITAL	PROVINCIAL	ATTRACTANT	CUTTLEFISH	RUBBERNECK	OVERWINTER
DREAMWORLD	PREMEDICAL	TRAJECTORY	ATTRACTION	DUMBWAITER	SUBCOMPACT	SWEETBREAD
ERGONOMICS	PREPACKAGE	TRAMPOLINE	OTHERWORLD	DUNDERHEAD	SUBJECTIVE	SWEETBRIER
ERGOSTEROL	PREPOSSESS	TRANSCRIBE	STAGECOACH	DUODECIMAL	SUBLIMINAL	SWEETHEART
ERYSIPELAS	PRESBYOPIA	TRANSCRIPT	STALACTITE	DUPLICATOR	SUBORBITAL	SWITCHBACK
FRANCHISEE	PRESBYTERY	TRANSDUCER	STALAGMITE	EUCALYPTUS	SUBROUTINE	EXACERBATE
FRANCHISER	PRESCIENCE	TRANSGRESS	STANDPOINT	EUPHONIOUS	SUBSEQUENT	EXACTITUDE
FRANCHISOR	PRESSURIZE	TRANSISTOR	STANDSTILL	EURODOLLAR	SUBSIDIARY	EXAGGERATE
FRATERNITY	PRESUPPOSE	TRANSITION	STARVELING	EUTHANASIA	SUBSTATION	EXASPERATE
FRATERNIZE	PRIMORDIAL	TRANSITIVE	STATECRAFT	FUSSBUDGET	SUBSTITUTE	EXCELLENCE
FRATRICIDE	PRINCELING	TRANSITORY	STATEHOUSE	FUTURISTIC	SUBSTRATUM	EXCELLENCY
FRAUDULENT	PRINCIPLED	TRANSPLANT	STATIONARY	GUARDHOUSE	SUBSURFACE	EXCITEMENT
FREEBOOTER	PRIVILEGED	TRANSPOLAR	STATIONERY	GUILLOTINE	SUBTERFUGE	EXCOGITATE
FRESHWATER	PRIZEFIGHT	TRANSVERSE	STATISTICS	GUNSLINGER	SUBTRAHEND	EXHAUSTION
GRADUALISM	PROCEEDING	TRAVELOGUE	STATUESQUE	HULLABALOO	SUBVENTION	EXHAUSTIVE
GRADUATION	PROCESSION	TRAVERTINE	STENTORIAN	HUSBANDMAN	SUCCESSION	EXHILARATE
GRAINFIELD	PROCLIVITY	TREMENDOUS	STEPFATHER	JUBILATION	SUCCESSIVE	EXOBIOLOGY
GRAMOPHONE	PROCURATOR	TRIFOLIATE	STEPLADDER	JUDICATURE	SUFFERANCE	EXORBITANT
GRANDCHILD	PRODIGIOUS	TRIMONTHLY	STEPMOTHER	JUGGERNAUT	SUFFICIENT	EXOTHERMIC
GRANDSTAND	PRODUCTION	TRIPARTITE	STEPPARENT	LUBRICIOUS	SUFFRAGIST	EXPATRIATE
GRAPEFRUIT	PROFESSION	TRIPLICATE	STEPSISTER	LUGUBRIOUS	SUGGESTION	EXPECTANCY
GRATUITOUS	PROFICIENT	TROLLEYBUS	STEREOTYPE	LUMBERJACK	SUGGESTIVE	EXPEDIENCE
GRAVESTONE	PROFLIGATE	TROUBADOUR	STIGMATIZE	LUMBERYARD	SUNGLASSES	EXPEDIENCY
GRAVIMETER	PROGENITOR	TRUNCATION	STILLBIRTH	MUDSLINGER	SUPERCARGO	EXPEDITION
GREENHOUSE	PROGNOSTIC	URETHRITIS	STOCHASTIC	MUHAMMADAN	SUPERSONIC	EXPERIENCE
GREENSWARD	PROGRAMMED	URINALYSIS	STOREHOUSE	MULTILEVEL	SUPERTWIST	EXPERIMENT

EXPLICABLE	CHANCELLOR	GRAVESTONE	STATEHOUSE	LUBRICIOUS	BACKSTROKE	MICROGRAPH
EXPOSITION	CHANDELIER	GRAVIMETER	STATIONARY	NEBULOSITY	BICHLORIDE	MICROMETER
EXPRESSION	CHANGELING	GUARDHOUSE	STATIONERY	PUBESCENCE	CACCIATORE	MICROPHONE
EXPRESSMAN	CHANGEOVER	HEADMASTER	STATISTICS	REBELLIOUS	COCKATRICE	MICROPROBE
EXPRESSWAY	CHANNELIZE	HEADSTRONG	STATUESQUE	RIBOFLAVIN	CYCLOMETER	MICROSCOPE
EXTINGUISH	CHAPFALLEN	HEADWAITER	TEARJERKER	RUBBERNECK	CYCLOPEDIA	MICROSTATE
EXTRAMURAL	CHARACTERY	HEARTBREAK	TRAJECTORY	SUBCOMPACT	DECAPITATE	NECROMANCY
EXTRANEOUS	CHARITABLE	HEARTHSIDE	TRAMPOLINE	SUBJECTIVE	DECELERATE	NECROPOLIS
EXURBANITE	CHARLESTON	HEARTTHROB	TRANSCRIBE	SUBLIMINAL	DECIMALIZE	NUCLEONICS
CYBERSPACE	CHARTREUSE	HEATSTROKE	TRANSCRIPT	SUBORBITAL	DECLASSIFY	OCCASIONAL
CYCLOMETER	CHATELAINE	IMAGINABLE	TRANSDUCER	SUBROUTINE	DECLENSION	OCCIDENTAL
CYCLOPEDIA	CHATTERBOX	INACTIVATE	TRANSGRESS	SUBSEQUENT	DECOLORIZE	OCCUPATION
DYSPROSIUM	CHAUVINISM	INADEQUATE	TRANSISTOR	SUBSIDIARY	DECOMPRESS	OCCURRENCE
EYEDROPPER	CLASSICISM	INAPTITUDE	TRANSITION	SUBSTATION	DECORATION	PACKSADDLE
EYEWITNESS	CLASSIFIED	INAUGURATE	TRANSITIVE	SUBSTITUTE	DECORATIVE	PACKTHREAD
GYMNASTICS	CLAVICHORD	LEAFHOPPER	TRANSITORY	SUBSTRATUM	DECRYPTION	PECCADILLO
GYMNOSPERM	CRADLESONG	MEADOWLARK	TRANSPLANT	SUBSURFACE	DICTIONARY	PICARESQUE
GYNECOLOGY	CRANKSHAFT	OPALESCENT	TRANSPOLAR	SUBTERFUGE	DOCKWORKER	PICCALILLI
HYDRAULICS	DEACTIVATE	ORATORICAL	TRANSVERSE	SUBTRAHEND	ENCRYPTION	PICKANINNY
HYDROLYSIS	DEADWEIGHT	PEACEMAKER	TRAVELOGUE	SUBVENTION	ENCYCLICAL	PICKPOCKET
HYDROMETER	DEALERSHIP	PEASHOOTER	TRAVERTINE	TABERNACLE	ESCARPMENT	PICOSECOND
HYDROPHONE	DEATHWATCH	PIANISSIMO	UNABRIDGED	TABLECLOTH	ESCRITOIRE	POCKETBOOK
HYDROPLANE	DIAPHANOUS	PIANOFORTE	UNAFFECTED	TABLESPOON	ESCUTCHEON	RACECOURSE
HYGROMETER	DRAWBRIDGE	PLAGIARIZE	UNASSUMING	TUBERCULAR	EUCALYPTUS	RECEIVABLE
HYPERBARIC	DRAWSTRING	PLANTATION	UNATTACHED	TUBERCULIN	EXCELLENCE	RECEPTACLE
HYPOCENTER	EMANCIPATE	PLAYACTING	UNAVAILING	UNBALANCED	EXCELLENCY	RECIDIVISM
HYPODERMIC	EMASCULATE	PLAYGROUND	WEAPONLESS	UNBEARABLE	EXCITEMENT	RECIPROCAL
HYPOTENUSE	ENAMELWARE	PLAYWRIGHT	WEATHERING	UNBEATABLE	EXCOGITATE	RECITATION
HYPOTHESIS	EVANESCENT	PRAGMATISM	WEATHERMAN	UNBECOMING	FACILITATE	RECOILLESS
MYRIAMETER	EVANGELISM	QUADRANGLE	WHARFINGER	UNBELIEVER	FACTITIOUS	RECOMPENSE
PYRIMIDINE	EVANGELIST	QUADRATICS	WHATSOEVER	UNBLUSHING	FICTITIOUS	RECONSIDER
SYMPATHIZE	EVANGELIZE	QUADRIVIUM	WRAPAROUND	UPBRINGING	HECTOLITER	RECREATION
TYPESCRIPT	EXACERBATE	QUADRUPLET	ABBREVIATE	VIBRAPHONE	HECTOMETER	RECUPERATE
TYPESETTER	EXACTITUDE	QUARANTINE	ALBUMINOUS	ACCELERATE	INCAPACITY	RICKETTSIA
TYPEWRITER	EXAGGERATE	QUATREFOIL	AMBASSADOR	ACCENTUATE	INCENDIARY	SACCHARINE
TYPOGRAPHY	EXASPERATE	REACTIVATE	AMBULATORY	ACCEPTABLE	INCIDENTAL	SACERDOTAL
TYRANNICAL	FLAGELLATE	READERSHIP	ARBITRATOR	ACCEPTANCE	INCINERATE	SACROILIAC
	FLAGITIOUS	REASONABLE	ARBORVITAE	ACCESSIBLE	INCIVILITY	SACROSANCT
	FLAMBOYANT	ROADRUNNER	CYBERSPACE	ACCIDENTAL	INCLINABLE	SECONDHAND
	FLASHLIGHT	SCAPEGRACE	DEBILITATE	ACCOMPLICE	INCOHERENT	SECULARISM
3RD LETTER	FRANCHISEE	SCARLATINA	EMBANKMENT	ACCOMPLISH	INCOMPLETE	SECULARIZE
	FRANCHISER	SEAMANSHIP	EMBONPOINT	ACCORDANCE	INCONSTANT	SUCCESSION
AMALGAMATE	FRANCHISOR	SEAMSTRESS	EMBOUCHURE	ACCOUNTANT	INCREDIBLE	SUCCESSIVE
AMANUENSIS	FRATERNITY	SEARCHWARE	EMBROIDERY	ACCOUNTING	INCULPABLE	TACHOMETER
BEAUJOLAIS	FRATERNIZE	SEASONABLE	EMBRYOLOGY	ACCUMULATE	INCUMBENCY	TECHNETIUM
BEAUTICIAN	FRATRICIDE	SHAMEFACED	FIBERBOARD	ACCUSATIVE	JACKANAPES	TECHNICIAN
BLACKAMOOR	FRAUDULENT	SKATEBOARD	FIBERGLASS	ACCUSTOMED	JACKHAMMER	TECHNOLOGY
BLACKBERRY	GLACIOLOGY	SMATTERING	FIBRINOGEN	ALCOHOLISM	JACKRABBIT	UNCRITICAL
BLACKBOARD	GOALKEEPER	SNAPDRAGON	HABILIMENT	ARCHBISHOP	LACHRYMOSE	VICEGERENT
BLACKGUARD	GRADUALISM	SPACECRAFT	HABITATION	ARCHDEACON	LACKLUSTER	VICTORIOUS
BLACKSMITH	GRADUATION	STAGECOACH	HOBBYHORSE	ARCHITRAVE	LICENTIATE	VICTUALLER
BLACKTHORN	GRAINFIELD	STALACTITE	IMBIBITION	ASCENDANCY	LICENTIOUS	VOCABULARY
BLANCMANGE	GRAMOPHONE	STALAGMITE	INBREEDING	AUCTIONEER	LOCOMOTION	VOCIFERATE
BRAHMANISM	GRANDCHILD	STANDPOINT	JUBILATION	BACKGAMMON	LOCOMOTIVE	VOCIFEROUS
BRAINCHILD	GRANDSTAND	STANDSTILL	LABORATORY	BACKGROUND	MACKINTOSH	WICKERWORK
BRAINSTORM	GRAPEFRUIT	STARVELING	LIBERALISM	BACKHANDED	MECHANICAL	ADDITIONAL
CHALCEDONY	GRATUITOUS	STATECRAFT	LIBIDINOUS	BACKSTAIRS	MICROFICHE	AUDIOPHILE

AUDITORIUM	RIDICULOUS	ELECTRONIC	PREPACKAGE	INFALLIBLE	MIGNONETTE	BOISTEROUS
BEDCLOTHES	SIDESTROKE	ELEMENTARY	PREPOSSESS	INFIDELITY	NEGATIVISM	BRICKLAYER
BEDRAGGLED	SIDEWINDER	EVENHANDED	PRESBYOPIA	INFIGHTING	NEGLIGIBLE	BRIDEGROOM
BUDGERIGAR	UNDENIABLE	EVERYTHING	PRESBYTERY	INFILTRATE	NIGHTDRESS	BRIDESMAID
CADAVEROUS	UNDERBELLY	EVERYWHERE	PRESCIENCE	INFINITIVE	NIGHTSHADE	BRIDGEHEAD
ELDERBERRY	UNDERBRUSH	EYEDROPPER	PRESSURIZE	INFINITUDE	NIGHTSHIRT	BRIDGEWORK
ENDANGERED	UNDERCOVER	EYEWITNESS	PRESUPPOSE	INFLECTION	NIGHTSTICK	BRIGANTINE
ENDEARMENT	UNDERCROFT	FIELDPIECE	PSEUDOCODE	INFLEXIBLE	ORGANGUTAN	CHIFFONIER
ENDOGENOUS	UNDERLYING	FREEBOOTER	RHEUMATISM	INFRACTION	PAGINATION	CHILDBIRTH
FEDERALISM	UNDERNEATH	FRESHWATER	SEERSUCKER	INFRASONIC	PIGEONHOLE	CHIMERICAL
FEDERALIST	UNDERPANTS	GREENHOUSE	SHENANIGAN	INFREQUENT	PUGNACIOUS	CHIMPANZEE
FEDERALIZE	UNDERSCORE	GREENSWARD	SKEPTICISM	LIFESAVING	RAGAMUFFIN	CHINCHILLA
FEDERATION	UNDERSEXED	GREGARIOUS	SLENDERIZE	REFERENDUM	REGENERACY	CHIROMANCY
GADOLINIUM	UNDERSHIRT	HIEROPHANT	SPECIALIST	REFINEMENT	REGENERATE	CHIVALROUS
HODGEPODGE	UNDERSHOOT	ICEBREAKER	SPECIALIZE	REFRACTION	REGISTRANT	CLINGSTONE
HYDRAULICS	UNDERSIZED	INELIGIBLE	SPELLBOUND	REFRACTORY	REGRESSION	COINCIDENT
HYDROLYSIS	UNDERSKIRT	INEQUALITY	STENTORIAN	REFRINGENT	REGULATION	CRISSCROSS
HYDROMETER	UNDERSLUNG	INEVITABLE	STEPFATHER	REFULGENCE	SUGGESTION	EPIGLOTTIS
HYDROPHONE	UNDERSTAND	INEXORABLE	STEPLADDER	SUFFERANCE	SUGGESTIVE	EPISCOPACY
HYDROPLANE	UNDERSTATE	INEXPIABLE	STEPMOTHER	SUFFICIENT	UNGENEROUS	EPISCOPATE
INDECISION	UNDERSTOOD	KIESELGUHR	STEPPARENT	SUFFRAGIST	UNGRACEFUL	EPITHELIUM
INDECISIVE	UNDERSTORY	LIEUTENANT	STEPSISTER	UNFAITHFUL	UNGRACIOUS	EVISCERATE
INDECOROUS	UNDERSTUDY	MEERSCHAUM	STEREOTYPE	UNFAMILIAR	UNGRATEFUL	FAIRGROUND
INDEFINITE	UNDERTAKER	NEEDLEWORK	SWEETBREAD	UNFRIENDLY	UNGROUNDED	GRINDSTONE
INDELICATE	UNDERTRICK	OCEANARIUM	SWEETBRIER	UNFRUITFUL	VEGETARIAN	GUILLOTINE
INDICATIVE	UNDERVALUE	OCEANFRONT	SWEETHEART	AGGRANDIZE	VEGETATION	IDIOPATHIC
INDIGENOUS	UNDERWAIST	OCEANGOING	TEETHRIDGE	AGGRESSION	VEGETATIVE	INIMITABLE
INDISCREET	UNDERWATER	OCEANOLOGY	THEATRICAL	AGGRESSIVE	ACHROMATIC	INITIATIVE
INDISPOSED	UNDERWORLD	OLEAGINOUS	THEMSELVES	ANGIOSPERM	BEHINDHAND	INITIATORY
INDISTINCT	UNDERWRITE	OVERCHARGE	THEREAFTER	ANGLOPHILE	DEHUMANIZE	KNICKKNACK
INDIVIDUAL	UNDULATION	OVERMASTER	THERMISTOR	ANGLOPHOBE	DEHUMIDIFY	KNIGHTHOOD
INDONESIAN	VIDEOPHONE	OVERSHADOW	THERMOSTAT	COGNIZANCE	EXHAUSTION	MAIDENHAIR
INDUCEMENT	WIDESPREAD	OVERSPREAD	TREMENDOUS	DEGENERACY	EXHAUSTIVE	MAIDENHEAD
INDUCTANCE	ABERRATION	OVERWINTER	UNEMPLOYED	DEGENERATE	EXHILARATE	MAIDENHOOD
INDULGENCE	AMELIORATE	PHENOMENON	UNEVENTFUL	DEGRADABLE	FAHRENHEIT	MAINSPRING
INDUSTRIAL	AMERINDIAN	PLEASANTRY	UNEXAMPLED	DOGCATCHER	INHABITANT	MAINSTREAM
JUDICATURE	ANEMOMETER	PLEBISCITE	UNEXPECTED	ENGAGEMENT	INHIBITION	MAISONETTE
LADYFINGER	ANESTHESIA	PREARRANGE	URETHRITIS	ERGONOMICS	INHUMANITY	NEIGHBORLY
LEDERHOSEN	ANESTHETIC	PREBENDARY	VIETNAMESE	ERGOSTEROL	MOHAMMEDAN	NOISEMAKER
MEDDLESOME	BREADBOARD	PRECARIOUS	WHEELCHAIR	FIGURATION	MUHAMMADAN	PAINKILLER
MEDICAMENT	BREADFRUIT	PRECAUTION	WHEELHORSE	FIGURATIVE	OPHTHALMIC	PAINTBRUSH
MIDDLEBROW	BREADSTUFF	PRECEDENCE	WHEELHOUSE	FIGUREHEAD	OTHERWORLD	PHILISTINE
MIDSHIPMAN	BREAKFRONT	PRECESSION	WHENSOEVER	HIGHLANDER	SCHISMATIC	PHILOSOPHY
MUDSLINGER	BREAKWATER	PRECIOSITY	AFFLICTIVE	HIGHWAYMAN	SCHOLASTIC	POINSETTIA
ORDINATION	BREASTBONE	PRECOCIOUS	BEFOREHAND	HYGROMETER	SCHOOLGIRL	PRIMORDIAL
PEDESTRIAN	BREASTWORK	PREDACEOUS	DEFINITION	INGLORIOUS	SCHOOLMARM	PRINCELING
PEDIATRICS	CHEAPSKATE	PREDECEASE	DEFINITIVE	INGRATIATE	SCHOOLMATE	PRINCIPLED
RADARSCOPE	CHECKPOINT	PREDESTINE	DEFLAGRATE	INGREDIENT	SCHOOLROOM	PRIVILEGED
RADICALIZE	CHEESECAKE	PREDICABLE	DIFFERENCE	JUGGERNAUT	UNHALLOWED	PRIZEFIGHT
RADIOGENIC	CLERESTORY	PREDISPOSE	DIFFICULTY	LEGITIMATE	UNHANDSOME	QUICKBASIC
RADIOGRAPH	CREDENTIAL	PREEMINENT	EFFECTUATE	LIGHTHOUSE	UPHOLSTERY	QUINTUPLET
RADIOMETER	CREDITABLE	PREEMPTIVE	EFFEMINATE	LIGHTPROOF	AFICIONADO	RAINMAKING
RADIOPHONE	CRENELLATE	PREFERENCE	EFFERVESCE	LOGANBERRY	ALIMENTARY	RHINESTONE
RADIOSONDE	CRETACEOUS	PREFERMENT	EFFICIENCY	LOGGERHEAD	ANIMADVERT	RHINOCEROS
REDEMPTION	DIELECTRIC	PREHENSILE	EFFLORESCE	LOGROLLING	ANIMALCULE	SEISMOGRAM
REDISTRICT	DREAMWORLD	PREMARITAL	EFFRONTERY	LUGUBRIOUS	ARITHMETIC	SEISMOLOGY
REDUNDANCY	ELECTORATE	PREMEDICAL	EFFULGENCE	MAGISTRATE	BLITZKRIEG	SHIBBOLETH

SHILLELAGH	COLLOQUIAL	PALATINATE	ATMOSPHERE	DOMINATION	UNMANNERLY	CONNECTION
SHIPFITTER	COLLOQUIUM	PALIMPSEST	BIMETALLIC	DUMBWAITER	UNMERCIFUL	CONNECTIVE
SHIPWRIGHT	COLORATION	PALINDROME	BOMBARDIER	FAMILARIZE	ANNIHILATE	CONNIPTION
SLIPSTREAM	COLORATURA	PALLBEARER	CAMELOPARD	GAMEKEEPER	ANNUNCIATE	CONSCIENCE
SPIRITUOUS	COLPORTEUR	PHLEBOTOMY	CAMOUFLAGE	GYMNASTICS	BENCHMARKS	CONSECRATE
SPIROCHETE	DELECTABLE	PHLEGMATIC	CAMPHORATE	GYMNOSPERM	BENEFACTOR	CONSEQUENT
SPITTLEBUG	DELEGATION	PILGRIMAGE	COMBUSTION	HAMMERHEAD	BENEFICENT	CONSISTORY
STIGMATIZE	DELIBERATE	PILLOWCASE	COMEDIENNE	HAMMERLOCK	BENEFICIAL	CONSONANCE
STILLBIRTH	DELINQUENT	PILOTHOUSE	COMESTIBLE	HEMATOLOGY	BONDHOLDER	CONSORTIUM
SWITCHBACK	DELIQUESCE	POLITICIAN	COMMANDANT	HEMISPHERE	CANDELABRA	CONSPECTUS
TRIFOLIATE	DELPHINIUM	POLYCLINIC	COMMANDEER	HEMOGLOBIN	CANDESCENT	CONSPIRACY
TRIMONTHLY	DILETTANTE	POLYHEDRON	COMMENTARY	HEMOPHILIA	CANDLEWICK	CONSTITUTE
TRIPARTITE	DILLYDALLY	POLYNESIAN	COMMERCIAL	HEMORRHAGE	CANKERWORM	CONSTRAINT
TRIPLICATE	FALLACIOUS	POLYTHEISM	COMMISSARY	HEMORRHOID	CANNONBALL	CONSUMMATE
UBIQUITOUS	FELICITATE	RELATIONAL	COMMISSION	HOMECOMING	CANONICALS	CONTAGIOUS
UNICAMERAL	FELICITOUS	RELATIVITY	COMMODIOUS	HOMEOPATHY	CANTALOUPE	CONTENTION
UNIFORMITY	FELLOWSHIP	RELAXATION	COMMONALTY	HOMOGENIZE	CANTILEVER	CONTIGUOUS
UNILATERAL	FILIBUSTER	RELENTLESS	COMMONWEAL	HOMOLOGOUS	CANTONMENT	CONTINENCE
UNIVERSITY	FOLKSINGER	RELINQUISH	COMMUNIQUE	HOMOSEXUAL	CANVASBACK	CONTINGENT
URINALYSIS	GOLDBEATER	RELUCTANCE	COMMUTATOR	IMMACULATE	CENSORIOUS	CONTINUITY
VOICEPRINT	HALLELUJAH	ROLLERBALL	COMPARABLE	IMMATERIAL	CENSORSHIP	CONTINUOUS
WAINWRIGHT	HELICOPTER	ROLLICKING	COMPARISON	IMMEMORIAL	CENTENNIAL	CONTRABAND
WEIGHTLESS	HELIOGRAPH	SALAMANDER	COMPASSION	IMMISCIBLE	CENTESIMAL	CONTRADICT
WHIRLYBIRD	HELIOTROPE	SALESWOMAN	COMPATIBLE	IMMOBILIZE	CENTIGRADE	CONTRAVENE
WHITSUNDAY	HOLLOWWARE	SALTCELLAR	COMPATRIOT	IMMODERATE	CENTILITER	CONTRIBUTE
WRISTWATCH	HOLOGRAPHY	SALUBRIOUS	COMPENDIUM	IMMORALITY	CENTIMETER	CONTROLLER
ADJUDICATE	HULLABALOO	SALUTATION	COMPENSATE	IMMUNOLOGY	CENTRALIZE	CONTROVERT
ENJAMBMENT	ILLITERATE	SELENOLOGY	COMPETENCE	JIMSONWEED	CENTRIFUGE	CONVALESCE
INJUNCTION	ILLUMINATE	SILHOUETTE	COMPETENCY	LUMBERJACK	CINERARIUM	CONVECTION
PEJORATIVE	ILLUSTRATE	SILVERFISH	COMPETITOR	LUMBERYARD	CINQUEFOIL	CONVENIENT
REJUVENATE	MALADAPTED	SILVERWARE	COMPLECTED	MEMBERSHIP	CONCENTRIC	CONVENTION
ALKALINIZE	MALAPROPOS	SOLICITOUS	COMPLEMENT	MEMORANDUM	CONCEPTION	CONVERSANT
LIKELIHOOD	MALCONTENT	SOLICITUDE	COMPLEXION	MIMEOGRAPH	CONCERNING	CONVERSION
ALLEGIANCE	MALEFACTOR	SOLIDARITY	COMPLIANCE	NOMINATIVE	CONCERTINA	CONVEYANCE
ALLHALLOWS	MALEFICENT	SPLASHDOWN	COMPLIANCY	NUMBERLESS	CONCESSION	CONVICTION
ALLITERATE	MALEVOLENT	TELEGRAPHY	COMPLICATE	NUMEROLOGY	CONCESSIVE	CONVOLUTED
BALBRIGGAN	MALODOROUS	TELESCOPIC	COMPLICITY	RAMSHACKLE	CONCILIATE	CONVULSION
BALDERDASH	MALTHUSIAN	TELEVISION	COMPLIMENT	REMARKABLE	CONCLUSION	DENDROLOGY
BALLISTICS	MELANCHOLY	UNLETTERED	COMPOSITOR	REMEDIABLE	CONCORDANT	DENOMINATE
BALUSTRADE	MELANESIAN	VELOCIPEDE	COMPREHEND	REMITTANCE	CONCRETION	DENOTATIVE
BELLADONNA	MILITARISM	VILLAINOUS	COMPROMISE	REMUNERATE	CONCURRENT	DENOUEMENT
BELLETRIST	MILITARIZE	VOLLEYBALL	COMPULSION	SEMIDRYING	CONCUSSION	DENTIFRICE
BELLWETHER	MILLENNIUM	VOLUMETRIC	COMPULSIVE	SEMPSTRESS	CONDENSATE	DINNERWARE
BELONGINGS	MILLILITER	VOLUMINOUS	COMPULSORY	SIMILITUDE	CONDESCEND	DONNYBROOK
BOLSHEVISM	MILLIMETER	VOLUPTUARY	COMPUSERVE	SIMPLICITY	CONDUCTIVE	DUNDERHEAD
BULLHEADED	MILLSTREAM	VOLUPTUOUS	CUMMERBUND	SIMPLISTIC	CONFECTION	FINGERLING
CALCAREOUS	MILLWRIGHT	VULNERABLE	CUMULATIVE	SOMERSAULT	CONFERENCE	FINGERNAIL
CALCULATED	MOLYBDENUM	WALLFLOWER	DEMOBILIZE	SYMPATHIZE	CONFESSION	GENERALITY
CALUMNIATE	MULTILEVEL	WELLSPRING	DEMOCRATIC	TAMBOURINE	CONFIDENCE	GENERALIZE
CELEBRATED	MULTIMEDIA	WILDEBEEST	DEMOGRAPHY	TEMPERANCE	CONFISCATE	GENERATION
CELLARETTE	MULTIPLIER	WILDERNESS	DEMOISELLE	TEMPTATION	CONFLUENCE	GENTLEFOLK
CELLOPHANE	MULTISENSE	WILLOWWARE	DEMOLITION	TIMBERLINE	CONFORMITY	GINGERSNAP
CHLORINATE	MULTISTAGE	ADMINISTER	DEMONETIZE	TIMEKEEPER	CONGENITAL	GINGIVITIS
CHLOROFORM	MULTISTORY	ADMISSIBLE	DEMONOLOGY	TOMFOOLERY	CONGREGATE	GONOCOCCUS
COLLARBONE	OBLIGATION	ADMITTANCE	DEMORALIZE	TUMBLEDOWN	CONGRUENCE	GUNSLINGER
COLLATERAL	OBLITERATE	AMMUNITION	DIMINUENDO	TUMBLEWEED	CONGRUENCY	GYNECOLOGY
COLLECTIVE	PALATALIZE	ARMAGEDDON	DIMINUTIVE	TUMULTUOUS	CONJECTURE	HANDBARROW

HANDICRAFT	PENMANSHIP	BOOKKEEPER	PHOTOMETER	STOREHOUSE	DIPSOMANIA	REPATRIATE
HANDLEBARS	PENNYROYAL	BOOKMOBILE	PHOTOMURAL	THOUGHTFUL	DUPLICATOR	REPERTOIRE
HANDMAIDEN	PENTAMETER	BOOKSELLER	PHOTOPAINT	TOOTHBRUSH	EMPIRICISM	REPETITION
HANDSPRING	PINCUSHION	BOONDOGGLE	PROCEEDING	TOOTHPASTE	EMPLOYMENT	REPETITIVE
HENCEFORTH	PINFEATHER	BROADCLOTH	PROCESSION	TROLLEYBUS	ESPADRILLE	REPORTEDLY
HINTERLAND	PUNISHMENT	BROADSWORD	PROCLIVITY	TROUBADOUR	EUPHONIOUS	REPOSITORY
HONORARIUM	RENASCENCE	BRONCHITIS	PROCURATOR	UNOCCUPIED	EXPATRIATE	REPUBLICAN
IGNORAMOUS	RENDEZVOUS	BRONTOSAUR	PRODIGIOUS	UROGENITAL	EXPECTANCY	REPUGNANCE
INNOMINATE	RINGLEADER	BROWNSTONE	PRODUCTION	WHOMSOEVER	EXPEDIENCE	REPUTATION
INNOVATION	RINGMASTER	CAOUTCHOUC	PROFESSION	WOODCUTTER	EXPEDIENCY	SAPROPHYTE
IONOSPHERE	SANATORIUM	CLODHOPPER	PROFICIENT	WOODENWARE	EXPEDITION	SEPARATION
JINRIKISHA	SANDALWOOD	CLOTHESPIN	PROFLIGATE	WOODPECKER	EXPERIENCE	SEPARATIST
KINEMATICS	SANGUINARY	CLOUDBURST	PROGENITOR	ALPHABETIC	EXPERIMENT	SEPARATIVE
KINGFISHER	SANITARIAN	CLOVERLEAF	PROGNOSTIC	AMPHIBIOUS	EXPLICABLE	SEPTICEMIA
LANDHOLDER	SANITARIUM	COORDINATE	PROGRAMMED	APPARITION	EXPOSITION	SEPTUAGINT
LANDLOCKED	SANITATION	CROSSBONES	PROGRAMMER	APPEARANCE	EXPRESSION	SEPULCHRAL
LANDLUBBER	SENEGALESE	CROSSBREED	PROJECTILE	APPETIZING	EXPRESSMAN	SOPHOMORIC
LENGTHWISE	SENESCENCE	CROSSPIECE	PROMETHIUM	APPLICABLE	EXPRESSWAY	SUPERCARGO
LINEBACKER	SINGLETREE	DOORKEEPER	PROMINENCE	APPLICATOR	HEPTAMETER	SUPERSONIC
MANAGEMENT	SUNGLASSES	DUODECIMAL	PROMISSORY	APPOINTIVE	HIPPODROME	SUPERTWIST
MANDELBROT	TANTAMOUNT	ECONOMICAL	PROMONTORY	APPOSITION	HYPERBARIC	SUPPLEMENT
MANDRAGORA	TENDERFOOT	EGOCENTRIC	PROMPTBOOK	APPOSITIVE	HYPOCENTER	SUPPLICANT
MANICURIST	TENDERLOIN	EXOBIOLOGY	PROMULGATE	APPRECIATE	HYPODERMIC	SUPPLICATE
MANIPULATE	TENEBRIOUS	EXORBITANT	PRONOUNCED	APPRENTICE	HYPOTENUSE	TOPOGRAPHY
MANSERVANT	UNNUMBERED	EXOTHERMIC	PROPAGANDA	ASPHYXIATE	HYPOTHESIS	TYPESCRIPT
MANSUETUDE	VINDICTIVE	FLOODLIGHT	PROPELLANT	ASPIRATION	IMPALPABLE	TYPESETTER
MANTLEROCK	WANDERLUST	FLOODPLAIN	PROPENSITY	BAPTISTERY	IMPASSABLE	TYPEWRITER
MANUSCRIPT	WINCHESTER	FLOODWATER	PROPERTIED	BIPARENTAL	IMPASSIBLE	TYPOGRAPHY
MENDACIOUS	WINDFLOWER	FLOORBOARD	PROPITIATE	BIPARIETAL	IMPATIENCE	UNPLEASANT
MENINGITIS	WINDJAMMER	FOOTBRIDGE	PROPITIOUS	BIPARTISAN	IMPECCABLE	INQUIETUDE
MENSURABLE	WINDOWPANE	FOOTLIGHTS	PROPORTION	CAPACITATE	IMPEDIMENT	LOQUACIOUS
MINERALIZE	WINDOWSILL	FOOTLOCKER	PROPRIETOR	CAPITALISM	IMPENITENT	ACROBATICS
MINERALOGY	WINDSHIELD	GEOCENTRIC	PROPRINTER	CAPITALIST	IMPERATIVE	ACROPHOBIA
MINESTRONE	WINEGROWER	GEOPHYSICS	PROPULSION	CAPITALIZE	IMPERSONAL	ADRENALINE
MINISCROLL	WINGSPREAD	GEOSCIENCE	PROSCENIUM	CAPITATION	IMPERVIOUS	AEROBATICS
MINISTRANT	WINTERTIDE	GEOTHERMAL	PROSPECTUS	CAPITULATE	IMPLACABLE	AIRFREIGHT
MONARCHIST	WINTERTIME	GHOSTWRITE	PROSPERITY	CAPOREGIME	IMPORTANCE	AURIFEROUS
MONOCHROME	WONDERLAND	GOOSEBERRY	PROSPEROUS	COPPERHEAD	IMPOSSIBLE	BAREHEADED
MONOPHONIC	WONDERMENT	GOOSEFLESH	PROSTHESIS	COPYREADER	IMPOVERISH	BIRTHPLACE
MONOTHEISM	XENOPHOBIA	GROUNDLING	PROSTITUTE	COPYWRITER	IMPREGNATE	BIRTHRIGHT
MONOTONOUS	ABOMINABLE	GROUNDMASS	PROTECTION	DEPARTMENT	IMPRESARIO	BIRTHSTONE
MONSTRANCE	ABORIGINAL	GROUNDWORK	PROTESTANT	DEPENDABLE	IMPRESSION	BORDERLAND
MONUMENTAL	ABOVEBOARD	HOOTENANNY	PROTOPLASM	DEPENDENCE	IMPRESSIVE	CARABINEER
MUNIFICENT	ALONGSHORE	ICONOCLASM	PROTRACTOR	DEPENDENCY	IMPRIMATUR	CARBOLATED
NANOSECOND	APOCALYPSE	ICONOCLAST	PROVENANCE	DEPILATORY	IMPROBABLE	CARBURETOR
NINCOMPOOP	APOCRYPHAL	INOPERABLE	PROVIDENCE	DEPLORABLE	LEPRECHAUN	CARCINOGEN
NONCHALANT	APOLITICAL	INORDINATE	PROVINCIAL	DEPOLARIZE	LIPREADING	CARDIOGRAM
NONDRINKER	APOLOGETIC	ISOMETRICS	SHOESTRING	DEPOPULATE	NAPOLEONIC	CARDIOLOGY
NONSTARTER	APOSTROPHE	ISOTHERMAL	SHOPKEEPER	DEPORTMENT	OPPRESSION	CARICATURE
NONSUPPORT	APOTHECARY	KNOCKWURST	SHORTENING	DEPOSITION	OPPROBRIUM	CEREBELLUM
OMNIPOTENT	APOTHEOSIS	MOONSTRUCK	SMOKESTACK	DEPOSITORY	PAPERBOARD	CEREMONIAL
OMNISCIENT	BIOMEDICAL	NEOCLASSIC	SNOWMOBILE	DEPRECIATE	PEPPERCORN	CHROMOSOME
OMNIVOROUS	BIOPHYSICS	PHONOGRAPH	SOOTHSAYER	DEPRESSANT	PEPPERMINT	CHRONOLOGY
PANJANDRUM	BLOCKHOUSE	PHOSPHORUS	SPOILSPORT	DEPRESSION	POPULATION	CHRYSOLITE
PANTALOONS	BLOODHOUND	PHOTOFLASH	SPOLIATION	DEPRESSIVE	REPAGINATE	CIRCUITOUS
PANTYWAIST	BLOODSTAIN	PHOTOGENIC	SPORTSCAST	DEPUTATION	REPARATION	CIRCUMCISE
PENICILLIN	BLOODSTONE	PHOTOGRAPH	STOCHASTIC	DIPHTHERIA	REPARATIVE	CIRCUMFLEX

CIRCUMVENT	MARGINALIA	SERVOMOTOR	AUSTRALIAN	EISTEDDFOD	RESOUNDING	ANTITHESIS
CORDILLERA	MARGUERITE	SPRINGTIME	BASKETBALL	FASTIDIOUS	RESPECTING	ARTICULATE
CORDWAINER	MARIONETTE	SPRINKLING	BASTARDIZE	FISTICUFFS	RESPECTIVE	ARTIFICIAL
CORNFLOWER	MARROWBONE	STRAIGHTEN	BESPRINKLE	FOSTERLING	RESPIRATOR	ASTRINGENT
CORNSTARCH	MARTINGALE	STRAWBERRY	BESTIALITY	FUSSBUDGET	RESPONDENT	ATTACHMENT
CORNUCOPIA	MERCANTILE	STRENGTHEN	BUSHMASTER	GASTRONOMY	RESPONSIVE	ATTAINMENT
CORONATION	MORATORIUM	STRINGENCY	COSMOPOLIS	GESUNDHEIT	RESTAURANT	ATTENDANCE
CORPULENCE	MORPHOLOGY	STRIPTEASE	DESALINATE	HISTRIONIC	RESTORABLE	ATTRACTANT
CORRESPOND	MYRIAMETER	STRONGHOLD	DESALINIZE	HOSPITABLE	RESTRAINED	ATTRACTION
CORRIGIBLE	NARCISSISM	STRYCHNINE	DESCENDANT	HUSBANDMAN	RESURGENCE	AUTHORSHIP
CURRICULUM	NURSERYMAN	SURREALISM	DESERVEDLY	INSATIABLE	RISIBILITY	AUTOMATION
CURVACEOUS	PARAMECIUM	TARANTELLA	DESOLATION	INSEMINATE	SISTERHOOD	AUTOMATIZE
DERIVATION	PARAPHRASE	TERMINATOR	DESPICABLE	INSENSIBLE	SUSPENSION	AUTOMOBILE
DERIVATIVE	PARAPLEGIA	THREADBARE	DESTRUCTOR	INSENTIENT	SUSPENSORY	AUTOMOTIVE
DERMATITIS	PARATROOPS	THREEPENCE	DISAPPOINT	INSISTENCE	SUSPICIOUS	AUTONOMOUS
DEROGATORY	PARLIAMENT	THREESCORE	DISAPPROVE	INSOLATION	SUSTENANCE	AUTOSTRADA
EARTHQUAKE	PARMIGIANA	THROMBOSIS	DISARRANGE	INSOLVABLE	TASKMASTER	BATHYSCAPH
EURODOLLAR	PARTICIPLE	THROUGHOUT	DISBELIEVE	INSTRUCTOR	TESSELLATE	BATRACHIAN
FARFETCHED	PARTICULAR	THROUGHPUT	DISCERNING	INSTRUMENT	UNSCHOOLED	BATTLEMENT
FARSIGHTED	PERCENTAGE	THROUGHWAY	DISCIPLINE	LASCIVIOUS	UNSCRAMBLE	BATTLESHIP
FERTILIZER	PERCENTILE	TORRENTIAL	DISCOMFORT	MASQUERADE	UNSKILLFUL	BETTERMENT
FORBIDDING	PERCEPTION	TURBULENCE	DISCOMMODE	MASTERMIND	UNSUITABLE	BITUMINOUS
FORECASTLE	PERCEPTIVE	TURNBUCKLE	DISCOMPOSE	MASTERSHIP	UPSTANDING	BOTTLENECK
FOREFATHER	PERCEPTUAL	TURPENTINE	DISCONCERT	MASTERWORK	VESPERTINE	BOTTOMLAND
FOREFINGER	PERCIPIENT	TURTLEDOVE	DISCONNECT	MESOSPHERE	VISIBILITY	BUTTERMILK
FOREGATHER	PERCUSSION	TURTLENECK	DISCONTENT	MISALIGNED	VISITATION	BUTTONHOLE
FOREGROUND	PERDURABLE	TYRANNICAL	DISCOURAGE	MISCELLANY	WASTEPAPER	BUTTONHOOK
FOREHANDED	PEREMPTORY	UNREASONED	DISCREPANT	MISCONDUCT	WESTERNIZE	CATABOLISM
FOREORDAIN	PERFECTION	UNRESERVED	DISCRETION	MISFORTUNE	YESTERYEAR	CATAFALQUE
FORERUNNER	PERIHELION	UPROARIOUS	DISCURSIVE	MISOGAMIST	ACTIONABLE	CATCHPENNY
FORESHADOW	PERIODICAL	VARICOSITY	DISCUSSANT	MISOGYNIST	AFTERBIRTH	CATECHUMEN
FORFEITURE	PERIPHERAL	VERMICELLI	DISEMBOWEL	MISSILEMAN	AFTERIMAGE	CATEGORIZE
FORMIDABLE	PERISHABLE	VERNACULAR	DISENCHANT	MISSIONARY	AFTERTASTE	CITRONELLA
FORTHRIGHT	PERITONEUM	VERTEBRATE	DISGRUNTLE	MISTAKABLE	ALTARPIECE	COTERMINAL
FORTISSIMO	PERIWINKLE	VIRTUOSITY	DISHABILLE	MUSICOLOGY	ALTERNATOR	COTTONSEED
FORTUITOUS	PERMAFROST	WIREHAIRED	DISHARMONY	NASTURTIUM	ALTOGETHER	COTTONTAIL
GARGANTUAN	PERMISSION	WORKBASKET	DISHEARTEN	OBSEQUIOUS	ANTAGONISM	COTTONWOOD
GERIATRICS	PERMISSIVE	WORKINGMAN	DISHWASHER	OBSERVABLE	ANTAGONIST	CUTTLEFISH
GORGONZOLA	PERNICIOUS	WORSHIPFUL	DISINCLINE	OBSERVANCE	ANTAGONIZE	DATAMATION
GORMANDIZE	PERORATION	WORTHWHILE	DISINHERIT	OBSTETRICS	ANTEBELLUM	DETACHMENT
HARDHEADED	PERPETRATE	XEROGRAPHY	DISJOINTED	OESOPHAGUS	ANTECEDENT	DETERMINED
HARMONIOUS	PERPETUATE	YARDMASTER	DISORDERLY	PASSAGEWAY	ANTEPENULT	DETERRENCE
HEREABOUTS	PERPETUITY	ABSCISSION	DISPENSARY	PASTEBOARD	ANTHRACITE	ENTERPRISE
HEREDITARY	PERQUISITE	ABSOLUTION	DISPOSABLE	PASTEURIZE	ANTHROPOID	ENTHUSIASM
HERETOFORE	PERSIFLAGE	ABSOLUTISM	DISPOSSESS	PESTILENCE	ANTIBIOTIC	ENTOMOLOGY
HORIZONTAL	PERSONABLE	ABSORPTION	DISQUALIFY	POSSESSION	ANTICANCER	ESTIMATION
HORRENDOUS	PERSONALTY	ABSTEMIOUS	DISRESPECT	POSSESSIVE	ANTICHRIST	EUTHANASIA
HORSEFLESH	PERSUASION	ABSTINENCE	DISSATISFY	POSTHUMOUS	ANTICIPATE	EXTINGUISH
HORSELAUGH	PERVERSION	AESTHETICS	DISSENSION	POSTMASTER	ANTICLIMAX	EXTRAMURAL
HORSEPOWER	PHRENOLOGY	ANSWERABLE	DISSERVICE	POSTMORTEM	ANTIFREEZE	EXTRANEOUS
HORSEWOMAN	PORTCULLIS	ASSEMBLAGE	DISSIMILAR	POSTPARTUM	ANTIMATTER	FATHERLAND
IRRATIONAL	PORTENTOUS	ASSEVERATE	DISSOCIATE	POSTSCRIPT	ANTINOMIAN	FATHOMLESS
IRRELEVANT	PORTUGUESE	ASSIGNMENT	DISSONANCE	RESILIENCE	ANTIPHONAL	FUTURISTIC
IRRESOLUTE	PYRIMIDINE	ASSIMILATE	DISTILLATE	RESILIENCY	ANTIPROTON	GATEKEEPER
JARDINIERE	SCRUTINIZE	ASSORTMENT	DISTRAUGHT	RESISTANCE	ANTIQUATED	INTANGIBLE
LARYNGITIS	SERPENTINE	ASSUMPTION	DISTRIBUTE	RESOLUTION	ANTISEPTIC	INTEGUMENT
MARASCHINO	SERVICEMAN	AUSPICIOUS	DYSPROSIUM	RESORPTION	ANTISOCIAL	INTERBLOCK

INTERBREED	OCTOTHORPE	BLUECOLLAR	TOURNIQUET	SKYSCRAPER	ESPADRILLE	PARATROOPS
INTERFAITH	OFTENTIMES	BLUEJACKET	TRUNCATION	SKYWRITING	EUCALYPTUS	PICARESQUE
INTERFERON	OSTENSIBLE	CHURCHGOER	VAUDEVILLE	UNYIELDING	EXHAUSTION	PLEASANTRY
INTERLEAVE	OSTEOPATHY	CHURCHLESS	ADVENTURER	MIZZENMAST	EXHAUSTIVE	PREARRANGE
INTERLUNAR	OUTBALANCE	CHURCHYARD	ADVISEMENT	MOZZARELLA	EXPATRIATE	RADARSCOPE
INTERMARRY	OUTGENERAL	COUNTERACT	CAVITATION		HEMATOLOGY	RAGAMUFFIN
INTERMEZZO	OUTLANDISH	COUNTERMAN	DEVITALIZE		IMMACULATE	RELATIONAL
INTERNMENT	OUTPATIENT	COUNTERSPY	DIVINATION		IMMATERIAL	RELATIVITY
INTERSTATE	OUTPERFORM	COUNTRYMAN	FAVORITISM	**4TH LETTER**	IMPALPABLE	RELAXATION
INTERSTICE	OUTPOURING	COURTHOUSE	GOVERNMENT		IMPASSABLE	REMARKABLE
INTERTIDAL	OUTRAGEOUS	CRUSTACEAN	INVALIDATE	ALKALINIZE	IMPASSIBLE	RENASCENCE
INTERTWINE	PATHFINDER	EBULLITION	INVALUABLE	ALTARPIECE	IMPATIENCE	REPAGINATE
INTERTWIST	PATRONYMIC	ECUMENICAL	INVARIABLE	AMBASSADOR	INCAPACITY	REPARATION
INTERURBAN	PETNAPPING	EMULSIFIER	INVESTMENT	ANTAGONISM	INFALLIBLE	REPARATIVE
INTERWEAVE	PETROLATUM	EQUANIMITY	INVETERATE	ANTAGONIST	INHABITANT	REPATRIATE
INTIMIDATE	POTENTIATE	EQUESTRIAN	INVIGORATE	ANTAGONIZE	INSATIABLE	SALAMANDER
INTINCTION	PUTRESCENT	EQUITATION	INVINCIBLE	APPARITION	INTANGIBLE	SANATORIUM
INTOLERANT	RATTLETRAP	EQUIVALENT	INVIOLABLE	AQUALUNGER	INVALIDATE	SEPARATION
INTONATION	RETRACTILE	EQUIVOCATE	INVOCATION	AQUAMARINE	INVALUABLE	SEPARATIST
INTOXICANT	RETROGRADE	EXURBANITE	INVOLUTION	ARMAGEDDON	INVARIABLE	SEPARATIVE
INTOXICATE	RETROGRESS	FLUIDOUNCE	LIVELIHOOD	ATTACHMENT	IRRATIONAL	SPLASHDOWN
INTRAMURAL	RETROSPECT	FLUORIDATE	LIVERWURST	ATTAINMENT	LOGANBERRY	STRAIGHTEN
INTRASTATE	ROTISSERIE	FLUORINATE	LOVEMAKING	BIPARENTAL	MALADAPTED	STRAWBERRY
KETTLEDRUM	SETTLEMENT	FOUNDATION	REVELATION	BIPARIETAL	MALAPROPOS	TARANTELLA
LETTERHEAD	TATTERSALL	FOURSQUARE	REVITALIZE	BIPARTISAN	MANAGEMENT	THEATRICAL
LITERALISM	TATTLETALE	HOUSECLEAN	REVOCATION	BREADBOARD	MARASCHINO	TYRANNICAL
LITERATURE	TETRAMETER	HOUSEWARES	REVOLUTION	BREADFRUIT	MELANCHOLY	UNBALANCED
LITHUANIAN	ULTRASHORT	JOURNALESE	VIVIPAROUS	BREADSTUFF	MELANESIAN	UNFAITHFUL
MATCHMAKER	ULTRASONIC	JOURNALISM	WAVELENGTH	BREAKFRONT	METABOLISM	UNFAMILIAR
MATURATION	ULTRASOUND	JOURNEYMAN	BOWDLERIZE	BREAKWATER	METABOLITE	UNHALLOWED
METABOLISM	UNTHINKING	KRUGERRAND	COWPUNCHER	BREASTBONE	METACARPUS	UNHANDSOME
METABOLITE	VETERINARY	MOUNTEBANK	DOWNSTAIRS	BREASTWORK	METAGALAXY	UNMANNERLY
METACARPUS	VITUPERATE	MOUTHPIECE	DOWNSTREAM	BROADCLOTH	METALLURGY	VOCABULARY
METAGALAXY	WATCHMAKER	NEUTRALISM	DOWNSTROKE	BROADSWORD	METASTASIS	BALBRIGGAN
METALLURGY	WATCHTOWER	NEUTRALITY	JAWBREAKER	CADAVEROUS	METATARSAL	BOMBARDIER
METASTASIS	WATERBORNE	NEUTRALIZE	LAWBREAKER	CAPACITATE	METATARSUS	CARBOLATED
METATARSAL	WATERCOLOR	NOURISHING	LAWRENCIUM	CARABINEER	MISALIGNED	CARBURETOR
METATARSUS	WATERCRAFT	PLUPERFECT	NEWFANGLED	CATABOLISM	MOHAMMEDAN	COMBUSTION
METICULOUS	WATERCRESS	PLUTOCRACY	NEWSGROUPS	CATAFALQUE	MONARCHIST	DISBELIEVE
METROPOLIS	WATERFRONT	POULTRYMAN	NEWSLETTER	CHEAPSKATE	MORATORIUM	DUMBWAITER
METTLESOME	WATERMELON	POURPARLER	NEWSWORTHY	DATAMATION	MUHAMMADAN	EXOBIOLOGY
MOTHERHOOD	WATERPOWER	ROUGHHOUSE	PAWNBROKER	DECAPITATE	NATATORIUM	FORBIDDING
MOTHERLAND	WATERPROOF	ROUNDABOUT	POWERHOUSE	DEPARTMENT	NEGATIVISM	HOBBYHORSE
MOTORCYCLE	WATERSPOUT	ROUNDHOUSE	POWERLINES	DESALINATE	NOTABILITY	HUSBANDMAN
MOTORTRUCK	WATERTIGHT	ROUSTABOUT	TOXICOLOGY	DESALINIZE	OCCASIONAL	ICEBREAKER
NATATORIUM	WATERWHEEL	SAUERKRAUT	ASYMMETRIC	DETACHMENT	OCEANARIUM	JAWBREAKER
NATIONWIDE	WATERWORKS	SCURRILOUS	CRYOGENICS	DISAPPOINT	OCEANFRONT	LAWBREAKER
NATURALISM	WITCHCRAFT	SHUNPIKING	CRYPTOGRAM	DISAPPROVE	OCEANGOING	LUMBERJACK
NATURALIST	WITCHGRASS	SHUTTERBUG	ERYSIPELAS	DISARRANGE	OCEANOLOGY	LUMBERYARD
NATURALIZE	WITHDRAWAL	SLUMBEROUS	FLYCATCHER	DREAMWORLD	OLEAGINOUS	MEMBERSHIP
NETHERMOST	ADULTERANT	STUPENDOUS	MAYONNAISE	EMBANKMENT	ORGANGUTAN	NUMBERLESS
NETTLESOME	ADULTERATE	THUMBSCREW	PHYLACTERY	ENDANGERED	PALATALIZE	OUTBALANCE
NOTABILITY	AQUALUNGER	THUNDEROUS	PHYSIOLOGY	ENGAGEMENT	PALATINATE	PLEBISCITE
NOTEWORTHY	AQUAMARINE	TOUCHSTONE	PSYCHIATRY	ENJAMBMENT	PARAMECIUM	PREBENDARY
NOTICEABLE	BLUEBONNET	TOURMALINE	PSYCHOLOGY	EQUANIMITY	PARAPHRASE	RUBBERNECK
NUTCRACKER	BLUEBOTTLE	TOURNAMENT	PSYCHOPATH	ESCARPMENT	PARAPLEGIA	SHIBBOLETH

TAMBOURINE	DISCUSSANT	SUBCOMPACT	LANDLOCKED	AFTERTASTE	EXPECTANCY	INTERFAITH
TIMBERLINE	DOGCATCHER	SUCCESSION	LANDLUBBER	ALLEGIANCE	EXPEDIENCE	INTERFERON
TUMBLEDOWN	EGOCENTRIC	SUCCESSIVE	MAIDENHAIR	ALTERNATOR	EXPEDIENCY	INTERLEAVE
TUMBLEWEED	ELECTORATE	TOUCHSTONE	MAIDENHEAD	ANTEBELLUM	EXPEDITION	INTERLUNAR
TURBULENCE	ELECTRONIC	UNICAMERAL	MAIDENHOOD	ANTECEDENT	EXPERIENCE	INTERMARRY
UNABRIDGED	EXACERBATE	UNOCCUPIED	MANDELBROT	ANTEPENULT	EXPERIMENT	INTERMEZZO
ABSCISSION	EXACTITUDE	UNSCHOOLED	MANDRAGORA	APPEARANCE	FEDERALISM	INTERNMENT
AFICIONADO	FLYCATCHER	UNSCRAMBLE	MEADOWLARK	APPETIZING	FEDERALIST	INTERSTATE
APOCALYPSE	GEOCENTRIC	VOICEPRINT	MEDDLESOME	ASCENDANCY	FEDERALIZE	INTERSTICE
APOCRYPHAL	GLACIOLOGY	WATCHMAKER	MENDACIOUS	ASSEMBLAGE	FEDERATION	INTERTIDAL
BEDCLOTHES	HENCEFORTH	WATCHTOWER	MIDDLEBROW	ASSEVERATE	FIBERBOARD	INTERTWINE
BENCHMARKS	INACTIVATE	WINCHESTER	NEEDLEWORK	ATTENDANCE	FIBERGLASS	INTERTWIST
BLACKAMOOR	KNICKKNACK	WITCHCRAFT	NONDRINKER	BAREHEADED	FORECASTLE	INTERURBAN
BLACKBERRY	KNOCKWURST	WITCHGRASS	PERDURABLE	BENEFACTOR	FOREFATHER	INTERWEAVE
BLACKBOARD	LASCIVIOUS	BALDERDASH	PREDACEOUS	BENEFICENT	FOREFINGER	INVESTMENT
BLACKGUARD	MALCONTENT	BONDHOLDER	PREDECEASE	BENEFICIAL	FOREGATHER	INVETERATE
BLACKSMITH	MATCHMAKER	BORDERLAND	PREDESTINE	BIMETALLIC	FOREGROUND	IRRELEVANT
BLACKTHORN	MERCANTILE	BOWDLERIZE	PREDICABLE	BLUEBONNET	FOREHANDED	IRRESOLUTE
BLOCKHOUSE	MISCELLANY	BRIDEGROOM	PREDISPOSE	BLUEBOTTLE	FOREORDAIN	KINEMATICS
BRICKLAYER	MISCONDUCT	BRIDESMAID	PRODIGIOUS	BLUECOLLAR	FORERUNNER	LEDERHOSEN
CACCIATORE	NARCISSISM	BRIDGEHEAD	PRODUCTION	BLUEJACKET	FORESHADOW	LIBERALISM
CALCAREOUS	NEOCLASSIC	BRIDGEWORK	QUADRANGLE	CAMELOPARD	FREEBOOTER	LICENTIATE
CALCULATED	NINCOMPOOP	CANDELABRA	QUADRATICS	CATECHUMEN	GAMEKEEPER	LICENTIOUS
CARCINOGEN	NONCHALANT	CANDESCENT	QUADRIVIUM	CATEGORIZE	GATEKEEPER	LIFESAVING
CATCHPENNY	NUTCRACKER	CANDLEWICK	QUADRUPLET	CELEBRATED	GENERALITY	LIKELIHOOD
CHECKPOINT	PEACEMAKER	CARDIOGRAM	READERSHIP	CEREBELLUM	GENERALIZE	LINEBACKER
CIRCUITOUS	PECCADILLO	CARDIOLOGY	RENDEZVOUS	CEREMONIAL	GENERATION	LITERALISM
CIRCUMCISE	PERCENTAGE	CLODHOPPER	ROADRUNNER	CHEESECAKE	GOVERNMENT	LITERATURE
CIRCUMFLEX	PERCENTILE	CONDENSATE	SANDALWOOD	CINERARIUM	GREENHOUSE	LIVELIHOOD
CIRCUMVENT	PERCEPTION	CONDESCEND	TENDERFOOT	COMEDIENNE	GREENSWARD	LIVERWURST
CONCENTRIC	PERCEPTIVE	CONDUCTIVE	TENDERLOIN	COMESTIBLE	GYNECOLOGY	LOVEMAKING
CONCEPTION	PERCEPTUAL	CORDILLERA	VAUDEVILLE	COTERMINAL	HEREABOUTS	MALEFACTOR
CONCERNING	PERCIPIENT	CORDWAINER	VINDICTIVE	CYBERSPACE	HEREDITARY	MALEFICENT
CONCERTINA	PERCUSSION	CRADLESONG	WANDERLUST	DECELERATE	HERETOFORE	MALEVOLENT
CONCESSION	PICCALILLI	CREDENTIAL	WILDEBEEST	DEGENERACY	HOMECOMING	MIMEOGRAPH
CONCESSIVE	PINCUSHION	CREDITABLE	WILDERNESS	DEGENERATE	HOMEOPATHY	MINERALIZE
CONCILIATE	PRECARIOUS	DEADWEIGHT	WINDFLOWER	DELECTABLE	HYPERBARIC	MINERALOGY
CONCLUSION	PRECAUTION	DENDROLOGY	WINDJAMMER	DELEGATION	IMMEMORIAL	MINESTRONE
CONCORDANT	PRECEDENCE	DUNDERHEAD	WINDOWPANE	DEPENDABLE	IMPECCABLE	NOTEWORTHY
CONCRETION	PRECESSION	DUODECIMAL	WINDOWSILL	DEPENDENCE	IMPEDIMENT	NUMEROLOGY
CONCURRENT	PRECIOSITY	EYEDROPPER	WINDSHIELD	DEPENDENCY	IMPENITENT	OBSEQUIOUS
CONCUSSION	PRECOCIOUS	GOLDBEATER	WONDERLAND	DESERVEDLY	IMPERATIVE	OBSERVABLE
DEACTIVATE	PROCEEDING	GRADUALISM	WONDERMENT	DETERMINED	IMPERSONAL	OBSERVANCE
DESCENDANT	PROCESSION	GRADUATION	WOODCUTTER	DETERRENCE	IMPERVIOUS	OFTENTIMES
DISCERNING	PROCLIVITY	HANDBARROW	WOODENWARE	DILETTANTE	INCENDIARY	OSTENSIBLE
DISCIPLINE	PROCURATOR	HANDICRAFT	WOODPECKER	DISEMBOWEL	INDECISION	OSTEOPATHY
DISCOMFORT	PSYCHIATRY	HANDLEBARS	YARDMASTER	DISENCHANT	INDECISIVE	OTHERWORLD
DISCOMMODE	PSYCHOLOGY	HANDMAIDEN	ACCELERATE	EFFECTUATE	INDECOROUS	PAPERBOARD
DISCOMPOSE	PSYCHOPATH	HANDSPRING	ACCENTUATE	EFFEMINATE	INDEFINITE	PEDESTRIAN
DISCONCERT	QUICKBASIC	HARDHEADED	ACCEPTABLE	EFFERVESCE	INDELICATE	PEREMPTORY
DISCONNECT	REACTIVATE	HEADMASTER	ACCEPTANCE	ELDERBERRY	INSEMINATE	PHLEBOTOMY
DISCONTENT	SACCHARINE	HEADSTRONG	ACCESSIBLE	ENDEARMENT	INSENSIBLE	PHLEGMATIC
DISCOURAGE	SPACECRAFT	HEADWAITER	ADRENALINE	ENTERPRISE	INSENTIENT	PHRENOLOGY
DISCREPANT	SPECIALIST	INADEQUATE	ADVENTURER	EQUESTRIAN	INTEGUMENT	PIGEONHOLE
DISCRETION	SPECIALIZE	JARDINIERE	AFTERBIRTH	EXCELLENCE	INTERBLOCK	POTENTIATE
DISCURSIVE	STOCHASTIC	LANDHOLDER	AFTERIMAGE	EXCELLENCY	INTERBREED	POWERHOUSE

POWERLINES	UNDERCROFT	CONFESSION	PLAGIARIZE	PATHFINDER	DELIBERATE	INTINCTION
PREEMINENT	UNDERLYING	CONFIDENCE	PRAGMATISM	PREHENSILE	DELINQUENT	INVIGORATE
PREEMPTIVE	UNDERNEATH	CONFISCATE	PROGENITOR	SILHOUETTE	DELIQUESCE	INVINCIBLE
PUBESCENCE	UNDERPANTS	CONFLUENCE	PROGNOSTIC	SOPHOMORIC	DEPILATORY	INVIOLABLE
RACECOURSE	UNDERSCORE	CONFORMITY	PROGRAMMED	TACHOMETER	DERIVATION	JUBILATION
REBELLIOUS	UNDERSEXED	DIFFERENCE	PROGRAMMER	TECHNETIUM	DERIVATIVE	JUDICATURE
RECEIVABLE	UNDERSHIRT	DIFFICULTY	RINGLEADER	TECHNICIAN	DEVITALIZE	LEGITIMATE
RECEPTACLE	UNDERSHOOT	FARFETCHED	RINGMASTER	TECHNOLOGY	DIMINUENDO	LIBIDINOUS
REDEMPTION	UNDERSIZED	FORFEITURE	ROUGHHOUSE	UNTHINKING	DIMINUTIVE	MAGISTRATE
REFERENDUM	UNDERSKIRT	LEAFHOPPER	SANGUINARY	WITHDRAWAL	DISINCLINE	MANICURIST
REGENERACY	UNDERSLUNG	MISFORTUNE	SINGLETREE	ACCIDENTAL	DISINHERIT	MANIPULATE
REGENERATE	UNDERSTAND	NEWFANGLED	STAGECOACH	ACTIONABLE	DIVINATION	MARIONETTE
RELENTLESS	UNDERSTATE	PERFECTION	STIGMATIZE	ADDITIONAL	DOMINATION	MEDICAMENT
REMEDIABLE	UNDERSTOOD	PINFEATHER	SUGGESTION	ADMINISTER	EFFICIENCY	MENINGITIS
REPERTOIRE	UNDERSTORY	PREFERENCE	SUGGESTIVE	ADMISSIBLE	EMPIRICISM	METICULOUS
REPETITION	UNDERSTUDY	PREFERMENT	SUNGLASSES	ADMITTANCE	EQUITATION	MILITARISM
REPETITIVE	UNDERTAKER	PROFESSION	UROGENITAL	ADVISEMENT	EQUIVALENT	MILITARIZE
REVELATION	UNDERTRICK	PROFICIENT	WEIGHTLESS	ALLITERATE	EQUIVOCATE	MINISCROLL
SACERDOTAL	UNDERVALUE	PROFLIGATE	WINGSPREAD	ANGIOSPERM	ESTIMATION	MINISTRANT
SALESWOMAN	UNDERWAIST	SUFFERANCE	ALLHALLOWS	ANNIHILATE	EXCITEMENT	MUNIFICENT
SAUERKRAUT	UNDERWATER	SUFFICIENT	ALPHABETIC	ANTIBIOTIC	EXHILARATE	MUSICOLOGY
SELENOLOGY	UNDERWORLD	SUFFRAGIST	AMPHIBIOUS	ANTICANCER	EXTINGUISH	MYRIAMETER
SENEGALESE	UNDERWRITE	TOMFOOLERY	ANTHRACITE	ANTICHRIST	FACILITATE	NATIONWIDE
SENESCENCE	UNGENEROUS	TRIFOLIATE	ANTHROPOID	ANTICIPATE	FAMILARIZE	NOMINATIVE
SHOESTRING	UNLETTERED	UNAFFECTED	ARCHBISHOP	ANTICLIMAX	FELICITATE	NOTICEABLE
SIDESTROKE	UNMERCIFUL	UNIFORMITY	ARCHDEACON	ANTIFREEZE	FELICITOUS	OBLIGATION
SIDEWINDER	UNREASONED	BRIGANTINE	ARCHITRAVE	ANTIMATTER	FILIBUSTER	OBLITERATE
SOMERSAULT	UNRESERVED	BUDGERIGAR	ASPHYXIATE	ANTINOMIAN	FLUIDOUNCE	OCCIDENTAL
STRENGTHEN	VEGETARIAN	CONGENITAL	AUTHORSHIP	ANTIPHONAL	GERIATRICS	OMNIPOTENT
SUPERCARGO	VEGETATION	CONGREGATE	BATHYSCAPH	ANTIPROTON	GRAINFIELD	OMNISCIENT
SUPERSONIC	VEGETATIVE	CONGRUENCE	BICHLORIDE	ANTIQUATED	HABILIMENT	OMNIVOROUS
SUPERTWIST	VETERINARY	CONGRUENCY	BRAHMANISM	ANTISEPTIC	HABITATION	ORDINATION
SWEETBREAD	VICEGERENT	DISGRUNTLE	BUSHMASTER	ANTISOCIAL	HELICOPTER	PAGINATION
SWEETBRIER	VIDEOPHONE	EPIGLOTTIS	DIPHTHERIA	ANTITHESIS	HELIOGRAPH	PALIMPSEST
SWEETHEART	WATERBORNE	EXAGGERATE	DISHABILLE	ARBITRATOR	HELIOTROPE	PALINDROME
TABERNACLE	WATERCOLOR	FINGERLING	DISHARMONY	ARTICULATE	HEMISPHERE	PEDIATRICS
TELEGRAPHY	WATERCRAFT	FINGERNAIL	DISHEARTEN	ARTIFICIAL	HORIZONTAL	PENICILLIN
TELESCOPIC	WATERCRESS	FLAGELLATE	DISHWASHER	ASPIRATION	ILLITERATE	PERIHELION
TELEVISION	WATERFRONT	FLAGITIOUS	ENTHUSIASM	ASSIGNMENT	IMBIBITION	PERIODICAL
TENEBRIOUS	WATERMELON	GARGANTUAN	EUPHONIOUS	ASSIMILATE	IMMISCIBLE	PERIPHERAL
THREADBARE	WATERPOWER	GINGERSNAP	EUTHANASIA	AUDIOPHILE	INCIDENTAL	PERISHABLE
THREEPENCE	WATERPROOF	GINGIVITIS	FATHERLAND	AUDITORIUM	INCINERATE	PERITONEUM
THREESCORE	WATERSPOUT	GORGONZOLA	FATHOMLESS	AURIFEROUS	INCIVILITY	PERIWINKLE
TIMEKEEPER	WATERTIGHT	GREGARIOUS	HIGHLANDER	BEHINDHAND	INDICATIVE	POLITICIAN
TUBERCULAR	WATERWHEEL	HODGEPODGE	HIGHWAYMAN	BRAINCHILD	INDIGENOUS	PUNISHMENT
TUBERCULIN	WATERWORKS	IMAGINABLE	LACHRYMOSE	BRAINSTORM	INDISCREET	PYRIMIDINE
TYPESCRIPT	WAVELENGTH	JUGGERNAUT	LIGHTHOUSE	CAPITALISM	INDISPOSED	RADICALIZE
TYPESETTER	WHEELCHAIR	KINGFISHER	LIGHTPROOF	CAPITALIST	INDISTINCT	RADIOGENIC
TYPEWRITER	WHEELHORSE	KNIGHTHOOD	LITHUANIAN	CAPITALIZE	INDIVIDUAL	RADIOGRAPH
UNBEARABLE	WHEELHOUSE	KRUGERRAND	MECHANICAL	CAPITATION	INFIDELITY	RADIOMETER
UNBEATABLE	WIDESPREAD	LENGTHWISE	MOTHERHOOD	CAPITULATE	INFIGHTING	RADIOPHONE
UNBECOMING	WINEGROWER	LOGGERHEAD	MOTHERLAND	CARICATURE	INFILTRATE	RADIOSONDE
UNBELIEVER	WIREHAIRED	MARGINALIA	NETHERMOST	CAVITATION	INFINITIVE	RECIDIVISM
UNDENIABLE	AIRFREIGHT	MARGUERITE	NIGHTDRESS	DEBILITATE	INFINITUDE	RECIPROCAL
UNDERBELLY	CHIFFONIER	NEIGHBORLY	NIGHTSHADE	DECIMALIZE	INHIBITION	RECITATION
UNDERBRUSH	CONFECTION	OUTGENERAL	NIGHTSHIRT	DEFINITION	INSISTENCE	REDISTRICT
UNDERCOVER	CONFERENCE	PILGRIMAGE	NIGHTSTICK	DEFINITIVE	INTIMIDATE	REFINEMENT

REGISTRANT	PACKTHREAD	HOLLOWWARE	COMMISSARY	CHANDELIER	PIANOFORTE	AUTOMATION
RELINQUISH	PICKANINNY	HULLABALOO	COMMISSION	CHANGELING	PLANTATION	AUTOMATIZE
REMITTANCE	PICKPOCKET	IMPLACABLE	COMMODIOUS	CHANGEOVER	POINSETTIA	AUTOMOBILE
RESILIENCE	POCKETBOOK	INCLINABLE	COMMONALTY	CHANNELIZE	PRINCELING	AUTOMOTIVE
RESILIENCY	RICKETTSIA	INELIGIBLE	COMMONWEAL	CHINCHILLA	PRINCIPLED	AUTONOMOUS
RESISTANCE	SMOKESTACK	INFLECTION	COMMUNIQUE	CLINGSTONE	PRONOUNCED	AUTOSTRADA
REVITALIZE	TASKMASTER	INFLEXIBLE	COMMUTATOR	COGNIZANCE	PUGNACIOUS	BEFOREHAND
RIDICULOUS	UNSKILLFUL	INGLORIOUS	COSMOPOLIS	COINCIDENT	QUINTUPLET	BELONGINGS
RISIBILITY	WICKERWORK	MILLENNIUM	CUMMERBUND	CONNECTION	RAINMAKING	BLOODHOUND
ROTISSERIE	WORKBASKET	MILLILITER	DERMATITIS	CONNECTIVE	RHINESTONE	BLOODSTAIN
SANITARIAN	WORKINGMAN	MILLIMETER	ECUMENICAL	CONNIPTION	RHINOCEROS	BLOODSTONE
SANITARIUM	ADULTERANT	MILLSTREAM	ELEMENTARY	CORNFLOWER	ROUNDABOUT	CAMOUFLAGE
SANITATION	ADULTERATE	MILLWRIGHT	ENAMELWARE	CORNSTARCH	ROUNDHOUSE	CANONICALS
SCHISMATIC	AFFLICTIVE	NEGLIGIBLE	FLAMBOYANT	CORNUCOPIA	SHENANIGAN	CAPOREGIME
SEMIDRYING	AMALGAMATE	NUCLEONICS	FORMIDABLE	COUNTERACT	SHUNPIKING	CHLORINATE
SIMILITUDE	AMELIORATE	OPALESCENT	GORMANDIZE	COUNTERMAN	SLENDERIZE	CHLOROFORM
SOLICITOUS	ANGLOPHILE	OUTLANDISH	GRAMOPHONE	COUNTERSPY	STANDPOINT	CHROMOSOME
SOLICITUDE	ANGLOPHOBE	PALLBEARER	HAMMERHEAD	COUNTRYMAN	STANDSTILL	CHRONOLOGY
SOLIDARITY	APOLITICAL	PARLIAMENT	HAMMERLOCK	CRANKSHAFT	STENTORIAN	COLORATION
SPOILSPORT	APOLOGETIC	PHILISTINE	HARMONIOUS	CRENELLATE	THUNDEROUS	COLORATURA
SPRINGTIME	APPLICABLE	PHILOSOPHY	INIMITABLE	DINNERWARE	TRANSCRIBE	CORONATION
SPRINKLING	APPLICATOR	PHYLACTERY	ISOMETRICS	DONNYBROOK	TRANSCRIPT	CRYOGENICS
STRINGENCY	BALLISTICS	PILLOWCASE	PARMIGIANA	DOWNSTAIRS	TRANSDUCER	DECOLORIZE
STRIPTEASE	BELLADONNA	POULTRYMAN	PENMANSHIP	DOWNSTREAM	TRANSGRESS	DECOMPRESS
TOXICOLOGY	BELLETRIST	ROLLERBALL	PERMAFROST	DOWNSTROKE	TRANSISTOR	DECORATION
UNYIELDING	BELLWETHER	ROLLICKING	PERMISSION	ECONOMICAL	TRANSITION	DECORATIVE
VARICOSITY	BULLHEADED	SHILLELAGH	PERMISSIVE	EMANCIPATE	TRANSITIVE	DEMOBILIZE
VISIBILITY	CELLARETTE	SPELLBOUND	PREMARITAL	EVANESCENT	TRANSITORY	DEMOCRATIC
VISITATION	CELLOPHANE	SPOLIATION	PREMEDICAL	EVANGELISM	TRANSPLANT	DEMOGRAPHY
VIVIPAROUS	CHALCEDONY	STALACTITE	PRIMORDIAL	EVANGELIST	TRANSPOLAR	DEMOISELLE
VOCIFERATE	CHILDBIRTH	STALAGMITE	PROMETHIUM	EVANGELIZE	TRANSVERSE	DEMOLITION
VOCIFEROUS	COLLARBONE	STILLBIRTH	PROMINENCE	EVENHANDED	TRUNCATION	DEMONETIZE
CONJECTURE	COLLATERAL	SUBLIMINAL	PROMISSORY	FOUNDATION	TURNBUCKLE	DEMONOLOGY
DISJOINTED	COLLECTIVE	TABLECLOTH	PROMONTORY	FRANCHISEE	URINALYSIS	DEMORALIZE
PANJANDRUM	COLLOQUIAL	TABLESPOON	PROMPTBOOK	FRANCHISER	VERNACULAR	DENOMINATE
PROJECTILE	COLLOQUIUM	TROLLEYBUS	PROMULGATE	FRANCHISOR	VULNERABLE	DENOTATIVE
SUBJECTIVE	CYCLOMETER	UNBLUSHING	SEAMANSHIP	GRANDCHILD	WAINWRIGHT	DENOUEMENT
TRAJECTORY	CYCLOPEDIA	UNILATERAL	SEAMSTRESS	GRANDSTAND	WHENSOEVER	DEPOLARIZE
BACKGAMMON	DEALERSHIP	UNPLEASANT	SHAMEFACED	GRINDSTONE	ABSOLUTION	DEPOPULATE
BACKGROUND	DECLASSIFY	VILLAINOUS	SLUMBEROUS	GYMNASTICS	ABSOLUTISM	DEPORTMENT
BACKHANDED	DECLENSION	VOLLEYBALL	TERMINATOR	GYMNOSPERM	ABSORPTION	DEPOSITION
BACKSTAIRS	DEFLAGRATE	WALLFLOWER	THEMSELVES	ICONOCLASM	ACCOMPLICE	DEPOSITORY
BACKSTROKE	DEPLORABLE	WELLSPRING	THUMBSCREW	ICONOCLAST	ACCOMPLISH	DEROGATORY
BASKETBALL	DIELECTRIC	WILLOWWARE	TRAMPOLINE	MAINSPRING	ACCORDANCE	DESOLATION
BOOKKEEPER	DILLYDALLY	ABOMINABLE	TREMENDOUS	MAINSTREAM	ACCOUNTANT	DISORDERLY
BOOKMOBILE	DUPLICATOR	ALIMENTARY	TRIMONTHLY	MIGNONETTE	ACCOUNTING	EMBONPOINT
BOOKSELLER	EBULLITION	ANEMOMETER	UNEMPLOYED	MOONSTRUCK	ACROBATICS	EMBOUCHURE
CANKERWORM	EFFLORESCE	ANIMADVERT	VERMICELLI	MOUNTEBANK	ACROPHOBIA	ENDOGENOUS
COCKATRICE	EMPLOYMENT	ANIMALCULE	WHOMSOEVER	PAINKILLER	AEROBATICS	ENTOMOLOGY
DOCKWORKER	EMULSIFIER	ASYMMETRIC	ALONGSHORE	PAINTBRUSH	ALCOHOLISM	ERGONOMICS
FOLKSINGER	EXPLICABLE	BIOMEDICAL	AMANUENSIS	PAWNBROKER	ALTOGETHER	ERGOSTEROL
JACKANAPES	FALLACIOUS	CHIMERICAL	BLANCMANGE	PENNYROYAL	APPOINTIVE	EURODOLLAR
JACKHAMMER	FELLOWSHIP	CHIMPANZEE	BOONDOGGLE	PERNICIOUS	APPOSITION	EXCOGITATE
JACKRABBIT	FIELDPIECE	COMMANDANT	BRONCHITIS	PETNAPPING	APPOSITIVE	EXPOSITION
LACKLUSTER	GOALKEEPER	COMMANDEER	BRONTOSAUR	PHENOMENON	ARBORVITAE	FAVORITISM
MACKINTOSH	GUILLOTINE	COMMENTARY	CANNONBALL	PHONOGRAPH	ASSORTMENT	FLOODLIGHT
PACKSADDLE	HALLELUJAH	COMMERCIAL	CHANCELLOR	PIANISSIMO	ATMOSPHERE	FLOODPLAIN

FLOODWATER	NANOSECOND	COMPLIANCE	SEMPSTRESS	CHURCHGOER	INFRASONIC	SEERSUCKER
FLOORBOARD	NAPOLEONIC	COMPLIANCY	SERPENTINE	CHURCHLESS	INFREQUENT	SHORTENING
FLUORIDATE	OCTOTHORPE	COMPLICATE	SHIPFITTER	CHURCHYARD	INGRATIATE	SPIRITUOUS
FLUORINATE	OESOPHAGUS	COMPLICITY	SHIPWRIGHT	CITRONELLA	INGREDIENT	SPIROCHETE
GADOLINIUM	PEJORATIVE	COMPLIMENT	SHOPKEEPER	CLERESTORY	INORDINATE	SPORTSCAST
GONOCOCCUS	PERORATION	COMPOSITOR	SIMPLICITY	COORDINATE	INTRAMURAL	STARVELING
HEMOGLOBIN	PICOSECOND	COMPREHEND	SIMPLISTIC	CORRESPOND	INTRASTATE	STEREOTYPE
HEMOPHILIA	PILOTHOUSE	COMPROMISE	SKEPTICISM	CORRIGIBLE	JINRIKISHA	STOREHOUSE
HEMORRHAGE	RECOILLESS	COMPULSION	SLIPSTREAM	COURTHOUSE	JOURNALESE	SUBROUTINE
HEMORRHOID	RECOMPENSE	COMPULSIVE	SNAPDRAGON	CURRICULUM	JOURNALISM	SURREALISM
HOLOGRAPHY	RECONSIDER	COMPULSORY	STEPFATHER	DECRYPTION	JOURNEYMAN	TEARJERKER
HOMOGENIZE	REPORTEDLY	COMPUSERVE	STEPLADDER	DEGRADABLE	LAWRENCIUM	TETRAMETER
HOMOLOGOUS	REPOSITORY	COPPERHEAD	STEPMOTHER	DEPRECIATE	LEPRECHAUN	THEREAFTER
HOMOSEXUAL	RESOLUTION	CORPULENCE	STEPPARENT	DEPRESSANT	LIPREADING	THERMISTOR
HONORARIUM	RESORPTION	COWPUNCHER	STEPSISTER	DEPRESSION	LOGROLLING	THERMOSTAT
HYPOCENTER	RESOUNDING	CRYPTOGRAM	STUPENDOUS	DEPRESSIVE	LUBRICIOUS	TORRENTIAL
HYPODERMIC	REVOCATION	DELPHINIUM	SUPPLEMENT	DISRESPECT	MARROWBONE	TOURMALINE
HYPOTENUSE	REVOLUTION	DESPICABLE	SUPPLICANT	DOORKEEPER	MEERSCHAUM	TOURNAMENT
HYPOTHESIS	RIBOFLAVIN	DIAPHANOUS	SUPPLICATE	EFFRONTERY	METROPOLIS	TOURNIQUET
IDIOPATHIC	SCHOLASTIC	DISPENSARY	SUSPENSION	EMBROIDERY	MICROFICHE	ULTRASHORT
IGNORAMOUS	SCHOOLGIRL	DISPOSABLE	SUSPENSORY	EMBRYOLOGY	MICROGRAPH	ULTRASONIC
IMMOBILIZE	SCHOOLMARM	DISPOSSESS	SUSPICIOUS	ENCRYPTION	MICROMETER	ULTRASOUND
IMMODERATE	SCHOOLMATE	DYSPROSIUM	SYMPATHIZE	ESCRITOIRE	MICROPHONE	UNCRITICAL
IMMORALITY	SCHOOLROOM	GEOPHYSICS	TEMPERANCE	EVERYTHING	MICROPROBE	UNFRIENDLY
IMPORTANCE	SECONDHAND	GRAPEFRUIT	TEMPTATION	EVERYWHERE	MICROSCOPE	UNFRUITFUL
IMPOSSIBLE	STRONGHOLD	HIPPODROME	TRIPARTITE	EXORBITANT	MICROSTATE	UNGRACEFUL
IMPOVERISH	SUBORBITAL	HOSPITABLE	TRIPLICATE	EXPRESSION	NECROMANCY	UNGRACIOUS
INCOHERENT	THROMBOSIS	INAPTITUDE	TURPENTINE	EXPRESSMAN	NECROPOLIS	UNGRATEFUL
INCOMPLETE	THROUGHOUT	INOPERABLE	VESPERTINE	EXPRESSWAY	NOURISHING	UNGROUNDED
INCONSTANT	THROUGHPUT	MORPHOLOGY	WEAPONLESS	EXTRAMURAL	OPPRESSION	UPBRINGING
INDONESIAN	THROUGHWAY	OUTPATIENT	WRAPAROUND	EXTRANEOUS	OPPROBRIUM	VIBRAPHONE
INNOMINATE	TOPOGRAPHY	OUTPERFORM	CINQUEFOIL	EXURBANITE	OUTRAGEOUS	WHARFINGER
INNOVATION	TYPOGRAPHY	OUTPOURING	DISQUALIFY	FAHRENHEIT	OVERCHARGE	WHIRLYBIRD
INSOLATION	UPHOLSTERY	PEPPERCORN	INEQUALITY	FAIRGROUND	OVERMASTER	ANESTHESIA
INSOLVABLE	UPROARIOUS	PEPPERMINT	MASQUERADE	FIBRINOGEN	OVERSHADOW	ANESTHETIC
INTOLERANT	VELOCIPEDE	PERPETRATE	PERQUISITE	FOURSQUARE	OVERSPREAD	APOSTROPHE
INTONATION	XENOPHOBIA	PERPETUATE	UBIQUITOUS	GUARDHOUSE	OVERWINTER	BOISTEROUS
INTOXICANT	XEROGRAPHY	PERPETUITY	ABBREVIATE	HEARTBREAK	PATRONYMIC	BOLSHEVISM
INTOXICATE	AUSPICIOUS	PLUPERFECT	ABERRATION	HEARTHSIDE	PETROLATUM	CENSORIOUS
INVOCATION	BESPRINKLE	PREPACKAGE	ABORIGINAL	HEARTTHROB	POURPARLER	CENSORSHIP
INVOLUTION	BIOPHYSICS	PREPOSSESS	ACHROMATIC	HIEROPHANT	PUTRESCENT	CLASSICISM
IONOSPHERE	CAMPHORATE	PROPAGANDA	AGGRANDIZE	HORRENDOUS	QUARANTINE	CLASSIFIED
LABORATORY	CHAPFALLEN	PROPELLANT	AGGRESSION	HYDRAULICS	RECREATION	CONSCIENCE
LOCOMOTION	COLPORTEUR	PROPENSITY	AGGRESSIVE	HYDROLYSIS	REFRACTION	CONSECRATE
LOCOMOTIVE	COMPARABLE	PROPERTIED	AMERINDIAN	HYDROMETER	REFRACTORY	CONSEQUENT
MALODOROUS	COMPARISON	PROPITIATE	APPRECIATE	HYDROPHONE	REFRINGENT	CONSISTORY
MAYONNAISE	COMPASSION	PROPITIOUS	APPRENTICE	HYDROPLANE	REGRESSION	CONSONANCE
MEMORANDUM	COMPATIBLE	PROPORTION	ASTRINGENT	HYGROMETER	RETRACTILE	CONSORTIUM
MESOSPHERE	COMPATRIOT	PROPRIETOR	ATTRACTANT	IMPREGNATE	RETROGRADE	CONSPECTUS
MISOGAMIST	COMPENDIUM	PROPRINTER	ATTRACTION	IMPRESARIO	RETROGRESS	CONSPIRACY
MISOGYNIST	COMPENSATE	PROPULSION	BATRACHIAN	IMPRESSION	RETROSPECT	CONSTITUTE
MONOCHROME	COMPETENCE	RESPECTING	BEDRAGGLED	IMPRESSIVE	SACROILIAC	CONSTRAINT
MONOPHONIC	COMPETENCY	RESPECTIVE	CHARACTERY	IMPRIMATUR	SACROSANCT	CONSUMMATE
MONOTHEISM	COMPETITOR	RESPIRATOR	CHARITABLE	IMPROBABLE	SAPROPHYTE	CRISSCROSS
MONOTONOUS	COMPLECTED	RESPONDENT	CHARLESTON	INBREEDING	SCARLATINA	CROSSBONES
MOTORCYCLE	COMPLEMENT	RESPONSIVE	CHARTREUSE	INCREDIBLE	SCURRILOUS	CROSSBREED
MOTORTRUCK	COMPLEXION	SCAPEGRACE	CHIROMANCY	INFRACTION	SEARCHWARE	CROSSPIECE

CRUSTACEAN	PRESBYOPIA	CENTILITER	HECTOMETER	POSTSCRIPT	ACCUSATIVE	PSEUDOCODE
DIPSOMANIA	PRESBYTERY	CENTIMETER	HEPTAMETER	PROTECTION	ACCUSTOMED	RECUPERATE
DISSATISFY	PRESCIENCE	CENTRALIZE	HINTERLAND	PROTESTANT	ADJUDICATE	REDUNDANCY
DISSENSION	PRESSURIZE	CENTRIFUGE	HISTRIONIC	PROTOPLASM	ALBUMINOUS	REFULGENCE
DISSERVICE	PRESUPPOSE	CHATELAINE	HOOTENANNY	PROTRACTOR	AMBULATORY	REGULATION
DISSIMILAR	PROSCENIUM	CHATTERBOX	INITIATIVE	QUATREFOIL	AMMUNITION	REJUVENATE
DISSOCIATE	PROSPECTUS	CLOTHESPIN	INITIATORY	RATTLETRAP	ANNUNCIATE	RELUCTANCE
DISSONANCE	PROSPERITY	CONTAGIOUS	INSTRUCTOR	RESTAURANT	ASSUMPTION	REMUNERATE
EMASCULATE	PROSPEROUS	CONTENTION	INSTRUMENT	RESTORABLE	BALUSTRADE	REPUBLICAN
EPISCOPACY	PROSTHESIS	CONTIGUOUS	ISOTHERMAL	RESTRAINED	BEAUJOLAIS	REPUGNANCE
EPISCOPATE	PROSTITUTE	CONTINENCE	KETTLEDRUM	SALTCELLAR	BEAUTICIAN	REPUTATION
ERYSIPELAS	RAMSHACKLE	CONTINGENT	LETTERHEAD	SEPTICEMIA	BITUMINOUS	RESURGENCE
EVISCERATE	REASONABLE	CONTINUITY	MALTHUSIAN	SEPTUAGINT	CALUMNIATE	RHEUMATISM
EXASPERATE	ROUSTABOUT	CONTINUOUS	MANTLEROCK	SETTLEMENT	CAOUTCHOUC	SALUBRIOUS
FARSIGHTED	SEASONABLE	CONTRABAND	MARTINGALE	SHUTTERBUG	CHAUVINISM	SALUTATION
FLASHLIGHT	SEISMOGRAM	CONTRADICT	MASTERMIND	SISTERHOOD	CLOUDBURST	SCRUTINIZE
FRESHWATER	SEISMOLOGY	CONTRAVENE	MASTERSHIP	SKATEBOARD	CUMULATIVE	SECULARISM
FUSSBUDGET	SKYSCRAPER	CONTRIBUTE	MASTERWORK	SMATTERING	DEHUMANIZE	SECULARIZE
GEOSCIENCE	SUBSEQUENT	CONTROLLER	METTLESOME	SOOTHSAYER	DEHUMIDIFY	SEPULCHRAL
GHOSTWRITE	SUBSIDIARY	CONTROVERT	MISTAKABLE	SPITTLEBUG	DEPUTATION	THOUGHTFUL
GOOSEBERRY	SUBSTATION	COTTONSEED	MOUTHPIECE	STATECRAFT	EFFULGENCE	TROUBADOUR
GOOSEFLESH	SUBSTITUTE	COTTONTAIL	MULTILEVEL	STATEHOUSE	ESCUTCHEON	TUMULTUOUS
GUNSLINGER	SUBSTRATUM	COTTONWOOD	MULTIMEDIA	STATIONARY	FIGURATION	UNDULATION
HORSEFLESH	SUBSURFACE	CRETACEOUS	MULTIPLIER	STATIONERY	FIGURATIVE	UNNUMBERED
HORSELAUGH	TESSELLATE	CUTTLEFISH	MULTISENSE	STATISTICS	FIGUREHEAD	UNSUITABLE
HORSEPOWER	UNASSUMING	DEATHWATCH	MULTISTAGE	STATUESQUE	FRAUDULENT	VITUPERATE
HORSEWOMAN	WORSHIPFUL	DENTIFRICE	MULTISTORY	SUBTERFUGE	FUTURISTIC	VOLUMETRIC
HOUSECLEAN	WRISTWATCH	DESTRUCTOR	NASTURTIUM	SUBTRAHEND	GESUNDHEIT	VOLUMINOUS
HOUSEWARES	ABSTEMIOUS	DICTIONARY	NETTLESOME	SUSTENANCE	GROUNDLING	VOLUPTUARY
JIMSONWEED	ABSTINENCE	DISTILLATE	NEUTRALISM	SWITCHBACK	GROUNDMASS	VOLUPTUOUS
KIESELGUHR	AESTHETICS	DISTRAUGHT	NEUTRALITY	TANTAMOUNT	GROUNDWORK	ABOVEBOARD
MAISONETTE	APOTHECARY	DISTRIBUTE	NEUTRALIZE	TATTERSALL	ILLUMINATE	CANVASBACK
MANSERVANT	APOTHEOSIS	EARTHQUAKE	OBSTETRICS	TATTLETALE	ILLUSTRATE	CHIVALROUS
MANSUETUDE	ARITHMETIC	EISTEDDFOD	OPHTHALMIC	TEETHRIDGE	IMMUNOLOGY	CLAVICHORD
MENSURABLE	AUCTIONEER	EPITHELIUM	ORATORICAL	TOOTHBRUSH	INAUGURATE	CLOVERLEAF
MIDSHIPMAN	AUSTRALIAN	EXOTHERMIC	PANTALOONS	TOOTHPASTE	INCULPABLE	CONVALESCE
MISSILEMAN	BAPTISTERY	FACTITIOUS	PANTYWAIST	TURTLEDOVE	INCUMBENCY	CONVECTION
MISSIONARY	BASTARDIZE	FASTIDIOUS	PARTICIPLE	TURTLENECK	INDUCEMENT	CONVENIENT
MONSTRANCE	BATTLEMENT	FERTILIZER	PARTICULAR	UNATTACHED	INDUCTANCE	CONVENTION
MUDSLINGER	BATTLESHIP	FICTITIOUS	PASTEBOARD	UPSTANDING	INDULGENCE	CONVERSANT
NEWSGROUPS	BESTIALITY	FISTICUFFS	PASTEURIZE	URETHRITIS	INDUSTRIAL	CONVERSION
NEWSLETTER	BETTERMENT	FOOTBRIDGE	PENTAMETER	VERTEBRATE	INHUMANITY	CONVEYANCE
NEWSWORTHY	BIRTHPLACE	FOOTLIGHTS	PESTILENCE	VICTORIOUS	INJUNCTION	CONVICTION
NOISEMAKER	BIRTHRIGHT	FOOTLOCKER	PHOTOFLASH	VICTUALLER	INQUIETUDE	CONVOLUTED
NONSTARTER	BIRTHSTONE	FORTHRIGHT	PHOTOGENIC	VIETNAMESE	LIEUTENANT	CONVULSION
NONSUPPORT	BLITZKRIEG	FORTISSIMO	PHOTOGRAPH	VIRTUOSITY	LOQUACIOUS	CURVACEOUS
NURSERYMAN	BOTTLENECK	FORTUITOUS	PHOTOMETER	WASTEPAPER	LUGUBRIOUS	GRAVESTONE
PASSAGEWAY	BOTTOMLAND	FOSTERLING	PHOTOMURAL	WEATHERING	MANUSCRIPT	GRAVIMETER
PEASHOOTER	BUTTERMILK	FRATERNITY	PHOTOPAINT	WEATHERMAN	MATURATION	INEVITABLE
PERSIFLAGE	BUTTONHOLE	FRATERNIZE	PLUTOCRACY	WESTERNIZE	MONUMENTAL	PERVERSION
PERSONABLE	BUTTONHOOK	FRATRICIDE	PORTCULLIS	WHATSOEVER	NATURALISM	PRIVILEGED
PERSONALTY	CANTALOUPE	GASTRONOMY	PORTENTOUS	WHITSUNDAY	NATURALIST	PROVENANCE
PERSUASION	CANTILEVER	GENTLEFOLK	PORTUGUESE	WINTERTIDE	NATURALIZE	PROVIDENCE
PHOSPHORUS	CANTONMENT	GEOTHERMAL	POSTHUMOUS	WINTERTIME	NEBULOSITY	PROVINCIAL
PHYSIOLOGY	CENTENNIAL	GRATUITOUS	POSTMASTER	WORTHWHILE	OCCUPATION	SERVICEMAN
POSSESSION	CENTESIMAL	HEATSTROKE	POSTMORTEM	YESTERYEAR	OCCURRENCE	SERVOMOTOR
POSSESSIVE	CENTIGRADE	HECTOLITER	POSTPARTUM	ACCUMULATE	POPULATION	SILVERFISH

SILVERWARE	CANTALOUPE	NEWFANGLED	VIBRAPHONE	ANTICLIMAX	NOTICEABLE	GRANDCHILD
SUBVENTION	CANVASBACK	OUTBALANCE	VILLAINOUS	ARTICULATE	OVERCHARGE	GRANDSTAND
TRAVELOGUE	CELLARETTE	OUTLANDISH	WRAPAROUND	ATTACHMENT	PENICILLIN	GRINDSTONE
TRAVERTINE	CHARACTERY	OUTPATIENT	ACROBATICS	BLANCMANGE	POLYCLINIC	GUARDHOUSE
UNAVAILING	CHIVALROUS	OUTRAGEOUS	AEROBATICS	BLUECOLLAR	PORTCULLIS	HEREDITARY
UNEVENTFUL	COCKATRICE	PANJANDRUM	ANTEBELLUM	BRONCHITIS	PRESCIENCE	HYPODERMIC
UNIVERSITY	COLLARBONE	PANTALOONS	ANTIBIOTIC	CAPACITATE	PRINCELING	IMMODERATE
ANSWERABLE	COLLATERAL	PASSAGEWAY	ARCHBISHOP	CARICATURE	PRINCIPLED	IMPEDIMENT
BROWNSTONE	COMMANDANT	PECCADILLO	BLUEBONNET	CATECHUMEN	PROSCENIUM	INCIDENTAL
DRAWBRIDGE	COMMANDEER	PEDIATRICS	BLUEBOTTLE	CHALCEDONY	RACECOURSE	INFIDELITY
DRAWSTRING	COMPARABLE	PENMANSHIP	CARABINEER	CHANCELLOR	RADICALIZE	INORDINATE
EYEWITNESS	COMPARISON	PENTAMETER	CATABOLISM	CHINCHILLA	RELUCTANCE	LIBIDINOUS
SKYWRITING	COMPASSION	PERMAFROST	CELEBRATED	CHURCHGOER	REVOCATION	MALADAPTED
SNOWMOBILE	COMPATIBLE	PETNAPPING	CEREBELLUM	CHURCHLESS	RIDICULOUS	MALODOROUS
INEXORABLE	COMPATRIOT	PHYLACTERY	DELIBERATE	CHURCHYARD	SALTCELLAR	OCCIDENTAL
INEXPIABLE	CONTAGIOUS	PICCALILLI	DEMOBILIZE	COINCIDENT	SEARCHWARE	PSEUDOCODE
UNEXAMPLED	CONVALESCE	PICKANINNY	DRAWBRIDGE	CONSCIENCE	SKYSCRAPER	RECIDIVISM
UNEXPECTED	CRETACEOUS	PLAYACTING	EXORBITANT	DELECTABLE	SOLICITOUS	REMEDIABLE
CHRYSOLITE	CURVACEOUS	PRECARIOUS	EXURBANITE	DEMOCRATIC	SOLICITUDE	ROUNDABOUT
COPYREADER	DECLASSIFY	PRECAUTION	FILIBUSTER	DETACHMENT	STRYCHNINE	ROUNDHOUSE
COPYWRITER	DEFLAGRATE	PREDACEOUS	FLAMBOYANT	EFFECTUATE	SWITCHBACK	SEMIDRYING
ENCYCLICAL	DEGRADABLE	PREMARITAL	FOOTBRIDGE	EFFICIENCY	TOXICOLOGY	SLENDERIZE
LADYFINGER	DERMATITIS	PREPACKAGE	FREEBOOTER	EMANCIPATE	TRUNCATION	SNAPDRAGON
LARYNGITIS	DISHABILLE	PROPAGANDA	FUSSBUDGET	EMASCULATE	UNBECOMING	SOLIDARITY
MOLYBDENUM	DISHARMONY	PUGNACIOUS	GOLDBEATER	ENCYCLICAL	UNOCCUPIED	STANDPOINT
PLAYACTING	DISSATISFY	QUARANTINE	HANDBARROW	EPISCOPACY	VARICOSITY	STANDSTILL
PLAYGROUND	DOGCATCHER	REFRACTION	IMBIBITION	EPISCOPATE	VELOCIPEDE	THUNDEROUS
PLAYWRIGHT	ENDEARMENT	REFRACTORY	IMMOBILIZE	EVISCERATE	WOODCUTTER	WITHDRAWAL
POLYCLINIC	EUTHANASIA	RESTAURANT	INHABITANT	EXPECTANCY	ACCIDENTAL	ABBREVIATE
POLYHEDRON	EXTRAMURAL	RETRACTILE	INHIBITION	FELICITATE	ADJUDICATE	ABOVEBOARD
POLYNESIAN	EXTRANEOUS	SANDALWOOD	LINEBACKER	FELICITOUS	ARCHDEACON	ABSTEMIOUS
POLYTHEISM	FALLACIOUS	SEAMANSHIP	LUGUBRIOUS	FORECASTLE	BLOODHOUND	AGGRESSION
STRYCHNINE	FLYCATCHER	SHENANIGAN	METABOLISM	FRANCHISEE	BLOODSTAIN	AGGRESSIVE
MIZZENMAST	GARGANTUAN	STALACTITE	METABOLITE	FRANCHISER	BLOODSTONE	ALIMENTARY
MOZZARELLA	GERIATRICS	STALAGMITE	MOLYBDENUM	FRANCHISOR	BOONDOGGLE	ANSWERABLE
PRIZEFIGHT	GORMANDIZE	SYMPATHIZE	NOTABILITY	GEOSCIENCE	BREADBOARD	APPRECIATE
	GREGARIOUS	TANTAMOUNT	PALLBEARER	GONOCOCCUS	BREADFRUIT	APPRENTICE
	GYMNASTICS	TETRAMETER	PAWNBROKER	GYNECOLOGY	BREADSTUFF	BALDERDASH
	HEPTAMETER	THREADBARE	PHLEBOTOMY	HELICOPTER	BROADCLOTH	BASKETBALL
	HEREABOUTS	TRIPARTITE	PRESBYOPIA	HOMECOMING	BROADSWORD	BELLETRIST
	HULLABALOO	ULTRASHORT	PRESBYTERY	HYPOCENTER	CHANDELIER	BETTERMENT

AGGRANDIZE	HUSBANDMAN	ULTRASONIC	REPUBLICAN	IMMACULATE	CHILDBIRTH	BIOMEDICAL
ALLHALLOWS	HYDRAULICS	ULTRASOUND	RISIBILITY	IMPECCABLE	CLOUDBURST	BORDERLAND
ALPHABETIC	IMPLACABLE	UNAVAILING	SALUBRIOUS	INDECISION	COMEDIENNE	BRIDEGROOM
ANIMADVERT	INFRACTION	UNBEARABLE	SHIBBOLETH	INDECISIVE	COORDINATE	BRIDESMAID
ANIMALCULE	INFRASONIC	UNBEATABLE	SLUMBEROUS	INDECOROUS	ESPADRILLE	BUDGERIGAR
APOCALYPSE	INGRATIATE	UNEXAMPLED	TENEBRIOUS	INDICATIVE	EURODOLLAR	BUTTERMILK
APPEARANCE	INTRAMURAL	UNGRACEFUL	THUMBSCREW	INDUCEMENT	EXPEDIENCE	CANDELABRA
ATTRACTANT	INTRASTATE	UNGRACIOUS	TROUBADOUR	INDUCTANCE	EXPEDIENCY	CANDESCENT
ATTRACTION	JACKANAPES	UNGRATEFUL	TURNBUCKLE	INVOCATION	EXPEDITION	CANKERWORM
BASTARDIZE	LOQUACIOUS	UNICAMERAL	VISIBILITY	JUDICATURE	FIELDPIECE	CENTENNIAL
BATRACHIAN	MECHANICAL	UNILATERAL	VOCABULARY	MANICURIST	FLOODLIGHT	CENTESIMAL
BEDRAGGLED	MENDACIOUS	UNREASONED	WORKBASKET	MEDICAMENT	FLOODPLAIN	CHATELAINE
BELLADONNA	MERCANTILE	UPROARIOUS	ANTECEDENT	METACARPUS	FLOODWATER	CHIMERICAL
BOMBARDIER	MISTAKABLE	UPSTANDING	ANTICANCER	METICULOUS	FLUIDOUNCE	CLERESTORY
BRIGANTINE	MOZZARELLA	URINALYSIS	ANTICHRIST	MONOCHROME	FOUNDATION	CLOVERLEAF
CALCAREOUS	MYRIAMETER	VERNACULAR	ANTICIPATE	MUSICOLOGY	FRAUDULENT	COLLECTIVE

COMMENTARY	EISTEDDFOD	LIPREADING	PREMEDICAL	TENDERFOOT	STEPFATHER	SENEGALESE
COMMERCIAL	ELEMENTARY	LOGGERHEAD	PRIZEFIGHT	TENDERLOIN	UNAFFECTED	TELEGRAPHY
COMPENDIUM	ENAMELWARE	LUMBERJACK	PROCEEDING	TESSELLATE	VOCIFERATE	THOUGHTFUL
COMPENSATE	EVANESCENT	LUMBERYARD	PROCESSION	THEREAFTER	VOCIFEROUS	TOPOGRAPHY
COMPETENCE	EXACERBATE	MAIDENHAIR	PROFESSION	THREEPENCE	WALLFLOWER	TYPOGRAPHY
COMPETENCY	EXPRESSION	MAIDENHEAD	PROGENITOR	THREESCORE	WHARFINGER	VICEGERENT
COMPETITOR	EXPRESSMAN	MAIDENHOOD	PROJECTILE	TIMBERLINE	WINDFLOWER	WINEGROWER
CONCENTRIC	EXPRESSWAY	MANDELBROT	PROMETHIUM	TORRENTIAL	ALLEGIANCE	XEROGRAPHY
CONCEPTION	FAHRENHEIT	MANSERVANT	PROPELLANT	TRAJECTORY	ALONGSHORE	AESTHETICS
CONCERNING	FARFETCHED	MASTERMIND	PROPENSITY	TRAVELOGUE	ALTOGETHER	ALCOHOLISM
CONCERTINA	FATHERLAND	MASTERSHIP	PROPERTIED	TRAVERTINE	AMALGAMATE	ANNIHILATE
CONCESSION	FINGERLING	MASTERWORK	PROTECTION	TREMENDOUS	ANTAGONISM	APOTHECARY
CONCESSIVE	FINGERNAIL	MEMBERSHIP	PROTESTANT	TURPENTINE	ANTAGONIST	APOTHEOSIS
CONDENSATE	FLAGELLATE	MILLENNIUM	PROVENANCE	UNEVENTFUL	ANTAGONIZE	ARITHMETIC
CONDESCEND	FORFEITURE	MISCELLANY	PUTRESCENT	UNIVERSITY	ARMAGEDDON	BACKHANDED
CONFECTION	FOSTERLING	MIZZENMAST	READERSHIP	UNPLEASANT	ASSIGNMENT	BAREHEADED
CONFERENCE	FRATERNITY	MOTHERHOOD	RECREATION	UNYIELDING	BACKGAMMON	BENCHMARKS
CONFESSION	FRATERNIZE	MOTHERLAND	REGRESSION	UROGENITAL	BACKGROUND	BIOPHYSICS
CONGENITAL	GEOCENTRIC	NETHERMOST	RENDEZVOUS	VAUDEVILLE	BRIDGEHEAD	BIRTHPLACE
CONJECTURE	GINGERSNAP	NOISEMAKER	RESPECTING	VERTEBRATE	BRIDGEWORK	BIRTHRIGHT
CONNECTION	GOOSEBERRY	NUCLEONICS	RESPECTIVE	VESPERTINE	CATEGORIZE	BIRTHSTONE
CONNECTIVE	GOOSEFLESH	NUMBERLESS	RHINESTONE	VOICEPRINT	CHANGELING	BOLSHEVISM
CONSECRATE	GRAPEFRUIT	NURSERYMAN	RICKETTSIA	VOLLEYBALL	CHANGEOVER	BONDHOLDER
CONSEQUENT	GRAVESTONE	OBSTETRICS	ROLLERBALL	VULNERABLE	CLINGSTONE	BULLHEADED
CONTENTION	HALLELUJAH	OPALESCENT	RUBBERNECK	WANDERLUST	CRYOGENICS	CAMPHORATE
CONVECTION	HAMMERHEAD	OPPRESSION	SCAPEGRACE	WASTEPAPER	DELEGATION	CATCHPENNY
CONVENIENT	HAMMERLOCK	OUTGENERAL	SERPENTINE	WESTERNIZE	DEMOGRAPHY	CLODHOPPER
CONVENTION	HENCEFORTH	OUTPERFORM	SHAMEFACED	WICKERWORK	DEROGATORY	CLOTHESPIN
CONVERSANT	HINTERLAND	PASTEBOARD	SILVERFISH	WILDEBEEST	ENDOGENOUS	DEATHWATCH
CONVERSION	HODGEPODGE	PASTEURIZE	SILVERWARE	WILDERNESS	ENGAGEMENT	DELPHINIUM
CONVEYANCE	HOOTENANNY	PEACEMAKER	SISTERHOOD	WINTERTIDE	EVANGELISM	DIAPHANOUS
COPPERHEAD	HORRENDOUS	PEPPERCORN	SKATEBOARD	WINTERTIME	EVANGELIST	EARTHQUAKE
CORRESPOND	HORSEFLESH	PEPPERMINT	SMOKESTACK	WONDERLAND	EVANGELIZE	EPITHELIUM
CREDENTIAL	HORSELAUGH	PERCENTAGE	SPACECRAFT	WONDERMENT	EXAGGERATE	EVENHANDED
CRENELLATE	HORSEPOWER	PERCENTILE	STAGECOACH	WOODENWARE	EXCOGITATE	EXOTHERMIC
CUMMERBUND	HORSEWOMAN	PERCEPTION	STATECRAFT	YESTERYEAR	FAIRGROUND	FLASHLIGHT
DEALERSHIP	HOUSECLEAN	PERCEPTIVE	STATEHOUSE	ANTIFREEZE	FOREGATHER	FOREHANDED
DECLENSION	HOUSEWARES	PERCEPTUAL	STEREOTYPE	ARTIFICIAL	FOREGROUND	FORTHRIGHT
DEPRECIATE	IMPREGNATE	PERFECTION	STOREHOUSE	AURIFEROUS	HEMOGLOBIN	FRESHWATER
DEPRESSANT	IMPRESARIO	PERPETRATE	STUPENDOUS	BENEFACTOR	HOLOGRAPHY	GEOPHYSICS
DEPRESSION	IMPRESSION	PERPETUATE	SUBJECTIVE	BENEFICENT	HOMOGENIZE	GEOTHERMAL
DEPRESSIVE	IMPRESSIVE	PERPETUITY	SUBSEQUENT	BENEFICIAL	INAUGURATE	HARDHEADED
DESCENDANT	INADEQUATE	PERVERSION	SUBTERFUGE	CATAFALQUE	INDIGENOUS	INCOHERENT
DIELECTRIC	INBREEDING	PINFEATHER	SUBVENTION	CHAPFALLEN	INFIGHTING	ISOTHERMAL
DIFFERENCE	INCREDIBLE	PLUPERFECT	SUCCESSION	CHIFFONIER	INTEGUMENT	JACKHAMMER
DINNERWARE	INFLECTION	POCKETBOOK	SUCCESSIVE	CORNFLOWER	INVIGORATE	KNIGHTHOOD
DISBELIEVE	INFLEXIBLE	PORTENTOUS	SUFFERANCE	FOREFATHER	MANAGEMENT	LANDHOLDER
DISCERNING	INFREQUENT	POSSESSION	SUGGESTION	FOREFINGER	METAGALAXY	LEAFHOPPER
DISHEARTEN	INGREDIENT	POSSESSIVE	SUGGESTIVE	INDEFINITE	MISOGAMIST	MALTHUSIAN
DISPENSARY	INOPERABLE	PREBENDARY	SURREALISM	KINGFISHER	MISOGYNIST	MATCHMAKER
DISRESPECT	ISOMETRICS	PRECEDENCE	SUSPENSION	LADYFINGER	NEWSGROUPS	MIDSHIPMAN
DISSENSION	JUGGERNAUT	PRECESSION	SUSPENSORY	MALEFACTOR	OBLIGATION	MORPHOLOGY
DISSERVICE	KIESELGUHR	PREDECEASE	SUSTENANCE	MALEFICENT	OLEAGINOUS	MOUTHPIECE
DUNDERHEAD	KRUGERRAND	PREDESTINE	TABLECLOTH	MUNIFICENT	PHLEGMATIC	NEIGHBORLY
DUODECIMAL	LAWRENCIUM	PREFERENCE	TABLESPOON	PATHFINDER	PLAYGROUND	NONCHALANT
ECUMENICAL	LEPRECHAUN	PREFERMENT	TATTERSALL	RIBOFLAVIN	REPAGINATE	OPHTHALMIC
EGOCENTRIC	LETTERHEAD	PREHENSILE	TEMPERANCE	SHIPFITTER	REPUGNANCE	PEASHOOTER

PERIHELION	CHARITABLE	INITIATORY	SPECIALIZE	BEDCLOTHES	INVALIDATE	TRIPLICATE
POLYHEDRON	CLAVICHORD	INQUIETUDE	SPIRITUOUS	BICHLORIDE	INVALUABLE	TROLLEYBUS
POSTHUMOUS	COGNIZANCE	JARDINIERE	SPOLIATION	BOTTLENECK	INVOLUTION	TUMBLEDOWN
PSYCHIATRY	COMMISSARY	JINRIKISHA	STATIONARY	BOWDLERIZE	IRRELEVANT	TUMBLEWEED
PSYCHOLOGY	COMMISSION	LASCIVIOUS	STATIONERY	CAMELOPARD	JUBILATION	TUMULTUOUS
PSYCHOPATH	CONCILIATE	LUBRICIOUS	STATISTICS	CANDLEWICK	KETTLEDRUM	TURTLEDOVE
RAMSHACKLE	CONFIDENCE	MACKINTOSH	STRAIGHTEN	CHARLESTON	LACKLUSTER	TURTLENECK
ROUGHHOUSE	CONFISCATE	MARGINALIA	SUBLIMINAL	COMPLECTED	LANDLOCKED	UNBALANCED
SACCHARINE	CONNIPTION	MARTINGALE	SUBSIDIARY	COMPLEMENT	LANDLUBBER	UNBELIEVER
SOOTHSAYER	CONSISTORY	MILLILITER	SUFFICIENT	COMPLEXION	LIKELIHOOD	UNDULATION
STOCHASTIC	CONTIGUOUS	MILLIMETER	SUSPICIOUS	COMPLIANCE	LIVELIHOOD	UNHALLOWED
TEETHRIDGE	CONTINENCE	MISSILEMAN	TERMINATOR	COMPLIANCY	MANTLEROCK	UPHOLSTERY
TOOTHBRUSH	CONTINGENT	MISSIONARY	UNCRITICAL	COMPLICATE	MEDDLESOME	WAVELENGTH
TOOTHPASTE	CONTINUITY	MULTILEVEL	UNFAITHFUL	COMPLICITY	METALLURGY	WHEELCHAIR
TOUCHSTONE	CONTINUOUS	MULTIMEDIA	UNFRIENDLY	COMPLIMENT	METTLESOME	WHEELHORSE
UNSCHOOLED	CONVICTION	MULTIPLIER	UNSKILLFUL	CONCLUSION	MIDDLEBROW	WHEELHOUSE
URETHRITIS	CORDILLERA	MULTISENSE	UNSUITABLE	CONFLUENCE	MISALIGNED	WHIRLYBIRD
WATCHMAKER	CORRIGIBLE	MULTISTAGE	UNTHINKING	CRADLESONG	MUDSLINGER	ACCOMPLICE
WATCHTOWER	CREDITABLE	MULTISTORY	UPBRINGING	CUMULATIVE	NAPOLEONIC	ACCOMPLISH
WEATHERING	CURRICULUM	NARCISSISM	VERMICELLI	CUTTLEFISH	NEBULOSITY	ACCUMULATE
WEATHERMAN	DEMOISELLE	NEGLIGIBLE	VINDICTIVE	DEBILITATE	NEEDLEWORK	ALBUMINOUS
WEIGHTLESS	DENTIFRICE	NOURISHING	WORKINGMAN	DECELERATE	NEOCLASSIC	ANTIMATTER
WINCHESTER	DESPICABLE	PARLIAMENT	BEAUJOLAIS	DECOLORIZE	NETTLESOME	AQUAMARINE
WIREHAIRED	DICTIONARY	PARMIGIANA	BLUEJACKET	DEMOLITION	NEWSLETTER	ASSEMBLAGE
WITCHCRAFT	DIFFICULTY	PARTICIPLE	TEARJERKER	DEPILATORY	POPULATION	ASSIMILATE
WITCHGRASS	DISCIPLINE	PARTICULAR	WINDJAMMER	DEPOLARIZE	PROCLIVITY	ASSUMPTION
WORSHIPFUL	DISSIMILAR	PERCIPIENT	BLACKAMOOR	DESALINATE	PROFLIGATE	ASYMMETRIC
WORTHWHILE	DISTILLATE	PERMISSION	BLACKBERRY	DESALINIZE	RATTLETRAP	AUTOMATION
ABOMINABLE	DUPLICATOR	PERMISSIVE	BLACKBOARD	DESOLATION	REBELLIOUS	AUTOMATIZE
ABORIGINAL	ERYSIPELAS	PERNICIOUS	BLACKGUARD	EBULLITION	REFULGENCE	AUTOMOBILE
ABSCISSION	ESCRITOIRE	PERSIFLAGE	BLACKSMITH	EFFULGENCE	REGULATION	AUTOMOTIVE
ABSTINENCE	EXOBIOLOGY	PESTILENCE	BLACKTHORN	EPIGLOTTIS	RESILIENCE	BITUMINOUS
AFFLICTIVE	EXPLICABLE	PHILISTINE	BLOCKHOUSE	EUCALYPTUS	RESILIENCY	BOOKMOBILE
AFICIONADO	EYEWITNESS	PHYSIOLOGY	BOOKKEEPER	EXCELLENCE	RESOLUTION	BRAHMANISM
AMELIORATE	FACTITIOUS	PIANISSIMO	BREAKFRONT	EXCELLENCY	REVELATION	BUSHMASTER
AMERINDIAN	FARSIGHTED	PLAGIARIZE	BREAKWATER	EXHILARATE	REVOLUTION	CALUMNIATE
AMPHIBIOUS	FASTIDIOUS	PLEBISCITE	BRICKLAYER	FACILITATE	RINGLEADER	CEREMONIAL
APOLITICAL	FERTILIZER	PRECIOSITY	CHECKPOINT	FAMILARIZE	SCARLATINA	CHROMOSOME
APPLICABLE	FIBRINOGEN	PREDICABLE	CRANKSHAFT	FOOTLIGHTS	SCHOLASTIC	DATAMATION
APPLICATOR	FICTITIOUS	PREDISPOSE	DOORKEEPER	FOOTLOCKER	SECULARISM	DECIMALIZE
APPOINTIVE	FISTICUFFS	PRIVILEGED	GAMEKEEPER	GADOLINIUM	SECULARIZE	DECOMPRESS
ARCHITRAVE	FLAGITIOUS	PRODIGIOUS	GATEKEEPER	GENTLEFOLK	SEPULCHRAL	DEHUMANIZE
ASTRINGENT	FORBIDDING	PROFICIENT	GOALKEEPER	GUILLOTINE	SETTLEMENT	DEHUMIDIFY
ATTAINMENT	FORMIDABLE	PROMINENCE	KNICKKNACK	GUNSLINGER	SHILLELAGH	DENOMINATE
AUCTIONEER	FORTISSIMO	PROMISSORY	KNOCKWURST	HABILIMENT	SIMILITUDE	DISEMBOWEL
AUSPICIOUS	GINGIVITIS	PROPITIATE	PAINKILLER	HANDLEBARS	SIMPLICITY	DREAMWORLD
BALLISTICS	GLACIOLOGY	PROPITIOUS	QUICKBASIC	HIGHLANDER	SIMPLISTIC	EFFEMINATE
BAPTISTERY	GRAVIMETER	PROVIDENCE	SHOPKEEPER	HOMOLOGOUS	SINGLETREE	ENJAMBMENT
BESTIALITY	HANDICRAFT	PROVINCIAL	TIMEKEEPER	IMPALPABLE	SPELLBOUND	ENTOMOLOGY
CACCIATORE	HOSPITABLE	RECEIVABLE	ABSOLUTION	INCULPABLE	SPOILSPORT	ESTIMATION
CANTILEVER	IMAGINABLE	RECOILLESS	ABSOLUTISM	INDELICATE	STEPLADDER	HANDMAIDEN
CARCINOGEN	IMPRIMATUR	REFRINGENT	ACCELERATE	INDULGENCE	STILLBIRTH	HEADMASTER
CARDIOGRAM	INCLINABLE	RESPIRATOR	ALKALINIZE	INFALLIBLE	SUNGLASSES	ILLUMINATE
CARDIOLOGY	INELIGIBLE	ROLLICKING	AMBULATORY	INFILTRATE	SUPPLEMENT	IMMEMORIAL
CENTIGRADE	INEVITABLE	SEPTICEMIA	AQUALUNGER	INSOLATION	SUPPLICANT	INCOMPLETE
CENTILITER	INIMITABLE	SERVICEMAN	BATTLEMENT	INSOLVABLE	SUPPLICATE	INCUMBENCY
CENTIMETER	INITIATIVE	SPECIALIST	BATTLESHIP	INTOLERANT	TATTLETALE	INHUMANITY

INNOMINATE	CANONICALS	MELANCHOLY	CANNONBALL	HIEROPHANT	PIGEONHOLE	CHIMPANZEE
INSEMINATE	CHANNELIZE	MELANESIAN	CANTONMENT	HIPPODROME	PILLOWCASE	CONSPECTUS
INTIMIDATE	CHRONOLOGY	MENINGITIS	CARBOLATED	HOLLOWWARE	PLUTOCRACY	CONSPIRACY
KINEMATICS	CORONATION	NOMINATIVE	CELLOPHANE	HOMEOPATHY	PRECOCIOUS	DECAPITATE
LOCOMOTION	DEFINITION	OCEANARIUM	CENSORIOUS	HYDROLYSIS	PREPOSSESS	DEPOPULATE
LOCOMOTIVE	DEFINITIVE	OCEANFRONT	CENSORSHIP	HYDROMETER	PRIMORDIAL	DISAPPOINT
LOVEMAKING	DEGENERACY	OCEANGOING	CHIROMANCY	HYDROPHONE	PROMONTORY	DISAPPROVE
MOHAMMEDAN	DEGENERATE	OCEANOLOGY	CITRONELLA	HYDROPLANE	PRONOUNCED	EXASPERATE
MONUMENTAL	DELINQUENT	OFTENTIMES	COLLOQUIAL	HYGROMETER	PROPORTION	HEMOPHILIA
MUHAMMADAN	DEMONETIZE	ORDINATION	COLLOQUIUM	ICONOCLASM	PROTOPLASM	IDIOPATHIC
OVERMASTER	DEMONOLOGY	ORGANGUTAN	COLPORTEUR	ICONOCLAST	RADIOGENIC	INCAPACITY
PALIMPSEST	DEPENDABLE	OSTENSIBLE	COMMODIOUS	IMPROBABLE	RADIOGRAPH	INEXPIABLE
PARAMECIUM	DEPENDENCE	PAGINATION	COMMONALTY	INEXORABLE	RADIOMETER	MALAPROPOS
PEREMPTORY	DEPENDENCY	PALINDROME	COMMONWEAL	INGLORIOUS	RADIOPHONE	MANIPULATE
POSTMASTER	DIMINUENDO	PHRENOLOGY	COMPOSITOR	INVIOLABLE	RADIOSONDE	MONOPHONIC
POSTMORTEM	DIMINUTIVE	POLYNESIAN	CONCORDANT	JIMSONWEED	REASONABLE	OCCUPATION
PRAGMATISM	DISENCHANT	POTENTIATE	CONFORMITY	LOGROLLING	RESPONDENT	OESOPHAGUS
PREEMINENT	DISINCLINE	PROGNOSTIC	CONSONANCE	MAISONETTE	RESPONSIVE	OMNIPOTENT
PREEMPTIVE	DISINHERIT	RECONSIDER	CONSORTIUM	MALCONTENT	RESTORABLE	PARAPHRASE
PYRIMIDINE	DIVINATION	REDUNDANCY	CONVOLUTED	MARIONETTE	RETROGRADE	PARAPLEGIA
RAGAMUFFIN	DOMINATION	REFINEMENT	COSMOPOLIS	MARROWBONE	RETROGRESS	PERIPHERAL
RAINMAKING	EMBANKMENT	REGENERACY	COTTONSEED	MEADOWLARK	RETROSPECT	PHOSPHORUS
RECOMPENSE	EMBONPOINT	REGENERATE	COTTONTAIL	METROPOLIS	RHINOCEROS	PICKPOCKET
REDEMPTION	ENDANGERED	RELENTLESS	COTTONWOOD	MICROFICHE	SACROILIAC	POSTPARTUM
RHEUMATISM	EQUANIMITY	RELINQUISH	CYCLOMETER	MICROGRAPH	SACROSANCT	POURPARLER
RINGMASTER	ERGONOMICS	REMUNERATE	CYCLOPEDIA	MICROMETER	SAPROPHYTE	PROMPTBOOK
SALAMANDER	EXTINGUISH	SECONDHAND	DEPLORABLE	MICROPHONE	SCHOOLGIRL	PROSPECTUS
SEISMOGRAM	GESUNDHEIT	SELENOLOGY	DIPSOMANIA	MICROPROBE	SCHOOLMARM	PROSPERITY
SEISMOLOGY	GRAINFIELD	SPRINGTIME	DISCOMFORT	MICROSCOPE	SCHOOLMATE	PROSPEROUS
SNOWMOBILE	GREENHOUSE	SPRINKLING	DISCOMMODE	MICROSTATE	SCHOOLROOM	RECEPTACLE
STEPMOTHER	GREENSWARD	STRENGTHEN	DISCOMPOSE	MIGNONETTE	SEASONABLE	RECIPROCAL
STIGMATIZE	GROUNDLING	STRINGENCY	DISCONCERT	MIMEOGRAPH	SERVOMOTOR	RECUPERATE
TASKMASTER	GROUNDMASS	STRONGHOLD	DISCONNECT	MISCONDUCT	SILHOUETTE	SHUNPIKING
THERMISTOR	GROUNDWORK	TARANTELLA	DISCONTENT	MISFORTUNE	SOPHOMORIC	STEPPARENT
THERMOSTAT	IMMUNOLOGY	TECHNETIUM	DISCOURAGE	NATIONWIDE	SPIROCHETE	STRIPTEASE
THROMBOSIS	IMPENITENT	TECHNICIAN	DISJOINTED	NECROMANCY	SUBCOMPACT	TRAMPOLINE
TOURMALINE	INCENDIARY	TECHNOLOGY	DISPOSABLE	NECROPOLIS	SUBROUTINE	UNEMPLOYED
UNFAMILIAR	INCINERATE	TOURNAMENT	DISPOSSESS	NINCOMPOOP	TACHOMETER	UNEXPECTED
UNNUMBERED	INCONSTANT	TOURNIQUET	DISSOCIATE	OPPROBRIUM	TAMBOURINE	VITUPERATE
VOLUMETRIC	INDONESIAN	TYRANNICAL	DISSONANCE	ORATORICAL	TOMFOOLERY	VIVIPAROUS
VOLUMINOUS	INFINITIVE	UNDENIABLE	ECONOMICAL	OSTEOPATHY	TRIFOLIATE	VOLUPTUARY
YARDMASTER	INFINITUDE	UNGENEROUS	EFFLORESCE	OUTPOURING	TRIMONTHLY	VOLUPTUOUS
ACCENTUATE	INJUNCTION	UNHANDSOME	EFFRONTERY	PATRONYMIC	UNGROUNDED	WOODPECKER
ADMINISTER	INSENSIBLE	UNMANNERLY	EMBROIDERY	PERIODICAL	UNIFORMITY	XENOPHOBIA
ADRENALINE	INSENTIENT	VIETNAMESE	EMPLOYMENT	PERSONABLE	VICTORIOUS	ANTIQUATED
ADVENTURER	INTANGIBLE	ACHROMATIC	EUPHONIOUS	PERSONALTY	VIDEOPHONE	DELIQUESCE
AMMUNITION	INTINCTION	ACTIONABLE	FATHOMLESS	PETROLATUM	WEAPONLESS	OBSEQUIOUS
ANNUNCIATE	INTONATION	ANEMOMETER	FELLOWSHIP	PHENOMENON	WILLOWWARE	ABERRATION
ANTINOMIAN	INVINCIBLE	ANGIOSPERM	FOREORDAIN	PHILOSOPHY	WINDOWPANE	ABSORPTION
ASCENDANCY	JOURNALESE	ANGLOPHILE	GORGONZOLA	PHONOGRAPH	WINDOWSILL	ACCORDANCE
ATTENDANCE	JOURNALISM	ANGLOPHOBE	GRAMOPHONE	PHOTOFLASH	ACCEPTABLE	AFTERBIRTH
AUTONOMOUS	JOURNEYMAN	APOLOGETIC	GYMNOSPERM	PHOTOGENIC	ACCEPTANCE	AFTERIMAGE
BEHINDHAND	LARYNGITIS	AUDIOPHILE	HARMONIOUS	PHOTOGRAPH	ACROPHOBIA	AFTERTASTE
BELONGINGS	LICENTIATE	AUTHORSHIP	HECTOLITER	PHOTOMETER	ANTEPENULT	AIRFREIGHT
BRAINCHILD	LICENTIOUS	BOTTOMLAND	HECTOMETER	PHOTOMURAL	ANTIPHONAL	ALTARPIECE
BRAINSTORM	LOGANBERRY	BUTTONHOLE	HELIOGRAPH	PHOTOPAINT	ANTIPROTON	ALTERNATOR
BROWNSTONE	MAYONNAISE	BUTTONHOOK	HELIOTROPE	PIANOFORTE	CHEAPSKATE	ANTHRACITE

ANTHROPOID	ENTERPRISE	JACKRABBIT	RESTRAINED	WATERPROOF	INDISPOSED	TRANSDUCER
APOCRYPHAL	ESCARPMENT	JAWBREAKER	RESURGENCE	WATERSPOUT	INDISTINCT	TRANSGRESS
APPARITION	EXPERIENCE	LABORATORY	ROADRUNNER	WATERTIGHT	INDUSTRIAL	TRANSISTOR
ARBORVITAE	EXPERIMENT	LACHRYMOSE	SACERDOTAL	WATERWHEEL	INSISTENCE	TRANSITION
ASPIRATION	EYEDROPPER	LAWBREAKER	SAUERKRAUT	WATERWORKS	INVESTMENT	TRANSITIVE
ASSORTMENT	FAVORITISM	LEDERHOSEN	SCURRILOUS	ACCESSIBLE	IONOSPHERE	TRANSITORY
AUSTRALIAN	FEDERALISM	LIBERALISM	SEPARATION	ACCUSATIVE	IRRESOLUTE	TRANSPLANT
BALBRIGGAN	FEDERALIST	LITERALISM	SEPARATIST	ACCUSTOMED	LIFESAVING	TRANSPOLAR
BEFOREHAND	FEDERALIZE	LITERATURE	SEPARATIVE	ADMISSIBLE	MAGISTRATE	TRANSVERSE
BESPRINKLE	FEDERATION	LIVERWURST	SKYWRITING	ADVISEMENT	MAINSPRING	TYPESCRIPT
BIPARENTAL	FIBERBOARD	MANDRAGORA	SOMERSAULT	AMBASSADOR	MAINSTREAM	TYPESETTER
BIPARIETAL	FIBERGLASS	MATURATION	SUBORBITAL	ANTISEPTIC	MANUSCRIPT	UNASSUMING
BIPARTISAN	FIGURATION	MEMORANDUM	SUBTRAHEND	ANTISOCIAL	MARASCHINO	UNRESERVED
CAPOREGIME	FIGURATIVE	MINERALIZE	SUFFRAGIST	APPOSITION	MEERSCHAUM	WELLSPRING
CENTRALIZE	FIGUREHEAD	MINERALOGY	SUPERCARGO	APPOSITIVE	MESOSPHERE	WHATSOEVER
CENTRIFUGE	FLOORBOARD	MONARCHIST	SUPERSONIC	ATMOSPHERE	METASTASIS	WHENSOEVER
CHLORINATE	FLUORIDATE	MOTORCYCLE	SUPERTWIST	AUTOSTRADA	MILLSTREAM	WHITSUNDAY
CHLOROFORM	FLUORINATE	MOTORTRUCK	TABERNACLE	BACKSTAIRS	MINESTRONE	WHOMSOEVER
CINERARIUM	FORERUNNER	NATURALISM	TUBERCULAR	BACKSTROKE	MINISCROLL	WIDESPREAD
COLORATION	FRATRICIDE	NATURALIST	TUBERCULIN	BALUSTRADE	MINISTRANT	WINDSHIELD
COLORATURA	FUTURISTIC	NATURALIZE	UNABRIDGED	BOOKSELLER	MOONSTRUCK	WINGSPREAD
COMPREHEND	GASTRONOMY	NEUTRALISM	UNDERBELLY	BREASTBONE	NANOSECOND	ADDITIONAL
COMPROMISE	GENERALITY	NEUTRALITY	UNDERBRUSH	BREASTWORK	OCCASIONAL	ADMITTANCE
CONCRETION	GENERALIZE	NEUTRALIZE	UNDERCOVER	CHEESECAKE	OMNISCIENT	ADULTERANT
CONGREGATE	GENERATION	NONDRINKER	UNDERCROFT	CHRYSOLITE	OVERSHADOW	ADULTERATE
CONGRUENCE	GOVERNMENT	NUMEROLOGY	UNDERLYING	CLASSICISM	OVERSPREAD	ALLITERATE
CONGRUENCY	HEMORRHAGE	NUTCRACKER	UNDERNEATH	CLASSIFIED	PACKSADDLE	ANESTHESIA
CONTRABAND	HEMORRHOID	OBSERVABLE	UNDERPANTS	COMESTIBLE	PEDESTRIAN	ANESTHETIC
CONTRADICT	HISTRIONIC	OBSERVANCE	UNDERSCORE	CORNSTARCH	PERISHABLE	ANTITHESIS
CONTRAVENE	HONORARIUM	OCCURRENCE	UNDERSEXED	CRISSCROSS	PICOSECOND	APOSTROPHE
CONTRIBUTE	HYPERBARIC	OTHERWORLD	UNDERSHIRT	CROSSBONES	PLEASANTRY	APPETIZING
CONTROLLER	ICEBREAKER	PAPERBOARD	UNDERSHOOT	CROSSBREED	POINSETTIA	ARBITRATOR
CONTROVERT	IGNORAMOUS	PEJORATIVE	UNDERSIZED	CROSSPIECE	POSTSCRIPT	AUDITORIUM
COPYREADER	IMMORALITY	PERORATION	UNDERSKIRT	DEPOSITION	PRESSURIZE	BEAUTICIAN
COTERMINAL	IMPERATIVE	PICARESQUE	UNDERSLUNG	DEPOSITORY	PUBESCENCE	BIMETALLIC
CYBERSPACE	IMPERSONAL	PILGRIMAGE	UNDERSTAND	DOWNSTAIRS	PUNISHMENT	BOISTEROUS
DECORATION	IMPERVIOUS	POWERHOUSE	UNDERSTATE	DOWNSTREAM	REDISTRICT	BRONTOSAUR
DECORATIVE	IMPORTANCE	POWERLINES	UNDERSTOOD	DOWNSTROKE	REGISTRANT	CAOUTCHOUC
DEMORALIZE	INSTRUCTOR	PREARRANGE	UNDERSTORY	DRAWSTRING	RENASCENCE	CAPITALISM
DENDROLOGY	INSTRUMENT	PROGRAMMED	UNDERSTUDY	EMULSIFIER	REPOSITORY	CAPITALIST
DEPARTMENT	INTERBLOCK	PROGRAMMER	UNDERTAKER	EQUESTRIAN	RESISTANCE	CAPITALIZE
DEPORTMENT	INTERBREED	PROPRIETOR	UNDERTRICK	ERGOSTEROL	ROTISSERIE	CAPITATION
DESERVEDLY	INTERFAITH	PROPRINTER	UNDERVALUE	EXPOSITION	SALESWOMAN	CAPITULATE
DESTRUCTOR	INTERFERON	PROTRACTOR	UNDERWAIST	FOLKSINGER	SCHISMATIC	CAVITATION
DETERMINED	INTERLEAVE	QUADRANGLE	UNDERWATER	FORESHADOW	SEAMSTRESS	CHARTREUSE
DETERRENCE	INTERLUNAR	QUADRATICS	UNDERWORLD	FOURSQUARE	SEERSUCKER	CHATTERBOX
DISARRANGE	INTERMARRY	QUADRIVIUM	UNDERWRITE	HANDSPRING	SEMPSTRESS	CONSTITUTE
DISCREPANT	INTERMEZZO	QUADRUPLET	UNMERCIFUL	HEADSTRONG	SENESCENCE	CONSTRAINT
DISCRETION	INTERNMENT	QUATREFOIL	UNSCRAMBLE	HEATSTROKE	SHOESTRING	COUNTERACT
DISGRUNTLE	INTERSTATE	RADARSCOPE	VETERINARY	HEMISPHERE	SIDESTROKE	COUNTERMAN
DISORDERLY	INTERSTICE	REFERENDUM	WATERBORNE	HOMOSEXUAL	SLIPSTREAM	COUNTERSPY
DISTRAUGHT	INTERTIDAL	REMARKABLE	WATERCOLOR	ILLUSTRATE	SPLASHDOWN	COUNTRYMAN
DISTRIBUTE	INTERTWINE	REPARATION	WATERCRAFT	IMMISCIBLE	STEPSISTER	COURTHOUSE
DYSPROSIUM	INTERTWIST	REPARATIVE	WATERCRESS	IMPASSABLE	TELESCOPIC	CRUSTACEAN
EFFERVESCE	INTERURBAN	REPERTOIRE	WATERFRONT	IMPASSIBLE	THEMSELVES	CRYPTOGRAM
ELDERBERRY	INTERWEAVE	REPORTEDLY	WATERMELON	IMPOSSIBLE	TRANSCRIBE	DEACTIVATE
EMPIRICISM	INVARIABLE	RESORPTION	WATERPOWER	INDISCREET	TRANSCRIPT	DENOTATIVE

				6TH LETTER		
DEPUTATION	PILOTHOUSE	CIRCUMVENT	UNBLUSHING	ABERRATION	DEPUTATION	INTONATION
DEVITALIZE	PLANTATION	COMBUSTION	UNFRUITFUL	ACCUSATIVE	DERIVATION	INVOCATION
DILETTANTE	POLITICIAN	COMMUNIQUE	VICTUALLER	ACROBATICS	DERIVATIVE	JACKHAMMER
DIPHTHERIA	POLYTHEISM	COMMUTATOR	VIRTUOSITY	ADRENALINE	DEROGATORY	JACKRABBIT
ELECTORATE	POULTRYMAN	COMPULSION	ASSEVERATE	AEROBATICS	DESOLATION	JOURNALESE
ELECTRONIC	PROSTHESIS	COMPULSIVE	CADAVEROUS	AMALGAMATE	DEVITALIZE	JOURNALISM
EQUITATION	PROSTITUTE	COMPULSORY	CHAUVINISM	AMBULATORY	DIAPHANOUS	JUBILATION
ESCUTCHEON	QUINTUPLET	COMPUSERVE	DERIVATION	ANTHRACITE	DISHEARTEN	JUDICATURE
EXACTITUDE	REACTIVATE	CONCURRENT	DERIVATIVE	ANTICANCER	DISHWASHER	KINEMATICS
EXCITEMENT	RECITATION	CONCUSSION	EQUIVALENT	ANTIMATTER	DISQUALIFY	LABORATORY
EXPATRIATE	RELATIONAL	CONDUCTIVE	EQUIVOCATE	AQUAMARINE	DISTRAUGHT	LIBERALISM
GHOSTWRITE	RELATIVITY	CONSUMMATE	IMPOVERISH	ASPIRATION	DIVINATION	LIFESAVING
HABITATION	REMITTANCE	CONVULSION	INCIVILITY	AUSTRALIAN	DOMINATION	LINEBACKER
HEARTBREAK	REPATRIATE	CORNUCOPIA	INDIVIDUAL	AUTOMATION	DUMBWAITER	LIPREADING
HEARTHSIDE	REPETITION	CORPULENCE	INNOVATION	AUTOMATIZE	EQUITATION	LITERALISM
HEARTTHROB	REPETITIVE	COWPUNCHER	MALEVOLENT	BACKGAMMON	EQUIVALENT	LITERATURE
HEMATOLOGY	REPUTATION	DENOUEMENT	OMNIVOROUS	BACKHANDED	ESTIMATION	LITHUANIAN
HERETOFORE	REVITALIZE	DISCURSIVE	REJUVENATE	BENEFACTOR	EVENHANDED	LOVEMAKING
HYPOTENUSE	ROUSTABOUT	DISCUSSANT	STARVELING	BESTIALITY	EXHILARATE	MALADAPTED
HYPOTHESIS	SALUTATION	DISQUALIFY	TELEVISION	BIMETALLIC	EXURBANITE	MALEFACTOR
ILLITERATE	SANATORIUM	EMBOUCHURE	BELLWETHER	BLACKAMOOR	FAMILARIZE	MANDRAGORA
IMMATERIAL	SANITARIAN	ENTHUSIASM	COPYWRITER	BLUEJACKET	FEDERALISM	MATURATION
IMPATIENCE	SANITARIUM	EXHAUSTION	CORDWAINER	BRAHMANISM	FEDERALIST	MEDICAMENT
INACTIVATE	SANITATION	EXHAUSTIVE	DEADWEIGHT	BUSHMASTER	FEDERALIZE	MEMORANDUM
INAPTITUDE	SCRUTINIZE	FORTUITOUS	DISHWASHER	CACCIATORE	FEDERATION	METACARPUS
INSATIABLE	SHORTENING	GRADUALISM	DOCKWORKER	CAPITALISM	FIGURATION	METAGALAXY
INVETERATE	SHUTTERBUG	GRADUATION	DUMBWAITER	CAPITALIST	FIGURATIVE	METATARSAL
IRRATIONAL	SKEPTICISM	GRATUITOUS	HEADWAITER	CAPITALIZE	FORECASTLE	METATARSUS
LEGITIMATE	SMATTERING	INEQUALITY	HIGHWAYMAN	CAPITATION	FOREFATHER	MILITARISM
LENGTHWISE	SPITTLEBUG	LITHUANIAN	MILLWRIGHT	CARICATURE	FOREGATHER	MILITARIZE
LIEUTENANT	SPORTSCAST	MANSUETUDE	NEWSWORTHY	CATAFALQUE	FOREHANDED	MINERALIZE
LIGHTHOUSE	STENTORIAN	MARGUERITE	NOTEWORTHY	CAVITATION	FOUNDATION	MINERALOGY
LIGHTPROOF	SUBSTATION	MASQUERADE	OVERWINTER	CENTRALIZE	GENERALITY	MISOGAMIST
METATARSAL	SUBSTITUTE	MENSURABLE	PERIWINKLE	CHAPFALLEN	GENERALIZE	NATURALISM
METATARSUS	SUBSTRATUM	NASTURTIUM	PLAYWRIGHT	CHIMPANZEE	GENERATION	NATURALIST
MILITARISM	SWEETBREAD	NONSUPPORT	SHIPWRIGHT	CINERARIUM	GRADUALISM	NATURALIZE
MILITARIZE	SWEETBRIER	PERCUSSION	SIDEWINDER	COLORATION	GRADUATION	NEOCLASSIC
MONOTHEISM	SWEETHEART	PERDURABLE	STRAWBERRY	COLORATURA	HABITATION	NEUTRALISM
MONOTONOUS	TEMPTATION	PERQUISITE	TYPEWRITER	CONTRABAND	HANDBARROW	NEUTRALITY
MONSTRANCE	THEATRICAL	PERSUASION	WAINWRIGHT	CONTRADICT	HANDMAIDEN	NEUTRALIZE
MORATORIUM	UNATTACHED	PINCUSHION	INTOXICANT	CONTRAVENE	HEADMASTER	NOMINATIVE
MOUNTEBANK	UNLETTERED	PORTUGUESE	INTOXICATE	CORDWAINER	HEADWAITER	NONCHALANT
NATATORIUM	VEGETARIAN	PRESUPPOSE	RELAXATION	CORONATION	HIGHLANDER	NONSTARTER
NEGATIVISM	VEGETATION	PROCURATOR	ASPHYXIATE	CRUSTACEAN	HIGHWAYMAN	NUTCRACKER
NIGHTDRESS	VEGETATIVE	PRODUCTION	BATHYSCAPH	CUMULATIVE	HONORARIUM	OBLIGATION
NIGHTSHADE	VISITATION	PROMULGATE	DECRYPTION	DATAMATION	IDIOPATHIC	OCCUPATION
NIGHTSHIRT	WRISTWATCH	PROPULSION	DILLYDALLY	DECIMALIZE	IGNORAMOUS	OCEANARIUM
NIGHTSTICK	ACCOUNTANT	RESOUNDING	DONNYBROOK	DECORATION	IMMORALITY	OPHTHALMIC
NONSTARTER	ACCOUNTING	SANGUINARY	EMBRYOLOGY	DECORATIVE	IMPERATIVE	ORDINATION
OBLITERATE	AMANUENSIS	SEPTUAGINT	ENCRYPTION	DEHUMANIZE	INCAPACITY	OVERMASTER
OCTOTHORPE	CALCULATED	STATUESQUE	EVERYTHING	DELEGATION	INDICATIVE	PACKSADDLE
PACKTHREAD	CAMOUFLAGE	SUBSURFACE	EVERYWHERE	DEMORALIZE	INEQUALITY	PAGINATION
PAINTBRUSH	CARBURETOR	THROUGHOUT	HOBBYHORSE	DENOTATIVE	INHUMANITY	PALATALIZE
PALATALIZE	CINQUEFOIL	THROUGHPUT	PANTYWAIST	DEPILATORY	INITIATIVE	PARLIAMENT
PALATINATE	CIRCUITOUS	THROUGHWAY	PENNYROYAL	DENOTATIVE	INITIATORY	PEJORATIVE
PARATROOPS	CIRCUMCISE	TURBULENCE	BLITZKRIEG	DEPILATORY	INNOVATION	PERORATION
PERITONEUM	CIRCUMFLEX	UBIQUITOUS	HORIZONTAL	DEPOLARIZE	INSOLATION	PERSUASION

PINFEATHER	SUBTRAHEND	OPPROBRIUM	EMBOUCHURE	ROLLICKING	GROUNDWORK	CANDLEWICK
PLAGIARIZE	SUFFRAGIST	PAINTBRUSH	ESCUTCHEON	SENESCENCE	HIPPODROME	CAPOREGIME
PLANTATION	SUNGLASSES	PAPERBOARD	EXPLICABLE	SEPTICEMIA	INCENDIARY	CEREBELLUM
PLEASANTRY	SURREALISM	PASTEBOARD	FALLACIOUS	SEPULCHRAL	INCREDIBLE	CHALCEDONY
POPULATION	TASKMASTER	QUICKBASIC	FISTICUFFS	SERVICEMAN	INGREDIENT	CHANCELLOR
POSTMASTER	TEMPTATION	SKATEBOARD	GRANDCHILD	SPACECRAFT	MOLYBDENUM	CHANDELIER
POSTPARTUM	THEREAFTER	SPELLBOUND	HANDICRAFT	SPIROCHETE	NIGHTDRESS	CHANGELING
POURPARLER	TOURMALINE	STILLBIRTH	HOUSECLEAN	STAGECOACH	PALINDROME	CHANGEOVER
PRAGMATISM	TOURNAMENT	STRAWBERRY	ICONOCLASM	STALACTITE	PECCADILLO	CHANNELIZE
PROGRAMMED	TROUBADOUR	SUBORBITAL	ICONOCLAST	STATECRAFT	PERIODICAL	CHARLESTON
PROGRAMMER	TRUNCATION	SWEETBREAD	IMMISCIBLE	SUBJECTIVE	PRECEDENCE	CHATTERBOX
PROTRACTOR	UNATTACHED	SWEETBRIER	IMPECCABLE	SUFFICIENT	PREMEDICAL	CHEESECAKE
QUADRANGLE	UNBALANCED	THROMBOSIS	IMPLACABLE	SUPERCARGO	PROVIDENCE	CINQUEFOIL
QUADRATICS	UNDULATION	TOOTHBRUSH	INDISCREET	SUSPICIOUS	REDUNDANCY	CLOTHESPIN
RADICALIZE	UNPLEASANT	UNDERBELLY	INFLECTION	TABLECLOTH	SACERDOTAL	COMPLECTED
RAINMAKING	UNSCRAMBLE	UNDERBRUSH	INFRACTION	TELESCOPIC	SECONDHAND	COMPLEMENT
RAMSHACKLE	VEGETARIAN	UNNUMBERED	INJUNCTION	TRAJECTORY	SUBSIDIARY	COMPLEXION
RECITATION	VEGETATION	VERTEBRATE	INTINCTION	TRANSCRIBE	THREADBARE	COMPREHEND
RECREATION	VEGETATIVE	WATERBORNE	INVINCIBLE	TRANSCRIPT	TRANSDUCER	CONCRETION
REGULATION	VICTUALLER	WILDEBEEST	LEPRECHAUN	TUBERCULAR	UNHANDSOME	CONGREGATE
RELAXATION	VIETNAMESE	AFFLICTIVE	LOQUACIOUS	TUBERCULIN	ACCELERATE	CONSPECTUS
REPARATION	VISITATION	ANNUNCIATE	LUBRICIOUS	TYPESCRIPT	ACCIDENTAL	COPYREADER
REPARATIVE	VIVIPAROUS	APPLICABLE	MANUSCRIPT	UNDERCOVER	ADULTERANT	COUNTERACT
REPUTATION	WINDJAMMER	APPLICATOR	MARASCHINO	UNDERCROFT	ADULTERATE	COUNTERMAN
RESTRAINED	WIREHAIRED	APPRECIATE	MEERSCHAUM	UNGRACEFUL	ADVISEMENT	COUNTERSPY
REVELATION	WORKBASKET	ATTRACTANT	MELANCHOLY	UNGRACIOUS	AESTHETICS	CRADLESONG
REVITALIZE	YARDMASTER	ATTRACTION	MENDACIOUS	UNMERCIFUL	AIRFREIGHT	CRYOGENICS
REVOCATION	ABOVEBOARD	AUSPICIOUS	MINISCROLL	VERMICELLI	ALLITERATE	CUTTLEFISH
RHEUMATISM	AFTERBIRTH	BATRACHIAN	MONARCHIST	VERNACULAR	ALTOGETHER	DEADWEIGHT
RINGMASTER	ALPHABETIC	BRAINCHILD	MOTORCYCLE	VINDICTIVE	AMANUENSIS	DECELERATE
ROUNDABOUT	AMPHIBIOUS	BROADCLOTH	OMNISCIENT	WATERCOLOR	ANTEBELLUM	DEGENERACY
ROUSTABOUT	ASSEMBLAGE	CAOUTCHOUC	PARTICIPLE	WATERCRAFT	ANTECEDENT	DEGENERATE
SACCHARINE	BLACKBERRY	CHARACTERY	PARTICULAR	WATERCRESS	ANTEPENULT	DELIBERATE
SALAMANDER	BLACKBOARD	CLAVICHORD	PERFECTION	WHEELCHAIR	ANTISEPTIC	DEMONETIZE
SALUTATION	BREADBOARD	COLLECTIVE	PERNICIOUS	WITCHCRAFT	APOTHECARY	DENOUEMENT
SANITARIAN	CHILDBIRTH	CONDUCTIVE	PHYLACTERY	ACCORDANCE	APOTHEOSIS	DISCREPANT
SANITARIUM	CLOUDBURST	CONFECTION	PLAYACTING	ANIMADVERT	ARCHDEACON	DISCRETION
SANITATION	CROSSBONES	CONJECTURE	PLUTOCRACY	ASCENDANCY	ARMAGEDDON	DOORKEEPER
SCARLATINA	CROSSBREED	CONNECTION	POSTSCRIPT	ATTENDANCE	ASSEVERATE	ENDOGENOUS
SCHOLASTIC	DISEMBOWEL	CONNECTIVE	PRECOCIOUS	BEHINDHAND	ASYMMETRIC	ENGAGEMENT
SECULARISM	DISHABILLE	CONSECRATE	PREDACEOUS	BELLADONNA	AURIFEROUS	EPITHELIUM
SECULARIZE	DONNYBROOK	CONVECTION	PREDECEASE	BIOMEDICAL	BAREHEADED	EVANGELISM
SENEGALESE	ELDERBERRY	CONVICTION	PREDICABLE	COMMODIOUS	BATTLEMENT	EVANGELIST
SEPARATION	ENJAMBMENT	CORNUCOPIA	PREPACKAGE	CONFIDENCE	BATTLESHIP	EVANGELIZE
SEPARATIST	FIBERBOARD	CRETACEOUS	PRODUCTION	DEGRADABLE	BEFOREHAND	EVISCERATE
SEPARATIVE	FLOORBOARD	CRISSCROSS	PROFICIENT	DEPENDABLE	BELLWETHER	EXAGGERATE
SEPTUAGINT	GOOSEBERRY	CURRICULUM	PROJECTILE	DEPENDENCE	BIPARENTAL	EXASPERATE
SOLIDARITY	HEARTBREAK	CURVACEOUS	PROTECTION	DEPENDENCY	BOISTEROUS	EXCITEMENT
SPECIALIST	HEREABOUTS	DEPRECIATE	PUBESCENCE	DILLYDALLY	BOLSHEVISM	EXOTHERMIC
SPECIALIZE	HULLABALOO	DESPICABLE	PUGNACIOUS	DISORDERLY	BOOKKEEPER	FIGUREHEAD
SPOLIATION	HYPERBARIC	DIELECTRIC	REFRACTION	EISTEDDFOD	BOOKSELLER	GAMEKEEPER
STEPFATHER	IMPROBABLE	DIFFICULTY	REFRACTORY	FASTIDIOUS	BOTTLENECK	GATEKEEPER
STEPLADDER	INCUMBENCY	DISENCHANT	RENASCENCE	FORBIDDING	BOWDLERIZE	GENTLEFOLK
STEPPARENT	INTERBLOCK	DISINCLINE	RESPECTING	FORMIDABLE	BRIDGEHEAD	GEOTHERMAL
STIGMATIZE	INTERBREED	DISSOCIATE	RESPECTIVE	GESUNDHEIT	BRIDGEWORK	GOALKEEPER
STOCHASTIC	LOGANBERRY	DUODECIMAL	RETRACTILE	GROUNDLING	BULLHEADED	GOLDBEATER
SUBSTATION	NEIGHBORLY	DUPLICATOR	RHINOCEROS	GROUNDMASS	CADAVEROUS	HANDLEBARS

HARDHEADED	PROCEEDING	CAMOUFLAGE	REFULGENCE	PARAPHRASE	COINCIDENT	FUTURISTIC
HOMOGENIZE	PROSCENIUM	DENTIFRICE	RESURGENCE	PERIPHERAL	COMEDIENNE	GADOLINIUM
HOMOSEXUAL	PROSPECTUS	GOOSEFLESH	RETROGRADE	PERISHABLE	COMPLIANCE	GEOSCIENCE
HYPOCENTER	PROSPERITY	GRAINFIELD	RETROGRESS	PHOSPHORUS	COMPLIANCY	GRATUITOUS
HYPODERMIC	PROSPEROUS	GRAPEFRUIT	SCAPEGRACE	PILOTHOUSE	COMPLICATE	GUNSLINGER
HYPOTENUSE	QUATREFOIL	HENCEFORTH	SPRINGTIME	POLYTHEISM	COMPLICITY	HABILIMENT
ICEBREAKER	RATTLETRAP	HORSEFLESH	STALAGMITE	POWERHOUSE	COMPLIMENT	HEREDITARY
ILLITERATE	RECUPERATE	INTERFAITH	STRAIGHTEN	PROSTHESIS	CONSCIENCE	HISTRIONIC
IMMATERIAL	REFERENDUM	INTERFERON	STRENGTHEN	PUNISHMENT	CONSPIRACY	ILLUMINATE
IMMODERATE	REFINEMENT	MICROFICHE	STRINGENCY	ROUGHHOUSE	CONSTITUTE	IMBIBITION
IMPOVERISH	REGENERACY	OCEANFRONT	STRONGHOLD	ROUNDHOUSE	CONTRIBUTE	IMMOBILIZE
INBREEDING	REGENERATE	PERMAFROST	THROUGHOUT	SEARCHWARE	COORDINATE	IMPATIENCE
INCIDENTAL	REJUVENATE	PERSIFLAGE	THROUGHPUT	SPLASHDOWN	DEACTIVATE	IMPEDIMENT
INCINERATE	REMUNERATE	PHOTOFLASH	THROUGHWAY	STATEHOUSE	DEBILITATE	IMPENITENT
INCOHERENT	RINGLEADER	PIANOFORTE	TRANSGRESS	STOREHOUSE	DECAPITATE	INACTIVATE
INDIGENOUS	SALTCELLAR	PRIZEFIGHT	WITCHGRASS	STRYCHNINE	DEFINITION	INAPTITUDE
INDONESIAN	SETTLEMENT	SHAMEFACED	ACROPHOBIA	SWEETHEART	DEFINITIVE	INCIVILITY
INDUCEMENT	SHILLELAGH	WATERFRONT	ANESTHESIA	SWITCHBACK	DEHUMIDIFY	INDECISION
INFIDELITY	SHOPKEEPER	ABORIGINAL	ANESTHETIC	THOUGHTFUL	DELPHINIUM	INDECISIVE
INQUIETUDE	SHORTENING	APOLOGETIC	ANTICHRIST	WHEELHORSE	DEMOBILIZE	INDEFINITE
INTOLERANT	SHUTTERBUG	BEDRAGGLED	ANTIPHONAL	WHEELHOUSE	DEMOLITION	INDELICATE
INVETERATE	SINGLETREE	BELONGINGS	ANTITHESIS	WINDSHIELD	DENOMINATE	INDIVIDUAL
IRRELEVANT	SLENDERIZE	BLACKGUARD	ATTACHMENT	XENOPHOBIA	DEPOSITION	INEXPIABLE
ISOTHERMAL	SLUMBEROUS	BRIDEGROOM	BLOCKHOUSE	ADDITIONAL	DEPOSITORY	INFINITIVE
JAWBREAKER	SMATTERING	CENTIGRADE	BLOODHOUND	ADJUDICATE	DESALINATE	INFINITUDE
JOURNEYMAN	STARVELING	CONTAGIOUS	BRONCHITIS	ADMINISTER	DESALINIZE	INHABITANT
KETTLEDRUM	STATUESQUE	CONTIGUOUS	CATECHUMEN	AFTERIMAGE	DISJOINTED	INHIBITION
LAWBREAKER	SUPPLEMENT	CORRIGIBLE	CHINCHILLA	ALBUMINOUS	DISTRIBUTE	INNOMINATE
LIEUTENANT	TATTLETALE	DEFLAGRATE	CHURCHGOER	ALKALINIZE	EBULLITION	INORDINATE
MANAGEMENT	TEARJERKER	EFFULGENCE	CHURCHLESS	ALLEGIANCE	EFFEMINATE	INSATIABLE
MANSUETUDE	TECHNETIUM	ENDANGERED	CHURCHYARD	AMMUNITION	EFFICIENCY	INSEMINATE
MANTLEROCK	THEMSELVES	EXTINGUISH	COURTHOUSE	ANNIHILATE	EMANCIPATE	INTIMIDATE
MARGUERITE	THUNDEROUS	FARSIGHTED	DETACHMENT	ANTIBIOTIC	EMBROIDERY	INTOXICANT
MASQUERADE	TIMEKEEPER	FIBERGLASS	DIPHTHERIA	ANTICIPATE	EMPIRICISM	INTOXICATE
MEDDLESOME	TROLLEYBUS	HELIOGRAPH	DISINHERIT	APPARITION	EMULSIFIER	INVALIDATE
MELANESIAN	TUMBLEDOWN	IMPREGNATE	FORESHADOW	APPETIZING	EQUANIMITY	INVARIABLE
METTLESOME	TUMBLEWEED	INDULGENCE	FRANCHISEE	APPOSITION	EXACTITUDE	IRRATIONAL
MIDDLEBROW	TURTLEDOVE	INELIGIBLE	FRANCHISER	APPOSITIVE	EXCOGITATE	KINGFISHER
MONUMENTAL	TURTLENECK	INTANGIBLE	FRANCHISOR	ARCHBISHOP	EXORBITANT	LADYFINGER
MOUNTEBANK	TYPESETTER	LARYNGITIS	GREENHOUSE	ARTIFICIAL	EXPEDIENCE	LEGITIMATE
NANOSECOND	UNAFFECTED	MENINGITIS	GUARDHOUSE	ASSIMILATE	EXPEDIENCY	LIBIDINOUS
NAPOLEONIC	UNEXPECTED	MICROGRAPH	HEARTHSIDE	BALBRIGGAN	EXPEDITION	LIKELIHOOD
NEEDLEWORK	UNFRIENDLY	MIMEOGRAPH	HEMOPHILIA	BEAUTICIAN	EXPERIENCE	LIVELIHOOD
NETTLESOME	UNGENEROUS	NEGLIGIBLE	HOBBYHORSE	BENEFICENT	EXPERIMENT	MALEFICENT
NEWSLETTER	UNRESERVED	OCEANGOING	HYPOTHESIS	BENEFICIAL	EXPOSITION	MIDSHIPMAN
NOTICEABLE	VICEGERENT	ORGANGUTAN	INFIGHTING	BESPRINKLE	FACILITATE	MISALIGNED
OBLITERATE	VITUPERATE	OUTRAGEOUS	LEDERHOSEN	BIPARIETAL	FAVORITISM	MUDSLINGER
OCCIDENTAL	VOCIFERATE	PARMIGIANA	LENGTHWISE	BITUMINOUS	FELICITATE	MUNIFICENT
PALLBEARER	VOCIFEROUS	PASSAGEWAY	LIGHTHOUSE	CANONICALS	FELICITOUS	NEGATIVISM
PARAMECIUM	VOLUMETRIC	PHONOGRAPH	MONOCHROME	CAPACITATE	FLUORIDATE	NONDRINKER
PERIHELION	WAVELENGTH	PHOTOGENIC	MONOPHONIC	CARABINEER	FLUORINATE	NOTABILITY
PICARESQUE	WEATHERING	PHOTOGRAPH	MONOTHEISM	CENTRIFUGE	FOLKSINGER	OCCASIONAL
PICOSECOND	WEATHERMAN	PORTUGUESE	OCTOTHORPE	CHAUVINISM	FOOTLIGHTS	OLEAGINOUS
POINSETTIA	WINCHESTER	PRODIGIOUS	OESOPHAGUS	CHLORINATE	FOREFINGER	OVERWINTER
POLYHEDRON	WOODPECKER	PROPAGANDA	OVERCHARGE	CIRCUITOUS	FORFEITURE	PAINKILLER
POLYNESIAN	BREADFRUIT	RADIOGENIC	OVERSHADOW	CLASSICISM	FORTUITOUS	PALATINATE
PRINCELING	BREAKFRONT	RADIOGRAPH	PACKTHREAD	CLASSIFIED	FRATRICIDE	PATHFINDER

PENICILLIN	UNAVAILING	HORSELAUGH	CIRCUMCISE	ACTIONABLE	EXTRANEOUS	QUARANTINE
PERIWINKLE	UNBELIEVER	HYDROLYSIS	CIRCUMFLEX	AGGRANDIZE	FAHRENHEIT	REASONABLE
PERQUISITE	UNDENIABLE	INFALLIBLE	CIRCUMVENT	ALIMENTARY	FIBRINOGEN	REFRINGENT
PILGRIMAGE	UNFAMILIAR	INTERLEAVE	CONSUMMATE	ALTERNATOR	GARGANTUAN	REPUGNANCE
POLITICIAN	UNFRUITFUL	INTERLUNAR	COTERMINAL	AMERINDIAN	GEOCENTRIC	RESOUNDING
PREEMINENT	VELOCIPEDE	INVIOLABLE	CYCLOMETER	APPOINTIVE	GORGONZOLA	RESPONDENT
PRESCIENCE	VETERINARY	KIESELGUHR	DETERMINED	APPRENTICE	GORMANDIZE	RESPONSIVE
PRINCIPLED	VILLAINOUS	LOGROLLING	DIPSOMANIA	ASSIGNMENT	GOVERNMENT	SEAMANSHIP
PROCLIVITY	VISIBILITY	MANDELBROT	DISCOMFORT	ASTRINGENT	HARMONIOUS	SEASONABLE
PROFLIGATE	VOLUMINOUS	METALLURGY	DISCOMMODE	ATTAINMENT	HOOTENANNY	SERPENTINE
PROPRIETOR	WHARFINGER	MILLILITER	DISCOMPOSE	BRIGANTINE	HORRENDOUS	SHENANIGAN
PROPRINTER	WORSHIPFUL	MISCELLANY	DISSIMILAR	BUTTONHOLE	HUSBANDMAN	STUPENDOUS
PROSTITUTE	BLITZKRIEG	MISSILEMAN	ECONOMICAL	BUTTONHOOK	IMAGINABLE	SUBVENTION
PSYCHIATRY	EMBANKMENT	MULTILEVEL	EXTRAMURAL	CALUMNIATE	INCLINABLE	SUSPENSION
PYRIMIDINE	JINRIKISHA	OUTBALANCE	FATHOMLESS	CANNONBALL	INTERNMENT	SUSPENSORY
QUADRIVIUM	KNICKKNACK	PANTALOONS	GRAVIMETER	CANTONMENT	JACKANAPES	SUSTENANCE
REACTIVATE	MISTAKABLE	PARAPLEGIA	HECTOMETER	CARCINOGEN	JARDINIERE	TABERNACLE
RECIDIVISM	REMARKABLE	PESTILENCE	HEPTAMETER	CENTENNIAL	JIMSONWEED	TERMINATOR
RELATIONAL	SAUERKRAUT	PETROLATUM	HYDROMETER	CITRONELLA	LAWRENCIUM	TORRENTIAL
RELATIVITY	SPRINKLING	PICCALILLI	HYGROMETER	COMMANDANT	MACKINTOSH	TREMENDOUS
REMEDIABLE	ALLHALLOWS	POLYCLINIC	IMPRIMATUR	COMMANDEER	MAIDENHAIR	TRIMONTHLY
REPAGINATE	ANIMALCULE	POWERLINES	INTERMARRY	COMMENTARY	MAIDENHEAD	TURPENTINE
REPETITION	ANTICLIMAX	PRIVILEGED	INTERMEZZO	COMMONALTY	MAIDENHOOD	TYRANNICAL
REPETITIVE	APOCALYPSE	PROMULGATE	INTRAMURAL	COMMONWEAL	MAISONETTE	UNDERNEATH
REPOSITORY	BRICKLAYER	PROPELLANT	MATCHMAKER	COMMUNIQUE	MALCONTENT	UNEVENTFUL
RESILIENCE	CALCULATED	PROPULSION	MICROMETER	COMPENDIUM	MARGINALIA	UNMANNERLY
RESILIENCY	CANDELABRA	REBELLIOUS	MILLIMETER	COMPENSATE	MARIONETTE	UNTHINKING
RISIBILITY	CANTALOUPE	RECOILLESS	MOHAMMEDAN	CONCENTRIC	MARTINGALE	UPBRINGING
SACROILIAC	CANTILEVER	REPUBLICAN	MUHAMMADAN	CONDENSATE	MAYONNAISE	UPSTANDING
SANGUINARY	CARBOLATED	RIBOFLAVIN	MULTIMEDIA	CONGENITAL	MECHANICAL	UROGENITAL
SCRUTINIZE	CENTILITER	SANDALWOOD	MYRIAMETER	CONSONANCE	MERCANTILE	WEAPONLESS
SCURRILOUS	CHATELAINE	SCHOOLGIRL	NECROMANCY	CONTENTION	MIGNONETTE	WOODENWARE
SHIPFITTER	CHIVALROUS	SCHOOLMARM	NINCOMPOOP	CONTINENCE	MILLENNIUM	WORKINGMAN
SHUNPIKING	COMPULSION	SCHOOLMATE	NOISEMAKER	CONTINGENT	MISCONDUCT	AFICIONADO
SIDEWINDER	COMPULSIVE	SCHOOLROOM	PEACEMAKER	CONTINUITY	MIZZENMAST	ALCOHOLISM
SIMILITUDE	COMPULSORY	SPITTLEBUG	PENTAMETER	CONTINUOUS	NATIONWIDE	AMELIORATE
SIMPLICITY	CONCILIATE	TESSELLATE	PHENOMENON	CONVENIENT	NEWFANGLED	ANTAGONISM
SIMPLISTIC	CONVALESCE	TRAVELOGUE	PHLEGMATIC	CONVENTION	OUTGENERAL	ANTAGONIST
SKEPTICISM	CONVOLUTED	TRIFOLIATE	PHOTOMETER	COTTONSEED	OUTLANDISH	ANTAGONIZE
SKYWRITING	CONVULSION	TURBULENCE	PHOTOMURAL	COTTONTAIL	PANJANDRUM	ANTHROPOID
SOLICITOUS	CORDILLERA	UNDERLYING	RADIOMETER	COTTONWOOD	PATRONYMIC	ANTINOMIAN
SOLICITUDE	CORNFLOWER	UNEMPLOYED	SCHISMATIC	COWPUNCHER	PENMANSHIP	ANTISOCIAL
STEPSISTER	CORPULENCE	UNHALLOWED	SERVOMOTOR	CREDENTIAL	PERCENTAGE	AUCTIONEER
SUBSTITUTE	CRENELLATE	UNSKILLFUL	SOPHOMORIC	DECLENSION	PERCENTILE	AUDITORIUM
SUPPLICANT	DISBELIEVE	UNYIELDING	SUBCOMPACT	DESCENDANT	PERSONABLE	AUTOMOBILE
SUPPLICATE	DISTILLATE	URINALYSIS	SUBLIMINAL	DISCONCERT	PERSONALTY	AUTOMOTIVE
TECHNICIAN	ENAMELWARE	WALLFLOWER	TACHOMETER	DISCONNECT	PICKANINNY	AUTONOMOUS
TELEVISION	ENCYCLICAL	WINDFLOWER	TANTAMOUNT	DISCONTENT	PIGEONHOLE	BEAUJOLAIS
THERMISTOR	EXCELLENCE	ABSTEMIOUS	TETRAMETER	DISPENSARY	PORTENTOUS	BEDCLOTHES
TOURNIQUET	EXCELLENCY	ACHROMATIC	UNEXAMPLED	DISSENSION	PREBENDARY	BICHLORIDE
TRANSISTOR	FERTILIZER	ANEMOMETER	UNICAMERAL	DISSONANCE	PREHENSILE	BLUEBONNET
TRANSITION	FLAGELLATE	ARITHMETIC	WATCHMAKER	ECUMENICAL	PROGENITOR	BLUEBOTTLE
TRANSITIVE	FLASHLIGHT	BENCHMARKS	WATERMELON	EFFRONTERY	PROMINENCE	BLUECOLLAR
TRANSITORY	FLOODLIGHT	BLANCMANGE	ABOMINABLE	EGOCENTRIC	PROMONTORY	BONDHOLDER
TRIPLICATE	HALLELUJAH	BOTTOMLAND	ABSTINENCE	ELEMENTARY	PROPENSITY	BOOKMOBILE
UBIQUITOUS	HECTOLITER	CENTIMETER	ACCOUNTANT	EUPHONIOUS	PROVENANCE	BOONDOGGLE
UNABRIDGED	HEMOGLOBIN	CHIROMANCY	ACCOUNTING	EUTHANASIA	PROVINCIAL	BRONTOSAUR

CAMELOPARD	LOCOMOTION	ACCOMPLICE	PERCEPTIVE	CARBURETOR	FRATERNIZE	PROCURATOR
CAMPHORATE	LOCOMOTIVE	ACCOMPLISH	PERCEPTUAL	CELEBRATED	GINGERSNAP	PROPERTIED
CARDIOGRAM	MALEVOLENT	ALTARPIECE	PERCIPIENT	CELLARETTE	GREGARIOUS	PROPORTION
CARDIOLOGY	MALODOROUS	ANGLOPHILE	PEREMPTORY	CENSORIOUS	HAMMERHEAD	READERSHIP
CATABOLISM	METABOLISM	ANGLOPHOBE	PETNAPPING	CENSORSHIP	HAMMERLOCK	RECIPROCAL
CATEGORIZE	METABOLITE	ASSUMPTION	PHOTOPAINT	CHARTREUSE	HEMORRHAGE	REPATRIATE
CEREMONIAL	MISSIONARY	ATMOSPHERE	PREEMPTIVE	CHIMERICAL	HEMORRHOID	RESPIRATOR
CHIFFONIER	MONOTONOUS	AUDIOPHILE	PRESUPPOSE	CLOVERLEAF	HINTERLAND	RESTORABLE
CHLOROFORM	MORATORIUM	BIRTHPLACE	PROTOPLASM	COLLARBONE	HOLOGRAPHY	ROLLERBALL
CHROMOSOME	MORPHOLOGY	CATCHPENNY	RADIOPHONE	COLPORTEUR	INEXORABLE	RUBBERNECK
CHRONOLOGY	MUSICOLOGY	CELLOPHANE	RECOMPENSE	COMMERCIAL	INGLORIOUS	SALUBRIOUS
CHRYSOLITE	NATATORIUM	CHECKPOINT	REDEMPTION	COMPARABLE	INOPERABLE	SEMIDRYING
CLODHOPPER	NEBULOSITY	CONCEPTION	RESORPTION	COMPARISON	JUGGERNAUT	SHIPWRIGHT
COMPROMISE	NEWSWORTHY	CONNIPTION	SAPROPHYTE	CONCERNING	KRUGERRAND	SILVERFISH
CONTROLLER	NOTEWORTHY	COSMOPOLIS	STANDPOINT	CONCERTINA	LETTERHEAD	SILVERWARE
CONTROVERT	NUCLEONICS	CROSSPIECE	THREEPENCE	CONCORDANT	LOGGERHEAD	SISTERHOOD
CRYPTOGRAM	NUMEROLOGY	CYCLOPEDIA	TOOTHPASTE	CONCURRENT	LUGUBRIOUS	SKYSCRAPER
DECOLORIZE	OCEANOLOGY	DECOMPRESS	TRANSPLANT	CONFERENCE	LUMBERJACK	SNAPDRAGON
DEMONOLOGY	OMNIPOTENT	DECRYPTION	TRANSPOLAR	CONFORMITY	LUMBERYARD	SUBSTRATUM
DENDROLOGY	OMNIVOROUS	DISAPPOINT	UNDERPANTS	CONSORTIUM	MALAPROPOS	SUBSURFACE
DICTIONARY	PEASHOOTER	DISAPPROVE	VIBRAPHONE	CONSTRAINT	MANSERVANT	SUBTERFUGE
DOCKWORKER	PERITONEUM	DISCIPLINE	VIDEOPHONE	CONVERSANT	MASTERMIND	SUFFERANCE
DYSPROSIUM	PHLEBOTOMY	EMBONPOINT	VOICEPRINT	CONVERSION	MASTERSHIP	TATTERSALL
ELECTORATE	PHRENOLOGY	ENCRYPTION	WASTEPAPER	COPPERHEAD	MASTERWORK	TEETHRIDGE
EMBRYOLOGY	PHYSIOLOGY	ENTERPRISE	WATERPOWER	COPYWRITER	MEMBERSHIP	TELEGRAPHY
ENTOMOLOGY	PICKPOCKET	ERYSIPELAS	WATERPROOF	COUNTRYMAN	MENSURABLE	TEMPERANCE
EPIGLOTTIS	POSTMORTEM	ESCARPMENT	WELLSPRING	CUMMERBUND	MILLWRIGHT	TENDERFOOT
EPISCOPACY	PRECIOSITY	FIELDPIECE	WIDESPREAD	DEALERSHIP	MISFORTUNE	TENDERLOIN
EPISCOPATE	PROGNOSTIC	FLOODPLAIN	WINGSPREAD	DEMOCRATIC	MONSTRANCE	TENEBRIOUS
EQUIVOCATE	PSEUDOCODE	GRAMOPHONE	COLLOQUIAL	DEMOGRAPHY	MOTHERHOOD	THEATRICAL
ERGONOMICS	PSYCHOLOGY	HANDSPRING	COLLOQUIUM	DEPLORABLE	MOTHERLAND	TIMBERLINE
EURODOLLAR	PSYCHOPATH	HEMISPHERE	CONSEQUENT	DETERRENCE	MOZZARELLA	TOPOGRAPHY
EXOBIOLOGY	RACECOURSE	HIEROPHANT	DELINQUENT	DIFFERENCE	NASTURTIUM	TRAVERTINE
EYEDROPPER	SANATORIUM	HODGEPODGE	EARTHQUAKE	DINNERWARE	NETHERMOST	TRIPARTITE
FLAMBOYANT	SEISMOGRAM	HOMEOPATHY	FOURSQUARE	DISARRANGE	NEWSGROUPS	TYPEWRITER
FLUIDOUNCE	SEISMOLOGY	HORSEPOWER	INADEQUATE	DISCERNING	NUMBERLESS	TYPOGRAPHY
FOOTLOCKER	SELENOLOGY	HYDROPHONE	INFREQUENT	DISCURSIVE	NURSERYMAN	UNBEARABLE
FREEBOOTER	SHIBBOLETH	HYDROPLANE	RELINQUISH	DISHARMONY	OCCURRENCE	UNIFORMITY
GASTRONOMY	SNOWMOBILE	IMPALPABLE	SUBSEQUENT	DISSERVICE	ORATORICAL	UNIVERSITY
GLACIOLOGY	STATIONARY	INCOMPLETE	ANSWERABLE	DRAWBRIDGE	OUTPERFORM	UPROARIOUS
GONOCOCCUS	STATIONERY	INCULPABLE	ANTIFREEZE	DUNDERHEAD	PARATROOPS	URETHRITIS
GUILLOTINE	STENTORIAN	INDISPOSED	ANTIPROTON	EFFLORESCE	PAWNBROKER	VESPERTINE
GYNECOLOGY	STEPMOTHER	IONOSPHERE	APOSTROPHE	ELECTRONIC	PENNYROYAL	VICTORIOUS
HELICOPTER	STEREOTYPE	LIGHTPROOF	APPEARANCE	ENDEARMENT	PEPPERCORN	VULNERABLE
HEMATOLOGY	TECHNOLOGY	MAINSPRING	ARBITRATOR	ESPADRILLE	PEPPERMINT	WAINWRIGHT
HERETOFORE	THERMOSTAT	MESOSPHERE	AUTHORSHIP	EXACERBATE	PERDURABLE	WANDERLUST
HOMECOMING	TOMFOOLERY	METROPOLIS	BACKGROUND	EXPATRIATE	PERVERSION	WESTERNIZE
HOMOLOGOUS	TOXICOLOGY	MICROPHONE	BALDERDASH	FAIRGROUND	PLAYGROUND	WICKERWORK
HORIZONTAL	TRAMPOLINE	MICROPROBE	BASTARDIZE	FATHERLAND	PLAYWRIGHT	WILDERNESS
IMMEMORIAL	UNBECOMING	MOUTHPIECE	BETTERMENT	FINGERLING	PLUPERFECT	WINEGROWER
IMMUNOLOGY	UNSCHOOLED	MULTIPLIER	BIRTHRIGHT	FINGERNAIL	POULTRYMAN	WINTERTIDE
INDECOROUS	VARICOSITY	NECROPOLIS	BOMBARDIER	FOOTBRIDGE	PREARRANGE	WINTERTIME
INVIGORATE	VIRTUOSITY	NONSUPPORT	BORDERLAND	FOREGROUND	PRECARIOUS	WITHDRAWAL
IRRESOLUTE	WHATSOEVER	OSTEOPATHY	BUDGERIGAR	FOREORDAIN	PREFERENCE	WONDERLAND
LANDHOLDER	WHENSOEVER	OVERSPREAD	BUTTERMILK	FORTHRIGHT	PREFERMENT	WONDERMENT
LANDLOCKED	WHOMSOEVER	PALIMPSEST	CALCAREOUS	FOSTERLING	PREMARITAL	WRAPAROUND
LEAFHOPPER	ABSORPTION	PERCEPTION	CANKERWORM	FRATERNITY	PRIMORDIAL	XEROGRAPHY

YESTERYEAR	EXPRESSMAN	REGRESSION	BLACKTHORN	INTERTWIST	UNSUITABLE	REVOLUTION
ABSCISSION	EXPRESSWAY	RETROSPECT	BREASTBONE	INVESTMENT	VOLUPTUARY	RIDICULOUS
ACCESSIBLE	FORTISSIMO	RHINESTONE	BREASTWORK	ISOMETRICS	VOLUPTUOUS	ROADRUNNER
ADMISSIBLE	GRANDSTAND	ROTISSERIE	CHARITABLE	KNIGHTHOOD	WATCHTOWER	SEERSUCKER
AGGRESSION	GRAVESTONE	SACROSANCT	COCKATRICE	LICENTIATE	WATERTIGHT	SILHOUETTE
AGGRESSIVE	GREENSWARD	SMOKESTACK	COLLATERAL	LICENTIOUS	WEIGHTLESS	SUBROUTINE
ALONGSHORE	GRINDSTONE	SOMERSAULT	COMESTIBLE	MAGISTRATE	ABSOLUTION	TAMBOURINE
AMBASSADOR	GYMNASTICS	SOOTHSAYER	COMMUTATOR	MAINSTREAM	ABSOLUTISM	TURNBUCKLE
ANGIOSPERM	GYMNOSPERM	SPOILSPORT	COMPATIBLE	METASTASIS	ACCUMULATE	UNASSUMING
BALLISTICS	IMPASSABLE	SPORTSCAST	COMPATRIOT	MILLSTREAM	ANTIQUATED	UNGROUNDED
BAPTISTERY	IMPASSIBLE	STANDSTILL	COMPETENCE	MINESTRONE	AQUALUNGER	UNOCCUPIED
BATHYSCAPH	IMPERSONAL	STATISTICS	COMPETENCY	MINISTRANT	ARTICULATE	VOCABULARY
BIRTHSTONE	IMPOSSIBLE	SUCCESSION	COMPETITOR	MOONSTRUCK	CAPITULATE	WHITSUNDAY
BLACKSMITH	IMPRESARIO	SUCCESSIVE	CORNSTARCH	MOTORTRUCK	CONCLUSION	WOODCUTTER
BLOODSTAIN	IMPRESSION	SUGGESTION	CREDITABLE	OBSTETRICS	CONFLUENCE	ABBREVIATE
BLOODSTONE	IMPRESSIVE	SUGGESTIVE	DELECTABLE	OFTENTIMES	CONGRUENCE	ARBORVITAE
BRAINSTORM	INCONSTANT	SUPERSONIC	DEPARTMENT	OUTPATIENT	CONGRUENCY	DESERVEDLY
BREADSTUFF	INFRASONIC	TABLESPOON	DEPORTMENT	PEDESTRIAN	DELIQUESCE	EFFERVESCE
BRIDESMAID	INSENSIBLE	THREESCORE	DERMATITIS	PEDIATRICS	DEPOPULATE	GINGIVITIS
BROADSWORD	INTERSTATE	THUMBSCREW	DILETTANTE	PERPETRATE	DESTRUCTOR	IMPERVIOUS
BROWNSTONE	INTERSTICE	TOUCHSTONE	DISSATISFY	PERPETUATE	DIMINUENDO	INSOLVABLE
CANDESCENT	INTRASTATE	ULTRASHORT	DOGCATCHER	PERPETUITY	DIMINUTIVE	LASCIVIOUS
CANVASBACK	MICROSCOPE	ULTRASONIC	DOWNSTAIRS	POCKETBOOK	DISCOURAGE	OBSERVABLE
CENTESIMAL	MICROSTATE	ULTRASOUND	DOWNSTREAM	POTENTIATE	DISGRUNTLE	OBSERVANCE
CHEAPSKATE	MULTISENSE	UNBLUSHING	DOWNSTROKE	PROMETHIUM	EMASCULATE	RECEIVABLE
CLERESTORY	MULTISTAGE	UNDERSCORE	DRAWSTRING	PROMPTBOOK	FILIBUSTER	TRANSVERSE
CLINGSTONE	MULTISTORY	UNDERSEXED	EFFECTUATE	PROPITIATE	FORERUNNER	UNDERVALUE
COMBUSTION	NARCISSISM	UNDERSHIRT	EQUESTRIAN	PROPITIOUS	FRAUDULENT	VAUDEVILLE
COMMISSARY	NIGHTSHADE	UNDERSHOOT	ERGOSTEROL	RECEPTACLE	FUSSBUDGET	BREAKWATER
COMMISSION	NIGHTSHIRT	UNDERSIZED	ESCRITOIRE	REDISTRICT	HYDRAULICS	DEATHWATCH
COMPASSION	NIGHTSTICK	UNDERSKIRT	EVERYTHING	REGISTRANT	IMMACULATE	DREAMWORLD
COMPOSITOR	NOURISHING	UNDERSLUNG	EXPECTANCY	RELENTLESS	INAUGURATE	EVERYWHERE
COMPUSERVE	OPALESCENT	UNDERSTAND	EYEWITNESS	RELUCTANCE	INSTRUCTOR	FELLOWSHIP
CONCESSION	OPPRESSION	UNDERSTATE	FACTITIOUS	REMITTANCE	INSTRUMENT	FLOODWATER
CONCESSIVE	OSTENSIBLE	UNDERSTOOD	FARFETCHED	REPERTOIRE	INTEGUMENT	FRESHWATER
CONCUSSION	PERCUSSION	UNDERSTORY	FICTITIOUS	REPORTEDLY	INTERURBAN	GHOSTWRITE
CONDESCEND	PERMISSION	UNDERSTUDY	FLAGITIOUS	RESISTANCE	INVALUABLE	HOLLOWWARE
CONFESSION	PERMISSIVE	UNREASONED	FLYCATCHER	RICKETTSIA	INVOLUTION	HORSEWOMAN
CONFISCATE	PHILISTINE	UPHOLSTERY	GERIATRICS	SEAMSTRESS	LACKLUSTER	HOUSEWARES
CONSISTORY	PHILOSOPHY	WATERSPOUT	HEADSTRONG	SEMPSTRESS	LANDLUBBER	INTERWEAVE
CORRESPOND	PIANISSIMO	ACCENTUATE	HEARTTHROB	SHOESTRING	MALTHUSIAN	KNOCKWURST
CRANKSHAFT	PINCUSHION	ACCEPTABLE	HEATSTROKE	SIDESTROKE	MANICURIST	LIVERWURST
CYBERSPACE	PLEBISCITE	ACCEPTANCE	HELIOTROPE	SLIPSTREAM	MANIPULATE	MARROWBONE
DECLASSIFY	POSSESSION	ACCUSTOMED	HOSPITABLE	SPIRITUOUS	METICULOUS	MEADOWLARK
DEMOISELLE	POSSESSIVE	ADMITTANCE	ILLUSTRATE	STRIPTEASE	OBSEQUIOUS	OTHERWORLD
DEPRESSANT	PRECESSION	ADVENTURER	IMPORTANCE	SUPERTWIST	OUTPOURING	PANTYWAIST
DEPRESSION	PREDESTINE	AFTERTASTE	INDISTINCT	SYMPATHIZE	PASTEURIZE	PILLOWCASE
DEPRESSIVE	PREDISPOSE	APOLITICAL	INDUCTANCE	TARANTELLA	PORTCULLIS	SALESWOMAN
DISCUSSANT	PREPOSSESS	ARCHITRAVE	INDUSTRIAL	TUMULTUOUS	POSTHUMOUS	UNDERWAIST
DISPOSABLE	PROCESSION	ASSORTMENT	INEVITABLE	UNBEATABLE	PRECAUTION	UNDERWATER
DISPOSSESS	PROFESSION	AUTOSTRADA	INFILTRATE	UNCRITICAL	PRESSURIZE	UNDERWORLD
DISRESPECT	PROMISSORY	BACKSTAIRS	INGRATIATE	UNDERTAKER	PRONOUNCED	UNDERWRITE
ENTHUSIASM	PROTESTANT	BACKSTROKE	INIMITABLE	UNDERTRICK	QUADRUPLET	WATERWHEEL
EVANESCENT	PUTRESCENT	BALUSTRADE	INSENTIENT	UNFAITHFUL	QUINTUPLET	WATERWORKS
EXHAUSTION	RADARSCOPE	BASKETBALL	INSISTENCE	UNGRATEFUL	RAGAMUFFIN	WILLOWWARE
EXHAUSTIVE	RADIOSONDE	BELLETRIST	INTERTIDAL	UNILATERAL	RESOLUTION	WINDOWPANE
EXPRESSION	RECONSIDER	BIPARTISAN	INTERTWINE	UNLETTERED	RESTAURANT	WINDOWSILL

WORTH**W**HILE	COGNIZ**A**NCE	INDUCT**A**NCE	REMEDI**A**BLE	MANDEL**B**ROT	LAWREN**C**IUM	FLUORI**D**ATE
WRIST**W**ATCH	COMMON**A**LTY	INEVIT**A**BLE	REMITT**A**NCE	MARROW**B**ONE	LINEBA**C**KER	FORBID**D**ING
ASPHY**X**IATE	COMMUT**A**TOR	INEXOR**A**BLE	REPUGN**A**NCE	MIDDLE**B**ROW	MALEFA**C**TOR	FOREOR**D**AIN
INFLE**X**IBLE	COMPAR**A**BLE	INEXPI**A**BLE	RESIST**A**NCE	MOUNTE**B**ANK	MALEFI**C**ENT	FUSSBU**D**GET
APOCR**Y**PHAL	COMPLI**A**NCE	INIMIT**A**BLE	RESPIR**A**TOR	POCKET**B**OOK	MICROS**C**OPE	GORMAN**D**IZE
BIOPH**Y**SICS	COMPLI**A**NCY	INOPER**A**BLE	RESTOR**A**BLE	PROMPT**B**OOK	MUNIFI**C**ENT	HORREN**D**OUS
CONVE**Y**ANCE	CONSON**A**NCE	INSATI**A**BLE	RIBOFL**A**VIN	ROLLER**B**ALL	NANOSE**C**OND	HUSBAN**D**MAN
EMPLO**Y**MENT	CONSTR**A**INT	INSOLV**A**BLE	RINGLE**A**DER	ROUND**A**BOUT	NUTCRA**C**KER	INBREE**D**ING
EUCAL**Y**PTUS	CONVEY**A**NCE	INTERF**A**ITH	SACROS**A**NCT	ROUSTA**B**OUT	OPALES**C**ENT	INDIVI**D**UAL
GEOPH**Y**SICS	COPYRE**A**DER	INTERM**A**RRY	SCHISM**A**TIC	SNOWMO**B**ILE	PARAME**C**IUM	INTIMI**D**ATE
LACHR**Y**MOSE	CORNST**A**RCH	INVALU**A**BLE	SEASON**A**BLE	SWITCH**B**ACK	PEPPER**C**ORN	INVALI**D**ATE
MISOG**Y**NIST	CREDIT**A**BLE	INVARI**A**BLE	SHAMEF**A**CED	THREAD**B**ARE	PICKPO**C**KET	KETTLE**D**RUM
PRESB**Y**OPIA	DEATHW**A**TCH	INVIOL**A**BLE	SKYSCR**A**PER	VOLLEY**B**ALL	PICOSE**C**OND	LIPREA**D**ING
PRESB**Y**TERY	DEGRAD**A**BLE	JACKAN**A**PES	SNAPDR**A**GON	WHIRLY**B**IRD	PILLOW**C**ASE	MISCON**D**UCT
VOLLE**Y**BALL	DELECT**A**BLE	JAWBRE**A**KER	SOMERS**A**ULT	ADJUDI**C**ATE	PLEBIS**C**ITE	OUTLAN**D**ISH
WHIRL**Y**BIRD	DEMOCR**A**TIC	LAWBRE**A**KER	SOOTHS**A**YER	ANIMAL**C**ULE	POLITI**C**IAN	PACKSA**D**DLE
COGNI**Z**ANCE	DEMOGR**A**PHY	MARGIN**A**LIA	SUBSTR**A**TUM	ANTHRA**C**ITE	PROSPE**C**TUS	PANJAN**D**RUM
RENDE**Z**VOUS	DEPEND**A**BLE	MATCHM**A**KER	SUFFER**A**NCE	ANTISO**C**IAL	PROTRA**C**TOR	POLYHE**D**RON
	DEPLOR**A**BLE	MAYONN**A**ISE	SUPERC**A**RGO	APOTHE**C**ARY	PROVIN**C**IAL	PREBEN**D**ARY
	DESPIC**A**BLE	MENSUR**A**BLE	SUSTEN**A**NCE	ARTIFI**C**IAL	PSEUDO**C**ODE	PRIMOR**D**IAL
	DILETT**A**NTE	METAST**A**SIS	TABERN**A**CLE	BATHYS**C**APH	PUTRES**C**ENT	PROCEE**D**ING
7TH LETTER	DILLYD**A**LLY	MISTAK**A**BLE	TELEGR**A**PHY	BEAUTI**C**IAN	RADARS**C**OPE	PYRIMI**D**INE
ABOMIN**A**BLE	DIPSOM**A**NIA	MONSTR**A**NCE	TEMPER**A**NCE	BENEFA**C**TOR	RAMSHA**C**KLE	RESOUN**D**ING
ACCEPT**A**BLE	DISARR**A**NGE	MUHAMM**A**DAN	TERMIN**A**TOR	BENEFI**C**ENT	SEERSU**C**KER	RESPON**D**ENT
ACCEPT**A**NCE	DISPOS**A**BLE	NECROM**A**NCY	TOOTHP**A**STE	BENEFI**C**IAL	SIMPLI**C**ITY	SPLASH**D**OWN
ACCORD**A**NCE	DISSON**A**NCE	NOISEM**A**KER	TOPOGR**A**PHY	BLUEJA**C**KET	SKEPTI**C**ISM	STEPLA**D**DER
ACHROM**A**TIC	DOWNST**A**IRS	NOTICE**A**BLE	TYPOGR**A**PHY	CANDES**C**ENT	SPORTS**C**AST	STUPEN**D**OUS
ACTION**A**BLE	DUPLIC**A**TOR	OBSERV**A**BLE	UNBEAR**A**BLE	CANONI**C**ALS	SUPPLI**C**ANT	TREMEN**D**OUS
ADMITT**A**NCE	EUTHAN**A**SIA	OBSERV**A**NCE	UNBEAT**A**BLE	CHEESE**C**AKE	SUPPLI**C**ATE	TROUBA**D**OUR
AFTERT**A**STE	EXPECT**A**NCY	OESOPH**A**GUS	UNDENI**A**BLE	CIRCUM**C**ISE	TECHNI**C**IAN	TUMBLE**D**OWN
ALLEGI**A**NCE	EXPLIC**A**LBE	OSTEOP**A**THY	UNDERP**A**NTS	CLASSI**C**ISM	THREES**C**ORE	TURTLE**D**OVE
ALTERN**A**TOR	FLOODW**A**TER	OUTBAL**A**NCE	UNDERT**A**KER	COMMER**C**IAL	THUMBS**C**REW	UNABRI**D**GED
AMBASS**A**DOR	FORESH**A**DOW	OVERCH**A**RGE	UNDERV**A**LUE	COMPLE**C**TED	TRIPLI**C**ATE	UNYIEL**D**ING
ANSWER**A**BLE	FORMID**A**BLE	OVERSH**A**DOW	UNDERW**A**IST	COMPLI**C**ATE	TURNBU**C**KLE	UPSTAN**D**ING
ANTIQU**A**TED	FRESHW**A**TER	PALLBE**A**RER	UNDERW**A**TER	COMPLI**C**ITY	UNAFFE**C**TED	ABSTIN**E**NCE
APPEAR**A**NCE	GOLDBE**A**TER	PANTYW**A**IST	UNSUIT**A**BLE	CONDES**C**END	UNATTA**C**HED	ALPHAB**E**TIC
APPLIC**A**BLE	HARDHE**A**DED	PEACEM**A**KER	VULNER**A**BLE	CONFIS**C**ATE	UNDERS**C**ORE	ANEMOM**E**TER
APPLIC**A**TOR	HOLOGR**A**PHY	PERDUR**A**BLE	WASTEP**A**PER	CONSPE**C**TUS	UNEXPE**C**TED	ANESTH**E**SIA
ARBITR**A**TOR	HOMEOP**A**THY	PERISH**A**BLE	WATCHM**A**KER	COWPUN**C**HER	WOODPE**C**KER	ANESTH**E**TIC
ARCHDE**A**CON	HOOTEN**A**NNY	PERSON**A**BLE	WITHDR**A**WAL	CRUSTA**C**EAN	AGGRAN**D**IZE	ANTIFR**E**EZE
ASCEND**A**NCY	HORSEL**A**UGH	PERSON**A**LTY	WRISTW**A**TCH	DESTRU**C**TOR	AMERIN**D**IAN	ANTITH**E**SIS
ATTEND**A**NCE	HOSPIT**A**BLE	PETROL**A**TUM	XEROGR**A**PHY	DISCON**C**ERT	ANTECE**D**ENT	APOLOG**E**TIC
BACKST**A**IRS	HOUSEW**A**RES	PHLEGM**A**TIC	AUTOMO**B**ILE	DOGCAT**C**HER	ARMAGE**D**DON	ARITHM**E**TIC
BAREHE**A**DED	HULLAB**A**LOO	PHOTOP**A**INT	BASKET**B**ALL	EMPIRI**C**ISM	BALDER**D**ASH	BIPARI**E**TAL
BENCHM**A**RKS	HYPERB**A**RIC	PREARR**A**NGE	BOOKMO**B**ILE	EQUIVO**C**ATE	BASTAR**D**IZE	BLACKB**E**RRY
BLANCM**A**NGE	ICEBRE**A**KER	PREDIC**A**BLE	BREAST**B**ONE	EVANES**C**ENT	BOMBAR**D**IER	BOOKKE**E**PER
BREAKW**A**TER	IMAGIN**A**BLE	PROCUR**A**TOR	CANNON**B**ALL	FARFET**C**HED	CHALCE**D**ONY	CALCAR**E**OUS
BRICKL**A**YER	IMPALP**A**BLE	PROPAG**A**NDA	CANVAS**B**ACK	FLYCAT**C**HER	COINCI**D**ENT	CANTIL**E**VER
BULLHE**A**DED	IMPASS**A**BLE	PROVEN**A**NCE	COLLAR**B**ONE	FOOTLO**C**KER	COMMAN**D**ANT	CARBUR**E**TOR
CALCUL**A**TED	IMPECC**A**BLE	PSYCHI**A**TRY	CONTRA**B**AND	FRATRI**C**IDE	COMMAN**D**EER	CATCHP**E**NNY
CANDEL**A**BRA	IMPLAC**A**BLE	QUICKB**A**SIC	CONTRI**B**UTE	GONOCO**C**CUS	COMPEN**D**IUM	CELLAR**E**TTE
CARBOL**A**TED	IMPORT**A**NCE	REASON**A**BLE	CUMMER**B**UND	INCAPA**C**ITY	CONCOR**D**ANT	CENTIM**E**TER
CELEBR**A**TED	IMPRES**A**RIO	RECEIV**A**BLE	DISTRI**B**UTE	INDELI**C**ATE	CONTRA**D**ICT	CHARTR**E**USE
CHARIT**A**BLE	IMPRIM**A**TUR	RECEPT**A**CLE	EXACER**B**ATE	INSTRU**C**TOR	DEHUMI**D**IFY	CITRON**E**LLA
CHATEL**A**INE	IMPROB**A**BLE	REDUND**A**NCY	HANDLE**B**ARS	INTOXI**C**ANT	DESCEN**D**ANT	COLLAT**E**RAL
CHIROM**A**NCY	INCLIN**A**BLE	RELUCT**A**NCE	JACKRA**B**BIT	INTOXI**C**ATE	EISTED**D**FOD	COMEDI**E**NNE
	INCULP**A**BLE	REMARK**A**BLE	LANDLU**B**BER	LANDLO**C**KED	EMBROI**D**ERY	COMPET**E**NCE

COMPETENCY	INTERLEAVE	SPITTLEBUG	CRYPTOGRAM	LEPRECHAUN	ARBORVITAE	FLAGITIOUS
COMPUSERVE	INTERMEZZO	STRAWBERRY	FOOTLIGHTS	LETTERHEAD	ASPHYXIATE	FLASHLIGHT
CONFERENCE	INTERWEAVE	STRINGENCY	HOMOLOGOUS	LIKELIHOOD	AUSPICIOUS	FLOODLIGHT
CONFIDENCE	LOGANBERRY	STRIPTEASE	KIESELGUHR	LIVELIHOOD	BELONGINGS	FOOTBRIDGE
CONFLUENCE	MAISONETTE	SWEETHEART	MANDRAGORA	LOGGERHEAD	BIOMEDICAL	FORTHRIGHT
CONGRUENCE	MARIONETTE	TACHOMETER	MARTINGALE	MAIDENHAIR	BIPARTISAN	FRANCHISEE
CONGRUENCY	MICROMETER	TARANTELLA	MISALIGNED	MAIDENHEAD	BIRTHRIGHT	FRANCHISER
CONSCIENCE	MIGNONETTE	TETRAMETER	NEWFANGLED	MAIDENHOOD	BRONCHITIS	FRANCHISOR
CONTINENCE	MILLIMETER	THREEPENCE	PROFLIGATE	MARASCHINO	BUDGERIGAR	GINGIVITIS
CONVALESCE	MISSILEMAN	TIMEKEEPER	PROMULGATE	MEERSCHAUM	CALUMNIATE	GRAINFIELD
CORPULENCE	MOHAMMEDAN	TRANSVERSE	REFRINGENT	MELANCHOLY	CENSORIOUS	GREGARIOUS
CRETACEOUS	MOLYBDENUM	TURBULENCE	SCHOOLGIRL	MESOSPHERE	CENTESIMAL	HANDMAIDEN
CURVACEOUS	MONOTHEISM	UNBELIEVER	SEISMOGRAM	MICROPHONE	CENTILITER	HARMONIOUS
CYCLOMETER	MOZZARELLA	UNDERBELLY	SEPTUAGINT	MONARCHIST	CHILDBIRTH	HEADWAITER
CYCLOPEDIA	MULTILEVEL	UNDERNEATH	SUFFRAGIST	MOTHERHOOD	CHIMERICAL	HECTOLITER
DELIQUESCE	MULTIMEDIA	UNDERSEXED	UPBRINGING	NIGHTSHADE	CHINCHILLA	HEMOPHILIA
DEMOISELLE	MULTISENSE	UNGRACEFUL	WORKINGMAN	NIGHTSHIRT	COMESTIBLE	IMMISCIBLE
DEPENDENCE	MYRIAMETER	UNGRATEFUL	ALONGSHORE	NOURISHING	COMMODIOUS	IMPASSIBLE
DEPENDENCY	OCCURRENCE	UNICAMERAL	ANGLOPHILE	PIGEONHOLE	COMMUNIQUE	IMPERVIOUS
DESERVEDLY	OUTGENERAL	UNILATERAL	ANGLOPHOBE	PINCUSHION	COMPARISON	IMPOSSIBLE
DETERRENCE	OUTRAGEOUS	UNLETTERED	ATMOSPHERE	PROMETHIUM	COMPATIBLE	INCENDIARY
DIFFERENCE	PARAPLEGIA	UNMANNERLY	AUDIOPHILE	RADIOPHONE	COMPETITOR	INCREDIBLE
DIMINUENDO	PASSAGEWAY	UNNUMBERED	BATRACHIAN	SAPROPHYTE	COMPOSITOR	INDISTINCT
DIPHTHERIA	PENTAMETER	VERMICELLI	BEFOREHAND	SECONDHAND	CONCILIATE	INELIGIBLE
DISINHERIT	PERIPHERAL	WATERMELON	BEHINDHAND	SEPULCHRAL	CONGENITAL	INFALLIBLE
DISORDERLY	PESTILENCE	WHATSOEVER	BLACKTHORN	SISTERHOOD	CONTAGIOUS	INFLEXIBLE
DOORKEEPER	PHENOMENON	WHENSOEVER	BRAINCHILD	SPIROCHETE	CONVENIENT	INGLORIOUS
EFFERVESCE	PHOTOGENIC	WHOMSOEVER	BRIDGEHEAD	STRAIGHTEN	COPYWRITER	INGRATIATE
EFFICIENCY	PHOTOMETER	WILDEBEEST	BUTTONHOLE	STRONGHOLD	CORDWAINER	INGREDIENT
EFFLORESCE	POLYTHEISM	CENTRIFUGE	BUTTONHOOK	SUBTRAHEND	CORRIGIBLE	INSENSIBLE
EFFULGENCE	PRECEDENCE	CHLOROFORM	CAOUTCHOUC	SYMPATHIZE	COTERMINAL	INSENTIENT
ELDERBERRY	PREDACEOUS	CINQUEFOIL	CELLOPHANE	THROUGHOUT	CROSSPIECE	INTANGIBLE
ENDANGERED	PREDECEASE	CIRCUMFLEX	CLAVICHORD	THROUGHPUT	DEADWEIGHT	INTERTIDAL
ERGOSTEROL	PREFERENCE	CLASSIFIED	COMPREHEND	THROUGHWAY	DEPRECIATE	INVINCIBLE
ERYSIPELAS	PRESCIENCE	CUTTLEFISH	COPPERHEAD	ULTRASHORT	DERMATITIS	JARDINIERE
EXCELLENCE	PRIVILEGED	DISCOMFORT	CRANKSHAFT	UNBLUSHING	DETERMINED	JINRIKISHA
EXCELLENCY	PROMINENCE	EMULSIFIER	DISENCHANT	UNDERSHIRT	DISBELIEVE	LARYNGITIS
EXPEDIENCE	PROPRIETOR	GENTLEFOLK	DUNDERHEAD	UNDERSHOOT	DISHABILLE	LASCIVIOUS
EXPEDIENCY	PROSTHESIS	HERETOFORE	EMBOUCHURE	UNFAITHFUL	DISSATISFY	LICENTIATE
EXPERIENCE	PROVIDENCE	OUTPERFORM	ESCUTCHEON	VIBRAPHONE	DISSIMILAR	LICENTIOUS
EXTRANEOUS	PUBESCENCE	PLUPERFECT	EVERYTHING	VIDEOPHONE	DISSOCIATE	LOQUACIOUS
GAMEKEEPER	RADIOGENIC	QUATREFOIL	EVERYWHERE	WATERWHEEL	DRAWBRIDGE	LUBRICIOUS
GATEKEEPER	RADIOMETER	RAGAMUFFIN	FAHRENHEIT	WHEELCHAIR	DUMBWAITER	LUGUBRIOUS
GEOSCIENCE	RECOMPENSE	SILVERFISH	FARSIGHTED	WORTHWHILE	DUODECIMAL	MECHANICAL
GOALKEEPER	REFULGENCE	SUBSURFACE	FIGUREHEAD	ABBREVIATE	ECONOMICAL	MENDACIOUS
GOOSEBERRY	RENASCENCE	SUBTERFUGE	GESUNDHEIT	ABORIGINAL	ECUMENICAL	MENINGITIS
GRAVIMETER	REPORTEDLY	TENDERFOOT	GRAMOPHONE	ABSTEMIOUS	ENCYCLICAL	MICROFICHE
HECTOMETER	RESILIENCE	THEREAFTER	GRANDCHILD	ACCESSIBLE	ENTHUSIASM	MILLILITER
HEPTAMETER	RESILIENCY	ASTRINGENT	HAMMERHEAD	ADMISSIBLE	ESPADRILLE	MILLWRIGHT
HYDROMETER	RESURGENCE	BALBRIGGAN	HEARTTHROB	AFTERBIRTH	EUPHONIOUS	MOUTHPIECE
HYGROMETER	RHINOCEROS	BEDRAGGLED	HEMISPHERE	AIRFREIGHT	EXPATRIATE	NEGLIGIBLE
HYPOTHESIS	ROTISSERIE	BOONDOGGLE	HEMORRHAGE	ALTARPIECE	FACTITIOUS	OBSEQUIOUS
IMPATIENCE	SENESCENCE	CAPOREGIME	HEMORRHOID	AMPHIBIOUS	FALLACIOUS	OFTENTIMES
INCUMBENCY	SEPTICEMIA	CARDIOGRAM	HIEROPHANT	ANNUNCIATE	FASTIDIOUS	OMNISCIENT
INDULGENCE	SERVICEMAN	CHURCHGOER	HYDROPHONE	ANTICLIMAX	FERTILIZER	ORATORICAL
INSISTENCE	SHOPKEEPER	CONGREGATE	IONOSPHERE	APOLITICAL	FICTITIOUS	OSTENSIBLE
INTERFERON	SILHOUETTE	CONTINGENT	KNIGHTHOOD	APPRECIATE	FIELDPIECE	OUTPATIENT

PARMIGIANA	CHEAPSKATE	DEPOPULATE	LITERALISM	SPRINKLING	ENJAMBMENT	ANTICANCER
PARTICIPLE	LOVEMAKING	DEVITALIZE	LOGROLLING	STARVELING	EQUANIMITY	AQUALUNGER
PECCADILLO	PREPACKAGE	DISCIPLINE	MALEVOLENT	SURREALISM	ERGONOMICS	AUCTIONEER
PERCIPIENT	RAINMAKING	DISINCLINE	MANIPULATE	TABLECLOTH	ESCARPMENT	BACKHANDED
PERIODICAL	ROLLICKING	DISQUALIFY	MEADOWLARK	TECHNOLOGY	EXCITEMENT	BESPRINKLE
PERNICIOUS	SHUNPIKING	DISTILLATE	METABOLISM	TENDERLOIN	EXPERIMENT	BIPARENTAL
PICCALILLI	UNDERSKIRT	EMASCULATE	METABOLITE	TESSELLATE	GOVERNMENT	BITUMINOUS
PICKANINNY	UNTHINKING	EMBRYOLOGY	METAGALAXY	THEMSELVES	GROUNDMASS	BLUEBONNET
PLAYWRIGHT	ACCOMPLICE	ENTOMOLOGY	METICULOUS	TIMBERLINE	HABILIMENT	BOTTLENECK
POLYCLINIC	ACCOMPLISH	EPITHELIUM	MINERALIZE	TOMFOOLERY	HOMECOMING	BRAHMANISM
POTENTIATE	ACCUMULATE	EQUIVALENT	MINERALOGY	TOURMALINE	IGNORAMOUS	CARABINEER
POWERLINES	ADRENALINE	EURODOLLAR	MISCELLANY	TOXICOLOGY	IMPEDIMENT	CENTENNIAL
PRECARIOUS	ALCOHOLISM	EVANGELISM	MORPHOLOGY	TRAMPOLINE	INDUCEMENT	CEREMONIAL
PRECOCIOUS	ALLHALLOWS	EVANGELIST	MOTHERLAND	TRANSPLANT	INSTRUMENT	CHAUVINISM
PREMARITAL	ANNIHILATE	EVANGELIZE	MULTIPLIER	UNAVAILING	INTEGUMENT	CHIFFONIER
PREMEDICAL	ANTEBELLUM	EXOBIOLOGY	MUSICOLOGY	UNDERSLUNG	INTERNMENT	CHIMPANZEE
PRIZEFIGHT	ARTICULATE	FATHERLAND	NATURALISM	UNFAMILIAR	INVESTMENT	CHLORINATE
PRODIGIOUS	ASSEMBLAGE	FATHOMLESS	NATURALIST	UNSKILLFUL	JACKHAMMER	CONCERNING
PROFICIENT	ASSIMILATE	FEDERALISM	NATURALIZE	VICTUALLER	LACHRYMOSE	COORDINATE
PROGENITOR	AUSTRALIAN	FEDERALIST	NEUTRALISM	VISIBILITY	LEGITIMATE	CRYOGENICS
PROPITIATE	BEAUJOLAIS	FEDERALIZE	NEUTRALITY	VOCABULARY	MANAGEMENT	DEHUMANIZE
PROPITIOUS	BESTIALITY	FIBERGLASS	NEUTRALIZE	WANDERLUST	MASTERMIND	DELPHINIUM
PUGNACIOUS	BIMETALLIC	FINGERLING	NONCHALANT	WEAPONLESS	MEDICAMENT	DENOMINATE
REBELLIOUS	BIRTHPLACE	FLAGELLATE	NOTABILITY	WEIGHTLESS	MISOGAMIST	DESALINATE
RECONSIDER	BLUECOLLAR	FLOODPLAIN	NUMBERLESS	WONDERLAND	MIZZENMAST	DESALINIZE
REPATRIATE	BONDHOLDER	FOSTERLING	NUMEROLOGY	ADVISEMENT	NETHERMOST	DIAPHANOUS
REPUBLICAN	BOOKSELLER	FRAUDULENT	OCEANOLOGY	AFTERIMAGE	PARLIAMENT	DICTIONARY
RESTRAINED	BORDERLAND	GENERALITY	OPHTHALMIC	AMALGAMATE	PEPPERMINT	DISCERNING
SALUBRIOUS	BOTTOMLAND	GENERALIZE	PAINKILLER	ANTINOMIAN	PILGRIMAGE	DISCONNECT
SHENANIGAN	BROADCLOTH	GLACIOLOGY	PALATALIZE	ASSIGNMENT	POSTHUMOUS	DISGRUNTLE
SHIPWRIGHT	CAMOUFLAGE	GOOSEFLESH	PENICILLIN	ASSORTMENT	PREFERMENT	DISJOINTED
STILLBIRTH	CAPITALISM	GRADUALISM	PERIHELION	ATTACHMENT	PROGRAMMED	EFFEMINATE
SUBLIMINAL	CAPITALIST	GROUNDLING	PERSIFLAGE	ATTAINMENT	PROGRAMMER	ENDOGENOUS
SUBORBITAL	CAPITALIZE	GYNECOLOGY	PHOTOFLASH	AUTONOMOUS	PUNISHMENT	EVENHANDED
SUBSIDIARY	CAPITULATE	HAMMERLOCK	PHRENOLOGY	BACKGAMMON	REFINEMENT	EXURBANITE
SUFFICIENT	CARDIOLOGY	HEMATOLOGY	PHYSIOLOGY	BATTLEMENT	SCHOOLMARM	EYEWITNESS
SUSPICIOUS	CATABOLISM	HINTERLAND	PORTCULLIS	BETTERMENT	SCHOOLMATE	FINGERNAIL
TEETHRIDGE	CATAFALQUE	HORSEFLESH	PRINCELING	BLACKAMOOR	SETTLEMENT	FLUORINATE
TENEBRIOUS	CENTRALIZE	HOUSECLEAN	PROPELLANT	BLACKSMITH	STALAGMITE	FOLKSINGER
THEATRICAL	CEREBELLUM	HYDRAULICS	PROTOPLASM	BRIDESMAID	SUPPLEMENT	FOREFINGER
TRIFOLIATE	CHANCELLOR	HYDROPLANE	PSYCHOLOGY	BUTTERMILK	TOURNAMENT	FOREHANDED
TYPEWRITER	CHANDELIER	ICONOCLASM	RADICALIZE	CANTONMENT	UNASSUMING	FORERUNNER
TYRANNICAL	CHANGELING	ICONOCLAST	RECOILLESS	COMPLEMENT	UNBECOMING	FRATERNITY
UNCRITICAL	CHANNELIZE	IMMACULATE	RELENTLESS	COMPLIMENT	UNIFORMITY	FRATERNIZE
UNDERSIZED	CHAPFALLEN	IMMOBILIZE	REVITALIZE	COMPROMISE	UNSCRAMBLE	GADOLINIUM
UNGRACIOUS	CHRONOLOGY	IMMORALITY	RIDICULOUS	CONFORMITY	VIETNAMESE	GASTRONOMY
UNMERCIFUL	CHRYSOLITE	IMMUNOLOGY	RISIBILITY	CONSUMMATE	WINDJAMMER	GUNSLINGER
UPROARIOUS	CHURCHLESS	INCIVILITY	SACROILIAC	DENOUEMENT	WONDERMENT	HIGHLANDER
URETHRITIS	CLOVERLEAF	INCOMPLETE	SALTCELLAR	DEPARTMENT	ACCIDENTAL	HOMOGENIZE
UROGENITAL	CONTROLLER	INEQUALITY	SCURRILOUS	DEPORTMENT	AFICIONADO	HORIZONTAL
VAUDEVILLE	CORDILLERA	INFIDELITY	SEISMOLOGY	DETACHMENT	ALBUMINOUS	HYPOCENTER
VICTORIOUS	CRENELLATE	INTERBLOCK	SELENOLOGY	DISCOMMODE	ALKALINIZE	HYPOTENUSE
WAINWRIGHT	DECIMALIZE	IRRESOLUTE	SENEGALESE	DISHARMONY	AMANUENSIS	ILLUMINATE
WATERTIGHT	DEMOBILIZE	JOURNALESE	SHIBBOLETH	EMBANKMENT	ANTAGONISM	IMPREGNATE
WINDSHIELD	DEMONOLOGY	JOURNALISM	SHILLELAGH	EMPLOYMENT	ANTAGONIST	INCIDENTAL
WIREHAIRED	DEMORALIZE	LANDHOLDER	SPECIALIST	ENDEARMENT	ANTAGONIZE	INDEFINITE
LUMBERJACK	DENDROLOGY	LIBERALISM	SPECIALIZE	ENGAGEMENT	ANTEPENULT	INDIGENOUS

INHUMANITY	ABOVEBOARD	NEIGHBORLY	WHEELHOUSE	AURIFEROUS	GHOSTWRITE	MOONSTRUCK
INNOMINATE	ACCUSTOMED	NEWSGROUPS	WINDFLOWER	AUTOSTRADA	GRAPEFRUIT	MORATORIUM
INORDINATE	ACROPHOBIA	OCCASIONAL	WINEGROWER	BACKSTROKE	HANDBARROW	MOTORTRUCK
INSEMINATE	ADDITIONAL	OCEANGOING	WRAPAROUND	BALUSTRADE	HANDICRAFT	NATATORIUM
JUGGERNAUT	ANTIBIOTIC	OCTOTHORPE	XENOPHOBIA	BELLETRIST	HANDSPRING	NEWSWORTHY
KNICKKNACK	ANTIPHONAL	OTHERWORLD	ANGIOSPERM	BICHLORIDE	HEADSTRONG	NIGHTDRESS
LADYFINGER	ANTIPROTON	PANTALOONS	ANTHROPOID	BLITZKRIEG	HEARTBREAK	NONSTARTER
LIBIDINOUS	APOSTROPHE	PAPERBOARD	ANTICIPATE	BOISTEROUS	HEATSTROKE	NOTEWORTHY
LIEUTENANT	APOTHEOSIS	PARATROOPS	ANTISEPTIC	BOWDLERIZE	HELIOGRAPH	OBLITERATE
LITHUANIAN	BACKGROUND	PASTEBOARD	APOCRYPHAL	BREADFRUIT	HELIOTROPE	OBSTETRICS
MEMORANDUM	BELLADONNA	PAWNBROKER	CAMELOPARD	BREAKFRONT	HIPPODROME	OCEANARIUM
MILLENNIUM	BLACKBOARD	PEASHOOTER	CLODHOPPER	BRIDEGROOM	HONORARIUM	OCEANFRONT
MISOGYNIST	BLOCKHOUSE	PENNYROYAL	CORRESPOND	CADAVEROUS	HYPODERMIC	OMNIVOROUS
MISSIONARY	BLOODHOUND	PHILOSOPHY	CYBERSPACE	CAMPHORATE	ILLITERATE	OPPROBRIUM
MONOTONOUS	BREADBOARD	PHOSPHORUS	DISCOMPOSE	CATEGORIZE	ILLUSTRATE	OUTPOURING
MONUMENTAL	CANTALOUPE	PIANOFORTE	DISCREPANT	CENTIGRADE	IMMATERIAL	OVERSPREAD
MUDSLINGER	CARCINOGEN	PILOTHOUSE	DISRESPECT	CHATTERBOX	IMMEMORIAL	PACKTHREAD
NONDRINKER	CHANGEOVER	PLAYGROUND	EMANCIPATE	CHIVALROUS	IMMODERATE	PAINTBRUSH
NUCLEONICS	CHECKPOINT	POWERHOUSE	EPISCOPACY	CINERARIUM	IMPOVERISH	PALINDROME
OCCIDENTAL	CORNFLOWER	PRESBYOPIA	EPISCOPATE	COCKATRICE	INAUGURATE	PARAPHRASE
OLEAGINOUS	CORNUCOPIA	RADIOSONDE	EUCALYPTUS	COMPATRIOT	INCINERATE	PASTEURIZE
OVERWINTER	COSMOPOLIS	RECIPROCAL	EYEDROPPER	CONCURRENT	INCOHERENT	PEDESTRIAN
PALATINATE	COURTHOUSE	RELATIONAL	GYMNOSPERM	CONSECRATE	INDECOROUS	PEDIATRICS
PATHFINDER	CROSSBONES	REPERTOIRE	HELICOPTER	CONSPIRACY	INDISCREET	PERMAFROST
PERITONEUM	DISAPPOINT	ROUGHHOUSE	LEAFHOPPER	COUNTERACT	INDUSTRIAL	PERPETRATE
PERIWINKLE	DISEMBOWEL	ROUNDHOUSE	MALADAPTED	COUNTERMAN	INFILTRATE	PHONOGRAPH
PLEASANTRY	DREAMWORLD	SACERDOTAL	MIDSHIPMAN	COUNTERSPY	INTERBREED	PHOTOGRAPH
PREEMINENT	ELECTRONIC	SALESWOMAN	NINCOMPOOP	CRISSCROSS	INTERURBAN	PLAGIARIZE
PRONOUNCED	EMBONPOINT	SERVOMOTOR	NONSUPPORT	CROSSBREED	INTOLERANT	PLUTOCRACY
PROPRINTER	ESCRITOIRE	SKATEBOARD	PETNAPPING	DECELERATE	INVETERATE	POSTMORTEM
PROSCENIUM	FAIRGROUND	SOPHOMORIC	PREDISPOSE	DECOLORIZE	INVIGORATE	POSTPARTUM
QUADRANGLE	FIBERBOARD	SPELLBOUND	PRESUPPOSE	DECOMPRESS	ISOMETRICS	POSTSCRIPT
REFERENDUM	FIBRINOGEN	STAGECOACH	PRINCIPLED	DEFLAGRATE	ISOTHERMAL	POURPARLER
REJUVENATE	FLOORBOARD	STANDPOINT	PSYCHOPATH	DEGENERACY	KRUGERRAND	PRESSURIZE
REPAGINATE	FOREGROUND	STATEHOUSE	QUADRUPLET	DEGENERATE	LIGHTPROOF	PROSPERITY
ROADRUNNER	FREEBOOTER	STOREHOUSE	QUINTUPLET	DELIBERATE	MAGISTRATE	PROSPEROUS
RUBBERNECK	GREENHOUSE	SUPERSONIC	RETROSPECT	DENTIFRICE	MAINSPRING	RADIOGRAPH
SALAMANDER	GUARDHOUSE	TANTAMOUNT	SPOILSPORT	DEPOLARIZE	MAINSTREAM	RECUPERATE
SANGUINARY	HEMOGLOBIN	TELESCOPIC	SUBCOMPACT	DISAPPROVE	MALODOROUS	REDISTRICT
SCRUTINIZE	HENCEFORTH	THROMBOSIS	TABLESPOON	DISCOURAGE	MANICURIST	REGENERACY
SHORTENING	HEREABOUTS	TRANSPOLAR	UNEXAMPLED	DISHEARTEN	MANTLEROCK	REGENERATE
SIDEWINDER	HISTRIONIC	TRAVELOGUE	UNOCCUPIED	DOCKWORKER	MANUSCRIPT	REGISTRANT
STATIONARY	HOBBYHORSE	ULTRASONIC	VELOCIPEDE	DONNYBROOK	MARGUERITE	REMUNERATE
STATIONERY	HODGEPODGE	ULTRASOUND	WATERSPOUT	DOWNSTREAM	MASQUERADE	RESTAURANT
STRYCHNINE	HORSEPOWER	UNDERCOVER	WINDOWPANE	DOWNSTROKE	METACARPUS	RETROGRADE
TURTLENECK	HORSEWOMAN	UNDERWORLD	WORSHIPFUL	DRAWSTRING	METATARSAL	RETROGRESS
UNBALANCED	IMPERSONAL	UNEMPLOYED	TOURNIQUET	ELECTORATE	METATARSUS	SACCHARINE
UNFRIENDLY	INDISPOSED	UNHALLOWED	ACCELERATE	ENTERPRISE	MICROGRAPH	SANATORIUM
UNGROUNDED	INFRASONIC	UNREASONED	ADULTERANT	EQUESTRIAN	MICROPROBE	SANITARIAN
VETERINARY	IRRATIONAL	UNSCHOOLED	ADULTERATE	EVISCERATE	MILITARISM	SANITARIUM
VILLAINOUS	LEDERHOSEN	WALLFLOWER	ALLITERATE	EXAGGERATE	MILITARIZE	SAUERKRAUT
VOLUMINOUS	LIGHTHOUSE	WATCHTOWER	AMELIORATE	EXASPERATE	MILLSTREAM	SCAPEGRACE
WAVELENGTH	MALAPROPOS	WATERBORNE	ANTICHRIST	EXHILARATE	MIMEOGRAPH	SCHOOLROOM
WESTERNIZE	METROPOLIS	WATERCOLOR	AQUAMARINE	EXOTHERMIC	MINESTRONE	SEAMSTRESS
WHARFINGER	MONOPHONIC	WATERPOWER	ARCHITRAVE	FAMILARIZE	MINISCROLL	SECULARISM
WHITSUNDAY	NAPOLEONIC	WATERWORKS	ASSEVERATE	GEOTHERMAL	MINISTRANT	SECULARIZE
WILDERNESS	NECROPOLIS	WHEELHORSE	AUDITORIUM	GERIATRICS	MONOCHROME	SEMPSTRESS

SHOESTRING	CENSORSHIP	MELANESIAN	VARICOSITY	COLORATION	EPIGLOTTIS	INTONATION
SHUTTERBUG	CHARLESTON	MEMBERSHIP	VIRTUOSITY	COLORATURA	EQUITATION	INTRASTATE
SIDESTROKE	CHROMOSOME	METTLESOME	WINCHESTER	COLPORTEUR	ESTIMATION	INVOCATION
SLENDERIZE	CLOTHESPIN	NARCISSISM	WINDOWSILL	COMBUSTION	EXACTITUDE	INVOLUTION
SLIPSTREAM	COMMISSARY	NEBULOSITY	WORKBASKET	COMMENTARY	EXCOGITATE	JUBILATION
SLUMBEROUS	COMMISSION	NEOCLASSIC	YARDMASTER	CONCENTRIC	EXHAUSTION	JUDICATURE
SMATTERING	COMPASSION	NETTLESOME	ABERRATION	CONCEPTION	EXHAUSTIVE	KINEMATICS
SOLIDARITY	COMPENSATE	OPPRESSION	ABSOLUTION	CONCERTINA	EXORBITANT	LABORATORY
SPACECRAFT	COMPULSION	OVERMASTER	ABSOLUTISM	CONCRETION	EXPEDITION	LITERATURE
STATECRAFT	COMPULSIVE	PALIMPSEST	ABSORPTION	CONDUCTIVE	EXPOSITION	LOCOMOTION
STENTORIAN	COMPULSORY	PENMANSHIP	ACCOUNTANT	CONFECTION	FACILITATE	LOCOMOTIVE
STEPPARENT	CONCESSION	PERCUSSION	ACCOUNTING	CONJECTURE	FAVORITISM	MACKINTOSH
SWEETBREAD	CONCESSIVE	PERMISSION	ACCUSATIVE	CONNECTION	FEDERATION	MALCONTENT
SWEETBRIER	CONCLUSION	PERMISSIVE	ACROBATICS	CONNECTIVE	FELICITATE	MANSUETUDE
TAMBOURINE	CONCUSSION	PERQUISITE	AEROBATICS	CONNIPTION	FELICITOUS	MATURATION
TEARJERKER	CONDENSATE	PERSUASION	AESTHETICS	CONSISTORY	FIGURATION	MERCANTILE
THUNDEROUS	CONFESSION	PERVERSION	AFFLICTIVE	CONSORTIUM	FIGURATIVE	MICROSTATE
TOOTHBRUSH	CONVERSANT	PIANISSIMO	ALIMENTARY	CONSTITUTE	FOREFATHER	MISFORTUNE
TRANSCRIBE	CONVERSION	PICARESQUE	ALTOGETHER	CONTENTION	FOREGATHER	MULTISTAGE
TRANSCRIPT	CONVULSION	POLYNESIAN	AMBULATORY	CONVECTION	FORFEITURE	MULTISTORY
TRANSGRESS	COTTONSEED	POSSESSION	AMMUNITION	CONVENTION	FORTUITOUS	NASTURTIUM
TYPESCRIPT	CRADLESONG	POSSESSIVE	ANTIMATTER	CONVICTION	FOUNDATION	NEWSLETTER
UNDERBRUSH	DEALERSHIP	POSTMASTER	APPARITION	CORONATION	GARGANTUAN	NIGHTSTICK
UNDERCROFT	DECLASSIFY	PRECESSION	APPOINTIVE	COTTONTAIL	GENERATION	NOMINATIVE
UNDERTRICK	DECLENSION	PRECIOSITY	APPOSITION	CREDENTIAL	GEOCENTRIC	OBLIGATION
UNDERWRITE	DEPRESSANT	PREHENSILE	APPOSITIVE	CUMULATIVE	GRADUATION	OCCUPATION
UNGENEROUS	DEPRESSION	PREPOSSESS	APPRENTICE	DATAMATION	GRANDSTAND	OMNIPOTENT
UNRESERVED	DEPRESSIVE	PROCESSION	ASPIRATION	DEBILITATE	GRATUITOUS	ORDINATION
VEGETARIAN	DISCURSIVE	PROFESSION	ASSUMPTION	DECAPITATE	GRAVESTONE	PAGINATION
VERTEBRATE	DISCUSSANT	PROGNOSTIC	ASYMMETRIC	DECORATION	GRINDSTONE	PEJORATIVE
VICEGERENT	DISHWASHER	PROMISSORY	ATTRACTANT	DECORATIVE	GUILLOTINE	PERCENTAGE
VITUPERATE	DISPENSARY	PROPENSITY	ATTRACTION	DECRYPTION	GYMNASTICS	PERCENTILE
VIVIPAROUS	DISPOSSESS	PROPULSION	AUTOMATION	DEFINITION	HABITATION	PERCEPTION
VOCIFERATE	DISSENSION	READERSHIP	AUTOMATIZE	DEFINITIVE	HEREDITARY	PERCEPTIVE
VOCIFEROUS	DYSPROSIUM	REGRESSION	AUTOMOTIVE	DELEGATION	IDIOPATHIC	PERCEPTUAL
VOICEPRINT	EXPRESSION	RESPONSIVE	BALLISTICS	DEMOLITION	IMBIBITION	PEREMPTORY
WATERCRAFT	EXPRESSMAN	RINGMASTER	BAPTISTERY	DEMONETIZE	IMPENITENT	PERFECTION
WATERCRESS	EXPRESSWAY	SCHOLASTIC	BEDCLOTHES	DENOTATIVE	IMPERATIVE	PERORATION
WATERFRONT	FELLOWSHIP	SEAMANSHIP	BELLWETHER	DEPILATORY	INAPTITUDE	PHILISTINE
WATERPROOF	FILIBUSTER	SIMPLISTIC	BIRTHSTONE	DEPOSITION	INCONSTANT	PHLEBOTOMY
WEATHERING	FORECASTLE	STATUESQUE	BLOODSTAIN	DEPOSITORY	INDICATIVE	PHYLACTERY
WEATHERMAN	FORTISSIMO	STEPSISTER	BLOODSTONE	DEPUTATION	INFIGHTING	PINFEATHER
WELLSPRING	FUTURISTIC	STOCHASTIC	BLUEBOTTLE	DERIVATION	INFINITIVE	PLANTATION
WIDESPREAD	GEOPHYSICS	SUCCESSION	BRAINSTORM	DERIVATIVE	INFINITUDE	PLAYACTING
WINGSPREAD	GINGERSNAP	SUCCESSIVE	BREADSTUFF	DEROGATORY	INFLECTION	POINSETTIA
WITCHCRAFT	HEADMASTER	SUNGLASSES	BRIGANTINE	DESOLATION	INFRACTION	POPULATION
WITCHGRASS	HEARTHSIDE	SUSPENSION	BROWNSTONE	DIELECTRIC	INHABITANT	PORTENTOUS
ABSCISSION	IMPRESSION	SUSPENSORY	CACCIATORE	DIMINUTIVE	INHIBITION	PRAGMATISM
ADMINISTER	IMPRESSIVE	TATTERSALL	CAPACITATE	DISCONTENT	INITIATIVE	PRECAUTION
AGGRESSION	INDECISION	TASKMASTER	CAPITATION	DISCRETION	INITIATORY	PREDESTINE
AGGRESSIVE	INDECISIVE	TELEVISION	CARICATURE	DIVINATION	INJUNCTION	PREEMPTIVE
ARCHBISHOP	INDONESIAN	THERMISTOR	CAVITATION	DOMINATION	INNOVATION	PRESBYTERY
AUTHORSHIP	KINGFISHER	THERMOSTAT	CHARACTERY	EBULLITION	INQUIETUDE	PRODUCTION
BATTLESHIP	LACKLUSTER	TRANSISTOR	CIRCUITOUS	EFFRONTERY	INSOLATION	PROJECTILE
BIOPHYSICS	MALTHUSIAN	UNHANDSOME	CLERESTORY	EGOCENTRIC	INTERSTATE	PROMONTORY
BRONTOSAUR	MASTERSHIP	UNIVERSITY	CLINGSTONE	ELEMENTARY	INTERSTICE	PROPERTIED
BUSHMASTER	MEDDLESOME	UNPLEASANT	COLLECTIVE	ENCRYPTION	INTINCTION	PROPORTION

PROSTITUTE	SUBSTITUTE	EXTINGUISH	GREENSWARD	AMALGAMATE	CONSPIRACY	FIBERGLASS
PROTECTION	SUBVENTION	EXTRAMURAL	GROUNDWORK	AMELIORATE	CONSUMMATE	FINGERNAIL
PROTESTANT	SUGGESTION	FISTICUFFS	HOLLOWWARE	ANNIHILATE	CONTRABAND	FLAGELLATE
QUADRATICS	SUGGESTIVE	FLUIDOUNCE	INTERTWINE	ANNUNCIATE	CONVERSANT	FLAMBOYANT
QUARANTINE	TATTLETALE	FOURSQUARE	INTERTWIST	ANTICIPATE	COORDINATE	FLOODPLAIN
RATTLETRAP	TECHNETIUM	HALLELUJAH	JIMSONWEED	APOTHECARY	COTTONTAIL	FLOORBOARD
RECITATION	TEMPTATION	INADEQUATE	LENGTHWISE	APPRECIATE	COUNTERACT	FLUORIDATE
RECREATION	THOUGHTFUL	INFREQUENT	MASTERWORK	ARCHITRAVE	CRANKSHAFT	FLUORINATE
REDEMPTION	TORRENTIAL	INTERLUNAR	NATIONWIDE	ARTICULATE	CRENELLATE	FOREORDAIN
REFRACTION	TOUCHSTONE	INTRAMURAL	NEEDLEWORK	ASPHYXIATE	CYBERSPACE	FOURSQUARE
REFRACTORY	TRAJECTORY	KNOCKWURST	SANDALWOOD	ASSEMBLAGE	DEACTIVATE	GRANDSTAND
REGULATION	TRANSITION	LIVERWURST	SEARCHWARE	ASSEVERATE	DEBILITATE	GREENSWARD
RELAXATION	TRANSITIVE	METALLURGY	SILVERWARE	ASSIMILATE	DECAPITATE	GROUNDMASS
REPARATION	TRANSITORY	ORGANGUTAN	SUPERTWIST	ATTRACTANT	DECELERATE	HANDICRAFT
REPARATIVE	TRAVERTINE	PARTICULAR	TUMBLEWEED	AUTOSTRADA	DEFLAGRATE	HANDLEBARS
REPETITION	TRIMONTHLY	PERPETUATE	WICKERWORK	BALDERDASH	DEGENERACY	HELIOGRAPH
REPETITIVE	TRIPARTITE	PERPETUITY	WILLOWWARE	BALUSTRADE	DEGENERATE	HEMORRHAGE
REPOSITORY	TRUNCATION	PHOTOMURAL	WOODENWARE	BASKETBALL	DELIBERATE	HEREDITARY
REPUTATION	TURPENTINE	PORTUGUESE	COMPLEXION	BATHYSCAPH	DENOMINATE	HIEROPHANT
RESOLUTION	TYPESETTER	RACECOURSE	HOMOSEXUAL	BEAUJOLAIS	DEPOPULATE	HINTERLAND
RESORPTION	UBIQUITOUS	RELINQUISH	APOCALYPSE	BEFOREHAND	DEPRECIATE	HOLLOWWARE
RESPECTING	UNDERSTAND	SPIRITUOUS	CHURCHYARD	BEHINDHAND	DEPRESSANT	HYDROPLANE
RESPECTIVE	UNDERSTATE	SUBSEQUENT	COUNTRYMAN	BIRTHPLACE	DESALINATE	ICONOCLASM
RETRACTILE	UNDERSTOOD	TRANSDUCER	FLAMBOYANT	BLACKBOARD	DESCENDANT	ICONOCLAST
REVELATION	UNDERSTORY	TUBERCULAR	HIGHWAYMAN	BLACKGUARD	DICTIONARY	ILLITERATE
REVOCATION	UNDERSTUDY	TUBERCULIN	HYDROLYSIS	BLOODSTAIN	DINNERWARE	ILLUMINATE
REVOLUTION	UNDULATION	TUMULTUOUS	JOURNEYMAN	BORDERLAND	DISCOURAGE	ILLUSTRATE
RHEUMATISM	UNEVENTFUL	VERNACULAR	LUMBERYARD	BOTTOMLAND	DISCREPANT	IMMACULATE
RHINESTONE	UNFRUITFUL	VOLUPTUARY	MOTORCYCLE	BREADBOARD	DISCUSSANT	IMMODERATE
RICKETTSIA	UPHOLSTERY	VOLUPTUOUS	NURSERYMAN	BRIDESMAID	DISENCHANT	IMPREGNATE
SALUTATION	VEGETATION	ANIMADVERT	PATRONYMIC	BRONTOSAUR	DISPENSARY	INACTIVATE
SANITATION	VEGETATIVE	BOLSHEVISM	POULTRYMAN	CALUMNIATE	DISSOCIATE	INADEQUATE
SCARLATINA	VESPERTINE	CIRCUMVENT	SEMIDRYING	CAMELOPARD	DISTILLATE	INAUGURATE
SEPARATION	VINDICTIVE	CONTRAVENE	TROLLEYBUS	CAMOUFLAGE	EARTHQUAKE	INCENDIARY
SEPARATIST	VISITATION	CONTROVERT	UNDERLYING	CAMPHORATE	EFFECTUATE	INCINERATE
SEPARATIVE	VOLUMETRIC	DEACTIVATE	URINALYSIS	CANNONBALL	EFFEMINATE	INCONSTANT
SERPENTINE	WINTERTIDE	DISSERVICE	YESTERYEAR	CANONICALS	ELECTORATE	INDELICATE
SHIPFITTER	WINTERTIME	INACTIVATE	APPETIZING	CANVASBACK	ELEMENTARY	INFILTRATE
SIMILITUDE	WOODCUTTER	IRRELEVANT	GORGONZOLA	CAPACITATE	EMANCIPATE	INGRATIATE
SINGLETREE	ACCENTUATE	LIFESAVING		CAPITULATE	EMASCULATE	INHABITANT
SKYWRITING	ADVENTURER	MANSERVANT		CELLOPHANE	ENAMELWARE	INNOMINATE
SMOKESTACK	BLACKGUARD	NEGATIVISM		CENTIGRADE	ENTHUSIASM	INORDINATE
SOLICITOUS	CATECHUMEN	PROCLIVITY	**8TH LETTER**	CHEAPSKATE	EPISCOPACY	INSEMINATE
SOLICITUDE	CLOUDBURST	QUADRIVIUM		CHEESECAKE	EPISCOPATE	INTERLEAVE
SPOLIATION	COLLOQUIAL	REACTIVATE	ABBREVIATE	CHLORINATE	EQUIVOCATE	INTERSTATE
SPRINGTIME	COLLOQUIUM	RECIDIVISM	ABOVEBOARD	CHURCHYARD	EVISCERATE	INTERWEAVE
STALACTITE	CONSEQUENT	RELATIVITY	ACCELERATE	COMMANDANT	EXACERBATE	INTIMIDATE
STANDSTILL	CONTIGUOUS	RENDEZVOUS	ACCENTUATE	COMMENTARY	EXAGGERATE	INTOLERANT
STATISTICS	CONTINUITY	BREASTWORK	ACCOUNTANT	COMMISSARY	EXASPERATE	INTOXICANT
STEPFATHER	CONTINUOUS	BRIDGEWORK	ACCUMULATE	COMPENSATE	EXCOGITATE	INTOXICATE
STEPMOTHER	CONVOLUTED	BROADSWORD	ADJUDICATE	COMPLICATE	EXHILARATE	INTRASTATE
STEREOTYPE	CURRICULUM	CANDLEWICK	ADULTERANT	CONCILIATE	EXORBITANT	INVALIDATE
STIGMATIZE	DELINQUENT	CANKERWORM	ADULTERATE	CONCORDANT	EXPATRIATE	INVETERATE
STRENGTHEN	DIFFICULTY	COMMONWEAL	AFICIONADO	CONDENSATE	FACILITATE	INVIGORATE
SUBJECTIVE	DISTRAUGHT	COTTONWOOD	AFTERIMAGE	CONFISCATE	FATHERLAND	IRRELEVANT
SUBROUTINE	EARTHQUAKE	DINNERWARE	ALIMENTARY	CONGREGATE	FELICITATE	JUGGERNAUT
SUBSTATION	EFFECTUATE	ENAMELWARE	ALLITERATE	CONSECRATE	FIBERBOARD	KNICKKNACK

KRUGERRAND	RECUPERATE	WITCHCRAFT	INVINCIBLE	ARMAGEDDON	CANTONMENT	FIELDPIECE
LEGITIMATE	REGENERACY	WITCHGRASS	INVIOLABLE	BACKHANDED	CARABINEER	FIGUREHEAD
LEPRECHAUN	REGENERATE	WONDERLAND	JACKRABBIT	BAREHEADED	CHARACTERY	FRAUDULENT
LICENTIATE	REGISTRANT	WOODENWARE	LANDLUBBER	BONDHOLDER	CHURCHLESS	GESUNDHEIT
LIEUTENANT	REJUVENATE	ABOMINABLE	MENSURABLE	BULLHEADED	CIRCUMVENT	GOOSEFLESH
LUMBERJACK	REMUNERATE	ACCEPTABLE	MISTAKABLE	COPYREADER	CLOVERLEAF	GOVERNMENT
LUMBERYARD	REPAGINATE	ACCESSIBLE	NEGLIGIBLE	CYCLOPEDIA	COINCIDENT	GRAINFIELD
MAGISTRATE	REPATRIATE	ACROPHOBIA	NOTICEABLE	DESERVEDLY	COLPORTEUR	GYMNOSPERM
MAIDENHAIR	RESTAURANT	ACTIONABLE	OBSERVABLE	DRAWBRIDGE	COMMANDEER	HABILIMENT
MANIPULATE	RETROGRADE	ADMISSIBLE	OSTENSIBLE	EVENHANDED	COMMONWEAL	HAMMERHEAD
MANSERVANT	ROLLERBALL	ANSWERABLE	PERDURABLE	FOOTBRIDGE	COMPLEMENT	HEARTBREAK
MARTINGALE	SANGUINARY	APPLICABLE	PERISHABLE	FOREHANDED	COMPLIMENT	HEMISPHERE
MASQUERADE	SAUERKRAUT	CANDELABRA	PERSONABLE	FORESHADOW	COMPREHEND	HORSEFLESH
MEADOWLARK	SCAPEGRACE	CHARITABLE	PREDICABLE	HANDMAIDEN	CONCURRENT	HOUSECLEAN
MEERSCHAUM	SCHOOLMARM	CHATTERBOX	REASONABLE	HARDHEADED	CONDESCEND	IMPEDIMENT
METAGALAXY	SCHOOLMATE	COMESTIBLE	RECEIVABLE	HIGHLANDER	CONSEQUENT	IMPENITENT
MICROGRAPH	SEARCHWARE	COMPARABLE	REMARKABLE	HODGEPODGE	CONTINGENT	INCOHERENT
MICROSTATE	SECONDHAND	COMPATIBLE	REMEDIABLE	INTERTIDAL	CONTRAVENE	INCOMPLETE
MIMEOGRAPH	SHILLELAGH	CORRIGIBLE	RESTORABLE	LANDHOLDER	CONTROVERT	INDISCREET
MINISTRANT	SILVERWARE	CREDITABLE	SEASONABLE	MEMORANDUM	CONVENIENT	INDUCEMENT
MISCELLANY	SKATEBOARD	DEGRADABLE	SHUTTERBUG	MOHAMMEDAN	COPPERHEAD	INFREQUENT
MISSIONARY	SMOKESTACK	DELECTABLE	SPITTLEBUG	MUHAMMADAN	CORDILLERA	INGREDIENT
MIZZENMAST	SPACECRAFT	DEPENDABLE	TROLLEYBUS	MULTIMEDIA	COTTONSEED	INSENTIENT
MOTHERLAND	SPORTSCAST	DEPLORABLE	UNBEARABLE	OVERSHADOW	CROSSBREED	INSTRUMENT
MOUNTEBANK	STAGECOACH	DESPICABLE	UNBEATABLE	PACKSADDLE	CROSSPIECE	INTEGUMENT
MULTISTAGE	STATECRAFT	DISPOSABLE	UNDENIABLE	PATHFINDER	CRUSTACEAN	INTERBREED
NIGHTSHADE	STATIONARY	EXPLICABLE	UNSCRAMBLE	RECONSIDER	DECOMPRESS	INTERNMENT
NONCHALANT	STRIPTEASE	FORMIDABLE	UNSUITABLE	REFERENDUM	DELINQUENT	INVESTMENT
OBLITERATE	SUBCOMPACT	HEMOGLOBIN	VULNERABLE	REPORTEDLY	DENOUEMENT	IONOSPHERE
PALATINATE	SUBSIDIARY	HOSPITABLE	XENOPHOBIA	RINGLEADER	DEPARTMENT	JARDINIERE
PAPERBOARD	SUBSURFACE	IMAGINABLE	ANTICANCER	SALAMANDER	DEPORTMENT	JIMSONWEED
PARAPHRASE	SUPPLICANT	IMMISCIBLE	APOLITICAL	SIDEWINDER	DETACHMENT	JOURNALESE
PARMIGIANA	SUPPLICATE	IMPALPABLE	ARCHDEACON	STEPLADDER	DISBELIEVE	LETTERHEAD
PASTEBOARD	SWEETHEART	IMPASSABLE	BIOMEDICAL	TEETHRIDGE	DISCONCERT	LOGGERHEAD
PERCENTAGE	SWITCHBACK	IMPASSIBLE	CHIMERICAL	UNFRIENDLY	DISCONNECT	MAIDENHEAD
PERPETRATE	TATTERSALL	IMPECCABLE	ECONOMICAL	UNGROUNDED	DISCONTENT	MAINSTREAM
PERPETUATE	TATTLETALE	IMPLACABLE	ECUMENICAL	WHITSUNDAY	DISPOSSESS	MALCONTENT
PERSIFLAGE	TESSELLATE	IMPOSSIBLE	ENCYCLICAL	ADVISEMENT	DISRESPECT	MALEFICENT
PHONOGRAPH	THREADBARE	IMPROBABLE	GONOCOCCUS	ALTARPIECE	DOWNSTREAM	MALEVOLENT
PHOTOFLASH	TRANSPLANT	INCLINABLE	MECHANICAL	ANGIOSPERM	DUNDERHEAD	MANAGEMENT
PHOTOGRAPH	TRIFOLIATE	INCREDIBLE	MICROFICHE	ANIMADVERT	EFFRONTERY	MEDICAMENT
PILGRIMAGE	TRIPLICATE	INCULPABLE	MOTORCYCLE	ANTECEDENT	EMBANKMENT	MESOSPHERE
PILLOWCASE	UNDERNEATH	INELIGIBLE	ORATORICAL	ANTIFREEZE	EMBROIDERY	MILLSTREAM
PLUTOCRACY	UNDERSTAND	INEVITABLE	PERIODICAL	ASSIGNMENT	EMPLOYMENT	MOUTHPIECE
POTENTIATE	UNDERSTATE	INEXORABLE	PREMEDICAL	ASSORTMENT	ENDEARMENT	MUNIFICENT
PREBENDARY	UNPLEASANT	INEXPIABLE	PRONOUNCED	ASTRINGENT	ENGAGEMENT	NIGHTDRESS
PREDECEASE	VERTEBRATE	INFALLIBLE	RECEPTACLE	ATMOSPHERE	ENJAMBMENT	NUMBERLESS
PREPACKAGE	VETERINARY	INFLEXIBLE	RECIPROCAL	ATTACHMENT	EQUIVALENT	OMNIPOTENT
PROFLIGATE	VITUPERATE	INIMITABLE	REPUBLICAN	ATTAINMENT	ESCARPMENT	OMNISCIENT
PROMULGATE	VOCABULARY	INOPERABLE	SHAMEFACED	AUCTIONEER	ESCUTCHEON	OPALESCENT
PROPELLANT	VOCIFERATE	INSATIABLE	TABERNACLE	BAPTISTERY	EVANESCENT	OUTPATIENT
PROPITIATE	VOLLEYBALL	INSENSIBLE	THEATRICAL	BATTLEMENT	EVERYWHERE	OVERSPREAD
PROTESTANT	VOLUPTUARY	INSOLVABLE	TRANSDUCER	BENEFICENT	EXCITEMENT	PACKTHREAD
PROTOPLASM	WATERCRAFT	INTANGIBLE	TYRANNICAL	BETTERMENT	EXPERIMENT	PALIMPSEST
PSYCHOPATH	WHEELCHAIR	INTERURBAN	UNBALANCED	BOTTLENECK	EYEWITNESS	PARLIAMENT
RADIOGRAPH	WILLOWWARE	INVALUABLE	UNCRITICAL	BRIDGEHEAD	FAHRENHEIT	PERCIPIENT
REACTIVATE	WINDOWPANE	INVARIABLE	AMBASSADOR	CANDESCENT	FATHOMLESS	PERITONEUM

PHYLACTERY	UNFAITHFUL	FOOTLIGHTS	AUDITORIUM	COMMISSION	DENOTATIVE	FIGURATION
PLUPERFECT	UNFRUITFUL	FOREFATHER	AUSTRALIAN	COMPASSION	DENTIFRICE	FIGURATIVE
PORTUGUESE	UNGRACEFUL	FOREGATHER	AUTOMATION	COMPATRIOT	DEPOLARIZE	FINGERLING
PREEMINENT	UNGRATEFUL	IDIOPATHIC	AUTOMATIZE	COMPENDIUM	DEPOSITION	FORBIDDING
PREFERMENT	UNMERCIFUL	KINGFISHER	AUTOMOBILE	COMPLEXION	DEPRESSION	FORTISSIMO
PREPOSSESS	UNSKILLFUL	MASTERSHIP	AUTOMOTIVE	COMPLICITY	DEPRESSIVE	FOSTERLING
PRESBYTERY	WORSHIPFUL	MEMBERSHIP	BACKSTAIRS	COMPROMISE	DEPUTATION	FOUNDATION
PROFICIENT	AIRFREIGHT	PENMANSHIP	BALLISTICS	COMPULSION	DERIVATION	FRATERNITY
PUNISHMENT	AQUALUNGER	PINFEATHER	BASTARDIZE	COMPULSIVE	DERIVATIVE	FRATERNIZE
PUTRESCENT	BALBRIGGAN	READERSHIP	BATRACHIAN	CONCEPTION	DESALINIZE	FRATRICIDE
RECOILLESS	BIRTHRIGHT	SEAMANSHIP	BEAUTICIAN	CONCERNING	DESOLATION	GADOLINIUM
REFINEMENT	BOONDOGGLE	STEPFATHER	BELLETRIST	CONCERTINA	DEVITALIZE	GENERALITY
REFRINGENT	BUDGERIGAR	STEPMOTHER	BENEFICIAL	CONCESSION	DIMINUTIVE	GENERALIZE
RELENTLESS	CARCINOGEN	STRENGTHEN	BESTIALITY	CONCESSIVE	DISAPPOINT	GENERATION
RESPONDENT	DEADWEIGHT	TRIMONTHLY	BICHLORIDE	CONCLUSION	DISCERNING	GEOPHYSICS
RETROGRESS	DISTRAUGHT	UNATTACHED	BIOPHYSICS	CONCRETION	DISCIPLINE	GERIATRICS
RETROSPECT	FIBRINOGEN	ABERRATION	BLACKSMITH	CONCUSSION	DISCRETION	GHOSTWRITE
RUBBERNECK	FLASHLIGHT	ABSCISSION	BLITZKRIEG	CONDUCTIVE	DISCURSIVE	GORMANDIZE
SEAMSTRESS	FLOODLIGHT	ABSOLUTION	BOLSHEVISM	CONFECTION	DISINCLINE	GRADUALISM
SEMPSTRESS	FOLKSINGER	ABSOLUTISM	BOMBARDIER	CONFESSION	DISQUALIFY	GRADUATION
SENEGALESE	FOREFINGER	ABSORPTION	BOOKMOBILE	CONFORMITY	DISSENSION	GRANDCHILD
SETTLEMENT	FORTHRIGHT	ACCOMPLICE	BOWDLERIZE	CONNECTION	DISSERVICE	GROUNDLING
SHIBBOLETH	FUSSBUDGET	ACCOMPLISH	BRAHMANISM	CONNECTIVE	DIVINATION	GUILLOTINE
SLIPSTREAM	GUNSLINGER	ACCOUNTING	BRAINCHILD	CONNIPTION	DOMINATION	GYMNASTICS
SPIROCHETE	LADYFINGER	ACCUSATIVE	BRIGANTINE	CONSORTIUM	DOWNSTAIRS	HABITATION
STATIONERY	MILLWRIGHT	ACROBATICS	BUTTERMILK	CONSTRAINT	DRAWSTRING	HANDSPRING
STEPPARENT	MUDSLINGER	ADRENALINE	CANDLEWICK	CONTENTION	DYSPROSIUM	HEARTHSIDE
SUBSEQUENT	OESOPHAGUS	AEROBATICS	CAPITALISM	CONTINUITY	EBULLITION	HOMECOMING
SUBTRAHEND	PARAPLEGIA	AESTHETICS	CAPITALIST	CONTRADICT	EMBONPOINT	HOMOGENIZE
SUFFICIENT	PLAYWRIGHT	AFFLICTIVE	CAPITALIZE	CONVECTION	EMPIRICISM	HONORARIUM
SUPPLEMENT	PRIVILEGED	AGGRANDIZE	CAPITATION	CONVENTION	EMULSIFIER	HYDRAULICS
SWEETBREAD	PRIZEFIGHT	AGGRESSION	CAPOREGIME	CONVERSION	ENCRYPTION	IMBIBITION
TOMFOOLERY	QUADRANGLE	AGGRESSIVE	CATABOLISM	CONVICTION	ENTERPRISE	IMMATERIAL
TOURNAMENT	SHENANIGAN	ALCOHOLISM	CATEGORIZE	CONVULSION	EPITHELIUM	IMMEMORIAL
TRANSGRESS	SHIPWRIGHT	ALKALINIZE	CAVITATION	CORONATION	EQUANIMITY	IMMOBILIZE
TUMBLEWEED	SNAPDRAGON	AMERINDIAN	CENTENNIAL	CREDENTIAL	EQUESTRIAN	IMMORALITY
TURTLENECK	TRAVELOGUE	AMMUNITION	CENTRALIZE	CRYOGENICS	EQUITATION	IMPERATIVE
UPHOLSTERY	UNABRIDGED	ANGLOPHILE	CEREMONIAL	CUMULATIVE	ERGONOMICS	IMPOVERISH
VELOCIPEDE	WAINWRIGHT	ANTAGONISM	CHANDELIER	CUTTLEFISH	ESCRITOIRE	IMPRESSION
VICEGERENT	WATERTIGHT	ANTAGONIST	CHANGELING	DATAMATION	ESTIMATION	IMPRESSIVE
VIETNAMESE	WAVELENGTH	ANTAGONIZE	CHANNELIZE	DECIMALIZE	EVANGELISM	INBREEDING
WATERCRESS	WHARFINGER	ANTHRACITE	CHATELAINE	DECLASSIFY	EVANGELIST	INCAPACITY
WATERWHEEL	ALTOGETHER	ANTICHRIST	CHAUVINISM	DECLENSION	EVANGELIZE	INCIVILITY
WEAPONLESS	APOCRYPHAL	ANTINOMIAN	CHECKPOINT	DECOLORIZE	EVERYTHING	INDECISION
WEIGHTLESS	ARCHBISHOP	ANTISOCIAL	CHIFFONIER	DECORATION	EXHAUSTION	INDECISIVE
WIDESPREAD	AUTHORSHIP	APPARITION	CHRYSOLITE	DECORATIVE	EXHAUSTIVE	INDEFINITE
WILDEBEEST	BATTLESHIP	APPETIZING	CINERARIUM	DECRYPTION	EXPEDITION	INDICATIVE
WILDERNESS	BEDCLOTHES	APPOINTIVE	CIRCUMCISE	DEFINITION	EXPOSITION	INDONESIAN
WINDSHIELD	BELLWETHER	APPOSITION	CLASSICISM	DEFINITIVE	EXPRESSION	INDUSTRIAL
WINGSPREAD	CENSORSHIP	APPOSITIVE	CLASSIFIED	DEHUMANIZE	EXTINGUISH	INEQUALITY
WONDERMENT	COWPUNCHER	APPRENTICE	COCKATRICE	DEHUMIDIFY	EXURBANITE	INFIDELITY
YESTERYEAR	DEALERSHIP	AQUAMARINE	COLLECTIVE	DELEGATION	FAMILARIZE	INFIGHTING
EISTEDDFOD	DISHWASHER	ARTIFICIAL	COLLOQUIAL	DELPHINIUM	FAVORITISM	INFINITIVE
FISTICUFFS	DOGCATCHER	ASPIRATION	COLLOQUIUM	DEMOBILIZE	FEDERALISM	INFLECTION
RAGAMUFFIN	FARFETCHED	ASSUMPTION	COLORATION	DEMOLITION	FEDERALIST	INFRACTION
THOUGHTFUL	FELLOWSHIP	ATTRACTION	COMBUSTION	DEMONETIZE	FEDERALIZE	INHIBITION
UNEVENTFUL	FLYCATCHER	AUDIOPHILE	COMMERCIAL	DEMORALIZE	FEDERATION	INHUMANITY

INITIATIVE	NEBULOSITY	POSSESSIVE	REVELATION	SUGGESTION	WHIRLYBIRD	METROPOLIS
INJUNCTION	NEGATIVISM	POSTSCRIPT	REVITALIZE	SUGGESTIVE	WINDOWSILL	MOZZARELLA
INNOVATION	NEUTRALISM	PRAGMATISM	REVOCATION	SUPERTWIST	WINTERTIDE	NECROPOLIS
INSOLATION	NEUTRALITY	PRECAUTION	REVOLUTION	SURREALISM	WINTERTIME	NEWFANGLED
INTERFAITH	NEUTRALIZE	PRECESSION	RHEUMATISM	SUSPENSION	WORTHWHILE	PAINKILLER
INTERSTICE	NIGHTSHIRT	PRECIOSITY	RISIBILITY	SWEETBRIER	HALLELUJAH	PARTICULAR
INTERTWINE	NIGHTSTICK	PREDESTINE	ROLLICKING	SYMPATHIZE	BESPRINKLE	PECCADILLO
INTERTWIST	NOMINATIVE	PREEMPTIVE	SACCHARINE	TAMBOURINE	BLUEJACKET	PENICILLIN
INTINCTION	NOTABILITY	PREHENSILE	SACROILIAC	TECHNETIUM	DOCKWORKER	PERSONALTY
INTONATION	NOURISHING	PRESSURIZE	SALUTATION	TECHNICIAN	FOOTLOCKER	PICCALILLI
INVOCATION	NUCLEONICS	PRIMORDIAL	SANATORIUM	TELEVISION	ICEBREAKER	PORTCULLIS
INVOLUTION	OBLIGATION	PRINCELING	SANITARIAN	TEMPTATION	JAWBREAKER	POURPARLER
ISOMETRICS	OBSTETRICS	PROCEEDING	SANITARIUM	TIMBERLINE	LANDLOCKED	PRINCIPLED
JOURNALISM	OCCUPATION	PROCESSION	SANITATION	TORRENTIAL	LAWBREAKER	QUADRUPLET
JUBILATION	OCEANARIUM	PROCLIVITY	SCARLATINA	TOURMALINE	LINEBACKER	QUINTUPLET
KINEMATICS	OCEANGOING	PRODUCTION	SCHOOLGIRL	TRAMPOLINE	MATCHMAKER	SALTCELLAR
LAWRENCIUM	OPPRESSION	PROFESSION	SCRUTINIZE	TRANSCRIBE	NOISEMAKER	TARANTELLA
LENGTHWISE	OPPROBRIUM	PROJECTILE	SECULARISM	TRANSCRIPT	NONDRINKER	TRANSPOLAR
LIBERALISM	ORDINATION	PROMETHIUM	SECULARIZE	TRANSITION	NUTCRACKER	TUBERCULAR
LIFESAVING	OUTLANDISH	PROPENSITY	SEMIDRYING	TRANSITIVE	PAWNBROKER	TUBERCULIN
LIPREADING	OUTPOURING	PROPERTIED	SEPARATION	TRAVERTINE	PEACEMAKER	UNDERBELLY
LITERALISM	PAGINATION	PROPORTION	SEPARATIST	TRIPARTITE	PERIWINKLE	UNDERVALUE
LITHUANIAN	PALATALIZE	PROPULSION	SEPARATIVE	TRUNCATION	PICKPOCKET	UNEXAMPLED
LOCOMOTION	PANTYWAIST	PROSCENIUM	SEPTUAGINT	TURPENTINE	RAMSHACKLE	UNSCHOOLED
LOCOMOTIVE	PARAMECIUM	PROSPERITY	SERPENTINE	TYPESCRIPT	SEERSUCKER	VAUDEVILLE
LOGROLLING	PASTEURIZE	PROTECTION	SHOESTRING	UNASSUMING	TEARJERKER	VERMICELLI
LOVEMAKING	PEDESTRIAN	PROVINCIAL	SHORTENING	UNAVAILING	TURNBUCKLE	VERNACULAR
MAINSPRING	PEDIATRICS	PYRIMIDINE	SHUNPIKING	UNBECOMING	UNDERTAKER	VICTUALLER
MALTHUSIAN	PEJORATIVE	QUADRATICS	SILVERFISH	UNBLUSHING	WATCHMAKER	WATERCOLOR
MANICURIST	PEPPERMINT	QUADRIVIUM	SIMPLICITY	UNDERLYING	WOODPECKER	WATERMELON
MANUSCRIPT	PERCENTILE	QUARANTINE	SKEPTICISM	UNDERSHIRT	WORKBASKET	ACCUSTOMED
MARASCHINO	PERCEPTION	RADICALIZE	SKYWRITING	UNDERSKIRT	ANTEBELLUM	ANTICLIMAX
MARGUERITE	PERCEPTIVE	RAINMAKING	SLENDERIZE	UNDERTRICK	BEDRAGGLED	BACKGAMMON
MASTERMIND	PERCUSSION	RECIDIVISM	SMATTERING	UNDERWAIST	BIMETALLIC	CATECHUMEN
MATURATION	PERFECTION	RECITATION	SNOWMOBILE	UNDERWRITE	BLUECOLLAR	CENTESIMAL
MAYONNAISE	PERIHELION	RECREATION	SOLIDARITY	UNDULATION	BOOKSELLER	COUNTERMAN
MELANESIAN	PERMISSION	REDEMPTION	SPECIALIST	UNFAMILIAR	CEREBELLUM	COUNTRYMAN
MERCANTILE	PERMISSIVE	REDISTRICT	SPECIALIZE	UNIFORMITY	CHANCELLOR	DUODECIMAL
METABOLISM	PERORATION	REFRACTION	SPOLIATION	UNIVERSITY	CHAPFALLEN	EXOTHERMIC
METABOLITE	PERPETUITY	REGRESSION	SPRINGTIME	UNOCCUPIED	CHINCHILLA	EXPRESSMAN
MILITARISM	PERQUISITE	REGULATION	SPRINKLING	UNTHINKING	CIRCUMFLEX	GEOTHERMAL
MILITARIZE	PERSUASION	RELATIVITY	STALACTITE	UNYIELDING	CITRONELLA	HIGHWAYMAN
MILLENNIUM	PERVERSION	RELAXATION	STALAGMITE	UPBRINGING	COMMONALTY	HORSEWOMAN
MINERALIZE	PETNAPPING	RELINQUISH	STANDPOINT	UPSTANDING	CONTROLLER	HUSBANDMAN
MISOGAMIST	PHILISTINE	REPARATION	STANDSTILL	VARICOSITY	COSMOPOLIS	HYPODERMIC
MISOGYNIST	PHOTOPAINT	REPARATIVE	STARVELING	VEGETARIAN	CURRICULUM	ISOTHERMAL
MONARCHIST	PIANISSIMO	REPERTOIRE	STATISTICS	VEGETATION	DEMOISELLE	JACKHAMMER
MONOTHEISM	PINCUSHION	REPETITION	STENTORIAN	VEGETATIVE	DIFFICULTY	JOURNEYMAN
MORATORIUM	PLAGIARIZE	REPETITIVE	STIGMATIZE	VESPERTINE	DILLYDALLY	MIDSHIPMAN
MULTIPLIER	PLANTATION	REPUTATION	STRYCHNINE	VINDICTIVE	DISHABILLE	MISSILEMAN
NARCISSISM	PLAYACTING	RESOLUTION	SUBJECTIVE	VIRTUOSITY	DISSIMILAR	NURSERYMAN
NASTURTIUM	PLEBISCITE	RESORPTION	SUBROUTINE	VISIBILITY	ERYSIPELAS	OFTENTIMES
NATATORIUM	POLITICIAN	RESOUNDING	SUBSTATION	VISITATION	ESPADRILLE	OPHTHALMIC
NATIONWIDE	POLYNESIAN	RESPECTING	SUBVENTION	VOICEPRINT	EURODOLLAR	PATRONYMIC
NATURALISM	POLYTHEISM	RESPECTIVE	SUCCESSION	WEATHERING	HEMOPHILIA	POULTRYMAN
NATURALIST	POPULATION	RESPONSIVE	SUCCESSIVE	WELLSPRING	HULLABALOO	PROGRAMMED
NATURALIZE	POSSESSION	RETRACTILE	SUFFRAGIST	WESTERNIZE	MARGINALIA	PROGRAMMER

SALESWOMAN	EXPECTANCY	RESILIENCE	CHLOROFORM	GROUNDWORK	MUSICOLOGY	SCHOOLROOM
SEPTICEMIA	EXPEDIENCE	RESILIENCY	CHROMOSOME	GYNECOLOGY	NANOSECOND	SCURRILOUS
SERVICEMAN	EXPEDIENCY	RESISTANCE	CHRONOLOGY	HAMMERLOCK	NEEDLEWORK	SEISMOLOGY
WEATHERMAN	EXPERIENCE	RESTRAINED	CHURCHGOER	HARMONIOUS	NETHERMOST	SELENOLOGY
WINDJAMMER	FLUIDOUNCE	RESURGENCE	CINQUEFOIL	HEADSTRONG	NETTLESOME	SIDESTROKE
WORKINGMAN	FORERUNNER	ROADRUNNER	CIRCUITOUS	HEATSTROKE	NINCOMPOOP	SISTERHOOD
ABORIGINAL	GEOSCIENCE	SACROSANCT	CLAVICHORD	HELIOTROPE	NONSUPPORT	SLUMBEROUS
ABSTINENCE	GINGERSNAP	SENESCENCE	CLERESTORY	HEMATOLOGY	NUMEROLOGY	SOLICITOUS
ACCEPTANCE	HISTRIONIC	STRINGENCY	CLINGSTONE	HEMORRHOID	OBSEQUIOUS	SPIRITUOUS
ACCORDANCE	HOOTENANNY	SUBLIMINAL	COLLARBONE	HERETOFORE	OCEANFRONT	SPLASHDOWN
ADDITIONAL	IMPATIENCE	SUFFERANCE	COMMODIOUS	HIPPODROME	OCEANOLOGY	SPOILSPORT
ADMITTANCE	IMPERSONAL	SUPERSONIC	COMPULSORY	HOMOLOGOUS	OLEAGINOUS	STRONGHOLD
ALLEGIANCE	IMPORTANCE	SUSTENANCE	CONSISTORY	HORRENDOUS	OMNIVOROUS	STUPENDOUS
ANTIPHONAL	INCUMBENCY	TEMPERANCE	CONTAGIOUS	HYDROPHONE	OUTPERFORM	SUSPENSORY
APPEARANCE	INDISTINCT	THREEPENCE	CONTIGUOUS	IGNORAMOUS	OUTRAGEOUS	SUSPICIOUS
ASCENDANCY	INDUCTANCE	TURBULENCE	CONTINUOUS	IMMUNOLOGY	PALINDROME	TABLECLOTH
ATTENDANCE	INDULGENCE	ULTRASONIC	CORRESPOND	IMPERVIOUS	PANTALOONS	TABLESPOON
BELLADONNA	INFRASONIC	UNDERPANTS	COTTONWOOD	INDECOROUS	PARATROOPS	TECHNOLOGY
BELONGINGS	INSISTENCE	UNREASONED	CRADLESONG	INDIGENOUS	PEPPERCORN	TENDERFOOT
BLANCMANGE	INTERLUNAR	ABSTEMIOUS	CRETACEOUS	INGLORIOUS	PEREMPTORY	TENDERLOIN
BLUEBONNET	IRRATIONAL	ALBUMINOUS	CRISSCROSS	INITIATORY	PERMAFROST	TENEBRIOUS
CATCHPENNY	MISALIGNED	ALLHALLOWS	CURVACEOUS	INTERBLOCK	PERNICIOUS	THREESCORE
CHIROMANCY	MOLYBDENUM	ALONGSHORE	DEMONOLOGY	KNIGHTHOOD	PHLEBOTOMY	THROUGHOUT
COGNIZANCE	MONOPHONIC	AMBULATORY	DENDROLOGY	LABORATORY	PHRENOLOGY	THUNDEROUS
COMEDIENNE	MONSTRANCE	AMPHIBIOUS	DEPILATORY	LACHRYMOSE	PHYSIOLOGY	TOUCHSTONE
COMPETENCE	MULTISENSE	ANGLOPHOBE	DEPOSITORY	LASCIVIOUS	PICOSECOND	TOXICOLOGY
COMPETENCY	NAPOLEONIC	ANTHROPOID	DEROGATORY	LIBIDINOUS	PIGEONHOLE	TRAJECTORY
COMPLIANCE	NECROMANCY	AURIFEROUS	DIAPHANOUS	LICENTIOUS	POCKETBOOK	TRANSITORY
COMPLIANCY	OBSERVANCE	AUSPICIOUS	DISAPPROVE	LIGHTPROOF	PORTENTOUS	TREMENDOUS
CONFERENCE	OCCASIONAL	AUTONOMOUS	DISCOMFORT	LIKELIHOOD	POSTHUMOUS	TROUBADOUR
CONFIDENCE	OCCURRENCE	BACKSTROKE	DISCOMMODE	LIVELIHOOD	PRECARIOUS	TUMBLEDOWN
CONFLUENCE	OUTBALANCE	BIRTHSTONE	DISCOMPOSE	LOQUACIOUS	PRECOCIOUS	TUMULTUOUS
CONGRUENCE	PESTILENCE	BITUMINOUS	DISHARMONY	LUBRICIOUS	PREDACEOUS	TURTLEDOVE
CONGRUENCY	PHENOMENON	BLACKAMOOR	DONNYBROOK	LUGUBRIOUS	PREDISPOSE	UBIQUITOUS
CONSCIENCE	PHOTOGENIC	BLACKTHORN	DOWNSTROKE	MACKINTOSH	PRESUPPOSE	ULTRASHORT
CONSONANCE	PICKANINNY	BLOODSTONE	EMBRYOLOGY	MAIDENHOOD	PRODIGIOUS	UNDERCROFT
CONTINENCE	POLYCLINIC	BOISTEROUS	ENDOGENOUS	MALODOROUS	PROMISSORY	UNDERSCORE
CONVEYANCE	POWERLINES	BRAINSTORM	ENTOMOLOGY	MANDRAGORA	PROMONTORY	UNDERSHOOT
CORDWAINER	PREARRANGE	BREAKFRONT	EUPHONIOUS	MANTLEROCK	PROMPTBOOK	UNDERSTOOD
CORPULENCE	PRECEDENCE	BREASTBONE	EXOBIOLOGY	MARROWBONE	PROPITIOUS	UNDERSTORY
COTERMINAL	PREFERENCE	BREASTWORK	EXTRANEOUS	MASTERWORK	PROSPEROUS	UNGENEROUS
CROSSBONES	PRESCIENCE	BRIDEGROOM	FACTITIOUS	MEDDLESOME	PSEUDOCODE	UNGRACIOUS
DEPENDENCE	PROMINENCE	BRIDGEWORK	FALLACIOUS	MELANCHOLY	PSYCHOLOGY	UNHANDSOME
DEPENDENCY	PROPAGANDA	BROADCLOTH	FASTIDIOUS	MENDACIOUS	PUGNACIOUS	UPROARIOUS
DETERMINED	PROVENANCE	BROADSWORD	FELICITOUS	METICULOUS	QUATREFOIL	VIBRAPHONE
DETERRENCE	PROVIDENCE	BROWNSTONE	FICTITIOUS	METTLESOME	RADARSCOPE	VICTORIOUS
DIFFERENCE	PUBESCENCE	BUTTONHOLE	FLAGITIOUS	MICROPHONE	RADIOPHONE	VIDEOPHONE
DILETTANTE	RADIOGENIC	BUTTONHOOK	FORTUITOUS	MICROPROBE	REBELLIOUS	VILLAINOUS
DIMINUENDO	RADIOSONDE	CACCIATORE	GASTRONOMY	MICROSCOPE	REFRACTORY	VIVIPAROUS
DIPSOMANIA	RECOMPENSE	CADAVEROUS	GENTLEFOLK	MINERALOGY	RENDEZVOUS	VOCIFEROUS
DISARRANGE	REDUNDANCY	CALCAREOUS	GLACIOLOGY	MINESTRONE	REPOSITORY	VOLUMINOUS
DISSONANCE	REFULGENCE	CANKERWORM	GORGONZOLA	MINISCROLL	RHINESTONE	VOLUPTUOUS
EFFICIENCY	RELATIONAL	CAOUTCHOUC	GRAMOPHONE	MONOCHROME	RIDICULOUS	WATERFRONT
EFFULGENCE	RELUCTANCE	CARDIOLOGY	GRATUITOUS	MONOTONOUS	ROUNDABOUT	WATERPROOF
ELECTRONIC	REMITTANCE	CENSORIOUS	GRAVESTONE	MORPHOLOGY	ROUSTABOUT	WATERSPOUT
EXCELLENCE	RENASCENCE	CHALCEDONY	GREGARIOUS	MOTHERHOOD	SALUBRIOUS	WICKERWORK
EXCELLENCY	REPUGNANCE	CHIVALROUS	GRINDSTONE	MULTISTORY	SANDALWOOD	APOCALYPSE

APOSTROPHE	GOOSEBERRY	ANTITHESIS	CELEBRATED	MIGNONETTE	TYPEWRITER	PERCEPTUAL
BOOKKEEPER	HANDBARROW	APOTHEOSIS	CELLARETTE	MILLILITER	UNAFFECTED	PILOTHOUSE
CLODHOPPER	HEARTTHROB	BIPARTISAN	CENTILITER	MILLIMETER	UNDERWATER	PLAYGROUND
CLOTHESPIN	HENCEFORTH	COMPARISON	CENTIMETER	MONUMENTAL	UNEXPECTED	POWERHOUSE
CORNUCOPIA	HOBBYHORSE	CONVALESCE	CHARLESTON	MYRIAMETER	URETHRITIS	PROSTITUTE
DEMOGRAPHY	HOUSEWARES	COUNTERSPY	COMMUTATOR	NEWSLETTER	UROGENITAL	ROUGHHOUSE
DOORKEEPER	HYPERBARIC	DELIQUESCE	COMPETITOR	NEWSWORTHY	WINCHESTER	ROUNDHOUSE
EYEDROPPER	IMPRESARIO	DISSATISFY	COMPLECTED	NONSTARTER	WOODCUTTER	SIMILITUDE
GAMEKEEPER	INTERFERON	EFFERVESCE	COMPOSITOR	NOTEWORTHY	WRISTWATCH	SOLICITUDE
GATEKEEPER	INTERMARRY	EFFLORESCE	CONGENITAL	OCCIDENTAL	YARDMASTER	SOMERSAULT
GOALKEEPER	INTRAMURAL	EUTHANASIA	CONSPECTUS	ORGANGUTAN	ANIMALCULE	SPELLBOUND
HOLOGRAPHY	KETTLEDRUM	FRANCHISEE	CONVOLUTED	OSTEOPATHY	ANTEPENULT	STATEHOUSE
JACKANAPES	KNOCKWURST	FRANCHISER	COPYWRITER	OVERMASTER	BACKGROUND	STOREHOUSE
LEAFHOPPER	LIVERWURST	FRANCHISOR	CYCLOMETER	OVERWINTER	BLOCKHOUSE	SUBSTITUTE
MALAPROPOS	LOGANBERRY	HYDROLYSIS	DEATHWATCH	PEASHOOTER	BLOODHOUND	SUBTERFUGE
METACARPUS	MANDELBROT	HYPOTHESIS	DEMOCRATIC	PENTAMETER	BREADFRUIT	TANTAMOUNT
PARTICIPLE	METALLURGY	INDISPOSED	DERMATITIS	PETROLATUM	BREADSTUFF	TOOTHBRUSH
PHILOSOPHY	MIDDLEBROW	JINRIKISHA	DESTRUCTOR	PHLEGMATIC	CANTALOUPE	TOURNIQUET
PRESBYOPIA	NEIGHBORLY	LEDERHOSEN	DISGRUNTLE	PHOTOMETER	CARICATURE	ULTRASOUND
SHOPKEEPER	OCTOTHORPE	METASTASIS	DISHEARTEN	PLEASANTRY	CENTRIFUGE	UNDERBRUSH
SKYSCRAPER	OTHERWORLD	METATARSAL	DISJOINTED	POINSETTIA	CHARTREUSE	UNDERSLUNG
TELEGRAPHY	OUTGENERAL	METATARSUS	DUMBWAITER	POSTMASTER	COLORATURA	UNDERSTUDY
TELESCOPIC	OVERCHARGE	NEOCLASSIC	DUPLICATOR	POSTMORTEM	CONJECTURE	WANDERLUST
THROUGHPUT	PALLBEARER	PROSTHESIS	EPIGLOTTIS	POSTPARTUM	CONSTITUTE	WHEELHOUSE
TIMEKEEPER	PANJANDRUM	QUICKBASIC	EUCALYPTUS	PREMARITAL	CONTRIBUTE	WRAPAROUND
TOPOGRAPHY	PERIPHERAL	RICKETTSIA	FARSIGHTED	PROCURATOR	COURTHOUSE	CANTILEVER
TYPOGRAPHY	PHOSPHORUS	SUNGLASSES	FILIBUSTER	PROGENITOR	CUMMERBUND	CHANGEOVER
WASTEPAPER	PHOTOMURAL	THROMBOSIS	FLOODWATER	PROGNOSTIC	DISTRIBUTE	MULTILEVEL
XEROGRAPHY	PIANOFORTE	TOOTHPASTE	FORECASTLE	PROPRIETOR	EMBOUCHURE	RIBOFLAVIN
CATAFALQUE	POLYHEDRON	URINALYSIS	FREEBOOTER	PROPRINTER	EXACTITUDE	THEMSELVES
COMMUNIQUE	RACECOURSE	ACCIDENTAL	FRESHWATER	PROSPECTUS	FAIRGROUND	UNBELIEVER
PICARESQUE	RATTLETRAP	ACHROMATIC	FUTURISTIC	PROTRACTOR	FOREGROUND	UNDERCOVER
STATUESQUE	RHINOCEROS	ADMINISTER	GINGIVITIS	PSYCHIATRY	FORFEITURE	UNRESERVED
ADVENTURER	ROTISSERIE	ALPHABETIC	GOLDBEATER	RADIOMETER	GARGANTUAN	WHATSOEVER
AFTERBIRTH	SEISMOGRAM	ALTERNATOR	GRAVIMETER	RESPIRATOR	GRAPEFRUIT	WHENSOEVER
ASYMMETRIC	SEPULCHRAL	ANEMOMETER	HEADMASTER	RINGMASTER	GREENHOUSE	WHOMSOEVER
BENCHMARKS	SINGLETREE	ANESTHETIC	HEADWAITER	SACERDOTAL	GUARDHOUSE	CORNFLOWER
BLACKBERRY	SOPHOMORIC	ANTIBIOTIC	HECTOLITER	SCHISMATIC	HEREABOUTS	DISEMBOWEL
CARDIOGRAM	STILLBIRTH	ANTIMATTER	HECTOMETER	SCHOLASTIC	HOMOSEXUAL	EXPRESSWAY
CHILDBIRTH	STRAWBERRY	ANTIPROTON	HELICOPTER	SERVOMOTOR	HORSELAUGH	HORSEPOWER
CLOUDBURST	SUPERCARGO	ANTIQUATED	HEPTAMETER	SHIPFITTER	HYPOTENUSE	PASSAGEWAY
COLLATERAL	THUMBSCREW	ANTISEPTIC	HOMEOPATHY	SILHOUETTE	INAPTITUDE	THROUGHWAY
COMPUSERVE	TRANSVERSE	APOLOGETIC	HORIZONTAL	SIMPLISTIC	INDIVIDUAL	UNHALLOWED
CONCENTRIC	UNDERWORLD	APPLICATOR	HYDROMETER	STEPSISTER	INFINITUDE	WALLFLOWER
CORNSTARCH	UNICAMERAL	ARBITRATOR	HYGROMETER	STOCHASTIC	INQUIETUDE	WATCHTOWER
CRYPTOGRAM	UNILATERAL	ARBORVITAE	HYPOCENTER	STRAIGHTEN	IRRESOLUTE	WATERPOWER
DIELECTRIC	UNLETTERED	ARITHMETIC	IMPRIMATUR	SUBORBITAL	JUDICATURE	WINDFLOWER
DIPHTHERIA	UNMANNERLY	BENEFACTOR	INCIDENTAL	SUBSTRATUM	KIESELGUHR	WINEGROWER
DISINHERIT	UNNUMBERED	BIPARENTAL	INSTRUCTOR	TACHOMETER	LIGHTHOUSE	WITHDRAWAL
DISORDERLY	VOLUMETRIC	BIPARIETAL	LACKLUSTER	TASKMASTER	LITERATURE	UNDERSEXED
DREAMWORLD	WATERBORNE	BLUEBOTTLE	LARYNGITIS	TERMINATOR	MANSUETUDE	BRICKLAYER
EGOCENTRIC	WATERWORKS	BREAKWATER	MAISONETTE	TETRAMETER	MISCONDUCT	PENNYROYAL
ELDERBERRY	WHEELHORSE	BRONCHITIS	MALADAPTED	THEREAFTER	MISFORTUNE	SAPROPHYTE
ENDANGERED	WIREHAIRED	BUSHMASTER	MALEFACTOR	THERMISTOR	MOONSTRUCK	SOOTHSAYER
ERGOSTEROL	AFTERTASTE	CALCULATED	MARIONETTE	THERMOSTAT	MOTORTRUCK	STEREOTYPE
EXTRAMURAL	AMANUENSIS	CARBOLATED	MENINGITIS	TRANSISTOR	NEWSGROUPS	UNEMPLOYED
GEOCENTRIC	ANESTHESIA	CARBURETOR	MICROMETER	TYPESETTER	PAINTBRUSH	CHIMPANZEE

FERTILIZER	EQUESTRIAN	PASSAGEWAY	ABSTINENCE	EFFERVESCE	QUADRATICS	VELOCIPEDE
INTERMEZZO	ERYSIPELAS	PEDESTRIAN	ACCEPTANCE	EFFICIENCY	REDISTRICT	WINTERTIDE
UNDERSIZED	EURODOLLAR	PENNYROYAL	ACCOMPLICE	EFFLORESCE	REDUNDANCY	ACCUSTOMED
	EXPRESSMAN	PERCEPTUAL	ACCORDANCE	EFFULGENCE	REFULGENCE	ADMINISTER
	EXPRESSWAY	PERIODICAL	ACROBATICS	EPISCOPACY	REGENERACY	ADVENTURER
	EXTRAMURAL	PERIPHERAL	ADMITTANCE	ERGONOMICS	RELUCTANCE	ALTOGETHER
9TH LETTER	FIGUREHEAD	PHOTOMURAL	AEROBATICS	EXCELLENCE	REMITTANCE	ANEMOMETER
	GARGANTUAN	POLITICIAN	AESTHETICS	EXCELLENCY	RENASCENCE	ANTICANCER
ABORIGINAL	GEOTHERMAL	POLYNESIAN	ALLEGIANCE	EXPECTANCY	REPUGNANCE	ANTIMATTER
ACCIDENTAL	GINGERSNAP	POULTRYMAN	ALTARPIECE	EXPEDIENCE	RESILIENCE	ANTIQUATED
ADDITIONAL	HALLELUJAH	PREMARITAL	APPEARANCE	EXPEDIENCY	RESILIENCY	AQUALUNGER
AMERINDIAN	HAMMERHEAD	PREMEDICAL	APPRENTICE	EXPERIENCE	RESISTANCE	AUCTIONEER
ANTICLIMAX	HEARTBREAK	PRIMORDIAL	ASCENDANCY	FIELDPIECE	RESURGENCE	BACKHANDED
ANTINOMIAN	HIGHWAYMAN	PROVINCIAL	ATTENDANCE	FLUIDOUNCE	RETROSPECT	BAREHEADED
ANTIPHONAL	HOMOSEXUAL	RATTLETRAP	BALLISTICS	GEOPHYSICS	RUBBERNECK	BEDCLOTHES
ANTISOCIAL	HORIZONTAL	RECIPROCAL	BIOPHYSICS	GEOSCIENCE	SACROSANCT	BEDRAGGLED
APOCRYPHAL	HORSEWOMAN	RELATIONAL	BIRTHPLACE	GERIATRICS	SCAPEGRACE	BELLWETHER
APOLITICAL	HOUSECLEAN	REPUBLICAN	BOTTLENECK	GYMNASTICS	SENESCENCE	BLITZKRIEG
ARBORVITAE	HUSBANDMAN	SACERDOTAL	CANDLEWICK	HAMMERLOCK	SMOKESTACK	BLUEBONNET
ARTIFICIAL	IMMATERIAL	SACROILIAC	CANVASBACK	HYDRAULICS	STAGECOACH	BLUEJACKET
AUSTRALIAN	IMMEMORIAL	SALESWOMAN	CHIROMANCY	IMPATIENCE	STATISTICS	BOMBARDIER
BALBRIGGAN	IMPERSONAL	SALTCELLAR	COCKATRICE	IMPORTANCE	STRINGENCY	BONDHOLDER
BATRACHIAN	INCIDENTAL	SANITARIAN	COGNIZANCE	INCUMBENCY	SUBCOMPACT	BOOKKEEPER
BEAUTICIAN	INDIVIDUAL	SEISMOGRAM	COMPETENCE	INDISTINCT	SUBSURFACE	BOOKSELLER
BENEFICIAL	INDONESIAN	SEPULCHRAL	COMPETENCY	INDUCTANCE	SUFFERANCE	BREAKWATER
BIOMEDICAL	INDUSTRIAL	SERVICEMAN	COMPLIANCE	INDULGENCE	SUSTENANCE	BRICKLAYER
BIPARENTAL	INTERLUNAR	SHENANIGAN	COMPLIANCY	INSISTENCE	SWITCHBACK	BULLHEADED
BIPARIETAL	INTERTIDAL	SLIPSTREAM	CONFERENCE	INTERBLOCK	TEMPERANCE	BUSHMASTER
BIPARTISAN	INTERURBAN	STENTORIAN	CONFIDENCE	INTERSTICE	THREEPENCE	CALCULATED
BLUECOLLAR	INTRAMURAL	SUBLIMINAL	CONFLUENCE	ISOMETRICS	TURBULENCE	CANTILEVER
BRIDGEHEAD	IRRATIONAL	SUBORBITAL	CONGRUENCE	KINEMATICS	TURTLENECK	CARABINEER
BUDGERIGAR	ISOTHERMAL	SWEETBREAD	CONGRUENCY	KNICKKNACK	UNDERTRICK	CARBOLATED
CARDIOGRAM	JOURNEYMAN	TECHNICIAN	CONSCIENCE	LUMBERJACK	WRISTWATCH	CARCINOGEN
CENTENNIAL	LETTERHEAD	THEATRICAL	CONSONANCE	MANTLEROCK	AFICIONADO	CATECHUMEN
CENTESIMAL	LITHUANIAN	THERMOSTAT	CONSPIRACY	MISCONDUCT	AUTOSTRADA	CELEBRATED
CEREMONIAL	LOGGERHEAD	THROUGHWAY	CONTINENCE	MONSTRANCE	BALUSTRADE	CENTILITER
CHIMERICAL	MAIDENHEAD	TORRENTIAL	CONTRADICT	MOONSTRUCK	BICHLORIDE	CENTIMETER
CLOVERLEAF	MAINSTREAM	TRANSPOLAR	CONVALESCE	MOTORTRUCK	CENTIGRADE	CHANDELIER
COLLATERAL	MALTHUSIAN	TUBERCULAR	CONVEYANCE	MOUTHPIECE	DIMINUENDO	CHANGEOVER
COLLOQUIAL	MECHANICAL	TYRANNICAL	CORNSTARCH	NECROMANCY	DISCOMMODE	CHAPFALLEN
COMMERCIAL	MELANESIAN	UNCRITICAL	CORPULENCE	NIGHTSTICK	EXACTITUDE	CHIFFONIER
COMMONWEAL	METATARSAL	UNFAMILIAR	COUNTERACT	NUCLEONICS	FRATRICIDE	CHIMPANZEE
CONGENITAL	MIDSHIPMAN	UNICAMERAL	CROSSPIECE	OBSERVANCE	HEARTHSIDE	CHURCHGOER
COPPERHEAD	MILLSTREAM	UNILATERAL	CRYOGENICS	OBSTETRICS	INAPTITUDE	CIRCUMFLEX
COTERMINAL	MISSILEMAN	UROGENITAL	CYBERSPACE	OCCURRENCE	INFINITUDE	CLASSIFIED
COUNTERMAN	MOHAMMEDAN	VEGETARIAN	DEATHWATCH	OUTBALANCE	INQUIETUDE	CLODHOPPER
COUNTRYMAN	MONUMENTAL	VERNACULAR	DEGENERACY	PEDIATRICS	MANSUETUDE	COMMANDEER
CREDENTIAL	MUHAMMADAN	WEATHERMAN	DELIQUESCE	PESTILENCE	MASQUERADE	COMPLECTED
CRUSTACEAN	NURSERYMAN	WHITSUNDAY	DENTIFRICE	PLUPERFECT	NATIONWIDE	CONTROLLER
CRYPTOGRAM	OCCASIONAL	WIDESPREAD	DEPENDENCE	PLUTOCRACY	NIGHTSHADE	CONVOLUTED
DISSIMILAR	OCCIDENTAL	WINGSPREAD	DEPENDENCY	PRECEDENCE	PROPAGANDA	COPYREADER
DOWNSTREAM	ORATORICAL	WITHDRAWAL	DETERRENCE	PREFERENCE	PSEUDOCODE	COPYWRITER
DUNDERHEAD	ORGANGUTAN	WORKINGMAN	DIFFERENCE	PRESCIENCE	RADIOSONDE	CORDWAINER
DUODECIMAL	OUTGENERAL	YESTERYEAR	DISCONNECT	PROMINENCE	RETROGRADE	CORNFLOWER
ECONOMICAL	OVERSPREAD	ANGLOPHOBE	DISRESPECT	PROVENANCE	SIMILITUDE	COTTONSEED
ECUMENICAL	PACKTHREAD	MICROPROBE	DISSERVICE	PROVIDENCE	SOLICITUDE	COWPUNCHER
ENCYCLICAL	PARTICULAR	TRANSCRIBE	DISSONANCE	PUBESCENCE	UNDERSTUDY	CROSSBONES

CROSSBREED	INTERBREED	RADIOMETER	VICTUALLER	METALLURGY	ANESTHETIC	INFRASONIC
CYCLOMETER	JACKANAPES	RECONSIDER	WALLFLOWER	MINERALOGY	ANTHROPOID	JACKRABBIT
DETERMINED	JACKHAMMER	RESTRAINED	WASTEPAPER	MORPHOLOGY	ANTIBIOTIC	LARYNGITIS
DISEMBOWEL	JAWBREAKER	RINGLEADER	WATCHMAKER	MULTISTAGE	ANTISEPTIC	MAIDENHAIR
DISHEARTEN	JIMSONWEED	RINGMASTER	WATCHTOWER	MUSICOLOGY	ANTITHESIS	MARGINALIA
DISHWASHER	KINGFISHER	ROADRUNNER	WATERPOWER	NUMEROLOGY	APOLOGETIC	MASTERSHIP
DISJOINTED	LACKLUSTER	SALAMANDER	WATERWHEEL	OCEANOLOGY	APOTHEOSIS	MEMBERSHIP
DOCKWORKER	LADYFINGER	SEERSUCKER	WHARFINGER	OVERCHARGE	ARITHMETIC	MENINGITIS
DOGCATCHER	LANDHOLDER	SHAMEFACED	WHATSOEVER	PERCENTAGE	ASYMMETRIC	METASTASIS
DOORKEEPER	LANDLOCKED	SHIPFITTER	WHENSOEVER	PERSIFLAGE	AUTHORSHIP	METROPOLIS
DUMBWAITER	LANDLUBBER	SHOPKEEPER	WHOMSOEVER	PHRENOLOGY	BATTLESHIP	MONOPHONIC
EMULSIFIER	LAWBREAKER	SIDEWINDER	WINCHESTER	PHYSIOLOGY	BEAUJOLAIS	MULTIMEDIA
ENDANGERED	LEAFHOPPER	SINGLETREE	WINDFLOWER	PILGRIMAGE	BIMETALLIC	NAPOLEONIC
EVENHANDED	LEDERHOSEN	SKYSCRAPER	WINDJAMMER	PREARRANGE	BLOODSTAIN	NECROPOLIS
EYEDROPPER	LINEBACKER	SOOTHSAYER	WINEGROWER	PREPACKAGE	BREADFRUIT	NEOCLASSIC
FARFETCHED	MALADAPTED	STEPFATHER	WIREHAIRED	PSYCHOLOGY	BRIDESMAID	OPHTHALMIC
FARSIGHTED	MATCHMAKER	STEPLADDER	WOODCUTTER	SEISMOLOGY	BRONCHITIS	PARAPLEGIA
FERTILIZER	MICROMETER	STEPMOTHER	WOODPECKER	SELENOLOGY	CENSORSHIP	PATRONYMIC
FIBRINOGEN	MILLILITER	STEPSISTER	WORKBASKET	SHILLELAGH	CINQUEFOIL	PENICILLIN
FILIBUSTER	MILLIMETER	STRAIGHTEN	YARDMASTER	SUBTERFUGE	CLOTHESPIN	PENMANSHIP
FLOODWATER	MISALIGNED	STRENGTHEN	BREADSTUFF	SUPERCARGO	CONCENTRIC	PHLEGMATIC
FLYCATCHER	MUDSLINGER	SUNGLASSES	CRANKSHAFT	TECHNOLOGY	CORNUCOPIA	PHOTOGENIC
FOLKSINGER	MULTILEVEL	SWEETBRIER	DECLASSIFY	TEETHRIDGE	COSMOPOLIS	POINSETTIA
FOOTLOCKER	MULTIPLIER	TACHOMETER	DEHUMIDIFY	TOXICOLOGY	COTTONTAIL	POLYCLINIC
FOREFATHER	MYRIAMETER	TASKMASTER	DISQUALIFY	AIRFREIGHT	CYCLOPEDIA	PORTCULLIS
FOREFINGER	NEWFANGLED	TEARJERKER	DISSATISFY	APOSTROPHE	DEALERSHIP	PRESBYOPIA
FOREGATHER	NEWSLETTER	TETRAMETER	FISTICUFFS	BIRTHRIGHT	DEMOCRATIC	PROGNOSTIC
FOREHANDED	NOISEMAKER	THEMSELVES	HANDICRAFT	DEADWEIGHT	DERMATITIS	PROSTHESIS
FORERUNNER	NONDRINKER	THEREAFTER	SPACECRAFT	DEMOGRAPHY	DIELECTRIC	QUATREFOIL
FRANCHISEE	NONSTARTER	THUMBSCREW	STATECRAFT	DISTRAUGHT	DIPHTHERIA	QUICKBASIC
FRANCHISER	NUTCRACKER	TIMEKEEPER	UNDERCROFT	FLASHLIGHT	DIPSOMANIA	RADIOGENIC
FREEBOOTER	OFTENTIMES	TOURNIQUET	WATERCRAFT	FLOODLIGHT	DISINHERIT	RAGAMUFFIN
FRESHWATER	OVERMASTER	TRANSDUCER	WITCHCRAFT	FORTHRIGHT	EGOCENTRIC	READERSHIP
FUSSBUDGET	OVERWINTER	TUMBLEWEED	AFTERIMAGE	HOLOGRAPHY	ELECTRONIC	RIBOFLAVIN
GAMEKEEPER	PAINKILLER	TYPESETTER	ASSEMBLAGE	HOMEOPATHY	EPIGLOTTIS	RICKETTSIA
GATEKEEPER	PALLBEARER	TYPEWRITER	BELONGINGS	JINRIKISHA	EUTHANASIA	ROTISSERIE
GOALKEEPER	PATHFINDER	UNABRIDGED	BLANCMANGE	KIESELGUHR	EXOTHERMIC	SCHISMATIC
GOLDBEATER	PAWNBROKER	UNAFFECTED	CAMOUFLAGE	MICROFICHE	FAHRENHEIT	SCHOLASTIC
GRAVIMETER	PEACEMAKER	UNATTACHED	CARDIOLOGY	MILLWRIGHT	FELLOWSHIP	SEAMANSHIP
GUNSLINGER	PEASHOOTER	UNBALANCED	CENTRIFUGE	NEWSWORTHY	FINGERNAIL	SEPTICEMIA
HANDMAIDEN	PENTAMETER	UNBELIEVER	CHRONOLOGY	NOTEWORTHY	FLOODPLAIN	SIMPLISTIC
HARDHEADED	PHOTOMETER	UNDERCOVER	DEMONOLOGY	OSTEOPATHY	FOREORDAIN	SOPHOMORIC
HEADMASTER	PICKPOCKET	UNDERSEXED	DENDROLOGY	PHILOSOPHY	FUTURISTIC	STOCHASTIC
HEADWAITER	PINFEATHER	UNDERSIZED	DISARRANGE	PLAYWRIGHT	GEOCENTRIC	SUPERSONIC
HECTOLITER	POSTMASTER	UNDERTAKER	DISCOURAGE	PRIZEFIGHT	GESUNDHEIT	TELESCOPIC
HECTOMETER	POSTMORTEM	UNDERWATER	DRAWBRIDGE	SHIPWRIGHT	GINGIVITIS	TENDERLOIN
HELICOPTER	POURPARLER	UNEMPLOYED	EMBRYOLOGY	TELEGRAPHY	GRAPEFRUIT	THROMBOSIS
HEPTAMETER	POWERLINES	UNEXAMPLED	ENTOMOLOGY	TOPOGRAPHY	HEMOGLOBIN	TUBERCULIN
HIGHLANDER	PRINCIPLED	UNEXPECTED	EXOBIOLOGY	TYPOGRAPHY	HEMOPHILIA	ULTRASONIC
HORSEPOWER	PRIVILEGED	UNGROUNDED	FOOTBRIDGE	WAINWRIGHT	HEMORRHOID	URETHRITIS
HOUSEWARES	PROGRAMMED	UNHALLOWED	GLACIOLOGY	WATERTIGHT	HISTRIONIC	URINALYSIS
HYDROMETER	PROGRAMMER	UNLETTERED	GYNECOLOGY	XEROGRAPHY	HYDROLYSIS	VOLUMETRIC
HYGROMETER	PRONOUNCED	UNNUMBERED	HEMATOLOGY	ACHROMATIC	HYPERBARIC	WHEELCHAIR
HYPOCENTER	PROPERTIED	UNOCCUPIED	HEMORRHAGE	ACROPHOBIA	HYPODERMIC	XENOPHOBIA
ICEBREAKER	PROPRINTER	UNREASONED	HODGEPODGE	ALPHABETIC	HYPOTHESIS	BACKSTROKE
INDISCREET	QUADRUPLET	UNRESERVED	HORSELAUGH	AMANUENSIS	IDIOPATHIC	BENCHMARKS
INDISPOSED	QUINTUPLET	UNSCHOOLED	IMMUNOLOGY	ANESTHESIA	IMPRESARIO	CHEESECAKE

DOWNSTROKE	IMAGINABLE	REASONABLE	APPETIZING	DENOUEMENT	INCONSTANT	PICOSECOND
EARTHQUAKE	IMMISCIBLE	RECEIVABLE	AQUAMARINE	DEPARTMENT	INDUCEMENT	PLAYACTING
HEATSTROKE	IMPALPABLE	RECEPTACLE	ASSIGNMENT	DEPORTMENT	INFIGHTING	PLAYGROUND
SIDESTROKE	IMPASSABLE	REMARKABLE	ASSORTMENT	DEPRESSANT	INFREQUENT	PREDESTINE
WATERWORKS	IMPASSIBLE	REMEDIABLE	ASTRINGENT	DESCENDANT	INGREDIENT	PREEMINENT
ABOMINABLE	IMPECCABLE	REPORTEDLY	ATTACHMENT	DETACHMENT	INHABITANT	PREFERMENT
ACCEPTABLE	IMPLACABLE	RESTORABLE	ATTAINMENT	DISAPPOINT	INSENTIENT	PRINCELING
ACCESSIBLE	IMPOSSIBLE	RETRACTILE	ATTRACTANT	DISCERNING	INSTRUMENT	PROCEEDING
ACTIONABLE	IMPROBABLE	ROLLERBALL	BACKGROUND	DISCIPLINE	INTEGUMENT	PROFICIENT
ADMISSIBLE	INCLINABLE	SEASONABLE	BATTLEMENT	DISCONTENT	INTERNMENT	PROPELLANT
ANGLOPHILE	INCREDIBLE	SNOWMOBILE	BEFOREHAND	DISCREPANT	INTERTWINE	PROTESTANT
ANIMALCULE	INCULPABLE	SOMERSAULT	BEHINDHAND	DISCUSSANT	INTOLERANT	PUNISHMENT
ANSWERABLE	INELIGIBLE	STANDSTILL	BELLADONNA	DISENCHANT	INTOXICANT	PUTRESCENT
ANTEPENULT	INEVITABLE	STRONGHOLD	BENEFICENT	DISHARMONY	INVESTMENT	PYRIMIDINE
APPLICABLE	INEXORABLE	TABERNACLE	BETTERMENT	DISINCLINE	IRRELEVANT	QUARANTINE
AUDIOPHILE	INEXPIABLE	TARANTELLA	BIRTHSTONE	DRAWSTRING	KRUGERRAND	RADIOPHONE
AUTOMOBILE	INFALLIBLE	TATTERSALL	BLOODHOUND	EMBANKMENT	LIEUTENANT	RAINMAKING
BASKETBALL	INFLEXIBLE	TATTLETALE	BLOODSTONE	EMBONPOINT	LIFESAVING	REFINEMENT
BESPRINKLE	INIMITABLE	TRIMONTHLY	BORDERLAND	EMPLOYMENT	LIPREADING	REFRINGENT
BLUEBOTTLE	INOPERABLE	TURNBUCKLE	BOTTOMLAND	ENDEARMENT	LOGROLLING	REGISTRANT
BOOKMOBILE	INSATIABLE	UNBEARABLE	BREAKFRONT	ENGAGEMENT	LOVEMAKING	RESOUNDING
BOONDOGGLE	INSENSIBLE	UNBEATABLE	BREASTBONE	ENJAMBMENT	MAINSPRING	RESPECTING
BRAINCHILD	INSOLVABLE	UNDENIABLE	BRIGANTINE	EQUIVALENT	MALCONTENT	RESPONDENT
BUTTERMILK	INTANGIBLE	UNDERBELLY	BROWNSTONE	ESCARPMENT	MALEFICENT	RESTAURANT
BUTTONHOLE	INVALUABLE	UNDERWORLD	CANDESCENT	EVANESCENT	MALEVOLENT	RHINESTONE
CANNONBALL	INVARIABLE	UNFRIENDLY	CANTONMENT	EVERYTHING	MANAGEMENT	ROLLICKING
CANONICALS	INVINCIBLE	UNMANNERLY	CATCHPENNY	EXCITEMENT	MANSERVANT	SACCHARINE
CHARITABLE	INVIOLABLE	UNSCRAMBLE	CELLOPHANE	EXORBITANT	MARASCHINO	SCARLATINA
CHINCHILLA	MARTINGALE	UNSUITABLE	CHALCEDONY	EXPERIMENT	MARROWBONE	SECONDHAND
CITRONELLA	MELANCHOLY	VAUDEVILLE	CHANGELING	FAIRGROUND	MASTERMIND	SEMIDRYING
COMESTIBLE	MENSURABLE	VERMICELLI	CHATELAINE	FATHERLAND	MEDICAMENT	SEPTUAGINT
COMPARABLE	MERCANTILE	VOLLEYBALL	CHECKPOINT	FINGERLING	MICROPHONE	SERPENTINE
COMPATIBLE	MINISCROLL	VULNERABLE	CIRCUMVENT	FLAMBOYANT	MINESTRONE	SETTLEMENT
CORRIGIBLE	MISTAKABLE	WINDOWSILL	CLINGSTONE	FORBIDDING	MINISTRANT	SHOESTRING
CREDITABLE	MOTORCYCLE	WINDSHIELD	COINCIDENT	FOREGROUND	MISCELLANY	SHORTENING
DEGRADABLE	MOZZARELLA	WORTHWHILE	COLLARBONE	FOSTERLING	MISFORTUNE	SHUNPIKING
DELECTABLE	NEGLIGIBLE	CAPOREGIME	COMEDIENNE	FRAUDULENT	MOTHERLAND	SKYWRITING
DEMOISELLE	NEIGHBORLY	CHROMOSOME	COMMANDANT	GOVERNMENT	MOUNTEBANK	SMATTERING
DEPENDABLE	NOTICEABLE	FORTISSIMO	COMPLEMENT	GRAMOPHONE	NANOSECOND	SPELLBOUND
DEPLORABLE	OBSERVABLE	GASTRONOMY	COMPLIMENT	GRANDSTAND	NONCHALANT	SPRINKLING
DESERVEDLY	OSTENSIBLE	HIPPODROME	COMPREHEND	GRAVESTONE	NOURISHING	STANDPOINT
DESPICABLE	OTHERWORLD	MEDDLESOME	CONCERNING	GRINDSTONE	OCEANFRONT	STARVELING
DILLYDALLY	PACKSADDLE	METTLESOME	CONCERTINA	GROUNDLING	OCEANGOING	STEPPARENT
DISGRUNTLE	PARTICIPLE	MONOCHROME	CONCORDANT	GUILLOTINE	OMNIPOTENT	STRYCHNINE
DISHABILLE	PECCADILLO	NETTLESOME	CONCURRENT	HABILIMENT	OMNISCIENT	SUBROUTINE
DISORDERLY	PERCENTILE	PALINDROME	CONDESCEND	HANDSPRING	OPALESCENT	SUBSEQUENT
DISPOSABLE	PERDURABLE	PHLEBOTOMY	CONSEQUENT	HEADSTRONG	OUTPATIENT	SUBTRAHEND
DREAMWORLD	PERISHABLE	PIANISSIMO	CONSTRAINT	HIEROPHANT	OUTPOURING	SUFFICIENT
ESPADRILLE	PERIWINKLE	SPRINGTIME	CONTINGENT	HINTERLAND	PANTALOONS	SUPPLEMENT
EXPLICABLE	PERSONABLE	UNHANDSOME	CONTRABAND	HOMECOMING	PARLIAMENT	SUPPLICANT
FORECASTLE	PICCALILLI	WINTERTIME	CONTRAVENE	HOOTENANNY	PARMIGIANA	TAMBOURINE
FORMIDABLE	PIGEONHOLE	ACCOUNTANT	CONVENIENT	HYDROPHONE	PEPPERMINT	TANTAMOUNT
GENTLEFOLK	PREDICABLE	ACCOUNTING	CONVERSANT	HYDROPLANE	PERCIPIENT	TIMBERLINE
GORGONZOLA	PREHENSILE	ADRENALINE	CORRESPOND	IMPEDIMENT	PETNAPPING	TOUCHSTONE
GRAINFIELD	PROJECTILE	ADULTERANT	CRADLESONG	IMPENITENT	PHILISTINE	TOURMALINE
GRANDCHILD	QUADRANGLE	ADVISEMENT	CUMMERBUND	INBREEDING	PHOTOPAINT	TOURNAMENT
HOSPITABLE	RAMSHACKLE	ANTECEDENT	DELINQUENT	INCOHERENT	PICKANINNY	TRAMPOLINE

TRANSPLANT	CHANCELLOR	EXHAUSTION	PERVERSION	THERMISTOR	CHLOROFORM	MULTISTORY
TRAVERTINE	CHARLESTON	EXPEDITION	PHENOMENON	TRANSISTOR	CHURCHYARD	NEEDLEWORK
TURPENTINE	CHATTERBOX	EXPOSITION	PINCUSHION	TRANSITION	CLAVICHORD	NIGHTSHIRT
ULTRASOUND	COLORATION	EXPRESSION	PLANTATION	TRUNCATION	CLERESTORY	NONSUPPORT
UNASSUMING	COMBUSTION	FEDERATION	POCKETBOOK	UNDERSHOOT	COLORATURA	OUTPERFORM
UNAVAILING	COMMISSION	FIGURATION	POLYHEDRON	UNDERSTOOD	COMMENTARY	PAPERBOARD
UNBECOMING	COMMUTATOR	FORESHADOW	POPULATION	UNDULATION	COMMISSARY	PASTEBOARD
UNBLUSHING	COMPARISON	FOUNDATION	POSSESSION	VEGETATION	COMPULSORY	PEPPERCORN
UNDERLYING	COMPASSION	FRANCHISOR	PRECAUTION	VISITATION	CONJECTURE	PEREMPTORY
UNDERSLUNG	COMPATRIOT	GENERATION	PRECESSION	WATERCOLOR	CONSISTORY	PHYLACTERY
UNDERSTAND	COMPETITOR	GRADUATION	PROCESSION	WATERMELON	CONTROVERT	PLEASANTRY
UNPLEASANT	COMPLEXION	HABITATION	PROCURATOR	WATERPROOF	CORDILLERA	PREBENDARY
UNTHINKING	COMPOSITOR	HANDBARROW	PRODUCTION	BATHYSCAPH	DEPILATORY	PRESBYTERY
UNYIELDING	COMPULSION	HEARTTHROB	PROFESSION	CANTALOUPE	DEPOSITORY	PROMISSORY
UPBRINGING	CONCEPTION	HULLABALOO	PROGENITOR	COUNTERSPY	DEROGATORY	PROMONTORY
UPSTANDING	CONCESSION	IMBIBITION	PROMPTBOOK	HELIOGRAPH	DICTIONARY	PSYCHIATRY
VESPERTINE	CONCLUSION	IMPRESSION	PROPORTION	HELIOTROPE	DINNERWARE	REFRACTORY
VIBRAPHONE	CONCRETION	INDECISION	PROPRIETOR	MANUSCRIPT	DISCOMFORT	REPERTOIRE
VICEGERENT	CONCUSSION	INFLECTION	PROPULSION	MICROGRAPH	DISCONCERT	REPOSITORY
VIDEOPHONE	CONFECTION	INFRACTION	PROTECTION	MICROSCOPE	DISPENSARY	SANGUINARY
VOICEPRINT	CONFESSION	INHIBITION	PROTRACTOR	MIMEOGRAPH	DOWNSTAIRS	SCHOOLGIRL
WATERBORNE	CONNECTION	INJUNCTION	RECITATION	NEWSGROUPS	EFFRONTERY	SCHOOLMARM
WATERFRONT	CONNIPTION	INNOVATION	RECREATION	OCTOTHORPE	ELDERBERRY	SEARCHWARE
WEATHERING	CONTENTION	INSOLATION	REDEMPTION	PARATROOPS	ELEMENTARY	SILVERWARE
WELLSPRING	CONVECTION	INSTRUCTOR	REFRACTION	PHONOGRAPH	EMBOUCHURE	SKATEBOARD
WINDOWPANE	CONVENTION	INTERFERON	REGRESSION	PHOTOGRAPH	EMBROIDERY	SPOILSPORT
WONDERLAND	CONVERSION	INTINCTION	REGULATION	POSTSCRIPT	ENAMELWARE	STATIONARY
WONDERMENT	CONVICTION	INTONATION	RELAXATION	RADARSCOPE	ESCRITOIRE	STATIONERY
WRAPAROUND	CONVULSION	INVOCATION	REPARATION	RADIOGRAPH	EVERYWHERE	STRAWBERRY
ABERRATION	CORONATION	INVOLUTION	REPETITION	STEREOTYPE	FIBERBOARD	SUBSIDIARY
ABSCISSION	COTTONWOOD	JUBILATION	REPUTATION	TRANSCRIPT	FLOORBOARD	SUSPENSORY
ABSOLUTION	DATAMATION	KNIGHTHOOD	RESOLUTION	TYPESCRIPT	FORFEITURE	SWEETHEART
ABSORPTION	DECLENSION	LIGHTPROOF	RESORPTION	ABOVEBOARD	FOURSQUARE	THREADBARE
AGGRESSION	DECORATION	LIKELIHOOD	RESPIRATOR	ALIMENTARY	GOOSEBERRY	THREESCORE
ALTERNATOR	DECRYPTION	LIVELIHOOD	REVELATION	ALONGSHORE	GREENSWARD	TOMFOOLERY
AMBASSADOR	DEFINITION	LOCOMOTION	REVOCATION	AMBULATORY	GROUNDWORK	TRAJECTORY
AMMUNITION	DELEGATION	MAIDENHOOD	REVOLUTION	ANGIOSPERM	GYMNOSPERM	TRANSITORY
ANTIPROTON	DEMOLITION	MALAPROPOS	RHINOCEROS	ANIMADVERT	HANDLEBARS	ULTRASHORT
APPARITION	DEPOSITION	MALEFACTOR	SALUTATION	APOTHECARY	HEMISPHERE	UNDERSCORE
APPLICATOR	DEPRESSION	MANDLEBROT	SANDALWOOD	ATMOSPHERE	HEREDITARY	UNDERSHIRT
APPOSITION	DEPUTATION	MATURATION	SANITATION	BACKSTAIRS	HERETOFORE	UNDERSKIRT
ARBITRATOR	DERIVATION	MIDDLEBROW	SCHOOLROOM	BAPTISTERY	HOLLOWWARE	UNDERSTORY
ARCHBISHOP	DESOLATION	MOTHERHOOD	SEPARATION	BLACKBERRY	INCENDIARY	UPHOLSTERY
ARCHDEACON	DESTRUCTOR	NINCOMPOOP	SERVOMOTOR	BLACKBOARD	INITIATORY	VETERINARY
ARMAGEDDON	DISCRETION	OBLIGATION	SISTERHOOD	BLACKGUARD	INTERMARRY	VOCABULARY
ASPIRATION	DISSENSION	OCCUPATION	SNAPDRAGON	BLACKTHORN	IONOSPHERE	VOLUPTUARY
ASSUMPTION	DIVINATION	OPPRESSION	SPOLIATION	BRAINSTORM	JARDINIERE	WHIRLYBIRD
ATTRACTION	DOMINATION	ORDINATION	SUBSTATION	BREADBOARD	JUDICATURE	WICKERWORK
AUTOMATION	DONNYBROOK	OVERSHADOW	SUBVENTION	BREASTWORK	LABORATORY	WILLOWWARE
BACKGAMMON	DUPLICATOR	PAGINATION	SUCCESSION	BRIDGEWORK	LITERATURE	WOODENWARE
BENEFACTOR	EBULLITION	PERCEPTION	SUGGESTION	BROADSWORD	LOGANBERRY	ABSOLUTISM
BLACKAMOOR	EISTEDDFOD	PERCUSSION	SUSPENSION	CACCIATORE	LUMBERYARD	ACCOMPLISH
BRIDEGROOM	ENCRYPTION	PERFECTION	TABLESPOON	CAMELOPARD	MANDRAGORA	ALCOHOLISM
BUTTONHOOK	EQUITATION	PERIHELION	TELEVISION	CANDELABRA	MASTERWORK	ANTAGONISM
CAPITATION	ERGOSTEROL	PERMISSION	TEMPTATION	CANKERWORM	MEADOWLARK	ANTAGONIST
CARBURETOR	ESCUTCHEON	PERORATION	TENDERFOOT	CARICATURE	MESOSPHERE	ANTICHRIST
CAVITATION	ESTIMATION	PERSUASION	TERMINATOR	CHARACTERY	MISSIONARY	APOCALYPSE

BALDERDASH	METABOLISM	SUPERTWIST	CONGREGATE	IMPREGNATE	PROSTITUTE	CENSORIOUS
BELLETRIST	MILITARISM	SURREALISM	CONSECRATE	INACTIVATE	PSYCHOPATH	CEREBELLUM
BLOCKHOUSE	MISOGAMIST	TOOTHBRUSH	CONSTITUTE	INADEQUATE	REACTIVATE	CHIVALROUS
BOLSHEVISM	MISOGYNIST	TRANSGRESS	CONSUMMATE	INAUGURATE	RECUPERATE	CINERARIUM
BRAHMANISM	MIZZENMAST	TRANSVERSE	CONTINUITY	INCAPACITY	REGENERATE	CIRCUITOUS
CAPITALISM	MONARCHIST	UNDERBRUSH	CONTRIBUTE	INCINERATE	REJUVENATE	COLLOQUIUM
CAPITALIST	MONOTHEISM	UNDERWAIST	COORDINATE	INCIVILITY	RELATIVITY	COLPORTEUR
CATABOLISM	MULTISENSE	VIETNAMESE	CRENELLATE	INCOMPLETE	REMUNERATE	COMMODIOUS
CHARTREUSE	NARCISSISM	WANDERLUST	DEACTIVATE	INDEFINITE	REPAGINATE	COMMUNIQUE
CHAUVINISM	NATURALISM	WATERCRESS	DEBILITATE	INDELICATE	REPATRIATE	COMPENDIUM
CHURCHLESS	NATURALIST	WEAPONLESS	DECAPITATE	INEQUALITY	RISIBILITY	CONSORTIUM
CIRCUMCISE	NEGATIVISM	WEIGHTLESS	DECELERATE	INFIDELITY	SAPROPHYTE	CONSPECTUS
CLASSICISM	NETHERMOST	WHEELHORSE	DEFLAGRATE	INFILTRATE	SCHOOLMATE	CONTAGIOUS
CLOUDBURST	NEUTRALISM	WHEELHOUSE	DEGENERATE	INGRATIATE	SHIBBOLETH	CONTIGUOUS
COMPROMISE	NIGHTDRESS	WILDEBEEST	DELIBERATE	INHUMANITY	SILHOUETTE	CONTINUOUS
COURTHOUSE	NUMBERLESS	WILDERNESS	DENOMINATE	INNOMINATE	SIMPLICITY	CRETACEOUS
CRISSCROSS	OUTLANDISH	WITCHGRASS	DEPOPULATE	INORDINATE	SOLIDARITY	CURRICULUM
CUTTLEFISH	PAINTBRUSH	ABBREVIATE	DEPRECIATE	INSEMINATE	SPIROCHETE	CURVACEOUS
DECOMPRESS	PALIMPSEST	ACCELERATE	DESALINATE	INTERFAITH	STALACTITE	DELPHINIUM
DISCOMPOSE	PANTYWAIST	ACCENTUATE	DIFFICULTY	INTERSTATE	STALAGMITE	DIAPHANOUS
DISPOSSESS	PARAPHRASE	ACCUMULATE	DILETTANTE	INTIMIDATE	STILLBIRTH	DYSPROSIUM
EMPIRICISM	PERMAFROST	ADJUDICATE	DISSOCIATE	INTOXICATE	SUBSTITUTE	ENDOGENOUS
ENTERPRISE	PHOTOFLASH	ADULTERATE	DISTILLATE	INTRASTATE	SUPPLICATE	EPITHELIUM
ENTHUSIASM	PILLOWCASE	AFTERBIRTH	DISTRIBUTE	INVALIDATE	TABLECLOTH	EUCALYPTUS
EVANGELISM	PILOTHOUSE	AFTERTASTE	EFFECTUATE	INVETERATE	TESSELLATE	EUPHONIOUS
EVANGELIST	POLYTHEISM	ALLITERATE	EFFEMINATE	INVIGORATE	TOOTHPASTE	EXTRANEOUS
EXTINGUISH	PORTUGUESE	AMALGAMATE	ELECTORATE	IRRESOLUTE	TRIFOLIATE	FACTITIOUS
EYEWITNESS	POWERHOUSE	AMELIORATE	EMANCIPATE	LEGITIMATE	TRIPARTITE	FALLACIOUS
FATHOMLESS	PRAGMATISM	ANNIHILATE	EMASCULATE	LICENTIATE	TRIPLICATE	FASTIDIOUS
FAVORITISM	PREDECEASE	ANNUNCIATE	EPISCOPATE	MAGISTRATE	UNDERNEATH	FELICITOUS
FEDERALISM	PREDISPOSE	ANTHRACITE	EQUANIMITY	MAISONETTE	UNDERPANTS	FICTITIOUS
FEDERALIST	PREPOSSESS	ANTICIPATE	EQUIVOCATE	MANIPULATE	UNDERSTATE	FLAGITIOUS
FIBERGLASS	PRESUPPOSE	APPRECIATE	EVISCERATE	MARGUERITE	UNDERWRITE	FORTUITOUS
GOOSEFLESH	PROTOPLASM	ARTICULATE	EXACERBATE	MARIONETTE	UNIFORMITY	GADOLINIUM
GRADUALISM	RACECOURSE	ASPHYXIATE	EXAGGERATE	METABOLITE	UNIVERSITY	GONOCOCCUS
GREENHOUSE	RECIDIVISM	ASSEVERATE	EXASPERATE	MICROSTATE	VARICOSITY	GRATUITOUS
GROUNDMASS	RECOILLESS	ASSIMILATE	EXCOGITATE	MIGNONETTE	VERTEBRATE	GREGARIOUS
GUARDHOUSE	RECOMPENSE	BESTIALITY	EXHILARATE	NEBULOSITY	VIRTUOSITY	HARMONIOUS
HOBBYHORSE	RELENTLESS	BLACKSMITH	EXPATRIATE	NEUTRALITY	VISIBILITY	HOMOLOGOUS
HORSEFLESH	RELINQUISH	BROADCLOTH	EXURBANITE	NOTABILITY	VITUPERATE	HONORARIUM
HYPOTENUSE	RETROGRESS	CALUMNIATE	FACILITATE	OBLITERATE	VOCIFERATE	HORRENDOUS
ICONOCLASM	RHEUMATISM	CAMPHORATE	FELICITATE	PALATINATE	WAVELENGTH	IGNORAMOUS
ICONOCLAST	ROUGHHOUSE	CAPACITATE	FLAGELLATE	PERPETRATE	ABSTEMIOUS	IMPERVIOUS
IMPOVERISH	ROUNDHOUSE	CAPITULATE	FLUORIDATE	PERPETUATE	ALBUMINOUS	IMPRIMATUR
INTERTWIST	SEAMSTRESS	CELLARETTE	FLUORINATE	PERPETUITY	AMPHIBIOUS	INDECOROUS
JOURNALESE	SECULARISM	CHEAPSKATE	FOOTLIGHTS	PERQUISITE	ANTEBELLUM	INDIGENOUS
JOURNALISM	SEMPSTRESS	CHILDBIRTH	FRATERNITY	PERSONALTY	AUDITORIUM	INGLORIOUS
KNOCKWURST	SENEGALESE	CHLORINATE	GENERALITY	PIANOFORTE	AURIFEROUS	JUGGERNAUT
LACHRYMOSE	SEPARATIST	CHRYSOLITE	GHOSTWRITE	PLEBISCITE	AUSPICIOUS	KETTLEDRUM
LENGTHWISE	SILVERFISH	COMMONALTY	HENCEFORTH	POTENTIATE	AUTONOMOUS	LASCIVIOUS
LIBERALISM	SKEPTICISM	COMPENSATE	HEREABOUTS	PRECIOSITY	BITUMINOUS	LAWRENCIUM
LIGHTHOUSE	SPECIALIST	COMPLICATE	ILLITERATE	PROCLIVITY	BOISTEROUS	LEPRECHAUN
LITERALISM	SPORTSCAST	COMPLICITY	ILLUMINATE	PROFLIGATE	BRONTOSAUR	LIBIDINOUS
LIVERWURST	STATEHOUSE	CONCILIATE	ILLUSTRATE	PROMULGATE	CADAVEROUS	LICENTIOUS
MACKINTOSH	STOREHOUSE	CONDENSATE	IMMACULATE	PROPENSITY	CALCAREOUS	LOQUACIOUS
MANICURIST	STRIPTEASE	CONFISCATE	IMMODERATE	PROPITIATE	CAOUTCHOUC	LUBRICIOUS
MAYONNAISE	SUFFRAGIST	CONFORMITY	IMMORALITY	PROSPERITY	CATAFALQUE	LUGUBRIOUS

MALODOROUS	STATUESQUE	DISCURSIVE	FRATERNIZE	SEPTICEMIA	BEHINDHAND	KNIGHTHOOD
MEERSCHAUM	STUPENDOUS	EXHAUSTIVE	GENERALIZE	TARANTELLA	BLACKBOARD	KRUGERRAND
MEMORANDUM	SUBSTRATUM	FIGURATIVE	GORMANDIZE	XENOPHOBIA	BLACKGUARD	LANDLOCKED
MENDACIOUS	SUSPICIOUS	IMPERATIVE	HOMOGENIZE	HEARTTHROB	BLOODHOUND	LETTERHEAD
METACARPUS	TECHNETIUM	IMPRESSIVE	IMMOBILIZE	ACHROMATIC	BORDERLAND	LIKELIHOOD
METATARSUS	TENEBRIOUS	INDECISIVE	INTERMEZZO	ALPHABETIC	BOTTOMLAND	LIVELIHOOD
METICULOUS	THOUGHTFUL	INDICATIVE	MILITARIZE	ANESTHETIC	BRAINCHILD	LOGGERHEAD
MILLENNIUM	THROUGHOUT	INFINITIVE	MINERALIZE	ANTIBIOTIC	BREADBOARD	LUMBERYARD
MOLYBDENUM	THROUGHPUT	INITIATIVE	NATURALIZE	ANTISEPTIC	BRIDESMAID	MAIDENHEAD
MONOTONOUS	THUNDEROUS	INTERLEAVE	NEUTRALIZE	APOLOGETIC	BRIDGEHEAD	MAIDENHOOD
MORATORIUM	TRAVELOGUE	INTERWEAVE	PALATALIZE	ARITHMETIC	BROADSWORD	MALADAPTED
NASTURTIUM	TREMENDOUS	LOCOMOTIVE	PASTEURIZE	ASYMMETRIC	BULLHEADED	MASTERMIND
NATATORIUM	TROLLEYBUS	NOMINATIVE	PLAGIARIZE	BIMETALLIC	CALCULATED	MISALIGNED
OBSEQUIOUS	TROUBADOUR	PEJORATIVE	PRESSURIZE	CAOUTCHOUC	CAMELOPARD	MOTHERHOOD
OCEANARIUM	TUMULTUOUS	PERCEPTIVE	RADICALIZE	CONCENTRIC	CARBOLATED	MOTHERLAND
OESOPHAGUS	UBIQUITOUS	PERMISSIVE	REVITALIZE	DEMOCRATIC	CELEBRATED	NANOSECOND
OLEAGINOUS	UNDERVALUE	POSSESSIVE	SCRUTINIZE	DIELECTRIC	CHURCHYARD	NEWFANGLED
OMNIVOROUS	UNEVENTFUL	PREEMPTIVE	SECULARIZE	EGOCENTRIC	CLASSIFIED	OTHERWORLD
OPPROBRIUM	UNFAITHFUL	REPARATIVE	SLENDERIZE	ELECTRONIC	CLAVICHORD	OVERSPREAD
OUTRAGEOUS	UNFRUITFUL	REPETITIVE	SPECIALIZE	EXOTHERMIC	COMPLECTED	PACKTHREAD
PANJANDRUM	UNGENEROUS	RESPECTIVE	STIGMATIZE	FUTURISTIC	COMPREHEND	PAPERBOARD
PARAMECIUM	UNGRACEFUL	RESPONSIVE	SYMPATHIZE	GEOCENTRIC	CONDESCEND	PASTEBOARD
PERITONEUM	UNGRACIOUS	SEPARATIVE	WESTERNIZE	HISTRIONIC	CONTRABAND	PICOSECOND
PERNICIOUS	UNGRATEFUL	SUBJECTIVE		HYPERBARIC	CONVOLUTED	PLAYGROUND
PETROLATUM	UNMERCIFUL	SUCCESSIVE		HYPODERMIC	COPPERHEAD	PRINCIPLED
PHOSPHORUS	UNSKILLFUL	SUGGESTIVE		IDIOPATHIC	CORRESPOND	PRIVILEGED
PICARESQUE	UPROARIOUS	TRANSITIVE	**10TH LETTER**	INFRASONIC	COTTONSEED	PROGRAMMED
PORTENTOUS	VICTORIOUS	TURTLEDOVE		MONOPHONIC	COTTONWOOD	PRONOUNCED
POSTHUMOUS	VILLAINOUS	VEGETATIVE	ACROPHOBIA	NAPOLEONIC	CROSSBREED	PROPERTIED
POSTPARTUM	VIVIPAROUS	VINDICTIVE	ANESTHESIA	NEOCLASSIC	CUMMERBUND	RESTRAINED
PRECARIOUS	VOCIFEROUS	ALLHALLOWS	AUTOSTRADA	OPHTHALMIC	DETERMINED	SANDALWOOD
PRECOCIOUS	VOLUMINOUS	SPLASHDOWN	BELLADONNA	PATRONYMIC	DISJOINTED	SECONDHAND
PREDACEOUS	VOLUPTUOUS	TUMBLEDOWN	CANDELABRA	PHLEGMATIC	DREAMWORLD	SHAMEFACED
PRODIGIOUS	WATERSPOUT	METAGALAXY	CHINCHILLA	PHOTOGENIC	DUNDERHEAD	SISTERHOOD
PROMETHIUM	WORSHIPFUL	AGGRANDIZE	CITRONELLA	POLYCLINIC	EISTEDDFOD	SKATEBOARD
PROPITIOUS	ACCUSATIVE	ALKALINIZE	COLORATURA	PROGNOSTIC	ENDANGERED	SPELLBOUND
PROSCENIUM	AFFLICTIVE	ANTAGONIZE	CONCERTINA	QUICKBASIC	EVENHANDED	STRONGHOLD
PROSPECTUS	AGGRESSIVE	ANTIFREEZE	CORDILLERA	RADIOGENIC	FAIRGROUND	SUBTRAHEND
PROSPEROUS	APPOINTIVE	AUTOMATIZE	CORNUCOPIA	SACROILIAC	FARFETCHED	SWEETBREAD
PUGNACIOUS	APPOSITIVE	BASTARDIZE	CYCLOPEDIA	SCHISMATIC	FARSIGHTED	TUMBLEWEED
QUADRIVIUM	ARCHITRAVE	BOWDLERIZE	DIPHTHERIA	SCHOLASTIC	FATHERLAND	ULTRASOUND
REBELLIOUS	AUTOMOTIVE	CAPITALIZE	DIPSOMANIA	SIMPLISTIC	FIBERBOARD	UNABRIDGED
REFERENDUM	COLLECTIVE	CATEGORIZE	EUTHANASIA	SOPHOMORIC	FIGUREHEAD	UNAFFECTED
RENDEZVOUS	COMPULSIVE	CENTRALIZE	GORGONZOLA	STOCHASTIC	FLOORBOARD	UNATTACHED
RIDICULOUS	COMPUSERVE	CHANNELIZE	HEMOPHILIA	SUPERSONIC	FOREGROUND	UNBALANCED
ROUNDABOUT	CONCESSIVE	DECIMALIZE	JINRIKISHA	TELESCOPIC	FOREHANDED	UNDERSEXED
ROUSTABOUT	CONDUCTIVE	DECOLORIZE	MANDRAGORA	ULTRASONIC	GRAINFIELD	UNDERSIZED
SALUBRIOUS	CONNECTIVE	DEHUMANIZE	MARGINALIA	VOLUMETRIC	GRANDCHILD	UNDERSTAND
SANATORIUM	CUMULATIVE	DEMOBILIZE	MOZZARELLA	ABOVEBOARD	GRANDSTAND	UNDERSTOOD
SANITARIUM	DECORATIVE	DEMONETIZE	MULTIMEDIA	ACCUSTOMED	GREENSWARD	UNDERWORLD
SAUERKRAUT	DEFINITIVE	DEMORALIZE	PARAPLEGIA	ANTHROPOID	HAMMERHEAD	UNEMPLOYED
SCURRILOUS	DENOTATIVE	DEPOLARIZE	PARMIGIANA	ANTIQUATED	HARDHEADED	UNEXAMPLED
SHUTTERBUG	DEPRESSIVE	DESALINIZE	POINSETTIA	BACKGROUND	HEMORRHOID	UNEXPECTED
SLUMBEROUS	DERIVATIVE	DEVITALIZE	PRESBYOPIA	BACKHANDED	HINTERLAND	UNGROUNDED
SOLICITOUS	DIMINUTIVE	EVANGELIZE	PROPAGANDA	BAREHEADED	INDISPOSED	UNHALLOWED
SPIRITUOUS	DISAPPROVE	FAMILARIZE	RICKETTSIA	BEDRAGGLED	INTERBREED	UNLETTERED
SPITTLEBUG	DISBELIEVE	FEDERALIZE	SCARLATINA	BEFOREHAND	JIMSONWEED	UNNUMBERED

UNOCCUPIED	APPRECIATE	CHIMPANZEE	DECIMALIZE	EFFERVESCE	HEARTHSIDE	INFINITUDE
UNREASONED	APPRENTICE	CHLORINATE	DECOLORIZE	EFFLORESCE	HEATSTROKE	INFLEXIBLE
UNRESERVED	AQUAMARINE	CHROMOSOME	DECORATIVE	EFFULGENCE	HELIOTROPE	INGRATIATE
UNSCHOOLED	ARBORVITAE	CHRYSOLITE	DEFINITIVE	ELECTORATE	HEMISPHERE	INIMITABLE
WHIRLYBIRD	ARCHITRAVE	CIRCUMCISE	DEFLAGRATE	EMANCIPATE	HEMORRHAGE	INITIATIVE
WIDESPREAD	ARTICULATE	CLINGSTONE	DEGENERATE	EMASCULATE	HERETOFORE	INNOMINATE
WINDSHIELD	ASPHYXIATE	COCKATRICE	DEGRADABLE	EMBOUCHURE	HIPPODROME	INOPERABLE
WINGSPREAD	ASSEMBLAGE	COGNIZANCE	DEHUMANIZE	ENAMELWARE	HOBBYHORSE	INORDINATE
WIREHAIRED	ASSEVERATE	COLLARBONE	DELECTABLE	ENTERPRISE	HODGEPODGE	INQUIETUDE
WONDERLAND	ASSIMILATE	COLLECTIVE	DELIBERATE	EPISCOPATE	HOLLOWWARE	INSATIABLE
WRAPAROUND	ATMOSPHERE	COMEDIENNE	DELIQUESCE	EQUIVOCATE	HOMOGENIZE	INSEMINATE
ABBREVIATE	ATTENDANCE	COMESTIBLE	DEMOBILIZE	ESCRITOIRE	HOSPITABLE	INSENSIBLE
ABOMINABLE	AUDIOPHILE	COMMUNIQUE	DEMOISELLE	ESPADRILLE	HYDROPHONE	INSISTENCE
ABSTINENCE	AUTOMATIZE	COMPARABLE	DEMONETIZE	EVANGELIZE	HYDROPLANE	INSOLVABLE
ACCELERATE	AUTOMOBILE	COMPATIBLE	DEMORALIZE	EVERYWHERE	HYPOTENUSE	INTANGIBLE
ACCENTUATE	AUTOMOTIVE	COMPENSATE	DENOMINATE	EVISCERATE	ILLITERATE	INTERLEAVE
ACCEPTABLE	BACKSTROKE	COMPETENCE	DENOTATIVE	EXACERBATE	ILLUMINATE	INTERSTATE
ACCEPTANCE	BALUSTRADE	COMPLIANCE	DENTIFRICE	EXACTITUDE	ILLUSTRATE	INTERSTICE
ACCESSIBLE	BASTARDIZE	COMPLICATE	DEPENDABLE	EXAGGERATE	IMAGINABLE	INTERTWINE
ACCOMPLICE	BESPRINKLE	COMPROMISE	DEPENDENCE	EXASPERATE	IMMACULATE	INTERWEAVE
ACCORDANCE	BICHLORIDE	COMPULSIVE	DEPLORABLE	EXCELLENCE	IMMISCIBLE	INTIMIDATE
ACCUMULATE	BIRTHPLACE	COMPUSERVE	DEPOLARIZE	EXCOGITATE	IMMOBILIZE	INTOXICATE
ACCUSATIVE	BIRTHSTONE	CONCESSIVE	DEPOPULATE	EXHAUSTIVE	IMMODERATE	INTRASTATE
ACTIONABLE	BLANCMANGE	CONCILIATE	DEPRECIATE	EXHILARATE	IMPALPABLE	INVALIDATE
ADJUDICATE	BLOCKHOUSE	CONDENSATE	DEPRESSIVE	EXPATRIATE	IMPASSABLE	INVALUABLE
ADMISSIBLE	BLOODSTONE	CONDUCTIVE	DERIVATIVE	EXPEDIENCE	IMPASSIBLE	INVARIABLE
ADMITTANCE	BLUEBOTTLE	CONFERENCE	DESALINATE	EXPERIENCE	IMPATIENCE	INVETERATE
ADRENALINE	BOOKMOBILE	CONFIDENCE	DESALINIZE	EXPLICABLE	IMPECCABLE	INVIGORATE
ADULTERATE	BOONDOGGLE	CONFISCATE	DESPICABLE	EXURBANITE	IMPERATIVE	INVINCIBLE
AFFLICTIVE	BOWDLERIZE	CONFLUENCE	DETERRENCE	FACILITATE	IMPLACABLE	INVIOLABLE
AFTERIMAGE	BREASTBONE	CONGREGATE	DEVITALIZE	FAMILARIZE	IMPORTANCE	IONOSPHERE
AFTERTASTE	BRIGANTINE	CONGRUENCE	DIFFERENCE	FEDERALIZE	IMPOSSIBLE	IRRESOLUTE
AGGRANDIZE	BROWNSTONE	CONJECTURE	DILETTANTE	FELICITATE	IMPREGNATE	JARDINIERE
AGGRESSIVE	BUTTONHOLE	CONNECTIVE	DIMINUTIVE	FIELDPIECE	IMPRESSIVE	JOURNALESE
ALKALINIZE	CACCIATORE	CONSCIENCE	DINNERWARE	FIGURATIVE	IMPROBABLE	JUDICATURE
ALLEGIANCE	CALUMNIATE	CONSECRATE	DISAPPROVE	FLAGELLATE	INACTIVATE	LACHRYMOSE
ALLITERATE	CAMOUFLAGE	CONSONANCE	DISARRANGE	FLUIDOUNCE	INADEQUATE	LEGITIMATE
ALONGSHORE	CAMPHORATE	CONSTITUTE	DISBELIEVE	FLUORIDATE	INAPTITUDE	LENGTHWISE
ALTARPIECE	CANTALOUPE	CONSUMMATE	DISCIPLINE	FLUORINATE	INAUGURATE	LICENTIATE
AMALGAMATE	CAPACITATE	CONTINENCE	DISCOMMODE	FOOTBRIDGE	INCINERATE	LIGHTHOUSE
AMELIORATE	CAPITALIZE	CONTRAVENE	DISCOMPOSE	FORECASTLE	INCLINABLE	LITERATURE
ANGLOPHILE	CAPITULATE	CONTRIBUTE	DISCOURAGE	FORFEITURE	INCOMPLETE	LOCOMOTIVE
ANGLOPHOBE	CAPOREGIME	CONVALESCE	DISCURSIVE	FORMIDABLE	INCREDIBLE	MAGISTRATE
ANIMALCULE	CARICATURE	CONVEYANCE	DISGRUNTLE	FOURSQUARE	INCULPABLE	MAISONETTE
ANNIHILATE	CATAFALQUE	COORDINATE	DISHABILLE	FRANCHISEE	INDECISIVE	MANIPULATE
ANNUNCIATE	CATEGORIZE	CORPULENCE	DISINCLINE	FRATERNIZE	INDEFINITE	MANSUETUDE
ANSWERABLE	CELLARETTE	CORRIGIBLE	DISPOSABLE	FRATRICIDE	INDELICATE	MARGUERITE
ANTAGONIZE	CELLOPHANE	COURTHOUSE	DISSERVICE	GENERALIZE	INDICATIVE	MARIONETTE
ANTHRACITE	CENTIGRADE	CREDITABLE	DISSOCIATE	GEOSCIENCE	INDUCTANCE	MARROWBONE
ANTICIPATE	CENTRALIZE	CRENELLATE	DISSONANCE	GHOSTWRITE	INDULGENCE	MARTINGALE
ANTIFREEZE	CENTRIFUGE	CROSSPIECE	DISTILLATE	GORMANDIZE	INELIGIBLE	MASQUERADE
APOCALYPSE	CHANNELIZE	CUMULATIVE	DISTRIBUTE	GRAMOPHONE	INEVITABLE	MAYONNAISE
APOSTROPHE	CHARITABLE	CYBERSPACE	DOWNSTROKE	GRAVESTONE	INEXORABLE	MEDDLESOME
APPEARANCE	CHARTREUSE	DEACTIVATE	DRAWBRIDGE	GREENHOUSE	INEXPIABLE	MENSURABLE
APPLICABLE	CHATELAINE	DEBILITATE	EARTHQUAKE	GRINDSTONE	INFALLIBLE	MERCANTILE
APPOINTIVE	CHEAPSKATE	DECAPITATE	EFFECTUATE	GUARDHOUSE	INFILTRATE	MESOSPHERE
APPOSITIVE	CHEESECAKE	DECELERATE	EFFEMINATE	GUILLOTINE	INFINITIVE	METABOLITE

METTLESOME	PICARESQUE	RENASCENCE	SUCCESSIVE	WHEELHOUSE	UNBECOMING	BUTTONHOOK
MICROFICHE	PIGEONHOLE	REPAGINATE	SUFFERANCE	WILLOWWARE	UNBLUSHING	CANDLEWICK
MICROPHONE	PILGRIMAGE	REPARATIVE	SUGGESTIVE	WINDOWPANE	UNDERLYING	CANVASBACK
MICROPROBE	PILLOWCASE	REPATRIATE	SUPPLICATE	WINTERTIDE	UNDERSLUNG	DONNYBROOK
MICROSCOPE	PILOTHOUSE	REPERTOIRE	SUSTENANCE	WINTERTIME	UNTHINKING	GENTLEFOLK
MICROSTATE	PLAGIARIZE	REPETITIVE	SYMPATHIZE	WOODENWARE	UNYIELDING	GROUNDWORK
MIGNONETTE	PLEBISCITE	REPUGNANCE	TABERNACLE	WORTHWHILE	UPBRINGING	HAMMERLOCK
MILITARIZE	PORTUGUESE	RESILIENCE	TAMBOURINE	BREADSTUFF	UPSTANDING	HEARTBREAK
MINERALIZE	POSSESSIVE	RESISTANCE	TATTLETALE	CLOVERLEAF	WEATHERING	INTERBLOCK
MINESTRONE	POTENTIATE	RESPECTIVE	TEETHRIDGE	LIGHTPROOF	WELLSPRING	KNICKKNACK
MISFORTUNE	POWERHOUSE	RESPONSIVE	TEMPERANCE	WATERPROOF	ACCOMPLISH	LUMBERJACK
MISTAKABLE	PREARRANGE	RESTORABLE	TESSELLATE	ACCOUNTING	AFTERBIRTH	MANTLEROCK
MONOCHROME	PRECEDENCE	RESURGENCE	THREADBARE	APPETIZING	BALDERDASH	MASTERWORK
MONSTRANCE	PREDECEASE	RETRACTILE	THREEPENCE	BLITZKRIEG	BATHYSCAPH	MEADOWLARK
MOTORCYCLE	PREDESTINE	RETROGRADE	THREESCORE	CHANGELING	BLACKSMITH	MOONSTRUCK
MOUTHPIECE	PREDICABLE	REVITALIZE	TIMBERLINE	CONCERNING	BROADCLOTH	MOTORTRUCK
MULTISENSE	PREDISPOSE	RHINESTONE	TOOTHPASTE	CRADLESONG	CHILDBIRTH	MOUNTEBANK
MULTISTAGE	PREEMPTIVE	ROTISSERIE	TOUCHSTONE	DISCERNING	CORNSTARCH	NEEDLEWORK
NATIONWIDE	PREFERENCE	ROUGHHOUSE	TOURMALINE	DRAWSTRING	CUTTLEFISH	NIGHTSTICK
NATURALIZE	PREHENSILE	ROUNDHOUSE	TRAMPOLINE	EVERYTHING	DEATHWATCH	POCKETBOOK
NEGLIGIBLE	PREPACKAGE	SACCHARINE	TRANSCRIBE	FINGERLING	EXTINGUISH	PROMPTBOOK
NETTLESOME	PRESCIENCE	SAPROPHYTE	TRANSITIVE	FORBIDDING	GOOSEFLESH	RUBBERNECK
NEUTRALIZE	PRESSURIZE	SCAPEGRACE	TRANSVERSE	FOSTERLING	HALLELUJAH	SMOKESTACK
NIGHTSHADE	PRESUPPOSE	SCHOOLMATE	TRAVELOGUE	GROUNDLING	HELIOGRAPH	SWITCHBACK
NOMINATIVE	PROFLIGATE	SCRUTINIZE	TRAVERTINE	HANDSPRING	HENCEFORTH	TURTLENECK
NOTICEABLE	PROJECTILE	SEARCHWARE	TRIFOLIATE	HEADSTRONG	HORSEFLESH	UNDERTRICK
OBLITERATE	PROMINENCE	SEASONABLE	TRIPARTITE	HOMECOMING	HORSELAUGH	WICKERWORK
OBSERVABLE	PROMULGATE	SECULARIZE	TRIPLICATE	INBREEDING	IMPOVERISH	ABORIGINAL
OBSERVANCE	PROPITIATE	SENEGALESE	TURBULENCE	INFIGHTING	INTERFAITH	ACCIDENTAL
OCCURRENCE	PROSTITUTE	SENESCENCE	TURNBUCKLE	LIFESAVING	MACKINTOSH	ADDITIONAL
OCTOTHORPE	PROVENANCE	SEPARATIVE	TURPENTINE	LIPREADING	MICROGRAPH	ANTIPHONAL
OSTENSIBLE	PROVIDENCE	SERPENTINE	TURTLEDOVE	LOGROLLING	MIMEOGRAPH	ANTISOCIAL
OUTBALANCE	PSEUDOCODE	SIDESTROKE	UNBEARABLE	LOVEMAKING	OUTLANDISH	APOCRYPHAL
OVERCHARGE	PUBESCENCE	SILHOUETTE	UNBEATABLE	MAINSPRING	PAINTBRUSH	APOLITICAL
PACKSADDLE	PYRIMIDINE	SILVERWARE	UNDENIABLE	NOURISHING	PHONOGRAPH	ARTIFICIAL
PALATALIZE	QUADRANGLE	SIMILITUDE	UNDERSCORE	OCEANGOING	PHOTOFLASH	BASKETBALL
PALATINATE	QUARANTINE	SINGLETREE	UNDERSTATE	OUTPOURING	PHOTOGRAPH	BENEFICIAL
PALINDROME	RACECOURSE	SLENDERIZE	UNDERVALUE	PETNAPPING	PSYCHOPATH	BIOMEDICAL
PARAPHRASE	RADARSCOPE	SNOWMOBILE	UNDERWRITE	PLAYACTING	RADIOGRAPH	BIPARENTAL
PARTICIPLE	RADICALIZE	SOLICITUDE	UNHANDSOME	PRINCELING	RELINQUISH	BIPARIETAL
PASTEURIZE	RADIOPHONE	SPECIALIZE	UNSCRAMBLE	PROCEEDING	SHIBBOLETH	CANNONBALL
PEJORATIVE	RADIOSONDE	SPIROCHETE	UNSUITABLE	RAINMAKING	SHILLELAGH	CENTENNIAL
PERCENTAGE	RAMSHACKLE	SPRINGTIME	VAUDEVILLE	RESOUNDING	SILVERFISH	CENTESIMAL
PERCENTILE	REACTIVATE	STALACTITE	VEGETATIVE	RESPECTING	STAGECOACH	CEREMONIAL
PERCEPTIVE	REASONABLE	STALAGMITE	VELOCIPEDE	ROLLICKING	STILLBIRTH	CHIMERICAL
PERDURABLE	RECEIVABLE	STATEHOUSE	VERTEBRATE	SEMIDRYING	TABLECLOTH	CINQUEFOIL
PERISHABLE	RECEPTACLE	STATUESQUE	VESPERTINE	SHOESTRING	TOOTHBRUSH	COLLATERAL
PERIWINKLE	RECOMPENSE	STEREOTYPE	VIBRAPHONE	SHORTENING	UNDERBRUSH	COLLOQUIAL
PERMISSIVE	RECUPERATE	STIGMATIZE	VIDEOPHONE	SHUNPIKING	UNDERNEATH	COMMERCIAL
PERPETRATE	REFULGENCE	STOREHOUSE	VIETNAMESE	SHUTTERBUG	WAVELENGTH	COMMONWEAL
PERPETUATE	REGENERATE	STRIPTEASE	VINDICTIVE	SKYWRITING	WRISTWATCH	CONGENITAL
PERQUISITE	REJUVENATE	STRYCHNINE	VITUPERATE	SMATTERING	PICCALILLI	COTERMINAL
PERSIFLAGE	RELUCTANCE	SUBJECTIVE	VOCIFERATE	SPITTLEBUG	VERMICELLI	COTTONTAIL
PERSONABLE	REMARKABLE	SUBROUTINE	VULNERABLE	SPRINKLING	BOTTLENECK	CREDENTIAL
PESTILENCE	REMEDIABLE	SUBSTITUTE	WATERBORNE	STARVELING	BREASTWORK	DISEMBOWEL
PHILISTINE	REMITTANCE	SUBSURFACE	WESTERNIZE	UNASSUMING	BRIDGEWORK	DUODECIMAL
PIANOFORTE	REMUNERATE	SUBTERFUGE	WHEELHORSE	UNAVAILING	BUTTERMILK	ECONOMICAL

ECUMENICAL	UNICAMERAL	MILITARISM	AUSTRALIAN	DIVINATION	MUHAMMADAN	SANITATION
ENCYCLICAL	UNILATERAL	MILLENNIUM	AUTOMATION	DOMINATION	NURSERYMAN	SEPARATION
ERGOSTEROL	UNMERCIFUL	MILLSTREAM	BACKGAMMON	EBULLITION	OBLIGATION	SERVICEMAN
EXTRAMURAL	UNSKILLFUL	MOLYBDENUM	BALBRIGGAN	ENCRYPTION	OCCUPATION	SHENANIGAN
FINGERNAIL	UROGENITAL	MONOTHEISM	BATRACHIAN	EQUESTRIAN	OPPRESSION	SNAPDRAGON
GEOTHERMAL	VOLLEYBALL	MORATORIUM	BEAUTICIAN	EQUITATION	ORDINATION	SPLASHDOWN
HOMOSEXUAL	WATERWHEEL	NARCISSISM	BIPARTISAN	ESCUTCHEON	ORGANGUTAN	SPOLIATION
HORIZONTAL	WINDOWSILL	NASTURTIUM	BLACKTHORN	ESTIMATION	PAGINATION	STENTORIAN
IMMATERIAL	WITHDRAWAL	NATATORIUM	BLOODSTAIN	EXHAUSTION	PEDESTRIAN	STRAIGHTEN
IMMEMORIAL	WORSHIPFUL	NATURALISM	CAPITATION	EXPEDITION	PENICILLIN	STRENGTHEN
IMPERSONAL	ABSOLUTISM	NEGATIVISM	CARCINOGEN	EXPOSITION	PEPPERCORN	SUBSTATION
INCIDENTAL	ALCOHOLISM	NEUTRALISM	CATECHUMEN	EXPRESSION	PERCEPTION	SUBVENTION
INDIVIDUAL	ANGIOSPERM	OCEANARIUM	CAVITATION	EXPRESSMAN	PERCUSSION	SUCCESSION
INDUSTRIAL	ANTAGONISM	OPPROBRIUM	CHAPFALLEN	FEDERATION	PERFECTION	SUGGESTION
INTERTIDAL	ANTEBELLUM	OUTPERFORM	CHARLESTON	FIBRINOGEN	PERIHELION	SUSPENSION
INTRAMURAL	AUDITORIUM	PANJANDRUM	CLOTHESPIN	FIGURATION	PERMISSION	TABLESPOON
IRRATIONAL	BOLSHEVISM	PARAMECIUM	COLORATION	FLOODPLAIN	PERORATION	TECHNICIAN
ISOTHERMAL	BRAHMANISM	PERITONEUM	COMBUSTION	FOREORDAIN	PERSUASION	TELEVISION
MECHANICAL	BRAINSTORM	PETROLATUM	COMMISSION	FOUNDATION	PERVERSION	TEMPTATION
METATARSAL	BRIDEGROOM	POLYTHEISM	COMPARISON	GARGANTUAN	PHENOMENON	TENDERLOIN
MINISCROLL	CANKERWORM	POSTMORTEM	COMPASSION	GENERATION	PINCUSHION	TRANSITION
MONUMENTAL	CAPITALISM	POSTPARTUM	COMPLEXION	GRADUATION	PLANTATION	TRUNCATION
MULTILEVEL	CARDIOGRAM	PRAGMATISM	COMPULSION	HABITATION	POLITICIAN	TUBERCULIN
OCCASIONAL	CATABOLISM	PROMETHIUM	CONCEPTION	HANDMAIDEN	POLYHEDRON	TUMBLEDOWN
OCCIDENTAL	CEREBELLUM	PROSCENIUM	CONCESSION	HEMOGLOBIN	POLYNESIAN	UNDULATION
ORATORICAL	CHAUVINISM	PROTOPLASM	CONCLUSION	HIGHWAYMAN	POPULATION	VEGETARIAN
OUTGENERAL	CHLOROFORM	QUADRIVIUM	CONCRETION	HORSEWOMAN	POSSESSION	VEGETATION
PENNYROYAL	CINERARIUM	RECIDIVISM	CONCUSSION	HOUSECLEAN	POULTRYMAN	VISITATION
PERCEPTUAL	CLASSICISM	REFERENDUM	CONFECTION	HUSBANDMAN	PRECAUTION	WATERMELON
PERIODICAL	COLLOQUIUM	RHEUMATISM	CONFESSION	IMBIBITION	PRECESSION	WEATHERMAN
PERIPHERAL	COMPENDIUM	SANATORIUM	CONNECTION	IMPRESSION	PROCESSION	WORKINGMAN
PHOTOMURAL	CONSORTIUM	SANITARIUM	CONNIPTION	INDECISION	PRODUCTION	AFICIONADO
PREMARITAL	CRYPTOGRAM	SCHOOLMARM	CONTENTION	INDONESIAN	PROFESSION	DIMINUENDO
PREMEDICAL	CURRICULUM	SCHOOLROOM	CONVECTION	INFLECTION	PROPORTION	FORTISSIMO
PRIMORDIAL	DELPHINIUM	SECULARISM	CONVENTION	INFRACTION	PROPULSION	HULLABALOO
PROVINCIAL	DOWNSTREAM	SEISMOGRAM	CONVERSION	INHIBITION	PROTECTION	IMPRESARIO
QUATREFOIL	DYSPROSIUM	SKEPTICISM	CONVICTION	INJUNCTION	RAGAMUFFIN	INTERMEZZO
RECIPROCAL	EMPIRICISM	SLIPSTREAM	CONVULSION	INNOVATION	RECITATION	MARASCHINO
RELATIONAL	ENTHUSIASM	SUBSTRATUM	CORONATION	INSOLATION	RECREATION	PECCADILLO
ROLLERBALL	EPITHELIUM	SURREALISM	COUNTERMAN	INTERFERON	REDEMPTION	PIANISSIMO
SACERDOTAL	EVANGELISM	TECHNETIUM	COUNTRYMAN	INTERURBAN	REFRACTION	SUPERCARGO
SCHOOLGIRL	FAVORITISM	ABERRATION	CRUSTACEAN	INTINCTION	REGRESSION	ARCHBISHOP
SEPULCHRAL	FEDERALISM	ABSCISSION	DATAMATION	INTONATION	REGULATION	AUTHORSHIP
STANDSTILL	GADOLINIUM	ABSOLUTION	DECLENSION	INVOCATION	RELAXATION	BATTLESHIP
SUBLIMINAL	GRADUALISM	ABSORPTION	DECORATION	INVOLUTION	REPARATION	CENSORSHIP
SUBORBITAL	GYMNOSPERM	AGGRESSION	DECRYPTION	JOURNEYMAN	REPETITION	DEALERSHIP
TATTERSALL	HONORARIUM	AMERINDIAN	DEFINITION	JUBILATION	REPUBLICAN	FELLOWSHIP
THEATRICAL	ICONOCLASM	AMMUNITION	DELEGATION	LEDERHOSEN	REPUTATION	GINGERSNAP
THOUGHTFUL	JOURNALISM	ANTINOMIAN	DEMOLITION	LEPRECHAUN	RESOLUTION	MASTERSHIP
TORRENTIAL	KETTLEDRUM	ANTIPROTON	DEPOSITION	LITHUANIAN	RESORPTION	MEMBERSHIP
TYRANNICAL	LAWRENCIUM	APPARITION	DEPRESSION	LOCOMOTION	REVELATION	NINCOMPOOP
UNCRITICAL	LIBERALISM	APPOSITION	DEPUTATION	MALTHUSIAN	REVOCATION	PENMANSHIP
UNEVENTFUL	LITERALISM	ARCHDEACON	DERIVATION	MATURATION	REVOLUTION	RATTLETRAP
UNFAITHFUL	MAINSTREAM	ARMAGEDDON	DESOLATION	MELANESIAN	RIBOFLAVIN	READERSHIP
UNFRUITFUL	MEERSCHAUM	ASPIRATION	DISCRETION	MIDSHIPMAN	SALESWOMAN	SEAMANSHIP
UNGRACEFUL	MEMORANDUM	ASSUMPTION	DISHEARTEN	MISSILEMAN	SALUTATION	ADMINISTER
UNGRATEFUL	METABOLISM	ATTRACTION	DISSENSION	MOHAMMEDAN	SANITARIAN	ADVENTURER

ALTERNATOR	FERTILIZER	NONDRINKER	TYPEWRITER	COMMODIOUS	ISOMETRICS	RHINOCEROS
ALTOGETHER	FILIBUSTER	NONSTARTER	UNBELIEVER	CONSPECTUS	JACKANAPES	RIDICULOUS
AMBASSADOR	FLOODWATER	NUTCRACKER	UNDERCOVER	CONTAGIOUS	KINEMATICS	SALUBRIOUS
ANEMOMETER	FLYCATCHER	OVERMASTER	UNDERTAKER	CONTIGUOUS	LARYNGITIS	SCURRILOUS
ANTICANCER	FOLKSINGER	OVERWINTER	UNDERWATER	CONTINUOUS	LASCIVIOUS	SEAMSTRESS
ANTIMATTER	FOOTLOCKER	PAINKILLER	UNFAMILIAR	COSMOPOLIS	LIBIDINOUS	SEMPSTRESS
APPLICATOR	FOREFATHER	PALLBEARER	VERNACULAR	CRETACEOUS	LICENTIOUS	SLUMBEROUS
AQUALUNGER	FOREFINGER	PARTICULAR	VICTUALLER	CRISSCROSS	LOQUACIOUS	SOLICITOUS
ARBITRATOR	FOREGATHER	PATHFINDER	WALLFLOWER	CROSSBONES	LUBRICIOUS	SPIRITUOUS
AUCTIONEER	FORERUNNER	PAWNBROKER	WASTEPAPER	CRYOGENICS	LUGUBRIOUS	STATISTICS
BELLWETHER	FRANCHISER	PEACEMAKER	WATCHMAKER	CURVACEOUS	MALAPROPOS	STUPENDOUS
BENEFACTOR	FRANCHISOR	PEASHOOTER	WATCHTOWER	DECOMPRESS	MALODOROUS	SUNGLASSES
BLACKAMOOR	FREEBOOTER	PENTAMETER	WATERCOLOR	DERMATITIS	MENDACIOUS	SUSPICIOUS
BLUECOLLAR	FRESHWATER	PHOTOMETER	WATERPOWER	DIAPHANOUS	MENINGITIS	TENEBRIOUS
BOMBARDIER	GAMEKEEPER	PINFEATHER	WHARFINGER	DISPOSSESS	METACARPUS	THEMSELVES
BONDHOLDER	GATEKEEPER	POSTMASTER	WHATSOEVER	DOWNSTAIRS	METASTASIS	THROMBOSIS
BOOKKEEPER	GOALKEEPER	POURPARLER	WHEELCHAIR	ENDOGENOUS	METATARSUS	THUNDEROUS
BOOKSELLER	GOLDBEATER	PROCURATOR	WHENSOEVER	EPIGLOTTIS	METICULOUS	TRANSGRESS
BREAKWATER	GRAVIMETER	PROGENITOR	WHOMSOEVER	ERGONOMICS	METROPOLIS	TREMENDOUS
BRICKLAYER	GUNSLINGER	PROGRAMMER	WINCHESTER	ERYSIPELAS	MONOTONOUS	TROLLEYBUS
BRONTOSAUR	HEADMASTER	PROPRIETOR	WINDFLOWER	EUCALYPTUS	NECROPOLIS	TUMULTUOUS
BUDGERIGAR	HEADWAITER	PROPRINTER	WINDJAMMER	EUPHONIOUS	NEWSGROUPS	UBIQUITOUS
BUSHMASTER	HECTOLITER	PROTRACTOR	WINEGROWER	EXTRANEOUS	NIGHTDRESS	UNDERPANTS
CANTILEVER	HECTOMETER	RADIOMETER	WOODCUTTER	EYEWITNESS	NUCLEONICS	UNGENEROUS
CARABINEER	HELICOPTER	RECONSIDER	WOODPECKER	FACTITIOUS	NUMBERLESS	UNGRACIOUS
CARBURETOR	HEPTAMETER	RESPIRATOR	YARDMASTER	FALLACIOUS	OBSEQUIOUS	UPROARIOUS
CENTILITER	HIGHLANDER	RINGLEADER	YESTERYEAR	FASTIDIOUS	OBSTETRICS	URETHRITIS
CENTIMETER	HORSEPOWER	RINGMASTER	ABSTEMIOUS	FATHOMLESS	OESOPHAGUS	URINALYSIS
CHANCELLOR	HYDROMETER	ROADRUNNER	ACROBATICS	FELICITOUS	OFTENTIMES	VICTORIOUS
CHANDELIER	HYGROMETER	SALAMANDER	AEROBATICS	FIBERGLASS	OLEAGINOUS	VILLAINOUS
CHANGEOVER	HYPOCENTER	SALTCELLAR	AESTHETICS	FICTITIOUS	OMNIVOROUS	VIVIPAROUS
CHIFFONIER	ICEBREAKER	SEERSUCKER	ALBUMINOUS	FISTICUFFS	OUTRAGEOUS	VOCIFEROUS
CHURCHGOER	IMPRIMATUR	SERVOMOTOR	ALLHALLOWS	FLAGITIOUS	PANTALOONS	VOLUMINOUS
CLODHOPPER	INSTRUCTOR	SHIPFITTER	AMANUENSIS	FOOTLIGHTS	PARATROOPS	VOLUPTUOUS
COLPORTEUR	INTERLUNAR	SHOPKEEPER	AMPHIBIOUS	FORTUITOUS	PEDIATRICS	WATERCRESS
COMMANDEER	JACKHAMMER	SIDEWINDER	ANTITHESIS	GEOPHYSICS	PERNICIOUS	WATERWORKS
COMMUTATOR	JAWBREAKER	SKYSCRAPER	APOTHEOSIS	GERIATRICS	PHOSPHORUS	WEAPONLESS
COMPETITOR	KIESELGUHR	SOOTHSAYER	AURIFEROUS	GINGIVITIS	PORTCULLIS	WEIGHTLESS
COMPOSITOR	KINGFISHER	STEPFATHER	AUSPICIOUS	GONOCOCCUS	PORTENTOUS	WILDERNESS
CONTROLLER	LACKLUSTER	STEPLADDER	AUTONOMOUS	GRATUITOUS	POSTHUMOUS	WITCHGRASS
COPYREADER	LADYFINGER	STEPMOTHER	BACKSTAIRS	GREGARIOUS	POWERLINES	ACCOUNTANT
COPYWRITER	LANDHOLDER	STEPSISTER	BALLISTICS	GROUNDMASS	PRECARIOUS	ADULTERANT
CORDWAINER	LANDLUBBER	SWEETBRIER	BEAUJOLAIS	GYMNASTICS	PRECOCIOUS	ADVISEMENT
CORNFLOWER	LAWBREAKER	TACHOMETER	BEDCLOTHES	HANDLEBARS	PREDACEOUS	AIRFREIGHT
COWPUNCHER	LEAFHOPPER	TASKMASTER	BELONGINGS	HARMONIOUS	PREPOSSESS	ANIMADVERT
CYCLOMETER	LINEBACKER	TEARJERKER	BENCHMARKS	HEREABOUTS	PRODIGIOUS	ANTAGONIST
DESTRUCTOR	MAIDENHAIR	TERMINATOR	BIOPHYSICS	HOMOLOGOUS	PROPITIOUS	ANTECEDENT
DISHWASHER	MALEFACTOR	TETRAMETER	BITUMINOUS	HORRENDOUS	PROSPECTUS	ANTEPENULT
DISSIMILAR	MATCHMAKER	THEREAFTER	BOISTEROUS	HOUSEWARES	PROSPEROUS	ANTICHRIST
DOCKWORKER	MICROMETER	THERMISTOR	BRONCHITIS	HYDRAULICS	PROSTHESIS	ASSIGNMENT
DOGCATCHER	MILLILITER	TIMEKEEPER	CADAVEROUS	HYDROLYSIS	PUGNACIOUS	ASSORTMENT
DOORKEEPER	MILLIMETER	TRANSDUCER	CALCAREOUS	HYPOTHESIS	QUADRATICS	ASTRINGENT
DUMBWAITER	MUDSLINGER	TRANSISTOR	CANONICALS	IGNORAMUS	REBELLIOUS	ATTACHMENT
DUPLICATOR	MULTIPLIER	TRANSPOLAR	CENSORIOUS	IMPERVIOUS	RECOILLESS	ATTAINMENT
EMULSIFIER	MYRIAMETER	TROUBADOUR	CHIVALROUS	INDECOROUS	RELENTLESS	ATTRACTANT
EURODOLLAR	NEWSLETTER	TUBERCULAR	CHURCHLESS	INDIGENOUS	RENDEZVOUS	BATTLEMENT
EYEDROPPER	NOISEMAKER	TYPESETTER	CIRCUITOUS	INGLORIOUS	RETROGRESS	BELLETRIST

BENEFICENT	EVANGELIST	MIZZENMAST	SUBCOMPACT	CHRONOLOGY	HOMEOPATHY	REFRACTORY
BETTERMENT	EXCITEMENT	MONARCHIST	SUBSEQUENT	CLERESTORY	HOOTENANNY	REGENERACY
BIRTHRIGHT	EXORBITANT	MUNIFICENT	SUFFICIENT	COMMENTARY	IMMORALITY	RELATIVITY
BLUEBONNET	EXPERIMENT	NATURALIST	SUFFRAGIST	COMMISSARY	IMMUNOLOGY	REPORTEDLY
BLUEJACKET	FAHRENHEIT	NETHERMOST	SUPERTWIST	COMMONALTY	INCAPACITY	REPOSITORY
BREADFRUIT	FEDERALIST	NIGHTSHIRT	SUPPLEMENT	COMPETENCY	INCENDIARY	RESILIENCY
BREAKFRONT	FLAMBOYANT	NONCHALANT	SUPPLICANT	COMPLIANCY	INCIVILITY	RISIBILITY
CANDESCENT	FLASHLIGHT	NONSUPPORT	SWEETHEART	COMPLICITY	INCUMBENCY	SANGUINARY
CANTONMENT	FLOODLIGHT	OCEANFRONT	TANTAMOUNT	COMPULSORY	INEQUALITY	SEISMOLOGY
CAPITALIST	FORTHRIGHT	OMNIPOTENT	TENDERFOOT	CONFORMITY	INFIDELITY	SELENOLOGY
CHECKPOINT	FRAUDULENT	OMNISCIENT	THERMOSTAT	CONGRUENCY	INHUMANITY	SIMPLICITY
CIRCUMVENT	FUSSBUDGET	OPALESCENT	THROUGHOUT	CONSISTORY	INITIATORY	SOLIDARITY
CLOUDBURST	GESUNDHEIT	OUTPATIENT	THROUGHPUT	CONSPIRACY	INTERMARRY	STATIONARY
COINCIDENT	GOVERNMENT	PALIMPSEST	TOURNAMENT	CONTINUITY	LABORATORY	STATIONERY
COMMANDANT	GRAPEFRUIT	PANTYWAIST	TOURNIQUET	COUNTERSPY	LOGANBERRY	STRAWBERRY
COMPATRIOT	HABILIMENT	PARLIAMENT	TRANSCRIPT	DECLASSIFY	MELANCHOLY	STRINGENCY
COMPLEMENT	HANDICRAFT	PEPPERMINT	TRANSPLANT	DEGENERACY	METAGALAXY	SUBSIDIARY
COMPLIMENT	HIEROPHANT	PERCIPIENT	TYPESCRIPT	DEHUMIDIFY	METALLURGY	SUSPENSORY
CONCORDANT	ICONOCLAST	PERMAFROST	ULTRASHORT	DEMOGRAPHY	MINERALOGY	TECHNOLOGY
CONCURRENT	IMPEDIMENT	PHOTOPAINT	UNDERCROFT	DEMONOLOGY	MISCELLANY	TELEGRAPHY
CONSEQUENT	IMPENITENT	PICKPOCKET	UNDERSHIRT	DENDROLOGY	MISSIONARY	THROUGHWAY
CONSTRAINT	INCOHERENT	PLAYWRIGHT	UNDERSHOOT	DEPENDENCY	MORPHOLOGY	TOMFOOLERY
CONTINGENT	INCONSTANT	PLUPERFECT	UNDERSKIRT	DEPILATORY	MULTISTORY	TOPOGRAPHY
CONTRADICT	INDISCREET	POSTSCRIPT	UNDERWAIST	DEPOSITORY	MUSICOLOGY	TOXICOLOGY
CONTROVERT	INDISTINCT	PREEMINENT	UNPLEASANT	DEROGATORY	NEBULOSITY	TRAJECTORY
CONVENIENT	INDUCEMENT	PREFERMENT	VICEGERENT	DESERVEDLY	NECROMANCY	TRANSITORY
CONVERSANT	INFREQUENT	PRIZEFIGHT	VOICEPRINT	DICTIONARY	NEIGHBORLY	TRIMONTHLY
COUNTERACT	INGREDIENT	PROFICIENT	WAINWRIGHT	DIFFICULTY	NEUTRALITY	TYPOGRAPHY
CRANKSHAFT	INHABITANT	PROPELLANT	WANDERLUST	DILLYDALLY	NEWSWORTHY	UNDERBELLY
DEADWEIGHT	INSENTIENT	PROTESTANT	WATERCRAFT	DISHARMONY	NOTABILITY	UNDERSTORY
DELINQUENT	INSTRUMENT	PUNISHMENT	WATERFRONT	DISORDERLY	NOTEWORTHY	UNDERSTUDY
DENOUEMENT	INTEGUMENT	PUTRESCENT	WATERSPOUT	DISPENSARY	NUMEROLOGY	UNFRIENDLY
DEPARTMENT	INTERNMENT	QUADRUPLET	WATERTIGHT	DISQUALIFY	OCEANOLOGY	UNIFORMITY
DEPORTMENT	INTERTWIST	QUINTUPLET	WILDEBEEST	DISSATISFY	OSTEOPATHY	UNIVERSITY
DEPRESSANT	INTOLERANT	REDISTRICT	WITCHCRAFT	EFFICIENCY	PASSAGEWAY	UNMANNERLY
DESCENDANT	INTOXICANT	REFINEMENT	WONDERMENT	EFFRONTERY	PEREMPTORY	UPHOLSTERY
DETACHMENT	INVESTMENT	REFRINGENT	WORKBASKET	ELDERBERRY	PERPETUITY	VARICOSITY
DISAPPOINT	IRRELEVANT	REGISTRANT	FORESHADOW	ELEMENTARY	PERSONALTY	VETERINARY
DISCOMFORT	JACKRABBIT	RESPONDENT	HANDBARROW	EMBROIDERY	PHILOSOPHY	VIRTUOSITY
DISCONCERT	JUGGERNAUT	RESTAURANT	MIDDLEBROW	EMBRYOLOGY	PHLEBOTOMY	VISIBILITY
DISCONNECT	KNOCKWURST	RETROSPECT	OVERSHADOW	ENTOMOLOGY	PHRENOLOGY	VOCABULARY
DISCONTENT	LIEUTENANT	ROUNDABOUT	THUMBSCREW	EPISCOPACY	PHYLACTERY	VOLUPTUARY
DISCREPANT	LIVERWURST	ROUSTABOUT	ANTICLIMAX	EQUANIMITY	PHYSIOLOGY	WHITSUNDAY
DISCUSSANT	MALCONTENT	SACROSANCT	CHATTERBOX	EXCELLENCY	PICKANINNY	XEROGRAPHY
DISENCHANT	MALEFICENT	SAUERKRAUT	CIRCUMFLEX	EXOBIOLOGY	PLEASANTRY	
DISINHERIT	MALEVOLENT	SEPARATIST	ALIMENTARY	EXPECTANCY	PLUTOCRACY	
DISRESPECT	MANAGEMENT	SEPTUAGINT	AMBULATORY	EXPEDIENCY	PREBENDARY	
DISTRAUGHT	MANDELBROT	SETTLEMENT	APOTHECARY	EXPRESSWAY	PRECIOSITY	
EMBANKMENT	MANICURIST	SHIPWRIGHT	ASCENDANCY	FRATERNITY	PRESBYTERY	
EMBONPOINT	MANSERVANT	SOMERSAULT	BAPTISTERY	GASTRONOMY	PROCLIVITY	
EMPLOYMENT	MANUSCRIPT	SPACECRAFT	BESTIALITY	GENERALITY	PROMISSORY	
ENDEARMENT	MEDICAMENT	SPECIALIST	BLACKBERRY	GLACIOLOGY	PROMONTORY	
ENGAGEMENT	MILLWRIGHT	SPOILSPORT	CARDIOLOGY	GOOSEBERRY	PROPENSITY	
ENJAMBMENT	MINISTRANT	SPORTSCAST	CATCHPENNY	GYNECOLOGY	PROSPERITY	
EQUIVALENT	MISCONDUCT	STANDPOINT	CHALCEDONY	HEMATOLOGY	PSYCHIATRY	
ESCARPMENT	MISOGAMIST	STATECRAFT	CHARACTERY	HEREDITARY	PSYCHOLOGY	
EVANESCENT	MISOGYNIST	STEPPARENT	CHIROMANCY	HOLOGRAPHY	REDUNDANCY	

11
LETTER WORDS

DISCOURTESY	EXHAUSTLESS	GEOMAGNETIC	HOSPITALIZE	INCARNATION	INTELLIGENT	LEATHERNECK
DISCREPANCY	EXPECTATION	GEOPOLITICS	HOUSEBROKEN	INCERTITUDE	INTENTIONAL	LEGERDEMAIN
DISENCUMBER	EXPECTORANT	GEOSYNCLINE	HOUSEKEEPER	INCINERATOR	INTERACTION	LEGISLATION
DISENTANGLE	EXPECTORATE	GERONTOLOGY	HOUSELIGHTS	INCLINATION	INTERACTIVE	LEGISLATIVE
DISILLUSION	EXPEDITIOUS	GERRYMANDER	HOUSEMOTHER	INCOMPETENT	INTERATOMIC	LEGISLATURE
DISORGANIZE	EXPENDITURE	GESTICULATE	HUCKLEBERRY	INCONGRUENT	INTERCALARY	LETTERPRESS
DISPENSABLE	EXPERIENCED	GINGERBREAD	HUMMINGBIRD	INCONGRUOUS	INTERCALATE	LEVELHEADED
DISPLEASURE	EXPOSTULATE	GLOSSOLALIA	HYDROCARBON	INCONTINENT	INTERCEPTOR	LIBERTARIAN
DISPOSITION	EXPROPRIATE	GODDAUGHTER	HYDROGENATE	INCORPORATE	INTERCHANGE	LICKSPITTLE
DISPUTATION	EXTEMPORARY	GRANDFATHER	HYDROGRAPHY	INCORPOREAL	INTERCOURSE	LIGHTWEIGHT
DISQUIETUDE	EXTEMPORIZE	GRANDMOTHER	HYDROPHOBIA	INCREDULOUS	INTERESTING	LILLIPUTIAN
DISSEMINATE	EXTERMINATE	GRANDPARENT	HYDROPONICS	INCREMENTAL	INTERLACING	LINGUISTICS
DISSIMULATE	EXTRADITION	GRANITEWARE	HYDROSPHERE	INCRIMINATE	INTERLINEAR	LIONHEARTED
DISSOLUTION	EXTRAPOLATE	GRASSHOPPER	HYDROSTATIC	INCUNABULUM	INTERLINING	LITHOGRAPHY
DISTINCTION	EXTRAVAGANT	GRAVITATION	HYGROSCOPIC	INDEFINABLE	INTERMEDDLE	LITHOSPHERE
DISTINCTIVE	FAMILIARITY	GREASEPAINT	HYPERACTIVE	INDENTATION	INTERMINGLE	LITTERATEUR
DISTINGUISH	FARINACEOUS	GREENGROCER	HYPERBOREAN	INDEPENDENT	INTERNECINE	LOUDMOUTHED
DISTRIBUTOR	FARTHERMOST	GROUNDSHEET	HYPERTROPHY	INDIFFERENT	INTERNUNCIO	LOUDSPEAKER
DOCTRINAIRE	FARTHINGALE	GROUNDWATER	HYPHENATION	INDIGESTION	INTEROFFICE	LUCUBRATION
DOCUMENTARY	FASHIONABLE	GUTTERSNIPE	HYPOTHECATE	INDIGNATION	INTERPOLATE	MACHINATION
DOMESTICATE	FAULTFINDER	GYROCOMPASS	HYPOTHESIZE	INDIVIDUATE	INTERPRETER	MACROBIOTIC
DOMESTICITY	FEATHEREDGE	HABERDASHER	ICHTHYOLOGY	INDIVISIBLE	INTERRACIAL	MACROSCOPIC
DOWNHEARTED	FIDDLESTICK	HABITUATION	IDENTIFIERS	INDOMITABLE	INTERREGNUM	MAGISTERIAL
DOWNTRODDEN	FILMOGRAPHY	HAEMORRHAGE	IGNOMINIOUS	INDUBITABLE	INTERRELATE	MAGNANIMOUS
DREADNOUGHT	FINGERBOARD	HAGIOGRAPHY	ILLIMITABLE	INDUSTRIOUS	INTERROGATE	MAGNIFICENT
DRILLMASTER	FINGERPRINT	HAIRBREADTH	ILLUSIONISM	INEFFECTIVE	INTERSPERSE	MAIDSERVANT
DYNAMOMETER	FIRECRACKER	HAIRDRESSER	ILLUSTRIOUS	INEFFECTUAL	INTOLERABLE	MALADJUSTED
EARTHENWARE	FLABBERGAST	HAIRSTYLIST	IMAGESETTER	INEFFICIENT	INTRACTABLE	MALAPROPISM
EDIFICATION	FLANNELETTE	HALFHEARTED	IMAGINATION	INELUCTABLE	INTRAVENOUS	MALEDICTION
EFFICACIOUS	FLOORWALKER	HALLUCINATE	IMBRICATION	INESCAPABLE	INVESTIGATE	MALFEASANCE
EINSTEINIUM	FLORESCENCE	HANDICAPPER	IMMITIGABLE	INESTIMABLE	INVESTITURE	MALFUNCTION
ELECTIONEER	FLUOROSCOPE	HANDSHAKING	IMMORTALITY	INEXCUSABLE	INVOLUNTARY	MALPRACTICE
ELECTRICIAN	FORECLOSURE	HANDWRITING	IMMORTALIZE	INFANTICIDE	IRIDESCENCE	MANTELPIECE
ELECTRICITY	FOREQUARTER	HARDHEARTED	IMPASSIONED	INFLAMMABLE	IRREDENTISM	MANUFACTORY
ELECTROCUTE	FORESHORTEN	HARDWORKING	IMPECUNIOUS	INFORMATION	IRREDUCIBLE	MANUFACTURE
ELECTROFORM	FORETHOUGHT	HAREBRAINED	IMPEDIMENTA	INFORMATIVE	IRREFUTABLE	MARCHIONESS
ELECTROLYTE	FOREVERMORE	HARPSICHORD	IMPERFORATE	INGATHERING	IRRELIGIOUS	MARKETPLACE
ELECTRONICS	FORMFITTING	HEARTBROKEN	IMPERIALISM	INGRATITUDE	IRREMOVABLE	MARQUISETTE
ELECTROTYPE	FORNICATION	HEARTHSTONE	IMPERMANENT	INNERSPRING	IRREPARABLE	MARSHMALLOW
ELEPHANTINE	FORTHCOMING	HEAVYWEIGHT	IMPERMEABLE	INNUMERABLE	IRREVERENCE	MASSACHUSET
ELIZABETHAN	FORTNIGHTLY	HELLENISTIC	IMPERSONATE	INOPERATIVE	IRREVOCABLE	MASTERPIECE
EMPLACEMENT	FOULMOUTHED	HERBIVOROUS	IMPERTINENT	INOPPORTUNE	JABBERWOCKY	MATERIALISM
ENCAPSULATE	FRAGMENTARY	HERPETOLOGY	IMPLAUSIBLE	INQUISITION	JUVENOCRACY	MATERIALIZE
ENDOTHERMIC	FRANKFURTER	HERRINGBONE	IMPORTATION	INQUISITIVE	KINDHEARTED	MATHEMATICS
ENFRANCHISE	FREETHINKER	HEXADECIMAL	IMPORTUNATE	INSCRUTABLE	KINESTHESIA	MATRICULATE
ENGINEERING	FUNCTIONARY	HIGHFALUTIN	IMPRACTICAL	INSECTICIDE	KITCHENETTE	MEADOWSWEET
ENVIRONMENT	FUNDAMENTAL	HINDQUARTER	IMPREGNABLE	INSEPARABLE	KITCHENWARE	MEASUREMENT
EPINEPHRINE	FURNISHINGS	HISTORICITY	IMPROPRIETY	INSINUATING	KLEPTOMANIA	MECHANISTIC
EQUIDISTANT	FURTHERMORE	HISTRIONICS	IMPROVEMENT	INSOUCIANCE	KNUCKLEBONE	MEDIUMISTIC
EQUILATERAL	FURTHERMOST	HOMEOSTASIS	IMPROVIDENT	INSPIRATION	KWASHIORKOR	MEGALOMANIA
EQUILIBRIUM	GALLBLADDER	HOMESTEADER	IMPUISSANCE	INSTABILITY	LABORSAVING	MEGALOPOLIS
EVANGELICAL	GALLIMAUFRY	HOMESTRETCH	INADVERTENT	INSTALLMENT	LABRADORITE	MELANCHOLIA
EVENTUALITY	GARNISHMENT	HOMOGENEOUS	INALIENABLE	INSTANTIATE	LACRIMATION	MELANCHOLIC
EVERLASTING	GEANTICLINE	HONEYSUCKLE	INATTENTION	INSTITUTION	LAMPLIGHTER	MELLIFLUOUS
EXCEEDINGLY	GENDARMERIE	HORSEPLAYER	INCANTATION	INSTRUCTION	LASERWRITER	MEMORABILIA
EXCEPTIONAL	GENERALSHIP	HORSERADISH	INCARCERATE	INSTRUCTIVE	LATCHSTRING	MENDELEVIUM
EXCRESCENCE	GENTLEWOMAN	HOSPITALITY	INCARNADINE	INSUPERABLE	LATTICEWORK	MENSURATION

MERCHANDISE	NECKERCHIEF	PARATYPHOID	PORTMANTEAU	PUNCTILIOUS	RESTORATION	STEPBROTHER
MERCHANTMAN	NEEDLEPOINT	PARENTHESIS	PORTRAITIST	PUNCTUATION	RESTORATIVE	STEREOSCOPE
MERITOCRACY	NEEDLEWOMAN	PARISHIONER	PORTRAITURE	QUACKSALVER	RESTRICTION	STEREOSCOPY
MERITORIOUS	NETHERWORLD	PARTICIPATE	PRACTICABLE	QUADRENNIAL	RESUSCITATE	STEREOTYPED
MERRYMAKING	NICKELODEON	PARTICULATE	PREASSIGNED	QUADRENNIUM	RETRIBUTION	STETHOSCOPE
MESALLIANCE	NIGHTINGALE	PARTURITION	PRECIPITATE	QUALITATIVE	RETROACTIVE	STOCKBROKER
METAPHYSICS	NIGHTWALKER	PATERNALISM	PRECIPITOUS	QUARTERBACK	REVERBERATE	STOCKHOLDER
METEOROLOGY	NINNYHAMMER	PENETRATING	PRECONCEIVE	QUARTERDECK	REVERENTIAL	STOCKINETTE
METHODOLOGY	NONDESCRIPT	PENNYWEIGHT	PREDECESSOR	QUICKSILVER	ROADABILITY	STOMACHACHE
METRICATION	NONDOCUMENT	PENTECOSTAL	PREDICAMENT	RADIOCARBON	ROMANTICISM	STOREKEEPER
MICROCAPSUL	NONETHELESS	PENULTIMATE	PREDOMINATE	RADIOMETRIC	ROTOGRAVURE	STORYTELLER
MICROSCOPIC	NONNEGATIVE	PERAMBULATE	PREHISTORIC	RAPSCALLION	ROTTENSTONE	STRAIGHTWAY
MICROSECOND	NONPARTISAN	PERCEPTIBLE	PREIGNITION	RATHSKELLER	SAFEKEEPING	STRAITLACED
MILLIAMPERE	NONRESIDENT	PERFECTIBLE	PRELIMINARY	RATIONALISM	SARCOPHAGUS	STRANGULATE
MILLIONAIRE	NONVIOLENCE	PERFORMANCE	PREMEDITATE	RATIONALITY	SCAFFOLDING	STRAWFLOWER
MILLISECOND	NORTHEASTER	PERFUNCTORY	PREMONITION	RATIONALIZE	SCHOLARSHIP	STREAMLINED
MINESWEEPER	NOTHINGNESS	PERIODONTAL	PREOCCUPIED	RATTLESNAKE	SCHOOLHOUSE	STREAMLINER
MINIATURIZE	NOURISHMENT	PERIPATETIC	PREPOSITION	REACTIONARY	SCINTILLATE	STROBOSCOPE
MINNESINGER	NUMISMATICS	PERIPHRASIS	PREROGATIVE	REALPOLITIK	SCREWDRIVER	SUBASSEMBLY
MISALLIANCE	NURSERYMAID	PERISTALSIS	PRESUMPTION	RECESSIONAL	SCRUMPTIOUS	SUBJUNCTIVE
MISANTHROPE	NYMPHOMANIA	PERITONITIS	PRETENTIOUS	RECIPROCATE	SCUTTLEBUTT	SUBMERSIBLE
MISBEGOTTEN	OBSERVATION	PERMISSIBLE	PRETERMINAL	RECIPROCITY	SEARCHLIGHT	SUBORDINATE
MISBELIEVER	OBSERVATORY	PERMUTATION	PREVARICATE	RECOGNITION	SEISMOGRAPH	SUBSISTENCE
MISCHIEVOUS	OBSTRUCTION	PERSNICKETY	PRIMITIVISM	RECONNOITER	SEISMOMETER	SUBSTANDARD
MISCONCEIVE	OBSOLESCENT	PERSONALITY	PRIZEWINNER	RECONSTRUCT	SEMITRAILER	SUBSTANTIAL
MISCONSTRUE	OFFICIALDOM	PERSONALIZE	PROBATIONER	RECRIMINATE	SENSATIONAL	SUBSTANTIVE
MISDEMEANOR	OFFICIALISM	PERSPECTIVE	PROBLEMATIC	RECTILINEAR	SENSIBILITY	SUBTROPICAL
MISFEASANCE	OMNIPRESENT	PERSPICUOUS	PROCRUSTEAN	REDOUBTABLE	SENTENTIOUS	SUBURBANITE
MISGUIDANCE	OPINIONATED	PESTIFEROUS	PROFANATORY	REFORMATION	SENTIMENTAL	SUFFICIENCY
MOCKINGBIRD	OPPORTUNISM	PETROGRAPHY	PROGNATHOUS	REFORMATORY	SEQUESTRATE	SUFFRAGETTE
MODULARIZED	OPPORTUNITY	PHARISAICAL	PROGRAMMING	REFRESHMENT	SERENDIPITY	SUMMERHOUSE
MOLLYCODDLE	OPPROBRIOUS	PHILOSOPHER	PROGRESSION	REFRIGERATE	SERVICEABLE	SUPERFICIAL
MOMENTARILY	ORCHESTRATE	PHOTOGRAPHY	PROGRESSIVE	REGIMENTALS	SHAREHOLDER	SUPERFLUOUS
MONASTICISM	ORNITHOLOGY	PHOTOSPHERE	PROHIBITION	REGURGITATE	SHELLACKING	SUPERIMPOSE
MONEYLENDER	ORTHODONTIA	PHRASEOLOGY	PROLETARIAN	REINFECTION	SHIPBUILDER	SUPERINTEND
MONKEYSHINE	ORTHOGRAPHY	PHYSIOGNOMY	PROLETARIAT	RELOCATABLE	SHORTCHANGE	SUPERLATIVE
MONOLINGUAL	ORTHOPEDICS	PICTURESQUE	PROLIFERATE	REMEMBRANCE	SHORTCOMING	SUPERMARKET
MONSEIGNEUR	OSTENTATION	PISCATORIAL	PROMISCUOUS	REMINISCENT	SHORTHANDED	SUPERSCRIBE
MORTARBOARD	OUTBUILDING	PITCHBLENDE	PROMPTITUDE	REMONSTRANT	SHUTTLECOCK	SUPERSCRIPT
MOTHERBOARD	OUTDISTANCE	PLACEHOLDER	PROPHYLAXIS	REMONSTRATE	SIGNIFICANT	SUPERSONICS
MOUNTAINEER	OUTMANEUVER	PLAINSPOKEN	PROPINQUITY	RENAISSANCE	SLEEPWALKER	SUPPOSITION
MOUNTAINTOP	OUTSTANDING	PLANETARIUM	PROPOSITION	REPETITIOUS	SMITHEREENS	SUPPOSITORY
MULTIFAMILY	OVERBALANCE	PLANETOLOGY	PROPRIETARY	REPLACEMENT	SMORGASBORD	SUPPRESSANT
MULTIRACIAL	OVERBEARING	PLEASURABLE	PROSELYTIZE	REPLICATION	SOLILOQUIZE	SUPREMACIST
MUSCULATURE	OVERSTUFFED	POCKETKNIFE	PROSTATITIS	REPROBATION	SOVEREIGNTY	SUSCEPTIBLE
MUSKELLUNGE	OVERWEENING	POINTILLISM	PROSTHETICS	REQUIREMENT	SPACEFLIGHT	SWALLOWTAIL
MUTTONCHOPS	OVERWROUGHT	POLLINATION	PROTAGONIST	REQUISITION	SPECTACULAR	SWEEPSTAKES
NAPHTHALENE	OZONOSPHERE	POLTERGEIST	PROTOMARTYR	RESEMBLANCE	SPECTROGRAM	SWITCHBLADE
NARRAGANSET	PACHYSANDRA	POLYNOMINAL	PROTUBERANT	RESERVATION	SPEEDOMETER	SWITCHBOARD
NATIONALISM	PAINSTAKING	POLYSTYRENE	PROVENIENCE	RESIDENTIAL	SPELLBINDER	SYNCHROMESH
NATIONALIST	PALEOGRAPHY	POLYTECHNIC	PROVISIONAL	RESIGNATION	SPENDTHRIFT	SYNCHRONIZE
NATIONALITY	PANDEMONIUM	POMEGRANATE	PSYCHEDELIA	RESISTIVITY	SPONTANEOUS	SYNCHRONOUS
NATIONALIZE	PAPERHANGER	PONTIFICALS	PSYCHEDELIC	RESPECTABLE	SPREADSHEET	SYNCOPATION
NEANDERTHAL	PAPERWEIGHT	PONTIFICATE	PSYCHODRAMA	RESPIRATION	SPRINGBOARD	SYNTHESIZER
NEARSIGHTED	PARAMEDICAL	PORNOGRAPHY	PSYCHOGENIC	RESPLENDENT	STANDARDIZE	SYSTEMATIZE
NECESSITATE	PARATHYROID	PORTERHOUSE	PUBLICATION	RESPONSIBLE	STEAMROLLER	TACHYCARDIA
NECESSITOUS	PARATROOPER	PORTIONLESS	PULCHRITUDE	RESTITUTION	STENOGRAPHY	TEASPOONFUL

TECHNOCRACY	TYPEFOUNDER	VALEDICTORY	CABINETWORK	HARDHEARTED	PARTICULATE	SCRUMPTIOUS
TELEPRINTER	TYPESETTING	VARICOLORED	CALCIFEROUS	HARDWORKING	PARTURITION	SCUTTLEBUTT
TEMPERAMENT	TYPEWRITING	VENTILATION	CALCULATING	HAREBRAINED	PATERNALISM	ADOLESCENCE
TEMPERATURE	TYPOGRAPHER	VENTRILOQUY	CALCULATION	HARPSICHORD	RADIOCARBON	ADVERSATIVE
TEMPESTUOUS	ULTRAMARINE	VENTURESOME	CALIFORNIUM	JABBERWOCKY	RADIOMETRIC	ADVERTISING
TENDENTIOUS	ULTRAMODERN	VERMICULITE	CALLIGRAPHY	LABORSAVING	RAPSCALLION	EDIFICATION
TERMINOLOGY	ULTRASONICS	VERTIGINOUS	CALORIMETER	LABRADORITE	RATHSKELLER	IDENTIFIERS
TERRESTRIAL	ULTRAVIOLET	VICHYSSOISE	CAMARADERIE	LACRIMATION	RATIONALISM	AERONAUTICS
TERRITORIAL	UNACCOUNTED	VICISSITUDE	CAMEROONIAN	LAMPLIGHTER	RATIONALITY	BEACHCOMBER
TESTIMONIAL	UNALIENABLE	VINAIGRETTE	CAMPANOLOGY	LASERWRITER	RATIONALIZE	BEHAVIORISM
THALIDOMIDE	UNAVOIDABLE	VINDICATION	CANDELABRUM	LATCHSTRING	RATTLESNAKE	BELLIGERENT
THEATRICALS	UNCERTAINTY	VIOLONCELLO	CANDIDATURE	LATTICEWORK	SAFEKEEPING	BENEDICTION
THENCEFORTH	UNCHRISTIAN	VIRIDESCENT	CANDLELIGHT	MACHINATION	SARCOPHAGUS	BENEFACTION
THEORETICAL	UNCIVILIZED	VITICULTURE	CANDLESTICK	MACROBIOTIC	TACHYCARDIA	BENEFICENCE
THERAPEUTIC	UNCOMMITTED	VIVISECTION	CANNIBALIZE	MACROSCOPIC	VACATIONIST	BENEFICIARY
THEREABOUTS	UNCONCERNED	VOLCANOLOGY	CAPACITANCE	MAGISTERIAL	VACCINATION	BENEVOLENCE
THEREWITHAL	UNCONSCIOUS	WAINSCOTING	CAPILLARITY	MAGNANIMOUS	VALEDICTION	CEMENTATION
THERMOCLINE	UNDERCHARGE	WARMHEARTED	CARAVANSARY	MAGNIFICENT	VALEDICTORY	CENTENARIAN
THERMOMETER	UNDEREXPOSE	WASHERWOMAN	CARDINALATE	MAIDSERVANT	VARICOLORED	CENTERBOARD
THISTLEDOWN	UNDERGROUND	WASTEBASKET	CARDINALITY	MALADJUSTED	WAINSCOTING	CENTERPIECE
THITHERWARD	UNDERGROWTH	WATERCOURSE	CARDIOGRAPH	MALAPROPISM	WARMHEARTED	CENTRIFUGAL
THOUGHTLESS	UNDERHANDED	WATERLOGGED	CARDSHARPER	MALEDICTION	WASHERWOMAN	CENTRIPETAL
THUNDERBOLT	UNDERSHORTS	WEATHERCOCK	CARMINATIVE	MALFEASANCE	WASTEBASKET	CEREMONIOUS
THUNDERCLAP	UNDERSIGNED	WEATHERWORN	CARNIVOROUS	MALFUNCTION	WATERCOURSE	CERTIFICATE
THUNDERHEAD	UNDERTAKING	WHEELBARROW	CARRAGEENAN	MALPRACTICE	WATERLOGGED	DECLARATIVE
TIGHTFISTED	UNDERWEIGHT	WHEELWRIGHT	CARTOGRAPHY	MANTELPIECE	ABECEDARIAN	DECRESCENDO
TIMESHARING	UNDESIGNING	WHEREABOUTS	CASSITERITE	MANUFACTORY	ABOMINATION	DEFALCATION
TOASTMASTER	UNDESIRABLE	WHERESOEVER	CASTELLATED	MANUFACTURE	ABORTIONIST	DEFLORATION
TOBACCONIST	UNDEVIATING	WHEREWITHAL	CATASTROPHE	MARCHIONESS	ABRACADABRA	DELECTATION
TONSILLITIS	UNEQUIVOCAL	WHICHSOEVER	CATEGORICAL	MARKETPLACE	ABSENTEEISM	DELETERIOUS
TOPDRESSING	UNFAVORABLE	WHIFFLETREE	CATERCORNER	MARQUISETTE	ABSTRACTION	DELINQUENCY
TOTALIZATOR	UNFLAPPABLE	WHIPPLETREE	CATERPILLAR	MARSHMALLOW	OBSERVATION	DEMAGNETIZE
TOWNSPEOPLE	UNFLINCHING	WIDEMOUTHED	CATHOLICITY	MASSACHUSET	OBSERVATORY	DEMOCRATIZE
TRAGEDIENNE	UNFORTUNATE	WINTERGREEN	CAULIFLOWER	MASTERPIECE	OBSOLESCENT	DEMONSTRATE
TRAILBLAZER	UNICELLULAR	WITENAGEMOT	EARTHENWARE	MATERIALISM	OBSTRUCTION	DENOMINATOR
TRANQUILIZE	UNIFICATION	WOODCHOPPER	FAMILIARITY	MATERIALIZE	ACADEMICIAN	DEPRECATORY
TRANSACTION	UNINHIBITED	WORDPERFECT	FARINACEOUS	MATHEMATICS	ACADEMICISM	DEPREDATION
TRANSCEIVER	UNMITIGATED	WORKMANLIKE	FARTHERMOST	MATRICULATE	ACCELERANDO	DEPRIVATION
TRANSFIGURE	UNOBTRUSIVE	WORKMANSHIP	FARTHINGALE	NAPHTHALENE	ACCELERATOR	DERELICTION
TRANSLUCENT	UNORGANIZED	WORKSTATION	FASHIONABLE	NARRAGANSET	ACCEPTATION	DERMATOLOGY
TRANSMITTER	UNPRINTABLE	WRONGHEADED	FAULTFINDER	NATIONALISM	ACCLAMATION	DESCRIPTION
TRANSPARENT	UNQUALIFIED	ZOOMORPHISM	GALLBLADDER	NATIONALIST	ACCLIMATIZE	DESEGREGATE
TREACHEROUS	UNREASONING	ZOOPLANKTON	GALLIMAUFRY	NATIONALITY	ACCOMMODATE	DESENSITIZE
TRENCHERMAN	UNRELENTING		GARNISHMENT	NATIONALIZE	ACCORDINGLY	DESIDERATUM
TREPIDATION	UNREMITTING		HABERDASHER	PACHYSANDRA	ACCOUNTABLE	DESPERATION
TRIANGULATE	UNRIGHTEOUS		HABITUATION	PAINSTAKING	ACCUMULATOR	DESPONDENCY
TRIBULATION	UNSATURATED	**2ND LETTER**	HAEMORRHAGE	PALEOGRAPHY	ACKNOWLEDGE	DESTINATION
TRICHINOSIS	UNSPEAKABLE		HAGIOGRAPHY	PANDEMONIUM	ACQUIREMENT	DESTRUCTION
TRINIDADIAN	UNTHINKABLE	BACCHANALIA	HAGIOGRAPHY	PAPERHANGER	ACQUISITION	DETERIORATE
TRINITARIAN	UNTOUCHABLE	BACKSTRETCH	HAIRBREADTH	PAPERWEIGHT	ACQUISITIVE	DETERMINANT
TRIUMVIRATE	UNUTTERABLE	BALLCARRIER	HAIRDRESSER	PARAMEDICAL	ACUPUNCTURE	DETERMINATE
TROPOSPHERE	UNVARNISHED	BALLETOMANE	HAIRSTYLIST	PARATHYROID	ICHTHYOLOGY	DETERMINISM
TRUEHEARTED	UNWHOLESOME	BARBITURATE	HALFHEARTED	PARATROOPER	SCAFFOLDING	FEATHEREDGE
TRUSTEESHIP	UTILITARIAN	BATHYSCAPHE	HALLUCINATE	PARATYPHOID	SCHOLARSHIP	GEANTICLINE
TRUSTWORTHY	VACATIONIST	BATHYSPHERE	HANDICAPPER	PARENTHESIS	SCHOOLHOUSE	GENDARMERIE
TUBERCULATE	VACCINATION	BATTLEFIELD	HANDSHAKING	PARISHIONER	SCINTILLATE	GENERALSHIP
TWELVEMONTH	VALEDICTION	BATTLEWAGON	HANDWRITING	PARTICIPATE	SCREWDRIVER	GENTLEWOMAN

GEOMAGNETIC	PERFECTIBLE	RESTORATION	CHIROGRAPHY	DIAMONDBACK	MILLIAMPERE	ELECTRICITY
GEOPOLITICS	PERFORMANCE	RESTORATIVE	CHLOROPHYLL	DIAPHORETIC	MILLIONAIRE	ELECTROCUTE
GEOSYNCLINE	PERFUNCTORY	RESTRICTION	CHOCKABLOCK	DICOTYLEDON	MILLISECOND	ELECTROFORM
GERONTOLOGY	PERIODONTAL	RESUSCITATE	CHOIRMASTER	DICTATORIAL	MINESWEEPER	ELECTROLYTE
GERRYMANDER	PERIPATETIC	RETRIBUTION	CHOLESTEROL	DIFFRACTION	MINIATURIZE	ELECTRONICS
GESTICULATE	PERIPHRASIS	RETROACTIVE	CHRISTENDOM	DILAPIDATED	MINNESINGER	ELECTROTYPE
HEARTBROKEN	PERISTALSIS	REVERBERATE	CHRISTIANIA	DIPLOMATIST	MISALLIANCE	ELEPHANTINE
HEARTHSTONE	PERITONITIS	REVERENTIAL	CHRONOGRAPH	DIRECTORATE	MISANTHROPE	ELIZABETHAN
HEAVYWEIGHT	PERMISSIBLE	SEARCHLIGHT	CHRONOMETER	DISAPPROVAL	MISBEGOTTEN	FLABBERGAST
HELLENISTIC	PERMUTATION	SEISMOGRAPH	PHARISAICAL	DISASSEMBLE	MISBELIEVER	FLANNELETTE
HERBIVOROUS	PERSNICKETY	SEISMOMETER	PHILOSOPHER	DISCONTINUE	MISCHIEVOUS	FLOORWALKER
HERPETOLOGY	PERSONALITY	SEMITRAILER	PHOTOGRAPHY	DISCOTHEQUE	MISCONCEIVE	FLORESCENCE
HERRINGBONE	PERSONALIZE	SENSATIONAL	PHOTOSPHERE	DISCOURTESY	MISCONSTRUE	FLUOROSCOPE
HEXADECIMAL	PERSPECTIVE	SENSIBILITY	PHRASEOLOGY	DISCREPANCY	MISDEMEANOR	GLOSSOLALIA
LEATHERNECK	PERSPICUOUS	SENTENTIOUS	PHYSIOGNOMY	DISENCUMBER	MISFEASANCE	ILLIMITABLE
LEGERDEMAIN	PESTIFEROUS	SENTIMENTAL	SHAREHOLDER	DISENTANGLE	MISGUIDANCE	ILLUSIONISM
LEGISLATION	PETROGRAPHY	SEQUESTRATE	SHELLACKING	DISILLUSION	NICKELODEON	ILLUSTRIOUS
LEGISLATIVE	REACTIONARY	SERENDIPITY	SHIPBUILDER	DISORGANIZE	NIGHTINGALE	KLEPTOMANIA
LEGISLATURE	REALPOLITIK	SERVICEABLE	SHORTCHANGE	DISPENSABLE	NIGHTWALKER	PLACEHOLDER
LETTERPRESS	RECESSIONAL	TEASPOONFUL	SHORTCOMING	DISPLEASURE	NINNYHAMMER	PLAINSPOKEN
LEVELHEADED	RECIPROCATE	TECHNOCRACY	SHORTHANDED	DISPOSITION	PICTURESQUE	PLANETARIUM
MEADOWSWEET	RECIPROCITY	TELEPRINTER	SHUTTLECOCK	DISPUTATION	PISCATORIAL	PLANETOLOGY
MEASUREMENT	RECOGNITION	TEMPERAMENT	THALIDOMIDE	DISQUIETUDE	PITCHBLENDE	PLEASURABLE
MECHANISTIC	RECONNOITER	TEMPERATURE	THEATRICALS	DISSEMINATE	SIGNIFICANT	SLEEPWALKER
MEDIUMISTIC	RECONSTRUCT	TEMPESTUOUS	THENCEFORTH	DISSIMULATE	TIGHTFISTED	ULTRAMARINE
MEGALOMANIA	RECRIMINATE	TENDENTIOUS	THEORETICAL	DISSOLUTION	TIMESHARING	ULTRAMODERN
MEGALOPOLIS	RECTILINEAR	TERMINOLOGY	THERAPEUTIC	DISTINCTION	VICHYSSOISE	ULTRASONICS
MELANCHOLIA	REDOUBTABLE	TERRESTRIAL	THEREABOUTS	DISTINCTIVE	VICISSITUDE	ULTRAVIOLET
MELANCHOLIC	REFORMATION	TERRITORIAL	THEREWITHAL	DISTINGUISH	VINAIGRETTE	AMBIVALENCE
MELLIFLUOUS	REFORMATORY	TESTIMONIAL	THERMOCLINE	DISTRIBUTOR	VINDICATION	AMONTILLADO
MEMORABILIA	REFRESHMENT	VENTILATION	THERMOMETER	EINSTEINIUM	VIOLONCELLO	AMPHETAMINE
MENDELEVIUM	REFRIGERATE	VENTRILOQUY	THISTLEDOWN	FIDDLESTICK	VIRIDESCENT	EMPLACEMENT
MENSURATION	REGIMENTALS	VENTURESOME	THITHERWARD	FILMOGRAPHY	VITICULTURE	IMAGESETTER
MERCHANDISE	REGURGITATE	VERMICULITE	THOUGHTLESS	FINGERBOARD	VIVISECTION	IMAGINATION
MERCHANTMAN	REINFECTION	VERTIGINOUS	THUNDERBOLT	FINGERPRINT	WIDEMOUTHED	IMBRICATION
MERITOCRACY	RELOCATABLE	WEATHERCOCK	THUNDERCLAP	FIRECRACKER	WINTERGREEN	IMMITIGABLE
MERITORIOUS	REMEMBRANCE	WEATHERWORN	THUNDERHEAD	GINGERBREAD	WITENAGEMOT	IMMORTALITY
MERRYMAKING	REMINISCENT	AFFECTATION	WHEELBARROW	HIGHFALUTIN	ALEXANDRIAN	IMMORTALIZE
MESALLIANCE	REMONSTRANT	AFFIRMATIVE	WHEELWRIGHT	HINDQUARTER	ALEXANDRINE	IMPASSIONED
METAPHYSICS	REMONSTRATE	AFTERBURNER	WHEREABOUTS	HISTORICITY	ALPHABETIZE	IMPECUNIOUS
METEOROLOGY	RENAISSANCE	AFTEREFFECT	WHERESOEVER	HISTRIONICS	ALTERCATION	IMPEDIMENTA
METHODOLOGY	REPETITIOUS	EFFICACIOUS	WHEREWITHAL	KINDHEARTED	ALTERNATIVE	IMPERFORATE
METRICATION	REPLACEMENT	OFFICIALDOM	WHICHSOEVER	KINESTHESIA	BLAMEWORTHY	IMPERIALISM
NEANDERTHAL	REPLICATION	OFFICIALISM	WHIFFLETREE	KITCHENETTE	BLOCKBUSTER	IMPERMANENT
NEARSIGHTED	REPROBATION	AGGLOMERATE	WHIPPLETREE	KITCHENWARE	BLOODMOBILE	IMPERMEABLE
NECESSITATE	REQUIREMENT	AGGLUTINATE	BIBLIOPHILE	LIBERTARIAN	BLOODSTREAM	IMPERSONATE
NECESSITOUS	REQUISITION	AGGREGATION	BICARBONATE	LICKSPITTLE	BLOODSUCKER	IMPERTINENT
NECKERCHIEF	RESEMBLANCE	AGORAPHOBIA	BICENTENARY	LIGHTWEIGHT	BLUNDERBUSS	IMPLAUSIBLE
NEEDLEPOINT	RESERVATION	AGRICULTURE	BIMETALLISM	LILLIPUTIAN	CLAIRVOYANT	IMPORTATION
NEEDLEWOMAN	RESIDENTIAL	IGNOMINIOUS	BIOFEEDBACK	LINGUISTICS	CLANDESTINE	IMPORTUNATE
NETHERWORLD	RESIGNATION	CHAMBERLAIN	BITTERSWEET	LIONHEARTED	CLEARHEADED	IMPRACTICAL
PENETRATING	RESISTIVITY	CHAMBERMAID	CIRCULARITY	LITHOGRAPHY	CLERICALISM	IMPREGNABLE
PENNYWEIGHT	RESPECTABLE	CHANCELLERY	CIRCULARIZE	LITHOSPHERE	CLIMACTERIC	IMPROPRIETY
PENTECOSTAL	RESPIRATION	CHANTICLEER	CIRCUMLUNAR	LITTERATEUR	CLIMATOLOGY	IMPROVEMENT
PENULTIMATE	RESPLENDENT	CHEERLEADER	CIRCUMPOLAR	MICROCAPSUL	CLOSEFISTED	IMPROVIDENT
PERAMBULATE	RESPONSIBLE	CHEESECLOTH	CIRCUMSPECT	MICROSCOPIC	ELECTIONEER	IMPUISSANCE
PERCEPTIBLE	RESTITUTION	CHIAROSCURO	DIAMAGNETIC	MICROSECOND	ELECTRICIAN	OMNIPRESENT

SMITHEREENS	INFANTICIDE	KNUCKLEBONE	COINCIDENCE	CONSIDERING	FORESHORTEN	PORNOGRAPHY
SMORGASBORD	INFLAMMABLE	UNACCOUNTED	COLLABORATE	CONSIGNMENT	FORETHOUGHT	PORTERHOUSE
ANACHRONISM	INFORMATION	UNALIENABLE	COLLOCATION	CONSISTENCE	FOREVERMORE	PORTIONLESS
ANAESTHESIA	INFORMATIVE	UNAVOIDABLE	COLONIALISM	CONSISTENCY	FORMFITTING	PORTMANTEAU
ANASTOMOSIS	INGATHERING	UNCERTAINTY	COLORCASTER	CONSOLIDATE	FORNICATION	PORTRAITIST
ANNIVERSARY	INGRATITUDE	UNCHRISTIAN	COMBINATION	CONSPICUOUS	FORTHCOMING	PORTRAITURE
ANNUNCIATOR	INNERSPRING	UNCIVILIZED	COMBUSTIBLE	CONSTITUENT	FORTNIGHTLY	ROADABILITY
ANTECHAMBER	INNUMERABLE	UNCOMMITTED	COMEUPPANCE	CONSUMERISM	FOULMOUTHED	ROMANTICISM
ANTICYCLONE	INOPERATIVE	UNCONCERNED	COMFORTABLE	CONSUMPTION	GODDAUGHTER	ROTOGRAVURE
ANTIGRAVITY	INOPPORTUNE	UNCONSCIOUS	COMMANDMENT	CONSUMPTIVE	HOMEOSTASIS	ROTTENSTONE
ANTINEUTRON	INQUISITION	UNDERCHARGE	COMMEMORATE	CONTAMINANT	HOMESTEADER	SOLILOQUIZE
ANTIOXIDANT	INQUISITIVE	UNDEREXPOSE	COMMENTATOR	CONTAMINATE	HOMESTRETCH	SOVEREIGNTY
ANTIPOVERTY	INSCRUTABLE	UNDERGROUND	COMMINATION	CONTEMPLATE	HOMOGENEOUS	TOASTMASTER
ANTIQUARIAN	INSECTICIDE	UNDERGROWTH	COMMISERATE	CONTENTMENT	HONEYSUCKLE	TOBACCONIST
ENCAPSULATE	INSEPARABLE	UNDERHANDED	COMMONPLACE	CONTINENTAL	HORSEPLAYER	TONSILLITIS
ENDOTHERMIC	INSINUATING	UNDERSHORTS	COMMUNICANT	CONTINGENCY	HORSERADISH	TOPDRESSING
ENFRANCHISE	INSOUCIANCE	UNDERSIGNED	COMMUNICATE	CONTINUANCE	HOSPITALITY	TOTALIZATOR
ENGINEERING	INSPIRATION	UNDERTAKING	COMMUTATION	CONTRACTILE	HOSPITALIZE	TOWNSPEOPLE
ENVIRONMENT	INSTABILITY	UNDERWEIGHT	COMMUTATIVE	CONTRAPTION	HOUSEBROKEN	VOLCANOLOGY
INADVERTENT	INSTALLMENT	UNDESIGNING	COMPARATIVE	CONTRARIETY	HOUSEKEEPER	WOODCHOPPER
INALIENABLE	INSTANTIATE	UNDESIRABLE	COMPARTMENT	CONTRETEMPS	HOUSELIGHTS	WORDPERFECT
INATTENTION	INSTITUTION	UNDEVIATING	COMPETITION	CONTRIVANCE	HOUSEMOTHER	WORKMANLIKE
INCANTATION	INSTRUCTION	UNEQUIVOCAL	COMPLACENCE	CONTROVERSY	LOUDMOUTHED	WORKMANSHIP
INCARCERATE	INSTRUCTIVE	UNFAVORABLE	COMPLACENCY	CONURBATION	LOUDSPEAKER	WORKSTATION
INCARNADINE	INSUPERABLE	UNFLAPPABLE	COMPLICATED	CONVENIENCE	MOCKINGBIRD	ZOOMORPHISM
INCARNATION	INTELLIGENT	UNFLINCHING	COMPORTMENT	CONVENTICLE	MODULARIZED	ZOOPLANKTON
INCERTITUDE	INTENTIONAL	UNFORTUNATE	COMPOSITION	CONVERTIBLE	MOLLYCODDLE	APHRODISIAC
INCINERATOR	INTERACTION	UNICELLULAR	COMPTROLLER	CONVOCATION	MOMENTARILY	APOCYNTHION
INCLINATION	INTERACTIVE	UNIFICATION	COMPUNCTION	CONVOLUTION	MONASTICISM	APPELLATION
INCOMPETENT	INTERATOMIC	UNINHIBITED	COMPUTERIZE	COOPERATIVE	MONEYLENDER	APPLICATION
INCONGRUENT	INTERCALARY	UNMITIGATED	CONCENTRATE	COPROCESSOR	MONKEYSHINE	APPOINTMENT
INCONGRUOUS	INTERCALATE	UNOBTRUSIVE	CONCERNMENT	CORNERSTONE	MONOLINGUAL	APPRECIABLE
INCONTINENT	INTERCEPTOR	UNORGANIZED	CONCOMITANT	CORPORATION	MONSEIGNEUR	APPROBATION
INCORPORATE	INTERCHANGE	UNPRINTABLE	CONCORDANCE	CORRELATIVE	MORTARBOARD	APPROPRIATE
INCORPOREAL	INTERCOURSE	UNQUALIFIED	CONCURRENCE	CORRIGENDUM	MOTHERBOARD	APPROXIMATE
INCREDULOUS	INTERESTING	UNREASONING	CONDITIONAL	CORROBORATE	MOUNTAINEER	EPINEPHRINE
INCREMENTAL	INTERLACING	UNRELENTING	CONDITIONED	COSIGNATORY	MOUNTAINTOP	OPINIONATED
INCRIMINATE	INTERLINEAR	UNREMITTING	CONDOMINIUM	COTERMINOUS	NONDESCRIPT	OPPORTUNISM
INCUNABULUM	INTERLINING	UNRIGHTEOUS	CONDUCTANCE	COTTONMOUTH	NONDOCUMENT	OPPORTUNITY
INDEFINABLE	INTERMEDDLE	UNSATURATED	CONFEDERACY	COUNTENANCE	NONETHELESS	OPPROBRIOUS
INDENTATION	INTERMINGLE	UNSPEAKABLE	CONFEDERATE	COUNTERFEIT	NONNEGATIVE	SPACEFLIGHT
INDEPENDENT	INTERNECINE	UNTHINKABLE	CONFESSEDLY	COUNTERMAND	NONPARTISAN	SPECTACULAR
INDIFFERENT	INTERNUNCIO	UNTOUCHABLE	CONFORMANCE	COUNTERPANE	NONRESIDENT	SPECTROGRAM
INDIGESTION	INTEROFFICE	UNUTTERABLE	CONGRESSMAN	COUNTERPART	NONVIOLENCE	SPEEDOMETER
INDIGNATION	INTERPOLATE	UNVARNISHED	CONJUGATION	COUNTERSIGN	NORTHEASTER	SPELLBINDER
INDIVIDUATE	INTERPRETER	UNWHOLESOME	CONJUNCTION	COUNTERSINK	NOTHINGNESS	SPENDTHRIFT
INDIVISIBLE	INTERRACIAL	BOILERMAKER	CONJUNCTIVA	COUNTERVAIL	NOURISHMENT	SPONTANEOUS
INDOMITABLE	INTERREGNUM	BOURGEOISIE	CONJUNCTIVE	COUNTRIFIED	POCKETKNIFE	SPREADSHEET
INDUBITABLE	INTERRELATE	BOUTONNIERE	CONJUNCTURE	COUNTRYSIDE	POINTILLISM	SPRINGBOARD
INDUSTRIOUS	INTERROGATE	BOYSENBERRY	CONNOISSEUR	DOCTRINAIRE	POLLINATION	AQUICULTURE
INEFFECTIVE	INTERSPERSE	COBBLESTONE	CONNOTATION	DOCUMENTARY	POLTERGEIST	EQUIDISTANT
INEFFECTUAL	INTOLERABLE	COCKLESHELL	CONNOTATIVE	DOMESTICATE	POLYNOMINAL	EQUILATERAL
INEFFICIENT	INTRACTABLE	COEDUCATION	CONSECUTIVE	DOMESTICITY	POLYSTYRENE	EQUILIBRIUM
INELUCTABLE	INTRAVENOUS	COEFFICIENT	CONSEQUENCE	DOWNHEARTED	POLYTECHNIC	ARBITRAMENT
INESCAPABLE	INVESTIGATE	COEXTENSIVE	CONSERVANCY	DOWNTRODDEN	POMEGRANATE	ARCHAEOLOGY
INESTIMABLE	INVESTITURE	COFFEEHOUSE	CONSERVATOR	FORECLOSURE	PONTIFICALS	ARCHDIOCESE
INEXCUSABLE	INVOLUNTARY	COGNOSCENTE	CONSIDERATE	FOREQUARTER	PONTIFICATE	ARCHIPELAGO

ARISTOCRACY	PREPOSITION	ASSASSINATE	OUTDISTANCE	EXCEEDINGLY	ANASTOMOSIS	SCAFFOLDING
BRAGGADOCIO	PREROGATIVE	ASSEMBLYMAN	OUTMANEUVER	EXCEPTIONAL	BEACHCOMBER	SEARCHLIGHT
BREADBASKET	PRESUMPTION	ASSIGNATION	OUTSTANDING	EXCRESCENCE	BLAMEWORTHY	SHAREHOLDER
BREADWINNER	PRETENTIOUS	ASSOCIATION	PUBLICATION	EXHAUSTLESS	BRAGGADOCIO	SPACEFLIGHT
BREAKPOINTS	PRETERMINAL	ASSOCIATIVE	PULCHRITUDE	EXPECTATION	CHAMBERLAIN	STANDARDIZE
BREASTPLATE	PREVARICATE	ASTIGMATISM	PUNCTILIOUS	EXPECTORANT	CHAMBERMAID	SWALLOWTAIL
BROTHERHOOD	PRIMITIVISM	OSTENTATION	PUNCTUATION	EXPECTORATE	CHANCELLERY	TEASPOONFUL
CRACKERJACK	PRIZEWINNER	PSYCHEDELIA	QUACKSALVER	EXPEDITIOUS	CHANTICLEER	THALIDOMIDE
CRAPSHOOTER	PROBATIONER	PSYCHEDELIC	QUADRENNIAL	EXPENDITURE	CLAIRVOYANT	TOASTMASTER
CREPUSCULAR	PROBLEMATIC	PSYCHODRAMA	QUADRENNIUM	EXPERIENCED	CLANDESTINE	TRAGEDIENNE
CRESTFALLEN	PROCRUSTEAN	PSYCHOGENIC	QUALITATIVE	EXPOSTULATE	CRACKERJACK	TRAILBLAZER
CRIMINOLOGY	PROFANATORY	ATTRIBUTIVE	QUARTERBACK	EXPROPRIATE	CRAPSHOOTER	TRANQUILIZE
CRUCIFIXION	PROGNATHOUS	STANDARDIZE	QUARTERDECK	EXTEMPORARY	DIAMAGNETIC	TRANSACTION
CRYSTALLIZE	PROGRAMMING	STEAMROLLER	QUICKSILVER	EXTEMPORIZE	DIAMONDBACK	TRANSCEIVER
DREADNOUGHT	PROGRESSION	STENOGRAPHY	SUBASSEMBLY	EXTERMINATE	DIAPHORETIC	TRANSFIGURE
DRILLMASTER	PROGRESSIVE	STEPBROTHER	SUBJUNCTIVE	EXTRADITION	EVANGELICAL	TRANSLUCENT
FRAGMENTARY	PROHIBITION	STEREOSCOPE	SUBMERSIBLE	EXTRAPOLATE	FEATHEREDGE	TRANSMITTER
FRANKFURTER	PROLETARIAN	STEREOSCOPY	SUBORDINATE	EXTRAVAGANT	FLABBERGAST	TRANSPARENT
FREETHINKER	PROLETARIAT	STEREOTYPED	SUBSISTENCE	CYBERNATION	FLANNELETTE	UNACCOUNTED
GRANDFATHER	PROLIFERATE	STETHOSCOPE	SUBSTANDARD	CYBERNETICS	FRAGMENTARY	UNALIENABLE
GRANDMOTHER	PROMISCUOUS	STOCKBROKER	SUBSTANTIAL	DYNAMOMETER	FRANKFURTER	UNAVOIDABLE
GRANDPARENT	PROMPTITUDE	STOCKHOLDER	SUBSTANTIVE	GYROCOMPASS	GEANTICLINE	WEATHERCOCK
GRANITEWARE	PROPHYLAXIS	STOCKINETTE	SUBTROPICAL	HYDROCARBON	GRANDFATHER	WEATHERWORN
GRASSHOPPER	PROPINQUITY	STOMACHACHE	SUBURBANITE	HYDROGENATE	GRANDMOTHER	AMBIVALENCE
GRAVITATION	PROPOSITION	STOREKEEPER	SUFFICIENCY	HYDROGRAPHY	GRANDPARENT	ARBITRAMENT
GREASEPAINT	PROPRIETARY	STORYTELLER	SUFFRAGETTE	HYDROPHOBIA	GRANITEWARE	BIBLIOPHILE
GREENGROCER	PROSELYTIZE	STRAIGHTWAY	SUMMERHOUSE	HYDROPONICS	GRASSHOPPER	CABINETWORK
GROUNDSHEET	PROSTATITIS	STRAITLACED	SUPERFICIAL	HYDROSPHERE	GRAVITATION	COBBLESTONE
GROUNDWATER	PROSTHETICS	STRANGULATE	SUPERFLUOUS	HYDROSTATIC	HEARTBROKEN	CYBERNATION
IRIDESCENCE	PROTAGONIST	STRAWFLOWER	SUPERIMPOSE	HYGROSCOPIC	HEARTHSTONE	CYBERNETICS
IRREDENTISM	PROTOMARTYR	STREAMLINED	SUPERINTEND	HYPERACTIVE	HEAVYWEIGHT	HABERDASHER
IRREDUCIBLE	PROTUBERANT	STREAMLINER	SUPERLATIVE	HYPERBOREAN	IMAGESETTER	HABITUATION
IRREFUTABLE	PROVENIENCE	STROBOSCOPE	SUPERMARKET	HYPERTROPHY	IMAGINATION	IMBRICATION
IRRELIGIOUS	PROVISIONAL	UTILITARIAN	SUPERSCRIBE	HYPHENATION	INADVERTENT	JABBERWOCKY
IRREMOVABLE	TRAGEDIENNE	AUDIOVISUAL	SUPERSCRIPT	HYPOTHECATE	INALIENABLE	LABORSAVING
IRREPARABLE	TRAILBLAZER	BUREAUCRACY	SUPERSONICS	HYPOTHESIZE	INATTENTION	LABRADORITE
IRREVERENCE	TRANQUILIZE	BURGOMASTER	SUPPOSITION	NYMPHOMANIA	KWASHIORKOR	LIBERTARIAN
IRREVOCABLE	TRANSACTION	BUSINESSMAN	SUPPOSITORY	SYNCHROMESH	LEATHERNECK	PUBLICATION
ORCHESTRATE	TRANSCEIVER	CUSTOMHOUSE	SUPPRESSANT	SYNCHRONIZE	MEADOWSWEET	SUBASSEMBLY
ORNITHOLOGY	TRANSFIGURE	FUNCTIONARY	SUPREMACIST	SYNCHRONOUS	MEASUREMENT	SUBJUNCTIVE
ORTHODONTIA	TRANSLUCENT	FUNDAMENTAL	SUSCEPTIBLE	SYNCOPATION	NEANDERTHAL	SUBMERSIBLE
ORTHOGRAPHY	TRANSMITTER	FURNISHINGS	TUBERCULATE	SYNTHESIZER	NEARSIGHTED	SUBORDINATE
ORTHOPEDICS	TRANSPARENT	FURTHERMORE	AVOIRDUPOIS	SYSTEMATIZE	PHARISAICAL	SUBSISTENCE
PRACTICABLE	TREACHEROUS	FURTHERMOST	EVANGELICAL	TYPEFOUNDER	PLACEHOLDER	SUBSTANDARD
PREASSIGNED	TRENCHERMAN	GUTTERSNIPE	EVENTUALITY	TYPESETTING	PLAINSPOKEN	SUBSTANTIAL
PRECIPITATE	TREPIDATION	HUCKLEBERRY	EVERLASTING	TYPEWRITING	PLANETARIUM	SUBSTANTIVE
PRECIPITOUS	TRIANGULATE	HUMMINGBIRD	OVERBALANCE	TYPOGRAPHER	PLANETOLOGY	SUBTROPICAL
PRECONCEIVE	TRIBULATION	JUVENOCRACY	OVERBEARING	OZONOSPHERE	PRACTICABLE	SUBURBANITE
PREDECESSOR	TRICHINOSIS	LUCUBRATION	OVERSTUFFED		QUACKSALVER	TOBACCONIST
PREDICAMENT	TRINIDADIAN	MULTIFAMILY	OVERWEENING		QUADRENNIAL	TUBERCULATE
PREDOMINATE	TRINITARIAN	MULTIRACIAL	OVERWROUGHT	**3RD LETTER**	QUADRENNIUM	ACCELERANDO
PREHISTORIC	TRIUMVIRATE	MUSCULATURE	KWASHIORKOR		QUALITATIVE	ACCELERATOR
PREIGNITION	TROPOSPHERE	MUSKELLUNGE	SWALLOWTAIL		QUARTERBACK	ACCEPTATION
PRELIMINARY	TRUEHEARTED	MUTTONCHOPS	SWEEPSTAKES	ACADEMICIAN	QUARTERDECK	ACCLAMATION
PREMEDITATE	TRUSTEESHIP	NUMISMATICS	SWITCHBLADE	ACADEMICISM	REACTIONARY	ACCLIMATIZE
PREMONITION	TRUSTWORTHY	NURSERYMAID	SWITCHBOARD	ANACHRONISM	REALPOLITIK	ACCOMMODATE
PREOCCUPIED	WRONGHEADED	OUTBUILDING	TWELVEMONTH	ANAESTHESIA	ROADABILITY	ACCORDINGLY

ACCOUNTABLE	RECESSIONAL	UNDESIRABLE	PREDICAMENT	INFORMATION	ELIZABETHAN	FILMOGRAPHY
ACCUMULATOR	RECIPROCATE	UNDEVIATING	PREDOMINATE	INFORMATIVE	EPINEPHRINE	GALLBLADDER
ARCHAEOLOGY	RECIPROCITY	WIDEMOUTHED	PREHISTORIC	OFFICIALDOM	HAIRBREADTH	GALLIMAUFRY
ARCHDIOCESE	RECOGNITION	ABECEDARIAN	PREIGNITION	OFFICIALISM	HAIRDRESSER	HALFHEARTED
ARCHIPELAGO	RECONNOITER	ALEXANDRIAN	PRELIMINARY	REFORMATION	HAIRSTYLIST	HALLUCINATE
BACCHANALIA	RECONSTRUCT	ALEXANDRINE	PREMEDITATE	REFORMATORY	IRIDESCENCE	HELLENISTIC
BACKSTRETCH	RECRIMINATE	BREADBASKET	PREMONITION	REFRESHMENT	MAIDSERVANT	ILLIMITABLE
BICARBONATE	RECTILINEAR	BREADWINNER	PREOCCUPIED	REFRIGERATE	OPINIONATED	ILLUSIONISM
BICENTENARY	TACHYCARDIA	BREAKPOINTS	PREPOSITION	SAFEKEEPING	PAINSTAKING	ILLUSTRIOUS
COCKLESHELL	TECHNOCRACY	BREASTPLATE	PREROGATIVE	SUFFICIENCY	PHILOSOPHER	LILLIPUTIAN
DECLARATIVE	UNCERTAINTY	CHEERLEADER	PRESUMPTION	SUFFRAGETTE	POINTILLISM	MALADJUSTED
DECRESCENDO	UNCHRISTIAN	CHEESECLOTH	PRETENTIOUS	UNFAVORABLE	PRIMITIVISM	MALAPROPISM
DICOTYLEDON	UNCIVILIZED	CLEARHEADED	PRETERMINAL	UNFLAPPABLE	PRIZEWINNER	MALEDICTION
DICTATORIAL	UNCOMMITTED	CLERICALISM	PREVARICATE	UNFLINCHING	QUICKSILVER	MALFEASANCE
DOCTRINAIRE	UNCONCERNED	COEDUCATION	SHELLACKING	UNFORTUNATE	REINFECTION	MALFUNCTION
DOCUMENTARY	UNCONSCIOUS	COEFFICIENT	SLEEPWALKER	AGGLOMERATE	SCINTILLATE	MALPRACTICE
ENCAPSULATE	VACATIONIST	COEXTENSIVE	SPECTACULAR	AGGLUTINATE	SEISMOGRAPH	MELANCHOLIA
EXCEEDINGLY	VACCINATION	CREPUSCULAR	SPECTROGRAM	AGGREGATION	SEISMOMETER	MELANCHOLIC
EXCEPTIONAL	VICHYSSOISE	CRESTFALLEN	SPEEDOMETER	COGNOSCENTE	SHIPBUILDER	MELLIFLUOUS
EXCRESCENCE	VICISSITUDE	DREADNOUGHT	SPELLBINDER	ENGINEERING	SMITHEREENS	MILLIAMPERE
HUCKLEBERRY	AUDIOVISUAL	ELECTIONEER	SPENDTHRIFT	HAGIOGRAPHY	SWITCHBLADE	MILLIONAIRE
INCANTATION	ENDOTHERMIC	ELECTRICIAN	STEAMROLLER	HIGHFALUTIN	SWITCHBOARD	MILLISECOND
INCARCERATE	FIDDLESTICK	ELECTRICITY	STENOGRAPHY	HYGROSCOPIC	THISTLEDOWN	MOLLYCODDLE
INCARNADINE	GODDAUGHTER	ELECTROCUTE	STEPBROTHER	INGATHERING	THITHERWARD	MULTIFAMILY
INCARNATION	HYDROCARBON	ELECTROFORM	STEREOSCOPE	INGRATITUDE	TRIANGULATE	MULTIRACIAL
INCERTITUDE	HYDROGENATE	ELECTROLYTE	STEREOSCOPY	LEGERDEMAIN	TRIBULATION	PALEOGRAPHY
INCINERATOR	HYDROGRAPHY	ELECTRONICS	STEREOTYPED	LEGISLATION	TRICHINOSIS	POLLINATION
INCLINATION	HYDROPHOBIA	ELECTROTYPE	STETHOSCOPE	LEGISLATIVE	TRINIDADIAN	POLTERGEIST
INCOMPETENT	HYDROPONICS	ELEPHANTINE	SWEEPSTAKES	LEGISLATURE	TRINITARIAN	POLYNOMINAL
INCONGRUENT	HYDROSPHERE	EVENTUALITY	THEATRICALS	LIGHTWEIGHT	TRIUMVIRATE	POLYSTYRENE
INCONGRUOUS	HYDROSTATIC	EVERLASTING	THENCEFORTH	MAGISTERIAL	UNICELLULAR	POLYTECHNIC
INCONTINENT	INDEFINABLE	FREETHINKER	THEORETICAL	MAGNANIMOUS	UNIFICATION	PULCHRITUDE
INCORPORATE	INDENTATION	GREASEPAINT	THERAPEUTIC	MAGNIFICENT	UNINHIBITED	RELOCATABLE
INCORPOREAL	INDEPENDENT	GREENGROCER	THEREABOUTS	MEGALOMANIA	UTILITARIAN	SOLILOQUIZE
INCREDULOUS	INDIFFERENT	HAEMORRHAGE	THEREWITHAL	MEGALOPOLIS	WAINSCOTING	TELEPRINTER
INCREMENTAL	INDIGESTION	IDENTIFIERS	THERMOCLINE	NIGHTINGALE	WHICHSOEVER	VALEDICTION
INCRIMINATE	INDIGNATION	INEFFECTIVE	THERMOMETER	NIGHTWALKER	WHIFFLETREE	VALEDICTORY
INCUNABULUM	INDIVIDUATE	INEFFECTUAL	TREACHEROUS	REGIMENTALS	WHIPPLETREE	VOLCANOLOGY
LACRIMATION	INDIVISIBLE	INEFFICIENT	TRENCHERMAN	REGURGITATE	ACKNOWLEDGE	BIMETALLISM
LICKSPITTLE	INDOMITABLE	INELUCTABLE	TREPIDATION	SIGNIFICANT	BALLCARRIER	CAMARADERIE
LUCUBRATION	INDUBITABLE	INESCAPABLE	TWELVEMONTH	TIGHTFISTED	BALLETOMANE	CAMEROONIAN
MACHINATION	INDUSTRIOUS	INESTIMABLE	UNEQUIVOCAL	APHRODISIAC	BELLIGERENT	CAMPANOLOGY
MACROBIOTIC	MEDIUMISTIC	INEXCUSABLE	WHEELBARROW	BEHAVIORISM	CALCIFEROUS	CEMENTATION
MACROSCOPIC	MODULARIZED	KLEPTOMANIA	WHEELWRIGHT	EXHAUSTLESS	CALCULATING	COMBINATION
MECHANISTIC	RADIOCARBON	NEEDLEPOINT	WHEREABOUTS	ICHTHYOLOGY	CALCULATION	COMBUSTIBLE
MICROCAPSUL	RADIOMETRIC	NEEDLEWOMAN	WHERESOEVER	SCHOLARSHIP	CALIFORNIUM	COMEUPPANCE
MICROSCOPIC	REDOUBTABLE	OVERBALANCE	WHEREWITHAL	SCHOOLHOUSE	CALLIGRAPHY	COMFORTABLE
MICROSECOND	UNDERCHARGE	OVERBEARING	AFFECTATION	ARISTOCRACY	CALORIMETER	COMMANDMENT
MOCKINGBIRD	UNDEREXPOSE	OVERSTUFFED	AFFIRMATIVE	BOILERMAKER	CHLOROPHYLL	COMMEMORATE
NECESSITATE	UNDERGROUND	OVERWEENING	COFFEEHOUSE	CHIAROSCURO	COLLABORATE	COMMENTATOR
NECESSITOUS	UNDERGROWTH	OVERWROUGHT	DEFALCATION	CHIROGRAPHY	COLLOCATION	COMMINATION
NECKERCHIEF	UNDERHANDED	PLEASURABLE	DEFLORATION	CLIMACTERIC	COLONIALISM	COMMISERATE
NICKELODEON	UNDERSHORTS	PREASSIGNED	DIFFRACTION	CLIMATOLOGY	COLORCASTER	COMMONPLACE
ORCHESTRATE	UNDERSIGNED	PRECIPITATE	EFFICACIOUS	COINCIDENCE	DELECTATION	COMMUNICANT
PACHYSANDRA	UNDERTAKING	PRECIPITOUS	ENFRANCHISE	CRIMINOLOGY	DELETERIOUS	COMMUNICATE
PICTURESQUE	UNDERWEIGHT	PRECONCEIVE	INFANTICIDE	DRILLMASTER	DELINQUENCY	COMMUTATION
POCKETKNIFE	UNDESIGNING	PREDECESSOR	INFLAMMABLE	EDIFICATION	DILAPIDATED	COMMUTATIVE

COMPARATIVE	CENTERPIECE	CONVOCATION	SENSATIONAL	PROHIBITION	EXPECTORATE	TYPEWRITING
COMPARTMENT	CENTRIFUGAL	CONVOLUTION	SENSIBILITY	PROLETARIAN	EXPEDITIOUS	TYPOGRAPHER
COMPETITION	CENTRIPETAL	DENOMINATOR	SENTENTIOUS	PROLETARIAT	EXPENDITURE	UNPRINTABLE
COMPLACENCE	CONCENTRATE	DYNAMOMETER	SENTIMENTAL	PROLIFERATE	EXPERIENCED	ACQUIREMENT
COMPLACENCY	CONCERNMENT	EINSTEINIUM	SYNCHROMESH	PROMISCUOUS	EXPOSTULATE	ACQUISITION
COMPLICATED	CONCOMITANT	FINGERBOARD	SYNCHRONIZE	PROMPTITUDE	EXPROPRIATE	ACQUISITIVE
COMPORTMENT	CONCORDANCE	FINGERPRINT	SYNCHRONOUS	PROPHYLAXIS	HYPERACTIVE	INQUISITION
COMPOSITION	CONCURRENCE	FUNCTIONARY	SYNCOPATION	PROPINQUITY	HYPERBOREAN	INQUISITIVE
COMPTROLLER	CONDITIONAL	FUNDAMENTAL	SYNTHESIZER	PROPOSITION	HYPERTROPHY	REQUIREMENT
COMPUNCTION	CONDITIONED	GENDARMERIE	TENDENTIOUS	PROPRIETARY	HYPHENATION	REQUISITION
COMPUTERIZE	CONDOMINIUM	GENERALSHIP	TONSILLITIS	PROSELYTIZE	HYPOTHECATE	SEQUESTRATE
DEMAGNETIZE	CONDUCTANCE	GENTLEWOMAN	VENTILATION	PROSTATITIS	HYPOTHESIZE	UNQUALIFIED
DEMOCRATIZE	CONFEDERACY	GINGERBREAD	VENTRILOQUY	PROSTHETICS	IMPASSIONED	ABRACADABRA
DEMONSTRATE	CONFEDERATE	HANDICAPPER	VENTURESOME	PROTAGONIST	IMPECUNIOUS	AERONAUTICS
DOMESTICATE	CONFESSEDLY	HANDSHAKING	VINAIGRETTE	PROTOMARTYR	IMPEDIMENTA	AGRICULTURE
DOMESTICITY	CONFORMANCE	HANDWRITING	VINDICATION	PROTUBERANT	IMPERFORATE	BARBITURATE
FAMILIARITY	CONGRESSMAN	HINDQUARTER	WINTERGREEN	PROVENIENCE	IMPERIALISM	BUREAUCRACY
HOMEOSTASIS	CONJUGATION	HONEYSUCKLE	ABOMINATION	PROVISIONAL	IMPERMANENT	BURGOMASTER
HOMESTEADER	CONJUNCTION	IGNOMINIOUS	ABORTIONIST	SHORTCHANGE	IMPERMEABLE	CARAVANSARY
HOMESTRETCH	CONJUNCTIVA	INNERSPRING	ADOLESCENCE	SHORTCOMING	IMPERSONATE	CARDINALATE
HOMOGENEOUS	CONJUNCTIVE	INNUMERABLE	AGORAPHOBIA	SHORTHANDED	IMPERTINENT	CARDINALITY
HUMMINGBIRD	CONJUNCTURE	KINDHEARTED	AMONTILLADO	SMORGASBORD	IMPLAUSIBLE	CARDIOGRAPH
IMMITIGABLE	CONNOISSEUR	KINESTHESIA	APOCYNTHION	SPONTANEOUS	IMPORTATION	CARDSHARPER
IMMORTALITY	CONNOTATION	LINGUISTICS	AVOIRDUPOIS	STOCKBROKER	IMPORTUNATE	CARMINATIVE
IMMORTALIZE	CONNOTATIVE	MANTELPIECE	BIOFEEDBACK	STOCKHOLDER	IMPRACTICAL	CARNIVOROUS
LAMPLIGHTER	CONSECUTIVE	MANUFACTORY	BLOCKBUSTER	STOCKINETTE	IMPREGNABLE	CARRAGEENAN
MEMORABILIA	CONSEQUENCE	MANUFACTURE	BLOODMOBILE	STOMACHACHE	IMPROPRIETY	CARTOGRAPHY
MOMENTARILY	CONSERVANCY	MENDELEVIUM	BLOODSTREAM	STOREKEEPER	IMPROVEMENT	CEREMONIOUS
NUMISMATICS	CONSERVATOR	MENSURATION	BLOODSUCKER	STORYTELLER	IMPROVIDENT	CERTIFICATE
NYMPHOMANIA	CONSIDERATE	MINESWEEPER	BROTHERHOOD	THOUGHTLESS	IMPUISSANCE	CHRISTENDOM
POMEGRANATE	CONSIDERING	MINIATURIZE	CHOCKABLOCK	TROPOSPHERE	NAPHTHALENE	CHRISTIANIA
REMEMBRANCE	CONSIGNMENT	MINNESINGER	CHOIRMASTER	UNOBTRUSIVE	OPPORTUNISM	CHRONOGRAPH
REMINISCENT	CONSISTENCE	MONASTICISM	CHOLESTEROL	UNORGANIZED	OPPORTUNITY	CHRONOMETER
REMONSTRANT	CONSISTENCY	MONEYLENDER	CLOSEFISTED	VIOLONCELLO	OPPROBRIOUS	CIRCULARITY
REMONSTRATE	CONSOLIDATE	MONKEYSHINE	COOPERATIVE	WOODCHOPPER	PAPERHANGER	CIRCULARIZE
ROMANTICISM	CONSPICUOUS	MONOLINGUAL	FLOORWALKER	WRONGHEADED	PAPERWEIGHT	CIRCUMLUNAR
SEMITRAILER	CONSTITUENT	MONSEIGNEUR	FLORESCENCE	ZOOMORPHISM	RAPSCALLION	CIRCUMPOLAR
SUMMERHOUSE	CONSUMERISM	NINNYHAMMER	GEOMAGNETIC	ZOOPLANKTON	REPETITIOUS	CIRCUMSPECT
TEMPERAMENT	CONSUMPTION	NONDESCRIPT	GEOPOLITICS	ALPHABETIZE	REPLACEMENT	CORNERSTONE
TEMPERATURE	CONSUMPTIVE	NONDOCUMENT	GEOSYNCLINE	AMPHETAMINE	REPLICATION	CORPORATION
TEMPESTUOUS	CONTAMINANT	NONETHELESS	GLOSSOLALIA	APPELLATION	REPROBATION	CORRELATIVE
TIMESHARING	CONTAMINATE	NONNEGATIVE	GROUNDSHEET	APPLICATION	SUPERFICIAL	CORRIGENDUM
UNMITIGATED	CONTEMPLATE	NONPARTISAN	GROUNDWATER	APPOINTMENT	SUPERFLUOUS	CORROBORATE
ANNIVERSARY	CONTENTMENT	NONRESIDENT	INOPERATIVE	APPRECIABLE	SUPERIMPOSE	DERELICTION
ANNUNCIATOR	CONTINENTAL	NONVIOLENCE	INOPPORTUNE	APPROBATION	SUPERINTEND	DERMATOLOGY
BENEDICTION	CONTINGENCY	OMNIPRESENT	LIONHEARTED	APPROPRIATE	SUPERLATIVE	DIRECTORATE
BENEFACTION	CONTINUANCE	ORNITHOLOGY	OZONOSPHERE	APPROXIMATE	SUPERMARKET	EARTHENWARE
BENEFICENCE	CONTRACTILE	PANDEMONIUM	PHOTOGRAPHY	CAPACITANCE	SUPERSCRIBE	FARINACEOUS
BENEFICIARY	CONTRAPTION	PENETRATING	PHOTOSPHERE	CAPILLARITY	SUPERSCRIPT	FARTHERMOST
BENEVOLENCE	CONTRARIETY	PENNYWEIGHT	PROBATIONER	COPROCESSOR	SUPERSONICS	FARTHINGALE
CANDELABRUM	CONTRETEMPS	PENTECOSTAL	PROBLEMATIC	DEPRECATORY	SUPPOSITION	FIRECRACKER
CANDIDATURE	CONTRIVANCE	PENULTIMATE	PROCRUSTEAN	DEPREDATION	SUPPOSITORY	FORECLOSURE
CANDLELIGHT	CONTROVERSY	PONTIFICALS	PROFANATORY	DEPRIVATION	SUPPRESSANT	FOREQUARTER
CANDLESTICK	CONURBATION	PONTIFICATE	PROGNATHOUS	DIPLOMATIST	SUPREMACIST	FORESHORTEN
CANNIBALIZE	CONVENIENCE	PUNCTILIOUS	PROGRAMMING	EMPLACEMENT	TOPDRESSING	FORETHOUGHT
CENTENARIAN	CONVENTICLE	PUNCTUATION	PROGRESSION	EXPECTATION	TYPEFOUNDER	FOREVERMORE
CENTERBOARD	CONVERTIBLE	RENAISSANCE	PROGRESSIVE	EXPECTORANT	TYPESETTING	FORMFITTING

FORNICATION	PERISTALSIS	CUSTOMHOUSE	MISBELIEVER	CATERPILLAR	METEOROLOGY	COUNTRYSIDE
FORTHCOMING	PERITONITIS	DESCRIPTION	MISCHIEVOUS	CATHOLICITY	METHODOLOGY	CRUCIFIXION
FORTNIGHTLY	PERMISSIBLE	DESEGREGATE	MISCONCEIVE	COTERMINOUS	METRICATION	EQUIDISTANT
FURNISHINGS	PERMUTATION	DESENSITIZE	MISCONSTRUE	COTTONMOUTH	MOTHERBOARD	EQUILATERAL
FURTHERMORE	PERSNICKETY	DESIDERATUM	MISDEMEANOR	DETERIORATE	MUTTONCHOPS	EQUILIBRIUM
FURTHERMOST	PERSONALITY	DESPERATION	MISFEASANCE	DETERMINANT	NATIONALISM	FAULTFINDER
GARNISHMENT	PERSONALIZE	DESPONDENCY	MISGUIDANCE	DETERMINATE	NATIONALIST	FLUOROSCOPE
GERONTOLOGY	PERSPECTIVE	DESTINATION	MUSCULATURE	DETERMINISM	NATIONALITY	FOULMOUTHED
GERRYMANDER	PERSPICUOUS	DESTRUCTION	MUSKELLUNGE	EXTEMPORARY	NATIONALIZE	HOUSEBROKEN
GYROCOMPASS	PHRASEOLOGY	DISAPPROVAL	OBSERVATION	EXTEMPORIZE	NETHERWORLD	HOUSEKEEPER
HARDHEARTED	PORNOGRAPHY	DISASSEMBLE	OBSERVATORY	EXTERMINATE	NOTHINGNESS	HOUSELIGHTS
HARDWORKING	PORTERHOUSE	DISCONTINUE	OBSOLESCENT	EXTRADITION	ORTHODONTIA	HOUSEMOTHER
HAREBRAINED	PORTIONLESS	DISCOTHEQUE	OBSTRUCTION	EXTRAPOLATE	ORTHOGRAPHY	KNUCKLEBONE
HARPSICHORD	PORTMANTEAU	DISCOURTESY	PESTIFEROUS	EXTRAVAGANT	ORTHOPEDICS	LOUDMOUTHED
HERBIVOROUS	PORTRAITIST	DISCREPANCY	PISCATORIAL	GUTTERSNIPE	OSTENTATION	LOUDSPEAKER
HERPETOLOGY	PORTRAITURE	DISENCUMBER	RESEMBLANCE	INTELLIGENT	OUTBUILDING	MOUNTAINEER
HERRINGBONE	SARCOPHAGUS	DISENTANGLE	RESERVATION	INTENTIONAL	OUTDISTANCE	MOUNTAINTOP
HORSEPLAYER	SCREWDRIVER	DISILLUSION	RESIDENTIAL	INTERACTION	OUTMANEUVER	NOURISHMENT
HORSERADISH	SCRUMPTIOUS	DISORGANIZE	RESIGNATION	INTERACTIVE	OUTSTANDING	SCUTTLEBUTT
IRREDENTISM	SERENDIPITY	DISPENSABLE	RESISTIVITY	INTERATOMIC	PATERNALISM	SHUTTLECOCK
IRREDUCIBLE	SERVICEABLE	DISPLEASURE	RESPECTABLE	INTERCALARY	PETROGRAPHY	THUNDERBOLT
IRREFUTABLE	SPREADSHEET	DISPOSITION	RESPIRATION	INTERCALATE	PITCHBLENDE	THUNDERCLAP
IRRELIGIOUS	SPRINGBOARD	DISPUTATION	RESPLENDENT	INTERCEPTOR	RATHSKELLER	THUNDERHEAD
IRREMOVABLE	STRAIGHTWAY	DISQUIETUDE	RESPONSIBLE	INTERCHANGE	RATIONALISM	TRUEHEARTED
IRREPARABLE	STRAITLACED	DISSEMINATE	RESTITUTION	INTERCOURSE	RATIONALITY	TRUSTEESHIP
IRREVERENCE	STRANGULATE	DISSIMULATE	RESTORATION	INTERESTING	RATIONALIZE	TRUSTWORTHY
IRREVOCABLE	STRAWFLOWER	DISSOLUTION	RESTORATIVE	INTERLACING	RATTLESNAKE	UNUTTERABLE
MARCHIONESS	STREAMLINED	DISTINCTION	RESTRICTION	INTERLINEAR	RETRIBUTION	ADVERSATIVE
MARKETPLACE	STREAMLINER	DISTINCTIVE	RESUSCITATE	INTERLINING	RETROACTIVE	ADVERTISING
MARQUISETTE	STROBOSCOPE	DISTINGUISH	SUSCEPTIBLE	INTERMEDDLE	ROTOGRAVURE	ENVIRONMENT
MARSHMALLOW	TERMINOLOGY	DISTRIBUTOR	SYSTEMATIZE	INTERMINGLE	ROTTENSTONE	INVESTIGATE
MERCHANDISE	TERRESTRIAL	FASHIONABLE	TESTIMONIAL	INTERNECINE	TOTALIZATOR	INVESTITURE
MERCHANTMAN	TERRITORIAL	GESTICULATE	UNSATURATED	INTERNUNCIO	ULTRAMARINE	INVOLUNTARY
MERITOCRACY	UNREASONING	HISTORICITY	UNSPEAKABLE	INTEROFFICE	ULTRAMODERN	JUVENOCRACY
MERITORIOUS	UNRELENTING	HISTRIONICS	WASHERWOMAN	INTERPOLATE	ULTRASONICS	LEVELHEADED
MERRYMAKING	UNREMITTING	HOSPITALITY	WASTEBASKET	INTERPRETER	ULTRAVIOLET	REVERBERATE
MORTARBOARD	UNRIGHTEOUS	HOSPITALIZE	AFTERBURNER	INTERRACIAL	UNTHINKABLE	REVERENTIAL
NARRAGANSET	VARICOLORED	INSCRUTABLE	AFTEREFFECT	INTERREGNUM	UNTOUCHABLE	SOVEREIGNTY
NORTHEASTER	VERMICULITE	INSECTICIDE	ALTERCATION	INTERRELATE	VITICULTURE	UNVARNISHED
NURSERYMAID	VERTIGINOUS	INSEPARABLE	ALTERNATIVE	INTERROGATE	WATERCOURSE	VIVISECTION
PARAMEDICAL	VIRIDESCENT	INSINUATING	ANTECHAMBER	INTERSPERSE	WATERLOGGED	DOWNHEARTED
PARATHYROID	WARMHEARTED	INSOUCIANCE	ANTICYCLONE	INTOLERABLE	WITENAGEMOT	DOWNTRODDEN
PARATROOPER	WORDPERFECT	INSPIRATION	ANTIGRAVITY	INTRACTABLE	ACUPUNCTURE	TOWNSPEOPLE
PARATYPHOID	WORKMANLIKE	INSTABILITY	ANTINEUTRON	INTRAVENOUS	AQUICULTURE	UNWHOLESOME
PARENTHESIS	WORKMANSHIP	INSTALLMENT	ANTIOXIDANT	KITCHENETTE	BLUNDERBUSS	HEXADECIMAL
PARISHIONER	WORKSTATION	INSTANTIATE	ANTIPOVERTY	KITCHENWARE	BOURGEOISIE	BOYSENBERRY
PARTICIPATE	ABSENTEEISM	INSTITUTION	ANTIQUARIAN	LATCHSTRING	BOUTONNIERE	CRYSTALLIZE
PARTICULATE	ABSTRACTION	INSTRUCTION	ASTIGMATISM	LATTICEWORK	CAULIFLOWER	PHYSIOGNOMY
PARTURITION	ASSASSINATE	INSTRUCTIVE	ATTRIBUTIVE	LETTERPRESS	COUNTENANCE	PSYCHEDELIA
PERAMBULATE	ASSEMBLYMAN	INSUPERABLE	BATHYSCAPHE	LITHOGRAPHY	COUNTERFEIT	PSYCHEDELIC
PERCEPTIBLE	ASSIGNATION	LASERWRITER	BATHYSPHERE	LITHOSPHERE	COUNTERMAND	PSYCHODRAMA
PERFECTIBLE	ASSOCIATION	MASSACHUSET	BATTLEFIELD	LITTERATEUR	COUNTERPANE	PSYCHOGENIC
PERFORMANCE	ASSOCIATIVE	MASTERPIECE	BATTLEWAGON	MATERIALISM	COUNTERPART	
PERFUNCTORY	BUSINESSMAN	MESALLIANCE	BITTERSWEET	MATERIALIZE	COUNTERSIGN	
PERIODONTAL	CASSITERITE	MISALLIANCE	CATASTROPHE	MATHEMATICS	COUNTERSINK	
PERIPATETIC	CASTELLATED	MISANTHROPE	CATEGORICAL	MATRICULATE	COUNTERVAIL	
PERIPHRASIS	COSIGNATORY	MISBEGOTTEN	CATERCORNER	METAPHYSICS	COUNTRIFIED	

4TH LETTER						
ABRACADABRA	STRAITLACED	ELECTRICITY	ACADEMICISM	AFTERBURNER	FORETHOUGHT	IRREDENTISM
ASSASSINATE	STRANGULATE	ELECTROCUTE	CANDELABRUM	AFTEREFFECT	FOREVERMORE	IRREDUCIBLE
BEHAVIORISM	STRAWFLOWER	ELECTROFORM	CANDIDATURE	ALTERCATION	FREETHINKER	IRREFUTABLE
BICARBONATE	SUBASSEMBLY	ELECTROLYTE	CANDLELIGHT	ALTERNATIVE	GENERALSHIP	IRRELIGIOUS
BREADBASKET	THEATRICALS	ELECTRONICS	CANDLESTICK	ANAESTHESIA	GREENGROCER	IRREMOVABLE
BREADWINNER	TOBACCONIST	ELECTROTYPE	CARDINALATE	ANTECHAMBER	HABERDASHER	IRREPARABLE
BREAKPOINTS	TOTALIZATOR	FUNCTIONARY	CARDINALITY	APPELLATION	HAREBRAINED	IRREVERENCE
BREASTPLATE	TREACHEROUS	INSCRUTABLE	CARDIOGRAPH	ASSEMBLYMAN	HOMEOSTASIS	IRREVOCABLE
CAMARADERIE	TRIANGULATE	KITCHENETTE	CARDSHARPER	BENEDICTION	HOMESTEADER	JUVENOCRACY
CAPACITANCE	UNFAVORABLE	KITCHENWARE	COEDUCATION	BENEFACTION	HOMESTRETCH	KINESTHESIA
CARAVANSARY	UNSATURATED	KNUCKLEBONE	CONDITIONAL	BENEFICENCE	HONEYSUCKLE	LASERWRITER
CATASTROPHE	UNVARNISHED	LATCHSTRING	CONDITIONED	BENEFICIARY	HYPERACTIVE	LEGERDEMAIN
CHIAROSCURO	VACATIONIST	MARCHIONESS	CONDOMINIUM	BENEVOLENCE	HYPERBOREAN	LEVELHEADED
CLEARHEADED	VINAIGRETTE	MERCHANDISE	CONDUCTANCE	BICENTENARY	HYPERTROPHY	LIBERTARIAN
DEFALCATION	BARBITURATE	MERCHANTMAN	FIDDLESTICK	BIMETALLISM	IMPECUNIOUS	MALEDICTION
DEMAGNETIZE	COBBLESTONE	MISCHIEVOUS	FUNDAMENTAL	BUREAUCRACY	IMPEDIMENTA	MATERIALISM
DILAPIDATED	COMBINATION	MISCONCEIVE	GENDARMERIE	CAMEROONIAN	IMPERFORATE	MATERIALIZE
DISAPPROVAL	COMBUSTIBLE	MISCONSTRUE	GODDAUGHTER	CATEGORICAL	IMPERIALISM	METEOROLOGY
DISASSEMBLE	FLABBERGAST	MUSCULATURE	HANDICAPPER	CATERCORNER	IMPERMANENT	MINESWEEPER
DREADNOUGHT	HERBIVOROUS	PERCEPTIBLE	HANDSHAKING	CATERPILLAR	IMPERMEABLE	MOMENTARILY
DYNAMOMETER	JABBERWOCKY	PISCATORIAL	HANDWRITING	CEMENTATION	IMPERSONATE	MONEYLENDER
ENCAPSULATE	MISBEGOTTEN	PITCHBLENDE	HARDHEARTED	CEREMONIOUS	IMPERTINENT	NECESSITATE
EXHAUSTLESS	MISBELIEVER	PLACEHOLDER	HARDWORKING	CHEERLEADER	INCERTITUDE	NECESSITOUS
GREASEPAINT	OUTBUILDING	PRACTICABLE	HINDQUARTER	CHEESECLOTH	INDEFINABLE	NONETHELESS
HEXADECIMAL	PROBATIONER	PRECIPITATE	INADVERTENT	COMEUPPANCE	INDENTATION	OBSERVATION
IMPASSIONED	PROBLEMATIC	PRECIPITOUS	IRIDESCENCE	COTERMINOUS	INDEPENDENT	OBSERVATORY
INCANTATION	TRIBULATION	PRECONCEIVE	KINDHEARTED	CYBERNATION	INNERSPRING	OSTENTATION
INCARCERATE	UNOBTRUSIVE	PROCRUSTEAN	LOUDMOUTHED	CYBERNETICS	INSECTICIDE	PALEOGRAPHY
INCARNADINE	ABECEDARIAN	PSYCHEDELIA	LOUDSPEAKER	DELECTATION	INSEPARABLE	PAPERHANGER
INCARNATION	ANACHRONISM	PSYCHEDELIC	MAIDSERVANT	DELETERIOUS	INTELLIGENT	PAPERWEIGHT
INFANTICIDE	APOCYNTHION	PSYCHODRAMA	MEADOWSWEET	DERELICTION	INTENTIONAL	PARENTHESIS
INGATHERING	BACCHANALIA	PSYCHOGENIC	MENDELEVIUM	DESEGREGATE	INTERACTION	PATERNALISM
MALADJUSTED	BEACHCOMBER	PULCHRITUDE	MISDEMEANOR	DESENSITIZE	INTERACTIVE	PENETRATING
MALAPROPISM	BLOCKBUSTER	PUNCTILIOUS	NEEDLEPOINT	DETERIORATE	INTERATOMIC	POMEGRANATE
MEGALOMANIA	CALCIFEROUS	PUNCTUATION	NEEDLEWOMAN	DETERMINANT	INTERCALARY	RECESSIONAL
MEGALOPOLIS	CALCULATING	QUACKSALVER	NONDESCRIPT	DETERMINATE	INTERCALATE	REMEMBRANCE
MELANCHOLIA	CALCULATION	QUICKSILVER	NONDOCUMENT	DETERMINISM	INTERCEPTOR	REPETITIOUS
MELANCHOLIC	CHOCKABLOCK	REACTIONARY	OUTDISTANCE	DIRECTORATE	INTERCHANGE	RESEMBLANCE
MESALLIANCE	CIRCULARITY	SARCOPHAGUS	PANDEMONIUM	DISENCUMBER	INTERCOURSE	RESERVATION
METAPHYSICS	CIRCULARIZE	SPACEFLIGHT	PREDECESSOR	DISENTANGLE	INTERESTING	REVERBERATE
MISALLIANCE	CIRCUMLUNAR	SPECTACULAR	PREDICAMENT	DOMESTICATE	INTERLACING	REVERENTIAL
MISANTHROPE	CIRCUMPOLAR	SPECTROGRAM	PREDOMINATE	DOMESTICITY	INTERLINEAR	SAFEKEEPING
MONASTICISM	CIRCUMSPECT	STOCKBROKER	QUADRENNIAL	EXCEEDINGLY	INTERLINING	SCREWDRIVER
PARAMEDICAL	CONCENTRATE	STOCKHOLDER	QUADRENNIUM	EXCEPTIONAL	INTERMEDDLE	SERENDIPITY
PARATHYROID	CONCERNMENT	STOCKINETTE	ROADABILITY	EXPECTATION	INTERMINGLE	SLEEPWALKER
PARATROOPER	CONCOMITANT	SUSCEPTIBLE	TENDENTIOUS	EXPECTORANT	INTERNECINE	SOVEREIGNTY
PARATYPHOID	CONCORDANCE	SYNCHROMESH	TOPDRESSING	EXPECTORATE	INTERNUNCIO	SPEEDOMETER
PERAMBULATE	CONCURRENCE	SYNCHRONIZE	VINDICATION	EXPEDITIOUS	INTEROFFICE	SPREADSHEET
PHRASEOLOGY	CRACKERJACK	SYNCHRONOUS	WOODCHOPPER	EXPENDITURE	INTERPOLATE	STREAMLINED
PLEASURABLE	CRUCIFIXION	SYNCOPATION	WORDPERFECT	EXPERIENCED	INTERPRETER	STREAMLINER
PREASSIGNED	DESCRIPTION	TRICHINOSIS	ABSENTEEISM	EXTEMPORARY	INTERRACIAL	SUPERFICIAL
RENAISSANCE	DISCONTINUE	UNACCOUNTED	ACCELERANDO	EXTEMPORIZE	INTERREGNUM	SUPERFLUOUS
ROMANTICISM	DISCOTHEQUE	UNICELLULAR	ACCELERATOR	EXTERMINATE	INTERRELATE	SUPERIMPOSE
STEAMROLLER	DISCOURTESY	VACCINATION	ACCEPTATION	FIRECRACKER	INTERROGATE	SUPERINTEND
STRAIGHTWAY	DISCREPANCY	VOLCANOLOGY	ADVERSATIVE	FORECLOSURE	INTERSPERSE	SUPERLATIVE
	ELECTIONEER	WHICHSOEVER	ADVERTISING	FOREQUARTER	INVESTIGATE	SUPERMARKET
	ELECTRICIAN	ACADEMICIAN	AFFECTATION	FORESHORTEN	INVESTITURE	SUPERSCRIBE

SUPERSCRIPT	SUFFRAGETTE	VICHYSSOISE	NATIONALISM	POCKETKNIFE	TWELVEMONTH	CONNOISSEUR
SUPERSONICS	UNIFICATION	WASHERWOMAN	NATIONALIST	WORKMANLIKE	UNALIENABLE	CONNOTATION
SWEEPSTAKES	WHIFFLETREE	AFFIRMATIVE	NATIONALITY	WORKMANSHIP	UNFLAPPABLE	CONNOTATIVE
TELEPRINTER	BRAGGADOCIO	AGRICULTURE	NATIONALIZE	WORKSTATION	UNFLINCHING	CORNERSTONE
TIMESHARING	BURGOMASTER	AMBIVALENCE	NUMISMATICS	ACCLAMATION	UTILITARIAN	COUNTENANCE
TRUEHEARTED	CONGRESSMAN	ANNIVERSARY	OFFICIALDOM	ACCLIMATIZE	VIOLONCELLO	COUNTERFEIT
TUBERCULATE	FINGERBOARD	ANTICYCLONE	OFFICIALISM	ADOLESCENCE	ABOMINATION	COUNTERMAND
TYPEFOUNDER	FINGERPRINT	ANTIGRAVITY	OMNIPRESENT	AGGLOMERATE	BLAMEWORTHY	COUNTERPANE
TYPESETTING	FRAGMENTARY	ANTINEUTRON	ORNITHOLOGY	AGGLUTINATE	CARMINATIVE	COUNTERPART
TYPEWRITING	GINGERBREAD	ANTIOXIDANT	PARISHIONER	APPLICATION	CHAMBERLAIN	COUNTERSIGN
UNCERTAINTY	IMAGESETTER	ANTIPOVERTY	PERIODONTAL	BALLCARRIER	CHAMBERMAID	COUNTERSINK
UNDERCHARGE	IMAGINATION	ANTIQUARIAN	PERIPATETIC	BALLETOMANE	CLIMACTERIC	COUNTERVAIL
UNDEREXPOSE	LINGUISTICS	AQUICULTURE	PERIPHRASIS	BELLIGERENT	CLIMATOLOGY	COUNTRIFIED
UNDERGROUND	MISGUIDANCE	ARBITRAMENT	PERISTALSIS	BIBLIOPHILE	COMMANDMENT	COUNTRYSIDE
UNDERGROWTH	PROGNATHOUS	ASSIGNATION	PERITONITIS	BOILERMAKER	COMMEMORATE	DOWNHEARTED
UNDERHANDED	PROGRAMMING	ASTIGMATISM	PLAINSPOKEN	CALLIGRAPHY	COMMENTATOR	DOWNTRODDEN
UNDERSHORTS	PROGRESSION	AUDIOVISUAL	PREIGNITION	CAULIFLOWER	COMMINATION	EPINEPHRINE
UNDERSIGNED	PROGRESSIVE	AVOIRDUPOIS	RADIOCARBON	CHOLESTEROL	COMMISERATE	EVANGELICAL
UNDERTAKING	TRAGEDIENNE	BUSINESSMAN	RADIOMETRIC	COLLABORATE	COMMONPLACE	EVENTUALITY
UNDERWEIGHT	ALPHABETIZE	CABINETWORK	RATIONALISM	COLLOCATION	COMMUNICANT	FLANNELETTE
UNDESIGNING	AMPHETAMINE	CALIFORNIUM	RATIONALITY	DECLARATIVE	COMMUNICATE	FORNICATION
UNDESIRABLE	ARCHAEOLOGY	CAPILLARITY	RATIONALIZE	DEFLORATION	COMMUTATION	FRANKFURTER
UNDEVIATING	ARCHDIOCESE	CHOIRMASTER	RECIPROCATE	DIPLOMATIST	COMMUTATIVE	FURNISHINGS
UNREASONING	ARCHIPELAGO	CHRISTENDOM	RECIPROCITY	DRILLMASTER	CRIMINOLOGY	GARNISHMENT
UNRELENTING	BATHYSCAPHE	CHRISTIANIA	REGIMENTALS	EMPLACEMENT	DERMATOLOGY	GEANTICLINE
UNREMITTING	BATHYSPHERE	CLAIRVOYANT	REMINISCENT	FAULTFINDER	DIAMAGNETIC	GRANDFATHER
VALEDICTION	CATHOLICITY	COSIGNATORY	RESIDENTIAL	FOULMOUTHED	DIAMONDBACK	GRANDMOTHER
VALEDICTORY	FASHIONABLE	DELINQUENCY	RESIGNATION	GALLBLADDER	FILMOGRAPHY	GRANDPARENT
WATERCOURSE	HIGHFALUTIN	DESIDERATUM	RESISTIVITY	GALLIMAUFRY	FORMFITTING	GRANITEWARE
WATERLOGGED	HYPHENATION	DISILLUSION	SEMITRAILER	HALLUCINATE	GEOMAGNETIC	IDENTIFIERS
WHEELBARROW	LIGHTWEIGHT	EFFICACIOUS	SOLILOQUIZE	HELLENISTIC	HAEMORRHAGE	LIONHEARTED
WHEELWRIGHT	LITHOGRAPHY	ENGINEERING	SPRINGBOARD	IMPLAUSIBLE	HUMMINGBIRD	MAGNANIMOUS
WIDEMOUTHED	LITHOSPHERE	ENVIRONMENT	TRAILBLAZER	INALIENABLE	OUTMANEUVER	MAGNIFICENT
WITENAGEMOT	MACHINATION	EQUIDISTANT	UNCIVILIZED	INCLINATION	PERMISSIBLE	MINNESINGER
BIOFEEDBACK	MATHEMATICS	EQUILATERAL	UNMITIGATED	INELUCTABLE	PERMUTATION	MOUNTAINEER
COEFFICIENT	MECHANISTIC	EQUILIBRIUM	UNRIGHTEOUS	INFLAMMABLE	PREMEDITATE	MOUNTAINTOP
COFFEEHOUSE	METHODOLOGY	FAMILIARITY	VARICOLORED	LILLIPUTIAN	PREMONITION	NEANDERTHAL
COMFORTABLE	MOTHERBOARD	FARINACEOUS	VICISSITUDE	MELLIFLUOUS	PRIMITIVISM	NINNYHAMMER
CONFEDERACY	NAPHTHALENE	HABITUATION	VIRIDESCENT	MILLIAMPERE	PROMISCUOUS	NONNEGATIVE
CONFEDERATE	NETHERWORLD	HAGIOGRAPHY	VITICULTURE	MILLIONAIRE	PROMPTITUDE	OPINIONATED
CONFESSEDLY	NIGHTINGALE	ILLIMITABLE	VIVISECTION	MILLISECOND	STOMACHACHE	OZONOSPHERE
CONFORMANCE	NIGHTWALKER	IMMITIGABLE	CONJUGATION	MOLLYCODDLE	SUBMERSIBLE	PAINSTAKING
DIFFRACTION	NOTHINGNESS	INCINERATOR	CONJUNCTION	PHILOSOPHER	SUMMERHOUSE	PENNYWEIGHT
EDIFICATION	ORCHESTRATE	INDIFFERENT	CONJUNCTIVA	POLLINATION	TERMINOLOGY	PLANETARIUM
HALFHEARTED	ORTHODONTIA	INDIGESTION	CONJUNCTIVE	PRELIMINARY	VERMICULITE	PLANETOLOGY
INEFFECTIVE	ORTHOGRAPHY	INDIGNATION	CONJUNCTURE	PROLETARIAN	WARMHEARTED	POINTILLISM
INEFFECTUAL	ORTHOPEDICS	INDIVIDUATE	SUBJUNCTIVE	PROLETARIAT	ZOOMORPHISM	PORNOGRAPHY
INEFFICIENT	PACHYSANDRA	INDIVISIBLE	BACKSTRETCH	PROLIFERATE	ACKNOWLEDGE	REINFECTION
MALFEASANCE	PREHISTORIC	INSINUATING	COCKLESHELL	PUBLICATION	AMONTILLADO	SCINTILLATE
MALFUNCTION	PROHIBITION	LEGISLATION	HUCKLEBERRY	QUALITATIVE	BLUNDERBUSS	SIGNIFICANT
MISFEASANCE	RATHSKELLER	LEGISLATIVE	LICKSPITTLE	REALPOLITIK	CANNIBALIZE	SPENDTHRIFT
PERFECTIBLE	TACHYCARDIA	LEGISLATURE	MARKETPLACE	REPLACEMENT	CARNIVOROUS	SPONTANEOUS
PERFORMANCE	TECHNOCRACY	MAGISTERIAL	MOCKINGBIRD	REPLICATION	CHANCELLERY	STANDARDIZE
PERFUNCTORY	TIGHTFISTED	MEDIUMISTIC	MONKEYSHINE	SHELLACKING	CHANTICLEER	STENOGRAPHY
PROFANATORY	UNCHRISTIAN	MERITOCRACY	MUSKELLUNGE	SPELLBINDER	CLANDESTINE	THENCEFORTH
SCAFFOLDING	UNTHINKABLE	MERITORIOUS	NECKERCHIEF	SWALLOWTAIL	COGNOSCENTE	THUNDERBOLT
SUFFICIENCY	UNWHOLESOME	MINIATURIZE	NICKELODEON	THALIDOMIDE	COINCIDENCE	THUNDERCLAP

THUNDERHEAD	INFORMATION	ELEPHANTINE	DEPRECATORY	OVERWROUGHT	CONSUMERISM	BOUTONNIERE
TOWNSPEOPLE	INFORMATIVE	GEOPOLITICS	DEPREDATION	PETROGRAPHY	CONSUMPTION	BROTHERHOOD
TRANQUILIZE	INSOUCIANCE	HARPSICHORD	DEPRIVATION	PHARISAICAL	CONSUMPTIVE	CARTOGRAPHY
TRANSACTION	INTOLERABLE	HERPETOLOGY	ENFRANCHISE	PREROGATIVE	CRESTFALLEN	CASTELLATED
TRANSCEIVER	INVOLUNTARY	HOSPITALITY	EVERLASTING	QUARTERBACK	CRYSTALLIZE	CENTENARIAN
TRANSFIGURE	LABORSAVING	HOSPITALIZE	EXCRESCENCE	QUARTERDECK	DISSEMINATE	CENTERBOARD
TRANSLUCENT	MEMORABILIA	INOPERATIVE	EXPROPRIATE	RECRIMINATE	DISSIMULATE	CENTERPIECE
TRANSMITTER	MONOLINGUAL	INOPPORTUNE	EXTRADITION	REFRESHMENT	DISSOLUTION	CENTRIFUGAL
TRANSPARENT	OBSOLESCENT	INSPIRATION	EXTRAPOLATE	REFRIGERATE	EINSTEINIUM	CENTRIPETAL
TRENCHERMAN	OPPORTUNISM	KLEPTOMANIA	EXTRAVAGANT	REPROBATION	GEOSYNCLINE	CERTIFICATE
TRINIDADIAN	OPPORTUNITY	LAMPLIGHTER	FLORESCENCE	RETRIBUTION	GLOSSOLALIA	CONTAMINANT
TRINITARIAN	PREOCCUPIED	MALPRACTICE	GERRYMANDER	RETROACTIVE	GRASSHOPPER	CONTAMINATE
UNINHIBITED	RECOGNITION	NONPARTISAN	HAIRBREADTH	SEARCHLIGHT	HORSEPLAYER	CONTEMPLATE
WAINSCOTING	RECONNOITER	NYMPHOMANIA	HAIRDRESSER	SHAREHOLDER	HORSERADISH	CONTENTMENT
WRONGHEADED	RECONSTRUCT	PREPOSITION	HAIRSTYLIST	SHORTCHANGE	HOUSEBROKEN	CONTINENTAL
ACCOMMODATE	REDOUBTABLE	PROPHYLAXIS	HEARTBROKEN	SHORTCOMING	HOUSEKEEPER	CONTINGENCY
ACCORDINGLY	REFORMATION	PROPINQUITY	HEARTHSTONE	SHORTHANDED	HOUSELIGHTS	CONTINUANCE
ACCOUNTABLE	REFORMATORY	PROPOSITION	HERRINGBONE	SMORGASBORD	HOUSEMOTHER	CONTRACTILE
AERONAUTICS	RELOCATABLE	PROPRIETARY	HYDROCARBON	STEREOSCOPE	INESCAPABLE	CONTRAPTION
APPOINTMENT	REMONSTRANT	RESPECTABLE	HYDROGENATE	STEREOSCOPY	INESTIMABLE	CONTRARIETY
ASSOCIATION	REMONSTRATE	RESPIRATION	HYDROGRAPHY	STEREOTYPED	KWASHIORKOR	CONTRETEMPS
ASSOCIATIVE	ROTOGRAVURE	RESPLENDENT	HYDROPHOBIA	STOREKEEPER	MARSHMALLOW	CONTRIVANCE
BLOODMOBILE	SCHOLARSHIP	RESPONSIBLE	HYDROPONICS	STORYTELLER	MASSACHUSET	CONTROVERSY
BLOODSTREAM	SCHOOLHOUSE	SHIPBUILDER	HYDROSPHERE	SUPREMACIST	MEASUREMENT	COTTONMOUTH
BLOODSUCKER	STROBOSCOPE	STEPBROTHER	HYDROSTATIC	TERRESTRIAL	MENSURATION	CUSTOMHOUSE
CALORIMETER	SUBORDINATE	SUPPOSITION	HYGROSCOPIC	TERRITORIAL	MONSEIGNEUR	DESTINATION
CHLOROPHYLL	THEORETICAL	SUPPOSITORY	IMBRICATION	THERAPEUTIC	NURSERYMAID	DESTRUCTION
CHRONOGRAPH	TYPOGRAPHER	SUPPRESSANT	IMPRACTICAL	THEREABOUTS	OUTSTANDING	DICTATORIAL
CHRONOMETER	UNCOMMITTED	TEMPERAMENT	IMPREGNABLE	THEREWITHAL	PERSNICKETY	DISTINCTION
COLONIALISM	UNCONCERNED	TEMPERATURE	IMPROPRIETY	THERMOCLINE	PERSONALITY	DISTINCTIVE
COLORCASTER	UNCONSCIOUS	TEMPESTUOUS	IMPROVEMENT	THERMOMETER	PERSONALIZE	DISTINGUISH
DEMOCRATIZE	UNFORTUNATE	TREPIDATION	IMPROVIDENT	ULTRAMARINE	PERSPECTIVE	DISTRIBUTOR
DEMONSTRATE	UNTOUCHABLE	TROPOSPHERE	INCREDULOUS	ULTRAMODERN	PERSPICUOUS	DOCTRINAIRE
DENOMINATOR	ACUPUNCTURE	UNSPEAKABLE	INCREMENTAL	ULTRASONICS	PHYSIOGNOMY	EARTHENWARE
DICOTYLEDON	CAMPANOLOGY	WHIPPLETREE	INCRIMINATE	ULTRAVIOLET	PRESUMPTION	FARTHERMOST
DISORGANIZE	COMPARATIVE	ZOOPLANKTON	INGRATITUDE	UNORGANIZED	PROSELYTIZE	FARTHINGALE
ENDOTHERMIC	COMPARTMENT	DISQUIETUDE	INTRACTABLE	UNPRINTABLE	PROSTATITIS	FEATHEREDGE
EXPOSTULATE	COMPETITION	MARQUISETTE	INTRAVENOUS	WHEREABOUTS	PROSTHETICS	FORTHCOMING
FLOORWALKER	COMPLACENCE	UNEQUIVOCAL	LABRADORITE	WHERESOEVER	RAPSCALLION	FORTNIGHTLY
FLUOROSCOPE	COMPLACENCY	ABORTIONIST	LACRIMATION	WHEREWITHAL	SEISMOGRAPH	FURTHERMORE
GERONTOLOGY	COMPLICATED	AGGREGATION	MACROBIOTIC	ANASTOMOSIS	SEISMOMETER	FURTHERMOST
GYROCOMPASS	COMPORTMENT	AGORAPHOBIA	MACROSCOPIC	ARISTOCRACY	SENSATIONAL	GENTLEWOMAN
HOMOGENEOUS	COMPOSITION	APHRODISIAC	MATRICULATE	BOYSENBERRY	SENSIBILITY	GESTICULATE
HYPOTHECATE	COMPTROLLER	APPRECIABLE	MERRYMAKING	CASSITERITE	SUBSISTENCE	GUTTERSNIPE
HYPOTHESIZE	COMPUNCTION	APPROBATION	METRICATION	CLOSEFISTED	SUBSTANDARD	HISTORICITY
IGNOMINIOUS	COMPUTERIZE	APPROPRIATE	MICROCAPSUL	CONSECUTIVE	SUBSTANTIAL	HISTRIONICS
IMMORTALITY	COOPERATIVE	APPROXIMATE	MICROSCOPIC	CONSEQUENCE	SUBSTANTIVE	ICHTHYOLOGY
IMMORTALIZE	CORPORATION	ATTRIBUTIVE	MICROSECOND	CONSERVANCY	TEASPOONFUL	INATTENTION
IMPORTATION	CRAPSHOOTER	BOURGEOISIE	NARRAGANSET	CONSERVATOR	THISTLEDOWN	INSTABILITY
IMPORTUNATE	CREPUSCULAR	CARRAGEENAN	NEARSIGHTED	CONSIDERATE	TOASTMASTER	INSTALLMENT
INCOMPETENT	DESPERATION	CHIROGRAPHY	NONRESIDENT	CONSIDERING	TONSILLITIS	INSTANTIATE
INCONGRUENT	DESPONDENCY	CLERICALISM	NOURISHMENT	CONSIGNMENT	TRUSTEESHIP	INSTITUTION
INCONGRUOUS	DIAPHORETIC	COPROCESSOR	OPPROBRIOUS	CONSISTENCE	TRUSTWORTHY	INSTRUCTION
INCONTINENT	DISPENSABLE	CORRELATIVE	OVERBALANCE	CONSISTENCY	ABSTRACTION	INSTRUCTIVE
INCORPORATE	DISPLEASURE	CORRIGENDUM	OVERBEARING	CONSOLIDATE	BATTLEFIELD	LATTICEWORK
INCORPOREAL	DISPOSITION	CORROBORATE	OVERSTUFFED	CONSPICUOUS	BATTLEWAGON	LEATHERNECK
INDOMITABLE	DISPUTATION	DECRESCENDO	OVERWEENING	CONSTITUENT	BITTERSWEET	LETTERPRESS

LITTERATEUR	WEATHERCOCK	POLYTECHNIC	OUTMANEUVER	GYROCOMPASS	ACADEMICIAN	HORSEPLAYER
MANTELPIECE	WEATHERWORN	ELIZABETHAN	PISCATORIAL	IMPECUNIOUS	ACADEMICISM	HORSERADISH
MASTERPIECE	WINTERGREEN	PRIZEWINNER	PREVARICATE	INESCAPABLE	ADOLESCENCE	HOUSEBROKEN
MORTARBOARD	ACCUMULATOR		PROBATIONER	INEXCUSABLE	AGGREGATION	HOUSEKEEPER
MULTIFAMILY	ACQUIREMENT		PROFANATORY	INSECTICIDE	AMPHETAMINE	HOUSELIGHTS
MULTIRACIAL	ACQUISITION	**5TH LETTER**	PROTAGONIST	OFFICIALDOM	APPRECIABLE	HOUSEMOTHER
MUTTONCHOPS	ACQUISITIVE		REPLACEMENT	OFFICIALISM	BALLETOMANE	HYPHENATION
NORTHEASTER	ANNUNCIATOR		ROADABILITY	PREOCCUPIED	BIOFEEDBACK	IMAGESETTER
OBSTRUCTION	CONURBATION	ACCLAMATION	SENSATIONAL	RAPSCALLION	BITTERSWEET	IMPREGNABLE
PARTICIPATE	DOCUMENTARY	AGORAPHOBIA	SPREADSHEET	RELOCATABLE	BLAMEWORTHY	INCREDULOUS
PARTICULATE	GROUNDSHEET	ALEXANDRIAN	STOMACHACHE	SEARCHLIGHT	BOILERMAKER	INCREMENTAL
PARTURITION	GROUNDWATER	ALEXANDRINE	STREAMLINED	SWITCHBLADE	BOYSENBERRY	INOPERATIVE
PENTECOSTAL	ILLUSIONISM	ALPHABETIZE	STREAMLINER	SWITCHBOARD	CANDELABRUM	IRIDESCENCE
PESTIFEROUS	ILLUSTRIOUS	ARCHAEOLOGY	THERAPEUTIC	THENCEFORTH	CASTELLATED	JABBERWOCKY
PHOTOGRAPHY	IMPUISSANCE	BUREAUCRACY	ULTRAMARINE	TOBACCONIST	CENTENARIAN	LETTERPRESS
PHOTOSPHERE	INCUNABULUM	CAMPANOLOGY	ULTRAMODERN	TREACHEROUS	CENTERBOARD	LITTERATEUR
PICTURESQUE	INDUBITABLE	CARRAGEENAN	ULTRASONICS	TRENCHERMAN	CENTERPIECE	MALFEASANCE
POLTERGEIST	INDUSTRIOUS	CLIMACTERIC	ULTRAVIOLET	UNACCOUNTED	CHOLESTEROL	MANTELPIECE
PONTIFICALS	INNUMERABLE	CLIMATOLOGY	UNFLAPPABLE	VARICOLORED	CLOSEFISTED	MARKETPLACE
PONTIFICATE	INQUISITION	COLLABORATE	UNREASONING	VITICULTURE	COFFEEHOUSE	MASTERPIECE
PORTERHOUSE	INQUISITIVE	COMMANDMENT	VOLCANOLOGY	WOODCHOPPER	COMMEMORATE	MATHEMATICS
PORTIONLESS	INSUPERABLE	COMPARATIVE	CHAMBERLAIN	ARCHDIOCESE	COMMENTATOR	MENDELEVIUM
PORTMANTEAU	LUCUBRATION	COMPARTMENT	CHAMBERMAID	BENEDICTION	COMPETITION	MINNESINGER
PORTRAITIST	MANUFACTORY	CONTAMINANT	FLABBERGAST	BLOODMOBILE	CONCENTRATE	MISBEGOTTEN
PORTRAITURE	MANUFACTURE	CONTAMINATE	GALLBLADDER	BLOODSTREAM	CONCERNMENT	MISBELIEVER
PRETENTIOUS	MODULARIZED	DECLARATIVE	HAIRBREADTH	BLOODSUCKER	CONFEDERACY	MISDEMEANOR
PRETERMINAL	PENULTIMATE	DERMATOLOGY	HAREBRAINED	BLUNDERBUSS	CONFEDERATE	MISFEASANCE
PROTAGONIST	REGURGITATE	DIAMAGNETIC	INDUBITABLE	BREADBASKET	CONFESSEDLY	MONKEYSHINE
PROTOMARTYR	REQUIREMENT	DICTATORIAL	LUCUBRATION	BREADWINNER	CONSECUTIVE	MONSEIGNEUR
PROTUBERANT	REQUISITION	ELIZABETHAN	OVERBALANCE	CLANDESTINE	CONSEQUENCE	MOTHERBOARD
RATTLESNAKE	RESUSCITATE	EMPLACEMENT	OVERBEARING	DESIDERATUM	CONSERVANCY	MUSKELLUNGE
RECTILINEAR	SCRUMPTIOUS	ENFRANCHISE	SHIPBUILDER	DREADNOUGHT	CONSERVATOR	NECKERCHIEF
RESTITUTION	SEQUESTRATE	EXTRADITION	STEPBROTHER	EQUIDISTANT	CONTEMPLATE	NETHERWORLD
RESTORATION	SUBURBANITE	EXTRAPOLATE	STROBOSCOPE	EXPEDITIOUS	CONTENTMENT	NICKELODEON
RESTORATIVE	THOUGHTLESS	EXTRAVAGANT	ABRACADABRA	GRANDFATHER	CONVENIENCE	NONDESCRIPT
RESTRICTION	TRIUMVIRATE	FUNDAMENTAL	AFFECTATION	GRANDMOTHER	CONVENTICLE	NONNEGATIVE
ROTTENSTONE	UNQUALIFIED	GENDARMERIE	AGRICULTURE	GRANDPARENT	CONVERTIBLE	NONRESIDENT
SCUTTLEBUTT	CONVENIENCE	GEOMAGNETIC	ANTECHAMBER	HAIRDRESSER	COOPERATIVE	NURSERYMAID
SENTENTIOUS	CONVENTICLE	GODDAUGHTER	ANTICYCLONE	HEXADECIMAL	CORNERSTONE	ORCHESTRATE
SENTIMENTAL	CONVERTIBLE	IMPLAUSIBLE	AQUICULTURE	IMPEDIMENTA	CORRELATIVE	PANDEMONIUM
SHUTTLECOCK	CONVOCATION	IMPRACTICAL	ASSOCIATION	IRREDENTISM	DECRESCENDO	PENTECOSTAL
SMITHEREENS	CONVOLUTION	INFLAMMABLE	ASSOCIATIVE	IRREDUCIBLE	DEPRECATORY	PERCEPTIBLE
STETHOSCOPE	GRAVITATION	INGRATITUDE	BALLCARRIER	MALADJUSTED	DEPREDATION	PERFECTIBLE
SUBTROPICAL	HEAVYWEIGHT	INSTABILITY	CAPACITANCE	MALEDICTION	DESPERATION	PLACEHOLDER
SWITCHBLADE	NONVIOLENCE	INSTALLMENT	CHANCELLERY	NEANDERTHAL	DISPENSABLE	PLANETARIUM
SWITCHBOARD	PREVARICATE	INSTANTIATE	COINCIDENCE	RESIDENTIAL	DISSEMINATE	PLANETOLOGY
SYNTHESIZER	PROVENIENCE	INTRACTABLE	DELECTATION	SPEEDOMETER	EPINEPHRINE	POCKETKNIFE
SYSTEMATIZE	PROVISIONAL	INTRAVENOUS	DEMOCRATIZE	SPENDTHRIFT	EXCEEDINGLY	POLTERGEIST
TESTIMONIAL	SERVICEABLE	LABRADORITE	DIRECTORATE	STANDARDIZE	EXCRESCENCE	PORTERHOUSE
THITHERWARD	UNAVOIDABLE	MAGNANIMOUS	EFFICACIOUS	THUNDERBOLT	FINGERBOARD	PREDECESSOR
UNUTTERABLE	ALEXANDRIAN	MASSACHUSET	EXPECTATION	THUNDERCLAP	FINGERPRINT	PREMEDITATE
VENTILATION	ALEXANDRINE	MECHANISTIC	EXPECTORANT	THUNDERHEAD	FLORESCENCE	PRETENTIOUS
VENTRILOQUY	COEXTENSIVE	MINIATURIZE	EXPECTORATE	VALEDICTION	GINGERBREAD	PRETERMINAL
VENTURESOME	INEXCUSABLE	MORTARBOARD	FIRECRACKER	VALEDICTORY	GUTTERSNIPE	PRIZEWINNER
VERTIGINOUS	POLYNOMINAL	NARRAGANSET	FORECLOSURE	VIRIDESCENT	HELLENISTIC	PROLETARIAN
WASTEBASKET	POLYSTYRENE	NONPARTISAN		ABECEDARIAN	HERPETOLOGY	PROLETARIAT

PROSELYTIZE	BOURGEOISIE	PSYCHODRAMA	CRIMINOLOGY	PHARISAICAL	VINDICATION	RESPLENDENT
PROVENIENCE	BRAGGADOCIO	PSYCHOGENIC	CRUCIFIXION	PHYSIOGNOMY	BLOCKBUSTER	SCHOLARSHIP
REFRESHMENT	CATEGORICAL	PULCHRITUDE	DEPRIVATION	POLLINATION	BREAKPOINTS	SHELLACKING
RESPECTABLE	COSIGNATORY	SMITHEREENS	DESTINATION	PONTIFICALS	CHOCKABLOCK	SOLILOQUIZE
ROTTENSTONE	DEMAGNETIZE	STETHOSCOPE	DISSIMULATE	PONTIFICATE	CRACKERJACK	SPELLBINDER
SENTENTIOUS	DESEGREGATE	SYNCHROMESH	DISTINCTION	PORTIONLESS	FRANKFURTER	SWALLOWTAIL
SEQUESTRATE	EVANGELICAL	SYNCHRONIZE	DISTINCTIVE	PRECIPITATE	KNUCKLEBONE	TOTALIZATOR
SHAREHOLDER	HOMOGENEOUS	SYNCHRONOUS	DISTINGUISH	PRECIPITOUS	QUACKSALVER	TRAILBLAZER
SPACEFLIGHT	INDIGESTION	SYNTHESIZER	EDIFICATION	PREDICAMENT	QUICKSILVER	UNRELENTING
STEREOSCOPE	INDIGNATION	THITHERWARD	FASHIONABLE	PREHISTORIC	SAFEKEEPING	WHEELBARROW
STEREOSCOPY	POMEGRANATE	TRICHINOSIS	FORNICATION	PRELIMINARY	STOCKBROKER	WHEELWRIGHT
STEREOTYPED	PREIGNITION	TRUEHEARTED	FURNISHINGS	PRIMITIVISM	STOCKHOLDER	ZOOPLANKTON
STOREKEEPER	RECOGNITION	UNINHIBITED	GALLIMAUFRY	PROHIBITION	STOCKINETTE	ACCOMMODATE
SUBMERSIBLE	RESIGNATION	WARMHEARTED	GARNISHMENT	PROLIFERATE	ACCELERANDO	ACCUMULATOR
SUMMERHOUSE	ROTOGRAVURE	WEATHERCOCK	GESTICULATE	PROMISCUOUS	ACCELERATOR	ASSEMBLYMAN
SUPREMACIST	SMORGASBORD	WEATHERWORN	GRANITEWARE	PROPINQUITY	APPELLATION	CEREMONIOUS
SUSCEPTIBLE	THOUGHTLESS	WHICHSOEVER	GRAVITATION	PROVISIONAL	BATTLEFIELD	DENOMINATOR
SYSTEMATIZE	TYPOGRAPHER	ABOMINATION	HANDICAPPER	PUBLICATION	BATTLEWAGON	DOCUMENTARY
TEMPERAMENT	UNORGANIZED	ACCLIMATIZE	HERBIVOROUS	QUALITATIVE	CANDLELIGHT	DYNAMOMETER
TEMPERATURE	UNRIGHTEOUS	ACQUIREMENT	HERRINGBONE	RECRIMINATE	CANDLESTICK	EXTEMPORARY
TEMPESTUOUS	WRONGHEADED	ACQUISITION	HOSPITALITY	RECTILINEAR	CAPILLARITY	EXTEMPORIZE
TENDENTIOUS	ANACHRONISM	ACQUISITIVE	HOSPITALIZE	REFRIGERATE	COBBLESTONE	FOULMOUTHED
TERRESTRIAL	BACCHANALIA	APPLICATION	HUMMINGBIRD	RENAISSANCE	COCKLESHELL	FRAGMENTARY
THEREABOUTS	BEACHCOMBER	APPOINTMENT	IMAGINATION	REPLICATION	COMPLACENCE	IGNOMINIOUS
THEREWITHAL	BROTHERHOOD	ARCHIPELAGO	IMBRICATION	REQUIREMENT	COMPLACENCY	ILLIMITABLE
TRAGEDIENNE	DIAPHORETIC	ATTRIBUTIVE	IMPUISSANCE	REQUISITION	COMPLICATED	INCOMPETENT
UNICELLULAR	DOWNHEARTED	BARBITURATE	INALIENABLE	RESPIRATION	DEFALCATION	INDOMITABLE
UNSPEAKABLE	EARTHENWARE	BELLIGERENT	INCLINATION	RESTITUTION	DERELICTION	INNUMERABLE
WASHERWOMAN	ELEPHANTINE	BIBLIOPHILE	INCRIMINATE	RETRIBUTION	DISILLUSION	IRREMOVABLE
WASTEBASKET	FARTHERMOST	CALCIFEROUS	INQUISITION	SENSIBILITY	DISPLEASURE	LOUDMOUTHED
WHEREABOUTS	FARTHINGALE	CALLIGRAPHY	INQUISITIVE	SENTIMENTAL	DRILLMASTER	PARAMEDICAL
WHERESOEVER	FEATHEREDGE	CANDIDATURE	INSPIRATION	SERVICEABLE	EQUILATERAL	PERAMBULATE
WHEREWITHAL	FORTHCOMING	CANNIBALIZE	INSTITUTION	SIGNIFICANT	EQUILIBRIUM	PORTMANTEAU
WINTERGREEN	FURTHERMORE	CARDINALATE	LACRIMATION	STRAIGHTWAY	EVERLASTING	REGIMENTALS
BENEFACTION	FURTHERMOST	CARDINALITY	LATTICEWORK	STRAITLACED	FAMILIARITY	REMEMBRANCE
BENEFICENCE	HALFHEARTED	CARDIOGRAPH	LILLIPUTIAN	SUBSISTENCE	FIDDLESTICK	RESEMBLANCE
BENEFICIARY	HARDHEARTED	CARMINATIVE	MACHINATION	SUFFICIENCY	GENTLEWOMAN	SCRUMPTIOUS
CALIFORNIUM	ICHTHYOLOGY	CARNIVOROUS	MAGNIFICENT	TERMINOLOGY	HUCKLEBERRY	SEISMOGRAPH
COEFFICIENT	KINDHEARTED	CASSITERITE	MATRICULATE	TERRITORIAL	INTELLIGENT	SEISMOMETER
FORMFITTING	KITCHENETTE	CAULIFLOWER	MELLIFLUOUS	TESTIMONIAL	INTOLERABLE	STEAMROLLER
HIGHFALUTIN	KITCHENWARE	CERTIFICATE	METRICATION	THALIDOMIDE	INVOLUNTARY	THERMOCLINE
INDEFINABLE	KWASHIORKOR	CLERICALISM	MILLIAMPERE	TONSILLITIS	IRRELIGIOUS	THERMOMETER
INDIFFERENT	LATCHSTRING	COMBINATION	MILLIONAIRE	TREPIDATION	LAMPLIGHTER	TRIUMVIRATE
INEFFECTIVE	LEATHERNECK	COMMINATION	MILLISECOND	TRINIDADIAN	LEVELHEADED	UNCOMMITTED
INEFFECTUAL	LIONHEARTED	COMMISERATE	MOCKINGBIRD	TRINITARIAN	MEGALOMANIA	UNREMITTING
INEFFICIENT	MARCHIONESS	CONDITIONAL	MULTIFAMILY	UNALIENABLE	MEGALOPOLIS	WIDEMOUTHED
IRREFUTABLE	MARSHMALLOW	CONDITIONED	MULTIRACIAL	UNFLINCHING	MESALLIANCE	WORKMANLIKE
MANUFACTORY	MERCHANDISE	CONSIDERATE	NONVIOLENCE	UNIFICATION	MISALLIANCE	WORKMANSHIP
MANUFACTURE	MERCHANTMAN	CONSIDERING	NOTHINGNESS	UNPRINTABLE	MODULARIZED	ABSENTEEISM
REINFECTION	MISCHIEVOUS	CONSIGNMENT	NOURISHMENT	UNTHINKABLE	MONOLINGUAL	AERONAUTICS
SCAFFOLDING	NORTHEASTER	CONSISTENCE	OPINIONATED	UTILITARIAN	NEEDLEPOINT	ANNUNCIATOR
TYPEFOUNDER	NYMPHOMANIA	CONSISTENCY	OUTDISTANCE	VACCINATION	NEEDLEWOMAN	ANTINEUTRON
WHIFFLETREE	PITCHBLENDE	CONTINENTAL	PARTICIPATE	VENTILATION	OBSOLESCENT	BICENTENARY
ANTIGRAVITY	PROPHYLAXIS	CONTINGENCY	PARTICULATE	VERMICULITE	PENULTIMATE	BUSINESSMAN
ASSIGNATION	PSYCHEDELIA	CONTINUANCE	PERMISSIBLE	VERTIGINOUS	PROBLEMATIC	CABINETWORK
ASTIGMATISM	PSYCHEDELIC	CORRIGENDUM	PESTIFEROUS	VINAIGRETTE	RATTLESNAKE	CEMENTATION

CHRONOGRAPH	APPROPRIATE	LITHOSPHERE	UNWHOLESOME	CHOIRMASTER	INSTRUCTION	REVERENTIAL
CHRONOMETER	APPROXIMATE	MACROBIOTIC	VIOLONCELLO	CLAIRVOYANT	INSTRUCTIVE	SOVEREIGNTY
COLONIALISM	AUDIOVISUAL	MACROSCOPIC	ZOOMORPHISM	CLEARHEADED	INTERACTION	SUBORDINATE
DELINQUENCY	BOUTONNIERE	MEADOWSWEET	ACCEPTATION	COLORCASTER	INTERACTIVE	SUBTROPICAL
DEMONSTRATE	BURGOMASTER	METEOROLOGY	ANTIPOVERTY	CONGRESSMAN	INTERATOMIC	SUBURBANITE
DESENSITIZE	CARTOGRAPHY	METHODOLOGY	CONSPICUOUS	CONTRACTILE	INTERCALARY	SUFFRAGETTE
DISENCUMBER	CATHOLICITY	MICROCAPSUL	DILAPIDATED	CONTRAPTION	INTERCALATE	SUPERFICIAL
DISENTANGLE	CHIROGRAPHY	MICROSCOPIC	DISAPPROVAL	CONTRARIETY	INTERCEPTOR	SUPERFLUOUS
ENGINEERING	COGNOSCENTE	MICROSECOND	ENCAPSULATE	CONTRETEMPS	INTERCHANGE	SUPERIMPOSE
EXPENDITURE	COLLOCATION	MISCONCEIVE	EXCEPTIONAL	CONTRIVANCE	INTERCOURSE	SUPERINTEND
FARINACEOUS	COMFORTABLE	MISCONSTRUE	INDEPENDENT	CONTROVERSY	INTERESTING	SUPERLATIVE
FLANNELETTE	COMMONPLACE	MUTTONCHOPS	INOPPORTUNE	CONURBATION	INTERLACING	SUPERMARKET
FORTNIGHTLY	COMPORTMENT	NATIONALISM	INSEPARABLE	COTERMINOUS	INTERLINEAR	SUPERSCRIBE
GERONTOLOGY	COMPOSITION	NATIONALIST	INSUPERABLE	CYBERNATION	INTERLINING	SUPERSCRIPT
GREENGROCER	CONCOMITANT	NATIONALITY	IRREPARABLE	CYBERNETICS	INTERMEDDLE	SUPERSONICS
GROUNDSHEET	CONCORDANCE	NATIONALIZE	MALAPROPISM	DESCRIPTION	INTERMINGLE	SUPPRESSANT
GROUNDWATER	CONDOMINIUM	NONDOCUMENT	METAPHYSICS	DESTRUCTION	INTERNECINE	THEORETICAL
INCANTATION	CONFORMANCE	OPPROBRIOUS	OMNIPRESENT	DETERIORATE	INTERNUNCIO	TOPDRESSING
INCINERATOR	CONNOISSEUR	ORTHODONTIA	PERIPATETIC	DETERMINANT	INTEROFFICE	TUBERCULATE
INCONGRUENT	CONNOTATION	ORTHOGRAPHY	PERIPHRASIS	DETERMINATE	INTERPOLATE	UNCERTAINTY
INCONGRUOUS	CONNOTATIVE	ORTHOPEDICS	PERSPECTIVE	DETERMINISM	INTERPRETER	UNCHRISTIAN
INCONTINENT	CONSOLIDATE	OZONOSPHERE	PERSPICUOUS	DIFFRACTION	INTERRACIAL	UNDERCHARGE
INCUNABULUM	CONVOCATION	PALEOGRAPHY	PROMPTITUDE	DISCREPANCY	INTERREGNUM	UNDEREXPOSE
INDENTATION	CONVOLUTION	PERFORMANCE	REALPOLITIK	DISORGANIZE	INTERRELATE	UNDERGROUND
INFANTICIDE	COPROCESSOR	PERIODONTAL	RECIPROCATE	DISTRIBUTOR	INTERROGATE	UNDERGROWTH
INSINUATING	CORPORATION	PERSONALITY	RECIPROCITY	DOCTRINAIRE	INTERSPERSE	UNDERHANDED
INTENTIONAL	CORROBORATE	PERSONALIZE	SLEEPWALKER	ENVIRONMENT	LABORSAVING	UNDERSHORTS
JUVENOCRACY	COTTONMOUTH	PETROGRAPHY	SWEEPSTAKES	EXPERIENCED	LASERWRITER	UNDERSIGNED
MELANCHOLIA	CUSTOMHOUSE	PHILOSOPHER	TEASPOONFUL	EXTERMINATE	LEGERDEMAIN	UNDERTAKING
MELANCHOLIC	DEFLORATION	PHOTOGRAPHY	TELEPRINTER	FLOORWALKER	LIBERTARIAN	UNDERWEIGHT
MISANTHROPE	DESPONDENCY	PHOTOSPHERE	WHIPPLETREE	FLUOROSCOPE	MALPRACTICE	UNFORTUNATE
MOMENTARILY	DIAMONDBACK	PORNOGRAPHY	WORDPERFECT	GENERALSHIP	MATERIALISM	UNVARNISHED
OSTENTATION	DIPLOMATIST	PRECONCEIVE	ANTIQUARIAN	HABERDASHER	MATERIALIZE	VENTRILOQUY
PARENTHESIS	DISCONTINUE	PREDOMINATE	FOREQUARTER	HISTRIONICS	MEMORABILIA	WATERCOURSE
PERSNICKETY	DISCOTHEQUE	PREMONITION	HINDQUARTER	HYPERACTIVE	OBSERVATION	WATERLOGGED
PLAINSPOKEN	DISCOURTESY	PREPOSITION	TRANQUILIZE	HYPERBOREAN	OBSERVATORY	ANAESTHESIA
POLYNOMINAL	DISPOSITION	PREROGATIVE	ABSTRACTION	HYPERTROPHY	OBSTRUCTION	ASSASSINATE
PROGNATHOUS	DISSOLUTION	PROPOSITION	ACCORDINGLY	IMMORTALITY	OPPORTUNISM	BACKSTRETCH
RECONNOITER	EXPROPRIATE	PROTOMARTYR	ADVERSATIVE	IMMORTALIZE	OPPORTUNITY	BREASTPLATE
RECONSTRUCT	FILMOGRAPHY	RADIOCARBON	ADVERTISING	IMPERFORATE	PAPERHANGER	CARDSHARPER
REMINISCENT	GEOPOLITICS	RADIOMETRIC	AFFIRMATIVE	IMPERIALISM	PAPERWEIGHT	CATASTROPHE
REMONSTRANT	HAEMORRHAGE	RATIONALISM	AFTERBURNER	IMPERMANENT	PATERNALISM	CHEESECLOTH
REMONSTRATE	HAGIOGRAPHY	RATIONALITY	AFTEREFFECT	IMPERMEABLE	PORTRAITIST	CHRISTENDOM
ROMANTICISM	HISTORICITY	RATIONALIZE	ALTERCATION	IMPERSONATE	PORTRAITURE	CHRISTIANIA
SERENDIPITY	HOMEOSTASIS	REPROBATION	ALTERNATIVE	IMPERTINENT	PROCRUSTEAN	CRAPSHOOTER
SPRINGBOARD	HYDROCARBON	RESPONSIBLE	AVOIRDUPOIS	IMPORTATION	PROGRAMMING	DISASSEMBLE
STRANGULATE	HYDROGENATE	RESTORATION	BICARBONATE	IMPORTUNATE	PROGRESSION	DOMESTICATE
TECHNOCRACY	HYDROGRAPHY	RESTORATIVE	CALORIMETER	INCARCERATE	PROGRESSIVE	DOMESTICITY
TRIANGULATE	HYDROPHOBIA	RETROACTIVE	CAMARADERIE	INCARNADINE	PROPRIETARY	EXPOSTULATE
UNCONCERNED	HYDROPONICS	SARCOPHAGUS	CAMEROONIAN	INCARNATION	QUADRENNIAL	FORESHORTEN
UNCONSCIOUS	HYDROSPHERE	SCHOOLHOUSE	CATERCORNER	INCERTITUDE	QUADRENNIUM	GLOSSOLALIA
WITENAGEMOT	HYDROSTATIC	STENOGRAPHY	CATERPILLAR	INCORPORATE	REFORMATION	GRASSHOPPER
ACKNOWLEDGE	HYGROSCOPIC	SUPPOSITION	CENTRIFUGAL	INCORPOREAL	REFORMATORY	GREASEPAINT
AGGLOMERATE	IMPROPRIETY	SUPPOSITORY	CENTRIPETAL	INFORMATION	REGURGITATE	HAIRSTYLIST
ANTIOXIDANT	IMPROVEMENT	SYNCOPATION	CHEERLEADER	INFORMATIVE	RESERVATION	HANDSHAKING
APHRODISIAC	IMPROVIDENT	TROPOSPHERE	CHIAROSCURO	INNERSPRING	RESTRICTION	HARPSICHORD
APPROBATION	LITHOGRAPHY	UNAVOIDABLE	CHLOROPHYLL	INSCRUTABLE	REVERBERATE	HOMESTEADER

HOMESTRETCH	COMPTROLLER	PARATYPHOID	CONCURRENCE	SCREWDRIVER	IRREPARABLE	HEARTBROKEN
ILLUSIONISM	CONSTITUENT	PENETRATING	CONDUCTANCE	STRAWFLOWER	MALFEASANCE	HOUSEBROKEN
ILLUSTRIOUS	COUNTENANCE	PERITONITIS	CONJUGATION	TYPEWRITING	MALPRACTICE	HYPERBOREAN
IMPASSIONED	COUNTERFEIT	POINTILLISM	CONJUNCTION	APOCYNTHION	MANUFACTORY	INSTABILITY
INDUSTRIOUS	COUNTERMAND	POLYTECHNIC	CONJUNCTIVA	BATHYSCAPHE	MANUFACTURE	MACROBIOTIC
INVESTIGATE	COUNTERPANE	PRACTICABLE	CONJUNCTIVE	BATHYSPHERE	MEMORABILIA	OPPROBRIOUS
INVESTITURE	COUNTERPART	PROSTATITIS	CONJUNCTURE	GEOSYNCLINE	MERCHANDISE	PERAMBULATE
KINESTHESIA	COUNTERSIGN	PROSTHETICS	CONSUMERISM	GERRYMANDER	MERCHANTMAN	PITCHBLENDE
LEGISLATION	COUNTERSINK	PUNCTILIOUS	CONSUMPTION	HEAVYWEIGHT	MILLIAMPERE	PROHIBITION
LEGISLATIVE	COUNTERVAIL	PUNCTUATION	CONSUMPTIVE	HONEYSUCKLE	MISFEASANCE	PROTUBERANT
LEGISLATURE	COUNTRIFIED	QUARTERBACK	CREPUSCULAR	MERRYMAKING	MODULARIZED	REDOUBTABLE
LICKSPITTLE	COUNTRYSIDE	QUARTERDECK	DISPUTATION	MOLLYCODDLE	MOUNTAINEER	REMEMBRANCE
LOUDSPEAKER	CRESTFALLEN	REACTIONARY	DISQUIETUDE	MONEYLENDER	MOUNTAINTOP	REPROBATION
MAGISTERIAL	CRYSTALLIZE	REPETITIOUS	EXHAUSTLESS	NINNYHAMMER	OUTSTANDING	RESEMBLANCE
MAIDSERVANT	DELETERIOUS	SCINTILLATE	HALLUCINATE	PACHYSANDRA	OVERBALANCE	RETRIBUTION
MINESWEEPER	DICOTYLEDON	SCUTTLEBUTT	INELUCTABLE	PENNYWEIGHT	PERIPATETIC	REVERBERATE
MONASTICISM	DOWNTRODDEN	SEMITRAILER	INSOUCIANCE	STORYTELLER	PORTMANTEAU	ROADABILITY
NEARSIGHTED	EINSTEINIUM	SHORTCHANGE	LINGUISTICS	TACHYCARDIA	PORTRAITIST	SENSIBILITY
NECESSITATE	ELECTIONEER	SHORTCOMING	MALFUNCTION	VICHYSSOISE	PORTRAITURE	SPELLBINDER
NECESSITOUS	ELECTRICIAN	SHORTHANDED	MARQUISETTE		PROGNATHOUS	STOCKBROKER
NUMISMATICS	ELECTRICITY	SHUTTLECOCK	MEASUREMENT		PROGRAMMING	SUBURBANITE
OVERSTUFFED	ELECTROCUTE	SPECTACULAR	MEDIUMISTIC		PROSTATITIS	TRAILBLAZER
PAINSTAKING	ELECTROFORM	SPECTROGRAM	MENSURATION	**6TH LETTER**	RAPSCALLION	WASTEBASKET
PARISHIONER	ELECTROLYTE	SPONTANEOUS	MISGUIDANCE		RELOCATABLE	WHEELBARROW
PERISTALSIS	ELECTRONICS	SUBSTANDARD	MUSCULATURE	ABRACADABRA	RETROACTIVE	ALTERCATION
PHRASEOLOGY	ELECTROTYPE	SUBSTANTIAL	OUTBUILDING	ABSTRACTION	SCHOLARSHIP	ANNUNCIATOR
PLEASURABLE	ENDOTHERMIC	SUBSTANTIVE	PARTURITION	AERONAUTICS	SHELLACKING	APPLICATION
POLYSTYRENE	EVENTUALITY	THEATRICALS	PERFUNCTORY	AMBIVALENCE	SMORGASBORD	APPRECIABLE
PREASSIGNED	FAULTFINDER	THISTLEDOWN	PERMUTATION	BACCHANALIA	SPECTACULAR	BEACHCOMBER
RATHSKELLER	FORETHOUGHT	TIGHTFISTED	PICTURESQUE	BALLCARRIER	SPONTANEOUS	CATERCORNER
RECESSIONAL	FREETHINKER	TOASTMASTER	PRESUMPTION	BENEFACTION	STANDARDIZE	CLERICALISM
RESISTIVITY	FUNCTIONARY	TRUSTEESHIP	PROTUBERANT	BIMETALLISM	SUBSTANDARD	CLIMACTERIC
RESUSCITATE	GEANTICLINE	TRUSTWORTHY	REDOUBTABLE	BRAGGADOCIO	SUBSTANTIAL	COEDUCATION
SUBASSEMBLY	HABITUATION	UNMITIGATED	SUBJUNCTIVE	CAMARADERIE	SUBSTANTIVE	COLLOCATION
TIMESHARING	HEARTBROKEN	UNOBTRUSIVE	TRIBULATION	CARAVANSARY	SUFFRAGETTE	COLORCASTER
TOWNSPEOPLE	HEARTHSTONE	UNSATURATED	UNEQUIVOCAL	CHOCKABLOCK	THEREABOUTS	CONDUCTANCE
TRANSACTION	HYPOTHECATE	UNUTTERABLE	UNTOUCHABLE	COMPLACENCE	TRANSACTION	CONSECUTIVE
TRANSCEIVER	HYPOTHESIZE	VACATIONIST	VENTURESOME	COMPLACENCY	UNORGANIZED	CONVOCATION
TRANSFIGURE	IDENTIFIERS	ACCOUNTABLE	AMBIVALENCE	CONTRACTILE	UNSPEAKABLE	COPROCESSOR
TRANSLUCENT	IMMITIGABLE	ACUPUNCTURE	ANNIVERSARY	CONTRAPTION	WHEREABOUTS	DEFALCATION
TRANSMITTER	INATTENTION	AGGLUTINATE	BEHAVIORISM	CONTRARIETY	WITENAGEMOT	DEPRECATORY
TRANSPARENT	INESTIMABLE	CALCULATING	BENEVOLENCE	CRYSTALLIZE	WORKMANLIKE	DISENCUMBER
TYPESETTING	INGATHERING	CALCULATION	CARAVANSARY	DIFFRACTION	WORKMANSHIP	EDIFICATION
UNDESIGNING	KLEPTOMANIA	CIRCULARITY	FOREVERMORE	EFFICACIOUS	ZOOPLANKTON	EMPLACEMENT
UNDESIRABLE	LIGHTWEIGHT	CIRCULARIZE	INADVERTENT	ELEPHANTINE	AFTERBURNER	FORNICATION
VICISSITUDE	MERITOCRACY	CIRCUMLUNAR	INDIVIDUATE	EQUILATERAL	ALPHABETIZE	FORTHCOMING
VIVISECTION	MERITORIOUS	CIRCUMPOLAR	INDIVISIBLE	EVERLASTING	APPROBATION	GESTICULATE
WAINSCOTING	MOUNTAINEER	CIRCUMSPECT	IRREVERENCE	FARINACEOUS	ASSEMBLYMAN	HALLUCINATE
WORKSTATION	MOUNTAINTOP	COEDUCATION	IRREVOCABLE	GENERALSHIP	ATTRIBUTIVE	HANDICAPPER
ABORTIONIST	NAPHTHALENE	COMBUSTIBLE	TWELVEMONTH	HIGHFALUTIN	BICARBONATE	HYDROCARBON
AMONTILLADO	NIGHTINGALE	COMEUPPANCE	UNCIVILIZED	HYPERACTIVE	BLOCKBUSTER	IMBRICATION
ANASTOMOSIS	NIGHTWALKER	COMMUNICANT	UNDEVIATING	INCUNABULUM	BREADBASKET	IMPRACTICAL
ARBITRAMENT	NONETHELESS	COMMUNICATE	UNFAVORABLE	INESCAPABLE	CANNIBALIZE	INCARCERATE
ARISTOCRACY	ORNITHOLOGY	COMMUTATION	HANDWRITING	INSEPARABLE	COLLABORATE	INELUCTABLE
BIMETALLISM	OUTSTANDING	COMMUTATIVE	HARDWORKING	INTERACTION	CONURBATION	INSOUCIANCE
CHANTICLEER	PARATHYROID	COMPUNCTION	OVERWEENING	INTERACTIVE	CORROBORATE	INTERCALARY
COEXTENSIVE	PARATROOPER	COMPUTERIZE	OVERWROUGHT	INTERATOMIC	ELIZABETHAN	INTERCALATE

INTERCEPTOR	GROUNDWATER	DOCUMENTARY	PSYCHEDELIC	STRAWFLOWER	HEARTHSTONE	DISQUIETUDE
INTERCHANGE	HABERDASHER	DOWNHEARTED	QUADRENNIAL	SUPERFICIAL	HYPOTHECATE	DISTRIBUTOR
INTERCOURSE	INCREDULOUS	EARTHENWARE	QUADRENNIUM	SUPERFLUOUS	HYPOTHESIZE	DOCTRINAIRE
INTRACTABLE	LABRADORITE	EINSTEINIUM	QUARTERBACK	TIGHTFISTED	INGATHERING	ELECTIONEER
LATTICEWORK	LEGERDEMAIN	ENGINEERING	QUARTERDECK	TRANSFIGURE	LEVELHEADED	EQUIDISTANT
MASSACHUSET	METHODOLOGY	EVANGELICAL	RATTLESNAKE	AGGREGATION	METAPHYSICS	EQUILIBRIUM
MATRICULATE	ORTHODONTIA	FARTHERMOST	REGIMENTALS	BELLIGERENT	NAPHTHALENE	EXPEDITIOUS
MELANCHOLIA	PERIODONTAL	FEATHEREDGE	REINFECTION	CALLIGRAPHY	NINNYHAMMER	EXPERIENCED
MELANCHOLIC	PREMEDITATE	FIDDLESTICK	RESIDENTIAL	CARRAGEENAN	NONETHELESS	FAMILIARITY
METRICATION	SCREWDRIVER	FLABBERGAST	RESPLENDENT	CARTOGRAPHY	ORNITHOLOGY	FARTHINGALE
MICROCAPSUL	SERENDIPITY	FLANNELETTE	REVERENTIAL	CHIROGRAPHY	PAPERHANGER	FORMFITTING
MOLLYCODDLE	SPREADSHEET	FOREVERMORE	SAFEKEEPING	CONJUGATION	PARATHYROID	FORTNIGHTLY
NONDOCUMENT	SUBORDINATE	FRAGMENTARY	SMITHEREENS	CONSIGNMENT	PARISHIONER	FUNCTIONARY
PARTICIPATE	THALIDOMIDE	FURTHERMORE	SOVEREIGNTY	CORRIGENDUM	PERIPHRASIS	GEANTICLINE
PARTICULATE	TRAGEDIENNE	FURTHERMOST	SUPPRESSANT	DIAMAGNETIC	PLACEHOLDER	HARPSICHORD
PENTECOSTAL	TREPIDATION	GENTLEWOMAN	SYNTHESIZER	DISORGANIZE	PROSTHETICS	HISTRIONICS
PERFECTIBLE	TRINIDADIAN	GREASEPAINT	THENCEFORTH	FILMOGRAPHY	SEARCHLIGHT	IDENTIFIERS
PREDECESSOR	ACCELERANDO	HALFHEARTED	THEORETICAL	GEOMAGNETIC	SHAREHOLDER	IGNOMINIOUS
PREDICAMENT	ACCELERATOR	HARDHEARTED	THITHERWARD	GREENGROCER	SHORTHANDED	ILLIMITABLE
PREOCCUPIED	AFTEREFFECT	HEXADECIMAL	THUNDERBOLT	HAGIOGRAPHY	STOCKHOLDER	ILLUSIONISM
PUBLICATION	ANNIVERSARY	HOMOGENEOUS	THUNDERCLAP	HYDROGENATE	SWITCHBLADE	IMMITIGABLE
RADIOCARBON	ANTINEUTRON	HUCKLEBERRY	THUNDERHEAD	HYDROGRAPHY	SWITCHBOARD	IMPEDIMENTA
REPLACEMENT	ARCHAEOLOGY	INADVERTENT	TOPDRESSING	IMPREGNABLE	THOUGHTLESS	IMPERIALISM
REPLICATION	BATTLEFIELD	INALIENABLE	TRUEHEARTED	INCONGRUENT	TIMESHARING	INDEFINABLE
RESPECTABLE	BATTLEWAGON	INATTENTION	TRUSTEESHIP	INCONGRUOUS	TREACHEROUS	INDIVIDUATE
RESUSCITATE	BIOFEEDBACK	INCINERATOR	TWELVEMONTH	LITHOGRAPHY	TRENCHERMAN	INDIVISIBLE
SERVICEABLE	BLUNDERBUSS	INDEPENDENT	TYPESETTING	MISBEGOTTEN	UNDERHANDED	INDOMITABLE
SHORTCHANGE	BOURGEOISIE	INDIGESTION	UNALIENABLE	NARRAGANSET	UNRIGHTEOUS	INDUBITABLE
SHORTCOMING	BROTHERHOOD	INEFFECTIVE	UNDEREXPOSE	NONNEGATIVE	WOODCHOPPER	INEFFICIENT
STOMACHACHE	BUSINESSMAN	INEFFECTUAL	UNRELENTING	ORTHOGRAPHY	WRONGHEADED	INESTIMABLE
SUFFICIENCY	CABINETWORK	INNUMERABLE	UNUTTERABLE	PALEOGRAPHY	ABORTIONIST	IRRELIGIOUS
TACHYCARDIA	CANDLELIGHT	INSUPERABLE	VIRIDESCENT	PETROGRAPHY	AMONTILLADO	KWASHIORKOR
TOBACCONIST	CANDLESTICK	INTERESTING	VIVISECTION	PHOTOGRAPHY	ARCHDIOCESE	LAMPLIGHTER
TRANSCEIVER	CHAMBERLAIN	INTOLERABLE	WARMHEARTED	PORNOGRAPHY	ASSOCIATION	LINGUISTICS
TUBERCULATE	CHAMBERMAID	IRREDENTISM	WEATHERCOCK	PREROGATIVE	ASSOCIATIVE	MALEDICTION
UNCONCERNED	CHANCELLERY	IRREVERENCE	WEATHERWORN	PROTAGONIST	BEHAVIORISM	MARCHIONESS
UNDERCHARGE	CHEESECLOTH	KINDHEARTED	WORDPERFECT	REFRIGERATE	BENEDICTION	MARQUISETTE
UNIFICATION	CLANDESTINE	KITCHENETTE	CALCIFEROUS	REGURGITATE	BENEFICENCE	MATERIALISM
UNTOUCHABLE	COBBLESTONE	KITCHENWARE	CAULIFLOWER	SPRINGBOARD	BENEFICIARY	MATERIALIZE
VERMICULITE	COCKLESHELL	LEATHERNECK	CERTIFICATE	STENOGRAPHY	CALORIMETER	MISCHIEVOUS
VINDICATION	COEXTENSIVE	LIONHEARTED	CLOSEFISTED	STRAIGHTWAY	CAPACITANCE	MISGUIDANCE
WAINSCOTING	COFFEEHOUSE	MAIDSERVANT	CRESTFALLEN	STRANGULATE	CENTRIFUGAL	MONOLINGUAL
WATERCOURSE	CONGRESSMAN	NEANDERTHAL	CRUCIFIXION	TRIANGULATE	CENTRIPETAL	MONSEIGNEUR
ABECEDARIAN	CONTRETEMPS	NEEDLEPOINT	FAULTFINDER	UNDERGROUND	CHANTICLEER	NEARSIGHTED
ACCORDINGLY	COUNTENANCE	NEEDLEWOMAN	FRANKFURTER	UNDERGROWTH	COEFFICIENT	NIGHTINGALE
APHRODISIAC	COUNTERFEIT	NORTHEASTER	GRANDFATHER	VERTIGINOUS	COINCIDENCE	OFFICIALDOM
AVOIRDUPOIS	COUNTERMAND	OBSOLESCENT	IMPERFORATE	VINAIGRETTE	COLONIALISM	OFFICIALISM
CANDIDATURE	COUNTERPANE	OVERBEARING	INDIFFERENT	ANTECHAMBER	COMPLICATED	OUTBUILDING
CONFEDERACY	COUNTERPART	OVERWEENING	MAGNIFICENT	CARDSHARPER	CONNOISSEUR	PERSNICKETY
CONFEDERATE	COUNTERSIGN	PARAMEDICAL	MELLIFLUOUS	CLEARHEADED	CONSPICUOUS	PERSPICUOUS
CONSIDERATE	COUNTERSINK	PERSPECTIVE	MULTIFAMILY	CRAPSHOOTER	CONSTITUENT	POINTILLISM
CONSIDERING	COUNTERVAIL	PHRASEOLOGY	PESTIFEROUS	ENDOTHERMIC	CONTRIVANCE	PRACTICABLE
DEPREDATION	CRACKERJACK	POLYTECHNIC	PONTIFICALS	FORESHORTEN	DENOMINATOR	PROPRIETARY
EXCEEDINGLY	DELETERIOUS	PROBLEMATIC	PONTIFICATE	FORETHOUGHT	DERELICTION	PUNCTILIOUS
EXPENDITURE	DESIDERATUM	PROGRESSION	PROLIFERATE	FREETHINKER	DESCRIPTION	REACTIONARY
EXTRADITION	DISCREPANCY	PROGRESSIVE	SIGNIFICANT	GRASSHOPPER	DETERIORATE	REMINISCENT
GROUNDSHEET	DISPLEASURE	PSYCHEDELIA	SPACEFLIGHT	HANDSHAKING	DILAPIDATED	REPETITIOUS

RESTRICTION	MISBELIEVER	GERRYMANDER	COMMANDMENT	NATIONALITY	GYROCOMPASS	GRANDPARENT
SCINTILLATE	MONEYLENDER	GRANDMOTHER	COMMENTATOR	NATIONALIZE	HARDWORKING	HORSEPLAYER
STOCKINETTE	MUSCULATURE	HOUSEMOTHER	COMMINATION	NOTHINGNESS	INOPPORTUNE	HYDROPHOBIA
SUPERIMPOSE	MUSKELLUNGE	IMPERMANENT	COMMONPLACE	OUTMANEUVER	INTEROFFICE	HYDROPONICS
SUPERINTEND	NICKELODEON	IMPERMEABLE	COMMUNICANT	PATERNALISM	IRREMOVABLE	IMPROPRIETY
TOTALIZATOR	PROSELYTIZE	INCREMENTAL	COMMUNICATE	PERFUNCTORY	IRREVOCABLE	INCOMPETENT
TRICHINOSIS	RECTILINEAR	INCRIMINATE	COMPUNCTION	PERSONALITY	JUVENOCRACY	INCORPORATE
UNAVOIDABLE	SCHOOLHOUSE	INFLAMMABLE	CONCENTRATE	PERSONALIZE	KLEPTOMANIA	INCORPOREAL
UNCHRISTIAN	SCUTTLEBUTT	INFORMATION	CONJUNCTION	POLLINATION	LOUDMOUTHED	INTERPOLATE
UNCIVILIZED	SHUTTLECOCK	INFORMATIVE	CONJUNCTIVA	PRECONCEIVE	MEGALOMANIA	INTERPRETER
UNDESIGNING	SUPERLATIVE	INTERMEDDLE	CONJUNCTIVE	PREIGNITION	MEGALOPOLIS	LICKSPITTLE
UNDESIRABLE	THISTLEDOWN	INTERMINGLE	CONJUNCTURE	PREMONITION	MERITOCRACY	LILLIPUTIAN
UNDEVIATING	TONSILLITIS	LACRIMATION	CONTENTMENT	PRETENTIOUS	MERITORIOUS	LOUDSPEAKER
UNEQUIVOCAL	TRANSLUCENT	MARSHMALLOW	CONTINENTAL	PROFANATORY	MILLIONAIRE	ORTHOPEDICS
UNINHIBITED	TRIBULATION	MATHEMATICS	CONTINGENCY	PROPINQUITY	NONVIOLENCE	PERCEPTIBLE
UNMITIGATED	UNICELLULAR	MEDIUMISTIC	CONTINUANCE	PROVENIENCE	NYMPHOMANIA	PRECIPITATE
UNREMITTING	UNQUALIFIED	MERRYMAKING	CONVENIENCE	RATIONALISM	OPINIONATED	PRECIPITOUS
VACATIONIST	UNWHOLESOME	MISDEMEANOR	CONVENTICLE	RATIONALITY	PERITONITIS	SARCOPHAGUS
VALEDICTION	VENTILATION	NUMISMATICS	COSIGNATORY	RATIONALIZE	PHYSIOGNOMY	SCRUMPTIOUS
VALEDICTORY	WATERLOGGED	PANDEMONIUM	COTTONMOUTH	RECOGNITION	POLYNOMINAL	SUSCEPTIBLE
VENTRILOQUY	WHIFFLETREE	PREDOMINATE	CRIMINOLOGY	RECONNOITER	PORTIONLESS	SYNCOPATION
MALADJUSTED	WHIPPLETREE	PRELIMINARY	CYBERNATION	RESIGNATION	PSYCHODRAMA	THERAPEUTIC
HOUSEKEEPER	ACADEMICIAN	PRESUMPTION	CYBERNETICS	RESPONSIBLE	PSYCHOGENIC	TOWNSPEOPLE
RATHSKELLER	ACADEMICISM	PROTOMARTYR	DEMAGNETIZE	ROTTENSTONE	REALPOLITIK	TRANSPARENT
STOREKEEPER	ACCLAMATION	RADIOMETRIC	DESPONDENCY	SENTENTIOUS	SCAFFOLDING	UNFLAPPABLE
APPELLATION	ACCLIMATIZE	RECRIMINATE	DESTINATION	SUBJUNCTIVE	SEISMOGRAPH	CONSEQUENCE
CALCULATING	ACCOMMODATE	REFORMATION	DIAMONDBACK	TENDENTIOUS	SEISMOMETER	DELINQUENCY
CALCULATION	AFFIRMATIVE	REFORMATORY	DISCONTINUE	TERMINOLOGY	SOLILOQUIZE	ACQUIREMENT
CANDELABRUM	AGGLOMERATE	SENTIMENTAL	DISPENSABLE	UNFLINCHING	SPEEDOMETER	ANACHRONISM
CAPILLARITY	ASTIGMATISM	STREAMLINED	DISTINCTION	UNPRINTABLE	STEREOSCOPE	ANTIGRAVITY
CASTELLATED	BLOODMOBILE	STREAMLINER	DISTINCTIVE	UNTHINKABLE	STEREOSCOPY	ARBITRAMENT
CATHOLICITY	BURGOMASTER	SUPERMARKET	DISTINGUISH	UNVARNISHED	STEREOTYPED	BITTERSWEET
CHEERLEADER	CHOIRMASTER	SUPREMACIST	DREADNOUGHT	VACCINATION	STETHOSCOPE	BOILERMAKER
CIRCULARITY	CIRCUMLUNAR	SYSTEMATIZE	ENFRANCHISE	VIOLONCELLO	STROBOSCOPE	CENTERBOARD
CIRCULARIZE	CIRCUMPOLAR	TESTIMONIAL	GEOSYNCLINE	VOLCANOLOGY	SUBTROPICAL	CENTERPIECE
CONSOLIDATE	CIRCUMSPECT	TOASTMASTER	HELLENISTIC	ANASTOMOSIS	SWALLOWTAIL	COMFORTABLE
CONVOLUTION	COMMEMORATE	TRANSMITTER	HERRINGBONE	ANTIPOVERTY	TEASPOONFUL	COMPARATIVE
CORRELATIVE	CONCOMITANT	ULTRAMARINE	HUMMINGBIRD	ARISTOCRACY	TECHNOCRACY	COMPARTMENT
DISILLUSION	CONDOMINIUM	ULTRAMODERN	HYPHENATION	BENEVOLENCE	THERMOCLINE	COMPORTMENT
DISSOLUTION	CONSUMERISM	UNCOMMITTED	IMAGINATION	BIBLIOPHILE	THERMOMETER	COMPTROLLER
FORECLOSURE	CONSUMPTION	ABOMINATION	INCARNADINE	CALIFORNIUM	TYPEFOUNDER	CONCERNMENT
GALLBLADDER	CONSUMPTIVE	ACCOUNTABLE	INCARNATION	CAMEROONIAN	UNACCOUNTED	CONCORDANCE
GEOPOLITICS	CONTAMINANT	ACUPUNCTURE	INCLINATION	CARDIOGRAPH	UNFAVORABLE	CONCURRENCE
HOUSELIGHTS	CONTAMINATE	ALEXANDRIAN	INDIGNATION	CATEGORICAL	VARICOLORED	CONFORMANCE
INSTALLMENT	CONTEMPLATE	ALEXANDRINE	INSTANTIATE	CEREMONIOUS	WIDEMOUTHED	CONSERVANCY
INTELLIGENT	COTERMINOUS	ALTERNATIVE	INTERNECINE	CHIAROSCURO	AGORAPHOBIA	CONSERVATOR
INTERLACING	CUSTOMHOUSE	APOCYNTHION	INTERNUNCIO	CHLOROPHYLL	APPROPRIATE	CONVERTIBLE
INTERLINEAR	DETERMINANT	APPOINTMENT	MACHINATION	CHRONOGRAPH	ARCHIPELAGO	COOPERATIVE
INTERLINING	DETERMINATE	ASSIGNATION	MAGNANIMOUS	CHRONOMETER	BREAKPOINTS	CORNERSTONE
KNUCKLEBONE	DETERMINISM	BOUTONNIERE	MALFUNCTION	CONTROVERSY	CATERPILLAR	CORPORATION
LEGISLATION	DIPLOMATIST	BOYSENBERRY	MECHANISTIC	DIAPHORETIC	COMEUPPANCE	COUNTRIFIED
LEGISLATIVE	DISSEMINATE	CAMPANOLOGY	MISCONCEIVE	DYNAMOMETER	DISAPPROVAL	COUNTRYSIDE
LEGISLATURE	DISSIMULATE	CARDINALATE	MISCONSTRUE	ENVIRONMENT	EPINEPHRINE	DECLARATIVE
MANTELPIECE	DRILLMASTER	CARDINALITY	MOCKINGBIRD	FASHIONABLE	EXPROPRIATE	DEFLORATION
MENDELEVIUM	EXTERMINATE	CARMINATIVE	MUTTONCHOPS	FLUOROSCOPE	EXTEMPORARY	DEMOCRATIZE
MESALLIANCE	FUNDAMENTAL	CENTENARIAN	NATIONALISM	FOULMOUTHED	EXTEMPORIZE	DESEGREGATE
MISALLIANCE	GALLIMAUFRY	COMBINATION	NATIONALIST	GLOSSOLALIA	EXTRAPOLATE	DESPERATION

DOWNTRODDEN	RECIPROCITY	HYDROSPHERE	SWEEPSTAKES	HERPETOLOGY	STORYTELLER	HEAVYWEIGHT
ELECTRICIAN	REQUIREMENT	HYDROSTATIC	TEMPESTUOUS	HOMESTEADER	STRAITLACED	LASERWRITER
ELECTRICITY	RESPIRATION	HYGROSCOPIC	TERRESTRIAL	HOMESTRETCH	TERRITORIAL	LIGHTWEIGHT
ELECTROCUTE	RESTORATION	IMAGESETTER	TROPOSPHERE	HOSPITALITY	TRINITARIAN	MEADOWSWEET
ELECTROFORM	RESTORATIVE	IMPASSIONED	ULTRASONICS	HOSPITALIZE	UNCERTAINTY	MINESWEEPER
ELECTROLYTE	ROTOGRAVURE	IMPERSONATE	UNCONSCIOUS	HYPERTROPHY	UNDERTAKING	NIGHTWALKER
ELECTRONICS	SEMITRAILER	IMPUISSANCE	UNDERSHORTS	ILLUSTRIOUS	UNFORTUNATE	PAPERWEIGHT
ELECTROTYPE	SPECTROGRAM	INNERSPRING	UNDERSIGNED	IMMORTALITY	UTILITARIAN	PENNYWEIGHT
FINGERBOARD	STEAMROLLER	INQUISITION	UNREASONING	IMMORTALIZE	WORKSTATION	PRIZEWINNER
FINGERPRINT	STEPBROTHER	INQUISITIVE	VICHYSSOISE	IMPERTINENT	ACCUMULATOR	SLEEPWALKER
FIRECRACKER	SUBMERSIBLE	INTERSPERSE	VICISSITUDE	IMPORTATION	AGRICULTURE	THEREWITHAL
GENDARMERIE	SUMMERHOUSE	IRIDESCENCE	WHERESOEVER	IMPORTUNATE	ANTIQUARIAN	TRUSTWORTHY
GINGERBREAD	SYNCHROMESH	LABORSAVING	WHICHSOEVER	INCANTATION	AQUICULTURE	UNDERWEIGHT
GUTTERSNIPE	SYNCHRONIZE	LATCHSTRING	ABSENTEEISM	INCERTITUDE	BUREAUCRACY	WHEELWRIGHT
HAEMORRHAGE	SYNCHRONOUS	LITHOSPHERE	ACCEPTATION	INCONTINENT	DESTRUCTION	WHEREWITHAL
HAIRBREADTH	TELEPRINTER	MACROSCOPIC	ADVERTISING	INDENTATION	DISCOURTESY	ANTIOXIDANT
HAIRDRESSER	TEMPERAMENT	MICROSCOPIC	AFFECTATION	INDUSTRIOUS	EVENTUALITY	APPROXIMATE
HANDWRITING	TEMPERATURE	MICROSECOND	AGGLUTINATE	INFANTICIDE	FOREQUARTER	ANTICYCLONE
HAREBRAINED	THEATRICALS	MILLISECOND	AMPHETAMINE	INGRATITUDE	GODDAUGHTER	DICOTYLEDON
HISTORICITY	TYPEWRITING	MINNESINGER	ANAESTHESIA	INSECTICIDE	HABITUATION	ICHTHYOLOGY
HORSERADISH	TYPOGRAPHER	NECESSITATE	BACKSTRETCH	INSTITUTION	HINDQUARTER	MONKEYSHINE
INOPERATIVE	UNOBTRUSIVE	NECESSITOUS	BALLETOMANE	INTENTIONAL	IMPECUNIOUS	PARATYPHOID
INSPIRATION	VENTURESOME	NONDESCRIPT	BARBITURATE	INVESTIGATE	IMPLAUSIBLE	PROPHYLAXIS
INTERRACIAL	WASHERWOMAN	NONRESIDENT	BICENTENARY	INVESTITURE	INEXCUSABLE	
INTERREGNUM	WINTERGREEN	NOURISHMENT	BREASTPLATE	KINESTHESIA	INSCRUTABLE	
INTERRELATE	ZOOMORPHISM	ORCHESTRATE	CASSITERITE	LIBERTARIAN	INSINUATING	
INTERROGATE	ACQUISITION	OUTDISTANCE	CATASTROPHE	MAGISTERIAL	INSTRUCTION	**7TH LETTER**
JABBERWOCKY	ACQUISITIVE	OZONOSPHERE	CEMENTATION	MARKETPLACE	INSTRUCTIVE	
LETTERPRESS	ADOLESCENCE	PACHYSANDRA	CHRISTENDOM	MINIATURIZE	INVOLUNTARY	ABECEDARIAN
LITTERATEUR	ADVERSATIVE	PERMISSIBLE	CHRISTIANIA	MISANTHROPE	IRREDUCIBLE	ABOMINATION
LUCUBRATION	ASSASSINATE	PHARISAICAL	CLIMATOLOGY	MOMENTARILY	IRREFUTABLE	ACCEPTATION
MALAPROPISM	BATHYSPHERE	PHILOSOPHER	COMMUTATION	MONASTICISM	OBSTRUCTION	ACCLAMATION
MASTERPIECE	BATHYSCAPHE	PHOTOSPHERE	COMMUTATIVE	OPPORTUNISM	PLEASURABLE	ACCLIMATIZE
MEASUREMENT	BLOODSTREAM	PLAINSPOKEN	COMPETITION	OPPORTUNITY	PROCRUSTEAN	ADVERSATIVE
MENSURATION	BLOODSUCKER	PREASSIGNED	COMPUTERIZE	OSTENTATION	PUNCTUATION	AFFECTATION
METEOROLOGY	CHOLESTEROL	PREHISTORIC	CONDITIONAL	OVERSTUFFED	SHIPBUILDER	AFFIRMATIVE
MORTARBOARD	COGNOSCENTE	PREPOSITION	CONDITIONED	PAINSTAKING	TRANQUILIZE	AGGREGATION
MOTHERBOARD	COMBUSTIBLE	PROMISCUOUS	CONNOTATION	PARENTHESIS	UNSATURATED	ALTERCATION
MULTIRACIAL	COMMISERATE	PROPOSITION	CONNOTATIVE	PENULTIMATE	VITICULTURE	ALTERNATIVE
NECKERCHIEF	COMPOSITION	PROVISIONAL	DELECTATION	PERISTALSIS	AUDIOVISUAL	AMPHETAMINE
NETHERWORLD	CONFESSEDLY	QUACKSALVER	DERMATOLOGY	PERMUTATION	CARNIVOROUS	ANTECHAMBER
NONPARTISAN	CONSISTENCE	QUICKSILVER	DICTATORIAL	PISCATORIAL	CLAIRVOYANT	ANTIGRAVITY
NURSERYMAID	CONSISTENCY	RECESSIONAL	DIRECTORATE	PLANETARIUM	DEPRIVATION	ANTIQUARIAN
OMNIPRESENT	CREPUSCULAR	RECONSTRUCT	DISCOTHEQUE	PLANETOLOGY	EXTRAVAGANT	APPELLATION
OVERWROUGHT	DECRESCENDO	REFRESHMENT	DISENTANGLE	POCKETKNIFE	HERBIVOROUS	APPLICATION
PARATROOPER	DEMONSTRATE	REMONSTRANT	DISPUTATION	POLYSTYRENE	IMPROVEMENT	APPROBATION
PARTURITION	DESENSITIZE	REMONSTRATE	DOMESTICATE	PRIMITIVISM	IMPROVIDENT	ARBITRAMENT
PENETRATING	DISASSEMBLE	RENAISSANCE	DOMESTICITY	PROBATIONER	INTRAVENOUS	ASSIGNATION
PERFORMANCE	DISPOSITION	REQUISITION	EXCEPTIONAL	PROLETARIAN	OBSERVATION	ASSOCIATION
PICTURESQUE	ENCAPSULATE	SEQUESTRATE	EXPECTATION	PROLETARIAT	OBSERVATORY	ASSOCIATIVE
POLTERGEIST	EXCRESCENCE	SUBASSEMBLY	EXPECTORANT	PROMPTITUDE	RESERVATION	ASTIGMATISM
POMEGRANATE	EXHAUSTLESS	SUBSISTENCE	EXPECTORATE	QUALITATIVE	TRIUMVIRATE	BREADBASKET
PORTERHOUSE	FLORESCENCE	SUPERSCRIBE	EXPOSTULATE	RESISTIVITY	ULTRAVIOLET	BURGOMASTER
PRETERMINAL	FURNISHINGS	SUPERSCRIPT	GERONTOLOGY	RESTITUTION	ACKNOWLEDGE	CALCULATING
PREVARICATE	GARNISHMENT	SUPERSONICS	GRANITEWARE	ROMANTICISM	BLAMEWORTHY	CALCULATION
PULCHRITUDE	HOMEOSTASIS	SUPPOSITION	GRAVITATION	SENSATIONAL	BREADWINNER	CANDELABRUM
RECIPROCATE	HONEYSUCKLE	SUPPOSITORY	HAIRSTYLIST	SPENDTHRIFT	FLOORWALKER	CANDIDATURE

CANNIBALIZE	FORNICATION	MENSURATION	RESIGNATION	WHEREABOUTS	MALFUNCTION	AGGLOMERATE
CAPILLARITY	GALLBLADDER	MERRYMAKING	RESPIRATION	ABSTRACTION	MALPRACTICE	ALPHABETIZE
CARDINALATE	GALLIMAUFRY	METRICATION	RESTORATION	ACUPUNCTURE	MANUFACTORY	ARCHIPELAGO
CARDINALITY	GERRYMANDER	MICROCAPSUL	RESTORATIVE	ADOLESCENCE	MANUFACTURE	BELLIGERENT
CARDSHARPER	GRANDFATHER	MOMENTARILY	ROTOGRAVURE	ANTICYCLONE	MERITOCRACY	BICENTENARY
CARMINATIVE	GRANDPARENT	MULTIFAMILY	SEMITRAILER	ARISTOCRACY	MICROSCOPIC	CALCIFEROUS
CEMENTATION	GRAVITATION	MULTIRACIAL	SHORTHANDED	BATHYSCAPHE	MISCONCEIVE	CARRAGEENAN
CENTENARIAN	HABERDASHER	MUSCULATURE	SLEEPWALKER	BENEDICTION	MUTTONCHOPS	CASSITERITE
CHOIRMASTER	HABITUATION	NAPHTHALENE	SUBURBANITE	BENEFACTION	NECKERCHIEF	CHEERLEADER
CIRCULARITY	HALFHEARTED	NARRAGANSET	SUPERLATIVE	BENEFICENCE	NONDESCRIPT	CHRISTENDOM
CIRCULARIZE	HANDICAPPER	NATIONALISM	SUPERMARKET	BENEFICIARY	OBSTRUCTION	CLEARHEADED
CLERICALISM	HANDSHAKING	NATIONALIST	SUPREMACIST	BUREAUCRACY	PERFUNCTORY	COMMISERATE
COEDUCATION	HARDHEARTED	NATIONALITY	SYNCOPATION	CHANTICLEER	PERSNICKETY	COMPUTERIZE
COLLOCATION	HAREBRAINED	NATIONALIZE	SYSTEMATIZE	CHEESECLOTH	PERSPECTIVE	CONFEDERACY
COLONIALISM	HINDQUARTER	NIGHTWALKER	TACHYCARDIA	COEFFICIENT	PERSPICUOUS	CONFEDERATE
COLORCASTER	HORSERADISH	NINNYHAMMER	TEMPERAMENT	COGNOSCENTE	POLYTECHNIC	CONSIDERATE
COMBINATION	HOSPITALITY	NONNEGATIVE	TEMPERATURE	COMPLACENCE	PRACTICABLE	CONSIDERING
COMMINATION	HOSPITALIZE	NORTHEASTER	TIMESHARING	COMPLACENCY	PRECONCEIVE	CONSUMERISM
COMMUTATION	HYDROCARBON	NUMISMATICS	TOASTMASTER	COMPLICATED	PROMISCUOUS	CONTINENTAL
COMMUTATIVE	HYPHENATION	OBSERVATION	TRANSPARENT	COMPUNCTION	REINFECTION	COPROCESSOR
COMPARATIVE	IMAGINATION	OBSERVATORY	TREPIDATION	CONJUNCTION	RESTRICTION	CORRIGENDUM
CONJUGATION	IMBRICATION	OFFICIALDOM	TRIBULATION	CONJUNCTIVA	RETROACTIVE	CYBERNETICS
CONNOTATION	IMMORTALITY	OFFICIALISM	TRINIDADIAN	CONJUNCTIVE	SHELLACKING	DEMAGNETIZE
CONNOTATIVE	IMMORTALIZE	OSTENTATION	TRINITARIAN	CONJUNCTURE	SPECTACULAR	DESEGREGATE
CONURBATION	IMPERIALISM	OVERBEARING	TRUEHEARTED	CONSPICUOUS	SUBJUNCTIVE	DISASSEMBLE
CONVOCATION	IMPERMANENT	PACHYSANDRA	TYPOGRAPHER	CONTRACTILE	SUPERSCRIBE	DISQUIETUDE
COOPERATIVE	IMPORTATION	PAINSTAKING	ULTRAMARINE	CREPUSCULAR	SUPERSCRIPT	ELIZABETHAN
CORPORATION	INCANTATION	PAPERHANGER	UNCERTAINTY	DECRESCENDO	TECHNOCRACY	EMPLACEMENT
CORRELATIVE	INCARNADINE	PATERNALISM	UNDERHANDED	DERELICTION	THERMOCLINE	ENDOTHERMIC
COSIGNATORY	INCARNATION	PENETRATING	UNDERTAKING	DESTRUCTION	TRANSACTION	ENGINEERING
CRESTFALLEN	INCLINATION	PERISTALSIS	UNDEVIATING	DIFFRACTION	UNCONSCIOUS	EXPERIENCED
CYBERNATION	INDENTATION	PERMUTATION	UNIFICATION	DISTINCTION	UNFLINCHING	FUNDAMENTAL
DECLARATIVE	INDIGNATION	PERSONALITY	UTILITARIAN	DISTINCTIVE	VALEDICTION	GRANITEWARE
DEFALCATION	INFORMATION	PERSONALIZE	VACCINATION	EFFICACIOUS	VALEDICTORY	HAIRBREADTH
DEFLORATION	INFORMATIVE	PHARISAICAL	VENTILATION	ENFRANCHISE	VIOLONCELLO	HAIRDRESSER
DELECTATION	INOPERATIVE	PLANETARIUM	VINDICATION	EXCRESCENCE	VIVISECTION	HEAVYWEIGHT
DEMOCRATIZE	INSINUATING	POLLINATION	WARMHEARTED	FARINACEOUS	ABRACADABRA	HOMESTEADER
DEPRECATORY	INSPIRATION	POMEGRANATE	WASTEBASKET	FLORESCENCE	ALEXANDRIAN	HOUSEKEEPER
DEPREDATION	INTERCALARY	PREDICAMENT	WHEELBARROW	GEANTICLINE	ALEXANDRINE	HYDROGENATE
DEPRIVATION	INTERCALATE	PREROGATIVE	WORKSTATION	GEOSYNCLINE	BIOFEEDBACK	HYPOTHECATE
DESPERATION	INTERLACING	PROFANATORY	BOYSENBERRY	HARPSICHORD	BRAGGADOCIO	HYPOTHESIZE
DESTINATION	INTERRACIAL	PROLETARIAN	CENTERBOARD	HEXADECIMAL	CAMARADERIE	IMAGESETTER
DIPLOMATIST	KINDHEARTED	PROLETARIAT	CHOCKABLOCK	HYGROSCOPIC	COINCIDENCE	IMPERMEABLE
DISENTANGLE	LABORSAVING	PROTOMARTYR	DISTRIBUTOR	HYPERACTIVE	COMMANDMENT	IMPROVEMENT
DISORGANIZE	LACRIMATION	PUBLICATION	EQUILIBRIUM	INEFFECTIVE	CONCORDANCE	INCARCERATE
DISPLEASURE	LEGISLATION	PUNCTUATION	FINGERBOARD	INEFFECTUAL	DESPONDENCY	INCOMPETENT
DISPUTATION	LEGISLATIVE	QUACKSALVER	GINGERBREAD	INEFFICIENT	DIAMONDBACK	INCREMENTAL
DOWNHEARTED	LEGISLATURE	QUALITATIVE	HUCKLEBERRY	INSTRUCTION	DILAPIDATED	INDIFFERENT
DRILLMASTER	LIBERTARIAN	RADIOCARBON	INCUNABULUM	INSTRUCTIVE	INDIVIDUATE	INGATHERING
EDIFICATION	LIONHEARTED	RATIONALISM	MEMORABILIA	INTERACTION	MISGUIDANCE	INTERCEPTOR
EVENTUALITY	LITTERATEUR	RATIONALITY	MORTARBOARD	INTERACTIVE	PARAMEDICAL	INTERMEDDLE
EXPECTATION	LUCUBRATION	RATIONALIZE	MOTHERBOARD	IRIDESCENCE	PSYCHEDELIA	INTERNECINE
EXTRAVAGANT	MACHINATION	REFORMATION	SPRINGBOARD	IRREDUCIBLE	PSYCHEDELIC	INTERREGNUM
FAMILIARITY	MARSHMALLOW	REFORMATORY	SWITCHBLADE	IRREVOCABLE	PSYCHODRAMA	INTERRELATE
FIRECRACKER	MATERIALISM	REPLICATION	SWITCHBOARD	JUVENOCRACY	UNAVOIDABLE	INTRAVENOUS
FLOORWALKER	MATERIALIZE	REPROBATION	THEREABOUTS	MACROSCOPIC	ABSENTEEISM	KNUCKLEBONE
FOREQUARTER	MATHEMATICS	RESERVATION	UNINHIBITED	MALEDICTION	ACQUIREMENT	LATTICEWORK

LEGERDEMAIN	CENTRIFUGAL	ACADEMICIAN	HISTORICITY	PRIZEWINNER	AQUICULTURE	INFLAMMABLE
LEVELHEADED	IDENTIFIERS	ACADEMICISM	HOUSELIGHTS	PROBATIONER	ASSEMBLYMAN	KLEPTOMANIA
LIGHTWEIGHT	INTEROFFICE	ACCORDINGLY	IMPASSIONED	PROHIBITION	BENEVOLENCE	MEGALOMANIA
LOUDSPEAKER	THENCEFORTH	ACQUISITION	IMPERTINENT	PROMPTITUDE	BIMETALLISM	MILLIAMPERE
MAGISTERIAL	CARDIOGRAPH	ACQUISITIVE	IMPROVIDENT	PROPOSITION	CANDLELIGHT	NYMPHOMANIA
MEASUREMENT	CHRONOGRAPH	ADVERTISING	INCERTITUDE	PROVENIENCE	CASTELLATED	PERFORMANCE
MENDELEVIUM	CONTINGENCY	AGGLUTINATE	INCONTINENT	PROVISIONAL	CAULIFLOWER	POLYNOMINAL
MICROSECOND	DISTINGUISH	ANNUNCIATOR	INCRIMINATE	PULCHRITUDE	CHANCELLERY	PRETERMINAL
MILLISECOND	FORTNIGHTLY	ANTIOXIDANT	INFANTICIDE	QUICKSILVER	CIRCUMLUNAR	PROBLEMATIC
MINESWEEPER	GODDAUGHTER	APHRODISIAC	INGRATITUDE	RECESSIONAL	CRYSTALLIZE	PROGRAMMING
MISCHIEVOUS	HERRINGBONE	APPRECIABLE	INQUISITION	RECOGNITION	DICOTYLEDON	SEISMOMETER
MISDEMEANOR	HUMMINGBIRD	APPROXIMATE	INQUISITIVE	RECRIMINATE	EVANGELICAL	SPEEDOMETER
MONEYLENDER	IMMITIGABLE	ASSASSINATE	INSECTICIDE	RECTILINEAR	FLANNELETTE	SUPERIMPOSE
NONETHELESS	IRRELIGIOUS	AUDIOVISUAL	INSOUCIANCE	REGURGITATE	GENERALSHIP	THERMOMETER
OMNIPRESENT	LAMPLIGHTER	BREADWINNER	INSTABILITY	REQUISITION	GLOSSOLALIA	TWELVEMONTH
ORTHOPEDICS	MOCKINGBIRD	CATERPILLAR	INTELLIGENT	RESISTIVITY	HIGHFALUTIN	BACCHANALIA
OUTMANEUVER	MONSEIGNEUR	CATHOLICITY	INTENTIONAL	RESUSCITATE	HORSEPLAYER	BOUTONNIERE
OVERWEENING	NEARSIGHTED	CERTIFICATE	INTERLINEAR	ROADABILITY	INSTALLMENT	CARAVANSARY
PAPERWEIGHT	NOTHINGNESS	CHRISTIANIA	INTERLINING	ROMANTICISM	MELLIFLUOUS	CEREMONIOUS
PENNYWEIGHT	PHYSIOGNOMY	CLOSEFISTED	INTERMINGLE	SENSATIONAL	MUSKELLUNGE	COEXTENSIVE
PESTIFEROUS	POLTERGEIST	COMMUNICANT	INVESTIGATE	SENSIBILITY	NONVIOLENCE	CONCERNMENT
PICTURESQUE	PSYCHOGENIC	COMMUNICATE	INVESTITURE	SERENDIPITY	OUTBUILDING	CONSIGNMENT
PREDECESSOR	SEISMOGRAPH	COMPETITION	LICKSPITTLE	SHIPBUILDER	OVERBALANCE	COUNTENANCE
PROLIFERATE	SUFFRAGETTE	COMPOSITION	MACROBIOTIC	SIGNIFICANT	PITCHBLENDE	DENOMINATOR
PROPRIETARY	UNDESIGNING	CONCOMITANT	MAGNANIMOUS	SOVEREIGNTY	POINTILLISM	DIAMAGNETIC
PROSTHETICS	UNMITIGATED	CONDITIONAL	MAGNIFICENT	SPELLBINDER	PROPHYLAXIS	DOCTRINAIRE
PROTUBERANT	WINTERGREEN	CONDITIONED	MECHANISTIC	SUBORDINATE	PUNCTILIOUS	DOCUMENTARY
RADIOMETRIC	WITENAGEMOT	CONDOMINIUM	MEDIUMISTIC	SUFFICIENCY	RAPSCALLION	EARTHENWARE
RATHSKELLER	AGORAPHOBIA	CONSOLIDATE	MESALLIANCE	SUPERFICIAL	REALPOLITIK	ELEPHANTINE
REFRIGERATE	ANAESTHESIA	CONTAMINANT	MINNESINGER	SUPPOSITION	RESEMBLANCE	ENVIRONMENT
REPLACEMENT	COFFEEHOUSE	CONTAMINATE	MISALLIANCE	SUPPOSITORY	SCAFFOLDING	FARTHINGALE
REQUIREMENT	CUSTOMHOUSE	CONVENIENCE	MISBELIEVER	TELEPRINTER	SCINTILLATE	FASHIONABLE
REVERBERATE	DISCOTHEQUE	COTERMINOUS	MONASTICISM	THEATRICALS	SEARCHLIGHT	FRAGMENTARY
SAFEKEEPING	EPINEPHRINE	COUNTRIFIED	MOUNTAINEER	THEREWITHAL	SPACEFLIGHT	GEOMAGNETIC
SCUTTLEBUTT	FURNISHINGS	CRUCIFIXION	MOUNTAINTOP	TIGHTFISTED	STRAITLACED	HOMOGENEOUS
SENTIMENTAL	GARNISHMENT	DESENSITIZE	NECESSITATE	TRAGEDIENNE	STRAWFLOWER	IGNOMINIOUS
SERVICEABLE	HYDROPHOBIA	DETERMINANT	NECESSITOUS	TRANQUILIZE	STREAMLINED	IMPECUNIOUS
SHUTTLECOCK	INTERCHANGE	DETERMINATE	NONRESIDENT	TRANSFIGURE	STREAMLINER	IMPREGNABLE
STOREKEEPER	KINESTHESIA	DETERMINISM	PARISHIONER	TRANSMITTER	SUPERFLUOUS	INALIENABLE
STORYTELLER	MASSACHUSET	DISPOSITION	PARTICIPATE	TRIUMVIRATE	TONSILLITIS	INATTENTION
SUBASSEMBLY	MELANCHOLIA	DISSEMINATE	PARTURITION	TYPEWRITING	TRAILBLAZER	INDEFINABLE
THERAPEUTIC	MELANCHOLIC	DOMESTICATE	PENULTIMATE	ULTRAVIOLET	UNCIVILIZED	INDEPENDENT
THISTLEDOWN	MISANTHROPE	DOMESTICITY	PONTIFICALS	UNCOMMITTED	UNICELLULAR	INVOLUNTARY
TOWNSPEOPLE	NOURISHMENT	EINSTEINIUM	PONTIFICATE	UNDERSIGNED	VARICOLORED	IRREDENTISM
TRANSCEIVER	PARENTHESIS	ELECTRICIAN	PORTRAITIST	UNQUALIFIED	VENTRILOQUY	KITCHENETTE
TREACHEROUS	PORTERHOUSE	ELECTRICITY	PORTRAITURE	UNVARNISHED	VITICULTURE	KITCHENWARE
TRENCHERMAN	REFRESHMENT	EXCEEDINGLY	PREASSIGNED	VERTIGINOUS	ANASTOMOSIS	MERCHANDISE
TRUSTEESHIP	SARCOPHAGUS	EXCEPTIONAL	PRECIPITATE	VICISSITUDE	BOILERMAKER	MERCHANTMAN
UNCONCERNED	SCHOOLHOUSE	EXPENDITURE	PRECIPITOUS	WHEREWITHAL	CALORIMETER	MILLIONAIRE
UNDERWEIGHT	SHORTCHANGE	EXTERMINATE	PREDOMINATE	POCKETKNIFE	CHRONOMETER	MONOLINGUAL
UNWHOLESOME	SPENDTHRIFT	EXTRADITION	PREIGNITION	UNSPEAKABLE	CONFORMANCE	NIGHTINGALE
VENTURESOME	STOMACHACHE	FAULTFINDER	PRELIMINARY	UNTHINKABLE	COTTONMOUTH	OPINIONATED
WHIFFLETREE	STRAIGHTWAY	FREETHINKER	PREMEDITATE	ACCUMULATOR	DYNAMOMETER	OUTSTANDING
WHIPPLETREE	SUMMERHOUSE	GEOPOLITICS	PREMONITION	ACKNOWLEDGE	GENDARMERIE	PERITONITIS
WRONGHEADED	UNDERCHARGE	HALLUCINATE	PREPOSITION	AGRICULTURE	GYROCOMPASS	PORTIONLESS
AFTEREFFECT	UNDERSHORTS	HANDWRITING	PREVARICATE	AMBIVALENCE	IMPEDIMENTA	PORTMANTEAU
BATTLEFIELD	UNTOUCHABLE	HELLENISTIC	PRIMITIVISM	AMONTILLADO	INESTIMABLE	QUADRENNIAL

QUADRENNIUM	EXTEMPORARY	STOCKHOLDER	TROPOSPHERE	INCONGRUENT	COCKLESHELL	COMBUSTIBLE
REGIMENTALS	EXTEMPORIZE	SUPERSONICS	UNFLAPPABLE	INCONGRUOUS	CONFESSEDLY	COMFORTABLE
RESIDENTIAL	EXTRAPOLATE	SYNCHROMESH	ZOOMORPHISM	INDUSTRIOUS	CONGRESSMAN	COMMENTATOR
RESPLENDENT	FORECLOSURE	SYNCHRONIZE	PROPINQUITY	INNUMERABLE	CONNOISSEUR	COMPARTMENT
REVERENTIAL	FORESHORTEN	SYNCHRONOUS	SOLILOQUIZE	INOPPORTUNE	CORNERSTONE	COMPORTMENT
SPONTANEOUS	FORETHOUGHT	TEASPOONFUL	ACCELERANDO	INSEPARABLE	DISPENSABLE	CONCENTRATE
STOCKINETTE	FORTHCOMING	TERMINOLOGY	ACCELERATOR	INSUPERABLE	EQUIDISTANT	CONDUCTANCE
SUBSTANDARD	FUNCTIONARY	TERRITORIAL	ANNIVERSARY	INTERPRETER	EVERLASTING	CONSISTENCE
SUBSTANTIAL	GERONTOLOGY	TESTIMONIAL	APPROPRIATE	INTOLERABLE	FIDDLESTICK	CONSISTENCY
SUBSTANTIVE	GRANDMOTHER	THALIDOMIDE	BACKSTRETCH	IRREPARABLE	FLUOROSCOPE	CONSTITUENT
SUPERINTEND	GRASSHOPPER	TOBACCONIST	BALLCARRIER	IRREVERENCE	GROUNDSHEET	CONTENTMENT
TRICHINOSIS	HERBIVOROUS	TRUSTWORTHY	BLUNDERBUSS	LASERWRITER	GUTTERSNIPE	CONTRETEMPS
UNALIENABLE	HERPETOLOGY	ULTRAMODERN	BROTHERHOOD	LEATHERNECK	HEARTHSTONE	CONVENTICLE
UNORGANIZED	HISTRIONICS	ULTRASONICS	CALIFORNIUM	LITHOGRAPHY	IMPLAUSIBLE	CONVERTIBLE
UNRELENTING	HOUSEMOTHER	UNREASONING	CALLIGRAPHY	MAIDSERVANT	IMPUISSANCE	DEMONSTRATE
WORKMANLIKE	HYDROPONICS	VACATIONIST	CARTOGRAPHY	MERITORIOUS	INDIGESTION	DISCONTINUE
WORKMANSHIP	HYPERBOREAN	VOLCANOLOGY	CATASTROPHE	MODULARIZED	INDIVISIBLE	EQUILATERAL
ZOOPLANKTON	ICHTHYOLOGY	WAINSCOTING	CATEGORICAL	NEANDERTHAL	INEXCUSABLE	EXHAUSTLESS
ABORTIONIST	ILLUSIONISM	WATERCOURSE	CHAMBERLAIN	OPPROBRIOUS	INTERESTING	EXPEDITIOUS
ACCOMMODATE	IMPERFORATE	WATERLOGGED	CHAMBERMAID	ORTHOGRAPHY	LINGUISTICS	FORMFITTING
ANACHRONISM	IMPERSONATE	WHERESOEVER	CHIROGRAPHY	PALEOGRAPHY	MALFEASANCE	HOMEOSTASIS
ARCHAEOLOGY	INCORPORATE	WHICHSOEVER	CONCURRENCE	PERIPHRASIS	MARQUISETTE	HYDROSTATIC
ARCHDIOCESE	INCORPOREAL	WOODCHOPPER	CONTRARIETY	PETROGRAPHY	MEADOWSWEET	ILLIMITABLE
BALLETOMANE	INTERCOURSE	BATHYSPHERE	COUNTERFEIT	PHOTOGRAPHY	MISCONSTRUE	IMPRACTICAL
BEACHCOMBER	INTERPOLATE	BIBLIOPHILE	COUNTERMAND	PLEASURABLE	MISFEASANCE	INDOMITABLE
BEHAVIORISM	INTERROGATE	BREASTPLATE	COUNTERPANE	PORNOGRAPHY	MONKEYSHINE	INDUBITABLE
BICARBONATE	KWASHIORKOR	CENTERPIECE	COUNTERPART	QUARTERBACK	OBSOLESCENT	INELUCTABLE
BLAMEWORTHY	LABRADORITE	CENTRIPETAL	COUNTERSIGN	QUARTERDECK	PERMISSIBLE	INSCRUTABLE
BLOODMOBILE	MALAPROPISM	CHLOROPHYLL	COUNTERSINK	REMEMBRANCE	PROCRUSTEAN	INSTANTIATE
BOURGEOISIE	MARCHIONESS	CIRCUMPOLAR	COUNTERVAIL	SCHOLARSHIP	PROGRESSION	INTERATOMIC
BREAKPOINTS	METEOROLOGY	COMEUPPANCE	CRACKERJACK	SCREWDRIVER	PROGRESSIVE	INTRACTABLE
CAMEROONIAN	METHODOLOGY	COMMONPLACE	DELETERIOUS	SMITHEREENS	RATTLESNAKE	IRREFUTABLE
CAMPANOLOGY	MISBEGOTTEN	CONSUMPTION	DESIDERATUM	STANDARDIZE	REMINISCENT	LATCHSTRING
CARNIVOROUS	MOLLYCODDLE	CONSUMPTIVE	DIAPHORETIC	STENOGRAPHY	RENAISSANCE	NONPARTISAN
CATERCORNER	NICKELODEON	CONTEMPLATE	DISAPPROVAL	STOCKBROKER	RESPONSIBLE	ORCHESTRATE
CLAIRVOYANT	ORNITHOLOGY	CONTRAPTION	DISCOURTESY	THITHERWARD	ROTTENSTONE	OUTDISTANCE
CLIMATOLOGY	ORTHODONTIA	DESCRIPTION	EXPROPRIATE	THUNDERBOLT	SMORGASBORD	PERCEPTIBLE
COLLABORATE	OVERWROUGHT	DISCREPANCY	FARTHERMOST	THUNDERCLAP	SPREADSHEET	PERFECTIBLE
COMMEMORATE	PANDEMONIUM	FINGERPRINT	FEATHEREDGE	THUNDERHEAD	STEREOSCOPE	PERIPATETIC
COMPTROLLER	PARATROOPER	GREASEPAINT	FILMOGRAPHY	UNDERGROUND	STEREOSCOPY	PREHISTORIC
CORROBORATE	PENTECOSTAL	HYDROSPHERE	FLABBERGAST	UNDERGROWTH	STETHOSCOPE	PRETENTIOUS
CRAPSHOOTER	PERIODONTAL	INESCAPABLE	FOREVERMORE	UNDESIRABLE	STROBOSCOPE	PROGNATHOUS
CRIMINOLOGY	PHILOSOPHER	INNERSPRING	FURTHERMORE	UNFAVORABLE	SUBMERSIBLE	PROSTATITIS
DERMATOLOGY	PHRASEOLOGY	INTERSPERSE	FURTHERMOST	UNSATURATED	SUPPRESSANT	RECONSTRUCT
DETERIORATE	PISCATORIAL	LETTERPRESS	GREENGROCER	UNUTTERABLE	SYNTHESIZER	REDOUBTABLE
DICTATORIAL	PLACEHOLDER	LITHOSPHERE	HAEMORRHAGE	VINAIGRETTE	TOPDRESSING	RELOCATABLE
DIRECTORATE	PLANETOLOGY	MANTELPIECE	HAGIOGRAPHY	WEATHERCOCK	UNCHRISTIAN	REMONSTRANT
DOWNTRODDEN	PROTAGONIST	MARKETPLACE	HARDWORKING	WEATHERWORN	VICHYSSOISE	REMONSTRATE
DREADNOUGHT	REACTIONARY	MASTERPIECE	HEARTBROKEN	WHEELWRIGHT	VIRIDESCENT	REPETITIOUS
ELECTIONEER	RECIPROCATE	MEGALOPOLIS	HOMESTRETCH	WORDPERFECT	ACCOUNTABLE	RESPECTABLE
ELECTROCUTE	RECIPROCITY	NEEDLEPOINT	HOUSEBROKEN	BITTERSWEET	APOCYNTHION	SCRUMPTIOUS
ELECTROFORM	RECONNOITER	OZONOSPHERE	HYDROGRAPHY	BUSINESSMAN	APPOINTMENT	SENTENTIOUS
ELECTROLYTE	SHAREHOLDER	PARATYPHOID	HYPERTROPHY	CANDLESTICK	BLOODSTREAM	SEQUESTRATE
ELECTRONICS	SHORTCOMING	PHOTOSPHERE	ILLUSTRIOUS	CHIAROSCURO	CABINETWORK	STEREOTYPED
ELECTROTYPE	SPECTROGRAM	PLAINSPOKEN	IMPROPRIETY	CIRCUMSPECT	CAPACITANCE	SUBSISTENCE
EXPECTORANT	STEAMROLLER	PRESUMPTION	INADVERTENT	CLANDESTINE	CHOLESTEROL	SUSCEPTIBLE
EXPECTORATE	STEPBROTHER	SUBTROPICAL	INCINERATOR	COBBLESTONE	CLIMACTERIC	SWEEPSTAKES

TEMPESTUOUS	UNOBTRUSIVE	CONFORMANCE	MESALLIANCE	KNUCKLEBONE	ANTIOXIDANT	DIAMAGNETIC
TENDENTIOUS	VERMICULITE	CONSERVANCY	MILLIONAIRE	MOCKINGBIRD	CONSOLIDATE	DIAPHORETIC
TERRESTRIAL	WIDEMOUTHED	CONSERVATOR	MISALLIANCE	QUARTERBACK	DOWNTRODDEN	DICOTYLEDON
THEORETICAL	ANTIPOVERTY	CONTINUANCE	MISDEMEANOR	SCUTTLEBUTT	GALLBLADDER	DISCOTHEQUE
THOUGHTLESS	CONSERVANCY	CONTRIVANCE	MISFEASANCE	SMORGASBORD	HORSERADISH	DYNAMOMETER
TYPESETTING	CONSERVATOR	COUNTENANCE	MISGUIDANCE	THUNDERBOLT	IMPROVIDENT	EQUILATERAL
UNPRINTABLE	CONTRIVANCE	DENOMINATOR	NYMPHOMANIA	ACADEMICIAN	INCARNADINE	EXCRESCENCE
UNREMITTING	CONTROVERSY	DESIDERATUM	OPINIONATED	ACADEMICISM	INDEPENDENT	FARINACEOUS
UNRIGHTEOUS	IRREMOVABLE	DILAPIDATED	ORTHOGRAPHY	ARCHDIOCESE	INTERMEDDLE	FEATHEREDGE
AERONAUTICS	UNEQUIVOCAL	DISCREPANCY	OUTDISTANCE	BLOODSUCKER	MERCHANDISE	FLANNELETTE
AFTERBURNER	BATTLEWAGON	DISPENSABLE	OVERBALANCE	CATHOLICITY	MOLLYCODDLE	FLORESCENCE
ANTINEUTRON	GENTLEWOMAN	DOCTRINAIRE	PALEOGRAPHY	CERTIFICATE	NICKELODEON	GENDARMERIE
ATTRIBUTIVE	GROUNDWATER	FASHIONABLE	PERFORMANCE	CHIAROSCURO	NONRESIDENT	GEOMAGNETIC
AVOIRDUPOIS	JABBERWOCKY	FILMOGRAPHY	PERIPHRASIS	COMMUNICANT	ORTHOPEDICS	HOMESTRETCH
BARBITURATE	NEEDLEWOMAN	GLOSSOLALIA	PETROGRAPHY	COMMUNICATE	OUTBUILDING	HOMOGENEOUS
BLOCKBUSTER	NETHERWORLD	GREASEPAINT	PHOTOGRAPHY	DOMESTICATE	OUTSTANDING	HOUSEKEEPER
BLOODSUCKER	SWALLOWTAIL	GROUNDWATER	PLEASURABLE	DOMESTICITY	QUARTERDECK	HUCKLEBERRY
CONSECUTIVE	WASHERWOMAN	HAGIOGRAPHY	PORNOGRAPHY	ELECTRICIAN	RESPLENDENT	IMPEDIMENTA
CONSEQUENCE	UNDEREXPOSE	HAIRBREADTH	PRACTICABLE	ELECTRICITY	SCAFFOLDING	INTERPRETER
CONTINUANCE	COUNTRYSIDE	HOMEOSTASIS	PROBLEMATIC	ELECTROCUTE	STANDARDIZE	INTERSPERSE
CONVOLUTION	HAIRSTYLIST	HOMESTEADER	PROPHYLAXIS	FIRECRACKER	SUBSTANDARD	IRIDESCENCE
DELINQUENCY	METAPHYSICS	HORSEPLAYER	REDOUBTABLE	FLUOROSCOPE	THISTLEDOWN	IRREVERENCE
DISENCUMBER	NURSERYMAID	HYDROGRAPHY	RELOCATABLE	HISTORICITY	TRINIDADIAN	KINESTHESIA
DISILLUSION	PARATHYROID	HYDROSTATIC	REMEMBRANCE	HONEYSUCKLE	ULTRAMODERN	KITCHENETTE
DISSIMULATE	POLYSTYRENE	ILLIMITABLE	RENAISSANCE	HYPOTHECATE	ABSENTEEISM	MARQUISETTE
DISSOLUTION	PROSELYTIZE	IMMITIGABLE	RESEMBLANCE	INFANTICIDE	ACKNOWLEDGE	MINESWEEPER
ENCAPSULATE	TOTALIZATOR	IMPERMEABLE	RESPECTABLE	INSECTICIDE	ADOLESCENCE	MISBELIEVER
EXPOSTULATE		IMPREGNABLE	SARCOPHAGUS	INTERLACING	AMBIVALENCE	MISCONCEIVE
FOULMOUTHED		IMPUISSANCE	SERVICEABLE	INTERNECINE	ANAESTHESIA	NONVIOLENCE
FRANKFURTER		INALIENABLE	SHORTCHANGE	INTERRACIAL	ANTIPOVERTY	PARENTHESIS
GESTICULATE	**8TH LETTER**	INCINERATOR	STENOGRAPHY	MAGNIFICENT	BACKSTRETCH	PERIPATETIC
HONEYSUCKLE		INDEFINABLE	STOMACHACHE	MICROSECOND	BENEFICENCE	PITCHBLENDE
IMPORTUNATE	ABRACADABRA	INDOMITABLE	STRAITLACED	MILLISECOND	BENEVOLENCE	POLTERGEIST
INCREDULOUS	ACCELERANDO	INDUBITABLE	SWEEPSTAKES	MONASTICISM	BOYSENBERRY	PRECONCEIVE
INSTITUTION	ACCELERATOR	INELUCTABLE	TOTALIZATOR	MULTIRACIAL	CALORIMETER	PROVENIENCE
INTERNUNCIO	ACCOUNTABLE	INESCAPABLE	TRAILBLAZER	OBSOLESCENT	CAMARADERIE	PSYCHEDELIA
LILLIPUTIAN	ACCUMULATOR	INESTIMABLE	UNALIENABLE	PONTIFICALS	CARRAGEENAN	PSYCHEDELIC
LOUDMOUTHED	ANNUNCIATOR	INEXCUSABLE	UNAVOIDABLE	PONTIFICATE	CENTRIPETAL	PSYCHOGENIC
MALADJUSTED	APPRECIABLE	INFLAMMABLE	UNDERCHARGE	PREVARICATE	CHOLESTEROL	SEISMOMETER
MATRICULATE	BACCHANALIA	INNUMERABLE	UNDESIRABLE	RECIPROCATE	CHRONOMETER	SMITHEREENS
MINIATURIZE	BATHYSCAPHE	INSCRUTABLE	UNFAVORABLE	RECIPROCITY	CLIMACTERIC	SPEEDOMETER
NONDOCUMENT	BATTLEWAGON	INSEPARABLE	UNFLAPPABLE	REMINISCENT	COGNOSCENTE	SPONTANEOUS
OPPORTUNISM	BOILERMAKER	INSOUCIANCE	UNMITIGATED	ROMANTICISM	COINCIDENCE	STOCKINETTE
OPPORTUNITY	CALLIGRAPHY	INSUPERABLE	UNPRINTABLE	SHUTTLECOCK	COMPLACENCE	STOREKEEPER
OVERSTUFFED	CAPACITANCE	INTERCHANGE	UNSATURATED	SIGNIFICANT	COMPLACENCY	SUBSISTENCE
PARTICULATE	CARTOGRAPHY	INTOLERABLE	UNSPEAKABLE	STEREOSCOPE	CONCURRENCE	SUFFICIENCY
PERAMBULATE	CASTELLATED	INTRACTABLE	UNTHINKABLE	STEREOSCOPY	CONFESSEDLY	SUFFRAGETTE
PREOCCUPIED	CHEERLEADER	IRREFUTABLE	UNTOUCHABLE	STETHOSCOPE	CONSEQUENCE	THERMOMETER
RESTITUTION	CHIROGRAPHY	IRREMOVABLE	UNUTTERABLE	STROBOSCOPE	CONSISTENCE	TRAGEDIENNE
RETRIBUTION	CHRISTIANIA	IRREPARABLE	WRONGHEADED	SUPERFICIAL	CONSISTENCY	UNRIGHTEOUS
STRANGULATE	CLEARHEADED	IRREVOCABLE	BIOFEEDBACK	SUPREMACIST	CONTINGENCY	VINAIGRETTE
TRANSLUCENT	COMEUPPANCE	KLEPTOMANIA	BLOODMOBILE	THEATRICALS	CONTRETEMPS	VIOLONCELLO
TRIANGULATE	COMFORTABLE	LEVELHEADED	BLUNDERBUSS	THUNDERCLAP	CONTROVERSY	WHERESOEVER
TUBERCULATE	COMMENTATOR	LITHOGRAPHY	CANDELABRUM	TRANSLUCENT	CONVENIENCE	WHICHSOEVER
TYPEFOUNDER	COMPLICATED	LOUDSPEAKER	DIAMONDBACK	VIRIDESCENT	DECRESCENDO	WITENAGEMOT
UNACCOUNTED	CONCORDANCE	MALFEASANCE	HERRINGBONE	WEATHERCOCK	DELINQUENCY	AFTEREFFECT
UNFORTUNATE	CONDUCTANCE	MEGALOMANIA	HUMMINGBIRD	ACCOMMODATE	DESPONDENCY	COUNTERFEIT

COUNTRIFIED	BREAKPOINTS	REPETITIOUS	CRIMINOLOGY	QUACKSALVER	MEASUREMENT	IMPERMANENT
ELECTROFORM	CANDLELIGHT	RESPONSIBLE	CRYSTALLIZE	QUICKSILVER	MULTIFAMILY	IMPERSONATE
INTEROFFICE	CATEGORICAL	SCREWDRIVER	DERMATOLOGY	RAPSCALLION	NINNYHAMMER	IMPERTINENT
OVERSTUFFED	CENTERPIECE	SCRUMPTIOUS	DISSIMULATE	RATHSKELLER	NONDOCUMENT	IMPORTUNATE
UNQUALIFIED	CEREMONIOUS	SEARCHLIGHT	ELECTROLYTE	RATIONALISM	NOURISHMENT	INCONTINENT
WORDPERFECT	COEFFICIENT	SEMITRAILER	ENCAPSULATE	RATIONALITY	NURSERYMAID	INCREMENTAL
DESEGREGATE	COMBUSTIBLE	SENTENTIOUS	EVENTUALITY	RATIONALIZE	PENULTIMATE	INCRIMINATE
EXTRAVAGANT	CONTRARIETY	SPACEFLIGHT	EXHAUSTLESS	ROADABILITY	PREDICAMENT	INTERLINEAR
FARTHINGALE	CONVENTICLE	STREAMLINED	EXPOSTULATE	SCINTILLATE	PROGRAMMING	INTERLINING
FLABBERGAST	CONVERTIBLE	STREAMLINER	EXTRAPOLATE	SENSIBILITY	REFRESHMENT	INTERMINGLE
HOUSELIGHTS	DELETERIOUS	SUBMERSIBLE	FLOORWALKER	SHAREHOLDER	REPLACEMENT	INTERNUNCIO
INTELLIGENT	DISCONTINUE	SUBTROPICAL	GEANTICLINE	SHIPBUILDER	REQUIREMENT	INTRAVENOUS
INTERREGNUM	EFFICACIOUS	SUSCEPTIBLE	GEOSYNCLINE	SLEEPWALKER	SHORTCOMING	LEATHERNECK
INTERROGATE	EVANGELICAL	SYNTHESIZER	GERONTOLOGY	STEAMROLLER	SUBASSEMBLY	MARCHIONESS
INVESTIGATE	EXPEDITIOUS	TENDENTIOUS	GESTICULATE	STOCKHOLDER	SYNCHROMESH	MINNESINGER
MONOLINGUAL	EXPROPRIATE	THEORETICAL	HAIRSTYLIST	STORYTELLER	TEMPERAMENT	MONEYLENDER
NIGHTINGALE	FURNISHINGS	TONSILLITIS	HERPETOLOGY	STRANGULATE	THALIDOMIDE	MONSEIGNEUR
PREASSIGNED	HAREBRAINED	TRANSCEIVER	HOSPITALITY	SWITCHBLADE	ABORTIONIST	MOUNTAINEER
SOVEREIGNTY	HEAVYWEIGHT	UNCERTAINTY	HOSPITALIZE	TERMINOLOGY	ACCORDINGLY	MOUNTAINTOP
SPECTROGRAM	HEXADECIMAL	UNCIVILIZED	ICHTHYOLOGY	THERMOCLINE	AGGLUTINATE	NARRAGANSET
TRANSFIGURE	IDENTIFIERS	UNCONSCIOUS	IMMORTALITY	THOUGHTLESS	ANACHRONISM	NOTHINGNESS
UNDERSIGNED	IGNOMINIOUS	UNDERWEIGHT	IMMORTALIZE	TRANQUILIZE	ASSASSINATE	OPPORTUNISM
WATERLOGGED	ILLUSTRIOUS	UNINHIBITED	IMPERIALISM	TRIANGULATE	BICARBONATE	OPPORTUNITY
APOCYNTHION	IMPECUNIOUS	UNORGANIZED	INCREDULOUS	TUBERCULATE	BICENTENARY	ORTHODONTIA
BATHYSPHERE	IMPLAUSIBLE	WHEELWRIGHT	INSTABILITY	VERMICULITE	BREADWINNER	OVERWEENING
BIBLIOPHILE	IMPRACTICAL	CRACKERJACK	INTERCALARY	VOLCANOLOGY	CALIFORNIUM	PACHYSANDRA
BROTHERHOOD	IMPROPRIETY	HANDSHAKING	INTERCALATE	WORKMANLIKE	CAMEROONIAN	PANDEMONIUM
CHLOROPHYLL	INDIVISIBLE	HARDWORKING	INTERPOLATE	ACQUIREMENT	CHRISTENDOM	PAPERHANGER
COCKLESHELL	INDUSTRIOUS	MERRYMAKING	INTERRELATE	AMPHETAMINE	CONDOMINIUM	PERIODONTAL
ENFRANCHISE	INEFFICIENT	PAINSTAKING	MARKETPLACE	ANTECHAMBER	CONTAMINANT	PHYSIOGNOMY
FORTNIGHTLY	INSTANTIATE	PERSNICKETY	MARSHMALLOW	APPOINTMENT	CONTAMINATE	POCKETKNIFE
GODDAUGHTER	IRREDUCIBLE	SHELLACKING	MATERIALISM	APPROXIMATE	CONTINENTAL	POMEGRANATE
GROUNDSHEET	IRRELIGIOUS	UNDERTAKING	MATERIALIZE	ARBITRAMENT	CORRIGENDUM	PREDOMINATE
HAEMORRHAGE	LASERWRITER	ZOOPLANKTON	MATRICULATE	BALLETOMANE	COTERMINOUS	PRELIMINARY
HARPSICHORD	LIGHTWEIGHT	AMONTILLADO	METEOROLOGY	BEACHCOMBER	DETERMINANT	PRIZEWINNER
HYDROSPHERE	MANTELPIECE	ANTICYCLONE	METHODOLOGY	CHAMBERMAID	DETERMINATE	PROTAGONIST
LAMPLIGHTER	MASTERPIECE	ARCHAEOLOGY	NAPHTHALENE	COMMANDMENT	DETERMINISM	QUADRENNIAL
LITHOSPHERE	MEMORABILIA	ARCHIPELAGO	NATIONALISM	COMPARTMENT	DISENTANGLE	QUADRENNIUM
MONKEYSHINE	MERITORIOUS	BIMETALLISM	NATIONALIST	COMPORTMENT	DISORGANIZE	RATTLESNAKE
MUTTONCHOPS	MODULARIZED	BREASTPLATE	NATIONALITY	CONCERNMENT	DISSEMINATE	REACTIONARY
NEARSIGHTED	NONPARTISAN	CAMPANOLOGY	NATIONALIZE	CONSIGNMENT	EINSTEINIUM	RECRIMINATE
NECKERCHIEF	OPPROBRIOUS	CANNIBALIZE	NIGHTWALKER	CONTENTMENT	ELECTIONEER	RECTILINEAR
OZONOSPHERE	PAPERWEIGHT	CARDINALATE	NONETHELESS	COUNTERMAND	ELECTRONICS	SENTIMENTAL
PARATYPHOID	PARAMEDICAL	CARDINALITY	OFFICIALDOM	DISASSEMBLE	EXCEEDINGLY	SHORTHANDED
PHOTOSPHERE	PENNYWEIGHT	CATERPILLAR	OFFICIALISM	DISENCUMBER	EXPERIENCED	SPELLBINDER
POLYTECHNIC	PERCEPTIBLE	CHAMBERLAIN	ORNITHOLOGY	EMPLACEMENT	EXTERMINATE	SUBORDINATE
PROGNATHOUS	PERFECTIBLE	CHANCELLERY	PARTICULATE	ENVIRONMENT	FAULTFINDER	SUBURBANITE
SPREADSHEET	PERITONITIS	CHANTICLEER	PATERNALISM	FARTHERMOST	FREETHINKER	SUPERSONICS
THUNDERHEAD	PERMISSIBLE	CHEESECLOTH	PERAMBULATE	FOREVERMORE	FUNCTIONARY	SYNCHRONIZE
TROPOSPHERE	PHARISAICAL	CHOCKABLOCK	PERISTALSIS	FORTHCOMING	FUNDAMENTAL	SYNCHRONOUS
UNFLINCHING	POLYNOMINAL	CLERICALISM	PERSONALITY	FURTHERMORE	GERRYMANDER	TEASPOONFUL
ZOOMORPHISM	PRETENTIOUS	CLIMATOLOGY	PERSONALIZE	FURTHERMOST	GUTTERSNIPE	TELEPRINTER
APPROPRIATE	PRETERMINAL	COLONIALISM	PHRASEOLOGY	GARNISHMENT	HALLUCINATE	TESTIMONIAL
BATTLEFIELD	PROSTATITIS	COMMONPLACE	PLACEHOLDER	IMPROVEMENT	HISTRIONICS	TOBACCONIST
BENEFICIARY	PUNCTILIOUS	COMPTROLLER	PLANETOLOGY	INSTALLMENT	HYDROGENATE	TYPEFOUNDER
BOURGEOISIE	REALPOLITIK	CONTEMPLATE	POINTILLISM	LEGERDEMAIN	HYDROPONICS	ULTRASONICS
BOUTONNIERE	RECONNOITER	CRESTFALLEN	PORTIONLESS	MAGNANIMOUS	ILLUSIONISM	UNACCOUNTED

UNDERHANDED	SUMMERHOUSE	CATERCORNER	MAGISTERIAL	CARAVANSARY	ALPHABETIZE	DEFALCATION
UNDESIGNING	SWITCHBOARD	CENTENARIAN	MERITOCRACY	CHOIRMASTER	ALTERCATION	DEFLORATION
UNFORTUNATE	THENCEFORTH	CHRONOGRAPH	MINIATURIZE	CLOSEFISTED	ALTERNATIVE	DELECTATION
UNREASONING	THEREABOUTS	CIRCULARITY	MISANTHROPE	COEXTENSIVE	ANTINEUTRON	DEMAGNETIZE
VACATIONIST	TOWNSPEOPLE	CIRCULARIZE	MOMENTARILY	COLORCASTER	APPELLATION	DEMOCRATIZE
VERTIGINOUS	TRICHINOSIS	COLLABORATE	NONDESCRIPT	CONGRESSMAN	APPLICATION	DEPRECATORY
AGORAPHOBIA	TWELVEMONTH	COMMEMORATE	ORCHESTRATE	CONNOISSEUR	APPROBATION	DEPREDATION
ANASTOMOSIS	ULTRAVIOLET	COMMISERATE	OVERBEARING	COPROCESSOR	AQUICULTURE	DEPRIVATION
BRAGGADOCIO	UNDERGROUND	COMPUTERIZE	PARATHYROID	COUNTERSIGN	ASSIGNATION	DERELICTION
CATASTROPHE	UNDERGROWTH	CONCENTRATE	PESTIFEROUS	COUNTERSINK	ASSOCIATION	DESCRIPTION
CAULIFLOWER	UNDERSHORTS	CONFEDERACY	PISCATORIAL	COUNTRYSIDE	ASSOCIATIVE	DESENSITIZE
CENTERBOARD	UNEQUIVOCAL	CONFEDERATE	PLANETARIUM	DISILLUSION	ASTIGMATISM	DESPERATION
CIRCUMPOLAR	VARICOLORED	CONSIDERATE	POLYSTYRENE	DISPLEASURE	ATTRIBUTIVE	DESTINATION
COFFEEHOUSE	VENTRILOQUY	CONSIDERING	PROLETARIAN	DRILLMASTER	BENEDICTION	DESTRUCTION
CONDITIONAL	VICHYSSOISE	CONSUMERISM	PROLETARIAT	FORECLOSURE	BENEFACTION	DIFFRACTION
CONDITIONED	WASHERWOMAN	CORROBORATE	PROLIFERATE	GENERALSHIP	CALCULATING	DIPLOMATIST
COTTONMOUTH	WHEREABOUTS	DEMONSTRATE	PROTOMARTYR	HABERDASHER	CALCULATION	DISCOURTESY
CRAPSHOOTER	AVOIRDUPOIS	DETERIORATE	PROTUBERANT	HAIRDRESSER	CANDIDATURE	DISPOSITION
CUSTOMHOUSE	CIRCUMSPECT	DICTATORIAL	PSYCHODRAMA	HELLENISTIC	CANDLESTICK	DISPUTATION
DISAPPROVAL	COUNTERPANE	DIRECTORATE	RADIOCARBON	HYPOTHESIZE	CARMINATIVE	DISQUIETUDE
EXCEPTIONAL	COUNTERPART	DOWNHEARTED	RECONSTRUCT	MALADJUSTED	CEMENTATION	DISSOLUTION
FINGERBOARD	GRASSHOPPER	ENDOTHERMIC	REFRIGERATE	MECHANISTIC	CLANDESTINE	DISTINCTION
GENTLEWOMAN	GYROCOMPASS	ENGINEERING	REMONSTRANT	MEDIUMISTIC	COBBLESTONE	DISTINCTIVE
GREENGROCER	HANDICAPPER	EPINEPHRINE	REMONSTRATE	METAPHYSICS	COEDUCATION	DOCUMENTARY
HEARTBROKEN	INTERCEPTOR	EQUILIBRIUM	REVERBERATE	NORTHEASTER	COLLOCATION	EDIFICATION
HOUSEBROKEN	MALAPROPISM	EXPECTORANT	SEISMOGRAPH	OMNIPRESENT	COMBINATION	ELECTROTYPE
HYDROPHOBIA	MICROCAPSUL	EXPECTORATE	SEQUESTRATE	PENTECOSTAL	COMMINATION	ELEPHANTINE
HYGROSCOPIC	MILLIAMPERE	EXTEMPORARY	SPENDTHRIFT	PICTURESQUE	COMMUTATION	ELIZABETHAN
HYPERTROPHY	PARTICIPATE	EXTEMPORIZE	SUPERMARKET	PREDECESSOR	COMMUTATIVE	EQUIDISTANT
IMPASSIONED	PHILOSOPHER	FAMILIARITY	SUPERSCRIBE	PROGRESSION	COMPARATIVE	EVERLASTING
INTENTIONAL	PREOCCUPIED	FINGERPRINT	SUPERSCRIPT	PROGRESSIVE	COMPETITION	EXPECTATION
INTERATOMIC	SAFEKEEPING	FOREQUARTER	TACHYCARDIA	SCHOLARSHIP	COMPOSITION	EXPENDITURE
JABBERWOCKY	SERENDIPITY	FORESHORTEN	TECHNOCRACY	SUPPRESSANT	COMPUNCTION	EXTRADITION
MACROBIOTIC	SUPERIMPOSE	FRANKFURTER	TERRESTRIAL	TIGHTFISTED	CONCOMITANT	FIDDLESTICK
MACROSCOPIC	TYPOGRAPHER	GINGERBREAD	TERRITORIAL	TOASTMASTER	CONJUGATION	FORMFITTING
MEGALOPOLIS	UNDEREXPOSE	GRANDPARENT	TIMESHARING	TOPDRESSING	CONJUNCTION	FORNICATION
MELANCHOLIA	WOODCHOPPER	HALFHEARTED	TRANSPARENT	TRUSTEESHIP	CONJUNCTIVA	FOULMOUTHED
MELANCHOLIC	ABECEDARIAN	HARDHEARTED	TREACHEROUS	UNOBTRUSIVE	CONJUNCTIVE	FRAGMENTARY
MICROSCOPIC	AFTERBURNER	HERBIVOROUS	TRENCHERMAN	UNVARNISHED	CONJUNCTURE	GEOPOLITICS
MORTARBOARD	AGGLOMERATE	HINDQUARTER	TRINITARIAN	UNWHOLESOME	CONNOTATION	GRANDFATHER
MOTHERBOARD	ALEXANDRIAN	HYDROCARBON	TRIUMVIRATE	VENTURESOME	CONNOTATIVE	GRANDMOTHER
NEEDLEPOINT	ALEXANDRINE	HYPERBOREAN	TRUEHEARTED	WASTEBASKET	CONSECUTIVE	GRAVITATION
NEEDLEWOMAN	ANTIQUARIAN	IMPERFORATE	TRUSTWORTHY	WORKMANSHIP	CONSUMPTION	HABITUATION
NETHERWORLD	ARISTOCRACY	INCARCERATE	ULTRAMARINE	ABOMINATION	CONSUMPTIVE	HANDWRITING
PARATROOPER	BALLCARRIER	INCORPORATE	UNCONCERNED	ABSTRACTION	CONTRACTILE	HEARTHSTONE
PARISHIONER	BARBITURATE	INCORPOREAL	UTILITARIAN	ACCEPTATION	CONTRAPTION	HOUSEMOTHER
PLAINSPOKEN	BEHAVIORISM	INDIFFERENT	WARMHEARTED	ACCLAMATION	CONURBATION	HYPERACTIVE
PORTERHOUSE	BELLIGERENT	INGATHERING	WHEELBARROW	ACCLIMATIZE	CONVOCATION	HYPHENATION
PREHISTORIC	BLAMEWORTHY	INNERSPRING	WINTERGREEN	ACQUISITION	CONVOLUTION	IMAGESETTER
PROBATIONER	BLOODSTREAM	JUVENOCRACY	ADVERTISING	ACQUISITIVE	COOPERATIVE	IMAGINATION
PROVISIONAL	BUREAUCRACY	KINDHEARTED	ANNIVERSARY	ACUPUNCTURE	CORNERSTONE	IMBRICATION
RECESSIONAL	CALCIFEROUS	KWASHIORKOR	APHRODISIAC	ADVERSATIVE	CORPORATION	IMPORTATION
SCHOOLHOUSE	CAPILLARITY	LABRADORITE	AUDIOVISUAL	AERONAUTICS	CORRELATIVE	INADVERTENT
SENSATIONAL	CARDIOGRAPH	LATCHSTRING	BLOCKBUSTER	AFFECTATION	COSIGNATORY	INATTENTION
SPRINGBOARD	CARDSHARPER	LETTERPRESS	BREADBASKET	AFFIRMATIVE	CYBERNATION	INCANTATION
STOCKBROKER	CARNIVOROUS	LIBERTARIAN	BURGOMASTER	AGGREGATION	CYBERNETICS	INCARNATION
STRAWFLOWER	CASSITERITE	LIONHEARTED	BUSINESSMAN	AGRICULTURE	DECLARATIVE	INCERTITUDE

INCLINATION	PARTURITION	SUPERINTEND	PROMISCUOUS	CARDIOGRAPH	GYROCOMPASS	REMONSTRANT
INCOMPETENT	PENETRATING	SUPERLATIVE	PROPINQUITY	CENTERBOARD	HAEMORRHAGE	REMONSTRATE
INDENTATION	PERFUNCTORY	SUPPOSITION	SOLILOQUIZE	CERTIFICATE	HALLUCINATE	RESUSCITATE
INDIGESTION	PERMUTATION	SUPPOSITORY	SPECTACULAR	CHAMBERLAIN	HYDROGENATE	REVERBERATE
INDIGNATION	PERSPECTIVE	SWALLOWTAIL	SUPERFLUOUS	CHAMBERMAID	HYPOTHECATE	SCINTILLATE
INEFFECTIVE	POLLINATION	SYNCOPATION	TEMPESTUOUS	CHRONOGRAPH	IMPERFORATE	SEISMOGRAPH
INEFFECTUAL	PORTMANTEAU	SYSTEMATIZE	THERAPEUTIC	CLAIRVOYANT	IMPERSONATE	SEQUESTRATE
INFORMATION	PORTRAITIST	TEMPERATURE	UNICELLULAR	COLLABORATE	IMPORTUNATE	SIGNIFICANT
INFORMATIVE	PORTRAITURE	THEREWITHAL	WATERCOURSE	COMMEMORATE	INCARCERATE	SPRINGBOARD
INGRATITUDE	PRECIPITATE	TRANSACTION	ANTIGRAVITY	COMMISERATE	INCORPORATE	STRANGULATE
INOPERATIVE	PRECIPITOUS	TRANSMITTER	COUNTERVAIL	COMMONPLACE	INCRIMINATE	SUBORDINATE
INOPPORTUNE	PREIGNITION	TREPIDATION	LABORSAVING	COMMUNICANT	INDIVIDUATE	SUBSTANDARD
INQUISITION	PREMEDITATE	TRIBULATION	MAIDSERVANT	COMMUNICATE	INSTANTIATE	SUPPRESSANT
INQUISITIVE	PREMONITION	TYPESETTING	MENDELEVIUM	CONCENTRATE	INTERCALARY	SWALLOWTAIL
INSINUATING	PREPOSITION	TYPEWRITING	MISCHIEVOUS	CONCOMITANT	INTERCALATE	SWITCHBLADE
INSPIRATION	PREROGATIVE	UNCHRISTIAN	PRIMITIVISM	CONFEDERACY	INTERPOLATE	SWITCHBOARD
INSTITUTION	PRESUMPTION	UNCOMMITTED	RESISTIVITY	CONFEDERATE	INTERRELATE	TECHNOCRACY
INSTRUCTION	PROCRUSTEAN	UNDEVIATING	ROTOGRAVURE	CONSIDERATE	INTERROGATE	THEATRICALS
INSTRUCTIVE	PROFANATORY	UNIFICATION	BITTERSWEET	CONSOLIDATE	INVESTIGATE	THITHERWARD
INTERACTION	PROHIBITION	UNRELENTING	CABINETWORK	CONTAMINANT	INVOLUNTARY	TRIANGULATE
INTERACTIVE	PROMPTITUDE	UNREMITTING	EARTHENWARE	CONTAMINATE	JUVENOCRACY	TRIUMVIRATE
INTERESTING	PROPOSITION	VACCINATION	GRANITEWARE	CONTEMPLATE	KITCHENWARE	TUBERCULATE
INVESTITURE	PROPRIETARY	VALEDICTION	KITCHENWARE	CORROBORATE	LEGERDEMAIN	UNFORTUNATE
INVOLUNTARY	PROSELYTIZE	VALEDICTORY	LATTICEWORK	COUNTERMAND	MAIDSERVANT	ABRACADABRA
IRREDENTISM	PROSTHETICS	VENTILATION	MEADOWSWEET	COUNTERPANE	MARKETPLACE	ACCOUNTABLE
LACRIMATION	PUBLICATION	VICISSITUDE	THITHERWARD	COUNTERPART	MATRICULATE	AGORAPHOBIA
LEGISLATION	PULCHRITUDE	VINDICATION	WEATHERWORN	COUNTERVAIL	MERITOCRACY	ANTECHAMBER
LEGISLATIVE	PUNCTUATION	VITICULTURE	CRUCIFIXION	CRACKERJACK	MORTARBOARD	APPRECIABLE
LEGISLATURE	QUALITATIVE	VIVISECTION	ASSEMBLYMAN	DEMONSTRATE	MOTHERBOARD	BEACHCOMBER
LICKSPITTLE	RADIOMETRIC	WAINSCOTING	CLAIRVOYANT	DESEGREGATE	NECESSITATE	COMBUSTIBLE
LILLIPUTIAN	RECOGNITION	WHEREWITHAL	STEREOTYPED	DETERIORATE	NIGHTINGALE	COMFORTABLE
LINGUISTICS	REFORMATION	WHIFFLETREE		DETERMINANT	NURSERYMAID	CONVERTIBLE
LITTERATEUR	REFORMATORY	WHIPPLETREE		DETERMINATE	ORCHESTRATE	DISASSEMBLE
LOUDMOUTHED	REGIMENTALS	WIDEMOUTHED		DIAMONDBACK	PARTICIPATE	DISENCUMBER
LUCUBRATION	REGURGITATE	WORKSTATION	**9TH LETTER**	DIRECTORATE	PARTICULATE	DISPENSABLE
MACHINATION	REINFECTION	CENTRIFUGAL		DISSEMINATE	PENULTIMATE	FASHIONABLE
MALEDICTION	REPLICATION	CIRCUMLUNAR	ACCOMMODATE	DISSIMULATE	PERAMBULATE	HYDROCARBON
MALFUNCTION	REPROBATION	CONSPICUOUS	AGGLOMERATE	DOCUMENTARY	POMEGRANATE	HYDROPHOBIA
MALPRACTICE	REQUISITION	CONSTITUENT	AGGLUTINATE	DOMESTICATE	PONTIFICALS	ILLIMITABLE
MANUFACTORY	RESERVATION	CREPUSCULAR	AMONTILLADO	EARTHENWARE	PONTIFICATE	IMMITIGABLE
MANUFACTURE	RESIDENTIAL	DISTINGUISH	ANNIVERSARY	ENCAPSULATE	PRECIPITATE	IMPERMEABLE
MATHEMATICS	RESIGNATION	DISTRIBUTOR	ANTIOXIDANT	EQUIDISTANT	PREDOMINATE	IMPLAUSIBLE
MENSURATION	RESPIRATION	DREADNOUGHT	APPROPRIATE	EXPECTORANT	PRELIMINARY	IMPREGNABLE
MERCHANTMAN	RESTITUTION	FORETHOUGHT	APPROXIMATE	EXPECTORATE	PREMEDITATE	INALIENABLE
METRICATION	RESTORATION	GALLIMAUFRY	ARCHIPELAGO	EXPOSTULATE	PREVARICATE	INDEFINABLE
MISBEGOTTEN	RESTORATIVE	HIGHFALUTIN	ARISTOCRACY	EXPROPRIATE	PROLIFERATE	INDIVISIBLE
MISCONSTRUE	RESTRICTION	INCONGRUENT	ASSASSINATE	EXTEMPORARY	PROPRIETARY	INDOMITABLE
MUSCULATURE	RESUSCITATE	INCONGRUOUS	BALLETOMANE	EXTERMINATE	PROTUBERANT	INDUBITABLE
NEANDERTHAL	RETRIBUTION	INCUNABULUM	BARBITURATE	EXTRAPOLATE	PSYCHODRAMA	INELUCTABLE
NECESSITATE	RETROACTIVE	INDIVIDUATE	BENEFICIARY	EXTRAVAGANT	QUARTERBACK	INESCAPABLE
NECESSITOUS	REVERENTIAL	INTERCOURSE	BICARBONATE	FARTHINGALE	RATTLESNAKE	INESTIMABLE
NONNEGATIVE	ROTTENSTONE	MASSACHUSET	BICENTENARY	FINGERBOARD	REACTIONARY	INEXCUSABLE
NUMISMATICS	STEPBROTHER	MELLIFLUOUS	BIOFEEDBACK	FLABBERGAST	RECIPROCATE	INFLAMMABLE
OBSERVATION	STRAIGHTWAY	MUSKELLUNGE	BREASTPLATE	FRAGMENTARY	RECRIMINATE	INNUMERABLE
OBSERVATORY	SUBJUNCTIVE	OUTMANEUVER	BUREAUCRACY	FUNCTIONARY	REFRIGERATE	INSCRUTABLE
OBSTRUCTION	SUBSTANTIAL	OVERWROUGHT	CARAVANSARY	GESTICULATE	REGIMENTALS	INSEPARABLE
OSTENTATION	SUBSTANTIVE	PERSPICUOUS	CARDINALATE	GRANITEWARE	REGURGITATE	INSUPERABLE

INTOLERABLE	GALLBLADDER	HYPERBOREAN	SUPERINTEND	ABECEDARIAN	CIRCULARITY	DESTINATION
INTRACTABLE	GERRYMANDER	IDENTIFIERS	SYNCHROMESH	ABOMINATION	CIRCULARIZE	DESTRUCTION
IRREDUCIBLE	HAIRBREADTH	IMPERMANENT	TEMPERAMENT	ABORTIONIST	CLANDESTINE	DETERMINISM
IRREFUTABLE	HOMESTEADER	IMPERTINENT	THOUGHTLESS	ABSENTEEISM	CLERICALISM	DICTATORIAL
IRREMOVABLE	INTERMEDDLE	IMPROPRIETY	THUNDERHEAD	ABSTRACTION	COEDUCATION	DIFFRACTION
IRREPARABLE	LEVELHEADED	IMPROVEMENT	TRANSLUCENT	ACADEMICIAN	COEXTENSIVE	DIPLOMATIST
IRREVOCABLE	MOLLYCODDLE	IMPROVIDENT	TRANSPARENT	ACADEMICISM	COLLOCATION	DISILLUSION
PERCEPTIBLE	MONEYLENDER	INADVERTENT	TROPOSPHERE	ACCEPTATION	COLONIALISM	DISORGANIZE
PERFECTIBLE	OFFICIALDOM	INCOMPETENT	ULTRAMODERN	ACCLAMATION	COMBINATION	DISPOSITION
PERMISSIBLE	PACHYSANDRA	INCONGRUENT	VIRIDESCENT	ACCLIMATIZE	COMMINATION	DISPUTATION
PLEASURABLE	PLACEHOLDER	INCONTINENT	WINTERGREEN	ACQUISITION	COMMUTATION	DISSOLUTION
PRACTICABLE	SHAREHOLDER	INCORPOREAL	WORDPERFECT	ACQUISITIVE	COMMUTATIVE	DISTINCTION
RADIOCARBON	SHIPBUILDER	INDEPENDENT	GALLIMAUFRY	ADVERSATIVE	COMPARATIVE	DISTINCTIVE
REDOUBTABLE	SHORTHANDED	INDIFFERENT	OVERSTUFFED	ADVERTISING	COMPETITION	DISTINGUISH
RELOCATABLE	SPELLBINDER	INEFFICIENT	TEASPOONFUL	AERONAUTICS	COMPOSITION	DOCTRINAIRE
RESPECTABLE	STOCKHOLDER	INSTALLMENT	ACCORDINGLY	AFFECTATION	COMPUNCTION	DOMESTICITY
RESPONSIBLE	TACHYCARDIA	INTELLIGENT	BATTLEWAGON	AFFIRMATIVE	COMPUTERIZE	EDIFICATION
SERVICEABLE	TYPEFOUNDER	INTERLINEAR	CANDLELIGHT	AGGREGATION	CONDOMINIUM	EINSTEINIUM
SUBASSEMBLY	UNDERHANDED	LEATHERNECK	CENTRIFUGAL	ALEXANDRIAN	CONJUGATION	ELECTRICIAN
SUBMERSIBLE	WRONGHEADED	LETTERPRESS	DISENTANGLE	ALEXANDRINE	CONJUNCTION	ELECTRICITY
SUSCEPTIBLE	ACQUIREMENT	LITHOSPHERE	DREADNOUGHT	ALPHABETIZE	CONJUNCTIVA	ELECTRONICS
UNALIENABLE	AFTEREFFECT	LITTERATEUR	EXCEEDINGLY	ALTERCATION	CONJUNCTIVE	ELEPHANTINE
UNAVOIDABLE	APPOINTMENT	MAGNIFICENT	FORETHOUGHT	ALTERNATIVE	CONNOTATION	ENFRANCHISE
UNDESIRABLE	ARBITRAMENT	MANTELPIECE	HEAVYWEIGHT	AMPHETAMINE	CONNOTATIVE	ENGINEERING
UNFAVORABLE	ARCHDIOCESE	MARCHIONESS	INTERMINGLE	ANACHRONISM	CONSECUTIVE	EPINEPHRINE
UNFLAPPABLE	BATHYSPHERE	MASTERPIECE	LIGHTWEIGHT	ANTIGRAVITY	CONSIDERING	EQUILIBRIUM
UNPRINTABLE	BATTLEFIELD	MEADOWSWEET	MINNESINGER	ANTIQUARIAN	CONSUMERISM	EVENTUALITY
UNSPEAKABLE	BELLIGERENT	MEASUREMENT	OVERWROUGHT	APHRODISIAC	CONSUMPTION	EVERLASTING
UNTHINKABLE	BITTERSWEET	MILLIAMPERE	PAPERHANGER	APOCYNTHION	CONSUMPTIVE	EXPECTATION
UNTOUCHABLE	BLOODSTREAM	MONSEIGNEUR	PAPERWEIGHT	APPELLATION	CONTRACTILE	EXTEMPORIZE
UNUTTERABLE	BOUTONNIERE	MOUNTAINEER	PENNYWEIGHT	APPLICATION	CONTRAPTION	EXTRADITION
BRAGGADOCIO	CENTERPIECE	NAPHTHALENE	SARCOPHAGUS	APPROBATION	CONURBATION	FAMILIARITY
CATEGORICAL	CHANCELLERY	NICKELODEON	SEARCHLIGHT	ASSIGNATION	CONVOCATION	FIDDLESTICK
CONVENTICLE	CHANTICLEER	NONDOCUMENT	SPACEFLIGHT	ASSOCIATION	CONVOLUTION	FINGERPRINT
EVANGELICAL	CIRCUMSPECT	NONETHELESS	UNDERWEIGHT	ASSOCIATIVE	COOPERATIVE	FORMFITTING
EXPERIENCED	COCKLESHELL	NONRESIDENT	WATERLOGGED	ASTIGMATISM	CORPORATION	FORNICATION
GREENGROCER	COEFFICIENT	NOTHINGNESS	WHEELWRIGHT	ATTRIBUTIVE	CORRELATIVE	FORTHCOMING
IMPRACTICAL	COMMANDMENT	NOURISHMENT	ELIZABETHAN	BALLCARRIER	COUNTERSIGN	GEANTICLINE
INTERNUNCIO	COMPARTMENT	OBSOLESCENT	FOULMOUTHED	BEHAVIORISM	COUNTERSINK	GEOPOLITICS
JABBERWOCKY	COMPORTMENT	OMNIPRESENT	GENERALSHIP	BENEDICTION	COUNTRIFIED	GEOSYNCLINE
PARAMEDICAL	CONCERNMENT	OZONOSPHERE	GRANDFATHER	BENEFACTION	COUNTRYSIDE	GRAVITATION
PHARISAICAL	CONNOISSEUR	PERSNICKETY	GRANDMOTHER	BIBLIOPHILE	CRUCIFIXION	GREASEPAINT
STOMACHACHE	CONSIGNMENT	PHOTOSPHERE	HABERDASHER	BIMETALLISM	CRYSTALLIZE	GUTTERSNIPE
STRAITLACED	CONSTITUENT	POLYSTYRENE	HOUSELIGHTS	BLOODMOBILE	CYBERNATION	HABITUATION
SUBTROPICAL	CONTENTMENT	PORTIONLESS	HOUSEMOTHER	CALCULATING	CYBERNETICS	HAIRSTYLIST
THEORETICAL	CONTRARIETY	PORTMANTEAU	LOUDMOUTHED	CALCULATION	DECLARATIVE	HANDSHAKING
UNEQUIVOCAL	COUNTERFEIT	PREDICAMENT	NEANDERTHAL	CALIFORNIUM	DEFALCATION	HANDWRITING
ACKNOWLEDGE	DISCOURTESY	PROCRUSTEAN	PHILOSOPHER	CAMEROONIAN	DEFLORATION	HARDWORKING
CHEERLEADER	ELECTIONEER	QUARTERDECK	SCHOLARSHIP	CANDLESTICK	DELECTATION	HISTORICITY
CHRISTENDOM	EMPLACEMENT	RECTILINEAR	STEPBROTHER	CANNIBALIZE	DEMAGNETIZE	HISTRIONICS
CLEARHEADED	ENVIRONMENT	REFRESHMENT	THEREWITHAL	CAPILLARITY	DEMOCRATIZE	HORSERADISH
CONFESSEDLY	EXHAUSTLESS	REMINISCENT	TRUSTEESHIP	CARDINALITY	DEPREDATION	HOSPITALITY
CORRIGENDUM	GARNISHMENT	REPLACEMENT	TYPOGRAPHER	CARMINATIVE	DEPRIVATION	HOSPITALIZE
DICOTYLEDON	GINGERBREAD	REQUIREMENT	UNVARNISHED	CASSITERITE	DERELICTION	HUMMINGBIRD
DOWNTRODDEN	GRANDPARENT	RESPLENDENT	WHEREWITHAL	CATHOLICITY	DESCRIPTION	HYDROPONICS
FAULTFINDER	GROUNDSHEET	SMITHEREENS	WIDEMOUTHED	CEMENTATION	DESENSITIZE	HYPERACTIVE
FEATHEREDGE	HYDROSPHERE	SPREADSHEET	WORKMANSHIP	CENTENARIAN	DESPERATION	HYPHENATION

HYPOTHESIZE	MATERIALISM	PREOCCUPIED	SUBSTANTIVE	FIRECRACKER	BENEFICENCE	NONVIOLENCE
ILLUSIONISM	MATERIALIZE	PREPOSITION	SUBURBANITE	FLOORWALKER	BENEVOLENCE	NYMPHOMANIA
IMAGINATION	MATHEMATICS	PREROGATIVE	SUPERFICIAL	FREETHINKER	BREADWINNER	OUTDISTANCE
IMBRICATION	MENDELEVIUM	PRESUMPTION	SUPERLATIVE	HEARTBROKEN	BREAKPOINTS	OVERBALANCE
IMMORTALITY	MENSURATION	PRIMITIVISM	SUPERSCRIBE	HONEYSUCKLE	CAPACITANCE	PARISHIONER
IMMORTALIZE	MERCHANDISE	PROGRAMMING	SUPERSCRIPT	HOUSEBROKEN	CARRAGEENAN	PERFORMANCE
IMPERIALISM	MERRYMAKING	PROGRESSION	SUPERSONICS	KWASHIORKOR	CATERCORNER	PITCHBLENDE
IMPORTATION	METAPHYSICS	PROGRESSIVE	SUPPOSITION	LOUDSPEAKER	CHRISTIANIA	POLYNOMINAL
INATTENTION	METRICATION	PROHIBITION	SUPREMACIST	NIGHTWALKER	CIRCUMLUNAR	POLYTECHNIC
INCANTATION	MILLIONAIRE	PROLETARIAN	SYNCHRONIZE	PLAINSPOKEN	COGNOSCENTE	PREASSIGNED
INCARNADINE	MINIATURIZE	PROLETARIAT	SYNCOPATION	SLEEPWALKER	COINCIDENCE	PRETERMINAL
INCARNATION	MISCONCEIVE	PROPINQUITY	SYSTEMATIZE	STOCKBROKER	COMEUPPANCE	PRIZEWINNER
INCLINATION	MOCKINGBIRD	PROPOSITION	TERRESTRIAL	SUPERMARKET	COMPLACENCE	PROBATIONER
INDENTATION	MOMENTARILY	PROSELYTIZE	TERRITORIAL	SWEEPSTAKES	COMPLACENCY	PROVENIENCE
INDIGESTION	MONASTICISM	PROSTHETICS	TESTIMONIAL	WASTEBASKET	CONCORDANCE	PROVISIONAL
INDIGNATION	MONKEYSHINE	PROTAGONIST	THALIDOMIDE	BACCHANALIA	CONCURRENCE	PSYCHOGENIC
INEFFECTIVE	MULTIFAMILY	PUBLICATION	THERMOCLINE	CATERPILLAR	CONDITIONAL	RECESSIONAL
INFANTICIDE	MULTIRACIAL	PUNCTUATION	TIMESHARING	CIRCUMPOLAR	CONDITIONED	REMEMBRANCE
INFORMATION	NATIONALISM	QUADRENNIAL	TOBACCONIST	COMPTROLLER	CONDUCTANCE	RENAISSANCE
INFORMATIVE	NATIONALIST	QUADRENNIUM	TOPDRESSING	CREPUSCULAR	CONFORMANCE	RESEMBLANCE
INGATHERING	NATIONALITY	QUALITATIVE	TRANQUILIZE	CRESTFALLEN	CONSEQUENCE	SENSATIONAL
INNERSPRING	NATIONALIZE	RAPSCALLION	TRANSACTION	GLOSSOLALIA	CONSERVANCY	SHORTCHANGE
INOPERATIVE	NECKERCHIEF	RATIONALISM	TREPIDATION	INCUNABULUM	CONSISTENCE	SOVEREIGNTY
INQUISITION	NEEDLEPOINT	RATIONALITY	TRIBULATION	MARSHMALLOW	CONSISTENCY	STREAMLINED
INQUISITIVE	NONDESCRIPT	RATIONALIZE	TRINIDADIAN	MEGALOPOLIS	CONTINGENCY	STREAMLINER
INSECTICIDE	NONNEGATIVE	RECIPROCITY	TRINITARIAN	MELANCHOLIA	CONTINUANCE	SUBSISTENCE
INSINUATING	NUMISMATICS	RECOGNITION	TYPESETTING	MELANCHOLIC	CONTRIVANCE	SUFFICIENCY
INSPIRATION	OBSERVATION	REFORMATION	TYPEWRITING	MEMORABILIA	CONVENIENCE	TRAGEDIENNE
INSTABILITY	OBSTRUCTION	REINFECTION	ULTRAMARINE	PSYCHEDELIA	COUNTENANCE	TWELVEMONTH
INSTITUTION	OFFICIALISM	REPLICATION	ULTRASONICS	PSYCHEDELIC	DECRESCENDO	UNCERTAINTY
INSTRUCTION	OPPORTUNISM	REPROBATION	UNCHRISTIAN	RATHSKELLER	DELINQUENCY	UNCONCERNED
INSTRUCTIVE	OPPORTUNITY	REQUISITION	UNDERTAKING	SEMITRAILER	DESPONDENCY	UNDERSIGNED
INTERACTION	ORTHOPEDICS	RESERVATION	UNDESIGNING	SPECTACULAR	DISCONTINUE	ANTICYCLONE
INTERACTIVE	OSTENTATION	RESIDENTIAL	UNDEVIATING	STEAMROLLER	DISCREPANCY	ARCHAEOLOGY
INTERESTING	OUTBUILDING	RESIGNATION	UNFLINCHING	STORYTELLER	EXCEPTIONAL	AVOIRDUPOIS
INTERLACING	OUTSTANDING	RESISTIVITY	UNIFICATION	THUNDERCLAP	EXCRESCENCE	BROTHERHOOD
INTERLINING	OVERBEARING	RESPIRATION	UNOBTRUSIVE	ULTRAVIOLET	FLORESCENCE	CABINETWORK
INTERNECINE	OVERWEENING	RESTITUTION	UNQUALIFIED	UNICELLULAR	FURNISHINGS	CALCIFEROUS
INTEROFFICE	PAINSTAKING	RESTORATION	UNREASONING	VIOLONCELLO	HAREBRAINED	CAMPANOLOGY
INTERRACIAL	PANDEMONIUM	RESTORATIVE	UNRELENTING	ASSEMBLYMAN	IMPASSIONED	CARNIVOROUS
IRREDENTISM	PARTURITION	RESTRICTION	UNREMITTING	BUSINESSMAN	IMPEDIMENTA	CEREMONIOUS
LABORSAVING	PATERNALISM	RETRIBUTION	UTILITARIAN	CONGRESSMAN	IMPUISSANCE	CHEESECLOTH
LABRADORITE	PENETRATING	RETROACTIVE	VACATIONIST	CONTRETEMPS	INSOUCIANCE	CHOCKABLOCK
LACRIMATION	PERMUTATION	REVERENTIAL	VACCINATION	ENDOTHERMIC	INTENTIONAL	CLIMATOLOGY
LATCHSTRING	PERSONALITY	ROADABILITY	VALEDICTION	GENTLEWOMAN	INTERCHANGE	COBBLESTONE
LEGISLATION	PERSONALIZE	ROMANTICISM	VENTILATION	HEXADECIMAL	INTERREGNUM	CONSPICUOUS
LEGISLATIVE	PERSPECTIVE	SAFEKEEPING	VERMICULITE	INTERATOMIC	IRIDESCENCE	CORNERSTONE
LIBERTARIAN	PISCATORIAL	SCAFFOLDING	VICHYSSOISE	MERCHANTMAN	IRREVERENCE	COSIGNATORY
LILLIPUTIAN	PLANETARIUM	SENSIBILITY	VINDICATION	NEEDLEWOMAN	KLEPTOMANIA	COTERMINOUS
LINGUISTICS	POCKETKNIFE	SERENDIPITY	VIVISECTION	NINNYHAMMER	MALFEASANCE	CRIMINOLOGY
LUCUBRATION	POINTILLISM	SHELLACKING	WAINSCOTING	TRENCHERMAN	MEGALOMANIA	DELETERIOUS
MACHINATION	POLLINATION	SHORTCOMING	WORKMANLIKE	WASHERWOMAN	MESALLIANCE	DEPRECATORY
MAGISTERIAL	POLTERGEIST	SOLILOQUIZE	WORKSTATION	WITENAGEMOT	MISALLIANCE	DERMATOLOGY
MALAPROPISM	PORTRAITIST	SPENDTHRIFT	ZOOMORPHISM	ACCELERANDO	MISDEMEANOR	EFFICACIOUS
MALEDICTION	PRECONCEIVE	STANDARDIZE	BLOODSUCKER	ADOLESCENCE	MISFEASANCE	ELECTROFORM
MALFUNCTION	PREIGNITION	SUBJUNCTIVE	BOILERMAKER	AFTERBURNER	MISGUIDANCE	EXPEDITIOUS
MALPRACTICE	PREMONITION	SUBSTANTIAL	BREADBASKET	AMBIVALENCE	MUSKELLUNGE	FARINACEOUS

FARTHERMOST	SHUTTLECOCK	PICTURESQUE	COLORCASTER	PROBLEMATIC	RECONSTRUCT	CIRCUMPOLAR	
FLUOROSCOPE	SMORGASBORD	VENTRILOQUY	COMMENTATOR	PROSTATITIS	ROTOGRAVURE	CONDITIONAL	
FOREVERMORE	SPONTANEOUS	ANTINEUTRON	COMPLICATED	PROTOMARTYR	SCHOOLHOUSE	CONGRESSMAN	
FURTHERMORE	STEREOSCOPE	ANTIPOVERTY	CONSERVATOR	REALPOLITIK	SCUTTLEBUTT	CONTINENTAL	
FURTHERMOST	STEREOSCOPY	BOYSENBERRY	CONTINENTAL	RECONNOITER	SUMMERHOUSE	CREPUSCULAR	
GERONTOLOGY	STETHOSCOPE	CAMARADERIE	CRAPSHOOTER	SEISMOMETER	TEMPERATURE	DICTATORIAL	
HARPSICHORD	STROBOSCOPE	CANDELABRUM	DENOMINATOR	SENTIMENTAL	THEREABOUTS	DISAPPROVAL	
HEARTHSTONE	SUPERFLUOUS	CHOLESTEROL	DESIDERATUM	SPEEDOMETER	TRANSFIGURE	ELECTRICIAN	
HERBIVOROUS	SUPERIMPOSE	CLIMACTERIC	DIAMAGNETIC	STOCKINETTE	UNDERGROUND	ELIZABETHAN	
HERPETOLOGY	SUPPOSITORY	CONTROVERSY	DIAPHORETIC	SUFFRAGETTE	VICISSITUDE	EQUILATERAL	
HERRINGBONE	SYNCHRONOUS	EQUILATERAL	DILAPIDATED	TELEPRINTER	VITICULTURE	EVANGELICAL	
HOMOGENEOUS	TEMPESTUOUS	GENDARMERIE	DISTRIBUTOR	THERAPEUTIC	WHEREABOUTS	EXCEPTIONAL	
ICHTHYOLOGY	TENDENTIOUS	HUCKLEBERRY	DOWNHEARTED	THERMOMETER	DISAPPROVAL	FUNDAMENTAL	
IGNOMINIOUS	TERMINOLOGY	INTERCOURSE	DRILLMASTER	TIGHTFISTED	MISBELIEVER	GENTLEWOMAN	
ILLUSTRIOUS	THISTLEDOWN	INTERSPERSE	DYNAMOMETER	TOASTMASTER	OUTMANEUVER	GINGERBREAD	
IMPECUNIOUS	THUNDERBOLT	MISCONSTRUE	FLANNELETTE	TONSILLITIS	QUACKSALVER	HEXADECIMAL	
INCONGRUOUS	TREACHEROUS	NETHERWORLD	FOREQUARTER	TOTALIZATOR	QUICKSILVER	HYPERBOREAN	
INCREDULOUS	UNCONSCIOUS	PREHISTORIC	FORESHORTEN	TRANSMITTER	SCREWDRIVER	IMPRACTICAL	
INDUSTRIOUS	UNDEREXPOSE	RADIOMETRIC	FORTNIGHTLY	TRUEHEARTED	TRANSCEIVER	INCORPOREAL	
INTRAVENOUS	UNRIGHTEOUS	SPECTROGRAM	FRANKFURTER	TRUSTWORTHY	WHERESOEVER	INCREMENTAL	
IRRELIGIOUS	UNWHOLESOME	THENCEFORTH	FUNDAMENTAL	UNACCOUNTED	WHICHSOEVER	INEFFECTUAL	
KNUCKLEBONE	VALEDICTORY	UNDERCHARGE	GEOMAGNETIC	UNCOMMITTED	CAULIFLOWER	INTENTIONAL	
LATTICEWORK	VENTURESOME	UNDERSHORTS	GODDAUGHTER	UNINHIBITED	STRAIGHTWAY	INTERLINEAR	
MAGNANIMOUS	VERTIGINOUS	VARICOLORED	GROUNDWATER	UNMITIGATED	STRAWFLOWER	INTERRACIAL	
MANUFACTORY	VOLCANOLOGY	WATERCOURSE	HALFHEARTED	UNSATURATED	UNDERGROWTH	LIBERTARIAN	
MELLIFLUOUS	WEATHERCOCK	WHEELBARROW	HARDHEARTED	VINAIGRETTE	PROPHYLAXIS	LILLIPUTIAN	
MERITORIOUS	WEATHERWORN	WHIFFLETREE	HELLENISTIC	WARMHEARTED	CHLOROPHYLL	MAGISTERIAL	
METEOROLOGY	BATHYSCAPHE	WHIPPLETREE	HIGHFALUTIN	ZOOPLANKTON	ELECTROLYTE	MERCHANTMAN	
METHODOLOGY	CALLIGRAPHY	ANAESTHESIA	HINDQUARTER	ACUPUNCTURE	ELECTROTYPE	MONOLINGUAL	
MICROSECOND	CARDSHARPER	ANASTOMOSIS	HOMESTRETCH	AGRICULTURE	HORSEPLAYER	MULTIRACIAL	
MILLISECOND	CARTOGRAPHY	BOURGEOISIE	HYDROSTATIC	AQUICULTURE	MODULARIZED	NEANDERTHAL	
MISANTHROPE	CATASTROPHE	COPROCESSOR	IMAGESETTER	AUDIOVISUAL	SYNTHESIZER	NEEDLEWOMAN	
MISCHIEVOUS	CHIROGRAPHY	HAIRDRESSER	INCINERATOR	BLUNDERBUSS	TRAILBLAZER	NONPARTISAN	
MUTTONCHOPS	FILMOGRAPHY	HOMEOSTASIS	INCREMENTAL	CANDIDATURE	UNCIVILIZED	PARAMEDICAL	
NECESSITOUS	GRASSHOPPER	KINESTHESIA	INTERCEPTOR	CHIAROSCURO	UNORGANIZED	PENTECOSTAL	
OBSERVATORY	HAGIOGRAPHY	MASSACHUSET	INTERPRETER	COFFEEHOUSE		PERIODONTAL	
OPPROBRIOUS	HANDICAPPER	MICROCAPSUL	KINDHEARTED	CONJUNCTURE		PHARISAICAL	
ORNITHOLOGY	HOUSEKEEPER	NARRAGANSET	KITCHENETTE	COTTONMOUTH		PISCATORIAL	
PARATHYROID	HYDROGRAPHY	NONPARTISAN	LAMPLIGHTER	CUSTOMHOUSE	**10TH LETTER**	POLYNOMINAL	
PARATYPHOID	HYGROSCOPIC	PARENTHESIS	LASERWRITER	DISPLEASURE		PORTMANTEAU	
PERFUNCTORY	HYPERTROPHY	PERIPHRASIS	LICKSPITTLE	DISQUIETUDE	ABECEDARIAN	PRETERMINAL	
PERSPICUOUS	LITHOGRAPHY	PERISTALSIS	LIONHEARTED	ELECTROCUTE	ACADEMICIAN	PROCRUSTEAN	
PESTIFEROUS	MACROSCOPIC	PREDECESSOR	MACROBIOTIC	EXPENDITURE	ALEXANDRIAN	PROLETARIAN	
PHRASEOLOGY	MICROSCOPIC	TRICHINOSIS	MALADJUSTED	FORECLOSURE	ANTIQUARIAN	PROLETARIAT	
PHYSIOGNOMY	MINESWEEPER	ACCELERATOR	MARQUISETTE	INCERTITUDE	APHRODISIAC	PROVISIONAL	
PLANETOLOGY	ORTHOGRAPHY	ACCUMULATOR	MECHANISTIC	INEFFECTUAL	ASSEMBLYMAN	QUADRENNIAL	
PRECIPITOUS	PALEOGRAPHY	ANNUNCIATOR	MEDIUMISTIC	INGRATITUDE	AUDIOVISUAL	RECESSIONAL	
PRETENTIOUS	PARATROOPER	BACKSTRETCH	MISBEGOTTEN	INOPPORTUNE	BLOODSTREAM	RECTILINEAR	
PROFANATORY	PETROGRAPHY	BLAMEWORTHY	MOUNTAINTOP	INVESTITURE	BUSINESSMAN	RESIDENTIAL	
PROGNATHOUS	PHOTOGRAPHY	BLOCKBUSTER	NEARSIGHTED	LEGISLATURE	CAMEROONIAN	REVERENTIAL	
PROMISCUOUS	PORNOGRAPHY	BURGOMASTER	NORTHEASTER	MANUFACTURE	CARRAGEENAN	SENSATIONAL	
PUNCTILIOUS	STENOGRAPHY	CALORIMETER	OPINIONATED	MONOLINGUAL	CATEGORICAL	SENTIMENTAL	
REFORMATORY	STEREOTYPED	CASTELLATED	ORTHODONTIA	MUSCULATURE	CATERPILLAR	SPECTACULAR	
REPETITIOUS	STOREKEEPER	CENTRIPETAL	PENTECOSTAL	PORTERHOUSE	CENTENARIAN	SPECTROGRAM	
ROTTENSTONE	TOWNSPEOPLE	CHOIRMASTER	PERIODONTAL	PORTRAITURE	CENTRIFUGAL	STRAIGHTWAY	
SCRUMPTIOUS	WOODCHOPPER	CHRONOMETER	PERIPATETIC	PROMPTITUDE	CENTRIPETAL	SUBSTANTIAL	
SENTENTIOUS	DISCOTHEQUE	CLOSEFISTED	PERITONITIS	PULCHRITUDE	CIRCUMLUNAR	SUBTROPICAL	

SUPERFICIAL	DISCREPANCY	INFANTICIDE	GRANDFATHER	PROBATIONER	WHICHSOEVER	PORNOGRAPHY
TERRESTRIAL	ELECTRONICS	INGRATITUDE	GRANDMOTHER	QUACKSALVER	WHIFFLETREE	SEARCHLIGHT
TERRITORIAL	EXCRESCENCE	INSECTICIDE	GRASSHOPPER	QUICKSILVER	WHIPPLETREE	SPACEFLIGHT
TESTIMONIAL	FIDDLESTICK	PITCHBLENDE	GREENGROCER	RATHSKELLER	WIDEMOUTHED	STENOGRAPHY
THEORETICAL	FLORESCENCE	PROMPTITUDE	GROUNDSHEET	RECONNOITER	WINTERGREEN	STOMACHACHE
THEREWITHAL	GEOPOLITICS	PULCHRITUDE	GROUNDWATER	SCREWDRIVER	WOODCHOPPER	TRUSTWORTHY
THUNDERCLAP	HISTRIONICS	SWITCHBLADE	HABERDASHER	SEISMOMETER	WRONGHEADED	UNDERWEIGHT
THUNDERHEAD	HOMESTRETCH	THALIDOMIDE	HAIRDRESSER	SEMITRAILER	POCKETKNIFE	WHEELWRIGHT
TRENCHERMAN	HYDROPONICS	VICISSITUDE	HALFHEARTED	SHAREHOLDER	SPENDTHRIFT	AGORAPHOBIA
TRINIDADIAN	IMPUISSANCE	AFTERBURNER	HANDICAPPER	SHIPBUILDER	ACKNOWLEDGE	ANAESTHESIA
TRINITARIAN	INSOUCIANCE	ANTECHAMBER	HARDHEARTED	SHORTHANDED	ARCHAEOLOGY	ANASTOMOSIS
UNCHRISTIAN	INTEROFFICE	BALLCARRIER	HAREBRAINED	SLEEPWALKER	ARCHIPELAGO	AVOIRDUPOIS
UNEQUIVOCAL	IRIDESCENCE	BEACHCOMBER	HEARTBROKEN	SPEEDOMETER	CAMPANOLOGY	BACCHANALIA
UNICELLULAR	IRREVERENCE	BITTERSWEET	HINDQUARTER	SPELLBINDER	CLIMATOLOGY	BOURGEOISIE
UTILITARIAN	JUVENOCRACY	BLOCKBUSTER	HOMESTEADER	SPREADSHEET	COUNTERSIGN	BRAGGADOCIO
WASHERWOMAN	LEATHERNECK	BLOODSUCKER	HORSEPLAYER	STEAMROLLER	CRIMINOLOGY	CAMARADERIE
WHEREWITHAL	LINGUISTICS	BOILERMAKER	HOUSEBROKEN	STEPBROTHER	DERMATOLOGY	CHAMBERLAIN
SUPERSCRIBE	MALFEASANCE	BREADBASKET	HOUSEKEEPER	STEREOTYPED	FEATHEREDGE	CHAMBERMAID
ADOLESCENCE	MALPRACTICE	BREADWINNER	HOUSEMOTHER	STOCKBROKER	FURNISHINGS	CHRISTIANIA
AERONAUTICS	MANTELPIECE	BURGOMASTER	IMAGESETTER	STOCKHOLDER	GERONTOLOGY	CLIMACTERIC
AFTEREFFECT	MARKETPLACE	CALORIMETER	IMPASSIONED	STOREKEEPER	HAEMORRHAGE	COUNTERFEIT
AMBIVALENCE	MASTERPIECE	CARDSHARPER	INTERPRETER	STORYTELLER	HERPETOLOGY	COUNTERVAIL
ARISTOCRACY	MATHEMATICS	CASTELLATED	KINDHEARTED	STRAITLACED	ICHTHYOLOGY	DIAMAGNETIC
BACKSTRETCH	MERITOCRACY	CATERCORNER	LAMPLIGHTER	STRAWFLOWER	INTERCHANGE	DIAPHORETIC
BENEFICENCE	MESALLIANCE	CAULIFLOWER	LASERWRITER	STREAMLINED	METEOROLOGY	ENDOTHERMIC
BENEVOLENCE	METAPHYSICS	CHANTICLEER	LEVELHEADED	STREAMLINER	METHODOLOGY	GENDARMERIE
BIOFEEDBACK	MISALLIANCE	CHEERLEADER	LIONHEARTED	SUPERMARKET	MUSKELLUNGE	GENERALSHIP
BUREAUCRACY	MISFEASANCE	CHOIRMASTER	LOUDMOUTHED	SWEEPSTAKES	ORNITHOLOGY	GEOMAGNETIC
CANDLESTICK	MISGUIDANCE	CHRONOMETER	LOUDSPEAKER	SYNTHESIZER	PHRASEOLOGY	GLOSSOLALIA
CAPACITANCE	NONVIOLENCE	CLEARHEADED	MALADJUSTED	TELEPRINTER	PLANETOLOGY	HELLENISTIC
CENTERPIECE	NUMISMATICS	CLOSEFISTED	MASSACHUSET	THERMOMETER	SHORTCHANGE	HIGHFALUTIN
CHOCKABLOCK	ORTHOPEDICS	COLORCASTER	MEADOWSWEET	TIGHTFISTED	TERMINOLOGY	HOMEOSTASIS
CIRCUMSPECT	OUTDISTANCE	COMPLICATED	MINESWEEPER	TOASTMASTER	UNDERCHARGE	HYDROPHOBIA
COINCIDENCE	OVERBALANCE	COMPTROLLER	MINNESINGER	TRAILBLAZER	VOLCANOLOGY	HYDROSTATIC
COMEUPPANCE	PERFORMANCE	CONDITIONED	MISBEGOTTEN	TRANSCEIVER	BATHYSCAPHE	HYGROSCOPIC
COMMONPLACE	PROSTHETICS	COUNTRIFIED	MISBELIEVER	TRANSMITTER	BLAMEWORTHY	INTERATOMIC
COMPLACENCE	PROVENIENCE	CRAPSHOOTER	MODULARIZED	TRUEHEARTED	CALLIGRAPHY	INTERNUNCIO
COMPLACENCY	QUARTERBACK	CRESTFALLEN	MONEYLENDER	TYPEFOUNDER	CANDLELIGHT	KINESTHESIA
CONCORDANCE	QUARTERDECK	DILAPIDATED	MOUNTAINEER	TYPOGRAPHER	CARTOGRAPHY	KLEPTOMANIA
CONCURRENCE	RECONSTRUCT	DISENCUMBER	NARRAGANSET	ULTRAVIOLET	CATASTROPHE	LEGERDEMAIN
CONDUCTANCE	REMEMBRANCE	DOWNHEARTED	NEARSIGHTED	UNACCOUNTED	CHIROGRAPHY	MACROBIOTIC
CONFEDERACY	RENAISSANCE	DOWNTRODDEN	NECKERCHIEF	UNCIVILIZED	DREADNOUGHT	MACROSCOPIC
CONFORMANCE	RESEMBLANCE	DRILLMASTER	NIGHTWALKER	UNCOMMITTED	FILMOGRAPHY	MECHANISTIC
CONSEQUENCE	SHUTTLECOCK	DYNAMOMETER	NINNYHAMMER	UNCONCERNED	FORETHOUGHT	MEDIUMISTIC
CONSERVANCY	SUBSISTENCE	ELECTIONEER	NORTHEASTER	UNDERHANDED	HAGIOGRAPHY	MEGALOMANIA
CONSISTENCE	SUFFICIENCY	EXPERIENCED	OPINIONATED	UNDERSIGNED	HEAVYWEIGHT	MEGALOPOLIS
CONSISTENCY	SUPERSONICS	FAULTFINDER	OUTMANEUVER	UNINHIBITED	HYDROGRAPHY	MELANCHOLIA
CONTINGENCY	TECHNOCRACY	FIRECRACKER	OVERSTUFFED	UNMITIGATED	HYPERTROPHY	MELANCHOLIC
CONTINUANCE	ULTRASONICS	FLOORWALKER	PAPERHANGER	UNORGANIZED	LIGHTWEIGHT	MEMORABILIA
CONTRIVANCE	WEATHERCOCK	FOREQUARTER	PARATROOPER	UNQUALIFIED	LITHOGRAPHY	MICROSCOPIC
CONVENIENCE	WORDPERFECT	FORESHORTEN	PARISHIONER	UNSATURATED	ORTHOGRAPHY	NURSERYMAID
COUNTENANCE	ACCELERANDO	FOULMOUTHED	PHILOSOPHER	UNVARNISHED	OVERWROUGHT	NYMPHOMANIA
CRACKERJACK	AMONTILLADO	FRANKFURTER	PLACEHOLDER	VARICOLORED	PALEOGRAPHY	ORTHODONTIA
CYBERNETICS	COUNTRYSIDE	FREETHINKER	PLAINSPOKEN	WARMHEARTED	PAPERWEIGHT	PARATHYROID
DELINQUENCY	DECRESCENDO	GALLBLADDER	PREASSIGNED	WASTEBASKET	PENNYWEIGHT	PARATYPHOID
DESPONDENCY	DISQUIETUDE	GERRYMANDER	PREOCCUPIED	WATERLOGGED	PETROGRAPHY	PARENTHESIS
DIAMONDBACK	INCERTITUDE	GODDAUGHTER	PRIZEWINNER	WHERESOEVER	PHOTOGRAPHY	PERIPATETIC

PERIPHRASIS	INESCAPABLE	ADVERTISING	INCARNADINE	SUPERINTEND	CONJUGATION	INTERCEPTOR
PERISTALSIS	INESTIMABLE	ALEXANDRINE	INCOMPETENT	SUPPRESSANT	CONJUNCTION	KWASHIORKOR
PERITONITIS	INEXCUSABLE	AMPHETAMINE	INCONGRUENT	TEMPERAMENT	CONNOTATION	LACRIMATION
POLYTECHNIC	INFLAMMABLE	ANTICYCLONE	INCONTINENT	THERMOCLINE	CONSERVATOR	LEGISLATION
PREHISTORIC	INNUMERABLE	ANTIOXIDANT	INDEPENDENT	TIMESHARING	CONSUMPTION	LUCUBRATION
PROBLEMATIC	INSCRUTABLE	APPOINTMENT	INDIFFERENT	TOPDRESSING	CONTRAPTION	MACHINATION
PROPHYLAXIS	INSEPARABLE	ARBITRAMENT	INEFFICIENT	TRAGEDIENNE	CONURBATION	MALEDICTION
PROSTATITIS	INSUPERABLE	BALLETOMANE	INGATHERING	TRANSLUCENT	CONVOCATION	MALFUNCTION
PSYCHEDELIA	INTERMEDDLE	BELLIGERENT	INNERSPRING	TRANSPARENT	CONVOLUTION	MARSHMALLOW
PSYCHEDELIC	INTERMINGLE	CALCULATING	INOPPORTUNE	TYPESETTING	COPROCESSOR	MENSURATION
PSYCHOGENIC	INTOLERABLE	CLAIRVOYANT	INSINUATING	TYPEWRITING	CORPORATION	METRICATION
RADIOMETRIC	INTRACTABLE	CLANDESTINE	INSTALLMENT	ULTRAMARINE	CRUCIFIXION	MISDEMEANOR
REALPOLITIK	IRREDUCIBLE	COBBLESTONE	INTELLIGENT	UNDERGROUND	CYBERNATION	MOUNTAINTOP
SCHOLARSHIP	IRREFUTABLE	COEFFICIENT	INTERESTING	UNDERTAKING	DEFALCATION	NICKELODEON
SWALLOWTAIL	IRREMOVABLE	COMMANDMENT	INTERLACING	UNDESIGNING	DEFLORATION	OBSERVATION
TACHYCARDIA	IRREPARABLE	COMMUNICANT	INTERLINING	UNDEVIATING	DELECTATION	OBSTRUCTION
THERAPEUTIC	IRREVOCABLE	COMPARTMENT	INTERNECINE	UNFLINCHING	DENOMINATOR	OFFICIALDOM
TONSILLITIS	LICKSPITTLE	COMPORTMENT	KNUCKLEBONE	UNREASONING	DEPREDATION	OSTENTATION
TRICHINOSIS	MOLLYCODDLE	CONCERNMENT	LABORSAVING	UNRELENTING	DEPRIVATION	PARTURITION
TRUSTEESHIP	MOMENTARILY	CONCOMITANT	LATCHSTRING	UNREMITTING	DERELICTION	PERMUTATION
WORKMANSHIP	MULTIFAMILY	CONSIDERING	MAGNIFICENT	VIRIDESCENT	DESCRIPTION	POLLINATION
JABBERWOCKY	NETHERWORLD	CONSIGNMENT	MAIDSERVANT	WAINSCOTING	DESPERATION	PREDECESSOR
RATTLESNAKE	NIGHTINGALE	CONSTITUENT	MEASUREMENT	ABOMINATION	DESTINATION	PREIGNITION
WORKMANLIKE	PERCEPTIBLE	CONTAMINANT	MERRYMAKING	ABSTRACTION	DESTRUCTION	PREMONITION
ACCORDINGLY	PERFECTIBLE	CONTENTMENT	MICROSECOND	ACCELERATOR	DICOTYLEDON	PREPOSITION
ACCOUNTABLE	PERMISSIBLE	CORNERSTONE	MILLISECOND	ACCEPTATION	DIFFRACTION	PRESUMPTION
APPRECIABLE	PLEASURABLE	COUNTERMAND	MONKEYSHINE	ACCLAMATION	DISILLUSION	PROGRESSION
BATTLEFIELD	PONTIFICALS	COUNTERPANE	NAPHTHALENE	ACCUMULATOR	DISPOSITION	PROHIBITION
BIBLIOPHILE	PRACTICABLE	COUNTERSINK	NEEDLEPOINT	ACQUISITION	DISPUTATION	PROPOSITION
BLOODMOBILE	REDOUBTABLE	DETERMINANT	NONDOCUMENT	AFFECTATION	DISSOLUTION	PUBLICATION
CHLOROPHYLL	REGIMENTALS	ELEPHANTINE	NONRESIDENT	AGGREGATION	DISTINCTION	PUNCTUATION
COCKLESHELL	RELOCATABLE	EMPLACEMENT	NOURISHMENT	ALTERCATION	DISTRIBUTOR	RADIOCARBON
COMBUSTIBLE	RESPECTABLE	ENGINEERING	OBSOLESCENT	ANNUNCIATOR	EDIFICATION	RAPSCALLION
COMFORTABLE	RESPONSIBLE	ENVIRONMENT	OMNIPRESENT	ANTINEUTRON	EXPECTATION	RECOGNITION
CONFESSEDLY	SERVICEABLE	EPINEPHRINE	OUTBUILDING	APOCYNTHION	EXTRADITION	REFORMATION
CONTRACTILE	SUBASSEMBLY	EQUIDISTANT	OUTSTANDING	APPELLATION	FORNICATION	REINFECTION
CONVENTICLE	SUBMERSIBLE	EVERLASTING	OVERBEARING	APPLICATION	GRAVITATION	REPLICATION
CONVERTIBLE	SUSCEPTIBLE	EXPECTORANT	OVERWEENING	APPROBATION	HABITUATION	REPROBATION
DISASSEMBLE	THEATRICALS	EXTRAVAGANT	PAINSTAKING	ASSIGNATION	HYDROCARBON	REQUISITION
DISENTANGLE	THUNDERBOLT	FINGERPRINT	PENETRATING	ASSOCIATION	HYPHENATION	RESERVATION
DISPENSABLE	TOWNSPEOPLE	FORMFITTING	POLYSTYRENE	BATTLEWAGON	IMAGINATION	RESIGNATION
EXCEEDINGLY	UNALIENABLE	FORTHCOMING	PREDICAMENT	BENEDICTION	IMBRICATION	RESPIRATION
FARTHINGALE	UNAVOIDABLE	GARNISHMENT	PROGRAMMING	BENEFACTION	IMPORTATION	RESTITUTION
FASHIONABLE	UNDESIRABLE	GEANTICLINE	PROTUBERANT	BROTHERHOOD	INATTENTION	RESTORATION
FORTNIGHTLY	UNFAVORABLE	GEOSYNCLINE	REFRESHMENT	CALCULATION	INCANTATION	RESTRICTION
HONEYSUCKLE	UNFLAPPABLE	GRANDPARENT	REMINISCENT	CEMENTATION	INCARNATION	RETRIBUTION
ILLIMITABLE	UNPRINTABLE	GREASEPAINT	REMONSTRANT	CHOLESTEROL	INCINERATOR	SUPPOSITION
IMMITIGABLE	UNSPEAKABLE	HANDSHAKING	REPLACEMENT	CHRISTENDOM	INCLINATION	SYNCOPATION
IMPERMEABLE	UNTHINKABLE	HANDWRITING	REQUIREMENT	COEDUCATION	INDENTATION	TOTALIZATOR
IMPLAUSIBLE	UNTOUCHABLE	HARDWORKING	RESPLENDENT	COLLOCATION	INDIGESTION	TRANSACTION
IMPREGNABLE	UNUTTERABLE	HEARTHSTONE	ROTTENSTONE	COMBINATION	INDIGNATION	TREPIDATION
INALIENABLE	VIOLONCELLO	HERRINGBONE	SAFEKEEPING	COMMENTATOR	INFORMATION	TRIBULATION
INDEFINABLE	PHYSIOGNOMY	IMPERMANENT	SCAFFOLDING	COMMINATION	INQUISITION	UNIFICATION
INDIVISIBLE	PSYCHODRAMA	IMPERTINENT	SHELLACKING	COMMUTATION	INSPIRATION	VACCINATION
INDOMITABLE	UNWHOLESOME	IMPROVEMENT	SHORTCOMING	COMPETITION	INSTITUTION	VALEDICTION
INDUBITABLE	VENTURESOME	IMPROVIDENT	SIGNIFICANT	COMPOSITION	INSTRUCTION	VENTILATION
INELUCTABLE	ACQUIREMENT	INADVERTENT	SMITHEREENS	COMPUNCTION	INTERACTION	VINDICATION

VIVISECTION	HUMMINGBIRD	CUSTOMHOUSE	APPROPRIATE	HYPOTHECATE	STOCKINETTE	MONSEIGNEUR
WHEELBARROW	HYDROSPHERE	DETERMINISM	APPROXIMATE	IMMORTALITY	STRANGULATE	NECESSITOUS
WITENAGEMOT	IDENTIFIERS	DIPLOMATIST	ASSASSINATE	IMPEDIMENTA	SUBORDINATE	OPPROBRIOUS
WORKSTATION	INTERCALARY	DISCOURTESY	BARBITURATE	IMPERFORATE	SUBURBANITE	PANDEMONIUM
ZOOPLANKTON	INVESTITURE	DISTINGUISH	BICARBONATE	IMPERSONATE	SUFFRAGETTE	PERSPICUOUS
CARDIOGRAPH	INVOLUNTARY	ENFRANCHISE	BREAKPOINTS	IMPORTUNATE	THENCEFORTH	PESTIFEROUS
CHRONOGRAPH	KITCHENWARE	EXHAUSTLESS	BREASTPLATE	IMPROPRIETY	THEREABOUTS	PICTURESQUE
CONTRETEMPS	LATTICEWORK	FARTHERMOST	CAPILLARITY	INCARCERATE	TRIANGULATE	PLANETARIUM
ELECTROTYPE	LEGISLATURE	FLABBERGAST	CARDINALATE	INCORPORATE	TRIUMVIRATE	PRECIPITOUS
FLUOROSCOPE	LITHOSPHERE	FURTHERMOST	CARDINALITY	INCRIMINATE	TUBERCULATE	PRETENTIOUS
GUTTERSNIPE	MANUFACTORY	GYROCOMPASS	CASSITERITE	INDIVIDUATE	TWELVEMONTH	PROGNATHOUS
MISANTHROPE	MANUFACTURE	HAIRSTYLIST	CATHOLICITY	INSTABILITY	UNCERTAINTY	PROMISCUOUS
MUTTONCHOPS	MILLIAMPERE	HORSERADISH	CERTIFICATE	INSTANTIATE	UNDERGROWTH	PUNCTILIOUS
NONDESCRIPT	MILLIONAIRE	ILLUSIONISM	CHEESECLOTH	INTERCALATE	UNDERSHORTS	QUADRENNIUM
SEISMOGRAPH	MOCKINGBIRD	IMPERIALISM	CIRCULARITY	INTERPOLATE	UNFORTUNATE	REPETITIOUS
STEREOSCOPE	MORTARBOARD	INTERCOURSE	COGNOSCENTE	INTERRELATE	VERMICULITE	SARCOPHAGUS
STEREOSCOPY	MOTHERBOARD	INTERSPERSE	COLLABORATE	INTERROGATE	VINAIGRETTE	SCRUMPTIOUS
STETHOSCOPE	MUSCULATURE	IRREDENTISM	COMMEMORATE	INVESTIGATE	WHEREABOUTS	SENTENTIOUS
STROBOSCOPE	OBSERVATORY	LETTERPRESS	COMMISERATE	KITCHENETTE	CALCIFEROUS	SPONTANEOUS
SUPERSCRIPT	OZONOSPHERE	MALAPROPISM	COMMUNICATE	LABRADORITE	CALIFORNIUM	SUPERFLUOUS
ABRACADABRA	PACHYSANDRA	MARCHIONESS	CONCENTRATE	MARQUISETTE	CANDELABRUM	SYNCHRONOUS
ACUPUNCTURE	PERFUNCTORY	MATERIALISM	CONFEDERATE	MATRICULATE	CARNIVOROUS	TEASPOONFUL
AGRICULTURE	PHOTOSPHERE	MERCHANDISE	CONSIDERATE	NATIONALITY	CEREMONIOUS	TEMPESTUOUS
ANNIVERSARY	PORTRAITURE	MONASTICISM	CONSOLIDATE	NECESSITATE	CONDOMINIUM	TENDENTIOUS
AQUICULTURE	PRELIMINARY	NATIONALISM	CONTAMINATE	OPPORTUNITY	CONNOISSEUR	TREACHEROUS
BATHYSPHERE	PROFANATORY	NATIONALIST	CONTEMPLATE	ORCHESTRATE	CONSPICUOUS	UNCONSCIOUS
BENEFICIARY	PROPRIETARY	NONETHELESS	CONTRARIETY	PARTICIPATE	CORRIGENDUM	UNRIGHTEOUS
BICENTENARY	REACTIONARY	NOTHINGNESS	CORROBORATE	PARTICULATE	COTERMINOUS	VENTRILOQUY
BOUTONNIERE	REFORMATORY	OFFICIALISM	COTTONMOUTH	PENULTIMATE	DELETERIOUS	VERTIGINOUS
BOYSENBERRY	ROTOGRAVURE	OPPORTUNISM	DEMONSTRATE	PERAMBULATE	DESIDERATUM	ACQUISITIVE
CABINETWORK	SMORGASBORD	PATERNALISM	DESEGREGATE	PERSNICKETY	DISCONTINUE	ADVERSATIVE
CANDIDATURE	SPRINGBOARD	POINTILLISM	DETERIORATE	PERSONALITY	DISCOTHEQUE	AFFIRMATIVE
CARAVANSARY	SUBSTANDARD	POLTERGEIST	DETERMINATE	POMEGRANATE	EFFICACIOUS	ALTERNATIVE
CENTERBOARD	SUPPOSITORY	PORTERHOUSE	DIRECTORATE	PONTIFICATE	EINSTEINIUM	ASSOCIATIVE
CHANCELLERY	SWITCHBOARD	PORTIONLESS	DISSEMINATE	PRECIPITATE	EQUILIBRIUM	ATTRIBUTIVE
CHIAROSCURO	TEMPERATURE	PORTRAITIST	DISSIMULATE	PREDOMINATE	EXPEDITIOUS	CARMINATIVE
CONJUNCTURE	THITHERWARD	PRIMITIVISM	DOMESTICATE	PREMEDITATE	FARINACEOUS	COEXTENSIVE
COSIGNATORY	TRANSFIGURE	PROTAGONIST	DOMESTICITY	PREVARICATE	HERBIVOROUS	COMMUTATIVE
COUNTERPART	TROPOSPHERE	RATIONALISM	ELECTRICITY	PROLIFERATE	HOMOGENEOUS	COMPARATIVE
DEPRECATORY	ULTRAMODERN	ROMANTICISM	ELECTROCUTE	PROPINQUITY	IGNOMINIOUS	CONJUNCTIVA
DISPLEASURE	VALEDICTORY	SCHOOLHOUSE	ELECTROLYTE	RATIONALITY	ILLUSTRIOUS	CONJUNCTIVE
DOCTRINAIRE	VITICULTURE	SUMMERHOUSE	ENCAPSULATE	RECIPROCATE	IMPECUNIOUS	CONNOTATIVE
DOCUMENTARY	WEATHERWORN	SUPERIMPOSE	EVENTUALITY	RECIPROCITY	INCONGRUOUS	CONSECUTIVE
EARTHENWARE	ABORTIONIST	SUPREMACIST	EXPECTORATE	RECRIMINATE	INCREDULOUS	CONSUMPTIVE
ELECTROFORM	ABSENTEEISM	SYNCHROMESH	EXPOSTULATE	REFRIGERATE	INCUNABULUM	COOPERATIVE
EXPENDITURE	ACADEMICISM	THOUGHTLESS	EXPROPRIATE	REGURGITATE	INDUSTRIOUS	CORRELATIVE
EXTEMPORARY	ANACHRONISM	TOBACCONIST	EXTERMINATE	REMONSTRATE	INTERREGNUM	DECLARATIVE
FINGERBOARD	ARCHDIOCESE	UNDEREXPOSE	EXTRAPOLATE	RESISTIVITY	INTRAVENOUS	DISTINCTIVE
FORECLOSURE	ASTIGMATISM	VACATIONIST	FAMILIARITY	RESUSCITATE	IRRELIGIOUS	HYPERACTIVE
FOREVERMORE	BEHAVIORISM	VICHYSSOISE	FLANNELETTE	REVERBERATE	LITTERATEUR	INEFFECTIVE
FRAGMENTARY	BIMETALLISM	WATERCOURSE	GESTICULATE	ROADABILITY	MAGNANIMOUS	INFORMATIVE
FUNCTIONARY	BLUNDERBUSS	ZOOMORPHISM	HAIRBREADTH	SCINTILLATE	MELLIFLUOUS	INOPERATIVE
FURTHERMORE	CLERICALISM	ACCOMMODATE	HALLUCINATE	SCUTTLEBUTT	MENDELEVIUM	INQUISITIVE
GALLIMAUFRY	COFFEEHOUSE	AGGLOMERATE	HISTORICITY	SENSIBILITY	MERITORIOUS	INSTRUCTIVE
GRANITEWARE	COLONIALISM	AGGLUTINATE	HOSPITALITY	SEQUESTRATE	MICROCAPSUL	INTERACTIVE
HARPSICHORD	CONSUMERISM	ANTIGRAVITY	HOUSELIGHTS	SERENDIPITY	MISCHIEVOUS	LEGISLATIVE
HUCKLEBERRY	CONTROVERSY	ANTIPOVERTY	HYDROGENATE	SOVEREIGNTY	MISCONSTRUE	MISCONCEIVE

NONNEGATIVE	MEMORABILIA	LOUDMOUTHED	AGGLUTINATE	CONCENTRATE	ELECTROTYPE	INDIVISIBLE
PERSPECTIVE	NYMPHOMANIA	MALADJUSTED	AGRICULTURE	CONCORDANCE	ELEPHANTINE	INDOMITABLE
PRECONCEIVE	ORTHODONTIA	MICROSECOND	ALEXANDRINE	CONCURRENCE	ENCAPSULATE	INDUBITABLE
PREROGATIVE	PACHYSANDRA	MILLISECOND	ALPHABETIZE	CONDUCTANCE	ENFRANCHISE	INEFFECTIVE
PROGRESSIVE	PSYCHEDELIA	MOCKINGBIRD	ALTERNATIVE	CONFEDERATE	EPINEPHRINE	INELUCTABLE
QUALITATIVE	PSYCHODRAMA	MODULARIZED	AMBIVALENCE	CONFORMANCE	EXCRESCENCE	INESCAPABLE
RESTORATIVE	TACHYCARDIA	MORTARBOARD	AMPHETAMINE	CONJUNCTIVE	EXPECTORATE	INESTIMABLE
RETROACTIVE	APHRODISIAC	MOTHERBOARD	ANTICYCLONE	CONJUNCTURE	EXPENDITURE	INEXCUSABLE
SUBJUNCTIVE	CLIMACTERIC	NEARSIGHTED	APPRECIABLE	CONNOTATIVE	EXPOSTULATE	INFANTICIDE
SUBSTANTIVE	DIAMAGNETIC	NETHERWORLD	APPROPRIATE	CONSECUTIVE	EXPROPRIATE	INFLAMMABLE
SUPERLATIVE	DIAPHORETIC	NURSERYMAID	APPROXIMATE	CONSEQUENCE	EXTEMPORIZE	INFORMATIVE
UNOBTRUSIVE	ENDOTHERMIC	OPINIONATED	AQUICULTURE	CONSIDERATE	EXTERMINATE	INGRATITUDE
THISTLEDOWN	GEOMAGNETIC	OVERSTUFFED	ARCHDIOCESE	CONSISTENCE	EXTRAPOLATE	INNUMERABLE
PROTOMARTYR	HELLENISTIC	PARATHYROID	ASSASSINATE	CONSOLIDATE	FARTHINGALE	INOPERATIVE
ACCLIMATIZE	HYDROSTATIC	PARATYPHOID	ASSOCIATIVE	CONSUMPTIVE	FASHIONABLE	INOPPORTUNE
ALPHABETIZE	HYGROSCOPIC	PREASSIGNED	ATTRIBUTIVE	CONTAMINATE	FEATHEREDGE	INQUISITIVE
CANNIBALIZE	INTERATOMIC	PREOCCUPIED	BALLETOMANE	CONTEMPLATE	FLANNELETTE	INSCRUTABLE
CIRCULARIZE	MACROBIOTIC	SHORTHANDED	BARBITURATE	CONTINUANCE	FLORESCENCE	INSECTICIDE
COMPUTERIZE	MACROSCOPIC	SMORGASBORD	BATHYSCAPHE	CONTRACTILE	FLUOROSCOPE	INSEPARABLE
CRYSTALLIZE	MECHANISTIC	SPRINGBOARD	BATHYSPHERE	CONTRIVANCE	FORECLOSURE	INSOUCIANCE
DEMAGNETIZE	MEDIUMISTIC	STEREOTYPED	BENEFICENCE	CONVENIENCE	FOREVERMORE	INSTANTIATE
DEMOCRATIZE	MELANCHOLIC	STRAITLACED	BENEVOLENCE	CONVENTICLE	FURTHERMORE	INSTRUCTIVE
DESENSITIZE	MICROSCOPIC	STREAMLINED	BIBLIOPHILE	CONVERTIBLE	GEANTICLINE	INSUPERABLE
DISORGANIZE	PERIPATETIC	SUBSTANDARD	BICARBONATE	COOPERATIVE	GENDARMERIE	INTERACTIVE
EXTEMPORIZE	POLYTECHNIC	SWITCHBOARD	BLOODMOBILE	CORNERSTONE	GEOSYNCLINE	INTERCALATE
HOSPITALIZE	PREHISTORIC	THITHERWARD	BOURGEOISIE	CORRELATIVE	GESTICULATE	INTERCHANGE
HYPOTHESIZE	PROBLEMATIC	THUNDERHEAD	BOUTONNIERE	CORROBORATE	GRANITEWARE	INTERCOURSE
IMMORTALIZE	PSYCHEDELIC	TIGHTFISTED	BREASTPLATE	COUNTENANCE	GUTTERSNIPE	INTERMEDDLE
MATERIALIZE	PSYCHOGENIC	TRUEHEARTED	CAMARADERIE	COUNTERPANE	HAEMORRHAGE	INTERMINGLE
MINIATURIZE	RADIOMETRIC	UNACCOUNTED	CANDIDATURE	COUNTRYSIDE	HALLUCINATE	INTERNECINE
NATIONALIZE	THERAPEUTIC	UNCIVILIZED	CANNIBALIZE	CRYSTALLIZE	HEARTHSTONE	INTEROFFICE
PERSONALIZE	BATTLEFIELD	UNCOMMITTED	CAPACITANCE	CUSTOMHOUSE	HERRINGBONE	INTERPOLATE
PROSELYTIZE	BROTHERHOOD	UNCONCERNED	CARDINALATE	DECLARATIVE	HONEYSUCKLE	INTERRELATE
RATIONALIZE	CASTELLATED	UNDERGROUND	CARMINATIVE	DEMAGNETIZE	HOSPITALIZE	INTERROGATE
SOLILOQUIZE	CENTERBOARD	UNDERHANDED	CASSITERITE	DEMOCRATIZE	HYDROGENATE	INTERSPERSE
STANDARDIZE	CHAMBERMAID	UNDERSIGNED	CATASTROPHE	DEMONSTRATE	HYDROSPHERE	INTOLERABLE
SYNCHRONIZE	CLEARHEADED	UNINHIBITED	CENTERPIECE	DESEGREGATE	HYPERACTIVE	INTRACTABLE
SYSTEMATIZE	CLOSEFISTED	UNMITIGATED	CERTIFICATE	DESENSITIZE	HYPOTHECATE	INVESTIGATE
TRANQUILIZE	COMPLICATED	UNORGANIZED	CIRCULARIZE	DETERIORATE	HYPOTHESIZE	INVESTITURE
	CONDITIONED	UNQUALIFIED	CLANDESTINE	DETERMINATE	ILLIMITABLE	IRIDESCENCE
	COUNTERMAND	UNSATURATED	COBBLESTONE	DIRECTORATE	IMMITIGABLE	IRREDUCIBLE
	COUNTRIFIED	UNVARNISHED	COEXTENSIVE	DISASSEMBLE	IMMORTALIZE	IRREFUTABLE
11TH LETTER	DILAPIDATED	VARICOLORED	COFFEEHOUSE	DISCONTINUE	IMPERFORATE	IRREMOVABLE
	DOWNHEARTED	WARMHEARTED	COGNOSCENTE	DISCOTHEQUE	IMPERMEABLE	IRREPARABLE
ABRACADABRA	EXPERIENCED	WATERLOGGED	COINCIDENCE	DISENTANGLE	IMPERSONATE	IRREVERENCE
AGORAPHOBIA	FINGERBOARD	WIDEMOUTHED	COLLABORATE	DISORGANIZE	IMPLAUSIBLE	IRREVOCABLE
ANAESTHESIA	FOULMOUTHED	WRONGHEADED	COMBUSTIBLE	DISPENSABLE	IMPORTUNATE	KITCHENETTE
BACCHANALIA	GINGERBREAD	ACCLIMATIZE	COMEUPPANCE	DISPLEASURE	IMPREGNABLE	KITCHENWARE
CHRISTIANIA	HALFHEARTED	ACCOMMODATE	COMFORTABLE	DISQUIETUDE	IMPUISSANCE	KNUCKLEBONE
CONJUNCTIVA	HARDHEARTED	ACCOUNTABLE	COMMEMORATE	DISSEMINATE	INALIENABLE	LABRADORITE
GLOSSOLALIA	HAREBRAINED	ACKNOWLEDGE	COMMISERATE	DISSIMULATE	INCARCERATE	LEGISLATIVE
HYDROPHOBIA	HARPSICHORD	ACQUISITIVE	COMMONPLACE	DISTINCTIVE	INCARNADINE	LEGISLATURE
IMPEDIMENTA	HUMMINGBIRD	ACUPUNCTURE	COMMUNICATE	DOCTRINAIRE	INCERTITUDE	LICKSPITTLE
KINESTHESIA	IMPASSIONED	ADOLESCENCE	COMMUTATIVE	DOMESTICATE	INCORPORATE	LITHOSPHERE
KLEPTOMANIA	KINDHEARTED	ADVERSATIVE	COMPARATIVE	EARTHENWARE	INCRIMINATE	MALFEASANCE
MEGALOMANIA	LEVELHEADED	AFFIRMATIVE	COMPLACENCE	ELECTROCUTE	INDEFINABLE	MALPRACTICE
MELANCHOLIA	LIONHEARTED	AGGLOMERATE	COMPUTERIZE	ELECTROLYTE	INDIVIDUATE	MANTELPIECE

MANUFACTURE	PREVARICATE	THALIDOMIDE	OUTSTANDING	COCKLESHELL	CHRISTENDOM	BUSINESSMAN
MARKETPLACE	PROGRESSIVE	THERMOCLINE	OVERBEARING	CONDITIONAL	CLERICALISM	CALCULATION
MARQUISETTE	PROLIFERATE	TOWNSPEOPLE	OVERWEENING	CONTINENTAL	COLONIALISM	CAMEROONIAN
MASTERPIECE	PROMPTITUDE	TRAGEDIENNE	PAINSTAKING	COUNTERVAIL	CONDOMINIUM	CARRAGEENAN
MATERIALIZE	PROSELYTIZE	TRANQUILIZE	PENETRATING	DICTATORIAL	CONSUMERISM	CEMENTATION
MATRICULATE	PROVENIENCE	TRANSFIGURE	PROGRAMMING	DISAPPROVAL	CORRIGENDUM	CENTENARIAN
MERCHANDISE	PULCHRITUDE	TRIANGULATE	SAFEKEEPING	EQUILATERAL	DESIDERATUM	CHAMBERLAIN
MESALLIANCE	QUALITATIVE	TRIUMVIRATE	SCAFFOLDING	EVANGELICAL	DETERMINISM	COEDUCATION
MILLIAMPERE	RATIONALIZE	TROPOSPHERE	SHELLACKING	EXCEPTIONAL	EINSTEINIUM	COLLOCATION
MILLIONAIRE	RATTLESNAKE	TUBERCULATE	SHORTCOMING	FUNDAMENTAL	ELECTROFORM	COMBINATION
MINIATURIZE	RECIPROCATE	ULTRAMARINE	TIMESHARING	HEXADECIMAL	EQUILIBRIUM	COMMINATION
MISALLIANCE	RECRIMINATE	UNALIENABLE	TOPDRESSING	IMPRACTICAL	ILLUSIONISM	COMMUTATION
MISANTHROPE	REDOUBTABLE	UNAVOIDABLE	TYPESETTING	INCORPOREAL	IMPERIALISM	COMPETITION
MISCONCEIVE	REFRIGERATE	UNDERCHARGE	TYPEWRITING	INCREMENTAL	INCUNABULUM	COMPOSITION
MISCONSTRUE	REGURGITATE	UNDEREXPOSE	UNDERTAKING	INEFFECTUAL	INTERREGNUM	COMPUNCTION
MISFEASANCE	RELOCATABLE	UNDESIRABLE	UNDESIGNING	INTENTIONAL	IRREDENTISM	CONGRESSMAN
MISGUIDANCE	REMEMBRANCE	UNFAVORABLE	UNDEVIATING	INTERRACIAL	MALAPROPISM	CONJUGATION
MOLLYCODDLE	REMONSTRATE	UNFLAPPABLE	UNFLINCHING	MAGISTERIAL	MATERIALISM	CONJUNCTION
MONKEYSHINE	RENAISSANCE	UNFORTUNATE	UNREASONING	MICROCAPSUL	MENDELEVIUM	CONNOTATION
MUSCULATURE	RESEMBLANCE	UNOBTRUSIVE	UNRELENTING	MONOLINGUAL	MONASTICISM	CONSUMPTION
MUSKELLUNGE	RESPECTABLE	UNPRINTABLE	UNREMITTING	MULTIRACIAL	NATIONALISM	CONTRAPTION
NAPHTHALENE	RESPONSIBLE	UNSPEAKABLE	WAINSCOTING	NEANDERTHAL	OFFICIALDOM	CONURBATION
NATIONALIZE	RESTORATIVE	UNTHINKABLE	BACKSTRETCH	PARAMEDICAL	OFFICIALISM	CONVOCATION
NECESSITATE	RESUSCITATE	UNTOUCHABLE	CARDIOGRAPH	PENTECOSTAL	OPPORTUNISM	CONVOLUTION
NIGHTINGALE	RETROACTIVE	UNUTTERABLE	CHEESECLOTH	PERIODONTAL	PANDEMONIUM	CORPORATION
NONNEGATIVE	REVERBERATE	UNWHOLESOME	CHRONOGRAPH	PHARISAICAL	PATERNALISM	COUNTERSIGN
NONVIOLENCE	ROTOGRAVURE	VENTURESOME	COTTONMOUTH	PISCATORIAL	PLANETARIUM	CRESTFALLEN
ORCHESTRATE	ROTTENSTONE	VERMICULITE	DISTINGUISH	POLYNOMINAL	POINTILLISM	CRUCIFIXION
OUTDISTANCE	SCHOOLHOUSE	VICHYSSOISE	HAIRBREADTH	PRETERMINAL	PRIMITIVISM	CYBERNATION
OVERBALANCE	SCINTILLATE	VICISSITUDE	HOMESTRETCH	PROVISIONAL	QUADRENNIUM	DEFALCATION
OZONOSPHERE	SEQUESTRATE	VINAIGRETTE	HORSERADISH	QUADRENNIAL	RATIONALISM	DEFLORATION
PARTICIPATE	SERVICEABLE	VITICULTURE	SEISMOGRAPH	RECESSIONAL	ROMANTICISM	DELECTATION
PARTICULATE	SHORTCHANGE	WATERCOURSE	SYNCHROMESH	RESIDENTIAL	SPECTROGRAM	DEPREDATION
PENULTIMATE	SOLILOQUIZE	WHIFFLETREE	THENCEFORTH	REVERENTIAL	ZOOMORPHISM	DEPRIVATION
PERAMBULATE	STANDARDIZE	WHIPPLETREE	TWELVEMONTH	SENSATIONAL	ABECEDARIAN	DERELICTION
PERCEPTIBLE	STEREOSCOPE	WORKMANLIKE	UNDERGROWTH	SENTIMENTAL	ABOMINATION	DESCRIPTION
PERFECTIBLE	STETHOSCOPE	NECKERCHIEF	BIOFEEDBACK	SUBSTANTIAL	ABSTRACTION	DESPERATION
PERFORMANCE	STOCKINETTE	ADVERTISING	CABINETWORK	SUBTROPICAL	ACADEMICIAN	DESTINATION
PERMISSIBLE	STOMACHACHE	CALCULATING	CANDLESTICK	SUPERFICIAL	ACCEPTATION	DESTRUCTION
PERSONALIZE	STRANGULATE	CONSIDERING	CHOCKABLOCK	SWALLOWTAIL	ACCLAMATION	DICOTYLEDON
PERSPECTIVE	STROBOSCOPE	ENGINEERING	COUNTERSINK	TEASPOONFUL	ACQUISITION	DIFFRACTION
PHOTOSPHERE	SUBJUNCTIVE	EVERLASTING	CRACKERJACK	TERRESTRIAL	AFFECTATION	DISILLUSION
PICTURESQUE	SUBMERSIBLE	FORMFITTING	DIAMONDBACK	TERRITORIAL	AGGREGATION	DISPOSITION
PITCHBLENDE	SUBORDINATE	FORTHCOMING	FIDDLESTICK	TESTIMONIAL	ALEXANDRIAN	DISPUTATION
PLEASURABLE	SUBSISTENCE	HANDSHAKING	LATTICEWORK	THEORETICAL	ALTERCATION	DISSOLUTION
POCKETKNIFE	SUBSTANTIVE	HANDWRITING	LEATHERNECK	THEREWITHAL	ANTINEUTRON	DISTINCTION
POLYSTYRENE	SUBURBANITE	HARDWORKING	QUARTERBACK	UNEQUIVOCAL	ANTIQUARIAN	DOWNTRODDEN
POMEGRANATE	SUFFRAGETTE	INGATHERING	QUARTERDECK	WHEREWITHAL	APOCYNTHION	EDIFICATION
PONTIFICATE	SUMMERHOUSE	INNERSPRING	REALPOLITIK	ABSENTEEISM	APPELLATION	ELECTRICIAN
PORTERHOUSE	SUPERIMPOSE	INSINUATING	SHUTTLECOCK	ACADEMICISM	APPLICATION	ELIZABETHAN
PORTRAITURE	SUPERLATIVE	INTERESTING	WEATHERCOCK	ANACHRONISM	APPROBATION	EXPECTATION
PRACTICABLE	SUPERSCRIBE	INTERLACING	AUDIOVISUAL	ASTIGMATISM	ASSEMBLYMAN	EXTRADITION
PRECIPITATE	SUSCEPTIBLE	INTERLINING	CATEGORICAL	BEHAVIORISM	ASSIGNATION	FORESHORTEN
PRECONCEIVE	SWITCHBLADE	LABORSAVING	CENTRIFUGAL	BIMETALLISM	ASSOCIATION	FORNICATION
PREDOMINATE	SYNCHRONIZE	LATCHSTRING	CENTRIPETAL	BLOODSTREAM	BATTLEWAGON	GENTLEWOMAN
PREMEDITATE	SYSTEMATIZE	MERRYMAKING	CHLOROPHYLL	CALIFORNIUM	BENEDICTION	GRAVITATION
PREROGATIVE	TEMPERATURE	OUTBUILDING	CHOLESTEROL	CANDELABRUM	BENEFACTION	HABITUATION

HEARTBROKEN	RAPSCALLION	BEACHCOMBER	INTERPRETER	TYPOGRAPHER	ORTHOPEDICS	COMPARTMENT
HIGHFALUTIN	RECOGNITION	BLOCKBUSTER	KWASHIORKOR	UNICELLULAR	PARENTHESIS	COMPORTMENT
HOUSEBROKEN	REFORMATION	BLOODSUCKER	LAMPLIGHTER	WHERESOEVER	PERIPHRASIS	CONCERNMENT
HYDROCARBON	REINFECTION	BOILERMAKER	LASERWRITER	WHICHSOEVER	PERISTALSIS	CONCOMITANT
HYPERBOREAN	REPLICATION	BREADWINNER	LITTERATEUR	WOODCHOPPER	PERITONITIS	CONSIGNMENT
HYPHENATION	REPROBATION	BURGOMASTER	LOUDSPEAKER	AERONAUTICS	PERSPICUOUS	CONSTITUENT
IMAGINATION	REQUISITION	CALORIMETER	MINESWEEPER	ANASTOMOSIS	PESTIFEROUS	CONTAMINANT
IMBRICATION	RESERVATION	CARDSHARPER	MINNESINGER	AVOIRDUPOIS	PONTIFICALS	CONTENTMENT
IMPORTATION	RESIGNATION	CATERCORNER	MISBELIEVER	BLUNDERBUSS	PORTIONLESS	COUNTERFEIT
INATTENTION	RESPIRATION	CATERPILLAR	MISDEMEANOR	BREAKPOINTS	PRECIPITOUS	COUNTERPART
INCANTATION	RESTITUTION	CAULIFLOWER	MONEYLENDER	CALCIFEROUS	PRETENTIOUS	DETERMINANT
INCARNATION	RESTORATION	CHANTICLEER	MONSEIGNEUR	CARNIVOROUS	PROGNATHOUS	DIPLOMATIST
INCLINATION	RESTRICTION	CHEERLEADER	MOUNTAINEER	CEREMONIOUS	PROMISCUOUS	DREADNOUGHT
INDENTATION	RETRIBUTION	CHOIRMASTER	NIGHTWALKER	CONSPICUOUS	PROPHYLAXIS	EMPLACEMENT
INDIGESTION	SUPPOSITION	CHRONOMETER	NINNYHAMMER	CONTRETEMPS	PROSTATITIS	ENVIRONMENT
INDIGNATION	SYNCOPATION	CIRCUMLUNAR	NORTHEASTER	COTERMINOUS	PROSTHETICS	EQUIDISTANT
INFORMATION	THISTLEDOWN	CIRCUMPOLAR	OUTMANEUVER	CYBERNETICS	PUNCTILIOUS	EXPECTORANT
INQUISITION	TRANSACTION	COLORCASTER	PAPERHANGER	DELETERIOUS	REGIMENTALS	EXTRAVAGANT
INSPIRATION	TRENCHERMAN	COMMENTATOR	PARATROOPER	EFFICACIOUS	REPETITIOUS	FARTHERMOST
INSTITUTION	TREPIDATION	COMPTROLLER	PARISHIONER	ELECTRONICS	SARCOPHAGUS	FINGERPRINT
INSTRUCTION	TRIBULATION	CONNOISSEUR	PHILOSOPHER	EXHAUSTLESS	SCRUMPTIOUS	FLABBERGAST
INTERACTION	TRINIDADIAN	CONSERVATOR	PLACEHOLDER	EXPEDITIOUS	SENTENTIOUS	FORETHOUGHT
LACRIMATION	TRINITARIAN	COPROCESSOR	PREDECESSOR	FARINACEOUS	SMITHEREENS	FURTHERMOST
LEGERDEMAIN	ULTRAMODERN	CRAPSHOOTER	PRIZEWINNER	FURNISHINGS	SPONTANEOUS	GARNISHMENT
LEGISLATION	UNCHRISTIAN	CREPUSCULAR	PROBATIONER	GEOPOLITICS	SUPERFLUOUS	GRANDPARENT
LIBERTARIAN	UNIFICATION	DENOMINATOR	PROTOMARTYR	GYROCOMPASS	SUPERSONICS	GREASEPAINT
LILLIPUTIAN	UTILITARIAN	DISENCUMBER	QUACKSALVER	HERBIVOROUS	SWEEPSTAKES	GROUNDSHEET
LUCUBRATION	VACCINATION	DISTRIBUTOR	QUICKSILVER	HISTRIONICS	SYNCHRONOUS	HAIRSTYLIST
MACHINATION	VALEDICTION	DRILLMASTER	RATHSKELLER	HOMEOSTASIS	TEMPESTUOUS	HEAVYWEIGHT
MALEDICTION	VENTILATION	DYNAMOMETER	RECONNOITER	HOMOGENEOUS	TENDENTIOUS	IMPERMANENT
MALFUNCTION	VINDICATION	ELECTIONEER	RECTILINEAR	HOUSELIGHTS	THEATRICALS	IMPERTINENT
MENSURATION	VIVISECTION	FAULTFINDER	SCREWDRIVER	HYDROPONICS	THEREABOUTS	IMPROVEMENT
MERCHANTMAN	WASHERWOMAN	FIRECRACKER	SEISMOMETER	IDENTIFIERS	THOUGHTLESS	IMPROVIDENT
METRICATION	WEATHERWORN	FLOORWALKER	SEMITRAILER	IGNOMINIOUS	TONSILLITIS	INADVERTENT
MISBEGOTTEN	WINTERGREEN	FOREQUARTER	SHAREHOLDER	ILLUSTRIOUS	TREACHEROUS	INCOMPETENT
NEEDLEWOMAN	WORKSTATION	FRANKFURTER	SHIPBUILDER	IMPECUNIOUS	TRICHINOSIS	INCONGRUENT
NICKELODEON	ZOOPLANKTON	FREETHINKER	SLEEPWALKER	INCONGRUOUS	ULTRASONICS	INCONTINENT
NONPARTISAN	ACCELERANDO	GALLBLADDER	SPECTACULAR	INCREDULOUS	UNCONSCIOUS	INDEPENDENT
OBSERVATION	AMONTILLADO	GERRYMANDER	SPEEDOMETER	INDUSTRIOUS	UNDERSHORTS	INDIFFERENT
OBSTRUCTION	ARCHIPELAGO	GODDAUGHTER	SPELLBINDER	INTRAVENOUS	UNRIGHTEOUS	INEFFICIENT
OSTENTATION	BRAGGADOCIO	GRANDFATHER	STEAMROLLER	IRRELIGIOUS	VERTIGINOUS	INSTALLMENT
PARTURITION	CHIAROSCURO	GRANDMOTHER	STEPBROTHER	LETTERPRESS	WHEREABOUTS	INTELLIGENT
PERMUTATION	DECRESCENDO	GRASSHOPPER	STOCKBROKER	LINGUISTICS	ABORTIONIST	LIGHTWEIGHT
PLAINSPOKEN	INTERNUNCIO	GREENGROCER	STOCKHOLDER	MAGNANIMOUS	ACQUIREMENT	MAGNIFICENT
POLLINATION	VIOLONCELLO	GROUNDWATER	STOREKEEPER	MARCHIONESS	AFTEREFFECT	MAIDSERVANT
PREIGNITION	GENERALSHIP	HABERDASHER	STORYTELLER	MATHEMATICS	ANTIOXIDANT	MASSACHUSET
PREMONITION	MOUNTAINTOP	HAIRDRESSER	STRAWFLOWER	MEGALOPOLIS	APPOINTMENT	MEADOWSWEET
PREPOSITION	SCHOLARSHIP	HANDICAPPER	STREAMLINER	MELLIFLUOUS	ARBITRAMENT	MEASUREMENT
PRESUMPTION	THUNDERCLAP	HINDQUARTER	SYNTHESIZER	MERITORIOUS	BELLIGERENT	NARRAGANSET
PROCRUSTEAN	TRUSTEESHIP	HOMESTEADER	TELEPRINTER	METAPHYSICS	BITTERSWEET	NATIONALIST
PROGRESSION	WORKMANSHIP	HORSEPLAYER	THERMOMETER	MISCHIEVOUS	BREADBASKET	NEEDLEPOINT
PROHIBITION	ACCELERATOR	HOUSEKEEPER	TOASTMASTER	MUTTONCHOPS	CANDLELIGHT	NONDESCRIPT
PROLETARIAN	ACCUMULATOR	HOUSEMOTHER	TOTALIZATOR	NECESSITOUS	CIRCUMSPECT	NONDOCUMENT
PROPOSITION	AFTERBURNER	IMAGESETTER	TRAILBLAZER	NONETHELESS	CLAIRVOYANT	NONRESIDENT
PUBLICATION	ANNUNCIATOR	INCINERATOR	TRANSCEIVER	NOTHINGNESS	COEFFICIENT	NOURISHMENT
PUNCTUATION	ANTECHAMBER	INTERCEPTOR	TRANSMITTER	NUMISMATICS	COMMANDMENT	OBSOLESCENT
RADIOCARBON	BALLCARRIER	INTERLINEAR	TYPEFOUNDER	OPPROBRIOUS	COMMUNICANT	OMNIPRESENT

OVERWROUGHT	CARDINALITY	MULTIFAMILY
PAPERWEIGHT	CARTOGRAPHY	NATIONALITY
PENNYWEIGHT	CATHOLICITY	OBSERVATORY
POLTERGEIST	CHANCELLERY	OPPORTUNITY
PORTRAITIST	CHIROGRAPHY	ORNITHOLOGY
PREDICAMENT	CIRCULARITY	ORTHOGRAPHY
PROLETARIAT	CLIMATOLOGY	PALEOGRAPHY
PROTAGONIST	COMPLACENCY	PERFUNCTORY
PROTUBERANT	CONFEDERACY	PERSNICKETY
RECONSTRUCT	CONFESSEDLY	PERSONALITY
REFRESHMENT	CONSERVANCY	PETROGRAPHY
REMINISCENT	CONSISTENCY	PHOTOGRAPHY
REMONSTRANT	CONTINGENCY	PHRASEOLOGY
REPLACEMENT	CONTRARIETY	PHYSIOGNOMY
REQUIREMENT	CONTROVERSY	PLANETOLOGY
RESPLENDENT	COSIGNATORY	PORNOGRAPHY
SCUTTLEBUTT	CRIMINOLOGY	PRELIMINARY
SEARCHLIGHT	DELINQUENCY	PROFANATORY
SIGNIFICANT	DEPRECATORY	PROPINQUITY
SPACEFLIGHT	DERMATOLOGY	PROPRIETARY
SPENDTHRIFT	DESPONDENCY	RATIONALITY
SPREADSHEET	DISCOURTESY	REACTIONARY
SUPERMARKET	DISCREPANCY	RECIPROCITY
SUPERSCRIPT	DOCUMENTARY	REFORMATORY
SUPPRESSANT	DOMESTICITY	RESISTIVITY
SUPREMACIST	ELECTRICITY	ROADABILITY
TEMPERAMENT	EVENTUALITY	SENSIBILITY
THUNDERBOLT	EXCEEDINGLY	SERENDIPITY
TOBACCONIST	EXTEMPORARY	SOVEREIGNTY
TRANSLUCENT	FAMILIARITY	STENOGRAPHY
TRANSPARENT	FILMOGRAPHY	STEREOSCOPY
ULTRAVIOLET	FORTNIGHTLY	STRAIGHTWAY
UNDERWEIGHT	FRAGMENTARY	SUBASSEMBLY
VACATIONIST	FUNCTIONARY	SUFFICIENCY
VIRIDESCENT	GALLIMAUFRY	SUPPOSITORY
WASTEBASKET	GERONTOLOGY	TECHNOCRACY
WHEELWRIGHT	HAGIOGRAPHY	TERMINOLOGY
WITENAGEMOT	HERPETOLOGY	TRUSTWORTHY
WORDPERFECT	HISTORICITY	UNCERTAINTY
PORTMANTEAU	HOSPITALITY	VALEDICTORY
MARSHMALLOW	HUCKLEBERRY	VENTRILOQUY
WHEELBARROW	HYDROGRAPHY	VOLCANOLOGY
ACCORDINGLY	HYPERTROPHY	
ANNIVERSARY	ICHTHYOLOGY	
ANTIGRAVITY	IMMORTALITY	
ANTIPOVERTY	IMPROPRIETY	
ARCHAEOLOGY	INSTABILITY	
ARISTOCRACY	INTERCALARY	
BENEFICIARY	INVOLUNTARY	
BICENTENARY	JABBERWOCKY	
BLAMEWORTHY	JUVENOCRACY	
BOYSENBERRY	LITHOGRAPHY	
BUREAUCRACY	MANUFACTORY	
CALLIGRAPHY	MERITOCRACY	
CAMPANOLOGY	METEOROLOGY	
CAPILLARITY	METHODOLOGY	
CARAVANSARY	MOMENTARILY	

12

LETTER WORDS

	BIOGEOGRAPHY	COMMENCEMENT	CUMULONIMBUS	ENCYCLOPEDIA	HUMANITARIAN
	BIOSATELLITE	COMMENSURATE	DECALCOMANIA	ENTERPRISING	HYDROTHERAPY
ABBREVIATION	BIOTELEMETRY	COMMISSARIAT	DECASYLLABIC	ENTREPRENEUR	HYDROTHERMAL
ABOLITIONISM	BLANDISHMENT	COMMISSIONER	DECOMMISSION	EPISCOPALIAN	HYPERACIDITY
ABSENTMINDED	BLATHERSKITE	COMMONWEALTH	DECONGESTANT	EPITHALAMIUM	HYPERTENSION
ACCOMPLISHED	BLOCKBUSTING	COMMUNICABLE	DELIBERATIVE	EQUESTRIENNE	HYPOCHONDRIA
ACQUAINTANCE	BLOODLETTING	COMPANIONWAY	DELICATESSEN	EVERBLOOMING	HYPOGLYCEMIA
ADVENTITIOUS	BLOODTHIRSTY	COMPLAISANCE	DEMILITARIZE	EXCRUCIATING	HYSTERECTOMY
AERODYNAMICS	BLUESTOCKING	CONCELEBRANT	DEMIMONDAINE	EXTORTIONATE	IDIOSYNCRASY
AFORETHOUGHT	BRAINWASHING	CONCRESCENCE	DEMINERALIZE	EXTRAMARITAL	ILLEGITIMATE
AFTERTHOUGHT	BREAKTHROUGH	CONFECTIONER	DEMONSTRABLE	EXTRASENSORY	ILLUSTRATION
ALLITERATION	BREASTSTROKE	CONFESSIONAL	DENOMINATION	EXTRAVAGANZA	ILLUSTRATIVE
ALPHANUMERIC	BREATHTAKING	CONFIDENTIAL	DENSITOMETER	FAINTHEARTED	IMMEASURABLE
AMBIDEXTROUS	BRILLIANTINE	CONFIRMATION	DENUNCIATION	FEEBLEMINDED	IMPENETRABLE
AMPHITHEATER	BUTTERSCOTCH	CONFORMATION	DESPOLIATION	FENESTRATION	IMPERCEPTIVE
ANATHEMATIZE	CABINETMAKER	CONFUCIANISM	DESTRUCTIBLE	FERMENTATION	IMPERCIPIENT
ANNUNCIATION	CALISTHENICS	CONGLOMERATE	DETERMINABLE	FIBRILLATION	IMPERFECTION
ANTEDILUVIAN	CANTANKEROUS	CONGRATULATE	DIASTROPHISM	FLAMETHROWER	IMPERISHABLE
ANTHROPOLOGY	CARBOHYDRATE	CONGREGATION	DICTATORSHIP	FLUORESCENCE	IMPONDERABLE
ANTIALIASING	CARBONACEOUS	CONQUISTADOR	DIFFERENTIAL	FLUOROCARBON	INARTICULATE
ANTIELECTRON	CARILLONNEUR	CONSERVATION	DISACCHARIDE	FORMALDEHYDE	INCALCULABLE
ANTIMACASSAR	CARPETBAGGER	CONSERVATISM	DISADVANTAGE	FOUNTAINHEAD	INCANDESCENT
ANTIMAGNETIC	CHALCOPYRITE	CONSERVATIVE	DISAGREEABLE	FRANKENSTEIN	INCAPACITATE
ANTIPARTICLE	CHAMPIONSHIP	CONSERVATORY	DISASSOCIATE	FRANKINCENSE	INCOMPARABLE
ANTITHETICAL	CHARACTERIZE	CONSIDERABLE	DISCIPLINARY	FREESTANDING	INCOMPATIBLE
APOSTROPHIZE	CHECKERBERRY	CONSTABULARY	DISCONNECTED	FRONTISPIECE	INCONSOLABLE
APPENDECTOMY	CHECKERBOARD	CONSTIPATION	DISCONSOLATE	GALVANOMETER	INCONVENIENT
APPENDICITIS	CHEESEBURGER	CONSTITUENCY	DISCOURTEOUS	GEOCHEMISTRY	INCORRIGIBLE
APPRECIATIVE	CHEESEPARING	CONSTITUTION	DISCRIMINATE	GLASSBLOWING	INCRUSTATION
APPREHENSIVE	CHEMOTHERAPY	CONSTITUTIVE	DISESTABLISH	GLOCKENSPIEL	INDECLINABLE
APPURTENANCE	CHESTERFIELD	CONSTRUCTION	DISFRANCHISE	GOBBLEDYGOOK	INDEFEASIBLE
ARCHITECTURE	CHILDBEARING	CONTAINERIZE	DISINGENUOUS	GREATHEARTED	INDEPENDENCE
ARGILLACEOUS	CHIROPRACTIC	CONTEMPORARY	DISINTEGRATE	HABERDASHERY	INDIGESTIBLE
ASTRONAUTICS	CHITTERLINGS	CONTEMPTIBLE	DISOBEDIENCE	HAIRSPLITTER	INDISPUTABLE
ASTRONOMICAL	CHOREOGRAPHY	CONTEMPTUOUS	DISPENSATION	HALLUCINOGEN	INDISSOLUBLE
ASTROPHYSICS	CHRISTIANITY	CONTERMINOUS	DISPLACEMENT	HANDKERCHIEF	INDOCTRINATE
ASYNCHRONOUS	CHRISTIANIZE	CONTINUATION	DISPUTATIOUS	HEADMISTRESS	INEFFACEABLE
ATMOSPHERICS	CHROMATICITY	CONTRAPUNTAL	DISQUISITION	HEADQUARTERS	INEXPERIENCE
ATTITUDINIZE	CHROMOSPHERE	CONTRARIWISE	DISREPUTABLE	HEARTRENDING	INEXPLICABLE
AUDIOVISUALS	CHURCHWARDEN	CONTUMACIOUS	DISSERTATION	HEARTSTRINGS	INEXTRICABLE
AUSTRONESIAN	CINEMATHEQUE	CONTUMELIOUS	DISTILLATION	HEARTWARMING	INFELICITOUS
AUTHENTICATE	CIRCUMSCRIBE	CONVENTIONAL	DISTRIBUTIVE	HEAVYHEARTED	INFLAMMATION
AVITAMINOSIS	CIRCUMSTANCE	CONVERSATION	EARSPLITTING	HELIOCENTRIC	INFLAMMATORY
BACKTRACKING	CIVILIZATION	CORESPONDENT	EARTHSHAKING	HELLGRAMMITE	INFLATIONARY
BACTERICIDAL	CLOSEMOUTHED	COSMOPOLITAN	ECCLESIASTIC	HENCEFORWARD	INFLATIONISM
BACTERIOLOGY	CLOTHESHORSE	COUNTERCLAIM	ECHOLOCATION	HETEROSEXUAL	INGRATIATING
BELLIGERENCY	CLOTHESPRESS	COUNTERPOINT	EDITORIALIZE	HIERARCHICAL	INSALUBRIOUS
BIBLIOGRAPHY	COELENTERATE	COUNTERPOISE	ELECTROLYSIS	HIEROGLYPHIC	INSTRUMENTAL
BICENTENNIAL	COLLECTIVISM	COUNTERTENOR	ELECTROPLATE	HIPPOPOTAMUS	INSUFFERABLE
BILLINGSGATE	COLLECTIVIZE	CROSSCURRENT	ELEEMOSYNARY	HORTICULTURE	INSUFFICIENT
BIOCHEMISTRY	COLLEGIALITY	CRYPTOGRAPHY	ENCEPHALITIS	HOUSEWARMING	INSURRECTION

INTELLECTUAL	MICROBIOLOGY	OXYACETYLENE	PREPOSTEROUS	SCANDINAVIAN	THANKSGIVING
INTELLIGENCE	MICROCIRCUIT	PACKINGHOUSE	PREREQUISITE	SCATOLOGICAL	THERAPEUTICS
INTELLIGIBLE	MICROCLIMATE	PALEONTOLOGY	PRESBYTERIAN	SCHOOLFELLOW	THERMOSPHERE
INTEMPERANCE	MICROSPACING	PANCHROMATIC	PRESCRIPTION	SCHOOLMASTER	THOROUGHBRED
INTERCESSION	MICROSURGERY	PARADISIACAL	PRESENTIMENT	SECRETARIATE	THOROUGHFARE
INTERFERENCE	MIDDLEWEIGHT	PARAMILITARY	PRESUMPTUOUS	SELENOGRAPHY	THUNDERCLOUD
INTERGLACIAL	MINICOMPUTER	PARASITOLOGY	PRIMOGENITOR	SENSITOMETER	THUNDERSTORM
INTERJECTION	MISADVENTURE	PARENTHESIZE	PRINCIPALITY	SEXAGENARIAN	TOTALITARIAN
INTERLOCUTOR	MISAPPREHEND	PEACEKEEPING	PROCATHEDRAL	SHARECROPPER	TRADESPEOPLE
INTERMEDIARY	MISCALCULATE	PENITENTIARY	PROCESSIONAL	SHARPSHOOTER	TRANQUILIZER
INTERMEDIATE	MISINTERPRET	PERADVENTURE	PROFESSIONAL	SHORTSIGHTED	TRANSCENDENT
INTERMINABLE	MISPRONOUNCE	PERAMBULATOR	PROGRAMMABLE	SHUFFLEBOARD	TRANSFERENCE
INTERMISSION	MISREPRESENT	PERICYNTHION	PROLEGOMENON	SIGNIFICANCE	TRANSMIGRATE
INTERMITTENT	MONOFILAMENT	PERSPICACITY	PROPAGANDIZE	SIMULTANEOUS	TRANSMISSION
INTERSECTION	MONOSYLLABLE	PERTINACIOUS	PROPHYLACTIC	SLEDGEHAMMER	TRANSMOGRIFY
INTERSTELLAR	MOUNTAINSIDE	PESTILENTIAL	PROPORTIONAL	SOMNAMBULISM	TRANSOCEANIC
INTERVOCALIC	MUDDLEHEADED	PHARMACOLOGY	PROTACTINIUM	SPECTROGRAPH	TRANSPACIFIC
INTRANSIGENT	MULLIGATAWNY	PHILANTHROPY	PROTECTORATE	SPECTROMETER	TRANSVESTISM
INTRANSITIVE	MULTICOLORED	PHILHARMONIC	PROTHALAMION	SPECTROSCOPE	TRAPSHOOTING
INVERTEBRATE	MULTIFACETED	PHILODENDRON	PROTUBERANCE	SPERMATOZOON	TRIGNOMETRIC
INVITATIONAL	MULTIFARIOUS	PHILOSOPHIZE	PROVIDENTIAL	SPIRITUALISM	TRIGONOMETRY
INVULNERABLE	MULTILATERAL	PHOTOCOMPOSE	PSYCHOACTIVE	SPORTSWRITER	TROUBLEMAKER
IRREDEEMABLE	MULTILINGUAL	PHOTOENGRAVE	PSYCHOSEXUAL	STEEPLECHASE	TUBERCULOSIS
IRREFRAGABLE	MULTIPLICAND	PHOTOGRAVURE	PSYCHOTROPIC	STEPDAUGHTER	ULTRAMONTANE
IRREMEDIABLE	MULTIPLICITY	PHYSIOGRAPHY	PUMPERNICKEL	STEREOPHONIC	UNACCUSTOMED
IRRESISTIBLE	MULTIPURPOSE	PICKERELWEED	PYROTECHNICS	STEREOSCOPIC	UNASSAILABLE
IRRESPECTIVE	MULTISESSION	PIGMENTATION	QUANTITATIVE	STRAIGHTAWAY	UNBELIEVABLE
IRREVERSIBLE	MULTITASKING	PLANETESIMAL	QUARTERSTAFF	STRAIGHTEDGE	UNCHARITABLE
ISOLATIONISM	MULTIVERSITY	PLASTERBOARD	QUESTIONABLE	STRAITJACKET	UNDERCLOTHES
JURISDICTION	MULTIVITAMIN	POLARIZATION	QUINTESSENCE	STRATIGRAPHY	UNDERCOATING
KALEIDOSCOPE	MUNICIPALITY	POLICYHOLDER	RADIOISOTOPE	STRATOSPHERE	UNDERCURRENT
KINDERGARTEN	NEIGHBORHOOD	POLYETHYLENE	RADIOTHERAPY	STREETWALKER	UNDERDRAWERS
LEXICOGRAPHY	NEURASTHENIA	POLYMORPHISM	RAMBUNCTIOUS	STREPTOMYCIN	UNDERGARMENT
LIGHTHEARTED	NEUROSCIENCE	POLYSYLLABIC	RECALCITRANT	SUBCOMMITTEE	UNDERPINNING
LONGITUDINAL	NEVERTHELESS	POLYSYLLABLE	RECAPITULATE	SUBCONSCIOUS	UNDERSURFACE
LONGSHOREMAN	NEWSMAGAZINE	PORCELAINIZE	RECEIVERSHIP	SUBCONTINENT	UNDOCUMENTED
LUMINESCENCE	NEWSPAPERMAN	POSTDOCTORAL	RECEPTIONIST	SUBCUTANEOUS	UNEMPLOYMENT
LUNCHEONETTE	NIGHTCLOTHES	POSTGRADUATE	RECOGNIZANCE	SUBDIRECTORY	UNFREQUENTED
MADEMOISELLE	NOMENCLATURE	POSTHYPNOTIC	RECOLLECTION	SUBMINIATURE	UNGOVERNABLE
MAGNETOMETER	NONAGENARIAN	POSTMISTRESS	RECONSTITUTE	SUBSCRIPTION	UNINTERESTED
MAGNILOQUENT	NONCOMBATANT	PRACTITIONER	REGISTRATION	SUBSERVIENCE	UNIVERSALIST
MALFORMATION	NONCOMMITTAL	PRASEODYMIUM	REHABILITATE	SUBSTANTIATE	UNIVERSALITY
MALNOURISHED	NONCONDUCTOR	PREAMPLIFIER	RELATIONSHIP	SUBSTRUCTURE	UNIVERSALIZE
MALNUTRITION	NONOBJECTIVE	PRECANCEROUS	RELATIVISTIC	SUBTERRANEAN	UNLIKELIHOOD
MALOCCLUSION	NONSCHEDULED	PRECIPITANCY	REMINISCENCE	SUPERANNUATE	UNMISTAKABLE
MANSLAUGHTER	OBSCURANTISM	PRECONCERTED	REMONSTRANCE	SUPERCHARGER	UNPARALLELED
MARLINESPIKE	OBSTREPEROUS	PRECONDITION	REMUNERATION	SUPERCILIOUS	UNPRINCIPLED
MASTERSTROKE	OCEANOGRAPHY	PREDESIGNATE	REMUNERATIVE	SUPERHIGHWAY	UNPROFITABLE
MASTURBATION	OCTOGENARIAN	PREDETERMINE	RENUNCIATION	SUPERNATURAL	UNREASONABLE
MEALYMOUTHED	OCTOSYLLABIC	PREDIGESTION	REPERCUSSION	SUPERSTITION	UNREGENERATE
MEETINGHOUSE	OFFICEHOLDER	PREDILECTION	RESPECTIVELY	SURROUNDINGS	UNRESTRAINED
MENSTRUATION	ONOMATOPOEIA	PREFABRICATE	RESTAURATEUR	SURVEILLANCE	UNSCIENTIFIC
MERCHANTABLE	ORGANIZATION	PREINDUCTION	RESURRECTION	SWASHBUCKLER	UNSCRUPULOUS
MERETRICIOUS	OSCILLOSCOPE	PREMENSTRUAL	RHODODENDRON	TECHNICALITY	UNSEARCHABLE
MESSEIGNEURS	OTHERWORLDLY	PREOPERATIVE	SARSAPARILLA	TENDEROMETER	UNSEASONABLE
METALANGUAGE	OUTSTRETCHED	PREPAREDNESS	SATISFACTION	TERCENTENARY	UNSEGREGATED
METAMORPHISM	OVEREXPOSURE	PREPONDERATE	SATISFACTORY	TESTOSTERONE	VACATIONLAND

VAINGLORIOUS	RAMBUNCTIOUS	HENCEFORWARD	WEATHERGLASS	CIVILIZATION	BLUESTOCKING
VALENCIENNES	SARSAPARILLA	HETEROSEXUAL	WEATHERPROOF	DIASTROPHISM	CLOSEMOUTHED
VALORIZATION	SATISFACTION	LEXICOGRAPHY	WELTERWEIGHT	DICTATORSHIP	CLOTHESHORSE
VENIPUNCTURE	SATISFACTORY	MEALYMOUTHED	AFORETHOUGHT	DIFFERENTIAL	CLOTHESPRESS
VERTICILLATE	VACATIONLAND	MEETINGHOUSE	AFTERTHOUGHT	DISACCHARIDE	ELECTROLYSIS
VETERINARIAN	VAINGLORIOUS	MENSTRUATION	OFFICEHOLDER	DISADVANTAGE	ELECTROPLATE
WEATHERBOARD	VALENCIENNES	MERCHANTABLE	CHALCOPYRITE	DISAGREEABLE	ELEEMOSYNARY
WEATHERGLASS	VALORIZATION	MERETRICIOUS	CHAMPIONSHIP	DISASSOCIATE	FLAMETHROWER
WEATHERPROOF	ABBREVIATION	MESSEIGNEURS	CHARACTERIZE	DISCIPLINARY	FLUORESCENCE
WELTERWEIGHT	ABOLITIONISM	METALANGUAGE	CHECKERBERRY	DISCONNECTED	FLUOROCARBON
WHIPPOORWILL	ABSENTMINDED	METAMORPHISM	CHECKERBOARD	DISCONSOLATE	GLASSBLOWING
WHOLEHEARTED	OBSCURANTISM	NEIGHBORHOOD	CHEESEBURGER	DISCOURTEOUS	GLOCKENSPIEL
ZOOGEOGRAPHY	OBSTREPEROUS	NEURASTHENIA	CHEESEPARING	DISCRIMINATE	ILLEGITIMATE
	ACCOMPLISHED	NEUROSCIENCE	CHEMOTHERAPY	DISESTABLISH	ILLUSTRATION
	ACQUAINTANCE	NEVERTHELESS	CHESTERFIELD	DISFRANCHISE	ILLUSTRATIVE
	ECCLESIASTIC	NEWSMAGAZINE	CHILDBEARING	DISINGENUOUS	PLANETESIMAL
	ECHOLOCATION	NEWSPAPERMAN	CHIROPRACTIC	DISINTEGRATE	PLASTERBOARD
	OCEANOGRAPHY	PEACEKEEPING	CHITTERLINGS	DISOBEDIENCE	SLEDGEHAMMER
2ND LETTER	OCTOGENARIAN	PENITENTIARY	CHOREOGRAPHY	DISPENSATION	ULTRAMONTANE
	OCTOSYLLABIC	PERADVENTURE	CHRISTIANITY	DISPLACEMENT	AMBIDEXTROUS
BACKTRACKING	SCANDINAVIAN	PERAMBULATOR	CHRISTIANIZE	DISPUTATIOUS	AMPHITHEATER
BACTERICIDAL	SCATOLOGICAL	PERICYNTHION	CHROMATICITY	DISQUISITION	IMMEASURABLE
BACTERIOLOGY	SCHOOLFELLOW	PERSPICACITY	CHROMOSPHERE	DISREPUTABLE	IMPENETRABLE
CABINETMAKER	SCHOOLMASTER	PERTINACIOUS	CHURCHWARDEN	DISSERTATION	IMPERCEPTIVE
CALISTHENICS	ADVENTITIOUS	PESTILENTIAL	PHARMACOLOGY	DISTILLATION	IMPERCIPIENT
CANTANKEROUS	EDITORIALIZE	RECALCITRANT	PHILANTHROPY	DISTRIBUTIVE	IMPERFECTION
CARBOHYDRATE	IDIOSYNCRASY	RECAPITULATE	PHILHARMONIC	FIBRILLATION	IMPERISHABLE
CARBONACEOUS	AERODYNAMICS	RECEIVERSHIP	PHILODENDRON	HIERARCHICAL	IMPONDERABLE
CARILLONNEUR	BELLIGERENCY	RECEPTIONIST	PHILOSOPHIZE	HIEROGLYPHIC	ANATHEMATIZE
CARPETBAGGER	DECALCOMANIA	RECOGNIZANCE	PHOTOCOMPOSE	HIPPOPOTAMUS	ANNUNCIATION
EARSPLITTING	DECASYLLABIC	RECOLLECTION	PHOTOENGRAVE	KINDERGARTEN	ANTEDILUVIAN
EARTHSHAKING	DECOMMISSION	RECONSTITUTE	PHOTOGRAVURE	LIGHTHEARTED	ANTHROPOLOGY
FAINTHEARTED	DECONGESTANT	REGISTRATION	PHYSIOGRAPHY	MICROBIOLOGY	ANTIALIASING
GALVANOMETER	DELIBERATIVE	REHABILITATE	RHODODENDRON	MICROCIRCUIT	ANTIELECTRON
HABERDASHERY	DELICATESSEN	RELATIONSHIP	SHARECROPPER	MICROCLIMATE	ANTIMACASSAR
HAIRSPLITTER	DEMILITARIZE	RELATIVISTIC	SHARPSHOOTER	MICROSPACING	ANTIMAGNETIC
HALLUCINOGEN	DEMIMONDAINE	REMINISCENCE	SHORTSIGHTED	MICROSURGERY	ANTIPARTICLE
HANDKERCHIEF	DEMINERALIZE	REMONSTRANCE	SHUFFLEBOARD	MIDDLEWEIGHT	ANTITHETICAL
KALEIDOSCOPE	DEMONSTRABLE	REMUNERATION	THANKSGIVING	MINICOMPUTER	ENCEPHALITIS
MADEMOISELLE	DENOMINATION	REMUNERATIVE	THERAPEUTICS	MISADVENTURE	ENCYCLOPEDIA
MAGNETOMETER	DENSITOMETER	RENUNCIATION	THERMOSPHERE	MISAPPREHEND	ENTERPRISING
MAGNILOQUENT	DENUNCIATION	REPERCUSSION	THOROUGHBRED	MISCALCULATE	ENTREPRENEUR
MALFORMATION	DESPOLIATION	RESPECTIVELY	THOROUGHFARE	MISINTERPRET	INARTICULATE
MALNOURISHED	DESTRUCTIBLE	RESTAURATEUR	THUNDERCLOUD	MISPRONOUNCE	INCALCULABLE
MALNUTRITION	DETERMINABLE	RESURRECTION	THUNDERSTORM	MISREPRESENT	INCANDESCENT
MALOCCLUSION	FEEBLEMINDED	SECRETARIATE	WHIPPOORWILL	NIGHTCLOTHES	INCAPACITATE
MANSLAUGHTER	FENESTRATION	SELENOGRAPHY	WHOLEHEARTED	PICKERELWEED	INCOMPARABLE
MARLINESPIKE	FERMENTATION	SENSITOMETER	BIBLIOGRAPHY	PIGMENTATION	INCOMPATIBLE
MASTERSTROKE	GEOCHEMISTRY	SEXAGENARIAN	BICENTENNIAL	SIGNIFICANCE	INCONSOLABLE
MASTURBATION	HEADMISTRESS	TECHNICALITY	BILLINGSGATE	SIMULTANEOUS	INCONVENIENT
PACKINGHOUSE	HEADQUARTERS	TENDEROMETER	BIOCHEMISTRY	ALLITERATION	INCORRIGIBLE
PALEONTOLOGY	HEARTRENDING	TERCENTENARY	BIOGEOGRAPHY	ALPHANUMERIC	INCRUSTATION
PANCHROMATIC	HEARTSTRINGS	TESTOSTERONE	BIOSATELLITE	BLANDISHMENT	INDECLINABLE
PARADISIACAL	HEARTWARMING	VENIPUNCTURE	BIOTELEMETRY	BLATHERSKITE	INDEFEASIBLE
PARAMILITARY	HEAVYHEARTED	VERTICILLATE	CINEMATHEQUE	BLOCKBUSTING	INDEPENDENCE
PARASITOLOGY	HELIOCENTRIC	VETERINARIAN	CIRCUMSCRIBE	BLOODLETTING	INDIGESTIBLE
PARENTHESIZE	HELLGRAMMITE	WEATHERBOARD	CIRCUMSTANCE	BLOODTHIRSTY	INDISPUTABLE
RADIOISOTOPE					
RADIOTHERAPY					

INDISSOLUBLE	UNIVERSALITY	CONTRARIWISE	ARCHITECTURE	PROTUBERANCE	MULTIPURPOSE
INDOCTRINATE	UNIVERSALIZE	CONTUMACIOUS	ARGILLACEOUS	PROVIDENTIAL	MULTISESSION
INEFFACEABLE	UNLIKELIHOOD	CONTUMELIOUS	BRAINWASHING	TRADESPEOPLE	MULTITASKING
INEXPERIENCE	UNMISTAKABLE	CONVENTIONAL	BREAKTHROUGH	TRANQUILIZER	MULTIVERSITY
INEXPLICABLE	UNPARALLELED	CONVERSATION	BREASTSTROKE	TRANSCENDENT	MULTIVITAMIN
INEXTRICABLE	UNPRINCIPLED	CORESPONDENT	BREATHTAKING	TRANSFERENCE	MUNICIPALITY
INFELICITOUS	UNPROFITABLE	COSMOPOLITAN	BRILLIANTINE	TRANSMIGRATE	OUTSTRETCHED
INFLAMMATION	UNREASONABLE	COUNTERCLAIM	CROSSCURRENT	TRANSMISSION	PUMPERNICKEL
INFLAMMATORY	UNREGENERATE	COUNTERPOINT	CRYPTOGRAPHY	TRANSMOGRIFY	QUANTITATIVE
INFLATIONARY	UNRESTRAINED	COUNTERPOISE	FRANKENSTEIN	TRANSOCEANIC	QUARTERSTAFF
INFLATIONISM	UNSCIENTIFIC	COUNTERTENOR	FRANKINCENSE	TRANSPACIFIC	QUESTIONABLE
INGRATIATING	UNSCRUPULOUS	FORMALDEHYDE	FREESTANDING	TRANSVESTISM	QUINTESSENCE
INSALUBRIOUS	UNSEARCHABLE	FOUNTAINHEAD	FRONTISPIECE	TRAPSHOOTING	SUBCOMMITTEE
INSTRUMENTAL	UNSEASONABLE	GOBBLEDYGOOK	GREATHEARTED	TRIGNOMETRIC	SUBCONSCIOUS
INSUFFERABLE	UNSEGREGATED	HORTICULTURE	IRREDEEMABLE	TRIGONOMETRY	SUBCONTINENT
INSUFFICIENT	COELENTERATE	HOUSEWARMING	IRREFRAGABLE	TROUBLEMAKER	SUBCUTANEOUS
INSURRECTION	COLLECTIVISM	LONGITUDINAL	IRREMEDIABLE	ASTRONAUTICS	SUBDIRECTORY
INTELLECTUAL	COLLECTIVIZE	LONGSHOREMAN	IRRESISTIBLE	ASTRONOMICAL	SUBMINIATURE
INTELLIGENCE	COLLEGIALITY	MONOFILAMENT	IRRESPECTIVE	ASTROPHYSICS	SUBSCRIPTION
INTELLIGIBLE	COMMENCEMENT	MONOSYLLABLE	IRREVERSIBLE	ASYNCHRONOUS	SUBSERVIENCE
INTEMPERANCE	COMMENSURATE	MOUNTAINSIDE	ORGANIZATION	ISOLATIONISM	SUBSTANTIATE
INTERCESSION	COMMISSARIAT	NOMENCLATURE	PRACTITIONER	OSCILLOSCOPE	SUBSTRUCTURE
INTERFERENCE	COMMISSIONER	NONAGENARIAN	PRASEODYMIUM	PSYCHOACTIVE	SUBTERRANEAN
INTERGLACIAL	COMMONWEALTH	NONCOMBATANT	PREAMPLIFIER	PSYCHOSEXUAL	SUPERANNUATE
INTERJECTION	COMMUNICABLE	NONCOMMITTAL	PRECANCEROUS	PSYCHOTROPIC	SUPERCHARGER
INTERLOCUTOR	COMPANIONWAY	NONCONDUCTOR	PRECIPITANCY	ATMOSPHERICS	SUPERCILIOUS
INTERMEDIARY	COMPLAISANCE	NONOBJECTIVE	PRECONCERTED	ATTITUDINIZE	SUPERHIGHWAY
INTERMEDIATE	CONCELEBRANT	NONSCHEDULED	PRECONDITION	OTHERWORLDLY	SUPERNATURAL
INTERMINABLE	CONCRESCENCE	POLARIZATION	PREDESIGNATE	STEEPLECHASE	SUPERSTITION
INTERMISSION	CONFECTIONER	POLICYHOLDER	PREDETERMINE	STEPDAUGHTER	SURROUNDINGS
INTERMITTENT	CONFESSIONAL	POLYETHYLENE	PREDIGESTION	STEREOPHONIC	SURVEILLANCE
INTERSECTION	CONFIDENTIAL	POLYMORPHISM	PREDILECTION	STEREOSCOPIC	TUBERCULOSIS
INTERSTELLAR	CONFIRMATION	POLYSYLLABIC	PREFABRICATE	STRAIGHTAWAY	AVITAMINOSIS
INTERVOCALIC	CONFORMATION	POLYSYLLABLE	PREINDUCTION	STRAIGHTEDGE	EVERBLOOMING
INTRANSIGENT	CONFUCIANISM	PORCELAINIZE	PREMENSTRUAL	STRAITJACKET	OVEREXPOSURE
INTRANSITIVE	CONGLOMERATE	POSTDOCTORAL	PREOPERATIVE	STRATIGRAPHY	SWASHBUCKLER
INVERTEBRATE	CONGRATULATE	POSTGRADUATE	PREPAREDNESS	STRATOSPHERE	EXCRUCIATING
INVITATIONAL	CONGREGATION	POSTHYPNOTIC	PREPONDERATE	STREETWALKER	EXTORTIONATE
INVULNERABLE	CONQUISTADOR	POSTMISTRESS	PREPOSTEROUS	STREPTOMYCIN	EXTRAMARITAL
ONOMATOPOEIA	CONSERVATION	SOMNAMBULISM	PREREQUISITE	AUDIOVISUALS	EXTRASENSORY
UNACCUSTOMED	CONSERVATISM	TOTALITARIAN	PRESBYTERIAN	AUSTRONESIAN	EXTRAVAGANZA
UNASSAILABLE	CONSERVATIVE	ZOOGEOGRAPHY	PRESCRIPTION	AUTHENTICATE	OXYACETYLENE
UNBELIEVABLE	CONSERVATORY	APOSTROPHIZE	PRESENTIMENT	BUTTERSCOTCH	HYDROTHERAPY
UNCHARITABLE	CONSIDERABLE	APPENDECTOMY	PRESUMPTUOUS	CUMULONIMBUS	HYDROTHERMAL
UNDERCLOTHES	CONSTABULARY	APPENDICITIS	PRIMOGENITOR	HUMANITARIAN	HYPERACIDITY
UNDERCOATING	CONSTIPATION	APPRECIATIVE	PRINCIPALITY	JURISDICTION	HYPERTENSION
UNDERCURRENT	CONSTITUENCY	APPREHENSIVE	PROCATHEDRAL	LUMINESCENCE	HYPOCHONDRIA
UNDERDRAWERS	CONSTITUTION	APPURTENANCE	PROCESSIONAL	LUNCHEONETTE	HYPOGLYCEMIA
UNDERGARMENT	CONSTITUTIVE	EPISCOPALIAN	PROFESSIONAL	MUDDLEHEADED	HYSTERECTOMY
UNDERPINNING	CONSTRUCTION	EPITHALAMIUM	PROGRAMMABLE	MULLIGATAWNY	PYROTECHNICS
UNDERSURFACE	CONTAINERIZE	SPECTROGRAPH	PROLEGOMENON	MULTICOLORED	
UNDOCUMENTED	CONTEMPORARY	SPECTROMETER	PROPAGANDIZE	MULTIFACETED	
UNEMPLOYMENT	CONTEMPTIBLE	SPECTROSCOPE	PROPHYLACTIC	MULTIFARIOUS	
UNFREQUENTED	CONTEMPTUOUS	SPERMATOZOON	PROPORTIONAL	MULTILATERAL	**3**RD **L**ETTER
UNGOVERNABLE	CONTERMINOUS	SPIRITUALISM	PROTACTINIUM	MULTILINGUAL	
UNINTERESTED	CONTINUATION	SPORTSWRITER	PROTECTORATE	MULTIPLICAND	ANATHEMATIZE
UNIVERSALIST	CONTRAPUNTAL	EQUESTRIENNE	PROTHALAMION	MULTIPLICITY	BLANDISHMENT

BLATHERSKITE	SUBCONTINENT	INDECLINABLE	PREMENSTRUAL	IDIOSYNCRASY	POLYSYLLABIC
BRAINWASHING	SUBCUTANEOUS	INDEFEASIBLE	PREOPERATIVE	NEIGHBORHOOD	POLYSYLLABLE
CHALCOPYRITE	SUBDIRECTORY	INDEPENDENCE	PREPAREDNESS	PHILANTHROPY	RELATIONSHIP
CHAMPIONSHIP	SUBMINIATURE	INDIGESTIBLE	PREPONDERATE	PHILHARMONIC	RELATIVISTIC
CHARACTERIZE	SUBSCRIPTION	INDISPUTABLE	PREPOSTEROUS	PHILODENDRON	SELENOGRAPHY
DIASTROPHISM	SUBSERVIENCE	INDISSOLUBLE	PREREQUISITE	PHILOSOPHIZE	UNLIKELIHOOD
FLAMETHROWER	SUBSTANTIATE	INDOCTRINATE	PRESBYTERIAN	PRIMOGENITOR	VALENCIENNES
FRANKENSTEIN	SUBSTRUCTURE	MADEMOISELLE	PRESCRIPTION	PRINCIPALITY	VALORIZATION
FRANKINCENSE	SUBTERRANEAN	MIDDLEWEIGHT	PRESENTIMENT	QUINTESSENCE	WELTERWEIGHT
GLASSBLOWING	TUBERCULOSIS	MUDDLEHEADED	PRESUMPTUOUS	SPIRITUALISM	ATMOSPHERICS
HEADMISTRESS	UNBELIEVABLE	RADIOISOTOPE	QUESTIONABLE	TRIGNOMETRIC	COMMENCEMENT
HEADQUARTERS	ACCOMPLISHED	RADIOTHERAPY	SLEDGEHAMMER	TRIGONOMETRY	COMMENSURATE
HEARTRENDING	ARCHITECTURE	UNDERCLOTHES	SPECTROGRAPH	UNINTERESTED	COMMISSARIAT
HEARTSTRINGS	BACKTRACKING	UNDERCOATING	SPECTROMETER	UNIVERSALIST	COMMISSIONER
HEARTWARMING	BACTERICIDAL	UNDERCURRENT	SPECTROSCOPE	UNIVERSALITY	COMMONWEALTH
HEAVYHEARTED	BACTERIOLOGY	UNDERDRAWERS	SPERMATOZOON	UNIVERSALIZE	COMMUNICABLE
INARTICULATE	BICENTENNIAL	UNDERGARMENT	STEEPLECHASE	VAINGLORIOUS	COMPANIONWAY
MEALYMOUTHED	DECALCOMANIA	UNDERPINNING	STEPDAUGHTER	WHIPPOORWILL	COMPLAISANCE
PEACEKEEPING	DECASYLLABIC	UNDERSURFACE	STEREOPHONIC	ALLITERATION	CUMULONIMBUS
PHARMACOLOGY	DECOMMISSION	UNDOCUMENTED	STEREOSCOPIC	BELLIGERENCY	DEMILITARIZE
PLANETESIMAL	DECONGESTANT	BREAKTHROUGH	THERAPEUTICS	BILLINGSGATE	DEMIMONDAINE
PLASTERBOARD	DICTATORSHIP	BREASTSTROKE	THERMOSPHERE	CALISTHENICS	DEMINERALIZE
PRACTITIONER	ECCLESIASTIC	BREATHTAKING	UNEMPLOYMENT	COLLECTIVISM	DEMONSTRABLE
PRASEODYMIUM	ENCEPHALITIS	CHECKERBERRY	DIFFERENTIAL	COLLECTIVIZE	HUMANITARIAN
QUANTITATIVE	ENCYCLOPEDIA	CHECKERBOARD	INFELICITOUS	COLLEGIALITY	IMMEASURABLE
QUARTERSTAFF	EXCRUCIATING	CHEESEBURGER	INFLAMMATION	DELIBERATIVE	LUMINESCENCE
SCANDINAVIAN	INCALCULABLE	CHEESEPARING	INFLAMMATORY	DELICATESSEN	NOMENCLATURE
SCATOLOGICAL	INCANDESCENT	CHEMOTHERAPY	INFLATIONARY	GALVANOMETER	PUMPERNICKEL
SHARECROPPER	INCAPACITATE	CHESTERFIELD	INFLATIONISM	HALLUCINOGEN	RAMBUNCTIOUS
SHARPSHOOTER	INCOMPARABLE	COELENTERATE	OFFICEHOLDER	HELIOCENTRIC	REMINISCENCE
SWASHBUCKLER	INCOMPATIBLE	ELECTROLYSIS	UNFREQUENTED	HELLGRAMMITE	REMONSTRANCE
THANKSGIVING	INCONSOLABLE	ELECTROPLATE	ARGILLACEOUS	ILLEGITIMATE	REMUNERATION
TRADESPEOPLE	INCONVENIENT	ELEEMOSYNARY	INGRATIATING	ILLUSTRATION	REMUNERATIVE
TRANQUILIZER	INCORRIGIBLE	EVERBLOOMING	LIGHTHEARTED	ILLUSTRATIVE	SIMULTANEOUS
TRANSCENDENT	INCRUSTATION	FEEBLEMINDED	MAGNETOMETER	KALEIDOSCOPE	SOMNAMBULISM
TRANSFERENCE	MICROBIOLOGY	FREESTANDING	MAGNILOQUENT	MALFORMATION	UNMISTAKABLE
TRANSMIGRATE	MICROCIRCUIT	GREATHEARTED	NIGHTCLOTHES	MALNOURISHED	ANNUNCIATION
TRANSMISSION	MICROCLIMATE	HIERARCHICAL	ORGANIZATION	MALNUTRITION	CANTANKEROUS
TRANSMOGRIFY	MICROSPACING	HIEROGLYPHIC	PIGMENTATION	MALOCCLUSION	CINEMATHEQUE
TRANSOCEANIC	MICROSURGERY	INEFFACEABLE	REGISTRATION	MULLIGATAWNY	CONCELEBRANT
TRANSPACIFIC	OSCILLOSCOPE	INEXPERIENCE	SIGNIFICANCE	MULTICOLORED	CONCRESCENCE
TRANSVESTISM	PACKINGHOUSE	INEXPLICABLE	UNGOVERNABLE	MULTIFACETED	CONFECTIONER
TRAPSHOOTING	PICKERELWEED	INEXTRICABLE	ECHOLOCATION	MULTIFARIOUS	CONFESSIONAL
UNACCUSTOMED	RECALCITRANT	MEETINGHOUSE	OTHERWORLDLY	MULTILATERAL	CONFIDENTIAL
UNASSAILABLE	RECAPITULATE	OCEANOGRAPHY	REHABILITATE	MULTILINGUAL	CONFIRMATION
WEATHERBOARD	RECEIVERSHIP	OVEREXPOSURE	SCHOOLFELLOW	MULTIPLICAND	CONFORMATION
WEATHERGLASS	RECEPTIONIST	PREAMPLIFIER	SCHOOLMASTER	MULTIPLICITY	CONFUCIANISM
WEATHERPROOF	RECOGNIZANCE	PRECANCEROUS	AVITAMINOSIS	MULTIPURPOSE	CONGLOMERATE
ABBREVIATION	RECOLLECTION	PRECIPITANCY	BRILLIANTINE	MULTISESSION	CONGRATULATE
AMBIDEXTROUS	RECONSTITUTE	PRECONCERTED	CHILDBEARING	MULTITASKING	CONGREGATION
BIBLIOGRAPHY	SECRETARIATE	PRECONDITION	CHIROPRACTIC	MULTIVERSITY	CONQUISTADOR
CABINETMAKER	TECHNICALITY	PREDESIGNATE	CHITTERLINGS	MULTIVITAMIN	CONSERVATION
FIBRILLATION	UNCHARITABLE	PREDETERMINE	EDITORIALIZE	PALEONTOLOGY	CONSERVATISM
GOBBLEDYGOOK	VACATIONLAND	PREDIGESTION	EPISCOPALIAN	POLARIZATION	CONSERVATIVE
HABERDASHERY	AUDIOVISUALS	PREDILECTION	EPITHALAMIUM	POLICYHOLDER	CONSERVATORY
SUBCOMMITTEE	HYDROTHERAPY	PREFABRICATE	FAINTHEARTED	POLYETHYLENE	CONSIDERABLE
SUBCONSCIOUS	HYDROTHERMAL	PREINDUCTION	HAIRSPLITTER	POLYMORPHISM	CONSTABULARY

CONSTIPATION	CLOTHESHORSE	UNPARALLELED	ABSENTMINDED	UNSEGREGATED	COUNTERPOISE
CONSTITUENCY	CLOTHESPRESS	UNPRINCIPLED	AUSTRONESIAN	AFTERTHOUGHT	COUNTERTENOR
CONSTITUTION	CROSSCURRENT	UNPROFITABLE	COSMOPOLITAN	ANTEDILUVIAN	EQUESTRIENNE
CONSTITUTIVE	FRONTISPIECE	ACQUAINTANCE	DESPOLIATION	ANTHROPOLOGY	FLUORESCENCE
CONSTRUCTION	GEOCHEMISTRY	AERODYNAMICS	DESTRUCTIBLE	ANTIALIASING	FLUOROCARBON
CONTAINERIZE	GLOCKENSPIEL	CARBOHYDRATE	DISACCHARIDE	ANTIELECTRON	FOUNTAINHEAD
CONTEMPORARY	ISOLATIONISM	CARBONACEOUS	DISADVANTAGE	ANTIMACASSAR	HOUSEWARMING
CONTEMPTIBLE	ONOMATOPOEIA	CARILLONNEUR	DISAGREEABLE	ANTIMAGNETIC	MOUNTAINSIDE
CONTEMPTUOUS	PHOTOCOMPOSE	CARPETBAGGER	DISASSOCIATE	ANTIPARTICLE	NEURASTHENIA
CONTERMINOUS	PHOTOENGRAVE	CHRISTIANITY	DISCIPLINARY	ANTITHETICAL	NEUROSCIENCE
CONTINUATION	PHOTOGRAVURE	CHRISTIANIZE	DISCONNECTED	ASTRONAUTICS	SHUFFLEBOARD
CONTRAPUNTAL	PROCATHEDRAL	CHROMATICITY	DISCONSOLATE	ASTRONOMICAL	THUNDERCLOUD
CONTRARIWISE	PROCESSIONAL	CHROMOSPHERE	DISCOURTEOUS	ASTROPHYSICS	THUNDERSTORM
CONTUMACIOUS	PROFESSIONAL	CIRCUMSCRIBE	DISCRIMINATE	ATTITUDINIZE	ADVENTITIOUS
CONTUMELIOUS	PROGRAMMABLE	CIRCUMSTANCE	DISESTABLISH	AUTHENTICATE	CIVILIZATION
CONVENTIONAL	PROLEGOMENON	CORESPONDENT	DISFRANCHISE	BUTTERSCOTCH	INVERTEBRATE
CONVERSATION	PROPAGANDIZE	EARSPLITTING	DISINGENUOUS	DETERMINABLE	INVITATIONAL
DENOMINATION	PROPHYLACTIC	EARTHSHAKING	DISINTEGRATE	ENTERPRISING	INVULNERABLE
DENSITOMETER	PROPORTIONAL	FERMENTATION	DISOBEDIENCE	ENTREPRENEUR	NEVERTHELESS
DENUNCIATION	PROTACTINIUM	FORMALDEHYDE	DISPENSATION	EXTORTIONATE	NEWSMAGAZINE
FENESTRATION	PROTECTORATE	HORTICULTURE	DISPLACEMENT	EXTRAMARITAL	NEWSPAPERMAN
HANDKERCHIEF	PROTHALAMION	IRREDEEMABLE	DISPUTATIOUS	EXTRASENSORY	LEXICOGRAPHY
HENCEFORWARD	PROTUBERANCE	IRREFRAGABLE	DISQUISITION	EXTRAVAGANZA	SEXAGENARIAN
KINDERGARTEN	PROVIDENTIAL	IRREMEDIABLE	DISREPUTABLE	HETEROSEXUAL	ASYNCHRONOUS
LONGITUDINAL	RHODODENDRON	IRRESISTIBLE	DISSERTATION	INTELLECTUAL	CRYPTOGRAPHY
LONGSHOREMAN	SHORTSIGHTED	IRRESPECTIVE	DISTILLATION	INTELLIGENCE	OXYACETYLENE
LUNCHEONETTE	SPORTSWRITER	IRREVERSIBLE	DISTRIBUTIVE	INTELLIGIBLE	PHYSIOGRAPHY
MANSLAUGHTER	THOROUGHBRED	JURISDICTION	HYSTERECTOMY	INTEMPERANCE	PSYCHOACTIVE
MENSTRUATION	THOROUGHFARE	MARLINESPIKE	INSALUBRIOUS	INTERCESSION	PSYCHOSEXUAL
MINICOMPUTER	TROUBLEMAKER	MERCHANTABLE	INSTRUMENTAL	INTERFERENCE	PSYCHOTROPIC
MONOFILAMENT	WHOLEHEARTED	MERETRICIOUS	INSUFFERABLE	INTERGLACIAL	
MONOSYLLABLE	ZOOGEOGRAPHY	PARADISIACAL	INSUFFICIENT	INTERJECTION	
MUNICIPALITY	ALPHANUMERIC	PARAMILITARY	INSURRECTION	INTERLOCUTOR	

NONAGENARIAN	AMPHITHEATER	PARASITOLOGY	MASTERSTROKE	INTERMEDIARY	
NONCOMBATANT	APPENDECTOMY	PARENTHESIZE	MASTURBATION	INTERMEDIATE	
NONCOMMITTAL	APPENDICITIS	PERADVENTURE	MESSEIGNEURS	INTERMINABLE	BREAKTHROUGH
NONCONDUCTOR	APPRECIATIVE	PERAMBULATOR	MISADVENTURE	INTERMISSION	BREASTSTROKE
NONOBJECTIVE	APPREHENSIVE	PERICYNTHION	MISAPPREHEND	INTERMITTENT	BREATHTAKING
NONSCHEDULED	APPURTENANCE	PERSPICACITY	MISCALCULATE	INTERSECTION	DECALCOMANIA
PANCHROMATIC	HIPPOPOTAMUS	PERTINACIOUS	MISINTERPRET	INTERSTELLAR	DECASYLLABIC
PENITENTIARY	HYPERACIDITY	PORCELAINIZE	MISPRONOUNCE	INTERVOCALIC	DISACCHARIDE
RENUNCIATION	HYPERTENSION	PYROTECHNICS	MISREPRESENT	INTRANSIGENT	DISADVANTAGE
SENSITOMETER	HYPOCHONDRIA	SARSAPARILLA	OBSCURANTISM	INTRANSITIVE	DISAGREEABLE
TENDEROMETER	HYPOGLYCEMIA	STRAIGHTAWAY	OBSTREPEROUS	METALANGUAGE	DISASSOCIATE
VENIPUNCTURE	IMPENETRABLE	STRAIGHTEDGE	PESTILENTIAL	METAMORPHISM	GREATHEARTED
ABOLITIONISM	IMPERCEPTIVE	STRAITJACKET	POSTDOCTORAL	OCTOGENARIAN	HUMANITARIAN
AFORETHOUGHT	IMPERCIPIENT	STRATIGRAPHY	POSTGRADUATE	OCTOSYLLABIC	INCALCULABLE
APOSTROPHIZE	IMPERFECTION	STRATOSPHERE	POSTHYPNOTIC	OUTSTRETCHED	INCANDESCENT
BIOCHEMISTRY	IMPERISHABLE	STREETWALKER	POSTMISTRESS	SATISFACTION	INCAPACITATE
BIOGEOGRAPHY	IMPONDERABLE	STREPTOMYCIN	RESPECTIVELY	SATISFACTORY	INSALUBRIOUS
BIOSATELLITE	REPERCUSSION	SURROUNDINGS	RESTAURATEUR	TOTALITARIAN	METALANGUAGE
BIOTELEMETRY	SUPERANNUATE	SURVEILLANCE	RESURRECTION	ULTRAMONTANE	METAMORPHISM
BLOCKBUSTING	SUPERCHARGER	TERCENTENARY	TESTOSTERONE	VETERINARIAN	MISADVENTURE
BLOODLETTING	SUPERCILIOUS	UNREASONABLE	UNSCIENTIFIC	BLUESTOCKING	MISAPPREHEND
BLOODTHIRSTY	SUPERHIGHWAY	UNREGENERATE	UNSCRUPULOUS	CHURCHWARDEN	NONAGENARIAN
CHOREOGRAPHY	SUPERNATURAL	UNRESTRAINED	UNSEARCHABLE	COUNTERCLAIM	OCEANOGRAPHY
CLOSEMOUTHED	SUPERSTITION	VERTICILLATE	UNSEASONABLE	COUNTERPOINT	ORGANIZATION

OXYACETYLENE	PRECIPITANCY	HYPERTENSION	TUBERCULOSIS	ANTITHETICAL	COLLEGIALITY
PARADISIACAL	PRECONCERTED	ILLEGITIMATE	UNBELIEVABLE	ARGILLACEOUS	ECCLESIASTIC
PARAMILITARY	PRECONDITION	IMMEASURABLE	UNDERCLOTHES	ATTITUDINIZE	HALLUCINOGEN
PARASITOLOGY	PROCATHEDRAL	IMPENETRABLE	UNDERCOATING	AUDIOVISUALS	HELLGRAMMITE
PERADVENTURE	PROCESSIONAL	IMPERCEPTIVE	UNDERCURRENT	BRAINWASHING	INFLAMMATION
PERAMBULATOR	PSYCHOACTIVE	IMPERCIPIENT	UNDERDRAWERS	CABINETMAKER	INFLAMMATORY
POLARIZATION	PSYCHOSEXUAL	IMPERFECTION	UNDERGARMENT	CALISTHENICS	INFLATIONARY
PREAMPLIFIER	PSYCHOTROPIC	IMPERISHABLE	UNDERPINNING	CARILLONNEUR	INFLATIONISM
RECALCITRANT	SPECTROGRAPH	INDECLINABLE	UNDERSURFACE	CHRISTIANITY	ISOLATIONISM
RECAPITULATE	SPECTROMETER	INDEFEASIBLE	UNREASONABLE	CHRISTIANIZE	MARLINESPIKE
REHABILITATE	SPECTROSCOPE	INDEPENDENCE	UNREGENERATE	CIVILIZATION	MEALYMOUTHED
RELATIONSHIP	SUBCOMMITTEE	INFELICITOUS	UNRESTRAINED	DELIBERATIVE	MULLIGATAWNY
RELATIVISTIC	SUBCONSCIOUS	INTELLECTUAL	UNSEARCHABLE	DELICATESSEN	PHILANTHROPY
SEXAGENARIAN	SUBCONTINENT	INTELLIGENCE	UNSEASONABLE	DEMILITARIZE	PHILHARMONIC
STRAIGHTAWAY	SUBCUTANEOUS	INTELLIGIBLE	UNSEGREGATED	DEMIMONDAINE	PHILODENDRON
STRAIGHTEDGE	TERCENTENARY	INTEMPERANCE	VALENCIENNES	DEMINERALIZE	PHILOSOPHIZE
STRAITJACKET	UNACCUSTOMED	INTERCESSION	VETERINARIAN	DISINGENUOUS	PROLEGOMENON
STRATIGRAPHY	UNSCIENTIFIC	INTERFERENCE	CONFECTIONER	DISINTEGRATE	WHOLEHEARTED
STRATOSPHERE	UNSCRUPULOUS	INTERGLACIAL	CONFESSIONAL	HELIOCENTRIC	CHAMPIONSHIP
TOTALITARIAN	HANDKERCHIEF	INTERJECTION	CONFIDENTIAL	INDIGESTIBLE	CHEMOTHERAPY
UNPARALLELED	HEADMISTRESS	INTERLOCUTOR	CONFIRMATION	INDISPUTABLE	COMMENCEMENT
VACATIONLAND	HEADQUARTERS	INTERMEDIARY	CONFORMATION	INDISSOLUBLE	COMMENSURATE
CARBOHYDRATE	KINDERGARTEN	INTERMEDIATE	CONFUCIANISM	INVITATIONAL	COMMISSARIAT
CARBONACEOUS	MIDDLEWEIGHT	INTERMINABLE	DIFFERENTIAL	JURISDICTION	COMMISSIONER
FEEBLEMINDED	MUDDLEHEADED	INTERMISSION	DISFRANCHISE	LEXICOGRAPHY	COMMONWEALTH
GOBBLEDYGOOK	PREDESIGNATE	INTERMITTENT	INEFFACEABLE	LUMINESCENCE	COMMUNICABLE
RAMBUNCTIOUS	PREDETERMINE	INTERSECTION	MALFORMATION	MINICOMPUTER	COSMOPOLITAN
BIOCHEMISTRY	PREDIGESTION	INTERSTELLAR	PREFABRICATE	MISINTERPRET	FERMENTATION
BLOCKBUSTING	PREDILECTION	INTERVOCALIC	PROFESSIONAL	MUNICIPALITY	FLAMETHROWER
CHECKERBERRY	RHODODENDRON	INVERTEBRATE	SHUFFLEBOARD	OFFICEHOLDER	FORMALDEHYDE
CHECKERBOARD	SLEDGEHAMMER	IRREDEEMABLE	BIOGEOGRAPHY	OSCILLOSCOPE	ONOMATOPOEIA
CIRCUMSCRIBE	SUBDIRECTORY	IRREFRAGABLE	CONGLOMERATE	PENITENTIARY	PIGMENTATION
CIRCUMSTANCE	TENDEROMETER	IRREMEDIABLE	CONGRATULATE	PERICYNTHION	PREMENSTRUAL
CONCELEBRANT	TRADESPEOPLE	IRRESISTIBLE	CONGREGATION	POLICYHOLDER	PRIMOGENITOR
CONCRESCENCE	ABSENTMINDED	IRRESPECTIVE	LONGITUDINAL	PREINDUCTION	SUBMINIATURE
DISCIPLINARY	ADVENTITIOUS	IRREVERSIBLE	LONGSHOREMAN	RADIOISOTOPE	UNEMPLOYMENT
DISCONNECTED	AFTERTHOUGHT	KALEIDOSCOPE	NEIGHBORHOOD	RADIOTHERAPY	ASYNCHRONOUS
DISCONSOLATE	ANTEDILUVIAN	MADEMOISELLE	PROGRAMMABLE	REGISTRATION	BLANDISHMENT
DISCOURTEOUS	APPENDECTOMY	MERETRICIOUS	TRIGNOMETRIC	REMINISCENCE	COUNTERCLAIM
DISCRIMINATE	APPENDICITIS	NEVERTHELESS	TRIGONOMETRY	SATISFACTION	COUNTERPOINT
ELECTROLYSIS	BICENTENNIAL	NOMENCLATURE	ZOOGEOGRAPHY	SATISFACTORY	COUNTERPOISE
ELECTROPLATE	BLUESTOCKING	OTHERWORLDLY	ALPHANUMERIC	UNLIKELIHOOD	COUNTERTENOR
GEOCHEMISTRY	CHEESEBURGER	PALEONTOLOGY	AMPHITHEATER	UNMISTAKABLE	FAINTHEARTED
GLOCKENSPIEL	CHEESEPARING	PARENTHESIZE	ANTHROPOLOGY	VENIPUNCTURE	FOUNTAINHEAD
HENCEFORWARD	CINEMATHEQUE	RECEIVERSHIP	ARCHITECTURE	BACKTRACKING	FRANKENSTEIN
LUNCHEONETTE	CORESPONDENT	RECEPTIONIST	AUTHENTICATE	PACKINGHOUSE	FRANKINCENSE
MERCHANTABLE	DETERMINABLE	REPERCUSSION	LIGHTHEARTED	PICKERELWEED	FRONTISPIECE
MISCALCULATE	DISESTABLISH	SELENOGRAPHY	NIGHTCLOTHES	ABOLITIONISM	MAGNETOMETER
NONCOMBATANT	ELEEMOSYNARY	STEEPLECHASE	TECHNICALITY	BELLIGERENCY	MAGNILOQUENT
NONCOMMITTAL	ENCEPHALITIS	STREETWALKER	UNCHARITABLE	BIBLIOGRAPHY	MALNOURISHED
NONCONDUCTOR	ENTERPRISING	STREPTOMYCIN	ALLITERATION	BILLINGSGATE	MALNUTRITION
OBSCURANTISM	EQUESTRIENNE	SUPERANNUATE	AMBIDEXTROUS	BRILLIANTINE	MOUNTAINSIDE
PANCHROMATIC	FENESTRATION	SUPERCHARGER	ANTIALIASING	CHALCOPYRITE	PLANETESIMAL
PEACEKEEPING	FREESTANDING	SUPERCILIOUS	ANTIELECTRON	CHILDBEARING	PRINCIPALITY
PORCELAINIZE	HABERDASHERY	SUPERHIGHWAY	ANTIMACASSAR	COELENTERATE	QUANTITATIVE
PRACTITIONER	HETEROSEXUAL	SUPERNATURAL	ANTIMAGNETIC	COLLECTIVISM	QUINTESSENCE
PRECANCEROUS	HYPERACIDITY	SUPERSTITION	ANTIPARTICLE	COLLECTIVIZE	SCANDINAVIAN

SIGNIFICANCE	UNGOVERNABLE	MICROBIOLOGY	NEWSPAPERMAN	MULTIFARIOUS	UNIVERSALITY
SOMNAMBULISM	VALORIZATION	MICROCIRCUIT	NONSCHEDULED	MULTILATERAL	UNIVERSALIZE
THANKSGIVING	CARPETBAGGER	MICROCLIMATE	OUTSTRETCHED	MULTILINGUAL	INEXPERIENCE
THUNDERCLOUD	COMPANIONWAY	MICROSPACING	PERSPICACITY	MULTIPLICAND	INEXPLICABLE
THUNDERSTORM	COMPLAISANCE	MICROSURGERY	PHYSIOGRAPHY	MULTIPLICITY	INEXTRICABLE
TRANQUILIZER	CRYPTOGRAPHY	MISREPRESENT	PLASTERBOARD	MULTIPURPOSE	ENCYCLOPEDIA
TRANSCENDENT	DESPOLIATION	NEURASTHENIA	PRASEODYMIUM	MULTISESSION	POLYETHYLENE
TRANSFERENCE	DISPENSATION	NEUROSCIENCE	PRESBYTERIAN	MULTITASKING	POLYMORPHISM
TRANSMIGRATE	DISPLACEMENT	OVEREXPOSURE	PRESCRIPTION	MULTIVERSITY	POLYSYLLABIC
TRANSMISSION	DISPUTATIOUS	PHARMACOLOGY	PRESENTIMENT	MULTIVITAMIN	POLYSYLLABLE
TRANSMOGRIFY	HIPPOPOTAMUS	PREREQUISITE	PRESUMPTUOUS	OBSTREPEROUS	
TRANSOCEANIC	MISPRONOUNCE	QUARTERSTAFF	QUESTIONABLE	PERTINACIOUS	
TRANSPACIFIC	PREPAREDNESS	SECRETARIATE	SARSAPARILLA	PESTILENTIAL	
TRANSVESTISM	PREPONDERATE	SHARECROPPER	SENSITOMETER	PHOTOCOMPOSE	**5TH LETTER**
UNINTERESTED	PREPOSTEROUS	SHARPSHOOTER	SUBSCRIPTION	PHOTOENGRAVE	
VAINGLORIOUS	PROPAGANDIZE	SHORTSIGHTED	SUBSERVIENCE	PHOTOGRAVURE	ACQUAINTANCE
ACCOMPLISHED	PROPHYLACTIC	SPERMATOZOON	SUBSTANTIATE	POSTDOCTORAL	ALPHANUMERIC
AERODYNAMICS	PROPORTIONAL	SPIRITUALISM	SUBSTRUCTURE	POSTGRADUATE	ANTIALIASING
ATMOSPHERICS	PUMPERNICKEL	SPORTSWRITER	SWASHBUCKLER	POSTHYPNOTIC	AVITAMINOSIS
BLOODLETTING	RESPECTIVELY	STEREOPHONIC	UNASSAILABLE	POSTMISTRESS	BIOSATELLITE
BLOODTHIRSTY	STEPDAUGHTER	STEREOSCOPIC	ANATHEMATIZE	PROTACTINIUM	CANTANKEROUS
CHROMATICITY	TRAPSHOOTING	SURROUNDINGS	AUSTRONESIAN	PROTECTORATE	CHARACTERIZE
CHROMOSPHERE	WHIPPOORWILL	THERAPEUTICS	AVITAMINOSIS	PROTHALAMION	COMPANIONWAY
DECOMMISSION	CONQUISTADOR	THERMOSPHERE	BACTERICIDAL	PROTUBERANCE	CONTAINERIZE
DECONGESTANT	DISQUISITION	THOROUGHBRED	BACTERIOLOGY	RESTAURATEUR	DICTATORSHIP
DEMONSTRABLE	ABBREVIATION	THOROUGHFARE	BIOTELEMETRY	SCATOLOGICAL	EXTRAMARITAL
DENOMINATION	AFORETHOUGHT	ULTRAMONTANE	BLATHERSKITE	SUBTERRANEAN	EXTRASENSORY
DISOBEDIENCE	APPRECIATIVE	UNFREQUENTED	BUTTERSCOTCH	TESTOSTERONE	EXTRAVAGANZA
ECHOLOCATION	APPREHENSIVE	UNPRINCIPLED	CANTANKEROUS	VERTICILLATE	FORMALDEHYDE
EXTORTIONATE	ASTRONAUTICS	UNPROFITABLE	CHITTERLINGS	WEATHERBOARD	GALVANOMETER
FLUORESCENCE	ASTRONOMICAL	APOSTROPHIZE	CLOTHESHORSE	WEATHERGLASS	HIERARCHICAL
FLUOROCARBON	ASTROPHYSICS	BIOSATELLITE	CLOTHESPRESS	WEATHERPROOF	IMMEASURABLE
HYPOCHONDRIA	CHARACTERIZE	CHESTERFIELD	CONTAINERIZE	WELTERWEIGHT	INFLAMMATION
HYPOGLYCEMIA	CHIROPRACTIC	CLOSEMOUTHED	CONTEMPORARY	ACQUAINTANCE	INFLAMMATORY
IDIOSYNCRASY	CHOREOGRAPHY	CONSERVATION	CONTEMPTIBLE	ANNUNCIATION	INFLATIONARY
IMPONDERABLE	CHURCHWARDEN	CONSERVATISM	CONTEMPTUOUS	APPURTENANCE	INFLATIONISM
INCOMPARABLE	DISREPUTABLE	CONSERVATIVE	CONTERMINOUS	CUMULONIMBUS	INGRATIATING
INCOMPATIBLE	ENTREPRENEUR	CONSERVATORY	CONTINUATION	DENUNCIATION	INTRANSIGENT
INCONSOLABLE	EVERBLOOMING	CONSIDERABLE	CONTRAPUNTAL	ILLUSTRATION	INTRANSITIVE
INCONVENIENT	EXCRUCIATING	CONSTABULARY	CONTRARIWISE	ILLUSTRATIVE	ISOLATIONISM
INCORRIGIBLE	EXTRAMARITAL	CONSTIPATION	CONTUMACIOUS	INSUFFERABLE	MISCALCULATE
INDOCTRINATE	EXTRASENSORY	CONSTITUENCY	CONTUMELIOUS	INSUFFICIENT	NEURASTHENIA
MALOCCLUSION	EXTRAVAGANZA	CONSTITUTION	DESTRUCTIBLE	INSURRECTION	ONOMATOPOEIA
MONOFILAMENT	FIBRILLATION	CONSTITUTIVE	DICTATORSHIP	INVULNERABLE	PHILANTHROPY
MONOSYLLABLE	HAIRSPLITTER	CONSTRUCTION	DISTILLATION	REMUNERATION	PRECANCEROUS
NONOBJECTIVE	HEARTRENDING	CROSSCURRENT	DISTRIBUTIVE	REMUNERATIVE	PREFABRICATE
OCTOGENARIAN	HEARTSTRINGS	DENSITOMETER	EARTHSHAKING	RENUNCIATION	PREPAREDNESS
OCTOSYLLABIC	HEARTWARMING	DIASTROPHISM	EDITORIALIZE	RESURRECTION	PROCATHEDRAL
PREOPERATIVE	HIERARCHICAL	DISSERTATION	EPITHALAMIUM	SIMULTANEOUS	PROPAGANDIZE
PYROTECHNICS	HIEROGLYPHIC	EARSPLITTING	HORTICULTURE	TROUBLEMAKER	PROTACTINIUM
RECOGNIZANCE	HYDROTHERAPY	EPISCOPALIAN	HYSTERECTOMY	CONVENTIONAL	RESTAURATEUR
RECOLLECTION	HYDROTHERMAL	GLASSBLOWING	INSTRUMENTAL	CONVERSATION	SARSAPARILLA
RECONSTITUTE	INARTICULATE	HOUSEWARMING	MASTERSTROKE	GALVANOMETER	SOMNAMBULISM
REMONSTRANCE	INCRUSTATION	MANSLAUGHTER	MASTURBATION	HEAVYHEARTED	THERAPEUTICS
SCHOOLFELLOW	INGRATIATING	MENSTRUATION	MEETINGHOUSE	PROVIDENTIAL	ULTRAMONTANE
SCHOOLMASTER	INTRANSIGENT	MESSEIGNEURS	MULTICOLORED	SURVEILLANCE	UNCHARITABLE
UNDOCUMENTED	INTRANSITIVE	NEWSMAGAZINE	MULTIFACETED	UNIVERSALIST	UNREASONABLE

UNSEARCHABLE	BACTERIOLOGY	PROLEGOMENON	PROPHYLACTIC	STRAIGHTEDGE	HEADMISTRESS
UNSEASONABLE	BIOGEOGRAPHY	PROTECTORATE	PROTHALAMION	STRAITJACKET	INCOMPARABLE
DELIBERATIVE	BIOTELEMETRY	PUMPERNICKEL	PSYCHOACTIVE	SUBDIRECTORY	INCOMPATIBLE
DISOBEDIENCE	BUTTERSCOTCH	RESPECTIVELY	PSYCHOSEXUAL	SUBMINIATURE	INTEMPERANCE
EVERBLOOMING	CARPETBAGGER	SECRETARIATE	PSYCHOTROPIC	UNPRINCIPLED	IRREMEDIABLE
NONOBJECTIVE	CHOREOGRAPHY	SHARECROPPER	SWASHBUCKLER	UNSCIENTIFIC	MADEMOISELLE
PRESBYTERIAN	CLOSEMOUTHED	STEREOPHONIC	WEATHERBOARD	VERTICILLATE	METAMORPHISM
REHABILITATE	COELENTERATE	STEREOSCOPIC	WEATHERGLASS	BLOCKBUSTING	NEWSMAGAZINE
TROUBLEMAKER	COLLECTIVISM	STREETWALKER	WEATHERPROOF	BREAKTHROUGH	PARAMILITARY
ASYNCHRONOUS	COLLECTIVIZE	SUBSERVIENCE	ABOLITIONISM	CHECKERBERRY	PERAMBULATOR
CHALCOPYRITE	COLLEGIALITY	SUBTERRANEAN	AMPHITHEATER	CHECKERBOARD	PHARMACOLOGY
CHURCHWARDEN	COMMENCEMENT	SURVEILLANCE	ARCHITECTURE	FRANKENSTEIN	POLYMORPHISM
DELICATESSEN	COMMENSURATE	TENDEROMETER	BELLIGERENCY	FRANKINCENSE	POSTMISTRESS
DISACCHARIDE	CONCELEBRANT	TERCENTENARY	BIBLIOGRAPHY	GLOCKENSPIEL	PREAMPLIFIER
ENCYCLOPEDIA	CONFECTIONER	TRADESPEOPLE	BILLINGSGATE	HANDKERCHIEF	SPERMATOZOON
EPISCOPALIAN	CONFESSIONAL	UNFREQUENTED	COMMISSARIAT	THANKSGIVING	THERMOSPHERE
HYPOCHONDRIA	CONSERVATION	UNIVERSALIST	COMMISSIONER	UNLIKELIHOOD	ABSENTMINDED
INDECLINABLE	CONSERVATISM	UNIVERSALITY	CONFIDENTIAL	ARGILLACEOUS	ADVENTITIOUS
INDOCTRINATE	CONSERVATIVE	UNIVERSALIZE	CONFIRMATION	BRILLIANTINE	ANNUNCIATION
LEXICOGRAPHY	CONSERVATORY	WELTERWEIGHT	CONSIDERABLE	CARILLONNEUR	APPENDECTOMY
MALOCCLUSION	CONTEMPORARY	WHOLEHEARTED	CONTINUATION	CIVILIZATION	APPENDICITIS
MINICOMPUTER	CONTEMPTIBLE	ZOOGEOGRAPHY	DENSITOMETER	COMPLAISANCE	BICENTENNIAL
MUNICIPALITY	CONTEMPTUOUS	INDEFEASIBLE	DISCIPLINARY	CONGLOMERATE	BRAINWASHING
NONSCHEDULED	CONTERMINOUS	INEFFACEABLE	DISTILLATION	CUMULONIMBUS	CABINETMAKER
OFFICEHOLDER	CONVENTIONAL	INSUFFERABLE	FIBRILLATION	DECALCOMANIA	DECONGESTANT
OXYACETYLENE	CONVERSATION	INSUFFICIENT	HORTICULTURE	DEMILITARIZE	DEMINERALIZE
PERICYNTHION	DIFFERENTIAL	IRREFRAGABLE	KALEIDOSCOPE	DISPLACEMENT	DEMONSTRABLE
POLICYHOLDER	DISPENSATION	MONOFILAMENT	LONGITUDINAL	ECHOLOCATION	DENUNCIATION
PRESCRIPTION	DISREPUTABLE	SHUFFLEBOARD	MAGNILOQUENT	FEEBLEMINDED	DISINGENUOUS
PRINCIPALITY	DISSERTATION	DISAGREEABLE	MARLINESPIKE	GOBBLEDYGOOK	DISINTEGRATE
SUBSCRIPTION	ECCLESIASTIC	HELLGRAMMITE	MEETINGHOUSE	INCALCULABLE	HUMANITARIAN
UNACCUSTOMED	ENTREPRENEUR	HYPOGLYCEMIA	MULLIGATAWNY	INFELICITOUS	IMPENETRABLE
UNDOCUMENTED	FERMENTATION	ILLEGITIMATE	MULTICOLORED	INSALUBRIOUS	IMPONDERABLE
AERODYNAMICS	FLAMETHROWER	INDIGESTIBLE	MULTIFACETED	INTELLECTUAL	INCANDESCENT
AMBIDEXTROUS	HENCEFORWARD	NONAGENARIAN	MULTIFARIOUS	INTELLIGENCE	INCONSOLABLE
ANTEDILUVIAN	HOUSEWARMING	OCTOGENARIAN	MULTILATERAL	INTELLIGIBLE	INCONVENIENT
BLANDISHMENT	HYSTERECTOMY	POSTGRADUATE	MULTILINGUAL	INVULNERABLE	LUMINESCENCE
BLOODLETTING	KINDERGARTEN	RECOGNIZANCE	MULTIPLICAND	MANSLAUGHTER	MISINTERPRET
BLOODTHIRSTY	MAGNETOMETER	SEXAGENARIAN	MULTIPLICITY	METALANGUAGE	NOMENCLATURE
CHILDBEARING	MASTERSTROKE	SLEDGEHAMMER	MULTIPURPOSE	MIDDLEWEIGHT	OCEANOGRAPHY
DISADVANTAGE	MESSEIGNEURS	UNREGENERATE	MULTISESSION	MUDDLEHEADED	ORGANIZATION
IRREDEEMABLE	MISREPRESENT	UNSEGREGATED	MULTITASKING	OSCILLOSCOPE	PARENTHESIZE
MISADVENTURE	OVEREXPOSURE	VAINGLORIOUS	MULTIVERSITY	RECALCITRANT	PREINDUCTION
PARADISIACAL	PEACEKEEPING	ANATHEMATIZE	MULTIVITAMIN	RECOLLECTION	RECONSTITUTE
PERADVENTURE	PICKERELWEED	BIOCHEMISTRY	PACKINGHOUSE	SIMULTANEOUS	REMINISCENCE
POSTDOCTORAL	PIGMENTATION	BLATHERSKITE	PERTINACIOUS	TOTALITARIAN	REMONSTRANCE
SCANDINAVIAN	PLANETESIMAL	CLOTHESHORSE	PESTILENTIAL	UNBELIEVABLE	REMUNERATION
STEPDAUGHTER	POLYETHYLENE	CLOTHESPRESS	PHYSIOGRAPHY	ACCOMPLISHED	REMUNERATIVE
THUNDERCLOUD	PORCELAINIZE	EARTHSHAKING	PRECIPITANCY	ANTIMACASSAR	RENUNCIATION
THUNDERSTORM	PRASEODYMIUM	EPITHALAMIUM	PREDIGESTION	ANTIMAGNETIC	SELENOGRAPHY
ABBREVIATION	PREDESIGNATE	GEOCHEMISTRY	PREDILECTION	CHROMATICITY	TECHNICALITY
AFORETHOUGHT	PREDETERMINE	LUNCHEONETTE	PROVIDENTIAL	CHROMOSPHERE	TRIGNOMETRIC
ANTIELECTRON	PREMENSTRUAL	MERCHANTABLE	RECEIVERSHIP	CINEMATHEQUE	VALENCIENNES
APPRECIATIVE	PREREQUISITE	NEIGHBORHOOD	SENSITOMETER	DECOMMISSION	ASTRONAUTICS
APPREHENSIVE	PRESENTIMENT	PANCHROMATIC	SIGNIFICANCE	DEMIMONDAINE	ASTRONOMICAL
AUTHENTICATE	PROCESSIONAL	PHILHARMONIC	SPIRITUALISM	DENOMINATION	ASTROPHYSICS
BACTERICIDAL	PROFESSIONAL	POSTHYPNOTIC	STRAIGHTAWAY	ELEEMOSYNARY	AUDIOVISUALS

CARBOHYDRATE	EARSPLITTING	INTERMISSION	JURISDICTION	MOUNTAINSIDE	COMPLAISANCE
CARBONACEOUS	ENCEPHALITIS	INTERMITTENT	LONGSHOREMAN	NIGHTCLOTHES	CONGRATULATE
CHEMOTHERAPY	INCAPACITATE	INTERSECTION	MONOSYLLABLE	OUTSTRETCHED	CONSTABULARY
CHIROPRACTIC	INDEPENDENCE	INTERSTELLAR	OCTOSYLLABIC	PENITENTIARY	CONTRAPUNTAL
COMMONWEALTH	INEXPERIENCE	INTERVOCALIC	PARASITOLOGY	PLASTERBOARD	CONTRARIWISE
CONFORMATION	INEXPLICABLE	INVERTEBRATE	POLYSYLLABIC	PRACTITIONER	DELICATESSEN
COSMOPOLITAN	MISAPPREHEND	MISPRONOUNCE	POLYSYLLABLE	PYROTECHNICS	DISFRANCHISE
DESPOLIATION	NEWSPAPERMAN	NEVERTHELESS	REGISTRATION	QUANTITATIVE	DISPLACEMENT
DISCONNECTED	PERSPICACITY	OBSTREPEROUS	SATISFACTION	QUARTERSTAFF	EPITHALAMIUM
DISCONSOLATE	PREOPERATIVE	OTHERWORLDLY	SATISFACTORY	QUESTIONABLE	FOUNTAINHEAD
DISCOURTEOUS	RECAPITULATE	POLARIZATION	TRANSCENDENT	QUINTESSENCE	HYPERACIDITY
EDITORIALIZE	RECEPTIONIST	PROGRAMMABLE	TRANSFERENCE	RELATIONSHIP	INCAPACITATE
HELIOCENTRIC	SHARPSHOOTER	REPERCUSSION	TRANSMIGRATE	RELATIVISTIC	INEFFACEABLE
HIEROGLYPHIC	STEEPLECHASE	RESURRECTION	TRANSMISSION	SHORTSIGHTED	INVITATIONAL
HIPPOPOTAMUS	STREPTOMYCIN	SUPERANNUATE	TRANSMOGRIFY	SPECTROGRAPH	MANSLAUGHTER
HYDROTHERAPY	UNEMPLOYMENT	SUPERCHARGER	TRANSOCEANIC	SPECTROMETER	MERCHANTABLE
HYDROTHERMAL	VENIPUNCTURE	SUPERCILIOUS	TRANSPACIFIC	SPECTROSCOPE	METALANGUAGE
MALFORMATION	WHIPPOORWILL	SUPERHIGHWAY	TRANSVESTISM	SPORTSWRITER	MOUNTAINSIDE
MALNOURISHED	HEADQUARTERS	SUPERNATURAL	TRAPSHOOTING	STRATIGRAPHY	NEWSMAGAZINE
MICROBIOLOGY	TRANQUILIZER	SUPERSTITION	UNASSAILABLE	STRATOSPHERE	NEWSPAPERMAN
MICROCIRCUIT	AFTERTHOUGHT	TUBERCULOSIS	UNMISTAKABLE	SUBSTANTIATE	PHARMACOLOGY
MICROCLIMATE	ANTHROPOLOGY	UNDERCLOTHES	UNRESTRAINED	SUBSTRUCTURE	PHILHARMONIC
MICROSPACING	APPURTENANCE	UNDERCOATING	ALLITERATION	UNINTERESTED	PROGRAMMABLE
MICROSURGERY	AUSTRONESIAN	UNDERCURRENT	ANTITHETICAL	VACATIONLAND	PROTHALAMION
NEUROSCIENCE	CONCRESCENCE	UNDERDRAWERS	APOSTROPHIZE	CIRCUMSCRIBE	SPERMATOZOON
NONCOMBATANT	CONGRATULATE	UNDERGARMENT	ATTITUDINIZE	CIRCUMSTANCE	STEPDAUGHTER
NONCOMMITTAL	CONGREGATION	UNDERPINNING	BACKTRACKING	COMMUNICABLE	SUBSTANTIATE
NONCONDUCTOR	CONTRAPUNTAL	UNDERSURFACE	BREATHTAKING	CONFUCIANISM	SUPERANNUATE
PALEONTOLOGY	CONTRARIWISE	UNPARALLELED	CHESTERFIELD	CONQUISTADOR	UNASSAILABLE
PHILODENDRON	DESTRUCTIBLE	UNSCRUPULOUS	CHITTERLINGS	CONTUMACIOUS	UNPARALLELED
PHILOSOPHIZE	DETERMINABLE	VALORIZATION	CONSTABULARY	CONTUMELIOUS	BLOCKBUSTING
PHOTOCOMPOSE	DISCRIMINATE	VETERINARIAN	CONSTIPATION	DISPUTATIOUS	CHILDBEARING
PHOTOENGRAVE	DISFRANCHISE	ATMOSPHERICS	CONSTITUENCY	DISQUISITION	GLASSBLOWING
PHOTOGRAVURE	DISTRIBUTIVE	BLUESTOCKING	CONSTITUTION	EXCRUCIATING	MICROBIOLOGY
PRECONCERTED	ENTERPRISING	BREASTSTROKE	CONSTITUTIVE	HALLUCINOGEN	NEIGHBORHOOD
PRECONDITION	EXTORTIONATE	CALISTHENICS	CONSTRUCTION	INCRUSTATION	PERAMBULATOR
PREPONDERATE	FLUORESCENCE	CHEESEBURGER	COUNTERCLAIM	MALNUTRITION	PREFABRICATE
PREPOSTEROUS	FLUOROCARBON	CHEESEPARING	COUNTERPOINT	MASTURBATION	PROTUBERANCE
PRIMOGENITOR	HABERDASHERY	CHRISTIANITY	COUNTERPOISE	OBSCURANTISM	SWASHBUCKLER
PROPORTIONAL	HETEROSEXUAL	CHRISTIANIZE	COUNTERTENOR	PRESUMPTUOUS	ANNUNCIATION
RADIOISOTOPE	HYPERACIDITY	CORESPONDENT	CRYPTOGRAPHY	PROTUBERANCE	APPRECIATIVE
RADIOTHERAPY	HYPERTENSION	CROSSCURRENT	DIASTROPHISM	RAMBUNCTIOUS	CHARACTERIZE
RHODODENDRON	IMPERCEPTIVE	DECASYLLABIC	ELECTROLYSIS	SUBCUTANEOUS	COLLECTIVISM
SCATOLOGICAL	IMPERCIPIENT	DISASSOCIATE	ELECTROPLATE	IRREVERSIBLE	COLLECTIVIZE
SCHOOLFELLOW	IMPERFECTION	DISESTABLISH	FAINTHEARTED	UNGOVERNABLE	CONFECTIONER
SCHOOLMASTER	IMPERISHABLE	EQUESTRIENNE	FOUNTAINHEAD	HEAVYHEARTED	CONFUCIANISM
SUBCOMMITTEE	INCORRIGIBLE	FENESTRATION	FRONTISPIECE	MEALYMOUTHED	CROSSCURRENT
SUBCONSCIOUS	INSTRUMENTAL	FREESTANDING	GREATHEARTED		DECALCOMANIA
SUBCONTINENT	INSURRECTION	GLASSBLOWING	HEARTRENDING		DENUNCIATION
SURROUNDINGS	INTERCESSION	HAIRSPLITTER	HEARTSTRINGS		DISACCHARIDE
TESTOSTERONE	INTERFERENCE	IDIOSYNCRASY	HEARTWARMING	**6TH LETTER**	EXCRUCIATING
THOROUGHBRED	INTERGLACIAL	ILLUSTRATION	INARTICULATE		HALLUCINOGEN
THOROUGHFARE	INTERJECTION	ILLUSTRATIVE	INEXTRICABLE	ANTIMACASSAR	HELIOCENTRIC
TRIGONOMETRY	INTERLOCUTOR	INDISPUTABLE	INVITATIONAL	ANTIMAGNETIC	HORTICULTURE
UNPROFITABLE	INTERMEDIARY	INDISSOLUBLE	LIGHTHEARTED	ANTIPARTICLE	IMPERCEPTIVE
ANTIPARTICLE	INTERMEDIATE	IRRESISTIBLE	MENSTRUATION	CHROMATICITY	IMPERCIPIENT
CHAMPIONSHIP	INTERMINABLE	IRRESPECTIVE	MERETRICIOUS	CINEMATHEQUE	INCALCULABLE

INTERCESSION	COUNTERTENOR	SATISFACTORY	ILLEGITIMATE	INTERLOCUTOR	COMMONWEALTH
MALOCCLUSION	DELIBERATIVE	SIGNIFICANCE	IMPERISHABLE	MAGNILOQUENT	COMMUNICABLE
MICROCIRCUIT	DEMINERALIZE	TRANSFERENCE	INARTICULATE	MISCALCULATE	COMPANIONWAY
MICROCLIMATE	DISOBEDIENCE	UNPROFITABLE	INFELICITOUS	MULTILATERAL	CONTINUATION
MULTICOLORED	FEEBLEMINDED	BELLIGERENCY	IRRESISTIBLE	MULTILINGUAL	CONVENTIONAL
NIGHTCLOTHES	FLUORESCENCE	COLLEGIALITY	MESSEIGNEURS	OSCILLOSCOPE	DISCONNECTED
NOMENCLATURE	FRANKENSTEIN	DECONGESTANT	MONOFILAMENT	PESTILENTIAL	DISCONSOLATE
PHOTOCOMPOSE	GEOCHEMISTRY	DISINGENUOUS	MUNICIPALITY	PORCELAINIZE	DISPENSATION
PROTACTINIUM	GLOCKENSPIEL	HIEROGLYPHIC	ORGANIZATION	PREDILECTION	FERMENTATION
PROTECTORATE	GOBBLEDYGOOK	INTERGLACIAL	PARADISIACAL	RECOLLECTION	GALVANOMETER
RECALCITRANT	HANDKERCHIEF	MULLIGATAWNY	PARAMILITARY	SCATOLOGICAL	INTRANSIGENT
RENUNCIATION	IMPENETRABLE	PHOTOGRAVURE	PARASITOLOGY	SCHOOLFELLOW	INTRANSITIVE
REPERCUSSION	INDEFEASIBLE	PREDIGESTION	PERSPICACITY	SCHOOLMASTER	INVULNERABLE
RESPECTIVELY	INDEPENDENCE	PRIMOGENITOR	POLARIZATION	SHUFFLEBOARD	MARLINESPIKE
SHARECROPPER	INDIGESTIBLE	PROLEGOMENON	POSTMISTRESS	STEEPLECHASE	MEETINGHOUSE
SUPERCHARGER	INEXPERIENCE	PROPAGANDIZE	PRACTITIONER	TROUBLEMAKER	NONCONDUCTOR
SUPERCILIOUS	IRREDEEMABLE	STRAIGHTAWAY	PRINCIPALITY	UNEMPLOYMENT	PACKINGHOUSE
TRANSCENDENT	IRREMEDIABLE	STRAIGHTEDGE	QUANTITATIVE	VAINGLORIOUS	PALEONTOLOGY
TUBERCULOSIS	IRREVERSIBLE	UNDERGARMENT	QUESTIONABLE	AVITAMINOSIS	PERTINACIOUS
UNDERCLOTHES	LUMINESCENCE	ANTITHETICAL	RADIOISOTOPE	CIRCUMSCRIBE	PHILANTHROPY
UNDERCOATING	LUNCHEONETTE	APPREHENSIVE	RECAPITULATE	CIRCUMSTANCE	PIGMENTATION
UNDERCURRENT	MIDDLEWEIGHT	ASYNCHRONOUS	REHABILITATE	CLOSEMOUTHED	PRECANCEROUS
VALENCIENNES	MUDDLEHEADED	BREATHTAKING	RELATIONSHIP	CONTEMPORARY	PRECONCERTED
VERTICILLATE	NONAGENARIAN	CARBOHYDRATE	RELATIVISTIC	CONTEMPTIBLE	PRECONDITION
APPENDECTOMY	OBSTREPEROUS	CHURCHWARDEN	REMINISCENCE	CONTEMPTUOUS	PREMENSTRUAL
APPENDICITIS	OCTOGENARIAN	ENCEPHALITIS	SCANDINAVIAN	CONTUMACIOUS	PREPONDERATE
CONFIDENTIAL	OFFICEHOLDER	FAINTHEARTED	STRATIGRAPHY	CONTUMELIOUS	PRESENTIMENT
CONSIDERABLE	OXYACETYLENE	GREATHEARTED	SURVEILLANCE	DECOMMISSION	RAMBUNCTIOUS
HABERDASHERY	PENITENTIARY	HEAVYHEARTED	TECHNICALITY	DETERMINABLE	RECOGNIZANCE
IMPONDERABLE	PHOTOENGRAVE	HYPOCHONDRIA	TOTALITARIAN	EXTRAMARITAL	SUBCONSCIOUS
INCANDESCENT	PLASTERBOARD	LIGHTHEARTED	UNBELIEVABLE	INFLAMMATION	SUBCONTINENT
JURISDICTION	PREOPERATIVE	LONGSHOREMAN	VACATIONLAND	INFLAMMATORY	SUBMINIATURE
KALEIDOSCOPE	PYROTECHNICS	NONSCHEDULED	VALORIZATION	INTERMEDIARY	SUPERNATURAL
PHILODENDRON	QUARTERSTAFF	SUPERHIGHWAY	VETERINARIAN	INTERMEDIATE	TERCENTENARY
PREINDUCTION	QUINTESSENCE	TRAPSHOOTING	INTERJECTION	INTERMINABLE	TRIGONOMETRY
PROVIDENTIAL	REMUNERATION	WHOLEHEARTED	NONOBJECTIVE	INTERMISSION	UNPRINCIPLED
RHODODENDRON	REMUNERATIVE	ACQUAINTANCE	PEACEKEEPING	INTERMITTENT	ANTHROPOLOGY
UNDERDRAWERS	SEXAGENARIAN	ANTEDILUVIAN	ANTIALIASING	MEALYMOUTHED	AUSTRONESIAN
ALLITERATION	SLEDGEHAMMER	BLANDISHMENT	ANTIELECTRON	NONCOMBATANT	BIBLIOGRAPHY
AMBIDEXTROUS	THUNDERCLOUD	BRILLIANTINE	ARGILLACEOUS	NONCOMMITTAL	BIOGEOGRAPHY
ANATHEMATIZE	THUNDERSTORM	CHAMPIONSHIP	BIOTELEMETRY	PRESUMPTUOUS	CHALCOPYRITE
BIOCHEMISTRY	UNGOVERNABLE	CIVILIZATION	BLOODLETTING	SOMNAMBULISM	CHOREOGRAPHY
BLATHERSKITE	UNINTERESTED	CONQUISTADOR	CARILLONNEUR	SUBCOMMITTEE	CHROMOSPHERE
CABINETMAKER	UNLIKELIHOOD	CONSTIPATION	CONCELEBRANT	TRANSMIGRATE	CONGLOMERATE
CHECKERBERRY	UNREGENERATE	CONSTITUENCY	DESPOLIATION	TRANSMISSION	CRYPTOGRAPHY
CHECKERBOARD	UNSCIENTIFIC	CONSTITUTION	DISTILLATION	TRANSMOGRIFY	CUMULONIMBUS
CHEESEBURGER	WEATHERBOARD	CONSTITUTIVE	EARSPLITTING	ULTRAMONTANE	DEMIMONDAINE
CHEESEPARING	WEATHERGLASS	CONTAINERIZE	ENCYCLOPEDIA	ALPHANUMERIC	ECHOLOCATION
CHESTERFIELD	WEATHERPROOF	DEMILITARIZE	EVERBLOOMING	ASTRONAUTICS	ELEEMOSYNARY
CHITTERLINGS	HENCEFORWARD	DENOMINATION	FIBRILLATION	ASTRONOMICAL	EPISCOPALIAN
CLOTHESHORSE	IMPERFECTION	DISCRIMINATE	FORMALDEHYDE	AUTHENTICATE	FLUOROCARBON
CLOTHESPRESS	INSUFFERABLE	DISQUISITION	HYPOGLYCEMIA	BILLINGSGATE	HETEROSEXUAL
CONCRESCENCE	INSUFFICIENT	DISTRIBUTIVE	INDECLINABLE	CANTANKEROUS	LEXICOGRAPHY
CONGREGATION	INTERFERENCE	FRANKINCENSE	INEXPLICABLE	CARBONACEOUS	MADEMOISELLE
COUNTERCLAIM	MULTIFACETED	FRONTISPIECE	INTELLECTUAL	COELENTERATE	METAMORPHISM
COUNTERPOINT	MULTIFARIOUS	HEADMISTRESS	INTELLIGENCE	COMMENCEMENT	MINICOMPUTER
COUNTERPOISE	SATISFACTION	HUMANITARIAN	INTELLIGIBLE	COMMENSURATE	MISPRONOUNCE

OCEANOGRAPHY	CONSERVATORY	ECCLESIASTIC	FENESTRATION	DISADVANTAGE	MULTIFARIOUS
PHYSIOGRAPHY	CONSTRUCTION	EXTRASENSORY	FLAMETHROWER	EXTRAVAGANZA	MULTILATERAL
POLYMORPHISM	CONTERMINOUS	HEARTSTRINGS	FREESTANDING	INCONVENIENT	MULTITASKING
POSTDOCTORAL	CONVERSATION	IMMEASURABLE	HYDROTHERAPY	INTERVOCALIC	OBSCURANTISM
PRASEODYMIUM	DIASTROPHISM	INCONSOLABLE	HYDROTHERMAL	MISADVENTURE	PERTINACIOUS
PSYCHOACTIVE	DIFFERENTIAL	INCRUSTATION	HYPERTENSION	MULTIVERSITY	PORCELAINIZE
PSYCHOSEXUAL	DISAGREEABLE	INDISSOLUBLE	ILLUSTRATION	MULTIVITAMIN	POSTGRADUATE
PSYCHOTROPIC	DISSERTATION	INTERSECTION	ILLUSTRATIVE	PERADVENTURE	PROPAGANDIZE
SELENOGRAPHY	EDITORIALIZE	INTERSTELLAR	INDOCTRINATE	RECEIVERSHIP	PSYCHOACTIVE
STEREOPHONIC	ELECTROLYSIS	MICROSPACING	INFLATIONARY	TRANSVESTISM	SARSAPARILLA
STEREOSCOPIC	ELECTROPLATE	MICROSURGERY	INFLATIONISM	BRAINWASHING	SATISFACTION
STRATOSPHERE	HEARTRENDING	MULTISESSION	INGRATIATING	HEARTWARMING	SATISFACTORY
THERMOSPHERE	HELLGRAMMITE	NEURASTHENIA	INVERTEBRATE	HOUSEWARMING	SECRETARIATE
TRANSOCEANIC	HIERARCHICAL	NEUROSCIENCE	ISOLATIONISM	OTHERWORLDLY	SIMULTANEOUS
TRIGNOMETRIC	HYSTERECTOMY	PHILOSOPHIZE	LONGITUDINAL	OVEREXPOSURE	SUBCUTANEOUS
WHIPPOORWILL	INCORRIGIBLE	PREDESIGNATE	MAGNETOMETER	AERODYNAMICS	SUPERNATURAL
ZOOGEOGRAPHY	INEXTRICABLE	PREPOSTEROUS	MALNUTRITION	DECASYLLABIC	TRANSPACIFIC
ACCOMPLISHED	INSURRECTION	PROCESSIONAL	MISINTERPRET	IDIOSYNCRASY	UNDERGARMENT
ASTROPHYSICS	IRREFRAGABLE	PROFESSIONAL	MULTITASKING	MONOSYLLABIC	UNMISTAKABLE
ATMOSPHERICS	KINDERGARTEN	RECONSTITUTE	NEVERTHELESS	OCTOSYLLABIC	CARPETBAGGER
CHIROPRACTIC	MALFORMATION	REMONSTRANCE	ONOMATOPOEIA	PERICYNTHION	CHEESEBURGER
CORESPONDENT	MASTERSTROKE	SHARPSHOOTER	PARENTHESIZE	POLICYHOLDER	CONSTABULARY
COSMOPOLITAN	MASTURBATION	SHORTSIGHTED	PLANETESIMAL	POLYSYLLABIC	DISTRIBUTIVE
DISCIPLINARY	MENSTRUATION	SPORTSWRITER	POLYETHYLENE	POLYSYLLABLE	INSALUBRIOUS
DISREPUTABLE	MERETRICIOUS	SUPERSTITION	PREDETERMINE	POSTHYPNOTIC	MASTURBATION
ENTERPRISING	OBSCURANTISM	TESTOSTERONE	PROCATHEDRAL	PRESBYTERIAN	NONCOMBATANT
ENTREPRENEUR	OUTSTRETCHED	THANKSGIVING	RADIOTHERAPY	PROPHYLACTIC	SOMNAMBULISM
HAIRSPLITTER	PANCHROMATIC	TRADESPEOPLE	RECEPTIONIST		ANTIMACASSAR
HIPPOPOTAMUS	PICKERELWEED	UNDERSURFACE	REGISTRATION		COMMENCEMENT
INCOMPARABLE	POSTGRADUATE	UNREASONABLE	SECRETARIATE		DESTRUCTIBLE
INCOMPATIBLE	PREPAREDNESS	UNSEASONABLE	SENSITOMETER	**7TH LETTER**	DISPLACEMENT
INDISPUTABLE	PRESCRIPTION	ABOLITIONISM	SIMULTANEOUS		ECHOLOCATION
INTEMPERANCE	PROPORTIONAL	ABSENTMINDED	SPIRITUALISM	ARGILLACEOUS	FLUOROCARBON
IRRESPECTIVE	PUMPERNICKEL	ADVENTITIOUS	STRAITJACKET	ASTRONAUTICS	HIERARCHICAL
MISAPPREHEND	RESURRECTION	AFORETHOUGHT	STREETWALKER	BACKTRACKING	HYPERACIDITY
MISREPRESENT	SPECTROGRAPH	AFTERTHOUGHT	STREPTOMYCIN	BRAINWASHING	INARTICULATE
MULTIPLICAND	SPECTROMETER	AMPHITHEATER	SUBCUTANEOUS	BRILLIANTINE	INCAPACITATE
MULTIPLICITY	SPECTROSCOPE	APPURTENANCE	UNMISTAKABLE	CARBONACEOUS	INEFFACEABLE
MULTIPURPOSE	SUBDIRECTORY	ARCHITECTURE	UNRESTRAINED	CONTUMACIOUS	INFELICITOUS
PREAMPLIFIER	SUBSCRIPTION	BICENTENNIAL	ATTITUDINIZE	DISADVANTAGE	MISCALCULATE
PRECIPITANCY	SUBSERVIENCE	BIOSATELLITE	DESTRUCTIBLE	DISESTABLISH	NEUROSCIENCE
SARSAPARILLA	SUBSTRUCTURE	BLOODTHIRSTY	DISCOURTEOUS	DISPUTATIOUS	PERSPICACITY
THERAPEUTICS	SUBTERRANEAN	BLUESTOCKING	HEADQUARTERS	ENCEPHALITIS	PHARMACOLOGY
TRANSPACIFIC	TENDEROMETER	BREAKTHROUGH	INSALUBRIOUS	EXTRAMARITAL	POSTDOCTORAL
UNDERPINNING	UNCHARITABLE	BREASTSTROKE	INSTRUMENTAL	EXTRAVAGANZA	PRECANCEROUS
PREREQUISITE	UNIVERSALIST	CALISTHENICS	MALNOURISHED	FREESTANDING	PRECONCERTED
UNFREQUENTED	UNIVERSALITY	CARPETBAGGER	RESTAURATEUR	HABERDASHERY	PYROTECHNICS
APOSTROPHIZE	UNIVERSALIZE	CHEMOTHERAPY	SURROUNDINGS	HEADQUARTERS	RAMBUNCTIOUS
BACKTRACKING	UNSEARCHABLE	CHRISTIANITY	THOROUGHBRED	HEARTWARMING	TECHNICALITY
BACTERICIDAL	UNSEGREGATED	CHRISTIANIZE	THOROUGHFARE	HELLGRAMMITE	TRANSOCEANIC
BACTERIOLOGY	WELTERWEIGHT	DENSITOMETER	TRANQUILIZER	HOUSEWARMING	UNPRINCIPLED
BUTTERSCOTCH	COMMISSARIAT	DICTATORSHIP	UNACCUSTOMED	INCOMPARABLE	UNSEARCHABLE
CONFIRMATION	COMMISSIONER	DISESTABLISH	UNDOCUMENTED	INCOMPATIBLE	ATTITUDINIZE
CONFORMATION	CONFESSIONAL	DISINTEGRATE	UNSCRUPULOUS	INDEFEASIBLE	DISOBEDIENCE
CONSERVATION	DEMONSTRABLE	DISPUTATIOUS	VENIPUNCTURE	IRREFRAGABLE	FORMALDEHYDE
CONSERVATISM	DISASSOCIATE	EQUESTRIENNE	ABBREVIATION	MULLIGATAWNY	GOBBLEDYGOOK
CONSERVATIVE	EARTHSHAKING	EXTORTIONATE	AUDIOVISUALS	MULTIFACETED	IRREMEDIABLE

NONCONDUCTOR	MULTIVERSITY	ASTROPHYSICS	INEXTRICABLE	MONOSYLLABLE	PENITENTIARY
PRASEODYMIUM	NONOBJECTIVE	ATMOSPHERICS	INFLATIONARY	MULTIPLICAND	PERICYNTHION
PRECONDITION	NONSCHEDULED	BLOODTHIRSTY	INFLATIONISM	MULTIPLICITY	PHOTOENGRAVE
PREPONDERATE	OUTSTRETCHED	BREAKTHROUGH	INGRATIATING	NIGHTCLOTHES	PUMPERNICKEL
ANTIELECTRON	PEACEKEEPING	CALISTHENICS	INSUFFICIENT	NOMENCLATURE	SCANDINAVIAN
ANTITHETICAL	PERADVENTURE	CHEMOTHERAPY	INTELLIGENCE	OCTOSYLLABIC	SEXAGENARIAN
APPENDECTOMY	PESTILENTIAL	DISACCHARIDE	INTELLIGIBLE	PARAMILITARY	SUBSTANTIATE
APPREHENSIVE	PHILODENDRON	EARTHSHAKING	INTERMINABLE	POLYSYLLABIC	SUPERANNUATE
APPURTENANCE	PICKERELWEED	FLAMETHROWER	INTERMISSION	POLYSYLLABLE	SURROUNDINGS
ARCHITECTURE	PLANETESIMAL	HYDROTHERAPY	INTERMITTENT	PREAMPLIFIER	UNREGENERATE
BELLIGERENCY	PREDETERMINE	HYDROTHERMAL	ISOLATIONISM	PROPHYLACTIC	UNSCIENTIFIC
BICENTENNIAL	PREDIGESTION	MUDDLEHEADED	JURISDICTION	PROTHALAMION	VENIPUNCTURE
BIOSATELLITE	PREDILECTION	NEVERTHELESS	MADEMOISELLE	REHABILITATE	VETERINARIAN
BIOTELEMETRY	PREPAREDNESS	OFFICEHOLDER	MERETRICIOUS	SURVEILLANCE	APOSTROPHIZE
BLOODLETTING	PRIMOGENITOR	PARENTHESIZE	MICROBIOLOGY	UNDERCLOTHES	ASTRONOMICAL
CHILDBEARING	PROTUBERANCE	POLICYHOLDER	MICROCIRCUIT	UNLIKELIHOOD	BLUESTOCKING
CONCELEBRANT	PROVIDENTIAL	POLYETHYLENE	MOUNTAINSIDE	UNPARALLELED	CARILLONNEUR
CONFIDENTIAL	RECEIVERSHIP	PROCATHEDRAL	MULTILINGUAL	ABSENTMINDED	CHAMPIONSHIP
CONSIDERABLE	RECOLLECTION	RADIOTHERAPY	MULTIVITAMIN	ANATHEMATIZE	CLOSEMOUTHED
CONTUMELIOUS	RESURRECTION	SHARPSHOOTER	PRECIPITANCY	BIOCHEMISTRY	CORESPONDENT
DECONGESTANT	RHODODENDRON	SLEDGEHAMMER	PREDESIGNATE	CONFIRMATION	COSMOPOLITAN
DIFFERENTIAL	SHUFFLEBOARD	STRAIGHTAWAY	PRESCRIPTION	CONFORMATION	DECALCOMANIA
DISAGREEABLE	STEEPLECHASE	STRAIGHTEDGE	RECALCITRANT	CONGLOMERATE	DENSITOMETER
DISINGENUOUS	SUBDIRECTORY	SUPERCHARGER	RECEPTIONIST	CONTERMINOUS	DIASTROPHISM
DISINTEGRATE	THERAPEUTICS	ABBREVIATION	RECOGNIZANCE	DISCRIMINATE	DICTATORSHIP
EXTRASENSORY	TRANSCENDENT	ABOLITIONISM	RENUNCIATION	FEEBLEMINDED	DISASSOCIATE
FAINTHEARTED	TRANSFERENCE	ADVENTITIOUS	SHORTSIGHTED	GEOCHEMISTRY	ELECTROLYSIS
GREATHEARTED	TRANSVESTISM	ANNUNCIATION	SIGNIFICANCE	INFLAMMATION	ELECTROPLATE
HEARTRENDING	TROUBLEMAKER	ANTIALIASING	SUBMINIATURE	INFLAMMATORY	ENCYCLOPEDIA
HEAVYHEARTED	UNBELIEVABLE	APPENDICITIS	SUBSCRIPTION	INSTRUMENTAL	EVERBLOOMING
HELIOCENTRIC	UNSEGREGATED	APPRECIATIVE	SUPERCILIOUS	MALFORMATION	GALVANOMETER
HYPERTENSION	WHOLEHEARTED	AUDIOVISUALS	SUPERHIGHWAY	MINICOMPUTER	HENCEFORWARD
HYSTERECTOMY	SCHOOLFELLOW	AVITAMINOSIS	TRANQUILIZER	NONCOMMITTAL	HIPPOPOTAMUS
IMPERCEPTIVE	ANTIMAGNETIC	BACTERICIDAL	TRANSMIGRATE	PROGRAMMABLE	HYPOCHONDRIA
IMPERFECTION	BIBLIOGRAPHY	BACTERIOLOGY	TRANSMISSION	SCHOOLMASTER	INCONSOLABLE
IMPONDERABLE	BILLINGSGATE	CHRISTIANITY	UNASSAILABLE	SUBCOMMITTEE	INDISSOLUBLE
INCANDESCENT	BIOGEOGRAPHY	CHRISTIANIZE	UNCHARITABLE	TRIGNOMETRIC	INTERLOCUTOR
INCONVENIENT	CHOREOGRAPHY	COLLEGIALITY	UNDERPINNING	UNDOCUMENTED	INTERVOCALIC
INSUFFERABLE	CONGREGATION	COMMUNICABLE	UNPROFITABLE	ACQUAINTANCE	KALEIDOSCOPE
INSURRECTION	CRYPTOGRAPHY	COMPANIONWAY	VALENCIENNES	AERODYNAMICS	LONGSHOREMAN
INTELLECTUAL	KINDERGARTEN	COMPLAISANCE	VERTICILLATE	AUSTRONESIAN	LUNCHEONETTE
INTEMPERANCE	LEXICOGRAPHY	CONFUCIANISM	STRAITJACKET	CONTAINERIZE	MAGNETOMETER
INTERCESSION	MEETINGHOUSE	DECOMMISSION	CANTANKEROUS	CUMULONIMBUS	MAGNILOQUENT
INTERFERENCE	MESSEIGNEURS	DENUNCIATION	ACCOMPLISHED	DEMIMONDAINE	MEALYMOUTHED
INTERJECTION	NEWSMAGAZINE	DESPOLIATION	ANTEDILUVIAN	DENOMINATION	MULTICOLORED
INTERMEDIARY	OCEANOGRAPHY	DETERMINABLE	DECASYLLABIC	DISCONNECTED	NEIGHBORHOOD
INTERMEDIATE	PACKINGHOUSE	EARSPLITTING	DISCIPLINARY	DISFRANCHISE	ONOMATOPOEIA
INTERSECTION	PHYSIOGRAPHY	ECCLESIASTIC	DISTILLATION	FRANKENSTEIN	OSCILLOSCOPE
INVERTEBRATE	SELENOGRAPHY	EDITORIALIZE	EPITHALAMIUM	FRANKINCENSE	OTHERWORLDLY
INVULNERABLE	STRATIGRAPHY	EXCRUCIATING	FIBRILLATION	GLOCKENSPIEL	PANCHROMATIC
IRREDEEMABLE	THANKSGIVING	EXTORTIONATE	GLASSBLOWING	IDIOSYNCRASY	PHILOSOPHIZE
IRRESPECTIVE	THOROUGHBRED	FOUNTAINHEAD	HAIRSPLITTER	INDEPENDENCE	PHOTOCOMPOSE
LIGHTHEARTED	THOROUGHFARE	HALLUCINOGEN	HIEROGLYPHIC	MERCHANTABLE	PROLEGOMENON
MARLINESPIKE	ZOOGEOGRAPHY	IMPERCIPIENT	INTERGLACIAL	METALANGUAGE	QUESTIONABLE
MISADVENTURE	AFORETHOUGHT	INCORRIGIBLE	MALOCCLUSION	MISPRONOUNCE	RELATIONSHIP
MISINTERPRET	AFTERTHOUGHT	INDECLINABLE	MICROCLIMATE	NONAGENARIAN	SCATOLOGICAL
MULTISESSION	AMPHITHEATER	INEXPLICABLE	MONOFILAMENT	OCTOGENARIAN	SENSITOMETER

SPECTROGRAPH	HANDKERCHIEF	INDIGESTIBLE	PREPOSTEROUS	AMBIDEXTROUS	EPITHALAMIUM
SPECTROMETER	ILLUSTRATION	INTRANSIGENT	PRESBYTERIAN	CARBOHYDRATE	EXCRUCIATING
SPECTROSCOPE	ILLUSTRATIVE	INTRANSITIVE	PRESENTIMENT	HYPOGLYCEMIA	FAINTHEARTED
STREPTOMYCIN	INDOCTRINATE	IRRESISTIBLE	PROPORTIONAL	CIVILIZATION	FENESTRATION
TENDEROMETER	INEXPERIENCE	LUMINESCENCE	PROTACTINIUM	ORGANIZATION	FERMENTATION
TRANSMOGRIFY	IRREVERSIBLE	MASTERSTROKE	PROTECTORATE	POLARIZATION	FIBRILLATION
TRAPSHOOTING	MALNOURISHED	PARADISIACAL	PSYCHOTROPIC	VALORIZATION	FLUOROCARBON
TRIGONOMETRY	MALNUTRITION	POSTMISTRESS	QUANTITATIVE		GREATHEARTED
ULTRAMONTANE	METAMORPHISM	PREMENSTRUAL	RECAPITULATE		HEAVYHEARTED
UNDERCOATING	MISAPPREHEND	PROCESSIONAL	RECONSTITUTE		HUMANITARIAN
UNEMPLOYMENT	MISREPRESENT	PROFESSIONAL	REMONSTRANCE	**8TH LETTER**	ILLUSTRATION
UNREASONABLE	PHILHARMONIC	PSYCHOSEXUAL	RESPECTIVELY		ILLUSTRATIVE
UNSEASONABLE	PHOTOGRAVURE	QUINTESSENCE	SPERMATOZOON	ABBREVIATION	INCRUSTATION
VACATIONLAND	PLASTERBOARD	RADIOISOTOPE	SUBCONTINENT	AERODYNAMICS	INFLAMMATION
VAINGLORIOUS	POLYMORPHISM	REMINISCENCE	SUPERSTITION	ALLITERATION	INFLAMMATORY
WHIPPOORWILL	PREFABRICATE	STEREOSCOPIC	TERCENTENARY	ANATHEMATIZE	INGRATIATING
ANTHROPOLOGY	PREOPERATIVE	STRATOSPHERE	TESTOSTERONE	ANNUNCIATION	INTERGLACIAL
CHALCOPYRITE	QUARTERSTAFF	SUBCONSCIOUS	TOTALITARIAN	ANTIALIASING	KINDERGARTEN
CHEESEPARING	REGISTRATION	THERMOSPHERE	ALPHANUMERIC	ANTIMACASSAR	LIGHTHEARTED
CONSTIPATION	REMUNERATION	UNACCUSTOMED	BLOCKBUSTING	APPRECIATIVE	MALFORMATION
CONTEMPORARY	REMUNERATIVE	UNIVERSALIST	CONSTRUCTION	BREATHTAKING	MASTURBATION
CONTEMPTIBLE	RESTAURATEUR	UNIVERSALITY	CONTINUATION	CARPETBAGGER	MENSTRUATION
CONTEMPTUOUS	SHARECROPPER	UNIVERSALIZE	CROSSCURRENT	CHEESEPARING	MICROSPACING
CONTRAPUNTAL	SUBTERRANEAN	AUTHENTICATE	DISREPUTABLE	CHILDBEARING	MONOFILAMENT
EPISCOPALIAN	THUNDERCLOUD	BREATHTAKING	HORTICULTURE	CHIROPRACTIC	MUNICIPALITY
MICROSPACING	THUNDERSTORM	CABINETMAKER	IMMEASURABLE	CHRISTIANITY	NEWSMAGAZINE
MUNICIPALITY	UNDERDRAWERS	CHARACTERIZE	INCALCULABLE	CHRISTIANIZE	NOMENCLATURE
NEWSPAPERMAN	UNGOVERNABLE	CHROMATICITY	INDISPUTABLE	CHURCHWARDEN	NONAGENARIAN
OBSTREPEROUS	UNINTERESTED	CINEMATHEQUE	LONGITUDINAL	CIVILIZATION	NONCOMBATANT
OVEREXPOSURE	UNRESTRAINED	COELENTERATE	MANSLAUGHTER	COLLEGIALITY	OCTOGENARIAN
POSTHYPNOTIC	WEATHERBOARD	COLLECTIVISM	MENSTRUATION	COMMISSARIAT	ORGANIZATION
PRESUMPTUOUS	WEATHERGLASS	COLLECTIVIZE	MICROSURGERY	CONFIRMATION	PERSPICACITY
PRINCIPALITY	WEATHERPROOF	CONFECTIONER	MULTIPURPOSE	CONFORMATION	PHOTOGRAVURE
STEREOPHONIC	BLANDISHMENT	CONGRATULATE	PERAMBULATOR	CONFUCIANISM	PIGMENTATION
TRADESPEOPLE	BREASTSTROKE	CONSTITUENCY	PREINDUCTION	CONGREGATION	POLARIZATION
UNSCRUPULOUS	BUTTERSCOTCH	CONSTITUTION	PREREQUISITE	CONSERVATION	PREOPERATIVE
ALLITERATION	CHROMOSPHERE	CONSTITUTIVE	REPERCUSSION	CONSERVATISM	PRINCIPALITY
ANTIPARTICLE	CIRCUMSCRIBE	CONVENTIONAL	SPIRITUALISM	CONSERVATIVE	PROPHYLACTIC
ASYNCHRONOUS	CIRCUMSTANCE	DELICATESSEN	STEPDAUGHTER	CONSERVATORY	PROTHALAMION
BLATHERSKITE	CLOTHESHORSE	DEMILITARIZE	SUBSTRUCTURE	CONSTIPATION	QUANTITATIVE
CHECKERBERRY	CLOTHESPRESS	DEMONSTRABLE	SWASHBUCKLER	CONTINUATION	REGISTRATION
CHECKERBOARD	COMMENSURATE	DISSERTATION	TUBERCULOSIS	CONVERSATION	REMUNERATION
CHESTERFIELD	COMMISSARIAT	FERMENTATION	UNDERCURRENT	DELIBERATIVE	REMUNERATIVE
CHIROPRACTIC	COMMISSIONER	HEARTSTRINGS	UNDERSURFACE	DEMILITARIZE	RENUNCIATION
CHITTERLINGS	CONCRESCENCE	HUMANITARIAN	UNFREQUENTED	DEMINERALIZE	RESTAURATEUR
CONTRARIWISE	CONFESSIONAL	ILLEGITIMATE	CONSERVATION	DENOMINATION	SCANDINAVIAN
COUNTERCLAIM	CONQUISTADOR	IMPENETRABLE	CONSERVATISM	DENUNCIATION	SCHOOLMASTER
COUNTERPOINT	CONVERSATION	INCRUSTATION	CONSERVATIVE	DESPOLIATION	SEXAGENARIAN
COUNTERPOISE	DISCONSOLATE	INTERSTELLAR	CONSERVATORY	DISACCHARIDE	SLEDGEHAMMER
COUNTERTENOR	DISPENSATION	INVITATIONAL	RELATIVISTIC	DISPENSATION	SPIRITUALISM
DELIBERATIVE	DISQUISITION	NEURASTHENIA	SUBSERVIENCE	DISSERTATION	STRAITJACKET
DEMINERALIZE	ELEEMOSYNARY	OXYACETYLENE	CHURCHWARDEN	DISTILLATION	STREETWALKER
DISCOURTEOUS	FLUORESCENCE	PALEONTOLOGY	COMMONWEALTH	EARTHSHAKING	SUBMINIATURE
ENTERPRISING	FRONTISPIECE	PARASITOLOGY	MIDDLEWEIGHT	ECCLESIASTIC	SUBTERRANEAN
ENTREPRENEUR	HEADMISTRESS	PHILANTHROPY	SPORTSWRITER	ECHOLOCATION	SUPERCHARGER
EQUESTRIENNE	HETEROSEXUAL	PIGMENTATION	STREETWALKER	EDITORIALIZE	TECHNICALITY
FENESTRATION	IMPERISHABLE	PRACTITIONER	WELTERWEIGHT	EPISCOPALIAN	TOTALITARIAN

UNDERCOATING	PERTINACIOUS	NEVERTHELESS	THOROUGHFARE	PUMPERNICKEL	TRIGONOMETRY
UNDERDRAWERS	PREDILECTION	NEWSPAPERMAN	UNSEARCHABLE	RECONSTITUTE	TROUBLEMAKER
UNIVERSALIST	PREINDUCTION	OBSTREPEROUS	ABSENTMINDED	REHABILITATE	ANTIMAGNETIC
UNIVERSALITY	PSYCHOACTIVE	PARENTHESIZE	ACCOMPLISHED	RELATIVISTIC	APPREHENSIVE
UNIVERSALIZE	RECOLLECTION	PEACEKEEPING	ATTITUDINIZE	RESPECTIVELY	APPURTENANCE
UNRESTRAINED	REMINISCENCE	PRECANCEROUS	AUTHENTICATE	SUBCOMMITTEE	AVITAMINOSIS
VALORIZATION	RESURRECTION	PRECONCERTED	BIOCHEMISTRY	SUBCONTINENT	BICENTENNIAL
VETERINARIAN	SATISFACTION	PREPONDERATE	BLOODTHIRSTY	SUBSERVIENCE	BRILLIANTINE
WHOLEHEARTED	SATISFACTORY	PREPOSTEROUS	CHROMATICITY	SUPERSTITION	CARILLONNEUR
CHECKERBERRY	SIGNIFICANCE	PRESBYTERIAN	COLLECTIVISM	THANKSGIVING	CHAMPIONSHIP
CHECKERBOARD	STEEPLECHASE	PROCATHEDRAL	COLLECTIVIZE	UNLIKELIHOOD	CONFIDENTIAL
CONCELEBRANT	STEREOSCOPIC	PSYCHOSEXUAL	COMMISSIONER	UNPRINCIPLED	CORESPONDENT
DISESTABLISH	SUBCONSCIOUS	RADIOTHERAPY	CONFECTIONER	UNMISTAKABLE	DETERMINABLE
INVERTEBRATE	SUBDIRECTORY	SCHOOLFELLOW	CONFESSIONAL	BIOSATELLITE	DIFFERENTIAL
PLASTERBOARD	SUBSTRUCTURE	TERCENTENARY	CONTERMINOUS	CHITTERLINGS	DISADVANTAGE
SHUFFLEBOARD	SWASHBUCKLER	TESTOSTERONE	CONTRARIWISE	CONTUMELIOUS	DISINGENUOUS
WEATHERBOARD	THUNDERCLOUD	TRADESPEOPLE	CONVENTIONAL	COSMOPOLITAN	EXTRASENSORY
ANTIELECTRON	TRANSPACIFIC	TRANSOCEANIC	CUMULONIMBUS	DECASYLLABIC	FOUNTAINHEAD
APPENDECTOMY	VENIPUNCTURE	TRIGNOMETRIC	DISCIPLINARY	ELECTROLYSIS	FREESTANDING
APPENDICITIS	CARBOHYDRATE	UNDOCUMENTED	DISCRIMINATE	ENCEPHALITIS	HALLUCINOGEN
ARCHITECTURE	DEMIMONDAINE	UNFREQUENTED	DISOBEDIENCE	HORTICULTURE	HEARTRENDING
ARGILLACEOUS	INDEPENDENCE	UNINTERESTED	DISQUISITION	INCALCULABLE	HELIOCENTRIC
BACKTRACKING	INTERMEDIARY	VALENCIENNES	ENTERPRISING	INCONSOLABLE	HYPERTENSION
BACTERICIDAL	INTERMEDIATE	WELTERWEIGHT	EQUESTRIENNE	INDISSOLUBLE	HYPOCHONDRIA
BLUESTOCKING	LONGITUDINAL	CHESTERFIELD	FEEBLEMINDED	MONOSYLLABLE	INCONVENIENT
BUTTERSCOTCH	NONSCHEDULED	DISINTEGRATE	GEOCHEMISTRY	MULTICOLORED	INDECLINABLE
CARBONACEOUS	POSTGRADUATE	EXTRAVAGANZA	HAIRSPLITTER	OCTOSYLLABIC	INTERMINABLE
CIRCUMSCRIBE	PREPAREDNESS	INCORRIGIBLE	HYPERACIDITY	PERAMBULATOR	LUNCHEONETTE
COMMUNICABLE	SURROUNDINGS	INTELLIGENCE	ILLEGITIMATE	PICKERELWEED	MESSEIGNEURS
CONCRESCENCE	AMPHITHEATER	INTELLIGIBLE	INCAPACITATE	POLYSYLLABIC	MISADVENTURE
CONSTRUCTION	ATMOSPHERICS	IRREFRAGABLE	INDOCTRINATE	POLYSYLLABLE	MOUNTAINSIDE
CONTUMACIOUS	AUSTRONESIAN	MANSLAUGHTER	INEXPERIENCE	SUPERCILIOUS	MULTILINGUAL
COUNTERCLAIM	CALISTHENICS	METALANGUAGE	INFELICITOUS	SURVEILLANCE	OBSCURANTISM
DISASSOCIATE	CANTANKEROUS	PHOTOENGRAVE	INTRANSIGENT	TRANQUILIZER	PERADVENTURE
DISFRANCHISE	CHARACTERIZE	PREDESIGNATE	INTRANSITIVE	TUBERCULOSIS	PESTILENTIAL
FLUORESCENCE	CHEMOTHERAPY	SCATOLOGICAL	INVITATIONAL	UNASSAILABLE	PHILODENDRON
FRANKINCENSE	COELENTERATE	SHORTSIGHTED	IRREMEDIABLE	UNPARALLELED	POSTHYPNOTIC
HANDKERCHIEF	COMMENCEMENT	SPECTROGRAPH	MALNOURISHED	VERTICILLATE	PRIMOGENITOR
HYPOGLYCEMIA	COMMONWEALTH	STEPDAUGHTER	MALNUTRITION	ALPHANUMERIC	PROPAGANDIZE
HYSTERECTOMY	CONGLOMERATE	SUPERHIGHWAY	MICROCLIMATE	ASTRONOMICAL	PROVIDENTIAL
IDIOSYNCRASY	CONTAINERIZE	TRANSMIGRATE	MULTIPLICAND	BIOTELEMETRY	QUESTIONABLE
IMPERFECTION	DELICATESSEN	TRANSMOGRIFY	MULTIPLICITY	CABINETMAKER	RELATIONSHIP
INEXPLICABLE	DISAGREEABLE	UNSEGREGATED	NEUROSCIENCE	DECALCOMANIA	RHODODENDRON
INEXTRICABLE	DISCONNECTED	WEATHERGLASS	NONCOMMITTAL	DENSITOMETER	SIMULTANEOUS
INSUFFICIENT	DISPLACEMENT	BLANDISHMENT	PARADISIACAL	GALVANOMETER	SUBCUTANEOUS
INSURRECTION	ENTREPRENEUR	CINEMATHEQUE	PARAMILITARY	HELLGRAMMITE	SUPERANNUATE
INTELLECTUAL	FORMALDEHYDE	CLOTHESHORSE	PORCELAINIZE	IRREDEEMABLE	TRANSCENDENT
INTERJECTION	HETEROSEXUAL	HIERARCHICAL	PRACTITIONER	MAGNETOMETER	ULTRAMONTANE
INTERLOCUTOR	HYDROTHERAPY	IMPERISHABLE	PREAMPLIFIER	PANCHROMATIC	UNDERPINNING
INTERSECTION	HYDROTHERMAL	MEETINGHOUSE	PRECONDITION	PHILHARMONIC	UNGOVERNABLE
INTERVOCALIC	INEFFACEABLE	NEURASTHENIA	PREFABRICATE	PHOTOCOMPOSE	UNREASONABLE
IRRESPECTIVE	INSTRUMENTAL	PACKINGHOUSE	PREREQUISITE	PROGRAMMABLE	UNSEASONABLE
JURISDICTION	INTERSTELLAR	PHILANTHROPY	PRESENTIMENT	PROLEGOMENON	VACATIONLAND
LUMINESCENCE	MIDDLEWEIGHT	PYROTECHNICS	PROCESSIONAL	SENSITOMETER	ABOLITIONISM
MERETRICIOUS	MISAPPREHEND	STEREOPHONIC	PROFESSIONAL	SPECTROMETER	AFORETHOUGHT
MULTIFACETED	MISREPRESENT	THOROUGHBRED	PROPORTIONAL	STREPTOMYCIN	AFTERTHOUGHT
NONOBJECTIVE	MUDDLEHEADED	THOROUGHBRED	PROTACTINIUM	TENDEROMETER	ANTHROPOLOGY

ASYNCHRONOUS	CRYPTOGRAPHY	GLOCKENSPIEL	PREMENSTRUAL	COMMONWEALTH	STRAIGHTAWAY
BACTERIOLOGY	DEMONSTRABLE	HABERDASHERY	PRESUMPTUOUS	COMMUNICABLE	STRATIGRAPHY
COMPANIONWAY	DICTATORSHIP	INCANDESCENT	RAMBUNCTIOUS	COMPLAISANCE	SURVEILLANCE
CONTEMPORARY	EXTRAMARITAL	INDEFEASIBLE	RECALCITRANT	CONQUISTADOR	TRANSOCEANIC
DISCONSOLATE	FLAMETHROWER	INTERCESSION	STRAIGHTAWAY	CONSIDERABLE	TROUBLEMAKER
EVERBLOOMING	HEADQUARTERS	INTERMISSION	STRAIGHTEDGE	CRYPTOGRAPHY	UNASSAILABLE
EXTORTIONATE	HEARTSTRINGS	IRREVERSIBLE	SUBSTANTIATE	DECALCOMANIA	UNBELIEVABLE
GLASSBLOWING	HEARTWARMING	KALEIDOSCOPE	SUPERNATURAL	DECASYLLABIC	UNCHARITABLE
INFLATIONARY	HENCEFORWARD	MADEMOISELLE	UNACCUSTOMED	DEMIMONDAINE	UNGOVERNABLE
INFLATIONISM	HOUSEWARMING	MARLINESPIKE	UNCHARITABLE	DEMONSTRABLE	UNMISTAKABLE
ISOLATIONISM	IMMEASURABLE	MULTISESSION	UNPROFITABLE	DETERMINABLE	UNPROFITABLE
MICROBIOLOGY	IMPENETRABLE	MULTITASKING	UNSCIENTIFIC	DISAGREEABLE	UNREASONABLE
MISPRONOUNCE	IMPONDERABLE	OSCILLOSCOPE	ANTEDILUVIAN	DISREPUTABLE	UNSEARCHABLE
NIGHTCLOTHES	INCOMPARABLE	PLANETESIMAL	ASTRONAUTICS	EXTRAVAGANZA	UNSEASONABLE
OFFICEHOLDER	INSALUBRIOUS	PREDIGESTION	CHEESEBURGER	HIPPOPOTAMUS	UNSEGREGATED
OVEREXPOSURE	INSUFFERABLE	QUARTERSTAFF	CLOSEMOUTHED	IMMEASURABLE	ZOOGEOGRAPHY
PALEONTOLOGY	INTEMPERANCE	QUINTESSENCE	COMMENSURATE	IMPENETRABLE	THOROUGHBRED
PARASITOLOGY	INTERFERENCE	REPERCUSSION	CONGRATULATE	IMPERISHABLE	AUTHENTICATE
PHARMACOLOGY	INVULNERABLE	SPECTROSCOPE	CONSTABULARY	IMPONDERABLE	CHIROPRACTIC
POLICYHOLDER	LEXICOGRAPHY	THUNDERSTORM	CONSTITUENCY	INCALCULABLE	CHROMATICITY
PROTECTORATE	LONGSHOREMAN	TRANSMISSION	CONSTITUTION	INCOMPARABLE	DISCONNECTED
RADIOISOTOPE	MICROCIRCUIT	TRANSVESTISM	CONSTITUTIVE	INCONSOLABLE	INCANDESCENT
RECEPTIONIST	MICROSURGERY	ACQUAINTANCE	CONTRAPUNTAL	INDECLINABLE	INTERGLACIAL
SHARECROPPER	MISINTERPRET	ADVENTITIOUS	DISTRIBUTIVE	INDISPUTABLE	KALEIDOSCOPE
SHARPSHOOTER	MULTIFARIOUS	AMBIDEXTROUS	INARTICULATE	INEFFACEABLE	MICROCIRCUIT
SPERMATOZOON	MULTIPURPOSE	ANTIPARTICLE	MALOCCLUSION	INEXPLICABLE	MICROSPACING
TRAPSHOOTING	MULTIVERSITY	ANTITHETICAL	MEALYMOUTHED	INEXTRICABLE	MULTIPLICAND
UNDERCLOTHES	NEIGHBORHOOD	BLOODLETTING	MISCALCULATE	INSUFFERABLE	MULTIPLICITY
APOSTROPHIZE	OCEANOGRAPHY	BREASTSTROKE	NONCONDUCTOR	INTEMPERANCE	NONCONDUCTOR
CHROMOSPHERE	OTHERWORLDLY	CIRCUMSTANCE	RECAPITULATE	INTERMINABLE	OSCILLOSCOPE
CLOTHESPRESS	PHYSIOGRAPHY	CONQUISTADOR	SOMNAMBULISM	INTERVOCALIC	OUTSTRETCHED
COUNTERPOINT	PREDETERMINE	CONTEMPTIBLE	THERAPEUTICS	INVULNERABLE	PERSPICACITY
COUNTERPOISE	PROTUBERANCE	CONTEMPTUOUS	UNSCRUPULOUS	IRREDEEMABLE	PREFABRICATE
DIASTROPHISM	PSYCHOTROPIC	COUNTERTENOR	UNBELIEVABLE	IRREFRAGABLE	PROPHYLACTIC
ELECTROPLATE	RECEIVERSHIP	DESTRUCTIBLE	ASTROPHYSICS	IRREMEDIABLE	PUMPERNICKEL
ENCYCLOPEDIA	REMONSTRANCE	DISCOURTEOUS	CHALCOPYRITE	LEXICOGRAPHY	SPECTROSCOPE
FRONTISPIECE	SARSAPARILLA	DISPUTATIOUS	ELEEMOSYNARY	MERCHANTABLE	STRAITJACKET
IMPERCEPTIVE	SECRETARIATE	DISREPUTABLE	GOBBLEDYGOOK	MONOSYLLABLE	CORESPONDENT
IMPERCIPIENT	SELENOGRAPHY	EARSPLITTING	HIEROGLYPHIC	MUDDLEHEADED	FREESTANDING
METAMORPHISM	SPORTSWRITER	HEADMISTRESS	OXYACETYLENE	MULLIGATAWNY	HEARTRENDING
MINICOMPUTER	STRATIGRAPHY	HIPPOPOTAMUS	POLYETHYLENE	MULTIVITAMIN	HYPERACIDITY
ONOMATOPOEIA	TRANSFERENCE	INCOMPATIBLE	PRASEODYMIUM	OCEANOGRAPHY	HYPOCHONDRIA
PHILOSOPHIZE	UNDERCURRENT	INDIGESTIBLE	UNEMPLOYMENT	OCTOSYLLABIC	PHILODENDRON
POLYMORPHISM	UNDERGARMENT	INDISPUTABLE	RECOGNIZANCE	PANCHROMATIC	PROCATHEDRAL
PRESCRIPTION	UNDERSURFACE	INTERMITTENT		PARADISIACAL	PROPAGANDIZE
STRATOSPHERE	VAINGLORIOUS	IRRESISTIBLE		PERAMBULATOR	RHODODENDRON
SUBSCRIPTION	WHIPPOORWILL	MASTERSTROKE		PHYSIOGRAPHY	TRANSCENDENT
THERMOSPHERE	ZOOGEOGRAPHY	MERCHANTABLE	**9TH LETTER**	POLYSYLLABIC	ALPHANUMERIC
WEATHERPROOF	AUDIOVISUALS	MULLIGATAWNY		POLYSYLLABLE	ANTIMAGNETIC
MAGNILOQUENT	BILLINGSGATE	MULTILATERAL	ACQUAINTANCE	PRECIPITANCY	ARGILLACEOUS
BELLIGERENCY	BLATHERSKITE	MULTIVITAMIN	AMPHITHEATER	PROGRAMMABLE	BELLIGERENCY
BIBLIOGRAPHY	BLOCKBUSTING	OUTSTRETCHED	APPURTENANCE	PROTUBERANCE	BIOTELEMETRY
BIOGEOGRAPHY	BRAINWASHING	PENITENTIARY	BIBLIOGRAPHY	QUESTIONABLE	CARBONACEOUS
BREAKTHROUGH	COMPLAISANCE	PERICYNTHION	BIOGEOGRAPHY	RECOGNIZANCE	CHECKERBERRY
CHOREOGRAPHY	DECOMMISSION	POSTDOCTORAL	CABINETMAKER	REMONSTRANCE	CINEMATHEQUE
CONSIDERABLE	DECONGESTANT	POSTMISTRESS	CHOREOGRAPHY	SELENOGRAPHY	CONCRESCENCE
CROSSCURRENT	FRANKENSTEIN	PRECIPITANCY	CIRCUMSTANCE	SIGNIFICANCE	CONSTITUENCY

COUNTERTENOR	MISAPPREHEND	SPORTSWRITER	VACATIONLAND	UNDOCUMENTED	CHEMOTHERAPY
DENSITOMETER	NEIGHBORHOOD	SUBCONSCIOUS	VERTICILLATE	UNFREQUENTED	CHILDBEARING
DISCOURTEOUS	PERICYNTHION	SUBSTANTIATE	WEATHERGLASS	VALENCIENNES	CHURCHWARDEN
DISOBEDIENCE	PHILOSOPHIZE	SUPERCILIOUS	AERODYNAMICS	AVITAMINOSIS	CIRCUMSCRIBE
ENCYCLOPEDIA	POLYMORPHISM	SURROUNDINGS	BLANDISHMENT	BREAKTHROUGH	CLOTHESPRESS
EQUESTRIENNE	SHORTSIGHTED	TRANQUILIZER	COMMENCEMENT	BUTTERSCOTCH	COELENTERATE
FLUORESCENCE	STEEPLECHASE	TRANSPACIFIC	CUMULONIMBUS	CHECKERBOARD	COMMENSURATE
FRANKINCENSE	STEPDAUGHTER	UNRESTRAINED	DISPLACEMENT	CLOTHESHORSE	COMMISSARIAT
GALVANOMETER	STRATOSPHERE	UNSCIENTIFIC	EPITHALAMIUM	COMMISSIONER	CONCELEBRANT
HYPOGLYCEMIA	SUPERHIGHWAY	VAINGLORIOUS	EVERBLOOMING	CONFECTIONER	CONGLOMERATE
INDEPENDENCE	THERMOSPHERE	WELTERWEIGHT	HEARTWARMING	CONFESSIONAL	CONTAINERIZE
INEXPERIENCE	UNLIKELIHOOD	BACKTRACKING	HELLGRAMMITE	CONVENTIONAL	CONTEMPORARY
INTELLIGENCE	ADVENTITIOUS	BLATHERSKITE	HOUSEWARMING	COUNTERPOINT	CROSSCURRENT
INTERFERENCE	ANTIPARTICLE	BLUESTOCKING	ILLEGITIMATE	COUNTERPOISE	DEMILITARIZE
LONGSHOREMAN	ANTITHETICAL	BREATHTAKING	MICROCLIMATE	FLAMETHROWER	DISACCHARIDE
LUMINESCENCE	APPENDICITIS	EARTHSHAKING	MONOFILAMENT	HALLUCINOGEN	DISINTEGRATE
LUNCHEONETTE	ASTRONOMICAL	MULTITASKING	PRASEODYMIUM	INVITATIONAL	FAINTHEARTED
MADEMOISELLE	BACTERICIDAL	SWASHBUCKLER	PREDETERMINE	MEETINGHOUSE	FLUOROCARBON
MAGNETOMETER	CHESTERFIELD	ANTHROPOLOGY	PRESENTIMENT	MULTICOLORED	GREATHEARTED
MESSEIGNEURS	CHITTERLINGS	BACTERIOLOGY	PROTHALAMION	ONOMATOPOEIA	HEADMISTRESS
MULTIFACETED	CONTEMPTIBLE	BIOSATELLITE	SLEDGEHAMMER	PACKINGHOUSE	HEAVYHEARTED
MULTILATERAL	CONTUMACIOUS	COLLEGIALITY	UNDERGARMENT	PHILHARMONIC	HUMANITARIAN
NEURASTHENIA	CONTUMELIOUS	CONGRATULATE	UNEMPLOYMENT	PLASTERBOARD	HYDROTHERAPY
NEUROSCIENCE	COSMOPOLITAN	CONSTABULARY	ABOLITIONISM	POSTDOCTORAL	HYDROTHERMAL
PROLEGOMENON	DESTRUCTIBLE	COUNTERCLAIM	ABSENTMINDED	POSTHYPNOTIC	IDIOSYNCRASY
QUINTESSENCE	DISASSOCIATE	DEMINERALIZE	ASYNCHRONOUS	PRACTITIONER	INVERTEBRATE
REMINISCENCE	DISPUTATIOUS	DISCONSOLATE	ATTITUDINIZE	PROCESSIONAL	KINDERGARTEN
SENSITOMETER	ENCEPHALITIS	DISESTABLISH	BICENTENNIAL	PROFESSIONAL	LIGHTHEARTED
SIMULTANEOUS	EXTRAMARITAL	EDITORIALIZE	CALISTHENICS	PROPORTIONAL	MASTERSTROKE
SPECTROMETER	FRONTISPIECE	ELECTROPLATE	CARILLONNEUR	PSYCHOTROPIC	NEWSPAPERMAN
STRAIGHTEDGE	HEARTSTRINGS	EPISCOPALIAN	CHRISTIANITY	SHARPSHOOTER	NONAGENARIAN
SUBCUTANEOUS	HIERARCHICAL	INARTICULATE	CHRISTIANIZE	SHUFFLEBOARD	OBSTREPEROUS
SUBSERVIENCE	IMPERCIPIENT	INTERSTELLAR	COMPANIONWAY	STEREOPHONIC	OCTOGENARIAN
TENDEROMETER	INCOMPATIBLE	MICROBIOLOGY	CONFUCIANISM	STEREOSCOPIC	PHILANTHROPY
TRANSFERENCE	INCONVENIENT	MISCALCULATE	CONTERMINOUS	TRADESPEOPLE	PHOTOENGRAVE
TRIGONOMETRY	INCORRIGIBLE	MUNICIPALITY	CONTRAPUNTAL	TUBERCULOSIS	POSTMISTRESS
UNPARALLELED	INDEFEASIBLE	NEVERTHELESS	DISCIPLINARY	UNACCUSTOMED	PRECANCEROUS
PREAMPLIFIER	INDIGESTIBLE	OFFICEHOLDER	DISCRIMINATE	WEATHERBOARD	PRECONCERTED
THOROUGHFARE	INSALUBRIOUS	OTHERWORLDLY	ELEEMOSYNARY	GLOCKENSPIEL	PREMENSTRUAL
UNDERSURFACE	INSUFFICIENT	OXYACETYLENE	ENTREPRENEUR	HIEROGLYPHIC	PREPONDERATE
BILLINGSGATE	INTELLIGIBLE	PALEONTOLOGY	EXTORTIONATE	MARLINESPIKE	PREPOSTEROUS
CARPETBAGGER	INTERMEDIARY	PARASITOLOGY	FEEBLEMINDED	MISINTERPRET	PRESBYTERIAN
GOBBLEDYGOOK	INTERMEDIATE	PHARMACOLOGY	INDOCTRINATE	MULTIPURPOSE	PROTECTORATE
INTRANSIGENT	IRRESISTIBLE	POLICYHOLDER	INFLATIONARY	PEACEKEEPING	RADIOTHERAPY
MICROSURGERY	IRREVERSIBLE	POLYETHYLENE	INFLATIONISM	PHOTOCOMPOSE	RECALCITRANT
MULTILINGUAL	LONGITUDINAL	PRINCIPALITY	INSTRUMENTAL	SHARECROPPER	SEXAGENARIAN
APOSTROPHIZE	MERETRICIOUS	RECAPITULATE	ISOLATIONISM	UNPRINCIPLED	SPECTROGRAPH
BRAINWASHING	MIDDLEWEIGHT	SCHOOLFELLOW	PORCELAINIZE	AMBIDEXTROUS	SUPERCHARGER
CHROMOSPHERE	MULTIFARIOUS	SOMNAMBULISM	PREDESIGNATE	ATMOSPHERICS	TESTOSTERONE
DIASTROPHISM	PENITENTIARY	SPIRITUALISM	PREPAREDNESS	BLOODTHIRSTY	TOTALITARIAN
DISFRANCHISE	PERTINACIOUS	STREETWALKER	PROTACTINIUM	BREASTSTROKE	TRANSMIGRATE
FORMALDEHYDE	PLANETESIMAL	TECHNICALITY	PYROTECHNICS	CANTANKEROUS	TRANSMOGRIFY
FOUNTAINHEAD	PRIMOGENITOR	THUNDERCLOUD	RECEPTIONIST	CARBOHYDRATE	UNDERCURRENT
HABERDASHERY	RAMBUNCTIOUS	UNIVERSALIST	SUBCONTINENT	CHALCOPYRITE	UNREGENERATE
HANDKERCHIEF	SARSAPARILLA	UNIVERSALITY	SUBTERRANEAN	CHARACTERIZE	VETERINARIAN
MANSLAUGHTER	SCATOLOGICAL	UNIVERSALIZE	TERCENTENARY	CHEESEBURGER	WEATHERPROOF
METAMORPHISM	SECRETARIATE	UNSCRUPULOUS	UNDERPINNING	CHEESEPARING	WHOLEHEARTED

ACCOMPLISHED	CONSTITUTION	NONOBJECTIVE	NONSCHEDULED	INARTICULATE	INCALCULABLE
ANTIALIASING	CONSTITUTIVE	OBSCURANTISM	POSTGRADUATE	INCAPACITATE	INCOMPARABLE
ANTIMACASSAR	CONSTRUCTION	ORGANIZATION	PRESUMPTUOUS	INDOCTRINATE	INCOMPATIBLE
APPREHENSIVE	CONTINUATION	PARAMILITARY	SUPERANNUATE	INFLATIONARY	INCONSOLABLE
ASTROPHYSICS	CONVERSATION	PERADVENTURE	SUPERNATURAL	INTERMEDIARY	INCORRIGIBLE
AUSTRONESIAN	DECONGESTANT	PESTILENTIAL	ANTEDILUVIAN	INTERMEDIATE	INDECLINABLE
BIOCHEMISTRY	DELIBERATIVE	PIGMENTATION	COLLECTIVISM	INVERTEBRATE	INDEFEASIBLE
CHAMPIONSHIP	DENOMINATION	POLARIZATION	COLLECTIVIZE	METALANGUAGE	INDIGESTIBLE
DECOMMISSION	DENUNCIATION	PRECONDITION	PHOTOGRAVURE	MICROCLIMATE	INDISPUTABLE
DELICATESSEN	DESPOLIATION	PREDIGESTION	RESPECTIVELY	MISCALCULATE	INDISSOLUBLE
DICTATORSHIP	DIFFERENTIAL	PREDILECTION	SCANDINAVIAN	MULTIPLICAND	INEFFACEABLE
ECCLESIASTIC	DISADVANTAGE	PREINDUCTION	THANKSGIVING	NONCOMBATANT	INEXPLICABLE
ENTERPRISING	DISPENSATION	PREOPERATIVE	CONTRARIWISE	PARAMILITARY	INEXTRICABLE
EXTRASENSORY	DISQUISITION	PRESCRIPTION	GLASSBLOWING	PENITENTIARY	INSUFFERABLE
GEOCHEMISTRY	DISSERTATION	PROVIDENTIAL	HENCEFORWARD	PHOTOENGRAVE	INTELLIGIBLE
HYPERTENSION	DISTILLATION	PSYCHOACTIVE	PICKERELWEED	PLASTERBOARD	INTERMINABLE
INTERCESSION	DISTRIBUTIVE	QUANTITATIVE	UNDERDRAWERS	POSTGRADUATE	INVULNERABLE
INTERMISSION	EARSPLITTING	QUARTERSTAFF	WHIPPOORWILL	PREDESIGNATE	IRREDEEMABLE
MALNOURISHED	ECHOLOCATION	RADIOISOTOPE	HETEROSEXUAL	PREFABRICATE	IRREFRAGABLE
MALOCCLUSION	EXCRUCIATING	RECOLLECTION	PSYCHOSEXUAL	PREPONDERATE	IRREMEDIABLE
MISREPRESENT	FENESTRATION	RECONSTITUTE	ELECTROLYSIS	PROTECTORATE	IRRESISTIBLE
MOUNTAINSIDE	FERMENTATION	REGISTRATION	STREPTOMYCIN	QUARTERSTAFF	IRREVERSIBLE
MULTISESSION	FIBRILLATION	REHABILITATE	NEWSMAGAZINE	RADIOTHERAPY	MERCHANTABLE
MULTIVERSITY	FRANKENSTEIN	REMUNERATION	SPERMATOZOON	RECALCITRANT	MONOSYLLABLE
OVEREXPOSURE	HAIRSPLITTER	REMUNERATIVE		RECAPITULATE	OCTOSYLLABIC
PARENTHESIZE	HEADQUARTERS	RENUNCIATION		REHABILITATE	POLYSYLLABIC
PREREQUISITE	HELIOCENTRIC	RESTAURATEUR		SECRETARIATE	POLYSYLLABLE
RECEIVERSHIP	HORTICULTURE	RESURRECTION	**10TH LETTER**	SHUFFLEBOARD	PROGRAMMABLE
RELATIONSHIP	HYSTERECTOMY	SATISFACTION		SPECTROGRAPH	QUESTIONABLE
RELATIVISTIC	ILLUSTRATION	SATISFACTORY	AUDIOVISUALS	STEEPLECHASE	UNASSAILABLE
REPERCUSSION	ILLUSTRATIVE	SUBCOMMITTEE	AUTHENTICATE	SUBSTANTIATE	UNBELIEVABLE
SCHOOLMASTER	IMPERCEPTIVE	SUBDIRECTORY	BILLINGSGATE	SUPERANNUATE	UNCHARITABLE
TRANSMISSION	IMPERFECTION	SUBMINIATURE	CARBOHYDRATE	TERCENTENARY	UNGOVERNABLE
UNINTERESTED	INCAPACITATE	SUBSCRIPTION	CHECKERBOARD	THOROUGHFARE	UNMISTAKABLE
ABBREVIATION	INCRUSTATION	SUBSTRUCTURE	CHEMOTHERAPY	TRANSMIGRATE	UNPROFITABLE
ALLITERATION	INFELICITOUS	SUPERSTITION	COELENTERATE	ULTRAMONTANE	UNREASONABLE
ANATHEMATIZE	INFLAMMATION	THERAPEUTICS	COMMENSURATE	UNDERSURFACE	UNSEARCHABLE
ANNUNCIATION	INFLAMMATORY	THUNDERSTORM	CONCELEBRANT	UNREGENERATE	UNSEASONABLE
ANTIELECTRON	INGRATIATING	TRANSVESTISM	CONGLOMERATE	VACATIONLAND	ANTIPARTICLE
APPENDECTOMY	INSURRECTION	TRAPSHOOTING	CONGRATULATE	VERTICILLATE	ANTITHETICAL
APPRECIATIVE	INTELLECTUAL	TRIGNOMETRIC	CONSTABULARY	WEATHERBOARD	ASTRONOMICAL
ARCHITECTURE	INTERJECTION	ULTRAMONTANE	CONTEMPORARY	WEATHERGLASS	HIERARCHICAL
ASTRONAUTICS	INTERMITTENT	UNDERCLOTHES	COUNTERCLAIM	COMMUNICABLE	PARADISIACAL
BLOCKBUSTING	INTERSECTION	UNDERCOATING	DECONGESTANT	CONSIDERABLE	SCATOLOGICAL
BLOODLETTING	INTRANSITIVE	VALORIZATION	DISADVANTAGE	CONTEMPTIBLE	STREPTOMYCIN
BRILLIANTINE	IRRESPECTIVE	VENIPUNCTURE	DISASSOCIATE	CUMULONIMBUS	ABSENTMINDED
CIVILIZATION	JURISDICTION	AFORETHOUGHT	DISCIPLINARY	DECASYLLABIC	BACTERICIDAL
CLOSEMOUTHED	MALFORMATION	AFTERTHOUGHT	DISCONSOLATE	DEMONSTRABLE	CHURCHWARDEN
CONFIDENTIAL	MALNUTRITION	AUDIOVISUALS	DISCRIMINATE	DESTRUCTIBLE	CONQUISTADOR
CONFIRMATION	MASTURBATION	CONTEMPTUOUS	DISINTEGRATE	DETERMINABLE	ENCYCLOPEDIA
CONFORMATION	MEALYMOUTHED	DISINGENUOUS	ELECTROPLATE	DISAGREEABLE	FEEBLEMINDED
CONGREGATION	MENSTRUATION	INDISSOLUBLE	ELEEMOSYNARY	DISREPUTABLE	MUDDLEHEADED
CONSERVATION	MISADVENTURE	INTERLOCUTOR	EXTORTIONATE	FLUOROCARBON	OFFICEHOLDER
CONSERVATISM	NIGHTCLOTHES	MAGNILOQUENT	HENCEFORWARD	IMMEASURABLE	OTHERWORLDLY
CONSERVATIVE	NOMENCLATURE	METALANGUAGE	HYDROTHERAPY	IMPENETRABLE	POLICYHOLDER
CONSERVATORY	NONCOMBATANT	MINICOMPUTER	IDIOSYNCRASY	IMPERISHABLE	STRAIGHTEDGE
CONSTIPATION	NONCOMMITTAL	MISPRONOUNCE	ILLEGITIMATE	IMPONDERABLE	BLANDISHMENT

CARILLONNEUR	CLOSEMOUTHED	CONSERVATIVE	INFLAMMATION	PROTHALAMION	PLANETESIMAL
CHESTERFIELD	DICTATORSHIP	CONSTIPATION	INFLATIONISM	PROVIDENTIAL	SLEDGEHAMMER
CHROMOSPHERE	HIEROGLYPHIC	CONSTITUTION	INGRATIATING	PSYCHOACTIVE	UNACCUSTOMED
CLOTHESPRESS	MALNOURISHED	CONSTITUTIVE	INSURRECTION	PYROTECHNICS	ACQUAINTANCE
COMMENCEMENT	MEALYMOUTHED	CONSTRUCTION	INTERCESSION	QUANTITATIVE	APPURTENANCE
CORESPONDENT	NIGHTCLOTHES	CONTAINERIZE	INTERGLACIAL	RECEPTIONIST	BELLIGERENCY
CROSSCURRENT	OUTSTRETCHED	CONTINUATION	INTERJECTION	RECOLLECTION	CHITTERLINGS
DISPLACEMENT	RECEIVERSHIP	CONTRARIWISE	INTERMISSION	REGISTRATION	CIRCUMSTANCE
ENTREPRENEUR	RELATIONSHIP	CONVERSATION	INTERSECTION	REMUNERATION	COMMISSIONER
FOUNTAINHEAD	UNDERCLOTHES	COUNTERPOINT	INTRANSITIVE	REMUNERATIVE	COMPLAISANCE
FRANKENSTEIN	ABBREVIATION	COUNTERPOISE	IRRESPECTIVE	RENUNCIATION	CONCRESCENCE
FRONTISPIECE	ABOLITIONISM	DECOMMISSION	ISOLATIONISM	REPERCUSSION	CONFECTIONER
HABERDASHERY	AERODYNAMICS	DELIBERATIVE	JURISDICTION	RESURRECTION	CONFESSIONAL
HEADMISTRESS	ALLITERATION	DEMILITARIZE	MALFORMATION	SATISFACTION	CONSTITUENCY
HEADQUARTERS	ANATHEMATIZE	DEMIMONDAINE	MALNUTRITION	SCANDINAVIAN	CONVENTIONAL
IMPERCIPIENT	ANNUNCIATION	DEMINERALIZE	MALOCCLUSION	SEXAGENARIAN	COUNTERTENOR
INCANDESCENT	ANTEDILUVIAN	DENOMINATION	MARLINESPIKE	SOMNAMBULISM	DECALCOMANIA
INCONVENIENT	ANTIALIASING	DENUNCIATION	MASTURBATION	SPIRITUALISM	DISOBEDIENCE
INSUFFICIENT	APOSTROPHIZE	DESPOLIATION	MENSTRUATION	SUBSCRIPTION	EQUESTRIENNE
INTERMITTENT	APPRECIATIVE	DIASTROPHISM	METAMORPHISM	SUPERSTITION	EXTRAVAGANZA
INTRANSIGENT	APPREHENSIVE	DIFFERENTIAL	MICROSPACING	TECHNICALITY	FLUORESCENCE
MAGNILOQUENT	ASTRONAUTICS	DISACCHARIDE	MOUNTAINSIDE	THANKSGIVING	FRANKINCENSE
MICROSURGERY	ASTROPHYSICS	DISESTABLISH	MULTIPLICITY	THERAPEUTICS	HEARTSTRINGS
MISAPPREHEND	ATMOSPHERICS	DISFRANCHISE	MULTISESSION	TOTALITARIAN	INDEPENDENCE
MISREPRESENT	ATTITUDINIZE	DISPENSATION	MULTITASKING	TRANSMISSION	INEXPERIENCE
MONOFILAMENT	AUSTRONESIAN	DISQUISITION	MULTIVERSITY	TRANSMOGRIFY	INTELLIGENCE
NEVERTHELESS	BACKTRACKING	DISSERTATION	MUNICIPALITY	TRANSVESTISM	INTEMPERANCE
ONOMATOPOEIA	BICENTENNIAL	DISTILLATION	NEWSMAGAZINE	TRAPSHOOTING	INTERFERENCE
OXYACETYLENE	BIOSATELLITE	DISTRIBUTIVE	NONAGENARIAN	UNDERCOATING	INVITATIONAL
PICKERELWEED	BLATHERSKITE	EARSPLITTING	NONOBJECTIVE	UNDERPINNING	LONGITUDINAL
POLYETHYLENE	BLOCKBUSTING	EARTHSHAKING	OBSCURANTISM	UNIVERSALIST	LUMINESCENCE
POSTMISTRESS	BLOODLETTING	ECHOLOCATION	OCTOGENARIAN	UNIVERSALITY	MISPRONOUNCE
PREPAREDNESS	BLUESTOCKING	EDITORIALIZE	ORGANIZATION	UNIVERSALIZE	NEURASTHENIA
PRESENTIMENT	BRAINWASHING	ENTERPRISING	PARENTHESIZE	VALORIZATION	NEUROSCIENCE
RESPECTIVELY	BREATHTAKING	EPISCOPALIAN	PEACEKEEPING	VETERINARIAN	PHILHARMONIC
RESTAURATEUR	BRILLIANTINE	EPITHALAMIUM	PERICYNTHION	WHIPPOORWILL	PRACTITIONER
STRATOSPHERE	CALISTHENICS	EVERBLOOMING	PERSPICACITY	CABINETMAKER	PRECIPITANCY
SUBCONTINENT	CHALCOPYRITE	EXCRUCIATING	PESTILENTIAL	PUMPERNICKEL	PROCESSIONAL
SUBTERRANEAN	CHARACTERIZE	FENESTRATION	PHILOSOPHIZE	STRAITJACKET	PROFESSIONAL
THERMOSPHERE	CHEESEPARING	FERMENTATION	PIGMENTATION	STREETWALKER	PROLEGOMENON
TRANSCENDENT	CHILDBEARING	FIBRILLATION	POLARIZATION	TROUBLEMAKER	PROPORTIONAL
UNDERCURRENT	CHRISTIANITY	FREESTANDING	POLYMORPHISM	COMMONWEALTH	PROTUBERANCE
UNDERDRAWERS	CHRISTIANIZE	GLASSBLOWING	PORCELAINIZE	INTERSTELLAR	QUINTESSENCE
UNDERGARMENT	CHROMATICITY	GLOCKENSPIEL	PRASEODYMIUM	INTERVOCALIC	RECOGNIZANCE
UNEMPLOYMENT	CIRCUMSCRIBE	HANDKERCHIEF	PREAMPLIFIER	MADEMOISELLE	REMINISCENCE
TRANSPACIFIC	CIVILIZATION	HEARTRENDING	PRECONDITION	NONSCHEDULED	REMONSTRANCE
UNSCIENTIFIC	COLLECTIVISM	HEARTWARMING	PREDETERMINE	SARSAPARILLA	SIGNIFICANCE
AFORETHOUGHT	COLLECTIVIZE	HELLGRAMMITE	PREDIGESTION	SCHOOLFELLOW	STEREOPHONIC
AFTERTHOUGHT	COLLEGIALITY	HOUSEWARMING	PREDILECTION	SWASHBUCKLER	SUBSERVIENCE
CARPETBAGGER	COMMISSARIAT	HUMANITARIAN	PREINDUCTION	UNPARALLELED	SURROUNDINGS
CHEESEBURGER	CONFIDENTIAL	HYPERACIDITY	PREOPERATIVE	UNPRINCIPLED	SURVEILLANCE
HALLUCINOGEN	CONFIRMATION	HYPERTENSION	PREREQUISITE	HIPPOPOTAMUS	TRANSFERENCE
MIDDLEWEIGHT	CONFORMATION	ILLUSTRATION	PRESBYTERIAN	HYDROTHERMAL	TRANSOCEANIC
SUPERCHARGER	CONFUCIANISM	ILLUSTRATIVE	PRESCRIPTION	HYPOGLYCEMIA	UNRESTRAINED
WELTERWEIGHT	CONGREGATION	IMPERCEPTIVE	PRINCIPALITY	LONGSHOREMAN	VALENCIENNES
ACCOMPLISHED	CONSERVATION	IMPERFECTION	PROPAGANDIZE	MULTIVITAMIN	ADVENTITIOUS
CHAMPIONSHIP	CONSERVATISM	INCRUSTATION	PROTACTINIUM	NEWSPAPERMAN	AMBIDEXTROUS

ANTHROPOLOGY	BIBLIOGRAPHY	INSTRUMENTAL	STRAIGHTAWAY	SCATOLOGICAL	COMMISSIONER
APPENDECTOMY	BIOGEOGRAPHY	INTERLOCUTOR	SUPERHIGHWAY	SEXAGENARIAN	CONFECTIONER
ARGILLACEOUS	CHOREOGRAPHY	KINDERGARTEN	FORMALDEHYDE	STRAIGHTAWAY	DELICATESSEN
ASYNCHRONOUS	CRYPTOGRAPHY	LIGHTHEARTED	TRANQUILIZER	SUBTERRANEAN	DENSITOMETER
BACTERIOLOGY	LEXICOGRAPHY	LUNCHEONETTE		SUPERHIGHWAY	DISCONNECTED
BREASTSTROKE	OCEANOGRAPHY	MAGNETOMETER		SUPERNATURAL	FAINTHEARTED
CANTANKEROUS	PHYSIOGRAPHY	MANSLAUGHTER		TOTALITARIAN	FEEBLEMINDED
CARBONACEOUS	PSYCHOTROPIC	MINICOMPUTER	**11TH LETTER**	VETERINARIAN	FLAMETHROWER
CONSERVATORY	SELENOGRAPHY	MULTIFACETED		CIRCUMSCRIBE	GALVANOMETER
CONTEMPTUOUS	SHARECROPPER	NONCOMMITTAL	ANTEDILUVIAN	ACQUAINTANCE	GLOCKENSPIEL
CONTERMINOUS	STEREOSCOPIC	NONCONDUCTOR	ANTIMACASSAR	AERODYNAMICS	GREATHEARTED
CONTUMACIOUS	STRATIGRAPHY	PANCHROMATIC	ANTITHETICAL	APPURTENANCE	HAIRSPLITTER
CONTUMELIOUS	TRADESPEOPLE	PERAMBULATOR	ASTRONOMICAL	ASTRONAUTICS	HALLUCINOGEN
DISCOURTEOUS	ZOOGEOGRAPHY	POSTHYPNOTIC	AUSTRONESIAN	ASTROPHYSICS	HANDKERCHIEF
DISINGENUOUS	CINEMATHEQUE	PRECONCERTED	BACTERICIDAL	ATMOSPHERICS	HEAVYHEARTED
DISPUTATIOUS	ALPHANUMERIC	PRIMOGENITOR	BICENTENNIAL	BELLIGERENCY	KINDERGARTEN
EXTRASENSORY	ANTIELECTRON	PROPHYLACTIC	COMMISSARIAT	BUTTERSCOTCH	LIGHTHEARTED
GOBBLEDYGOOK	CHECKERBERRY	RELATIVISTIC	COMPANIONWAY	CALISTHENICS	MAGNETOMETER
HYSTERECTOMY	CLOTHESHORSE	SCHOOLMASTER	CONFESSIONAL	CIRCUMSTANCE	MALNOURISHED
INFELICITOUS	HELIOCENTRIC	SENSITOMETER	CONFIDENTIAL	COMPLAISANCE	MANSLAUGHTER
INFLAMMATORY	HYPOCHONDRIA	SHARPSHOOTER	CONTRAPUNTAL	CONCRESCENCE	MEALYMOUTHED
INSALUBRIOUS	MISINTERPRET	SHORTSIGHTED	CONVENTIONAL	CONSTITUENCY	MINICOMPUTER
KALEIDOSCOPE	MULTICOLORED	SPECTROMETER	COSMOPOLITAN	DISOBEDIENCE	MISINTERPRET
MASTERSTROKE	MULTILATERAL	SPORTSWRITER	DIFFERENTIAL	FLUORESCENCE	MUDDLEHEADED
MERETRICIOUS	PHILODENDRON	STEPDAUGHTER	EPISCOPALIAN	FRONTISPIECE	MULTICOLORED
MICROBIOLOGY	POSTDOCTORAL	SUBCOMMITTEE	EXTRAMARITAL	INDEPENDENCE	MULTIFACETED
MULTIFARIOUS	PROCATHEDRAL	TENDEROMETER	FOUNTAINHEAD	INEXPERIENCE	NIGHTCLOTHES
MULTIPURPOSE	RHODODENDRON	TRIGONOMETRY	HETEROSEXUAL	INTELLIGENCE	NONSCHEDULED
NEIGHBORHOOD	SUPERNATURAL	UNDOCUMENTED	HIERARCHICAL	INTEMPERANCE	OFFICEHOLDER
OBSTREPEROUS	THOROUGHBRED	UNFREQUENTED	HUMANITARIAN	INTERFERENCE	OUTSTRETCHED
OSCILLOSCOPE	TRIGNOMETRIC	UNINTERESTED	HYDROTHERMAL	LUMINESCENCE	PICKERELWEED
PALEONTOLOGY	ANTIMACASSAR	UNSEGREGATED	INSTRUMENTAL	MISPRONOUNCE	POLICYHOLDER
PARASITOLOGY	AVITAMINOSIS	WHOLEHEARTED	INTELLECTUAL	NEUROSCIENCE	PRACTITIONER
PERTINACIOUS	BLOODTHIRSTY	ARCHITECTURE	INTERGLACIAL	PRECIPITANCY	PREAMPLIFIER
PHARMACOLOGY	DELICATESSEN	BREAKTHROUGH	INTERSTELLAR	PROTUBERANCE	PRECONCERTED
PHILANTHROPY	ELECTROLYSIS	HETEROSEXUAL	INVITATIONAL	PYROTECHNICS	PUMPERNICKEL
PHOTOCOMPOSE	TUBERCULOSIS	HORTICULTURE	LONGITUDINAL	QUINTESSENCE	SCHOOLMASTER
PRECANCEROUS	AMPHITHEATER	INTELLECTUAL	LONGSHOREMAN	RECOGNIZANCE	SENSITOMETER
PREPOSTEROUS	ANTIMAGNETIC	MEETINGHOUSE	MULTILATERAL	REMINISCENCE	SHARECROPPER
PRESUMPTUOUS	APPENDICITIS	MESSEIGNEURS	MULTILINGUAL	REMONSTRANCE	SHARPSHOOTER
RADIOISOTOPE	BIOCHEMISTRY	MICROCIRCUIT	NEWSPAPERMAN	SIGNIFICANCE	SHORTSIGHTED
RAMBUNCTIOUS	BIOTELEMETRY	MISADVENTURE	NONAGENARIAN	SUBSERVIENCE	SLEDGEHAMMER
SATISFACTORY	BUTTERSCOTCH	MULTILINGUAL	NONCOMMITTAL	SURVEILLANCE	SPECTROMETER
SIMULTANEOUS	CHIROPRACTIC	NOMENCLATURE	OCTOGENARIAN	THERAPEUTICS	SPORTSWRITER
SPECTROSCOPE	CONTRAPUNTAL	OVEREXPOSURE	PARADISIACAL	TRANSFERENCE	STEPDAUGHTER
SPERMATOZOON	COSMOPOLITAN	PACKINGHOUSE	PESTILENTIAL	UNDERSURFACE	STRAITJACKET
SUBCONSCIOUS	DENSITOMETER	PERADVENTURE	PLANETESIMAL	DISACCHARIDE	STREETWALKER
SUBCUTANEOUS	DISCONNECTED	PHOTOGRAVURE	POSTDOCTORAL	FORMALDEHYDE	SUBCOMMITTEE
SUBDIRECTORY	ECCLESIASTIC	PREMENSTRUAL	PREMENSTRUAL	MOUNTAINSIDE	SUPERCHARGER
SUPERCILIOUS	ENCEPHALITIS	PSYCHOSEXUAL	PRESBYTERIAN	ABSENTMINDED	SWASHBUCKLER
TESTOSTERONE	EXTRAMARITAL	RECONSTITUTE	PROCATHEDRAL	ACCOMPLISHED	TENDEROMETER
THUNDERCLOUD	FAINTHEARTED	SUBMINIATURE	PROCESSIONAL	AMPHITHEATER	THOROUGHBRED
THUNDERSTORM	GALVANOMETER	SUBSTRUCTURE	PROFESSIONAL	CABINETMAKER	TRANQUILIZER
UNLIKELIHOOD	GEOCHEMISTRY	VENIPUNCTURE	PROPORTIONAL	CARPETBAGGER	TROUBLEMAKER
UNSCRUPULOUS	GREATHEARTED	COMPANIONWAY	PROVIDENTIAL	CHEESEBURGER	UNACCUSTOMED
VAINGLORIOUS	HAIRSPLITTER	FLAMETHROWER	PSYCHOSEXUAL	CHURCHWARDEN	UNDERCLOTHES
WEATHERPROOF	HEAVYHEARTED	MULLIGATAWNY	SCANDINAVIAN	CLOSEMOUTHED	UNDOCUMENTED

UNFREQUENTED	MICROCIRCUIT	IRREDEEMABLE	IMPERCIPIENT	DISSERTATION	WEATHERPROOF
UNINTERESTED	MULTIVITAMIN	IRREFRAGABLE	INCANDESCENT	DISTILLATION	CHEMOTHERAPY
UNPARALLELED	NEURASTHENIA	IRREMEDIABLE	INCONVENIENT	ECHOLOCATION	HYDROTHERAPY
UNPRINCIPLED	OCTOSYLLABIC	IRRESISTIBLE	INGRATIATING	FENESTRATION	KALEIDOSCOPE
UNRESTRAINED	ONOMATOPEIA	IRREVERSIBLE	INSUFFICIENT	FERMENTATION	OSCILLOSCOPE
UNSEGREGATED	PANCHROMATIC	MADEMOISELLE	INTERMITTENT	FIBRILLATION	PHILANTHROPY
VALENCIENNES	PHILHARMONIC	MERCHANTABLE	INTRANSIGENT	FLUOROCARBON	RADIOISOTOPE
WHOLEHEARTED	POLYSYLLABIC	MONOSYLLABLE	MAGNILOQUENT	GOBBLEDYGOOK	RADIOTHERAPY
QUARTERSTAFF	POSTHYPNOTIC	OTHERWORLDLY	MICROSPACING	HYPERTENSION	SPECTROGRAPH
TRANSMOGRIFY	PROPHYLACTIC	POLYSYLLABLE	MISAPPREHEND	ILLUSTRATION	SPECTROSCOPE
ANTHROPOLOGY	PSYCHOTROPIC	PROGRAMMABLE	MISREPRESENT	IMPERFECTION	ARCHITECTURE
BACTERIOLOGY	RECEIVERSHIP	QUESTIONABLE	MONOFILAMENT	INCRUSTATION	BIOCHEMISTRY
BREAKTHROUGH	RELATIONSHIP	RESPECTIVELY	MULLIGATAWNY	INFLAMMATION	BIOTELEMETRY
CHITTERLINGS	RELATIVISTIC	SARSAPARILLA	MULTIPLICAND	INSURRECTION	CHECKERBERRY
DISADVANTAGE	STEREOPHONIC	TRADESPEOPLE	MULTITASKING	INTERCESSION	CHECKERBOARD
HEARTSTRINGS	STEREOSCOPIC	UNASSAILABLE	NEWSMAGAZINE	INTERJECTION	CHROMOSPHERE
METALANGUAGE	STREPTOMYCIN	UNBELIEVABLE	NONCOMBATANT	INTERLOCUTOR	CONSERVATORY
MICROBIOLOGY	TRANSOCEANIC	UNCHARITABLE	OXYACETYLENE	INTERMISSION	CONSTABULARY
PALEONTOLOGY	TRANSPACIFIC	UNGOVERNABLE	PEACEKEEPING	INTERSECTION	CONTEMPORARY
PARASITOLOGY	TRIGNOMETRIC	UNMISTAKABLE	POLYETHYLENE	JURISDICTION	DISCIPLINARY
PHARMACOLOGY	TUBERCULOSIS	UNPROFITABLE	PREDETERMINE	MALFORMATION	ELEEMOSYNARY
STRAIGHTEDGE	UNSCIENTIFIC	UNREASONABLE	PRESENTIMENT	MALNUTRITION	EXTRASENSORY
SURROUNDINGS	BREASTSTROKE	UNSEARCHABLE	RECALCITRANT	MALOCCLUSION	GEOCHEMISTRY
AFORETHOUGHT	MARLINESPIKE	UNSEASONABLE	SUBCONTINENT	MASTURBATION	HABERDASHERY
AFTERTHOUGHT	MASTERSTROKE	WHIPPOORWILL	TESTOSTERONE	MENSTRUATION	HEADQUARTERS
BIBLIOGRAPHY	ANTIPARTICLE	APPENDECTOMY	THANKSGIVING	MULTISESSION	HENCEFORWARD
BIOGEOGRAPHY	AUDIOVISUALS	HYSTERECTOMY	TRANSCENDENT	NEIGHBORHOOD	HORTICULTURE
CHOREOGRAPHY	CHESTERFIELD	ANTIALIASING	TRAPSHOOTING	NONCONDUCTOR	INFLAMMATORY
CRYPTOGRAPHY	COMMUNICABLE	BACKTRACKING	ULTRAMONTANE	ORGANIZATION	INFLATIONARY
LEXICOGRAPHY	CONSIDERABLE	BLANDISHMENT	UNDERCOATING	PERAMBULATOR	INTERMEDIARY
MIDDLEWEIGHT	CONTEMPTIBLE	BLOCKBUSTING	UNDERCURRENT	PERICYNTHION	MESSEIGNEURS
OCEANOGRAPHY	DEMONSTRABLE	BLOODLETTING	UNDERGARMENT	PHILODENDRON	MICROSURGERY
PHYSIOGRAPHY	DESTRUCTIBLE	BLUESTOCKING	UNDERPINNING	PIGMENTATION	MISADVENTURE
SELENOGRAPHY	DETERMINABLE	BRAINWASHING	UNEMPLOYMENT	POLARIZATION	NOMENCLATURE
STRATIGRAPHY	DISAGREEABLE	BREATHTAKING	VACATIONLAND	PRECONDITION	OVEREXPOSURE
WELTERWEIGHT	DISREPUTABLE	BRILLIANTINE	ABBREVIATION	PREDIGESTION	PARAMILITARY
ZOOGEOGRAPHY	IMMEASURABLE	CHEESEPARING	ALLITERATION	PREDILECTION	PENITENTIARY
ALPHANUMERIC	IMPENETRABLE	CHILDBEARING	ANNUNCIATION	PREINDUCTION	PERADVENTURE
ANTIMAGNETIC	IMPERISHABLE	COMMENCEMENT	ANTIELECTRON	PRESCRIPTION	PHOTOGRAVURE
APPENDICITIS	IMPONDERABLE	CONCELEBRANT	CIVILIZATION	PRIMOGENITOR	PLASTERBOARD
AVITAMINOSIS	INCALCULABLE	CORESPONDENT	CONFIRMATION	PROLEGOMENON	SATISFACTORY
CHAMPIONSHIP	INCOMPARABLE	COUNTERPOINT	CONFORMATION	PROTHALAMION	SHUFFLEBOARD
CHIROPRACTIC	INCOMPATIBLE	CROSSCURRENT	CONGREGATION	RECOLLECTION	STRATOSPHERE
COUNTERCLAIM	INCONSOLABLE	DECONGESTANT	CONQUISTADOR	REGISTRATION	SUBDIRECTORY
DECALCOMANIA	INCORRIGIBLE	DEMIMONDAINE	CONSERVATION	REMUNERATION	SUBMINIATURE
DECASYLLABIC	INDECLINABLE	DISPLACEMENT	CONSTIPATION	RENUNCIATION	SUBSTRUCTURE
DICTATORSHIP	INDEFEASIBLE	EARSPLITTING	CONSTITUTION	REPERCUSSION	TERCENTENARY
ECCLESIASTIC	INDIGESTIBLE	EARTHSHAKING	CONSTRUCTION	RESURRECTION	THERMOSPHERE
ELECTROLYSIS	INDISPUTABLE	ENTERPRISING	CONTINUATION	RHODODENDRON	THOROUGHFARE
ENCEPHALITIS	INDISSOLUBLE	EQUESTRIENNE	CONVERSATION	SATISFACTION	THUNDERSTORM
ENCYCLOPEDIA	INEFFACEABLE	EVERBLOOMING	COUNTERTENOR	SCHOOLFELLOW	TRIGONOMETRY
FRANKENSTEIN	INEXPLICABLE	EXCRUCIATING	DECOMMISSION	SPERMATOZOON	UNDERDRAWERS
HELIOCENTRIC	INEXTRICABLE	FREESTANDING	DENOMINATION	SUBSCRIPTION	VENIPUNCTURE
HIEROGLYPHIC	INSUFFERABLE	GLASSBLOWING	DENUNCIATION	SUPERSTITION	WEATHERBOARD
HYPOCHONDRIA	INTELLIGIBLE	HEARTRENDING	DESPOLIATION	TRANSMISSION	ABOLITIONISM
HYPOGLYCEMIA	INTERMINABLE	HEARTWARMING	DISPENSATION	UNLIKELIHOOD	CLOTHESHORSE
INTERVOCALIC	INVULNERABLE	HOUSEWARMING	DISQUISITION	VALORIZATION	CLOTHESPRESS

COLLECTIVISM	INTERMEDIATE	RAMBUNCTIOUS	DECASYLLABIC	UNSEGREGATED	DISINTEGRATE
CONFUCIANISM	INVERTEBRATE	RESTAURATEUR	ECCLESIASTIC	VACATIONLAND	DISOBEDIENCE
CONSERVATISM	LUNCHEONETTE	SIMULTANEOUS	HELIOCENTRIC	WEATHERBOARD	DISREPUTABLE
CONTRARIWISE	MICROCLIMATE	SUBCONSCIOUS	HIEROGLYPHIC	WHOLEHEARTED	DISTRIBUTIVE
COUNTERPOISE	MISCALCULATE	SUBCUTANEOUS	INTERVOCALIC	ACQUAINTANCE	EDITORIALIZE
DIASTROPHISM	MULTIPLICITY	SUPERCILIOUS	OCTOSYLLABIC	ANATHEMATIZE	ELECTROPLATE
DISESTABLISH	MULTIVERSITY	THUNDERCLOUD	PANCHROMATIC	ANTIPARTICLE	EQUESTRIENNE
DISFRANCHISE	MUNICIPALITY	UNSCRUPULOUS	PHILHARMONIC	APOSTROPHIZE	EXTORTIONATE
FRANKINCENSE	PERSPICACITY	VAINGLORIOUS	POLYSYLLABIC	APPRECIATIVE	FLUORESCENCE
HEADMISTRESS	POSTGRADUATE	APPRECIATIVE	POSTHYPNOTIC	APPREHENSIVE	FORMALDEHYDE
IDIOSYNCRASY	PREDESIGNATE	APPREHENSIVE	PROPHYLACTIC	APPURTENANCE	FRANKINCENSE
INFLATIONISM	PREFABRICATE	CONSERVATIVE	PSYCHOTROPIC	ARCHITECTURE	FRONTISPIECE
ISOLATIONISM	PREPONDERATE	CONSTITUTIVE	RELATIVISTIC	ATTITUDINIZE	HELLGRAMMITE
MEETINGHOUSE	PREREQUISITE	DELIBERATIVE	STEREOPHONIC	AUTHENTICATE	HORTICULTURE
METAMORPHISM	PRINCIPALITY	DISTRIBUTIVE	STEREOSCOPIC	BILLINGSGATE	ILLEGITIMATE
MULTIPURPOSE	PROTECTORATE	ILLUSTRATIVE	TRANSOCEANIC	BIOSATELLITE	ILLUSTRATIVE
NEVERTHELESS	RECAPITULATE	IMPERCEPTIVE	TRANSPACIFIC	BLATHERSKITE	IMMEASURABLE
OBSCURANTISM	RECONSTITUTE	INTRANSITIVE	TRIGNOMETRIC	BREASTSTROKE	IMPENETRABLE
PACKINGHOUSE	REHABILITATE	IRRESPECTIVE	UNSCIENTIFIC	BRILLIANTINE	IMPERCEPTIVE
PHOTOCOMPOSE	SECRETARIATE	NONOBJECTIVE	ABSENTMINDED	CARBOHYDRATE	IMPERISHABLE
POLYMORPHISM	SUBSTANTIATE	PHOTOENGRAVE	ACCOMPLISHED	CHALCOPYRITE	IMPONDERABLE
POSTMISTRESS	SUPERANNUATE	PREOPERATIVE	CHECKERBOARD	CHARACTERIZE	INARTICULATE
PREPAREDNESS	TECHNICALITY	PSYCHOACTIVE	CHESTERFIELD	CHRISTIANIZE	INCALCULABLE
RECEPTIONIST	TRANSMIGRATE	QUANTITATIVE	CLOSEMOUTHED	CHROMOSPHERE	INCAPACITATE
SOMNAMBULISM	UNIVERSALITY	REMUNERATIVE	DISCONNECTED	CINEMATHEQUE	INCOMPARABLE
SPIRITUALISM	UNREGENERATE	ANATHEMATIZE	FAINTHEARTED	CIRCUMSCRIBE	INCOMPATIBLE
STEEPLECHASE	VERTICILLATE	APOSTROPHIZE	FEEBLEMINDED	CIRCUMSTANCE	INCONSOLABLE
TRANSVESTISM	ADVENTITIOUS	ATTITUDINIZE	FOUNTAINHEAD	CLOTHESHORSE	INCORRIGIBLE
UNIVERSALIST	AMBIDEXTROUS	CHARACTERIZE	GREATHEARTED	COELENTERATE	INDECLINABLE
WEATHERGLASS	ARGILLACEOUS	CHRISTIANIZE	HEAVYHEARTED	COLLECTIVIZE	INDEFEASIBLE
AUTHENTICATE	ASYNCHRONOUS	COLLECTIVIZE	HENCEFORWARD	COMMENSURATE	INDEPENDENCE
BILLINGSGATE	CANTANKEROUS	CONTAINERIZE	LIGHTHEARTED	COMMUNICABLE	INDIGESTIBLE
BIOSATELLITE	CARBONACEOUS	DEMILITARIZE	MALNOURISHED	COMPLAISANCE	INDISPUTABLE
BLATHERSKITE	CARILLONNEUR	DEMINERALIZE	MEALYMOUTHED	CONCRESCENCE	INDISSOLUBLE
BLOODTHIRSTY	CINEMATHEQUE	EDITORIALIZE	MISAPPREHEND	CONGLOMERATE	INDOCTRINATE
CARBOHYDRATE	CONTEMPTUOUS	EXTRAVAGANZA	MUDDLEHEADED	CONGRATULATE	INEFFACEABLE
CHALCOPYRITE	CONTERMINOUS	PARENTHESIZE	MULTICOLORED	CONSERVATIVE	INEXPERIENCE
CHRISTIANITY	CONTUMACIOUS	PHILOSOPHIZE	MULTIFACETED	CONSIDERABLE	INEXPLICABLE
CHROMATICITY	CONTUMELIOUS	PORCELAINIZE	MULTIPLICAND	CONSTITUTIVE	INEXTRICABLE
COELENTERATE	CUMULONIMBUS	PROPAGANDIZE	NEIGHBORHOOD	CONTAINERIZE	INSUFFERABLE
COLLEGIALITY	DISCOURTEOUS	UNIVERSALIZE	NONSCHEDULED	CONTEMPTIBLE	INTELLIGENCE
COMMENSURATE	DISINGENUOUS		OUTSTRETCHED	CONTRARIWISE	INTELLIGIBLE
COMMONWEALTH	DISPUTATIOUS		PICKERELWEED	COUNTERPOISE	INTEMPERANCE
CONGLOMERATE	ENTREPRENEUR		PLASTERBOARD	DELIBERATIVE	INTERFERENCE
CONGRATULATE	EPITHALAMIUM	**12TH LETTER**	PRECONCERTED	DEMILITARIZE	INTERMEDIATE
DISASSOCIATE	HIPPOPOTAMUS		SHORTSIGHTED	DEMIMONDAINE	INTERMINABLE
DISCONSOLATE	INFELICITOUS	DECALCOMANIA	SHUFFLEBOARD	DEMINERALIZE	INTRANSITIVE
DISCRIMINATE	INSALUBRIOUS	ENCYCLOPEDIA	THOROUGHBRED	DEMONSTRABLE	INVERTEBRATE
DISINTEGRATE	MERETRICIOUS	EXTRAVAGANZA	THUNDERCLOUD	DESTRUCTIBLE	INVULNERABLE
ELECTROPLATE	MULTIFARIOUS	HYPOCHONDRIA	UNACCUSTOMED	DETERMINABLE	IRREDEEMABLE
EXTORTIONATE	OBSTREPEROUS	HYPOGLYCEMIA	UNDOCUMENTED	DISACCHARIDE	IRREFRAGABLE
HELLGRAMMITE	PERTINACIOUS	NEURASTHENIA	UNFREQUENTED	DISADVANTAGE	IRREMEDIABLE
HYPERACIDITY	PRASEODYMIUM	ONOMATOPOEIA	UNINTERESTED	DISAGREEABLE	IRRESISTIBLE
ILLEGITIMATE	PRECANCEROUS	SARSAPARILLA	UNLIKELIHOOD	DISASSOCIATE	IRRESPECTIVE
INARTICULATE	PREPOSTEROUS	ALPHANUMERIC	UNPARALLELED	DISCONSOLATE	IRREVERSIBLE
INCAPACITATE	PRESUMPTUOUS	ANTIMAGNETIC	UNPRINCIPLED	DISCRIMINATE	KALEIDOSCOPE
INDOCTRINATE	PROTACTINIUM	CHIROPRACTIC	UNRESTRAINED	DISFRANCHISE	LUMINESCENCE

LUNCHEONETTE	STEEPLECHASE	THANKSGIVING	OBSCURANTISM	MALFORMATION	ENTREPRENEUR
MADEMOISELLE	STRAIGHTEDGE	TRAPSHOOTING	POLYMORPHISM	MALNUTRITION	FLAMETHROWER
MARLINESPIKE	STRATOSPHERE	UNDERCOATING	PRASEODYMIUM	MALOCCLUSION	GALVANOMETER
MASTERSTROKE	SUBCOMMITTEE	UNDERPINNING	PROTACTINIUM	MASTURBATION	HAIRSPLITTER
MEETINGHOUSE	SUBMINIATURE	BREAKTHROUGH	SOMNAMBULISM	MENSTRUATION	INTERLOCUTOR
MERCHANTABLE	SUBSERVIENCE	BUTTERSCOTCH	SPIRITUALISM	MULTISESSION	INTERSTELLAR
METALANGUAGE	SUBSTANTIATE	COMMONWEALTH	THUNDERSTORM	MULTIVITAMIN	MAGNETOMETER
MICROCLIMATE	SUBSTRUCTURE	DISESTABLISH	TRANSVESTISM	NEWSPAPERMAN	MANSLAUGHTER
MISADVENTURE	SUPERANNUATE	SPECTROGRAPH	ABBREVIATION	NONAGENARIAN	MINICOMPUTER
MISCALCULATE	SURVEILLANCE	GOBBLEDYGOOK	ALLITERATION	OCTOGENARIAN	NONCONDUCTOR
MISPRONOUNCE	TESTOSTERONE	ANTITHETICAL	ANNUNCIATION	ORGANIZATION	OFFICEHOLDER
MONOSYLLABLE	THERMOSPHERE	ASTRONOMICAL	ANTEDILUVIAN	PERICYNTHION	PERAMBULATOR
MOUNTAINSIDE	THOROUGHFARE	BACTERICIDAL	ANTIELECTRON	PHILODENDRON	POLICYHOLDER
MULTIPURPOSE	TRADESPEOPLE	BICENTENNIAL	AUSTRONESIAN	PIGMENTATION	PRACTITIONER
NEUROSCIENCE	TRANSFERENCE	CONFESSIONAL	CHURCHWARDEN	POLARIZATION	PREAMPLIFIER
NEWSMAGAZINE	TRANSMIGRATE	CONFIDENTIAL	CIVILIZATION	PRECONDITION	PRIMOGENITOR
NOMENCLATURE	ULTRAMONTANE	CONTRAPUNTAL	CONFIRMATION	PREDIGESTION	RESTAURATEUR
NONOBJECTIVE	UNASSAILABLE	CONVENTIONAL	CONFORMATION	PREDILECTION	SCHOOLMASTER
OSCILLOSCOPE	UNBELIEVABLE	DIFFERENTIAL	CONGREGATION	PREINDUCTION	SENSITOMETER
OVEREXPOSURE	UNCHARITABLE	EXTRAMARITAL	CONSERVATION	PRESBYTERIAN	SHARECROPPER
OXYACETYLENE	UNDERSURFACE	GLOCKENSPIEL	CONSTIPATION	PRESCRIPTION	SHARPSHOOTER
PACKINGHOUSE	UNGOVERNABLE	HETEROSEXUAL	CONSTITUTION	PROLEGOMENON	SLEDGEHAMMER
PARENTHESIZE	UNIVERSALIZE	HIERARCHICAL	CONSTRUCTION	PROTHALAMION	SPECTROMETER
PERADVENTURE	UNMISTAKABLE	HYDROTHERMAL	CONTINUATION	RECOLLECTION	SPORTSWRITER
PHILOSOPHIZE	UNPROFITABLE	INSTRUMENTAL	CONVERSATION	REGISTRATION	STEPDAUGHTER
PHOTOCOMPOSE	UNREASONABLE	INTELLECTUAL	COSMOPOLITAN	REMUNERATION	STREETWALKER
PHOTOENGRAVE	UNREGENERATE	INTERGLACIAL	DECOMMISSION	RENUNCIATION	SUPERCHARGER
PHOTOGRAVURE	UNSEARCHABLE	INVITATIONAL	DELICATESSEN	REPERCUSSION	SWASHBUCKLER
POLYETHYLENE	UNSEASONABLE	LONGITUDINAL	DENOMINATION	RESURRECTION	TENDEROMETER
POLYSYLLABLE	VENIPUNCTURE	MULTILATERAL	DENUNCIATION	RHODODENDRON	TRANQUILIZER
PORCELAINIZE	VERTICILLATE	MULTILINGUAL	DESPOLIATION	SATISFACTION	TROUBLEMAKER
POSTGRADUATE	HANDKERCHIEF	NONCOMMITTAL	DISPENSATION	SCANDINAVIAN	ADVENTITIOUS
PREDESIGNATE	QUARTERSTAFF	PARADISIACAL	DISQUISITION	SEXAGENARIAN	AERODYNAMICS
PREDETERMINE	WEATHERPROOF	PESTILENTIAL	DISSERTATION	SPERMATOZOON	AMBIDEXTROUS
PREFABRICATE	ANTIALIASING	PLANETESIMAL	DISTILLATION	STREPTOMYCIN	APPENDICITIS
PREOPERATIVE	BACKTRACKING	POSTDOCTORAL	ECHOLOCATION	SUBSCRIPTION	ARGILLACEOUS
PREPONDERATE	BLOCKBUSTING	PREMENSTRUAL	EPISCOPALIAN	SUBTERRANEAN	ASTRONAUTICS
PREREQUISITE	BLOODLETTING	PROCATHEDRAL	FENESTRATION	SUPERSTITION	ASTROPHYSICS
PROGRAMMABLE	BLUESTOCKING	PROCESSIONAL	FERMENTATION	TOTALITARIAN	ASYNCHRONOUS
PROPAGANDIZE	BRAINWASHING	PROFESSIONAL	FIBRILLATION	TRANSMISSION	ATMOSPHERICS
PROTECTORATE	BREATHTAKING	PROPORTIONAL	FLUOROCARBON	VALORIZATION	AUDIOVISUALS
PROTUBERANCE	CHEESEPARING	PROVIDENTIAL	FRANKENSTEIN	VETERINARIAN	AVITAMINOSIS
PSYCHOACTIVE	CHILDBEARING	PSYCHOSEXUAL	HALLUCINOGEN	CHAMPIONSHIP	CALISTHENICS
QUANTITATIVE	EARSPLITTING	PUMPERNICKEL	HUMANITARIAN	DICTATORSHIP	CANTANKEROUS
QUESTIONABLE	EARTHSHAKING	SCATOLOGICAL	HYPERTENSION	RECEIVERSHIP	CARBONACEOUS
QUINTESSENCE	ENTERPRISING	SUPERNATURAL	ILLUSTRATION	RELATIONSHIP	CHITTERLINGS
RADIOISOTOPE	EVERBLOOMING	WHIPPOORWILL	IMPERFECTION	AMPHITHEATER	CLOTHESPRESS
RECAPITULATE	EXCRUCIATING	ABOLITIONISM	INCRUSTATION	ANTIMACASSAR	CONTEMPTUOUS
RECOGNIZANCE	FREESTANDING	COLLECTIVISM	INFLAMMATION	CABINETMAKER	CONTERMINOUS
RECONSTITUTE	GLASSBLOWING	CONFUCIANISM	INSURRECTION	CARILLONNEUR	CONTUMACIOUS
REHABILITATE	HEARTRENDING	CONSERVATISM	INTERCESSION	CARPETBAGGER	CONTUMELIOUS
REMINISCENCE	HEARTWARMING	COUNTERCLAIM	INTERJECTION	CHEESEBURGER	CUMULONIMBUS
REMONSTRANCE	HOUSEWARMING	DIASTROPHISM	INTERMISSION	COMMISSIONER	DISCOURTEOUS
REMUNERATIVE	INGRATIATING	EPITHALAMIUM	INTERSECTION	CONFECTIONER	DISINGENUOUS
SECRETARIATE	MICROSPACING	INFLATIONISM	JURISDICTION	CONQUISTADOR	DISPUTATIOUS
SIGNIFICANCE	MULTITASKING	ISOLATIONISM	KINDERGARTEN	COUNTERTENOR	ELECTROLYSIS
SPECTROSCOPE	PEACEKEEPING	METAMORPHISM	LONGSHOREMAN	DENSITOMETER	ENCEPHALITIS

HEADMISTRES**S**	PRESENTIMEN**T**	PENITENTIAR**Y**
HEADQUARTER**S**	RECALCITRAN**T**	PERSPICACIT**Y**
HEARTSTRING**S**	RECEPTIONIS**T**	PHARMACOLOG**Y**
HIPPOPOTAMU**S**	STRAITJACKE**T**	PHILANTHROP**Y**
INFELICITOU**S**	SUBCONTINEN**T**	PHYSIOGRAPH**Y**
INSALUBRIOU**S**	TRANSCENDEN**T**	PRECIPITANC**Y**
MERETRICIOU**S**	UNDERCURREN**T**	PRINCIPALIT**Y**
MESSEIGNEUR**S**	UNDERGARMEN**T**	RADIOTHERAP**Y**
MULTIFARIOU**S**	UNEMPLOYMEN**T**	RESPECTIVEL**Y**
NEVERTHELES**S**	UNIVERSALIS**T**	SATISFACTOR**Y**
NIGHTCLOTHE**S**	WELTERWEIGH**T**	SELENOGRAPH**Y**
OBSTREPEROU**S**	SCHOOLFELLO**W**	STRAIGHTAWA**Y**
PERTINACIOU**S**	ANTHROPOLOG**Y**	STRATIGRAPH**Y**
POSTMISTRES**S**	APPENDECTOM**Y**	SUBDIRECTOR**Y**
PRECANCEROU**S**	BACTERIOLOG**Y**	SUPERHIGHWA**Y**
PREPAREDNES**S**	BELLIGERENC**Y**	TECHNICALIT**Y**
PREPOSTEROU**S**	BIBLIOGRAPH**Y**	TERCENTENAR**Y**
PRESUMPTUOU**S**	BIOCHEMISTR**Y**	TRANSMOGRIF**Y**
PYROTECHNIC**S**	BIOGEOGRAPH**Y**	TRIGONOMETR**Y**
RAMBUNCTIOU**S**	BIOTELEMETR**Y**	UNIVERSALIT**Y**
SIMULTANEOU**S**	BLOODTHIRST**Y**	ZOOGEOGRAPH**Y**
SUBCONSCIOU**S**	CHECKERBERR**Y**	
SUBCUTANEOU**S**	CHEMOTHERAP**Y**	
SUPERCILIOU**S**	CHOREOGRAPH**Y**	
SURROUNDING**S**	CHRISTIANIT**Y**	
THERAPEUTIC**S**	CHROMATICIT**Y**	
TUBERCULOSI**S**	COLLEGIALIT**Y**	
UNDERCLOTHE**S**	COMPANIONWA**Y**	
UNDERDRAWER**S**	CONSERVATOR**Y**	
UNSCRUPULOU**S**	CONSTABULAR**Y**	
VAINGLORIOU**S**	CONSTITUENC**Y**	
VALENCIENNE**S**	CONTEMPORAR**Y**	
WEATHERGLAS**S**	CRYPTOGRAPH**Y**	
AFORETHOUGH**T**	DISCIPLINAR**Y**	
AFTERTHOUGH**T**	ELEEMOSYNAR**Y**	
BLANDISHMEN**T**	EXTRASENSOR**Y**	
COMMENCEMEN**T**	GEOCHEMISTR**Y**	
COMMISSARIA**T**	HABERDASHER**Y**	
CONCELEBRAN**T**	HYDROTHERAP**Y**	
CORESPONDEN**T**	HYPERACIDIT**Y**	
COUNTERPOIN**T**	HYSTERECTOM**Y**	
CROSSCURREN**T**	IDIOSYNCRAS**Y**	
DECONGESTAN**T**	INFLAMMATOR**Y**	
DISPLACEMEN**T**	INFLATIONAR**Y**	
IMPERCIPIEN**T**	INTERMEDIAR**Y**	
INCANDESCEN**T**	LEXICOGRAPH**Y**	
INCONVENIEN**T**	MICROBIOLOG**Y**	
INSUFFICIEN**T**	MICROSURGER**Y**	
INTERMITTEN**T**	MULLIGATAWN**Y**	
INTRANSIGEN**T**	MULTIPLICIT**Y**	
MAGNILOQUEN**T**	MULTIVERSIT**Y**	
MICROCIRCUI**T**	MUNICIPALIT**Y**	
MIDDLEWEIGH**T**	OCEANOGRAPH**Y**	
MISINTERPRE**T**	OTHERWORLDL**Y**	
MISREPRESEN**T**	PALEONTOLOG**Y**	
MONOFILAMEN**T**	PARAMILITAR**Y**	
NONCOMBATAN**T**	PARASITOLOG**Y**	

13
LETTER WORDS

UNDERGRADUATE	**SC**HOOLTEACHER	**CI**NEMATOGRAPH	**INS**ECTIVOROUS	**C**ONCENTRATION	**IR**REPRESSIBLE
UNDERSTANDING	**AD**MINISTRATOR	**CI**RCUMABULATE	**INS**TANTANEOUS	**C**ONCEPTUALIZE	**IR**RESPONSIBLE
UNFORGETTABLE	**AD**VENTURESOME	**CI**RCUMFERENCE	**INS**UBORDINATE	**C**ONCERTMASTER	**IR**RETRIEVABLE
UNIMPEACHABLE	**AD**VERTISEMENT	**DI**FFERENTIATE	**INS**UBSTANTIAL	**C**ONCUPISCENCE	**OR**THONDONTICS
UNINTELLIGENT	**CE**RTIFICATION	**DI**SINTERESTED	**INS**UPPORTABLE	**C**ONFABULATION	**PR**ECIPITATION
UNINTENTIONAL	**DE**CONTAMINATE	**DI**SPASSIONATE	**INT**ERCULTURAL	**C**ONFECTIONERY	**PR**EOCCUPATION
UNINTERRUPTED	**DE**HYDROGENATE	**DI**SPROPORTION	**INT**ERGALACTIC	**C**ONFEDERATION	**PR**EPOSSESSING
UNMENTIONABLE	**DE**MONSTRATIVE	**DI**STINGUISHED	**INT**ERLOCUTORY	**C**ONFIGURATION	**PR**EPOSSESSION
UNNECESSARILY	**DE**TERMINATION	**MI**CROCOMPUTER	**INT**ERMARRIAGE	**C**ONFLAGRATION	**PR**ETERNATURAL
UNPRECEDENTED	**FE**ATHERWEIGHT	**MI**CROORGANISM	**INT**ERNATIONAL	**C**ONFRATERNITY	**PR**IMOGENITURE
UNPREDICTABLE	**FE**RROMAGNETIC	**MI**SALLOCATION	**INT**ERPERSONAL	**C**ONSANGUINITY	**PR**OCRASTINATE
UNPRETENTIOUS	**GE**NERALISSIMO	**MI**SCEGENATION	**INT**ERROGATIVE	**C**ONSCIENTIOUS	**PR**OFESSORIATE
UNQUESTIONING	**GE**NITOURINARY	**MI**SCELLANEOUS	**INT**ERROGATORY	**C**ONSEQUENTIAL	**PR**OGNOSTICATE
UNSUBSTANTIAL	**GE**OCHRONOLOGY	**MI**SUNDERSTAND	**INT**RAMUSCULAR	**C**ONSIDERATION	**PR**OJECTIONIST
UNWARRANTABLE	**GE**OMORPHOLOGY	**NI**TRIFICATION	**INT**RANSIGENCE	**C**ONSTELLATION	**PR**ONOUNCEMENT
UPPERCLASSMAN	**GE**OSTATIONARY	**NI**TROGLYCERIN	**INT**ROSPECTION	**C**ONSTERNATION	**PR**ONUNCIATION
VALEDICTORIAN	**HE**ARTBREAKING	**BL**OODCURDLING	**K**NOWLEDGEABLE	**C**ONTAINERSHIP	**PR**OTECTIONIST
VENTRILOQUISM	**HE**RMAPHRODITE	**CL**EARINGHOUSE	**UNA**CCOMPANIED	**C**ONTORTIONIST	**TRANSA**TLANTIC
VERSIFICATION	**HE**TEROGENEOUS	**EL**ECTROLOGIST	**UNA**CCOUNTABLE	**C**ONTRACEPTION	**TRANS**CRIPTION
VOCATIONALISM	**ME**TAMORPHOSIS	**EL**ECTROMAGNET	**UNA**DULTERATED	**C**ORRESPONDENT	**TRANS**ISTORIZE
WHITHERSOEVER	**PE**REGRINATION	**EL**EPHANTIASIS	**UNC**EREMONIOUS	**C**OSMETOLOGIST	**TRANSN**ATIONAL
WOOLGATHERING	**PE**RFECTIONIST	**OL**EOMARGARINE	**UNC**IRCUMCISED	**C**OUNTERATTACK	**ES**TABLISHMENT
	PERPENDICULAR	**AM**NIOCENTESIS	**UNC**OMFORTABLE	**C**OUNTERWEIGHT	**PS**YCHOSOMATIC
	PETROCHEMICAL	**IMP**ERCEPTIBLE	**UNC**ONDITIONAL	**C**OUNTINGHOUSE	**PS**YCHOTHERAPY
	RECRUDESCENCE	**IMP**ERMISSIBLE	**UNC**ONDITIONED	**G**ONADOTROPHIC	**STR**ANGULATION
	REINCARNATION	**IMP**ERTURBABLE	**UNC**ONQUERABLE	**G**ONADOTROPHIN	**STR**EPTOCOCCUS
	REPREHENSIBLE	**IMP**RACTICABLE	**UND**ERACHIEVER	**H**OUSEBREAKING	**STR**IKEBREAKER
2ND LETTER	**RE**VOLUTIONARY	**IMP**RESSIONISM	**UND**ERCARRIAGE	**J**OLLIFICATION	**AU**THORITARIAN
	REVOLUTIONIST	**IMP**RESSIONIST	**UND**ERCLASSMAN	**M**ONOCHROMATIC	**AU**THORITATIVE
BACCALAUREATE	**RE**VOLUTIONIZE	**ANT**ICOAGULANT	**UND**ERCLOTHING	**M**ONOCOTYLEDON	**AU**TOBIOGRAPHY
BACTERIOPHAGE	**SE**MIAUTOMATIC	**ANT**IFERTILITY	**UND**EREMPLOYED	**M**ONONUCLEOSIS	**AU**TOCHTHONOUS
CARBONIFEROUS	**SE**MICONDUCTOR	**ANT**IHISTAMINE	**UND**ERESTIMATE	**N**ONCONFORMIST	**EU**ROPOCENTRIC
DAGUERREOTYPE	**SE**MIPERMEABLE	**ANT**ILOGARITHM	**UND**ERGRADUATE	**N**ONINTERLACED	**GU**BERNATORIAL
HALLUCINATION	**TE**NDERHEARTED	**ANT**IPERSONNEL	**UND**ERSTANDING	**N**ONRESISTANCE	**HU**NDREDWEIGHT
KAFFEEKLATSCH	**TE**RCENTENNIAL	**ANT**IPOLLUTION	**UNF**ORGETTABLE	**P**OLIOMYELITIS	**JU**RISPRUDENCE
LACKADAISICAL	**VE**NTRILOQUISM	**INA**PPRECIABLE	**UNI**MPEACHABLE	**P**OSTOPERATIVE	**JU**STIFICATION
LAUGHINGSTOCK	**VE**RSIFICATION	**INC**OMBUSTIBLE	**UNI**NTELLIGENT	**R**OENTGENOLOGY	**MU**LTINATIONAL
MACHICOLATION	**AF**FORESTATION	**INC**OMMUNICADO	**UNI**NTENTIONAL	**S**OPHISTICATED	**PU**SILLANIMOUS
MAGNETOSPHERE	**EF**FLORESCENCE	**INC**ONSIDERATE	**UNI**NTERRUPTED	**T**ONSILLECTOMY	**QU**ADRILATERAL
MALADMINISTER	**AG**GIORNAMENTO	**INC**ONSPICUOUS	**UNM**ENTIONABLE	**T**ORTOISESHELL	**QU**ADRIPARTITE
MANIFESTATION	**CH**RISTMASTIDE	**INC**ONTESTABLE	**UNN**ECESSARILY	**V**OCATIONALISM	**QU**ADRUPLICATE
PARALLELOGRAM	**CH**RYSANTHEMUM	**INC**ONVENIENCE	**UNP**RECEDENTED	**W**OOLGATHERING	**QU**ALIFICATION
PARAPHERNALIA	**PH**ARMACOPOEIA	**INC**ORRUPTIBLE	**UNP**REDICTABLE	**AP**PROPRIATION	**QU**ARTERMASTER
PARTICULARIZE	**PH**ENOBARBITAL	**IND**EFATIGABLE	**UNP**RETENTIOUS	**OP**HTHALMOLOGY	**QU**ESTIONNAIRE
PATERFAMILIAS	**PH**OTOCHEMICAL	**IND**ESCRIBABLE	**UNQ**UESTIONING	**SP**ECIFICATION	**QU**INTUPLICATE
RADIOACTIVITY	**PH**OTOELECTRIC	**IND**ETERMINATE	**UNS**UBSTANTIAL	**UP**PERCLASSMAN	**SU**BDISCIPLINE
RAPPROCHEMENT	**PH**OTOELECTRON	**IND**ISPENSABLE	**UNW**ARRANTABLE	**AR**CHIMANDRITE	**SU**LFANILAMIDE
RATIOCINATION	**PH**OTOEMISSION	**IND**IVIDUALISM	**BO**ARDINGHOUSE	**AR**CHITECTONIC	**SU**PERABUNDANT
SANCTIMONIOUS	**PH**YSIOTHERAPY	**IND**IVIDUALIST	**BO**UILLABAISSE	**AR**GUMENTATION	**SU**PERCOMPUTER
TABLESPOONFUL	**TH**ENCEFORWARD	**IND**IVIDUALITY	**CO**LLOQUIALISM	**AR**GUMENTATIVE	**SU**PERNUMERARY
VALEDICTORIAN	**TH**ERMONUCLEAR	**IND**IVIDUALIZE	**CO**MMEMORATIVE	**BR**OKENHEARTED	**SU**PRANATIONAL
ACCELEROMETER	**TH**ERMOPLASTIC	**IND**USTRIALIST	**CO**MMENSURABLE	**FR**AGMENTATION	**SU**RREPTITIOUS
ACCOMMODATING	**TH**OROUGHGOING	**IND**USTRIALIZE	**CO**MMERCIALISM	**GR**ANDDAUGHTER	**TU**RBOELECTRIC
ACCOMMODATION	**TH**UNDERSHOWER	**INE**XHAUSTIBLE	**CO**MMERCIALIZE	**GR**ANTSMANSHIP	**OV**ERQUALIFIED
ACCOMPANIMENT	**TH**UNDERSTRUCK	**INE**XPRESSIBLE	**CO**MMUNICATION	**IR**RECLAIMABLE	**OV**ERSUBSCRIBE
ACCULTURATION	**WH**ITHERSOEVER	**INF**INITESIMAL	**CO**MPLIMENTARY	**IR**RECOVERABLE	**EX**CEPTIONABLE
ACETYLCHOLINE	**BI**ODEGRADABLE	**INF**LORESCENCE	**CO**NCATENATION	**IR**REPLACEABLE	**EX**COMMUNICATE
SCANDALMONGER					
SCHIZOPHRENIA					

EXHIBITIONISM	INCONVENIENCE	THERMOPLASTIC	CONFIGURATION	IMPRACTICABLE	MISALLOCATION
EXPEDITIONARY	INCORRUPTIBLE	AFFORESTATION	CONFLAGRATION	IMPRESSIONISM	MISCEGENATION
EXPRESSIONISM	LACKADAISICAL	DIFFERENTIATE	CONFRATERNITY	IMPRESSIONIST	MISCELLANEOUS
EXTRAGALACTIC	MACHICOLATION	EFFLORESCENCE	CONSANGUINITY	RAPPROCHEMENT	MISUNDERSTAND
EXTRAORDINARY	MICROCOMPUTER	INFINITESIMAL	CONSCIENTIOUS	REPREHENSIBLE	POSTOPERATIVE
HYDROCEPHALUS	MICROORGANISM	INFLORESCENCE	CONSEQUENTIAL	SOPHISTICATED	PUSILLANIMOUS
HYDRODYNAMICS	RECRUDESCENCE	KAFFEEKLATSCH	CONSIDERATION	SUPERABUNDANT	UNSUBSTANTIAL
HYDROELECTRIC	UNCEREMONIOUS	UNFORGETTABLE	CONSTELLATION	SUPERCOMPUTER	ANTICOAGULANT
HYPERCRITICAL	UNCIRCUMCISED	AGGIORNAMENTO	CONSTERNATION	SUPERNUMERARY	ANTIFERTILITY
HYPERDOCUMENT	UNCOMFORTABLE	ARGUMENTATION	CONTAINERSHIP	SUPRANATIONAL	ANTIHISTAMINE
SYLLABICATION	UNCONDITIONAL	ARGUMENTATIVE	CONTORTIONIST	UNPRECEDENTED	ANTILOGARITHM
	UNCONDITIONED	DAGUERREOTYPE	CONTRACEPTION	UNPREDICTABLE	ANTIPERSONNEL
	UNCONQUERABLE	MAGNETOSPHERE	GENERALISSIMO	UNPRETENTIOUS	ANTIPOLLUTION
	VOCATIONALISM	DEHYDROGENATE	GENITOURINARY	UPPERCLASSMAN	AUTHORITARIAN
3RD LETTER	HYDROCEPHALUS	EXHIBITIONISM	GONADOTROPHIC	UNQUESTIONING	AUTHORITATIVE
	HYDRODYNAMICS	OPHTHALMOLOGY	GONADOTROPHIN	CARBONIFEROUS	AUTOBIOGRAPHY
BOARDINGHOUSE	HYDROELECTRIC	SCHIZOPHRENIA	HUNDREDWEIGHT	CERTIFICATION	AUTOCHTHONOUS
FEATHERWEIGHT	INDEFATIGABLE	SCHOOLTEACHER	MANIFESTATION	CHRISTMASTIDE	DETERMINATION
FRAGMENTATION	INDESCRIBABLE	PRIMOGENITURE	MONOCHROMATIC	CHRYSANTHEMUM	ESTABLISHMENT
GRANDDAUGHTER	INDETERMINATE	QUINTUPLICATE	MONOCOTYLEDON	CIRCUMABULATE	EXTRAGALACTIC
GRANTSMANSHIP	INDISPENSABLE	REINCARNATION	MONONUCLEOSIS	CIRCUMFERENCE	EXTRAORDINARY
HEARTBREAKING	INDIVIDUALISM	UNIMPEACHABLE	NONCONFORMIST	CORRESPONDENT	HETEROGENEOUS
INAPPRECIABLE	INDIVIDUALIST	UNINTELLIGENT	NONINTERLACED	EUROPOCENTRIC	INTERCULTURAL
PHARMACOPOEIA	INDIVIDUALITY	UNINTENTIONAL	NONRESISTANCE	FERROMAGNETIC	INTERGALACTIC
QUADRILATERAL	INDIVIDUALIZE	UNINTERRUPTED	SANCTIMONIOUS	HERMAPHRODITE	INTERLOCUTORY
QUADRIPARTITE	INDUSTRIALIST	WHITHERSOEVER	TENDERHEARTED	IRRECLAIMABLE	INTERMARRIAGE
QUADRUPLICATE	INDUSTRIALIZE	COLLOQUIALISM	TONSILLECTOMY	IRRECOVERABLE	INTERNATIONAL
QUALIFICATION	RADIOACTIVITY	HALLUCINATION	UNNECESSARILY	IRREPLACEABLE	INTERPERSONAL
QUARTERMASTER	UNDERACHIEVER	JOLLIFICATION	VENTRILOQUISM	IRREPRESSIBLE	INTERROGATIVE
SCANDALMONGER	UNDERCARRIAGE	MALADMINISTER	BIODEGRADABLE	IRRESPONSIBLE	INTERROGATORY
TRANSATLANTIC	UNDERCLASSMAN	MULTINATIONAL	BLOODCURDLING	IRRETRIEVABLE	INTRAMUSCULAR
TRANSCRIPTION	UNDERCLOTHING	POLIOMYELITIS	BROKENHEARTED	JURISPRUDENCE	INTRANSIGENCE
TRANSISTORIZE	UNDEREMPLOYED	SULFANILAMIDE	GEOCHRONOLOGY	PARALLELOGRAM	INTROSPECTION
TRANSNATIONAL	UNDERESTIMATE	SYLLABICATION	GEOMORPHOLOGY	PARAPHERNALIA	METAMORPHOSIS
UNACCOMPANIED	UNDERGRADUATE	VALEDICTORIAN	GEOSTATIONARY	PARTICULARIZE	NITRIFICATION
UNACCOUNTABLE	UNDERSTANDING	ADMINISTRATOR	KNOWLEDGEABLE	PEREGRINATION	NITROGLYCERIN
UNADULTERATED	ACETYLCHOLINE	COMMEMORATIVE	PHOTOCHEMICAL	PERFECTIONIST	ORTHONDONTICS
GUBERNATORIAL	CLEARINGHOUSE	COMMENSURABLE	PHOTOELECTRIC	PERPENDICULAR	PATERFAMILIAS
SUBDISCIPLINE	ELECTROLOGIST	COMMERCIALISM	PHOTOELECTRON	STRANGULATION	PETROCHEMICAL
TABLESPOONFUL	ELECTROMAGNET	COMMERCIALIZE	PHOTOEMISSION	STREPTOCOCCUS	RATIOCINATION
ACCELEROMETER	ELEPHANTIASIS	COMMUNICATION	PROCRASTINATE	STRIKEBREAKER	BOUILLABAISSE
ACCOMMODATING	INEXHAUSTIBLE	COMPLIMENTARY	PROFESSORIATE	SURREPTITIOUS	COUNTERATTACK
ACCOMMODATION	INEXPRESSIBLE	DEMONSTRATIVE	PROGNOSTICATE	TERCENTENNIAL	COUNTERWEIGHT
ACCOMPANIMENT	OLEOMARGARINE	SEMIAUTOMATIC	PROJECTIONIST	TORTOISESHELL	COUNTINGHOUSE
ACCULTURATION	OVERQUALIFIED	SEMICONDUCTOR	PRONOUNCEMENT	TURBOELECTRIC	HOUSEBREAKING
ARCHIMANDRITE	OVERSUBSCRIBE	SEMIPERMEABLE	PRONUNCIATION	VERSIFICATION	LAUGHINGSTOCK
ARCHITECTONIC	PHENOBARBITAL	UNMENTIONABLE	PROTECTIONIST	COSMETOLOGIST	THUNDERSHOWER
BACCALAUREATE	PRECIPITATION	AMNIOCENTESIS	THOROUGHGOING	DISINTERESTED	THUNDERSTRUCK
BACTERIOPHAGE	PREOCCUPATION	CINEMATOGRAPH	WOOLGATHERING	DISPASSIONATE	ADVENTURESOME
DECONTAMINATE	PREPOSSESSING	CONCATENATION	APPROPRIATION	DISPROPORTION	ADVERTISEMENT
EXCEPTIONABLE	PREPOSSESSION	CONCENTRATION	EXPEDITIONARY	DISTINGUISHED	REVOLUTIONARY
EXCOMMUNICATE	PRETERNATURAL	CONCEPTUALIZE	EXPRESSIONISM	INSECTIVOROUS	REVOLUTIONIST
INCOMBUSTIBLE	QUESTIONNAIRE	CONCERTMASTER	HYPERCRITICAL	INSTANTANEOUS	REVOLUTIONIZE
INCOMMUNICADO	ROENTGENOLOGY	CONCUPISCENCE	HYPERDOCUMENT	INSUBORDINATE	UNWARRANTABLE
INCONSIDERATE	SPECIFICATION	CONFABULATION	IMPERCEPTIBLE	INSUBSTANTIAL	PHYSIOTHERAPY
INCONSPICUOUS	THENCEFORWARD	CONFECTIONERY	IMPERMISSIBLE	INSUPPORTABLE	PSYCHOSOMATIC
INCONTESTABLE	THERMONUCLEAR	CONFEDERATION	IMPERTURBABLE	JUSTIFICATION	PSYCHOTHERAPY

4TH LETTER

CLEARINGHOUSE
ESTABLISHMENT
GONADOTROPHIC
GONADOTROPHIN
MALADMINISTER
METAMORPHOSIS
MISALLOCATION
PARALLELOGRAM
PARAPHERNALIA
STRANGULATION
UNWARRANTABLE
VOCATIONALISM
CARBONIFEROUS
TURBOELECTRIC
BACCALAUREATE
CIRCUMABULATE
CIRCUMFERENCE
CONCATENATION
CONCENTRATION
CONCEPTUALIZE
CONCERTMASTER
CONCUPISCENCE
ELECTROLOGIST
ELECTROMAGNET
GEOCHRONOLOGY
MISCEGENATION
MISCELLANEOUS
NONCONFORMIST
PRECIPITATION
PROCRASTINATE
PSYCHOSOMATIC
PSYCHOTHERAPY
SANCTIMONIOUS
SPECIFICATION
TERCENTENNIAL
UNACCOMPANIED
UNACCOUNTABLE
BIODEGRADABLE
HUNDREDWEIGHT
QUADRILATERAL
QUADRIPARTITE
QUADRUPLICATE
SUBDISCIPLINE
TENDERHEARTED
UNADULTERATED
ACCELEROMETER
ADVENTURESOME
ADVERTISEMENT
CINEMATOGRAPH
DETERMINATION
EXCEPTIONABLE
EXPEDITIONARY
GENERALISSIMO
GUBERNATORIAL
HETEROGENEOUS

HYPERCRITICAL
HYPERDOCUMENT
IMPERCEPTIBLE
IMPERMISSIBLE
IMPERTURBABLE
INDEFATIGABLE
INDESCRIBABLE
INDETERMINATE
INSECTIVOROUS
INTERCULTURAL
INTERGALACTIC
INTERLOCUTORY
INTERMARRIAGE
INTERNATIONAL
INTERPERSONAL
INTERROGATIVE
INTERROGATORY
IRRECLAIMABLE
IRRECOVERABLE
IRREPLACEABLE
IRREPRESSIBLE
IRRESPONSIBLE
IRRETRIEVABLE
PATERFAMILIAS
PEREGRINATION
STREPTOCOCCUS
SUPERABUNDANT
SUPERCOMPUTER
SUPERNUMERARY
UNCEREMONIOUS
UNDERACHIEVER
UNDERCARRIAGE
UNDERCLASSMAN
UNDERCLOTHING
UNDEREMPLOYED
UNDERESTIMATE
UNDERGRADUATE
UNDERSTANDING
UNMENTIONABLE
UNNECESSARILY
UPPERCLASSMAN
VALEDICTORIAN
CONFABULATION
CONFECTIONERY
CONFEDERATION
CONFIGURATION
CONFLAGRATION
CONFRATERNITY
DIFFERENTIATE
KAFFEEKLATSCH
PERFECTIONIST
PROFESSORIATE
SULFANILAMIDE
FRAGMENTATION
LAUGHINGSTOCK
PROGNOSTICATE
ARCHIMANDRITE

ARCHITECTONIC
AUTHORITARIAN
AUTHORITATIVE
MACHICOLATION
ORTHONDONTICS
SOPHISTICATED
ADMINISTRATOR
AGGIORNAMENTO
AMNIOCENTESIS
ANTICOAGULANT
ANTIFERTILITY
ANTIHISTAMINE
ANTILOGARITHM
ANTIPERSONNEL
ANTIPOLLUTION
BOUILLABAISSE
CHRISTMASTIDE
DISINTERESTED
EXHIBITIONISM
GENITOURINARY
INDISPENSABLE
INDIVIDUALISM
INDIVIDUALIST
INDIVIDUALITY
INDIVIDUALIZE
INFINITESIMAL
JURISPRUDENCE
MANIFESTATION
NONINTERLACED
POLIOMYELITIS
PUSILLANIMOUS
RADIOACTIVITY
RATIOCINATION
SCHIZOPHRENIA
SEMIAUTOMATIC
SEMICONDUCTOR
SEMIPERMEABLE
STRIKEBREAKER
UNCIRCUMCISED
PROJECTIONIST
BROKENHEARTED
LACKADAISICAL
COLLOQUIALISM
EFFLORESCENCE
HALLUCINATION
INFLORESCENCE
JOLLIFICATION
QUALIFICATION
SYLLABICATION
TABLESPOONFUL
WOOLGATHERING
COMMEMORATIVE
COMMENSURABLE
COMMERCIALISM
COMMERCIALIZE
COMMUNICATION
COSMETOLOGIST

GEOMORPHOLOGY
HERMAPHRODITE
PRIMOGENITURE
UNIMPEACHABLE
COUNTERATTACK
COUNTERWEIGHT
COUNTINGHOUSE
GRANDDAUGHTER
GRANTSMANSHIP
MAGNETOSPHERE
PHENOBARBITAL
PRONOUNCEMENT
PRONUNCIATION
QUINTUPLICATE
REINCARNATION
ROENTGENOLOGY
SCANDALMONGER
THENCEFORWARD
THUNDERSHOWER
THUNDERSTRUCK
TRANSATLANTIC
TRANSCRIPTION
TRANSISTORIZE
TRANSNATIONAL
UNINTELLIGENT
UNINTENTIONAL
UNINTERRUPTED
ACCOMMODATING
ACCOMMODATION
ACCOMPANIMENT
AFFORESTATION
AUTOBIOGRAPHY
AUTOCHTHONOUS
BLOODCURDLING
DECONTAMINATE
DEMONSTRATIVE
EUROPOCENTRIC
EXCOMMUNICATE
INCOMBUSTIBLE
INCOMMUNICADO
INCONSIDERATE
INCONSPICUOUS
INCONTESTABLE
INCONVENIENCE
INCORRUPTIBLE
MONOCHROMATIC
MONOCOTYLEDON
MONONUCLEOSIS
OLEOMARGARINE
PREOCCUPATION
REVOLUTIONARY
REVOLUTIONIST
REVOLUTIONIZE
SCHOOLTEACHER
UNCOMFORTABLE
UNCONDITIONAL
UNCONDITIONED

UNCONQUERABLE
UNFORGETTABLE
COMPLIMENTARY
DISPASSIONATE
DISPROPORTION
ELEPHANTIASIS
INAPPRECIABLE
PERPENDICULAR
PREPOSSESSING
PREPOSSESSION
RAPPROCHEMENT
APPROPRIATION
BOARDINGHOUSE
CORRESPONDENT
EXPRESSIONISM
EXTRAGALACTIC
EXTRAORDINARY
FERROMAGNETIC
HEARTBREAKING
HYDROCEPHALUS
HYDRODYNAMICS
HYDROELECTRIC
IMPRACTICABLE
IMPRESSIONISM
IMPRESSIONIST
INTRAMUSCULAR
INTRANSIGENCE
INTROSPECTION
MICROCOMPUTER
MICROORGANISM
NITRIFICATION
NITROGLYCERIN
NONRESISTANCE
OVERQUALIFIED
OVERSUBSCRIBE
PETROCHEMICAL
PHARMACOPOEIA
QUARTERMASTER
RECRUDESCENCE
REPREHENSIBLE
SUPRANATIONAL
SURREPTITIOUS
THERMONUCLEAR
THERMOPLASTIC
THOROUGHGOING
UNPRECEDENTED
UNPREDICTABLE
UNPRETENTIOUS
CONSANGUINITY
CONSCIENTIOUS
CONSEQUENTIAL
CONSIDERATION
CONSTELLATION
CONSTERNATION
GEOSTATIONARY
HOUSEBREAKING
PHYSIOTHERAPY

QUESTIONNAIRE
TONSILLECTOMY
VERSIFICATION
ACETYLCHOLINE
BACTERIOPHAGE
CERTIFICATION
CONTAINERSHIP
CONTORTIONIST
CONTRACEPTION
DISTINGUISHED
FEATHERWEIGHT
INSTANTANEOUS
JUSTIFICATION
MULTINATIONAL
OPHTHALMOLOGY
PARTICULARIZE
PHOTOCHEMICAL
PHOTOELECTRIC
PHOTOELECTRON
PHOTOEMISSION
POSTOPERATIVE
PRETERNATURAL
PROTECTIONIST
TORTOISESHELL
VENTRILOQUISM
WHITHERSOEVER
ACCULTURATION
ARGUMENTATION
ARGUMENTATIVE
DAGUERREOTYPE
INDUSTRIALIST
INDUSTRIALIZE
INSUBORDINATE
INSUBSTANTIAL
INSUPPORTABLE
MISUNDERSTAND
UNQUESTIONING
UNSUBSTANTIAL
KNOWLEDGEABLE
INEXHAUSTIBLE
INEXPRESSIBLE
CHRYSANTHEMUM
DEHYDROGENATE

5TH LETTER

BACCALAUREATE
CONCATENATION
CONFABULATION
CONSANGUINITY
CONTAINERSHIP
DISPASSIONATE
EXTRAGALACTIC
EXTRAORDINARY
HERMAPHRODITE

IMPRACTICABLE	DAGUERREOTYPE	SPECIFICATION	AUTHORITATIVE	GUBERNATORIAL	COUNTINGHOUSE
INSTANTANEOUS	DIFFERENTIATE	SUBDISCIPLINE	CARBONIFEROUS	HETEROGENEOUS	ELECTROLOGIST
INTRAMUSCULAR	EXPRESSIONISM	TONSILLECTOMY	COLLOQUIALISM	HUNDREDWEIGHT	ELECTROMAGNET
INTRANSIGENCE	HOUSEBREAKING	VERSIFICATION	CONTORTIONIST	HYPERCRITICAL	GENITOURINARY
LACKADAISICAL	IMPRESSIONISM	STRIKEBREAKER	EFFLORESCENCE	HYPERDOCUMENT	GEOSTATIONARY
SEMIAUTOMATIC	IMPRESSIONIST	ACCELEROMETER	FERROMAGNETIC	IMPERCEPTIBLE	GRANTSMANSHIP
SULFANILAMIDE	KAFFEEKLATSCH	ACCULTURATION	GEOMORPHOLOGY	IMPERMISSIBLE	HEARTBREAKING
SUPRANATIONAL	MAGNETOSPHERE	ANTILOGARITHM	HYDROCEPHALUS	IMPERTURBABLE	INDETERMINATE
SYLLABICATION	MISCEGENATION	BOUILLABAISSE	HYDRODYNAMICS	INCORRUPTIBLE	IRRETRIEVABLE
AUTOBIOGRAPHY	MISCELLANEOUS	COMPLIMENTARY	HYDROELECTRIC	INTERCULTURAL	QUARTERMASTER
ESTABLISHMENT	NONRESISTANCE	CONFLAGRATION	INFLORESCENCE	INTERGALACTIC	QUESTIONNAIRE
EXHIBITIONISM	PERFECTIONIST	KNOWLEDGEABLE	INTROSPECTION	INTERLOCUTORY	QUINTUPLICATE
INSUBORDINATE	PERPENDICULAR	MISALLOCATION	MICROCOMPUTER	INTERMARRIAGE	ROENTGENOLOGY
INSUBSTANTIAL	PRETERNATURAL	PARALLELOGRAM	MICROORGANISM	INTERNATIONAL	SANCTIMONIOUS
UNSUBSTANTIAL	PROFESSORIATE	PUSILLANIMOUS	NITROGLYCERIN	INTERPERSONAL	UNINTELLIGENT
ANTICOAGULANT	PROJECTIONIST	REVOLUTIONARY	NONCONFORMIST	INTERROGATIVE	UNINTENTIONAL
AUTOCHTHONOUS	PROTECTIONIST	REVOLUTIONIST	ORTHODONTICS	INTERROGATORY	UNINTERRUPTED
CONSCIENTIOUS	REPREHENSIBLE	REVOLUTIONIZE	PETROCHEMICAL	PATERFAMILIAS	VOCATIONALISM
INSECTIVOROUS	SURREPTITIOUS	ACCOMMODATING	PHENOBARBITAL	PROCRASTINATE	CIRCUMABULATE
IRRECLAIMABLE	TABLESPOONFUL	ACCOMMODATION	PHOTOCHEMICAL	QUADRILATERAL	CIRCUMFERENCE
IRRECOVERABLE	TENDERHEARTED	ACCOMPANIMENT	PHOTOELECTRIC	QUADRIPARTITE	COMMUNICATION
MONOCHROMATIC	TERCENTENNIAL	ARGUMENTATION	PHOTOELECTRON	QUADRUPLICATE	CONCUPISCENCE
MONOCOTYLEDON	UNPRECEDENTED	ARGUMENTATIVE	PHOTOEMISSION	RAPPROCHEMENT	HALLUCINATION
PREOCCUPATION	UNPREDICTABLE	CINEMATOGRAPH	POLIOMYELITIS	SUPERABUNDANT	PRONUNCIATION
REINCARNATION	UNPRETENTIOUS	EXCOMMUNICATE	POSTOPERATIVE	SUPERCOMPUTER	RECRUDESCENCE
SEMICONDUCTOR	UNQUESTIONING	FRAGMENTATION	PREPOSSESSING	SUPERNUMERARY	UNADULTERATED
THENCEFORWARD	ANTIFERTILITY	INCOMBUSTIBLE	PREPOSSESSION	UNCEREMONIOUS	INDIVIDUALISM
UNACCOMPANIED	INDEFATIGABLE	INCOMMUNICADO	PRIMOGENITURE	UNCIRCUMCISED	INDIVIDUALIST
UNACCOUNTABLE	MANIFESTATION	METAMORPHOSIS	PRONOUNCEMENT	UNDERACHIEVER	INDIVIDUALITY
UNNECESSARILY	PEREGRINATION	OLEOMARGARINE	RADIOACTIVITY	UNDERCARRIAGE	INDIVIDUALIZE
BLOODCURDLING	WOOLGATHERING	PHARMACOPOEIA	RATIOCINATION	UNDERCLASSMAN	ACETYLCHOLINE
BOARDINGHOUSE	ANTIHISTAMINE	THERMONUCLEAR	SCHOOLTEACHER	UNDERCLOTHING	SCHIZOPHRENIA
DEHYDROGENATE	ELEPHANTIASIS	THERMOPLASTIC	THOROUGHGOING	UNDEREMPLOYED	
EXPEDITIONARY	FEATHERWEIGHT	UNCOMFORTABLE	TORTOISESHELL	UNDERESTIMATE	
GONADOTROPHIC	GEOCHRONOLOGY	ADMINISTRATOR	TURBOELECTRIC	UNDERGRADUATE	
GONADOTROPHIN	INEXHAUSTIBLE	ADVENTURESOME	ANTIPERSONNEL	UNDERSTANDING	

GRANDDAUGHTER	LAUGHINGSTOCK	DECONTAMINATE	ANTIPOLLUTION	UNFORGETTABLE	
MALADMINISTER	OPHTHALMOLOGY	DEMONSTRATIVE	EUROPOCENTRIC	UNWARRANTABLE	CHRYSANTHEMUM
SCANDALMONGER	PSYCHOSOMATIC	DISINTERESTED	EXCEPTIONABLE	UPPERCLASSMAN	CINEMATOGRAPH
THUNDERSHOWER	PSYCHOTHERAPY	INCONSIDERATE	INAPPRECIABLE	VENTRILOQUISM	CONFLAGRATION
THUNDERSTRUCK	WHITHERSOEVER	INCONSPICUOUS	INEXPRESSIBLE	CHRISTMASTIDE	CONFRATERNITY
VALEDICTORIAN	ARCHIMANDRITE	INCONTESTABLE	INSUPPORTABLE	CHRYSANTHEMUM	CONTRACEPTION
BACTERIOPHAGE	ARCHITECTONIC	INCONVENIENCE	IRREPLACEABLE	INDESCRIBABLE	ELEPHANTIASIS
BIODEGRADABLE	CERTIFICATION	INFINITESIMAL	IRREPRESSIBLE	INDISPENSABLE	GENERALISSIMO
BROKENHEARTED	CONFIGURATION	MISUNDERSTAND	PARAPHERNALIA	INDUSTRIALIST	GEOSTATIONARY
COMMEMORATIVE	CONSIDERATION	MONONUCLEOSIS	SEMIPERMEABLE	INDUSTRIALIZE	INDEFATIGABLE
COMMENSURABLE	DISTINGUISHED	NONINTERLACED	STREPTOCOCCUS	IRRESPONSIBLE	INEXHAUSTIBLE
COMMERCIALISM	JOLLIFICATION	PROGNOSTICATE	UNIMPEACHABLE	JURISPRUDENCE	OLEOMARGARINE
COMMERCIALIZE	JUSTIFICATION	STRANGULATION	OVERQUALIFIED	OVERSUBSCRIBE	OPHTHAMOLOGY
CONCENTRATION	MACHICOLATION	UNCONDITIONAL	ADVERTISEMENT	TRANSATLANTIC	PHARMACOPOEIA
CONCEPTUALIZE	MULTINATIONAL	UNCONDITIONED	AFFORESTATION	TRANSCRIPTION	PROCRASTINATE
CONCERTMASTER	NITRIFICATION	UNCONQUERABLE	CLEARINGHOUSE	TRANSISTORIZE	RADIOACTIVITY
CONFECTIONERY	PARTICULARIZE	UNMENTIONABLE	CONFRATERNITY	TRANSNATIONAL	REINCARNATION
CONFEDERATION	PHYSIOTHERAPY	AGGIORNAMENTO	CONTRACEPTION	CONSTELLATION	SCANDALMONGER
CONSEQUENTIAL	PRECIPITATION	AMNIOCENTESIS	DETERMINATION	CONSTERNATION	SUPERABUNDANT
CORRESPONDENT	QUALIFICATION	APPROPRIATION	DISPROPORTION	COUNTERATTACK	TRANSATLANTIC
COSMETOLOGIST	SOPHISTICATED	AUTHORITARIAN	GENERALISSIMO	COUNTERWEIGHT	UNDERACHIEVER

WOOLGATHERING	FRAGMENTATION	CONTAINERSHIP	INTERNATIONAL	BACTERIOPHAGE	INCONTESTABLE
CONFABULATION	HUNDREDWEIGHT	COUNTINGHOUSE	INTRANSIGENCE	COMMERCIALISM	INDUSTRIALIST
HEARTBREAKING	HYDROELECTRIC	EXHIBITIONISM	MULTINATIONAL	COMMERCIALIZE	INDUSTRIALIZE
HOUSEBREAKING	INDETERMINATE	EXPEDITIONARY	NONCONFORMIST	CONCERTMASTER	INSECTIVOROUS
INCOMBUSTIBLE	KAFFEEKLATSCH	INDIVIDUALISM	ORTHODONTICS	CONTORTIONIST	MAGNETOSPHERE
PHENOBARBITAL	KNOWLEDGEABLE	INDIVIDUALIST	PERPENDICULAR	DAGUERREOTYPE	NONINTERLACED
SYLLABICATION	MANIFESTATION	INDIVIDUALITY	PRONUNCIATION	DEHYDROGENATE	STREPTOCOCCUS
AMNIOCENTESIS	PHOTOELECTRIC	INDIVIDUALIZE	SULFANILAMIDE	DIFFERENTIATE	UNMENTIONABLE
BLOODCURDLING	PHOTOELECTRON	INFINITESIMAL	SUPERNUMERARY	EFFLORESCENCE	UNPRETENTIOUS
CONFECTIONERY	PHOTOEMISSION	LAUGHINGSTOCK	SUPRANATIONAL	ELECTROLOGIST	MONONUCLEOSIS
HALLUCINATION	QUARTERMASTER	QUADRILATERAL	TERCENTENNIAL	ELECTROMAGNET	OVERQUALIFIED
HYDROCEPHALUS	SEMIPERMEABLE	QUADRIPARTITE	TRANSNATIONAL	GEOCHRONOLOGY	OVERSUBSCRIBE
HYPERCRITICAL	STRIKEBREAKER	QUESTIONNAIRE	ANTICOAGULANT	GEOMORPHOLOGY	PRONOUNCEMENT
IMPERCEPTIBLE	THENCEFORWARD	SANCTIMONIOUS	ANTILOGARITHM	INAPPRECIABLE	QUADRUPLICATE
IMPRACTICABLE	THUNDERSHOWER	TORTOISESHELL	ANTIPOLLUTION	INCORRUPTIBLE	QUINTUPLICATE
INDESCRIBABLE	THUNDERSTRUCK	TRANSISTORIZE	DISPROPORTION	INEXPRESSIBLE	REVOLUTIONARY
INTERCULTURAL	TURBOELECTRIC	VALEDICTORIAN	EUROPOCENTRIC	INFLORESCENCE	REVOLUTIONIST
MACHICOLATION	UNCEREMONIOUS	VENTRILOQUISM	EXTRAORDINARY	INTERROGATIVE	REVOLUTIONIZE
MICROCOMPUTER	UNDEREMPLOYED	VOCATIONALISM	GENITOURINARY	INTERROGATORY	SEMIAUTOMATIC
PARTICULARIZE	UNDERESTIMATE	ACETYLCHOLINE	GONADOTROPHIC	IRREPRESSIBLE	THOROUGHGOING
PERFECTIONIST	UNIMPEACHABLE	BACCALAUREATE	GONADOTROPHIN	IRRETRIEVABLE	INCONVENIENCE
PETROCHEMICAL	UNINTELLIGENT	BOUILLABAISSE	HETEROGENEOUS	PEREGRINATION	
PHOTOCHEMICAL	UNINTENTIONAL	ESTABLISHMENT	INSUBORDINATE	PRETERNATURAL	
PREOCCUPATION	UNINTERRUPTED	INTERLOCUTORY	IRRECOVERABLE	TENDERHEARTED	
PROJECTIONIST	UNNECESSARILY	IRRECLAIMABLE	METAMORPHOSIS	UNWARRANTABLE	
PROTECTIONIST	WHITHERSOEVER	IRREPLACEABLE	MICROORGANISM	CORRESPONDENT	**7TH LETTER**
RATIOCINATION	CERTIFICATION	MISALLOCATION	MONOCOTYLEDON	DEMONSTRATIVE	
SUPERCOMPUTER	JOLLIFICATION	MISCELLANEOUS	PHYSIOTHERAPY	DISPASSIONATE	ACCOMPANIMENT
TRANSCRIPTION	JUSTIFICATION	PARALLELOGRAM	PROGNOSTICATE	EXPRESSIONISM	ANTICOAGULANT
UNCIRCUMCISED	NITRIFICATION	PUSILLANIMOUS	PSYCHOSOMATIC	GRANTSMANSHIP	ARCHIMANDRITE
UNDERCARRIAGE	PATERFAMILIAS	SCHOOLTEACHER	PSYCHOTHERAPY	IMPRESSIONISM	BACCALAUREATE
UNDERCLASSMAN	QUALIFICATION	TONSILLECTOMY	RAPPROCHEMENT	IMPRESSIONIST	BOUILLABAISSE
UNDERCLOTHING	SPECIFICATION	UNADULTERATED	SCHIZOPHRENIA	INCONSIDERATE	CIRCUMABULATE
UNPRECEDENTED	UNCOMFORTABLE	ACCOMMODATING	SEMICONDUCTOR	INCONSPICUOUS	DECONTAMINATE
UPPERCLASSMAN	VERSIFICATION	ACCOMMODATION	THERMONUCLEAR	INSUBSTANTIAL	EXTRAGALACTIC
CONFEDERATION	BIODEGRADABLE	ARCHIMANDRITE	THERMOPLASTIC	INTROSPECTION	FERROMAGNETIC
CONSIDERATION	CONFIGURATION	CIRCUMABULATE	UNACCOMPANIED	NONRESISTANCE	GRANDDAUGHTER
GRANDDAUGHTER	EXTRAGALACTIC	CIRCUMFERENCE	UNACCOUNTABLE	PREPOSSESSING	GUBERNATORIAL
HYDRODYNAMICS	INTERGALACTIC	COMMEMORATIVE	ACCOMPANIMENT	PREPOSSESSION	INTERGALACTIC
HYPERDOCUMENT	MISCEGENATION	DETERMINATION	APPROPRIATION	PROFESSORIATE	INTERMARRIAGE
LACKADAISICAL	NITROGLYCERIN	EXCOMMUNICATE	CONCEPTUALIZE	SOPHISTICATED	INTERNATIONAL
MISUNDERSTAND	PRIMOGENITURE	FERROMAGNETIC	CONCUPISCENCE	SUBDISCIPLINE	IRRECLAIMABLE
RECRUDESCENCE	ROENTGENOLOGY	IMPERMISSIBLE	HERMAPHRODITE	TABLESPOONFUL	IRREPLACEABLE
UNCONDITIONAL	STRANGULATION	INCOMMUNICADO	INDISPENSABLE	UNDERSTANDING	LACKADAISICAL
UNCONDITIONED	UNDERGRADUATE	INTERMARRIAGE	INSUPPORTABLE	UNQUESTIONING	MULTINATIONAL
UNPREDICTABLE	UNFORGETTABLE	INTRAMUSCULAR	INTERPERSONAL	UNSUBSTANTIAL	OVERQUALIFIED
ACCELEROMETER	AUTOCHTHONOUS	MALADMINISTER	IRRESPONSIBLE	ACCULTURATION	PATERFAMILIAS
AFFORESTATION	MONOCHROMATIC	POLIOMYELITIS	JURISPRUDENCE	ADVENTURESOME	PHENOBARBITAL
ANTIFERTILITY	PARAPHERNALIA	BROKENHEARTED	POSTOPERATIVE	ADVERTISEMENT	PUSILLANIMOUS
ANTIPERSONNEL	REPREHENSIBLE	CARBONIFEROUS	PRECIPITATION	ARCHITECTONIC	SUPRANATIONAL
ARGUMENTATION	ADMINISTRATOR	COMMENSURABLE	SURREPTITIOUS	CHRISTMASTIDE	TRANSNATIONAL
ARGUMENTATIVE	ANTIHISTAMINE	COMMUNICATION	COLLOQUIALISM	CONCATENATION	UNDERCARRIAGE
CONSTELLATION	AUTOBIOGRAPHY	CONCENTRATION	CONSEQUENTIAL	COSMETOLOGIST	UNIMPEACHABLE
CONSTERNATION	BOARDINGHOUSE	CONSANGUINITY	UNCONQUERABLE	DECONTAMINATE	UNWARRANTABLE
COUNTERATTACK	CLEARINGHOUSE	DISTINGUISHED	AGGIORNAMENTO	DISINTERESTED	OVERSUBSCRIBE
COUNTERWEIGHT	COMPLIMENTARY	GUBERNATORIAL	AUTHORITARIAN	EXCEPTIONABLE	STRIKEBREAKER
FEATHERWEIGHT	CONSCIENTIOUS	INSTANTANEOUS	AUTHORITATIVE	IMPERTURBABLE	SUPERABUNDANT
					ACETYLCHOLINE

COMMERCIALISM	CONSANGUINITY	UNDERCLOTHING	QUADRIPARTITE	UNDERESTIMATE	PARTICULARIZE
COMMERCIALIZE	DISTINGUISHED	UNINTELLIGENT	QUADRUPLICATE	UNNECESSARILY	PREOCCUPATION
CONTRACEPTION	HETEROGENEOUS	UPPERCLASSMAN	QUINTUPLICATE	AUTOCHTHONOUS	STRANGULATION
EUROPOCENTRIC	THOROUGHGOING	VENTRILOQUISM	SCHIZOPHRENIA	CINEMATOGRAPH	SUPERNUMERARY
MONONUCLEOSIS	BROKENHEARTED	CHRISTMASTIDE	TABLESPOONFUL	CONCENTRATION	UNACCOUNTABLE
PHARMACOPOEIA	HERMAPHRODITE	COMPLIMENTARY	THERMOPLASTIC	CONCEPTUALIZE	UNCIRCUMCISED
PRONUNCIATION	PETROCHEMICAL	GRANTSMANSHIP	ACCELEROMETER	CONCERTMASTER	UNCONQUERABLE
RADIOACTIVITY	PHOTOCHEMICAL	PHOTOEMISSION	ANTIFERTILITY	CONFECTIONERY	IRRECOVERABLE
RAPPROCHEMENT	TENDERHEARTED	SANCTIMONIOUS	ANTIPERSONNEL	CONFRATERNITY	HYDRODYNAMICS
SUBDISCIPLINE	ADVERTISEMENT	UNACCOMPANIED	APPROPRIATION	CONTORTIONIST	POLIOMYELITIS
UNDERACHIEVER	AUTHORITARIAN	UNCEREMONIOUS	BIODEGRADABLE	DEMONSTRATIVE	
VALEDICTORIAN	AUTHORITATIVE	UNDEREMPLOYED	CONSTERNATION	EXHIBITIONISM	
HUNDREDWEIGHT	BACTERIOPHAGE	AGGIORNAMENTO	COUNTERATTACK	EXPEDITIONARY	

8TH LETTER

INDIVIDUALISM	CARBONIFEROUS	ARGUMENTATION	COUNTERWEIGHT	GEOSTATIONARY	
INDIVIDUALIST	CERTIFICATION	ARGUMENTATIVE	DAGUERREOTYPE	GONADOTROPHIC	AGGIORNAMENTO
INDIVIDUALITY	COMMUNICATION	BOARDINGHOUSE	EXTRAORDINARY	GONADOTROPHIN	ANTILOGARITHM
INDIVIDUALIZE	CONCUPISCENCE	CHRYSANTHEMUM	FEATHERWEIGHT	IMPRACTICABLE	BIODEGRADABLE
KNOWLEDGEABLE	DETERMINATION	CLEARINGHOUSE	HEARTBREAKING	INDEFATIGABLE	CHRISTMASTIDE
ORTHODONTICS	ESTABLISHMENT	CONTAINERSHIP	HOUSEBREAKING	INFINITESIMAL	COUNTERATTACK
PERPENDICULAR	EXCEPTIONABLE	COUNTINGHOUSE	HYPERCRITICAL	INSTANTANEOUS	GRANTSMANSHIP
AMNIOCENTESIS	HALLUCINATION	ELEPHANTIASIS	INDESCRIBABLE	INSUBSTANTIAL	INSTANTANEOUS
ARCHITECTONIC	IMPERMISSIBLE	FRAGMENTATION	INDETERMINATE	MONOCOTYLEDON	INSUBSTANTIAL
CONCATENATION	INCONSIDERATE	LAUGHINGSTOCK	INDUSTRIALIST	PERFECTIONIST	MISCELLANEOUS
CONFEDERATION	INSECTIVOROUS	PRETERNATURAL	INDUSTRIALIZE	PHYSIOTHERAPY	PRETERNATURAL
CONSCIENTIOUS	IRRETRIEVABLE	PRONOUNCEMENT	INSUBORDINATE	PSYCHOTHERAPY	QUADRILATERAL
CONSIDERATION	JOLLIFICATION	SEMICONDUCTOR	JURISPRUDENCE	PROJECTIONIST	QUADRIPARTITE
DIFFERENTIATE	JUSTIFICATION	THERMONUCLEAR	METAMORPHOSIS	PROTECTIONIST	UNDERCLASSMAN
DISINTERESTED	MALADMINISTER	UNINTENTIONAL	MICROORGANISM	REVOLUTIONARY	UNDERGRADUATE
EFFLORESCENCE	NITRIFICATION	ACCOMMODATING	MONOCHROMATIC	REVOLUTIONIST	UNDERSTANDING
HYDROCEPHALUS	NONRESISTANCE	ACCOMMODATION	OLEOMARGARINE	REVOLUTIONIZE	UNSUBSTANTIAL
IMPERCEPTIBLE	PEREGRINATION	AUTOBIOGRAPHY	QUARTERMASTER	SCHOOLTEACHER	UPPERCLASSMAN
INAPPRECIABLE	PRECIPITATION	COMMEMORATIVE	REINCARNATION	SEMIAUTOMATIC	BOUILLABAISSE
INCONTESTABLE	QUALIFICATION	COSMETOLOGIST	SEMIPERMEABLE	SOPHISTICATED	CIRCUMABULATE
INCONVENIENCE	RATIOCINATION	DEHYDROGENATE	THUNDERSHOWER	SURREPTITIOUS	ARCHITECTONIC
INDISPENSABLE	SPECIFICATION	ELECTROLOGIST	THUNDERSTRUCK	TERCENTENNIAL	CERTIFICATION
INEXPRESSIBLE	SULFANILAMIDE	ELECTROMAGNET	TRANSCRIPTION	TRANSATLANTIC	COMMUNICATION
INFLORESCENCE	SYLLABICATION	GEOCHRONOLOGY	UNDERGRADUATE	UNADULTERATED	HYPERDOCUMENT
INTERPERSONAL	UNCONDITIONAL	HYPERDOCUMENT	UNINTERRUPTED	UNDERSTANDING	INAPPRECIABLE
IRREPRESSIBLE	UNCONDITIONED	INSUPPORTABLE	WHITHERSOEVER	UNQUESTIONING	INTERLOCUTORY
MISCEGENATION	UNMENTIONABLE	INTERLOCUTORY	ADMINISTRATOR	UNSUBSTANTIAL	IRREPLACEABLE
MISUNDERSTAND	UNPREDICTABLE	INTERROGATIVE	AFFORESTATION	WOOLGATHERING	JOLLIFICATION
NONINTERLACED	VERSIFICATION	INTERROGATORY	ANTIHISTAMINE	ACCULTURATION	JUSTIFICATION
PARALLELOGRAM	KAFFEEKLATSCH	IRRESPONSIBLE	COMMENSURABLE	ADVENTURESOME	MISALLOCATION
PARAPHERNALIA	ANTIPOLLUTION	MACHICOLATION	DISPASSIONATE	BLOODCURDLING	NITRIFICATION
POSTOPERATIVE	CONSTELLATION	MAGNETOSPHERE	EXPRESSIONISM	COLLOQUIALISM	PRONOUNCEMENT
PRIMOGENITURE	GENERALISSIMO	MICROCOMPUTER	IMPRESSIONISM	CONFABULATION	QUALIFICATION
RECRUDESCENCE	HYDROELECTRIC	MISALLOCATION	IMPRESSIONIST	CONFIGURATION	SPECIFICATION
REPREHENSIBLE	MISCELLANEOUS	QUESTIONNAIRE	INTRANSIGENCE	CONSEQUENTIAL	STREPTOCOCCUS
ROENTGENOLOGY	NITROGLYCERIN	STREPTOCOCCUS	MANIFESTATION	EXCOMMUNICATE	SYLLABICATION
UNFORGETTABLE	OPHTHALMOLOGY	SUPERCOMPUTER	PREPOSSESSING	GENITOURINARY	UNIMPEACHABLE
UNPRECEDENTED	PHOTOELECTRIC	UNCOMFORTABLE	PREPOSSESSION	IMPERTURBABLE	UNPREDICTABLE
UNPRETENTIOUS	PHOTOELECTRON	VOCATIONALISM	PROCRASTINATE	INCOMBUSTIBLE	VERSIFICATION
CIRCUMFERENCE	QUADRILATERAL	CORRESPONDENT	PROFESSORIATE	INCOMMUNICADO	ACCOMMODATING
NONCONFORMIST	SCANDALMONGER	DISPROPORTION	PROGNOSTICATE	INCORRUPTIBLE	ACCOMMODATION
THENCEFORWARD	TONSILLECTOMY	GEOMORPHOLOGY	PSYCHOSOMATIC	INEXHAUSTIBLE	EXTRAORDINARY
ANTILOGARITHM	TURBOELECTRIC	INCONSPICUOUS	TORTOISESHELL	INTERCULTURAL	INCONSIDERATE
CONFLAGRATION	UNDERCLASSMAN	INTROSPECTION	TRANSISTORIZE	INTRAMUSCULAR	

INSUBORDINATE	UNDERACHIEVER	SULFANILAMIDE	PROFESSORIATE	IRREPRESSIBLE	**9TH LETTER**
SEMICONDUCTOR	WOOLGATHERING	THERMOPLASTIC	PSYCHOSOMATIC	MAGNETOSPHERE	
UNPRECEDENTED	APPROPRIATION	TRANSATLANTIC	SANCTIMONIOUS	NONRESISTANCE	ACCOMMODATING
BROKENHEARTED	COLLOQUIALISM	UNINTELLIGENT	SEMIAUTOMATIC	OVERSUBSCRIBE	ACCOMMODATION
CIRCUMFERENCE	COMMERCIALISM	CONCERTMASTER	TABLESPOONFUL	RECRUDESCENCE	ACCULTURATION
COMPLIMENTARY	COMMERCIALIZE	DECONTAMINATE	THENCEFORWARD	THUNDERSHOWER	AFFORESTATION
CONFRATERNITY	CONFECTIONERY	ELECTROMAGNET	UNCEREMONIOUS	THUNDERSTRUCK	ANTIHISTAMINE
CONSEQUENTIAL	CONTORTIONIST	INDETERMINATE	UNDERCLOTHING	UNNECESSARILY	APPROPRIATION
CONTAINERSHIP	DISPASSIONATE	MICROCOMPUTER	UNMENTIONABLE	WHITHERSOEVER	ARGUMENTATION
CONTRACEPTION	EXHIBITIONISM	OPHTHALMOLOGY	VENTRILOQUISM	ADMINISTRATOR	ARGUMENTATIVE
DAGUERREOTYPE	EXPEDITIONARY	PATERFAMILIAS	HYDROCEPHALUS	AFFORESTATION	AUTHORITARIAN
EUROPOCENTRIC	EXPRESSIONISM	QUARTERMASTER	IMPERCEPTIBLE	ANTIFERTILITY	AUTHORITATIVE
HEARTBREAKING	GENERALISSIMO	SCANDALMONGER	INCORRUPTIBLE	ANTIHISTAMINE	BOUILLABAISSE
HETEROGENEOUS	GEOSTATIONARY	SEMIPERMEABLE	METAMORPHOSIS	ARGUMENTATION	BROKENHEARTED
HOUSEBREAKING	HYPERCRITICAL	SUPERCOMPUTER	PREOCCUPATION	ARGUMENTATIVE	CERTIFICATION
HYDROELECTRIC	IMPRACTICABLE	SUPERNUMERARY	UNACCOMPANIED	AUTHORITARIAN	COLLOQUIALISM
INFINITESIMAL	IMPRESSIONISM	UNCIRCUMCISED	UNDEREMPLOYED	AUTHORITATIVE	COMMEMORATIVE
INTROSPECTION	IMPRESSIONIST	ACCOMPANIMENT	ACCULTURATION	CHRYSANTHEMUM	COMMERCIALISM
IRRECOVERABLE	INCONSPICUOUS	AMNIOCENTESIS	ADVENTURESOME	ELEPHANTIASIS	COMMERCIALIZE
IRRETRIEVABLE	INDEFATIGABLE	ARCHIMANDRITE	BLOODCURDLING	FRAGMENTATION	COMMUNICATION
PETROCHEMICAL	INDESCRIBABLE	CONCATENATION	COMMEMORATIVE	GUBERNATORIAL	CONCATENATION
PHOTOCHEMICAL	INDUSTRIALIST	CONSCIENTIOUS	CONCENTRATION	INTERNATIONAL	CONCENTRATION
PHOTOELECTRIC	INDUSTRIALIZE	CONSTERNATION	CONFEDERATION	MANIFESTATION	CONCEPTUALIZE
PHOTOELECTRON	INTRANSIGENCE	DETERMINATION	CONFIGURATION	MULTINATIONAL	CONCERTMASTER
POLIOMYELITIS	IRRECLAIMABLE	DIFFERENTIATE	CONFLAGRATION	PRECIPITATION	CONFABULATION
PREPOSSESSING	LACKADAISICAL	EXCOMMUNICATE	CONSIDERATION	PROCRASTINATE	CONFEDERATION
PREPOSSESSION	PERFECTIONIST	GEOCHRONOLOGY	DEMONSTRATIVE	PROGNOSTICATE	CONFIGURATION
SCHOOLTEACHER	PERPENDICULAR	HALLUCINATION	DISINTERESTED	RADIOACTIVITY	CONFLAGRATION
TENDERHEARTED	PHOTOEMISSION	HYDRODYNAMICS	GENITOURINARY	SUPRANATIONAL	CONSIDERATION
TERCENTENNIAL	PROJECTIONIST	INCOMMUNICADO	GONADOTROPHIC	TRANSISTORIZE	CONSTELLATION
TONSILLECTOMY	PRONUNCIATION	INCONVENIENCE	GONADOTROPHIN	TRANSNATIONAL	CONSTERNATION
TORTOISESHELL	PROTECTIONIST	INDISPENSABLE	HERMAPHRODITE	UNCONDITIONAL	DEMONSTRATIVE
TURBOELECTRIC	REVOLUTIONARY	IRRESPONSIBLE	IMPERTURBABLE	UNCONDITIONED	DETERMINATION
UNADULTERATED	REVOLUTIONIST	MALADMINISTER	INSUPPORTABLE	UNDERESTIMATE	ELECTROMAGNET
UNCONQUERABLE	REVOLUTIONIZE	MISCEGENATION	INTERMARRIAGE	UNFORGETTABLE	EXTRAGALACTIC
CARBONIFEROUS	SOPHISTICATED	PEREGRINATION	INTERPERSONAL	UNINTENTIONAL	FRAGMENTATION
ANTICOAGULANT	SUBDISCIPLINE	PRIMOGENITURE	MISUNDERSTAND	VALEDICTORIAN	HALLUCINATION
AUTOBIOGRAPHY	SURREPTITIOUS	PUSILLANIMOUS	NONINTERLACED	BACCALAUREATE	HEARTBREAKING
BOARDINGHOUSE	TRANSCRIPTION	QUESTIONNAIRE	PARAPHERNALIA	COMMENSURABLE	HOUSEBREAKING
CLEARINGHOUSE	UNQUESTIONING	RATIOCINATION	PHENOBARBITAL	CONCEPTUALIZE	HYDRODYNAMICS
COUNTINGHOUSE	ANTIPOLLUTION	REINCARNATION	POSTOPERATIVE	CONSANGUINITY	INDIVIDUALISM
DEHYDROGENATE	CONFABULATION	REPREHENSIBLE	STRIKEBREAKER	DISTINGUISHED	INDIVIDUALIST
FERROMAGNETIC	CONSTELLATION	ROENTGENOLOGY	UNCOMFORTABLE	GRANDDAUGHTER	INDIVIDUALITY
INTERROGATIVE	COSMETOLOGIST	UNACCOUNTABLE	UNDERCARRIAGE	INDIVIDUALISM	INDIVIDUALIZE
INTERROGATORY	ELECTROLOGIST	UNPRETENTIOUS	UNINTERRUPTED	INDIVIDUALIST	INDUSTRIALIST
KNOWLEDGEABLE	EXTRAGALACTIC	UNWARRANTABLE	ADVERTISEMENT	INDIVIDUALITY	INDUSTRIALIZE
LAUGHINGSTOCK	INTERCULTURAL	VOCATIONALISM	ANTIPERSONNEL	INDIVIDUALIZE	INTERGALACTIC
MICROORGANISM	INTERGALACTIC	ACCELEROMETER	CONCUPISCENCE	JURISPRUDENCE	INTERROGATIVE
OLEOMARGARINE	KAFFEEKLATSCH	BACTERIOPHAGE	EFFLORESCENCE	SUPERABUNDANT	INTERROGATORY
ACETYLCHOLINE	MACHICOLATION	CINEMATOGRAPH	ESTABLISHMENT	THERMONUCLEAR	JOLLIFICATION
AUTOCHTHONOUS	MONONUCLEOSIS	CORRESPONDENT	IMPERMISSIBLE	INSECTIVOROUS	JUSTIFICATION
GEOMORPHOLOGY	OVERQUALIFIED	DISPROPORTION	INCOMBUSTIBLE	COUNTERWEIGHT	KAFFEEKLATSCH
PHYSIOTHERAPY	PARALLELOGRAM	EXCEPTIONABLE	INCONTESTABLE	FEATHERWEIGHT	MACHICOLATION
PSYCHOTHERAPY	PARTICULARIZE	MONOCHROMATIC	INEXHAUSTIBLE	HUNDREDWEIGHT	MANIFESTATION
RAPPROCHEMENT	QUADRUPLICATE	NONCONFORMIST	INEXPRESSIBLE	MONOCOTYLEDON	MICROORGANISM
SCHIZOPHRENIA	QUINTUPLICATE	ORTHONDONTICS	INFLORESCENCE	NITROGLYCERIN	MISALLOCATION
THOROUGHGOING	STRANGULATION	PHARMACOPOEIA	INTRAMUSCULAR		MISCEGENATION

NITRIFICATION	FEATHERWEIGHT	UNCONDITIONAL	HERMAPHRODITE	LACKADAISICAL	INAPPRECIABLE
OLEOMARGARINE	HUNDREDWEIGHT	UNCONDITIONED	IMPRESSIONISM	LAUGHINGSTOCK	INCONTESTABLE
PARTICULARIZE	INCONSIDERATE	UNDERACHIEVER	IMPRESSIONIST	MISUNDERSTAND	INDEFATIGABLE
PEREGRINATION	IRREPLACEABLE	UNDERESTIMATE	INSECTIVOROUS	PHOTOEMISSION	INDESCRIBABLE
POSTOPERATIVE	KNOWLEDGEABLE	UNINTELLIGENT	OPHTHALMOLOGY	PREPOSSESSING	INDISPENSABLE
PRECIPITATION	MONONUCLEOSIS	UNINTENTIONAL	PARALLELOGRAM	PREPOSSESSION	INSUPPORTABLE
PREOCCUPATION	PHYSIOTHERAPY	MONOCOTYLEDON	PERFECTIONIST	REPREHENSIBLE	IRRECLAIMABLE
PRONUNCIATION	PSYCHOTHERAPY	NONINTERLACED	PROJECTIONIST	TORTOISESHELL	IRRECOVERABLE
QUALIFICATION	PRONOUNCEMENT	POLIOMYELITIS	PROTECTIONIST	UNDERCLASSMAN	IRREPLACEABLE
QUARTERMASTER	RAPPROCHEMENT	UNDEREMPLOYED	REVOLUTIONARY	UPPERCLASSMAN	IRRETRIEVABLE
RATIOCINATION	SEMIPERMEABLE	ACCELEROMETER	REVOLUTIONIST	AMNIOCENTESIS	KNOWLEDGEABLE
REINCARNATION	STRIKEBREAKER	AGGIORNAMENTO	REVOLUTIONIZE	ARCHITECTONIC	MONOCHROMATIC
SCHOOLTEACHER	SUPERNUMERARY	IRRECLAIMABLE	ROENTGENOLOGY	CONSCIENTIOUS	NONINTERLACED
SPECIFICATION	UNPRECEDENTED	MONOCHROMATIC	SCANDALMONGER	COUNTERATTACK	NONRESISTANCE
STRANGULATION	WOOLGATHERING	PETROCHEMICAL	STREPTOCOCCUS	DIFFERENTIATE	PARAPHERNALIA
SULFANILAMIDE	CINEMATOGRAPH	PHOTOCHEMICAL	TABLESPOONFUL	HYPERCRITICAL	PSYCHOSOMATIC
SYLLABICATION	GRANDDAUGHTER	PSYCHOSOMATIC	TRANSISTORIZE	IMPERCEPTIBLE	QUESTIONNAIRE
TENDERHEARTED	INDEFATIGABLE	SEMIAUTOMATIC	UNQUESTIONING	INCOMBUSTIBLE	SEMIAUTOMATIC
THERMOPLASTIC	INTRANSIGENCE	COMPLIMENTARY	VALEDICTORIAN	INCONTESTABLE	SEMIPERMEABLE
TRANSATLANTIC	THOROUGHGOING	CONSEQUENTIAL	WHITHERSOEVER	INCORRUPTIBLE	SOPHISTICATED
UNACCOMPANIED	BOARDINGHOUSE	CORRESPONDENT	BACTERIOPHAGE	INEXHAUSTIBLE	STRIKEBREAKER
UNNECESSARILY	CHRYSANTHEMUM	EUROPOCENTRIC	CONTRACEPTION	INSUPPORTABLE	UNACCOUNTABLE
VERSIFICATION	CLEARINGHOUSE	EXCEPTIONABLE	MAGNETOSPHERE	INTERCULTURAL	UNADULTERATED
VOCATIONALISM	COUNTINGHOUSE	FERROMAGNETIC	MICROCOMPUTER	NONRESISTANCE	UNCOMFORTABLE
IMPERTURBABLE	ESTABLISHMENT	GRANTSMANSHIP	PHARMACOPOEIA	PRETERNATURAL	UNCONQUERABLE
INDESCRIBABLE	HYDROCEPHALUS	HETEROGENEOUS	SUBDISCIPLINE	QUADRILATERAL	UNFORGETTABLE
PHENOBARBITAL	METAMORPHOSIS	INSTANTANEOUS	SUPERCOMPUTER	SURREPTITIOUS	UNIMPEACHABLE
CONCUPISCENCE	THUNDERSHOWER	INSUBSTANTIAL	TRANSCRIPTION	THUNDERSTRUCK	UNMENTIONABLE
EFFLORESCENCE	UNIMPEACHABLE	MISCELLANEOUS	VENTRILOQUISM	UNACCOUNTABLE	UNPREDICTABLE
HYDROELECTRIC	ACCOMPANIMENT	ORTHONDONTICS	ADMINISTRATOR	UNCOMFORTABLE	UNWARRANTABLE
IMPRACTICABLE	ANTIFERTILITY	PARAPHERNALIA	ANTILOGARITHM	UNDERCLOTHING	EXCOMMUNICATE
INCONSPICUOUS	CONSANGUINITY	QUESTIONNAIRE	AUTOBIOGRAPHY	UNFORGETTABLE	EXTRAGALACTIC
INFLORESCENCE	DECONTAMINATE	SANCTIMONIOUS	BACCALAUREATE	UNPREDICTABLE	INCOMMUNICADO
INTRAMUSCULAR	DISTINGUISHED	SUPERABUNDANT	CIRCUMFERENCE	UNPRETENTIOUS	INTERGALACTIC
INTROSPECTION	ELEPHANTIASIS	TERCENTENNIAL	COMMENSURABLE	UNWARRANTABLE	PROGNOSTICATE
NITROGLYCERIN	EXCOMMUNICATE	UNCEREMONIOUS	CONFRATERNITY	ANTICOAGULANT	QUADRUPLICATE
OVERSUBSCRIBE	EXTRAORDINARY	UNDERSTANDING	CONTAINERSHIP	ANTIPOLLUTION	QUINTUPLICATE
PERPENDICULAR	GENITOURINARY	UNMENTIONABLE	DISPROPORTION	CIRCUMABULATE	SCHOOLTEACHER
PHOTOELECTRIC	INAPPRECIABLE	UNSUBSTANTIAL	INTERMARRIAGE	HYPERDOCUMENT	SEMICONDUCTOR
PHOTOELECTRON	INCOMMUNICADO	ACETYLCHOLINE	IRRECOVERABLE	INTERLOCUTORY	STREPTOCOCCUS
RECRUDESCENCE	INCONVENIENCE	ANTIPERSONNEL	NONCONFORMIST	SEMICONDUCTOR	CORRESPONDENT
SOPHISTICATED	INDETERMINATE	AUTOCHTHONOUS	PROFESSORIATE	UNINTERRUPTED	HERMAPHRODITE
THERMONUCLEAR	INSUBORDINATE	CONFECTIONERY	QUADRIPARTITE	IRRETRIEVABLE	SUPERABUNDANT
TONSILLECTOMY	INTERNATIONAL	CONTORTIONIST	SCHIZOPHRENIA		UNDERSTANDING
TURBOELECTRIC	MALADMINISTER	COSMETOLOGIST	THENCEFORWARD		ACCELEROMETER
UNCIRCUMCISED	MULTINATIONAL	DAGUERREOTYPE	UNADULTERATED	**10TH LETTER**	AGGIORNAMENTO
ARCHIMANDRITE	OVERQUALIFIED	DISPASSIONATE	UNCONQUERABLE		AMNIOCENTESIS
BIODEGRADABLE	PATERFAMILIAS	ELECTROLOGIST	UNDERCARRIAGE		BACCALAUREATE
BLOODCURDLING	PRIMOGENITURE	EXHIBITIONISM	CHRISTMASTIDE	ADMINISTRATOR	CHRYSANTHEMUM
JURISPRUDENCE	PROCRASTINATE	EXPEDITIONARY	GENERALISSIMO	AUTOBIOGRAPHY	CIRCUMFERENCE
UNDERGRADUATE	PROGNOSTICATE	EXPRESSIONISM	IMPERMISSIBLE	BIODEGRADABLE	CONCUPISCENCE
ADVENTURESOME	PUSILLANIMOUS	GEOCHRONOLOGY	INDISPENSABLE	COMMENSURABLE	EFFLORESCENCE
ADVERTISEMENT	QUADRUPLICATE	GEOMORPHOLOGY	INEXPRESSIBLE	ELEPHANTIASIS	FERROMAGNETIC
CARBONIFEROUS	QUINTUPLICATE	GEOSTATIONARY	INFINITESIMAL	EXCEPTIONABLE	HETEROGENEOUS
COUNTERWEIGHT	RADIOACTIVITY	GONADOTROPHIC	INTERPERSONAL	HYDROCEPHALUS	INCONVENIENCE
DEHYDROGENATE	SUPRANATIONAL	GONADOTROPHIN	IRREPRESSIBLE	IMPERTURBABLE	INFLORESCENCE
DISINTERESTED	TRANSNATIONAL	GUBERNATORIAL	IRRESPONSIBLE	IMPRACTICABLE	INSTANTANEOUS

INTRANSIGENCE	BLOODCURDLING	REVOLUTIONIST	MALADMINISTER	ORTHONDONTICS	INTERMARRIAGE
JURISPRUDENCE	CIRCUMABULATE	REVOLUTIONIZE	PHOTOEMISSION	PEREGRINATION	MISUNDERSTAND
MISCELLANEOUS	COLLOQUIALISM	SCANDALMONGER	PREPOSSESSING	PHOTOELECTRIC	PHYSIOTHERAPY
MONOCOTYLEDON	COMMERCIALISM	TABLESPOONFUL	PREPOSSESSION	PHOTOELECTRON	PSYCHOTHERAPY
NITROGLYCERIN	COMMERCIALIZE	TERCENTENNIAL	QUARTERMASTER	POSTOPERATIVE	PROCRASTINATE
QUADRILATERAL	CONCEPTUALIZE	TRANSATLANTIC	THERMOPLASTIC	PRECIPITATION	PROFESSORIATE
RECRUDESCENCE	GEOCHRONOLOGY	UNACCOMPANIED	UNDERCLASSMAN	PREOCCUPATION	PROGNOSTICATE
SCHIZOPHRENIA	GEOMORPHOLOGY	UNPRECEDENTED	UPPERCLASSMAN	PRIMOGENITURE	QUADRUPLICATE
UNDERACHIEVER	INDIVIDUALISM	UNQUESTIONING	ACCOMMODATING	PRONUNCIATION	QUINTUPLICATE
WHITHERSOEVER	INDIVIDUALIST	ARCHITECTONIC	ACCOMMODATION	QUADRIPARTITE	REVOLUTIONARY
OVERQUALIFIED	INDIVIDUALITY	BOARDINGHOUSE	ACCULTURATION	QUALIFICATION	SUPERABUNDANT
COSMETOLOGIST	INDIVIDUALIZE	CLEARINGHOUSE	AFFORESTATION	RATIOCINATION	SUPERNUMERARY
ELECTROLOGIST	OPHTHALMOLOGY	COUNTINGHOUSE	ANTIPOLLUTION	REINCARNATION	THENCEFORWARD
ELECTROMAGNET	INDUSTRIALIST	INTERNATIONAL	APPROPRIATION	SPECIFICATION	UNDERCARRIAGE
PARALLELOGRAM	INDUSTRIALIZE	INTERPERSONAL	ARGUMENTATION	STRANGULATION	UNDERESTIMATE
UNINTELLIGENT	PATERFAMILIAS	METAMORPHOSIS	ARGUMENTATIVE	SYLLABICATION	UNDERGRADUATE
BACTERIOPHAGE	ROENTGENOLOGY	MONONUCLEOSIS	AUTHORITATIVE	TONSILLECTOMY	BIODEGRADABLE
GRANDDAUGHTER	SUBDISCIPLINE	MULTINATIONAL	CERTIFICATION	TRANSCRIPTION	COMMENSURABLE
MAGNETOSPHERE	THERMONUCLEAR	PHARMACOPOEIA	CHRISTMASTIDE	TURBOELECTRIC	EXCEPTIONABLE
TORTOISESHELL	VOCATIONALISM	SUPRANATIONAL	COMMEMORATIVE	UNSUBSTANTIAL	IMPERCEPTIBLE
UNDERCLOTHING	ACCOMPANIMENT	THOROUGHGOING	COMMUNICATION	VERSIFICATION	IMPERMISSIBLE
ANTILOGARITHM	ADVERTISEMENT	THUNDERSHOWER	COMPLIMENTARY	INCONSPICUOUS	IMPERTURBABLE
BOUILLABAISSE	ANTIHISTAMINE	TRANSNATIONAL	CONCATENATION	INTERCULTURAL	IMPRACTICABLE
CONSCIENTIOUS	ESTABLISHMENT	UNCONDITIONAL	CONCENTRATION	INTRAMUSCULAR	INAPPRECIABLE
COUNTERWEIGHT	HYDRODYNAMICS	UNCONDITIONED	CONFABULATION	MICROCOMPUTER	INCOMBUSTIBLE
DIFFERENTIATE	HYPERDOCUMENT	UNDEREMPLOYED	CONFEDERATION	PERPENDICULAR	INCONTESTABLE
FEATHERWEIGHT	NONCONFORMIST	UNINTENTIONAL	CONFIGURATION	PRETERNATURAL	INCORRUPTIBLE
HUNDREDWEIGHT	PRONOUNCEMENT	GONADOTROPHIC	CONFLAGRATION	SUPERCOMPUTER	INDEFATIGABLE
HYPERCRITICAL	PUSILLANIMOUS	GONADOTROPHIN	CONSEQUENTIAL	UNDERGRADUATE	INDESCRIBABLE
IMPERCEPTIBLE	RAPPROCHEMENT	UNINTERRUPTED	CONSIDERATION	VENTRILOQUISM	INDISPENSABLE
IMPERMISSIBLE	SULFANILAMIDE	ARCHIMANDRITE	CONSTELLATION	RADIOACTIVITY	INEXHAUSTIBLE
INCOMBUSTIBLE	UNDERESTIMATE	AUTHORITARIAN	CONSTERNATION	THENCEFORWARD	INEXPRESSIBLE
INCORRUPTIBLE	ANTIPERSONNEL	BROKENHEARTED	CONTRACEPTION		INSUPPORTABLE
INEXHAUSTIBLE	AUTOCHTHONOUS	CARBONIFEROUS	COUNTERATTACK		IRRECLAIMABLE
INEXPRESSIBLE	CONFECTIONERY	CINEMATOGRAPH	DAGUERREOTYPE		IRRECOVERABLE
INFINITESIMAL	CONFRATERNITY	GUBERNATORIAL	DEMONSTRATIVE	**11TH LETTER**	IRREPLACEABLE
INTERMARRIAGE	CONSANGUINITY	INCONSIDERATE	DETERMINATION		IRREPRESSIBLE
IRREPRESSIBLE	CONTORTIONIST	INSECTIVOROUS	DISPROPORTION	ANTICOAGULANT	IRRESPONSIBLE
IRRESPONSIBLE	DECONTAMINATE	OLEOMARGARINE	EUROPOCENTRIC	BACCALAUREATE	IRRETRIEVABLE
LACKADAISICAL	DEHYDROGENATE	OVERSUBSCRIBE	FRAGMENTATION	BACTERIOPHAGE	KNOWLEDGEABLE
PETROCHEMICAL	DISPASSIONATE	PARTICULARIZE	HALLUCINATION	CINEMATOGRAPH	REPREHENSIBLE
PHENOBARBITAL	EXHIBITIONISM	PHYSIOTHERAPY	HYDROELECTRIC	CIRCUMABULATE	SEMIPERMEABLE
PHOTOCHEMICAL	EXPEDITIONARY	PSYCHOTHERAPY	INSUBSTANTIAL	COMPLIMENTARY	UNACCOUNTABLE
POLIOMYELITIS	EXPRESSIONISM	SUPERNUMERARY	INTERLOCUTORY	COUNTERATTACK	UNCOMFORTABLE
PROFESSORIATE	EXTRAORDINARY	TENDERHEARTED	INTERROGATIVE	DECONTAMINATE	UNCONQUERABLE
REPREHENSIBLE	GENITOURINARY	THUNDERSTRUCK	INTERROGATORY	DEHYDROGENATE	UNFORGETTABLE
SANCTIMONIOUS	GEOSTATIONARY	TRANSISTORIZE	INTROSPECTION	DIFFERENTIATE	UNIMPEACHABLE
SURREPTITIOUS	IMPRESSIONISM	UNNECESSARILY	JOLLIFICATION	DISPASSIONATE	UNMENTIONABLE
UNCEREMONIOUS	IMPRESSIONIST	VALEDICTORIAN	JUSTIFICATION	EXCOMMUNICATE	UNPREDICTABLE
UNCIRCUMCISED	INDETERMINATE	WOOLGATHERING	KAFFEEKLATSCH	EXPEDITIONARY	UNWARRANTABLE
UNDERCARRIAGE	INSUBORDINATE	ADVENTURESOME	LAUGHINGSTOCK	EXTRAORDINARY	HYPERCRITICAL
UNPRETENTIOUS	MICROORGANISM	CONCERTMASTER	MACHICOLATION	GENITOURINARY	LACKADAISICAL
HEARTBREAKING	PERFECTIONIST	CONTAINERSHIP	MANIFESTATION	GEOSTATIONARY	NONINTERLACED
HOUSEBREAKING	PROCRASTINATE	DISINTERESTED	MISALLOCATION	INCOMMUNICADO	PETROCHEMICAL
ACETYLCHOLINE	PROJECTIONIST	DISTINGUISHED	MISCEGENATION	INCONSIDERATE	PHOTOCHEMICAL
ANTICOAGULANT	PROTECTIONIST	GENERALISSIMO	MISUNDERSTAND	INDETERMINATE	STREPTOCOCCUS
ANTIFERTILITY	REVOLUTIONARY	GRANTSMANSHIP	NITRIFICATION	INSUBORDINATE	MONOCOTYLEDON

ACCOMPANIMENT	CONSTELLATION	QUALIFICATION	UNINTENTIONAL	QUARTERMASTER	CIRCUMFERENCE
ADVERTISEMENT	CONSTERNATION	QUESTIONNAIRE	ADVENTURESOME	SEMIAUTOMATIC	CONCUPISCENCE
CONFECTIONERY	CONTORTIONIST	RADIOACTIVITY	AUTOCHTHONOUS	SEMICONDUCTOR	COUNTERATTACK
CORRESPONDENT	CONTRACEPTION	RATIOCINATION	CARBONIFEROUS	SOPHISTICATED	EFFLORESCENCE
ESTABLISHMENT	COSMETOLOGIST	REINCARNATION	CONSCIENTIOUS	SUPERCOMPUTER	HYDRODYNAMICS
HYPERDOCUMENT	DEMONSTRATIVE	REVOLUTIONIST	GEOCHRONOLOGY	TENDERHEARTED	INCONVENIENCE
MAGNETOSPHERE	DETERMINATION	REVOLUTIONIZE	GEOMORPHOLOGY	THERMOPLASTIC	INFLORESCENCE
PHARMACOPOEIA	DISPROPORTION	SPECIFICATION	HETEROGENEOUS	TRANSATLANTIC	INTRANSIGENCE
PRONOUNCEMENT	ELECTROLOGIST	STRANGULATION	INCONSPICUOUS	UNADULTERATED	JURISPRUDENCE
RAPPROCHEMENT	EXHIBITIONISM	SUBDISCIPLINE	INSECTIVOROUS	UNINTERRUPTED	KAFFEEKLATSCH
THERMONUCLEAR	EXPRESSIONISM	SULFANILAMIDE	INSTANTANEOUS	UNPRECEDENTED	LAUGHINGSTOCK
TORTOISESHELL	FRAGMENTATION	SYLLABICATION	INTERLOCUTORY	BOARDINGHOUSE	NONRESISTANCE
UNINTELLIGENT	GENERALISSIMO	TERCENTENNIAL	INTERROGATORY	CLEARINGHOUSE	ORTHONDONTICS
TABLESPOONFUL	GUBERNATORIAL	THOROUGHGOING	LAUGHINGSTOCK	COUNTINGHOUSE	RECRUDESCENCE
COUNTERWEIGHT	HALLUCINATION	TRANSCRIPTION	MISCELLANEOUS	PRIMOGENITURE	THUNDERSTRUCK
FEATHERWEIGHT	HEARTBREAKING	TRANSISTORIZE	OPHTHALMOLOGY	THUNDERSTRUCK	CHRISTMASTIDE
HUNDREDWEIGHT	HERMAPHRODITE	UNACCOMPANIED	PUSILLANIMOUS	UNDERACHIEVER	INCOMMUNICADO
SCANDALMONGER	HOUSEBREAKING	UNDERCLOTHING	ROENTGENOLOGY	WHITHERSOEVER	SULFANILAMIDE
CONTAINERSHIP	HYDRODYNAMICS	UNDERSTANDING	SANCTIMONIOUS	THUNDERSHOWER	ACCELEROMETER
DISTINGUISHED	IMPRESSIONISM	UNNECESSARILY	SURREPTITIOUS	DAGUERREOTYPE	ANTIPERSONNEL
GONADOTROPHIC	IMPRESSIONIST	UNQUESTIONING	TONSILLECTOMY	UNDEREMPLOYED	BROKENHEARTED
GONADOTROPHIN	INDIVIDUALISM	UNSUBSTANTIAL	UNCEREMONIOUS		CONCERTMASTER
GRANTSMANSHIP	INDIVIDUALIST	VALEDICTORIAN	UNPRETENTIOUS		DISINTERESTED
SCHOOLTEACHER	INDIVIDUALITY	VENTRILOQUISM	AUTOBIOGRAPHY		DISTINGUISHED
ACCOMMODATING	INDIVIDUALIZE	VERSIFICATION	EUROPOCENTRIC	**12TH**	ELECTROMAGNET
ACCOMMODATION	INDUSTRIALIST	VOCATIONALISM	HYDROELECTRIC	**LETTER**	GRANDDAUGHTER
ACCULTURATION	INDUSTRIALIZE	WOOLGATHERING	INTERCULTURAL	AUTHORITARIAN	MALADMINISTER
ACETYLCHOLINE	INSUBSTANTIAL	STRIKEBREAKER	NITROGLYCERIN	CONSEQUENTIAL	MICROCOMPUTER
AFFORESTATION	INTERROGATIVE	HYDROCEPHALUS	PARALLELOGRAM	GUBERNATORIAL	NONINTERLACED
ANTIFERTILITY	INTROSPECTION	INTRAMUSCULAR	PHOTOELECTRIC	HYPERCRITICAL	OVERQUALIFIED
ANTIHISTAMINE	JOLLIFICATION	PARAPHERNALIA	PHOTOELECTRON	INFINITESIMAL	QUARTERMASTER
ANTIPOLLUTION	JUSTIFICATION	PERPENDICULAR	PRETERNATURAL	INSUBSTANTIAL	SCANDALMONGER
APPROPRIATION	MACHICOLATION	CHRYSANTHEMUM	QUADRILATERAL	INTERCULTURAL	SCHOOLTEACHER
ARCHIMANDRITE	MANIFESTATION	INFINITESIMAL	TURBOELECTRIC	INTERNATIONAL	SOPHISTICATED
ARGUMENTATION	MICROORGANISM	UNDERCLASSMAN	AMNIOCENTESIS	INTERPERSONAL	STRIKEBREAKER
ARGUMENTATIVE	MISALLOCATION	UPPERCLASSMAN	BOUILLABAISSE	INTRAMUSCULAR	SUPERCOMPUTER
AUTHORITARIAN	MISCEGENATION	AGGIORNAMENTO	ELEPHANTIASIS	LACKADAISICAL	TENDERHEARTED
AUTHORITATIVE	NITRIFICATION	ANTIPERSONNEL	KAFFEEKLATSCH	MULTINATIONAL	THUNDERSHOWER
BLOODCURDLING	NONCONFORMIST	ARCHITECTONIC	METAMORPHOSIS	PARALLELOGRAM	UNACCOMPANIED
CERTIFICATION	OLEOMARGARINE	CIRCUMFERENCE	MONONUCLEOSIS	PATERFAMILIAS	UNADULTERATED
CHRISTMASTIDE	ORTHONDONTICS	CONCUPISCENCE	UNCIRCUMCISED	PERPENDICULAR	UNCIRCUMCISED
COLLOQUIALISM	OVERQUALIFIED	EFFLORESCENCE	ACCELEROMETER	PETROCHEMICAL	UNCONDITIONED
COMMEMORATIVE	OVERSUBSCRIBE	ELECTROMAGNET	ADMINISTRATOR	PHENOBARBITAL	UNDERACHIEVER
COMMERCIALISM	PARTICULARIZE	INCONVENIENCE	ANTILOGARITHM	PHOTOCHEMICAL	UNDEREMPLOYED
COMMERCIALIZE	PATERFAMILIAS	INFLORESCENCE	BROKENHEARTED	PRETERNATURAL	UNINTERRUPTED
COMMUNICATION	PEREGRINATION	INTERNATIONAL	CONCERTMASTER	QUADRILATERAL	UNPRECEDENTED
CONCATENATION	PERFECTIONIST	INTERPERSONAL	DISINTERESTED	SUPRANATIONAL	WHITHERSOEVER
CONCENTRATION	PHOTOEMISSION	INTRANSIGENCE	EXTRAGALACTIC	TERCENTENNIAL	BACTERIOPHAGE
CONCEPTUALIZE	POSTOPERATIVE	JURISPRUDENCE	FERROMAGNETIC	THERMONUCLEAR	GEOCHRONOLOGY
CONFABULATION	PRECIPITATION	MULTINATIONAL	GRANDDAUGHTER	TRANSNATIONAL	GEOMORPHOLOGY
CONFEDERATION	PREOCCUPATION	NONRESISTANCE	INTERGALACTIC	UNCONDITIONAL	INTERMARRIAGE
CONFIGURATION	PREPOSSESSING	RECRUDESCENCE	MALADMINISTER	UNDERCLASSMAN	OPHTHALMOLOGY
CONFLAGRATION	PREPOSSESSION	SCHIZOPHRENIA	MICROCOMPUTER	UNINTENTIONAL	ROENTGENOLOGY
CONFRATERNITY	PROJECTIONIST	SUPRANATIONAL	MONOCHROMATIC	UNSUBSTANTIAL	UNDERCARRIAGE
CONSANGUINITY	PRONUNCIATION	TRANSNATIONAL	PHENOBARBITAL	UPPERCLASSMAN	ANTILOGARITHM
CONSEQUENTIAL	PROTECTIONIST	UNCONDITIONAL	POLIOMYELITIS	VALEDICTORIAN	AUTOBIOGRAPHY
CONSIDERATION	QUADRIPARTITE	UNCONDITIONED	PSYCHOSOMATIC	OVERSUBSCRIBE	COUNTERWEIGHT

FEATHERWEIGHT	UNCONQUERABLE	HALLUCINATION	INDIVIDUALISM	DEMONSTRATIVE	BOARDINGHOUSE
HUNDREDWEIGHT	UNFORGETTABLE	INTROSPECTION	INDIVIDUALIST	INTERROGATIVE	BOUILLABAISSE
AMNIOCENTESIS	UNIMPEACHABLE	JOLLIFICATION	INDUSTRIALIST	POSTOPERATIVE	CHRISTMASTIDE
ARCHITECTONIC	UNMENTIONABLE	JUSTIFICATION	MICROORGANISM	COMMERCIALIZE	CIRCUMABULATE
CONTAINERSHIP	UNNECESSARILY	MACHICOLATION	NONCONFORMIST	CONCEPTUALIZE	CIRCUMFERENCE
ELEPHANTIASIS	UNPREDICTABLE	MANIFESTATION	PERFECTIONIST	INDIVIDUALIZE	CLEARINGHOUSE
EUROPOCENTRIC	UNWARRANTABLE	MISALLOCATION	PROJECTIONIST	INDUSTRIALIZE	COMMEMORATIVE
EXTRAGALACTIC	ADVENTURESOME	MISCEGENATION	PROTECTIONIST	PARTICULARIZE	COMMENSURABLE
FERROMAGNETIC	GENERALISSIMO	MONOCOTYLEDON	REVOLUTIONIST	REVOLUTIONIZE	COMMERCIALIZE
GONADOTROPHIC	TONSILLECTOMY	NITRIFICATION	VENTRILOQUISM	TRANSISTORIZE	CONCEPTUALIZE
GONADOTROPHIN	ACCOMMODATING	PEREGRINATION	VOCATIONALISM		CONCUPISCENCE
GRANTSMANSHIP	ACCOMPANIMENT	PHOTOELECTRON	AGGIORNAMENTO		COUNTINGHOUSE
HYDROELECTRIC	ACETYLCHOLINE	PHOTOEMISSION	ANTIFERTILITY		DAGUERREOTYPE
INTERGALACTIC	ADVERTISEMENT	PRECIPITATION	ARCHIMANDRITE	**13TH LETTER**	DECONTAMINATE
METAMORPHOSIS	ANTICOAGULANT	PREOCCUPATION	BACCALAUREATE		DEHYDROGENATE
MONOCHROMATIC	ANTIHISTAMINE	PREPOSSESSION	CIRCUMABULATE	PARAPHERNALIA	DEMONSTRATIVE
MONONUCLEOSIS	BLOODCURDLING	PRONUNCIATION	CONFRATERNITY	PHARMACOPOEIA	DIFFERENTIATE
NITROGLYCERIN	CORRESPONDENT	QUALIFICATION	CONSANGUINITY	SCHIZOPHRENIA	DISPASSIONATE
PARAPHERNALIA	ESTABLISHMENT	RATIOCINATION	DECONTAMINATE	ARCHITECTONIC	EFFLORESCENCE
PHARMACOPOEIA	HEARTBREAKING	REINCARNATION	DEHYDROGENATE	EUROPOCENTRIC	EXCEPTIONABLE
PHOTOELECTRIC	HOUSEBREAKING	SEMICONDUCTOR	DIFFERENTIATE	EXTRAGALACTIC	EXCOMMUNICATE
POLIOMYELITIS	HYPERDOCUMENT	SPECIFICATION	DISPASSIONATE	FERROMAGNETIC	HERMAPHRODITE
PSYCHOSOMATIC	MISUNDERSTAND	STRANGULATION	EXCOMMUNICATE	GONADOTROPHIC	IMPERCEPTIBLE
SCHIZOPHRENIA	OLEOMARGARINE	SYLLABICATION	HERMAPHRODITE	HYDROELECTRIC	IMPERMISSIBLE
SEMIAUTOMATIC	PREPOSSESSING	TRANSCRIPTION	INCONSIDERATE	INTERGALACTIC	IMPERTURBABLE
THERMOPLASTIC	PRONOUNCEMENT	VERSIFICATION	INDETERMINATE	MONOCHROMATIC	IMPRACTICABLE
TRANSATLANTIC	RAPPROCHEMENT	CINEMATOGRAPH	INDIVIDUALITY	PHOTOELECTRIC	INAPPRECIABLE
TURBOELECTRIC	SUBDISCIPLINE	DAGUERREOTYPE	INSUBORDINATE	PSYCHOSOMATIC	INCOMBUSTIBLE
BIODEGRADABLE	SUPERABUNDANT	PHYSIOTHERAPY	PROCRASTINATE	SEMIAUTOMATIC	INCONSIDERATE
COMMENSURABLE	THOROUGHGOING	PSCHOTHERAPY	PROFESSORIATE	THERMOPLASTIC	INCONTESTABLE
EXCEPTIONABLE	UNDERCLOTHING	COMPLIMENTARY	PROGNOSTICATE	TRANSATLANTIC	INCONVENIENCE
IMPERCEPTIBLE	UNDERSTANDING	CONFECTIONERY	QUADRIPARTITE	TURBOELECTRIC	INCORRUPTIBLE
IMPERMISSIBLE	UNINTELLIGENT	EXPEDITIONARY	QUADRUPLICATE	BROKENHEARTED	INDEFATIGABLE
IMPERTURBABLE	UNQUESTIONING	EXTRAORDINARY	QUINTUPLICATE	DISINTERESTED	INDESCRIBABLE
IMPRACTICABLE	WOOLGATHERING	GENITOURINARY	RADIOACTIVITY	DISTINGUISHED	INDETERMINATE
INAPPRECIABLE	ACCOMMODATION	GEOSTATIONARY	UNDERESTIMATE	MISUNDERSTAND	INDISPENSABLE
INCOMBUSTIBLE	ACCULTURATION	INTERLOCUTORY	UNDERGRADUATE	NONINTERLACED	INDIVIDUALIZE
INCONTESTABLE	ADMINISTRATOR	INTERROGATORY	AUTOCHTHONOUS	OVERQUALIFIED	INDUSTRIALIZE
INCORRUPTIBLE	AFFORESTATION	MAGNETOSPHERE	CARBONIFEROUS	SOPHISTICATED	INEXHAUSTIBLE
INDEFATIGABLE	ANTIPOLLUTION	PRIMOGENITURE	CHRYSANTHEMUM	TENDERHEARTED	INEXPRESSIBLE
INDESCRIBABLE	APPROPRIATION	QUESTIONNAIRE	CONSCIENTIOUS	THENCEFORWARD	INFLORESCENCE
INDISPENSABLE	ARGUMENTATION	REVOLUTIONARY	HETEROGENEOUS	UNACCOMPANIED	INSUBORDINATE
INEXHAUSTIBLE	CERTIFICATION	SUPERNUMERARY	HYDROCEPHALUS	UNADULTERATED	INSUPPORTABLE
INEXPRESSIBLE	COMMUNICATION	THENCEFORWARD	INCONSPICUOUS	UNCIRCUMCISED	INTERMARRIAGE
INSUPPORTABLE	CONCATENATION	BOARDINGHOUSE	INSECTIVOROUS	UNCONDITIONED	INTERROGATIVE
IRRECLAIMABLE	CONCENTRATION	BOUILLABAISSE	INSTANTANEOUS	UNDEREMPLOYED	INTRANSIGENCE
IRRECOVERABLE	CONFABULATION	CLEARINGHOUSE	MISCELLANEOUS	UNINTERRUPTED	IRRECLAIMABLE
IRREPLACEABLE	CONFEDERATION	COLLOQUIALISM	PUSILLANIMOUS	UNPRECEDENTED	IRRECOVERABLE
IRREPRESSIBLE	CONFIGURATION	COMMERCIALISM	SANCTIMONIOUS	ACETYLCHOLINE	IRREPLACEABLE
IRRESPONSIBLE	CONFLAGRATION	CONTORTIONIST	STREPTOCOCCUS	ADVENTURESOME	IRREPRESSIBLE
IRRETRIEVABLE	CONSIDERATION	COSMETOLOGIST	SURREPTITIOUS	ANTIHISTAMINE	IRRESPONSIBLE
KNOWLEDGEABLE	CONSTELLATION	COUNTINGHOUSE	TABLESPOONFUL	ARCHIMANDRITE	IRRETRIEVABLE
REPREHENSIBLE	CONSTERNATION	ELECTROLOGIST	UNCEREMONIOUS	ARGUMENTATIVE	JURISPRUDENCE
SEMIPERMEABLE	CONTRACEPTION	EXHIBITIONISM	UNPRETENTIOUS	AUTHORITATIVE	KNOWLEDGEABLE
TORTOISESHELL	DETERMINATION	EXPRESSIONISM	ARGUMENTATIVE	BACCALAUREATE	MAGNETOSPHERE
UNACCOUNTABLE	DISPROPORTION	IMPRESSIONISM	AUTHORITATIVE	BACTERIOPHAGE	NONRESISTANCE
UNCOMFORTABLE	FRAGMENTATION	IMPRESSIONIST	COMMEMORATIVE	BIODEGRADABLE	OLEOMARGARINE

OVERSUBSCRIBE	PHOTOCHEMICAL	PEREGRINATION	POLIOMYELITIS
PARTICULARIZE	PRETERNATURAL	PHOTOELECTRON	PUSILLANIMOUS
POSTOPERATIVE	QUADRILATERAL	PHOTOEMISSION	SANCTIMONIOUS
PRIMOGENITURE	SUPRANATIONAL	PRECIPITATION	STREPTOCOCCUS
PROCRASTINATE	TABLESPOONFUL	PREOCCUPATION	SURREPTITIOUS
PROFESSORIATE	TERCENTENNIAL	PREPOSSESSION	UNCEREMONIOUS
PROGNOSTICATE	TORTOISESHELL	PRONUNCIATION	UNPRETENTIOUS
QUADRIPARTITE	TRANSNATIONAL	QUALIFICATION	ACCOMPANIMENT
QUADRUPLICATE	UNCONDITIONAL	RATIOCINATION	ADVERTISEMENT
QUESTIONNAIRE	UNINTENTIONAL	REINCARNATION	ANTICOAGULANT
QUINTUPLICATE	UNSUBSTANTIAL	SPECIFICATION	CONTORTIONIST
RECRUDESCENCE	ANTILOGARITHM	STRANGULATION	CORRESPONDENT
REPREHENSIBLE	CHRYSANTHEMUM	SYLLABICATION	COSMETOLOGIST
REVOLUTIONIZE	COLLOQUIALISM	TRANSCRIPTION	COUNTERWEIGHT
SEMIPERMEABLE	COMMERCIALISM	UNDERCLASSMAN	ELECTROLOGIST
SUBDISCIPLINE	EXHIBITIONISM	UPPERCLASSMAN	ELECTROMAGNET
SULFANILAMIDE	EXPRESSIONISM	VALEDICTORIAN	ESTABLISHMENT
TRANSISTORIZE	IMPRESSIONISM	VERSIFICATION	FEATHERWEIGHT
UNACCOUNTABLE	INDIVIDUALISM	AGGIORNAMENTO	HUNDREDWEIGHT
UNCOMFORTABLE	MICROORGANISM	GENERALISSIMO	HYPERDOCUMENT
UNCONQUERABLE	PARALLELOGRAM	INCOMMUNICADO	IMPRESSIONIST
UNDERCARRIAGE	VENTRILOQUISM	CONTAINERSHIP	INDIVIDUALIST
UNDERESTIMATE	VOCATIONALISM	GRANTSMANSHIP	INDUSTRIALIST
UNDERGRADUATE	ACCOMMODATION	ACCELEROMETER	NONCONFORMIST
UNFORGETTABLE	ACCULTURATION	ADMINISTRATOR	PERFECTIONIST
UNIMPEACHABLE	AFFORESTATION	CONCERTMASTER	PROJECTIONIST
UNMENTIONABLE	ANTIPOLLUTION	GRANDDAUGHTER	PRONOUNCEMENT
UNPREDICTABLE	APPROPRIATION	INTRAMUSCULAR	PROTECTIONIST
UNWARRANTABLE	ARGUMENTATION	MALADMINISTER	RAPPROCHEMENT
ACCOMMODATING	AUTHORITARIAN	MICROCOMPUTER	REVOLUTIONIST
BLOODCURDLING	CERTIFICATION	PERPENDICULAR	SUPERABUNDANT
HEARTBREAKING	COMMUNICATION	QUARTERMASTER	UNINTELLIGENT
HOUSEBREAKING	CONCATENATION	SCANDALMONGER	ANTIFERTILITY
PREPOSSESSING	CONCENTRATION	SCHOOLTEACHER	AUTOBIOGRAPHY
THOROUGHGOING	CONFABULATION	SEMICONDUCTOR	COMPLIMENTARY
UNDERCLOTHING	CONFEDERATION	STRIKEBREAKER	CONFECTIONERY
UNDERSTANDING	CONFIGURATION	SUPERCOMPUTER	CONFRATERNITY
UNQUESTIONING	CONFLAGRATION	THERMONUCLEAR	CONSANGUINITY
WOOLGATHERING	CONSIDERATION	THUNDERSHOWER	EXPEDITIONARY
CINEMATOGRAPH	CONSTELLATION	UNDERACHIEVER	EXTRAORDINARY
KAFFEEKLATSCH	CONSTERNATION	WHITHERSOEVER	GENITOURINARY
COUNTERATTACK	CONTRACEPTION	AMNIOCENTESIS	GEOCHRONOLOGY
LAUGHINGSTOCK	DETERMINATION	AUTOCHTHONOUS	GEOMORPHOLOGY
THUNDERSTRUCK	DISPROPORTION	CARBONIFEROUS	GEOSTATIONARY
ANTIPERSONNEL	FRAGMENTATION	CONSCIENTIOUS	INDIVIDUALITY
CONSEQUENTIAL	GONADOTROPHIN	ELEPHANTIASIS	INTERLOCUTORY
GUBERNATORIAL	HALLUCINATION	HETEROGENEOUS	INTERROGATORY
HYPERCRITICAL	INTROSPECTION	HYDROCEPHALUS	OPHTHALMOLOGY
INFINITESIMAL	JOLLIFICATION	HYDRODYNAMICS	PHYSIOTHERAPY
INSUBSTANTIAL	JUSTIFICATION	INCONSPICUOUS	RADIOACTIVITY
INTERCULTURAL	MACHICOLATION	INSECTIVOROUS	PSYCHOTHERAPY
INTERNATIONAL	MANIFESTATION	INSTANTANEOUS	REVOLUTIONARY
INTERPERSONAL	MISALLOCATION	METAMORPHOSIS	ROENTGENOLOGY
LACKADAISICAL	MISCEGENATION	MISCELLANEOUS	SUPERNUMERARY
MULTINATIONAL	MONOCOTYLEDON	MONONUCLEOSIS	TONSILLECTOMY
PETROCHEMICAL	NITRIFICATION	ORTHODONTICS	UNNECESSARILY
PHENOBARBITAL	NITROGLYCERIN	PATERFAMILIAS	

14
LETTER WORDS

ACCOMPLISHMENT
ADMINISTRATION
AFOREMENTIONED
ANESTHESIOLOGY
ANTIDEPRESSANT
ANTINEOPLASTIC
ANTIPERSPIRANT
ARCHIEPISCOPAL
ARCHITECTONICS
BUTTERFINGERED
CAPITALIZATION
CARDIOVASCULAR
CHARACTERISTIC
CHEMOSTERILANT
CHICKENHEARTED
CHROMATOGRAPHY
CINEMATOGRAPHY
CIRCUMLOCUTION
CIRCUMNAVIGATE
CIRCUMSTANTIAL
CLAUSTROPHOBIA
CONGREGATIONAL
CONJUNCTIVITIS
CONSTITUTIONAL
CORRESPONDENCE
COSMOCHEMISTRY
COUNTERBALANCE
COUNTERCULTURE
COUNTERMEASURE
DECOMPENSATION
DINOFLAGELLATE
DISAPPROBATION
DISCIPLINARIAN
DISCOMBOBULATE
DISCOUNTENANCE
DISCRIMINATING
DISCRIMINATORY
DISENFRANCHISE
DISEQUILIBRIUM
DISINCLINATION
ECCLESIASTICAL
EGALITARIANISM
ELECTRODEPOSIT
ELECTROSTATICS
EXISTENTIALISM
EXTEMPORANEOUS
EXTRAVEHICULAR
FEATHERBEDDING
FUNDAMENTALISM

GENERALIZATION
GRANDILOQUENCE
HYPERSENSITIVE
HYPOTHYROIDISM
IDENTIFICATION
IMPRESSIONABLE
INCOMMENSURATE
INCOMMUNICABLE
INCOMPRESSIBLE
INCONSIDERABLE
INDISCRIMINATE
INSURMOUNTABLE
INTELLIGENTSIA
INTERDEPENDENT
INTERFEROMETER
INTERMOLECULAR
INTERPLANETARY
INTERPRETATION
INTRAMOLECULAR
INTRANSIGEANCE
IRRECONCILABLE
IRREPROACHABLE
KINDERGARTENER
KREMLINOLOGIST
LATITUDINARIAN
MESDEMOISELLES
METEMPSYCHOSIS
MICROMETEORITE
MICROMETEOROID
MICROMINIATURE
MICROPROCESSOR
MISAPPROPRIATE
MULTIPLICATION
NEOCOLONIALISM
NITROCELLULOSE
NONCOOPERATION
NONRESTRICTIVE
OBSTRUCTIONIST
OPHTHALMOSCOPE
ORGANOCHLORINE
OTOLARYNGOLOGY
PALEOMAGNETISM
PARAPSYCHOLOGY
PHANTASMAGORIA
PHARMACEUTICAL
PHOTOENGRAVING
PHOTOSENSITIVE
PHOTOSYNTHESIS
PNEUMOCONIOSIS
PREADOLESCENCE
PREDESTINATION

PRONUNCIAMENTO
PSYCHOANALYSIS
PSYCHOCHEMICAL
RADIOTELEGRAPH
RADIOTELEMETRY
RADIOTELEPHONE
RECOMMENDATION
RECONNAISSANCE
RECONSTRUCTION
REPRESENTATION
REPRESENTATIVE
RESPONSIBILITY
SCHOOLMISTRESS
SEGREGATIONIST
SENSATIONALISM
SENTIMENTALIZE
SEPTUAGENARIAN
SERVOMECHANISM
SESQUIPEDALIAN
SLAUGHTERHOUSE
SOCIORELIGIOUS
STAPHYLOCOCCUS
SUBMICROSCOPIC
SUPERSTRUCTURE
TATTERDEMALION
TELETYPEWRITER
THERMODYNAMICS
TRANSCENDENTAL
TROUBLESHOOTER
ULTRAMINIATURE
UNCOMPROMISING
UNCONSCIONABLE
UNCONTROLLABLE
UNCONVENTIONAL
UNDERDEVELOPED
UNDEREMPHASIZE
UNDERNOURISHED
UNDERSECRETARY
UNIDIRECTIONAL
UNINTELLIGIBLE
UNPROFESSIONAL
UNQUESTIONABLE
UTILITARIANISM
VALETUDINARIAN
VERISIMILITUDE
VIETNAMIZATION
WEATHERABILITY
WHIPPERSNAPPER
ZOROASTRIANISM

CAPITALIZATION
CARDIOVASCULAR
LATITUDINARIAN
PALEOMAGNETISM
PARAPSYCHOLOGY
RADIOTELEGRAPH
RADIOTELEMETRY
RADIOTELEPHONE
TATTERDEMALION
VALETUDINARIAN
OBSTRUCTIONIST
ACCOMPLISHMENT
ECCLESIASTICAL
SCHOOLMISTRESS
ADMINISTRATION
IDENTIFICATION
DECOMPENSATION
FEATHERBEDDING
GENERALIZATION
MESDEMOISELLES
METEMPSYCHOSIS
NEOCOLONIALISM
RECOMMENDATION
RECONNAISSANCE
RECONSTRUCTION
REPRESENTATION
REPRESENTATIVE
RESPONSIBILITY
SEGREGATIONIST
SENSATIONALISM
SENTIMENTALIZE
SEPTUAGENARIAN
SERVOMECHANISM
SESQUIPEDALIAN
TELETYPEWRITER
VERISIMILITUDE
WEATHERABILITY
AFOREMENTIONED
EGALITARIANISM
CHARACTERISTIC
CHEMOSTERILANT
CHICKENHEARTED
CHROMATOGRAPHY
PHANTASMAGORIA
PHARMACEUTICAL
PHOTOENGRAVING
PHOTOSENSITIVE
PHOTOSYNTHESIS
THERMODYNAMICS

WHIPPERSNAPPER
CINEMATOGRAPHY
CIRCUMLOCUTION
CIRCUMNAVIGATE
CIRCUMSTANTIAL
DINOFLAGELLATE
DISAPPROBATION
DISCIPLINARIAN
DISCOMBOBULATE
DISCOUNTENANCE
DISCRIMINATING
DISCRIMINATORY
DISENFRANCHISE
DISEQUILIBRIUM
DISINCLINATION
KINDERGARTENER
MICROMETEORITE
MICROMETEOROID
MICROMINIATURE
MICROPROCESSOR
MISAPPROPRIATE
NITROCELLULOSE
VIETNAMIZATION
CLAUSTROPHOBIA
ELECTRODEPOSIT
ELECTROSTATICS
SLAUGHTERHOUSE
ULTRAMINIATURE
IMPRESSIONABLE
ANESTHESIOLOGY
ANTIDEPRESSANT
ANTINEOPLASTIC
ANTIPERSPIRANT
INCOMMENSURATE
INCOMMUNICABLE
INCOMPRESSIBLE
INCONSIDERABLE
INDISCRIMINATE
INSURMOUNTABLE
INTELLIGENTSIA
INTERDEPENDENT
INTERFEROMETER
INTERMOLECULAR
INTERPLANETARY
INTERPRETATION
INTRAMOLECULAR
INTRANSIGEANCE
PNEUMOCONIOSIS
UNCOMPROMISING
UNCONSCIONABLE
UNCONTROLLABLE

UNCONVENTIONAL	FEATHERBEDDING	UTILITARIANISM	DISEQUILIBRIUM	CARDIOVASCULAR
UNDERDEVELOPED	GRANDILOQUENCE	WHIPPERSNAPPER	DISINCLINATION	FUNDAMENTALISM
UNDEREMPHASIZE	PHANTASMAGORIA	MULTIPLICATION	INSURMOUNTABLE	KINDERGARTENER
UNDERNOURISHED	PHARMACEUTICAL	PALEOMAGNETISM	MESDEMOISELLES	MESDEMOISELLES
UNDERSECRETARY	SLAUGHTERHOUSE	TELETYPEWRITER	MISAPPROPRIATE	PREDESTINATION
UNIDIRECTIONAL	STAPHYLOCOCCUS	VALETUDINARIAN	OBSTRUCTIONIST	UNIDIRECTIONAL
UNINTELLIGIBLE	TRANSCENDENTAL	ADMINISTRATION	RESPONSIBILITY	CINEMATOGRAPHY
UNPROFESSIONAL	WEATHERABILITY	CINEMATOGRAPHY	SESQUIPEDALIAN	DISENFRANCHISE
UNQUESTIONABLE	SUBMICROSCOPIC	CONGREGATIONAL	ANTIDEPRESSANT	DISEQUILIBRIUM
CONGREGATIONAL	ACCOMPLISHMENT	CONJUNCTIVITIS	ANTINEOPLASTIC	EXTEMPORANEOUS
CONJUNCTIVITIS	ARCHIEPISCOPAL	CONSTITUTIONAL	ANTIPERSPIRANT	GENERALIZATION
CONSTITUTIONAL	ARCHITECTONICS	DINOFLAGELLATE	BUTTERFINGERED	HYPERSENSITIVE
CORRESPONDENCE	DECOMPENSATION	FUNDAMENTALISM	EXTEMPORANEOUS	INTELLIGENTSIA
COSMOCHEMISTRY	ECCLESIASTICAL	GENERALIZATION	EXTRAVEHICULAR	INTERDEPENDENT
COUNTERBALANCE	INCOMMENSURATE	KINDERGARTENER	INTELLIGENTSIA	INTERFEROMETER
COUNTERCULTURE	INCOMMUNICABLE	NONCOOPERATION	INTERDEPENDENT	INTERMOLECULAR
COUNTERMEASURE	INCOMPRESSIBLE	NONRESTRICTIVE	INTERFEROMETER	INTERPLANETARY
NONCOOPERATION	INCONSIDERABLE	SENSATIONALISM	INTERMOLECULAR	INTERPRETATION
NONRESTRICTIVE	MICROMETEORITE	SENTIMENTALIZE	INTERPLANETARY	IRRECONCILABLE
SOCIORELIGIOUS	MICROMETEOROID	AFOREMENTIONED	INTERPRETATION	IRREPROACHABLE
ZOROASTRIANISM	MICROMINIATURE	NEOCOLONIALISM	INTRAMOLECULAR	METEMPSYCHOSIS
OPHTHALMOSCOPE	MICROPROCESSOR	OTOLARYNGOLOGY	INTRANSIGEANCE	PALEOMAGNETISM
ARCHIEPISCOPAL	RECOMMENDATION	PHOTOENGRAVING	LATITUDINARIAN	SUPERSTRUCTURE
ARCHITECTONICS	RECONNAISSANCE	PHOTOSENSITIVE	METEMPSYCHOSIS	TELETYPEWRITER
GRANDILOQUENCE	RECONSTRUCTION	PHOTOSYNTHESIS	NITROCELLULOSE	UNDERDEVELOPED
IRRECONCILABLE	SOCIORELIGIOUS	PRONUNCIAMENTO	TATTERDEMALION	UNDEREMPHASIZE
IRREPROACHABLE	UNCOMPROMISING	TROUBLESHOOTER	ULTRAMINIATURE	UNDERNOURISHED
KREMLINOLOGIST	UNCONSCIONABLE	CAPITALIZATION	COUNTERBALANCE	UNDERSECRETARY
ORGANOCHLORINE	UNCONTROLLABLE	HYPERSENSITIVE	COUNTERCULTURE	VALETUDINARIAN
PREADOLESCENCE	UNCONVENTIONAL	HYPOTHYROIDISM	COUNTERMEASURE	CONGREGATIONAL
PREDESTINATION	INDISCRIMINATE	IMPRESSIONABLE	PSYCHOANALYSIS	ARCHIEPISCOPAL
PRONUNCIAMENTO	RADIOTELEGRAPH	REPRESENTATION	PSYCHOCHEMICAL	ARCHITECTONICS
TRANSCENDENTAL	RADIOTELEMETRY	REPRESENTATIVE		ADMINISTRATION
TROUBLESHOOTER	RADIOTELEPHONE	SEPTUAGENARIAN		ANTIDEPRESSANT
PSYCHOANALYSIS	UNDERDEVELOPED	SUPERSTRUCTURE		ANTINEOPLASTIC
PSYCHOCHEMICAL	UNDEREMPHASIZE	UNPROFESSIONAL	**4TH LETTER**	ANTIPERSPIRANT
OTOLARYNGOLOGY	UNDERNOURISHED	UNQUESTIONABLE		CAPITALIZATION
STAPHYLOCOCCUS	UNDERSECRETARY	CARDIOVASCULAR	DISAPPROBATION	DISINCLINATION
UTILITARIANISM	ANESTHESIOLOGY	CHROMATOGRAPHY	MISAPPROPRIATE	INDISCRIMINATE
BUTTERFINGERED	CHEMOSTERILANT	CIRCUMLOCUTION	ORGANOCHLORINE	LATITUDINARIAN
FUNDAMENTALISM	ELECTRODEPOSIT	CIRCUMNAVIGATE	PARAPSYCHOLOGY	RADIOTELEGRAPH
MULTIPLICATION	ELECTROSTATICS	CIRCUMSTANTIAL	PREADOLESCENCE	RADIOTELEMETRY
SUBMICROSCOPIC	IDENTIFICATION	CORRESPONDENCE	CHICKENHEARTED	RADIOTELEPHONE
SUPERSTRUCTURE	KREMLINOLOGIST	IRRECONCILABLE	CIRCUMLOCUTION	SOCIORELIGIOUS
EXISTENTIALISM	PNEUMOCONIOSIS	IRREPROACHABLE	CIRCUMNAVIGATE	VERISIMILITUDE
EXTEMPORANEOUS	PREADOLESCENCE	PARAPSYCHOLOGY	CIRCUMSTANTIAL	CONJUNCTIVITIS
EXTRAVEHICULAR	PREDESTINATION	SERVOMECHANISM	DISCIPLINARIAN	ECCLESIASTICAL
HYPERSENSITIVE	THERMODYNAMICS	VERISIMILITUDE	DISCOMBOBULATE	EGALITARIANISM
HYPOTHYROIDISM	VIETNAMIZATION	ZOROASTRIANISM	DISCOUNTENANCE	OTOLARYNGOLOGY
	ORGANOCHLORINE	COSMOCHEMISTRY	DISCRIMINATING	UTILITARIANISM
	SEGREGATIONIST	DISAPPROBATION	DISCRIMINATORY	CHEMOSTERILANT
	OPHTHALMOSCOPE	DISCIPLINARIAN	ELECTRODEPOSIT	COSMOCHEMISTRY
3RD LETTER	SCHOOLMISTRESS	DISCOMBOBULATE	ELECTROSTATICS	KREMLINOLOGIST
	CHICKENHEARTED	DISCOUNTENANCE	NEOCOLONIALISM	SUBMICROSCOPIC
CHARACTERISTIC	EXISTENTIALISM	DISCRIMINATING	NONCOOPERATION	COUNTERBALANCE
CLAUSTROPHOBIA	UNIDIRECTIONAL	DISCRIMINATORY	PSYCHOANALYSIS	COUNTERCULTURE
EGALITARIANISM	UNINTELLIGIBLE	DISENFRANCHISE	PSYCHOCHEMICAL	COUNTERMEASURE

GRANDILOQUENCE	PHOTOENGRAVING	ARCHITECTONICS	SCHOOLMISTRESS	**6**TH **LETTER**
IDENTIFICATION	PHOTOSENSITIVE	CARDIOVASCULAR	SERVOMECHANISM	
PHANTASMAGORIA	PHOTOSYNTHESIS	DISCIPLINARIAN	SOCIORELIGIOUS	CAPITALIZATION
PRONUNCIAMENTO	SENTIMENTALIZE	EGALITARIANISM	UNPROFESSIONAL	CHROMATOGRAPHY
TRANSCENDENTAL	SEPTUAGENARIAN	MULTIPLICATION	ANTIPERSPIRANT	CINEMATOGRAPHY
UNINTELLIGIBLE	TATTERDEMALION	SENTIMENTALIZE	DISAPPROBATION	GENERALIZATION
ACCOMPLISHMENT	VIETNAMIZATION	SUBMICROSCOPIC	IRREPROACHABLE	OPHTHALMOSCOPE
CHROMATOGRAPHY	WEATHERABILITY	UNIDIRECTIONAL	MISAPPROPRIATE	PHANTASMAGORIA
DECOMPENSATION	CLAUSTROPHOBIA	UTILITARIANISM	PARAPSYCHOLOGY	PHARMACEUTICAL
DINOFLAGELLATE	INSURMOUNTABLE	CHICKENHEARTED	WHIPPERSNAPPER	SEPTUAGENARIAN
HYPOTHYROIDISM	PNEUMOCONIOSIS	INTELLIGENTSIA	DISEQUILIBRIUM	VIETNAMIZATION
INCOMMENSURATE	SLAUGHTERHOUSE	KREMLINOLOGIST	CONGREGATIONAL	CHARACTERISTIC
INCOMMUNICABLE	TROUBLESHOOTER	ACCOMPLISHMENT	DISCRIMINATING	COSMOCHEMISTRY
INCOMPRESSIBLE	UNQUESTIONABLE	CHROMATOGRAPHY	DISCRIMINATORY	DISINCLINATION
INCONSIDERABLE	SERVOMECHANISM	CINEMATOGRAPHY	GENERALIZATION	INDISCRIMINATE
RECOMMENDATION		DECOMPENSATION	HYPERSENSITIVE	NITROCELLULOSE
RECONNAISSANCE		EXTEMPORANEOUS	INSURMOUNTABLE	SUBMICROSCOPIC
RECONSTRUCTION	**5**TH	INCOMMENSURATE	INTERDEPENDENT	TRANSCENDENTAL
SCHOOLMISTRESS	**LETTER**	INCOMMUNICABLE	INTERFEROMETER	INTERDEPENDENT
UNCOMPROMISING		INCOMPRESSIBLE	INTERMOLECULAR	UNDERDEVELOPED
UNCONSCIONABLE	CHARACTERISTIC	METEMPSYCHOSIS	INTERPLANETARY	ANTIDEPRESSANT
UNCONTROLLABLE	EXTRAVEHICULAR	PHARMACEUTICAL	INTERPRETATION	ANTINEOPLASTIC
UNCONVENTIONAL	FUNDAMENTALISM	PNEUMOCONIOSIS	OBSTRUCTIONIST	ANTIPERSPIRANT
ZOROASTRIANISM	INTRAMOLECULAR	RECOMMENDATION	SUPERSTRUCTURE	ARCHIEPISCOPAL
RESPONSIBILITY	INTRANSIGEANCE	THERMODYNAMICS	UNDERDEVELOPED	CHICKENHEARTED
STAPHYLOCOCCUS	OTOLARYNGOLOGY	UNCOMPROMISING	UNDEREMPHASIZE	CONGREGATIONAL
WHIPPERSNAPPER	SENSATIONALISM	ADMINISTRATION	UNDERNOURISHED	COUNTERBALANCE
SESQUIPEDALIAN	ULTRAMINIATURE	ANTINEOPLASTIC	UNDERSECRETARY	COUNTERCULTURE
AFOREMENTIONED	ZOROASTRIANISM	DISENFRANCHISE	CLAUSTROPHOBIA	COUNTERMEASURE
CHARACTERISTIC	TROUBLESHOOTER	DISINCLINATION	INDISCRIMINATE	EXISTENTIALISM
CORRESPONDENCE	IRRECONCILABLE	INCONSIDERABLE	TRANSCENDENTAL	FEATHERBEDDING
EXTRAVEHICULAR	ANTIDEPRESSANT	ORGANOCHLORINE	VERISIMILITUDE	PHOTOENGRAVING
IMPRESSIONABLE	GRANDILOQUENCE	RECONNAISSANCE	ANESTHESIOLOGY	UNDEREMPHASIZE
INTRAMOLECULAR	PREADOLESCENCE	RECONSTRUCTION	CAPITALIZATION	UNINTELLIGIBLE
INTRANSIGEANCE	AFOREMENTIONED	UNCONSCIONABLE	CONSTITUTIONAL	WEATHERABILITY
MICROMETEORITE	BUTTERFINGERED	UNCONTROLLABLE	COUNTERBALANCE	WHIPPERSNAPPER
MICROMETEOROID	CORRESPONDENCE	UNCONVENTIONAL	COUNTERCULTURE	DISENFRANCHISE
MICROMINIATURE	ECCLESIASTICAL	VIETNAMIZATION	COUNTERMEASURE	INTERFEROMETER
MICROPROCESSOR	IMPRESSIONABLE	CHEMOSTERILANT	ELECTRODEPOSIT	UNPROFESSIONAL
NITROCELLULOSE	KINDERGARTENER	COSMOCHEMISTRY	ELECTROSTATICS	SEGREGATIONIST
NONRESTRICTIVE	MESDEMOISELLES	DISCOMBOBULATE	EXISTENTIALISM	ANESTHESIOLOGY
PHARMACEUTICAL	NONRESTRICTIVE	DISCOUNTENANCE	HYPOTHYROIDISM	HYPOTHYROIDISM
REPRESENTATION	PREDESTINATION	MICROMETEORITE	IDENTIFICATION	SLAUGHTERHOUSE
REPRESENTATIVE	REPRESENTATION	MICROMETEOROID	LATITUDINARIAN	ADMINISTRATION
SEGREGATIONIST	REPRESENTATIVE	MICROMINIATURE	PHANTASMAGORIA	CONSTITUTIONAL
THERMODYNAMICS	SEGREGATIONIST	MICROPROCESSOR	TELETYPEWRITER	DISCRIMINATING
ULTRAMINIATURE	TATTERDEMALION	NEOCOLONIALISM	UNINTELLIGIBLE	DISCRIMINATORY
UNPROFESSIONAL	UNQUESTIONABLE	NITROCELLULOSE	VALETUDINARIAN	GRANDILOQUENCE
ANESTHESIOLOGY	DINOFLAGELLATE	NONCOOPERATION	CIRCUMLOCUTION	IDENTIFICATION
CONSTITUTIONAL	SLAUGHTERHOUSE	PALEOMAGNETISM	CIRCUMNAVIGATE	KREMLINOLOGIST
EXISTENTIALISM	FEATHERBEDDING	PHOTOENGRAVING	CIRCUMSTANTIAL	SESQUIPEDALIAN
SENSATIONALISM	OPHTHALMOSCOPE	PHOTOSENSITIVE	CONJUNCTIVITIS	VERISIMILITUDE
BUTTERFINGERED	PSYCHOANALYSIS	PHOTOSYNTHESIS	PRONUNCIAMENTO	DINOFLAGELLATE
FEATHERBEDDING	PSYCHOCHEMICAL	RADIOTELEGRAPH	SEPTUAGENARIAN	INTELLIGENTSIA
MULTIPLICATION	STAPHYLOCOCCUS	RADIOTELEMETRY	SESQUIPEDALIAN	NEOCOLONIALISM
OBSTRUCTIONIST	WEATHERABILITY	RADIOTELEPHONE		SCHOOLMISTRESS
OPHTHALMOSCOPE	ARCHIEPISCOPAL	RESPONSIBILITY		TROUBLESHOOTER

AFOREMENTIONED
CIRCUMLOCUTION
CIRCUMNAVIGATE
CIRCUMSTANTIAL
DISCOMBOBULATE
FUNDAMENTALISM
INCOMMENSURATE
INCOMMUNICABLE
INSURMOUNTABLE
INTERMOLECULAR
INTRAMOLECULAR
MESDEMOISELLES
MICROMETEORITE
MICROMETEOROID
MICROMINIATURE
PALEOMAGNETISM
RECOMMENDATION
SENTIMENTALIZE
SERVOMECHANISM
ULTRAMINIATURE
CONJUNCTIVITIS
INTRANSIGEANCE
PRONUNCIAMENTO
RECONNAISSANCE
RESPONSIBILITY
UNDERNOURISHED
CARDIOVASCULAR
IRRECONCILABLE
NONCOOPERATION
ORGANOCHLORINE
PNEUMOCONIOSIS
PREADOLESCENCE
PSYCHOANALYSIS
PSYCHOCHEMICAL
THERMODYNAMICS
ACCOMPLISHMENT
DECOMPENSATION
DISAPPROBATION
DISCIPLINARIAN
EXTEMPORANEOUS
INCOMPRESSIBLE
INTERPLANETARY
INTERPRETATION
METEMPSYCHOSIS
MICROPROCESSOR
MISAPPROPRIATE
MULTIPLICATION
UNCOMPROMISING
BUTTERFINGERED
ELECTRODEPOSIT
ELECTROSTATICS
IRREPROACHABLE
KINDERGARTENER
OTOLARYNGOLOGY
SOCIORELIGIOUS
TATTERDEMALION
UNIDIRECTIONAL

CHEMOSTERILANT
CORRESPONDENCE
ECCLESIASTICAL
HYPERSENSITIVE
IMPRESSIONABLE
INCONSIDERABLE
NONRESTRICTIVE
PARAPSYCHOLOGY
PHOTOSENSITIVE
PHOTOSYNTHESIS
PREDESTINATION
RECONSTRUCTION
REPRESENTATION
REPRESENTATIVE
SUPERSTRUCTURE
UNCONSCIONABLE
UNDERSECRETARY
UNQUESTIONABLE
ZOROASTRIANISM
ARCHITECTONICS
CLAUSTROPHOBIA
EGALITARIANISM
RADIOTELEGRAPH
RADIOTELEMETRY
RADIOTELEPHONE
SENSATIONALISM
UNCONTROLLABLE
UTILITARIANISM
DISCOUNTENANCE
DISEQUILIBRIUM
LATITUDINARIAN
OBSTRUCTIONIST
VALETUDINARIAN
EXTRAVEHICULAR
UNCONVENTIONAL
STAPHYLOCOCCUS
TELETYPEWRITER

7TH LETTER

DINOFLAGELLATE
EGALITARIANISM
PALEOMAGNETISM
PSYCHOANALYSIS
RECONNAISSANCE
SEGREGATIONIST
UTILITARIANISM
DISCOMBOBULATE
CONJUNCTIVITIS
OBSTRUCTIONIST
ORGANOCHLORINE
PHARMACEUTICAL
PNEUMOCONIOSIS
PRONUNCIAMENTO
PSYCHOCHEMICAL

UNCONSCIONABLE
LATITUDINARIAN
TATTERDEMALION
THERMODYNAMICS
VALETUDINARIAN
AFOREMENTIONED
ANESTHESIOLOGY
ARCHITECTONICS
DECOMPENSATION
EXTRAVEHICULAR
FUNDAMENTALISM
HYPERSENSITIVE
INCOMMENSURATE
INTERDEPENDENT
INTERFEROMETER
MICROMETEORITE
MICROMETEOROID
NITROCELLULOSE
PHOTOSENSITIVE
RADIOTELEGRAPH
RADIOTELEMETRY
RADIOTELEPHONE
RECOMMENDATION
REPRESENTATION
REPRESENTATIVE
SENTIMENTALIZE
SERVOMECHANISM
SOCIORELIGIOUS
TRANSCENDENTAL
TROUBLESHOOTER
UNCONVENTIONAL
UNDERDEVELOPED
UNDERSECRETARY
UNIDIRECTIONAL
UNPROFESSIONAL
BUTTERFINGERED
IDENTIFICATION
CONGREGATIONAL
KINDERGARTENER
SEPTUAGENARIAN
COSMOCHEMISTRY
DISEQUILIBRIUM
ECCLESIASTICAL
INCONSIDERABLE
INTELLIGENTSIA
MICROMINIATURE
SENSATIONALISM
ULTRAMINIATURE
ACCOMPLISHMENT
CAPITALIZATION
CIRCUMLOCUTION
DISCIPLINARIAN
DISINCLINATION
GENERALIZATION
GRANDILOQUENCE
INTERPLANETARY
MULTIPLICATION

OPHTHALMOSCOPE
PREADOLESCENCE
STAPHYLOCOCCUS
UNINTELLIGIBLE
DISCRIMINATING
DISCRIMINATORY
SCHOOLMISTRESS
UNDEREMPHASIZE
VERISIMILITUDE
VIETNAMIZATION
CHICKENHEARTED
CIRCUMNAVIGATE
DISCOUNTENANCE
EXISTENTIALISM
IRRECONCILABLE
KREMLINOLOGIST
PHOTOENGRAVING
ANTINEOPLASTIC
ELECTRODEPOSIT
ELECTROSTATICS
EXTEMPORANEOUS
INSURMOUNTABLE
INTERMOLECULAR
INTRAMOLECULAR
IRREPROACHABLE
MESDEMOISELLES
NEOCOLONIALISM
UNDERNOURISHED
ANTIDEPRESSANT
ARCHIEPISCOPAL
CORRESPONDENCE
NONCOOPERATION
SESQUIPEDALIAN
TELETYPEWRITER
ANTIPERSPIRANT
CLAUSTROPHOBIA
COUNTERBALANCE
COUNTERCULTURE
COUNTERMEASURE
DISAPPROBATION
DISENFRANCHISE
FEATHERBEDDING
INCOMPRESSIBLE
INDISCRIMINATE
INTERPRETATION
MICROPROCESSOR
MISAPPROPRIATE
SUBMICROSCOPIC
UNCOMPROMISING
UNCONTROLLABLE
WEATHERABILITY
WHIPPERSNAPPER
ADMINISTRATION
CIRCUMSTANTIAL
IMPRESSIONABLE
INTRANSIGEANCE
METEMPSYCHOSIS

PHANTASMAGORIA
RESPONSIBILITY
CHARACTERISTIC
CHEMOSTERILANT
CHROMATOGRAPHY
CINEMATOGRAPHY
CONSTITUTIONAL
NONRESTRICTIVE
PREDESTINATION
RECONSTRUCTION
SLAUGHTERHOUSE
SUPERSTRUCTURE
UNQUESTIONABLE
ZOROASTRIANISM
INCOMMUNICABLE
CARDIOVASCULAR
HYPOTHYROIDISM
OTOLARYNGOLOGY
PARAPSYCHOLOGY
PHOTOSYNTHESIS

8TH LETTER

CARDIOVASCULAR
CIRCUMNAVIGATE
CONGREGATIONAL
DISENFRANCHISE
ECCLESIASTICAL
INTERPLANETARY
IRREPROACHABLE
KINDERGARTENER
WEATHERABILITY
COUNTERBALANCE
FEATHERBEDDING
ARCHITECTONICS
COUNTERCULTURE
IRRECONCILABLE
PARAPSYCHOLOGY
SERVOMECHANISM
UNDERSECRETARY
UNIDIRECTIONAL
ELECTRODEPOSIT
INCONSIDERABLE
CHARACTERISTIC
CHEMOSTERILANT
COSMOCHEMISTRY
INCOMPRESSIBLE
INTERPRETATION
NONCOOPERATION
PHARMACEUTICAL
PREADOLESCENCE
SEPTUAGENARIAN
SESQUIPEDALIAN
SLAUGHTERHOUSE
TATTERDEMALION

TELETYPEWRITER	PHOTOSYNTHESIS	UNDERDEVELOPED	DISEQUILIBRIUM	KINDERGARTENER
DINOFLAGELLATE	PSYCHOANALYSIS	METEMPSYCHOSIS	EGALITARIANISM	NONCOOPERATION
INTELLIGENTSIA	RECOMMENDATION	THERMODYNAMICS	EXISTENTIALISM	PHOTOENGRAVING
PALEOMAGNETISM	REPRESENTATION		EXTRAVEHICULAR	SLAUGHTERHOUSE
PHOTOENGRAVING	REPRESENTATIVE		INCOMMUNICABLE	UNDERNOURISHED
CHICKENHEARTED	SENTIMENTALIZE		IRRECONCILABLE	UNDERSECRETARY
EXTRAVEHICULAR	TRANSCENDENTAL	**9TH LETTER**	MICROMINIATURE	ACCOMPLISHMENT
ORGANOCHLORINE	ULTRAMINIATURE		NEOCOLONIALISM	ARCHIEPISCOPAL
PSYCHOCHEMICAL	UNCONVENTIONAL	CIRCUMSTANTIAL	NONRESTRICTIVE	CARDIOVASCULAR
ACCOMPLISHMENT	CHROMATOGRAPHY	COUNTERBALANCE	OBSTRUCTIONIST	DECOMPENSATION
ARCHIEPISCOPAL	CINEMATOGRAPHY	EXTEMPORANEOUS	SEGREGATIONIST	ECCLESIASTICAL
BUTTERFINGERED	CIRCUMLOCUTION	PHANTASMAGORIA	SOCIORELIGIOUS	HYPERSENSITIVE
CAPITALIZATION	CLAUSTROPHOBIA	PRONUNCIAMENTO	ULTRAMINIATURE	INCOMMENSURATE
DISCIPLINARIAN	CORRESPONDENCE	PSYCHOANALYSIS	UNINTELLIGIBLE	INCOMPRESSIBLE
DISCRIMINATING	DISAPPROBATION	DISAPPROBATION	UTILITARIANISM	MESDEMOISELLES
DISCRIMINATORY	DISCOMBOBULATE	DISCOMBOBULATE	ZOROASTRIANISM	PHOTOSENSITIVE
DISINCLINATION	GRANDILOQUENCE	RESPONSIBILITY	ANTINEOPLASTIC	PREADOLESCENCE
GENERALIZATION	KREMLINOLOGIST	WEATHERABILITY	KREMLINOLOGIST	RECONNAISSANCE
IDENTIFICATION	MICROPROCESSOR	CIRCUMLOCUTION	NITROCELLULOSE	SCHOOLMISTRESS
IMPRESSIONABLE	MISAPPROPRIATE	IDENTIFICATION	ORGANOCHLORINE	SUBMICROSCOPIC
INDISCRIMINATE	PNEUMOCONIOSIS	IRREPROACHABLE	UNCONTROLLABLE	UNPROFESSIONAL
INTRANSIGEANCE	SENSATIONALISM	METEMPSYCHOSIS	VERISIMILITUDE	AFOREMENTIONED
LATITUDINARIAN	STAPHYLOCOCCUS	MICROPROCESSOR	COSMOCHEMISTRY	ARCHITECTONICS
MESDEMOISELLES	SUBMICROSCOPIC	MULTIPLICATION	INDISCRIMINATE	CONGREGATIONAL
MULTIPLICATION	UNCOMPROMISING	STAPHYLOCOCCUS	TATTERDEMALION	CONSTITUTIONAL
PREDESTINATION	UNCONTROLLABLE	RECOMMENDATION	UNCOMPROMISING	ELECTROSTATICS
PRONUNCIAMENTO	ANTINEOPLASTIC	SESQUIPEDALIAN	BUTTERFINGERED	FUNDAMENTALISM
RECONNAISSANCE	INTERDEPENDENT	TRANSCENDENTAL	CORRESPONDENCE	INTERPRETATION
RESPONSIBILITY	UNDEREMPHASIZE	ANTIDEPRESSANT	DISCIPLINARIAN	PHOTOSYNTHESIS
SCHOOLMISTRESS	ANTIDEPRESSANT	CHICKENHEARTED	DISCRIMINATING	REPRESENTATION
UNCONSCIONABLE	EGALITARIANISM	COUNTERMEASURE	DISCRIMINATORY	REPRESENTATIVE
UNQUESTIONABLE	EXTEMPORANEOUS	DINOFLAGELLATE	DISENFRANCHISE	SENTIMENTALIZE
VALETUDINARIAN	HYPOTHYROIDISM	DISCOUNTENANCE	DISINCLINATION	UNCONVENTIONAL
VERISIMILITUDE	INTERFEROMETER	ELECTRODEPOSIT	INSURMOUNTABLE	UNIDIRECTIONAL
VIETNAMIZATION	NONRESTRICTIVE	FEATHERBEDDING	INTERPLANETARY	COUNTERCULTURE
DISEQUILIBRIUM	RECONSTRUCTION	INCONSIDERABLE	LATITUDINARIAN	PHARMACEUTICAL
INTERMOLECULAR	SUPERSTRUCTURE	INTELLIGENTSIA	PALEOMAGNETISM	RECONSTRUCTION
INTRAMOLECULAR	UTILITARIANISM	INTERDEPENDENT	PNEUMOCONIOSIS	SUPERSTRUCTURE
NITROCELLULOSE	ZOROASTRIANISM	INTERMOLECULAR	PREDESTINATION	CIRCUMNAVIGATE
RADIOTELEGRAPH	ANESTHESIOLOGY	INTRAMOLECULAR	SENSATIONALISM	TELETYPEWRITER
RADIOTELEMETRY	ANTIPERSPIRANT	MICROMETEORITE	SEPTUAGENARIAN	CAPITALIZATION
RADIOTELEPHONE	ELECTROSTATICS	MICROMETEOROID	THERMODYNAMICS	GENERALIZATION
SOCIORELIGIOUS	TROUBLESHOOTER	PSYCHOCHEMICAL	VALETUDINARIAN	VIETNAMIZATION
UNINTELLIGIBLE	UNPROFESSIONAL	RADIOTELEGRAPH	WHIPPERSNAPPER	
COUNTERMEASURE	WHIPPERSNAPPER	RADIOTELEMETRY	HYPOTHYROIDISM	
OPHTHALMOSCOPE	ADMINISTRATION	RADIOTELEPHONE	IMPRESSIONABLE	**10TH LETTER**
PHANTASMAGORIA	CIRCUMSTANTIAL	UNDERDEVELOPED	INTERFEROMETER	
AFOREMENTIONED	CONJUNCTIVITIS	CHROMATOGRAPHY	OPHTHALMOSCOPE	ADMINISTRATION
DECOMPENSATION	DISCOUNTENANCE	CINEMATOGRAPHY	UNCONSCIONABLE	ANTINEOPLASTIC
FUNDAMENTALISM	EXISTENTIALISM	INTRANSIGEANCE	UNQUESTIONABLE	CAPITALIZATION
HYPERSENSITIVE	MICROMETEORITE	OTOLARYNGOLOGY	ANTIPERSPIRANT	CHICKENHEARTED
INCOMMENSURATE	MICROMETEOROID	PARAPSYCHOLOGY	CLAUSTROPHOBIA	COUNTERMEASURE
INCOMMUNICABLE	OBSTRUCTIONIST	SERVOMECHANISM	MISAPPROPRIATE	DECOMPENSATION
MICROMINIATURE	SEGREGATIONIST	TROUBLESHOOTER	GRANDILOQUENCE	DISAPPROBATION
NEOCOLONIALISM	CONSTITUTIONAL	UNDEREMPHASIZE	ADMINISTRATION	DISCIPLINARIAN
OTOLARYNGOLOGY	INSURMOUNTABLE	ANESTHESIOLOGY	CHARACTERISTIC	DISCRIMINATING
PHOTOSENSITIVE	UNDERNOURISHED	CONJUNCTIVITIS	CHEMOSTERILANT	DISCRIMINATING

DISCRIMINATORY	RADIOTELEGRAPH	PARAPSYCHOLOGY	PHOTOSYNTHESIS	UNCONVENTIONAL
DISINCLINATION	SOCIORELIGIOUS	SEGREGATIONIST	PREADOLESCENCE	UNDERDEVELOPED
EGALITARIANISM	UNINTELLIGIBLE	STAPHYLOCOCCUS	PRONUNCIAMENTO	UNIDIRECTIONAL
ELECTROSTATICS	ACCOMPLISHMENT	TROUBLESHOOTER	RADIOTELEMETRY	UNPROFESSIONAL
EXISTENTIALISM	CLAUSTROPHOBIA	ELECTRODEPOSIT	CIRCUMNAVIGATE	WHIPPERSNAPPER
FUNDAMENTALISM	IRREPROACHABLE	RADIOTELEPHONE	KREMLINOLOGIST	ANTIPERSPIRANT
GENERALIZATION	METEMPSYCHOSIS	CHROMATOGRAPHY	DISENFRANCHISE	CHICKENHEARTED
IDENTIFICATION	PHOTOSYNTHESIS	CINEMATOGRAPHY	RADIOTELEPHONE	DISCIPLINARIAN
INTERPRETATION	SLAUGHTERHOUSE	INCONSIDERABLE	CONJUNCTIVITIS	DISEQUILIBRIUM
LATITUDINARIAN	AFOREMENTIONED	MISAPPROPRIATE	ECCLESIASTICAL	INCOMMENSURATE
MICROMINIATURE	ANTIPERSPIRANT	TELETYPEWRITER	INCOMPRESSIBLE	LATITUDINARIAN
MULTIPLICATION	CHARACTERISTIC	ANTIDEPRESSANT	MISAPPROPRIATE	MICROMETEORITE
NEOCOLONIALISM	CHEMOSTERILANT	INCOMPRESSIBLE	PHARMACEUTICAL	MICROMETEOROID
NONCOOPERATION	CIRCUMNAVIGATE	OPHTHALMOSCOPE	PSYCHOCHEMICAL	ORGANOCHLORINE
PHOTOENGRAVING	CONGREGATIONAL	RECONNAISSANCE	SOCIORELIGIOUS	RADIOTELEGRAPH
PREDESTINATION	CONSTITUTIONAL	ECCLESIASTICAL	TELETYPEWRITER	SCHOOLMISTRESS
RECOMMENDATION	COSMOCHEMISTRY	INSURMOUNTABLE	UNINTELLIGIBLE	SEPTUAGENARIAN
REPRESENTATION	HYPERSENSITIVE	KINDERGARTENER	ANESTHESIOLOGY	VALETUDINARIAN
REPRESENTATIVE	HYPOTHYROIDISM	PHARMACEUTICAL	CHEMOSTERILANT	ANTIDEPRESSANT
SENSATIONALISM	INDISCRIMINATE	SCHOOLMISTRESS	DINOFLAGELLATE	ANTINEOPLASTIC
SENTIMENTALIZE	PHOTOSENSITIVE	CIRCUMLOCUTION	DISCOMBOBULATE	CHARACTERISTIC
SEPTUAGENARIAN	PNEUMOCONIOSIS	DISCOMBOBULATE	EXISTENTIALISM	COSMOCHEMISTRY
SERVOMECHANISM	RESPONSIBILITY	GRANDILOQUENCE	FUNDAMENTALISM	COUNTERMEASURE
SESQUIPEDALIAN	UNCOMPROMISING	INCOMMENSURATE	MESDEMOISELLES	MICROPROCESSOR
TATTERDEMALION	UNCONVENTIONAL	NITROCELLULOSE	NEOCOLONIALISM	UNCOMPROMISING
THERMODYNAMICS	UNDERNOURISHED	CONJUNCTIVITIS	NITROCELLULOSE	UNDEREMPHASIZE
ULTRAMINIATURE	UNIDIRECTIONAL		OTOLARYNGOLOGY	UNDERNOURISHED
UNDEREMPHASIZE	UNPROFESSIONAL		PARAPSYCHOLOGY	ADMINISTRATION
UTILITARIANISM	VERISIMILITUDE		RESPONSIBILITY	CAPITALIZATION
VALETUDINARIAN	WEATHERABILITY	**11TH LETTER**	SENSATIONALISM	CIRCUMLOCUTION
VIETNAMIZATION	COUNTERBALANCE		SENTIMENTALIZE	CIRCUMSTANTIAL
WHIPPERSNAPPER	COUNTERCULTURE	CHROMATOGRAPHY	SESQUIPEDALIAN	COUNTERCULTURE
ZOROASTRIANISM	DINOFLAGELLATE	CINEMATOGRAPHY	TATTERDEMALION	DECOMPENSATION
DISEQUILIBRIUM	IRRECONCILABLE	COUNTERBALANCE	WEATHERABILITY	DISAPPROBATION
ARCHIEPISCOPAL	PSYCHOANALYSIS	DISCOUNTENANCE	ACCOMPLISHMENT	DISCRIMINATING
CARDIOVASCULAR	UNCONTROLLABLE	IMPRESSIONABLE	THERMODYNAMICS	DISCRIMINATORY
DISENFRANCHISE	UNDERDEVELOPED	INCOMMUNICABLE	ARCHITECTONICS	DISINCLINATION
EXTRAVEHICULAR	INTERFEROMETER	INCONSIDERABLE	EGALITARIANISM	ELECTROSTATICS
INCOMMUNICABLE	PRONUNCIAMENTO	INSURMOUNTABLE	INDISCRIMINATE	GENERALIZATION
INTERMOLECULAR	PSYCHOCHEMICAL	INTRANSIGEANCE	OBSTRUCTIONIST	HYPERSENSITIVE
INTRAMOLECULAR	RADIOTELEMETRY	IRRECONCILABLE	SEGREGATIONIST	IDENTIFICATION
NONRESTRICTIVE	CIRCUMSTANTIAL	IRREPROACHABLE	SERVOMECHANISM	INTELLIGENTSIA
PREADOLESCENCE	DISCOUNTENANCE	RECONNAISSANCE	TRANSCENDENTAL	INTERPLANETARY
RECONSTRUCTION	EXTEMPORANEOUS	UNCONSCIONABLE	UTILITARIANISM	INTERPRETATION
SUBMICROSCOPIC	IMPRESSIONABLE	UNCONTROLLABLE	ZOROASTRIANISM	MICROMINIATURE
SUPERSTRUCTURE	INTELLIGENTSIA	UNQUESTIONABLE	AFOREMENTIONED	MULTIPLICATION
CORRESPONDENCE	INTERDEPENDENT	OPHTHALMOSCOPE	ARCHIEPISCOPAL	NONCOOPERATION
FEATHERBEDDING	UNCONSCIONABLE	STAPHYLOCOCCUS	CLAUSTROPHOBIA	NONRESTRICTIVE
INTERPLANETARY	UNQUESTIONABLE	FEATHERBEDDING	CONGREGATIONAL	PALEOMAGNETISM
INTRANSIGEANCE	ANESTHESIOLOGY	HYPOTHYROIDISM	CONSTITUTIONAL	PHOTOSENSITIVE
MESDEMOISELLES	ARCHITECTONICS	INTERDEPENDENT	ELECTRODEPOSIT	PREDESTINATION
MICROPROCESSOR	KREMLINOLOGIST	BUTTERFINGERED	METEMPSYCHOSIS	RECOMMENDATION
PALEOMAGNETISM	MICROMETEORITE	CORRESPONDENCE	PHANTASMAGORIA	RECONSTRUCTION
TRANSCENDENTAL	MICROMETEOROID	EXTEMPORANEOUS	PNEUMOCONIOSIS	REPRESENTATION
UNDERSECRETARY	OBSTRUCTIONIST	GRANDILOQUENCE	SLAUGHTERHOUSE	REPRESENTATIVE
BUTTERFINGERED	ORGANOCHLORINE	INTERFEROMETER	SUBMICROSCOPIC	SUPERSTRUCTURE
PHANTASMAGORIA	OTOLARYNGOLOGY	KINDERGARTENER	TROUBLESHOOTER	ULTRAMINIATURE

UNDERSECRETARY
VERISIMILITUDE
VIETNAMIZATION
CARDIOVASCULAR
EXTRAVEHICULAR
INTERMOLECULAR
INTRAMOLECULAR
PHOTOENGRAVING
PSYCHOANALYSIS

12TH LETTER

ANTIDEPRESSANT
ANTIPERSPIRANT
CHEMOSTERILANT
CIRCUMNAVIGATE
DINOFLAGELLATE
DISCOMBOBULATE
INCOMMENSURATE
INDISCRIMINATE
INTERPLANETARY
MISAPPROPRIATE
RADIOTELEGRAPH
UNDERSECRETARY
CLAUSTROPHOBIA
IMPRESSIONABLE
INCOMMUNICABLE
INCOMPRESSIBLE
INCONSIDERABLE
INSURMOUNTABLE
IRRECONCILABLE
IRREPROACHABLE
UNCONSCIONABLE
UNCONTROLLABLE
UNINTELLIGIBLE
UNQUESTIONABLE
ECCLESIASTICAL
PHARMACEUTICAL
PSYCHOCHEMICAL
STAPHYLOCOCCUS
ACCOMPLISHMENT
INTERDEPENDENT
SCHOOLMISTRESS
UNDERNOURISHED
ADMINISTRATION
ARCHITECTONICS
CAPITALIZATION
CIRCUMLOCUTION
CIRCUMSTANTIAL
DECOMPENSATION
DISAPPROBATION
DISCIPLINARIAN
DISCRIMINATING
DISENFRANCHISE
DISEQUILIBRIUM

DISINCLINATION
EGALITARIANISM
ELECTROSTATICS
EXISTENTIALISM
FEATHERBEDDING
FUNDAMENTALISM
GENERALIZATION
HYPERSENSITIVE
HYPOTHYROIDISM
IDENTIFICATION
INTERPRETATION
KREMLINOLOGIST
LATITUDINARIAN
MICROMETEORITE
MULTIPLICATION
NEOCOLONIALISM
NONCOOPERATION
NONRESTRICTIVE
OBSTRUCTIONIST
ORGANOCHLORINE
PALEOMAGNETISM
PHOTOENGRAVING
PHOTOSENSITIVE
PREDESTINATION
RECOMMENDATION
RECONSTRUCTION
REPRESENTATION
REPRESENTATIVE
RESPONSIBILITY
SEGREGATIONIST
SENSATIONALISM
SENTIMENTALIZE
SEPTUAGENARIAN
SERVOMECHANISM
SESQUIPEDALIAN
TATTERDEMALION
THERMODYNAMICS
UNCOMPROMISING
UNDEREMPHASIZE
UTILITARIANISM
VALETUDINARIAN
VIETNAMIZATION
WEATHERABILITY
ZOROASTRIANISM
CARDIOVASCULAR
EXTRAVEHICULAR
INTERMOLECULAR
INTRAMOLECULAR
MESDEMOISELLES
AFOREMENTIONED
CONGREGATIONAL
CONSTITUTIONAL
CORRESPONDENCE
COUNTERBALANCE
DISCOUNTENANCE
GRANDILOQUENCE
INTRANSIGEANCE

KINDERGARTENER
PREADOLESCENCE
PRONUNCIAMENTO
RECONNAISSANCE
UNCONVENTIONAL
UNIDIRECTIONAL
UNPROFESSIONAL
ANESTHESIOLOGY
DISCRIMINATORY
EXTEMPORANEOUS
MICROMETEOROID
NITROCELLULOSE
OPHTHALMOSCOPE
OTOLARYNGOLOGY
PARAPSYCHOLOGY
RADIOTELEPHONE
SOCIORELIGIOUS
ARCHIEPISCOPAL
CHROMATOGRAPHY
CINEMATOGRAPHY
SUBMICROSCOPIC
UNDERDEVELOPED
WHIPPERSNAPPER
BUTTERFINGERED
PHANTASMAGORIA
ELECTRODEPOSIT
INTELLIGENTSIA
METEMPSYCHOSIS
MICROPROCESSOR
PHOTOSYNTHESIS
PNEUMOCONIOSIS
PSYCHOANALYSIS
ANTINEOPLASTIC
CHARACTERISTIC
CHICKENHEARTED
CONJUNCTIVITIS
COSMOCHEMISTRY
INTERFEROMETER
RADIOTELEMETRY
TELETYPEWRITER
TRANSCENDENTAL
TROUBLESHOOTER
COUNTERCULTURE
COUNTERMEASURE
MICROMINIATURE
SLAUGHTERHOUSE
SUPERSTRUCTURE
ULTRAMINIATURE
VERISIMILITUDE

13TH LETTER

ARCHIEPISCOPAL
CARDIOVASCULAR
CIRCUMSTANTIAL

CONGREGATIONAL
CONSTITUTIONAL
DISCIPLINARIAN
ECCLESIASTICAL
EXTRAVEHICULAR
INTERMOLECULAR
INTRAMOLECULAR
LATITUDINARIAN
PHARMACEUTICAL
PSYCHOCHEMICAL
SEPTUAGENARIAN
SESQUIPEDALIAN
TRANSCENDENTAL
UNCONVENTIONAL
UNIDIRECTIONAL
UNPROFESSIONAL
VALETUDINARIAN
ARCHITECTONICS
CORRESPONDENCE
COUNTERBALANCE
DISCOUNTENANCE
ELECTROSTATICS
GRANDILOQUENCE
INTRANSIGEANCE
PREADOLESCENCE
RECONNAISSANCE
THERMODYNAMICS
VERISIMILITUDE
AFOREMENTIONED
BUTTERFINGERED
CHICKENHEARTED
INTERFEROMETER
KINDERGARTENER
MESDEMOISELLES
TELETYPEWRITER
TROUBLESHOOTER
UNDERDEVELOPED
UNDERNOURISHED
WHIPPERSNAPPER
ANESTHESIOLOGY
OTOLARYNGOLOGY
PARAPSYCHOLOGY
CHROMATOGRAPHY
CINEMATOGRAPHY
ANTINEOPLASTIC
CHARACTERISTIC
CLAUSTROPHOBIA
CONJUNCTIVITIS
ELECTRODEPOSIT
INTELLIGENTSIA
METEMPSYCHOSIS
MICROMETEOROID
PHANTASMAGORIA
PHOTOSYNTHESIS
PNEUMOCONIOSIS
PSYCHOANALYSIS
SUBMICROSCOPIC

IMPRESSIONABLE
INCOMMUNICABLE
INCOMPRESSIBLE
INCONSIDERABLE
INSURMOUNTABLE
IRRECONCILABLE
IRREPROACHABLE
UNCONSCIONABLE
UNCONTROLLABLE
UNINTELLIGIBLE
UNQUESTIONABLE
ACCOMPLISHMENT
ANTIDEPRESSANT
ANTIPERSPIRANT
CHEMOSTERILANT
DISCRIMINATING
FEATHERBEDDING
INTERDEPENDENT
ORGANOCHLORINE
PHOTOENGRAVING
RADIOTELEPHONE
UNCOMPROMISING
ADMINISTRATION
CAPITALIZATION
CIRCUMLOCUTION
DECOMPENSATION
DISAPPROBATION
DISINCLINATION
GENERALIZATION
IDENTIFICATION
INTERPRETATION
MICROPROCESSOR
MULTIPLICATION
NONCOOPERATION
PREDESTINATION
RECOMMENDATION
RECONSTRUCTION
REPRESENTATION
TATTERDEMALION
VIETNAMIZATION
OPHTHALMOSCOPE
RADIOTELEGRAPH
COSMOCHEMISTRY
COUNTERCULTURE
COUNTERMEASURE
DISCRIMINATORY
INTERPLANETARY
MICROMINIATURE
RADIOTELEMETRY
SUPERSTRUCTURE
ULTRAMINIATURE
UNDERSECRETARY
DISENFRANCHISE
EGALITARIANISM
EXISTENTIALISM
FUNDAMENTALISM
HYPOTHYROIDISM

KREMLINOLOGIST	DISENFRANCHISE	PALEOMAGNETISM	KREMLINOLOGIST
NEOCOLONIALISM	GRANDILOQUENCE	SENSATIONALISM	OBSTRUCTIONIST
NITROCELLULOSE	HYPERSENSITIVE	SERVOMECHANISM	SEGREGATIONIST
OBSTRUCTIONIST	IMPRESSIONABLE	UTILITARIANISM	ANESTHESIOLOGY
PALEOMAGNETISM	INCOMMENSURATE	ZOROASTRIANISM	CHROMATOGRAPHY
SCHOOLMISTRESS	INCOMMUNICABLE	ADMINISTRATION	CINEMATOGRAPHY
SEGREGATIONIST	INCOMPRESSIBLE	CAPITALIZATION	COSMOCHEMISTRY
SENSATIONALISM	INCONSIDERABLE	CIRCUMLOCUTION	DISCRIMINATORY
SERVOMECHANISM	INDISCRIMINATE	DECOMPENSATION	INTERPLANETARY
SLAUGHTERHOUSE	INSURMOUNTABLE	DISAPPROBATION	OTOLARYNGOLOGY
UTILITARIANISM	INTRANSIGEANCE	DISCIPLINARIAN	PARAPSYCHOLOGY
ZOROASTRIANISM	IRRECONCILABLE	DISINCLINATION	RADIOTELEMETRY
CIRCUMNAVIGATE	IRREPROACHABLE	GENERALIZATION	RESPONSIBILITY
DINOFLAGELLATE	MICROMETEORITE	IDENTIFICATION	UNDERSECRETARY
DISCOMBOBULATE	MICROMINIATURE	INTERPRETATION	WEATHERABILITY
INCOMMENSURATE	MISAPPROPRIATE	LATITUDINARIAN	
INDISCRIMINATE	NITROCELLULOSE	MULTIPLICATION	
MICROMETEORITE	NONRESTRICTIVE	NONCOOPERATION	
MISAPPROPRIATE	OPHTHALMOSCOPE	PREDESTINATION	
PRONUNCIAMENTO	ORGANOCHLORINE	RECOMMENDATION	
RESPONSIBILITY	PHOTOSENSITIVE	RECONSTRUCTION	
WEATHERABILITY	PREADOLESCENCE	REPRESENTATION	
DISEQUILIBRIUM	RADIOTELEPHONE	SEPTUAGENARIAN	
EXTEMPORANEOUS	RECONNAISSANCE	SESQUIPEDALIAN	
SOCIORELIGIOUS	REPRESENTATIVE	TATTERDEMALION	
STAPHYLOCOCCUS	SENTIMENTALIZE	VALETUDINARIAN	
HYPERSENSITIVE	SLAUGHTERHOUSE	VIETNAMIZATION	
NONRESTRICTIVE	SUPERSTRUCTURE	PRONUNCIAMENTO	
PHOTOSENSITIVE	ULTRAMINIATURE	CARDIOVASCULAR	
REPRESENTATIVE	UNCONSCIONABLE	EXTRAVEHICULAR	
SENTIMENTALIZE	UNCONTROLLABLE	INTERFEROMETER	
UNDEREMPHASIZE	UNDEREMPHASIZE	INTERMOLECULAR	
	UNINTELLIGIBLE	INTRAMOLECULAR	
	UNQUESTIONABLE	KINDERGARTENER	
	VERISIMILITUDE	MICROPROCESSOR	
14TH LETTER	DISCRIMINATING	TELETYPEWRITER	
	FEATHERBEDDING	TROUBLESHOOTER	
CLAUSTROPHOBIA	PHOTOENGRAVING	WHIPPERSNAPPER	
INTELLIGENTSIA	UNCOMPROMISING	ARCHITECTONICS	
PHANTASMAGORIA	RADIOTELEGRAPH	CONJUNCTIVITIS	
ANTINEOPLASTIC	ARCHIEPISCOPAL	ELECTROSTATICS	
CHARACTERISTIC	CIRCUMSTANTIAL	EXTEMPORANEOUS	
SUBMICROSCOPIC	CONGREGATIONAL	MESDEMOISELLES	
AFOREMENTIONED	CONSTITUTIONAL	METEMPSYCHOSIS	
BUTTERFINGERED	ECCLESIASTICAL	PHOTOSYNTHESIS	
CHICKENHEARTED	PHARMACEUTICAL	PNEUMOCONIOSIS	
MICROMETEOROID	PSYCHOCHEMICAL	PSYCHOANALYSIS	
UNDERDEVELOPED	TRANSCENDENTAL	SCHOOLMISTRESS	
UNDERNOURISHED	UNCONVENTIONAL	SOCIORELIGIOUS	
CIRCUMNAVIGATE	UNIDIRECTIONAL	STAPHYLOCOCCUS	
CORRESPONDENCE	UNPROFESSIONAL	THERMODYNAMICS	
COUNTERBALANCE	DISEQUILIBRIUM	ACCOMPLISHMENT	
COUNTERCULTURE	EGALITARIANISM	ANTIDEPRESSANT	
COUNTERMEASURE	EXISTENTIALISM	ANTIPERSPIRANT	
DINOFLAGELLATE	FUNDAMENTALISM	CHEMOSTERILANT	
DISCOMBOBULATE	HYPOTHYROIDISM	ELECTRODEPOSIT	
DISCOUNTENANCE	NEOCOLONIALISM	INTERDEPENDENT	

15

LETTER WORDS

1ST LETTER

ANTHROPOCENTRIC
ATHEROSCLEROSIS
CONSERVATIONIST
CONSTRUCTIONIST
CONTEMPORANEOUS
CONVENTIONALIZE
CRYSTALLOGRAPHY
DISINTOXICATION
DISSATISFACTION
ELECTRODYNAMICS
ELECTROMAGNETIC
ELECTROPHORESIS
EXTRACURRICULAR
FLIBBERTIGIBBET
HISTORIOGRAPHER
HYPERTHYROIDISM
INCONSEQUENTIAL
INSTRUMENTALIST
INSTRUMENTALITY
INSTRUMENTATION
INTELLECTUALISM
INTERCOLLEGIATE
INTERSCHOLASTIC
INTERVENTIONISM
METHAMPHETAMINE
MICROCONTROLLER
MICROPHOTOGRAPH
MULTIPROCESSING
NONINTERVENTION
NONPRESCRIPTION
NOTWITHSTANDING
ORGANOPHOSPHATE
PARLIAMENTARIAN
PARTHENOGENESIS
PHOSPHORESCENCE
PHOTOMICROGRAPH
PITHECANTHROPUS
PLAINCLOTHESMAN
PLENIPOTENTIARY
POLYCRYSTALLINE
POLYUNSATURATED
POSTCONSONANTAL
PROFESSIONALISM
PROFESSIONALIZE
STRAIGHTFORWARD
THERMOREGULATOR
ULTRACENTRIFUGE
ULTRAMICROSCOPE
UNCOMMUNICATIVE

UNDEMONSTRATIVE
UNDERPRIVILEGED
UNDERPRODUCTION
UNEXCEPTIONABLE
UNINTERRUPTIBLE
UNPARLIAMENTARY
UNRECONSTRUCTED
UNSOPHISTICATED
VASOCONSTRICTOR
WEATHERBOARDING

2ND LETTER

PARLIAMENTARIAN
PARTHENOGENESIS
VASOCONSTRICTOR
METHAMPHETAMINE
WEATHERBOARDING
PHOSPHORESCENCE
PHOTOMICROGRAPH
THERMOREGULATOR
DISINTOXICATION
DISSATISFACTION
HISTORIOGRAPHER
MICROCONTROLLER
MICROPHOTOGRAPH
PITHECANTHROPUS
ELECTRODYNAMICS
ELECTROMAGNETIC
ELECTROPHORESIS
FLIBBERTIGIBBET
PLAINCLOTHESMAN
PLENIPOTENTIARY
ULTRACENTRIFUGE
ULTRAMICROSCOPE
ANTHROPOCENTRIC
INCONSEQUENTIAL
INSTRUMENTALIST
INSTRUMENTALITY
INSTRUMENTATION
INTELLECTUALISM
INTERCOLLEGIATE
INTERSCHOLASTIC
INTERVENTIONISM
UNCOMMUNICATIVE
UNDEMONSTRATIVE
UNDERPRIVILEGED
UNDERPRODUCTION
UNEXCEPTIONABLE

UNINTERRUPTIBLE
UNPARLIAMENTARY
UNRECONSTRUCTED
UNSOPHISTICATED
CONSERVATIONIST
CONSTRUCTIONIST
CONTEMPORANEOUS
CONVENTIONALIZE
NONINTERVENTION
NONPRESCRIPTION
NOTWITHSTANDING
POLYCRYSTALLINE
POLYUNSATURATED
POSTCONSONANTAL
CRYSTALLOGRAPHY
ORGANOPHOSPHATE
PROFESSIONALISM
PROFESSIONALIZE
ATHEROSCLEROSIS
STRAIGHTFORWARD
MULTIPROCESSING
EXTRACURRICULAR
HYPERTHYROIDISM

3RD LETTER

PLAINCLOTHESMAN
WEATHERBOARDING
INCONSEQUENTIAL
MICROCONTROLLER
MICROPHOTOGRAPH
UNCOMMUNICATIVE
UNDEMONSTRATIVE
UNDERPRIVILEGED
UNDERPRODUCTION
ELECTRODYNAMICS
ELECTROMAGNETIC
ELECTROPHORESIS
PLENIPOTENTIARY
THERMOREGULATOR
UNEXCEPTIONABLE
ORGANOPHOSPHATE
ATHEROSCLEROSIS
FLIBBERTIGIBBET
UNINTERRUPTIBLE
MULTIPROCESSING
POLYCRYSTALLINE
POLYUNSATURATED
CONSERVATIONIST

CONSTRUCTIONIST
CONTEMPORANEOUS
CONVENTIONALIZE
NONINTERVENTION
NONPRESCRIPTION
PHOSPHORESCENCE
PHOTOMICROGRAPH
PROFESSIONALISM
PROFESSIONALIZE
HYPERTHYROIDISM
UNPARLIAMENTARY
PARLIAMENTARIAN
PARTHENOGENESIS
STRAIGHTFORWARD
UNRECONSTRUCTED
DISINTOXICATION
DISSATISFACTION
HISTORIOGRAPHER
INSTRUMENTALIST
INSTRUMENTALITY
INSTRUMENTATION
POSTCONSONANTAL
UNSOPHISTICATED
VASOCONSTRICTOR
ANTHROPOCENTRIC
EXTRACURRICULAR
INTELLECTUALISM
INTERCOLLEGIATE
INTERSCHOLASTIC
INTERVENTIONISM
METHAMPHETAMINE
NOTWITHSTANDING
PITHECANTHROPUS
ULTRACENTRIFUGE
ULTRAMICROSCOPE
CRYSTALLOGRAPHY

4TH LETTER

ORGANOPHOSPHATE
STRAIGHTFORWARD
UNPARLIAMENTARY
FLIBBERTIGIBBET
ELECTRODYNAMICS
ELECTROMAGNETIC
ELECTROPHORESIS
ATHEROSCLEROSIS
HYPERTHYROIDISM
INTELLECTUALISM

INTERCOLLEGIATE
INTERSCHOLASTIC
INTERVENTIONISM
UNDEMONSTRATIVE
UNDERPRIVILEGED
UNDERPRODUCTION
UNRECONSTRUCTED
PROFESSIONALISM
PROFESSIONALIZE
ANTHROPOCENTRIC
METHAMPHETAMINE
PITHECANTHROPUS
DISINTOXICATION
NONINTERVENTION
PLAINCLOTHESMAN
PARLIAMENTARIAN
PLENIPOTENTIARY
UNINTERRUPTIBLE
INCONSEQUENTIAL
UNCOMMUNICATIVE
UNSOPHISTICATED
VASOCONSTRICTOR
NONPRESCRIPTION
EXTRACURRICULAR
MICROCONTROLLER
MICROPHOTOGRAPH
THERMOREGULATOR
ULTRACENTRIFUGE
ULTRAMICROSCOPE
CONSERVATIONIST
CONSTRUCTIONIST
CRYSTALLOGRAPHY
DISSATISFACTION
PHOSPHORESCENCE
CONTEMPORANEOUS
HISTORIOGRAPHER
INSTRUMENTALIST
INSTRUMENTALITY
INSTRUMENTATION
MULTIPROCESSING
PARTHENOGENESIS
PHOTOMICROGRAPH
POSTCONSONANTAL
WEATHERBOARDING
CONVENTIONALIZE
NOTWITHSTANDING
UNEXCEPTIONABLE
POLYCRYSTALLINE
POLYUNSATURATED

5TH LETTER

DISSATISFACTION
EXTRACURRICULAR
METHAMPHETAMINE
ULTRACENTRIFUGE
ULTRAMICROSCOPE
FLIBBERTIGIBBET
POLYCRYSTALLINE
POSTCONSONANTAL
UNEXCEPTIONABLE
UNRECONSTRUCTED
VASOCONSTRICTOR
CONSERVATIONIST
CONTEMPORANEOUS
CONVENTIONALIZE
PITHECANTHROPUS
PROFESSIONALISM
PROFESSIONALIZE
PARTHENOGENESIS
WEATHERBOARDING
MULTIPROCESSING
NOTWITHSTANDING
PARLIAMENTARIAN
PLENIPOTENTIARY
STRAIGHTFORWARD
INTELLECTUALISM
THERMOREGULATOR
UNCOMMUNICATIVE
UNDEMONSTRATIVE
DISINTOXICATION
INCONSEQUENTIAL
NONINTERVENTION
ORGANOPHOSPHATE
PLAINCLOTHESMAN
HISTORIOGRAPHER
MICROCONTROLLER
MICROPHOTOGRAPH
PHOTOMICROGRAPH
PHOSPHORESCENCE
UNSOPHISTICATED
ANTHROPOCENTRIC
ATHEROSCLEROSIS
HYPERTHYROIDISM
INSTRUMENTALIST
INSTRUMENTALITY
INSTRUMENTATION
INTERCOLLEGIATE
INTERSCHOLASTIC
INTERVENTIONISM
NONPRESCRIPTION
UNDERPRIVILEGED
UNDERPRODUCTION
UNPARLIAMENTARY
CONSTRUCTIONIST
CRYSTALLOGRAPHY
ELECTRODYNAMICS

ELECTROMAGNETIC
ELECTROPHORESIS
UNINTERRUPTIBLE
POLYUNSATURATED

6TH LETTER

CRYSTALLOGRAPHY
PARLIAMENTARIAN
EXTRACURRICULAR
INTERCOLLEGIATE
MICROCONTROLLER
PITHECANTHROPUS
PLAINCLOTHESMAN
ULTRACENTRIFUGE
FLIBBERTIGIBBET
NONPRESCRIPTION
PARTHENOGENESIS
UNEXCEPTIONABLE
UNINTERRUPTIBLE
WEATHERBOARDING
STRAIGHTFORWARD
PHOSPHORESCENCE
UNSOPHISTICATED
INTELLECTUALISM
UNPARLIAMENTARY
CONTEMPORANEOUS
METHAMPHETAMINE
PHOTOMICROGRAPH
ULTRAMICROSCOPE
UNCOMMUNICATIVE
CONVENTIONALIZE
POLYUNSATURATED
ANTHROPOCENTRIC
ATHEROSCLEROSIS
ORGANOPHOSPHATE
POSTCONSONANTAL
THERMOREGULATOR
UNDEMONSTRATIVE
UNRECONSTRUCTED
VASOCONSTRICTOR
MICROPHOTOGRAPH
MULTIPROCESSING
PLENIPOTENTIARY
UNDERPRIVILEGED
UNDERPRODUCTION
CONSERVATIONIST
CONSTRUCTIONIST
ELECTRODYNAMICS
ELECTROMAGNETIC
ELECTROPHORESIS
HISTORIOGRAPHER
POLYCRYSTALLINE
INCONSEQUENTIAL
INTERSCHOLASTIC

PROFESSIONALISM
PROFESSIONALIZE
DISINTOXICATION
DISSATISFACTION
HYPERTHYROIDISM
NONINTERVENTION
NOTWITHSTANDING
INSTRUMENTALIST
INSTRUMENTALITY
INSTRUMENTATION
INTERVENTIONISM

7TH LETTER

PITHECANTHROPUS
INTERSCHOLASTIC
INCONSEQUENTIAL
INTELLECTUALISM
INTERVENTIONISM
NONINTERVENTION
ULTRACENTRIFUGE
HYPERTHYROIDISM
MICROPHOTOGRAPH
NOTWITHSTANDING
STRAIGHTFORWARD
DISSATISFACTION
HISTORIOGRAPHER
PHOTOMICROGRAPH
ULTRAMICROSCOPE
UNPARLIAMENTARY
UNSOPHISTICATED
CRYSTALLOGRAPHY
PLAINCLOTHESMAN
INSTRUMENTALIST
INSTRUMENTALITY
INSTRUMENTATION
PARLIAMENTARIAN
PARTHENOGENESIS
POSTCONSONANTAL
UNDEMONSTRATIVE
UNRECONSTRUCTED
VASOCONSTRICTOR
DISINTOXICATION
ELECTRODYNAMICS
ELECTROMAGNETIC
ELECTROPHORESIS
INTERCOLLEGIATE
MICROCONTROLLER
PHOSPHORESCENCE
PLENIPOTENTIARY
ANTHROPOCENTRIC
CONTEMPORANEOUS
METHAMPHETAMINE
ORGANOPHOSPHATE
UNEXCEPTIONABLE

FLIBBERTIGIBBET
MULTIPROCESSING
THERMOREGULATOR
UNDERPRIVILEGED
UNDERPRODUCTION
UNINTERRUPTIBLE
WEATHERBOARDING
ATHEROSCLEROSIS
NONPRESCRIPTION
POLYUNSATURATED
PROFESSIONALISM
PROFESSIONALIZE
CONVENTIONALIZE
CONSTRUCTIONIST
EXTRACURRICULAR
UNCOMMUNICATIVE
CONSERVATIONIST
POLYCRYSTALLINE

8TH LETTER

CONSERVATIONIST
POLYUNSATURATED
UNPARLIAMENTARY
WEATHERBOARDING
ATHEROSCLEROSIS
CONSTRUCTIONIST
INTELLECTUALISM
NONPRESCRIPTION
PHOTOMICROGRAPH
ULTRAMICROSCOPE
ELECTRODYNAMICS
INSTRUMENTALIST
INSTRUMENTALITY
INSTRUMENTATION
PARLIAMENTARIAN
THERMOREGULATOR
INTERSCHOLASTIC
METHAMPHETAMINE
ORGANOPHOSPHATE
CONVENTIONALIZE
PROFESSIONALISM
PROFESSIONALIZE
UNDERPRIVILEGED
CRYSTALLOGRAPHY
INTERCOLLEGIATE
ELECTROMAGNETIC
INTERVENTIONISM
MICROCONTROLLER
PITHECANTHROPUS
ULTRACENTRIFUGE
UNCOMMUNICATIVE
ANTHROPOCENTRIC
CONTEMPORANEOUS
HISTORIOGRAPHER

MICROPHOTOGRAPH
MULTIPROCESSING
PARTHENOGENESIS
PLAINCLOTHESMAN
UNDERPRODUCTION
ELECTROPHORESIS
INCONSEQUENTIAL
EXTRACURRICULAR
NONINTERVENTION
PHOSPHORESCENCE
UNINTERRUPTIBLE
DISSATISFACTION
NOTWITHSTANDING
POLYCRYSTALLINE
POSTCONSONANTAL
UNDEMONSTRATIVE
UNRECONSTRUCTED
UNSOPHISTICATED
VASOCONSTRICTOR
FLIBBERTIGIBBET
PLENIPOTENTIARY
STRAIGHTFORWARD
UNEXCEPTIONABLE
DISINTOXICATION
HYPERTHYROIDISM

9TH LETTER

ELECTROMAGNETIC
ANTHROPOCENTRIC
MULTIPROCESSING
UNDERPRODUCTION
METHAMPHETAMINE
PHOSPHORESCENCE
PLENIPOTENTIARY
DISSATISFACTION
STRAIGHTFORWARD
HISTORIOGRAPHER
PARTHENOGENESIS
THERMOREGULATOR
ELECTROPHORESIS
DISINTOXICATION
FLIBBERTIGIBBET
UNCOMMUNICATIVE
UNEXCEPTIONABLE
ATHEROSCLEROSIS
INTERCOLLEGIATE
UNPARLIAMENTARY
INSTRUMENTALIST
INSTRUMENTALITY
INSTRUMENTATION
PARLIAMENTARIAN
CONVENTIONALIZE
CRYSTALLOGRAPHY
INTERSCHOLASTIC

ORGANOPHOSPHATE
POSTCONSONANTAL
PROFESSIONALISM
PROFESSIONALIZE
WEATHERBOARDING
CONTEMPORANEOUS
EXTRACURRICULAR
HYPERTHYROIDISM
NONPRESCRIPTION
PHOTOMICROGRAPH
ULTRAMICROSCOPE
CONSERVATIONIST
CONSTRUCTIONIST
INTELLECTUALISM
INTERVENTIONISM
MICROCONTROLLER
MICROPHOTOGRAPH
NOTWITHSTANDING
PITHECANTHROPUS
PLAINCLOTHESMAN
POLYCRYSTALLINE
POLYUNSATURATED
ULTRACENTRIFUGE
UNDEMONSTRATIVE
UNRECONSTRUCTED
UNSOPHISTICATED
VASOCONSTRICTOR
INCONSEQUENTIAL
UNINTERRUPTIBLE
NONINTERVENTION
UNDERPRIVILEGED
ELECTRODYNAMICS

10TH LETTER

CONTEMPORANEOUS
DISSATISFACTION
NOTWITHSTANDING
POLYCRYSTALLINE
WEATHERBOARDING
DISINTOXICATION
UNCOMMUNICATIVE
ANTHROPOCENTRIC
ATHEROSCLEROSIS
INCONSEQUENTIAL
INTERCOLLEGIATE
MULTIPROCESSING
NONINTERVENTION
PARTHENOGENESIS
UNPARLIAMENTARY
CRYSTALLOGRAPHY
ELECTROMAGNETIC
FLIBBERTIGIBBET
PITHECANTHROPUS
PLAINCLOTHESMAN

CONSERVATIONIST
CONSTRUCTIONIST
EXTRACURRICULAR
INTERVENTIONISM
NONPRESCRIPTION
UNDERPRIVILEGED
UNSOPHISTICATED
INTERSCHOLASTIC
CONVENTIONALIZE
ELECTRODYNAMICS
PLENIPOTENTIARY
POSTCONSONANTAL
PROFESSIONALISM
PROFESSIONALIZE
ELECTROPHORESIS
HYPERTHYROIDISM
MICROPHOTOGRAPH
PHOTOMICROGRAPH
STRAIGHTFORWARD
ULTRAMICROSCOPE
UNEXCEPTIONABLE
UNINTERRUPTIBLE
HISTORIOGRAPHER
MICROCONTROLLER
ULTRACENTRIFUGE
UNDEMONSTRATIVE
UNRECONSTRUCTED
VASOCONSTRICTOR
ORGANOPHOSPHATE
PHOSPHORESCENCE
INSTRUMENTALIST
INSTRUMENTALITY
INSTRUMENTATION
METHAMPHETAMINE
PARLIAMENTARIAN
INTELLECTUALISM
POLYUNSATURATED
THERMOREGULATOR
UNDERPRODUCTION

11TH LETTER

CONVENTIONALIZE
DISINTOXICATION
ELECTRODYNAMICS
HISTORIOGRAPHER
INSTRUMENTALIST
INSTRUMENTALITY
INSTRUMENTATION
INTELLECTUALISM
INTERSCHOLASTIC
METHAMPHETAMINE
PARLIAMENTARIAN
POSTCONSONANTAL
PROFESSIONALISM

PROFESSIONALIZE
UNCOMMUNICATIVE
UNDEMONSTRATIVE
DISSATISFACTION
EXTRACURRICULAR
PHOSPHORESCENCE
UNDERPRODUCTION
UNSOPHISTICATED
PLAINCLOTHESMAN
INTERCOLLEGIATE
MICROPHOTOGRAPH
PHOTOMICROGRAPH
FLIBBERTIGIBBET
HYPERTHYROIDISM
ULTRACENTRIFUGE
VASOCONSTRICTOR
POLYCRYSTALLINE
THERMOREGULATOR
UNDERPRIVILEGED
ANTHROPOCENTRIC
CONTEMPORANEOUS
ELECTROMAGNETIC
INCONSEQUENTIAL
NONINTERVENTION
NOTWITHSTANDING
PARTHENOGENESIS
UNEXCEPTIONABLE
UNPARLIAMENTARY
CONSERVATIONIST
CONSTRUCTIONIST
INTERVENTIONISM
MICROCONTROLLER
NONPRESCRIPTION
ORGANOPHOSPHATE
ATHEROSCLEROSIS
CRYSTALLOGRAPHY
ELECTROPHORESIS
PITHECANTHROPUS
POLYUNSATURATED
STRAIGHTFORWARD
WEATHERBOARDING
MULTIPROCESSING
ULTRAMICROSCOPE
PLENIPOTENTIARY
UNINTERRUPTIBLE
UNRECONSTRUCTED

12TH LETTER

CRYSTALLOGRAPHY
POLYUNSATURATED
THERMOREGULATOR
UNEXCEPTIONABLE
UNSOPHISTICATED
FLIBBERTIGIBBET

PROFESSIONALIZE
UNCOMMUNICATIVE
UNDEMONSTRATIVE
DISSATISFACTION
EXTRACURRICULAR
PHOSPHORESCENCE
UNDERPRODUCTION
UNSOPHISTICATED
PLAINCLOTHESMAN
INTERCOLLEGIATE
MICROPHOTOGRAPH
PHOTOMICROGRAPH
FLIBBERTIGIBBET
HYPERTHYROIDISM
ULTRACENTRIFUGE
VASOCONSTRICTOR
POLYCRYSTALLINE
THERMOREGULATOR
UNDERPRIVILEGED
ANTHROPOCENTRIC
CONTEMPORANEOUS
ELECTROMAGNETIC
INCONSEQUENTIAL
NONINTERVENTION
NOTWITHSTANDING
PARTHENOGENESIS
UNEXCEPTIONABLE
UNPARLIAMENTARY
CONSERVATIONIST
CONSTRUCTIONIST
INTERVENTIONISM
MICROCONTROLLER
NONPRESCRIPTION
ORGANOPHOSPHATE
ATHEROSCLEROSIS
CRYSTALLOGRAPHY
ELECTROPHORESIS
PITHECANTHROPUS
POLYUNSATURATED
STRAIGHTFORWARD
WEATHERBOARDING
MULTIPROCESSING
ULTRAMICROSCOPE
PLENIPOTENTIARY
UNINTERRUPTIBLE
UNRECONSTRUCTED

ULTRAMICROSCOPE
UNRECONSTRUCTED
VASOCONSTRICTOR
HYPERTHYROIDISM
NOTWITHSTANDING
WEATHERBOARDING
CONTEMPORANEOUS
ELECTROMAGNETIC
ELECTROPHORESIS
PARTHENOGENESIS
PHOSPHORESCENCE
UNDERPRIVILEGED
ULTRACENTRIFUGE
ORGANOPHOSPHATE
INTERCOLLEGIATE
PLENIPOTENTIARY
UNINTERRUPTIBLE
CONVENTIONALIZE
INSTRUMENTALIST
INSTRUMENTALITY
INTELLECTUALISM
MICROCONTROLLER
POLYCRYSTALLINE
PROFESSIONALISM
PROFESSIONALIZE
ELECTRODYNAMICS
METHAMPHETAMINE
CONSERVATIONIST
CONSTRUCTIONIST
INTERVENTIONISM
POSTCONSONANTAL
ATHEROSCLEROSIS
PITHECANTHROPUS
HISTORIOGRAPHER
MICROPHOTOGRAPH
PARLIAMENTARIAN
PHOTOMICROGRAPH
INTERSCHOLASTIC
MULTIPROCESSING
PLAINCLOTHESMAN
ANTHROPOCENTRIC
DISINTOXICATION
DISSATISFACTION
INCONSEQUENTIAL
INSTRUMENTATION
NONINTERVENTION
NONPRESCRIPTION
UNCOMMUNICATIVE
UNDEMONSTRATIVE
UNDERPRODUCTION
UNPARLIAMENTARY
EXTRACURRICULAR
STRAIGHTFORWARD

13TH LETTER

INTERCOLLEGIATE
MICROPHOTOGRAPH
ORGANOPHOSPHATE
PHOTOMICROGRAPH
PLENIPOTENTIARY
STRAIGHTFORWARD
UNPARLIAMENTARY
FLIBBERTIGIBBET
UNEXCEPTIONABLE
UNINTERRUPTIBLE
UNDERPRIVILEGED
HISTORIOGRAPHER
CONSERVATIONIST
CONSTRUCTIONIST
CONVENTIONALIZE
DISINTOXICATION
DISSATISFACTION
ELECTRODYNAMICS
HYPERTHYROIDISM
INCONSEQUENTIAL
INSTRUMENTALIST
INSTRUMENTALITY
INSTRUMENTATION
INTELLECTUALISM
INTERVENTIONISM
METHAMPHETAMINE
MULTIPROCESSING
NONINTERVENTION
NONPRESCRIPTION
NOTWITHSTANDING
PARLIAMENTARIAN
POLYCRYSTALLINE
PROFESSIONALISM
PROFESSIONALIZE
UNCOMMUNICATIVE
UNDEMONSTRATIVE
UNDERPRODUCTION
WEATHERBOARDING
EXTRACURRICULAR
MICROCONTROLLER
PLAINCLOTHESMAN
PHOSPHORESCENCE
CONTEMPORANEOUS
ULTRAMICROSCOPE
CRYSTALLOGRAPHY
PITHECANTHROPUS
ANTHROPOCENTRIC
ATHEROSCLEROSIS
ELECTROPHORESIS
PARTHENOGENESIS
ELECTROMAGNETIC
INTERSCHOLASTIC
POLYUNSATURATED
POSTCONSONANTAL
THERMOREGULATOR

UNRECONSTRUCTED
UNSOPHISTICATED
VASOCONSTRICTOR
ULTRACENTRIFUGE

14th Letter

EXTRACURRICULAR
INCONSEQUENTIAL
PARLIAMENTARIAN
PLAINCLOTHESMAN
POSTCONSONANTAL
ELECTRODYNAMICS
PHOSPHORESCENCE
FLIBBERTIGIBBET
HISTORIOGRAPHER
MICROCONTROLLER
POLYUNSATURATED
UNDERPRIVILEGED
UNRECONSTRUCTED
UNSOPHISTICATED
ULTRACENTRIFUGE
CRYSTALLOGRAPHY
ANTHROPOCENTRIC
ATHEROSCLEROSIS
ELECTROMAGNETIC
ELECTROPHORESIS
INTERSCHOLASTIC
PARTHENOGENESIS
UNEXCEPTIONABLE
UNINTERRUPTIBLE
METHAMPHETAMINE
MULTIPROCESSING
NOTWITHSTANDING
POLYCRYSTALLINE
WEATHERBOARDING
DISINTOXICATION
DISSATISFACTION
INSTRUMENTATION
NONINTERVENTION
NONPRESCRIPTION
THERMOREGULATOR
UNDERPRODUCTION
VASOCONSTRICTOR
MICROPHOTOGRAPH
PHOTOMICROGRAPH
ULTRAMICROSCOPE
PLENIPOTENTIARY
STRAIGHTFORWARD
UNPARLIAMENTARY
CONSERVATIONIST
CONSTRUCTIONIST
HYPERTHYROIDISM
INSTRUMENTALIST
INTELLECTUALISM

INTERVENTIONISM
PROFESSIONALISM
INSTRUMENTALITY
INTERCOLLEGIATE
ORGANOPHOSPHATE
CONTEMPORANEOUS
PITHECANTHROPUS
UNCOMMUNICATIVE
UNDEMONSTRATIVE
CONVENTIONALIZE
PROFESSIONALIZE

15th Letter

ANTHROPOCENTRIC
ELECTROMAGNETIC
INTERSCHOLASTIC
POLYUNSATURATED
STRAIGHTFORWARD
UNDERPRIVILEGED
UNRECONSTRUCTED
UNSOPHISTICATED
CONVENTIONALIZE
INTERCOLLEGIATE
METHAMPHETAMINE
ORGANOPHOSPHATE
PHOSPHORESCENCE
POLYCRYSTALLINE
PROFESSIONALIZE
ULTRACENTRIFUGE
ULTRAMICROSCOPE
UNCOMMUNICATIVE
UNDEMONSTRATIVE
UNEXCEPTIONABLE
UNINTERRUPTIBLE
MULTIPROCESSING
NOTWITHSTANDING
WEATHERBOARDING
MICROPHOTOGRAPH
PHOTOMICROGRAPH
INCONSEQUENTIAL
POSTCONSONANTAL
HYPERTHYROIDISM
INTELLECTUALISM
INTERVENTIONISM
PROFESSIONALISM
DISINTOXICATION
DISSATISFACTION
INSTRUMENTATION
NONINTERVENTION
NONPRESCRIPTION
PARLIAMENTARIAN
PLAINCLOTHESMAN
UNDERPRODUCTION
EXTRACURRICULAR

HISTORIOGRAPHER
MICROCONTROLLER
THERMOREGULATOR
VASOCONSTRICTOR
ATHEROSCLEROSIS
CONTEMPORANEOUS
ELECTRODYNAMICS
ELECTROPHORESIS
PARTHENOGENESIS
PITHECANTHROPUS
CONSERVATIONIST
CONSTRUCTIONIST
FLIBBERTIGIBBET
INSTRUMENTALIST
CRYSTALLOGRAPHY
INSTRUMENTALITY
PLENIPOTENTIARY
UNPARLIAMENTARY

16
LETTER WORDS

MULTI**P**ROGRAMMING
TINTIN**N**ABULATION
INCO**M**PREHENSIBLE
DECE**N**TRALIZATION
INCO**N**TROVERTIBLE
MISU**N**DERSTANDING
ORGA**N**OPHOSPHORUS
UNCO**N**STITUTIONAL
MICR**O**ELECTRONICS
MICR**O**ENCAPSULATE
MISC**O**MMUNICATION
PIEZ**O**ELECTRICITY
PARA**P**ROFESSIONAL
ANTH**R**OPOMORPHISM
ARTE**R**IOSCLEROSIS
ENVI**R**ONMENTALIST
GAST**R**OENTEROLOGY
GAST**R**OINTESTINAL
INTE**R**CONTINENTAL
INTE**R**NATIONALISM
INTE**R**NATIONALIZE
NONP**R**OLIFERATION
UNDE**R**REPRESENTED
TRAN**S**CONTINENTAL
COUN**T**ERCLOCKWISE
COUN**T**ERESPIONAGE
COUN**T**EROFFENSIVE
ELEC**T**ROCHEMISTRY
ELEC**T**ROHYDRAULIC
ELEC**T**ROMAGNETISM
PRES**T**IDIGITATION
SESQ**U**ICENTENNIAL

INTER**C**ONTINENTAL
TRANS**C**ONTINENTAL
MISUN**D**ERSTANDING
MULTI**D**IMENSIONAL
COUNT**E**RCLOCKWISE
COUNT**E**RESPIONAGE
COUNT**E**ROFFENSIVE
MICRO**E**LECTRONICS
MICRO**E**NCAPSULATE
PIEZO**E**LECTRICITY
ULTRA**F**ASHIONABLE
ARTER**I**OSCLEROSIS
CONTA**I**NERIZATION
PREST**I**DIGITATION
SESQU**I**CENTENNIAL
MISCO**M**MUNICATION
MULTI**M**ILLIONAIRE
ULTRA**M**ICROSCOPIC
AUTOI**N**TOXICATION
INTER**N**ATIONALISM

INTER**N**ATIONALIZE
TINTIN**N**ABULATION
ANTHR**O**POMORPHISM
ENVIR**O**NMENTALIST
GASTR**O**ENTEROLOGY
GASTR**O**INTESTINAL
NONPR**O**LIFERATION
ORGAN**O**PHOSPHORUS
VASOC**O**NSTRICTION
INCOM**P**REHENSIBLE
MULTI**P**ROGRAMMING
COMPA**R**TMENTALIZE
ELECT**R**OCHEMISTRY
ELECT**R**OHYDRAULIC
ELECT**R**OMAGNETISM
PARAP**R**OFESSIONAL
UNDER**R**EPRESENTED
UNCON**S**TITUTIONAL
DECEN**T**RALIZATION
EXTRA**T**ERRESTRIAL
EXTRA**T**ERRITORIAL
INCON**T**ROVERTIBLE
ANTIH**Y**PERTENSIVE

INTERN**A**TIONALISM
INTERN**A**TIONALIZE
ULTRAF**A**SHIONABLE
SESQUI**C**ENTENNIAL
PRESTI**D**IGITATION
EXTRAT**E**RRESTRIAL
EXTRAT**E**RRITORIAL
GASTRO**E**NTEROLOGY
MISUND**E**RSTANDING
UNDERR**E**PRESENTED
GASTRO**I**NTESTINAL
MULTID**I**MENSIONAL
MULTIM**I**LLIONAIRE
ULTRAM**I**CROSCOPIC
MICROE**L**ECTRONICS
NONPRO**L**IFERATION
PIEZOE**L**ECTRICITY
MISCOM**M**UNICATION
CONTAI**N**ERIZATION
ENVIRO**N**MENTALIST
MICROE**N**CAPSULATE
TINTIN**N**ABULATION
VASOCO**N**STRICTION
ARTERI**O**SCLEROSIS
ELECTR**O**CHEMISTRY
ELECTR**O**HYDRAULIC
ELECTR**O**MAGNETISM
INTERC**O**NTINENTAL
PARAPR**O**FESSIONAL

INTER**N**ATIONALIZE
TINTIN**N**ABULATION
ANTHR**O**POMORPHISM
ENVIR**O**NMENTALIST
GASTR**O**ENTEROLOGY
GASTR**O**INTESTINAL
NONPR**O**LIFERATION
ORGAN**O**PHOSPHORUS
VASOC**O**NSTRICTION
INCOM**P**REHENSIBLE
MULTI**P**ROGRAMMING
COMPA**R**TMENTALIZE
ELECT**R**OCHEMISTRY
ELECT**R**OHYDRAULIC
ELECT**R**OMAGNETISM
PARAP**R**OFESSIONAL
UNDER**R**EPRESENTED
UNCON**S**TITUTIONAL
DECEN**T**RALIZATION
EXTRA**T**ERRESTRIAL
EXTRA**T**ERRITORIAL
INCON**T**ROVERTIBLE
ANTIH**Y**PERTENSIVE

TRANSC**O**NTINENTAL
ANTHRO**P**OMORPHISM
ANTIHY**P**ERTENSIVE
ORGANO**P**HOSPHORUS
COUNTE**R**CLOCKWISE
COUNTE**R**ESPIONAGE
COUNTE**R**OFFENSIVE
DECENT**R**ALIZATION
INCOMP**R**EHENSIBLE
INCONT**R**OVERTIBLE
MULTIP**R**OGRAMMING
AUTOIN**T**OXICATION
COMPAR**T**MENTALIZE
UNCONS**T**ITUTIONAL

DECENTR**A**LIZATION
TINTINN**A**BULATION
COUNTER**C**LOCKWISE
ELECTRO**C**HEMISTRY
MICROEN**C**APSULATE
ULTRAMI**C**ROSCOPIC
ANTIHYP**E**RTENSIVE
CONTAIN**E**RIZATION
COUNTER**E**SPIONAGE
INCOMPR**E**HENSIBLE
MICROEL**E**CTRONICS
PIEZOEL**E**CTRICITY
SESQUIC**E**NTENNIAL
PARAPRO**F**ESSIONAL
ELECTRO**H**YDRAULIC
ORGANOP**H**OSPHORUS
NONPROL**I**FERATION
PRESTID**I**GITATION
UNCONST**I**TUTIONAL
MULTIMI**L**LIONAIRE
COMPART**M**ENTALIZE
ELECTRO**M**AGNETISM
ENVIRON**M**ENTALIST
MULTIDI**M**ENSIONAL
GASTROE**N**TEROLOGY
GASTROI**N**TESTINAL
INTERCO**N**TINENTAL
TRANSCO**N**TINENTAL
ANTHROP**O**MORPHISM
AUTOINT**O**XICATION
COUNTER**O**FFENSIVE
INCONTR**O**VERTIBLE
MULTIPR**O**GRAMMING
UNDERRE**P**RESENTED
EXTRATE**R**RESTRIAL
EXTRATE**R**RITORIAL
MISUNDE**R**STANDING
ARTERIO**S**CLEROSIS

ULTRAFA**S**HIONABLE
VASOCON**S**TRICTION
INTERNA**T**IONALISM
INTERNA**T**IONALIZE
MISCOMM**U**NICATION

ELECTROM**A**GNETISM
MICROENC**A**PSULATE
TINTINNA**B**ULATION
ARTERIOS**C**LEROSIS
MICROELE**C**TRONICS
PIEZOELE**C**TRICITY
COMPARTM**E**NTALIZE
ENVIRONM**E**NTALIST
MULTIDIM**E**NSIONAL
PARAPROF**E**SSIONAL
COUNTERO**F**FENSIVE
NONPROLI**F**ERATION
MULTIPRO**G**RAMMING
PRESTIDI**G**ITATION
ELECTROC**H**EMISTRY
INCOMPRE**H**ENSIBLE
ULTRAFAS**H**IONABLE
INTERNAT**I**ONALISM
INTERNAT**I**ONALIZE
COUNTERC**L**OCKWISE
DECENTRA**L**IZATION
MULTIMIL**L**IONAIRE
ANTHROPO**M**ORPHISM
MISCOMMU**N**ICATION
SESQUICE**N**TENNIAL
ORGANOPH**O**SPHORUS
ANTIHYPE**R**TENSIVE
CONTAINE**R**IZATION
EXTRATER**R**ESTRIAL
EXTRATER**R**ITORIAL
ULTRAMIC**R**OSCOPIC
UNDERREP**R**ESENTED
COUNTERE**S**PIONAGE
MISUNDER**S**TANDING
GASTROEN**T**EROLOGY
GASTROIN**T**ESTINAL
INTERCON**T**INENTAL
TRANSCON**T**INENTAL
UNCONSTI**T**UTIONAL
VASOCONS**T**RICTION
INCONTRO**V**ERTIBLE
AUTOINTO**X**ICATION
ELECTROH**Y**DRAULIC

10TH LETTER

ELECTROHY**D**RAULIC
ELECTROC**H**EMISTRY
EXTRATERRE**S**TRIAL
GASTROENTE**R**OLOGY
GASTROINTE**S**TINAL
INCOMPREHE**N**SIBLE
INCONTROV**E**RTIBLE
NONPROLIF**E**RATION
UNDERREPR**E**SENTED
COUNTEROF**F**ENSIVE
ELECTROMA**G**NETISM
AUTOINTO**X**ICATION
CONTAINER**I**ZATION
DECENTRAL**I**ZATION
EXTRATERR**I**TORIAL
INTERCONTI**N**ENTAL
MISCOMMUN**I**CATION
MULTIMILL**I**ONAIRE
PRESTIDIG**I**TATION
TRANSCONTI**N**ENTAL
ULTRAFASH**I**ONABLE
ARTERIOSCL**E**ROSIS
COMPARTME**N**TALIZE
ENVIRONME**N**TALIST
MULTIDIME**N**SIONAL
ANTHROPOM**O**RPHISM
COUNTERCL**O**CKWISE
INTERNATI**O**NALISM
INTERNATI**O**NALIZE
ULTRAMICR**O**SCOPIC
COUNTERES**P**IONAGE
MICROENCA**P**SULATE
MULTIPROG**R**AMMING
VASOCONST**R**ICTION
ORGANOPHO**S**PHORUS
PARAPROFE**S**SIONAL
ANTIHYPER**T**ENSIVE
MICROELEC**T**RONICS
MISUNDERS**T**ANDING
PIEZOELEC**T**RICITY
SESQUICEN**T**ENNIAL
TINTINNAB**U**LATION
UNCONSTIT**U**TIONAL

11TH LETTER

MISUNDERST**A**NDING
MULTIPROGR**A**MMING
AUTOINTOXI**C**ATION
COUNTERCLO**C**KWISE
MISCOMMUNI**C**ATION
ANTIHYPERT**E**NSIVE
ARTERIOSCL**E**ROSIS

COUNTEROFF**E**NSIVE
SESQUICENT**E**NNIAL
COUNTERESP**I**ONAGE
VASOCONSTR**I**CTION
TINTINNABU**L**ATION
ELECTROCHE**M**ISTRY
ELECTROMAG**N**ETISM
INCOMPREHE**N**SIBLE
INTERCONTI**N**ENTAL
INTERNATIO**N**ALISM
INTERNATIO**N**ALIZE
TRANSCONTI**N**ENTAL
MULTIMILLI**O**NAIRE
ULTRAFASHI**O**NABLE
ORGANOPHOS**P**HORUS
ANTHROPOMO**R**PHISM
ELECTROHYD**R**AULIC
GASTROENTE**R**OLOGY
INCONTROVE**R**TIBLE
MICROELECT**R**ONICS
NONPROLIFE**R**ATION
PIEZOELECT**R**ICITY
EXTRATERRE**S**TRIAL
GASTROINTE**S**TINAL
MICROENCAP**S**ULATE
MULTIDIMEN**S**IONAL
PARAPROFES**S**IONAL
ULTRAMICRO**S**COPIC
UNDERREPRE**S**ENTED
COMPARTMEN**T**ALIZE
ENVIRONMEN**T**ALIST
EXTRATERRI**T**ORIAL
PRESTIDIGI**T**ATION
UNCONSTITU**T**IONAL
CONTAINERI**Z**ATION
DECENTRALI**Z**ATION

12TH LETTER

AUTOINTOXIC**A**TION
COMPARTMENT**A**LIZE
CONTAINERIZ**A**TION
DECENTRALIZ**A**TION
ELECTROHYDR**A**ULIC
ENVIRONMENT**A**LIST
INTERNATION**A**LISM
INTERNATION**A**LIZE
MISCOMMUNIC**A**TION
NONPROLIFER**A**TION
PRESTIDIGIT**A**TION
TINTINNABUL**A**TION
ULTRAMICROS**C**OPIC
VASOCONSTRI**C**TION
ELECTROMAGN**E**TISM
INTERCONTIN**E**NTAL

TRANSCONTIN**E**NTAL
UNDERREPRES**E**NTED
ORGANOPHOSP**H**ORUS
ELECTROCHEM**I**STRY
MULTIDIMENS**I**ONAL
PARAPROFESS**I**ONAL
PIEZOELECTR**I**CITY
UNCONSTITUT**I**ONAL
COUNTERCLOC**K**WISE
MULTIPROGRA**M**MING
ANTIHYPERTE**N**SIVE
COUNTEROFFE**N**SIVE
MISUNDERSTA**N**DING
MULTIMILLIO**N**AIRE
SESQUICENTE**N**NIAL
ULTRAFASHIO**N**ABLE
COUNTERESPI**O**NAGE
EXTRATERRIT**O**RIAL
GASTROENTER**O**LOGY
MICROELECTR**O**NICS
ANTHROPOMOR**P**HISM
ARTERIOSCLE**R**OSIS
INCOMPREHEN**S**IBLE
EXTRATERRES**T**RIAL
GASTROINTES**T**INAL
INCONTROVER**T**IBLE
MICROENCAPS**U**LATE

13TH LETTER

MULTIMILLIO**N**AIRE
ULTRAFASHIO**N**ABLE
PIEZOELECTR**I**CITY
MISUNDERSTA**N**DING
ANTHROPOMOR**P**HISM
GASTROINTES**T**INAL
INCOMPREHEN**S**IBLE
INCONTROVER**T**IBLE
COMPARTMENT**A**LIZE
ENVIRONMENT**A**LIST
GASTROENTER**O**LOGY
INTERNATION**A**LISM
INTERNATION**A**LIZE
MICROENCAPS**U**LATE
MULTIPROGRA**M**MING
COUNTERESPI**O**NAGE
INTERCONTIN**E**NTAL
MICROELECTR**O**NICS
SESQUICENTE**N**NIAL
TRANSCONTIN**E**NTAL
UNDERREPRES**E**NTED
ARTERIOSCLE**R**OSIS
MULTIDIMENS**I**ONAL
ORGANOPHOSP**H**ORUS
PARAPROFESS**I**ONAL

14TH LETTER

COUNTERESPION**A**GE
MICROENCAPSUL**A**TE
INCOMPREHENSI**B**LE
INCONTROVERTI**B**LE
ULTRAFASHIONA**B**LE
ANTHROPOMORPHISM
ANTIHYPERTENS**I**VE
AUTOINTOXICAT**I**ON
COMPARTMENTAL**I**ZE
CONTAINERIZAT**I**ON
COUNTERCLOCKW**I**SE
COUNTEROFFENS**I**VE
DECENTRALIZAT**I**ON
ELECTROMAGNET**I**SM
ENVIRONMENTAL**I**ST
EXTRATERRESTR**I**AL
EXTRATERRITOR**I**AL
INTERNATIONAL**I**SM
INTERNATIONAL**I**ZE
MICROELECTRON**I**CS
MISCOMMUNICAT**I**ON
MISUNDERSTAND**I**NG
MULTIMILLIONA**I**RE
MULTIPROGRAMM**I**NG
NONPROLIFERAT**I**ON
PIEZOELECTRIC**I**TY
PRESTIDIGITAT**I**ON
SESQUICENTENN**I**AL
TINTINNABULAT**I**ON
VASOCONSTRICT**I**ON
ELECTROHYDRAU**L**IC
GASTROINTESTI**N**AL
MULTIDIMENSIO**N**AL
PARAPROFESSIO**N**AL

UNCONSTITUTIO**N**AL
GASTROENTEROL**O**GY
ULTRAMICROSCO**P**IC
ORGANOPHOSPHO**R**US
ARTERIOSCLERO**S**IS
ELECTROCHEMIS**T**RY
INTERCONTINEN**T**AL
TRANSCONTINEN**T**AL
UNDERREPRESEN**T**ED

15TH LETTER

EXTRATERRESTRI**A**L
EXTRATERRITORI**A**L
GASTROINTESTIN**A**L
INTERCONTINEN**T**AL
MULTIDIMENSION**A**L
PARAPROFESSION**A**L
SESQUICENTENNI**A**L
TRANSCONTINEN**T**AL
UNCONSTITUTION**A**L
MICROELECTRONI**C**S
UNDERREPRESEN**T**ED
COUNTERESPIONA**G**E
GASTROENTEROLO**G**Y
ARTERIOSCLEROS**I**S
ELECTROHYDRAULI**C**
ULTRAMICROSCOPI**C**
INCOMPREHENSIB**L**E
INCONTROVERTIB**L**E
ULTRAFASHIONAB**L**E
MISUNDERSTANDI**N**G
MULTIPROGRAMMI**N**G
AUTOINTOXICATI**O**N
CONTAINERIZATI**O**N
DECENTRALIZATI**O**N
MISCOMMUNICATI**O**N
NONPROLIFERATI**O**N
PRESTIDIGITATI**O**N
TINTINNABULATI**O**N
VASOCONSTRICTI**O**N
ELECTROCHEMIST**R**Y
MULTIMILLIONAI**R**E
ANTHROPOMORPHI**S**M
COUNTERCLOCKWI**S**E
ELECTROMAGNETI**S**M
ENVIRONMENTALI**S**T
INTERNATIONALI**S**M
MICROENCAPSULA**T**E
PIEZOELECTRICI**T**Y
ORGANOPHOSPHOR**U**S
ANTIHYPERTENSI**V**E
COUNTEROFFENSI**V**E
COMPARTMENTALI**Z**E
INTERNATIONALI**Z**E

16TH LETTER

ELECTROHYDRAULI**C**
ULTRAMICROSCOPI**C**
UNDERREPRESENTE**D**
ANTIHYPERTENSIV**E**
COMPARTMENTALIZ**E**
COUNTERCLOCKWIS**E**
COUNTERESPIONAG**E**
COUNTEROFFENSIV**E**
INCOMPREHENSIBL**E**
INCONTROVERTIBL**E**
INTERNATIONALIZ**E**
MICROENCAPSULAT**E**
MULTIMILLIONAIR**E**
ULTRAFASHIONABL**E**
MISUNDERSTANDIN**G**
MULTIPROGRAMMIN**G**
EXTRATERRESTRIA**L**
EXTRATERRITORIA**L**
GASTROINTESTINA**L**
INTERCONTINENTA**L**
MULTIDIMENSIONA**L**
PARAPROFESSIONA**L**
SESQUICENTENNIA**L**
TRANSCONTINENTA**L**
UNCONSTITUTIONA**L**
ANTHROPOMORPHIS**M**
ELECTROMAGNETIS**M**
INTERNATIONALIS**M**
AUTOINTOXICATIO**N**
CONTAINERIZATIO**N**
DECENTRALIZATIO**N**
MISCOMMUNICATIO**N**
NONPROLIFERATIO**N**
PRESTIDIGITATIO**N**
TINTINNABULATIO**N**
VASOCONSTRICTIO**N**
ARTERIOSCLEROSI**S**
MICROELECTRONIC**S**
ORGANOPHOSPHORU**S**
ENVIRONMENTALIS**T**
ELECTROCHEMISTR**Y**
GASTROENTEROLOG**Y**
PIEZOELECTRICIT**Y**

17
LETTER WORDS

1ST LETTER

CONGREGATIONALIST
CONSTITUTIONALITY
CONSUBSTANTIATION
CONTRADISTINCTION
COUNTERINSURGENCY
COUNTERREVOLUTION
ELECTROCARDIOGRAM
ENCEPHALOMYELITIS
IMMUNOSUPPRESSIVE
INTERDEPARTMENTAL
INTERDISCIPLINARY
INTERGENERATIONAL
INTERGOVERNMENTAL
MICROMINIATURIZED
POSTIMPRESSIONISM
SUPERCONDUCTIVITY
TELECOMMUNICATION
TRANSCENDENTALISM
ULTRACONSERVATIVE

2ND LETTER

T**E**LECOMMUNICATION
M**I**CROMINIATURIZED
E**L**ECTROCARDIOGRAM
U**L**TRACONSERVATIVE
I**M**MUNOSUPPRESSIVE
E**N**CEPHALOMYELITIS
I**N**TERDEPARTMENTAL
I**N**TERDISCIPLINARY
I**N**TERGENERATIONAL
I**N**TERGOVERNMENTAL
C**O**NGREGATIONALIST
C**O**NSTITUTIONALITY
C**O**NSUBSTANTIATION
C**O**NTRADISTINCTION
C**O**UNTERINSURGENCY
C**O**UNTERREVOLUTION
P**O**STIMPRESSIONISM
T**R**ANSCENDENTALISM
S**U**PERCONDUCTIVITY

3RD LETTER

TR**A**NSCENDENTALISM
EN**C**EPHALOMYELITIS

MIC**R**OMINIATURIZED
EL**E**CTROCARDIOGRAM
TE**L**ECOMMUNICATION
IM**M**UNOSUPPRESSIVE
CON**G**REGATIONALIST
CON**S**TITUTIONALITY
CON**S**UBSTANTIATION
CON**T**RADISTINCTION
SU**P**ERCONDUCTIVITY
PO**S**TIMPRESSIONISM
INT**E**RDEPARTMENTAL
INT**E**RDISCIPLINARY
INT**E**RGENERATIONAL
INT**E**RGOVERNMENTAL
UL**T**RACONSERVATIVE
COU**N**TERINSURGENCY
COU**N**TERREVOLUTION

4TH LETTER

ELE**C**TROCARDIOGRAM
ENC**E**PHALOMYELITIS
INT**E**RDEPARTMENTAL
INT**E**RDISCIPLINARY
INT**E**RGENERATIONAL
INT**E**RGOVERNMENTAL
SUP**E**RCONDUCTIVITY
TEL**E**COMMUNICATION
CON**G**REGATIONALIST
COU**N**TERINSURGENCY
COU**N**TERREVOLUTION
TRA**N**SCENDENTALISM
MIC**R**OMINIATURIZED
ULT**R**ACONSERVATIVE
CON**S**TITUTIONALITY
CON**S**UBSTANTIATION
CON**T**RADISTINCTION
POS**T**IMPRESSIONISM
IMM**U**NOSUPPRESSIVE

5TH LETTER

ULTR**A**CONSERVATIVE
TELE**C**OMMUNICATION
POST**I**MPRESSIONISM
IMMU**N**OSUPPRESSIVE
MICR**O**MINIATURIZED

ENCE**P**HALOMYELITIS
CONG**R**EGATIONALIST
CONT**R**ADISTINCTION
INTE**R**DEPARTMENTAL
INTE**R**DISCIPLINARY
INTE**R**GENERATIONAL
INTE**R**GOVERNMENTAL
SUPE**R**CONDUCTIVITY
TRAN**S**CENDENTALISM
CONS**T**ITUTIONALITY
COUN**T**ERINSURGENCY
COUN**T**ERREVOLUTION
ELEC**T**ROCARDIOGRAM
CONS**U**BSTANTIATION

6TH LETTER

CONTR**A**DISTINCTION
CONSU**B**STANTIATION
SUPER**C**ONDUCTIVITY
TRANS**C**ENDENTALISM
ULTRA**C**ONSERVATIVE
INTER**D**EPARTMENTAL
INTER**D**ISCIPLINARY
CONGR**E**GATIONALIST
COUNT**E**RINSURGENCY
COUNT**E**RREVOLUTION
INTER**G**ENERATIONAL
INTER**G**OVERNMENTAL
ENCEP**H**ALOMYELITIS
CONST**I**TUTIONALITY
MICRO**M**INIATURIZED
POSTI**M**PRESSIONISM
IMMUN**O**SUPPRESSIVE
TELEC**O**MMUNICATION
ELECT**R**OCARDIOGRAM

7TH LETTER

ENCEPH**A**LOMYELITIS
CONTRA**D**ISTINCTION
INTERD**E**PARTMENTAL
INTERG**E**NERATIONAL
TRANSC**E**NDENTALISM
CONGRE**G**ATIONALIST
INTERD**I**SCIPLINARY
MICROM**I**NIATURIZED

TELECOM**M**UNICATION
ELECTRO**C**ARDIOGRAM
INTERG**O**VERNMENTAL
SUPERC**O**NDUCTIVITY
ULTRAC**O**NSERVATIVE
POSTIM**P**RESSIONISM
COUNTE**R**INSURGENCY
COUNTE**R**REVOLUTION
CONSUB**S**TANTIATION
IMMUNO**S**UPPRESSIVE
CONSTI**T**UTIONALITY

8TH LETTER

CONGREG**A**TIONALIST
ELECTRO**C**ARDIOGRAM
CONTRAD**I**STINCTION
COUNTER**I**NSURGENCY
ENCEPHA**L**OMYELITIS
TELECOM**M**UNICATION
INTERGE**N**ERATIONAL
MICROMIN**I**ATURIZED
SUPERCON**D**UCTIVITY
TRANSCEN**D**ENTALISM
ULTRACON**S**ERVATIVE
INTERDEP**A**RTMENTAL
COUNTERR**E**VOLUTION
POSTIMPR**E**SSIONISM
INTERDIS**C**IPLINARY
CONSUBST**A**NTIATION
CONSTITU**T**IONALITY
IMMUNOSU**P**PRESSIVE
INTERGOV**E**RNMENTAL

9TH LETTER

CONSUBSTA**N**TIATION
ELECTROCA**R**DIOGRAM
INTERDEPA**R**TMENTAL
INTERDISC**I**PLINARY
SUPERCOND**U**CTIVITY
TRANSCEND**E**NTALISM
COUNTERRE**V**OLUTION
INTERGENE**R**ATIONAL
INTERGOVE**R**NMENTAL
POSTIMPRE**S**SIONISM
MICROMINI**A**TURIZED

COUNTERINSURGENCY
ENCEPHALOMYELITIS
IMMUNOSUPPRESSIVE
CONTRADISTINCTION
ULTRACONSERVATIVE
CONGREGATIONALIST
CONSTITUTIONALITY
TELECOMMUNICATION

10TH LETTER

MICROMINIATURIZED
TRANSCENDENTALISM
ULTRACONSERVATIVE
CONGREGATIONALIST
CONSTITUTIONALITY
INTERDISCIPLINARY
ENCEPHALOMYELITIS
CONSUBSTANTIATION
TELECOMMUNICATION
IMMUNOSUPPRESSIVE
ELECTROCARDIOGRAM
INTERDEPARTMENTAL
INTERGENERATIONAL
INTERGOVERNMENTAL
COUNTERINSURGENCY
POSTIMPRESSIONISM
CONTRADISTINCTION
SUPERCONDUCTIVITY
COUNTERREVOLUTION

11TH LETTER

INTERGENERATIONAL
SUPERCONDUCTIVITY
ELECTROCARDIOGRAM
CONTRADISTINCTION
TELECOMMUNICATION
INTERGOVERNMENTAL
TRANSCENDENTALISM
CONGREGATIONALIST
CONSTITUTIONALITY
COUNTERREVOLUTION
INTERDISCIPLINARY
IMMUNOSUPPRESSIVE
ULTRACONSERVATIVE
POSTIMPRESSIONISM
CONSUBSTANTIATION
INTERDEPARTMENTAL
MICROMINIATURIZED
COUNTERINSURGENCY
ENCEPHALOMYELITIS

12TH LETTER

TELECOMMUNICATION
ENCEPHALOMYELITIS
IMMUNOSUPPRESSIVE
CONSUBSTANTIATION
ELECTROCARDIOGRAM
POSTIMPRESSIONISM
COUNTERREVOLUTION
INTERDISCIPLINARY
INTERDEPARTMENTAL
INTERGOVERNMENTAL
CONGREGATIONALIST
CONSTITUTIONALITY
CONTRADISTINCTION
COUNTERINSURGENCY
INTERGENERATIONAL
SUPERCONDUCTIVITY
TRANSCENDENTALISM
MICROMINIATURIZED
ULTRACONSERVATIVE

13TH LETTER

CONGREGATIONALIST
CONSTITUTIONALITY
CONSUBSTANTIATION
TELECOMMUNICATION
TRANSCENDENTALISM
ULTRACONSERVATIVE
CONTRADISTINCTION
INTERDEPARTMENTAL
INTERGOVERNMENTAL
COUNTERINSURGENCY
INTERDISCIPLINARY
INTERGENERATIONAL
SUPERCONDUCTIVITY
ENCEPHALOMYELITIS
ELECTROCARDIOGRAM
POSTIMPRESSIONISM
MICROMINIATURIZED
IMMUNOSUPPRESSIVE
COUNTERREVOLUTION

14TH LETTER

COUNTERINSURGENCY
ELECTROCARDIOGRAM
ENCEPHALOMYELITIS
MICROMINIATURIZED
CONGREGATIONALIST
CONSTITUTIONALITY

TRANSCENDENTALISM
INTERDEPARTMENTAL
INTERDISCIPLINARY
INTERGOVERNMENTAL
POSTIMPRESSIONISM
INTERGENERATIONAL
IMMUNOSUPPRESSIVE
CONSUBSTANTIATION
CONTRADISTINCTION
COUNTERREVOLUTION
TELECOMMUNICATION
ULTRACONSERVATIVE
SUPERCONDUCTIVITY

15TH LETTER

INTERDISCIPLINARY
CONGREGATIONALIST
CONSTITUTIONALITY
CONSUBSTANTIATION
CONTRADISTINCTION
COUNTERREVOLUTION
IMMUNOSUPPRESSIVE
POSTIMPRESSIONISM
SUPERCONDUCTIVITY
TELECOMMUNICATION
TRANSCENDENTALISM
ULTRACONSERVATIVE
COUNTERINSURGENCY
INTERGENERATIONAL
ELECTROCARDIOGRAM
ENCEPHALOMYELITIS
INTERDEPARTMENTAL
INTERGOVERNMENTAL
MICROMINIATURIZED

16TH LETTER

ELECTROCARDIOGRAM
INTERDEPARTMENTAL
INTERGENERATIONAL
INTERGOVERNMENTAL
COUNTERINSURGENCY
MICROMINIATURIZED
ENCEPHALOMYELITIS
CONSUBSTANTIATION
CONTRADISTINCTION
COUNTERREVOLUTION
TELECOMMUNICATION
INTERDISCIPLINARY
CONGREGATIONALIST
POSTIMPRESSIONISM

TRANSCENDENTALISM
CONSTITUTIONALITY
SUPERCONDUCTIVITY
IMMUNOSUPPRESSIVE
ULTRACONSERVATIVE

17TH LETTER

MICROMINIATURIZED
IMMUNOSUPPRESSIVE
ULTRACONSERVATIVE
INTERDEPARTMENTAL
INTERGENERATIONAL
INTERGOVERNMENTAL
ELECTROCARDIOGRAM
POSTIMPRESSIONISM
TRANSCENDENTALISM
CONSUBSTANTIATION
CONTRADISTINCTION
COUNTERREVOLUTION
TELECOMMUNICATION
ENCEPHALOMYELITIS
CONGREGATIONALIST
CONSTITUTIONALITY
COUNTERINSURGENCY
INTERDISCIPLINARY
SUPERCONDUCTIVITY

18
LETTER WORDS

ELECTROCARDIOGRAPH
PHOTODECOMPOSITION
TRANSUBSTANTIATION

TRANSU**B**STANTIATION
PHOTOD**E**COMPOSITION
ELECTR**O**CARDIOGRAPH

TRANSUBSTANT**I**ATION
ELECTROCARDI**O**GRAPH
PHOTODECOMPO**S**ITION

P**H**OTODECOMPOSITION
E**L**ECTROCARDIOGRAPH
T**R**ANSUBSTANTIATION

ELECTRO**C**ARDIOGRAPH
PHOTODE**C**OMPOSITION
TRANSUB**S**TANTIATION

TRANSUBSTANTI**A**TION
ELECTROCARDIO**G**RAPH
PHOTODECOMPOSITION

TR**A**NSUBSTANTIATION
EL**E**CTROCARDIOGRAPH
PH**O**TODECOMPOSITION

ELECTROCA**R**DIOGRAPH
PHOTODEC**O**MPOSITION
TRANSUB**S**TANTIATION

ELECTROCARDIOG**R**APH
PHOTODECOMPOSI**T**ION
TRANSUBSTANTIA**T**ION

ELE**C**TROCARDIOGRAPH
TRA**N**SUBSTANTIATION
PHO**T**ODECOMPOSITION

TRANSUBST**A**NTIATION
PHOTODECO**M**POSITION
ELECTROCA**R**DIOGRAPH

ELECTROCARDIOGR**A**PH
PHOTODECOMPOSIT**I**ON
TRANSUBSTANTIAT**I**ON

PHOT**O**DECOMPOSITION
TRAN**S**UBSTANTIATION
ELEC**T**ROCARDIOGRAPH

ELECTROCAR**D**IOGRAPH
TRANSUBSTAN**T**IATION
PHOTODECOM**P**OSITION

PHOTODECOMPOSITI**O**N
TRANSUBSTANTIATIO**N**
ELECTROCARDIOGRAP**H**

PHOTO**D**ECOMPOSITION
ELECT**R**OCARDIOGRAPH
TRANS**U**BSTANTIATION

ELECTROCARD**I**OGRAPH
PHOTODECOMP**O**SITION
TRANSUBSTAN**T**IATION

ELECTROCARDIOGRAP**H**
PHOTODECOMPOSITIO**N**
TRANSUBSTANTIATIO**N**

19

LETTER WORDS

COUNTERINTELLIGENCE
DEINDUSTRIALIZATION
EXTRATERRITORIALITY
INTERDENOMINATIONAL
NONREPRESENTATIONAL

INTER**D**ENOMINATIONAL
COUNT**E**RINTELLIGENCE
NONRE**P**RESENTATIONAL
EXTRA**T**ERRITORIALITY
DEIND**U**STRIALIZATION

DEINDUSTRI**A**LIZATION
COUNTERINT**E**LLIGENCE
INTERDENOM**I**NATIONAL
NONREPRESE**N**TATIONAL
EXTRATERRI**T**ORIALITY

COUNTERINTELLI**G**ENCE
EXTRATERRITORIA**L**ITY
INTERDENOMINATI**O**NAL
NONREPRESENTATI**O**NAL
DEINDUSTRIALIZA**T**ION

D**E**INDUSTRIALIZATION
I**N**TERDENOMINATIONAL
C**O**UNTERINTELLIGENCE
N**O**NREPRESENTATIONAL
EX**T**RATERRITORIALITY

EXTRAT**E**RRITORIALITY
INTERD**E**NOMINATIONAL
COUNTE**R**INTELLIGENCE
NONREP**R**ESENTATIONAL
DEINDU**S**TRIALIZATION

COUNTERINTEL**L**IGENCE
DEINDUSTRIA**L**IZATION
INTERDENOMIN**A**TIONAL
EXTRATERRITO**R**IALITY
NONREPRESENT**A**TIONAL

DEINDUSTRIALIZA**T**ION
EXTRATERRITORIA**L**ITY
COUNTERINTELLIGE**N**CE
INTERDENOMINATIO**N**AL
NONREPRESENTATIO**N**AL

DE**I**NDUSTRIALIZATION
NO**N**REPRESENTATIONAL
EX**T**RATERRITORIALITY
IN**T**ERDENOMINATIONAL
CO**U**NTERINTELLIGENCE

NONREPR**E**SENTATIONAL
COUNTER**I**NTELLIGENCE
INTERDE**N**OMINATIONAL
EXTRATER**R**ITORIALITY
DEINDUS**T**RIALIZATION

INTERDENOMIN**A**TIONAL
NONREPRESENT**A**TIONAL
DEINDUSTRIALI**Z**ATION
COUNTERINTELL**I**GENCE
EXTRATERRITOR**I**ALITY

INTERDENOMINATIONA**L**
NONREPRESENTATIONA**L**
COUNTERINTELLIGENC**E**
DEINDUSTRIALIZATIO**N**
EXTRATERRITORIALIT**Y**

INT**E**RDENOMINATIONAL
COU**N**TERINTELLIGENCE
DEI**N**DUSTRIALIZATION
EXT**R**ATERRITORIALITY
NON**R**EPRESENTATIONAL

COUNTERI**N**TELLIGENCE
INTERDEN**O**MINATIONAL
DEINDUST**R**IALIZATION
EXTRATERR**I**TORIALITY
NONREPRE**S**ENTATIONAL

COUNTERINTELLI**G**ENCE
EXTRATERRITOR**I**ALITY
INTERDENOMINA**T**IONAL
NONREPRESENTA**T**IONAL
DEINDUSTRIALI**Z**ATION

COUNTERINTELLIGENC**E**
INTERDENOMINATIONA**L**
NONREPRESENTATIONA**L**
DEINDUSTRIALIZATIO**N**
EXTRATERRITORIALIT**Y**

EXTR**A**TERRITORIALITY
DEIN**D**USTRIALIZATION
NONR**E**PRESENTATIONAL
INTE**R**DENOMINATIONAL
COUN**T**ERINTELLIGENCE

NONREPRES**E**NTATIONAL
DEINDUSTRI**A**LIZATION
EXTRATERRI**T**ORIALITY
INTERDENO**M**INATIONAL
COUNTERINT**E**LLIGENCE

DEINDUSTRIALIZ**A**TION
EXTRATERRITORI**A**LITY
COUNTERINTELLI**G**ENCE
INTERDENOMINAT**I**ONAL
NONREPRESENTAT**I**ONAL

1ST LETTER

ELECTROENCEPHALOGRAM
MICROMINIATURIZATION
TETRAHYDROCANNABINOL

2ND LETTER

T**E**TRAHYDROCANNABINOL
M**I**CROMINIATURIZATION
E**L**ECTROENCEPHALOGRAM

3RD LETTER

MI**C**ROMINIATURIZATION
EL**E**CTROENCEPHALOGRAM
TE**T**RAHYDROCANNABINOL

4TH LETTER

ELE**C**TROENCEPHALOGRAM
MIC**R**OMINIATURIZATION
TET**R**AHYDROCANNABINOL

5TH LETTER

TETR**A**HYDROCANNABINOL
MICR**O**MINIATURIZATION
ELEC**T**ROENCEPHALOGRAM

6TH LETTER

TETRA**H**YDROCANNABINOL
MICRO**M**INIATURIZATION
ELECT**R**OENCEPHALOGRAM

7TH LETTER

MICROM**I**NIATURIZATION
ELECTR**O**ENCEPHALOGRAM
TETRAH**Y**DROCANNABINOL

8TH LETTER

TETRAHY**D**ROCANNABINOL
ELECTRO**E**NCEPHALOGRAM
MICROMIN**I**ATURIZATION

9TH LETTER

MICROMIN**I**ATURIZATION
ELECTROE**N**CEPHALOGRAM
TETRAHYD**R**OCANNABINOL

10TH LETTER

MICROMINI**A**TURIZATION
ELECTROEN**C**EPHALOGRAM
TETRAHYDR**O**CANNABINOL

11TH LETTER

TETRAHYDRO**C**ANNABINOL
ELECTROENC**E**PHALOGRAM
MICROMINIA**T**URIZATION

12TH LETTER

TETRAHYDROC**A**NNABINOL
ELECTROENCE**P**HALOGRAM
MICROMINIAT**U**RIZATION

13TH LETTER

ELECTROENCEP**H**ALOGRAM
TETRAHYDROCA**N**NABINOL
MICROMINIATU**R**IZATION

14TH LETTER

ELECTROENCEPH**A**LOGRAM
MICROMINIATURIZATION
TETRAHYDROCAN**N**ABINOL

15TH LETTER

TETRAHYDROCANN**A**BINOL
ELECTROENCEPHA**L**OGRAM
MICROMINIATURI**Z**ATION

16TH LETTER

MICROMINIATURIZ**A**TION
TETRAHYDROCANNA**B**INOL
ELECTROENCEPHAL**O**GRAM

17TH LETTER

ELECTROENCEPHALO**G**RAM
TETRAHYDROCANNABI**N**OL
MICROMINIATURIZAT**I**ON

18TH LETTER

MICROMINIATURIZATI**O**N
TETRAHYDROCANNABIN**O**L
ELECTROENCEPHALOGR**A**M

19TH LETTER

ELECTROENCEPHALOGR**A**M
MICROMINIATURIZATI**O**N
TETRAHYDROCANNABIN**O**L

20TH LETTER

TETRAHYDROCANNABINO**L**
ELECTROENCEPHALOGRA**M**
MICROMINIATURIZATIO**N**

ELECTROENCEPHALOGRAPH

Since there are no other words of 21 letters, this one stands alone. At least two words of the same length are required in order to sort them alphabetically by any position.

SECTION 2 · NAMES OF PEOPLE

2-14
LETTER WORDS

2 LETTER / 1ST LETTER										4 LETTER / 1ST LETTER			
2 LETTER	JO	EMI	LUN	VAN	BEG	OLE	SUU	GIG	DAO	HEY	BELL	CHER	DUNS
1ST LETTER	MO	EVA	MAX	VOS	BEN	ULF	TUM	SIH	HAO	JAY	BELO	CHEW	EADS
AL	YO	EWA	MEL	WAN	DEI	AMY	YUL	ADI	IVO	JOY	BENA	CHIA	EARL
AN	FU	FAY	MOE	WEI	DEL	EMI	EVA	DEI	KUO	KAY	BENO	CHIH	EDME
BO	HU	FOX	MOO	XIE	HEY	ANN	IVO	ELI	LEO	LEY	BENZ	CHIU	EDNA
XC	LU	GAY	NEF	YAN	KEN	BOB	EWA	EMI	MOO	RAY	BERG	CHOH	EIKO
ST	SU	GIG	ODD	YIN	LEE	BOK	UWE	HSI	RIO	ROY	BERN	CHOU	ELEK
CS	TU	GIL	OHM	YUL	LEO	BOX	KYI	HUI	THO	PAZ	BERT	CHUN	ELIA
ED	WU	GUS	OLE	ZAN	LEV	CON	TZU	KYI	UGO		BEST	CLAY	ELIE
FU	YU	GUY	ORR	ZHI	LEW	COX		SHI	ARP		BILL	CLEM	ELIO
HU	ZU	HAL	PAN	ZOU	LEY	DON		WEI	ASP		BING	CODE	ELMO
JO	·	HAN	PAR	**2ND LETTER**	MEL	FOX		ZHI	HAR	**4 LETTER**	BINI	COHN	ELSO
LI	**3 LETTER**	HAO	PAZ		NEF	HOE	**3RD LETTER**	BOK	ORR	**1ST LETTER**	BIOT	COKE	EMIL
LU	**1ST LETTER**	HAR	PDE	BAY	PER	HOU		DEL	PAR	AAGE	BIRO	COLE	EMMA
MA	ABU	HEY	PER	DAG	RED	JOE	ASA	GIL	PER	ABBE	BLAS	COLT	EMMY
MO	ADI	HIN	POE	DAM	REE	JON	EVA	SIR	SIR	ABBY	BOAS	COOK	ERIC
OE	AKE	HOE	RAY	DAO	REX	JOY	EWA	GUS	GUS	ABEL	BODE	COPE	ERIK
PI	ALF	HOU	RED	DAY	SEE	LON	IRA	RIS	RIS	ADAM	BOHR	CORI	EWEN
SU	AMY	HSI	REE	FAY	TED	LOW	JIA	VOS	VOS	AGNE	BOIS	CORT	FADL
TI	ANN	HUI	REX	GAY	WEI	MOE	KUA	ART	ART	AIME	BOLL	CRAM	FAPP
TU	ARP	IAN	RIO	HAL	UGO	MOO	BOB	KIT	KIT	AIRY	BOLT	CURL	FARR
VE	ART	IRA	RIS	HAN	CHU	POE	DUD	ABU	ABU	ALAN	BOND	DALE	FASH
WU	ASA	IVO	ROD	HAO	OHM	ROD	ODD	CHU	CHU	ALCA	BORN	DANA	FATH
YA	ASP	JAN	ROY	HAR	SHI	ROY	RED	HOU	HOU	ALEC	BOSE	DANE	FAYE
YO	BAY	JAY	SAM	IAN	THO	TOM	ROD	LIU	LIU	ALEX	BOSS	DANY	FELT
YU	BEG	JIA	SAN	JAN	ZHI	VOS	TED	SSU	SSU	ALVA	BOYD	DART	FINK
ZI	BEN	JIM	SEE	JAY	GIG	ZOU	TOM	STU	STU	AMES	BUCK	DAVE	FITZ
ZU	BOB	JOE	SHI	KAY	GIL	ARP	TIM	SUU	SUU	ANDY	BUDD	DAVY	FORD
2ND LETTER	BOK	JON	SIH	MAX	HIN	ART	TOM	TSU	TSU	ANEL	BURL	DAWN	FRED
MA	BOX	JOY	SIR	PAN	JIA	IRA	TED	TUM	ZOU	ANNA	BURT	DEAN	FUNK
YA	CHU	KAY	SSU	PAR	JIM	ORR	ROD	SUU	TZU	ANNE	BUSH	DEHN	FUST
ED	CON	KEN	STU	PAZ	KIM	URE	SAM	ANN	ANN	ARNE	BYRD	DIAS	GAHN
OE	COX	KIM	SUU	RAY	KIT	ASA	VAN	BEN	BEN	ARNO	CAGE	DIAZ	GAIL
VE	DAG	KIT	TED	SAM	LIE	ASP	WAN	CON	CON	AUER	CAMP	DICK	GALE
LI	DAM	KUA	THO	SAN	LIU	PDE	YAN	DON	DON	AUNG	CANN	DIOR	GALL
PI	DAO	KUO	TIM	VAL	RIO	POE	YIN	HAN	HAN	AXEL	CANO	DIRK.	GARY
TI	DAY	KYI	TOM	VAN	RIS	SSU	ZAN	IAN	HIN	BAKR	CARL	DODD	GAWA
ZI	DEI	LEE	TSE	WAN	SIH	SEE	DAG	JAN	IAN	BARR	CARO	DONN	GELL
AL	DEL	LEO	TSU	XIE	SIR	TSE	ALF	KEN	JAN	BART	CARR	DORE	GENE
AN	DON	LEV	TUM	YAN	TIM	TSU	NEF	LON	BOX	BAY	CATO	DORN	GENG
BO	DUD	LEW	TZU	YIN	XIE	URE	ULF	JON	COX	BASS	CECH	DORR	GERD
	ELI	LEY	UGO	AKE	YIN	UWE	YAN	JAN	FOX	BEAL	CELA	DOUG	GEZA
	ELY	LIE	ULF	ALF	AKE	XIE	WAN	JIA	KEN	BEAN	CEVA	DOVE	GIDE
		LIU	URE	ADI	ALF	YIN	ULF	HUI	LON	BEDE	CHAN	DOWD	GILE
		LON	UWE	ODD	ELI	KUO	KUA	YIN	PAN	BEER	CHAO	DUKE	GILL
		LOW	VAL	PDE	ELY	LUN	ZAN	GUY	GUY	BELA	CHEN	DUNN	GOLD

GRAM	JUAN	LOEB	OPIK	SCOT	WEYL	GAIL	WALD	LENZ	BING	OKUN	DORE
GRAY	JUDY	LOIS	ORRY	SEAN	WIEN	GALE	WANG	LEON	BINI	ALAN	DORN
GREG	JUMP	LONG	OTIS	SEKI	WILM	GALL	WARD	LEVI	BIOT	ALCA	DORR
GREN	JUNG	LORD	OTTO	SETH	WING	GARY	WATT	MEAD	BIRO	ALEC	DOUG
GREW	JUST	LORY	OWEN	SHAO	WISE	GAWA	YAGA	MELA	DIAS	ALEX	DOVE
GREY	KAHN	LOUS	PAGE	SHAW	WOLE	HAHN	YANG	NEAL	DIAZ	ALVA	DOWD
GUTH	KALR	LOVE	PAIS	SHEN	WONG	HALE	ABBE	NEIL	DICK	BLAS	FORD
GWEN	KANT	LOYS	PANE	SHIH	WOOD	HALL	ABBY	PECK	DIOR	CLAY	GOLD
HAHN	KARK	LUAN	PARE	SHIN	WREN	HANS	ABEL	PERE	DIRK	CLEM	HOCH
HALE	KARL	LUCA	PATI	SHOU	XIEN	HARD	SCOT	PERL	EIKO	ELEK	HOLM
HALL	KARY	LUIS	PAUL	SNOW	YAGA	HARE	ADAM	READ	FINK	ELIA	HOMI
HANS	KEIR	LUNG	PECK	STAN	YANG	HAUY	EDME	REDI	FITZ	ELIE	HOPE
HARD	KENG	LYLE	PERE	STAS	YING	HAWN	EDNA	REED	GIDE	ELIO	HOWE
HARE	KERN	LYNN	PERL	SUNE	YUAN	JAAP	BEAL	REES	GILE	ELMO	HOYT
HAUY	KIDD	LYON	PHIL	SUNG	YURI	JACK	BEAN	REID	GILL	ELSO	JOAN
HAWN	KING	LYOT	PIRE	SVEN	YVES	JANE	BEDE	RENE	HIGH	ILYA	JOEL
HEAD	KIRK	MACH	POLK	SWAN	ZENO	KAHN	BEER	SEAN	HILL	KLAS	JOHN
HEBB	KISH	MANN	POLO	TAFT	ZHOU	KALR	BELA	SEKI	KIDD	KLUG	JOSE
HEIM	KLAS	MARC	PONS	TAMM	ZHUO	KANT	BELL	SETH	KING	OLAH	KOCH
HENG	KLUG	MARK	POPE	TATE	ZING	KARK	BELO	VEHE	KIRK	OLEN	KOPP
HERB	KNOW	MARX	POTT	THOM	ZINN	KARL	BENA	VENN	KISH	OLOF	KORN
HERO	KNUT	MARY	PUZO	TINA	ZUSE	KARY	BENO	VERA	LILA	ULAM	KOSA
HESS	KOCH	MEAD	QUTB	TING		LADY	BENZ	WEBB	LILY	AMES	KOWA
HIGH	KOPP	MELA	RABE	TJIO		LAMB	BERG	WEFA	LIND	EMIL	LOEB
HILL	KORN	MIKE	RABI	TODD	2ND LETTER	LAME	BERN	WEIN	LING	EMMA	LOIS
HOCH	KOSA	MILL	RADO	TOLL		LAND	BERT	WEST	LINK	EMMY	LONG
HOLM	KOWA	MILO	RAHN	TONE	AAGE	LANE	BEST	WEYL	LISA	OMAR	LORD
HOMI	KUEI	MING	RAPU	TONI	BAKR	LANG	CECH	ZENO	LISE	ANDY	LORY
HOPE	KUHN	MIRA	READ	TONY	BARR	LARS	CELA	LFRY	LIZA	ANEL	LOUS
HOWE	KUNG	MOHR	REDI	TREG	BART	MACH	CEVA	AGNE	MIKE	ANNA	LOVE
HOYT	KURI	MOHS	REED	TSAI	BASS	MANN	DEAN	IGOR	MILL	ANNE	LOYS
HSIN	KURT	MONA	REES	TULL	CAGE	MARC	DEHN	NGOR	MILO	INGE	MOHR
HSUN	LADY	MONK	REID	TULP	CAMP	MARK	FELT	CHAN	MING	KNOW	MOHS
HUGH	LAMB	MOON	RENE	TUTU	CANN	MARX	GELL	CHAO	MIRA	KNUT	MONA
HUGO	LAME	MORE	RICK	TUVE	CANO	MARY	GENE	CHEN	NICK	SNOW	MONK
HULL	LAND	MORO	RING	TUZO	CARL	PAGE	GENG	CHER	NIEL	BOAS	MOON
HUME	LANE	MOTT	RITA	UHRY	CARO	PAIS	GERD	CHEW	NILS	BODE	MORE
HUNT	LANG	MUNI	ROCK	ULAM	CARR	PANE	GEZA	CHIA	NING	BOHR	MORO
HURT	LARS	MUSA	ROLF	UREY	CATO	PARE	HEAD	CHIH	NINO	BOIS	MOTT
HYDE	LEAH	NEAL	ROME	URIE	DALE	PATI	HEBB	CHIU	PIRE	BOLL	NOAM
HYOK	LEAN	NEIL	RONA	VANE	DANA	PAUL	HEIM	CHOH	RICK	BOLT	NOEL
IGOR	LECH	NGOR	ROOT	VEHE	DANE	RABE	HENG	CHOU	RING	BOND	OORT
ILYA	LEHN	NICK	ROSE	VENN	DANY	RABI	HERB	CHUN	RITA	BORN	POLK
INGE	LEIF	NIEL	ROSS	VERA	DART	RADO	HERO	PHIL	TINA	BOSE	POLO
IVAN	LENT	NILS	ROTH	VINE	DAVE	RAHN	HESS	SHAO	TING	BOSS	PONS
IVAR	LENZ	NING	ROUS	VITO	DAVY	RAPU	JEAN	SHAW	VINE	BOYD	POPE
IVES	LEON	NINO	ROUX	VOCK	DAWN	SADI	JEFF	SHEN	VITO	CODE	POTT
JAAP	LEVI	NOAM	RUSH	VOGT	EADS	SAHA	JEON	SHIH	WIEN	COHN	ROCK
JACK	LFRY	NOEL	RUTH	WADA	EARL	SALK	KEIR	SHIN	WILM	COKE	ROLF
JANE	LILA	OKEN	RYAN	WALD	FADL	SALT	KENG	SHOU	WING	COLE	ROME
JEAN	LILY	OLAH	RYLE	WANG	FAPP	SATO	KERN	THOM	WISE	COLT	RONA
JEFF	LIND	OLEN	SADI	WARD	FARR	SAUL	LEAH	UHRY	XIEN	COOK	ROOT
JEON	LING	OLOF	SAHA	WATT	FASH	TAFT	LEAN	ZHOU	YING	COPE	ROSE
JOAN	LINK	OMAR	SALK	WEBB	FATH	TAMM	LECH	ZHUO	ZING	CORI	ROSS
JOEL	LISA	OORT	SALT	WEFA	FAYE	TATE	LEHN	AIME	ZINN	CORT	ROTH
JOHN	LISE	OPIE	SATO	WEIN	GAHN	VANE	LEIF	AIRY	TJIO	DODD	ROUS
JOSE	LIZA	OPIE	SAUL	WEST	GAHN	WADA	LENT	BILL	OKEN	DONN	ROUX

TODD	JUDY	BLAS	ROCK	XIEN	BAKR	LAMB	PONS	BORN	BOSS	TUVE	LAMB
TOLL	JUMP	BOAS	VOCK	YVES	COKE	LAME	RENE	BURL	BUSH	DAWN	LOEB
TONE	JUNG	CHAN	ANDY	JEFF	DUKE	ROME	RING	BURT	ELSO	DOWD	QUTB
TONI	JUST	CHAO	BEDE	TAFT	EIKO	TAMM	RONA	BYRD	FASH	GAWA	WEBB
TONY	KUEI	CLAY	BODE	WEFA	MIKE	AGNE	SUNE	CARL	FUST	HAWN	ALEC
VOCK	KUHN	CRAM	BUDD	AAGE	SEKI	ANNA	SUNG	CARO	HESS	HOWE	ERIC
VOGT	KUNG	DEAN	CODE	CAGE	BELA	ANNE	TINA	CARR	JOSE	KOWA	MARC
WOLE	KURI	DIAS	DODD	HIGH	BELL	ARNE	TING	CORI	JUST	BOYD	BOND
WONG	KURT	DIAZ	EADS	HUGH	BELO	ARNO	TONE	CORT	KISH	FAYE	BOYD
WOOD	LUAN	GRAM	FADL	HUGO	BILL	AUNG	TONI	CURL	KOSA	HOYT	BUDD
OPIE	LUCA	GRAY	GIDE	INGE	BOLL	BENA	TONY	DART	LISA	ILYA	BYRD
OPIK	LUIS	HEAD	HYDE	PAGE	BOLT	BENO	VANE	DIRK	LISE	LOYS	DODD
ARNE	LUNG	IVAN	JUDY	VOGT	CELA	BENZ	VENN	DORE	MUSA	WEYL	DOWD
ARNO	MUNI	IVAR	KIDD	YAGA	COLE	BING	VINE	DORN	ROSE	GEZA	FORD
CRAM	MUSA	JAAP	LADY	BOHR	COLT	BINI	WANG	DORR	ROSS	LIZA	FRED
ERIC	PUZO	JEAN	RADO	COHN	DALE	BOND	WING	EARL	RUSH	PUZO	GERD
ERIK	QUTB	JOAN	REDI	DEHN	FELT	CANN	WONG	FARR	WEST	TUZO	GOLD
FRED	RUSH	JUAN	SADI	GAHN	GALE	CANO	YANG	FORD	WISE		HARD
GRAM	RUTH	KLAS	TODD	HAHN	GALL	DANA	YING	GARY	ZUSE		HEAD
GRAY	SUNE	LEAH	WADA	JOHN	GELL	DANE	ZENO	GERD	CATO		KIDD
GREG	SUNG	LEAN	ABEL	KAHN	GILE	DANY	ZING	HARD	FATH	**4TH LETTER**	LAND
GREN	TULL	LUAN	ALEC	KUHN	GILL	DONN	ZINN	HARE	FITZ		LIND
GREW	TULP	MEAD	ALEX	LEHN	GOLD	DUNN	BIOT	HERB	GUTH	ALCA	LORD
GREY	TUTU	NEAL	AMES	MOHR	HALE	DUNS	CHOH	HERO	MOTT	ALVA	MEAD
ORRY	TUVE	NOAM	ANEL	MOHS	HALL	EDNA	CHOU	HURT	OTTO	ANNA	READ
TREG	TUZO	OLAH	AUER	RAHN	HILL	FINK	COOK	KARK	PATI	BELA	REED
UREY	YUAN	OMAR	AXEL	SAHA	HOLM	FUNK	DIOR	KARL	POTT	BENA	REID
URIE	YURI	READ	BEER	VEHE	HULL	GENE	HYOK	KARY	QUTB	CELA	TODD
WREN	ZUSE	RYAN	CHEN	BOIS	KALR	GENG	IGOR	KERN	RITA	CEVA	WALD
HSIN	IVAN	SEAN	CHER	CHIA	LILA	HANS	JEON	KIRK	ROTH	CHIA	WARD
HSUN	IVAR	SHAO	CHEW	CHIH	LILY	HENG	KNOW	KORN	RUTH	DANA	WOOD
TSAI	IVES	SHAW	CLEM	CHIU	LYLE	HUNT	LEON	KURI	SATO	EDNA	AAGE
OTIS	SVEN	STAN	ELEK	ELIA	MELA	JANE	LYON	KURT	SETH	ELIA	ABBE
OTTO	YVES	STAS	EWEN	ELIE	MILL	JUNG	LYOT	LARS	TATE	EMMA	AGNE
STAN	EWEN	SWAN	FRED	ELIO	MILO	KANT	MOON	LFRY	TUTU	GAWA	AIME
STAS	GWEN	TSAI	GREG	EMIL	NILS	KENG	NGOR	LORD	VITO	GEZA	ANNE
AUER	OWEN	ULAM	GREN	ERIC	POLK	KING	OLOF	LORY	WATT	ILYA	ARNE
AUNG	SWAN	YUAN	GREW	ERIK	POLO	KUNG	ROOT	MARC	CHUN	KOSA	BEDE
BUCK	AXEL	ABBE	GREY	GAIL	ROLF	LAND	SCOT	MARK	DOUG	KOWA	BODE
BUDD	BYRD	ABBY	GWEN	HEIM	RYLE	LANE	SHOU	MARX	HAUY	LILA	BOSE
BURL	HYDE	HEBB	IVES	HSIN	SALK	LANG	SNOW	MARY	HSUN	LISA	CAGE
BURT	HYOK	RABE	JOEL	KEIR	SALT	LENT	THOM	MIRA	KLUG	LIZA	CODE
BUSH	LYLE	RABI	KUEI	LEIF	TOLL	LENZ	WOOD	MORE	KNUT	LUCA	COKE
CURL	LYNN	WEBB	LOEB	LOIS	TULL	LIND	ZHOU	MORO	LOUS	MELA	COLE
DUKE	LYON	ALCA	NIEL	LUIS	TULP	LING	COPE	OORT	OKUN	MIRA	COPE
DUNN	LYOT	BUCK	NOEL	NEIL	WALD	LINK	FAPP	ORRY	PAUL	MONA	DALE
DUNS	RYAN	CECH	OKEN	OPIE	WILM	LONG	HOPE	PARE	ROUS	MUSA	DANE
FUNK	RYLE	DICK	OLEN	OPIK	WOLE	LUNG	KOPP	PERE	ROUX	RITA	DAVE
FUST		HOCH	OWEN	OTIS	AIME	LYNN	POPE	PERL	SAUL	RONA	DORE
GUTH		JACK	REED	PAIS	CAMP	MANN	RAPU	PIRE	ZHUO	SAHA	DOVE
HUGH		KOCH	REES	PHIL	EDME	MING	AIRY	UHRY	ALVA	TINA	DUKE
HUGO	**3RD LETTER**	LECH	SHEN	REID	ELMO	MONA	BARR	VERA	CEVA	VERA	EDME
HULL		LUCA	SVEN	SHIH	EMMA	MONK	BART	WARD	DAVE	WADA	ELIE
HUME	ADAM	MACH	TREG	SHIN	EMMY	MUNI	BERG	YURI	DAVY	WEFA	FAYE
HUNT	ALAN	NICK	UREY	TJIO	HOMI	NING	BERN	BASS	DOVE	YAGA	GALE
HURT	BEAL	PECK	WIEN	URIE	HUME	NINO	BERT	BEST	LEVI	HEBB	GENE
JUAN	BEAN	RICK	WREN	WEIN	JUMP	PANE	BIRO	BOSE	LOVE	HERB	GIDE

GILE	LING	FINK	NOAM	SWAN	NGOR	VOGT	ADOLF	BERRY	BYRON	CYRUS	ELMER
HALE	LONG	FUNK	TAMM	VENN	OMAR	WATT	AGNON	BETHE	CABLE	DALEN	ELVEN
HARE	LUNG	HYOK	THOM	WEIN	AMES	WEST	AHMAD	BETTE	CAINE	DANBY	ELWYN
HOPE	MING	JACK	ULAM	WIEN	BASS	CHIU	AHMES	BETTY	CAJAL	DANNY	EMERT
HOWE	NING	KARK	WILM	WREN	BLAS	CHOU	AIKEN	BEVIS	CAMUS	DANTE	EMILE
HUME	RING	KIRK	ALAN	XIEN	BOAS	RAPU	AKIRA	BHANU	CAPEK	DARBY	EMILY
HYDE	SUNG	LINK	BEAN	YUAN	BOIS	SHOU	ALDER	BILLY	CAPRA	DARIO	ENCKE
INGE	TING	MARK	BERN	ZINN	BOSS	TUTU	ALDUS	BINET	CAREL	DAVID	ENNIO
JANE	TREG	MONK	BORN	ARNO	DIAS	ZHOU	ALEXI	BIROC	CARLO	DAVIS	ERICH
JOSE	WANG	NICK	CANN	BELO	DUNS	CHEW	ALICE	BLACK	CAROL	DAWES	ERMAN
LAME	WING	OPIK	CHAN	BENO	EADS	GREW	ALICK	BLAKE	CAROL	DEBYE	ERNST
LANE	WONG	PECK	CHEN	BIRO	HANS	KNOW	ALLAN	BLANE	CECIL	DELLA	ERWIN
LISE	YANG	POLK	CHUN	CANO	HESS	SHAW	ALLEN	BLISS	CELVE	DEMME	ESAKI
LOVE	YING	RICK	COHN	CARO	IVES	SNOW	ALMON	BLOCH	CERNY	DENIS	ETHEL
LYLE	ZING	ROCK	DAWN	CATO	KLAS	ALEX	ALOYS	BLOCK	CESAR	DEREK	EUGEN
MIKE	BUSH	SALK	DEAN	CHAO	LARS	MARX	ALTER	BLOOM	CHACE	DERVA	EULER
MORE	CECH	VOCK	DEHN	EIKO	LOIS	ROUX	ALTON	BODEN	CHAIM	DEWAR	EVANS
OPIE	CHIH	ABEL	DONN	ELIO	LOUS	ABBY	ALVAN	BONDI	CHAIN	DEWEY	EWALD
PAGE	CHOH	ANEL	DORN	ELMO	LOYS	AIRY	ALVIN	BOOLE	CHANG	DIANE	EWING
PANE	FASH	AXEL	DUNN	ELSO	LUIS	ANDY	AMICI	BOOTH	CHENG	DICKE	FABRI
PARE	FATH	BEAL	EWEN	HERO	MOHS	CLAY	ANDRE	BOREL	CHIAO	DIELS	FABRY
PERE	GUTH	BELL	GAHN	HUGO	NILS	DANY	ANGEL	BORIS	CHIEH	DIRAC	FALSE
PIRE	HIGH	BILL	GREN	MILO	OTIS	DAVY	ANNIE	BOSCH	CHIEN	DIXON	FAZAN
POPE	HOCH	BOLL	GWEN	MORO	PAIS	EMMY	ANTON	BOTHE	CHING	DOELL	FEGTE
RABE	HUGH	BURL	HAHN	NINO	PONS	GARY	ANWAR	BOTTA	CHONG	DOISY	FELIX
RENE	KISH	CARL	HAWN	OTTO	REES	GRAY	APIAN	BOULE	CHRIS	DOLBY	FERMI
ROME	KOCH	CURL	HSIN	POLO	ROSS	GREY	ARAGO	BOVET	CHUBB	DONAT	FERRO
ROSE	LEAH	EARL	HSUN	PUZO	ROUS	HAUY	ARBER	BOWEN	CHUCK	DONNA	FIELD
RYLE	LECH	EMIL	IVAN	RADO	STAS	JUDY	ARIAS	BOYER	CHUNG	DORIS	FINCH
SUNE	MACH	FADL	JEAN	SATO	YVES	KARY	ARLEN	BOYLE	CLARA	DOUST	FIORE
TATE	OLAH	GAIL	JEON	SHAO	BART	LADY	ARVID	BOYSE	CLARK	DRACH	FITCH
TONE	ROTH	GALL	JOAN	TJIO	BERT	LFRY	ASAPH	BRADY	CLAUS	DRAKE	FLORY
TUVE	RUSH	GELL	JOHN	TUZO	BEST	LILY	ASHBY	BRAGG	CLERK	DRESS	FLOYD
URIE	RUTH	GILL	JUAN	VITO	BIOT	LORY	ASSER	BRAHE	CLIFF	DRUDE	FOCKE
VANE	SETH	HALL	KAHN	ZENO	BOLT	MARY	ASTON	BRAID	CLINE	DUBIN	FONDA
VEHE	SHIH	HILL	KERN	ZHUO	BURT	ORRY	ASTOR	BRAJA	CLINT	DUBOS	FOOTE
VINE	BINI	HULL	KORN	CAMP	COLT	TONY	AVARY	BRAND	CLYDE	DUMAS	FORTT
WISE	CORI	JOEL	KUHN	FAPP	CORT	UHRY	AVERY	BRAUN	COHEN	DURER	FOSSE
WOLE	HOMI	KARL	LEAN	JAAP	DART	UREY	BAKER	BREEN	COLIN	DYSON	FOWLE
ZUSE	KUEI	MILL	LEHN	JUMP	FELT	BENZ	BANKS	BRENT	COMER	EBERS	FRANK
JEFF	KURI	NEAL	LEON	KOPP	FUST	DIAZ	BARON	BRIAN	COMTE	EBING	FRANS
LEIF	LEVI	NEIL	LUAN	TULP	HOYT	FITZ	BARRY	BRINK	CONON	EDDIE	FRANZ
OLOF	MUNI	NIEL	LYNN	AUER	HUNT	LENZ	BARUJ	BROCA	CONTI	EDGAR	FREGE
ROLF	PATI	NOEL	LYON	BAKR	HURT		BASIL	BROOK	COREY	EDITH	FREMY
AUNG	RABI	PAUL	MANN	BARR	JUST		BASOV	BROOM	CORNU	EDLEN	FRERE
BERG	REDI	PERL	MOON	BEER	KANT		BASSI	BROWN	COSTA	EDWIN	FREUD
BING	SADI	PHIL	OKEN	BOHR	KNUT	**5 LETTER**	BATES	BRUCE	COTES	EEMIL	FRIED
DOUG	SEKI	SAUL	OKUN	CARR	KURT	**1st LETTER**	BAUME	BRUNO	COUNT	EIGEN	FRIES
GENG	TONI	TOLL	OLEN	CHER	LENT		BAYER	BRYAN	COURT	EJNAR	FRITZ
GREG	TSAI	TULL	OWEN	DIOR	LYOT	AARON	BEACH	BUELL	COWAN	ELERT	FROSH
HENG	YURI	WEYL	RAHN	DORR	MOTT	ABDUS	BEAMS	BUNIN	CRAIG	ELIAS	FUCHS
JUNG	BUCK	ADAM	RYAN	FARR	OORT	ABEGG	BEEBE	BURGI	CRICK	ELIHU	FUKUI
KENG	COOK	CLEM	SEAN	IGOR	POTT	ABNEY	BEERY	BURKE	CRISP	ELION	FURSE
KING	DICK	CRAM	SHEN	IVAR	ROOT	ABNEY	BEGIN	BURKS	CROSS	ELIOT	FURST
KLUG	DIRK	GRAM	SHIN	KALR	SALT	ADAIR	BELON	BURNS	CUKOR	ELLEN	GABLE
KUNG	ELEK	HEIM	STAN	KEIR	SCOT	ADAMS	BENGT	BURTT	CURIE	ELLET	GABOR
LANG	ERIK	HOLM	SVEN	MOHR	TAFT	ADLER	BEPPO	BYRAM	CYRIL	ELLIS	GAEDE

GALEN	HEMAN	JORIE	LEIGH	MCKAY	OWENS	REICH	SOREN	VITUS	CAPRA	LAMAS	SAINT
GALLE	HENCH	JOSEF	LEONE	MENES	PABLO	REISS	SPIES	VOGEL	CAREL	LANDE	SAKEL
GAMOW	HENLE	JOSIE	LEVAN	MERAY	PABST	REMAK	SPORN	VOLTA	CARLO	LANGE	SALAM
GARRY	HENRI	JOULE	LEVEN	MERLE	PACKE	RENIE	SSUMA	WAAGE	CAROL	LARRY	SALLY
GATES	HENRY	JUDAH	LEWIS	MERYL	PADDY	RHIND	STAIN	WALAS	DALEN	LAURA	SANDY
GAUSS	HEROD	JULES	LIANG	METON	PAGET	RHINE	STARK	WALDO	DANBY	LAWES	SANZO
GEBER	HERON	JULIA	LIBBY	METTY	PANUM	RICCI	STEEN	WALSH	DANNY	LAZLO	SARAH
GEENA	HERTZ	JULIE	LINDA	MEYER	PAOLO	RIGHI	STENO	WAYNE	DANTE	MABEL	SAYED
GEMMA	HESSE	JUNGE	LINDE	MILES	PAPIN	RINIO	STERN	WEBER	DARBY	MAEVE	TAIEB
GEORG	HEYSE	JURAN	LINUS	MILLS	PARRY	ROALD	STEVE	WEISS	DARIO	MALEY	TALLY
GERMI	HIGGS	KAMAL	LIZZY	MILNE	PASCH	ROBIN	STOCK	WELLS	DAVID	MALUS	TALVA
GEROG	HIRAM	KAMEN	LLOYD	MILOS	PASSY	ROCHE	STOLL	WENDY	DAVIS	MARCH	TAMBI
GERRY	HOKIN	KANIN	LOCKE	MINOS	PATTY	ROGER	STONE	WHITE	DAWES	MARCO	TANDY
GERTY	HOLLY	KAREL	LODGE	MINOT	PAULI	ROLLE	STOUT	WHYTT	FABRI	MAREY	TATUM
GIBBS	HONDA	KARLE	LOEWI	MOLLO	PAVEL	ROMER	STRHL	WIARD	FABRY	MARIA	TAUBE
GIGER	HOOKE	KATHY	LOGIE	MONGE	PAYEN	ROOKE	SUESS	WIEST	FALSE	MARIE	VASCO
GILES	HOPPE	KAZAN	LOREN	MONIZ	PAYNE	ROSSE	SUGER	WILDT	FAZAN	MARIK	WAAGE
GILKS	HORTA	KEIKE	LORNE	MONOD	PEANO	ROSSI	SULLY	WILES	GABLE	MARIN	WALAS
GLENN	HOUCK	KEITH	LOTKA	MOORE	PEARL	ROUSE	SUSAN	WILEY	GABOR	MARIO	WALDO
GLUCK	HOYLE	KELLY	LOUIS	MORSE	PEARY	ROWAN	SYNGE	WILLY	GAEDE	MARKO	WALSH
GOBAT	HUANG	KEOGH	LOWER	MOSES	PEDRO	ROYDS	SZENT	WIRTH	GALEN	MARSH	WAYNE
GODEL	HUBEL	KERST	LOWIG	MOTTE	PEGGY	RUBEL	TAIEB	WOLFF	GALLE	MASON	YALOW
GODOY	HUBER	KEVIN	LOYAL	MOULD	PERCY	RUBIN	TALLY	WOODY	GAMOW	MAURY	ABDUS
GOERG	HULSE	KIRSH	LUCAS	MOYER	PERES	RUEHL	TALVA	WUNDT	GARRY	MAXIM	ABEGG
GOLGI	HYATT	KLAUS	LUCIO	MPILO	PEREY	RUNGE	TAMBI	WURTZ	GATES	MAYER	ABNEY
GOMPF	HYMAN	KLEBS	LUIGI	MUREN	PEREZ	RUSKA	TANDY	WYLER	GAUSS	MAYOW	EBERS
GOULD	HYMNS	KLEIN	LUISE	NAMBU	PERSE	SABIN	TATUM	WYMAN	HABER	NAMBU	EBING
GRACE	HYRON	KLINE	LUKAS	NANCY	PESCI	SACHS	TAUBE	YALOW	HAIGH	NANCY	ICIRO
GRANT	ICIRO	KOLBE	LULLY	NASIR	PETER	SAGAN	TEMIN	YEATS	HAING	NASIR	MCKAY
GREEN	IGNAZ	KOLFF	LUNDH	NATTA	PETIT	SAINT	TESLA	YOSEF	HAISE	NATTA	OCHOA
GREER	IHNEN	KORDA	LURIA	NEELY	PFAFF	SAKEL	THAER	YOUNG	HALES	PABLO	SCOTT
GREGG	ILICH	KOSMA	LUSKE	NEHER	PIERO	SALAM	THEON	YUANG	HAMAO	PABST	ADAIR
GROSS	INNES	KOWAL	LUZZI	NEILL	PINEL	SALLY	THIEL	YUSEF	HANEY	PACKE	ADAMS
GROTE	INOUE	KRAMS	LWOFF	NELLY	PIXII	SANDY	TIBOR	ZENER	HANKS	PADDY	ADLER
GROVE	IRENE	KREBS	LYELL	NEVIL	PLATO	SANZO	TITOV	ZHANG	HANNO	PAGET	ADOLF
GUYOT	IRONS	KRESS	LYMAN	NICOL	PLATT	SARAH	TOLDY		HANNS	PANUM	EDDIE
GWENN	IRVIN	KROGH	LYNDS	NIELS	PLAUT	SAYED	TOMEI		HARDY	PAOLO	EDGAR
HABER	IRWIN	KROTO	LYNEN	NILES	PLINY	SCOTT	TOMMY		HARRY	PAPIN	EDITH
HAIGH	ISAAC	KRUPP	MABEL	NIVEN	POPOV	SEGRE	TOWNE	**2ND LETTER**	HARTZ	PARRY	EDLEN
HAING	JABIR	KUHNE	MAEVE	NIXON	PORTA	SELMA	TRACY		HAUGE	PASCH	EDWIN
HAISE	JACOB	KUNDT	MALEY	NOBEL	PREGL	SELYE	TRETZ	AARON	HAYES	PASSY	BEACH
HALES	JAKOB	KUNIO	MALUS	NOBLE	PROUT	SETON	TRYON	BAKER	JABIR	PATTY	BEAMS
HAMAO	JAMES	KURTZ	MARCH	NORMA	PUPIN	SHARP	TSENG	BANKS	JACOB	PAULI	BEEBE
HANEY	JANET	KUSCH	MARCO	NORTH	PYOTR	SHENG	TSUNG	BARON	JAKOB	PAVEL	BEERY
HANKS	JANOS	LAING	MAREY	NUFER	QUEEN	SHORT	TULLY	BARRY	JAMES	PAYEN	BEGIN
HANNO	JASON	LAMAR	MARIA	NUNES	QUICK	SHULL	TUROK	BARUJ	JANET	PAYNE	BELON
HANNS	JEANS	LAMAS	MARIE	NUNEZ	RABIN	SIMIC	TWORT	BASIL	JANOS	RABIN	BENGT
HARDY	JENNY	LANDE	MARIK	OCHOA	RAINE	SIMON	TYCHO	BASOV	JASON	RAINE	BEPPO
HARRY	JERNE	LANGE	MARIN	OGAWA	RALPH	SISSY	TYLER	BASSI	KAMAL	RALPH	BERRY
HARTZ	JESSE	LARRY	MARIO	OGDEN	RAMAN	SKALL	TYLOR	BATES	KAMEN	RAMAN	BETHE
HAUGE	JIMMY	LAURA	MARKO	OLSON	RAMON	SMALL	TYTUS	BAUME	KANIN	RAMON	BETTE
HAYES	JODIE	LAWES	MARSH	ONNES	RAMOS	SMITH	ULUGH	BAYER	KAREL	RAMOS	BETTY
HEBER	JOHAN	LAZLO	MASON	ORBOM	RAMUS	SNELL	UMEKI	CABLE	KARLE	RAMUS	BEVIS
HECHT	JOHNS	LEBON	MAURY	ORSON	RAOUL	SODDY	VASCO	CAINE	KATHY	RAOUL	CECIL
HEINE	JONAS	LECOQ	MAXIM	OSCAR	REBER	SOLON	VERNA	CAJAL	KAZAN	SABIN	CELVE
HEINZ	JONES	LEDER	MAYER	OSKAR	REESE	SONYA	VESTO	CAMUS	LAING	SACHS	CERNY
HELEN	JOOST	LEGER	MAYOW	OSLER	REGAN	SORBY	VIETA	CAPEK	LAMAR	SAGAN	CESAR

DEBYE	MERLE	CHIAO	NIELS	ELIHU	BOYSE	KOWAL	SPIES	IRONS	FUKUI	LWOFF	DRACH
DELLA	MERYL	CHIEH	NILES	ELION	COHEN	LOCKE	SPORN	IRVIN	FURSE	OWENS	DRAKE
DEMME	METON	CHIEN	NIVEN	ELIOT	COLIN	LODGE	ARAGO	IRWIN	FURST	TWORT	ESAKI
DENIS	METTY	CHING	NIXON	ELLEN	COMER	LOEWI	ARBER	KRAMS	GUYOT	BYRAM	EVANS
DEREK	MEYER	CHONG	PIERO	ELLET	COMTE	LOGIE	ARIAS	KREBS	HUANG	BYRON	EWALD
DERVA	NEELY	CHRIS	PINEL	ELLIS	CONON	LOREN	ARLEN	KRESS	HUBEL	CYRIL	FRANK
DEWAR	NEHER	CHUBB	PIXII	ELMER	CONTI	LORNE	ARVID	KROGH	HUBER	CYRUS	FRANS
DEWEY	NEILL	CHUCK	RICCI	ELVEN	COREY	LOTKA	BRADY	KR'OTO	HULSE	DYSON	FRANZ
EEMIL	NELLY	CHUNG	RIGHI	ELWYN	CORNU	LOUIS	BRAGG	KRUPP	JUDAH	HYATT	GRACE
FEGTE	NEVIL	IHNEN	RINIO	FLORY	COSTA	LOWER	BRAHE	ORBOM	JULES	HYMAN	GRANT
FELIX	PEANO	RHIND	SIMIC	FLOYD	COTES	LOWIG	BRAID	ORSON	JULIA	HYMNS	HUANG
FERMI	PEARL	RHINE	SIMON	GLENN	COUCH	LOYAL	BRAJA	PREGL	JULIE	HYRON	HYATT
FERRO	PEARY	SHARP	SISSY	GLUCK	COUNT	MOLLO	BRAND	PROUT	JUNGE	LYELL	ISAAC
GEBER	PEDRO	SHENG	TIBOR	ILICH	COURT	MONGE	BRAUN	TRACY	JURAN	LYMAN	JEANS
GEENA	PEGGY	SHORT	TITOV	KLAUS	COWAN	MONIZ	BREEN	TRETZ	KUHNE	LYNDS	KLAUS
GEMMA	PERCY	SHULL	VIETA	KLEBS	DOELL	MONOD	BRENT	TRYON	KUNDT	LYNEN	KRAMS
GEORG	PERES	THAER	VITUS	KLEIN	DOISY	MOORE	BRIAN	ASAPH	KUNIO	PYOTR	LIANG
GERMI	PEREY	THEON	WIARD	KLINE	DOLBY	MORSE	BRINK	ASHBY	KURTZ	SYNGE	OGAWA
GEROG	PEREZ	THIEL	WIEST	LLOYD	DONAT	MOSES	BROCA	ASSER	KUSCH	TYCHO	PEANO
GERRY	PERSE	WHITE	WILDT	OLSON	DONNA	MOTTE	BROOK	ASTON	LUCAS	TYLER	PEARL
GERTY	PESCI	WHYTT	WILES	PLATO	DORIS	MOULD	BROOM	ASTOR	LUCIO	TYLOR	PEARY
HEBER	PETER	ZHANG	WILEY	PLATT	DOUST	MOYER	BROWN	ESAKI	LUIGI	TYTUS	PFAFF
HECHT	PETIT	AIKEN	WILLY	PLAUT	FOCKE	NOBEL	BRUCE	ISAAC	LUISE	WYLER	PLATO
HEINE	REBER	BILLY	WIRTH	PLINY	FONDA	NOBLE	BRUNO	OSCAR	LUKAS	WYMAN	PLATT
HEINZ	REESE	BINET	EJNAR	ULUGH	FOOTE	NORMA	BRYAN	OSKAR	LULLY	SZENT	PLAUT
HELEN	REGAN	BIROC	AKIRA	AMICI	FORTT	NORTH	CRAIG	OSLER	LUNDH		ROALD
HEMAN	REICH	DIANE	SKALL	EMERT	FOSSE	POPOV	CRICK	SSUMA	LURIA		SHARP
HENCH	REISS	DICKE	ALDER	EMILE	FOWLE	PORTA	CRISP	TSENG	LUSKE		SKALL
HENLE	REMAK	DIELS	ALDUS	EMILY	GOBAT	ROALD	CROSS	TSUNG	LUZZI	**3RD LETTER**	SMALL
HENRI	RENIE	DIRAC	ALEXI	SMALL	GODEL	ROBIN	DRACH	ETHEL	MUREN		STAIN
HENRY	SEGRE	DIXON	ALICE	SMITH	GODOY	ROGER	DRAKE	STAIN	NUFER	ADAIR	STARK
HEROD	SELMA	EIGEN	ALICK	UMEKI	GOERG	ROLLE	DRESS	STARK	NUNES	ADAMS	THAER
HERON	SELYE	FIELD	ALLAN	ANDRE	GOLGI	ROMER	DRUDE	STEEN	NUNEZ	ARAGO	TRACY
HERTZ	SETON	FINCH	ALLEN	ANGEL	GOMPF	ROOKE	ERICH	STENO	PUPIN	ASAPH	WAAGE
HESSE	TEMIN	FIORE	ALMON	ANNIE	GOULD	ROSSE	ERMAN	STERN	QUEEN	AVARY	WIARD
HEYSE	TESLA	FITCH	ALOYS	ANTON	HOKIN	ROSSI	ERNST	STEVE	QUICK	BEACH	YEATS
JEANS	VERNA	GIBBS	ALTER	ANWAR	HOLLY	ROSSI	ERWIN	STOCK	RUBEL	BEAMS	YUANG
JENNY	VESTO	GIGER	ALTON	ENCKE	HONDA	ROUSE	FRANK	STOLL	RUBIN	BHANU	ZHANG
JERNE	WEBER	GILES	ALVAN	ENNIO	HOOKE	ROWAN	FRANS	STONE	RUEHL	BLACK	ARBER
JESSE	WEISS	GILKS	ALVIN	INNES	HOPPE	ROYDS	FRANZ	STOUT	RUNGE	BLAKE	CABLE
KEIKE	WELLS	HIGGS	BLACK	INOUE	HORTA	SODDY	FREGE	STRHL	RUSKA	BLANE	DEBYE
KEITH	WENDY	HIRAM	BLAKE	ONNES	HOUCK	SOLON	FREMY	BUELL	SUESS	BRADY	DUBIN
KELLY	YEATS	JIMMY	BLANE	SNELL	HOYLE	SONYA	FRERE	BUNIN	SUGER	BRAGG	DUBOS
KEOGH	ZENER	KIRSH	BLISS	BODEN	JODIE	SORBY	FREUD	BURGI	SULLY	BRAHE	FABRI
KERST	PFAFF	LIANG	BLOCH	BONDI	JOHAN	SOREN	FRIED	BURKE	SUSAN	BRAID	FABRY
KEVIN	AGNON	LIBBY	BLOCK	BOOLE	JOHNS	TOLDY	FRIES	BURKS	TULLY	BRAJA	GABLE
LEBON	IGNAZ	LINDA	BLOOM	BOOTH	JONAS	TOMEI	FRITZ	BURNS	TUROK	BRAND	GABOR
LECOQ	OGAWA	LINDE	CLARA	BOREL	JONES	TOMMY	FROSH	BURTT	WUNDT	BRAUN	GEBER
LEDER	OGDEN	LINUS	CLARK	BORIS	JOOST	TOWNE	GRACE	CUKOR	WURTZ	CHACE	GIBBS
LEGER	AHMAD	LIZZY	CLAUS	BOSCH	JORIE	VOGEL	GRANT	CURIE	YUANG	CHAIM	GOBAT
LEIGH	AHMES	MILES	CLERK	BOTHE	JOSEF	VOLTA	GREEN	DUBIN	YUSEF	CHAIN	HABER
LEONE	BHANU	MILLS	CLIFF	BOTTA	JOSIE	WOLFF	GREER	DUBOS	AVARY	CHANG	HEBER
LEVAN	CHACE	MILNE	CLINE	BOULE	JOULE	WOODY	GREGG	DUMAS	AVERY	CLARA	HUBEL
LEVEN	CHAIM	MILOS	CLINT	BOVET	KOLBE	YOSEF	GROSS	DURER	EVANS	CLARK	HUBER
LEWIS	CHAIN	MINOS	CLYDE	BOWEN	KOLFF	YOUNG	GROTE	EUGEN	EWALD	CLAUS	JABIR
MENES	CHANG	MINOT	ELERT	BOYER	KORDA	APIAN	GROVE	EULER	EWING	CRAIG	LEBON
MERAY	CHENG	NICOL	ELIAS	BOYLE	KOSMA	MPILO	IRENE	FUCHS	GWENN	DIANE	LIBBY

MABEL	CLERK	GIGER	HEINE	GALLE	DEMME	HANNS	BROOK	BURNS	MARIE	SUSAN	PAULI
NOBEL	DIELS	HIGGS	HEINZ	GILES	DUMAS	HENCH	BROOM	BURTT	MARIK	TESLA	ROUSE
NOBLE	DOELL	LEGER	ICIRO	GILKS	EEMIL	HENLE	BROWN	BYRAM	MARIN	VASCO	SHULL
ORBOM	DRESS	LOGIE	ILICH	GOLGI	ELMER	HENRI	CHONG	BYRON	MARIO	VESTO	SSUMA
PABLO	EBERS	PAGET	KEIKE	HALES	ERMAN	HENRY	CROSS	CAREL	MARKO	YOSEF	TAUBE
PABST	ELERT	PEGGY	KEITH	HELEN	GAMOW	HONDA	FIORE	CARLO	MARSH	YUSEF	TSUNG
RABIN	EMERT	REGAN	KLINE	HOLLY	GEMMA	IGNAZ	FLORY	CAROL	MERAY	ALTER	ULUGH
REBER	FIELD	RIGHI	LAING	HULSE	GOMPF	IHNEN	FLOYD	CERNY	MERLE	ALTON	YOUNG
ROBIN	FREGE	ROGER	LEIGH	JULES	HAMAO	INNES	FOOTE	CHRIS	MERYL	ANTON	ALVAN
RUBEL	FREMY	SAGAN	LUIGI	JULIA	HEMAN	JANET	FROSH	COREY	MORSE	ASTON	ALVIN
RUBIN	FRERE	SEGRE	LUISE	JULIE	HYMAN	JANOS	GEORG	CORNU	MUREN	ASTOR	ARVID
SABIN	FREUD	SUGER	MPILO	KELLY	HYMNS	JENNY	GROSS	CURIE	NORMA	BATES	BEVIS
TIBOR	GAEDE	VOGEL	NEILL	KOLBE	JAMES	JONAS	GROTE	CYRIL	NORTH	BETHE	BOVET
WEBER	GEENA	ASHBY	PLINY	KOLFF	JIMMY	JONES	GROVE	CYRUS	PARRY	BETTE	DAVID
CECIL	GLENN	COHEN	QUICK	LULLY	KAMAL	JUNGE	HOOKE	DARBY	PERCY	BETTY	DAVIS
DICKE	GOERG	ETHEL	RAINE	MALEY	KAMEN	KANIN	INOUE	DARIO	PERES	BOTHE	ELVEN
ENCKE	GREEN	JOHAN	REICH	MALUS	LAMAR	KUNDT	IRONS	DEREK	PEREY	BOTTA	IRVIN
FOCKE	GREER	JOHNS	REISS	MILES	LAMAS	KUNIO	JOOST	DERVA	PEREZ	COTES	KEVIN
FUCHS	GREGG	KUHNE	RHIND	MILLS	LYMAN	LANDE	KEOGH	DIRAC	PERSE	FITCH	LEVAN
HECHT	GWENN	NEHER	RHINE	MILNE	NAMBU	LANGE	KROGH	DORIS	PORTA	GATES	LEVEN
JACOB	IRENE	OCHOA	SAINT	MILOS	RAMAN	LINDA	KROTO	DURER	SARAH	KATHY	NEVIL
LECOQ	KLEBS	AKIRA	SMITH	MOLLO	RAMON	LINDE	LEONE	FERMI	SORBY	LOTKA	NIVEN
LOCKE	KLEIN	ALICE	SPIES	NELLY	RAMOS	LINUS	LLOYD	FERRO	SOREN	METON	PAVEL
LUCAS	KREBS	ALICK	TAIEB	NILES	RAMUS	LUNDH	LWOFF	FORTT	STRHL	METTY	ANWAR
LUCIO	KRESS	AMICI	THIEL	OSLER	REMAK	LYNDS	MOORE	FURSE	TUROK	MOTTE	BOWEN
NICOL	LOEWI	APIAN	WEISS	RALPH	ROMER	LYNEN	PAOLO	FURST	VERNA	NATTA	COWAN
OSCAR	LYELL	ARIAS	WHITE	ROLLE	SIMIC	MENES	PROUT	GARRY	WIRTH	PATTY	DAWES
PACKE	MAEVE	BLISS	CAJAL	SALAM	SIMON	MINOS	PYOTR	GERMI	WURTZ	PETER	DEWAR
RICCI	NEELY	BRIAN	AIKEN	SALLY	TAMBI	MINOT	RAOUL	GEROG	ASSER	PETIT	DEWEY
ROCHE	NIELS	BRINK	BAKER	SELMA	TEMIN	MONGE	ROOKE	GERRY	BASIL	SETON	EDWIN
SACHS	OWENS	CAINE	CUKOR	SELYE	TOMEI	MONIZ	SCOTT	GERTY	BASOV	TATUM	ELWYN
TYCHO	PIERO	CHIAO	FUKUI	SOLON	TOMMY	MONOD	SHORT	HARDY	BASSI	TITOV	ERWIN
ABDUS	PREGL	CHIEH	HOKIN	SULLY	WYMAN	NANCY	SPORN	HARRY	BOSCH	TYTUS	FOWLE
ALDER	QUEEN	CHIEN	JAKOB	TALLY	ABNEY	NUNES	STOCK	HARTZ	CESAR	VITUS	IRWIN
ALDUS	REESE	CHING	LUKAS	TALVA	AGNON	NUNEZ	STOLL	HEROD	COSTA	BAUME	KOWAL
ANDRE	RUEHL	CLIFF	MCKAY	TOLDY	ANNIE	ONNES	STONE	HERON	DYSON	BOULE	LAWES
BODEN	SHENG	CLINE	OSKAR	TULLY	BANKS	PANUM	STOUT	HERTZ	FOSSE	BRUCE	LEWIS
EDDIE	SNELL	CLINT	SAKEL	TYLER	BENGT	PINEL	TWORT	HIRAM	HESSE	BRUNO	LOWER
GODEL	STEEN	CRICK	ADLER	TYLOR	BINET	RENIE	WOODY	HORTA	JASON	CHUBB	LOWIG
GODOY	STENO	CRISP	ALLAN	VOLTA	BONDI	RINIO	BEPPO	HYRON	JESSE	CHUCK	ROWAN
JODIE	STERN	DOISY	ALLEN	WALAS	BUNIN	RUNGE	CAPEK	JERNE	JOSEF	CHUNG	TOWNE
JUDAH	STEVE	EBING	ARLEN	WALDO	CONON	SANDY	CAPRA	JORIE	JOSIE	COUCH	DIXON
LEDER	SUESS	EDITH	BELON	WALSH	CONTI	SANZO	HOPPE	JURAN	KOSMA	COUNT	MAXIM
LODGE	SZENT	ELIAS	BILLY	WELLS	DANBY	SONYA	PAPIN	KAREL	KUSCH	COURT	NIXON
OGDEN	THEON	ELIHU	CELVE	WILDT	DANNY	SYNGE	POPOV	KARLE	LUSKE	DOUST	PIXII
PADDY	TRETZ	ELION	COLIN	WILES	DANTE	TANDY	PUPIN	KERST	MASON	DRUDE	BAYER
PEDRO	TSENG	ELIOT	DALEN	WILEY	DENIS	WENDY	AARON	KIRSH	MOSES	GAUSS	BOYER
SODDY	UMEKI	EMILE	DELLA	WILLY	DONAT	WUNDT	BARON	KORDA	NASIR	GLUCK	BOYLE
ABEGG	VIETA	EMILY	DOLBY	WOLFF	DONNA	ZENER	BARRY	KURTZ	OLSON	GOULD	BOYSE
ALEXI	WIEST	ERICH	EDLEN	WYLER	EJNAR	ADOLF	BARUJ	LARRY	ORSON	HAUGE	BRYAN
AVERY	NUFER	EWING	ELLEN	YALOW	ENNIO	ALOYS	BERRY	LOREN	PASCH	HOUCK	CLYDE
BEEBE	ANGEL	FRIED	ELLET	AHMAD	ERNST	BLOCH	BIROC	LORNE	PASSY	JOULE	GUYOT
BEERY	BEGIN	FRIES	ELLIS	AHMES	FINCH	BLOCK	BOREL	LURIA	PESCI	KRUPP	HAYES
BREEN	EDGAR	FRITZ	EULER	ALMON	FONDA	BLOOM	BORIS	MARCH	ROSSE	LAURA	HEYSE
BRENT	EIGEN	HAIGH	FALSE	CAMUS	HANEY	BOOLE	BURGI	MARCO	ROSSI	LOUIS	HOYLE
BUELL	EUGEN	HAING	FELIX	COMER	HANKS	BOOTH	BURKE	MAREY	RUSKA	MAURY	LOYAL
CHENG	FEGTE	HAISE	GALEN	COMTE	HANNO	BROCA	BURKS	MARIA	SISSY	MOULD	MAYER

MAYOW	LAMAS	ILICH	BOVET	LOREN	LWOFF	CURIE	BANKS	NIELS	EWING	BELON	HOPPE
MEYER	LEVAN	KUSCH	BOWEN	LOWER	PFAFF	CYRIL	BLAKE	NOBLE	FRANK	BIROC	KRUPP
MOYER	LOYAL	MARCH	BOYER	LYNEN	WOLFF	DARIO	BURKE	PABLO	FRANS	BLOOM	RALPH
PAYEN	LUCAS	MARCO	BREEN	MABEL	ABEGG	DAVID	BURKS	PAOLO	FRANZ	BROOK	AKIRA
PAYNE	LUKAS	NANCY	CAPEK	MALEY	ARAGO	DAVIS	DICKE	PAULI	GEENA	BROOM	ANDRE
ROYDS	LYMAN	PASCH	CAREL	MAREY	BENGT	DENIS	DRAKE	ROALD	GLENN	BYRON	AVARY
SAYED	MCKAY	PERCY	CHIEH	MAYER	BRAGG	DORIS	ENCKE	ROLLE	GRANT	CAROL	AVERY
TRYON	MERAY	PESCI	CHIEN	MENES	BURGI	DUBIN	ESAKI	SALLY	GWENN	CONON	BARRY
WAYNE	OSCAR	QUICK	COHEN	MEYER	FREGE	EDDIE	FOCKE	SHULL	HAING	CUKOR	BEERY
WHYTT	OSKAR	REICH	COMER	MILES	GOLGI	EDWIN	GILKS	SKALL	HANNO	DIXON	BERRY
FAZAN	RAMAN	RICCI	COREY	MOSES	GREGG	EEMIL	HANKS	SMALL	HANNS	DUBOS	CAPRA
KAZAN	REGAN	STOCK	COTES	MOYER	HAIGH	ELLIS	HOOKE	SNELL	HEINE	DYSON	CLARA
LAZLO	REMAK	TRACY	DALEN	MUREN	HAUGE	ENNIO	KEIKE	STOLL	HEINZ	ELION	CLARK
LIZZY	ROWAN	VASCO	DAWES	NEHER	HIGGS	ERWIN	LOCKE	SULLY	HUANG	ELIOT	CLERK
LUZZI	SAGAN	BONDI	DEREK	NILES	JUNGE	FELIX	LOTKA	TALLY	HYMNS	GABOR	COURT
	SALAM	BRADY	DEWEY	NIVEN	KEOGH	HOKIN	LUSKE	TESLA	IRENE	GAMOW	EBERS
	SARAH	CLYDE	DURER	NOBEL	KROGH	IRVIN	MARKO	TULLY	IRONS	GEROG	ELERT
	SUSAN	DRUDE	EDLEN	NUFER	LANGE	IRWIN	PACKE	WELLS	JEANS	GODOY	EMERT
4TH LETTER	WALAS	FONDA	EIGEN	NUNES	LEIGH	JABIR	ROOKE	WILLY	JENNY	GUYOT	FABRI
	WYMAN	GAEDE	ELLEN	NUNEZ	LODGE	JODIE	RUSKA	ADAMS	JERNE	HEROD	FABRY
AHMAD	ASHBY	HARDY	ELLET	OGDEN	LUIGI	JORIE	UMEKI	BAUME	JOHNS	HERON	FERRO
ALLAN	BEEBE	HONDA	ELMER	ONNES	MONGE	JOSIE	ADOLF	BEAMS	KLINE	HYRON	FIORE
ALVAN	CHUBB	KORDA	ELVEN	OSLER	PEGGY	JULIA	BILLY	DEMME	KUHNE	JACOB	FLORY
ANWAR	DANBY	KUNDT	ETHEL	PAGET	PREGL	JULIE	BOOLE	FERMI	LAING	JAKOB	FRERE
APIAN	DARBY	LANDE	EUGEN	PAVEL	RUNGE	KANIN	BOULE	FREMY	LEONE	JANOS	GARRY
ARIAS	DOLBY	LINDA	EULER	PAYEN	SYNGE	KEVIN	BOYLE	GEMMA	LIANG	JASON	GEORG
BRIAN	GIBBS	LINDE	FRIED	PERES	ULUGH	KLEIN	BUELL	GERMI	LORNE	LEBON	GERRY
BRYAN	KLEBS	LUNDH	FRIES	PEREY	WAAGE	KUNIO	CABLE	JIMMY	MILNE	LECOQ	GOERG
BYRAM	KOLBE	LYNDS	GALEN	PEREZ	BETHE	LEWIS	CARLO	KOSMA	OWENS	MASON	HARRY
CAJAL	KREBS	PADDY	GATES	PETER	BOTHE	LOGIE	DELLA	KRAMS	PAYNE	MAYOW	HENRI
CESAR	LIBBY	ROYDS	GEBER	PINEL	BRAHE	LOUIS	DIELS	NORMA	PEANO	METON	HENRY
CHIAO	NAMBU	SANDY	GIGER	QUEEN	ELIHU	LOWIG	DOELL	SELMA	PLINY	MILOS	ICIRO
COWAN	SORBY	SODDY	GILES	REBER	FUCHS	LUCIO	EMILE	SSUMA	RAINE	MINOS	LARRY
DEWAR	TAMBI	TANDY	GODEL	ROGER	HECHT	LURIA	EMILY	TOMMY	RHIND	MINOT	LAURA
DIRAC	TAUBE	TOLDY	GREEN	ROMER	KATHY	MARIA	EWALD	BHANU	RHINE	MONOD	MAURY
DONAT	ALICE	WALDO	GREER	RUBEL	RIGHI	MARIE	FIELD	BLANE	SAINT	NICOL	MOORE
DUMAS	ALICK	WENDY	HABER	SAKEL	ROCHE	MARIK	FOWLE	BRAND	SHENG	NIXON	PARRY
EDGAR	AMICI	WILDT	HALES	SAYED	RUEHL	MARIN	GABLE	BRENT	STENO	OCHOA	PEARL
EJNAR	BEACH	WOODY	HANEY	SOREN	SACHS	MARIO	GALLE	BRINK	STONE	OLSON	PEARY
ELIAS	BLACK	WUNDT	HAYES	SPIES	STRHL	MAXIM	GOULD	BRUNO	SZENT	ORBOM	PEDRO
ERMAN	BLOCH	ABNEY	HEBER	STEEN	TYCHO	MONIZ	HENLE	BURNS	TOWNE	ORSON	PIERO
FAZAN	BLOCK	ADLER	HELEN	SUGER	ADAIR	NASIR	HOLLY	CAINE	TSENG	POPOV	SEGRE
GOBAT	BOSCH	AHMES	HUBEL	TAIEB	ALVIN	NEVIL	HOYLE	CERNY	TSUNG	RAMON	SHARP
HAMAO	BROCA	AIKEN	HUBER	THAER	ANNIE	PAPIN	JOULE	CHANG	VERNA	RAMOS	SHORT
HEMAN	BRUCE	ALDER	IHNEN	THIEL	ARVID	PETIT	KARLE	CHENG	WAYNE	SETON	SPORN
HIRAM	CHACE	ALLEN	INNES	TOMEI	BASIL	PIXII	KELLY	CHING	YOUNG	SIMON	STARK
HYMAN	CHUCK	ALTER	JAMES	TYLER	BEGIN	PUPIN	LAZLO	CHONG	YUANG	SOLON	STERN
IGNAZ	COUCH	ANGEL	JANET	VOGEL	BEVIS	RABIN	LULLY	CHUNG	ZHANG	THEON	TWORT
ISAAC	CRICK	ARBER	JONES	WEBER	BORIS	RENIE	LYELL	CLINE	AARON	TIBOR	WIARD
JOHAN	DRACH	ARLEN	JOSEF	WILES	BRAID	RINIO	MERLE	CLINT	AGNON	TITOV	BASSI
JONAS	ERICH	ASSER	JULES	WILEY	BUNIN	ROBIN	MILLS	CORNU	ALMON	TRYON	BLISS
JUDAH	FINCH	BAKER	KAMEN	WYLER	CECIL	RUBIN	MOLLO	COUNT	ALTON	TUROK	BOYSE
JURAN	FITCH	BATES	KAREL	YOSEF	CHAIM	SABIN	MOULD	DANNY	ANTON	TYLOR	CRISP
KAMAL	GLUCK	BAYER	LAWES	YUSEF	CHAIN	SIMIC	MPILO	DIANE	ASTON	YALOW	CROSS
KAZAN	GRACE	BINET	LEDER	ZENER	CHRIS	STAIN	NEELY	DONNA	ASTOR	ASAPH	DOISY
KOWAL	HENCH	BODEN	LEGER	CLIFF	COLIN	TEMIN	NEILL	EBING	BARON	BEPPO	DOUST
LAMAR	HOUCK	BOREL	LEVEN	KOLFF	CRAIG	BRAJA	NELLY	EVANS	BASOV	GOMPF	DRESS

ERNST	MOTTE	SELYE	BRAID	FOSSE	PERSE	BEACH	TOMEI	SKALL	ELVEN	SOLON	BAYER
FALSE	NATTA	SONYA	BRAND	FOWLE	RAINE	BLOCH	UMEKI	SMALL	ELWYN	SOREN	BOYER
FOSSE	NORTH	LIZZY	DAVID	FREGE	REESE	BOOTH	BARUJ	SNELL	ERMAN	SPORN	CESAR
FROSH	PATTY	LUZZI	EWALD	FRERE	RENIE	BOSCH	ALICK	STOLL	ERWIN	STAIN	COMER
FURSE	PLATO	SANZO	FIELD	FURSE	RHINE	CHIEH	BLACK	STRHL	EUGEN	STEEN	CUKOR
FURST	PLATT		FLOYD	GABLE	ROCHE	COUCH	BLOCK	THIEL	FAZAN	STERN	DEWAR
GAUSS	PORTA		FREUD	GAEDE	ROLLE	DRACH	BRINK	VOGEL	GALEN	SUSAN	DURER
GROSS	PYOTR		FRIED	GALLE	ROOKE	EDITH	BROOK	BLOOM	GLENN	TEMIN	EDGAR
HAISE	SCOTT	**5TH**	GOULD	GRACE	ROSSE	ERICH	CAPEK	BROOM	GREEN	THEON	EJNAR
HESSE	SMITH	**LETTER**	HEROD	GROTE	ROUSE	FINCH	CHUCK	BYRAM	GWENN	TRYON	ELMER
HEYSE	TRETZ	AKIRA	LLOYD	GROVE	RUNGE	FITCH	CLARK	CHAIM	HELEN	WYMAN	EULER
HULSE	VESTO	BOTTA	MONOD	HAISE	SEGRE	FROSH	CLERK	HIRAM	HEMAN	ARAGO	GABOR
JESSE	VIETA	BRAJA	MOULD	HAUGE	SELYE	HAIGH	CRICK	MAXIM	HERON	BEPPO	GEBER
JOOST	VOLTA	BROCA	RHIND	HEINE	STEVE	HENCH	DEREK	TATUM	HYRON	BRUNO	GIGER
KERST	WHITE	CAPRA	ROALD	HENLE	STONE	ILICH	FRANK	PANUM	HYMAN	CARLO	GREER
KIRSH	WHYTT	CLARA	SAYED	HESSE	SYNGE	JUDAH	GLUCK	SALAM	HYRON	CHIAO	HABER
KRESS	WIRTH	COSTA	WIARD	HEYSE	TAUBE	KEITH	HOUCK	TATUM	IHNEN	DARIO	HEBER
LUISE	WURTZ	DELLA	ALICE	HOOKE	TOWNE	KEOGH	MARIK	AARON	IRVIN	ENNIO	HUBER
MARSH	YEATS	DERVA	ANDRE	HOPPE	WAAGE	KIRSH	QUICK	AGNON	IRWIN	FERRO	JABIR
MORSE	ABDUS	DONNA	ANNIE	HOYLE	WAYNE	KROGH	REMAK	AIKEN	JASON	HAMAO	LAMAR
PABST	ALDUS	FONDA	BAUME	HULSE	WHITE	KUSCH	STARK	ALLAN	JOHAN	HANNO	LEDER
PASSY	BARUJ	GEENA	BEEBE	INOUE	ADOLF	LEIGH	STOCK	ALLEN	JURAN	ICIRO	LEGER
PERSE	BRAUN	GEMMA	BETHE	IRENE	CLIFF	LUNDH	TUROK	ALMON	KAMEN	KROTO	LOWER
REESE	CAMUS	HONDA	BETTE	JERNE	GOMPF	MARCH	ANGEL	ALTON	KANIN	KUNIO	MAYER
REISS	CLAUS	HORTA	BLAKE	JESSE	JOSEF	MARSH	BASIL	ALVAN	KAZAN	LAZLO	MEYER
ROSSE	CYRUS	JULIA	BLANE	JODIE	KOLFF	NORTH	BOREL	ALVIN	KEVIN	LUCIO	MOYER
ROSSI	FREUD	KORDA	BOOLE	JORIE	LWOFF	PASCH	BUELL	ANTON	KLEIN	MARCO	NASIR
ROUSE	FUKUI	KOSMA	BOTHE	JOSIE	PFAFF	RALPH	CAJAL	APIAN	LEBON	MARIO	NEHER
SISSY	INOUE	LAURA	BOULE	JOULE	WOLFF	REICH	CAREL	ARLEN	LEVAN	MARKO	NUFER
SUESS	KLAUS	LINDA	BOYLE	JULIE	YOSEF	SARAH	CAROL	ASTON	LEVEN	MOLLO	OSCAR
WALSH	LINUS	LOTKA	BOYSE	JUNGE	YUSEF	SMITH	CECIL	BARON	LOREN	MPILO	OSKAR
WEISS	MALUS	LURIA	BRAHE	KARLE	ABEGG	ULUGH	CYRIL	BEGIN	LYMAN	PABLO	OSLER
WIEST	PANUM	MARIA	BRUCE	KEIKE	BRAGG	WALSH	DOELL	BELON	LYNEN	PAOLO	PETER
BETTE	PLAUT	NATTA	BURKE	KLINE	CHANG	WIRTH	EEMIL	BODEN	MARIN	PEANO	PYOTR
BETTY	PROUT	NORMA	CABLE	KOLBE	CHENG	ALEXI	ETHEL	BOWEN	MASON	PEDRO	REBER
BOOTH	RAMUS	OCHOA	CAINE	KUHNE	CHING	AMICI	GODEL	BRAUN	METON	PIERO	ROGER
BOTTA	RAOUL	OGAWA	CELVE	LANDE	CHONG	BASSI	HUBEL	BREEN	MUREN	PLATO	ROMER
BURTT	STOUT	PORTA	CHACE	LANGE	CHUNG	BONDI	KAMAL	BRIAN	NIVEN	RINIO	SUGER
COMTE	TATUM	RUSKA	CLINE	LEONE	CRAIG	BURGI	KAREL	BROWN	NIXON	SANZO	THAER
CONTI	TYTUS	SELMA	CLYDE	LINDE	EBING	CONTI	KOWAL	BRYAN	OGDEN	STENO	TIBOR
COSTA	VITUS	SONYA	COMTE	LOCKE	EWING	ESAKI	LOYAL	BUNIN	OLSON	TYCHO	TYLER
DANTE	CELVE	SSUMA	CURIE	LODGE	GEORG	FABRI	LYELL	BYRON	ORSON	VASCO	TYLOR
EDITH	DERVA	TALVA	DANTE	LOGIE	GEROG	FERMI	MABEL	CHAIN	PAPIN	VESTO	WEBER
FEGTE	GROVE	TESLA	DEBYE	LORNE	GOERG	FUKUI	MERYL	CHIEN	PAYEN	WALDO	WYLER
FOOTE	MAEVE	VERNA	DEMME	LUISE	GREGG	GERMI	NEILL	COHEN	PUPIN	CRISP	ZENER
FORTT	STEVE	VIETA	DIANE	LUSKE	HAING	GOLGI	NEVIL	COLIN	QUEEN	KRUPP	ABDUS
FRITZ	TALVA	VOLTA	DICKE	MAEVE	HUANG	HENRI	NICOL	CONON	RABIN	SHARP	ADAMS
GERTY	BROWN	CHUBB	DRAKE	MARIE	LAING	LOEWI	NOBEL	COWAN	RAMAN	LECOQ	AHMES
GROTE	LOEWI	JACOB	DRUDE	MERLE	LIANG	LUIGI	PAVEL	DALEN	RAMON	ADAIR	ALDUS
HARTZ	OGAWA	JAKOB	EDDIE	MILNE	LOWIG	LUZZI	PEARL	DIXON	REGAN	ADLER	ALOYS
HERTZ	ALEXI	TAIEB	EMILE	MONGE	SHENG	PAULI	PINEL	DUBIN	ROBIN	ALDER	ARIAS
HORTA	ALOYS	BIROC	ENCKE	MOORE	TSENG	PESCI	PREGL	DYSON	ROWAN	ALTER	BANKS
HYATT	DEBYE	DIRAC	FALSE	MORSE	TSUNG	PIXII	RAOUL	EDLEN	RUBIN	ANWAR	BATES
KEITH	ELWYN	ISAAC	FEGTE	MOTTE	YOUNG	RICCI	RUBEL	EDWIN	SABIN	ARBER	BEAMS
KROTO	FLOYD	SIMIC	FIORE	NOBLE	YUANG	RIGHI	RUEHL	EIGEN	SAGAN	ASSER	BEVIS
KURTZ	LLOYD	AHMAD	FOCKE	PACKE	ZHANG	ROSSI	SAKEL	ELION	SETON	ASTOR	BLISS
METTY	MERYL	ARVID	FOOTE	PAYNE	ASAPH	TAMBI	SHULL	ELLEN	SIMON	BAKER	BORIS

6 LETTER · 1ST LETTER

BURKS	LYNDS	PAGET	HOLLY	ARNAUD	BESSEL	CANNOM	CORDUS	DUFOUR
BURNS	MALUS	PETIT	JENNY	ARNOLD	BHABHA	CANNON	CORNER	DUGGAR
CAMUS	MENES	PLATT	JIMMY	ARREST	BICHAT	CANTIN	CORTES	DULONG
CHRIS	MILES	PLAUT	KATHY	ARTEDI	BIDDEL	CANTON	COSTER	DUNANT
CLAUS	MILLS	PROUT	KELLY	ARTHUR	BINNIG	CANTOR	COTTON	DUNBAR
COTES	MILOS	SAINT	LARRY	ASHKIN	BISHOP	CAPMAN	COUPER	DUNCAN
CROSS	MINOS	SCOTT	LIBBY	ASPDIN	BIZIOU	CARAKA	COWLES	DUNHAM
CYRUS	MOSES	SHORT	LIZZY	ATWOOD	BLAAUW	CARBON	CRAFTS	DUNLOP
DAVIS	NIELS	STOUT	LULLY	AUBREY	BLAISE	CARLOS	CRAGOE	DUPUIS
DAWES	NILES	SZENT	MALEY	AUDREY	BLATTY	CARMEN	CRAMER	DUSTIN
DENIS	NUNES	TWORT	MAREY	AUGUST	BODMER	CARNEY	CRANCH	DUTTON
DIELS	ONNES	WHYTT	MAURY	AUSTEN	BOGART	CARNOT	CRELLE	DUVALL
DORIS	OWENS	WIEST	MCKAY	AUSTIN	BOHLIN	CARREL	CREMER	DWIGHT
DRESS	PERES	WILDT	MERAY	AUZOUT	BOLTON	CARSON	CRONIN	EAGLER
DUBOS	RAMOS	WUNDT	METTY	AYLING	BOLYAI	CARTAN	CROSBY	ECCLES
DUMAS	RAMUS	BHANU	NANCY	AYLMER	BONNER	CARTER	CUGNOT	ECKERT
EBERS	REISS	CORNU	NEELY	AYMAND	BONNET	CARVER	CULLEN	EDISON
ELIAS	ROYDS	ELIHU	NELLY	BAINES	BONNOT	CASKEY	CURTIS	EDLUND
ELLIS	SACHS	NAMBU	PADDY	BANACH	BORDEN	CASPAR	CURTIZ	EDMOND
EVANS	SPIES	BASOV	PARRY	BARANY	BORDET	CASSIN	CUVIER	EDUARD
FRANS	SUESS	POPOV	PASSY	BARBER	BORDEU	CASTEL	CYRANO	EDWARD
FRIES	TYTUS	TITOV	PATTY	BARBRA	BORMAN	CAUCHY	DAFFOS	EIFFEL
FUCHS	VITUS	GAMOW	PEARY	BARKLA	BOUGHN	CAVETT	DALTON	EILEEN
GATES	WALAS	MAYOW	PEGGY	BARNES	BOULLE	CAXTON	DANIEL	EISAKU
GAUSS	WEISS	YALOW	PERCY	BARNEY	BOVERI	CAYLEY	DANILO	EISELE
GIBBS	WELLS	FELIX	PEREY	BARROW	BOWLES	CEDRIC	DARWIN	ELISHA
GILES	WILES	ABNEY	PLINY	BARTON	BRAMAH	CELSUS	DAVIES	ELLERY
GILKS	YEATS	ASHBY	SALLY	BARUCH	BRANCA	CERNAN	DAWSON	ELLIOT
GROSS	BENGT	AVARY	SANDY	BASEVI	BRANDO	CERRAF	DAYTON	ELOISE
HALES	BINET	AVERY	SISSY	BAUHIN	BRANDT	CESARE	DECUIR	ELSTER
HANKS	BOVET	BARRY	SODDY	BAWDEN	BRENDA	CESARI	DELANO	ELYTIS
HANNS	BRENT	BEERY	SORBY	BAXTER	BREUER	CHABRY	DELANY	EMERIC
HAYES	BURTT	BERRY	SULLY	BEADLE	BRIAND	CHANCE	DENJOY	EMILIE
HIGGS	CLINT	BETTY	TALLY	BEATON	BRIDGE	CHAPPE	DENNIS	EMILIO
HYMNS	COUNT	BILLY	TANDY	BEATTY	BRIGGS	CHEOPS	DENTON	ENDERS
INNES	COURT	BRADY	TOLDY	BEAVAN	BRIGHT	CHEYNE	DENZEL	ENGELS
IRONS	DONAT	CERNY	TOMMY	BECHER	BRILEY	CHIANG	DERHAM	ENRICO
JAMES	DOUST	COREY	TRACY	BECKET	BROOKE	CHURCH	DESIRE	ERCKER
JANOS	ELERT	DANBY	TULLY	BEGLEY	BROOKS	CIMINO	DIANNE	ERLICH
JEANS	ELIOT	DANNY	WENDY	BEGUIN	BRUNEL	CIVITA	DIBBLE	ERNEST
JOHNS	ELLET	DARBY	WILEY	BEHAIM	BRUTUS	CLAIRE	DIESEL	ETIENE
JONAS	EMERT	DEWEY	WILLY	BELLOW	BUDDHA	CLARKE	DIETER	EUCKEN
JONES	ERNST	DOISY	WOODY	BENDER	BULLEN	CLAUDE	DIGGES	EUCLID
JULES	FORTT	DOLBY	FRANZ	BENITO	BUNCHE	CLORIS	DILLEY	EUGENE
KLAUS	FURST	EMILY	FRITZ	BENNET	BUNSEN	CLOVIS	DILLON	EVARTS
KLEBS	GOBAT	FABRY	HARTZ	BENOIT	BURALI	COATES	DINTIS	EVELYN
KRAMS	GRANT	FLORY	HEINZ	BENSON	BURNET	COBURN	DMITRI	EYVIND
KREBS	GUYOT	FREMY	HERTZ	BENTON	BURTON	COCKER	DOMAGK	FABIAN
KRESS	HECHT	GARRY	IGNAZ	BERGER	BUSSEY	COFFIN	DONALD	FAIRLY
LAMAS	HYATT	GERRY	KURTZ	BERING	BUSTER	COLLIP	DONATI	FAJANS
LAWES	JANET	GERTY	MONIZ	BERMAN	BUTLER	COLMAN	DONATO	FARADY
LEWIS	JOOST	GODOY	NUNEZ	BERNAL	CABRAL	CONRAD	DORIAN	FARFAX
LINUS	KERST	HANEY	PEREZ	BEROZA	CAESAR	CONRAT	DRAPER	FARMAN
LOUIS	KUNDT	HARDY	TRETZ	BERTHA	CAGNEY	COOLEY	DREIER	FARMER
LUCAS	MINOT	HARRY	WURTZ	BERTIL	CALLIE	COOPER	DREYER	FAROUK
LUKAS	PABST	HENRY		ARMAND	BESLER	CALVIN	COPLEY	DUDLEY	FARRAR

FARROW	GERMAN	HALDAN	HORACE	KEATON	LEONOV	MARLEE	MURIEL	PALMER	RAKINE
FAUSTO	GEROGE	HALLER	HORNER	KEELER	LERNER	MARLON	MURPHY	PAMELA	RAMSAY
FELIPE	GERRIT	HALLEY	HORTON	KEESOM	LESLEY	MARTEL	MURRAY	PANDER	RAMSEY
FEODOR	GERSON	HALSEY	HOWARD	KEFFER	LESLIE	MARTIN	MUSSET	PAPPUS	RANDAL
FERNEL	GESELL	HALTON	HSIUNG	KEILIN	LESTER	MARVIN	MYRDAL	PAQUIN	RAOULT
FERRER	GESNER	HAMSUN	HUBBLE	KEKULE	LEVENE	MATEOS	NADINE	PARKER	REAGAN
FIELDS	GIANNI	HANLEY	HUBERT	KELLER	LEVIEN	MATLIN	NAGANO	PARKES	REALDO
FIESER	GIBBON	HANNES	HUGHES	KELLEY	LEVINE	MAYALL	NAGELI	PASCAL	REGIUS
FINLAY	GIBNEY	HANSEN	HUNTER	KELVIN	LEXELL	MCADAM	NAGUIB	PAVLOV	REILLY
FINNEY	GIBSON	HARALD	HUSTON	KEMENY	LINDER	MCCORD	NAIFEH	PAXTON	REINER
FINSEN	GIDEON	HARDEN	HUTTON	KEMMER	LINDON	MCCUNE	NAKANO	PELLOS	REINES
FISHER	GIESEL	HARLEY	HUXLEY	KEPLER	LIONEL	MCKEEN	NANSEN	PEPLOE	REISCH
FIZEAU	GILLES	HARLOW	IGNATZ	KEYNES	LIOTTA	MCLEAN	NAPIER	PERKIN	REMSEN
FLEROV	GILMAN	HAROLD	ILMARI	KHOURI	LIPPES	MCLEOD	NARMER	PERRIN	RENFEW
FLOREY	GINGER	HARRIS	INGRAM	KIBBLE	LISTER	MEDICI	NATHAN	PERUTZ	RENNIE
FLOYER	GIOSUE	HARUNA	INGRID	KILJAN	LITTLE	MEEHAN	NAUDIN	PETERS	REVERE
FORBES	GIRARD	HARVEY	IRVING	KINSKY	LOFTUS	MEIKLE	NECKAM	PETRIE	RHAZES
FOREST	GIULIO	HASDAI	ISAACS	KIRWAN	LOLOIR	MELLOR	NELSON	PETRUS	RHODES
FORMAN	GLADYS	HASSEL	ISADOR	KOCHER	LONDON	MELVIN	NERNST	PETTIT	RICHER
FOSTER	GLASER	HATTIE	ISIDOR	KOHLER	LOOMIS	MELVYN	NERUDA	PEYTON	RICHET
FOWLER	GLAZER	HAUBEN	ISMAEL	KOLLER	LORENZ	MENCHU	NERVIG	PHILIP	RINGER
FRANCA	GLENDA	HAVERS	IVANOV	KONRAD	LOTHAR	MENDEL	NESTOR	PHILON	RIQUET
FRANCE	GLORIA	HAZARD	JACOBI	KOPPEN	LOUDON	MENGES	NEVILL	PIAZZI	RISKIN
FRANCK	GLOVER	HEANEY	JACOBS	KOSMAS	LOUISE	MENKEN	NEWCOM	PICARD	RITTER
FRANCO	GMELIN	HEDGES	JACOPO	KOSSEL	LOVELL	MENZEL	NEWMAN	PICTET	RIVEST
FRANKE	GOBIND	HEEGER	JAGGER	KOSTER	LOVISA	MERCER	NEWTON	PIERCE	ROBBIE
FRASCH	GOERGE	HEEZEN	JANSKY	KOTARO	LOWELL	MERRIT	NICOLA	PIERRE	ROBERT
FRAZER	GOLDIE	HEFLIN	JANUSZ	KRAELY	LOWITZ	MESMER	NICOLE	PIETER	ROBINS
FRENCH	GOOSEN	HELLER	JEANNE	KRASNA	LUCILA	MICALI	NICOLO	PIETRO	ROBLEY
FREUND	GORDON	HENCKE	JENNER	KUIPER	LUCIUS	MICHEL	NIEPCE	PINCUS	RODNEY
FRICKE	GORGAS	HENNIG	JENSEN	KUMMER	LUDERS	MIGUEL	NIKOLA	PIROSH	ROGERS
FROSCH	GOSSET	HENRIK	JEREMY	KUNKEL	LUDWIG	MILENA	NILSON	PISTEK	ROHRER
FSCOTT	GRAEBE	HENSEN	JEROME	KYESER	LUSSAC	MILLAN	NIPKOW	PLANCK	ROLAND
FULLER	GRAHAM	HERALD	JESSUP	LANDAU	LUTHER	MILLER	NOBILI	PLANTE	ROMAIN
FULTON	GRAMME	HERBIG	JETHRO	LANDON	LUTULI	MILNER	NOLLET	PLUCHE	ROMANO
GAINES	GRANIT	HERMAN	JOANNE	LARMOR	LYCETT	MILOSZ	NORGAY	POGSON	RONALD
GALOIS	GRAUNT	HERMES	JOGESH	LARNER	LYNDON	MILTON	NORMAN	POLHEM	RONNIE
GALTON	GRAVES	HESTON	JOHANN	LARSEN	MADLER	MOBIUS	NORRIS	PORTER	ROOSBY
GARCIA	GRAZIA	HEVESY	JOLIOT	LARSON	MAFFEO	MOLINA	NOSSAL	POWELL	ROSHER
GARDAY	GREENE	HEWISH	JORDAN	LARTET	MAGGIE	MONETA	OAKLEY	POYNER	ROTTER
GARMES	GREGOR	HEWITT	JOSEPH	LASEAR	MAGNUS	MONROE	OBERTH	PRAWER	ROZIER
GARROD	GRIESS	HIDEKI	JOSHUA	LASKER	MAHLON	MONTEL	OFFROY	PREBUS	RUBBIA
GARROW	GRIGGS	HILLER	JOSIAH	LASZLO	MAIMAN	MOREAU	OLBERS	PREVIN	RUBNER
GARSON	GRIJNS	HILTON	JULIAN	LATTES	MALAKH	MORENO	OLDHAM	PRINCE	RUCKER
GASSER	GRIMES	HINTON	JULIEN	LAUREL	MALDEN	MORGAN	OLIVER	PROULX	RUDOLF
GASTON	GROVER	HIRSCH	JULIUS	LAUREN	MALONE	MORITZ	OLIVIA	PROUST	RUEBEN
GAUDIO	GUERIN	HITLER	JURAGA	LAWRIE	MANABA	MORLEY	OPARIN	PSEUDO	RUMKER
GAVRAS	GUFFEY	HITNER	JUSTUS	LAYARD	MANLIO	MORRIS	ORESME	PULLER	RUPERT
GAYNOR	GUNTER	HITZIG	KALUZA	LAZARE	MANSON	MORROW	ORVILL	PUNNET	RUSSEL
GEIGER	GURNEY	HOBBES	KANADA	LAZEAR	MARCEL	MORTON	OSWALD	QUIDDE	RYBERG
GEISEL	GUSTAF	HOLDEN	KAPARY	LEAKEY	MARCIA	MOTHER	OTHMAN	QUINCY	SABINE
GEITEL	GUSTAV	HOLLEY	KARNOW	LEIBER	MARCUS	MOUTON	OTTMAR	RACHEL	SAINTE
GEORGE	GUYTON	HOLMES	KARRER	LEMERY	MARION	MOYERS	PACINI	RACINE	SAKATA
GEORGI	GYATSO	HONOLD	KASPAR	LEMMON	MARISA	MULLER	PACINO	RAFAEL	SALEEN
GERALD	GYORGY	HOOVER	KATINA	LENOIR	MARIUS	MULLIS	PALADE	RAGNAR	SAMUAL
GERARD	HADLEY	HOPPER	KEARNS	LEONOR	MARKOV	MUNGLE	PALFYN	RAINER	SAMUEL

SANGER	SOPHUS	TOBIAS	WATKIN	BARBRA	FAROUK	LARMOR	PALFYN	WALTER	BERGER
SANTEL	SPACEK	TOLAND	WATSON	BARKLA	FARRAR	LARNER	PALMER	WALTON	BERING
SAPPHO	SPACEY	TOLMAN	WEAVER	BARNES	FARROW	LARSEN	PAMELA	WANKEL	BERMAN
SARGON	SPENCE	TOPHAM	WEINER	BARNEY	FAUSTO	LARSON	PANDER	WARING	BERNAL
SARTRE	SPERRY	TORREY	WELLER	BARROW	GAINES	LARTET	PAPPUS	WARNER	BEROZA
SAURIA	SQUIER	TOWNES	WELLES	BARTON	GALOIS	LASEAR	PAQUIN	WARREN	BERTHA
SAVAGE	STALIN	TRAJAN	WENZEL	BARUCH	GALTON	LASKER	PARKER	WATERS	BERTIL
SAVARY	STEARN	TRAVIS	WERNER	BASEVI	GARCIA	LASZLO	PARKES	WATKIN	BESLER
SAVERY	STEARS	TREVOR	WESLEY	BAUHIN	GARDAY	LATTES	PASCAL	WATSON	BESSEL
SCARPA	STEELE	TROFIM	WESSEL	BAWDEN	GARMES	LAUREL	PAVLOV	YASSER	CEDRIC
SCHACK	STEFAN	TROTTI	WEXLER	BAXTER	GARROD	LAUREN	PAXTON	ZARNKE	CELSUS
SCHARY	STEVEN	TRUMAN	WHOOPI	CABRAL	GARROW	LAWRIE	RACHEL	ZAVIER	CERNAN
SCHELL	STIFEL	TRUMBO	WIENER	CAESAR	GARSON	LAYARD	RACINE	ZAVITZ	CERRAF
SCHICK	STILES	TSVETT	WIESEL	CAGNEY	GASSER	LAZARE	RAFAEL	ABBOTT	CESARE
SCHNEE	STOCKE	TULLIO	WIGNER	CALLIE	GASTON	LAZEAR	RAGNAR	OBERTH	CESARI
SCOPES	STOKES	TUMMEL	WILBER	CALVIN	GAUDIO	MADLER	RAINER	ECCLES	DECUIR
SCOTUS	STONEY	TURING	WILCKE	CANNOM	GAVRAS	MAFFEO	RAKINE	ECKERT	DELANO
SEAMUS	STRABO	ULISSE	WILDER	CANNON	GAYNOR	MAGGIE	RAMSAY	MCADAM	DELANY
SEATON	STRATO	ULPIUS	WILKES	CANTIN	HADLEY	MAGNUS	RAMSEY	MCCORD	DENJOY
SECCHI	STREEP	ULRICH	WILLEM	CANTON	HALDAN	MAHLON	RANDAL	MCCUNE	DENNIS
SEGALL	STREET	UNDSET	WILLIS	CANTOR	HALLER	MAIMAN	RAOULT	MCKEEN	DENTON
SELMAN	STRONG	UNSOLD	WILSON	CAPMAN	HALLEY	MALAKH	SABINE	MCLEAN	DENZEL
SEMJON	STRUSS	UPDIKE	WILTER	CARAKA	HALSEY	MALDEN	SAINTE	MCLEOD	DERHAM
SEMLER	STRUTT	URBAIN	WINSOR	CARBON	HALTON	MALONE	SAKATA	SCARPA	DESIRE
SENECA	STRUVE	USSHER	WINTON	CARLOS	HAMSUN	MANABA	SALEEN	SCHACK	FELIPE
SERSEN	STUART	VALENS	WITELO	CARMEN	HANLEY	MANLIO	SAMUAL	SCHARY	FEODOR
SEVERO	STUMPF	VALLEE	WITTIG	CARNEY	HANNES	MANSON	SAMUEL	SCHELL	FERNEL
SEWALL	SUMNER	VALLES	WOHLER	CARNOT	HANSEN	MARCEL	SANGER	SCHICK	FERRER
SEYLER	SUSUME	VARMUS	WOLSKY	CARREL	HARALD	MARCIA	SANTEL	SCHNEE	GEIGER
SHAMIR	SUSUMU	VAUBAN	WOOLEY	CARSON	HARDEN	MARCUS	SAPPHO	SCOPES	GEISEL
SHANKS	SUTTON	VENETZ	WRIGHT	CARTAN	HARLEY	MARION	SARGON	SCOTUS	GEITEL
SHARPE	SUZUKI	VENING	WYDNER	CARTER	HARLOW	MARISA	SARTRE	ADDAMS	GEORGE
SHEMIN	SVANTE	VERNER	YASSER	CARVER	HAROLD	MARIUS	SAURIA	ADOLFO	GEORGI
SHIMON	SYDNEY	VERNON	YERGIN	CASKEY	HARRIS	MARKOV	SAVAGE	ADOLPH	GERALD
SHIUNG	TADDEO	VERTES	YERKES	CASPAR	HARUNA	MARLEE	SAVARY	ADRIAN	GERARD
SHMUEL	TAGORE	VICTOR	YERSIN	CASSIN	HARVEY	MARLON	SAVERY	ADRIEN	GERMAN
SHOVEL	TALBOT	VIKTOR	YOICHI	CASTEL	HASDAI	MARTEL	TADDEO	EDISON	GEROGE
SHUKEN	TANAKA	VILMOS	YORDAN	CAUCHY	HASSEL	MARTIN	TAGORE	EDLUND	GERRIT
SIBLEY	TARSKI	VIRGIL	YUKAWA	CAVETT	HATTIE	MARVIN	TALBOT	EDMOND	GERSON
SIDNEY	TASMAN	VIVIAN	YVONNE	CAXTON	HAUBEN	MATEOS	TANAKA	EDUARD	GESELL
SIGRID	TAUBES	VIVIEN	ZARNKE	CAYLEY	HAVERS	MATLIN	TARSKI	EDWARD	GESNER
SILVIO	TAUROG	VOIGHT	ZAVIER	DAFFOS	HAZARD	MAYALL	TASMAN	BEADLE	HEANEY
SIMEON	TAYLOR	VOISIN	ZAVITZ	DALTON	JACOBI	NADINE	TAUBES	BEATON	HEDGES
SIMOND	TELLER	WAGNER	ZEEMAN	DANIEL	JACOBS	NAGANO	TAUROG	BEATTY	HEEGER
SIMONE	TEODOR	WALDEN	ZENOBE	DANILO	JACOPO	NAGELI	TAYLOR	BEAVAN	HEEZEN
SIMONI	TERESA	WALESA	ZINNER	DARWIN	JAGGER	NAGUIB	VALENS	BECHER	HEFLIN
SIMONS	TESICH	WALKEN	ZOLTAN	DAVIES	JANSKY	NAIFEH	VALLEE	BECKET	HELLER
SINGER	TEWFIK	WALKER	ZWICKY	DAWSON	JANUSZ	NAKANO	VALLES	BEGLEY	HENCKE
SKOTAK	THABIT	WALLIS		DAYTON	KALUZA	NANSEN	VARMUS	BEGUIN	HENNIG
SLIFER	THALES	WALSON		EAGLER	KANADA	NAPIER	VAUBAN	BEHAIM	HENRIK
SLOANE	THELMA	WALTER		FABIAN	KAPARY	NARMER	WAGNER	BELLOW	HENSEN
SMAUEL	THEONI	WALTON	**2ND LETTER**	FAIRLY	KARNOW	NATHAN	WALDEN	BENDER	HERALD
SMILEY	THIOUT	WANKEL		FAJANS	KARRER	NAUDIN	WALESA	BENITO	HERBIG
SMYTHE	THOLDE	WARING	BAINES	FARADY	KASPAR	OAKLEY	WALKEN	BENNET	HERMAN
SOLVAY	THOMAS	WARNER	BANACH	FARFAX	KATINA	PACINI	WALKER	BENOIT	HERMES
SOPHIA	TIMONI	WARREN	BARANY	FARMAN	LANDAU	PACINO	WALLIS	BENSON	HESTON
SOPHIE	TITIUS	WATERS	BARBER	FARMER	LANDON	PALADE	WALSON	BENTON	HEVESY

HEWISH	NESTOR	YERGIN	EISELE	PICTET	ALFRED	SMILEY	DONATI	MONETA	YORDAN
HEWITT	NEVILL	YERKES	FIELDS	PIERCE	ALFVEN	SMYTHE	DONATO	MONROE	ZOLTAN
JEANNE	NEWCOM	YERSIN	FIESER	PIERRE	ALISON	ANDERS	DORIAN	MONTEL	APPERT
JENNER	NEWMAN	ZEEMAN	FINLAY	PIETER	ALLDER	ANDREA	FORBES	MOREAU	APPOLT
JENSEN	NEWTON	ZENOBE	FINNEY	PIETRO	ALLVAR	ANDREI	FOREST	MORENO	OPARIN
JEREMY	PELLOS	OFFROY	FINSEN	PINCUS	ALONZO	ANDRES	FORMAN	MORGAN	SPACEK
JEROME	PEPLOE	AGNETA	FISHER	PIROSH	ALPHER	ANDREW	FOSTER	MORITZ	SPACEY
JESSUP	PERKIN	IGNATZ	FIZEAU	PISTEK	ALPINI	ANDREY	FOWLER	MORLEY	SPENCE
JETHRO	PERRIN	BHABHA	GIANNI	RICHER	ALTMAN	ANDRIC	GOBIND	MORRIS	SPERRY
KEARNS	PERUTZ	CHABRY	GIBBON	RICHET	BLAAUW	ANGELL	GOERGE	MORROW	UPDIKE
KEATON	PETERS	CHANCE	GIBNEY	RINGER	BLAISE	ANGELO	GOLDIE	MORTON	SQUIER
KEELER	PETRIE	CHAPPE	GIBSON	RIQUET	BLATTY	ANHALT	GOOSEN	MOTHER	ARAFAT
KEESOM	PETRUS	CHEOPS	GIDEON	RISKIN	CLAIRE	ANNING	GORDON	MOUTON	ARCHER
KEFFER	PETTIT	CHEYNE	GIESEL	RITTER	CLARKE	ANTONY	GORGAS	MOYERS	ARCHIE
KEILIN	PEYTON	CHIANG	GILLES	RIVEST	CLAUDE	ENDERS	GOSSET	NOBILI	ARDREY
KEKULE	REAGAN	CHURCH	GILMAN	SIBLEY	CLORIS	ENGELS	HOBBES	NOLLET	ARGAND
KELLER	REALDO	KHOURI	GINGER	SIDNEY	CLOVIS	ENRICO	HOLDEN	NORGAY	ARLING
KELLEY	REGIUS	PHILIP	GIOSUE	SIGRID	ELISHA	INGRAM	HOLLEY	NORMAN	ARLISS
KELVIN	REILLY	PHILON	GIRARD	SILVIO	ELLERY	INGRID	HOLMES	NORRIS	ARMAND
KEMENY	REINER	RHAZES	GIULIO	SIMEON	ELLIOT	UNDSET	HONOLD	NOSSAL	ARNAUD
KEMMER	REINES	RHODES	HIDEKI	SIMOND	ELOISE	UNSOLD	HOOVER	POGSON	ARNOLD
KEPLER	REISCH	SHAMIR	HILLER	SIMONE	ELSTER	BODMER	HOPPER	POLHEM	ARREST
KEYNES	REMSEN	SHANKS	HILTON	SIMONI	ELYTIS	BOGART	HORACE	PORTER	ARTEDI
LEAKEY	RENFEW	SHARPE	HINTON	SIMONS	FLEROV	BOHLIN	HORNER	POWELL	ARTHUR
LEIBER	RENNIE	SHEMIN	HIRSCH	SINGER	FLOREY	BOLTON	HORTON	POYNER	BRAMAH
LEMERY	REVERE	SHIMON	HITLER	TIMONI	FLOYER	BOLYAI	HOWARD	ROBBIE	BRANCA
LEMMON	SEAMUS	SHIUNG	HITNER	TITIUS	GLADYS	BONNER	JOANNE	ROBERT	BRANDO
LENOIR	SEATON	SHMUEL	HITZIG	VICTOR	GLASER	BONNET	JOGESH	ROBINS	BRANDT
LEONOR	SECCHI	SHOVEL	KIBBLE	VIKTOR	GLAZER	BONNOT	JOHANN	ROBLEY	BRENDA
LEONOV	SEGALL	SHUKEN	KILJAN	VILMOS	GLENDA	BORDEN	JOLIOT	RODNEY	BREUER
LERNER	SELMAN	THABIT	KINSKY	VIRGIL	GLORIA	BORDET	JORDAN	ROGERS	BRIAND
LESLEY	SEMJON	THALES	KIRWAN	VIVIAN	GLOVER	BORDEU	JOSEPH	ROHRER	BRIDGE
LESLIE	SEMLER	THELMA	LINDER	VIVIEN	ILMARI	BORMAN	JOSHUA	ROLAND	BRIGGS
LESTER	SENECA	THEONI	LINDON	WIENER	OLBERS	BOUGHN	JOSIAH	ROMAIN	BRIGHT
LEVENE	SERSEN	THIOUT	LIONEL	WIESEL	OLDHAM	BOULLE	KOCHER	ROMANO	BRILEY
LEVIEN	SEVERO	THOLDE	LIOTTA	WIGNER	OLIVER	BOVERI	KOHLER	RONALD	BROOKE
LEVINE	SEWALL	THOMAS	LIPPES	WILBER	OLIVIA	BOWLES	KOLLER	RONNIE	BROOKS
LEXELL	SEYLER	WHOOPI	LISTER	WILCKE	PLANCK	COATES	KONRAD	ROOSBY	BRUNEL
MEDICI	TELLER	AITKEN	LITTLE	WILDER	PLANTE	COBURN	KOPPEN	ROSHER	BRUTUS
MEEHAN	TEODOR	BICHAT	MICALI	WILKES	PLUCHE	COCKER	KOSMAS	ROTTER	CRAFTS
MEIKLE	TERESA	BIDDEL	MICHEL	WILLEM	SLIFER	COFFIN	KOSSEL	ROZIER	CRAGOE
MELLOR	TESICH	BINNIG	MIGUEL	WILLIS	SLOANE	COLLIP	KOSTER	SOLVAY	CRAMER
MELVIN	TEWFIK	BISHOP	MILENA	WILSON	ULISSE	COLMAN	KOTARO	SOPHIA	CRANCH
MELVYN	VENETZ	BIZIOU	MILLAN	WILTER	ULPIUS	CONRAD	LOFTUS	SOPHIE	CRELLE
MENCHU	VENING	CIMINO	MILLER	WINSOR	ULRICH	CONRAT	LOLOIR	SOPHUS	CREMER
MENDEL	VERNER	CIVITA	MILNER	WINTON	AMAGAT	COOLEY	LONDON	TOBIAS	CRONIN
MENGES	VERNON	DIANNE	MILOSZ	WITELO	AMDAHL	COOPER	LOOMIS	TOLAND	CROSBY
MENKEN	VERTES	DIBBLE	MILTON	WITTIG	AMECHE	COPLEY	LORENZ	TOLMAN	DRAPER
MENZEL	WEAVER	DIESEL	NICOLA	ZINNER	AMEDEO	CORDUS	LOTHAR	TOPHAM	DREIER
MERCER	WEINER	DIETER	NICOLE	SKOTAK	AMPERE	CORNER	LOUDON	TORREY	DREYER
MERRIT	WELLER	DIGGES	NICOLO	ALARIC	AMTHOR	CORTES	LOUISE	TOWNES	ERCKER
MESMER	WELLES	DILLEY	NIEPCE	ALBERT	DMITRI	COSTER	LOVELL	VOIGHT	ERLICH
NECKAM	WENZEL	DILLON	NIKOLA	ALCOCK	EMERIC	COTTON	LOVISA	VOISIN	ERNEST
NELSON	WERNER	DINTIS	NILSON	ALCOTT	EMILIE	COUPER	LOWELL	WOHLER	FRANCA
NERNST	WESLEY	EIFFEL	NIPKOW	ALCUIN	EMILIO	COWLES	LOWITZ	WOLSKY	FRANCE
NERUDA	WESSEL	EILEEN	PIAZZI	ALDRIN	GMELIN	DOMAGK	MOBIUS	WOOLEY	FRANCK
NERVIG	WEXLER	EISAKU	PICARD	ALEXIS	SMAUEL	DONALD	MOLINA	YOICHI	FRANCO

			3RD LETTER						
FRANKE	STALIN	EUGENE	TUMMEL	EVARTS	ALBERT	NICOLO	CREMER	HEFLIN	BRIAND
FRASCH	STEARN	FULLER	TURING	FRANCA	AUBREY	PACINI	DIESEL	KEFFER	BRIDGE
FRAZER	STEARS	FULTON	YUKAWA	FRANCE	CABRAL	PACINO	DIETER	LOFTUS	BRIGGS
FRENCH	STEELE	GUERIN	EVARTS	FRANCK	COBURN	PICARD	DREIER	MAFFEO	BRIGHT
FREUND	STEFAN	GUFFEY	EVELYN	FRANCO	DIBBLE	PICTET	DREYER	OFFROY	BRILEY
FRICKE	STEVEN	GUNTER	IVANOV	FRANKE	FABIAN	RACHEL	EMERIC	RAFAEL	CHIANG
FROSCH	STIFEL	GURNEY	SVANTE	FRASCH	GIBBON	RACINE	EVELYN	ANGELL	DMITRI
GRAEBE	STILES	GUSTAF	YVONNE	FRAZER	GIBNEY	RICHER	FIELDS	ANGELO	DWIGHT
GRAHAM	STOCKE	GUSTAV	DWIGHT	GIANNI	GIBSON	RICHET	FIESER	ARGAND	EDISON
GRAMME	STOKES	GUYTON	ZWICKY	GLADYS	GOBIND	RUCKER	FLEROV	AUGUST	ELISHA
GRANIT	STONEY	HUBBLE	AYLING	GLASER	HOBBES	SECCHI	FRENCH	BEGLEY	EMILIE
GRAUNT	STRABO	HUBERT	AYLMER	GLAZER	HUBBLE	VICTOR	FREUND	BEGUIN	EMILIO
GRAVES	STRATO	HUGHES	AYMAND	GRAEBE	HUBERT	ADDAMS	GIESEL	BOGART	ETIENE
GRAZIA	STREEP	HUNTER	CYRANO	GRAHAM	KIBBLE	ALDRIN	GLENDA	CAGNEY	FAIRLY
GREENE	STREET	HUSTON	EYVIND	GRAMME	MOBIUS	AMDAHL	GMELIN	CUGNOT	FRICKE
GREGOR	STRONG	HUTTON	GYATSO	GRANIT	NOBILI	ANDERS	GOERGE	DIGGES	GAINES
GRIESS	STRUSS	HUXLEY	GYORGY	GRAUNT	OLBERS	ANDREA	GREENE	DUGGAR	GEIGER
GRIGGS	STRUTT	JULIAN	KYESER	GRAVES	ROBBIE	ANDREI	GREGOR	EAGLER	GEISEL
GRIJNS	STRUVE	JULIEN	LYCETT	GRAZIA	ROBERT	ANDRES	GUERIN	ENGELS	GEITEL
GRIMES	STUART	JULIUS	LYNDON	GYATSO	ROBINS	ANDREW	HEEGER	EUGENE	GRIESS
GROVER	STUMPF	JURAGA	MYRDAL	HEANEY	ROBLEY	ANDREY	HEEZEN	HUGHES	GRIGGS
IRVING	AUBREY	JUSTUS	RYBERG	ISAACS	RUBBIA	ANDRIC	KEELER	INGRAM	GRIJNS
KRAELY	AUDREY	KUIPER	SYDNEY	ISADOR	RUBNER	ARDREY	KEESOM	INGRID	GRIMES
KRASNA	AUGUST	KUMMER	WYDNER	IVANOV	RYBERG	AUDREY	KYESER	JAGGER	HSIUNG
ORESME	AUSTEN	KUNKEL		JEANNE	SABINE	BIDDEL	MEEHAN	JOGESH	ISIDOR
ORVILL	AUSTIN	LUCILA		JOANNE	SIBLEY	BODMER	NIEPCE	MAGGIE	KEILIN
PRAWER	AUZOUT	LUCIUS		KEARNS	TOBIAS	BUDDHA	OBERTH	MAGNUS	KUIPER
PREBUS	BUDDHA	LUDERS	**3RD LETTER**	KEATON	URBAIN	CEDRIC	ORESME	MIGUEL	LEIBER
PREVIN	BULLEN	LUDWIG		KRAELY	ALCOCK	DUDLEY	PIERCE	NAGANO	MAIMAN
PRINCE	BUNCHE	LUSSAC	ALARIC	KRASNA	ALCOTT	ENDERS	PIERRE	NAGELI	MEIKLE
PROULX	BUNSEN	LUTHER	AMAGAT	LEAKEY	ALCUIN	GIDEON	PIETER	NAGUIB	NAIFEH
PROUST	BURALI	LUTULI	ARAFAT	MCADAM	ARCHER	HADLEY	PIETRO	POGSON	OLIVER
TRAJAN	BURNET	MULLER	BEADLE	OPARIN	ARCHIE	HEDGES	PREBUS	RAGNAR	OLIVIA
TRAVIS	BURTON	MULLIS	BEATON	PIAZZI	BECHER	HIDEKI	PREVIN	REGIUS	PHILIP
TREVOR	BUSSEY	MUNGLE	BEATTY	PLANCK	BECKET	LUDERS	PSEUDO	ROGERS	PHILON
TROFIM	BUSTER	MURIEL	BEAVAN	PLANTE	BICHAT	LUDWIG	RUEBEN	SEGALL	PRINCE
TROTTI	BUTLER	MURPHY	BHABHA	PRAWER	COCKER	MADLER	SHEMIN	SIGRID	QUIDDE
TRUMAN	CUGNOT	MURRAY	BLAAUW	REAGAN	DECUIR	MEDICI	SPENCE	TAGORE	QUINCY
TRUMBO	CULLEN	MUSSET	BLAISE	REALDO	ECCLES	NADINE	SPERRY	WAGNER	RAINER
URBAIN	CURTIS	PULLER	BLATTY	RHAZES	ERCKER	OLDHAM	STEARN	WIGNER	REILLY
WRIGHT	CURTIZ	PUNNET	BRAMAH	SCARPA	EUCKEN	RODNEY	STEARS	ANHALT	REINER
ASHKIN	CUVIER	QUIDDE	BRANCA	SEAMUS	EUCLID	RUDOLF	STEELE	ASHKIN	REINES
ASPDIN	DUDLEY	QUINCY	BRANDO	SEATON	FSCOTT	SIDNEY	STEFAN	BEHAIM	REISCH
FSCOTT	DUFOUR	RUBBIA	BRANDT	SHAMIR	JACOBI	SYDNEY	STEVEN	BOHLIN	SAINTE
HSIUNG	DUGGAR	RUBNER	CHABRY	SHANKS	JACOBS	TADDEO	THELMA	JOHANN	SHIMON
ISAACS	DULONG	RUCKER	CHANCE	SHARPE	JACOPO	UNDSET	THEONI	KOHLER	SHIUNG
ISADOR	DUNANT	RUDOLF	CHAPPE	SMAUEL	KOCHER	UPDIKE	TREVOR	MAHLON	SLIFER
ISIDOR	DUNBAR	RUEBEN	CLAIRE	SPACEK	LUCILA	WYDNER	WIENER	OTHMAN	STIFEL
ISMAEL	DUNCAN	RUMKER	CLARKE	SPACEY	LUCIUS	ALEXIS	WIESEL	ROHRER	SMILEY
OSWALD	DUNHAM	RUPERT	CLAUDE	STALIN	LYCETT	AMECHE	ZEEMAN	SCHACK	STILES
PSEUDO	DUNLOP	RUSSEL	COATES	SVANTE	MCCORD	AMEDEO	ALFRED	SCHARY	THIOUT
TSVETT	DUPUIS	SUMNER	CRAFTS	THABIT	MCCUNE	BRENDA	ALFVEN	SCHELL	ULISSE
USSHER	DUSTIN	SUSUME	CRAGOE	THALES	MICALI	BREUER	COFFIN	SCHICK	VOIGHT
ATWOOD	DUTTON	SUSUMU	CRAMER	TRAJAN	MICHEL	CAESAR	DAFFOS	SCHNEE	VOISIN
ETIENE	DUVALL	SUTTON	CRANCH	TRAVIS	NECKAM	CHEOPS	DUFOUR	WOHLER	WEINER
OTHMAN	EUCKEN	SUZUKI	DIANNE	WEAVER	NICOLA	CHEYNE	EIFFEL	ALISON	WRIGHT
OTTMAR	EUCLID	TULLIO	DRAPER	ABBOTT	NICOLE	CRELLE	GUFFEY	BAINES	YOICHI

ZWICKY	HOLMES	WALSON	BENSON	LENOIR	GEORGI	SOPHUS	FARMER	MARCUS	VERTES
FAJANS	JOLIOT	WALTER	BENTON	LINDER	GIOSUE	TOPHAM	FAROUK	MARION	VIRGIL
ECKERT	JULIAN	WALTON	BINNIG	LINDON	GLORIA	ULPIUS	FARRAR	MARISA	WARING
KEKULE	JULIEN	WELLER	BONNER	LONDON	GLOVER	PAQUIN	FARROW	MARIUS	WARNER
MCKEEN	JULIUS	WELLES	BONNET	LYNDON	GOOSEN	RIQUET	FERNEL	MARKOV	WARREN
NAKANO	KALUZA	WILBER	BONNOT	MANABA	GROVER	ADRIAN	FERRER	MARLEE	WERNER
NIKOLA	KELLER	WILCKE	BUNCHE	MANLIO	GYORGY	ADRIEN	FORBES	MARLON	YERGIN
OAKLEY	KELLEY	WILDER	BUNSEN	MANSON	HOOVER	ARREST	FOREST	MARTEL	YERKES
RAKINE	KELVIN	WILKES	CANNOM	MENCHU	KHOURI	BARANY	FORMAN	MARTIN	YERSIN
SAKATA	KILJAN	WILLEM	CANNON	MENDEL	LEONOR	BARBER	GARCIA	MARVIN	YORDAN
VIKTOR	KOLLER	WILLIS	CANTIN	MENGES	LEONOV	BARBRA	GARDAY	MERCER	ZARNKE
YUKAWA	LOLOIR	WILSON	CANTON	MENKEN	LIONEL	BARKLA	GARMES	MERRIT	AUSTEN
ALLDER	MALAKH	WILTER	CANTOR	MENZEL	LIOTTA	BARNES	GARROD	MOREAU	AUSTIN
ALLVAR	MALDEN	WOLSKY	CONRAD	MONETA	LOOMIS	BARNEY	GARROW	MORENO	BASEVI
ARLING	MALONE	ZOLTAN	CONRAT	MONROE	PROULX	BARROW	GARSON	MORGAN	BESLER
ARLISS	MCLEAN	ARMAND	DANIEL	MONTEL	PROUST	BARTON	GERALD	MORITZ	BESSEL
AYLING	MCLEOD	AYMAND	DANILO	MUNGLE	RAOULT	BARUCH	GERARD	MORLEY	BISHOP
AYLMER	MELLOR	CIMINO	DENJOY	NANSEN	RHODES	BERGER	GERMAN	MORRIS	BUSSEY
BELLOW	MELVIN	DOMAGK	DENNIS	PANDER	ROOSBY	BERING	GEROGE	MORROW	BUSTER
BOLTON	MELVYN	EDMOND	DENTON	PINCUS	SCOPES	BERMAN	GERRIT	MORTON	CASKEY
BOLYAI	MILENA	HAMSUN	DENZEL	PUNNET	SCOTUS	BERNAL	GERSON	MURIEL	CASPAR
BULLEN	MILLAN	ILMARI	DINTIS	RANDAL	SHOVEL	BEROZA	GIRARD	MURPHY	CASSIN
CALLIE	MILLER	ISMAEL	DONALD	RENFEW	SKOTAK	BERTHA	GORDON	MURRAY	CASTEL
CALVIN	MILNER	KEMENY	DONATI	RENNIE	SLOANE	BERTIL	GORGAS	MYRDAL	CESARE
CELSUS	MILOSZ	KEMMER	DONATO	RINGER	STOCKE	BORDEN	GURNEY	NARMER	CESARI
COLLIP	MILTON	KUMMER	DUNANT	RONALD	STOKES	BORDET	HARALD	NERNST	COSTER
COLMAN	MOLINA	LEMERY	DUNBAR	RONNIE	STONEY	BORDEU	HARDEN	NERUDA	DESIRE
CULLEN	MULLER	LEMMON	DUNCAN	SANGER	TEODOR	BORMAN	HARLEY	NERVIG	DUSTIN
DALTON	MULLIS	PAMELA	DUNHAM	SANTEL	THOLDE	BURALI	HARLOW	NORGAY	EISAKU
DELANO	NELSON	RAMSAY	DUNLOP	SENECA	THOMAS	BURNET	HAROLD	NORMAN	EISELE
DELANY	NILSON	RAMSEY	ERNEST	SINGER	TROFIM	BURTON	HARRIS	NORRIS	ELSTER
DILLEY	NOLLET	REMSEN	FINLAY	TANAKA	TROTTI	CARAKA	HARUNA	PARKER	FISHER
DILLON	PALADE	ROMAIN	FINNEY	VENETZ	WHOOPI	CARBON	HARVEY	PARKES	FOSTER
DULONG	PALFYN	ROMANO	FINSEN	VENING	WOOLEY	CARLOS	HERALD	PERKIN	GASSER
EDLUND	PALMER	RUMKER	GINGER	WANKEL	YVONNE	CARMEN	HERBIG	PERRIN	GASTON
EILEEN	PELLOS	SAMUAL	GUNTER	WENZEL	ALPHER	CARNEY	HERMAN	PERUTZ	GESELL
ELLERY	POLHEM	SAMUEL	HANLEY	WINSOR	ALPINI	CARNOT	HERMES	PIROSH	GESNER
ELLIOT	PULLER	SEMJON	HANNES	WINTON	AMPERE	CARREL	HIRSCH	PORTER	GOSSET
ERLICH	ROLAND	SEMLER	HANSEN	ZENOBE	APPERT	CARSON	HORACE	SARGON	GUSTAF
FELIPE	SALEEN	SHMUEL	HENCKE	ZINNER	APPOLT	CARTAN	HORNER	SARTRE	GUSTAV
FULLER	SELMAN	SIMEON	HENNIG	ADOLFO	ASPDIN	CARTER	HORTON	SERSEN	HASDAI
FULTON	SILVIO	SIMOND	HENRIK	ADOLPH	CAPMAN	CARVER	JEREMY	STRABO	HASSEL
GALOIS	SOLVAY	SIMONE	HENSEN	ALONZO	COPLEY	CERNAN	JEROME	STRATO	HESTON
GALTON	TALBOT	SIMONI	HINTON	BROOKE	DUPUIS	CERRAF	JORDAN	STREEP	HUSTON
GILLES	TELLER	SIMONS	HONOLD	BROOKS	HOPPER	CORDUS	JURAGA	STREET	JESSUP
GILMAN	TOLAND	SUMNER	HUNTER	CLORIS	KAPARY	CORNER	KARNOW	STRONG	JOSEPH
GOLDIE	TOLMAN	TIMONI	IGNATZ	CLOVIS	KEPLER	CORTES	KARRER	STRUSS	JOSHUA
HALDAN	TULLIO	TUMMEL	JANSKY	COOLEY	KOPPEN	CURTIS	KIRWAN	STRUTT	JOSIAH
HALLER	VALENS	AGNETA	JANUSZ	COOPER	LIPPES	CURTIZ	LARMOR	STRUVE	JUSTUS
HALLEY	VALLEE	ANNING	JENNER	CRONIN	NAPIER	CYRANO	LARNER	TARSKI	KASPAR
HALSEY	VALLES	ARNAUD	JENSEN	CROSBY	NIPKOW	DARWIN	LARSEN	TERESA	KOSMAS
HALTON	VILMOS	ARNOLD	KANADA	ELOISE	PAPPUS	DERHAM	LARSON	TORREY	KOSSEL
HELLER	WALDEN	BANACH	KINSKY	FEODOR	PEPLOE	DORIAN	LARTET	TURING	KOSTER
HILLER	WALESA	BENDER	KONRAD	FLOREY	RUPERT	ENRICO	LERNER	ULRICH	LASEAR
HILTON	WALKEN	BENITO	KUNKEL	FLOYER	SAPPHO	FARADY	LORENZ	VARMUS	LASKER
HOLDEN	WALKER	BENNET	LANDAU	FROSCH	SOPHIA	FARFAX	MARCEL	VERNER	LASZLO
HOLLEY	WALLIS	BENOIT	LANDON	GEORGE	SOPHIE	FARMAN	MARCIA	VERNON	LESLEY

			4TH LETTER						
LESLIE	WATERS	SAVARY	ADDAMS	NAGANO	HENCKE	RANDAL	MCLEOD	DUGGAR	USSHER
LESTER	WATKIN	SAVERY	AMDAHL	NAKANO	MARCEL	RHODES	MILENA	DWIGHT	ADRIAN
LISTER	WATSON	SEVERO	ANHALT	OSWALD	MARCIA	TADDEO	MONETA	GEIGER	ADRIEN
LUSSAC	WITELO	TSVETT	ARGAND	PALADE	MARCUS	TEODOR	MOREAU	GINGER	ALPINI
MESMER	WITTIG	VIVIAN	ARMAND	PICARD	MENCHU	WALDEN	MORENO	GORGAS	ANNING
MUSSET	BAUHIN	VIVIEN	ARNAUD	RAFAEL	MERCER	WILDER	MOYERS	GREGOR	ARLING
NESTOR	BOUGHN	ZAVIER	AYMAND	ROLAND	NEWCOM	YORDAN	NAGELI	GRIGGS	ARLISS
NOSSAL	BOULLE	ZAVITZ	BANACH	ROMAIN	PASCAL	AGNETA	OLBERS	HEDGES	AYLING
PASCAL	BRUNEL	ATWOOD	BARANY	ROMANO	PINCUS	ALBERT	PAMELA	HEEGER	BENITO
PISTEK	BRUTUS	BAWDEN	BEHAIM	RONALD	PLUCHE	AMPERE	PETERS	JAGGER	BERING
RISKIN	CAUCHY	BOWLES	BLAAUW	SAKATA	SECCHI	ANDERS	POWELL	MAGGIE	BIZIOU
ROSHER	CHURCH	COWLES	BOGART	SAVAGE	SPACEK	ANGELL	REVERE	MENGES	BLAISE
RUSSEL	COUPER	DAWSON	BRIAND	SAVARY	SPACEY	ANGELO	RIVEST	MORGAN	CIMINO
SUSUME	EDUARD	EDWARD	BURALI	SCHACK	STOCKE	APPERT	ROBERT	MUNGLE	CIVITA
SUSUMU	FAUSTO	FOWLER	CARAKA	SCHARY	WILCKE	ARREST	ROGERS	NORGAY	CLAIRE
TASMAN	GAUDIO	HEWISH	CESARE	SEGALL	YOICHI	ARTEDI	RUPERT	REAGAN	CUVIER
TESICH	GIULIO	HEWITT	CESARI	SEWALL	ZWICKY	BASEVI	RYBERG	RINGER	DANIEL
UNSOLD	HAUBEN	HOWARD	CHIANG	SLOANE	ALLDER	BOVERI	SALEEN	SANGER	DANILO
USSHER	LAUREL	LAWRIE	CYRANO	STEARN	AMEDEO	CAVETT	SAVERY	SARGON	DAVIES
WESLEY	LAUREN	LOWELL	DELANO	STEARS	ASPDIN	ECKERT	SCHELL	SINGER	DESIRE
WESSEL	LOUDON	LOWITZ	DELANY	STRABO	BAWDEN	EILEEN	SENECA	VIRGIL	DORIAN
YASSER	LOUISE	NEWCOM	DOMAGK	STRATO	BEADLE	EISELE	SEVERO	VOIGHT	DREIER
AITKEN	MOUTON	NEWMAN	DONALD	STUART	BENDER	ELLERY	SIMEON	WRIGHT	ELLIOT
ALTMAN	NAUDIN	NEWTON	DONATI	TANAKA	BIDDEL	ENDERS	STEELE	YERGIN	ELOISE
AMTHOR	PLUCHE	OSWALD	DONATO	TOLAND	BORDEN	ENGELS	STREEP	ALPHER	ENRICO
ANTONY	SAURIA	POWELL	DUNANT	URBAIN	BORDET	ERNEST	STREET	AMTHOR	ERLICH
ARTEDI	SHUKEN	SEWALL	DUVALL	YUKAWA	BORDEU	ETIENE	TERESA	ARCHER	EYVIND
ARTHUR	SQUIER	TEWFIK	EDUARD	BARBER	BRIDGE	EUGENE	TSVETT	ARCHIE	FABIAN
BUTLER	STUART	TOWNES	EDWARD	BARBRA	BUDDHA	FIZEAU	VALENS	ARTHUR	FELIPE
COTTON	STUMPF	BAXTER	EISAKU	BHABHA	CORDUS	FOREST	VENETZ	BAUHIN	GOBIND
DUTTON	TAUBES	CAXTON	FAJANS	CARBON	FEODOR	GESELL	WALESA	BECHER	HEWISH
HATTIE	TAUROG	HUXLEY	FARADY	CHABRY	GARDAY	GIDEON	WATERS	BICHAT	HEWITT
HITLER	TRUMAN	LEXELL	GERALD	DIBBLE	GAUDIO	GRAEBE	WITELO	BISHOP	IRVING
HITNER	TRUMBO	PAXTON	GERARD	DUNBAR	GLADYS	GREENE	ARAFAT	DERHAM	JOLIOT
HITZIG	VAUBAN	WEXLER	GIRARD	FORBES	GOLDIE	GRIESS	COFFIN	DUNHAM	JOSIAH
HUTTON	BOVERI	CAYLEY	HARALD	GIBBON	GORDON	HAVERS	CRAFTS	FISHER	JULIAN
JETHRO	CAVETT	DAYTON	HAZARD	HAUBEN	HALDAN	HEVESY	DAFFOS	GRAHAM	JULIEN
KATINA	CIVITA	ELYTIS	HERALD	HERBIG	HARDEN	HIDEKI	EIFFEL	HUGHES	JULIUS
KOTARO	CUVIER	GAYNOR	HORACE	HOBBES	HASDAI	HUBERT	FARFAX	JETHRO	KATINA
LATTES	DAVIES	GUYTON	HOWARD	HUBBLE	HOLDEN	JEREMY	GUFFEY	JOSHUA	LEVIEN
LITTLE	DUVALL	KEYNES	IGNATZ	KIBBLE	ISADOR	JOGESH	KEFFER	KOCHER	LEVINE
LOTHAR	EYVIND	LAYARD	ILMARI	LEIBER	ISIDOR	JOSEPH	MAFFEO	LOTHAR	LOUISE
LUTHER	GAVRAS	MAYALL	ISAACS	PREBUS	JORDAN	KEMENY	NAIFEH	LUTHER	LOVISA
LUTULI	HAVERS	MOYERS	ISMAEL	ROBBIE	LANDAU	KRAELY	PALFYN	MEEHAN	LOWITZ
MATEOS	HEVESY	PEYTON	JOHANN	RUBBIA	LANDON	LASEAR	RENFEW	MICHEL	LUCILA
MATLIN	IRVING	POYNER	JURAGA	RUEBEN	LINDER	LAZEAR	SLIFER	MOTHER	LUCIUS
MOTHER	LEVENE	SEYLER	KANADA	TALBOT	LINDON	LEMERY	STEFAN	NATHAN	MARION
NATHAN	LEVIEN	SMYTHE	KAPARY	TAUBES	LONDON	LEVENE	STIFEL	OLDHAM	MARISA
OTTMAR	LEVINE	TAYLOR	KOTARO	THABIT	LOUDON	LEXELL	TEWFIK	POLHEM	MARIUS
PETERS	LOVELL	AUZOUT	LAYARD	VAUBAN	LYNDON	LORENZ	TROFIM	RACHEL	MEDICI
PETRIE	LOVISA	BIZIOU	LAZARE	WILBER	MALDEN	LOVELL	AMAGAT	RICHER	MOBIUS
PETRUS	NEVILL	FIZEAU	LAZARE	AMECHE	MCADAM	LOWELL	BERGER	RICHET	MOLINA
PETTIT	ORVILL	HAZARD	LAZARE	BUNCHE	MENDEL	LUDERS	BOUGHN	ROSHER	MORITZ
RITTER	PAVLOV	LAZARE	MALAKH	CAUCHY	MYRDAL	LYCETT	BRIGGS	SOPHIA	MURIEL
ROTTER	REVERE	LAZEAR	MANABA	DUNCAN	NAUDIN	MATEOS	BRIGHT	SOPHIE	NADINE
SUTTON	RIVEST	ROZIER	MAYALL	FRICKE	PANDER	MCKEEN	CRAGOE	SOPHUS	NAPIER
TITIUS	SAVAGE	SUZUKI	MICALI	GARCIA	QUIDDE	MCLEAN	DIGGES	TOPHAM	NEVILL

NOBILI	WATKIN	KOHLER	CARMEN	BRENDA	RAGNAR	LOLOIR	CONRAD	BUSSEY	TARSKI
ORVILL	WILKES	KOLLER	COLMAN	BRUNEL	RAINER	MALONE	CONRAT	CAESAR	ULISSE
PACINI	YERKES	LESLEY	CRAMER	BURNET	REINER	MCCORD	EMERIC	CARSON	UNDSET
PACINO	ADOLFO	LESLIE	CREMER	CAGNEY	REINES	MILOSZ	EVARTS	CASSIN	VOISIN
RACINE	ADOLPH	MADLER	FARMAN	CANNOM	RENNIE	NICOLA	FAIRLY	CELSUS	WALSON
RAKINE	BEGLEY	MAHLON	FARMER	CANNON	RODNEY	NICOLE	FARRAR	CROSBY	WATSON
REGIUS	BELLOW	MANLIO	FORMAN	CARNEY	RONNIE	NICOLO	FARROW	DAWSON	WESSEL
ROBINS	BESLER	MARLEE	GARMES	CARNOT	RUBNER	NIKOLA	FERRER	DIESEL	WIESEL
ROZIER	BOHLIN	MARLON	GERMAN	CERNAN	SAINTE	PIROSH	FLEROV	EDISON	WILSON
SABINE	BOULLE	MATLIN	GILMAN	CHANCE	SCHNEE	RUDOLF	FLOREY	ELISHA	WINSOR
SCHICK	BOWLES	MELLOR	GRAMME	CORNER	SHANKS	SIMOND	GARROD	FAUSTO	WOLSKY
SQUIER	BRILEY	MILLAN	GRIMES	CRANCH	SIDNEY	SIMONE	GARROW	FIESER	YASSER
TESICH	BULLEN	MILLER	HERMAN	CRONIN	SPENCE	SIMONI	GAVRAS	FINSEN	YERSIN
TITIUS	BUTLER	MORLEY	HERMES	CUGNOT	STONEY	SIMONS	GEORGE	FRASCH	AUSTEN
TOBIAS	CALLIE	MULLER	HOLMES	DENNIS	SUMNER	STRONG	GEORGI	FROSCH	AUSTIN
TURING	CARLOS	MULLIS	KEMMER	DIANNE	SVANTE	TAGORE	GERRIT	GARSON	BARTON
ULPIUS	CAYLEY	NOLLET	KOSMAS	FERNEL	SYDNEY	THEONI	GLORIA	GASSER	BAXTER
ULRICH	COLLIP	OAKLEY	KUMMER	FINNEY	TOWNES	THIOUT	GOERGE	GEISEL	BEATON
UPDIKE	COOLEY	PAVLOV	LARMOR	FRANCA	VERNER	TIMONI	GUERIN	GERSON	BEATTY
VENING	COPLEY	PELLOS	LEMMON	FRANCE	VERNON	UNSOLD	GYORGY	GIBSON	BENTON
VIVIAN	COWLES	PEPLOE	LOOMIS	FRANCK	WAGNER	WHOOPI	HARRIS	GIESEL	BERTHA
VIVIEN	CRELLE	PHILIP	MAIMAN	FRANCO	WARNER	ZENOBE	HENRIK	GIOSUE	BERTIL
WARING	CULLEN	PHILON	MESMER	FRANKE	WEINER	CASPAR	INGRAM	GLASER	BLATTY
ZAVIER	DILLEY	PULLER	NARMER	FRENCH	WERNER	CHAPPE	INGRID	GOOSEN	BOLTON
ZAVITZ	DILLON	REALDO	NEWMAN	GAINES	WIENER	COOPER	KARRER	GOSSET	BRUTUS
DENJOY	DUDLEY	REILLY	NORMAN	GAYNOR	WIGNER	COUPER	KEARNS	HALSEY	BURTON
GRIJNS	DUNLOP	ROBLEY	OTHMAN	GESNER	WYDNER	DRAPER	KONRAD	HAMSUN	BUSTER
KILJAN	EAGLER	SEMLER	OTTMAR	GIANNI	YVONNE	HOPPER	LAUREL	HANSEN	CANTIN
SEMJON	ECCLES	SEYLER	PALMER	GIBNEY	ZARNKE	KASPAR	LAUREN	HASSEL	CANTON
TRAJAN	EMILIE	SIBLEY	SEAMUS	GLENDA	ZINNER	KOPPEN	LAWRIE	HENSEN	CANTOR
AITKEN	EMILIO	SMILEY	SELMAN	GRANIT	ABBOTT	KUIPER	MERRIT	HIRSCH	CARTAN
ASHKIN	EUCLID	STALIN	SHAMIR	GURNEY	ALCOCK	LIPPES	MONROE	JANSKY	CARTER
BARKLA	EVELYN	STILES	SHEMIN	HANNES	ALCOTT	MURPHY	MORRIS	JENSEN	CASTEL
BECKET	FIELDS	TAYLOR	SHIMON	HEANEY	ANTONY	NIEPCE	MORROW	JESSUP	CAXTON
CASKEY	FINLAY	TELLER	STUMPF	HENNIG	APPOLT	PAPPUS	MURRAY	KEESOM	COATES
COCKER	FOWLER	THALES	TASMAN	HITNER	ARNOLD	SAPPHO	NORRIS	KINSKY	CORTES
ERCKER	FULLER	THELMA	THOMAS	HORNER	ATWOOD	SCOPES	OBERTH	KOSSEL	COSTER
EUCKEN	GILLES	THOLDE	TOLMAN	IVANOV	AUZOUT	ALARIC	OFFROY	KRASNA	COTTON
KUNKEL	GIULIO	TULLIO	TRUMAN	JEANNE	BENOIT	ALDRIN	OPARIN	KYESER	CURTIS
LASKER	GMELIN	VALLEE	TRUMBO	JENNER	BEROZA	ALFRED	PERRIN	LARSEN	CURTIZ
LEAKEY	HADLEY	VALLES	TUMMEL	JOANNE	BROOKE	ANDREA	PETRIE	LARSON	DALTON
MARKOV	HALLER	WALLIS	VARMUS	KARNOW	BROOKS	ANDREI	PETRUS	LUSSAC	DAYTON
MEIKLE	HALLEY	WELLER	VILMOS	KEYNES	CHEOPS	ANDRES	PIERCE	MANSON	DENTON
MENKEN	HANLEY	WELLES	ZEEMAN	LARNER	DUFOUR	ANDREW	PIERRE	MUSSET	DIETER
NECKAM	HARLEY	WESLEY	ALONZO	LEONOR	DULONG	ANDREY	ROHRER	NANSEN	DINTIS
NIPKOW	HARLOW	WEXLER	BAINES	LEONOV	EDMOND	ANDRIC	SAURIA	NELSON	DMITRI
PARKER	HEFLIN	WILLEM	BARNES	LERNER	FAROUK	ARDREY	SCARPA	NILSON	DUSTIN
PARKES	HELLER	WILLIS	BARNEY	LIONEL	FSCOTT	AUBREY	SHARPE	NOSSAL	DUTTON
PERKIN	HILLER	WOHLER	BENNET	MAGNUS	GALOIS	AUDREY	SIGRID	ORESME	ELSTER
RISKIN	HITLER	WOOLEY	BERNAL	MILNER	GEROGE	BARROW	SPERRY	POGSON	ELYTIS
RUCKER	HOLLEY	ALTMAN	BINNIG	NERNST	HAROLD	CABRAL	TAUROG	RAMSAY	FOSTER
RUMKER	HUXLEY	AYLMER	BONNER	PLANCK	HONOLD	CARREL	TORREY	RAMSEY	FULTON
SHUKEN	KEELER	BERMAN	BONNET	PLANTE	JACOBI	CEDRIC	WARREN	REISCH	GALTON
STOKES	KEILIN	BODMER	BONNOT	POYNER	JACOBS	CERRAF	ALISON	REMSEN	GASTON
WALKEN	KELLER	BORMAN	BRANCA	PRINCE	JACOPO	CHURCH	BENSON	ROOSBY	GEITEL
WALKER	KELLEY	BRAMAH	BRANDO	PUNNET	JEROME	CLARKE	BESSEL	RUSSEL	GUNTER
WANKEL	KEPLER	CAPMAN	BRANDT	QUINCY	LENOIR	CLORIS	BUNSEN	SERSEN	GUSTAF

GUSTAV	ALCUIN	OLIVER	DERHAM	RAGNAR	SCHICK	BORDET	FINNEY	HOLMES	MENKEN
GUYTON	AUGUST	OLIVIA	DORIAN	RAMSAY	SENECA	BORDEU	FINSEN	HOOVER	MENZEL
GYATSO	BARUCH	PREVIN	DUGGAR	RANDAL	SPENCE	BOWLES	FISHER	HOPPER	MERCER
HALTON	BEGUIN	SHOVEL	DUNBAR	REAGAN	TESICH	BREUER	FLOREY	HORNER	MESMER
HATTIE	BREUER	SILVIO	DUNCAN	SAMUAL	ULRICH	BRILEY	FLOYER	HUGHES	MICHEL
HESTON	CLAUDE	SOLVAY	DUNHAM	SELMAN	ARTEDI	BRUNEL	FORBES	HUNTER	MIGUEL
HILTON	COBURN	STEVEN	FABIAN	SKOTAK	BRANDO	BULLEN	FOSTER	HUXLEY	MILLER
HINTON	DECUIR	TRAVIS	FARFAX	SOLVAY	BRANDT	BUNSEN	FOWLER	ISMAEL	MILNER
HORTON	DUPUIS	TREVOR	FARMAN	STEFAN	BRENDA	BURNET	FRAZER	JAGGER	MONTEL
HUNTER	EDLUND	WEAVER	FARRAR	TASMAN	CLAUDE	BUSSEY	FULLER	JENNER	MORLEY
HUSTON	FREUND	DARWIN	FINLAY	THOMAS	FARADY	BUSTER	GAINES	JENSEN	MOTHER
HUTTON	GRAUNT	KIRWAN	FIZEAU	TOBIAS	FIELDS	BUTLER	GARMES	JULIEN	MULLER
JUSTUS	HARUNA	LUDWIG	FORMAN	TOLMAN	GLENDA	CAGNEY	GASSER	KARRER	MURIEL
KEATON	HSIUNG	PRAWER	GARDAY	TOPHAM	KANADA	CARMEN	GEIGER	KEELER	MUSSET
KOSTER	JANUSZ	ALEXIS	GAVRAS	TRAJAN	NERUDA	CARNEY	GEISEL	KEFFER	NAIFEH
LARTET	KALUZA	BOLYAI	GERMAN	TRUMAN	PALADE	CARREL	GEITEL	KELLER	NANSEN
LATTES	KEKULE	CHEYNE	GILMAN	VAUBAN	PSEUDO	CARTER	GESNER	KELLEY	NAPIER
LESTER	KHOURI	DREYER	GORGAS	VIVIAN	QUIDDE	CARVER	GIBNEY	KEMMER	NARMER
LIOTTA	LUTULI	FLOYER	GRAHAM	YORDAN	REALDO	CASKEY	GIESEL	KEPLER	NOLLET
LISTER	MCCUNE	DENZEL	GUSTAF	ZEEMAN	THOLDE	CASTEL	GILLES	KEYNES	OAKLEY
LITTLE	MIGUEL	FRAZER	GUSTAV	ZOLTAN	ADRIEN	CAYLEY	GINGER	KOCHER	OLIVER
LOFTUS	NAGUIB	GLAZER	HALDAN	CROSBY	AITKEN	COATES	GLASER	KOHLER	PALMER
MARTEL	NERUDA	GRAZIA	HASDAI	GRAEBE	ALFRED	COCKER	GLAZER	KOLLER	PANDER
MARTIN	PAQUIN	HEEZEN	HERMAN	JACOBI	ALFVEN	COOLEY	GLOVER	KOPPEN	PARKER
MILTON	PERUTZ	HITZIG	INGRAM	JACOBS	ALLDER	COOPER	GOOSEN	KOSSEL	PARKES
MONTEL	PROULX	LASZLO	JORDAN	MANABA	ALPHER	COPLEY	GOSSET	KOSTER	PICTET
MORTON	PROUST	MENZEL	JOSIAH	ROOSBY	AMEDEO	CORNER	GRAVES	KUIPER	PIETER
MOUTON	PSEUDO	PIAZZI	JULIAN	STRABO	ANDREA	CORTES	GRIMES	KUMMER	PISTEK
NESTOR	RAOULT	RHAZES	KASPAR	TRUMBO	ANDREI	COSTER	GROVER	KUNKEL	POLHEM
NEWTON	RIQUET	WENZEL	KILJAN	ZENOBE	ANDRES	COUPER	GUFFEY	KYESER	PORTER
PAXTON	SAMUAL		KIRWAN	ALCOCK	ANDREW	COWLES	GUNTER	LARNER	POYNER
PETTIT	SAMUAL		KONRAD	BANACH	ANDREY	CRAMER	GURNEY	LARSEN	PRAWER
PEYTON	SHIUNG		KOSMAS	BARUCH	ARCHER	CREMER	HADLEY	LARTET	PULLER
PICTET	SHMUEL	**5TH LETTER**	LANDAU	BRANCA	ARDREY	CULLEN	HALLER	LASKER	PUNNET
PIETER	SMAUEL		LASEAR	CHANCE	AUBREY	CUVIER	HALLEY	LATTES	RACHEL
PIETRO	STRUSS	ADRIAN	LAZEAR	CHURCH	AUDREY	DANIEL	HALSEY	LAUREL	RAFAEL
PISTEK	STRUTT	ALLVAR	LOTHAR	CRANCH	AUSTEN	DAVIES	HANLEY	LAUREN	RAINER
PORTER	STRUVE	ALTMAN	LUSSAC	ENRICO	AYLMER	DENZEL	HANNES	LEAKEY	RAMSEY
RITTER	SUSUME	AMAGAT	MAIMAN	ERLICH	BAINES	DIESEL	HANSEN	LEIBER	REINER
ROTTER	SUSUMU	ARAFAT	MCADAM	FRANCA	BARBER	DIETER	HARDEN	LERNER	REINES
SANTEL	SUZUKI	BEAVAN	MCLEAN	FRANCE	BARNES	DIGGES	HARLEY	LESLEY	REMSEN
SARTRE	ALFVEN	BERMAN	MEEHAN	FRANCK	BARNEY	DILLEY	HARVEY	LESTER	RENFEW
SCOTUS	ALLVAR	BERNAL	MILLAN	FRANCO	BAWDEN	DRAPER	HASSEL	LEVIEN	RHAZES
SEATON	BEAVAN	BICHAT	MOREAU	FRASCH	BAXTER	DREIER	HAUBEN	LINDER	RHODES
SKOTAK	CALVIN	BOLYAI	MORGAN	FRENCH	BECHER	DREYER	HEANEY	LIONEL	RICHER
SMYTHE	CARVER	BORMAN	MURRAY	FROSCH	BECKET	DUDLEY	HEDGES	LIPPES	RICHET
SUTTON	CLOVIS	BRAMAH	MYRDAL	HIRSCH	BEGLEY	EAGLER	HEEGER	LISTER	RINGER
TROTTI	GLOVER	CABRAL	NATHAN	HORACE	BENDER	ECCLES	HEEZEN	LUTHER	RIQUET
VERTES	GRAVES	CAESAR	NECKAM	ISAACS	BENNET	EIFFEL	HELLER	MADLER	RITTER
VICTOR	GROVER	CAPMAN	NEWMAN	MEDICI	BERGER	EILEEN	HENSEN	MAFFEO	ROBLEY
VIKTOR	HARVEY	CARTAN	NORGAY	NIEPCE	BESLER	ELSTER	HERMES	MALDEN	RODNEY
WALTER	HOOVER	CASPAR	NORMAN	PIERCE	BESSEL	ERCKER	HILLER	MARCEL	ROHRER
WALTON	KELVIN	CERNAN	NOSSAL	PLANCK	BIDDEL	EUCKEN	HITLER	MARLEE	ROSHER
WILTER	MARVIN	CERRAF	OLDHAM	PRINCE	BODMER	FARMER	HITNER	MARTEL	ROTTER
WINTON	MELVIN	COLMAN	OTHMAN	QUINCY	BONNER	FERNEL	HOBBES	MCKEEN	ROZIER
WITTIG	MELVYN	CONRAD	OTTMAR	REISCH	BONNET	FERRER	HOLDEN	MENDEL	RUBNER
ZOLTAN	NERVIG	CONRAT	PASCAL	SCHACK	BORDEN	FIESER	HOLLEY	MENGES	RUCKER

RUEBEN	WELLER	ALEXIS	LAWRIE	BROOKE	MEIKLE	EYVIND	BEATON	ISADOR	VIKTOR
RUMKER	WELLES	ANDRIC	LENOIR	BROOKS	MICALI	FAJANS	BELLOW	ISIDOR	VILMOS
RUSSEL	WENZEL	ARCHIE	LESLIE	CARAKA	MUNGLE	FREUND	BENSON	IVANOV	WALSON
SALEEN	WERNER	ASHKIN	LOLOIR	CLARKE	NAGELI	GIANNI	BENTON	JOLIOT	WALTON
SAMUEL	WESLEY	ASPDIN	LOOMIS	EISAKU	NEVILL	GOBIND	BISHOP	KARNOW	WATSON
SANGER	WESSEL	AUSTIN	LUDWIG	FRANKE	NICOLA	GRAUNT	BIZIOU	KEATON	WILSON
SANTEL	WEXLER	BAUHIN	MAGGIE	FRICKE	NICOLE	GREENE	BOLTON	KEESOM	WINSOR
SCHNEE	WIENER	BEGUIN	MANLIO	HENCKE	NICOLO	GRIJNS	BONNOT	LANDON	WINTON
SCOPES	WIESEL	BEHAIM	MARCIA	HIDEKI	NIKOLA	HARUNA	BURTON	LARMOR	ADOLPH
SEMLER	WIGNER	BENOIT	MARTIN	JANSKY	NOBILI	HSIUNG	CANNOM	LARSON	CHAPPE
SERSEN	WILBER	BERTIL	MARVIN	KINSKY	ORVILL	IRVING	CANNON	LEMMON	CHEOPS
SEYLER	WILDER	BINNIG	MATLIN	MALAKH	OSWALD	JEANNE	CANTON	LEONOR	FELIPE
SHMUEL	WILKES	BOHLIN	MELVIN	SHANKS	PAMELA	JOANNE	CANTOR	LEONOV	JACOPO
SHOVEL	WILLEM	CALLIE	MERRIT	STOCKE	POWELL	JOHANN	CARBON	LINDON	JOSEPH
SHUKEN	WILTER	CALVIN	MORRIS	SUZUKI	PROULX	KATINA	CARLOS	LONDON	SCARPA
SIBLEY	WOHLER	CANTIN	MULLIS	TANAKA	RAOULT	KEARNS	CARNOT	LOUDON	SHARPE
SIDNEY	WOOLEY	CASSIN	NAGUIB	TARSKI	REILLY	KEMENY	CARSON	LYNDON	STUMPF
SINGER	WYDNER	CEDRIC	NAUDIN	UPDIKE	RONALD	KRASNA	CAXTON	MAHLON	WHOOPI
SLIFER	YASSER	CLORIS	NERVIG	WILCKE	RUDOLF	LEVENE	COTTON	MANSON	ALBERT
SMAUEL	YERKES	CLOVIS	NORRIS	WOLSKY	SCHELL	LEVINE	CRAGOE	MARION	AMPERE
SMILEY	ZAVIER	COFFIN	OLIVIA	ZARNKE	SEGALL	LORENZ	CUGNOT	MARKOV	ANDERS
SPACEK	ZINNER	COLLIP	OPARIN	ZWICKY	SEWALL	MALONE	DAFFOS	MARLON	APPERT
SPACEY	ADOLFO	CRONIN	PAQUIN	ANGELL	STEELE	MCCUNE	DALTON	MATEOS	BARBRA
SQUIER	BRIDGE	CURTIS	PERKIN	ANGELO	UNSOLD	MILENA	DAWSON	MCLEOD	BOGART
STEVEN	BRIGGS	CURTIZ	PERRIN	ANHALT	WITELO	MOLINA	DAYTON	MELLOR	BOVERI
STIFEL	DOMAGK	DARWIN	PETRIE	APPOLT	ADDAMS	MORENO	DENJOY	MILTON	CESARE
STILES	GEORGE	DECUIR	PETTIT	ARNOLD	GRAMME	NADINE	DENTON	MONROE	CESARI
STOKES	GEORGI	DENNIS	PHILIP	BARKLA	JEREMY	NAGANO	DILLON	MORROW	CHABRY
STONEY	GEROGE	DINTIS	PREVIN	BEADLE	JEROME	NAKANO	DUNLOP	MORTON	CLAIRE
STREEP	GOERGE	DUPUIS	RENNIE	BOULLE	ORESME	PACINI	DUTTON	MOUTON	COBURN
STREET	GRIGGS	DUSTIN	RISKIN	BURALI	SUSUME	PACINO	EDISON	NELSON	DESIRE
SUMNER	GYORGY	ELYTIS	ROBBIE	CRELLE	SUSUMU	RACINE	ELLIOT	NESTOR	DMITRI
SYDNEY	JURAGA	EMERIC	ROMAIN	DANILO	THELMA	RAKINE	FARROW	NEWCOM	ECKERT
TADDEO	SAVAGE	EMILIE	RONNIE	DIBBLE	ALPINI	ROBINS	FEODOR	NEWTON	EDUARD
TAUBES	AMDAHL	EMILIO	RUBBIA	DONALD	ANNING	ROLAND	FLEROV	NILSON	EDWARD
TELLER	AMECHE	EUCLID	SAURIA	DUVALL	ANTONY	ROMANO	FULTON	NIPKOW	ELLERY
THALES	BERTHA	GALOIS	SHAMIR	EISELE	ARGAND	SABINE	GALTON	OFFROY	ENDERS
TORREY	BHABHA	GARCIA	SHEMIN	ENGELS	ARLING	SHIUNG	GARROD	PAVLOV	GERARD
TOWNES	BOUGHN	GAUDIO	SIGRID	FAIRLY	ARMAND	SIMOND	GARROW	PAXTON	GIRARD
TUMMEL	BRIGHT	GERRIT	SILVIO	GERALD	AYLING	SIMONE	GARSON	PELLOS	HAVERS
UNDSET	BUDDHA	GIULIO	SOPHIA	GESELL	AYMAND	SIMONI	GASTON	PEPLOE	HAZARD
USSHER	BUNCHE	GLORIA	SOPHIE	HARALD	BARANY	SIMONS	GAYNOR	PEYTON	HOWARD
VALLEE	CAUCHY	GMELIN	STALIN	HAROLD	BERING	SLOANE	GERSON	PHILON	HUBERT
VALLES	DWIGHT	GOLDIE	TEWFIK	HERALD	BRIAND	STRONG	GIBBON	POGSON	ILMARI
VERNER	ELISHA	GRANIT	THABIT	HONOLD	CHEYNE	THEONI	GIBSON	SARGON	JETHRO
VERTES	MENCHU	GRAZIA	TRAVIS	HUBBLE	CHIANG	TIMONI	GIDEON	SEATON	KAPARY
VIVIEN	MURPHY	GUERIN	TROFIM	KEKULE	CIMINO	TOLAND	GORDON	SEMJON	KHOURI
WAGNER	PLUCHE	HARRIS	TULLIO	KIBBLE	CYRANO	TURING	GREGOR	SHIMON	KOTARO
WALDEN	SAPPHO	HATTIE	URBAIN	KRAELY	DELANO	VALENS	GUYTON	SIMEON	LAYARD
WALKEN	SECCHI	HEFLIN	VIRGIL	LASZLO	DELANY	VENING	HALTON	SUTTON	LAZARE
WALKER	SMYTHE	HENNIG	VOISIN	LEXELL	DIANNE	WARING	HARLOW	TALBOT	LEMERY
WALTER	VOIGHT	HENRIK	WALLIS	LITTLE	DULONG	YVONNE	HESTON	TAUROG	LUDERS
WANKEL	WRIGHT	HERBIG	WATKIN	LOVELL	DUNANT	ALISON	HILTON	TAYLOR	MCCORD
WARNER	YOICHI	HITZIG	WILLIS	LOWELL	EDLUND	AMTHOR	HINTON	TEODOR	MOYERS
WARREN	ALARIC	INGRID	WITTIG	LUCILA	EDMOND	ATWOOD	HORTON	TREVOR	OLBERS
WEAVER	ALCUIN	KEILIN	YERGIN	LUTULI	ETIENE	BARROW	HUSTON	VERNON	PETERS
WEINER	ALDRIN	KELVIN	YERSIN	MAYALL	EUGENE	BARTON	HUTTON	VICTOR	PICARD

PIERRE	HEWITT	MELVYN	TERESA	BRIDGE	NICOLE	HSIUNG	PIAZZI	MIGUEL	BAUHIN
PIETRO	IGNATZ	PALFYN	THELMA	BROOKE	NIEPCE	IRVING	SECCHI	MONTEL	BAWDEN
REVERE	LIOTTA	ALONZO	WALESA	BUNCHE	ORESME	LUDWIG	SIMONI	MURIEL	BEATON
ROBERT	LOWITZ	BEROZA	YUKAWA	CALLIE	PALADE	NERVIG	SUZUKI	MYRDAL	BEAVAN
ROGERS	LYCETT	KALUZA	NAGUIB	CESARE	PEPLOE	RYBERG	TARSKI	NEVILL	BEGUIN
RUPERT	MONETA	PIAZZI	ALARIC	CHANCE	PETRIE	SHIUNG	THEONI	NOSSAL	BENSON
RYBERG	MORITZ		ANDRIC	CHAPPE	PIERCE	STRONG	TIMONI	ORVILL	BENTON
SARTRE	OBERTH		CEDRIC	CHEYNE	PIERRE	TAUROG	TROTTI	PASCAL	BERMAN
SAVARY	PERUTZ		EMERIC	CLAIRE	PLANTE	TURING	WHOOPI	POWELL	BOHLIN
SAVERY	PLANTE	**6TH LETTER**	LUSSAC	CLARKE	PLUCHE	VENING	YOICHI	RACHEL	BOLTON
SCHARY	SAINTE		ALFRED	CLAUDE	PRINCE	WARING	ALCOCK	RAFAEL	BORDEN
SEVERO	SAKATA	AGNETA	ARGAND	CRAGOE	QUIDDE	WITTIG	DOMAGK	RANDAL	BORMAN
SPERRY	STRATO	ANDREA	ARMAND	CRELLE	RACINE	ADOLPH	FAROUK	RUSSEL	BOUGHN
STEARN	STRUTT	BARBRA	ARNAUD	DESIRE	RAKINE	BANACH	FRANCK	SAMUAL	BULLEN
STEARS	SVANTE	BARKLA	ARNOLD	DIANNE	RENNIE	BARUCH	HENRIK	SAMUEL	BUNSEN
STUART	BEROZA	BEROZA	ATWOOD	DIBBLE	REVERE	BRAMAH	PISTEK	SANTEL	BURTON
TAGORE	TROTTI	BERTHA	AYMAND	EISELE	ROBBIE	CHURCH	PLANCK	SCHELL	CALVIN
WATERS	TSVETT	BHABHA	BRIAND	ELOISE	RONNIE	CRANCH	SCHACK	SEGALL	CANNON
ARLISS	VENETZ	BRANCA	CONRAD	EMILIE	SABINE	ERLICH	SCHICK	SEWALL	CANTIN
ARREST	ZAVITZ	BRENDA	DONALD	ETIENE	SAINTE	FRASCH	SKOTAK	SHMUEL	CANTON
AUGUST	ARNAUD	BUDDHA	EDLUND	EUGENE	SARTRE	FRENCH	SPACEK	SHOVEL	CAPMAN
BLAISE	ARTHUR	CARAKA	EDMOND	FELIPE	SAVAGE	FROSCH	TEWFIK	SMAUEL	CARBON
ELOISE	AUZOUT	CIVITA	EDUARD	FRANCE	SCHNEE	HEWISH	AMDAHL	STIFEL	CARMEN
ERNEST	BLAAUW	ELISHA	EDWARD	FRANKE	SHARPE	HIRSCH	ANGELL	TUMMEL	CARSON
FOREST	BRUTUS	FRANCA	EUCLID	FRICKE	SIMONE	JOGESH	BERNAL	VIRGIL	CARTAN
GRIESS	CELSUS	GARCIA	EYVIND	GEORGE	SLOANE	JOSEPH	BERTIL	WANKEL	CASSIN
GYATSO	CORDUS	GLENDA	FREUND	GEROGE	SMYTHE	JOSIAH	BESSEL	WENZEL	CAXTON
HEVESY	DUFOUR	GLORIA	GARROD	GIOSUE	SOPHIE	MALAKH	BIDDEL	WESSEL	CERNAN
HEWISH	FAROUK	GRAZIA	GERALD	GOERGE	SPENCE	NAIFEH	BRUNEL	WIESEL	COBURN
JANUSZ	GIOSUE	HARUNA	GERARD	GOLDIE	STEELE	OBERTH	CABRAL	BEHAIM	COFFIN
JOGESH	HAMSUN	JOSHUA	GIRARD	GRAEBE	STOCKE	PIROSH	CARREL	CANNOM	COLMAN
LOUISE	JESSUP	JURAGA	GOBIND	GRAMME	STRUVE	REISCH	CASTEL	DERHAM	COTTON
LOVISA	JOSHUA	KALUZA	HARALD	GREENE	SUSUME	TESICH	DANIEL	DUNHAM	CRONIN
MARISA	JULIUS	KANADA	HAROLD	HATTIE	SVANTE	ULRICH	DENZEL	GRAHAM	CULLEN
MILOSZ	JUSTUS	KATINA	HAZARD	HENCKE	TAGORE	ALPINI	DIESEL	INGRAM	DALTON
NERNST	LOFTUS	KRASNA	HERALD	HORACE	THOLDE	ANDREI	DUVALL	KEESOM	DARWIN
PIROSH	LUCIUS	LIOTTA	HONOLD	HUBBLE	ULISSE	ARTEDI	EIFFEL	MCADAM	DAWSON
PROUST	MAGNUS	LOVISA	HOWARD	JEANNE	UPDIKE	BASEVI	FERNEL	NECKAM	DAYTON
RIVEST	MARCUS	LUCILA	INGRID	JEROME	VALLEE	BOLYAI	GEISEL	NEWCOM	DENTON
STRUSS	MARIUS	MANABA	KONRAD	JOANNE	WILCKE	BOVERI	GEITEL	OLDHAM	DILLON
TERESA	MOBIUS	MARCIA	LAYARD	KEKULE	YVONNE	BURALI	GESELL	POLHEM	DORIAN
ULISSE	PAPPUS	MARISA	MCCORD	KIBBLE	ZARNKE	CESARI	GIESEL	TOPHAM	DUNCAN
WALESA	PETRUS	MILENA	MCLEOD	LAWRIE	ZENOBE	DMITRI	HASSEL	TROFIM	DUSTIN
ABBOTT	PINCUS	MOLINA	OSWALD	LAZARE	CERRAF	DONATI	ISMAEL	WILLEM	DUTTON
AGNETA	PREBUS	MONETA	PICARD	LESLIE	GUSTAF	GEORGI	KOSSEL	ADRIAN	EDISON
ALCOTT	REGIUS	NERUDA	ROLAND	LEVENE	RUDOLF	GIANNI	KUNKEL	ADRIEN	EILEEN
BEATTY	SCOTUS	NICOLA	RONALD	LEVINE	STUMPF	HASDAI	LAUREL	AITKEN	EUCKEN
BENITO	SEAMUS	NIKOLA	SIGRID	LITTLE	ANNING	HIDEKI	LEXELL	ALCUIN	EVELYN
BLATTY	SOPHUS	OLIVIA	SIMOND	LOUISE	ARLING	ILMARI	LIONEL	ALDRIN	FABIAN
CAVETT	THIOUT	PAMELA	TOLAND	MAGGIE	AYLING	JACOBI	LOVELL	ALFVEN	FARMAN
CIVITA	TITIUS	RUBBIA	UNSOLD	MALONE	BERING	KHOURI	LOWELL	ALISON	FINSEN
CRAFTS	ULPIUS	SAKATA	AMECHE	MARLEE	BINNIG	LUTULI	MARCEL	ALTMAN	FORMAN
DONATI	VARMUS	SAURIA	AMPERE	MCCUNE	CHIANG	MEDICI	MARTEL	ASHKIN	FULTON
DONATO	BASEVI	SCARPA	ARCHIE	MEIKLE	DULONG	MICALI	MAYALL	ASPDIN	GALTON
EVARTS	STRUVE	SENECA	BEADLE	MONROE	HENNIG	NAGELI	MENDEL	AUSTEN	GARSON
FAUSTO	YUKAWA	SOPHIA	BLAISE	MUNGLE	HERBIG	NOBILI	MENZEL	AUSTIN	GASTON
FSCOTT	GLADYS	TANAKA	BOULLE	NADINE	HITZIG	PACINI	MICHEL	BARTON	GERMAN

GERSON	MCKEEN	VIVIAN	TULLIO	FOSTER	LUTHER	WELLER	GRAVES	STILES	GRANIT
GIBBON	MCLEAN	VIVIEN	WITELO	FOWLER	MADLER	WERNER	GRIESS	STOKES	GRAUNT
GIBSON	MEEHAN	VOISIN	BISHOP	FRAZER	MELLOR	WEXLER	GRIGGS	STRUSS	HEWITT
GIDEON	MELVIN	WALDEN	COLLIP	FULLER	MERCER	WIENER	GRIJNS	TAUBES	HUBERT
GILMAN	MELVYN	WALKEN	DUNLOP	GASSER	MESMER	WIGNER	GRIMES	THALES	JOLIOT
GMELIN	MENKEN	WALSON	JESSUP	GAYNOR	MILLER	WILBER	HANNES	THOMAS	LARTET
GOOSEN	MILLAN	WALTON	PHILIP	GEIGER	MILNER	WILDER	HARRIS	TITIUS	LYCETT
GORDON	MILTON	WARREN	STREEP	GESNER	MOTHER	WILTER	HAVERS	TOBIAS	MERRIT
GUERIN	MORGAN	WATKIN	ALLDER	GINGER	MULLER	WINSOR	HEDGES	TOWNES	MUSSET
GUYTON	MORTON	WATSON	ALLVAR	GLASER	NAPIER	WOHLER	HERMES	TRAVIS	NERNST
HALDAN	MOUTON	WILSON	ALPHER	GLAZER	NARMER	WYDNER	HOBBES	ULPIUS	NOLLET
HALTON	NANSEN	WINTON	AMTHOR	GLOVER	NESTOR	YASSER	HOLMES	VALENS	PETTIT
HAMSUN	NATHAN	YERGIN	ARCHER	GREGOR	OLIVER	ZAVIER	HUGHES	VALLES	PICTET
HANSEN	NAUDIN	YERSIN	ARTHUR	GROVER	OTTMAR	ZINNER	ISAACS	VARMUS	PROUST
HARDEN	NELSON	YORDAN	AYLMER	GUNTER	PALMER	ADDAMS	JACOBS	VERTES	PUNNET
HAUBEN	NEWMAN	ZEEMAN	BARBER	HALLER	PANDER	ALEXIS	JULIUS	VILMOS	RAOULT
HEEZEN	NEWTON	ZOLTAN	BAXTER	HEEGER	PARKER	ANDERS	JUSTUS	WALLIS	RICHET
HEFLIN	NILSON	ADOLFO	BECHER	HELLER	PIETER	ANDRES	KEARNS	WATERS	RIQUET
HENSEN	NORMAN	ALONZO	BENDER	HILLER	PORTER	ARLISS	KEYNES	WELLES	RIVEST
HERMAN	OPARIN	AMEDEO	BERGER	HITLER	POYNER	BAINES	KOSMAS	WILKES	ROBERT
HESTON	OTHMAN	ANGELO	BESLER	HITNER	PRAWER	BARNES	LATTES	WILLIS	RUPERT
HILTON	PALFYN	BENITO	BODMER	HOOVER	PULLER	BOWLES	LIPPES	YERKES	STREET
HINTON	PAQUIN	BRANDO	BONNER	HOPPER	RAGNAR	BRIGGS	LOFTUS	ABBOTT	STRUTT
HOLDEN	PAXTON	CIMINO	BREUER	HORNER	RAINER	BROOKS	LOOMIS	ALBERT	STUART
HORTON	PERKIN	CYRANO	BUSTER	HUNTER	REINER	BRUTUS	LUCIUS	ALCOTT	TALBOT
HUSTON	PERRIN	DANILO	BUTLER	ISADOR	RICHER	CARLOS	LUDERS	AMAGAT	THABIT
HUTTON	PEYTON	DELANO	CAESAR	ISIDOR	RINGER	CELSUS	MAGNUS	ANHALT	THIOUT
JENSEN	PHILON	DONATO	CANTOR	JAGGER	RITTER	CHEOPS	MARCUS	APPERT	TSVETT
JOHANN	POGSON	EMILIO	CARTER	JENNER	ROHRER	CLORIS	MARIUS	APPOLT	UNDSET
JORDAN	PREVIN	ENRICO	CARVER	KARRER	ROSHER	CLOVIS	MATEOS	ARAFAT	VOIGHT
JULIAN	REAGAN	FAUSTO	CASPAR	KASPAR	ROTTER	COATES	MENGES	ARREST	WRIGHT
JULIEN	REMSEN	FRANCO	COCKER	KEELER	ROZIER	CORDUS	MOBIUS	AUGUST	BIZIOU
KEATON	RISKIN	GAUDIO	COOPER	KEFFER	RUBNER	CORTES	MORRIS	AUZOUT	BORDEU
KEILIN	ROMAIN	GIULIO	CORNER	KELLER	RUCKER	COWLES	MOYERS	BECKET	EISAKU
KELVIN	RUEBEN	GYATSO	COSTER	KEMMER	RUMKER	CRAFTS	MULLIS	BENNET	FIZEAU
KILJAN	SALEEN	JACOPO	COUPER	KEPLER	SANGER	CURTIS	NORRIS	BENOIT	LANDAU
KIRWAN	SARGON	JETHRO	CRAMER	KOCHER	SEMLER	DAFFOS	OLBERS	BICHAT	MENCHU
KOPPEN	SEATON	KOTARO	CREMER	KOHLER	SEYLER	DAVIES	PAPPUS	BOGART	MOREAU
LANDON	SELMAN	LASZLO	CUVIER	KOLLER	SHAMIR	DENNIS	PARKES	BONNET	SUSUMU
LARSEN	SEMJON	MAFFEO	DECUIR	KOSTER	SINGER	DIGGES	PELLOS	BONNOT	FLEROV
LARSON	SERSEN	MANLIO	DIETER	KUIPER	SLIFER	DINTIS	PETERS	BORDET	GUSTAV
LAUREN	SHEMIN	MORENO	DRAPER	KUMMER	SQUIER	DUPUIS	PETRUS	BRANDT	IVANOV
LEMMON	SHIMON	NAGANO	DREIER	KYESER	SUMNER	ECCLES	PINCUS	BRIGHT	LEONOV
LEVIEN	SHUKEN	NAKANO	DREYER	LARMOR	TAYLOR	ELYTIS	PREBUS	BURNET	MARKOV
LINDON	SIMEON	NICOLO	DUFOUR	LARNER	TELLER	ENDERS	REGIUS	CARNOT	PAVLOV
LONDON	STALIN	PACINO	DUGGAR	LASEAR	TEODOR	ENGELS	REINES	CAVETT	ANDREW
LOUDON	STEARN	PIETRO	DUNBAR	LASKER	TREVOR	EVARTS	RHAZES	CONRAT	BARROW
LYNDON	STEFAN	PSEUDO	EAGLER	LAZEAR	USSHER	FAJANS	RHODES	CUGNOT	BELLOW
MAHLON	STEVEN	REALDO	ELSTER	LEIBER	VERNER	FIELDS	ROBINS	DUNANT	BLAAUW
MAIMAN	SUTTON	ROMANO	ERCKER	LENOIR	VICTOR	FORBES	ROGERS	DWIGHT	FARROW
MALDEN	TASMAN	SAPPHO	FARMER	LEONOR	VIKTOR	GAINES	SCOPES	ECKERT	GARROW
MANSON	TOLMAN	SEVERO	FARRAR	LERNER	WAGNER	GALOIS	SCOTUS	ELLIOT	HARLOW
MARION	TRAJAN	SILVIO	FEODOR	LESTER	WALKER	GARMES	SEAMUS	ERNEST	KARNOW
MARLON	TRUMAN	STRABO	FERRER	LINDER	WALTER	GAVRAS	SHANKS	FOREST	MORROW
MARTIN	URBAIN	STRATO	FIESER	LISTER	WARNER	GILLES	SIMONS	FSCOTT	NIPKOW
MARVIN	VAUBAN	TADDEO	FISHER	LOLOIR	WEAVER	GLADYS	SOPHUS	GERRIT	RENFEW
MATLIN	VERNON	TRUMBO	FLOYER	LOTHAR	WEINER	GORGAS	STEARS	GOSSET	FARFAX

PROULX	MORLEY	ADOLPHO	BELLINI	BUTTONS	COLLINS	DREBBEL	FRANCIS
ANDREY	MURPHY	ADRIAAN	BELZONI	CABAEUS	COLOMBO	DREXLER	FRECHET
ANTONY	MURRAY	ADRIAEN	BENNETT	CABIBBO	COLUMBO	DRINKER	FREDDIE
ARDREY	NORGAY	AEPINUS	BENTHAM	CABRERA	COMPTON	DUHAMEL	FREDRIC
AUBREY	OAKLEY	AGASSIZ	BERGIUS	CAMERON	CONNERY	DUILLER	FREDRIK
AUDREY	OFFROY	AGRIPPA	BERGMAN	CAMILLE	CONYERS	DUKAKIS	FREEMAN
BARANY	QUINCY	AIKICHI	BERGSON	CAMILLO	COPPOLA	DUNAWAY	FRESNEL
BARNEY	RAMSAY	ALBERTI	BERNARD	CAMPION	CORDELL	DUNNING	FRICKER
BEATTY	RAMSEY	ALBINUS	BERTRAM	CANETTI	CORLISS	DYKSTRA	FRIEDEL
BEGLEY	REILLY	ALCAEUS	BERWICK	CARDANO	CORMACK	EASTMAN	FRISIUS
BLATTY	ROBLEY	ALFONSO	BEYRICH	CARDIFF	CORRENS	EDELMAN	FRITIOF
BRILEY	RODNEY	ALFREDO	BIGELOW	CARLSON	COSTNER	EDEMANN	FRITSCH
BUSSEY	ROOSBY	ALHAZEN	BINGHAM	CARLYLE	COTTELL	EDOUARD	GABRIEL
CAGNEY	SAVARY	ALLBUTT	BITTNER	CAROLUS	COULTER	EDOUART	GADOLIN
CARNEY	SAVERY	ALVAREZ	BJORKEN	CAROLYN	COULUMB	EHRLICH	GAGARIN
CASKEY	SCHARY	AMBROSE	BJORNST	CARRERE	CREMMER	EIJKMAN	GALILEO
CAUCHY	SIBLEY	ANATOLE	BLAGDEN	CARRIER	CRESCAS	EINHORN	GALVANI
CAYLEY	SIDNEY	ANDREAS	BLALACK	CARROLL	CRETIEN	EKEBERG	GARBETT
CHABRY	SMILEY	ANDREWS	BLALOCK	CASIMIR	CRIPPEN	ELLIOTT	GARDNER
COOLEY	SOLVAY	ANDRIJA	BLERIOT	CASSINI	CROOKES	ELLMANN	GARMIRE
COPLEY	SPACEY	ANGELOS	BOEHMER	CASTELI	CRUTZEN	EMANUAL	GASPARD
CROSBY	SPERRY	ANNAEUS	BOLZANO	CASTNER	CUMMING	EMANUEL	GASSNER
DELANY	STONEY	ANSELME	BORDERS	CATALDI	CURTISS	EMERSON	GATLING
DENJOY	SYDNEY	ANTHONY	BORELLI	CATESBY	CUSHING	EMPEROR	GAUSMAN
DILLEY	TORREY	ANTOINE	BORLAUG	CATLETT	CZESLAW	EPHRAIM	GEHRING
DUDLEY	WESLEY	ANTONIO	BORZAGE	CATTELL	DAIMLER	EPSTEIN	GELFAND
ELLERY	WOLSKY	APTHROP	BOTTGER	CECELIA	DANGEAU	ERASMUS	GELLERT
FAIRLY	WOOLEY	AQUINAS	BOUCHER	CELESTE	DANIELE	ERNESTO	GEMINUS
FARADY	ZWICKY	AROBLES	BOUGUER	CELSIUS	DANIELL	ESTELLE	GEORGES
FINLAY	CURTIZ	ARRIGHI	BOULTON	CERLUTI	DANIELS	ETIENNE	GEORGII
FINNEY	IGNATZ	ARTTURI	BOURATT	CHAFFEE	DARLING	EUDEMUS	GERBERT
FLOREY	JANUSZ	ASHMOLE	BOUVARD	CHAPMAN	DARWELL	EUDOXUS	GERHARD
GARDAY	LORENZ	ASTBURY	BRADLEY	CHAPPEL	DAUBREE	EUGENIO	GERHART
GIBNEY	LOWITZ	ATHAIYA	BRANDES	CHAPTAL	DAUSSET	EUSTACE	GERMAIN
GUFFEY	MILOSZ	AUDUBON	BRANTON	CHARCOT	DEHMELT	EXIGUUS	GERSTAD
GURNEY	MORITZ	AUGUSTE	BRENNAN	CHARLES	DELBERT	EZEKIEL	GHIORSO
GYORGY	PERUTZ	AUGUSTO	BRENNER	CHARNAY	DELEDDA	FARACHI	GIACOMO
HADLEY	VENETZ	AXELROD	BRETTON	CHARPAK	DELIGNE	FARCIOT	GIAUQUE
HALLEY	ZAVITZ	BAKHUIS	BRIDGES	CHASLES	DELISLE	FARNHAM	GIBBONS
HALSEY		BANGHAM	BRITTON	CHAUCER	DENISON	FECHNER	GIELGUD
HANLEY		BANTING	BROADUS	CHELPIN	DESAULT	FERNAND	GIFFARD
HARLEY		BARBARA	BRODSKY	CHESTER	DESMOND	FERRARI	GILBERT
HARVEY	**7 LETTER / 1st LETTER**	BARDEEN	BROUWER	CHLADNI	DEVILLE	FERRIER	GIORGOS
HEANEY		BARNARD	BRUGSCH	CHOMSKY	DEVRIES	FEYNMAN	GIOVANI
HEVESY		BARNETT	BRUNHES	CHRISTY	DIAMOND	FIBIGER	GLAEVER
HOLLEY		BATESON	BRYNNER	CHUQUET	DICKSON	FILIPPO	GLASHOW
HUXLEY	ABELARD	BATFOUR	BUCHMAN	CLAVIUS	DIDERIK	FISCHER	GLAUBER
JANSKY	ABELSON	BAUMANN	BUCHNER	CLAYTON	DIDEROT	FITZROY	GLAUCUS
JEREMY	ABRAHAM	BECKETT	BUISSON	CLEMENS	DIOCLES	FLEMING	GLEASON
KAPARY	ACHESON	BECKLIN	BULLOCK	CLEMENT	DOHERTY	FLOWERS	GLISSON
KELLEY	ACHILLE	BECKMAN	BURBANK	CLEWALL	DOLLOND	FOLKERS	GODDARD
KEMENY	ACKLAND	BEDDOES	BURIDAN	CLINTON	DOMINGO	FOLKMAN	GODFREY
KINSKY	ACTINUS	BEDNARZ	BURNELL	CLOPTON	DONDERS	FONTANA	GOERGES
KRAELY	ADDISON	BEDNORZ	BURNETT	CLOQUET	DONNALL	FOREMAN	GOLDING
LEAKEY	ADELARD	BEECHER	BURROWS	CLOUSER	DOPPLER	FORREST	GOLDMAN
LEMERY	ADLEMAN	BEGUYER	BURSTYN	COLBERT	DOROTHY	FOURIER	GOMBERG
LESLEY	ADOLPHE	BELKNAP	BURWELL	COLDITZ	DOUGLAS	FRANCES	GONZALO

GOODHUE	HENRICK	JOACHIM	LEBLANC	MAURIAC	NYKVIST	POITIER	RUDYARD
GOODMAN	HEPBURN	JOCELYN	LECLERC	MAURICE	OCTAVIO	POLANYI	RUFFINI
GOODWIN	HERBERT	JODOCUS	LEHMANN	MAXSTED	OERSTED	POLLACK	RUMFORD
GOOSSON	HERCZEG	JOHNSON	LEIBNIZ	MAXWELL	OLIVIER	POMEROY	RUNNELS
GORGIAS	HERMANN	JOKICHI	LEIPOLD	MAYNARD	OLMSTED	PORSCHE	RUSSELL
GOSSAGE	HERMITE	JOUHAUX	LELOUCH	MCCAREY	OLYMPIA	PORSILD	RUZICKA
GOSSETT	HEROULT	JUERGEN	LEONARD	MCCLUNG	ONSAGER	POULSEN	RYDBERG
GOTTLOB	HERRING	KAEMPFE	LEOPOLD	MEGHNAD	ORLANDO	PRACHAR	SAKMANN
GRAHAME	HERSHEY	KAPITZA	LEUPOLD	MEINESZ	OSBORNE	PRANDTL	SALILEI
GREGORY	HEYMANS	KAPTEYN	LINACRE	MEITNER	OSTWALD	PRESPER	SALOMEN
GRESHAM	HICKMAN	KASIMIR	LINCOLN	MELLONI	OSVALDO	PRESTON	SANCHEZ
GRIFFIN	HIGUCHI	KASTLER	LIPMANN	MENGOLI	OTHNIEL	PREVOST	SANDAGE
GRISSOM	HILAIRE	KAUFMAN	LOCKYER	MENZIES	OTTILIA	PROCLUS	SANDERS
GROESSE	HILBERT	KAZAKOV	LOFFLER	MERRIAM	PACCARD	PROCTOR	SARGENT
GUFFROY	HILLARY	KEDROVA	LORENTZ	MERRILL	PACIOLI	PTASHNE	SAROYAN
GUILLET	HILLIER	KELLOGG	LORENZO	MESSIER	PALANCE	PTOLEMY	SAUVEUR
GUSELLA	HILYARD	KENDALL	LORETTA	MICHAEL	PALISSY	PULLMAN	SAVEGAR
GUSTAVE	HIPPIAS	KENDREW	LORIMER	MICHAIL	PANCINI	PURCELL	SCANLAN
GUTHRIE	HIROSHI	KENICHI	LORRAIN	MICHELE	PAOLINI	PYTHEAS	SCHAFER
GYORGYI	HITTORF	KENNEDY	LUCIANA	MICHELL	PARESCE	QUENTIN	SCHALLY
HACKMAN	HJALMAR	KENNETH	LUEDTKE	MIDGLEY	PARRISH	RADNITZ	SCHEELE
HADDOCK	HODGKIN	KHAYYAM	LUITZEN	MIKHAIL	PARSONS	RAINGER	SCHIRRA
HAECKEL	HOFFMAN	KHORANA	LUMIERE	MILFORD	PASCHEN	RALEIGH	SCHLACK
HAFSTAD	HOFMANN	KIDDINU	LUNARDI	MILLAND	PASTEUR	RALSTON	SCHMIDT
HAGEMAN	HOKFELT	KIEBACH	LURSSEN	MISTRAL	PATRICK	RAMSDEN	SCHMITT
HALDANE	HOMBERG	KINGDOM	LYSENKO	MIYOAKA	PAULING	RAPHAEL	SCHONER
HALLDOR	HOMEYER	KIPLING	MAARTEN	MIYOSHI	PAXINOU	RAYMOND	SCHURER
HALPERN	HOPKINS	KIPPING	MACAVIN	MOHAMED	PEACOCK	RECORDE	SCHWABE
HALSTED	HOPWOOD	KIRCHER	MACLURE	MOISSAN	PEARSON	REDFORD	SCHWANN
HAMMANN	HORNING	KIYOSHI	MACQUER	MOMMSEN	PECQUET	REGNIER	SEABORG
HAMMOND	HORSLEY	KNIFTON	MADISON	MONDINO	PELIGOT	REIMANN	SEBOKHT
HAMPSON	HOUSSAY	KOLSTER	MADRAZO	MONTAGU	PELLING	REMNICK	SEEBECK
HAMPTON	HUGGINS	KOMAROV	MAELZEL	MONTALE	PELTIER	RENAULT	SEFERIS
HANTARO	HUMASON	KOZYREV	MAGNANI	MONZANI	PENROSE	RETZIUS	SEIFERT
HARBURG	HUMPHRY	KRAMERS	MAHFOUZ	MOSELEY	PENZIAS	REYMOND	SEIRTON
HARDING	HUYGENS	KRASKER	MAIREAD	MOULTON	PEOPPEL	REYMONT	SEMENOV
HARKINS	HYPATIA	KRASNER	MALCOLM	MUELLER	PEREIRA	RICCATI	SEQUARD
HARLING	ICHBIAH	KROEKEL	MALLAND	MUNSTER	PERINAL	RICHARD	SERVAIS
HARRIOT	IGNACIO	KUBRICK	MALLORY	MURDOCK	PERNIER	RICHLIN	SEVERIN
HARTLEY	IMHOTEP	KUNCKEL	MALTHUS	NAGAOKA	PERRINE	RICHTER	SEVERUS
HARTMAN	ISADORE	LAENNEC	MANDELA	NATHANS	PERTHES	ROBARDS	SEYMOUR
HARTMUT	ISHIOKA	LAMBERT	MANDELL	NEEDHAM	PEVONAK	ROBBINS	SHAFFER
HASKELL	ISIDORE	LAMRACK	MANFRED	NEISSER	PFEFFER	ROBERTO	SHAMROY
HATTORI	JACINTO	LANCISI	MANTELL	NEWCOMB	PHIDIAS	ROBERTS	SHANLEY
HAVLICK	JACKSON	LANGLEY	MARALDI	NICCOLO	PHILIPP	ROBINET	SHANNON
HAWKING	JACOBUS	LANSTON	MARCONI	NICHOLS	PHILIPS	ROBISON	SHAPIRO
HAWKINS	JACQUES	LAPLACE	MARQUEZ	NICOLAS	PHILLIP	RODBELL	SHAPLEY
HAWORTH	JAHRAUS	LAPORTE	MARQUIS	NICOLLE	PHOEBUS	ROEBUCK	SHARAFF
HAYFORD	JANSSEN	LARDNER	MARSHAK	NIELSON	PHYLLIS	ROLLAND	SHEARER
HAYWARD	JARCHUS	LASSELL	MARTINE	NIKITIN	PICCARD	ROMANES	SHEEHAN
HECKART	JEAKINS	LAURENT	MASASHI	NIKLAUS	PICKARD	ROSALYN	SHELDON
HEDRICK	JEFFERY	LAVERAN	MATTHAU	NIKOLAI	PIERSON	ROTBLAT	SHELLEY
HEERMAN	JEMISON	LAXNESS	MATTHEW	NIKOLAY	PILATRE	ROUELLE	SHELTON
HEITLER	JENKINS	LAZARUS	MAUCHLY	NODDACK	PILBEAM	ROWLAND	SHEPARD
HENDRIK	JENSSON	LAZZARO	MAUMONT	NOETHER	PIZARRO	RUDBECK	SHERIFF
HENLEIN	JESSICA	LEAVITT	MAUNDER	NORBERT	PLUCKER	RUDOLFF	SHERMAN
HENNESY	JIMENEZ	LEBEDEV	MAUREEN	NORRISH	POISSON	RUDOLPH	SHIELDS

SHIPLER	TARLOFF	WERNHER	BARNETT	HAFSTAD	MACAVIN	RAYMOND	ADOLPHE
SHIRLEY	TEDESCO	WHARTON	BATESON	HAGEMAN	MACLURE	SAKMANN	ADOLPHO
SHOICHI	TELESIO	WHEELER	BATFOUR	HALDANE	MACQUER	SALILEI	ADRIAAN
SHUFTAN	TELFORD	WHEWELL	BAUMANN	HALLDOR	MADISON	SALOMEN	ADRIAEN
SHUNPEI	TENNANT	WHIPPLE	CABAEUS	HALPERN	MADRAZO	SANCHEZ	EDELMAN
SIEMENS	TENZING	WHISTON	CABIBBO	HALSTED	MAELZEL	SANDAGE	EDEMANN
SIGMUND	TEODORO	WHITNEY	CABRERA	HAMMANN	MAGNANI	SANDERS	EDOUARD
SIMPSON	TERENCE	WHITTLE	CAMERON	HAMMOND	MAHFOUZ	SARGENT	EDOUART
SINATRA	TERRILE	WIDMANN	CAMILLE	HAMPSON	MAIREAD	SAROYAN	AEPINUS
SJOBERG	THADEUS	WIELAND	CAMILLO	HAMPTON	MALCOLM	SAUVEUR	BECKETT
SKINNER	THEILER	WILCZEL	CAMPION	HANTARO	MALLAND	SAVEGAR	BECKLIN
SLIPHER	THENARD	WILFRED	CANETTI	HARBURG	MALLORY	TADASHI	BECKMAN
SMALLEY	THEODOR	WILHELM	CARDANO	HARDING	MALTHUS	TADEUSZ	BEDDOES
SMEATON	THEURER	WILKINS	CARDIFF	HARKINS	MANDELA	TAINTER	BEDNARZ
SMELLIE	THOMSEN	WILLANS	CARLSON	HARLING	MANDELL	TAKASHI	BEDNORZ
SOLOMON	THOMSON	WILLARD	CARLYLE	HARRIOT	MANFRED	TARAGAY	BEECHER
SOLOVAY	TIDYMAN	WILLIAM	CAROLUS	HARTLEY	MANTELL	TARLOFF	BEGUYER
SORVINO	TIMOTHY	WINDAUS	CAROLYN	HARTMAN	MARALDI	VALMONT	BELKNAP
SOYINKA	TIPPETT	WINKLER	CARRERE	HARTMUT	MARCONI	VANESSA	BELLINI
SPECTOR	TORBERN	WINSLOW	CARRIER	HASKELL	MARQUEZ	VAUGHAN	BELZONI
SPEISER	TORELLO	WINSTON	CARROLL	HATTORI	MARQUIS	VAVILOV	BENNETT
SPEMANN	TORSTEN	WINTERS	CASIMIR	HAVLICK	MARSHAK	WAKSMAN	BENTHAM
SPENCER	TRAUNER	WISLAWA	CASSINI	HAWKING	MARTINE	WALCOTT	BERGIUS
SPINRAD	TRAVERS	WOODGER	CASTELI	HAWKINS	MASASHI	WALLACE	BERGMAN
SPITZER	TYNDALL	WOODROW	CASTNER	HAWORTH	MATTHAU	WALLACH	BERGSON
SPRAGUE	ULYSSES	WOOLLEY	CATALDI	HAYFORD	MATTHEW	WALTHER	BERNARD
STANLEY	UMEZAWA	WOOSTER	CATESBY	HAYWARD	MAUCHLY	WANTZEL	BERTRAM
STARKEY	USTINOV	WORTLEY	CATLETT	JACINTO	MAUMONT	WARBURG	BERWICK
STARSKI	VALMONT	WOTTITZ	CATTELL	JACKSON	MAUNDER	ZABDIEL	BEYRICH
STEARNS	VANESSA	WUERZER	DAIMLER	JACOBUS	MAUREEN	ZACHARY	CECELIA
STEIGER	VAUGHAN	WYCKOFF	DANGEAU	JACQUES	MAURIAC	ZANETTI	CELESTE
STEINER	VAVILOV	WYVILLE	DANIELE	JAHRAUS	MAURICE	ABELARD	CELSIUS
STENDEL	VEKSLER	XIMENES	DANIELL	JANSSEN	MAXSTED	ABELSON	CERLUTI
STEPHAN	VENKATA	YEATMAN	DANIELS	JARCHUS	MAXWELL	ABRAHAM	DEHMELT
STEPHEN	VENTRIS	YITZHAK	DARLING	KAEMPFE	MAYNARD	ACHESON	DELBERT
STEPVEN	VERNIER	YOLANDA	DARWELL	KAPITZA	NAGAOKA	ACHILLE	DELEDDA
STEVENS	VICENTE	YOSHIDA	DAUBREE	KAPTEYN	NATHANS	ACKLAND	DELIGNE
STEWART	VILHELM	ZABDIEL	DAUSSET	KASIMIR	PACCARD	ACTINUS	DELISLE
STORARO	VILLARD	ZACHARY	EASTMAN	KASTLER	PACIOLI	ICHBIAH	DENISON
STRABEL	VINCENT	ZANETTI	FARACHI	KAUFMAN	PALANCE	MCCAREY	DESAULT
STURGES	VIRCHOW	ZEIDLER	FARCIOT	KAZAKOV	PALISSY	MCCLUNG	DESMOND
SUMMERS	VIVIANI	ZERMELO	FARNHAM	LAENNEC	PANCINI	OCTAVIO	DEVILLE
SURTEES	VOLHARD	ZERNIKE	GABRIEL	LAMBERT	PAOLINI	SCANLAN	DEVRIES
SUSANNE	VOLKOFF	ZIEGLER	GADOLIN	LAMRACK	PARESCE	SCHAFER	FECHNER
SUSRATA	WAKSMAN	ZINSSER	GAGARIN	LANCISI	PARRISH	SCHALLY	FERNAND
SUSSMAN	WALCOTT	ZYGMUNT	GALILEO	LANGLEY	PARSONS	SCHEELE	FERRARI
SUZANNE	WALLACE		GALVANI	LANSTON	PASCHEN	SCHIRRA	FERRIER
SWIGERT	WALLACH		GARBETT	LAPLACE	PASTEUR	SCHLACK	FEYNMAN
SYLBERT	WALTHER		GARDNER	LAPORTE	PATRICK	SCHMIDT	GEHRING
SYLVIUS	WANTZEL	**2ND LETTER**	GARMIRE	LARDNER	PAULING	SCHMITT	GELFAND
SZILARD	WARBURG		GASPARD	LASSELL	PAXINOU	SCHONER	GELLERT
SZOSTAK	WEGENER	BAKHUIS	GASSNER	LAURENT	RADNITZ	SCHURER	GEMINUS
TADASHI	WEIZMAN	BANGHAM	GATLING	LAVERAN	RAINGER	SCHWABE	GEORGES
TADEUSZ	WELLAND	BANTING	GAUSMAN	LAXNESS	RALEIGH	SCHWANN	GEORGII
TAINTER	WELLMAN	BARBARA	HACKMAN	LAZARUS	RALSTON	ADDISON	GERBERT
TAKASHI	WENDELL	BARDEEN	HADDOCK	LAZZARO	RAMSDEN	ADELARD	GERHARD
TARAGAY	WENTZEL	BARNARD	HAECKEL	MAARTEN	RAPHAEL	ADLEMAN	GERHART

GERMAIN	PEARSON	ZERNIKE	THOMSEN	MIDGLEY	ZINSSER	ANDRIJA	GOMBERG
GERSTAD	PECQUET	PFEFFER	THOMSON	MIKHAIL	BJORKEN	ANGELOS	GONZALO
HECKART	PELIGOT	AGASSIZ	WHARTON	MILFORD	BJORNST	ANNAEUS	GOODHUE
HEDRICK	PELLING	AGRIPPA	WHEELER	MILLAND	HJALMAR	ANSELME	GOODMAN
HEERMAN	PELTIER	IGNACIO	WHEWELL	MISTRAL	SJOBERG	ANTHONY	GOODWIN
HEITLER	PENROSE	CHAFFEE	WHIPPLE	MIYOAKA	EKEBERG	ANTOINE	GOOSSON
HENDRIK	PENZIAS	CHAPMAN	WHISTON	MIYOSHI	SKINNER	ANTONIO	GORGIAS
HENLEIN	PEOPPEL	CHAPPEL	WHITNEY	NICCOLO	ALBERTI	KNIFTON	GOSSAGE
HENNESY	PEREIRA	CHAPTAL	WHITTLE	NICHOLS	ALBINUS	ONSAGER	GOSSETT
HENRICK	PERINAL	CHARCOT	AIKICHI	NICOLAS	ALCAEUS	BOEHMER	GOTTLOB
HEPBURN	PERNIER	CHARLES	BIGELOW	NICOLLE	ALFONSO	BOLZANO	HODGKIN
HERBERT	PERRINE	CHARNAY	BINGHAM	NIELSON	ALFREDO	BORDERS	HOFFMAN
HERCZEG	PERTHES	CHARPAK	BITTNER	NIKITIN	ALHAZEN	BORELLI	HOFMANN
HERMANN	PEVONAK	CHASLES	DIAMOND	NIKLAUS	ALLBUTT	BORLAUG	HOKFELT
HERMITE	RECORDE	CHAUCER	DICKSON	NIKOLAI	ALVAREZ	BORZAGE	HOMBERG
HEROULT	REDFORD	CHELPIN	DIDERIK	NIKOLAY	BLAGDEN	BOTTGER	HOMEYER
HERRING	REGNIER	CHESTER	DIDEROT	PICCARD	BLALACK	BOUCHER	HOPKINS
HERSHEY	REIMANN	CHLADNI	DIOCLES	PICKARD	BLALOCK	BOUGUER	HOPWOOD
HEYMANS	REMNICK	CHOMSKY	EIJKMAN	PIERSON	BLERIOT	BOULTON	HORNING
JEAKINS	RENAULT	CHRISTY	EINHORN	PILATRE	CLAVIUS	BOURATT	HORSLEY
JEFFERY	RETZIUS	CHUQUET	FIBIGER	PILBEAM	CLAYTON	BOUVARD	HOUSSAY
JEMISON	REYMOND	EHRLICH	FILIPPO	PIZARRO	CLEMENS	COLBERT	JOACHIM
JENKINS	REYMONT	GHIORSO	FISCHER	RICCATI	CLEMENT	COLDITZ	JOCELYN
JENSSON	SEABORG	KHAYYAM	FITZROY	RICHARD	CLEWALL	COLLINS	JODOCUS
JESSICA	SEBOKHT	KHORANA	GIACOMO	RICHLIN	CLINTON	COLOMBO	JOHNSON
KEDROVA	SEEBECK	PHIDIAS	GIAUQUE	RICHTER	CLOPTON	COLUMBO	JOKICHI
KELLOGG	SEFERIS	PHILIPP	GIBBONS	SIEMENS	CLOQUET	COMPTON	JOUHAUX
KENDALL	SEIFERT	PHILIPS	GIELGUD	SIGMUND	CLOUSER	CONNERY	KOLSTER
KENDREW	SEIRTON	PHILLIP	GIFFARD	SIMPSON	ELLIOTT	CONYERS	KOMAROV
KENICHI	SEMENOV	PHOEBUS	GILBERT	SINATRA	ELLMANN	COPPOLA	KOZYREV
KENNEDY	SEQUARD	PHYLLIS	GIORGOS	TIDYMAN	FLEMING	CORDELL	LOCKYER
KENNETH	SERVAIS	SHAFFER	GIOVANI	TIMOTHY	FLOWERS	CORLISS	LOFFLER
LEAVITT	SEVERIN	SHAMROY	HICKMAN	TIPPETT	GLAEVER	CORMACK	LORENTZ
LEBEDEV	SEVERUS	SHANLEY	HIGUCHI	VICENTE	GLASHOW	CORRENS	LORENZO
LEBLANC	SEYMOUR	SHANNON	HILAIRE	VILHELM	GLAUBER	COSTNER	LORETTA
LECLERC	TEDESCO	SHAPIRO	HILBERT	VILLARD	GLAUCUS	COTTELL	LORIMER
LEHMANN	TELESIO	SHAPLEY	HILLARY	VINCENT	GLEASON	COULTER	LORRAIN
LEIBNIZ	TELFORD	SHARAFF	HILLIER	VIRCHOW	GLISSON	COULUMB	MOHAMED
LEIPOLD	TENNANT	SHEARER	HILYARD	VIVIANI	OLIVIER	DOHERTY	MOISSAN
LELOUCH	TENZING	SHEEHAN	HIPPIAS	WIDMANN	OLMSTED	DOLLOND	MOMMSEN
LEONARD	TEODORO	SHELDON	HIROSHI	WIELAND	OLYMPIA	DOMINGO	MONDINO
LEOPOLD	TERENCE	SHELLEY	HITTORF	WILCZEL	PLUCKER	DONDERS	MONTAGU
LEUPOLD	TERRILE	SHELTON	JIMENEZ	WILFRED	SLIPHER	DONNALL	MONTALE
MEGHNAD	VEKSLER	SHEPARD	KIDDINU	WILHELM	ULYSSES	DOPPLER	MONZANI
MEINESZ	VENKATA	SHERIFF	KIEBACH	WILKINS	AMBROSE	DOROTHY	MOSELEY
MEITNER	VENTRIS	SHERMAN	KINGDOM	WILLANS	EMANUAL	DOUGLAS	MOULTON
MELLONI	VERNIER	SHIELDS	KIPLING	WILLARD	EMANUEL	FOLKERS	NODDACK
MENGOLI	WEGENER	SHIPLER	KIPPING	WILLIAM	EMERSON	FOLKMAN	NOETHER
MENZIES	WEIZMAN	SHIRLEY	KIRCHER	WINDAUS	EMPEROR	FONTANA	NORBERT
MERRIAM	WELLAND	SHOICHI	KIYOSHI	WINKLER	IMHOTEP	FOREMAN	NORRISH
MERRILL	WELLMAN	SHUFTAN	LINACRE	WINSLOW	SMALLEY	FORREST	POISSON
MESSIER	WENDELL	SHUNPEI	LINCOLN	WINSTON	SMEATON	FOURIER	POITIER
NEEDHAM	WENTZEL	THADEUS	LIPMANN	WINTERS	SMELLIE	GODDARD	POLANYI
NEISSER	WERNHER	THEILER	MICHAEL	WISLAWA	UMEZAWA	GODFREY	POLLACK
NEWCOMB	YEATMAN	THENARD	MICHAIL	XIMENES	ANATOLE	GOERGES	POMEROY
OERSTED	ZEIDLER	THEODOR	MICHELE	YITZHAK	ANDREAS	GOLDING	PORSCHE
PEACOCK	ZERMELO	THEURER	MICHELL	ZIEGLER	ANDREWS	GOLDMAN	PORSILD

				3RD LETTER				
POULSEN	BROUWER	OSVALDO	HUMASON	AGASSIZ	SHAPIRO	MCCAREY	TADASHI
ROBARDS	BRUGSCH	USTINOV	HUMPHRY	ANATOLE	SHAPLEY	MCCLUNG	TADEUSZ
ROBBINS	BRUNHES	ATHAIYA	HUYGENS	BLAGDEN	SHARAFF	MICHAEL	TEDESCO
ROBERTO	BRYNNER	ETIENNE	JUERGEN	BLALACK	SMALLEY	MICHAIL	TIDYMAN
ROBERTS	CREMMER	OTHNIEL	KUBRICK	BLALOCK	STANLEY	MICHELE	WIDMANN
ROBINET	CRESCAS	OTTILIA	KUNCKEL	BRADLEY	STARKEY	MICHELL	ABELARD
ROBISON	CRETIEN	PTASHNE	LUCIANA	BRANDES	STARSKI	NICCOLO	ABELSON
RODBELL	CRIPPEN	PTOLEMY	LUEDTKE	BRANTON	THADEUS	NICHOLS	ADELARD
ROEBUCK	CROOKES	STANLEY	LUITZEN	CHAFFEE	TRAUNER	NICOLAS	AXELROD
ROLLAND	CRUTZEN	STARKEY	LUMIERE	CHAPMAN	TRAVERS	NICOLLE	BEECHER
ROMANES	DREBBEL	STARSKI	LUNARDI	CHAPPEL	WHARTON	PACCARD	BLERIOT
ROSALYN	DREXLER	STEARNS	LURSSEN	CHAPTAL	YEATMAN	PACIOLI	BOEHMER
ROTBLAT	DRINKER	STEIGER	MUELLER	CHARCOT	ALBERTI	PECQUET	BRENNAN
ROUELLE	ERASMUS	STEINER	MUNSTER	CHARLES	ALBINUS	PICCARD	BRENNER
ROWLAND	ERNESTO	STENDEL	MURDOCK	CHARNAY	AMBROSE	PICKARD	BRETTON
SOLOMON	FRANCES	STEPHAN	PULLMAN	CHARPAK	CABAEUS	RECORDE	CHELPIN
SOLOVAY	FRANCIS	STEPHEN	PURCELL	CHASLES	CABIBBO	RICCATI	CHESTER
SORVINO	FRECHET	STEPVEN	QUENTIN	CHAUCER	CABRERA	RICHARD	CLEMENS
SOYINKA	FREDDIE	STEVENS	RUDBECK	CLAVIUS	FIBIGER	RICHLIN	CLEMENT
TORBERN	FREDRIC	STEWART	RUDOLFF	CLAYTON	GABRIEL	RICHTER	CLEWALL
TORELLO	FREDRIK	STORARO	RUDOLPH	DIAMOND	GIBBONS	VICENTE	CREMMER
TORSTEN	FREEMAN	STRABEL	RUDYARD	EMANUAL	KUBRICK	WYCKOFF	CRESCAS
VOLHARD	FRESNEL	STURGES	RUFFINI	EMANUEL	LEBEDEV	ZACHARY	CRETIEN
VOLKOFF	FRICKER	AUDUBON	RUMFORD	ERASMUS	LEBLANC	ADDISON	CZESLAW
WOODGER	FRIEDEL	AUGUSTE	RUNNELS	FRANCES	OSBORNE	ANDREAS	DREBBEL
WOODROW	FRISIUS	AUGUSTO	RUSSELL	FRANCIS	ROBARDS	ANDREWS	DREXLER
WOOLLEY	FRITIOF	BUCHMAN	RUZICKA	GIACOMO	ROBBINS	ANDRIJA	EDELMAN
WOOSTER	FRITSCH	BUCHNER	SUMMERS	GIAUQUE	ROBERTO	AUDUBON	EDEMANN
WORTLEY	GRAHAME	BUISSON	SURTEES	GLAEVER	ROBERTS	BEDDOES	EKEBERG
WOTTITZ	GREGORY	BULLOCK	SUSANNE	GLASHOW	ROBINET	BEDNARZ	EMERSON
YOLANDA	GRESHAM	BURBANK	SUSRATA	GLAUBER	ROBISON	BEDNORZ	EZEKIEL
YOSHIDA	GRIFFIN	BURIDAN	SUSSMAN	GLAUCUS	SEBOKHT	DIDERIK	FLEMING
APTHROP	GRISSOM	BURNELL	SUZANNE	GRAHAME	ZABDIEL	DIDEROT	FRECHET
EPHRAIM	GROESSE	BURNETT	WUERZER	HJALMAR	ALCAEUS	EUDEMUS	FREDDIE
EPSTEIN	KRAMERS	BURROWS	SWIGERT	ISADORE	BECKETT	EUDOXUS	FREDRIC
SPECTOR	KRASKER	BURSTYN	AXELROD	JEAKINS	BECKLIN	GADOLIN	FREDRIK
SPEISER	KRASNER	BURWELL	EXIGUUS	JOACHIM	BECKMAN	GODDARD	FREEMAN
SPEMANN	KROEKEL	BUTTONS	DYKSTRA	KHAYYAM	BUCHMAN	GODFREY	FRESNEL
SPENCER	ORLANDO	CUMMING	GYORGYI	KRAMERS	BUCHNER	HADDOCK	GIELGUD
SPINRAD	PRACHAR	CURTISS	HYPATIA	KRASKER	CECELIA	HEDRICK	GLEASON
SPITZER	PRANDTL	CUSHING	LYSENKO	KRASNER	DICKSON	HODGKIN	GOERGES
SPRAGUE	PRESPER	DUHAMEL	NYKVIST	LEAVITT	FECHNER	JODOCUS	GREGORY
AQUINAS	PRESTON	DUILLER	PYTHEAS	MAARTEN	HACKMAN	KEDROVA	GRESHAM
AROBLES	PREVOST	DUKAKIS	RYDBERG	PEACOCK	HECKART	KIDDINU	HAECKEL
ARRIGHI	PROCLUS	DUNAWAY	SYLBERT	PEARSON	HICKMAN	MADISON	HEERMAN
ARTTURI	PROCTOR	DUNNING	SYLVIUS	PRACHAR	JACINTO	MADRAZO	JUERGEN
BRADLEY	TRAUNER	EUDEMUS	TYNDALL	PRANDTL	JACKSON	MIDGLEY	KAEMPFE
BRANDES	TRAVERS	EUDOXUS	WYCKOFF	PTASHNE	JACOBUS	NODDACK	KIEBACH
BRANTON	ASHMOLE	EUGENIO	WYVILLE	SCANLAN	JACQUES	RADNITZ	LAENNEC
BRENNAN	ASTBURY	EUSTACE	ZYGMUNT	SEABORG	JOCELYN	REDFORD	LUEDTKE
BRENNER	ESTELLE	GUFFROY	CZESLAW	SHAFFER	LECLERC	RODBELL	MAELZEL
BRETTON	ISADORE	GUILLET	EZEKIEL	SHAMROY	LOCKYER	RUDBECK	MUELLER
BRIDGES	ISHIOKA	GUSELLA	SZILARD	SHANLEY	LUCIANA	RUDOLFF	NEEDHAM
BRITTON	ISIDORE	GUSTAVE	SZOSTAK	SHAMROY	MACAVIN	RUDOLPH	NIELSON
BROADUS	OSBORNE	GUTHRIE		SHANLEY	MACLURE	RUDYARD	NOETHER
BRODSKY	OSTWALD	HUGGINS		SHANNON	MACQUER	RYDBERG	PFEFFER

PIERSON	BIGELOW	FRITIOF	NIKOLAI	MILFORD	HOMBERG	KENNEDY	CLOPTON
PRESPER	EUGENIO	FRITSCH	NIKOLAY	MILLAND	HOMEYER	KENNETH	CLOQUET
PRESTON	GAGARIN	GHIORSO	NYKVIST	ORLANDO	HUMASON	KINGDOM	CLOUSER
PREVOST	HAGEMAN	GLISSON	SAKMANN	PALANCE	HUMPHRY	KUNCKEL	CROOKES
QUENTIN	HIGUCHI	GRIFFIN	TAKASHI	PALISSY	JEMISON	LANCISI	DIOCLES
ROEBUCK	HUGGINS	GRISSOM	VEKSLER	PELIGOT	JIMENEZ	LANGLEY	EDOUARD
SEEBECK	MAGNANI	GUILLET	WAKSMAN	PELLING	KOMAROV	LANSTON	EDOUART
SHEARER	MEGHNAD	HEITLER	ADLEMAN	PELTIER	LAMBERT	LINACRE	FLOWERS
SHEEHAN	NAGAOKA	ISIDORE	ALLBUTT	PILATRE	LAMRACK	LINCOLN	GEORGES
SHELDON	REGNIER	KNIFTON	BELKNAP	PILBEAM	LUMIERE	LUNARDI	GEORGII
SHELLEY	SIGMUND	LEIBNIZ	BELLINI	POLANYI	MOMMSEN	MANDELA	GIORGOS
SHELTON	WEGENER	LEIPOLD	BELZONI	POLLACK	OLMSTED	MANDELL	GIOVANI
SHEPARD	ZYGMUNT	LUITZEN	BOLZANO	PULLMAN	POMEROY	MANFRED	GOODHUE
SHERIFF	ACHESON	MAIREAD	BULLOCK	RALEIGH	RAMSDEN	MANTELL	GOODMAN
SHERMAN	ACHILLE	MEINESZ	CELESTE	RALSTON	REMNICK	MENGOLI	GOODWIN
SIEMENS	ALHAZEN	MEITNER	CELSIUS	ROLLAND	ROMANES	MENZIES	GOOSSON
SMEATON	ASHMOLE	MOISSAN	CHLADNI	SALILEI	RUMFORD	MONDINO	GROESSE
SMELLIE	ATHAIYA	NEISSER	COLBERT	SALOMEN	SEMENOV	MONTAGU	GYORGYI
SPECTOR	DEHMELT	OLIVIER	COLDITZ	SOLOMON	SIMPSON	MONTALE	KHORANA
SPEISER	DOHERTY	PHIDIAS	COLLINS	SOLOVAY	SUMMERS	MONZANI	KROEKEL
SPEMANN	DUHAMEL	PHILIPP	COLOMBO	SYLBERT	TIMOTHY	MUNSTER	LEONARD
SPENCER	EPHRAIM	PHILIPS	COLOMBO	SYLVIUS	XIMENES	PANCINI	LEOPOLD
STEARNS	GEHRING	PHILLIP	DELBERT	TELESIO	ANNAEUS	PENROSE	PAOLINI
STEIGER	ICHBIAH	POISSON	DELEDDA	TELFORD	BANGHAM	PENZIAS	PEOPPEL
STEINER	IMHOTEP	POITIER	DELIGNE	VALMONT	BANTING	RENAULT	PHOEBUS
STENDEL	ISHIOKA	RAINGER	DELISLE	VILHELM	BENNETT	RUNNELS	PROCLUS
STEPHAN	JAHRAUS	REIMANN	DOLLOND	VILLARD	BENTHAM	SANCHEZ	PROCTOR
STEPHEN	JOHNSON	SEIFERT	ELLIOTT	VOLHARD	BINGHAM	SANDAGE	PTOLEMY
STEPVEN	LEHMANN	SEIRTON	ELLMANN	VOLKOFF	CANETTI	SANDERS	SHOICHI
STEVENS	MAHFOUZ	SHIELDS	FILIPPO	WALCOTT	CONNERY	SINATRA	SJOBERG
STEWART	MOHAMED	SHIPLER	FOLKERS	WALLACE	CONYERS	TENNANT	STORARO
THEILER	OTHNIEL	SHIRLEY	FOLKMAN	WALLACH	DANGEAU	TENZING	SZOSTAK
THENARD	SCHAFER	SKINNER	GALILEO	WALTHER	DANIELE	TYNDALL	TEODORO
THEODOR	SCHALLY	SLIPHER	GALVANI	WELLAND	DANIELL	VANESSA	THOMSEN
THEURER	SCHEELE	SPINRAD	GELFAND	WELLMAN	DANIELS	VENKATA	THOMSON
UMEZAWA	SCHIRRA	SPITZER	GELLERT	WILCZEL	DENISON	VENTRIS	WOODGER
WHEELER	SCHLACK	SWIGERT	GILBERT	WILFRED	DONDERS	VINCENT	WOODROW
WHEWELL	SCHMIDT	SZILARD	GOLDING	WILHELM	DONNALL	WANTZEL	WOOLLEY
WIELAND	SCHMITT	TAINTER	GOLDMAN	WILKINS	DUNAWAY	WENDELL	WOOSTER
WUERZER	SCHONER	WEIZMAN	HALDANE	WILLANS	DUNNING	WENTZEL	AEPINUS
ZIEGLER	SCHURER	WHIPPLE	HALLDOR	WILLARD	EINHORN	WINDAUS	COPPOLA
ALFONSO	SCHWABE	WHISTON	HALPERN	WILLIAM	ERNESTO	WINKLER	DOPPLER
ALFREDO	SCHWANN	WHITNEY	HALSTED	YOLANDA	FONTANA	WINSLOW	EMPEROR
GIFFARD	BRIDGES	WHITTLE	HILAIRE	CAMERON	GONZALO	WINSTON	HEPBURN
GUFFROY	BRITTON	ZEIDLER	HILBERT	CAMILLE	HANTARO	WINTERS	HIPPIAS
HAFSTAD	BUISSON	EIJKMAN	HILLARY	CAMILLO	HENDRIK	ZANETTI	HOPKINS
HOFFMAN	CLINTON	ACKLAND	HILLIER	CAMPION	HENLEIN	ZINSSER	HOPWOOD
HOFMANN	CRIPPEN	AIKICHI	HILYARD	COMPTON	HENNESY	ADOLPHE	HYPATIA
JEFFERY	DAIMLER	BAKHUIS	KELLOGG	CUMMING	HENRICK	ADOLPHO	KAPITZA
LOFFLER	DRINKER	DUKAKIS	KOLSTER	DOMINGO	IGNACIO	AROBLES	KAPTEYN
RUFFINI	DUILLER	DYKSTRA	LELOUCH	GEMINUS	JANSSEN	BJORKEN	KIPLING
SEFERIS	ETIENNE	HOKFELT	MALCOLM	GOMBERG	JENKINS	BJORNST	KIPPING
ANGELOS	EXIGUUS	JOKICHI	MALLAND	HAMMANN	JENSSON	BROADUS	LAPLACE
AUGUSTE	FRICKER	MIKHAIL	MALLORY	HAMMOND	KENDALL	BRODSKY	LAPORTE
AUGUSTO	FRIEDEL	NIKITIN	MALTHUS	HAMPSON	KENDREW	BROUWER	LIPMANN
BEGUYER	FRISIUS	NIKLAUS	MELLONI	HAMPTON	KENICHI	CHOMSKY	RAPHAEL

TIPPETT	GARDNER	PURCELL	SUSRATA	FOURIER	PHYLLIS	PIZARRO	WARBURG
SEQUARD	GARMIRE	SARGENT	SUSSMAN	GAUSMAN	RAYMOND	POLANYI	BEECHER
ABRAHAM	GERBERT	SAROYAN	WISLAWA	HOUSSAY	REYMOND	RENAULT	BOUCHER
ADRIAAN	GERHARD	SERVAIS	YOSHIDA	JOUHAUX	REYMONT	ROBARDS	DIOCLES
ADRIAEN	GERHART	SORVINO	ACTINUS	KAUFMAN	SEYMOUR	ROMANES	FARCIOT
AGRIPPA	GERMAIN	SPRAGUE	ANTHONY	LAURENT	SOYINKA	ROSALYN	FISCHER
ARRIGHI	GERSTAD	STRABEL	ANTOINE	LEUPOLD	ULYSSES	SCHAFER	FRECHET
BARBARA	GORGIAS	SURTEES	ANTONIO	MAUCHLY	KAZAKOV	SCHALLY	FRICKER
BARDEEN	HARBURG	TARAGAY	APTHROP	MAUMONT	KOZYREV	SHEARER	GIACOMO
BARNARD	HARDING	TARLOFF	ARTTURI	MAUNDER	LAZARUS	SINATRA	HAECKEL
BARNETT	HARKINS	TERENCE	ASTBURY	MAUREEN	LAZZARO	SMEATON	HERCZEG
BERGIUS	HARLING	TERRILE	BATESON	MAURIAC	PIZARRO	SPRAGUE	JARCHUS
BERGMAN	HARRIOT	TORBERN	BATFOUR	MAURICE	RUZICKA	STEARNS	JOACHIM
BERGSON	HARTLEY	TORELLO	BITTNER	MOULTON	SUZANNE	STRABEL	KIRCHER
BERNARD	HARTMAN	TORSTEN	BOTTGER	PAULING	**4TH LETTER**	SUSANNE	KUNCKEL
BERTRAM	HARTMUT	VERNIER	BUTTONS	PLUCKER		SUZANNE	LANCISI
BERWICK	HERBERT	VIRCHOW	CATALDI	POULSEN	ABRAHAM	TADASHI	LINCOLN
BORDERS	HERCZEG	WARBURG	CATESBY	ROUELLE	ALCAEUS	TAKASHI	MALCOLM
BORELLI	HERMANN	WERNHER	CATLETT	SAUVEUR	ALHAZEN	TARAGAY	MARCONI
BORLAUG	HERMITE	WORTLEY	CATTELL	SHUFTAN	ALVAREZ	YOLANDA	MAUCHLY
BORZAGE	HEROULT	ZERMELO	COTTELL	SHUNPEI	ANNAEUS	ALLBUTT	NEWCOMB
BURBANK	HERRING	ZERNIKE	ESTELLE	STURGES	ATHAIYA	AROBLES	NICCOLO
BURIDAN	HERSHEY	ANSELME	FITZROY	VAUGHAN	BROADUS	ASTBURY	PACCARD
BURNELL	HIROSHI	CASIMIR	GATLING	ALVAREZ	CABAEUS	BARBARA	PANCINI
BURNETT	HORNING	CASSINI	GOTTLOB	DEVILLE	CATALDI	BURBANK	PASCHEN
BURROWS	HORSLEY	CASTELI	GUTHRIE	DEVRIES	CHLADNI	COLBERT	PEACOCK
BURSTYN	JARCHUS	CASTNER	HATTORI	HAVLICK	DESAULT	DAUBREE	PICCARD
BURWELL	KIRCHER	COSTNER	HITTORF	LAVERAN	DUHAMEL	DELBERT	PLUCKER
CARDANO	LARDNER	CUSHING	MATTHAU	OSVALDO	DUKAKIS	DREBBEL	PRACHAR
CARDIFF	LORENTZ	DESAULT	MATTHEW	PEVONAK	DUNAWAY	EKEBERG	PROCLUS
CARLSON	LORENZO	DESMOND	NATHANS	SAVEGAR	FARACHI	GARBETT	PROCTOR
CARLYLE	LORETTA	EASTMAN	OCTAVIO	SEVERIN	GAGARIN	GERBERT	PURCELL
CAROLUS	LORIMER	EPSTEIN	OSTWALD	SEVERUS	GLEASON	GIBBONS	RICCATI
CAROLYN	LORRAIN	EUSTACE	OTTILIA	VAVILOV	HILAIRE	GILBERT	SANCHEZ
CARRERE	LURSSEN	FISCHER	PATRICK	VIVIANI	HUMASON	GOMBERG	SPECTOR
CARRIER	MARALDI	GASPARD	PYTHEAS	WYVILLE	HYPATIA	HARBURG	VINCENT
CARROLL	MARCONI	GASSNER	RETZIUS	HAWKING	IGNACIO	HEPBURN	VIRCHOW
CERLUTI	MARQUEZ	GOSSAGE	ROTBLAT	HAWKINS	KAZAKOV	HERBERT	WALCOTT
CHRISTY	MARQUIS	GOSSETT	USTINOV	HAWORTH	KOMAROV	HILBERT	WILCZEL
CORDELL	MARSHAK	GUSELLA	WOTTITZ	NEWCOMB	LAZARUS	HOMBERG	BARDEEN
CORLISS	MARTINE	GUSTAVE	YITZHAK	ROWLAND	LINACRE	ICHBIAH	BEDDOES
CORMACK	MERRIAM	HASKELL	AQUINAS	LAXNESS	LUNARDI	KIEBACH	BORDERS
CORRENS	MERRILL	JESSICA	BAUMANN	MAXSTED	MACAVIN	LAMBERT	BRADLEY
CURTISS	MURDOCK	KASIMIR	BOUCHER	MAXWELL	MARALDI	LEIBNIZ	BRIDGES
DARLING	NORBERT	KASTLER	BOUGUER	PAXINOU	MASASHI	NORBERT	BRODSKY
DARWELL	NORRISH	LASSELL	BOULTON	BEYRICH	MCCAREY	PILBEAM	CARDANO
DOROTHY	OERSTED	LYSENKO	BOURATT	BRYNNER	MOHAMED	ROBBINS	CARDIFF
EHRLICH	PARESCE	MASASHI	BOUVARD	FEYNMAN	NAGAOKA	RODBELL	COLDITZ
FARACHI	PARRISH	MESSIER	BRUGSCH	HAYFORD	OCTAVIO	ROEBUCK	CORDELL
FARCIOT	PARSONS	MISTRAL	BRUNHES	HAYWARD	ONSAGER	ROTBLAT	DONDERS
FARNHAM	PEREIRA	MOSELEY	CHUQUET	HEYMANS	ORLANDO	RUDBECK	FREDDIE
FERNAND	PERINAL	ONSAGER	COULTER	HUYGENS	OSVALDO	RYDBERG	FREDRIC
FERRARI	PERNIER	PASCHEN	COULUMB	KIYOSHI	PALANCE	SEABORG	FREDRIK
FERRIER	PERRINE	PASTEUR	CRUTZEN	MAYNARD	PILATRE	SEEBECK	GARDNER
FOREMAN	PERTHES	ROSALYN	DAUBREE	MIYOAKA		SJOBERG	GODDARD
FORREST	PORSCHE	RUSSELL	DAUSSET	MIYOSHI		SYLBERT	GOLDING
GARBETT	PORSILD	SUSANNE	DOUGLAS	OLYMPIA		TORBERN	GOLDMAN

GOODHUE	FRIEDEL	MAHFOUZ	NICHOLS	PELIGOT	CARLSON	SHELTON	SPEMANN
GOODMAN	GLAEVER	MANFRED	PYTHEAS	PERINAL	CARLYLE	SMALLEY	SUMMERS
GOODWIN	GROESSE	MILFORD	RAPHAEL	ROBINET	CATLETT	SMELLIE	THOMSEN
HADDOCK	GUSELLA	PFEFFER	RICHARD	ROBISON	CERLUTI	SZILARD	THOMSON
HALDANE	HAGEMAN	REDFORD	RICHLIN	RUZICKA	CHELPIN	TARLOFF	VALMONT
HARDING	HOMEYER	RUFFINI	RICHTER	SALILEI	COLLINS	VILLARD	WIDMANN
HENDRIK	JIMENEZ	RUMFORD	VILHELM	SCHIRRA	CORLISS	WALLACE	ZERMELO
ISADORE	JOCELYN	SEIFERT	VOLHARD	SHOICHI	COULTER	WALLACH	ZYGMUNT
ISIDORE	KROEKEL	SHAFFER	WILHELM	SOYINKA	COULUMB	WELLAND	BARNARD
KENDALL	LAVERAN	SHUFTAN	YOSHIDA	SPEISER	DARLING	WELLMAN	BARNETT
KENDREW	LEBEDEV	TELFORD	ZACHARY	STEIGER	DOLLOND	WIELAND	BEDNARZ
KIDDINU	LORENTZ	WILFRED	ACHILLE	STEINER	DUILLER	WILLANS	BEDNORZ
LARDNER	LORENZO	BANGHAM	ACTINUS	THEILER	EDELMAN	WILLARD	BENNETT
LUEDTKE	LORETTA	BERGIUS	ADDISON	USTINOV	EHRLICH	WILLIAM	BERNARD
MANDELA	LYSENKO	BERGMAN	ADRIAAN	VAVILOV	GATLING	WISLAWA	BRANDES
MANDELL	MOSELEY	BERGSON	ADRIAEN	VIVIANI	GELLERT	WOOLLEY	BRANTON
MONDINO	PARESCE	BINGHAM	AEPINUS	WYVILLE	GIELGUD	ASHMOLE	BRENNAN
MURDOCK	PEREIRA	BLAGDEN	AGRIPPA	BECKETT	GUILLET	BAUMANN	BRENNER
NEEDHAM	PHOEBUS	BOUGUER	AIKICHI	BECKLIN	HALLDOR	CHOMSKY	BRUNHES
NODDACK	POMEROY	BRUGSCH	ALBINUS	BECKMAN	HARLING	CLEMENS	BRYNNER
PHIDIAS	RALEIGH	DANGEAU	AQUINAS	BELKNAP	HAVLICK	CLEMENT	BURNELL
SANDAGE	ROBERTO	DOUGLAS	ARRIGHI	DICKSON	HENLEIN	CORMACK	BURNETT
SANDERS	ROBERTS	EXIGUUS	BURIDAN	EIJKMAN	HILLARY	CREMMER	CLINTON
TEODORO	ROUELLE	GORGIAS	CABIBBO	EZEKIEL	HILLIER	CUMMING	CONNERY
THADEUS	SAVEGAR	GREGORY	CAMILLE	FOLKERS	HJALMAR	DAIMLER	DONNALL
TYNDALL	SCHEELE	HODGKIN	CAMILLO	FOLKMAN	KELLOGG	DEHMELT	DRINKER
WENDELL	SEFERIS	HUGGINS	CASIMIR	HACKMAN	KIPLING	DESMOND	DUNNING
WINDAUS	SEMENOV	HUYGENS	CHRISTY	HARKINS	LAPLACE	DIAMOND	EMANUAL
WOODGER	SEVERIN	KINGDOM	DANIELE	HASKELL	LEBLANC	EDEMANN	EMANUEL
WOODROW	SEVERUS	LANGLEY	DANIELL	HAWKING	LECLERC	ELLMANN	FARNHAM
ZABDIEL	SHEEHAN	MENGOLI	DANIELS	HAWKINS	MACLURE	FLEMING	FERNAND
ZEIDLER	SHIELDS	MIDGLEY	DELIGNE	HECKART	MAELZEL	GARMIRE	FEYNMAN
ACHESON	TADEUSZ	SARGENT	DELISLE	HICKMAN	MALLAND	GERMAIN	FRANCES
ADLEMAN	TEDESCO	SWIGERT	DENISON	HOPKINS	MALLORY	HAMMANN	FRANCIS
ALBERTI	TELESIO	VAUGHAN	DEVILLE	JACKSON	MCCLUNG	HAMMOND	HENNESY
ANGELOS	TERENCE	ZIEGLER	DOMINGO	JEAKINS	MELLONI	HERMANN	HORNING
ANSELME	TORELLO	ANTHONY	ELLIOTT	JENKINS	MILLAND	HERMITE	JOHNSON
BATESON	VANESSA	APTHROP	FIBIGER	LOCKYER	MOULTON	HEYMANS	KENNEDY
BIGELOW	VICENTE	BAKHUIS	FILIPPO	PICKARD	MUELLER	HOFMANN	KENNETH
BORELLI	WEGENER	BOEHMER	GALILEO	VENKATA	NIELSON	KAEMPFE	LAENNEC
CAMERON	WHEELER	BUCHMAN	GEMINUS	VOLKOFF	NIKLAUS	KRAMERS	LAXNESS
CANETTI	XIMENES	BUCHNER	ISHIOKA	WILKINS	PAOLINI	LEHMANN	LEONARD
CATESBY	ZANETTI	CUSHING	JACINTO	WINKLER	PAULING	LIPMANN	MAGNANI
CECELIA	BATFOUR	EINHORN	JEMISON	WYCKOFF	PELLING	MAUMONT	MAUNDER
CELESTE	CHAFFEE	FECHNER	JOKICHI	ABELARD	PHILIPP	MOMMSEN	MAYNARD
DELEDDA	GELFAND	GERHARD	KAPITZA	ABELSON	PHILIPS	OLYMPIA	MEINESZ
DIDERIK	GIFFARD	GERHART	KASIMIR	ACKLAND	PHILLIP	RAYMOND	OTHNIEL
DIDEROT	GODFREY	GRAHAME	KENICHI	ADELARD	PHYLLIS	REIMANN	PERNIER
DOHERTY	GRIFFIN	GUTHRIE	LORIMER	ADOLPHE	POLLACK	REYMOND	PRANDTL
EMPEROR	GUFFROY	JOUHAUX	LUCIANA	ADOLPHO	POULSEN	REYMONT	QUENTIN
ERNESTO	HAYFORD	MEGHNAD	LUMIERE	AXELROD	PTOLEMY	SAKMANN	RADNITZ
ESTELLE	HOFFMAN	MICHAEL	MADISON	BELLINI	PULLMAN	SCHMIDT	RAINGER
ETIENNE	HOKFELT	MICHAIL	NIKITIN	BLALACK	ROLLAND	SCHMITT	REGNIER
EUDEMUS	JEFFERY	MICHELE	OTTILIA	BLALOCK	ROWLAND	SEYMOUR	REMNICK
EUGENIO	KAUFMAN	MICHELL	PACIOLI	BORLAUG	SCHLACK	SHAMROY	RUNNELS
FOREMAN	KNIFTON	MIKHAIL	PALISSY	BOULTON	SHELDON	SIEMENS	SCANLAN
FREEMAN	LOFFLER	NATHANS	PAXINOU	BULLOCK	SHELLEY	SIGMUND	SHANLEY

SHANNON	COMPTON	FERRIER	CHESTER	WINSLOW	WALTHER	HILYARD		GERHARD
SHUNPEI	COPPOLA	FORREST	CRESCAS	WINSTON	WANTZEL	KHAYYAM		GERHART
SKINNER	CRIPPEN	FOURIER	CZESLAW	WOOSTER	WENTZEL	KOZYREV		GERMAIN
SPENCER	DOPPLER	GABRIEL	DAUSSET	ZINSSER	WHITNEY	RUDYARD		GIFFARD
SPINRAD	GASPARD	GEHRING	DYKSTRA	ANATOLE	WHITTLE	TIDYMAN		GIOVANI
STANLEY	HALPERN	GEORGES	ERASMUS	ARTTURI	WINTERS	BELZONI		GODDARD
STENDEL	HAMPSON	GEORGII	FRESNEL	BANTING	WORTLEY	BOLZANO		GONZALO
TAINTER	HAMPTON	GIORGOS	FRISIUS	BENTHAM	WOTTITZ	BORZAGE		GOSSAGE
TENNANT	HIPPIAS	GOERGES	GASSNER	BERTRAM	YEATMAN	FITZROY		GRAHAME
THENARD	HUMPHRY	GYORGYI	GAUSMAN	BITTNER	AUDUBON	GONZALO		GUSTAVE
VERNIER	KIPPING	HARRIOT	GERSTAD	BOTTGER	AUGUSTE	LAZZARO		HALDANE
WERNHER	LEIPOLD	HEDRICK	GLASHOW	BRETTON	AUGUSTO	MENZIES		HAMMANN
ZERNIKE	LEOPOLD	HEERMAN	GLISSON	BRITTON	BEGUYER	MONZANI		HANTARO
ALFONSO	LEUPOLD	HENRICK	GOOSSON	BUTTONS	BROUWER	PENZIAS		HAYWARD
ANTOINE	PEOPPEL	HERRING	GOSSAGE	CASTELI	CHAUCER	RETZIUS		HECKART
ANTONIO	SHAPIRO	JAHRAUS	GOSSETT	CASTNER	CLOUSER	TENZING		HERMANN
CAROLUS	SHAPLEY	JUERGEN	GRESHAM	CATTELL	COLUMBO	UMEZAWA		HEYMANS
CAROLYN	SHEPARD	KEDROVA	GRISSOM	COSTNER	EDOUARD	WEIZMAN		HILLARY
COLOMBO	SHIPLER	KHORANA	HAFSTAD	COTTELL	EDOUART	YITZHAK		HILYARD
CROOKES	SIMPSON	KUBRICK	HALSTED	CRETIEN	GIAUQUE			HOFMANN
DOROTHY	SLIPHER	LAMRACK	HERSHEY	CRUTZEN	GLAUBER			JAHRAUS
EUDOXUS	STEPHAN	LAURENT	HORSLEY	CURTISS	GLAUCUS			JOUHAUX
GADOLIN	STEPHEN	LORRAIN	HOUSSAY	EASTMAN	HIGUCHI	**5TH**		KENDALL
GHIORSO	STEPVEN	MAARTEN	JANSSEN	EPSTEIN	SCHURER	**LETTER**		KHORANA
HAWORTH	TIPPETT	MADRAZO	JENSSON	EUSTACE	SEQUARD	ABELARD		KIEBACH
HEROULT	WHIPPLE	MAIREAD	JESSICA	FONTANA	THEURER	ACKLAND		LAMRACK
HIROSHI	CHUQUET	MAUREEN	KOLSTER	FRITIOF	TRAUNER	ADELARD		LAPLACE
IMHOTEP	CLOQUET	MAURIAC	KRASKER	FRITSCH	BOUVARD	ADRIAAN		LAZZARO
JACOBUS	JACQUES	MAURICE	KRASNER	GOTTLOB	CLAVIUS	ADRIAEN		LEBLANC
JODOCUS	MACQUER	MERRIAM	LANSTON	GUSTAVE	GALVANI	BARBARA		LEHMANN
KIYOSHI	MARQUEZ	MERRILL	LASSELL	HANTARO	GIOVANI	BARNARD		LEONARD
LAPORTE	MARQUIS	NORRISH	LURSSEN	HARTLEY	LEAVITT	BAUMANN		LIPMANN
LELOUCH	PECQUET	PARRISH	MARSHAK	HARTMAN	NYKVIST	BEDNARZ		LORRAIN
MIYOAKA	ALFREDO	PATRICK	MAXSTED	HARTMUT	OLIVIER	BERNARD		LUCIANA
MIYOSHI	AMBROSE	PEARSON	MESSIER	HATTORI	PREVOST	BLALACK		MADRAZO
NICOLAS	ANDREAS	PENROSE	MOISSAN	HEITLER	SAUVEUR	BOLZANO		MAGNANI
NICOLLE	ANDREWS	PERRINE	MUNSTER	HITTORF	SERVAIS	BORLAUG		MALLAND
NIKOLAI	ANDRIJA	PIERSON	NEISSER	KAPTEYN	SORVINO	BORZAGE		MAYNARD
NIKOLAY	BEYRICH	SEIRTON	OERSTED	KASTLER	STEVENS	BOURATT		MICHAEL
OSBORNE	BJORKEN	SHARAFF	OLMSTED	LUITZEN	SYLVIUS	BOUVARD		MICHAIL
PEVONAK	BJORNST	SHERIFF	PARSONS	MALTHUS	TRAVERS	BURBANK		MIKHAIL
RECORDE	BLERIOT	SHERMAN	POISSON	MANTELL	BERWICK	CARDANO		MILLAND
RUDOLFF	BOURATT	SHIRLEY	PORSCHE	MARTINE	BURWELL	CLEWALL		MIYOAKA
RUDOLPH	BURROWS	STARKEY	PORSILD	MATTHAU	CLEWALL	CORMACK		MONTAGU
SALOMEN	CABRERA	STARSKI	PRESPER	MATTHEW	DARWELL	DONNALL		MONTALE
SAROYAN	CARRERE	STORARO	PRESTON	MEITNER	FLOWERS	EDEMANN		MONZANI
SCHONER	CARRIER	STURGES	PTASHNE	MISTRAL	HAYWARD	EDOUARD		NATHANS
SEBOKHT	CARROLL	SUSRATA	RALSTON	MONTAGU	HOPWOOD	EDOUART		NIKLAUS
SOLOMON	CHARCOT	TERRILE	RAMSDEN	MONTALE	MAXWELL	ELLMANN		NODDACK
SOLOVAY	CHARLES	WHARTON	RUSSELL	NOETHER	OSTWALD	EPHRAIM		OSTWALD
THEODOR	CHARNAY	WUERZER	SUSSMAN	PASTEUR	SCHWABE	EUSTACE		PACCARD
TIMOTHY	CHARPAK	AGASSIZ	SZOSTAK	PELTIER	SCHWANN	FERNAND		PICCARD
CAMPION	CORRENS	BUISSON	TORSTEN	PERTHES	STEWART	FERRARI		PICKARD
CHAPMAN	DEVRIES	BURSTYN	ULYSSES	POITIER	WHEWELL	FONTANA		POLLACK
CHAPPEL	EMERSON	CASSINI	VEKSLER	SPITZER	DREXLER	GALVANI		RAPHAEL
CHAPTAL	EPHRAIM	CELSIUS	WAKSMAN	SURTEES	CLAYTON	GASPARD		REIMANN
CLOPTON	FERRARI	CHASLES	WHISTON	VENTRIS	CONYERS	GELFAND		RICCATI

RICHARD	PORSCHE	EPSTEIN	SJOBERG	HUMPHRY	FRITIOF	PHIDIAS	CZESLAW
ROLLAND	RUZICKA	FLOWERS	STEVENS	JARCHUS	GABRIEL	PHILIPP	DAIMLER
ROWLAND	SHOICHI	FOLKERS	SUMMERS	JOACHIM	GARMIRE	PHILIPS	DEVILLE
RUDYARD	SPENCER	FORREST	SURTEES	KIRCHER	GATLING	POITIER	DIOCLES
SAKMANN	BLAGDEN	GARBETT	SWIGERT	MALTHUS	GEHRING	PORSILD	DOPPLER
SANDAGE	BRANDES	GELLERT	SYLBERT	MARSHAK	GOLDING	RADNITZ	DOUGLAS
SCHLACK	BROADUS	GERBERT	THADEUS	MATTHAU	GORGIAS	RALEIGH	DREXLER
SCHWABE	BURIDAN	GILBERT	TIPPETT	MATTHEW	HARDING	REGNIER	DUILLER
SCHWANN	CHLADNI	GOMBERG	TORBERN	MAUCHLY	HARKINS	REMNICK	ESTELLE
SEQUARD	DELEDDA	GOSSETT	TRAVERS	NEEDHAM	HARLING	RETZIUS	GADOLIN
SERVAIS	FREDDIE	HALPERN	VILHELM	NOETHER	HARRIOT	ROBBINS	GALILEO
SHARAFF	FRIEDEL	HASKELL	VINCENT	PASCHEN	HAVLICK	RUFFINI	GOTTLOB
SHEPARD	HALLDOR	HENLEIN	WENDELL	PERTHES	HAWKING	SCHMIDT	GUILLET
SPEMANN	KINGDOM	HENNESY	WHEWELL	PRACHAR	HAWKINS	SCHMITT	GUSELLA
STEWART	LEBEDEV	HERBERT	WILHELM	PTASHNE	HEDRICK	SHAPIRO	HARTLEY
STORARO	MAUNDER	HILBERT	WINTERS	SANCHEZ	HENRICK	SHERIFF	HEITLER
SUSRATA	PRANDTL	HOKFELT	ZERMELO	SHEEHAN	HERMITE	SORVINO	HORSLEY
SZILARD	RAMSDEN	HOMBERG	CHAFFEE	SLIPHER	HERRING	SYLVIUS	JOCELYN
TENNANT	SHELDON	HUYGENS	GRIFFIN	STEPHAN	HILAIRE	TENZING	KASTLER
THENARD	STENDEL	JEFFERY	PFEFFER	STEPHEN	HILLIER	TERRILE	LANGLEY
TYNDALL	THEODOR	KAPTEYN	SCHAFER	VAUGHAN	HIPPIAS	VERNIER	LOFFLER
UMEZAWA	ALCAEUS	KENNEDY	SHAFFER	VIRCHOW	HOPKINS	WILKINS	MARALDI
VENKATA	ALFREDO	KENNETH	ARRIGHI	WALTHER	HORNING	WILLIAM	MIDGLEY
VILLARD	ANDREAS	KRAMERS	BOTTGER	WERNHER	HUGGINS	WOTTITZ	MOSELEY
VIVIANI	ANDREWS	LAMBERT	BRIDGES	YITZHAK	ICHBIAH	YOSHIDA	MUELLER
VOLHARD	ANNAEUS	LASSELL	DELIGNE	ANDRIJA	JEAKINS	ZABDIEL	NICOLAS
WALLACE	BARDEEN	LAURENT	FIBIGER	ANTOINE	JENKINS	ZERNIKE	NICOLLE
WALLACH	BARNETT	LAXNESS	GEORGES	ATHAIYA	JESSICA	BJORKEN	NIKOLAI
WELLAND	BECKETT	LECLERC	GEORGII	BANTING	KIDDINU	CROOKES	NIKOLAY
WIDMANN	BENNETT	LUMIERE	GIELGUD	BELLINI	KIPLING	DRINKER	OSVALDO
WIELAND	BORDERS	MAIREAD	GIORGOS	BERGIUS	KIPPING	DUKAKIS	OTTILIA
WILLANS	BURNELL	MANDELA	GOERGES	BERWICK	KUBRICK	FRICKER	PHILLIP
WILLARD	BURNETT	MANDELL	GYORGYI	BEYRICH	LANCISI	HAECKEL	PHYLLIS
WINDAUS	BURWELL	MANTELL	JUERGEN	BLERIOT	LEAVITT	HODGKIN	PROCLUS
WISLAWA	CABAEUS	MAUREEN	ONSAGER	CAMPION	MARTINE	KAZAKOV	RICHLIN
ZACHARY	CABRERA	MAXWELL	PELIGOT	CARDIFF	MAURIAC	KRASKER	ROSALYN
AUDUBON	CARRERE	MEINESZ	RAINGER	CARRIER	MAURICE	KROEKEL	ROTBLAT
CABIBBO	CASTELI	MICHELE	SAVEGAR	CASSINI	MENZIES	KUNCKEL	ROUELLE
DREBBEL	CATLETT	MICHELL	SPRAGUE	CELSIUS	MERRIAM	PLUCKER	RUDOLFF
GLAUBER	CATTELL	NORBERT	STEIGER	CLAVIUS	MERRILL	SEBOKHT	RUDOLPH
JACOBUS	CLEMENS	PASTEUR	STURGES	COLDITZ	MESSIER	STARKEY	SALILEI
PHOEBUS	CLEMENT	PILBEAM	TARAGAY	COLLINS	MONDINO	ACHILLE	SCANLAN
STRABEL	COLBERT	PTOLEMY	WOODGER	CORLISS	NORRISH	ANGELOS	SCHALLY
AIKICHI	CONNERY	PURCELL	ABRAHAM	CRETIEN	NYKVIST	ANSELME	SHANLEY
CHARCOT	CONYERS	PYTHEAS	BANGHAM	CUMMING	OLIVIER	AROBLES	SHAPLEY
CHAUCER	CORDELL	RODBELL	BEECHER	CURTISS	OTHNIEL	BECKLIN	SHELLEY
CRESCAS	CORRENS	RUDBECK	BENTHAM	CUSHING	PANCINI	BIGELOW	SHIELDS
FARACHI	COTTELL	RUNNELS	BINGHAM	DARLING	PAOLINI	BORELLI	SHIPLER
FRANCES	DANGEAU	RUSSELL	BOUCHER	DEVRIES	PARRISH	BRADLEY	SHIRLEY
FRANCIS	DANIELE	RYDBERG	BRUNHES	DUNNING	PATRICK	CAMILLE	SMALLEY
GLAUCUS	DANIELL	SANDERS	FARNHAM	EHRLICH	PAULING	CAMILLO	SMELLIE
HIGUCHI	DANIELS	SARGENT	FISCHER	EZEKIEL	PELLING	CAROLUS	STANLEY
IGNACIO	DARWELL	SAUVEUR	FRECHET	FARCIOT	PELTIER	CAROLYN	THEILER
JODOCUS	DEHMELT	SCHEELE	GLASHOW	FERRIER	PENZIAS	CATALDI	TORELLO
JOKICHI	DELBERT	SEEBECK	GOODHUE	FLEMING	PEREIRA	CECELIA	VAVILOV
KENICHI	DONDERS	SEIFERT	GRESHAM	FOURIER	PERNIER	CHARLES	VEKSLER
LINACRE	EKEBERG	SIEMENS	HERSHEY	FRISIUS	PERRINE	CHASLES	WHEELER

WINKLER	AQUINAS	ASHMOLE	SEABORG	POMEROY	LURSSEN	MUNSTER	MACAVIN
WINSLOW	BELKNAP	BATFOUR	SEYMOUR	RECORDE	MADISON	NIKITIN	OCTAVIO
WOOLLEY	BITTNER	BEDDOES	TARLOFF	ROBARDS	MASASHI	OERSTED	SOLOVAY
WORTLEY	BJORNST	BEDNORZ	TELFORD	ROBERTO	MIYOSHI	OLMSTED	STEPVEN
WYVILLE	BRENNAN	BELZONI	TEODORO	ROBERTS	MOISSAN	PILATRE	BROUWER
ZEIDLER	BRENNER	BLALOCK	VALMONT	SCHIRRA	MOMMSEN	PRESTON	DUNAWAY
ZIEGLER	BRYNNER	BULLOCK	VOLKOFF	SCHURER	NEISSER	PROCTOR	GOODWIN
ADLEMAN	BUCHNER	BURROWS	WALCOTT	SEFERIS	NIELSON	QUENTIN	EUDOXUS
BECKMAN	CASTNER	BUTTONS	WYCKOFF	SEVERIN	PALISSY	RALSTON	BEGUYER
BERGMAN	CHARNAY	CARROLL	ADOLPHE	SEVERUS	PARESCE	RICHTER	CARLYLE
BOEHMER	COSTNER	COPPOLA	ADOLPHO	SHAMROY	PEARSON	SEIRTON	HOMEYER
BUCHMAN	DOMINGO	DESMOND	AGRIPPA	SHEARER	PIERSON	SHELTON	KHAYYAM
CASIMIR	ETIENNE	DIAMOND	CHAPPEL	SPINRAD	POISSON	SHUFTAN	LOCKYER
CHAPMAN	EUGENIO	DOLLOND	CHARPAK	STEARNS	POULSEN	SINATRA	SAROYAN
COLOMBO	FECHNER	EINHORN	CHELPIN	THEURER	ROBISON	SMEATON	ALHAZEN
COLUMBO	FRESNEL	ELLIOTT	CRIPPEN	VENTRIS	SIMPSON	SPECTOR	CRUTZEN
CREMMER	GARDNER	GIACOMO	FILIPPO	WILFRED	SPEISER	SZOSTAK	HERCZEG
DUHAMEL	GASSNER	GIBBONS	KAEMPFE	WOODROW	STARSKI	TAINTER	LUITZEN
EASTMAN	GEMINUS	GREGORY	OLYMPIA	ABELSON	TADASHI	TIMOTHY	MAELZEL
EDELMAN	JACINTO	HADDOCK	PEOPPEL	ACHESON	TAKASHI	TORSTEN	SPITZER
EIJKMAN	JIMENEZ	HAMMOND	PRESPER	ADDISON	TEDESCO	WHARTON	WANTZEL
ERASMUS	KRASNER	HATTORI	SHUNPEI	AGASSIZ	TELESIO	WHISTON	WENTZEL
EUDEMUS	LAENNEC	HAYFORD	WHIPPLE	AUGUSTE	THOMSEN	WHITTLE	WILCZEL
FEYNMAN	LARDNER	HITTORF	GIAUQUE	AUGUSTO	THOMSON	WINSTON	WUERZER
FOLKMAN	LEIBNIZ	HOPWOOD	ALBERTI	BATESON	ULYSSES	WOOSTER	
FOREMAN	LORENTZ	ISADORE	ALVAREZ	BERGSON	VANESSA	ZANETTI	
FREEMAN	LORENZO	ISHIOKA	APTHROP	BRODSKY	ZINSSER	ALLBUTT	
GAUSMAN	LYSENKO	ISIDORE	AXELROD	BRUGSCH	BOULTON	ARTTURI	**6TH LETTER**
GOLDMAN	MEGHNAD	KEDROVA	BERTRAM	BUISSON	BRANTON	ASTBURY	
GOODMAN	MEITNER	KELLOGG	CAMERON	CARLSON	BRETTON	BAKHUIS	ABRAHAM
HACKMAN	ORLANDO	LEIPOLD	DAUBREE	CATESBY	BRITTON	BOUGUER	ADLEMAN
HAGEMAN	PALANCE	LEOPOLD	DIDERIK	CELESTE	BURSTYN	CERLUTI	ADRIAAN
HARTMAN	PAXINOU	LEUPOLD	DIDEROT	CHOMSKY	CANETTI	CHUQUET	ANDREAS
HARTMUT	PERINAL	LINCOLN	DOHERTY	CHRISTY	CHAPTAL	CLOQUET	AQUINAS
HEERMAN	PEVONAK	MAHFOUZ	EMPEROR	CLOUSER	CHESTER	COULUMB	BANGHAM
HICKMAN	POLANYI	MALCOLM	FITZROY	DAUSSET	CLAYTON	DESAULT	BECKMAN
HJALMAR	ROBINET	MALLORY	FREDRIC	DELISLE	CLINTON	EMANUAL	BELKNAP
HOFFMAN	ROMANES	MARCONI	FREDRIK	DENISON	CLOPTON	EMANUEL	BENTHAM
KASIMIR	SCHONER	MAUMONT	GAGARIN	DICKSON	COMPTON	EXIGUUS	BERGMAN
KAUFMAN	SEMENOV	MELLONI	GHIORSO	EMERSON	COULTER	HARBURG	BERTRAM
LORIMER	SHANNON	MENGOLI	GODFREY	ERNESTO	DOROTHY	HEPBURN	BINGHAM
MOHAMED	SKINNER	MILFORD	GUFFROY	FRITSCH	DYKSTRA	HEROULT	BRENNAN
PULLMAN	SOYINKA	MURDOCK	GUTHRIE	GLEASON	GERSTAD	JACQUES	BUCHMAN
SALOMEN	STEINER	NAGAOKA	HAWORTH	GLISSON	HAFSTAD	LELOUCH	BURIDAN
SHERMAN	SUSANNE	NEWCOMB	HENDRIK	GOOSSON	HALSTED	MACLURE	CHAPMAN
SOLOMON	SUZANNE	NICCOLO	KENDREW	GRISSOM	HAMPTON	MACQUER	CHAPTAL
SUSSMAN	TERENCE	NICHOLS	KOMAROV	GROESSE	HYPATIA	MARQUEZ	CHARNAY
TIDYMAN	TRAUNER	PACIOLI	KOZYREV	HAMPSON	IMHOTEP	MARQUIS	CHARPAK
WAKSMAN	USTINOV	PARSONS	LAPORTE	HIROSHI	KAPITZA	MCCLUNG	CRESCAS
WEIZMAN	VICENTE	PEACOCK	LAVERAN	HOUSSAY	KNIFTON	PECQUET	CZESLAW
WELLMAN	WEGENER	PENROSE	LAZARUS	HUMASON	KOLSTER	RENAULT	DANGEAU
YEATMAN	WHITNEY	PREVOST	LUNARDI	JACKSON	LANSTON	ROEBUCK	DOUGLAS
ACTINUS	XIMENES	RAYMOND	MANFRED	JANSSEN	LORETTA	SIGMUND	DUNAWAY
AEPINUS	YOLANDA	REDFORD	MCCAREY	JEMISON	LUEDTKE	TADEUSZ	EASTMAN
ALBINUS	AMBROSE	REYMOND	MISTRAL	JENSSON	MAARTEN	WARBURG	EDELMAN
ALFONSO	ANATOLE	REYMONT	OSBORNE	JOHNSON	MAXSTED	ZYGMUNT	EIJKMAN
ANTONIO	ANTHONY	RUMFORD	PIZARRO	KIYOSHI	MOULTON	GLAEVER	EMANUAL

FARNHAM	TARAGAY	ORLANDO	DRINKER	MAARTEN	SHIRLEY	GOSSAGE	MARQUIS
FEYNMAN	TIDYMAN	OSVALDO	DUHAMEL	MACQUER	SHUNPEI	KELLOGG	MICHAIL
FOLKMAN	VAUGHAN	RECORDE	DUILLER	MAELZEL	SKINNER	MONTAGU	MIKHAIL
FOREMAN	WAKSMAN	ROBARDS	EMANUEL	MANFRED	SLIPHER	RALEIGH	NIKITIN
FREEMAN	WEIZMAN	SCHMIDT	EZEKIEL	MARQUEZ	SMALLEY	SANDAGE	OCTAVIO
GAUSMAN	WELLMAN	SHIELDS	FECHNER	MATTHEW	SPEISER	ADOLPHE	OLYMPIA
GERSTAD	WILLIAM	YOLANDA	FERRIER	MAUNDER	SPENCER	ADOLPHO	OTTILIA
GOLDMAN	YEATMAN	YOSHIDA	FIBIGER	MAUREEN	SPITZER	AIKICHI	PHILLIP
GOODMAN	YITZHAK	ADRIAEN	FISCHER	MAXSTED	STANLEY	ARRIGHI	PHYLLIS
GORGIAS	CABIBBO	ALHAZEN	FOURIER	MCCAREY	STARKEY	DOROTHY	QUENTIN
GRESHAM	CATESBY	ALVAREZ	FRANCES	MEITNER	STEIGER	FARACHI	RICHLIN
HACKMAN	COLOMBO	AROBLES	FRECHET	MENZIES	STEINER	HIGUCHI	SEFERIS
HAFSTAD	COLUMBO	BARDEEN	FRESNEL	MESSIER	STENDEL	HIROSHI	SERVAIS
HAGEMAN	SCHWABE	BEDDOES	FRICKER	MICHAEL	STEPHEN	JOKICHI	SEVERIN
HARTMAN	BERWICK	BEECHER	FRIEDEL	MIDGLEY	STEPVEN	KENICHI	SMELLIE
HEERMAN	BEYRICH	BEGUYER	GABRIEL	MOHAMED	STRABEL	KIYOSHI	TELESIO
HICKMAN	BLALACK	BITTNER	GALILEO	MOMMSEN	STURGES	MASASHI	VENTRIS
HIPPIAS	BLALOCK	BJORKEN	GARDNER	MOSELEY	SURTEES	MIYOSHI	ANDRIJA
HJALMAR	BRUGSCH	BLAGDEN	GASSNER	MUELLER	TAINTER	PORSCHE	BRODSKY
HOFFMAN	BULLOCK	BOEHMER	GEORGES	MUNSTER	THEILER	SEBOKHT	CHOMSKY
HOUSSAY	CORMACK	BOTTGER	GLAEVER	NEISSER	THEURER	SHOICHI	ISHIOKA
ICHBIAH	EHRLICH	BOUCHER	GLAUBER	NOETHER	THOMSEN	TADASHI	LUEDTKE
KAUFMAN	EUSTACE	BOUGUER	GODFREY	OERSTED	TORSTEN	TAKASHI	LYSENKO
KHAYYAM	FRITSCH	BRADLEY	GOERGES	OLIVIER	TRAUNER	TIMOTHY	MIYOAKA
LAVERAN	HADDOCK	BRANDES	GUILLET	OLMSTED	ULYSSES	AGASSIZ	NAGAOKA
MAIREAD	HAVLICK	BRENNER	HAECKEL	ONSAGER	VEKSLER	ANTONIO	RUZICKA
MARSHAK	HEDRICK	BRIDGES	HALSTED	OTHNIEL	VERNIER	BAKHUIS	SOYINKA
MATTHAU	HENRICK	BROUWER	HARTLEY	PASCHEN	WALTHER	BECKLIN	STARSKI
MAURIAC	JESSICA	BRUNHES	HEITLER	PECQUET	WANTZEL	CASIMIR	ZERNIKE
MEGHNAD	KIEBACH	BRYNNER	HERCZEG	PELTIER	WEGENER	CECELIA	ACHILLE
MERRIAM	KUBRICK	BUCHNER	HERSHEY	PEOPPEL	WENTZEL	CHELPIN	ANATOLE
MISTRAL	LAMRACK	CARRIER	HILLIER	PERNIER	WERNHER	DIDERIK	ASHMOLE
MOISSAN	LAPLACE	CASTNER	HOMEYER	PERTHES	WHEELER	DUKAKIS	BORELLI
NEEDHAM	LELOUCH	CHAFFEE	HORSLEY	PFEFFER	WHITNEY	EPHRAIM	BURNELL
NICOLAS	MAURICE	CHAPPEL	IMHOTEP	PLUCKER	WILCZEL	EPSTEIN	BURWELL
NIKOLAI	MURDOCK	CHARLES	JACQUES	POITIER	WILFRED	EUGENIO	CAMILLE
NIKOLAY	NODDACK	CHASLES	JANSSEN	POULSEN	WINKLER	FRANCIS	CAMILLO
PENZIAS	PALANCE	CHAUCER	JIMENEZ	PRESPER	WOODGER	FREDDIE	CARLYLE
PERINAL	PARESCE	CHESTER	JUERGEN	RAINGER	WOOLLEY	FREDRIC	CARROLL
PEVONAK	PATRICK	CHUQUET	KASTLER	RAMSDEN	WOOSTER	FREDRIK	CASTELI
PHIDIAS	PEACOCK	CLOQUET	KENDREW	RAPHAEL	WORTLEY	GADOLIN	CATTELL
PILBEAM	POLLACK	CLOUSER	KIRCHER	REGNIER	WUERZER	GAGARIN	CLEWALL
PRACHAR	REMNICK	COSTNER	KOLSTER	RICHTER	XIMENES	GEORGII	COPPOLA
PULLMAN	ROEBUCK	COULTER	KOZYREV	ROBINET	ZABDIEL	GERMAIN	CORDELL
PYTHEAS	RUDBECK	CREMMER	KRASKER	ROMANES	ZEIDLER	GOODWIN	COTTELL
ROTBLAT	SCHLACK	CRETIEN	KRASNER	SALILEI	ZIEGLER	GRIFFIN	DANIELE
SAROYAN	SEEBECK	CRIPPEN	KROEKEL	SALOMEN	ZINSSER	GUTHRIE	DANIELL
SAVEGAR	TEDESCO	CROOKES	KUNCKEL	SANCHEZ	CARDIFF	HENDRIK	DANIELS
SCANLAN	TERENCE	CRUTZEN	LAENNEC	SCHAFER	KAEMPFE	HENLEIN	DARWELL
SHEEHAN	WALLACE	DAIMLER	LANGLEY	SCHONER	RUDOLFF	HODGKIN	DEHMELT
SHERMAN	WALLACH	DAUBREE	LARDNER	SCHURER	SHARAFF	HYPATIA	DELISLE
SHUFTAN	ALFREDO	DAUSSET	LEBEDEV	SHAFFER	SHERIFF	IGNACIO	DESAULT
SOLOVAY	CATALDI	DEVRIES	LOCKYER	SHANLEY	TARLOFF	JOACHIM	DEVILLE
SPINRAD	DELEDDA	DIOCLES	LOFFLER	SHAPLEY	VOLKOFF	KASIMIR	DONNALL
STEPHAN	KENNEDY	DOPPLER	LORIMER	SHEARER	WYCKOFF	LEIBNIZ	ESTELLE
SUSSMAN	LUNARDI	DREBBEL	LUITZEN	SHELLEY	BORZAGE	LORRAIN	GONZALO
SZOSTAK	MARALDI	DREXLER	LURSSEN	SHIPLER	DOMINGO	MACAVIN	GUSELLA

HASKELL	BELZONI	LIPMANN	AXELROD	POMEROY	GASPARD	SHAPIRO	ELLIOTT
HEROULT	BOLZANO	LUCIANA	BATESON	PRESTON	GELLERT	SHEPARD	ERNESTO
HOKFELT	BURBANK	MAGNANI	BERGSON	PROCTOR	GERBERT	SINATRA	GARBETT
KENDALL	BUTTONS	MALLAND	BIGELOW	RALSTON	GERHARD	SJOBERG	GOSSETT
LASSELL	CARDANO	MARCONI	BLERIOT	ROBISON	GERHART	STEWART	HAWORTH
LEIPOLD	CASSINI	MARTINE	BOULTON	SEIRTON	GIFFARD	STORARO	HERMITE
LEOPOLD	CHLADNI	MAUMONT	BRANTON	SEMENOV	GILBERT	SUMMERS	JACINTO
LEUPOLD	CLEMENS	MCCLUNG	BRETTON	SHAMROY	GODDARD	SWIGERT	KENNETH
LINCOLN	CLEMENT	MELLONI	BRITTON	SHANNON	GOMBERG	SYLBERT	LAPORTE
MALCOLM	COLLINS	MILLAND	BUISSON	SHELDON	GREGORY	SZILARD	LEAVITT
MANDELA	CORRENS	MONDINO	CAMERON	SHELTON	HALPERN	TELFORD	LORENTZ
MANDELL	CUMMING	MONZANI	CAMPION	SIMPSON	HANTARO	TEODORO	LORETTA
MANTELL	CUSHING	NATHANS	CARLSON	SMEATON	HARBURG	THENARD	PRANDTL
MAUCHLY	DARLING	OSBORNE	CHARCOT	SOLOMON	HATTORI	TORBERN	RADNITZ
MAXWELL	DELIGNE	PANCINI	CLAYTON	SPECTOR	HAYFORD	TRAVERS	RICCATI
MENGOLI	DESMOND	PAOLINI	CLINTON	THEODOR	HAYWARD	VILLARD	ROBERTO
MERRILL	DIAMOND	PARSONS	CLOPTON	THOMSON	HECKART	VOLHARD	ROBERTS
MICHELE	DOLLOND	PAULING	COMPTON	USTINOV	HEPBURN	WARBURG	SCHMITT
MICHELL	DUNNING	PELLING	DENISON	VAVILOV	HERBERT	WILLARD	SUSRATA
MONTALE	EDEMANN	PERRINE	DICKSON	VIRCHOW	HILAIRE	WINTERS	TIPPETT
NICCOLO	ELLMANN	PTASHNE	DIDEROT	WHARTON	HILBERT	ZACHARY	VENKATA
NICHOLS	ETIENNE	RAYMOND	EMERSON	WHISTON	HILLARY	ALFONSO	VICENTE
NICOLLE	FERNAND	REIMANN	EMPEROR	WINSLOW	HILYARD	AMBROSE	WALCOTT
OSTWALD	FLEMING	REYMOND	FARCIOT	WINSTON	HITTORF	BJORNST	WOTTITZ
PACIOLI	FONTANA	REYMONT	FITZROY	WOODROW	HOMBERG	CORLISS	ZANETTI
PORSILD	GALVANI	ROBBINS	FRITIOF	AGRIPPA	HUMPHRY	CURTISS	ACTINUS
PURCELL	GATLING	ROLLAND	GIORGOS	FILIPPO	ISADORE	FORREST	AEPINUS
RENAULT	GEHRING	ROWLAND	GLASHOW	PHILIPP	ISIDORE	GHIORSO	ALBINUS
RODBELL	GELFAND	RUFFINI	GLEASON	PHILIPS	JEFFERY	GROESSE	ALCAEUS
ROUELLE	GIBBONS	SAKMANN	GLISSON	RUDOLPH	KRAMERS	HENNESY	ANNAEUS
RUNNELS	GIOVANI	SARGENT	GOOSSON	ABELARD	LAMBERT	LANCISI	BATFOUR
RUSSELL	GOLDING	SCHWANN	GOTTLOB	ADELARD	LAZZARO	LAXNESS	BERGIUS
SCHALLY	HALDANE	SIEMENS	GRISSOM	ARTTURI	LECLERC	MEINESZ	BORLAUG
SCHEELE	HAMMANN	SIGMUND	GUFFROY	ASTBURY	LEONARD	NORRISH	BROADUS
TERRILE	HAMMOND	SORVINO	HALLDOR	BARBARA	LINACRE	NYKVIST	CABAEUS
TORELLO	HARDING	SPEMANN	HAMPSON	BARNARD	LUMIERE	PALISSY	CAROLUS
TYNDALL	HARKINS	STEARNS	HAMPTON	BEDNARZ	MACLURE	PARRISH	CELSIUS
VILHELM	HARLING	STEVENS	HARRIOT	BEDNORZ	MALLORY	PENROSE	CLAVIUS
WENDELL	HAWKING	SUSANNE	HOPWOOD	BERNARD	MAYNARD	PREVOST	ERASMUS
WHEWELL	HAWKINS	SUZANNE	HUMASON	BORDERS	MILFORD	TADEUSZ	EUDEMUS
WHIPPLE	HERMANN	TENNANT	JACKSON	BOUVARD	NORBERT	VANESSA	EUDOXUS
WHITTLE	HERRING	TENZING	JEMISON	CABRERA	PACCARD	ALBERTI	EXIGUUS
WILHELM	HEYMANS	VALMONT	JENSSON	CARRERE	PEREIRA	ALLBUTT	FRISIUS
WYVILLE	HOFMANN	VINCENT	JOHNSON	COLBERT	PICCARD	AUGUSTE	GEMINUS
ZERMELO	HOPKINS	VIVIANI	KAZAKOV	CONNERY	PICKARD	AUGUSTO	GIAUQUE
ANSELME	HORNING	WELLAND	KINGDOM	CONYERS	PILATRE	BARNETT	GIELGUD
COULUMB	HUGGINS	WIDMANN	KNIFTON	DELBERT	PIZARRO	BECKETT	GLAUCUS
GIACOMO	HUYGENS	WIELAND	KOMAROV	DONDERS	REDFORD	BENNETT	GOODHUE
GRAHAME	JEAKINS	WILKINS	LANSTON	DYKSTRA	RICHARD	BOURATT	HARTMUT
NEWCOMB	JENKINS	WILLANS	MADISON	EDOUARD	RUDYARD	BURNETT	JACOBUS
PTOLEMY	KHORANA	ZYGMUNT	MOULTON	EDOUART	RUMFORD	CANETTI	JAHRAUS
ACKLAND	KIDDINU	ABELSON	NIELSON	EINHORN	RYDBERG	CATLETT	JARCHUS
ANTHONY	KIPLING	ACHESON	PAXINOU	EKEBERG	SANDERS	CELESTE	JODOCUS
ANTOINE	KIPPING	ADDISON	PEARSON	FERRARI	SCHIRRA	CERLUTI	JOUHAUX
BANTING	LAURENT	ANGELOS	PELIGOT	FLOWERS	SEABORG	CHRISTY	LAZARUS
BAUMANN	LEBLANC	APTHROP	PIERSON	FOLKERS	SEIFERT	COLDITZ	MAHFOUZ
BELLINI	LEHMANN	AUDUBON	POISSON	GARMIRE	SEQUARD	DOHERTY	MALTHUS

NIKLAUS	OTTILIA	MILFORD	GOSSAGE	BORLAUG	FARACHI	PEACOCK	WANTZEL
PASTEUR	PEREIRA	MILLAND	GRAHAME	CUMMING	FERRARI	PEVONAK	WENDELL
PHOEBUS	RUZICKA	MOHAMED	GROESSE	CUSHING	GALVANI	POLLACK	WENTZEL
PROCLUS	SCHIRRA	OERSTED	GUSTAVE	DARLING	GEORGII	REMNICK	WHEWELL
RETZIUS	SINATRA	OLMSTED	GUTHRIE	DUNNING	GIOVANI	ROEBUCK	WILCZEL
SAUVEUR	SOYINKA	OSTWALD	HALDANE	EKEBERG	GYORGYI	RUDBECK	ZABDIEL
SEVERUS	SUSRATA	PACCARD	HERMITE	FLEMING	HATTORI	SCHLACK	ABRAHAM
SEYMOUR	UMEZAWA	PICCARD	HILAIRE	GATLING	HIGUCHI	SEEBECK	BANGHAM
SPRAGUE	VANESSA	PICKARD	ISADORE	GEHRING	HIROSHI	SZOSTAK	BENTHAM
SYLVIUS	VENKATA	PORSILD	ISIDORE	GOLDING	JOKICHI	YITZHAK	BERTRAM
THADEUS	WISLAWA	RAYMOND	KAEMPFE	GOMBERG	KENICHI	BURNELL	BINGHAM
WINDAUS	YOLANDA	REDFORD	LAPLACE	HARBURG	KIYOSHI	BURWELL	EPHRAIM
GUSTAVE	YOSHIDA	REYMOND	LAPORTE	HARDING	LANCISI	CARROLL	FARNHAM
KEDROVA	COULUMB	RICHARD	LINACRE	HARLING	LUNARDI	CATTELL	GRESHAM
ANDREWS	GOTTLOB	ROLLAND	LUEDTKE	HAWKING	MAGNANI	CHAPPEL	GRISSOM
BURROWS	NEWCOMB	ROWLAND	LUMIERE	HERCZEG	MARALDI	CHAPTAL	JOACHIM
UMEZAWA	FREDRIC	RUDYARD	MACLURE	HERRING	MARCONI	CLEWALL	KHAYYAM
WISLAWA	LAENNEC	RUMFORD	MARTINE	HOMBERG	MASASHI	CORDELL	KINGDOM
ATHAIYA	LEBLANC	SEQUARD	MAURICE	HORNING	MELLONI	COTTELL	MALCOLM
BURSTYN	LECLERC	SHEPARD	MICHELE	KELLOGG	MENGOLI	DANIELL	MERRIAM
CAROLYN	MAURIAC	SIGMUND	MONTALE	KIPLING	MIYOSHI	DARWELL	NEEDHAM
GYORGYI	ABELARD	SPINRAD	NICOLLE	KiPPING	MONZANI	DONNALL	PILBEAM
JOCELYN	ACKLAND	SZILARD	OSBORNE	MCCLUNG	NIKOLAI	DREBBEL	VILHELM
KAPTEYN	ADELARD	TELFORD	PALANCE	PAULING	PACIOLI	DUHAMEL	WILHELM
POLANYI	AXELROD	THENARD	PARESCE	PELLING	PANCINI	EMANUAL	WILLIAM
ROSALYN	BARNARD	VILLARD	PENROSE	RYDBERG	PAOLINI	EMANUEL	ABELSON
KAPITZA	BERNARD	VOLHARD	PERRINE	SEABORG	POLANYI	EZEKIEL	ACHESON
LORENZO	BOUVARD	WELLAND	PILATRE	SJOBERG	RICCATI	FRESNEL	ADDISON
MADRAZO	DESMOND	WIELAND	PORSCHE	TENZING	RUFFINI	FRIEDEL	ADLEMAN
	DIAMOND	WILFRED	PTASHNE	WARBURG	SALILEI	GABRIEL	ADRIAAN
	DOLLOND	WILLARD	RECORDE	BEYRICH	SHOICHI	HAECKEL	ADRIAEN
	EDOUARD	ACHILLE	ROUELLE	BRUGSCH	SHUNPEI	HASKELL	ALHAZEN
7TH LETTER	FERNAND	ADOLPHE	SANDAGE	EHRLICH	STARSKI	KENDALL	AUDUBON
	GASPARD	AMBROSE	SCHEELE	FRITSCH	TADASHI	KROEKEL	BARDEEN
AGRIPPA	GELFAND	ANATOLE	SCHWABE	HAWORTH	TAKASHI	KUNCKEL	BATESON
ANDRIJA	GERHARD	ANSELME	SMELLIE	ICHBIAH	VIVIANI	LASSELL	BAUMANN
ATHAIYA	GERSTAD	ANTOINE	SPRAGUE	KENNETH	ZANETTI	MAELZEL	BECKLIN
BARBARA	GIELGUD	ASHMOLE	SUSANNE	KIEBACH	BERWICK	MANDELL	BECKMAN
CABRERA	GIFFARD	AUGUSTE	SUZANNE	LELOUCH	BLALACK	MANTELL	BERGMAN
CECELIA	GODDARD	BORZAGE	TERENCE	NORRISH	BLALOCK	MAXWELL	BERGSON
COPPOLA	HAFSTAD	CAMILLE	TERRILE	PARRISH	BULLOCK	MERRILL	BJORKEN
DELEDDA	HALSTED	CARLYLE	VICENTE	RALEIGH	BURBANK	MICHAEL	BLAGDEN
DYKSTRA	HAMMOND	CARRERE	WALLACE	RUDOLPH	CHARPAK	MICHAIL	BOULTON
FONTANA	HAYFORD	CELESTE	WHIPPLE	WALLACH	CORMACK	MICHELL	BRANTON
GUSELLA	HAYWARD	CHAFFEE	WHITTLE	AIKICHI	DIDERIK	MIKHAIL	BRENNAN
HYPATIA	HILYARD	DANIELE	WYVILLE	ALBERTI	FREDRIK	MISTRAL	BRETTON
ISHIOKA	HOPWOOD	DAUBREE	ZERNIKE	ARRIGHI	HADDOCK	OTHNIEL	BRITTON
JESSICA	LEIPOLD	DELIGNE	CARDIFF	ARTTURI	HAVLICK	PEOPPEL	BUCHMAN
KAPITZA	LEONARD	DELISLE	FRITIOF	BELLINI	HEDRICK	PERINAL	BUISSON
KEDROVA	LEOPOLD	DEVILLE	HITTORF	BELZONI	HENDRIK	PRANDTL	BURIDAN
KHORANA	LEUPOLD	ESTELLE	RUDOLFF	BORELLI	HENRICK	PURCELL	BURSTYN
LORETTA	MAIREAD	ETIENNE	SHARAFF	CANETTI	KUBRICK	RAPHAEL	CAMERON
LUCIANA	MALLAND	EUSTACE	SHERIFF	CASSINI	LAMRACK	RODBELL	CAMPION
MANDELA	MANFRED	FREDDIE	TARLOFF	CASTELI	MARSHAK	RUSSELL	CARLSON
MIYOAKA	MAXSTED	GARMIRE	VOLKOFF	CATALDI	MURDOCK	STENDEL	CAROLYN
NAGAOKA	MAYNARD	GIAUQUE	WYCKOFF	CERLUTI	NODDACK	STRABEL	CHAPMAN
OLYMPIA	MEGHNAD	GOODHUE	BANTING	CHLADNI	PATRICK	TYNDALL	CHELPIN

CLAYTON	KNIFTON	TORSTEN	BEECHER	NEISSER	ANGELOS	JACOBUS	BJORNST
CLINTON	LANSTON	VAUGHAN	BEGUYER	NOETHER	ANNAEUS	JACQUES	BLERIOT
CLOPTON	LAVERAN	WAKSMAN	BITTNER	OLIVIER	AQUINAS	JAHRAUS	BOURATT
COMPTON	LEHMANN	WEIZMAN	BOEHMER	ONSAGER	AROBLES	JARCHUS	BURNETT
CRETIEN	LINCOLN	WELLMAN	BOTTGER	PASTEUR	BAKHUIS	JEAKINS	CATLETT
CRIPPEN	LIPMANN	WHARTON	BOUCHER	PELTIER	BEDDOES	JENKINS	CHARCOT
CRUTZEN	LORRAIN	WHISTON	BOUGUER	PERNIER	BERGIUS	JODOCUS	CHUQUET
DENISON	LUITZEN	WIDMANN	BRENNER	PFEFFER	BORDERS	KRAMERS	CLEMENT
DICKSON	LURSSEN	WINSTON	BROUWER	PLUCKER	BRANDES	LAXNESS	CLOQUET
EASTMAN	MAARTEN	YEATMAN	BRYNNER	POITIER	BRIDGES	LAZARUS	COLBERT
EDELMAN	MACAVIN	ADOLPHO	BUCHNER	PRACHAR	BROADUS	MALTHUS	DAUSSET
EDEMANN	MADISON	ALFONSO	CARRIER	PRESPER	BRUNHES	MARQUIS	DEHMELT
EIJKMAN	MAUREEN	ALFREDO	CASIMIR	PROCTOR	BURROWS	MENZIES	DELBERT
EINHORN	MOISSAN	ANTONIO	CASTNER	RAINGER	BUTTONS	NATHANS	DESAULT
ELLMANN	MOMMSEN	AUGUSTO	CHAUCER	REGNIER	CABAEUS	NICHOLS	DIDEROT
EMERSON	MOULTON	BOLZANO	CHESTER	RICHTER	CAROLUS	NICOLAS	EDOUART
EPSTEIN	NIELSON	CABIBBO	CLOUSER	SAUVEUR	CELSIUS	NIKLAUS	ELLIOTT
FEYNMAN	NIKITIN	CAMILLO	COSTNER	SAVEGAR	CHARLES	PARSONS	FARCIOT
FOLKMAN	PASCHEN	CARDANO	COULTER	SCHAFER	CHASLES	PENZIAS	FORREST
FOREMAN	PEARSON	COLOMBO	CREMMER	SCHONER	CLAVIUS	PERTHES	FRECHET
FREEMAN	PIERSON	COLUMBO	DAIMLER	SCHURER	CLEMENS	PHIDIAS	GARBETT
GADOLIN	POISSON	DOMINGO	DOPPLER	SEYMOUR	COLLINS	PHILIPS	GELLERT
GAGARIN	POULSEN	ERNESTO	DREXLER	SHAFFER	CONYERS	PHOEBUS	GERBERT
GAUSMAN	PRESTON	EUGENIO	DRINKER	SHEARER	CORLISS	PHYLLIS	GERHART
GERMAIN	PULLMAN	FILIPPO	DUILLER	SHIPLER	CORRENS	PROCLUS	GILBERT
GLEASON	QUENTIN	GALILEO	EMPEROR	SKINNER	CRESCAS	PYTHEAS	GOSSETT
GLISSON	RALSTON	GHIORSO	FECHNER	SLIPHER	CROOKES	RETZIUS	GUILLET
GOLDMAN	RAMSDEN	GIACOMO	FERRIER	SPECTOR	CURTISS	ROBARDS	HARRIOT
GOODMAN	REIMANN	GONZALO	FIBIGER	SPEISER	DANIELS	ROBBINS	HARTMUT
GOODWIN	RICHLIN	HANTARO	FISCHER	SPENCER	DEVRIES	ROBERTS	HECKART
GOOSSON	ROBISON	IGNACIO	FOURIER	SPITZER	DIOCLES	ROMANES	HERBERT
GRIFFIN	ROSALYN	JACINTO	FRICKER	STEIGER	DONDERS	RUNNELS	HEROULT
HACKMAN	SAKMANN	LAZZARO	GARDNER	STEINER	DOUGLAS	SANDERS	HILBERT
HAGEMAN	SALOMEN	LORENZO	GASSNER	TAINTER	DUKAKIS	SEFERIS	HOKFELT
HALPERN	SAROYAN	LYSENKO	GLAEVER	THEILER	ERASMUS	SERVAIS	LAMBERT
HAMMANN	SCANLAN	MADRAZO	GLAUBER	THEODOR	EUDEMUS	SEVERUS	LAURENT
HAMPSON	SCHWANN	MONDINO	HALLDOR	THEURER	EUDOXUS	SHIELDS	LEAVITT
HAMPTON	SEIRTON	NICCOLO	HEITLER	TRAUNER	EXIGUUS	SIEMENS	MAUMONT
HARTMAN	SEVERIN	OCTAVIO	HILLIER	VEKSLER	FLOWERS	STEARNS	NORBERT
HEERMAN	SHANNON	ORLANDO	HJALMAR	VERNIER	FOLKERS	STEVENS	NYKVIST
HENLEIN	SHEEHAN	OSVALDO	HOMEYER	WALTHER	FRANCES	STURGES	PECQUET
HEPBURN	SHELDON	PIZARRO	KASIMIR	WEGENER	FRANCIS	SUMMERS	PELIGOT
HERMANN	SHELTON	ROBERTO	KASTLER	WERNHER	FRISIUS	SURTEES	PREVOST
HICKMAN	SHERMAN	SHAPIRO	KIRCHER	WHEELER	GEMINUS	SYLVIUS	RENAULT
HODGKIN	SHUFTAN	SORVINO	KOLSTER	WINKLER	GEORGES	THADEUS	REYMONT
HOFFMAN	SIMPSON	STORARO	KRASKER	WOODGER	GIBBONS	TRAVERS	ROBINET
HOFMANN	SMEATON	TEDESCO	KRASNER	WOOSTER	GIORGOS	ULYSSES	ROTBLAT
HUMASON	SOLOMON	TELESIO	LARDNER	WUERZER	GLAUCUS	VENTRIS	SARGENT
JACKSON	SPEMANN	TEODORO	LOCKYER	ZEIDLER	GOERGES	WILKINS	SCHMIDT
JANSSEN	STEPHAN	TORELLO	LOFFLER	ZIEGLER	GORGIAS	WILLANS	SCHMITT
JEMISON	STEPHEN	ZERMELO	LORIMER	ZINSSER	HARKINS	WINDAUS	SEBOKHT
JENSSON	STEPVEN	APTHROP	MACQUER	ACTINUS	HAWKINS	WINTERS	SEIFERT
JOCELYN	SUSSMAN	BELKNAP	MAUNDER	AEPINUS	HEYMANS	XIMENES	STEWART
JOHNSON	THOMSEN	IMHOTEP	MEITNER	ALBINUS	HIPPIAS	ALLBUTT	SWIGERT
JUERGEN	THOMSON	PHILIPP	MESSIER	ALCAEUS	HOPKINS	BARNETT	SYLBERT
KAPTEYN	TIDYMAN	PHILLIP	MUELLER	ANDREAS	HUGGINS	BECKETT	TENNANT
KAUFMAN	TORBERN	BATFOUR	MUNSTER	ANDREWS	HUYGENS	BENNETT	TIPPETT

VALMONT	PALISSY	AMONTONS	BOMBELLI	CHROWDER	EMMANUEL	GERHARDT	HILDYARD
VINCENT	POMEROY	AMUNDSEN	BORGNINE	CLAIRAUT	EPALINUS	GERTRUDE	HIPPACOS
WALCOTT	PTOLEMY	ANDERSON	BOTSTEIN	CLARENCE	EPICURUS	GHERARDI	HIPPALUS
ZYGMUNT	SCHALLY	ANFINSEN	BOULLIAU	CLAUDINE	ERICKSON	GHISLAIN	HIPPASUS
DANGEAU	SHAMROY	ANGSTROM	BOURBAKI	CLAUDIUS	ERICSSON	GIACCONI	HIRAYAMA
KIDDINU	SHANLEY	ANJELICA	BOURGOIN	CLAUSIUS	ERLANGER	GILLETTE	HISINGER
MATTHAU	SHAPLEY	ANSCHUTZ	BOWDITCH	CLEMENCE	ESQUIVEL	GIORDANO	HOAGLAND
MONTAGU	SHELLEY	ANTONIO	BOYLSTON	CLIFFORD	EUGENIUS	GIOVANNI	HOFFMANN
PAXINOU	SHIRLEY	APPLETON	BRACKETT	COBLENTZ	EUTOCIUS	GIROLAMO	HOLLIDAY
KAZAKOV	SMALLEY	ARCHYTAS	BRADFORD	COLLINGS	EVARISTE	GIUSEPPE	HOLWARDA
KOMAROV	SOLOVAY	ARISTIDE	BRAMANTE	COLUMBUS	FAHLBERG	GODEFROY	HORNBECK
KOZYREV	STANLEY	ARZACHEL	BRANTING	CONVERSI	FAUCHARD	GOEPPERT	HORROCKS
LEBEDEV	STARKEY	ASHCROFT	BRATTAIN	COOLIDGE	FAULKNER	GOLDBACH	HORSFALL
SEMENOV	TARAGAY	ASTURIAS	BRENTANO	CORNELIS	FAVALORO	GOLDBERG	HOUSEMAN
USTINOV	TIMOTHY	AUGUSTIN	BREWSTER	CORONADO	FEILDING	GOLDMARK	HOUTGAST
VAVILOV	WHITNEY	AUGUSTUS	BRICKMAN	CORRIGAN	FELICITA	GOLITZEN	HUFELAND
BIGELOW	WOOLLEY	AURELIUS	BRIDGMAN	COTTRELL	FILLMORE	GOODRICH	HUMPHREY
CZESLAW	WORTLEY	AVERROES	BRINDLEY	COUNTESS	FISHBACH	GOODYEAR	HUNTSMAN
GLASHOW	ZACHARY	AVICENNA	BRONSTED	COURNAND	FLANNERY	GORDIMER	HURLBERT
KENDREW	AGASSIZ	AVILDSEN	BRUNFELS	COURTOIS	FLEMMING	GOTTLIEB	HUTSHING
MATTHEW	ALVAREZ	AVOGADRO	BUCHANAN	COUSTEAU	FLETCHER	GOUDSMIT	IMMANUEL
VIRCHOW	BEDNARZ	BANCROFT	BUCKLAND	CRAWFORD	FLINDERS	GRANTLEY	INGEBORG
WINSLOW	BEDNORZ	BAPTISTA	BUMSTEAD	CRISTIAN	FLORENCE	GREENHAM	IPATIEFF
WOODROW	COLDITZ	BAPTISTE	BUSCHING	CROMPTON	FLOURENS	GRIFFITH	ISAEVICH
JOUHAUX	JIMENEZ	BARONESS	BUSHNELL	CROWFOOT	FONTAINE	GRIGNARD	ISAMBARD
ANTHONY	LEIBNIZ	BARTHOUD	BUSTILLO	CUTHBERT	FOUCAULT	GRIMALDI	JACOBSON
ASTBURY	LORENTZ	BARTLETT	BUTLEROV	DAGUERRE	FOURCROY	GROTRIAN	JACQUARD
BRADLEY	MAHFOUZ	BASHEVIS	CAGLIONE	DAREVSKY	FOURNIER	GUETTARD	JAENISCH
BRODSKY	MARQUEZ	BASILIUS	CALANDRI	DAVIDSON	FRAENKEL	GUINNESS	JANNINGS
CATESBY	MEINESZ	BATTISTA	CALLAHAN	DAVISSON	FRAMPTON	GUISEPPE	JAROSLAV
CHARNAY	RADNITZ	BAUCHENS	CALMETTE	DEBIERNE	FRANCOIS	GULDBERG	JEANETTE
CHOMSKY	SANCHEZ	BEATRICE	CAMPANUS	DEDEKIND	FRANKLIN	HADAMARD	JEDEDIAH
CHRISTY	TADEUSZ	BEAUMONT	CAMPBELL	DELAMBRE	FREDERIC	HADFIELD	JEFFREYS
CONNERY	WOTTITZ	BECCARIA	CANONERO	DELBRUCK	FREDHOLM	HAFFKINE	JEFFRIES
DOHERTY		BECKWITH	CAPELLER	DEMARCAY	FREDRICH	HAGGERTY	JENNIFER
DOROTHY		BEECKMAN	CARADINI	DEMPSTER	FREEDMAN	HALLBERG	JENNINGS
DUNAWAY		BELTRAMI	CARDUCCI	DESHNJOV	FRENICLE	HAMILTON	JENNISON
FITZROY	**8 LETTER**	BENEDICT	CARFAGNO	DESIDERI	FRIDTJOF	HANNIBAL	JEREMIAH
GODFREY	**1ST LETTER**	BENJAMIN	CARLETON	DESORMES	FRIEDKIN	HARCOURT	JEREMIAS
GREGORY		BENNETTI	CARLISLE	DILLEHAY	FRIEDMAN	HARKNESS	JHABVALA
GUFFROY		BERKELEY	CARNEGIE	DOMENICO	FRUEHAUF	HARRISON	JOHANNES
HARTLEY	ADELBERT	BERLINER	CAROLINE	DOUGLASS	GABRIELA	HARTLINE	JOHANSON
HENNESY	ADOVASIO	BERNARDO	CASTILLO	DRESSLER	GAERTNER	HARTMANN	JOHNSTON
HERSHEY	ADRIENNE	BERNHARD	CHADWICK	DREYFUSS	GAJDUSEK	HATCHETT	JONATHAN
HILLARY	AECHYLUS	BEROULLI	CHAKIRIS	DRUMMOND	GAMALIEL	HAUKSBEE	JORDANUS
HORSLEY	AFANASSI	BERTRAND	CHALONGE	DUCOMMUN	GANGELIN	HAUPTMAN	JOUFFROY
HOUSSAY	AGOSTINO	BESSEMER	CHAMBERS	DUJARDIN	GARDINER	HAVELOCK	JUNGHANS
HUMPHRY	AGRICOLA	BILLINGS	CHANDLER	EASTWOOD	GARFIELD	HEINEMAN	KAMINSKI
JEFFERY	AHLQUIST	BIRDSEYE	CHANNING	EBERHARD	GARNERIN	HEINRICH	KAMMERER
KENNEDY	ALBERTUS	BIRKHOFF	CHARGAFF	EGBERTUS	GASCOYNE	HEMPHREY	KANELLOS
LANGLEY	ALBRECHT	BJERKNES	CHARLIER	EILHARDT	GASSENDI	HENDRICK	KAUFMANN
MALLORY	ALCMAEON	BJORNSON	CHARLTON	EINSTEIN	GEISSLER	HENRICUS	KAWABATA
MAUCHLY	ALDREDGE	BLACKETT	CHATELET	ELDREDGE	GEOFFORY	HERANADO	KAZUHIKO
MCCAREY	ALGERNON	BLANFORD	CHEVREUL	ELEANORE	GEOFFREY	HERSCHEL	KENNELLY
MIDGLEY	ALISTAIR	BLUMBERG	CHIRIKOV	ELLICOTT	GEORGIUS	HERZBERG	KINGSLEY
MOSELEY	AMBROISE	BOETHIUS	CHISHOLM	ELSASSER	GERARDUS	HEVELIUS	KIRCHHOF
NIKOLAY	AMERICUS	BOLTWOOD	CHRISTIE	ELVEHJEM	GERGONNE	HIJUELOS	KIRKWOOD

KITASATO	MARSIGLI	NORDHEIM	RICCARDO	SINCLAIR	VANNEVAR	BARTHOUD	JACOBSON
KJELDAHL	MARTINUS	NORTHROP	RICCIOLI	SKOLNICK	VASSILIS	BARTLETT	JACQUARD
KLAPROTH	MATHISON	NOVARESE	RICHARDS	SMITHSON	VESALIUS	BASHEVIS	JAENISCH
KORNBERG	MATTHIAS	NUSSLEIN	RICHMANN	SOCRATES	VILLEMIN	BASILIUS	JANNINGS
KORNGOLD	MATUYAMA	ODYSSEUS	RICHMOND	SORENSEN	VINCENTE	BATTISTA	JAROSLAV
KUBOYAMA	MAUDSLAY	OLIPHANT	RICKETTS	SOUFFLOT	VINCENZO	BAUCHENS	KAMINSKI
LAGERLOF	MCCARTHY	OSHEROFF	RICKOVER	SOUTHERN	VIRTANEN	CAGLIONE	KAMMERER
LAGRANGE	MCCLEARY	OSIANDER	ROBERTUS	SPEDDING	VITTORIO	CALANDRI	KANELLOS
LANGEVIN	MCCOLLUM	OUGHTRED	ROBINSON	SPITTLER	VLADIMIR	CALLAHAN	KAUFMANN
LANGMUIR	MCDANIEL	PAGANINI	RODERICK	SPRECKER	VOLTAIRE	CALMETTE	KAWABATA
LANTIERI	MCDIVITT	PALITZSH	ROEBLING	SPRENGEL	VOLTERRA	CAMPANUS	KAZUHIKO
LAPWORTH	MCEVILLY	PALMIERI	ROENTGEN	STAFFORD	VONNEGUT	CAMPBELL	LAGERLOF
LASHELLE	MCKINLEY	PARRONDO	ROSALIND	STANFORD	WAKELING	CANONERO	LAGRANGE
LASSALLY	MCLAGLEN	PATERSON	ROUSSEAU	STARLING	WALDEMAR	CAPELLER	LANGEVIN
LASSETER	MCLELLAN	PATRICIA	RUDOLPHE	STAUFFER	WALDEYER	CARADINI	LANGMUIR
LAUGHTON	MCMILLAN	PATRIZIA	RUGGIERO	STEINITZ	WANSTALL	CARDUCCI	LANTIERI
LAURENCE	MCMURTRY	PATTISON	RUTLEDGE	STEINORE	WATANABE	CARFAGNO	LAPWORTH
LAWRENCE	MEISSNER	PEDERSEN	RYDSTROM	STEPHENS	WATERMAN	CARLETON	LASHELLE
LEACHMAN	MELCHIOR	PEDERSON	SAAVEDRA	STEVINUS	WECHSLER	CARLISLE	LASSALLY
LEBESGUE	MELLANBY	PERCIVAL	SABATIER	STIRLING	WEHINGER	CARNEGIE	LASSETER
LEDERMAN	MENACHEM	PERELMAN	SACCHERI	STOTHART	WEINBERG	CAROLINE	LAUGHTON
LEGENDRE	MENELAUS	PERICLES	SAKHAROV	STRAIGHT	WEISMANN	CASTILLO	LAURENCE
LEISHMAN	MENGHINI	PERRAULT	SALVADOR	STROWGER	WELSBACH	DAGUERRE	LAWRENCE
LEMAITRE	MERCATOR	PERSONNE	SANTIAGO	STURGEON	WENDELIN	DAREVSKY	MACBRIDE
LEMELSON	MERCEDES	PESCUCCI	SANTILLO	SULEIMAN	WESTMORE	DAVIDSON	MACLAINE
LEONARDO	MEREDITH	PETERSON	SARANDON	SULLIVAN	WHISTLER	DAVISSON	MACQUORN
LEONHARD	MERSENNE	PETRUCCI	SAUNDERS	SUNDMANN	WHITFORD	EASTWOOD	MADESANI
LEOPOLDO	MESENKOP	PHILIPPE	SAUTUOLA	SVEDBERG	WIECHERT	FAHLBERG	MAGELLAN
LEUCKART	MEYERHOF	PHILLIPE	SCALIGER	SYDENHAM	WILLHELM	FAUCHARD	MAGENDIE
LEVINSON	MIESCHER	PICKFORD	SCHAEFER	TAKAMINE	WILLIAMS	FAULKNER	MAGIDSON
LIBAVIUS	MILLIKAN	PIERPONT	SCHALLER	TARADASH	WIMPERIS	FAVALORO	MAITLAND
LINDBLAD	MILSTEIN	PITISCUS	SCHAWLOW	TERENIUS	WINTHROP	GABRIELA	MALPIGHI
LINDHEIM	MINNAERT	PLASKETT	SCHEINER	THATCHER	WOLFGANG	GAERTNER	MANUTIUS
LINNAEUS	MINNELLI	PLAYFAIR	SCHIMMEL	THEEUWES	WOODBURY	GAJDUSEK	MARCELIN
LIPPMANN	MITCHELL	PLUNKETT	SCHIMPER	THEOBALD	WOODRUFF	GAMALIEL	MARCELLO
LIPSCOMB	MOHAMMED	POINCARE	SCHROTER	THEODORE	WOODWARD	GANGELIN	MARGARET
LJAPUNOW	MONNARTZ	POLIDORE	SCHULMAN	THEORELL	YAMAMOTO	GARDINER	MARGGRAF
LOBASHOV	MORGAGNI	POLITZER	SCHULTES	THEVENET	YAMAZAKE	GARFIELD	MARIOTTE
LUNDBERG	MORRISON	POLYKARP	SCHULTZE	THIBAULT	YAMAZAKI	GARNERIN	MARJORIE
MACBRIDE	MOSANDER	PONCELET	SCHUSTER	THIMOTHY	YANOFSKY	GASCOYNE	MARSHALL
MACLAINE	MUHAMMAD	PRESCOTT	SCHWARTZ	THOMPSON	YASUMASA	GASSENDI	MARSHMAN
MACQUORN	MULLIKEN	PROSPERO	SCIPIONE	THUNBERG	YASUNARI	HADAMARD	MARSIGLI
MADESANI	NAARMANN	PURKINJE	SCOFIELD	TISELIUS	YOICHIRO	HADFIELD	MARTINUS
MAGELLAN	NAPOLEON	PYLARINI	SEDGWICK	TOMBAUGH	ZAILLIAN	HAFFKINE	MATHISON
MAGENDIE	NARINDER	QUARANTA	SEFSTROM	TOMMASON	ZEMECKIS	HAGGERTY	MATTHIAS
MAGIDSON	NEHEMIAH	QUETELET	SELEUCUS	TOMONAGA	ZEPPELIN	HALLBERG	MATUYAMA
MAITLAND	NEWCOMBE	RAMBALDI	SEPKOSKI	TONEGAWA	ZSIGMOND	HAMILTON	MAUDSLAY
MALPIGHI	NEWCOMEN	RAYLEIGH	SERVETUS	TOWNSEND	ZWORYKIN	HANNIBAL	NAARMANN
MANUTIUS	NEWLANDS	REDFIELD	SHEARMAN	TRAJANUS		HARCOURT	NAPOLEON
MARCELIN	NICHOLAS	REDGRAVE	SHERIDAN	TREMBLEY		HARKNESS	NARINDER
MARCELLO	NICKOLAI	REGINALD	SHERWOOD	TRUMPLER		HARRISON	PAGANINI
MARGARET	NICOLAAS	REGNAULT	SHOCKLEY	TRUSCOTT	**2ND LETTER**	HARTLINE	PALITZSH
MARGGRAF	NICOLASS	REINHOLD	SHRAPNEL	UNSWORTH		HARTMANN	PALMIERI
MARIOTTE	NICOLAUS	REITSEMA	SIEGBAHN	VALDEMAR	BANCROFT	HATCHETT	PARRONDO
MARJORIE	NIKOLASS	RENNAHAN	SIGNORET	VALENTIN	BAPTISTA	HAUKSBEE	PATERSON
MARSHALL	NIKOLAUS	REYNOLDS	SIKORSKI	VALERIUS	BAPTISTE	HAUPTMAN	PATRICIA
MARSHMAN	NOBUYUKI	RHETICUS	SILLIMAN	VALSALVA	BARONESS	HAVELOCK	PATRIZIA

PATTISON	SCHUSTER	JENNIFER	TERENIUS	DILLEHAY	VILLEMIN	ANGSTROM	JOHNSTON
RAMBALDI	SCHWARTZ	JENNINGS	VESALIUS	EILHARDT	VINCENTE	ANJELICA	JONATHAN
RAYLEIGH	SCIPIONE	JENNISON	WECHSLER	EINSTEIN	VINCENZO	ANSCHUTZ	JORDANUS
SAAVEDRA	SCOFIELD	JEREMIAH	WEHINGER	FILLMORE	VIRTANEN	ANTIONIO	JOUFFROY
SABATIER	ADELBERT	JEREMIAS	WEINBERG	FISHBACH	VITTORIO	INGEBORG	KORNBERG
SACCHERI	ADOVASIO	KENNELLY	WEISMANN	GIACCONI	WIECHERT	UNSWORTH	KORNGOLD
SAKHAROV	ADRIENNE	LEACHMAN	WELSBACH	GILLETTE	WILLHELM	BOETHIUS	LOBASHOV
SALVADOR	ODYSSEUS	LEBESGUE	WENDELIN	GIORDANO	WILLIAMS	BOLTWOOD	MOHAMMED
SANTIAGO	AECHYLUS	LEDERMAN	WESTMORE	GIOVANNI	WIMPERIS	BOMBELLI	MONNARTZ
SANTILLO	BEATRICE	LEGENDRE	ZEMECKIS	GIROLAMO	WINTHROP	BORGNINE	MORGAGNI
SARANDON	BEAUMONT	LEISHMAN	ZEPPELIN	GIUSEPPE	BJERKNES	BOTSTEIN	MORRISON
SAUNDERS	BECCARIA	LEMAITRE	AFANASSI	HIJUELOS	BJORNSON	BOULLIAU	MOSANDER
SAUTUOLA	BECKWITH	LEMELSON	AGOSTINO	HILDYARD	KJELDAHL	BOURBAKI	NOBUYUKI
TAKAMINE	BEECKMAN	LEONARDO	AGRICOLA	HIPPACOS	LJAPUNOW	BOURGOIN	NORDHEIM
TARADASH	BELTRAMI	LEONHARD	EGBERTUS	HIPPALUS	SKOLNICK	BOWDITCH	NORTHROP
VALDEMAR	BENEDICT	LEOPOLDO	AHLQUIST	HIPPASUS	ALBERTUS	BOYLSTON	NOVARESE
VALENTIN	BENJAMIN	LEUCKART	CHADWICK	HIRAYAMA	ALBRECHT	COBLENTZ	POINCARE
VALERIUS	BENNETTI	LEVINSON	CHAKIRIS	HISINGER	ALCMAEON	COLLINGS	POLIDORE
VALSALVA	BERKELEY	MEISSNER	CHALONGE	KINGSLEY	ALDREDGE	COLUMBUS	POLITZER
VANNEVAR	BERLINER	MELCHIOR	CHAMBERS	KIRCHHOF	ALGERNON	CONVERSI	POLYKARP
VASSILIS	BERNARDO	MELLANBY	CHANDLER	KIRKWOOD	ALISTAIR	COOLIDGE	PONCELET
WAKELING	BERNHARD	MENACHEM	CHANNING	KITASATO	BLACKETT	CORNELIS	ROBERTUS
WALDEMAR	BEROULLI	MENELAUS	CHARGAFF	LIBAVIUS	BLANFORD	CORONADO	ROBINSON
WALDEYER	BERTRAND	MENGHINI	CHARLIER	LINDBLAD	BLUMBERG	CORRIGAN	RODERICK
WANSTALL	BESSEMER	MERCATOR	CHARLTON	LINDHEIM	CLAIRAUT	COTTRELL	ROEBLING
WATANABE	DEBIERNE	MERCEDES	CHATELET	LINNAEUS	CLARENCE	COUNTESS	ROENTGEN
WATERMAN	DEDEKIND	MEREDITH	CHEVREUL	LIPPMANN	CLAUDINE	COURNAND	ROSALIND
YAMAMOTO	DELAMBRE	MERSENNE	CHIRIKOV	LIPSCOMB	CLAUDIUS	COURTOIS	ROUSSEAU
YAMAZAKE	DELBRUCK	MESENKOP	CHISHOLM	MIESCHER	CLAUSIUS	COUSTEAU	SOCRATES
YAMAZAKI	DEMARCAY	MEYERHOF	CHRISTIE	MILLIKAN	CLEMENCE	DOMENICO	SORENSEN
YANOFSKY	DEMPSTER	NEHEMIAH	CHROWDER	MILSTEIN	CLIFFORD	DOUGLASS	SOUFFLOT
YASUMASA	DESHNJOV	NEWCOMBE	GHERARDI	MINNAERT	ELDREDGE	FONTAINE	SOUTHERN
YASUNARI	DESIDERI	NEWCOMEN	GHISLAIN	MINNELLI	ELEANORE	FOUCAULT	TOMBAUGH
ZAILLIAN	DESORMES	NEWLANDS	JHABVALA	MITCHELL	ELLICOTT	FOURCROY	TOMMASON
EBERHARD	FEILDING	PEDERSEN	PHILIPPE	NICHOLAS	ELSASSER	FOURNIER	TOMONAGA
MCCARTHY	FELICITA	PEDERSON	PHILLIPE	NICKOLAI	ELVEHJEM	GODEFROY	TONEGAWA
MCCLEARY	GEISSLER	PERCIVAL	RHETICUS	NICOLAAS	FLANNERY	GOEPPERT	TOWNSEND
MCCOLLUM	GEOFFORY	PERELMAN	SHEARMAN	NICOLASS	FLEMMING	GOLDBACH	VOLTAIRE
MCDANIEL	GEOFFREY	PERICLES	SHERIDAN	NICOLAUS	FLETCHER	GOLDBERG	VOLTERRA
MCDIVITT	GEORGIUS	PERRAULT	SHERWOOD	NIKOLASS	FLINDERS	GOLDMARK	VONNEGUT
MCEVILLY	GERARDUS	PERSONNE	SHOCKLEY	NIKOLAUS	FLORENCE	GOLITZEN	WOLFGANG
MCKINLEY	GERGONNE	PESCUCCI	SHRAPNEL	PICKFORD	FLOURENS	GOODRICH	WOODBURY
MCLAGLEN	GERHARDT	PETERSON	THATCHER	PIERPONT	KLAPROTH	GOODYEAR	WOODRUFF
MCLELLAN	GERTRUDE	PETRUCCI	THEEUWES	PITISCUS	OLIPHANT	GORDIMER	WOODWARD
MCMILLAN	HEINEMAN	REDFIELD	THEOBALD	RICCARDO	PLASKETT	GOTTLIEB	YOICHIRO
MCMURTRY	HEINRICH	REDGRAVE	THEODORE	RICCIOLI	PLAYFAIR	GOUDSMIT	APPLETON
SCALIGER	HEMPHREY	REGINALD	THEORELL	RICHARDS	PLUNKETT	HOAGLAND	EPALINUS
SCHAEFER	HENDRICK	REGNAULT	THEVENET	RICHMANN	VLADIMIR	HOFFMANN	EPICURUS
SCHALLER	HENRICUS	REINHOLD	THIBAULT	RICHMOND	AMBROISE	HOLLIDAY	IPATIEFF
SCHAWLOW	HERANADO	REITSEMA	THIMOTHY	RICKETTS	AMERICUS	HOLWARDA	SPEDDING
SCHEINER	HERSCHEL	RENNAHAN	THOMPSON	RICKOVER	AMONTONS	HORNBECK	SPITTLER
SCHIMMEL	HERZBERG	REYNOLDS	THUNBERG	SIEGBAHN	AMUNDSEN	HORROCKS	SPRECKER
SCHIMPER	HEVELIUS	SEDGWICK	WHISTLER	SIGNORET	EMMANUEL	HORSFALL	SPRENGEL
SCHROTER	JEANETTE	SEFSTROM	WHITFORD	SIKORSKI	IMMANUEL	HOUSEMAN	ARCHYTAS
SCHULMAN	JEDEDIAH	SELEUCUS	BILLINGS	SILLIMAN	SMITHSON	HOUTGAST	ARISTIDE
SCHULTES	JEFFREYS	SEPKOSKI	BIRDSEYE	SINCLAIR	ANDERSON	JOHANNES	ARZACHEL
SCHULTZE	JEFFRIES	SERVETUS	BIRKHOFF	TISELIUS	ANFINSEN	JOHANSON	BRACKETT

		3RD LETTER					
BRADFORD	STAUFFER	PYLARINI	SCALIGER	DEDEKIND	SHERWOOD	SCHIMPER	ZAILLIAN
BRAMANTE	STEINITZ	RYDSTROM	STAFFORD	ELDREDGE	SIEGBAHN	SCHROTER	ZSIGMOND
BRANTING	STEINORE	SYDENHAM	STANFORD	GODEFROY	SPEDDING	SCHULMAN	ANJELICA
BRATTAIN	STEPHENS		STARLING	HADAMARD	STEINITZ	SCHULTES	DUJARDIN
BRENTANO	STEVINUS		STAUFFER	HADFIELD	STEINORE	SCHULTZE	GAJDUSEK
BREWSTER	STIRLING		THATCHER	JEDEDIAH	STEPHENS	SCHUSTER	HIJUELOS
BRICKMAN	STOTHART		TRAJANUS	LEDERMAN	STEVINUS	SCHWARTZ	MCKINLEY
BRIDGMAN	STRAIGHT		VLADIMIR	MADESANI	SVEDBERG	WEHINGER	NIKOLASS
BRINDLEY	STROWGER	AFANASSI	ALBERTUS	MCDANIEL	THEEUWES	ALISTAIR	NIKOLAUS
BRONSTED	STURGEON	BEATRICE	ALBRECHT	MCDIVITT	THEOBALD	ARISTIDE	SAKHAROV
BRUNFELS	AUGUSTIN	BEAUMONT	AMBROISE	PEDERSEN	THEODORE	AVICENNA	SIKORSKI
CRAWFORD	AUGUSTUS	BLACKETT	COBLENTZ	PEDERSON	THEORELL	AVILDSEN	TAKAMINE
CRISTIAN	AURELIUS	BLANFORD	DEBIERNE	REDFIELD	THEVENET	BRICKMAN	WAKELING
CROMPTON	BUCHANAN	BRACKETT	EGBERTUS	REDGRAVE	TREMBLEY	BRIDGMAN	AHLQUIST
CROWFOOT	BUCKLAND	BRADFORD	GABRIELA	RODERICK	WIECHERT	BRINDLEY	BELTRAMI
DRESSLER	BUMSTEAD	BRAMANTE	KUBOYAMA	RUDOLPHE	ANFINSEN	CHIRIKOV	BILLINGS
DREYFUSS	BUSCHING	BRANTING	LEBESGUE	RYDSTROM	HAFFKINE	CHISHOLM	BOLTWOOD
DRUMMOND	BUSHNELL	BRATTAIN	LIBAVIUS	SEDGWICK	HOFFMANN	CLIFFORD	CALANDRI
ERICKSON	BUSTILLO	CHADWICK	LOBASHOV	SYDENHAM	HUFELAND	CRISTIAN	CALLAHAN
ERICSSON	BUTLEROV	CHAKIRIS	NOBUYUKI	ADELBERT	JEFFREYS	EPICURUS	CALMETTE
ERLANGER	CUTHBERT	CHALONGE	ROBERTUS	AMERICUS	JEFFRIES	ERICKSON	COLLINGS
FRAENKEL	DUCOMMUN	CHAMBERS	ROBINSON	AVERROES	SEFSTROM	ERICSSON	COLUMBUS
FRAMPTON	DUJARDIN	CHANDLER	SABATIER	BEECKMAN	ALGERNON	FEILDING	DELAMBRE
FRANCOIS	EUGENIUS	CHANNING	AECHYLUS	BJERKNES	ANGSTROM	FLINDERS	DELBRUCK
FRANKLIN	EUTOCIUS	CHARGAFF	ALCMAEON	BOETHIUS	AUGUSTIN	FRIDTJOF	DILLEHAY
FREDERIC	GUETTARD	CHARLIER	ARCHYTAS	BRENTANO	AUGUSTUS	FRIEDKIN	EILHARDT
FREDHOLM	GUINNESS	CHARLTON	BECCARIA	BREWSTER	CAGLIONE	FRIEDMAN	ELLICOTT
FREDRICH	GUISEPPE	CHATELET	BECKWITH	CHEVREUL	DAGUERRE	GEISSLER	ERLANGER
FREEDMAN	GULDBERG	CLAIRAUT	BUCHANAN	CLEMENCE	EUGENIUS	GHISLAIN	FELICITA
FRENICLE	HUFELAND	CLARENCE	BUCKLAND	DRESSLER	HAGGERTY	GRIFFITH	FILLMORE
FRIDTJOF	HUMPHREY	CLAUDINE	DUCOMMUN	DREYFUSS	INGEBORG	GRIGNARD	GILLETTE
FRIEDKIN	HUNTSMAN	CLAUDIUS	JACOBSON	EBERHARD	LAGERLOF	GRIMALDI	GOLDBACH
FRIEDMAN	HURLBERT	CLAUSIUS	JACQUARD	ELEANORE	LAGRANGE	GUINNESS	GOLDBERG
FRUEHAUF	HUTSHING	CRAWFORD	MACBRIDE	FLEMMING	LEGENDRE	GUISEPPE	GOLDMARK
GRANTLEY	JUNGHANS	EPALINUS	MACLAINE	FLETCHER	MAGELLAN	HEINEMAN	GOLITZEN
GREENHAM	KUBOYAMA	EVARISTE	MACQUORN	FREDERIC	MAGENDIE	HEINRICH	GULDBERG
GRIFFITH	LUNDBERG	FLANNERY	MCCARTHY	FREDHOLM	MAGIDSON	LEISHMAN	HALLBERG
GRIGNARD	MUHAMMAD	FRAENKEL	MCCLEARY	FREDRICH	OUGHTRED	MAITLAND	HILDYARD
GRIMALDI	MULLIKEN	FRAMPTON	MCCOLLUM	FREEDMAN	PAGANINI	MEISSNER	HOLLIDAY
GROTRIAN	NUSSLEIN	FRANCOIS	NICHOLAS	FRENICLE	REGINALD	OLIPHANT	HOLWARDA
PRESCOTT	OUGHTRED	FRANKLIN	NICKOLAI	GAERTNER	REGNAULT	OSIANDER	MALPIGHI
PROSPERO	PURKINJE	GIACCONI	NICOLAAS	GHERARDI	RUGGIERO	PHILIPPE	MCLAGLEN
TRAJANUS	QUARANTA	GRANTLEY	NICOLASS	GOEPPERT	SIGNORET	PHILLIPE	MCLELLAN
TREMBLEY	QUETELET	HOAGLAND	NICOLAUS	GREENHAM	ASHCROFT	POINCARE	MELCHIOR
TRUMPLER	RUDOLPHE	IPATIEFF	PICKFORD	GUETTARD	FAHLBERG	REINHOLD	MELLANBY
TRUSCOTT	RUGGIERO	ISAEVICH	RICCARDO	JAENISCH	JOHANNES	REITSEMA	MILLIKAN
ASHCROFT	RUTLEDGE	ISAMBARD	RICCIOLI	KJELDAHL	JOHANSON	SCIPIONE	MILSTEIN
ASTURIAS	SULEIMAN	JEANETTE	RICHARDS	MCEVILLY	JOHNSTON	SMITHSON	MULLIKEN
ESQUIVEL	SULLIVAN	JHABVALA	RICHMANN	MIESCHER	MOHAMMED	SPITTLER	PALITZSH
ISAEVICH	SUNDMANN	KLAPROTH	RICHMOND	PIERPONT	MUHAMMAD	STIRLING	PALMIERI
ISAMBARD	AVERROES	LEACHMAN	RICKETTS	PRESCOTT	NEHEMIAH	THIBAULT	POLIDORE
OSHEROFF	AVICENNA	LJAPUNOW	RICKOVER	QUETELET	OSHEROFF	THIMOTHY	POLITZER
OSIANDER	AVILDSEN	NAARMANN	SACCHERI	RHETICUS	SCHAEFER	WEINBERG	POLYKARP
ZSIGMOND	AVOGADRO	PLASKETT	SOCRATES	ROEBLING	SCHALLER	WEISMANN	PYLARINI
STAFFORD	EVARISTE	PLAYFAIR	WECHSLER	ROENTGEN	SCHAWLOW	WHISTLER	SALVADOR
STANFORD	SVEDBERG	QUARANTA	ALDREDGE	SHEARMAN	SCHEINER	WHITFORD	SELEUCUS
STARLING	ZWORYKIN	SAAVEDRA	ANDERSON	SHERIDAN	SCHIMMEL	YOICHIRO	SILLIMAN

SULEIMAN	JENNIFER	LEONHARD	GERARDUS	SPRECKER	PATRIZIA	NOVARESE	SABATIER
SULLIVAN	JENNINGS	LEOPOLDO	GERGONNE	SPRENGEL	PATTISON	BOWDITCH	SARANDON
VALDEMAR	JENNISON	PROSPERO	GERHARDT	STRAIGHT	PETERSON	KAWABATA	SCHAEFER
VALENTIN	JONATHAN	SCOFIELD	GERTRUDE	STROWGER	PETRUCCI	LAWRENCE	SCHALLER
VALERIUS	JUNGHANS	SHOCKLEY	GIROLAMO	TARADASH	PITISCUS	NEWCOMBE	SCHAWLOW
VALSALVA	KANELLOS	SKOLNICK	GORDIMER	TERENIUS	RUTLEDGE	NEWCOMEN	SHEARMAN
VILLEMIN	KENNELLY	STOTHART	HARCOURT	VIRTANEN	VITTORIO	NEWLANDS	SHRAPNEL
VOLTAIRE	KINGSLEY	THOMPSON	HARKNESS	ANSCHUTZ	WATANABE	TOWNSEND	STRAIGHT
VOLTERRA	LANGEVIN	WOODBURY	HARRISON	BASHEVIS	WATERMAN	BOYLSTON	TAKAMINE
WALDEMAR	LANGMUIR	WOODRUFF	HARTLINE	BASILIUS	AMUNDSEN	MEYERHOF	TARADASH
WALDEYER	LANTIERI	WOODWARD	HARTMANN	BESSEMER	BAUCHENS	ODYSSEUS	VESALIUS
WELSBACH	LINDBLAD	ZWORYKIN	HERANADO	BUSCHING	BLUMBERG	RAYLEIGH	WATANABE
WILLHELM	LINDHEIM	APPLETON	HERSCHEL	BUSHNELL	BOULLIAU	REYNOLDS	YAMAMOTO
WILLIAMS	LINNAEUS	BAPTISTA	HERZBERG	BUSTILLO	BOURBAKI	ARZACHEL	YAMAZAKE
WOLFGANG	LUNDBERG	BAPTISTE	HIRAYAMA	CASTILLO	BOURGOIN	KAZUHIKO	YAMAZAKI
BOMBELLI	MANUTIUS	CAPELLER	HORNBECK	DESHNJOV	BRUNFELS		BOMBELLI
BUMSTEAD	MENACHEM	HIPPACOS	HORROCKS	DESIDERI	COUNTESS		DELBRUCK
CAMPANUS	MENELAUS	HIPPALUS	HORSFALL	DESORMES	COURNAND		JHABVALA
CAMPBELL	MENGHINI	HIPPASUS	HURLBERT	EASTWOOD	COURTOIS	**4TH LETTER**	MACBRIDE
DEMARCAY	MINNAERT	LAPWORTH	JAROSLAV	ELSASSER	COUSTEAU		RAMBALDI
DEMPSTER	MINNELLI	LIPPMANN	JEREMIAH	FISHBACH	DOUGLASS	ARZACHEL	ROEBLING
DOMENICO	MONNARTZ	LIPSCOMB	JEREMIAS	GASCOYNE	DRUMMOND	CALANDRI	THIBAULT
EMMANUEL	PONCELET	NAPOLEON	JORDANUS	GASSENDI	FAUCHARD	CARADINI	TOMBAUGH
GAMALIEL	RENNAHAN	SEPKOSKI	KIRCHHOF	HISINGER	FAULKNER	DELAMBRE	ANSCHUTZ
HAMILTON	SANTIAGO	ZEPPELIN	KIRKWOOD	LASHELLE	FOUCAULT	DEMARCAY	ASHCROFT
HEMPHREY	SANTILLO	ESQUIVEL	KORNBERG	LASSALLY	FOURCROY	DUJARDIN	AVICENNA
HUMPHREY	SINCLAIR	ADRIENNE	KORNGOLD	LASSETER	FOURNIER	ELEANORE	BANCROFT
IMMANUEL	SUNDMANN	AGRICOLA	MARCELIN	MESENKOP	FRUEHAUF	ELSASSER	BAUCHENS
KAMINSKI	TONEGAWA	AURELIUS	MARCELLO	MOSANDER	GIUSEPPE	EMMANUEL	BECCARIA
KAMMERER	VANNEVAR	BARONESS	MARGARET	NUSSLEIN	GOUDSMIT	ERLANGER	BEECKMAN
LEMAITRE	VINCENTE	BARTHOUD	MARGGRAF	PESCUCCI	HAUKSBEE	FAVALORO	BLACKETT
LEMELSON	VINCENZO	BARTLETT	MARIOTTE	ROSALIND	HAUPTMAN	GAMALIEL	BRACKETT
MCMILLAN	VONNEGUT	BERKELEY	MARJORIE	TISELIUS	HOUSEMAN	GERARDUS	BRICKMAN
MCMURTRY	WANSTALL	BERLINER	MARSHALL	UNSWORTH	HOUTGAST	HADAMARD	BUSCHING
RAMBALDI	WENDELIN	BERNARDO	MARSHMAN	VASSILIS	JOUFFROY	HERANADO	EPICURUS
TOMBAUGH	WINTHROP	BERNHARD	MARSIGLI	VESALIUS	KAUFMANN	HIRAYAMA	ERICKSON
TOMMASON	YANOFSKY	BEROULLI	MARTINUS	WESTMORE	LAUGHTON	IMMANUEL	ERICSSON
TOMONAGA	ADOVASIO	BERTRAND	MERCATOR	YASUMASA	LAURENCE	JOHANNES	FAUCHARD
WIMPERIS	AGOSTINO	BIRDSEYE	MERCEDES	YASUNARI	LEUCKART	JOHANSON	FOUCAULT
YAMAMOTO	AMONTONS	BIRKHOFF	MEREDITH	ANTIONIO	MAUDSLAY	JONATHAN	GASCOYNE
YAMAZAKE	AVOGADRO	BORGNINE	MERSENNE	ASTURIAS	PLUNKETT	KAWABATA	GIACCONI
YAMAZAKI	BJORNSON	CARADINI	MORGAGNI	BATTISTA	ROUSSEAU	KITASATO	HARCOURT
ZEMECKIS	BRONSTED	CARDUCCI	MORRISON	BOTSTEIN	SAUNDERS	LEMAITRE	HATCHETT
BANCROFT	COOLIDGE	CARFAGNO	NARINDER	BUTLEROV	SAUTUOLA	LIBAVIUS	KIRCHHOF
BENEDICT	CROMPTON	CARLETON	NORDHEIM	COTTRELL	SOUFFLOT	LOBASHOV	LEACHMAN
BENJAMIN	CROWFOOT	CARLISLE	NORTHROP	CUTHBERT	SOUTHERN	MCCARTHY	LEUCKART
BENNETTI	FLORENCE	CARNEGIE	PARRONDO	EUTOCIUS	STURGEON	MCDANIEL	MARCELIN
CANONERO	FLOURENS	CAROLINE	PERCIVAL	GOTTLIEB	THUNBERG	MCLAGLEN	MARCELLO
CONVERSI	GEOFFORY	CHRISTIE	PERELMAN	HATCHETT	TRUMPLER	MENACHEM	MELCHIOR
EINSTEIN	GEOFFREY	CHROWDER	PERICLES	HUTSHING	TRUSCOTT	MOHAMMED	MERCATOR
FONTAINE	GEORGIUS	CORNELIS	PERRAULT	KITASATO	DAVIDSON	MOSANDER	MERCEDES
GANGELIN	GIORDANO	CORONADO	PERSONNE	MATHISON	DAVISSON	MUHAMMAD	MITCHELL
HANNIBAL	GIOVANNI	CORRIGAN	PURKINJE	MATTHIAS	ELVEHJEM	NOVARESE	NEWCOMBE
HENDRICK	GOODRICH	DAREVSKY	SARANDON	MATUYAMA	FAVALORO	OSIANDER	NEWCOMEN
HENRICUS	GOODYEAR	GARDINER	SERVETUS	MITCHELL	HAVELOCK	PAGANINI	PERCIVAL
HUNTSMAN	GROTRIAN	GARFIELD	SHRAPNEL	PATERSON	HEVELIUS	PYLARINI	PESCUCCI
JANNINGS	LEONARDO	GARNERIN	SORENSEN	PATRICIA	LEVINSON	ROSALIND	PONCELET

RICCARDO	DOMENICO	ZEMECKIS	RICHMOND	APPLETON	PALMIERI	ROENTGEN	AHLQUIST
RICCIOLI	EGBERTUS	CARFAGNO	SAKHAROV	AVILDSEN	THIMOTHY	SAUNDERS	JACQUARD
SACCHERI	ELVEHJEM	CLIFFORD	WECHSLER	BERLINER	THOMPSON	SIGNORET	MACQUORN
SHOCKLEY	EUGENIUS	GARFIELD	ADRIENNE	BILLINGS	TOMMASON	STANFORD	ALBRECHT
SINCLAIR	FRAENKEL	GEOFFORY	AGRICOLA	BOULLIAU	TREMBLEY	THUNBERG	ALDREDGE
VINCENTE	FREEDMAN	GEOFFREY	ANFINSEN	BOYLSTON	TRUMPLER	TOWNSEND	AMBROISE
VINCENZO	FRIEDKIN	GRIFFITH	ANTONIO	BUTLEROV	AFANASSI	VANNEVAR	AMERICUS
WIECHERT	FRIEDMAN	HADFIELD	BASILIUS	CAGLIONE	AMONTONS	VONNEGUT	AVERROES
YOICHIRO	FRUEHAUF	HAFFKINE	CHRISTIE	CALLAHAN	AMUNDSEN	WEINBERG	BJERKNES
BIRDSEYE	GODEFROY	HOFFMANN	CLAIRAUT	CARLETON	BENNETTI	BARONESS	BJORNSON
BOWDITCH	GREENHAM	JEFFREYS	DAVIDSON	CARLISLE	BERNARDO	BEROULLI	BOURBAKI
BRADFORD	HAVELOCK	JEFFRIES	DAVISSON	CHALONGE	BERNHARD	CANONERO	BOURGOIN
BRIDGMAN	HEVELIUS	JOUFFROY	DEBIERNE	COBLENTZ	BLANFORD	CAROLINE	CHARGAFF
CARDUCCI	HUFELAND	KAUFMANN	DESIDERI	COLLINGS	BRANTING	CHROWDER	CHARLIER
CHADWICK	INGEBORG	REDFIELD	ELLICOTT	COOLIDGE	BRENTANO	CORONADO	CHARLTON
FREDERIC	ISAEVICH	SCOFIELD	FELICITA	DILLEHAY	BRINDLEY	DESORMES	CHIRIKOV
FREDHOLM	JEDEDIAH	SOUFFLOT	GOLITZEN	EPALINUS	BRONSTED	DUCOMMUN	CLARENCE
FREDRICH	JEREMIAH	STAFFORD	HAMILTON	FAHLBERG	BRUNFELS	EUTOCIUS	CORRIGAN
FRIDTJOF	JEREMIAS	WOLFGANG	HISINGER	FAULKNER	CARNEGIE	GIROLAMO	COURNAND
GAJDUSEK	KANELLOS	AVOGADRO	KAMINSKI	FEILDING	CHANDLER	JACOBSON	COURTOIS
GARDINER	LAGERLOF	BORGNINE	LEVINSON	FILLMORE	CHANNING	JAROSLAV	EBERHARD
GOLDBACH	LEBESGUE	DOUGLASS	MAGIDSON	GILLETTE	CORNELIS	KUBOYAMA	ELDREDGE
GOLDBERG	LEDERMAN	GANGELIN	MARIOTTE	HALLBERG	COUNTESS	MCCOLLUM	EVARISTE
GOLDMARK	LEGENDRE	GERGONNE	MCDIVITT	HOLLIDAY	FLANNERY	NAPOLEON	FLORENCE
GOODRICH	LEMELSON	GRIGNARD	MCKINLEY	HURLBERT	FLINDERS	NICOLAAS	FOURCROY
GOODYEAR	MADESANI	HAGGERTY	MCMILLAN	KJELDAHL	FRANCOIS	NICOLASS	FOURNIER
GORDIMER	MAGELLAN	HOAGLAND	NARINDER	MACLAINE	FRANKLIN	NICOLASS	GABRIELA
GOUDSMIT	MAGENDIE	JUNGHANS	PALITZSH	MCCLEARY	FRENICLE	NIKOLASS	GAERTNER
GULDBERG	MCLELLAN	KINGSLEY	PERICLES	MELLANBY	GARNERIN	NIKOLAUS	GEORGIUS
HENDRICK	MENELAUS	LANGEVIN	PITISCUS	MILLIKAN	GRANTLEY	RUDOLPHE	GHERARDI
HILDYARD	MEREDITH	LANGMUIR	POLIDORE	MULLIKEN	GUINNESS	SIKORSKI	GIORDANO
JORDANUS	MESENKOP	LAUGHTON	POLITZER	NEWLANDS	HANNIBAL	STROWGER	HARRISON
LINDBLAD	MEYERHOF	MARGARET	REGINALD	PHILIPPE	HEINEMAN	THEOBALD	HENRICUS
LINDHEIM	NEHEMIAH	MARGGRAF	ROBINSON	PHILLIPE	HEINRICH	THEODORE	HORROCKS
LUNDBERG	OSHEROFF	MENGHINI	SCHIMMEL	RAYLEIGH	HORNBECK	THEORELL	LAGRANGE
MAUDSLAY	PATERSON	MORGAGNI	SCHIMPER	RUTLEDGE	JAENISCH	TOMONAGA	LAURENCE
NORDHEIM	PEDERSEN	REDGRAVE	STEINITZ	SCALIGER	JANNINGS	YANOFSKY	LAWRENCE
SPEDDING	PEDERSON	RUGGIERO	STEINORE	SILLIMAN	JEANETTE	CAMPANUS	MORRISON
SUNDMANN	PERELMAN	SEDGWICK	WEHINGER	SKOLNICK	JENNIFER	CAMPBELL	NAARMANN
SVEDBERG	PETERSON	SIEGBAHN	BENJAMIN	SULLIVAN	JENNINGS	DEMPSTER	PARRONDO
VALDEMAR	ROBERTUS	ZSIGMOND	MARJORIE	VILLEMIN	JENNISON	GOEPPERT	PATRICIA
VLADIMIR	RODERICK	AECHYLUS	TRAJANUS	WILLHELM	JOHNSTON	HAUPTMAN	PATRIZIA
WALDEMAR	SCHEINER	ARCHYTAS	BECKWITH	WILLIAMS	KENNELLY	HEMPHREY	PERRAULT
WALDEYER	SELEUCUS	BASHEVIS	BERKELEY	ZAILLIAN	KORNBERG	HIPPACOS	PETRUCCI
WENDELIN	SORENSEN	BUCHANAN	BIRKHOFF	ALCMAEON	KORNGOLD	HIPPALUS	PIERPONT
WOODBURY	SPRECKER	BUSHNELL	BUCKLAND	BLUMBERG	LEONARDO	HIPPASUS	QUARANTA
WOODRUFF	SPRENGEL	CUTHBERT	CHAKIRIS	BRAMANTE	LEONHARD	HUMPHREY	SCHROTER
WOODWARD	SULEIMAN	DESHNJOV	HARKNESS	CALMETTE	LINNAEUS	KLAPROTH	SHERIDAN
ALBERTUS	SYDENHAM	EILHARDT	HAUKSBEE	CHAMBERS	MINNAERT	LEOPOLDO	SHERWOOD
ALGERNON	TERENIUS	FISHBACH	KIRKWOOD	CLEMENCE	MINNELLI	LIPPMANN	SOCRATES
ANDERSON	THEEUWES	GERHARDT	NICKOLAI	CROMPTON	MONNARTZ	LJAPUNOW	STARLING
ANJELICA	TISELIUS	LASHELLE	PICKFORD	DRUMMOND	PLUNKETT	MALPIGHI	STIRLING
AURELIUS	TONEGAWA	MATHISON	PURKINJE	FLEMMING	POINCARE	OLIPHANT	STURGEON
BENEDICT	VALENTIN	NICHOLAS	RICKETTS	FRAMPTON	REGNAULT	SCIPIONE	ZWORYKIN
CAPELLER	VALERIUS	OUGHTRED	RICKOVER	GRIMALDI	REINHOLD	STEPHENS	AGOSTINO
DAREVSKY	WAKELING	RICHARDS	SEPKOSKI	ISAMBARD	RENNAHAN	WIMPERIS	ALISTAIR
DEDEKIND	WATERMAN	RICHMANN	ADELBERT	KAMMERER	REYNOLDS	ZEPPELIN	ANGSTROM

ARISTIDE	CHATELET	SCHULTZE	LEONARDO	WOODBURY	CALMETTE	WIMPERIS	LEONHARD
BESSEMER	COTTRELL	SCHUSTER	LINNAEUS	AGRICOLA	CARLETON	ZEPPELIN	LINDHEIM
BOTSTEIN	EASTWOOD	STAUFFER	MACLAINE	ARZACHEL	CARNEGIE	BLANFORD	MARSHALL
BUMSTEAD	FLETCHER	YASUMASA	MARGARET	ELLICOTT	CHATELET	BRADFORD	MARSHMAN
CHISHOLM	FONTAINE	YASUNARI	MELLANBY	EUTOCIUS	CLARENCE	BRUNFELS	MATTHIAS
COUSTEAU	GERTRUDE	ADOVASIO	MERCATOR	FELICITA	CLEMENCE	CLIFFORD	MELCHIOR
CRISTIAN	GOTTLIEB	CHEVREUL	MINNAERT	FLETCHER	COBLENTZ	CRAWFORD	MENGHINI
DRESSLER	GROTRIAN	CONVERSI	MONNARTZ	FOURCROY	CONVERSI	CROWFOOT	MITCHELL
EINSTEIN	GUETTARD	GIOVANNI	MORGAGNI	FRANCOIS	CORNELIS	DREYFUSS	NORDHEIM
GASSENDI	HARTLINE	MCEVILLY	NEWLANDS	GIACCONI	DAGUERRE	GEOFFORY	NORTHROP
GEISSLER	HARTMANN	SAAVEDRA	PERRAULT	HERSCHEL	DEBIERNE	GEOFFREY	OLIPHANT
GHISLAIN	HOUTGAST	SALVADOR	QUARANTA	LIPSCOMB	DILLEHAY	GODEFROY	REINHOLD
GIUSEPPE	HUNTSMAN	SERVETUS	RAMBALDI	MENACHEM	ELDREDGE	GRIFFITH	SACCHERI
HERSCHEL	IPATIEFF	STEVINUS	REGNAULT	MIESCHER	FLORENCE	HORSFALL	SMITHSON
HORSFALL	LANTIERI	THEVENET	RENNAHAN	PERICLES	FREDERIC	JOUFFROY	SOUTHERN
HOUSEMAN	MAITLAND	BREWSTER	RICCARDO	POINCARE	GANGELIN	PICKFORD	STEPHENS
HUTSHING	MARTINUS	CRAWFORD	RICHARDS	PRESCOTT	GARNERIN	PLAYFAIR	STOTHART
LASSALLY	MATTHIAS	CROWFOOT	SAKHAROV	SPRECKER	GASSENDI	SOUFFLOT	WIECHERT
LASSETER	NORTHROP	HOLWARDA	SALVADOR	THATCHER	GILLETTE	STAFFORD	WILLHELM
LEISHMAN	PATTISON	LAPWORTH	SCHWARTZ	TRUSCOTT	GIUSEPPE	STANFORD	WINTHROP
LIPSCOMB	QUETELET	SCHWARTZ	SOCRATES	ZEMECKIS	HAGGERTY	STAUFFER	YOICHIRO
MARSHALL	REITSEMA	UNSWORTH	THIBAULT	AMUNDSEN	HEINEMAN	WHITFORD	AMERICUS
MARSHMAN	RHETICUS	DREYFUSS	TOMBAUGH	AVILDSEN	HIJUELOS	YANOFSKY	BAPTISTA
MARSIGLI	SANTIAGO	PLAYFAIR	TOMMASON	BENEDICT	HOUSEMAN	BOURGOIN	BAPTISTE
MEISSNER	SANTILLO	POLYKARP	TRAJANUS	BRINDLEY	JEANETTE	BRIDGMAN	BATTISTA
MERSENNE	SAUTUOLA	HERZBERG	VALSALVA	CARADINI	KAMMERER	CHARGAFF	BERLINER
MIESCHER	SMITHSON		VIRTANEN	CHANDLER	KENNELLY	GEORGIUS	BILLINGS
MILSTEIN	SOUTHERN		VOLTAIRE	CLAUDINE	LANGEVIN	HOUTGAST	BOWDITCH
NUSSLEIN	SPITTLER		ADELBERT	CLAUDIUS	LASHELLE	KORNGOLD	BUSTILLO
ODYSSEUS	STOTHART	**5TH LETTER**	BLUMBERG	DAVIDSON	LASSETER	MARGGRAF	CAGLIONE
PERSONNE	THATCHER		BOURBAKI	DESIDERI	LAURENCE	MCLAGLEN	CARLISLE
PLASKETT	VIRTANEN	ADOVASIO	CAMPBELL	FEILDING	LAWRENCE	STURGEON	CASTILLO
PRESCOTT	VITTORIO	AFANASSI	CHAMBERS	FLINDERS	MARCELIN	TONEGAWA	CHAKIRIS
PROSPERO	VOLTAIRE	ALCMAEON	CUTHBERT	FREEDMAN	MARCELLO	WOLFGANG	CHIRIKOV
ROUSSEAU	VOLTERRA	AVOGADRO	FAHLBERG	FRIEDKIN	MCCLEARY	ANSCHUTZ	COLLINGS
RYDSTROM	WESTMORE	BECCARIA	FISHBACH	FRIEDMAN	MERCEDES	BARTHOUD	COOLIDGE
SEFSTROM	WHITFORD	BENJAMIN	GOLDBACH	GIORDANO	MERSENNE	BAUCHENS	CORRIGAN
TRUSCOTT	WINTHROP	BERNARDO	GOLDBERG	JEDEDIAH	MINNELLI	BERNHARD	EPALINUS
VALSALVA	ASTURIAS	BRAMANTE	GULDBERG	KJELDAHL	PONCELET	BIRKHOFF	ESQUIVEL
VASSILIS	AUGUSTIN	BUCHANAN	HALLBERG	MAGIDSON	QUETELET	BOETHIUS	EVARISTE
WANSTALL	AUGUSTUS	CALLAHAN	HERZBERG	MEREDITH	RAYLEIGH	BUSCHING	FRENICLE
WEISMANN	BEAUMONT	CAMPANUS	HORNBECK	POLIDORE	RICKETTS	CHISHOLM	GABRIELA
WELSBACH	CLAUDINE	CARFAGNO	HURLBERT	SAUNDERS	RUTLEDGE	EBERHARD	GARDINER
WHISTLER	CLAUDIUS	EILHARDT	INGEBORG	SPEDDING	SAAVEDRA	ELVEHJEM	GARFIELD
BAPTISTA	CLAUSIUS	FONTAINE	ISAMBARD	TARADASH	SCHAEFER	FAUCHARD	GORDIMER
BAPTISTE	COLUMBUS	FOUCAULT	JACOBSON	THEODORE	SERVETUS	FREDHOLM	HADFIELD
BARTHOUD	DAGUERRE	GERHARDT	KAWABATA	ADRIENNE	THEVENET	FRUEHAUF	HANNIBAL
BARTLETT	ESQUIVEL	GHERARDI	KORNBERG	ALBRECHT	VALDEMAR	HATCHETT	HARRISON
BATTISTA	FLOURENS	GIOVANNI	LINDBLAD	ALDREDGE	VANNEVAR	HEMPHREY	HENRICUS
BEATRICE	HIJUELOS	GRIMALDI	LUNDBERG	APPLETON	VILLEMIN	HUMPHREY	HOLLIDAY
BELTRAMI	KAZUHIKO	HIPPACOS	SIEGBAHN	AVICENNA	VINCENTE	HUTSHING	IPATIEFF
BERTRAND	MANUTIUS	HIPPALUS	SVEDBERG	BASHEVIS	VINCENZO	JUNGHANS	JAENISCH
BOETHIUS	MATUYAMA	HIPPASUS	THEOBALD	BENNETTI	VOLTERRA	KAZUHIKO	JANNINGS
BOLTWOOD	MCMURTRY	HOLWARDA	THUNBERG	BERKELEY	VONNEGUT	KIRCHHOF	JENNIFER
BRATTAIN	NOBUYUKI	JORDANUS	TREMBLEY	BESSEMER	WALDEMAR	LAUGHTON	JENNINGS
BUSTILLO	SCHULMAN	LAGRANGE	WEINBERG	BOMBELLI	WALDEYER	LEACHMAN	JENNISON
CASTILLO	SCHULTES	LASSALLY	WELSBACH	BUTLEROV	WENDELIN	LEISHMAN	LANTIERI

LEMAITRE	CAROLINE	JEREMIAH	OSIANDER	BEATRICE	GEISSLER	EPICURUS	FISHBACH
MALPIGHI	CHARLIER	JEREMIAS	PAGANINI	BELTRAMI	GOUDSMIT	GAJDUSEK	FRUEHAUF
MARSIGLI	CHARLTON	KAUFMANN	REGINALD	BERTRAND	HAUKSBEE	JACQUARD	GHISLAIN
MARTINUS	DOUGLASS	LANGMUIR	ROBINSON	CHEVREUL	HUNTSMAN	LJAPUNOW	GIORDANO
MATHISON	FAVALORO	LIPPMANN	SARANDON	CLAIRAUT	JAROSLAV	MACQUORN	GIROLAMO
MCEVILLY	GAMALIEL	MOHAMMED	SKOLNICK	COTTRELL	JOHNSTON	PESCUCCI	GOLDBACH
MILLIKAN	GHISLAIN	MUHAMMAD	SORENSEN	DELBRUCK	KINGSLEY	PETRUCCI	GOLDMARK
MORRISON	GIROLAMO	NAARMANN	SPRENGEL	DEMARCAY	KITASATO	SAUTUOLA	GRIGNARD
MULLIKEN	GOTTLIEB	NEHEMIAH	STEINITZ	DESORMES	LEBESGUE	SELEUCUS	GUETTARD
PALMIERI	HAMILTON	RICHMANN	STEINORE	DUJARDIN	LOBASHOV	THEEUWES	HADAMARD
PATRICIA	HARTLINE	RICHMOND	SYDENHAM	EGBERTUS	MADESANI	DAREVSKY	HARTMANN
PATRIZIA	HAVELOCK	SCHIMMEL	TERENIUS	FLOURENS	MAUDSLAY	ISAEVICH	HERANADO
PATTISON	HEVELIUS	SCHIMPER	TOMONAGA	FREDRICH	MEISSNER	JHABVALA	HILDYARD
PERCIVAL	HOAGLAND	SUNDMANN	VALENTIN	GERARDUS	ODYSSEUS	LIBAVIUS	HIRAYAMA
PHILIPPE	HUFELAND	TAKAMINE	WATANABE	GERTRUDE	PITISCUS	MCDIVITT	HOAGLAND
PURKINJE	KANELLOS	WEISMANN	WEHINGER	GOODRICH	REITSEMA	BECKWITH	HOFFMANN
REDFIELD	LEMELSON	WESTMORE	YASUNARI	GROTRIAN	ROUSSEAU	BOLTWOOD	HORSFALL
RHETICUS	MAGELLAN	YAMAMOTO	AMBROISE	HEINRICH	SCHUSTER	CHADWICK	HOUTGAST
RICCIOLI	MAITLAND	YASUMASA	ANTONIO	HENDRICK	TOWNSEND	CHROWDER	HUFELAND
RUGGIERO	MCCOLLUM	ZSIGMOND	CHALONGE	JEFFREYS	WECHSLER	EASTWOOD	ISAMBARD
SANTIAGO	MCLELLAN	ANFINSEN	GASCOYNE	JEFFRIES	AGOSTINO	KIRKWOOD	JACQUARD
SANTILLO	MCMILLAN	BARONESS	GERGONNE	KLAPROTH	ALISTAIR	SCHAWLOW	JHABVALA
SCALIGER	MENELAUS	BJORNSON	HARCOURT	LAGERLOF	AMONTONS	SEDGWICK	JUNGHANS
SCHEINER	NAPOLEON	BORGNINE	HORROCKS	LEDERMAN	ANGSTROM	SHERWOOD	KAUFMANN
SCIPIONE	NICOLAAS	BUSHNELL	LAPWORTH	MACBRIDE	ARISTIDE	STROWGER	KAWABATA
SCOFIELD	NICOLAUS	CALANDRI	LEOPOLDO	MCCARTHY	BOTSTEIN	WOODWARD	KITASATO
SHERIDAN	NICOLAUS	CANONERO	MARIOTTE	MCMURTRY	BRANTING	AECHYLUS	KJELDAHL
SILLIMAN	NIKOLASS	CHANNING	MARJORIE	MEYERHOF	BRATTAIN	ARCHYTAS	KUBOYAMA
STEVINUS	NIKOLAUS	CORONADO	NEWCOMBE	NOVARESE	BRENTANO	GOODYEAR	LEONHARD
STRAIGHT	NUSSLEIN	COURNAND	NEWCOMEN	OSHEROFF	BUMSTEAD	HILDYARD	LEUCKART
SULEIMAN	PERELMAN	DESHNJOV	NICHOLAS	PATERSON	COUNTESS	HIRAYAMA	LIPPMANN
SULLIVAN	PHILLIPE	DOMENICO	NICKOLAI	PEDERSEN	COURTOIS	KUBOYAMA	MADESANI
VASSILIS	ROEBLING	ELEANORE	PARRONDO	PEDERSON	COUSTEAU	MATUYAMA	MAITLAND
VLADIMIR	ROSALIND	EMMANUEL	PERSONNE	PETERSON	CRISTIAN	NOBUYUKI	MARSHALL
WILLIAMS	RUDOLPHE	ERLANGER	REYNOLDS	PYLARINI	EINSTEIN	ZWORYKIN	MATUYAMA
BEECKMAN	SCHALLER	EUGENIUS	RICKOVER	REDGRAVE	FRIDTJOF	YAMAZAKE	MCCLEARY
BJERKNES	SCHULMAN	FLANNERY	SCHROTER	ROBERTUS	GAERTNER	YAMAZAKI	MENELAUS
BLACKETT	SCHULTES	FOURNIER	SEPKOSKI	RODERICK	GOLITZEN		NAARMANN
BRACKETT	SCHULTZE	FRAENKEL	SIGNORET	SHEARMAN	GRANTLEY		NICOLAAS
BRICKMAN	SINCLAIR	GREENHAM	THIMOTHY	SIKORSKI	GUETTARD		NICOLASS
DEDEKIND	STARLING	GRIGNARD	UNSWORTH	THEORELL	HAUPTMAN	**6TH LETTER**	NICOLAUS
ERICKSON	STIRLING	GUINNESS	VITTORIO	VALERIUS	JONATHAN		NIKOLASS
FAULKNER	TISELIUS	HARKNESS	CROMPTON	WATERMAN	MANUTIUS	ALISTAIR	NIKOLAUS
FRANKLIN	VESALIUS	HERANADO	FRAMPTON	WOODRUFF	MILSTEIN	BELTRAMI	OLIPHANT
HAFFKINE	WAKELING	HISINGER	GOEPPERT	AUGUSTIN	OUGHTRED	BERNHARD	PLAYFAIR
LEUCKART	ZAILLIAN	IMMANUEL	PIERPONT	AUGUSTUS	PALITZSH	BERTRAND	POINCARE
PLASKETT	BEAUMONT	JOHANNES	PROSPERO	BIRDSEYE	POLITZER	BOURBAKI	POLYKARP
PLUNKETT	COLUMBUS	JOHANSON	SHRAPNEL	BOYLSTON	ROENTGEN	BRATTAIN	REDGRAVE
POLYKARP	DELAMBRE	KAMINSKI	THOMPSON	BREWSTER	RYDSTROM	BRENTANO	REGINALD
SHOCKLEY	DRUMMOND	LEGENDRE	TRUMPLER	BRONSTED	SABATIER	BUCKLAND	RICHMANN
ANJELICA	DUCOMMUN	LEVINSON	ALBERTUS	CHRISTIE	SEFSTROM	CHARGAFF	SANTIAGO
AURELIUS	FILLMORE	MAGENDIE	ALGERNON	CLAUSIUS	SPITTLER	CLAIRAUT	SIEGBAHN
BARTLETT	FLEMMING	MCDANIEL	ANDERSON	DAVISSON	WANSTALL	CORONADO	SINCLAIR
BASILIUS	GOLDMARK	MCKINLEY	ASHCROFT	DEMPSTER	WHISTLER	COURNAND	STOTHART
BOULLIAU	HADAMARD	MESENKOP	ASTURIAS	DRESSLER	AHLQUIST	DOUGLASS	SUNDMANN
BUCKLAND	HARTMANN	MOSANDER	AVERROES	ELSASSER	BEROULLI	EBERHARD	TARADASH
CAPELLER	HOFFMANN	NARINDER	BANCROFT	ERICSSON	CARDUCCI	FAUCHARD	THEOBALD

TOMONAGA	BLACKETT	RUGGIERO	BECKWITH	PYLARINI	LASHELLE	NEWCOMBE	TRAJANUS
TONEGAWA	BLUMBERG	SACCHERI	BENEDICT	RAYLEIGH	LASSALLY	NEWCOMEN	VINCENTE
WANSTALL	BOTSTEIN	SAUNDERS	BOETHIUS	RODERICK	LEOPOLDO	PERELMAN	VINCENZO
WATANABE	BRACKETT	SCOFIELD	BORGNINE	ROEBLING	LINDBLAD	SCHIMMEL	VIRTANEN
WEISMANN	BRUNFELS	SOUTHERN	BOULLIAU	ROSALIND	MAGELLAN	SCHULMAN	AGRICOLA
WELSBACH	BUMSTEAD	STEPHENS	BRANTING	SABATIER	MARCELIN	SHEARMAN	AMONTONS
WILLIAMS	BUSHNELL	STURGEON	BUSCHING	SEDGWICK	MARCELLO	SILLIMAN	ASHCROFT
WOLFGANG	CAMPBELL	SVEDBERG	CARADINI	SKOLNICK	MAUDSLAY	SULEIMAN	AVERROES
WOODWARD	CANONERO	THEORELL	CAROLINE	SPEDDING	MCCOLLUM	VALDEMAR	BANCROFT
YAMAZAKE	CHAMBERS	THUNBERG	CHADWICK	STARLING	MCEVILLY	VILLEMIN	BARTHOUD
YAMAZAKI	CHEVREUL	TOWNSEND	CHANNING	STEINITZ	MCKINLEY	VLADIMIR	BEAUMONT
YASUMASA	COTTRELL	WEINBERG	CHARLIER	STIRLING	MCLAGLEN	WALDEMAR	BIRKHOFF
YASUNARI	COUNTESS	WIECHERT	CLAUDINE	TAKAMINE	MCLELLAN	WATERMAN	BLANFORD
COLUMBUS	COUSTEAU	WILLHELM	CLAUDIUS	TERENIUS	MCMILLAN	ADRIENNE	BOLTWOOD
DELAMBRE	CUTHBERT	JENNIFER	CLAUSIUS	TISELIUS	MINNELLI	ALGERNON	BOURGOIN
HANNIBAL	DESIDERI	SCHAEFER	CRISTIAN	VALERIUS	NICHOLAS	ANTIONIO	BRADFORD
HAUKSBEE	EINSTEIN	STAUFFER	DEDEKIND	VESALIUS	NICKOLAI	AVICENNA	CAGLIONE
ALBRECHT	FAHLBERG	CARFAGNO	DOMENICO	VOLTAIRE	PERICLES	BERLINER	CHISHOLM
AMERICUS	FLANNERY	CARNEGIE	EUGENIUS	WAKELING	PONCELET	BILLINGS	CLIFFORD
CARDUCCI	FLINDERS	CORRIGAN	EUTOCIUS	YOICHIRO	QUETELET	BJERKNES	COURTOIS
DEMARCAY	FLOURENS	ERLANGER	FEILDING	ZAILLIAN	RAMBALDI	BRAMANTE	CRAWFORD
FRENICLE	GABRIELA	HISINGER	FELICITA	DESHNJOV	REYNOLDS	BUCHANAN	CROWFOOT
HENRICUS	GARFIELD	LEBESGUE	FLEMMING	ELVEHJEM	SANTILLO	CAMPANUS	DRUMMOND
HIPPACOS	GOEPPERT	MALPIGHI	FONTAINE	FRIDTJOF	SCHALLER	CHALONGE	EASTWOOD
HORROCKS	GOLDBERG	MARSIGLI	FOURNIER	CHIRIKOV	SCHAWLOW	CLARENCE	ELEANORE
PATRICIA	GOODYEAR	MORGAGNI	FREDRICH	FRAENKEL	SHOCKLEY	CLEMENCE	ELLICOTT
PESCUCCI	GUINNESS	ROENTGEN	GAMALIEL	FRIEDKIN	SOUFFLOT	COBLENTZ	FAVALORO
PETRUCCI	GULDBERG	SCALIGER	GEORGIUS	MESENKOP	SPITTLER	COLLINGS	FILLMORE
PITISCUS	HADFIELD	SPRENGEL	GOODRICH	MILLIKAN	TREMBLEY	EPALINUS	FRANCOIS
RHETICUS	HALLBERG	STRAIGHT	GOTTLIEB	MULLIKEN	TRUMPLER	FAULKNER	FREDHOLM
SELEUCUS	HARKNESS	STROWGER	GRIFFITH	SPRECKER	VALSALVA	FLORENCE	GEOFFORY
ALDREDGE	HATCHETT	VONNEGUT	GROTRIAN	ZEMECKIS	VASSILIS	GAERTNER	GIACCONI
AVOGADRO	HERZBERG	WEHINGER	HAFFKINE	ZWORYKIN	WECHSLER	GARDINER	HAVELOCK
CALANDRI	HORNBECK	ARZACHEL	HARTLINE	AECHYLUS	WENDELIN	GASSENDI	INGEBORG
CHROWDER	HURLBERT	CALLAHAN	HEINRICH	BERKELEY	WHISTLER	GERGONNE	KIRKWOOD
COOLIDGE	IPATIEFF	DILLEHAY	HENDRICK	BEROULLI	ZEPPELIN	GIOVANNI	KLAPROTH
DUJARDIN	JEFFREYS	FLETCHER	HEVELIUS	BOMBELLI	BEECKMAN	JANNINGS	KORNGOLD
ELDREDGE	KORNBERG	GREENHAM	HUTSHING	BRINDLEY	BENJAMIN	JENNINGS	LIPSCOMB
GERARDUS	LANTIERI	HERSCHEL	ISAEVICH	BUSTILLO	BESSEMER	JOHANNES	MACQUORN
HOLLIDAY	LINDHEIM	JONATHAN	JEDEDIAH	CAPELLER	BRICKMAN	JORDANUS	OSHEROFF
LEGENDRE	LINNAEUS	KIRCHHOF	JEFFRIES	CASTILLO	BRIDGMAN	LAGRANGE	PICKFORD
MAGENDIE	LUNDBERG	LOBASHOV	JEREMIAH	CHANDLER	DESORMES	LAURENCE	PIERPONT
MERCEDES	MILSTEIN	MENACHEM	JEREMIAS	CHATELET	DUCOMMUN	LAWRENCE	POLIDORE
MOSANDER	MINNAERT	MEYERHOF	KAZUHIKO	CORNELIS	FREEDMAN	LJAPUNOW	PRESCOTT
NARINDER	MITCHELL	MIESCHER	LIBAVIUS	DRESSLER	FRIEDMAN	MARTINUS	REINHOLD
OSIANDER	NAPOLEON	RENNAHAN	MACBRIDE	FRANKLIN	GORDIMER	MEISSNER	RICCIOLI
RUTLEDGE	NORDHEIM	SYDENHAM	MACLAINE	GANGELIN	GOUDSMIT	MELLANBY	RICHMOND
SAAVEDRA	NOVARESE	THATCHER	MANUTIUS	GEISSLER	HAUPTMAN	MERSENNE	SAUTUOLA
SALVADOR	NUSSLEIN	AGOSTINO	MATTHIAS	GRANTLEY	HEINEMAN	NEWLANDS	SCIPIONE
SARANDON	ODYSSEUS	AHLQUIST	MCDANIEL	GRIMALDI	HOUSEMAN	PARRONDO	SHERWOOD
SHERIDAN	PALMIERI	AMBROISE	MCDIVITT	HIJUELOS	HUNTSMAN	PERSONNE	STAFFORD
ADELBERT	PLASKETT	ANJELICA	MELCHIOR	HIPPALUS	LEACHMAN	PURKINJE	STANFORD
ALCMAEON	PLUNKETT	ARISTIDE	MENGHINI	JAROSLAV	LEDERMAN	QUARANTA	STEINORE
BARONESS	PROSPERO	ASTURIAS	MEREDITH	KANELLOS	LEISHMAN	SCHEINER	THEODORE
BARTLETT	REDFIELD	AURELIUS	NEHEMIAH	KENNELLY	MARSHMAN	SHRAPNEL	TRUSCOTT
BAUCHENS	REITSEMA	BASILIUS	PAGANINI	KINGSLEY	MOHAMMED	STEVINUS	WESTMORE
BIRDSEYE	ROUSSEAU	BEATRICE	PHILLIPE	LAGERLOF	MUHAMMAD	THEVENET	WHITFORD

YAMAMOTO	BATTISTA	JOHNSTON	BRICKMAN	WATERMAN	AVERROES	MOSANDER	JENNINGS
ZSIGMOND	BJORNSON	LASSETER	BRIDGMAN	ZAILLIAN	AVILDSEN	MULLIKEN	LAGRANGE
GIUSEPPE	CARLISLE	LAUGHTON	BUCHANAN	MELLANBY	BERKELEY	NARINDER	RAYLEIGH
PHILIPPE	DAREVSKY	LEMAITRE	BUMSTEAD	NEWCOMBE	BERLINER	NEWCOMEN	RUTLEDGE
RUDOLPHE	DAVIDSON	MARIOTTE	CALLAHAN	WATANABE	BESSEMER	OSIANDER	SANTIAGO
SCHIMPER	DAVISSON	MCCARTHY	CORRIGAN	ANJELICA	BJERKNES	OUGHTRED	TOMBAUGH
ANGSTROM	ELSASSER	MCMURTRY	COUSTEAU	BEATRICE	BREWSTER	PEDERSEN	TOMONAGA
BECCARIA	ERICKSON	MERCATOR	CRISTIAN	BENEDICT	BRINDLEY	PERICLES	ALBRECHT
BERNARDO	ERICSSON	RICKETTS	DEMARCAY	BOWDITCH	BRONSTED	POLITZER	KJELDAHL
BUTLEROV	EVARISTE	ROBERTUS	DILLEHAY	CARDUCCI	CAPELLER	PONCELET	MALPIGHI
CHAKIRIS	GAJDUSEK	SCHROTER	FREEDMAN	CHADWICK	CHANDLER	QUETELET	MCCARTHY
CONVERSI	HARRISON	SCHULTES	FRIEDMAN	CLARENCE	CHARLIER	RICKOVER	RUDOLPHE
DAGUERRE	HIPPASUS	SCHULTZE	GOODYEAR	CLEMENCE	CHATELET	ROENTGEN	SIEGBAHN
DEBIERNE	JACOBSON	SCHUSTER	GREENHAM	DELBRUCK	CHROWDER	SABATIER	STRAIGHT
EILHARDT	JAENISCH	SERVETUS	GROTRIAN	DOMENICO	DEMPSTER	SCALIGER	THIMOTHY
EPICURUS	JENNISON	SOCRATES	HANNIBAL	FISHBACH	DESORMES	SCHAEFER	ADOVASIO
FOURCROY	JOHANSON	THIMOTHY	HAUPTMAN	FLORENCE	DRESSLER	SCHALLER	ALISTAIR
FREDERIC	KAMINSKI	VALENTIN	HEINEMAN	FREDRICH	ELSASSER	SCHEINER	ANTONIO
GARNERIN	LEMELSON	ANSCHUTZ	HOLLIDAY	GOLDBACH	ELVEHJEM	SCHIMMEL	AUGUSTIN
GEOFFREY	LEVINSON	DELBRUCK	HOUSEMAN	GOODRICH	EMMANUEL	SCHIMPER	BASHEVIS
GERHARDT	MAGIDSON	DREYFUSS	HUNTSMAN	HAVELOCK	ERLANGER	SCHROTER	BECCARIA
GHERARDI	MATHISON	EMMANUEL	JAROSLAV	HEINRICH	ESQUIVEL	SCHULTES	BENJAMIN
GODEFROY	MORRISON	FOUCAULT	JEDEDIAH	HENDRICK	FAULKNER	SCHUSTER	BOTSTEIN
HAGGERTY	PATERSON	GERTRUDE	JEREMIAH	HORNBECK	FLETCHER	SHOCKLEY	BOURGOIN
HEMPHREY	PATTISON	HARCOURT	JEREMIAS	ISAEVICH	FOURNIER	SHRAPNEL	BRATTAIN
HOLWARDA	PEDERSEN	IMMANUEL	JONATHAN	JAENISCH	FRAENKEL	SIGNORET	CARNEGIE
HUMPHREY	PEDERSON	LANGMUIR	LEACHMAN	LAURENCE	GAERTNER	SOCRATES	CHAKIRIS
JOUFFROY	PETERSON	NOBUYUKI	LEDERMAN	LAWRENCE	GAJDUSEK	SORENSEN	CHRISTIE
KAMMERER	ROBINSON	PERRAULT	LEISHMAN	PESCUCCI	GAMALIEL	SPITTLER	CORNELIS
LAPWORTH	SEPKOSKI	REGNAULT	LINDBLAD	PETRUCCI	GARDINER	SPRECKER	COURTOIS
LEONARDO	SIKORSKI	THIBAULT	MAGELLAN	RODERICK	GEISSLER	SPRENGEL	DUJARDIN
MARGARET	SMITHSON	TOMBAUGH	MARGGRAF	SEDGWICK	GEOFFREY	STAUFFER	EINSTEIN
MARGGRAF	SORENSEN	WOODBURY	MARSHMAN	SKOLNICK	GOLITZEN	STROWGER	FRANCOIS
MARJORIE	THOMPSON	WOODRUFF	MATTHIAS	WELSBACH	GORDIMER	THATCHER	FRANKLIN
MONNARTZ	TOMMASON	BASHEVIS	MAUDSLAY	ARISTIDE	GOTTLIEB	THEEUWES	FREDERIC
NORTHROP	YANOFSKY	ESQUIVEL	MCLELLAN	BERNARDO	GRANTLEY	THEVENET	FRIEDKIN
OUGHTRED	ALBERTUS	LANGEVIN	MCMILLAN	CORONADO	HAUKSBEE	TREMBLEY	GANGELIN
RICCARDO	APPLETON	PERCIVAL	MILLIKAN	EILHARDT	HEMPHREY	TRUMPLER	GARNERIN
RICHARDS	ARCHYTAS	RICKOVER	MUHAMMAD	GASSENDI	HERSCHEL	VIRTANEN	GHISLAIN
RYDSTROM	AUGUSTIN	SULLIVAN	NEHEMIAH	GERHARDT	HISINGER	WALDEYER	GOUDSMIT
SAKHAROV	AUGUSTUS	VANNEVAR	NICHOLAS	GERTRUDE	HUMPHREY	WECHSLER	LANGEVIN
SCHWARTZ	BENNETTI	THEEUWES	NICKOLAI	GHERARDI	IMMANUEL	WEHINGER	LANGMUIR
SEFSTROM	BOWDITCH	GASCOYNE	NICOLAAS	GRIMALDI	JEFFRIES	WHISTLER	LINDHEIM
SIGNORET	BOYLSTON	WALDEYER	PERCIVAL	HERANADO	JENNIFER	ASHCROFT	MAGENDIE
UNSWORTH	BREWSTER	GOLITZEN	PERELMAN	HOLWARDA	JOHANNES	BANCROFT	MARCELIN
VITTORIO	BRONSTED	PALITZSH	RENNAHAN	LEONARDO	KAMMERER	BIRKHOFF	MARJORIE
VOLTERRA	CALMETTE	PATRIZIA	ROUSSEAU	LEOPOLDO	KINGSLEY	CHARGAFF	MILSTEIN
WIMPERIS	CARLETON	POLITZER	SCHULMAN	MACBRIDE	LASSETER	IPATIEFF	NORDHEIM
WINTHROP	CHARLTON		SHEARMAN	NEWLANDS	MARGARET	OSHEROFF	NUSSLEIN
ADOVASIO	CHRISTIE		SHERIDAN	PARRONDO	MCDANIEL	WOODRUFF	PATRICIA
AFANASSI	CROMPTON		SILLIMAN	RAMBALDI	MCKINLEY	ALDREDGE	PATRIZIA
AMUNDSEN	DEMPSTER	**7TH LETTER**	SULEIMAN	REYNOLDS	MCLAGLEN	BILLINGS	PLAYFAIR
ANDERSON	EGBERTUS		SULLIVAN	RICCARDO	MEISSNER	CHALONGE	SINCLAIR
ANFINSEN	FRAMPTON	ARCHYTAS	SYDENHAM	RICHARDS	MENACHEM	COLLINGS	VALENTIN
AVILDSEN	GILLETTE	ASTURIAS	VALDEMAR	AMUNDSEN	MERCEDES	COOLIDGE	VASSILIS
BAPTISTA	HAMILTON	BEECKMAN	VANNEVAR	ANFINSEN	MIESCHER	ELDREDGE	VILLEMIN
BAPTISTE	JEANETTE	BOULLIAU	WALDEMAR	ARZACHEL	MOHAMMED	JANNINGS	VITTORIO

VLADIMIR	THEORELL	MERSENNE	KANELLOS	FAUCHARD	WOODWARD	VINCENTE	SCHULTZE
WENDELIN	THIBAULT	MORGAGNI	KIRCHHOF	FAVALORO	YASUNARI	YAMAMOTO	VINCENZO
WIMPERIS	WANSTALL	NAARMANN	KIRKWOOD	FILLMORE	YOICHIRO	AECHYLUS	
ZEMECKIS	WILLHELM	OLIPHANT	LAGERLOF	FLANNERY	AFANASSI	ALBERTUS	
ZEPPELIN	BELTRAMI	PAGANINI	LAUGHTON	FLINDERS	AHLQUIST	AMERICUS	
ZWORYKIN	GIROLAMO	PERSONNE	LEMELSON	GEOFFORY	AMBROISE	AUGUSTUS	**8TH LETTER**
PURKINJE	HIRAYAMA	PIERPONT	LEVINSON	GOEPPERT	BARONESS	AURELIUS	
BOURBAKI	KUBOYAMA	PYLARINI	LJAPUNOW	GOLDBERG	CONVERSI	BARTHOUD	AGRICOLA
DAREVSKY	LIPSCOMB	RICHMANN	LOBASHOV	GOLDMARK	COUNTESS	BASILIUS	ANJELICA
HORROCKS	MATUYAMA	RICHMOND	MAGIDSON	GRIGNARD	DOUGLASS	BOETHIUS	AVICENNA
KAMINSKI	REITSEMA	ROEBLING	MATHISON	GUETTARD	DREYFUSS	CAMPANUS	BAPTISTA
KAZUHIKO	WILLIAMS	ROSALIND	MELCHIOR	GULDBERG	GUINNESS	CHEVREUL	BATTISTA
NOBUYUKI	ADRIENNE	SCIPIONE	MERCATOR	HADAMARD	HARKNESS	CLAIRAUT	BECCARIA
SEPKOSKI	AGOSTINO	SPEDDING	MESENKOP	HALLBERG	HOUTGAST	CLAUDIUS	FELICITA
SIKORSKI	AMONTONS	STARLING	MEYERHOF	HARCOURT	NICOLASS	CLAUSIUS	GABRIELA
YAMAZAKE	AVICENNA	STEPHENS	MORRISON	HERZBERG	NIKOLASS	COLUMBUS	HIRAYAMA
YAMAZAKI	BAUCHENS	STIRLING	NAPOLEON	HILDYARD	NOVARESE	DUCOMMUN	HOLWARDA
YANOFSKY	BEAUMONT	SUNDMANN	NORTHROP	HURLBERT	PALITZSH	EGBERTUS	JHABVALA
AGRICOLA	BERTRAND	TAKAMINE	PATERSON	INGEBORG	TARADASH	EPALINUS	KAWABATA
BEROULLI	BORGNINE	TOWNSEND	PATTISON	ISAMBARD	YASUMASA	EPICURUS	KUBOYAMA
BOMBELLI	BRANTING	WAKELING	PEDERSON	JACQUARD	ANSCHUTZ	EUGENIUS	MATUYAMA
BRUNFELS	BRENTANO	WEISMANN	PETERSON	KORNBERG	BAPTISTA	EUTOCIUS	PATRICIA
BUSHNELL	BUCKLAND	WOLFGANG	ROBINSON	LANTIERI	BAPTISTE	FRUEHAUF	PATRIZIA
BUSTILLO	BUSCHING	ZSIGMOND	RYDSTROM	LEGENDRE	BARTLETT	GEORGIUS	QUARANTA
CAMPBELL	CAGLIONE	ALCMAEON	SAKHAROV	LEMAITRE	BATTISTA	GERARDUS	REITSEMA
CARLISLE	CARADINI	ALGERNON	SALVADOR	LEONHARD	BECKWITH	HENRICUS	SAAVEDRA
CASTILLO	CARFAGNO	ANDERSON	SARANDON	LEUCKART	BENNETTI	HEVELIUS	SAUTUOLA
CHISHOLM	CAROLINE	ANGSTROM	SCHAWLOW	LUNDBERG	BLACKETT	HIPPALUS	TOMONAGA
COTTRELL	CHANNING	APPLETON	SEFSTROM	MACQUORN	BRACKETT	HIPPASUS	TONEGAWA
FOUCAULT	CLAUDINE	BJORNSON	SHERWOOD	MCCLEARY	BRAMANTE	JORDANUS	VALSALVA
FREDHOLM	COURNAND	BOLTWOOD	SMITHSON	MCMURTRY	CALMETTE	LEBESGUE	VOLTERRA
FRENICLE	DEBIERNE	BOYLSTON	SOUFFLOT	MINNAERT	COBLENTZ	LIBAVIUS	YASUMASA
GABRIELA	DEDEKIND	BUTLEROV	STURGEON	PALMIERI	ELLICOTT	LINNAEUS	GOTTLIEB
GARFIELD	DRUMMOND	CARLETON	THOMPSON	PICKFORD	EVARISTE	MANUTIUS	LIPSCOMB
HADFIELD	FEILDING	CHARLTON	TOMMASON	POINCARE	FELICITA	MARTINUS	FREDERIC
HORSFALL	FLEMMING	CHIRIKOV	WINTHROP	POLIDORE	GILLETTE	MCCOLLUM	BARTHOUD
JHABVALA	FLOURENS	CROMPTON	GIUSEPPE	POLYKARP	GRIFFITH	MENELAUS	BERNHARD
KENNELLY	FONTAINE	CROWFOOT	PHILIPPE	PROSPERO	HAGGERTY	NICOLAUS	BERTRAND
KORNGOLD	GASCOYNE	DAVIDSON	PHILLIPE	RUGGIERO	HATCHETT	NIKOLAUS	BLANFORD
LASHELLE	GERGONNE	DAVISSON	ADELBERT	SAAVEDRA	JEANETTE	ODYSSEUS	BOLTWOOD
LASSALLY	GIACCONI	DESHNJOV	AVOGADRO	SACCHERI	KAWABATA	PITISCUS	BRADFORD
MARCELLO	GIORDANO	EASTWOOD	BERNHARD	SAUNDERS	KITASATO	RHETICUS	BRONSTED
MARSHALL	GIOVANNI	ERICKSON	BLANFORD	SOUTHERN	KLAPROTH	ROBERTUS	BUCKLAND
MARSIGLI	HAFFKINE	ERICSSON	BLUMBERG	STAFFORD	LAPWORTH	SELEUCUS	BUMSTEAD
MCEVILLY	HARTLINE	FOURCROY	BRADFORD	STANFORD	MARIOTTE	SERVETUS	CLIFFORD
MINNELLI	HARTMANN	FRAMPTON	CALANDRI	STEINORE	MCDIVITT	STEVINUS	COURNAND
MITCHELL	HOAGLAND	FRIDTJOF	CANONERO	STOTHART	MEREDITH	TERENIUS	CRAWFORD
PERRAULT	HOFFMANN	GODEFROY	CHAMBERS	SVEDBERG	MONNARTZ	TISELIUS	DEDEKIND
REDFIELD	HUFELAND	HAMILTON	CLIFFORD	THEODORE	PLASKETT	TRAJANUS	DRUMMOND
REGINALD	HUTSHING	HARRISON	CRAWFORD	THUNBERG	PLUNKETT	VALERIUS	EASTWOOD
REGNAULT	JUNGHANS	HIJUELOS	CUTHBERT	VOLTAIRE	PRESCOTT	VESALIUS	EBERHARD
REINHOLD	KAUFMANN	HIPPACOS	DAGUERRE	VOLTERRA	QUARANTA	VONNEGUT	FAUCHARD
RICCIOLI	LIPPMANN	JACOBSON	DELAMBRE	WEINBERG	RICKETTS	REDGRAVE	GARFIELD
SANTILLO	MACLAINE	JENNISON	DESIDERI	WESTMORE	SCHWARTZ	VALSALVA	GRIGNARD
SAUTUOLA	MADESANI	JOHANSON	EBERHARD	WHITFORD	STEINITZ	TONEGAWA	GUETTARD
SCOFIELD	MAITLAND	JOHNSTON	ELEANORE	WIECHERT	TRUSCOTT	BIRDSEYE	HADAMARD
THEOBALD	MENGHINI	JOUFFROY	FAHLBERG	WOODBURY	UNSWORTH	JEFFREYS	HADFIELD

HILDYARD	FRENICLE	BUSCHING	GIACCONI	WANSTALL	HARTMANN	SULEIMAN	DEMPSTER
HOAGLAND	GASCOYNE	CHANNING	GIOVANNI	ANGSTROM	HAUPTMAN	SULLIVAN	DRESSLER
HUFELAND	GERGONNE	FAHLBERG	GRIMALDI	CHISHOLM	HEINEMAN	SUNDMANN	ELSASSER
ISAMBARD	GERTRUDE	FEILDING	KAMINSKI	ELVEHJEM	HOFFMANN	THOMPSON	ERLANGER
JACQUARD	GILLETTE	FLEMMING	LANTIERI	FREDHOLM	HOUSEMAN	TOMMASON	FAULKNER
KIRKWOOD	GIUSEPPE	GOLDBERG	MADESANI	GREENHAM	HUNTSMAN	VALENTIN	FLETCHER
KORNGOLD	HAFFKINE	GULDBERG	MALPIGHI	LINDHEIM	JACOBSON	VILLEMIN	FOURNIER
LEONHARD	HARTLINE	HALLBERG	MARSIGLI	MCCOLLUM	JENNISON	VIRTANEN	GAERTNER
LINDBLAD	HAUKSBEE	HERZBERG	MENGHINI	MENACHEM	JOHANSON	WATERMAN	GARDINER
MAITLAND	JEANETTE	HUTSHING	MINNELLI	NORDHEIM	JOHNSTON	WEISMANN	GEISSLER
MOHAMMED	LAGRANGE	INGEBORG	MORGAGNI	RYDSTROM	JONATHAN	WENDELIN	GOODYEAR
MUHAMMAD	LASHELLE	KORNBERG	NICKOLAI	SEFSTROM	KAUFMANN	ZAILLIAN	GORDIMER
OUGHTRED	LAURENCE	LUNDBERG	NOBUYUKI	SYDENHAM	LANGEVIN	ZEPPELIN	HISINGER
PICKFORD	LAWRENCE	ROEBLING	PAGANINI	WILLHELM	LAUGHTON	ZWORYKIN	JENNIFER
REDFIELD	LEBESGUE	SPEDDING	PALMIERI	ALCMAEON	LEACHMAN	ADOVASIO	KAMMERER
REGINALD	LEGENDRE	STARLING	PESCUCCI	ALGERNON	LEDERMAN	AGOSTINO	LANGMUIR
REINHOLD	LEMAITRE	STIRLING	PETRUCCI	AMUNDSEN	LEISHMAN	ANTIONIO	LASSETER
RICHMOND	MACBRIDE	SVEDBERG	PYLARINI	ANDERSON	LEMELSON	AVOGADRO	MEISSNER
ROSALIND	MACLAINE	THUNBERG	RAMBALDI	ANFINSEN	LEVINSON	BERNARDO	MELCHIOR
SCOFIELD	MAGENDIE	WAKELING	RICCIOLI	APPLETON	LIPPMANN	BRENTANO	MERCATOR
SHERWOOD	MARIOTTE	WEINBERG	SACCHERI	AUGUSTIN	MACQUORN	BUSTILLO	MIESCHER
STAFFORD	MARJORIE	WOLFGANG	SEPKOSKI	AVILDSEN	MAGELLAN	CANONERO	MOSANDER
STANFORD	MERSENNE	BECKWITH	SIKORSKI	BEECKMAN	MAGIDSON	CARFAGNO	NARINDER
THEOBALD	NEWCOMBE	BOWDITCH	YAMAZAKI	BENJAMIN	MARCELIN	CASTILLO	OSIANDER
TOWNSEND	NOVARESE	FISHBACH	YASUNARI	BJORNSON	MARSHMAN	CORONADO	PLAYFAIR
WHITFORD	PERSONNE	FREDRICH	CHADWICK	BOTSTEIN	MATHISON	DOMENICO	POLITZER
WOODWARD	PHILIPPE	GOLDBACH	DELBRUCK	BOURGOIN	MCLAGLEN	FAVALORO	RICKOVER
ZSIGMOND	PHILLIPE	GOODRICH	GAJDUSEK	BOYLSTON	MCLELLAN	GIORDANO	SABATIER
ADRIENNE	POINCARE	GRIFFITH	GOLDMARK	BRATTAIN	MCMILLAN	GIROLAMO	SALVADOR
ALDREDGE	POLIDORE	HEINRICH	HAVELOCK	BRICKMAN	MILLIKAN	HERANADO	SCALIGER
AMBROISE	PURKINJE	ISAEVICH	HENDRICK	BRIDGMAN	MILSTEIN	KAZUHIKO	SCHAEFER
ARISTIDE	REDGRAVE	JAENISCH	HORNBECK	BUCHANAN	MORRISON	KITASATO	SCHALLER
BAPTISTE	RUDOLPHE	JEDEDIAH	RODERICK	CALLAHAN	MULLIKEN	LEONARDO	SCHEINER
BEATRICE	RUTLEDGE	JEREMIAH	SEDGWICK	CARLETON	NAARMANN	LEOPOLDO	SCHIMPER
BIRDSEYE	SCHULTZE	KLAPROTH	SKOLNICK	CHARLTON	NAPOLEON	MARCELLO	SCHROTER
BORGNINE	SCIPIONE	LAPWORTH	ARZACHEL	CORRIGAN	NEWCOMEN	PARRONDO	SCHUSTER
BRAMANTE	STEINORE	MEREDITH	BUSHNELL	CRISTIAN	NUSSLEIN	PROSPERO	SINCLAIR
CAGLIONE	TAKAMINE	NEHEMIAH	CAMPBELL	CROMPTON	PATERSON	RICCARDO	SPITTLER
CALMETTE	THEODORE	PALITZSH	CHEVREUL	DAVIDSON	PATTISON	RUGGIERO	SPRECKER
CARLISLE	VINCENTE	RAYLEIGH	COTTRELL	DAVISSON	PEDERSEN	SANTIAGO	STAUFFER
CARNEGIE	VOLTAIRE	TARADASH	EMMANUEL	DUCOMMUN	PEDERSON	SANTILLO	STROWGER
CAROLINE	WATANABE	TOMBAUGH	ESQUIVEL	DUJARDIN	PERELMAN	VINCENZO	THATCHER
CHALONGE	WESTMORE	UNSWORTH	FRAENKEL	EINSTEIN	PETERSON	VITTORIO	TRUMPLER
CHRISTIE	YAMAZAKE	WELSBACH	GAMALIEL	ERICKSON	RENNAHAN	YAMAMOTO	VALDEMAR
CLARENCE	BIRKHOFF	AFANASSI	HANNIBAL	ERICSSON	RICHMANN	YOICHIRO	VANNEVAR
CLAUDINE	CHARGAFF	BELTRAMI	HERSCHEL	FRAMPTON	ROBINSON	MESENKOP	VLADIMIR
CLEMENCE	FRIDTJOF	BENNETTI	HORSFALL	FRANKLIN	ROENTGEN	NORTHROP	WALDEMAR
COOLIDGE	FRUEHAUF	BEROULLI	IMMANUEL	FREEDMAN	SARANDON	POLYKARP	WALDEYER
DAGUERRE	IPATIEFF	BOMBELLI	KJELDAHL	FRIEDKIN	SCHULMAN	WINTHROP	WECHSLER
DEBIERNE	KIRCHHOF	BOURBAKI	MARSHALL	FRIEDMAN	SHEARMAN	ALISTAIR	WEHINGER
DELAMBRE	LAGERLOF	CALANDRI	MCDANIEL	GANGELIN	SHERIDAN	BERLINER	WHISTLER
ELDREDGE	MARGGRAF	CARADINI	MITCHELL	GARNERIN	SIEGBAHN	BESSEMER	AECHYLUS
ELEANORE	MEYERHOF	CARDUCCI	PERCIVAL	GHISLAIN	SILLIMAN	BREWSTER	ALBERTUS
EVARISTE	OSHEROFF	CONVERSI	SCHIMMEL	GOLITZEN	SMITHSON	CAPELLER	AMERICUS
FILLMORE	WOODRUFF	DESIDERI	SHRAPNEL	GROTRIAN	SORENSEN	CHANDLER	AMONTONS
FLORENCE	BLUMBERG	GASSENDI	SPRENGEL	HAMILTON	SOUTHERN	CHARLIER	ARCHYTAS
FONTAINE	BRANTING	GHERARDI	THEORELL	HARRISON	STURGEON	CHROWDER	ASTURIAS

AUGUSTUS	MENELAUS	HURLBERT	MCKINLEY	BENAVENTE	CORNELIUS	GABRIELLA	JOHNSTONE
AURELIUS	MERCEDES	LEUCKART	MCMURTRY	BENEDETTO	CORNFORTH	GABRIELLE	JORGENSEN
AVERROES	NEWLANDS	MARGARET	MELLANBY	BENEDICKS	CRESWICKE	GANSWINDT	JORGENSON
BARONESS	NICHOLAS	MCDIVITT	SHOCKLEY	BENZELIUS	CRISTIANI	GASCOIGNE	JOSEPHINE
BASHEVIS	NICOLAAS	MINNAERT	THIMOTHY	BERGSTROM	CRONSTEDT	GAZZANIGA	JOSEPHSON
BASILIUS	NICOLASS	OLIPHANT	TREMBLEY	BERNIGAUD	CTESIBIUS	GEGENBAUR	JUSTINIAN
BAUCHENS	NICOLAUS	PERRAULT	WOODBURY	BERNOULLI	DALRYMPLE	GEMINIANO	KARDASHEV
BILLINGS	NIKOLASS	PIERPONT	YANOFSKY	BERNSTEIN	DAMOISEAU	GERALDINE	KARLFELDT
BJERKNES	NIKOLAUS	PLASKETT	ANSCHUTZ	BERTHELOT	DAUBENTON	GIANNETTI	KATHARINE
BOETHIUS	ODYSSEUS	PLUNKETT	COBLENTZ	BERZELIUS	DECONCINI	GILLESPIE	KENZABURO
BRUNFELS	PERICLES	PONCELET	MONNARTZ	BESSARION	DELEZENNE	GJELLERUP	KETTERING
CAMPANUS	PITISCUS	PRESCOTT	SCHWARTZ	BIANCHINI	DEMESTRAL	GLADSTONE	KIRCHHOFF
CHAKIRIS	REYNOLDS	QUETELET	STEINITZ	BIRKELAND	DESARGUES	GOLDHABER	KISSINGER
CHAMBERS	RHETICUS	REGNAULT		BJORKHOLM	DESCARTES	GOLDSTEIN	KOBREUTER
CLAUDIUS	RICHARDS	SIGNORET		BLAKESLEE	DESMAREST	GOLDSTINE	KOENEKAMP
CLAUSIUS	RICKETTS	SOUFFLOT		BLANCHARD	DICKINSON	GOLDSTONE	KOLREUTER
COLLINGS	ROBERTUS	STOTHART	**9 LETTER**	BOCCACCIO	DIEUDONNE	GOODRICKE	KRAUSHAAR
COLUMBUS	SAUNDERS	STRAIGHT	**1ST LETTER**	BOERHAAVE	DIONYSIUS	GORBACHEV	KRONECKER
CORNELIS	SCHULTES	THEVENET		BOLTZMANN	DIRICHLET	GOTTFRIED	KURCHATOV
COUNTESS	SELEUCUS	THIBAULT		BORNSTEIN	DOMINIQUE	GRANVILLE	LAMORISSE
COURTOIS	SERVETUS	TRUSCOTT	AFRAGAMUS	BOSCOVICH	DONALDSON	GRASSMANN	LANCASTER
DESORMES	SOCRATES	VONNEGUT	AGRAMONTE	BOURGEOIS	DUNALDSON	GREENBERG	LATREILLE
DOUGLASS	STEPHENS	WIECHERT	ALBERTSON	BRACEWELL	DUTROCHET	GREENWOOD	LAVOISIER
DREYFUSS	STEVINUS	BOULLIAU	ALDEROTTI	BRACONNOT	ECHEGARAY	GROTEFEND	LECLANCHE
EGBERTUS	TERENIUS	COUSTEAU	ALEKSANDR	BRODERICK	EDDINGTON	GROTTHUSS	LEDERBERG
EPALINUS	THEEUWES	ROUSSEAU	ALEXANDER	BROUNCKER	EHRENBERG	GRUENTZIG	LEMONOSOV
EPICURUS	TISELIUS	BUTLEROV	ALEXANDRE	BURGUNDIO	EILENBERG	GUGLIELMO	LENORMAND
EUGENIUS	TRAJANUS	CHIRIKOV	ALGAROTTI	BURKHARDT	EINTHOVEN	GUILLAUME	LEUCIPPUS
EUTOCIUS	VALERIUS	DESHNJOV	ALMENDROS	BURROUGHS	ELIZABETH	GUILLEMIN	LEVERRIER
FLINDERS	VASSILIS	JAROSLAV	ALTRAMURA	BUTENANDT	ELLENSHAW	GUSTAFSON	LINDBERGH
FLOURENS	VESALIUS	LOBASHOV	AMMERMANN	CAILLETET	ESTABROOK	GUTENBERG	LIOUVILLE
FRANCOIS	WILLIAMS	SAKHAROV	ANACHARIS	CALLENDAR	EUPALINUS	HAFFENDEN	LLEWELLYN
GEORGIUS	WIMPERIS	LJAPUNOW	ARBUTHNOT	CALLIPPUS	EURIPIDES	HAHNEMANN	LOMONOSOV
GERARDUS	ZEMECKIS	SCHAWLOW	ARCHIBALD	CAROTHERS	EUSTACHIO	HAMMURABI	LOSCHMIDT
GUINNESS	ADELBERT	BERKELEY	ARFWEDSON	CARPENTER	FABRICIUS	HASBROUCK	LUCRETIUS
HARKNESS	AHLQUIST	BRINDLEY	ARISTIDES	CASCARDIO	FAIRBAIRN	HAUPTMANN	MACARTHUR
HENRICUS	ALBRECHT	DAREVSKY	ARISTOTLE	CASSERIUS	FALLOPIUS	HAUSDORFF	MACDONALD
HEVELIUS	ASHCROFT	DEMARCAY	ARKWRIGHT	CAVALIERI	FERCHAULT	HEAVISIDE	MACEDONIO
HIJUELOS	BANCROFT	DILLEHAY	ARMSTRONG	CAVENDISH	FERDINAND	HECATAEUS	MACMILLAN
HIPPACOS	BARTLETT	FLANNERY	ARNOLDSON	CESALPINO	FESSENDEN	HELVETIUS	MAHARIDGE
HIPPALUS	BEAUMONT	FOURCROY	ARRHENIUS	CHAYEFSKY	FEUERBACH	HEMINGWAY	MARTINSON
HIPPASUS	BENEDICT	GEOFFORY	ARYABHATA	CHERENKOV	FIBONACCI	HENDERSON	MASKELYNE
HORROCKS	BLACKETT	GEOFFREY	ASERINSKY	CHRISTAIN	FLAMSTEED	HENRIETTA	MAUROLICO
JANNINGS	BRACKETT	GODEFROY	ATANASOFF	CHRISTIAN	FLORIMOND	HERODOTUS	MCALISTER
JEFFREYS	CHATELET	GRANTLEY	AULENBACK	CHRISTINE	FORLANINI	HEYROVSKY	MCCONNELL
JEFFRIES	CLAIRAUT	HAGGERTY	BALTIMORE	CHRISTOFF	FORSSMANN	HIPPOLYTE	MCCORMICK
JENNINGS	CROWFOOT	HEMPHREY	BAMBERGER	CHRISTOPH	FRANCESCO	HITCHINGS	MCDOUGALL
JEREMIAS	CUTHBERT	HOLLIDAY	BARGHOORN	CHURCHILL	FRANCISCO	HOLLERITH	MCPHERSON
JOHANNES	EILHARDT	HUMPHREY	BARRINGER	CLAPEYRON	FRANCOISE	HORODYSKY	MCQUARRIE
JORDANUS	ELLICOTT	JOUFFROY	BARRYMORE	CLAUDETTE	FRANKLAND	HUTCHINGS	MECHNIKOV
JUNGHANS	FOUCAULT	KENNELLY	BARTHOLIN	CLEOPATRA	FREDERICK	HUTCHISON	MEHRINGER
KANELLOS	GERHARDT	KINGSLEY	BATAILLON	CLEVELAND	FRIEDMANN	HYACINTHE	MENDELEEV
LIBAVIUS	GOEPPERT	LASSALLY	BEAUCHAMP	COCKCROFT	FRIEDRICH	IVANOVICH	MICHAELIS
LINNAEUS	GOUDSMIT	MAUDSLAY	BECQUEREL	COCKERELL	FROESCHEL	IVANOVSKY	MICHELSON
MANUTIUS	HARCOURT	MCCARTHY	BEERNAERT	CONDORCET	FRONTINUS	JARNOWSKY	MIELZINER
MARTINUS	HATCHETT	MCCLEARY	BEILSTEIN	CONYBEARE	FRUCHTMAN	JEFFERSON	MILESTONE
MATTHIAS	HOUTGAST	MCEVILLY	BEKTHEREV	CORNEILLE	FULLERTON	JOHANNSEN	MINKOWSKI

MONTANARI	SCHONLEIN	VESPASIAN	GASCOIGNE	SCHOEFFER	NEETHLING	MICHAELIS	BOSCOVICH
MORTILLET	SCHULBERG	VESPUSIUS	GAZZANIGA	SCHONBEIN	OENOPIDES	MICHELSON	BOURGEOIS
MOSSBAUER	SCHWEIZER	VIEUSSENS	HAFFENDEN	SCHONLEIN	PELLETIER	MIELZINER	COCKCROFT
MURCHISON	SCHWINGER	VINCENZIO	HAHNEMANN	SCHULBERG	PERCIVALL	MILESTONE	COCKERELL
MUSSOLINI	SEBASTIAN	VITRUVIUS	HAMMURABI	SCHWEIZER	PETROSIAN	MINKOWSKI	CONDORCET
NATHANAEL	SEMIRAMIS	WAHLSTROM	HASBROUCK	SCHWINGER	REVEILLON	NICEPHORE	CONYBEARE
NATHANIEL	SERTURNER	WARBURTON	HAUPTMANN	EDDINGTON	SEBASTIAN	NICHOLSON	CORNEILLE
NEETHLING	SHECHTMAN	WASSERMAN	HAUSDORFF	BEAUCHAMP	SEMIRAMIS	NICKERSON	CORNELIUS
NICEPHORE	SHOLOKHOV	WEDGEWOOD	JARNOWSKY	BECQUEREL	SERTURNER	NICOLAIER	CORNFORTH
NICHOLSON	SIEGFRIED	WEISSKOPF	KARDASHEV	BEERNAERT	VERNADSKY	NIEUWLAND	DOMINIQUE
NICKERSON	SILLANPAA	WEISSMANN	KARLFELDT	BEILSTEIN	VESPASIAN	NIRENBERG	DONALDSON
NICOLAIER	SODERBLOM	WETHERALD	KATHARINE	BEKTHEREV	VESPUSIUS	NISHIJIMA	FORLANINI
NIEUWLAND	SOMERFELD	WHINFIELD	LAMORISSE	BENAVENTE	WEDGEWOOD	PICKERING	FORSSMANN
NIRENBERG	SOPHOCLES	WHITEHEAD	LANCASTER	BENEDETTO	WEISSKOPF	RIGOBERTA	GOLDHABER
NISHIJIMA	SOSIGENES	WHITTAKER	LATREILLE	BENEDICKS	WEISSMANN	SIEGFRIED	GOLDSTEIN
OENOPIDES	SOUBEIRAN	WHITWORTH	LAVOISIER	BENZELIUS	WETHERALD	SILLANPAA	GOLDSTINE
OLDENBURG	SOUTHGATE	WIESCHAUS	MACARTHUR	BERGSTROM	AFRAGAMUS	TINBERGEN	GOLDSTONE
PARKINSON	SPIELBERG	WILKINSON	MACDONALD	BERNIGAUD	AGRAMONTE	TITCHENER	GOODRICKE
PASTERNAK	SPITTELER	WILLADSEN	MACEDONIO	BERNOULLI	CHAYEFSKY	VIEUSSENS	GORBACHEV
PELLETIER	SRINIVASA	WILLUGHBY	MACMILLAN	BERNSTEIN	CHERENKOV	VINCENZIO	GOTTFRIED
PERCIVALL	STANISLAO	WITHERING	MAHARIDGE	BERTHELOT	CHRISTAIN	VITRUVIUS	HOLLERITH
PETROSIAN	STANISLAW	WLADYSLAW	MARTINSON	BERZELIUS	CHRISTIAN	WIESCHAUS	HORODYSKY
PHILIPPUS	STAPLETON	WOLFSKEHL	MASKELYNE	BESSARION	CHRISTINE	WILKINSON	JOHANNSEN
PHILOLAUS	STEENBERG	WOLLASTON	MAUROLICO	CESALPINO	CHRISTOFF	WILLADSEN	JOHNSTONE
PICKERING	STEENBOCK	ZACHERIAS	NATHANAEL	DECONCINI	CHRISTOPH	WILLUGHBY	JORGENSEN
POLLENDER	STEINBECK	ZINNEMANN	NATHANIEL	DELEZENNE	CHURCHILL	WITHERING	JORGENSON
PRIESTLEY	STEINKAMP	ZSIGMONDY	PARKINSON	DEMESTRAL	EHRENBERG	ZINNEMANN	JOSEPHINE
PRIGOGINE	STEINMETZ		PASTERNAK	DESARGUES	PHILIPPUS	BJORKHOLM	JOSEPHSON
PRITCHARD	STEVENSON		RAINWATER	DESCARTES	PHILOLAUS	GJELLERUP	KOBREUTER
PROKHOROV	STOICHEFF		RAMANUJAN	DESMAREST	SHECHTMAN	ALBERTSON	KOENEKAMP
PRUDHOMME	STONEHILL	**2ND LETTER**	RAWLINSON	FERCHAULT	SHOLOKHOV	ALDEROTTI	KOLREUTER
QUASIMODO	STRADLING		SABASTIAN	FERDINAND	THEODORIC	ALEKSANDR	LOMONOSOV
RAINWATER	STRASSMAN	BALTIMORE	SALVATORE	FESSENDEN	THEODORUS	ALEXANDER	LOSCHMIDT
RAMANUJAN	STREISAND	BAMBERGER	TACHENIUS	FEUERBACH	THEOPHILE	ALEXANDRE	MONTANARI
RAWLINSON	STROMGREN	BARGHOORN	TAKAHASHI	GEGENBAUR	THORNDIKE	ALGAROTTI	MORTILLET
REVEILLON	SUSSMILCH	BARRINGER	TANIGUCHI	GEMINIANO	UHLENBECK	ALMENDROS	MOSSBAUER
RIGOBERTA	SYLVESTER	BARRYMORE	TARANTINO	GERALDINE	WHINFIELD	ALTRAMURA	POLLENDER
ROBERTSON	TACHENIUS	BARTHOLIN	TARTAGLIA	HEAVISIDE	WHITEHEAD	BLAKESLEE	ROBERTSON
ROCCHETTI	TAKAHASHI	BATAILLON	VALENTINA	HECATAEUS	WHITTAKER	BLANCHARD	ROCCHETTI
ROCHESTER	TANIGUCHI	CAILLETET	VALENTINE	HELVETIUS	WHITWORTH	CLAPEYRON	ROCHESTER
ROGGEVEEN	TARANTINO	CALLENDAR	VANNOCCIO	HEMINGWAY	BIANCHINI	CLAUDETTE	ROGGEVEEN
ROMANENKO	TARTAGLIA	CALLIPPUS	VAUQUELIN	HENDERSON	BIRKELAND	CLEOPATRA	ROMANENKO
ROOSEVELT	THEODORIC	CAROTHERS	WAHLSTROM	HENRIETTA	DICKINSON	CLEVELAND	ROOSEVELT
ROOZEBOOM	THEODORUS	CARPENTER	WARBURTON	HERODOTUS	DIEUDONNE	ELIZABETH	ROOZEBOOM
RORSCHACH	THEOPHILE	CASCARDIO	WASSERMAN	HEYROVSKY	DIONYSIUS	ELLENSHAW	RORSCHACH
ROSENBAUM	THORNDIKE	CASSERIUS	ZACHERIAS	JEFFERSON	DIRICHLET	FLAMSTEED	ROSENBAUM
ROSENBERG	TINBERGEN	CAVALIERI	ECHEGARAY	KENZABURO	EILENBERG	FLORIMOND	ROSENBERG
ROUSSELOT	TITCHENER	CAVENDISH	MCALISTER	KETTERING	EINTHOVEN	GLADSTONE	ROUSSELOT
RUHMKORFF	TOUSSIENG	DALRYMPLE	MCCONNELL	LECLANCHE	FIBONACCI	LLEWELLYN	SODERBLOM
SABASTIAN	TSCHERMAK	DAMOISEAU	MCCORMICK	LEDERBERG	GIANNETTI	OLDENBURG	SOMERFELD
SALVATORE	TUNNSTALL	DAUBENTON	MCDOUGALL	LEMONOSOV	GILLESPIE	WLADYSLAW	SOPHOCLES
SCAEBERLE	UHLENBECK	FABRICIUS	MCPHERSON	LENORMAND	HIPPOLYTE	AMMERMANN	SOSIGENES
SCHAFFNER	VALENTINA	FAIRBAIRN	MCQUARRIE	LEUCIPPUS	HITCHINGS	ANACHARIS	SOUBEIRAN
SCHAUDINN	VALENTINE	FALLOPIUS	SCAEBERLE	LEVERRIER	KIRCHHOFF	BOCCACCIO	SOUTHGATE
SCHLEIDEN	VANNOCCIO	GABRIELLA	SCHAFFNER	MECHNIKOV	KISSINGER	BOERHAAVE	TOUSSIENG
SCHOEFFER	VAUQUELIN	GABRIELLE	SCHAUDINN	MEHRINGER	LINDBERGH	BOLTZMANN	WOLFSKEHL
SCHONBEIN	VERNADSKY	GANSWINDT	SCHLEIDEN	MENDELEEV	LIOUVILLE	BORNSTEIN	WOLLASTON

SPIELBERG	STEINMETZ	FRANCISCO	ZACHERIAS	SCHAFFNER	HOLLERITH	VANNOCCIO	EHRENBERG
SPITTELER	STEVENSON	FRANCOISE	ALDEROTTI	SCHAUDINN	KOLREUTER	VINCENZIO	EURIPIDES
ARBUTHNOT	STOICHEFF	FRANKLAND	EDDINGTON	SCHLEIDEN	MILESTONE	ZINNEMANN	FERCHAULT
ARCHIBALD	STONEHILL	GIANNETTI	LEDERBERG	SCHOEFFER	PELLETIER	BJORKHOLM	FERDINAND
ARFWEDSON	STRADLING	GLADSTONE	MCDOUGALL	SCHONBEIN	POLLENDER	BRODERICK	FORLANINI
ARISTIDES	STRASSMAN	GRANVILLE	OLDENBURG	SCHONLEIN	SALVATORE	BROUNCKER	FORSSMANN
ARISTOTLE	STREISAND	GRASSMANN	SODERBLOM	SCHULBERG	SILLANPAA	CRONSTEDT	GERALDINE
ARKWRIGHT	STROMGREN	HEAVISIDE	WEDGEWOOD	SCHWEIZER	SYLVESTER	DIONYSIUS	GORBACHEV
ARMSTRONG	AULENBACK	HYACINTHE	ALEKSANDR	SCHWINGER	UHLENBECK	FLORIMOND	HERODOTUS
ARNOLDSON	BURGUNDIO	IVANOVICH	ALEXANDER	WAHLSTROM	VALENTINA	FROESCHEL	HORODYSKY
ARRHENIUS	BURKHARDT	IVANOVSKY	ALEXANDRE	ARISTIDES	VALENTINE	FRONTINUS	JARNOWSKY
ARYABHATA	BURROUGHS	KRAUSHAAR	ASERINSKY	ARISTOTLE	WILKINSON	GOODRICKE	JORGENSEN
BRACEWELL	BUTENANDT	MCALISTER	BEERNAERT	BEILSTEIN	WILLADSEN	GROTEFEND	JORGENSON
BRACONNOT	DUNALDSON	QUASIMODO	BOERHAAVE	CAILLETET	WILLUGHBY	GROTTHUSS	KARDASHEV
BRODERICK	DUTROCHET	SCAEBERLE	CHERENKOV	CRISTIANI	WOLFSKEHL	KRONECKER	KARLFELDT
BROUNCKER	EUPALINUS	STANISLAO	CLEOPATRA	ELIZABETH	WOLLASTON	LIOUVILLE	KIRCHHOFF
CRESWICKE	EURIPIDES	STANISLAW	CLEVELAND	FAIRBAIRN	ALMENDROS	PROKHOROV	KURCHATOV
CRISTIANI	EUSTACHIO	STAPLETON	CRESWICKE	FRIEDMANN	AMMERMANN	ROOSEVELT	MARTINSON
CRONSTEDT	FULLERTON	WLADYSLAW	CTESIBIUS	FRIEDRICH	ARMSTRONG	ROOZEBOOM	MORTILLET
FRANCESCO	GUGLIELMO	ALBERTSON	DIEUDONNE	GUILLAUME	BAMBERGER	SHOLOKHOV	MURCHISON
FRANCISCO	GUILLAUME	ARBUTHNOT	FREDERICK	GUILLEMIN	DAMOISEAU	STOICHEFF	NIRENBERG
FRANCOISE	GUILLEMIN	FABRICIUS	GJELLERUP	PHILIPPUS	DEMESTRAL	STONEHILL	PARKINSON
FRANKLAND	GUSTAFSON	FIBONACCI	GREENBERG	PHILOLAUS	DOMINIQUE	THORNDIKE	PERCIVALL
FREDERICK	GUTENBERG	GABRIELLA	GREENWOOD	PRIESTLEY	GEMINIANO	EUPALINUS	RORSCHACH
FRIEDMANN	HUTCHINGS	GABRIELLE	KOENEKAMP	PRIGOGINE	HAMMURABI	HIPPOLYTE	SERTURNER
FRIEDRICH	HUTCHISON	KOBREUTER	LLEWELLYN	PRITCHARD	HEMINGWAY	MCPHERSON	STRADLING
FROESCHEL	JUSTINIAN	ROBERTSON	MIELZINER	RAINWATER	LAMORISSE	SOPHOCLES	STRASSMAN
FRONTINUS	KURCHATOV	SABASTIAN	NEETHLING	SPIELBERG	LEMONOSOV	MCQUARRIE	STREISAND
FRUCHTMAN	LUCRETIUS	SEBASTIAN	NIEUWLAND	SPITTELER	LOMONOSOV	AFRAGAMUS	STROMGREN
GRANVILLE	MURCHISON	ARCHIBALD	SHECHTMAN	SRINIVASA	RAMANUJAN	AGRAMONTE	TARANTINO
GRASSMANN	MUSSOLINI	BECQUEREL	SIEGFRIED	WEISSKOPF	ROMANENKO	ARRHENIUS	TARTAGLIA
GREENBERG	QUASIMODO	BOCCACCIO	STEENBERG	WEISSMANN	SEMIRAMIS	BARGHOORN	VERNADSKY
GREENWOOD	RUHMKORFF	COCKCROFT	STEENBOCK	WHINFIELD	SOMERFELD	BARRINGER	WARBURTON
GROTEFEND	SUSSMILCH	COCKERELL	STEINBECK	WHITEHEAD	ARNOLDSON	BARRYMORE	BESSARION
GROTTHUSS	TUNNSTALL	DECONCINI	STEINKAMP	WHITTAKER	BENAVENTE	BARTHOLIN	BOSCOVICH
GRUENTZIG	IVANOVICH	DICKINSON	STEINMETZ	WHITWORTH	BENEDETTO	BERGSTROM	CASCARDIO
KRAUSHAAR	IVANOVSKY	HECATAEUS	STEVENSON	ZSIGMONDY	BENEDICKS	BERNIGAUD	CASSERIUS
KRONECKER	HYACINTHE	LECLANCHE	THEODORIC	ARKWRIGHT	BENZELIUS	BERNOULLI	CESALPINO
PRIESTLEY	SYLVESTER	LUCRETIUS	THEODORUS	BEKTHEREV	CONDORCET	BERNSTEIN	DESARGUES
PRIGOGINE		MACARTHUR	THEOPHILE	TAKAHASHI	CONYBEARE	BERTHELOT	DESCARTES
PRITCHARD		MACDONALD	VIEUSSENS	AULENBACK	DONALDSON	BERZELIUS	DESMAREST
PROKHOROV		MACEDONIO	WIESCHAUS	BALTIMORE	DUNALDSON	BIRKELAND	EUSTACHIO
PRUDHOMME	3RD LETTER	MACMILLAN	ARFWEDSON	BOLTZMANN	EINTHOVEN	BORNSTEIN	FESSENDEN
SRINIVASA		MCCONNELL	HAFFENDEN	CALLENDAR	GANSWINDT	BURGUNDIO	GASCOIGNE
ASERINSKY	ANACHARIS	MCCORMICK	JEFFERSON	CALLIPPUS	HENDERSON	BURKHARDT	GUSTAFSON
ESTABROOK	ATANASOFF	MECHNIKOV	ALGAROTTI	DALRYMPLE	HENRIETTA	BURROUGHS	HASBROUCK
TSCHERMAK	BEAUCHAMP	MICHAELIS	GEGENBAUR	DELEZENNE	KENZABURO	CAROTHERS	JOSEPHINE
ZSIGMONDY	BIANCHINI	MICHELSON	GUGLIELMO	EILENBERG	LANCASTER	CARPENTER	JOSEPHSON
ATANASOFF	BLAKESLEE	NICEPHORE	RIGOBERTA	ELLENSHAW	LENORMAND	CHRISTAIN	JUSTINIAN
CTESIBIUS	BLANCHARD	NICHOLSON	ROGGEVEEN	FALLOPIUS	LINDBERGH	CHRISTIAN	KISSINGER
STANISLAO	BRACEWELL	NICKERSON	ECHEGARAY	FULLERTON	MENDELEEV	CHRISTINE	LOSCHMIDT
STANISLAW	BRACONNOT	NICOLAIER	HAHNEMANN	GILLESPIE	MINKOWSKI	CHRISTOFF	MASKELYNE
STAPLETON	CHAYEFSKY	PICKERING	JOHANNSEN	GOLDHABER	MONTANARI	CHRISTOPH	MOSSBAUER
STEENBERG	CLAPEYRON	ROCCHETTI	JOHNSTONE	GOLDSTEIN	OENOPIDES	CORNEILLE	MUSSOLINI
STEENBOCK	CLAUDETTE	ROCHESTER	MAHARIDGE	GOLDSTINE	TANIGUCHI	CORNELIUS	NISHIJIMA
STEINBECK	FLAMSTEED	TACHENIUS	MEHRINGER	GOLDSTONE	TINBERGEN	CORNFORTH	PASTERNAK
STEINKAMP	FRANCESCO	TSCHERMAK	RUHMKORFF	HELVETIUS	TUNNSTALL	DIRICHLET	ROSENBAUM

ROSENBERG	ALGAROTTI	VINCENZIO	SODERBLOM	TANIGUCHI	CORNELIUS	HIPPOLYTE	WASSERMAN
SOSIGENES	ARYABHATA	BRODERICK	SOMERFELD	ALEKSANDR	CORNFORTH	STAPLETON	WEISSKOPF
SUSSMILCH	BATAILLON	CONDORCET	SPIELBERG	BIRKELAND	CRONSTEDT	VESPASIAN	WEISSMANN
VESPASIAN	BENAVENTE	FERDINAND	STEENBERG	BLAKESLEE	DIONYSIUS	VESPUSIUS	WIESCHAUS
VESPUSIUS	CAVALIERI	FREDERICK	STEENBOCK	BURKHARDT	FRANCESCO	BECQUEREL	BALTIMORE
WASSERMAN	CESALPINO	GLADSTONE	STREISAND	COCKCROFT	FRANCISCO	VAUQUELIN	BARTHOLIN
ALTRAMURA	DESARGUES	GOLDHABER	UHLENBECK	COCKERELL	FRANCOISE	ALTRAMURA	BEKTHEREV
BATAILLON	DONALDSON	GOLDSTEIN	VALENTINA	DICKINSON	FRANKLAND	ASERINSKY	BERTHELOT
BUTENANDT	DUNALDSON	GOLDSTINE	VALENTINE	MASKELYNE	FRONTINUS	BARRINGER	BOLTZMANN
DUTROCHET	ESTABROOK	GOLDSTONE	HAFFENDEN	MINKOWSKI	GIANNETTI	BARRYMORE	EINTHOVEN
ESTABROOK	EUPALINUS	GOODRICKE	JEFFERSON	NICKERSON	GRANVILLE	BEERNAERT	EUSTACHIO
GOTTFRIED	GERALDINE	HENDERSON	WOLFSKEHL	PARKINSON	HAHNEMANN	BJORKHOLM	GOTTFRIED
GUTENBERG	HECATAEUS	KARDASHEV	BARGHOORN	PICKERING	IVANOVICH	BOERHAAVE	GROTEFEND
HITCHINGS	JOHANNSEN	LINDBERGH	BERGSTROM	PROKHOROV	IVANOVSKY	BOURGEOIS	GROTTHUSS
HUTCHINGS	MACARTHUR	MACDONALD	BURGUNDIO	WILKINSON	JARNOWSKY	BURROUGHS	GUSTAFSON
HUTCHISON	MACDONALD	MENDELEEV	JORGENSEN	BEILSTEIN	JOHNSTONE	CHERENKOV	JUSTINIAN
KATHARINE	MAHARIDGE	PRUDHOMME	JORGENSON	CAILLETET	KOENEKAMP	CHURCHILL	KETTERING
KETTERING	RAMANUJAN	WLADYSLAW	PRIGOGINE	CALLENDAR	KRONECKER	DALRYMPLE	MARTINSON
LATREILLE	ROMANENKO	ALBERTSON	ROGGEVEEN	CALLIPPUS	RAINWATER	DUTROCHET	MONTANARI
NATHANAEL	SABASTIAN	ALDEROTTI	SIEGFRIED	FALLOPIUS	SRINIVASA	FABRICIUS	MORTILLET
NATHANIEL	SCHAFFNER	ALMENDROS	WEDGEWOOD	FORLANINI	STANISLAO	FAIRBAIRN	NEETHLING
PETROSIAN	SCHAUDINN	AMMERMANN	ZSIGMONDY	FULLERTON	STANISLAW	FLORIMOND	PASTERNAK
TITCHENER	SEBASTIAN	AULENBACK	ARCHIBALD	GILLESPIE	STONEHILL	GABRIELLA	PRITCHARD
VITRUVIUS	STRADLING	BENEDETTO	ARRHENIUS	GJELLERUP	TUNNSTALL	GABRIELLE	SERTURNER
WETHERALD	STRASSMAN	BENEDICKS	KATHARINE	GUGLIELMO	VANNOCCIO	HENRIETTA	SOUTHGATE
WITHERING	TAKAHASHI	BUTENANDT	MCPHERSON	GUILLAUME	VERNADSKY	HEYROVSKY	SPITTELER
BOURGEOIS	TARANTINO	CAVENDISH	MECHNIKOV	GUILLEMIN	WHINFIELD	KOBREUTER	TARTAGLIA
CHURCHILL	BAMBERGER	DELEZENNE	MICHAELIS	HOLLERITH	ZINNEMANN	KOLREUTER	WHITEHEAD
DAUBENTON	DAUBENTON	DEMESTRAL	MICHELSON	KARLFELDT	ARNOLDSON	LATREILLE	WHITTAKER
FEUERBACH	GORBACHEV	ECHEGARAY	NATHANAEL	LECLANCHE	CAROTHERS	LUCRETIUS	WHITWORTH
FRUCHTMAN	HASBROUCK	EHRENBERG	NATHANIEL	MCALISTER	CLEOPATRA	MAUROLICO	ARBUTHNOT
GRUENTZIG	SOUBEIRAN	EILENBERG	NICHOLSON	MIELZINER	DAMOISEAU	MEHRINGER	BEAUCHAMP
HAUPTMANN	TINBERGEN	ELLENSHAW	NISHIJIMA	PELLETIER	DECONCINI	PETROSIAN	BROUNCKER
HAUSDORFF	ANACHARIS	FEUERBACH	ROCHESTER	PHILIPPUS	FIBONACCI	THORNDIKE	CLAUDETTE
LEUCIPPUS	BOCCACCIO	FRIEDMANN	SOPHOCLES	PHILOLAUS	HERODOTUS	VITRUVIUS	DIEUDONNE
MAUROLICO	BOSCOVICH	FRIEDRICH	TACHENIUS	POLLENDER	HORODYSKY	ARISTIDES	KRAUSHAAR
PRUDHOMME	BRACEWELL	FROESCHEL	TSCHERMAK	RAWLINSON	LAMORISSE	ARISTOTLE	LIOUVILLE
ROUSSELOT	BRACONNOT	GEGENBAUR	WETHERALD	SCHLEIDEN	LAVOISIER	ARMSTRONG	MCQUARRIE
SOUBEIRAN	CASCARDIO	GREENBERG	WITHERING	SHOLOKHOV	LEMONOSOV	BESSARION	NIEUWLAND
SOUTHGATE	DESCARTES	GREENWOOD	ZACHERIAS	SILLANPAA	LENORMAND	CASSERIUS	SCHULBERG
TOUSSIENG	FERCHAULT	GRUENTZIG	CHRISTAIN	WAHLSTROM	LOMONOSOV	CRESWICKE	VIEUSSENS
VAUQUELIN	FRUCHTMAN	GUTENBERG	CHRISTIAN	WILLADSEN	MCCONNELL	CRISTIANI	CLEVELAND
CAVALIERI	GASCOIGNE	JOSEPHINE	CHRISTINE	WILLUGHBY	MCCORMICK	CTESIBIUS	HEAVISIDE
CAVENDISH	HITCHINGS	JOSEPHSON	CHRISTOFF	WOLLASTON	MCDOUGALL	FESSENDEN	HELVETIUS
LAVOISIER	HUTCHINGS	LEDERBERG	CHRISTOPH	DESMAREST	NICOLAIER	FORSSMANN	SALVATORE
LEVERRIER	HUTCHISON	LEVERRIER	DIRICHLET	FLAMSTEED	OENOPIDES	GANSWINDT	STEVENSON
REVEILLON	HYACINTHE	MACEDONIO	DOMINIQUE	HAMMURABI	RIGOBERTA	GRASSMANN	SYLVESTER
RAWLINSON	KIRCHHOFF	MILESTONE	EDDINGTON	MACMILLAN	SCHOEFFER	HAUSDORFF	ARFWEDSON
ARYABHATA	KURCHATOV	NICEPHORE	EURIPIDES	RUHMKORFF	SCHONBEIN	KISSINGER	ARKWRIGHT
HEYROVSKY	LANCASTER	NIRENBERG	GEMINIANO	ATANASOFF	SCHONLEIN	MOSSBAUER	LLEWELLYN
GAZZANIGA	LEUCIPPUS	OLDENBURG	HEMINGWAY	BERNIGAUD	STROMGREN	MUSSOLINI	SCHWEIZER
	LOSCHMIDT	PRIESTLEY	SEMIRAMIS	BERNOULLI	THEODORIC	QUASIMODO	SCHWINGER
	MURCHISON	REVEILLON	SOSIGENES	BERNSTEIN	THEODORUS	ROOSEVELT	ALEXANDER
4TH LETTER	PERCIVALL	ROBERTSON	STEINBECK	BIANCHINI	THEOPHILE	RORSCHACH	ALEXANDRE
	ROCCHETTI	ROSENBAUM	STEINKAMP	BLANCHARD	CARPENTER	ROUSSELOT	CHAYEFSKY
AFRAGAMUS	SHECHTMAN	ROSENBERG	STEINMETZ	BORNSTEIN	CLAPEYRON	SUSSMILCH	CONYBEARE
AGRAMONTE	TITCHENER	SCAEBERLE	STOICHEFF	CORNEILLE	HAUPTMANN	TOUSSIENG	BENZELIUS

BERZELIUS	FRANCISCO	LATREILLE	HUTCHINGS	RUHMKORFF	STEINKAMP	SOMERFELD	WARBURTON
ELIZABETH	FRANCOISE	LLEWELLYN	HUTCHISON	ARNOLDSON	STEINMETZ	ALEKSANDR	WILLUGHBY
GAZZANIGA	PRITCHARD	LUCRETIUS	KIRCHHOFF	CAILLETET	TARANTINO	BEILSTEIN	BENAVENTE
KENZABURO	RORSCHACH	MASKELYNE	KURCHATOV	CAVALIERI	THORNDIKE	BERGSTROM	GRANVILLE
ROOZEBOOM	STOICHEFF	MCPHERSON	LOSCHMIDT	CESALPINO	UHLENBECK	BERNSTEIN	LIOUVILLE
	WIESCHAUS	MENDELEEV	MURCHISON	DONALDSON	VALENTINA	BORNSTEIN	CRESWICKE
	BENEDETTO	MICHELSON	NEETHLING	DUNALDSON	VALENTINE	CHRISTAIN	GANSWINDT
	BENEDICKS	NICKERSON	PROKHOROV	EUPALINUS	BERNOULLI	CHRISTIAN	NIEUWLAND
5TH LETTER	CLAUDETTE	PASTERNAK	PRUDHOMME	GERALDINE	BOSCOVICH	CHRISTINE	RAINWATER
	DIEUDONNE	PELLETIER	ROCCHETTI	GJELLERUP	BRACONNOT	CHRISTOFF	WHITWORTH
ALEXANDER	FRIEDMANN	PICKERING	SHECHTMAN	GUILLAUME	BURROUGHS	CHRISTOPH	BARRYMORE
ALEXANDRE	FRIEDRICH	POLLENDER	SOUTHGATE	GUILLEMIN	CONDORCET	CRONSTEDT	DALRYMPLE
ALTRAMURA	HAUSDORFF	ROCHESTER	TAKAHASHI	NICOLAIER	DUTROCHET	DEMESTRAL	DIONYSIUS
ATANASOFF	HERODOTUS	ROGGEVEEN	TITCHENER	SCHULBERG	FALLOPIUS	FLAMSTEED	WLADYSLAW
BESSARION	HORODYSKY	ROOSEVELT	ARCHIBALD	SPIELBERG	GASCOIGNE	FORSSMANN	BOLTZMANN
BOCCACCIO	MACEDONIO	ROOZEBOOM	ASERINSKY	STAPLETON	HEYROVSKY	FROESCHEL	DELEZENNE
CASCARDIO	STRADLING	SCHLEIDEN	BALTIMORE	AGRAMONTE	HIPPOLYTE	GLADSTONE	MIELZINER
DESCARTES	THEODORIC	SCHOEFFER	BARRINGER	STROMGREN	IVANOVICH	GOLDSTEIN	
DESMAREST	THEODORUS	SCHWEIZER	BATAILLON	SUSSMILCH	IVANOVSKY	GOLDSTINE	
ELIZABETH	ARFWEDSON	SOUBEIRAN	BERNIGAUD	ZSIGMONDY	JARNOWSKY	GOLDSTONE	**6TH LETTER**
EUSTACHIO	ARRHENIUS	STEVENSON	CALLIPPUS	ALMENDROS	MACDONALD	GRASSMANN	
FORLANINI	BAMBERGER	STONEHILL	CTESIBIUS	AULENBACK	MAUROLICO	JOHNSTONE	AFRAGAMUS
GAZZANIGA	BENZELIUS	SYLVESTER	DAMOISEAU	BEERNAERT	MINKOWSKI	KRAUSHAAR	ALEKSANDR
GORBACHEV	BERZELIUS	TACHENIUS	DICKINSON	BROUNCKER	MUSSOLINI	MILESTONE	ANACHARIS
GUSTAFSON	BIRKELAND	TINBERGEN	FABRICIUS	BUTENANDT	NICHOLSON	PRIESTLEY	BEERNAERT
KARDASHEV	BLAKESLEE	TSCHERMAK	FERDINAND	CAVENDISH	PETROSIAN	ROUSSELOT	BOERHAAVE
KATHARINE	BRACEWELL	VINCENZIO	FLORIMOND	DECONCINI	PHILOLAUS	SABASTIAN	BURKHARDT
KENZABURO	BRODERICK	WASSERMAN	GABRIELLA	DOMINIQUE	PRIGOGINE	SEBASTIAN	BUTENANDT
LANCASTER	CALLENDAR	WEDGEWOOD	GABRIELLE	EDDINGTON	SHOLOKHOV	STRASSMAN	CLEOPATRA
LECLANCHE	CARPENTER	WETHERALD	GUGLIELMO	EHRENBERG	SOPHOCLES	TOUSSIENG	ECHEGARAY
MCQUARRIE	CASSERIUS	WHITEHEAD	HEAVISIDE	EILENBERG	VANNOCCIO	TUNNSTALL	FAIRBAIRN
MICHAELIS	CHAYEFSKY	WITHERING	HENRIETTA	ELLENSHAW	CLEOPATRA	VIEUSSENS	FERCHAULT
MONTANARI	CHERENKOV	ZACHERIAS	HYACINTHE	FIBONACCI	EURIPIDES	WAHLSTROM	FIBONACCI
NATHANAEL	CLAPEYRON	ZINNEMANN	JUSTINIAN	GEGENBAUR	JOSEPHINE	WEISSKOPF	GOLDHABER
NATHANIEL	CLEVELAND	CORNFORTH	KISSINGER	GEMINIANO	JOSEPHSON	WEISSMANN	GUILLAUME
SALVATORE	COCKERELL	GOTTFRIED	LAVOISIER	GIANNETTI	NICEPHORE	WOLFSKEHL	HECATAEUS
SILLANPAA	CORNEILLE	KARLFELDT	LEUCIPPUS	GREENBERG	OENOPIDES	ARBUTHNOT	KURCHATOV
TARTAGLIA	CORNELIUS	SCHAFFNER	MACMILLAN	GREENWOOD	THEOPHILE	ARISTIDES	MOSSBAUER
VERNADSKY	DAUBENTON	SIEGFRIED	MARTINSON	GRUENTZIG	ALBERTSON	ARISTOTLE	NICOLAIER
VESPASIAN	FESSENDEN	WHINFIELD	MCALISTER	GUTENBERG	ALDEROTTI	ARMSTRONG	RAINWATER
WILLADSEN	FREDERICK	AFRAGAMUS	MEHRINGER	HEMINGWAY	ALGAROTTI	CAROTHERS	SEMIRAMIS
WOLLASTON	FULLERTON	BOURGEOIS	MORTILLET	JOHANNSEN	AMMERMANN	CRISTIANI	TAKAHASHI
ARYABHATA	GILLESPIE	ECHEGARAY	NISHIJIMA	LEMONOSOV	ARKWRIGHT	FRONTINUS	WHITTAKER
CONYBEARE	GROTEFEND	SOSIGENES	PARKINSON	LOMONOSOV	DESARGUES	GROTTHUSS	ARCHIBALD
ESTABROOK	HAFFENDEN	TANIGUCHI	PERCIVALL	MCCONNELL	FEUERBACH	HAUPTMANN	AULENBACK
FAIRBAIRN	HAHNEMANN	ANACHARIS	PHILIPPUS	MECHNIKOV	GOODRICKE	HECATAEUS	CTESIBIUS
LINDBERGH	HELVETIUS	BARGHOORN	QUASIMODO	NIRENBERG	HASBROUCK	SPITTELER	EHRENBERG
MOSSBAUER	HENDERSON	BARTHOLIN	RAWLINSON	OLDENBURG	LAMORISSE	WHITTAKER	EILENBERG
RIGOBERTA	HOLLERITH	BEKTHEREV	REVEILLON	RAMANUJAN	LEDERBERG	BECQUEREL	ELIZABETH
SCAEBERLE	JEFFERSON	BERTHELOT	SCHWINGER	ROMANENKO	LENORMAND	BURGUNDIO	FEUERBACH
BEAUCHAMP	JORGENSEN	BOERHAAVE	SRINIVASA	ROSENBAUM	LEVERRIER	HAMMURABI	GEGENBAUR
BIANCHINI	JORGENSON	BURKHARDT	STANISLAO	ROSENBERG	MACARTHUR	MCDOUGALL	GREENBERG
BLANCHARD	KETTERING	EINTHOVEN	STANISLAW	SCHONBEIN	MAHARIDGE	SCHAUDINN	GUTENBERG
CHURCHILL	KOBREUTER	FERCHAULT	STREISAND	SCHONLEIN	MCCORMICK	SERTURNER	KENZABURO
COCKCROFT	KOENEKAMP	FRUCHTMAN	WILKINSON	STEENBERG	ROBERTSON	VAUQUELIN	LEDERBERG
DIRICHLET	KOLREUTER	GOLDHABER	BJORKHOLM	STEENBOCK	SEMIRAMIS	VESPUSIUS	NIRENBERG
FRANCESCO	KRONECKER	HITCHINGS	FRANKLAND	STEINBECK	SODERBLOM	VITRUVIUS	

							7TH LETTER	
OLDENBURG	ROMANENKO	FRONTINUS	DALRYMPLE	ARISTOTLE	WARBURTON	SEBASTIAN		HAMMURABI
ROOZEBOOM	ROUSSELOT	GANSWINDT	FLORIMOND	BARGHOORN	WASSERMAN	SHECHTMAN		HAUPTMANN
ROSENBAUM	SCAEBERLE	GASCOIGNE	FORSSMANN	BARTHOLIN	WETHERALD	TARANTINO		KOENEKAMP
ROSENBERG	SOSIGENES	GEMINIANO	FRIEDMANN	CORNFORTH	WITHERING	TUNNSTALL		KRAUSHAAR
SCHONBEIN	SPITTELER	GOODRICKE	GRASSMANN	DIEUDONNE	ZACHERIAS	VALENTINA		LENORMAND
SCHULBERG	STAPLETON	GRANVILLE	HAHNEMANN	EINTHOVEN	ATANASOFF	VALENTINE		MACDONALD
SODERBLOM	TITCHENER	HITCHINGS	HAUPTMANN	FRANCOISE	BLAKESLEE	WAHLSTROM		MCDOUGALL
SPIELBERG	VAUQUELIN	HUTCHINGS	LENORMAND	HASBROUCK	DAMOISEAU	BERNOULLI		MONTANARI
STEENBERG	CHAYEFSKY	HUTCHISON	LOSCHMIDT	HAUSDORFF	DIONYSIUS	BURROUGHS		NATHANAEL
STEENBOCK	GROTEFEND	LAMORISSE	MCCORMICK	HERODOTUS	ELLENSHAW	KOBREUTER		NIEUWLAND
STEINBECK	GUSTAFSON	LATREILLE	QUASIMODO	LEMONOSOV	GILLESPIE	KOLREUTER		PERCIVALL
UHLENBECK	SCHAFFNER	LIOUVILLE	STEINMETZ	LOMONOSOV	HEAVISIDE	RAMANUJAN		PHILOLAUS
BOCCACCIO	SCHOEFFER	MAHARIDGE	WEISSMANN	MACEDONIO	KARDASHEV	TANIGUCHI		PRITCHARD
BROUNCKER	SOMERFELD	MECHNIKOV	ZINNEMANN	PROKHOROV	LANCASTER	BOSCOVICH		RORSCHACH
DECONCINI	BERNIGAUD	MIELZINER	ALEXANDER	PRUDHOMME	LAVOISIER	HEYROVSKY		ROSENBAUM
DUTROCHET	DESARGUES	MURCHISON	ALEXANDRE	RUHMKORFF	MCALISTER	IVANOVICH		SOUTHGATE
EUSTACHIO	EDDINGTON	OENOPIDES	ARRHENIUS	THEODORIC	PETROSIAN	IVANOVSKY		SRINIVASA
FABRICIUS	HEMINGWAY	SCHLEIDEN	ASERINSKY	THEODORUS	ROCHESTER	PERCIVALL		STEINKAMP
FROESCHEL	MCDOUGALL	SCHWEIZER	BARRINGER	WHITWORTH	STANISLAO	ROGGEVEEN		STREISAND
GORBACHEV	PRIGOGINE	SOUBEIRAN	BRACONNOT	ZSIGMONDY	STANISLAW	ROOSEVELT		TUNNSTALL
KRONECKER	SOUTHGATE	SUSSMILCH	BURGUNDIO	CALLIPPUS	STRASSMAN	SRINIVASA		WEISSMANN
SOPHOCLES	STROMGREN	TOUSSIENG	CALLENDAR	CESALPINO	STREISAND	VITRUVIUS		WETHERALD
VANNOCCIO	TARTAGLIA	WHINFIELD	CARPENTER	FALLOPIUS	SYLVESTER	BRACEWELL		WIESCHAUS
ALMENDROS	WILLUGHBY	NISHIJIMA	CHERENKOV	LEUCIPPUS	VESPASIAN	GREENWOOD		ZINNEMANN
ARFWEDSON	ARBUTHNOT	KOENEKAMP	DAUBENTON	PHILIPPUS	VESPUSIUS	JARNOWSKY		GOLDHABER
ARNOLDSON	ARYABHATA	SHOLOKHOV	DICKINSON	ARMSTRONG	VIEUSSENS	MINKOWSKI		BENEDICKS
CAVENDISH	BEAUCHAMP	STEINKAMP	FERDINAND	BAMBERGER	WLADYSLAW	WEDGEWOOD		BOCCACCIO
DONALDSON	BIANCHINI	WEISSKOPF	FESSENDEN	BESSARION	WOLLASTON	CLAPEYRON		CONDORCET
DUNALDSON	BJORKHOLM	WOLFSKEHL	FORLANINI	BRODERICK	ALBERTSON	HORODYSKY		CRESWICKE
GERALDINE	BLANCHARD	BATAILLON	GAZZANIGA	CASCARDIO	BEILSTEIN			FIBONACCI
SCHAUDINN	CAROTHERS	BENZELIUS	HAFFENDEN	CASSERIUS	BERGSTROM			GOODRICKE
THORNDIKE	CHURCHILL	BERZELIUS	HYACINTHE	COCKCROFT	BERNSTEIN			LECLANCHE
VERNADSKY	DIRICHLET	BIRKELAND	JOHANNSEN	COCKERELL	BORNSTEIN			TANIGUCHI
WILLADSEN	GROTTHUSS	CLEVELAND	JORGENSEN	CONDORCET	CHRISTAIN			VANNOCCIO
BECQUEREL	JOSEPHINE	CORNELIUS	JORGENSON	DESCARTES	CHRISTIAN		AMMERMANN	ALEXANDER
BEKTHEREV	JOSEPHSON	FRANKLAND	JUSTINIAN	DESMAREST	CHRISTINE		ARCHIBALD	ALEXANDRE
BENAVENTE	KIRCHHOFF	HIPPOLYTE	KISSINGER	ESTABROOK	CHRISTOFF		ARYABHATA	ARISTIDES
BENEDETTO	KRAUSHAAR	LLEWELLYN	LECLANCHE	FREDERICK	CHRISTOPH		AULENBACK	BURGUNDIO
BERTHELOT	NICEPHORE	MACMILLAN	MACDONALD	FRIEDRICH	CRONSTEDT		BEAUCHAMP	CALLENDAR
BOURGEOIS	PRITCHARD	MASKELYNE	MARTINSON	FULLERTON	DEMESTRAL		BERNIGAUD	CASCARDIO
CAILLETET	RORSCHACH	MAUROLICO	MCCONNELL	GOTTFRIED	FLAMSTEED		BIRKELAND	EURIPIDES
CLAUDETTE	STOICHEFF	MENDELEEV	MEHRINGER	HAMMURABI	FRUCHTMAN		BLANCHARD	FESSENDEN
CONYBEARE	STONEHILL	MICHELSON	MONTANARI	HENDERSON	GLADSTONE		BOERHAAVE	HAFFENDEN
DELEZENNE	THEOPHILE	MORTILLET	NATHANAEL	HOLLERITH	GOLDSTEIN		BOLTZMANN	MAHARIDGE
FRANCESCO	WHITEHEAD	MUSSOLINI	NATHANIEL	JEFFERSON	GOLDSTINE		CHRISTAIN	OENOPIDES
GABRIELLA	WIESCHAUS	NEETHLING	PARKINSON	KATHARINE	GOLDSTONE		CLEVELAND	POLLENDER
GABRIELLE	ARISTIDES	NICHOLSON	POLLENDER	KETTERING	GRUENTZIG		CONYBEARE	SCHLEIDEN
GIANNETTI	ARKWRIGHT	NIEUWLAND	RAWLINSON	LEVERRIER	HELVETIUS		CRISTIANI	BEERNAERT
GJELLERUP	BENEDICKS	PHILOLAUS	SCHWINGER	MCPHERSON	JOHNSTONE		FERDINAND	BEILSTEIN
GUGLIELMO	CAVALIERI	REVEILLON	SILLANPAA	MCQUARRIE	LUCRETIUS		FEUERBACH	BERNSTEIN
GUILLEMIN	CORNEILLE	SCHONLEIN	STEVENSON	NICKERSON	MACARTHUR		FORSSMANN	BORNSTEIN
HENRIETTA	CRESWICKE	STRADLING	TACHENIUS	PASTERNAK	MILESTONE		FRANKLAND	BRACEWELL
KARLFELDT	CRISTIANI	ALTRAMURA	VINCENZIO	PICKERING	PELLETIER		FRIEDMANN	CAROTHERS
LINDBERGH	DOMINIQUE	AMMERMANN	WILKINSON	SERTURNER	PRIESTLEY		GEGENBAUR	CAVALIERI
MICHAELIS	EUPALINUS	BALTIMORE	AGRAMONTE	SIEGFRIED	ROBERTSON		GEMINIANO	COCKERELL
RIGOBERTA	EURIPIDES	BARRYMORE	ALDEROTTI	TINBERGEN	SABASTIAN		GRASSMANN	CRONSTEDT
ROCCHETTI	FRANCISCO	BOLTZMANN	ALGAROTTI	TSCHERMAK	SALVATORE		HAHNEMANN	DAMOISEAU

DESMAREST	BRODERICK	VESPASIAN	DIEUDONNE	GJELLERUP	BENEDETTO	PASTERNAK	CONDORCET
EHRENBERG	CASSERIUS	VESPUSIUS	EUPALINUS	HAUSDORFF	CAILLETET	PETROSIAN	DESARGUES
EILENBERG	CAVENDISH	VITRUVIUS	FRONTINUS	LINDBERGH	CARPENTER	RAMANUJAN	DESCARTES
ELIZABETH	CESALPINO	WITHERING	GANSWINDT	MCQUARRIE	CLAUDETTE	SABASTIAN	DIRICHLET
FLAMSTEED	CHRISTIAN	ZACHERIAS	HITCHINGS	PROKHOROV	CLEOPATRA	SEBASTIAN	DUTROCHET
GOLDSTEIN	CHRISTINE	RAMANUJAN	HUTCHINGS	RIGOBERTA	DAUBENTON	SHECHTMAN	EINTHOVEN
GREENBERG	CHURCHILL	BROUNCKER	MACEDONIO	RUHMKORFF	DESCARTES	SILLANPAA	EURIPIDES
GROTEFEND	CORNELIUS	CHERENKOV	MIELZINER	SCAEBERLE	EDDINGTON	SOUBEIRAN	FESSENDEN
GUTENBERG	CTESIBIUS	KRONECKER	PASTERNAK	SOUBEIRAN	FULLERTON	STANISLAO	FLAMSTEED
HECATAEUS	DECONCINI	MECHNIKOV	ROMANENKO	STROMGREN	GIANNETTI	STANISLAW	FROESCHEL
LEDERBERG	DIONYSIUS	WHITTAKER	SCHAFFNER	THEODORIC	HENRIETTA	STRASSMAN	GOLDHABER
MCCONNELL	FABRICIUS	BARTHOLIN	SERTURNER	THEODORUS	HERODOTUS	TSCHERMAK	GORBACHEV
MENDELEEV	FAIRBAIRN	BATAILLON	SOSIGENES	WAHLSTROM	HYACINTHE	VESPASIAN	GOTTFRIED
NIRENBERG	FALLOPIUS	BERNOULLI	TITCHENER	WHITWORTH	KOBREUTER	WASSERMAN	HAFFENDEN
ROGGEVEEN	FORLANINI	BERTHELOT	ZSIGMONDY	ALBERTSON	KOLREUTER	WHITEHEAD	JOHANNSEN
ROOSEVELT	FRANCOISE	BLAKESLEE	ARMSTRONG	ARFWEDSON	KURCHATOV	WLADYSLAW	JORGENSEN
ROSENBERG	FREDERICK	CORNEILLE	ATANASOFF	ARNOLDSON	LANCASTER	ZACHERIAS	KARDASHEV
SCHONBEIN	FRIEDRICH	DIRICHLET	BALTIMORE	ASERINSKY	MCALISTER	HAMMURABI	KISSINGER
SCHONLEIN	GAZZANIGA	GABRIELLA	BARGHOORN	CHAYEFSKY	RAINWATER	WILLUGHBY	KOBREUTER
SCHULBERG	GERALDINE	GABRIELLE	BARRYMORE	DICKINSON	ROCCHETTI	AULENBACK	KOLREUTER
SOMERFELD	GOLDSTINE	GRANVILLE	BJORKHOLM	DONALDSON	ROCHESTER	BOSCOVICH	KRONECKER
SPIELBERG	GOTTFRIED	GUGLIELMO	BOURGEOIS	DUNALDSON	STAPLETON	BRODERICK	LANCASTER
STEENBERG	HEAVISIDE	KARLFELDT	CHRISTOFF	FRANCESCO	SYLVESTER	FEUERBACH	LAVOISIER
STEINBECK	HELVETIUS	LATREILLE	CHRISTOPH	FRANCISCO	WARBURTON	FIBONACCI	LEVERRIER
STEINMETZ	HOLLERITH	LIOUVILLE	COCKCROFT	GUSTAFSON	WOLLASTON	FRANCESCO	MCALISTER
STOICHEFF	IVANOVICH	LLEWELLYN	ESTABROOK	HENDERSON	ALTRAMURA	FRANCISCO	MEHRINGER
TOUSSIENG	JOSEPHINE	MACMILLAN	FLORIMOND	HEYROVSKY	DESARGUES	FREDERICK	MENDELEEV
UHLENBECK	JUSTINIAN	MICHAELIS	GLADSTONE	HORODYSKY	FERCHAULT	FRIEDRICH	MIELZINER
VIEUSSENS	KATHARINE	MORTILLET	GOLDSTONE	HUTCHISON	GROTTHUSS	HASBROUCK	MORTILLET
WHINFIELD	KETTERING	PRIESTLEY	GREENWOOD	IVANOVSKY	GUILLAUME	IVANOVICH	MOSSBAUER
WHITEHEAD	LAVOISIER	REVEILLON	JOHNSTONE	JARNOWSKY	HASBROUCK	MAUROLICO	NATHANAEL
WOLFSKEHL	LEVERRIER	ROUSSELOT	KIRCHHOFF	JEFFERSON	KENZABURO	MCCORMICK	NATHANIEL
SCHOEFFER	LOSCHMIDT	SODERBLOM	MILESTONE	JOHANNSEN	MOSSBAUER	RORSCHACH	NICOLAIER
ARKWRIGHT	LUCRETIUS	SOPHOCLES	NICEPHORE	JORGENSEN	OLDENBURG	STEENBOCK	OENOPIDES
BAMBERGER	MAUROLICO	SPITTELER	QUASIMODO	JORGENSON	EINTHOVEN	STEINBECK	PELLETIER
BARRINGER	MCCORMICK	STANISLAO	ROOZEBOOM	JOSEPHSON	HEMINGWAY	SUSSMILCH	POLLENDER
BURROUGHS	MUSSOLINI	STANISLAW	SALVATORE	LAMORISSE	HIPPOLYTE	UHLENBECK	PRIESTLEY
GASCOIGNE	NATHANIEL	SUSSMILCH	STEENBOCK	LEMONOSOV	MASKELYNE	ALEKSANDR	RAINWATER
KISSINGER	NEETHLING	TARTAGLIA	WEDGEWOOD	LOMONOSOV	GRUENTZIG	BURKHARDT	ROCHESTER
MEHRINGER	NICOLAIER	VAUQUELIN	WEISSKOPF	MARTINSON	SCHWEIZER	BUTENANDT	ROGGEVEEN
SCHWINGER	NISHIJIMA	WLADYSLAW	CALLIPPUS	MCPHERSON	VINCENZIO	CRONSTEDT	SCHAFFNER
TINBERGEN	PELLETIER	AFRAGAMUS	DALRYMPLE	MICHELSON		GANSWINDT	SCHLEIDEN
DUTROCHET	PETROSIAN	FRUCHTMAN	GILLESPIE	MINKOWSKI		HEAVISIDE	SCHOEFFER
ELLENSHAW	PICKERING	GUILLEMIN	LEUCIPPUS	MURCHISON		KARLFELDT	SCHWEIZER
EUSTACHIO	PRIGOGINE	PRUDHOMME	PHILIPPUS	NICHOLSON	**8TH LETTER**	LOSCHMIDT	SCHWINGER
FROESCHEL	SABASTIAN	SEMIRAMIS	SILLANPAA	NICKERSON		QUASIMODO	SERTURNER
GORBACHEV	SCHAUDINN	SHECHTMAN	DOMINIQUE	PARKINSON	CALLENDAR	ZSIGMONDY	SIEGFRIED
KARDASHEV	SEBASTIAN	STRASSMAN	ALMENDROS	RAWLINSON	CHRISTIAN	ALEXANDER	SOPHOCLES
MACARTHUR	SIEGFRIED	TSCHERMAK	ANACHARIS	ROBERTSON	DAMOISEAU	ARISTIDES	SOSIGENES
SHOLOKHOV	STONEHILL	WASSERMAN	BECQUEREL	STEVENSON	DEMESTRAL	BAMBERGER	SPITTELER
WILLUGHBY	STRADLING	AGRAMONTE	BEKTHEREV	TAKAHASHI	ECHEGARAY	BARRINGER	STROMGREN
ARRHENIUS	TACHENIUS	ALEKSANDR	BERGSTROM	VERNADSKY	ELLENSHAW	BECQUEREL	SYLVESTER
BENZELIUS	TARANTINO	ARBUTHNOT	BURKHARDT	WILKINSON	FRUCHTMAN	BEKTHEREV	TINBERGEN
BERZELIUS	THEOPHILE	BENAVENTE	CLAPEYRON	WILLADSEN	HEMINGWAY	BLAKESLEE	TITCHENER
BESSARION	THORNDIKE	BRACONNOT	CORNFORTH	ALDEROTTI	JUSTINIAN	BROUNCKER	WHITTAKER
BIANCHINI	VALENTINA	BUTENANDT	DEMESTRAL	ALGAROTTI	KRAUSHAAR	CAILLETET	WILLADSEN
BOSCOVICH	VALENTINE	DELEZENNE	ECHEGARAY	ARISTOTLE	MACMILLAN	CARPENTER	ATANASOFF

					9TH LETTER		
CHRISTOFF	ARCHIBALD	GOLDSTONE	MARTINSON	LAMORISSE	ALTRAMURA	GASCOIGNE	WITHERING
COCKCROFT	ARISTOTLE	GRASSMANN	MCPHERSON	SRINIVASA	ARYABHATA	GERALDINE	BOSCOVICH
HAUSDORFF	BERNOULLI	GROTEFEND	MECHNIKOV	AGRAMONTE	CLEOPATRA	GILLESPIE	CAVENDISH
KIRCHHOFF	BJORKHOLM	HAHNEMANN	MICHELSON	ALDEROTTI	GABRIELLA	GLADSTONE	CHRISTOPH
RUHMKORFF	BRACEWELL	HAUPTMANN	MURCHISON	ALGAROTTI	GAZZANIGA	GOLDSTINE	CORNFORTH
STOICHEFF	CHURCHILL	JOHNSTONE	NICHOLSON	ARYABHATA	HENRIETTA	GOLDSTONE	ELIZABETH
GAZZANIGA	COCKERELL	JOSEPHINE	NICKERSON	BENAVENTE	NISHIJIMA	GOODRICKE	FEUERBACH
HITCHINGS	CORNEILLE	KATHARINE	PARKINSON	BENEDETTO	RIGOBERTA	GRANVILLE	FRIEDRICH
HUTCHINGS	DALRYMPLE	KETTERING	PROKHOROV	CLAUDETTE	SILLANPAA	GUILLAUME	HOLLERITH
LINDBERGH	FERCHAULT	LENORMAND	RAWLINSON	CORNFORTH	SRINIVASA	HEAVISIDE	IVANOVICH
MAHARIDGE	GABRIELLA	MASKELYNE	REVEILLON	ELIZABETH	TARTAGLIA	HIPPOLYTE	LINDBERGH
ARKWRIGHT	GABRIELLE	MILESTONE	ROBERTSON	GIANNETTI	VALENTINA	HYACINTHE	RORSCHACH
BURROUGHS	GRANVILLE	MUSSOLINI	ROOZEBOOM	HENRIETTA	THEODORIC	JOHNSTONE	SUSSMILCH
HYACINTHE	LATREILLE	NEETHLING	ROUSSELOT	HIPPOLYTE	ARCHIBALD	JOSEPHINE	WHITWORTH
LECLANCHE	LIOUVILLE	NIEUWLAND	SHOLOKHOV	HOLLERITH	BERNIGAUD	KATHARINE	ALDEROTTI
TAKAHASHI	MACDONALD	PICKERING	SODERBLOM	RIGOBERTA	BIRKELAND	LAMORISSE	ALGAROTTI
TANIGUCHI	MCCONNELL	PRIGOGINE	STAPLETON	ROCCHETTI	BLANCHARD	LATREILLE	BERNOULLI
WOLFSKEHL	MCDOUGALL	SCHAUDINN	STEVENSON	SOUTHGATE	BIRKELAND	LECLANCHE	BIANCHINI
ANACHARIS	PERCIVALL	STRADLING	WAHLSTROM	STEINMETZ	BLANCHARD	LIOUVILLE	CAVALIERI
BARTHOLIN	ROOSEVELT	STREISAND	WARBURTON	WHITWORTH	CLEVELAND	MAHARIDGE	CRISTIANI
BEILSTEIN	SCAEBERLE	TARANTINO	WEDGEWOOD	AFRAGAMUS	FERDINAND	MASKELYNE	DECONCINI
BERNSTEIN	SOMERFELD	TOUSSIENG	WILKINSON	ARRHENIUS	FLAMSTEED	MCQUARRIE	FIBONACCI
BOCCACCIO	STONEHILL	VALENTINA	WOLLASTON	BENZELIUS	FLORIMOND	MILESTONE	FORLANINI
BORNSTEIN	THEOPHILE	VALENTINE	CHRISTOPH	BERNIGAUD	FRANKLAND	NICEPHORE	GIANNETTI
BOURGEOIS	TUNNSTALL	VIEUSSENS	WEISSKOPF	BERZELIUS	GOTTFRIED	PRIGOGINE	HAMMURABI
BURGUNDIO	WETHERALD	WEISSMANN	ALEXANDRE	CALLIPPUS	GREENWOOD	PRUDHOMME	MINKOWSKI
CASCARDIO	WHINFIELD	WITHERING	ALTRAMURA	CASSERIUS	GROTEFEND	SALVATORE	MONTANARI
CHRISTAIN	BEAUCHAMP	ZINNEMANN	BALTIMORE	CORNELIUS	LENORMAND	SCAEBERLE	MUSSOLINI
EUSTACHIO	GUGLIELMO	ALBERTSON	BARGHOORN	CTESIBIUS	MACDONALD	SOUTHGATE	ROCCHETTI
GILLESPIE	GUILLAUME	ALMENDROS	BARRYMORE	DIONYSIUS	NIEUWLAND	THEOPHILE	TAKAHASHI
GOLDSTEIN	KOENEKAMP	ARBUTHNOT	BEERNAERT	DOMINIQUE	PRITCHARD	THORNDIKE	TANIGUCHI
GRUENTZIG	NISHIJIMA	ARFWEDSON	BLANCHARD	EUPALINUS	SIEGFRIED	VALENTINE	AULENBACK
GUILLEMIN	PRUDHOMME	ARNOLDSON	CAROTHERS	FABRICIUS	SOMERFELD	ATANASOFF	BRODERICK
MACEDONIO	STEINKAMP	BATAILLON	CAVALIERI	FALLOPIUS	STREISAND	CHRISTOFF	ESTABROOK
MCQUARRIE	AMMERMANN	BERGSTROM	CLEOPATRA	FRONTINUS	WEDGEWOOD	HAUSDORFF	FREDERICK
MICHAELIS	ARMSTRONG	BERTHELOT	CONYBEARE	GEGENBAUR	WETHERALD	KIRCHHOFF	HASBROUCK
SCHONBEIN	BIANCHINI	BESSARION	EHRENBERG	GJELLERUP	WHINFIELD	RUHMKORFF	MCCORMICK
SCHONLEIN	BIRKELAND	BRACONNOT	EILENBERG	HECATAEUS	WHITEHEAD	STOICHEFF	PASTERNAK
SEMIRAMIS	BOLTZMANN	CHERENKOV	FAIRBAIRN	HELVETIUS	AGRAMONTE	WEISSKOPF	STEENBOCK
TARTAGLIA	CESALPINO	CLAPEYRON	GREENBERG	HERODOTUS	ALEXANDRE	ARMSTRONG	STEINBECK
THEODORIC	CHRISTINE	DAUBENTON	GUTENBERG	LEUCIPPUS	ARISTOTLE	EHRENBERG	TSCHERMAK
VANNOCCIO	CLEVELAND	DICKINSON	KENZABURO	LUCRETIUS	BALTIMORE	EILENBERG	UHLENBECK
VAUQUELIN	CRISTIANI	DONALDSON	LEDERBERG	MACARTHUR	BARRYMORE	GREENBERG	BECQUEREL
VINCENZIO	DECONCINI	DUNALDSON	MONTANARI	PHILIPPUS	BENAVENTE	GRUENTZIG	BRACEWELL
ASERINSKY	DELEZENNE	EDDINGTON	NICEPHORE	PHILOLAUS	BLAKESLEE	GUTENBERG	CHURCHILL
BENEDICKS	DIEUDONNE	ESTABROOK	NIRENBERG	ROSENBAUM	BOERHAAVE	KETTERING	COCKERELL
CHAYEFSKY	FERDINAND	FULLERTON	OLDENBURG	TACHENIUS	CHRISTINE	LEDERBERG	DEMESTRAL
CRESWICKE	FLORIMOND	GREENWOOD	PRITCHARD	THEODORUS	CLAUDETTE	NEETHLING	FROESCHEL
GOODRICKE	FORLANINI	GUSTAFSON	ROSENBERG	VESPUSIUS	CONYBEARE	NIRENBERG	MCCONNELL
HEYROVSKY	FORSSMANN	HENDERSON	SALVATORE	VITRUVIUS	CORNEILLE	OLDENBURG	MCDOUGALL
HORODYSKY	FRANKLAND	HUTCHISON	SCHULBERG	WIESCHAUS	CRESWICKE	PICKERING	NATHANAEL
IVANOVSKY	FRIEDMANN	JEFFERSON	SPIELBERG	BOERHAAVE	DALRYMPLE	ROSENBERG	NATHANIEL
JARNOWSKY	GASCOIGNE	JORGENSON	STEENBERG	LLEWELLYN	DELEZENNE	SCHULBERG	PERCIVALL
MINKOWSKI	GEMINIANO	JOSEPHSON	CAVENDISH		DIEUDONNE	SPIELBERG	STONEHILL
ROMANENKO	GERALDINE	KURCHATOV	DESMAREST		DOMINIQUE	STEENBERG	TUNNSTALL
THORNDIKE	GLADSTONE	LEMONOSOV	FRANCOISE		FRANCOISE	STRADLING	WOLFSKEHL
VERNADSKY	GOLDSTINE	LOMONOSOV	GROTTHUSS		GABRIELLE	TOUSSIENG	BERGSTROM

BJORKHOLM	RAMANUJAN	GEGENBAUR	HUTCHINGS	HEYROVSKY	CAVANILLES	KAMERLINGH
ROOZEBOOM	RAWLINSON	GOLDHABER	LEUCIPPUS	HORODYSKY	CHAMBERLIN	KLEBESADEL
ROSENBAUM	REVEILLON	KISSINGER	LUCRETIUS	IVANOVSKY	CHARDONNET	KOMUNYAKAA
SODERBLOM	ROBERTSON	KOBREUTER	MICHAELIS	JARNOWSKY	CHRISTIAAN	KONSTANTIN
WAHLSTROM	ROGGEVEEN	KOLREUTER	OENOPIDES	PRIESTLEY	CHRISTIANE	KOURGANOFF
ALBERTSON	SABASTIAN	KRAUSHAAR	PHILIPPUS	VERNADSKY	CHRISTOPHE	KOVALEVSKI
AMMERMANN	SCHAUDINN	KRONECKER	PHILOLAUS	WILLUGHBY	CLATWORTHY	KOVALEVSKY
ARFWEDSON	SCHLEIDEN	LANCASTER	SEMIRAMIS	ZSIGMONDY	CLOUDESLEY	KRETSCHMER
ARNOLDSON	SCHONBEIN	LAVOISIER	SOPHOCLES	STEINMETZ	COPERNICUS	LAGERKVIST
BARGHOORN	SCHONLEIN	LEVERRIER	SOSIGENES		COURCHESNE	LAMBERTSON
BARTHOLIN	SEBASTIAN	MACARTHUR	TACHENIUS		CRUIKSHANK	LANGERHANS
BATAILLON	SHECHTMAN	MCALISTER	THEODORUS		CUNNINGHAM	LAURENTINE
BEILSTEIN	SOUBEIRAN	MEHRINGER	VESPUSIUS		DEMOCRITUS	LILIENTHAL
BERNSTEIN	STAPLETON	MIELZINER	VIEUSSENS	**10 LETTER**	DESIDERIUS	LIPPERSHEY
BESSARION	STEVENSON	MOSSBAUER	VITRUVIUS	**1ST LETTER**	DIOPHANTUS	MACFARLANE
BOLTZMANN	STRASSMAN	NICOLAIER	WIESCHAUS		DOBEREINER	MAIMONIDES
BORNSTEIN	STROMGREN	PELLETIER	ZACHERIAS	ALDROVANDI	DOBZHANSKY	MANCHESTER
CHRISTAIN	TINBERGEN	POLLENDER	ARBUTHNOT	ALEIXANDRE	DORNBERGER	MANDELBROT
CHRISTIAN	VAUQUELIN	RAINWATER	ARKWRIGHT	ALESSANDRO	EBBINGHAUS	MANKIEWICZ
CLAPEYRON	VESPASIAN	ROCHESTER	BEERNAERT	ALLESANDRO	EHRENFRIED	MARGUERITE
DAUBENTON	WARBURTON	SCHAFFNER	BERTHELOT	ANAXAGORAS	EISENHOWER	MASCHERONI
DICKINSON	WASSERMAN	SCHOEFFER	BRACONNOT	ANAXIMENES	EIZAGUIRRE	MAXIMILIAN
DONALDSON	WEISSMANN	SCHWEIZER	BURKHARDT	ANDREEVICH	EMPEDOCLES	MCCLINTOCK
DUNALDSON	WILKINSON	SCHWINGER	BUTENANDT	ANDRONIKOS	ENGELBREGT	MCCULLOUGH
EDDINGTON	WILLADSEN	SERTURNER	CAILLETET	APOLLONIUS	ERLENMEYER	MENAECHMUS
EINTHOVEN	WOLLASTON	SPITTELER	COCKCROFT	ARCHDEACON	FAHRENHEIT	MERRIFIELD
FAIRBAIRN	ZINNEMANN	SYLVESTER	CONDORCET	ARCHIMEDES	FEIGENBAUM	MONTALCINI
FESSENDEN	BENEDETTO	TITCHENER	CRONSTEDT	ARGELANDER	FERDINANDO	MOOKHERJEE
FORSSMANN	BOCCACCIO	WHITTAKER	DESMAREST	ARISTIPPUS	FITZGERALD	MUGGLESTON
FRIEDMANN	BURGUNDIO	AFRAGAMUS	DIRICHLET	ATHANASIUS	FOETTINGER	NEMORARIUS
FRUCHTMAN	CASCARDIO	ALMENDROS	DUTROCHET	BARKHAUSEN	FOTHERGILL	NEUGEBAUER
FULLERTON	CESALPINO	ANACHARIS	FERCHAULT	BARTOLEMEO	FOTOPOULOS	NIKOLAYEVA
GOLDSTEIN	EUSTACHIO	ARISTIDES	GANSWINDT	BARTOLOMEU	FRACASTORO	OTTAVIOANO
GRASSMANN	FRANCESCO	ARRHENIUS	KARLFELDT	BEIJERINCK	FRANCISCUS	PACHACUTEC
GUILLEMIN	FRANCISCO	BENEDICKS	LOSCHMIDT	BELOZERSKY	FRIEDERICH	PARACELSUS
GUSTAFSON	GEMINIANO	BENZELIUS	MORTILLET	BENZENBERG	GALSWORTHY	PARMENIDES
HAFFENDEN	GUGLIELMO	BERZELIUS	ROOSEVELT	BERNARDINO	GELLIBRAND	PASQUALINO
HAHNEMANN	KENZABURO	BOURGEOIS	ROUSSELOT	BERTHOLLET	GIORDMAINE	PHILOPONUS
HAUPTMANN	MACEDONIO	BURROUGHS	DAMOISEAU	BERTOLUCCI	GOLDBERGER	PIRANDELLO
HENDERSON	MAUROLICO	CALLIPPUS	BEKTHEREV	BIGELEISEN	GREENSTEIN	POCAHONTAS
HUTCHISON	QUASIMODO	CAROTHERS	CHERENKOV	BLUMENBACH	GULLSTRAND	POGGENDORF
JEFFERSON	ROMANENKO	CASSERIUS	GORBACHEV	BLUMENTHAL	HARGREAVES	POISEUILLE
JOHANNSEN	STANISLAO	CORNELIUS	KARDASHEV	BODENSTEIN	HARRINGTON	PRAXAGORAS
JORGENSEN	TARANTINO	CTESIBIUS	KURCHATOV	BRANSFIELD	HEISENBERG	PRINGSHEIM
JORGENSON	VANNOCCIO	DESARGUES	LEMONOSOV	BRETHERTON	HELLRIEGEL	PROTAGORAS
JOSEPHSON	VINCENZIO	DESCARTES	LOMONOSOV	BRETONNEAU	HERACLITUS	PYTHAGORAS
JUSTINIAN	BEAUCHAMP	DIONYSIUS	MECHNIKOV	BROCKHOUSE	HEROPHILUS	RAMMAZZINI
LLEWELLYN	GJELLERUP	EUPALINUS	MENDELEEV	CALLINICUS	HERSCHBACH	REICHSTEIN
MACMILLAN	KOENEKAMP	EURIPIDES	PROKHOROV	CAMERARIUS	HEYDENBERG	RICHARDSON
MARTINSON	STEINKAMP	FABRICIUS	SHOLOKHOV	CAMPANELLA	HIERONYMUS	ROKITANSKY
MCPHERSON	ALEKSANDR	FALLOPIUS	ELLENSHAW	CANNIZZARO	HIPPARCHUS	RUTHERFORD
MICHELSON	ALEXANDER	FRONTINUS	STANISLAW	CARMICHAEL	HOFMESITER	RUTTENBERG
MURCHISON	BAMBERGER	GROTTHUSS	WLADYSLAW	CARRINGTON	HOFSTADTER	SACROBOSCO
NICHOLSON	BARRINGER	HECATAEUS	ASERINSKY	CARTWRIGHT	HOLLDOBLER	SAMUELSSON
NICKERSON	BROUNCKER	HELVETIUS	CHAYEFSKY	CASSEGRAIN	HOUNSFIELD	SANCTORIUS
PARKINSON	CALLENDAR	HERODOTUS	ECHEGARAY	CASSINELLI	INGENHOUSZ	SCARFIOTTI
PETROSIAN	CARPENTER	HITCHINGS	HEMINGWAY	CATHERWOOD	IOSIFOVICH	SCHEUCHZER

SCHICKARDT
SCHLIEMANN
SCHRIEFFER
SCHUMACHER
SCHWEIGGER
SCHWEITZER
SEFERIADIS
SEMENOVICH
SENEFELDER
SHINGLETON
SHKLOVSKII
SILLIPHANT
SKLODOWSKA
SKOBELTZYN
SOMERVILLE
SOMMEILLER
SONNENBERG
SPIEGELMAN
STAHLECKER
STAUDINGER
STEINHARDT
STEPHENSON
STRESEMANN
STROHMEYER
STROMINGER
STURTEVANT
SUTHERLAND
SWAMMERDAM
SWEDENBORG
SZYMBORSKA
TAVOULARIS
TEISSERENC
TERESHKOVA
THEAETETUS
THEODOSIUS
THUCYDIDES
TISSANDIER
TORRICELLI
TOSCANELLI
TREVITHICK
TRUTFETTER
TSCHIRIKOV
VERROCCHIO
VINOGRADOV
WARRINGTON
WATERHOUSE
WEATHERWAX
WEIZSACKER
WETHERHILL
WHEATSTONE
WILLEBRORD
WILLIAMSON
WISLICENUS
WROBLEWSKI
WUNDERLICH
XENOPHANES
ZEHETBAUER

Column 2 — 2ND LETTER

BARKHAUSEN
BARTOLEMEO
BARTOLOMEU
CALLINICUS
CAMERARIUS
CAMPANELLA
CANNIZZARO
CARMICHAEL
CARRINGTON
CARTWRIGHT
CASSEGRAIN
CASSINELLI
CATHERWOOD
CAVANILLES
FAHRENHEIT
GALSWORTHY
HARGREAVES
HARRINGTON
KAMERLINGH
LAGERKVIST
LAMBERTSON
LANGERHANS
LAURENTINE
MACFARLANE
MAIMONIDES
MANCHESTER
MANDELBROT
MANKIEWICZ
MARGUERITE
MASCHERONI
MAXIMILIAN
PACHACUTEC
PARACELSUS
PARMENIDES
PASQUALINO
RAMMAZZINI
SACROBOSCO
SAMUELSSON
SANCTORIUS
TAVOULARIS
WARRINGTON
WATERHOUSE
EBBINGHAUS
MCCLINTOCK
MCCULLOUGH
SCARFIOTTI
SCHEUCHZER
SCHICKARDT
SCHLIEMANN
SCHRIEFFER
SCHUMACHER
SCHWEIGGER
SCHWEITZER
BEIJERINCK
BELOZERSKY

BENZENBERG
BERNARDINO
BERTHOLLET
BERTOLUCCI
DEMOCRITUS
DESIDERIUS
FEIGENBAUM
FERDINANDO
GELLIBRAND
HEISENBERG
HELLRIEGEL
HERACLITUS
HEROPHILUS
HERSCHBACH
HEYDENBERG
MENAECHMUS
MERRIFIELD
NEMORARIUS
NEUGEBAUER
REICHSTEIN
SEFERIADIS
SEMENOVICH
SENEFELDER
TEISSERENC
TERESHKOVA
VERROCCHIO
WEATHERWAX
WEIZSACKER
WETHERHILL
XENOPHANES
ZEHETBAUER
CHAMBERLIN
CHARDONNET
CHRISTIAAN
CHRISTIANE
CHRISTOPHE
EHRENFRIED
PHILOPONUS
SHINGLETON
SHKLOVSKII
THEAETETUS
THEODOSIUS
THUCYDIDES
WHEATSTONE
BIGELEISEN
DIOPHANTUS
EISENHOWER
EIZAGUIRRE
FITZGERALD
GIORDMAINE
HIERONYMUS
HIPPARCHUS
LILIENTHAL
LIPPERSHEY
NIKOLAYEVA
PIRANDELLO
RICHARDSON

SILLIPHANT
TISSANDIER
VINOGRADOV
WILLEBRORD
WILLIAMSON
WISLICENUS
SKLODOWSKA
SKOBELTZYN
ALDROVANDI
ALEIXANDRE
ALESSANDRO
ALLESANDRO
BLUMENBACH
BLUMENTHAL
CLATWORTHY
CLOUDESLEY
KLEBESADEL
EMPEDOCLES
ANAXAGORAS
ANAXIMENES
ANDREEVICH
ANDRONIKOS
ENGELBREGT
INGENHOUSZ
BODENSTEIN
COPERNICUS
COURCHESNE
DOBEREINER
DOBZHANSKY
DORNBERGER
FOETTINGER
FOTHERGILL
FOTOPOULOS
GOLDBERGER
HOFMESITER
HOFSTADTER
HOLLDOBLER
HOUNSFIELD
IOSIFOVICH
KOMUNYAKAA
KONSTANTIN
KOURGANOFF
KOVALEVSKI
KOVALEVSKY
MONTALCINI
MOOKHERJEE
POCAHONTAS
POGGENDORF
POISEUILLE
ROKITANSKY
SOMERVILLE
SOMMEILLER
SONNENBERG
TORRICELLI
TOSCANELLI
APOLLONIUS
SPIEGELMAN

ARCHDEACON
ARCHIMEDES
ARGELANDER
ARISTIPPUS
BRANSFIELD
BRETHERTON
BRETONNEAU
BROCKHOUSE
CRUIKSHANK
ERLENMEYER
FRACASTORO
FRANCISCUS
FRIEDERICH
GREENSTEIN
KRETSCHMER
PRAXAGORAS
PRINGSHEIM
PROTAGORAS
TREVITHICK
TRUTFETTER
WROBLEWSKI
TSCHIRIKOV
ATHANASIUS
OTTAVIOANO
STAHLECKER
STAUDINGER
STEINHARDT
STEPHENSON
STRESEMANN
STROHMEYER
STROMINGER
STURTEVANT
CUNNINGHAM
GULLSTRAND
MUGGLESTON
RUTHERFORD
RUTTENBERG
SUTHERLAND
WUNDERLICH
SWAMMERDAM
SWEDENBORG
PYTHAGORAS
SZYMBORSKA

3RD LETTER

ANAXAGORAS
ANAXIMENES
BRANSFIELD
CHAMBERLIN
CHARDONNET
CLATWORTHY
FRACASTORO
FRANCISCUS
PRAXAGORAS

SCARFIOTTI
STAHLECKER
STAUDINGER
SWAMMERDAM
WEATHERWAX
DOBEREINER
DOBZHANSKY
EBBINGHAUS
ARCHDEACON
ARCHIMEDES
MACFARLANE
MCCLINTOCK
MCCULLOUGH
PACHACUTEC
POCAHONTAS
RICHARDSON
SACROBOSCO
TSCHIRIKOV
ALDROVANDI
ANDREEVICH
ANDRONIKOS
BODENSTEIN
ALEIXANDRE
ALESSANDRO
BRETHERTON
BRETONNEAU
FOETTINGER
GREENSTEIN
HIERONYMUS
KLEBESADEL
KRETSCHMER
STEINHARDT
STEPHENSON
SWEDENBORG
THEAETETUS
THEODOSIUS
TREVITHICK
WHEATSTONE
HOFMESITER
HOFSTADTER
SEFERIADIS
ARGELANDER
BIGELEISEN
ENGELBREGT
INGENHOUSZ
LAGERKVIST
MUGGLESTON
POGGENDORF
ATHANASIUS
FAHRENHEIT
SCHEUCHZER
SCHICKARDT
SCHLIEMANN
SCHRIEFFER
SCHUMACHER
SCHWEIGGER
SCHWEITZER

ZEHETBAUER
ARISTIPPUS
BEIJERINCK
FEIGENBAUM
FRIEDERICH
HEISENBERG
MAIMONIDES
PHILOPONUS
POISEUILLE
PRINGSHEIM
REICHSTEIN
SHINGLETON
SPIEGELMAN
TEISSERENC
WEIZSACKER
NIKOLAYEVA
ROKITANSKY
SHKLOVSKII
ALLESANDRO
BELOZERSKY
CALLINICUS
ERLENMEYER
GALSWORTHY
GELLIBRAND
GOLDBERGER
GULLSTRAND
HELLRIEGEL
HOLLDOBLER
LILIENTHAL
SILLIPHANT
SKLODOWSKA
WILLEBRORD
WILLIAMSON
CAMERARIUS
CAMPANELLA
DEMOCRITUS
KAMERLINGH
KOMUNYAKAA
LAMBERTSON
NEMORARIUS
RAMMAZZINI
SAMUELSSON
SEMENOVICH
SOMERVILLE
SOMMEILLER
BENZENBERG
CANNIZZARO
CUNNINGHAM
KONSTANTIN
LANGERHANS
MANCHESTER
MANDELBROT
MANKIEWICZ
MENAECHMUS
MONTALCINI
SANCTORIUS
SENEFELDER

SONNENBERG	TOSCANELLI	MASCHERONI	WETHERHILL	NEMORARIUS	MONTALCINI	FRIEDERICH
VINOGRADOV	WISLICENUS	REICHSTEIN	ALEIXANDRE	NIKOLAYEVA	PROTAGORAS	GIORDMAINE
WUNDERLICH	CATHERWOOD	SANCTORIUS	CHRISTIAAN	SKLODOWSKA	RUTTENBERG	HOLLDOBLER
XENOPHANES	FITZGERALD	THUCYDIDES	CHRISTIANE	STROHMEYER	TRUTFETTER	SKLODOWSKA
APOLLONIUS	FOTHERGILL	TOSCANELLI	CHRISTOPHE	STROMINGER	WEATHERWAX	STAUDINGER
BROCKHOUSE	FOTOPOULOS	FERDINANDO	CRUIKSHANK	TAVOULARIS	CLOUDESLEY	THEODOSIUS
CLOUDESLEY	OTTAVIOANO	GOLDBERGER	DESIDERIUS	THEODOSIUS	KOMUNYAKAA	ANDREEVICH
DIOPHANTUS	PYTHAGORAS	HEYDENBERG	EBBINGHAUS	VINOGRADOV	MCCULLOUGH	BEIJERINCK
GIORDMAINE	RUTHERFORD	MANDELBROT	IOSIFOVICH	XENOPHANES	SAMUELSSON	BENZENBERG
MOOKHERJEE	RUTTENBERG	SWEDENBORG	LILIENTHAL	CAMPANELLA	SCHUMACHER	BLUMENBACH
PROTAGORAS	SUTHERLAND	WUNDERLICH	MAXIMILIAN	DIOPHANTUS	STAUDINGER	BLUMENTHAL
SKOBELTZYN	WATERHOUSE	ALLESANDRO	ROKITANSKY	HIPPARCHUS	TREVITHICK	CASSEGRAIN
WROBLEWSKI	WETHERHILL	ARGELANDER	SCHICKARDT	LIPPERSHEY	SCHWEIGGER	CATHERWOOD
COPERNICUS	BLUMENBACH	BIGELEISEN	STEINHARDT	STEPHENSON	SCHWEITZER	FAHRENHEIT
EMPEDOCLES	BLUMENTHAL	BODENSTEIN	BEIJERINCK	PASQUALINO	ANAXAGORAS	FEIGENBAUM
HIPPARCHUS	COURCHESNE	CAMERARIUS	BARKHAUSEN	ALDROVANDI	ANAXIMENES	FOTHERGILL
LIPPERSHEY	CRUIKSHANK	COPERNICUS	MANKIEWICZ	ANDREEVICH	PRAXAGORAS	HEISENBERG
BARKHAUSEN	HOUNSFIELD	DOBEREINER	MOOKHERJEE	ANDRONIKOS	BENZENBERG	HEYDENBERG
BARTOLEMEO	KOURGANOFF	EHRENFRIED	APOLLONIUS	CARRINGTON	DOBZHANSKY	HOFMESITER
BARTOLOMEU	LAURENTINE	EISENHOWER	CALLINICUS	CHARDONNET	FITZGERALD	KLEBESADEL
BERNARDINO	NEUGEBAUER	EMPEDOCLES	GELLIBRAND	COURCHESNE	WEIZSACKER	LAMBERTSON
BERTHOLLET	STURTEVANT	ENGELBREGT	GULLSTRAND	FAHRENHEIT		LANGERHANS
BERTOLUCCI	THUCYDIDES	ERLENMEYER	HELLRIEGEL	GIORDMAINE		LAURENTINE
CARMICHAEL	TRUTFETTER	FRIEDERICH	HOLLDOBLER	HARRINGTON		LILIENTHAL
CARRINGTON	CAVANILLES	GREENSTEIN	MCCLINTOCK	HIERONYMUS	**5TH LETTER**	LIPPERSHEY
CARTWRIGHT	KOVALEVSKI	INGENHOUSZ	PHILOPONUS	KOURGANOFF		MANDELBROT
CHRISTIAAN	KOVALEVSKY	KAMERLINGH	SCHLIEMANN	LAURENTINE	ANAXAGORAS	MENAECHMUS
CHRISTIANE	TAVOULARIS	LAGERKVIST	SHKLOVSKII	MERRIFIELD	BERNARDINO	NEUGEBAUER
CHRISTOPHE	MAXIMILIAN	SCHEUCHZER	SILLIPHANT	SACROBOSCO	CAMPANELLA	PARMENIDES
DORNBERGER	HEYDENBERG	SEFERIADIS	WILLEBRORD	SCARFIOTTI	FRACASTORO	POGGENDORF
EHRENFRIED	SZYMBORSKA	SEMENOVICH	WILLIAMSON	SCHRIEFFER	HIPPARCHUS	POISEUILLE
FERDINANDO	EIZAGUIRRE	SENEFELDER	WISLICENUS	STURTEVANT	MACFARLANE	RUTHERFORD
HARGREAVES		SOMERVILLE	BLUMENBACH	TORRICELLI	MONTALCINI	RUTTENBERG
HARRINGTON		SPIEGELMAN	BLUMENTHAL	VERROCCHIO	PACHACUTEC	SAMUELSSON
HERACLITUS		STRESEMANN	CARMICHAEL	WARRINGTON	PRAXAGORAS	SCHWEIGGER
HEROPHILUS	**4TH LETTER**	TERESHKOVA	CHAMBERLIN	ALESSANDRO	PROTAGORAS	SCHWEITZER
HERSCHBACH		WATERHOUSE	HOFMESITER	ARISTIPPUS	PYTHAGORAS	SKOBELTZYN
MARGUERITE	ATHANASIUS	ZEHETBAUER	MAIMONIDES	CASSEGRAIN	RAMMAZZINI	SOMMEILLER
MERRIFIELD	CAVANILLES	MACFARLANE	PARMENIDES	CASSINELLI	RICHARDSON	SONNENBERG
PARACELSUS	EIZAGUIRRE	FEIGENBAUM	RAMMAZZINI	GALSWORTHY	TISSANDIER	SUTHERLAND
PARMENIDES	HERACLITUS	HARGREAVES	SOMMEILLER	HEISENBERG	TOSCANELLI	SWEDENBORG
PIRANDELLO	KOVALEVSKI	LANGERHANS	SWAMMERDAM	HERSCHBACH	CHAMBERLIN	THEAETETUS
STRESEMANN	KOVALEVSKY	MARGUERITE	SZYMBORSKA	HOFSTADTER	DORNBERGER	WETHERHILL
STROHMEYER	MENAECHMUS	MUGGLESTON	BERNARDINO	KONSTANTIN	GOLDBERGER	WILLEBRORD
STROMINGER	OTTAVIOANO	NEUGEBAUER	BRANSFIELD	POISEUILLE	SZYMBORSKA	WUNDERLICH
TERESHKOVA	PARACELSUS	POGGENDORF	CANNIZZARO	TEISSERENC	COURCHESNE	IOSIFOVICH
TORRICELLI	PIRANDELLO	ARCHDEACON	CUNNINGHAM	TISSANDIER	DEMOCRITUS	SCARFIOTTI
VERROCCHIO	POCAHONTAS	ARCHIMEDES	DORNBERGER	BARTOLEMEO	FRANCISCUS	SENEFELDER
WARRINGTON	THEAETETUS	CATHERWOOD	FRANCISCUS	BARTOLOMEU	HERACLITUS	TRUTFETTER
CASSEGRAIN	WHEATSTONE	FOTHERGILL	HOUNSFIELD	BERTHOLLET	HERSCHBACH	EIZAGUIRRE
CASSINELLI	KLEBESADEL	PACHACUTEC	PRINGSHEIM	BERTOLUCCI	PARACELSUS	FITZGERALD
DESIDERIUS	LAMBERTSON	PYTHAGORAS	SHINGLETON	BRETHERTON	SCHICKARDT	KOURGANOFF
EISENHOWER	SKOBELTZYN	RICHARDSON	SONNENBERG	BRETONNEAU	ARCHDEACON	PRINGSHEIM
IOSIFOVICH	WROBLEWSKI	RUTHERFORD	BELOZERSKY	CARTWRIGHT	CHARDONNET	SHINGLETON
MASCHERONI	BROCKHOUSE	STAHLECKER	DEMOCRITUS	CLATWORTHY	CLOUDESLEY	SPIEGELMAN
PASQUALINO	FRACASTORO	SUTHERLAND	FOTOPOULOS	FOETTINGER	DESIDERIUS	VINOGRADOV
TISSANDIER	MANCHESTER	TSCHIRIKOV	HEROPHILUS	KRETSCHMER	EMPEDOCLES	BARKHAUSEN

BERTHOLLET	EISENHOWER	PASQUALINO	DESIDERIUS	SCHWEIGGER	CHARDONNET	**7TH LETTER**
BRETHERTON	ERLENMEYER	SCHEUCHZER	DOBEREJNER	SCHWEITZER	CLATWORTHY	ALDROVANDI
DIOPHANTUS	GREENSTEIN	TAVOULARIS	DORNBERGER	SEFERIADIS	EMPEDOCLES	ARCHDEACON
DOBZHANSKY	INGENHOUSZ	OTTAVIOANO	FITZGERALD	SOMMEILLER	FOTOPOULOS	FERDINANDO
MANCHESTER	KOMUNYAKAA	CARTWRIGHT	FRIEDERICH	STAUDINGER	GALSWORTHY	GIORDMAINE
MASCHERONI	PIRANDELLO	CLATWORTHY	GOLDBERGER	STROMINGER	HOLLDOBLER	HARGREAVES
MOOKHERJEE	SEMENOVICH	GALSWORTHY	HARGREAVES	LAGERKVIST	IOSIFOVICH	KLEBESADEL
POCAHONTAS	STEINHARDT	ALEIXANDRE	KOVALEVSKI	SCHICKARDT	POCAHONTAS	KOMUNYAKAA
REICHSTEIN	ALDROVANDI	THUCYDIDES	KOVALEVSKY	BARTOLEMEO	SANCTORIUS	NEUGEBAUER
STEPHENSON	ANDRONIKOS	BELOZERSKY	MANCHESTER	BARTOLOMEU	SEMENOVICH	SCHICKARDT
STROHMEYER	BARTOLEMEO	**6TH LETTER**	MANKIEWICZ	BERTOLUCCI	SKLODOWSKA	SEFERIADIS
WEATHERWAX	BARTOLOMEU	ALEIXANDRE	MARGUERITE	HERACLITUS	SZYMBORSKA	STEINHARDT
ANAXIMENES	BERTOLUCCI	ALESSANDRO	MASCHERONI	KAMERLINGH	THEODOSIUS	TAVOULARIS
ARCHIMEDES	BRETONNEAU	ALLESANDRO	MOOKHERJEE	MANDELBROT	PHILOPONUS	VINOGRADOV
CALLINICUS	HIERONYMUS	ARGELANDER	MUGGLESTON	MCCULLOUGH	SILLIPHANT	XENOPHANES
CANNIZZARO	MAIMONIDES	ATHANASIUS	PARACELSUS	MONTALCINI	BEIJERINCK	ZEHETBAUER
CARMICHAEL	PHILOPONUS	BARKHAUSEN	SCHLIEMANN	SAMUELSSON	BERNARDINO	BENZENBERG
CARRINGTON	SACROBOSCO	CAMERARIUS	SCHRIEFFER	SHINGLETON	CARTWRIGHT	BLUMENBACH
CASSINELLI	SHKLOVSKII	DIOPHANTUS	SENEFELDER	SKOBELTZYN	CATHERWOOD	FEIGENBAUM
CUNNINGHAM	VERROCCHIO	DOBZHANSKY	SPIEGELMAN	TAVOULARIS	DEMOCRITUS	HEISENBERG
FERDINANDO	FOTOPOULOS	HOFSTADTER	STAHLECKER	ANAXIMENES	FOTHERGILL	HERSCHBACH
GELLIBRAND	HEROPHILUS	KONSTANTIN	STEPHENSON	ARCHIMEDES	HIPPARCHUS	HEYDENBERG
HARRINGTON	XENOPHANES	KOURGANOFF	STRESEMANN	ERLENMEYER	LAMBERTSON	HOLLDOBLER
MANKIEWICZ	CAMERARIUS	NEMORARIUS	STURTEVANT	GIORDMAINE	LANGERHANS	MANDELBROT
MCCLINTOCK	COPERNICUS	NIKOLAYEVA	SWAMMERDAM	STROHMEYER	LIPPERSHEY	RUTTENBERG
MERRIFIELD	DOBEREINER	PASQUALINO	TEISSERENC	ANDRONIKOS	MACFARLANE	SONNENBERG
SCHLIEMANN	HARGREAVES	ROKITANSKY	TRUTFETTER	BENZENBERG	RICHARDSON	SWEDENBORG
SCHRIEFFER	HELLRIEGEL	SCHUMACHER	WEATHERWAX	BLUMENBACH	RUTHERFORD	EMPEDOCLES
SILLIPHANT	KAMERLINGH	WEIZSACKER	WROBLEWSKI	BLUMENTHAL	SUTHERLAND	HIPPARCHUS
TORRICELLI	LAGERKVIST	WILLIAMSON	BRANSFIELD	BRETONNEAU	TSCHIRIKOV	MONTALCINI
TREVITHICK	NEMORARIUS	ENGELBREGT	EHRENFRIED	CALLINICUS	VINOGRADOV	SCHUMACHER
TSCHIRIKOV	SEFERIADIS	GELLIBRAND	HOUNSFIELD	CAMPANELLA	WETHERHILL	STAHLECKER
WARRINGTON	SOMERVILLE	NEUGEBAUER	MERRIFIELD	CARRINGTON	WUNDERLICH	VERROCCHIO
WILLIAMSON	WATERHOUSE	SACROBOSCO	ANAXAGORAS	CASSINELLI	BODENSTEIN	WEIZSACKER
WISLICENUS	ALESSANDRO	WILLEBRORD	CASSEGRAIN	COPERNICUS	CRUIKSHANK	BERNARDINO
BROCKHOUSE	ALLESANDRO	ZEHETBAUER	EBBINGHAUS	CUNNINGHAM	FRACASTORO	HOFSTADTER
CRUIKSHANK	BRANSFIELD	CARMICHAEL	PRAXAGORAS	FAHRENHEIT	GREENSTEIN	POGGENDORF
APOLLONIUS	CHRISTIAAN	KRETSCHMER	PROTAGORAS	FEIGENBAUM	HOFMESITER	RICHARDSON
ARGELANDER	CHRISTIANE	MENAECHMUS	PYTHAGORAS	FERDINANDO	KLEBESADEL	TISSANDIER
BIGELEISEN	CHRISTOPHE	PACHACUTEC	BROCKHOUSE	HARRINGTON	PRINGSHEIM	ANAXIMENES
ENGELBREGT	GULLSTRAND	SCHEUCHZER	COURCHESNE	HEISENBERG	REICHSTEIN	ARCHIMEDES
KOVALEVSKI	HOUNSFIELD	TORRICELLI	EISENHOWER	HEYDENBERG	WHEATSTONE	BARTOLEMEO
KOVALEVSKY	KRETSCHMER	VERROCCHIO	HEROPHILUS	HIERONYMUS	CHRISTIAAN	CAMPANELLA
MCCULLOUGH	STRESEMANN	WISLICENUS	HERSCHBACH	LAURENTINE	CHRISTIANE	CASSINELLI
MUGGLESTON	TEISSERENC	PIRANDELLO	INGENHOUSZ	LILIENTHAL	CHRISTOPHE	COURCHESNE
NIKOLAYEVA	TERESHKOVA	THUCYDIDES	STEINHARDT	MAIMONIDES	GULLSTRAND	ERLENMEYER
STAHLECKER	WEIZSACKER	ANDREEVICH	TERESHKOVA	MCCLINTOCK	THEAETETUS	HELLRIEGEL
WROBLEWSKI	ARISTIPPUS	ARCHDEACON	WATERHOUSE	PARMENIDES	TREVITHICK	PIRANDELLO
MAXIMILIAN	FOETTINGER	BELOZERSKY	XENOPHANES	POGGENDORF	EIZAGUIRRE	SHINGLETON
SCHUMACHER	HOFSTADTER	BIGELEISEN	ARISTIPPUS	RUTTENBERG	POISEUILLE	STROHMEYER
STROMINGER	KONSTANTIN	BRETHERTON	POGGENDORF	SONNENBERG	ALDROVANDI	THEAETETUS
SWAMMERDAM	ROKITANSKY	CHAMBERLIN	RUTTENBERG	SWEDENBORG	SHKLOVSKII	TORRICELLI
ATHANASIUS	SANCTORIUS	CLOUDESLEY	CAVANILLES	TISSANDIER	SOMERVILLE	TOSCANELLI
BODENSTEIN	STURTEVANT		FOETTINGER	TOSCANELLI	KOMUNYAKAA	WISLICENUS
CAVANILLES	WHEATSTONE		FRANCISCUS	WARRINGTON	CANNIZZARO	RUTHERFORD
EBBINGHAUS	ZEHETBAUER		HELLRIEGEL	APOLLONIUS	RAMMAZZINI	SCHRIEFFER
EHRENFRIED	MARGUERITE		MAXIMILIAN	BERTHOLLET		
			OTTAVIOANO			
			SCARFIOTTI			

CARRINGTON	ALEIXANDRE	WEATHERWAX	FITZGERALD	CUNNINGHAM	BARTOLOMEU	CLATWORTHY
CUNNINGHAM	ALESSANDRO	WILLEBRORD	GELLIBRAND	HIPPARCHUS	HIERONYMUS	DEMOCRITUS
FOTHERGILL	ALLESANDRO	ATHANASIUS	GULLSTRAND	LILIENTHAL	KRETSCHMER	DIOPHANTUS
HARRINGTON	APOLLONIUS	CLOUDESLEY	HERSCHBACH	LIPPERSHEY	MENAECHMUS	GALSWORTHY
SCHWEIGGER	ARGELANDER	FRANCISCUS	LANGERHANS	SCHUMACHER	SPIEGELMAN	HARRINGTON
WARRINGTON	BRETONNEAU	LIPPERSHEY	MACFARLANE	VERROCCHIO	ALDROVANDI	HERACLITUS
CARMICHAEL	CHARDONNET	MANCHESTER	OTTAVIOANO	ANDREEVICH	ANAXIMENES	HOFMESITER
CRUIKSHANK	DIOPHANTUS	MUGGLESTON	SCHLIEMANN	APOLLONIUS	BEIJERINCK	HOFSTADTER
EBBINGHAUS	DOBZHANSKY	SAMUELSSON	SILLIPHANT	ATHANASIUS	CHARDONNET	KONSTANTIN
FAHRENHEIT	FOETTINGER	SHKLOVSKII	STRESEMANN	BERNARDINO	DOBEREINER	MANCHESTER
KRETSCHMER	KONSTANTIN	THEODOSIUS	STURTEVANT	CAMERARIUS	FERDINANDO	MUGGLESTON
LANGERHANS	KOURGANOFF	BLUMENTHAL	SUTHERLAND	DESIDERIUS	KAMERLINGH	PACHACUTEC
MENAECHMUS	POCAHONTAS	BODENSTEIN	ARCHDEACON	EHRENFRIED	PHILOPONUS	POCAHONTAS
PRINGSHEIM	ROKITANSKY	FRACASTORO	BERTOLUCCI	FOTHERGILL	WISLICENUS	SCARFIOTTI
SCHEUCHZER	STAUDINGER	GREENSTEIN	CALLINICUS	FRIEDERICH	XENOPHANES	SHINGLETON
SILLIPHANT	STEPHENSON	LAMBERTSON	COPERNICUS	GIORDMAINE	CATHERWOOD	THEAETETUS
TREVITHICK	STROMINGER	LAURENTINE	FRANCISCUS	IOSIFOVICH	FRACASTORO	TRUTFETTER
WETHERHILL	ANAXAGORAS	LILIENTHAL	ALEIXANDRE	LAGERKVIST	KOURGANOFF	WARRINGTON
ANDRONIKOS	BARTOLOMEU	MCCLINTOCK	ALESSANDRO	LAURENTINE	MASCHERONI	BROCKHOUSE
BEIJERINCK	BROCKHOUSE	REICHSTEIN	ALLESANDRO	MANKIEWICZ	MCCLINTOCK	INGENHOUSZ
BIGELEISEN	CHRISTOPHE	SCHWEITZER	ARCHIMEDES	MARGUERITE	POGGENDORF	MCCULLOUGH
BRANSFIELD	EISENHOWER	SKOBELTZYN	ARGELANDER	MAXIMILIAN	RUTHERFORD	NEUGEBAUER
CALLINICUS	INGENHOUSZ	TRUTFETTER	KLEBESADEL	MONTALCINI	SWEDENBORG	WATERHOUSE
CARTWRIGHT	MCCULLOUGH	WHEATSTONE	MAIMONIDES	NEMORARIUS	TERESHKOVA	ZEHETBAUER
CHRISTIAAN	OTTAVIOANO	BARKHAUSEN	PARMENIDES	PASQUALINO	WHEATSTONE	HARGREAVES
CHRISTIANE	PHILOPONUS	BERTOLUCCI	SEFERIADIS	RAMMAZZINI	WILLEBRORD	EISENHOWER
COPERNICUS	PRAXAGORAS	FOTOPOULOS	SENEFELDER	SANCTORIUS	ARISTIPPUS	WEATHERWAX
DEMOCRITUS	PROTAGORAS	PACHACUTEC	SWAMMERDAM	SEMENOVICH	CHRISTOPHE	ERLENMEYER
DOBEREINER	PYTHAGORAS	ANDREEVICH	THUCYDIDES	THEODOSIUS	ANAXAGORAS	STROHMEYER
EIZAGUIRRE	SACROBOSCO	IOSIFOVICH	VINOGRADOV	TISSANDIER	EIZAGUIRRE	SCHEUCHZER
HERACLITUS	SCARFIOTTI	KOVALEVSKI	BENZENBERG	TREVITHICK	MANDELBROT	SCHWEITZER
HEROPHILUS	WATERHOUSE	KOVALEVSKY	BODENSTEIN	WETHERHILL	PRAXAGORAS	SKOBELTZYN
HOFMESITER	ARISTIPPUS	LAGERKVIST	BRANSFIELD	WUNDERLICH	PROTAGORAS	
HOUNSFIELD	BELOZERSKY	SEMENOVICH	BRETONNEAU	MOOKHERJEE	PYTHAGORAS	
KAMERLINGH	BRETHERTON	STURTEVANT	ENGELBREGT	ANDRONIKOS	SCHICKARDT	**9TH LETTER**
MAIMONIDES	CAMERARIUS	CATHERWOOD	FAHRENHEIT	KOMUNYAKAA	STEINHARDT	
MERRIFIELD	CASSEGRAIN	MANKIEWICZ	GREENSTEIN	SHKLOVSKII	TAVOULARIS	ANAXAGORAS
PARMENIDES	CHAMBERLIN	SKLODOWSKA	HEISENBERG	STAHLECKER	BARKHAUSEN	BLUMENTHAL
POISEUILLE	CLATWORTHY	WROBLEWSKI	HEYDENBERG	TSCHIRIKOV	BELOZERSKY	BRETONNEAU
SOMERVILLE	DESIDERIUS	HIERONYMUS	HOUNSFIELD	WEIZSACKER	BIGELEISEN	CHRISTIAAN
THUCYDIDES	DORNBERGER	NIKOLAYEVA	MERRIFIELD	BERTHOLLET	COURCHESNE	CUNNINGHAM
TSCHIRIKOV	EHRENFRIED	CANNIZZARO	NIKOLAYEVA	CAMPANELLA	DOBZHANSKY	KOMUNYAKAA
TERESHKOVA	ENGELBREGT	RAMMAZZINI	PRINGSHEIM	CASSINELLI	KOVALEVSKI	LILIENTHAL
BERTHOLLET	FITZGERALD		REICHSTEIN	CAVANILLES	KOVALEVSKY	MAXIMILIAN
CAVANILLES	FRIEDERICH		RUTTENBERG	CHAMBERLIN	LAMBERTSON	POCAHONTAS
MACFARLANE	GALSWORTHY		SONNENBERG	CLOUDESLEY	PARACELSUS	PRAXAGORAS
MAXIMILIAN	GELLIBRAND	**8TH LETTER**	TEISSERENC	EMPEDOCLES	RICHARDSON	PROTAGORAS
PARACELSUS	GOLDBERGER		SCHRIEFFER	FOTOPOULOS	ROKITANSKY	PYTHAGORAS
PASQUALINO	GULLSTRAND	BLUMENBACH	CARTWRIGHT	HEROPHILUS	SACROBOSCO	SPIEGELMAN
SENEFELDER	MARGUERITE	CANNIZZARO	DORNBERGER	HOLLDOBLER	SAMUELSSON	SWAMMERDAM
SOMMEILLER	MASCHERONI	CARMICHAEL	FOETTINGER	PIRANDELLO	SKLODOWSKA	WEATHERWAX
SPIEGELMAN	MOOKHERJEE	CASSEGRAIN	GOLDBERGER	POISEUILLE	STEPHENSON	ANDREEVICH
SUTHERLAND	NEMORARIUS	CHRISTIAAN	HELLRIEGEL	SOMERVILLE	SZYMBORSKA	BEIJERINCK
WUNDERLICH	SANCTORIUS	CHRISTIANE	SCHWEIGGER	SOMMEILLER	WILLIAMSON	BERTOLUCCI
SCHLIEMANN	SWAMMERDAM	CRUIKSHANK	STAUDINGER	TORRICELLI	WROBLEWSKI	BLUMENBACH
STRESEMANN	SZYMBORSKA	EBBINGHAUS	STROMINGER	TOSCANELLI	BRETHERTON	FRIEDERICH
WILLIAMSON	TEISSERENC	FEIGENBAUM	BLUMENTHAL	BARTOLEMEO	CARRINGTON	

HERSCHBACH	THUCYDIDES	MASCHERONI	DEMOCRITUS	SOMERVILLE	HARRINGTON	ANAXIMENES
IOSIFOVICH	TISSANDIER	MONTALCINI	DESIDERIUS	WATERHOUSE	KONSTANTIN	ANDRONIKOS
MANKIEWICZ	TRUTFETTER	OTTAVIOANO	DIOPHANTUS	WHEATSTONE	LAMBERTSON	APOLLONIUS
MCCLINTOCK	WEIZSACKER	PASQUALINO	EBBINGHAUS	KOURGANOFF	MAXIMILIAN	ARCHIMEDES
SACROBOSCO	XENOPHANES	RAMMAZZINI	FEIGENBAUM	POGGENDORF	MUGGLESTON	ARISTIPPUS
SEMENOVICH	ZEHETBAUER	SCHLIEMANN	FRANCISCUS	BENZENBERG	REICHSTEIN	ATHANASIUS
TREVITHICK	KOURGANOFF	SILLIPHANT	HERACLITUS	HEISENBERG	RICHARDSON	CALLINICUS
WUNDERLICH	ENGELBREGT	STRESEMANN	HEROPHILUS	HEYDENBERG	SAMUELSSON	CAMERARIUS
ALDROVANDI	KAMERLINGH	STURTEVANT	HIERONYMUS	RUTTENBERG	SCHLIEMANN	CAVANILLES
FERDINANDO	MCCULLOUGH	SUTHERLAND	HIPPARCHUS	SONNENBERG	SHINGLETON	COPERNICUS
SCHICKARDT	CARTWRIGHT	TEISSERENC	MENAECHMUS	SWEDENBORG	SKOBELTZYN	DEMOCRITUS
STEINHARDT	CHRISTOPHE	WHEATSTONE	NEMORARIUS	ANDREEVICH	SPIEGELMAN	DESIDERIUS
ANAXIMENES	CLATWORTHY	ANDRONIKOS	PARACELSUS	BLUMENBACH	STEPHENSON	DIOPHANTUS
ARCHIMEDES	GALSWORTHY	ARCHDEACON	PHILOPONUS	FRIEDERICH	STRESEMANN	EBBINGHAUS
ARGELANDER	BODENSTEIN	BRETHERTON	SANCTORIUS	HERSCHBACH	WARRINGTON	EMPEDOCLES
BARKHAUSEN	CASSEGRAIN	CARRINGTON	THEAETETUS	IOSIFOVICH	WILLIAMSON	FOTOPOULOS
BARTOLEMEO	CHAMBERLIN	CATHERWOOD	THEODOSIUS	KAMERLINGH	ALESSANDRO	FRANCISCUS
BARTOLOMEU	FAHRENHEIT	FOTOPOULOS	WISLICENUS	MCCULLOUGH	ALLESANDRO	HARGREAVES
BERTHOLLET	GREENSTEIN	HARRINGTON	NIKOLAYEVA	SEMENOVICH	BARTOLEMEO	HERACLITUS
BIGELEISEN	KONSTANTIN	LAMBERTSON	TERESHKOVA	WUNDERLICH	BERNARDINO	HEROPHILUS
CARMICHAEL	PRINGSHEIM	MANDELBROT	SKOBELTZYN	ALDROVANDI	CANNIZZARO	HIERONYMUS
CAVANILLES	REICHSTEIN	MUGGLESTON		BERTOLUCCI	FERDINANDO	HIPPARCHUS
CHARDONNET	SEFERIADIS	RICHARDSON	**10TH LETTER**	CASSINELLI	FRACASTORO	LANGERHANS
CLOUDESLEY	SHKLOVSKII	SAMUELSSON		KOVALEVSKI	OTTAVIOANO	MAIMONIDES
DOBEREINER	TAVOULARIS	SHINGLETON		MASCHERONI	PASQUALINO	MENAECHMUS
DORNBERGER	VERROCCHIO	STEPHENSON		MONTALCINI	PIRANDELLO	NEMORARIUS
EHRENFRIED	BELOZERSKY	TSCHIRIKOV	CAMPANELLA	PIRANDELLO	SACROBOSCO	PARACELSUS
EISENHOWER	DOBZHANSKY	VINOGRADOV	KOMUNYAKAA	RAMMAZZINI	VERROCCHIO	PARMENIDES
EMPEDOCLES	KOVALEVSKI	WARRINGTON	NIKOLAYEVA	SCARFIOTTI	ARGELANDER	PHILOPONUS
ERLENMEYER	KOVALEVSKY	WILLIAMSON	SKLODOWSKA	SHKLOVSKII	DOBEREINER	POCAHONTAS
FOETTINGER	ROKITANSKY	ALEIXANDRE	SZYMBORSKA	TORRICELLI	DORNBERGER	PRAXAGORAS
GOLDBERGER	SKLODOWSKA	ALESSANDRO	TERESHKOVA	TOSCANELLI	EISENHOWER	PROTAGORAS
HARGREAVES	SZYMBORSKA	ALLESANDRO	PACHACUTEC	WROBLEWSKI	ERLENMEYER	PYTHAGORAS
HELLRIEGEL	WROBLEWSKI	BENZENBERG	TEISSERENC	BEIJERINCK	FOETTINGER	SANCTORIUS
HOFMESITER	BRANSFIELD	CANNIZZARO	BRANSFIELD	CRUIKSHANK	GOLDBERGER	SEFERIADIS
HOFSTADTER	CAMPANELLA	EIZAGUIRRE	CATHERWOOD	MCCLINTOCK	HOFMESITER	TAVOULARIS
HOLLDOBLER	CASSINELLI	FRACASTORO	EHRENFRIED	TREVITHICK	HOFSTADTER	THEAETETUS
KLEBESADEL	FITZGERALD	HEISENBERG	FITZGERALD	BLUMENTHAL	KRETSCHMER	THEODOSIUS
KRETSCHMER	FOTHERGILL	HEYDENBERG	GELLIBRAND	CARMICHAEL	MANCHESTER	THUCYDIDES
LIPPERSHEY	HOUNSFIELD	POGGENDORF	GULLSTRAND	FOTHERGILL	NEUGEBAUER	WISLICENUS
MAIMONIDES	MERRIFIELD	RUTHERFORD	HOUNSFIELD	HELLRIEGEL	SCHEUCHZER	XENOPHANES
MANCHESTER	PIRANDELLO	RUTTENBERG	MERRIFIELD	KLEBESADEL	SCHRIEFFER	BERTHOLLET
MOOKHERJEE	POISEUILLE	SONNENBERG	RUTHERFORD	LILIENTHAL	SCHUMACHER	CARTWRIGHT
NEUGEBAUER	SOMERVILLE	SWEDENBORG	SUTHERLAND	WETHERHILL	SCHWEIGGER	CHARDONNET
PACHACUTEC	TORRICELLI	WILLEBRORD	WILLEBRORD	CUNNINGHAM	SCHWEITZER	ENGELBREGT
PARMENIDES	TOSCANELLI	BROCKHOUSE	ALEIXANDRE	FEIGENBAUM	SENEFELDER	FAHRENHEIT
SCHEUCHZER	WETHERHILL	INGENHOUSZ	BROCKHOUSE	PRINGSHEIM	SOMMEILLER	LAGERKVIST
SCHRIEFFER	BERNARDINO	LAGERKVIST	CHRISTIANE	SWAMMERDAM	STAHLECKER	MANDELBROT
SCHUMACHER	CHRISTIANE	WATERHOUSE	CHRISTOPHE	ARCHDEACON	STAUDINGER	SCHICKARDT
SCHWEIGGER	COURCHESNE	MARGUERITE	COURCHESNE	BARKHAUSEN	STROHMEYER	SILLIPHANT
SCHWEITZER	CRUIKSHANK	SCARFIOTTI	EIZAGUIRRE	BIGELEISEN	STROMINGER	STEINHARDT
SENEFELDER	GELLIBRAND	APOLLONIUS	GIORDMAINE	BODENSTEIN	TISSANDIER	STURTEVANT
SOMMEILLER	GIORDMAINE	ARISTIPPUS	LAURENTINE	BRETHERTON	TRUTFETTER	BARTOLOMEU
STAHLECKER	GULLSTRAND	ATHANASIUS	MACFARLANE	CARRINGTON	WEIZSACKER	BRETONNEAU
STAUDINGER	LANGERHANS	CALLINICUS	MARGUERITE	CASSEGRAIN	ZEHETBAUER	TSCHIRIKOV
STROHMEYER	LAURENTINE	CAMERARIUS	MOOKHERJEE	CHAMBERLIN	ANAXAGORAS	VINOGRADOV
STROMINGER	MACFARLANE	COPERNICUS	POISEUILLE	CHRISTIAAN		WEATHERWAX
				GREENSTEIN		

BELOZERSKY
CLATWORTHY
CLOUDESLEY
DOBZHANSKY
GALSWORTHY
KOVALEVSKY
LIPPERSHEY
ROKITANSKY
INGENHOUSZ
MANKIEWICZ

11 LETTER

1ST LETTER

ALBATEGNIUS
ANAXIMANDER
ARISTARCHUS
ARTSIMOVICH
ASCLEPIADES
AUENBRUGGER
BARTHOLOMEW
BIRINGUCCIO
BLOEMBERGEN
BOEKELHEIDE
BONAVENTURA
BRADWARDINE
BRAHMAGUPTA
BRUNSCHWYGK
BUCKMINSTER
CAESALPINUS
CALLICRATES
CHAMBERLAIN
CHAMBERLAND
CHAMPOLLION
CHARLEMAGNE
CHRISTOFFEL
CHRISTOPHER
CRUICKSHANK
DEISENHOFER
DESAGULIERS
DICAEARCHUS
DIOSCORIDES
DMITRIEVICH
EVANGELISTA
GIAMBATISTA
GOLDSCHMIDT
GOODPASTURE
GROSSETESTE
HASELBERGER
HATZIDHAKIS
HERACLEIDES
HERTZSPRUNG
HINSHELWOOD
HIPPOCRATES

HUDALRICHUS
JABLOCHKOFF
KIBALCHITCH
LANDSTEINER
LEONIDOVICH
LOBACHEVSKI
MACHIAVELLI
MAETERLINCK
MARKOVNIKOV
MCCAMBRIDGE
MOHNOROVCIC
MONTGOLFIER
MORGENSTERN
NEDDERMEYER
NICHOMACHUS
NIGHTINGALE
NUSSENZWEIG
OPPENHEIMER
PAPANICOLAU
PHOCYCLIDES
PICCOLOMINI
PONTOPPIDAN
POSEIDONIUS
PRESSBURGER
PRZHEVALSKY
REICHENBACH
SCHILDKRAUT
SCHLESINGER
SCHNIRELMAN
SCHOONMAKER
SCHRODINGER
SCHWEICKART
SEMMELWEISS
SENNACHERIB
SERGEYEVICH
SHAKESPEARE
SHERRINGTON
SHIBASABURO
SIENKIEWICZ
SONDERGAARD
SPALLANZANI
STEENBURGEN
STEINBERGER
STERRENBERG
STRASBURGER
TSIOLKOVKSY
UNVERDORBEN
WEIERSTRASS
WILLSTATTER
ZINKERNAGEL

2ND LETTER

BARTHOLOMEW
CAESALPINUS

CALLICRATES
HASELBERGER
HATZIDHAKIS
JABLOCHKOFF
LANDSTEINER
MACHIAVELLI
MAETERLINCK
MARKOVNIKOV
PAPANICOLAU
MCCAMBRIDGE
SCHILDKRAUT
SCHLESINGER
SCHNIRELMAN
SCHOONMAKER
SCHRODINGER
SCHWEICKART
DEISENHOFER
DESAGULIERS
HERACLEIDES
HERTZSPRUNG
LEONIDOVICH
NEDDERMEYER
REICHENBACH
SEMMELWEISS
SENNACHERIB
SERGEYEVICH
WEIERSTRASS
CHAMBERLAIN
CHAMBERLAND
CHAMPOLLION
CHARLEMAGNE
CHRISTOFFEL
CHRISTOPHER
PHOCYCLIDES
SHAKESPEARE
SHERRINGTON
SHIBASABURO
BIRINGUCCIO
DICAEARCHUS
DIOSCORIDES
GIAMBATISTA
HINSHELWOOD
HIPPOCRATES
KIBALCHITCH
NICHOMACHUS
NIGHTINGALE
PICCOLOMINI
SIENKIEWICZ
WILLSTATTER
ZINKERNAGEL
ALBATEGNIUS
BLOEMBERGEN
DMITRIEVICH
ANAXIMANDER
UNVERDORBEN
BOEKELHEIDE
BONAVENTURA

GOLDSCHMIDT
GOODPASTURE
LOBACHEVSKI
MOHNOROVCIC
MONTGOLFIER
MORGENSTERN
PONTOPPIDAN
POSEIDONIUS
SONDERGAARD
OPPENHEIMER
SPALLANZANI
ARISTARCHUS
ARTSIMOVICH
BRADWARDINE
BRAHMAGUPTA
BRUNSCHWYGK
CRUICKSHANK
GROSSETESTE
PRESSBURGER
PRZHEVALSKY
ASCLEPIADES
TSIOLKOVKSY
STEENBURGEN
STEINBERGER
STERRENBERG
STRASBURGER
AUENBRUGGER
BUCKMINSTER
HUDALRICHUS
NUSSENZWEIG
EVANGELISTA

3RD LETTER

ANAXIMANDER
BRADWARDINE
BRAHMAGUPTA
CHAMBERLAIN
CHAMBERLAND
CHAMPOLLION
CHARLEMAGNE
EVANGELISTA
GIAMBATISTA
SHAKESPEARE
SPALLANZANI
ALBATEGNIUS
JABLOCHKOFF
KIBALCHITCH
LOBACHEVSKI
ASCLEPIADES
BUCKMINSTER
DICAEARCHUS
MACHIAVELLI
MCCAMBRIDGE
NICHOMACHUS

PICCOLOMINI
HUDALRICHUS
NEDDERMEYER
AUENBRUGGER
BOEKELHEIDE
CAESALPINUS
MAETERLINCK
PRESSBURGER
SHERRINGTON
SIENKIEWICZ
STEENBURGEN
STEINBERGER
STERRENBERG
NIGHTINGALE
MOHNOROVCIC
SCHILDKRAUT
SCHLESINGER
SCHNIRELMAN
SCHOONMAKER
SCHRODINGER
SCHWEICKART
ARISTARCHUS
DEISENHOFER
DMITRIEVICH
REICHENBACH
SHIBASABURO
TSIOLKOVKSY
WEIERSTRASS
CALLICRATES
GOLDSCHMIDT
WILLSTATTER
SEMMELWEISS
BONAVENTURA
HINSHELWOOD
LANDSTEINER
MONTGOLFIER
PONTOPPIDAN
SENNACHERIB
SONDERGAARD
ZINKERNAGEL
BLOEMBERGEN
DIOSCORIDES
GOODPASTURE
GROSSETESTE
LEONIDOVICH
PHOCYCLIDES
HIPPOCRATES
OPPENHEIMER
PAPANICOLAU
BARTHOLOMEW
BIRINGUCCIO
CHRISTOFFEL
CHRISTOPHER
HERACLEIDES
HERTZSPRUNG
MARKOVNIKOV
MORGENSTERN

SERGEYEVICH
STRASBURGER
DESAGULIERS
HASELBERGER
NUSSENZWEIG
POSEIDONIUS
ARTSIMOVICH
HATZIDHAKIS
BRUNSCHWYGK
CRUICKSHANK
UNVERDORBEN
PRZHEVALSKY

4TH LETTER

ALBATEGNIUS
BONAVENTURA
DESAGULIERS
DICAEARCHUS
HERACLEIDES
HUDALRICHUS
KIBALCHITCH
LOBACHEVSKI
MCCAMBRIDGE
PAPANICOLAU
STRASBURGER
SHIBASABURO
PHOCYCLIDES
PICCOLOMINI
REICHENBACH
BRADWARDINE
GOLDSCHMIDT
GOODPASTURE
LANDSTEINER
NEDDERMEYER
SONDERGAARD
BLOEMBERGEN
HASELBERGER
OPPENHEIMER
POSEIDONIUS
STEENBURGEN
UNVERDORBEN
WEIERSTRASS
MORGENSTERN
SERGEYEVICH
BRAHMAGUPTA
MACHIAVELLI
NICHOMACHUS
NIGHTINGALE
PRZHEVALSKY
BIRINGUCCIO
CHRISTOFFEL
CHRISTOPHER
CRUICKSHANK
SCHILDKRAUT

5TH LETTER

CAESALPINUS
SENNACHERIB

STEINBERGER
BOEKELHEIDE
BUCKMINSTER
MARKOVNIKOV
SHAKESPEARE
ZINKERNAGEL
ASCLEPIADES
CALLICRATES
JABLOCHKOFF
SCHLESINGER
SPALLANZANI
WILLSTATTER
CHAMBERLAIN
CHAMBERLAND
CHAMPOLLION
GIAMBATISTA
SEMMELWEISS
AUENBRUGGER
BRUNSCHWYGK
EVANGELISTA
LEONIDOVICH
MOHNOROVCIC
SCHNIRELMAN
SENNACHERIB
SIENKIEWICZ
SCHOONMAKER
TSIOLKOVKSY
HIPPOCRATES
CHARLEMAGNE
SCHRODINGER
SHERRINGTON
STERRENBERG
ARISTARCHUS
ARTSIMOVICH
CAESALPINUS
DEISENHOFER
DIOSCORIDES
GROSSETESTE
HINSHELWOOD
NUSSENZWEIG
PRESSBURGER
BARTHOLOMEW
DMITRIEVICH
HERTZSPRUNG
MAETERLINCK
MONTGOLFIER
PONTOPPIDAN
SCHWEICKART
ANAXIMANDER
HATZIDHAKIS

SHIBASABURO
AUENBRUGGER
CHAMBERLAIN
CHAMBERLAND
GIAMBATISTA
CRUICKSHANK
DIOSCORIDES
HERACLEIDES
LOBACHEVSKI
ASCLEPIADES
BOEKELHEIDE
DEISENHOFER
DICAEARCHUS
MAETERLINCK
MORGENSTERN
NEDDERMEYER
NUSSENZWEIG
PRZHEVALSKY
SCHLESINGER
SCHWEICKART
SEMMELWEISS
SERGEYEVICH
SHAKESPEARE
SONDERGAARD
ZINKERNAGEL
DESAGULIERS
EVANGELISTA
MONTGOLFIER
BARTHOLOMEW
HINSHELWOOD
REICHENBACH
ANAXIMANDER
ARTSIMOVICH
CALLICRATES
HATZIDHAKIS
LEONIDOVICH
MACHIAVELLI
POSEIDONIUS
SCHNIRELMAN
SIENKIEWICZ
CHARLEMAGNE
HASELBERGER
HUDALRICHUS
KIBALCHITCH
SCHILDKRAUT
SPALLANZANI
TSIOLKOVKSY
BLOEMBERGEN
BRAHMAGUPTA
BUCKMINSTER
MCCAMBRIDGE
BIRINGUCCIO
OPPENHEIMER
PAPANICOLAU
STEENBURGEN
STEINBERGER
HIPPOCRATES

JABLOCHKOFF
MARKOVNIKOV
MOHNOROVCIC
NICHOMACHUS
PICCOLOMINI
PONTOPPIDAN
SCHOONMAKER
SCHRODINGER
CHAMPOLLION
GOODPASTURE
DMITRIEVICH
SHERRINGTON
STERRENBERG
UNVERDORBEN
WEIERSTRASS
BRUNSCHWYGK
CHRISTOFFEL
CHRISTOPHER
GOLDSCHMIDT
GROSSETESTE
LANDSTEINER
PRESSBURGER
STRASBURGER
WILLSTATTER
ALBATEGNIUS
ARISTARCHUS
NIGHTINGALE
BONAVENTURA
BRADWARDINE
PHOCYCLIDES
HERTZSPRUNG

6TH LETTER

ARISTARCHUS
BRADWARDINE
BRAHMAGUPTA
DICAEARCHUS
GIAMBATISTA
GOODPASTURE
MACHIAVELLI
SPALLANZANI
BLOEMBERGEN
HASELBERGER
MCCAMBRIDGE
PRESSBURGER
STEENBURGEN
STEINBERGER
STRASBURGER
BRUNSCHWYGK
CALLICRATES
GOLDSCHMIDT
HIPPOCRATES
JABLOCHKOFF
KIBALCHITCH

PHOCYCLIDES
SENNACHERIB
HATZIDHAKIS
LEONIDOVICH
POSEIDONIUS
SCHILDKRAUT
SCHRODINGER
UNVERDORBEN
ALBATEGNIUS
BONAVENTURA
CHAMBERLAIN
CHAMBERLAND
CHARLEMAGNE
EVANGELISTA
GROSSETESTE
HINSHELWOOD
REICHENBACH
STERRENBERG
BIRINGUCCIO
LOBACHEVSKI
OPPENHEIMER
BUCKMINSTER
DMITRIEVICH
NIGHTINGALE
PAPANICOLAU
SCHWEICKART
SHERRINGTON
SIENKIEWICZ
CRUICKSHANK
TSIOLKOVKSY
BOEKELHEIDE
CAESALPINUS
HERACLEIDES
PICCOLOMINI
SEMMELWEISS
ANAXIMANDER
ARTSIMOVICH
NICHOMACHUS
DEISENHOFER
MORGENSTERN
NUSSENZWEIG
SCHOONMAKER
BARTHOLOMEW
CHAMPOLLION
DIOSCORIDES
MONTGOLFIER
ASCLEPIADES
PONTOPPIDAN
AUENBRUGGER
HUDALRICHUS
MAETERLINCK
MOHNOROVCIC
NEDDERMEYER
SCHNIRELMAN
SONDERGAARD
ZINKERNAGEL
HERTZSPRUNG

SCHLESINGER
SHAKESPEARE
SHIBASABURO
WEIERSTRASS
CHRISTOFFEL
CHRISTOPHER
LANDSTEINER
WILLSTATTER
DESAGULIERS
MARKOVNIKOV
PRZHEVALSKY
SERGEYEVICH

7TH LETTER

ANAXIMANDER
NICHOMACHUS
PRZHEVALSKY
SHIBASABURO
WILLSTATTER
PAPANICOLAU
SCHWEICKART
BLOEMBERGEN
DMITRIEVICH
HASELBERGER
HERACLEIDES
LANDSTEINER
LOBACHEVSKI
OPPENHEIMER
SCHNIRELMAN
SERGEYEVICH
SIENKIEWICZ
STEINBERGER
ALBATEGNIUS
BRAHMAGUPTA
SONDERGAARD
BOEKELHEIDE
BRUNSCHWYGK
DEISENHOFER
GOLDSCHMIDT
HATZIDHAKIS
JABLOCHKOFF
KIBALCHITCH
SENNACHERIB
ASCLEPIADES
HUDALRICHUS
SCHLESINGER
SCHRODINGER
SCHILDKRAUT
BARTHOLOMEW
CHAMPOLLION
DESAGULIERS
EVANGELISTA
HINSHELWOOD
MAETERLINCK

MONTGOLFIER
PHOCYCLIDES
CHARLEMAGNE
NEDDERMEYER
SCHOONMAKER
BONAVENTURA
BUCKMINSTER
MARKOVNIKOV
NIGHTINGALE
REICHENBACH
SHERRINGTON
SPALLANZANI
STERRENBERG
ZINKERNAGEL
ARTSIMOVICH
CHRISTOFFEL
CHRISTOPHER
LEONIDOVICH
MOHNOROVCIC
PICCOLOMINI
POSEIDONIUS
TSIOLKOVKSY
UNVERDORBEN
CAESALPINUS
HERTZSPRUNG
PONTOPPIDAN
SHAKESPEARE
ARISTARCHUS
BRADWARDINE
CALLICRATES
CHAMBERLAIN
CHAMBERLAND
DICAEARCHUS
DIOSCORIDES
HIPPOCRATES
MCCAMBRIDGE
CRUICKSHANK
GOODPASTURE
MORGENSTERN
GIAMBATISTA
GROSSETESTE
WEIERSTRASS
AUENBRUGGER
BIRINGUCCIO
PRESSBURGER
STEENBURGEN
STRASBURGER
MACHIAVELLI
SEMMELWEISS
NUSSENZWEIG

8TH LETTER

ASCLEPIADES
CALLICRATES

CHARLEMAGNE
HATZIDHAKIS
HIPPOCRATES
SCHOONMAKER
SONDERGAARD
ZINKERNAGEL
REICHENBACH
SHIBASABURO
STERRENBERG
ARISTARCHUS
BIRINGUCCIO
DICAEARCHUS
HUDALRICHUS
NICHOMACHUS
BRADWARDINE
BOEKELHEIDE
GROSSETESTE
MACHIAVELLI
NEDDERMEYER
SEMMELWEISS
SENNACHERIB
SHAKESPEARE
CHRISTOFFEL
MONTGOLFIER
AUENBRUGGER
NIGHTINGALE
SHERRINGTON
CRUICKSHANK
CAESALPINUS
DESAGULIERS
DIOSCORIDES
EVANGELISTA
GIAMBATISTA
HERACLEIDES
KIBALCHITCH
LANDSTEINER
MAETERLINCK
MARKOVNIKOV
MCCAMBRIDGE
OPPENHEIMER
PHOCYCLIDES
PONTOPPIDAN
JABLOCHKOFF
SCHWEICKART
CHAMBERLAIN
CHAMBERLAND
CHAMPOLLION
PRZHEVALSKY
SCHNIRELMAN
GOLDSCHMIDT
PICCOLOMINI
ALBATEGNIUS
ANAXIMANDER
POSEIDONIUS
SCHLESINGER
SCHRODINGER
BARTHOLOMEW

DEISENHOFER
PAPANICOLAU
CHRISTOPHER
BLOEMBERGEN
HASELBERGER
HERTZSPRUNG
PRESSBURGER
SCHILDKRAUT
STEENBURGEN
STEINBERGER
STRASBURGER
UNVERDORBEN
WEIERSTRASS
BUCKMINSTER
BONAVENTURA
GOODPASTURE
MORGENSTERN
WILLSTATTER
BRAHMAGUPTA
ARTSIMOVICH
DMITRIEVICH
LEONIDOVICH
LOBACHEVSKI
MOHNOROVCIC
SERGEYEVICH
TSIOLKOVKSY
BRUNSCHWYGK
HINSHELWOOD
NUSSENZWEIG
SIENKIEWICZ
SPALLANZANI

9TH LETTER

CHAMBERLAIN
CHAMBERLAND
CRUICKSHANK
NIGHTINGALE
REICHENBACH
SCHILDKRAUT
SCHWEICKART
SHAKESPEARE
SONDERGAARD
SPALLANZANI
WEIERSTRASS
UNVERDORBEN
BIRINGUCCIO
MOHNOROVCIC
ANAXIMANDER
ASCLEPIADES
DIOSCORIDES
HERACLEIDES
MCCAMBRIDGE
PHOCYCLIDES
PONTOPPIDAN

DESAGULIERS
MORGENSTERN
NUSSENZWEIG
STERRENBERG
CHRISTOFFEL
DEISENHOFER
AUENBRUGGER
BLOEMBERGEN
CHARLEMAGNE
HASELBERGER
PRESSBURGER
SCHLESINGER
SCHRODINGER
STEENBURGEN
STEINBERGER
STRASBURGER
ZINKERNAGEL
ARISTARCHUS
CHRISTOPHER
DICAEARCHUS
HUDALRICHUS
NICHOMACHUS
ALBATEGNIUS
ARTSIMOVICH
BOEKELHEIDE
BRADWARDINE
CHAMPOLLION
DMITRIEVICH
GOLDSCHMIDT
LEONIDOVICH
MONTGOLFIER
PICCOLOMINI
POSEIDONIUS
SEMMELWEISS
SERGEYEVICH
SIENKIEWICZ
HATZIDHAKIS
MARKOVNIKOV
SCHOONMAKER
TSIOLKOVKSY
MACHIAVELLI
PAPANICOLAU
BARTHOLOMEW
OPPENHEIMER
SCHNIRELMAN
CAESALPINUS
LANDSTEINER
MAETERLINCK
HINSHELWOOD
JABLOCHKOFF
BRAHMAGUPTA
SENNACHERIB
EVANGELISTA
GIAMBATISTA
GROSSETESTE
LOBACHEVSKI
PRZHEVALSKY

BUCKMINSTER
CALLICRATES
HIPPOCRATES
KIBALCHITCH
SHERRINGTON
WILLSTATTER
BONAVENTURA
GOODPASTURE
HERTZSPRUNG
SHIBASABURO
BRUNSCHWYGK
NEDDERMEYER

10TH LETTER

PAPANICOLAU
PONTOPPIDAN
SCHNIRELMAN
ARTSIMOVICH
DMITRIEVICH
KIBALCHITCH
LEONIDOVICH
MAETERLINCK
REICHENBACH
SERGEYEVICH
SIENKIEWICZ
BOEKELHEIDE
GOLDSCHMIDT
ANAXIMANDER
ASCLEPIADES
AUENBRUGGER
BARTHOLOMEW
BLOEMBERGEN
BUCKMINSTER
CALLICRATES
CHRISTOFFEL
CHRISTOPHER
DEISENHOFER
DIOSCORIDES
HASELBERGER
HERACLEIDES
HIPPOCRATES
LANDSTEINER
MONTGOLFIER
NEDDERMEYER
OPPENHEIMER
PHOCYCLIDES
PRESSBURGER
SCHLESINGER
SCHOONMAKER
SCHRODINGER
STEENBURGEN
STEINBERGER
STRASBURGER
UNVERDORBEN

WILLSTATTER
ZINKERNAGEL
JABLOCHKOFF
BRUNSCHWYGK
MCCAMBRIDGE
BIRINGUCCIO
CHAMBERLAIN
HATZIDHAKIS
MOHNOROVCIC
NUSSENZWEIG
SENNACHERIB
LOBACHEVSKI
PRZHEVALSKY
MACHIAVELLI
NIGHTINGALE
BRADWARDINE
CHAMBERLAND
CHARLEMAGNE
CRUICKSHANK
HERTZSPRUNG
PICCOLOMINI
SPALLANZANI
CHAMPOLLION
HINSHELWOOD
MARKOVNIKOV
SHERRINGTON
BONAVENTURA
DESAGULIERS
GOODPASTURE
MORGENSTERN
SCHWEICKART
SHAKESPEARE
SHIBASABURO
SONDERGAARD
STERRENBERG
SEMMELWEISS
TSIOLKOVKSY
WEIERSTRASS
BRAHMAGUPTA
EVANGELISTA
GIAMBATISTA
GROSSETESTE
ALBATEGNIUS
ARISTARCHUS
CAESALPINUS
DICAEARCHUS
HUDALRICHUS
NICHOMACHUS
POSEIDONIUS
SCHILDKRAUT

11TH LETTER

BONAVENTURA
BRAHMAGUPTA

EVANGELISTA
GIAMBATISTA
SENNACHERIB
MOHNOROVCIC
CHAMBERLAND
HINSHELWOOD
SONDERGAARD
BOEKELHEIDE
BRADWARDINE
CHARLEMAGNE
GOODPASTURE
GROSSETESTE
MCCAMBRIDGE
NIGHTINGALE
SHAKESPEARE
JABLOCHKOFF
HERTZSPRUNG
NUSSENZWEIG
STERRENBERG
ARTSIMOVICH
DMITRIEVICH
KIBALCHITCH
LEONIDOVICH
REICHENBACH
SERGEYEVICH
LOBACHEVSKI
MACHIAVELLI
PICCOLOMINI
SPALLANZANI
BRUNSCHWYGK
CRUICKSHANK
MAETERLINCK
CHRISTOFFEL
ZINKERNAGEL
BLOEMBERGEN

12 LETTER
1ST LETTER

CHAMBERLAIN
CHAMPOLLION
MORGENSTERN
PONTOPPIDAN
SCHNIRELMAN
SHERRINGTON
STEENBURGEN
UNVERDORBEN
BIRINGUCCIO
SHIBASABURO
ANAXIMANDER
AUENBRUGGER
BUCKMINSTER
CHRISTOPHER
DEISENHOFER
HASELBERGER
LANDSTEINER
MONTGOLFIER
NEDDERMEYER
OPPENHEIMER
PRESSBURGER
SCHLESINGER

SCHOONMAKER
SCHRODINGER
STEINBERGER
STRASBURGER
WILLSTATTER
ALBATEGNIUS
ARISTARCHUS
ASCLEPIADES
CAESALPINUS
CALLICRATES
DESAGULIERS
DICAEARCHUS
DIOSCORIDES
HATZIDHAKIS
HERACLEIDES
HIPPOCRATES
HUDALRICHUS
NICHOMACHUS
PHOCYCLIDES
POSEIDONIUS
SEMMELWEISS
WEIERSTRASS
GOLDSCHMIDT
SCHILDKRAUT
SCHWEICKART
PAPANICOLAU
MARKOVNIKOV
BARTHOLOMEW
PRZHEVALSKY
TSIOLKOVKSY
SIENKIEWICZ

12 LETTER
1ST LETTER

ALEKSEYEVICH
ALEPOUDHELIS
AMAZASPOVICH
AMBARTSUMIAN
ANTHONISZOON
ATTENBOROUGH
BOUSSINGAULT
COLLINGRIDGE
DESHOUILLERS
ERASISTRATUS
ERATOSTHENES
GALANOPOULOS
HAMMARSKJOLD
HOLLINGSHEAD
HULDSCHINSKY
KLEINSCHMIDT
MERGENTHALER
MICHELANGELO
MITSCHERLICH

NIKOLAEVITCH
NORDENSKIOLD
OSTROGRADSKI
RABINDRANATH
RAMACHANDRAN
SATYENDRANTH
SCHERTZINGER
SCHIAPARELLI
SCHOENHEIMER
SOLZHENITSYN
SQUARCIAPINO
SUBRAHMANYAN
THEOPHRASTUS
UYTTERHOEVEN
WEINDENREICH
WESTINGHOUSE

2ND LETTER

GALANOPOULOS
HAMMARSKJOLD
RABINDRANATH
RAMACHANDRAN
SATYENDRANTH
SCHERTZINGER
SCHIAPARELLI
SCHOENHEIMER
DESHOUILLERS
MERGENTHALER
WEINDENREICH
WESTINGHOUSE
THEOPHRASTUS
MICHELANGELO
MITSCHERLICH
NIKOLAEVITCH
ALEKSEYEVICH
ALEPOUDHELIS
KLEINSCHMIDT
AMAZASPOVICH
AMBARTSUMIAN
ANTHONISZOON
BOUSSINGAULT
COLLINGRIDGE
HOLLINGSHEAD
NORDENSKIOLD
SOLZHENITSYN
SQUARCIAPINO
ERASISTRATUS
ERATOSTHENES
OSTROGRADSKI
ATTENBOROUGH
HULDSCHINSKY
SUBRAHMANYAN
UYTTERHOEVEN

3RD LETTER

AMAZASPOVICH
ERASISTRATUS
ERATOSTHENES
AMBARTSUMIAN
RABINDRANATH
SUBRAHMANYAN
MICHELANGELO
ALEKSEYEVICH
ALEPOUDHELIS
KLEINSCHMIDT
THEOPHRASTUS
SCHERTZINGER
SCHIAPARELLI
SCHOENHEIMER
WEINDENREICH
NIKOLAEVITCH
COLLINGRIDGE
GALANOPOULOS
HOLLINGSHEAD
HULDSCHINSKY
SOLZHENITSYN
HAMMARSKJOLD
RAMACHANDRAN
MERGENTHALER
NORDENSKIOLD
DESHOUILLERS
WESTINGHOUSE
ANTHONISZOON
ATTENBOROUGH
MITSCHERLICH
OSTROGRADSKI
SATYENDRANTH
UYTTERHOEVEN
BOUSSINGAULT
SQUARCIAPINO

4TH LETTER

AMBARTSUMIAN
GALANOPOULOS
RAMACHANDRAN
SQUARCIAPINO
HULDSCHINSKY
NORDENSKIOLD
ATTENBOROUGH
SCHERTZINGER
MERGENTHALER
ANTHONISZOON
DESHOUILLERS
MICHELANGELO
KLEINSCHMIDT
RABINDRANATH
SCHIAPARELLI

ALEKSEYEVICH
COLLINGRIDGE
HOLLINGSHEAD
HAMMARSKJOLD
WEINDENREICH
NIKOLAEVITCH
SCHOENHEIMER
THEOPHRASTUS
ALEPOUDHELIS
OSTROGRADSKI
SUBRAHMANYAN
BOUSSINGAULT
ERASISTRATUS
MITSCHERLICH
ERATOSTHENES
UYTTERHOEVEN
WESTINGHOUSE
SATYENDRANTH
AMAZASPOVICH
SOLZHENITSYN

5TH LETTER

AMAZASPOVICH
HAMMARSKJOLD
SCHIAPARELLI
SUBRAHMANYAN
MITSCHERLICH
RAMACHANDRAN
WEINDENREICH
MERGENTHALER
MICHELANGELO
NORDENSKIOLD
SATYENDRANTH
SCHOENHEIMER
UYTTERHOEVEN
SOLZHENITSYN
COLLINGRIDGE
ERASISTRATUS
HOLLINGSHEAD
WESTINGHOUSE
NIKOLAEVITCH
ATTENBOROUGH
GALANOPOULOS
KLEINSCHMIDT
RABINDRANATH
ALEPOUDHELIS
ANTHONISZOON
DESHOUILLERS
ERATOSTHENES
OSTROGRADSKI
THEOPHRASTUS
AMBARTSUMIAN
SCHERTZINGER
SQUARCIAPINO

ALEKSEYEVICH
BOUSSINGAULT
HULDSCHINSKY

6TH LETTER

NIKOLAEVITCH
ATTENBOROUGH
HULDSCHINSKY
SQUARCIAPINO
RABINDRANATH
ALEKSEYEVICH
SOLZHENITSYN
WEINDENREICH
OSTROGRADSKI
MITSCHERLICH
RAMACHANDRAN
SUBRAHMANYAN
THEOPHRASTUS
BOUSSINGAULT
MICHELANGELO
ANTHONISZOON
COLLINGRIDGE
HOLLINGSHEAD
MERGENTHALER
NORDENSKIOLD
SATYENDRANTH
SCHOENHEIMER
WESTINGHOUSE
GALANOPOULOS
SCHIAPARELLI
HAMMARSKJOLD
UYTTERHOEVEN
AMAZASPOVICH
ERASISTRATUS
ERATOSTHENES
KLEINSCHMIDT
AMBARTSUMIAN
SCHERTZINGER
ALEPOUDHELIS
DESHOUILLERS

7TH LETTER

MICHELANGELO
RAMACHANDRAN
SCHIAPARELLI
KLEINSCHMIDT
ALEPOUDHELIS
SATYENDRANTH
MITSCHERLICH
NIKOLAEVITCH
COLLINGRIDGE

HOLLINGSHEAD
WESTINGHOUSE
HULDSCHINSKY
SCHOENHEIMER
UYTTERHOEVEN
ANTHONISZOON
DESHOUILLERS
SQUARCIAPINO
SUBRAHMANYAN
BOUSSINGAULT
SOLZHENITSYN
WEINDENREICH
ATTENBOROUGH
AMAZASPOVICH
GALANOPOULOS
OSTROGRADSKI
RABINDRANATH
THEOPHRASTUS
AMBARTSUMIAN
HAMMARSKJOLD
NORDENSKIOLD
ERASISTRATUS
ERATOSTHENES
MERGENTHALER
ALEKSEYEVICH
SCHERTZINGER

8TH LETTER

OSTROGRADSKI
RABINDRANATH
SQUARCIAPINO
SUBRAHMANYAN
THEOPHRASTUS
ALEKSEYEVICH
SCHOENHEIMER
BOUSSINGAULT
ALEPOUDHELIS
ERATOSTHENES
KLEINSCHMIDT
MERGENTHALER
WESTINGHOUSE
HULDSCHINSKY
SCHERTZINGER
SOLZHENITSYN
HAMMARSKJOLD
NORDENSKIOLD
DESHOUILLERS
MICHELANGELO
RAMACHANDRAN
AMAZASPOVICH
GALANOPOULOS
UYTTERHOEVEN
ATTENBOROUGH
COLLINGRIDGE

ERASISTRATUS
MITSCHERLICH
SATYENDRANTH
SCHIAPARELLI
WEINDENREICH
ANTHONISZOON
HOLLINGSHEAD
AMBARTSUMIAN
NIKOLAEVITCH

9TH LETTER

BOUSSINGAULT
ERASISTRATUS
MERGENTHALER
SATYENDRANTH
OSTROGRADSKI
RAMACHANDRAN
ALEPOUDHELIS
ERATOSTHENES
SCHIAPARELLI
UYTTERHOEVEN
WEINDENREICH
MICHELANGELO
HOLLINGSHEAD
COLLINGRIDGE
NIKOLAEVITCH
NORDENSKIOLD
SCHOENHEIMER
HAMMARSKJOLD
DESHOUILLERS
MITSCHERLICH
AMBARTSUMIAN
KLEINSCHMIDT
HULDSCHINSKY
RABINDRANATH
SCHERTZINGER
SUBRAHMANYAN
ATTENBOROUGH
WESTINGHOUSE
SQUARCIAPINO
THEOPHRASTUS
SOLZHENITSYN
GALANOPOULOS
ALEKSEYEVICH
AMAZASPOVICH
ANTHONISZOON

10TH LETTER

RABINDRANATH
COLLINGRIDGE
DESHOUILLERS

HOLLINGSHEAD
MICHELANGELO
SCHERTZINGER
ALEKSEYEVICH
AMAZASPOVICH
AMBARTSUMIAN
KLEINSCHMIDT
MITSCHERLICH
SQUARCIAPINO
WEINDENREICH
ALEPOUDHELIS
GALANOPOULOS
MERGENTHALER
SCHIAPARELLI
SCHOENHEIMER
ERATOSTHENES
SATYENDRANTH
ANTHONISZOON
HAMMARSKJOLD
NORDENSKIOLD
RAMACHANDRAN
HULDSCHINSKY
OSTROGRADSKI
SOLZHENITSYN
ERASISTRATUS
NIKOLAEVITCH
THEOPHRASTUS
ATTENBOROUGH
BOUSSINGAULT
WESTINGHOUSE
UYTTERHOEVEN
SUBRAHMANYAN

11TH LETTER

AMBARTSUMIAN
HOLLINGSHEAD
RAMACHANDRAN
SUBRAHMANYAN
ALEKSEYEVICH
AMAZASPOVICH
MITSCHERLICH
NIKOLAEVITCH
WEINDENREICH
KLEINSCHMIDT
ERATOSTHENES
MERGENTHALER
SCHERTZINGER
SCHOENHEIMER
UYTTERHOEVEN
ATTENBOROUGH
COLLINGRIDGE
ALEPOUDHELIS
HULDSCHINSKY
OSTROGRADSKI

BOUSSINGAULT
HAMMARSKJOLD
MICHELANGELO
NORDENSKIOLD
SCHIAPARELLI
SQUARCIAPINO
ANTHONISZOON
GALANOPOULOS
DESHOUILLERS
WESTINGHOUSE
RABINDRANATH
SATYENDRANTH
ERASISTRATUS
THEOPHRASTUS
SOLZHENITSYN

12TH LETTER

HAMMARSKJOLD
HOLLINGSHEAD
NORDENSKIOLD
COLLINGRIDGE
WESTINGHOUSE
ALEKSEYEVICH
AMAZASPOVICH
ATTENBOROUGH
MITSCHERLICH
NIKOLAEVITCH
RABINDRANATH
SATYENDRANTH
WEINDENREICH
OSTROGRADSKI
SCHIAPARELLI
AMBARTSUMIAN
ANTHONISZOON
RAMACHANDRAN
SOLZHENITSYN
SUBRAHMANYAN
UYTTERHOEVEN
MICHELANGELO
SQUARCIAPINO
MERGENTHALER
SCHERTZINGER
SCHOENHEIMER
ALEPOUDHELIS
DESHOUILLERS
ERASISTRATUS
ERATOSTHENES
GALANOPOULOS
THEOPHRASTUS
BOUSSINGAULT
KLEINSCHMIDT
HULDSCHINSKY

13 LETTER

1ST LETTER	2ND LETTER	3RD LETTER	4TH LETTER
BARTHOLOMAEUS	BARTHOLOMAEUS	BHATTACHARYYA	REICHELDERFER
BHATTACHARYYA	KANELLOPOULOS	BRANDENBURGER	WALDSEEMULLER
BRANDENBURGER	WALDSEEMULLER	CHANDRASEKHAR	KANELLOPOULOS
CHANDRASEKHAR	SCHWARZSCHILD	REGIOMONTANUS	REGIOMONTANUS
KANELLOPOULOS	REGIOMONTANUS	SCHWARZSCHILD	BRANDENBURGER
REGIOMONTANUS	REICHELDERFER	REICHELDERFER	CHANDRASEKHAR
REICHELDERFER	BHATTACHARYYA	WALDSEEMULLER	BARTHOLOMAEUS
SCHWARZSCHILD	CHANDRASEKHAR	KANELLOPOULOS	BHATTACHARYYA
WALDSEEMULLER	BRANDENBURGER	BARTHOLOMAEUS	SCHWARZSCHILD

5TH LETTER	6TH LETTER	7TH LETTER	8TH LETTER
SCHWARZSCHILD	BHATTACHARYYA	CHANDRASEKHAR	BRANDENBURGER
BRANDENBURGER	BRANDENBURGER	BHATTACHARYYA	REICHELDERFER
CHANDRASEKHAR	REICHELDERFER	WALDSEEMULLER	BHATTACHARYYA
BARTHOLOMAEUS	WALDSEEMULLER	BARTHOLOMAEUS	WALDSEEMULLER
REICHELDERFER	KANELLOPOULOS	REICHELDERFER	REGIOMONTANUS
KANELLOPOULOS	REGIOMONTANUS	BRANDENBURGER	BARTHOLOMAEUS
REGIOMONTANUS	BARTHOLOMAEUS	KANELLOPOULOS	KANELLOPOULOS
WALDSEEMULLER	CHANDRASEKHAR	REGIOMONTANUS	CHANDRASEKHAR
BHATTACHARYYA	SCHWARZSCHILD	SCHWARZSCHILD	SCHWARZSCHILD

9TH LETTER	10TH LETTER	11TH LETTER	12TH LETTER
BHATTACHARYYA	BARTHOLOMAEUS	BARTHOLOMAEUS	CHANDRASEKHAR
SCHWARZSCHILD	REGIOMONTANUS	REICHELDERFER	BRANDENBURGER
CHANDRASEKHAR	SCHWARZSCHILD	BRANDENBURGER	REICHELDERFER
REICHELDERFER	CHANDRASEKHAR	CHANDRASEKHAR	WALDSEEMULLER
BARTHOLOMAEUS	WALDSEEMULLER	SCHWARZSCHILD	SCHWARZSCHILD
KANELLOPOULOS	BHATTACHARYYA	KANELLOPOULOS	KANELLOPOULOS
REGIOMONTANUS	BRANDENBURGER	WALDSEEMULLER	BARTHOLOMAEUS
BRANDENBURGER	REICHELDERFER	REGIOMONTANUS	REGIOMONTANUS
WALDSEEMULLER	KANELLOPOULOS	BHATTACHARYYA	BHATTACHARYYA

13TH LETTER
BHATTACHARYYA
SCHWARZSCHILD
BRANDENBURGER
CHANDRASEKHAR
REICHELDERFER
WALDSEEMULLER
BARTHOLOMAEUS
KANELLOPOULOS
REGIOMONTANUS

14 LETTER

1ST LETTER	2ND LETTER	3RD LETTER	4TH LETTER
ALEKSANDROVICH	JAGADISCHANDRA	CHANDRASEKHARA	JAGADISCHANDRA
CHANDRASEKHARA	SCHALLENBERGER	ALEKSANDROVICH	SCHALLENBERGER
JAGADISCHANDRA	CHANDRASEKHARA	JAGADISCHANDRA	ALEKSANDROVICH
KLINGENSTIERNA	ALEKSANDROVICH	SCHALLENBERGER	CHANDRASEKHARA
SCHALLENBERGER	KLINGENSTIERNA	KLINGENSTIERNA	KLINGENSTIERNA

5TH LETTER	6TH LETTER	7TH LETTER	8TH LETTER
CHANDRASEKHARA	ALEKSANDROVICH	CHANDRASEKHARA	JAGADISCHANDRA
JAGADISCHANDRA	KLINGENSTIERNA	SCHALLENBERGER	ALEKSANDROVICH
KLINGENSTIERNA	JAGADISCHANDRA	ALEKSANDROVICH	SCHALLENBERGER
SCHALLENBERGER	SCHALLENBERGER	KLINGENSTIERNA	CHANDRASEKHARA
ALEKSANDROVICH	CHANDRASEKHARA	JAGADISCHANDRA	KLINGENSTIERNA

9TH LETTER	10TH LETTER
SCHALLENBERGER	JAGADISCHANDRA
CHANDRASEKHARA	SCHALLENBERGER
JAGADISCHANDRA	KLINGENSTIERNA
ALEKSANDROVICH	CHANDRASEKHARA
KLINGENSTIERNA	ALEKSANDROVICH

11TH Letter

KLINGENSTI**E**RNA
CHANDRASEK**H**ARA
JAGADISCHA**N**DRA
SCHALLENBE**R**GER
ALEKSANDRO**V**ICH

12TH Letter

CHANDRASEKH**A**RA
JAGADISCHAN**D**RA
SCHALLENBER**G**ER
ALEKSANDROV**I**CH
KLINGENSTIE**R**NA

13TH Letter

ALEKSANDROVI**C**H
SCHALLENBERG**E**R
KLINGENSTIER**N**A
CHANDRASEKHA**R**A
JAGADISCHAND**R**A

14TH Letter

CHANDRASEKHAR**A**
JAGADISCHANDR**A**
KLINGENSTIERN**A**
ALEKSANDROVIC**H**
SCHALLENBERGE**R**

SECTION 3 · GEOGRAPHIC NAMES

— 2-13 — LETTER WORDS

2 LETTER — 1ST LETTER

AD, AE, AF, AG, AI, AK, AL, AM, AN, AO, AQ, AR, AS, AT, AU, AW, AZ, BA, BB, BD, BE, BF, BG, BH, BI, BJ, BM, BN, BO, BR, BS, BT, BV, BW, BY, BZ, CA, CC, CF, CG, CH, CI

CK, CL, CM, CN, CO, CR, CT, CU, CV, CX, CY, CZ, DA, DC, DE, DJ, DK, DM, DO, DZ, EC, EE, EG, EH, EL, ER, ES, ET, FE, FI, FJ, FK, FL, FM, FO, FR, GA, GD, GE, GF, GG, GH, GI, GL, GM, GN

GP, GQ, GR, GS, GT, GU, GW, GY, HI, HK, HM, HN, HR, HT, HU, IA, ID, IE, IL, IM, IN, IQ, IR, IS, IT, JE, JM, JO, JP, KE, KG, KH, KI, KM, KN, KP, KR, KS, KW, KY, KZ, LA, LB, LC, LI

LK, LR, LS, LT, LU, LV, LY, MA, MC, MD, ME, MG, MH, MI, MK, ML, MN, MO, MP, MQ, MR, MS, MT, MU, MV, MW, MX, MY, MZ, NA, NC, ND, NE, NF, NG, NH, NI, NJ, NL, NM, NO, NP, NR, NU, NV, NY

NZ, OF, OH, OK, OM, OR, PA, PE, PF, PG, PH, PK, PL, PM, PN, PR, PT, PW, PY, QA, RE, RI, RO, RU, RW, SA, SB, SC, SD, SE, SG, SH, SI, SJ, SK, SL, SM, SN, SO, SP, SR, ST, SV, SY, SZ

TD, TF, TG, TH, TJ, TK, TM, TN, TO, TR, TT, TW, TX, TZ, UA, UG, UK, UM, US, UT, UY, UZ, VA, VC, VE, VG, VI, VS, VU, WA, WF, WI, WS, WV, WY, YE, YT, YU, ZA, ZM, ZR, ZW

2ND LETTER

BA, CA, DA, GA, IA, LA, MA, NA, PA, QA, SA, UA, VA, WA, ZA, BB, LB, SB, CC, DC, EC, LC, MC, NC, SC, TC, VC, AD, BD, GD, ID, ND, SD, TD, AE, BE, DE, EE, FE, GE, IE, JE, KE

ME, NE, PE, RE, SE, VE, YE, AF, BF, CF, GF, NF, OF, PF, TF, WF, AG, BG, CG, EG, GG, KG, MG, NG, PG, SG, TG, UG, VG, CH, EH, GH, IH, KH, MH, NH, SH, TH, AI, BI, CI, FI, GI, HI

KI, LI, MI, NI, RI, SI, VI, WI, BJ, DJ, FJ, NJ, SJ, TJ, AK, CK, DK, FK, HK, LK, MK, OK, PK, SK, TK, UK, AL, CL, EL, FL, GL, IL, ML, NL, PL, SL, AM, BM, CM, DM, FM, GM, HM, IM, JM, KM

NM, OM, PM, SM, TM, UM, ZM, AN, BN, CN, GN, HN, IN, KN, MN, PN, SN, TN, VN, AO, BO, CO, DO, FO, IO, JO, MO, NO, RO, SO, AP, GP, JP, KP, MP, NP, SP, AQ, GQ, IQ, MQ, AR, BR, CR, ER, FR

GR, HR, IR, KR, LR, MR, NR, OR, PR, SR, TR, ZR, AS, BS, ES, GS, IS, KS, LS, MS, US, WS, AT, BT, CT, ET, GT, HT, IT, LT, MT, PT, ST, TT, UT, VT, YT, AU, CU, GU, HU, LU, MU, NU, RU, VU

YU, BV, CV, LV, MV, NV, SV, AW, BW, GW, KW, MW, PW, RW, TW, ZW, CX, MX, TX, BY, CY, GY, KY, LY, MY, NY, PY, SY, UY, WY, AZ, BZ, CZ, DZ, KZ, MZ, NZ, SZ, TZ, UZ

3 LETTER

1ST LETTER:
ABU, AND, BAY, DES, INO, JAN, MAN, NEW, PAZ, RED, SAN, SAO, SEA, SRI, THE

2ND LETTER:
BAY, JAN, MAN, PAZ, SAN, SAO, ABU, DES, NEW, RED, SEA, THE, AND, INO, SRI

3RD LETTER:
SEA, AND, RED, THE, SRI, JAN, MAN, SAN, INO, SAO, DES, ABU, NEW, BAY, PAZ

4 LETTER

1ST LETTER:
ADEN, APAN, APIA, ARAB, ARAL, AVES, BAKU, BASS, BEAR, BERN, CAPE, CHAD, CITY, COOK, CUBA, DEAD, EAST, ERIE, FIJI, FOXE, GUAM, GULF, HONG, IOWA, IRAN, IRAQ

JAVA	**2ND LETTER**	TOME	LAKE	RIGA	LAOS	DHAKA	SANAA	QATAR	BLACK	GRAND	CUNHA
JOSE		TOWN	NUKU	SUVA	ROSS	DOVER	SANTA	RABAT	SLAVE	HEARD	DENIS
JUAN	BAKU	YORK	WAKE	VILA	EAST	EGYPT	SANTO	SAINT	AMMAN	IDAHO	FUNDI
KANE	BASS	APAN	GULF	ARAB	PORT	FAROE	SAUDI	SALEM	SMITH	ITALY	HANOI
KARA	CAPE	APIA	MALE	CHAD	SALT	FUNDI	SEOUL	SAMOA	INDIA	KUALA	KENYA
KIEV	EAST	ARAB	MALI	DEAD	WEST	GABON	SIDRA	SANAA	BOISE	PEARY	LANKA
KONG	JAVA	ARAL	OSLO	MAUD	BAKU	GHANA	SLAVE	COAST		PRAIA	MINSK
LAGO	KANE	ERIE	SALT	ROAD	NUKU	GRAND	SMITH	SANTO	COCOS	SLAVE	PHNOM
LAKE	KARA	IRAN	SULU	CAPE	PERU	GREAT	SOFIA	SAUDI	CONGO	SPAIN	SANAA
LAOS	LAGO	IRAQ	VILA	ERIE	SULU	HAITI	SOUND	VADUZ	CORAL	GABON	SANTA
LIMA	LAKE	OSLO	LIMA	FOXE	KIEV	HANOI	SOUTH	WALES	COSTA	KABUL	SANTO
LINE	LAOS	UTAH	LOME	JOSE	CITY	HEARD	SPAIN	YAREN	DOVER	LIBYA	TONGA
LOME	MALE	CUBA	ROME	KANE		HURON	SUDAN	ZAIRE	JOHNS	RABAT	TUNIS
MALE	MALI	GUAM	TOME	LAKE		IDAHO	SYRIA	ABABA	KOREA	ACCRA	ALOFA
MALI	MAUD	GULF	HONG	LINE		INDIA	ABUJA	LOUIS	COCOS	ALOFI	
MAUD	MAUI	JUAN	KANE	LOME	**5 LETTER**	IRISH	TERRE	ACCRA	NORTH	LUCIA	ATOLL
MAUI	PAGO	NUKU	KONG	MALE	**1ST LETTER**	ITALY	TEXAS	OCEAN	PORTO	MACAO	IVORY
NIUE	PAUL	SULU	LINE	NIUE		IVORY	TIMOR	ADDIS	ROUGE	ADDIS	LEONE
NOVO	SALT	SUVA	PENH	ROME		JAPAN	TONGA	IDAHO	SOFIA	INDIA	RHODE
NUKU	WAKE	TURK	COOK	TOME	ABABA	JOHNS	TUNIS	BENIN	SOUND	SIDRA	SEOUL
OHIO	ADEN	AVES	LAOS	WAKE	ABUJA	KABUL	TURKS	CEUTA	SOUTH	SUDAN	JAPAN
OMAN	BEAR		CAPE	GULF	ACCRA	KENYA	VADUZ	DELHI	TONGA	VADUZ	NEPAL
OSLO	BERN		BERN	REEF	ADDIS	KITTS	VELLA	DENIS	TOYKO	CZECH	PAPUA
PAGO	DEAD		KARA	HONG	AGANA	KOREA	VERDE	HEARD	SPAIN	GREAT	AIRES
PAUL	PENH	**3RD LETTER**	PERU	KONG	AIRES	KUALA	WALES	KENYA	ARUBA	OCEAN	CORAL
PENH	PERU		PORT	PENH	ALAND	LANKA	WHITE	LEONE	GRAND	QUEEN	FAROE
PERU	REEF	APAN	SERI	UTAH	ALGER	LEONE	YAREN	NEPAL	GREAT	SOFIA	HURON
PORT	SERI	ARAB	TURK	FIJI	ALOFA	LIBYA	YEMEN	NEVIS	IRISH	ALGER	KOREA
REEF	WEST	ARAL	YORK	MALI	ALOFI	LOUIS	ZAIRE	PEARY	PRAIA	BIGHT	NORTH
RICA	CHAD	BEAR	BASS	MAUI	AMMAN	LUCIA		SEOUL	ATOLL	NIGER	PARIS
RICO	OHIO	CHAD	EAST	SERI	ARUBA	MACAO		TERRE	ITALY	JOHNS	PORTO
RIGA	CITY	DEAD	JOSE	COOK	ATOLL	MAINE		TEXAS	CUNHA	BOISE	SYRIA
ROAD	FIJI	GUAM	ROSS	ROCK	BANDA	MALTA	**2ND LETTER**	VELLA	FUNDI	CAIRO	TERRE
ROCK	KIEV	IRAN	WEST	TURK	BASIN	MAYEN		VERDE	HURON	CHILE	TURKS
ROME	LIMA	IRAQ	CITY	YORK	BASSE	MINSK	BANDA	YEMEN	KUALA	CHINA	VERDE
ROSS	LINE	JUAN	MAUD	ARAL	BATON	NAURU	BASIN	KUALA	LUCIA	HAITI	YAREN
SALT	NIUE	OMAN	MAUI	PAUL	BATOR	NEPAL	BASSE	AGANA	IRISH	IRISH	BASIN
SERI	RICA	ROAD	NIUE	GUAM	BENIN	NEVIS	EGYPT	QUEEN	MAINE	QUITO	BASSE
SULU	RICO	ULAN	PAUL	ADEN	BIGHT	NIGER	BASSE	QUITO	QUITO	SAINT	COSTA
SUVA	RIGA	UTAH	JAVA	APAN	BLACK	NORTH	BATON	QUITO	SAINT	SMITH	BATON
TOGO	VILA	CUBA	NOVO	BERN	BOISE	OCEAN	CAIRO	SAINT	SMITH	WHITE	KITTS
TOME	ULAN	RICA	SUVA	IRAN	CAIRO	PALAU	DAKAR	TUNIS	IVORY	ZAIRE	QATAR
TOWN	OMAN	RICO	IOWA	JUAN	CEUTA	PAPUA	DAVIS	TURKS	SYRIA	DAKAR	ABUJA
TURK	COOK	ROCK	TOWN	OMAN	CHILE	PARIS	FAROE	SMITH	ZAIRE	QATAR	ARUBA
ULAN	FOXE	ADEN	FOXE	TOWN	CHINA	PEARY	PHNOM	WHITE	CZECH	DELHI	CEUTA
UTAH	HONG	AVES		ULAN	COAST	PHNOM	RHODE	ZAIRE		MALTA	LOUIS
VILA	IOWA	KIEV		LAGO	COCOS	PORTO	HAITI	AIRES		PALAU	NAURU
WAKE	JOSE	REEF		NOVO	CONGO	PRAIA	HANOI	BIGHT		SALEM	ROUGE
WEST	KONG	LAGO	**4TH LETTER**	OHIO	CORAL	QATAR	JAPAN	KITTS	**3RD LETTER**	VELLA	SAUDI
YORK	LOME	PAGO		OSLO	COSTA	QUEEN	KABUL	LIBYA		WALES	SOUND
	NOVO	RIGA	APIA	PAGO	CUNHA	QUITO	KITTS	MINSK	ABABA	AMMAN	SOUTH
	PORT	TOGO	CUBA	RICO	CZECH	RABAT	LANKA	MAINE	AGANA	SAMOA	DAVIS
	ROAD	APIA	IOWA	TOGO	DAKAR	RHODE	MACAO	NIGER	ALAND	TIMOR	DOVER
	ROCK	ERIE	JAVA	IRAQ	DAVIS	ROUGE	MAINE	SIDRA	BLACK	TIMOR	NEVIS
	ROME	OHIO	KARA	BEAR	DELHI	SAINT	MALTA	TIMOR	ALAND	YEMEN	TEXAS
	ROSS	FIJI	LIMA	AVES	DENIS	SALEM	MAYEN	BLACK	DHABI	BENIN	EGYPT
	TOGO	BAKU	RICA	BASS	DHABI	SAMOA	NAURU	ALAND	DHAKA	CONGO	
							PARIS	ALOFI	GHANA		

MAYEN	LOUIS	KITTS	BASSE	BATOR	BAMAKO	JORDAN	TARAWA	MAPUTO	ALBERT
TOYKO	LUCIA	MALTA	BOISE	DAKAR	BANABA	JUNEAU	TASMAN	MARINO	ALMATY
	NEVIS	NORTH	CHILE	DOVER	BANDAR	KANSAS	TEHRAN	MARTIN	AMALIE
	PARIS	PORTO	FAROE	NIGER	BANGUI	KIGALI	THIMBU	MASERU	ANGOLA
	PRAIA	QUITO	LEONE	QATAR	BANJUL	KUWAIT	TIRANA	NANSEN	ANKARA
[4TH LETTER]	SOFIA	SANTA	MAINE	TIMOR	BEIRUT	LADOGA	TOBAGO	NASSAU	INDIAN
	SPAIN	SANTO	RHODE	ADDIS	BELIZE	LAPTEV	TONKIN	PANAMA	UNGAVA
AMMAN	SYRIA	SMITH	ROUGE	AIRES	BENGAL	LATVIA	TOPEKA	SAHARA	UNITED
CORAL	TUNIS	SOUTH	SLAVE	COCOS	BERING	LISBON	TURKEY	TAIWAN	BOGOTA
DAKAR	ABUJA	WHITE	TERRE	DAVIS	BERLIN	LITTLE	UGANDA	TARAWA	BOSNIA
GREAT	DHAKA	KABUL	VERDE	DENIS	BHUTAN	LONDON	UNGAVA	TASMAN	BOSTON
JAPAN	LANKA	PAPUA	WHITE	JOHNS	BISCAY	LUANDA	UNITED	VALLEY	BOUVET
MACAO	TOYKO	SEOUL	ZAIRE	KITTS	BISSAU	LUMPUR	VALLEY	WALLIS	DODOMA
NEPAL	TURKS	VADUZ	CZECH	LOUIS	BOGOTA	LUSAKA	VIENNA	WARSAW	HORMUZ
OCEAN	ATOLL	SLAVE	IRISH	NEVIS	BOSNIA	MADRID	VIRGIN	YANGON	JORDAN
PALAU	CHILE	KENYA	NORTH	PARIS	BOSTON	MALABO	WALLIS	ZAGREB	LONDON
QATAR	ITALY	LIBYA	SMITH	TEXAS	BOUVET	MALAWI	WARSAW	ZAMBIA	MOINES
RABAT	KUALA		SOUTH	TUNIS	BRAZIL	MANAMA	YANGON	SCOTIA	MONACO
SANAA	VELLA		ALOFI	TURKS	BRUNEI	MANILA	YELLOW	EDWARD	MORONI
SUDAN	AGANA	**[5TH LETTER]**	DELHI	WALES	BUENOS	MAPUTO	ZAGREB	AEGEAN	MOSCOW
TEXAS	ALAND		DHABI	BIGHT	CAICOS	MARINO	ZAMBIA	BEIRUT	NORWAY
ABABA	CHINA	ABABA	FUNDI	COAST	CANADA	MARTIN		BELIZE	NOUMEA
ARUBA	GHANA	ABUJA	HAITI	EGYPT	CANARY	MASERU		BENGAL	POLAND
DHABI	GRAND	ACCRA	HANOI	GREAT	CARSON	MEXICO		BERING	ROSEAU
BLACK	JOHNS	AGANA	SAUDI	RABAT	CAYMAN	MIDWAY	**[2ND LETTER]**	BERLIN	TOBAGO
CZECH	LEONE	ALOFA	BLACK	SAINT	CELTIC	MINAMI		CELTIC	TONKIN
BANDA	MAINE	ALOFI	MINSK	NAURU	CROZET	MOINES	BAFFIN	DENVER	TOPEKA
FUNDI	SAINT	ARUBA	ATOLL	PALAU	CYPRUS	MONACO	BAGDAD	GEORGE	ARABIA
RHODE	SOUND	BANDA	CORAL	ITALY	DAKOTA	MORONI	BAIKAL	HECATE	BRAZIL
SAUDI	BATON	CEUTA	KABUL	IVORY	DAWHAH	MOSCOW	BALTIC	HELENA	BRUNEI
VERDE	BATOR	CHINA	NEPAL	PEARY	DENVER	MUSCAT	BAMAKO	JERSEY	CROZET
AIRES	COCOS	COSTA	SEOUL	VADUZ	DODOMA	NANSEN	BANABA	MEXICO	FRANCE
ALGER	FAROE	CUNHA	PHNOM		DUBLIN	NASSAU	BANDAR	NEVADA	FRENCH
DOVER	GABON	DHAKA	SALEM		EASTER	NEVADA	BANGUI	SERBIA	GREECE
KOREA	HANOI	GHANA	AMMAN		EDWARD	NIAMEY	BANJUL	TEHRAN	OREGON
MAYEN	HURON	INDIA	BASIN	**[6 LETTER]**	FRANCE	NORWAY	CAICOS	YELLOW	PRAGUE
NIGER	PHNOM	KENYA	BATON		FRENCH	NOUMEA	CANADA	AFRICA	PRINCE
QUEEN	SAMOA	KOREA	BENIN	**[1ST LETTER]**	FUTANA	OREGON	CANARY	UGANDA	ASMARA
SALEM	TIMOR	KUALA	GABON		GAMBIA	OTTAWA	CARSON	BHUTAN	ISLAND
WALES	EGYPT	LANKA	HURON	AEGEAN	GEORGE	PANAMA	CAYMAN	THIMBU	ISRAEL
YAREN	ACCRA	LIBYA	JAPAN	AFRICA	GIGEDO	PIERRE	DAKOTA	BISCAY	ATHENS
YEMEN	CAIRO	LUCIA	MAYEN	ALASKA	GREECE	POLAND	DAWHAH	BISSAU	OTTAWA
ALOFA	HEARD	MALTA	OCEAN	ALBANY	GUIANA	PRAGUE	EASTER	GIGEDO	STATES
ALOFI	IVORY	PAPUA	QUEEN	ALBERT	GUINEA	PRINCE	GAMBIA	KIGALI	STRAIT
CONGO	NAURU	PRAIA	SPAIN	ALMATY	GUYANA	PUERTO	HARARE	LISBON	AUSTIN
ROUGE	PEARY	SAMOA	SUDAN	AMALIE	HARARE	RIYADH	HAVANA	LITTLE	BUENOS
TONGA	SIDRA	SANAA	YAREN	ANGOLA	HAVANA	ROSEAU	HAWAII	MIDWAY	DUBLIN
BIGHT	TERRE	SANTA	YEMEN	ANKARA	HAWAII	RUSSIA	JALUIT	MINAMI	FUTANA
CUNHA	ZAIRE	SIDRA	CAIRO	ARABIA	HECATE	RWANDA	KANSAS	NIAMEY	GUIANA
DELHI	BASSE	SOFIA	CONGO	ASMARA	HELENA	SAHARA	LADOGA	PIERRE	GUINEA
IDAHO	BOISE	SYRIA	IDAHO	ATHENS	HORMUZ	SCOTIA	LAPTEV	RIYADH	GUYANA
ADDIS	COAST	TONGA	MACAO	AUSTIN	HUDSON	SERBIA	LATVIA	SIERRA	HUDSON
BASIN	IRISH	VELLA	PORTO	AZORES	INDIAN	SIERRA	MADRID	TIRANA	JUNEAU
BENIN	MINSK	ALAND	QUITO	BAFFIN	ISLAND	STATES	MALABO	VIENNA	KUWAIT
DAVIS	CEUTA	GRAND	SANTO	BAGDAD	ISRAEL	STRAIT	MALAWI	VIRGIN	LUANDA
DENIS	COSTA	HEARD	TOYKO	BAIKAL	JALUIT	SWEDEN	MANAMA	ALASKA	LUMPUR
INDIA	HAITI	SOUND	ALGER	BALTIC	JERSEY	TAIWAN	MANILA	ALBANY	LUSAKA

			4TH LETTER						
MUSCAT	BEIRUT	BERING		GREECE	BEIRUT	JORDAN	BERLIN	ALBERT	MANILA
PUERTO	CAICOS	BERLIN		HELENA	CYPRUS	JUNEAU	BOSNIA	ANKARA	NEVADA
RUSSIA	GUIANA	CARSON	ALBANY	JUNEAU	GEORGE	KANSAS	BRAZIL	ASMARA	NOUMEA
TURKEY	GUINEA	HARARE	ALMATY	MASERU	MADRID	MIDWAY	CELTIC	CANARY	OTTAWA
RWANDA	MOINES	HORMUZ	ANKARA	ROSEAU	PIERRE	MUSCAT	DUBLIN	EDWARD	PANAMA
SWEDEN	PRINCE	ISRAEL	ASMARA	TOPEKA	PUERTO	NASSAU	GAMBIA	HARARE	RUSSIA
CYPRUS	TAIWAN	JERSEY	BAMAKO	BAFFIN	SIERRA	NORWAY	HAWAII	MASERU	RWANDA
AZORES	THIMBU	JORDAN	BANABA	BANGUI	TEHRAN	ROSEAU	JALUIT	PIERRE	SAHARA
	UNITED	MARINO	CANADA	BENGAL	ZAGREB	TAIWAN	KUWAIT	SAHARA	SCOTIA
	ANKARA	MARTIN	CANARY	OREGON	ALASKA	TASMAN	LATVIA	SIERRA	SERBIA
	DAKOTA	MORONI	EDWARD	PRAGUE	BISSAU	TEHRAN	MADRID	ALMATY	SIERRA
3RD LETTER	BALTIC	NORWAY	FUTANA	VIRGIN	CARSON	WARSAW	MARTIN	BOGOTA	TARAWA
	BELIZE	SERBIA	GUIANA	YANGON	HUDSON	BANABA	RUSSIA	DAKOTA	TIRANA
ALASKA	CELTIC	STRAIT	GUYANA	DAWHAH	JERSEY	MALABO	SCOTIA	HECATE	TOPEKA
AMALIE	HELENA	TARAWA	HARARE	AFRICA	KANSAS	THIMBU	SERBIA	MAPUTO	UGANDA
ARABIA	ISLAND	TIRANA	HAVANA	BELIZE	NANSEN	AFRICA	STRAIT	PUERTO	UNGAVA
BRAZIL	JALUIT	TURKEY	HAWAII	BERING	NASSAU	FRANCE	TONKIN	BANGUI	VIENNA
FRANCE	MALABO	VIRGIN	HECATE	INDIAN	RUSSIA	FRENCH	VIRGIN	BANJUL	ZAMBIA
LUANDA	MALAWI	WARSAW	ISLAND	MANILA	WARSAW	GREECE	WALLIS	BEIRUT	ZAGREB
NIAMEY	POLAND	AUSTIN	ISRAEL	MARINO	AUSTIN	MEXICO	ZAMBIA	CYPRUS	BALTIC
PRAGUE	VALLEY	BISCAY	KIGALI	MEXICO	BALTIC	MONACO	ALASKA	HORMUZ	CELTIC
RWANDA	WALLIS	BISSAU	KUWAIT	BANJUL	BHUTAN	PRINCE	BAMAKO	LUMPUR	BAGDAD
STATES	YELLOW	BOSNIA	LUSAKA	BAIKAL	BOSTON	CANADA	LUSAKA	PRAGUE	EDWARD
UGANDA	ALMATY	BOSTON	MALABO	TONKIN	CELTIC	GIGEDO	TOPEKA	UNGAVA	ISLAND
ALBANY	ASMARA	EASTER	MALAWI	TURKEY	EASTER	LUANDA	ANGOLA	MALAWI	MADRID
ALBERT	BAMAKO	LISBON	MANAMA	AMALIE	LAPTEV	NEVADA	KIGALI	OTTAWA	POLAND
DUBLIN	GAMBIA	LUSAKA	MINAMI	BERLIN	LITTLE	RIYADH	LITTLE	TARAWA	UNITED
TOBAGO	LUMPUR	MASERU	MONACO	DUBLIN	MARTIN	RWANDA	MANILA	BELIZE	AMALIE
HECATE	ZAMBIA	MOSCOW	NEVADA	VALLEY	SCOTIA	UGANDA	DODOMA		BELIZE
DODOMA	BANABA	MUSCAT	OTTAWA	WALLIS	STATES	AZORES	MANAMA		FRANCE
HUDSON	BANDAR	NASSAU	PANAMA	YELLOW	UNITED	BOUVET	MINAMI		GEORGE
INDIAN	BANGUI	ROSEAU	POLAND	CAYMAN	JALUIT	BRUNEI	PANAMA	6TH LETTER	GREECE
LADOGA	BANJUL	RUSSIA	RIYADH	HORMUZ	MAPUTO	CROZET	ALBANY		HARARE
MADRID	BENGAL	TASMAN	SAHARA	NIAMEY	BOUVET	DENVER	ATHENS	AFRICA	HECATE
MIDWAY	CANADA	FUTANA	STRAIT	NOUMEA	DENVER	EASTER	BERING	ALASKA	LITTLE
BUENOS	CANARY	LATVIA	TARAWA	TASMAN	DENVER	GUINEA	FUTANA	ANGOLA	PIERRE
FRENCH	DENVER	LITTLE	TIRANA	THIMBU	LATVIA	ISRAEL	GUIANA	ANKARA	PRAGUE
GREECE	JUNEAU	OTTAWA	TOBAGO	BOSNIA	MIDWAY	JERSEY	GUYANA	ARABIA	PRINCE
OREGON	KANSAS	BHUTAN	UNGAVA	BRUNEI	NORWAY	LAPTEV	HAVANA	ASMARA	BERING
PIERRE	LONDON	BOUVET	ARABIA	BUENOS	TAIWAN	MOINES	HELENA	BANABA	DAWHAH
PUERTO	MANAMA	BRUNEI	GAMBIA	FRANCE	BRAZIL	NANSEN	ISLAND	BOGOTA	FRENCH
SIERRA	MANILA	NOUMEA	LISBON	FRENCH	CROZET	NIAMEY	MARINO	BOSNIA	RIYADH
SWEDEN	MINAMI	HAVANA	SERBIA	GUINEA		NOUMEA	MORONI	CANADA	BANGUI
VIENNA	MONACO	NEVADA	ZAMBIA	LUANDA		STATES	POLAND	DAKOTA	BRUNEI
BAFFIN	NANSEN	DAWHAH	BISCAY	MOINES	5TH LETTER	SWEDEN	TIRANA	DODOMA	HAWAII
AEGEAN	PANAMA	EDWARD	CAICOS	PRINCE		TURKEY	VIENNA	FUTANA	KIGALI
ANGOLA	TONKIN	HAWAII	MOSCOW	RWANDA	AEGEAN	UNITED	BOSTON	GAMBIA	MALAWI
BAGDAD	YANGON	KUWAIT	MUSCAT	UGANDA	BAGDAD	VALLEY	BUENOS	GUIANA	MINAMI
BOGOTA	AZORES	MEXICO	BAGDAD	VIENNA	BAIKAL	ZAGREB	CAICOS	GUINEA	MORONI
GIGEDO	CROZET	CAYMAN	BANDAR	ANGOLA	BANDAR	GEORGE	CARSON	GUYANA	BAIKAL
KIGALI	GEORGE	GUYANA	JORDAN	BOGOTA	BENGAL	LADOGA	HUDSON	HAVANA	BANJUL
UNGAVA	SCOTIA	RIYADH	LONDON	DAKOTA	BHUTAN	TOBAGO	LISBON	HELENA	BENGAL
ZAGREB	CYPRUS		SWEDEN	DODOMA	BISCAY	AMALIE	LONDON	LADOGA	BRAZIL
ATHENS	LAPTEV		AEGEAN	LADOGA	BISSAU	ARABIA	MOSCOW	LATVIA	ISRAEL
SAHARA	MAPUTO		ALBERT	MORONI	CAYMAN	AUSTIN	OREGON	LUANDA	AEGEAN
TEHRAN	TOPEKA		ATHENS	LUMPUR	DAWHAH	BAFFIN	YANGON	LUSAKA	AUSTIN
BAIKAL	AFRICA		GIGEDO	AZORES	INDIAN	BALTIC	YELLOW	MANAMA	BAFFIN

BERLIN	LAPTEV	BURUNDI	MONTANA	**2ND LETTER**	WEDDELL	ROMANIA	ANDAMAN
BHUTAN	MOSCOW	CARACAS	MORESBY		WESTERN	SOLOMON	ANDORRA
BOSTON	WARSAW	CASPIAN	MOROCCO	BAHAMAS	YEREVAN	SOMALIA	ANDREAS
CARSON	YELLOW	CAYENNE	MYANMAR	BAHRAIN	ZEALAND	TOKELAU	INDIANA
CAYMAN	ALBANY	CELEBES	NAIROBI	BANGKOK	AFRICAN	TORTOLA	MADEIRA
DUBLIN	ALMATY	CENTRAL	NAMIBIA	BARBUDA	AGULHAS	SPENCER	MADISON
HUDSON	BISCAY	CHANNEL	NAVASSA	BARENTS	CHANNEL	ARABIAN	WEDDELL
INDIAN	CANARY	CHATHAM	NICOSIA	CARACAS	CHATHAM	ARAFURA	AMERICA
JORDAN	JERSEY	CHUKCHI	NIGERIA	CASPIAN	CHUKCHI	ARIZONA	GRENADA
LISBON	MIDWAY	COLOMBO	NORFOLK	CAYENNE	PHOENIX	ARMENIA	ICELAND
LONDON	NIAMEY	COMOROS	NORONHA	JACKSON	THIMPHU	BRISTOL	IRELAND
MARTIN	NORWAY	CONAKRY	OKHOTSK	JAKARTA	WHARTON	BRITISH	SPENCER
NANSEN	TURKEY	CONCORD	OLYMPIA	JAMAICA	BISHKEK	CROATIA	TRENTON
OREGON	VALLEY	CROATIA	ONTARIO	LANSING	FINLAND	ERITREA	VIETNAM
SWEDEN	HORMUZ	DENMARK	PACIFIC	MAARTEN	KINGDOM	GRENADA	ALGERIA
TAIWAN		DOMINGO	PAPEETE	MADEIRA	KINGMAN	IRELAND	AUGUSTA
TONKIN		ECUADOR	PEOPLES	MADISON	LIBERIA	TRENTON	BEGAWAN
TASMAN		ENGLAND	PERSIAN	MAKAROV	LINCOLN	TRIPOLI	ENGLAND
TEHRAN	**7 LETTER**	ENGLISH	PHOENIX	MALPELO	NICOSIA	TRISTAN	ENGLISH
VIRGIN	**1ST LETTER**	ERITREA	RALEIGH	MANAGUA	NIGERIA	URAGUAY	NIGERIA
YANGON		ESTONIA	REUNION	MARIANA	VIETNAM	ESTONIA	BAHAMAS
BAMAKO	ABIDJAN	FINLAND	REVILLA	MAYOTTE	VILNIUS	ISLANDS	BAHRAIN
GIGEDO	AFRICAN	FLORIDA	ROMANIA	NAIROBI	VINCENT	ATLANTA	OKHOTSK
MALABO	AGULHAS	GEORGES	SENEGAL	NAMIBIA	OKHOTSK	STANLEY	ABIDJAN
MAPUTO	ALABAMA	GEORGIA	SOLOMON	NAVASSA	UKRAINE	STRAITS	ARIZONA
MARINO	ALBANIA	GERMANY	SOMALIA	PACIFIC	ALABAMA	AUGUSTA	BEIJING
MEXICO	ALGERIA	GODTHAR	SPENCER	PAPEETE	ALBANIA	AUSTRIA	BRISTOL
MONACO	AMERICA	GRENADA	STANLEY	RALEIGH	ALGERIA	BURKINA	BRITISH
PUERTO	ANDAMAN	HONIARA	STRAITS	TALLINN	FLORIDA	BURUNDI	ERITREA
TOBAGO	ANDORRA	HOWLAND	SURINAM	VANUATU	OLYMPIA	HUNGARY	NAIROBI
BANDAR	ANDREAS	HUNGARY	TALLINN	VATICAN	AMERICA	SURINAM	TBILISI
DENVER	ANNOBON	ICELAND	TBILISI	YAOUNDE	ANDAMAN	TUNISIA	THIMPHU
EASTER	ANTIGUA	INDIANA	THIMPHU	ABIDJAN	ANDORRA	MYANMAR	TRIPOLI
LUMPUR	ARABIAN	IRELAND	TOKELAU	MBABANE	ANDREAS	WYOMING	TRISTAN
ATHENS	ARAFURA	ISLANDS	TORTOLA	TBILISI	ANNOBON		JAKARTA
AZORES	ARIZONA	JACKSON	TRENTON	ECUADOR	ANTIGUA		MAKAROV
BUENOS	ARMENIA	JAKARTA	TRIPOLI	ICELAND	ENGLAND		TOKELAU
CAICOS	ATLANTA	JAMAICA	TRISTAN	BEGAWAN	ENGLISH	**3RD LETTER**	ATLANTA
CYPRUS	AUGUSTA	KINGDOM	TUNISIA	BEIJING	INDIANA		BELARUS
KANSAS	AUSTRIA	KINGMAN	UKRAINE	BELARUS	ONTARIO	ALABAMA	BELGIUM
MOINES	BAHAMAS	KOLONIA	URAGUAY	BELGIUM	BOLIVIA	ARABIAN	BOLIVIA
STATES	BAHRAIN	LANSING	VANUATU	BERMUDA	BOOTHIA	ARAFURA	CELEBES
WALLIS	BANGKOK	LEBANON	VATICAN	CELEBES	COLOMBO	CHANNEL	COLOMBO
ALBERT	BARBUDA	LESOTHO	VERMONT	CENTRAL	COMOROS	CHATHAM	ISLANDS
BEIRUT	BARENTS	LIBERIA	VIETNAM	DENMARK	CONAKRY	MAARTEN	KOLONIA
BOUVET	BEGAWAN	LINCOLN	VILNIUS	GEORGES	CONCORD	MBABANE	MALPELO
CROZET	BEIJING	MAARTEN	VINCENT	GEORGIA	DOMINGO	MYANMAR	MELILLA
JALUIT	BELARUS	MADEIRA	WEDDELL	GERMANY	GODTHAR	STANLEY	MOLDOVA
KUWAIT	BELGIUM	MADISON	WESTERN	LEBANON	HONIARA	URAGUAY	RALEIGH
MUSCAT	BERMUDA	MAKAROV	WHARTON	LESOTHO	HOWLAND	WHARTON	SOLOMON
STRAIT	BISHKEK	MALPELO	WYOMING	MELILLA	KOLONIA	ZEALAND	TALLINN
BISSAU	BOLIVIA	MANAGUA	YAOUNDE	PEOPLES	MOLDOVA	ALBANIA	VILNIUS
JUNEAU	BOOTHIA	MARIANA	YEREVAN	PERSIAN	MONTANA	LEBANON	ARMENIA
MASERU	BRISTOL	MAYOTTE	ZEALAND	REUNION	MORESBY	LIBERIA	COMOROS
NASSAU	BRITISH	MBABANE		REVILLA	MOROCCO	JACKSON	DOMINGO
ROSEAU	BURKINA	MELILLA		SENEGAL	NORFOLK	NICOSIA	JAMAICA
THIMBU		MOLDOVA		VERMONT	NORONHA	PACIFIC	NAMIBIA

	(4TH LETTER)					(6TH LETTER)	
ROMANIA	ESTONIA	MORESBY	SPENCER	DENMARK	REUNION	COMOROS	VIETNAM
SOMALIA	ONTARIO	NIGERIA	STANLEY	ENGLAND	STRAITS	ERITREA	YEREVAN
ANNOBON	VATICAN	PAPEETE	TRENTON	FINLAND	TALLINN	JAKARTA	COLOMBO
BANGKOK	AGULHAS	PHOENIX	VILNIUS	GERMANY	TBILISI	LIBERIA	MORESBY
CENTRAL	CHUKCHI	RALEIGH	ANDORRA	GRENADA	UKRAINE	MAKAROV	NAIROBI
CONAKRY	ECUADOR	SENEGAL	ANNOBON	HONIARA	VILNIUS	NIGERIA	AMERICA
CONCORD	REUNION	TOKELAU	COLOMBO	HOWLAND	WYOMING	ONTARIO	JAMAICA
DENMARK	NAVASSA	YEREVAN	COMOROS	HUNGARY	ABIDJAN	AUGUSTA	MOROCCO
FINLAND	REVILLA	ARAFURA	ESTONIA	ICELAND	BANGKOK	JACKSON	BARBUDA
HONIARA	HOWLAND	NORFOLK	KOLONIA	INDIANA	BISHKEK	MADISON	BERMUDA
HUNGARY	CAYENNE	BANGKOK	LESOTHO	IRELAND	CONAKRY	MORESBY	BURUNDI
KINGDOM	MAYOTTE	BELGIUM	MAYOTTE	MARIANA	MELILLA	NAVASSA	FLORIDA
KINGMAN	OLYMPIA	HUNGARY	MOROCCO	MBABANE	PEOPLES	NICOSIA	GRENADA
LANSING	**4TH LETTER**	KINGDOM	NICOSIA	MONTANA	REVILLA	TUNISIA	ISLANDS
LINCOLN	ALBANIA	KINGMAN	NORONHA	VANUATU	SOMALIA	BRISTOL	YAOUNDE
MANAGUA	ANDAMAN	URAGUAY	OKHOTSK	ZEALAND	STANLEY	CROATIA	BISHKEK
MONTANA	ATLANTA	BISHKEK	SOLOMON	ANNOBON	TOKELAU	LESOTHO	CELEBES
SENEGAL	BAHAMAS	AFRICAN	CASPIAN	CELEBES	ANDAMAN	MAARTEN	CHANNEL
TUNISIA	BEGAWAN	ANTIGUA	MALPELO	NAMIBIA	BAHAMAS	MAYOTTE	ERITREA
VANUATU	BELARUS	BOLIVIA	PEOPLES	AFRICAN	COLOMBO	OKHOTSK	GEORGES
VINCENT	CARACAS	DOMINGO	TRIPOLI	CARACAS	KINGMAN	TRENTON	MAARTEN
BOOTHIA	CONAKRY	HONIARA	AMERICA	CHUKCHI	MYANMAR	TRISTAN	PEOPLES
CROATIA	CROATIA	INDIANA	ANDREAS	MOROCCO	SOLOMON	WHARTON	SPENCER
FLORIDA	ECUADOR	MADISON	BAHRAIN	SPENCER	ALBANIA	ARAFURA	STANLEY
GEORGES	ISLANDS	MARIANA	FLORIDA	VATICAN	ARMENIA	BARBUDA	DOMINGO
GEORGIA	JAKARTA	MELILLA	GEORGES	ECUADOR	ATLANTA	BERMUDA	RALEIGH
PEOPLES	JAMAICA	NAMIBIA	GEORGIA	KINGDOM	BARENTS	URAGUAY	CHUKCHI
PHOENIX	LEBANON	PACIFIC	MAARTEN	ANDREAS	BURUNDI	BOLIVIA	LESOTHO
WYOMING	MAKAROV	REVILLA	NAIROBI	MALPELO	CAYENNE	YEREVAN	NORONHA
YAOUNDE	MANAGUA	SURINAM	WHARTON	PAPEETE	CHANNEL	BEGAWAN	THIMPHU
PAPEETE	NAVASSA	TUNISIA	BRISTOL	VINCENT	DOMINGO	**6TH LETTER**	ALBANIA
AFRICAN	ONTARIO	VATICAN	LANSING	WEDDELL	ESTONIA	ABIDJAN	ALGERIA
BARBUDA	ROMANIA	BEIJING	PERSIAN	WESTERN	ISLANDS	AFRICAN	ARMENIA
BARENTS	SOMALIA	BURKINA	TRISTAN	PACIFIC	KOLONIA	AGULHAS	AUSTRIA
BERMUDA	STRAITS	CHUKCHI	AUSTRIA	ANTIGUA	LEBANON	ANDAMAN	BAHRAIN
BURKINA	UKRAINE	JACKSON	BOOTHIA	GEORGES	NORONHA	ANDREAS	BOLIVIA
BURUNDI	ALABAMA	AGULHAS	BRITISH	GEORGIA	PHOENIX	ARABIAN	BOOTHIA
CARACAS	ARABIAN	ENGLAND	CENTRAL	MANAGUA	ROMANIA	BAHAMAS	CROATIA
GERMANY	BARBUDA	ENGLISH	CHATHAM	SENEGAL	SURINAM	BEGAWAN	ESTONIA
MARIANA	MBABANE	FINLAND	ERITREA	AGULHAS	VIETNAM	CARACAS	GEORGIA
MORESBY	CONCORD	HOWLAND	GODTHAR	BOOTHIA	YAOUNDE	CASPIAN	KOLONIA
MOROCCO	LINCOLN	ICELAND	MONTANA	CHATHAM	ARIZONA	CENTRAL	LIBERIA
NORFOLK	VINCENT	IRELAND	TORTOLA	GODTHAR	CONCORD	CHATHAM	NAMIBIA
NORONHA	ABIDJAN	TALLINN	VIETNAM	AMERICA	LINCOLN	GODTHAR	NICOSIA
PERSIAN	MOLDOVA	TBILISI	WESTERN	ARABIAN	MOLDOVA	KINGMAN	NIGERIA
STRAITS	WEDDELL	ZEALAND	AUGUSTA	BEIJING	NAIROBI	MYANMAR	OLYMPIA
SURINAM	ALGERIA	BERMUDA	BURUNDI	BELGIUM	NORFOLK	PERSIAN	ONTARIO
TORTOLA	ARMENIA	DENMARK	VANUATU	BRITISH	TORTOLA	SENEGAL	PACIFIC
UKRAINE	BARENTS	GERMANY	YAOUNDE	BURKINA	TRIPOLI	SURINAM	PHOENIX
VERMONT	CAYENNE	OLYMPIA	ARIZONA	CASPIAN	VERMONT	TOKELAU	ROMANIA
YEREVAN	CELEBES	THIMPHU		ENGLISH	OLYMPIA	TRISTAN	SOMALIA
AUSTRIA	LIBERIA	VERMONT		FLORIDA	THIMPHU	URAGUAY	TUNISIA
BISHKEK	MADEIRA	WYOMING		JAMAICA	ALGERIA	VATICAN	LINCOLN
CASPIAN		CHANNEL		LANSING	ANDORRA		MALPELO
LESOTHO		**5TH LETTER**		MADEIRA	AUSTRIA		MELILLA
WESTERN		GRENADA		PERSIAN	BELARUS		NORFOLK
ANTIGUA		MYANMAR		RALEIGH	CENTRAL		REVILLA
		REUNION					

TORTOLA	MAYOTTE	ROMANIA	MADISON	AMUNDSEN	LAWRENCE	**2ND LETTER**		PITCAIRN
TRIPOLI	PAPEETE	SOMALIA	PERSIAN	ANGUILLA	LILONGWE	BALKHASH		RICHMOND
WEDDELL	STRAITS	TORTOLA	REUNION	ANTILLES	LONGYEAR	BARBADOS		SIBERIAN
ALABAMA	VANUATU	TUNISIA	SOLOMON	ARKANSAS	MAGELLAN	CAMBODIA		TITICACA
ARIZONA	ANTIGUA	PACIFIC	TALLINN	ASHGABAT	MALAYSIA	CAMEROON		VICTORIA
BEIJING	BELARUS	CONCORD	TRENTON	ASUNCION	MALDIVES	CANBERRA		VIRGINIA
BURKINA	BELGIUM	ENGLAND	TRISTAN	ATLANTIC	MARSHALL	CAROLINA		VISCOUNT
CAYENNE	MANAGUA	FINLAND	VATICAN	BALKHASH	MARYLAND	CAROLINE		WINDHOEK
ENGLAND	VILNIUS	HOWLAND	WESTERN	BARBADOS	MCDONALD	CASTRIES		WINNIPEG
FINLAND	MOLDOVA	ICELAND	WHARTON	BEAUFORD	MELVILLE	DAMASCUS		ZIMBABWE
GERMANY		IRELAND	YEREVAN	BELGRADE	MICHIGAN	FALKLAND		DJIBOUTI
HOWLAND		ZEALAND	COLOMBO	BELMOPAN	MIQUELON	GABORONE		OKLAHOMA
ICELAND		CAYENNE	DOMINGO	BISMARCK	MISSOURI	HAMILTON		ALEUTIAN
INDIANA	**7TH LETTER**	MAYOTTE	LESOTHO	BOTSWANA	MONGOLIA	HARTFORD		ILLINOIS
IRELAND		MBABANE	MALPELO	BRASILIA	MONROVIA	LABRADOR		PLYMOUTH
LANSING	ALABAMA	PAPEETE	MOROCCO	BRUSSELS	NEBRASKA	LAWRENCE		SLOVAKIA
MARIANA	ALBANIA	UKRAINE	ONTARIO	BUDAPEST	NORTHERN	MAGELLAN		SLOVENIA
MBABANE	ALGERIA	YAOUNDE	ECUADOR	BULGARIA	OKLAHOMA	MALAYSIA		AMERICAN
MONTANA	AMERICA	BEIJING	GODTHAR	CAMBODIA	PAKISTAN	MALDIVES		AMUNDSEN
TALLINN	ANDORRA	LANSING	MYANMAR	CAMEROON	PARAGUAY	MARSHALL		EMIRATES
UKRAINE	ANTIGUA	WYOMING	SPENCER	CANBERRA	PITCAIRN	MARYLAND		ANGUILLA
VERMONT	ARAFURA	BRITISH	AGULHAS	CAROLINA	PLYMOUTH	PAKISTAN		ANTILLES
VINCENT	ARIZONA	ENGLISH	ANDREAS	CAROLINE	PORTUGAL	PARAGUAY		BOTSWANA
WYOMING	ARMENIA	RALEIGH	BAHAMAS	CASTRIES	PRINCIPE	SALVADOR		COCKBURN
ZEALAND	ATLANTA	BURUNDI	BARENTS	CHEYENNE	PROVEDEN	SANTIAGO		COLOMBIA
ANNOBON	AUGUSTA	CHUKCHI	BELARUS	COCKBURN	REINDEER	TANZANIA		COLORADO
BANGKOK	AUSTRIA	NAIROBI	CARACAS	COLOMBIA	REPUBLIC	TASHKENT		COLUMBIA
BRISTOL	BARBUDA	TBILISI	CELEBES	COLORADO	RICHMOND	VALLETTA		COLUMBUS
COMOROS	BERMUDA	TRIPOLI	COMOROS	COLUMBIA	SALVADOR	ZANZIBAR		DOMINICA
ECUADOR	BOLIVIA	BANGKOK	GEORGES	COLUMBUS	SANTIAGO	MCDONALD		GODTHAAB
JACKSON	BOOTHIA	BISHKEK	ISLANDS	DAMASCUS	TANZANIA	SCORESBY		HONDURAS
KINGDOM	BURKINA	DENMARK	PEOPLES	DELAWARE	TASHKENT	SCOTLAND		HONOLULU
LEBANON	CROATIA	NORFOLK	STRAITS	DJIBOUTI	THAILAND	ADRIATIC		JOHNSTON
MADISON	ERITREA	OKHOTSK	VILNIUS	DOMINICA	TITICACA	BEAUFORD		LONGYEAR
MAKAROV	ESTONIA	BRISTOL	VERMONT	DUSHANBE	TRINIDAD	BELGRADE		MONGOLIA
REUNION	FLORIDA	CENTRAL	VINCENT	EMIRATES	VALLETTA	BELMOPAN		MONROVIA
SOLOMON	GEORGIA	CHANNEL	THIMPHU	ETHIOPIA	VICTORIA	DELAWARE		NORTHERN
TRENTON	GRENADA	SENEGAL	TOKELAU	FALKLAND	VIRGINIA	FERNANDO		PORTUGAL
WHARTON	HONIARA	WEDDELL	VANUATU	FERNANDO	VISCOUNT	HELSINKI		SOUTHERN
ANDORRA	INDIANA	BELGIUM	MAKAROV	FREETOWN	WINDHOEK	KENTUCKY		ARKANSAS
ARAFURA	JAKARTA	CHATHAM	PHOENIX	GABORONE	WINNIPEG	MELVILLE		BRASILIA
CONAKRY	JAMAICA	KINGDOM	CONAKRY	GODTHAAB	ZANZIBAR	NEBRASKA		BRUSSELS
CONCORD	KOLONIA	SURINAM	GERMANY	GUERNSEY	ZIMBABWE	REINDEER		FREETOWN
DENMARK	LIBERIA	VIETNAM	HUNGARY	HAMILTON		REPUBLIC		PRINCIPE
HONIARA	MADEIRA	ABIDJAN	MORESBY	HARTFORD		CHEYENNE		PROVEDEN
HUNGARY	MANAGUA	AFRICAN	STANLEY	HELSINKI		KHARTOUM		TRINIDAD
MADEIRA	MARIANA	ANDAMAN	URAGUAY	HONDURAS		KINGSTON		ASHGABAT
WESTERN	MELILLA	ANNOBON		HONOLULU		KINSHASA		ASUNCION
BRITISH	MOLDOVA	ARABIAN		ILLINOIS		KIRIBATI		ATLANTIC
ENGLISH	MONTANA	BAHRAIN		JOHNSTON		KISHINEV		ETHIOPIA
NAVASSA	NAMIBIA	BEGAWAN	**8 LETTER**	KENTUCKY		LILONGWE		BUDAPEST
OKHOTSK	NAVASSA	CASPIAN		KHARTOUM		MICHIGAN		BULGARIA
TBILISI	NICOSIA	JACKSON	**1ST LETTER**	KINGSTON		MIQUELON		DUSHANBE
ATLANTA	NIGERIA	KINGMAN		KINSHASA		MISSOURI		GUERNSEY
AUGUSTA	NORONHA	LEBANON	ADRIATIC	KIRIBATI				SUPERIOR
BARENTS	OLYMPIA	LINCOLN	ALEUTIAN	KISHINEV				SVALBARD
JAKARTA	REVILLA	MAARTEN	AMERICAN	LABRADOR				

3RD LETTER		**4TH LETTER**		**5TH LETTER**		**6TH LETTER**	
	DAMASCUS		FERNANDO		ZANZIBAR		BRASILIA
	DOMINICA		JOHNSTON		TASHKENT		MAGELLAN
BEAUFORD	HAMILTON	ARKANSAS	PRINCIPE	ADRIATIC	ANTILLES	BALKHASH	MELVILLE
BRASILIA	ZIMBABWE	ATLANTIC	REINDEER	ASHGABAT	CAROLINA	BELGRADE	MIQUELON
KHARTOUM	CANBERRA	BUDAPEST	TRINIDAD	BARBADOS	CAROLINE	BOTSWANA	MONGOLIA
SVALBARD	HONDURAS	DAMASCUS	WINNIPEG	BISMARCK	FALKLAND	COLORADO	REPUBLIC
THAILAND	HONOLULU	DELAWARE	CAROLINA	BULGARIA	HAMILTON	DELAWARE	CHEYENNE
GABORONE	KENTUCKY	MALAYSIA	CAROLINE	DUSHANBE	HONOLULU	FALKLAND	DUSHANBE
LABRADOR	KINGSTON	OKLAHOMA	COLOMBIA	EMIRATES	MAGELLAN	GODTHAAB	FERNANDO
NEBRASKA	KINSHASA	PARAGUAY	COLORADO	FERNANDO	MARYLAND	KINSHASA	HELSINKI
SIBERIAN	LONGYEAR	BARBADOS	GABORONE	LABRADOR	SCOTLAND	KIRIBATI	KISHINEV
COCKBURN	MONGOLIA	CAMBODIA	HONOLULU	NEBRASKA	THAILAND	MARSHALL	LAWRENCE
MICHIGAN	MONROVIA	CANBERRA	LILONGWE	PITCAIRN	COLOMBIA	MARYLAND	SLOVENIA
RICHMOND	SANTIAGO	DJIBOUTI	MCDONALD	SALVADOR	COLUMBIA	MCDONALD	TANZANIA
VICTORIA	TANZANIA	ZIMBABWE	AMERICAN	SLOVAKIA	COLUMBUS	SANTIAGO	VIRGINIA
BUDAPEST	WINDHOEK	PITCAIRN	EMIRATES	TANZANIA	RICHMOND	SCOTLAND	BEAUFORD
GODTHAAB	WINNIPEG	VISCOUNT	GUERNSEY	ZIMBABWE	ARKANSAS	SVALBARD	CAMEROON
MCDONALD	ZANZIBAR	HONDURAS	KHARTOUM	COCKBURN	ATLANTIC	THAILAND	FREETOWN
ALEUTIAN	PROVEDEN	MALDIVES	LABRADOR	KIRIBATI	DOMINICA	TITICACA	GABORONE
AMERICAN	SCORESBY	WINDHOEK	LAWRENCE	REPUBLIC	GUERNSEY	ASHGABAT	HARTFORD
CHEYENNE	SCOTLAND	CAMEROON	MONROVIA	SVALBARD	ILLINOIS	COLOMBIA	ILLINOIS
FREETOWN	SLOVAKIA	FREETOWN	NEBRASKA	ASUNCION	LILONGWE	COLUMBIA	KHARTOUM
GUERNSEY	SLOVENIA	MAGELLAN	SCORESBY	PRINCIPE	MCDONALD	COLUMBUS	OKLAHOMA
ANGUILLA	REPUBLIC	SIBERIAN	BOTSWANA	TITICACA	BELMOPAN	ZANZIBAR	RICHMOND
MAGELLAN	SUPERIOR	SUPERIOR	BRASILIA	AMUNDSEN	CAMBODIA	ZIMBABWE	WINDHOEK
ASHGABAT	MIQUELON	ASHGABAT	BRUSSELS	REINDEER	DJIBOUTI	AMERICAN	BELMOPAN
ETHIOPIA	ADRIATIC	BELGRADE	HELSINKI	CANBERRA	ETHIOPIA	DAMASCUS	ETHIOPIA
JOHNSTON	BARBADOS	BULGARIA	KINSHASA	CHEYENNE	MISSOURI	KENTUCKY	WINNIPEG
DJIBOUTI	CAROLINA	KINGSTON	MARSHALL	LAWRENCE	MONGOLIA	BARBADOS	BISMARCK
EMIRATES	CAROLINE	LONGYEAR	MISSOURI	MIQUELON	MONROVIA	CAMBODIA	BULGARIA
PRINCIPE	FERNANDO	MONGOLIA	CASTRIES	PROVEDEN	PLYMOUTH	LABRADOR	CANBERRA
REINDEER	HARTFORD	VIRGINIA	GODTHAAB	SCORESBY	VICTORIA	PROVEDEN	HONDURAS
TRINIDAD	KIRIBATI	DUSHANBE	HARTFORD	SLOVENIA	VISCOUNT	SALVADOR	VICTORIA
ARKANSAS	MARSHALL	KISHINEV	KENTUCKY	VALLETTA	BUDAPEST	TRINIDAD	AMUNDSEN
PAKISTAN	MARYLAND	MICHIGAN	NORTHERN	BEAUFORD	BELGRADE	BRUSSELS	ARKANSAS
ATLANTIC	NORTHERN	RICHMOND	PORTUGAL	HARTFORD	CAMEROON	BUDAPEST	GUERNSEY
BALKHASH	PARAGUAY	TASHKENT	SANTIAGO	PARAGUAY	CASTRIES	LONGYEAR	MALAYSIA
BELGRADE	PORTUGAL	ADRIATIC	SCOTLAND	BALKHASH	COLORADO	NORTHERN	NEBRASKA
BELMOPAN	VIRGINIA	ANTILLES	SOUTHERN	GODTHAAB	GABORONE	REINDEER	SCORESBY
BULGARIA	BISMARCK	DOMINICA	VICTORIA	KINSHASA	SIBERIAN	SOUTHERN	ADRIATIC
COLOMBIA	CASTRIES	ETHIOPIA	ALEUTIAN	MARSHALL	SUPERIOR	TASHKENT	ATLANTIC
COLORADO	DUSHANBE	HAMILTON	ANGUILLA	NORTHERN	BRUSSELS	LILONGWE	EMIRATES
COLUMBIA	KISHINEV	ILLINOIS	BEAUFORD	OKLAHOMA	DAMASCUS	MICHIGAN	HAMILTON
COLUMBUS	MISSOURI	KIRIBATI	COLUMBIA	SOUTHERN	JOHNSTON	PORTUGAL	JOHNSTON
DELAWARE	TASHKENT	PAKISTAN	COLUMBUS	WINDHOEK	KINGSTON	ALEUTIAN	KINGSTON
FALKLAND	VISCOUNT	THAILAND	MIQUELON	AMERICAN	PAKISTAN	ASUNCION	PAKISTAN
HELSINKI	ANTILLES	TITICACA	REPUBLIC	ANGUILLA	ALEUTIAN	CAROLINA	VALLETTA
ILLINOIS	BOTSWANA	BALKHASH	MELVILLE	BRASILIA	FREETOWN	CAROLINE	COCKBURN
LILONGWE	PITCAIRN	COCKBURN	PROVEDEN	HELSINKI	KHARTOUM	CASTRIES	DJIBOUTI
MALAYSIA	TITICACA	FALKLAND	SALVADOR	KISHINEV	HONDURAS	DOMINICA	HONOLULU
MALDIVES	AMUNDSEN	SVALBARD	SLOVAKIA	MALDIVES	KENTUCKY	PITCAIRN	MISSOURI
MELVILLE	ASUNCION	VALLETTA	SLOVENIA	MELVILLE	PORTUGAL	PRINCIPE	PARAGUAY
OKLAHOMA	BRUSSELS	BELMOPAN	CHEYENNE	MICHIGAN	BOTSWANA	SIBERIAN	PLYMOUTH
SALVADOR	SOUTHERN	BISMARCK	MARYLAND	SANTIAGO	DELAWARE	SUPERIOR	VISCOUNT
VALLETTA	LAWRENCE	PLYMOUTH	TANZANIA	TRINIDAD	LONGYEAR	SLOVAKIA	MALDIVES
CAMBODIA	PLYMOUTH	AMUNDSEN	ZANZIBAR	VIRGINIA	MALAYSIA	ANGUILLA	MONROVIA
CAMEROON		ASUNCION		WINNIPEG		ANTILLES	

7TH LETTER

ALEUTIAN
AMERICAN
ARKANSAS
ASHGABAT
BELMOPAN
GODTHAAB
HONDURAS
LONGYEAR
MAGELLAN
MICHIGAN
PAKISTAN
PARAGUAY
PORTUGAL
SIBERIAN
TRINIDAD
ZANZIBAR
DUSHANBE
SCORESBY
BISMARCK
DOMINICA
LAWRENCE
TITICACA
BELGRADE
COLORADO
FERNANDO
AMUNDSEN
ANTILLES
CASTRIES
EMIRATES
GUERNSEY
KISHINEV
MALDIVES
PROVEDEN
REINDEER
WINDHOEK
WINNIPEG
SANTIAGO
ADRIATIC
ATLANTIC
BRASILIA
BULGARIA
CAMBODIA
COLOMBIA
COLUMBIA
ETHIOPIA
ILLINOIS
MALAYSIA
MONGOLIA
MONROVIA
REPUBLIC
SLOVAKIA
SLOVENIA
TANZANIA
VICTORIA
VIRGINIA

HELSINKI
KENTUCKY

8TH LETTER

NEBRASKA
ANGUILLA
BRUSSELS
HONOLULU
MARSHALL
MCDONALD
MELVILLE
OKLAHOMA
BOTSWANA
CAROLINA
CAROLINE
CHEYENNE
FALKLAND
GABORONE
MARYLAND
RICHMOND
SCOTLAND
TASHKENT
THAILAND
VISCOUNT
ASUNCION
BARBADOS
CAMEROON
HAMILTON
JOHNSTON
KINGSTON
LABRADOR
MIQUELON
SALVADOR
SUPERIOR
PRINCIPE
BEAUFORD
CANBERRA
COCKBURN
DELAWARE
HARTFORD
MISSOURI
NORTHERN
PITCAIRN
SOUTHERN
SVALBARD
BALKHASH
BUDAPEST
KINSHASA
DJIBOUTI
KIRIBATI
PLYMOUTH
VALLETTA
COLUMBUS
DAMASCUS
KHARTOUM
FREETOWN
LILONGWE
ZIMBABWE

8TH LETTER

ANGUILLA
BOTSWANA
BRASILIA
BULGARIA
CAMBODIA
CANBERRA
CAROLINA
COLOMBIA
COLUMBIA
DOMINICA
ETHIOPIA
KINSHASA
MALAYSIA
MONGOLIA
MONROVIA
NEBRASKA
OKLAHOMA
SLOVAKIA
SLOVENIA
TANZANIA
TITICACA
VALLETTA
VICTORIA
VIRGINIA
GODTHAAB
ADRIATIC
ATLANTIC
REPUBLIC
BEAUFORD
FALKLAND
HARTFORD
SALVADOR
MARYLAND
MCDONALD
RICHMOND
SCOTLAND
SVALBARD
THAILAND
TRINIDAD
BELGRADE
CAROLINE
CHEYENNE
DELAWARE
DUSHANBE
GABORONE
LAWRENCE
LILONGWE
MELVILLE
PRINCIPE
ZIMBABWE
WINNIPEG
KISHINEV
BALKHASH
PLYMOUTH
DJIBOUTI
HELSINKI
KIRIBATI

MISSOURI
BISMARCK
WINDHOEK
MARSHALL
PORTUGAL
KHARTOUM
ALEUTIAN
AMERICAN
AMUNDSEN
ASUNCION
BELMOPAN
CAMEROON
COCKBURN
FREETOWN
HAMILTON
JOHNSTON
KINGSTON
MAGELLAN
MICHIGAN
MIQUELON
NORTHERN
PAKISTAN
PITCAIRN
PROVEDEN
SIBERIAN
SOUTHERN
COLORADO
FERNANDO
SANTIAGO
LABRADOR
LONGYEAR
REINDEER
SALVADOR
SUPERIOR
ZANZIBAR
ANTILLES
ARKANSAS
BARBADOS
BRUSSELS
CASTRIES
COLUMBUS
DAMASCUS
EMIRATES
HONDURAS
ILLINOIS
MALDIVES
ASHGABAT
BUDAPEST
TASHKENT
VISCOUNT
HONOLULU
KISHINEV
GUERNSEY
KENTUCKY
PARAGUAY
SCORESBY

9 LETTER

1ST LETTER

AMSTERDAM
ANNAPOLIS
ARGENTINA
ARGENTINE
ASCENSION
ASHKHABAD
ATHABASCA
AUSTRALIA
BAILIWICK
BUCHAREST
BUJUMBURA
CALEDONIA
CARIBBEAN
CHARLOTTE
CHRISTMAS
CHURCHILL
DOMINICAN
FRANKFORT
GALAPAGOS
GIBRALTAR
GREENLAND
GUATEMALA
HAMPSHIRE
INDONESIA
ISLAMABAD
JAMESTOWN
JEFFERSON
JERUSALEM
KATHMANDU
KERGUELEN
KINGSTOWN
KUSKOKWIM
KYRGYSTAN
LANCASTER
LITHUANIA
LJUBLJANA
LOUISIANA
MACEDONIA
MACQUARIE
MASCARENE
MAURITIUS
MINNESOTA
MOGADISHU
NASHVILLE
NICARAGUA
NORTHWEST
NORWEGIAN
OGASAWARA
POLYNESIA
RAROTONGA
REYKJAVIK
RODRIGUES
SHELIKHOV

SINGAPORE
STOCKHOLM
SWAZILAND
TENNESSEE
TERRITORY
THORSHAVN
TORISHIMA
VENEZUELA
VIENTIANE
WISCONSIN

2ND LETTER

BAILIWICK
CALEDONIA
CARIBBEAN
GALAPAGOS
HAMPSHIRE
JAMESTOWN
KATHMANDU
LANCASTER
MACEDONIA
MACQUARIE
MASCARENE
MAURITIUS
NASHVILLE
RAROTONGA
JEFFERSON
JERUSALEM
KERGUELEN
REYKJAVIK
TENNESSEE
TERRITORY
VENEZUELA
KINGSTOWN
KUSKOKWIM
KYRGYSTAN
LANCASTER
LITHUANIA
LJUBLJANA
LOUISIANA
MACEDONIA
MACQUARIE
MASCARENE
MAURITIUS
MINNESOTA
NICARAGUA
SINGAPORE
VIENTIANE
WISCONSIN
LJUBLJANA
AMSTERDAM
ANNAPOLIS
INDONESIA
DOMINICAN
LOUISIANA
MOGADISHU

NORTHWEST
NORWEGIAN
POLYNESIA
RODRIGUES
TORISHIMA
ARGENTINA
ARGENTINE
FRANKFORT
GREENLAND
ASCENSION
ASHKHABAD
ISLAMABAD
ATHABASCA
STOCKHOLM
AUSTRALIA
BUCHAREST
BUJUMBURA
GUATEMALA
KUSKOKWIM
SWAZILAND
KYRGYSTAN

3RD LETTER

CHARLOTTE
FRANKFORT
GUATEMALA
OGASAWARA
SWAZILAND
GIBRALTAR
ASCENSION
BUCHAREST
MACEDONIA
MACQUARIE
NICARAGUA
INDONESIA
RODRIGUES
GREENLAND
SHELIKHOV
VIENTIANE
JEFFERSON
ARGENTINA
ARGENTINE
MOGADISHU
ASHKHABAD
ATHABASCA
BAILIWICK
BUJUMBURA
CALEDONIA
GALAPAGOS
ISLAMABAD
POLYNESIA
DOMINICAN
HAMPSHIRE
JAMESTOWN

ANNAPOLIS
KINGSTOWN
LANCASTER
MINNESOTA
SINGAPORE
TENNESSEE
VENEZUELA
STOCKHOLM
THORSHAVN
CARIBBEAN
CHRISTMAS
JERUSALEM
KERGUELEN
KYRGYSTAN
NORTHWEST
NORWEGIAN
RAROTONGA
TERRITORY
TORISHIMA
AMSTERDAM
AUSTRALIA
KUSKOKWIM
MASCARENE
NASHVILLE
WISCONSIN
KATHMANDU
LITHUANIA
CHURCHILL
LJUBLJANA
LOUISIANA
MAURITIUS
REYKJAVIK

4TH LETTER

ANNAPOLIS
ATHABASCA
GALAPAGOS
ISLAMABAD
MOGADISHU
NICARAGUA
LJUBLJANA
LANCASTER
MASCARENE
STOCKHOLM
WISCONSIN
ARGENTINA
ARGENTINE
ASCENSION
CALEDONIA
GREENLAND
JAMESTOWN
MACEDONIA
VENEZUELA
JEFFERSON

		6TH LETTER		7TH LETTER		8TH LETTER

KERGUELEN
KINGSTOWN
KYRGYSTAN
SINGAPORE
BUCHAREST
KATHMANDU
LITHUANIA
NASHVILLE
CARIBBEAN
CHRISTMAS
DOMINICAN
LOUISIANA
TORISHIMA
ASHKHABAD
KUSKOKWIM
REYKJAVIK
BAILIWICK
SHELIKHOV
FRANKFORT
MINNESOTA
TENNESSEE
INDONESIA
RAROTONGA
HAMPSHIRE
MACQUARIE
CHARLOTTE
CHURCHILL
GIBRALTAR
MAURITIUS
RODRIGUES
TERRITORY
THORSHAVN
OGASAWARA
AMSTERDAM
AUSTRALIA
GUATEMALA
NORTHWEST
BUJUMBURA
JERUSALEM
NORWEGIAN
POLYNESIA
SWAZILAND

5TH LETTER

BUCHAREST
GIBRALTAR
LANCASTER
MASCARENE
OGASAWARA
SINGAPORE
ATHABASCA
CARIBBEAN
CHURCHILL
CALEDONIA

MACEDONIA
MOGADISHU
AMSTERDAM
GUATEMALA
JEFFERSON
MINNESOTA
NORWEGIAN
TENNESSEE
ASHKHABAD
NORTHWEST
BAILIWICK
MAURITIUS
RODRIGUES
SHELIKHOV
SWAZILAND
TERRITORY
REYKJAVIK
FRANKFORT
STOCKHOLM
CHARLOTTE
LJUBLJANA
BUJUMBURA
ISLAMABAD
KATHMANDU
ARGENTINA
ARGENTINE
ASCENSION
DOMINICAN
GREENLAND
INDONESIA
POLYNESIA
KUSKOKWIM
WISCONSIN
ANNAPOLIS
GALAPAGOS
AUSTRALIA
NICARAGUA
CHRISTMAS
HAMPSHIRE
JAMESTOWN
JERUSALEM
KINGSTOWN
LOUISIANA
THORSHAVN
TORISHIMA
RAROTONGA
VIENTIANE
KERGUELEN
LITHUANIA
MACQUARIE
NASHVILLE
KYRGYSTAN
VENEZUELA

6TH LETTER

ASHKHABAD
ATHABASCA
AUSTRALIA
GALAPAGOS
ISLAMABAD
JERUSALEM
KATHMANDU
LITHUANIA
MACQUARIE
NICARAGUA
REYKJAVIK
BUJUMBURA
CARIBBEAN
INDONESIA
KERGUELEN
POLYNESIA
FRANKFORT
NORWEGIAN
RODRIGUES
CHURCHILL
HAMPSHIRE
STOCKHOLM
THORSHAVN
TORISHIMA
DOMINICAN
LOUISIANA
MOGADISHU
NASHVILLE
VIENTIANE
LJUBLJANA
KUSKOKWIM
SHELIKHOV
GIBRALTER
GREENLAND
SWAZILAND
GUATEMALA
WISCONSIN
ANNAPOLIS
CALEDONIA
CHARLOTTE
MACEDONIA
RAROTONGA
SINGAPORE
AMSTERDAM
BUCHAREST
JEFFERSON
MASCARENE
ASCENSION
KYRGYSTAN
LANCASTER
MINNESOTA
TENNESSEE
ARGENTINA
ARGENTINE
CHRISTMAS

JAMESTOWN
KINGSTOWN
MAURITIUS
TERRITORY
VENEZUELA
BAILIWICK
NORTHWEST
OGASAWARA

7TH LETTER

GREENLAND
GUATEMALA
LJUBLJANA
LOUISIANA
OGASAWARA
THORSHAVN
SWAZILAND
VIENTIANE
ASHKHABAD
ISLAMABAD
DOMINICAN
AMSTERDAM
BUCHAREST
CARIBBEAN
MASCARENE
NORTHWEST
VENEZUELA
GALAPAGOS
NICARAGUA
SHELIKHOV
ARGENTINA
ARGENTINE
ASCENSION
BAILIWICK
CHURCHILL
HAMPSHIRE
MAURITIUS
NORWEGIAN
TORISHIMA
ANNAPOLIS
AUSTRALIA
JERUSALEM
KERGUELEN
NASHVILLE
CHRISTMAS
CALEDONIA
KATHMANDU
LITHUANIA
MACEDONIA
RAROTONGA
FRANKFORT
JAMESTOWN
KINGSTOWN
MINNESOTA

SINGAPORE
STOCKHOLM
TERRITORY
MACQUARIE
ATHABASCA
INDONESIA
JEFFERSON
MOGADISHU
POLYNESIA
TENNESSEE
WISCONSIN
CHARLOTTE
GIBRALTAR
KYRGYSTAN
LANCASTER
BUJUMBURA
RODRIGUES
REYKJAVIK
KUSKOKWIM

8TH LETTER

AMSTERDAM
ASKHABAD
CARIBBEAN
CHRISTMAS
DOMINICAN
GIBRALTAR
ISLAMABAD
KYRGYSTAN
NORWEGIAN
ATHABASCA
BAILIWICK
KATHMANDU
JERUSALEM
KERGUELEN
LANCASTER
RODRIGUES
TENNESSEE
RAROTONGA
MOGADISHU
ANNAPOLIS
AUSTRALIA
CALEDONIA
INDONESIA
KUSKOKWIM
LITHUANIA
MACEDONIA
MACQUARIE
POLYNESIA
REYKJAVIK
WISCONSIN
CHURCHILL
GUATEMALA
NASHVILLE

STOCKHOLM
VENEZUELA
TORISHIMA
ARGENTINA
ARGENTINE
GREENLAND
LJUBLJANA
LOUISIANA
MASCARENE
SWAZILAND
VIENTIANE
ASCENSION
GALAPAGOS
JEFFERSON
SHELIKHOV
BUJUMBURA
FRANKFORT
HAMPSHIRE
OGASAWARA
SINGAPORE
TERRITORY
BUCHAREST
NORTHWEST
CHARLOTTE
MINNESOTA
MAURITIUS
NICARAGUA
THORSHAVN
JAMESTOWN
KINGSTOWN

9TH LETTER

ARGENTINA
ATHABASCA
AUSTRALIA
BUJUMBURA
CALEDONIA
GUATEMALA
INDONESIA
LITHUANIA
LJUBLJANA
LOUISIANA
MACEDONIA
MINNESOTA
NICARAGUA
OGASAWARA
POLYNESIA
RAROTONGA
TORISHIMA
VENEZUELA
ASHKHABAD
GREENLAND
ISLAMABAD
SWAZILAND

ARGENTINE
CHARLOTTE
HAMPSHIRE
MACQUARIE
MASCARENE
NASHVILLE
SINGAPORE
TENNESSEE
VIENTIANE
BAILIWICK
REYKJAVIK
CHURCHILL
AMSTERDAM
JERUSALEM
KUSKOKWIM
STOCKHOLM
ASCENSION
CARIBBEAN
DOMINICAN
JAMESTOWN
JEFFERSON
KERGUELEN
KINGSTOWN
KYRGYSTAN
NORWEGIAN
THORSHAVN
WISCONSIN
GIBRALTAR
LANCASTER
ANNAPOLIS
CHRISTMAS
GALAPAGOS
MAURITIUS
RODRIGUES
BUCHAREST
FRANKFORT
NORTHWEST
KATHMANDU
MOGADISHU
SHELIKHOV
TERRITORY

10 LETTER

1ST LETTER

ANTARCTICA
AUSTRALIAN
AZERBAIJAN
BANGLADESH
BASSETERRE
BRATISLAVA
BRIDGETOWN
CALIFORNIA
CHARLESTON

CLIPPERTON	DEMOCRATIC	DEMOCRATIC	DEMOCRATIC	TAJIKISTAN	WELLINGTON	TAJIKISTAN
COPENHAGEN	GEORGETOWN	BANGLADESH	YUGOSLAVIA	UZBEKISTAN	CALIFORNIA	UZBEKISTAN
CORONATION	SEYCHELLES	MONTENEGRO	CLIPPERTON	BANGLADESH	EQUATORIAL	WILLEMSTAD
DARUSSALAM	WELLINGTON	MONTEVIDEO	AZERBAIJAN	CHARLESTON	MONTGOMERY	ANTARCTICA
DEMOCRATIC	CHARLESTON	MONTGOMERY	CHARLESTON	LUXEMBOURG	PHILIPPINE	BRIDGETOWN
EQUATORIAL	PHILIPPINE	MONTPELIER	GEORGETOWN	MOZAMBIQUE	DEMOCRATIC	CORONATION
GEORGETOWN	LIBREVILLE	MONTSERRAT	HARRISBURG	PARAMARIBO	BRATISLAVA	GEORGETOWN
GRENADINES	MICRONESIA	TANGANYIKA	LIBREVILLE	COPENHAGEN	DARUSSALAM	TANGANYIKA
GUADELOUPE	WILLEMSTAD	GEORGETOWN	MAURITANIA	CORONATION	HARRISBURG	
HARRISBURG	CLIPPERTON	PROVIDENCE	MICRONESIA	MICRONESIA	BASSETERRE	
KAZAKHSTAN	ANTARCTICA	COPENHAGEN	SACRAMENTO	CLIPPERTON	MAURITANIA	**8TH LETTER**
LIBREVILLE	COPENHAGEN	CORONATION	TYRRHENIAN	MONTPELIER	LIBREVILLE	
LUXEMBOURG	CORONATION	DARUSSALAM	BASSETERRE	ANTARCTICA	MONTEVIDEO	BRATISLAVA
MADAGASCAR	MONTENEGRO	HARRISBURG	AUSTRALIAN	AUSTRALIAN		MADAGASCAR
MARTINIQUE	MONTEVIDEO	MARTINIQUE	BRATISLAVA	DARUSSALAM		MONTEVIDEO
MAURITANIA	MONTGOMERY	PARAMARIBO	MARTINIQUE	MONTSERRAT		BANGLADESH
MICRONESIA	MONTPELIER	TYRRHENIAN	MONTENEGRO	YUGOSLAVIA	**7TH LETTER**	MONTGOMERY
MONTENEGRO	MONTSERRAT	AUSTRALIAN	MONTEVIDEO	EQUATORIAL		COPENHAGEN
MONTEVIDEO	MOZAMBIQUE	BASSETERRE	MONTGOMERY		COPENHAGEN	MONTENEGRO
MONTGOMERY	NOUAKCHOTT	WASHINGTON	MONTPELIER		DARUSSALAM	ANTARCTICA
MONTPELIER	EQUATORIAL	ANTARCTICA	MONTSERRAT		DEMOCRATIC	AUSTRALIAN
MONTSERRAT	BRATISLAVA	EQUATORIAL	DARUSSALAM	**6TH LETTER**	MAURITANIA	CORONATION
MOZAMBIQUE	BRIDGETOWN	MAURITANIA	PROVIDENCE		YUGOSLAVIA	EQUATORIAL
NOUAKCHOTT	GRENADINES	NOUAKCHOTT		AUSTRALIAN	HARRISBURG	MONTPELIER
ORANJESTAD	ORANJESTAD	LUXEMBOURG		AZERBAIJAN	BANGLADESH	PARAMARIBO
PARAMARIBO	PROVIDENCE	SEYCHELLES		BANGLADESH	BASSETERRE	PHILIPPINE
PHILIPPINE	AUSTRALIAN	KAZAKHSTAN	**5TH LETTER**	CORONATION	MICRONESIA	TANGANYIKA
PROVIDENCE	GUADELOUPE	MOZAMBIQUE		MADAGASCAR	MONTENEGRO	TYRRHENIAN
SACRAMENTO	LUXEMBOURG		GRENADINES	PARAMARIBO	PROVIDENCE	AZERBAIJAN
SEYCHELLES	YUGOSLAVIA		SACRAMENTO	LUXEMBOURG	SACRAMENTO	DARUSSALAM
TAJIKISTAN	TYRRHENIAN		TANGANYIKA	MOZAMBIQUE	WASHINGTON	LIBREVILLE
TANGANYIKA	AZERBAIJAN	**4TH LETTER**	AZERBAIJAN	ANTARCTICA	WELLINGTON	SEYCHELLES
TYRRHENIAN	UZBEKISTAN		DEMOCRATIC	NOUAKCHOTT	NOUAKCHOTT	CALIFORNIA
UZBEKISTAN		ANTARCTICA	BASSETERRE	GRENADINES	AZERBAIJAN	GRENADINES
WASHINGTON		EQUATORIAL	GUADELOUPE	PROVIDENCE	GRENADINES	MAURITANIA
WELLINGTON		KAZAKHSTAN	LIBREVILLE	BRIDGETOWN	LIBREVILLE	PROVIDENCE
WILLEMSTAD	**3RD LETTER**	MADAGASCAR	MONTENEGRO	CHARLESTON	MARTINIQUE	SACRAMENTO
YUGOSLAVIA		MOZAMBIQUE	MONTEVIDEO	CLIPPERTON	MONTEVIDEO	BRIDGETOWN
	BRATISLAVA	NOUAKCHOTT	WILLEMSTAD	GEORGETOWN	MOZAMBIQUE	GEORGETOWN
	CHARLESTON	PARAMARIBO	CALIFORNIA	MONTSERRAT	AUSTRALIAN	NOUAKCHOTT
	GUADELOUPE	SEYCHELLES	BRIDGETOWN	MONTPELIER	BRATISLAVA	MARTINIQUE
2ND LETTER	ORANJESTAD	BRIDGETOWN	GEORGETOWN	ORANJESTAD	MONTPELIER	MOZAMBIQUE
	LIBREVILLE	GUADELOUPE	MADAGASCAR	SEYCHELLES	SEYCHELLES	BASSETERRE
BANGLADESH	UZBEKISTAN	COPENHAGEN	MONTGOMERY	TYRRHENIAN	MONTGOMERY	MONTSERRAT
BASSETERRE	MICRONESIA	LUXEMBOURG	SEYCHELLES	COPENHAGEN	TYRRHENIAN	MICRONESIA
CALIFORNIA	SACRAMENTO	UZBEKISTAN	TYRRHENIAN	KAZAKHSTAN	GUADELOUPE	CHARLESTON
DARUSSALAM	MADAGASCAR	BANGLADESH	BRATISLAVA	TAJIKISTAN	LUXEMBOURG	CLIPPERTON
HARRISBURG	AZERBAIJAN	TANGANYIKA	HARRISBURG	UZBEKISTAN	PHILIPPINE	DEMOCRATIC
KAZAKHSTAN	GRENADINES	WASHINGTON	MARTINIQUE	GUADELOUPE	CALIFORNIA	KAZAKHSTAN
MADAGASCAR	YUGOSLAVIA	CALIFORNIA	MAURITANIA	YUGOSLAVIA	CLIPPERTON	ORANJESTAD
MARTINIQUE	BRIDGETOWN	TAJIKISTAN	PHILIPPINE	SACRAMENTO	EQUATORIAL	TAJIKISTAN
MAURITANIA	CLIPPERTON	PHILIPPINE	PROVIDENCE	WILLEMSTAD	MONTSERRAT	UZBEKISTAN
PARAMARIBO	PHILIPPINE	WELLINGTON	WASHINGTON	MARTINIQUE	PARAMARIBO	WASHINGTON
SACRAMENTO	TAJIKISTAN	WILLEMSTAD	WELLINGTON	MICRONESIA	CHARLESTON	WELLINGTON
TAJIKISTAN	CALIFORNIA	GRENADINES	ORANJESTAD	MONTENEGRO	KAZAKHSTAN	WILLEMSTAD
TANGANYIKA	WELLINGTON	ORANJESTAD	KAZAKHSTAN	TANGANYIKA	MADAGASCAR	GUADELOUPE
WASHINGTON	WILLEMSTAD	CORONATION	NOUAKCHOTT	WASHINGTON	ORANJESTAD	

HARRISBURG
LUXEMBOURG
YUGOSLAVIA

9TH LETTER

AUSTRALIAN
AZERBAIJAN
DARUSSALAM
EQUATORIAL
KAZAKHSTAN
MADAGASCAR
MONTSERRAT
ORANJESTAD
TAJIKISTAN
TYRRHENIAN
UZBEKISTAN
WILLEMSTAD
PARAMARIBO
ANTARCTICA
PROVIDENCE
COPENHAGEN
GRENADINES
MONTEVIDEO
MONTPELIER
SEYCHELLES
CALIFORNIA
DEMOCRATIC
MAURITANIA
MICRONESIA
YUGOSLAVIA
TANGANYIKA
LIBREVILLE
PHILIPPINE
CHARLESTON
CLIPPERTON
CORONATION
WASHINGTON
WELLINGTON
GUADELOUPE
BASSETERRE
HARRISBURG
LUXEMBOURG
MONTENEGRO
MONTGOMERY
BANGLADESH
NOUAKCHOTT
SACRAMENTO
MARTINIQUE
MOZAMBIQUE
BRATISLAVA
BRIDGETOWN
GEORGETOWN

10TH LETTER

ANTARCTICA
BRATISLAVA
CALIFORNIA
MAURITANIA
MICRONESIA
TANGANYIKA
YUGOSLAVIA
DEMOCRATIC
ORANJESTAD
WILLEMSTAD
BASSETERRE
GUADELOUPE
LIBREVILLE
MARTINIQUE
MOZAMBIQUE
PHILIPPINE
PROVIDENCE
HARRISBURG
LUXEMBOURG
BANGLADESH
EQUATORIAL
DARUSSALAM
AUSTRALIAN
AZERBAIJAN
BRIDGETOWN
CHARLESTON
CLIPPERTON
COPENHAGEN
CORONATION
GEORGETOWN
KAZAKHSTAN
TAJIKISTAN
TYRRHENIAN
UZBEKISTAN
WASHINGTON
WELLINGTON
MONTENEGRO
MONTEVIDEO
PARAMARIBO
SACRAMENTO
MADAGASCAR
MONTPELIER
GRENADINES
SEYCHELLES
MONTSERRAT
NOUAKCHOTT
MONTGOMERY

11 LETTER

1ST LETTER

AFGHANISTAN
BRAZZAVILLE
CARPENTARIA
CHRISTOPHER
CONNECTICUT
HERZEGOVINA
LAKSHADWEEP
MISSISSIPPI
MONTPELLIER
NETHERLANDS
OUAGADOUGOU
PHILIPPINES
SPRINGFIELD
SWITZERLAND
TALLAHASSEE
TEGUCIGALPA
TERRITORIES

2ND LETTER

CARPENTARIA
LAKSHADWEEP
TALLAHASSEE
HERZEGOVINA
NETHERLANDS
TEGUCIGALPA
TERRITORIES
AFGHANISTAN
CHRISTOPHER
PHILIPPINES
MISSISSIPPI
CONNECTICUT
MONTPELLIER
SPRINGFIELD
BRAZZAVILLE
OUAGADOUGOU
SWITZERLAND

3RD LETTER

BRAZZAVILLE
OUAGADOUGOU
AFGHANISTAN
TEGUCIGALPA
PHILIPPINES
SWITZERLAND
LAKSHADWEEP
TALLAHASSEE
CONNECTICUT

MONTPELLIER
CARPENTARIA
CHRISTOPHER
HERZEGOVINA
SPRINGFIELD
TERRITORIES
MISSISSIPPI
NETHERLANDS

4TH LETTER

OUAGADOUGOU
AFGHANISTAN
NETHERLANDS
CHRISTOPHER
SPRINGFIELD
PHILIPPINES
TALLAHASSEE
CONNECTICUT
CARPENTARIA
TERRITORIES
LAKSHADWEEP
MISSISSIPPI
MONTPELLIER
SWITZERLAND
TEGUCIGALPA
BRAZZAVILLE
HERZEGOVINA

5TH LETTER

AFGHANISTAN
OUAGADOUGOU
TALLAHASSEE
TEGUCIGALPA
CARPENTARIA
CONNECTICUT
HERZEGOVINA
NETHERLANDS
LAKSHADWEEP
MISSISSIPPI
PHILIPPINES
TERRITORIES
SPRINGFIELD
MONTPELLIER
CHRISTOPHER
BRAZZAVILLE
SWITZERLAND

6TH LETTER

BRAZZAVILLE
LAKSHADWEEP
CONNECTICUT
OUAGADOUGOU
MONTPELLIER
SWITZERLAND
HERZEGOVINA
SPRINGFIELD
TALLAHASSEE
TEGUCIGALPA
AFGHANISTAN
CARPENTARIA
PHILIPPINES
NETHERLANDS
MISSISSIPPI
CHRISTOPHER
TERRITORIES

7TH LETTER

TALLAHASSEE
LAKSHADWEEP
SPRINGFIELD
TEGUCIGALPA
AFGHANISTAN
MONTPELLIER
NETHERLANDS
CHRISTOPHER
HERZEGOVINA
OUAGADOUGOU
TERRITORIES
PHILIPPINES
SWITZERLAND
MISSISSIPPI
CARPENTARIA
CONNECTICUT
BRAZZAVILLE

8TH LETTER

CARPENTARIA
NETHERLANDS
TEGUCIGALPA
BRAZZAVILLE
CONNECTICUT
MISSISSIPPI
PHILIPPINES
SPRINGFIELD
MONTPELLIER
SWITZERLAND
CHRISTOPHER

TERRITORIES
AFGHANISTAN
TALLAHASSEE
OUAGADOUGOU
HERZEGOVINA
LAKSHADWEEP

9TH LETTER

SWITZERLAND
CONNECTICUT
LAKSHADWEEP
SPRINGFIELD
OUAGADOUGOU
CHRISTOPHER
HERZEGOVINA
MONTPELLIER
TERRITORIES
BRAZZAVILLE
TEGUCIGALPA
NETHERLANDS
PHILIPPINES
MISSISSIPPI
CARPENTARIA
TALLAHASSEE
AFGHANISTAN

10TH LETTER

AFGHANISTAN
NETHERLANDS
CHRISTOPHER
LAKSHADWEEP
MONTPELLIER
PHILIPPINES
TALLAHASSEE
TERRITORIES
CARPENTARIA
BRAZZAVILLE
SPRINGFIELD
HERZEGOVINA
SWITZERLAND
OUAGADOUGOU
MISSISSIPPI
TEGUCIGALPA
CONNECTICUT

11TH LETTER

CARPENTARIA
HERZEGOVINA

TEGUCIGALPA
SPRINGFIELD
SWITZERLAND
BRAZZAVILLE
TALLAHASSEE
MISSISSIPPI
AFGHANISTAN
LAKSHADWEEP
CHRISTOPHER
MONTPELLIER
NETHERLANDS
PHILIPPINES
TERRITORIES
CONNECTICUT
OUAGADOUGOU

TURKMENISTAN
PENNSYLVANIA
YAMOUSSOUKRO
FORTDEFRANCE

5TH LETTER
INDIANAPOLIS
FORTDEFRANCE
TURKMENISTAN
ANTANANARIVO
PENNSYLVANIA
YAMOUSSOUKRO

6TH LETTER
ANTANANARIVO
FORTDEFRANCE
TURKMENISTAN
INDIANAPOLIS
YAMOUSSOUKRO
PENNSYLVANIA

7TH LETTER
INDIANAPOLIS
FORTDEFRANCE
PENNSYLVANIA
ANTANANARIVO
TURKMENISTAN
YAMOUSSOUKRO

8TH LETTER
ANTANANARIVO
TURKMENISTAN
YAMOUSSOUKRO
INDIANAPOLIS
FORTDEFRANCE
PENNSYLVANIA

9TH LETTER
FORTDEFRANCE
PENNSYLVANIA
INDIANAPOLIS
ANTANANARIVO

12 LETTER
1ST LETTER
ANTANANARIVO
FORTDEFRANCE
INDIANAPOLIS
PENNSYLVANIA
TURKMENISTAN
YAMOUSSOUKRO

2ND LETTER
YAMOUSSOUKRO
PENNSYLVANIA
ANTANANARIVO
INDIANAPOLIS
FORTDEFRANCE
TURKMENISTAN

3RD LETTER
INDIANAPOLIS
YAMOUSSOUKRO
PENNSYLVANIA
FORTDEFRANCE
TURKMENISTAN
ANTANANARIVO

4TH LETTER
ANTANANARIVO
INDIANAPOLIS

TURKMENISTAN
YAMOUSSOUKRO

10TH LETTER
ANTANANARIVO
YAMOUSSOUKRO
INDIANAPOLIS
FORTDEFRANCE
PENNSYLVANIA
TURKMENISTAN

11TH LETTER
TURKMENISTAN
FORTDEFRANCE
INDIANAPOLIS
PENNSYLVANIA
YAMOUSSOUKRO
ANTANANARIVO

12TH LETTER
PENNSYLVANIA
FORTDEFRANCE
TURKMENISTAN
ANTANANARIVO
YAMOUSSOUKRO
INDIANAPOLIS

13 LETTER
1ST LETTER
LIECHTENSTEIN
MASSACHUSETTS
MEDITERRANEAN

2ND LETTER
MASSACHUSETTS
MEDITERRANEAN
LIECHTENSTEIN

3RD LETTER
MEDITERRANEAN
LIECHTENSTEIN
MASSACHUSETTS

4TH LETTER
LIECHTENSTEIN
MEDITERRANEAN
MASSACHUSETTS

5TH LETTER
MASSACHUSETTS
MEDITERRANEAN
LIECHTENSTEIN

6TH LETTER
MEDITERRANEAN
MASSACHUSETTS
LIECHTENSTEIN

7TH LETTER
LIECHTENSTEIN
MASSACHUSETTS
MEDITERRANEAN

8TH LETTER
LIECHTENSTEIN
MEDITERRANEAN
MASSACHUSETTS

9TH LETTER
MEDITERRANEAN
LIECHTENSTEIN
MASSACHUSETTS

10TH LETTER
MASSACHUSETTS
MEDITERRANEAN
LIECHTENSTEIN

11TH LETTER
LIECHTENSTEIN
MEDITERRANEAN
MASSACHUSETTS

12TH LETTER
MEDITERRANEAN
LIECHTENSTEIN
MASSACHUSETTS

13TH LETTER
LIECHTENSTEIN
MEDITERRANEAN
MASSACHUSETTS

TABLE OF COUNTRIES,
WITH ABBREVIATIONS AND CAPITAL CITIES

COUNTRY	ABBR.	CAPITAL	COUNTRY	ABBR.	CAPITAL	COUNTRY	ABBR.	CAPITAL
AFGHANISTAN	AF	KABUL	BENIN	BJ	PORTO NOVO	CHILE	CL	SANTIAGO
ALAND ISLANDS	—	—	BERMUDA	BM	HAMILTON	CHINA	CN	BEIJING
ALBANIA	AL	TIRANA	BHUTAN	BT	THIMPHU	CHRISTMAS ISLAND	CX	—
ALGERIA	DZ	ALGER			(THIMBU)	CLIPPERTON ISLAND	IT	—
AMERICAN SAMOA	AS	PAGO PAGO	BOLIVIA	BO	LA PAZ	COCOS ISLANDS	CC	—
AMSTERDAM ISLANDS	—	—	BOSNIA	BA		COLOMBIA	CO	BOGOTA
ANDORRA	AD	ANDORRA LA	BOTSWANA	BW	GABORONE	COMOROS	KM	MORONI
		VELLA	BOUVET ISLAND	BV	—	CONGO	CG	BRAZZAVILLE
ANGOLA	AO	LUANDA	BRAZIL	BR	BRASILIA	COOK ISLANDS	CK	RAROTONGA
ANGUILLA	AI	THE VALLEY	BRITISH INDIAN			COSTA RICA	CR	SAN JOSE
ANDAMAN ISLANDS	US	—	OCEAN TERRITORY	IO		CROATIA	HR	ZAGREB
ANNOBON ISLAND	IT	—	BRITISH VIRGIN			CROZET		—
ANTARCTICA	AQ	—	ISLANDS	VG	ROAD TOWN,	CUBA	CU	HAVANA
ANTIGUA	AG	SAINT JOHNS			TORTOLA	CYPRUS	CY	NICOSIA
ARGENTINA	AR	BUENOS	BRUNEI DARUSSALAM	BN	BANDAR SERI	CZECH REPUBLIC	CZ	PRAGUE
		AIRES			BEGAWAN	DEMOCRATIC		
ARMENIA	AM	YEREVAN	BULGARIA	BG	SOFIA	PEOPLE'S REPUBLIC		
ARUBA	AW	ORANJESTAD	BURKINA FASO	BF	OUAGADOUGOU	OF KOREA	KP	P'YONGYANG
ASCENSION ISLAND	UK	—	BURUNDI	BI	BUJUMBURA	DEMOCRATIC		KINSHASA
AUSTRALIA	AU	CANBERRA				REPUBLIC OF		
AUSTRIA	AT	VIENNA	CAICOS ISLANDS	TC	COCKBURN	CONGO (ZAIRE)		
AVES ISLAND	IT	—			TOWN,	DENMARK	DK	COPENHAGEN
AZERBAIJAN	AZ	BAKU			GRANDTURK	DJIBOUTI	DJ	DJIBOUTI
AZORES ISLANDS	PT	—	CAMBODIA	KH	PHNOM PENH	DOMINICA	DM	ROSEAU
BAHAMAS	BS	NASSAU	CAMEROON	CM	YAOUNDE	DOMINICAN	DO	SANTO
BAHRAIN	BH	MANAMA	CANADA	CA	OTTAWA	REPUBLIC		DOMINGO
BAILIWICK OF JERSEY	JE	—	CANARY ISLANDS	ES	—	EASTER ISLAND	US	—
BANABA ISLAND	JP	—	CAPE VERDE	CV	PRAIA	EAST TIMOR	TP	—
BANGLADESH	BD	DHAKA	CAYMAN ISLANDS	KY	GEORGE TOWN	ECUADOR	EC	QUITO
BARBADOS	BB	BRIDGETOWN	CENTRAL AFRICAN			EGYPT	EG	CAIRO
BARBUDA	AG	SAINT JOHN'S	REPUBLIC	CF	BANGUI	EL SALVADOR	SV	SAN
BELARUS	BY	MINSK	CEUTA ISLAND	ES	—			SALVADOR
BELGIUM	BE	BRUSSELS	CHAD	TD	N'DJAMENA	ENGLAND	EN	LONDON
BELIZE	BZ	BELMOPAN	CHATHAM ISLAND	IT	—	EQUATORIAL GUINEA	GQ	MALABO

COUNTRY	ABBR.	CAPITAL	COUNTRY	ABBR.	CAPITAL	COUNTRY	ABBR.	CAPITAL
ERITREA	ER	ASMARA	HERZEGOVINA	BA	——	LITHUANIA	LT	VILNIUS
ESTONIA	EE	TALLINN	HONDURAS	HN	TEGUCIGALPA	LUXEMBOURG	LU	LUXEMBOURG
ETHIOPIA	ET	ADDIS ABABA	HONG KONG	HK	VICTORIA	MACAO	MO	MACAO
FAEROE ISLANDS	FO	THORSHAVN	HOWLAND ISLAND	UM	——	MACEDONIA	MK	——
FALKLAND ISLANDS	FK	STANLEY	HUNGARY	HU	BUDAPEST	MACQUARIE ISLAND	NF	——
FERNANDO			ICELAND	IS	REYKJAVIK	MADAGASCAR	MG	ANTANA-
DE NORONHA			ISLAND OF MAN	IM	——			NARIVO
ISLAND	BR	——	INDIA	IN	NEW DELHI	MADEIRA ISLANDS	PT	——
FIJI	FJ	SUVA	INDONESIA	ID	JAKARTA	MALAWI	MW	LILONGWE
FINLAND	FI	HELSINKI	IRAN	IR	TEHRAN	MALAYSIA	MY	KUALA
FRANCE	FR	PARIS	IRAQ	IQ	BAGDAD			LUMPUR
FRENCH GUIANA	GF	CAYENNE	IRELAND	IE	DUBLIN	MALDIVES	MV	MALE
FRENCH POLYNESIA	PF	PAPEETE	ISRAEL	IL	JERUSALEM	MALI	ML	BAMAKO
FRENCH			ITALY	IT	ROME	MALPELO PACIFIC		
SOUTHERN			IVORY COAST	CI	ABIDJAN	ISLAND	IT	——
TERRITORIES	TF	——	JAMAICA	JM	KINGSTON	MALTA	MT	VALLETTA
FUTANA ISLANDS	WF	——	JAN MAYEN ISLANDS	SJ	——	MARIANA ISLANDS	MP	——
GABON	GA	LIBREVILLE	JAPAN	JP	TOYKO	MARSHALL ISLANDS	MH	JALUIT
GALAPAGOS ISLANDS	EC	——	JOHNSTON ATOLL	UM	——	MARTINIQUE	MQ	FORT-DE-
GAMBIA	GM	BANJUL	JORDAN	JO	AMMAN			FRANCE
GEORGIA	GE	TBILISI	KAZAKHSTAN	KZ	ALMATY	MAURITANIA	MR	NOUAKCHOTT
GERMANY	DE	BERLIN	KENYA	KE	NAIROBI	MAURITIUS	MU	PORT LOUIS
GHANA	GH	ACCRA	KERGUELEN ISLANDS	FR	——	MAYOTTE	YT	——
GIBRALTAR	GI	GIBRALTER	KINGMAN REEF			MCDONALD ISLANDS	HM	——
GREECE	GR	ATHENS	ISLAND	UM	——	MELILLA ISLAND	ES	——
GREENLAND	GL	GODTHAR	KIRIBATI	KI	TARAWA	MEXICO	MX	MEXICO
GRENADA	GD	SAINT	KUWAIT	KW	KUWAIT CITY			CITY
		GEORGE'S	KYRGYSTAN	KG	BISHKEK	MICRONESIA	FM	KOLONIA
GRENADINES	VC	——	LAKSHADWEEP			MIDWAY ISLANDS	UM	——
GUADELOUPE	GP	BASSE TERRE	ISLAND	CA	——	MINAMI TORISHIMA		
GUAM	GU	AGANA	LAOS DEMOCRATIC			ISLAND	SP	——
GUATEMALA	GT	GUATEMALA	REPUBLIC	LA	VIENTIANE	MOLDOVA	MD	KISHINEV
GUERNSEY	GG	——	LATVIA	LV	RIGA	MONACO	MC	MONACO
GUINEA	GN	CONAKRY	LEBANON	LB	BEIRUT	MONGOLIA	MN	ULAN BATOR
GUINEA-BISSAU	GW	BISSAU	LESOTHO	LS	MASERU	MONTENEGRO	YU	——
GUYANA	GY	GEORGETOWN	LIBERIA	LR	MONROVIA	MONTSERRAT	MS	PLYMOUTH
HAITI	HT	PORT-	LIBYA	LY	TRIPOLI	MOROCCO	MA	RABAT
		AU-PRINCE	LIECHTENSTEIN	LI	VADUZ	MOZAMBIQUE	MZ	MAPUTO
HEARD ISLANDS	HM	——	LINE ISLANDS	JP	——	MYANMAR	BM	YANGON

COUNTRY	ABBR.	CAPITAL	COUNTRY	ABBR.	CAPITAL	COUNTRY	ABBR.	CAPITAL
NAMIBIA	NA	WINDHOEK	REVILLA GIGEDO			SOUTH GEORGIA	GS	——
NAURU	NR	YAREN	ISLANDS	US	——	SPAIN	ES	MADRID
NAVASSA ISLAND	UM	——	RODRIGUES ISLAND	US	——	SRI LANKA	LK	COLOMBO
NEPAL	NP	KATHMANDU	ROMANIA	RO	BUCHAREST	SUDAN	SD	KHARTOUM
NETHERLANDS	NL	AMSTERDAM	RUSSIA	RU	MOSCOW	SURINAM	SR	PARAMARIBO
NETHERLANDS			RWANDA	RW	KIGALI	SVALBARD ISLANDS	SJ	LONGYEAR
ANTILLES	AN	WILLEMSTAD	SAINT CHRISTOPHER					CITY
NEW CALEDONIA	NC	NOUMEA	ISLAND	KN	——	SWAZILAND	SZ	MBABANE
NEW ZEALAND	NZ	WELLINGTON	SAINT HELENA	SH	JAMESTOWN	SWEDEN	SE	STOCKHOLM
NICARAGUA	NI	MANAGUA	SAINT KITTS	KN	BASSETERRE	SWITZERLAND	CH	BERN
NIGER	NE	NIAMEY	SAINT LUCIA	LC	CASTRIES	SYRIA	SY	DAMASCUS
NIGERIA	NG	ABUJA	SAINT MAARTEN	SM	——	TAIWAN	TW	T'AI-PEI
NIUE	NU	ALOFI	SAINT MARTIN	SM	——	TAJIKISTAN	TJ	DUSHANBE
NORFOLK ISLAND	NF	——	SAINT MIQUELON	PM	——	TANZANIA	TZ	DODOMA
NORTHERN MARIANA			SAINT NEVIS	KN	BASSETERRE	THAILAND	TH	BANGKOK
ISLANDS	NP		SAINT PAUL	——	——	TOBAGO	TT	PORT OF SPAIN
NORWAY	NO	OSLO	SAINT PIERRE	PM	——	TOGO	TG	LOME
OGASAWARA ISLAND	US	——	SAINT VINCENT	VC	KINGSTOWN	TOKELAU	TK	——
OMAN	OM	MUSCAT	SAMOA	WS	APIA	TONGA	TO	NUKUALOFA
PAKISTAN	PK	ISLAMABAD	SAN INO	SM	——	TRINIDAD	TT	PORT OF SPAIN
PALAU	PW	——	SAN MARINO	SM	SAN MARINO	TRISTAN DA CUNHA		
PANAMA	PA	PANAMA	SAN ANDREAS			ISLAND	UK	——
PAPUA NEW GUINEA	PG	PORT	ISLAND	CO		TUNISIA	TN	TUNIS
		MORESBY	SAO TOME AND			TURKEY	TR	ANKARA
PARAGUAY	PY	ASUNCION	PRINCIPE	ST	SAO TOME	TURKMENISTAN	TM	ASHGABAT
PERU	PE	LIMA	SAUDI ARABIA	SA	RIYADH	TURKS ISLANDS	TC	
PHILIPPINES	PH	MANILA	SCOTLAND	UK	——	UGANDA	UG	KAMPALA
PITCAIRN	PN	——	SENEGAL	SN	DAKAR	UKRAINE	UA	KIEV
POLAND	PL	WARSAW	SERBIA	YU	——	UNITED ARAB		
PORTUGAL	PT	LISBON	SEYCHELLES	SC	VICTORIA	EMIRATES	AE	ABU DHABI
PRINCE EDWARD			SIERRA LEONE	SL	FREETOWN	UNITED KINGDOM	UK	LONDON
ISLAND	UK	——	SINGAPORE	SG	SINGAPORE	UNITED STATES		
PROVEDEN ISLAND	CO	——	SLOVAKIA	SK	BRATISLAVA	OF AMERICA	US	WASHINGTON
PUERTO RICO	PR	SAN JUAN	SLOVENIA	SI	LJUBLJANA	URAGUAY	UY	MONTEVIDEO
QATAR	QA	AD DAWHAH	SOLOMON ISLANDS	SB	HONIARA	US VIRGIN ISLANDS	VI	CHARLOTTE
REPUBLIC OF KOREA	KR	SEOUL	SOMALIA	SO	MOGADISHU			AMALIE
REUNION	RE	SAINT-DENIS	SOUTH AFRICA	ZA	CAPE TOWN	UZBEKISTAN	UZ	TASHKENT

COUNTRY	ABBR.	CAPITAL
VANUATU	VU	VILA
VATICAN CITY	VA	VATICAN CITY
VENEZUELA	VE	CARACAS
VIETNAM	VN	HANOI
VIRGIN ISLANDS	VI	——
WAKE ISLAND	UM	——
WALES	UK	——
WALLIS ISLANDS	WF	——
WESTERN SAHARA	EH	——
YEMEN	YE	SANAA
YUGOSLAVIA	YU	BELGRADE
ZAMBIA	ZM	LUSAKA
ZANZIBAR	US	——
ZIMBABWE	ZW	HARARE

TABLE OF STATES,
WITH ABBREVIATIONS AND CAPITAL CITIES

STATE	ABBR.	CAPITAL	STATE	ABBR.	CAPITAL
ALABAMA	AL	MONTGOMERY	NORTH DAKOTA	ND	BISMARCK
ALASKA	AK	JUNEAU	OHIO	OH	COLUMBUS
ARIZONA	AZ	PHOENIX	OKLAHOMA	OK	OKLAHOMA
ARKANSAS	AR	LITTLE ROCK			CITY
CALIFORNIA	CA	SACRAMENTO	OREGON	OR	SALEM
COLORADO	CO	DENVER	PENNSYLVANIA	PA	HARRISBURG
CONNECTICUT	CT	HARTFORD	RHODE ISLAND	RI	PROVIDENCE
DELAWARE	DE	DOVER	SOUTH CAROLINA	SC	COLUMBIA
FLORIDA	FL	TALLAHASSEE	SOUTH DAKOTA	SD	PIERRE
GEORGIA	GA	ATLANTA	TENNESSEE	TN	NASHVILLE
HAWAII	HI	HONOLULU	TEXAS	TX	AUSTIN
IDAHO	ID	BOISE	UTAH	UT	SALT LAKE
ILLINOIS	IL	SPRINGFIELD			CITY
INDIANA	IN	INDIANAPOLIS	VERMONT	VT	MONTPELIER
IOWA	IA	DES MOINES	VIRGINIA	VA	RICHMOND
KANSAS	KS	TOPEKA	WASHINGTON	WA	OLYMPIA
KENTUCKY	KY	FRANKFORT	WEST VIRGINIA	WV	CHARLESTON
LOUISIANA	LA	BATON ROUGE	WISCONSIN	WI	MADISON
MAINE	ME	AUGUSTA	WYOMING	WY	CHEYENNE
MARYLAND	MD	ANNAPOLIS			
MASSACHUSETTS	MA	BOSTON			
MICHIGAN	MI	LANSING			
MINNESOTA	MN	SAINT PAUL			
MISSISSIPPI	MS	JACKSON			
MISSOURI	MO	JEFFERSON			
		CITY			
MONTANA	MT	HELENA			
NEBRASKA	NE	LINCOLN			
NEVADA	NV	CARSON CITY			
NEW HAMPSHIRE	NH	CONCORD			
NEW JERSEY	NJ	TRENTON			
NEW MEXICO	NM	SANTA FE			
NEW YORK	NY	ALBANY			
NORTH CAROLINA	NC	RALEIGH			

MAJOR BODIES OF WATER

ADRIATIC SEA
AEGEAN SEA
AGULHAS BASIN
ALEUTIAN BASIN
ALEUTIAN ISLANDS
AMUNDSEN GULF
ARABIAN SEA
ARAFURA SEA
ARAL SEA
ARGENTINE BASIN
ATLANTIC OCEAN
ATLANTIC-INDIAN BASIN
BAFFIN BAY
BALTIC SEA
BANDA SEA
BARENTS SEA
BASS STRAIT
BAY OF BENGAL
BAY OF BISCAY
BAY OF FUNDI
BEAUFORD SEA
BERING SEA
BERING STRAIT
BLACK SEA
BRAZIL BASIN
BRISTOL BAY
CANADA BASIN
CARIBBEAN SEA
CASPIAN SEA
CELEBES SEA
CELTIC SEA
CENTRAL PACIFIC BASIN
CHUKCHI SEA
CHURCHILL LAKE
CORAL SEA
CORONATION GULF
CROZET BASIN
DAVIS STRAIT
DEAD SEA
DENMARK STRAIT
EAST CAROLINE BASIN
EAST CHINA SEA
EAST MARIANA BASIN
EAST SIBERIAN SEA
ENGLISH CHANNEL
FOXE CHANNEL
FOXE BASIN
GREAT AUSTRALIAN BIGHT
GREAT BEAR LAKE
GREAT SALT LAKE
GREAT SLAVE LAKE

GUINEA BASIN
GULF OF ADEN
GULF OF BAHRAIN
GULF OF BOOTHIA
GULF OF CALIFORNIA
GULF OF CARPENTARIA
GULF OF FINLAND
GULF OF GUINEA
GULF OF MEXICO
GULF OF PANAMA
GULF OF SAINT LAWRENCE
GULF OF SIDRA
GULF OF TONKIN
GULF OF THAILAND
HECATE STRAIT
HUDSON BAY
HUDSON STRAIT
INDIAN OCEAN
IRISH SEA
JAVA SEA
KANE BASIN
KARA SEA
KOREA STRAIT
KUSKOKWIM BAY
LABRADOR SEA
LAKE ALBERT
LAKE ATHABASCA
LAKE BAIKAL
LAKE BALKHASH
LAKE EDWARD
LAKE ERIE
LAKE HURON
LAKE LADOGA
LAKE MALAWI
LAKE MICHIGAN
LAKE ONTARIO
LAKE SUPERIOR
LAKE TANGANYIKA
LAKE TITICACA
LAKE VICTORIA
LAKE WINNIPEG
LANCASTER SOUND
LAPTEV SEA
LINCOLN SEA
M'CLINTOCK CHANNEL
M'CLURE STRAIT
MADAGASCAR BASIN
MAKAROV BASIN
MASCARENE BASIN
MEDITERRANEAN SEA
MOZAMBIQUE CHANNEL

NANSEN BASIN
NORTH AMERICAN BASIN
NORTH SEA
NORTHWEST PACIFIC BASIN
NORWEGIAN SEA
NORWEGIAN BAY
PACIFIC OCEAN
PEARY CHANNEL
PERSIAN GULF
PERU BASIN
PHILIPPINE SEA
QUEEN CHARLOTTE SOUND
QUEEN MAUD GULF
RED SEA
REINDEER LAKE
ROSS SEA
SCORESBY SOUND
SCOTIA SEA
SEA OF JAPAN
SEA OF OKHOTSK
SHELIKHOV GULF
SIERRA LEONE BASIN
SMITH BAY
SOLOMON SEA
SOUTH CHINA SEA
SPENCER GULF
STRAIT OF HORMUZ
STRAIT OF MAGELLAN
STRAITS OF FLORIDA
SULU SEA
TAIWAN STRAIT
TASMAN SEA
TIMOR SEA
TYRRHENIAN SEA
UNGAVA BAY
VISCOUNT MELVILLE SOUND
WEDDELL SEA
WEST CAROLINE BASIN
WHARTON BASIN
WHITE SEA
YELLOW SEA

BIBLIOGRAPHY

Section 1. Words

The Merriam-Webster Dictionary, Simon & Schuster

Funk & Wagnalls New Comprehensive International Dictionary of the English Language, deluxe reference edition, International Press, 1982

Dictionary of Computer Terms, fourth edition, by Douglas Downing, Michael A. Covington & Melody Mauldin Covington, Barron's Educational Series, 1992

Section 2. Names of People

The Timetables of Science: A Chronology of the Most Important People and Events in the History of Science, by Alexander Hellemans and Byran Bunch, Simon & Schuster, 1988

Nobel Prize Women in Science: Their Lives, Struggles and Momentous Discoveries, by Sharon Bertsch McGrayne, Carol Publishing, 1992

CHI Research Inc., Haddon Heights, New Jersey.
http://www.chiresearch.com

Nobel Prize Awards Archives, 1901–1996
http://www.almaz.com/nobel/alpha.html

Academy Award winners. http://www.academyawards.com
Also refer to http://us. imbd.com/oscars

Grammy Award Hall of Fame. http://www.grammy/highlights/hallfame.htlm

Pulitzer Prize winners, 1986–1996. http://www.pulitzer.org/winners

Section 3. Geographic Names

Illustrated Atlas of the World, Reader's Digest, 1992

World map, National Geographic Society, revised November 1995

U.S. Postal Service Manual

Maps on the Internet. http://www.guernsey.net